TWENTIETH EDITION

SCHROEDER'S
ANTIQUES
PRICE GUIDE

Edited by Sharon & Bob Huxford

COLLECTOR BOOKS

A Division of Schroeder Publishing Co., Inc.

The current values in this book should be used only as a guide. They are not intended to set prices, which vary from one section of the country to another. Auction prices as well as dealer prices vary greatly and are affected by condition as well as demand. Neither the editors nor the publisher assumes responsibility for any losses that might be incurred as a result of consulting this guide.

Searching For A Publisher?

We are always looking for people knowledgeable within their fields. If you feel that there is a real need for a book on your collectible subject and have a large comprehensive collection, please contact Collector Books.

COLLECTOR BOOKS
P.O. Box 3009
Paducah, Kentucky 42002-3009
www.collectorbooks.com

Copyright © 2002 Schroeder Publishing Co., Inc.

Introduction

As the editors and staff of *Schroeder's*, our goal is to compile the most useful, comprehensive, and accurate background and pricing information possible. We strive to suggest values based on traditional market sales rather than Internet auctions which are notoriously erratic. Our guide encompasses nearly five hundred categories, many of which you will not find in other price guide. Our sources are varied; we use auction results and dealer lists, and we consult with national collectors' clubs, recognized authorities, researchers, and appraisers. We have by far the largest Advisory Board of any similar publication on the market. Each year we add several new advisors and now have over 450 who cover almost all our categories. They go over our computer print-outs line by line, deleting listings that are misleading or too vague to be of merit; they often send background information and photos. We appreciate their assistance very much. Only through their expertise and experience in their special fields are we able to offer with confidence what we feel are useful, accurate evaluations that provide a sound understanding of the dealings in the marketplace today. Correspondence with so large an advisory panel adds months of extra work to an already monumental task, but we feel that to a very large extent this is the foundation that makes *Schroeder's* the success that it has become.

Our Directory, which you will find in the back of the book, lists each contributor by state. These are people who have allowed us to photograph various examples of merchandise from their show booths, sent us pricing information, or in any way have contributed to this year's book. If you happen to be traveling, consult the Directory for shops along your way. We also list clubs who have worked with us and auction houses who have allowed us to use photographs from their catalogs.

Our Advisory Board lists only names and home states, so check the Directory for addresses and telephone numbers should you want to correspond with one of our experts. Remember, when you do, *always* enclose a self-addressed, stamped envelope (SASE). Thousands of people buy our guide, and hundreds contact our advisors. The only agreement we have with our advisors is that they edit their categories. They are in no way obligated to answer mail. Some are dealers who do many shows a month. The time they spend at home may be very limited, and they may not be open to contacts. There's no doubt that the reason behind the success of our book is their assistance. We regret seeing them become more and more burdened by phone and mail inquiries. We have lost some of our good advisors for this reason, and when we do, the book suffers and consequently, so do our readers. Many of our listed reference sources report that they constantly receive long distance calls (at all hours) that are really valuation requests. If they are registered appraisers, they make their living at providing such information and expect a fee for their service and expertise.

If you find you need more information than *Schroeder's* provides, there are other sources available to you. Go to your local library; check their section on reference books. Museums are public facilities that are willing and able help you establish the origin and possibly even the value of your particular treasure. In today's world of e-commerce, there are many websites you may visit that are full of pertinent, up-to-date information. Check the yellow pages of your phone book. Other cities' phone books are available from either your library or from the telephone company office. Look under the heading *Antique Dealers*. Those who are qualified appraisers will mention this credit in their advertisement. But remember that if you sell to a dealer, he will expect to buy your merchandise at a price low enough that he will be able to make an appreciable profit when he sells it. Once you decide to contact one of these appraisers, unless you intend to see them directly, you'll need to take photographs. Don't send photos that are under- or overexposed, out of focus, or shot against a background that detracts from important details you want to emphasize. It is almost impossible for them to give you a value judgement on items they've not seen when your photos are of poor quality. Shoot the front, top, and the bottom; describe any marks and numbers (or send a pencil rubbing), explain how and when you acquired the article, and give accurate measurements and any further background information that may be helpful.

The auction houses listed in the Directory nearly all have a staff of appraisal experts. If the item you're attempting to research is of the caliber of material they deal with, they can offer extremely accurate evaluations. Of course, most have a fee. Be sure to send them only professional-quality photographs. Tell them if you expect to consign your item to their auction. If you disagree with the value they suggest, you are under no obligation to do so.

Nearly five hundred categories are included in our book. We have organized our topics alphabetically, following the most simple logic, usually either by manufacturer or by type of product. If you have difficulty in locating your subject, consult the index. Our guide is unique in that much more space has been allotted to background information than in any other publication of this type. Our readers tell us that these are features they enjoy. To be able to do this, we have adopted a format of one-line listings wherein we describe the items to the fullest extent possible by using several common-sense abbreviations; they will be easy to read and understand if you will first take the time to quickly scan through them.

The Editors

Editorial Staff

Editors
Sharon and Bob Huxford

Research and Editorial Assistants
Michael Drollinger, Donna Newnum, Loretta Suiters

Layout
Beth Ray, Terri Hunter, and Donna Ballard

Cover Design
Beth Summers

On the front cover: Gibbs horse and rider, 8" long, excellent condition, $350.00; Krammer and Reinhardt doll, 21", $6,000.00; Occasional table, carved mahogany and marquetry inlaid, 30½", $5,000.00 – 7,000.00; Azure vase, 7", $145.00; Nippon vase, molded roses, 9", $880.00; 1950s wreath pin and earring set, light pink, dark pink, ruby red, and clear Austrian crystal rhinestones, pin is 2¼" in diameter, earrings are 1½" long, $425.00 – 525.00; Snow King Baking Powder, figural diecut, $550.00.

On the back cover: Nippon urn, 18", $7,700.00.

Listing of Standard Abbreviations

The following is a list of abbreviations that have been used throughout this book in order to provide you with the most detailed descriptions possible in the limited space available. No periods are used after initials or abbreviations. When two dimensions are given, height is noted first. If only one dimension is listed, it will be height, except in the case of bowls, dishes, plates, or platters, when it will be diameter. The standard two-letter state abbreviations apply.

For glassware, if no color is noted, the glass is clear. Hyphenated colors, for example blue-green, olive-amber, etc., describe a single color tone; colors divided by a slash mark indicate two or more colors, i.e. blue/white. Teapots, sugar bowls, and butter dishes are assumed to be 'with cover.' Condition is extremely important in determining market value. Common sense suggests that art pottery, china, and glassware values would be given for examples in pristine, mint condition, while suggested prices for utility wares such as Redware, Mocha, and Blue and White Stoneware, for example, reflect the probability that since such items were subjected to everyday use in the home they may show minor wear (which is acceptable) but no notable damage. Values for other categories reflect the best average condition in which the particular collectible is apt to be offered for sale without the dealer feeling it necessary to mention wear or damage. For instance, advertising items are assumed to be in excellent condition since mint items are scarce enough that when one is offered for sale the dealer will most likely make mention of that fact. The same holds true for toys, banks, coin-operated machines, and the like. A basic rule of thumb is that an item listed as VG (very good) will bring 40% to 60% of its mint price — a first-hand, personal evaluation will enable you to make the final judgement; EX (excellent) is a condition midway between mint and very good, and values would correspond.

Am ....American	dvtl ....dovetail	litho ....lithograph	re ....regarding
appl ....applied	emb............embossed, embossing	lt.....................................light	rfn ....refinished
att ....attributed to	embr ....embroidered	M ....mint	rnd ....round
bbl ....barrel	Emp..............................Empire	mahog ....mahogany	rpl ....replaced
bk ....back	eng ....engraved, engraving	mc ....multicolor	rpr ....repaired
bl ....blue	EPNS...electroplated nickel silver	MIB ....mint in box	rpt ....repainted
blk ....black	EX ....excellent	MIG ....Made in Germany	rstr ....restored
brn ....brown	Fed ....Federal	MIP ....mint in package	rtcl ....reticulated
bulb ....bulbous	fr ....frame, framed	mk ....mark	rvpt ....reverse painted
bsk ....bisque	Fr ....French	MOC ....mint on card	s&p ....salt and pepper
b3m ....blown 3-mold	ft, ftd ....foot, feet, footed	MOP ....mother-of-pearl	sgn ....signed
C ....century	G ....good	mt, mtd.............mount, mounted	SP ....silverplated
c ....copyright	gr....................................green	NE ....New England	sq ....square
ca ....circa	grad ....graduated	NM ....near mint	std ....standard
cb ....cardboard	grpt ....grain painted	NRFB....never removed from box	str ....straight
Chpndl ....Chippendale	H.......................high, height	NP ....nickel plated	sz ....size
CI ....cast iron	Hplwht ....Hepplewhite	opal.........................opalescent	trn ....turned, turning
compo....................composition	hdl, hdld............handle, handled	orig...............................original	turq ....turquoise
cr/sug ....creamer and sugar	HP ....hand painted	o/l.................................overlay	uphl ....upholstered
c/s.........................cup and saucer	illus ......illustration, illustrated by	o/w ....otherwise	VG.........................very good
cvd ....carved	imp ....impressed	Pat ....patented	Vict ....Victorian
cvg ....carving	ind ....individual	pc ....piece	W ....width
dbl..............................double	int.................................interior	ped............................pedestal	wht ....white
decor ....decoration	Invt T'print ..Inverted Thumbprint	pk ....pink	w/ ....with
dk ....dark	irid ....iridescent	pnt..................................paint	w/o ....without
Dmn Quilt ....Diamond Quilted	L...........................length, long	porc ....porcelain	X, Xd.............cross, crossed
drw ....drawer	lav ....lavender	prof ....professional	yel ....yellow
dtd ....dated	ldgl ....leaded glass	QA ....Queen Anne	(+)..............has been reproduced

A B C Plates

Children's plates featuring the alphabet as part of the design were popular from as early as 1820 until after the turn of the century. The earliest English creamware plates were decorated with embossed letters and prim moralistic verses, but the later Staffordshire products were conducive to a more relaxed mealtime atmosphere, often depicting playful animals and riddles or scenes of pleasant leisure-time activities. They were made around the turn of the century by American potters as well. All featured transfer prints, but color was sometimes brushed on by hand to add interest to the design.

Be sure to inspect these plates carefully for damage, since condition is a key price-assessing factor, and aside from obvious chips and hairlines, even wear can substantially reduce their values. Another problem for collectors is the fact that there are current reproductions of glass and tin plates, particulary the glass plate referred to as Emma (child's face in center) and a tin plate showing children with hoops. These plates are so common as to be worthless as a collectible.

For further information we recommend *A B C Plates & Mugs, Identification and Value Guide,* by Irene and Ralph Lindsay (Collector Books). Our advisor for this category is Dr. Joan George; she is listed in the Directory under New Jersey.

Ceramic

Franklin's Proverbs, Keep Thy Shop and Thy Shop Will Keep Thee, black with multicolor, Meakin, 6¼", $185.00.

Aesop's Fable, man & boy carry donkey, bl transfer, unmk, 7"....135.00
April, boy among flowers, mc transfer, unmk, 6¾" 140.00
Baby, blk transfer, Powel & Bishop, 7" 140.00
Baby Bunting Lifts..., mc transfer, DE McNicol...OH, 7", $75 to ..135.00
Boys playing marbles, mc transfer, unmk, 5½" 145.00
Bulldog, My Face Is My Fortune, bl transfer, CA & Son, 7½"....140.00
Buster Brown, mc transfer on hard paste, Germany, unmk, 7" 135.00
Camel, Wild Animals, mc transfer, BP Co, 8½" 225.00
Child on chair w/puppet, blk transfer, unmk, 6" 135.00
Children under umbrella, mc transfer, Edge Malkin & Co, 6¼".145.00
Crusoe Teaching Friday, pk transfer, BP Co, England, 6" 140.00
Dove, ABCs right of mc transfer, #154 (Brownhills Pottery), 6½" ..150.00
Dutch girls (2), mc transfer, pk lustre rim, Germany, unmk, 7" ..125.00
Evening Bathing Scene at Manhattan Beach, brn transfer, unmk, 7".135.00
Fencing, mc transfer, unmk, 7½" 300.00
Ferret, blk transfer, Wm Adams & Co, 7" 150.00
Flowers That Never Fade, Cheerfulness, blk transfer, Meakin, 5¾" ..150.00
Franklin's Proverbs, Experience Keeps, mc transfer, unmk, 5".....150.00
Franklin's Proverbs, Sloth Like Rust, brn transfer, unmk, 6⅛"....140.00
Girl w/dog & puppy, mc transfer on hard paste, Germany, unmk, 6"...120.00
Girls w/ducks, mc transfer, Elsmore & Son, England, 7" 145.00
Highland Dance, mc transfer, unmk, 5½".....................................145.00
Horse, bl transfer w/blk ABC rim, W Adams & Co, 1891, 7¼" .125.00

How Doth the Little Busy Bee..., mc transfer, unmk, 5½" 140.00
Kestrel, mc transfer, red line along rim, unmk, 7"........................140.00
Leaves w/flowers & buds, brn transfer, unmk, 5".........................130.00
Little Bo Peep, bl transfer, HC Edmiston, England, 6" 135.00
Major General NP Banks, mc transfer, unmk, 5" 300.00
Mischief, cat & papers, mc transfer, unmk, 7¼" 165.00
Nightingale, red transfer, Edge Malkin & Co, 6¼".......................130.00
Rider rents horse (in dmn reserve), bl transfer, CA & Sons, 7½" .135.00
Stag & hounds, mc transfer, unmk, 6" 150.00
Sunbonnet girls making pie crust, Smith Phillips, 7"....................125.00
There Was a Crooked Man, mc transfer, unmk, 7½" 185.00
Whittington & His Cat, mc transfer, brn ABCs, England, #75,500, 8"..230.00
Woman feeding chicken, mc transfer, red line along rim, unmk, 8"..140.00
Women on bridge, mc transfer, Edge Malkin & Co, 7" 140.00

Glass

Christmas Eve, unmk, 6", from $175 to.......................................200.00
Clock face, ABCs & numerals, scalloped rim, unmk, 7", from $50 to ..60.00
Clock face, months, days, ABCs, unmk, 7", from $50 to...............60.00
Diamond center (resembling snowflake), ABC rim, unmk, 6¼", $50 to ..60.00
Ducks, deep yel, unmk, 6", from $60 to...70.00
Fan center, scalloped rim, unmk, 6", from $65 to...........................75.00
Milk glass w/brn enameling on raised letters & beads at rim, unmk, 7"..60.00
Rooster, smooth rim, unmk, 6", from $65 to 75.00
Sancho Panza & Dapple, smooth rim, 6", from $60 to 70.00

Tin

ABCs around rim, numerals in center, mc litho, unmk, 6", from $110 to...125.00
ABCs around rim, unmk, 2¾", from $65 to...................................100.00
ABCs around rim, unmk, 6¼", from $60 to 95.00
After Supper Run a Mile, mc litho, Kemp Mfg, 6", from $150 to...200.00
General Tom Thumb, mc enamel, unmk, 3", from $200 to.........300.00
Her Majesty Queen Victoria, unmk, 8" 375.00
Hi Diddle Diddle, unmk, 8¾", from $80 to...................................100.00
Horse, unmk, 5½", from $160 to 120.00
Jumbo, unmk, 5½", from $100 to 160.00
Mary Had a Little Lamb, unmk, 7¾", from $130 to 160.00
Peter Rabbit, mc litho, unmk, 7¾", from $200 to 350.00
Victoria & Albert, unmk, 3¼", from $300 to 450.00
Who Killed Cock Robin, unmk, 7¾", from $130 to....................150.00

Abingdon

From 1934 until 1950, the Abingdon Pottery Co. of Abingdon, Ill., made a line of art pottery with a white vitrified body decorated with various types of glazes in many lovely colors. Novelties, cookie jars, utility ware, and lamps were made in addition to several lines of simple yet striking art ware. Fern Leaf, introduced in 1937, featured molded vertical feathering. La Fleur, in 1939, consisted of flowerpots and flower-arranger bowls with rows of vertical ribbing. Classic, 1939 – 40, was a line of vases, many with evidence of Chinese influence. Several marks were used, most of which employed the company name. In 1950 the company reverted to the manufacture of sanitary ware that had been their mainstay before the art ware division was formed.

Highly decorated examples and those with black, bronze, or red glaze usually command at least 25% higher prices.

For further information we recommend *Abingdon Pottery Artware 1934 – 1950, Stepchild of the Great Depression,* by Joe Paradis (Schiffer).

#030, vase, Chang, bronze...225.00
#098, figurine, upright goose, 3½" 40.00

#103, vase, Gamma, 10" 36.00
#108, vase, Delta, 8" 40.00
#112, vase, Delta, 6" 38.00
#117, vase, Classic, gr, 10" 35.00
#119, vase, Classic, 10" 30.00
#120, planter w/bow, bl 20.00
#127, bowl, Classic, 6½x14" 45.00
#133, vase, Classic, 8" 25.00
#142, vase, Classic, 5½" 30.00
#150, flowerpot, La Fleur, 4" 15.00
#152, vase, yel, 8¾" 22.00
#153, vase, Classic, 9" 30.00
#154, lamp base, Draped Shaft, 21½" 110.00
#155, vase, Classic, 9" 20.00
#158, candle holder, La Fleur, 2x3½" 14.00
#177, vase, Floral, 10" 50.00
#181, vase, Floral, 10" 50.00
#304, vase, Sang, 9½" 65.00
#307, ashtray, Abingdon, 3x8" 50.00
#310, jar, Chang, 10½" 100.00
#315, vase, Athenian, 1947, 9" 35.00
#320, vase, Tulip, 4" 45.00
#321, bookends, Cossack/Russian, blk, 6½" or 8½", pr 95.00
#326, ashtray, Greek, 3x4¼" 45.00
#337, dessert dish, Square, 5x5" 25.00
#351, vase, Capri, 5¾" 120.00
#357, vase, Salon, 14" 100.00
#367, flowerpot, Egg & Dart, 4½" 20.00
#370, bookends, Cactus, 6", pr 50.00
#374, bookend, Cactus Planter, 7" 100.00
#377, wall pocket, Morning Glory, ivory, 9x6¼" 40.00
#379, wall pocket, Daisy, 7¾" 50.00
#383, bowl, Daisy, 9½" 40.00
#389, vase, Geranium, 7" 40.00
#3906, figurine, shepherdess & faun, blk, 11½" 250.00
#393, bowl, Morning Glory, 7" 35.00
#401, vase, Box, 5½" 50.00
#408, bowl, leaf, beige, 6½" 50.00
#411, vase, Volute, 10½" 75.00
#416, figurine, peacock, 7" 95.00
#421, vase, Fern Leaf, 8¾" 50.00
#428, bookend, Fern Leaf, 5½" 45.00
#432, fruit boat, Fern Leaf, 6½x15" 50.00
#435, wall pocket, Tri-Fern, 9" 100.00
#442, vase, Laurel, 5½" 50.00
#448, window box, Sunburst, 9" L 30.00
#450, bowl, Asters, flared rim, oval, 11½" L 50.00
#453, vase, Asters, 8" 25.00
#455, vase, Asters, 11½" 35.00
#463, vase, Star, 7" 18.00
#463, vase, Star, 7½" 25.00
#466, vase, Wheel Handle, 8" 40.00
#473, bowl, Combination, 7x12" 100.00
#474, cornucopia, yel, 5½" 18.00
#481, bowl, Ivy, 7x12" 48.00
#482, dbl cornucopia, peach, 11" 50.00
#486, vase, Acanthus, silver o/l birds on peach, 11" 125.00
#489, wall pocket, Dutch Boy, 10", from $75 to 100.00
#493, wall pocket, dbl; horn shaped, 8½" 75.00
#497, figurine, Blackamoor, w/decor, 7½" 95.00
#504, vase, Shell, 7½" 25.00
#505, candle holder, Shell, dbl, 4" 20.00
#509, ashtray, elephant, 5½" 50.00
#512, vase, Swirl, gr, 9" 20.00

#514, vase, Swirl, chartreuse, 11", from $25 to 35.00
#517, vase, Arden, 7" 28.00
#520, vase, gr, 9" 25.00
#528, bowl, Hibiscus, bl, 15" 40.00
#530, bowl, Traveler's Palm, 6½x16" 40.00
#532 & #575, console set, bl, 3-pc 25.00
#536, bowl, Regency, gr, 7x9x5" 35.00
#537, vase, Tassel, 9" 50.00
#544, bowl, Streamliner, 6x9" 20.00
#552, vase, squatty, 13" 40.00
#555, ashtray, 8" dia 18.00
#559, cache pot, 5½" 25.00
#559, planter, donkey, 7½" 75.00
#562, figurine, gull, 5" 70.00
#563, urn, coral w/wht decor, 9" 35.00
#567, vase, 5" 20.00
#568, mint compote, pk, ftd, 1942-47, 6" dia 25.00
#571, figurine, goose, blk, 5" 30.00
#573, figurine, penguin, decor, 5½" 30.00
#575, candle holders, dbl, 5", pr 20.00
#581, vase, dbl cornucopia; bl, 8½" 40.00
#587, wall pocket, Cherub, 7½" 60.00
#594, vase, Hour Glass, 9" 32.00
#596, vase, sea horse 50.00
#600, vase, Laurel, 12", from $45 to 50.00
#616D, vase, Cactus, w/sleeping Mexican man, 6½" 38.00
#629, vase, Poppy, 6½" 30.00
#630, vase, hdld, 9", from $25 to 30.00
#634, vase, Heirloom, 6½" 45.00
#639, vase, Calla, 8½" 35.00
#647, urn, 13½" 50.00
#654, vase, Tulip, 6½" 20.00
#657, figurine, swordfish, 4½" 50.00
#659, vase, Hackney, 8½" 30.00
#675D, wall pocket, matchbox form, 5½" 50.00
#681/#682, sugar bowl & creamer, Daisy, from $40 to 45.00
#685, bowl, Ribbed, 13¾" 20.00
#698, vase, Chinese Terrace, 6" 40.00
#706, vase, Oak Leaf, 9¼" 40.00
#711, wall vase, carriage lamp, 10" 35.00
#99, figurine, leaning goose, 1948-50, 2½" 40.00

Cookie jar, #674, Pumpkin, minimum value $325.00. (Photo courtesy Joyce Roerig)

Cookie jar, #471, Old Lady, decor, minimum value 300.00
Cookie jar, #495, Fat Boy 250.00
Cookie jar, #549, Hippo, decor, 1942 ....250.00
Cookie jar, #588, Money Bag 75.00
Cookie jar, #602, Hobby Horse 185.00
Cookie jar, #611, Jack-in-Box 275.00
Cookie jar, #622, Miss Muffet 205.00
Cookie jar, #651, Choo Choo (Locomotive) 150.00
Cookie jar, #653, Clock, 1949 ....100.00

Cookie jar, #663, Humpty Dumpty, decor 250.00
Cookie jar, #664, Pineapple 95.00
Cookie jar, #665, Wigwam 250.00
Cookie jar, #677, Daisy, 1949..50.00
Cookie jar, #678, Windmill, from $200 to 225.00
Cookie jar, #693, Little Girl, from $60 to...............................75.00
Cookie jar, #694, Bo Peep, from $250 to...............................275.00
Cookie jar, #695, Mother Goose, from $295 to 295.00
Cookie jar, #696, Three Bears, from $90 to 100.00

Adams

Wm. Adams, whose potting skills were developed under the tutelage of Josiah Wedgwood, founded the Greengates Pottery at Tunstall, England, in 1769. Many types of wares including basalt, ironstone, parian, and jasper were produced; and various impressed or printed marks were employed. Until 1800 'Adams Co.' or 'Adams' impressed in block letters identified the company's earthenwares and a fine type of jasper similar in color and decoration to Wedgwood's. The latter mark was used again from 1845 to 1864 on parian figures. Most examples of their product found on today's market are transfer-printed dinnerwares with ornate backstamps which often include the pattern name and the initials 'W.A. & S.' This type of product was made from 1820 until about 1920. After 1890 the word 'England' was included in the mark; 'Tunstall' was added after 1896. From 1914 through 1940, a printed crown with 'Adams, Estbd 1657, England,' identified their products. From 1900 to 1965, they produced souvenir plates with transfers of American scenes, many of which were marketed in this country by Roth Importers of Peoria, Illinois. In 1965 the company affiliated with Wedgwood. Although there were other Adams potteries in Staffordshire, their marks incorporate either the first name initial or a partner's name and so are easily distinguished from those of this company.

See also Adams Rose; Flow Blue; Spatter; Staffordshire; Tea Leaf.

Pitcher,   Dellarobia,
two-quart, $85.00.
(Photo courtesy Dave Boykin)

Cup & saucer, Cyrene, pk transfer, NM 95.00
Cup plate, courting couple, lav transfer, 4½", NM 35.00
Plate, Andalusia, pk transfer, mk, ca 1830, 8", M 145.00
Plate, China Bird, bl transfer, ca 1913, tab hdls, 2x9x10", NM.....90.00
Plate, China Bird, bl transfer, 10", NM 50.00
Plate, Cupid & Psyche, bl transfer, scalloped, 9", NM...............275.00
Plate, General Captured..., red transfer, train on tracks, 10½"......75.00
Plate, Isola Bella, bl transfer, ladies in classical garden, 9", NM....45.00
Plate, Pickwick Papers, Sam Weller, 9½", NM 60.00
Platter, Blue Willow, bl transfer, 13½", M 100.00
Platter, Fairy Villas, 16" L, M..250.00
Teapot, Tower, pk, dolphin hdl, 7¼" 250.00

Adams, Matthew

In the 1950s a trading post located in Alaska contacted Sascha Brastoff to design a line of porcelain with scenes of Eskimos, Alaskan motifs, and animals indigenous to that country. These items were to be sold in Alaska to the tourist trade.

Brastoff selected Matthew Adams to design the Alaska series. Pieces from the line he produced have the Sascha B mark on the front; some have a pattern number on the reverse. They did not have the rooster backstamp. (See the Sascha Brastoff category for information on this mark.)

After the Alaska series was introduced and proved to be successful, Matthew Adams left the employment of Sascha Brastoff and opened his own studio. Pieces made in his studio are signed Matthew Adams in script and may have the word Alaska on the front. Where his studio (or studios) was located is unknown at the present time, but a 'Made in Alaska' paper label has been found, suggesting that he may have worked from that location. Our advisor for this category is Marty Webster; he is listed in the Directory under Michigan. Feel free to contact Mr. Webster if you have any further information.

Ashtray, Eskimo face, hollow star shape, 13" 75.00
Ashtray, Eskimo family, 8½" 40.00
Ashtray, Husky, 13x10" 40.00
Ashtray, Walrus, star shape, walrus, 10x12" 95.00
Ashtray, Walrus on gr, 6" dia...25.00
Bowl, console; Glacier on bl, 12x20"..................................165.00
Bowl, Eskimo on blk, 9" 45.00
Bowl, Grizzly Bear on brn, free-form, 6½" L 55.00
Bowl, Husky, 6"...40.00
Bowl, Igloo & Dog, #138 boat shape, 9½" 50.00
Bowl, Polar Bear on gr, free-form, 7½" L..............................50.00
Bowl, Ram on gr, free-form, 7" 55.00
Bowl, Seal, oval, 9"..50.00
Bowl, Seal on blk, free-form, w/lid, #145, 7½" L 75.00
Bowl, Walrus, yel, w/lid, 7" 75.00
Bowl, Walrus & Glacier on brn, free-form, 8"........................65.00
Bowl, Walrus on blk, free-form, #104, 6½" L 50.00
Box, Glacier on bl, w/lid, 12" 95.00
Box, Seal, wht, 2¼x6"...50.00
Charger, Caribou on dk bl, 18"...150.00
Charger, Eskimo w/Harpoon, 16" 135.00
Charger, Walrus on dk bl, 17"...150.00
Coffeepot, Ram on gr, 11½", +6 4½" mugs...........................180.00
Cookie jar, Mother & Child on brn 75.00
Creamer, Polar Bear on blk 35.00
Cup & saucer, Sled on bl...25.00
Dish, Eskimo Lady on gr, elbow shape, 12" 50.00
Ginger jar, Seal on brn/wht, #095, 6½" 45.00
Humidor, Seal on gr, #025, 5¾" 85.00
Jar, Eskimo on ice bl, 6" 30.00
Jar, Eskimo woman on brn, w/lid, 7½" 50.00
Jar, Polar Bear on gr, w/lid, 7½" 65.00
Jar, Walrus on lt bl, w/lid, #1492, 7½" 50.00
Lighter, Glacier, 6" 40.00
Mug, Husky, #112A, 4½x4¾" 45.00
Pitcher, Eskimo, 13" 90.00
Pitcher, Eskimo Mother & Child, 13", +6 5½" mugs 195.00
Pitcher, Grizzly Bear, 11", +6 4" tumblers............................200.00
Pitcher, Husky, wht on teal, bulbous, 5" 65.00
Plate, Eskimo Girl, #162, 7½"..30.00
Platter, House, 12"...45.00
Pot, Walrus, w/lid, 12" 55.00
Shakers, Rams on gr, 4", pr..40.00
Tankard, Man on brn, 19", +6 mugs...................................250.00
Tankard, Polar Bear on blk, w/lid, 13" 200.00
Teapot, Walrus on ice bl, 6½"..75.00

Tile, Eskimo Mother & Child, 12¾x10½"......................125.00
Tile, Mountains & Glacier on blk, 10x8½".....................75.00
Tile, Walrus on bl, 10x8½"...75.00
Tumbler, Cabin...20.00
Vase, Glacier on gray, #143, 5½"................................50.00
Vase, House on yel, 11½"...100.00
Vase, Iceberg on gray, 7"...40.00
Vase, Mother & Child on teal, cylindrical, 17"............165.00
Vase, Mountain & Glacier on blk, #114, 12"..................80.00
Vase, Polar Bear on gr, 10"......................................100.00
Vase, Reindeer, 4½"..45.00
Vase, Sea Lion & Seaweed, oval, #128, 8"....................95.00
Vase, Seal & Glacier on brn, free-form, #911, 11"........125.00
Vase, Walrus on ice on bl, 10"..................................110.00

Adams Rose, Early and Late

In the second quarter of the nineteenth century, the Adams and Son Pottery produced a line of hand-painted dinnerware decorated in large, red brush-stroke roses with green leaves on whiteware, which collectors call Adams Rose. Later, G. Jones and Son (and possibly others) made a similar ware with less brilliant colors on a gray-white surface.

Note: Early English dinnerware values have softened considerably due to the influence of the Internet which makes good examples that once were hard to find much more accessible. Unless otherwise noted, our values are for items in mint condition or nearly so; be sure to discount prices for damage.

Creamer, late, 4½" 135.00
Pitcher, water; late, 3-color, emb at spout/hdl, 7½".....300.00
Plate, early, scalloped rim, ca 1825, 9", M.................150.00
Plate, late, scalloped rim, mk, ca 1840, 8½", M..........135.00
Plate, scalloped rim, early, 10¾", VG.........................45.00
Plate, scalloped rim w/beaded band, 10½", EX.............65.00
Plate, stick spatter, mk England, lion/unicorn crest, 7".......65.00
Saucer, red/gr/bl w/red rim band, England, 6"............30.00
Wash bowl & pitcher, early, prof rstr, 12", 4½x13½"..........2,100.00
Waste bowl, early, no mk, 3¼x6½", EX.......................85.00

Advertising

The advertising world has always been a fiercely competitive field. In an effort to present their product to the customer, every imaginable gimmick was put into play. Colorful and artfully decorated signs and posters, thermometers, tape measures, fans, hand mirrors, and attractive tin containers (all with catchy slogans, familiar logos, and often-bogus claims) are only a few of the many examples of early advertising memorabilia that are of interest to today's collectors.

Porcelain signs were made as early as 1890 and are highly prized for their artistic portrayal of life as it was then . . . often allowing amusing insights into the tastes, humor, and way of life of a bygone era. As a general rule, older signs are made from a heavier gauge metal. Those with three or more fired-on colors are especially desirable.

Tin containers were used to package consumer goods ranging from crackers and coffee to tobacco and talcum. After 1880 can companies began to decorate their containers by the method of lithography. Though colors were still subdued, intricate designs were used to attract the eye of the consumer. False labeling and unfounded claims were curtailed by the Pure Food and Drug Administration in 1906, and the name of the manufacturer as well as the brand name of the product had to be printed on the label. By 1910 color was rampant with more than a dozen hues printed on the tin or on paper labels. The tins themselves were often designed with a second use in mind, such as canisters, lunch boxes, even toy trains. As a general rule, tobacco-related tins are the most desirable, though personal preference may direct the interest of the collector to peanut butter pails with illustrations of children, or talcum tins with irresistible babies or beautiful ladies. Coffee tins are popular, as are those made to contain a particularly successful or well-known product.

Perhaps the most visual of the early advertising gimmicks were the character logos, the Fairbank Company's Gold Dust Twins, the goose trademark of the Red Goose Shoe Company, Nabisco's ZuZu Clown and Uneeda Kid, the Campbell Kids, the RCA dog Nipper, and Mr. Peanut, to name only a few. Many early examples of these bring high prices on the market today.

Our listings are alphabetized by product name or, in lieu of that information, by word content or other pertinent description. When no condition is indicated, the items listed below are assumed to be in excellent condition, except glass and ceramic items, which are assumed mint. Remember that condition greatly affects value (especially true for tin items). For instance, a sign in excellent or mint condition may bring twice as much as the same one in only very good condition, sometimes even more. On today's market, items in good to very good condition are slow to sell, unless they are extremely rare. Mint (or near-mint) examples are high.

We have several advertising advisors; see specific subheadings. For further information we recommend *General Store Collectibles I* and *II* by David L. Wilson; *Hake's Price Guide to Character Toys, 3rd Edition*, by Ted Hake; *Advertising Thermometers* by Curtis Merritt; *Victorian Trade Cards* by Dave Cheadle; *Advertising Character Collectibles* by Warren Dotz; *Value Guide to Advertising Memorabilia, Second Edition*, by B.J. Summers; *The World of Beer Memorabilia* by Herb and Helon Haydock; and *Encyclopedia of Advertising Tins, Vol. II*, by David Zimmerman. *Huxford's Collectible Advertising* and *Garage Sale and Flea Market Annual* by Sharon and Bob Huxford are other good references. All of these books are available at your local bookstore or from Collector Books. See also Advertising Dolls; Advertising Cards; Automobilia; Coca-Cola; Banks; Calendars; Cookbooks; Paperweights; Posters; Sewing Items.

Key:
cb — cardboard
cl — celluloid
fs — flange sign
lcs — litho on canvas sign

pp — pre-prohibition
ps — porcelain sign
tc — tin container
ts — tin sign

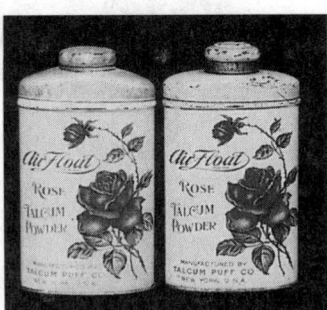

Air-Float Rose, tin container, Talcum Puff Co, NY, 4¾", from $25.00 to $30.00 each.
(Courtesy Bill and June Mason)

Adam's Blackjack Chewing Gum, ts, dc stand-up, elephant, 1916, 10", G...1,300.00
Adams' Tutti Frutti Pepsin Gum, sign, cb dc, Victorian lady, 14", VG.550.00
Adriance Platt & Co, sign, paper, lady/vignettes, 1904, 29x21", EX 950.00
Amaco Gas, blotter, Watch Him Grow in '41, 2½x5⅜", EX 15.00
Angelus Marshmallows, tape measure, cl, 1¼" dia, NM+ 75.00
Anheuser-Busch, sign, rvpt, On Draught, eagle logo, 10" dia, VG...900.00
Anheuser-Busch, tray, cherubs/logo, oval, 14x17", EX+...........1,000.00
Anheuser-Busch, tray, factory, hops/logo rim, oval, 15x18", G+ .650.00
Apache Trail Cigars, tc, 6x5½x4¼", EX 650.00
Araban Coffee, tc, 1929, 6", EX+ 300.00
Armour's Veribest Dried Beef, sign, tin/cb, casserole, 9x13", EX.180.00
Atlantic White Lead, string holder, boy on swing, 1925, 26x14", NM .5,200.00

Aunt Jemima Butter Lite, clipboard, yel, for store use, unused, M .75.00
Aunt Jemima Pancake Flour, sign, dc cb, holding plate, 16", VG .200.00
Aunt Jemima Pancake Flour/Self-Rising/Ready Mix, cb stand-up, 20", VG...375.00
Ayer's Cherry Pectoral, sign, dc stand-up, St Nick, 1890s, 13", EX ...1,050.00
Baker's Delight Baking Powder, tc, paper label, ring hdls, 14", G .80.00
Baker's Nursery Talcum Powder, tc, baby on stork, 6", EX+ 470.00
Banner Cigars, dice shaker w/5 miniature bone dice, 1¼", EX+ .150.00
Barq's, menu board, tin, red/wht/blk, 28x20", NM...........................90.00
Bartholomay Beers Ales & Porter, tip tray, C Shonk litho, 4" dia, EX.130.00
Bartlett Spring Mineral Water, tray, deer/bottle, 13" dia, NM 475.00
Bayer Asprin, display, asprin form, plaster, 7" dia, NM 50.00
Bayer Asprin, sign, dc cb trifold, exotic woman, 34x42", VG 160.00
BB French Corsets, sign, cb, shows 2 corsets, 1875-90, 10x15", NM ..600.00
Beechnut Chewing Gum, valentine, mechanical, 5x7", EX+ 55.00
Beeman's Pepsin Gum, sign, emb dc sf cb, lady in profile, 18x14", NM..3,600.00
Bettendorf Wagons, ashtray, tin, HD Beach litho, 1902, 3x5", NM..110.00
Blue Ribbon Coffee, tc, 2½-lb, 7¼", EX+ 525.00
Borden's Milk & Ice Cream, clock, Elsie in daisy, 21" dia, VG...150.00
Boston Belting Co, sign, paper, factory/vignettes, 18x13", EX 400.00
Bradshaw's 3 Bears Honey, tc, pry lid, 1949, 5-lb, EX+ 50.00
Breakfast Call Coffee, tc, rnd, slip lid, red/wht/gold, 9", EX........150.00
Budweiser, sign, rvpt, We Feature...Bottled Beer, red, 11" dia, NM..135.00
Buell's Brighton Blend Coffee, tc, paper label, screw lid, 6", G...160.00
Buffalo ALO Paints, ps, wht lettering on blk, 1905, 7x46", NM+ ..275.00
Bull Dog Cut Plug, match holder, dc tin, bulldog image, 6½", G+.135.00
Bull Dog Smoking De Luxe, pocket container, cb, vertical, EX+ ..700.00

Buster Brown

Buster Brown was the creation of cartoonist Richard Felton; his comic strip first appeared in the *New York Herald* on May 4, 1902. Since then Buster and his dog Tige (short for Tiger) have adorned sundry commercial products but are probably best known as the trademark for the Brown Shoe Company established early in this century. Today hundreds of Buster Brown premiums, store articles, and advertising items bring substantial prices from many serious collectors.

Shoe stand, tin litho diecut counter display, 13x8", EX+, $3,000.00. (Photo courtesy Buffalo Bay Auction Co.)

Display figure, compo, Buster (in store clothes)/Tige on base, 19", VG .225.00
Pin-bk button, BB Bread, Resolved That the Best Bread..., 1½", EX 25.00
Pin-bk button, BB Hose Supporter, Whitehead & Hoag, ⅞", VG...10.00
Pocket mirror, The Little Girl on the Other Side..., 1¾" dia, G.150.00
Shoe stretcher, plastic, figural, spring-loaded, 5x9" L, G 15.00
Sign, light-up, America's Favorite..., Buster/Tige, 6x15", EX 200.00
Sign, silk-screened cloth image of Buster/Tige on dc wood, 20", EX .350.00
Sign, tin, Authorized...Dealer, Buster & Tige portrait, 14x15", G+ 60.00
Sign, tin, Branch of Golden Sheaf Bakery/BB Bread/images, 29x28", G..350.00
Whistle, cylindrical, wht w/graphics, 1¼", VG 42.00

Whistle, tin keyhole shape, yel w/graphics, 1½", EX 42.00

Cadette Talcum Powder, tc, tin soldier figure, 7", EX..................140.00
Calumet Baking Powder, clock, Regulator, Sessions, 39x16", G .400.00
Calumet Baking Powder, table, child's; porc top/wood legs, 18", G 650.00
Candee Rubbers, sign, dc cb hanger, girl in hammock, 12x27", EX ..2,500.00
Chase & Sanborn's Coffee, milk pail, wht on red, bail hdl, 4-lb, VG ..130.00
Chauncy Olcott Cigar, blotter, It's Quality..., 3¾x8", EX 40.00
Cherry Blossom, bottle topper, girl's head in dc cherry blossom, NM...135.00
Chicklets Chewing Gum, ts, dc stand-up, raccoon, 1916, 10", G......2,300.00
Colgans Taffy Tolu, jar, emb glass, smiling man finial, 11", NM .260.00
Colgate's Talc Powder, sign, paperboard, Violet tin on blk, 18", VG+ .120.00
Colonial Club 5¢ Cigars, fs, steel, 2-sided, red/wht/bl, 9x19", EX 180.00
Comfort Talcum Powder, tc, baby/nurse, dtd 1891, 4x2½" dia, EX+.425.00
Continental Cubes Pipe Tobacco, pocket mirror, cl, oval, VG ...130.00
Continental Ins, sign, paper, 3 sections/3 scenes, fr, 35x69", VG..1,450.00
Continental Life Ins Co of New York, sign, paper, soldier, 32x25", NM.925.00
Corn King Manure Spreaders, poster, 2 scenes/2 spreaders, 26x20", G ...500.00
Cross-Country Bottled Beer, ts, hunt scene, oval hanger, 16x20", VG+.325.00
Daisy Air Rifles, poster, kid w/rifle & flag, 1911, 22x14", EX+...4,150.00
Daisy Air Rifles, poster, Two Daisies, 23x16", NM 4,200.00
Dead Shot Powder, sign, cb stand-up, bird hunt scene, 11x19", EX+...525.00
DeKalb, weather vane, emb dc tin corncob w/wings, 8x18", NM...50.00
DeLaval, match safe, separator form, dtd 1908, 7", MIB 380.00
Derby's Peter Pan Peanut Butter, sample tin, 2-oz, EX+ 70.00
Diamond Book Matches, dispenser, 2 For 1¢, metal, Pat 1928, 13", VG ...200.00
Diamond Cleaners, Scotty dog vase giveaway, ca 1920-30, 5", NM+ 180.00
Diamond Dyes, cabinet, wood/tin front (lady dying clothes), 30", EX ..1,200.00
Diplomat Whiskey, pocket knife, emb metal, 3¼", NM..............185.00
Dixie Kid Cut Plug, lunch box, Black child, 4x8x5", EX+ 325.00
Dolly Madison Ice Cream, automated doll in cloth dress, 39", VG ..1,000.00
Domestic Sewing Machine, The Little Savage (island girl), 32x18", NM ..480.00
Double Cola, menu board, tin, red oval logo on gr, 28x20", VG ..70.00
Double Cola, ts, Drink... on yel sunburst on red, diagonal, 45", VG...150.00

Dr. Pepper

A young pharmacist, Charles C. Alderton, was hired by W.B. Morrison, owner of Morrison's Old Corner Drug Store in Waco, Texas, around 1884. Alderton, an observant sort, noticed that the drugstore's patrons could never quite make up their minds as to which flavor of extract to order. He concocted a formula that combined many flavors, and Dr. Pepper was born. The name was chosen by Morrison in honor of a beautiful young girl with whom he had once been in love. The girl's father, a Virginia doctor by the name of Pepper, had discouraged the relationship due to their youth, but Morrison had never forgotten her. On December 1, 1885, a U.S. patent was issued to the creators of Dr. Pepper. Our advisor for Dr. Pepper is Craig Stifter; he is listed in the Directory under Illinois. See also Soda Fountain Collectibles.

Art plate, frontal portrait, decorative rim, 10" dia, G.................650.00
Clock, Good for Life! logo, Telechron (not a light-up), 15" dia, EX+...250.00
Clock, 10-2-4 bottle cap, emb tin, 18½" dia, NM 450.00
Clock, 10-2-4 bottle cap light-up, plastic front, 12" dia, VG 150.00
Match holder, tin, gr, 6", EX 80.00
Pencil holder, ceramic dispenser, wht w/gold trim, 1970s, NM+...60.00
Sign, cb, Certainly!, lady at football game, sf, 19x32", NM 400.00
Sign, cb, I'd Give.../WWII tank soldier, sf, 19x29", EX..............350.00
Sign, cb, Join Me!, girl in car, 28x21", NM...............................350.00
Sign, cb, Smart Lift, girl w/dog, wood fr, 21x33", EX+ 250.00
Sign, paper, Frosty Man Frosty!, lady w/groceries, 1957, 15x25", NM...30.00

Sign, porc, Drink DP on red, wht sf border, 9x24", EX..................**65.00**
Sign, porc, 10-2-4 disk w/DP center band, red/wht, 10" dia, NM..**225.00**
Sign, tin, Drink A-Bite To Eat/logo/At 10-2-4 on yel, 4x19", NM+...**160.00**
Sign, tin, 10-2-4 clock/tilted bottle/logo on yel, sf, 54x18", G+ .**225.00**
Thermometer, bottle cap, plastic, 10-2-4 logo, wht, 11 dia, NM ...**150.00**
Thermometer, dial, Hot or Cold, oval logo, 18" dia, EX+ **175.00**
Thermometer, tin, Hot or Cold, oval logo, red, 27", EX **200.00**

Duke's Best Cigarettes, sign, paper, lady standing w/fan, 47x16", VG..**1,230.00**
DuPont, letter opener, emb aluminum, 9", EX+ **100.00**
DuPont, spoon, sterling, trap shooting, mk Tiffany, EX+ **145.00**
DuPont, stickpin, figural dog, ca 1880-90, 2¼", EX+ **190.00**
DuPont, ts, Generations, Edw H Osthaus art, sf, 1903, 33x23", NM+....**1,350.00**
Dutch Boy White Lead, statue, papier-mache figure w/bucket, 28", EX ...**650.00**
Dutch Masters Paints, sign, porc, trademark image, 26" dia, VG...**325.00**
Edison Mazda Lamps, playhouse, cb, ca 1930, 9½x5x8", EX+ **65.00**
Edward F Heidenreich & Sons Leather, blotter, No Stares, Elvgren, EX ..**10.00**
Elkins Brewing Co, mug, wht ceramic bbl form, 1-pt, EX+.........**375.00**
Emilia Garcia, trifold, paper on cb, 3 scenes, 1930, 42x31", EX+ ...**135.00**
Everready, poster, man/2 kids at globe, ca 1930, 33x22", VG.....**175.00**
Fairy Soap, trolley sign, cb, For Toilet & Bath 5¢, 11x21", EX+.**200.00**
Falstaff Beer, An Old Friend!, Irene Patten art, 10x21", EX..........**70.00**
Fast Mail, pocket tin, flat, Pat'd 1878,½x3½x2¼", EX **250.00**
Fast Mail Tobacco, pail, red, Ginna litho, 5", NM **2,225.00**
Federal Cartridge, cb stand-up, 3 dogs, Rosseau art, 22x28", EX+ ..**575.00**
Fitch's Standard Heart Chewing Gum, sign, cb, lady/roses, 11x8", EX..**425.00**
Flec Bros Co, ashtray, CI, Indian head on rnd dish, 6x4", NM+.**165.00**
Fort Pitt Coffee, tc, red/wht/gold, 5½", VG+................................**425.00**
Freihoffer's Quality Cakes, cabinet, tin/glass, 22x17x15", EX+ ...**500.00**
Gallagher & Burton Fine Whiskey, ashtray, tin litho, 4½" dia, EX+ .**80.00**
Gibson Rye Whiskey, paperweight, glass, 5 dice inside, 3", EX...**170.00**
Gold Dust, ts, Let the Gold Dust Twins Do Your Work, 5x28", M ..**550.00**
Gold Dust Scouring Cleanser, tc, unopened, 4½", EX+ **50.00**
Gold Shield Coffee, sailboat, wood hull/metal keel/cl sail, 6", EX.....**180.00**
Golden West Brewing Co, tray, factory scene, 1911-20, 13" dia, EX+...**500.00**
Grain Belt Beer, cb, hunt scene, JF Kernan art, 1947, 24x27", NM ..**250.00**
Green River Soda, display, bottle on ad card, 11¼", EX+ **65.00**
Green River Whiskey, blotter, Blots Out All Your Troubles, 4x10", VG ..**25.00**
Green River Whiskey, blotter, ca 1899, unused, 4x10, NM+ **80.00**
Greensmith's Derby Dog Biscuits, sign, cb, circus, 1920s, 19x24", NM...**535.00**
Guardian Assurance Co of London, page mark, litho tin, 12", EX ..**75.00**
Hamm's Beer, display, keg/roll-over paper signs, light-up, 9" L, NM ...**110.00**
Harvey's Coffee, sign, rvpt hanger, red/gold, 6x11", NM+ **170.00**
Heath & Milligan Paints, tip tray, C Shonk litho, 4" dia, EX.....**210.00**
Heinz's Keystone Pickles, sign, emb cb, blk ground, 4x11", NM+....**170.00**
Highland Brand Evaporated Cream, sign, dc cb razor, 1903, 15", NM..**4,200.00**

Hires

Charles E. Hires, a drugstore owner in Philadelphia, became interested in natural teas. He began experimenting with roots and herbs and soon developed his own special formula. Hires introduced his product to his own patrons and began selling concentrated syrup to other soda fountains and grocery stores. Samples of his 'root beer' were offered for the public's approval at the 1876 Philadelphia Centennial. Today's collectors are often able to date their advertising items by observing the Hires boy on the logo. From 1891 to 1906, he wore a dress. From 1906 until 1914, he was shown in a bathrobe; and from 1915 until 1926, he was depicted in a dinner jacket. The apostrophe may or may not appear in the Hires name; this seems to have no bearing on dating an item. Our advisor for Hires is Craig Stifter; he is listed in the Directory under Illinois. See also Soda Fountain Collectibles.

Booklet, The Hires Story, 10x7", EX..**600.00**
Bottle, amber glass, emb around bottom, orig stopper, 9", EX **75.00**
Bottle, clear glass, Hires emb on bottom, orig stopper, 11", EX.....**50.00**
Bottle, syrup; red Hires on wht label w/gold border, w/lid, 12", EX ..**1,300.00**
Bottle carrier, aluminum case w/rod dividers, open hdls, 12x17", EX....**125.00**
Bottle opener, litho tin, It's Pure/Say Hires in blk on yel, 3", EX...**575.00**
Bottle topper, dc cb, 3-bottle, R-J logo/For All Occasions, 12", VG ..**25.00**
Checkerboard, cb, It Pays To Sell It, pointing kid, 12x12", EX ..**300.00**
Dispenser, china bbl, Drink Hires 5¢, w/spigot, dtd 1908, 15", EX ..**2,300.00**
Dispenser, wooden keg w/brass bands & ft, 5¢ sign, 26", EX.......**900.00**
Door push, metal, bottle on bl/wht stripes, 13½x2½", VG.........**180.00**
Door push, tin, tilted bottle/text on yel, 11x3", EX **375.00**
Drinking glass, tapered, etched, Hires/Champagne/Ginger Ale, 3", EX..**750.00**
Drinking glass, thick stem, etched, Hires Ginger Champanade, 5", EX..**600.00**
Festoon, bottles flanking scrolled banner w/R-J logo, 111x49", EX..**400.00**
Festoon, What More Could You Ask, winter girl, 11x50", G......**800.00**
Jug holder, metal counter model w/emb emblem, 12x5" dia, EX.**200.00**
Menu board, tin chalkboard, R-J logo/Ice Cold 5¢ Bottles, 29", NM...**350.00**
Mug, ceramic, Mettlach #3095, kid pointing, 4½", EX+.............**375.00**
Napkin, kid pointing flanked by 5¢/Hires script border, fr, 14x14", EX.**700.00**
Sign, cb, bottle shape (str, w/paper label), 2-sided, 11", EX **200.00**
Sign, cb, Drink...Delicious- Bracing-, bottle/glass, 11", EX **250.00**
Sign, cb, Enjoy Hires, lady on red, sgn Bradshaw Crandell, 11x8", EX.**700.00**
Sign, cb dc, Victorian couple at fountain table, 1915, 29x20", EX.**2,750.00**
Sign, glass light-up, Drink...Here/check-mark logo, 17" dia, EX.....**2,500.00**
Sign, paper, Say: Drink Hires 5¢, wht on red, early, 4x16", NM .**550.00**
Sign, paper, Thirst Gently Suffocated.../Josh Slinger, 7x11", EX ...**350.00**
Sign, rvpt, Hires R-J logo on gold crinkled ground, 12x16"VG **1,050.00**
Sign, rvpt, Hires Root Beer, wht/gold on blk, chain border, 3x6", EX ...**1,350.00**
Sign, tin, ...For Pleasure & Thirst, tilted bottle, 18x55", EX.......**750.00**
Sign, tin dc, kid pointing, Drink...It's Pure, chain hanger, 8", EX..**20,000.00**
Straw dispenser, CI, Drink Hires (cut-out letters), 1911, 6x10x5", EX..**5,250.00**
Straw dispenser, CI, ftd, 4 litho ads, 1911, 6x10x5", EX........**13,750.00**
String holder, R-J logo, 12" dia, EX..**800.00**

Thermometer, tin diecut, minor spotting, 28½", EX+, $150.00. (Photo courtesy Buffalo Bay Auction Co.)

Trade card, Put Roses in Your Cheeks, lady w/roses, 5x3", EX **90.00**
Trade card, Say Mama I Want Another Glass of..., kid, 5x3", EX.....**250.00**
Tray, Drink Hires, portrait/wood-grain, Haskell Coffin, 13x10", EX .**600.00**
Tray, Hires to Your Health, kid on blk w/red rim, 13" dia, EX .**2,200.00**
Tray, Hires 5¢, sgn Josh Slinger w/image, dtd 1915, 13" dia, EX ..**1,300.00**
Tray, Say: Drink Hires Root Beer 5¢, kid pointing, 12" dia, EX ...**2,750.00**

Hoosier Beer, ts on cb, fisherman in boat, Am Art Works, 15x13", EX..**600.00**
Horlicks Malted Milk Mirror, pocket mirror, 2" dia, VG+ **110.00**
Huntley & Palmers Biscuits, ts, beach scene, 29x24", G.............**425.00**

Ideal Chocolate & Cocoa, tip tray, 3¼x2½", EX.............................**90.00**

Infallible Smokeless, sign, paper, ducks in mist, 1920s, 25x15", EX **775.00**

Ingersoll Dollar Stropping Outfit, sign, cb dc stand-up, man, 8", EX..**200.00**

Interwoven Socks, dc cb stand-up, Santa on ladder, 1934, 32", EX **425.00**

Iroquois Beer/Ale, clock, 2-sided light-up, 15" dia, NM..............**800.00**

JA Folger & Co/Young Hyson Tea, store bin, tin, ornate, 20", EX ..**1,900.00**

Jap Rose Soap, tip tray, tin, kids bathing doll, 4" dia, EX+ **235.00**

JC Stevens/Old Judson, match holder, tin litho, 5", NM+..........**450.00**

John Deere, sign, paper, stag pulling carriage, fr, 24x32", EX+ ..**1,600.00**

Jumbo Peanut Butter, bank/jar, green glass elephant, 3½-oz, EX+ **350.00**

Kayo, menu board, tin chalkboard, Tops in Taste, yel top, 27", NM...**100.00**

Kayo, sign, ts, Tops..., boy pointing/bottle, red/yel, 14x27", NM ...**200.00**

King Cole Tea & Coffee, ps, keyhole shape, king w/cup, 15x9", VG...**1,300.00**

Kirk's Soap, shipping box, wood, stamped graphics, 8x16x20", EX ...**50.00**

Kis-Me Gum, sign, emb dc cb depicting lady, fr, 18x13", G **500.00**

Kondon's Catarrhal Jelly, thermometer, wood, yel, 24x6", EX+ ..**170.00**

Kool Cigarettes, sign, dc cb stand-up, Willie/trumpet, 13", NM+ **115.00**

La Flor De Carvalho Havana Cigars, ts, portrait on brn, 15x21", EX....**120.00**

Laflin & Rand Smokeless Powder, sign, paper, man w/gun, 14x9", NM...**525.00**

Lash's Kidney & Liver Bitters, cribbage board, wood, 13", EX+ **80.00**

Lash's Kidney & Liver Bitters, sign, dc cb stand-up, puppy, 7", EX+...**110.00**

LC Smith Gun, paperweight, glass, gun graphic, 1x2½x4", EX+....**375.00**

League Brand Tomatoes w/Puree, tc, ball player, 4½", EX...........**400.00**

Lily White Flour, ts, emb, curved, detailed, red/wht/bl, 36", VG+....**4,800.00**

Love Tobacco, sign, paper, Yankee & Reb trading, fr, VG **3,500.00**

Loylhanna Brewing Co, ts, factory & corner scenes, fr, 35x47", EX..**3,200.00**

Lucky Strike, pocket mirror, cigarette pack, 1938, 3x2", NM **190.00**

Magnolia Motor Oil/Gasoline, watch fob, enameled brass, 1½", NM..**300.00**

Marlin, poster, canoe scene, PR Goodwin art, 1907, 24x14", EX+ ...**1,950.00**

Marlin, sign, paper, hunter in woolie chaps, 24x14", EX+ **1,750.00**

Master Mason Smoking Tobacco, pocket tin, vertical, bl, 4½", EX...**925.00**

McLaughlin's Coffee, store bin, tin, slant top, 19x17x13", G+ ...**220.00**

Missing Miss 5¢ Cigar, tray, Viola, rolled edge, 1908, 15x15", EX ..**600.00**

Model Smoking Tobacco, ts, mc Indian on blk, 15x6", EX+.......**185.00**

Morton's Salt, display container, 1911, 5½x3", NM+....................**40.00**

Mountain Maid Coffee, tc, paper label, pry lid, 1-lb, EX+ **1,500.00**

Moxie

The Moxie Company was organized in 1884 by George Archer of Boston, Massachusetts. It was at first touted as a 'nerve food' to improve the appetite, promote restful sleep, and in general to make one 'feel better'! Emphasis was soon shifted, however, to the good taste of the brew, and extensive advertising campaigns rivaling those of such giant competitors as Coca-Cola and Hires resulted in successful marketing through the 1930s. Today the term Moxie has become synonymous with courage and audacity, traits displayed by the company who dared compete with such well-established rivals. Our advisor for Moxie is Craig Stifter; he is listed in the Directory under Illinois.

Display bottle, 3-D wood w/paper label, 36", VG....................**1,300.00**

Match holder, dc litho tin bottle, EX+..**550.00**

Sign, tin, Of Course You'll Have Some, girl pouring, 28x20", Poor...**450.00**

Sign, tin, wht horse in car passing billboard, 1933, 13x24", VG+....**480.00**

Thermometer, tin, Drink...Good at Any Temperature, 26", EX..............**1,100.00**

Munsingwear, paper dolls, w/advertising on bk, uncut, 5x15", NM ..**50.00**

Nabisco, letter opener, dc image of Uneeda boy, 8", EX **55.00**

Nabisco, sign, dc paper, Santa holding products, 1940s, 17x25", EX...**170.00**

National Biscuit Co, display case, wood/glass cathedral, 38", VG....**800.00**

Nehi, sign, dc cb hanger, lady seated w/legs crossed, 23x15", EX+...**200.00**

Nine O'Clock Washing Tea, ts, lady/clock/box, 1895-1901, 13", EX .**1,800.00**

NV Van Melle's Toffee, store bin, tin, bl w/exotic birds, 10", VG+........**600.00**

Oilzum, blotter, Now For Your Protection, 3x6", EX **15.00**

Old Crow

Old Crow Whiskey items have become popular with collectors primarily because of the dapper crow dressed in a tuxedo, top hat, etc., that was used by the company for promotional purposes during the 1940s through the 1960s. However, there is a vast variety of Old Crow collectibles, some of which carry only the whiskey's name. In the 1970s ceramic decanters shaped like chess pieces were available; these carried nothing more than a paper label and a presentation box to identify them. In 1985, the 150th anniversary of Old Crow, the realistic crow that had been extensively used prior to 1950 re-emerged.

Very little Old Crow memorabilia has been issued since National Distillers Products Corporations, the parent company since 1933, was purchased by Jim Beam Brands in 1987. No reproductions have surfaced, although a few fantasies have been found where the character crow was borrowed for private use. Our advisors for Old Crow collectibles are Judith and Robert Walthall; they are listed in the Directory under Alabama.

Statuette, composition, Carbondale Toy & Novelty Co., 1940, M in dated box, $200.00. (Photo courtesy Judith and Robert Walthall)

Ashtray, ceramic, blk w/'Old Crow,' etc, 5" dia.............................**35.00**

Bank, wooden bbl, 1985, 6", EX **15.00**

Bingo card, 100 proof, late 1940s, 7½x8¼".................................**45.00**

Bkbar display, ceramic Broken Leg mug holds bottle, 5¼", NM .**200.00**

Bottle display, glass cylinder w/gold plastic crow....................**50.00**

Bottle pourer, plastic figure, sm **5.00**

Chess set (32 decanters), ltd ed, empty, w/orig boxes & rug **200.00**

Cocktail glass, crow stem, Morgantown or Libbey, 1970s, from $10 to ..**15.00**

Decanter, Old Crow Distillery Co of Frankfort KY, 13½" **50.00**

Decanter, orange vest, Royal Doulton, 12½" **125.00**

Dice, I Buy, You Buy, crow on 1, ½", pr..................................**45.00**

Dice cup, Bakelite, blk w/yel lettering, felt-lined, NM **100.00**

Doorstop, cut-out wood crow, 21", EX..**125.00**

Figure, brass, on rnd ftd wood base, 11".....................................**85.00**

Figure, compo, name emb on base, 1940s, 27½", VG.................**450.00**

Figure, compo, 1950s, 11¼", EX...**125.00**

Figure, plastic, Advertising Novelty & Sign Co, 32", EX...........**200.00**

Figure, plastic, in birdcage, 9" **125.00**

Key chain, figural Old Crow **10.00**

Label, paper, gold, shows 1930 Hermitage Distillery, bbl, 4+x4+".**25.00**

Lighter, 14k gold-plated, Florentine, from $25 to **30.00**

Lipstick tissue booklet, 1950s, 1⅞x3" **20.00**

Money clip, chromed metal, emb disc w/crow on 2" clip, EX........**35.00**

Phone dialer, figural hard plastic crow, bk emb Call For, EX.........**10.00**

Pitcher, ceramic, Broken Leg decor, NM...................................**100.00**

Pitcher, ceramic, olive gr w/emb crow in reserve, McCoy, 7" **35.00**

Pitcher, glass w/metal ring & hdl, 5".......................................**25.00**

Pocketknife, pearlized hdls, 2 blades..................................**30.00**
Roly-poly, plastic, 9"...**95.00**
Shot glass, Old Crow & crow fired on in blk....................**20.00**
Stirrer, plastic, full-figure crow on end, from $1 to............**3.00**
Thermometer, rnd dial, 1950s, 9x13", EX........................**150.00**
Thermometer, Taste the Greatness, 1960, 5¾x13½", from $75 to...**100.00**

Old Reliable Coffee, picket mirror, cl, 2" dia, EX............**85.00**
Orange Julip, tray, beach girl w/umbrella, 13x11", EX+.............**325.00**
Orange Kist, ts, Drink..., bottle/oranges on blk, 28x10", NM+....**350.00**
Orange-Crush, baseball score board, tin, sf, dtd 10/39, 18x58", EX.**600.00**
Orange-Crush, calendar, 1947, young girl w/bottle, 31", NM.....**250.00**
Orange-Crush, sign, cb, So Refreshing! 5¢, girl, 1937, 19x12", EX+..**60.00**
Orange-Crush, sign, cl button, Enjoy.../Naturally..., 9", NM+.....**150.00**
Orange-Crush, thermometer, porc, brn bottle on wht, curved, 15", EX+.**120.00**
Ox-Heart Peanut Butter, pail, tin, slip lid, bail hdl, 1-lb, EX+....**240.00**
Oxydol, sign, dc cb hanger, box shape, 8x6", NM....................**100.00**
Packer's Tar Soap, sign, paper, man seated, 14x11", EX............**65.00**
Peg Top, The Old Reliable...5¢, door push, porc, 13x4", EX+....**375.00**

Pepsi-Cola

Pepsi-Cola was first served in the early 1890s to customers of Caleb D. Bradham, a young pharmacist who touted his concoction to be medicinal as well as delicious. It was first called 'Brad's Drink' but was renamed Pepsi-Cola in 1898. Various logos have been registered over the years. The familiar oval was first used in the early 1940s. At about the same time, the two 'dots' (indicated in our listings by '=') between the words Pepsi and Cola became one, though more recent items may carry the double-dot logo as well, especially when they're designed to be reminiscent of the old ones. The bottle cap logo came along in 1943 and with variations was used through the early 1960s. Our advisor for Pepsi is Craig Stifter; he is listed in the Directory under Illinois. See also Soda Fountain Collectibles.

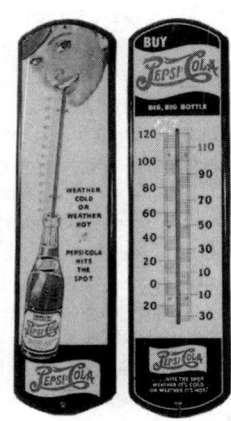

Thermometers, multicolor stencil on white sheet metal, 27", EX, $625.00 (left) and $425.00 (right).

Bottle carrier, wood, 6-pack, triangular w/cut-out hdl, 12x8", EX.**65.00**
Bottle display, bottle w/cb ad card, P=C Double Size 5¢, NM....**340.00**
Bottle display, bottle w/chalkware lady in red gown, 1940s, 11", EX+.**3,400.00**
Bottle display, dc cb w/bottle, Pepsi & Pete, 1940s, 14x12", EX.**290.00**
Calendar, 1911, 20", VG **3,200.00**
Calendar, 1944, Our America, fr, 22", VG **30.00**
Door push bar, Have a Pepsi flanked by logos on yel, 32", EX....**130.00**
Menu board, tin, Enjoy P=C/Bigger-Better, rope-like border, 30", VG+..**110.00**
Menu board, tin, Have a Pepsi, yel stripes, 30", EX...............**110.00**
Sign, cl over tin, P=C/5¢/12 Ounces, shows bottle on wht, 12x5", NM..**950.00**
Sign, cl stand-up, bottle cap form, Drink P-C, 9" dia, EX.........**100.00**

Sign, flange, Buy P=C Here on red, wht & bl disk, 16x17", NM.**1,300.00**
Sign, porc, Enjoy P=C 5¢/Hits the Spot, 2-sided, 32x56", EX....**700.00**
Sign, porc, Enjoy Pepsi, bottle cap on yel on tan, 13x29", VG...**125.00**
Sign, tin, More Bounce to the Ounce/cap/ribbon, wht, sf, 33x57", G...**150.00**
Sign, tin, Say Pepsi Please, swirl bottle on lime gr, sf, 47x17", EX...**200.00**
Sign, tin, Sold Here/P=C 5¢/Bigger-Better, 28x20", VG............**325.00**
Sign, tin bottle, Sparkling P=C/12 Fl oz label, 45x12", NM+.**1,350.00**
Sign, tin bottle cap, P-C logo, 37" dia, EX........................**275.00**
Sign, tin/cb, Say Pepsi Please, bottle/cap logo, sf, 9x11", VG......**90.00**
Syrup dispenser, metal, streamline, Ice Cold P=C 5¢ logo, 23", G...**190.00**
Syrup dispenser, wooden bbl w/2 taps, 3-ftd, 30", VG.............**415.00**
Thermometer, dial, Drink P=C Ice Cold, 1951, 12" dia, NM+..**1,000.00**
Thermometer, dial, Hot or Cold, maroon/red, 12" dia, EX.........**120.00**
Thermometer, tin, More Bounce to the Ounce, wht, 27", VG...**200.00**
Thermometer, tin, Pepsi top/bottom, wht, sq corners, 28", EX.....**50.00**
Thermometer, tin, The Light Refreshment, cap logo on yel, 28", NM..**165.00**
Tip tray, 1909, oval, EX...**765.00**
Vending machine, Vendorlator model #27, 52", Fair................**500.00**
Whistle, plastic dbl bottle shape, 3", EX.........................**80.00**

Perry Davis Pain Killer, sign, paper/cloth, girl/horseman, 28", NM..**280.00**
Peters, tray, wood, 3 mallards in flight, 1940s-50s, 11x18", NM+....**120.00**
Peters Ammunition, poster, moose/moon, Wm Schmetdgen art, 1920s, EX+.**550.00**
Pickaninny Peanut Butter, tin pail, slip lid, bail hdl, 1-lb, VG+.**270.00**

Planters Peanuts

The Planters Peanut Co. was founded in 1906. Mr. Peanut, the dashing peanut man with top hat, spats, monocle, and cane, has represented Planters since 1916. He took on his modern-day appearance after the company was purchased by Standard Brands in November 1960. He remains perhaps the most highly recognized logo of any company in the world. Mr. Peanut has promoted the company's products by appearing in ads; on product packaging; on or as store displays, novelties, and premiums; and even in character at promotional events (thanks to a special Mr. Peanut costume).

Among the favorite items of collectors today are the glass display jars which were sent to retailers nationwide to stimulate 'point-of-sale' trade. They come in a variety of shapes and styles. The first, distributed in the early 1920s, was a large universal candy jar (round covered bowl on a pedestal) with only a narrow paper label affixed at the neck to identify it as 'Planters.' In 1924 an octagonal jar was produced, all eight sides embossed, with Mr. Peanut on the narrow corner panels. On a second octagon jar, only seven sides were embossed, leaving one of the large panels blank to accommodate a paper label.

In late 1929 a fishbowl jar was introduced, and in 1932 a beautiful jar with a blown-out peanut on each of the four corners was issued. The football shape was also made in the 1930s, as were the square jar, the large barrel jar, and the hexagon jar with yellow fired-on designs alternating on each of the six sides. All of these early jars had glass lids which after 1930 had peanut finials.

In 1937 jars with lithographed tin lids were introduced. The first of these was the slant-front streamline jar, which is also found with screened yellow lettering. Next was a squat version, the clipper jar, then the upright rectangular 1940 leap year jar, and last, another upright rectangular jar with a screened, fired-on design similar to the red, white, and blue design on the cellophane 5¢ bags of peanuts of the period. This last jar was issued again after WWII with a plain red tin lid.

In 1959 Planters first used a stock Anchor Hocking one-gallon round jar with a 'customer-special' decoration in red. As the design was not plainly evident when the jar was full, the decoration was modified with a white under-panel. The two jars we've just described are perhaps the rarest of them all due to their limited production. After Standard Brands purchased Planters, they changed the red-on-white panel to show their more modern Mr. Peanut and in 1963 introduced this most plentiful, thus very common, Planters jar. In 1966 the last counter display jar was distributed: the Anchor Hocking jar with a fired-on large four-color design such as that which appeared on peanut bags of the period. Prior to this, a plain jar with a transfer decal in an almost identical but smaller design was used.

Some Planters jars have been reproduced: the octagon jar (with only six of the sides embossed), a small version of the barrel jar, and the four peanut corner jar. Some of the first were made in clear glass with 'Made in Italy' embossed on the bottom, but most have been made in Asia, many in various colors of glass (a dead giveaway) as well as clear, and carrying only small paper stickers, easily removed, identifying the country of origin. At least two reproductions of the Anchor Hocking jar with a four-color design have been made, one circa 1978, the other in 1989. Both, using the stock jar, are difficult to detect, but there are small differences between them and the original that will enable you to make an accurate identification. With the exception of several of the earliest and the Anchor Hocking, all authentic Planters jars have 'Made in USA' embossed on the bottom, and all, without exception, are clear glass. Unfortunately, several paper labels have also been reproduced, no doubt due to the fact that an original label or decal will greatly increase the value of an original jar. Jar prices continue to remain stable in today's market.

In the late 1920s, the first premiums were introduced in the form of story and paint books. Late in the 1930s, the tin nut set (which was still available into the 1960s) was distributed. A wood-jointed doll was available from Planters Peanuts stores at that time. Many post-WWII items were made of plastic: banks, salt and pepper shakers, cups, cookie cutters, small cars and trucks, charms, whistles, various pens and mechanical pencils, and almost any other item imaginable. In recent years the company, now a division of Nabisco, has continued to distribute a wide variety of novelties.

Note that there are many unauthorized Planters/Mr. Peanut items. Although several are reproductions or 'copycats,' most are fantasies and fakes. Our advisors for Planters Planters are Judith and Robert Walthall; they are in the Directory under Alabama.

Key:
MrP — Mr. Peanut
okl — octagon knob lid
pfl — peanut finial lid
pl — plastic

pm — papier-mache
pnut — peanut
shp — shipping

Scale, cast aluminum Mr. Peanut figure, mounted on cast-iron base, original paint, 46", VG, from $14,000.00 to $16,000.00. (Has been reproduced.)

Apron, Gold Measure, bl, 1991, M 6.00
Badge, NP, space for name, PLANTERS in red, 1¼x2¼" 300.00

Bank, MrP figure, pl, clear, 1950s-70s, EX, from $125 to 150.00
Blotter, truck w/MrP, Nickel Lunch, etc, 3x6" (Fake!) 4.00
Box, cb shp, 24-5¢ bags, roasted in the shell, NRA....................250.00
Container, pnt pm MrP figure against lg pnut, 12½", VG 500.00
Cup, ceramic, rhinestone in monocle, 1950s, 4".....................350.00
Display rack, tin, 3 products, 14" W, from $900 to..................1,200.00
Doll, stuffed cloth, Chase Bag Co, 1967, 21", EX 30.00
Doll, stuffed cloth, Chase Bag Co, 1970, 18", NM 25.00
Glass, circus acts, lg Mr P, EX 300.00
Glass, circus acts, MrP on stilts, EX...150.00
Glass, cocktail, V shape, MrP stem, 1940s, EX 650.00
Glass, Golden Jubilee, 50th Anniversary, 1956, EX....................250.00
Jar, Barrel, pfl, paper label, 1935, 12¼", EX 250.00
Jar, Fishbowl, okl, no label, 1929, 12½", EX 75.00
Jar, Fishbowl, okl, Planters on base, orig label, 12½", VG, $150 to .175.00
Jar, Football, pfl, 1931, 8½", EX 225.00
Jar, Four Peanut Corner, pfl, 1932, 14" (+) 225.00
Jar, Octagon, 6 sides emb, pfl, clear & colors, repro.....................35.00
Jar, Octagon, 7 sides emb, okl, no label, 12", EX 85.00
Jar, Octagon, 8 sides emb, okl, 1924, 12", EX 250.00
Nodder, clayware, Lego, 6½", MIB..150.00
Punchboard, cb, 1940s, unused, 8" sq, EX (+)..............................85.00
Shakers, MrP, bent knee, pk pl, 1960s, 3", MIP 18.00
Shakers, MrP, str legs, gr pl, 1950s, 4", NMIB..............................35.00
Sign, tin, emb PLANTERS, MrP w/pnut fingers, from $350 to ..500.00
Sign, trolley car, cb, Delicious w/cocktails, 1950s 300.00
Sign, trolley car, cb, The World Goes Nuts, 1930s 550.00
Standee, cb MrP figure, 12", M..10.00
Tankard, metal pewter type, Wilton, 1983, 4¾", M......................15.00
Thermometer for deep fryer, al w/MrP in chef's garb, MIB 275.00
Tin, Pennant Salted Peanuts, red, bl w/gold trim, 10-lb, VG+......40.00

Poll Parrot Shoes, display, ceramic parrot on stump, 12", EX......190.00
Poll Parrot Shoes, display, revolving, parrot in cage, 33", EX......150.00
Poll Parrot Shoes, lamp, figural, plastic shade, metal base, 19", VG 70.00
Poll Parrot Shoes, radio, compo parrot on GE tube radio, 11x4", VG..100.00
Poll Parrot Shoes, whistle, tin keyhole shape, yel w/graphics, G...25.00
Post Toasties, sign, 2-sided dc cb hanger, letters atop boxes, NM...3,200.00
Primley's California Fruit Chewing Gum, bear, dc cb, 1890s, 4x7", NM+ .165.00
Prince Albert Tobacco, tin, Chief Josef Nez Perce, 26x19", NM ..2,850.00
Punch Havana Cigars, cabinet, wood/glass, 3-shelf/marquee, 23x8", EX..200.00
Quaker Oats, sign, Today the Dionne Quints..., 5 photos, 14x32", VG ...100.00
Queen Quality Shoes, shoehorn, cl w/advertising, 8", NM 60.00

RCA Victor

Nipper, the RCA Victor trademark, was the creation of Francis Barraud, an English artist. His pet's intense fascination with the music of the phonograph seemed to him a worthy subject for his canvas. Although he failed to find a publishing house who would buy his work, the Gramophone Co. in England saw its potential and adopted Nipper to advertise their product. The painting was later acquired and trademarked in the United States by the Victor Talking Machine Co., which was purchased by RCA in 1929. The trademark is owned today by EMI in England and by General Electric in the U.S. Nipper's image appeared on packages, accessories, ads, brochures, and in three-dimensional form. You may find a life-size statue of him, but all are not old. They have been manufactured for the owner throughout RCA history and are marketed currently by licensees, BMG Inc. and Thomson Consumer Electronics (dba RCA). Except for the years between 1968 and 1976, Nipper has seen active duty, and with his image spruced up only a bit for the present day, the ageless symbol for RCA still listens intently to 'His Master's Voice.' Many of the items have been reproduced in recent years. Exercise care before you buy.

The recent phenomenon of Internet auctions has played havoc with prices paid for Victor and RCA Victor collectibles. Often prices paid for online sales bear little resemblance to the true value of the item. Reproductions are often sold as old on the Internet and bring prices accordingly. It is common knowledge that auction prices, more often than not, are inflated over sales made through traditional sales outlets. The Internet has exacerbated the situation by focusing a very large number of buyers and sellers through the narrow portal of a modem. The prices here are intended to reflect what one might expect to pay through traditional sales. Our advisor for RCA Victor is Roger R. Scott; he is listed in the Directory under Oklahoma.

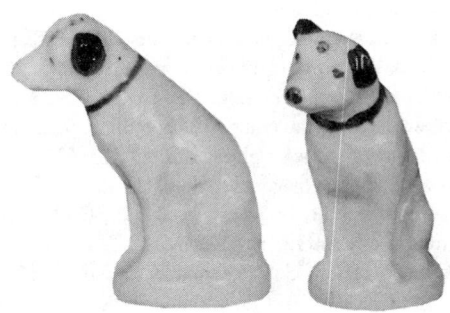

Shakers, Nipper figural, earthenware with glossy white glaze, 3", EX, pair, $55.00.

Bank, flocked, metal, 9" 125.00
Buckle, His Master's Voice, brass, Nash Tiffany London................25.00
Clock, RCA Victor Records, w/Nipper 350.00
Doll, Radio Man, jtd wood, Maxfield Parrish, M 900.00
Figure, Nipper, crystal, Fenton, 4"...................................50.00
Figure, Nipper, papier-mache, 11".....................................50.00
Figure, Nipper, papier-mache, 18"....................................350.00
Figure, Nipper, papier-mache, 36"....................................600.00
Figure, Nipper, plaster, 14½x7½x5", VG 200.00
Necktie, Nipper, M..20.00
Pin-back button, I Support Nipper, 1930s..............................45.00
Plater, Nipper, collector's edition...................................50.00
Puzzle, assembled..100.00
Record brush, Lucite hdl, in faux leather snap case 30.00
Shakers, Nipper, Lenox, pr..50.00
Sign, canvas, His Master's Voice, 26x19"............................1,500.00
Sign, plastic/metal, ...Radio, light-up, 1940s, 15x37", EX...........180.00
Sign, porc, record shape w/trademark image on red label, 24", VG .300.00
Snow globe..50.00
Thermometer, porc, NM 485.00
Watch fob, EX 30.00

Ramon's Quality Medicine, jar, glass w/yel tin lid, 8", NM+ 70.00
RC Cola, thermometer, tin, dmn logo/bottle, wht, 14", NM 185.00
Reading Brewing Co, sign, paper on cb, pictorial, 1890s, 21x14", EX ...2,650.00

Red Goose Shoes

Realizing that his last name was difficult to pronounce, Herman Giesceke, a shoe company owner resolved to give the public a modified, shortened version that would be better suited to the business world. The results suggested the use of the goose trademark with the last two letters, 'ke,' represented by the key that this early goose held in his mouth. Upon observing an employee casually coloring in the goose trademark with a red pencil, Giesceke saw new advertising potential and renamed the company Red Goose Shoes. Although the company has changed hands down through the years, the Red Goose emblem has remained. Collectors of this desirable fowl increase in number yearly, as do prices. Beware of reproductions; new chalkware figures are prevalent.

Clock, light-up, Pam, dtd Nov 1954, 15" dia, NM+ 550.00
Display egg layer, plastic goose on cb box, 27x22", G................200.00
Whistle, tin bow-tie shape, wht w/Red Goose logo, 4", EX...........42.00
Whistle, tin goose shape, red, EX 85.00
Whistle, tin keyhole shape, yel, EX 27.00
Whistle, wood w/metal goose figure, paper label, EX...................33.00

Red Raven, tip tray, Ask the Man, girl at window, 4" dia, EX 400.00
Red Raven, tray, red raven w/ft on bottle, 12" dia, EX+.............440.00
Red Ribbon Beer, tray, On the Square (bear), 13x13", Fair 700.00
Red Top Rye, dispenser, plated bbl form, ca 1900, 12", EX+.......240.00
Remington-UMC, poster, HG Edwards art, 26x18", EX+........1,700.00
Rexall Foot Bath Tablets, sign, paper, lady in ft bath, 47x22", VG ..300.00
Robin's Best Flour, menu board, hanger or stand-up, 21x14", EX.315.00

Rolling Rock Premium Beer, tan and cream plaster horse, raised white letters, 11x10½", EX, $45.00.

Round Oak Stoves & Ranges, display plate, Doe-Wah-Jack, 1900, 9", EX+..170.00
Roundup Grocery Co Sweet June Peas, tc, paper label, full, 4", EX+ ...275.00
Royal Crown Cola, sign, cb, patriotic girl, 1940s-50s, 22x18", EX+ 270.00
Royal Crown Cola, sign, cb, Shirley Temple Says..., 12x30", EX...225.00
Royal Crown Cola, sign, cb, Yes...Bring RC!, girl/phone, 11x28", EX..75.00
Royal Crown Cola, ts, Drink...Take Home a Carton, 22x58", EX ..375.00
Royal Crown Cola, ts, Enjoy..., red/wht/bl, sf, 12x32", M..............80.00
Royal Violet Borated Talcum Powder, tc, rnd, slip lid, 4", EX+ ..200.00
Roza De Luzon Cigars, paper, Battle of Chattanooga, 1888, 21x28", NM...650.00
Ruhstaller Gilt Edge Lager, sign, Vitrolite, curved, 21x15", EX+ ..525.00
Sailors Brand Alaska Pink Salmon, can, paper label, 4½", VG+...200.00
Samoset Chocolates, logo/lettering on red, 11x36", VG 400.00
Sander's Candy, pail, tin w/slip pry lid, bail hdl, 2½-lb, EX+ 300.00
Santa Fe Pure Ground Mustard, tc, paper label, 3¼", EX+ 60.00
Saplin Stove Pipe Enamel, sign, dc cb stand-up, domino game, 11", VG+ ..170.00
Satin Skin Cream & Powder, sign, dc cb stand-up, cherub/lady, 1911, EX...600.00
Sauer's Flavoring Extracts, thermometer, wood, 24", G 175.00
Sauer's Vanilla, thermometer, wood box shape, c 1918-19, 8", G.100.00
Schenley Whiskey, ts, I've Struck the Trail, wood fr, 33x25", NM .2,300.00
Seminola, sign, emb cl, beveled gold sf, 6x9", NM 180.00

Seven-Up

The Howdy Company of St. Louis, Missouri, was founded in 1920 by Charles L. Grigg. His first creation was an orange drink called Howdy.

In the late 1920s Howdy's popularity began to wane, so in 1929 Grigg invented a lemon-lime soda called Seven-Up as an alternative to colas. Grigg's Seven-Up became a widely accepted favorite. Our advisor for this category is Craig Stifter; he is listed in the Directory under Illinois. See also Soda Fountain Collectibles.

Sign, tin litho, 12x16", NM, $125.00.

Badge, hat; cloisonne 7-Up/bubbles logo, paper holder, 1½" dia, NM..**800.00**
Bottle topper, dc cb, Top O' The Mornin', leprechaun, NM.........**15.00**
Calendar, 1954, bust image of lady in low-cut top, 21", VG+.......**120.00**
Clock, light-up, 7-Up logo in center, Pam, 15" dia, NM+ **350.00**
Clock, rotating light-up, w/privilege panel, 16x11x6", EX+........**160.00**
Door push bar, porc, Fresh up w/Seven-Up!, wht, 32", EX+ **220.00**
Menu board, tin, hand-held bottle/logo, curved corners, 28x20", EX...**180.00**
Sign, cb, Make It a Case..., bottle/logo, 1945, 11x14", EX **35.00**
Sign, cb, Time Out/Fresh Up..., 2 hockey boys, ornate sf, 15x22", VG ..**35.00**
Sign, cb stand-up, grocer holding case, dtd 1948, 12x10", M **50.00**
Sign, cb w/wire fr, golf theme w/bottle, 21x34", EX...................**175.00**
Sign, flange, tin, bubble girl bottle/logo, 20x18", VG/EX...........**650.00**
Sign, light-up, Fresh Up With...In a Cup/You Like It..., 13x21", EX...**475.00**
Sign, porc, Fresh Up..., bottle/logo, dtd 9-5-51, 12x30", EX+ **750.00**
Sign, porc, 7-Up logo, wht/blk on red, 36x31x1", NM................**275.00**
Sign, rvpt, On Duty, spin wheel to change name, 6x11", EX+ ...**170.00**
Sign, tin, Fresh Up, bubble girl bottle, 54x18", EX...................**600.00**
Sign, tin, Fresh Up oval w/wings, silver fr, 41", VG **300.00**
Sign, tin, Fresh Up phrase & logo, dtd 54-3, 18x54", EX............**375.00**
Sign, tin, Fresh Up!, hand-held bottle, dtd 9-47, fr, 60x30", EX+ ..**525.00**
Sign, tin, Fresh Up/Nothing Does It, striped, dtd 1-59, 43", EX.**450.00**
Sign, tin, Get Real Action!/Your Thirst Away, dtd 7-63, 43", NM ...**350.00**
Sign, tin, 7-Up logo w/phrase, wht/blk on red, dtd 11-53, 28", NM..**325.00**
Sign, tin bottle shape, dtd 7-62, 45x13", EX+ **525.00**
Sign, tin dc, 7-Up/The Uncola sunrise logo, 12x24", EX **80.00**
Thermometer, dial, Fresh Clean Taste!, 12" dia, NM **325.00**
Thermometer, dial, The Quality Drink, 10" dia, VG+ **225.00**
Thermometer, dial, 7-Up Likes You, 12" dia, EX **120.00**
Thermometer, porc, The Fresh Up Family Drink, wht, curved, 15", EX ..**185.00**

Sharples Cream Separators, match holder, dc litho tin, 7", VG+ ...**285.00**
Sharples Spectator Co, ts, sf, girl/milkmaid/cow, 39x28", VG .**2,100.00**
Shredded Wheat Biscuit, sign, paper hanger, girl chef, 16x12", EX+.....**600.00**
Smith Bros Cough Drops, blotter, 3x6", EX **32.00**
Smith Bros Cough Drops, dispenser, tin, blk, 10x4x4", NM+ **400.00**
Snider's Catsup, mechanical dc, man watches bottle, 1891, 6", NM ..**130.00**
Sparrow Chocolates, tip tray, colorful graphics, 8x6½", VG+.....**130.00**
Squirrel Brand Peanuts, sign, dc cb, squirrel atop sign, 12x11", EX .**210.00**
Squirrel Peanut Butter, pail, bail hdl, yel, 1-lb, EX+....................**300.00**
Standard Oil, badge, Station Manager, red/wht/bl chevrons, 1", EX...**200.00**
Star Brand Shoes, sign, cb stand-up, lady, 1920s, 14x10", NM ...**275.00**
Star Soap, ps, Extra Lg/Extra Good/Save the Panels, 28x20", G.**390.00**
Stephenson Union Suits, thermometer, porc, red/wht, 1915, 39", EX...**875.00**
Sternemann Bros & Haysen, thermometer, wooden leaf shape, 24", VG+ ..**235.00**

Strong-Heart Coffee, tc, Indian portrait, screw lid, 6", VG+ **200.00**
Sultana Coffee, fan, dc cb dog in bonnet, 1892, 13", EX...............**30.00**
Sun Crest Beverages, clock, electric, Swihart, 8x6½", EX **100.00**
Swamp Root/The Listie Variety Store, blotter, 4x9", EX **30.00**
Sweet Cuba Fine Cut, store bin, cb w/tin base & top, 11x8x7", EX+ ..**500.00**
Swell Blend Chautauqua Brand Coffee, tc, pry lid, 6", VG+ **200.00**
Trilafon Prescription Tranquilizer, paperweight, porc bust, 5", NM+ .**60.00**
Tucketts Orinco Cut Fine, pocket tin, flat, ½x2¾x3½", NM+ ..**135.00**
Turkey Brand Coffee, tc, sm screw lid, red/wht on gold, 3-lb, EX+ ..**775.00**
Tuxedo Club Havana Cigars, change tray, leather, 6½" dia, EX+ **225.00**
Van Dam Cigars, ts, sf, profile portrait on wht, vertical, EX **280.00**
Van Dam Cigars (Little), cigar pocket tin, vertical, 25 ct, 5", EX ..**80.00**
WA Lagey Sour Mash, sign, etched brass, King of Kentucky, 24x17", EX...**400.00**
Wabash Cocoa, tc, red/wht/blk, 6", EX **200.00**
Wampum Coffee, tc, slip lid, 3-lb, 9¼", EX+ **650.00**
Warwick Whiskey, sign, rvpt hanger, bottle, scalloped, 16x10", EX+....**600.00**
Wayne Feed Dealer, thermometer, dc tin chick on feed bag, 6x4", EX..**315.00**
Weatherbird Shoes, whistle, tin rooster shape, EX **108.00**
Wedding Bouquet Cigar, ts, Climax of Perfection, 20x28", EX...**475.00**
Weinard's Beers, watch fob, Souvenir to Visiting Elks, 1912, NM+ **80.00**
West Hair Nets, cabinet, wht w/graphics, 1921, 20x13x12", EX+ ..**2,200.00**
Western Candy, sign, emb dc diagonal, girl's portrait, 11x12", EX+....**275.00**
Whistle, bag rack, tin, graphics on wht, curved ends, 17x37", VG **625.00**
Whistle, ts, Thirsty?...5¢, 1939, 3x12", NM **150.00**
White King Washing Machine Soap, ts, product on red, 14x10", EX..**235.00**
White Lion, tc, gr, Liberty Can Co, 4x6x5½", EX+ **200.00**
White Rock Table Water, tip tray, tin, Chas Shonk litho, 6x4", VG+ ...**70.00**
White Sewing Machines, puzzle, cb jigsaw, ca 1910, 16x11", EX+ **215.00**
Wildroot, sign, paper, gazing couple on bl, 1940s, fr, 36x25", EX+ **100.00**
Williams' Shaving Powder, tc, brn, 4", EX+ **225.00**
Winner Cut Plug Smoke & Chew, lunch box, 4¼x7¾x5", EX+ **450.00**
Witter's Laundry, sign, emb dc cb baby in pouch, 12x5", EX+ **530.00**
Wolverine Soap, shipping box, wood, stamped graphics, 7x21x14", EX+ .**100.00**
Woodland Whiskey, tip tray, shows Victorian lady, 4" dia, VG+ ...**325.00**
Woolrich Rugged Outdoorwear, hanging birch-bark canoe, 18", NM+ ..**550.00**
Wrigleys Chewing Gum, change tray, glass, 1¾x18x17", EX+ **60.00**
Yellowstone Whiskey, ashtray/match holder, ceramic, 1930-40, NM ...**185.00**
Yosemite Lager/Enterprise Brewing Co, ts, sf, scenic, 26x38", G.**800.00**
Yuenling's Bottled Beer, tip tray, girl in bonnet, 4¼" dia, EX+ ...**275.00**
Zenith Long Distance Radio, thermometer, tin, tower graphic, 71", VG...**475.00**

Advertising Cards

Advertising trade cards enjoyed great popularity during the last quarter of the nineteenth century when the chromolithography printing process was refined and put into common use. The purpose of the trade card was to acquaint the public with a business, product, service, or event. Most trade cards range in size from 2" x 3" to 4" x 6"; however, many are found in both smaller and larger sizes.

There are two classifications of trade cards: 'private design' and 'stock.' Private design cards were used by a single company or individual; the images on the cards were designed for only that company. Stock cards were generics that any individual or company could purchase from a printer's inventory. These cards usually had a blank space on the front for the company to overprint with their own name and product information.

Four categories of particular interest to collectors are:
Mechanical — a card which achieves movement through the use of a pull tab, fold-out side, or movable part.

Hold-to-light — a card that reveals its design only when viewed before a strong light.

Diecut — a card in the form of something like a box, a piece of clothing, etc.

Metamorphic — a card that by folding down a flap shows a transformed image, such as a white beard turning black after use of a product.

For a more thorough study of the subject, we recommend *Reflections 1* and *Reflections 2* by Kit Barry; his address can be found in the Directory under Vermont. *Victorian Trade Cards* by Dave Cheadle (Collector Books) is another fine reference. Values are given for cards in near-mint condition.

Acorn Stoves, die-cut acorn w/woman looking left 16.00
Alden Fruit Vinegar, Evangeline..12.00
Allan Fly Brick, 3 men around dish w/flies........................25.00
Allis & Co Clothes, setter dog at point facing right 10.00
American Breakfast Cereal, bobwhite bird in wheat 20.00
American Cereal Co, factory scene w/railroad tracks 25.00
Andes Stoves, woman in straw hat w/flowers.......................10.00
Andrew Gem Folding Bed, woman by bed............................35.00
Argand Stove, woman, child on floor, stove in parlor 35.00
Argand Stove, woman seated in parlor, stove 35.00
Ariosa Coffee, A Gloomy Outlook 10.00
Art Royal Stove, woman pushing aside drapes, stove 25.00
Austen's Forest Flower Cologne, girl holding roses 9.00
Barlow's Browned Flour, 3 chicks pulling at wheat stalk 6.00
Boss Watch Case, man playing croquet 20.00
Boston Electric Co, thief, thief climbing window 35.00
Bousemeem Spices, man, woman walking, flower garland...........12.00
Bugbee & Brownell, 1886 calendar, pimento stalk 18.00
Bugbee & Brownell Flavoring Extract, lemon stalk 18.00
Chas II Davis Clothes, girl w/basket in red outfit & hat............10.00
Clipper ship, Radiant, non-illustrated 175.00
Clipper ship, SC Grant, non-illustrated 150.00
Deluth Imperial flour, US Weather & Wind Signal Flags 12.00
Dr Price Flavoring Extract, boy & girl w/ice cream.................12.00
Dunham Cocoanut, nut w/6 monkeys at table 35.00
Edison Phonograph, product w/4 babies 60.00
Epsey's Fragrant Cream, girl w/fan, flowers at ft 18.00
Erdman Industry Stove Works, man & woman overheated...........25.00
Fairbank Canning Co, dressed lion holding product.................45.00
Fairbank Soap, Barbers Prefer..., barber shaving man................25.00
Fairbank soap, Our Artist..20.00
Fisk, Clark & Hagg Gloves for Coaching, 2 men w/horses...........10.00
Florence Lamp Stove, man w/nurser, mom w/baby, stove............20.00
Foster, Higgins Clothes, Press the Button & Get a Great............15.00
Garland Oil Stove, girl w/fan looking left 8.00
Gold Coin Stoves, 1893 Expo Electrical Building 18.00
Hagan Magnolia Balm, ship captain w/4 women on deck 35.00
Harishorn Root Beer, Brownies around giant glass.................45.00
Henderson Shoes, 1893 Expo Fisheries Building, boy fishing........20.00
Horsmann Bros, military regalia w/armored knight..................50.00
Imperial Granum, 10 children w/product on shelves 25.00
Inman Steamship Co, tug towing ship in harbor 35.00
Jennings Flavoring Extract, woman picking grapes 9.00
John Wanamaker Clothes, boy by stone wall w/sign...............12.00
John Wanamaker Clothes, country flag series - Sweden...........12.00
John Wanamaker Clothes, 2 boys shaking hands.................12.00
Kemp's Manure Spreader, image of spreader......................35.00
Keystone Watch Case, die-cut keystone, astronomer.............20.00
Kopf Soup, child in lg tureen, cook in doorway....................25.00
Lazell Persian Bouquet Perfume, woman, stairs, wreath.............12.00
Magee Stove, aproned woman holding loaf of bread 20.00
Magee Stove, boy baker w/7 loaves of bread under arms 20.00
Magee Stove, Mystic range, 3 children in kitchen, stove 25.00
Maltex Cereal, 7 silhouetted children in front of fence............35.00
Max Stadler Clothes, man leading boy on pony....................18.00
Mennen Talcum Powder, 2 children, 1 w/flag, & product 25.00
Metropolitan Life Ins Co, baby w/spoon in highchair 20.00

Metropolitan Life Ins Co, girl in garden holding leaf 10.00
Metropolitan Life Ins Co, 4 children playing w/toys....................25.00
Moir Preserved Food, 5 cooks holding products, London 25.00
Montgomery Ward Co, 1893 Expo Agricultural Building 20.00
Mumm Co Champagne, costume ball scene........................45.00
NY Erie & Western RR, woman boarding end car..................50.00
Ottmann Lith Co, Murray Hill Station, NYC, 1893 Expo...........45.00
Partridge Dining Rooms, man falling bk in rowboat.................10.00
Peckham Artisan Stove, stove in paint pallet, children 35.00
Peckham Rosedale Stove, 2 man on highwheels, stove 35.00
Peckham Saratoga Stove, woman & stove by window................35.00
Penn Mutual Life Ins Co, apple blossoms, bee 8.00
Petrie Face Powder, man & lute, woman w/fan 9.00
Petrie Face Powder, man holding woman on steps 9.00
Prudential Ins Co, boy & girl flying kite 15.00
Ritter Preserved Fruit, jam, child tipping table over 20.00
Rosenthal Boys' Clothes, 2 boys, 1 naked 12.00
Rough on Coughs, woman giving child medicine 45.00
Round Oak Stove, child w/toy horse, woman, boy, stove 20.00
Smith's Brass Ladles, Black cook at stove, woman in doorway......45.00
Spencerian Pen, boy, head on school desk 30.00
Stickney & Poor spices, woman stirring, 2 cans of product 9.00
Swift Co Wool Soap, woman w/basket on arm, umbrella..............20.00
Swinborne Isinglass Gelatin, girl holding product 10.00
Thomson Corset, woman dressing, lily pads on pond 15.00
Thurber Canned Vegetables, tomato, The Baldwin 15.00
Thurber Hominy, red-winged blackbird over nest...................15.00
Tnadzai's Russian Beer, banner w/rose stem 15.00
Uncle Sam's Condition Powder, 2 horses, cattle in field 25.00
Union Pacific Tea Co, 2 boys w/sailboat.............................8.00
Universal Fashion Co, sailor boy w/boat & girl 10.00
Wanamaker & Brown Clothes, Autumn Leaves 10.00
Weir Stove Co, boy & girl holding cake by stove 25.00
Weir Stove Co, girl in red dress, bouquet, stove to left..................15.00
Withington Cooley Rakes, rake & text................................35.00
Yates Clothes, man posting billboard w/3 onlookers.................12.00

Advertising Dolls and Figures

Whether your interest in ad dolls is fueled by nostalgia or strictly because of their amusing, often clever advertising impact, there are several points that should be considered before making your purchases. Condition is of utmost importance; never pay book price for dolls in poor condition, whether they are cloth or of another material. Restoring fabric dolls is usually unsatisfactory and involves a good deal of work. Seams must be opened, stuffing removed, the doll washed and dried, and then reassembled. Washing old fabrics may prove to be disastrous. Colors may fade or run, and most stains are totally resistant to washing. It's usually best to leave the fabric doll as it is.

Watch for new dolls as they become available. Save related advertising literature, extra coupons, etc., and keep these along with the doll to further enhance your collection. Old dolls with no marks are sometimes challenging to identify. While some products may use the same familiar trademark figures for a number of years (the Jolly Green Giant, Pillsbury's Poppin' Fresh, and the Keebler Elf, for example) others appear on the market for a short time only and may be difficult to trace. Most libraries have reference books with trademarks and logos that might provide a clue in tracking down your doll's identity. Children see advertising figures on Saturday morning cartoons that are often unfamiliar to adults, or other ad doll collectors may have the information you seek.

Some advertising dolls are still easy to find and relatively inexpensive, ranging in cost from $1.00 to $100.00. The hard plastic and early composition dolls are bringing the higher prices. Advertising dolls are popular with children as well as adults. For a more thorough study of the subject, we recommend *Advertising Character Collectibles* by Warren Dotz and *Advertising Dolls with Values* by Myra Yellin Outwater (Schiffer). Values apply only to examples in the condition given in the descriptions; you may have to adjust your prices up or down. Just be sure to discount prices for soil, missing parts, wear, or damage of any type.

AC Spark Plugs, doll, AC man w/AC on chest, rubber, 6", EXIB ..160.00
AC Spark Plugs, Sparky the Horse, inflatable, Ideal, 1960s, 15", EX..160.00
Adams Tutti Frutti Gum, girl, cb stand-up, early premium, 6", NM+.150.00
Aunt Jemima, Breakfast Bear, bl plush in chef's garb, 13", M 175.00
Bosco Chocolate, Bosco the Clown, vinyl, NM..................................25.00
Buster Brown Shoes, Buster Brown, stuffed cloth, 1974, 14", NM .20.00
Butterfinger, Butterfinger Bear, plush, 1987, 15", M 10.00
Cheer Detergent, Cheer girl, plastic/cloth clothes, 1960, 10", NM .25.00
Cheetos, Chester Cheetah, plush, 18", EX....................................15.00
Crayola Crayons, Crayola Bear, plush, Graphics Int, 1986, 6", NM...10.00

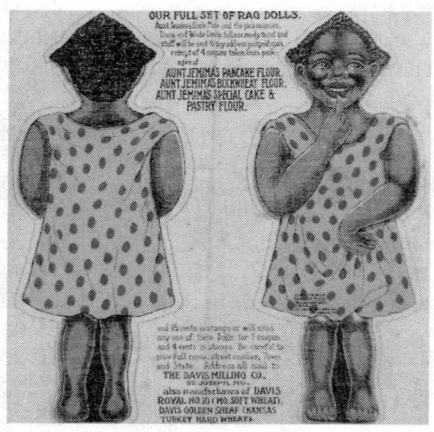

Davis Milling Co. (Now Quaker Oats), Diana (Aunt Jemima's daughter), uncut cloth, ca 1905, 12x12", $300.00. (Photo courtesy Myla Perkins)

Del Monte, Country Yumkin, Fruits or Veggies, plush, 1980s, M, ea .15.00
Del Monte, Shoo Shoo Scarecrow, plush, 1983, NM.....................15.00
Energizer Batteries, Energizer Bunny, plush, b/o, 24", M...............45.00
GE, drum major, pnt jtd wood, by Maxfield Parrish, 18½", EX+ ...550.00
Gerber, baby w/diaper & bib, 1965 premium, MIB 65.00
Green Giant, Jolly Green Giant, vinyl, ca 1975, 9", EX................75.00
Green Giant, Little Sprout, stuffed cloth, 1874, 10½", NM..........15.00
Kellogg's, Snap!, Crackle! & Pop!, uncut cloth, 1948, NM+, set .160.00
Kellogg's, Tony the Tiger, plush, premium, 1997, 8", NM................5.00
Kellogg's, Tony the Tiger, stuffed cloth, 1973, 14", EX 40.00
Kentucky Fried Chicken, nodder, Col Sanders, bsk, 1960s, 7½", M..75.00
Kodak, Colorkins, stuffed, ca 1990, 8" to 10", ea 10.00
Lee Jeans, Buddy Lee in overalls & striped hat, 13", EX 180.00
Malto Rice, Miss Malto Rice, uncut cloth, c 1899, 35x18", EX..130.00
Mott's, Apple of My Eye Bear, plush, 1988, M..............................15.00
Nestle, Chocolate Man, stuffed cloth, Chase Bag Co, 1970, 15", EX..20.00
Nestle Quik, Quik Bunny, plush, premium, 1980s, M....................35.00
Ralston, Magic Pup, plastic/cloth ears, mouth moves, 1951, 3", NM..100.00
Sprite, Lucky Lymon, vinyl talker, 1990s, 7½", M 25.00
Stollwerck's Cocoa, Jack the Giant Killer, cb, premium, 5", EX+ ...120.00
Sunbeam Bread, Miss Sunbeam, vinyl/rooted hair, Eegee, 1959, 17", NM ..50.00
Swiss Miss Chocolate, Swiss Miss, stuffed/vinyl face/yarn hair, EX ..30.00
Tropicana Orange Juice, Tropic-Ana, stuffed cloth, 1977, 17", NM...35.00
Tyson Chicken, Chicken Quick, stuffed cloth, 13", VG................15.00
Vlasic Pickles, Stork, wht fur w/glasses & bow tie, 1989, 22", NM ...40.00

African Art

African art does not consist of a single class of objects. Rather, these often-powerful images and objects are carved by many varying African tribes and groups across the central continent; each item represents specific cultural and spiritual functions and meanings. Many kinds of materials are used including wood, metal, fiber, ivory, and bone. Large numbers of these items are now being produced and sold to the tourist trade, but 'authentic' African art is generally considered to consist of objects which were used in cultural and/or religious activities. The items listed here are authentic, in good condition, without provenance, and considered to be of average aesthetic quality. Scott Nelson, a collector of African art, is our advisor; his address is listed in the Directory under New Mexico.

Basket, Nigeria, open fiber w/cowrie shells, 8x10" 175.00
Beads, trade; ceramic, string of 20 ....100.00
Bracelet, Ashanti, bronze, knobs...35.00
Cloth, Kuba, geometric design, 18" sq.......................................175.00
Comb, Ashanti, bird's head surmount, 4"...................................200.00
Container, Luba, gourd, wooden figural stopper...........................90.00
Divination board, Yoruba, animals, 20" dia...............................475.00
Doll, Ashanti, figural, 7" 275.00
Doll, Mossi, abstract human figure 275.00
Door, Dogon, granary, human figures, 26"...............................1,200.00
Drum, Hemba, geometric designs, 22".......................................275.00
Earrings, Masai, beaded, 6"...175.00
Figure, Dogon, crouched male, 10"..650.00
Figure, Senufo, standing female, 12"...275.00
Figure, Yoruba, pnt colonial, 12"..175.00
Goldweight, Ashanti, bronze figure..125.00
Hat, Kuba, fibre, blk pnt 175.00
Headdress, Bamana, Tchi-wara (antelope), horizontal................675.00
Heddle pulley, Senufo, bird surmount, 5" 275.00
Ibejis, Yoruba, 9", pr 375.00
Lock, Bamana, door, 2 figural surmounts, 14" 675.00
Mask, Bamana, N'Tomo, 14" 375.00
Mask, Dan, human face, 15" 375.00
Mask, Dogon, Kanaga, 26"...500.00
Mask, Karumba, polychrome, antelope, 21"...............................475.00
Mask, Mende, helmet, female initiation, 12" 875.00
Mask, Pende, human face, 8" 375.00
Pendant, Yoruba, ivory human figure, 4" 900.00
Pipe, Cameroons, elephant, brass, 14".......................................275.00
Ring, Dogon, bronze, horse & rider..275.00
Slingshot, Baule, animal head, 5"..85.00
Stool, Lega, human figural supports, 13"....................................675.00
Whisk, Yoruba, human figure, wood & horsehair, 12"................275.00

Agata

Agata is New England peachblow (the factory called it 'Wild Rose') with an applied metallic stain which produces gold tracery and dark blue mottling. The stain is subject to wear, and the amount of remaining stain greatly affects the value. It is especially valuable (and rare) on satin-finish items when found on peachblow of intense color. Caution! Be sure to use only gentle cleaning methods.

Currently rare types of art glass have been realizing erratic prices at auction; until they stabilize, we can only suggest an average range of values. In the listings that follow, examples are glossy unless noted otherwise. A condition rating of 'EX' indicates that the stain shows a slight amount of wear. Our advisors for this category are Betty and Clarence Maier; they are listed in the Directory under Pennsylvania. See also Green Opaque.

Bowl, EX mottling, waisted, tri-ruffled rim, 3½x5".....................450.00
Bowl, finger; EX coloring, 2x5"..700.00

Bowl, sauce; G color & mottling 350.00
Creamer & sugar bowl, loop hdls, 3x6" 3,750.00
Pitcher, reeded hdl, water sz 2,500.00
Toothpick holder, tricorner, EX mottling, 2⅜" 450.00

Tumbler, EX color and mottling, 3¾", from $750.00 to $1,000.00.

Tumbler, lemonade 750.00
Vase, lily; EX mottling, paper label, 24", pr 4,000.00
Vase, lily; EX mottling, 7¾" 850.00
Vase, lily; in cattail & reed Tufts fr, 11" 1,500.00

Agate Ware

Clays of various natural or artificially dyed colors combined to produce agate ware, a procedure similar to the methods used by Niloak in potting their Mission Ware. It was made by many Staffordshire potteries from about 1740 until about 1825.

Fork, steel tines, Staffordshire, 1760s, rpr, 7" 230.00
Teapot, bl & brn to cream, 1760s, 3¾", NM 925.00
Teapot, brn & rust to cream, globular, mid-1700s, rstr, 4¾" 500.00
Teapot, globular, 3 paw ft, arched hdl, stick spout, 4⅝x6¾", VG 220.00
Vase, scroll hdls w/goat masks at shoulders, festoons, 18th C, 15" ..1,375.00

Akro Agate

The Akro Agate Co., founded in 1914 primarily as a marble maker, operated in Clarksburg, West Virginia, until 1951. Their popular wares included children's dishes, powder jars, flowerpots, and novelty items along with the famous 'Akro Aggies.' Much of their glass was produced in the distinctive marbleized colors they called Red Onyx, Blue Onyx, etc.; solid opaque and transparent colors were also produced. Most of the wares are marked with their trademark, a crow flying through the letter 'A' holding an Aggie in its beak and one in each claw. Other marks include 'J.P.' on children's pieces, 'J.V. Co., Inc.,' 'Braun & Corwin,' 'N.Y.C. Vogue Merc Co. U.S.A.,' 'Hamilton Match Co.,' and 'Mexicali Pickwick Cosmetic Corp.' on novelty items. In 1936 Akro obtained the molds from the Balmer-Westite Co. of Weston, West Virginia. Westite produced a similar line of products for several years. Their ware is drab in color when compared to Akro and is generally unmarked. The embossed Westite logo does appear occasionally on the bottoms of some pieces. Westite is commonly accepted as a companion collectible of Akro.

Our advisor for miscellaneous Akro Agate is Albert Morin; he is listed in the Directory under Massachusetts.

Chiquita

Creamer, baked-on colors, 1½" 8.00

Cup, cobalt transparent, 1½" 8.00
Cup, gr opaque, 1½" 6.00
Saucer, baked-on colors, 3⅛" 2.00
Set, baked-on colors, 16-pc , MIB 90.00
Sugar bowl, gr opaque, 1½" 7.00
Sugar bowl (open), transparent cobalt, 1½" 16.00
Teapot, gr opaque, wlid, 3" 18.00

Concentric Rib

Creamer, sm, gr or wht opaque, 1¼" 8.00
Plate, sm, opaque colors other than gr or wht, 3¼" 7.00
Set, sm, gr or wht opaque, 8-pc, MIB 45.00
Sugar bowl (open), sm, opaque colors other than gr or wht, 1¼" .16.00
Teapot, sm, opaque colors, other than gr or wht, 3⅜" ...30.00

Concentric Ring

Cereal, lg, opaque colors, 3⅜" 25.00
Creamer, sm, opaque colors, 1¼" 20.00
Cup, lg, yel, 1⅜" 50.00
Cup, sm, yel & lav, 1¼" 30.00
Saucer, lg, bl marbleized, 3⅛" 15.00
Set, sm, opaque colors, 16-pc set, MIB 175.00
Teapot, sm, cobalt transparent, 3⅜" 50.00

Interior Panel, Stippled Interior Panel

Set, small, twelve-piece set (six pieces shown), blue and white marbleized, $220.00.

Cereal, lg, azure bl, 3⅜" 30.00
Cereal, lg, gr & wht marbleized, 3⅜" 30.00
Creamer, sm, azure bl, 1¼" 32.00
Creamer, sm, red & wht marbleized, 1¼" 35.00
Cup, lg, bl & wht marbleized, 2⅜" 25.00
Cup, sm, pumpkin, 1¼" 20.00
Plate, lg, lemonade & oxblood, 4¼" 15.00
Plate, lg, yel, 4¼" 10.00
Plate, sm, red & wht, 3¼" 12.00
Saucer, lg lemonade & oxblood, 3⅛" 10.00
Set, lg, topaz transparent, 21-pc, MIP 225.00
Sugar bowl, sm, azure bl, 1¼" 35.00
Teapot, lg, lemonade & oxblood, w/lid, 3¾" 85.00
Teapot, sm, gr & wht marbleized, 3⅜" 35.00
Tumbler, sm, gr lustre, 2" 12.00

J.P. (Made for J. Pressman Company)

Creamer, lg, lt bl transparent or crystal, 1½" 32.00
Cup, lg, bl transparent, ribbed, 1½" 18.00
Plate, lg, gr transparent, 4¼" 15.00

Set, lg, gr or brn transparent, 16-pc, MIB 350.00
Sugar bowl, lg, lt bl or crystal, 1½" 32.00
Teapot, lg, lt bl or crystal, w/lid, 2¾" 50.00

Miss America

Creamer, forest gr, 1¼" 65.00
Creamer, wht w/decal, 1¼" 65.00
Plate, decal or forest gr, 4½" 45.00
Plate, forest gr, 4½" 45.00
Saucer, wht, 3⅝" 15.00
Sugar bowl, forest gr, w/lid 80.00
Sugar bowl, wht w/decal, w/lid, 2" 85.00
Teapot, wht w/decal, w/lid, 3¼" 140.00

Octagonal

Tea set, opaque American Maid, large, seventeen-piece set, MIB, $200.00. (Photo courtesy Doris Lechler)

Cereal, lg, beige or pumpkin, 3⅜" 20.00
Creamer, lg, lemonade & oxblood, closed hdl, 1½" 30.00
Creamer, sm, any opaque color, open hdl, 1¼" 16.00
Creamer, sm, dk gr, 1¼" 16.00
Cup, lg, pumpkin, closed hdl, 1½" 20.00
Cup, sm, bl or wht, 1¼" 10.00
Plate, lg, yel, 4¼" 6.50
Plate, sm, yel, 3⅜" 8.00
Set, lg, gr or wht, 21-pc, MIB 160.00
Set, lg, lemonade & oxblood, 17-pc, MIB 350.00
Set, sm, gr & wht, 16-pc, MIB 140.00
Sugar bowl, lg, beige or pumpkin, closed hdl, w/lid, 1½" 18.00
Tumbler, sm, bl or wht, 2" 14.00

Raised Daisy

Creamer, sm, yel, 1¼" 50.00
Plate, sm, bl, 3" 14.00
Saucer, sm, yel, 2½" 10.00
Teapot, sm, gr, no lid, 2⅜" 35.00
Teapot, sm, yel, no lid, 2⅜" 45.00
Tumbler, sm, yel, 2" 27.00

Stacked Disc

Creamer, sm, gr or wht, 1¼" 12.00
Cup, sm, any opaque color other than gr or wht, 1¼" 14.00
Cup, sm, wht, 1¼" 6.00
Plate, sm, any opaque color other than gr or wht, 3¼" 5.00
Saucer, sm, gr or wht, 2¾" 3.00
Set, sm, gr, 21-pc, MIB 145.00
Tumbler, sm, any opaque color other than gr or wht, 2" 14.00

Stacked Disc and Interior Panel

Cereal, lg, any solid color, 3⅜" 25.00
Creamer, lg, cobalt transparent, 1⅜" 32.00
Cup, sm, gr transparent, 1¼" 22.00
Pitcher, sm, gr, 2⅞" 18.00
Plate, lg, cobalt transparent, 4¾" 15.00
Plate, sm, gr transparent, 3¼" 8.00
Set, lg, any solid color, 21-pc set, MIB 370.00
Set, sm, bl marbleized, 8-pc, MIB 275.00
Sugar bowl, sm, bl marbleized, 1¼" 45.00
Teapot, lg, gr transparent, w/lid, 3¾" 55.00
Tumbler, sm, cobalt, 2" 18.00
Tumbler, sm, gr transparent, 2" 14.00
Water set, sm, gr, 7-pc, MIB 100.00

Stippled Band

Creamer, lg, azure transparent, 1½" 35.00
Creamer, sm, amber transparent, 1¼" 30.00
Cup, sm, topaz transparent, 1¼" 7.00
Pitcher, sm, gr transparent, 2⅞" 15.00
Plate, lg, gr transparent, 4¼" 6.00
Saucer, sm, amber transparent, 2¾" 2.50
Set, lg, gr transparent, 17-pc, MIB 165.00
Set, sm, gr transparent, 7-pc, MIB 70.00
Sugar bowl, lg, azure transparent, w/lid, 1½" 55.00
Teapot, lg, amber transparent, w/lid, 3¾" 40.00
Teapot, lg, gr transparent, w/lid, 3¾" 40.00

Miscellaneous

J. Vivaudou, shaving mug, black, $65.00. (Photo courtesy Albert Morin)

Ashtray, Gypsy Smoker Set, MIB 225.00
Ashtray, Hotel Edison, orange 125.00
Ashtray, Hotel Lincoln, gr, w/matchbook holder 95.00
Ashtray, leaf, leaf, gr/wht 12.00
Ashtray, oxblood, hexagonal 65.00
Ashtray, rectangular, no tab, any color 250.00
Ashtray, Victory Star, rare 300.00
Basket, bl/wht, 2-hdl 45.00
Basket, orange/wht, 2-hdl 40.00
Bell, gr 350.00
Bell, yel, rare 400.00
Bowl, fruit; cobalt, ftd 450.00
Bowl, Graduated Dart, blk, #320 ....200.00
Candlesticks, ivory, lamp parts, pr 40.00
Candlesticks, orange, 3¼", pr 400.00
Cornucopia, gr/wht, #765 ....16.00
Cornucopia, NYC Vogue Merc, crystal rare 200.00

Creamer & sugar bowl, mk w/crow trademark, rare, 3", ea..........300.00
Flowerpot, gr, #1308..200.00
Flowerpot, gr, #1309..165.00
Flowerpot, orange, #1310..225.00
Flowerpot, Ribs & Flutes, orange, #296..............................30.00
Flowerpot, Ribs & Flutes, yel, #305...................................28.00
Flowerpot, Thumpots, marbleized, #290.............................28.00
J Vivaudou, apothecary, pk, #329....................................145.00
J Vivaudou, puff box, pk, rare...250.00
J Vivaudou, shaving mug, beige, rare...............................200.00
Jardiniere, Narrow Ledge, gr, #314....................................45.00
Jardiniere, Ribs & Flutes, bl, #306CF.................................45.00
Knife, grid style, crystal, #739..65.00
Knife, grid style, pk transparent, #739.............................125.00
Lamp, crystal, 5-pc...45.00
Lamp, marbleized, 5-pc...95.00
Lamp shade, marbleized...225.00
Marble box, Akro Chinese Checkers...................................35.00
Marble box, tin, #150...350.00
Marble box, 100 #0 Hero marbles....................................350.00
Pitcher, milk; bl, X-14, rare...800.00
Planter, factory decor, #654..45.00
Planter, Lily, #658..24.00
Planter, oval, orange/wht, #654..12.00
Planter, rectangular, bl, #653..35.00
Powder jar, apple form, ivory..400.00
Powder jar, Mexicali, bl/wht..75.00
Urn, floral, NYC Vogue Merc, bl.......................................18.00
Urn, Grecian, Niagara Falls, #764......................................35.00
Vase, Graduated Dart, gr, tab hdls, #317...........................85.00
Vase, Ribs & Flutes, orange/wht, #311.............................250.00
Vase, Ribs & Flutes, yel, #311...225.00
Westite, bud vase, marbleized, #310.................................400.00
Westite, cigar ashtray, NASM..75.00
Westite, flowerpot, gr, #301..40.00
Westite, Japanese planter, gr/wht.....................................500.00

Alamo Pottery

Alamo art pottery (1945 – 1951) was a division of the Alamo Pottery of San Antonio, Texas, which was primarily a maker of sanitary ware (bathroom fixtures). The art pottery division was founded by Jake Rowe, Richard Potter, and Bruce Blunt, and produced vitreous china items which have survived the decades without crazing and with the high gloss glazes still gleaming as if new. (Mrs. Potter was a valuable resource in compiling information about Alamo history.)

Rowe, Potter, and Blunt developed glazes, processes, and mold shapes from which came styles and colors that ran the gamut from elegant, classically styled vases to whimsical figurals, and from pale translucent aquas and yellows to bold crayon greens, blues, and yellows. The vast majority of the pieces are monochromatic, and the rare sponge- or spatter-ware pieces are at a premium.

Alamo is usually marked with a mold number (from 701 to 908, and P-2, P-3, and presumably P-1). Many also have an oval Alamo Pottery ink stamp in either black or blue. Bottoms are generally unglazed, although a few pitchers with glazed bottoms exist. Flea bites in the glaze are fairly common and unless excessive are tolerated by most collectors. Crazing and staining are nonexistent, and virtually all interiors are fully glazed. These items were originally intended for the floral trade, and most sold for less than $3.00.

The art pottery division of Alamo closed in 1951 due to high costs of storing and shipping. Rowe, Potter, and Blunt moved to Gilmer, Texas, and founded Gilmer Pottery (see Gilmer listing), which produced many

items often mistaken for Alamo. Our advisor for this category is Suzanne Knight; she is listed in the Directory under Texas.

Ashtray, #800..18.00
Bowl, #730, duck, rabbit & bear..33.00
Bowl, #766, rings, 2¾x6"...30.00
Bowl, #767, rings, 3x7"...15.00
Bowl, #772, tulip form, 2¾x3½".......................................16.00
Bowl, #777, tulip form, 2¾x6½".......................................18.00
Bowl, console; Delphinium Blue, #775, 3¼x9"....................22.50
Figural, baby diaper w/hole for pin..................................113.00
Figural, bunny...90.00
Figural, high-top baby shoe..40.00
Figural, swan, #725, 5½x5"..40.00
Figural, toilet, 4½"...60.00
Flowerpot, #829-10, diagonal waves, 10"...........................70.00
Flowerpot, #829-5, diagonal waves, 5"...............................10.00
Pitcher, #759, modified octagon, 7¼x7½"..........................40.00
Pitcher, #760, 4 diagonal sweep indentations, 7½x8½".........40.00
Planter, #734, oval, 2x8½x4"..14.00
Planter, #735, oval, 2¼x11½x6½"......................................14.00
Planter, #736, oval, 2¾x15x10"...20.00
Planter, #737, 3¾x6x6"..20.00
Planter, #769, rings, 2¼x8"..26.00
Planter, #770, rings, 3x9½x6"...18.00
Planter, #771, 3¼x12x7"...34.00
Shakers, modified octagonal, 4½", pr.................................47.00
Shakers, pr...90.00
Vase, #701, grapes & Pan, hdls, 5¾x6½"............................45.00
Vase, #703, 12½"...375.00
Vase, #704, bottom smaller than top, 8x4".........................175.00
Vase, #704, wht w/bl sponging (rare), 8x4".........................236.00
Vase, #705, 8"...18.00
Vase, #706, 12x6"..58.00
Vase, #707, 21½"...225.00
Vase, #708, 12½"...300.00
Vase, #709, 11½x6½"...92.00
Vase, #716, 11"..41.00
Vase, #717, 9"..130.00
Vase, #718, rnd base, sq top, 8½x5½"................................45.00
Vase, #719, rnd base, sq top, 9¾x5½"................................43.00
Vase, #720, 9½"...90.00
Vase, #721, 6x4"...15.00
Vase, #723, 9"..33.00
Vase, #732, hdls, 7½x8"...48.00
Vase, #733 (1 of 2 fan vases), 7x7"....................................80.00
Vase, #741, 10"..50.00
Vase, #742, 12"..130.00
Vase, #743, 15x6", from $77 to..180.00
Vase, #746, cornucopia, 7¾"..45.00
Vase, #761, octagon, 10x8"...285.00
Vase, #900-10, flares to 5¼" at top, 10"..............................44.00
Vase, #900-5, flares to 6¼" at top, 5".................................20.00
Vase, #901-7...52.00
Vase, #902-10...45.00
Vase, #902-5..8.00
Vase, #903-5, 5"..50.00
Vase, #904-5, 5"..166.00
Vase, #907, 10"...240.00
Vase, #939 (1 of 2 fan vases), 6x12"..................................30.00
Vase, not numbered, stretch bud.......................................57.00
Vase, P-2, ink stamped #, 6½"..48.00
Vase, P-2, yel w/blk spatters (rare), 6½".............................83.00
Vase, P-3, str sides, vertical ribs, 12½"..............................66.00

Vase/oil jar, #810, 18".................................550.00
Wall pocket, fish figural...............................60.00

Alexandrite

Alexandrite is a type of art glass introduced around the turn of the century by Thomas Webb and Sons of England. It is recognized by its characteristic shading, pale yellow to rose and blue at the edge of the item. Although other companies (Moser, for example) produced glass they called alexandrite, only examples made by Webb possess all the described characteristics and command premium prices. Amount and intensity of blue determines value. Our advisors for this category are Betty and Clarence Maier; they are listed in the Directory under Pennsylvania.

**Finger bowl and underplate, crimped and ruffled, 8",
$1,450.00.** (Photo courtesy Jackson's)

Bowl, ruffled, 2½x5", w/6" underplate 1,450.00
Pitcher, appl shaded hdl, 7-petal top, 5¼x4" 1,435.00
Vase, floriform, bl rim, amethyst ribs & stem, bl ft, 8" 2,100.00
Vase, floriform, 8 optic ribs, 6½" 1,345.00
Vase, floriform petal top, #RD SP 164, 3¼"..................650.00
Vase, Raindrop, pinched/ruffled top, 4¼" 700.00
Wine, 4¼" 900.00

Almanacs

The earliest evidence indicates that almanacs were used as long ago as Ancient Egypt. Throughout the Dark Ages they were circulated in great volume and were referred to by more people than any other book except the Bible. *The Old Farmer's Almanac* first appeared in 1793 and has been issued annually since that time. Usually more of a pamphlet than a book (only a few have hard covers), the almanac provided planting and harvesting information to farmers, weather forecasts for seamen, medical advice, household hints, mathematical tutoring, postal rates, railroad schedules, weights and measures, 'receipts,' and jokes. Before 1800 the information was unscientific and based entirely on astrology and folklore. The first almanac in America was printed in 1639 by William Pierce Mariner; it contained data of this nature. One of the best-known editions, Ben Franklin's *Poor Richard's Almanac*, was introduced in 1732 and continued to be printed for twenty-five years.

By the nineteenth century, merchants saw the advertising potential in a publication so widely distributed, and the advertising almanac evolved. These were distributed free of charge by drug stores and mercantiles and were usually somewhat lacking in information, containing simply a calendar, a few jokes, and a variety of ads for quick remedies and quack cures.

Today their concept and informative, often amusing text make

almanacs popular collectibles that may usually be had at reasonable prices. Because they were printed in such large numbers and often saved from year to year, their prices are still low. Most fall within a range of $4.00 to $15.00. Very common examples may be virtually worthless; those printed before 1860 are especially collectible. Quite rare and highly prized are the Kate Greenaway 'Almanacks,' printed in London from 1883 to 1897. These are illustrated with her drawings of children, one for each calendar month. See also Greenaway, Kate.

1791, Weatherwife's, stains/tears, 17-pg............17.50
1804, Houghton's Genuine..., Prentiss, 48-pg, VG 25.00
1805, New-England, Bickerstaff, Providence RI, 24-pg 35.00
1806, Farmer's, Robert B Thomas, 42-pg.........32.00
1808, Farmer's, Robert B Thomas, 44 of 48 pgs 26.00
1809, New-England Diary &, J Parkhurst Jun, MA, 48-pg........24.00
1814, Farmer's, Robert B Thomas, 46 of 48 pgs 27.50
1835, Farmer's, Robert B Thomas 22.50
1852, Horace Greeley's WHIG, 64 pgs of faces/comments/etc 22.50
1860, Methodist, many illustrations & ads, 74-pg............22.00
1860, Sketch of the Progress of Waterbury (CT), Cooke, 55 pgs ..24.00
1862, Der Nen Reading Calendar, in German, PA, 39-pg...........27.00
1871, Cassell's Illustrated..., color cover, 80-pg, 10½x7½" 25.00
1875, Boston...& Business Directory, 535-pg, EX 37.50
1881, Horsford... & Cook Book, Rumford, softcover, 47-pg, 7x4½"...35.00
1887, Barker's Illustrated...Farmer's Guide..., G 25.00
1887, Bradley's Fertilizer, Indian cover, 8x5¼" 23.00
1887, Wright's Pictorial Family, Ferrett, 24-pg, G 13.50
1888, Diamond Dye... & Household Guide, Wells, Richardson & Co...22.00
1892, Dr Harter's, 32-pg, 7½x5" 12.50
1898, Radway's...New York City, 32-pg 20.00
1906, Northrop & Lyman Medical..., EX advertising.........27.50
1907, Dr Ayer's American 8.00
1908, Studebaker's Farmer's... & Weather..., 48-pg, 8½x5", G 17.50

1909, Bliss Native Herbs, EX, $5.00.

1911, Chicago Daily News...& Year Book 35.00
1911, Dr Miles New Weather... & Hand Book, Elkhart IN, 32-pg ..27.50
1912, International Harvester Co, 96-pg, 5x8", VG 26.00
1915, Watkins...Home Doctor & Cook Book, 48th Year, 96-pg....16.00
1916, Dr JH McLean's Medical..., 63rd edition, 32-pg...........32.00
1916, International Harvester, many machines pictured 17.50
1917, Metropolitan Life Insurance..........12.00
1917, Watkins Home Doctor & Cook Book, 64-pg, 6x9", EX+ 37.50
1920, Chicago Daily News...& Yearbook..........22.50
1935, Illinois Herb Co, 80-pg, 8¼x5½" 12.50
1936, Dallas Morning News Texas Centennial, 512-pg, VG.........17.50
1937, Lum & Abner's Family, Horlick's Malted Milk premium.....35.00
1940, Goodrich, ED Barton & Sons, Youngsville PA 12.00
1948, McLean's Volcanic Oil Medicine, 34-pg, 8x5½"..................14.00
1959, International Television, w/index, 745-pg, 9½x7½"............22.50

Aluminum

Aluminum, though being the most abundant metal in the earth's crust, always occurs in combination with other elements. Before a practical method for its refinement was developed in the late nineteenth century, articles made of aluminum were very expensive. After the process for commercial smelting was perfected in 1916, it became profitable to adapt the ductile, nontarnishing material to many uses.

By the late '30s, novelties, trays, pitchers, and many other tableware items were being produced. They were often handcrafted with elaborate decoration. Russel Wright designed a line of lovely pieces such as lamps, vases, and desk accessories that are becoming very collectible. Many who crafted the ware marked it with their company logo, and these signed pieces are attracting the most interest. Wendell August Forge (Grove City, PA) is a mark to watch for; this firm was the first to produce hammered aluminum (it is still made there today), and some of their examples are particularly nice. Upwardly mobile market values reflect their popularity with today's collectors. In general, 'spun' aluminum is from the '30s or early '40s, and 'hammered' aluminum is from the '30s to the '60s.

For further information, refer to Collectible Aluminum by Everett Grist, listed in the Directory under Tennessee; Affordable Art Deco by Ken Hutchison and Greg Johnson; Vintage Bar Ware by Stephen Visakay; and Collector's Encyclopedia of Russel Wright by Ann Kerr. Another excellent reference is Hammered Aluminum, Hand Wrought Collectibles, by our advisor, Dannie Woodard, see the Directory for Texas.

Patio cart, Everlast, fitted with accessories with Fallen Leaves pattern by Mary Wright, from $650.00 to $850.00. (Photo courtesy Dannie Woodard)

Ashtray, bamboo, single rest, Everlast, 5" dia 30.00
Ashtray, sailboat on water, W August Forge, 4½" sq 20.00
Basket, apple; tray w/serrated rim, sq-knot hdl, Everlast, 11" 10.00
Basket, hammered, beaded rim, twist hdl, Buenilum, 5x9"............20.00
Basket, poinsettia, fluted bowl, rnd hdl, Farber/Shelvin, 7"...........10.00
Beverage server, concentric circles, Kromax, 11x5" dia 25.00
Bowl, bittersweet, notched rim, W August Forge, 2x7" 20.00
Bowl, Deco style, plain, Kensington, 5" dia.................................16.00
Bowl, dessert; anodized, w/glass insert, 3½", set of 8, NM 50.00
Bowl, hammered, serrated rim, 3-loop hdls, Buenilum, 2x12".......10.00
Bowl, wheat, plain rim, Palmer/Smith, 14" dia 90.00
Bowl, wild roses/geometrics, scalloped rim, Continental, 3x11"....15.00
Cake salver, hot pk w/blk hdl on cover, Regal, 13" plate, EX........30.00
Cake stand, shields band/serrated rim/ped ft, Wilson metal, 8x12" ...10.00
Candlesticks, beaded S-shape tulip form, II Farberware, 8", pr......45.00
Candy dish, bird-&-grape side hdl on oval, M Bowman, 13" 15.00
Candy dish, fruit & flowers, 2 joined bowls, center hdl, 13" L......25.00
Casserole, bamboo, bamboo finial on lid, no hdls, Everlast, 4x7" .10.00
Casserole, floral band on lid, rolled hdls, Everlast, 9" 25.00
Casserole holder, sailing ships, clip-type hdls, Forman, 3x9" 20.00

Cigarette box, bittersweet, hinged lid, W August Forge, 1½x3x5" ..75.00
Coasters, bamboo, set of 8 w/ftd hdld holder, Everlast...................30.00
Coasters, set of 8, M 25.00
Coffeepot, mums, petal finial, Continental, 10"............................85.00
Creamer & sugar bowl on tray, gold w/blk Bakelite hdls, Neocraft, EX..40.00
Crumb tray & brush, flowers w/ribbons on hammered ground, unmk....25.00
Dip server, bamboo structure w/hammered bowls, Everlast, 11" 60.00
Gravy boat, plain w/serrated lip & base rim, Buenilum, 3x6" dia..25.00
Hurricane lamp, 2 glass chimneys w/twisted hdl, Buenilum, 10x9"...30.00
Ice bucket, hammered, beaded lip, twisted hdl, Buenilum, 6x5" ...25.00
Ice bucket (open), acorn/leaf, cane-shaped hdls, Continental 25.00
Lazy Susan, fruit & flowers, serrated edge, Cromwell, 16" 10.00
Lazy Susan, glass inserts, Continental #1021................................35.00
Leaf tray, Bruce Fox, Fox L-34, 7¼x10" 125.00
Lemonade set, Gailstyn, hammered 64-oz pitcher, 6 16-oz tumblers ..30.00
Matchbox cover, shotgun/flying ducks/clouds, W August Forge....75.00
Napkin holder, thistle, crimped edge, unmk, 4x2x6" 10.00
Napkin rings, anodized, wide, in orig plastic box, set of 4, M 50.00
Nut bowl, flowers/leaves, ruffled/serrated rim, ped ft, Wilson, 7" ..10.00
Pitcher, gr anodized, w/8 5" tumblers, Colorcraft, Indpls Ind, NM ..60.00
Pitcher, tulips, hammered, Rodney Kent, 10" 30.00
Plate, dogwood, plain edge, W August Forge, 9".........................30.00
Rolling pin, anodized, w/stand, EX 30.00
Silent butler, berries, Everlast, 6" 20.00
Spoons, iced tea; anodized, 8", NM, set of 6 ....25.00
Tidbit, mums, crimped edges, 2-tier, Continental, 9¼" 35.00
Tray, bar; tulips, Rodney Kent..40.00
Tray, berry/leaf, Victorian ladies on china insert, Cromwell, 16" dia..45.00
Tray, bread; acorns/grapes, oval, W August Forge, 7x11"..............45.00
Tray, floral, hammered, ball ft, Everlast 65.00
Tray, goldfish, hammered rim w/beaded edge, unmk, 10x14" 45.00
Tray, larkspur, W August Forge, 20x13".......................................75.00
Tray, sandwich; crane/bamboo/hammered, appl hdls, Hand Forge, 9"...30.00
Tray, sandwich; tennis player, Hyman Blum, 10x16" 45.00
Tree ornaments, anodized twisted icicles, 15 in box, NM..............25.00
Trivet, grapevine band, Everlast, 10" dia 15.00
Tumblers, anodized, 5", set of 6, M 25.00
Tumblers, anodized, 5", w/matching 9" straws, set of 6, NM 45.00
Umbrella stand, larkspur, W August Forge, 22" 285.00
Vase, gold laurel-leaf base, Kensington, 10" 50.00
Wastebasket, emb floral, Everlast, 11x11" dia 60.00

AMACO, American Art Clay Co.

AMACO is the logo of the American Art Clay Co. Inc., founded in Indianapolis, Indiana, in 1919, by Ted O. Philpot. They produced a line of art pottery from 1931 through 1938. The company is still in business but now produces only supplies, implements, and tools for the ceramic trade.

Values for AMACO have risen sharply, especially those for figurals, items with Art Deco styling, and pieces with uncommon shapes. Our advisor for this category is Virginia Heiss; she is listed in the Directory under Indiana.

Bust, lady's head, bl, #159, 8"...175.00
Bust, lady's head, wht, #144, 5½" 155.00
Bust, lady's head, wht, #158, 8"...160.00
Vase, blk gloss w/2 hdls, #39, 6x4½"...95.00
Vase, gr & silver, 4 spheres stack, Deco style, #1, 9"....................125.00
Vase, gr matt w/2 lg hdls, #6, 9"...125.00
Vase, lt bl gloss, #S-1, 5½"...65.00
Vase, matt gr, #80, 6¼x5½"...85.00
Vase, metallic gr, #46, 6½"..100.00

Vase, yel matt w/hdls, #2, 4½" 60.00

Amberina

Amberina, one of the earliest types of art glass, was developed in 1883 by Joseph Locke of the New England Glass Company. The trademark was registered by W.L. Libbey, who often signed his name in script within the pontil.

Amberina was made by adding gold powder to the batch, which produced glass in the basic amber hue. Part of the item, usually the top, was simply reheated to develop the characteristic deep red or fuchsia shading. Early amberina was mold blown, but cut and pressed amberina was also produced. The rarest type is plated amberina, made by New England for a short time after 1886. It has been estimated that less than 2,000 pieces were ever produced. Other companies, among them Hobbs and Brockunier, Mt. Washington Glass Company, and Sowerby's Ellison Glassworks of England, made their own versions, being careful to change the name of their product to avoid infringing on Libbey's patent. Prices realized at auction seem to be erratic, to say the least, and dealers appear to be 'testing the waters' with prices that start out very high only to be reduced later if the item does not sell at the original asking price. A lot of amberina glassware is of a more recent vintage — look for evidence of an early production, since the later wares are worth much less than glassware that can be attributed to the older makers. Generic amberina with hand-painted flowers will bring lower prices as well. Our values are taken from auction results and dealer lists, omitting the extremely high and low ends of the range. Our advisor is Debbie Maggard; she is listed in the Directory under Ohio. See also Libbey.

Beverage set, Invt T'print, amber fluted hdl, w/10 6½" tumblers...**900.00**
Bowl, centerpc; HP florals, amber ft, 9½x16x11" **2,500.00**
Bowl, finger; ruffled rim, 2½x5½" **200.00**
Bowl, floriform, flanged/scalloped rim, fuchsia, 3¾x7", NM **550.00**
Bowl, swirled w/crimped/ruffled rim, 3¾x5½" **175.00**
Celery vase, Dmn Quilt, cylinder w/sq scalloped rim, 6⅛"..........**200.00**
Creamer, Daisy & Button, str sides, 5" **275.00**
Creamer, Invt T'print, amber hdl, 4¼" **150.00**
Creamer, melon shape..**130.00**
Creamer, squatty, waisted neck, amber hdl, fuchsia, NE Glass, 4"...**300.00**
Cruet, trifold rim, amber faceted stopper, 5½" **275.00**
Cup, amber hdl, ribbed, 2¾"..**135.00**
Cup, punch; Dmn Quilt, reeded amber hdl, 2½"..........................**120.00**
Ewer, amberina, HP florals w/gold, amber hdl, 18" **1,250.00**
Mug, Invt T'print...**90.00**
Pitcher, amber hdl, sq rim, 6¾" **160.00**
Pitcher, Dmn Quilt, water sz..**150.00**
Pitcher, Invt T'print, reeded amber hdl, 5" **110.00**
Pitcher, Lincoln Drape, reverse coloring, ruffled top, 5¼" **115.00**
Pitcher, pinched, amber hdl extends beyond top, sq mouth, 6¾"..**160.00**
Pitcher, reverse color, Invt T'print, reeded amber hdl, 5"............**110.00**
Pitcher, trifold, amberina hdl, Midwest, 4½" **100.00**
Pitcher, Wheeling Drape, melon shaped, water sz **175.00**
Tankard, Dmn Quilt, flared cylinder, appl hdl, 7".......................**450.00**
Tankard, elongated Dmn Quilt, NE Glass, 8½"...........................**675.00**
Tankard, 10-panel cylinder, reeded hdl, 6⅝"..............................**325.00**
Toothpick holder, tricorner, 2½" **285.00**
Tumbler, Dmn Quilt, fuchsia, 3¾"...**60.00**
Tumbler, juice; tapered cylinder, reeded hdl, 3½", 10 for **700.00**
Tumbler, lemonade; amber reeded hdl, 5¼", pr **250.00**
Tumbler, lemonade; Swirl, amber reeded hdl, 5½" **125.00**
Vase, HP maidenhair ferns, crimped rim, Webb, 4¼"...................**475.00**
Vase, lily; trifold top, 9" **550.00**
Wine, 4¾" **300.00**

Plated Amberina

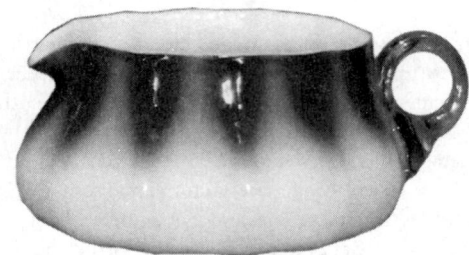

Creamer, 3x4½", $9,200.00.

Bowl, 8" **5,250.00**
Cruet, amber hdl, faceted stopper, 6¾" **3,750.00**
Pitcher, tankard, amber loop hdl, 8¾" **16,675.00**
Sugar bowl, 2 appl amber hdls, 2x6" **16,000.00**
Tumbler, 3¾" **1,700.00**
Vase, lily, trifold rim, 8" **7,000.00**

American Encaustic Tiling Co.

A.E. Tile was organized in 1879 in Zanesville, Ohio. Until its closing in 1935, they produced beautiful ornamental and architectural tile equal to the best European imports. They also made vases, figurines, and novelty items with exceptionally fine modeling and glazes. For a more thorough study we recommend *American Art Pottery* by Dick Sigafoose. See also Tiles.

Bookends, girl & rabbit emb, beige & bl matt, 1926, 4½", pr.....**150.00**
Bookends, putti play w/rabbit, matt blk & silver, mk **325.00**
Box, Oriental garden, figures, animals, emb emb on red-orange, lid, 7"....**165.00**
Desk pc, ram on stepped base w/pen troughs, 1922, 5½" **200.00**
Figurine, elephant walking, gray/ivory matt, rpr, 6½x11".............**70.00**
Paperweight, ram w/lg horns, orange matt & gloss, 3½x5½" **125.00**
Plaque, lion & lioness, dusty rose, 12x6", pr **695.00**
Vase, lime crystalline w/violet & bl irid, hdls, #734, 9" **150.00**

American Indian Art

That time when the American Indian was free to practice the crafts and culture that was his heritage has always held a fascination for many. They were a people who appreciated beauty of design and colorful decoration in their furnishings and clothing; and because instruction in their crafts was a routine part of their rearing, they were well accomplished. Several tribes developed areas in which they excelled. The Navajo were weavers and silversmiths, the Zuni, lapidaries. Examples of their craftsmanship are very valuable. Today even the work of contemporary Indian artists — weavers, silversmiths, carvers, and others — is highly collectible. Unless otherwise noted, values are for items with no obvious damage or excessive wear (EX/NM). For a more thorough study we recommend *Arrowheads and Projectile Points*, *Indian Axes*, *Indian Artifacts of the Midwest*, and *Collector's Guide to Indian Pipes, Identification and Values*. All four have been written by our advisor, Lar Hothem; you will find his address in the Directory under Ohio.

Key:
bw — beadwork   p-h — prehistoric
dmn — diamond   s-s — sinew sewn

Apparel and Accessories

Before the white traders brought the Indian women cloth from which to sew their garments and beads to use for decorating them, clothing was made from skins sewn together with sinew, usually made of animal tendon. Porcupine quills were dyed bright colors and woven into bags and armbands and used to decorate clothing and moccasins. Examples of early quillwork are scarce today and highly collectible.

Early in the nineteenth century, beads were being transported via pony pack trains. These 'pony' beads were irregular shapes of opaque glass imported from Venice. Nearly always blue or white, they were twice as large as the later 'seed' beads. By 1870 translucent beads in many sizes and colors had been made available, and Indian beadwork had become commercialized. Each tribe developed its own distinctive methods and preferred decorations, making it possible for collectors today to determine the origin of many items. Soon after the turn of the century, the craft of beadworking began to diminish.

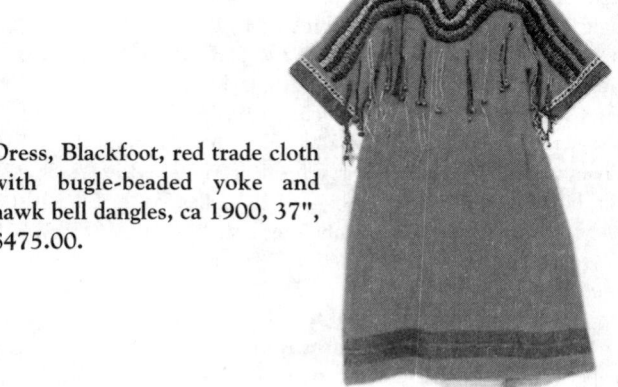

Dress, Blackfoot, red trade cloth with bugle-beaded yoke and hawk bell dangles, ca 1900, 37", $475.00.

Belt, Crow, brass-tacked leather w/bw, 1910s, 46x12" **200.00**
Belt, Navajo lady's, silver conchos w/turq stones, 1940s, 30" **70.00**
Belt, Sioux, bw geometrics on old pnt parfleche, 1900, 43x2"...**225.00**
Blouse, Navajo, blk velvet w/silver buttons, +lg satin skirt, 1940s.....**475.00**
Bonnet, Sioux baby's, full bw/s-s/velvet lined/satin trim, 1880s, 6"....**850.00**
Cap, Sioux child's, geometric bw, calico lining, 1910s, 8" **715.00**
Cuffs, Sioux boy's, s-s on buffalo w/bw geometrics, 1890s, 5x5"..**500.00**
Dress, Navajo, traditional, hand-loomed, 2-part, 1930s, 38x23".**225.00**
Dress, Nez Perce, bw yoke/shoulders on hide w/fringe, 1880s, 42" .**1,500.00**
Dress, Nez Perce, bw yoke/sleeves on tradecloth, fringe, 1940s, 45" ..**300.00**
Dress, Nez Perce, gr corduroy w/line bw, cvd shells, 1940s, 47x25" ...**200.00**
Dress, Nez Perce, purple trade cloth w/floral bw, 1900s, 44x38" .**900.00**
Dress, Plateau child's, bw yoke on tanned buckskin, 1890s, NM ...**800.00**
Gauntlets, Crow, buckskin, high-top w/floral bw, fringe, 1940s, 13" ...**225.00**
Gauntlets, Nez Perce, floral bw on ochre hide, 1900s, 15x8" **600.00**
Gauntlets, Plateau, hide w/deer & geometric bw, 1940s, 18x7"..**600.00**
Gloves, Cree, high-top hide w/floral bw & fringe, 1900s, 11".....**150.00**
Gloves, wht buckskin, full bw ea side, 20th C, M........................**700.00**
Hat, Crow 'Reservation' bw band, appl bw buffalo head, 1935 ...**600.00**
Hat, Nez Perce lady's, twined corn husk w/mc Vs, fez style, 1890s, 6" .**1,300.00**
Jacket, Cree, tanned moose hide w/fringe/bw stars, 1920s............**170.00**
Jacket, Flathead, buckskin w/fringe/stylized floral bw, 1920s, 27"...**120.00**
Legging strips, Nez Perce, buffalo hide w/bw/fringe, 1930s, 3x30", pr...**500.00**
Leggings, Crow, mc bw on leather, attached to trade cloth, 1920s........**880.00**
Leggings, Nez Perce, bw leather panels (1900s) on newer trade cloth..**475.00**
Leggings, Pawnee, trade cloth w/geometric bw strip, 1900s, 28x14".....**750.00**
Leggings, Ute, geometric bw on gr trade cloth w/red trim, 1900s, 31x3".**300.00**
Mittens, Cree, moosehide w/mc floral embr, blanket lining, 13", pr....**140.00**
Moccasins, Algonquin child's, red velvet uppers w/floral bw, 4½" ...**85.00**
Moccasins, Assiniboine, buffalo hide w/bl bw, quills, 1920s, 11"..**200.00**
Moccasins, Blackfeet, s-s buffalo hide w/parfleche soles, 1880s, 11" ..**800.00**
Moccasins, burial; Arapaho, full bw (even soles), 1890s, 6"........**900.00**

Moccasins, burial; Sioux, full bw (even soles), 1920s, 6x3".........**375.00**
Moccasins, Cheyenne lady's, full bw ft/top, yel-ochred hide, 1890s ..**2,000.00**
Moccasins, Cree, hide w/floral bw on blk velvet, puckered toes, 1900s..**130.00**
Moccasins, Crow, antelope hide w/bw toes, rawhide soles, 1890s, 10"...**225.00**
Moccasins, Hopi, thick-soled boot style w/concho closure, 1880s, 5"....**375.00**
Moccasins, Mandan/Hidatso, hide w/quilled disc on toes, 1870s, 9½" ..**950.00**
Moccasins, Nez perce, hide w/full geometric/floral bw, 1920s, 11x4".....**500.00**
Moccasins, Nez Perce, s-s, soft soles, floral bw toes, 1890s, 5".....**375.00**
Moccasins, Osage, heavy bw w/star motif, 10½" **600.00**
Moccasins, Seneca, allover bw, 1850s, 10½" **400.00**
Moccasins, Sioux, hide w/full bw geometrics, 1920s, 11x4" **475.00**
Moccasins, Sioux, red/wht/bl bw w/parfleche soles, 1890s, 10½"...**550.00**
Sash, Navaho, hand-woven wool w/fringe, 1970s, 62x3"..............**25.00**
Shirt, Blackfoot, classic red stroud w/basket bw yoke, 1900s, 31x16"..**475.00**
Shirt, Iroquois, floral bw on canvas, 1890s, 30x23" **375.00**
Shirt, Nez Perce child's war, #16 cut beads on red stroud, 1885...**4,750.00**
Shirt, Plateau, trade cloth w/heavy floral bw, fringe, 1920s, 27" .**850.00**
Shirt, Potowatami, blk velvet w/mc floral bw, 1890s, 31x24"......**600.00**
Shirt, war; Sioux, bw buckskin w/scalp locks, 1940s, lg **2,750.00**
Snowshoes, E Woodlands child's, wood & rawhide, 1900s, 32x10"...**225.00**
Vest, Crow, s-s beaded buckskin, Tobacco Society, 1890s, lg.......**850.00**
Vest, Sioux, full bw, Pine Ridge Reservation, 1940s.................**2,350.00**
Vest, Sioux, full bw front & bk w/flag & teepee design, 1930s, sm ..**900.00**

Bags and Cases

The Indians used bags for many purposes, and most display excellent form and workmanship. Of the types listed below, many collectors consider the pipe bag to be the most desirable form. Pipe bags were long, narrow, leather and bead or quillwork creations made to hold tobacco in a compartment at the bottom and the pipe, with the bowl removed from the stem, in the top. Long buckskin fringe was used as trim and complemented the quilled and beaded design to make the bag a masterpiece of Indian art.

Sioux, knife case, sinew-sewn hide with geometric beadwork, 1880s, 12x3½", $450.00.

Assiniboine, teepee, full bw/elk hide, mini (toy), 1910, 6", pr....**850.00**
Cheyenne, pipe, much bw, quilled slats, fringe, 1920s, 40x5" ..**1,500.00**
Cheyenne, pipe, s-s, bar pattern, bw/fringe, 20th C, 43x5"......**1,800.00**
Cheyenne, pipe, tab-top bar pattern, bw on ochred elk hide, 1900s, 37".**1,200.00**
Cheyenne-style, bonnet, mineral pnt on parfleche, 20th C, 24x7" .**120.00**
Chippewa, bandolier, full bw florals/animals, 20th C, 48x14" .**1,400.00**
Cree, tanned moose hide w/bw & fringe, 1890s, 7x9" **300.00**
Crow, awl case, full bw w/brass teads/tin cone dangles, 1880s, 16"...**275.00**
Crow, medicine, full bw, s-s, w/tin case/horsehair drops, 18801, 8x6" .**550.00**
Crow, parfleche, miner-pnt on elk hide, 1880s, 27x14" **900.00**
Crow, teepee, hide w/line bw, beaded ends/tin cones, 1920s, 14x12" ...**325.00**
Flathead, pipe, smoked buckskin w/horse & rider, fringe, 1978, 30" **300.00**
Great Lakes, pony & seed beads on Fr velvet, 1890s, 6x8" **110.00**
Gros Ventre, mc w/ornate bw ea side, 1880s, 6", M **1,400.00**
Maidu, bandolier, olive shell & trade cloth, 1-pc, 1900s.............**170.00**
N Plains, parfleche envelope, elk hide, red/gr pnt, 1900s, 26x14" ..**450.00**

Nez Perce, belt pouch, full geometric bw, flap top, 1920s, 5x4" ..150.00
Nez Perce, heart-shape w/floral bw ea side, 1920s, 10x9" 325.00
Nez Perce, parfleche, classic pnt designs, 1900s, 29x13" 500.00
Nez Perce, parfleche, pnt geometrics, fold-over, 1920s, 12x25" ..325.00
Nez Perce, parfleche, pnt geometrics on rawhide, 1880s, 17x6"..475.00
Nez Perce, twined corn husk w/geometrics, 1880s, 14x18".........950.00
Ojibway, medicine, loomed w/bw, bead & tin cone fringe, 1890s, 23x8" .400.00
Oto, bandolier, much bw w/ribbon-work neck strap, 1940s, 36x10" ...350.00
Plains, parfleche, strong mc, missing tie, 9½x6¾" 495.00
Plateau, flat w/full bw of warrior on horse, 1930s, lg 2,250.00
Plateau, full bw floral & foliage, 1930s, 9x8" 400.00
Plateau, full bw w/deer head & floral designs, 1930s, 11x12"......600.00
Plateau, full bw w/deer in forest, flat, 1920s, 12x14" 375.00
Plateau, full bw w/florals & foliage, flat, 1930s, 11x13"..............800.00
Shoshone, bw Indian head & torso, oval, 1950s, 12x7" 250.00
Sioux, bladder, w/mc porcupine quills, 1880s, 9x3" 110.00
Sioux, doctor, bw warriors on all sides, 1930s, 15x20", M........6,000.00
Sioux, pipe, deer hide, s-s, bw sides, 1880s, 7½x17"..................800.00
Sioux, pipe, geometric bw/quillwork/fringe on buckskin, 20th C, 29" ...475.00
Sioux, pipe, s-s buffalo hide w/geometric bw/quills/fringe, 1890, 33"..2,500.00
Sioux, strike-a-lite, traditional bw, fringe, 1890s, 8" 300.00
Ute, full geometric bw w/flap, ca 1900, 19x6".........................500.00
Ute, tail, full bw on ochred mtn sheep hide, 19th C, 19x2½" 750.00
Wasco, tobacco, bw on deer hide, 1940s, 10x3½" 140.00

Baskets

In the following listings, examples are basket form and coiled unless noted otherwise.

Pima, olla, ladder design,
1920s, 10x12", $900.00.

Apache, bowl, animals & checkerboard, 1900s, 4x20"............2,250.00
Apache, bowl, blk quadrants/red Xs/arrow parts, 1920, 2x8½" ...225.00
Apache, bowl, ornate checkerboard, 1900s, 4x14" 1,200.00
Apache, bowl, plain, 1920s, 2x9" 180.00
Apache, bowl, swastikas/Xs/triangles, 1920s, 3x11"................1,000.00
Apache, burden, twined, buckskin trim, fringe, cones, 1930s, 14x10".350.00
Apache, burden, twined, buckskin trim & fringe, 1930s, 14x18" ..700.00
Apache, pitched tus (water), 1975, 10x13"...............................350.00
Athabascan, bark, cut-out decor, w/lid, 1930, 5x6" 130.00
CA Mission, diagonal checkered design, lt wear, 2⅛x4⅜"..........440.00
Cherokee, dbl-weave, Eva Wolfe, ca 1940, w/documentation, 4x7" .225.00
Eastern Woodlands, baby carrier, ca 1900, mini, 2½x7"............300.00
Hopi, tray, mc majestic eagle, 1920s, 15".................................550.00
Hopi, tray, wicker w/sunflower design, 1950s, 9½" 140.00
Hupa, cooking, hourglass design, 1890s, 6x18"..........................450.00
Klickitat, embricated, base & rim loops, geometrics, 1900, 6x9x4"..275.00
Klickitat, embricated, conical w/rim loops & geometrics, 1910, 12x12"..1,400.00
Klickitat, embricated, rim loops, arrowhead design, 1910s, 10x8"..1,100.00
Maidu, bowl, blk parallelograms, 1920s, 8x4½".......................1,100.00
Maidu, complicated geometrics & flames, 1920s, 6x12" 2,500.00
Maidu, winnowing, willow & red bud, 1930s, 6x15" 325.00

Mission, basket, snake type w/mc dmns, 1920s, 5x10"................500.00
Mission, tray, fine weave w/blossom design, 1940s, 11¼" 750.00
Navajo, wedding, mc decor, tight weave, 1920s, 12½"...............300.00
NW Coast, hat, conical w/dome, whaling figures, analine dyes, 7x9"..360.00
Panamint, mc w/butterflies rim ticking, 1940s, 3x6" 800.00
Papago, bowl, radiating lines, 1930s, 3x11"...............................70.00
Pima, bowl, checker-dmns w/overcast stitched dk martynia rim, 5x7"..825.00
Pima, classic design, 1890s, 4½x13" 450.00
Pima, horsehair Friendship design w/27 figures, C Juan, 20th C, 3"..500.00
Pima, tray, expanded maze, dk martynia center, G age, 2¾x9⅞"...385.00
Pomo, bowl, fine weave, blk stacked design, ca 1900, 2⅜x5½"..935.00
Skokomish, twined w/quail, topknot & V formation, 1920s, 13x9"..850.00
Tlingit, bowl, gold 'I' and red X design, 1910, 6x8" 575.00
Tlingit, mc geometrics, 1920s, 9x14" 5,000.00
Tlingit, mc stepped design, fine weave, 1920s, 4x3".................350.00
Tlingit, mc stepped design, 1920s, 9x10" 1,600.00
Tlingit, rattle top, brn/orange decor, provenance, 1910s, 4x6"...2,500.00
Tlingit, rattle top w/brn & gold fret design, 1910, 3x7" 400.00
Tlingit, rattle top w/mc chevrons, 1920s, 5x8" 1,000.00
Tulare, mc arrow points & dmns, 1920s, 6x13" 1,300.00
Washo, single rod, mc lightning decor, 1910, 3x7".....................140.00
Washo, vessel, Great Basin 1-rod coil, oblong, w/lid, 3x7½x3½" 715.00
Whilkut, bowl, half-twist/full-twist o/l maidenhair fern decor, 3x5"..275.00
Yokut, bowl, mc rectangular design, ca 1930, 6x15½" 1,200.00
Yurok, bowl, bear grass & maidenhair fern, slight wear, 3½x5½" ..825.00

Blades and Points

Relics of this type usually display characteristics of a general area, time period, or a particular location. With study, those made by the Plains Indians are easily discerned from those of the West Coast. Because modern man has imitated the art of the Indian by reproducing these artifacts through modern means, use caution before investing your money in 'too good to be authentic' specimens. For a more thorough study we recommend *Flint Arrowheads and Knives of the North American Indian* by Lawrence N. and Steven N. Tulley, and *Arrowheads and Projectile Points* and *Indian Artifacts of the Midwest*, Books I through IV, by Lar Hothem.

Adena, high-grade Flintridge, Woodland, OH, 5½x2"...............900.00
Bi-pointed, Burlington chert, Mississipian, 6⅞x2x½"................150.00
Bifurcate, blk/red/orange flint, early Archaic, IL, 1⅛x1¼" 25.00
Corner-notch, Coshocton flint, well chipped, Archaic, OH, 2¼"...65.00
Corner-notch, 2-tone gray Flintridge, Archaic, 3¾", $325 to.....450.00
Cupp, maroon flint, late Mississippian, MO, 1¾".......................25.00
Dickson, Burlington chert, middle Woodland, 3½x1⅛", $150 to...225.00
Dickson, ultra-thin, wht material, middle Woodland, IL, 6".......750.00
Etley, Burlington chert, slightly twisted, Archaic, 4⅝", $225 to.350.00
Hardin, mc heat-treated flint, early Archaic, IL, 3x1⅛" 60.00
Hopewell, blk Upper Mercer flint, middle Woodland, 3¾x1¼" .225.00
Scallorn, tan chert, middle Mississippian, 2½" 65.00
Side-notch, bl-gray gem-quality Flintridge, Archaic, OH, 3¼"...100.00
Snyders, Burlington chert, well chipped, Woodland, 3¾x2⅝", up to.400.00
Stemmed, wht flint, Archaic, IL, 5x1" 450.00
Stilwell, IN hornstone, heavy serrations, Archaic, 3⅝", up to....425.00
Table rock/bottleneck, Flintridge, Archaic, 2½x1⅜".....................60.00
Thebes, wht flint, early Archaic, IL, 4x2"..................................300.00
Turkey-tail, dbl-notched, hornstone, early Woodland, 3¼" 175.00
Turkey-tail, striped flint, Woodland, IN, 4x1½"........................200.00
Waubesa, Burlington chert, middle Woodland, IA, 5x1⅝", $150 to...200.00
Waubesa, gray chert, Woodland, EX flaking/grinding, 3x1¼".....195.00

Ceremonial Items

Amulet, Great Lakes, Midi Society, bw, 20th C, 5x7".................110.00

Bonnet, Arapaho, horned, ermine decor, beaded band, 1880s, 17x10"..3,750.00
Club, medicine; Blackfoot, 1880s, 12x1"......................................450.00
Cross, silver on hand-wrought metal, heavy beads, 20th C, 36" .200.00
Drum, Plains, pnt rawhide w/stylized horse & 4-winds design, 1930, 21"..425.00
Drum, Sioux, pnt buffalo hand-held type w/beaded/pnt beater, 1890s...950.00
Drum, WN Coast, hide, red/blk pnt totems, 1900, 1x10" dia 225.00
Drum strip, bw floral band from drum top, 1890s, 69x4"............600.00
Feast dish, cvd cedar w/yel decor, 1930s, 13" 275.00
Fetish, Cheyenne, turtle umbilical cord, spot-stiched bw, 5".......330.00
Fetish, Plains, snake, allover bw, 1910, 6" 120.00
Fetish, Sioux, lizard, allover bw, tin cones/horsehair, 1920s, 6"...600.00
Fetish, Sioux, turtle, s-s w/tin cones, 1920s, 4" 110.00
Fetish, Sioux cradlebrd; lizard w/mc bw, stitched border, 6¼".....440.00
Helmet, NW Coast, cvd/pnt bear & eagle decor, 1930s, 12x9"..600.00
Mask, Iroquois, False Face, braided/coiled corn husks, 1920s 225.00
Mask, Iroquois, False Face, cvd wood/horsehair/metal, 20th C, 13x7"..350.00
Maskette, Haida, cvd argillite, 1930s, 5x3".................................200.00
Maskette, Tlingit shaman's, cvd ivory w/abalone inlay, 1900, 2x3" .2,000.00
Medicine pc, Haida, cvd ivory skull, 1920s, 2½x1" 75.00
Medicine wheel, hide/trade cloth w/animal suspensions, 1880s, 14x9" .700.00
Paddles, Kwakiutl, cvd/pnt, ca 1900, 18", pr............................225.00
Pipe tomahawk, brass w/tacked & file-burned hdl, hide grip, 1890s, 18"..950.00
Pipe tomahawk, iron w/heart cutout, brass-tacked wood hdl, 19th C, 19"..700.00
Rattle, dance; Hopi, parfleche top, horsehair attachments, 8¼".110.00
Rattle, Kiowa, gourd w/bw, 1890s, 16" 550.00
Rattle, NW Coast, cvd/pnt bear w/twine-wrapped hdl, 1930s, 12x5" .400.00
Roach, dance; Crow, dyed porcupine & deer hair, 1970, 20x7" 30.00
Soul catcher, NW Coast, cvd ivory w/abalone inlay, 1920s, 6x2x2"...300.00
Spoon, Haida, horn w/mtn goat cvd hdl w/abalone inlay, 1900s, 13x3"...450.00
Tabletta, handmade/HP cottonwood butterfly, 20th C, 19x22" ..650.00
Wand, dance, cvd horn, bull bw hdl, 20th C, 30x12" 200.00

Dolls

Apache, cloth, handmade, w/Apache dress, ca 1960, 15x4"..........50.00
Apache, Devil Dancer, hand cvd, ca 1950, 13x5" 160.00
Cheyenne, s-s buckskin w/buffalo hair, full costume, 20th C...1,000.00
Hopi, Kachina, Hoote Ogre, cvd cottonwood root, 1930s, 6½"..475.00
Hopi, Kachina, Hoote Ogre, kilt & leather cloak, 1950s, 13".....200.00
Hopi, Kachina, Mo Mo, 1910s, 12x3" 500.00
Hopi, Kachina, Rain Dancer, sgn, HB, 1940s, 13x6"...................225.00
Hopi, Kachina, Squirrel, cvd cottonwood, 1930s, 6½"................450.00
Hopi, Kachina, Sunflower, 1-pc, 1940s, 14x5"............................225.00
Hopi, Kachina, Tasop, Geraldine Shongra, 1970s, 10x4" 130.00
Hopi, Kachina, 1-pc cvg, rare, 1940, 10x6"................................300.00
Hopi, Morning Singer Kachina, EX detail, 1950s, 7½x2½"........225.00
Navajo, handmade male in full ceremonial dress, 1940s, 12x5" 60.00
Seminole, palm frond w/ribbon-work outfit, 1940s, 17x6" 160.00
Tulalip, basketry type w/long braids, 1920s, 8x3½"......................210.00

Domestics

Baby carrier, Cree, buckskin & birchbark w/bw, 1940s, mini, 11x4"...250.00
Baby carrier, Salish, embricated geometrics, 1900s, 28x11x6".....650.00
Blanket, Chimayo, blk/wht/gray, fringed, 1940s, 72x48" 275.00
Blanket, Navajo, chinle w/banded design, 1910s, 84x72" 650.00
Blanket, Navajo, Transitional Eye Dazzler, 1900s, 80x54" 1,600.00
Blanket, Nez Perce, bw on trade cloth w/buckskin fringe, 1890s, 35x53"..700.00
Bucket, Plateau, rawhide container, rnd, 1940s, 12x10"...............100.00
Cradle, Nez Perce, hide & buckskin w/bw & human hair, mini, 1900, 8x3"..450.00
Cradle, Ponca, full-loom w/bw, orig tacked boards, 1900s, 33x9"..2,000.00
Cradleboard, doll; Apache, s-s leather w/splint boards, 1910s, 15"..1,150.00
Drape, saddle; Nez Perce, buffalo hide w/bw/fringe, 1900s, 110x11"..800.00
Flag, teepee; quilled buffalo hide, 1870s, 18x10" 550.00

Pestle, Chumash, cvd/grooved stone, p-h, 8" 140.00
Saddle, Sioux, rawhide over antlers/wood, s-s, 1880s, 12x18".....140.00
Spoon, Cheyenne, buffalo horn, horse effigy bw hdl/fringe, 1870s, 12"..550.00
Spoon, cvd horn w/animal effigy, bw hdl, 20th C, 14x2" 150.00
Spoon, Plains, cvd horn w/animal effigy, bw hdl, 20th C, 10x4"...180.00
Tamper, Sioux, cvd wood w/human effigy & quill decor, 1920s, 20"...300.00
Tamper, Sioux, hand/cvd/pnt, puzzle type, 19th C, 15½"............200.00

Jewelry and Adornments

As early as 500 A.D., Indians in the Southwest drilled turquoise nuggets and strung them on cords made of sinew or braided hair. The Spanish introduced them to coral, and it became a popular item of jewelry; abalone and clam shells were favored by the Coastal Indians. Not until the last half of the nineteenth century did the Indians learn to work with silver. Each tribe developed its own distinctive style and preferred design, which until about 1920 made it possible to determine tribal origin with some degree of accuracy. Since that time, because of modern means of communication and travel, motifs have become less distinct.

Quality Indian silver jewelry may be antique or contemporary. Age, though certainly to be considered, is not as important a factor as fine workmanship and good stones. Pre-1910 silver will show evidence of hammer marks, and designs are usually simple. Beads have sometimes been shaped from coins. Stones tend to be small; when silver wire was used, it is usually square. To insure your investment, choose a reputable dealer.

Belt, Navajo lady's, silver & turq cluster conchos, 20th C 450.00
Bolo, Navajo, silver Eagle Dancer w/turq & bear-claw hook, 1970s..300.00
Bracelet, Haida, hand-cvd, silver w/Beaver design, 1970s, 6x1¾"...150.00
Bracelet, Navajo, silver w/lg turq stone, sgn, 1950s, 9x3"............350.00
Bracelet, Navajo, silver w/turq/coral inlay, T Singer, 1980, 7x1½" ..375.00
Bracelet, Zuni, silver row type w/98 turq stones, 1940s, 6x½" 225.00
Bracelet, Zuni, silver w/inlaid Devil Dancer center, 1970, 6x2" 80.00
Breastplate, Sioux, leather fr w/hairpipe bone beads/claw drops, 1890s ..900.00
Earrings, Navajo, free-form turq & silver, 1940s, 1x¾", pr..........100.00
Earrings, Navajo, turq & silver, 3-part, 1940s, 2x½", pr..............120.00
Earrings, Navajo, turq & silver drop clusters, 1940s, 4x1", pr 195.00
Hat band, Navajo, hammered silver w/dbl turq buckle/tips, 1970s, 25"..80.00
Necklace, Hopi, silver choker w/handmade chain, 1970s, 5½x1"....225.00
Necklace, Hupa, 2-strand, matched dentalia band & abalone, 195h C, 38"..275.00
Necklace, Navajo, graduated silver 'melon' beads, 1970s, 22".......80.00
Necklace, Santo Domingo, inlaid shell pendant, shell beads, 1970s, 23"..80.00
Necklace, Santo Domingo, triple jackla, turq & shell, 1970s, 48" ...90.00
Necklace, Sioux, bone hairpipe w/brass/glass bead breastplate, 1930s ..350.00
Ring, Navajo, silver w/red branch coral/lg turq stone, Hawks, 1970s......50.00
Squash, Zuni, petit point on dbl-row beads w/155 turq stones, 1950s.130.00
Trade beads, Lewis & Clark style, Venetian beads, 1840s, 32" 200.00

Pipes

Pipe bowls were usually carved from soft stone, such as catlinite or red pipestone, an argilaceous sedimentary rock composed mainly of hardened clay. Steatite was also used. Some ceremonial pipes were simply styled, while others were intricately designed naturalistic figurals, sometimes in bird or frog forms called effigies. Their stems, made of wood and often covered with leather, were sometimes nearly a yard in length. For a more thorough study we recommend *Collector's Guide to Indian Pipes* by Lar Hothem.

Argillite, carved bird with birds and humans, Haida, 6¾x2", $325.00.
(Photo courtesy Allard Auctions)

Banded slate, oval w/flared rim, Mississippian, 2x2" 450.00
Catlinite, axe-shape head w/Indian head inscription, Sioux, 1920s ..110.00
Catlinite, eagle claw cvg, orig cvd stem, Sioux, 1880s, 18" 950.00
Catlinite bowl w/pewter inlay, cvd/pnt stem, Sioux, 1940s, 24"..300.00
Catlinite T-bowl, lead/pewter spirals, Plains, late historic, 3x5" .550.00
Catlinite T-bowl w/inlay, ermine/hair dangles, Nez Perce, 1920s, 28"..400.00
Catlinite T-bowl w/lg plain ash stem, Sioux, 1880s, 26x4".........300.00
Catlinite T-bowl w/pewter inlay, cvd coiled snake, Sioux, 1920s, 10"..300.00
Clay elbow, shell tempered, Mississippian, 4½" L......................150.00
Effigy (bird), blk stone, Mound Builder, p-h, 10x3" 60.00
Effigy (bird), tan pipestone, Mississippian, 4" 2,800.00
Effigy (buffalo), catlinite, Sioux, 1890s, 8½x4" 425.00
Effigy (fish), catlinite, late historic, 7½x2x1" 685.00
Effigy (fish), catlinite, sgn W Ward, 1950s, 10¼" 700.00
Effigy (human head), blk steatite, stem emerges from mouth, 2x2½" 750.00
Effigy (pinched-face blower), pottery, Huron-Petun, 4¼" H, 4" stem .1,500.00
Effigy (pregnant woman), maroon catlinite, 1840s, 4½x4" 1,800.00
Forged iron, hammered, Iroquois, 1850-1750, 1¾x2", from $300 to ...400.00
Pipestone, Dis, polished, late p-h, 1½x4½" 1,000.00
Pipestone platform, Hopewell, Middle Woodland, 1¼x2¼"....1,000.00
Pottery, dot designs, flared rim, Iroquois, 1600-50, 1½x2¼" 300.00
Pottery, tan/gray trumpet form, pre-Iroquois, 1550-80, 3x6", $350 to ..450.00
Steatite (blk) platform, polished, Woodland, 3⅛x4⅜" 2,700.00
Steatite (brn) elbow, Iroquois, 1700-1800, 2¼x2", from $300 to 450.00
Steatite (dk), shaman's medicine tube, raised center ring, 5¾"....3,500.00
Steatite elbow, gray-gr, late Woodland, 3½x5⅝x2" 900.00
Steatite/wood, tubular, Hupa, ca 1900, ⅞" dia, 4¼" L 800.00
Stone (blk), Hupa, cvd, 1920s, 8x1½", in cvd wood case 180.00
Stone (blk) Cloud Blower, lizard cvg on top, Mound Builder, 3x2"...160.00
Stone (dk), tubular, Archaic, 1" dia, 3¼" L, from $400 to..........500.00

Pottery

Indian pottery is nearly always decorated in such a manner as to indicate the tribe that produced it or the pueblo in which it was made. For instance, the designs of Cochiti potters were usually scattered forms from nature or sacred symbols. The Zuni preferred an ornate repetitive decoration of a closer configuration. They often used stylized deer and bird forms, sometimes in dimensional applications.

Jedito, olla, black on buff geometric designs, prehistoric, 8x12", $400.00.

Acoma, canteen, bird design, 1930s, 6x5"....................................400.00
Acoma, canteen, mc bird, leather thong, ca 1958, 7x8½" 400.00
Acoma, jar, foliate & curvilinear decor, 1935, 8x7"....................750.00
Acoma, pot, mc, att Lucy Lewis, 1920s, 9x10" 1,000.00
Acoma, pot, 3-banded traditional design, Lewis Family, 1930s, 9x11"..1,200.00
Anasazi, bowl, blk geometrics on wht, p-h, 3x6" 225.00
Anasazi, jar, mc geometrics, bulbous, p-h, 6x3" 120.00
Anasazi, jar, seed; blk & wht w/linear decor, p-h, 5x6" 450.00
Anasazi, mug, snowflake design, no rstr, p-h, 6" dia 800.00
Anasazi, olla, blk geometrics on wht, p-h, 12x15" 400.00

Anasazi, olla, blk on buff, p-h, 9x12" 500.00
Anasazi, olla, plainware, p-h, 17x14" 200.00
Blue Corn, bowl, blkware, dmns on rim, 1970s, 1½x2½" 250.00
Casas Grandes, olla, mc geometrics, p-h, 5x6" 110.00
Casas Grandes, olla, mc geometrics, p-h, 8x8½" 500.00
Cochiti, canteen, cream slip, brn band on bottom, 1890s, 6x6" .550.00
Hopi, jar, fingernail design, redware, G Pavatea, 1960s, 3¾x5"..160.00
Hopi, plate, mc Kachina & bird, att Nampeyo, 1940s, 8½"........300.00
Hopi, wedding jar, EX design, sgn Erma Tawyesva, 1930s, 9½x6½" .425.00
Laguna, wedding vase, handmade, 20th C, 9x9"........................275.00
Santa Clara, blkware, water serpent, Donna Tafoya, 6x6"...........330.00
Santa Clara, figure, mc cat w/2 kittens, S Naranjo, 5x2½" 110.00
Santa Clara, jar, Avenu, blkware, Barbara, 1950s, 6x7".............150.00
Santa Clara, red w/cvd Avenu, sgn Severa, 1950s, 4x5" 140.00
Santa Clara, wedding vase, Pablita, 1950s, 9x4½".....................400.00
Santo Domingo, bowl, dough; blk dmns on gray slip w/red base, 3x9"...225.00
Santo Domingo, bowl, dough; sgn V Aguilar, 1960s, 6½x14".....300.00
Santo Domingo, olla, open star decor, 1935, 12x10" 900.00
SW Pueblo, bowl, dough; geometrics, red/umber on cream, rprs, 4x7".....85.00

Pottery, San Ildefonso

The pottery of the San Ildefonso pueblo is especially sought after by collectors today. Under the leadership of Maria Martinez and her husband Julian, experiments began about 1918 which led to the development of the 'black-on-black' design achieved through exacting methods of firing the ware. They discovered that by smothering the fire at a specified temperature, the carbon in the smoke that ensued caused the pottery to blacken. Maria signed her work (often 'Marie') from the late teens to the 1960s; she died in 1980. Today a piece with her signature may bring prices in the $500.00 to $4,500.00 range.

Plate, blackware, feather motif, signed Marie and Julian, minor surface abrasions, 13", $2,100.00.

Bowl, Avenu on redware, polished, Marie & Julian, 1935, 3x6"..2,500.00
Bowl, blkware, feathers, Maria & Santana, 1970s, 6¾x7" 2,500.00
Bowl, blkware w/design, Rosalie & Joe, 1935, 2x8x6" 110.00
Jar, blkware, feathers, Marie & Julian, 1940s, 5x6" 1,500.00
Jar, blkware, simple shoulder decor, Marie & Julian, 1940s, 5½x4" .800.00
Olla, blkware, polished, Lupita Martinez, 1980, 8x6" 200.00

Rugs, Navajo

Boxed & banded design, hand-spun, natural/vegetal dyes, 1930s, 60x31" ...500.00
Chinle, banded design, vegetal dyes on wool, 37x64" 330.00
Crystal, hook/border/feather design, hand-spun, natural, 1930s, 73x42"...2,500.00
Crystal, intricate geometrics, natural wool, 1935, 63x30" 450.00
Crystal area, looped terrace & dmns, mc on wht & carded tan, 49x86"...660.00
Crystal area, vegetal dye, 1970s, 108x75"...................................600.00
Dmn twill weaving, natural hand-spun wool, 1950s, 34x51" 100.00
Dmns & Spirit Lines, hand-spun, 1950s, 80x50" 400.00

Ganado, hooks border, hand-spun, 1940s, 80x60" 1,700.00
Ganado, red/wht/blk on gray w/blk & wht border, 38x53" 440.00
Ganado area, Klagetoh dmns, mc on dbl-dye red, 28x45" 395.00
Geometric dmns on wht, hand-spun, 1950s, 60x32" 300.00
Klagetoh, geometrics & swastikas, heavy, 1940s, 72x52" 900.00
Klagetoh, red/blk/gray geometrics, 1940s, 72x48" 500.00
Klagetoh area, serrated dmns, hand-spun, 1920s, 63x44" 300.00
Modified Storm pattern w/Teec Nos Pos border, mc on red, 1935, 41x56" ..415.00
Pictorial by Isabel John, vegetal dyes, hand-spun, 1974, 42x27" .325.00
Rainbow Yei, natural/aniline-colored wool, 1940s, 37x51" 325.00
Serrated dmns, hand-spun, Classic, 69x42" 750.00
Stepped blocks & dmns, red/brn/gray/natural, lt stains, 57x34" ..465.00
Stepped dmns, red/brn/gray/natural, carded wool, 72x32" 600.00
Tec Nos Pos, fine weave, Thelma Begay, 1970s, 72x54" 2,250.00
Transitional, Eye-Dazzler, 4-color, minor red bleeding, 51x80" ...770.00
Transitional, Ganado Red, stepped dmns, 5-color, 52x66" 220.00
Transitional, gray & red bands w/terraces in gold/gray, 54x70", EX .330.00
Transitional, Optical Eye-Dazzler, 4-color, late 1800s, 49x64", EX...715.00
Transitional, serrated dmns, 4-color w/red & blk border, ca '25, 80" L .275.00
Transitional, serrated dmns & whirling logs, 3-color, 1900s, 56x92" 770.00
Western Reservation, mc geometrics, ca 1970, 48x32" 110.00
Western Reservation, Storm pattern, 1950s, 51x36" 375.00
Western Reservation, 4-color geometrics, 1940s, 66x41" 425.00
Wide Ruins, banded dmns, natural/vegetal dyes, 1950s, 56x30" .375.00
Wide Ruins, Vera Spencer/Hubbell Trading Post, 1970s, 46x30" ..350.00
Yei, 6-figure, old style, ca 1950, 28x45" 200.00
Yei, 7-figure, aniline red/natural dyes, wool, 28x38" 448.00
2 Gray Hills, hand-spun, natural tight weave, 1940s, 68x40" 950.00

Shaped Stone Artifacts

Bannerstone, dk banded slate, winged, Archaic, 3½x1¾", up to...600.00
Bannerstone, gr-tan chlorite, tube type, Archaic, 2⅝x1½", up to ..2,750.00
Bannerstone, tan pipestone, pick type, Archaic, 4½x1⅛" 900.00
Bannerstone, tan/gr chlorite, pick type, Archaic, 3¼x1½", up to..2,250.00
Boatstone, blk hematite w/red streaks, grooved, Woodland, 4½" ..850.00
Cone, hematite, Woodland, 1¼x2" dia 175.00
Discoidal, swirled agate, late Woodlands, 2½" dia.......................850.00
Gorget, gr banded slate, late Archaic, 2¼x6" 640.00
Gorget, quadriconcave, lt/dk brn slate, polished, Adena, 3⅛x2⅛"..375.00
Gorget, semi-keeled type, banded slate, Adena, 2⅞x1⅝" 600.00
Pendant, banded hardstone, Archaic, IN, 1½" dia 40.00
Pendant, gr hardstone, drilled, Archaic, IN, 1⅞x2" 25.00
Pendant, stylized anchor type, banded slate, Woodland, 3⅝x1½" ..400.00
Pestle, blk stone, dbl-ended phallic shape, p-h, 5x2" 80.00

Tools

Adz blade, hematite, Adena, OH, 2¼"...50.00
Axe, Ho Ho Kam, dk gray stone, ¾-groove, p-h, 7x2½" 130.00
Axe, mc granitic diorite, ¾-groove, Archaic, 7x3⅝", minimum value..1,000.00
Axe, speckled hardstone, full groove, Archaic, 7¼x4¼".............400.00
Axe, tan hardstone, full groove, Archaic, 2½x2"...........................50.00
Celt, cream & blk hardstone, polished, Woodland, IL, 4¼x2⅜" ...125.00
Celt, gray hardstone, Woodland (probably Adena), 4⅜x2⅜".....100.00
Celt, mixed hardstone, well polished, Woodland, 8x3⅛"............450.00
Celt, mixed hardstone, Woodland (probably Hopewell), 3½x2" ..80.00
Celt/chisel, gray-wht chert, Mississippian, 8⅜x1¾" 375.00
Chisel, gray hardstone, Mississippian tradition, 4¾x1⅝" 65.00
Chisel, greenstone, fire-blackened/polished, 4½x1x¾" 40.00
Drill, tan chert, Woodland, MO, 4" 150.00
Gouge, dk hardstone, well scooped, 5⅞" 85.00
Gouge, hardstone, ME, 9¼x1½", from $150 to 175.00
Pestle, lt gr hardstone, hoof type, Archaic, OH, 4⅛" 60.00
Pestle, wht quartzite, bell shape, Archaic, OH, 6½", from $325 to..400.00
Pestle/maul, gray-blk hardstone, expanded top, Archaic, 5x3⅜" ...225.00
Plummet, hematite, ungrooved, Archaic, IL, 2¾x1⅜", $200 to .250.00
Plummet, hematite conglomerate, top groove, Archaic, 2½x1⅛" ...300.00
Plummet, red hematite, wide groove, Archaic, OH, 2¼x1" 150.00
Quirt, Sioux, antler w/leather whip, s-s hide hdl, 1900, 37x2"....375.00
Spud/celtiform-axe blade, clear quartz Crystal, Mississippian, 4¾" ..2,000.00
Spud/flared-bit celt, polished hematite, Mississippian, 6½" 450.00

Weapons

Bow, Cheyenne, pnt, recurve, orig sinew string, 1850s, 44" 500.00
Bow, Woodlands, cvd hardwood, 19th C, 78", +provenance 500.00
Bow, Yurok, sinew string, ca 1900, 42x3", +3 arrows 450.00
Club, egg-shaped stone w/cvg & yel pigment, 1880s, 26x8" w/wood hdl...300.00
Club, egg-shaped stone w/full bw hdl, 20th C, 22x3" 110.00
Club, heavy wood w/cvg & inlay, 1900s, 29x4" 70.00
Club, pnt catlinite w/bw hdl, 1890s, 31x6" 325.00
Club, Shoshone, egg-shaped stone, hide-covered bw hdl, 1900s, 20"...150.00
Club, Sioux, egg-shaped catlinite, rawhide hdl w/bw drop, 1880s.........800.00
Knife, fighting; copper w/cvd wood effigy hdl, 1930s, M.............350.00
Tomahawk, Great Lakes, eng steel head, cvd/pnt shaft, 19th C, 21" ..275.00
Tomahawk, handmade brass head, tiger maple shaft, 19th C......425.00
Tomahawk, iron pipe w/star cutout, tacked wooden stem, 1900s, 21x7" ..500.00
Tomahawk, Osage, wrought-iron head, cvd haft, 19th C, 19".....350.00

American Painted Porcelain

The American china-painting movement can be traced back to an extracurricular class attended by art students at the McMicken School of Design in Cincinnati. These students, who were the wives and daughters of the city's financial elite, managed to successfully paint numerous porcelains for display in the Woman's Pavilion of the 1876 United States Centennial Exposition held in Philadelphia — an amazing feat considering the high technical skill required for proficiency, as well as the length of time and multiple firings necessary to finish the ware. From then until 1917 when the United States entered World War I, china painting was a profession as well as a popular amateur pursuit for many people, particularly women. In fact, over 25,000 people were involved in this art form at the turn of the last century.

Collectors and antique dealers have discovered American hand-painted porcelain, and they have become aware of its history, beauty, and potential value. Until now, there was no all-inclusive source to turn to for information on this subject. *American Painted Porcelain: Collector's Identification & Value Guide* and *Antique Trader's Comprehensive Guide to American Painted Porcelain* by Dorothy Kamm are the culmination of a decade of research; we recommend them highly for further study.

Though American pieces are of high quality and commensurate with their European counterparts, they are much less costly today. Generally, you will pay as little as $10.00 for a 6" plate and less than $50.00 for many other items. Values are based on aesthetic appeal, quality of the workmanship, size, rarity of the piece and of the subject matter, and condition. Age is the least important factor, because most American painted porcelains are not dated. (Factory backstamps are helpful in establishing the approximate time period an item was decorated, but they aren't totally reliable.) See Clubs, Newsletters, and Catalogs for information regarding *Dorothy's Kamm's Porcelain Collector's Companion*, each issue of which contains comprehensive material expounding on artists, patterns, dating, and functions of china.

Our advisor for this category is Dorothy Kamm; she is listed in the Directory under Florida.

Bar pin, brass-plated bezel, 1½" W, from $25 to............................45.00

Belt buckle brooch, oval, 1¾x2⅛", from $90 to 125.00
Bonbon bowl (depending on size), from $18 to 85.00
Bowl, fruit; from $60 to 80.00
Box, 4¾" dia, from $50 to 75.00
Brooch, brass-plated bezel, oval, 2x1½", from $55 to 75.00
Brooch, gold-plated bezel, 1½" dia, from $35 to 55.00
Brooch/pendant, heart shape, gold-plated bezel, 2x1¾", from $50 to....85.00
Cake plate, from $35 to 75.00
Candlestick, from $45 to 125.00
Celery tray, from $35 to 75.00
Creamer & sugar bowl, from $30 to 65.00
Cruet, from $60 to 80.00
Cuff pin, rectangular, brass-plated bezel, ¼x1⅛", from $12 to 18.00
Cup & saucer 45.00
Cup & saucer, bouillon; from $35 to 45.00
Ewer (depending on size), from $100 to 175.00
Gravy boat, from $55 to 75.00
Handy pin, brass-plated bezel, 1½", from $30 to...........................40.00
Hatpin holder, from $88 to 125.00
Jam jar, from $30 to 50.00
Jardiniere (depending on size), from $65 to 375.00
Mug, from $30 to 75.00
Napkin ring, from $10 to..25.00
Pendant, gold-plated bezel, 1" dia, from $50 to 75.00
Pin tray, from $30 to 50.00
Pitcher, lemonade; from $175 to...225.00
Plate, 6", from $10 to..35.00
Plate, 8", from $45 to..65.00
Salt cellar, from $20 to 40.00
Scarf pin, medallion, brass-plated bezel & shank, 1¼" dia, $35 to...65.00
Shakers, pr, from $25 to 40.00
Shirtwaist button, 1" dia, from $20 to 40.00
Shirtwaist set, brooch, brass-plated mts, 1¾"+cuff links, $150 to ..250.00
Stein, from $75 to 115.00

Tea set, overglaze painting with gold trim, Bavaria blank, ca 1908 – 1918, from $175.00 to $300.00. (Photo courtesy Dorothy Kamm)

Vase, 6-7", ea, from $45 to 75.00
Whiskey set, ears of corn, sgn, Surquist, 1903-17, 8-pc, $300 to ..400.00

Amphora

The Amphora Porcelain Works in the Teplitz-Turn area of Bohemia produced Art Nouveau-styled vases and figurines during the latter part of the 1800s through the first few decades of the twentieth century. They marked their wares with various stamps, some incorporating the name and location of the pottery with a crown or a shield. Because Bohemia was part of the Austro-Hungarian empire prior to WWI, some examples are marked Austria; items marked with the Czechoslovakia designation were made after the war. All decoration described in the listings that follow is hand painted unless otherwise indicated.

Figurine, Arab on camel, realistic mc, detailed, mk, 34" 3,000.00
Pitcher, flower reserve on bl, cobalt gloss hdl, 7½" 85.00
Vase, blown-out mc flowers, Imperial mk, 6" 130.00
Vase, boy & girl stand on curve of gourd shape, 11" 800.00
Vase, cherry branches in relief, mc w/gold on gr irid, waisted, 15" ...350.00
Vase, dbl; regal person w/crown, Czecho-Slovakia Amphora, 6½" ..200.00
Vase, Egyptian figures, brn tones & blk, bulbous, 14½" 450.00
Vase, exotic birds & flowers, hdls, Holland mk, 19⅛", EX 1,000.00
Vase, goats pastoral scene, ovoid, ftd, #32 59, 10¾" 925.00
Vase, gr tones w/wraparound snake, emb floral, 7½", NM 325.00
Vase, gr w/8 lg/8 sm jewels at center, jeweled rim, stick neck, 5" ...100.00
Vase, mc enameling on dull gray, hdls, #11798 over 64, 11" 150.00
Vase, molded stylized trees, gourd shape w/hdls, 9" 350.00
Vase, Nouveau leaves, turq/cream w/gold, pierced rim, bulbous, 7"...525.00
Vase, tree limbs, gold-brn on dk brn, shouldered, 10", NM.........200.00
Vase, trees w/heart-shaped leaves, #2929, prof rpr, 22⅜" 3,300.00
Vase, village scene/Medieval lady, loop hdls, mk, 9¾" 150.00

Animal Dishes With Covers

Covered animal dishes have been produced for nearly two centuries and are as varied as their manufacturers. They were made in many types of glass (slag, colored, clear, and milk glass) as well as china and pottery. On bases of nests and baskets, you will find animals and birds of every sort. The most common was the hen.

Some of the smaller versions made by McKee, Indiana Tumbler and Goblet Company, and Westmoreland Specialty Glass of Pittsburgh, Pennsylvania, were sold to food-processing companies who filled them with prepared mustard, baking powder, etc. Occasionally one will be found with the paper label identifying the product and processing company still intact.

Many of the glass versions produced during the latter part of the nineteenth century have been recently reproduced. In the 1960s, the Kemple Glass Company made the rooster, fox, lion, cat, lamb, hen, horse, turkey, duck, dove, and rabbit on split-ribbed or basketweave bases. They were made in amethyst, blue, amber, and milk glass, as well as a variegated slag. Kanawha, L.G. Wright, and Imperial made several as well. It is sometimes necessary to compare items in question to verified examples of older glass in order to recognize reproductions. Reproduction is continued today.

For more information, we recommend *Covered Animal Dishes* by Everett Grist, whose address is in the Directory under Tennessee; *Collector's Encyclopedia of Milk Glass* by Betty and Bill Newbound; *Westmoreland Glass* by Charles West Wilson; and *American Slag Glass* by Ruth Grizel. In the listings below, when only one dimension is given, it is the greater one, usually length. See also Greentown and other specific companies.

Baby Moses, milk glass, cattail or reed base, unmk, 6¼" 220.00
Bambi, carnival glass powder jar, Jeannette, 1950s 25.00
Bird w/berry, clear, Kemple or St Clair repro 300.00
Boar's head, milk glass, Atterbury, Pat May 29, 1888, 9½" 1,500.00
Cat, milk glass, split-rib base, unmk McKee, 5½" 175.00
Chick on eggs, pnt on bl frost, 2-hdld basket base......................100.00
Chicks in oblong basket, milk glass w/pnt details, 2¼x4¼" 325.00
Dolphin, milk glass, sawtooth edge, Kemple or St Clair 75.00
Duck, Atterbury; colored repro by Wright, 11" 70.00
Duck, Atterbury; milk glass, Patent Apld for, 11".......................245.00
Duck, Dominecker; pnt on milk glass..350.00
Duck, milk glass, cattail base, unmk, 5½" 120.00

Duck, swimming; yel, Vallerysthal, 5" or 5¾", ea 120.00
Eagle, Mother; color other than milk glass, mk WG 125.00
Fish, Entwined; milk glass, lacy base, Atterbury, 6" dia 225.00
Fish, frosted, collared base, Central Glass Co 150.00
Fox, milk glass, ribbed lid & base, dtd 275.00
Hen, Atterbury; milk glass w/bl opaque head, lacy base 275.00
Hen, Str-Headed; clear w/pnt comb & waddle, beaded edge, Indiana ..15.00
Hen, Str-Headed; marigold carnival, beaded edge, Indiana 25.00
Hen on sleigh, milk glass, Westmoreland, 5½" 85.00
Hen w/chicks, milk glass, unmk McKee, 5½" 165.00
Horse, milk glass, split-rib base, unmk Mckee, 5½" 185.00
Lamb, milk glass, bl opaque, picket base, Westmoreland 95.00
Lion, British; milk glass, emb title on base, 6¼" 195.00
Quail, milk glass, scroll base, 5½" 85.00
Rabbit, clear, basketweave base, US Glass, 8" 65.00
Rabbit emerging from horizontal egg, milk glass w/HP details 65.00
Rat on lg egg, milk glass, Vallerysthal..225.00
Robin on nest, milk glass, unknown maker, 6½" 200.00
Rooster, bl opaque, basketweave base, Westmoreland, lg 125.00
Rooster, color other than wht, wide-rib base, Westmoreland, 5¼" ...95.00
Rooster, milk glass, wide-rib base, Westmoreland, 5¼" 40.00
Rooster, milk glass head/bl opaque body, wide-rib base, Westmoreland...95.00
Squirrel, milk glass, split-rib base, unmk McKee, 5½" 185.00
Swan, Block; clear frosted, Challinor Taylor & Co, 7" 145.00
Swan, Closed-Neck, bl opaque, Westmoreland Specialty Co......110.00
Swan, Raised-Wing; milk glass, eye sockets for glass eyes............225.00
Swan, Raised-Wing; milk glass, molded eyes, Westmoreland repro....85.00
Swan, Vallerysthal, clear frosted, 5½" (+) 65.00
Turkey, Standing; frosted, LE Smith 55.00
Turkey, Standing; milk glass, LE Smith 130.00
Turtle, dk amber, knobby-bk, LG Wright 45.00
Turtle, milk glass, scroll base w/2 hdls, 7½" 185.00
Water buffalo, milk glass, recumbent..350.00

Appliances, Electric

Antique electric appliances represent a diverse field and are always being sought after by collectors. There were over one hundred different companies manufacturing electric appliances in the first half of the twentieth century; some were making over ten different models under several different names at any given time in all fields: coffeepots, toasters, waffle irons, etc., while others were making only one or two models for extended periods of time. Today collectors and decorators alike are seeking those items to add to a collection or to use as accent pieces in a period kitchen. Refer to *Toasters and Small Kitchen Appliances* published by L-W Book Sales for more information. If you're especially interested in vintage fans, we recommend *The Collector's Guide to Electric Fans* by John Witt. Toaster collectors will enjoy *Collector's Guide to Toasters & Accessories* by Helen Greguire. (The latter two books are published by Collector Books.)

Always check the cord before using and make sure the appliance is in good condition, free of rust and pitting. The prices below are for appliances in good to excellent condition. Prices may vary around the country.

If you have any questions regarding antique appliances, feel free to contact our advisor, Jim Barker; he is listed in the Directory under Pennsylvania.

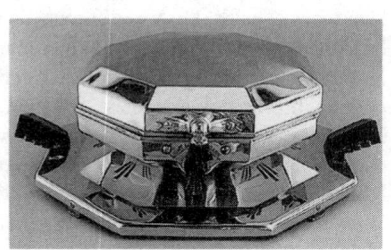

Waffle iron, chrome with Bakelite handles, 5x13x11", $100.00. (Photo courtesy Leslie Zysman)

Bread mixer/juicer, Vita-Mix 3600, M............................140.00
Broiler, Farberware, lg fr, 1960s, cooking surface: 8½x12" 24.00
Broiler, Holliwood Electric #60, Finders Mfg Chicago, 1950s, MIB..20.00
Broiler, Maxim Barbeque Model EB-7, stainless, MIB 12.50
Can opener, Libby's Can-O-Matic, Amsco, 1950s, MIB................30.00
Can opener, Rival All Crome Can-O-Mat AD 345 w/magnet, 1950s, MIB..50.00
Can opener, Sunbeam, pk & chrome, counter-top style, 6½x6"....30.00
Chafing dish, Universal E-921, Pat 1913, rpl cord (EX fit) 15.00
Coffee maker, Corning Ware, 10-cup 17.50
Coffee maker, Deco-style chrome, glass finial, 9" 18.00
Coffee maker, International Heartland, Proctor-Silex, 12-cup 70.00
Coffee maker, Silex, glass & chrome, 3-pc, cloth cord................70.00
Coffee maker, Wear-Ever, aluminum, 1965, MIB........................35.00
Coffee urn, Farberware, stainless steel, ped ft, 55-cup 70.00
Coffee urn, Manning-Bowman, chrome w/Bakelite hdl, 15" 55.00
Coffee urn, stainless steel, gr glass lid, unmk 25.00
Coffee urn, Universal, Pat dates 1912 to 1924, 12" 50.00
Coffee urn, Westinghouse, ca 1914, EX....................................25.00
Coffeepot, Sunbeam Coffeemaster, chrome & Bakelite, 8-cup......17.50
Egg cooker, Hankscraft, aluminum, ca 1950, NM......................15.00
Egg cooker, Sunbeam, aluminum, 4-leg, blk plastic finial, 7x5¼"..35.00
Egg cooker, Sunbeam #2, 8x7" 15.00
Fan, brass w/CI base, Wesco, 12" cage, EX................................575.00
Fan, floor; Westinghouse, quatrefoil metal std, CI base, 1950s, 58".....175.00
Fan, General Electric, brass, 16x13¼" 170.00
Heater, America's Favorite, submersible, NMIB..........................45.00
Heater, Gilbert, stainless steel, 660 watts, 13"............................35.00
Heater, Radia Health Heater, Shepler Mfg, CI base, 5.7 amps......37.50
Heater, Rome, copper & stainless steel, 660 watts, 19" 45.00
Heater, Sofono, chromium front, Bakelite hdls, 1950s, 26" dia.....80.00
Heater, Universal E-9955, ceramic cone, CI base, 1922 ....60.00
Hot plate, Rival, single burner, 750 watt, std 110 volt plug...........35.00
Hot plate & magnetic stirrer, Corning PC-351, 7½x6" top...........90.00
Hot plate & stirrer, Troemner #980, 850 watts, 7½x9½" top........60.00
Kettle, General Electric, chrome half-oval w/creme hdl, 1950s, 11" L ...25.00
Kettle, General Electric K48A, 1950s, 9" L................................20.00
Mixer, Canfield Power Mix, chrome, 10 settings, 12x12x6½" 40.00
Mixer, Chrome-Ever, Wade-Youman's Co, 8½" 45.00
Mixer, Dormeyer, 1950s, w/accessories, NM..............................30.00
Mixer, General Electric Home, 3-blade, plastic, 14" 35.00
Mixer, Handy Hanna, pk plastic, 3-speed, hand-held, NM in G box..35.00
Mixer, Kitchenaid 3-C, 10-speed, complete w/bowls 45.00
Mixer, Manning-Bowman, 115 volt, .75 amps, on stand, 13x6"....80.00
Mixer, Mary Dunbar Handymix, 1940s, 11x8", VG......................30.00
Mixer, Sunbeam Mixmaster, w/Jade-ite bowls............................150.00
Percolator, General Electric, mirror finish, Bakelite hdl, 115 volts ...40.00
Percolator, General Mills GM8-A, pump attached to pot 18.00
Percolator, Kenmore Automatic, Bakelite hdl, 1950s 22.50
Percolator, Manning-Bowman, chrome w/glass finial, 1948, 8-cup..27.50
Percolator, Mirro-Matic, Bakelite hdl, 4-cup..............................22.50
Percolator, United, chrome w/glass lid, 1940s, switch on cord 25.00
Popcorn popper, aluminum w/sapphire bl lid, ca 1950s 30.00
Popcorn popper, Dominion, aluminum, glass lid..........................15.00
Popcorn popper, Kenmore, aluminum, glass finial, 1951 ....10.00
Popcorn popper, Knapp-Monarch, glass lid, 10x8" dia..................25.00
Skillet, Lustre Craft, 110-120 volts, w/egg poacher insert, 10" dia, M.....30.00
Skillet, Sunbeam, w/metal rack, chrome w/blk hdls, w/instructions/etc..25.00
Toaster, Bee-Vac #12, Birtman Electric Co 55.00
Toaster, El Tosto, Pacific Heating Co, 7x6½x5¾" 88.00
Toaster, Estate Stove Co #177, chrome, Bakelite switch on cord..55.00
Toaster, General Electric D-12, porc 240.00
Toaster, General Electric, wht enamel porc base, Pat Dec 28, 1909 70.00
Toaster, Hotpoint #156t25, 8x6¾x5" 30.00
Toaster, marshmallow; Angelus Campfire Co, toasts 1, 1930s........30.00

Toaster, Son Chief, 1930s..**40.00**
Toaster, Star Electric, Fitzgerald Mfg, sides drop, 9¼x7" at base ...**50.00**
Toaster, Universal #E9410...**525.00**
Toaster/oven, General Electric, chrome, 1950s **70.00**
Vacuum cleaner, Filter Queen #500, 1950s, w/accessories **70.00**
Vacuum cleaner, Hoover #541, die-cast aluminum, ca 1923-26 ....**85.00**
Waffle iron, GE Hotpoint, chrome w/butterscotch Bakelite hdls..**25.00**
Waffle iron, Manning-Bowman, chrome, Deco style **15.00**
Waffle iron, Rogers Electric Laboratories Co, red wood hdls.........**22.50**

Arequipa

The Arequipa Pottery operated from 1911 until 1918 at a sanitorium near Fairfax, California. Its purpose was two-fold: therapy for the patients and financial support for the institution. Frederick H. Rhead was the originator and director. The ware, made from local clays, was often hand thrown, simply styled and decorated. Marks were varied but always incorporated the name of the pottery and the state. A circular arrangement encompassing the negative image of a vase beside a tree is most common.

Examples are evaluated according to quality of artwork; size and shape are less important. Those done by Rhead himself are most desirable.

Tile, Nouveau leaves & flowers, 4-color cuenca technique, 6x7"....**350.00**
Vase, repetitive Deco flower neck band, 3-color, 4¾x4½" **650.00**
Vase, slip-trailed floral neck band, gray mottle, thrown, #23, 7"...**6,600.00**

Argy-Rousseau, G.

Gabriel Argy-Rousseau produced both fine art glass and quality commercial ware in Paris, France, in 1918. He favored Art Nouveau as well as Art Deco and in the '20s produced a line of vases in the Egyptian manner, made popular by the discovery of King Tut's tomb. One of the most important types of glass he made was pate-de-verre. Most of his work is signed. Items listed below are pate-de-verre unless noted otherwise.

Night light, three repeating purple blossoms with black V-shaped devices on mottled gray-lavender, in footed wrought frame, 8¼", $7,000.00.

Bowl, berries & vines, brick red/gr/plum/gray, 2½x3¼" **2,900.00**
Box, flower & foliage, mc on gray w/purple/pk splashes, 5" dia ..**4,300.00**
Figure, Baigneuse, nude w/drape between legs, pate-de-cristal, 10" ...**7,000.00**
Pendant, cicada, red & blk on wine, orig silk cord, 2½x2" **1,100.00**
Pendant, edelweiss, purple w/raspberry center, 2⅝" dia............**1,035.00**
Pendant, moth, red-amber/blk/yel/red on pebbly gray, 2½x1¾"...**1,300.00**
Tray, berries & leaves, brick red/purple/gray, 1½x3½"..............**1,000.00**
Vase, anemones, purple/wht/blk w/mc vertical streaks, 5½" **5,300.00**

Vase, foliage over chevrons, gray w/purple/bl splashes, 7½" **4,000.00**
Vase, leaves/webs/spiders on gray & purple, wide mouth, 4¾x4½" ...**5,000.00**

Art Deco

To the uninformed observer, 'Art Deco' evokes images of chrome and glass, streamlined curves and aerodynamic shapes, mirrored prints of pink flamingos, and statues of slender nudes and greyhound dogs. Though the Deco movement began in 1925 at the Paris International Exposition and lasted to some extent into the 1950s, within that period of time the evolution of fashion and taste continued as it always has, resulting in subtle variations.

The French Deco look was one of opulence — exotic inlaid woods, rich material, lush fur, and leather. Lines tended toward symmetrical curves. American designers adapted the concept to cover every aspect of fashion and home furnishings from small inexpensive picture frames, cigarette lighters, and costume jewelry to high-fashion designer clothing and exquisite massive furniture with squared or circular lines. Vinyl was a popular covering, and chrome-plated brass was used for chairs, cocktail shakers, lamps, and tables. Dinnerware, glassware, theaters, and train stations were designed to reflect the new 'Modernism.'

The Deco movement made itself apparent into the '50s in wrought iron lamps with stepped pink plastic shades and Venetian blinds. The sheer volume of production during those twenty-five years provides collectors today with fine examples of the period that can be bought for as little as $10.00 or $20.00 up to the thousands. Chrome items signed 'Chase' are prized by collectors, and blue glass radios and tables with blue glass tops are high on the list of desirability in many areas.

Those interested in learning more about this subject will want to read *Collector's Guide to Art Deco* by Mary Frank Gaston; and *Affordable Art Deco, Identification and Value Guide*, by Hutchinson and Johnson. (Both are published by Collector Books.) See also Bronzes; Chase; Frankart; Jewelry; Lalique; Radios; etc.

Bookends, dancing nudes, patinated metal, #203, 1930s, 6½", pr....**235.00**
Bookends, stylized figure w/ball, brass & Bakelite, 7", pr............**375.00**
Box, cigarette; brass w/sliding red Bakelite top, Von Nessen.........**60.00**
Box, dresser; gr & blk Bakelite, knob ft, 2½x5", from $75 to........**95.00**
Box, powder; seminude figural, gr frosted glass, unmk, 8½" **90.00**
Cabinet, display; burl walnut w/3 doors (center: glass), 62x47"....**5,275.00**
Candle holder, lady holds 2 cups w/hands out, silver-tone metal, 15" ..**400.00**
Candle holders, sterling on bronze, Heintz Art Metal, 5", pr.......**265.00**
Car mascot, draped lady w/arm out, topaz, att Etling, 1927, 11x14"........**1,150.00**
Carpet, earth tones w/cloud bands & abstract center, 1925, 127x105"...**3,450.00**
Carpet, earth tones w/lt bl & mauve, stylized water/rocks, 143x105"......**2,585.00**
Chandelier, dbl support holds wrought floral fr, 16-light, 40" **975.00**
Chandelier, frosted glass in triform wrought fr, 3-light w/center bowl..**1,725.00**
Chandelier, wht opaque panels, 3 cast brackets w/silver gilt, 28x18" **275.00**
Clock, alarm; brushed aluminum w/off-center crystal face, Gilbert, 6"....**350.00**
Clock, boudoir; peach-colored glass, mirror base, Am, 7x6" dia .**250.00**
Clock, desk; bronze w/blk enamel, mk JAZ, Fr, 1930s, 4x5½" **225.00**
Figurine, dancer w/fan, flowing skirt, Herwig, 1930s, 12"...........**300.00**
Figurine, draped nude sitting, chrome on onyx base, 1920s, 4"...**125.00**
Figurine, girl holds skirt wide, chrome on marble base, unmk, 4½" ..**135.00**
Figurine, lady w/2 wolfhounds, faux marble, Santini, 12x14"......**475.00**
Frame, alumimum & dk walnut stand, 8x6".................................**200.00**
Frame, chrome holder w/glass, 5½" sq..**375.00**
Gate, oval reserve amid wrought scrollwork, 72x52"................**1,850.00**
Hall rack, chromed metal fr w/center mirror & shelf, 72x43x7"...**3,750.00**
Holder, cigarette; blk plastic trimmed w/gold band, 2½" **25.00**
Holder, cigarette; chrome & glass, 2 sections, unmk, from $125 to .**150.00**
Holder, cigarette; dk red plastic w/amber stones, 3", from $50 to..**60.00**

Ice bucket, chrome w/cobalt glass Hazel Atlas insert, 11x8" **95.00**
Incense burner, ceramic, Egyptian lady w/bowl, Lisne, French, 6½" ...**375.00**
Incense burner, CI w/molded florals/geometrics, Made in France, 6½"..**175.00**
Lamp, alabaster domical shade on wrought pierced floral fr, 19"..**700.00**
Lamp, ceramic sphere w/in cube, cream/gray crackle, Guillard, 17"..**700.00**
Lamp, draped nude w/tambourine light, marble base, Fayral, 21" ..**2,100.00**
Lamp, gilt-bronze & onyx gazebo form, Bouraine, 17¾".........**2,300.00**
Lamp, HP geometric mushroom shade, wrought-iron std, Faure, 14x9" dia..**2,900.00**
Lamp, nude figure w/gr patina, frosted glass panel behind, Fayral, 17"..**2,300.00**
Lamp, perfume; orange satin glass, stepped design, 1920s, 7" **365.00**
Lamps, aluminum/Bakelite/brass, Von Nessen/Pattyn, 1930, 20", pr ..**4,850.00**
Mirror, floor; tubular chrome fr on caster, Germany, 1930s, 71x23" ..**1,300.00**
Pedestal, sq patterned shagreen form on maple/brass base, 54x10" sq..**2,100.00**
Table, marble inset top, wrought-iron base, Fr, 1920s, 20x19" sq .**550.00**
Tea cart, chrome curvilinear fr w/smoky glass top & shelf, 26x32x19" ..**800.00**
Toothpick holder, chrome swan, unmk, from $30 to **35.00**
Vial, perfume; glass w/ceramic head stopper, Germany, 3¼" **115.00**

Art Glass Baskets

Popular novelty and gift items during the Victorian era, these one-of-a-kind works of art were produced in just about any type of art glass in use at that time. They were never marked. Many were not true production pieces but 'whimsies' made by glassworkers to relieve the tedium of the long work day. Some were made as special gifts. The more decorative and imaginative the design, the more valuable the basket. Our advisor for this category is Deborah Maggard; she is listed in the Directory under Ohio.

Note: Prices on art glass baskets have softened due to the influence of the Internet which has made them much more accessible.

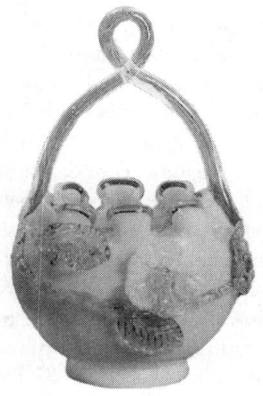

White opaque with applied amber leaves, handle, and pink flower, 7½", $225.00

Amberina w/amber thorn hdl & ruffle, 7¼x5" **335.00**
Bl Dmn MOP, frosted hdl, ruffled rim, 7x4½" **400.00**
Bl spatter over wht w/mica, ruffled, twisted loop hdl, 6½x6½" ..**100.00**
Bl/red/yel spatter w/gold mica, pk int, amber hdl, 11x10" **300.00**
Brn & yel o/l, mc & gold decor, clear twist hdl, 8x7¼x5½" **225.00**
Cream/opal irid w/decor, attached metal fr, Austria, 9½x9" **1,380.00**
Electric bl w/appl ribbon edge, twisted hdl, 6½" **115.00**
Hobnail, chartreuse, 5x3¼" **100.00**
Lt gr opaque w/appl flowers, gr twist hdl **115.00**
Mc spatter w/mica, wht int, 6 pointed ruffles, clear thorn hdl, 8x8"..**125.00**
Mc spatter w/silver mica, clear ruffle & reeded hdl, 11½x8".......**275.00**
Peachblow, appl amber ft, amber thorn hdl, 6" **175.00**
Pk Dmn Quilt MOP, frosted rope hdl, 6½x6½" **400.00**
Pk Herringbone MOP, ribbed body, pk int, frosted thorn hdl, 7x6" .**200.00**
Pk opal w/wht appl flower, ruffled, clear twist hdl, 7x5"...............**165.00**
Pk to wht cased, ruffled rim, clear rope hdl, 6½" **125.00**
Pk w/mica, ruffled rim, clear hdl, 5x5½" **110.00**

Wht w/pk to wht int, ribbed, shiny, thorn hdl, 7x7" **125.00**
Yel-gold spatter w/mica, reeded/pointed hdl, 7x7" **100.00**

Art Nouveau

From the famous 'L'Art Nouveau' shop in the Rue de Provence in Paris, 'New Art' spread across the continent and belatedly arrived in America in time to add its curvilinear elements and asymmetrical ornamentations to the ostentatious remains of the Rococo revival of the 1800s. Nouveau manifested itself in every facet of decorative art. In glassware Tiffany turned the concept into a commercial success that lasted well into the second decade of this century and created a style that inspired other American glassmakers for decades. Furniture, lamps, bronzes, jewelry, and automobiles were designed within the realm of its dictates. Today's market abounds with lovely examples of Art Nouveau, allowing the collector to choose one or several areas that hold a special interest. Our advisor for this category is Steven Whysel; he is listed in the Directory under Florida. See also Bronzes; Galle; Jewelry; Loetz; Tiffany; Silver; specific manufacturers.

Belt buckle, gilt brass lady, in fr, 4x2"...**100.00**
Box, brass covered wood w/emb florals, Daguet, 5½x14½x8" **350.00**
Buttons, sterling, lady, English hallmk, 4 for................................**100.00**
Candelabrum, dore bronze, 3-arm, scrolling vines/boy/lizard, 27".**4,500.00**
Candlesticks, gilt metal draped nudes, DP Muller, 10½", pr **375.00**
Gong, mahog, 5 grad bronze bells, floral marquetry, 10x12x11"..**450.00**
Inkwell, bronze, dbl wells (w/o inserts), vines..............................**250.00**
Lamp, desk, bronze helmet shade w/flared base, 13⅞"................**865.00**
Lavabo, brass w/emb dogs & linear decor, spigot center, 19x14x14" ...**230.00**
Lithograph, Les Eglantines, lady & roses, P Berthon, Paris, 15x21" **650.00**
Plaque, dore bronze, ¾-view of lady, fr: ebony/gilt, 20x10", pr ...**1,150.00**
Tray, brass & copper, eng floral, English, 14x8" **150.00**
Tray, porc insert w/HP iris/lily pads w/in mixed metal fr **575.00**

Arts and Crafts

The Arts and Crafts movement began in England during the last quarter of the nineteenth century, and its influence was soon felt in this country. Among its proponents in America were Elbert Hubbard (see Roycroft) and Gustav Stickley (see Stickley). They rebelled against the mechanized mass production of the Industrial Revolution and against the cumulative influence of hundreds of years of man's changing taste. They subscribed to a theory of purification of style: that designs be geared strictly to necessity. At the same time they sought to elevate these basic ideals to the level of accepted 'art.' Simplicity was their virtue; to their critics it was a fault.

The type of furniture they promoted was squarely built, usually of heavy oak, and so simple was its appearance that as a result many began to copy the style which became known as 'Mission.' Soon factories had geared production toward making cheap copies of their designs. In 1915 Stickley's own operation failed, a victim of changing styles and tastes. Hubbard lost his life that same year on the ill-fated *Lusitania*. By the end of the decade the style had lost its popularity.

Metalware was produced by numerous crafts people, from experts such as Dirk van Erp and Albert Berry to unknown novices. Metal items or hardware should not be scrubbed or scoured; to do so could remove or damage the rich, dark patina typical of this period. Collectors have become increasingly fussy, rejecting outright pieces with damage or alteration to their original condition (such as refinishing, patina loss, repairs, and replacements). As is true for other categories of antiques and collectibles, premium prices have been paid for objects in mint original and untouched condition. Our advisor for this category is Bruce Austin; he is listed in the Directory under New York. See also Roycroft; Silver; Stickley; specific manufacturers.

    Note: Values for metal items reflect the worth of examples that retain their original patina, unless otherwise indicated in the description.

    Key: h/cp — hammered copper

Armchair, Old Hickory, woven bk/seat, brand, brass tag, 34", VG...**600.00**
Armchair, wide crest rail, 3 wide slats, spring cushion, 35x29x24"..**450.00**
Ashtray, van Erp, h/cp, 3 rests, dk brn patina, 7½" dia **300.00**
Bed, trundle; slatted sides & bk, in style of Gustav Stickley, 78"..**4,250.00**
Bench, hall; curved rail on panel bk, lift seat, 37x39x18" **400.00**
Bench, hall; Limbert, #92, lift seat, arched top, 41¼x42x18"..**4,250.00**
Bookcase, Lifetime, Puritan, 3 doors, arched toe board, 52x56".....**4,000.00**
Bookcase, Limbert, #315, dbl doors w/ldgl, keyed tenons, 55x45".**5,500.00**
Bookends, Frost, brass w/cut-bk trees & house, 6" W, pr **400.00**
Bowl, Heintz, sterling floral on bronze, 8" dia............................**350.00**
Bowl, Jarvie, hammered brass, 7" **300.00**
Bowl, Jarvie, hammered silver, #2122, 9½", EX......................**1,500.00**
Bowl, Kalo, h/cp w/SP int, #323, 7" **1,000.00**
Bowl, M Zimmerman, polished copper, 4" dia............................**125.00**
Bowl, van Erp, h/cp, brn patina, ca 1911, 12¾" **1,400.00**
Box, Silvercrest, bronze, geometrics, 6x10" **200.00**
Buffet, Limbert, 2 doors flank drw, drop-front door over drw, 48x59"..**2,300.00**
Cabinet, china; Limbert, #1146, 2 arched 8-pane doors, 59x48x17".......**6,000.00**
Cabinet, china; Limbert, #452, 4-pane door, open shelves at sides, 59"..**4,500.00**
Cabinet, Limbert, 5-drw w/bksplash, flush top, curved apron, 44x33" **2,000.00**
Candlestick, Jarvie, Alpha, brass, cleaned patina, unmk, 11", VG.....**500.00**
Candlesticks, Benedict, h/cp, 9½", pr.................................**325.00**
Candlesticks, ET Hurley, bronze, sea-horse base, 1914, 13", pr ..**1,100.00**
Candlesticks, Heintz, silver decor on bronze, #3074, 14½" **1,000.00**
Candlesticks, Heintz, sterling geometrics on bronze, 11½", pr....**700.00**
Candlesticks, Jarvie, Lambda, bronze, unmk, 6", pr..................**1,600.00**
Candlesticks, M Zimmerman, h/cp, scalloped ft, flared bobeche, 12", pr..**1,500.00**
Cellarette, flat top, 1-door, canted sides, cut-out base, 30x26"....**400.00**
Cellarette, Lakeside Crafters, zinc-lined section, 2 doors, 32".....**650.00**
Chair, child's; Ford & Johnson, mahog finish, 3-slat bk, 19".......**200.00**
Chair, desk; Limbert, #84, slatted bk, saddle seat, rfn, 40" **500.00**
Chair, side; Austrian, mahog w/floral inlay MOP in spindled bk, 41" ..**1,000.00**
Chair, tall single slat bk, plank seat, arched stretchers, 50".........**250.00**
Chairs, dining; Limbert, #1845/#1951, saddle seats, 2 arm+4 sides **1,500.00**
Chairs, dining; Limbert, wide slat over 3 narrow, rpl rush seat, 6 for..**2,900.00**
Chamberstick, Arts Crafts Shop, copper w/enameled flowers, #3004, 5" **700.00**
Chamberstick, Jarvie, Zeta, brass, unmk, 6", VG **700.00**
Chandelier, Prairie School, center box/4 ldgl lanterns, 23x16x16" **4,750.00**
Chandelier, 3 sq-link oak chains, 3 slag lanterns, 23½" drop......**800.00**
Coal scuttle, h/cp w/brass hdls, unmk, sm rprs, 23½x10" **425.00**
Cookie tin, Louis Chalon, h/cp, emb crab w/mc enameling, 2¾x10¼"....**1,000.00**
Curtain rods, S Yellin, wrought iron w/brass wash, scrolled top, 18" ...**600.00**
Desk, drop-front; Limbert, drw, sq copper pulls, 34½x33x18" .**1,100.00**
Desk set, Heintz, sterling decor on bronze, 4-pc **350.00**
Door, ldgl upper half w/long-stem rose & Gothic Arch, oak, 78x28"..**635.00**
Doors, Prairie School, ldgl floral panes, cvd roses, 80x24", pr..**4,250.00**
Footstool, Harden, arched seat rail, rfn, missing cushion, 14x20x14"...**325.00**
Footstool, Old Hickory, woven splint top on twig base, 17x16" sq **300.00**
Hall bench, McHugh, high bk w/3 dbl-key tenons at seat, 57x49x29", VG..**1,500.00**
Hall chair, slab bk & seat, splayed base w/cutouts, 39" **2,000.00**
Humidor, Carence Crafters, copper, etch swans, pagoda shape, 6¾"........**750.00**
Humidor, Shreve, h/cp, riveted to oak base w/leaves on sterling bands ..**800.00**
Humidor, Silvercrest, silver decor on bronze, golfer finial, 9½" ..**300.00**
Jardiniere, unmk, gr matt w/emb pyramids/oxen/sphinx, 11" W .225.00
Jardiniere, unmk, h/cp w/emb floral, 30" **850.00**
Lamp, Benedict, h/cp, mica 6-sided 20" shade, 26" **5,000.00**
Lamp, Heintz, bell shade; flared NP base w/geometrics, 10" **850.00**

Lamp, Heintz, silver decor on bronze, 3-arm spider, 10" **1,300.00**
Lamp, Heintz, sterling on bronze, mushroom-cap shade, 15x14"..**1,100.00**
Lamp, Prairie School, 15" sq ldgl linear shade; tiered base, 20....**800.00**
Lamp, van Erp, h/cp, conical mica shade, 2-light trumpet base, 18"..**35,000.00**
Lamp, van Erp, h/cp, conical mica shade, 3-arm, att, 20x18¾"...........**5,465.00**
Lamp, van Erp, h/cp, 3-panel mica shade, globular, 20x21"...**40,000.00**
Lamp, van Erp, h/cp, 3-panel mica shade, riveted shaft, 18x18"..**35,000.00**
Lamp, van Erp, h/cp, 3-panel mica shade, tapered base, 21"..**11,500.00**
Lamp, van Erp, h/cp, 4-panel mica shade, baluster, 11x11" **7,000.00**
Letter holder, G Twichell, h/cp, HP sailing ship, 4¼x5½"..........**375.00**
Letter opener, Handicraft Guild (att), wrought copper, cleaned, 6"....**225.00**
Mirror, Limbert, #21, arched top, vertical slats, rfn, 26x36"........**850.00**
Painting, CA mtn scene, W Dorsey, oil on canvas, 9½x7½"+fr **1,000.00**
Paperweight, Yellin, wrought iron, flower on curled hdl, 1933, 3½" .**800.00**
Piano shawl, stylized flowers, earth tones, frayed fringe, 108x48" ..**500.00**
Pillows, embr stylized flowers, tassels, 11½x17", EX, pr...............**300.00**
Pitcher, water; Eicher, hammered sterling, 10x6" **1,600.00**
Print, woodblock; Helen Hyde, Moonlight Trail, 1904, 12x14"..**700.00**
Rocker, Harden, att; 4-slat bk, thru-tenons, reuphl spring seat, 38" ..**375.00**
Rocker, Lifetime, bow arms, wing bk, reuphl seat, 37x31x29" .**1,000.00**
Rocker, Old Hickory, twig type, orig splint seat/bk, unsgn, 32"...**475.00**
Rocker, Paine, 4-slat bk, plank armrests, thru tenons, 36" **750.00**
Rocker, sewing; curved crest over 3 vertical slats, ca 1912, 32" ..**125.00**
Rocker, 4-slat bk, arms adjust, reuphl bk/seat, 42" **800.00**
Rug, Druggett, bright flowers on oatmeal, 171x111", VG **275.00**
Screen, Helen Bridges, 3-panel pyrographic scene, ea panel: 72x24"..**2,000.00**
Screen, 3-panel, oak w/poppy pyrography, unmk, ea panel: 70x20"....**1,200.00**
Server, Lifetime, #5295½, 2-drw/2-door, thru-tenons, rfn, 45x66" **1,500.00**
Settle, deep floral cvg on crest, 9-slat bk, leather uphl, 47x84x33" **3,500.00**
Settle, Lifetime, broad paneled bk, arms mortised through legs, 72"..**3,250.00**
Settle, Paine, drop-arm, curved rail, 6 vertical slats, 28x74"........**2,400.00**
Sideboard, arched/mirrored bksplash, 3-drw/2-door, linen drws, 72"....**2,000.00**
Sideboard, Limbert, #1445, arched paneled door & bk rail, 46x60" **8,000.00**
Sideboard, Limbert, mirror bk, 2 drws over 2 doors over drw, 57x60"..**7,000.00**
Sideboard, Limbert, plate rail, drop-front, drw, 2-door, 40x60"..**4,000.00**
Sideboard, mirrored bksplash, 2-drw/2-door, linen drw, rfn, 55x60" ..**1,400.00**
Smoke set, Benedict Studios, h/cp, brass ft, cleaned, 4-pc............**400.00**
Stand, magazine; Ford & Johnson, 4-shelf, ebonized, 42x18x13" ..**650.00**
Stand, magazine; Limbert, 4-shelf, flared sides, med brn, 42x20".......**1,100.00**
Stand, magazine; 4-shelf, 3-slat sides, arched toe board, 40x21x12"..**1,000.00**
Stool, Limbert, tacked leather seat, shelf, orig finish, 18x20"..**1,300.00**
Stool, Thebes, in style of Liberty, slatted seat, trn legs, 13x16" sq.....**450.00**
Table, cafe; Limbert, #117, X-stretcher, thru-tenons, rfn, 36" dia ..**1,100.00**
Table, dining; Lifetime, att; ped base w/curved supports, 54" **900.00**
Table, dining; Limbert, #1487, Prairie School, 3 leaves, 54" dia, VG..**6,000.00**
Table, dining; Limbert, #423, 4-leg, brand/#d, rfn, 54" dia+4 leaves..**4,250.00**
Table, dining; Limbert, cut-out base, rfn top, 48" dia+2 leaves..**2,600.00**
Table, library; Limbert, #1131 (similar), drw, arched skirt, 29x48x28" ..**1,100.00**
Table, library; Limbert, blind lift-top drw, arched sides/bk, rfn, 48"...**1,400.00**
Table, library; Limbert, drw, sq copper pulls, arched apron, 48".........**1,400.00**
Table, library; Limbert, ebon-oak, 1-drw, arched apron, 42" **1,400.00**
Table, Limbert, #148, X-stretcher w/cutouts, brand, 29x30"......**3,750.00**
Table, Limbert, 4 extended ft, brand, 29x54" dia+1 leaf **1,800.00**
Table, lunch; Limbert; #1172, ca 1910, 29x42x28" **1,200.00**
Table, rnd top w/sq legs, X-stretcher/platform, 30x42" dia.........**1,500.00**
Table, telephone; Limbert, drw, arched front, shelf, rfn, 39x24x22" ..**1,300.00**
Table runner, embr mc floral on linen, 42x21½", VG.................**100.00**
Tile, poppies on whiplash stems, in orig fr, 6" sq........................**300.00**
Tray, Frost, h/cp, etched birds, unmk, 13" **425.00**
Tray, Frost, h/cp, etched poppies, 14x12" **700.00**
Tray, Kalo, h/cp, hdls, EX orig patina, 14" W, VG.....................**700.00**
Tray, LeBolt, hammered silver w/glass bottom, 10x5".................**100.00**
Tumbler, Kalo, hammered sterling, monogram, 1916, EX **300.00**
Vase, h/cp, Am Beauty style, lt patina, unmk, 21x9".................**600.00**

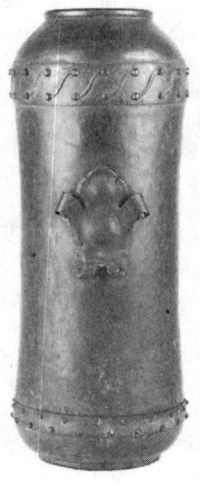

Umbrella stand, hammered iron, riveted band and applied medallion, 24½", $400.00.

Vase, Heintz, sterling branch on bronze, corseted, 8x3½" 450.00
Vase, Heintz, sterling daffodils on bronze cylinder, 12" 750.00
Vase, Heintz, sterling Dutch landscape on bronze, unmk, 12" 500.00
Vase, Heintz, sterling floral on bronze, 3½" 200.00
Vase, Heintz, sterling floral on bronze, 4½" 375.00
Vase, Heintz, sterling pine cones on bronze, 9½" 750.00
Vase, Heintz, sterling rose on bronze, rstr ft, 12½" 600.00
Vase, Kalo, h/cp, closed low form, old cleaning, 7½" W 500.00
Vase, silver bird on branch on bronze, dent/wear, 10x3" 150.00
Wall sconce, Benedict Studio, h/cp, 12" 350.00
Window seat, Limbert, #243½, slab sides w/cutouts, 24x25x18", VG ...5,000.00
Woodblock print, C Weston, By the Sea, coastal scene, 6x8½"+fr.....425.00
Woodblock print, H Hyde, Asian children, 1913, matted/fr, 4½x4"...500.00
Woodblock print, snowy mtn scene, dbl matted in orig fr, 18x14"......600.00
Woodblock print, stylized floral, dbl matted in orig fr, 5½x7" 200.00

Attwell, Mabel Lucie

Born in London in 1879, Mabel Lucie Attwell put her talent in illustration and design toward many outlets. Merchandise ranging from children's books and dinnerware, postcards, advertising, dolls, calendars, and greeting cards were marketed under her direction. She also designed a line of china called Nursery Ware for the Shelley China Company (see also Shelley). Our advisor for this category is David Ehrhard; he is listed in the Directory under California.

Beaker, girl w/doll & parasol w/pixies, orange trim, hdl, 3½" 150.00
Biscuit tin, Mushroom House, Wm Crawford & Sons, EX..........215.00
Book, Lucie Attwell's Bed Time Tales, Partridge, 1920s, 10x8½" ...200.00
Egg cup, pixie in gr on wht, unmk, 2½"......................................200.00
Figurine, Boo Boo, LA 11, 1920s, 2¾".......................................825.00
Jug, Boo Boo figural, 1926, milk sz 100.00
Jug, Pixie Mushroom, orange hdl, 4" 375.00
Mug, boy & girl on tricycle followed by 2 pixies.........................90.00
Mug, Fairies Love Motoring..., Shelley..155.00
Music box, Good Morning Mister Snowman, MIB......................80.00
Plate, Here's Cowboy James..., Shelley, 6½"...............................98.00
Sugar bowl, Mushroom, orange dots, gr grassy ft, 3¾x4¼" 155.00
Teapot, Boo Boo, Shelley, #d, 4½x6", NM 235.00
Teapot, Mushroom House, part of Boo Boo set, orange hdl, 4½" ..300.00

Autographs

Autograph collecting, also known as 'philography' or 'love of writ-ing,' used to be a hobby shared by a few thousand dedicated collectors. But in recent years, autograph collecting has become a serious pursuit for more than 2,000,000 collectors worldwide. And in the past decade, more investors are adding rare and valuable autograph portfolios to their traditional investments. One reason for this sudden interest in autograph investing relates to the simple economic law of supply and demand. Rare autographs have a 'fixed' supply, meaning that unlike diamonds, gold, silver, stock certificates, etc., no more are being produced. There are only so many Abraham Lincoln, Marilyn Monroe, and Charles Lindbergh autographs available. In the meantime, it's estimated that more than 20,000 new collectors enter the market each year, thus creating an ever-increasing demand. Hence, the rare autographs generally rise steadily in value each year. Because of this scarcity, a serious collector will pay over $10,000.00 for a photograph signed by both Wilbur and Orville Wright, or as much as $25,000.00 for a handwritten letter of George Washington.

But by far, the majority of autograph collectors in the country do it for the love of the hobby. A polite letter and self-addressed, stamped envelope sent to a famous person will often bring the desired result. And occasionally one receives not only an autograph but a nice handwritten letter thanking the fan as well!

In terms of value, there are five general types of autographs: 1) mere signatures on an album page or card; 2) signed photographs; 3) signed documents; 4) typed letters signed; and 5) handwritten letters. The signatures are the least valuable, and handwritten letters the most valuable. The reasoning here is simple: with a handwritten letter, not only do you get an autograph but the handwritten message of the person as well. And this content can sometimes increase the value many times over. A handwritten letter of Babe Ruth's thanking a fan for a gift might fetch a few thousand dollars. But if the letter were to mention Ruth's feelings on the day he retired, it could easily sell for $10,000.00 or more.

Today the Internet has become a popular way to buy and sell autographs. A word of warning: be very careful when buying over the Internet. It is an easy way for unscrupulous forgers to sell their fakes and disappear. Teenagers need to be especially aware that many of the 'signed' photos on the Internet of Sarah Michelle Gellar, Brad Pitt, Katie Holmes, Leonardo DeCaprio, Kate Winslett, and many others are either signed by secretaries or are outright forgeries. Make sure the Internet dealer offers a full money-back guarantee of authenticity and belongs to one of the major autograph organizations. Ask how long the dealer has been in business and for personal references if possible. Remember the old Latin warning, 'caveat emptor,' let the buyer beware.

There are several major autograph collector organizations where members can exchange celebrity addresses or buy, sell, and trade their autographed wares. Philography can be a fun and rewarding hobby. And who knows! In ten or twenty years, those autographs you got for free could be worth a small fortune!

In the listings below, photos are assumed black and white unless noted color. Our advisor for autographs is Tim Anderson; he is listed in the Directory under Utah.

Key:
ADS — handwritten document signed	ins — inscription
	ISP — inscribed signed photo
ALS — handwritten letter signed	LH — letterhead
	LS — signed letter, typed or written by someone else
ANS — handwritten note signed	
AQS — autograph quotation signed	PLH — personal letterhead
	sig — signature
CS — counter signed	SP — signed photo
DS — document signed	

Anthony, Susan B; cut sig, Yours sincerely, 2¾x5½" 220.00
Barton, Clara; sig on card, 1¾x3¾" 110.00

Bergen, Edgar; LS, 1938 ....100.00
Berry, Noah; sig on contract re trout farm....................125.00
Bisset, Jacqueline; sig on The Deep lobby card 50.00
Bradley, Omar N; SP, official Army photo, 8x10".........150.00
Burke, Billie; SP, sepia-tone portrait, 5x7", VG 150.00
Butler, Benj F; DS, as Major General, partly printed, 1864......1,250.00
Christie, Julie; SP, w/matt...30.00
Clinton, George; DS, land grant, as Governor of NY, dtd 1790 .550.00
Curtis, Jamie; SP, w/matt 70.00
Dempsey, Jack; SP, in workout suit, w/Seasons' Greetings..., 1937 .80.00
Earhart, Amelia; sig on album pg, 4¼x6" 550.00
Edison, Thos A; sig on card, bold, w/certificate of authenticity..265.00
Ford, Gerald R; TLS on White House stationery...........85.00
Ford, Gerald; TLS on White House stationery, Gerry Ford sig ...300.00
Fremont, John C; LS, to wife of Gen Townsend, 8x5"....................25.00
Garner, James; SP, w/matt...250.00
Goldberg, Whoopie; SP, w/matt....................................70.00
Goodyear, Charles; LS, re meeting w/Lord Hardringe, 1853....1,250.00
Harrison, William Henry; DS, as aide de camp to Anthony Wayne, 1795...1,300.00
Hayes, Rutherford B; DS, as Governor, 1869, 8½x14" 300.00
Hoover, J Edgar; sig in book: Masters of Deceit..., M in jacket ...200.00
Howe, Julia Ward; sig on card, 1901, 2½x4", w/mtd photo...........70.00
Huston, Anjelica, SP, w/matt...30.00
Jackson, Andrew; sig on captain's passport, vellum, 183?, EX..1,700.00
Keller, Helen; sig on card, block letters, dtd 1901, 2½x3½" 150.00
Lee, Fitzhugh; sig on card, 2½x3½"..............................125.00
Lemmon, Jack; SP, w/matt..30.00
Lewis, Jerry; SP, w/matt 30.00
Loren, Sophia; SP, w/matt...40.00
McGwire, Mark; SP, 8x10"..95.00
Moore, Thomas O; sig on Confederate bond as governor, 1862..460.00
Newmar, Julie; SP, as Cat Woman 35.00
Polk, James K; cut sig, bold w/flourishes, 1½x4½" 500.00
Reynolds, Burt; SP, w/matt..30.00
Rogers, Roy; SP, w/matt...125.00
Roosevelt, Eleanor; sig cut from letter mtd w/WWII-era photo..125.00
Sosa, Sammy; SP, 8x10" 95.00
Stone, Lucy; sig on card, bold/clear, 2x3½" 90.00
Schwarzeneggar, Arnold; SP, w/matt 125.00
Travolta, John; SP, w/matt...70.00

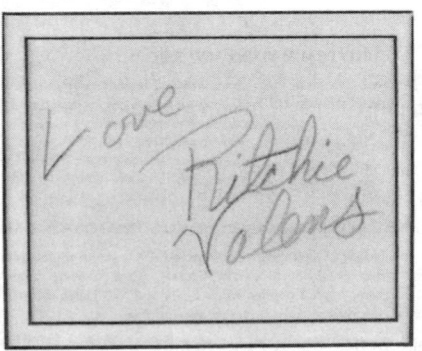

Richie Valens, signature in pencil on single sheet (with certificate of authenticity), matted and framed with black and white 5x7" photograph (not shown), overall size: 11x17", NM, $415.00.

Whitman, Walt; sig in book: Leaves of Grass, McKay, 1900 ....800.00

Automobilia

While some automobilia buffs are primarily concerned with restoring vintage cars, others concentrate on only one area of collecting. For instance, hood ornaments were often quite spectacular. Made of chrome or nickel plate on brass or bronze, they were designed to represent the 'winged maiden' Victory, flying bats, sleek greyhounds, soaring eagles,

and a host of other creatures. Today they often bring prices in the $75.00 to $200.00 range. R. Lalique glass ornaments go much higher!

Horns, radios, clocks, gear shift knobs, and key chains with company emblems are other areas of interest. Generally, items pertaining to the classics of the '30s are most in demand. Paper advertising material, manuals, and catalogs in excellent condition are also collectible.

License plate collectors search for the early porcelain-on-cast-iron examples. First year plates (e.g., Massachusetts, 1903; Wisconsin, 1905; Indiana, 1913) are especially valuable. The last of the states to issue regulation plates were South Carolina and Texas in 1917, and Florida in 1918. While many northeastern states had registered hundreds of thousands of vehicles by the 1920s making these plates relatively common, those from the southern and western states of that period are considered rare. Naturally, condition is important. While a pair in mint condition might sell for as much as $100.00 to $125.00, a pair with chipped or otherwise damaged porcelain may sometimes be had for as little as $25.00 to $30.00.

Our advisor for this category is Leonard Needham; he is listed in the Directory under California. For more information we recommend *American Automobilia: An Illustrated History and Price Guide* by Jim and Nancy Schaut. See also Gas Globes and Panels.

Brochure, Grand Central Palace Auto Show, 1914, EX, $325.00. (Photo courtesy Dunbar Auction Gallery)

Air dispenser, Eco, CI, Deco style, retractable hose, 53x19" sq, rstr ..1,150.00
Badge, cap; US Post Office Vehicle Service, metal eagle shield, EX........22.00
Badge, chauffeur; 1923 Registered..., metal arrowhead, 2", NM 28.00
Badge, chauffeur; 1952 Alberta..., bronze-tone metal shield, EX...45.00
Banner, 1954 Studebaker/World's Finest...V-8, silk/fringe, 40", VG ...80.00
Book, Rolling Thunder, The Harley-Davidson Legend; M Norris, 1992, M..13.00
Calendar, Chevrolet Motor Cars, 1920, paper litho, fr, 34x20", EX+...170.00
Calendar, Greyhound, 1953, Biscayne Key, Miami photo, 32", EX+....100.00
Chain tightener, Harley-Davidson, chrome...................................35.00
Change purse, leather hat w/NP bill, emb scene, 1910, 2½" dia, EX.....120.00
Clock, Chevrolet, desk type w/sq metal face, rnd marble base, 4", EX ..260.00
Clock, Chevrolet Super Service, metal, sq w/rnded corners, 15", VG...300.00
Clock, GMC Truck Sales & Service, neon/tin, octagonal, VG...800.00
Clock, Pontiac Service, plastic, wht on bl, 15" dia, EX...............350.00
Desk accessory, GMC truck ('40s-'50s), bronzed, lettered base, 7", EX...100.00
Fan, Frigid, vacuum op, for steering wheel, early 55.00
Grille, center; Chrysler 300, 1963, NM..195.00
Grille badge, tin oval, Farmer Mutual Auto Ins Co, 3x4", NM+...300.00
Hood ornament, flying horse, 6x6", EX+ 250.00
Hood ornament, Packard, Goddess of Speed figure, chrome, 1932-37 ..130.00
Hood ornament, Studebaker, rocket, 1948-50, EX.........................70.00
Jacket, Harley-Davidson, cloth, dealer advertising on bk, med, EX..35.00
Lamp, brass Chevy truck on wooden base, burlap shade, 23", EX.30.00
License plate, CA, 1919, red star tab 250.00
License plate, PA, 1913, porc, wht on gr, VG+ 100.00
Manual, Chevrolet, 1927 ....75.00
Manual, Ford V8, 1933...65.00
Manual, Graham-Paige Model 612 ....90.00
Manual, Indian Motorcycle, 1950s, EX 65.00
Manual, Model A Ford, 1928...95.00

Manual, Nash Standard Six Series 320...60.00
Manual, Studebaker - The Light Six 40.00
Manual, Studebaker Standard Six, 1926 ....40.00
Motometer, American La France, atop winged cap, NP, EX........250.00
Motometer, Duesenberg Model A, atop monogram eagle cap, EX...750.00
Pamphlet, Diamond T Introduces Four Great Sixes, 1928, NM ...40.00
Pamphlet, Nash '400,' full color, 12 pgs, 8x10½", EX....................28.00
Pamphlet, Studebaker Models & Prices, Aug 1, 1922, 13x10", EX......20.00
Paperweight, Chalmers Motor Co, brass, emb factory scene, 2x4", EX...120.00
Paperweight, shaped like chrome GMC Art Deco hood ornament, 6½", G ..85.00
Picnic set, Ford, case w/service for 4, shakers, etc, 18x5", VG 275.00
Poster, Ford, Smart New Interiors..., 1946, 35x46", G 80.00
Poster, Impala Convertible, car/couple/building, fr, 21x35", VG...35.00
Poster, We Airline Check When We Chevy Tune, 44x17", EX..100.00
Promotional car, Corvette Mako Shark, Stingray prototype, MIB...15.00
Promotional car, 1989 Silver Anniversary Corvette, MIB.............75.00
Promotional car, 1994 Brickyard 400 Monte Carlo Pacecar, MIB.70.00
Promotional car, 1996 Viper, 3-car set, ea car exclusive to set, MIB..55.00
Promotional car, 1999 Beetle, yel, 1:25 scale, MIB......................65.00
Radiator cap, lady's head, brass, Ternstedt...USA, 4½x2⅝" 385.00
Radiator mascot, Chevy, Viking, 1930, EX 195.00
Sign, cb, Auto Dept/Fireman's Fund Insurance Co, fr, 13x23", EX+.......500.00
Sign, cb, Chevrolet diecut bow tie emblem, wht on bl, 11x30", VG 80.00
Sign, neon, DeSoto, emb bust image on geometric ground, 38" dia, G ..300.00
Sign, neon, Dodge/Plymouth, porc emblem, wht on bl, 28x60", VG+...850.00
Sign, neon, Pontiac, logo flanked by 6-8, name below, 28x38", EX.......220.00
Sign, porc, Approved by Federal Hi-way Tourist Guide, 2-sided, VG..100.00
Sign, porc, Ford script logo, bl & wht, 26x40", VG......................325.00
Sign, porc, Ford/Genuine Parts, 2-sided oval, 17x24", EX/VG+ .300.00
Sign, porc, Greyhound Bus Depot, 18x72", EX.............................425.00
Sign, porc, Huile Bugatti, oval logo above, 19x27", NM+ 2,000.00
Sign, tin, Buick/Authorized Service, 2-sided, 18" dia, VG..........220.00
Sign, tin, Licenses & General Motor Insurance, graphics, 29x19", G...200.00
Sign, tin, We Use An Overland Motor Car, chalkboard-look, 10x14", EX..170.00
Sign, tin wheel w/wooden spokes, Kwickwork Auto Enamel, 28" dia, VG...250.00
Thermometer, dial, Mack Trucks, bulldog logo, rnd, VG+..........200.00
Thermometer, dial, Studebaker Batteries, Pam, 1963, 12x12", EX...200.00
Thermometer, plastic pole sign, Chevrolet, red on wht, 6½", NM ..150.00
Thermometer, porc, Buick Motor Cars, bl & wht, 27x7", G 450.00

Autumn Leaf

In 1933 the Hall China Company designed a line of dinnerware for the Jewel Tea Company, who offered it to their customers as premiums. Although you may hear the ware referred to as 'Jewel Tea,' it was officially named Autumn Leaf in the 1940s. In addition to the dinnerware, frosted Libbey glass tumblers, stemware, and a melmac service with the orange and gold bittersweet pod were available over the years, as were tablecloths, plastic covers for bowls and mixers, and metal items such as cake safes, hot pads, coasters, wastebaskets, and canisters. Even shelf paper and playing cards were made to coordinate. In 1958 the International Silver Company designed silverplated flatware in a pattern called Autumn which was to be used with dishes in the Autumn Leaf pattern. A year later, a line of stainless flatware was introduced. These accessory lines are prized by collectors today.

One of the most fascinating aspects of collecting the Autumn Leaf pattern has been the wonderful discoveries of previously unlisted pieces. Among these items are two different bud-ray lid one-pound butter dishes; most recently a one-pound butter dish in the 'Zephyr' or 'Bingo' style; a miniature set of the 'Casper' salt and pepper shakers; coffee, tea, and sugar canisters; a pair of candlesticks; an experimental condiment jar; and a covered candy dish. All of these china pieces are attributed to the Hall China Company. Other unusual items have turned up in the acces-

sory lines as well and include a Libbey frosted tumbler in a pilsner shape, a wooden serving bowl, and an apron made from the oilcloth (plastic) material that was used in the 1950s tablecloth. These latter items appear to be professionally done, and we can only speculate as to their origin. Collectors believe that the Hall items were sample pieces that were never meant to be distributed.

Hall discontinued the Autumn Leaf line in 1978. At that time the date was added to the backstamp to mark ware still in stock in the Hall warehouse. A special promotion by Jewel saw the reintroduction of basic dinnerware and serving pieces with the 1978 backstamp. These pieces have made their way into many collections. Additionally, in 1979 Jewel released a line of enamel-clad cookware and a Vellux blanket made by Martex which were decorated with the Autumn Leaf pattern. They continued to offer these items for a few years only, then all distribution of Autumn Leaf items was discontinued.

It should be noted that the Hall China Company has produced several limited edition items for the National Autumn Leaf Collectors Club (NALCC): a New York-style teapot (1984); an Edgewater vase (1987, different than the original shape); candlesticks (1988); a Philadelphia-style teapot, creamer and sugar set (1990); a tea-for-two set and a Solo tea set (1991), a donut jug, and a large oval casserole. Later came the small ball jug, one-cup French teapot, and a set of four chocolate mugs. Other special items over the past few years made for them by Hall China include a sugar packet holder, a chamberstick, and an oyster cocktail. Additional items are scheduled for production. All of these are plainly marked as having been made for the NALCC and are appropriately dated. A few other pieces have been made by Hall as limited editions for an Ohio company, but these are easily identified: the Airflow teapot and the Norris refrigerator pitcher (neither of which was previously decorated with the Autumn Leaf decal), a square-handled beverage mug, and the new-style Irish mug. A production problem with the square-handled mugs halted their production. The company then issued a regular conic-style mug with a round handle. Additional items available now are a covered onion soup, tall bud vase, china kitchen memo board, and egg drop-style salt and pepper shakers with a mustard pot. They have also issued a deck of playing cards and Libbey tumblers. See *Garage Sale & Flea Market Annual* (Collector Books) for suggested values for club pieces. Our advisor for this category is Gwynne Harrison; she is listed in the Directory under California. For more information we recommend *Collector's Encyclopedia of Hall China, Third Edition*, by Margaret and Kenn Whitmyer.

Marmalade, three-piece set, from $100.00 to $125.00.

Apron, oilcloth..700.00
Baker, cake; Heatflow clear glass, Mary Dunbar, 1½-qt.................85.00
Baker, French; 3-pt...20.00
Baker, oval, Fort Pitt, 12-oz ind..225.00
Baker/souffle, 4½"...80.00
Bean pot, 1-hdl...1,000.00
Bean pot, 2-hdl, 2¼-qt..250.00

Blanket, Vellux, bl, full sz...200.00
Book, Mary Dunbar Cookbook 30.00
Bottle, Jim Beam, w/stand 130.00
Bowl, cereal; 6" 12.00
Bowl, cream soup; 2-hdl 40.00
Bowl, flat soup; 8½" 20.00
Bowl, fruit; 5½" 6.00
Bowl, grease; w/lid 20.00
Bowl, mixing; New Metal, 3-pc set..........................275.00
Bowl, refrigerator; metal w/plastic lids, 3 for 275.00
Bowl, Royal Glas-Bake, set of 4 ....500.00
Bowl, soup; Melmac...20.00
Bowl, vegetable; divided, oval..................................125.00
Bowl, vegetable; oval, w/lid, 10" 75.00
Bowl, vegetable; rnd, 9" 175.00
Bowl, vegetable; Royal Glasbake, milk wht, divided 150.00
Bowl cover set, plastic, 8-pc: 7 assorted covers in pouch.............100.00
Bread box, metal, from $400 to 800.00
Butter dish, 1-lb, ruffled top, regular.......................500.00
Butter dish, ¼-lb, regular, ruffled top, from $175 to 250.00
Butter dish, ¼-lb, sq top, rare 2,000.00
Butter dish, ¼-lb, wings top 2,000.00
Cake safe, metal, motif on top or sides, 5", ea..........50.00
Candle holder, Chamber, club gift, 1991..................125.00
Candle holder, club pc, 892 made, 1989, pr.............250.00
Candlestick, metal, Douglas, 4", pr..........................100.00
Canister, brn & gold, wht plastic lid..........................30.00
Canister, metal, rnd, w/coppertone lid, set of 4, from $600 to .1,000.00
Canister, metal, rnd, w/matching lids, set of 3, from $200 to......300.00
Casserole, Heatflow, w/lid, rnd, 2-qt.........................85.00
Casserole, Royal Glas-Bake, rnd, milk wht w/clear glass lid 90.00
Catalog, Jewel, hardbound 50.00
Clock, electric 550.00
Coaster, metal, 3⅛" 8.00
Coffee dispenser, metal..400.00
Coffee percolator, electric, all china, 4-pc...............400.00
Coffeepot, Jewel's Best, 30-cup 600.00
Coffeepot, Rayed, 8-cup 45.00
Coffeepot, 9-cup, Rayed 45.00
Cookware, New Metal, 7-pc set..................................650.00
Creamer & sugar bowl, Nautilus...............................125.00
Creamer & sugar bowl, Rayed, 1930s style...............80.00
Cup & saucer, regular, Ruffled-D 9.00
Custard cup, Heatflow clear glass, Mary Dunbar, from $40 to.......60.00
Custard cup, Radiance..10.00
Dripper, metal, for coffeepot, 8- or 9-cup, ea..........25.00
Flatware, silverplated, ea 35.00
Flatware, silverplated, serving pc, ea........................175.00
Fork, pickle; Jewel Tea..75.00
Gravy boat, w/underplate (pickle dish) 55.00
Hot pad, metal, oval, 10¾", from $12 to....................15.00
Hot pad, metal, red or gr felt-like bking, rnd............20.00
Hurricane lamp, Douglas, w/metal base, pr, minimum value.......500.00
Jug, utility; Rayed, 2½-pt, 6" 25.00
Loaf pan, Mary Dunbar, from $90 to........................125.00
Mug, chocolate; club pc, 1,500 made, 1992, 4-pc set................100.00
Mug, conic 65.00
Mustard, condiment set, 3-pc....................................125.00
Napkin, ecru muslin, 16" sq 50.00
Pickle dish or gravy liner, oval, 9".............................25.00
Pie plate, Heatflow, clear glass, Mary Dunbar, from $45 to 60.00
Pie plate, 9½" 35.00
Pitcher, syrup; club pc, 1995 ....95.00
Place mat, paper, scalloped, set of 8, from $150 to......325.00

Plate, salad; Melmac, 7" 20.00
Plate, 10"...18.00
Plate, 7¼" 10.00
Plate, 8"...18.00
Plate, 9"...12.00
Platter, oval, 11½" 28.00
Platter, oval, 13½" 28.00
Pressure cooker, Mary Dunbar, metal........................225.00
Sauce dish, serving; Douglas, Bakelite hdl, w/warmer base..........600.00
Saucepan, w/lid, metal, 2-qt......................................100.00
Shakers, Casper, ruffled, regular, pr............................30.00
Shakers, range, hdl, pr..30.00
Shelf liner, paper, 108" roll...50.00
Sifter, metal 400.00
Tablecloth, cotton sailcloth w/gold stripe, 54x54"...........140.00
Tablecloth, cotton sailcloth w/gold stripe, 54x72"...........140.00
Tablecloth, muslin, 56x81" 300.00
Tablecloth, plastic 150.00
Teapot, Aladdin 70.00
Teapot, long spout, Rayed, 1935 ....95.00
Teapot, Newport, dtd 1978, from $175 to 250.00
Teapot, Rayed, long spout, 1978, from $800 to 1,600.00
Teapot, Solo, club pc, 1,400 made, 1991...................100.00
Tidbit tray, 3-tier..100.00
Tin, fruitcake; wht or tan 10.00
Toaster cover, plastic, Mary Dunbar...........................50.00
Towel, tea; cotton, 16x33" 60.00
Toy, Jewel Truck, gr, from $350 to 425.00
Toy, Jewel Truck Semi Trailer, brn, from $1,000 to 1,500.00
Toy, Jewel Van, brn, Buddy L, from $400 to..............650.00
Tray, glass, wood hdl 140.00
Tray, metal, oval 100.00
Tumbler, Brockway, 9-oz, 13-oz or 16-oz, ea..............45.00
Tumbler, Libbey, frosted, 14-oz, 5½" 20.00
Tumbler, Libbey, frosted, 9-oz, 3¾" 32.00
Tumbler, Libbey, gold & frost on clear, 10-oz 75.00
Tumbler, Libbey, gold frost etched, flat or ftd, 10-oz, ea 65.00
Tumbler, Libbey, gold frost etched, flat or ftd, 15-oz, ea 65.00
Vase, bud; regular decal, 6" 275.00
Vase, Edgewater, club pc, 626 made, 1987 ....350.00
Warmer base, oval 200.00

Aviation

Aviation buffs are interested in any phase of flying, from early developments with gliders, balloons, airships, and flying machines to more modern innovations. Books, catalogs, photos, patents, lithographs, ad cards, and posters are among the paper ephemera they treasure alongside models of unlikely flying contraptions, propellers and rudders, insignia and equipment from WWI and WWII, and memorabilia from the flights of the Wright Brothers, Lindbergh, Earhart, and the Zeppelins. See also Militaria. Our advisor for this category is John R. Joiner; he is listed in the Directory under Georgia.

Ashtray, Piedmont Airlines, wht ceramic, 4 rests 57.50
Bag, Aloha Airlines, yel/orange/wht floral, 1970s, 14x12", EX 80.00
Bag, carry-on; Canadian Pacific Airlines, 15x10x4½", EX............55.00
Bag, duffel; Pan Am Airlines, canvas, zipper closure, 22" L 70.00
Beret, hostess'; Golden Falcon Eastern Airlines, gold velvet.........70.00
Blanket, Delta, gold w/brn logo, 53x54"....................80.00
Blanket, Mawhawk, blk lettering on lt bl, 40x56" 70.00
Blanket, Transcontinental Airlines, blk w/bl edging, 55x62" 85.00
Book, system map; United Airlines, DC-4 cover, 1946, 35-pg......40.00

Brochure, Scandinavian Airlines system, w/map, 1948, 20-pg **55.00**
Cachet cover, Hindenburg, from Germany to NY, 1936, VG **65.00**
Cocktail glass, Braniff Airlines..**12.50**
Cocktail glass, National Airlines, 1970s...**10.00**

**Cup, Spirit of St. Louis, ceram-
ic, blue and brown background,
inscribed and dated 1930, 3½",
NM, $100.00.**

Cup & saucer, Trans Canada Airlines, maple leaf logo..................**50.00**
Doll, Am Airlines Stewardess, Mattel #984, 1961, NRFB **225.00**
Insignia, pilot's hat; Delta Airlines, enamel on gold-tone **38.00**
Jacket, flight; Type B-3, sheepskin lining **400.00**
Label, bag; Pan Am Airways, Deco scene, 1930s, 3x3"..................**35.00**
Label, baggage; Am Airlines World's 1st Sleeper Plane Service, 1930s..**80.00**
Manual, pilot's; Am Airlines 757/767 operational, EX................**150.00**
Map, promotional; United Airlines, Hawaiian Islands, 3-D, fr, 36x26" ..**160.00**
Medal, Eastern Airlines, 50 Years of Service **35.00**
Model, United Airlines Airbus A340, w/stand, 25" L **190.00**
Model kit, Am Airlines Turboprop Electra Airliner, Revell, MIB ..**235.00**
Photo, Eddie Rickenbacker near prop of his Spad, autographed, 8x10"..**525.00**
Pin, employee; Hawaiian Airlines, shield & wings, 1940s............**55.00**
Pitcher, water; Eastern Airlines, Legion Utensils, 1951, 8" **50.00**
Postcard, early view of lady at controls of 2-seater biplane, EX...**215.00**
Program, Internat'l Air Races, OH, 1924, 64-pg, 8½x11", VG...**150.00**
Propeller, solid wood, 31" L...**95.00**
Spoon, Pan Am Airlines, Internat'l Silver, 4"...............................**17.50**
Stamp, Graf Zeppelin, First Flight Air Mail, 1928, 7x3⅞" **50.00**
Swizzle stick, Eastern Airlines, clear glass, 4¾", 3 for **42.00**
Timetable, Am Airlines, shows DC-8s, 1971, EX **80.00**
Timetable, Capital Airlines, 1960...**42.00**
Timetable, Mid-Continent Airlines, 1938......................................**42.50**
Timetable, Pan Am World Airlines, 1948-49................................**16.50**
Utensils, serving; Eastern Airlines, fork & spoon, M in orig bag...**32.50**
Wings, flight attendant's; Am Airlines, AA w/eagle......................**32.50**
Wings, Mohawk Airlines, pilot's, 1950s, EX **162.50**
Wings, pilot's; Channel Express Airlines, gold metal....................**24.00**
Wings, pilot's; Eastern Airlines, gold metal, 1985, NM..............**155.00**
Wings, United Airlines, metal, minor pnt wear...........................**225.00**
Wings, United Airlines, sterling, enameled crest w/4 gold stars..**100.00**
Wristwatch, Delta Airlines, dual dial, M in case............................**40.00**

Baccarat

The Baccarat Glass company was founded in 1765 near Luneville,
France, and continues to this day to produce quality crystal tableware,
vases, perfume bottles, and figurines. The firm became famous for the
high-quality millefiori and caned paperweights produced there from
1845 until about 1860. Examples of these range from $300.00 to as much
as several thousand. Since 1953 they have resumed the production of
paperweights on a limited edition basis. Our advisors for this category are
Randall Monsen and Rod Baer; their address is listed in the Directory

under Virginia. See also Bottles, Commercial Perfume; Paperweights.

Bell, plain w/6 t'prints at shoulder, faceted ball terminal, 6" **65.00**
Bottle, Rose Tiente Swirl, 5½", pr...**125.00**
Bowl, Harcourt, 4½x10" **400.00**

**Box, cut crystal with
ormolu mounts, marked,
5½x7x4", $770.00.**

Candelabra, crystal shaft, 5-light, prisms, bl bobeches, 27x19", pr...**3,850.00**
Candelabrum, faceted shaft, 4 candle cups, bobeches/prisms, 1850s, 24" ...**750.00**
Candelabrum, Swirl, 2 arms, ea w/9 cut prisms, 13x9", EX **450.00**
Candelsticks, ribbed, slim w/bun base & thick rim, 6x3", pr.......**225.00**
Centerpc, rim w/8 long points, 2 curve up as hdls, 15" L **95.00**
Champagne, Capri, 7x2", set of 6...**350.00**
Cordial, Massena, 5"..**125.00**
Decanter, Nouveau vines/coat-of-arms etching, ftd disk, 10x6" ..**300.00**
Decanter, ovoid w/fluted stick neck, 12" **245.00**
Decanter, Zipper, Rose Tiente, cut paneled neck, 10¼x5" **225.00**
Dish, 8-pointed swirled rim, 6" dia **65.00**
Goblet, water; Compiegne, panels w/rnded tops, plain rim, 8"......**60.00**
Goblet, water; Medicis, etched, 7"...**60.00**
Goblet, wine; Lafayette, etched, 6"...**35.00**
Goblet, wine; Lagny, 5¾"...**75.00**
Goblet, wine; Mercure, 5⅞", set of 6..**400.00**
Ice bucket, flared/octagonal, silver hdls, ca 1940s, 9x8" **600.00**
Obelisk, swan in flight attached, ltd ed, Mansau, 11".................**275.00**
Obelisk, 10" **225.00**
Sculpture, eagle, sgn R Rigot, 10x5½" **700.00**
Tumbler, old fashioned; Harcourt, 3¾", set of 8.........................**700.00**
Vase, octagonal panels, flared rim, 8x5" **350.00**

Badges

The breast badge came into general usage in this country about
1840. Since most are not marked and styles have changed very little to
the present day, they are often difficult to date. The most reliable clue
is the pin and catch. One of the earliest types, used primarily before the
turn of the century, involved a 't-pin' and a 'shell' catch. In a second
style, the pin was hinged with a small square of sheet metal, and the
clasp was cylindrical. From the late 1800s until about 1940, the pin and
clasp were made from one continuous piece of thin metal wire. The
same type, with the addition of a flat back plate, was used a little later.
There are exceptions to these findings, and other types of clasps were
also used. Hallmarks and inscriptions may also help pinpoint an
approximate age.

Badges have been made from a variety of materials, usually brass or
nickel silver; but even solid silver and gold were used for special orders.
They are found in many basic shapes and variations — stars with five to
seven points, shields, disks, ovals, and octagonals being most often
encountered. Of prime importance to collectors, however, is that the
title and/or location appear on the badge. Those with designations of

positions no longer existing (City Constable, for example) and names of early western states and towns are most valuable.

Badges are among the most commonly reproduced (and faked) types of antiques on the market. At any flea market, ten fakes can be found for every authentic example. Genuine law badges start at $30.00 to $40.00 for recent examples (1950 – 1970); earlier pieces (1910 – 1930) usually bring $50.00 to $90.00. Pre-1900 badges often sell for more than $100.00. Authentic gold badges are usually priced at a minimum of scrap value (karat, weight, spot price for gold); fine gold badges from before 1900 can sell for $400.00 to $800.00, and a few will bring even more. A fire badge is usually valued at about half the price of a law badge from the same era and material. Our advisor for this category is Gene Matzke; he is listed in the Directory under Wisconsin.

Apache Police San Carlos AZ, 5-pointed silver star w/Chief's head...**440.00**
Chicago Relief Engineer, silver-tone, CH Hanson Co Chicago, 2⅛"...**135.00**
Civil Defense Auxilary Police, Kent OH, 2¼x1½" **32.50**
Commercial Union Tel Co, NP shield, 1930s, 1⅝x2⅛" **85.00**
County Police Richmond Co GA, NP shield, 1940s, EX **27.50**
DC Metro Police 1993 Inauguration of President Commemorative..**165.00**
Deputy Sheriff, brass, Century RS Wks...NY, 1920s, 2½x1¾" **110.00**
Deputy Sheriff, SP brass shield w/blk lettering, early 1900s, 2x1¾" ..**160.00**

Deputy U.S. Marshall, 1920s, type #3 variation, worn original finish, safety-pin style clasp, $770.00.

GA Dept of Corrections, NP w/eagle, bl enameling, 1980s...............**32.50**
Greyhound Lines, greyhound, bl enamel on silver-tone, 2½x2½" ...**78.00**
Hermosa Beach Police, 6-pointed star, 1980s..............................**160.00**
Inauguration of President of US...Metropolitan..., bronze/enamel, 1989 ..**359.99**
LAFD, gold-tone, hat badge, 1950s, 2" **20.00**
Marianao (Cuba) Policia, NP copper shield w/bee, 1910-20, EX ..**100.00**
MO chauffeur, metal, pin-bk, 1932, 1½x1¾"..................................**40.00**
New England Ship Building Corp, photo ID, ca 1940s, 2½x1¾" .**40.00**
Normandie French Lines Transatlantic, brass & enamel, 1x¾" **32.50**
Pinkerton, eagle on shield, SP, screw bk **35.00**
Police, silver-tone shield, mk Mitchell Mfg Co Boston, 2½x2¼" .**70.00**
School Sheriff, MN, heavy NP metal, 1930s-40s, 2⅛x1¾"...........**32.50**
St Louis Co MO Deputy Sheriff, state seal, silver, 3" 6-pointed star ...**150.00**
Tucson Cornelia & Gila Bend AZ RR Co Police, eagle over shield...............**185.00**
US Marshall, genuine gold, ball finials on star, ca 1910, 44mm dia, EX...**950.00**

Banks

As always true, the continuing impact of auctions shows in the listings. Again, condition, condition, condition is what is driving the market. The spread between a bank in good condition and an excellent or original condition example continues to widen. It is imperative that you realize the importance of paint and the completeness of a bank. Also

some banks have a wide margin of value based on color variations. It becomes more and more important that you attend as many shows and auctions as possible. Direct contact with collectors and knowledgeable dealers is the only way you can get a feel for prices and the desirability of banks, both mechanical and still. Banks continue to hold their value. However, it is becoming extremely important for collectors to understand the market.

Let's take a look at the price variations possible on an Uncle Sam mechanical bank. If you find one with considerable paint missing but with some good color showing, the price would be around $1,000.00. If it has repairs or restoration, the value would drop to something like $800.00 or less. If you had another example, and it had two thirds of its original paint and no repairs, it would be priced around $1,800.00. One with minor nicks and 90% of the original paint could go as high as $3,500.00. Or if you find one that is in near-original paint and has no repairs, $5,000.00 would not be out of line. This should help you see what causes price variations. After considering all of these factors, remember the final price is always determined by what a willing buyer and seller agree on for a specific bank.

The category of mechanical banks is unique. Along with cast-iron toys, they are among the most outstanding products of the Industrial Revolution and are recognized as some of the most successful of the mass-produced products of the nineteenth century. The earliest mechanicals were made of wood or lead, but when John Hall introduced Hall's Excelsior, a cast-iron mechanical bank, it was an immediate success. J. & E. Stevens produced the bank for Hall and soon began to make their own designs. Several companies followed suit, most of which were already in the hardware business. They used newly developed iron-molding techniques to produce these novelty savings devices for the emerging toy market. Mechanical banks reflect the social and political attitudes of the times, racial prejudices, the excitement of the circus, and humorous everyday events. Their designers made the most of simple mechanics to produce banks with captivating actions that served not only to amuse but to promote the concept of thrift to the children. The quality of detail in the castings are truly remarkable. The most collectible examples were made during the period of 1870 to 1900; however, they continued to be made until the early days of World War II. J. & E. Stevens, Shepard Hardware, and Kyser and Rex are some of the more well-known manufacturers; most made still banks as well.

Still banks are widely collected, and you can literally choose from thousands of banks. No one knows exactly how many different banks were made, but at least three thousand have been identified in the various books published on the subject. Cast-iron examples still dominate the market, but the lead banks from Europe are growing in value. Tin and early pottery banks are drawing more interest as well. American pottery banks which were primarily collected by Americana collectors are becoming more important in the still bank field. This market has not been as volatile as the mechanical banks, but the number of collectors is growing. The auction market on still banks is not as extensive as with the mechanicals, but some nice examples do turn up. Collectors and dealers are still the best source.

Book of Knowledge Banks were produced by John Wright (Pennsylvania) from circa 1950 until 1975. Of the thirty models they made during those years, a few continued to be made in very limited numbers until the late 1980s; these they referred to as the 'Medallion' series. (Today the Medallion banks command the same prices as the earlier Book of Knowledge series.) Each bank was a handcrafted, hand-painted duplicate of an original as was found in the collection of The Book of Knowledge, the first children's encyclopedia in this country. Because the antique banks are often priced out of the range of many of today's collectors, these banks are being sought out as affordable substitutes for their very expensive counterparts. It should also be noted that China has reproduced banks with the Book of Knowledge inscription on them. Buyers should take extra caution when investing in Book of Knowledge banks and purchase through a reputable dealer who offers a satisfaction guarantee as well as a guarantee that the bank is authentic.

As both value and interest continue on the increase, it becomes even more important to educate one's self to the fullest extent possible. We recommend these books for your library: *The Dictionary of Still Banks* by Long and Pitman, *The Penny Bank Book* by Moore, *Penny Banks Around the World* by Don Duer, *The Bank Book* by Norman, *Collector's Guide to Glass Banks* by Charles V. Reynolds, and *Collector's Guide to Banks* by Beverly and Jim Mangus. If you are primarily interested in mechanicals, *Penny Lane*, a book by Davidson, is considered the most complete reference available. It contains a cross-reference listing of numbers from all other publications on mechanical banks.

Our advisor for mechanicals is Diane Patalano, listed in the Directory under New Jersey; Dan Iannotti (for Book of Knowledge), is listed under Michigan.

Key:
CI — cast iron   NPCI — nickel-plated cast iron
EPCI — electroplated cast iron

Advertising

Fobrux Furnace, tin & CI, 5½", EX...175.00
GE Radio, Arcade, gr, 4", G..250.00
GE Refrigerator, cream, 4", VG...200.00
Hot Point Electric Stove, Arcade, wht w/gray trim, 6", VG.......525.00
Kelvinator Ice Box, Arcade, wht, 4", NMIB.........................2,000.00
Magic Chef Stove, Save w/Magic Shef, wht-pnt metal, 3½", EX 200.00
Marietta Silo, gold, 5½", EX...625.00

Rival Dog Food, tin litho, light rust, 2¾x2¼", $15.00.

Sears Tower, wht metal, 7½", NM...45.00
Singer Sewing Machine, Germany, table w/Singer label, 5", NM (VG box)...1,000.00

Book of Knowledge Banks

Artillery Bank, NM...335.00
Auto, John Wright, ltd ed of 250, NM..600.00
Boy on Trapeze, M..495.00
Butting Buffalo, M..350.00
Cabin, NM...325.00
Cat & Mouse, NM...325.00
Dentist, EX..175.00
Eagle & Eaglets, M...395.00
Humpty Dumpty, M..325.00
Leap Frog, NM..335.00
Magician, MIB..325.00

Milking Cow, NM..295.00
Organ Bank, boy & girl, NM..375.00
Owl, turns head, NM...250.00
Paddy & The Pig, NM..375.00
Punch & Judy, NM..325.00
Tammany, NMIB...325.00
Teddy & the Bear, NM...300.00
Trick Pony, NM...350.00
Uncle Remus, M..375.00
US & Spain, M..335.00
William Tell, NM...325.00
World's Fair, mc version, NM...450.00

Mechanical

Afghanistan Bank, Mechanical Novelty Works, EX 4,950.00
Always Did 'Spise a Mule (boy on bench), J&E Stevens, G 750.00
Always Did 'Spise a Mule (jockey), J&E Stevens, G-.................500.00
Artillery Bank, J&E Stevens, EX+ 2,000.00
Auto, John Wright, ltd edition of 250, NM...............................600.00
Bad Accident, J&E Stevens, VG...2,100.00
Bad Accident, James Capron, M..759.00
Betsy Ross, Davidson/Imswiller, bl or yel dress, M.....................875.00
Bill E Grin, pnt aluminum, EX...325.00
Boy Robbing Bird's Nest, J&E Stevens, NM..........................6,100.00
Boy Stealing Watermelon, Kyser & Rex, VG..........................1,650.00
Butting Goat, Judd Mfg, G...450.00
Cabin, J&E Stevens, NM..1,100.00
Calamity, J&E Stevens, VG..12,100.00
Cat Boat, Richards/Wilton, NM...695.00
Chief Big Moon, J&E Stevens, EX+ 4,400.00
Circus Ticket Collector, Judd, EX...475.00
Columbian Magic Savings, Introduction Co, ca 1892, G............450.00
Creedmoor Bank, J&E Stevens, VG, from $500 to 650.00
Dentist Bank, J&E Stevens, EX 18,000.00
Eagle & Eaglets, J&E Stevens, NM.......................................3,300.00
Elephant, James Capron, M..250.00
Elephant, John Wright, NM 175.00
Elephant (Jumbo on Wheels), J&E Stevens, VG 550.00
Ferris Wheel, Hubley, EX..5,000.00
Frog on Rnd Base, J&E Stevens, VG..550.00
Girl Skipping Rope, J&E Stevens, VG..................................14,300.00
Harold Lloyd, Germany, tin, EX..1,100.00
Home Bank, Judd, NM..2,200.00
Horse Race, J&E Stevens, str base, VG+..............................6,600.00
Humpty Dumpty, Shepard Hardware, VG, from $800 to 1,000.00
Indian Shooting Bear, J&E Stevens, rpl feathers, VG 1,600.00
John Deere Anvil, CI, NM..325.00
Leap Frog, Shepard Hardware, G..1,500.00
Lion & Monkeys, James Capron, M..875.00
Lion & Monkeys, Kyser & Rex, VG+ 950.00
Magician, J&E Stevens, VG..1,600.00
Minstrel, Saalheimer & Strauss, litho tin, EX............................385.00
Monkey, James Capron, MIB..395.00
Monkey & Coconut, J&E Stevens, VG..................................2,700.00
Motor Bank, Kyser & Rex, VG...3,450.00
Mule Entering Barn, J&E Stevens, G.......................................600.00
Mule Entering Barn, James Capron, NM..................................495.00
Organ Bank (boy & girl), Kyser & Rex, G, from $600 to 800.00
Owl (Turns Head), J&E Stevens, brn w/yel eyes, EX.................700.00
Pay Phone, J&E Stevens, NP, EX 700.00
Penny Pineapple, Richards/Wilton, commemorates Hawaii 50th state, NM...450.00
Picture Gallery, Shepard Hardware, VG 9,900.00
Pistol, Kyser & Rex, rpl trap, G...275.00

Professor Pug frog, J&E Stevens, VG 6,050.00
Punch & Judy, Shepard Hardware, EX, from $2,800 to 3,100.00
Rabbit in Cabbage, Kilgore, VG, from $400 to 500.00
Race Course, James Capron, NM 575.00
Rooster, Kyser & Rex, NM 1,100.00
Trick Dog, Hubley, bl base, VG 500.00
Trick Dog, James Capron, NM 400.00
Uncle Remus, Kyser & Rex, VG+ 2,100.00
Uncle Sam, Richards/Wilton, rear trap, scarce, NM 450.00
Uncle Sam, Shepard Hardware, VG 1,600.00
Vending Bank (Pinball), Germany, tin litho, VG 750.00
William Tell, J&E Stevens, NM 3,100.00
World's Fair, J&E Stevens, EX 1,200.00
Zoo Bank, Kyser & Rex, VG 825.00

Registering

Bank of America, cash register shape, tin litho, 4", EX 50.00
Captain Marvel Magic Dime Saver, tin litho, EX 300.00
Davy Crockett Frontier Dime Bank, tin litho, EX 400.00
Dime Register Trunk, CI, 4", EX 225.00
Five Coin Economy Bank, cash register shape, tin litho, 4, EX 40.00
Jackie Robinson Daily Dime Register, tin litho, EX 600.00
Keep 'Em Flying Dime Register, tin litho, EX 400.00
Popeye Daily Quarter, tin litho, NM, from $150 to 200.00
Prince Valiant Dime Register, tin litho, EX 250.00
Prudential Dime Savings, NP CI, 7¼", EX 150.00
Snow White & 7 Dwarfs Dime Register, WDE, 1938, tin litho, NM .350.00
Thrifty Elf Dime Register, tin litho, 2½" sq 175.00
Uncle Sam's Nickel Register, cash register shape, tin litho, 3", EX 35.00

Still

Alamo, Alamo Iron Works, 2¾x3½", VG 325.00
Apple, Kyser & Rex, reddish-yel, 5", EX 900.00
Bank Building w/Horse Atop (Savings Bank), wht metal, 6", NM ..125.00
Bank of Commerce Safe, Kenton, 6¾", VG 250.00
Bankers Trust Building, wht metal, 6½", M 50.00
Basset Hound, blk (rare color), 3", G 1,050.00
Battleship Maine, Grey Iron, bl w/gold detail, 5", EX 325.00
Battleship Maine, Grey Iron, silver, 4½", G 100.00
Bean Pot, red w/NP top & wire hdl, 3" dia, VG 250.00
Bear w/Honey Pot, Hubley, 6½", NM 225.00
Bird Cage, CI & tin, 3⅞", VG 100.00
Boy Scout, AC Williams, gold w/red hat band, 6", EX 200.00
Broadway Saving Bank, tin litho, 4", EX 75.00
Buster Brown & Tige, AC Williams, bl w/red scarf, 5½", NM 550.00
Cadet Officer hat, Hubley, bl w/gold trim, 5¾", VG 1,000.00
Camel Kneeling w/Backpack, Kyser & Rex, japanned, 2½", EX .550.00
Campbell Kids, AC Williams, gold, 4", EX 300.00
Cat on Tub, 4⅛", G 150.00
Cat w/Ball, AC Williams, 5½", EX 350.00
Century of Progress Bank, Arcade, wht w/bl roof, 7" L, NM ..2,200.00
Church w/Steeple, tin litho, 3", NM 225.00
Columbia Bank, Kenton, wht, 6", VG 500.00
Conch Shell (shell out), J&E Stevens, wht, 4¾", EX 600.00
County Bank, Harper, japanned, 4", EX 300.00
Cow on Base, NP brass, 4¼", EX 325.00
Cupola, J&E Stevens, wht w/red & bl trim, 3¼", EX 375.00
Daisy Safe, 3½", NM 75.00
Dog on Ball, brass, 3", EX 60.00
Donkey, AC Williams, gray w/brn saddle, 6", NM 400.00
Dutch Girl, Grey Iron, gold, 6½", VG 385.00
Elephant w/Blanket Standing on Tub, silver & red, 5", EX 225.00

Elk, AC Williams, gold, 9½", NM 300.00
Feed My Sheep (Lamb), lead, 3" L, NM 250.00
Fidelity Safe, Kyser & Rex, emb dog, gr w/gold, 3½", EX 250.00
Fidelity Trust Vault w/Lord Fauntleroy, J Barton Smith, NM 850.00
Fido, Hubley, wht w/blk ears & red collar, 5", EX 100.00
Foxy Grandpa, Hubley, 5½", VG 325.00
German Grenade, tin, 3½", EX 250.00
Globe on Arc, Grey Iron, red, 5¼", EX 400.00
Happy Days Barrel, tin litho, w/1933 Chicago sticker, 4", EX 45.00
Harper Stork Safe, blk w/gold stork, 6", NM 1,500.00
Home Savings Bank, yel, 3½", VG 225.00
Horse w/Blanket on Tub, blk w/red saddle, 5", NM 300.00
Humpty Dumpty, Shepard Hardware, VG 825.00
Independence Hall Tower, 9½", NM 325.00
Indian w/Tomahawk, Hubley, brn, 6", G 150.00
Liberty Bell Hat, tin litho, 2", EX 95.00
Liberty Head Dime Safe, 3", EX 250.00
Lindbergh Bust, lead, 5½", NM 115.00
Lion on Tub, AC Williams, gold/bl/red, 5½", NM 200.00
Log Cabin, Kyser & Rex, red, 2½", EX 350.00
Main Street Trolley w/People, gold, 3", NM 225.00
Mammy w/Spoon, AC Williams, 6", VG 175.00
Mermaid (Girl in Boat), US, gold, 4½", VG 650.00
My Pet (Horse), Arcade, 4", NM 250.00
My Secret Safe, red-pnt tin, 5", EX 40.00
Oriental Camel, US, blk w/gr rocking base, 4", EX 935.00
Owl, Vindex, orange & wht, 4", VG 150.00
Palace, Ives, japanned & HP w/gold, ca 1885, 7½x8x5", EX, minimum...2,000.00
Pirates, tin litho book shape, 6", EX 50.00

Policeman Safe, cast iron, worn black paint, J.M. Harper, 5¼", G, $1,455.00.

Post Office, tin litho, tower w/peaked roof, people graphics, 7", EX...325.00
Rabbit Begging, gold w/red eyes, 5", EX 150.00
Reindeer, gr, 6", EX 175.00
Roller Safe, Kyser & Rex, japanned, 1882, 3½", EX+ 165.00
Roly Poly Monkey, tin litho, 6", M 500.00
Rumplestiltskin, US gold w/red hat, 6", EX 350.00
Sailor Saluting, Hubley, silver w/bl scarf, 5", NM 300.00
Santa Standing w/Toys, US Ceramic, reddish brn, 6¾", EX 275.00
Seal on Rock, Arcade, blk, 3½", NM 350.00
Security Safe Deposit, Ives, blk w/gold, brass dial, 8¼", VG 135.00
Sharecropper, mk Made in Canada, blk w/gold trim, 5½", VG...300.00
Skyscraper (6 Finials), AC Williams, silver w/gold, 6½", EX+ ...550.00
Spaniel w/Pack, blk w/gold details, 5½", NM 100.00
State Bank, Kenton, japanned w/bronze trim, 9", EX+ 800.00

Teapot, wood & tin w/floral design, 3", EX **55.00**
Three Wise Monkeys, AC Williams, gold, 3½", EX **225.00**
Thrift Bank (Safe), Champion, red w/bl, NP combination lock, 4", EX ..**200.00**
Tower Bank, Kyser & Rex, red/brn/gold/bl, 9¼", EX+ **9,300.00**
Trolley, japanned, 4½", NM...**500.00**
US Airmail (Mailbox), red w/bl & wht details, 6½", EX **500.00**
Victory Ship, chalkware, 4", NMIB..**100.00**
Washington Monument, AC Williams, gold, 6⅛", VG **250.00**
West Side Presbyterian Church, gr, 4", VG, from $300 to **400.00**
Westward Ho, tin litho book shape, 6", EX...............................**50.00**
White City Puzzle Safe No 12, 5", NM.....................................**150.00**
Winston Churchill Bust, compo & wood, 4", EX.......................**35.00**

Barber Shop Collectibles

Even for the stranger in town, the local barber shop was easy to find, its location vividly marked with the traditional red and white striped barber pole that for centuries identified such establishments. As far back as the twelfth century, the barber has had a place in recorded history. At one time he not only groomed the beards and cut the hair of his gentlemen clients but was known as the 'blood-letter' as well, hence the red stripe for blood and the white for the bandages. Many early barbers even pulled teeth! Later, laws were enacted that divided the practices of barbering and surgery.

The Victorian barber shop reflected the charm of that era with fancy barber chairs upholstered in rich wine-colored velvet; rows of bottles made from colored art glass held hair tonics and shaving lotion. Backbars of richly carved oak with beveled mirrors lined the wall behind the barber's station. During the late nineteenth century, the barber pole with a blue stripe added to the standard red and white as a patriotic gesture came into vogue.

Today the barber shop has all but disappeared from the American scene, replaced by modern unisex salons. Collectors search for the barber poles, the fancy chairs, and the tonic bottles of an era gone but not forgotten. See also Bottles; Razors; Shaving Mugs.

Blade bank, ceramic barber chair form, 6".......................................**55.00**
Bowl, bleeding; La Francaise Porcelain, Sebring Ohio, 1905, 11"...**100.00**
Cabinet, chrome w/Bakelite hdls, 1930s, 42x26x12" **450.00**
Cabinet, comb; wooden w/glass door & shelf, 12½x12½x9¼" **60.00**
Chair, Belmont, red uphl, stainless fr, 1920s, EX **650.00**
Chair, Berninghaus, Hercules, old rstr, Pat 1901, G **500.00**
Chair, Berninghaus, reuphl, wht porc, rstr, 1920s **585.00**
Chair, child's, carousel-type horse, cvd wood, EX pnt, 17"..........**225.00**
Chair, GW Archer, wooden swan w/cast-metal seat, March 1874..**700.00**

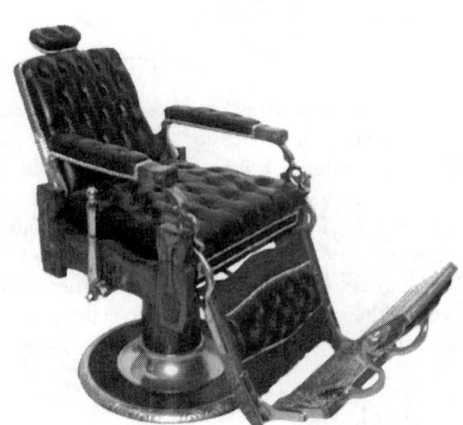

Chair, Koken, oak with leather upholstery, professional restoration, 44x27", $2,300.00.

Chair, Koken, oak & chestnut, leather reuphl, Pat 1888.............**750.00**
Chair, Koken, oak w/cvd owls, leather-like reuphl, ca 1920........**850.00**
Chair, Koken, red leather, brass tacks, rfn oak, M rstr..............**4,500.00**
Chair, Koken, wht oak/NP & brass, reuphl, Pat 1891, 1895, 1901 ..**2,400.00**
Chair, Theo A Kochs Co, red w/wht porc, 1940s **575.00**
Chair, waiting; red leather & chrome, Deco style, 1930s...............**75.00**
Hot leather dispenser, Campbell JJ 86566, chrome & blk, electric ...**110.00**
Jar, Germicidal Disinfectant Comb, Marvy #3, 9"........................**55.00**
Massager, Oster #M-1A J, hand-held, 1950s **55.00**
Mug cabinet, quartersawn oak, glass door, 33x26x5½" **550.00**
Mug rack, oak, 35-compartment, 47x41x8", VG **925.00**
Pole, CI & tin, sidewalk style, John Rieder, 1912, 96", EX **550.00**
Pole, Loch #7, glass/porc, globe light, 1930s era **525.00**
Pole, Marvy #055, plastic lens, metal trim, EX **280.00**
Pole, Marvy #066, lights up/rotates, wood base...........................**450.00**
Pole, Marvy #607, glass cylinder, 1950s, 24" **360.00**
Pole, porc, w/rotating panel in glass tube, electric, 47x12", EX ..**600.00**
Pole, trn laminated wood w/worn/weathered mc rpt, 49½", G......**85.00**
Pole, trn wood, weathered mc pnt, rpl base, 81" **700.00**
Pole, wood, red/wht stripes w/bl balls at top & bottom, 58x6"....**415.00**
Pole, wood floor model, red & wht w/gold ball finial, 85x8", VG..**1,650.00**
Shaving brush, Simpson 86 Pure Badger, 1935, 3¾".....................**30.00**
Shaving stand, NP, beveled mirror, removable bowl w/glass insert, 22" ...**45.00**
Shoe-shine stand, metal & wrought iron, old rpt, 52x22", +stool...**110.00**
Shoe-shine stool, twisted wire, wooden seat, 28x20x10", EX **70.00**
Sign, CI & tin w/lighted milk glass globe, red/wht pnt, 27"".........**85.00**
Sign, Union Shop, tin on cb, eagle/AFL, 9⅜x8" **55.00**
Sign, Wild Root & barber pole, emb self-fr tin, 39½x13½", NM ...**200.00**
Sterilizer, hot towels, gas fired, floor model, 1912, EX.................**525.00**
Strop, Romo #731, EX..**45.00**
Strop, Winchester, leather, EX..**200.00**
Wall pocket/bank/tip jar, barber figural, ceramic, Japan, EX **50.00**
Waste jar (shaving paper); amethyst glass w/floral, 1890s, 8x5½"...**600.00**

Barometers

Barometers are instruments designed to measure the weight or pressure of the atmosphere in order to anticipate approaching weather changes. They have a glorious history. Some of the foremost thinkers of the seventeenth century developed the mercury barometer, as the discovery of the natural laws of the universe progressed. Working in 1644 from experiments by Galileo, Evangelista Torricelli used a glass tube and a jar of mercury to create a vacuum and therefore prove that air has weight. Four years later, Rene Descartes added a paper scale to the top of Torricelli's mercury tube and created the basic barometer. Blaise Pascal, working with Descartes, used it to determine the heights of mountains; indeed, only later was the correlation between changes in air pressure and changes in the weather observed and the term 'weather-glass' applied. Robert Boyle introduced it to England, and Robert Hook modified the form and designed the wheel barometer.

The most common type of barometer is the wheel or banjo type. Second is the stick type. Modifications of the plain stick would be the marine gimballed type, followed by the laboratory or Kew or Fortin type. Others are the Admiral Fitzroys of which there are twelve or more types. The above all have mercury contained in either glass tubing or woodbox cisterns.

Another type of barometer is the aneroid, working on atmospheric pressure changes. They come in all sizes ranging from 1" in diameter to 12" or larger. They may be in metal or wood cases. There is a Barograph which records on a graph that rotates around a drum powered by a seven-day clock mechanism. Pocket barometers (altimeters) vary in sizes from 1" diameter up to 6" diameter. One final type of barometer is the symphisometer, a modification of the stick barometer used for a limited time and not as accurate as a conventional marine barometer. Our advisor for this category is Bob Elsner; he is listed in the Directory under Florida.

American

B Pike & Sons, NY, silvered scale, 14" thermometer, 1880s **2,450.00**
Charles Wilder...NH/Woodruff's...1860, curly mahog, stick type, 37" ..**825.00**
DE Lent, Rochester NY...**950.00**
FD McKay Jr, Elmira NY, dbl-trn wood columns......................**3,100.00**
Henry Green NY, brass, lacks mercury, VG **400.00**

English

Admiral Fitzroy's, mercury tube/thermometer, 48", VG..............**475.00**
Angelenetta & Bregazzi, London, heavy cvg, 10" wheel..........**1,650.00**
Fortin-type (Kew or laboratory), metal on board w/milk glass **750.00**
L Casella, London, rosewood, stick type **1,650.00**
Scurr Thirsk, mahog veneer w/inlay, silvered dial, 38¼", EX......**660.00**
Stanley, Peterborough, silvered scale/thermometer, 6" wheel...**1,450.00**
Troutman/Simms, bow-front mahog urn-shape cistern cover, stick type...**5,000.00**
Woodruff's Pat, June 5 1860, mahog, stick type, 41" **2,145.00**

Other Types

Aneroid, w/½-rnd thermometer **250.00**
Aneroid, 4-6" dia, brass case **150.00**
Barograph reading barometer, mahog, Negretti & Zambra..........**950.00**
Pocket barometer (altimeter), w/case, from $200 to **300.00**

Barware

Back in the thirties when social soirees were very elegant affairs thanks to the influence of Hollywood in all its glamour and mystique, cocktails were often served up in shakers styled as miniature airplanes, zeppelins, skyscrapers, ladies' legs, penguins, roosters, bowling pins, etc. Some were by top designers such as Norman Bel Geddes and Russel Wright. They were made of silverplate, glass, and chrome, often trimmed with colorful Bakelite handles. Today these are hot collectibles, and even the more common Deco-styled chrome cylinders are often priced at $25.00 and up. Ice buckets, trays, and other bar accessories are also included in this area of collecting.

For further information we recommend *Vintage Bar Ware Identification & Value Guide* by Stephen Visakay, our advisor for this category; he is listed in the Directory under New Jersey.

Manhattan cocktail set, Revere Copper & Brass Co., designed by Norman Bel Geddes, chrome, 13" shaker, from $350.00 to $400.00; Complete four-piece set (shaker, tray, and two cups): $1,250.00.
(Photo courtesy Stephen Visakay)

Cocktail cup, Catalin w/chrome stem, mk NUDAWN USA, 6¾x3¼" dia ...**27.50**

Cocktail cup, Manhattan, chrome over copper, Revere, 4¼x2½ ..**500.00**
Cocktail glass, amber w/pierced chrome holder, Farber Bros, 3½" ...**30.00**
Cocktail glass, rooster figural, red enamel on clear, '30s, 3¼" **17.50**
Cocktail set, Diana, chrome, Manning-Bowman, shaker+8 cups+tray...**95.00**
Decanter, bowling ball form, bowler finial, '40-'50s, 13x8½" **115.00**
Drink muddler, glass **10.00**
Drink stirrer, plastic female form, 1930s, 7"...............................**30.00**
Ice bucket, Ships, wht on cobalt, Hazel Atlas, 4¼x5½" **55.00**
Ice chopper, cobalt w/silk-screened recipes, 1930s, 11½" **110.00**
Mixer set, Derby SP #1921, golfing theme, tray+shaker+6 cups..**7,500.00**
Napkins, orange & brn linen, tuxedoed man & shaker, 8 for......**130.00**
Roly-poly, Ships, wht on bl, Hazel Atlas, 2½" **10.00**
Serving rack, gyroscope, holds 8 glasses, 20x8¼" dia..................**400.00**
Shaker, Caribbean, bl, crystal, amber or red, 10½", from $275 to...**325.00**
Shaker, chrome w/orange Catalin trim, Krome Kraft, 12¾"..........**80.00**
Shaker, Clown/Jingle-Bell, chrome w/wooden hdl, ca 1935, 14x5" ..**425.00**
Shaker, cobalt skyscraper w/ribs, silkscreened recipes, 13½" **350.00**
Shaker, Dumbbell, cobalt glass, West Virginia Specialty, 13"......**400.00**
Shaker, extinguisher form, ruby glass/copper lid, recipes, 11½" ..**450.00**
Shaker, fighting cocks, silver on ruby glass, 1930s, 12"...............**500.00**
Shaker, football player, sterling on cobalt glass, 1930s, 12½"......**335.00**
Shaker, frosted glass w/appl sterling rim, 1930s, 12"...................**185.00**
Shaker, Frosty Polar Bear, bl & wht enamel on clear, 1930s-40s, 10" ...**125.00**
Shaker, gr glass w/chrome lid, Catalin finial, Cambridge, 13".....**275.00**
Shaker, Lady's Leg, ruby glass w/chrome, Derby Shelton Silver **2,000.00**
Shaker, lantern, SP/cranberry glass, Made in England, 1930s, 10" .**2,000.00**
Shaker, Manhattan, chrome over brass, Revere, 12¾" **525.00**
Shaker, NP, hammered & plain, Expressware NY Stamping Co, 17½"...**300.00**
Shaker, Penguin, SP, Napier, ca 1936, 12" **15,000.00**
Shaker, pewter, hammered/handmade, Reig for Mary Ryan, 1935, 13½"...**450.00**
Shaker, pnt/lacquered leather over wood, metal insert, Fr, '30s, 12"..**1,250.00**
Shaker, rooster, NP, eng/enameled, Meriden, Pat Jan 11, 1927...**215.00**
Shaker, rooster's head, SP brass on clear base, w/strainer, '20s, 11" ..**650.00**
Shaker, ruby glass, ftd, chrome lid, 11½" **100.00**
Shaker, skyscraper type, SP, Lurelle Guild, 16x3½"...................**3,250.00**
Shaker, spatter glass, 1930s, 7"...**110.00**
Shot set, 6 glasses in chrome fr, Farberware, 1935, 5x6" dia..........**85.00**
Stem, ruby glass on chrome base, SW Farber Co, 5"....................**10.00**
Stopper, horse head, Heisey, 13½", from $350 to **450.00**
Swizzle sticks, tuxedoed men, glass, 1930s, 7¼", set of 6 ....**55.00**
Traveling bar, NP shaker form, Germany, 2 decanters+7 pcs, 1930s, 14"...**525.00**
Traveling bar, zeppelin, chrome-plated, Germany, 11-pc, 9" **2,000.00**
Tray, cut/etched olives on clear, Lucite hdls, 1950s, 12x18" **90.00**
Tray, Manhattan, chrome over brass, Revere, 14½x11½" **250.00**
Tray, metal & glass w/pnt peacock, 1930s, 12¼x20"....................**70.00**
Tray, Norseman, satin chrome, Norman Bel Geddes, 1935, 15½x9"..**100.00**

Basalt

Basalt is a type of unglazed black pottery developed by Josiah Wedgwood and copied by many other companies during the late eighteenth and early nineteenth centuries. It is also called 'Egyptian Black.' See also Wedgwood.

Coffeepot, trn lower body, foliate hdl, Sybil finial, Turner, 8".....**700.00**
Creamer, incised scrolls, English, 19th C **120.00**
Mug, emb face bordered w/grapevines, Turner, early 1800s, 4¼" ...**3,225.00**
Vase, children at play central frieze/foliage/zodiac, hdls, w/lid, 9" ..**2,000.00**
Vase, grapevine festoons, mask hdls, Wedgwood & Bently, 5⅜".**925.00**

Baskets

Basket weaving is a craft as old as ancient history. Baskets have been used to harvest crops, for domestic chores, and to contain the catch of fishermen. Materials at hand were utilized, and baskets from a specific region are often distinguishable simply by analyzing the natural fibers used in their construction. Early Indian baskets were made of corn husks or woven grasses. Willow splint, straw, rope, and paper were also used. Until the invention of the veneering machine in the late 1800s, splint was made by water-soaking a split log until the fibers were softened and flexible. Long strips were pulled out by hand and, while still wet and pliable, woven into baskets in either a cross-hatch or hexagonal weave.

Most handcrafted baskets on the market today were made between 1860 and the early 1900s. Factory baskets with a thick, wide splint cut by machine are of little interest to collectors. The more popular baskets are those designed for a specific purpose, rather than the more commonly found utility baskets that had multiple uses. Among the most costly forms are the Nantucket Lighthouse baskets, which were basically copied from those made there for centuries by aboriginal Indians. They were designed in the style of whale-oil barrels and named for the South Shoal Nantucket Lightship where many were made during the last half of the nineteenth century. Cheese baskets (used to separate curds from whey), herb-gathering baskets, and finely woven Shaker miniatures are other highly-prized examples of the basket-weaver's art.

In the listings that follow, assume that each has a center bentwood handle (unless handles of another type are noted) that is not included in the height. Unless another type of material is indicated, assume that each is made of splint. Prices are subjective and hinge on several factors: construction, age, color, and general appearance.

See also American Indian; Eskimo; Sewing; Shaker.

Melon, woven wicker, some age, EX patina, 3¾x4x5", $300.00.

Bread, flat bottom, flared sides, 19th C, 3¾x9¾"	85.00
Bread, flat bottom, woven-in loop on rim, 19th C, 4⅝x11⅛"	150.00
Bread, rye straw, flared at rim, 19th C, 4⅝x11¾"	60.00
Buttocks, 14-rib, EX form & detail, 2½x3"	350.00
Buttocks, 19th C, 6¼x4⅝"	100.00
Buttocks, 19th C, 7½x10½", EX	285.00
Buttocks, 20-rib, worn patina, minor damage, 4x8x8"	165.00
Buttocks, 22-rib, EX old patina, minor damage, 4x8x8"	185.00
Buttocks, 22-rib, 3½x5½x5¾"	200.00
Buttocks, 23-rib, 3x6"	165.00
Buttocks, 24-rib, dmn-design hdl, sun bleached w/gr stripes, 4x9x7"	185.00
Buttocks, 24-rib, lt patina, twisted hdl w/dmn at ends, 3x7x5"	150.00
Buttocks, 34-rib, varnished, minor damage, 10x17x15"	100.00
Buttocks, 36-rib, EX old patina, 7x10¾x9½"	400.00
Buttocks, 38-rib, late stained finish, 8¼"	220.00
Cheese, hexagonal base, rnd top, EX color, rpr, 7½x22½"	270.00
Cheese, scrubbed, minor damage, 6½x18"	225.00
Feather, gr pnt w/wht pnt traces, 19th C, 34½"	500.00
Feather, rys straw, 18" H	140.00
Field, cvd knotched hdls, rnd w/sq base, 1890s, 14x25" dia	350.00
Gathering, ca 1900, 7x7⅝" dia	250.00
Gathering, coiled band forms ft, PA, 19th C, 8¾x14" dia	250.00

Gathering, coiled rye straw & splint, flat bottom, 8x24x18"	225.00
Gathering, flat bottom w/2 exposed ribs, 12⅜x29x26"	300.00
Gathering, X-weave design, bentwood top & bottom, oval, 9x20x15"	200.00
Half, 8-rib, 7"	125.00
Half, 9-rib, dk finish, minor damage, 7½"	200.00
Half, 11-rib, gr pnt, 4½x9"	175.00
Half, 16-rib, med patina, minor wear, 9x13"	200.00
Hamper, coiled rye cylinder, rnd ft, flat lid, 19th C, 12x12¾"	350.00
Hickory cvd ft, pierced hdls, oval top, sq base, scrubbed, 16x21x20"	200.00
Laundry, reed/cane, mc pnt w/stars & stripes, wood/wire hdls, 25" L	250.00
Market, iron tacks at hdl, flat hdl, 7x26x14"	175.00
Market, iron tacks at hdl, hinged lid, Bellefonte, ca 1900, 6x13x9"	140.00
Market, iron tacks hold bottom, Bellefonte, ca 1900, 7½x21x11"	250.00
Melon, ca 1850s, 4½x9x8¼"	200.00
Melon, tight weave, 16 flat bentwood staves, 13½", VG	175.00
Melon, tight weave w/designs beneath arched hdl, 8⅛x9¼"	100.00
Melon, 12-rib, coarse weave, EX color, 6½"	100.00
Melon, 20-rib, 2 bl-gr stained lines at base, 6½"	175.00
Nantucket, trn wood base, brass ears, MA, 5x13¼", G	300.00
Nantucket, worn rim, 10", EX	375.00
Picnic, hinged lid, metal strap w/catch on lid, iron hdl, 9x21x11"	125.00
Rectangular, tightly woven base, loosely woven at top, 6x13x11"	110.00
Round, coiled rye, flat bottom, 3⅛x9¼"	75.00
Round, dbl hdls, EX patina, minor crack in hdl, 14½"	175.00
Round, swivel hdl, EX rprs in base, dk brn varnish, 8x16"	195.00
Sewing, rye straw, ftd, flared sides, 4x11⅝", VG	50.00
Sq, tightly woven, minor breaks, orig dk gr pnt, 4½x12x12"	275.00
Sq base & rnd top, red & bl geometric potato stamps, 4x5"	450.00
Storage, pnt rye straw, swollen oval, losses, PA, 18" H	315.00

Batchelder

Ernest A. Batchelder was a leading exponent of the Arts and Crafts movement in the United States. His influential book, *Design in Theory and Practice,* was originally published in 1910. He is best known, however, for his artistic tiles which he first produced in Pasadena, California, from 1909 to 1916. In 1916 the business was relocated to Los Angeles where it continued until 1932, closing because of the Depression.

In 1938 Batchelder resumed production in Pasadena under the name of 'Kinneola Kiln.' Output of the new pottery consisted of delicately cast bowls and vases in an Oriental style. This business closed in 1951. Tiles carry a die-stamped mark; vases and bowls are hand incised. For more information we recommend *Collector's Encyclopedia of California Pottery, Second Edition,* by Jack Chipman (Collector Books).

Vase, oblong, 6¼x8", $175.00; Bowl, low, shaped rim, 1½x7", $125.00. (Photo courtesy Jack Chipman)

Bookends, monk sitting, unglazed patina, mk, ca 1923, 4½", pr.**500.00**
Bowl, flower; #72, incised mk, 3x6"...**125.00**
Bowl, Kinneloa Kiln floral artware, #218, incised mk, 8½".........**125.00**
Jardiniere, unglazed, base mk, 12x13", minimum value............**1,000.00**
Vase, yel, incised mk, 6"..**175.00**

Battersea

Battersea is a term that refers to enameling on copper or other metal. Though originally produced at Battersea, England, in the mid-eighteenth century, the craft was later practiced throughout the Staffordshire district. Boxes are the most common examples. Some are figurals, and many bear an inscription. Values are given for examples with only minimal damage, which is normal. Our advisor for this category is John Harrigan; he is listed in the Directory under Minnesota.

Opera glasses, children hunting and fishing in bright and pastel colors, 4¼" wide in velvet case, EX, $425.00.

Box, courting couple in landscape, ca 1760, 1⅛x3x1¾", EX **300.00**
Box, I Love Thee Too Well..., ca 1760, 1¼x1¾", EX..................**225.00**
Box, mc floral, 1790s-1810, 2" dia...**260.00**
Box, Remember Me When This You See, ¾x1½"........................**310.00**
Candlesticks, exotic bird & flowers, scalloped bobeches, 1770s, 9", pr....**3,000.00**

Bauer

Originally founded in Paducah, Kentucky, in 1885, the J.A. Bauer Company moved to Los Angeles where it was re-established in 1910. Until the 1920s their major products were terra cotta gardenware, flowerpots, and stoneware and yellow ware bowls. During prohibition they produced crocks for home use. A more artful form of product began to develop with the addition of designer Louis Ipsen to the staff circa 1915. Some of his work, a line of molded vases, flowerpots, bowls, etc., was awarded a bronze medal at the Pacific International Exposition in 1916.

In 1930 the first of many dinnerware lines was tested on the market. Their initial pattern, Plain Ware, was well accepted and led the way to the introduction of the most popular dinnerware in their history and with today's collectors, Ring Ware. It was produced from 1932 into the early 1960s in solid colors of jade green, royal blue, dusty burgundy, ivory, Chinese Yellow, Delph Blue, orange-red, and (in very limited quantities) black or white. Its simple pattern was a design of closely-spaced concentric ribs, either convex or concave. Over the years, more than one hundred shapes were available. Some were made in limited quantities, resulting in rare items to whet the appetites of Bauer buffs today. Other patterns were La Linda, produced during the 1940s and 1950s, and Monterey Moderne, introduced in 1948 and remaining popular into the 1950s (made in pink, black, gray, brown, and green).

After WWII a flood of foreign imports and loss of key employees

drastically curtailed their sales, and the pottery began a steady decline that ended in failure in 1962. Prices listed below reflect the California market. For more information we recommend *Collector's Encyclopedia of Bauer Pottery: Identification & Values* (Collector Books) and *The Collector's Encyclopedia of California Pottery, Second Edition*, both by Jack Chipman, our advisor for this category. Mr. Chipman's address may be found in the Directory under California.

In the lines of Ring and Plain ware, pricing depends to some extent on color. Use the low end of our range of values for light brown, Chinese Yellow, orange-red, jade green, red-brown, olive green, light blue, turquoise, and gray; the high-end colors are Delph Blue, ivory, dusty burgundy, cobalt, chartreuse, papaya, and burgundy. Black is 50% higher than the high end; to evaluate white, double the high side. Use the low end of the range to evaluate Monterey items in all colors but Monterey Blue, burgundy, and white — those are high-end colors. You'll need to double the high end for black in this line as well as Monterey Moderne. An in-depth study of colors may be found in the books referenced above.

Art Pottery

Carnation jar, gr semimatt w/blk or irid spots, 24", minimum value..**1,500.00**
Flower bowl, dk gr overdrip, low, 10", minimum value...............**800.00**
Jardiniere, craggy mossy gr, raised filigree design, 10" **500.00**
Tray, yellowware, 12" **50.00**

Brusche Al Fresco and Contempo

Bowl, soup/cereal; Contempo, pk, deep, 5½" **15.00**
Bowl, vegetable; Al Fresco, Hemlock Green, divided, 9¼" **30.00**
Bowl, vegetable; Contempo, yel, rnd, 7½" **24.00**
Pitcher, Al Fresco, Dubonnet, w/ice lip, raffia-wrapped hdl, 2-qt..**75.00**
Sugar bowl, Al Fresco, Hemlock Green, w/lid **18.00**
Sugar bowl, Contempo, gray, w/lid..**20.00**

Cal-Art Pottery

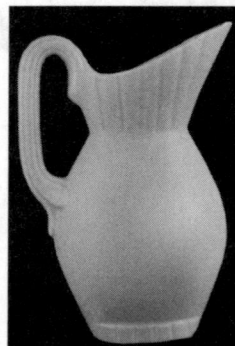

Ewer, blue, 10", $125.00.
(Photo courtesy Jack Chipman)

Bowl, matt gr, sq, 9¾" **45.00**
Candlestick, triple; matt wht **50.00**
Figurine, Madonna, matt bl, 8", minimum value **250.00**
Teapot, Contempo, dk gr, 7x10" **65.00**
Vase, bud; burgundy (uncommon color), 7½", minimum value **80.00**
Vase, horn-of-plenty; matt bl, 6½" **45.00**
Vase, robot midget; matt bl, 4"..**40.00**

Matt Carlton

Ashtray, Mexican; Delph Blue, 3", minimum value......................**250.00**
Bowl, gr, ruffled rim, 3½x7" **85.00**
Match holder, orange-red, 2" **150.00**
Sugar bowl, orange-red, sq, 2½x6"..**75.00**

Vase, California; yel, 10¼", minimum value 450.00
Vase, carnation; gr, 5¾" 200.00
Vase, carnation; jade gr, 10" 350.00
Vase, orange-red, Matt Carlton's signature style, 18½", minimum...1,800.00
Vase, orange-red, ribbed, in iron stand, 5¼", minimum value.....325.00
Vase, Rebekah; Chinese Yellow, 12", minimum value 900.00
Vase, royal bl, twisted hdl, 9½", minimum value...............1,200.00
Vase, striated fan; wht (uncommon color), 6x8", minimum value...500.00
Vase, wht, handmade, 9½", minimum value...........................1,500.00

Florist and Garden Pottery

Basket, hanging; orange-red, 8" 225.00
Bowl, Chinese Yellow, oval, 10½" L 85.00
Cactus jar, jade gr, handmade, 6-cup, 4", minimum value...........150.00
Oil jar, bl, 16", minimum value 500.00
Pedestal pot, conical, blk matt, 11½x11", pr 375.00
Pot, Italian; orange-red, 5" 50.00
Pot, lion; orange-red, 8", minimum value............................200.00
Pot, Spanish; gr, Hi-Fire, 10" 100.00
Pot, stepped; dmn shape, minimum value 150.00

Hi-Fire Pottery

Ashtray, turq, handmade, scarce, 1x4", minimum value..............100.00
Bowl, bulb; red-brn, 5" 35.00
Bowl, flower; lt bl, #209, low, 6" 50.00
Bowl, flower; turq, #211, deep, 6" 45.00
Bowl, rose; wht, 5½" 45.00
Bowl, rose; yel, 6" 50.00
Vase, #214, Monterey Blue, 6" 60.00
Vase, #214, red-brn, 7½" 65.00
Vase, stock; olive gr, 9"..100.00

La Linda

Bowl, fruit; matt bl, 5" 18.00
Creamer, old style, burgundy..15.00
Cup, matt bl..18.00
Gravy boat, matt pk...35.00
Pitcher, gr pastel gloss, ice lip, 2-qt, 6¼".........................155.00
Platter, matt bl, oval, 10" 22.50
Saucer, turq 4.00

Monterey

Beverage dispenser, refrigerator; w/lid, from $200 to 300.00
Bowl, fruit; ftd, 9", from $45 to......................................65.00
Bowl, fruit; 5", from $12 to...18.00
Bowl, serving; blk, very rare, 9", minimum value....................150.00
Bowl, vegetable; oval, 10", from $55 to................................80.00
Centerpc, Monterey Blue, w/2 detachable candle holders, minimum..250.00
Coffee server, w/lid, from $45 to......................................65.00
Creamer, from $12 to...18.00
Plate, dinner; 10½", from $30 to.......................................45.00
Plate, relish; 3-section, 10", from $60 to.............................90.00
Platter, oval, 10", from $30 to..45.00
Saucer, from $6 to...9.00
Teapot, old style, 6-cup, from $75 to.................................100.00

Monterey Moderne and Related Kitchenware

Bowl, batter; yel, 1-qt 50.00
Bowl, mixing; olive gr, #9...45.00

Bowl, salad; barnyard scene, low 40.00
Bowl, salad; brn, 8½" 35.00
Bowl, serving; chartreuse, 7" 25.00
Butter dish, pk, rnd, w/lid...65.00
Canister, barnyard scene, wood/metal lid, 4x4½" 30.00
Cookie jar, chartreuse, ceramic lid, 8" 95.00
Creamer, pk...12.50
Pitcher, beater; bl, 1-qt...35.00
Pitcher, chartreuse, 2½-qt..85.00
Plate, bread & butter; olive gr, 6½" 8.00
Plate, chop; chartreuse 40.00
Plate, dinner; pk, 10½" 25.00
Plate, salad; gray, 7½" 10.00
Platter, chartreuse, 12"..25.00
Saucer..6.00
Sugar bowl, chartreuse, w/lid, 2-hdld.................................20.00
Teapot, pk, 2-cup 40.00
Tray, hors d'oeuvre; 3-tiered, bottom blk 9½" plate...................65.00

Plain Ware

Ashtray, sq, 3", from $45 to..65.00
Bean pot, 2-qt, from $75 to..100.00
Beer mug, from $125 to...175.00
Bottle, water; 7", minimum value.....................................200.00
Bowl, mixing; #4, 1½-gal, minimum value..............................200.00
Bowl, mixing; #6, 1¼-gal, blk, minimum value 337.50
Bowl, salad; 8¼", from $60 to...90.00
Carafe, 9", minimum value..250.00
Coffee server, w/lid, from $65 to.....................................95.00
Mug, handmade, 3", from $45 to 65.00
Plate, bread & butter; colors other than blk, 6½", from $10 to.....15.00
Plate, butter; 4½", minimum value.....................................60.00
Plate, salad; 8½", minimum value......................................45.00
Pudding dish, #4, 8¼", from $60 to 90.00
Pudding dish, #6, 10¼", from $80 to 120.00
Ramekin, colors other than blk, from $15 to 20.00
Saucer, from $10 to...15.00
Sugar bowl, blk, w/lid, minimum value 135.00
Tumbler, 2¾", minimum value..30.00

Red, White, and Yellow Ware

Bean pot, brn glaze, 4-qt..65.00
Churn, whtware, stamp mk, w/lid, 7x12½" 100.00
Flower frog, frog shape, cobalt, 2x4½"...............................45.00
Jap tub, redware, 11" 125.00
Jug, brn glaze, 5-gal, 17"...180.00
Mug, yelware, handmade, 3", minimum value............................45.00
Pitcher, yelware, handmade, 3-qt, 12", minimum value 300.00
Plate, butter; cobalt, inscription, 4½", minimum value...............350.00
Porch pot, redware, laurel wreath, 10"...............................150.00
Vase, swirl pnt, 6¼"..250.00

Ring Ware

Ashtray, 2" dia, from $50 to 75.00
Baking dish, w/lid, 4", from $35 to..................................50.00
Beer mug, minimum value...150.00
Bowl, batter; 1-qt, rare, minimum value.............................400.00
Bowl, batter; 2-qt, from $85 to 125.00
Bowl, berry; 4", from $20 to...30.00
Bowl, cereal; 4½", from $35 to.......................................50.00
Bowl, fruit; 5", from $25 to...35.00

Bowl, lug soup; from $60 to...75.00
Bowl, mixing; #24, from $35 to..50.00
Bowl, mixing; #9, from $150 to 175.00
Bowl, vegetable; oval, 8", from $85 to.............................125.00
Coffee server, wht w/blk lid, metal hdl, 8-cup, minimum value ..190.00
Coffee server, 6-cup, open, wood hdl, from $90 to 120.00
Cookie jar, from $400 to 600.00
Creamer, restyled, from $50 to..75.00
Cup & saucer, from $45 to..65.00
Mug, barrel shape, from $135 to......................................165.00
Plate, bread & butter; 5", minimum value......................60.00
Plate, bread & butter; 6", from $20 to............................35.00
Plate, chop; 14", from $125 to 160.00
Plate, chop; 17", minimum value....................................200.00
Plate, dinner; 10½", from $85 to 100.00
Plate, luncheon; 9", from $45 to 55.00
Plate, relish; from $85 to..125.00
Platter, 12", from $90 to...125.00

Teapot, black, six-cup,
$300.00 minimum value.
(Photo courtesy Jack Chipman)

Teapot, 2-cup, from $85 to..120.00
Tumbler, barrel shape, metal hdl, from $50 to...............75.00
Tumbler, barrel shape, metal hdl, ivory, rare 175.00
Tumbler, 12-oz, from $50 to...75.00

Bavaria

Bavaria, Germany, was long the center of that country's pottery industry; in the 1800s, many firms operated in and around the area. Chinaware vases, novelties, and table accessories were decorated with transfer prints as well as by hand by artists who sometimes signed their work. The examples listed here are marked with 'Bavaria' and the logos of some of the various companies which were located there.

Bowl, Blue Floral, scalloped edge, w/lid, 5x8½" 45.00
Bowl, chrysanthemums & roses w/gold, emb scrolls, 3x10½"........45.00
Bowl, roses (2 lg) w/gr leaves, emb rim w/gold, RC mk, 10" 57.50
Coffee set, floral w/gold, melon ribs, mk, 9½" pot+cr/sug 110.00
Jar, jam; Prince Regent, daisies w/gold, 6¼", +underplate, 3-pc .130.00
Plate, angels reserves w/gold, pierced hdls, mk, 9¾" 32.00
Plate, flowers/game birds, Schumann, rtcl rim, 10-sided, 10" 35.00
Plate, roses, gold trim, mk MR Sevres..., 12½" 45.00
Teacup & saucer, red & gold decor, Alboth & Kaiser, 1927-53.....65.00
Teacup & saucer, roses, Lady Linda, 6 for.....................................35.00

Beer Cans

In the early 1930s one of America's largest can-manufacturing companies approached an East Coast brewery with a novel concept — beer in cans. The brewery decided to take a chance on the idea, and in January 1935, the beer can was born.

The 'church key' style can opener was invented at the same time, and early flat top cans actually had instructions on how to use it to open a can.

Canned beer soared in popularity, and breweries scrambled to meet the canning challenge. Since many companies did not have a machine to fill a flat-top can, the cone top was invented. Brewery executives believed its shape would be more acceptable to consumers used to buying bottled beer, and it easily passed through existing bottling machinery. The more compact flat-top can dominated sales, and by the 1950s cone tops were obsolete.

About values: Condition is critical when determining the value of a beer can. Prices quoted are for like-new condition cans, free of rust, dents, scratches, and other damage. Like any collectible, value drops in direct proportion to condition, and off-grade cans are often worth no more than one-half of retail value. Our advisor for this category is Dan Andrews; he is listed in the Directory under California. Information in our descriptions is given in this specific order: 1.) name of brew; 2.) company — may be simply repetitive; and 3.) city/state or state.

A-1 Pilsner, Arizona Brg, Phoenix AZ, flat top, 10-oz..................45.00
A-1 Premium, Arizona Brg, Phoenix AZ, flat top..........................20.00
Acme Beer, Acme Brg, San Francisco CA, flat top 20.00
Balboa Export, Southern Brg, Los Angeles CA, flat top.............100.00
Bartels Extra Light, Bartels Brg, Edwardsville PA, flat top 90.00
Bay State Ale, Commonwealth Brg, Springfield MN, instructional.....150.00
Beverwyck Famous Ale, Beverwyck Brg, Albany NY, cone top (low)..120.00
Billy Beer, various breweries, tab top 1.00
Bohemian Club Beer, Bohemian Brg, Boise ID, cone top..............75.00
Buckeye Sparkling Dry, Buckeye Brg, Toledo OH, cone top 150.00
Carling's Ale, Brg Corp of America, Cleveland OH, cone top......85.00
Chief Oshkosh Beer, Oshkosh Brg, Oshkosh WI, flat top 70.00
Club House Premium, Grace Bros Brg, Santa Rosa CA, flat top ..90.00
Corona Cerceza, Five Star Brg, New York NY, flat top..................70.00
Dart Premium Light Beer, Bavarian Brg, Reading PA, zip tab.......65.00
Davidson Premium, Coldwial Brg, Hammonton NJ, flat top.........60.00
Duquesne Pilsner, Duquesne Brg, Pittsburg PA, flat top 30.00
Ebling Premium Beer, Ebling Brg, New York NY, crowntainer......75.00
El Rancho Beer, General Brg, Los Angeles CA, pull tab...............10.00
Esslinger Parti-Quiz, Esslinger Brg, Philadelphia PA, flat top......125.00
Fitzgerald's Burgomaster, Fitzgerald, Troy NY, crowntainer (enamel)...80.00
Fort Schuylar Lager, Utica Brg, Utica NY, cone top.....................105.00
Frankenmuth Mel-O-Dry, Frankenmuth Brg, Frankenmuth MI, flat top ...50.00
Gibbons Season's Best, Lion Inc, Wilkes-Barre PA, zip tab.........185.00
Goebel Beer, Goebel Brg, Detroit MI, instructional 50.00
Goetz Country Club, Goetz Brg, St Joseph MO, cone top 50.00
Grain Belt Beer, Minneapolis Brg, Minneapolis MN, cone top (low)..200.00
Grain Belt Premium Strong, Minneapolis Brg, Minneapolis MN, cone top...40.00
Grand Prize Beer, Gulf Brewing, Houston TX, instructional.........60.00
Gretz Tooner Schooner Beer, Gretz Brg, Philadelphia PA, bank top ..220.00
Hamm's Preferred Stock, Hamm Brg, St Paul MN, flat top..........25.00
Hanley's Extra Pale Ale, Hanley Brg, Providence RI, crowntainer ..75.00
Hochburg Bock, Neuweiler Brg, Allentown PA, pull tab 75.00
Hudepohl Chevy Ale, Hudephol Brg, Cincinnati OH, crowntainer...750.00
Hudson House Beer, Maier Brg, Los Angeles CA, pull tab............15.00
Jacob Ruppert Ale, J Ruppert Brg, New York NY, flat top 160.00
Jacob Ruppert Knickerbocker, J Ruppert Brg, New York, instructional...175.00
Jax Draft, Jackson Brg, New Orleans LA, zip tab 20.00
Kentucky Malt Liquor, Oerytel Brg, Louisville KY, zip tab............40.00
Kessler Beer, Kessler Brg, Helens MT, cone top 60.00
Krueger Cream Ale, Krueger Brg, Newwark NJ, flat top................80.00
Krueger Finest Beer, Krueger Brg, Newark NJ, instructional 175.00
Kuebler Cream Ale, Kuebler Brg, Easton PA, cone top (J-spout) ...250.00
Lone Star Beer, Lone Star Brg, San Francisco CA, flat top...........20.00
Martin's Beer, Yakina Valley Brewing, Selah WA, cone top........265.00
Milwaukee Club Beer, Schlitz Brg, Milwaukee WI, cone top......500.00
Old Bohemian Draft, Eastern Brg, Hammonton NJ, pull tab 50.00
Old Dutch Lager, Maier Brg, Los Angeles CA, flat top 50.00

Old England Cream Ale, Old England Brg, Derby CT, cone top (low)..575.00
Old German Brand, Queen City Brg, Cumberland MD, cone top...75.00
Old Ox Head Ale, Standard Brg, Rochester NY, crowntainer 190.00
Old Rainier Beer, Hornell Brg, Trenton NJ, pull tab 50.00
Old Reading Beer, Old Reading Brg, Reading PA, cone top 245.00
Old Reading Golden Dry, Old Reading Brg, Reading PA, cone top.....150.00
Old Shay Beer, Fort Pitt Brg, Pittsburg PA, crowntainer............100.00
Old Virginia Special Export, Virginia Brg, Roanoke VA, cone top...75.00
Pacific Lager Beer, Rainier Brg, San Francisco CA, cone top 200.00
Peerless Beer, LaCrosse Brg, LaCrosse WI, cone top.....................50.00
Pilser's Maltcrest Brew, Metropolis Brg, Trenton NJ, flat top 60.00
Rainier Special Export, Rainier Brg, San Francisco, cone top (low)..40.00
Regal Bock Beer, Regal Amber Brg, San Francisco CA, flat top...65.00
Schaefer Light Beer, Schaefer Brg, New York NY, flat top 25.00
Sebewaing Beer, Sebewaing Brg, Sebewaing MI, zip tab...............45.00
Senator's Club Premium, Columbus Brg, Shenandoah PA, flat top..75.00
Stroz Gole Crest Beer, Stroz Brg, Omaha NE, flat top.................325.00
Tam O'Shanter Dry Hopped, American Brg, Rochester NY, instructional ...75.00
Trophy Beer, Birk Bros Brg, Chicago IL, cone top 100.00
Uchtorff Beer, Uchtorff Brg, Davenport IA, cone top 200.00
Weber Waukesha Beer, W Waukesha Brg, Waukesha WI, cone top ..210.00
White Cap Beer, Two Rivers Brg, Two Rivers WI, cone top 120.00
Wiedland's Extra Pale, Pacific Brew & Malt, San Jose CA, cone top ..130.00
Yoerg's Cave Aged Beer, Yoerg Brg, St Paul MN, crowntainer....250.00

Bellaire, Marc

Marc Bellaire, originally Donald Edmund Fleischman, was born in Toledo, Ohio, in 1925. He studied at the Toledo Museum of Art under Ernest Spring while employed as a designer for the Libbey Glass Company. During World War II while serving in the Navy, he travelled extensively throughout the Pacific, resulting in his enriched sense of design and color.

Marc settled in California in the 1950s where his work attracted the attention of national buyers and agencies who persuaded him to create ceramic lines of his own, employing hand-decorating techniques throughout. This resulted in the building of a studio in Culver City. He produced high-quality ceramics, often decorated with ultramodern figures or geometric patterns and executed with a distinctive flair. His most famous line was Mardi Gras, decorated with slim dancers in spattered and striped colors of black, blue, pink, and white. Other major patterns were Jamaica, Balinese, Beachcomber, Friendly Island, Cave Painting, Hawaiian, Bird Isle, Oriental, Jungle Dancer, and Kashmir. Kashmir usually has the name Ingle on the front and Ballaire on the reverse.

It is to be noted that Marc was employed by Sascha Brastoff during the 1950s. Many believe that he was hired for his creative imagination and style.

During the period of 1951 – 1956, Marc was named one of the top ten artware designers by *Giftwares Magazine*. After 1956 he taught and lectured on art, design, and ceramic decorating techniques from coast to coast. Many pieces were one of a kind, commissioned throughout the United States.

During the 1970s he set up a studio in Marin County, California, and eventually moved to Palm Springs where he opened his final studio/gallery. There he produced large pieces with a Southwestern style. Mr. Bellaire died in 1994. Our advisor for this category is Marty Webster; he is listed in the Directory under Michigan.

Ashtray, Bird Isle, blk birds on cream, 8" 85.00
Ashtray, Bird Isle, blk birds on wht, 9x8".....................................150.00
Ashtray, Clown, mc on cream, 7"...65.00
Ashtray, Jamaica, musicians on brn, 10x14"..................................85.00
Ashtray, Mardi Gras, figures on blk, rolled rim, 9" 100.00

Ashtray, Mardi Gras, figures on blk, 14x14"...................................225.00
Ashtray, Still Life, matt fruits & leaves, 10x15"............................100.00
Bowl, Beachcomber, low teardrop shape, 12" L.............................100.00
Bowl, Cortillian, lady w/bl bird, 13x9" 125.00
Bowl, Fruit - Three Pears, yel & gr 45.00
Bowl, Jungle Dancer, 11½x5½"...150.00
Box, African Figures on lid, 6" 95.00
Box, Jamaica, man w/guitar, free-form, B46, 8".............................115.00
Box, Mardi Gras, 10" dia...150.00
Candlestick, Jamaica Man, 10½"..125.00
Charger, Stylized Bird on branch, 15" 165.00
Compote, Cave Painting, 4-ftd, 6x12" 100.00
Compote, Cotillian, 4-ftd, 8x17" 200.00
Cookie jar, Stick People, wood lid, 10" 150.00
Ewer, Mardi Gras, figures on blk, hdl, 18".....................................400.00

Mardi Gras figures on metal stands, 24", minimum value: $1,000.00; 30", from $800.00 to $1,000.00. (Photo courtesy Jack Chipman)

Figurine, Bird w/long neck, 17"...250.00
Figurine, Buffalo, brn & blk, 9½" L...465.00
Figurine, Bull, 9"...345.00
Figurine, Jamaica, man playing guitar..300.00
Figurine, Mardi Gras, reclining man, very slim, 18" 800.00
Figurine, Polynesian, man standing, 12"..500.00
Lamp, Mardi Gras, long-neck vase on wood base, 28"..................450.00
Platter, Fisherman w/net, 16" dia..150.00
Platter, Friendly Island, 10"..135.00
Platter, Hawaiian, 3 figures on orange, 13x7" 100.00
Platter, Mardi Gras, figures on blk, 18x12" 250.00
Platter, Polynesian Dancer, egg shape, 15x11" 250.00
Platter, Underwater design in sea gr, 16" 100.00
Switch plate, Dancer on blk, B-26, 3x4¾" 150.00
Tray, Hawaiian figures, peach & blk, 14x10"................................145.00
Tray, Jungle Dancer, figure on blk/gr, 12" dia 145.00
Vase, Balinese Women, hourglass shape, 8" 100.00
Vase, Black Cats, hourglass shape, 8" 100.00
Vase, Mardi Gras, figures on blk, 18"...250.00
Vase, Mardi Gras, hourglass shape on 3 ft, 11"............................125.00
Vase, Polynesian Woman, 9"..100.00
Vase, Stick People, irregular beak-like opening, 12" 250.00

Belleek, American

From 1883 until 1930, several American potteries located in New Jersey and Ohio manufactured a type of china similar to the famous Irish Belleek soft-paste porcelain. The American manufacturers identified their porcelain by using 'Belleek' or 'Beleek' in their marks. American

Belleek is considered the highest achievement of the American porcelain industry. Production centered around artistic cabinet pieces and luxury tablewares. Many examples emulated Irish shapes and decor with marine themes and other naturalistic styles. While all are highly collectible, some companies' products are rarer than others. The best-known manufacturers are Ott and Brewer, Willets, The Ceramic Art Company (CAC), and Lenox. You will find more detailed information in those specific categories. Our advisor for this category is Mary Frank Gaston.

Key: AAC — American Art China

Cream soup, Bouquet, Coxon, w/underplate **175.00**
Creamer, floral (dainty), mc on wht w/gold, Coxon, 4¾" **125.00**
Cup, peony & flowers, Coxon, ca 1926-30, 2¼x4" **75.00**
Plate, bread; wht w/gold rim, Morgan, ca 1926, 5¾", 5 for **250.00**
Salt cellar, sponged gold on scalloped rim & base, AAC, 2½" ...**125.00**
Teapot, gold-paste decor on dragon shape, red CAP mk, 9" W ..**1,500.00**
Vase, orchids, EX art, sgn, 1903, 13" **395.00**

Belleek, Irish

Belleek is a very thin translucent porcelain that takes its name from the village in Ireland where it originated in 1859. The glaze is a creamy ivory color with a pearl-like lustre. The tablewares, baskets, figurines, and vases that have always been made there are being crafted yet today. Shamrock, Tridacna, Echinus, and Thorn are but a few of the many patterns of tableware which have been made during some periods of the pottery's history. Throughout the years, their most popular pattern has been Shamrock.

It is possible to date an example to within twenty to thirty years of crafting by the mark. Pieces with an early stamp often bring prices nearly triple that of a similar but current item. With some variation, the marks have always incorporated the Irish wolfhound, Celtic round tower, harp, and shamrocks. The first three marks (usually in black) were used from 1863 to 1946. A series of green marks identified the pottery's offerings from 1946 until the seventh mark (in gold/brown) was introduced in 1980 (it was discontinued in 1992). The most current mark, the eighth, is blue. Belleek Collector's International Society limited edition pieces are designated with a special mark in red. In the listings below, numbers designated with the prefix 'D' relate to the book *Belleek, The Complete Collector's Guide and Illustrated Reference, Second Edition*, by Richard K. Degenhardt (published by Wallace-Homestead Book Company, One Chilton Way, Radnor, PA 19098-0230). 'B' numbers refer to stock numbers of recent pieces that do not have a 'D' number, but may be given one at a future time. Our advisor for this category is Liz Stillwell; she is listed in the Directory under California.

Key:
A — plain (glazed only)
B — cob lustre
C — hand tinted
D — hand painted
E — hand-painted shamrocks
F — hand gilted
G — hand tinted and gilted
H — hand-painted shamrocks and gilted
J — mother-of-pearl
K — hand painted and gilted
L — bisque and plain
M — decalcomania
N — special hand-painted decoration
T — transfer design

I — 1863 – 1890
II — 1891 – 1926
III — 1926 – 1946
IV — 1946 – 1955
V — 1955 – 1965
VI — 1965 – 3/31/1980
VII — 4/1/1980 – 12/22/1992
VIII — 1/4/1993 – current

Further information concerning Periods of Crafting (Baskets):
1 — 1865 – 1890, BELLEEK (three strand)
2 — 1865 – 1890, BELLEEK CO. FERMANAGH (three strand)
3 — 1891 – 1920, BELLEEK CO. FERMANAGH IRELAND (three strand)
4 — 1921 – 1954, BELLEEK CO. FERMANAGH IRELAND (four strand)
5 — 1955 – 1979, BELLEEK® CO. FERMANAGH IRELAND (four strand)
6 — 1980 – 1985, BELLEEK® IRELAND (four strand)
7 — 1985 – 1989, BELLEEK® IRELAND 'ID NUMBER' (four strand)
8 – 12 — 1990 to present (Refer to *Belleek, The Complete Collector's Guide and Illustrated Reference, 2nd Edition*, Chapter 5)

Aberdeen Cup & Saucer, D489-II, A..................................**550.00**
Aberdeen Vase Flowered, D59-V, A, sm.............................**235.00**
Achilles Vase, D1154-V...**150.00**
Allingham Spill, B908-VI...**25.00**
Ampanida Creamer, D1291-II, A...**275.00**
Bamboo Teapot, D515-I..**600.00**
Belleek Merchant Sign, D1805-VII.......................................**125.00**
Bird's Nest Basket, D123-IV, B&C......................................**250.00**
Blarney Demi Cup & Saucer, D1821-VII, C, BCIS...............**120.00**
Blarney Teapot, D568-II, C..**700.00**
Brooch - Precious Heart, B2107-VIII, C.................................**35.00**
Butterfly Photo Frame, D1905-VII, A.....................................**85.00**
Charter Member Trademark Plaque, D1810-VII, G, 1979.........**165.00**
Cherub Candelabra, D341-II, rstr......................................**2,800.00**
Claddagh Makeup Bell, B2050-VII, A....................................**25.00**
Cleary Cream & Sugar, D249-V, B...**90.00**
Cleary Mug, D218-II, B..**225.00**
Cone Cup & Saucer, D432-II, A...**350.00**
Cone Sugar, D434-II, C..**250.00**
Corn Spill, D190-VI, D...**100.00**
Dairy Sugar & Cream, D251-II, A..**350.00**
Double Shell Flower Pot, D226-II, C....................................**275.00**
Dragonfly Trinket Box, D1914-VII, D.....................................**60.00**
Earthenware Bread Tray, D2081-II, A..................................**600.00**
Earthenware Chamber Pot, D929-II, T..................................**400.00**
Erne Cup & Saucer, D445-II, C...**300.00**
Erne Vase, D83-III, B...**300.00**
Fan Teacup & Saucer, D694-II, C..**425.00**
Finner Cream & Sugar, D671 & 672-II, G............................**500.00**
Flowered Crate, D268-II, B..**650.00**
Georgian Shell Bowl, B-2277-VIII, C, 8"...............................**65.00**
Girl's Baby Cup, B2351-VIII..**25.00**
Grass Mug, D214-II, D...**250.00**
Greyhound Male & Female, D1138-VI..................................**450.00**
Harp Shamrock Bell, D1364-VII, E..**55.00**
Harp Shamrock Kettle, D1359-V..**275.00**
Heart Cup & Saucer, D2805-VII, A......................................**175.00**
Hexagon Basket, D1265, A, 4...**2,000.00**
Hexagon Cream, D393-II, C, sm..**200.00**
Hexagon Teapot, D407-II, G..**500.00**
Holly Cup & Saucer, D1954-56-VII, D..................................**110.00**
Holly Plate, D1962-VII, D, 5"...**30.00**
Imperial Shell, D138-VI...**425.00**
Institute Breakfast Cup & Daucer, D723-II, B......................**350.00**
Institute Plate, D724-II, C..**170.00**
Irish Pot, D205-II, C, 5"...**300.00**
Irish Wolfhound Orig, D1823-VII, 1987................................**375.00**
Jack on Shore Trinket Box, D24, A, rstr...............................**500.00**
Lagen Planter, B676-VII, B..**60.00**
Liffey Vase, B1221-VIII, E..**56.00**

Lily Coffee Cup & Saucer, D548-II, A 300.00
Lily Cream & Sugar, D235-VI, B..................................90.00
Lovers at Table Lithophane, D1540, B.........................350.00
Marine Vase, D95-V, A, sm...200.00
Mask Cup & Saucer, D1494-III, A&B 150.00
Mask Teapot, D1495-VI, A&B 150.00
Mask Tobacco Box, D1549-III, B...................................500.00
Neptune Cake Plate, D425-VI, C...................................160.00
Neptune Water Kettle, D431-V, C, lg 300.00
Nickel Flower Pot, D209-V, A&B 60.00
Oval Coral Frame, B1939-VII, C.....................................75.00
Papillion Vase, D 'BCIS' limited 200..............................450.00
Princess Vase, D60-III, C 450.00
Queen of Hope, D1130-II, L.......................................4,750.00

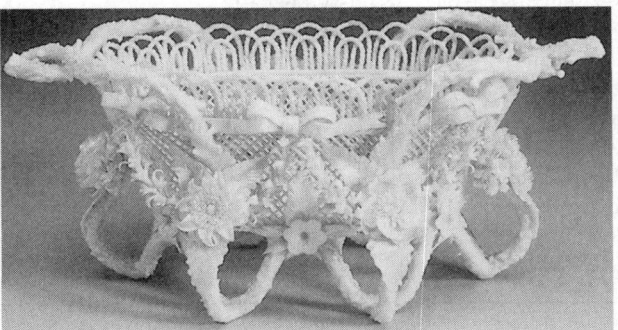

Rathmore Oval Basket, three-strand, restored, D117-3, D, ca 1890, 5½x8", $8,000.00.

Rope Handle Mug, D215-II, A 225.00
Serenity Dinner Plate, B2147, A, 11¼" 45.00
Serenity Tea & Saucer, B2141 & 42-VIII, A 45.00
Shamrock Mustache Cup & Saucer, D374-II, E 550.00
Stilton Cheese Dish Earthenware, I 3,600.00
Tridacna Breakfast Cup & Saucer, D460-II 300.00

Bells

Some areas of interest represented in the study of bells are history, religion, and geography. Since Biblical times, bells have announced morning church services, vespers, deaths, christenings, school hours, fires, and community events. Countries have used them en masse to peal out the good news of Christmas, New Year's, and the endings of World Wars I and II. They've been rung in times of great sorrow, such as the death of Abraham Lincoln.

Dorothy Malone Anthony is the author of a series of ten books entitled *World of Bells*. Her address is in the Directory under Kansas. All have over two hundred colored pictures covering many bell categories. See also Nodders; Schoolhouse Collectibles.

Ornate nickeled bronze bell with Atlas holding world on his shoulders, fancy bronze knob taps to ring bell, marked Dep. French, 6", $250.00. (Photo courtesy Dorothy Malone Anthony)

Brass, cherub holding up tap-type bell, 10x3½"..........................135.00
Brass, crowned bear w/shield forms hdl, Hemony, 5⅝"...............250.00
Brass, Jacobean head finial, emb figures around sides, 4x3¼"........95.00
Brass, lady in long gown holds dbl-twist hotel bell, 1800s, 8½"..295.00
Brass, Lucy Locket, fancy clothes & hat, 4¾" 85.00
Brass, tap type, flying goose top, 2 dragons on base, 3x3"............315.00
Brass, Tony Weller figural...70.00
Bronze, bell on tree w/2 sparrows by fence w/flowers, 1890s, 7½" .385.00
China, cherub figural hdl, emb floral on wht, unmk Italy 38.00
China, lady figural, gold lustre, Germany 40.00
Dinner, brass, youth on top w/stick & rope, Victorian, 7½" 425.00
Door, brass/CI, emb hdl w/porc knob, Taylor's Pat...1860, 5" dia...185.00
Door, cast brass w/ornate design, iron bk plate, 5" dia 90.00
Gong, brass, on stand w/wooden striker, 7" 15.00
Metal, Holstein Bell No 1 label, Blum Mfg, 7" w/hdl, EX...........100.00
NP brass, dog stands beside bell, ca 1930, 6x5x3", EX.................225.00
Sheep, brass, 3 on leather strap..45.00
Silver, squirrel figural hdl, Spratling, 5x2"................................700.00
Sleigh, bell-metal, set of 21, on new 86" strap 250.00
Sleigh, brass, graduated set of 21, center bell: 2½", on strap.......220.00
Sleigh, brass, graduated set of 6, largest: 2½", on 27" strap 200.00
Sleigh, brass, set of 23, ea 1½", on strap, EX.............................200.00
Sleigh, NP brass, set of 70, ea 1½", on 41" strap.........................185.00
Sleigh, NP-steel, graduated set of 37, on 80" strap 140.00
SP brass, queen figurals (6), Gorham series, 1970, 5", complete set..425.00
Sterling, Red Riding Hood figural hdl, chrome bell, 4½"..............30.00
Tea, silver, winged angel figural hdl, mk 800................................75.00

Bennington

Although the term has become a generic one for the mottled brown ware produced there, Bennington is not a type of pottery, but rather a town in Vermont where two important potteries were located. The Norton Company, founded in 1793, produced mainly redware and salt-glazed stoneware; only during a brief partnership with Fenton (1845 – 47) was any Rockingham attempted. The Norton Company endured until 1894, operated by succeeding generations of the Norton family. Fenton organized his own pottery in 1847. There he manufactured not only redware and stoneware, but more artistic types as well — graniteware, scroddled ware, flint enamel, a fine parian, and vast amounts of their famous Rockingham. Though from an esthetic standpoint his work rated highly among the country's finest ceramic achievements, he was economically unsuccessful. His pottery closed in 1858.

It is estimated that only one in five Fenton pieces were marked; and although it has become a common practice to link any fine piece of Rockingham to this area, careful study is vital in order to be able to distinguish Bennington's from the similar wares of many other American and Staffordshire potteries. Although the practice was without the permission of the proprietor, it was nevertheless a common occurrence for a potter to take his molds with him when moving from one pottery to the next, so particularly well-received designs were often reproduced at several locations. Of eight known Fenton marks, four are variations of the '1849' impressed stamp: 'Lyman Fenton Co., Fenton's Enamel Patented 1849, Bennington, Vermont.' These are generally found on examples of Rockingham and flint enamel. A raised, rectangular scroll with 'Fenton's Works, Bennington, Vermont,' was used on early examples of porcelain. From 1852 to 1858, the company operated under the title of the United States Pottery Company. Three marks — the ribbon mark with the initials USP, the oval with a scrollwork border and the name in full, and the plain oval with the name in full — were used during that period.

Among the more sought-after examples are the bird and animal figurines, novelty pitchers, figural bottles, and all of the more finely modeled items. Recumbent deer, cows, standing lions with one forepaw on a ball, and opposing pairs of poodles with baskets in their mouths and 'coleslaw' fur were made in Rockingham, flint enamel, and occasionally in parian. Numbers in the listings below refer to the book *Bennington Pottery and Porcelain* by Barret. Our advisors for Bennington (except for parian and stoneware) are Barbara and Charles Adams; they are listed in the Directory under Massachusetts.

Key: c/s — cobalt on salt glaze

Bank, Uncle Sam, Rockingham, 4" **400.00**
Book flask, Bennington Battle, flint enamel, EX rstr, 11" **3,000.00**
Book flask, Departed Spirits, brn & yel, 5⅝" **675.00**
Book flask, Departed Spirits, flint enamel, brn/gr/yel, 5½" **650.00**
Book flask, Wonders of Earth, brn & bl, chips, 6¾" **600.00**
Bottle, Coachman, Rockingham, 1849 mk, chips, 11", VG **550.00**
Bottle, Coachman, Rockingham, 1849 mk, 10⅜" **900.00**
Box, flint enamel, Alternate Rib, M w/VG lid, 3x8" L **650.00**
Candlestick, flint enamel, 6⅝" **900.00**
Candlestick, Rockingham, 7¾" **750.00**
Candlesticks, gr & amber runs, 7⅞", pr **1,700.00**
Coffeepot, flint enamel, helmet shape, rstr, 12¾" **1,800.00**
Creamer, Rockingham, cow form, mk F under base, 7" L **600.00**
Cuspidor, Rockingham, 1849 mk, 9¾" **300.00**
Frame, flint enamel, plain scalloped edge, crack, 11" **1,100.00**
Humidor, Rockingham, EX color, Alternate Rib, 1849 mk, 7", EX **650.00**
Inkwell, Rockingham, shoe shape, surface chip, att, ca 1880, 5½" L ..**250.00**
Lamp base, flint enamel, olive w/brn stepped base, 9" **2,000.00**
Name plate, Rockingham w/1 wht letter, 7⅜" L........................**400.00**

Picture frame, Rockingham, minor restoration, 10x10½", $2,200.00.

Pie plate, Rockingham w/yel highlights, 1849 mk, 11", EX+ **500.00**
Pitcher, brn lead glaze, hound hdl, 9" **465.00**
Pitcher, flint enamel, scalloped ribs, 12½" **900.00**
Pitcher, flint enamel w/EX color, Alternate Rib, 11", EX **1,400.00**
Pitcher, Rockingham, bust of Gen Stark form, EX rstr, 6" **1,850.00**
Pitcher, Rockingham, Franklin's bust form, boot hdl, mk, 6", EX ...**895.00**
Pitcher, Rockingham, grape relief, mk, 1845, rpr, 7" **700.00**
Poodle, olive flint, w/basket in mouth, no base, 8½" **6,500.00**
Soap dish, flint enamel, Alternate Rib, w/lid, 1849 mk, 5⅝", EX...**800.00**
Tiebk, Rockingham, att, 1850s, 4½" dia, pr **300.00**
Toby jug, Rockingham, imp mk, 6¼" **375.00**
Wash bowl, flint enamel, emb dmns, wear/line, 4½x13" **600.00**
Whiskey bbl, flint enamel, Rockingham Whiskey, 6" **350.00**

Stoneware

Churn, #2/leaf (dotted), c/s, E&LP Norton, rpr, 13½" **550.00**
Crock, #1½/leaf, c/s, J&E Norton, 10" **470.00**
Crock, #1/brushed plume, c/s, E&LP Norton, hairline, ca 1880, 7" ..**175.00**

Crock, #2/bird on plume, c/s, E&LP Norton, 1870s, 9", EX........**600.00**
Crock, #3/deer/tree/fence, c/s, J&E Norton, rpr, 10½" **4,800.00**
Crock, #4/floral spray, cobalt on tan clay, E&LP Norton, 1880s, 11", G ..**100.00**
Crock, #4/running rabbit, c/s, Norton & Fenton, rstr, 14½" **900.00**
Crock, chicken pecking corn, c/s, J Norton, 2-gal..................**1,600.00**
Crock, leafy floral, c/s, ovoid, L Norton & Co, 1-gal, EX...........**250.00**
Jar, preserve; #2/floral, c/s, E&LP Norton, prof rstr, 1880s, 11"...**415.00**
Jar, preserve; #2/floral, c/s, J&E Norton, ca 1855, 11", EX **745.00**
Jar, preserve; #3/flowers in vase, c/s, J&E Norton, ca 1855, 13", EX..**1,200.00**
Jar, preserve; #3/thistle floral (lg), c/s, J&E Norton, 1855, 12", VG......**415.00**
Jug, #1/bird, c/s, J Norton & Co, prof rstr, ca 1861, 10" **770.00**
Jug, #1/bird on stump, c/s, J&E Norton, chips, ca 1855, 11" **650.00**
Jug, #2/bird on branch w/worm, c/s, J&E Norton, rstr, 13½"...**1,980.00**
Jug, #2/floral, c/s, J&E Norton, ca 1855, 13", EX...................**360.00**
Jug, #2/LWC in script, c/s, Norton & Co, chip, 13½" **175.00**
Jug, #2/standing deer, c/s, J&E Norton, ca 1855, 14" **6,600.00**
Jug, #3/deer among pines, c/s, J&E Norton, rstr, 15½" **6,875.00**
Jug, #3/floral, c/s, J&E Norton, ca 1855, 15" **600.00**
Jug, #3/geometrics, c/s, J&E Norton, line, 15" **225.00**
Jug, #3/triple flower, c/s, Julius Norton, stain, ca 1848, 16"........**165.00**
Jug, #4/floral, c/s, E&LP Norton, ca 1880, 17½", EX **1,045.00**
Pitcher, #2/plume, FB Norton..., chip/line, 1870s, 13½" **575.00**
Pitcher, Albany slip, E&LP, 1½-gal..................................**275.00**

Beswick

In the early 1890s, James Wright Beswick operated a pottery in Longston, England, where he produced fine dinnerware as well as ornamental ceramics. Today's collectors are most interested in the figurines made since 1936 by a later generation Beswick firm, John Beswick, Ltd. They specialize in reproducing accurately detailed bone-china models of authentic breeds of animals. Their Fireside Series includes dogs, cats, elephants, horses, the Huntsman, and an Indian figure, which measure up to 14" in height. The Connoisseur line is modeled after the likenesses of famous racing horses. Beatrix Potter's characters and some of Walt Disney's are charmingly re-created and appeal to children and adults alike. Other items, such as character Tobys, have also been produced. The Beswick name is stamped on each piece. The firm was absorbed by the Doulton group in 1973. Our advisor for this category is Nicki Budin; she is listed in the Directory under Ohio.

Beatrix Potter, Amiable Guinea Pig, B-3, needs rpr **300.00**
Beatrix Potter, Anna Maria, B3a **450.00**
Beatrix Potter, Aunt Petitoes, B6.......................................**75.00**
Beatrix Potter, Benjamin Bank, head trn, 3B.........................**115.00**
Beatrix Potter, Benjamin Bunny Bank, B6 ....**45.00**
Beatrix Potter, Benjamin Wakes Up, B6 ....**75.00**
Beatrix Potter, Christmas Stocking, B6................................**250.00**
Beatrix Potter, Cousin Ribby, B3 ....**55.00**
Beatrix Potter, Duchess, 3B...**450.00**
Beatrix Potter, Flopsy, Mopsy, Cottontail, 2B **195.00**
Beatrix Potter, Gentleman Mouse Made Bow, B6a..................**200.00**
Beatrix Potter, Goody & Timmy Tiptoes, C3........................**275.00**
Beatrix Potter, Hunca Munca, gold, 2B..............................**175.00**
Beatrix Potter, Hunca Munca Sweeping, B3 ....**75.00**
Beatrix Potter, Jemima & Foxy Gentleman, B6 ....**65.00**
Beatrix Potter, Jemima Puddleduck/Nest, B3 ....**65.00**
Beatrix Potter, Little Black Rabbit, B3 ....**65.00**
Beatrix Potter, Little Pig Robinson Spying, B6 ....**135.00**
Beatrix Potter, Mother Ladybird, B6 ....**115.00**
Beatrix Potter, Mr Drake Puddleduck, B3 ....**65.00**
Beatrix Potter, Mr Jeremy Fisher, B3 ....**65.00**
Beatrix Potter, Mr Tod, B6..**200.00**

Beatrix Potter, Mrs Rabbit, umbrella out, 2B 450.00
Beatrix Potter, Mrs Rabbit w/Peter, B6 ....65.00
Beatrix Potter, Mrs Tiggy Winkle Takes Tea, B3 ....85.00
Beatrix Potter, No More Twists, B6 ....55.00
Beatrix Potter, Old Mr Brown, B3 ....60.00
Beatrix Potter, Old Woman in Shoe, knitting, B3 ....95.00
Beatrix Potter, Peter in Bed, B6 ....55.00
Beatrix Potter, Peter w/Postbag, B6 ....50.00
Beatrix Potter, Pigling Eats Porridge, B6 ....195.00
Beatrix Potter, Rebecca Puddleduck, B3 ....40.00
Beatrix Potter, Samuel Whiskers, B3 ....45.00
Beatrix Potter, Tabitha Twitchit, B6 ....40.00
Beatrix Potter, Timmy Tiptoes, 3B 65.00
Beatrix Potter, Tom Kitten, B10 ....50.00
Bird, American Robin, #2187, 4⅜x5" 165.00
Bird, Bobwhite Quail, #2191, 1970-73, 4⅞" 195.00
Bird, Cedar Waxwing, #2184, 4½" 165.00
Bird, Goldeneye Duck, #1524, 3½" L 165.00
Bird, Green Woodpecker, #1218B, 1967-89, 9" 220.00
Bird, Mallard, wings wide, #749, 6½" 185.00
Bird, Ring-Neck Pheasant, no flowers on base, #1225B, 1967-77, NM..185.00

Cat, bone china, 1950s, 6½", $20.00.

(Photo courtesy Marbena 'Jean' Fyke)

Disney, Alice in Wonderland, #2476, 1973-83 ....500.00
Disney, Cheshire Cat, #3480, 1973-82, 1½" 300.00
Disney, Mad Hatter, 1957-81, 4¼" 250.00
Disney, Mock Turtle, #2478, 1973-83 ....175.00
Disney, Zimmy Lion, #1150, 1949-55, 4" 215.00
Dog, Basset Hound, #2045B, 1970-89, 6" 130.00
Dog, Old English Sheepdog, Fireside series, #2232, 12" 125.00
Farm animal, Ayrshire calf, brn & wht glossy, #1249, 2¾"..........100.00
Farm animal, Friesian bull, #2580, blk & wht matt, 7½" 250.00
Farm animal, Friesian cow, brn & wht matt, #1362, 4½" L 285.00
Farm animal, Hereford calf, roan (rare), #854, 4½" 650.00
Farm animal, Hereford cow, brn & wht, #948, 5x8½" 400.00
Fish, Golden Trout, #1246, 6x9½" 185.00
Fish, Perch, #1975, 1963-71, 6¼" 200.00
Horse, Clydesdale, orig leather harness & blanket, 10x11" 350.00
Horse, Highland Pony, dun color, #1544, 1961-69 ....145.00
Horse, Hunter, brn w/2 wht stockings, 11¾" 185.00
Horse, Shire mare, recumbent, brn, #2459, 5x8" 300.00
Huntsman Series, lady on jumping horse, #32, 9¾" 400.00
Huntsman Series, lady on standing gray horse, #1730 ....215.00
Huntsman Series, man on rearing brn horse, #868, 9½" 200.00
Huntsman Series, man on standing brn horse, #1501, 8¼" 175.00
Wild animal, elephant, long tusks, trumpeting, 15" L 225.00
Wild animal, leopard, seated, #841, 6¼x9½" 300.00
Wild animal, lion on rocky base, #2554A, 8½x12" 215.00
Wild animal, zebra, tan & blk, #845A, 7¼" 235.00

Bicycles

The time frame of collecting cycling items extends from the days of ancient manumotive transport to the present. The eras most interesting to collectors are (simplistically) the 1860s, with the Velocipede; 1875 – 89, famous for the High Wheel; 1890 – 1900, when the Safety bicycle was developed; 1920 – 1955, for the Balloon Tire. Virtually every aspect of collecting is encompassed — everything from late eighteenth-century prints to jerseys worn in last year's Tour de France. The collector can break the field down to a particular category, medium, or history. One can make special collections of cycling photographs, the bikes themselves, porcelains, lithographs, related toys, etc. There are over fifteen different circa 1819 Hobby horse plates which in themselves would make a most wonderful and challenging collection. Cycliana encompasses virtually every aspect of art, antiques, and collectibles. Any one of these fields could relate to social, sport, financial, or mechanical history. Below is a select group of items from a few of these categories.

Our advisor for this category is Lorne Shields; he is listed in the Directory under Ohio. (Mr. Shields is interested in the acquisition of early cycliana and offers to help evaluate early bicycle-related items.)

Bicycles

Barnes White Flyer, lady's model, pneumatic tires, ca 1895, NM orig....**950.00**
Columbia High Wheel 50" Expert model, NP, 1887, w/brake hdw, VG metal..**3,000.00**
Hobby Horse/Draisienne, 31" front wheel/no pedals, crude, 1819, VG.**10,000.00**
Pickering Velocipede/Boneshaker, 32" front wheel, orig pnt, 1869, VG..**2,500.00**
Pierce Arrow Racer, Buffalo NY, 28" wood wheels, complete, EX orig **1,500.00**
Schwinn Black Phantom, 26" balloon tires, ca 1950, NM orig...**750.00**
Victor Spring Fork Safety, hard tires/28" wheels, 1889, brakes gone .**3,500.00**

Related Memorabilia

Bar pin, Safety Bicycle in filigree, sterling hallmk, British, 1902 ...**150.00**
Bell, emb Am flag, working, ca 1920, as found, VG **35.00**
Bell, high-wheel era, narrow mt, NP bronze, Lucas, ca 1882, VG ..**350.00**
Blotter, Pope Columbia Bicycles, ca 1900, as found, G **25.00**
Bottle, lady velocipede rider, bluish clear, various types, 1869, EX **350.00**
Cabinet card, couple w/Safety Cycles, studio shot, ca 1900, 4x6", EX.**25.00**
Calendar, Victor Bicycle chromolitho top, no pages, 1897, 16x11"...**150.00**
Carte de visite, man on high-wheeler (outside), 1882, 2½x4", VG.....**75.00**
Catalog, Remington Bicycles of Ilion NY, 1893, EX....................**125.00**
Catalog, Star Bicycles, HB Smith...Smithfield NJ, 1885, NM **175.00**
Cigar cutter, figural regular safety-style bicycle, ca 1895, VG **750.00**
Cigar cutter, full table Model w/high-wheelers, NP CI, ca 1886, 3", G ..**600.00**
Clock, Automata, man w/bicycle, +barometer/thermometer, 1890, 16", EX...**10,000.00**
Clock, man/bicycle, gilt bronze, British United Clock, 1893, 7", VG..**600.00**
Cyclometer, NY Std w/League of Am Wheelmen symbol, ca 1896, MIB...**325.00**
Cyclometer, Seth thomas, cracked glass cover, 1898 ....**50.00**
Ice cream mold, man & lady on Safety Cycles, ca 1900, EX, pr .**225.00**
Lamp, oil; fits hub of high-wheeler, Columbia, complete, VG.**1,750.00**
Lamp, oil; fits Safety Bike, 20th C brand, w/font, compete, 1900 ....**175.00**
Match safe, gutta percha, cyclists on 2 sides, ca 1900, 2x1¼", VG ..**150.00**
Medal, Cycling Club group ride, dtd/identified, no eng, bronze, 1897 ..**50.00**
Medal, race participant, Philadelpha, enamel on gold, 1885, 4" .**500.00**
Paperweight, Colonel AA Pope, Columbia Bicycles, glass w/photo, 1893...**50.00**
Pipe, meerschaum, cvd lady on high-wheeler, ca 1885, VG........**400.00**
Pitcher, pattern glass, lady on Safety Bike, Am, ca 1897, 11", M .**1,000.00**
Plate, velocipede comic mc transfer on soft paste, ca 1868, 6½" ...**350.00**
Plate, 4 assorted cycling & sport thematic, H Gray, ca 1904, EX ..**300.00**
Poster, Am Crescent Bicycles, Ramsdell, Art Nouveau, 42x63", EX...**3,500.00**
Poster, E Penfield for October, Harper's Magazine, 1897, 21x17", EX .**1,000.00**
Poster, Lady on Hard Tired Cycle, J Chert, Fr, 1891, 35x48", VG.......**2,500.00**

Poster, monkey/parrot on Columbia Bike, CM Coolidge, 1895, 20x25", VG..**500.00**
Print, AB Frost, ca 1895, 73x110" in fr...**125.00**
Print, hobby horse (pre pedal), mc etching, Tegg, 1819, 12x18", VG..**325.00**
Print, lady racers on velocipedes, hand colored, Fr, 1868, 22x15", EX..**1,000.00**
Sign, Singer Cycles, bl/wht enamel, England, 1890s, 24x18", EX....**500.00**
Stevengraph, Last Lap, high-wheeler race, orig mt, ca 1878, M..**300.00**
Tin container, Huntley & Palmer, scenes w/cyclists, 1900, VG ..**150.00**
Toothbrush holder, Daisy Bell by Shorter, England, ca 1940, EX..**45.00**
Trophy, Club Race, SP, Buffalo NY, eng/dtd 1932, 14", VG..........**30.00**
Watch, silvery metal, open face w/racing cyclists, ca 1905, 1¾".**250.00**

Big Little Books

The first Big Little Book was published in 1933 and copyrighted in 1932 by the Whitman Publishing Company of Racine, Wisconsin. Its hero was Dick Tracy. The concept was so well accepted that others soon followed Whitman's example; and though the 'Big Little Book' phrase became a trademark of the Whitman Company, the formats of his competitors (Saalfield, Goldsmith, Van Wiseman, Lynn, and World Syndicate) were exact copies. Today's Big Little Book buffs collect them all.

These hand-sized sagas of adventure were illustrated with full-page cartoons on the right-hand page and the story narration on the left. Colorful cardboard covers contained hundreds of pages, usually totaling over an inch in thickness. Big Little Books originally sold for 10¢ at the dime store; as late as the mid-1950s when the popularity of comic books caused sales to decline, signaling an end to production, their price had risen to a mere 20¢. Their appeal was directed toward the pre-teens who bought, traded, and hoarded Big Little Books. Because so many were stored in attics and closets, many have survived. Among the super heroes are G-Men, Flash Gordon, Tarzan, the Lone Ranger, and Red Ryder; in a lighter vein, you'll find such lovable characters as Blondie and Dagwood, Mickey Mouse, Little Orphan Annie, and Felix the Cat.

In the early to mid-'30s, Whitman published several Big Little Books as advertising premiums for the Coco Malt Company, who packed them in boxes of their cereal. These are highly prized by today's collectors, as are Disney stories and super-hero adventures.

For more information we recommend *Big Little Books, A Collector's Reference and Value Guide*, by Larry Jacobs; and *Collector's Guide to Children's Books, Volumes 1, 2, and 3*, by Diane McClure Jones and Rosemary Jones (Collector Books). Our advisor for this category is Ron Donnelly; he is listed in the Directory under Alabama.

Note: At the present time, the market for these books is fairly stable — values for common examples are actually dropping. Only the rare, character-related titles are increasing.

Air Fighters of America, Whitman #1448, EX...........................**35.00**
Andy Panda in the City of Ice, Whitman #1441, NM **40.00**
Apple Mary & Dennie Fool the Swindlers, Whitman #1130, NM..**35.00**
Bambi, Whitman #1469, EX...**70.00**
Bambi's Children, Whitman #1497, NM..................................**70.00**
Betty Boop in Miss Gulliver's Travels, Whitman #1158, EX.......**100.00**
Black Silver Pirate Crew, Whitman #1414, EX.........................**25.00**
Blondie & Bouncing Baby Dumpling, Whitman #1476, NM........**40.00**
Bonanza, The Bubble Gum Kid, Whitman #2002, EX **15.00**
Brenda Star & the Masked Imposter, Whitman #1427, NM.........**45.00**
Buck Jones in the Roaring West, Whitman #1174, VG **35.00**
Buck Rogers & the Planetoid Plot, Whitman #1197, NM **100.00**
Bugs Bunny in Risky Business, Whitman #1440, VG **35.00**
Captain Easy Soldier of Fortune, Whitman #1128, NM..............**45.00**
Captain Midnight & Sheik Joman Khan, Whitman #1402, EX....**60.00**
Charlie McCarthy & Edgar Bergen, Whitman #1456, EX **25.00**
Chester Gump at Silver Creek Ranch, Whitman #734, EX..........**35.00**
Dan Dunn on the Trail of Wu Fang, Whitman #1454, EX............**30.00**

David Copperfield, Whitman #1148, VG **35.00**
Dick Tracy & the Racketeer Gang, Whitman #1112, EX.............**55.00**
Dick Tracy in Chains of Crime, Whitman #1185, NM **75.00**
Don Winslow & the Giant Girl Spy, Whitman #1408, EX...........**35.00**
Donald Duck Gets Fed Up, Whitman #1462, EX **50.00**
Ella Cinders & the Mysterious House, Whitman #1106, EX.........**40.00**
Eric Noble & the Forty Niners, Whitman #772, EX....................**20.00**
Flame Boy & the Indians' Secret, Whitman #1464, VG **25.00**
Flash Gordon & the Red Sword Invaders, Whitman #1479, NM.**85.00**
Frank Merriwell at Yale, Whitman #1121, EX **20.00**
Freckles & the Lost Diamond Mine, Whitman #1164, EX...........**35.00**
G-Man Breaking the Gambling Ring, Whitman #1493, 1938, NM ..**50.00**
G-Man Vs the Fifth Column, Whitman #1470, VG **35.00**
G-Men on the Job, Whitman #1168, EX **20.00**
Gang Busters in Action, Whitman #1451, EX..........................**25.00**
Gene Autry & the Hawk of the Hills, Whitman #1493, NM **50.00**
Gene Autry Cowboy Detective, Whitman #1494, EX...............**35.00**
George O'Brien in Gun Law, Whitman #1418, EX **30.00**
Green Hornet Cracks Down, Whitman #1480, NM...................**135.00**
Hairbreath Harry in Dept QT, Whitman #1101, EX...................**35.00**
In the Name of the Law, Whitman #1155, VG **25.00**
Jack Armstrong & the Mystery of the Iron Key, Whitman #1432, VG..**30.00**
Jack Swift & His Rocket Ship, Whitman #1102, EX....................**40.00**
Jungle Jim & the Vampire Woman, Whitman #1139, NM **75.00**
Just Kids, Whitman #1401, EX **35.00**
Kayo in the Land of Sunshine, Whitman #1180, EX....................**35.00**
Kazan in Revenge of the North, Whitman #1105, EX.................**20.00**
Laughing Dragon of Oz, Whitman #1126, EX **125.00**
Little Annie Roonie & the Orphan House, Whitman #1117, VG..**30.00**
Little Orphan Annie & the Gooneyville Mystery, Whitman #1435, NM...**50.00**
Little Women, Whitman #757, EX..**45.00**
Lone Ranger & the Red Renegades, Whitman #1489, EX **50.00**
Lone Ranger & the Secret Killer, Whitman #1431, EX **45.00**
Mandrake the Magician, Whitman #1167, EX **50.00**
Mandrake the Magician & the Flame Pearls, Whitman #1418, VG..**40.00**

Marge's Little Lulu, Alvin, and Tubby, Whitman, 1947, EX, $35.00.

Mickey Mouse & the Magic Lamp, Whitman #1429, NM............**70.00**
Mickey Mouse on the Cave-Man Island, Whitman #1499, VG....**50.00**
Mutt & Jeff, Whitman #1113, NM..**90.00**
Myra North Special Nurse & Foreign Spies, Whitman #1497, EX..**25.00**
Nancy Has Fun, Whitman #1487, EX **25.00**
Og Son of Fire, Whitman #1115, EX.......................................**25.00**
Once Upon a Time, Whitman #718, EX...................................**50.00**
Our Gang on the March, Whitman #1451, EX...........................**30.00**
Peggy Brown & the Jewel of Fire, Whitman #1463, EX **20.00**
Perry Winkle & the Rinkeydinks Get a Horse, Whitman #1487, NM..**45.00**
Phantom & the Sky Pirates, Whitman #1468, NM......................**65.00**
Popeye & Castor Oyl the Detective, Whitman #1497, EX............**50.00**

Popeye and Queen Olive Oyl, 1949, Bud Sagendorf, EX, $35.00.

Porky Pig & His Gang, Whitman #1404, VG...................................45.00
Prairie Bill & the Covered Wagon, Whitman #758, EX...............25.00
Punch Davis of the Aircraft Carrier, Whitman #1440, EX............20.00
Ray Land of the Tank Corps USA, Whitman #1447, EX.............25.00
Red Berry Under Cover Man, Whitman #1426, EX......................30.00
Red Ryder & the Little Beaver on Hoofs of Thunder, Whitman #1400, EX ..50.00
Roy Rogers & the Deadly Treasure, Whitman #1437, VG............40.00
Secret Agent X-9 & the Mad Assassin, Whitman #1472, EX.......45.00
Shazzam — The Glass Princess, Whitman #2024, EX.................5.00
Skeezix at the Military Academy, Whitman #1408, EX 30.00
Skippy, Whitman #761, EX..30.00
Skyroads w/Hurricane Hawk, Whitman #1127, EX.......................30.00
Smilin' Jack & the Escape From Death Rock, Whitman #1445, NM...50.00
Smilin' Jack Speed Pilot, Whitman #1473, EX 35.00
Sombrero Pete, Whitman #1136, VG 25.00
SOS Coast Guard, Whitman #1191, EX 25.00
Tailspin Tommy in the Famous Pay-Roll Mystery, Whitman #747, NM ..65.00
Tarzan & the Golden Lion, Whitman #1448, NM 75.00
Tarzan in the Land of the Apes, Whitman #1467, EX...................50.00
Tarzan's Revenge, Whitman #1488, EX..40.00
Tillie the Toiler & the Wild Man of Desert Island, Whitman #1442, NM ...40.00
Tom Mix & the Stranger From the South, Whitman #1183, EX..40.00
Tom Swift & His Magnetic Silencer, Whitman #1437, EX...........35.00
Treasure Island, Whitman #720, EX 30.00
Two-Gun Montana, Whitman #1104, EX.......................................20.00
Uncle Don's Strange Adventures, Whitman #1114, VG................30.00
Union Pacific, Whitman #1411, EX...25.00
Wash Tubbs & Captain Easy Hunting for Whales, Whitman #1455, EX ..30.00
Wells Fargo, Whitman #1471, EX 25.00
Wimpy the Hamburger Eater, Whitman #1458, EX.......................40.00
Wings of the USA, Whitman #1407, EX 20.00
Zane Grey's Tex Thorne Comes Out of the West, Whitman #1440, EX ..25.00

Bing and Grondahl

In 1853 brothers M.H. and J.H. Bing formed a partnership with Frederick Vilhelm Grondahl in Copenhagen, Denmark. Their early wares were porcelain plaques and figurines designed by the noted sculptor Thorvaldsen of Denmark. Dinnerware production began in 1863, and by 1889 their underglaze color 'Copenhagen Blue' had earned them worldwide acclaim. They are perhaps most famous today for their Christmas plates, the first of which was made in 1895. See also Limited Edition Plates.

Bowl, cream soup; Sea Gull, +7" saucer...60.00
Bowl, rim soup; 8", from $20 to 25.00
Bowl, Sea Gull, 3-lobed shell form, 6½" 25.00
Bowl, serving; Cornflower, 3¼x8½" 48.00
Brooch, Sea Gull, 1/20 12KTGF, 2" dia, on 24" chain 50.00

Coffeepot, Sea Gull, 10½", from $125 to...................................150.00
Creamer & sugar bowl, 3¼", 3½" 50.00
Cup & saucer, Sea Gull, w/gold trim, 2x4", 5¾" dia...................25.00
Figurine, boy & girl, #1781, 8¼"..80.00
Figurine, boy & girl reading book, #1567, 4x4", from $130 to 165.00
Figurine, boy & girl sitting holding glasses, #2175, 5½x4¾" 150.00
Figurine, boy & starfish, #22265, 1957, 4½"............................135.00
Figurine, boy hugging bulldog, #1790, 4x4¾", from $145 to.......190.00
Figurine, boy w/puppy, #2334, 5" 130.00
Figurine, clown, #2353, 9½" 85.00
Figurine, cockatoo, #2178, 5½" 95.00
Figurine, Collie dog, ca 1950s, 6x11½"....................................350.00
Figurine, First Kiss, #2162, 7½x5", from $90 to 125.00
Figurine, fisherman, #2370, 8½" 195.00
Figurine, fox terrier, #2099, 9x8" 140.00
Figurine, girl lying down reading book, #2304, 7½" L, from $100 to ..135.00
Figurine, girl sewing, sitting on bench, long brn braids, 7¾" 125.00
Figurine, girl w/2 calves, #2270, 9x7" 235.00
Figurine, kingfisher on rock slab, #1619, 4½" 70.00
Figurine, little girl w/doll, #1526, 3½", from $80 to 100.00
Figurine, Love Refused, #1614, 7", from $150 to 175.00
Figurine, mother, baby & cat, #1829, 12"..................................310.00
Figurine, nude boy w/flippers on ft holding starfish, #2265, 4½" ...130.00
Figurine, snow seal, 6" L, from $70 to 90.00
Figurine, Spilt Milk, #2246, 6¾"...160.00
Figurine, Springer Spaniel, #2095, 6½x8" 80.00
Figurine, Tom & Willy, boy on box, 2nd w/knife, #1648, 8" 275.00
Napkin rings, Sea Gull, set of 6 ....185.00
Plate, Blue Fluted, 9½"..30.00

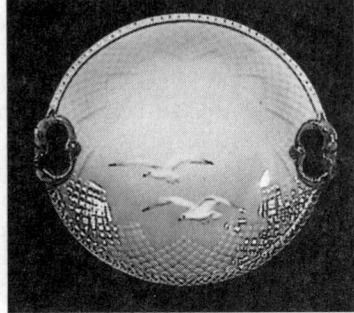

Plate, Sea Gull, handles, #304, 10", $100.00.

Plate, dinner; Sea Gull, 9½", from $40 to 50.00
Plate, Mother's Day, Spaniel & puppies, 1st in series, 1969, MIB...185.00
Plate, Mother's Day Jubilee, 1969-89, mare & foal decor, 9", MIB ...80.00
Platter, Sea Gull, 16"...150.00
Teapot, Sea Gull, #654, snail hdld lid, 6" 90.00
Vase, Blue Fluted, #208/32, 2½x2" 40.00
Vase, pansies, #8752/243, Artium label, 9½"............................105.00
Vase, river scene w/trees, bls & grays, 10x17" 260.00
Vase, Sea Gull, #678, gold at top & bottom rim, 5½" 80.00

Binoculars

There are several types of binoculars, and the terminology used to refers to them is not consistent or precise. Generally, 'field glasses' refer to simple Galilean optics, where the lens next to the eye (the ocular) is concave and dished away from the eye. By looking through the large lens (the objective), it is easy to see that the light goes straight through the two lenses. These are lower power, have a very small field of view, and do not work nearly as well as prism binoculars. In a smaller size, they are opera glasses, and their price increases if they are covered with mother-of-pearl (fairly common but very attractive), abalone shell (more colorful), ivory (quite scarce), or other exotic materials. Field glasses are not valuable unless very unusual or by the best makers, such as Zeiss or Leitz. Prism binoculars have the objective lens offset from the eyepiece and give a much better view. This is the standard binocular form, called Porro prisms, and dates from around 1900. Another type of prism binocular is the roof prism, which at first resembles the straight-through field glasses, with two simple cylinders or cones, here containing very small prisms. These can be distinguished by the high quality views they give and by a thin diagonal line that can be seen when looking backwards through the objective. In general, German binoculars are the most desirable, followed by American, English, and finally French, which can be of good quality but are very common unless of unusual configuration. Japanese optics of WWII or before are often of very high quality. 'Made in Occupied Japan' binoculars are very common, but collectors prize those by Nippon Kogaku (Nikon). Some binoculars are center focus (CF), with one central wheel that focuses both sides at once. These are much easier to use but more difficult to seal against dirt and moisture. Individual focus (IF) binoculars are adjusted by rotating each eyepiece and tend to be cleaner inside in older optics. Each type is preferred by different collectors. Very large binoculars are always of great interest. All binoculars are numbered according to their magnifying power and the diameter of the objective in millimeters. For example, 6 x 30 optics magnify six times and have 30 millimeter objectives.

Prisms are easily knocked out of alignment, requiring an expensive and difficult repair. If severe, this misalignment is immediately noticeable on use by the double-image scene. Minor damage can be seen by focusing on a small object and slowly moving the binoculars away from the eye, which will cause the images to appear to separate. Overall cleanliness should be checked by looking backwards (through the objective) at a light or the sky, when any film or dirt on the lenses or prisms can easily be seen. Pristine binoculars are worth far more than when dirty or misaligned, and broken or cracked optics lower the value far more. Cases help keep binoculars clean but do not add materially to the value.

As of 2001, any significant changes in value are due to Internet sales. Some of the prices listed here are lower than would be reached at an online auction. Revisions of these values would be inappropriate at this point for these reasons: First, values are fluctuating wildly on the Internet; 'auction fever' is extreme. Second, some common instruments can fetch a high price at an Internet sale, and it is clear that the price will not be supported as more of them are placed at auction. In fact, an overlooked collectible like the binocular will be subject to a great increase in supply as they are retrieved from closets in response to the values people see at an online auction. Third, sellers who have access to these Internet auctions can use them for price guides if they wish, but the values in this listing have to reflect what can be obtained at an average large antique show. The following listings assume a very good overall condition, with generally clean and aligned optics.

Our advisor for this category is Peter Abrahams, who studies and collects binoculars and other optics. Please contact, especially to exchange reference material (SASE required with written questions). Mr. Abrahams is listed in the Directory under Oregon.

Field Glasses

Fernglas 08, German WWI, 6x39, military gr, many makers 50.00
Folding, modern, hinged flat case, oculars outside 10.00
Folding or telescoping, no bbls, old 125.00
Ivory covered, various sm szs & makers 200.00
LeMaire, bl leather/brass, various szs, other Fr same 25.00
Metal, emb hunting scene, various sm szs & makers 45.00

Pearl covered, various sm szs & makers 90.00
Porc covered, delicate painting, various sm szs & makers 200.00
US Naval Gun Factory Optical Shop 6x30.....................................75.00
Zeiss 'Galan' 2.5x34, modern design look, early 1920s 120.00

Prism Binoculars (Porro)

Barr & Stroud, 7x50, Porro II prisms, IF, WWII 120.00
Bausch & Lomb, 6x30, IF, WWI, Signal Corps...........................50.00
Bausch & Lomb, 7x50, IF, WWII, other makers same 90.00
Bausch & Lomb Zephyr, 7x35 & other, CF..................................140.00
Bausch & Lomb/Zeiss, 8x17, CF, Pat 1897................................140.00
Crown Optical, 6x30, IF, WWI, filters 50.00
France, various makers & szs, if not unusual 30.00
German WWII 10x80, eyepcs at 45 degrees 500.00
German WWII 6x30, 3-letter code for various makers.................60.00
Goertz Trieder Binocle, various szs, unusual adjustment 85.00
Huet, Paris 7x22, other sm szs, unusual shapes..........................80.00
Leitz 6x30 Dienstglas, IF, good optics 75.00
Leitz 8x30 Binuxit, CF, outstanding optics................................150.00
M19, US military 7x50, ca 1980...150.00
Nikon 9x35, 7x35, CF, 1950s..100.00
Nippon Kogaku, 7x50, IF, Made in Occupied Japan...................150.00
Ross Stepnada, 7x30, CF, wide angle, 1930s 250.00
Ross 6x30, standard British WWI issue 50.00
Sard, 6x42, IF, very wide angle, WWII..900.00
Toko (Tokyo Opt Co) 7x50, IF, Made in Occupied Japan...........45.00
Universal Camera 6x30, IF, WWII, other makers same................50.00
US Naval Gun Factory Optical Shop 6x30, IF, filters, WWI 70.00
US Naval Gun Factory Optical 10x45, IF, WWI.........................200.00
US Navy, 20x120, various makers, WWII & later 2,200.00
Warner & Swasey (important maker) 8x20, CF, 1902.................200.00
Wollensak 6x30, ca 1940...50.00
Zeiss Deltrintem 8x30, CF, 1930s..95.00
Zeiss DF 95, 6x18, sq shoulder, very early 160.00
Zeiss Starmorbi 12/24/42x60, turret eyepcs, 1920s 2,500.00
Zeiss Teleater 3x13, CF, bl leather 120.00
Zeiss 15x60, CF or IF, various models...700.00
Zeiss 8x40 Delactis, CF or IF, 1930s 230.00

Roof Prism Binoculars

Hensoldt Dialyt, various szs, 1930s-80s 140.00
Hensoldt Universal Dialyt, 6x26, 3.5x26, 1920s........................120.00
Leitz Trinovid, 7x42 & other, CF, 1960s-80s, EX.......................500.00
Zeiss Dialyt, 8x30, CF, 1960s 400.00

Birdcages

Birdcages can be found in various architectural styles and in a range of materials such as wood, wicker, brass, and gilt metal with ormolu mounts. Those that once belonged to the wealthy are sometimes inlaid with silver or jewels. In the 1800s, it became fashionable to keep birds, and some of the most beautiful examples found today date back to that era. Musical cages that contained automated bird figures became popular; today these command prices of several thousand dollars. In the latter 1800s, wicker styles came into vogue. Collectors still appreciate their graceful lines and find they adapt easily to modern homes.

Brass, Hendryx, 1930s, 12x10", EX 35.00
Brass, simple wire dome, EX patina, 13¼" 70.00
Cvd wood & wirework, Art Nouveau style, 36" 550.00
Tin, sliding door, tubular bars, curved panels, dome top, 21x13" ...700.00

Bisque

Bisque is a term referring to unglazed earthenware or porcelain that has been fired only once. During the Victorian era, bisque figurines became very popular. Most were highly decorated in pastels and gilt and demonstrated a fine degree of workmanship in the quality of their modeling. Few were marked. See also Heubach; Nodders; Dolls; Piano Babies.

Three children playing with ornate cart, pastels with gold trim, marked DEP 9918 (Karl Schneider symbol), 7", $145.00.

Angel kneeling, wht, A Godard, late 19th C, 22x15x11" 865.00
Bathing beauty, nude w/bl swim cap, Germany, 1920s, 3¼" L ...165.00
Boy & girl w/baskets, floral attire, Germany, 15", pr...................450.00
Boy w/feeding dish, girl w/dog in apron, mc, 13x4", pr...............395.00
Boy w/flower basket by fence, pastels, Fr, 7¼" 125.00
Boy w/watch & girl w/berries in apron, pastels, 11", pr 150.00
Bust, young woman w/2 braids, shades of bl, 13½" 180.00
Bust, youthful blond man w/gray hat, mk MB, 11x6½"..............295.00
Cat, blk, crying w/wht kerchief, basket at side, 4¾" 70.00
Colonial boy, #d, sgn, 10"..95.00
Couple under umbrella, pastels, 6x3⅜"...135.00
Girl in nightie w/kittens, dog & cat, Germany, 8½" 165.00
Girl on swing w/dog, gold trim, 4⅝x3"..95.00
Girl w/book & dog, You Can't Read, 11½" 175.00
Lady in 18th-C dress, mk Expositon de Londres...a Paris, 1860s, 15" ..1,150.00
Peasant man & lady scanning horizon, 23", pr 1,200.00
Pug dog, seated, pastels, Germany, pre-1900, 3¼" 85.00
Vase, boy in hat holds tennis racquet/stands by tree trunk, 8" 90.00
Vase, googly-eyed baby w/hands on gr bag, #d, 3¾".......................40.00
Wall pocket, boy & girl in balcony, scrolling, mc, 7"....................75.00
Witch beside house w/elf hiding at side, Germany, #8398, 2½"..100.00

Black Americana

Black memorabilia is without a doubt a field that encompasses the most widely exploited ethnic group in our history. But within this field there are many levels of interest: arts and achievements such as folk music and literature, caricatures in advertising, souvenirs, toys, fine art, and legitimate research into the days of their enslavement and enduring struggle for equality. The list is endless.

In the listings below are some with a derogatory connotation. Thankfully, these are from a bygone era and represent the mores of a culture that existed nearly a century ago. They are included only to convey the fact that they are a part of this growing area of collecting interest. Black Americana catalogs featuring a wide variety of items for sale are available; see the Directory under Clubs, Newsletters, and Catalogs for more information. We also recommend *Black Collectibles* by P.J. Gibbs published by Collector Books. See also Cookie Jars; Postcards; Posters; Sheet Music.

Ashtray stand, CI butler figural, EX pnt, 35", VG 500.00

Bank, golliwog, Let Golly Save Your Lolly, ceramic, 1920s, 6", EX.....350.00
Bank, golliwog, pnt wood/mink hair/wht coat, label, German, '20s, 5" ...185.00
Bank, log cabin w/banjo playing & dancing, tin, Chein, 1930s, 4", M....400.00
Banner, Martin Luther King memorial, blk & wht, 40x46", EX .440.00

Book, Ezekiel's Travels, Elvira Garner, Henry Holt and Company, New York, 1938, EX, from $80.00 to $125.00. (Photo courtesy P.J. Gibbs)

Book, Little Alexander, Besse Schiff, 1955, hardbk, EX 100.00
Book, Little Black Sambo, diecut figure, 12 illus, 25 pgs, EX+....490.00
Book, Little Black Sambo, Helen Bannerman, 1st ed, 1945, hardbk, VG ...100.00
Book, Topsy, McLoughlin, 1880s, diecut Topsy figure, 14 pgs, EX+......425.00
Booklet, Kellogg's Story Book of Games/Little Black Sambo, 1931, EX.85.00
Bottle opener, man's head w/open mouth, pnt CI, 4¼", VG.........70.00
Clicker, Minstrel Sam, litho tin, 1920s, 1¾", EX 100.00
Clock, head w/moving eyes atop clock w/watermelon slice, cvd, 7", VG.560.00
Coin-op automated machine, The Five Pence Jazz Band, 66x44", G 2,000.00
Coloring book, Little Brown Koko, D Wadstaff illus, 1941, unused, EX...125.00
Cookie jar, Aunt Jemima, plastic, F&F 500.00
Creamer & sugar bowl, Aunt Jemima & Uncle Mose, plastic, F&F.175.00
Dart board, Sambo, tin/cb, Wyandotte, 23x14", G+ 80.00
Dart board, Target Beer, tin over cb, Black boy in center, 14x11", VG ..225.00
Doll, golliwog, stuffed cloth, tuxedo w/striped pants, 26", EX+ ..125.00
Doll, golliwog, yarn w/felt features, 1930s, 17", EX.....................150.00
Doll, Tod-L-Tot, Sun Rubber, 1930s, 10", EX 75.00
Doll kit, Sambo, Bucilla Needlework, 1950s, complete, EX........100.00
Figure, baby, bsk/pnt features/real hair/cloth clothes, 1910, 5", EX..75.00
Figure, girl singing, ceramic, yel trim, Japan, 1930s, 6", EX..........65.00
Figure, slave, wood/glass eyes/ivory teeth/jtd arms, 1870s, 18", NM ..630.00
Figure, 3 boys at fence/cockfight, chalkware, c 1898, 12", Fair ...500.00
Game, Chuck, litho cb, Ottman/USA, 1890s, rare, NM (EX box)..365.00
Game, Four Frisky Darkies, 1880s, complete, rare, VG 300.00
Game, Noddy's Ring Toss, England, 1960s, EXIB.......................100.00
Game, Picaninny Bowling Spears, 1928, complete, rare, EX........450.00
Jack-in-the box, stuffed cloth golliwog in tuxedo, England, 10", NM......75.00
Lamp, oil; wick comes out of man's mouth, bronze, early, 5", EX+ 260.00
Letter opener/pencil, boy/gator, pnt celluloid, Germany, 1880s, NM 140.00
Marionette, Jambo the Jiver, jtd wood, Talent Prod, 1948, 14", VG 225.00
Marionette, minstrel w/banjo, wood/cloth clothes, Pelham, 13", MIB..200.00
Match holder, figure w/open/close mouth, bsk, Japan, prewar, 4", NM .190.00
Match holder, Johnny Griffin head, pnt bsk, Austria, 1880s, 4", NM ...375.00
Measuring cup set, 4 stacked heads, ceramic, Japan, prewar, 7", NM 165.00
Mechanical figure, Stepping Tom, pnt wood, White Mfg, 13", NM ..55.00
Memo board, Mammy, We Needs 85.00
Menu, Coon Chicken Inn, diecut cb smiling head, M 125.00
Music box, man standing on base, tin, Germany, 1920, 8", EX...700.00
Music box, rnd litho tin w/top hand crank, Germany, 1890s, 4¼", EX+....200.00
Nodder, man on elephant, papier-mache, 8", VG........................300.00
Note pad, Aunt Jemima, F&F, 1950s 95.00
Pillow cover, humorous exterior wedding scene, 22x22", EX 225.00
Pillow cover, 3 shoeshine boys playing craps, 22x22", VG 250.00
Pincushion, stuffed pillow shape w/embroidered golliwog, lace trim, NM ..35.00

Pitcher, ceramic, scenes both sides, gold trim, Grafton, 3½", NM ...**400.00**
Plaque, molded bronze female figure from waist up, 25x16", VG .**400.00**
Plate, ceramic, mk Dixie Land, 3 boys eating watermelon, 5" dia, M...**175.00**
Poster, Amos 'N Andy in Check & Double Check, cb, fr, 18x14", EX.**175.00**
Poster, Colored Man Is No Slacker, c 1918, 20x16", VG **75.00**
Poster, Geo Evans' 'Honey Boy' Minstrels, detailed, 77x39", EX...**1,700.00**
Poster, McNish, Johnson & Slavin's Refined Minstrels, 42x31", VG..**425.00**
Poster, Uncle Tom's Cabin, lg bearded face/curtain, 40x88", VG......**1,000.00**
Powder box, tortoise shell celluloid w/dude lid, 1920s, 4" dia, M.**140.00**
Print, exterior cabin scene/banjo player/family, c 1898, 16x20", VG.**150.00**
Roly Poly, golliwog, compo, gr outfit/bl tie/red trim, EX **500.00**
Roly Poly, man, papier-mache, yel jacket & hat/bl vest, 10", EX...**425.00**
Shakers, Aunt Jemima & Uncle Mose, plastic, F&F, 3½", pr........**65.00**
Shakers, Aunt Jemima & Uncle Mose, plastic, F&F, 5", pr **75.00**
Shakers, Mammy & Rastus, porc, pr...**50.00**
Shaving mug, ceramic, I'm Not Greedy.../fat man, Germany, 1900s, NM...**110.00**
Signs, 5 Miles To.. to 1 Mile To.., Ithaca, set of 5, 48x12" ea, EX..**1,700.00**
Soap holder, Mammy w/removable basket on head, pnt CI, 5", EX ..**125.00**
Spice jar, Aunt Jemima, plastic, F&F, from set of 6, ea.................**50.00**
Spice shelf, Mammy, HP diecut wood w/scalloped trim, prewar, 11", NM...**75.00**
Syrup, Aunt Jemima, plastic, F&F, 5½" **70.00**
Towel, 2 Mammies w/umbrella & fruit, print on cotton, 14x26", EX..**45.00**
Toy, pull-string; litho tin face w/movable eyes, 2" dia, VG.............**45.00**
Toy, w/up; goose appears to bite boy, pnt plastic, USA, 1930s, 9", NM...**280.00**
Trivet, chef w/bowl & spoon, CI, Toledo Stove & Range, 1920s, 8", NM...**155.00**
Vending machine, Smiling Sam the Voo Doo Man, vends cb charm, 76", G.**1,500.00**
Ventriloquist doll, in bowler hat, papier-mache/wood/stuffed, 35", VG ..**850.00**
Window card, silhouette band/seated minstrels/dancing couple, 24", VG...**170.00**

Black Cats

Made in Japan during the '50s, these novelty cats may be found bearing the labels of several different importers, all with their own particular characteristics. The best known and most collectible of these cats are from the Shafford line. Even when unmarked, they are easily identified by their red bows, green eyes, and white whiskers, eyeliners, and eyebrows. Relco/Royal Sealy cats are tall and slender, and their bow ties are gold with red dots. Wales is a wonderful line with yellow eyes and gold detailing; Enesco cats have blue eyes, and there are other lines as well. When evaluating your black cats, be sure to inspect their paint and judge them accordingly. For example 50% paint should relate to 50% of our suggested values, which are given for cats in mint (or nearly mint) paint. Enthusiastic bidding on Internet auctions has resulted in much higher prices on the more hard-to-find items as reflected in our listings.

For more information we recommend *Collectible Cats, Book II,* by Marbena 'Jean' Fyke.

Condiment set, 6" oil and vinegar cruets and 2¾" shakers in metal frame, $85.00.

Ashtray, flat face, Shafford, hard-to-find sz, 3¾"........................**45.00**

Ashtray, head shape, not Shafford, several variants, ea, from $12 to..**15.00**
Ashtray, 3-D head, open mouth w/cigarette rest, Shafford **22.00**
Bank, seated, coin slot in top of head, Shafford, from $225 to....**275.00**
Bank, upright, Shafford-like features, mk Tommy, 2-part, from $150 to .**175.00**
Cigarette lighter, sm cat stands on book by table lamp.................**65.00**
Condiment set, 2 joined heads, J&M bows w/spoons, Shafford, 4"..**95.00**
Cookie jar, head w/fierce look, yel eyes, brn-blk glaze, red clay, lg ...**250.00**
Cookie jar, lg head, Shafford, from $80 to **100.00**
Creamer & sugar bowl, head lids are shakers, yel eyes, 5⅜" **50.00**
Creamer & sugar bowl, Shafford..**45.00**
Cruet, upright, yel eyes, open mouth, paw spout..........................**30.00**
Cruets, he w/O eyes, she w/V eyes & hair bow, Shafford, pr, $60 to ..**75.00**
Decanter, long, red fish in mouth as stopper **60.00**
Desk caddy, pen forms tail, spring body holds letters, 6½".............**8.00**
Egg cup, cat face on bowl, ped ft, Shafford, from $95 to **125.00**
Fork, emb cat face, gr eyes, from wall-hanging utensil set, Shafford..**125.00**
Grease jar, sm head, Shafford, from $95 to..................................**110.00**
Measuring cups, 4 szs on wood rack w/pnt cat face, Shafford, $350 to ..**400.00**
Mug, Shafford, rare lg sz, 4¼", from $70 to..................................**80.00**
Mug, Shafford, 3½" **55.00**
Paperweight, head on stepped chrome base, open mouth, yel eyes, rare..**75.00**
Pincushion, cushion on bk, tongue measure.................................**25.00**
Pitcher, milk; upright, Shafford...**150.00**
Pot holder caddy, 'teapot' cat, 3 hooks, Shafford, from $170 to ..**195.00**
Shakers, long & crouching, shaker ea end, Shafford, 10" **165.00**
Shakers, rnd-bodied 'teapot' cat, Shafford, pr, from $125 to **140.00**
Shakers, round-bodied teapot type, Shafford, pr, from $125 to ...**140.00**
Shakers, upright, Shafford, 3¾" (also slightly smaller), pr............**25.00**
Spice set, 6 sq shakers in wooden fr, yel eyes **175.00**
Teapot, ball-shaped body, gr eyes, Shafford, 4-4½" **30.00**
Teapot, ball-shaped body, head lid, gr eyes, Shafford, med sz **45.00**
Teapot, ball-shaped body, head lid, gr eyes, Shafford, 7"...............**75.00**
Teapot, panther-like appearance, gold eyes, sm.............................**20.00**
Teapot, upright, slim w/lift-off head, Shafford, rare, 8"................**250.00**
Teapot, yel eyes, 1-cup...**30.00**
Tray, flat face, wicker hdl, Shafford, rare **185.00**
Wall pocket, flattened 'teapot' cat, Shafford, scarce, $125 to......**150.00**
Wine, emb face, gr eyes, Shafford, sm..**75.00**

Black Glass

Black glass is a type of colored glass that when held to strong light usually appears deep purple, though since each glasshouse had its own formula, tones may vary. It was sometimes etched or given a satin finish; and occasionally it was decorated with silver, gold, enamel, coralene, or any of these in combination. The decoration was done either by the glasshouse or by firms that specialized in decorating glassware. Crystal, jade, colored glass, or milk glass was sometimes used with the black as an accent. Black glass has been made by many companies since the seventeenth century. Contemporary glasshouses produced black glass during the Depression, seldom signing their product. It is still being made today.

To learn more about the subject, we recommend *A Collector's Guide to Black Glass, Books I and II,* written by our advisor, Marlena Toohey; she is listed in the Directory under Colorado. Look for her newly updated value guide. See also Tiffin, L.E. Smith, and other specific manufacturers.

Ashtray, sq, Cambridge, #151, ca 1922, 3½" **20.00**
Basin, enamel decor, Italy, early 1900s, 14"..................................**135.00**
Basket, Sawtooth or Cameo, Tiara Exclusives, 10" **50.00**
Bowl, console; Lotus or Stockholm, Dalzell mk, 13½" **45.00**
Bowl, Dolphin Shell, from Westmoreland #1049 mold, Viking, 8"...**65.00**
Box, glove; scallops, early 1900s, 4x10½" **145.00**
Candlestick, #63 pillar, blk satin, US Glass, 1924-34, 7½" **35.00**

Candlestick, 3-light, 1930s-30s, 9" **45.00**
Candlesticks, Sawtooth or Cameo, Tiara Exclusives, 4¼x3¼", pr **15.00**
Candy dish, shallow, 1930s-30s, 6" dia **25.00**
Cigarette box, eng monogram, 1930s, 4½" W **35.00**
Cigarette holder, 1930s-40s, 3" **25.00**
Clock, wall; Tiara Exclusives by Indiana Glass, 1980s, 12" **75.00**
Decanter, pewter o/l, ca 1930s, 9½" **95.00**
Drink caddy w/chrome holder, Bake-O-Lite hdl, unmk, 1930s, 5½x4" ..**25.00**
Flower frog, emb floral, Greensburg, 1930s, 4½" dia **15.00**
Goblet, champagne, crystal bowl, Italy label, 1966, 6-oz **20.00**
Honey dish, Beehive, Tiara Exclusives, 6" **45.00**
Knife rest, hollow, faceted, 6" L **35.00**
Planter, penguin figural, 4" **32.00**
Plate, Cloverleaf, Hazel-Atlas, 1930-36, 8" **20.00**
Plate, Geo Washington Bicentennial, LE Smith, 1932, 8¼" **85.00**
Shakers, horizontal ribs, ftd, Hazel-Atlas, 1930s, 3½", pr **45.00**
Stand, Beaumont Glass Co, 1920s, 4½" W **65.00**
Stand, punch bowl; 1930s-30s, 7" **30.00**
Stand, 1920s-30s, 3-5" dia, ea **15.00**
Sugar bowl, invt cone, angle hdls, ftd, 1920-30s, 4" **15.00**
Toothpick holder, Indian chief, V in circle, Summit, 1980s, 2½" .**20.00**
Tray, dresser; early 1900s, 9½" **85.00**
Vase, bud; decor, 1930s, 10" **35.00**
Vase, emb daffodil, flared rim, ftd, 1930s, 4¾" **28.00**
Vase, Fern & Holly, ftd, early 1900s, 3½" **38.00**
Vase, fluted, 1930s, 6¼" **30.00**

Blown Glass

Blown glass is rather difficult to date; eighteenth and nineteenth century examples vary little as to technique or style. It ranges from the primitive to the sophisticated, but the metallic content of very early glass caused tiny imperfections that are obvious upon examination, and these are often indicative of age.

In America, Stiegel introduced the English technique of using a patterned, part-size mold, a practice which was generally followed by many glasshouses after the Revolution. From 1820 to about 1850, glass was blown into full-size three-part molds. In the listings below, glass is assumed clear unless color is mentioned. For further information you may refer to the standard reference book, *American Glass*, by Helen and George McKearin. See also Bottles and specific manufacturers. Our advisor for this category is Mark Vuono; he is listed in the Directory under Connecticut. See also Bottles.

Pitcher, golden amber, tooled spout, applied solid foot with pontil, American, 5¾x7¼", $400.00.

Bank, lt bl, sheared coin slot, 2 appl rings, appl button front, 5"..**450.00**
Bottle, gemel, aquamarine, sheared mouth/base, 8½"..................**130.00**
Bowl, amethyst, folded rim, wear, 3⅞x6¼" **550.00**
Bowl, aqua, flared sides, folded rim, pontil scar, Am, 1800s, 8x10"..**575.00**
Bowl, cobalt, kicked-up pontil base, rolled rim, 11⅛" **880.00**
Bowl, dk bl-gr, pontil scar, folded rim, high sides, 4½" H **1,150.00**

Bowl, med amber, pontil scar, folded rim, potstone, 5x8½" **275.00**
Bowl, med amber, pontil scar, rolled lip, high sides, 6½" H **110.00**
Bowl, med gr, pontil scar, outward folded rim, 6¼x7⅜" **825.00**
Bowl, mixing; aqua, pontil scar, folded rim, 8½" H **600.00**
Bowl, yel-olive gr, pontil scar, folded rim, 3x6¾" **850.00**
Creamer, aquamarine, tooled rim/spout, appl threading, 5¼", NM ...**550.00**
Creamer, clear w/mercurial decor, pinched rim/spout, 1813-35, 5"....**275.00**
Creamer, dk amethyst, tooled/shaped rim, pear shape/curled hdl, 4".**450.00**
Creamer, mercurial ring decor, curled hdl, 1813-35, 4¾" **300.00**
Cuspidor, bright turq, 12-rib, 1950s, 4½" **150.00**
Darner, mc spatter cased in clear, 6⅛" **150.00**
Decanter, cobalt, brass neck rim, pontil, MOP & brass stopper, 7¾" ...**150.00**
Decanter, cobalt w/wht spirals & swirls, pontil scar, 8⅞" **300.00**
Decanter, tapered, orig stopper, ground pontil, 11½"..................**50.00**
Flask, clear w/bl & red spots, sheared lip & pontil, 5¾".............**150.00**
Flip, cut/etch, scalloped bands, Dutch inscription, 6".................**165.00**
Flip, soda-lime, eng decor at rim, pontil, 6½".........................**250.00**
Flower arranger, clear w/cobalt filigree, 12-rib, 4¾".................**160.00**
Fly trap, aqua, tooled open base, 3 appl ft, 1890-1930, 6".........**75.00**
Fly trap, cranberry flashing on inside, tooled open base, 3 ft, 6".**300.00**
Pan, aquamarine, flared/folded rim, 4⅜x11¾"............................**1,250.00**
Pan, aquamarine, folded rim, pontil, mini, 4"...........................**120.00**
Pan, lt gr-aqua, crimped pour spout, folded rim, 3x10¾".............**475.00**
Pan, med amber, flared-out rim, heavy base, 4⅞x13"..................**975.00**
Pan, med cobalt, outward folded rim, pontil scar, 2x5⅝"............**150.00**
Pan, med sapphire bl, 16 vertical ribs, 2" H...............................**325.00**
Pan, milk; aqua, crimped pour spout, folded rim, 4½x14½"........**625.00**
Pitcher, amber, appl hdl, crimped base, open pontil, 1790s, 9"...**1,955.00**
Pitcher, aquamarine, Lily Pad, appl ribbed hdl, 4⅞"...............**3,750.00**
Pitcher, olive-amber, appl threading below rim, early 1800s, 3¼"..**1,265.00**
Pitcher/creamer, dk red-amber, solid hdl w/curl, tooled rim, 5½"....**750.00**
Rolling pin, med cobalt w/gold pnt decor, 1875-1900, 14"..........**110.00**
Rolling pin, olive-amber w/wht splotches, 1860-75, 14½"..........**160.00**
Rolling pin, wht opal, sheared open pontil, 1875-1900, 16".......**100.00**
Salt cellar, cobalt, pontil scar on ft, flared rim, 1-pc, 1¾"..........**95.00**
Spittoon, lt bl opaque, 1880-1910, 4½x7⅝"............................**125.00**
Sugar bowl, dk amethyst, milk glass banded rim, 1825-45..........**825.00**
Sugar bowl, emerald gr, gauffered rim, bulbous, appl ft, w/lid, 5½".....**5,000.00**
Sugar bowl/compote, flared/folded rim, 10-pattern body, stem, 4x5½"..**300.00**
Sweetmeat/sugar bowl, teardrop stem, w/lid, 1820-30, 9".........**225.00**
Vase, amethyst, pontil scarred ft, folded rim, 1820-50, 12" **200.00**
Vase, Hyacinth, cobalt, pontil scar, tooled rim, 9"......................**300.00**
Wine, dk purple amethyst, pontil scar on ft, folded/tooled rim, 5"...**180.00**

Blown Three-Mold Glass

A popular collectible in the '20s, '30s, and '40s, blown three-mold glass has again gained the attention of many. Produced from approximately 1815 to 1840 in various New York, New England, and Midwestern glasshouses, it was a cheaper alternative to the expensive imported Irish cut glass.

Distinguishing features of blown three-mold glass are the three distinct mold marks and the concave-convex appearance of the glass. For every indentation on the inner surface of the ware, there will be a corresponding protuberance on the outside. Blown three-mold glass is most often clear with the exception of inkwells and a few known decanters. Any colored three-mold glass commands a premium price.

The numbers in the listings that follow refer to the book *American Glass* by George and Helen McKearin. Our advisor for this category is Mark Vuono; he is listed in the Directory under Connecticut.

Bowl, GII-22, turned-over lip, 1⅜x6¼" **245.00**
Bowl, GIII-4, 3⅛x5½" **990.00**

Compote, GV-24 invt variant, Baroque, knop stem, trn lip, 4x4", NM..385.00
Condiment, GII-44, pontil scar, tooled lip, 1815-30, 4⅝" 100.00
Condiment, GIII-27, 9-sided, pontil scar, flared lip, 4⅝" 160.00
Creamer, GI-30, aquamarine, solid hdl w/curl, pontil, 3¾".........400.00

Creamer, GIII-26, purple-blue, flared mouth with tooled rim, rayed base, applied handle with curl terminal, Boston & Sandwich, 4¼", $3,500.00.

Decanter, cobalt w/emb florals & beads, European, 1825-45, 9½"..325.00
Decanter, GII-16, med olive gr w/amber tone, 1815-30, 7¼" 650.00
Decanter, GII-45, med olive gr, dmns, dbl collar mouth, 8¼" 4,600.00
Decanter, GII-6, aquamarine, flared-out lip, pontil scar, chip, 7" ..900.00
Decanter, GII-6 (similar), tooled mouth, solid hdl, stopper, 12".225.00
Decanter, GIII-19, med olive gr, 1815-35, qt, 9¼" 1,650.00
Decanter, GIII-2, mismatched ball stopper, 11" 150.00
Flip, GII-18, amethystine, potstone w/star, 4½"...........................110.00
Flip, GII-22, pontil scar, tooled rim, 5¾" 200.00
Flip hat, GII-7, pontil scar, folded rim, 2⅜" 65.00
Hat, GIII-23, cobalt, Sunburst-in-Sq, 2¼x2½" 715.00
Inkwell, GIII-29, amber, some wear, 1½x2⅜" 165.00
Pan, GIII-20, lt wear, 1½x5¾" 165.00
Pan, GIII-20, lt wear, 1⅞x7⅞" 275.00
Pan, GIII-22, pontil scar, folded rim, 1815-35, 1½x6¼" 100.00
Pan, GIII-24, wear at kick-up, 1½x6" 165.00
Pitcher, GIII-21, appl hdl, mini, 2⅞" 200.00
Syrup, GV-11, pewter lid, star-pressed base, solid hdl, 7½", NM ...225.00

Blue and White Stoneware

Salt glaze or molded stoneware was most commonly produced in a blue and white coloration, much of which was also decorated with numerous 'in-mold' designs (some 150 plus patterns). It was made by practically every American pottery from the turn of the century until the mid-1930s. Crocks, pitchers, wash sets, rolling pins, and other household wares are only a few of the items that may be found in this type of 'country' pottery, now one of today's popular collectibles.

Logan, Brush-McCoy, Uhl Co., and Burley Winter were among those who produced it; but very few pieces were ever signed. Naturally, condition must be a prime consideration, especially if one is buying for resale; pieces with good, strong color and fully molded patterns bring premium prices. Normal wear and signs of age are to be expected, since this was utility ware and received heavy use in busy households.

In the listings that follow, crocks, salts, and butter holders are assumed to be without lids unless noted otherwise. Items are in near-mint condition unless noted otherwise. Though common pieces seem to have softened to some degree, scarce items and those in outstanding mint condition are stronger than ever. For further information we recommend *Blue and White Stoneware* (1981) by Kathryn McNerny and *Collector's Encyclopedia of Salt Glaze Stoneware* (1997) by Terry Taylor and Terry and Kay Lowrance. See also specific manufacturers.

Bank w/Money Bank stencil, coin slot, break to open, 4x3" 1,200.00
Bowl, Apricot, 9½"..95.00
Bowl, Daisy on Lattice, 10¾"...100.00
Bowl, milk; Flying Bird shoulder, 3¾x9½", w/matching lid...1,000.00
Bowl, mixing; Flying Bird, 4x7½"..350.00
Bowl, Reverse Pyramids w/Reverse Picket Fence, 2½x4½" 65.00
Bowl, Wedding Ring, 6 szs, $150 ea, or set of 6 for....................800.00
Bowl (milk crock), Apricot, w/hdl..225.00
Box, powder; Wildflower & Fishscale, w/lid................................275.00
Butter crock, Apricot, appl wood & wire hdl, w/lid, 4x7" 275.00
Butter crock, Basketweave & Morning Glory, w/lid, 4x7½" 425.00
Butter crock, Butterfly, orig lid & bail, 6½"...............................225.00
Butter crock, Cows, appl wood & wire hdl, w/lid, 4½x7¼" 500.00
Butter crock, Dragon Fly & Flower, no lid, 4½x7" 125.00
Butter crock, Draped Windows, 4½x8"....................................225.00
Butter crock, Eagle, orig lid & bail, M 1,080.00
Butter crock, Grapes & Leaves, dbl ring around rim, 3x6½" 175.00
Butter crock, Peacock, w/lid, 6x6"...675.00
Butter crock, Wild Flower (stenciled), w/lid, 6½x7¼" 175.00
Butter jar, Wildflower, appl wood & wire hdl, 5x7"...................275.00
Canister, Basketweave, Cloves, orig lid, 4½"............................200.00
Canister, Basketweave, Coffee, orig lid, 7½"............................350.00
Canister, Basketweave, Put Your Fist In, orig lid, 7½"...............750.00
Canister, Basketweave, Salt, orig lid, 7½"...............................350.00
Canister, Basketweave, Sugar, orig lid, 7½".............................350.00
Canister, Basketweave, Tobacco, orig lid, 7½"..........................750.00
Canister set, Basketweave, 9-pc...5,000.00
Chamberpot, Fishscale & Wild Rose, no lid, 5½x9¼" 250.00
Chamberpot, Peacock, 9¾" 1,250.00
Chamberpot, Wildflower & Fishscale, w/lid..............................400.00
Coffeepot, Bull's Eye, rim chips, 9¾x3¾" (base)....................2,550.00
Coffeepot, Peacock, patterned sloped sides, 7x10" 3,500.00
Coffeepot, Swirl, w/lid...900.00
Cookie jar, Brickers, flat button finial, 8x8".............................500.00
Cooler, iced tea;, Blue Band, flat lid, complete, 13x11" 295.00
Cooler, water; Blue Band, orig lid..250.00
Cooler, water; Cupid, brass spigot, patterned lid, 15x12" 700.00
Cooler, water; Polar Bear, Ice Water, no lid, 15¼" 500.00
Crock, Lovebird, rstr bail & handgrip, 5½x9"...........................400.00
Cup, Wildflower w/emb Ribbon & Bow, 4½x2½"........................85.00
Cuspidor, Basketweave & Morning Glory, 5x7½" 150.00
Cuspidor, Flower Panels & Arches, 7x7½" 250.00
Custard cup, Fishscale, 5x2½"...150.00
Grease jar, Flying Bird, orig lid, 4x4½"................................1,200.00
Ice crock, Barrel Staves, rope/tongs/ice block emb, 4½x6" 225.00
Jardiniere, Flowers, hairline, 7x7⅞" (complete w/stand & crock) ...800.00
Meat tenderizer, Wildflower...650.00
Mug, beer; advertising, Diffused Blue, sqd hdl 150.00
Mug, Flying Bird, 5x3" 200.00
Mug, Windy City (Fannie Flagg), Robinson Clay Products 200.00
Pie plate, Blue Walled Brick-Edge star emb base, 10½" 225.00
Pitcher, Acorns, stenciled, 8x6½" 175.00
Pitcher, Apricot, 8" 250.00
Pitcher, Barrel, +6 mugs...395.00
Pitcher, Basketweave & Morning Glory, 9" 300.00
Pitcher, Blue Band, plain 200.00
Pitcher, Bluebird, 9x7"...450.00
Pitcher, Butterfly, 9x7"...500.00
Pitcher, Cattails, stenciled design, bulbous, 7".........................225.00
Pitcher, Cattails, 10" 300.00
Pitcher, Cattails, 9½"..275.00
Pitcher, Cherry Cluster, 7½"..650.00
Pitcher, Columns & Arches, 8¾x5"..425.00
Pitcher, Daisy Cluster, rare, 7x7" 800.00

Pitcher, Doe & Fawn, bl, 8½" 185.00
Pitcher, Dutch Landscape, stenciled, Diffused Blue, tall.............225.00
Pitcher, Eagle w/Shield & Arrows, rare, 8" 800.00
Pitcher, Fishscale & Wild Rose (part of wash set), 10".............160.00
Pitcher, Garden Rose, 9" 500.00
Pitcher, Garden Rose Sponge, 9" 800.00
Pitcher, Girl & Dog, regular bl, 9" 675.00

Pitcher, Grape with Leaf Band, medium blue, 9", $200.00.

Pitcher, Grape & Shield, 8½x5" 150.00
Pitcher, Grape w/Rickrack, any sz......................250.00
Pitcher, Grazing Cows, bl, 7½" 400.00
Pitcher, Grazing Cows, 6½" 500.00
Pitcher, hot water; Wildflower & Fishscale, sm 150.00
Pitcher, Indian Boy & Girl (Capt John Smith & Pocahontas), 6"...300.00
Pitcher, Iris, 9" 375.00
Pitcher, Leaping Deer, sponge, 8" 1,200.00
Pitcher, Leaping Deer in 1 oval, Swan in other (mfg error), 8" ..1,500.00
Pitcher, Lincoln, allover deep bl, 4¾x4¾" 250.00
Pitcher, Lincoln, allover deep bl, 6x4" 300.00
Pitcher, Lincoln, allover deep bl, 7x5" 400.00
Pitcher, Lovebird, arc bands, deep color, 8½", EX 500.00
Pitcher, Lovebird, pale color, 8½" 300.00
Pitcher, Monk, dk cobalt................................350.00
Pitcher, Peacock..1,500.00
Pitcher, Pine Cone, sponge, rare, 9½" 850.00
Pitcher, Pine Cone, 9½" 750.00
Pitcher, Poinsettia, 6½" 275.00
Pitcher, Scroll & Leaf, advertising, 8" 450.00
Pitcher, Shield, prof rpr, 8" 200.00
Pitcher, Stag & Pine Trees, 9" 350.00
Pitcher, Tulip, 8x4" 300.00
Pitcher, Wild Rose, solid bl, 9x6" 450.00
Pitcher, Wild Rose, sponged bands, 9" 500.00
Pitcher, Windmills, 7¼", EX 195.00
Pitcher, Windy City (Fannie Flagg), Robinson Clay, 8½"...........450.00
Roaster, Wildflower, domed lid, 8½x12" 225.00
Rolling pin, Blue Band, advertising, Andka, Nebr, 14x4" 900.00
Rolling pin, Blue Band, no advertising, 14x4" 350.00
Rolling pin, Swirl, orig wooden hdls, 13" 1,200.00
Rolling pin, Wild Flower, advertising, Analomink PA, dtd 1905 .1,100.00
Rolling pin, Wildflower, plain...........................375.00
Salt crock, Apricot, no lid 130.00
Salt crock, Butterfly, orig lid 275.00
Salt crock, Eagle, w/lid 575.00
Salt crock, Peacock, w/lid 550.00
Soap dish, Beaded Rose 150.00
Soap dish, cat's head..................................200.00
Soap dish, Indian in War Bonnet 250.00
Spice set, Basketweave, 6-pc, w/lids 2,000.00
Teapot, Swirl, dbl wire bail hdl, ball shape, 9x6½" 1,200.00

Toothbrush holder, Bow Tie, stenciled flower 50.00
Vinegar cruet, rare, 4½x3" 300.00
Wash bowl & pitcher, Rose on Trellis 300.00
Wash bowl & pitcher, Wildflower & Fishscale 500.00
Wash set, Wildflower & Fishscale, complete, 7-pc 2,000.00
Washboard, sponge......................................400.00
Water bottle, Diffused Blue Swirl, stopper w/cork, 10x5½" 800.00

Blue Ridge

Blue Ridge dinnerware was produced by Southern Potteries of Erwin, Tennessee, from the late 1930s until 1956 in twelve basic styles and two thousand different patterns, all of which were hand decorated under the glaze. Vivid colors lit up floral arrangements of seemingly endless variation, fruit of every sort from simple clusters to lush assortments, barnyard fowl, peasant figures, and unpretentious textured patterns. Although it is these dinnerware lines for which they are best known, collectors prize the artist-signed plates from the '40s and the limited line of character jugs made during the '50s most highly. Examples of the French Peasant pattern are valued at double the prices listed below; very simple patterns will bring 25% to 50% less.

Our advisors, Betty and Bill Newbound, have compiled three lovely books, *Blue Ridge Dinnerware, Revised Third Edition*, and *The Collector's Encyclopedia of Blue Ridge, Volumes I and II*, all with beautiful color illustrations and current market values. They are listed in the Directory under North Carolina. For information concerning the National Blue Ridge Newsletter, see the Clubs, Newsletters, and Catalogs section of the Directory.

Ashtray, advertising, Railroad, from $65 to 75.00
Ashtray, ind, from $20 to 24.00
Ashtray, Mallard, box shape, 3½x2½", from $40 to 45.00
Baking dish, divided, 8x13", from $25 to................30.00
Baking dish, plain, 8x13", from $22 to 25.00
Basket, aluminum edge, 10", from $30 to 35.00
Bonbon, Charm House, china, from $100 to 125.00
Bonbon, flat shell, china, from $75 to 80.00
Bowl, cereal soup (coupe); 6", from $14 to.............16.00
Bowl, fruit; 5¼", from $6 to 8.00
Bowl, hot cereal; from $14 to 17.00
Bowl, mixing; med, from $20 to 25.00
Bowl, vegetable; w/lid, from $60 to....................65.00
Box, Mallard Duck, from $650 to 700.00
Box, Sherman Lily, from $700 to........................750.00

Butter dish, from $35.00 to $45.00.

Cake lifter, from $30 to 35.00
Casserole, w/lid, from $50 to..........................55.00
Child's play tea set, complete, from $375 to 400.00
Chocolate tray, from $450 to 500.00
Creamer, Charm House, china, from $70 to...............85.00
Creamer, Colonial, lg, open, from $18 to 20.00
Creamer, regular shape, from $15 to 18.00

Cup & saucer, demi; earthenware, from $40 to **45.00**

Cup & saucer, demi; premium, from $60 to **65.00**

Cup & saucer, Turkey & Acorns, from $60 to.............................**65.00**

Egg cup, dbl, from $25 to **30.00**

Jug, character; Daniel Boone, Indian, or Paul Revere, ea, from $725 to...**750.00**

Jug, character; Pioneer Woman, from $575 to **600.00**

Lamp, china, from $250 to **300.00**

Lazy susan center bowl, w/lid, from $150 to **180.00**

Leftover w/lid, sm, med, or lg, ea, from $25 to **30.00**

Pitcher, Abby, china, from $175 to......................................**180.00**

Pitcher, Antique, china, 5", from $85 to **95.00**

Pitcher, Chick, china, from $120 to....................................**125.00**

Pitcher, Sculptured Fruit, petite, from $80 to **85.00**

Pitcher, Watuga, from $375 to..**400.00**

Plate, advertising, lg, from $400 to.....................................**450.00**

Plate, artist sgn, 10¼", from $575 to **626.00**

Plate, Christmas Tree, from $75 to **80.00**

Plate, dinner; premium, 10½", from $50 to **60.00**

Plate, party; w/cup & well, premium, from $80 to **85.00**

Plate, 11½-12", from $45 to **50.00**

Platter, Turkey pattern, lg, from $260 to **275.00**

Platter, 12½-13", ea, from $22 to..**25.00**

Ramekin, w/lid, 5", from $25 to **30.00**

Relish, deep shell, china, from $80 to....................................**85.00**

Relish, Mod Leaf, china, from $70 to **75.00**

Salad fork, china, from $45 to..**50.00**

Server, wood or metal hdl, from $25 to **30.00**

Shakers, Apple, 1¾", pr, from $25 to **30.00**

Shakers, Bud Top, pr, from $50 to...**55.00**

Shakers, Chickens, pr, from $140 to......................................**150.00**

Shakers, Mallard Ducks, pr, from $300 to **350.00**

Shakers, range; pr, from $45 to...**50.00**

Shakers, Skyline, pr, from $20 to...**25.00**

Shakers, Twig, pr, from $20 to...**22.00**

Sugar bowl, Charm House, china, from $75 to **850.00**

Sugar bowl, Colonial, sm, from $18 to **20.00**

Sugar bowl, regular shape, w/lid, from $20 to **22.00**

Tea tile, rnd or sq, 6", ea, from $50 to **60.00**

Teapot, Ball shape, premium, from $200 to..............................**225.00**

Teapot, Good Housekeeping, from $175 to...............................**180.00**

Tidbit, 3-tier, from $40 to...**45.00**

Toast, w/lid, premium, from $200 to **210.00**

Tray, demi; Skyline, 9½x7½", from $90 to.................................**95.00**

Vase, Boot form, 8", from $95 to...**98.00**

Vase, tapered, china, from $100 to **110.00**

Blue Willow

Blue Willow, inspired no doubt by the numerous patterns of the blue and white Nanking imports, has been popular since the late eighteenth century and has been made in as many variations as there were manufacturers. English transfer wares by such notable firms as Allerton and Ridgway are the most sought after and the most expensive. Japanese potters have been producing Willow-patterned dinnerware since the late 1800s, and American manufacturers have followed suit. Although blue is the color most commonly used, mauve and black lines have also been made. For further study we recommend the book *Blue Willow*, with full-color photos and current prices, by Mary Frank Gaston, our advisor for this category. In the following listings, if no manufacturer is noted, the ware is unmarked. See also Buffalo.

Ashtray, Royal China, 5½" **12.00**

Baking dish, oven proof, mk Japan, 2½x5" **40.00**

Bank, stacking pig figures (3), Japan, 7", from $65 to **75.00**

Biscuit jar, metal hdl, unmk Japan, 6", from $150 to **175.00**

Biscuit jar, Two Temples II, Traditional border, cane hdl, Adderly ..**200.00**

Bone dish, kidney shape, Bourne & Leigh, 6¼", from $45 to **55.00**

Bowl, chestnut; rtcl sides, unmk English, 10", from $800 to....**1,000.00**

Bowl, cream soup; Homer Laughlin, from $25 to............................**30.00**

Bowl, lug soup; Homer Laughlin, from $25 to **30.00**

Bowl, ped ft, John Tams Ltd, 5x9¼", from $150 to **175.00**

Bowl, soup; Allerton's, ca 1903-12, 9", 3 for **90.00**

Bowl, soup; Royal China, 8¼" **15.00**

Bowl, soup; unmk English, early 1900s, 9⅝" **45.00**

Bowl, soup/cereal; scalloped, flow bl, Doulton, 7½", from $100 to ..**120.00**

Bowl, vegetable; hdls, Davenport, late 1700s, 11" L, from $400 to..**500.00**

Bowl, vegetable; hdls, w/lid, Japan, 9", from $75 to....................**100.00**

Bowl, vegetable; sq, hdls, unmk English, 8¾x7", from $80 to.....**100.00**

Bowl, vegetable; sq, w/lid, Ridgway's, 1912-27 mk, 10" **250.00**

Bowl, vegetable; variant center scene, reserves in border, unmk, 10"....**25.00**

Bowl, vegetable; w/lid, Adderly, 6x10", from $175 to.................**200.00**

Box, dresser; porc, unmk English, ca 1880s, 2x4", from $175 to.**200.00**

Breakfast set, ind; Spode/Copeland, toast rack+c/s+cr/sug, 5-pc.**225.00**

Butter dish, Royal China, ¼-lb...**35.00**

Butter dish, unidentified English mk, 3x8", from $150 to **175.00**

Butter pat, Ridgway's, 1912-27 mk, 3¾", 4 for **60.00**

Cake stand, Traditional pattern, unmk English, 4x10½", $300 to ...**325.00**

Candle holders, sq, Doulton, 7½", pr, from $400 to **500.00**

Canisters, sq, tin, unmk, 7", 5½", 5", 4½", set of 4, $120 to **140.00**

Casserole, Empress, w/lid, Homer Laughlin, from $70 to..............**75.00**

Casserole, w/lid, Royal China **95.00**

Cheese dish, Burleigh pattern, scroll & flower border, Burgess & Leigh ...**275.00**

Cheese keeper, slant lid, numbered, 7¾", $185.00.

Clock, Traditional pattern/pictorial border, 8-day, German works, tin......**165.00**

Coffeepot, Booths, gold trim, mk Real Old Willow, 8½" **210.00**

Coffeepot, graniteware, unmk, 6½", from $90 to........................**110.00**

Condiment shaker, pierced silver lid, Taylor, Tunnicliffe & Co, 2" **50.00**

Creamer, Two Temples II, butterfly border, ftd, unmk, 4x6", $75 to....**85.00**

Creamer & sugar bowl, w/lid, Steventon & Sons, 3", 4", from $70 to.**80.00**

Cruets (2)/condiments (3), on matching stand, Japan, 6½"........**140.00**

Cup, handleless; Pountney & Co, 3½", from $75 to **85.00**

Cup & saucer, jumbo; Homer Laughlin, from $20 to....................**25.00**

Cup & saucer, Royal China..**6.00**

Cup & saucer, tea; Pictorial border, porc, Noritake, 3", from $40 to..**50.00**

Cup & saucer, Washington Pottery, 3" cup, from $5 to **10.00**

Dinnerware, child's; Japan, tureen/platter+teapot+s/cr, serves 6 .**200.00**

Dish, child's; Ridgway, w/lid, 5" **175.00**

Drainer, meat; Turner Center pattern, unmk English, 14¼x10¼" ...**375.00**

Gravy boat, Homer Laughlin, from $20 to..............................**25.00**

Gravy boat, Ridgway's, 8" L, from $70 to **80.00**

Invalid feeder, Wood & Sons, 2½x6x2", from $150 to...............**175.00**

Jug, milk; Homer Laughlin, from $125 to...............................**150.00**

Ladle, unmk, 7" L, from $140 to...**160.00**

Lamp, kerosene; ceramic shade, Japan, 11½", from $125 to........**150.00**

Match safe, slotted cylinder w/saucer base, Shenango China Co, 2"..80.00
Measuring cups, Japan (label), 4 on wall-mt 'dipper' rack, 8" L..165.00
Mug, unmk Japan, 3½", from $10 to 15.00
Mustard pot, bbl shape, unmk, 2½", from $65 to........................75.00
Pie plate, Royal China, 10" 30.00
Pitcher, Burleigh pattern, cylindrical, Burgess & Leigh, 7" 350.00
Pitcher, milk; Allerton's, tankard form, 7", EX 125.00
Pitcher, squat, Ridgway's, 1890s, 5½x6", from $80 to....................100.00
Pitcher, Traditional center, Wedgwood, 1929+ mk, 11¼"............150.00
Plate, Booth's Variant center, gold trim, 8-sided, Booth's, 8¾" 60.00
Plate, dinner; Royal China, 10" 6.00
Plate, grill; Booth's center, Bow-Knot border, Booth's, 10¾" 40.00
Plate, Traditional center, Ridgway's, 9½", 4 for..........................80.00
Plate, Traditional center, rtcl rim, unmk English, 7¼" 165.00
Platter, Allerton's, 16x12"...275.00
Platter, Staffordshire, mk Warranted, 18", NM 165.00
Platter, Traditional center, 1912-1927, 15½x12½"......................225.00
Platter, Two Temples II (simplified), floral border, unmk Am, 12x9"....45.00
Relish, Booth's center pattern, Bow-Knot border, Wood & Sons, 9" 30.00
Salt box, unmk Japan, wall mt, wood lid, 5" 110.00
Shakers, Royal China, pr..25.00
Spoon rest, dbl (2 rests), Japan, 9", from $40 to...........................50.00
Sugar bowl, rope & anchor finial, unmk, 6", from $45 to..............55.00
Sugar bowl, w/lid, Royal China...15.00
Tea set, child's; Occupied Japan, +6 3¾" plates/c&s, 22-pc 200.00
Teapot, Allerton's, 6", NM...225.00
Teapot, Doulton, 4x7½" (spout to hdl), from $225 to.................250.00
Teapot, Well's shape, Homer Laughlin, from $80 to....................100.00
Toast rack, Grimwades, 6", from $80 to......................................100.00
Tureen, soup; Traditional center, Ridgway's, 1912-27 mk, 7¾x11" ..450.00
Tureen, w/lid & ladle, unidentified English mk, 15x11", from $800 to...1,000.00
Waste bowl, Doulton mk, 3½x6½", from $125 to 150.00

Bluebird China

Made from 1910 to 1934, Bluebird China is lovely ware most often decorated with bluebirds flying among pink flowering branches. Another style depicts larger, more slender bluebirds in flight. The latter variety was made by Knowles, Taylor, Knowles; W.S. George (Derwood); French Co.; Sterling Colonial; and Pope Gosser. All of it was inexpensive dinnerware and reached the height of its popularity in the second decade of the twentieth century. Many potteries produced it, and shapes differ from one manufacturer to another. Besides the companies we've already mentioned, you'll find the trademarks of Cleveland; Carrolton; Homer Laughlin (today the most expensive, most collected and most available of all the lines); Limoges China of Sebring, Ohio; Salem; Taylor, Smith, Taylor; and there are others.

Our advisor for this category is Kenna Rosen; she is listed in the Directory under Texas.

Casserole with lid, from $100.00 to $125.00.

Bowl, berry; Cleveland, ind...12.50

Bowl, deep, Derwood, WS George, 4¾".......................................25.00
Bowl, deep, Homer Laughlin, 5½"..35.00
Bowl, gravy; w/saucer, Hopewell China..50.00
Bowl, sauce; SP Co, 4½"..12.50
Bowl, soup; PMC Co, 8"...30.00
Bowl, vegetable; Cleveland, 9¾"...45.00
Butter dish, Carrollton, 6¼" sq...85.00
Butter dish, 4½" holder w/in 7" dish, Steubenville.......................175.00
Butter pat, unmk..15.00
Calendar plate, 1921 advertising pc, ELPCO, 8" 95.00
Canister set, rnd, unmk, 6½x5", 6 for..300.00
Casserole, Homer Laughlin Empress, rnd, w/lid, 8½".....................150.00
Casserole, Ostro China, 10½" dia..95.00
Casserole, Pope Gosser, w/lid, 10½x10½"...................................100.00
Casserole, Royal China Internat'l, 7x11½"..................................125.00
Casserole, Taylor Smith & Taylor, w/lid, 11x7½".........................130.00
Chocolate cup, ftd, no mk, 3½"..35.00
Coffeepot, Sterling Colonial...150.00
Creamer, Derwood, WS George...30.00
Creamer, no mk, 4¼"...25.00
Creamer & sugar bowl, Knowles Taylor Knowles............................75.00
Creamer & sugar bowl, SP Co, w/lid...85.00
Creamer & sugar bowl, w/lid, Homer Laughlin.............................100.00
Cup, coffee; unmk, 3½"...25.00
Cup, tea; unmk..15.00
Cup & saucer, from $35 to...45.00
Dish, oval, Hudson, Homer Laughlin, 1x5¼x4".............................20.00
Gravy w/underplate, Homer Laughlin, 4x9¾"................................75.00
Ladle, sauce; gold scrolling..40.00
Pitcher, water; Salem China, 10"..125.00
Plate, baby's, ELP Co China, 7½x7½"...150.00
Plate, bread; hdls, gold trim, unmk, 10"......................................150.00
Plate, dessert; Limoges, 6"..8.00
Plate, dinner; Cleveland, 9"...25.00
Plate, dinner; Knowles Taylor Knowles, 9¾"................................22.50
Plate, dinner; Wilmer Ware..20.00
Plate, Homer Laughlin, 8½"...35.00
Plate, National China, 8"...22.50
Plate, rtcl, sq, unmk, 9"...35.00
Plate, scalloped, Homer Laughlin, 7¼"...35.00
Plate, Steubenville, 9"...22.50
Platter, Edwin M Knowles, 14½x11"..75.00
Platter, Hopewell China, 13x10"...75.00
Platter, Hopewell China, 17½x13"..100.00
Platter, sqd oval, Carrollton, 17¾x12¾".......................................95.00
Platter, Thompson Glenwood, 13x10"...75.00
Platter, unmk, 9x7"...45.00
Platter, West End Pottery Co, 15½x11".......................................100.00
Platter, 10 bluebirds, gold trim at rim, DE McNichol, 15¼x11¼"...75.00
Saucer, Homer Laughlin 5.00
Sugar bowl, Illinois China Co, w/lid, 7x6"....................................50.00
Syrup, Homer Laughlin, 6½"...150.00
Syrup, unmk, 4"...35.00
Tea set, CPCo, child sz, 21-pc..400.00
Teapot, Carrollton..250.00
Teapot, ELP Co, 8½x8½"..250.00
Teapot, Homer Laughlin..400.00
Teapot, KT&K mk, 3½x7¼"...250.00

Boch Freres

Founded in the early 1840s in La Louviere, Boch Freres Keramis became the foremost producer of art pottery in Belgium. Though primarily they served a localized market, in 1844 they earned worldwide recognition for some of their sculptural works on display at the International Exposition in Paris.

In 1907 Charles Catteau of France was appointed head of the art department. Before that time, the firm had concentrated on developing glazes and perfecting elegant forms. The style they pursued was traditional, favoring the re-creation of established eighteenth-century ceramics. Catteau brought with him to Boch Freres the New Wave (or Art Nouveau) influence in form and decoration. His designs won him international acclaim at the Exhibition d'Art Decoratif in Paris in 1925, and it is for his work that Boch Freres is so highly regarded today. He occasionally signed his work as well as that of others who under his direct supervision carried out his preconceived designs. He was associated with the company until 1950 and lived the remainder of his life in Nice, France, where he died in 1966. The Boch Freres Keramis factory continues to operate today, producing bathroom fixtures and other utilitarian wares. A variety of marks have been used, most incorporating some combination of 'Boch Freres,' 'Keramis,' 'BFK,' or 'Ch Catteau.' A shield topped by a crown and flanked by a 'B' and an 'F' was used as well.

Ginger jar, allover chintz floral, red/wht, gilt finial, 15" **325.00**
Lamp base, floral on bl/gr drip, dbl gourd, metal mts, D700/#904, 10" ..**575.00**
Lamp base, geometrics, 6-sided, mk, 12½" **200.00**
Lamp base, roses on lg lobe of dbl gourd form, w/mts: 20" **550.00**
Lamp base, turq gloss, invt funnel shape w/3 sm neck hdls, 18" **80.00**
Vase, bright bl crackle, mk, 9½x6" **65.00**
Vase, concentric circles, mc scattered on wht, dbl gourd, 7x6" ...**345.00**
Vase, floral, brn/bl on lt tan, ca 1925, 9½" **400.00**
Vase, floral, mc on gray crackle, #d, 7" **300.00**
Vase, floral, mc on stoneware, Gres Keramis, #897, 9¾" **800.00**
Vase, floral, mc on wht, bl rim/base, U-form, '40s, 9x6" **375.00**
Vase, floral, mc on wide lt gr band, Keramis/#d, 1932, 12" **675.00**
Vase, flying birds in bands, Catteau, #1073, ca 1925, 9¾" **1,000.00**
Vase, seed pods/stems, tan/gr/brn on med bl, 13x6" **385.00**
Vase, 3-color motif on crackle, 3 hdls, Catteau, 13" **675.00**
Vase, 4 gazelles, bl/turq/blk on gray crackle, Catteau, 9½x9" ..**1,200.00**
Wash bowl+pitcher, yel/floral rim bands on wht, BFK, NM........**185.00**

Boehm

Boehm sculptures were the creation of Edward Marshall Boehm, a ceramic artist who coupled his love of the art with his love of nature to produce figurines of birds, animals, and flowers in lovely background settings accurate to the smallest detail. Sculptures of historical figures and those representing the fine arts were also made, and along with many of the bird figurines, have established secondary-market values many times their original prices. His first pieces were made in the very early 1950s in Trenton, New Jersey, under the name of Osso Ceramics. Mr. Boehm died in 1969, and the firm has since been managed by his wife. Today known as Edward Marshall Boehm, Inc., the private family-held corporation produces not only porcelain sculptures but collector plates as well. Both limited and non-limited editions of their works have been issued. Examples are marked with various backstamps, all of which have incorporated the Boehm name since 1951. 'Osso Ceramics' in upper case lettering was used in 1950 and 1951. Our advisor for this category is Leon Reimert; he is listed in the Directory under Pennsylvania.

African Elephant, #200-44, 10x7x5¾", from $410 to................**425.00**
African Elephant, 8", from $265 to **300.00**
Allen's Hummingbird w/Trumpet Vine **345.00**
Basset Hound Dog, #127, 7x6" **800.00**
Black-Capped Chickadee, #438C, 8½x2⅝" **185.00**
Black-Tailed Bantams, 1957, pr, 13x8", 9½x5".................**1,800.00**

Boxer dog, standing at attention, 8½x9"....................**575.00**
Bridled Tit, #200-24, 5x5x10"..............................**240.00**
Brown Pelican w/Mangrove, #40342, 22", minimum value......**3,600.00**
Canada Geese, #408L, 7½", pr **500.00**
Cat Playing w/Ball, #124, ca 1950s, 3x5½"..................**425.00**
Cheetah Head, Treasures of Tutankhamun, 7"................**215.00**
Chipmunk, Friends of the Forest series, #HS5, 3x4½" **105.00**
Cinderella Camellia, 3x6x5"................................**245.00**
Dachshund, #40156, 6" L...................................**300.00**
Flicker w/Chipmunk & Mushroom, 13x11"...................**1,700.00**
Giant Panda Cub, lying on bk, #400-47, 1974................**270.00**
Goddess Basket (Egyptian cat), 10½".......................**285.00**
Green Jays, #480R, 18", 14", pr **1,300.00**
Grosbeak, #489, 11½x9", from $400 to......................**450.00**
Hooded Mergansers, #496, 10½", pr **1,600.00**
Hummingbird w/Snow Queen Camellia, #40501................**350.00**
Indigo Bunting on Flower, 10", from $280 to................**300.00**
Killer Whale, leaping, 1990s, 10".........................**425.00**
King Tut on Leopard, gold figure on leopard's bk, ltd ed, 17½x15"..**2,600.00**
Kingfisher Fledgling, #449, 6¼"...........................**200.00**
Linnet w/Gentians, #200-45, 7"............................**300.00**
Long-Horned Bull, 10x14"..................................**1,300.00**
Lovebird Fledglings on Tree Branches, 6" **235.00**
Lucifer Hummingbird w/Hibiscus, #40428, 11x7"............**235.00**
Mallard Ducklings, #400-797, 5½"..........................**145.00**

Marsh Harrier with Water Lilies, #53, 25", $1,150.00.

Mockingbirds (3) & Flowers, #95, 1977, 10x12", from $900 to **1,100.00**
Orchard Orioles on Blossoming Tulip, #400-11, 1970s, 11x7".**1,350.00**
Panda, reclining, 1974, 5x7"...............................**350.00**
Panda, seated, #40237, 5".................................**105.00**
Panda Cub, #400, 1954, 9", NMIB...........................**325.00**
Penguin Fledgling, 3½".....................................**235.00**
Peregrine Falcon on Gloved Hand, #10207, 17x10" **2,100.00**
Poinsettia, 6x5x2½"..**300.00**
Polar Bear, #200-87, 5¼x5⅞"...............................**170.00**
Polar Bear w/Cubs (2), #20114, 6x11" **400.00**
Presidential Eagle, Ronald Reagan, #393, 9"...............**500.00**
Presidential Eagle, 14x12x12" **1,000.00**
Rhino Cub, 12½x7x5¾".......................................**400.00**
Robin Fledgling, #402-51, from $150 to....................**175.00**
Robin w/Daffodils, #472, 1965, 13x8".......................**1,550.00**
Ruby-Throated Hummingbird w/Chrysanthemum Petal Camellia, #40434..**300.00**
Rufous Hummingbirds w/Catteya Orchids, #40440, 9x9x5"........**725.00**
Saw-Whet Owl, #200-38, 6".................................**180.00**
Springer Spaniel, liver & wht, #112, 6¾x8½", from $1,000 to ...**1,250.00**

St Joseph w/Infant, ca 1960s, 14" 650.00
St Patrick's Rose, 5¾" W 300.00
Swan (male), #40534, 9½x16½x6¾" 345.00
Tree Peony w/Wild Rose 850.00
Western Bluebird Fledglings, #49413, 6¼" 155.00
Western Meadowlark, on rock w/lichens, ca 1970s.................625.00
White Owl, #40122, 4¾" 150.00
Yellow-Throated Warbler, #431, 10", from $250 to 300.00

Scissor-tailed Flycatcher, #11, 1977, 13½", $1,380.00.

Bohemian Glass

The term 'Bohemian glass' has come to refer to a type of glass developed in Bohemia in the late sixteenth century at the Imperial Court of Rudolf II, the Hapsburg Emperor. The popular artistic pursuit of the day was stone carving, and it naturally followed to transfer familiar procedures to the glassmaking industry. During the next century, a formula was discovered that produced a glass with a fine crystal appearance which lent itself well to deep, intricate engraving, and the art was further advanced.

Although many other kinds of art glass were made there, collectors today use the term 'Bohemian glass' to often indicate clear glass overlaid or stained with color through which a design is cut or etched. (Unless otherwise described, the items in the listings that follow are of this type.) Red or yellow on clear glass is common, but other colors may also be found. Another type of Bohemian glass involves cutting through and exposing two layers of color in patterns that are often very intricate. Items such as these are sometimes further decorated with enamel and/or gilt work.

Candlesticks, red, one with stag, the other with birds, gold paper label, 9", pair, $150.00.

Beaker, bl, cameo-cut fawn scene, 1850s, 4½" 1,450.00
Beaker, red, faceted, ca 1875, 5" 135.00
Beaker, red & amber, wheel-cut florals, 1930s, 5½" 100.00
Bottle, scent; cobalt, faceted body/stopper, 1850s, 5" 300.00
Bottle, scent; ruby, faceted, dbl-ended, silver caps, 4½" 350.00
Box, dresser; gr, geometrics w/gold & wht enameling, ftd, 5" 175.00
Decanter, red, florals/scrolls, 1930s, 12½", +6 cordials 175.00
Goblet, ruby, stags in landscape, 10x4¼" 275.00
Goblet, wine; red, deer & castle, 1900, 5⅛" 40.00
Pokal, ruby, woodland deer, 11½", pr 475.00
Stein, bl opaline, HP florals w/gold, inlaid lid, 1840s, 6" 2,500.00
Urn, amber, nature scene, tall knob std w/eng base, 20" 1,250.00
Vase, amber, cut decor, hobnail center band, gold flowers, 10" ...230.00
Vase, cobalt/wht opal, cut/HP foliage, 19th C, 12½" 450.00
Vase, cranberry, cut floral/foliage w/gold, 8½" 400.00
Vase, gr, cut/HP florals, gilt scrolls, 13" 300.00
Vase, red, X-hatching, HP floral panels, 12" 350.00

Bookends

Though a few were produced before 1880, bookends became a necessary library accessory and a popular commodity after the printing industry was revolutionized by Mergenthaler's invention, the linotype. Books became abundantly available at such affordable prices that almost every home suddenly had need for bookends. They were carved from wood; cast in iron, bronze, or brass; or cut from stone. Chalkware and glass were used as well. Today's collectors may find such designs as ships, animals, flowers, and children. Patriotic themes, art reproductions, and those with Art Nouveau and Art Deco styling provide a basis for a diverse and interesting collection.

Currently, figural cast-iron pieces are in demand, especially examples with good original polychrome paint. This has driven the value of painted cast-iron bookends up considerably.

For further information we recommend *Collector's Guide to Bookends, Identification and Values,* by Louis Kuritzky, our advisor for this category; he is listed in the Directory under Florida. See also Arts and Crafts; Bradley and Hubbard.

Asleep at Mid-Story, man in chair, gray metal, K&O, ca 1929, 4¼" ..165.00
Atlas, chalk on polished stone base, JB Hirsch, ca 1940, 7¾" 135.00
Auld Lang Syne, Robert Burns seated, gray metal, K&O, 1926, 4¾"...110.00
Beethoven, at piano, gray metal on marble, JBH 1932, 4½" 250.00
Blacksmith, man at anvil, CI, Littco, ca 1925, 5" 175.00
Borglum's Lincoln, gray metal, Ronson, tag #14149, 1931, 4½" ...90.00
Butterfly Dancer, nude w/wings, bronze, ca 1925, 7½" 475.00
Charioteer, gray metal on polished stone, att Hirsch, 1925, 5" ...375.00
Cherub Reading, bronze clad, Morani, Armor Bronze, ca 1925, 6"..150.00
Companions, child w/dog, gray metal, WB, ca 1929, 7" 275.00
Curtseying Girl, bronze, Austria, ca 1920, 5½" 650.00
Dante's Inferno, gray metal/celluloid/stone, Hirsch, 1925, 8½" ..225.00
Egyptian Face, bronze, ca 1930, 6"...175.00
Elephant Challenge, trunk up, gray metal, Ronson, ca 1926, 6".175.00
Elephant Heads, gray metal, Jenning Bros, #1531, ca 1928, 7" ..210.00
End of Trail, mc on gray metal, Ronson, ca 1930, 6" 90.00
Facing the Lion, lion in relief, CI, Judd, ca 1928, 4½" 100.00
Fisherman w/Net, CI, Littco, ca 1928, 6¾" 125.00
Girl in Wreath (stylized nude), CI, X-1, ca 1919, 6¼" 195.00
Gleaners, mc on gray metal, K&O, ca 1925, 4½" 125.00
Guarding the Flock, dog relief, gray metal, X-1, #610, ca 1925, 5½" 195.00
Huck Finn, bronze clad w/enameling, Armor Bronze, ca 1930, 7¾" ..225.00
Indian Brave, profile in relief, CI, Judd, #9964, ca 1926, 5"........150.00
John Harvard, gray metal, mk Daniel C French, #2654, ca 1928, 7" 450.00
Knowledge, Classic lady w/books relief, metal, Pompeian Bronze, 1925.150.00

Lancelette, lady lancer, gray metal/celluloid/stone, Hirsch, 1929, 6".......**275.00**
Lincoln's Monument, bronze, WB, ca 1930, 5½" **150.00**
Minstrel Clown, gray metal on marble base, K&O, ca 1929, 5¼" ..**175.00**
Mixed Bouquet, pnt CI, Albany Advertising Co, ca 1925, 5¾" .**125.00**
Moose Revenge, scene in relief, amber glass, ca 1930, 7" **175.00**
Nouveau Dance, 2 nudes in relief, CI, #306, ca 1920, 5⅛".........**175.00**
Nude w/Mirror, kneeling, bronze clad, Pompeian Bronze, ca 1922, 6½" ..**175.00**
Outrageous, draped nude, bronze clad, Gotham Art Bronze, 1930s, 6½".**250.00**
Owl in Archway, Durez resin, Fleuron, ca 1930......................**125.00**
Parrot on book, mc on gray metal, K&O, ca 1928, 6" **125.00**
Pine Cone, bronze w/silver o/l, Heintz Art Metal, ca 1914, 5", up to...**400.00**
Pocahontas & Smith, bronze, ca 1929, 5¾"............................**175.00**
Puritan, Colonial man w/clock & musket, gray metal, ca 1924, 9¼"......**375.00**
Read to Me, woman & child, gray metal, X-1, #509, ca 1925, 5½".........**125.00**
Robin & Marian, gray metal on polished stone, JB Hirsch, ca 1924, 7" .**295.00**
Setter Dog, gray metal, Ronson, LVA 1922, 3¼".........................**125.00**
Three Graduates, gray metal, K&O, ca 1932 ....**110.00**
Trout, leaping, gray metal, ca 1934, 6½" **125.00**
Weather-Beaten Mariner, gray metal, Ronson, ca 1930, 6" **150.00**
Well of Widsom, kneeling nude, CI, Connecticut Foundry, 1929, 6" ..**250.00**

Bootjacks and Bootscrapers

Bootjacks were made from metal or wood. Some were fancy figural shapes, others strictly business! Their purpose was to facilitate the otherwise awkward process of removing one's boots. Bootscrapers were handy gadgets that provided an effective way to clean the soles of mud and such. Our advisor for this category is Louis Picek; he is listed in the Directory under Iowa.

Bootjacks

Am Bull Dog, pistol shape, CI, blk pnt, 8"......................................**75.00**
Beetle, CI, orig pnt, Reading PA, 4x11x3", EX............................**120.00**
Beetle-shaped jaws, CI, no pnt, ca 1880 ....**50.00**
Fish (stylized), cvd wood, worn finish, 22" L................................**135.00**
Heart figural, scalloped sides, CI, 13" L.......................................**225.00**
Lever action, wood & CI, EX **150.00**
Naughty Nellie, CI, EX pnt, no rust, 11x5x2½", EX...................**375.00**
Naughty Nellie, CI, worn mc w/gold, pnt losses, 19th C, 11½"...**250.00**
Openwork between hexagonal supports, CI w/blk pnt, 6" L..........**65.00**
Pine w/sq nails, lg, early **80.00**
Try Me, CI, openwork, ca 1890s, 12x4x1¾" **100.00**

Bootscrapers

Mammy with hands on hips stands above wire brushes, cast iron with original paint, 15x16x9", VG, $425.00.

Baroque scrollwork, CI, set in marble block, 14" **95.00**
Black shoe-shine boy atop, CI, oval base, 13", VG......................**140.00**
CI, base pushes into ground, Holcraft & Sons label, 19"...............**60.00**

Dachshund, CI, EX pnt, full bodied, 21" L, EX..........................**330.00**
Dachshund, rpt CI, 21½" **120.00**
Duck, full body, CI, 14½" L **350.00**
Griffins, CI, EX cast detail, oval dish base, 10x14x9½" **220.00**
Lyre on oval scalloped base, CI, 9x11" **125.00**
Ornate scroll finial, wrought iron, 21x24"..................................**500.00**
Pig silhouette, cut-out eye, CI, 8½x12"......................................**215.00**
Quails (2) ea end, rectangular pan, CI w/pnt traces, 7x16".........**295.00**
Ribbon curls on atop ea end, wrought iron, 7x7", EX..................**40.00**
Scottie dog, CI, orig pnt, EX..**65.00**
Sq bars on lg scrolls, CI, rprs, 11x7⅜".......................................**150.00**
Wall type w/twisting support braces, wrought iron, 18th C, 12x10"..**230.00**

Borsato, Antonio

Borsato was a remarkable artist/sculptor who produced some of the most intricately modeled and executed figurines ever made. He was born in Italy and at an early age enjoyed modeling wildlife from clay he dug from the river banks near his home. At age eleven, he became an apprentice of Guido Cacciapuotti of Milan, who helped him develop his skills. During the late '20s and '30s, he continued to concentrate on wildlife studies. Because of his resistance to the fascist government, he was interred at Sardinia from 1940 until the end of the war, after which he returned to Milan where he focused his attention on religious subjects. He entered the export market in 1948 and began to design pieces featuring children and more romantic themes. By the 1960s his work had become very popular in this country. His talent for creating lifelike figures has seldom been rivaled. He contributed much of his success to the fact that each of his figures, though built from the same molded pieces, had its own personality, due the unique way he would tilt a head or position an arm. All had eyelashes, fingernails, and defined musculature; and each piece was painted by hand with antiquated colors and signed 'A. Borsato.' He made over six hundred different models, with some of his groups requiring more than one hundred and sixty components and several months of work to reach completion.

Borsato died in 1982. Today, some of his work is displayed in the Vatican Museum as well private collections.

Prices vary according to size and the amount of work involved. Single figures often fetch $1,000.00. Larger pieces, for instance, 'Gypsy Camp' or 'Revelry,' may go from $12,000.00 to as high as $15,000.00. 'Play Gypsy Play' was originally made in the early '30s; a second version followed in the late '40s, and a limited edition was created to mark the 30th anniversary of the date he began his work. Though he planned to make thirty of these limited edition groupings, he died after only thirteen had been completed. This version was larger than the first two and has sold on the secondary market for more than $50,000.00. Various pieces were made in two mediums, gres and porcelain, with porcelain being double the cost of gres. In the listings that follow, our suggested values should be regarded as conservative.

Our advisor for this category is Elizabeth Langtree, she is listed in the Directory under California.

Caner, The; man caning chairs w/supplies **1,900.00**
Christ's Resurrection, 13th Station of the Cross, 7 figures, 19" ..**5,000.00**
Excursion, 4 figures in early open-air auto, 12x18x8", from $4,000 to **4,500.00**
Farmer toting wood on bk w/goat, 8½x11½"..................................**1,200.00**
Fisherman catching a fish w/fish in creel, 6¼x8¼" **900.00**
Grandparents, Grandma doing needlework, Grandpa smoking pipe, 8".**1,100.00**
Man & woman on bench w/dog, 5⅜x7⅝".....................................**1,200.00**
Mother w/child (naked) on bk, tree trunk w/flower on base, 9" ..**1,100.00**
Play Gypsy Play, #1274, 17¼x18", minimum value **50,000.00**
Siesta's Price, fruit card, peddlar asleep while cash drw is robbed....**2,700.00**
Sylvan Beauty, lady w/flowers..**1,100.00**

Bossons Artware

Bossons closed operations December 1996. The company (located in England) was founded by the late William Henry Bossons in 1944; his son W. Ray Bossons (now deceased) was manager from 1951 until he retired in 1994. It was always owned and managed by the Bossons family, who have stored the only remaining molds (many have been destroyed) and at the present time have no intention of selling them or the Bossons name.

With the company's closing, all Bossons are now categorized as discontinued; as stock holdings are depleted, some are appreciating at a very fast rate. Many that sold in the US for under $5.00 are now in the range of $100.00 to $300.00. Bossons were exported to nearly forty countries around the globe with Canada and the U.S. being the most important importers, and as a result, collector interest is widespread. In the past few years added interest has been given to the wide variety of Bossons subjects including wildlife, wall figures, birds of prey figures, high-relief floral and scenic plaques (from 4" to 14"), and The Cats of Character and Dogs of Distinction.

Major points to remember:

1) Not all will have the name incised under the collar (e.g., Syrian, Smuggler, Tibetan, and Tyrolean, see *Schroeder's* 17th Ed. for pictures).

2) Many character studies in gypsum plaster are produced in England that are not Bossons; to be specific, Legends, Naturecraft, and those incised 'Made in England.' Fraser-Art products are Bossons, so are products marked Briar Rose and Bossons Ivorex. Osborne Ivorex is not Bossons. For pictures and technical details about plaster faces that are *not* Bossons, typical trademarks, Bossons Ivorex and Bossons Briar Rose Products, link on the net directly to this URL: www.donsbossons.com/page2.html.

3) Except in very rare cases, all carry the incised copyright: Bossons, Congleton, England, World copyright reserved' on the back *and* in most cases under the collars, along with that particular Bossons' specific name. The Fraser-Art Division (named for Mrs. Ruth Fraser Bossons) is becoming one of the most popular areas of collecting for experienced and avid Bossons collectors for these reasons, termed by Bossons to be 'five-star wall ornaments:' 1) exhibition, quality models, 2) bold designs for effect, 3) fine detail to add interest, 4) shockproof and lightweight (made of hard PVC/Stonite® substance, 5) colorfully hand-painted as are all Bossons (see photo). **Important:** The copyright date is a mold release date; each Beefeater, for example, will carry the date 1966. This is not the date of manufacture, so it has no bearing on value.

Though they can be used for authentication, a signature is not a critical consideration when determining value; most are the initials of painters, e.g., PB is Phyllis Brightwell. FW (Fred Wright), AB (Alice Brindley), and WRB (W. Ray Bossons) are sculptor/modelers. Mold makers' marks include K (Ken Potts), P (George Proudlove), and D (Damen Smith). In extremely rare instances where the Bossons copyright does not appear, it is sometimes possible to make positive identification using these initials.

Suggestions for evaluating Bossons based on rarity and condition:

A. Determine the copyright (release) date from under the collar or on the back.

B. Length of production helps determine rarity; with few exceptions, the earlier (1958 – 63) and latest (1986 – 98) are found in fewer numbers. This information can be found in *Imagical World of Bossons*, Vol. 1, 1946 – 82, and Vol. II, 1982 – 94, by Dr. Robert E. Davis. (See advisor's Directory listing for information on this publication.) Examples in rare color combinations may be valued at 200% to 300% of retail as indicated in the line listings that follow.

C. Condition is a major factor. If mint and in original colors, a Bossons is worth 100% of its retail value. Premium prices are obtained for only pristine, mint condition Bossons, either factory mint in original boxes or perfectly returned to their original structural and coloring beauty by a professional restoration artist recommended by Bossons. For restoration and purchasing questions answered by our advisor, Don Hardisty, link on the 'net to: www.donsbossons.com/page3/html. For the 'Do's and Don'ts of Bossons Repairing,' link directly to www/donsbossons.com/restoration2/html.

Beware of fakes and look-alikes; above all, know your dealer. Be aware that Internet auctions are flooded with plaster 'faces' and figures claiming to be Bossons in mint condition which are neither mint nor Bossons.

See Clubs, Newsletters, and Catalogs in the Directory for information about *Bossons Briefs*, the quarterly magazine of the International Bossons Collector' Society (IBCS). Our advisor for this category is Dr. Don Hardisty; since 1984 he has been recommended by Bossons to restore their products. He is listed in the Directory under New Mexico. Visit his website for more information.

Fraser-Art Stag's Head, Fraser-Art sticker (otherwise unmarked), ca 1970 – 72, 13", M, $1,000.00 at auction. (Photo courtesy Dr. Don Hardisty)

Abduhl, 1961-86, widely available today, M, minimum value.......**55.00**
Aruja Barbarossa, 1994-96 (2-yr production), MIB, from $145 to.**250.00**
Espana (male & female), very desirable, poor condition **600.00**
Espana (male & female), very desirable, prof rstr, minimum value ..**6,000.00**
Examples originally valued at $5, many models, from $100 to....**300.00**
Examples released ca 1959, rare, from $500 to **1,000.00**
Examples released ca 1959, very rare (few examples), minimum value ...**10,000.00**
Punjabi, gr hat (standard color), from $65 to..............................**100.00**
Punjabi, yel hat (rare), from $200 to **300.00**
Snake Charmer, 1959-64 (once $700-900), EX, now from $300 to ..**500.00**

Bottle Openers

At the beginning of the nineteenth century, manufacturers began to seal bottles with a metal cap that required a new type of bottle opener. Now the screw cap and the flip top have made bottle openers nearly obsolete. There are many variations, some in combination with other tools. Many openers were used as means of advertising a product. Various materials were used, including silver and brass.

A figural bottle opener is defined as a figure designed for the sole purpose of lifting a bottle cap. The actual opener must be an integral part of the figure itself. A base-plate opener is one where the lifter is a separate metal piece attached to the underside of the figure. The major producers of iron figurals were Wilton Products, John Wright Inc., Gadzik Sales, and L & L Favors. Openers may be free-standing and three-dimensional, wall hung or flat. They can be made of cast iron (often painted), brass, bronze, or aluminum.

Numbers within the listings refer to a reference book printed by the FBOC (Figural Bottle Opener Collectors) organization. Those seeking additional information are encouraged to contact FBOC, whose address can be found in the Directory under Clubs, Newsletters, and Catalogs. The items below are all in excellent original condition unless noted otherwise.

Alligator, CI, no pnt, curved tail, F-136c, 1¼x6⅛" 30.00
Alligator & boy, CI, Wilton, F-134 ....125.00
Bar Bum, no tools, aluminum alloy, no pnt, F-190a, 6¾" 45.00
Bear head, brass, Wright, F-426, 3¾" 130.00
Bulldog head, CI, wall mt, F-425, 4", NM 75.00
Canada goose, CI, Wilton, F-105...................................85.00
Clown head, brass, wall mt, Wright, F-417a, 4⅛x3⅝" 60.00
Cowboy w/guitar, aluminum, F-27a 15.00
Dachshund, brass, F-83..40.00
Donkey, brass, F-60b, 3½x3¼" 45.00
Drunk at lamppost, CI, EX pnt, Wright, F-1, 4⅛" 15.00
Drunk at lamppost, CI, mk Germantown OH 1804-1954, F-1, mtd on tray ..25.00
Drunk at lamppost, CI, Wilton, F-2, 4⅛"..........................12.00
Drunk at sign post, CI, mk Youngstown OH, F-11, mtd on tray ...20.00
Drunk in high hat at sign post, CI, Wright, 4¼" 12.00
Elephant, CI, pk, Wright, F-49, 3" 50.00
Elephant, CI, Wilton, F-48, 3½" 25.00
Foundry man, F-29, brass, 3⅛" 15.00
Four-eyed lady, CI, wall mt, Wright, F-407, 4x3¾" 130.00
Four-eyed man, CI, wall mt, Wright, F-413........................40.00
Hanging drunk, CI, wall mt, Wilton, F-415, 5x3½" 70.00
Hockey skate, pot metal 50.00
Horse's rear end, pot metal, base plate opener...................45.00
Indian boy, Iroquois Beverages, pnt aluminum, F-197 ....55.00

Laughing man's face, brass with some soiling and tarnish, F-403a, 4¼x3¾", $35.00.

Lobster, CI, Wilton, F-167, 1¼x3⅜" 35.00
Mr Dry, CI, wall mt, Wilton, F-416, 5½x3½" 85.00
Negro, aluminum, no pnt, F-402a...................................60.00
Negro, brass, smooth eye pupils, Wilton, 4¼" 45.00
Negro, chrome, smooth eye pupils, F-402b, 4¼"....................70.00
Negro, CI, pupils indented, wall mt, Wilton, F-402, 4⅛"..........75.00
Old Snifter, brass, w/corkscrew, F-198 ....80.00
Parrot, brass, Riverside, F-112a, 3"..............................40.00
Parrot, CI, orig mc pnt, John Wright, F-111, 3¼" 110.00
Parrot, CI, Wilton, F-112, sm, 3" 45.00
Parrot w/box, chrome, Negbauer USA, F-116a, 5⅛x2½"...............30.00
Pretzel, aluminum, EX pnt, F-230 ....70.00
Sea gull, Ci, EX pnt, Wright, F-123...............................45.00
Setter dog, CI, Wright, F-79, 2½", mtd on tray 80.00

Squirrel, brass, F-93, 2⅝x1⅝" 20.00
Squirrel, NP CI, Norlin Enterprises, F-91d, 1¾x3" 50.00

Bottles and Flasks

As far back as the first century B.C., the Romans preferred blown glass containers for their pills and potions. Though you're not apt to find many of those, you will find bottles of every size, shape, and color made to hold perfume, ink, medicine, soda, spirits, vinegar, and many other liquids. American business firms preferred glass bottles in which to package their commercial products and used them extensively from the late eighteenth century on. Bitters bottles contained 'medicine' (actually herb-flavored alcohol), and judging from the number of these found today, their contents found favor with many! Because of a heavy tax imposed on the sale of liquor in seventeenth-century England by King George, who hoped to curtail alcohol abuse among his subjects, bottlers simply added 'curative' herbs to their brew and thus avoided taxation. Since gin was taxed in America as well, the practice continued in this country. Scores of brands were sold; among the most popular were Dr. H.S. Flint & Co. Quaker Bitters, Dr. Kaufman's Anti-Cholera Bitters, and Dr. J. Hostetter's Stomach Bitters. Most bitters bottles were made in shades of amber, brown, and aquamarine. Clear glass was used to a lesser extent, as were green tones. Blue, amethyst, red-brown, and milk glass examples are rare. (Please note that color is a strong factor when pricing bottles. For example, an amber Hostetter's bitters sells for $25.00 or less, but a green variant can bring hundreds of dollars. An aqua scroll flask may bring $50.00, but a cobalt blue variation will command over $1,000.00.)

Perfume or scent bottles were produced abroad by companies all over Europe from the late sixteenth century on. Perfume making became such a prolific trade that as a result beautifully decorated bottles were fashionable. In America they were produced in great quantities by Stiegel in 1770 and by Boston and Sandwich in the early nineteenth century. Cologne bottles were first made in about 1830 and toilet-water bottles in the 1880s. Rene Lalique produced fine scent bottles from as early as the turn of the century. The first were one-of-a-kind creations done in the cire perdue method. He later designed bottles for the Coty Perfume Company with a different style for each Coty fragrance.

Spirit flasks from the nineteenth century were blown in specially designed molds with varied motifs including political subjects, railroad trains, and symbolic devices. The most commonly used colors were amber, dark brown, and green.

From the twentieth century, early pop and beer bottles are very collectible as is nearly every extinct commercial container. Dairy bottles are a relatively new area of interest; look for round bottles in good condition with both city and state as well as a nice graphic relating to the farm or the dairy.

Bottles may be dated by the methods used in their production. For instance, a rough pontil indicates a date before 1845. After the bottle was blown, a pontil rod was attached to the bottom with a glob of molten glass acting as the 'glue.' This allowed the glassblower to continue to manipulate the extremely hot bottle until it was finished. From about 1845 until approximately 1860, the molten glass 'glue' was omitted. The rod was simply heated to a temperature high enough to cause it to afix itself to the bottle. When the rod was snapped off, a metallic residue was left on the base of the bottle; this is called an 'iron pontil.' (The presence of a pontil scar thus indicates early manufacture and increases the value of a bottle.) A seam that reaches from base to lip marks a machine-made bottle from after 1903, while an applied or hand-finished lip points to an early mold-blown bottle. The Industrial Revolution saw keen competition between manufacturers, and as a result, scores of patents were issued. Many concentrated on various types of closures; the crown bottle cap, for instance, was patented in 1892. If a manufacturer's name is present, consulting a book on marks may help you date your bottle. For more information we recommend *Bottle Pricing Guide, 3rd Edition*, by Hugh Cleveland.

Among our advisors for this category are Madeleine France (see the Directory under Florida), Mark Vuono (Connecticut), Steve Ketcham (Minnesota), Monsen and Baer (Virginia), and John Shaw (Florida/Maine). In the listings that follow (most of which have been taken from auction catalogs), glass is assumed to be clear unless color is indicated. Numbers refer to a standard reference book, *American Glass*, by George and Helen McKearin. See also Advertising, various companies; Avon; Barber Shop Collectibles; Blown Glass; Blown Three-Mold Glass; California Perfume Company; Czechoslovakia; De Vilbiss; Fire Fighting; Lalique; Medical Collectibles; Sandwich Glass; Steuben; Zanesville Glass.

Key:
am — applied mouth	grd — ground pontil
bbl — barrel	GW — Glass Works
bt — blob top	ip — iron pontil
b3m — blown 3-mold	ps — pontil scar
cm — collared mouth	rm — rolled mouth
fl — filigree	sb — smooth base
fm — flared mouth	sl — sloping
gm — ground mouth	sm — sheared mouth
gp — graphite pontil	tm — tooled mouth

Barber Bottles

Amethyst, corset waist, emb ribs, wht enamel, ps, 7¾" 100.00
Amethyst, mallet form w/mc enamel, ps, tm, 1885-1925, 8".......150.00
Amethyst, ribbed bell form w/mc stag scene in wht reserve, ps, 7⅞" ..375.00
Brilliantine, cobalt w/2 sets of indented panels, sb, tm, 3⅛".......375.00
Brilliantine, dk amethyst, emb ribs w/wht & gold decor, 3" 325.00
Brilliantine, milk glass w/mc geometrics, sb, ps, 4½" 425.00
Clear w/heavy mc floral & overall pk to lav ground, ps, tm, 8" ..825.00
Cobalt frost w/emb ribs, heavy mc roses, sb, tm, 8⅛" 500.00
Cobalt w/emb ribs, mc florals, ps, tm, 7⅝".................................325.00
Cobalt w/emb ribs, waisted, mc florals, ps, rm, 7⅝" 250.00
Cobalt w/emb ribs & allover elaborate florals, ps, tm, 7¼" 925.00
Cobalt w/emb ribs & mc floral spray, bell form, ps, tm, 7⅞" 210.00
Cranberry w/emb ribs, bl & wht florals, ps, tm, 7¼" 500.00
Gr fiery opal w/mc boy & girl, ps, rm, 8½" 500.00
Gr opaque w/mc cottage scene, sb, 1890-1925, 7¼" 255.00
Gr-aqua frost w/emb ribs & mc floral, ps, tm, 7⅞" 375.00
Grape amethyst w/ribs & mc stag in oval fr, bell form, ps, tm, 8" ..650.00
Hobnail, cranberry opal, tm, 8" 150.00
Hobnail, orange-amber, sb, tm, 7"...65.00
Mary Gregory, cobalt, girl, emb ribs, ps, tm, 7" 300.00
Mary Gregory, med yel-gr, boy, ps, tm, 8" 220.00
Milk glass, Bay Rum, mc horseshoe & floral, sb, rm, 9⅛" 200.00
Milk glass, Bay Rum, mc roses, August Kern..., sb, rm, 9", EX 135.00
Milk glass cased in pk satin, emb dmns, sb, 7⅛", NM 475.00
Milk glass w/cherubs on bl & yel, ps, tm, 7¾" 450.00
Milk glass w/mc floral, sb, tm, orig chrome spout, 7" 110.00
Milk glass w/mc floral, Toilet Water, sb, rm, 7" 400.00
Pk opaque w/mc floral, flared neck, 1890-1930, 7⅝".................220.00
Purple amethyst w/emb ribs, mc floral, bell form, ps, 8" 425.00
Ruby-stain shoulder w/etched Sea Foam, sb, tm, 6¾" 275.00
Teal gr, ribbed w/wht enameling, corset waist, ps, tm, 7" 200.00
Teal gr frost w/emb ribs, wht & gold strawberries, ps, tm, 7⅞"...375.00
Thumbprint, lt to med cobalt w/orange & wht enamel, ps, rm, 8" ..110.00
Turq bl w/wht loopings, polished p, fm, 7⅜".............................140.00
Venetian, 4-color bands, thin fishnet pattern, 8⅝" 350.00
Wht fiery opal, Hair Oil, mc sailboats on water, ps, rm, 9" 575.00
Wht opal, Bay Rum, mc tulips, sb, am, 8⅝" 375.00

Wht opal, Sea Foam & mc clovers, ps, am, 8¾" 220.00
Wht opal, Witch Hazel, sparrow & mc floral, 9¼" 325.00
Wht opal, Witch Hazel & mc tulips, sb, am, 8⅝" 450.00
Yel-gr w/emb ribs, wht & gold decor, ps, sm, 6¾", NM 90.00

Bitters Bottles

Hall's Bitters – E.E. Hall New Haven..., medium amber barrel, smooth base, 9⅛", $180.00; **Holtzermann's Patent Stomach Bitters**, medium amber four-roof log cabin, smooth base, original label, 9⅞", $275.00.

Atwood's Jaundice...Georgetown MA, dk bl-aqua, 12-sided, ps, 6⅛" ...180.00
Atwood's Jaundice...Gerogetown MA, dk bl-aqua, 12-sided, sb, 6⅛" 20.00
Baker's Orange Grove, med topaz-puce, sb, sl cm, flake, 9¼" 825.00
Big Bill Best, med amber, sb, tm, EX labels/contents, 12⅛" 120.00
Brown's Celebrated Indian Herb...1866, golden-amber, queen, 12¼" ..325.00
Brown's Celebrated Indian Herb...1867, amber, queen, 12⅜" 675.00
Brown's Celebrated Indian Herb...1867, chocolate-amber, queen, 12" ...800.00
Brown's Celebrated Indian Herb...1868, med to yel amber, queen, 12" ..750.00
California Herb...GW Frazier, med amber, sb, cm, 9⅜", NM 2,000.00
Canton (star) Bitters, med amber, sb, lady's leg, 12⅛" 400.00
Damiana...Manuf'r Lewis Hess, deep aqua, sb, sl dbl cm, 11½" 95.00
David Andrews Vegetable...Providence RI, aqua tombstone, ps, 8¼" .1,500.00
Dimmitt's 50 Cts...Saint Louis, yel-amber, strap sided, sb, 6½"...600.00
Doyle's Hop...1872 (berries & leaves), yel-amber, semi-cabin, 10"...275.00
Dr AS Hopkin's Union Stomach, golden yel-amber, sb, cm, 9¾", NM...65.00
Dr Bell's Liver/Kidney (emb 2 sides), aqua, sb, sl cm, flake, 9"......85.00
Dr Blake's Aromatic...NY, bl-aqua, ps, sl cm, 7", NM 160.00
DR CD Warner's German...1880 Reading MI, amber, semi-cabin, 9¾"...100.00
Dr CW Roback's...Cincinnati O, amber bbl, red ip, cm, 9⅞", NM..350.00
Dr J Hostetter's Stomach, amber, sb, 8¾"..................................20.00
Dr J Hostetter's Stomach, dk olive amber, sb, bubbles, 9¼" 300.00
Dr J Hostetter's Stomach, golden yel w/olive tone, sb, 8¾" 575.00
Dr J Hostetter's Stomach, yel w/olive tone, sb, sl cm, EX labels, 9"...850.00
Dr Soule's Hop...1872, med copper topaz, sb, semi-cabin, 7¾" ...375.00
Dr Soule's Hop...1872 (berries/leaves), gasoline puce, semi-cabin, 10"..160.00
Eagle Angostura Aromatic, amber, sb, tm, lt haze, 3⅝" 175.00
Frisco Hop...Co, aqua, semi-cabin, scratches, 9¼"......................210.00
Greeley's Bourbon, dk smoky puce, sb, bbl, 9¼" 700.00
Greeley's Bourbon, smoky copper puce, sb, bbl, 9⅜"...............1,200.00
Greeley's Bourbon Whiskey..., med smoky pk puce, bbl, 9½"..1,200.00
Hartwig Kantorowicz, red-amber, squat onion form, sb w/kick-up, 7¾"....200.00
Hercules...1 Quart, dk gr, sb, tm, orig label, crude, 7⅜".........1,200.00
Hertrichs Gesundheits...Geschutzt, lt to med yel-olive gr, sb, 12"...700.00
Hertrichs...Einzigerfabrikant...Geschutzt, med olive gr, sb, 9⅜"..400.00
Jno Moffat...NY Price 1$, dk tobacco amber (near blk), ps, rm, 5½" .1,000.00
Jones Universal Stomach...Penn, med amber, sb, sl cm, 9¼" 375.00
Kimball's Jaundice... Troy NH, med yel-amber w/olive tone, ip, 7", NM..1,000.00
Moulton's Oloroso...Trade Mark, dk bl-aqua, sl dbl cm, 11¼" 300.00
St Drake's 1860 Plant'n X Pat 1862, cherry puce, 6-log, 10".......100.00
St Drake's 1860 Plant'n X Pat 1862, yel-celery, cabin, 10", NM.900.00
St Drake's 1860 Plant'n X Pat 1862, yel-olive, 4-log, 10" 1,200.00
The Fish...WH Ware Pat 1866, dk amber, fish, sb, am, label, 11⅝"...275.00

William Allen's Congress Bitters, yel-amber semi-cabin, label, 10" .1,200.00
XXX E Dexter Loveridge...1863, med amber, semi-cabin, 10¼" .800.00

Black Glass Bottles

Many early European and American bottles are deep, dark green or amber in color. Collectors refer to such coloring as black glass. Before held to light, the glass is so dark it appears to be black.

Kidney, dk olive gr w/amber tone, ps, am, 6¾", NM 700.00
Mallet, olive gr, ps, appl sq string lip, English, 1760-80, 8" 160.00
Mallet, olive-amber, ps, deep kick-up, appl string lip, 1750s, 8⅝" ..160.00
Onion, dk bl-gr, ps, appl string lip (prof rpr), 6⅜x4" 1,500.00
Onion, dk olive gr, ps, appl string lip, chip, 6¼x5⅜" 300.00
Onion, olive gr, ps, appl string lip, crack, 1720-30, 6x5" base.....300.00
Seal: Class of 1846 W, olive-gr w/amber tone, Dyottville GW Phila, 11"....375.00
Seal: Eman Coll, dk olive gr, ps, pointed kick-up, dbl cm, 11½" ..80.00
Seal: fox beneath baron's coronet, olive-gr, ½-sz onion, 5⅛" ..2,100.00
Seal: I Smith 1706, olive-amber onion, ps, am, stain, 6⅝" 7,000.00
Seal: Jas Oakes Bury 1793, olive gr, ps, am, spider, 10" 625.00
Seal: John Wills 1818, dk olive-amber, ps, am, 9⅝" 525.00
Seal: Redges & Butler, dk tobacco-amber, ps, am, b3m, 8½" 230.00

Blown Glass Bottles and Flasks

Chestnut flask, dk violet-bl, 16 broken-swirl ribs, 4½", EX.........500.00
Chestnut flask, med olive gr, ps, rm, bubbles, 5⅜" 240.00
Chestnut flask, med olive gr w/amber tone, ps, am, 1780-1820, 8¾" ...275.00
Chestnut flask, med orange-amber, 24 vertical ribs, ps, tm, 5" 275.00
Chestnut flask, med yel-olive, ps, am, bubbles, 1780-1820, 10¾" 375.00
Chestnut flask, olive gr, ps, am, seed bubbles/swirls, 6⅜" 325.00
Chestnut flask, yel w/olive tone, ps, am, 1780-1810, 5⅞" 275.00
Chestnut flask, 16 broken-swirl ribs, att Mantua OH, 5⅛" 360.00
Globular, yel-olive, ps, appl string lip, 1780-1820, 10¼" 550.00
Ludlow, gr, many bubbles, a/m, 5½", pr 330.00
Ludlow, olive-amber, am, minor wear, 8½" 220.00
Pitkin flask, med olive gr, 36 broken left-swirl ribs, ps, 4⅞" 400.00
Pitkin flask, med olive gr, 36 left-swirl ribs, ps, tm, 5½" 875.00
Saddle flask, olive amber, flattened sides, ps, sm, 9¼", NM 140.00

Cologne, Perfume, and Toilet Water Bottles

Sandwich-type cologne, bright orange-amber, octagonal, tooled lip, original stopper, ca 1860 – 80, 3⅝", $375.00.

Blk glass & gold-etch flowers, long dauber, Pyramid label, 6¼" ..300.00
Bsk, Mannekin-Pis of Brussels, crown stopper, #2710, Germany, 5" ..350.00
Ceramic, cat w/violin, gr & yel, crown top, Germany, #417, 2½" 165.00
Ceramic, dog w/googly eyes, metal crown stopper, #15295, Germany ...100.00
Ceramic, flapper baby, mc, metal crown stopper, Germany, 3½" ...135.00
Ceramic, Pierrot w/roses, metal crown stopper, Germany, #24627, 4" ...325.00
Clear, monument, ps, rm, rare, 1845-55, mini, 2⅝" 325.00
Clear, violin form, emb crown/hearts/fleur-de-lis, ps, 3" 150.00
Clear, 12-sided, sb, am, 1850-70, mini, 2⅜"....................................350.00
Cobalt, monument (tapered/4 sided), rm, crude, 8⅛" 450.00
Cobalt, right-swirl ribs, ps, tm, Am, 1845-55, 3" 160.00
Cobalt cut to clear, Sandwich type, am, 1850-70, 8⅞" 475.00
Cobalt w/HP florals, bullet form, sb, metal threads, 2¼" 80.00
Dk cobalt, sunburst, ps, tm, 1845-65, 3¼" 3,100.00
Dk purple-amethyst, 12-sided, sl shoulders, ps, 1855-75, 4¾" 160.00
Dk sapphire bl, emb florals/lattice, shouldered, waisted, ftd, 5⅝" ...1,550.00
Dk teal gr, vertical ribs, ps, tm, Am, 1845-65, 3" 140.00
Lt ice bl, herringbone corners, sb, rm, Am, 1855-70, 6¼" 500.00
Med pk amethyst, sunburst, ps, tm, lt haze, 1850-70, 2⅞" 975.00
Milk glass, 8-sided, sb, rm, EX label, Am, 1855-75, 4¼" 150.00
Peacock bl, 8-sided, corset waist, st, rm, Am, 1865-75, 4¾" 675.00
Pk amethyst, 12-sided, sl shoulders, st, tm, Am, 1865-75, 6⅛" ...140.00
Purple amethyst, 8-sided, waisted, sb, 4½" 375.00

Commercial Perfume Bottles

One of the most popular and growing areas of perfume bottle collecting is what are called 'commercial' perfume bottles. They are called commercial because they were sold with perfume in them — in a sense one pays for the perfume and the bottle is free. Collectors especially value bottles that retain their original label and box, called a perfume presentation. If the bottle is unopened, so much the better. Rare fragrances and those from the 1920s are highly prized. 'Tis a sweet, sweet hobby. Our advisors are Randy Monsen and Rod Baer; they are listed in the Directory under Virginia.

Bourjois, Evening in Paris, cobalt w/frosted stopper, label, 4", +box ...225.00
Bourjois, Kobako, emb leaves, metallic label, 3½", +box 355.00
Bryenne, Chu Chin Chow, fat Oriental man w/fan, mc enamel, 2½" ..2,300.00
Caron, Le Tabac Blond, gold flower label, full/sealed, 3½", MIB...150.00
Ciro, Chevalier de Nuit, blk stylized knight, 4½", +box 450.00
Corday, Jet Parfume, clear/frosted fountain, rare, 5¾"..............2,300.00
Corday, Toujours Moi, emb vegetal decor, brn patina, 3", +brn box ...155.00
Coty, Meteor, clear flask w/blk label, 1¾", + plastic case 100.00
D'Orsay, Intoxication, pleated w/gold label at neck, empty, 5", MIB....175.00
Forest, Ming Toy, Oriental lady w/fan, mc on clear, Baccarat, 4½" ...2,750.00
Fragonard, Belle de Nuit, clear w/gold cap, M label, full, 2", MIB 150.00
G Monteil, Laughter, gold label, clear/frosted top, 2¾", +box 100.00
Guerlain, Coque d'Or, cobalt/gold bow tie form, Baccarat #770, 3" ..465.00
Guerlain, Parure, clear w/gr plastic lid, full, 1957, 1⅛" 225.00
Guerlain, Shalimar, mk Baccarat, M, unopened in 7½x5" box...330.00
Hattie Carnegie, Perfume No 7, lady's head & shoulders, 3½", MIB ..935.00
Helen of Troy, Pour la Brunette, blk w/silver label, 3¼", +half box 225.00
Houbigant, La Rose, clear w/gold label, Baccarat #29, 4", +box .385.00
Houbigant, Presence, intersecting pleats, 1930s, 4", +gr box 150.00
Houbigant, Subtilite, clear Buddha, brass ring, Baccarat, 3½", +box ...500.00
Isabey, Jasmin, pearlized enamel stopper, 2½", +old box 225.00
Jean Patou, Caline, clear w/gold cap, gold enamel, 2¼", +wht box ..45.00
L Lelong, Jabot, frosted jabot shape w/lg bow overcap, 3" 385.00
L Lelong, Parfume, sq w/protrusions, logo top, 3½", +box 715.00
L Lelong, Taglio, clear w/emb medallion, empty, 1½", +Lucite box 135.00
Lentheric, Tweed, gold metal compact, wht cameo on gr, 1¾", MIB......65.00
M Rochas, Femme, bl opaque w/blk lace, dauber, empty, 2½", +purse .125.00
Matchabelli, Wind Song, gold/gr enamel crown, 1½", MIB........125.00
N Ricci, L'Air du Temps, clear w/emb swirls, gold cap, Lalique, MIB....400.00

Renaud, Sweet Pea Ambre, gr opaque w/gold labels, empty, 4", +box...**320.00**
Roger et Gallet, Le Jade, bird on branches, RL France, 3".......**2,185.00**
Rose Valois, Aigrette, clear w/wht head-like cap, 2¼", +case.....**250.00**
Schiaparelli, Zut, lady's torso, clear/frosted, unopened, 5½".......**715.00**
Schiaparelli, Zut, lady's torso in wave base, clear w/gold/gr, 4¾" ...**300.00**
Suzy, Ecarlate de Suzy, clear w/red enamel, ⅛-oz, 2", MIB **450.00**
Woodworth, Viegay, frosted fishscales, red stopper, 3¼", +box ...**500.00**

Dairy Bottles

Alta Crest Farms, Spencer MA, bl pyro, 10-oz...............................**42.50**
Beacon Light Dairy, wht pyro, sq qt..**8.00**
Beltz Dairy, Palmerton PA, red pyro, tall rnd qt.............................**35.00**
Booth Bros Modern Dairy, Barre VT, orange pyro, qt.....................**10.00**
Candlelight Goat Dairy, New Milford CT, gr pyro, tall rnd qt....**125.00**
Cloverleaf Blue Ribbon Farms...CA, red pyro, cream top, qt **22.50**
DA Delano, Norway ME, emb, tall rnd qt **105.00**
Dairimaid, orange pyro, squat, ½-pt **10.00**
Dias Dairy, So Dartmouth MA, brn pyro, tall rnd qt **45.00**
Essex Junction VT, wht pyro on amber, qt **10.00**
Florida Dairy, wht pyro, sq qt..**12.00**
Footman's Dairy, Brewer ME, orange pyro, sq qt............................**10.00**
Gamage All Jersey Farms Augusta ME, orange & red pyro, sq qt..**18.00**
Gossholme Farms...VT, orange pyro, sq qt......................................**10.00**
Hillside Dairy, Salisbury MA, red pyro, sq qt **14.00**
Kenwood Farms, Burlington VT, orange pyro, sq qt........................**10.00**
Kribel's Dairy, Hereford PA, red pyro, sq qt...................................**14.00**
Marble Farms Dairy, yel pyro on amber, sq qt.................................**10.00**
Pine Ridge Dairy, Leesburg FL, red pyro, tall rnd qt **110.00**
Sawyer's Dairy, orange pyro, sq qt...**20.00**
Silver Springs Farms, Drums PA, orange pyro, sq qt **17.00**
Smith's Dairy Farm, Crystal River FL, gr pyro, sq qt......................**10.00**
Snyder's Jersey Dairy, WI, red pyro, tall rnd qt..............................**40.00**
Sunlight Dairy, Upper Peninsula...MI, red pyro, sq qt **12.00**
Sunshine Milk, Bridgeport CT, orange pyro, rnd qt.......................**28.00**

Figural Bottles

Atterbury Duck, milk glass, sb, gm, 1871-85, 11⅝" **230.00**
Barrel, milk glass, sb, tm, emb staves, oval label panel, 11".........**275.00**
Bear, blk amethyst, appl face, tm, 11¼" **375.00**

Bear, Distrie Mercator Sa/Anvers Belcique/Depose (on reverse), clear with smooth base, tooled mouth, French, ca 1900, 9⅞", $170.00; Lady in flowing dress, medium green, Depose (reverse), pontil scar, rolled mouth, ca 1900, 13⅛", $600.00.

Bear, dk bl-aqua, appl face, sb, tm, ANT 1890 on side of base, 8⅛" ...**550.00**
Bear, dk bl-aqua, appl face, sb, tm, 10⅜"......................................**325.00**
Bunker Hill monument, milk glass, sb, rm, 1865-80, 12" **200.00**
Bust of crying baby, PS&Co NY on sb, tm, flake, 6"......................**55.00**
Cannon, dk amber w/overall outside frost, sb, tm, bubbles, 9⅝".**375.00**

Cat, frosted clear, emb Depose on side at sb, 1⅞"......................**160.00**
Chinaman, Billiken The God of Things..., milk glass, 4"............**110.00**
Christmas tree, sb, tm, glass star topper, 13¾" **100.00**
Cigar, med amber, tm, Am, 1890-1910, 5½"..................................**80.00**
Clam, bl-aqua, sb, gm, orig metal screw cap, 1890-1910, 4¾".......**80.00**
Clock, D&D on face, ps, tm, orig stopper, 16¼"...........................**350.00**
Coachman, Van Dunck's Zgenever..., orange-amber, sb, am, 8¾", NM ...**75.00**
Columbus monument, cast metal on milk glass base, sm, 18¼"..**575.00**
Ear of corn, frontal panel for label, sb, tm, 10⅝", NM **55.00**
Ear of corn, med gr carnival, sb, gm, 1900-20, 4¾" **300.00**
Ear of corn, orange carnival, sb, gm, 1900-20, 4¾" **300.00**
Ear of corn, purple carnival, sb, gm, 1900-20, 4¾" **400.00**
Egyptian woman, ps, fm, shallow chip, 1890-1910, 6"..................**150.00**
Fish, Fischer's Oil...KY, sb, tm, haze, 5" L...................................**300.00**
Grant's Tomb, cast metal bust on milk glass base, 10" **875.00**
Hand holding dagger, turq, Depose at side of base, ps, tm, 11½" ...**350.00**
Hand pointing, W Zeige & Sohn Berlin..., med yel-olive, sb, 10¾".......**85.00**
Helmet w/plume, emb star on front, Haselhorst Dresden on sb, 3⅜" ...**180.00**
Hot air balloon, Ballon Captif 1878, Depose on sb, 9⅛" **450.00**
Hot air balloon, Ballon Captif 1878, sb, tm, Fr, 1890-1910, 9¼" ..**185.00**
Jeanne d'Arc, bon Bons John Tavernier on shield, milk glass, 16½"...**400.00**
Jester, sb, tm, 1890-1920, 6⅞"..**65.00**
Joan of Arc, ps, Depose emb on side at base, no stopper, 14" **65.00**
Jolly golfer, cobalt frost, Pat Appld For on sb, 11½"...................**450.00**
Kummel Bear, grape amethyst, tm, sb, 11⅝" **100.00**
Kummel Bear, milk glass, am, sb, 10⅞" **100.00**
Moses in bullrushes, sb, tm, 1890-1910, 5", NM **85.00**
Piece of coal, blk amethyst, sb, metal screw cap, chip, 3½" **120.00**
Pig, CF Knapp Philada on sb, tm, 1890-1910, 3⅞".......................**55.00**
Pig w/corncob in mouth, sb, tm, ca 1890-1910, 6¼" **100.00**
Pistol, yel-amber, gm, metal screw cap, 9⅝"................................**70.00**
Policeman, med yel-amber to yel, sb, sm, sm chips, 9⅛" **300.00**
Policeman, milk glass w/partial gold pnt, ps, tm, 9½" **725.00**
Radio, cobalt, sb, emb dials/numbers, 3" **100.00**
Revolver, amber, CPPCo Pat-d App For (on butt of hdl), screw cap, 8"...**50.00**
Roasted turkey, med amber, gm, orig metal screw cap, 4¾"...........**85.00**
Sailor & Chinaman on tower, Depose on ps base, orig pnt, 12½" ..**175.00**
Santa Claus, mc pnt on clear, sb, tm, 1890-1910, 7½" **500.00**
Shoe, Wales Goodyear, sb, gm, 2⅛" **110.00**
Statue of Liberty, cast metal on milk glass base, 15½".................**500.00**
Uncle Sam, Pat Apl'd For on sb, tm, 1890-1910, missing hat, 9½" ..**80.00**
Woman's torso, sb, gm, metal screw cap, 1890-1910, 6½", NM **40.00**
Woman w/muff, sb, tm, 1890-1910, 6⅜" **70.00**

Flasks

Byron/Scott, GI-114, med yel-olive, ps, tm, potstone, ½-pt........**160.00**
Byron/Scott, GI-114, yel-amber w/olive tone, ps, tm, ½-pt **220.00**
Corn for World/Monument, GVI-4, bright golden amber, st, dbl cm, qt...**825.00**
Cornucopia/Urn, GII-4, olive gr, ps, tm, seed bubbles, pt **130.00**
Cornucopia/Urn, GII-7, med olive gr w/amber tone, ps, tm, ½-pt **95.00**
Eagle w/Banner, GII-143, med 7-Up gr, ip, sl cm, whittled calabash...**500.00**
Eagle/Clasped Hands, GXII-13, amber, sb, am, some haze, qt.....**500.00**
Eagle/Columbia, GI-121, aqua, ps, tm, pt....................................**400.00**
Eagle/Cornucopia, GII-72, bright golden yel-amber w/olive, tm, pt.......**350.00**
Eagle/Eagle, GI-224, dk gray-clambroth, ps, rm, pt, NM..........**1,100.00**
Eagle/Eagle, GII-70, dk tobacco-amber, ps, sm, crude, pt **375.00**
Eagle/Eagle, GII-71, med olive gr w/amber tone, open/p, tm, ½-pt...**275.00**
Eagle/Eagle, GII-78, med olive-amber, ps, tm, qt **450.00**
Eagle/Eagle, GII-81, med olive-amber, ps, tm, pt **325.00**
Eagle/Eagle, GII-84, med olive-amber, ps, tm, pt **160.00**
Eagle/Eagle, GII-86, olive-amber, ps, tm, ½-pt **130.00**
Eagle/Franklin, GII-42, aqua, ps, tm, pt, NM..............................**300.00**
Eagle/Masonic Arch, GIV-17, yel olive-amber, ps, tm, pt **250.00**

Eagle/Masonic Arch, GIV-27, aqua, ps, tm, pt............................230.00
Eagle/Masonic Arch, GIV-27, bl-aqua w/olive striations, ps, tm, pt..275.00
Eagle/Masonic Arch, GIV-32, deep reddish amber, ps, tm, pt..1,050.00
Eagle/Morning Glory, GII-19, bl-aqua, ps, dbl cm, pt.................350.00
Eagle/Prospector, GXI-17, lt to med citron, sb, am, crude, pt 825.00
Franklin/Dyott, GI-94, golden amber, ps, sm, crude, pt, NM...2,300.00
Franklin/Dyott, GI-94, golden amber, ps, tm, pt......................3,800.00
Franklin/Dyott, GI-98, aqua, ps, tm, pt....................................675.00
Hunter/Fisherman, GXIII-4, dk strawberry puce, ip, am, calabash, NM...750.00
Kossuth/S Huffsey, GI-112, bl-aqua, ps, sl cm, calabash 275.00
Lafayette/Clinton, GI-80, yel-amber w/olive tone, ps, sm, crude, pt ...925.00
Liberty/Eagle, GII-63, med yel-amber, sb, dbl cm, pt..................575.00
Masonic/Eagle, GIV-3, med copper topaz w/yel-gr tone, ps, rm, pt....5,750.00
Sailor/Banjo Player, GXIII-8, med amber, sb, am, ½-pt................425.00
Scroll, GIX-02, med apple gr, open p, sm, sm stain, qt................625.00
Scroll, GIX-02, moonstone w/amethystine tint, ps, tm, qt, NM .825.00
Scroll, GIX-10, milky jade gr, ps, tm, stress crack, pt.................625.00
Scroll, GIX-10a, dk olive gr w/yel tone, red ip, am, pt............1,000.00
Scroll, GIX-11, dk yel-amber, ip, am, pt...................................875.00
Scroll, GIX-11, med yel-amber, open p, tm, shallow chip, pt......275.00
Scroll, GIX-11, med yel-gr, open p, sm, shallow flake, crude, pt.475.00
Scroll, GIX-11a, lt to med bl-gr, ps, tm, pt..............................700.00
Scroll, GIX-11a, olive gr, red ip, am, shallow ship at lip, pt........475.00
Scroll, GIX-14, med yel-gr, open p, tm, pt...............................750.00
Scroll, GIX-15, med apple gr, ps, sm, crude, chips, pt................525.00
Scroll, GIX-31, yel-gr, ps, sm, pt...900.00
Scroll, GIX-34, yel-gr, open p, sm, ½-pt 900.00
Sheaf of Wheat, GXIII-33, sb, tm, 1885-1895, pt....................170.00
Sheaf of Wheat/Star, GXIII-45, dk amber, ip, am, hdl, calabash, NM...250.00
Sheaf of Wheat/Tree, GXIII-46, dk burgundy puce, ps, calabash ...700.00
Soldier/Hound, GXIII-16, straw yel w/olive tone, sb, dbl cm, qt ...650.00
Stag/Tree, GX-1, bl-aqua, ps, tm, haze spots, pt.......................220.00
Steamboat/Sheaf of Wheat, GX-21, dk gr-aqua, ps, sm, pt 6,500.00
Success to RR/Horse Pulling Cart, GV-6, yel olive-amber, ps, tm, pt...325.00
Sunburst, GVIII-2, med gr, ps, tm, pt......................................525.00
Sunburst, GVIII-8, med olive gr w/amber tone, ps, tm, ½-pt......650.00
Traveler's Companion/Sheaf of Wheat, GXIV-1, dk olive-amber, sb, qt...500.00
Washington/Eagle, GI-07, aqua, ps, tm, pt................................600.00
Washington/Eagle, GI-11, dk bl-aqua, ps, sm, lt wear, pt 450.00
Washington/Eagle, GI-14, aqua, ps, sm, mfg bruise, pt................275.00
Washington/Jackson, GI-31, dk yel-olive gr, ps, tm, pt 375.00
Washington/Jackson, GI-32, yel-amber w/olive tone, ps, sm, bubbles, pt...220.00
Washington/Taylor, GI-38, med yel to copper, sb, sq cm, bubbles, qt......1,400.00
Washington/Taylor, GI-39, smoky topaz w/olive tone, sb, pt ...1,250.00

Food Bottles and Jars

Berry, deep tobacco-amber, 10 petals at shoulder & neck, sb, 11⅛"..400.00
Honey, emb beehive & bees, aqua, rm, whittled, 7⅛"................200.00
Ketchup, Shriver's Oyster...Baltimore, emerald gr, sb, sl cm, 7⅝"...1,150.00
Peppersauce, cathedral, aqua, 6-sided, dbl cm, sm stain, 10¾" ...150.00
Peppersauce, cathedral, lt aqua, ps, dbl cm, 9⅛"......................375.00
Peppersauce, cathedral, lt to med bl-gr, open p, dbl cm, NM......200.00
Peppersauce, Western Spice Mills, cathedral, golden yel, 8¾"..3,500.00
Pickle, aquamarine, petals/flutes on base/shoulder, rm, ip, 12½"..100.00
Pickle, cathedral, aqua, rm, ip, 8⅞"..525.00
Pickle, cathedral, bl-aqua, ps, rm, stain, 8⅞"...........................325.00
Pickle, cathedral, bright med gr, tm, sb, 11¾"..........................350.00
Pickle, cathedral, deep ice bl, 3 X-hatch panels, sb, 13¼"..........800.00
Pickle, cathedral, gr-aqua, sb, rm, faint haze, 11⅝" 160.00
Pickle, cathedral, lt to apple gr, sb, am, 11¾"...........................350.00
Pickle, cathedral, med bl-gr, rm, ip, 9¼"..............................1,150.00
Pickle, cathedral, med bl-gr, sb, am, 7⅜"................................400.00
Pickle, cathedral, med emerald gr, tm, ip, 11½" 950.00

Pickle, cathedral, med gr, clock faces 2 sides/clam shells, 11⅛" 1,800.00
Pickle, cathedral, WK Lewis & Co Boston, med gr, 5-panel, 10¾"...775.00
Pickle, Cloverleaf, med orange-amber, am, sb, 1860s, 8⅜" 550.00
Pickle, Milwaukee...Wauwatosa WI, orange-amber, ½-gal, 9⅝".130.00
Pickle, Skilton Foote...Bunker Hill..., golden yel-amber, 7½".......70.00
Pickle, TB Smith & Co Philada, cathedral, bl-aqua, ps, am, 9¼"...500.00
Pickle, WD Smith NY, cathedral, lt to med teal, rm, 8½" 600.00
Tomato sauce, TA Bryan & Co's...MD, golden yel-amber, 8¼" ..240.00
Utility, med olive gr, wide mouth, ps, tm, 10½"......................190.00
Wide mouth, lt olive gr, ps, fm, 8¾x3¾"...............................650.00

Ink Bottles

Blown, fiery opal milk glass w/HP florals, ps, 2¼" 525.00
Ca-rt-er, cobalt, 6-sided, sb, 9¾"...85.00
Cabin, sb, tm, rare, 2⅜"..775.00
Carter's, cathedral master, med cobalt, 6-sided, sb, am, 6¼" 220.00
Carter's, dk bl-gr, sb, am, tooled pour spout, 8"......................110.00
Cathedral master, med cobalt, sb, am, 6¼", NM......................230.00
Cone, med gr, ps, rm, 2⅝"..220.00
Cottage, dk bl-aqua, st, sm, 2⅝"...325.00
Davids, med teal, sb, tm, 1⅞"...525.00

Fine Black Ink Prepared By Baum & Hawley, 301 River St. Troy, medium olive-amber, pontil scar, 98% original label, sloping collar mouth, 5½", $300.00.

Geometric, dk olive gr, ps, tm, 1½x2¼".................................180.00
Geometric, dk olive-amber, ps, tm, 2x2⅝"..............................170.00
Harrison's Columbian, bl-aqua, 8-sided turtle, sm, 1⅞"............350.00
Harrison's Columbian, cobalt, ps, am, 5¾"...........................1,550.00
Harrison's Columbian, dk sapphire bl, open p, am, cleaned, 7¼"..1,250.00
Igloo, cobalt, sb, gm, Am, 1⅞"...1,400.00
Igloo, lt bl-gr, sb, gm, Am, 1⅞"..130.00
Igloo, med bl-gr, sb, gm, Am, 1¾"..220.00
Igloo, med purple amethyst, sb, gm, Am, crack, 2"...................575.00
Igloo, root beer-amber, sb, gm, Am, 1⅞"................................750.00
J&IEM, lt bl-gr, sb, gm, shallow chip, 1⅝"...............................120.00
J&IEM, lt to med electric cobalt, sb, gm, lt haze, 1⅝"...........2,200.00
J&IEM, med tobacco amber, sb, gm, whittled, 1¾"...................450.00
J&IEM, vaseline, sb, tm, lt stain, 1⅝" 700.00
J&IEM, yel-amber, sb, gm, 1⅝"..220.00
JB Davids & Co, aqua, sb, tm, 1⅞"..325.00
Jones' Empire...NY, dk emerald gr, 12-sided, ip, am, 5⅞", NM...2,800.00
Ma & Pa Carter's Inx, wht china w/mc enamel, Germany, 3½", pr...150.00
Pitkin, med yel-amber w/olive tone, ps, tm, 1½", NM 650.00
Pitkin, med yel-olive, 36 left-swirl ribs, ps, disk tm, 1½x2⅛" ...575.00
Pressed glass, sq w/emb dmns, orig ring & cover, 1¾" 230.00
Ross's (in slug plate) Excelsior, med emerald gr, 12-sided, 7⅜"...4,200.00
SMFG Co, aqua, sb, gm, flake/haze, 1⅞" 300.00
Teakettle, cobalt, sb, rough sm, stain, 2⅛"...............................57.00
Teakettle, cobalt, 6-sided, elongated loops, brass collar, 19th C, 2" ...400.00

Teakettle, dk purple amethyst, sb, gm, orig brass ring, 2" **350.00**
Teakettle, dk purple amethyst, sb, sm, orig metal band, hinged lid, 2" ..**400.00**
Teakettle, med gr, 8-sided, sb, brass neck ring, 2⅛" **625.00**
Umbrella, dk olive gr, 8-sided, ps, tm, whittled, 2½".................**250.00**
Use Shipman's...Utica NY, aqua, sb, tm, 1⅝" **300.00**
12-sided, med bl-gr, open p, rm, minor grinding lines, 1⅞"...........**90.00**

Medicine Bottles

Alan's Anti Fat Botanic...NY, dk sapphire bl, sb, sl cm, 7½", NM...**200.00**
Alexander's Silameau, med sapphire bl, ps, tm, stain, 6¼"..........**500.00**
Brown's Blood Treatment Philadelphia, med 7-Up gr, sb, tm, stain, 6"..**180.00**
C Brinckerhoff's Health Restorative...NY, dk yel olive-amber, 7⅝"....**1,000.00**
C Heimstreet & Co Troy NY, med cobalt, 8-sided, ps, dbl cm, 7⅛" **300.00**
Carter's Spanish Mixture, dk yel-olive, ip, sl dbl cm, 8" **525.00**
Climax Syrup Owego NY, lt aqua, 12-sided, ps, fm, nick, 4¾" ...**180.00**
Craig's Kidney & Liver Cure..., med amber, sb, tm, flake, 9¾"...**120.00**
Dr Hawk's Universal Stimulant, aqua, am, 80% label, 3⅞" **190.00**
Dr JS Wood's...NY, dk bl-gr, tombstone, ip, sl cm, 8⅞", NM...**4,900.00**
Dr Kennedy Salt Rheum Ointment, bl-aqua, open p, rm, 3⅝"...**120.00**
Dr Roger's Liverwort & Tar, med sapphire bl, ps, rm, 8⅜", NM...**13,500.00**
EH Flagg's Instantaneous Relief Phila, bl-aqua, ps, rm, 3⅞" **325.00**
GW Merchant Chemist Lockport NY, med bl-gr, ip, am, 7".......**300.00**
GW Merchant Lockport NY, dk Lockport gr, ps, sl cm, whittled, 5"...**325.00**
I Covert's Balm of Life, dk olive gr, open p, sl cm, 6"...............**2,350.00**
I Covert's Balm of Life, dk olive gr, ps, sl cm, 6" **2,900.00**
Indian Panacea, dk gr w/yel tint, ps, sl dbl cm, crude/swirled, 8"....**4,800.00**
J Starkweather's Hepatic Elixer Upton Mass, gr-aqua, 6-sided, ps.......**120.00**
JB Wheatley Compound Syrup Dallasburgh KY, dk aqua, ps, am, 6" .**140.00**
John J Smith Louisville KY, dk bl-gr, sl cm, 5⅜" **1,800.00**
Log Cabin Cough & Consumption Remedy...1887, amber, sb, tm, 6¾"...**180.00**
LP Dodge Reumatic Liniment Newburg, dk yel-amber, sl cm, 6", NM.**3,000.00**
LQC Wishart's Pine Tree...1859, dk yel-tobacco amber, sb, 10"..**400.00**
LQC Wishart's Pine Tree...1859, lt bl-gr, sb, sl cm, flake, 7⅞"....**120.00**
LQC Wishart's Pine Tree...1859, med emerald gr, sb, sl cm, 7½", NM..**235.00**
LQC Wishart's Pine Tree...1859, med ice bl, sb, sl cm, chip, 7½" ...**185.00**
Morse's Celebrated Prov RI, bl-aqua, lg red ip, cm, 9⅜" **190.00**
NW Seat MD Negative Electric Fluid NY, aqua, rm, 1845-55, 4"........**190.00**
Original Balm of Thousand Flowers Jules Hauel Philada, ps, 5", NM ..**140.00**
Primley's Iron & Wahoo Tonic...IN, bright straw yel, sb, tm, 9½"........**400.00**
Pure Cod Liver Oil Reed Carnrick & Andrus..., cobalt, sb, cm, 9¾"...**250.00**
Reed's Gilt 1878 Edge Tonic, amber, sb, am, 8⅝" **85.00**
Rheumatic Trade Mk Syrup...NY, med amber, sb, sl cm, dullness, 9¾"..**150.00**
Rohrer's Expectorial Cherry...PA, amber, ip, sl dbl cm, 10½"......**325.00**
Smith's Gr Mtn Renovator...VT, dk yel-amber, ip, sl cm, 7⅛"..**1,800.00**
Swaim's Panacea Philada, med apple gr, ps, sl dbl cm, 7¾".........**400.00**
Trade Mk Sparks Perfect...NJ, yel-amber, sb, tm, cleaned, 9⅜"....**190.00**
University Free Medicine Philadelphia, bl-aqua, 6-sided, ps, 4⅞" ..**130.00**
USA Hosp Dept, med cobalt, cylindrical, b3m, tm, 7⅜", NM ...**550.00**
USA Hosp Dept, med yel-olive gr, sb, dbl cm, bubbles, 9¼" ...**550.00**
Wayne's Diuretic Elixer FE Suir & Co Cincinnati, cobalt, sb, 7⅜" **300.00**
Wm S Merrell & Co Druggists Cincinnati, bl-aqua, ip, am, stain, 8⅛"...**275.00**

Mineral Water and Soda Bottles

Artesian Spring Co...Ballston Spa..., med emerald gr, sb, pt **110.00**
Beard's...F&B Boston, bl-gr, sb, bt, 7" **65.00**
Blue Lick Water Co KY, dk chocolate-amber, mug base, ip, dbl cm, pt..**750.00**
Buffalo Lithia Water..., med teal bl, sb, am, ½-gal......................**230.00**
C Cleminshaw...Troy NY, lt sapphire bl, ip, am, faint bruise, 7½" **80.00**
C Norris & Co City Bottling...Detroit Mich, cobalt, st, am, 6¾"...**125.00**
Clarke & Co NY, med bl-gr, ip, sl dbl cm, cleaned, pt **210.00**
Congress & Empire Spring Co Hotchkiss Sons..., root beer-amber, pt.....**350.00**
Congress & Empire Spring Co...Saratoga NY, emerald gr, sb, dbl cm, pt.**625.00**

Crystal...Patented Nov 12-1872..., med cobalt, chip, 7⅝"............**55.00**
Deep Rock Spring Oswego NY, orange-amber, sb, dbl cm, qt **825.00**
E Harley 802 Market St, lt bl-gr, ip, bt, lt stain, 7⅛"..................**120.00**
EM Gatchell & Co Charleston SC..., med gr, ip, sl cm, cleaned, 7⅞"..**300.00**
Franklin Spring...Ballston Spa...NY, emerald gr, sb, am, pt, EX ..**160.00**
Guilford Mineral Spring Water GMWS..., emerald gr, sb, dbl cm, qt **75.00**
Highrock Congress Spring 1767...NY, dk root beer-amber, bubbles, pt..**325.00**
Highrock Congress Spring 1767...NY, golden amber, sb, dbl cm, qt.......**325.00**
Highrock Congress Spring...Saratoga NY, lt to med teal bl, pt ...**450.00**
Highrock Congress Spring...Saratoga NY, yel-olive gr, sb, dbl cm, pt...**300.00**
Highrock Congress Spring...Saratoga NY, yel-olive gr, sb, pt **235.00**
Lancaster GW, med cobalt, ip, sl cm, whittled, 7½" **220.00**
Middletown Healing Springs Grays & Clark...VT, med yel-amber, sb, qt...**85.00**
MM Battelle Brooklyn...Union GW, med teal, ip, bt, 7½" **180.00**
Ogemaw Spring Water (chief) Bay City MI, aqua, st, ½-gal.......**160.00**
Saratoga (star) Spring, olive gr, sb, dbl cm, bubbles, qt **120.00**
Saratoga A Hathorn Carl H Schultz NY, bl-gr, sb, dbl cm, pt, NM ..**525.00**
SJ Estern (lg letters), dk emerald gr, sb, bt, 7¼"............................**90.00**
Syracuse Springs D...NY, yel-amber, sb, dbl cm, ½-pt **675.00**
Tweddle's Celebrated...NY, med bl-gr, open p, sl cm, stain, 7½".**300.00**
Union Lava Works Conshohocken Patented 1852, dk sapphire bl, ip, 7"...**525.00**
W Eagle Vestry Varick...Union GW Phila, med bl-gr, ip, bt, 7⅜"....**190.00**

Poison Bottles

Columbian Pharmacy...NJ, med gr, irregular hexagon, 5" **1,100.00**
Contents 4 Fl Oz...Toronto (inside heart), cobalt, sb, tm, 5" **500.00**
Gift (skull & X bones) Vorsicht, 250 on sb, tm, 7½"................**200.00**
Gift Flasche (skull & X bones), med amber, 6-sided, sb, tm, 9½"....**120.00**
Gift Flasche (skull & X bones), med yel-gr, 6-sided, 9½"...........**140.00**
JG Godding & Co...Boston MA, cobalt, mk on sb, scarce, 6¼" ..**375.00**
Lattice & Dmn, cobalt, sb, tm, 4" **85.00**
Lyon's Powder B&P NY, golden yel-amber, open p, rm, 4¼", NM...**450.00**
Lyon's Powder B&P NY, olive gr, open p, rm, 4¼" **375.00**
Owl Drug (owl on mortar & pestle), cobalt, triangular, sb, tm, 9⅝".....**975.00**
Owl Drug (owl on mortar & pestle), med amber, beer bottle form, 8" ...**80.00**
Pat Amtl Gesch, orange-amber, sb, stain, orig glass stopper, 6¼" .**55.00**
Poison, Lattice & Dmn, cobalt, sb, tm, 5½" **130.00**
Poison, med amber coffin, sb, tm, 3½" **275.00**
Poison (owl on mortar & pestal), cobalt, triangular, sb, tm, 8"...**400.00**
TOD Co Trade Mk (owl on martar & pestal), cobalt, sb, 6¼" ...**240.00**
Vorsicht Gift/skull & Xbones, olive gr, 6-sided, sb, 6⅞", NM.....**110.00**

Sarsaparilla Bottles

Dr Townsend's...NY, dk olive amber, ps, sl cm, 9½" **300.00**
Log Cabin...Rochester/Pat...1887, deep amber, sb, 9" **170.00**
Old Dr Townsend's...NY, lt gr, sb, sl cm, 9½" **130.00**
Wynkoop's Katharismic Honduras, cobalt, sl cm, scratches/flake, 10" ...**4,000.00**

Spirits Bottles

Phoenix Old Trade Mark Bourbon..., light amber, tooled lip, smooth base, ca 1879 – 1888, one-pint, $300.00.

AM Bininger...NY, yel-amber, sb, dbl cm, hdl, whittled, 8" **300.00**
Bininger's Regulator 19 Broad St NY, golden yel-amber, clock, 6" **500.00**
Booth & Sedgwick's London Cordial Gin, dk emerald gr, ip, sl cm, 10"..**450.00**
Casper's Whiskey Made By Honest...People, cobalt, sb, tm, 12".**400.00**
Griffith Hyatt & Co Baltimore, dk olive gr jug, ps, 7¼" **975.00**
H Pharazyn Phila Right Secured, golden amber, Indian Queen, 12⅜" ...**1,300.00**
Henry Chapman & Co...Montreal, bright straw yel, teardrop, 5¾", NM ..**500.00**
Landsberg's Pure Blackberry Brandy...NY, dk bl-aqua, sb, 11¼" **1,500.00**
London Jockey Club House Gin (jockey/horse), dk olive gr, 9⅜", NM ..**350.00**
London Jockey Club House Gin (jockey/horse), emerald gr, 9⅝" **450.00**
Mohawk Whiskey Pure Rye...1868, golden amber, Indian queen, 12⅜"...**2,350.00**
Pure Cognac on appl seal, med amber, ps, dbl cm, hdl, 8⅞" **775.00**
RB Cutter Louisville KY, golden yel-amber, sb, am, hdl, 8⅝" **725.00**
RB Cutter Louisville KY, root beer-amber, hdld jug, 8½" **325.00**
RB Cutter's Pure Bourbon, dk cherry puce, hdld jug, ps, am, 8½" **450.00**
Vivard & Sheehan, med yel-gr, sb, am, tooled pour spout/hdl, 9⅞"..**1,500.00**
Voldner's Aromatic Schnapps..., dk yel olive-amber, ps, 9⅞"......**150.00**
Vonthofen's Aromatic Scheidam Schnapps, med emerald gr, ip, 8⅛" ..**170.00**
Wharton's...1850 Chestnut Grove, amber, hdl, 10" **400.00**
Wharton's...1850 Chestnut Grove, amber, teardrop, 5⅜" **185.00**
Wharton's...1850 Chestnut Grove, golden yel-amber, hdl, 10" ...**850.00**

Boxes

Boxes have been used by civilized man since ancient Egypt and Rome. Down through the centuries, specifically designed containers have been made from every conceivable material. Precious metals, papier-mache, Battersea, Oriental lacquer, and wood have held riches from the treasuries of kings, snuff for the fashionable set of the last century, China tea, and countless other commodities. In the following descriptions, when only one dimension is given, it is length. See also Toleware; specific manufacturers.

Apple, poplar w/old red rpt, 7x10½" **360.00**
Ash burl, old varnish, hinged lid, brass closure, 2x4x2½" **330.00**

Band box with original wallpaper covering with scene of Castle Carden, multicolor on blue, 23" long, EX, $3,300.00 at auction.

Bentwood, lapped seams, worn gr pnt, 13" L, EX.......................**600.00**
Bentwood, lapped seams w/iron tacks, dk gr pnt, 5x10" **440.00**
Bentwood, lt gr rpt w/some wear, lapped seams, 10" **130.00**
Bentwood, lt varnish, 1-finger w/steel tacks, 6" L.......................**100.00**
Bentwood, old dk rpt, lapped seams on base, finger on lid, 8¾" L ..**750.00**
Bentwood, worn gr pnt, 2-finger, steel tacks, 4" L **360.00**
Bible, dvtl walnut, breadboard ends, CI bail hdls, 12x21x14".....**350.00**
Birch bark, oval, sawtooth edges, cutout triangles, 4½x6" **140.00**
Bride's, pine w/mc florals, angel on lid, lt wear, 17" L **1,450.00**
Bride's, pine w/mc florals, couple on lid, worn, 19" L **440.00**
Bride's, pine w/mc florals & hunt scene on red, 18", EX..........**1,300.00**
Candle, mahog, dvtl drw w/beaded edge, scalloped crst, 18x11x5"..**600.00**
Candle, mahog, dvtl w/slant lid, scallop crest, age cracks, 10x6x9" .**165.00**
Candle, pine w/old red-brn stain, blk stencil initials, dvtl, 20" L....**300.00**
Candle, pine w/orig brn grpt, mc reserves on sides, dvtl, 5x13x8" **2,400.00**

Candle, poplar w/old yel layers, 2-section, hanging crest, 17x12x6"..**3,300.00**
Cherry, dvtl, wire nails, old finish, 12" L................................**80.00**
Chip-cvd, hardwood w/cherry stain, 20th C, 6¼"......................**85.00**
Document, pine w/orig red & blk rosewood-like decor, dvtl, 7x12x7" ..**300.00**
Dome top, gr sponging on wood, hinged lid, iron hdls, 1800s, 24".....**2,500.00**
Dough, pine w/old red, chip-cvd & molded edge details, 11x27x12" **275.00**
Dough, poplar w/old red rpt, splayed base, sq legs, dvtl, 29x40x21".......**465.00**
File, desk top, antique leather book spines facade, 8x13x7" **385.00**
Knife, hardwood w/natural varnish, brass screws, dvtl, 8½x18" **85.00**
Pantry, lap seam, old yel pnt, age crack, bail hdl, 5½x9"............**465.00**
Pine w/brn grpt & yel striping, appl base, wear, 8x21x8¼".........**220.00**
Pipe, mahog stained poplar, nailed, wall mt, 1800s, 22x5x5"......**2,650.00**
Pipe, pine w/heart-shaped bkbrd, old red pnt, ca 1800, 16x5x5" ..**3,100.00**
Pipe, pine w/old blk rpt, scrolled crest, w/3 clay pipes, 16" **220.00**
Poplar w/blk checkerboard top, dvtl, 6x14x7" **275.00**
Salt, pine w/old worn gr pnt, cross-member crest, hinged lid, 19"....**220.00**
Sewing, cherry/mahog, 2-drw/compartment, rpr/worn cushion top, 7x7x5"...**165.00**
Sewing, floral/fruit stencil on mustard, Am, 1800s, 6x8x10".......**1,150.00**
Spice, poplar w/old red, dvtl drw w/dividers, crest, wall mt, 15x11x7"..**550.00**
Storage, leather covered, hinged, brass tack decor, 19th C, 7x17x13"..**430.00**
Strong, steel w/bl pnt & mc floral decor, NP hdl, w/lock/key, 8" L........**150.00**
Work, figured veneer w/marquetry inlay, drw/lift-out tray, 6x14x10"....**275.00**
Writing, pine/poplar w/old blk pnt, lock removed, 8¼x19x15" ..**110.00**

Boyd Crystal Art Glass

This small but productive glasshouse has more than 300 molds and has produced more than 350 colors. They are very collector oriented and alter their mark every five years. In 1978 they used a simple B in a diamond. Today, with four changes behind them, the original mark is now encompassed by four additional lines. Vaseline collectors have increased in number, and many of Boyd's Vaseline pieces (variations include Firefly and Citron) are increasing in value rapidly. Many of Boyd's colors — Golden Delight, Peridot, Pippin Green, and others — fluoresce under black light, and are now highly sought after.

In the near future, watch for price increases for Joey the Horse, as the mold has recently been converted to a carousel horse, preventing further production. Li'l Joe the Horse has met the same fate and is now very limited. As always, satins and hand-painted pieces are commanding 10 – 50% more than the same items in the regular finish. Also worth mentioning is the fact that when this glasshouse retires a design, they select a color of their choosing once a year and make that item with a 'R' on it so that collectors that choose to can still collect that design.

Internet exposure and the heightened awareness of Boyd collectibles that resulted have caused an increase in prices of from 5% to 85% in some cases. We will wait to see where they level off before endorsing what may be erratic values. Our advisor for this category is Joyce Pringle; she is listed in the Directory under Texas.

Key: (R) — retired

Airplane (R), Classic Black..**22.00**
Airplane (R), Nile Green...**19.00**
Airplane (R), Primrose..**18.50**
Angel, Marshmallow **24.00**
Angel, Rosie Pink..**20.00**
Angel, Vaseline Carnival **22.50**
Artie Penguin (R), Cardinal Red...**21.00**
Artie Penguin (R), Columbus White **22.00**
Artie Penguin (R), Waterloo **12.00**
Bernie the Eagle (R), Cobalt Carnival **15.00**
Bernie the Eagle (R), Royal Plum Carnival **12.00**
Bernie the Eagle (R), Vanilla Coral.....................................**10.00**

Bingo the Deer, Cashmire Pink.................................10.00
Bingo the Deer, Potpourri..28.00
Bingo the Deer, Winter Swirl....................................30.00
Bow Slipper, Golden Delight.....................................15.00
Bow Slipper, Magic Marble.......................................12.50
Bow Slipper, Millenneum White...................................9.50
Bow Slipper, Rubina..22.50
Brian Bunny (R), Pearl...18.00
Brian Bunny (R), Toffee Slag......................................8.50
Brian Bunny (R), Waterloo..12.00
Bunny Salt, Alice Blue...20.00
Bunny Salt, Platinum Carnival....................................25.00
Bunny Salt, Spring Surprise......................................11.00
Bunny Salt, Teal...10.00
Candy the Carousel Horse (R), Auba Slag...........................8.50
Candy the Carousel Horse (R), Maverick Blue......................13.00
Candy the Carousel Horse (R), Sunkist Carnival....................9.00
Cat Slipper, Apricot...35.00
Cat Slipper, Candy Swirl...15.00
Cat Slipper, Harvest Gold...9.00
Cat Slipper, Spinnaker Carnival..................................13.50
Chick Salt, Cobalt...60.00
Chick Salt, Copper Glo...45.00
Chick Salt, Lemonade...12.00
Chick Salt, Nightwatch Black......................................9.00
Chick Salt, Shasta White...18.00
Elizabeth (R), Banana Cream......................................10.00
Elizabeth (R), Classic Black.....................................12.50
Elizabeth (R), Lemon Splash.......................................9.00
JB Scotty (R), Cobalt...130.00
JB Scotty (R), Confetti...225.00
JB Scotty (R), Daffodil..45.00
JB Scotty (R), Mirage..10.00
JB Scotty (R), Rosewood..35.00
Jennifer, Cobalt...12.00
Jennifer, Crystal Carnival.......................................10.00
Jeremy Frog (R), Nile Green......................................10.00
Jeremy Frog (R), Sunkist Carnival................................12.00
Jeremy Frog (R), Vaseline Carnival...............................15.00
Joey the Horse (R), Bermuda Carnival.............................80.00
Joey the Horse (R), Crown Tuscan Carnival........................42.50
Joey the Horse (R), Delphinium...................................30.00
Joey the Horse (R), Furr Green...................................22.50
Joey the Horse (R), Ruby...60.00
Kitten on Pillow (R), Butterscotch...............................26.50
Kitten on Pillow (R), Delphinium.................................25.00
Kitten on Pillow (R), Firefly....................................40.00
Lil Joe (R), Autumn Beige..18.00
Lil Joe (R), Enchantment...22.00
Lil Joe (R), Pistachio...27.00
Little Luck (R), Mulberry Carnival...............................18.00
Little Luck (R), Mystique Carnival...............................10.00
Little Luck (R), Orange Spice....................................11.00
Little Luck (R), Pacifica Green..................................15.00
Louise Doll, Capri Blue, HP decor................................22.00
Louise Doll, Flame...52.50
Louise Doll, Mardigras...22.00
Lucky the Unicorn, Bermuda.......................................24.50
Lucky the Unicorn, Ebony Carnival................................60.00
Lucky the Unicorn, Fantasia......................................16.50
Lucky the Unicorn, Winter Swirl..................................45.00
Mabel the Cow, Harvest Gold......................................10.00
Mabel the Cow, Purple Fizz..8.00
Melissa Doll, Avocado...7.50

Melissa Doll, Lemon Splash..7.50
Melissa Doll, Vaseline Carnival..................................10.00
Miss Cotton the Cat, Buckeye......................................9.00
Miss Cotton the Cat, Ginger......................................28.50
Miss Cotton the Cat, Millennium Surprise.........................10.00
Miss Cotton the Cat, Oleander....................................25.00
Nancy Doll, Aruba Slag..9.00
Nancy Doll, Milk Chocolate.......................................10.00
Nancy Doll, Tangy Lime..9.50
Pooch the Dog, Cobalt Swirl......................................25.00
Pooch the Dog, Grape Parfait.....................................22.50
Pooch the Dog, John's Surprise...................................45.00
Pooch the Dog, Royalty...30.00
Pooch the Dog, Vaseline Surprise.................................12.50
Taffy the Carousel Horse, Cobalt Carnival........................25.00
Taffy the Carousel Horse, Jade...................................19.00
Taffy the Carousel Horse, Moss Green.............................22.00
Taffy the Carousel Horse, Purple Frost Carnival..................21.50
Tucker the Car (R), Dijon..15.00
Tucker the Car (R), Maverick Blue................................20.00
Tucker the Car (R), Peach..25.50
Zack the Elephant (R), Autumn Splendor...........................60.00
Zack the Elephant (R), December Swirl............................65.00
Zack the Elephant (R), Peacock Blue Swirl........................21.00
Zack the Elephant (R), Plum Slag.................................28.00

Bradley and Hubbard

The Bradley and Hubbard Mfg. Company was a firm which produced metal accessories for the home. They operated from about 1860 until the early part of this century, and their products reflected both the Arts and Crafts and Art Nouveau influence. Their logo was a device with a triangular arrangement of the company name containing a smaller triangle and an Aladdin lamp.

Lamps

Banquet, pk satin dome shade; ornate #20413 base, dtd 1895, 20" ..275.00
Kitchen, milk glass shade w/HP flowers; ornate CI fr, smoke bell 375.00
Student, lt gr ribbed shade w/milk glass int, adjustable, 21"........825.00
8" etched ball shade; brass-urn base dtd 1892, 17"+chimney 350.00
12" slag glass & brass 3-panel shade; bronze std, 19" 2,200.00
15" slag glass 8-sided metal o/l shade; metal stick base, 18" 750.00
16" slag glass metal o/l dome shade; cast column, 23", EX 700.00
16" slag glass 8-sided metal o/l shade; stick base, rprs 600.00
17" slag glass & bronze 8-panel shade; fluted iron base, 20" 1,200.00
18" rvpt floral shade; oak leaves emb on bronze std, 26"..........2,300.00
20" slag glass dome shade; Celtic knot bronze std, 23" 2,700.00

Miscellaneous

Wall plaque, lady in flowing blue, cast iron, #1821, $485.00.

Andirons, Deco geometric finial, CI, #9531, 24¼", pr 225.00
Ashtray, man's profile, CI w/gold pnt, #3596, 6¼" 90.00
Ashtray, parrot on perch beside tray on tall stand, bronze, 33" ...175.00
Bookends, Buddha, CI, orig pnt, 1920s, 5½", pr 225.00
Bookends, bulldog, bronze, 5¼x5", pr 170.00
Bookends, cat on open book, CI w/mc pnt, 5x3¾", pr 300.00
Bookends, elephant, pnt CI, unmk, 6x6½", pr 225.00
Bookends, homestead scene in relief, bronze, 5¼x3¾", pr 75.00
Bookends, Sphinx & flowers, CI, orig pnt, 4¾", pr 125.00
Calling card pedestal, classical scene, spelter & CI, ca 1870.......465.00
Candle holder, brass, Arts & Crafts style, 8⅜x5¼x4¼" 75.00
Candlesticks, orig gr patina, heavy, sgn, 15½", pr 525.00
Desk set, brass, blotter/letter opener, pen tray, triangle mks 70.00
Desk set, bronze, Mission-style decor, 8-pc, EX....................400.00
Inkwell, Arts & Crafts style, crackle finish on metal, 1900s 125.00
Inkwell, stag figure beside glass well, EX patina, #2340, 5½" 315.00
Match safe, CI, birds, musical instruments, wall mt, 9x4¾"..........225.00
Plaque, Nouveau lady's portrait, #1820, 13¾x10¼", w/chain 525.00
Statuette, Don Juan flexing sword, patinated metal, 1911/label, 21"...175.00
Tray, CI, kittens in relief, #1640, 7" 110.00

Brass

Brass is an alloy consisting essentially of copper and zinc in variable proportions. It is a medium that has been used for both utilitarian items and objects of artistic merit. Today, with the inflated price of copper and the popular use of plastics, almost anything made of brass is collectible, though right now, at least, there is little interest in items made after 1950. Our advisor, Mary Frank Gaston, has compiled a lovely book, *Antique Brass and Copper*, with full-color photos. See also Candlesticks.

Ashtray, naughty lady w/skirt up at side, 6x4" 35.00
Billikin, mk USP, 1908, DRGM, 1¾"...50.00
Box, slipper, emb tavern scene, mtd on casters, 14x17x11", $175 to ..200.00
Box, stamp; enameled/emb pagoda scene lid, China, 1¼x2x1½" .40.00
Can, watering; hinged lid, European, 8x11", from $120 to..........135.00
Candelabrum, ornate, 3-light, English, mid-1800s, 20x16", $1,000 to.1,200.00
Candle holder, 8-sided base, English, 1850s, 7x2½", pr, $325 to ...375.00
Chestnut roaster, pierced lid & hdl, English, 19½" L 300.00
Coal bucket, 13½"..100.00
Crucifix, ornate, 13½x6" 100.00
Cue rest, spider type, 3-slot top, 4x3¼", EX...............................80.00
Dipper, 4½" bowl, 13", from $80 to 90.00
Figurine, Deco nude dancer, 8x6½ on 2½" dia weighted base 50.00
Hinges, ornate design, Victorian era, lg, pr 50.00
Holder, hand towel; hand holder w/spring, Japan, 7x3" 35.00
Kettle, cast brass hdl mts, iron swing hdls, 19th C, 9⅝".............75.00
Kettle, jelly; iron bail, Am, late 1800s, 7x13", from $275 to.......325.00
Kettle, preserving; 1880s, 9x14"..150.00
Kettle, spun, iron swing hdl, HW Hayden, 6⅛x9⅞" 50.00
Kettle, spun, wrought-iron bail hdl, Hayden's Pat, 18x24½".......195.00
Kettle, str sides, rolled rim, brass hdl mts/copper rivets, 11" dia....65.00
Kettle, str sides, rolled rim, cast hdl mts, 1850s, 10⅜x15¾" 200.00
Ladle, tasting; wrought-iron hdl, FBS Canton O...86, 14" 170.00
Ladle, wrought-iron hdl, 5" bowl, 3 copper rivets, 19"................80.00
Mailbox, Arts & Crafts style, 1930s.......................................95.00
Pail, milk/water; rim forms loops for bail, 9", from $125 to 150.00
Pan, candy making; hdls, Am, 16" dia, from $200 to 225.00
Paper clip, duck form w/glass eyes, hook for hanging, 6½" L 50.00
Sconces, cast bow & roses, 2-light, 1920-30, 8¼x7¾", pr............65.00
Stand, music; lyre-shaped rest, 40", EX...................................40.00
Teakettle, removable base, G age, dents, 14" 200.00
Teakettle & stand, curved spout, arched hinged hdl, wood grip, ca 1895...250.00

Tiebacks, cast brass, griffin shapes w/scrolls, 7¼", pr 200.00
Umbrella stand, inside tray removes, 18½", 7-lb 125.00
Vase, classic form w/Nouveau leafy branches, Fr, 10½" 225.00
Wall sconce, emb bird & landscape, 2-light, English, 19x15" 650.00

Brastoff, Sascha

The son of immigrant parents, Sascha Brastoff was encouraged to develop his artistic talents to the fullest, encouragement that was well taken, as his achievements aptly attest. Though at various times he was a dancer, sculptor, Hollywood costume designer, jeweler, and painter, it is his ceramics that are today becoming highly regarded collectibles.

Sascha began his career in the United States in the late 1940s. In a beautiful studio built for him by his friend and mentor, Winthrop Rockefeller, he designed innovative wares that even then were among the most expensive on the market. All designing was done personally by Brastoff; he also supervised the staff which at the height of production numbered approximately 150. Wares signed with his full signature (not merely backstamped 'Sascha Brastoff') were personally crafted by him and are valued much more highly than those signed 'Sascha B.,' indicating work done under his supervision. Until his death in 1993, he continued his work in Los Angeles, in his latter years producing 'Sascha Holograms,' which were distributed by the Hummelwerk Company.

Though the resin animals signed 'Sascha B.' were neither made nor designed by Brastoff, collectors of these pieces value them highly. After he left the factory in the 1960s, the company retained the use of the name to be used on reissues of earlier pieces or merchandise purchased at trade shows.

In the listings that follow, items are ceramic and signed 'Sascha B.' unless 'full signature' or another medium is indicated. For further information we recommend *Collector's Encyclopedia of California Pottery, Second Edition*, by Jack Chipman, available from Collector Books or your local book store. Our advisor for this category is Susan Cox; she is listed in the Directory under California.

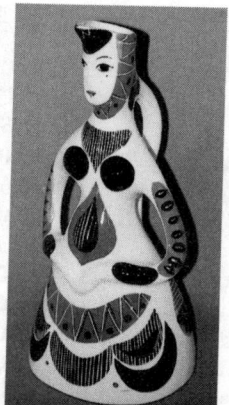

Pitcher, woman figural, 13", $525.00.

Ashtray, leaves on forest gr, sq w/pulled corners, 7½"...................45.00
Ashtray, Star Steed, curved platter shape, 17½x9".......................125.00
Ashtray, Star Steed, pk w/wht & gold on dk gray, 3x8" dia..........50.00
Bowl, carousel horse on bl, hdls, 11" 70.00
Bowl vase, Roof Tops, bl-gray matt, 5x6½"................................55.00
Box, Smoke Tree, pk, 2x7¼x4½" 50.00
Candle holder, amber resin, dmn shape w/emb dmns, 6"..............35.00
Chocolate pot, Roof Tops, slim cylinder, 15½"..........................200.00
Cup & saucer, lav Surf Ballet, 2x4", 6"....................................35.00
Figurine, elephant, platinum on pk Surf Ballet ground, 8½".......155.00
Figurine, fox, solid bronze, 1970s, 5" 200.00
Figurine, Merbaby, bl w/smoke gray & gold, 6¾x5".....................85.00
Figurine, seal, emerald gr resin, 2 blk beaded eyes, 7x9½" 275.00

Figurine, water buffalo, resin, red w/yel tones, 3¾x7½" 315.00
Lamp, angelic dancers, gray/blk/wht/gold, 14x15", w/shade: 29".175.00
Lamp, patio; Tiki figure w/mask-like ft, wht w/platinum & gold, 9¾" ...165.00
Pendant, rooster, gold-plated sterling, Sascha, 2¼x3" 200.00
Pitcher, gold ewer w/brushed gold spoked wheel decor, 10½" 150.00
Plate, chop; grape clusters enameled on metal w/gold, 13¾" 85.00
Plate, Surf Ballet, platinum on turq, 6¾", 4 for 32.00
Plate, Surf Ballet, platinum on turq, 8½", 6 for 50.00
Platter, Star Steed, gold-tone metal, wall hanging, 11½" 125.00
Tray, gr grapes enameled on metal, 17¾" 100.00
Tray, Surf Ballet, pk/gold on wht, 3-compartment, 10¾" sq 55.00
Vase, African linear decor, brns/rust/cream/blk, 5⅝x3⅝" 45.00
Vase, Aztec Horse, gold on wht, flared rim, 5" 55.00
Vase, chartreuse resin w/grapes in relief, cylindrical, 5¾" 55.00
Vase, Roof Tops, F20, 5x7x3" 55.00
Vase, Star Steed, ovoid, #F46, 11¼" 155.00
Vase/candle holder, gold w/fleur-de-lis pattern, 8-sided, 10" 80.00
Vase/candle holder, yel-gold resin w/abstract pattern, sticker, 11".80.00

Brayton Laguna

A few short years after Durlin Brayton married Ellen Webster Grieve, his small pottery, which he had opened in 1927, became highly successful. Extensive lines were created and all of them flourished. Hand-turned pieces were done in the early years; today these are the most difficult to find. Durlin Brayton hand incised ashtrays, vases, and dinnerware (plates in assorted sizes, pitchers, cups and saucers, and creamers and sugar bowls.) These early items were marked 'Laguna Pottery,' incised on unglazed bases.

Brayton's childrens' series is highly collected today as is the Walt Disney line. Also popular are the Circus line, Calasia (art pottery decorated with stylized feathers and circles), Webton Ware, the Blackamoor series, and the Gay Nineties line. Each seemed to prove more profitable than the lines before it. Both white and pink clays were utilized in production. At its peak, the pottery employed more than 150 people. After World War II when imports began to flood the market, Brayton Laguna was one of the companies that managed to hold their own. By 1968, however, it was necessary to cease production.

For more information on this as well as many other potteries in the state, we recommend *The Collector's Encyclopedia of California Pottery* by Jack Chipman; he is listed in the Directory under California. Our advisor for this category is Susan Cox; she is listed in the Directory under California.

Ashtray, cigarette rest, bl, incised Brayton, rare, 4½" dia............100.00
Bowl, man in sombrero smoking cigarette, 4" dia 275.00
Candle holder, seated Blackamoor, 5"..95.00
Figurine, Alice in Wonderland, 6"..300.00
Figurine, bird, stylized, blk w/gold trim, 9½x11"........................155.00
Figurine, Black dice player w/gr gloves & pk hat 85.00
Figurine, Black prince feeding grapes to tropical bird, 18½"....1,250.00
Figurine, bust of gypsy woman, 9"..250.00
Figurine, cow, purple, 9x5½"...195.00
Figurine, doe, Disney Snow White series, 9" 80.00
Figurine, donkey & cart, ceramic & wood, set............................150.00
Figurine, elephant, 1 front leg raised, trunk in air, 13½"............225.00
Figurine, Ferdinand the Bull, 7½x8" 500.00
Figurine, Gay Nineties, lovers in cab, 7½x11"............................350.00
Figurine, Gay Nineties, 3 men at bar, 7½x8½"............................100.00
Figurine, Gepetto, 8"...800.00
Figurine, Hawaiian hula girl, 4½"..150.00
Figurine, head & shoulders in blk matt, 12x13", minimum value...600.00
Figurine, Jiminy Cricket, 3" 600.00
Figurine, jockey on horse, 11"..370.00

Figurine, lady in undergarments, talks on phone/stands by chair, 9" ...275.00
Figurine, lady w/2 Russian Wolfhounds, 11" 115.00
Figurine, Little Boy Blue 275.00
Figurine, Little Red Riding Hood 275.00
Figurine, Mad Hatter, 7" 350.00
Figurine, Mexican peasant couple, 12½".....................................255.00
Figurine, Millie bent at waist looking through legs, 3¾"..............145.00
Figurine, native musician, stained/wht crackle glaze, 11" 175.00
Figurine, peasant woman w/baskets, 7¾"......................................55.00
Figurine, Pedro, 6½"...200.00
Figurine, Peruvian native man, 9¼" 350.00
Figurine, Petunia, little Black girl w/basket, 6¼" 175.00
Figurine, Pinnochio, 6" 500.00
Figurine, pirate sitting on treasure chest, 9" 450.00
Figurine, Pluto, howling, 6" 180.00
Figurine, red fox, seated/upright, H-57, lg 175.00
Figurine, rooster, H-47, 6x17" 115.00
Figurine, Rosita, 5½"...100.00

Figurine, rooster, ink stamp: Brayton – Calif USA, 8", $75.00. (Photo courtesy Lee Garmon)

Figurine, Sambo, little Black boy w/hands in pocket, 7¾"..........300.00
Figurine, squirrel, crouched, head tilted, wht crackle, T-14, 7½"...100.00
Figurine, St Bernard 200.00
Figurine, swan, gray & wht, 6x4½"..75.00
Figurine, Toucan, polychrome high glaze, 9"................................200.00
Figurine, Toucan, woodtone w/high glaze, 9"...............................125.00
Figurine, voodoo drummer, 13"...450.00
Figurines, Eric & Inger (Swedish boy & girl), pr 300.00
Figurines, fighting pirates, brn-stained bsk, 9", pr........................650.00
Figurines, Hillbilly Shotgun Wedding, set of 6 ....1,500.00
Figurines, Zizi & Fifi, maroon & gr, pr..495.00
Flower holder, Swedish peasant woman, 11 /2".............................350.00
Lamp base, little girl holding doll, rare...400.00
Mug, yel & brn, pretzel-shaped hdl...15.00
Pitcher, brn w/wht tulips, J-7, 5", w/5 matching mugs, set 130.00
Planter, fruits (pk) & leaves on turq, 12"..30.00
Shakers, mammy & chef, bl & wht, 5", pr....................................195.00
Shakers, man & woman, Webton Ware, pr....................................140.00
Tray, yel & brn, pretzel-shaped hdls, 10" 25.00
Vase, Calasia, raised circles & feathers, A-6, 9" 65.00
Vase, sea horse figural, wht rubbing w/turq trim, 8½" 225.00

Bread Plates and Trays

Bread plates and trays have been produced not only in many types of glass but in metal and pottery as well. Those considered most collectible were made during the last quarter of the nineteenth century from pressed glass with well-detailed embossed designs, many of them portraying a particularly significant historical event. A great number of these plates were sold at the 1876 Philadelphia Centennial Exposition by various glass manufacturers who exhibited their wares on the grounds. Among the themes depicted are the Declaration of Independence, the Constitution, McKinley's memorial 'It Is God's Way,' Remembrance of Three Presidents, the Purchase of Alaska, and various presidential campaigns, to mention only a few.

'L' numbers correspond with a reference book by Lindsey; 'S' refers to a book by Stuart. Our advisor for this category is Darlene Yohe; she is listed in the Directory under Arkansas.

Actress (Miss Neilson)	120.00
American Flag, 38 stars, L-51, 11x8"	235.00
Banner Baking Powder, shield center, 11"	155.00
Barley	65.00
Bishop, L-201	200.00
Canadian, amber, rnd	45.00
Cleveland/Thurman, clear/frosted, L-325, 9½x8½"	215.00
Columbus, milk glass, cut-out rim	80.00
Constitution w/eagle	60.00
Cupid & Venus, 10½" dia	55.00
Deer & Pine Tree, apple gr	125.00
Deer & Pine Tree, bl	65.00
Double Hands w/Grapes, milk glass	45.00
Egyptian, Cleopatra center, 13" L	80.00
Frosted Lion, Give Us This Day, 12½x9"	175.00
GAR	265.00
Garfield Drape, dtd	75.00
Garfield Drape, We Mourn Our Nation's Loss, L-303, 11½"	75.00
Garfield Memorial, 101 border	85.00
Good Luck, dbl horseshoe hdls	120.00
Grant Maple Leaf, Let Us Have Peace	95.00
Grant Maple Leaf, Let Us Have Peace, amber	110.00
Grant Maple Leaf, Let Us Have Peace, gr	160.00
Grape (It's a Pleasure)	55.00
Heroes of Bunker Hill	95.00
Jewel & Dewdrop (Kansas)	55.00
Lotus (Garden of Eden)	45.00
Maple Leaf, Gillinder, oval	75.00
McCormick's Reaper	160.00
McKinley, His Will Be Done, oval	55.00
Merry Christmas, bells in center, shallow bowl shape	75.00

McKinley, It Is God's Way His Will Be Done, $70.00.

Minerva	75.00
Moses Montifiore, L-239	75.00
Nellie Bly, oval, L-136, 12"	200.00
Niagara Falls, frosted, L489, 16" L	135.00
Old State House, L-32	55.00
Pioneer White Wings Flour 90th Anniversary, bundle of wheat hdls	175.00
Polar Bear, ship, L-486, 16"	165.00
Preparedness, L-481	300.00
Prescott Stark	60.00

Retriever, milk glass	80.00
Sheaf of Wheat, ftd oval, maple leaf hdls, Give Us This Day, NM	95.00
Sheraton	45.00
Three Graces, Pat dtd 1865	65.00
Three Presidents, In Remembrance, 12½x10"	95.00
Transcontinental Railroad, 9x12"	95.00
Washington Centennial, Washington center, frosted	140.00

Bretby

Bretby art pottery was made by Tooth & Co., at Woodville, near Burton-on-Trent, Derbyshire, from as early in 1884 until well into the twentieth century. Marks containing the 'Made in England' designation indicate twentieth-century examples.

Clock, female head surmount, HP bird & flowers on gray, 1900s, 10"	1,500.00
Jardiniere, gr over brn, scalloped rim, 1920s, sm	40.00
Pitcher, streaky gr, waisted, Nerton Ware, ca 1910, 7½x5½"	70.00
Vase, blk drip on cobalt, bulbous, #20E, 4⅞"	60.00
Vase, Clanta, dimpled decor, 4-hdl, ca 1900, 10x6", from $85 to	100.00
Vase, hammered copper look, #1688, 3", pr	70.00
Vase, Mr Pickwick relief, mc on brn, ca 1920, 10", from $60 to	85.00
Vase, Nouveau iris & Celtic scrolls, faux jewels, #1729, 20x9½"	550.00
Vase, Nouveau riveted copper look w/faux jewels, conical, hdls, 9"	425.00
Vase, stork & bamboo figural, ca 1891-1900, prof rstr, 11¾"	225.00

Bride's Baskets and Bowls

Victorian brides were showered with gifts, as brides have always been; one of the most popular gift items was the bride's basket. Art glass inserts from both European and American glasshouses, some in lovely transparent hues with dainty enameled florals, others of Peachblow, Vasa Murrhina, satin or cased glass, were cradled in complementary silverplated holders. While many of these holders were simply engraved or delicately embossed, others (such as those from Pairpoint and Wilcox) were wonderfully ornate, often with figurals of cherubs or animals or birds. The bride's basket was no longer in fashion after the turn of the century.

Watch for 'marriages' of bowls and frames. To warrant the best price, the two pieces should be the original pairing. If you can't be certain of this, at least check to see that the bowl fits snugly into the frame. Beware of later-made bowls (such as Fenton's) in Victorian holders and new frames being produced in Taiwan.

Our advisor for this category is Deborah Maggard; she is listed in the Directory under Ohio. In the listings that follow, if no frame is described, the price is for a bowl only.

Amberina w/HP daisies, Dmn Quilt/melon ribs, petal rim, 5x9¾"	800.00
Chartruse w/gold & wht daisies, pk int, ruffled, 10½"	300.00
Cranberry, ruffled rim; ornate SP fr (lt wear), 11½x10½"	225.00
Cranberry opal Coin Spot; ornate SP fr, 11"	425.00
Frosted w/ruffled gr enamel rim, HP wht flowers, 11"	100.00
Mahog-red ruffled rim w/HP decor, chartreuse oil spots; Tufts fr, 8"	500.00
Opal w/vaseline rim, gold enamel, opal threads, 4¼x11½"	400.00
Peachblow, melon ribs, crystal ruffled rim, HP floral, 5¼x11"	750.00
Peachblow, sq ruffled rim, HP florals w/gold; SP Pelton Bros fr, 14"	2,150.00
Pk cased, HP roses, clear ruffled trim; 4-footed SP fr, 12x10"	325.00
Pk cased opal w/amber rim/HP peaches/gold; SP cherub 2-hdl fr, 17" L	1,800.00
Pk MOP Dmn Quilt; ornate Rockford SP #8020 fr, 13x10x6"	215.00
Pk MOP Herringbone; Homan SP fr w/cupids/lattice/etc, 4¾x10"	850.00
Pk o/l w/hobnails, clear ruffle; brass fr w/emb decor, 7¾x9½"	175.00
Pk satin w/HP florals, ruffled; rstr SP fr w/dolphins, 8¼x7½"	325.00

Pk to yel on wht (like burmese), dbl griffins/flowers, Mt WA, 4x9"....750.00
Pk w/HP petals & gold leaves; Austria SP fr, 10½" 200.00
Pk w/vaseline ruffled rim, gold trim, opal threading, 4¼x11½" ..300.00
Pk w/wht int, HP floral, scalloped; mk Poole SP fr, 12" dia 425.00
Tomato red w/yel int, sq rim, emb drapes, clear edge, 3½x10¾"..200.00
Wht w/lt to deep pk int, ruffled rim; Colonial Silver SP fr, 12"..275.00
Wht w/pk int, crimped citron rim, triangular, 3x9" 150.00
Wht w/pk int & amber ruffled rim; Wilcox SP fr, 11" 275.00

Bristol Glass

Bristol is a type of semi-opaque opaline glass whose name was derived from the area in England where it was first produced. Similar glass was made in France, Germany, and Italy. In this country, it was made by the New England Glass Company and to a lesser extent by its contemporaries. During the eighteenth and nineteenth centuries, Bristol glass was imported in large amounts and sold cheaply, thereby contributing to the demise of the earlier glasshouses here in America. It is very difficult to distinguish the English Bristol from other opaline types. Style, design, and decoration serve as clues to its origin; but often only those well versed in the field can spot these subtle variations.

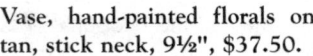

Vase, hand-painted florals on tan, stick neck, 9½", $37.50.

Biscuit jar, turq w/floral, resilvered top/rim/hdl, 6¾" 195.00
Box, wht, children building snowman, 2⅜x4½" 145.00
Cheese dish, wht w/floral, scalloped base, 7¾x9½" 195.00
Lamp, amethyst w/floral, Krono Model 1914, 2-pc, 23¾" 150.00
Lamp, bright bl w/wht florals & gold, brass collar, burner, 12"....220.00
Mug, cobalt w/grapes & gold, ftd, appl hdl, 4x3¼" 25.00
Sweetmeat jar, gr, HP birds, SP lid/rim/hdl, 4⅜x3¼" 125.00
Teapot, cream opaque, water birds in grasses, 5¼" 295.00
Vase, wht w/mc floral, bulbous, 6¼" 30.00
Wine, clear, mc floral w/gold, 4½" 25.00

British Royalty Commemoratives

Commemoratives have been issued for royal events since Edward VI's 1547 coronation through modern-day occasions, so it's possible to start collecting at any period of history. Many collectors begin with Queen Victoria's reign, collecting examples for each succeeding monarch and continuing through modern events.

Some collectors identify with a particular royal personage and limit their collecting to that era, ie., Queen Elizabeth's life and reign. Other collectors look to the future, expanding their collection to include the heir apparents Prince Charles and his first-born son, Prince William.

Royalty commemorative collecting is often further refined around a particular type of collectible. Nearly any item with room for a portrait

and a description has been manufactured as a souvenir. Thus royalty commemoratives are available in glass, ceramic, metal, fabric, plastic, and paper. This wide variety of material lends itself to any pocketbook. The range covers expensive limited edition ceramics to inexpensive souvenir key chains, puzzles, matchbooks, etc.

Many recent royalty headline events have been commemorated in a variety of souvenirs. Buying some of these modern commemoratives at the moderate issue prices could be a good investment. After all, today's events are tomorrow's history.

For further study we recommend *British Royal Commemoratives* by our advisor for this category, Audrey Zeder; she is listed in the Directory under Washington.

Key:
A/S — Andrew/Sarah
ann — anniversary
BD — birthday
C/D — Charles/Diana
chr — christening
Chs — Charles
com — commemorative
cor — coronation
EPNS — electro-plated nickel silver
ILN — Illustrated London News
inscr — inscribed
invest — investiture
jub — jubilee
K/Q — King/Queen
LE — limited edition
mem — memorial
Pr — Prince
Prs — Princess
QM — Queen Mother
wed — wedding
Wm — William
vis — visit

Baby dish, George VI cor, mc portrait/decor, raised sides, 6½"......80.00
Beaker, C/D '81 vis Wales, mc decor, lion hdl, Caverswall 185.00
Beaker, Edward VII, sepia portrait, mc official design, 1937, 4" 55.00
Beaker, Edward VII cor, King's Dinner, gr portrait/decor, Doulton....150.00
Beaker, Edward VII cor, mc portrait/decor, enamel......................175.00
Beaker, George VI '39 vis, clear glass, bl portrait K/Q+2 Prs.........35.00
Beaker, George V jub, sepia portrait, mc official design, 4" 55.00
Beaker, George VI cor, clear glass, bl portrait/decor, 4¾" 20.00
Beaker, George VI cor, gray portrait, mc decor, Doulton, 4" 85.00
Biscuit bbl, George VI cor, mc decor, brass hdl, 5" 125.00
Book, Royal Tour Canada, arrangements, 1959, 7x5"....................25.00
Book, Victoria '97 jub, Book of Common Prayer, 5x4"..................55.00
Booklet, C/D vis Canada, portrait cover/foldout, Methuen, 1983.35.00
Booklet, C/D wed, Royal Engagement Official Souvenir...............45.00
Booklet, Earl Harewood wed, Pitkins, 1949 ....20.00
Booklet, Pr Chs, Country & Sporting Pub, 1940s, set of 3 ....50.00
Booklet, Prs Elizabeth, Royal Tour Kenya, Daily Graphic, 1952 ...25.00
Booklet, Prs Elizabeth, Wife & Mother, Thomas Pub, 1948..........25.00
Bookmark, Pr Wm birth, bl leather w/gold decor 25.00
Bookmark, QM 100 BD, woven portrait/decor, on com card, Cash ...30.00
Bottle, beer; C/D wed, mc label, Courage, unopened 45.00
Bowl, C/D wed, mc portrait/decor, Royal Grafton, 4½" 40.00
Bowl, crystal, w/rose candle, Prs Diana mem, Stuart......................35.00
Bowl, Edward VI cor, relief portrait, rtcl rim, metal, 3½"..............45.00
Bowl, Elizabeth II cor, brn portrait, mc Tudor rose decor, 6" 35.00
Bowl, George VI cor, insc portrait/decor, chrome, 1½x9¾"..........30.00
Bust, Edward VIII, soapstone, 1937, 5½" 55.00
Cake tin, Victoria '97 jub, relief portrait/decor, 4x2½".................75.00
Compact, Elizabeth II cor, mc portrait, 3¾"..................................60.00
Compact, George VI cor, pastel K/Q portrait, Rachel, 1¾" 80.00
Covered dish, George VI '39 vis, blk/wht K/Q w/capital buildings..60.00
Cup & saucer, Edward VII cor, mc K/Q portrait in cor robe/crown...165.00
Cup & saucer, Edward VIII, blk/wht portrait, Japan, 1937............35.00
Cup & saucer, George V cor, mc portrait/decor, bone china.......150.00
Cup & saucer, George VI 1939 vis, blk/wht family portrait, Meakin...55.00
Cup & saucer, Victoria '97 jub, sepia portrait/sports events 175.00
Doll, Pr Wm, bsk, wht sailor suit, Danbury, 1986, 12" 295.00

Doll, Prs Diana 5-pc nesting doll family set, HP wood **95.00**

Doll, Prs Elizabeth, compo, glass eyes, Alexander, 1939, 20" **650.00**

Egg cup, Edward VIII, mc portrait/decor, gold rim, ftd, 1937 ....**55.00**

Ephemera, Elizabeth II, ad Christmas card, mc portrait, 1953, 9x6" ..**20.00**

Ephemera, Elizabeth II cor coloring book, unused, 14x10"............**35.00**

Ephemera, George VI cor paper napkin, mc flags/date decor **12.00**

Ephemera, Pr George ad card, Milward Needles, 1880, 3x2½" **15.00**

Figure, C/D on base, Dapol, 1984, 5"....................................**75.00**

Figure, Elizabeth II & Philip on base, Dapol, 1984, 5".................**75.00**

Figure, Prs Diana, HP, dk bl dress, 1997, 11¾"......................**85.00**

Figure, Q Victoria, young, in plaid dress, 1870, 7"....................**135.00**

Horse brass, C/D wed, relief portrait/decor, scallop rim, 3"............**45.00**

Horse brass, Elizabeth II cor, Derby Cor Horse Race **45.00**

Horse brass, George V cor, relief portrait/decor, woven ribbon **35.00**

ILN Record No Elizabeth II cor, bl cover, gold decor, 14x10".......**75.00**

ILN Record No Elizabeth II jub, bl cover/silver decor, 14x10"......**60.00**

ILN Record No George V jub, red cover/silver decor, 14x10" **125.00**

ILN Royal Silver Wed No, George VI, May 1, 1948 ....**45.00**

ILN Royal Wed No, Prs Elizabeth, November 29, 1947 ....**35.00**

Jewelry, Edward VII 3-generation cuff links, sepia portrait **50.00**

Jewelry, Prs Diana pin, blk lacquer, HP portrait, LE, 2¼"..............**55.00**

Jewelry, Victoria pendant, Canada coin, enameled, in gold bezel .**25.00**

Medallion, Elizabeth II '76 US vis, bronze, 1¼"........................**35.00**

Medallion, Prs Diana mem, 14k gold plate on silver,¾", MIB.......**55.00**

Medallion, Victoria '87 jub, brass w/red enamel decor, 1½".........**95.00**

Medallion, Victoria '87 jub, brass w/silver relief portrait, 2½" **45.00**

Medallion, Year of 3 Kings Ann 1936-86, in display holder.........**55.00**

Miniature, George V cor jug, mc K/Q decor, T&K, 3" **75.00**

Miniature, George VI cor bowl, mc portrait/decor, 2½x½"...........**35.00**

Miniature, George VI cor decanter, gold portrait on glass, 4¼" **45.00**

Miniature, George VI cor tray, mc portrait/decor, china, 3x2" **45.00**

Miniature, Prs Elizabath/Margaret dish, mc portrait w/lustre, 5" ...**65.00**

Miniature, Prs Elizabeth/Margaret c/s, mc portrait w/lustre **40.00**

Miniature, Prs Elizabeth/Margaret platter, mc portrait w/lustre, 5" ..**65.00**

Miniature, Prs Elizabeth/Margaret sugar bowl, mc portrait w/lustre, 3"..**45.00**

Miniature, Q Mary cor vase, mc portrait, 2¼" **75.00**

Miniature, QM '80 plate, mc portrait, purple hat/dress, 2¼".........**30.00**

Miniature, Victoria mem tray, mc portrait/decor, tin, 4x3" **125.00**

Movie film, Elizabeth II 1953 Birthday Parade, 8mm **50.00**

Mug, C/D engagement, lion/unicorn/announcement, Mays.........**150.00**

Mug, C/D wed, mc pastel portrait/decor, china, Royal Grafton.....**45.00**

Mug, C/D wed, milk glass, mc portrait/decor **25.00**

Mug, Edward VII cor, mc K/Q portrait/decor, angular hdl, 3" **145.00**

Mug, Elizabeth II '91 Washington vis, blk/wht Q/Bush portrait, Chown ...**155.00**

Mug, Elizabeth II cor, mc decor, Official Design **25.00**

Mug, Elizabeth II 50th wed ann, mc portrait/decor, Cantree of Wales ..**45.00**

Mug, George V cor, mc portrait, dbl pierced hdl, 2⅝"..................**60.00**

Mug, George V jub, sepia portrait, mc decor, silver rim/hdl, 3" **55.00**

Mug, George VI cor, royal family sepia portrait by Marcus Adam.**65.00**

Mug, Pr Chs 50th BD, mc portrait/decor, LE 50, Chown **75.00**

Mug, Pr Wales '27 vis Canada, sepia portrait, Paragon **75.00**

Mug, Pr Wm '82 birth, C/D/Wm portrait, mc decor, Creemore....**35.00**

Mug, Pr Wm '82 birth, mc portrait, ftd, Crown Staffordshire **45.00**

Mug, QM 99 BD, mc portrait/decor, LE 80, Chown.....................**100.00**

Mug, Victoria '97 jug, mc portrait/castle decor, thumb-grip hdl..**175.00**

Newspaper, Duke of Kent wed, Daily Dispatch, November 29, 1934..**20.00**

Newspaper, Edward VII funeral, The Queen, May 21, 1910..........**30.00**

Newspaper, King Abdicates, Daily Herald, December 11, 1936....**35.00**

Newspaper, King His People Hail Victory, Daily Sketch, 1918 .....**20.00**

Newspaper, Prs Elizabeth wed, Daily Graphic, November 21, 1947..**25.00**

Newspaper, Prs Louise wed, The Scotsman, March 22, 1871 ....**20.00**

Novelty, C/D slippers, Splitting Image, 1988, unused...................**95.00**

Novelty, C/d wed house key blank, relief portrait/decor, 2¾" **35.00**

Novelty, Edward VII cor pipe, relief portrait, wht clay, 4¼"...........**75.00**

Novelty, Elizabeth II cor fold-out needle book, mc protrait/decor.**25.00**

Novelty, Elizabeth II cor letter opener, relief portrait, 7¾" **25.00**

Novelty, Elizabeth II cor periscope, cb................................**75.00**

Novelty, Elizabeth II jub key chain/coin purse, 3½" dia **15.00**

Novelty, Elizabeth II jub soap dish, plastic, mc portrait/decor.......**25.00**

Novelty, George VI '39 Canada vis coat hanger, portrait on wood..**45.00**

Novelty, George VI cor pocketknife, portrait/decor, 2-blade, 3" ...**50.00**

Novelty, George VI purse mirror, mc portrait/decor, 3" dia **35.00**

Novelty, Prs Diana phone cards, 8 different versions **40.00**

Novelty, Prs Elizabeth '52 vis Canada bottle cap, mc portrait/decor ..**12.00**

Paperweight, Elizabeth '77 jub, cameo portrait on amber, Baccarat .**165.00**

Paperweight, Elizabeth II '77 jub, marble w/enamel decor, 3x2" ...**25.00**

Photograph, Elizabeth II w/Churchill, blk/wht, 1955, 9x7"...........**25.00**

Photograph, Prs Elizabeth '47 wed, Elizabeth/Philip, blk/wht, 8x10" .**35.00**

Pin-bk, Edward VII cor, blk/wht portrait, mc decor, 1¼" **45.00**

Pin-bk, Prs Elizabeth/Margaret, blk portrait/decor, 1937, 1¼".......**35.00**

Pin-bk, Victoria mem, blk/wht portrait, brass bezel, 1¾"............**50.00**

Pitcher, Elizabeth II cor, sepia portrait w/mc decor, Doulton, 6½"..**475.00**

Pitcher, Victoria 1860 Review, relief portrait/decor, Sanford, 10"...**825.00**

Plaque, Victoria '87 jub, wood w/relief profile portrait, 5x4".......**195.00**

Plate, C/D wed, mc portrait, relief inscription, Myott, 10"............**75.00**

Plate, Edward VII cor, mc portrait, cobalt border, 8½"................**165.00**

Plate, Edward VII cor, mc portrait, pierced border, 8¼"...............**150.00**

Plate, Edward VII mem, mo portrait, silver rim, 9½"..................**225.00**

Plate, Elizabeth II '54 Australia vis, relief portrait/decor, 5½".......**45.00**

Plate, George V cor, mc K/Q portrait/decor, cobalt border, 6" **65.00**

Plate, George V jub, Art Deco shape, Doulton, 4x2".................**65.00**

Plate, Pr Wm '82 birth, mc C/D portrait, octagonal, 8"...............**65.00**

Plate, Pr Wm 12th BD & Pr Henry 10th BD, mc decor, 3½".......**55.00**

Plate, Prs Diana, 3 portraits, Royal Doulton, 1987, 10½"............**325.00**

Plate, Victoria '87 jub, Balance of Power theme, octagonal, 9"...**295.00**

Plate, Victoria '87 jub, blk/wht portrait, relief basketweave border ..**195.00**

Plate, Victoria '97 jub, mc portrait, scallop rim, Doulton, 10" **225.00**

Plate, Victoria 97 jub, bl portrait/decor, scalloped edge, 9" **195.00**

Playing cards, George VI cor, mc portrait, dbl deck.....................**75.00**

Postcard, C/D Royal Honeymoon, bl portrait/decor, Faga **20.00**

Postcard, QM 100 BD, mc portrait, royal residences....................**5.00**

Poster, Prs Diana mem, blk/wht portrait, Elton John poem, 36x24"..**30.00**

Pressed glass, C/D wed plate, portrait/decor, lav, 3½"................**35.00**

Pressed glass, Elizabeth II cor bowl, crown shape, 4x7"...............**45.00**

Pressed glass, George VI cor plate, relief portrait, clear, 9½"..........**95.00**

Pressed glass, Pr Wm 10 BD plate, portrait, amber, 3½"..............**35.00**

Pressed glass, Prs Diana 30 BD plate, portrait, gr, 3½"...............**35.00**

Pressed glass, Victoria '40 wed vase, blk relief portrait, 3¼".......**135.00**

Pressed glass, Victoria '87 jub compote, amber, ftd, 5x5"............**110.00**

Pressed glass, Victoria '87 jub plate, amber, 10" **95.00**

Program, George VI '39 Saskatchewan Canada vis, Official **25.00**

Puzzle, Prs Anne '50 chr, mc family portrait, Tower......................**75.00**

Puzzle, Prs Diana, beige hat/raincoat, Waddingtons, 1988............**45.00**

Record, George V 1928 opening ceremonies, Columbia, 78 rpm..**55.00**

Ribbon, Elizabeth II cor ribbon, mc decor, 1½ yards **15.00**

Ribbon, Victoria '87 jub, bl w/woven profile, decor, 5x¾"............**75.00**

Ribbon, Victoria mem, wht w/blk portrait/inscr, Victoria Day, 5" .**60.00**

Scrapbook, C/D wed, sb mc portrait cover, unused, 16x11" **35.00**

Scrapbook, Prs Elizabeth '51 Canada vis, mc portrait cover, unused ..**45.00**

Sheet music, Will the King Be Proud of Canada, 1915 ....**30.00**

Sheet music, 1863 wed, God Bless the Prince of Wales................**50.00**

Spoon, Elizabeth II jub, figural seated Q on throne, SP, 4"............**25.00**

Spoon, QM 100 BD, mc portrait/decor, SP, 4½" **15.00**

Stamps, Prs Diana mem, Cuba, 7 different, cancelled...................**5.00**

Stamps, Prs Diana 21 BD, 4 stamp block, Korea, 7x4" **25.00**

Tea caddy, George VI cor, mc decor, ceramic, Mailing, 7x6" **225.00**

Tea set, Elizabeth II cor, dk bl jasper, Wedgwood, 3-pc............**1,050.00**

Teapot, Edward VII cor, mc portrait, pk lustre, 2-cup...................**195.00**

Teapot, George V cor, sepia portrait, mc decor, brn trim, 2-cup .175.00
Teapot, George VI '39 vis, mc portrait/decor, yel, 4-cup 150.00
Teapot, Pr Chs/Wm/Harry 2000 Mil, LE 10, Chown, 2-cup 150.00
Textile, C/D wed tea towel, blk/wht portrait, bl decor, 30x19" **35.00**
Textile, Edward VIII banner, portrait on red/wht/bl, 1937, 36x24" ...55.00
Textile, Victoria '87 handkerchief, mc hand embr, 13x13"...........35.00
Textile, Victoria '97 handkerchief, silk-like w/mc portrait, 11x11" ..95.00
Thimble, Pr Wm 18th BD, mc portrait/decor, bone china 10.00
Tin, C/D wed, mc portrait/decor, attached brass hdl, 11" 75.00
Tin, Edward VIII '36 accession, mc portrait/decor, 6x3x1¼"........75.00
Tin, Elizabeth II cor, mc portrait, Collin St Bakery, 3x8" dia 35.00
Tin, George V cor, mc portrait/decor, Rowntree, 5¼x2¼" 95.00
Tin, George VI cor, mc portrait/decor, bl border, octagonal, 6x5".35.00
Tin, George VI cor, mc portrait/decor, Cleves, 10x7" 45.00
Tin, Pr Wm birth, portrait C/D as children & adults, upright.......55.00
Tin, Prs Mary 1914 gift to WWI troops, relief decor, brass............95.00
Toby mug, Elizabeth II, seated w/Dog, Kevin Frances, 1992........325.00
Tray, C/D wed, mc portrait/decor, Canadian Sunset, 11" dia.........35.00
Tray, Victoria '87 jub, impressed portrait/decor, brass, 12" dia.......75.00

Broadmoor

In October of 1933, the Broadmoor Art Pottery was formed and space rented at 217 East Pikes Peak Avenue, Colorado Springs, Colorado. Most of the pottery they produced would not be considered elaborate, and only a handful was decorated. Many pieces were signed by P.H. Genter, J.B. Hunt, Eric Hellman, and Cecil Jones. It is reported that this plant closed in 1936, and Genter moved his operations to Denver.

Broadmoor pottery is marked in several ways: a Greek or Egyptian-type label depicting two potters (one at the wheel and one at a tile-pressing machine) and the word Broadmoor; an ink-stamped 'Broadmoor Pottery, Colorado Springs (or Denver), Colorado'; and an incised version of the latter.

The bottoms of all pieces are always white and can be either glazed or unglazed. Glaze colors are turquoise, green, yellow, cobalt blue, light blue, white, pink, pink with blue, maroon red, black, and copper lustre. Both matt and high gloss finishes were used.

The company produced many advertising tiles, novelty items, coasters, ashtrays, and vases for local establishments around Denver and as far away as Wyoming. An Indian head was incised into many of the advertising items, which also often bear a company or a product name. A series of small animals (horses, dogs, elephants, lambs, squirrels, a toucan bird, and a hippo), each about 2" high, are easily recognized by the style of their modeling and glaze treatments, though all are unmarked.

Vase, embossed Egyptian figure on turquoise, signed PH Genter, dated 1936, 10½x7", $500.00. (Photo courtesy Carol and Jim Carlton)

Ashtray, Creditors Collection Bureau...Colo, turq 40.00
Bookend, Art Deco head, crackle finish, minimum value 165.00
Bowl, red, incurvate rim, low, 15" 60.00
Candle holder, 3 metal flower forms on scrolling base, w/inserts...85.00
Creamer & sugar bowl, bl matt, 2" 40.00
Figurine, squirrel, mk, 2" 50.00
Lamp base, creamy wht swirl, sgn C Jones, 15", rare, minimum value...225.00
Paperweight, Indian head, bl matt, rare..65.00
Pitcher, cobalt, slim, 12"..125.00
Vase, bl spongeware, bulbous, 5" 50.00
Vase, cobalt, pleated look w/incurvate rim, w/sticker, 15" 195.00
Vase, cobalt w/shiny pyrite flecks, shouldered, 12" 140.00
Vase, cornucopia; bl to mauve, 6" 50.00
Vase, gr, sm raised rim, slightly bulbous, PH Genter, 4"................70.00
Vase, gr matt, rectangular w/rnd ft, orig sticker, 15", minimum value .200.00
Vase, red, appl hdls, 6½"...65.00
Vase, red, 3 rim-to-hip hdls, sgn E Hellman, 8" 137.50
Vase, turq, flared rim, 2"...22.50
Vase, wht w/emb floral, ball shape, 6"..50.00

Broadsides

Webster defines a broadside as simply a large sheet of paper printed on one side. During the 1880s, they were the most practical means of mass communication. By the middle of the century, they had become elaborate and lengthy with information, illustrations, portraits, and fancy border designs. Those printed on coated stock are usually worth more.

Battalion orders, sgn in type by Joseph E Smith, 1818, 18¾x14" ..**900.00**
Declaration of individual as notorious liar, 1868, 4¾x9½" 175.00
Erklarung der Unabhangigkeit...July 1776, Washington reserve, 24x19" .45.00
General orders from Boston headquarters, 1791, 7¾x13" 700.00
MA resolution, type set, sgn in type by John Hancock, 1778, 13x8½"..2,000.00
Meeting in MO courthouse re nominations to citizen's ticket, 6x9" 85.00
Memorial poem to fine lady, 26 verses, 1800s, 12x9" 85.00
Message of President Jackson to Congress on silk, 1830, 26x20" ..4,000.00

Old Style Minstrel Show..., December 5th, 1928, with detailed specifics, 20x13½", EX, $70.00.

Paddock-Hawley Iron Co, St Louis MO advertising, 1895, 13x6" ...50.00
Pequea Assoc for Detection of Thieves..., routes/names, PA, 1859 ....35.00
Poem, Maiden's Lamentation, Revolutionary War, British, 1776, 14x5" .3,500.00
Public sale in MO, 1868, 12¼x9½"...85.00
Revolutionary war enlistment for Continental Army, 1871, 10x7" ...2,750.00
1812 Anti-War message, NY, 1812, 13x9½" 550.00

Bronzes

Thomas Ball, George Bessell, and Leonard Volk were some of the earliest American sculptors who produced figures in bronze for home decor during the 1840s. Pieces of historical significance were the most popular, but by the 1880s a more fanciful type of artwork took hold. Some of the fine sculptors of the day were Daniel Chester French, Augustus St. Gaudens, and John Quincy Adams Ward. Bronzes reached the height of their popularity at the turn of the century. The American West was portrayed to its fullest by Remington, Russell, James Frazier, Hermon MacNeil, and Solon Borglum. Animals of every species were modeled by A.P. Proctor, Paul Bartlett, and Albert Laellele, to name but a few.

Art Nouveau and Art Deco influenced the medium during the '20s, evidenced by the works of Allen Clark, Harriet Frismuth, E.F. Sanford, and Bessie P. Vonnoh.

Be aware that recasts abound. While often esthetically satisfactory, they are not original and should be priced accordingly. In much the same manner as prints are evaluated, the original castings made under the direction of the artist are the most valuable. Later castings from the original mold are worth less. A recast is not made from the original mold. Instead, a rubber-like substance is applied to the bronze, peeled away, and filled with wax. Then, using the same 'lost wax' procedure as the artist uses on completion of his original wax model, a clay-like substance is formed around the wax figure and the whole fired to vitrify the clay. The wax, of course, melts away, hence the term 'lost wax.' Recast bronzes lose detail and are somewhat smaller than the original due to the shrinkage of the clay mold.

Moigniez, Jules (1835 – 1895); sheep grouping, 11x16", $3,000.00. (Photo courtesy Jackson's Auctioneers and Appraisers of Fine Art)

Austria, nude seated on cvd marble base, 14½" 800.00
Austrian, harlequin-style lady dancer, ivory inlay, 9¾" 980.00
Barillot, E; Court Jester, ivory inlay & cold pnt, marble socle, 11"....600.00
Bergman, Franz Xavier; cameleer group, gold pnt, ca 1900, 8¼"....1,380.00
Bergman, Franz Xavier; Orientalist dancer seated, polychrome, 11"...1,980.00
Chevaux de Marli, trainer & rearing horse, 23½x18½x8½".......990.00
Chiparus, dancer, ivory inlay, onyx base, late 19th C, 16¾"....6,600.00
Chiparus, girl, ivory face, winter attire, #1138, ca 1925, 7¾"..2,300.00
Chiparus, Scarf Dancer, mc details, ca 1925, 26" 7,475.00
Clark, Balinese dancer, nude w/headdress, 8⅞" 5,175.00
Continental, eagle on marble plinth, late 1800s, 13x5¼" 140.00
Drouot, Eduoard; Indian on horseback, gr-gold patina, 1900, 21"..4,750.00
Eisenberger, L; medieval knight on horsebk, marble plinth, 22x14x8"...1,980.00
Erte, lady among butterflies, stepped base, 20½" 1,850.00
French, classical youth w/animal skin on shoulder, Barbedienne, 25" ...1,600.00
French, shepherd w/sheep, 19th C, 7½x9x4½" 400.00
Frishmuth, Harrite; nude dancer, blk marble base, Gorham, 1927, 15"...9,500.00
Godard, A; untitled woman seated w/knees bent, marble base, 15x24"..3,165.00
Granger, nude dancing w/grapes, gr patina, 1930s, 19" 1,265.00
Kernalan, flapper girl, ivory inlay face & limbs, 1925, 15¼" ...4,400.00
Kitson, HH; Jefferson Davis, dk patina, ca 1927, 26¾x9¼x8" ...5,775.00
Lippmann, A; French Cavalier, 1874, 24" 1,650.00
Longman, Victory in form of classical athlete, marble base 3,750.00
Lorenzl, lady dancing, gr marble base, EX patina, 1925, 9" 500.00
Meier, lady w/flowers, ivory face, HP details, 8".............................60.00

Muller, H; Diana, verde patina, sienna marble base, 19th C, 12¼"....330.00
Pierrot Charol, ivory face & hands, oval marble base, 12⅜" ...1,400.00
Poertzel, snake charmer, ivory inlay, ca 1930, 21" 9,200.00
Robert Fres, woman on chariot w/cherubs, rouge marble base, 22x25" ...6,000.00
Ron Sauvage after A Bagoet, Venus de Milo, 20th C, 22" 550.00
SM Devolterra, Roman warrior on horsebk, marble base, 20th C, 20x40" ...1,045.00
Somme, maiden in long gown w/sword, ivory mts, 9" 1,000.00
Toussaint, Armand; Roman Slave, Barbedienne foundry mk, 1850, 28" .3,000.00
Trodoux, pheasants (2) in underbrush, on wooden stand, 23½".650.00
Unknown, classical woman, 11½x15½"..................................660.00
Unknown, lion, recumbent, detailed mane, 20x36", pr...........2,000.00
Vannetti, tiger roaring w/2 cubs, lt brn patina, 10½x25".........1,600.00
Villanis, bust of lady in turban, agate base, 5½" 185.00

Brouwer

Theophilis A. Brouwer, an accomplished artist even before his interests turned to the medium of pottery, started a small one-man operation in 1894 in East Hampton, New York. Two years later he relocated in Westhampton, where he perfected the technique of fire-painting, learning to control the effects of the kiln to produce the best possible results. In 1925 he founded the Ceramic Flame Company in New York, but it is for his earlier work that he is best known. Brouwer died in 1932.

Vase, dk brn metallic w/some copper, gr & purple irid, 5x6".......825.00
Vase, flame-pnt yel/orange/brn organic lustre, 7½x4", EX..........650.00
Vase, yel & gunmetal lustre flame, 12¼x8" 1,400.00

Brownies by Palmer Cox

Created by Palmer Cox in 1883, the Brownies charmed children through the pages of books and magazines, as dolls, on their dinnerware, in advertising material, and on souvenirs. Each had his own personality, among them The Bellhop, The London Bobby, The Chairman, and Uncle Sam. But the oversized, triangular face with the startled expression, the protruding tummy, and the spindle legs were characteristics of them all. They were inspired by the Scottish legends related to Cox as a child by his parents, who were of English descent. His introduction of the Brownies to the world was accomplished by a poem called *The Brownies Ride*. Books followed in rapid succession, thirteen in the series, all written as well as illustrated by Palmer Cox.

By the late 1890s, the Brownies were active in advertising. They promoted such products as games, coffee, toys, patent medicines, and rubber boots. 'Greenies' were the Brownies' first cousins, created by Cox to charm and to woo through the pages of the advertising almanacs of the G.G. Green Company of New Jersey. Perhaps the best-known endorsement in the Brownies' career was for the Kodak Brownie, which became so popular and sold in such volume that their name became synonymous with this type of camera. Our advisor for this category is Anne Kier; she is listed in the Directory under Ohio.

Ashtray, Brownie scene, RS Germany, 1913 ....75.00
Basket, SP, Brownies w/chocolate advertising, Tufts 225.00
Book, Another Brownie Book, NY, 1890, 1st ed, VG 150.00
Book, Brownies & Goblins, Grosset Dunlap, no date, VG...........45.00
Book, Brownies & Other Stories, ca 1900, VG............................55.00
Book, Brownies & Prince Florimel, Century, 1918, VG 95.00
Book, Brownies at Home, laminated cover, Dover, 1968, EX........35.00
Book, Brownies at Home, w/dust cover, 1942, VG 35.00
Book, Brownies in Fairyland, Century Co 45.00
Book, Funny Stories About Funny People, 1905, EX...................35.00
Book, Little Goody Two Shoes, 1903, EX..................................40.00

Book, Querie Queers, color plates, EX 125.00
Book, The Brownies, Their Book, 1897, EX 175.00
Bottle, soda; emb Brownies, M...30.00
Brownie Portrait Cubes, McLoughlin Bros, c Cox 1892, VG......300.00
Candlestick, Bobby, majolica, 7½" 300.00
Candy dish, 15 Brownies, ball ft, Tufts SP, 7x5½" 210.00
Cigar holder/ashtray, full-figure Brownie, Pairpoint SP 350.00
Creamer, Little Boy Blue verse & 4 Brownies, gold trim, china....80.00
Creamer, Scottsman head, majolica, 3¼" 80.00
Cup & saucer, demi; comical action Brownies, Ceramic Art Co...110.00
Figure, Chinaman, papier-mache head, 9", EX 450.00
Figures, papier-mache w/stick legs, jtd arms, 1900s, 5", EX, 4 for..1,250.00
Fruit crate label, Brownies collect/distribute orange juice, 10" 45.00
Game, 9-Pins, 1883, MIB 1,800.00
Humidor, Bobby head figural, majolica, 6" 165.00
Ice cream bag, Cox illus, 5¢ orig value, 1930s, M 40.00
Magazine page, Ladies' Home Journal, Cox illus, ca 1890 ....18.00
Match holder, Brownie on striker, majolica 185.00
Needle book, Brownies, 1892 World's Fair, rare 64.00
Paper doll, Indian Brownie, Lion Coffee, EX 40.00
Paperweight, Brownie figural, SP...125.00
Pencil box, rolling pin shape, 15 Brownies in boat 95.00
Pitcher, china, Brownies playing golf on tan, 6" 155.00
Pitcher, china, 2 Brownies on front, 3 on bk, 4½" 75.00
Plate, porc, mk La Francaise, 7"...85.00
Plate, SP, Brownies on rim, 8½" 75.00
Rubber stamp, set of 12 ....100.00
Sheet music, Dance of the Brownies...30.00
Sign, emb Brownies on tin, Howell's Root Beer, EX...................185.00
Table set, brass, emb Brownies, 3-pc (knife/fork/spoon), no box...75.00
Table set, brass, emb Brownies, 6", in orig box...........................90.00
Trade card, Sheriff's Sale Segars, Brownies & product, 5x3" 25.00
Tray, 2 fencing Brownies, self hdls, china, 6¼x4½" 95.00

Brush-McCoy

George Brush began his career in the pottery industry in 1901 working for the J.B. Owens Pottery Co. in Zanesville, Ohio. He left the company in 1907 to go into business for himself, only to have fire completely destroy his pottery less than one year after it was founded. In 1909 he became associated with J.W. McCoy, who had operated a pottery of his own in Roseville, Ohio, since 1899. The two men formed the Brush-McCoy Pottery in 1911, locating their headquarters in Zanesville. After the merger, the company expanded and produced not only staple commercial wares but also fine artware. Lines of the highest quality such as Navarre, Venetian, Oriental, and Sylvan were equal to that of their larger competitors. Because very little of the ware was marked, it is often mistaken for Weller, Roseville, or Peters and Reed.

In 1918 after a fire in Zanesville had destroyed the manufacturing portion of that plant, all production was contained in their Roseville (Ohio) plant #2. A stoneware type of clay was used there, and as a result the artware lines of Jewel, Zuniart, King Tut, Florastone, Jetwood, Krakle-Kraft, and Panelart are so distinctive that they are more easily recognizable. Examples of these lines are unique and very beautiful, also quite rare and highly prized!

After McCoy died, the family withdrew their interests, and in 1925 the name of the firm was changed to The Brush Pottery. The era of hand-decorated art pottery production had passed for the most part, having been almost completely replaced by commercial lines. The Brush-Barnett family retained their interest in the pottery until 1981 when it was purchased by the Dearborn Company.

For more information we recommend *The Collector's Encyclopedia of Brush-McCoy Pottery* by Sharon and Bob Huxford, and *Sanford's Guide to*

Brush-McCoy Pottery, Books I and *II*, written by Martha and Steve Sanford, our advisors for this category, and edited by David P. Sanford. They are listed in the Directory under California.

Of all the wares bearing the later Brush script mark, their figural cookie jars are the most collectible, and several have been reproduced. Information on Brush cookie jars (as well as confusing reproductions) can be found in *The Collector's Encyclopedia of Cookie Jars* by Joyce and Fred Roerig; they are listed in the Directory under South Carolina. Beware! Cookie jars marked Brush-McCoy are not authentic.

Cookie Jars

Antique Touring Car...700.00
Boy w/Balloons 800.00
Chick in Nest (+) 400.00
Cinderella Pumpkin, #W32, from $200 to 275.00
Circus Horse, gr (+) 950.00

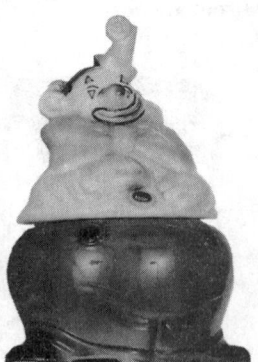

Clown, red pants, W 22 Brush USA, from $175.00 to $200.00.
(Photo courtesy Joyce and Fred Roerig)

Clown, yel pants..250.00
Clown Bust, #W49, minimum value 325.00
Cookie House, #W31 ....125.00
Covered Wagon, dog finial, #W30, minimum value (+) 550.00
Cow w/Cat on Bk, brn, #W10 (+)...125.00
Cow w/Cat on Bk, purple, minimum value (+) 1,000.00
Davy Crockett, no gold, mk USA (+)..300.00
Dog & Basket 250.00
Donkey Cart, ears down, gray, #W33 ....400.00
Donkey Cart, ears up, #W33, minimum value 800.00
Elephant w/Ice Cream Cone (+) 500.00
Elephant w/Monkey on Bk, minimum value.............................5,000.00
Fish, #W52 (+)..500.00
Formal Pig, gold trim, #W7 Brush USA (+) 475.00
Formal Pig, no gold, gr hat & coat (+)..300.00
Gas Lamp, #K1 ....75.00
Granny, pk apron, bl dots on skirt 325.00
Granny, plain skirt, minimum value (+) 400.00
Happy Bunny, wht, #W25..225.00
Hen on Basket, unmk 125.00
Hillbilly Frog, minimum value (+)..4,500.00
Humpty Dumpty, w/beany & bow tie (+) 275.00
Humpty Dumpty, w/peaked hat & shoes, from $250 to 350.00
Laughing Hippo, #W27 (+), from $750 to 850.00
Little Angel (+) 800.00
Little Boy Blue, gold trim, #K25, sm 700.00
Little Boy Blue, no gold, #K24 Brush USA, lg (+) 800.00
Little Girl, #017 (+) 550.00
Little Red Riding Hood, gold trim, mk lg, minimum value (+) ..850.00
Little Red Riding Hood, no gold, #K24 USA, sm 550.00
Night Owl...125.00
Old Clock, #W10 ....165.00

Old Shoe, #W23 (+)	125.00
Panda, #W21 (+)	250.00
Peter, Peter Pumpkin Eater, #W24	300.00
Peter Pan, gold trim, lg (+)	800.00
Peter Pan, no gold, sm	550.00
Puppy Police (+)	585.00
Raggedy Ann, #W16, from $475 to	525.00
Sitting Pig (+), from $400 to	450.00
Smiling Bear, #W46 (+)	350.00
Squirrel on Log, #W26	100.00
Squirrel w/Top Hat, blk coat & hat	275.00
Squirrel w/Top Hat, gr coat	250.00
Stylized Owl	350.00
Stylized Siamese, #W41, from $400 to	500.00
Teddy Bear, ft apart	250.00
Teddy Bear, ft together	200.00
Treasure Chest, #W28	170.00

Miscellaneous

Jardiniere and pedestal, Matt Green Ware, #2500, 1926, 36½", $2,500.00.
(Photo courtesy Martha and Steve Sanford)

Ashtray, turtle, late, 5", from $55 to	70.00
Bank, hobo, #069, 1916, 6", from $75 to	125.00
Bookends, elephant heads, #0126, 1928, pr, from $150 to	225.00
Bookends, Wise Bird (owl), 1927, 7", ea, from $200 to	250.00
Bottle, Onyx (bl), pinch type, 1910-30s, 10½"	100.00
Bowl, Berries & Leaves (Bittersweet), #756, 1945, from $50 to	75.00
Bowl, Jetwood, #01, 4", from $225 to	325.00
Bowl, Jewel, #055, 1923, 2½", from $250 to	350.00
Bowl, Mt Pelee, 1902, 3½x12", from $2,500 to	4,000.00
Bread jar, Kolorkraft, #350, 1931, 10", from $75 to	150.00
Candle holder, Christmas tree, 1969, from $30 to	45.00
Candlesticks, Jewel, #032, 1923, 10", pr, from $600 to	900.00
Candlesticks, Onyx (bl), #032, 10½", pr, from $125 to	175.00
Casserole, Perfection, 1920s, 4x10", from $25 to	60.00
Chamber pot, Lucile Ware, #17, from $75 to	125.00
Clock, Moderne Kolorkraft (Sweetheart), #338K, 1929, 5", from $275 to	400.00
Cornucopia, Berries & Leaves (Bittersweet), #753, 1945, 4x6", $30 to	45.00
Creamer & sugar bowl, Kolorkraft, #378, 1930, from $40 to	75.00
Cuspidor, frog, #3, 1912, 7½", from $50 to	100.00
Flower frog, Florastone, #05, 3½", from $125 to	150.00
Flowerpot, Rockkraft, 1933, 8", from $50 to	75.00
Hanging pot, Floradora, 1928, 5x7", from $65 to	100.00
Hanging pot, Stardust Flying Saucer, 1957, from $75 to	100.00
Jardiniere, Bluebird, 1915, 7½", from $200 to	350.00
Jardiniere, Bon-Ton, 1916, 7", from $150 to	200.00
Jardiniere, Cameo, #273, 1933, 11", from $150 to	175.00

Jardiniere, Decorated Autumn Leaf, #29, 1915, 10½", from $300 to	400.00
Jardiniere, Duotone Cameo, 1933, 10", from $150 to	175.00
Jardiniere, HP daisies, #215, 1915, 8½", from $225 to	325.00
Jardiniere, Majolica (brn), #252, 9", from $95 to	175.00
Jardiniere, New Blended, #242, 1928, 9½", from $75 to	125.00
Jardiniere, Onyx (bl), #240, 10", from $125 to	150.00
Jardiniere, Stonecraft, 10", from $150 to	200.00
Jardiniere, Sylvan II, #280, 1930s, 4½", from $25 to	35.00
Jug, Corn Line, #519, 1918, 9", from $75 to	135.00
Jug, figural head, #88A, gold on wht, 7½", from $150 to	200.00
Lamp, Wise Bird (owl), 1927, 8", from $175 to	200.00
Lamp, Wise Bird (owl), 1927, 9", from $195 to	225.00
Match holder, Kolorkraft, 1932, 6", from $40 to	65.00
Mug, Art Glazed Dutch, #347, 1928, 4-pt, from $75 to	175.00
Oil jar, Squeeze Bag, 1928-31, 19", from $1,000 to	1,500.00
Oil lamp, Ivotint, 1929, 4x8", from $450 to	600.00
Ornament, frog, 1967, 11½", from $150 to	250.00
Ornament, frog on stump, 1920s-30s, 8", from $275 to	375.00
Ornament, Wise Bird (owl), 1927, 9", from $200 to	300.00
Patio ashtray, 10", from $50 to	65.00
Patio lantern, owl, 9½", from $40 to	60.00
Pitcher, Old Mill, 1916, 7", from $150 to	175.00
Planter, bull, #138, 1940, 4½x6", from $35 to	45.00
Planter, fan shape w/lovebirds, 1941, 5", from $30 to	45.00
Planter, Floradora bulb log, #0124, glossy, 1928, 6", from $40 to	70.00
Planter, frog, lt bl matt, 1920s-30s, 3", from $25 to	40.00
Planter, Little Red Riding Hood, #619, 1941, from $25 to	50.00
Planter, mermaid, #245, late 1940s, from $20 to	40.00
Salt box, Old Mill, 1918, 4½x6½", from $95 to	125.00
Tea jar, Kolorkraft, #380, 1931, 6", from $75 to	100.00
Teapot, Mirror Black, 1920s, 4", from $35 to	65.00
TV light, sailing ship form, late 1950s, from $40 to	65.00
Umbrella stand, New Blended Basketweave, #402, 1915, 21", from $375 to	500.00
Umbrella stand, Onyx, #74, 1910, 22½", from $450 to	650.00
Vase, Cleo, #044, 1915, 11", from $250 to	400.00
Vase, fan shape w/bird motif, #734, 1960, 10½", from $35 to	45.00
Vase, Glo Art, #769, 1939, 8", from $50 to	75.00
Vase, HP by Cusick, #049, 1933, 8", from $235 to	325.00
Vase, Jewel, 1923, 3", from $300 to	400.00
Vase, King Tut, #41, 8", from $1,000 to	1,600.00
Vase, King Tut, #56, 1920s, 8", from $1,200 to	1,800.00
Vase, Moderne Kolorkraft, 1929, 12", from $125 to	185.00
Vase, Rosewood, #10, 1904, 9", from $175 to	300.00
Vase, tall pitcher shape, #609, 1940, 12", from $40 to	75.00
Vase, vertical stripes, #514, 1954, 18½", from $75 to	100.00
Vase, Vogue, 1916, 10", from $175 to	250.00
Vase, Wise Bird (owl/tree trunk), glossy, 1927, 8", from $175 to	250.00

Buffalo Pottery

The founding of the Buffalo Pottery in Buffalo, New York, in 1901, was a direct result of the success achieved by John Larkin through his innovative methods of marketing 'Sweet Home Soap.' Choosing to omit 'middle-man' profits, Larkin preferred to deal directly with the consumer and offered premiums as an enticement for sales. The pottery soon proved a success in its own right and began producing advertising and commemorative items for other companies, as well as commercial tableware. In 1905 they introduced their Blue Willow line after extensive experimentation resulted in the development of the first successful underglaze cobalt achieved by an American company. Between 1905 and 1909, a line of pitchers and jugs were hand decorated in historical, literary, floral, and outdoor themes. Twenty-nine styles are known to have been made.

Their most famous line was Deldare Ware, the bulk of which was made from 1908 to 1909. It was hand decorated after illustrations by Cecil Aldin. Views of English life were portrayed in detail through unusual use of color against the natural olive green cast of the body. Today the 'Fallowfield Hunt' scenes are more difficult to locate than 'Scenes of Village Life in Ye Olden Days.' A Deldare calendar plate was made in 1910. These are very rare and are highly valued by collectors. The line was revived in 1923 and dropped again in 1925. Every piece was marked 'Made at Ye Buffalo Pottery, Deldare Ware Underglaze.' Most are dated, though date has no bearing on the value. Emerald Deldare was made on the same olive body and on standard Deldare Ware shapes and featured historical scenes and Art Nouveau decorations. Most pieces are found with a 1911 date stamp. Production was very limited due to the intricate, time-consuming detail. Needless to say, it is very rare and extremely desirable.

Abino Ware, most of which was made in 1912, also used standard Deldare shapes, but its colors were earthy and the decorations more delicately applied. Sailboats, windmills, and country scenes were favored motifs. These designs were achieved by overpainting transfer prints and were often signed by the artist. The ware is marked 'Abino' in hand-printed block letters. Production was limited; and as a result, examples of this line are scarce today.

Commercial or institutional ware was another of Buffalo Pottery's crowning achievements. In 1917 vitrified china production began, and the firm produced for accounts worldwide. After 1956 all of their wares bore the name Buffalo China. Buffalo China (commercial and institutional ware) is being produced today by Oneida Silver Company.

Our advisors for this category are Fred and Lila Shrader; they are listed in the Directory under California.

Key: C — commercial ware marked

Abino

Cup & saucer, moonlight harbor scene	410.00
Tea tile, moonlight harbor scene, 6"	420.00
Tray, lake scene w/windmill & sm boats, 9½x12"	2,100.00
Vase, cylindrical w/Abino scene & Deldare colors, 13½"	3,875.00

Deldare

Ashtray/match holder, Fallowfield Hunt, 3½x6"	985.00
Bowl, cereal; The Fallowfield Hunt, no rim, 6¼"	360.00
Bowl, cereal; Ye Olden Days, no rim, 6¼"	170.00
Bowl, fruit; The Fallowfield Hunt, The Death, 9", from $460 to	525.00
Bowl, fruit; Ye Village Tavern, 3¾x9"	335.00
Bowl, nut; Ye Lion Inn, rolled rim, 3¼x8"	685.00
Bowl, soup; Ye Olden Days, flat rim, 9"	265.00
Candlestick, Villate Street scene, shield bk, 7"	1,280.00
Candlesticks, Emerald, bayberry motif, sgn Sauter, 9", pr	1,255.00
Creamer, Dr Syntax w/the Dairy Maid, 3½"	775.00
Creamer, Fallowfield, Breaking Cover, 3"	485.00
Cup & saucer, chocolate; Ye Village Street	400.00
Cup & saucer, The Fallowfield Hunt	435.00
Cup & saucer, Ye Olden Days	235.00
Humidor, Emerald, Dr Syntax, 7"	1,090.00
Humidor, There Was an Old Sailor, 8", from $925 to	1,400.00
Mug, child's; Village LIfe in Ye Olden Days, 2½"	935.00
Mug, The Fallowfield Hunt, Breaking Cover, 3½", from $340 to	425.00
Mug, The Fallowfield Hunt, 2½", from $285 to	495.00
Pitcher, Robin Hood (on Deldare body), 8"	995.00
Pitcher, The Fallowfield Hunt, The Return, 8"	585.00
Pitcher, To Demand My Annual Rent, 8"	520.00

Plaque, Fallowfield Hunt Breakfast, 12"	785.00
Plate, chop; Emerald, Dr Syntax Sells Grizzle, 13½"	1,320.00
Plate, Dr Syntax Making a Discovery, 10", from $900 to	1,050.00
Plate, The Fallofield Hunt, 6¼"	175.00
Plate, The Fallowfield Hunt, The Death, 8¼"	135.00
Plate, The Fallowfield Hunt, The Start, 9½"	225.00
Plate, Ye Town Crier, 8¼"	120.00
Plate, Ye Village Street, 7¼"	90.00
Relish dish, The Fallowfield Hunt, The Dash, 12x6½"	785.00
Tea tile, The Fallowfield Hunt, Breaking Cover, 6", from $290 to	450.00
Tea tile, Traveling in Ye Olden Days, 6½"	290.00
Teapot, Emerald, Dr Syntax Disputing Bill..., 4½"	1,250.00
Teapot, Fallowfield Hunt scene, 3¾"	625.00
Teapot, Scenes of Village Life, 3¾"	385.00
Teapot, Scenes of Village Life, 5¾"	490.00
Toothpick holder, Emerald, Art Nouveau floral, 2¼"	580.00
Tray, calling card; Dr Syntax Robbed of..., 7¼", from $825 to	1,000.00
Tray, pin; Ye Olden Days, 6½x3x3¾"	200.00
Tray, tea; Dr Syntax Mistakes a Gentleman's..., 13½x10½"	1,920.00
Vase, City scenes (untitled), 7"	395.00
Vase, Emerald Deldare, American Beauty, 13½"	2,200.00
Vase, Ye Village Parson/Schoolmaster, 8½"	845.00

Miscellaneous

Pitcher, Geranium, cobalt and white, 6½", $475.00; Dutch jug, castle and landscape, woman and child, coat of arms on white, 1907, 6½", $600.00.

Bowl, Blue Willow, C, 2½x6"	20.00
Bowl, Blue Willow, 3½x5½"	55.00
Bowl, chili; Fallen Leaf Lodge, CA, C, 5¼"	38.00
Bowl, chili; US Forest Service, C, 5¼"	48.00
Bowl, fruit; Blue Willow, 5½", from $9 to	19.00
Bowl, salad; natural wood design, C, 8½"	125.00
Bowl, salad; Tea Rose, 6"	15.00
Bowl, US Navy, Captain's Mess, flat, C, 9½"	39.00
Bowl, vegetable; Blue Bird, hdls, w/lid, 5½x10"	165.00
Bowl, vegetable; Blue Willow, hdls, w/lid, 8½x10"	215.00
Bowl, vegetable; Blue Willow, w/lid, 8½" sq	175.00
Bowl, vegetable; various '20s dinnerware patterns, w/lid, from $35 to	130.00
Bowl, vegetable; Vienna, deep bl & rich gold, oval, 9x6"	85.00
Butter dish, Blue Willow, ice ring, 4¾x8½" dia	225.00
Butter dish, Blue Willow, 7⅝" dia	145.00
Butter pat, Blue Willow, 3½", from $15 to	38.00
Butter pat, GH, Greenbrier Hotel, C, 3¾"	55.00
Butter pat, Palace Hotel (SF), C, 3½"	25.00
Butter pat, Princess, 3½", from $10 to	15.00
Butter pat, US Military Academy, West Point, C, 3¼", from $18 to	35.00
Butter pat, Veteran's Adm, C, 3¼"	26.00
Butter pat, WSF or SWF, pine tree decor, C, 3½"	18.00
Butter pat, YMCA, C, 3½"	45.00
Candlestick, pk, blk & gold, 9"	45.00

Canisters, Tea, Coffee & Flour, brn lettering on ivory, 3-pc set ..200.00
Chamber pot, pk, blk & gold, w/lid..100.00
Child's feeding dish, Blue Bird, w/hot water chamber, 7½".........210.00
Child's tea set, floral decor, pot+2 c/s+2 5" plates......................110.00
Chocolate pot, floral spray, good gold, 8"....................................95.00
Condiment jar, blk & wht checks, C, 5½"......................................25.00
Condiment set, Oil & Vinegar, cork-wrapped stoppers, C, 9", pr..55.00
Creamer, crossed golf clubs, FCC, no hdl, C, 3"...........................26.00
Creamer, Ft Lewis Officer's Mess, hdl, C, 3½"..............................42.00
Creamer, KC, w/religious cross, hdl, C, 3"....................................35.00
Creamer, Mandalay, no hdl, C, 2¾"...18.00
Creamer, Multifleure, no hdl, C, 3½"..58.00
Creamer, Roosevelt Bears, 2¾"...400.00
Creamer, Roycroft logo, no hdl, C, 3"..275.00
Creamer, Yosemite Park, Ahwahnee, geometrics, C, ind sz 55.00
Creamer & sugar bowl, Blue Bird, w/lid......................................115.00
Cruet, w/hdl, orig cork-wrapped stopper, 9¼"..............................18.00
Cup & saucer, demitasse; Palace Hotel (SF), C 22.00
Cup & saucer, demitasse; sterling cup holder & saucer, C............48.00
Cup & saucer, Fallen Leaf Lodge, C 55.00
Cup & saucer, Trocadero Hotel (FL), Colorido ware, C................32.00
Egg cup, blk & wht checkerboard band, C, 4¼".............................20.00
Fruit set, floral w/gold, 8" bowl+4 5" bowls 95.00
Game set, good gold, 15x11" platter+6 9½" plates, from $185 to...320.00
Gravy boat, Kenmore, good gold, no liner 24.00
Gravy boat, Tahoe Tavern...45.00
Jug, Blue Willow, C, 8"..55.00
Jug, Blue Willow, Chicago style, 4¾"...325.00
Jug, Blue Willow, Chicago style, 7"...260.00
Jug, Buffalo Hunt, w/gold banding, 6", from $225 to 325.00
Jug, Gaudy Willow, Chicago style, 7"...595.00
Jug, Orchid Spray, w/lid, 5¾"..300.00
Jug, Robin Hood, 8½"..495.00
Mug, advertising, Bing & Nathan/Friar, good gold, 5½" 75.00
Mug, coffee; US Military Academy, West Point, C 55.00
Mug, Indian Hatti Tom portrait, good gold, 5¾"..........................125.00
Mug, Roosevelt Bears, 3¼"..390.00
Pitcher, cream; Veteran's Adm, C, 4¾"...17.00
Pitcher, poppies, lav on pk w/gold, from toilet set, 8½" 105.00
Pitcher, Sailor, w/sailors & lighthouse, 9¼"..................................485.00
Pitcher, Salvation Army, C, 7"...145.00
Plate, advertising; Home Furniture...Co, Toledo, teal gr, 7½".........22.00
Plate, advertising; LL Milring, Advance, Commerce..., 7½".........65.00
Plate, advertising; Wanamaker's Jubilee 1911, teal gr, 4"..............25.00
Plate, Biltmore Hotel, Los Angeles, B logo/BS, C 32.00
Plate, Christmas, Spirit of Christmas Past, 1956, C, 9½".............28.00
Plate, Dr Syntax Disputing..., bl & wht, 9½".................................185.00
Plate, game; RK Beck design, deer w/gold border, 9" 50.00
Plate, Gaudy Willow w/rich cobalt, gr, brn & gold, 9½"...............180.00
Plate, grill; Blue Willow, C, 10"..25.00
Plate, Patrons of Husbandry, w/logo, 9½".....................................26.00
Plate, Red Willow, C, 8"..9.00

Plate, Roosevelt Bears, teddy bear reserves, 8", from $1,000.00 to $1,500.00.

Plate, Salvation Army, 1926, C, 9½" 95.00
Plate, Tahoe Tavern, C, 5½"..30.00
Plate, US Bureau of Fisheries, C, 9½" 65.00
Platter, Blue Willow, 14x11", from $65 to....................................120.00
Platter, Hotel Montclaire, 1925, C, 7x9".......................................14.00
Platter, Solari's, brn & blk bands, C, 7x9".....................................17.00
Relish dish, Seneca, 9½x5½"..22.00
Shakers, Roycroft Inn, cylindrical, 1995, C, 3", pr........................26.00
Shakers, Roycroft Inn, 1925, 3½", pr..670.00
Shaving mug, dbl; Wildroot, w/metal hdl, C..................................88.00
Soup, Blue Willow, w/1⅛" rim, 1917, 8½".....................................50.00
Soup plate, Blue Willow, rimless, C, 8"..12.00
Sugar bowl, Blue Bird, hdls, w/lid, 3¾"..55.00
Sugar bowl, Seneca, w/lid, 5¼"...35.00
Teapot, Baby Bunting, child sz, 3½"...85.00
Teapot, Cairo, rnd, C, ind sz 30.00
Teapot, Geranium, bl & wht, w/orig & complete tea infusor.......275.00
Teapot, Red Willow, C, ind sz 26.00
Toilet set, Chrysanthemum, pitcher+bowl+chamber pot w/lid+jar w/lid...300.00
Vase, red & blk vertical columns, C, 6x3¾"....................................35.00
Vase, Roycroft; by Buffalo China, 1995, 5".....................................25.00

Buggy Steps

The recent increased interest in western collectibles has stimulated a renewed awareness in all horse-drawn memorabilia. A good example of this is the buggy step. This device allowed the passenger to enter or exit the vehicle without the driver's assistance. Steps may be hinged, pivoted, adjustable, folding, and spring loaded. The elaborate handwork of the blacksmiths who created them was equal to that of the finest wheelwrights, carpenters, and leather workers involved in the manufacture of early wheeled vehicles (1865 – 1910). For listings of no-name steps with multiple designs, see previous editions of this book. Prices suggested here are for steps in mint to good condition. Rust, breaks, and pitting reduce their value. The following name steps are listed as they appear on the buggy step tread. Our advisor for this category is John Waddell; he is listed in the Directory under Texas.

A B Co...55.00
Abbot Buggy Co 55.00
Beebe Cart 55.00
C & W Co 55.00
Cadillac...70.00
Cole...55.00
Columbia 70.00
Creamer Scott Co..65.00
Dean & Co 75.00
Deere...75.00
Easy...65.00
Eckhart..60.00
Emerson...75.00
Ferguson..55.00
Freeport...60.00
Harper...65.00
Henney Buggy Co..70.00
L Burg Mfg Co 55.00
M & L Co 50.00
M & T w/elephant...75.00
Moon Bro 70.00
Ney, Canton, Ohio..70.00
Parsons & Goodfellow 55.00
Peerless..55.00
Peru..70.00

Racine W & C Co...**65.00**
Rambler..**70.00**
Rockford...**70.00**
S Frazier & Co..**60.00**
Sattley, Racine..**70.00**
Scott Cart...**60.00**
Selle Co..**55.00**
Spaulding..**70.00**
Staver...**70.00**
Stoughton...**55.00**
Studebaker..**75.00**
Thompson...**60.00**
Tiger...**70.00**
W O Hesse & Son..**65.00**
W S Frazier & Co..**65.00**

Burmese

Burmese glass was patented in 1885 by the Mount Washington Glass Co. It is typically shaded from canary yellow to a rosy salmon color. The yellow is produced by the addition of uranium oxide to the mix. The salmon color comes from the addition of gold salts and is achieved by reheating the object (partially) in the furnace. It is thus called 'heat sensitive' glass. Thomas Webb of England was licensed to produce Burmese and often added more gold, giving an almost fuchsia tinge to the salmon in some cases. They called their glass 'Queen's Burmese,' and this is sometimes etched on the base of the object. This is not to be confused with Mount Washington's 'Queen's Design,' which refers to the design painted on the object. Both companies added decoration to many pieces. Mount Washington-Pairpoint produced some Burmese in the late 1920s and Gundersen and Bryden in the 1950s and 1970s, but the color and shapes are different.

Our advisors for this category are Dolli and Wilfred Cohen; they are listed in the Directory under California. In the listings that follow, examples are assumed to have the satin finish unless noted 'shiny.' See also Lamps, Fairy.

Bonbon, Mt WA, rectangular, turned-in edges, 1½x5¼".............**185.00**
Bonbon, Mt WA, shiny, 3 appl prunts, hdl, 2⅜x6½x4¾".............**695.00**
Bonbon, shiny, rigaree collar, SP fr.......................................**650.00**
Bowl, bride's; Mt WA, red leaves/wht berries/bl flowers, SP fr, 9"..**1,650.00**
Bowl, finger; Mt WA, shiny, 2¾" H.......................................**350.00**
Bowl, ice cream; Mt WA, ruffled, 4¾".....................................**250.00**
Bowl, 16 vertical ribs, deep color, appl burmese border, 7½x7"....**2,500.00**
Celery vase, Mt WA, pinched rim, 6½".....................................**350.00**
Condiment set, Mt WA, ribbed shakers/cruet in mk silver fr...**1,750.00**
Creamer & sugar bowl, shiny, 2-hdl, urn-shaped bodies, 3½".....**595.00**
Cruet, Mt WA, 30 ribs, 7"..**1,250.00**
Cup, Mt WA, 2 birds on branch, 2½".......................................**250.00**
Cup, punch; Mt WA, waisted, 2½"...**250.00**
Epergne, Webb, flower-form center, 3 sm bud vases in brass fr, 8"..**1,950.00**
Epergne, 3 domed shades on Clarke bases, burmese & brass holder, 11"...**2,750.00**
Ewer, dragons & flowers (later decor, EX art), bulbous, 10".....**1,500.00**
Ginger jar, camel rider/pyramids, hdls, 6⅜"........................**3,500.00**
Lamp, fairy; Webb, clear Clarke cup, 3¾"................................**650.00**
Lamp, fairy; Webb, Queen's, 5½x5¾".......................................**995.00**
Pitcher, dragons & flowers (later decor, EX art), 12½"...........**1,550.00**
Pitcher, Mt WA, ruffled top, 5½"...**600.00**
Pitcher, Mt WA, 6¾x8½"..**950.00**
Plate, Gundersen, EX color, 9"..**375.00**
Plate, Pairpoint, shiny, ca 1920s, 10".....................................**265.00**
Rose bowl, appl gr matsu-no-ke vines, ruffled rim, 3¼x3½"....**225.00**
Rose bowl, Webb, lav-bl floral/fall-color leaves, 3"..................**325.00**

Saucer, shiny..**85.00**
Shaker, Mt WA, cylindrical w/emb ribs, 2-part metal lid, 4¼"..**265.00**
Toothpick holder, Mt WA, berries, tricorn rim, low................**850.00**
Toothpick holder, Mt WA, pine cones/needles, sq rim, 3".........**650.00**
Toothpick holder, Webb, ball shape w/short neck, 2½"..............**385.00**
Tumbler, Mt WA, ivy, 3¾"...**495.00**
Tumbler, Mt WA, 3¾"..**200.00**
Tumbler, whiskey; Mt WA, sq rim, 2½"..................................**175.00**
Vase, flared rim, SP fr, 10½"...**1,300.00**
Vase, Gundersen, man in balloon flight, stylized flowers, 8".....**500.00**
Vase, jack-in-pulpit; Pairpoint, shiny, 5x6¾"...........................**535.00**
Vase, jack-in-pulpit; Webb, prunus blossoms w/gold, 12½".....**1,250.00**
Vase, lily; Egyptian jeweled florals, 14", pr...........................**2,500.00**
Vase, lily; Gundersen, 9½"...**365.00**
Vase, lily; Mt WA, 12"..**750.00**
Vase, mc leaves & vines, tricorn, 10"..................................**1,500.00**
Vase, Mt WA, Egyptian pyramid scene w/gold, oviform, 11½"..**2,500.00**
Vase, Mt WA, fern leaves, in sgn Dunham holder, 6"...............**545.00**
Vase, Mt WA, floral w/mc leaves & pods, stick neck, 10".......**1,250.00**
Vase, Mt WA, overall gold tracery, gourd shape, 12"............**1,250.00**
Vase, Mt WA, roses, stick neck, 10¼".....................................**800.00**
Vase, Mt WA, shiny, #52½S, 6½"..**565.00**
Vase, Mt WA, shiny, cylindrical neck, scalloped rim, 4½".........**585.00**
Vase, Mt WA, wht asters, bulbous, 13", NM...........................**1,750.00**
Vase, Pairpoint, ruffled goblet form, ca 1920s, 10x7"..............**595.00**
Vase, ruffled top, pale ribbed panels, 5½".................................**600.00**
Vase, shiny, flared top, SP fr, 10½".....................................**1,000.00**
Vase, shiny, pale ribbed panels, 8½".......................................**600.00**
Vase, Webb, leafy vines/pods in gold, gold ringed hdls, 3¾x6"...**1,150.00**
Vase, Webb, lilac (rare color, ca 1888), petal top, 3"................**650.00**
Vase, Webb, melon ribs, waisted, 3"..**250.00**
Vase, Webb, Queen's, stick neck, #1139/4 V48F, 10¾".............**850.00**

Butter Molds and Stamps

The art of decorating butter began in Europe during the reign of Charles II. This practice was continued in America by the farmer's wife who sold her homemade butter at the weekly market to earn extra money during hard times. A mold or stamp with a special design, hand carved either by her husband or a local craftsman, not only made her product more attractive but also helped identify it as hers. The pattern became the trademark of Mrs. Smith, and all who saw it knew that this was her butter. It was usually the rule that no two farms used the same mold within a certain area, thus the many variations and patterns available to the collector today. The most valuable are those which have animals, birds, or odd shapes. The most sought-after motifs are the eagle, cow, fish, and rooster. These works of early folk art are quickly disappearing from the market.

Pedestal-form double butter stamp with good chip-carved stylized eagle and rose designs, early, $500.00.
(Photo courtesy Aston Macek Auctioneers and Appraisers)

Molds

Acorns & leaves, EX cvg, 4¼x3¾"..85.00
Acorns & oak leaves, 2-pc w/stick hdl, 5⅛x4¾" 80.00
Compass flower, hexagonal, chamfered lollipop hdl, 4⅞" dia 770.00
Rooster, fruitwood, EX patina, 3½x3½"+hdl.....................75.00
Rose & leaves, scalloped rectangle, PA, 1860s, 10¾" L 165.00
Roses/wheat/corn/grapes/etc, 8 presses in all, 11x5x½" fr............200.00
Sheaf of wheat, EX patina, 1866, EX..............................145.00
Sheaf of wheat, 2-pc w/stick hdl, 4¼x4½"........................75.00

Stamps

Concentric circular lines/swirled outer band, 3⅝" 180.00
Cow, deep cvg, 4x2¼" dia...110.00
Cow & ornamental edge, worn, age crack, 3½x4⅞" 175.00
Cow & tree, 2-pc w/trn hdls, scrubbed, 4½" dia 165.00
Eagle, good detail, 3⅝" dia..450.00
Eagle w/shield, EX patina, 2⅝" 225.00
Eagles (2) w/wings wide, chip-cvd, ca 1840-70, no hdl, 4½" L ...250.00
Flower w/chip-cvd details, compass flower below, 4½" dia..........200.00
Flower w/chip-cvd details, 3¾" 190.00
Pomegranate, 1-pc trn hdl..75.00
Sheaf of wheat, half-rnd, hdl, 3⅜x6⅜" 350.00
Sheaf of wheat, 1-pc trn hdl, 4¼" dia...............................75.00
Thistle, 1-pc, trn hdl, 3½" dia..75.00
Tulip (stylized), EX detail, 1-pc w/trn hdl, scrubbed, 3¼" 250.00
Tulip & leaves, stick hdl, 3¾" dia.....................................150.00

Buttonhooks

The earliest known written reference to buttonhooks (shoe hooks, glove hooks, or collar buttoners) is dated 1611. They became a necessary implement in the 1850s when tight-fitting high-button shoes became fashionable. Later in the nineteenth century, ladies' button gloves and men's button-on collars and cuffs dictated specific types of buttoners, some with a closed wire loop instead of a hook end. Both shoes and gloves used as many as twenty-four buttons each. Usage began to wane in the late 1920s following a fashion change to low-cut laced shoes and the invention of the zipper. There was a brief resurgence of use following the 1948 movie *High Button Shoes*. For a simple, needed utilitarian device, buttonhook handles were made from a surprising variety of materials: natural wood, bone, ivory, agate, and mother-of-pearl to plain steel, celluloid, aluminum, iron, lead and pewter, artistic copper, brass, silver, gold, and many other materials, in lengths that varied from under 2" to over 20". Many designs folded or retracted, and buttonhooks were often combined with shoehorns and other useful implements. Stamped steel buttonhooks often came free with the purchase of shoes, gloves, or collars. Material, design, workmanship, condition, and relative scarcity are the primary market value factors. Prices range from $1.00 to over $500.00, with most being in the $10.00 to $100.00 range. Buttonhooks are fairly easy to find, and they are interesting to display.

Our advisor for this category is Richard Mathes; he is listed in the Directory under Ohio. See also The Buttonhook Society listing in the Directory under Clubs, Newsletters, and Catalogs.

Buttonhook/penknife, ivory side plates, man's 50.00
Collar buttoner, stamped steel, advertising, closed end, 3"............20.00
Glove hook, gold-plated, retractable, 3"...............................90.00
Glove hook, loop end, agate hdl, 2½".................................60.00
Shoe hook, colored celluloid hdl, 8".................................15.00
Shoe hook, lathe-trn hardwood hdl, dk finish, 8" 15.00
Shoe hook, SP w/blade, repousse hdl, Pat Jan 5 1892, 5" 40.00

Shoe hook, stamped steel, advertising, 5"................................8.00
Shoe hook, sterling, floral & geometrics, 8" 55.00
Shoe hook, sterling, Nouveau lady's face, 6½".........................75.00
Shoe hook, sterling, W w/arrow, hammered Florentine decor, mk 55.00
Shoe hook/shoehorn, combination, steel & celluloid, 9" 35.00

Bybee

The Bybee Pottery was founded in 1845 in the small town of Bybee, Kentucky, by the Cornelison family. Their earliest wares were primarily stoneware churns and jars. Today the work is carried on by sixth-generation Cornelison potters who still use the same facilities and production methods to make a more diversified line of pottery. From a fine white clay mined only a few miles from the potting shed itself, the shop produces vases, jugs, dinnerware, and banks in a variety of colors, some of which are shipped to the larger cities to be sold in department stores and specialty shops. The bulk of their wares, however, is sold to the thousands of tourists who are attracted to the pottery each year.

Pitcher, sky blue glossy glaze, signed BB by Walter Cornelison, ca 1981, 8⅞", $70.00.
(Photo courtesy Southern Folk Pottery Collectors Society)

Pitcher, chick figural, feldspathic sky bl, BB, after 1969, 5½" 90.00
Teapot, feldspathic gold, pre-1969, 4⅞x8½"................................110.00
Teapot, feldspathic sky bl, BB, after 1969, 5¼x9".........................100.00
Vase, tan semigloss, flared cylinder, 1927, 5⅝" 150.00

Cabat

From beginning experimentation with pottery in New York City around 1940, through several different types of clay, designs, and glazes, and relocation to Arizona, the Rose Cabat 'Feelie,' so named because 'it feels so good,' evolved into present forms and glazes in the late 1950s. Rose was aided and encouraged through the years by her late husband Erni. Their small 'weed pots' are readily recognizable by their light weight, tiny thin necks, and soft glazes. Pieces are marked with a hand-incised 'Cabat' on the bottom.

Plate, incised/pnt Modern design, gr/bl/brn, 8½".......................200.00
Vase, Feelie, bl & gr crystalline on brn clay, 4"............................375.00
Vase, Feelie, bl & ivory mat on charcoal clay, 3½".....................175.00
Vase, Feelie, gr & mauve semigloss, 2⅝" 200.00
Vase, Feelie, mc pk matt on brn, sm, broad, 2½" W....................110.00
Vase, Feelie, multi-tone purple on black clay, 3" 160.00
Vase, Feelie, pk/purple/charcoal/ivory on charcoal clay, 3" 260.00
Vase, Feelie, yel & gr crystalline on brn clay, cylindrical, 3" 325.00

Calendar Plates

Calendar plates were advertising giveaways most popular from about 1906 until the late twenties. They were decorated with colorful underglaze decals of lovely ladies, flowers, animals, birds and, of course, the twelve months of the year of their issue. During the 1950s they came into vogue again but never to the extent they were originally. Those with exceptional detailing, or those with scenes of a particular activity are most desirable, so are any from before 1906.

1909, Gibson girl bathing beauty, 9", from $50 to 65.00
1909, Harrison Fisher girl, 9" 30.00
1909, horse's portrait w/harness & bridle 150.00
1910, holly, 8½", EX...30.00
1910, Indian chief, worn gold, 7½" 65.00
1910, lady w/horse, worn gold...70.00
1910, Niagara Falls 32.50
1911, cherub & bl sky 35.00
1911, fruit & flowers, 8¼"...32.50
1911, Gibson girl & cherubs, 9", from $50 to 65.00
1912, football player w/2 lovely ladies, 8¼" 80.00
1912, Indian maiden, NM 35.00
1913, biplane, dbl gold line at rim, 8¼", from $50 to 65.00
1913, Victorian lady overlooking lake, worn gold, 7½" 60.00
1914, lady in buggy...52.50
1914, map of Panama Canal, flags & presidents form border 125.00
1914, Washington's Old Home at Mt Vernon, from $65 to...........85.00
1917, turkeys, 9" 35.00
1917, violets, 9"..35.00
1921, partridges in center, bluebirds along rim, 8¼", EX..............60.00
1922, 48-star flag, 9¼", from $45 to 55.00
1928, deer in winter scene, Harker, 9", from $40 to......................50.00
1928, pk roses, calendar pgs at top, 8", from $45 to 60.00

Calendars

Calendars are collected for their colorful prints, often attributed to a well-recognized artist of the period. Advertising calendars from the turn of the century often have a double appeal when representing a company whose tins, signs, store displays, etc., are also collectible. See also Parrish, Maxfield.

1886, Hood's Sarsaparilla, girl in bonnet, 7", EX+ 70.00
1892, Hood's Sarsaparilla, The Sewing Circle, 7" dia, EX...........120.00
1893, Hires, History of Hires sales since 1878, unused, 9", NM .1,800.00
1893, Horsford's, diecut image of child on sled, 9x8", EX+ 60.00
1895, Hood's Sarsaparilla, heart shape, winter/summer girls, 8", EX .100.00
1896, Deere & Co, diecut, deer family, sepia/bl, 15", EX+ 110.00
1898, Hood's Sarsaparilla Coupon Calendar, 7", NM 70.00
1899, Union Metallic Cartridge Co, Rough Riders depictions, 28", EX+ ..750.00
1899, Youth Companion, 5-fold diecut, ladies/lilacs, 11x23", EX+ ..45.00
1900, DuPont, gun boat in action, Strobridge litho, 28", EX 325.00
1900, Hood's Sarsaparilla, 2 girls holding pad, 6½", VG 45.00
1900, John G Watts, cb, lady customers in meat market, 18", VG+ ...165.00
1900, Laflin & Rand Powder Co, elk, 6x3", NM+ 450.00
1900, United States Rubbers, diecut trifold, EX+ 100.00
1901, Hood's Sarsaparilla, Patience, 7", EX+ 100.00
1901, Sinclair's Fidelity, triangular, w/envelope, 6", EX+..............80.00
1902, Champion Binders Mowers & Rakes, 6", NM 200.00
1903, DuPont Explosives, EH Osthaus art, 31", VG 1,100.00
1903, Ferndell Pure Foods, lady's portrait, 8½", NM 25.00
1903, Hood's Sarsaparilla, girl/donkey/2 dogs, 17x6", VG 90.00
1903, Marguerite Havana Cigar, cb w/cut-out cameo center, 15", VG+ ...60.00
1903, Shelter Top Co, aluminum, 5x3½", EX+ 70.00
1904, DuPont, The First Day of the Opening Season, 28", EX 2,800.00
1905, Harrington & Richardson, woman/dog on bench, 26", NM ..1,750.00

1905, Hawley & Hoops, farm girl, 12", NM.................................100.00
1905, NA Jordan Sporting Goods, 14", EX+.................................90.00
1906, Companion, trifold, Spirit of '76 images, 11x24" (open), EX ...40.00
1906, Libby, McNeill & Libby, cb, girl in straw hat, 17", Fair.....100.00

1907, Scherling Bros., girl talking to doll on stump, 17x10½", VG+, $250.00.

1910, Harrington & Richardson Arms, G Muss Arnolt art, 27", EX+....1,425.00
1911, Holden's Shoes, diecut, boy/girl/chicks, 9x7", VG+ 90.00
1911, Syracuse Boat Mfg, Critical Moment, HC Edwards art, 21", EX+ ...1,100.00
1911, Whitehead & Hoag Co Badges Emblems & Banners, lady driver, EX....40.00
1911, Wrigley's Chewing Gum, boy teasing dog, 9", EX+ 55.00
1913, Fox Bread, boy/girl at stone wall, EX................................110.00
1913, Selby Loads, quail, Ed Wilson Curner art, 28", EX+ 3,500.00
1914, Harrington & Richardson Arms, 2 dogs w/hunter, 26x14", EX..850.00
1914, Luteys Grocers & Coffee Roasters, self-fr tin, 5x7", NM 30.00
1915, Peters, setters in field, Arnolt, 10x14½", EX 625.00
1916, Hercules Powder, shorebirds, w/single pg, 27x12", EX.......275.00
1916, Peters, moonlit ducks in flight, Frank Stick art, 20", EX+...1,750.00
1916, Weiss girl beside flowers diecut, 20½x10½", EX...............360.00
1916, 3 girls w/doll on balcony, 16½x9½", EX 330.00
1917, Hall's Chocolates, couple pictured, 30", G........................110.00
1917, Peters, G Muss Arnolt art, 27", EX...................................500.00
1918, lovely lady, stone litho, full pad, 15½x11½" 175.00
1920, Sharples, mother watching children, 22", VG+ 50.00
1922, Anxious Moment (hunter stalking deer), 15", EX+.............50.00
1922, Remington, Phillip R Goodwin art, 29", EX+ 1,000.00
1922, US Cartridges, grizzly holding box, 36", EX 425.00
1924, Let'er Rain, fr, 29", NM+...1,200.00
1924, McCormick Deering, farm lady's portrait, 24", EX+ 25.00
1924, Western, dog getting hunter out of bed, 31", EX 400.00
1928, Lydia Pinkham's Vegetable Compound, biplane 23", G.....110.00
1929, Rumford Baking Powder, lady/horse/collie, 16", VG...........50.00
1929, Shell Gasoline/Motor Oil, Roxana, 17", NM+ 200.00
1930, Western Ammunition, Parsons art, canoe scene, 27", EX+ .250.00
1931, DeLaval, 15", NM 35.00
1931, Get the Wolves First/Consult Your Vet, snowy hunt, 16", EX ..55.00
1931, Louis Dow Co, woman's portrait by J Knowles, 34", NM 60.00
1931, Peters, pheasants, LB Hunt, 32½x13½", EX.......................225.00
1932, Buick on Redwood Empire Road, complete, EX 28.00
1932, Hercules, Stowaways, 1 pg, 30x13", EX.............................325.00
1932, Western Ammunition, Champion Mars Guy, Osthaus art, 28", NM+ ..525.00
1934, Perfection Oak Flooring, nude in pond, 48x26", EX 135.00
1936, Bartell's Corners, bighorn hunt, P Goodwin art, 16", NM ...200.00
1937, DuPont Explosives, EH Osthaus art, 28", G.......................275.00
1938, Will Rogers, Dependable, A D'elia art, 28", NM 40.00
1938, Will Rogers talking to dog, full pad, 46x21", EX...............95.00
1940, Hercules Powder, pioneers in Conastoga wagon, 30", EX..160.00
1942, Maas & Steffen, Otters Playground, 26", EX+ 160.00

1942, 3 bears on cliff watch loggers on river, 43x29", G..............110.00
1943, A Modern Eve, Earl Moran pinup art, 24", EX+ 225.00
1943, Maas & Steffen, Treasure of the Marshlands, 26", EX 220.00
1943, Shaw-Barton, Girl of the Golden West, 44", EX 30.00
1944, Esquire, Varga art, 12", EX..45.00
1944, Myers Pumps, sm pad on vertical sign, kids/pump, 51", EX...275.00
1944, Shaw-Barton, Highroad to Happiness, 18", NM 30.00
1945, Maas & Steffen, The Surprise Attack, 27", EX..................250.00
1945, Shaw-Barton, Blue Ribbon Pair, 20", EX.............................25.00
1946, Esquire, Varga girl ea month, 8½x12", EX in sleeve..........250.00
1946, Hercules, The Spirit of '46, NC Wyeth art, 31", Fair 250.00
1946, Kist Beverages, garden girl, 26", NM...............................180.00
1946, Maas & Steffen, A Bear Chance, 26", EX+ 425.00
1947, Am De-Luxe Art Calendars, Thrilling Adventure, 26", EX....30.00
1947, Moon Glow, Zoe Mozert pinup art, 35", NM+ 260.00
1947, Orange-Crush, girl w/bottle, 31", NM...............................250.00
1948, Am De-Luxe Art Calendars, Rounding Up Herd, 27", NM ..40.00
1948, Maas & Steffen, Wandering Herd, 26", EX+ 170.00
1949, Maas & Steffen, When Strangers Meet, 27", EX+.............170.00
1950, Lone Ranger on silver, bread promotion, 15x8¼", VG 150.00
1952, Esquire, Chiriaka art, w/orig envelope, 11", EX 40.00
1953, DuPont, Champion Warhoop Jake, Lougheed, 31", NM+ .130.00
1953, Zoe Mozert pinup art, 34", NM..30.00
1954, Esquire, Chiriaka art, w/orig envelope, 11", EX 50.00
1954, Mission Orange, 25", EX..75.00
1955, Esquire, Petty art, 11", EX...38.00

Caliente

Caliente was a line of colored dinnerware made by the Paden City Pottery Company in Paden City, West Virginia. It was produced during the 1930s and 1940s in tangerine, yellow, blue, green, and cobalt blue.

Bowl, cream soup..18.00
Bowl, salad; 10"...28.00
Bowl, 5¼"...10.00
Bowl, 9"...20.00
Candle holder...20.00
Casserole...40.00
Creamer...18.00
Cup & saucer..15.00
Plate, dinner; 10"..17.50
Plate, 6"...5.00
Plate, 9½"...10.00
Platter, 12"...25.00
Platter, 14"...28.00
Shakers, pr...25.00
Sugar bowl, w/lid..20.00
Teapot...50.00

California Faience

California Faience was the trade name used by William V. Bragdon and Chauncy R. Thomas on vases, bowls, and other artware produced at their pottery known as 'The Tile Shop' in Berkeley, California, from 1920 to 1930. Faience tile was the principal product of the business during these years and is the favorite with today's collectors. Items in a glossy glaze are rare and therefore more valuable. Tiles were marked 'California Faience' with a die stamp.

Ashtray, stylized dog spans length, orange-yel matt, 6x5x4" 225.00
Book block, bear, plum-brn matt, 4x4½x6" 350.00

Bowl, burgundy gloss, incurvate, 3¾x6½".....................................250.00
Bowl vase, tobacco matt, low, 5½" W 170.00
Charger, golf scene, brn emb on celadon, VS on front, 11" 500.00

Trivet, multicolor sailing vessel in stormy sea, four-color gloss and matt glazes, 5⅜x5⅜", $450.00.

Vase, bl matt on red clay, 3"...275.00
Vase, gr w/silver crystalline over buff clay, shouldered, 9¾".....1,200.00
Vase, mustard matt, trumpet shape, 6¾x5", EX 200.00
Vase, stylized floral, wht slip trail on turq gloss, sgn, 4x4"...........900.00

California Perfume Company

D.H. McConnell, Sr., founded the California Perfume Company (C.P. Company; C.P.C.) in 1886 in New York City. He had previously been a salesman for a book company, which he later purchased. His door-to-door sales usually involved the lady of the house, to whom he presented a complimentary bottle of inexpensive perfume. Upon determining his perfume to be more popular than his books, he decided that the manufacture of perfume might be more lucrative. He bottled toiletries under the name 'California Perfume Company' and a line of household products called 'Perfection.' In 1928 the name 'Avon' appeared on the label, and in 1939 the C.P.C. name was entirely removed from the product. The success of the company is attributed to the door-to-door sales approach and 'money back' guarantee offered by his first 'Depot Agent,' Mrs. P.F.E. Albee, known today as the 'Avon Lady.'

The company's containers are quite collectible today, especially the older, hard-to-find items. Advanced collectors seek 'go with' items labeled Goetting & Co., New York; Goetting's; or Savoi Et Cie, Paris. Such examples date from 1871 to 1896. The Goetting Company was purchased by D.H. McConnell; Savoi Et Cie was a line which they imported to sell through department stores. Also of special interest are packaging and advertising with the Ambrosia or Hinze Ambrosia Company label. This was a subsidiary company whose objective seems to have been to produce a line of face creams, etc., for sale through drugstores and other such commercial outlets. They operated in New York from about 1875 until 1954. Because very little is known about these companies and since only a few examples of their product containers and advertising material have been found, market values for such items have not yet been established. Other items sought by the collector include products marked Gertrude Recordon, Marvel Electric Silver Cleaner, Easy Day Automatic Clothes Washer, pre-1915 catalogs, California Perfume Company 1909 and 1910 calendars, and 1916 Calopad Sanitary Napkins.

There are hundreds of local Avon Collector Clubs throughout the world that also have C.P.C. collectors in their membership. If you are interested in joining, locating, or starting a new club, contact the National Association of Avon Collectors, Inc., listed in the Directory under Clubs, Newsletters, and Catalogs. Those wanting a National Newsletter Club or price guides may contact Avon Times, listed in the same section. Inquiries concerning California Perfume Company items and the companies or items mentioned in the previous paragraphs should be directed toward our advisor, Dick Pardini, whose address is given under California. (Please send a large SASE and be sure to request clearly the information you are seeking; not interested in Avons, 'Perfection' marked C.P.C.'s, or Anniversary Keepsakes.) For more information we recommend *Bud Hastin's New 16th Edition Avon Collector's Encylopedia.*

Note: Our values are for items in mint condition. A very rare item or one in super mint condition might go for 10% more. Damage, wear, missing parts, etc., must be considered; items judged to be in only good to very good condition should be priced at up to 50% of listed values, with fair to good at 25% and excellent at 75%. Parts (labels, stoppers, caps, etc.) might be evaluated at 10% of these prices.

American Ideal Lipstick, 1929, CPC on tube, M............................45.00
American Ideal Perfume, wood box, introductory sz, 1910, M....210.00
American Ideal Perfume, 1929, gr satin box, 1-oz, MIB..............145.00
Baby Set, 1916, 3-pc, MIB...350.00
Bandolene Hair Dressing, 1923, 4-oz, M..................................45.00
Bay Rum, 1908, 4-oz, M..80.00
Boudoir Manicure Set, 1929, 4-pc, w/booklet, M 85.00
California Tooth Tablet, metal lid, glass bottom, ca 1900, M........70.00
Catalog, color, w/tabs, 1915-29, M...60.00
CPC Sample Case, basketweave w/label, 1915, M...................100.00
Cut Glass Perfume, sq label, 1915, MIB.................................235.00
Daphne Bath Salts, glass jar w/gold label, 1925, 10-oz, MIB 70.00
Daphne Talcum Powder, tin container, gr can, 1923, 4-oz, M.......70.00
Depilatory, 1915, 1-oz, M..100.00
Eau De Quinine, 1923, 6-oz, M..80.00
Elite Powder, Perfect Foot Powder, oval can, 1923, sm, M 25.00
Elite Powder, Perfect Foot Powder, tin can, 1923, 1-lb, M 55.00
Gentleman's Shaving Set, 1917, 7-pc, MIB 405.00
Gertrude Recordon's Introductory Facial Treatment Set, MIB....305.00
Juvenile Set, 1915, MIB...435.00
Lavender Salts, gr glass, 1910, MIB 225.00
Lemonal Cleansing Cream, jar, 1926, M..................................55.00
Lilac Vegetal, ribbed glass, 1925, 2-oz, M................................55.00
Liquid Shampoo, 1923, 6-oz, M..65.00
Little Folks Set, 4-bottle, 1905, MIB......................................260.00
Lotus Cream, 1917, 12-oz, MIB...160.00
Lotus Cream, 1925, 4-oz, MIB..90.00
Mission Garden Dbl Compact, brass, 1922, M..........................50.00
Nail Cream, tin container, 1924, M 10.00

Calling Cards, Cases, and Receivers

The practice of announcing one's arrival with a calling card borne by the maid to the mistress of the house was a social grace of the Victorian era. Different messages (condolences, a personal visit, or a good-by) were related by turning down one corner or another. The custom was forgotten by WWI. Fashionable ladies and gents carried their personally engraved cards in elaborate cases made of such materials as embossed silver, mother-of-pearl with intricate inlay, tortoise shell, and ivory. Card receivers held cards left by visitors who called while the mistress was out or 'not receiving.' Calling cards with fringe, die-cut flaps that cover the name, or an unusual decoration are worth about $3.00 to $4.00, while plain cards usually sell for around $1.00.

Cases

Abalone shell inlay, cvd wht floral medallion, 3⅝".......................85.00
Continental sterling w/chased body & gr enameling, ca 1911 ....385.00
Ivory, cvd figures in garden, 1800s, 3¾x2¾"...........................195.00
Sterling, chinoiserie relief, grapevines, 3¾".............................215.00

Sterling w/chased borders & red enameling, 1910 mks 250.00

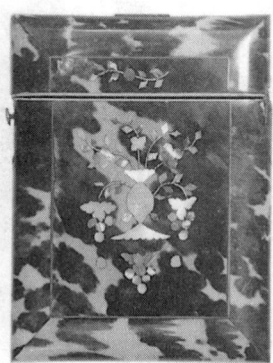

Tortoise shell with ivory and mother-of-pearl inlay, $135.00.

Tortoise shell, ivory mts, English, 1800s......................................85.00
Tunbridge, mosaic florals, mid-1800s, EX....................................85.00

Receivers

Brass, Nouveau lady across front, 3½x7"....................................125.00
Patinated metal exotic lady holds tray on sq base, 44"...........3,400.00
Porcelain, bust of armored knight, Derby, 3¾x5"...........................90.00
Silverplate, stag's head hdl, Middleton......................................195.00
White metal, Nouveau lady emb on fan shape, 5x6"....................85.00

Camark

The Camden Art and Tile Company (commonly known as Camark) of Camden, Arkansas, was organized in the fall of 1926 by Samuel J. 'Jack' Carnes. Using clays from Arkansas, John Lessell, who had been hired as art director by Carnes, produced the initial lustre and iridescent Lessell wares for Camark ('CAM'den, 'ARK'ansas) before his death in December 1926. Before the plant opened in the spring of 1927, Carnes brought John's wife, Jeanne, and stepdaughter Billie to oversee the art department's manufacture of Le-Camark. Production by the Lessell family included variations of J.B. Owens' Soudanese and Opalesce and Weller's Marengo and Lamar. Camark's version of Marengo was called Old English. They also made wares identical to Weller's LaSa. Pieces made by John Lessell back in Ohio were signed 'Lessell,' while those made by Jeanne and Billie in Arkansas during 1927 were signed 'Le-Camark.' By 1928 Camark's production centered on traditional glazes. Drip glazes similar to Muncie Pottery were produced, in particular the green drip over pink. In the 1930s commercial castware with simple glossy and matt finishes became the primary focus and would continue so until Camark closed in the early 1960s. Between the 1960s and 1980s the company operated mainly as a retail store selling existing inventory, but some limited production occurred. In 1986 the company was purchased by the Ashcraft family of Camden, but no pottery has yet been made at the factory.

For further information we recommend *Collector's Encyclopedia of Camark Pottery, Book I* and *II*, by David Edwin Gifford. Our advisor for this category is Tony Freyaldenhoven; he is listed in the Directory under Arkansas.

Covered dish, hen on nest, wht/pk/brn, #R55, 7½x7½", NM.......85.00
Figurine, cat, climbing, wht, 15" L...70.00
Figurine, hound dog, sitting, head down, pk w/souvenir label, sm...65.00
Fishbowl cat, cinnamon...40.00
Jug, ball; brn mottle, no stopper, 6" 50.00
Jug, ball; yel w/blk speckles, orig cork in cap, 7½" 48.00

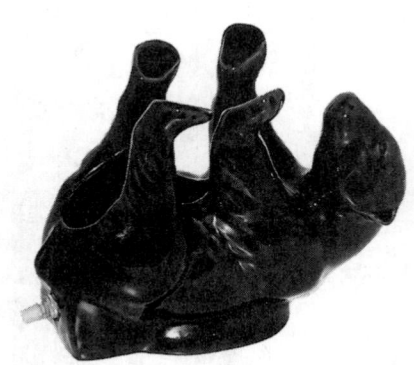

Lamp, bear figural, bur-
gundy, $180.00.

Lamp base, Old English, trees landscape, gray-bl, Lessell, 8".......550.00
Pitcher, bl & gr drip, slim neck, trifold top, 9½" 215.00
Pitcher, drip glaze, bulbous, 1928, 7x8" 110.00
Pitcher, lemonade; lemon & leaves on cream, 7¾" 55.00
Pitcher, parrot hdl, paper label, #131, 7" 175.00
Scouring pad holder, Humpty Dumpty, 6½" 135.00
Vase, brn stipple, shouldered, unmk, 10", from $250 to..............300.00
Vase, Celestial Blue w/blk overflow, cylindrical, 10¾" 275.00
Vase, Deco-style emb deer on mottled gr & yel, unmk, 9¾".......600.00
Vase, Festoon of Roses, Lechner, #272, 9½".................................150.00
Vase, frosted gr, bulbous, 4¼", from $30 to 40.00
Vase, gr overflow on orange, bulbous, sm rim, 4½", from $50 to...70.00
Vase, gr overflow on rose, rim-to-hip hdls, 4½", from $60 to........80.00
Vase, Lessell, palm scenic, mk LeCamark/sticker, 7", from $500 to.700.00
Vase, Modernistic, Yel Crackle Bright, bottle neck, 16¼" 1,200.00
Vase, pale bl, ruffled rim, low hdls, 7¾x6", pr.............................52.50
Vase, rose & bl matt, slightly bulbous, unmk, 6" 80.00
Vase, turq tulip shape, 3-sided, 1930s, 8x6" 75.00
Vase, yel top w/drips over bl, ring hdls, unmk, 5¾" 300.00

Cambridge Glass

The Cambridge Glass Company began operations in 1901 in Cambridge, Ohio. Primarily they made crystal dinnerware and well-designed
accessory pieces until the 1920s when they introduced the concept of
color that was to become so popular on the American dinnerware market. Always maintaining high standards of quality and elegance, they
produced many lines that became bestsellers; through the '20s and '30s
they were recognized as the largest manufacturer of this type of glassware
in the world.

Of the various marks the company used, the 'C in triangle' is the
most familiar. Production stopped in 1958. For a more thorough study of
the subject, we recommend *Colors in Cambridge Glass* by the National
Cambridge Collectors, Inc.; their address may be found in the Directory
under Clubs. *Glass Animals and Figural Flower Frogs of the Depression Era*
by Lee Garmon and Dick Spencer is a wonderful source for an in-depth
view of their particular aspect of glass collecting. They are both listed in
the Directory under Illinois. See also Carnival Glass; Glass Animals.

Apple Blossom, crystal, ashtray, heavy, 6" 50.00
Apple Blossom, crystal, butter dish, w/lid, 5½"............................145.00
Apple Blossom, crystal, stem, sherbet; #3135, tall, 6-oz................18.00
Apple Blossom, pk or gr, bowl, mayonnaise; 4-ftd, w/liner & ladle..80.00
Apple Blossom, pk or gr, bowl, pickle; 9" 60.00
Apple Blossom, pk or gr, stem, parfait; #1066 ....150.00
Apple Blossom, pk or gr, tumbler, #3135, ftd, 8-oz.........................40.00
Apple Blossom, yel or amber, bowl, bonbon; 2-hdl, 5½"...............40.00
Apple Blossom, yel or amber, comport, fruit cocktail; 4"...............28.00
Apple Blossom, yel or amber, plate, salad; sq 22.00

Apple Blossom, yel or amber, tumbler, #3025, 4-oz.........................24.00
Candelight, bowl, #3900/34, 2-hdl, 11" 90.00
Candelight, candle holder, #3900/67, 5" 60.00
Candelight, creamer, #3900/41 ....25.00
Candelight, mayonnaise, #3900/129, 3-pc.....................................75.00
Candelight, plate, #3900/20, 6½" 14.00
Candelight, relish, #3400/91, 3-part, 8"..65.00
Candelight, stem, water; #3776, 9-oz..45.00
Candelight, vase, #6004, ftd, 8"..120.00
Caprice, bl, pk or crystal, tumbler, #184, flat, 12-oz.......................53.00
Caprice, bl, pk or crystal, vase, ball; #237, 4½" 175.00
Caprice, bl or pk, bowl, pickle; #102, 9".......................................60.00
Caprice, bl or pk, candy, #168, divided, w/lid, 6"........................150.00
Caprice, bl or pk, plate, #28, 4-ftd, 14" 85.00
Caprice, bl or pk, stem, wine; #6, 3-oz...140.00
Caprice, crystal, bonbon, #155, ftd, oval, 6"..................................20.00
Caprice, crystal, bowl, salad; #80, cupped, 13" 75.00
Caprice, crystal, candle reflector, #73..350.00
Caprice, crystal, creamer, #38, med 11.00
Caprice, crystal, plate, bread & butter; #20, 5½" 12.00
Caprice, crystal, stem, cocktail; #300, blown, 3-oz.........................22.00
Caprice, crystal, tumbler, #12, ftd, 3-oz..27.50
Cascade, crystal, ashtray, 4½"...6.00
Cascade, crystal, plate, 4-ftd, 11½"...17.50
Cascade, gr or yel, candlestick, 5" 35.00
Cascade, gr or yel, creamer...20.00
Cascade, gr or yel, sugar bowl...20.00
Cascade, gr or yel, vase 9½"...75.00
Chantilly, bowl, flared, 4-ftd, 10" 50.00
Chantilly, butter dish, ¼-lb...250.00
Chantilly, comport, blown, 5⅜"...40.00
Chantilly, hurricane lamp, candlestick base 130.00
Chantilly, pitcher, ball 195.00
Chantilly, salad dressing bottle 150.00
Chantilly, stem, cordial; #3600, 1-oz..60.00
Chantilly, stem, sherbet; #3775, tall, 6-oz 20.00
Chantilly, stem, water; #3600, 10-oz..28.00
Chantilly, stem, water; #3625, 10-oz..28.00
Chantilly, stem, water; #3779, 9-oz..28.00
Chantilly, tumbler, tea; #3625, ftd, 12-oz.....................................26.00
Chantilly, vase, flower; high ftd, 8"...55.00

Charter Oak, Moonlight Blue,
pitcher, #3362, $75.00. (Photo
courtesy Gene Florence)

Cleo, bl, bowl, relish; 2-part...40.00
Cleo, bl, bowl, soup; tab hdld, 7½"...55.00
Cleo, bl, candlestick, 2-light 110.00
Cleo, bl, plate, luncheon; Decagon, 8½"..40.00
Cleo, bl, saucer, Decagon..8.00
Cleo, bl, sugar sifter, ftd, 6¾"...750.00
Cleo, bl, tumbler, #3077, ftd, 10-oz..65.00
Cleo, pk, gr, yel or amber, #3115, ftd, 12-oz.................................35.00
Cleo, pk, gr, yel or amber, bowl, cereal; Decagon, 6" 35.00
Cleo, pk, gr, yel or amber, bowl, oval, 11" 75.00

Cleo, pk, gr, yel or amber, ice pail..............................**95.00**
Cleo, pk, gr, yel or amber, stem, cocktail; #3115, 3½-oz..............**25.00**
Cleo, pk, gr, yel or amber, tray, serving; hdld, 12"..............**155.00**
Daffodil, candlestick, #628, 3½..............................**50.00**
Daffodil, cup, #11770..............................**25.00**
Daffodil, shakers, #360, squat, pr..............................**65.00**
Daffodil, stem, cordial; #3779, 1-oz..............................**85.00**
Daffodil, stem, wine; #1937, 3-oz..............................**55.00**
Daffodil, vase, #278, ftd, 11"..............................**125.00**
Decagon, bl, bowl, cranberry; belled, 3½"..............................**32.00**
Decagon, bl, comport, low ftd, 6½"..............................**35.00**
Decagon, bl, plate, dinner; 9½"..............................**70.00**
Decagon, bl, stem, sherbet; low, 6-oz..............................**18.00**
Decagon, bl, tray, service; oval, 12"..............................**45.00**
Decagon, pastel colors, bowl, cereal; belled, 6"..............................**20.00**
Decagon, pastel colors, bowl, vegetable; oval, 10½"..............................**35.00**
Decagon, pastel colors, creamer, lightning-bolt hdls..............................**10.00**
Decagon, pastel colors, plate, bread & butter; 6¼"..............................**5.00**
Decagon, pastel colors, salt dip, ftd, 1½"..............................**25.00**
Decagon, pastel colors, sugar bowl, lg ftd, tall..............................**20.00**
Decagon, pastel colors, tumbler, ftd, 12-oz..............................**25.00**
Diane, basket, ftd, 2-hdl, 6"..............................**30.00**
Diane, bowl, bonbon; ftd, 2-hdl, 6"..............................**25.00**
Diane, bowl, celery & relish; 5-part, 12"..............................**65.00**
Diane, bowl, relish; 2-part, 7"..............................**35.00**
Diane, bowl, 4-ftd, 11"..............................**65.00**
Diane, candlestick, 5"..............................**20.00**
Diane, comport, 5½"..............................**35.00**
Diane, hurricane lamp, candlestick base..............................**175.00**
Diane, mayonnaise, w/ladle & liner..............................**50.00**
Diane, plate, salad; 8"..............................**14.00**
Diane, stem, cocktail; #1066, 3-oz..............................**25.00**
Diane, stem, cocktail; #3122, 3-oz..............................**20.00**
Diane, stem, sherbet; #1066, low, 7-oz..............................**18.00**
Diane, sugar bowl, #3900, scalloped edge, ind..............................**20.00**
Diane, tumbler, #3122, 2½-oz..............................**33.00**
Diane, tumbler, juice; #1066, 5-oz..............................**20.00**
Diane, tumbler, sham bottom, 10-oz..............................**35.00**
Diane, vase, flower; high ft, 6"..............................**55.00**
Diane, vase, keyhole base, 12"..............................**95.00**
Elaine, bowl, finger; #3104, w/liner..............................**40.00**
Elaine, bowl, relish; 3-part, 6½"..............................**25.00**
Elaine, bowl, tab hdls, 11"..............................**75.00**
Elaine, candy box, w/lid, rnd..............................**100.00**
Elaine, hat, 9"..............................**395.00**
Elaine, plate, ftd, 2-hdl, 8"..............................**22.00**
Elaine, stem, brandy; #3104 (very sm stems), ¾-oz..............................**195.00**
Elaine, stem, cocktail; #3104, 3½-oz..............................**100.00**
Elaine, stem, cordial; #1402, 1-oz..............................**65.00**
Elaine, stem, cordial; #3121, 1-oz..............................**65.00**
Elaine, stem, water; #3121, 10-oz..............................**28.00**
Elaine, sugar bowl, ind..............................**20.00**
Elaine, vase, ftd, 6"..............................**75.00**
Gloria, crystal, bowl, bonbon; crimped edge, ftd, 5"..............................**30.00**
Gloria, crystal, bowl, fruit; 2-hdl, 11"..............................**60.00**
Gloria, crystal, comport, fruit cocktail; 4"..............................**18.00**
Gloria, crystal, icer, w/insert..............................**65.00**
Gloria, crystal, plate, cake; ftd, sq, 11"..............................**100.00**
Gloria, crystal, saucer, rnd..............................**4.00**
Gloria, crystal, stem, water; #3130, 8-oz..............................**28.00**
Gloria, crystal, stem, water; #3135, 8-oz..............................**28.00**
Gloria, crystal, tumbler, #3115, ftd, 10oz..............................**25.00**
Gloria, crystal, tumbler, #3120, ftd, 10-oz..............................**22.00**
Gloria, crystal, vase, squarish top, 12"..............................**185.00**

Gloria, gr, pk or yel, bowl, cereal; sq, 6"..............................**50.00**
Gloria, gr, pk or yel, bowl, finger; ftd..............................**60.00**
Gloria, gr, pk or yel, cup, 4-ftd, sq..............................**100.00**
Gloria, gr, pk or yel, plate, 2-hdl, 6"..............................**20.00**
Gloria, gr, pk or yel, stem, cocktail; #3035, 3-oz..............................**35.00**
Gloria, gr, pk or yel, stem, water; #3135, 10-oz..............................**40.00**
Gloria, gr, pk or yel, tray, relish; center hdl, 2-part..............................**50.00**
Imperial Hunt Scene, colors, creamer, flat..............................**50.00**
Imperial Hunt Scene, colors, stem, claret; #3085, 4½-oz..............................**67.50**
Imperial Hunt Scene, colors, stem, water; #3085, 9-oz..............................**55.00**
Imperial Hunt Scene, colors, tumbler, #3085, ftd, 5-oz, 3⅞"..............................**35.00**
Imperial Hunt Scene, crystal, bowl, 3-part, 8½"..............................**45.00**
Imperial Hunt Scene, crystal, ice tub..............................**55.00**
Imperial Hunt Scene, crystal, shakers, pr..............................**175.00**
Imperial Hunt Scene, crystal, stem, #1402, 14-oz..............................**55.00**
Imperial Hunt Scene, crystal, stem, tomato; #1402, 6-oz..............................**45.00**
Imperial Hunt Scene, crystal, tumbler, #1402, flat, tall, 10-oz..............................**25.00**
Imperial Hunt Scene, crystal, tumbler, #1402, flat, 5-oz..............................**20.00**
Marjorie, comport, #4004, 5"..............................**35.00**
Marjorie, jug, #106, w/lid, 30-oz..............................**225.00**
Marjorie, nappy, #5000, ftd, 4"..............................**22.50**
Marjorie, stem, water; #7606, 10-oz..............................**22.00**
Marjorie, stem, wine; #7606, 2½-oz..............................**65.00**
Marjorie, tumbler, #3750, ftd, 10-oz..............................**25.00**

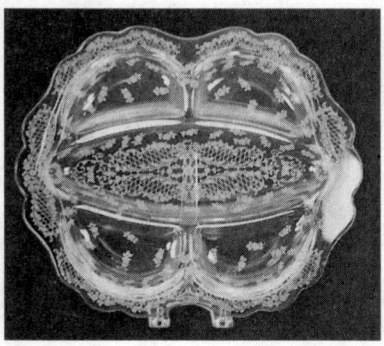

Minerva, five-part relish, $65.00.

Mt Vernon, amber or crystal, ashtray, #63, 3½"..............................**8.00**
Mt Vernon, amber or crystal, bottle, bitters; #62, 2½-oz..............................**65.00**
Mt Vernon, amber or crystal, bowl, #129, flanged, rolled edge, 12"..............................**32.50**
Mt Vernon, amber or crystal, bowl, #136, 4-ftd, oval, 11"..............................**27.50**
Mt Vernon, amber or crystal, bowl, ivy ball/rose; #12, ftd, 4½"..............................**27.50**
Mt Vernon, amber or crystal, bowl, pickle; #65, 8"..............................**17.50**
Mt Vernon, amber or crystal, bowl, preserve; #76, 6"..............................**12.00**
Mt Vernon, amber or crystal, cake stand, #150, ftd, 10½"..............................**35.00**
Mt Vernon, amber or crystal, cigarette holder, #66..............................**15.00**
Mt Vernon, amber or crystal, comport, #96, belled, 6½"..............................**22.50**
Mt Vernon, amber or crystal, creamer, #4, ind..............................**10.00**
Mt Vernon, amber or crystal, mug, #84, 14-oz..............................**30.00**
Mt Vernon, amber or crystal, pitcher, #95, ball shape, 80-oz..............................**105.00**
Mt Vernon, amber or crystal, plate, dinner; #40, 10½"..............................**35.00**
Mt Vernon, amber or crystal, relish, #200, 3-part, 11"..............................**25.00**
Mt Vernon, amber or crystal, salt cellar, #24..............................**75.00**
Mt Vernon, amber or crystal, sugar bowl, #86..............................**10.00**
Mt Vernon, amber or crystal, tumbler, tea; #20, ftd, 12-oz..............................**17.00**
No 520 Byzantine, Peach Blo or gr, bowl, finger; #3060..............................**25.00**
No 520 Byzantine, Peach Blo or gr, creamer, #138, rim ft..............................**20.00**
No 520 Byzantine, Peach Blo or gr, plate, dinner; #810, 9½"..............................**60.00**
No 520 Byzantine, Peach Blo or gr, saucer, #933..............................**7.00**
No 520 Byzantine, Peach Blo or gr, stem, sherbet; #3060, 7-oz..............................**22.50**
No 520 Byzantine, Peach Blo or gr, tumbler, #3060, ftd, 5-oz..............................**22.50**
No 704 Windows Border, colors, bowl, cereal; 6"..............................**25.00**

No 704 Windows Border, colors, bowl, finger; #3075 ....35.00
No 704 Windows Border, colors, celery tray, #652, 11" 45.00
No 704 Windows Border, colors, cologne, #198 or #199, 1-oz 125.00
No 704 Windows Border, colors, cup, #933.................................15.00
No 704 Windows Border, colors, jug, #124, w/lid, 68-oz 195.00
No 704 Windows Border, colors, plate, 6"....................................6.00
No 704 Windows Border, colors, platter, #904, oval, 16" 95.00
No 704 Windows Border, colors, stem, parfait; #3060, 5-oz.........40.00
No 704 Windows Border, colors, sugar bowl, #137, flat...............20.00
No 704 Windows Border, colors, tumbler, #3060, flat, 10-oz........20.00
No 704 Windows Border, colors, tumbler, whiskey; #3075, 2-oz ...35.00

Nude stem, Crown Tuscan, candlesticks, with gold decoration, 8½", $650.00 for the pair.

Portia, bowl, cranberry; 3½"...40.00
Portia, bowl, pickle; ftd 9½"...35.00
Portia, bowl, relish; 3-part, 6½"...30.00
Portia, candlestick, 3-light, 6"..55.00
Portia, comport, blown, 5⅜"...65.00
Portia, ice bucket, w/chrome hdl 95.00
Portia, plate, bread & butter; 6½"...7.50
Portia, shakers, flat, pr 30.00
Portia, stem, fruit/oyster cocktail; #3130, 4½-oz 20.00
Portia, stem, goblet; #3126, 9-oz...28.00
Portia, stem, sherbet; #3121, low, 6-oz....................................20.00
Portia, tumbler, juice; #3121, ftd, 5-oz....................................20.00
Portia, tumbler, tea; #3126, 12-oz..30.00
Portia, vase, flower; 11"..75.00
Rosalie, amber, bowl, cranberry; 3½"...35.00
Rosalie, amber, bowl, decagon; 14"..195.00
Rosalie, amber, bowl, soup; 8½"..35.00
Rosalie, amber, candlestick, keyhole shape, 3-light, 6" 45.00
Rosalie, amber, comport, 6¾" 35.00
Rosalie, amber, mayonnaise, ftd, w/liner...................................25.00
Rosalie, amber, platter, 12"...50.00
Rosalie, amber, saucer..4.00
Rosalie, amber, vase, 6" 55.00
Rosalie, bl, pk or gr, bowl, basket; 2-hdl, 11" 75.00
Rosalie, bl, pk or gr, bowl, bonbon; 2-hdl, 5½" 25.00
Rosalie, bl, pk or gr, bowl, cream soup......................................30.00
Rosalie, bl, pk or gr, bowl, oval, 15½".....................................135.00
Rosalie, bl, pk or gr, comport, 5¾" 30.00
Rosalie, bl, pk or gr, ice bucket/pail 85.00
Rosalie, bl, pk or gr, plate, 8⅜"...20.00
Rosalie, bl, pk or gr, platter, 15"..150.00
Rosalie, bl, pk or gr, stem, goblet; #801, 10-oz 35.00
Rosalie, bl, pk or gr, tray, for sugar shaker & creamer 20.00
Rosalie, bl, pk or gr, tumbler, #3077, ftd, 8-oz..........................35.00
Rose Point, ashtray, #1715, stack set on metal pole...................255.00
Rose Point, ashtray, #3500/130, oval, 4"...................................90.00
Rose Point, basket, #3500/52, 1-hdl, 6"...................................350.00
Rose Point, bowl, #1247, 4-ftd, crimped edge, oblong, 14" 165.00
Rose Point, bowl, #3400/3, low ft, 11".....................................175.00

Rose Point, bowl, #3500/118, ftd, oblong, 12" 175.00
Rose Point, bowl, #3500/27, ram's head, sq, 8" 395.00
Rose Point, bowl, #3500/28, 2-hdl, 10"....................................77.50
Rose Point, bowl, cereal; #3400/53, 6" 110.00
Rose Point, bowl, cranberry; #3400/70, 3½" 95.00
Rose Point, butter dish, #3900/52, ¼-lb..................................395.00
Rose Point, candle, torchere; #3500/88, flat ftd 195.00
Rose Point, candlestick, #3121, 7"...100.00
Rose Point, candlestick, #3500/31, 6".......................................95.00
Rose Point, candy box, #3400/9, w/lid, 7"...............................165.00
Rose Point, cigarette holder, #1066, oval, w/ashtray ft 195.00
Rose Point, comport, #3400/28, keyhole shape, low, 7".............95.00
Rose Point, comport, #3900/135, 5"..50.00
Rose Point, decanter, #1380, sq, 26-oz....................................495.00
Rose Point, grapefruit, #187, w/liner..125.00
Rose Point, hurricane lamp, #1617, candlestick base 275.00
Rose Point, icer, cocktail; #968 or #18......................................80.00
Rose Point, mayonnaise, #3900/129, 3-pc 75.00
Rose Point, oil, #3900/100, loop hdl, w/stopper, 6-oz 155.00
Rose Point, pitcher, #3900/116, ball shape, 80-oz......................250.00
Rose Point, pithcer, martini; #1408, 60-oz............................1,995.00
Rose Point, plate, #1397, rolled edge, 13½".................................75.00
Rose Point, plate, #3400/35, 2-hdl, 11" 65.00
Rose Point, plate, #3500/4, 7½"..20.00
Rose Point, relish, #3400/90, 2-part, 6" 35.00
Rose Point, relish, #3500/65, 4-ftd, 4-part, 10" 65.00
Rose Point, relish, #419, Pristine, 5-part, 12" 275.00
Rose Point, sandwich tray, #3400/10, center hdl, 11" 145.00
Rose Point, shakers, #395, w/chrome lids, pr 185.00
Rose Point, stem, cocktail; #7801, plain stem, 4-oz 45.00
Rose Point, stem, cordial; #3106, 1-oz......................................135.00
Rose Point, stem, cordial; #3500, 1-oz..73.00
Rose Point, stem, water goblet; #3106, 10-oz 40.00
Rose Point, sugar bowl, #3900/41, ftd......................................22.00
Rose Point, tray, #3500/72, 2-hdl, rnd, 13" 195.00
Rose Point, tumbler, #3106, ftd, 3-oz...40.00
Rose Point, tumbler, #3900/115, 13-oz.......................................50.00
Rose Point, urn, #3500/41, w/lid, 10".......................................695.00
Rose Point, urn, #3500/42, w/lid, 12".......................................795.00
Rose Point, vase, #1301, ftd, 10"..85.00
Rose Point, vase, #3500/44, ftd, 8"...135.00
Rose Point, vase, flower; #279, ftd, 13".....................................225.00
Square, ashtray, #3797/150, 6½"...11.00
Square, candle holder, #3797/492, block shape, 1¾", pr.............25.00
Square, decanter, #3797/85, 32-oz..90.00
Square, plate, #3797/26, 11½"..25.00
Square, plate, dinner/luncheon; #3797/25, 9½"..........................28.00
Square, stem, water goblet; #3798..12.00
Square, tumbler, wine; #3797, low..15.00
Square, vase, #3797/79, ftd, 11"...40.00
Tally Ho, amber or crystal, ash well, center hdl, 2-pc 20.00
Tally Ho, amber or crystal, bowl, finger 17.50
Tally Ho, amber or crystal, bowl, 3-part, 10½"............................55.00
Tally Ho, amber or crystal, comport, mint; low ft 17.50
Tally Ho, amber or crystal, goblet, sherbet; tall 15.00
Tally Ho, amber or crystal, plate, lunch; 9½"..............................45.00
Tally Ho, amber or crystal, stem, sherbet; high, 7½-oz 20.00
Tally Ho, Carmen or Royal, bowl, flat rim, 12½" 110.00
Tally Ho, Carmen or Royal, bowl, nappy; 2-hdl, 6" 27.50
Tally Ho, Carmen or Royal, cheese & cracker, 17½" 165.00
Tally Ho, Carmen or Royal, cup, punch; ftd 20.00
Tally Ho, Carmen or Royal, mug, 12-oz.......................................40.00
Tally Ho, Carmen or Royal, plate, buffet lunch; 18" 125.00
Tally Ho, Carmen or Royal, sugar bowl, ftd 27.50

Tally Ho, Forest Green, bowl, pan shape, 17" 175.00
Tally Ho, Forest Green, bowl, 9" 65.00
Tally Ho, Forest Green, comport, tall, 4½" 25.00
Tally Ho, Forest Green, goblet, cordial............................50.00
Tally Ho, Forest Green, plate, bread & butter; 6" 12.50
Tally Ho, Forest Green, relish, 4-part, 10" 65.00
Tally Ho, Forest Green, tumbler, short, 10-oz 20.00
Valencia, ashtray, #3500/124, rnd, 3¼" 12.00
Valencia, bowl, #500/115, ftd, 2-hdl, 9½" 38.00
Valencia, comport, #3500/37, 7" 45.00
Valencia, nut, #3400/71, 4-ftd, 3" 65.00
Valencia, relish, #3500/67, 6-pc, 12" 195.00
Valencia, relish, #3500/69, 3-part, 6½" 30.00
Valencia, stem, cocktail; #3500, 3-oz................................22.00
Valencia, stem, wine; #1402...40.00
Valencia, sugar bowl, #3500/15, ind..................................20.00
Valencia, tumbler, #3500, ftd, 12-oz 25.00
Wildflower, bowl, #3400/4, 4-ftd, flared, 12" 40.00
Wildflower, bowl, relish; 3-part, 6½" 25.00
Wildflower, candy box, #3900/165, rnd, w/lid.................75.00
Wildflower, ice bucket, #3900/671, w/chrome hdl 70.00
Wildflower, plate, bread & butter; #3900/20, 6½" 7.50
Wildflower, plate, cake; #3900/35, 2-hdl, 13½" 45.00
Wildflower, stem, cordial; #3121, 1-oz.............................57.50
Wildflower, sugar bowl, #3900/41 ....14.00
Wildflower, vase, #1237, keyhole ftd, 9" 100.00

Cambridge Pottery

The Cambridge Art Pottery operated in Cambridge, Ohio, from 1900 until 1909. During that time, several lines of artware were developed under the direction of C.B. Upjohn, an established ceramic artist of the period. Their standard brown-glazed line was Terrhea, examples of which are often found bearing the signature of the artist responsible for the underglaze decoration. Oakwood was a second brown-glazed line, without the slip painting. Other lines were Acorn (introduced in 1904) and Otoe, a matt green ware (introduced in 1907) that utilized already existing shapes from earlier lines. However, their most successful product was a line of cookware called Gurnsey, made from a red-brown clay with a white-glazed interior. Sales proved to be so profitable that by 1908 all artware was discontinued in favor of its exclusive production. By the following year, the firm had elected to change the name of their pottery to the Gurnsey Earthenware Company. Marks varied, but all incorporated a device composed of the letters 'CAP'; with the cojoined 'AP' usually contained within a larger-scale 'C.'

Note: Cambridge's brown-glazed artware is compatible in value to Roseville's Rozane line or Weller's Louwelsa.

Vase, girl's portrait on brown, orange, and green shaded ground, A. Williams, #211, 24", NM, $3,750.00.

Bottle, scent; gr matt, long neck, flattened base, mk, 6⅛x5" 175.00
Casserole, Guernsey, crows, blk/yel on brn, CAP, +underplate, EX..125.00
Jardiniere & ped, irises on brn, rprs, att, 27½"............................500.00
Vase, Alexander Dumas portrait, Williams, 1912, 24", from $1,700 to .2,000.00
Vase, clovers on brn, 3", EX..50.00
Vase, emb florals, earth tones, bulbous, sm neck, 3½" 80.00

Cameo

The technique of glass carving was perfected 2,000 years ago in ancient Rome and Greece. The most famous ancient example of cameo glass is the Portland Vase, made in Rome around 100 A.D. After glass blowing was developed, glassmakers devised a method of casing several layers of colored glass together, often with a light color over a darker base, to enhance the design. Skilled carvers meticulously worked the fragile glass to produce incredibly detailed classic scenes. In the eighteenth and nineteenth centuries Oriental and Near-Eastern artisans used the technique more extensively. European glassmakers revived the art during the last quarter of the nineteenth century. In France, Galle and Daum produced some of the finest examples of modern times, using as many as five layers of glass to develop their designs, usually scenics or subjects from nature. Hand carving was supplemented by the use of a copper engraving wheel, and acid was used to cut away the layers more quickly.

In England, Thomas Webb and Sons used modern machinery and technology to eliminate many of the problems that plagued early glass carvers. One of Webb's best-known carvers, George Woodall, is credited with producing over four hundred pieces. Woodall was trained in the art by John Northwood, famous for reproducing the Portland Vase in 1876. Cameo glass became very popular during the late 1800s, resulting in a market that demanded more than could be produced, due to the tedious procedures involved. In an effort to produce greater volume, less elaborate pieces with simple floral or geometric designs were made, often entirely acid etched with little or no hand carving. While very little cameo glass was made in this country, a few pieces were produced by James Gillinder, Tiffany, and the Libbey Glass Company. Though some continued to be made on a limited scale into the 1900s (and until about 1920 in France), for the most part, inferior products caused a marked reduction in its manufacture by the turn of the century. Beware of new 'French' cameo glass from Romania and Taiwan. Some of it is very good and may be signed with 'old' signatures. Know your dealer! Our advisor for this category is Don Williams; he is listed in the Directory under Missouri. See also specific manufactures.

English

Purse bottle, duck head, wht feathers, citron bill, RD1109, 9" ...7,000.00
Purse bottle, floral, wht on red, crystal stopper, 7" 2,800.00
Purse bottle, roses/buds/butterfly, wht on bl, Gorham cap, 8½" .3,000.00
Vase, floral, wht & pk on bl, stick neck, 2x2½" 1,200.00
Vase, flower branch, wht on Prussian bl, bulbous, 7"................2,100.00
Vase, flower/bud/leaves, cattails beyond, wht on raisin, 5".......2,000.00
Vase, flowers/buds, wht on magenta, 6" 1,235.00
Vase, honeysuckle vine/flower, wht on pk, can neck, 5" 1,100.00
Vase, lilies/foliage, clear/amber/gold, ftd, Richardson, 8" 1,350.00
Vase, magnolia, wht on Prussian bl, silver decor, 4¼" 700.00
Vase, morning glories, wht on gr, stick neck, 2" 1,050.00
Vase, trumpet flower/butterfly, wht on citron, beaker shape, 7" ..950.00

French

Bottle, floral branches, cranberry/textured, att St Louis, 5".........150.00
Bottle, nasturtiums, gr/burgundy/chartreuse/gray, D Christian, 6" ..4,800.00
Bottle, trailing wild roses, yel/clear, cylindrical, 1900s, 6½".........175.00

Bowl, wisteria pods, dk & lt amethyst, ftd, 5x11½" 575.00
Vase, bayou at sunset, cream frost/yel/orange/brn/bl, Michel, 14" ..980.00
Vase, branch & berries, rose-red/frost w/gold, slim, St Louis, 10" ..600.00
Vase, bridge/foliage/sea/mtns, burgundy/rose/gr/citron, 8" 750.00
Vase, floral, gr/red/clear, 4-fold top, att St Louis, 10¾" 400.00
Vase, floral, purple/martele/gold, Burgun, Schwerer & Cie, 3" ...2,000.00
Vase, forest/mtns/sky, brn/gr/pk, slight shoulder, Lamartine, 6½"...950.00
Vase, fuchsia/branches/flowers, red/opal, Cristallerie de Pantin, 14"...1,800.00
Vase, leafy vines & flowers, opal/plum/chartreuse, Delatte, 4¼".750.00
Vase, morning glories/leaves, blk/brn/lilac/pk/apricot, Arsal, 8" ..900.00
Vase, mtns/forest, brn/gr/pk, Lamartine, 6½" 950.00
Vase, mythological scene, amber/rose, hdls, Berugn & Schverer, 11"..9,000.00
Vase, Nouveau floral spray, pk/frost, cylindrical, att St Louis, 6" ...200.00
Vase, oasis scene, orange frost/dk brn, Degue, 5½" 750.00
Vase, orchids/leaves, purple/gray w/gold, Lorraine/thistle mk, 6" .1,725.00
Vase, poppies, blk/brn/turq/yel, ftd stick form, Lasage, 17¼".......500.00
Vase, sailboats/branch, gr/burgundy on citron, Michel, 12½"...1,000.00
Vase, trees/lake/sun, brn/yel/orange, bulbous, 8¼"....................2,000.00
Vase, trees/sun, brn/yel/burnt orange/lt orange, intaglio mk, 8¼"...1,800.00
Vase, Venetian scene/flowers, bl/gr/yel frost, Dewey, 15" 1,600.00
Vase, violets, burgundy on frost, Cristallerie, 6¼" 565.00

Candle Holders

The earliest type of candlestick, called a pricket, was constructed with a sharp point on which the candle was impaled. The socket type, first used in the sixteenth century, consisted of the socket and a short stem with a wide drip pan and base. These were made from sheets of silver or other metal; not until late in the seventeenth century were candlesticks made by casting. By the 1700s, styles began to vary from the traditional fluted column or baluster form and became more elaborate. A Rococo style with scrolls, shellwork, and naturalistic leaves and flowers came into vogue that afforded the individual silversmith the opportunity to exhibit his skill and artistry. The last half of the eighteenth century brought a return to fluted columns with neoclassic motifs. Because they were made of thin sheet silver, weighted bases were used to add stability. The Rococo styles of the Regency period were heavily encrusted with applied figures and flowers. Candelabra with six to nine branches became popular. By the Victorian era when lamps came into general use, there was less innovation and more adaptation of the earlier styles. See also Silver; Tinware; specific manufacturers.

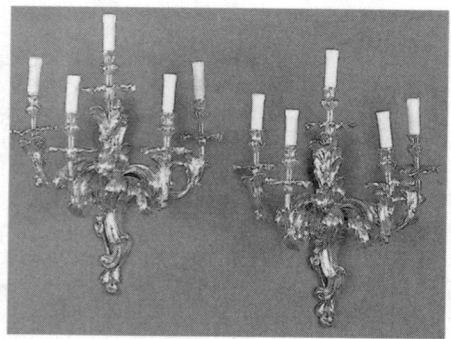

Sconces, bronze dorè, Rococo style, five-light, scrolling foliage, 24x18½x9½", $1,650.00 for the pair. (Photo courtesy Neal Auction Company)

Brass, beehive detail, pushups, 7¾", pr..........................110.00
Brass, beehive/baluster columns, scalloped hex base, 1850s, 10", pr ..225.00
Brass, CI weight in base, early 1900s, 9½", pr.........................165.00

Brass, English QA, scalloped base, baluster stem, rpr, 6¼"..........300.00
Brass, hexagonal, heavy, old but not period, 10¼", pr 110.00
Brass, hexagonal, w/pushups, 20th C, 12¼", pr.......................125.00
Brass, Neoclassical, side pushup, 6⅜" 750.00
Brass, petal base, conforming bobeche, 1750s, 8½", pr 1,380.00
Brass, QA, petal base & socket, baluster stem, rpr, 7¾" 330.00
Brass, QA, scroll ft, baluster stem, scalloped lip, 8½", pr 935.00
Brass, side pushup, English, early, 7" 220.00
Brass, 8-sided base & stem, 5¾"..100.00
Brass, 8-sided base mk: King of Dmns, w/pushup, 12½", pr.......495.00
Brass, 8-sided domed base, 8-sided stem & socket, 9" 660.00
Candelabra, brass, Fr Renaissance Revival style, 6-light, 21x14", pr ..1,100.00
Candelabra, clear press cut w/gilt fittings, prisms, rpr, 15", pr 330.00
Candelabrum, bronze dorè Louis XVI-style, 5-light, 19th C, 18x5" base ...880.00
Candelabrum, Rococo Revival bronze dorè, 7-light, ornate scrolls, 28"..1,400.00
Chandelier, maple & chestnut w/EX finish, 4 tin sockets, 31x30" dia...1,750.00
Glass, amethyst, optic-ribbed shaft, cupped ped, 12", pr..............235.00
Glass, clambroth, stepped base, fluted column, petal socket, 9¼"...250.00
Glass, clambroth/alabaster, pressed crucifix form, 9⅛", EX 150.00
Glass, pressed base, free-blown deep socket & extension, 9".......150.00
Glass, wht opaque, crucifix form, flint, 11¼" 90.00
Hogscraper, sheet iron, brass ring, pushup mk Shaw, 6½"...........350.00
Oak, open spiral stem, brass sockets, English, 12", pr 330.00
Sconce, brass, scrolled arm, stepped base, 19th C, 11½" 375.00
Sconce, brass Louis XVI-style, 7-light, 19th C, 12x12", pr.........375.00
Sconce, bronze Louis XVI-style, 4-light, vintage decor, 27x18", pr ...4,000.00
Sconce, CI, Iberian style, 7-light, 34".......................................175.00
Sconce, CI Rococo w/gilt, mirrored bk, rpr, 15½" 150.00
Sticking tommy, wrought steel, w/match compartment, 12".......400.00

Candlewick

Candlewick crystal was made by the Imperial Glass Corporation, a division of Lenox Inc., Bellaire, Ohio. It was introduced in 1936, and though never marked except for paper labels, it is easily recognized by the beaded crystal rims, stems, and handles inspired by the tufted needlework called candlewicking, practiced by our pioneer women. During its production, more than 741 items were designed and produced. In September 1982 when Imperial closed its doors, thirty-four pieces were still being made.

Identification numbers and mold numbers used by the company help collectors recognize the various styles and shapes. Most of the pieces are from the #400 series, though other series numbers were also used. Stemware was made in eight styles — five from the #400 series made from 1941 to 1962, one from #3400 series made in 1937, another from #3800 series made in 1941, and the eighth style from the #4000 series made in 1947. In the listings that follow, some #400 items lack the mold number because that information was not found in the company files.

A few pieces have been made in color or with a gold wash. At least two lines, Valley Lily and Floral, utilized Candlewick with floral patterns cut into the crystal. These are scarce today. Other rare items include gifts such as the desk calendar made by the company for its employees and customers; the dresser set comprised of a mirror, clock, puff jar, and cologne; and the chip and dip set.

Ashtray, #400/173, heart shape, 5½" 12.00
Ashtray, #400/33, rnd, 4" 11.00
Ashtray, #400/650, 3-pc nesting set, sq 130.00
Bowl, #400/124A, oval, 11" 275.00
Bowl, #400/17F, shallow, 12" 47.50
Bowl, #400/183, 3-ftd, 6"...60.00
Bowl, #400/49H, heart shape, 9" 135.00
Bowl, #400/5F, rnd, 7"..25.00

Bowl, #400/51H, heart shape w/hand, 6".............30.00

Bowl, #400/52, divided, two handles, 6", $25.00.

Bowl, #400/53H, heart shape, 5½"......................22.00
Bowl, #400/75F, cupped edge, 10".....................45.00
Bowl, finger; #3400, ftd...............................35.00
Bowl, fruit; #400/1F, 5"...............................12.00
Bowl, pickle/celery; #400/58, 8½".....................20.00
Bowl, relish; #400/209, 5-part, 13½"..................82.50
Bowl, relish; #400/217, 2-hdl, oval, 10"..............40.00
Bowl, relish; #400/268, 2-part, 8"....................20.00
Bowl, relish; #400/60, 7".............................25.00
Bowl, salad; #400/75B, 10½"...........................40.00
Cake stand, #400/67D, low ftd, 10"....................60.00
Candle holder, #400/100, 2-light......................24.00
Candle holder, #400/40HC, heart shape, 5".............85.00
Candle holder, flower; #400/40F, rnd, 6"..............25.00
Candle holder, flower; #400/66F, 2-bead stem, 4".....60.00
Candy box, #400/259, w/lid, 7".......................165.00
Candy box, #400/59, rnd, 5½"..........................45.00
Cigarette box, #400/134, w/lid........................35.00
Clock, rnd, 4".......................................295.00
Compote, #400/48F, bead stem, 8"......................90.00
Compote, #400/63B, 4½"................................40.00
Creamer, #400/18, domed ftd..........................135.00
Cup, #400/77, AD......................................17.50
Egg cup, #400/19, bead ft.............................47.50
Hurricane lamp, #400/79, candle base, 2-pc...........135.00
Ice tub, #400/63, 5½" deep, 8" dia...................110.00
Icer, seafood/fruit cocktail; #400/53/3, 2-pc.........95.00
Knife, butter; #4000.................................350.00
Ladle, mayonnaise; #400/135, 6¼".......................12.00
Mirror, standing, rnd, 4½"...........................135.00
Oil, #400/166, bead base, 6-oz........................65.00
Oil, #400/275, bulbous bottom, 6-oz...................60.00
Pitcher, #400/24, 80-oz..............................150.00
Pitcher, #400/330, short, rnd, 14-oz.................195.00
Pitcher, #400/419, plain, 40-oz.......................40.00
Plate, #400/34, 4½".....................................6.00
Plate, #400/62D, 2-hdl, 8½"...........................13.00
Plate, #400/72D, 2-hdl, 10"...........................27.50
Plate, luncheon; #400/7D, 9"..........................13.50
Plate, salad; #400/3D, 7"..............................8.00
Plate, salad; #400/5D, 8"..............................9.00
Plate, service; #400/13D, 12".........................33.00
Plate, service; #400/92D, 14".........................40.00
Plate, torte; #400/20D, 17"...........................95.00
Platter, #400/124D, 13".............................110.00
Punch ladle, #400/91..................................30.00
Salt dip, #400/61, 2".................................10.00
Sauce boat, #400/169.................................115.00
Shakers, #400/109, ind, pr............................11.00
Shakers, #400/190, bead base, ftd, pr.................47.50
Stem, brandy; #3800...................................35.00

Stem, claret; #3800...................................75.00
Stem, cocktail; #3400, 4-oz...........................18.00
Stem, cordial; #400/190, 1-oz.........................70.00
Stem, parfait; #3400, 6-oz............................58.00
Stem, wine; #4000, 5-oz...............................28.00
Stem, wine; #4001/90, 5-oz............................22.50
Sugar bowl, #400/30, bead hdl, 6-oz....................7.00
Tidbit, #400/18TB, 3-pc..............................225.00
Tray, #400/113E, hdls, 14"............................45.00
Tray, #400/29, 6½"....................................15.00
Tray, party; #400/68D, center hdl, 11½"...............33.00
Tumbler, #3400, ftd, 9-oz.............................16.00
Tumbler, old fashioned; #400/19, 7-oz.................38.00
Tumbler, parfait; #400/18, 7-oz.......................55.00
Tumbler, wine; #400/19, ftd, 3-oz.....................22.00
Vase, #400/193, ftd, 10".............................185.00
Vase, #400/198, 6" dia...............................300.00
Vase, bud; #400/28C, bead ft, 8½".....................85.00
Vase, ivy bowl; #400/74J, 7".........................135.00
Vase, rose bowl; #400/132, ftd, 7½".................425.00

Candy Containers

Figural glass candy containers were first created in 1876 when ingenious candy manufacturers began to use them to package their products. Two of the first containers, the Liberty Bell and Independence Hall, were distributed for our country's centennial celebration. Children found these toys appealing, and an industry was launched that lasted into the mid-1960s.

Figural candy containers include animals, comic characters, guns, telephones, transportation vehicles, household appliances, and many other intriguing designs. The oldest (those made prior to 1920) were usually hand painted and often contained extra metal parts in addition to the metal strip or screw closures. During the 1950s these metal parts were replaced with plastic, a practice that continued until candy containers met their demise in the 1960s. While predominantly clear, they are found in nearly all colors of glass including milk glass, green, amber, pink, emerald, cobalt, ruby flashed, and light blue. Usually the color was intentional, but leftover glass was used as well and resulted in unplanned colors. Various examples are found in light or ice blue, and new finds are always being discovered. Production of the glass portion of candy containers was centered around the western Pennsylvania city of Jeannette. Major producers include Westmoreland Glass, West Bros., Victory Glass, J.H. Millstein, J.C. Crosetti, L.E. Smith, Jack Stough, and T.H. Stough. While 90% of all glass candies were made in the Jeannette area, other companies such as Eagle Glass, Play Toy, and Geo. Borgfeldt Co. have a few to their credit as well.

Buyer beware! Many candy containers have been reproduced. Some, including the Camera and the Rabbit Pushing Wheelbarrow, come already painted from distributors. Others may have a slick or oily feel to the touch. The following list may also alert you to possible reproductions:

Amber Pistol, L #144 (first sold full in the 1970s, not listed in E&A)

Auto, D&P #173/E&A #33/L #377

Auto, D&P #163/E&A #60/L #356

Black and White Taxi, D&P #182/L #353 (A number of metal roofs have appeared. They are different from originals because the white section is more silvery in color than the original cream. These closures are put on original bases and often priced for hundreds of dollars.)

Camera, D&P #419/E&A #121/L #238 (original says 'Pat Apld For' on bottom, reproduction says 'B. Shakman' or is ground off)

Carpet Sweeper, D&P 296/E&A #133/L #243 (currently being sold with no metal parts)

Carpet Sweeper, E&A #132/L #242 (currently being sold with no metal parts)

Charlie Chaplin, D&P 195/E&A #137/L #83 (original has 'Geo. Borgfeldt' on base; reproduction comes in pink and blue)

Chicken on Nest, D&P #10/E&A #149/L #12

Display Case, D&P #422/E&A #177/L #246 (original should be painted silver and brown)

Dog, D&P #21/E&A #180/L #24 (clear and cobalt)

Drum Mug, D&P #431/E&A #543/L #255

Happifats on Drum, D&P #199/E&A #208/L #89 (no notches on repro for closure to hook into)

Fire Engine, D&P 258/E&A #213/L #386 (repros in green and blue glass)

Independence Hall, D&P #130/E&A #342/L #76 (original is rectangular; repro has offset base with red felt-lined closure)

Jackie Coogan, D&P #202/E&A #345/L #90 (marked inside 'B')

Kewpie, D&P #204/E&A #349/L #91 (must have Geo. Borgfeldt on base to be original)

Mailbox, D&P #216/E&A #521/L #254 (repro marked Taiwan)

Mantel Clock, D&P #483/E&A #162/L #114 (originally in ruby flashed, milk glass, clear, and frosted only)

Mule and Waterwagon, D&P #51/E&A #539/L #38 (original marked Jeannette, PA)

Naked Child, E&A 546/L #94

Owl, D&P #52/E&A #566/L #37, (original in clear only, often painted; repro found in clear, blue, green, and pink, with a higher threaded base and less detail)

Peter Rabbit, D&P #60/E&A #618/L #55

Piano, D&P #460/E&A #577/L #289 (original in only clear and milk glass, both painted)

Rabbit Pushing Wheelbarrow, D&P #72/E&A #601/L #47 (eggs are speckled on the repro; solid on the original)

Rocking Horse, D&P #46/E&A #651/L #58 (original in clear only, repro marked 'Rocky')

Safe, D&P #311/E&A #661/L #268 (original in clear, ruby flashed, and milk glass only)

Santa, D&P 284/E&A #674/L #103 (Original has plastic head; repro {1970s} is all glass and opens at bottom.)

Santa's Boot, D&P #273/E&A #111/L #233

Scottie Dog, D&P #35/E&A #184/L #17 (Repro has a ice-like color and is often slick and oily.)

Station Wagon, D&P #178/E&A #56/L #378

Stough Rabbit, D&P #53/E&A #617/L #54

Uncle Sam's Hat, D&P #428/E&A #303/L #168

Wagon, U.S. Express D&P #530 (Glass is being reproduced without any metal parts.)

Others are possible. If in doubt, do not buy without a guarantee from the dealer and return privilege in writing.

Our advisor for glass containers is Jeff Bradfield; he is listed in the Directory under Virginia. You may contact him with questions, if you will include an SASE. See Clubs, Newsletters, and Catalogs for the address of the Candy Container Collectors of America. A bimonthly newsletter offers insight into new finds, reproductions, updates, and articles from over four hundred collectors and members, including all authors of books on candy containers. Dues are $18.00 yearly. The club holds an annual convention in June in Reading, Pennsylvania, for collectors of candy containers.

'L' numbers used in this guide refer to a standard reference series, *An Album of Candy Containers, Vols 1 and 2*, by Jennie Long. 'E&A' numbers correlate with *The Compleat American Glass Candy Containers Handbook* by Eikelberner and Agadjanian, revised by Adele Bowden. D&P numbers refer to *The Collector's Guide to Candy Containers* by Doug Dezso and Leon and Rose Poirier (Collector Books).

Airplane, Boyd; various colors, D&P 77 ....**28.00**
Airplane, Passenger; 6-window, pnt accents, D&P 80/E&A 7 ....**445.00**
Airplane, Patent 113053, tin propeller, D&P 81/E&A 4 ....**105.00**

Airplane, Red Plastic Wing; Musical Toy on cap, D&P 83/E&A 3 ..**55.00**
Airplane, US P-51, star-in-circle insignia, D&P 87/E&A 5 ....**65.00**
Barney Google on Pedestal, w/red apple, EX pnt, D&P 189/E&A 72 ...**300.00**
Baseball Player on Base, gold w/pnt accents, D&P 191/E&A 78 ...**700.00**
Bell, Liberty Bank; various colors, D&P 94/E&A 87 ....**110.00**
Binoculars, Victor; brass-plated tin fr, D&P 98/E&A 560 ....**450.00**
Boat, Battleship; variations, D&P 99/E&A 97 ....**30.00**
Boat, Queen Mary; emb lifeboats/portholes/anchor, D&P 103 ...**350.00**

Boat, Submarine; clear with gray tin bottom, all original, Geo. Borgfelt & Co., ca 1915, D&P 104, 5½" long, from $550.00 ($200.00 with replaced tin parts).
(Photo courtesy Dezso, Poirier, and Poirier)

Boot, Santa's - Plastic; label: Merry Christmas, D&P 274 ....**8.00**
Bottle, Apothecary - Lg; 5¼", D&P 113 ....**80.00**
Bottle, Dairy Sweets; 3 in metal cloverleaf fr, D&P 108/E&A 532 ..**225.00**
Bottle, Dolly's Milk; mk Jenet, PA, D&P 109/E&A 527 ....**65.00**
Bus, Country Club; spoke wheels, D&P 150/E&A 117 ....**1,300.00**
Bus, Victory Stages; 8 side windows, D&P 157/E&A 118-1 ....**425.00**
Candelabrum, 2 cylinders in metal holder, D&P 317/E&A 174-1 ....**40.00**
Candlestick w/Hdls, ruby flashed, gilt accents, D&P 321/E&A 119 ...**310.00**
Cannon, 2-Wheel Mt #1; red tin carriage, D&P 384/E&A 123 .**400.00**
Cannon, 2-Wheel Mt #3, 1-pc barrel & carriage, D&P 386/E&A 127 ..**800.00**
Cannon on Truck, no mk, D&P 382/E&A 126 ....**2,350.00**
Car, Air Flow; modernistic/streamlined, EX pnt, D&P 158/E&A 61 ...**550.00**
Car, Electric Coupe - Pat Feb 18, 1913; D&P 162/E&A 48 ....**100.00**
Car, Lg Flat Top Hearse; tassles side/front, D&P 166/E&A 59 ....**600.00**
Car, Reo; spare tire on left side, D&P 175/E&A 62 ....**500.00**
Car, Sedan w/12 Vents; no radiator cap, D&P 177/E&A 36 ....**110.00**
Car, Yellow Taxi; wall behind driver extends to top, D&P 184/E&A 43 .**1,300.00**
Carpet Sweeper, Dolly; twisted wire hdl, D&P 296/E&A 133 ....**475.00**
Cash Register, 4 rows of keys, D&P 420/E&A 135/L 244 ....**550.00**
Charlie Chaplin by Curved Barrel, D&P 195/E&A 137 ....**95.00**
Chick, Baby Standing; D&P 7/E&A 145 ....**110.00**
Chicken on Nest, oval woven basket, D&P 10/E&A 149 ....**30.00**
Child, Naked Elfin; pointed head, blk eyes, D&P 198/E&A 545 ..**225.00**
Clock, Betty Barker Time Teacher; D&P 478 ....**150.00**
Clock, Mantel; scroll-emb front, D&P 482/E&A 164 ....**200.00**
Clock, Octagon; reads 8:17 o'clock, D&P 484/E&A 163 ....**225.00**
Coach, Angeline - No Couplers; D&P 519/E&A 166 ....**500.00**
Coal Car - W/Couplers; Overland Limited, D&P 522/E&A 171 ..**350.00**
Dog, Bulldog w/Round Base, spiked collar, D&P 18/E&A 189/L 15 ...**85.00**
Dog, Circus Clown Salt & Pepper, pr joined w/cb, D&P 20 ....**65.00**
Dog, Hound w/Lg Glass Hat, seated, D&P 27/E&A 182/L 22 ......**20.00**
Dog, Mutt; sm stippled glass hat, tooled fur, D&P 32/E&A 194 ...**85.00**
Don't Park Here USA, parking meter, D&P 423/E&A 196/L 314 ..**275.00**
Duck on Rope Top Basket, rectangular, D&P 39/E&A 198 ....**80.00**
Felix by Barrel, D&P 200/E&A 211 ....**625.00**
Fire Engine, Fire Dept #90; rounded grill/bk sloped, D&P 252/E&A 214 ...**135.00**
Fire Engine, Little Boiler #2, sq grid grill, D&P 257/E&A 218-1 ..**125.00**

Fire Engine, VG Co Little Boiler; pnt details, D&P 261/E&A 217 .**115.00**
Flossie Fisher's Chair, seat slides open, D&P 300/E&A 232/L 128...**700.00**
Flossie Fisher's Table, mk Helene Nyce, D&P 304/E&A 233 ..**1,900.00**
Fox, Learned; seated/holding book, E&A 470....................**85.00**
Gun, Kolt; dmn-emb grip, D&P 393/E&A 285 ....**125.00**
Gun, Sm Revolver; grip emb w/lg dmns, D&P 398/E&A 253......**28.00**
Gun, VG Co Revolver; 8-sided barrel, D&P 404/E&A 255...........**30.00**
Gun, Waffle Grip; waffle grid grip pattern, D&P 406/E&A 247-1 ..**25.00**
Helicopter, 4-blade rotor, mk Patent 113053, D&P 91/E&A 305 ..**275.00**
Horn, Musical Clarinet #515a; 3 sides stippled, D&P 452/E&A 315...**135.00**
Horn, 3-Valve; loop hdl, D&P 455/E&A 312..........................**300.00**
Horse, Rocking, w/Rider; pnt clown & horse, D&P 47/E&A 652..**200.00**
Iron, Electric; temperature dial, D&P 305/E&A 343 ....**55.00**
Jeep, many variations/colors, D&P 410/E&A 350 ....**30.00**
Kettle, Wee Soup; no tripod fr, D&P 308/E&A 356..................**20.00**
Kettle, Wee Soup; on tripod fr, complete, D&P 308/E&A 356 ..**100.00**
Kiddie Kar, horse's head above front wheel, D&P 430/E&A 360 ..**250.00**
Lamp, Hobnail; cb shade w/animals & people, D&P 329/E&A 365 ..**300.00**
Lamp, Kerosene; metal base w/screw cap, D&P 332/E&A 371 ...**100.00**
Lamp, Monkey; red plastic shade, D&P 338/E&A 533 ....**450.00**
Lamp, Monkey; yel plastic shade, D&P 338/E&A 533.................**525.00**
Lantern, Aluminum Top & Bottom, D&P 343/E&A 449/L 560...**50.00**
Lantern, Barn Type #3; w/legend, ruby flashed, D&P 346/E&A 427..**140.00**
Lantern, Beveled Panel, sq, D&P 349/E&A 396 ....**115.00**
Lantern, Dec 20 '04 - Med; shaker top, D&P 351/E&A 470/L 173 ..**30.00**
Lantern, Diamond Marked; flared metal base, D&P 353/E&A 441..**35.00**
Lantern, K600; aluminum reflector/base, D&P 355/E&A 445 ......**22.50**
Lantern, Stough's All Glass; stepped base/reflector, D&P 364/E&A 406....**25.00**
Lantern, Stough's No 81; tin shade/base, D&P 366/E&A 447 ......**48.00**
Lanterns, Twins on Anchor; D&P 370/E&A 385 ....**35.00**
Locomotive, American Type 23; bl, D&P 489/E&A 480............**170.00**
Locomotive, Dbl Window 888; 4-4-0 wheel arrangement, D&P 491/E&A 482....**35.00**
Locomotive, Sm Plain Screw Cap; 4-4-O arrangement, D&P 502/E&A 493 ..**165.00**
Locomotive, Stough's E3W Wide Cab; D&P 505/E&A 490 ....**30.00**
Locomotive, Stough's Tiny One; 1 window, D&P 509/E&A 475..**30.00**
Luggage, Trunk w/Rnd Top; milk glass, D&P 378/E&A 789.......**135.00**
Mug, Child's; screw bore, D&P 432/E&A 541 ....**325.00**
Nurser, Baby Dear; rnd front, flat bk, D&P 117/E&A 555 ....**30.00**
Nurser, Plain; rubber nipple, D&P 123/E&A 549 ....**30.00**
Oil Can, Independence Bell; D&P 435/E&A 556 ....**600.00**
Parlor Car, mk top of windows: NY Central, D&P 516/E&A 169..**325.00**
Piano, tin closure w/coin slot, D&P 460/E&A 577 ....**225.00**
Pumpkin-Head Witch, holds broom, NM pnt, D&P 272/E&A 594 ..**900.00**
Purse, gr, simulated alligator, D&P 379/E&A 599 ....**525.00**
Rabbit on Dome, holds handleless basket, D&P 65/E&A 607 ....**500.00**

Rabbit Family, gilt paint, marked V.G. Co. / Jeannette, PA / Avor. Oz, red tin snap-on closure, D&P 56, E&A 604, L 43, 1920s, 3⁷⁄₁₆x3⁷⁄₁₆x1³⁄₈", $900.00. (Photo courtesy Dezso, Poirer, and Poirer)

Rabbit Running on Log, heavy cvd fur, mk ½-oz AVOR, D&P 62/E&A 603....**350.00**
Racer, Pointed Front; 9 vents ea side, all orig, D&P 471/E&A 638 ..**3,000.00**
Racer, Stough's; wheels mtd on axles, D&P 473/E&A 640 ....**80.00**
Racer w/Number on Grill; balloon tires/spoked wheels, D&P 475/E&A 641 ...**125.00**

Rolling Pin, red tin caps/wood hdls, D&P 310/E&A 660............**300.00**
Rooster, Crowing; on tall reeds/grasses, D&P 73/E&A 151.........**325.00**
Santa Claus by Sq Chimney, top of chimney is threaded, D&P 275/E&A 672 ..**2,000.00**
Santa Claus in Banded Coat, pnt face/attire, D&P 277/E&A 669...**300.00**
Santa Claus in Long Coat, mk REGDNO716934, D&P 279......**300.00**
Santa Claus w/Skis, plastic, Rosen Co, D&P 287 ....**18.00**
Snowman, Sears; styrofoam head, D&P 289/E&A 681-1 ....**18.00**
Swan Boat, holds rabbit & chick, D&P 74/E&A 713 ....**950.00**
Swing, lawn; in red/wht striped canopy, D&P 314/E&A 469/L 135 ...**800.00**
Tank, Man in Turret; emb treads/geared wheels, D&P 412/E&A 722 ..**55.00**
Tank, WWI; sq turret w/pyramid-shaped cap, D&P 415/E&A 721 ....**150.00**
Telephone, Cog in Neck; partial groove at top, D&P 220/E&A ...**65.00**
Telephone, Glass Receiver, 2-fingered wire hook, D&P 226/E&A 736...**65.00**
Telephone, Pewter Top #1; Here's Your Party sticker, D&P 236/E&A 756 ..**125.00**
Telephone, Redlich's Screw Top #1; wood/metal mts, D&P 241/E&A 742 ...**425.00**
Telephone, Redlich's Tiny; pewter closure, D&P 245/E&A 758 .**210.00**
Top, Sm; mk Made in USA, ½-Oz AVOR, D&P 443/E&A 776/L272 ..**125.00**
Village Drug Store, w/liner, D&P 137/E&A 810 ....**135.00**
Wagon, Circus; lower half of wheels visible, D&P 527/L 439 .....**375.00**
Windmill, Dutch; emb bricks, 6-sided, w/blade, D&P 534/E&A 843..**95.00**
World Globe, pewter stand, D&P 445/E&A 860.........................**500.00**

Miscellaneous

These types of candy containers are generally figural. Many are holiday related. Our advisor for this category is Jenny Tarrant; she is listed in the Directory under Missouri. See also Christmas; Easter; Halloween.

Key: pm — papier-mache

Bulldog, compo, cream w/orange hat, Germany, 4", VG **100.00**
Cat, pm w/gesso, mc pnt, glass eyes, red ribbon, rpr, 6" **190.00**
Cat, seated, pm w/gesso, worn flocking, glass eyes, old rpr, 4".....**100.00**
Cat in shoe, compo & gesso w/mc pnt, rpr to ears, 4" **150.00**
Cat in shoe, pm & gesso, mc pnt, glass eyes, rprs, 4" **100.00**
Doll, bsk open dome head, crepe-paper/cb cylinder body, Germany, 6"....**225.00**
Elephant, pm, glass tusks, Germany, ca 1885-1920, 6" L **155.00**
English Bobby, pm, EX pnt, Pat No 208063, 12" **60.00**
Geo WA, compo, stands on rnd box w/silk flag, Germany, 5".....**225.00**
Geo WA bust, bottom plug, compo, 2-3" **75.00**
Geo WA bust, bottom plug, compo, 4-6" **150.00**
Geo WA w/tree stump, compo, Germany, 3-4" **55.00**
Geo WA w/tree stump, compo, Germany, 5-7" **85.00**
Horse, pm, head removes, 4½", VG **85.00**
Pig, pm, gr w/HP features, Made in Germany, 5¼x5½x3" **135.00**
Pig, pm, sleeping, worn/soiled pk flocking, 5⅝".............................**165.00**
Rooster, pm, lg red comb, Made in Japan, 1950s, 7", EX **75.00**
St Patrick's Day, Irish man bust, w/plug, compo, Germany, 3-4".**125.00**
St Patrick's Day, Irish man bust, w/plug, compo, Germany, 5-6".**150.00**
St Patrick's Day, Irish man on candy box, compo, Germany, 3½" ..**125.00**
St Patrick's Day, pig, flocked gr, plug in tummy, wood legs, 3-5".**165.00**
St Patrick's Day, pig, pk w/shamrock, compo, Germany, 4-6"......**155.00**
St Patrick's Day, potato, compo, Germany, 3-4" **75.00**
Stork w/baby, spun cotton & paper, lifts leg, Germany, 1950s, 6½"..**95.00**
Turkey, compo w/metal ft, head removes, Germany, 5" **195.00**
Turkey, compo w/metal legs, head removes, Germany, 3½" **125.00**
Turkey, pm, cb base, 5½", EX **170.00**
Watermelon w/face, molded cb, Made in Austria, 4¼x2¾", EX.**160.00**
Wheelbarrow, tin (held sm bag in bed), 7¾" **60.00**

Canes

Fancy canes and walking sticks were once the mark of a gentleman.

Hand-carved examples are collected and admired as folk art from the past. The glass canes that never could have been practical are unique whimseys of the glass-blower's profession. Gadget and container sticks, which were produced in a wide variety, are highly desirable. Character, political, and novelty types are also sought after as are those with handles made of precious metals.

For more information we recommend *American Folk Art Canes, Personal Sculpture*, by George H. Meyer, Sandringham Press, 100 West Long Lake Rd., Suite 100, Bloomfield Hills, MI 48304. Other possible references are *Canes in the United States* by Catherine Dike and *Canes From the 17th – 20th Century* by Jeffrey Snyder. For information concerning the Cane Collectors Club, see the Directory under Clubs, Newsletters, and Catalogs. Our advisor for this category is Bruce Thalberg.

Agate ball on SP collar, rosewood shaft, iron ferrule, 1890s........**425.00**
Alpaca panther-head curved hdl, glass eyes, 1920s......................**250.00**
Bamboo w/cvd figures from Punch, silver band, brass ferrule, 1878...**650.00**
Boar's tusk on silver mt, ebony shaft, brass ferrule, 1896.............**475.00**
Brass, toad hdl, cherrywood shaft, horn ferrule, 1890s.................**550.00**
Brigg sterling pop-up pencil gadget ball hdl, bamboo shaft, 1890s...**900.00**
Corkscrew inside removable metal hdl, malacca shaft, English, 1900s..**575.00**
Fruitwood, cvd shoe w/brass posts, shaft depicts pant leg, 1910s.**700.00**
Harmonica in hardwood shaft, hdl cvd as miner's ax, ca 1910 ...**1,100.00**

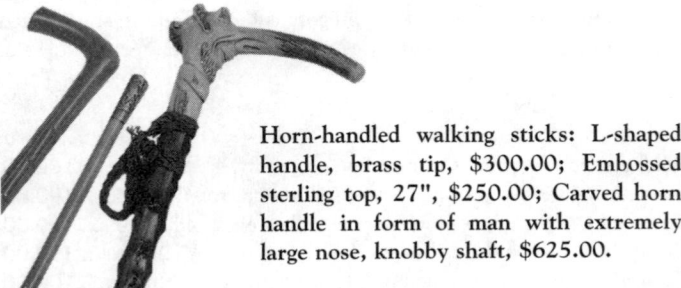

Horn-handled walking sticks: L-shaped handle, brass tip, $300.00; Embossed sterling top, 27", $250.00; Carved horn handle in form of man with extremely large nose, knobby shaft, $625.00.

Horn L-hdl w/7" dagger, thick bamboo shaft w/burnt decor, 1850s..**650.00**
Ivory, ball w/cvd dragons in foliage, hardwood shaft, Am, 1890s...**550.00**
Ivory, bulldog w/quartz eyes, rosewood shaft, brass ferrule, 1900s...**500.00**
Ivory, circus elephant ball hdl w/glass eyes, walnut shaft, 1890s.**750.00**
Ivory, dunce L-shaped hdl w/MOP eyes, ebony shaft, ca 1898.**1,000.00**
Ivory, fist/ball/snake, ebony/ivory separators, rosewood shaft, 1900s **650.00**
Ivory, horse w/silver bridle hdl, horn ferrule, rosewood shaft, 1880s..**2,000.00**
Ivory, lady's leg w/garter forms L-hdl, ebony shaft, 1860s **350.00**
Ivory, reclining draped nude, silver collar, hardwood shaft, 1900s....**2,500.00**
Ivory, Robin Hood hdl, figured snakewood shaft, horn ferrule, 1890s..**950.00**
Ivory, skull w/o lower jaw, chestnut shaft, horn ferrule, 1880s .**1,000.00**
Ivory, Thousand Faces hdl, silver collar, partridgewood shaft, 1890s...**525.00**
Ivory, whippet w/glass eyes, silver collar, bamboo shaft, 1890s....**650.00**
Ivory, 3 Scottish lions in relief on L hdl, ebonized shaft, 1890s ...**1,200.00**
Ivory & whalebone w/baleen inlay, L-shape, Am, 1850s..........**1,500.00**
Ivory knob hdl, punched silver collar, malacca shaft, 18th C......**950.00**
Ivory pique w/scrolls/flowers/dmns, rpl brass collar, malacca, 1690s ..**2,000.00**
Jade w/floral silver o/l, ebonized hardwood shaft, horn ferrule.**2,000.00**
Silver, horse as crook hdl, briarwood shaft w/strap collar, 1880s .**700.00**
Silver & enamel w/rose quartz inlay top & seed pearls, hardwood shaft...**1,200.00**
Silver Art Nouveau crook hdl, mahog shaft, wht metal ferrule, 1900s.**400.00**
Silver Art Nouveau floral hdl w/vermeil, partridgewood shaft, 1900s ..**550.00**
Snuff box in turban of Indian man ivory hdl, ebony shaft, 1880s......**1,000.00**
Staghorn, girl w/blown hair, silver collar, hardwood shaft, 1860s.......**1,000.00**
Staghorn, man's face cvg, whistle in hdl, gold-plated ferrule, 1870s......**750.00**
Staghorn, man w/lg mustache, malacca shaft, rpl ferrule, 1870s .**900.00**
Tortoise shell, pug dog in niche, glass eyes, ebonized shaft, 1890s ..**1,000.00**

WH Baker telescope, rosewood knob hdl w/swing cover, hardwood shaft...**2,700.00**
Whalebone, Victorian lady L hdl, baleen ring, whalebone shaft, 1860s...**2,800.00**
Wood, animal w/human ft in mouth, wht metal/iron ferrule, 1-pc, 1880s...**525.00**
Wood, Black dandy, cvd/pnt, 1880s, 1-pc **750.00**
Wood, bust of man, EX facial details, nubby shaft, 1-pc, 1890s ..**800.00**
Wood, cvd man/monkey 2-head hdl, inlaid eyes, EX patina, 38" .**660.00**

Canton

Canton is a blue and white porcelain that was first exported in the 1790s by clipper ships from China to the United States. Importation continued into the 1920s. Canton became very popular along the east coast where the major ports were located. Its popularity was due to several factors: it was readily available, inexpensive, and (due to the fact that it came in many different forms) appealing to homeowners.

The porcelain's blue and white color and simple motif (teahouse, trees, bridge, and a rain-cloud border) have made it a favorite of people who collect early American furniture and accessories. Buyers of Canton should shop at large outdoor shows and up-scale antique shows. Collections are regularly sold at auction and many examples may be found on eBay. Collectors usually prefer a rich, deep tone rather than a lighter blue. Cracks, large chips, and major repairs will substantially affect values. Prices of Canton have escalated sharply over the last twenty years, and rare forms are highly sought after by advanced collectors. Our advisor for this category is Hobart D. Van Deusen; he is listed in the Directory under Connecticut.

Basket, fruit; rtcl oval, w/undertray, 19th C, 4½x8⅝", 9⅞".....**1,150.00**
Basket, fruit; rtcl rim, w/undertray, 3¾x10", 10¼" **800.00**
Bowl, canted corners, 19th C, 4⅝x10¼", pr..............................**1,950.00**
Bowl, serving; boars' head hdls, mismatched lid, 11½" **275.00**
Dish, vegetable; almond shape, pine-cone finial, chips, 10¼" L .**385.00**
Dish, vegetable; rectangular, 19th C, 4½x7½x8¾", EX **345.00**
Ginger jar, drilled/mtd as lamp, brass base, 7½", 19" overall.......**275.00**
Jug, cider; dbl-woven strap hdl w/flower ends, foo dog finial, 8" ..**1,950.00**
Plate, dessert; 19th/20th C, 7⅜", EX, 6 for **435.00**
Plate, hot water; late, sm flakes, 9⅜"..**200.00**
Plate, hot water; orange peel, 9½", EX......................................**200.00**
Plate, hot water; 20th C, 10⅞"...**200.00**
Plate, luncheon; 19th/20th C, 8½", 6 for....................................**400.00**
Platter, canted corners, 19th C, 21⅛x17".................................**1,200.00**
Platter, octagonal w/central strainer, 19th C, 13¾x17⅛" **1,300.00**
Platter, orange peel, wear, chip on bk of rim, 13" **385.00**
Platter, oval, 19th C, 11½"..**515.00**
Platter, oval, 19th C, 17⅞x14¾"...**1,100.00**
Soup tureen, octagonal, boar's head hdls, +lid/tray, 8½x14¼" ...**1,950.00**
Tea caddy, octagonal, rare, 5½"...**2,645.00**
Teapot, domed top, prof rpr, 8⅛"..**500.00**
Undertray, fruit basket; rtcl rim, early 19th C, 10⅛x8¾"...........**230.00**

Capodimonte

The relief style, highly colored and defined porcelain pieces in this listing are commonly called and identified in our current marketplace as Capodimonte. It was King Ferdinand IV, son of King Charles who opened a factory in Naples in 1771 and began to use the mark of the blue crown N (BCN). When the factory closed in 1834, the Ginori family at Doccia near Florence, Italy, acquired what was left of the factory and continued using its mark. The factory continued until 1896 when it was then combined with Societa Ceramica Richard of Milan which continues today to manufacture fine porcelain pieces marked with a crest and wreaths under a blue crown with R. Capodimonte.

Boxes and steins are highly sought after as they are cross collectibles. Figurines, figure groupings, flowery vases, urns, and the like are also highly collectible, but most items on the market today are of recent manufacture. In the past several years, Europeans have been attending U.S. antique shows and auctions in order to purchase Capodimonte items to take back home, since many pieces were destroyed during the two world wars. This has driven up prices of the older ware. Our advisor for this category is James Highfield; he is listed in the Directory under Indiana.

Ashtray, mother & naked child, R Capo mk, 6" sq.........................**35.00**
Bottle, scent; cherubs & flowers, bronze corkstopper, BCN, 7"...**278.00**
Box, Cupid shooting arrow at cherub pr, BCN, 9x5½x4½" **500.00**
Box, figures (2) w/wine cup, heart shape, BCN, 3x2½x1" **140.00**
Candlesticks, maidens (3, partially draped), Rococo base, BCN, 13½"..**250.00**
Charger, men & women at war, BCN, 25" dia..........................**1,225.00**
Compote, eagle crest in center, BCN, 7x10½" **225.00**
Cup & saucer, chocolate; relief scenes, putti finial, 1870s...........**350.00**
Cup & saucer, demi; cavorting cherubs, twig hdl, 1890s **125.00**
Figurine, coach+4 horses, open carriage w/driver & couple, 14x35x14"..**2,800.00**
Figurine, David by Michaelangelo, 18x14x14" **1,000.00**
Figurine, Last Supper, 12x15" **3,000.00**
Figurine, Resurrection, 33x29x19" **3,700.00**
Figurine, Roman ladies (2) & cherub, harp & horns, BCN, 8x5¾x4¾"....**315.00**
Figurine, Romeo & Juliet, 18x10x10"..............................**575.00**
Humidor, outdoor tavern scene, BCN, 5x4" dia **100.00**
Jewel chest, Gloria in Excelsis Deo on lid, blk CN, 9½x5½x5" ...**1,000.00**
Monkey band, Meissen quality, BCN, 6-pc............................**600.00**
Planter, dolphin ft, BCN, ca 1850, 12x8x8" **1,400.00**
Planter, 4 rams' heads, cherubs & garland, BCN, 3¼x4" dia.........**75.00**
Platter, peasant scene, dogs, swans, Apollo on chariot, 15½x11¼"...**210.00**
Stein, drunken Bacchus in chariot, boar finial, BCN, 8".............**600.00**
Stein, lion hunt, lion finial, BCN, lg 2-litre, 10½" **1,000.00**
Tankard, camel-face hdl, wine bbl & partying, BCN, 8" **235.00**
Triptych, Fr Revolution street scenes, BCN, 9½x10"................**750.00**
Urn, fluted body, crown on lid, BCN, 18½x4".......................**510.00**
Urn, full lion hdls, BCN France, 9x6", pr **400.00**
Vase, Fr Champleve, solid lid, 9x2½"..............................**210.00**

Carlton Ware

Carlton Ware was the product of Wiltshaw and Robinson, who operated in the Staffordshire district of England from about 1890. During the 1920s, they produced ornamental ware with enameled and gilded decorations such as flowers and birds, often on a black background. In 1958 the firm was renamed Carlton Ware Ltd. Their trademark was a crown over a circular stamp with 'W & R, Stoke on Trent,' surrounding a swallow. 'Carlton Ware' was sometimes added by hand.

Demitasse cup and saucer, flowers on dark red lustre, gilt inside cup, ca 1925+, from $125.00 to $150.00. (Photo courtesy Susan and Jim Harran)

Bowl, Fantasia, lt bl ground, #3388/c/3621, 3x8" **1,000.00**
Bowl, Rouge Royale, flowers & exotic bird, ca 1930, 7⅛x11⅝" ..**300.00**
Bowl, salad; Lobster Ware, 1935+, 5x8" **85.00**
Bowl, spider web/berries on wht, gold hdls, 2x10½x8½", NM....**135.00**
Bowl, Tutankhamen, gold trim, 1922, 3¼x8¾"......................**1,150.00**
Candlesticks, Persian, minor wear to gold, 4", pr......................**235.00**
Casket, Iceland Poppy, #3507, 2½x6¼x4½".........................**465.00**
Charger, New Mikado, lustre, #2919, 15½" **325.00**
Coffeepot, Rouge Royal, spider web/berries/leaves, 7½"............**265.00**
Cup, chocolate; Apple Blossom on lt gr, #11687, 5", w/lid **145.00**
Cup & saucer, demi; wisteria/birds on cobalt lustre, gilt int/hdl...**100.00**
Ewer, foxglove, rose/gr on cream, branch hdl, 10" **195.00**
Jug, Spangled Tree, #4163, bulbous, 7¼" **365.00**
Plaque, fairy castle, 12½" dia.....................................**350.00**
Plate, Bleu Royale, flowers & ducks, ca 1930, 10⅞"................**300.00**
Plate, dragon & clouds, #3331, 9" **185.00**
Plate, Fantasia, purple, 5½".......................................**325.00**
Plate, Lobster Ware, red/lime gr, mk Australian design, 9"............**30.00**
Tea set, blkberries/leaves on cream, pot+cr/sug+2 c/s **300.00**
Tea set, cream w/blk Deco hdls, 6" pot+cr/sug+2 c/s **325.00**
Teapot, Buttercup, pk, #1522/2, ca 1936-45, 5" **525.00**
Teapot, shoes/striped socks as base, 7", +cr/sug **200.00**
Vase, Bleu Royal, birds w/gold filigree, #326, 6" **265.00**
Vase, Bleu Royale, grapes & leaves, 7¼".............................**215.00**
Vase, Bleu Royale, spider web/berries, 3-lobe gold hdls, 8".........**365.00**
Vase, Chinese Tea Garden, #2936, ca 1925, 10x4½" **365.00**
Vase, hollyhocks, Deco-style, 1930s, 6½"...........................**135.00**
Vase, Jazz Stitch, orange lustre, shouldered ovoid, 5½" **450.00**
Vase, Moonlight Cameo, dancing sprites, 1920s, 5" **235.00**
Vase, Prickly Pansy on rouge, fine lustre, 4¼x4¼", NM **275.00**
Vase, Secretary Bird, 4¾"..**1,300.00**
Vase, Spangled Tree variant on rouge, hdls, 4" **215.00**
Vase, Tutankhamen, gilt on blk, ca 1922, 8¼".......................**525.00**

Carnival Collectibles

Carnival items from the early part of this century represent the lighter side of an America that was alternately prospering and sophisticated or devastated by war and domestic conflict. But whatever the country's condition, the carnival's thrilling rides and shooting galleries were a sure way of letting it all go by — at least for an evening.

For further information on chalkware figures, we recommend *The Carnival Chalk Prize* by our advisor, Thomas G. Morris, who is listed in the Directory under Oregon.

In the shooting gallery target listings below, items are rated for availability from 1, commonly found, to 10, rarely found (these numbers appear just before the size), and all are made of cast iron. Richard and Valerie Tucker are our advisors; their address is listed in the Directory under Texas.

Chalkware Figures

Air raid warden holding US flag, 1940s, 14"................................**120.00**
Bear, bank, ca 1940-50, 11" **40.00**
Bird & nest, ca 1940-50, 9½" **40.00**
Black boy w/slice of watermelon, mk By Buelah, ca 1930-40, 7½" ..**95.00**
Boy & dog (Pals), ca 1935-45, 10x9" **45.00**
Boy standing by table talking on phone, ca 1940-50, 9"................**65.00**
Cat w/ball, ca 1930-45, 7" **20.00**
Cave girl holding club, HP pk chalk, ca 1920-30 ....**95.00**
China Girl, ca 1930-40, 5½"...**45.00**
Chinaman (Chinky), ca 1920-30, 9½"................................**110.00**
Chinese Lady (Tin Toy & Declaration Day), ca 1920, 14".........**195.00**
Cowboy, ashtray, ca 1930-40, 8¼"..................................**45.00**

Dog, bookends, ca 1935-40, 6½", pr......................................45.00
Dog bank, sitting w/flower, ca 1935-45, 10¾"......................40.00
Donkey seated w/toothy grin, ca 1940-50, 12"....................40.00
Elephant, bank, mk El Segundo, ca 1955, 12½".....................65.00
Fan dancer, ashtray, ca 1940, 10½"....................................95.00
Ferdinand the Bull, ca 1940-50, 10½".................................75.00
Girl & goat, ca 1930, 9½"...45.00
Girl in horseshoe (Baby Luck), 1947, 10½"..........................95.00
Girl in sombrero standing w/hands in pockets, ca 1930, 14"........85.00
Girl sitting in a flower, ca 1920, 11"..................................125.00
Girl sitting w/knees up & hands clasped, lg head bow, 1920s, 10"...95.00
Girl sitting winking, sticker mk Winkie 1919, Nick Navarra, 6"..75.00
Horse head in horseshoe, flat bk, ca 1940-50, 10"................35.00
Horse rearing, flat bk, ca 1940-50, 6½".............................15.00
Horse w/saddle, ca 1940-50, 10½"....................................45.00
Indian, ashtray, ca 1930-40, 6"..20.00
Lion, growling, standing w/front legs on rocks, 1935-40, 6"..........30.00
Little Lady, mohair wig/crepe-paper dress, Navarra, ca 1920-30, 12"..195.00
Maggie & Jiggs, ca 1920-35, 8¼x9½", pr...........................285.00
Newsboy hawking papers, ca 1935-45, 7".............................30.00
Nude island girl w/lei seated w/hands behind neck, 1935-45, 5½"..65.00
Nude kneeling covering breasts, sleek design, ca 1940-50, 12".....70.00
Nude standing w/banjo, ca 1935-45, 13"..............................90.00
Parrot, ca 1935-45, 13½"...45.00
Penguin in top hat, glass eyes, ca 1935-45, 7¼"...................50.00
Piano baby, ca 1910-25, 9½x10½".....................................120.00
Pigs (Mamma/Papa/Baby), flat bk, ca 1940-50, 6½" to 7", set....45.00
Pinocchio, ca 1940-50, 15"...175.00
Popeye, ca 1930-40, 10"...115.00
Rooster, mk RN, ca 1935-45, 12x10"...................................60.00
Sailor girl, mk Jenkins, ca 1934, 13½"................................95.00
Scottie w/ball, ca 1935-45, 8¾"...40.00
Sheba girl, hair tufts, c Jenkins, ca 1923, 13½"..................165.00
Shriner (Kewpie type) w/hands in pockets, mk Portland 1920, 10½"..130.00
Soldier boy (Remember Pearl Harbor), 1942, 13½"............185.00
Three Little Pigs, flat bk, 1930s-50s, 5x5½".........................30.00
Tom & Jerry, ca 1939, 8½"..55.00
Windmill, ca 1935-40, 10¾"..25.00

Shooting Gallery Targets

Battleship, worn wht pnt, Mangels, 5, 6¼x11⅜", $200 to..........300.00
Birds (8) on bar, worn pnt, Mangels, 9, 3½x41½", $700 to........800.00
Bull's eye w/pop-up duck, old pnt, Quackenbush, 7, 12" dia, $500 to..600.00
Dog running, worn pnt, Smith or Evans, 6, 6x11", $100 to........200.00
Duck, detailed feathers, old pnt, Parker, 8, 3¾x5½", $100 to.....200.00
Duck, detailed feathers, worn pnt, Evans, 4, 5½x8½", $100 to..200.00
Eagle w/wings wide, mc pnt, Smith or Evans, 6, 14¾", $650 to..750.00
Greyhound, bull's-eye, old patina, Parker, 8, 26" W, minimum..1,000.00
Monkey, standing, worn pnt, 10, 9¾x8½", $300 to....................400.00
Owl, bull's-eye, wht traces, Evans, 6, 10¾x5⅛", $400 to...........500.00
Pipe, old patina, Smith, 1, 5⅜x1¾", value less than..................50.00
Rabbit running, bull's eye, old patina, Parker, 8, 12x25x1", minimum..1,000.00
Rabbit standing, worn pnt, Smith or Mueller, 8, 18x10", $900 to..1,000.00
Reindeer (elk), worn pnt over wht, 7, 10x9", $300 to...............400.00
Saber-tooth tiger, old patina, Mangels, 7, 7¾x13", $300 to........400.00
Soldier w/rifle, pnt traces/old patina, Mueller, 5, 9x5", $100 to..200.00
Squirrel running, old patina, Smith, 4, 5⅛x9¼", $100 to...........200.00
Swan, worn wht pnt, Mueller, 6, 5¾x5", $100 to.....................200.00

Carnival Glass

Carnival glass is pressed glass that has been coated with a sodium solution and fired to give it an exterior lustre. First made in America in 1905, it was produced until the late 1920s and had great popularity in the average American household, for unlike the costly art glass produced by Tiffany, carnival glass could be mass produced at a small cost. Colors most found are marigold, green, blue, and purple; but others exist in lesser quantities and include white, clear, red, aqua opalescent, peach opalescent, ice blue, ice green, amber, lavender, and smoke.

Companies mainly responsible for its production in America include the Fenton Art Glass Company, Williamstown, West Virginia; the Northwood Glass Company, Wheeling, West Virginia; the Imperial Glass Company, Bellaire, Ohio; the Millersburg Glass Company, Millersburg, Ohio; and the Dugan Glass Company (Diamond Glass), Indiana, Pennsylvania. In addition to these major manufacturers, lesser producers included the U.S. Glass Company, the Cambridge Glass Company, the Westmoreland Glass Company, and the McKee Glass Company.

Carnival glass has been highly collectible since the 1950s and has been reproduced for the last twenty-five years. Several national and state collectors' organizations exist, and many fine books are available on old carnival glass, including *The Standard Encyclopedia of Carnival Glass* by Bill Edwards and Mike Carwile and *Dugan & Diamond Carnival Glass, 1909 – 1931*, by Carl O. Burns.

Absentee Dragon (Fenton), plate, marigold, rare.....................3,600.00
Acorn Burrs (Northwood), pitcher, gr....................................950.00
Amaryllis (Northwood), compote, bl, sm................................625.00
American (Fostoria), tumbler, gr, rare....................................140.00
Apple Blossom Twigs (Dugan), bowl, wht, 8"-9".....................125.00

April Showers, vase, amethyst, $55.00. (Photo courtesy Bill Edwards and Mike Carwile)

April Showers (Fenton), vase, vaseline....................................400.00
Aramis (Dunbar Glass Corp), pitcher, marigold, 2 styles, late.......60.00
Arcs (Imperial), bowl, wht, 8½"..175.00
Asters, bowl, bl..125.00
Aurora Pearls, bowl, amethyst, decor, 2 szs, ea.......................700.00
Australian Panels (Crystal), creamer, marigold..........................50.00
Autumn Acorns (Fenton), bowl, bl, 8½".................................100.00
Aztec (McKee), rose bowl, clambroth.....................................400.00
Ballons (Imperial), vase, smoke, 3 szs, ea...............................100.00
Banded Diamonds (Crystal), pitcher, amethyst, rare...............1,250.00
Banded Drape (Fenton), tumbler, bl..50.00
Barbella (Northwood), bowl, vaseline.......................................70.00
Barrel, tumbler, vaseline, scarce..150.00
Basket (Northwood), ice bl, ftd, 2 styles................................600.00
Basketweave & Cable (Westmoreland), creamer, marigold, w/lid..50.00
Beaded Basket (Dugan), bl...300.00
Beaded Cable (Northwood), candy dish, aqua opal or wht.........200.00
Beaded Hearts (Northwood), bowl, amethyst.............................85.00
Beaded Shell (Dugan), mug, marigold or bl.............................200.00
Beaded Shell (Dugan), tumbler, amethyst.................................70.00
Beaded Swirl (English), compote, bl..60.00
Bells & Beads (Dugan), compote, marigold...............................70.00

Bernheimer (Millersburg), bowl, bl, scarce, 8¾" 2,500.00
Big Basketweave (Dugan), vase, wht, squat, 4"-7" 150.00
Big Fish (Millersburg), bowl, vaseline, sq, rare 5,800.00
Bird of Paradise (Northwood), bowl, advertising; amethyst 400.00
Birds & Cherries (Fenton), plate, marigold, rare, 10" 1,200.00
Blackberry (Fenton), vase, whimsey; bl, rare 1,200.00
Blackberry Wreath (Millersburg), bowl, ice cream; marigold, 10"..95.00
Blackberry Wreath (Millersburg), spittoon whimsey, gr, rare ...4,000.00
Blueberry (Fenton), pitcher, bl, scarce 900.00
Booker, pitcher, cider; marigold 600.00
Border Plants (Dugan), bowl, peach opal, flat, 8½" 180.00
Boutonere (Millersburg), compote, amethyst 225.00
Briar Patch, hat shape, marigold 40.00
Britt (Kahula), tumbler, bl, very rare 1,000.00
Brocaded Base, vase, marigold 65.00
Brocaded Daffodils (Fostoria), bonbon, ice gr 90.00
Brocaded Palms (Fostoria), bonbon, ice gr 55.00
Brocaded Summer Gardens, bonbon, ice bl 65.00
Broken Arches (Imperial), bowl, gr, 8½"-10" 75.00
Brooklyn Bridge (Dugan), bowl, marigold, unlettered, rare 1,600.00
Bull's Eye & Beads (Fenton), vase, marigold, 14"-18" 125.00
Bull's Eye & Loop (Millersburg), vase, amethyst, rare, 7"-11" 450.00
Butterfly (Jeannette), pintray, teal 20.00
Butterfly & Berry (Fenton), sugar bowl, gr, w/lid 200.00
Butterfly & Corn, vase, marigold, rare 6,500.00

Butterfly and Tulip (Dugan), footed bowl, marigold, 10½", $400.00. (Photo courtesy Bill Edwards and Mike Carwile)

Butterfly Bower (Crystal), compote, amethyst 350.00
Buzz Saw & Fil Framed, bowl, marigold, 5½" 100.00
Cameo (Fenton), vase, Celeste Blue, scarce, 11"-17" 250.00
Cameo Pendant, cameo pc, amethyst..250.00
Cannon Ball Variant, pitcher, wht 400.00
Capitol (Westmoreland), bowl, amethyst or bl, ftd, sm 70.00
Captive Rose (Fenton), plate, gr, 9"...1,100.00
Cartwheel, #411 (Heisey), goblet, marigold 75.00
Channeled Flute (Northwood), vase, gr, 10"-16" 125.00
Chatelaine (Imperial), tumbler, amethyst, rare 400.00
Cherokee, tumbler, bl 65.00
Cherry (Dugan), bowl, wht, flat, 5"-7" 125.00
Cherry (Millersburg)(aka Hanging Cherries), bowl, gr, 5½" 90.00
Cherry & Cable (Northwood), pitcher, marigold, rare.............1,300.00
Cherry Chain (Fenton), bonbon, gr 65.00
Cherry Chain Variant (Fenton), plate, bl, 9½" 225.00
Cherubs, toothpick holder, marigold, mini...................................200.00
Chesterfield (Imperial), pitcher, marigold, w/lid 150.00
Chesterfield (Imperial), table salt, marigold 85.00
Circle Scroll (Dugan), vase whimsey, amethyst, rare 265.00
Cloverleaf, goldfish bowl, marigold, mini......................................45.00
Cobblestones (Imperial), bowl, bl, 8½"..500.00
Colonial Tulip (Northwood), compote, teal, rayed interior...........85.00
Columbia (Imperial), vase, gr...75.00

Columns & Rings, hat whimsey, marigold..65.00
Concave Diamonds (Northwood), tumble-up, olive gr, complete, rare ..115.00
Connie (Northwood), pitcher, wht 750.00
Corinth (Westmoreland), vase, peach opal 150.00
Corn Vase (Northwood), mold, marigold, regular 1,700.00
Cosmos (Millersburg), bowl, gr, ruffled, scarce, 6½" 150.00
Cosmos & Cane (US Glass), chop plate, wht, rare 1,350.00
Cosmos Variant, bowl, bl, 9"-10" 75.00
Covered Frog (Cooperative Flint), ice gr, 1 sz............................325.00
Covered Swan (English), marigold 300.00
Crab Claw (Imperial), bowl, amethyst, 10" 75.00
Crackle (Imperial), bowl, amethyst or gr, 9" 30.00
Crackle (Imperial), sherbet, marigold 20.00
Curved Star/Cathedral, pitcher, bl, rare 3,200.00
Cut Arches (Fenton), compote, bl 55.00
Cut Crystal (US Glass), water bottle, marigold 185.00
Cut Sprays (Imperial), vase, iridized moonstone, 10½" 175.00
Dagny (Sweden), vase, marigold 100.00
Dahlia (Dugan), tumbler, amethyst, rare 185.00
Daisy & Drape (Northwood), vase, aqua opal...............................625.00
Daisy & Plume (Northwood & Dugan), candy dish, marigold, ftd..70.00
Daisy Block (English), rowboat, amethyst, scarce 300.00
Daisy Web (Dugan), hat, marigold, rare 300.00
Dandelion (Northwood), mug, bl opal 750.00
Davisons Society Chocolates, plate, amethyst, w/handgrip......1,100.00
Desert Goddess, epergne, gr 475.00
Diamante (Sweden), vase, marigold 135.00
Diamond & Daisy Cut (US Glass), compote, bl 75.00
Diamond & Rib (Fenton), jardiniere whimsey, bl 1,300.00
Diamond Band (Crystal), float set, marigold, scarce...................400.00
Diamond Checkerboard, bowl, marigold, 9".................................40.00
Diamond Fountain (Higbee), cruet, marigold, very scarce 425.00
Diamond Lace (Imperial), bowl, gr, 5"...50.00
Diamond Lace (Imperial), tumbler, wht 250.00
Diamond Points (Northwood), basket, marigold, rare..............1,400.00
Diamond Ring (Imperial), bowl, smoke, 5" 30.00
Diamond Star, vase, marigold, 8" 80.00
Dianthus (Fenton), pitcher, ice gr 350.00
Diving Dolphins (English), bowl, amethyst, ftd, 7" 275.00
Dolphins (Millersburg), compote, bl, rare.................................5,700.00
Double Diamonds, perfume, marigold...60.00
Double Loop (Northwood), creamer, bl 350.00
Double Stem Rose (Dugan), bowl, ice gr, dome base, 8½" 1,750.00
Dragon Vase, vase, amethyst, sq...250.00
Drapery (Northwood), candy dish, marigold 80.00
Drapery Variant (Northwood), vase, bl, scarce 175.00
Dugan's Trumpet (Dugan), vase, bl, very scarce, 14"-16" 125.00
Dugan-Diamonds Rainbow, candy jar, wht, ftd, w/lid 90.00
Dutch Mill, ashtray, marigold 65.00
Egyptian Lustre (Dugan), vase, blk amethyst 100.00
Elephant, paperweight, marigold 1,250.00
Elfs (Fenton), plate, Atlantic City; gr, rare 1,700.00
Embroidered Mums (Northwood), bowl, aqua opal, 9" 3,500.00
Enameled Chrysanthemum w/Prism Band, pitcher, ice gr 265.00
Enameled Double Daisy, pitcher, wht...170.00
Enameled Prism Band, pitcher, marigold......................................200.00
Encore, bottle, marigold, late 10.00
English Hob & Button (English), bowl, bl, 7"-10"........................70.00
Engraved Zinnia (Fenton), tumbler, marigold 50.00
Estate (Westmoreland), creamer or sugar bowl, aqua opal...........290.00
Etched Leaves, oil bottle, marigold, 6⅞" 80.00
Fan (Dugan), bowl, sauce; peach opal, 5"....................................150.00
Fan-Tail (Fenton), plate, marigold, ftd, rare 5,600.00
Fanciful (Dugan), plate, lav, 9"...950.00

Feather Stitch (Fenton), bowl, red, 8½"-10" **7,500.00**

Feathered Serpent (Fenton), bowl, amethyst or bl, 5" **40.00**

Fenton #643, plate, ice gr, 7" **40.00**

Fenton #9, candy jar, marigold, w/lid **35.00**

Fenton's Smooth Rays, bowl, ice gr, 5"-6" **55.00**

Fentonia Fruit (Fenton), bowl, bl, ftd, 6" **120.00**

Field Thistle (US Glass), vase, marigold **600.00**

File & Fan, bowl, peach opal, ftd, 6" **160.00**

Fine Cut & Roses (Northwood), candy dish, ice gr, ftd **1,550.00**

Fine Cut Rings (English), butter dish, marigold **170.00**

Fine Cut Rings (English), jam jar, marigold, w/lid.....................**165.00**

Fine Rib (Dugan), vase, amethyst, 8"-15" **70.00**

Fishscale & Beads (Dugan), plate, wht, 7" **145.00**

Five Petals, compote, amber, rare...**90.00**

Fleur-De-Lis and Variant (Millersburg), bowl, amethyst, flat, 8½"...**550.00**

Floating Hens, candy, marigold, ftd, w/lid **400.00**

Flora (English), vase, marigold...**100.00**

Floral & Grape (Dugan), pitcher, wht...**325.00**

Floral & Grape Variant (Dugan), pitcher, ice gr, 2 styles **600.00**

Floral & Optic (Imperial), bowl, marigold milk glass, ft, 8"-10" .**150.00**

Florentine (Fenton & Northwood), candlesticks, bl, lg, pr **700.00**

Flowering Dill (Fenton), hat, marigold..**40.00**

Fluffy Peacock (Fenton), pitcher, gr **750.00**

Flute & Cane (Imperial), champagne, marigold, rare..................**150.00**

Flute & Honeycomb (Imperial), bowl, amethyst, rare, 5" **95.00**

Flute #700 (Imperial), custard bowl, gr, 11" **400.00**

Fostoria #1299 (Fostoria), tumbler, marigold.............................**150.00**

Four Flowers (Dugan), bowl, vaseline, 8"-10" **600.00**

Free Fold (Imperial), vase, wht **70.00**

Frosted Block (Imperial), bowl, marigold, 9"................................**30.00**

Frosted Block (Imperial), rose bowl, marigold..............................**80.00**

Fruit Salad (Westmoreland), punch bowl, peach opal, w/base, rare..**3,900.00**

Fruits & Flowers (Northwood), bonbon, marigold, amethyst or gr ...**75.00**

Fruits & Flowers Variant, bowl, gr, very scarce, 7"-8" **225.00**

Garden Path (Dugan), plate, peach opal, rare, 6" **425.00**

Gay 90s (Millersburg), pitcher, gr, rare **9,500.00**

Gevurtz Brothers (Fenton), bowl, advertising; amethyst, scarce...**800.00**

Goergia Belle (Dugan), card tray, peach opal, ftd, rare................**175.00**

Golden Grapes (Diamond), bowl, clambroth, 7" **50.00**

Golden Honeycomb, bowls, marigold, various, from $20 to **35.00**

Good Luck (Northwood), plate, bl, 9" **2,300.00**

Gooseberry Spray (US Glass), compote, wht, rare.......................**300.00**

Grape & Cable (Fenton), bowl, aqua opal, flat, 8" **850.00**

Grape & Cable (Northwood), bowl, bl, ruffled, 5½" **75.00**

Grape & Cable (Northwood), candle lamp, amethyst, complete .**600.00**

Grape & Cable (Northwood), cup & saucer, amethyst, rare **450.00**

Grape & Cable (Northwood), punch bowl, banquet; bl, w/base..**4,300.00**

Grape & Cable Variant (Northwood), bowl, ice bl, 6"-8" **900.00**

Grape & Cable w/Thumbprint (Northwood), tobacco jar, ice bl ...**625.00**

Grape Arbor (Northwood), hat, bl **145.00**

Grape Wreath (Millersburg), bowl, bl, 7½"-9" **800.00**

Grape Wreath Variant (Millersburg), bowl, marigold, 7½" **50.00**

Greek Key (Northwood), bowl, gr, 7"-8½" **175.00**

Ground Cherries, tumbler, bl **50.00**

Halloween, pitcher, marigold, 2 szs, ea **375.00**

Hawaiian Lei (Higbee), sugar bowl, marigold **75.00**

Headdress Variant (Cosmos & Cane Exterior), bowl, bl, 9"-10" ...**85.00**

Hearts & Flowers (Northwood), bowl, ice gr, 8½" **775.00**

Heavy Grape (Imperial), plate, marigold, 6" **300.00**

Heavy Hobnail (Fenton), vase, amethyst, rare.............................**600.00**

Heavy Honeycomb (Fenton), vase, amethyst, rare **600.00**

Heavy Prisms (English), vase, celery; bl, 6"..................................**100.00**

Heavy Web (Dugan), peach opal, rare, 11" **2,400.00**

Heinz Tomato Juice, juice glass, marigold......................................**75.00**

Heisey Puritan (#341), compote, marigold...................................**100.00**

Heron (Dugan), mug, amethyst, rare..**425.00**

Hex Base, candlesticks, gr, pr **110.00**

Hobnail (Millersburg), sugar bowl, bl, w/lid, rare.......................**750.00**

Hobnail Variant (Millersburg), jardiniere, amethyst, rare **950.00**

Hobstar (Imperial), sugar bowl, clambroth, w/lid..........................**60.00**

Hobstar & Feather (Millersburg), compote, marigold, rare, 6" ...**1,500.00**

Hobstar & Feather (Millersburg), punch cup, gr, scarce **75.00**

Hobstar & Fruit (Westmoreland), bowl, peach opal, rare, 6" **115.00**

Hobstar Band, celery, gr, scarce..**325.00**

Hobstar FLower (Imperial), cruet, marigold, rare.......................**400.00**

Hobstar Whirl (Finland), compote, bl, 4½"....................................**65.00**

Holly (Fenton), hat, aqua opal **1,200.00**

Holly Sprig (Millersburg), bowl, gr, sq, scarce, 7"-8" **400.00**

Holly Whirl (Millersbirg), bowl, gr, tri-corner, lg.......................**525.00**

Honeycomb Panels, tumbler, amethyst...**175.00**

Horse's Head (Fenton)(Horse Medallion), plate, gr, 6½"-8½"..**4,000.00**

Howard Advertising (Four Pillars)(Northwood), vase, gr...........**100.00**

Ice Crystals, salt, wht, ftd **65.00**

Imperial #107, goblet, amber **100.00**

Imperial #3939, punch bowl, marigold, w/base, scarce **300.00**

Imperial Grape (Imperial), bowl, smoke, flared, 10"-11" **200.00**

Imperial Grape (Imperial), plate, bl, 6½" **1,800.00**

Imperial Grape (Imperial), rose bowl, amethyst, rare.................**800.00**

Imperial Paperweight, advertising weight, amethyst, rare **1,200.00**

Indiana Statehouse (Fenton), plate, marigold, rare..................**16,000.00**

Intaglio Ovals (US Glass), plate, pastel marigold, 7½" **100.00**

Inverted Strawberry, sugar bowl, green, $480.00. (Photo courtesy Bill Edwards and Mike Carwile)

Jacob's Ladder, perfume, marigold **60.00**

Jester's Cap (Dugan/Diamond), vase, amethyst **75.00**

Jester's Cap (Westmoreland), vase, peach opal **200.00**

Jewels & Pearls (Fenton), basket, wht, 4"....................................**200.00**

Jockey Club (Northwood), plate, amethyst, flat or handgrip, scarce..**1,500.00**

Keg, toothpick holder, marigold...**20.00**

Kittens (Fenton), bowl, cereal; bl, scarce **400.00**

Kiwi & Variant (Australian), bowl, marigold, rare, 10"..............**850.00**

Kulor (Sweden), vase, bl, scarce...**295.00**

Large Kangaroo (Australian), bowl, amethyst, 10" **500.00**

Late Strawberry, pitcher, marigold **225.00**

Lattice (Crystal), bowl, amethyst, 7"-8" **145.00**

Lattice & Points (Dugan), vase, wht..**100.00**

Laurel & Grape, vase, peach opal, 6" **120.00**

Laurel Leaves (Imperial), plate, marigold.......................................**40.00**

Leaf Chain (Fenton), bowl, aqua opal, 7"-9" **1,800.00**

Leaf Rays (Dugan), nappy, ice gr, spade shape **225.00**

Leaf Swirl (Westmoreland), compote, bl..**80.00**

Liberty Bell, cookie jar, marigold, w/lid **40.00**

Lined Lattice (Dugan), vase, peach opal, squat, 5"-7"..................**250.00**

Little Beads, bowl, marigold, 8" **20.00**

Little Flowers (Fenton), plate, marigold, rare, 10".....................**2,100.00**

Little Stars (Millersburg), plate, gr, rare, 7½" **1,600.00**

Long Hobstar (Imperial), punch bowl, marigold, w/base.............**125.00**

Lotus & Grape (Fenton), bonbon, red 1,200.00
Lotus & Grape Variant (Fenton), rose bowl, bl, ftd, scarce 500.00
Louisa (Westmoreland), plate, marigold, ftd, rare, 8" 60.00
Lucky Bank, marigold 35.00
Lustre & Clear (Fenton), fan vase, ice gr 90.00
Lustre & Clear (Imperial), creamer, clambroth 30.00
Lustre Flute (Northwood), nappy, marigold, from punch cup 50.00
Lustre Rose (Imperial), bowl, berry; bl, ftd, 5" 125.00
Lutz (McKee), mug, marigold, ftd 60.00
Majestic (McKee), tumbler, marigold, rare 500.00
Many Fruits (Dugan), punch bowl, wht, w/base 1,550.00
Many Ribs (Model Flint Northwood), vase, aqua opal, very rare, 8" ...2,500.00
Marilyn (Millersburg), pitcher, amethyst, rare 1,000.00
Massachusetts (US Glass), mug, marigold, rare 150.00
Mayan (Millersburg), bowl, gr, 8½"-10" 125.00
Memphis (Northwood), bowl, fruit; amethyst, w/base 425.00
Meydam (Leerdam), butter dish, marigold 90.00
Mikado (Fenton), compote, bl, lg 950.00
Miniature Candelabra (Cambridge), marigold, 1 sz 500.00
Miniature Flower Basket (Westmoreland), bl opal 300.00
Mirrored Lotus (Fenton), bowl, bl, 7"-8½" 125.00
Mitered Ovals (Millersburg), vase, gr, rare 8,000.00
Moderne, cup & saucer, marigold 15.00
Moongleam (Heisey), tumbler, gr, rare 30.00
Morning Glory (Imperial), vase, amethyst, squat shape, 4"-7" 110.00
Morning Glory (Millersburg), pitcher, gr, rare 11,000.00
Multi-Fruits & Flowers (Millersburg), punch cup, bl, rare 2,000.00
Mystery Grape, bowl, gr 175.00
Napoli (Italy), wine, bl, ice bl or vaseline 25.00
Nesting Swan (Millersburg), bowl, gr, sq, rare 1,000.00
Nippon (Northwood), bowl, bl, 8½" 525.00
Nola (Scandinavian), powder box, marigold, w/lid, 2 szs 75.00
Northern Star (Fenton), bowl, marigold, 6" 30.00
Nu-Art (Chrysanthemum)(Imperial), plate, gr, rare 4,000.00
Number 2351 (Cambridge), punch cup, amethyst or gr, scarce 65.00
O'Hara (Loop), pitcher, marigold 120.00

Octagon (Imperial), vase, marigold, 7", $100.00. (Photo courtesy Bill Edwards and Mike Carwile)

Octet (Northwood), bowl, gr, scarce, 8½" 175.00
Ohio Star (Millersburg), vase whimsey, gr, rare.....................14,000.00
Omera (Imperial), bowl, wht, 10" 75.00
Open Edge Basket (Basketweave)(Fenton), bowl, bl, sq, scarce 80.00
Open Rose (Imperial), bowl, marigold, flat, 5½" 15.00
Optic (Imperial), bowl, amethyst, 9" 75.00
Optic Variant, bowl, amethyst, 6" 90.00
Orange Peel (Westmoreland), dessert, Russet Green, stemmed, scarce ..80.00
Orange Tree (Fenton), compote, marigold or bl, sm 50.00
Orange Tree (Fenton), wine, gr 300.00
Orchid Variant, pitcher, marigold 275.00

Oriental Poppy (Northwood), pitcher, bl 6,000.00
Pacifica (US Glass), tumbler, marigold 400.00
Palace Gates (Jain), tumbler, marigold 300.00
Palm Beach (US Glass), plate, amethyst, rare, 9" 275.00
Paneled Dandelion (Fenton), candle lamp whimsey, bl, rare ...3,200.00
Paneled Diamond & Bow (Fenton), vase, red, 5"-14" 700.00
Paneled Prism, jam jar, marigold, w/lid 55.00
Pansy (Imperial), bowl, gr, 8¼" 125.00
Panther (Fenton), bowl, marigold, ftd, 10" 150.00
Paradise Soda (Fenton), plate, advertising; amethyst, scarce 800.00
Peach (Northwood), pitcher, bl..1,300.00
Peaches, wine bottle, marigold...45.00
Peacock (Millersburg), bowl, ice cream; gr, scarce, 10" 2,200.00
Peacock & Urn (Fenton), goblet, bl, scarce.................................200.00
Peacock & Urn (Northwood), bowl, ice cream; aqua opal, 10" ...31,000.00
Peacock at the Fountain (Dugan), pitcher, bl 425.00
Peacock Tail (Fenton), bowl, peach opal, 5"-7".............................650.00
Peacocks (on fence)(Northwood), plate, marigold, 9"..................625.00
Pebbles (Fenton), bonbon, gr 65.00
Persian Garden (Dugan), plate, bl, scarce, 6"...............................900.00
Persian Garden (Fenton), plate, amethyst, 9½"...........................450.00
Persian Medallions (Fenton), compote, gr, sm 425.00
Petal & Fan (Dugan), bowl, marigold, 10" 155.00
Petals (Northwood), compote, ice bl 900.00
Pillar & Drape, shade, red..625.00
Pillar & Sunburst (Westmoreland), bowl, amethyst, 7½"-9".........50.00
Pine Cone (Fenton), bowl, wht, 6" 265.00
Pineapple & Fan, tumble-up set, bl, 3-pc.....................................600.00
Pipe Humidor (Millersburg), tobacco jar, marigold, w/lid, rare..12,000.00
Plain Pilsner, glass, marigold, stemmed, 6" 25.00
Plume Panels (Fenton), vase, gr, 7"-12" 250.00
Plums & Cherries (Northwood), sugar bowl, bl, rare 1,800.00
Poppy (Millersburg), compote, gr, scarce......................................800.00
Poppy Show (Northwood), bowl, bl, 8½".................................1,700.00
Powder Horn (Cambridge), candy holder, marigold 200.00
Primrose (Millersburg), bowl, bl, ruffled, 8¾".........................4,500.00
Primrose & Ribbon (Imperial), light shade, marigold...................90.00
Prism, shakers, marigold, pr...60.00
Prism Panels, bowl, marigold, 8"-9" 60.00
Prisms (Westmoreland), compote, amethyst, scarce, 5" 90.00
Provence (aka Bars & Cross Box), pitcher, marigold, rare 800.00
Puzzle (Dugan), bonbon, amethyst or peach opal 85.00
Question Marks (Dugan), bonbon, peach opal 50.00
Rabbit Bank, marigold, sm 90.00
Ranger (Imperial), breakfast set, marigold, 2-pc 100.00
Raspberry (Northwood), gravy boat, teal, ftd...............................400.00
Rays (Dugan), bowl, amethyst or gr, 5" 50.00
Regal Iris (Consolidated), Gone w/the Wind lamp, marigold, rare...3,750.00
Rib & Panel, vase, peach opal 400.00
Ribbed Holly (Fenton), goblet, red..1,150.00
Ribbon Tie (Fenton), bowl, marigold, 8¼" 100.00
Ripple (Imperial), vase, funeral; smoke, 15"-21"........................425.00
Rising Sun (US Glass), tumbler, juice; marigold, rare 550.00
Roll, pitcher, clambroth, rare..300.00
Rosalind (Millersburg), compote, jelly; bl, rare, 9"................15,000.00
Rose Column (Millersburg), vase, gr, rare................................3,900.00
Rose Show Variant (Northwood), plate, gr, 9" 3,000.00
Rose Tree (Fenton), bowl, bl, very rare, 10" 3,300.00
Roses & Greek Key, plate, marigold, sq, very rare......................5,000.00
Royal Swans (Sowerby), vase, marigold, rare............................1,500.00
Ruffles & Rings (Northwood), bowl, amethyst, scarce, 8½" 150.00
Rustic (Fenton), vase, peach opal, 10"-14" 1,400.00
Sailing Ship (Belmont), plate, marigold, 8" 25.00
Sawtooth Band, tumbler, marigold, rare.......................................400.00

Scale Band (Fenton), pitcher, gr..............................650.00
Scroll Embossed (Imperial), compote, amethyst, sm..............225.00
Seacoast (Millersburg), pin tray, marigold, scarce..............700.00
Seaweed (Millersburg), bowl, bl, rare, 5"-6½"..............3,000.00
Serrated Flute, vase, marigold, scarce, 8"-13"..............30.00
Shasta Daisy, pitcher, bl..............................500.00
Shell & Jewel (Westmoreland), sugar bowl, amethyst, w/lid.........65.00
Shrine (US Glass), toothpick holder, amethyst..............650.00
Simple Simon (Northwood), vase, gr..............................90.00
Singing Birds (Northwood), mug, bl, stippled..............525.00
Six Petals (Dugan), bowl, wht, 8½"..............................85.00
Ski Star (Dugan), bowl, amethyst, 8"-10"..............225.00
Small Blackberry (Northwood), compote, gr..............75.00
Small Rib (Fenton), spittoon whimsey, amethyst, stemmed, rare...150.00
Smooth Panels (Imperial), vase, peach opal, 8"-14"..............200.00
Smooth Rays (Northwood), bonbon, gr..............55.00
Soldiers & Sailors (Fenton), plate, bl, Indiana, very rare.......13,000.00
Soldiers & Sailors (Fenton), plate, marigold, Illinois, scarce...2,300.00
Souvenir Banded, mug, marigold..............................85.00
Spanish Moss, hatpin holder, marigold, rare, 5½"..............200.00
Spider Web (Northwood, Dugan), vase, gr, 2 styles..............75.00
Spiral (Imperial), candlesticks, amethyst, pr..............185.00
Springtime (Northwood), bowl, gr, 9"..............250.00
Spun Flowers, plate, wht, very scarce, 10"..............75.00
Square Diamond, vase, bl, rare..............................750.00
Star, goblet, buttermilk; marigold..............................25.00
Star & File (Imperial), bonbon, marigold..............35.00
Star & File (Imperial), decanter, marigold, w/stopper.................100.00
Star Medallion (Imperial), tumbler, gr, 2 szs...............50.00
Star Medallion (Imperial), compote, marigold..............45.00
Star of David (Imperial), bowl, gr, 8¾"..............125.00
Starburst (Finland), tumbler, bl..............................325.00
Starflower, pitcher, bl, rare..............................2,500.00
Stars Over India (Jain), tumbler, marigold..............200.00
Stippled Diamond Swag (English), compote, gr..............60.00
Stippled Flower (Dugan), bowl, peach opal, 8½"..............85.00
Stippled Rays (Fenton), creamer, red..............300.00
Stippled Strawberry (US Glass), pitcher, marigold, rare..............350.00
Strawberry (Fenton), bonbon, marigold..............50.00
Strawberry (Intaglio)(Northwood), bowl, marigold, 5½"..............30.00
Strawberry (Northwood), plate, gr, 9"..............325.00
Strawberry Scroll (Fenton, pitcher, bl, rare..............1,800.00
Stream of Hearts (Fenton), goblet, marigold, rare..............225.00
Sun Punch, bottle, marigold..............................30.00
Sunflower (Northwood), bowl, ice bl, 8½"..............1,750.00
Sungold Flora (Brockwitz), bowl, marigold, rare, 9"..............350.00
Sweetheart (Cambridge), cookie jar, gr, w/lid, rare..............1,100.00
Swirl Hobnail (Millersburg), spittoon, gr, rare..............4,000.00
Swirl Variant (Imperial), pitcher, marigold, 7½"..............100.00
Taffeta Lustre (Fostoria), candlesticks, bl, rare, pr..............400.00
Target (Dugan), vase, amethyst, 8"-13"..............300.00
Ten Mums (Fenton), bowl, marigold, 8"-11"..............325.00
Thin & Wide Rib (Northwood), vase, amethyst or gr, ruffled.......60.00
Thistle (English), vase, marigold, 6"..............45.00
Thistle (Fenton), plate, amethyst or gr, rare, 9"..............4,100.00
Three Diamonds (Dugan), vase, bl or peach opal, 6"-10"..............75.00
Three Fruits (Northwood), plate, ice bl, 9"..............9,000.00
Three Rivers, pickle castor, marigold..............225.00
Three-In-One (Imperial), bowl, gr, 4½"..............30.00
Tiered Thumbprint, candlesticks, marigold, pr..............120.00
Tiger Lily (Finland), pitcher, bl, rare..............950.00
Tornado (Northwood), vase, bl, ribbed, 2 szs, ea..............2,000.00
Tracery (Millersburg), bonbon, gr, rare..............1,100.00
Tree Bark (Imperial), bowl, console; marigold..............35.00

Tree Trunk (Northwood), vase, funeral; amethyst, 12"-22".....2,900.00
Triplets (Dugan), bowl, marigold, 6"-8"..............25.00
Tropicana, vase, marigold, rare..............................1,600.00
Tulip Panels, ginger jar, marigold..............125.00
Tuscan Column, vase whimsey, gr, 3"..............125.00
Twigs Vase (Dugan), vase, amethyst, tall..............70.00
Two Flowers (Fenton), plate, marigold, rare, 13"..............2,900.00
Universal (Northwood), bowl, ice bl, scarce..............100.00
US #310, bowl, ice gr, 10"..............................75.00
Utility, lamp, marigold, complete, 8"..............90.00
Venetian, creamer, marigold, rare..............550.00
Victorian (Dugan), bowl, peach opal, rare, 10"-12"..............2,500.00
Vintage (Dugan), powder jar, bl, w/lid..............300.00
Vintage (Fenton), compote, amethyst..............50.00
Vintage (Imperial), tray, marigold, center hdl..............35.00
Vintage Variant (Dugan), bowl, bl, ftd, 8½"..............200.00
Voltec (McKee), butter dish, amethyst, w/lid..............150.00
Waffle Block (Imperial), nappy, marigold..............40.00
Waffle Block & Hobnail (Imperial), basket, marigold, hdld.......250.00
Water Lily (Fenton), bowl, gr, ftd, 10"..............400.00
Water Lily & Cattails (Northwood), pitcher, marigold..............400.00
Western Thistle, pitcher, cider; bl..............350.00
Wheat (Northwood), sweetmeat, gr, w/lid, very rare..............9,500.00
Whirling Hobstar, cup, marigold..............40.00
White Elephant, ornament, wht, rare..............350.00
Wide Panel (Fenton), vase, amethyst, 7"-9"..............40.00
Wide Panel (Northwood), candy dish, ice bl, w/lid..............90.00
Wide Panel Variant (Northwood), pitcher, tankard; amethyst...275.00
Wide Rib (Northwood), vase, aqua opal, standard shape, 8"-14"..1,300.00
Wild Berry, powder jar, marigold, w/lid..............250.00

Wild Rose, syrup, marigold, rare, $700.00. (Photo courtesy Bill Edwards and Mike Carwile)

Wild Rose (Northwood), bowl, amethyst, ftd, open edge, 6"......100.00
Windflower (Dugan), nappy, bl, hdld..............250.00
Windmill (Imperial), pitcher, gr..............175.00
Wine & Rose (Fenton), wine, bl..............100.00
Wishbone (Northwood), bowl, amethyst, flat, 8"-10"..............200.00
Wisteria (Northwood), vase whimsey, gr, rare..............17,000.00
Wreath of Rose (Dugan), bowl, nut; marigold..............70.00
Wreath of Rose (Fenton), punch bowl, gr, w/base..............700.00
Zig Zag (Millersburg), bowl, marigold, tricornered, 10"..............575.00
Zipper Loop (Imperial), lamp, hand; marigold, 2 styles, rare....1,000.00
Zipper Variant, sugar bowl, marigold, w/lid..............35.00
474 (Imperial), bowl, gr, 8"-9"..............85.00
474 (Imperial), tumbler, marigold, scarce..............30.00
49'er, pitcher, marigold, squat..............225.00

Carousel Figures

For generations of Americans, visions of carousel horses revolving majestically around lively band organs rekindle wonderful childhood experiences. These nostalgic memories are the legacy of the creative talent from a dozen carving shops that created America's carousel art. Skilled craftsmen brought their trade from Europe where American carvers took the carousel animal from a folk art creation to a true art form. The golden age of carousel art lasted from 1880 to 1929.

There are two basic types of American carousels. The largest and most impressive is the 'park style' carousel built for permanent installation in major amusement centers. These were created in Philadelphia by Gustav and William Dentzel, Muller Brothers, and E. Joy Morris who became the Philadelphia Toboggan Company in 1902. A more flamboyant group of carousel animals was carved in Coney Island, New York, by Charles Looff, Marcus Illions, Charles Carmel, and Stein & Goldstein's Artistic Carousel Company. These park-style carousels were typically three, four, and even five rows with forty-five to sixty-eight animals on a platform. Collectors often pay a premium for the carvings by these men. The outside row animals are larger and more ornate and command higher prices. The horses on the inside rows are smaller, less decorated, and of lesser value.

The most popular style of carousel art is the 'country fair style.' These carousels were portable affairs created for mobility. The horses are smaller and less ornate with leg and head positions that allow for stacking and easy loading. These were built primarily for North Tonawanda, New York, near Niagara Falls, by Armitage Herschell Company, Herschell Spillman Company, Spillman Engineering Company, and Allen Herschell. Charles W. Parker was also well known for his portable merry-go-rounds. He was based in Leavenworth, Kansas. Parker and Herschell Spillman both created a few large park-style carousels as well, but they are better known for their portable models.

Horses are by far the most common figure found, but there are two dozen other animals that were created for the carousel platform. Carousel animals, unlike most other antiques, are oftentimes worth more in a restored condition. Figures found with original factory paint are extraordinarily rare and bring premium amounts. Typically, carousel horses are found in garish, poorly applied 'park paint' and are often missing legs or ears. Carousel horses are hollow. They were glued up from several blocks for greater strength and lighter weight. Bass and poplar woods were used extensively.

If you have an antique carousel animal you would like to have identified, send a clear photograph and description along with a LSASE to our advisor, William Manns, who is listed in the Directory under New Mexico. Mr. Manns is the author of *Painted Ponies*, containing many full-color photographs, guides, charts, and directories for the collector.

Key:
IR — inside row   OR — outside row
MR — middle row   PTC — Philadelphia Toboggan
                         Company

Coney Island-Style Horses

Carmel, IR jumper, unrstr 4,800.00

Carmel jumper, second row, 1918, restored, from $11,500.00 to $13,000.00.

Carmel, MR jumper, unrstr........8,500.00
Carmel, OR jumper w/cherub, rstr............26,500.00
Illions, IR jumper, rstr............5,200.00
Illions, MR stander, rstr............9,200.00
Looff, IR jumper unrstr............3,200.00
Looff, OR jumper, unrstr............17,000.00
Stein & Goldstein, IR jumper, unrstr............4,700.00
Stein & Goldstein, MR jumper, rstr............9,000.00
Stein & Goldstein, OR stander w/bells, unrstr............29,000.00

European Horses

Anderson, English, unrstr............3,500.00
Bayol, French, unrstr............3,000.00
Heyn, German, unrstr............3,500.00
Hubner, Belgian, unrstr............2,200.00
Savage, English, unrstr............2,900.00

Menagerie Animals (Non-Horses)

Dentzel, bear, unrstr............21,000.00
Dentzel, cat, unrstr............24,000.00
Dentzel, deer, unrstr............13,500.00
Dentzel, lion, unrstr............45,000.00
Dentzel, pig, unrstr............9,000.00
E Joy Morris, deer, unrstr............10,000.00
Herschell Spillman, cat, unrstr............12,500.00
Herschell Spillman, chicken, portable, unrstr............7,000.00
Herschell Spillman, dog, portable, unrstr............6,500.00
Herschell Spillman, frog, unrstr............20,000.00
Looff, camel, unrstr............10,000.00
Looff, goat, rstr............15,000.00
Muller, tiger, rstr............32,000.00

Philadelphia-Style Horses

Dentzel, IR 'topknot' jumper, unrstr............4,500.00
Dentzel, MR jumper, unrstr............9,500.00
Dentzel, OR stander, female cvg on shoulder, rstr............28,000.00
Dentzel, prancer, rstr............9,500.00
Morris, IR prancer, rstr............7,000.00
Morris, MR stander, unrstr............9,500.00
Morris, OR stander, rstr............15,000.00
Muller, IR jumper, rstr............5,700.00
Muller, MR jumper, rstr............12,000.00
Muller, OR stander, rstr............24,000.00
Muller, OR stander w/military trappings............40,000.00
PTC, chariot (bench-like seat), rstr............8,900.00
PTC, IR jumper, rstr............4,000.00
PTC, MR jumper, rstr............12,800.00
PTC, OR stander, armored, rstr............52,000.00
PTC, OR stander, unrstr............29,500.00

Portable Carousel Horses

Allan Herschell, all aluminum, ca 1950............500.00
Allan Herschell, half & half, wood & aluminum head............1,300.00
Allan Herschell, IR Indian pony, unrstr............2,500.00
Allan Herschell, OR, rstr............3,200.00
Allan Herschell, OR Trojan-style jumper............3,800.00
Armitage Herschell, track-machine jumper............2,800.00
Dare, jumper, unrstr............3,000.00
Herschell Spillman, chariot (bench-like seat)............3,800.00
Herschell Spillman, IR jumper, unrstr............2,400.00

Herschell Spillman, MR jumper, unrstr	2,900.00
Herschell Spillman, OR, eagle decor	4,500.00
Herschell Spillman, OR, park machine	10,000.00
Parker, MR jumper, unrstr	4,200.00
Parker, OR jumper, park machine, unrstr	7,500.00
Parker, OR jumper, rstr	5,800.00

Cartoon Art

Collectors of cartoon art are interested in many forms of original art — animation cels, sports, political or editorial cartoons, syndicated comic strip panels, and caricature. To produce even a short animated cartoon strip, hundreds of original drawings are required, each showing the characters in slightly advancing positions. Called 'cels' because those made prior to the 1950s were made from a celluloid material, collectors often pay hundreds of dollars for a frame from a favorite movie. Prices of Disney cels with backgrounds vary widely. Background paintings, model sheets, storyboards, and preliminary sketches are also collectible — so are comic book drawings executed in India ink and signed by the artist. Daily 'funnies' originals, especially the earlier ones portraying super heroes and Sunday comic strips, the early as well as the later ones, are collected. Cartoon art has become recognized and valued as a novel yet valid form of contemporary art. In the listings below all cells are gouache on celluloid unless noted otherwise.

Key
WB — Warner Brothers   WD — Walt Disney Productions

Animation Cel, Full Color

Aquaman & Aqualad on sea horses, Filmation, 1968, 13x9" +fr	100.00
Fantasia, dancing ostrich w/pk bow, WD, in fr	1,100.00
Fox & Hound, Tod & Vixie, Disney, 1981, matted & fr	400.00
Frankenberry, Booberry & Count Chocula characters on bicycle, 1960s	175.00
Lion King, Simba/Mufasa/Scar/others, Disney Ltd Ed, 1993	335.00
Little Mermaid, Ariel to waist, artist sgn, Disney, 5½x8" image	65.00
Little Mermaid, Flotsom & Jetsom (eels), Disney, 1988, full sz	575.00
Marvin the Martian, Model Sheet Series, WB Ltd Ed, 1996	515.00
Peanuts, Snoopy, 5½x8½" image, matted in 10x13" fr	325.00
Peanuts, Snoopy & Woodstock, HP orig, 1980s, 10x12"	330.00
Peter Pan, Mr Darling, Disney, 1953, 6½x7¼" image	515.00
Rabbit Romeo, Bugs Bunny, WB, 1957, 10½x12½"	985.00
Scooby Doo, all characters in speedboat, full bkground, 1980s	175.00
Scooby Doo, Hanna-Barbera, sgn/#d, 1997 issue, in 21x24" fr	585.00
Tom & Jerry, Tom, Jerry & Tuffy, HP orig, MGM, 1950s	355.00
Yellow Submarine, Paul w/2 octopus, in 21x17" fr	400.00

Animation Drawing

Bambi, Flower & son, crayon & charcoal pencil, 1942, in fr	415.00
Chilly Willy, graphite/bl/red pencil, Lantz, 1960s, 3¼x3¼" image	80.00
Fantasia, Bacchus & Jacchus (steed), sgn Ward Kimball, 1940	500.00
Peanuts, Snoopy, nice shading/notes, 2½x3" image on full sheet	85.00
Sleeping Beauty, Briar Rose, Disney, 1959, 12½x15½" sheet	85.00
Tom & Jerry, Part Time Pal, 1947, pr	140.00

Miscellaneous

Book, Art of Animation, Disney, Bob Thomas, 1958	130.00
Daily strip, Flash Gordon, Resse/Jones, 1991	50.00
Daily strip, Peanuts, January 24, 1963, M in fr	3,800.00
Daily strip, Peanuts, United Feature Syndicate, 1972, 10½x33"	4,500.00
Lithograph, Betty Boop, Big Date, G Natwick, 13x16", w/certificate	200.00

Model sheet, Jiminy Cricket, 32 images, 1939, +letter of authenticity	625.00
Model sheet, Mickey's Grand Opera, Donald w/sword, Disney, 1937	185.00
Model sheet, Mickey's Grand Opera, Mickey Mouse, Disney, 1937	155.00
Sunday strip, Flash Gordon, sgn Mac Raboy, notes in margins, May 1960	400.00
Sunday strip, Peanuts, Charlie & Sally, January 24, 1993	6,150.00
Sunday strip, Pogo, Walt Kelly, December 28, 1952, VG+	1,650.00

Cartoon Books

'Books of cartoons' were printed during the first decade of the twentieth century and remained popular until the advent of the modern comic book in the late '30s. Cartoon books, printed in both color and black and white, were merely reprints of current newspaper comic strips. The books, ranging from thirty to seventy pages and in sizes from 3½" x 8" up to 11" x 17", were usually bound with cardboard covers and were often distributed as premiums in exchange for coupons saved from the daily paper. One of the largest of the companies who printed these books was Cupples and Leon, producer of nearly half of the two hundred titles on record. Among the most popular sellers were *Mutt and Jeff, Bringing Up Father,* and *Little Orphan Annie.*

Blondie, #12, Chic Young, David McKay, 1937, 35-pg, 11¼x8½", VG	110.00
Bringing Up Father, #2, Cupples & Leon, EX	85.00
Captain Easy & Wash Tubbs, Whitman, Famous Comics, EX	55.00
Charlie Chaplin in the Army, Donohue, EX	110.00

The Gumps, Book No. 2, EX, from $30.00 to $45.00.

Jazz Era, #7, JN Darling, 1920, 12x9", 96-pg, VG	57.50
Little Orphan Annie in Cosmic City, Cupples & Leon, VG	65.00
Moon Mullins, 2nd series, 1920s, EX	110.00
Mutt & Jeff, Bud Fisher, 1914, 32-pg, 5½x15½", VG	45.00
Popeye, boxing cover, Saalfield, 1934, 8x13", VG	105.00
Smitty, Cupples & Leon, 1928, VG	40.00
Tricks of Katzenjammer Kids, 1905, EX	80.00

Cash Registers

From 1884 until 1916, the National Cash Register Company dominated the field with a massive over-choice of styles and functions. There were 1,600,000 registers built before the termination of the 'antique styles.' An inexpensive, painted-on woodgrain patterned steel cabinet replaced the ornate plates, though the mechanisms remained unchanged. Serial numbers were consecutive, making dating simple. Many registers were chopped up for brass shell casings in the two world wars, and as a result, those that remained became more attractive to collectors. Of the NCRs, scholars speculate that about half of them survive. Add to that the many other existing brands, and it is estimated that there are nearly two million registers to discover.

Register values are fixed by a machine's scarcity and charm, including add-on fixtures such as brass or glass topsigns, clocks, and personalized nameplates. National used eight designs on metal registers and four on inlaid wood machines.

The condition code of registers in this column is quite simple: good (G), very good (VG), and mint (M), restored by a professional. About 20% variation in prices can be attributed to geography and buyer/seller differences.

Internet web pages have jumped into the pricing fray, sometimes creating a carnival-like frenzy when prices aren't fixed. *Schroeder's* will provide a standard but also be mindful of permanent changes generated by the 'net.

An excellent book on cash registers is *Antique Cash Registers, 1880 – 1920*, by Bartsch and Sanchez. (Mr. Bartsch's address may be found in our Directory under Oregon.)

Dial, emb brass, emb pattern on drw, 25", EX............................**6,500.00**
Monitor #1A, wood w/CI Amount of Sale sign, ca 1900, 9x13x14", VG...**415.00**
NCR #1, Am detail adder, VG...**2,650.00**
NCR #2 or #3, inlaid oak or mahog, scarce **2,250.00**
NCR #3, mahog inlay, deep wood drw, ca 1886, VG **4,500.00**
NCR #5, narrow scroll, glass topsign, M **2,750.00**
NCR #7 or #8, detail adder, fleur-de-lis, VG...............................**850.00**
NCR #13 or #14, Ionic CI, 1899, G..**750.00**

NCR #30, bronze, fine scroll, total adder, thirteen keys, ca 1900, VG, $2,000.00. (Photo courtesy Henry Bartsch)

NCR #33, 1903, VG **900.00**
NCR #47, oak w/mahog inlay, up to $6, VG...........................**2,250.00**
NCR #50, Renaissance design, orig clock, M **2,500.00**
NCR #52, Renaissance design, orig clock, extended base, VG...**2,900.00**
NCR #52 or #52¼, Renaissance design, extended base, no clock, VG ..**2,500.00**
NCR #64, Bohemian pattern, iron, 25-key, 1901, VG **600.00**
NCR #78, custom built to eliminate bk window, NP, 1902, VG.**950.00**
NCR #129-130, bronze, VG **950.00**
NCR #130, Art Nouveau cabinet, M..**1,600.00**
NCR #135, Art Nouveau pattern, CI, 31-key, 1905, VG...........**600.00**
NCR #215 or #216, bronze fleur-de-lis, VG..............................**1,200.00**
NCR #226, rare bilingual topsign, VG **900.00**
NCR #250 or #251, bronze, VG...**1,200.00**
NCR #312, #313, or #317, dolphin pattern, VG **800.00**
NCR #322, #323, or #327, marble 3 sides, extended base, M ..**2,500.00**
NCR #322, #323, or #327, marble 3 sides, extended base, VG ...**1,500.00**
NCR #324, bronze plated, wood base, $2 till, rstr, 21x16x13½" ..**920.00**
NCR #324, VG **700.00**
NCR #332, #333 or #349, orig topsign, M................................**1,150.00**
NCR #332, #333 or #349, orig topsign, VG...............................**550.00**
NCR #336, brass, M...**950.00**
NCR #337, dolphin design, M...**950.00**
NCR #338, dogwood pattern, English numerals, CA, 1910-16, VG ..**475.00**
NCR #359-G, fleur-de-lis, dolphin pattern, 1908, EX+ **1,200.00**

NCR #360, 37 keys, rings to $60, 1908-09, M.........................**1,500.00**
NCR #441 or #442, Empire design w/quartered-oak base, M...**1,750.00**
NCR #441E, electric, VG..**1,250.00**
NCR #442E-L, EX orig...**1,800.00**
NCR #452E, electric, M **2,000.00**
NCR #522, 2-drw, electric bar model, 1910-16, M................**2,500.00**
NCR #522, 2-drw, electric bar model, 1910-16, VG **1,800.00**
NCR #711-#717, mahog-grain finish on steel, M **275.00**
NCR #1054, glass automatic w/box attachment, 1910-16, M..**1,200.00**

Cast Iron

In the mid-1800s, the cast-iron industry was raging in the United States. It was recognized as a medium extremely adaptable for uses ranging from ornamental architectural filigree to actual building construction. It could be cast from a mold into any conceivable design that could be reproduced over and over at a relatively small cost. It could be painted to give an entirely versatile appearance. Furniture with openwork designs of grapevines and leaves and intricate lacy scrollwork was cast for gardens as well as inside use. Figural doorstops of every sort, bootjacks, trivets, and a host of other useful and decorative items were made before the 'ferromania' had run its course. See also Kitchen, Cast-Iron Bakers and Kettles; and other specific categories.

Bank, seated pig, coin slot on top of head, old rpt, ca 1900, 3x5x2" ..**90.00**
Bench, foliate seat, cabriole legs, 19th C, 35x43x20"...............**1,750.00**
Bench, geometrics & scrolls, gr rpt, 1895, 33" **600.00**
Bench, Minerva head & flowers, cream rpt, rprs, modern, 46" ...**220.00**
Bench, scrolling foliage & fishscale bk w/floral crest, rpt, 46".....**880.00**
Bench, twig & branch design, old bl pnt, 33x35".....................**1,450.00**
Cupsidor, top-hat shape, old blk rpt, 7¼" **175.00**
Fern stand, 3 elephant heads support top, 30" **1,045.00**
Figure, eagle, att Peter Derr, 13½"...**250.00**
Figure, eagle, old gold pnt, modern wooden base, 15x23" **550.00**
Figure, quail, fat body w/pnt traces, 6¾" **300.00**
Figure, rabbit, wht rpt, 10¾"..**165.00**
Fountain, 3 herons support basin w/shell & lily pad lip, 49x41" dia...**1,650.00**
Fountain figure, swan, wht w/blk beak, gr ped, 1890s, 38x18" .**5,750.00**
Gate, 8 sq spindles, semicircular elements, 1890s, 38x35", VG ..**635.00**
Hitching post, horse head, old bl-gr rpt, some rust, 19th C, 70" .**800.00**
Kettle, sugar; Am, 19x35"...**440.00**
Kettle, sugar; Kehye's Ironworks Savannah GA, 14x50"..........**1,155.00**
Kettle, sugar; 23x43"..**900.00**
Pitcher, wrought-iron hdl, 7½"..**500.00**
Shutter dog, floral decor, old pnt, 4 for......................................**40.00**
Umbrella stand, w/drip pan, old wht pnt, 19th C, 27x17" **250.00**
Urn, foliage/vines/basketweave, old gr pnt, 28x21", pr.............**1,500.00**
Urn, grotesque faces on bowl, Fiske, 1875, 16½x17½" **465.00**
Urn, old blk rpt, 20"...**200.00**

Castor Sets

Castor sets became popular during the early years of the eighteenth century and continued to be used through the late Victorian era. Their purpose was to hold various condiments for table use. The most common type was a circular arrangement with a center handle on a revolving pedestal base that held three, four, five, or six bottles. A few were equipped with a bell for calling the servant. Frames were made of silverplate, glass, or pewter. Though most bottles were of pressed glass, some of the designs were cut, and on rare occasion, colored glass with enameled decorations was used as well. To maintain authenticity and value, castor sets should have matching bottles. Prices listed below are for those with matching bottles and in frames with plating that is in excellent condition (unless noted otherwise). Note: Watch for new frames and bottles in clear, cranberry, cobalt, and vaseline Inverted Thumbprint as well as reproductions of Czechoslovakian cut glass bottles. These have recently been appearing on the market. Our advisor for this category is Deborah Maggard; she is listed in the Directory under Ohio.

3-bottle, Am Shield; pewter fr w/eagle, mini, child sz 150.00
3-bottle, blown, Gothic Arch, orig stoppers; pewter fr 110.00
3-bottle, rubena, cut dmns; SP fr, 5½x4" 215.00
4-bottle, Coin Spot, cranberry w/HP floral; ormolu fr, 12" 1,350.00
4-bottle, cranberry, orig stoppers; pressed glass holder 265.00

Four bottles and two lidded jars, cut crystal in Continental silver frame with paw feet, 11", $990.00.

4-bottle, cut glass; SP Walker & Hall fr, Sheffield 150.00
4-bottle, King's Crown, ruby stain; orig glass stand 350.00
4-bottle, Log & Star, amber; orig ped-base fr 145.00
5-bottle, etched & wheel cut; orig SP fr, EX 250.00
5-bottle, Honeycomb; ornate Wilcox fr 295.00
5-bottle, opaque, HP floral, att Mt WA; rstr Middleton fr 425.00
6-bottle, cut vintage; SP Rogers Smith & Co fr 250.00
6-bottle, D&B, pressed; oversz 18" decor Meriden fr 395.00
6-bottle, etched wreath; lg Reed & Barton fr w/Cupid 365.00
6-bottle, Sawtooth; ornate Meriden fr, call bell, dtd 1888, EX....450.00
7-bottle, cut crystal; gadrooned/shell-border Geo III fr 495.00
7-bottle, cut crystal; lg ped-ft Gleason fr w/doors 1,550.00

Catalina Island

Catalina Island pottery was made on the island of the same name, which is about twenty-six miles off the coast of Los Angeles. The pottery was started in 1927 at Pebble Beach, by Wm. Wrigley, Jr., who was instrumental in developing and using the native clays. Its principal products were brick and tile to be used for construction on the island. Garden pieces were first produced, then vases, bookends, lamps, ashtrays, novelty items, and finally dinnerware. The ware became very popular and was soon being shipped to the mainland as well.

Some of the pottery was hand thrown; some was made in molds. Most pieces are marked Catalina Island or Catalina with a printed incised stamp or handwritten with a pointed tool. Cast items were sometimes marked in the mold, a few have an ink stamp, and a paper label was also used. The most favored colors in tableware and accessories are 1) black (rare), 2) Seafoam and Monterey Brown (uncommon), 3) matt blue and green , 4) Toyon Red (orange), 5) other brights, and 6) pastels with a matt finish.

The color of the clay can help to identify approximately when a piece was made: 1927 to 1932, brown to red (Island) clay (very popular with collectors, tends to increase values); 1931 to 1932, an experimental period with various colors; 1932 to 1937, mainly white clay, though tan to brown clays were also used on occasion.

Items marked Catalina Pottery are listed in Gladding McBean. For further information we recommend *The Collector's Encyclopedia of California Pottery, Second Edition*, by Jack Chipman (Collector Books). Our advisor is Steven Hoefs; he is listed in the Directory under Georgia.

Dinnerware

Catalina Island, bowl, berry 45.00
Catalina Island, bowl, cereal 75.00
Catalina Island, bowl, vegetable; rnd, 8½" 145.00
Catalina Island, coffee server, slanted opening, w/lid, rare 300.00
Catalina Island, compote, ftd, lg..225.00
Catalina Island, cup mug, demi 45.00
Catalina Island, mug, 6" 55.00
Catalina Island, plate, bread & butter; coupe design, 6" 25.00
Catalina Island, plate, chop; #622, 17½" 200.00
Catalina Island, plate, chop; 12½"..85.00
Catalina Island, saucer, 6½" 20.00
Catalina Island, teapot, traditional English style 275.00
Catalina Island, wine cup, hdld 35.00
Rope Edge, casserole, w/lid...95.00
Rope Edge, creamer 40.00
Rope Edge, cup & saucer 50.00
Rope Edge, plate, chop; 13½" 95.00
Rope Edge, plate, dinner; 10½" 35.00
Rope Edge, plate, salad; 8½" 30.00
Rope Edge, sugar bowl 50.00
Rope Edge, teapot..225.00

Miscellaneous

Bowl, Descanso Green, red clay, 3x9½" 85.00
Bowl, yel gloss, oval, #703, 15x10½", NM....................................200.00

Charger, hand-painted Carmel Mission bell tower, C.M. Graham, 14", from $750.00 to $950.00.

Jar, Bay Leaves, sponge-pnt type glaze, 3x3"...................................40.00
Pitcher, water; turq, wht clay, 7½" 275.00
Plaque, Submarine Gardens, fish, 13½" 1,450.00
Plate, Indian children & geese, red clay, 14"................................600.00
Tile, Deco-style flora, saracen, cuerda seca, mc, 6x6" 250.00
Vase, Mandarin Yellow, glossy, Deco hdls, 5¾x4".........................100.00
Vase, pearly wht, sq, #639, 5½" 88.00

Catalogs

Catalogs are not only intriguing to collect on their own merit, but for the collector with a specific interest, they are often the only remaining source of background information available, and as such they offer a wealth of otherwise unrecorded data. The mail-order industry can be traced as far back as the mid-1800s. Even before Aaron Montgomery Ward began his career in 1872, Laacke and Joys of Wisconsin and the Orvis Company of Vermont, both dealers in sporting goods, had been well established for many years. The E.C. Allen Company sold household necessities and novelties by mail on a broad scale in the 1870s. By the end of the Civil War, sewing machines, garden seed, musical instruments, even medicine, were available from catalogs. In the 1880s Macy's of New York issued a 127-page catalog; Sears and Spiegel followed suit in about 1890. Craft and art supply catalogs were first available about 1880 and covered such varied fields as china painting, stenciling, wood burning, brass embossing, hair weaving, and shellcraft. Today some collectors confine their interests not only to craft catalogs in general but often to just one subject. There are several factors besides rarity which make a catalog valuable: age, condition, profuse illustrations, how collectible the field is that it deals with, the amount of color used in its printing, its size (format and number of pages), and whether it is a manufacturer's catalog verses a jobber's catalog (the former being the most desirable).

Key:
F/W — Fall/Winter   S/S — Spring/Summer

Acme Blueprint Paper Co, drafting supplies, 1928, 384 pgs, VG ..**60.00**
Aladdin Porthal Lamps, #28, 1928, 32 pgs, VG..........................**185.00**
Allied Radio Corp, #630, 1963, 664 pgs, VG...............................**45.00**
American Separator Co, ca 1910, 72 pgs, VG **125.00**
Au Dilley & Co Inc, Oriental rugs, 1909, 81 pgs, G......................**38.00**
Baird North Co, jewelry/watches/silverware/leather, 1917, 198 pgs, VG....**125.00**
Barcalo Mfg Co, furniture, 1927, 36 pgs, G...................................**31.00**
Bellis Cycle Co, 1898, 16 pgs, EX...**125.00**
Besse-Sprague Co, F/W clothing, 1918, 20 pgs, G+.....................**19.00**
Boll Bros Mfg Co, furniture, 1914, 120 pgs, G...........................**48.00**
Bond Shoe Makers, F/W footwear, 1918-19, 16 pgs, EX................**20.00**
Buffalo Army Store, camping equipment, 1927, 32 pgs, G+ **18.00**
Carson Pirie Scott & Co, #35, 1926, 346 pgs, VG **135.00**
Cash Buyers Union Baby Carriage Catalogue, #371, 1900, 64 pgs, VG ..**90.00**
Charles Williams Stores, clothing, 1926, 500 pgs, G **31.00**
Chicago Mail Order, #30, F/W fashions, 1920, 264 pgs, VG.......**125.00**
Chicago Mail Order, S/S bicentennial ed, fashions, 1932, 312 pgs, VG...**60.00**
Cleveland Metal Products Co, #25, 1925, 64 pgs w/inserts, VG ...**65.00**
Cleveland Window Glass, windows/doors/etc, 1929, 139 pgs, G+ ...**37.00**
Consolidated Lamp & Glass Co, 1901, 44 pgs, EX.....................**185.00**
D Eddy & Sons, pre-electric wooden iceboxes, 1901, 44 pgs, VG ...**50.00**
Dazey Churn & Mfg Co, directions for use, ca 1929, 12 pgs, G **13.00**
Dent Hardware Co, CI toys, ca 1930, 39 pgs, EX **175.00**
Dixie Wood Co, garden/porch furniture, ca 1929, 34 pgs, VG......**89.00**
DR AC Daniels, canine remedies, 1936, 62 pgs, VG+ **26.00**
Eagle Lock Co, Vol 46, 1930, 773 pgs, EX **275.00**
Farmer Co, #11, 1899, 144 pgs, EX **125.00**
Firestone, auto supplies/appliances/sporting/etc, 1948, 100 pgs, VG ..**40.00**
Ford Motor Co, The Edsel, 1957, 4 pgs, VG...............................**28.00**
Gateway Sporting Goods Co, 1942, 146 pgs, VG **90.00**
Gehl Bros Mfg Co, agricultural silos, 1919, 3-fold, G **10.00**
Girl Scouts National Equipment Service, Fall, 1941, 40 pgs, VG.**50.00**
Goulds Mfg Co, Water Supply for Country Home, 1912, 20 pgs, VG **34.00**
Harry & David of Bear Creek Orchards, Christmas, 1960, 24 pgs, VG...**35.00**
Hartman Furniture Co, 1915, 64 pgs, VG **60.00**
Hertzler & Zook Co, #30, farm machinery, 1934-35, 40 pgs, VG .**60.00**
Hibbard, Spencer, Bartlett & Co, #77, ca 1932, 1,800 pgs, VG..**125.00**
Hill Brothers, women's millinery goods, 1899, 32 pgs, G..............**43.00**
HS Eckers & Co, embalmer's supplies, 1930, 324 pgs, VG..........**100.00**
International Merchandise Co, wholesale, 1942, 190 pgs, VG......**90.00**
Ithaca Guns, fox/pheasant graphics, 1919, 10 pgs, EX+ **120.00**
J Stevens Arms & Tool Co, settlers graphics, 1908, 160 pgs, NM.**85.00**

Jay C Wemple Co, window shades, 1890, 32 pgs, VG+.................**43.00**
JC Penney Co, Christmas, 1964, 298 pgs, EX..............................**125.00**
JI Case, Centennial Plow, Racine WI, 1936, 16 pgs, EX **22.50**
Jim Brown's Bargin Book, farm related, 128 pgs, 1930, NM.........**40.00**
John Wannamaker, china & glass, early, 52 pgs, G......................**58.00**
Kelvinator Refrigerators, color, 1941, 24 pgs, VG.......................**35.00**
Lakeside Trimmed Hat Co, S/S, 1911, 8 pgs, VG........................**32.00**
Lane Bryant, S/S, 1925, 104 pgs, VG **50.00**
Maher & Grosh Cutlery, price list #18, ca 1900, 80 pgs, G.........**47.00**
Mandel Brothers, hair products, ca 1906, 28 pgs, VG...................**68.00**
Mantle Lamp Co, Aladdin kerosene lamps, ca 1923, 27 pgs, G **14.00**
Margarette Steiff LTD, #KE68, 1968, 32 pgs, VG.......................**60.00**
Marlin Fire Arms Co, covers models 1892 (3, 4, 5 & 7), 1898, EX+ ...**160.00**
Marlin Repeaters/Rifles/Shotguns, models 1892-98, 1911, EX+ .**450.00**
MG Stoneman & Son, wholesale pnts, 1923, 48 pgs, G- **18.00**
Milton Bradley Co, arts & crafts, 1927, 31 pgs, G **34.00**
Montgomery Ward, #F, organs/pianos/sewing machines, 1895, 56 pgs, VG ..**75.00**
Montgomery Ward, Power-Kraft tools, 1935, 24 pgs, G................**24.00**
Montgomery Ward, S/S, 1956, 972 pgs, EX.................................**65.00**
Monumental Sales & Mfg Co, memorials, ca 1934, 8 pgs, VG **5.00**
MW Savage, clothing & general merchandise, 1928, 521 pgs, VG....**50.00**
National Bella Hess, F/W, 1946-47, 198 pgs, VG.........................**35.00**
National Cycle Mfg Co, bicycles, 1900, 32 pgs, G+ **43.00**
National Phonograh Co, 1905, 32 pgs, EX...................................**80.00**
Percy Ewing Supply House, puzzles/tricks/toys/etc, 1908, 42 pgs, VG..**50.00**
Pick's General Catalogue, #E47, hotel supply, 1945, 32 pgs, VG ..**35.00**
Quality Stove & Range Co, #29, 1927, 84 pgs, VG......................**80.00**
Rawlings Implement Co, agricultural supplies, 1922, 152 pgs, G ..**28.00**
Red Wing Shoe Co, Miss Red Wing Shoes, 1947, 8 pgs, VG **25.00**
Rolls-Royce Inc, new engine w/specifications, ca 1940, 5 pgs, G..**15.00**
Scranton Hardware & Iron Co, 1902, 294 pgs, EX.....................**190.00**
Sears, Roebuck & Co, #91R, bicycles, 1st ed, 1902, 20 pgs, VG ...**185.00**

Sears, Roebuck and Co., Philadelphia; Rockwell couple with dog, ca 1922, from $120.00 to $150.00. (Photo courtesy Candace Sten Davis and Patricia J. Baugh)

Sears, Roebuck & Co, Southern ed #252G, F/W, 1975, 1490 pgs, VG..**50.00**
Sears, Roebuck & Co, Waterwitch boats, ca 1924, 15 pgs, G **48.00**
Sethness Candy Maker, #5, ingredients/supplies, 1927, 64 pgs, VG...**75.00**
Simmons Hardware Co, #V, Keen Kutter/tools/etc, 1935, 2118 pgs, VG...**550.00**
Spiegel, Summer fashions/general, 1947, 180 pgs, VG **25.00**
Springall & Co Inc, floor plans for homes, 1921, 36 pgs, G-.........**26.00**
Stickley of Fayetteville, #25, 1928, 100 pgs w/2-pg insert, EX **150.00**
Taylor Instrument Companies, thermometers/etc, 1922, 24 pgs, EX ..**65.00**
Temington Bicycles, 1896, 32 pgs, EX+ **145.00**
Underwood Typewriters Co, typist guide, 1912, 24 pgs, VG **13.00**
W Stanley Marshall Jr, slide rule instructions, 1939, 24 pgs, G+ ..**24.00**
Western Electric, #5, telephone supplies, 1911, 336 pgs, VG......**125.00**
Williamsburg Restoration Reproductions, 1942, 32 pgs, VG.........**42.00**
Withington & Cooly Mfg Co, farm/garden tools, 1900, 96 pgs, VG ..**100.00**
WT Grant Co, Christmas, 1951, 40 pgs, VG................................**40.00**

Ceramic Art Company

Jonathan Coxon, Sr., and Walter Scott Lenox established the Ceramic Art Company in 1889 in Trenton, New Jersey, where they produced fine belleek porcelain. Both were experienced in its production, having previously worked for Ott and Brewer. They hired artists to hand paint their wares with portraits, scenes, and lovely florals. Today artist-signed examples bring the highest prices. Several marks were used, three of which contain the 'CAC' monogram. A green wreath surrounding the company name in full was used on special-order wares, but these are not often encountered. Coxon eventually left the company, and it was later reorganized under the Lenox name. See also Lenox. Our advisor for this category is Mary Frank Gaston.

Bell, tulip shape, wht w/silver decor, unmk 160.00
Bowl, gold florals, pastel sponging, ruffled, 2x4½" 135.00
Butter pat, gr leaves, emb scrolled rim, 1894-1906, 3¼" 27.50
Clock, HP florals & gold, bl beading, Ansonia works, mk, 9" .1,200.00
Coffeepot, floral on wht, long-neck Persian style, ca 1895, 8¼".235.00
Cup, chocolate; bl beading & gold on ivory, ped ft........................90.00
Cup & saucer, floral (2-color gold) on lt pk, ribbed, 1894-1906.125.00
Ewer, gold-paste florals on wht, ring hdl, mk, 7½" 550.00
Jug, pharmacy; Rx silver o/l on brn glossy, 4½" 425.00
Loving cup, 3 HP scenes, 3-hdl, 1889-1906, 7¼x3¾"................150.00
Mug, cider; apples on leafy branch, 4¾" 45.00
Pitcher, cider; apples, artist sgn, mk, ca 1900, 6" 295.00

Pitcher, floral on white with ribbed and embossed designs, spattered gold work on base, CAC mark, 4", $150.00. (Photo courtesy Mary Frank Gaston)

Pitcher, strawberries & leaves w/gold, sgn Leroy, 6".....................400.00
Spoon warmer, gold & mc apple blossoms on ivory, mk, 7x6" 375.00
Stein, HP monk, mk CAC/Lenox, copper & silver lid, ½-litre ..470.00
Vase, HP lav & wht flowers, ewer form, gold hdls, mk, 18" 900.00
Vase, landscape in Arts & Crafts style, shouldered, mk, 10x4½" 800.00
Vase, wht neck w/purple lustre body, gr mk, 3¾".........................125.00
Vase, 3 heron reserves, iris on blk at neck, mk, 22" 550.00

Ceramic Arts Studio, Madison

The Ceramic Arts Studio Company began operations sometime prior to the 1940s, but it was about then that Betty Harrington started marketing her goods through this company. Betty Harrington was the designer primarily responsible for creating the line of figurines and knickknacks that has become so popular with collectors. There were two others — Ulli Rebus, who not only designed several of the animals and various other pieces but taught Betty the art of mold-making as well; and Ruth Planter, who's work may have been limited to 'Sonny' and 'Honey.' About 65% of these items are marked, but even unmarked items become easily recognizable after only a brief study of their distinctive styling and glaze colors. At least eight different marks were used, among them the

black ink stamp and the incised mark: 'Ceramic Arts Studio, Madison, Wisc.' A paper sticker was used in the early years.

After the 1955 demise of the company in Madison, the owner (Ruben Sand) went to Japan where he continued production under the same name using many of the same molds. After a short time, the old molds were retired, and new and quite different items were produced. Most of the Japanese pieces can be found with a Ceramic Arts Studio backstamp. The Japanese identification was often on a paper label and can be missing. Japanese pieces are never marked Madison, Wisc., but not all Madison pieces are either. Red or blue backstamps are exclusively Japanese.

Another company that also produced figurines operated at about the same time as the Madison studio. It was called Ceramic Art (no 's') Studio; do not confuse the two.

A second and larger building in the C.A.S. complex in Madison was for the exclusive production of metal accessories. The creator and designer of this related line was Zona Liberace, Liberace's stepmother, who was art director for the line of figurines as well. These pieces are rising fast in value and because they weren't marked can sometimes be found at bargain prices. They were so popular that other ceramic companies bought them to complement their own lines, so they may also be found with ceramic figures other than C.A.S.'s.

Our advisor for this category is BA Wellman; his address can be found under Massachusetts. Mr. Wellman encourages collectors to e-mail him with any new information concerning company history and/or production. He sends John Canfield a 'thank you' for helping us with this year's updates. See also Clubs, Newsletters, and Catalogs.

Bank, Mrs Blankety Blank, 4½" 125.00
Bank, Paisley Pig, 3x5½"..150.00
Bell, Lillibelle, 6½"..95.00
Bell, Winter Bell, 5¼"..90.00
Candle holder, Bedtime Boy, 4¾"...95.00
Candle holder, Triad Girl, left or right, 7", ea, from $110 to.......125.00
Doll, Rene, adult lady, 14"...650.00
Figurine, Al the Hunter, 6¼"..100.00
Figurine, Aphrodite, 7¾"..225.00
Figurine, Bali-Hai, standing, 8", from $75 to 125.00
Figurine, Balinese Man, 9½", from $125 to................................135.00
Figurine, Beth, 5", from $55 to..75.00
Figurine, Burmese Man, 4½"...125.00
Figurine, Calico Cat, 3"...40.00
Figurine, Carmen, 7¼"...85.00
Figurine, child w/towel, 5" 120.00
Figurine, chipmunk, 2"...45.00
Figurine, Chubby St Francis, 8½"..130.00
Figurine, Colonial Woman, 6½"..75.00
Figurine, dachshund, standing, 3½", from $90 to 120.00
Figurine, Daisy, 5½"...150.00
Figurine, Dinky Girl, 2"..38.00
Figurine, doe, stylized, 3¾"...90.00
Figurine, Drum Girl, 4½"...75.00
Figurine, Elsie, 5"...95.00
Figurine, Fire Man, 11¼", from $185 to 200.00
Figurine, Frisky, lamb, garland, 3"...35.00
Figurine, frog, singing, 2"..35.00
Figurine, Guitar Man, sitting, 6½"..225.00
Figurine, Hans, Dance Boy, 5½" 70.00
Figurine, Harem Girl, kneeling, 4½"..80.00
Figurine, Imp, lying, 3½"...150.00
Figurine, Isaac, 10"...165.00
Figurine, Japanese Kabuki Man, 8½"..300.00
Figurine, Jester Flutist Man, 12", from $90 to 225.00
Figurine, lion, 5½" L...200.00
Figurine, Little Jack Horner #2, 4"...80.00

Figurine, lovebirds, 1-pc, 2¾" 45.00
Figurine, Lover Boy, 4½" 65.00
Figurine, Lucindy, 7" 60.00
Figurine, Manchu, Lantern Man, 9", from $60 to 90.00
Figurine, Mary, 6¼" 65.00
Figurine, Mermaid on rock, 4" 165.00
Figurine, Mexican boy w/cactus, 7" 80.00
Figurine, Modern Colt, stylized, 7¼" 125.00
Figurine, Modern Jaguar, stylized, 5" 200.00
Figurine, mother donkey, 3¼" 100.00
Figurine, Mr & Mrs Penguin, 3¾", pr 45.00
Figurine, Mrs Monkey, 3½" 95.00
Figurine, panda w/hat, 2½" 125.00
Figurine, Pekingese, 3" 95.00
Figurine, Peter Pan, 5¼" 95.00
Figurine, Petrov, Russian, 5" 50.00
Figurine, Pioneer Sam, 5½" 50.00
Figurine, Praise Angel, hand up, 6" 90.00
Figurine, Ralph the Goat, 4" 95.00
Figurine, rooster, sm, 3" 75.00
Figurine, Sambo, 3½" 325.00
Figurine, seal mother, 6" 235.00
Figurine, Shepherd & Shepherdess, 8½", pr 275.00
Figurine, Sleeping Girl Angel, 3¼" 85.00
Figurine, Spaniel pup, sitting, 2" 45.00

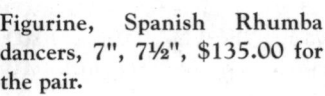

Figurine, Spanish Rhumba dancers, 7", 7½", $135.00 for the pair.

Figurine, spring colt, 3½" 125.00
Figurine, St Agnes w/Lamb, 6" 125.00
Figurine, St George on Charger, 8½" 225.00
Figurine, Sung-Tu, kneeling woman, 4" 30.00
Figurine, swan, neck up, 6" 110.00
Figurine, Swan Lake Man, 7" 250.00
Figurine, Tembo, realistic elephant, 6½" 250.00
Figurine, Temple Dance Man, 6½" 225.00
Figurine, tom cat, standing, 5", from $90 to 120.00
Figurine, tortoise w/cane, standing, 2¼" 95.00
Figurine, Wee Chinese Girl, 3" 15.00
Figurine, Wee French Girl, 3" 35.00
Figurine, Wee Scottish Girl, 3" 45.00
Figurine, Wing Sang, woman, 6", from $40 to 60.00
Figurine, Winter Willie, 4" 65.00
Figurine, zebra, 5", from $165 to 195.00
Figurine, Zulu Man, 5½" 225.00
Head vase, Becky, 5¼" 165.00
Head vase, Mei-Ling, 5" 150.00
Honey pot, w/bee, 4" 150.00
Lamp, Jester Flutist, very scarce 450.00
Lamp, Manchu, lantern holder 350.00
Lamps, Zor & Zorina, both on base, pr 700.00
Mug, Barber Shop Quartet, 3½" 150.00

Pitcher, Adam & Eve, mini, 3" 60.00
Pitcher, Pine Cone, mini, 3¾" 65.00
Plaque, cockatoo, 7½", from $50 to 85.00
Plaque, Dutch Dance Boy, 8", from $70 to 85.00
Plaque, Goosey Gander, 4½" 165.00
Plaque, Greg & Grace, 9", 9½", pr 135.00
Plaque, Hamlet, 8" 225.00
Plaque, Jack Be Nimble, 5" 125.00
Plaque, Sprite, tail down, 4½" 185.00
Plaque, striped fish mother, 5" 85.00
Plaque, Tragedy Mask, 5", from $80 to 90.00
Shakers, bear & cub, brn, snuggle type, pr 90.00
Shakers, clown & dog, snuggle type, pr 235.00
Shakers, cocks fighting, pr, from $70 to 80.00
Shakers, Dutch boy & girl, 4", pr 50.00
Shakers, fish on tail, pr 125.00
Shakers, fox & goose, snuggle type, pr 225.00
Shakers, frog & toadstool, pr, from $75 to 90.00
Shakers, girl kneeling in chair, snuggle type, pr 95.00
Shakers, mouse & cheese, snuggle type, pr 65.00
Shakers, Mr & Mrs Penguin, pr, from $80 to 100.00
Shakers, Peek & Boo, Siamese cats, snuggle type, pr ..185.00
Shakers, Sabu & elephant, snuggle type, pr 285.00
Shakers, sea horse & seaweed, snuggle type, pr 185.00
Shakers, Suzette the poodle on pillow, snuggle type, pr ..250.00
Shakers, Wee Chinese Boy & Girl, pr 35.00
Shakers, Wee Pigs, pr 95.00
Shakers, Wee Swedish Boy & Girl, pr 75.00
Shelf sitter, Banjo Girl, 4", from $80 to 100.00
Shelf sitter, canary, singing, 5" 90.00
Shelf sitter, Dutch Girl, 4½" 35.00
Shelf sitter, Farm Boy, fishing, w/pole & fish, 5" ..100.00
Shelf sitter, girl w/cat, 4¼" 75.00
Shelf sitter, Michelle, 7", from $75 to 85.00
Shelf sitter, Persian mother, gr eyes, 4¼" 125.00
Shelf sitter, tom cat, bl eyes, 4¾" 100.00
Shelf sitter, Wee Chinese Boy, 3½" 20.00
Shelf sitter, White Willy, ball down, 4½" 225.00

Metal Accessories

Arched window for religious figure, 6½" 75.00
Artist palette w/shelves, left & right, 13" W 95.00
Beanstalk for Jack, rare 165.00
Birdcage w/perch, 14" 85.00
Box, dmn shape, 15½x14" 55.00
Corner spider web for Miss Muffet, flat blk, 4" 95.00
Frame w/shelf, 22" sq 55.00
Garden shelf, for Mary Contrary, 4x12" 95.00
Musical score, flat blk, 14x12" 90.00
Pocket step shelf, w/planter, rnd, 8" 75.00
Pyramid shelf 75.00
Rainbow arch w/shelf, blk, 13½x19x5½" 120.00
Sofa, for Maurice & Michelle, from $60 to 80.00
Star for angel, flat blk 80.00
Triple ring for birds (shelf sitting), 15" 75.00

Chalkware

Chalkware figures were a popular commodity from approximately 1860 until 1890. They were made from gypsum or plaster of Paris formed in a mold and then hand painted in oils or watercolors. Items such as animals and birds, figures, banks, toys, and religious ornaments modeled after more expensive Staffordshire wares were often sold door to door. Their origin is attributed to Italian immigrants. Today regarded as a form of folk art, nineteenth century American pieces bring prices in the hundreds of dollars. Carnival chalkware from this century is also collectible, especially figures that are personality related. For those, see Carnival Collectibles.

Bird on plinth, blk & goldenrod pnt, 6½", EX 880.00
Cat, bank, slot on bk, mc pnt, 7¼x4x3⅛", EX+.....................350.00
Cat, seated, worn mc pnt, wear & edge damage, 5⅛" 385.00
Cat on base, mc pnt, rpr break, 1870s, 4½" 165.00
Dog, mc pnt, minor wear, 2 open blisters, 4½" 415.00
Dog, mc pnt, some wear, 8½" 650.00
Dog, seated, molded details, worn mc pnt, 5¾", VG 385.00
Ewe & lamb, worn mc pnt, rprs, 9¼" 360.00
Lamb, red/bl/yel/blk, some wear, 4⅛" L 935.00
Parrot on ball plinth, mc pnt, some wear, 8¼" 750.00
Parrot on plinth, very worn pnt, stains, 7⅛" 85.00
Pear bank, red & yel pnt, rpl wooden stem, 5½" 360.00
Poodle, blk rpt w/red base & tail, 7⅝x5¾x3", VG 300.00
Rabbit, seated, worn red/yel/blk pnt, 5¼" 520.00
Rooster, mc pnt, strong colors, old rpr, 5¾" 715.00
Rooster, worn mc pnt, 5½" 360.00
Squirrel, red & blk pnt, old brn varnish, wear, 8" 750.00
Stag, recumbent, worn pnt, prof rpr at bk, 10½x9⅜x2⅝"...........135.00
Stags (facing), worn mc pnt, damage/rprs to antlers, 8½", pr.....935.00
Urn w/fruit, mc pnt & brn varnish, touch ups/rpr, 11"............1,100.00

Chase Brass & Copper Company

Chase introduced this logo in 1928. The company incorporated in 1876 as the Waterbury Manufacturing Company. It was located in Waterbury, Connecticut. This location remained Chase's principal fabrication plant, and it was here that the 'Specialties' were made.

In 1900 the company chose the name Chase Companies Inc., in honor of their founder, Augustus Sabin Chase. The name encompassed Chase's many factories. Only the New York City sales division was called Chase Brass and Copper Co., but from 1936 on, that name was used exclusively.

In 1930 the sales division invited people to visit their new Specialties Sales Showroom in New York City 'where an interesting assortment of decorative and utilitarian pieces in brass and copper in a variety of designs and treatments are offered for your consideration.' Like several other large companies, Chase hired well-known designers such as Walter Von Nessen, Lurelle Guild, the Gerths, Russel Wright, and Dr. A Reimann. Harry Laylon, an in-house designer, created much of the new line.

From 1930 to 1942 Chase offered lamps, smoking accessories, and housewares similar to those Americans were seeing on the Hollywood screen — generally at prices the average person could afford.

Besides chromium, Chase manufactured many products in a variety of finishes, some even in silver plate. Many objects were polished or satin-finished brass and/or copper.

After World War II Chase no longer made the Specialties line. It had represented only a tiny fraction of this huge company's production. Instead they concentrated on a variety of fabricated mill items. Some dedicated Chase collectors even have shower heads, faucet aerators, gutter pipe, and metal samples. Is anyone using Chase window screening?

Chase products are marked either on the item itself or on a screw or rivet. Because Chase sold screws, rivets, nails, etc. (all with their logo), not all items having these Chase-marked components were actually made at Chase. It should also be noted that during the 1930s, China produced good quality chromium copies; so when you're not absolutely positive an item is Chase, buy it because you like it, understanding that its authenticity may be in question. Remember that if a magnet sticks to it, it's not Chase. Brass and copper are not magnetic, and Chase did not use steel.

Prior to 1933 Chase made smoking accessories for the Park Sherman Co. Some are marked 'Park Sherman, Chicago, Illinois, Made of Chase Brass.' Others carry a Park Sherman logo. It is believed that the 'heraldic emblem' was also used during this period. Many items are identical or very similar to Chase-marked pieces. Produced in the 1950s, National Silver's 'Emerald Glo' wares look very similar to Chase pieces, but Chase did not make them. It is very possible that National purchased Chase tooling after the Chase Specialties line was discontinued.

For further study we recommend *Chase Complete, Chase Catalogs 1934 & 1935, 1930s Lighting - Deco & Traditional by Chase*, all by Donald-Brian Johnson and Leslie Pina (Schiffer); *Art Deco Chrome, the Chase Era; Art Deco Chrome, Book 2, A Collectors Guide to Industrial Design in the Chase Era*, both by Richard Kilbride (Mrs. Kilbride is listed in the Directory under Connecticut); and *Art Deco Chrome* by James Linz (Schiffer).

In the listings that follow, examples are polished unless noted satin. Our advisor for this category is Barbara Endter; she is listed in the Directory under New York.

Key:
LG — designed by Lurelle Guild   VN — designed by Von Nessen

Airalite, #22003, pocket flashlight, nickel w/mc inlay, 2½", $75 to...85.00
Ashtray, Globe; #17068, chrome, VN, from $50 to 60.00
Ashtray, Humpty Dump; #500, copper or triangle metal w/glass, from $50...60.00
Ashtray, Swan; #837, chrome, VN, 3x5½", from $80 to 90.00
Basket, Fruit; #27028, wireware, Guild, 12½", from $200 to.......300.00
Bookends, Horse; #17044, brass, very stylized, VN, 6", from $600 to....650.00
Bowl, Fruit; #17007, chrome or copper, ftd/flared, 9½", VN, $100 to ...120.00
Bowl, Imperial; #15003, copper or chrome w/blk nickel, 8½", $120 to.130.00
Bowl, Pendant Plant; #04004, brass, copper or bronze, 6" dia, $40 to......45.00
Bowl, Viking Sauce; #17046, chrome, w/ladle & tray, VN, from $45 to..50.00
Box, Mirror Top; #21003, satin silver w/mirror, 5¾" dia, $900 to.......1,000.00
Box, Occassional; #90144, chrome w/plastic hearts/glass insert, $35 to...45.00
Breakfast Set, #26003, blk/chrome/wht, Gerths, cr/sug+tray, $40 to........50.00
Bud Holder, 4-Tube; #11230, brass/copper or chrome, Gerths, $25 to ..35.00
Candle Holder, Bubble; #17063, chrome or copper w/glass base, 2½"...40.00
Candlestick, Taurex, #24003, chrome or copper, VN, 7⅛", from $75 to..80.00
Centerpiece, Architext; #27009, rectangular, from $50 to 60.00
Centerpiece set, Architext; #27012, LG, 10-pc, from $550 to....600.00
Cigarette Box, Floral; #17097, gold/mc enamel inlay, from $125 to 150.00
Cigarette Lighter, Automatic Table; #825, chrome, 3¼", from $40 to.....50.00
Cigarette Server, Compact; #822, mc enamel, chrome lid/trays, $60 to..70.00
Cocktail Mixer, Stirring; #17049, chrome, w/spoon, VN, 8¾", $90 to..110.00
Cocktail Set, Gaiety; #90064, chrome, shaker+4 cups+tray, $100 to 110.00
Cocktail Shaker, Blue Moon; #90066, chrome w/bl ball top, from $100 to..125.00
Coffee Service, Comet; #90120, chrome, percolator+cr/sug+tray, $225 to ...275.00
Coffeepot, Continental; #17052, chrome, VN, 9¾", from $175 to..200.00
Cruet Set, #26009, ribbed glass w/chrome trim, 8", from $250 to 275.00
Dish, Tulip; #90095, chrome, scroll hdl, from $40 to....................50.00
Foot Scraper, #90033, brass, from $275 to.................................300.00
Ice Crusher, #90135, chrome, 6", from $40 to.............................50.00
Lamp, Glow, #01001, chrome w/blk, cone shade, 8", from $100 to...125.00
Lamp, Glow, #01001, copper & brass, cone shade, 8", from $50 to.....60.00
Lamp, Glow, #01001, copper w/wht, cone shade, 8", from $100 to...125.00
Light, Binnacle; #25001, brass lantern w/frosted globe, 5½", $30 to..35.00
Light, Binnacle; #25002, wired, colored glass, from $50 to...........65.00
Light, Binnacle; #25002, wired, from $35 to 45.00
Light, Binnacle; #25002, wired, 1933-34 Chicago Expo, from $100 to ..120.00
Light, Colonel's Lady; #27014, head is bulb, 9⅜", from $250 to.275.00
Light, Ship Ahoy; #01006, brass lantern w/colored globe, 10½", $75 ......95.00

Lighter, Fireball; #851, chrome, Schulze, 2½", from $50 to...........**60.00**
Pancake/Corn Set, #28003, chrome pitcher+s/p+bl glass tray, $200 to...**250.00**
Pitcher, Sparta; #9055, chrome w/wht plastic hdl, 8", from $75....**85.00**
Pitcher, Tavern; #17026, copper/brass, VN, 10¼", from $230 to..**250.00**
Plate, Service; #27002, chrome w/etched rings, 10½", from $40 to..**50.00**
Shakers, Skyway; #17095, chrome w/wht Bakelite bases, pr..........**35.00**
Sugar Bowl, Continental; #17052, chrome, VN, 3⅝", from $20 to..**25.00**
Syrup Jug, Jubilee; #26004, glass/chrome, +tray, from $65 to.........**75.00**
Table Bell, Ming; #13007, chrome w/ball knob, 3", from $50 to.....**60.00**
Table Bell, Rondo; #13003, brass or chrome/blk, 4", from $70 to .**80.00**

Table Chef, #17087, electric, Von Nessen, 10" diameter, from $150.00 to $175.00. (Photo by Dale Endter/courtesy Barbara Endter)

Tray, Bread; #27005, chrome w/etched rings, LG, 13½" L, from $50 to ..**60.00**
Tray, Cheese Server; #09010, chrome w/dome lid, 14" dia, from $65 to..**75.00**
Tray, Diplomat; #17030, blk w/chrome or copper edge, VN, 10", $230 to..**250.00**
Tray, Tiffin; #17027, chrome (or copper), blk hdls, VN, 18" L, $180 to..**200.00**
Tray, Triple; #9001, chrome, folding, +lid/plastic hdl cover, $55 to....**65.00**
Tray, Triple; #9001, chrome, folding, w/lid, 7½x11", from $55 to.**65.00**
Vase, Victorian; #03006, copper, bulbous w/flared neck, 6⅜", $40 to..**50.00**
Watering Can, Niagara; #05004, Gerths, 8⅜", from $65 to **75.00**
Wine Cooler, #27015, chrome, Bacchus relief, R Kent, 9¼", $550 to...**600.00**

Chelsea Dinnerware

Made from about 1830 to 1880 in the Staffordshire district of England, this white dinnerware is decorated with lustre embossings in the grape, thistle, sprig, or fruit and cornucopia patterns. The relief designs vary from lavender to blue, and the body of the ware may be porcelain, ironstone, or earthenware. Because it was not produced in Chelsea as the name would suggest, dealers often prefer to call it 'Grandmother's Ware.' Our advisor for this category is Mary Frank Gaston.

Grape, bowl, 8" **35.00**
Grape, coffeepot, stick hdl, 2-cup, 7"....................................**75.00**
Grape, creamer..**35.00**
Grape, cup & saucer **35.00**
Grape, egg cup **25.00**
Grape, pitcher, milk, 40-oz..**60.00**
Grape, plate, 6" **12.00**
Grape, plate, 7" **18.00**
Grape, plate, 8" **20.00**
Grape, sugar bowl, w/lid **50.00**
Grape, teapot, octagonal, 10"...**125.00**
Grape, teapot, 2-cup..**75.00**
Grape, waste bowl..**40.00**
Sprig, cake plate, 9"..**40.00**
Sprig, cup & saucer...**40.00**
Sprig, pitcher, milk **60.00**
Sprig, plate, dinner **25.00**
Sprig, plate, 7" **18.00**
Thistle, butter pat..**15.00**

Thistle, cup & saucer...**35.00**
Thistle, plate, 7" **15.00**
Thistle, sugar bowl, 8-sided, w/lid, 7½" **45.00**

Chelsea Keramic Art Works

The Chelsea Keramic Art Works Robertson and Sons Pottery was established in 1872 in Chelsea, Massachusetts, by several members of the Robertson family, including Hugh C. Robertson who later formed the Dedham Pottery. Though their very early artware utilized a redware body, by the late 1870s it was replaced with yellow or buff burning clay. A line called Bourg-la-Reine (underglazed slip-decorated ware with primarily blue and green backgrounds) was produced, though not to any great extent. Other pieces were designed in imitation of Asian metalware, even to the extent that surfaces were 'hammered' to further enhance the effect. Occasionally live flora was pressed into the damp vessel walls to leave a decorative impression. They also made glazed plaques and tiles. Hugh C. Robertson ran the pottery alone after 1884 and labored to re-create the ancient Ming-era blood-red glaze. Although world acclaim greeted his rediscovery of what he then called 'Robertson's Blood,' his red-glazed vases cost too much to produce and bankruptcy followed in 1889. Supported by wealthy Boston art patrons, Hugh's pottery reopened in 1891 as the Chelsea Pottery U.S., and began using his other 1880s rediscovery, the crackle glaze, producing cobalt blue-decorated dinnerware. When this firm moved to Dedham in 1895 the ware became known as Dedham Pottery. From 1875 to 1880 the pottery was marked Chelsea Keramic Art Works Robertson and Sons in either two or three impressed lines. Earlier pieces were not marked. The impressed mark CKAW in a diamond formation was also used between 1875 and 1889. From 1891 through 1895 the impressed letters CPUS in a cloverleaf was utilized for the new firm. After the move to Dedham, only new Dedham Pottery marks were used. See also Dedham Pottery.

Bottle, abstract leaves, clear olive-gr, GW Fenety, 7¼x3¼" **600.00**
Bottle, flowers, clear brn, Josephine Day, 6x3".....................**750.00**
Ewer, hammered honeycomb, clear gr, metal shape, 9½x6¼" .**1,200.00**
Flask, pilgrim; pilgrim in landscape, teal/olive, Robertson, 6¾"..**650.00**
Flask, pilgrim; streaky bl-gr & brn, scroll hdls, ftd, CKAW, 9"....**635.00**
Match holder, man's face w/open pocket, bl gloss, CKAW, 6".....**550.00**
Medallion, boy trumpeting, Robertson, 4¾x4" **750.00**
Plate, experimental gr, w/emb cloverleaves, CPUS, 10¼"..........**925.00**
Plate, Pineapple, CPUS, 8½", NM..**325.00**
Plate, Upside Down Dolphin & Baby, CPUS, 10¼" **950.00**
Vase, oxblood gloss, gourd shape, CKAW, 9", EX **300.00**
Vase, Terra Cotta, urn form w/leaf hdls, CKAW, ca 1880, 5¾"...**635.00**

Chicago Crucible

For only a few years during the 1920s, the Chicago (Illinois) Crucible Company made a limited amount of decorative pottery in addition to their regular line of architectural wares. Examples are very scarce today; they carry a variety of marks, all with the company name and location.

Vase, beige to pk, 2 sm open angle hdls, sm rpr, 5½" **475.00**
Vase, brn & gr matt, stick neck, 8"...**240.00**
Vase, floral, multitone gr, rpr, 9"..**400.00**
Vase, gr, open angle hdls, squat, 4"...**600.00**
Vase, gr, tulip supported by 4 buttresses, 11½".......................**2,300.00**
Vase, gr, 4 vertical buttresses, flared rim, 10½", NM..............**2,200.00**
Vase, gr semimatt w/emb broad leaves, 5½x6"..........................**450.00**
Vase, pk to lav, 4 cut-out hdls, cylindrical, 11".......................**5,500.00**

Children's Books

Children's books, especially those from the Victorian era, are charming collectibles. Colorful lithographic illustrations that once delighted little boys in long curls and tiny girls in long stockings and a lot of ribbons and lace have lost none of their appeal. Some collectors limit themselves to a specific subject, while others may be far more interested in the illustrations. First editions are more valuable than later issues, and condition and rarity are very important factors to consider before making your purchase. For further information we recommend *Collector's Guide to Children's Books, 1850 – 1950, Volumes I, II, and III*, by Diane McClure Jones and Rosemary Jones; and *Whitman Juvenile Books Reference & Value Guide* by David and Virginia Brown. Both are available from Collector Books or your local bookstore.

Key:
brd — board   ed — edition
dj — dust jacket

Abu Kassim's Slippers, N Green, WT Mars illus, pictorial brds, 1963...**10.00**
Al Alligator, RW Eschmeyer, Fisherman Press 1st ed, 1953, 49-pg...**10.00**
Alice's Adventures in Wonderland, Carroll, Ward Lock, 1920...**150.00**
Angry Waters, W Morey, Dutton, Cuffari illus, 1969, w/dj **20.00**
Apple Strudel Soldier, T McGowen, Follett 1st ed, 1968.............**15.00**
Army in Pigtails, Harriet Evatt, Bobbs-Merrill 1st ed, 1962, w/dj .**30.00**
Art for Children, E Raboff, Garden City 1st ed, oversz, 1968 ....**10.00**
Basement Clown, K James, V Golancz London 1st ed, 1972, w/dj...**15.00**
Blacky, Bartbrug, McLoughlin, Bracker illus, illus cover, 1939, sm ...**35.00**
Blubber, Judy Blume, Bradbury Press, 1974 1st ed, w/dj.................**90.00**
Boys' Book of Airmen, Crump, illus, Dodd Mead, 1927 ....**15.00**
Bunnikin's Picnic Party, AJ MacGregor, Wills & Hepworth, ca 1960s ...**10.00**
Campfire Stories, Cheley, Greenburg, 1942, 329-pg **20.00**
Cats for Kansas, H LeGrand, Abingdon, 1948 ....**15.00**
Child's Book of Planes, T Sinnickson, Caston Publishers, 1950s ...**15.00**
Children's Bells, Eleanor Farjeon, Walck 1st Am ed, 1960 ....**10.00**
Church Mice at Bay, G Oakley, Macmillan London 1st ed, 1978.**10.00**
Circus Baby, Maud & Miska Pertersham, Macmillan, oversz, 1950....**20.00**
Debutante Hill, Lois Duncan, Dodd Mead 1st ed, hardcover, 1958 ...**10.00**
Dick Deadeye, R Searle, Harcourt Brace Jovanovich 1st Am ed, 1975..**20.00**
Dog So Small, P Pearce, Maitland illus, Constable 1st ed, 1962 ...**15.00**
Dwarf on Blk Mountain, Bill Knott, Steck-Vaughn, 1967.............**10.00**
Eskimo Birthday, TD Robinson, Coalson illus, Dodd Mead, 1975...**15.00**
Everything Book, EG Vance, Golden Book, oversz, 174, 140+ pgs.**40.00**
Far Wilderness, Jean Yorty, WB Eerdmans 1st ed, 1966, w/dj........**15.00**
Felice, Marcia Brown, Scribner, oversz hardcover, 1958 ....**20.00**
Fun of Being Good, E Childs, Platt Munk, hardcover, 1954 ....**20.00**
Gentle Knight, R Schickel, Abelard-Schuman 1st Am ed, 1950, 26-pg...**15.00**
Giving Tree, S Silverstein, Harper 1st ed, 1964, w/dj **50.00**
Gold for Grahams, AC Fuller, Morse illus, Messner, 1948 ....**10.00**
Good Fairy, GB Steware, Adams illus, Reilly Lee, 1930, 128-pg...**10.00**
Good Old James, J Donovan, Harper, 1975 1st ed, w/dj **15.00**
Granny's Wonderful Chair, F Browne, Dutton, 1924 ed, 280-pg...**20.00**
Haven of Brace, E Yates, Knopf 1st ed, 1941, 262-pg **15.00**
Horses & Folks, CW Anderson, Harper, oversz w/dj, 1949 ....**50.00**
Hour in the Morning, Gordon Cooper, Dutton, hardcover, 1974, w/dj...**20.00**
House w/o Windows, BN Follett, Knopf 1st ed, 1927....................**70.00**
Jumping Lions of Bornei, JW Dunne, Robinson illus, Holt, 1938, oversz...**20.00**
Kiddie Rhymes, M Hays, Wiederseim (Drayton) illus, Jacobs, 1911 ..**60.00**
King of Doll House, P Clapp, Lothrop Lee, hardcover, 1974, 94-pg...**20.00**
Lassie Lost in Snow, S Frazee, Harris illus, Whitman, 1969 ....**10.00**
Little Brown Jug, M Nicholson, Flagg illus, Bobbs Merrill, 1908 ..**25.00**
Little Girl Who Curtsied, M Baker, Duffield 2nd ed, 1926 ....**40.00**
Little Lost Sioux, M Raabe, Howe illus, Whitman, 1942 ....**25.00**

Little Mommy, Sharon Kane, Golden Press, 1967 ....**20.00**

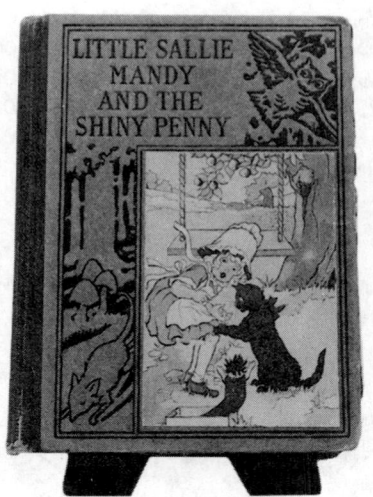

Little Sallie Mandy and the Shiny Penny, **by Helen R. Van Derveer, Henry Altemus Co. publishers, 1926, 5½x4½", VG, $15.00.** (Photo courtesy Diane McClure Jones and Rosemary Jones)

Lost Slipper, IL Johnson, Autustana, 1928, 89-pg, sm **20.00**
Meg & Melissa, Elizabeth Ladd, Morrow, 1964, w/dj **20.00**
Mouse Named Mus, I Brady, Houghton Mifflin 1st ed, 1972, w/dj ..**15.00**
Mr Grumpy's Motor Car, J Burningham, Harper-Collins 1st Am ed, 1976 ...**20.00**
My Father Was Uncle Wiggily, R Garis, McGraw-Hill 1st ed, 1966..**20.00**
Nigerian Holiday, MP Williams, Pickering & Inglis, 1959, w/dj ...**15.00**
Pride of Possession, James Street, Lippincott 1st ed, 1960, w/dj....**25.00**
Prince Yellowtop, KW Patch, illus cover, Page, 1903, sm..............**20.00**
Prize to Hardy, A Winter, illus cover, Bobbs Merrill, 1905 ....**15.00**
Shirley Temple's Fairyland, S Temple, Random House, oversz, 1958...**15.00**
Side Show Studies, F Metcalfe, Herford Illus, Outing co, 1906.....**25.00**
Stories To Live By, M Vetter, Platt Munk, 1960 ....**20.00**
Teenie Weenie Neighbors, Donahey, 1st ed, picture brds, 1945..**175.00**
Ten Brave Men, Sonia Daugherty, Lippincott, 1951, w/dj.............**30.00**
Three Birthday Wishes, RL Holberg, Weil blk/wht illus, Crowell, 1953...**10.00**
Trailer Tribe, F Musgrave, Ariel Books 1st ed, 1955 ....**15.00**
Viking Prince, A MacKaye, Thieme illus, Page, gr cover, 1928 ....**15.00**
We Are Seven, C Birley, Dutton, red cover, 1881, 136-pg............**25.00**
Young Viking of Brooklyn, H Carr, Morse illus, Viking, 1961, w/dj ...**15.00**

Children's Things

Nearly every item devised for adult furnishings has been reduced to child size — furniture, dishes, sporting goods, even some tools. All are very collectible. During the late seventeenth and early eighteenth centuries, miniature china dinnerware sets were made both in China and in England. They were not intended primarily as children's playthings, however, but instead were made to furnish miniature rooms and cabinets that provided a popular diversion for the adults of that period. By the nineteenth century, the emphasis had shifted, and most of the small-scaled dinnerware and tea sets were made for children's play.

Late in the nineteenth century and well into the twentieth, toy pressed glass dishes were made, many in the same pattern as full-scale glassware. Today these toy dishes often fetch prices in the same range as those for the 'grown-ups'!

See also A B C Plates; Blue Willow; Clothing; Stickley; etc.

Key: ds — doll size

China

Bowl, berry; Pastel Blue Rib & Floral, KT&K **6.00**

Bowl, Blue-Banded Ironstone, 8-sided, Iron Stone, 4" 20.00
Bowl, Miniature Blue Willow, England, 2" 35.00
Bowl, Myrtle Wreath, oval, JM&S, 5" 27.00
Bowl, Scenes From House That Jack Built, Florence Cook, 5¼" ..10.00
Bowl, Twin Flower, flow bl, oval, England, 4¾" 80.00
Bowl, vegetable (open); Gaudy Floral, England, 4" 55.00
Canister, Blue Banded, Coffee, Germany, 3⅝" 28.00
Canister, Mickey Mouse, tan lustre, Japan, 1½" 50.00
Casserole, Blue Willow, Japan, 4¾" 48.00
Casserole, Bluebird, Noritake, w/lid, 6" 45.00
Casserole, Forget-Me-Not, flow-bl type, England, 4¾" 145.00
Casserole, Gold Floral, bl w/gold & blk, England, 5½" 45.00
Casserole, Maiden-Hair-Fern, England, 5¼" 35.00
Casserole, Moss Rose, Made in Japan, w/lid, 5" 22.00
Comport, Pastel Blue Majolica, England, 3¼" 125.00
Creamer, Angel w/Shining Star, Germany, 3¾" 37.00
Creamer, Basket, flow bl, England 55.00
Creamer, Brundage Girls, Germany, 4" 32.00
Creamer, Butterfly, Made in Japan, 2¼" 9.00
Creamer, By the Mill, brn transfer, D Methvin & Sons 27.00
Creamer, Chinaman (figural), Japan, 2¼" 42.00
Creamer, Daffodil, Southern Potteries, 3" 20.00
Creamer, Elephant (figural), tan lustre, Made in Japan, 2" 20.00
Creamer, Embossed Leaf, burgundy, Made in Japan, 2" 7.00
Creamer, Girl w/Pets, Allerton & Sons, 3⅛" 17.00
Creamer, Holly, Germany, early 1900s 35.00
Creamer, Joseph, Mary & Donkey, Germany, 3" 40.00
Creamer, Kewpies, c Mrs Rose O'Neill Wilson, Bavaria 65.00
Creamer, Merry Christmas, pk or gr lustre, Germany, 2⅞" 35.00
Creamer, Nursery Rhymes, W&Co Hanley 25.00
Creamer, Old Moss Rose, brn & wht, Am 18.00
Creamer, Pagoda, Made in Japan 3.00
Creamer, Pink Rose, Homer Laughlin Eggshell, 2¼" 15.00
Creamer, Roman Chariots, bl & wht, Cauldon, England, 2" 40.00
Creamer, Silhouette Children, Victoria/Czechoslovakia, 2⅛" 12.00
Creamer, Snow White, Japan, WD Ent, c 1937, 2" 28.00
Creamer, Tan Lustre & White, England, 3¼" 12.00
Creamer, Water Hen, bl & wht, England, 3⅛" 35.00
Gravy boat, Blue Marble, England, 1½" 75.00
Gravy boat, Kite Fliers, England, 3¼" 125.00
Gravy boat, Livesley Fern & Floral, Livesley Powell, mid-1800s, 2½" ..55.00
Gravy boat, Rosamond, flow bl, Bistro, 2½" 65.00
Ladle, Greek Key, mk RSR (Ridgway, Sparks & Ridgway), 5" 15.00
Meat tenderizer, Blue Onion, wood hdl, Germany, 7" 180.00
Mug, Blue Willow, Coalport (Made in England), 1⅞" 22.00
Plate, Basket, flow bl, England, 5" 20.00
Plate, Buster Brown, Germany, 5" 30.00
Plate, Butterfly, England, 5" 6.00
Plate, Chauffeur w/Lady, pk lustre 12.00
Plate, Circus, Edwin M Knowles, 6½" 7.00
Plate, Colonial American, Am Ceramic Co, late 1930s 5.00
Plate, Dutch Figures, bl & wht, Japan 5.00
Plate, Floral, mc on cream w/yel band, Nippon, 5" 5.00
Plate, Flow Blue Dogwood, Minton, 4" 27.00
Plate, Friends, Germany 15.00
Plate, Gaudy Ironstone, England, 6" 45.00
Plate, Girl w/Pets, Allerton & Sons, 5¼" 10.00
Plate, Godey Prints, Salem China, 6¼" 5.00
Plate, grill; Blue Willow, Japan, 5" 45.00
Plate, House That Jack Built, Germany, 5¼" 8.00
Plate, Humphrey's Clock, Ridgway's England, 3⅞" 12.00
Plate, Mary Had a Little Lamb, Warwick, 6¼" 6.00
Plate, Mickey Mouse, c Walt Disney, Made in Japan, 4¼" 14.00
Plate, Myrtle Wreath, JM&S, 3¼" 8.00

Plate, Pembroke, Bistro, 4½" 10.00
Plate, Punch & Judy, bl & wht, England, 5¾" 25.00
Plate, Sunset, Made in Japan, 4¼" 5.00
Platter, Athens, England, 5½" 35.00
Platter, Fancy Loop, England, 6" 30.00
Platter, Forget-Me-Not, flow-bl type, England, 6½" 110.00
Platter, Gold Floral, bl w/gold & blk, England, 7" 32.00
Platter, Humphrey's Clock, Ridgway's England, 8" 47.00
Platter, Pagodas, England, 5⅛" 28.00
Platter, Rosamond, flow bl, Bistro, 5¼" 50.00
Rolling pin, Mary Had a Little Lamb, 9" 165.00
Soup bowl, Blue Acorn, mk RSR (Ridgway, Sparks & Ridgway), 4½" ..18.00
Soup bowl, Bluebird, Choisy & LeRoi, 4" 22.00
Soup bowl, Flow Blue Dogwood, Minton, 4⅛" 45.00
Soup bowl, Kite Fliers, England, 3½" 65.00
Sugar bowl, Amherst Japan, England, w/lid, 2½" 65.00
Sugar bowl, Banded Floral, England, w/lid, 4½" 20.00
Sugar bowl, Basket, PP Salem China, 2¼" 7.00
Sugar bowl, Lady Standing by Urn, England, w/lid, 3½" 55.00
Sugar bowl, Playful Cats, Germany, w/lid, 2¾" 45.00
Sugar bowl, Punch & Judy, bl & wht, England, w/lid, 4½" 30.00
Sugar bowl, Standing Pony, gr lustre, Germany, w/lid 30.00
Teacup & saucer, Acorn, England, 2", 4¾" 18.00
Teacup & saucer, Blue Onion, England 25.00
Teacup & saucer, Dutch Figures, Edwin M Knowles, 2⅛", 4¾" 10.00
Teacup & saucer, Dutch Windmill, Germany, 2¼", 4⅝" 25.00
Teacup & saucer, Father Christmas & Children, Germany, 2¼", 4¼" 35.00
Teacup & saucer, Orient, bl on cream, England, 3", 4¼" 28.00
Teacup & saucer, Peter Pan, Japan, 1¼", 3½" 12.00
Teacup & saucer, Red & White Rose, Germany, 2¼", 4½" 14.00
Teacup & saucer, Water Hen, bl & wht, England, 2", 4⅜" 23.00
Teapot, Banded Floral, England, 5½" 40.00
Teapot, Children w/Teddy Bear, lustre, Germany, 4½" 150.00
Teapot, Dimmocks' Blue Banded, Thomas Dimmock & Co, 3¾" .75.00
Teapot, Dutch Children on tan lustre, Made in Japan 27.00
Teapot, Holly, Germany, early 1900s 125.00
Teapot, Hunt Scene, pk lustre, Germany 110.00
Teapot, May, bl & wht, bulbous, England, 5" 75.00
Teapot, Mini Floral, England, 6½" 50.00

Teapot, Silhouette, marked Made in Japan, 4⅛", $30.00.
(Photo courtesy Margaret and Kenn Whitmyer)

Teapot, Silhouette Children, Victoria/Czechoslovakia, 3½" 37.00
Teapot, St Nicholas, Germany, 5½" 200.00
Tray, Dimity, rectangular, England, 4⅝" 18.00
Tray, Pink Open Rose, Made in England, 6" 10.00
Tureen, Athens, England, 3½" 55.00
Tureen, Flow Blue Dogwood, Minton, 6½" 135.00
Tureen, Livesley Fern & Floral, Livesley Powell, mid-1800s, 3½" .65.00
Underplate, Blue Marble, England, 5 /12" 50.00
Wash bowl & pitcher, Blue Floral, England 225.00
Wash bowl & pitcher, Pink Lustre, England, 4½", 3" 85.00
Waste bowl, Gaudy Ironstone, England, 2⅞" 110.00

Waste bowl, Lady Standing by Urn, England, 2⅞" **55.00**
Waste bowl, Nursery Rhymes, W&Co Hanley, 3½" **60.00**

Furniture

Examples with no dimensions given are child size unless noted doll size.

Armchair, crest, 5 spindles, bamboo-trn arms & legs, old bl pnt, 21" ...**300.00**
Armchair, maple QA, serpentine crest & arms, vasiform splat, 23" **600.00**
Armchair, maple/ash bow-bk Windsor, rfn/rprs, 19th C, 22½" ...**850.00**
Armchair, trn legs, scrolled arms, reuphl seat, Victorian, 24x11"...**225.00**
Armchair, trn/cvd rosewood grpt, 1850s, child sz.........................**440.00**
Armchair, 2-slat ladder-bk, arched crest, wood seat, 20th C, 20"...**80.00**
Armchair, 2-slat ladder-bk, brn pnt over red, rpl tape seat, 19" ..**200.00**
Armchair, 3-slat ladder-bk, cord seat, trn finials, 22" **350.00**
Bed, CI w/scrollwork/birds/etc, bl/wht rpt, rpr, ds, 13x22x16" **220.00**
Bed, soft wood, vertical spindles, sq rail below & above, ds, 22" L...**100.00**
Bureau, grained/pnt Emp, 2 glove/3 full drws, 19th C, 12x13x8"...**700.00**
Bureau, grpt, 3 drws/2 glove drws, serpentine columns, 10x9x6" ...**750.00**
Chair, mahog Chippendale-style wing-bk, worn uphl, 1900s, 29"....**350.00**
Chair, PA rod-bk Windsor, step-down crest, bamboo trns, old stencil...**120.00**
Chair, pnt bow-bk Windsor, H-stretchers, 1800s, 20"...............**500.00**
Chest, pine, 6-brd, hinged top, old cream pnt, 1800s, 16x29x13"....**600.00**
Chest, walnut w/old varnish, scrolled crest, 4-drw, 12x13x8"......**550.00**
Chest, walnut w/shaped aprons, 4 dvtl drw, rfn, 23x21x14" **385.00**
Chest, 6-brd, red pnt, cut-out ft, 1790s, 14x21x9" **1,150.00**

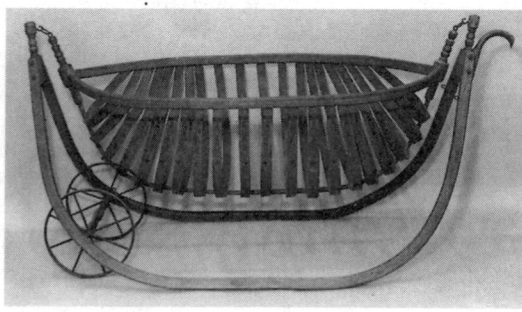

Cradle, bentwood, original red paint with silver striping and gold stencil, on wheels, Ford Johnson & Co., Patent Oct. 17th '76, 54", EX, $600.00. (Photo Courtesy Garth's Auctions, Inc.)

Cradle, cherry, sq corner posts w/acorn finials, cutouts, 20x35x16"...**350.00**
Cradle, grpt pine, hooded, dvtl, Am, 9x11x5" **150.00**
Cradle, mahog, mortised rockers, dvtl, flamed veneer hood, 40" ...**330.00**
Cradle, orange pnt wood w/dk gr trim/decor, Am, 19th C, 11x14x18"...**350.00**
Cradle, pine w/blk rpt over red w/yel striping, dvtl, rprs, 18" **120.00**
Cradle, poplar w/worn blk sponging on yel, old bl int, rprs, 42" .**275.00**
Crib, cherry w/red stain, spindled sides, ca 1800, 44x28x44" **515.00**
Crib, stencil on yel pnt, spindled sides, early 1800s, 33x25x52" .**435.00**
Cupboard, chip-cvd pine w/dk varnish, dbl doors, 7 drws, 21x15" **415.00**
Cupboard, jelly; pine/butternut w/varnish, 2 panel doors/crest, 14" ..**440.00**
Cupboard, pine w/gr rpt, red int, open shelfs, rstr drw, 27x19x9" ..**275.00**
Cupboard, pine w/worn finish, panel door, shelves, 17x13x6" **175.00**
Desk, cherry/tiger maple QA, slant lid, 1750s, 20¾x19" **3,500.00**
Dry sink, pine w/old grpt, 2-doors/drw, bracket ft, 13x13x8".......**650.00**
Dry sink, poplar/pine w/old brn pnt, drw, porc pulls, wire nails, 34" .**660.00**
Highchair, bamboo Windsor w/pnt stencil decor, spindle bk, 34" **350.00**
Highchair, Country Windsor, cleaned to red traces, 33½", EX ...**150.00**
Highchair, hard & softwood w/pnt traces, spindle bk, 31" **220.00**
Highchair, mixed woods, arrow-bk, bamboo-trn legs, rpl ft rest, 34"...**200.00**

Highchair, rabbit-ear Windsor w/bamboo trns, old rpt w/decor, 36" ...**450.00**
Highchair, trn legs/spindles, brn pnt w/yel stripes & mc flowers, 27"..**250.00**
Rocker, arm; blk pnt w/mc floral crest, red arms, NY, 26½".......**220.00**
Rocker, arm; 2-slat ladder-bk, worn red pnt w/worn decor, 25" ...**165.00**
Rocker, arrow-bk, orig red pnt w/gr & yel trim, 19" **245.00**
Rocker, bent elements intertwined, solid splat, plank seat, 1900s....**250.00**
Rocker, platform, walnut, folding, 1880s, 23x16" **300.00**
Settee, grpt w/gold stripe, rectangular crest, trn legs, 25" L....**1,200.00**
Settee, orig pnt/stencil, spindle bk, plank seat, 1800s, 22x26x9"...**3,000.00**
Table, drop-leaf; pine w/dk finish, trn legs, 22x22x14"+7" leaves ...**385.00**

Glass

Acorn, butter dish, frosted, 4"...**350.00**
Acorn, spooner, 3⅛"..**125.00**
Arched Panel, pitcher, amber, Westmoreland, 3¾" **110.00**
Arched Panel, water set, cobalt, 3¾" pitcher+6 2" tumblers.......**300.00**
Austrian No 200, creamer, canary, Greentown, 3¼"...............**200.00**
Austrian No 200, sugar bowl, chocolate, Greentown, w/lid, 3¾" ...**550.00**
Baby Thumbprint, cake stand, US Glass, 3"..........................**110.00**
Baby Thumbprint, compote, flared rim, US Glass **200.00**
Bead & Scroll, spooner, dk gr, 2¾"......................................**140.00**
Beaded Swirl, butter dish, amber or cobalt, Westmoreland, 2⅜"...**150.00**
Beaded Swirl, sugar bowl, Westmoreland, w/lid, 3¾" **42.00**
Betty Jane, casserole, McKee, red trim, #209, w/lid **40.00**
Betty Jane, pie plate, McKee, #97, 4½" **12.00**
Braided Belt, spooner, wht w/decal, 2⅝"...............................**125.00**
Bucket, butter dish, Bryce Bros...**280.00**
Bucket, spooner, Bryce Bros, 2½" **180.00**
Butterfly, mug, 3¼"...**50.00**
Cherry Blossom, creamer, pk, 2¾" (+) **35.00**
Cherry Blossom, plate, Delphite, 5⅞" (+) **8.00**
Chimo, butter dish **125.00**
Chimo, creamer, 2" (+)..**50.00**
Cloud Band, butter dish, milk glass w/pnt decor, Gillinder, 3¾" ...**200.00**
Cloud Band, spooner, Gillinder, 2⅜"....................................**45.00**
Diamond Ridge/D&M No 48, butter dish, Duncan & Sons........**195.00**
Diamond Ridge/D&M No 48, creamer, Duncan & Sons, 2½".....**85.00**
Fernland, butter dish, cobalt, Cambridge, 2⅝"......................**60.00**
Fernland, sugar bowl, emerald or olive gr, Cambridge, w/lid, 3" **45.00**
Fine Cut Star & Fan, butter dish, Higbee, 2½" **35.00**
Flattened Diamond & Sunburst 'Thumbellina,' butter dish, Westmoreland...**30.00**
Galloway, pitcher, US Glass, 3⅞"...**30.00**
Galloway, tumbler, blush, US Glass, 2" **20.00**
Grapevine w/Ovals, butter dish, McKee, 1½"........................**110.00**
Homespun, cup, pk, Jeannette, 1⅝".....................................**32.00**
Homespun, teapot, pk, w/lid, Jeannette.................................**125.00**
Inverted Strawberry, bowl, master berry; Cambridge, 1⅝"............**65.00**
Inverted Strawberry, punch bowl, Cambridge, 3⅜" **52.00**
Kidibake, bread baker, Fry, clear opal, #1928, 5" **65.00**
Kidibake, plate, grill; Fry, clear opal, 8½"..............................**27.50**
Kittens, bowl, cereal; marigold, Fenton, 3½" **125.00**
Kittens, cup & saucer, marigold, Fenton, 2⅛", 4½"................**140.00**
Lamb, butter dish..**175.00**
Lamb, creamer, rim roughness **40.00**
Lamb, spooner, 2⅛"...**110.00**
Laurel, plate, French Ivory, McKee, 5⅞" **8.00**
Laurel, sugar bowl, Jade Green, McKee, 2⅝"........................**32.00**
Liberty Bell, butter dish, 2¼"..**225.00**
Liberty Bell, spooner, 2⅜"..**150.00**
Lion, butter dish, frosted, Gillinder, 4¼" **140.00**
Lion, cup & saucer, crystal w/frosted head, Gillinder, 1¾", 3¼" ...**80.00**
Little Bo Peep, mug, etched **95.00**
Michigan, butter dish, red & gr flashed, US Glass, 3½".............**175.00**

Michigan, butter dish, US Glass, 3½" **95.00**
Michigan, stein, crystal w/gold, US Glass, 2⅞" **55.00**
Moderntone, creamer, beige, aqua or rose, 1¾" **9.00**
Moderntone, cup, pk, 1¾" **6.00**
Moderntone, teapot, wht, 3½" **110.00**
Nearcut, pitcher, Cambridge, 3⅛" **30.00**
Nearcut, tumbler, Cambridge, 2" **6.50**
Nursery Rhyme, pitcher, US Glass, 4¼" **120.00**
Nursery Rhyme, punch bowl, bl opaque **310.00**
Nursery Rhyme, punch cup, bl opaque, US Glass **45.00**
Pattee Cross, bowl, berry; US Glass, 1" **12.00**
Pattee Cross, pitcher, US Glass, 4½" **65.00**
Pennsylvania, butter dish, gr, US Glass, 3½" **225.00**
Pennsylvania, creamer, crystal w/gold, US Glass, 2½" **56.00**
Plain Pattern No 13, butter dish, milk glass, King Glass, 1⅞" **175.00**
Plain Pattern No 13, sugar bowl, cobalt, King Glass, w/lid, 3¼" ..**150.00**
Rex (Fancy Cut), butter dish, 2⅜" **42.00**
Rex (Fancy Cut), pitcher, 3½" **60.00**
Rooster No 140, butter dish, King Glass, 2¾" **200.00**
Rooster No 140, nappy, King Glass, 3" **140.00**
Sawtooth, butter dish, 3" **50.00**
Sawtooth, spooner, 3¼" **40.00**
Sawtooth Band No 1225, creamer, Heisey, 2½" **60.00**
Sawtooth Band No 1225, sugar bowl, red flashed, Heisey, w/lid, 4⅛" ..**150.00**
Standing Lamb, butter dish **900.00**
Standing Lamb, spooner, frosted **1,100.00**
Stippled Diamond, butter dish, bl or amber, 2¼" **160.00**
Stippled Diamond, spooner, 2⅛" **75.00**
Stippled Vine & Bead, creamer, NM **35.00**
Stippled Vine & Bead, sugar bowl, w/lid **85.00**
Sultan, butter dish, gr frosted, McKee, 3¾" **300.00**
Sultan, creamer, chocolate, McKee, 2½" **320.00**
Sunbeam No 15139 (Twin Snowshoes), butter dish, US Glass, 2" ..**140.00**
Sunny Suzy Baking Set #261, baker, hdls, Anchor-Hocking, 10-oz **10.00**
Sweetheart, creamer, Cambridge, 2¼" **12.00**
Twist No 137, butter dish, bl opal, Albany, 3⅝" **200.00**
Twist No 137, spooner, Albany, 2⅜" **22.00**
Two Band, creamer **40.00**
Two Band, sugar bowl, w/lid, 3¾" **65.00**
Whirligig, butter dish, US Glass, 2½" **27.00**
Whirligig, punch bowl, US Glass, 4¾" **35.00**

Miscellaneous

Baby walker, primitive, various woods w/old patina, 16x22x22" ...**40.00**
Bean pot, stoneware, Albany slip, 2¾" **50.00**
Carriage, cvd/bentwood body w/trn ball decor, metal fr & wheels, 1900s....**385.00**
Carriage, wood & metal w/orig mc pnt, wood spoke wheels, ds, 26x34" ..**330.00**
Coffeepot, aluminum, 3-pc **16.50**
Colander, aluminum **5.00**
Creamer, Frolicking Children, graniteware, Germany, 2½" **50.00**
Creamer, pewter, 3¼" **35.00**
Drum, dk gr pnt w/gold stencil, 9⅜x10", G **275.00**
Drum, tin w/wooden bands, Am flags in worn mc on gold japanning, 12"...**360.00**
Easel/slate, chromolitho paper top, Richmond School Furniture, 1939 ..**165.00**
Egg fryer, cobalt speckled graniteware, 4½" **75.00**
Fork, knife or spoon, bone hdl, ea **12.00**
Fork, knife or spoon, metal, Austria/Germany, ea **2.50**
Fork, knife or spoon, pewter, ea......................................**2.50**
Funnel, bl graniteware w/wht int **55.00**
Funnel, gray speckled graniteware, 2¼" **70.00**
Kaleidoscope, wood, interchangeable lenses, Peaches Browning, EXIB.**325.00**
Ladle, lt bl speckled graniteware, 4½" **40.00**
Rocking horse, burlap covered, horsehair mane/tail, hide ears, 30x38" ..**450.00**

Rocking horse, cvd w/old pnt, leather saddle, 1860-90, 39x73", VG...**1,725.00**
Rocking horse, dapple gray, brn leather saddle, stenciled base, 30x35"..**715.00**
Rocking horse, laminated wood, orig pnt, glass eyes, 36", EX **550.00**
Rocking horse, pine w/worn pk & wht pnt, nailed rprs, 44" **415.00**
Sled, dk bl rpt w/gold scrolls & mc stencil, iron runners, 29" **415.00**
Sleigh, worn blk, old velvet uphl, rpr, horse-drawn, 74"...............**225.00**
Sugar bowl, bl graniteware **30.00**
Sugar bowl, wht graniteware w/bl band **28.00**
Teacup & saucer, bl-speckled graniteware **35.00**
Teapot, wht graniteware w/bl band & gold trim, 5" **120.00**
Teapot & lid, Her Pet, graniteware................................**120.00**
Wheelbarrow, dk bl rpt w/striping, orange wheels, sq nails, 12" ..**435.00**

Chintz

'Chintz' is the generic name for English china with an allover floral transfer design. This eye-catching china is reminiscent of chintz dress fabric. It is colorful, bright, and cheery with its many floral designs and reminds one of an English garden in full bloom. It was produced in England during the first half of this century and stands out among other styles of china. Pattern names often found with the manufacturer's name on the bottom of pieces include Florence, Blue Chintz, English Roses, Delphinium, June Roses, Hazel, Eversham, Royalty, Sweet Pea, Summertime, and Welbeck, among others.

The older patterns tend to be composed of larger flowers, while the later, more popular lines can be quite intricate in design. And while the first collectors preferred the earthenware lines, many are now searching for the bone china dinnerware made by such firms as Shelley. You can concentrate on reassembling a favorite pattern, or you can mix two or more designs together for a charming, eclectic look. Another choice may be to limit your collection to teapots (the stacking ones are especially nice), breakfast sets, or cups and saucers.

Though the Chintz market remains very active, prices for some pieces have been significantly compromised due to their having been reproduced. For further information we recommend *Charlton Book of Chintz, I, II,* and *II,* by Susan Scott. Our advisor is Mary Jane Hastings; she is listed in the Directory under Illinois. See also Shelley.

Apple Blossom, plate, James Kent, 10" **110.00**
Balmoral, teapot, stacking; 3-pc set, Royal Winton **665.00**
Beeston, teapot, Royal Winton, 6-cup **925.00**
Blue Chintz, bowl, serving; 8-sided, ftd, Crown Ducal, lg **200.00**
Butterfly, sweet set, Wade Heath **185.00**
Butterfly, teapot, Wade Heath, 5¾" **395.00**
Carnation, compote, ftd, Royal Winton, 3½x5½" **125.00**
Cheadle, breakfast set, Royal Winton, 6-pc **710.00**
Chelsea, teapot, stacking; 3-pc set, Royal Winton **765.00**
Clyde, lamp, Royal Winton, 10x5" **335.00**
Cotswold, breakfast set, Royal Winton, 6-pc **675.00**
Country Lane, jug, Lord Nelson, 7" **150.00**
Crocus, teapot, stacking; Royal Winton **400.00**
DuBarry, breakfast set, James Kent, 6-pc **295.00**
DuBarry, chocolate pot, Granville shape, James Kent, 6¼" **395.00**
DuBarry, plate, dinner; James Kent, 9⅞" **145.00**
Eleanor, teapot, stacking; 3-pc, Royal Winton **495.00**
English Rose, bowl, hdls, Royal Winton, 5½x5" **150.00**
English Rose, breakfast set, Royal Winton, 6-pc **675.00**
Esther, compote, Royal Winton, 7½" **270.00**
Evesham, breakfast set, Royal Winton, 6-pc **1,400.00**
Evesham, butter dish, Royal Winton **250.00**
Evesham, hot water pot, Royal Winton, 7¼" **750.00**
Evesham, plate, Royal Winton, 8", 4 for **295.00**
Evesham, teapot, Athena shape, Royal Winton, 4" **650.00**

Florence, basket, Rowsley shape, Royal Winton, 5¼x5¼x3⅜" ..175.00
Florence, tray, Royal Winton, 7¾x5" 185.00
Florence, vase, Royal Winton, 12x6½" 195.00
Florida, jardiniere, Crown Ducal, 6½x7¾" 250.00
Hazel, bonbon, Royal Winton, 2½x7¼x6" 145.00
Hazel, cheese dish, Royal Winton 185.00
Hazel, compote, Royal Winton, 6½" 185.00
Hazel, egg cup & underplate, Royal Winton........................195.00
Hazel, teapot, Royal Winton, 6-cup 595.00
Heather, teapot, stacking; 3-pc set, Lord Nelson 495.00
Hydrangea, breakfast set, James Kent, 6-pc 750.00
Hydrangea, tea set, James Kent, 7-pc 850.00
Ivory Chintz, bowl, 8-sided, Crown Ducal, 5⅜x8⅜" 270.00
Ivory Chintz, condiment set, Crown Ducal..........................265.00
Ivory Chintz, jardiniere, Crown Ducal, 6¾x7¾" 295.00
Ivory Chintz, vase, 8-sided, Crown Ducal, 11½x6½" 395.00
Julia, candy box, Royal Winton, ...450.00
Julia, cheese keeper, Royal Winton 385.00
Julia, creamer & sugar bowl, Royal Winton 395.00
Julia, cup & saucer, Royal Winton 135.00
Julia, jug, Ascot shape, Royal Winton 260.00
Julia, jug & liner, Royal Winton, 5½", 5½" 400.00
June Roses, breakfast set, Royal Winton, pot+cr/sug+cup+toast+tray ..1,250.00
Kew, coffeepot, Royal Winton 495.00
Kew, jug, Royal Winton, 4" 350.00
Kew, teapot, Royal Winton, 6-cup 395.00
Lilac Time, coffeepot, Empire, 7½" 450.00
Lorna Doone, sugar shaker, Midwinter, 6½" 295.00
Marguerite, breakfast set, Royal Winton, 20-pc 395.00
Marguerite, teapot, Royal Winton, 6" 395.00
Marguerite, wash bowl & pitcher, Royal Winton, 5x16", 10½" ..550.00
Marina, teapot, Lord Nelson, 6-cup....................................385.00
Marina, teapot, stacking; 3-pc, Lord Nelson 360.00
Marion, cake plate, Royal Winton 350.00
Marion, canoe, Royal Winton 250.00
Marion, music box, Royal Winton, 3x5¼x3¼" 550.00
Nantwich, plate, Royal Winton, 10½" 145.00
Nantwich, teapot, stacking; 3-pc, Royal Winton...................600.00
Old Cottage, biscuit barrel, Royal Winton...........................350.00
Old Cottage, breakfast set, Royal Winton, 6-pc....................400.00
Old Cottage, cup & saucer, demitasse; Royal Winton 100.00
Old Cottage, hot water pot, Royal Winton...........................260.00
Old Cottage, jug, Royal Winton, 4⅝" 215.00
Old Cottage, jug, Royal Winton, 6½" 235.00
Old Cottage, lamp, Royal Winton, 16" overall 525.00
Old Cottage, teapot, Royal Winton, mini 220.00
Old Cottage, teapot, Royal Winton, 5½" 200.00
Orient, cake plate, Royal Winton, 12" 175.00
Paisley, breakfast set, Empire, 8-pc...................................300.00
Paisley, teapot, Wade, 5¼x7" 170.00
Pekin, bowl, salad; w/servers, Royal Winton 365.00
Pink Chintz, butter dish, Crown Ducal, 6" 215.00
Pink Chintz, condiment set, Crown Ducal, shakers+mustard+tray ...265.00
Pink Chintz, plate, Crown Ducal, 8½".................................215.00
Queen Anne, biscuit barrel, Royal Winton 280.00
Queen Anne, breakfast set, Royal Winton, 6-pc 300.00
Queen Anne, coffee set, Royal Winton, 10-pc set, serves 4........365.00
Rock Garden, tea set, Shelley, 15-pc..................................565.00
Rosetime, coffeepot, Royal Albert, 7" 165.00
Rosetime, teapot, Lord Nelson, 6-cup 195.00
Royalty, biscuit box, Royal Winton, 7½x7x5".......................500.00
Royalty, plate, dinner; Royal Winton, 10" 230.00
Royalty, sauce boat, Royal Winton....................................140.00
Royalty, teapot, Royal Winton, 5½".....................................215.00

Shrewsbury, teapot, Royal Winton, 8½" 500.00
Skylark, sandwich set, serving plate+6 sm...........................175.00
Spring, compote, ftd, Royal Winton, 3¼x5½" 150.00
Spring Flower, tray, sandwich; Myott, 12x6½" 185.00
Springtime, sardine box, Midwinter, 2x5x4"..........................165.00
Summer Flower, teapot, Myott, 4-cup 200.00
Summertime, bowl, vegetable; Royal Winton, 9½" 265.00
Summertime, bowl, vegetable; w/lid, Royal Winton, 10½" 380.00
Summertime, butter dish, Royal Winton 185.00
Summertime, cake plate, 3-tier, Royal Winton.....................185.00
Summertime, coffeepot, Ascot shape, Royal Winton, 8" 595.00
Summertime, creamer & sugar bowl on tray, Royal Winton 185.00
Summertime, gravy boat, Royal Winton, 8" 215.00
Summertime, jam pot, Royal Winton...................................185.00
Summertime, jug, water; Royal Winton, 7½" 350.00
Summertime, platter, Royal Winton, 13x10".........................225.00
Summertime, relish, 3-part, Royal Winton, 9½x9" 220.00
Summertime, teapot, stacking; 3-pc set, Royal Winton...........525.00
Summertime, vase, bud; Royal Winton, 5½"..........................195.00
Sunshine, teapot, Countess shape, Royal Winton, 4"..............385.00
Sweet Pea, bowl, 3-part, Royal Winton, 9½"........................155.00
Sweet Pea, breakfast set, Royal Winton, 6-pc.......................900.00
Sweet Pea, creamer & sugar bowl, Royal Winton 180.00
Sweet Pea, nut dish, Royal Winton, 4 for............................115.00
Sweet Pea, plate, Royal Winton, 6¼", 4 for 110.00
Sweet Pea, teapot, Royal Winton, 5" 450.00
Sweet Pea, teapot, Royal Winton, 6-cup 500.00
Sweet Pea, toast rack, Royal Winton 165.00
Thistle, teapot, Wade Heath, 6-cup 190.00
Tiger Lily, teapot, Royal Winton 235.00
Triumph, bowl, Royal Winton, 2x4½" 145.00
Triumph, breakfast set, Royal Winton, 6-pc.........................350.00
Welbeck, butter dish, Ascot shape, Royal Winton 235.00
Welbeck, teapot, stacking; 3-pc set, Royal Winton 925.00
Welbeck, tray, sandwich; Royal Winton...............................185.00

Chocolate Glass

Jacob Rosenthal developed chocolate glass, a rich shaded opaque brown sometimes referred to as caramel slag, in 1900 at the Indiana Tumbler and Goblet Company of Greentown, Indiana. Later, other companies produced similar ware. Only the latter is listed here. See also Greentown. Our advisors for this category are Jerry and Sandi Garrett; they are listed in the Directory under Indiana.

Butter dish, Cattail and Water Lily (Fenton), $1,250.00.

Bowl, Beaded Triangle, 4½" 350.00
Bowl, Chrysanthemum Leaf, 7" 575.00
Bowl, Geneva, oval, 8¼x5¼" 200.00
Bowl, Wild Rose w/Bowknot, 8½" 250.00
Box, dresser; Venetian...400.00

Butter dish, File...2,500.00
Butter dish, Geneva..650.00
Butter dish, Wild Rose w/Scrolling, child sz..............750.00
Celery holder, Chrysanthemum Leaf, 6"...................875.00
Celery holder, Fleur-de-Lis, 5¾"..............................365.00
Compote, Melrose, 7¾"..300.00
Creamer, Aldine, chocolate..................................1,300.00
Cruet, Shield w/Daisy & Button 5,000.00
Nappy, Navare...300.00
Novelty, griffin candle holder.............................2,475.00
Novelty, kingfisher toothpick holder....................1,000.00
Novelty, smoking set, McKee & Bros, 3-pc set........1,000.00
Pickle dish, Aurora, pickle dish, violin shape 225.00
Pitcher, Chrysanthem Leaf..................................3,000.00
Pitcher, Rose Garland...3,000.00
Salt dip, Honeycomb, 1¾".......................................450.00
Shaker, Wild Rose w/Bowknot................................250.00
Spooner, Chrysanthemum Leaf................................600.00
Spooner, Fleur-de-Lis..240.00
Sugar bowl, Aldine, w/lid 1,750.00
Syrup, Geneva, metal lid..650.00
Toothpick holder, Chrysanthemum Leaf 900.00
Tumbler, File..600.00
Tumbler, Wild Rose w/Bowknot..............................165.00

Christmas Collectibles

Christmas past . . . lovely mementos from long ago attest to the ostentatious Victorian celebrations of the season.

St. Nicholas, better known as Santa, has changed much since 300 A.D. when the good Bishop Nicholas showered needy children with gifts and kindnesses. During the early eighteenth century, Santa was portrayed as the kind gift-giver to well-behaved children and the stern switch-bearing disciplinarian to those who were bad. In 1822 Clement Clark Moore, a New York poet, wrote his famous *Night Before Christmas*, and the Santa he described was jolly and jovial — a lovable old elf who was stern with no one. Early Santas wore robes of yellow, brown, blue, green, red, white, or even purple. But Thomas Nast, who worked as an illustrator for *Harper's Weekly*, was the first to depict Santa in a red suit instead of the traditional robe and to locate him the entire year at the North Pole headquarters.

Today's collectors prize early Santa figures, especially those in robes of fur or mohair or those dressed in an unusual color. Some early examples of Christmas memorabilia are the pre-1870 ornaments from Dresden, Germany. These cardboard figures — angels, gondolas, umbrellas, dirigibles, and countless others — sparkle with gold and silver trim. Late in the 1870s, blown glass ornaments were imported from Germany. There were over 6,000 recorded designs, all painted inside with silvery colors. From 1890 through 1910, blown glass spheres were often decorated with beads, tassels, and tinsel rope.

Christmas lights, made by Sandwich and some of their contemporaries, were either pressed or mold-blown glass shaped into a form similar to a water tumbler. They were filled with water and then hung from the tree by a wire handle; oil floating on the surface of the water served as fuel for the lighted wick.

Kugels are glass ornaments that were made as early as 1820 and as late as 1890. Ball-shaped examples are more common than the fruit and vegetable forms and have been found in sizes ranging from 1" to 14" in diameter. They were made of thick glass with heavy brass caps, in cobalt, green, gold, silver, red, and occasionally in amethyst.

Although experiments involving the use of electric light bulbs for the Christmas tree occurred before 1900, it was 1903 before the first manufactured socket set was marketed. These were very expensive and often proved a safety hazard. In 1921 safety regulations were established, and products were guaranteed safety approved. The early bulbs were smaller replicas of Edison's household bulb. By 1910 G.E. bulbs were rounded with a pointed end, and until 1919 all bulbs were hand blown. The first figural bulbs were made around 1910 in Austria. Japan soon followed, but their product was never of the high quality of the Austrian wares. American manufacturers produced their first machine-made figurals after 1919. Today figural bulbs (especially character-related examples) are very popular collectibles. Bubble lights were popular from about 1945 to 1960 when miniature lights were introduced. These tiny lamps dampened the public's enthusiasm for the bubblers, and manufacturers stopped providing replacement bulbs.

Feather trees were made from 1850 to 1950. All are collectible. Watch for newly manufactured feather trees that have been reintroduced.

For further information concerning Christmas collectibles, we recommend *Christmas Ornaments, Lights, and Decorations, A Collector's Identification and Value Guide, Volumes I* through *III*, by George Johnson, available from Collector Books or your local bookstore.

Note: Values are given for bulbs that are in good paint, with no breaks or cracks, and in working order. Examples termed 'mini' measure no more than 1½". When no condition is mentioned in the description, assume values are for examples in EX/NM condition except paper items; those should be assumed NM/M.

Bulbs

Jester pointing to a playing card, milk glass, $90.00; Dutch girl, milk glass, $60.00; Snowman on skis, clear glass, $45.00.
(Photo courtesy Margaret and Kenn Whitmyer)

Angel w/violin, milk glass, 2½", from $80 to................................100.00
Baby in bathtub, celluloid, 3", from $75 to 80.00
Baby in clown suit, milk glass, 3¼", from $75 to 85.00
Baby in stocking, milk glass, mini, from $25 to.............................30.00
Ball, faceted, clear, 2", from $15 to..20.00
Ball, indented, Germany, 2½", from $30 to....................................40.00
Ball w/skull & crossbones, 2.5 volt, 2", from $12 to......................15.00
Bear in dress, celluloid, 3¾", from $70 to...80.00
Bell, faceted, Mazda, 2", from $60 to...70.00
Bell, milk glass, Christmas Greeting, 1950s, 1¼", from $10 to......15.00
Betty Boop, milk glass, Type 1, 2½", from $30 to 35.00
Bird in cage, milk glass, mini, from $45 to 65.00
Birds in chimney, clear, 2½", from $90 to 100.00
Bubble light, glass base, Alps, 1954, working, from $45 to............55.00
Bubble light, Noma, ca 1976-77, from $1 to 1.50
Bubble light, Noma Biscuit, 1946-60, from $3 to............................5.00
Bubble light, Paramount, from $30 to 40.00
Bubble light, Reliance Spark-L-Light, 1949-51, from $6 to............8.00
Bubble light, Snowman, Noma, 1985, from $8 to 9.00
Bubble light, Sterling, 1988, from $1 to 1.50

Candle, smooth flame, std base, sm, 4", from $30 to....................35.00
Candle, twisted, clear, 2¾", from $10 to 15.00
Charlie Chan, milk glass, ca 1950, 2¾", from $300 to 325.00
Church w/bell, milk glass, 2½", from $50 to...............................60.00
Cross, clear, exhaust tip, std base, 5½x3½", from $90 to 100.00
Cross on egg shape, clear, 2¼", from $35 to................................40.00
Cross w/star center, clear, 2¾", from $30 to...............................35.00
Dog, walking, celluloid, 3¾", from $65 to..................................75.00
Elephant, milk glass, trunk up, 3", from $20 to...........................30.00
Grapes, milk glass, 2", from $5 to..7.00
Humpty Dumpty, milk glass, ribbed bottom, 2", from $100 to 125.00
Indian lady w/baby on bk, milk glass, 3", from $300 to 350.00
Jack-o'-lantern w/leaves, milk glass, ca 1950, 1¾", from $45 to....55.00
Kewpie, milk glass, mini, from $20 to......................................25.00
Kewpie girl w/hat, milk glass, 2½", from $25 to..........................35.00
Kewpie w/lg head, milk glass, ca 1950, 2½", from $25 to.............35.00
Lantern, Japanese Odawara, milk glass, cylindrical, 3", from $3 to .5.00
Lantern, 6-panel, milk glass, 1950s, 2", from $10 to.....................12.00
Man w/hat, dbl-faced egg-shaped head, milk glass, ca 1950, $150 to ...175.00
Minnie Mouse, Disney, from $200 to 225.00
Monkey w/vine, clear, Germany, 2¼" 100.00
Old Woman in Shoe, milk glass, ca 1950, from $50 to...................75.00
Penguin, milk glass, mini, from $50 to 75.00
Pig playing drum, clear, 2¾", from $175 to 200.00
Polar bear, milk glass, mini, from $20 to...................................25.00
Putti angel, clear, Germany, 2¼", from $225 to 250.00
Rabbit, milk glass, sits, paws on hips, Germany, 2½" 85.00
Rooster, celluloid, 2½", from $50 to 60.00
Sailor boy w/parrot, celluloid, 4", from $45 to...........................50.00
Santa, clear, dbl-sided, common, 2½", from $10 to 15.00
Santa atop house, milk glass, 2¼", from $75 to...........................85.00
Santa face on dmn, milk glass, mini, from $50 to 70.00
Santa w/bag, dbl, milk glass, mini, from $20 to...........................25.00
Santa w/tree, clear, exhaust tip, 4", from $275 to 300.00
Snowman w/bag, clear or milk glass, 2½", ea, from $10 to............12.00
Songbird, clear, w/exhaust tip, Germany, 3½", from $25 to 35.00
Star, Matchless Wonder, single row type, from $20 to 25.00
Star w/Santa face, milk glass, 1950s, 2", from $55 to...................65.00
Statue of Liberty, milk glass, 4½", from $650 to 750.00
Trumpet flower, Mazda, 2¼", from $60 to 75.00
Turkey by house, clear, Germany, 3", from $300 to......................375.00

Candy Containers

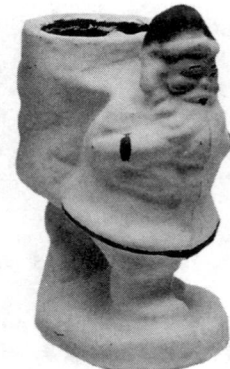

Santa with sack on back, papier-mache, painted details, 8", $80.00. (Photo courtesy Margaret and Kenn Whitmyer)

Birdcage, Dresden, gold/silver, flat, 4½x2½", from $75 to..............95.00
Clock, alarm; Dresden, gold/silver, 3-D, 2½", from $250 to........275.00
Clock, printed paper, Czar on horse, Russian lettering, 1930s, 4" ...125.00
Cornucopia, Dresden, gold/silver, 3-D, 4½", from $275 to..........300.00
Deer, Dresden, natural, 3-D, sack inside neck, 3", from $325 to ..350.00

Fan, Dresden, gold/silver or pnt, flat, 2x3½", from $30 to............40.00
Globe, paper map on cb, opens at equator, 3" dia, from $150 to.175.00
Heart, Dresden, gold/silver, 3-D, Type I, 2x2", from $140 to.......160.00
Parasol, paper w/wood hdl, fabric & lace trim, 2½" dia, $150 to ...175.00
Ram, Dresden, gold/silver, 3-D, 3¾", from $375 to 425.00
Rooster head, Dresden, natural, 3-D, Type 1, 3", from $325 to...350.00
Santa, felt coat, fur beard, opens at waist, compo, Germany, 4"..325.00
Santa, felt coat, fur beard, opens at waist, compo, Germany, 5"..375.00
Santa, felt coat, fur beard, opens at waist, compo, Germany, 6"..425.00
Santa, felt coat, fur beard, opens at waist, compo, Germany, 8"..525.00
Santa, felt coat, fur beard, opens at waist, compo, Germany, 10" ..625.00
Santa, molded cb, pot belly, spring neck, West Germany, 9".........85.00
Santa, papier-mache face, fur beard, felt coat, Germany, 5" 265.00
Santa, papier-mache face, fur beard, felt coat, wood base, Germany, 7"....425.00
Santa standing, hard plastic, Irwin, 1950s, 4", from $18 to 20.00
Slipper, red fabric on cb, appl Dresden trim, 5½", from $275 to ..300.00
Tambourine, printed paper, 5 sm brass bells, lid lifts, 2½"...........125.00
Turkey (roasted), paper, early 1900s, 3-4½", from $45 to 55.00
Turtle, Dresden, natural 3-D, Type II, 3½", from $350 to 375.00

Ornaments

Angel, Dresden, flying, gold/silver, 3-D, Type II, 4¼", $450 to...475.00
Angel child, hard plastic, Germany, 2-4", ea, from $8 to.................9.00
Angel child w/lily, scrap w/tinsel, Germany, 7", from $40 to.........50.00
Baby in buggy, Dresden, gold/silver, flat, 5¾x5½", from $125 to .135.00
Bear, Dresden, dancing w/stick, gold/silver, 3-D, 3", from $400 to..425.00
Bell, Dresden-like, foil on papier-mache, 3-D, ca 1935, 1¾", from $10 to ...15.00
Bird on branch, Dresden, natural, 3-D, appl feathers, 3", $275 to ..300.00
Bulldog, Dresden, gold/silver, dbl, barking, 3¾" W, from $295 to...325.00
Carp, Dresden, natural, 3-D, 1 lg/2 sm fins, 7½" L, from $500 to ...550.00
Cat w/ball of yarn, diecut paper w/crepe-paper trim, 18", from $200 to ...225.00
Cow w/milk pail, Dresden, gold/silver, flat, 3x5", from $95 to 115.00
Donkey, Dresden, gold/silver or natural, dbl, 2½x2½", $175 to..200.00
Dragonfly, Dresden, gold/silver or natural, flat, 2¾" wingspan......50.00
Father Christmas, Dresden, natural, 3-D, 5", from $375 to 400.00
Girl w/earrings, Dresden-like, pnt, 3-D, 1920s, 5¼", from $275 to...300.00
Honey bee, Dresden, gold/silver, flat, 3¼", from $100 to 120.00
Horse w/jockey, Dresden, gold/silver or natural, 3-D, 3¼x3" 400.00
Icicle, Dresden, gold/silver, dbl, 5", from $85 to..........................95.00
Ladder to star w/angels, cb w/glitter, Montgomery Ward, 1926, 7¾"...30.00
Nativity scene w/angels, scrap only, 5 figures, 6¼", from $20 to ...25.00
Paddle wheeler, Dresden, gold/silver, 3-D, 4¼", from $450 to 500.00
Roly poly Santa in chimney, celluloid, metal loop, 3", from $100 to...125.00
Rooster, Dresden, natural, crepe-paper clothes, 3-D, 2¼", $300 to 350.00
Salamander, Dresden, natural, 3-D, 4", from $300 to 325.00
Santa in sleigh, scrap only, old, 13¾" (+), from $125 to.............150.00
Santa w/girl & lamb, scrap w/tinsel, 6", from $20 to....................25.00
Santa w/tree & toys, scrap only, walking to right, 4¾x2", $15 to .25.00
Snow angel girl w/flower basket, scrap only, Germany, 10½", $35 to....45.00
Snowman, Dresden, gold/silver, flat, old, 4" (+), from $70 to.......80.00
Sunburst, Dresden, gold/silver, dbl, old, 5" dia (+), from $80 to ...95.00

Miscellaneous

Candle holder, acorn, heavy tin, clip-on, 2", from $40 to 45.00
Candle holder, Am Eagle, led pendulum weight, drip pan, 5¼" ...85.00
Candle holder, angel w/trumpet, tin litho, clip, 3", from $125 to.140.00
Candle holder, apple, blown counterweight type, clip, 3", $30 to.35.00
Candle holder, aviator head glass shade, clip, 3", from $350 to ..400.00
Candle holder, Bavarian boy, emb heavy tin, clip, 2¾", $80 to 90.00
Candle holder, butterfly (Type I), emb heavy tin, clip, 3x2", $60 to..70.00
Candle holder, dbl-weighted pendulum, clay ball, 4-6", ea, $15 to..25.00
Candle holder, partridge in pear tree, tin litho, clip, 2½" 125.00

Candle holder, pine cone, soldered wire weight, clamp, old, 6", $30 to ...40.00
Candle holder, poinsettia, emb heavy tin, clip, 1¾", from $40 to .45.00
Candle holder, squirrel, emb heavy tin, clip, 1¾", from $85 to 95.00
Christmas light, bust of Queen Mary, dk cobalt, Eclipse, 4¼" 375.00
Christmas light, bust of Queen Victoria, pk-puce, 4¼" 160.00
Christmas light, Daisy, cobalt, 3¾", from $60 to........................65.00
Christmas light, Dmn Quilt, clear, 3¾", from $12 to....................17.00
Christmas light, Dmn Quilt, lt bl, 3¾", from $40 to 45.00
Christmas light, Harlequin, bl, single row, 3½", from $80 to 90.00
Christmas light, head of Queen Mary, any color, 4", from $300 to ..350.00
Christmas light, Hobnail, amethyst, mini, 2", from $140 to........150.00
Christmas light, lantern, Chicago Lamp Candle, yel, wire hdl, 4¼" ...120.00
Christmas light, pineapple, cobalt, 1890-1910, 4⅛" 135.00
Christmas light, Thousand Eye, gr or amber, 3¾", from $80 to.....85.00
Christmas light, tulip, yel-amber, Hearn Wright..., 3½" 90.00
Decoration, angel doll, celluloid, tinsel dress/foil wings, 1920s, 4"...30.00
Decoration, elf, vinyl head, felt body, Japan, 1970s, 4-6", $2 to 3.00
Fence, feather, per section, from $25 to...35.00
Kugel, artichoke shape, 3", from $350 to......................................400.00
Kugel, ball, end-of day glass, 3", from $350 to 450.00
Kugel, ball w/dbl hanger, red, 2-3", from $175 to.......................200.00
Kugel, ball w/zig-zag pattern, 2", from $300 to...........................350.00
Kugel, egg, pear or teardrop, red, 3-4", from $400 to 500.00
Kugel, grape cluster, unsilvered gr, 7", from $275 to 300.00
Kugel, orange or lemon, amethyst, 3½", from $450 to 500.00
Kugel, orange or lemon, silver, 3½", from $200 to.......................225.00
Kugel, pacifier shape, unusual, 2½", from $275 to.......................325.00
Kugel, ribbed, bl, 1-2", from $150 to 175.00
Kugel, strawberry, cobalt, 4¼", from $600 to 700.00
Lantern, celluloid w/brass fr, folds up, 1920s, 6½" dia 25.00
Lantern, pierced metal, sq w/arched windows, Germany, 1930s, 1½"..50.00
Lantern, stained glass in metal fr, 4-sided, 1890s, 4¾", $40 to......60.00
Light cover, ball of yarn, clear glass, Germany/USA, 3", from $65 to ...75.00
Light cover, star on disk, clear glass, blown, Germany/USA, 4½" ...60.00
Light shade, bell (plain), plastic, Am, 2"...1.00
Light shade, paper, Whirl-Glo, US, ca 1936, 2", from $4 to............6.00
Santa, celluloid, w/lantern, Japan, 5½", EX 95.00
Santa, chalkware, purple-brn coat w/gold, 1800s, 18" 950.00
Santa, papier-mache, Belsnickle, pk-wht coat w/mica, 10½" 440.00
Santa, plastic, hands on stomach, jaunty pose, Am, 3¾", $12 to..15.00
Santa in sleigh, compo & wire, felt clothes, Germany, 7", EX 225.00
Santa in sleigh w/3 reindeer, papier-mache wood, Germany, 25"...300.00
Tree, feather; Germany, Japan or US, 7-12", from $75 to.............90.00
Tree, feather; Germany, Japan or US, 13-23", from $95 to..........120.00
Tree, feather; Germany, Japan or US, 32-36", from $155 to........185.00
Tree, feather; Germany, Japan or US, 48-54", from $300 to........350.00
Tree, feather; Germany, Japan or US, 56-62", from $355 to........450.00
Tree stand, metal, common type, 3 or 4 legs, 1950s-90s, lg, up to ...6.00
Tree stand, Santa head, concrete/plaster, 11½", from $300 to 350.00
Tree top, angel kneeling, blown glass, Germany, old, 10", $150 to ..175.00
Tree top, angel on ball, compo w/foil wings, non-electric, 6½".....15.00
Tree top, candelabra w/dangles, metal, Mayer, 1910s, 8", $175 to ..200.00
Tree top, rosette, spun glass, scrap 1 side only, 7½", $50 to..........60.00
Tree top, star (12-point, light ring), metal, Am, 1910s, 8½".......300.00

Chrysanthemum Sprig, Blue

This is the blue opaque version of Northwood's popular pattern, Chrysanthemum Sprig. It was made at the turn of the century and is today very rare, as its values indicate. Prices are influenced by the amount of gold remaining on the raised designs. Our advisors for this category are Betty and Clarence Maier; they're listed in the Directory under Pennsylvania.

Bowl, berry; sm 325.00
Bowl, master fruit; 10½" W 600.00
Butter dish...1,250.00
Butter dish, lt in color..500.00
Celery, from $400 to..550.00
Compote, jelly 600.00
Condiment tray, rare, VG gold 750.00
Creamer, from $285 to 350.00
Cruet, EX gold, from $975 to 1,200.00

Pitcher, 8", $1,100.00.

Shakers, pr 450.00
Spooner, from $300 to...350.00
Sugar bowl, M gold, w/lid, 7", from $350 to 450.00
Toothpick holder 450.00
Tumbler, EX gold, 3¾", from $185 to.......................................250.00

Circus Collectibles

The 1890s were the golden age of the circus. Barnum and Bailey's parades transformed mundane city streets into an exotic never-never land inhabited by trumpeting elephants with jeweled gold headgear strutting by to the strains of the calliope that issued from a fine red- and gilt-painted wagon extravagantly decorated with carved wooden animals of every description. It was an exciting experience. Is it any wonder that collectors today treasure the mementos of that golden era? See also Posters.

Key:
B&B — Barnum & Bailey   RB — Ringling Bros.

Carte de visite, Bearded Girl 7 Yrs Old, B&B, Anthony, VG.....140.00
Christmas card, RB, 1941..50.00
Herald, printed paper, 2-sided, Van Amburg, 1879, 8¾x26", G..140.00
Loud speaker assembly, Altec Lansing Corp, 1950s, 23½x25" ...175.00
Metrocard, RB, Gebel atop elephant, bl, M 70.00
Postcard, Ritter Midgets (troupe of 10), Berlin, VG+...................45.00
Prod, elephant...35.00
Program, Clyde Beatty, 1940s...30.00
Program, Hagenbeck-Wallace, 1927 ....30.00
Program, RB, 1937..35.00
Program, RB, 1977..25.00
Route book, RB, daily events/photos/etc, 1897, 136-pg, EX 100.00
Route book, RB, photos/etc, 1942, EX 35.00
Stereoview cards, circus parade, dtd 1884, pr...............................145.00

Cleminson

A hobby turned to enterprise, Cleminson is one of several California potteries whose clever hand-decorated wares are attracting the attention of today's collectors. The Cleminsons started their business at their El Monte home in 1941 and were so successful that eventually they expanded to a modern plant that employed more than 150 workers. They produced not only dinnerware and kitchen items such as cookie jars, canisters, and accessories, but novelty wall vases, small trays, plaques, etc., as well. Though nearly always marked, Cleminson wares are easy to spot as you become familiar with their distinctive glaze colors. Their grayed-down blue and green, berry red, and dusty pink say 'Cleminson' as clearly as their trademark. Unable to compete with foreign imports, the pottery closed in 1963. For more information we recommend *The Collector's Encyclopedia of California Pottery, Second Edition*, by Jack Chipman (Collector Books).

Bank, Let's Pay Off the Mortgage, wall mt 32.00
Bowl, Gram's, w/lid, 2½" H...30.00
Bread plate, Distkefink, bird shape, 5x6¼x12¾" 25.00
Child's mug, clown head, clown's hat is lid 80.00
Cleanser shaker, Katrina, girl in apron, 6"...................................35.00
Creamer, rooster, 5½"...45.00
Darner, lady figural, Darn It, 5", from $45 to 55.00
Egg cups, bride, groom, preacher, boy w/slingshot, 4", 4 for 150.00
Head vase, lady w/curlers, 4x3¾", NM..40.00
Lazy susan, Galagray, 7-pc, in wooden base, 16" dia, from $55 to .70.00
Match/toothpick holder, bird/flowers, 2-compartment, wall mt 40.00
Pitcher, Distlefink, 9", from $45 to 60.00
Plaque, baby, family tree & bunny, 9½x7½" 50.00
Plate, flowers, wall hanging, 5" 27.50
Razor bank, man shaving on front, from $40 to.............................55.00
Ring holder, Chef, from $25 to 30.00
Ring holder, dog, ring goes on tail 30.00
Ring holder, hand figural, 2¼"...42.50
Shakers, Old Salt & Hot Stuff, bowling pin shape, 5⅛", pr 45.00
Sprinkler, Oriental man, Sprinkle Plenty, 9"................................40.00
String holder, heart, You'll Always Have Pull w/Me.....................42.50
String holder, String Along With Me, 5½x6" 50.00

Wall pockets: Let's Pay Off the Mortgage, 7⅛", $30.00.; No Matter...My Kitchen Best, 7x8½", $30.00. (Photo courtesy Betty Newbound)

Wall pocket, bathtub...35.00
Wall pocket, bellows, Harmony & Understanding...Happy Hearth ...40.00
Wall pocket, Bonds for Baby, 7"...38.00
Wall pocket, coffee grinder, Time Out for Coffee 38.00
Wall pocket, flour scoop, mc floral decor 35.00
Wall pocket, Home Sweet Home, 6x7¾"......................................38.00
Wall pocket, kettle, Penny Saved, flowers on brn, 8x5" 45.00
Wall pocket, paint palette, Cooking Is an Art 45.00
Wall pocket, Pot Luck, lt gr, 8x6" 27.50
Wall pocket, spinning wheel, 8½" 42.50

Wall pocket, teapot, Penny Saved Is a Penny Earned...................40.00

Clewell

Charles Walter Clewell was a metal worker who perfected the technique of plating an entire ceramic vessel with a thin layer of copper or bronze treated with an oxidizing agent to produce a natural deterioration of the surface. Through trial and error, he was able to control the degree of patina achieved. In the early stages, the metal darkened and if allowed to develop further formed a natural turquoise-blue or green corrosion. He worked alone in his small Akron, Ohio, studio from about 1906, buying undecorated pottery from several Ohio firms, among them Weller, Owens, and Cambridge. His work is usually marked. Clewell died in 1965, having never revealed his secret process to others.

Prices for Clewell have advanced rapidly during the past few years along with the arts and crafts market in general. Right now, good examples are bringing whatever the traffic will bear.

Bowl, brn patina, rivets/panels, 3x9" 265.00

Candlesticks, #414-2-6, copper and green patina, 9½", $1,200.00 for the pair; Vase, #412-6, original green and blue patina, cylindrical, 9", $475.00.

Candlesticks, orange/gr patina (exceptional), #415-3-6, 10", pr ...1,650.00
Mug, #1035, Utopian, gr/gold bronze patina, emb vines 215.00
Tankard, riveted, inscr/1908, minor separation, 10" 365.00
Vase, #290-2-6, bronze to verdigris, bulbous, 7½x3½" 600.00
Vase, #295, copper clad w/crusty gr on brn, 7⅝" 325.00
Vase, #321-24, verdigris to bronze, flakes at rim, 6¼x3½" 550.00
Vase, #378-26, bronze to verdigris, some splits to copper, 14½" ..2,300.00
Vase, #520-220, gr/brn patina, urn form, 9x4½".........................1,800.00
Vase, copper clad w/verdigris, EX patina, ovoid, 10½" 550.00
Vase, gr/brn/orange patina, shouldered/incurvate, 6x3½"............400.00
Vase, striated gold, gr & copper patina, flat shoulder, 11x7¾" 950.00

Clews

Brothers Ralph and James Clews were potters who operated in Cobridge in the Staffordshire district from 1817 to 1835. They are best known for their blue and white transfer-printed earthenwares, which included American views, moral maxims, picturesque views, and English views. A series called Three Tours of Dr. Syntax contained thirty-one different scenes with each piece bearing a descriptive title. Another popular series was Pictures of Sir David Wilkie with seven prints. (Though we once thought that the Don Quixote series was made by Clews, new information seems to indicate that it was made instead by Davenport.) Both printed and impressed marks were used, often incorporating the pattern name as well as the pottery. See also Staffordshire, Historical.

Cup & saucer, Christmas Eve, Wilkie, dk bl transfer....................230.00
Cup & saucer, Water Girl, dk bl transfer.......................225.00
Plate, Coronation, floral, dk bl transfer, 10⅛"........................200.00
Plate, Letter of Introduction, dk bl transfer, 5½"....................235.00
Plate, Sancho, Priest & Barger, dk bl transfer, unmk, 7⅝", NM .140.00
Platter, Advertisement for a Wife, dk bl transfer, 15¼"...........1,550.00
Platter, Genevese, brn transfer, 1818-34 mk, 19¼x16".............600.00
Teapot, Setters, dk bl transfer, EX....................335.00
Vase, Chameleon Ware, HP geometrics, conical, 5⅜"...............140.00

Cliff, Clarice

Between 1928 and 1935 in Burslem, England, as the director and part owner of Wilkinson and Newport Pottery Companies, Clarice Cliff and her 'paintresses' created a body of hand-painted pottery whose influence is felt to the present time.

The name for the oevre was Bizarre Ware, and the predominant sensibility, style, and appearance was Deco. Almost all pieces are signed. There were over 160 patterns and more than 400 shapes, all of which are illustrated in A Bizarre Affair — The Life and Work of Clarice Cliff, published by Harry N. Abrams, Inc., written by Len Griffen and Susan and Louis Meisel.

Note: Non-hand-painted work (transfer printed) was produced after World War II and into the 1950s. Some of the most common names are 'Tonquin' and 'Charlotte.' These items, while attractive and enjoyable to own, have little value in the collector market. Our advisors for this category are Wilfred and Dolli Cohen; they are listed in the Directory under California.

Biscuit jar, Celtic Harvest, wheat sheaves/fruit, chrome lid, 6½"..175.00
Bowl, Autumn Crocus, flared rim, mc floral band inside rim, 3x5"...350.00
Bowl, Fantasque Range, cone shape in X base, 4x7½" 750.00
Bowl, Keyhole, mc geometrics, 1929, 3½x8⅜"............................375.00
Cake plate, Celtic Harvest, wheat sheaves/fruit, scalloped, 8" 125.00
Cup, Chintz, orange/brn/blk, ca 1932, 3⅝"...................................460.00
Honey pot, Melon, overlapping fruit, w/lid, 4" 850.00
Jam jar, Crocus, mc w/gr stems on brn, B Rigers, 3½x3¼"..........450.00
Jug, Lotus; Autumn, house & landscape, 11¾x8".....................2,250.00
Jug, Lotus; Gardenia, mc floral bands, 11¾x7⅛" 2,250.00
Jug, Rhodanthe, stylized plants, mc on cream, 6⅝x3⅝".............795.00
Plate, Autumn, Cafe-Au-Lait, 8½" 750.00
Sugar sifter, Marguerite, orange flower on gr, conical, 5½" 950.00
Teapot, Bizarre, trees on invt cone, orange/yel/blk, 4½", NM .2,185.00
Vase, Delecia Poppy, mc w/random drips on yel, Pat #25535, 8" ...850.00
Vase, Milano, tan w/orange bands, #264, 8", EX.....................350.00
Vase, pansies, mc on yel w/mc drips, 10½x4½" 995.00

Clifton

Clifton Art Pottery of Clifton, New Jersey, was organized ca. 1903. Until 1911 when they turned to the production of wall and floor tile, they made artware of several varieties. The founders were Fred Tschirner and William A. Long. Long had developed the method for underglaze slip painting that had been used at the Lonhuda Pottery in Steubenville, Ohio, in the 1890s. Crystal Patina, the first artware made by the small company, utilized a fine white body and flowing, blended colors, the earliest a green crystalline. Indian Ware, copied from the pottery of the American Indians, was usually decorated in black geometric designs on red clay. (On the occasions when white was used in addition to the black, the ware was often not as well executed; so even though two-color decoration is very rare, it is normally not as desirable to the collector.) Robin's Egg Blue, pale blue on the white body, and Tirrube, a slip-decorated matt ware, were also produced.

Jardiniere, Indian Ware, Four Mile Ruin, Arizona, buff and black on brown, 8½x11", $500.00.

Teapot, Crystal Patina, squat, 3½"...165.00
Teapot, Indian Ware, geometrics, brn & brick red, 4x8½"..........175.00
Vase, Crystal Patina, yel/buff mottle, 4-sided flared neck, 7" 275.00
Vase, gr matt, emb stylized lily pads, ftd sphere, 2½".................365.00
Vase, Indian Ware, blk/tan/rust geometrics, #206, 4⅜"..............125.00
Vase, Tirrube, jonquils, yel/wht/gr on brick red, 8x4" 325.00

Clocks

In the early days of our country's history, clock makers were influenced by styles imported from Europe. They copied the European's cabinets and reconstructed their movements — needed materials were in short supply; modifications had to be made. Of necessity was born mainspring motive power and spring clocks. Wooden movements were made on a mass-production basis as early as 1808. Before the middle of the century, brass movements had been developed.

Today's collectors prefer clocks from the eighteenth and nineteenth centuries with pendulum-regulated movements. Bracket clocks made during this period utilized the shorter pendulum improvised in 1658 by Fromentiel, a prominent English clock maker. These smaller square-face clocks usually were made with a dome top fitted with a handle or a decorative finial. The case was usually walnut or ebony and was sometimes decorated with pierced brass mountings. Brackets were often mounted on the wall to accommodate the clock, hence the name. The banjo clock was patented in 1802 by Simon Willard. It derived its descriptive name from its banjo-like shape. A similar but more elaborate style was called the lyre clock.

The first electric novelty clocks were developed in the 1940s. Lux, who was the major producer, had been in business since 1912, making wind-up novelties during the '20s and '30s. Another company, Mastercrafter Novelty Clocks, first obtained a patent to produce these clocks in the late 1940s. Other manufacturers were Keebler, Westclox, and Columbia Time. The cases were made of china, Syroco, wood, and plastic; most were animated and some had pendulettes. Prices vary according to condition and rarity.

Except for the novelty clocks whose values are on the increase, clock prices have been stable for several years. Unless noted otherwise, values are given for eight-day time only clocks in excellent condition. Clocks that have been altered, damaged, or have had parts replaced are worth considerably less.

Our advisor is Bruce A. Austin; he is listed in the Directory under New York. Our novelty clock advisors is Anita Levi (Allegheny Mountain Antiques Gallery); she is listed in the Directory under Pennsylvania.

Key:
br — brass
dl — dial
esc — escapement
mcr — mercury
mvt — movement
OG — ogee
pnd — pendulum

reg — regulator
rswd — rosewood
TS — time & strike
wt — weight
vnr — veneer
2nds — seconds

Calendar Clocks

Feishtinger/Waterbury, gingerbread walnut, Hebron, rfn, 1895, 22"...**1,100.00**
Fr crystal reg, 7" dl+3 sm dls, mrc pnd, coiled gong, 1890, 16¼"..**2,400.00**
Gilbert Octagon Drop, rfn mahog, weak orig tablet, 1870, 25"...**800.00**
Ingraham Dew Drop, rstr walnut, repapered dl, 1890, 23"...........**325.00**
Ingraham Round Drop, paper dl, old rfn case, 1890, 24", G........**425.00**
Ithaca #2 Shelf Cottage, NP pnd, repapered top dl, 1874, 22", VG..**625.00**
Ithaca #8 Shelf Library, walnut, dbl dl, rpl older finial, 1900, 26" **850.00**
Ithaca Farmer's, walnut w/cvd top, dbl-dl, 2 labels, 1875, 25"......**800.00**
Waterbury #25, oak (plain), 2-wt trapezoid mvt, orig dls, 1910, 35"..**2,000.00**
Waterbury #28, oak, dbl dl, 2 rear/1 int blk label, 1891, 41" ...**2,500.00**
Welch Arditi perpetual, dbl dl, rfn walnut, inner label, 1886, 27"...**1,250.00**
Welch Spring & Co #2 Reg, rswd vnr, orig dl, 1878, 35½", VG......**1,200.00**

Novelty Clocks

Nanny, eyes move with pendulum, Germany, H. Euk on
back, EX in box, $325.00.

Airplane, Bakelite & chrome, Mastercrafters, from $175 to........**225.00**
Ballerina, wooden, United, from $75 to......................................**100.00**
Carousel, plastic, carousel front, Mastercrafters, from $175 to....**225.00**
Cat w/flirty eyes, plastic, Spartus, from $25 to **40.00**
Clock Peddlar, whistler, 30-hr, wag pnd, Germany, 1960, 12" .**1,500.00**
Continental man, eyes blink, pnt CI, Bradley & Hubbard, 1860, 16½"...**800.00**
Cowboy w/Rope, metal, wooden base, United, from $100 to......**150.00**
Drunk, whistler, cvd figure w/wooden bottle, Germany, 1960, 18½"..**450.00**
Father Time, cast brass, Am, 1890s, 9½"......................................**400.00**
Fireplace, plastic, Mastercrafters, from $60 to **90.00**
God Bless America, flag waves, from $75 to **100.00**
Huck Finn, fishing pole & fish move, United, from $150 to.......**175.00**
Owl, blinking crossed eyes, pewter or spelter, Am, 1910, 6½" **500.00**
Rocking horse (Rancho), compo, Haddon, from $150 to............**200.00**
Singing Bird in Cage (2 birds), Fr, 1890, 22"...........................**1,500.00**
Swinging Girl, plastic, Mastercrafters, from $100 to...................**125.00**
Teeter Totter, children on seesaw, Haddon, from $125 to **175.00**
Waterfall & Wheel, plastic, Spartus, from $50 to **75.00**
Windmill, pk plastic case w/minor cracks, United, from $75 to..**100.00**

Shelf Clocks

Am Clock Turret #11, walnut, bbl pnd, 1875, 20½", VG **325.00**
Ansonia,#1241, br over CI, br dl, Nouveau numerals, 11".........**150.00**
Ansonia Barbelite #8, rpt hard rubber case & dl, NP mvt, 1883, 15½"..**500.00**
Ansonia Cabinet E, rfn oak w/br, rpl minute hand, clean mvt, 1894, 18".**1,100.00**
Ansonia Crystal Reg #3, floral on dk gr, open esc, porc dl, 1914, 18"..**2,500.00**
Ansonia Epsom, walnut, floral tablet, fancy pnd, 8-day, 1885, 18"......**300.00**
Ansonia Excelsior, br & bronze crystal reg, gold rpt, 1904, 20½" **1,600.00**
Ansonia Fisherman swinger, NP canister, paper dl, 1890, 21" .**3,400.00**
Ansonia Huntress swinger, bronzed statue, 1890, 24½", EX+..**3,000.00**

Ansonia La Chapelle, Royal Bonn porc, tricolor w/gold, 1904, 12"..**900.00**
Ansonia La Clairmont, Royal Bonn china, chipped dl, 1905, 11" **425.00**
Ansonia La Manche, Royal Bonn porc, floral, 1904, VG...........**450.00**
Ansonia La Moselle, Royal Bonn porc, lovers/doves, 1910, 14¼" ..**1,260.00**
Ansonia La Orb, Royal Bonn china, 3-color, chipped dl, 1905, 12½"..**700.00**
Ansonia Norma, bronzed spelter crystal reg, 1905, 14", G **775.00**
Ansonia Parisian, walnut, dbl bbl pnd, orig dl, 1880, rstr, 23" **450.00**
Ansonia Warlock, porc, floral on gr, porc dl, 1900, 10¼" **400.00**
Black Forest Cuckoo, br & shell inlay, dbl fusee, 1880, 18¼"...**2,300.00**
Brewster & Ingraham, br spring/onion top/4 candlestands, 1850, 20"...**850.00**
Brewster & Ingraham, mahog w/gilt, Gothic arch, pnd, 19" **400.00**
Brewster & Ingraham Fusee Steeple, 30-hr, prof full rstr, 1845, 19"..**600.00**
Briggs by GW Brown, rotary pnd, shaped pillar, 1865, 8" **1,325.00**
Bristol, CI front w/gilt, paper dl, br bezel, orig hands, 1855, 17"..**240.00**
English 1-fusee skeleton, rafter fr w/3 spires, 1900, 15½"+dome **1,000.00**
Fr architectural, eng gilt bronze, #d strike/gong, porc dl, 1875, 14"...**650.00**
Fr Big Ben architectural, bronze, porc dl, 1900, 22" **1,200.00**
Fr Cercles Tournants, annular dl, Louis XVI style, pnd, 1875, 20" **8,000.00**
Fr Forgeman (Industry Series), TS mystery, old patina, 1880, 17".....**9,000.00**
Fr Lyre, rswd w/satin inlay, peacock finial, bell strike, 1850, 21"........**3,100.00**
Fr Oarsman (Industrial series), 3-point mystery suspension, 1880, 17"...**14,000.00**
Fr Pendule, mvt w/in pnd, outer lyre case w/griffins, 1850, 23" **14,000.00**
Fr Riderless Horse ormolu figural, porc dl, silk thread mvt, 1840, 12"..**600.00**
Fr Windmill (Industrial Series), rpl fan, marble base, 1880, 17½".....**1,900.00**
Fr 400-day, glass/br, complex/compound pnd, 1880, 14" **5,000.00**
Gilbert Curfew, br mask on dl, orig hands/pnd, 1900, 17¾", G ..**275.00**
Gilbert Luna, walnut w/ebony, all orig, 1885, 21¼" **800.00**
Ingraham, scalloped/stenciled rswd, rstr dl, 30-hr TS/alarm, 1855, 17"..**475.00**
Ingraham Cabinet C, oak, paper dl/mask, wire gong in base, 1900, 16".**350.00**
Ingraham Doric, bird tablet, prof cleaned, 1880, 16", VG..........**175.00**
Ives, wagon spring, rpl dl (fine), strap brass design, 1829, 24" **12,500.00**
Ives, wagon spring, rpl 1955 mvt, rpt tablet & dl, 1828, 27" .**11,000.00**
Japy, onyx & ormolu crystal reg, bow front, pnt moldings, 1900, 13"..**2,000.00**
JC Brown Mini Ripple Beehive, 30-hr TS, old rfn, 1855, 15¼" **2,000.00**
JC Brown Ripple Steeple, rswd, mansion tablet, rstr dl, 1850, 20" ..**2,000.00**
Junghans Batboy, spelter statue, swinging arm, porc dl, 1910, 17½" ...**900.00**
Junghans Dog & Cat swinging arm, gold overpnt, porc dl, 1910, 9", VG..**2,500.00**
Junghans Doll swinger, pottery doll/walnut, porc dl, 30-hr, 1910, 13" ...**1,150.00**
Junghans Westminster chime bracket w/mahog case, 1920, 17" .**350.00**
Kroeber Langtry, walnut, rnd columns/blocks w/cvg, 1878, 23" ..**675.00**
Le Coultre Atmos Self-Winding, sq dl, lift-out door, 1979, 9¼", M...**550.00**
Mitchell, mahog vnr Emp triple-decker, pnd, 37" **1,500.00**
New Haven Fairfield, blk on CI, outside count wheel mvt, 11"..**370.00**
New Haven Hyperion, porc, pk orchids/bird, gilt dl center, 1900, 12"..**325.00**
New Haven Norwich Line A, oak gingerbread (rfn), alarm, 1905, 25", G...**185.00**
New Haven Westminster bracket, oak (sm molding gone), 1896, 17½"....**950.00**
One Hand Clock Co, minor stain on 6" dl, 1919, 9"...................**325.00**
S Thomas, mahog tambour, rubs on dl, 1920, 9" **130.00**
S Thomas, off-center pillar & scroll, rpl rvpt tablet, 1820, 30"....**3,000.00**
S Thomas Arch Top, rpl dl & pnd, rfn case, 1860, 15½"............**350.00**
S Thomas Chime #211, 8-bell, Westminster/Whittington, 1920, 13" .**2,000.00**
S Thomas Chime #255, 8 cup bells, crazed mahog, 1915, 9½"...**1,200.00**
S Thomas Chime #261, 8-bell, mahog vnr w/inlay, rstr, 1920, 14" ..**1,900.00**
S Thomas Garfield, walnut, damascene pnd, G orig dl, 1875, 24" **1,500.00**
S Thomas Long Alarm, br/spelter, orig dl, 15 minute alarm, 9"..**125.00**
S Thomas Octagon Top, rstr dl & rswd case, 1868, 9¼" **400.00**
S Thomas Plymouth Hollow Octagon, 1-day, TS/alarm, 1860, 14¼".....**475.00**
S Thomas Plymouth Pillar & Scroll, rstr Mt Vernon tablet, 1924, 24" ..**275.00**
S Thomas Queen Anne, ebonized walnut, rpt dl, 1890, 36" **700.00**
S Thomas Rnd Gothic, rswd, rpt dl, TS/alarm, 1868, 15", G......**270.00**
S Thomas Severn, Am eagle & shield inlay, cathedral gong, 1930, 10"..**325.00**
S Thomas Tudor #1, orig hands/dl/label, 1868, 16", VG **400.00**
Smith & Goodrich mini fusee, rpl dl, strawberry tablet, 1850, 15", VG...**275.00**
Stewart Limerick Paris, br works, cloisonne, w/key/pnd, 12" ...**1,155.00**

Terry, mahog vnr/ebonized pilasters/crest, pnd, 29", VG **825.00**

Terry & Andrews, beehive w/br springs, varnished, 1845, 19" **225.00**

Waterbury, CI front, orig dl, G label, 30-hr, 1860s, 16" **135.00**

Waterbury Conductor, TS/repeat, NM porc dl, 1912, 4½" **150.00**

Waterbury Parlor #55, Delft case, NP mvt, 1895, 13" **550.00**

Waterbury Romance figural, repapered dl, rfn, 1865, 21" **360.00**

Wedgwood, angels on gr mist, Fr open esc, 1910, 11¼" **850.00**

Welch, 8-day beehive, St Louis courthouse tablet, 1860, 19" **250.00**

Welch Patti VP, rswd w/orig buttons/finials, label, 1880, 18¾" ..**1,700.00**

Westclox, bronzed CI, paper dl, alarm, 1910, 5¼" **70.00**

Winterhalder & Hofmeier 3-train bracket, 5-gong, cvd oak, 1890, 18" ..**2,200.00**

Wm L Gilbert, mahog, 4-column, celluloid dl, gong, 1913, 16½" ...**250.00**

Tall Case Clocks

Aaron Smith...1871, pine w/old color, pnd, cannon-ball wt, 84"..**7,150.00**

AB Griswold, Fed-style mahog, pnt dl, Westminster chimes, 1890s, 94"..**3,650.00**

Blaylock Longtown, mahog Geo III, br face, 1780s, 77" **2,750.00**

David Wood, rfn mahog, rolling moon mvt, cvd molding, 1820, 92", G ..**3,500.00**

E Howard #87, cvd mahog, 14" silvered dl, 2-wt, 1881, 106" **15,000.00**

Emperor Oakridge, oak, 3-chime mvt, 1982, 80½" **300.00**

EO Stennes, cherry, TS, HP dl, bird in arch, pnd, 1961, 60" ...**1,500.00**

JE Stretcher, cherry Fed w/X-banding, arched ped, pnd, ca 1829, 94"..**6,000.00**

John Field, Cumberland RI, cvd cherry, eng arch, 1760-80, 95"....**62,000.00**

L Watson Cincinnati, pine w/orig vinegar grpt, fretwork cornice, 91"..**27,500.00**

Mahog Fed, swan's neck crest, tombstone door, mc & gilt decor, 98"..**6,900.00**

Midlands, oak/mahog vnr, br dl, eng 2nds dl, early 1800s, 91"..**3,500.00**

MW Campbell, cherry Hplwht, pnd, Shippensburg PA, 96", EX..**6,600.00**

S Hoadley Plymouth on face, arched cornice, rfn pine, 80".....**1,650.00**

Scottish, mixed woods, pnt 13" dl, broken arch, rprs, 1840, 90"........**1,850.00**

Walnut Hplwht w/figured vnr & inlay, dvtl bonnet, Fr ft, 98", EX ...**3,100.00**

Wm Cummens, Fed mahog w/inlay, pierced fretwork, old rfn, 97".**34,500.00**

Wall Clocks

Ansonia Queen Elizabeth, walnut, TS, sm tear in paper dl, 1890, 37"..**950.00**

Atkins Whiting Drop Octagon, rswd, 30-day wagon spring mvt, 1855, 25"..**2,500.00**

Austrian Grand Sonnerie Late Biedermeier, 3-wt, 72-beat, 1855, 47" ..**3,100.00**

Austrian Grand Sonnerie Late Biedermeier, 30-day spring, 1855, 26" ..**2,800.00**

Austrian Grand Sonnerie Reg, serpentine, 72-beat, 3-wt, 1860, 53" ..**3,750.00**

Austrian Grand Sonnerie walnut Baroque, etch dl, 3-wt, 1890, 54"..**4,200.00**

Austrian Vienna Reg, Alt Detsch walnut w/roof, eng dl, 2-25, 1890, 52"...**700.00**

Becker Grand Sonnerie, gesso on wood w/blk & gold, 3-wt, 1885, 39"..**1,750.00**

Becker Vienna-style reg, walnut, fleur-de-lis on dl, 2-wt, 1890, 52"..**1,700.00**

Black Forest, cuckoo, 3-wt, cvd game/firearms, EX **3,500.00**

E Howard Reg #9, figure-8 walnut, rpt baffle, orig tablets, 1890, 37"..**5,650.00**

E Howard Reg #10, walnut figure-8, damascene pnd, 1880, 34"..**3,000.00**

E Howard Reg #70, oak, damascene pnd, rstr, 1900, 31½" **2,000.00**

EN Welch, rswd octagon w/gold leaf, 9" drop, 1890s, 19" **200.00**

Fr, gilt spelter, conical, rotary pnd, cherub finial, 1890, 14"....**3,000.00**

Fr, walnut picture fr, rvpt glass dl, gong, 1880, 19" **125.00**

Fr walnut cartel, cvd lion top, ribbons/scrolls below, gong, 1890, 26"..**675.00**

Gebruder Resch-Remember Grand Sonnerie reg, 3-wt, 1880, 49"....**2,750.00**

German Gerliner, Nouveau florals on arch dl, br pnd, 1900, 41" **1,100.00**

Gilbert Admiral, pressed oak short drop, orig dl, rpl pnd, 1910, 27".....**235.00**

Gilbert Hollywood, beveled glass, NP pnd, dong-dong rods, 1925, 25" ...**300.00**

Gilbert Reg #10, rstr walnut, rstr paper dl, 1888, 53" **1,750.00**

Gustav Becker Grand Sonnerie reg, walnut Baroque, etch dl, 1890, 50"..**3,000.00**

Hamilton-Sangamo banjo, electric TS, patriotic tablets, 1930, 29"....**200.00**

Henry Adams London, dvtl wood, br works, eng face, 14¼" dia ...**550.00**

Howard-style banjo, cherry w/rswd grpt, rvpt panel, 29", VG **600.00**

Ingraham Landau w/advertising, improper pnd bob, 1925, 38" ...**400.00**

Ingraham Milford, golden oak, paper dl, 1925, 16¾" **225.00**

Ingraham Nyanza banjo, paper dl, 1915, 39"................................**275.00**

Ingraham Nyanza banjo, TS, paper dl, 1915, 39".........................**275.00**

Ingraham spring banjo, wood bezel, rstr dl, old rprs, 1855, 31" ...**500.00**

Junghans 'box style' reg, oak case, 2-wt, 1915, 33", G **300.00**

Junghans Uhren Fabrik reg, Alt Deutsch walnut, TS, pnd, 1895, 42"..**450.00**

JW Benson London, fusee drop dl, mahog vnrs, long pnd, 1920, 19"...**950.00**

New Haven Admiral 30-day, 2nds beat reg, 30" door, 1890, 62"........**2,700.00**

New Haven Manor, pastel gr, orig dl/hands, G label, 1925, 11½" **250.00**

New Haven Waring banjo, Deco screened tablets, 1925, 37" **250.00**

New Haven Welton banjo, rpr to eagle, pnd, G label, 1930, 24½", VG ..**150.00**

New Haven Whitney Westminster chime banjo, short pnd, orig finish, 31"...**200.00**

New Haven Willard banjo, 30-day, mahog, ship tablet, 1928, 45½"...**525.00**

S Thomas, oak octagon, 12" drop, EX label/dl/hands/pnd, 24" ...**300.00**

S Thomas Monitor ship's bell, polished br, 1936, 10½" **450.00**

S Thomas Reg #2, oak, flat door, stapled label, 1936, 34"........**1,300.00**

S Thomas Reg #6, mahog, rpl wt/pulley, door rpr, 1900, 48" ...**1,900.00**

Sessions Reg #4, mahog, advertising tablet (flaked), 1915, 38½", VG ..**400.00**

Sessions Reg E, oak, star pattern door, 1915, 39" **275.00**

Terry & Andrews, mahog, wooden dl, east-west mvt, 1847, 15" .**900.00**

Terry & Andrews Cottage, stenciled rswd vnr, flaking tablet, 1849, 16" ..**475.00**

Terry short drop dl, iron front, gold decor, orig tablet, 1870, 22"..**4,550.00**

Waltham Willard #1500 banjo, mahog, Perry's Victory rvpt, 1925, 42"..**1,800.00**

Waterbury Perth, orig mk dl, cathredal gong, NP pnd, rfn, 1890, 42" **1,500.00**

Waterbury Rennes reg, solid 2-pc dl, ring sash, pnd, 1905, 13½" ..**425.00**

Waterbury Toulon reg, br & glass, porc dl w/pinwheels, 1912, 11"...**400.00**

Cloisonne

Cloisonne is a method of decorating metal with enameling. Fine metal wires are soldered onto the metal body following the lines of a pre-determined design. The resulting channels are filled in with enamels of various colors, and the item is fired. The final step is a smoothing process that assures even exposure of the wire pattern. The art is predominately Oriental and has been practiced continuously, except during war years, since the sixteenth century. The most excellent examples date from 1865 until the turn of the century. The early twentieth century export variety is usually lightweight and the workmanship inferior. Modern wares are of good quality and are produced in Taiwan as well as China.

Several variations of the basic art include plique-a-jour, achieved by removing the metal body after firing, leaving only the transparent enamel work; foil cloisonne, using transparent or semitranslucent enameling over a layer of embossed silver covering the metal body of the vessel; wireless cloisonne, made by removing the wire dividers prior to firing; and cloisonne executed on ceramic, wood, or lacquer rather than metal.

Box, floral w/goldstone, bird finial on lift-off lid, 1½x3" **195.00**

Candlesticks, crane figural, mc w/pricket holders, 36", pr........**1,200.00**

Charger, cranes in landscape, various reserves form border of foliate-shaped rim, 23", VG+, $475.00.

Charger, heron & flowers on bl, China, 11½" **280.00**

Figure, bull, mc dragons & scrolls on bl over bronze, China, 22" ..**250.00**

Figure, camel, dragons & scrolls on bl, repousse/incised mane, 18"..**350.00**
Figure, water buffalo, dragons/roosters/scrolls on bl, China, 11" .**150.00**
Jar, flowers & feather-like decor on pk, Japan, 4½x3¾"..............**295.00**
Plaque, scrolled floral rosette border, flower center, China, 12"..**150.00**
Vase, birds in flowering cherry tree on maroon, Japan, 10".........**150.00**
Vase, butterflies, rooster & flowers in medallions, Japan, 8½"....**115.00**
Vase, butterflies & flowers in medallions, Japan, 10"..................**145.00**
Vase, cranes & waves on pk, elongated baluster, Meiji, 9¾", pr .**800.00**
Vase, dragons & intricate scrolls, petal rim, late, 14", pr..........**200.00**
Vase, hinoki on mustard, foliage at ft, att Namikawa, 1890, w/lid, 6"..**1,950.00**

Clothing and Accessories

More and more collectors are getting involved in the fascinating field of antique, vintage, and collectible clothing, once considered the realm of museum curators and historical societies. Today's collector is highly discriminating; most specialize in certain types of clothing or certain historical periods. This makes it important to know exactly how old an item is before determining a value. Gone are the days when it was sufficient to broadly categorize a dress as simply 'Victorian' or 'old,' as clothing from certain historical periods has increased in value faster than examples from other eras. A mistake in dating an item can cause a loss of several hundreds of dollars on the collectors' market. For example, prices for special-occasion dresses of the Civil War era have skyrocketed in recent years. Another big jump in market value is being seen in dresses of the late 1870s and early 1880s. Meanwhile, prices of dresses from the 1890s and 1900s have remained fairly stable.

Once the age of an item of clothing is ascertained, three other factors come into play in determining a price. The first is condition, as a noticeable rip or stain will devalue an item just as surely as a crack will devalue a glass vase. The second factor is quality: is it well made or made by a famous designer? Were fabrics and trimmings expensive or elaborate? Generally speaking, the more elaborate the item, the higher the value. The third factor is size. Today a large portion of collectors are searching for items which they can wear, therefore extremely small sizes are somewhat less valuable than larger ones.

For further information as well as an easy-to-use guide for dating women's clothing, we recommend *Collector's Guide to Vintage Fashions* by Kristina Harris, *Vintage Hats and Bonnets, 1770 – 1970*, by Susan Langley, *Ladies' Vintage Accessories*, by LaRee Johnson Bruton, and *Antique & Vintage Clothing: A Guide to Dating and Valuation of Women's Clothing, 1850 – 1940*, by our advisor, Diane Snyder-Haug, available from Collector Books or your local bookstore. Our values are for items of ladies' clothing unless noted 'man's' or 'child's.' Assume them to be in excellent condition unless otherwise described.

Key:
cap/s — cap sleeves   ms — machine sewn
embr — embroidery   n/s — no sleeves
hs — hand sewn   plt — pleated
l/s — long sleeves   s/s — short sleeves

Bathing suit, velvet w/ruched accents, 1940s, from $65 to...........**95.00**
Bathing suit, wool crepe, bodice w/attached bloomers, skirt, 1890s ..**100.00**
Blouse, cotton w/rows of embr, l/s, w/lace trim, 1910s, from $45 to.....**75.00**
Blouse, girl's, wht cotton, pinch plt/crochet trim, s/s.....................**22.50**
Blouse, rayon, lace inserts/ruching, ruffled/s, 1920s, from $10 to ..**30.00**
Blouse, wht linen, Peter Pan collar/silver trim, l/s, 1930s..............**12.00**
Bodice, beaded scoop neck, puff/s, 1900s, from $30 to **50.00**
Bodice, bl muslin w/emb roses, ruffled s/s, 1850s, from $65 to **120.00**
Bodice, bl silk w/blk lace o/l, lace yoke, l/s, 1900s, from $95 to..**120.00**
Bonnet, brn & lt bl silk, ms quilting, worn **60.00**
Bustle, various designs & shapes, 1880s, from $25 to....................**45.00**

Cap, boudoir; crochet daisies w/Fr-knot centers & tulle, 1930s, $35 to ...**55.00**
Cape, bl & blk silk w/velvet, full length, 1920s **135.00**
Coat, Battenberg lace, crochet buttons, 1910s...........................**500.00**
Coat, man's frock, Prince Albert style, mid-calf length, 1900s, $65 to...**95.00**
Coat, man's morning; bottle gr wool, 1910s, from $65 to **95.00**
Collar, blk jet overall beading, lg, NM **55.00**
Collar & cuff set, lady's, gold linen w/scallop trim **12.00**
Corset, button front, wide shoulder straps, Vict, from $85 to......**150.00**
Corset, elasticized panels, waist tie, 1880s, from $150 to............**200.00**
Drawers, wht cotton w/machine lace trim, 1890-1908, from $20 to ..**30.00**
Dress, bl wool w/blk lace collar/cuffs, beaded fringe, 1910s, $75 to..**150.00**
Dress, bl/wht cotton, sq neck, flare skirt, n/s, 1950s....................**35.00**
Dress, blk & red bodice, blk gored skirt, much embr, 1890s, $175 to...**275.00**
Dress, blk beads/sequins on silk chiffon, n/s, ca 1926, 38" L **250.00**
Dress, blk chiffon, sequin trim, n/s, flapper style **75.00**
Dress, blk crepe, V-front, 3-tier skirt, l/s, 1940s.........................**50.00**
Dress, blk velvet, l/s, jewel neck, 1920s...................................**70.00**
Dress, blk velvet w/beaded flowers, lace collar, s/s, 1920s, $50 to..**95.00**
Dress, boned bodice, pagoda/s w/attached under/s, hoop skirt, 1860s...**450.00**
Dress, child's, gold linen w/embr, lace trim, l/s, 1930s..................**40.00**
Dress, child's, wht w/pk floral embr & tucks, s/s, 1920s **35.00**
Dress, christening; cotton w/crochet buttons, Fr seams, 1900s, $65 to..**100.00**
Dress, christening; lace, eyelet inserts, ca 1900 ....**80.00**
Dress, cream crepe, rhinestones at top, s/s, 1930s........................**65.00**
Dress, cream lawn, pin tucks, lace inserts, 1910s.........................**135.00**
Dress, cream linen, lace inserts, crochet buttons, 1915.................**125.00**
Dress, embr blk silk w/gold & silver collar, 1910s.........................**90.00**
Dress, evening; embr net over silk muslin w/beads, low cut, 1910s ...**200.00**

Dress, evening; satin with lace bodice, beaded sleeves, ca 1912, $295.00. (Photo courtesy Diane Snyder-Haug)

Dress, gr plaid silk, l/s, full skirt, 1860s, VG................................**225.00**
Dress, gray net, rhinestones/beads, long skirt, lined, 1920s..........**250.00**
Dress, ivory rayon w/mc floral, jewel neck, cap/s, 1930s, EX **45.00**
Dress, lingerie; embr/scalloped hem, puffed bodice, 1904-07, $95 to ..**140.00**
Dress, lingerie; gauzy muslin, lace inserts, tucks, 1904-06, $95 to..**175.00**
Dress, plaid taffeta, bias-cut skirt, s/s, lace trim, 1940s, $20 to **30.00**
Dress, printed cotton w/braid, tucks/flounces, l/s, made for bustle ..**200.00**
Dress, red/wht cotton stripe, kick plt w/sash, s/s, 1950s **25.00**
Dress, rose & cream silk lace, chemise style, 1920s......................**75.00**
Dress, sateen print w/matching ruffled petticoat, embr l/s............**275.00**
Dress, silk faille, n/s, self bow at neck, 1950s.............................**50.00**
Dress, wedding; batiste, lace & tucks, high neck, Victorian........**400.00**
Dress, wedding; heavy cotton, fits over bustle, 1870s, EX **275.00**
Dress, wedding; ivory lace, taffeta slip, 1920s, +silk hose **265.00**

Dress, wedding; satin, Emp waist, puff/s, ribbon, 1960s, from $30 to..**75.00**
Dress, wht cotton gauze, peasant style, 1940s.....................................**35.00**
Dress, wht lawn, high neck, train skirt, Irish lace, 1910s.............**365.00**
Fur hat, beaver, wide brim, feathers/faux grapes, 1900s, from $75 to..**125.00**
Fur hat, ermine pillbox w/satin crown, Gimbels label, 1940s, $45 to ..**75.00**
Fur hat, toque w/faux animal face, ca 1900, from $75 to.............**150.00**
Gloves, wht nylon w/dainty machine embr, 1950s, from $3 to....**10.00**
Hat, brn velvet w/jet trim & dangles, velvet flowers, 1870s, $125 to ..**225.00**
Hat, child's straw bonnet, openwork loops, ca 1836, from $175 to.......**300.00**
Hat, drawn silk bonnet, plt bk, plume & bowl, 1820s, $300 to..**600.00**
Hat, fine straw Breton w/turned-up brim & ribbon, 1930s, from $85 to...**125.00**
Hat, lady's top hat w/tulle scarf & ostrich plume, 1870s, $75 to .**125.00**
Hat, natural straw, modified cloche style, 1930s, from $25 to **45.00**
Hat, pk ostrich feathers, 1950s, from $20 to.................................**40.00**
Hat, plush fur felt wide-brim w/plumes, 1900s, from $175 to......**250.00**
Hat, Sally Victor's Air Waves, bl felt, 1950s, from $65 to **85.00**
Hat, straw boater w/blk velvet band, Paris label, 1900s, from $150 to ...**200.00**
Hat, straw bonnet w/'modesty pc' at bk, 1850s, from $200 to.....**350.00**
Hat, toque bonnet, gathered Chantilly lace/blk sequins, 1890s, $100 to ..**175.00**
Hat, velvet helmet cloche w/mc smocked bands, 1930s, from $175 to.....**250.00**
Hat, wide-brim straw woven in lace pattern, 1920s, from $225 to..**300.00**
Hoop, metal rows held by fabric tape, 1858-63, EX, from $75 to ..**110.00**
Housecoat, lined brocade w/velvet trim, Mandarin collar, EX **50.00**
Jacket, blk cut velvet w/bead trim, dolman/s, 1900s **180.00**
Jacket, man's, buckskin, fringed sleeves, lined, 1930s **90.00**
Jacket, motorcycle; horsehide, 1920s...**385.00**
Jacket-bodice, bl silk velvet, 1890s, from $65 to **95.00**
Knickers, boy's, wool, 1930s, NM **20.00**
Nightgown, child's, wht linen w/pk trim, V-neck, n/s **20.00**
Pantaloons, lace trim, EX **50.00**
Petticoat, quilted blk sateen, EX quilting/feather meandering, 36"..**165.00**
Petticoat, quilted wht cotton, machine sewn/hand quilted, 26"..**220.00**
Petticoat, wht w/crochet insert, Vict **95.00**
Shawl, blk Chantilly lace w/overall floral pattern, 115x77x77"..**220.00**
Shawl, blk wool, blk satin embr, long silk fringe **75.00**
Shoes, blk fabric, 1850s, pr..**60.00**
Shoes, blk leather w/toe-to-ankle cutwork/jet beads, 1900, pr, $110 to ..**185.00**
Shoes, child's boots, high-button over-the-calf style, pr.................**75.00**
Shoes, high button; blk leather, pr...**55.00**
Shoes, linen high-top boots, 1900-09, pr, from $40 to...................**65.00**
Shoes, patent leather w/embr toe, 1860s, pr, from $150 to..........**250.00**
Skirt, blk taffeta, plt skirt, wide sweep hem, 1950s **25.00**
Skirt, tan cotton, walking type, ankle-length, 1910s, from $30 to..**65.00**
Slip, blk satin, 1930s, full-sz..**25.00**
Slip, wht cotton, tucks/embr top & punchwork straps, 1920s **65.00**
Sweater, bolero style, lav & gray wool, 1950s...............................**35.00**
Vest, man's, blk satin w/embr flowers, 1850s, from $45 to **75.00**
Vest, man's, wht linen, lined, pockets, EX......................................**25.00**

Cluthra

The name cluthra is derived from the Scottish word 'clutha,' meaning cloudy. Glassware by this name was first produced by J. Couper and Sons, England. Frederick Carder developed cluthra while at the Steuben Glass Works, and similar types of glassware were also made by Durand and Kimball. It is found in both solid and shaded colors and is characterized by a spotty appearance resulting from small air pockets trapped between its two layers.

Plate, pk to opal mottle, att Monart, 7"...**35.00**
Vase, bl w/clear ft, tapered, Kimball, #2011, 8½" **300.00**
Vase, gr bubbles on wht mottle, shouldered, Kimball, 6½" **250.00**
Vase, opal & amethyst mottle, att Kimball, 4¾" **250.00**

Vase, orange & wht mottle, invt baluster, Kimball, K37, 17½" ..**575.00**
Vase, orange/brn/opal mottle, tapered, Kimball, 12", pr **600.00**
Vase, spring gr, tapered, flared rim, Kimball, #1812, 12" **175.00**
Vase, yel & wht in clear, long neck, Kimball, 1949, 16" **350.00**

Coalport

In 1745 in Caughley, England, Squire Brown began a modest business fashioning crude pots and jugs from clay mined in his own fields. Tom Turner, a young potter who had apprenticed his trade at Worcester, was hired in 1772 to plan and oversee the construction of a 'proper' factory. Three years later he bought the business, which he named Caughley Coalport Porcelain Manufactory. Though the dinnerware he produced was meant to be only everyday china, the hand-painted florals, birds, and landscapes used to decorate the ware were done in exquisite detail and in a wide range of colors. In 1780 Turner introduced the Willow pattern which he produced using a newly perfected method of transfer printing. (Wares from the period between 1775 and 1799 are termed 'Caughley' or 'Salopian'; see section on Caughley.) John Rose purchased the Caughley factory from Thomas Turner in 1799, adding that holding to his own pottery which he had built two years before in Coalport. (It is from this point that the pottery's history that the wares are termed 'Coalport.') The porcelain produced there before 1814 was unmarked with very few exceptions. After 1820 some examples were marked with a '2' with an oversize top loop. The term 'Coalbrookdale' refers to a fine type of porcelain decorated in floral bas relief, similar to the work of Dresden.

After 1835 highly decorated ware with rich ground colors imitated the work of Sevres and Chelsea, even going so far as to copy their marks. From about 1895 until the 1920s, the mark in use was 'Coalport' over a crown with 'England A.D. 1750' indicating the date claimed as the founding, not the date of manufacture. From the 1920s until 1945, 'Made in England' over a crown and 'Coalport' below was used. Later the mark was 'Coalport' over a smaller crown with 'Made in England' in a curve below.

Each of the major English porcelain companies excelled in certain areas of manufacture. Coalport produced the finest 'jeweled' porcelain, made by picking up a heavy mixture of slip and color and dropping it onto the surface of the ware. These 'jewels' are perfectly spaced and are often graduated in size with the smaller 'jewels' at the neck or base of the vase. Some ware was decorated with very large 'jewels' resembling black opals or other polished stones. Such pieces are in demand by the advanced collector.

It is common to find considerable crazing in old Coalport, since the glaze was thinly applied to increase the brilliance of the colors. Many early vases had covers; look for a flat surface that would have supported a lid (just because it is gilded does not mean the vase never had one). Pieces whose lids are missing are worth about 40% less. Most lids had finials which have been broken and restored. You should deduct about 10% for a professional restoration on a finial.

In 1926 the Coalport Company moved to Shelton in Staffordshire and today belongs to a group headed by the Wedgwood Company. See also Indian Tree.

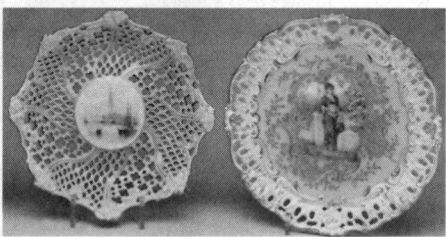

Plate, view of Venice, jewelled and pierced lobed and lozenge pattern border with foliate scrolls, ca 1900, 9½", $1,000.00; Plate, allegorical maiden at fountain, gilt foliate scrolls, and diapered panels along pierced and gilded rim, signed F.N. Sutton, ca 1900, 9¾", $550.00.

Cup & saucer, coral petals w/gold, 1948-59, from $100 to 125.00
Cup & saucer, demi; dk red w/turq & wht jewels, gold int, 1891-1939 ..225.00
Figurine, Christine, lady w/fan, bl dress, 20th C, 7⅜" 95.00
Teapot, flowers on 'marble,' dog spout, bird hdl, rpr, 8" 175.00
Trophy vase, bicentenary of St Leger 1776-1976, horseman, 12½"..300.00
Urn, floral w/gold lattice, bolted, 1914, 8½", NM......................175.00
Vase, turq & wht jewels in gilt on pk, gold scroll hdls, 7½" 1,150.00

Coca-Cola

    J.S. Pemberton, creator of Coca-Cola, originated his world-famous drink in 1886. From its inception the Coca-Cola Company began an incredible advertising campaign which has proven to be one of the most successful promotions in history. The quantity and diversity of advertising material put out by Coca-Cola in the last one hundred years is literally mind-boggling. From the beginning, the company has projected an image of wholesomeness and Americana. Beautiful women in Victorian costumes, teenagers and schoolchildren, blue- and white-collar workers, the men and women of the Armed Forces, and even Santa Claus have appeared in advertisements with a Coke in their hands. Some of the earliest collectibles include trays, syrup dispensers, gum jars, pocket mirrors, and calendars. Many of these items fetch prices in the thousands of dollars. Later examples include radios, signs, lighters, thermometers, playing cards, clocks, and toys — particularly toy trucks.

    In 1970 the Coca-Cola Company initialed a multimillion-dollar 'image-refurbishing campaign' which introduced the new 'Dynamic Contour' logo, a twisting white ribbon under the Coca-Cola and Coke trademarks. The new logo often serves as a cut-off point to the purist collector. Newer and very ardent collectors, however, relish the myriad of items marketed since that date, as they often cannot afford the high prices that the vintage pieces command. For more information we recommend *Petretti's Coca-Cola Collectibles Price Guide* (available from Nostalgia Publications whose address you will find under Auctions in the Directory); *BJ Summers' Guide to Coca-Cola, Third Edition,* and *B.J. Summers' Pocket Guide to Coca-Cola;* also *Coca-Cola Commemorative Bottles, Second Edition,* by Bob and Debra Henrich. You may wish to call our advisor for this category, Craig Stifter, at 630-789-5780; he is listed in the Directory under Illinois.

Key:
CC — Coca-Cola   tm — trademark
dc — diecut

Reproductions and Fantasies

    Beware of reproductions! Prices are given for the genuine original articles, but the symbol (+) at the end of some of the following lines indicate items that have been reproduced. Warning! The 1924, 1925, and 1935 calendars have been reproduced. They are identical in almost every way; only a professional can tell them apart. These are *very* deceiving! Watch for frauds: genuinely old celluloid items ranging from combs, mirrors, knives, and forks to doorknobs that have been recently etched with a new double-lined trademark. Still another area of concern deals with reproduction and fantasy items. A fantasy item is a novelty made to appear authentic with inscriptions such as 'Tiffany Studios,' 'Trans Pan Expo,' 'World's Fair,' etc. In reality, these items never existed as originals. For instance, don't be fooled by a Coca-Cola cash register; no originals are known to exist! Large mirrors for bars are being reproduced and are often selling for $10.00 to $50.00.

    Of the hundreds of reproductions (designated 'R' in the following examples) and fantasies (designated 'F') on the market today, these are the most deceiving.

Belt buckle, no originals thought to exist (F), up to 10.00
Bottle, dk amber, w/arrows, heavy, narrow spout (R)....................10.00

Bottle carrier, wood, yel w/red logo, holds 6 bottles (R)................10.00
Clock, Gilbert, regulator, battery-op, ¾-sz, NM+ (R)................175.00
Cooler, Glascock Jr, made by Coca-Cola USA (R) 350.00
Doorknob, glass etched w/tm (F) 3.00
Knife, bottle shape, 1970s, many variations (F), ea........................5.00
Knife, fork or spoon w/celluloid hdl, newly etched tm (F)................5.00
Letter opener, stamped metal, Coca-Cola for 5¢ (F) 3.00
Pocket watch, often old watch w/new face (R)...........................10.00
Pocketknife, yel & red, 1933 World's Fair (F)..............................2.00
Sign, cb, lady w/fur, dtd 1911, 9x11" (F) 3.00
Soda fountain glass holder, word 'Drink' no orig (R)......................5.00
Thermometer, bottle form, DONASCO, 17" (R)...........................10.00
Trade card, copy of 1905 'Bathtub' foldout, emb 1978 (R)...........25.00

    The following items have been reproduced and are among the most deceptive of all:
    Pocket mirrors from 1905, 1906, 1908, 1909, 1910, 1911, 1916, and 1920
    Trays from 1899, 1910, 1913, 1914, 1917, 1920, 1923, 1925, 1926, 1934, and 1937
    Tip trays from 1907, 1909, 1910, 1913, 1914, 1917, and 1920
    Knives: many versions of the German brass model
    Cartons: wood versions, yellow with logo
    Calendars: 1924, 1925, and 1935
    These items have been marketed:
    Brass thermometer, bottle shape, Taiwan, 24"
    Cast-iron toys (none ever made)
    Cast-iron door pull, bottle shape, made to look old
    Poster, Yes Girl (R)
    Button sign, has one round hole while original has four slots, most have bottle logo, 12", 16", 20" (R)
    Bullet trash receptacles (old cans with decals)
    Paperweight, rectangular, with Pepsin Gum insert
    1930 Bakelite radio, 24" tall, repro is lighter in weight than the original, of poor quality, and cheaply made
    1949 cooler radio (reproduced with tape deck)
    Tin bottle sign, 40"
    Fishtail die-cut tin sign, 20" long
    Straw holders (no originals exist)
    Coca-Cola bicycle with cooler, fantasy item: the piece has been totally made-up, no such original exists
    1914 calendar top, reproduction, 11¼x23¾", printed on smooth-finish heavy ivory paper
    Countless trays — most unauthorized (must read 'American Artworks; Coshocton, OH.')

Centennial Items

    The Coca-Cola Company celebrated its 100th birthday in 1986, and amidst all the fanfare came many new collectible items, all sporting the 100th-anniversary logo. These items are destined to become an important part of the total Coca-Cola collectible spectrum. The following pieces are among the most popular centennial items.

Bottle, gold-dipped, in velvet sleeve, 6½-oz....................................75.00
Bottle, Hutchinson, amber, Root Co, ½-oz, 3 in case..................375.00
Bottle, International, set of 9 in plexiglas case.............................500.00
Bottle, leaded crystal, 100th logo, 6½-oz, MIB.........................150.00
Medallion, bronze, 3" dia, w/box 100.00
Pin set, wood fr, 101 pins 300.00
Scarf, silk, 30x30"...40.00
Thermometer, glass cover, 14" dia, M................................35.00

Coca-Cola Originals

Ashtray, ceramic, rnd w/bottle lighter, 1950s, NM...................250.00

Ashtray, red Bakelite dish w/center rests, 1940s, NM+....................60.00
Award, Salesman of the Month, figure on bottle cap, 1930s, 6", EX..675.00
Badge, Bottlers' Conference, celluloid/tin, 1930s, 2½x2¾", EX+........125.00
Blotter, Cold Refreshment, bottle, 1937, NM....................35.00
Blotter, Play Refreshed, sporting theme, 1951, EX+ 18.00
Bookmark, cl heart shape, 1900, NM....................750.00
Bottle, display; glass 1923 Christmas, 1930s, 20", NM 375.00
Bottle, seltzer; 10-sided cobalt bl glass, w/top, 12¼", EX+ 400.00
Bottle carrier, aluminum 24-bottle, w/ad-on steel hdl, 4x12x17", EX+...150.00
Bottle carrier, cb 17¢ 4-pack, w/bottles, EX......................50.00
Bottle carrier, cb 25¢ 6-pack, Season's Greetings, 1930s, EX+....150.00
Bottle carrier, cb 6-pack w/wood grip on bail hdl, red, NM+ 50.00
Bottle holder, cb, red/wht, used in car, 1950s, NM+...............10.00
Bottle topper, We Let You See the Bottle, plastic button emblem, EX...750.00

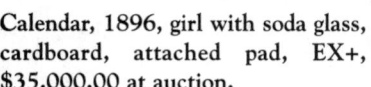

Calendar, 1896, girl with soda glass, cardboard, attached pad, EX+, $35,000.00 at auction.

Calendar, 1905, incomplete, EX+ 7,500.00
Calendar, 1907, complete, EX+..17,000.00
Calendar, 1908, incomplete, EX+ 4,200.00
Calendar, 1917, w/glass, complete, EX+..............................2,000.00
Calendar, 1925, complete, VG 425.00
Calendar, 1937, complete, NM 1,000.00
Calendar, 1945, complete, EX+..375.00
Carton display, pedestal w/sign, 1930s, 60", NM.....................825.00
Carton insert, dc cb Santa, Stock Up..., 1952, 22x13", NM 75.00
Clock, CC button, wht w/red dots, metal, 16", EX.....................500.00
Clock, CC in Bottles on dot, neon/rvpt/motion wheel, 1939, rnd, VG...1,500.00
Clock, Drink CC, serrated red dot decal, plastic, 13" sq, EX 200.00
Clock, Drink CC fishtail logo, gr ground, 15" sq, EX+................200.00
Clock, Drink CC in Bottles, rnd, Seth Thomas, 1930s, EX.....1,100.00
Clock, Things Go Better....button, plastic/metal, 16" sq, EX+....175.00
Cooler, airline; red, hinged lid/hdl/opener, 1950s, VG+..............235.00
Cuff links, bottle form, gold, mk 1/10 10k, ¾", NM, pr................50.00
Cutout for Children, Uncle Remus Story, uncut, 14x19", NM+..400.00
Decal, Drink CC in Bottles, red, curved corners, 9x15", NM 45.00
Dispenser, syrup; arched top, red, Drink C-C on sides, 1930s, NM+ ..1,500.00
Dispenser, syrup; frosted glass top w/ red porc base, 17", NM ..6,200.00
Display, cb, Friends for Life, fishing boy, Rockwell, 1935, 36", VG...2,500.00
Doll, Buddy Lee in uniform w/hat, compo, 1950s, EX+...............875.00
Door plate, porc, Come In! Have a CC, yel/wht script on red, 12", EX...325.00
Door pull, plastic bottle on metal bracket, 1950s, 8x2", NMIB ..425.00
Door push bar, Drink CC/D&R, silhouette girl, tin, 1939, 28", NM ..600.00
Fan, cb w/wood hdl, Have a Coke, Sprite Boy/bottle, 1950s, 9", EX.....80.00
Festoon, nautical, 9-pc, 1930s, EX+ 4,700.00
Festoon, sq dance, 5-pc, 1957, VG+ (in orig envelope)...........1,400.00
Game, Age Cards, 1928, NM (in orig envelope)......................600.00
Game, Safety & Danger, 1938, complete, EX+............................100.00
Glass, modified flare, no tm on tail of C, 1923-25, EX+................50.00
Light fixture, milk glass globe w/tassel, 1930s, all orig, NM+ ..3,500.00
Lighter, Blue-Bird musical, by Hadson, 2¼", NMIB....................200.00

Match holder, vending machine replica holds 12 packs, NM 160.00
Menu board, tin, silhouette girl, 1941, 28x20", EX....................425.00
Menu board, wood Kay Displays w/metal bottle, 8 slots, 17x35", NM..1,875.00
Needle case, cb, 1924, 3x2" (closed), EX+................................35.00
Pin, Safe Driver, cloisonne fishtail logo, mk 1/20 GF, 1", NM+..185.00
Playing cards, Be Really Refreshed, masquerade party, 1960, NMIB......165.00
Playing cards, Welcome Friend, Old Man Winter, 1958, M (VG box).100.00
Pocket mirror, cat's head, cb, 1920s, 2½", NM 600.00
Pocket mirror, girl w/bottle, 1916, oval, EX............................200.00
Pocketknife, brass, 2-blade w/corkscrew, Kaster, 1905-15, EX....385.00
Postcard, CC girl, 1910, NM+...775.00
Poster, Dancing Lady, Joan Crawford/Clark Gable, 1930s, EX.1,900.00
Puzzle, jigsaw; 2000 pcs, NMIB...25.00
Radio, floor cooler form, red plastic, 1950s, 10", EX+.................700.00
Radio, vending machine form, Drink CC, 1963, VG 65.00
Sign, arrow, dc tin, 2-sided, Ice Cold CC Sold Here, 1927, 30", G...380.00
Sign, bottle, dc porc, 12½", VG+...145.00
Sign, bottle carton (6), dc tin, D&R, dtd 6-51, 13x11", VG+....525.00
Sign, button, porc, CC lettered over bottle, red, 24" dia, EX+ 560.00
Sign, button, tin, Drink CC in Bottles, red, 16" dia, EX+...........400.00
Sign, button, tin, Drink CC/Sign of Good Taste, red, 16" dia, EX+..375.00
Sign, cb, Betty, 1914, 41x26", VG...650.00

Sign, cardboard, diving board girl, 1939, 50x29", EX, $650.00.
(Photo courtesy Craig Stifter)

Sign, cb, Drink CC/D&R, dbl bottles, tin fr, 1920s, 21x60", NM..1,450.00
Sign, cb, Friendly Pause, 3 girls w/bottles, 1948, 27x16", NM+ 1,550.00
Sign, cb, Have a Coke, bottle on iceberg, 1944, 20x36", NM.....300.00
Sign, cb, Hello Refreshment, girl being served, 1942, 20x36", NM+...1,800.00
Sign, cb, Hospitality, couples at open fridge, fr, 1948, 26x16", EX ...375.00
Sign, cb, Pause!, clown & ice skater, 1950s, 27x16", NM+ 2,800.00
Sign, cb, Shop Refreshed!, lady shopper, fr, 1949, 11x13", NM..500.00
Sign, cb, Sign of Good Taste, 2 bottles/saddle, 1956, 27x16", NM+..450.00
Sign, cb, The Gift for Thirst, Santa/family, 1952, 11x23", EX+....40.00
Sign, cb, Things Go Better..., phone girl, fr, 1960s, 27x16", VG+..250.00
Sign, cb, Tingling Refreshment, girl w/bottle, 1931, 40x23", EX ...1,500.00
Sign, cb, Wallace Berry, 1934, 30x14", VG+ 1,730.00
Sign, cb, You Taste It's Quality, girl/blossoms, 1942, 20x36", NM...1,150.00
Sign, cb cutout, Stop for a Pause/Go Refreshed, cop, 1937, 32x42", G+..1,050.00
Sign, cb hanger, Cold Refreshment, diagonal, 1937, 24" sq, NM...1,500.00
Sign, cb stand-up, Navy service girl w/bottle, 1943, 18", NM .1,000.00
Sign, cb stand-up, Santa, For Food/Fun/Friends, 1950s, 20", EX+....130.00
Sign, cb stand-up, Santa, Greetings, w/letter, 1945, 14", NM+ ..375.00
Sign, cb stand-up, Santa, Greetings From CC, 1948, 14", NM+ ...350.00
Sign, cb stand-up, Wayne Gretsky, life-sz, NM+ 75.00
Sign, cb stand-up, woman riding aquaplane, dc trifold, 1922, EX ..6,000.00
Sign, cb trolley, Around the Corner..., 1927, 11x21", EX+.......2,600.00
Sign, cb trolley, 4 seasons, 1923, 10x20", NM 4,000.00

Sign, cl, Drink CC/Coke/Ask for..., 1940s, 9" dia, NM **575.00**
Sign, Edgebrite light-up clock (rnd or sq), 1950s, 9x20", EX **700.00**
Sign, Edgebrite motion light-up, Pause, 1950s, 9x20", VG **850.00**
Sign, fishtail, dc tin, CC, wht on red, 12x26", NM **250.00**
Sign, flange, tin, Drink CC emblem, filigree top, 1937, 13x20", EX...**425.00**
Sign, flange, tin, Drink CC w/bottle on yel dot, 1949, 21x24", EX...**400.00**
Sign, flange, tin, Enjoy CC in Bottles, red, 1950s, 18" dia, NM .**770.00**
Sign, glass, Refresh Yourself/Drink CC, 1927, 6x12", VG+..........**325.00**
Sign, neon, CC Classic..., palm tree, 1980s, 28" dia, NM+ ...**1,700.00**
Sign, paper, Refreshing, button/bottle in snow/icicles, 19x57", EX **450.00**
Sign, paper, Treat Yourself Right, man w/bottle, 1920s, 20x12", EX **550.00**
Sign, porc, CC Sold Here Ice Cold, curved corners, 1955, 12x29", EX.**200.00**
Sign, porc, Drink CC, wht on red, 1910s, 18x45", EX+..........**1,000.00**
Sign, porc, Fountain Service emblem w/taps, 1930s, 14x27", VG+ ..**1,500.00**
Sign, ribbon, dc tin, Sign of Good Taste, red on yel, 10x42", EX .**75.00**
Sign, tin, Drink CC/D&R, couple w/bottle, 1942, 20x28", EX+ ...**550.00**
Sign, tin, Enjoy CC on red/bottle on wht inset, wht sf, 12x32", EX......**320.00**
Sign, tin, Ice Cold CC Sold Here, shows bottle, 1914, 20x28", NM .**2,400.00**
Sign, tin, Ice Cold CC Sold Here, 1932, 20" dia, NM+ **1,250.00**
Sign, tin, Sign of Good Taste fishtail/bottle, sf, 12x32", EX........**175.00**
Sign, tin, Sprite Boy/bottle/button on gold, 1950s, 12" dia, M ..**2,100.00**
Sign, tin, 6-Bottle Carton 27¢, shows 6-pack, 1930s, 60x36", VG+ ...**1,000.00**
String holder, Take Home in Cartons, red, 1930s, NM............**1,000.00**
Syrup can, 1-gal, paper label, CC on wht dot on red, EX+ **120.00**
Syrup jug, stoneware w/paper label, early 1900s, rare, NM **2,750.00**
Thermometer, dial, Drink CC, bottle outline, 1948, 12" dia, NM+ ...**700.00**
Thermometer, porc, Coke Refreshes, 1950s, 36", EX+ **1,450.00**
Thermometer, tin, bottle form, 29", NM......................**100.00**
Thermometer, tin, dbl bottles, 1941, 16", G..................**100.00**
Thermometer, tin, silhouette girl, 1939, 16", EX+................**400.00**
Thermometer, 1923 Christmas bottle shape, 1931, 17", G..........**150.00**
Tie bar, deliveryman figure w/case at 1 end, SP, 1930s, 1¾", EX+..**50.00**
Tip tray, 1903, VG...**900.00**
Tip tray, 1909, EX+..**875.00**
Tip tray, 1910, NM+ **1,540.00**
Tip tray, 1916, EX+ **275.00**
Toy bus, tin friction, Ashi Toys (ATC)/Japan, 14½", NM.......**1,300.00**
Toy dispneser, #16, w/4 plastic flared glasses, NMIB....................**135.00**
Toy picnic set, red plastic 6x5x4" cooler w/accessories, EX+.......**375.00**
Toy truck, A-frame, pressed steel, Metalcraft #171, 1932, 11", EX+ ...**800.00**
Toy truck, friction delivery, tin, Marusan #3431, 1956-57, NM+ ..**750.00**
Toy truck, friction squash cab, tin, yel, Linemar, 1950s, 3", EX+...**140.00**
Toy truck, stake bed w/Sprite Boy logo, tin, Marx #1088, 1956, NMIB..**1,150.00**
Trade card, folding, girl in tub/girl serving 2 gents, 1907, VG+ **1,250.00**
Whistle, cb bottle shape, 3¾", EX.........................**445.00**
Whistle, metal, Pure as Sunlight, red on yel, 2", EX...................**140.00**
Whistle, wood, cylindrical, Pure as Sunlight, 1½", EX..............**150.00**

Trays

Values are given for trays in excellent plus condition (C8+). Those that have been reproduced are marked with a (+). The 1934 Weismuller and O'Sullivan tray has been reproduced at least three times. To be original, it will have a black back and must say 'American Artworks, Coshocton, Ohio.' It was not reproduced by Coca-Cola in the 1950s.

All 10½x13½" original serving trays produced from 1910 to 1942 are marked with a date, Made in USA, and the American Artworks Inc., Coshocton Ohio. All original trays of this format (1910 – 40) had REG TM in the tail of the C.

1897, Victorian Lady, 9¼" dia, VG.......................**15,000.00**
1901, Hilda Clark, 9¾", VG...............................**4,000.00**
1903, Hilda Clark, oval, 18½x15", EX.....................**6,000.00**
1905, Lillian Russell, glass or bottle, 10½x13¼", EX..............**3,500.00**

1906, Juanita, glass or bottle, oval, 13¼x10½", EX.............**2,200.00**
1907, Relieves Fatigue, 10½x13¼", NM **4,000.00**
1907, Relieves Fatigue, 13½x16½", EX **3,600.00**
1908, Topless, Wherever Ginger Ale..., 12¼" dia, NM **10,000.00**
1909, St Louis Fair, 10½x13¼", EX **1,800.00**
1909, St Louis Fair, 13½x16½", NM **3,000.00**
1910, Coca-Cola Girl, Hamilton King, 10½x13¼", VG............**850.00**
1914, Betty, oval, 12¼x15¼", EX+...........................**575.00**
1914, Betty, 10½x13¼", EX.................................**600.00**
1916, Elaine, 8½x19", NM..................................**600.00**
1920, Garden Girl, oval, 10½x13¼", EX+.....................**800.00**
1921, Autumn Girl, oval, 10½x13¼", EX+.....................**800.00**
1922, Summer Girl, 10½x13¼", NM...........................**1,100.00**
1923, Flapper Girl, 10½x13¼", NM..........................**500.00**
1924, Smiling Girl, brn rim, 10½x13¼", EX **650.00**
1924, Smiling Girl, maroon rim, 10½x13¼", EX **850.00**
1925, Party, 10½x13¼", NM.................................**600.00**
1926, Golfers, 10½x13¼", VG...............................**700.00**
1927, Curbside Service, 10½x13¼", EX.......................**750.00**

1928, Bobbed Hair, 10½x13¼", EX+, $650.00.

1929, Girl in Swimsuit w/Glass, 10½x13¼", EX+................**450.00**
1930, Swimmer, 10½x13¼", EX...............................**425.00**
1930, Telephone, 10½x13¼", NM.............................**650.00**
1931, Boy w/Sandwich & Dog, 10½x13¼", NM....................**1,100.00**
1932, Girl in Swimsuit on Beach, Hayden, 10½x13¼", EX+ **625.00**
1933, Francis Dee, 10½x13¼", NM...........................**700.00**
1934, Weismuller & O'Sullivan, 10½x13¼", NM................**1,100.00**
1935, Madge Evans, 10½x13¼", NM...........................**500.00**
1936, Hostess, 10½x13¼", NM...............................**575.00**
1937, Running Girl, 10½x13¼", NM..........................**350.00**
1938, Girl in the Afternoon, 10½x13¼", NM **300.00**
1939, Springboard Girl, 10½x13¼", NM......................**350.00**
1940, Sailor Girl, 10½x13¼", NM...........................**400.00**
1941, Ice Skater, 10½x13¼", NM............................**450.00**
1942, Roadster, 10½x13¼", NM+.............................**500.00**
1950s, Girl w/Wind in Hair, screen bkground, 10½x13¼", M....**100.00**
1950s, Girl w/Wind in Hair, solid bkground, 10½x13¼", NM ...**225.00**
1955, Menu Girl, 10½x13¼", M..............................**65.00**
1957, Rooster, 10½x13¼", NM...............................**175.00**
1957, Umbrella Girl, 10½x13¼", M..........................**375.00**
1961, Pansy Garden, 10½x13¼", NM..........................**30.00**

Vendors

Though interest in Coca-Cola machines of the 1949 – 1959 era rose dramatically over the last few years, values currently seem to have leveled off and actually dropped 15% to 20%. The major manufacturers of these curved-top, 5¢ and 10¢ machines were Vendo (V), Vendorlator (VMC), Cavalier (C or CS), and Jacobs. Prices are for machines in excellent or better condition, complete and working. They vary greatly according to geographical location.

Cavalier, model #CS72, EX orig	**1,400.00**
Cavalier, model #CS72, M rstr	**3,200.00**
Cavalier, model #C27, M rstr	**2,800.00**
Cavalier, model #C27, orig	**1,200.00**
Cavalier, model #C51, EX orig	**850.00**
Cavalier, model #C51, M rstr	**1,800.00**
Jacobs, model #26, EX	**1,200.00**
Jacobs, model #26, M rstr	**2,500.00**
Vendo, model #23, EX orig	**900.00**
Vendo, model #39, EX orig	**900.00**
Vendo, model #39, M, rstr	**2,500.00**
Vendo, model #44, EX orig	**2,500.00**
Vendo, model #44, M rstr	**3,750.00**
Vendo, model #56, EX orig	**1,400.00**
Vendo, model #56, M rstr	**3,200.00**
Vendo, model #80, EX orig	**600.00**
Vendo, model #80, M rstr	**1,250.00**
Vendo, model #81, EX orig	**1,400.00**
Vendo, model #81, M rstr	**3,200.00**
Vendorlator, model #27, EX orig	**1,200.00**
Vendorlator, model #27, rstr (w/stand)	**2,750.00**
Vendorlator, model #27A, EX orig	**900.00**
Vendorlator, model #27A, M rstr	**2,000.00**
Vendorlator, model #33, EX orig	**1,100.00**
Vendorlator, model #33, M rstr	**2,250.00**
Vendorlator, model #44, EX orig	**1,500.00**
Vendorlator, model #44, M rstr	**3,200.00**
Vendorlator, model #72, EX orig	**1,000.00**
Vendorlator, model #72, M rstr	**1,800.00**

Coffee Grinders

Coffee mills, also called grinders, are becoming more and more popular with eager collectors and those simply wishing to add to their antique kitchen motif. Coffee mills fall into several basic types and the same mill can sometimes be referred to in various ways. Box mills, also called lap, or table mills are generally made of wood. True wall mills are usually of iron and have a cup or receiver of some kind to catch the ground coffee. Side mills, really made to be mounted to a post or the side of a cabinet are usually made completely of iron, or iron with a tin hopper. Canister mills have grinding mechanisms made of iron and can have hoppers made of either tin, sheet metal, glass, or porcelain. Upright iron mills can have one wheel, two wheels, one wheel and one crank, or just one crank alone, and can range in height from around twelve inches up to six or seven feet in height and weigh in excess of three hundred pounds. Some mills were made to be clamped to the edge of a table. And of cource, the final incarnation came with the advent of electricity in the form of small electric mills available to the homemaker up to the large industrial models for commercial use.

The advent of the Internet and online auctions has brought out both the good and bad among collectible coffee mills. Doing your homework is the most important factor when purchasing coffee mills online. Many reproductions and modern examples are found online that are represented as genuine old coffee mills. It should also be remembered that many companies produced certain models in the hundreds of thousands that still exist in vast numbers and therefore are quite common. Few mills are actually scarce or rare, and there are no known miniature salesmen's samples. Mills most often identified as salesmen's samples are in fact toys. This does not, however, diminish their desirability. Grist mills, for corn or other grains, are often incorrectly identified as coffee mills. While generally not as valuable as coffee mills, they are often found in the collections of coffee mill enthusiasts. Our advisor for this category is Shane Branchcomb; he is listed in the Directory under Virginia.

Key: adj — adjustment

Left to right: All-iron table mills, Russell & Erwin box mill #90 with two patent dates: Sept 28, 1875, and June 11, 1878, 5½", EX, $600.00; A. Kedrick & Sons, English, ca 1860, 6½", NM, $525.00; Landers, Frary & Clark, ca 1880, 4½", EX, $425.00. (Photo courtesy Shane Branchcomb)

A Kenrick & Sons No 1, lap, CI w/brass hopper, CI drw, EX	125.00
Adams Pat, lap, pewter hopper, wood w/orig knob	155.00
Arcade, Favorite No 7, side, CI w/orig lid, grind adj front, VG	95.00
Arcade, Imperial No 999, decal, 1-lb box, EX	155.00
Arcade, IXL, table, ornate CI hopper, hdl on side, 1-lb, EX	325.00
Arcade, Jewel, canister, rectangular glass hopper, w/lid, EX	695.00
Arcade, Our Baby (toy), label, mini, EX	95.00
Arcade, Queen, glass canister & receiver, CI works, EX	325.00
Arcade, Royal, canister, CI cup, tin hopper, EX	95.00
Arcade, X-Ray, CI works, wood hopper w/glass, EX	175.00
Arcade Crystal, #9010, CI, Art Deco, glass hopper, EX	175.00
Arcade No 3, canister, CI w/glass hopper, orig lid, EX	155.00
Arcade No 4, canister, CI, glass hopper, orig lid, wall mt, EX	175.00
Arcade No 5, side, CI, Pat June '94, VG	95.00
Arcade No 700, lap, w/dust cover, Sears 1908 catalog, EX	155.00
Bell, canister, similar to Golden Rule, CI & wood, EX	475.00
Belmont, Lightning No 23, canister, tin & CI, EX	225.00
Blackmsith-made, funnel shape, 1-hdl, open hopper, wall mt	345.00
Bronson-Walton, Ever Ready No 2, w/cup, Pat 1905, EX	165.00
Bronson-Walton, Silver Lake, canister, glass hopper, EX	485.00
Cavanaugh Bros, table, front fill, 1-lb, EX	225.00
Cavanaugh's, table, CI, ornate legs, wood box, EX	525.00
Clawson & Clark No 1, CI, dbl grind, Pat 1886, 6" wheel	525.00
Coles Mfg No 7, counter, CI, Pat 1887, 16" wheels, 27", EX	825.00
Coles No 00, CI, wall mt w/CI cup, NM	295.00
Daisy No 867 (toy), CI top, wood box & drw, orig decal, mini, EX	85.00
Elgin Nat'l, floor, silver hopper, 24" wheels	1,500.00
Elgin Nat'l No 44, CI, red, w/eagle & pan, 15" wheels, 24"	775.00
Elgin Nat'l No 46, orig pnt/decals, 12" wheels, EX	675.00
Enterprise, Boss, floor, CI, closed hopper, 1873, 39" wheels	3,675.00
Enterprise No 1, counter, open hopper, hdl, Pat 1873, 11", VG	225.00
Enterprise No 1, counter, orig pnt/decals, side hdl, 1898	235.00
Enterprise No 2, orig pnt/decal, 2 8¾" wheels, EX	825.00
Enterprise No 3, counter, CI, wood drw, orig pnt/decals	625.00
Enterprise No 7, counter, CI, orig pnt, 17" wheel w/eagle, VG	825.00
Enterprise No 16, floor, CI, orig pnt, CI hopper	4,100.00
Enterprise No 50, single-wheel grist mill, NM	100.00
Enterprise No 212, floor, CI, 2 wheels, orig pnt, 30½", EX	3,000.00
Enterprise No 300, very heavy, wall mt, w/catcher, EX	495.00
Fairbanks Morse, floor, CI, brass hopper, 2 wheels, 27", EX	3,100.00
Golden Rule, canister, w/orig glass, CI front, wood box, EX	425.00
Grand Union Tea, table, CI sq base, rnd hopper, mfg Griswold	495.00
Hart, Henry C; Detroit Mich, CI, wall mt, NM	95.00
Hobart No 265, electric, covered hopper	375.00

J Fisher Warranted, lap, dvtl walnut, pewter hopper, unique.......**265.00**
L'il Tot (toy), CI hopper & drw front, wood box, decal, mini.......**95.00**
Landers, Frary & Clark, canister, CI & tin, Pat 1905, VG...........**80.00**
Landers, Frary & Clark, CI, rnd, sq base, ornate, Pat 1875.........**600.00**
Landers, Frary & Clark, Crown #11, CI, decals, side crank, EX.......**225.00**
Landers, Frary & Clark, Crown #20, counter, 8" wheels, EX......**900.00**
Landers, Frary & Clark #24, w/orig mk hopper, NM...................**155.00**
Logan & Strobridge, Franco-American, lap, ornate CI hopper...**125.00**
Luther, side, CI, tin hopper, brass plate, Pat 1843........................**225.00**
MJB, tin canister, wall mt w/lid & cup, EX................................**165.00**
Nat'l Specialty, CI, brass hopper, 2 12½" wheels.....................**1,100.00**
Nat'l Specialty, CI, single crank, 12", EX..................................**375.00**
Nat'l Specialty No 0, table, CI, covered hopper, clamps on........**165.00**
Nat'l Specialty No 7, CI, 16½" wheels, EX...............................**1,000.00**
None Such, Bronson Co Cleveland OH, table, tin, pnt, EX.........**95.00**
Olde Thompson, lap, orig drw, EX...**65.00**
Parker, Challenge Fast Grind No 555, table, orig, 1-lb, EX.........**125.00**
Parker, Eagle No 50, side, CI, Pat 1860, EX.............................**85.00**
Parker (mk CPCo) No 1350, CI, wall mt, NM............................**85.00**
Parker No 260 Columbia, table, side grind, 1-lb, EX...................**350.00**
Parker No 350, side, orig lid, Pat 4/1876, EX............................**165.00**
Parker No 446, wall mt..**185.00**
Parker No 3000, drw, eagle on top, 11" wheels, orig.................**725.00**
Parker No 5000, counter, CI, Pat 1897, 12" wheels, 17", VG.....**750.00**
Parker Union, side, CI, gear drive, Pat 1855, EX.........................**135.00**
Peck, Stow & Wilcox Internat'l #360, lap..................................**155.00**
PS&W No 3500, side, CI, orig lid, EX.......................................**145.00**
Queen (toy), CI hopper & drw front, wood box, decal, mini........**95.00**
Richmond, side, CI, Chatham Conn (2 szs made), EX, ea..........**295.00**
Royal Blue, Supplee Hdwe Co, CI, tin hopper, EX.....................**195.00**
Russell & Erwin, Diamond, CI, bronze finish, rare......................**350.00**
Russell & Erwin Mfg Co No 1008, CI hopper, wood box..............**95.00**
Selsor, Cook & Co, lap, name on hdl, Pat 1859.........................**165.00**
Silvers No 1, CI, dbl-grind, w/cup, EX......................................**600.00**
Simmon's Hdwe, Delmar Coffee, table, CI cover.......................**295.00**
Simmons Defiance, label, CI fill lid, 1-lb box, EX.......................**125.00**
Star, canister, tin w/CI works, Pat 1910, VG..............................**90.00**
Star No 7, counter, CI, w/pan, 2-wheel, VG...............................**525.00**
Steinfield, canister, CI works, glass jar, orig lid, EX....................**165.00**
Stuttle, Henry; #2, CI, tin hopper, Pat 2/20/77, EX...................**295.00**
Sun, Success No 25, cylinder, 2 different szs, EX, ea..................**275.00**
Sun Mfg No 1080, orig lid & drw, 1-lb box, EX/NM....................**125.00**
Swift No 13, counter, orig tin drw, red pnt, 12" wheels, 19".......**475.00**
Swift No 15, counter, orig decals/pnt, Pat 1875, 19" wheels....**1,100.00**
Swift No 26, Lane Brothers, floor, CI, 2 wheels........................**2,500.00**
Tillmann's, Hawaiian Coffee, CI, wall mt, EX.............................**195.00**
Universal No 109, blk tin w/gr decal, Pat 1905, NM....................**75.00**
Vandergrift, side hinged, CI, ca 1870, complete, EX..................**185.00**
Waddel, A-17, CI, sunflower design, wall mt, EX........................**250.00**
Waddel, A-9, orig drw & label, box type, EX..............................**125.00**
Wilson, Increase, side, CI & tin...**70.00**
Wright, John; CI, red or gr, ca 1968, 2 6¾" wheels, NM............**350.00**
Wrightsville Hdwe, Brighton, label, 1-lb box, EX.......................**95.00**
Wrightsville Hdwe, Peerless No 200, canister, CI/glass, EX........**160.00**
WW Weaver Warranted, dvtl walnut, pewter hopper, ca 1830...**225.00**

Coin-Operated Machines

Coin-operated machines may be the fastest-growing area of collector interest in today's market. Many machines are bought, restored, and used for home entertainment. Older examples from the turn of the century and those with especially elaborate decoration and innovative features are most desirable.

The www.GameRoomAntiques.com website and *Antique Amusements, Slot Machine, and Jukebox Gazette* are excellent sources of information for those interested in coin-operated machines; see the Clubs, Newsletters, and Catalogs section of the Directory for publishing information. Jackie and Ken Durham are our advisors; they are listed in the Directory under the District of Columbia.

Arcade Machines

ABT Challenger, wood & aluminum case, 10x24x15", G..........**395.00**
Ask Me Another Question, 1939, EX...**900.00**
Caille Happy Home, VG...**1,500.00**
Chicago Coin Pistol, 1950s, EX orig...**1,400.00**
Chicago Coin Steam Shovel, EX...**2,295.00**
Clam Shell Mutoscope, orig marquee, Caught in Act reel, EX...**5,500.00**
Digger, floor model, orig Erie crane, new cabinet, EX..............**2,000.00**
Exhibit Supply Little Gypsy, penny drop, 1920s/30s, EX..........**1,450.00**
Gatter 1¢ Ten-Pin Bowling, 1930s, 9x22½x8½", VG................**715.00**
Grip Tester, table top, rpt case, 1940s......................................**495.00**
Hoops Ball Flip, ping-pong ball game, countertop, EX orig.....**1,300.00**
Internat'l Mutoscope 1¢ Shoot-a-Scope, CI, 8½x16x18½", G...**2,300.00**
Jr Deputy Sheriff Pistol Ranges, 1940-50s, EX orig...................**900.00**
Kissin Kupid Fortune Teller, lights up, EX................................**1,800.00**
Lindy Striker, EX...**300.00**
Mills Seal flip, 1390s, 32", EX...**2,500.00**
Miniature Steam Shovel, floor model w/marquee, EX..............**3,500.00**
Novelty Merchandiser, floor model, EX orig.............................**3,800.00**
Over the Top, skill game, wall type, 1930s, rstr, 20"................**1,295.00**
Peeping Tom House, EX...**1,500.00**
Sidewalk Engineer Crane, EX...**1,795.00**
Wee Gee Fortune Teller, wall machine, penny drop, EX.........**1,350.00**

Jukeboxes

The coin-operated phonograph of the early 1900s paved the way for the jukeboxes of the '20s. Seeburg was first on the market with an automatic eight-tune phonograph. By the 1930s Wurlitzer was the top name in the industry with dealerships all over the country. As a result of the growing ranks of competitors, the '40s produced the most beautiful machines made. Wurlitzers from this era are probably the most popularly sought-after models on the market today. The model #1015 of 1946 is considered the all-time classic and often brings prices in excess of $8,000.00.

Rockola #1422, light-up plastics and flashing lights, 1940s, EX original, $4,000.00.

AMI Continental II, 1962, rstr................................6,500.00
AMI MM-4, 200 selections, 1970, EX 1,000.00
Mills Panoram Movie, 1930s, rstr........................16,500.00
Rockola #1422, rstr..6,000.00
Rockola #1426, ca 1947, EX orig 3,300.00
Rockola #1428, red & gr w/grated front, 60", VG 2,500.00
Rockola #1493 Princess, EX orig..........................4,500.00
Rockola #490 Supersound, EX orig 1,500.00
Seeburg #100A, 1949-50, EX orig.........................4,500.00
Seeburg #100B Select-O-Matic 100, 1950, 54", EX 3,500.00
Seeburg #100W, 1953, EX orig..............................4,000.00
Seeburg B, rstr...6,000.00
Seeburg C, rstr...7,000.00
Seeburg G, rstr...6,600.00
Seeburg J, rstr..6,400.00
Seeburg M100-A, zebra wood, ca 1949, rstr...........5,000.00
Seeburg Q160, 1959, G...1,800.00
Seeburg SPS2 Matador, EX orig 2,000.00
Seeburg STD4 Mardi Gras, 1977, rstr 2,000.00
Seeburg Sunstar, EX orig......................................2,000.00
Seeburg USC1 Bandshell, EX orig 1,800.00
Supotone 25¢ Movie, 1960s, EX 4,000.00
Wurlitzer #1015, Bubbler, plays 78s, 60", VG..........7,500.00
Wurlitzer #1015, rstr..8,900.00
Wurlitzer #1050, colorful Plexiglas, plays 45s, 60", EX 2,300.00
Wurlitzer #2304, 1955, EX....................................3,000.00
Wurlitzer #2610, 33 & 45 rpms, VG 2,400.00

Slot Machines

Jennings 1¢ Little Duke, 1933, rstr........................3,200.00
Jennings 5¢ Duchess, w/mint vendor, 1934, rstr 2,600.00
Jennings 5¢ Good Luck, console, 1930s, 44", rstr.......2,800.00
Jennings 5¢ Light-Up Sun Chief, EX orig..................3,300.00
Jennings 5¢ Victory Chief, gold-pnt wood front on oak base, 28", G ..1,380.00
Jennings 10¢ Club Chief, rstr 3,700.00

Jennings Sun Chief 25¢, wood cased cast aluminum front, three-reel, lighted front, 28x15½", EX original, $2,500.00.

Keeney 5¢ Black Dragon, plays up to 7 coins, EX orig.............1,800.00
Keeney 25¢ Sweet Shawnee, plays up to 7 coins, 1960s, EX orig ..800.00
Mills Dewey Jackpot, CI w/roaring griffin head, Pat 1898, 66", VG..12,000.00
Mills Futurity, EX 4,000.00
Mills Hole-In-One, EX rstr....................................3,000.00
Mills 1¢ Skyscraper, 1936, EX orig.........................3,000.00
Mills 5¢ Blue-Bell Hightop, 3-reel, Deco style, CI/wood, 26", VG ...2,500.00
Mills 5¢ Chrome Front Hightop 777, 1948-51, M 3,200.00
Mills 5¢ Firebird QT, 1930s, rstr............................3,000.00
Mills 5¢ Horse Head Bonus, CI, 1937, EX orig 3,500.00
Mills 5¢ Lion's Head (Wolf's Head), 1932, EX orig 3,500.00
Mills 5¢ Vest Pocket, 1938, EX orig........................750.00

Mills 10¢ Buckley Criss Cross, 1948, EX orig, w/tokens...........3,000.00
Mills 25¢ Castle Front, 1933-38, rstr 3,000.00
Mills 25¢ Golden Nugget, 1947, prof rstr 3,000.00
Mills 25¢ Lion's Head, 1932, M rstr........................3,000.00
Mills 25¢ Roman Head, 1932, M rstr.......................3,000.00
Mills 25¢ Silver Place (Glorified Hightop), rstr..........2,900.00
Mills 25¢ War Eagle, 1931, rstr..............................3,200.00
Pace 10¢ Pocket-Rocket Comet, 1940, EX orig.........2,495.00
United Coin 25¢ Big Six, console, 1960s, EX orig.....2,000.00
Watling 10¢ Rol-A-Top Checkerboard (Castlefront), 1947, EX orig..6,000.00

Trade Stimulators

Bell Boy, 1930s, rstr..2,495.00
Bluebird, penny flip, w/gum vendor, ca 1920, EX 695.00
BT Mfg Big Game Hunter, quarter-sawn oak, 18", VG............1,375.00
Cent-a-Pat, aluminum case, 3-reel, w/gumball vendor, EX.........450.00
Comet, Art Deco, 3-reel, EX orig............................395.00
Daval Bell Slide, orig award card & reel strips, rstr, rare 975.00
Daval 5¢ Free Play, cigarette reels, gum vendor, 1940s, EX.........695.00
Depose Match Dispenser, CI w/rotating brass game wheel, 12½" ..2,000.00
Exhibit Half Mile, horse race, 8x13x19", EX orig.".............1,950.00
Fey 3-in-1 Dice, scarce, 1927, EX...........................2,750.00
Five Jacks Penny Drop, oak/aluminum, rstr, 16x15x9".............1,250.00
Garden City Pick-a-Pack, windmill front, 1930s, EX.............1,795.00
Groetchen High Stakers, horse race, 5-reel, 11", rstr case.........900.00
Jennings Grandstand, w/token dispenser & gum vendor, 1930s, 14", EX..1,300.00
Jennings Superior Confection, cigarette reels, w/vendor, EX 895.00
Keeney Steeple Chase, marble race, CI base, 1931, 18", EX 800.00
Lattimore Game O Skill, coin flip, late 1890s, rstr...................1,950.00
Liberty 5¢, cast aluminum, 3-reel, w/gumball vendor, 9x10½", G ..395.00
Mills Kounter King, w/reel window shutters & gum vendor, 1930s, EX ...975.00
Never Lose, penny drop, rpt case, ca 1940, 20", EX 395.00
Rockola Radio Wizard, single reel, w/cards, 1930s, EX orig.....1,295.00
Saratoga 1¢ Horse Race, glass dome top, orig decal, VG+.........2,300.00
Skipper, penny drop, clipper ship on front, 1940s-50s, EX 395.00
Standard Games Windmill, penny drop, ca 1946, 17", EX orig...875.00
Turf Flash, horse race, w/gumball vendor, 18", EX orig 2,450.00
5 Jacks, cast aluminum/glass, 16x18", EX................................1,495.00

Vendors

Vending machines sold a product or a service. They were already in common usage by 1900 selling gum, cigars, matches, and a host of other commodities. Peanut and gum-ball machines are especially popular today. The most valuable are those with their original finish and decals. Older machines made of cast iron are especially desirable, while those with plastic globes have little collector value. When buying unrestored peanut machines, beware of salt damage.

Basketball 1¢ Gum, gumball shoots into basket & down chute, G..300.00
Columbus Model 25 Ohio Blue Tip 1¢ Matches, 2-column, CI/metal, EX ..225.00
Jumbo 1¢, peanuts, circus elephant, 15", NM 400.00
Lil' Abner & Daisy Mae Vendor Bar, 22¾x12½x12½", EX........650.00
Macke 1¢ Cigarettes, aluminum, single vendor, 3½x6¼", EX 230.00
Mansfield Automatic Clerk 5¢, bell rings, dispenses stick gum, 12"....900.00
Master 1¢ Gumball, metal case w/cast aluminum front, 8x16", VG ...350.00
Morell 1¢ Match, metal case w/2 glass windows, 10x19½", EX ..600.00
Pepsi Vendorlator VMC #81, rstr bl & wht pnt, 58", M..........4,995.00
Pepsin 1¢ Gum, 2-column, clockwork, 1903, 10½" 5,650.00
Play Baseball 1¢, glass globe, rstr, 14"...................................195.00
Pulver Chewing Gum, cop variation, porc, 9", EX 850.00
Pulver 1¢ Gum, clown figure, rstr, 21x9"...............................750.00

Radio 1¢, hot nuts, 1950s, 18", EX.................................**500.00**
Ryede Specialty Works Model F, 4-column, oak case, 34", VG...**750.00**
Seven-Up Vendorlator VMC #81, gr & wht, late 1950s, rstr, 58"..**6,600.00**
Silver King 5¢, peanuts, glass globe, 11", rstr..............................**275.00**
Smilin' Sam From Alabam', peanuts. 1931, 11", +CI stand, EX **3,500.00**
Somerville's 1¢ Pepsin Gum, clockwork, aluminum base, glass dome, EX...**1,000.00**
Stollwerk's 1¢ Chocolate & Gum, oak, 4-column, porc marquee, 1892, 33"...**3,565.00**
Sun 5¢ Peanuts, aluminum base w/glass, LA Mfg, 8x14", VG.....**175.00**
Vendo Coin Changer, 10 & 25¢, upright, 60x12".....................**1,995.00**
World's Fair Card 1¢, wood case, 22x17", G **330.00**

Miscellaneous

Detroit Medical Battery 1¢ Electricty Is Life shock tester, EX .**3,300.00**
Mills 1¢ Std Weight, bl & wht porc face, CI marquee, 69" **2,000.00**
Mills 1¢ Std Weight, CI, EX orig pnt, 67" **800.00**
Mutual 1¢ Scale, CI, rstr, 78x20" **1,300.00**
Peerless 1¢ Scale, porc lollipop type, 69", EX **475.00**
Select Your Weight 1¢, Deco front, metal case, 1940s, 72", G....**250.00**
Watline 1¢ Scale, porc, mirror front, 49½x18", VG.....................**295.00**

Cole, A. R.

A second generation North Carolina potter, Arthur Ray Cole opened his own shop in 1926, operating under the name Rainbow Pottery until 1941 when he adopted his own name for the title of his business. He remained active until he died in 1974. He was skilled in modeling the pottery and highly recognized for his fine glazes.

Vase, mottled yellow on mirror-black, rim-to-shoulder handles, ca late 1920s – early 1930s, NM, 24", $325.00. (Photo courtesy Southern Folk Pottery Collectors Society)

Bowl, mc splotches on wht, earthenware, 1941-62, 2⅞x11" **150.00**
Bowl, yel-cream, earthenware, att J Kiser, 1930s, 4x9¾x13½".......**40.00**
Pie dish, gr-brn, fluted edge, earthenware, 1941-62, 2x10"............**50.00**
Pitcher, bl sponging on wht, thumb-grooved hdl, 8¼" **60.00**
Pitcher, gr varigated matt, earthenware, w/lid, 1941-62, 11½" ...**100.00**
Vase, gloppy raspberry & wht semigloss, hdls, mk, 5⅞" **100.00**
Vase, gr crystalline over brn, cylindrical neck, att, 9½" **110.00**

Compacts

The use of cosmetics before WWI was looked upon with disdain. After the war women became liberated, entered the work force, and started to use makeup. The compact, a portable container for cosmetics, became a necessity. The basic compact contains a mirror and a powder puff.

The vintage compacts were fashioned in a myriad of shapes, styles, materials, and motifs. They were made of precious metals, fabrics, plas-

tics, and in almost any other conceivable medium. Commemorative, premium, patriotic, figural, Art Deco, plastic, and gadgetry compacts are just a few of the most sought-after types available today. Those that are combined with other accessories (music/compact, watch/compact, cane/compact) are also very much in demand. Vintage compacts are an especially desirable collectible since the workmanship, design, techniques, and materials used in their execution would be very expensive and virtually impossible to duplicate today.

For more information we recommend *Collector's Encyclopedia of Compacts, Carryalls, and Face Powder Boxes, Volumes I* and *II*, by Laura M. Mueller. Our advisor, Roselyn Gerson, has written these highly informative books: *Vintage and Contemporary Purse Accessories* and *Vintage and Vogue Ladies' Compacts*. She is listed in the Directory under the state of New York. See Clubs, Newsletters, and Catalogs for information concerning the compact collectors' club and their periodical publication, *The Powder Puff*.

Apple, Volupte, gold-tone stylized form w/radiating lines, 3" **185.00**
Basket, Henriette, blk enamel w/gold-tone trim, no hdl, 2" dia..**100.00**
Bolster, Dorset Fifth Ave, gold-tone **60.00**
Butterfly, Wadsworth, 'Crystelle Luminous Lightweight,' 4" **225.00**
Carryall, Evans 'Park Lane,' gold-tone w/radiating ribs, ruby bijou ..**200.00**
Carryall, mini gun-metal book form w/chain, 4 faux amethysts ..**225.00**
Carryall, Volupte 'Sophisticase,'gold-tone w/blk moire slip case .**125.00**
Carryall, Zell 'Round Towner,' blk & lurex damask w/mesh strap, 4x3" ..**90.00**
Clamshell, Napier, sterling silver, 1940s.....................................**250.00**
Egg, gold-tone upright form w/blk ftd base, 3" **100.00**
Envelope, Coty, gold-tone, 1940s...**80.00**
Fan, Melissa, cracked eggshell w/enameled gondola decor, 2½x4¼" ...**125.00**
Finger-ring chain, rnd, copper-tone w/blk-enameled cat, 1½" ...**125.00**
Finger-ring chain, rnd, gr marbelized Bakelite/pk cvd roses, 2½" **200.00**
Half-moon, scalloped gold-tone w/2 hand-stitched puppies, 4x2" ...**175.00**
Hand, Volupte, gold-tone w/wht enameled lace mitt, 4½" **250.00**
Hat, dk bl & blk plastic w/gold-tone US Navy insignia, 3"...........**90.00**
Heart, gold-tone w/purple orchid on inlaid plastic........................**90.00**
Hexagonal, engine-trn brass tango chain w/lipstick case.............**125.00**
Jingle Bells, Coty, gold-tone w/scalloped row of bells, 1940s.......**175.00**
Mask, Elizabeth Arden, polished gold-tone harlequin form, 3"...**175.00**
Musical, Elgin Am, brushed gold-tone w/musical decor, 1¾x2¾"....**150.00**
Oblong, Volupte, gold-tone basketweave w/red stones, sliding lipstick **60.00**
Oval, Dorothy Gray, brushed gold-tone w/harlequin mask decor, 4".**125.00**
Oval, Evans, antique gold-tone w/faux cabochon jade & pearls....**60.00**
Oval, P Page Fifth Avenue, scalloped Lucite tortoise-shell w/flamingos ...**175.00**
Pendant, rnd gilt & enamel compact w/gold-tone chain, 1⅜" **150.00**
Pendant, sterling silver ball form w/eng design, w/chain, 1"........**250.00**
Petit-point, B Altman Co box, sq, couple walking hand-in-hand, 3¼" ..**225.00**
Petit-point, Elgin Am, fan shape, gold-tone trim, 3½x3"............**120.00**
Photo, sq, clear Lucite, rnd photo, 3¼"...**90.00**
Photo, sq, leather w/gold-trimmed fr, sq photo, 1940s, 3" **120.00**
Pocket watch, Italy, gold-tone w/Roman numerals & pnt country scene...**250.00**
Purse, Volupte, gold-tone, rnd photo under flap, lipstick on chain ..**160.00**
Rnd, Elizabeth Arden, silver-tone w/eng design, 2½".................**100.00**
Rnd, Estee Lauder, silver-tone w/3-tone Deco design, 4".............**225.00**
Rnd, sterling w/emb paisley & mc enamel swirl design, 2¾" **350.00**
Rnd, Volupte 'Baby Grand,' segments radiating from center, 5"..**150.00**
Rnd, Volupte, wht enamel w/red anchor & bl rope decor, 2½".....**70.00**
Souvenir, heart, Washington DC sites in gold-tone on silver-tone ...**60.00**
Souvenir, oblong, Paris in gold-tone on blk enamel, 2¾x3½" **175.00**
Souvenir, octagonal, Canada, chrome w/flags, 2½" **120.00**
Sq, Eisenberg, brushed gold-tone w/emerald-colored stones , 3" .**200.00**
Sq, G Vanderbuilt, gold-tone, Apres la pluie le beau temps, 3¾" ...**225.00**
Sq, gold scalloped edges/center w/Marine insignia, wht enamel trim, 2"...**60.00**
Sq, gold-tone w/HP enamel Japanese scene, 2¾x2½" **75.00**
Sq, gold-tone w/pnt tropical scene on encased Lucite lid.............**60.00**

Sq, Heyco Fifth Ave, SP w/gold-tone emb ducks/cattails, 3½" 90.00
Suitcase, Atomette, tan leather w/gold-tone trim, 3" 120.00
Suitcase, marbleized tortoise color w/gold-tone trim, 2½x3".......175.00
Sunburst medallion, Roger & Gallet, gold-tone Lucite, 4" dia....225.00
Telephone dial, wht w/gold-tone trim, 2¾" dia 125.00
Triangular, Schiaparelli, gold-tone w/female figure on dk pk, 2".100.00
Vanity, belt buckle, Coty, gold-tone w/wht enamel buckle, 1940s..125.00
Vanity, oblong, blk Bakelite w/clear/gr rhinestone decor, 4x2¼" 475.00
Vanity, oblong, gold w/Oriental scene, w/chain & ring, 3½x3" ...275.00
Vanity, oval, salmon Bakelite w/pnt flowers & rhinestones, 3" ...300.00
Vanity, photo, rnd gold-tone trim, 1920s, 2" 100.00
Vanity, rnd, Chatain, red Bakelite w/cvd gold-tone highlights, 4" ..350.00
Vanity, rnd, Evans, bl enamel w/silver-tone mesh trim, 4" 80.00
Vanity, saddlebag, red lizard, 3½x2½" 125.00
Vanity, triangular, blk Bakelite w/pnt silver leaves/rhinestones...225.00
Vanity/cigarette case, oblong blk Bakelite case/rnd tapestry compact ..175.00
Vanity/Trio-ette, Plate, plastic hand-mirror, from $125 to 250.00

Consolidated Lamp and Glass

The Consolidated Lamp and Glass Company of Coraopolis, Pennsylvania, was incorporated in 1894. For many years their primary business was the manufacture of lighting glass such as oil lamps and shades for both gas and electric lighting. The popular 'Cosmos' line of lamps and tableware was produced from 1894 to 1915. (See also Cosmos.) In 1926 Consolidated introduced their Martele line, a type of 'sculptured' ware closely resembling Lalique glassware of France. (Compare Consolidated's 'Lovebirds' vase with the Lalique 'Perruches' vase.) It is this line of vases, lamps, and tableware which is often mistaken for a very similar type of glassware produced by the Phoenix Glass Company, located nearby in Monaca, Pennsylvania. For example, the so-called Phoenix 'Grasshopper' vases are actually Consolidated's 'Katydid' vases.

Items in the Martele line were produced in blue, pink, green, crystal, white, or custard glass decorated with various fired-on color treatments or a satin finish. For the most part, their colors were distinctively different from those used by Phoenix. Although not foolproof, one of the ways of distinguishing Consolidated's wares from those of Phoenix is that most of the time Consolidated applied color to the raised portion of the design, leaving the background plain, while Phoenix usually applied color to the background, leaving the raised surfaces undecorated. This is particularly true of those pieces in white or custard glass.

In 1928 Consolidated introduced their Ruba Rombic line, which was their Art Deco or Art Moderne line of glassware. It was only produced from 1928 to 1932 and is quite scarce. Today it is highly sought after by both Consolidated and Art Deco collectors.

Consolidated closed its doors for good in 1964. Subsequently a few of the molds passed into the hands of other glass companies that later reproduced certain patterns; one such reissue is the 'Chickadee' vase, found in avocado green, satin-finish custard, or milk glass. Our advisor for this category is Jack D. Wilson, author of *Phoenix and Consolidated Art Glass, 1926 – 1980*; he is listed in the Directory under Arizona.

Key: mg — milk glass

Bird of Paradise, sepia wash, fan form, 6" 135.00
Bird of Paradise, vase, gr wash, 10"...275.00
Bird of Paradise, vase, heavy straw opal, 10" 400.00
Bittersweet, vase, amber irid over mg casing 295.00
Bittersweet, vase, bl berries, gr vines, orange leaves on satin mg.....125.00
Bittersweet, vase, gr cased 275.00
Blackberry, umbrella vase, red 2,000.00
Blackberry, umbrella vase, wht wash...550.00
Catalonian, bowl, salad; amethyst, str sided 40.00

Catalonian, candlestick, rainbow bl to crystal.............................75.00
Catalonian, flower bowl, yel..85.00
Catalonian, vase, bl irid stretch, cased, fan shape.......................175.00
Catalonian, voilet vase, ruby stain..75.00
Chickadee, vase, gr wash on crystal..110.00
Chintz, vase, amethyst & blk, 7" 300.00
Cockatoo, candlestick, purple wash..165.00
Cockatoo, vase, reverse gr highlights on crystal, Martele label ...275.00
Con-Cora, cookie jar, violets on mg, 6½".....................................85.00
Dancing Girls, lamp, red w/gold highlights 950.00
Dancing Girls, vase, bl highlights on satin mg............................475.00
Dancing Nymph, goblet, frosted 85.00
Dancing Nymph, plate, frosted, 8"...75.00
Dancing Nymph, plate, pk frost, 10"..175.00
Dancing Nymph, platter, bl wash, palace sz, 18" dia 2,500.00
Dancing Nymph, vase, crystal, fan form......................................125.00
Dancing Nymph, vase, reverse ruby-stain highlights, fan form ...250.00
Dogwood, lamp, 3-color highlights on satin mg..........................125.00
Dogwood, vase, bl transparent over wht irid casing.....................400.00
Dolphin, candlestick, gr wash, Santa Maria line.........................250.00
Dragon Fly, vase, gold on glossy custard 175.00
Dragon Fly, vase, lt bl (no highlights) 70.00
Dragon Fly, vase, reverse bl highlights on satin mg 135.00
Fish, bowl, gr wash w/frosted design, 15".....................................375.00
Fish, tray, reverse ruby-stain highlights on crystal.......................275.00
Five Fruits, plate, russet wash (rare), ormolu mts, 12" 295.00
Five Fruits, plate, sepia wash, 12"...110.00
Five Fruits, sundae, yel wash..25.00
Five Fruits, tumbler, gr wash, ftd..30.00
Florentine, vase, gr, urn shape..250.00
Florentine, vase, gr, 7"..195.00
Foxglove, vase, transparent amber over wht irid casing..............300.00
Foxglove, vase, 2-color highlights on satin custard.....................145.00
Hollyhock, lamp vase, reverse gr highlights on crystal 150.00
Hummingbird, compote, yel wash...85.00
Hummingbird, puff box, mc highlights on mg, 7".........................110.00
Hummingbird, puff box, sepia wash, 7".......................................100.00
Hummingbird & Orchids, bowl, console; bl wash (rare), sm 125.00
Hummingbird & Orchids, candlestick, purple wash 115.00
Iris, candlestick, gr wash, tall...75.00
Iris, jug, gr transparent over wht casing, ½-gal 350.00
Iris, jug, sepia wash..200.00
Iris, tumbler, gr transparent over wht casing...............................90.00
Jonquil, yel & gr highlights on satin custard 75.00
Katydid, vase, bl on satin mg, ovoid...165.00
Katydid, vase, gr wash, fan shape...165.00

Katydid, vase, green with brown stalks on milk glass, 7", $225.00.

Line 700, plate, service; bl frost, 10"..145.00
Line 700, vase, French crystal, 6½" 75.00
Line 700, vase, gold highlights on custard, 10" 425.00
Line 700, vase, red w/satin bkground, 7".....................................375.00
Love Birds, banana boat, reverse bl highlights on crystal............450.00

Love Birds, banana boat, 3-color highlights on custard, ormolu mts...550.00
Love Birds, vase, ruby stain on crystal, surmount, 11" 475.00
Love Birds, vase, straw opal, ornate ormolu mts 375.00
Nuthatch, vase, 2-color highlights on satin custard......................200.00
Olive, bowl, reverse bl highlighting (rare color).........................125.00
Olive, lamp, 3-color highlights, very rare...................................300.00
Olive, plate, ruby-stain highlights, 8".......................................45.00
Olive, vase, gold highlights on glossy mg 125.00
Pine Cone, vase, gold highlights on glossy custard 175.00
Pine Cone, vase, reverse rose highlights on glossy custard 150.00
Poppy, vase, bl wash 300.00
Poppy, vase, irid metallic red & gold on glossy custard...............400.00
Regent Line, cookie jar (florette), ash-rose pk over wht opal casing...250.00
Regent Line, vase, ash-rose pk over wht opal casing, #1174-B, 4½" ...125.00
Regent Line, vase, violets decor...45.00
Ruba Rombic, ashtray, lav opal..950.00
Ruba Rombic, bouillon, Sunshine 300.00
Ruba Rombic, bowl, jade, oblong, 12" 2,000.00
Ruba Rombic, jug, Jungle Green...2,500.00
Ruba Rombic, nut dish, Jungle Green, very rare.........................275.00
Ruba Rombic, sherbet, silver 250.00
Santa Maria, boudoir light, orange & blk 550.00
Santa Maria, cigarette box, amber wash 175.00
Sea Gull, vase, blk & gold irid highlights on custard gloss, 11" ..850.00
Sea Gull, vase, gold highlights on red, 11".................................850.00
Sea Gull, vase, gr cased, 11"...650.00
Spanish Knobs, pinch vase, red 125.00
Spanish Knobs, sundae, yel 30.00
Tropical Fish, vase, gr cased, 9"...525.00
Tropical Fish, vase, orange on gr satin, 9" 325.00
Tropical Fish, vase, red, 9"..750.00
Tropical Fish, vase, rose & bl on mg, 9" 300.00

Cookbooks

Cookbooks from the nineteenth century, though often hard to find, are a delight to today's collectors both for their quaint formats and printing methods as well as for their outmoded, often humorous views on nutrition. Recipes required a 'pinch' of salt, butter 'the size of an egg' or a 'walnut,' or a 'handful' of flour. Collectors sometimes specialize in cookbooks issued as advertising premiums. Especially desirable are the figurals that were shaped like a jar, a slice of bread, or some other form relative to the product. Others with unique features such as illustrations by well-known artists or references to famous people or places are priced in accordance. Cookbooks written earlier than 1874 are the most valuable and when found command prices as high as $200.00; figurals usually sell in the $10.00 to $15.00 range.

As is true with all other books, if the original dust jacket is present and in nice condition, a cookbook's value goes up by at least $5.00. Right now, books on Italian cooking from before 1940 are in demand, and bread-baking is important this year. For further information we recommend *A Guide to Collecting Cookbooks* by Col. Bob Allen and *Price Guide to Cookbooks and Recipe Leaflets* by Linda Dickinson. Our advisor for this category is Charlotte Safir; she is listed in the Directory under New York.

Key:
CB — cookbook   dj — dust jacket

Alice Bradley Menu CB, Bradley, 1944, hardbk, VG.....................12.00
America's CB, Home Institute, NY, 1937, hardbk, EX 16.00
Apple-Dore CB, A Graves, 1872, paperbk, EX 45.00
Art of Good Cooking, P Peck, 1966, paperbk, EX 10.00
Baker's Chocolate, 1923, paperbk, EX 25.00

Bamberger's CB, McClaire, 1932, EX 12.00
Betty Crocker CB, 1959, hardbk, EX...25.00
Big Boy Barbecue Book, 1957, hardbk, EX 8.00
Blondie Soup & Sandwich CB, 1947, VG 12.00
Boston School Kitchen Test Book, Lincoln, 1886, VG 75.00
Bride's Favorite Recipes, Indianapolis, 1909, hardbk, VG 20.00
Calumet CB, Kewpie cover, VG..20.00
Candy Making at Home, M Wright, 1920, VG 20.00

Chez Maxim's Secrets & Recipes...Famous Restaurant in Paris, Countess of Toulouse Lautrec, 1962, first edition, 253 pages, $25.00. (Photo courtesy Colonel Bob Allen)

Cooking for Two, J Hill, 1906, paperbk, VG...............................20.00
Cross Creek Cookery, Rawlings, 1942, VG 28.00
Daughter-in-Law CB, H Burnett, 1969, EX...............................10.00
Delineator CB, Delineator Home Institute, 1928, hardbk, VG.....30.00
Dinner at Omar Khyyam's, G Mardikian, 1944, hardbk, sgn, EX..12.00
Encyclopedia of Cooking, M Ginesn, 1947, EX 18.00
Escoffier CB, A Escoffier, 1941, EX 10.00
Fannie Farmer Catering for Special Occasions, 1922, VG..............50.00
Fannie Farmer Jr CB, Perkins, 1942, hardbk, VG 6.00
Fannie Farmer New Book of Cookery, 1912, VG.........................22.00
Fleischmann's Recipes, 1910, paperbk, VG 30.00
Ford Times CB, Kennedy, 1968, hardbk, EX..............................20.00
Fruit & Their Cookery, H Nelson, 1921, EX...............................18.00
General Foods Chocolate Cookery, 1929, leaflet, VG 6.50
General Foods Cooking School of the Air, 1932 & 1934, VG........8.00
Golden Rule CB, I Allen, 1916, paperbk, VG 25.00
Gone w/the Wind Famous Southern Recipes CB, Pebeco Toothpaste, VG ...38.00
Good Meals & How To Prepare Them, K Fisher, 1927, hardbk, VG ..18.00
Gorton — Codfish Recipes, Gorton Pew, 1906, leaflet, VG 4.00
Heinz Salad Book, J Gibson, ca 1933, paperbk, VG 12.00
Here Let Us Feast, M Fisher, 1946, EX 15.00
How To Cook w/Budweiser, Anheuser-Busch, 1952, VG 30.00
Ideal Cookery Book — 1,349 Recipes, 1891, EX 30.00
James Beard's Menu for Entertaining, 1965, hardbk, VG...............8.50
Jell-O Girl Gives a Party, Rose O'Neill illus, leaflet, EX 30.00
Jewel Tea CB, ca 1940, VG...12.00
Kerr Home Canning, Chicago World's Fair, 1933, paperbk, VG...20.00
Knox Dainty Desserts for Dainty People, 1915, leaflet, VG 8.00
LL Bean Game & Fish CB, A Cameron, 1983, hardbk, EX 12.00
Malleable Iron Range, Monarch, 1906, VG 25.00
Margaret Rudkin Pepperidge Farm CB, 1963, EX 20.00
Metropolitan CB, Metropolitan Life, 1914, paperbk, VG...............6.00
Modern Cooking, M Wilson, 1920, VG 15.00
My Better Homes & Gardens CB, 1940, hardbk, VG....................15.00
New Butterwick CB, 1924, EX..16.00
New England Butt'ry Shelf CB, M Campbell, 1969, VG..............13.00
New System of Domestic Cookery, London, 1849, VG 175.00
Old Mr Boston, 1940, hardbk, VG 15.00
Pennsylvania Dutch, sunbonnet girl cover, 1936, paperbk, VG 15.00
Polish Cookery, M Monatowa, 1958, hardbk, VG 6.00
Quality Grocer, March 1931, paperbk, EX 11.00

Rawleigh's Almanac CB, 1915, VG................................16.00
Royal Pudding, Ginger Rogers, 1940, EX....................13.00
Rumford Complete CB, L Wallace, 1946, hardbk, VG.......8.00
Scandinavian Cookery for Americans, F Brobeck, 1948, hardbk, EX...10.00
Simplified Cooking, A Peterson, 1926, hardbk, VG.......18.00
Swans Down Cake Book, 1934, paperbk, EX 5.00
Time-Life Picture CB, 1958, hardbk, VG....................20.00
Twentieth Century CB, 1921, VG...............................18.00
Uncle Sam's CB, C Woods, 1904, leather-bound, VG.......13.00
Victory Garden CB, M Morash, 1982, paperbk, EX.......18.00
Walter Baker Choice Recipes, 1914, leaflet, VG 12.00
Women's Institute Library of Cookery, 1919, hardbk, set of 5, VG....25.00
Your Home CB, Dane, 1929, 1st edition, VG 10.00
Zane Grey CB, B Rieger, 1976, EX............................20.00

Cookie Cutters

Early hand-fashioned cookie cutters have recently been commanding stiff prices at country auctions, and the ranks of interested collectors
are growing steadily. Especially valuable are the figural cutters; and the
more complicated the design, the higher the price. A follow-up of the
carved wooden cookie boards, the first cutters were probably made by
itinerant tinkers from leftover or recycled pieces of tin. Though most of
the eighteenth-century examples are now in museums or collections, it
is still possible to find some good cutters from the late 1800s when
changes in the manufacture of tin resulted in a thinner, less expensive
material. The width of the cutting strip is often a good indicator of age;
the wider the strip, the older the cutter. While the very early cutters were
1" to 1½" deep, by the '20s and '30s, many were less than ½" deep.
Crude, spotty soldering indicates an older cutter, while a thin line of solder usually tends to suggest a much later manufacture. The shape of the
backplate is another clue. Later cutters will have oval, round, or rectangular backs, while on the earlier type the back was cut to follow the lines
of the design. Cookie cutters usually vary from 2" to 4" in size, but gingerbread men were often made as tall as 12". Birds, fish, hearts, and tulips
are common; simple versions can be purchased for as little as $12.00 to
$15.00. The larger figurals, especially those with more imaginative
details, often bring $75.00 and up. The cookie cutters listed here are tin
and handmade unless noted otherwise.

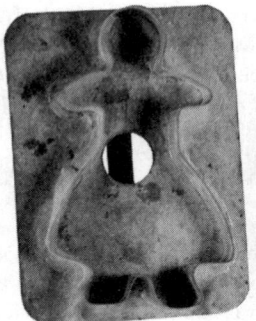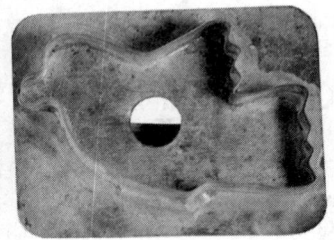

Girl, flat back, 4", $25.00; Bird, flat back, 4¼", $25.00.

Abraham Lincoln w/beard, ¾-view w/hand out, flat bk, 5x4¼" .100.00
Amish man w/beard & big nose, appl hdl, 3x2¼" 30.00
Amish woman w/inset arms, flat bk, 6x4¼" 50.00
Angel w/crimped hair, arm raised, 6x3½" 130.00
Bird in flight, rectangular bk, arched handle, 2¼x4½"..................35.00
Bird standing w/head bk, 4⅜x3¾" 35.00

Boot, flat bk, 3⅛x2"..25.00
Cat seated, arched hdl, 3⅜x2⅞"..................................20.00
Dagger, flat bk, 5⅜x2"..5.00
Dog, hdl, 3x4"...20.00
Eagle, flat bk, folded rims, 5¼x5¾"...........................100.00
Eagle w/crimped wings, flat bk, 3½x5⅛"....................50.00
Eagle w/sm rnd hole in bk, appl arched hdl, 3½x3".....40.00
Elephant, 3 sm holes in bk, appl arched hdl, 2¾x4"...100.00
Fish, flat bk, appl hdl, 3x4"..20.00
Fish, flat bk, 3⅜x7½"...40.00
Fox, long crimped tail curved over bk, flat bk.............50.00
Gooney bird, lg hole in bk, appl hdl, 6⅞x5½"...........120.00
Goose, flat bk, 3x4¾"..40.00
Hand w/pointing finger, crimped cuff, flat bk, 2½x6"...100.00
Hatchet, flat bk, appl arched hdl, 3⅜x2" 20.00
Horse, no hdl, 5¾x5⅞"..30.00
Horse w/bobbed tail prancing, folded rim/flat bk, crude, 4⅞x7¼" ...35.00
Indian w/feather in hair, tomahawk in hand, 7¾x4¾"..............625.00
Lady (Victorian) w/muff & hat, flat bk, 7¼x2⅞".....125.00
Lady w/crimped hair, lg nose, arm up, flat bk, 6x3"...150.00
Lady w/hair in bun, lg nose/chin, flat bk, arched hdl, 9¾x4¼" ..350.00
Lady w/hair in bun, long dress, flat bk, 6½x4"...........275.00
Man drinking from bottle, inset eye & arms, 2 lg holes in bk, hdl, 6" ..130.00
Man in the Moon, flat bk, broken solder, 5¼x3⅝".....350.00
Man riding horse, flat bk, poorly made, 5¾x5¾".........50.00
Man riding pig, 3 sm rnd holes punched in bk, 5¾x4¾".............575.00
Man w/cap, arm raised, 6x3"......................................150.00
Man wearing top hat, long coat, pointing, flat bk, 5¾"...300.00
Mermaid, flat bk, 3x6"...50.00
Moose w/lg antlers, inset legs, flat bk, 5⅞x4⅝"........270.00
Peacock w/crimped tail, pieced flat bk, 4x7¾"...........150.00
Pear, hdl missing, 2¾x2⅜"..10.00
Pear w/stem & crimped leaf, flat bk, 4¼x2½"...........25.00
Penguin, arched hdl, 3⅛x2"...45.00
Rat w/long body & tail, flat bk, 2⅛x5⅞".....................50.00
Rocking horse on flat rockers, flat bk, 3¾x4¼".........300.00
Rooster, flat bk, 5x4¼"..40.00
Star-like form w/pierced dmn in bk, arched hdl, 3⅝"...15.00
Swan, arched hdl, 3x3¼"...20.00
Tulip w/flat bk, 3x2⅛"...25.00
Turkey, crimped fan-shaped tail, flat bk, 4¾x5¼".......50.00
Viola, flat bk, appl arched hdl, 3½x2¼"......................25.00

Cookie Jars

The appeal of the cookie jar is universal; folks of all ages, both male
and female, love to collect 'em! The early '30s heavy stoneware jars of a
rather nondescript nature quickly gave way to figurals of every type
imaginable. Those from the mid to late '30s were often decorated over
the glaze with 'cold paint,' but by the early '40s underglaze decorating
resulted in cheerful, bright, permanent colors and cookie jars that still
have a new look fifty years later.

Stimulated by the high prices commanded by desirable cookie jars, a
broad spectrum of 'new' cookie jars are flooding the marketplace in three
categories: 1) Manufactures have expanded their lines with exciting new
designs specifically geared toward attracting the collector market. 2) Limited editions and artist-designed jars have proliferated. 3) Reproductions,
signed and unsigned, have pervaded the market, creating uncertainty
among new collectors and inexperienced dealers. One of the most trou-
blesome reproductions is the Little Red Riding Hood jar marked McCoy.
Several Brush jars are being reproduced, and because the old molds are
being used, these are especially deceptive. In addition to these reproductions, we've also been alerted to watch for cookie jars marked Brush-

McCoy made from molds that Brush never used. Remember that none of Brush's cookie jars were marked Brush-McCoy, so any bearing the compound name is fraudulent. For more information on cookie jars and reproductions, we recommend *The Collector's Encyclopedia of Cookie Jars, Books I, II,* and *III,* by Fred and Joyce Roerig; they are listed in the Directory under South Carolina. Another good source is *An Illustrated Guide to Cookie Jars, Books I* and *II,* by Ermagene Westfall. Our advisors for this category are Fred and Joyce Roerig; they are listed in the Directory under South Carolina.

The examples listed below were made by companies other than those found elsewhere in this book; see also specific manufacturers.

Alf, Handpainted Made in USA, from $90 to 110.00
Alpo Dan the Dog, USA, from $50 to 60.00
Baby Huey, American Bisque, USA (+), minimum value........2,500.00
Baby Huey, USA, American Bisque (+), minimum value........2,500.00
Barrel Mammy, Made in Taiwan paper label, from $30 to 40.00
Baseball Boy, CA originals, 875 USA on lid & base, from $35 to ...45.00
Beachbound Woody, ACC -6 c 1986 NAC USA, from $300 to...350.00
Big Al, c Disney on bk, from $50 to 60.00
Big Boy, Elias Bros ltd ed, 1992, from $475 to 525.00
Blanket Couple, A Little Co c 87, 12" 180.00
Blue Bonnet Sue, c 1989 Nabisco, from $60 to..............................80.00
Captain, USA, American Bisque..175.00
Chef Nerd, c 1984 Willie Wonka Brands, Taiwan, from $55 to....65.00
Christmas Car, Fitz & Floyd, FF Japan label, 8", from $450 to....500.00
Christmas Churn Mammy, Rick Wisecarver c 89, minimum value .300.00
Christmas Tree Mammy, Erwin Pottery...Tenn, from $150 to......175.00
Churn, USA, American Bisque...25.00
City Cab, Japan, from $175 to 225.00
Clown, Lane and Co Los Angeles c 1950, from $175 to 200.00
Clown, Maurice C Calif USA on base, from $225 to.................275.00

Clown riding elephant, marked c1957, Yona Original, from $300.00 to $325.00. (Photo courtesy Ermagene Westfall)

Coach Lamp, USA, American Bisque...125.00
Cookie Factory, Fitz & Floyd c FF 1987, FF Japan label, from $115 to..125.00
Cookiesaurus, c Treasure Craft in lid, from $35 to 40.00
Cream of Wheat Chef, Japan, 8", from $1,100 to....................1,200.00
Delicious Cookies, milk can, ...Made in Taiwan ROC label, from $35 to ..45.00
Duck w/Yarmulke, Doranne of California (unmk), from $50 to....60.00
Earth Goddess, A Little Co 1991 ....150.00
Edmund, A Little Co c 1992, 19" 175.00
Famous Amos, bsk, Treasure Craft c Made in USA, from $45 to..55.00
Fire Chief, USA, American Bisque 150.00
Fire Truck, CA Originals, 841 on base, from $175 to 225.00
French Poodle, burgundy, American Bisque, mk USA, from $100 to..125.00
Frog, Doranne of California (unmk), ca 1980s, from $45 to..........50.00
Garfield, c 1978, 1981 United Features Syndicate..., Made in Indonesia..125.00
Grandma's Cookies, Momonth Ill USA w/maple leaf mk, from $40 to...50.00
Grandmother w/Child, A Little Co, ltd ed, 1992, 13"................180.00

Halloween Witch, Exclusively for Lotus...Taiwan c 1989, from $50 to ..60.00
Harley-Davidson Gas Tank, Taiwan, from $75 to 95.00
Herman & Katnip, Harvey Famous Cartoons c 1960 USA, American Bisque....3,800.00
Indian Maiden, Wihoa's Limited...1989 Rick Wisecarver, from $175 to ..225.00
Jeep, Doranne Calif CJ 115, from $125 to 150.00
Jukebox, orig release (taller), Treasure Craft...USA, from $100 to...125.00
Kitten & Beehive, USA, brn/bl on wht (unusual), USA, American Bisque....75.00
Kooky Klown, Newhauser, Pat Pending...Cleveland, from $100 to...125.00
Liberty Bell, CA Originals, #883 in lid, #884 on base, from $35 to ...45.00
Liberty Bell, USa, American Bisque 125.00
Lil Ole Schoolhouse, CA Originals, 869 on lid & base, from $50 to ..60.00
Mammy Bust, Rick Wisecarver...R Sims, from $225 to 250.00
Mexican Bandito, Treasure Craft c Made in USA, from $40 to....50.00
Milk Bone Dog Biscuits, Roman Made in Thailand label, from $100 to ...125.00
Mona Lisa, Vandor 1992 Pelzman...Sri Lanka, from $50 to...........55.00
Mother Goose, decor, Doranne of California, mk USA, from $150 to...175.00
Mushrooms, Sierra Vista Ceramics...USA c 1957, from $40 to.....50.00
Noah's Ark, Pat Pend Starnes Calif c, from $225 to...................250.00
Oaken Water Bucket w/Gourd Dipper, American Bisque, mk USA, $100 to ..125.00
Oliver Hardy, mk C through W USA, from $600 to 650.00
Pegapuss, A Little Co 1992, minimum value 110.00
Peter Panda, DCJ-24 c 1985...NAC, from $30 to 35.00
Pick-Up Truck, orig issue, Treasure Craft...USA in lid, from $275 to ..325.00
Pig, A Little Co 1992, sm, med or lg, ea, minimum value...........110.00
Pinocchio, WH Hirsch...USA c 60 on base, from $200 to..........225.00
Planetary Pal, ...Hyman for Sigma...c MCMLXXXIV, from $125 to ...150.00
Popeye, USA, American Bisque 350.00
Popeye Spinach Can, Shirley Corl, from $100 to 125.00
Raggedy Ann, CA Originals, 859 on lid & base, from $100 to ...125.00
Roly-Poly Santa, Made in Taiwan label, from $20 to 30.00
Rooster, USA, American Bisque...60.00
Rudolph, c RLM, American Bisque (+) 400.00
Santa, Wihoa's...Rick Wisecarver 1990, minimum value 300.00
Scarecrow Turnabout, CA Originals, 858 on lid & base, from $75 to...90.00
Sears Strawberry, Sears Exclusively USA, American Bisque 40.00
Snappy Gingerbread Boy, DeForest of California C #6 Made in USA ..225.00
Snow White, CA Originals, C Walt Disney Prod 866 USA, minimum value ...2,000.00
Snowman, Doranne of California, mk J 52 USA, from $200 to..225.00
Space Ship, Sierra Vista (unmk), from $375 to 425.00
Tepee, Wihoa's...Rick Wisecarver...No 1 89..., from $250 to.......300.00
Thanksgiving Turkey Mammy, Erwin Pottery...Tenn, from $150 to....175.00
Toothache Dog, American Bisque, mk USA, from $400 to 425.00
Upside Down Turtle, CA Originals, 2627 USA on lid & base, from $100 to...125.00
Winnie the Pooh's Treats, c MCMLXIV Walt Disney Productions, $150 to...175.00
Yarn Doll, gold trim, unmk American Bisque 200.00
3-D Mickey, Treasure Craft...c Walt Disney Productions, from $100 to ...125.00

Cooper, Susie

A twentieth-century ceramic designer whose works are now attracting the attention of collectors, Susie Cooper was first affiliated with the A.E. Gray Pottery in Henley, England, in 1922 where she designed in lustres and painted items with her own ideas as well. (Examples of Gray's lustreware is rare and costly.) By 1930 she and her brother-in-law, Jack Beeson, had established a family business. Her pottery soon became a success, and she was subsequently offered space at Crown Works, Burslem. In 1940 she received the honorary title of Royal Designer for Industry, the only such distinction ever awarded by the Royal Society of Arts solely for pottery design. Miss Cooper received the Order of the British Empire in the New Year's Honors List of 1979. She was the chief designer for the Wedgwood group from 1966 until she resigned in 1972. After 1980 she worked on a free-lance basis until her death in July 1995. Our advisor is J. David Ehrhard; he is listed in the Directory under California.

Bowl, Cockerel, 4-color w/copper lustre, Gray's Period, 9"..........400.00
Bowl, cream soup; Gardenias, 1960s.................................20.00
Bowl, mc bands, Gray's Period, 9" 125.00
Bowl, Orchid, bl/brn on gray/bl, incurvate rim, 1932, 4½" H.....300.00
Charger, HP leaves, 14"...280.00
Coffeepot, yel wash, blk lines, 7¾"..............................150.00
Creamer & sugar bowl, Gardenias, 1960s, w/lid....................45.00
Cup & saucer, Black Fruit (for Wedgwood), 6 for.................225.00
Jam pot, Amaryllis, pk & gr, 4"..................................90.00
Jam pot, Crayon Line, red & brn lines, w/lid, 4" 60.00
Jug, Tulip (cvd), ochre, ca 1932, 7"............................600.00
Jug, Tulip (cvd), olive gr, 6½".................................200.00
Meat dish, Nosegay, yel-wash border, oval, 14" 70.00
Plate, Gray Leaf, brn-wash border, 10"...........................30.00
Plate, Pear in Pompadour, gr/blk/red/yel, 6" 40.00
Plate, Swansea Spray, gr wash band, 7"...........................20.00
Platter, Gray's Period, Sunbuff Coronal, oxblood bands, oval.....225.00
Vase, Orchid, mc on cream, M42, 1932, 5½" 350.00
Vase, pk, appl buttons, 7½" 400.00

Coors

The firm that became known as Coors Porcelain Company in 1920 was founded in 1908 by John J. Herold, originally of the Roseville Pottery in Zanesville, Ohio. Though still in business today, they are best known for their artware vases and Rosebud dinnerware produced before 1939.

Coors vases produced before the late '30s were made in a matt finish; by the latter years of the decade, high-gloss glazes were also being used. Nearly fifty shapes were in production, and some of the more common forms were made in three sizes. Typical colors in matt are white, orange, blue, green, yellow, and tan. Yellow, blue, maroon, pink, and green are found in high gloss. All vases are marked with a triangular arrangement of the words 'Coors Colorado Pottery' enclosing the word 'Golden.' You may find vases (usually 6" to 6½") marked with the Colorado State Fair stamp and dated 1939. For such a vase, add $10.00 to the suggested values given below.

Our advisor for this category is Jo Ellen Winther; she is listed in the Directory under Colorado.

Rosebud

Apple baker, w/lid..55.00
Ashtray 300.00
Baker, 9¼" 60.00
Bean pot, sm 65.00
Bowl, mixing; 2-hdld, 1½-pt......................................40.00
Bowl, mixing; 8-pt...75.00
Bowl, pudding; 2 sm ear hdls, 2-pt, from $35 to..................40.00
Cake plate, from $40 to..45.00
Casserole, Dutch; lg...95.00
Casserole, str sides, 8"...65.00
Cookie jar, Deluxe, 8-pt...110.00
Creamer..30.00
Cup & saucer 45.00
Custard set, 6 w/wire rack 125.00
Dish, oatmeal..25.00
Egg cup..50.00
Loaf pan...50.00
Muffin set, w/lid, rare 225.00
Pitcher, w/lid, lg...150.00
Plate, dinner; 10¼"..95.00
Plate, dinner; 9¼"...15.00
Plate, used under muffin cover, 6"...............................35.00

Plate, 7¼"...8.00
Refrigerator set 130.00
Shakers, table, pr 35.00
Shirred egg dish 35.00
Sugar shaker..75.00
Teapot, 2-cup, rare...200.00
Tumbler, ftd 125.00
Water server, w/stopper 120.00

Miscellaneous

Whip, Coors Malted Milk, red and black lettering on white, $300.00.

Cake knife, Hawthorne, decalcomania..............................90.00
Cake plate, Floree...55.00
Casserole, Coorado, ind, w/lid, 2x2" 45.00
Creamer, Mello-Tone or Rockmount.................................15.00
Figurine, Laughing or Crying Monk, 6", ea 300.00
Gravy boat, Mello-Tone or Rockmount 45.00
Lamp base, bl 200.00
Mortar & pestle, cobalt..55.00
Pie plate, Coorado 55.00
Plate, dinner; Tulip, decalcomania 100.00
Shakers, Coorado, gr, pr 50.00
Teapot, Chrysanthemum, decalcomania..............................150.00
Teapot, Tulip, decalcomania......................................150.00
Tumbler, Mello-Tone or Rockmount.................................35.00
Vase, Brighton, yel matt, bulbous, 8"............................70.00
Vase, bud; yel high gloss, 8"....................................30.00
Vase, Empire, yel matt, stepped form, 10"........................110.00
Vase, Florence, bl matt, trumpet neck, uptrn hdls, 12"...........125.00
Vase, Florence, matt tan, 12"....................................125.00
Vase, Golden, bl matt, integral hdls, 6".........................55.00
Vase, Matchless, gr matt, emb ribs, 8" 70.00
Vase, Montrose, bl matt, neck-to-shoulder hdls, 12" 125.00
Vase, Trinidad, wht matt w/turq int, hdls, 12"...................125.00
Water server, Mello-Tone or Rockmount 45.00

Copper

Handcrafted copper was made in America from early in the eighteenth century until about 1850, with the center of its production in Pennsylvania. Examples have been found signed by such notable coppersmiths as Kidd, Buchanan, Babb, Bently, and Harbeson. Of the many utilitarian items made, teakettles are the most desirable. Early examples from the eighteenth century were made with a dovetailed joint which was hammered and smoothed to a uniform thickness. Pots from the nineteenth century were seamed. Coffeepots were made in many shapes and sizes and along with mugs, kettles, warming pans, and measures are easiest to find. Stills ranging in sizes of up to fifty-gallon are popular with collectors today.

Mary Frank Gaston has compiled a lovely book, *Antique Brass and Copper*, with many full-color photos and current market values.

Bowl, ribbed, scalloped rim, Marie Zimmerman, 7½x9¾" **1,500.00**
Can, water; tinned int, iron hdls, brass spigot & mts, 12x10" **140.00**
Can w/spout, handmade w/some soldered rpr, OH, 17" **195.00**
Chestnut roaster, iron hdl, pierced lid, 16", from $120 to **140.00**
Coffee table, faux bamboo hdls & legs, Arts & Crafts period **400.00**
Coffeepot, wood hdl, hinged brass spout cover, Majestic, 11½"..**130.00**
Figure, eagle on ball, old gilt, Am, 19th C, rprs, 14½" **1,495.00**
Kettle, apple butter; rolled rim, dvtl, 14x23½" **400.00**
Kettle, brass mts & rivets, iron swing hdl, 19th C, 4½x6¾" **110.00**
Kettle, candy; wrought steel hdls, dvtl, polished, 6½x13" **195.00**
Kettle, heavy iron bail hdl, dvtl, polished, 22" dia......................**225.00**
Kettle, preserving; iron hdls, visible soldering, 25", from $300 to..**350.00**
Kettle, rnd bottom, sturdy CI hdls, dvtl, 7½x17½" dia **250.00**
Kettle, rolled rim, iron swing hdl, dvtl, 11x15", EX....................**250.00**
Kettle, stewing; dvtl, 8½x13½", from $150 to **175.00**
Kettle, stewing; Mid-Eastern, 6x9", from $75 to **100.00**
Measure, mk ½ (cup), 2½", from $20 to **25.00**
Pan, baking; 3x4½", from $60 to **80.00**
Pan, cast steel hdl, dvtl, Henry Trottman Philada label, 8" dia...**150.00**
Pan, sauce; iron hdls, w/lid, dvtl, 19th C, 11x14", from $400 to.**450.00**

Pan, stamped Charles Dennery/New Orleans, 20½" wide, $265.00.

Planter, brass lion heads & paw ft, 19th C, English, 15x13" **1,300.00**
Planter, flower form, mk China, 4x5½", from $30 to....................**40.00**
Syrup jug, funnel spout, Am, 19th C, from $200 to **225.00**
Vegetable steamer, brass hdl, English, 8½x14" dia, from $225 to...**275.00**
Wall pocket/letter holder, simple corner style, 9", from $55 to **65.00**
Wash boiler, mk Atlantic 11 Gallon, from $175 to **195.00**
Wash boiler, tin lid, mk Rochester, 13½x26½", from $140 to **165.00**

Copper Lustre

Copper lustre is a term referring to a type of pottery made in Staffordshire after the turn of the nineteenth century. It is finished in a metallic rusty-brown glaze resembling true copper. Pitchers are found in abundance, ranging from simple styles with dull bands of color to those with fancy handles and bands of embossed, polychromed flowers. Bowls are common; goblets, mugs, teapots, and sugar bowls much less so. It's easy to find, but not in good condition. Pieces with hand-painted decoration and those with historical transfers are the most valuable.

Creamer, HP flowers encircle body, 4½" **80.00**
Creamer & sugar bowl, bl stripes, Made in England, 3½", 2"........**80.00**
Mug, bl band, 3" **100.00**
Mug, bl floral band, ca 1840-50, 4x4½" **165.00**
Pitcher, bl band, 4¼"...**80.00**
Pitcher, brn transfer, AJ Wilkinston Ltd, 3½"...............................**70.00**

Pitcher, cottage band, ca 1820-30, 5" **275.00**
Pitcher, emb dmns in lower body, England, 6½".........................**120.00**
Pitcher, HP lady playing badminton reserve, ca 1820, 7" **350.00**
Pitcher, mk BCM Nelson Ware MIE, 2¾x4¾".............................**40.00**
Pitcher, pk stripes, 4x6"..**60.00**
Pitcher, wide floral band on lower body, 4" **90.00**

Coralene Glass

Coralene is a unique type of art glass easily recognized by the tiny grains of glass that form its decoration. Lacy allover patterns of seaweed, geometrics, and florals were used, as well as solid forms such as fish, plants, and single blossoms. (Seaweed is most commonly found and not as valuable as the other types of decoration.) It was made by several glasshouses both here and abroad. Values are based to a considerable extent on the amount of beading that remains. Our advisors for this category are Betty and Clarence Maier; they are listed in the Directory under Pennsylvania.

Bowl, wht opaque w/yel seaweed, 2x3" **60.00**
Lamp, perfume; pk MOP Dmn Quilt w/seaweed, orig burner, 5½x3½"..**650.00**
Rose bowl, peachblow w/yel seaweed, webb, 2⅞x4½".................**385.00**
Sugar shaker, royal bl Raindrop MOP w/seaweed, Patent, 6"...**1,085.00**
Vase, amber w/flower branch, ruffled rim, 4½" **115.00**
Vase, amethyst w/scrolls & flowers, slim w/flared rim, 8" **125.00**
Vase, bl to wht w/floral & HP, clear hdls, Webb, 8½" **350.00**
Vase, blk amethyst w/gold leafy branch, 5½", NM.........................**75.00**
Vase, fuchsia to pale pk w/yel seaweed, 7¼" **350.00**
Vase, gr w/coral-colored seaweed & clear shell, HP floral, slim, 10"..**155.00**
Vase, peachblow w/yel seaweed, cylindrical, 8¼", NM...............**500.00**
Vase, pk satin cased w/yel seaweed, stick neck, 12" **1,195.00**
Vase, rainbow Dmn Quilt w/bl seaweed, ca 1890, 6¼"...............**895.00**
Vase, red w/flowers & leaves, gold trim, cylindrical, 9½" **200.00**

Cordey

The Cordey China Company was founded in 1942 in Trenton, New Jersey, by Boleslaw Cybis. The operation was small with less than a dozen workers. They produced figurines, vases, lamps, and similar wares, much of which was marketed through gift shops both nationwide and abroad. Though the earlier wares were made of plaster, Cybis soon developed his own formula for a porcelain composition which he called 'Papka.' Cordey figurines and busts were characterized by old-world charm, Rococo scrolls, delicate floral appliqués, ruffles, and real lace which was dipped in liquefied clay to add dimension to the work.

Although on rare occasions some items were not numbered or signed, the 'basic' figure was cast both with numbers and the Cordey signature. The molded pieces were then individually decorated and each marked with its own impressed identification number as well as a mark to indicate the artist-decorator. Their numbering system began with 200 and in later years progressed into the 8000s. As can best be established, Cordey continued production until sometime in the mid-1950s. Boleslaw Cybis died in 1957, his wife in 1958.

Due to the increased availability of Cordey on the Internet over the last year, values of the more common pieces have fallen off. Our advisor for this category is Sharon A. Payne; she is listed in the Directory under Washington.

Key: ff — full figure

#302, lady, full-figure, flowing dress, 16" **125.00**
#313, bust of woman, sgn MB Cybis..**225.00**
#914, clock, mantel; Rococo, Lanshire Electric, 9½" **100.00**

#1023, bowl, console; lg roses w/gold, oblong, 6x15x8" 85.00
#3241, Oriental duck, wht, 14½" 200.00
#4002, man, ruffles at neck, bow at nape, 7" 85.00
#4014, bust of lady, 7¼" 60.00
#4020, bust of lady, flowers in hair & at waist, 6½" 45.00
#4027, lady w/parasol, slight lace damage, 8" 95.00
#4050-A, man, blk top hat, cape & scarf, 7" 90.00
#4129, courting group, man & lady on rnd base, lacy, rare 250.00
#5002/5032, figures, pr 135.00
#5013, bust of lady, wht shawl, bl bonnet w/ long pk ribbons 80.00
#5015, bust of lady, 6" 60.00
#5026, bust of lady w/mantilla, Jr Miss Group.......................65.00
#5027, bust of lady 50.00
#5028, bust of lady, textured bonnet & collar, scroll base..........65.00
#5034, bust of Raleigh, 8" 55.00
#5038, bust of Colonial lady 50.00
#5040, soldier figure, rare 90.00
#5043, man in Colonial attire, full figure 125.00
#5044, Colonial dbl figure, bl 190.00
#5045, boy figures w/basket of breadsticks, 9½" 95.00
#5066, Carmen, Spanish dress & mantilla, full figure, 14" 150.00
#5069, Marcele ¾ bust, much lace & roses...........................150.00
#5086, Victorian lady, full figure, 11" 100.00
#5088, lady, full figure, HP roses on dress, 11" 100.00
#5089, Fr dame, full figure, fancy, rare, 11" 135.00
#5089, Fr lady, full figure w/bustle 100.00
#6004, bluebird on stump, lg 90.00
#6087, bowl, cherubs & flowers, ftd, 7½x5¼x8¾".....................200.00
#7000, plaque, primrose, Colonial Lady, full figure 100.00
#7004, tray (or shallow bowl), 13x9" 80.00
#7028, wall shelf, Art Nouveau nude w/cornucopia, 8x6½"............75.00
#7094, vase, Oriental figures & flowers, gourd form, 9x8"..........100.00
#8002, pin/ashtray, 4" sq...20.00
Bust, fully draped in lace, no mk, 14" 170.00
Bust, Neopolitan squire, lace damage, 14"..........................120.00
Cat, wht w/gr eyes & pk ears, recumbent 125.00
Cat, wht w/gr eyes & pk ears, sitting, script mk, 8½" 95.00
Dresser tray & 2 perfumes w/hdls, appl roses/morning glories 200.00
Lamp, Chinese goddess, 12" figure on wooden base, 26" 130.00

Corkscrews

The history of the corkscrew dates back to the mid-1600s, when wine makers concluded that the best-aged wine was that stored in smaller containers, either stoneware or glass. Since plugs left unsealed were often damaged by rodents, corks were cut off flush with the bottle top and sealed with wax or a metal cover. Removing the cork cleanly with none left to grasp became a problem. The task was found to be relatively simple using the worm on the end of a flintlock gun rod. So the corkscrew evolved. Endless patents have been issued for mechanized models. Handles range from carved wood, ivory, and bone to porcelain and repoussé silver. Exotic materials such as agate, mother-of-pearl, and gold plate were also used on occasion. Celluloid lady's legs are popular.

For further information we recommend *The Ultimate Corkscrew Book* and *Bull's Pocket Guide to Corkscrews* by Donald Bull, our advisor for this category. He is listed in the Directory under Virginia. In the following descriptions, values are for examples in excellent condition, unless noted otherwise.

Anri figure, sailor seated on barrel w/bottle, cvd wood.............85.00
Bow, ornate silver stipple 150.00
Bow, w/foil cutter..175.00
Clough, wire 2-finger eyeglass type.................................115.00

Collapsing type, metal, w/brewery advertising 100.00
Cvd tusk hdl, boar's head w/silver fitting, w/1893 Walker bell....450.00
Dbl lever, Eterno, Ettore Cardini's 1945 Italian Pat 250.00
Dbl lever, Hootch Owl..1,800.00
Dbl lever, Magic Lever Cork Drawer................................115.00
Figural, anchor, metal, w/friction-fit sheath, mk HMS Victory 30.00
Figural, English bulldog, brass, 1930s, 6" 52.50
Figural, fish swallowing worm, cast metal, mk JB 60.00
Figural, golf bag mk Hook & Slice Club, w/worm as club, silver ...450.00
Figural, horse head, emb metal w/folding worm 40.00
Figural, owl, brass, 2-finger pull, English 35.00
Figural, teepee, pewter, mk Roux 75.00
Figural, terrier, cvd wood w/wire worm 25.00
Figural, Viking ship, pewter, sail mk Zero 90.00
Figural, winged creature (nude imp? w/bottle), brass, 6" 70.00
Figural, woman w/toothache, pnt metal 60.00
Finger pull, 3-finger, leather-wrapped 100.00
Flynut, The Victor, metal...160.00
Flynut, Valezina, brass-colored metal, 1943-44 Pat................115.00
Picnic, metal Pickwick figure w/Bakelite sheath 225.00
Picnic, metal w/wood sheath, rare 250.00
Pocket folder, metal, mk So-Ezy Made in USA Pat Pend..............50.00
Pocket folder, metal pea-pod shape, by Perille/Paris 250.00
Roundlet, sterling, sliding action 250.00
Scissors, metal, mk GMS No 10983 Germany 325.00
Single lever, Royal Club, C Hull, 1864 England Pat, from $2,500 to....4,500.00
Single lever, Sperry, 1878 Pat, from $2,500 to....................3,500.00
Single lever, Tucker, metal, 1878 Pat, from $1,800 to.............3,000.00
Spoon, SP, Walker & Orr, 1932 American Pat 125.00
Syroco, clown figure 450.00
Syroco, Pickwick head...130.00
Syroco, Scottie dog opener/corkscrew set..........................200.00
T-hdl, bone, NP brass fr w/lifting & centering button on worm...300.00
T-hdl, chrome, w/closed barrel, mk Italy 35.00
T-hdl, silver w/hammered design 450.00
T-hdl, wood, sleek, Murphy, mk Pat Apr 23 '01.....................100.00
T-hdl, wood, w/cast metal barrel, w/German mk, c 1932 ....110.00
T-hdl, wood, w/spring, Richard Recknagel's 1899 German Pat...275.00
Tap, New Century by Williamson Co, chrome 60.00
Thomason, wood T-hdl w/brush, ornate brass-colored barrel 650.00
Waiter's Friend, steel w/2-hook neck stand, w/beer advertising.....90.00
Whistle, metal roundlet, parts unscrew to form opener............325.00

Cosmos

Cosmos, sometimes called Stemless Daisy, is a patterned glass tableware produced from 1894 through 1915 by Consolidated Lamp and Glass Company. Relief-molded flowers on a finely crosscut background were painted in soft colors of pink, blue, and yellow. Though nearly all were made of milk glass, a few items may be found in clear glass with the designs painted on. In addition to the tableware, lamps were also made.

Sugar bowl (open) and creamer, $150.00 each.

Bottle, cologne; orig stopper, rare, from $275 to 300.00
Butter dish, 5x8" 275.00
Lamp, bouquet; kerosene, 24" 575.00
Lamp, bouquet; slender base, rnd globe, all orig, 16" 525.00
Lamp, mini, 7½", EX..275.00
Lamp, 10" 450.00
Pickle castor, mk SP fr, from $600 to.....................700.00
Pitcher, milk; 5" 250.00
Pitcher, syrup; 6" 300.00
Pitcher, water 350.00
Shakers, tall, orig lids, pr............................175.00
Spooner...125.00
Sugar bowl, w/lid 185.00
Sugar shaker...400.00
Tumbler, 3¾" 75.00

Cottageware

You'll find a varied assortment of novelty dinnerware items, all styled as cozy little English cottages or huts with cone-shaped roofs; some may have a waterwheel or a windmill. Marks will vary. English-made Price Brothers or Beswick pieces are valued in the same range as those marked Occupied Japan, while items marked simply Japan are considerably less pricey. Our advisor for this category is Grace Klender; she is listed in the Directory under Ohio. All of the following examples are Price Brothers/Kensington unless noted otherwise.

Salad bowl, $70.00.

Bank, dbl slot, 4½x3½x5" 95.00
Bell, minimum value 55.00
Biscuit jar, wicker hdl, Maruhon Ware, Occupied Japan, 6½" ..92.50
Butter dish..65.00
Butter dish, oval, Burlington Ware, 6"...................60.00
Butter pat, emb cottage, rectangular, Occupied Japan 20.00
Chocolate pot 148.00
Condiment set, mustard, 2½" s&p on 5" hdld leaf tray 85.00
Condiment set, mustard pot, s&p, tray, row arrangement, 6" 50.00
Condiment set, mustard pot, s&p, tray, row arrangement, 7¾" 50.00
Condinment set, 3-part cottage on shaped tray w/appl bush, 4½" ...85.00
Cookie jar, pk/brn/gr, sq, Japan, 8½x5½" 75.00
Cookie jar, windmill, wicker hdl..........................165.00
Cookie jar/canister, cylindrical, rare sz, 8x3¾" 275.00
Cookie jar/canister, cylindrical, 8½x5"..................140.00
Cookie/biscuit jar, Occupied Japan 95.00
Creamer, windmill, Occupied Japan, 2⅝" 30.00
Creamer & sugar bowl, 2½x4½".........................50.00
Cup & saucer, chocolate; str-sided cup, 3½x2¾", 5½" 45.00
Cup & saucer, 2½, 4½"......................................50.00
Demitasse pot 110.00
Dish w/cover, Occupied Japan, sm......................40.00
Egg cup set, 4 on 6" sq tray................................65.00
Gravy boat & tray, rare 275.00
Grease jar, Occupied Japan, from $25 to 38.50
Marmalade 45.00
Mug, 3⅞" 55.00

Pin tray, 4" dia 22.00
Pitcher, emb cottage, lg flower on hdl, lg...............150.00
Pitcher, tankard; rnd, 7⅞"................................138.00
Pitcher, water; 8" 165.00
Platter, oval, 11¾x7½".....................................65.00
Reamer, Japan..65.00
Sugar box, for cubes, 5¾" L...............................50.00
Tea set, child's, serves 4, Japan.........................165.00
Teapot, Occupied Japan, 6½"..............................55.00
Teapot, 6¼" 80.00
Teapot w/creamer & sugar bowl, Keele Street...........55.00
Toast rack, 3-slot, 3½"......................................75.00
Toast rack, 4-slot, 5½".......................................85.00
Tumbler, Occupied Japan, 3½", set of 6................65.00

Coverlets

The Jacquard attachment for hand looms represented a culmination of weaving developments made in France. Introduced to America by the early 1820s, it gave professional weavers the ability to easily create complex patterns with curved lines. Those who could afford the new loom adaptation could now use hole-punched pasteboard cards to weave floral patterns that before could only be achieved with intense labor on a draw-loom.

Before the Jacquard mechanism, most weavers made their coverlets in geometric patterns. Use of indigo-blue and brightly colored wools often livened the twills and overshot patterns available to the small-loom home weaver. Those who had larger multiple-harness looms could produce warm double-woven, twill-block, or summer-and-winter designs.

While the new floral and pictorial patterns' popularity had displaced the geometrics in urban areas, the mid-Atlantic, and the Midwest by the 1840s, even factory production of the Jacquard coverlets was disrupted by cotton and wool shortages during the Civil War. A revived production in the 1870s saw a style change to a center-medallion motif, but a new fad for white 'Marseilles' spreads soon halted sales of Jacquard-woven coverlets. Production of Jacquard carpets continued to the turn of the century.

Rural and frontier weavers continued to make geometric-design coverlets through the nineteenth century, and local craft revivals have continued the tradition through this century. All-cotton overshots were factory produced in Kentucky from the 1940s, and factories and professional weavers made cotton-and-wool overshots during the past decade. Many Jacquard-woven coverlets have dates and names of places and people (often the intended owner — not the weaver) woven into corners or borders. In the listings that follow, examples are blue and white and in excellent condition unless noted otherwise. When dates are included, they appear on the coverlet itself as part of the woven design.

Key: mdl — medallion

Jacquard

Compass star/4 mdls, 4-color, 1839, 2-pc, 80x88" 500.00
Floral mdl/eagle corners/zigzags, 66x82" 440.00
Floral mdls, red/natural, 1835, rpr, 90x98" 415.00
Floral mdls, red/natural, 2-pc/single weave, 77x93" 385.00
Floral mdls, 1851, dbl weave, rpr, 79x88" 250.00
Floral mdls, 4-color, 1853, 2-pc, 78x76", VG...............400.00
Floral mdls w/starflowers, 4-color, 1841, 2-pc, 97x80" 900.00
Floral mdls/buildings/chickens, 3-color, 2-pc, 84x74", VG...........550.00
Floral mdls/buildings/chickens, 4-color, 2-pc, 74x86"..............700.00
Floral panels/plant borders, 4-color, 1834, 1-pc/single weave, 96x82" ..600.00
Geometric, dbl-weave, 1830, 2-pc, 70x92", VG 450.00

Geometrics/tree border, summer/winter, 86x86", VG 110.00
Leaf panels/foliage borders, 1834, 2-pc/dbl weave, 72x89" 450.00
Lion corner block/eagle & tree border, single weave, 34x84", G......300.00
Rose center/eagle & tree border, PA, 1833, 94x86" 880.00
Rose mdls (4), 2-pc, rebound at top, 94x77"..........................415.00
Rose mdls (4), 4-color, 1838, 1-pc, 70x78", NM 1,450.00
Rose mdls (4)/stars/vines, 3-color, 1838, 2-pc, 99x76"................935.00
Rose mdls/men's faces/chain links, 2-pc/dbl weave, 70x75", G ...300.00
Rose mdls/starflowers, 2-pc, 76x78", VG..............................385.00
Star mdl w/flowers, eagle spandrels, 3-color, 80x102", G.............135.00
Star mdls/building borders, 3-color, OH, 1846, 1-pc, 90x76" 880.00
Stars/rose mdls w/eagles/trees, 4-color, 1833, 78x96" 600.00

Overshot

Dmns, bl/red/wht, stains/wear, 2-pc, 66x84".............................200.00
Geometrics, corners cut for bed posts, 92x21" 175.00
Geometrics, tomato red/brn/wht, 2-pc, wear, 69x61"..................225.00
Optical, 2 woven bands in fringe, 2-pc, 80x96", VG....................300.00
Stars/dmns/herringbone, 4-color, 2-pc, 74x84", VG 200.00

Cowan

Guy Cowan opened a small pottery near Cleveland, Ohio, in 1913, where he made tile and artware on a small scale from the natural red clay available there. He developed distinctive glazes — necessary, he felt, to cover the dark red body. After the war and a temporary halt in production, Cowan moved his pottery to Rocky River, where he made a commercial line of artware utilizing a highly-fired white porcelain. Although he acquiesced to the necessity of mass production, every effort was made to insure a product of highest quality. Fine artists, among them Waylande Gregory, Thelma Frazier, and Viktor Schreckengost, designed pieces which were often produced in limited editions, some of which sell today for prices in the thousands. Most of the ware was marked 'Cowan,' except for the 1930 mass-produced line called 'Lakeware.' Falling under the crunch of the Great Depression, the pottery closed in 1931.

The use of an asterisk (*) in the listing below indicates a nonfactory name that is being provided as a suggested name for the convenience of present-day collectors. One example is the glaze *Original Ivory, which is a high-gloss white that resembles undecorated porcelain. It was used on many of Cowan's lady 'flower figures' (Cowan's more graceful term for what some collectors call frogs).

Our advisor for this category is Mark Bassett; he is listed in the Directory under Ohio. With Victoria Naumann, Mark is the author of *Cowan Pottery and the Cleveland School*, a detailed history of Cowan Pottery and of Guy Cowan's students, colleagues, and designers. Prices quoted are for examples in mint condition, unless noted otherwise.

Bookends, Push-Pull elephants, designed by Margaret Postgate, bronze glaze, two Pull elephants shown, $1,500.00 for the pair. (If pair consists of one Push and one Pull, value would be $2,000.00 in this glaze.)

Ashtray, #774, duck, April Green, RG Cowan, 2¾" 95.00
Ashtray, #925, unicorn, Oriental Red, W Gregory 95.00
Bookends, #E-3, ram, Oriental Red, W Gregory, 7⅜", pr 2,000.00
Bookends, #E-961, unicorn, Foliage, W Gregory, 6¾", pr........1,250.00
Bookends, #519, boy-girl, *Original Ivory, FN Wilcox, pr 300.00
Bookends, #748, camels, Russet Brown, A Blazys, pr 2,500.00
Bowl, #713-B, Columbine, 13" 95.00
Bowl, #741-B, Hyancinth, ftd, 17"..65.00
Bowl, pterodactyl-head hdls, April, 9x15".................................85.00
Cake plate, #X-1, Caramel, scalloped, ftd 60.00
Candlesticks, #716, sea horse, Special Ivory, 4¼", pr..................50.00
Candlesticks, #744-L/#744-R, Special Ivory, figures, pr 1,500.00
Candlesticks, #782, Knickerbocker, Special Ivory, 3¾", pr............50.00
Creamer, #525, kitten hdl, Jet & *Original Ivory 200.00
Figure, #D-2-D, Flamingo, Special Ivory, W Gregory, 11"..........550.00
Figure, #793, Spanish Dancer (lady), Primrose, 8½" 700.00
Flower frog, #685, Duet, 2 ladies dancing, Special Ivory 600.00
Flower frog, #805, Tambourine Dancer, Special Ivory, W Gregory ..2,500.00
Lamp, #501-B, Jet, candlestick shape, 10¾"................................85.00
Lamp, squirrel/flamingo, Peach, W Gregory, 10" 500.00
Pitcher, #623, Delphinium, bulbous, 5" 85.00
Plaque, Atalanta & Hound, Guava & Egyptian Blue..............1,250.00
Sculpture, Colonial Head, Terra Cotta, W Gregory, 14".......4,000.00
Sculpture, Russian Peasants, Terra Cotta, Blazys, set of 4 ....6,000.00
Strawberry jar, #SJ-2, Azure, attached saucer, 10¾"...................500.00
Tea tile, fish & Deco flowers, hand decor, rnd 350.00
Vase, #V-75, Oriental Red, ribbed, RG Cowan, 8" 250.00
Vase, #V-91, Dry Point fish, Melon Green & Black, VS, 6" 1,500.00
Vase, #585, *Gunmetal drip on Marigold, 9½"..........................500.00
Vase, #649-A, pillow form, Marigold, RG Cowan, 6½"................50.00
Vase, #747, Chinese Bird, Egypt Blue, RG Cowan, 11".............600.00

Cracker Jack

Kids have been buying Cracker Jack since it was first introduced in the 1890s. By 1912 it was packaged with a free toy inside. Before the first kernel was crunched, eager fingers had retrieved the surprise from the depth of the box — actually no easy task, considering the care required to keep the contents so swiftly displaced from spilling over the side! Though a little older, perhaps, many of those same kids still are looking — just as eagerly — for the Cracker Jack prizes. Point of sale, company collectibles, and the prizes as well have over the years reflected America's changing culture. Grocer sales and incentives from around the turn of the century — paper dolls, postcards, and song books — were often marked Rueckheim Brothers (the inventors of Cracker Jack) or Reliable Confections. Over the years the company made some changes, leaving a trail of clues that often help collectors date their items. The company's name changed in 1922 from Rueckheim Brothers & Eckstein (who had been made a partner for inventing a method for keeping the caramelized kernels from sticking together) to The Cracker Jack Company. Their Brooklyn office was open from 1914 until it closed in 1923. The first time the sailor Jack logo was used on their packaging was in 1919. The sailor image of a Rueckheim child (with red, white, and blue colors) was introduced by these German immigrants in an attempt to show support during the time of heightened patriotism after WW I. For packages and 'point of sale' dating, note that the word 'prize' was used from 1912 to 1925, 'novelty' from 1925 to 1932, and 'toy' from 1933 on.

The first loose-packed prizes were toys made of wood, clay, tin, metal, and lithographed paper (the reason some early prizes are stained). Plastic toys were introduced in 1946. Paper wrapped for safety purposes in 1948, subjects echo the 'hype' of the day — yo-yos, tops, whistles, and sports cards in the simple, peaceful days of our country, propaganda and war toys in the '40s, games in the '50s, and space toys in the '60s. Few of the estimated 15 billion prizes were marked. Advertising items from Angelus Marshmallow and Checkers Confections (cousins of the Cracker Jack family) are also collectible. When no condition is indicated, the items listed below are assumed to be in excellent to mint condition. 'CJ' indicates that the item is marked. Note: An often-asked question concerns the tin Toonerville Trolley called 'CJ.' No data has been found in the factory archives to authenticate this item; it is assumed that the 'CJ' merely refers to its small size. For further information see *Cracker Jack Toys, The Complete, Unofficial Guide for Collectors*, by Larry White. Our co-advisors for this category are Wes Johnson (listed in the Directory under Kentucky) and Harriet Joyce (under Florida). Also look for *The Prize Insider* newsletter listed in the Directory under Clubs, Newsletters, and Catalogs.

Dealer Incentives and Premiums

Badge, pin-bk, celluloid, lady w/CJ label reverse, 1905, 1¼"........**85.00**
Blotter, CJ question mk box, yel, 7¾x3¾"........**185.00**
Book, pocket; jester on cover, CJ Riddles........**45.00**
Book, recipe; Angelus, 1930s........**22.00**
Book, Uncle Sam Song Book, CJ, 1911, ea........**55.00**
Corkscrew/opener, metal plated, CJ/Angelus, 3¾" tube case........**85.00**
Golf tee set, wood tees in paper 'matchbook' folder, CJ, 1920s...**725.00**
Jigsaw puzzle, CJ or Checkers, 1 of 4, 7x10", in envelope........**35.00**
Marbles, Akro set of 12 in box w/instructions, CJ, 1929........**950.00**
Match holder, hinged, eng gold-tone case, CJ, 2½x1⅞"........**650.00**
Mirror, oval, Angelus (redhead or blond) on box........**89.00**
Pen, ink; w/nib, tin litho bbl, CJ........**485.00**
Pencil top clip, metal/celluloid, oval boy & dog logo........**220.00**
Postcard, bear, 1 of 16, CJ, 1907, ea........**35.00**
Puzzle, metal, CJ/Angelus, 1 of 15, '34, in envelope, ea........**14.00**
Riddle card, 2 series of 20, w/pkg/from factory, CJ, 1907, ea........**10.00**
Thimble, aluminum, CJ Co/Angelus, red pnt, rare, ea........**165.00**
Truck, steel, wood wheels for CJ pkg, unmk........**85.00**

Packaging

Box, popcorn; Question Mark box end for CJ 'Toy,' 1933-34......**250.00**
Box, popcorn; red scroll border, CJ 'Prize,' 1912-25, ea........**150.00**
Box, popcorn; store display, CJ 'Novelty,' 1925-32, ea........**90.00**
Canister, tin, CJ Cocoanut Corn Crisp, 1-lb........**55.00**
Canister, tin, CJ Cocoanut Corn Crisp, 10-oz........**65.00**

Tin container, Cracker Jack Cocoanut Corn Crisp, Chicago, IL, 8½x5½", NM, from $100.00 to $150.00. (Photo courtesy Fred Dodge)

CJ Commemorative canister, wht w/red scroll, 1980s, ea........**8.00**
Crate, shipping; wood, CJ, Rueckheim Bros Eck, 1902-22, lg.....**165.00**

Prizes, Cast Metal

Badge, 6-point star, mc CJ Police, silver, 1931, 1¼"........**55.00**
Button, stud bk, Me for Cracker Jack, boy & dog, oval........**55.00**
Chair, T (Tootsie), 3 different sectional pcs, pnt, mini, ea........**12.00**
Coins, Presidents, 31 series, CJ, 1933, ea........**9.00**
Horse & wagon, CJ, 3-D, silver or gold, early, 2½", ea........**250.00**
Pistol, soft lead, inked, CJ on bbl, early, rare, 2⅛"........**180.00**
Rocking horse, no rider, 3-D, inked, early, 1⅛"........**25.00**
Rocking horse w/boy, 3-D, inked, early, 1½"........**32.00**
Tootsietoy series: boats, cars, animals; 1931, ¾"-1½", ea........**7.00**

Prizes, Paper

Book, Animals (or Birds), to color, Makatoy, unmk, 1949, mini...**35.00**
Book, Bess & Bill on CJ Hill, series of 12, 1937, mini........**105.00**
Book, Chaplin flip book, CJ, 1920s, ea........**140.00**
Book, drawing w/tracing paper, CJ, 1920s, mini........**110.00**
Booklet, stickers/wisecracks/riddles, Borden, CJ, 1965 on........**3.00**
Disguise, ears, red (out of carrier), unmk, 1950, pr........**30.00**
Disguise, glasses, hinged, cello lenses, CJ Where Ever..., 1933......**65.00**
Disguise, mustache, blk/brn, in carrier, CJ, 1949........**55.00**
Fan, lady's, folding, mc, unmk........**45.00**
Fortune wheel, 2-pc litho, turn for fortune, CJ, 1¾"........**70.00**
Game, Midget Auto Race, wheel spins, CJ, 1949, 3⅜" H........**25.00**
Game spinner, ...baseball at home, unmk, 1946, 1½" dia........**60.00**
Hat, Indian headdress, CJ, 1931, 2½" H........**125.00**
Hat, Indian headdress, CJ, 1950s, 5⅝" H........**275.00**
Hat, Me for CJ, early, ea........**120.00**
Magic game book, erasable slate, CJ, series of 13, 1946, ea........**25.00**
Movie, boy at blkboard, turn wheel: draws/erases, CJ, 1931, 2"..**175.00**
Movie, Goofy Zoo, trn wheel(s): change animals, unmk, 1939.....**25.00**
Movie, pull tab for 2nd picture, yel, early, 3", in envelope........**125.00**
Sand toy pictures, pours for action, series of 14, 1967, ea........**25.00**
Top, string; Rainbow Spinner, 2-pc, cb, different designs, ea........**45.00**
Transfer, iron-on, sport figure or patriotic, CJ, 1939, ea........**22.00**
Transfer, iron-on, sport figure or patriotic, unmk, 1939, ea........**6.00**
Whistle, Blow for More, CJ box/boy/dog, yel, 1931, ea........**55.00**
Whistle, pressed paper, series of 10, 1948-49, CJ, 1¼x2", ea........**34.00**
Whistle, Razz Zooka, C Carey Cloud design, CJ, 1949........**32.00**

Prizes, Plastic

Animals, standup on base, assorted, Nosco or CJ, 1947 on, ea........**2.00**
Baseball players, 3-D, bl or gray team, 1948, 1½", ea........**8.00**
Disc, emb fish plaque, oval, series of 10, 1956, unmk, ea........**14.00**
Dog, 3-D, hollow base, series of 10, CJCO, 1954, ea........**6.00**
Figure on rocking base, semi-flat, 1 of 9, Cloud design, '56........**4.00**
Fob, alphabet letter w/loop on top, 1 of 26, 1954, 1½"........**4.00**
Magnifying glass, many designs/shapes, from 1961, ea........**1.00**
Palm puzzle, ball(s) roll into holes, rectangle, CJ, 1920s, ea........**55.00**
Palm puzzle, ball(s) roll into holes, sq, CJ, 1920s, ea........**45.00**
Pinball game, lever shoots ball/score in holes, 1964 to recent........**5.00**
Signs, road; Stop, Caution, etc, yel, series of 10, 1954-60, ea........**5.00**
Toys, take apart/assemble, variety, from '62, assembled, ea........**2.00**
Toys, take apart/assemble, variety, from '62, unassembled, ea........**5.00**

Prizes, Tin

Badge, boy & dog diecut, w/o tab at top, CJ........**95.00**
Badge, litho, red/wht/bl, boy/dog, CJ, 1920s, 1¼" dia........**150.00**
Bank, 3-D book form, red/gr/or blk, CJ Bank, early, 2"........**120.00**
Bookmark, dogs, 4 different, 1941, 3", ea........**18.00**
Cash register, litho, More You Eat, CJ, early, 1⅞"........**275.00**
Clicker, 'Noisy CJ Snapper,' pear shape, aluminum, 1949........**20.00**
Clicker, CJ Telegraph, Pat 1897, inked, 1¾" dia, ea........**145.00**
Fortune Wheel, 2-pc litho, CJ, 1939-41, 1¾"........**105.00**

Horse & wagon, litho diecut, CJ & Angelus, 2⅛" **65.00**
Model T Ford, License: NY 1915 #999, blk/wht, CJ, rare, 2" **410.00**
Pocket watch, silver or gold, CJ as numerals, 1931, 1½" **55.00**
Small box shape: Elect Alarm Clock litho, unmk, 1⅛" **75.00**
Small box shape: electric stove litho, unmk, 1⅛" **80.00**
Small box shape: radio litho, bl, unmk, 1⅛" **60.00**
Soldier, litho, die-cut standup, officer/private/etc, unmk, ea **17.00**
Spinner, wood stick, Always on Top, red/wht/bl, CJ, 1½" dia **25.00**
Spinner, wood stick, Question Mark Box at center, CJ **50.00**
Spinner, wood stick, 2 Toppers, red/wht/bl, Angelus/Jack, 1½" **85.00**
Stand up, comic character, 1 of 10, CJ, 1936-46, ea **80.00**
Stand up, rectangle litho, boy & dog, ca 1916, lg or sm, ea **155.00**
Tall box shape: grandfather clock, unmk, 1947, 1¾" **65.00**
Tall box shape: radio, Tune in w/CJ, brn/yel, 1939, 1¾" **125.00**
Train, engine & tender, litho, CJ Line/512 ....**125.00**
Train, litho engine only, red, 1941, unmk **20.00**
Train, Lone Eagle Flyer engine, unmk **60.00**
Tray, emb, litho w/early pkg, 2¼x1¾" **95.00**
Wagon shape: Caterpillar tractor, unmk, 1931, 1¾" L..................**35.00**
Wagon shape: CJ Shows, yel circus wagon, series of 5, ea **175.00**
Wagon shape: tank, orange/red/gr camouflage, unmk **65.00**
Wheelbarrow, tin plated, bk leg in place, CJ, 1931, 2½" L **35.00**

Miscellaneous

Ad, Saturday Evening Post, mc, CJ, 1919, 11x14" **18.00**
Hat, ball park vendor cap, CJ, 1930s **30.00**
Lunch box, tin, 2 hdls, CJ, 1980s, 4½x5x6" **40.00**
Medal, CJ salesman award, brass, 1939, scarce..............................**125.00**
Sign, boy or girl w/box of CJ, 5-color cb, early, 17x22", ea **460.00**
Sign, Jack & Bingo, die-cut litho, easel standup, CJ, early..........**450.00**
Sign, Jack & Bingo, standing on early CJ pkg, mc cb, rare **520.00**
Sign, Santa & prizes, mc cb, Checkers, early, lg **1,000.00**

Crackle Glass

Though this type of glassware was introduced as early as the 1880s (by the New England Glass Co.), it was made primarily from 1930 until about 1980. It was produced by more than five hundred companies here (by Benko, Rainbow, and Kanawah, among others) and abroad (by such renown companies as Moser, for example), and its name is descriptive. The surface looks as though the glass has been heated then plunged into cold water, thus producing a network of tight cracks. It was made in a variety of colors; among the more expensive today are ruby red, amberina, cobalt, cranberry, and gray. For more information we recommend *Crackle Glass, Identification and Value Guide, Book I* and *Book II* (Collector Books), by Stan and Arlene Weitman, our advisors this category; they are listed in the Directory under New York. See also Moser.

Apple, gold peanut shell crackle w/gold leaf, 3½" **125.00**
Basket, dk orange w/crystal hdl, Hamon, 1940s-70s, 4¾" **75.00**
Candlesticks, bl, flat rim, Rainbow, 1940s-60s, 6", pr..................**150.00**
Creamer & sugar bowl, amber, smooth rim, Bonita, 1931-53, 2¾", pr..**85.00**
Cruet, orange pitcher form, clear dbl-ball stopper, Rainbow, 6¾".**85.00**
Decanter, amberina, invt cone w/long thin neck, Blenko, 17"....**200.00**
Decanter, amethyst, ball stopper, Rainbow, 1940s-60s, 8½" **125.00**
Decanter, crystal, appl crystal decor, teardrop stopper, Bonita, 7"..**100.00**
Decanter, smoke gray, slim, Pilgrim, 1950s, 11" **125.00**
Goblet, amber, long stem, att Blenko, 1960s, 11½" **125.00**
Patio light, topaz, Viking, 1944-60, 5x3"..**50.00**
Pitcher, amberina, pulled-bk hdl, 5" **60.00**
Pitcher, crystal w/bl serpentine at top, bl hdl, Blenko, 12¾" **150.00**
Rose bowl, tangerine, Pilgrim, 1949-69, 5¼x4½" **125.00**

Tumbler, crystal w/gr serpentine, European, 1920s, 8" **85.00**
Vase, amethyst, ruffled/crimped rim, Bischoff, 1940-63, 7½" **175.00**
Vase, bud; vaseline, stick neck, 6" **75.00**
Vase, clear w/faint gr tint, wht metal decor, ruffled rim, 8¾"......**150.00**
Vase, cobalt satin, bulbous, sm opening w/flared rim, 6" **110.00**
Vase, cobalt w/appl serpentine decor, ca 1940s, 4"........................**55.00**
Vase, olive gr, long cylindrical neck w/appl serpentine, Pilgrim, 7"...**75.00**
Vase, smoke gray, ruffled rim, Rainbow, 1940-60s, 4¾" **75.00**

Cranberry Glass

Cranberry glass is named for its resemblance to the color of cranberry juice. It was made by many companies both here and abroad, becoming popular in America soon after the Civil War. It was made in free-blown ware as well as mold-blown. Today cranberry glass is being reproduced, and it is sometimes difficult to distinguish the old from the new. Ask a reputable dealer if you are unsure.

For further information we recommend *American Art Glass* by John A. Shumann III, available from Collector Books or your local bookstore. See also Cruets; Salts; Sugar Shakers; Syrups.

Vase, ruffled rim, three indents in body, gold and enameled floral decor, 11", $275.00.

Basket, ruffled rim, clear twist hdl **230.00**
Biscuit jar, Invt T'print, floral decor, emb SP lid, 7½" **615.00**
Bottle, gold stars, star cut in base, w/stopper, 6x3"......................**165.00**
Bowl, clear scallops, mc florals w/gold, brass ft, 5x6⅜"................**195.00**
Bowl, finger; amber threading on ruffled rim **135.00**
Celery vase, Invt T'print, HP birds & flowers, SP Aurora hdld fr, 8"...**895.00**
Compote, mc florals & gold berries, clear ped, 4x6⅛" **135.00**
Cruet, craquelle, cut stopper, clear appl hdl **260.00**
Decanter, clear wafer ft, rope hdl, clear finial, 10¾" **195.00**
Decanter, floral decor, ribbed, flared rim, hollow stopper, 9¼" ...**175.00**
Ewer, floral decor, clear hdl, 8½x4¼"..**300.00**
Hat, SP brim, 2⅝" **190.00**
Pitcher, clear glass ice bladder, 10x5" **210.00**
Pitcher, waisted, clear ribbon hdl..**125.00**
Pitcher, water; Invt T'print, bulbous, 8" **215.00**
Pitcher, water; Invt T'print w/HP decor **325.00**
Plate, 8" **55.00**
Shade, Dmn Quilt, 4x6x8" **290.00**
Shakers, floral decor, orig lids, pr..**215.00**
Sugar bowl, clear ft, clear bubble finial, 6x4" **110.00**
Sweetmeat jar, HP decor, rstr SP lid/hdl, 4½" dia........................**250.00**
Syrup, SP hdl & spout, 6¾" **435.00**
Tankard, HP decor, 14" **125.00**
Tumbler, Invt T'print, 4¼"..**65.00**
Vase, wht lilies of the valley w/gold leaves, 7½" **135.00**

Crown Ducal

The Crown Ducal mark was first used by the A.G. Richardson &

Co. Pottery of Tunstall, England, in 1925. The items collectors are taking a particular interest in were decorated by Charlotte Rhead, a contemporary of Suzie Cooper and Clarice Cliff, and a member of the esteemed family of English pottery designers and artists.

Bowl, dragonflies on blk, bl int, 2x4¾" 70.00
Bowl, Rosalie, flower finial on lid, hdls, 10¼" 130.00
Charger, Pattern #5983, Charlotte Rhead, ca 1938, 12½" 335.00
Colonial Times, platter, Crown Ducal, 14" 165.00
Creamer & sugar bowl, Gainsborough, 3", 3¼" 60.00
Cup & saucer, fruits & flowers w/gold trim, ...30.00
Jug, Pattern #4100, orange/brn/cream, C Rhead, 5x4" 145.00
Plate, New Orleans, bl transfer, 10" 100.00
Platter, Pattern #762055, red birds & flowers, 10¼x9", NM 80.00
Toast rack, Peony Rose, sm rpr, 6x3" 120.00
Vase, Chinese Lantern, 9x5" 215.00
Vase, Pattern #2682, brn lotus leaves, C Rhead, ca 1932, 8½x4½" ...175.00

Crown Milano

Crown Milano was a line of decorated milk glass (or opal ware) introduced by the Mt. Washington Glass Co. of New Bedford, Massachussetts, in the early 1890s. It had previously been called Albertine Ware. Some pieces are marked with a 'CM,' and many had paper labels. This ware is usually highly decorated and will most likely have a significant amount of gold painted on it. The shiny pieces were recently discovered to have been called 'Colonial Ware' and have a laurel wreath and a crown. This ware was well received in its day, and outstanding pieces bring high prices on today's market. Advisors for this category are Wilfred and Dolli Cohen; they are listed in the Directory under California.

Biscuit jar, floral w/gold, SP rim/bail/lid, #4404, 6¾" 750.00
Bonbon, Colonial Ware, mc pansies, #3610, 1¾x5¼" 275.00
Bride's basket, gold & orange flowers, sq top, Pairpoint fr, 10x10" ...1,600.00
Cup & saucer, demi; dainty flowers w/much gold/blk dots, 2", 5" 1,750.00
Ewer, Colonial Ware, floral w/gold, rope hdl, 6½x7½" 835.00
Ewer, farmyard scene cartouche w/gold, rope hdl, #504, 10½" 2,250.00
Lamp, banquet; Colonial Ware, roses/gold, globe shade, 23x9" ...2,500.00
Pitcher, gold mums in blown-out reserves, reeded hdl, 8¼" 800.00
Sugar shaker, daisies/swags, tomato shape, metal collar, emb lid, 3x4" ..535.00
Sweetmeat, bl & wht diagonal stripes intaglio, gold floral, 4x5½" ...1,025.00
Sweetmeat, Dmn Quilt w/gold oak leaves/jewels, SP lid, branch hdl, 5" ...900.00
Syrup, netting, gold on pk, florals, melon ribs, 6" 1,850.00
Tumbler, Colonial Ware, gold bows/flower garlands, 3¾" 400.00
Vase, cherubs w/gold/jewels, #503, sm rstr, 19x8" 1,725.00
Vase, Colonial Ware, dancing couple, gold scrolls, #1029, 17½" ...1,150.00
Vase, Colonial Ware, mixed flowers w/gold, #0615, 9" 945.00
Vase, Colonial Ware, poppies w/gold net/scrolls on wht, hdls, 10" ..925.00
Vase, floral, mc w/gold scrolls, tricorner stick form, 8¼" 1,200.00
Vase, forget-me-nots, bulbous, 4-fold top, 24 swirling ribs, 6x5¾" ..1,350.00
Vase, Ginko, gold & gr leaves on wht, 6½x7½", NM 700.00
Vase, jack-in-the -pulpit; floral on pnt burmese, 9¾" 775.00
Vase, Nouveau peonies/buds/etc, 24 swirled ribs, 6x5¾" 1,250.00
Vase, pansies w/gold, petticoat shape, 10½" 750.00
Vase, peonies on soft lemon w/much gold, shouldered, 8" 765.00
Vase, sailboats w/Venetian scene beyond, bulbous, decor rim, 10" ...2,000.00
Vase, thistles w/gold, 3-hdl, triangular stick form, 9¼" 1,000.00

Cruets

Cruets, containers made to hold oil or vinegar, are usually bulbous with tall, narrow throats, a handle, and a stopper. During the nineteenth century and for several years after, they were produced in abundance in virtually every type of glassware available. Those listed below are assumed to be with stopper and mint unless noted otherwise. Our advisor for this category is Elaine Ezell; she is listed in the Directory under Maryland. See also Specific manufacturers.

Ada...60.00
Amazon, amber, w/orig Bar-in-Hand stopper, 1880-95, 8" 500.00
Amazon, w/orig Bar-in-Hand stopper, 1880-95, 8" 125.00
Arched Ovals, gr 130.00
Argonaut Shell, custard w/EX gold, 6½", from $800 to.............850.00
Bead Swag, milk glass w/gold beading 250.00
Beaded Swirl & Lens, ruby stain 195.00
Bubble Lattice Paneled Sprig, wht opal 325.00
Button Arches, ruby stain, bulbous, ribbed stopper 250.00
Cathedral, amber 125.00
Chrysanthemum Base Swirl, bl opal 250.00
Cranberry, threaded, clear reed hdl & bubble stopper, 7" 195.00
Cranberry spatter, ruffled top, clear stopper, 5¾" 95.00
Cut Log, lg 70.00
Daisy & Fern, bl opal, swirled, bl hdl, cut stopper, 6¾" 195.00
Daisy & Fern, wht opal, Northwood 225.00
Delaware, gr w/gold 495.00
Delaware, rose w/gold 550.00
Dewey, canary 195.00
Dmn Quilt, apricot MOP, frosted stopper, NM 350.00
Everglades, bl opal 500.00
Everglades, vaseline opal 595.00
Feather 60.00
Feather, gr 250.00
Fine Cut, vaseline..195.00
Flora, bl opal 795.00
Florette, pk satin, frosted hdl & stopper 235.00
Georgia Gem, custard w/gold 295.00
Hidalgo, frosted..70.00

Hobnail, cranberry opalescent, faceted crystal stopper, Hobbs & Brockunier, 7¼", $495.00.

Hobnail, rubena verde, Hobbs & Brockunier..........................595.00
Intaglio, vaseline opal 795.00
Inverted T'print, amber, amber hdl, cut stopper, 6½" 225.00
Inverted T'print, amberina, amber stopper, 6" 325.00
Inverted T'print, amberina, 5½" 300.00
Inverted T'print, cranberry 295.00
Inverted T'print, reverse amberina, amber hdl & stopper, 7½" 400.00
Ivy Scroll, gr 125.00
Jackson, vaseline opal..225.00
Massachusetts...50.00
Medallion Sprig, bl 450.00
Michigan..65.00
Nailhead, rose stain 295.00
New Jersey..50.00

Paneled Forget-Me-Not	55.00	R-37, now scarce, VG-	40.00
Paneled Herringbone, gr	125.00	R-39, VG	30.00
Paneled Thistle	60.00	R-41, scarce, G+	38.00
Pennsylvania	45.00	R-47, VG	30.00
Pillow Encircled, ruby stain, sm	150.00	R-48, G-	23.00
Plume	40.00	R-49, VG	30.00
Portland	65.00	R-53, now scarce, EX	60.00
Prize, gr	225.00	R-54, now scarce, VG-	48.00
Radiant Daisy, frosted w/amber stain	150.00	R-55, EX	85.00
Royal Crystal, ruby stain, sm	295.00	R-56, scarce, G	42.00
Sapphire bl crackle, bl reeded hdl, bl ball stopper, 7½x3½"	145.00	R-62-A, VG-	48.00
Seaweed, bl opal satin	475.00	R-65, scarce, G	42.00
Spanish Lace, bl opal, Northwood, clear cut stopper	595.00	R-79, G	32.00
Spanish Lace, wht opal, clear cut stopper	325.00	R-97, scarce, VG-	48.00
Stripe, wht opal	175.00	R-101, scarce, VG	51.00
Tiny Optic, amethyst w/decor	125.00	R-104, VG	35.00
Torpedo, faceted stopper	90.00	R-124-A, VG-	37.00
Tortoise shell, melon ribbed, clear hdl, faceted stopper, 7"	225.00	R-136-A, now rare, G+	68.00
Truncated Cube, ruby flashed & clear, pressed cube stopper	200.00	R-145-C, G+	30.00
Wild Bouquet, bl opal, opal hdl, clear stopper, 7¼"	395.00	R-150, G	31.00
Wisconsin	95.00	R-154-B, VG	35.00
Zipper	45.00	R-158-B, scarce, EX-	50.00

Cup Plates, Glass

Before the middle 1850s, it was socially acceptable to pour hot tea into a deep saucer to cool. The tea was sipped from the saucer rather than the cup, which frequently was handleless and too hot to hold. The cup plate served as a coaster for the cup. It is generally agreed that the first examples of pressed glass cup plates were made about 1826 at the Boston and Sandwich Glass Co. in Sandwich, Cape Cod, Massachusetts. Other glassworks in three major areas (New England, Philadelphia, and the Midwest, especially Pittsburgh) quickly followed suit.

Antique glass cup plates range in size from 2⅝" up to 4¼" in diameter. The earliest plates had simple designs inspired by cut glass patterns, but by 1829 they had become more complex. The span from then until about 1845 is known as the 'Lacy Period,' when cup plate designs and pressing techniques were at their peak. To cover pressing imperfections, the backgrounds of the plates were often covered with fine stippling which endowed them with a glittering brilliance called 'laciness.' They were made in a multitude of designs — some purely decorative, others commemorative. Subjects include the American eagle, hearts, sunbursts, log cabins, ships, George Washington, the political candidates Clay and Harrison, plows, beehives, etc. Of all the patterns, the round George Washington plate is the rarest and most valuable — only four are known to exist today.

Authenticity is most important. Collectors must be aware that contemporary plates which have no antique counterparts and fakes modeled after antique patterns have had wide distribution. Condition is also important, though it is the exceptional plate that does not have some rim roughness. More important considerations are scarcity of design and color.

Our advisor for this category is John Bilane; he is listed in the Directory under New Jersey. The book *American Glass* by George and Helen McKearin has a section on glass cup plates. The definitive book is *American Glass Cup Plates* by Ruth Webb Lee and James H. Rose. Numbers in the listings that follow refer to the latter. When attempting to evaluate a cup plate, remember that minor rim roughness is normal. See also Staffordshire; Pairpoint.

		R-159-A, scarce, G	39.00
		R-159-B, EX	40.00
		R-162-A, VG	35.00
		R-169-B, EX	40.00
		R-172-A, EX	40.00
		R-172-B, VG	34.00
		R-174, EX	45.00
		R-176-A, EX	43.00
		R-177, VG	43.00
		R-216, G	53.00
		R-235, VG	35.00
		R-236, G	28.00
		R-242-A, VG	34.00
		R-243, VG+	37.00
		R-245, G-	24.00
		R-255, VG	20.00
		R-256-A, rare, G+	75.00
		R-257, VG-	32.00
		R-258, VG	30.00
		R-269, VG	30.00
		R-269-B, G+	34.00
		R-271-A, VG	30.00
		R-272, VG+	31.00
		R-275, VG-	32.00
		R-285, VG	37.00
		R-291, VG-	26.00
		R-311, VG-	20.00
		R-313, G	18.00
		R-323, VG-	18.00
		R-324, VG	19.00
		R-327, G-	12.00
		R-332-B, G-	12.00
		R-333, VG	19.00
		R-334, G+	17.00
		R-334-A, G	15.00
		R-339, VG	19.00
		R-340, G	15.00
		R-343-B, scarce, VG	35.00
R-20, VG	30.00	R-365, VG	16.00
R-22, VG	30.00	R-367, G-	10.00
R-27, VG	30.00	R-370, EX-	16.00
R-28, VG	28.00	R-371, VG+	16.00

R-379, G 11.00
R-381, VG 14.00
R-390-A, G+ 11.00
R-391, VG 13.00
R-396, VG 13.00
R-402, VG 14.00
R-425, G 21.00
R-439-C, scarce, G 28.00
R-447, G 22.00
R-449, G- 39.00
R-458-A, VG- 28.00
R-465-F, VG 19.00
R-465-H, VG 23.00
R-465-N, G 16.00
R-467, VG 19.00
R-467-A, G 15.00
R-476, G- 13.00
R-479, VG 20.00
R-508, G+ 15.00
R-516, VG 17.00
R-524, scarce, G 20.00
R-531, VG- 20.00
R-546, G+ 15.00
R-562-A, very rare, G 245.00
R-564, G+ 26.00
R-565-A, G+ 26.00
R-569, VG 43.00
R-576, scarce, G 45.00
R-593, scarce, G 42.00
R-605-A, scarce, G+ 135.00
R-610-A, VG 34.00
R-610-C, VG- 40.00
R-612-A, rare, G- 165.00
R-619, G 35.00
R-636, VG- 42.00
R-643-A, VG 26.00
R-645-A, VG 21.00

R-654-A, eagle, 3", mold roughness, chip, $170.00;
R-694, beehive, roughness, $130.00

R-656, very rare, G 280.00
R-661, VG 39.00
R-665-A, G+ 34.00
R-666, VG 35.00
R-666-A, scarce, VG 48.00
R-667-A, G 32.00
R-670-A, VG 39.00
R-676-C, G 47.00
R-677, VG 38.00
R-679, VG 34.00
R-680, VG 34.00
R-691, scarce, G 70.00

R-693, scarce, G+ 75.00

Cups and Saucers

The earliest utensils for drinking were small porcelain and stoneware bowls imported from China by the East Indian Company in the early seventeenth century. European and English tea bowls and saucers, imitating Chinese and Japanese originals, were produced from the early eighteenth century and often decorated with Chinese-type motifs. By about 1810, handles were fitted to the bowl to form the now familiar teacup, and this form became almost universal. Coffee in England and on the continent was often served in a can — a straight-sided cylinder with a handle. After 1820 the coffee can gave way to the more fanciful form of the coffee cup.

An infinite variety of cups and saucers are available for both the new and experienced collector, and they can be found in all price ranges. There is probably no better way to thoroughly know and understand the various ceramic manufacturers than to study cups and saucers. Our advisors for this category, Susan and Jim Harran, have written two books, entitled *Collectible Cups and Saucers, Identification and Values, Books I* and *II*, published by Collector Books. Over 800 full-color photos fill book II which is divided into six collectible categories: early years (1700 – 1875), cabinet cups, nineteenth and twentieth century dinnerware, English tablewares, miniatures, and mustache cups and saucers. The Harrans are listed in the Directory under New Jersey.

Coffee, #3770, landscapes & bamboo, att Bodley, ca 1875, from $60 to ...**80.00**
Coffee, HP roses w/gold, Ahrenfeld, 1886-1910, from $100 to ...**125.00**
Coffee, mc flowers & insects, Lomonosov, 1930s-50s, from $45 to..**60.00**
Coffee, mums on wht to rose-pk, Royal Bayreuth, 1902, from $55 to .**65.00**
Coffee, portrait medallion, 3 paw ft, snake hdl, Riedl, 1890-1918.....**125.00**
Coffee can, Basalt, putto, loop hdl, Wedgwood, 1780-1820, from $400 to......**450.00**
Demi, beaded & hand-gilded decor on gr, Minton, 1891-1901, from $75 to.**100.00**
Demi, gilt scrolls & figures on dk red, Kuba, 1900-45, from $125 to...**150.00**
Demi, mc florals, paneled/ftd cup, Schumann, 1918-29, from $45 to....**55.00**
Demi, mc HP flowers, Von Schierholz, 1907, from $50 to **60.00**
Snack set, daisies, ribbed/waisted cup, Crown Staffordshire, 1930s+ ...**40.00**
Tea, bl floral transfer, ftd/scalloped, Taylor & Kent Ltd, 1939-49 **.40.00**
Tea, Brocade, Adams Titian Ware, 1924, from $25 to **35.00**
Tea, cobalt w/butterfly inside cup, Aynsley, 1950s, from $100 to .**125.00**
Tea, Cottage, Queen Anne shape, Shelley, 1925-45, from $50 to.**75.00**
Tea, Fence, underglaze bl, Worcester, 1780, from $250 to...........**300.00**
Tea, Florentine, ftd, kicked loop hdl, Wedgwood, 1901-19, from $50 to .**75.00**
Tea, HP portrait medallion, Royal Flute, Dresden, 1887-91, $350 to ...**400.00**
Tea, moriage flowers, Japan, 1920s, from $40 to **50.00**
Tea, pk pastoral transfer, ftd bowl, unmk Staffordshire, 1830s, up to...**150.00**
Tea, rose transfer on wht, Fr loop hdl, Crown Staffordshire, 1908-29 ...**45.00**
Tea, roses on lt gr, Old Royal Bone China, 1930-41, from $30 to.**40.00**
Tea, water scene/tartan ribbon, Royal Winton, 1934-50, from $60 to ..**75.00**

Currier & Ives by Royal

During the 1950s dinnerware decorated with transfer-printed scenes taken from prints by Currier and Ives was manufactured by Royal China and given as premiums through A&P stores. Though it was also made in pink and green, the blue is by far the most popular. Pie plates in black and brown can be found, but no china sets in these colors have been reported. Occasionally pieces are being found that have hand-painted colors on them with the same blue backgrounds. It has become a very popular collectible at malls and flea markets around the country. Included in our listings are pieces from Hostess sets, which should be of great interest to collectors. New pieces which have been added to the price list include the clock, coffee mug with round handle, tall cup, snack plate, spoon rest/wall plaque, second-type gravy and underplate, and third-type sugar bowl with no handles. Also, the 11½" round platter with the 'Rocky Mountains' scene has been added (very rare). Currier and Ives by Royal is one of the fastest growing collectibles on the market today. Our advisors for this category are Treva and Jack Hamlin; they are listed in the Directory under Ohio.

Ashtray, 5½", from $15 to 18.00
Bowl, cereal; tab hdl, 6¼" 48.00
Bowl, cereal; 6¼" 15.00
Bowl, dessert; 5½" 5.00
Bowl, soup; 8" 14.00
Bowl, vegetable, 9" 25.00
Bowl, vegetable; deep, 10" 30.00
Butter dish, Fashionable decal 55.00
Butter dish, Road Winter decal 40.00
Casserole, angle hdls 115.00
Casserole, tab hdls, knob turned 90 degrees 250.00
Clock, 10" plate, bl #s, 2 decals 200.00
Creamer, angle hdl 8.00
Creamer, rnd hdl, tall 48.00
Cup, angle hdl 4.00
Cup, rnd hdl, tall, 9" 10.00
Gravy boat, pour spout 20.00
Gravy boat, tab hdls 58.00
Ladle, gravy; all wht 50.00
Lamp, candle; w/globe 300.00
Mug, coffee; reg 35.00
Mug, coffee; rnd hdl 35.00
Pie baker, 9 decals, 10" 30.00
Plate, bread; 6½" 5.00
Plate, calendar; 10" 20.00
Plate, chop; Getting Ice, 11½" 38.00
Plate, chop; Rocky Mountains, 11½" 65.00
Plate, chop; 12¼" 35.00
Plate, dinner; 10" 7.00
Plate, luncheon; 9" 25.00
Plate, salad; 7¼" 15.00
Plate, snack; w/cup well, 9" 75.00
Platter, oval, 13" 35.00
Platter, tab hdls, 10½" dia 22.00
Platter, 13" dia 75.00
Saucer, 6⅛" 2.00
Shakers, pr 35.00
Spoon rest, wall hanging 75.00
Sugar bowl, hdld, w/lid 18.00
Sugar bowl, no hdls, flared top 48.00
Sugar bowl, no hdls, w/lid 35.00

Tab gravy and white tab underplate, rare, $125.00.
(Photo courtesy Jack and Treva Hamlin)

Teapot 150.00
Tidbit tray, 3-tier, orig only 75.00
Tray, gravy boat; like 7" plate 75.00
Tray, gravy boat; regular 20.00
Tumbler, iced tea; 12-oz, 5½" 17.50
Tumbler, juice; 5-oz, 3½" 17.50
Tumbler, old fashion; 7-oz, 3¼" 17.50
Tumbler, water; 8½-oz, 4¾" 17.50

Hostess Set Pieces

Bowl, candy; 7¾" 25.00
Bowl, dip; 4⅜" 20.00
Pie baker, 11" 45.00
Plate, cake; flat, 10" 40.00
Plate, cake; ftd, 10" 125.00
Plate, serving; 7" 18.00
Tray, deviled egg 150.00

Custard Glass

As early as the 1880s, custard glass was produced in England. Migrating glassmakers brought the formula for the creamy ivory ware to America. One of them was Harry Northwood, who in 1898 founded his company in Indiana, Pennsylvania, and introduced the glassware to the American market. Soon other companies were producing custard, among them Heisey, Tarentum, Fenton, and McKee. Not only dinnerware patterns but souvenir items were made. Today custard is the most expensive of the colored pressed glassware patterns. The formula for producing the luminous glass contains uranium salts which imparts the cream color to the batch and causes it to glow when it is examined under a black light.

Argonaut Shell, bowl, master berry; gold & decor, 10½" L 275.00
Argonaut Shell, bowl, sauce; ftd, gold & decor 75.00
Argonaut Shell, butter dish, gold & decor 350.00
Argonaut Shell, butter dish, no gold 300.00
Argonaut Shell, compote, jelly; gold & decor, scarce 165.00
Argonaut Shell, creamer, gold & decor 155.00
Argonaut Shell, creamer, no gold 110.00
Argonaut Shell, cruet, gold & decor 850.00
Argonaut Shell, pitcher, water; gold & decor 475.00
Argonaut Shell, shakers, gold & decor, pr 435.00
Argonaut Shell, spooner, gold & decor 200.00
Argonaut Shell, sugar bowl, w/lid, gold & decor 235.00
Argonaut Shell, tumbler, gold & decor 110.00
Bead Swag, bowl, sauce; floral & gold 50.00
Bead Swag, goblet, floral & gold 65.00
Bead Swag, tray, pickle; floral & gold, rare 300.00
Bead Swag, wine, floral & gold 60.00
Beaded Circle, bowl, master berry; floral & gold 275.00
Beaded Circle, butter dish, floral & gold 500.00
Beaded Circle, creamer, floral & gold 180.00
Beaded Circle, pitcher, water; floral & gold 750.00
Beaded Circle, shakers, floral & gold, pr 1,000.00
Beaded Circle, spooner, floral & gold 185.00
Beaded Circle, tumbler, floral & gold, very rare 150.00
Cane Insert, berry set, 7-pc 450.00
Cane Insert, table set, 4-pc 450.00
Cherry & Scales, bowl, master berry; nutmeg stain 145.00
Cherry & Scales, butter dish, nutmeg stain 250.00
Cherry & Scales, creamer, nutmeg stain 125.00
Cherry & Scales, pitcher, water; nutmeg stain, scarce 350.00

Cherry & Scales, spooner, nutmeg stain, scarce	125.00
Cherry & Scales, sugar bowl, w/lid, nutmeg stain, scarce	150.00
Cherry & Scales, tumbler, nutmeg stain, scarce	75.00
Chrysanthemum Sprig, bowl, master berry; gold & decor	300.00
Chrysanthemum Sprig, bowl, master berry; no gold	175.00
Chrysanthemum Sprig, bowl, sauce; ftd, gold & decor	60.00
Chrysanthemum Sprig, butter dish, gold & decor	375.00
Chrysanthemum Sprig, celery vase, gold & decor, rare	700.00
Chrysanthemum Sprig, compote, jelly; gold & decor	150.00
Chrysanthemum Sprig, compote, jelly; no decor	100.00
Chrysanthemum Sprig, creamer, gold & decor	135.00
Chrysanthemum Sprig, cruet, gold & decor, 6¾"	495.00
Chrysanthemum Sprig, pitcher, water; gold & decor	485.00
Chrysanthemum Sprig, pitcher, water; no decor	350.00
Chrysanthemum Sprig, shakers, gold & decor, pr	300.00
Chrysanthemum Sprig, spooner, gold & decor	135.00
Chrysanthemum Sprig, spooner, no gold	75.00
Chrysanthemum Sprig, sugar bowl, gold & decor	250.00
Chrysanthemum Sprig, toothpick holder, gold & decor	375.00
Chrysanthemum Sprig, toothpick holder, no decor	175.00
Chrysanthemum Sprig, tray, condiment; gold & decor, rare	595.00
Chrysanthemum Sprig, tumbler, gold & decor	80.00
Dandelion, mug, nutmeg stain	175.00
Delaware, bowl, sauce; pk stain	65.00
Delaware, creamer, breakfast; pk stain	75.00
Delaware, tray, pin; gr stain	85.00
Delaware, tumbler, pk stain	65.00
Diamond w/Peg, bowl, master berry; roses & gold	225.00
Diamond w/Peg, bowl, sauce; roses & gold	50.00
Diamond w/Peg, butter dish, roses & gold	275.00
Diamond w/Peg, creamer, ind; no decor	35.00
Diamond w/Peg, creamer, ind; souvenir	50.00
Diamond w/Peg, creamer, roses & gold	85.00
Diamond w/Peg, mug, souvenir	50.00
Diamond w/Peg, napkin ring, roses & gold, rare	175.00
Diamond w/Peg, pitcher, roses & gold, 5½"	275.00
Diamond w/Peg, sugar bowl, w/lid, roses & gold	175.00
Diamond w/Peg, toothpick holder, roses & gold	175.00
Diamond w/Peg, tumbler, roses & gold	75.00
Diamond w/Peg, water set, souvenir, 7-pc	650.00
Diamond w/Peg, wine, roses & gold	65.00
Diamond w/Peg, wine, souvenir	55.00
Everglades, bowl, master berry; gold & decor	215.00
Everglades, bowl, saucer; gold & decor	60.00
Everglades, butter dish, gold & decor	395.00
Everglades, creamer, gold & decor	155.00
Everglades, shakers, gold & decor, pr	375.00
Everglades, spooner, gold & decor	160.00
Everglades, sugar bowl, w/lid, gold & decor	235.00
Everglades, tumbler, gold & decor	100.00
Fan, bowl, master berry; good gold	200.00
Fan, bowl, sauce; good gold	60.00
Fan, butter dish, good gold	345.00
Fan, creamer, good gold	110.00
Fan, ice cream set, good gold, 7-pc	500.00
Fan, pitcher, water; good gold	300.00
Fan, spooner, good gold	100.00
Fan, sugar bowl, w/lid, good gold	175.00
Fan, tumbler, good gold	85.00
Fan, water set, good gold, 7-pc	725.00
Fine Cut & Roses, rose bowl, fancy int, nutmeg stain	100.00
Fine Cut & Roses, rose bowl, plain int	85.00
Geneva, bowl, master berry; floral decor, ftd, oval, 9" L	110.00
Geneva, bowl, master berry; floral decor, rnd, 9"	130.00
Geneva, bowl, sauce; floral decor, oval	50.00
Geneva, bowl, sauce; floral decor, rnd	50.00
Geneva, butter dish, floral decor	250.00
Geneva, butter dish, no decor	145.00
Geneva, compote, jelly; floral decor	95.00
Geneva, creamer, floral decor	115.00
Geneva, cruet, floral decor	475.00
Geneva, pitcher, water; floral decor	275.00
Geneva, shakers, floral decor, pr	280.00
Geneva, spooner, floral decor	100.00
Geneva, sugar bowl, open, floral decor	85.00
Geneva, sugar bowl, w/lid, floral decor	175.00
Geneva, syrup, floral decor	500.00
Geneva, toothpick holder, floral w/M gold	375.00
Geneva, tumbler, floral decor	60.00
Georgia Gem, bowl, master berry; good gold	135.00
Georgia Gem, bowl, master berry; gr opaque	115.00
Georgia Gem, butter dish, good gold	200.00
Georgia Gem, celery vase, good gold	145.00
Georgia Gem, creamer, good gold	100.00
Georgia Gem, creamer, no gold	60.00
Georgia Gem, cruet, good gold	295.00
Georgia Gem, mug, good gold	45.00
Georgia Gem, powder jar, w/lid, good gold	80.00
Georgia Gem, shakers, good gold, pr	140.00
Georgia Gem, spooner, souvenir	55.00
Georgia Gem, sugar bowl, w/lid, no gold	95.00
Grape (& Cable), bottle, scent; orig stopper, nutmeg stain	650.00
Grape (& Cable), bowl, banana; ftd, nutmeg stain	350.00
Grape (& Cable), bowl, centerpc; ftd, nutmeg stain	450.00
Grape (& Cable), bowl, master berry; flat, nutmeg stain	200.00
Grape (& Cable), bowl, nutmeg stain, 7½"	60.00
Grape (& Cable), bowl, orange; ftd, flat top, nutmeg stain	400.00
Grape (& Cable), bowl, orange; ftd, nutmeg stain	500.00
Grape (& Cable), bowl, sauce; nutmeg stain, ftd	50.00
Grape (& Cable), butter dish, nutmeg stain	300.00
Grape (& Cable), compote, jelly; open, nutmeg stain	150.00
Grape (& Cable), compote, nutmeg stain, 4½x8"	300.00
Grape (& Cable), cracker jar, nutmeg stain	850.00
Grape (& Cable), creamer, breakfast; nutmeg stain	80.00
Grape (& Cable), humidor, bl stain, rare	950.00
Grape (& Cable), humidor, nutmeg stain, rare	900.00
Grape (& Cable), nappy, nutmet stain, rare	60.00
Grape (& Cable), pitcher, water; nutmeg stain	550.00
Grape (& Cable), plate, nutmeg stain, 7"	50.00
Grape (& Cable), plate, nutmeg stain, 8"	65.00
Grape (& Cable), powder jar, nutmeg stain	350.00
Grape (& Cable), punch bowl, w/base, nutmeg stain	1,900.00
Grape (& Cable), spooner, nutmeg stain	155.00
Grape (& Cable), sugar bowl, breakfast; open, nutmeg stain	85.00
Grape (& Cable), sugar bowl, w/lid, nutmeg stain	225.00
Grape (& Cable), tray, dresser; nutmeg stain, scarce, lg	375.00
Grape (& Cable), tray, pin; nutmeg stain	150.00
Grape (& Cable), tumbler, nutmeg stain	75.00
Grape & Gothic Arches, bowl, master berry; pearl w/gold	200.00
Grape & Gothic Arches, bowl, sauce; pearl w/gold, rare	80.00
Grape & Gothic Arches, butter dish, pearl w/gold	235.00
Grape & Gothic Arches, creamer, pearl w/gold, rare	100.00
Grape & Gothic Arches, favor vase, nutmeg stain	80.00
Grape & Gothic Arches, goblet, pearl w/gold	75.00
Grape & Gothic Arches, pitcher, water; pearl w/gold	300.00
Grape & Gothic Arches, spooner, pearl w/gold	85.00
Grape & Gothic Arches, sugar bowl, w/lid, pearl w/gold	135.00
Grape & Gothic Arches, tumbler, pearl w/gold	65.00

Grape Arbor, vase, hat form..90.00
Heart w/Thumbprint, creamer 90.00
Heart w/Thumbprint, lamp, good pnt, scarce, 8" 450.00
Heart w/Thumbprint, sugar bowl, ind...............................95.00
Honeycomb, wine...65.00
Horse Medallion, bowl, gr stain, 7"..................................85.00
Intaglio, bowl, master berry; gold & decor, ftd, 9" 250.00
Intaglio, bowl, sauce; gold & decor.....................................50.00
Intaglio, butter dish, gold & decor, scarce 300.00
Intaglio, compote, jelly; gold & decor 125.00
Intaglio, creamer, gold & decor 125.00
Intaglio, cruet, gold & decor..475.00
Intaglio, pitcher, water; gold & decor...............................395.00
Intaglio, shakers, gold & decor, pr 250.00
Intaglio, spooner, gold & decor...135.00
Intaglio, sugar bowl, w/lid, gold & decor.........................180.00
Intaglio, tumbler, gold & decor...95.00
Inverted Fan & Feather, bowl, master berry; gold & decor..........275.00
Inverted Fan & Feather, bowl, sauce; gold & decor 75.00
Inverted Fan & Feather, butter dish, gold & decor.....................400.00
Inverted Fan & Feather, compote, jelly; gold & decor, rare 500.00
Inverted Fan & Feather, creamer, gold & decor............................175.00
Inverted Fan & Feather, cruet, gold & decor, scarce, 6½" 1,100.00
Inverted Fan & Feather, pitcher, water; gold & decor.................700.00
Inverted Fan & Feather, punch cup, gold & decor 250.00
Inverted Fan & Feather, shakers, gold & decor, pr 750.00
Inverted Fan & Feather, spooner, gold & decor............................165.00
Inverted Fan & Feather, sugar bowl, w/lid, gold & decor 250.00
Inverted Fan & Feather, tumbler, gold & decor............................115.00
Jackson (Alaska Variant), bowl, master berry; good gold, ftd......150.00
Jackson (Alaska Variant), bowl, sauce; good gold.........................50.00
Jackson (Alaska Variant), creamer, good gold...............................85.00
Jackson (Alaska Variant), pitcher, water; good gold..................250.00
Jackson (Alaska Variant), pitcher, water; no decor.....................175.00
Jackson (Alaska Variant), shakers, good gold, pr 195.00
Jackson (Alaska Variant), tumbler, good gold................................50.00

Louis XV, master berry bowl, four-footed, gold tracery, 10½" long, $250.00.

Louis XV, bowl, sauce; good gold, ftd..............................50.00
Louis XV, butter dish, good gold 250.00
Louis XV, creamer, good gold...85.00
Louis XV, pitcher, water; good gold 250.00
Louis XV, spooner, good gold..110.00
Louis XV, sugar bowl, w/lid, good gold.............................165.00
Louis XV, tumbler, good gold 65.00
Maple Leaf, bowl, master berry; gold & decor, scarce 350.00
Maple Leaf, bowl, sauce; gold & decor, scarce...............................50.00
Maple Leaf, butter dish, gold & decor 350.00
Maple Leaf, compote, jelly; gold & decor, rare 475.00
Maple Leaf, creamer, gold & decor....................................150.00
Maple Leaf, cruet, gold & decor, rare............................3,000.00
Maple Leaf, pitcher, water; gold & decor 400.00

Maple Leaf, shakers, gold & decor, very rare, pr.....1,000.00
Maple Leaf, spooner, gold & decor 175.00
Maple Leaf, sugar bowl, w/lid, gold & decor..................250.00
Maple Leaf, tumbler, gold & decor....................................100.00
Panelled Poppy, lamp shade, nutmeg stain, scarce 900.00
Peacock & Urn, bowl, ice cream; nutmeg stain, sm...80.00
Peacock & Urn, bowl, ice cream; nutmeg stain, 10" ...350.00
Punty Band, shakers, pr 175.00
Punty Band, spooner, floral decor.....................................100.00
Punty Band, tumbler, floral decor, souvenir.....................65.00
Ribbed Drape, bowl, sauce; roses & gold 45.00
Ribbed Drape, butter dish, scalloped, roses & gold.......400.00
Ribbed Drape, compote, jelly; roses & gold, rare 200.00
Ribbed Drape, creamer, roses & gold, scarce..................180.00
Ribbed Drape, cruet, roses & gold, rare 700.00
Ribbed Drape, pitcher, water; roses & gold, rare 365.00
Ribbed Drape, shakers, roses & gold, rare, pr................400.00
Ribbed Drape, spooner, roses & gold................................195.00
Ribbed Drape, sugar bowl, w/lid, roses & gold 250.00
Ribbed Drape, toothpick holder, roses & gold................475.00
Ribbed Drape, tumbler, roses & gold..................................75.00
Ribbed Thumbprint, wine, floral decor 80.00
Ring Band, bowl, master berry; roses & gold..................200.00
Ring Band, bowl, sauce; roses & gold..................................50.00
Ring Band, butter dish, roses & gold................................300.00
Ring Band, compote, jelly; roses & gold, scarce.............195.00
Ring Band, creamer, roses & gold......................................125.00
Ring Band, cruet, roses & gold, scarce 500.00
Ring Band, cruet, roses decor, clear stopper 175.00
Ring Band, pitcher, roses & gold, 7½" 375.00
Ring Band, shakers, roses & gold, pr 155.00
Ring Band, spooner, roses & gold......................................125.00
Ring Band, syrup, roses & gold, scarce 475.00
Ring Band, table set, 4-pc 450.00
Ring Band, toothpick holder, roses & gold 155.00
Ring Band, tray, condiment; roses & gold........................200.00
Singing Birds, mug, nutmeg stain.......................................85.00
Tarentum's Victoria, bowl, master berry; gold & decor...............200.00
Tarentum's Victoria, butter dish, gold & decor, rare 350.00
Tarentum's Victoria, celery vase, gold & decor, rare 300.00
Tarentum's Victoria, creamer, gold & decor, scarce 135.00
Tarentum's Victoria, pitcher, water; gold & decor, rare 375.00
Tarentum's Victoria, spooner, gold & decor.................................135.00
Tarentum's Victoria, sugar bowl, w/lid, gold & decor..................175.00
Tarentum's Victoria, tumbler, gold & decor...................................75.00
Vermont, butter dish, bl decor 195.00
Vermont, toothpick holder, bl decor.................................175.00
Vermont, vase, floral decor, jeweled.................................125.00
Wide Band, bell, roses 195.00
Wild Bouquet, bowl, sauce; gold & decor...........................60.00
Wild Bouquet, butter dish, gold & decor, rare 750.00
Wild Bouquet, creamer, no gold 145.00
Wild Bouquet, cruet, gold & decor....................................995.00
Wild Bouquet, spooner, gold & decor...............................175.00
Wild Bouquet, tumbler, no decor......................................100.00
Winged Scroll, bowl, master berry; gold & decor, 11" L.............250.00
Winged Scroll, bowl, sauce; good gold................................50.00
Winged Scroll, butter dish, good gold 235.00
Winged Scroll, butter dish, no decor.................................175.00
Winged Scroll, celery vase, good gold, rare 400.00
Winged Scroll, cigarette jar, scarce 195.00
Winged Scroll, compote, ruffled, rare, 6¾x10¾"...........495.00
Winged Scroll, cruet, good gold, rpl clear stopper 400.00
Winged Scroll, hair receiver, good gold.............................135.00

Winged Scroll, pitcher, water; bulbous, good gold......................**400.00**
Winged Scroll, shakers, bulbous, good gold, rare, pr...................**400.00**
Winged Scroll, shakers, str sides, good gold, pr.........................**300.00**

Winged Scroll, creamer and sugar bowl, with lid (not shown), gold trim, $325.00.

Winged Scroll, syrup, good gold **450.00**
Winged Scroll, tumbler, good gold..**75.00**

Cut Glass

The earliest documented evidence of commercial glass cutting in the United States was in 1810; the producers were Bakewell and Page of Pittsburgh. These first efforts resulted in simple patterns with only a moderate amount of cutting. By the middle of the century, glass cutters began experimenting with a thicker glass which enabled them to use deeper cuttings, though patterns remained much the same. This period is usually referred to as Rich Cut. Using three types of wheels — a flat edge, a mitered edge, and a convex edge — facets, miters, and depressions were combined to produce various designs. In the late 1870s, a curved miter was developed which greatly expanded design potential. Patterns became more elaborate, often covering the entire surface. The Brilliant Period of cut glass covered a span from about 1880 until 1915. Because of the pressure necessary to achieve the deeply cut patterns, only glass containing a high grade of metal could withstand the process. For this reason and the amount of handwork involved, cut glass has always been expensive. Bowls cut with pinwheels may be either foreign or of a newer vintage, beware! Identifiable patterns and signed pieces that are well cut and in excellent condition bring the higher prices on today's market. For more information, we recommend *Evers' Standard Cut Glass Value Guide* (Collector Books). See also Dorflinger; Hawkes; Libbey; Tuthill; Val St. Lambert; other specific manufacturers.

Basket, Pansy, Pitkins & Brooks, 8"..**425.00**
Bell, Premier, JD Bergen, 6"..**200.00**
Bonbon, Emblem, heart shape, JD Bergen, from $90 to **110.00**
Bonbon, Jewel, TB Clark & Co, from $60 to......................................**75.00**
Bonbon, Saratoga, Averbeck, from $65 to...**80.00**
Bonbon, Thelma, JD Bergen, 9", from $60 to.....................................**75.00**
Bottle, cologne; Wagner, JD Bergen, 8½", from $100 to.............**125.00**
Bowl, Ambrose, JD Bergen, 9", from $200 to...................................**225.00**
Bowl, berry; & undertray, Peerless, Higgins & Seiter, from $300 to ..**400.00**
Bowl, Empress, Pitkins & Brooks, 8", from $125 to.....................**150.00**
Bowl, finger; Occident, Averbeck, from $35 to...............................**40.00**
Bowl, Golf, JD Bergen, 7", from $65 to **80.00**
Bowl, Jubilee, rich cut, Higgins & Seiter, 9", from $150 to.........**200.00**
Bowl, nappy; Mikado, hdl, std grade, Pitkins & Brooks, 5", from $40 to...**50.00**
Bowl, nappy; Progress, JD Bergen, 6", from $70 to.........................**80.00**
Bowl, Nellore, Pitkins & Brooks, 8", from $150 to.....................**200.00**
Bowl, nut; Sparkle, std grade, Pitkins & Brooks, 6", from $75 to..**90.00**
Bowl, punch; Heart, Pitkins & Brooks, 12", from $800 to.......**1,000.00**
Bowl, Ruby, Averbeck, 9", from $125 to **150.00**
Bowl, salted almond; Webster, Higgins & Seiter, 6", from $40 to .**55.00**

Bowl, Winola, TB Clark & Co, 6", from $60 to **75.00**
Box, jewel; Delmar, Pitkins & Brooks, 7", from $150 to............**200.00**
Box, puff; Northern Star, Pitkins & Brooks, 6¾", from $150 to .**200.00**
Butter tub & plate, Seaside, JD Bergen, 2-pc, from $250 to........**300.00**
Candlestick, Victoria, JD Bergen, 7", from $125 to **150.00**
Carafe, Jewel, TB Clark, qt, from $100 to...................................**125.00**
Carafe, Liberty, Averbeck, qt, from $175 to **200.00**
Carafe, Progress, J D Bergen, qt, from $200 to **250.00**
Celery tray, American Beauty, Averbeck, 11¼", from $175 to....**200.00**
Celery tray, Belvidere, JD Bergen, 5x11", from $200 to..............**225.00**
Celery tray, Dorrance, TB Clark & Co, from $40 to....................**50.00**
Cheese dish, Webster, Higgins & Seiter, from $250 to...............**300.00**
Clock, Topaz, Pitkins & Brooks, 5½", from $350 to...................**400.00**
Comport, Bermuda, tall std, JD Bergen, 8", from $125 to **150.00**
Comport, Marcus, JD Bergen, 9", from $250 to **300.00**
Comport, McKinley, Pitkins & Brooks, 7", from $175 to............**200.00**
Compote, Monarch, scalloped base, teardrop stem, Hoare, 7x8" **395.00**
Cordial set, Webster, Higgins & Seiter, 8-pc set, from $600 to ...**750.00**
Creamer, Golf, JD Bergen, ½-pt, from $35 to **40.00**
Creamer & sugar bowl, Melba, Averbeck, from $85 to..............**100.00**
Creamer & sugar bowl, Oriole, Pitkins & Brooks, from $85 to...**100.00**
Creamer & sugar bowl, Pluto, Hoare, 3½x4".............................**395.00**
Cruet, Huron, TB Clark & Co, from $75 to **90.00**
Cruet, Waverly, JD Bergen, ½-pt, from $125 to..........................**150.00**
Cup, Vienna, Averbeck, from $20 to..**22.00**
Decanter, Ansonia, JD Bergen, 1-qt, from $225 to **250.00**
Decanter, Florentine, Higgins & Seiter, qt, from $150 to...........**175.00**
Decanter, Radium, Averbeck, 1-qt, from $200 to **250.00**

Decanter, Russian, three-ringed faceted neck on bulbous body, starred base, teardrop stopper, 11½", NM, $935.00.

Goblet, Alabama, Averbeck, from $40 to......................................**50.00**
Goblet, Cut Star, Higgins & Seiter, from $18 to............................**20.00**
Goblet, Marie, JD Bergen, from $55 to...**65.00**
Goblet, Premier, JD Bergen, from $50 to.....................................**60.00**
Hair receiver, Aladdin, Pitkins & Brooks, 4½", from $150 to.....**200.00**
Horseradish jar, Golf, JD Bergen, 6", from $100 to...................**125.00**
Ice tub, Admiral, Higgins & Seiter, 4x6", from $150 to..............**175.00**
Jug, Desdemona, TB Clark & Co, from $250 to **300.00**
Jug, Georgia, Averbeck, 3-pt, 9¾x7½", from $175 to **200.00**
Jug, Winola, TB Clark & Co, from $150 to..................................**175.00**
Ladle, SP w/cut glass hdl, Higgins & Seiter, from $100 to **125.00**
Lamp, Aurora Borealis, electric, Pitkins & Brooks, 12½x6", up to ..**800.00**
Lamp, Daisy, electric, 32 prisms, Pitkins & Brooks, 17", up to..**1,750.00**
Lamp, Poppy, electrified, eng, prisms, Pitkins & Brooks, 22", up to ..**1,750.00**
Mustard jar, Premier, JD Bergen, from $65 to............................**85.00**
Pickle dish, Saratoga, Averbeck, 8" L, from $80 to....................**100.00**
Pitcher, claret; Syrott, Higgins & Seiter, 1-qt, from #200 to.......**225.00**
Pitcher, tankard; Allyn, JD Bergen, 2-qt, from $175 to..............**200.00**
Pitcher, Vienna, Averbeck, 3-pt, from $225 to **250.00**

Pitcher, water tankard; Genoa, Averbeck, 3-pt, from $250 to.....300.00
Plate, Columbia, Blackmer, 7" 575.00
Plate/dish, White Rose, Bergen, 8" 595.00
Punch bowl, Elgin, JD Bergen, 14", from $500 to.......................600.00
Punch bowl, Sunburst, Pitkins & Brooks, 12", from $500 to.......750.00
Saucer, Bedford, JD Bergen, 5", from $60 to..............................70.00
Saucer, Webster, JD Bergen, 5", from $60 to 70.00
Shaker, cut shoulders, std grade, Pitkins & Brooks, from $15 to ...18.00
Shaker, floral cutting, paneled sides, JD Bergen, from $30 to........35.00
Shaker, unnamed pattern, fancy cutting, JD Bergen, from $22 to.25.00
Shaker, unnamed pattern, simple cutting, Pitkins & Brooks, from $12 to....15.00
Sherbet, Merlin, ftd, Pitkins & Brooks, from $20 to......................25.00
Spoon holder, Jewel, TB Clark & Co, from $100 to....................125.00
Spooner, Diamond, Averbeck, from $125 to 150.00
Spooner, Venice, Pitkins & Brooks, from $90 to 110.00
Tea caddy, Henry VIII, TB Clark & Co, w/sterling top, from $125 to...150.00
Tray, Azalea, 14" dia, from $500 to......................................600.00
Tray, ice cream; Arlington, Higgins & Seiter, 13½" L, from $250 to..300.00
Tray, ice cream; std grade, Pitkins & Brooks, 15" L, from $400 to......500.00
Tray, Monarch, Hoare, 12" dia......................................975.00
Tumbler, Boston, Averbeck, from $22 to 25.00
Tumbler, Evans, JD Bergen, from $22 to................................25.00
Tumbler, Marie, JD Bergen, from $25 to...............................30.00
Tumbler, Savoy, JD Bergen, from $22 to...............................25.00
Vase, Ashland, Averbeck, 5", from $75 to.................................90.00
Vase, Florentine, ped ft, Higgins & Seiter, 14" 775.00
Vase, Liberty, slim, flared scalloped rim, Averbeck, 8", from $100 to ...125.00
Vase, Palmetto, cylindrical, TB Clark & Co, lg, from $175 to....200.00
Vase, Star, plain ft, Pitkins & Brooks, 10", from $300 to.............400.00
Vase, Trophy, slim, JD Bergen, 10", from $60 to 80.00
Vase, Vienna, bulbous, Averbeck, 8", from $150 to 200.00
Water set, Golf, JD Bergen, decanter+6 tumblers+tray, from $350 to..400.00

Cut Overlay Glass

Glassware with one or more overlying colors through which a design has been cut is called Cut Overlay. It was made both here and abroad. Watch for new imitations!

Bottle, cordial; cranberry/clear, late 1800s, 14x4½".....................450.00
Bottle, scent; gr/clear, 3" 270.00

Cologne bottle, white to ruby with gold, matching stopper, 6½", $240.00. (Photo courtesy John A. Shumann III)

Compote, cobalt/clear, geometrics, appl clear stem, flint, 4½x9"...275.00
Compote, wht/clear, panels, star-cut pontil, 6x8½" 250.00
Flacon, bl/wht/red, long windows, metal neck & lid, 4⅛".........935.00
Jug, whiskey; cranberry/clear, orig stopper 785.00

Pitcher, caramel/wht/clear, 4¾" 90.00

Cut Velvet

Cut Velvet glassware was made during the late 1800s. It is characterized by the effect achieved through the execution of relief-molded patterns, often ribbing or diamond quilting, which allows its white inner casing to show through the outer layer.

Pitcher, Dmn Quilt, rose to wht, ewer form, 11" 425.00
Rose bowl, Ribbon (swirled), bl, 4" 230.00
Tumbler, yel to wht, rose lining, scarce 130.00
Vase, Dmn Quilt, gr, 6¼" 185.00
Vase, Dmn Quilt, pk, bottle form, 7¼" 250.00
Vase, Dmn Quilt, pk, gold coralene, red jewels, 11½" 300.00
Vase, Dmn Quilt, pk, 9¼x4¼" 175.00
Vase, Herringbone, pk, bulbous, 11" 330.00
Vase, vertical ribs, bl, 8" 285.00

Cybis

Boleslaw Cybis was a graduate of the Academy of Fine Arts in Warsaw, Poland, and was well recognized as a fine artist by the time he was commissioned by his government to paint murals in the Polish Pavilion's Hall of Honor at the 1939 World's Fair. Finding themselves stranded in America at the outbreak of WWII, the Cybises founded an artists' studio, first in Astoria, New York, and later in Trenton, New Jersey, where they made fine figurines and plaques with exacting artistry and craftsmanship entailing extensive handwork. The studio still operates today producing exquisite porcelains on a limited edition basis.

Betty, bl, 8¾"..210.00
Cally Lily, #515, 1968, 16½"...400.00
Cat, bl ribbon, 5¾x8"..225.00
Cat Topaz, sleeping, 2½x5½"..125.00
Charmaine, 1978, 13"..1,000.00
Circus dancing dog Dandy, 1977, 8".....................................195.00
Circus elephant, 1975, 6x7"..425.00
Clown, boy w/puppy, 1979, 6½"...285.00
Clown Funny Face, 1976, 10½"..245.00
Cotton, Puff & Snow, 3 bunnies lying in berry vines, 4½x5" 245.00
Deer mouse in clover, 3½"..75.00
Dolphin rider, #422, 7x10"...600.00
Egbert & Brewster, pr of playful beavers, #6010.......................310.00
Elizabeth Ann, seated w/rag doll...170.00
Eros (Cupid), 1974, 9½"..300.00
Eskimo boy (head portrait), in fur-lined hood, 10½"...................165.00
Free Spirit, pegasus colt, #74, 6x6".....................................430.00
Girl sitting, legs crossed, reading book.................................200.00
Indian boy (bust), full headdress, 13"..................................330.00
Lady & unicorn, #5038..2,025.00
Lady holding rabbit, 10"...300.00
Little Red Riding Hood, 1975, 6½".......................................165.00
Lullaby, baby in crescent moon, 1986, 6¾"...............................95.00
Madonna (bust) holding lily, #62, 12"...................................890.00
Madonna w/bird, 8x12"...265.00
Mary, Mary; bust-length girl in lg hat holds flowers, 1970s, 10½"....425.00
Meadowlarks, 8x8", pr...385.00
Narcissus, sprig of 3 blossoms, 11¾"....................................335.00
Nashua, race horse, 1971, 19x13".....................................1,100.00
Pandora, seated, legs out to side, 1967, 5"............................190.00
Rabbit, looking over left shoulder, 3¾"..................................80.00

Rabbit, lying down, ears laid bk, 2½x4¾" **90.00**
Rebecca, 6½x5" **375.00**
Sand Pipers, 8x6", pr **400.00**
Snail on rock, 1968, 4x3¾" **150.00**
Wood Duck, on driftwood branch, 9½x8½" **375.00**

Czechoslovakian Collectibles

Czechoslovakia came into being as a country in 1918. Located in the heart of Europe, it was a land with the natural resources necessary to support a glass industry that dated back to the mid-fourteenth century. The glass that was produced there has captured the attention of today's collectors, and for good reason. There are beautiful vases — cased, ruffled, applied with rigaree or silver overlay — fine enough to rival those of the best glasshouses. Czechoslovakian art glass baskets are quite as attractive as Victorian America's, and the elegant cut glass perfumes made in colors as well as crystal are unrivaled. There are also pressed glass perfumes, molded in lovely Deco shapes, of various types of art glass. Some are overlaid with gold filigree set with 'jewels.' Jewelry, lamps, porcelains, and fine art pottery are also included in the field.

More than seventy marks have been recorded, including those in the mold, ink stamped, acid etched, or on a small metal nameplate. The newer marks are incised, stamped 'Royal Dux Made in Czechoslovakia' (see Royal Dux), or printed on a paper label which reads 'Bohemian Glass Made in Czechoslovakia.' (Communist controlled from 1948, Czechoslovakia once again was made a free country in December 1989. Today it no longer exists; after 1993 it was divided to form two countries, the Czech Republic and the Slovak Republic.) For a more thorough study of the subject, we recommend *Made in Czechoslovakia* and *Made in Czechoslovakia, Book 2*, by our advisor, Ruth A. Forsythe. Other fine books are *Czechoslovakian Glass & Collectibles, Volumes I* and *II*, by Dale and Diane Barta and Helen M. Rose; *Czechoslovakian Perfume Bottles and Boudoir Accessories* by Jacquelyne Y. Jones North, and *Czechoslovakian Pottery* by Bowers, Closser, and Ellis. In the listings that follow, when one dimension is given, it refers to height; decoration is enamel unless noted otherwise. See also Amphora; Erphila.

Candy Containers

Bl & yel mottle, yel ruffled rim, blk twisted hdl, 8" **250.00**
Bl opaque, blk appl at ruffled rim, clear hdl, 6½" **125.00**
Gr, tangerine & yel mottle, cased, blk hdl & rim, 7" **250.00**
Gr varicolored w/red opaque o/l, gr hdl, 8½" **250.00**
Pk cased, bl appl hdl & threading, 9" **250.00**
Red & gr mottle, ruffled rim, clear twisted thorn hdl, 6½" **240.00**
Red & yel mottle, ruffled rim, clear hdl w/str top, 8½" **150.00**
Red cased, blk appl at ruffled rim, blk hdl, 6½" **125.00**
Yel w/blk trim, clear arched hdl, 6½" **200.00**
Yel/clear/red spatter, cased, twisted thorn hdl, 6¼" **125.00**

Cased Art Glass

Bowl, wht opaque w/fluted crystal rim, 3" **45.00**
Bride's basket, variegated/mottled orange/yel/brn, 4x9"+silver-tone fr...**200.00**
Candle holder, orange w/blk at rim, wide flared ft, 3½" **45.00**
Candolier, wht w/gold & cranberry rim, HP roses, crystal drops, 9¼"..**150.00**
Compote, orange, blk buttressed ft, 5¾" **90.00**
Flower holder, burnt orange w/mottled brn, metal top, 5½"..........**85.00**
Pitcher, red & yel hdl, 3-spout, cobalt hdl & rim, 4" **75.00**
Vase, bud; bl variegated, slim neck w/wide flared base, 8½"..........**65.00**
Vase, bud; rose pk w/gold trim, long neck, 9½"..............................**50.00**
Vase, cream w/bl o/l, cobalt ped ft, 10"...**100.00**
Vase, gr w/blk serpentine decor, waisted cylinder, 6½" **60.00**

Vase, jack-in-the-pulpit, orange, 7" **65.00**
Vase, jack-in-the-pulpit; orange multi-variegated, 9½" **85.00**
Vase, mc mottle w/turq aventurine, flared ft, 10¾" **85.00**
Vase, mottled autumn colors, slim, sm ft, 13¼" **85.00**
Vase, orange w/brn & bl mottling in lower half, 9½" **75.00**
Vase, orange w/Roman man pnt in blk, blk trim, ftd, 6"...............**70.00**
Vase, pk w/fluted top, flared ft, red rim, 9" **65.00**
Vase, red w/fluted blk rim, long trumpet neck, 11¾"...................**100.00**
Vase, red w/reddish-purple swirling design, spherical, 7½"..........**200.00**
Vase, vaseline w/red & yel canes, bl details, emb ribs, ftd, 9¾" ..**185.00**

Cut Glass Perfume Bottles

Highly cut square base with intaglio lady tambourine player in long dress in stopper, with dauber, signed, $375.00.
(Photo courtesy Monsen and Baer)

Bl, dmn-like facets, dancing nude male/female intaglio stopper, 7¼" ..**1,400.00**
Bl, faceted stars resembling wheels, couple figural stopper, 6¾"..**750.00**
Bl, fan shape w/overall polished facets, crystal fan stopper, 5½" .**185.00**
Bl, flower intaglio, spire stopper w/emb bird in rose bush, 5½"...**275.00**
Bl, sleigh form w/many facets, roses intaglio stopper, 5¼x8¼" ...**600.00**
Bl w/metal o/l & cvd bl & red flowers, dancer intaglio stopper, 5½" ..**935.00**
Charcoal crystal w/gold filigree, red/blk opaque stones, 5½".......**750.00**
Clear w/metal & porc couple medallion & gold, faceted stopper, 6"...**450.00**
Crystal, faceted fan shape, red grapes intaglio stopper, 5½" **300.00**
Crystal, oblong w/faceted shoulders, star-form stopper, 6" **350.00**
Crystal, shouldered w/facets, roses/ribbons tall stopper, 6" **300.00**
Crystal & frosted, cherubim & roses, couple intaglio stopper, 7¼"..**650.00**
Crystal ball shape w/dmn-like facets, red spire stopper, 4"...........**200.00**
Gr, abstract intaglio decor, scarf dancer intaglio stopper, 5".........**275.00**
Gr w/geometric cuttings, faceted spire top w/dauber, 2½"...........**155.00**
Gr w/leaf-like facets, gr stopper w/cut-out hearts, 4½" **200.00**
Pk, gold metal filigree w/faux jewels, maiden intaglio stopper, 6"..**825.00**
Pk w/cut facets, spire floral intaglio stopper w/dauber, 3½".........**200.00**
Violet, traiangular w/metal medallion w/gr stones, triangle top, 4"..**650.00**
Violet w/gold & jewels, rose intaglio stopper, 5" **550.00**
Yel, faceted pyramid, abstract vertical stopper, 6¾".....................**385.00**

Lamps

Boudoir, lady figural (Goebel), glass-flower skirt, 10¼" **1,200.00**
Kerosene, pnt milk glass, 12¾" **200.00**
Perfume, bl, cut bl shade, 4"..**350.00**
Perfume, enamel decor, 4" **150.00**
Sconce, crystal, 2-light (candle bulbs), prisms, 14½" **250.00**
Student, metal base, acid-cut shade, 21" **1,000.00**
Table, Art Deco base w/matching conical shade, 9"................**1,000.00**
Table, basket form, crystal beads, bl glass flowers, 8½" **800.00**
Table, Deco dancer beside bubbly paperweight globe, 9"............**800.00**
Table, dk bl lustre, rpl shade, 13¼" **200.00**
Table, mc mottled satin base & shade, 12½" **800.00**
Table, peacock figural, beaded tail, brass body, onyx base, 12¼"...**1,400.00**

Mold-Blown and Pressed Bottles

Amber, 6-sided w/3 ridge design at base, amber drop stopper, 4¾" ...**60.00**
Amethyst & crystal w/pnt daisies, 7".............................**125.00**
Atomizer, gr cased w/red mottle o/l at base, metal top, 5¾"..........**90.00**
Atomizer, gr w/appl serpentine decor, 8"....................**375.00**
Atomizer, orange cased w/mc mottled base, complete, 8"............**125.00**
Blk 4-sided base w/clear 4-sided drop stopper, mini, 2¾" **115.00**
Clear w/bl pnt stars & bands, bl pnt ball stopper, 4¼" **40.00**
Clear w/bubble design, shouldered, ball stopper, 4¾" **40.00**
Clear w/emb decor & chain dangles w/jewels, 2½".................**70.00**
Clear w/frosted & gold bands, frosted top, matching stopper, 4¼"....**40.00**
Topaz tinted, pillow form, blk stopper, 5" **45.00**

Opaque, Crystal, Colored Transparent Glass

Art Deco water set, orange and green, 12½" covered pitcher and four 4⅞" tumblers, $500.00 for all five pieces.
(Photo courtesy Guy S. Forsythe)

Beverage set, pnt egg form w/coraline, holds decanter/glasses, 9"...**150.00**
Beverage set, pnt egg form w/gold, holds 7" decanter/6 sm shots ...**150.00**
Box, amethyst w/HP decor, gold-tone metal band & closure, 1¼x2"....**50.00**
Candle holder, mc mottled satin, 4¼", pr **70.00**
Figurine, doctor in wht coat, amber pants, red stethoscope, 8¼"...**225.00**
Pitcher, amber w/gr & bl o/l, cobalt hdl & threading, 10¼" **185.00**
Pitcher, smoke color w/red threading, conical, blk angle hdl, 6"...**90.00**
Plate, blk amethyst w/silver floral o/l, 9½" **45.00**
Shakers, cut crystal, 2", pr **25.00**
Stem, champagne; cranberry swirled bowl, crystal stem, 6" **45.00**
Vase, bud; gr w/appl purple base, 11¾".........................**75.00**
Vase, bud; pk w/wht threading, bulbous/swirled body, sm neck, 5¼" .**35.00**
Vase, gr w/blk/gr/yel mottle at base, blk serpentine decor, 8¼" **95.00**
Vase, lt bl w/cream/bk flecks, cobalt o/l, ped ft, 9½" **130.00**
Vase, mc mottle w/cobalt serpentine, 8".......................**110.00**
Vase, orange w/cobalt threading at rim, wht hdl, 6" **75.00**
Vase, variegated autumn colors, cobalt buttressed ft, 8¼" **75.00**

Pottery, Porcelain, Semiporcelain

Animal dish, duck, muted colors, 4¼"..........................**45.00**
Basket, airbrushed sqs & circles, bl/orange/wht, 4¾"...............**45.00**
Bowl, nut; mc flower shape, 6"..................................**20.00**
Creamer, moose (recumbent) figural, wht w/bl hdl, blk eyes, 3" ...**55.00**
Creamer, orange lustre w/gr int, 2" **25.00**
Creamer, pearlescent lustreware w/gr rim & hdl, 3¾" **25.00**
Figurine, cat, wht w/pk details, 5"...........................**45.00**
Figurine, girl w/grapes, blk & wht, glazed, 9½" **100.00**
Flower holder, bird on stump w/3 holes, mc, 4½" **45.00**
Honey pot & saucer, vining red flowers & leaves, 6¼" **45.00**
Match holder, HP oriental scene/goldfish scene, ftd, 5" **70.00**
Pitcher, burgundy & wht w/blk mottling, tricorner, blk hdl/rim, 5¼" ...**50.00**
Pitcher, chicken figural, red, wht & blk, 7½"....................**55.00**
Pitcher, yel w/bl rim & hdl, trumpet neck, 7½" **45.00**
Toby mug, Bumble, red coat, blk hat, 5¼" **55.00**
Vase, angel w/horn of plenty, 5"...............................**25.00**

Vase, bl pearlescent mottle, 8" **50.00**
Vase, bright variegated pastels, glossy, hdls, 4¾"...................**50.00**

D'Argental

D'Argental cameo glass was produced in France from the 1870s until about 1920 in the Art Nouveau style. Browns and tans were favored colors used to complement floral and scenic designs developed through acid cuttings. Our advisor for this category is Don Williams; he is listed in the Directory under Missouri.

Cameo

Bowl, floral branches, burgundy on citron, ftd, 3¾x6¼" **900.00**
Box, orchids/moths, lt bl on amethyst, 4x6" **800.00**
Dish, leaves/flowers, wine/caramel on tan frost, w/lid, 7" **750.00**
Vase, ginko branches, bl on yel, elongated ovoid, 8"...............**1,150.00**
Vase, trees/lake/birds/sky, amethyst/rose/burgundy/frost, 10"...**1,500.00**
Vase, trees/river, fortress beyond, rose on yel, ftd, 14" **1,250.00**
Vase, treese/geese/mtns/lake, burgundy/maroon/amber/frost, 4½"..**700.00**
Vase, vineyard, orange-amber/brns, classic form, 13½" **1,050.00**

Daum Nancy

Daum was an important producer of French cameo glass, operating from the late 1800s until after the turn of the century. They used various techniques — acid cutting, wheel engraving, and handwork — to create beautiful scenic designs and nature subjects in the Art Nouveau manner. Virtually all examples are signed. Daum is still in production, producing many figural items. Our advisor for this category is Don Williams; he is listed in the Directory under Missouri.

Cameo

Ashtray, coastal scene, blk on gr, 3x5" **950.00**
Bottle, scent; courting scene, cut/pnt, 4-color w/silver o/l, 5½"..**2,000.00**
Bottle, scent; thistles, bl/yel/frost, rpl ball, 7"..................**850.00**
Bowl, cockscombs/leaves, red/blk/citron, hdls, 6x7" **2,000.00**
Bowl, daisies, cut/pnt, mottled wht/pk/purple/yel, 3x7¾" **2,000.00**
Bowl, daisies, gr/amethyst w/gold, 4-ruffle top, 2¾x5½" **1,150.00**
Bowl, foliage, gr/peach on gray frost, 6"......................**1,380.00**
Bowl, mistletoe, gr to clear, repousse holly ft, 4⅛" **1,150.00**
Bowl, roses, orange/yel/red/gr, 1¾x4" sq......................**500.00**
Bowl, snowflakes, gray/wht, triangular, rolled rim, 1¾x6½x4½"..**750.00**
Bowl, snowy trees, cut/pnt, orange/yel, 4 blown-out ridges, 5½x6" ...**3,100.00**
Bowl, sunflowers, cut/pnt, yel/rust/gr/amethyst/mottled frost, 6"...**1,350.00**
Bowl, thistle/dragonflies, cut/pnt on frost, gr shaded rim, 9"....**1,350.00**
Bowl, tomatoes & foliage on gray frost, 6".......................**1,380.00**
Bowl, trees/lake, yel/gr/burgundy/rose, 1½x5" sq.........................**800.00**
Box, landscape, fiery red/orange mottle, 4x6x6" w/5" dia lid ...**2,500.00**
Box, poppy/stem/leaves/halo, yel-orange/gray-gr/plum/yel, 6" sq..**3,700.00**
Chandelier, 4 seasons, 3-arm, dome center, complete, 15" dia.**6,750.00**
Ewer, foliage/blueberries on yel to brn mottle, bulbous, 8½" ...**6,325.00**
Inkwell, water lilies & dragonflies on streaked ground, 3½" **4,000.00**
Jar, thistles, cut/pnt on gilt, wedge stopper, 3" **800.00**
Lamp, boudoir; rainy landscape, cut/pnt, pk to gr, domed ft, 13¼" ..**12,500.00**
Lamp base, trumpet flowers, orange/dk orange/brn, w/mts, 23¼" .**1,400.00**
Letter opener, mistletoe/berries, cut/pnt on gr w/gilt, 8¾" **700.00**
Night light, trees in rain, cut/pnt, pk/gr/blk, metal stand, 8¾" .**5,500.00**
Pitcher, clover, clear & frost w/gold bands & decor, 9½".........**3,500.00**
Pitcher, orchids/foliage, cut/pnt, gold-orange/mocha/cream/gr, 4¼" ...**2,500.00**
Salt cellar, floral, gold/textrued to frost, ftd, 1¼x2" **1,200.00**

Salt cellar, rain scene, pk/gr, 2x1¼" **2,500.00**
Salt cellar, trees/shore/ruins, cut/pnt, blk/frost/gold, 1⅜" **600.00**
Toothpick holder, mistletoe, gold/wht/gr, 2" **650.00**
Vase, autumn oak leaves, amethyst/yel/frosty mottle, 14" **4,750.00**
Vase, autumn scene, cut/pnt, 7-color, shouldered, 8" **5,500.00**
Vase, berries/leaves/grasses, cut/pnt on frost, 15⅛", NM **1,495.00**
Vase, birches/lake/mtns, bl/yel/amethyst/frost, shouldered, 11¼"..**6,500.00**
Vase, classical couple/laurel wreath, cut/pnt, orange donut form, 6" ..**2,300.00**
Vase, cornflowers, cut/pnt, mottled gray to gr to cobalt, 7½" ..**4,600.00**
Vase, cyclamen, cut/pnt, gr/pk/clear, gold trim, 8½" **2,400.00**
Vase, dandelion puffs, rose pk/gr/opal martele, ftd, 8½" **4,000.00**
Vase, Dutch village winter scene, cut/pnt on bl, pillow form, 4¼" ..**3,000.00**
Vase, Dutch winter scene, cut/pnt, bl/wht/tan/blk, 11½x6"........**6,325.00**
Vase, farmer w/leafy fr, cut/pnt, gr frost w/clear drips, 13½" **4,000.00**
Vase, flowers (3-petal), gr on chipped ice w/gold, 3¼" **335.00**
Vase, flowers/butterflies, wht/gr/yel/bl/gray/orange, hdld urn, 7"..**4,500.00**
Vase, flowers/stalks/sunset, red-brn/amber/frost, shouldered, 12"..**2,950.00**
Vase, fuchsia/foliage, cut/pnt on gray frost, bulbous, 8⅝".........**3,450.00**
Vase, irises, gr/clear w/gold, sq cylinder, 4⅞"...............................**450.00**
Vase, irises, grape/gray-yel/gr, ftd cylinder, 9¾", NM................**2,600.00**
Vase, irises, mottled yel/wht/gr, cut/pnt, slim, ftd, 15¼" **3,750.00**
Vase, landscape (simple), gr on raspberry & peach streaks, 4¾"..**1,150.00**
Vase, leaves & branches, 4-color w/gold, 4 appl hdls, 8¾" **3,250.00**
Vase, leaves/pods, mulberry/frosted mottle, cut/pnt, stick, 4¾" ..**1,000.00**
Vase, lily of the valley, gr/purple/martele, 4x3¾" **3,225.00**
Vase, mums/leaves, red-brn/brn/amber/frost, shouldered, 15½" ..**3,300.00**
Vase, oak leaves, amethyst/yel frosty mottle, 14" **1,750.00**
Vase, oak leaves/acorns, orange-brn/frost, stick form, 14¾".....**1,150.00**
Vase, orchids/webs, red/yel/frost/brn, stick neck, 6¾" **3,500.00**
Vase, Parlant, floral, cut/pnt on amethyst, waisted, 7⅛" **1,500.00**
Vase, pines/sailboats, gray/textured opal, pillow form, 1½x2¼"..**1,500.00**
Vase, poppies, amber, in gilt-metal foliage-pierced base, 7½"......**975.00**
Vase, raspberries/leaves/branches, bl/marmalade/yel opal, 4½"..**1,200.00**
Vase, river scene, red/orange/gr/olive, bbl form, 4⅞"................**1,200.00**
Vase, sailboats, cut/pnt, orange/yel, pillow form, 3½x4½" **1,665.00**
Vase, sailboats, cut/pnt, orange/yel, pillow form, 5x6½" **2,125.00**
Vase, snowberries, cut/pnt, chipped ice to emerald gr w/gold, 10"..**500.00**
Vase, summer scenic, cut/pnt, bl/gr, pillow form, 5x6" **3,450.00**
Vase, summer scenic, cut/pnt, mottled gr/yel, flared top, 8¼x4"..**3,500.00**
Vase, summer scenic, flat sided, bulbous, 1½x1½" **1,400.00**
Vase, thistles, amber/red/gold, stick neck, 5"................................**825.00**
Vase, thistles, pk/grass gr on martele, elongated bell, 9"...........**1,600.00**
Vase, trees/lake, blk/gr/mauve/opal, cylindrical, 11¾"..............**2,800.00**
Vase, trees/lake, yel/red/bl/gr/gray/chartreuse/amethyst/frost, 8"..**2,500.00**
Vase, trees/mtns, cut/pnt, bl/gr/purple, 5½x2½"......................**1,325.00**
Vase, trees/mtns, lav on frost, conical w/flared rim, 5¼"...........**1,200.00**
Vase, trees/tower/lake/mtn, bl/yel/frost, shouldered, 11¼" **6,500.00**
Vase, trees/vegetation/sky/waters, ebony/marmalade, 6".........**1,300.00**
Vase, tulips, pk on frost w/gold, flattened ovoid, 9⅜" **1,725.00**
Vase, violets, cut/pnt, apricot/purple/gr/wht, 4¾x2½" **1,800.00**
Vase, violets on long stems, cut/pnt, purple/frost, stick neck, 8¾" ...**3,500.00**
Vase, winter forest/sunset, gray/yel/frost, pillow form, 4¾x5½"..**3,000.00**
Vase, winter scenic, cut/pnt, orange & yel mottle, ovoid, 11".**4,500.00**
Vase, winter trees, gray/yel/frost, pillow form, 5½x4¾".............**3,000.00**
Vase, woodbine berries/leaves, gr/pk opal martele, gourd, 5¼"..**2,900.00**

Enameled Glass

Atomizer, cyclamen & leaves on frost w/etch leaves/berries, 4" ..**500.00**
Goblet, thistles/foliage, ribbed bucket form, 5¼"........................**630.00**
Liqueur set, mustard/red horizontal stripes, decanter+4 liqueurs..**1,265.00**
Tumbler, daisies on wht opal & purple mottle, 4" **1,450.00**
Vase, birch branches/lake, gray frost, long neck, 9⅞".............**2,585.00**
Vase, Dutch lowlands scenes, mc on opal w/gold, 3½x5½".........**800.00**

Vase, figure on road/windmill/sailing ship, bulbous, 5¾" **1,035.00**
Vase, floral/butterflies on wht to gr, jewels, trumpet form, 13" ...**3,500.00**
Vase, harbor scene w/ships & windmills, ftd, 4¾" **1,300.00**
Vase, peasant lady/tree-lined hill on snowy wht, 2⅝"................**950.00**
Vase, swan & shield over Geneve on frost, broken egg form, 5¼"...**2,000.00**

Miscellaneous

Lamp, mc mottle mushroom shade; wrought iron pillar base, 12" **1,265.00**
Lamp, wht mottle dome shade w/tendrils, wrought Robj base, 9½" ..**1,600.00**
Lamp, 2 bell-form mottled glass shades; sq floral wrought fr, 17" **2,500.00**
Liqueur set, crystal w/tangerine trim, decanter/4 cordials/tray.....**900.00**
Vase, burgundy/crimson-pk/gray mottle, stick neck, 11¼" **300.00**

De Vez

De Vez was a type of acid-cut French cameo glass produced by Cristallerie de Pantin in Paris around the turn of the century. Our advisor for this
category is Don Williams; he is listed in the Directory under Missouri.

Cameo

Vase, A la Gloire de la Roumanie, yel/bl/opal, 10½x4½"........**1,725.00**
Vase, branches/lake/islands/mtns, bl frost to gr, 7½x3¾".........**1,000.00**
Vase, castle landscape, pk/yel/gr, 8¼x5"...................................**1,175.00**
Vase, cottages/mother/child, maroon/fiery amber, ovoid, 6" **865.00**
Vase, Moroccan waterfront, burgundy on vaseline opal, 4¼"......**675.00**
Vase, mtn scene, bl on yel/lav, shouldered, 6¼" **1,000.00**
Vase, mtn scene, blk/burgundy on vaseline opal, gourd shape, 7"..**785.00**
Vase, poppies/butterfly, dk persimmon on textured opal, 8"...**1,380.00**
Vase, trees/village/mtns, amber/olive/bl/frost, ovoid, 10"..........**1,150.00**
Vase, trumpet flowers/leaves, rose/gr/citron, cylindrical, 10¼"....**950.00**
Vase, Venetian harbor/foliage/pillars, rust/rose/bl, 7½" **1,500.00**
Vase, windmills/ships/clouds, brn/orange/frost/yel, 7½"...............**900.00**

De Vilbiss

Perfume bottles, atomizers, and dresser accessories marketed by the
De Vilbiss Company are appreciated by collectors today for the various
types of lovely glassware used in their manufacture as well as for their
pleasing shapes. Various companies provided the glass, while De Vilbiss
made only the metal tops. They marketed their merchandise not only
here but in Paris, England, Canada, and Havana as well. Their marks
were acid stamped, ink stamped, in gold script, molded in, or on paper
labels. One is no more significant than another. Our advisor for this category is Randy Monsen; he is listed in the Directory under Virginia.

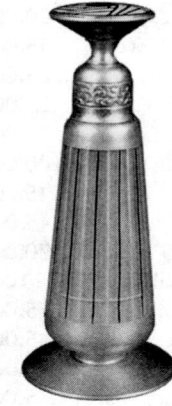

'Dropper' bottle, pink and gold, signed,
4½", $175.00. (Photo courtesy Monsen and Baer)

Atomizer, amber, long stem w/disk ft, gold top/bulb, 6½" 110.00
Atomizer, amber w/gold ft, baluster, acorn finial, all orig, 10¼" .550.00
Atomizer, blk w/coral & gold abstract design, all orig, 9½" 900.00
Atomizer, clear oval windows w/much gold, blk trim, all orig, 6" ..500.00
Atomizer, forget-me-nots emb on frost, cylindrical, 5½", MIB ...225.00
Atomizer, frosted orange, orig hdw, rpl ball/tassel, 6½" 175.00
Atomizer, Gold Aurene w/bl irid, Steuben, orig hdw/ball, 9½"..650.00
Atomizer, gold enamel on frost, orig hdw & ball, 5" 125.00
Atomizer, gold speckles on turq opaque, all orig, 6¼", MIB........400.00
Atomizer, gr enamel, disk ft, orig hdw/ball/cord, 6½" 100.00
Atomizer, hearts & vines, orange-gold on cobalt w/lustre, 10" ...1,500.00
Atomizer, orange frost w/gold flowers, gold ft, all orig, 6¾" 525.00
Atomizer, sky bl enamel, orig gold hdw & ball, 7" 150.00
Atomizer, triangular windows & gold, orig top/bulb, 8¼" 300.00
Atomizer, yel/blk/gold Deco design on clear, rpl ball/tassle, 7¼" ...525.00
Bottle, cranberry swirl, metal neck, long dauber, 6¼" 350.00
Bottle, lt gr w/5 oval windows, much gold w/blk details, 7¼" 325.00
Bottle, wht opal w/gold & blk, Fry, orig metal neck, glass dauber, 6" ...600.00
Ginger jar, chinoiserie trees & birds, gold on beige, 4½" 600.00
Lamp, perfume; dancing fairies on red-orange sky, metal fr, 12"....1,000.00
Lamp, perfume; windswept tree/moon, w/finial cap, complete, 8"....650.00
Pin tray, gr enamel on clear, metal holder w/bear, 3¼" 95.00

Decanters

Ceramic whiskey decanters were brought into prominence in 1955 by the James Beam Distilling Company. Few other companies besides Beam produced these decanters during the next ten years or so; however, other companies did eventually follow suit. At its peak in 1975, at least twenty prominent companies and several on a lesser scale made these decanters. Beam stopped making decanters in mid-1992. Now only a couple of companies are still producing these collectibles.

Liquor dealers have told collectors for years that ceramic decanters are not as valuable, and in some cases worthless, if emptied or if the federal tax stamp has been broken. Nothing is further from the truth. Following are but a few of many reasons you should consider emptying ceramic decanters:

1) If the thin glaze on the inside ever cracks (and it does in a small percentage of decanters), the contents will push through to the outside. It is then referred to as a 'leaker' and worth a fraction of its original value.

2) A large number of decanters left full in one area of your house poses a fire hazard.

3) A burglar, after stealing jewelry and electronics, may make off with some of your decanters just to enjoy the contents. If they are empty, chances are they will not be bothered.

4) It is illegal in most states for collectors to sell a full decanter without a liquor license.

Unlike years ago, few collectors now collect all types of decanters. Most now specialize. For example, they may collect trains, cars, owls, Indians, clowns, or any number of different things that have been depicted on or as a decanter. They are finding exceptional quality available at reasonable prices, especially when compared with many other types of collectibles.

We have tried to list those brands that are the most popular with collectors. Likewise, individual decanters listed are the ones (or representative of the ones) most commonly found. The following listing is but a small fraction of the thousands of decanters that have been produced.

These decanters come from all over the world. While Jim Beam owned its own china factory in the U.S., some of the others have been imported from Mexico, Taiwan, Japan, and elsewhere. They vary in size from miniatures (approximately two-ounce) to gallons. Values range from a few dollars to more than $3,000.00 per decanter.

Most collectors and dealers define a 'mint' decanter as one with no chips, no cracks, and label intact. A missing federal tax stamp or lack of contents have no bearing on value. All values are given for 'mint' decanters. A 'mini' behind a listing indicates a miniature. All others are fifth or 750 ml unless noted otherwise. Our advisor for this category is Roy Willis; he is listed in the Directory under Kentucky.

Aesthetic Specialties (ASI)

Cadillac, 1903, bl or wht 65.00
Chevrolet, 1914 ....75.00
Golf, Bing Crosby 38th 18.00

Beam

Casino Series, Golden Gate, 1970 ....18.00
Casino Series, Harold's Club, Pinwheel...40.00
Casino Series, Reno; Horseshoe, Primadonna or Cal-Neva...........10.00
Centennial Series, Alaska Purchase 10.00
Centennial Series, Cheyenne 10.00
Centennial Series, Key West 8.00
Centennial Series, Lombard 8.00
Centennial Series, Statue of Liberty, 1975 ....20.00
Executive Series, 1979 Mother of Pearl 20.00
Executive Series, 1980 Titan 15.00
Executive Series, 1981 Royal Filigree 18.00
Executive Series, 1982, America Pitcher..24.00
Executive Series, 1983, Partridge Bell 35.00
Executive Series, 1984 Carolers Bell 28.00
Foreign Series, Australia, Galah Bird...25.00
Foreign Series, Australia, Kangaroo 18.00
Foreign Series, Australia, Koala 18.00
Foreign Series, Fuji Islands 10.00
Foreign Series, Kiwi Bird 10.00
Foreign Series, Samoa 10.00
Organization Series, Ducks Unlimited #06, 1980 ....50.00
Organization Series, Ducks Unlimited #07, 1981 ....40.00
Organization Series, Ducks Unlimited #08, 1982 ....65.00
Organization Series, Ducks Unlimited #09, 1983 ....65.00
Organization Series, Ducks Unlimited #10, 1984 ....95.00
Organization Series, Elks, 1968 ....6.00
Organization Series, Legion Music...8.00
Organization Series, Phi Sigma Kappa..15.00
Organization Series, Shriner, Raja Temple 25.00
Organization Series, VFW 10.00
Organization Series, 101st Airborne 12.00
People Series, Cowboy..20.00
People Series, Emmet Kelly 35.00
People Series, George Washington 20.00
People Series, Hank Williams, Jr 38.00
People Series, Martha Washington 14.00
People Series, Mr Goodwrench 40.00
State Series, Delaware 10.00
State Series, Kentucky, blk stopper 18.00
State Series, Maine 8.00
State Series, New Hampshire 7.00
State Series, Ohio 12.00
Wheel Sereis, Harold's Club Covered Wagon (1974)....................45.00
Wheel Series, Cable Car, 1968...7.00
Wheel Series, Cable Car, 1983 ....60.00
Wheel Series, Corvette, 1954, bl 125.00
Wheel Series, Corvette, 1955, bronze 115.00
Wheel Series, Corvette, 1963, red or silver......................................85.00
Wheel Series, Corvette, 1978, yel, red or wht.................................75.00
Wheel Series, Ford, 1913 Model T, blk or gr 65.00
Wheel Series, Ford, 1964 Mustang, blk 135.00

Wheel Series, Ford, 1964 Mustang, red 90.00
Wheel Series, Ford, 1964 Mustang, wht 80.00
Wheel Series, Golf Car 50.00
Wheel Series, Mack Fire Engine 130.00
Wheel Series, Train, Caboose, gray 75.00
Wheel Series, Train, Caboose, red 70.00
Wheel Series, Train, Locomotive, General 125.00
Wheel Series, Train, Locomotive, Grant 80.00
Wheel Series, Train, Locomotive, JB Turner........................150.00
Wheel Series, Train, Passenger Car 55.00
Wheel Series, Train, Tender, Coal for Grant..........................70.00
Wheel Series, Train, Tender, Wood for (for General) 140.00
Wheel Series, Train, Tender, Wood for Turner.......................75.00

Brooks

American Legion, Denver, 1971 ....15.00
Amvets 10.00
Car, '62 Mako Shark..35.00
Car, Auburn...25.00
Car, Dusenberg...35.00
Dog w/bird, 1970 ....15.00
Elk 25.00
Fire Engine..25.00
Hambletonian...18.00
Indy Racer, #21 (1970)..65.00
Keystone Cops 75.00
Man 'O War 25.00
Panda 18.00
Phonograph..25.00
Pistol, Dueling 12.00
Shrine, King Tut Guard 22.00
Tennis Player..15.00
Ticker Tape 10.00
Trail Bike...25.00
Train, Iron Horse 10.00
Vermont Skier...12.00
Whale, Killer 22.00
Wichita Centennial...10.00

Dant, J.W.

American Legion 12.00
Field Birds, 8 different, ea..12.00
Indy 500 ....10.00

The Dickensian Collection

Golf Club (glass)...12.00
Powder Horn, amber, qt 15.00
Powder Horn, dk, ⅘-qt...12.00

Famous Firsts

Coffee Mill...38.00
Roulette Wheel..35.00
Scales, Lombardy 30.00
Spirit of St Louis...125.00
Spirit of St Louis, midi 70.00
Spirit of St Louis, mini 48.00

Hoffman

Big Red Machine 50.00

Cats, 6 different, mini, ea..15.00
Children of the World, 6 different, ea 28.00
College Series, Helmet, Auburn 28.00
College Series, Helmet, Missouri 28.00
College Series, Mascot, 'Ol Miss Rebel...................................50.00
College Series, Mascot, Nevada Wolfpack 50.00
Mr Lucky Series, Mr Blacksmith..40.00
Mr Lucky Series, Mr Blacksmith, mini 15.00
Mr Lucky Series, Mr Fireman..75.00
Mr Lucky Series, Mr Fireman, mini 25.00
Mr Lucky Series, Mr Policeman 50.00
Mr Lucky Series, Mr Policeman, mini 20.00
Racecar, Foyt #2 ....120.00
Wildlife Series, Doe & Fawn...50.00
Wildlife Series, Fox & Rabbit 50.00

Kontinental

Dentist...35.00
Dockworker...30.00
Innkeeper 30.00
Statue of Liberty 25.00
Stephen Foster 28.00
Surveyor...35.00

Lionstone

Backpacker..28.00
Barber 45.00
Barber, mini 20.00
Buffalo Hunter 35.00
Camp Cook..30.00
Camp Follower...30.00
Canada Goose..55.00
Clown, 6 different, ea 40.00
Dancehall Girl, mini 20.00
Doctor, Country...22.00

Firefighter #1, 1972, $95.00.

Fisherman...40.00
Football Player 60.00
Goldpanner, mini...20.00
Johnny Lightning #1 ....100.00
Johnny Lightning #2..90.00
Laundryman, Chinese...22.00
Meadowlark...28.00
Photographer...60.00
Photographer, mini 24.00
Rainmaker...35.00

Rainmaker, mini 20.00
Revere, Paul 30.00
Riverboat Captain 25.00
Sheepherder 42.00
Sheepherder, mini 20.00
Telegrapher 26.00
Turbo Car STP, red 60.00

McCormick

Bell, Alexander 30.00
Bunyan, Paul 35.00
Durante, Jimmy 65.00
Elvis, 1978, plays Love Me Tender, 750 ml 125.00
Elvis, 1979, plays Love Me Tender, mini 55.00
Elvis, 1980, plays Can't Help Falling in Love 125.00
Elvis, 1981, plays Can't Help Falling in Love, mini 55.00
Elvis, 1982, Elvis Karate, plays Don't Be Cruel 350.00
Elvis, 1983, Gold, plays My Way, mini 125.00
Elvis, 1984, Designer Gold, plays It's Now or Never 195.00
Elvis, 1984, 50th Anniversary, plays I Want You, I Need You, I Love You ..495.00
Elvis, 1985, Teddy Bear, plays Let Me Be Your Teddy Bear 695.00
Elvis, 1986, Designer I Silver, plays Are You Lonesome Tonight, mini ...135.00

Frontiersman Series, Jim Bowie, 1975, $35.00.

Iwo Jima 175.00
Iwo Jima, mini 75.00
King Arthur's Court, King Arthur 65.00
Lincoln, Abe 40.00
Monroe, Marilyn 650.00
Monroe, Marilyn; mini 175.00
Peary, Robert 35.00
Pony Express 60.00
Rogers, Will 35.00
Shrine Dune Buggy 45.00
Telephone Operator 65.00
Williams, Hank Sr 140.00

O.B.R.

Engine, General 20.00
Fields, WC; Bank Dick 45.00
Fields, WC; Top Hat 45.00
Guitar, Music City 18.00
Hockey Players 30.00

Old Commonwealth

Coal Miner #1, w/Shovel 95.00

Coal Miner #1, w/Shovel, mini 25.00
Coal Miner #2, w/Pick 45.00
Coal Miner #2, w/Pick, mini 20.00
Firefighter, Fallen Comrade 70.00
Firefighter, Fallen Comrade, mini 30.00
Firefighter, Modern Hero #1 ......75.00
Firefighter, Modern Hero #1, mini 25.00
Firefighter, Nozzleman #2 ......75.00
Firefighter, Nozzleman #2, mini 28.00

Old Fitzgerald

Irish, Blarney 12.00
Irish, Leprechaun, 'Plase God' 30.00
Irish, Leprechaun, 'Prase Be' 23.00
Irish, Luck 1972 ......28.00
Irish, Wish 1975 ......22.00
Rip Van Winkle 30.00

Ski Country

Barrel Racer 80.00
Barrel Racer, mini 35.00
Bear, Brown 35.00
Birth of Freedom 100.00
Birth of Freedom, mini 80.00
Birth of Freedom, 1-gal 1,900.00
Bob Cratchit 60.00
Bob Cratchit, mini 34.00
Cardinals, Holiday 1991 ......85.00
Cardinals, Holiday 1991, mini 35.00
Deer, Whitetail 175.00
Deer, Whitetail, mini 50.00
Ducks Unlimited, Pintail, 1978 ......95.00
Ducks Unlimited, Pintail, 1978, mini 30.00
Ducks Unlimited, Pintail, 1978, ½-gal 225.00
Ducks Unlimited, Widgeon, 1979 ......60.00
Ducks Unlimited, Widgeon, 1979, mini 30.00
Ducks Unlimited, Widgeon, 1979, ½-gal 175.00
Eagle, Majestic 300.00
Eagle, Majestic, mini 140.00
Eagle, Majestic, 1-gal 1,700.00
Elk 195.00
Elk, mini 65.00
Indian, Cigar Store 50.00
Indian, Cigar Store, mini 32.00
Indian, North American, mini, set of 6 ......150.00
Indian, North American, set of 6 ......225.00
Indian, Southwest Dancers, mini, set of 6 ......220.00
Indian, Southwest Dancers, set of 6 ......350.00
Jaguar 160.00
Jaguar, mini 50.00
Koala 50.00
Owl, Barred; wall plaque 130.00
Owl, Barred; wall plaque, mini 40.00
Owl, Great Gray 80.00
Owl, Great Gray, mini 35.00
Pelican 55.00
Pelican, mini 35.00
Pheasant, Standing; mini 60.00
Phoenix Bird 60.00
Ram, Bighorn 65.00
Ram, Bighorn, mini 30.00
Ruffed Grouse 60.00

Ruffed Grouse, mini..**28.00**
Skunk Family..**50.00**
Skunk Family, mini...**30.00**
Wild Turkey..**130.00**
Wild Turkey, mini..**125.00**

Wild Turkey

Series I, #1, #2, #3 or #4, mini, ea **18.00**
Series I, #1, 1971 ....**200.00**
Series I, #2 ....**150.00**
Series I, #3 ....**65.00**
Series I, #4 ....**65.00**
Series I, #5 ....**30.00**

Series I, #6, striding, 1976, $30.00.

Series I, #6 ....**30.00**
Series I, #7 ....**30.00**
Series I, #8 ....**45.00**
Series I, set of #5, #6, #7 & #8, mini **170.00**
Series II, Lore #1 ....**25.00**
Series II, Lore #2 ....**38.00**
Series II, Lore #3 ....**45.00**
Series II, Lore #4 ....**50.00**
Series III, #1, In Flight **120.00**
Series III, #1, In Flight, mini **45.00**
Series III, #2, Turkey & Bobcat **140.00**
Series III, #2, Turkey & Bobcat, mini **45.00**
Series III, #3, Fighting Turkeys **150.00**
Series III, #3, Fighting Turkeys, mini **50.00**
Series III, #4, Turkey & Eagle **95.00**
Series III, #4, Turkey & Eagle, mini **80.00**
Series III, #5, Turkey & Raccoon **95.00**
Series III, #5, Turkey & Raccoon, mini **45.00**
Series III, #6, Turkey & Poults **95.00**
Series III, #6, Turkey & Poults, mini **45.00**
Series III, #7, Turkey & Red Fox **95.00**
Series III, #7, Turkey & Red Fox, mini **50.00**
Series III, #8, Turkey & Owl **95.00**
Series III, #8, Turkey & Owl, mini **50.00**
Series III, #9, Turkey & Bear Cubs **95.00**
Series III, #9, Turkey & Bear Cubs, mini **50.00**
Series III, #10, Turkey & Coyote **95.00**
Series III, #10, Turkey & Coyote, mini **45.00**
Series III, #11, Turkey & Falcon **95.00**
Series III, #11, Turkey & Falcon, mini **50.00**
Series III, #12, Turkey & Skunks **95.00**
Series III, #12, Turkey & Skunks, mini **50.00**

Decoys

American colonists learned the craft of decoy making from the

Indians who used them to lure birds out of the sky as an important food source. Early models were carved from wood such as pine, cedar, balsa, etc., and a few were made of canvas or papier-mache. There are two basic types of decoys: water floaters and shorebirds (also called 'stick-ups'). Within each type are many different species, ducks being the most plentiful since they migrated along all four of America's great waterways. Market hunting became big business around 1880, resulting in large-scale commercial production of decoys which continued until about 1910 when such hunting was outlawed by the Migratory Bird Treaty.

Today decoys are one of the most collectible types of American folk art. The most valuable are those carved by such artists as Laing, Crowell, Ward, and Wheeler, to name only a few. Each area, such as Massachusetts, Connecticut, Maine, the Illinois River, and the Delaware River, produces decoys with distinctive regional characteristics. Examples of commercial decoys produced by well-known factories — among them Mason, Stevens, and Dodge — are also prized by collectors. Though mass produced, these nevertheless required a certain amount of hand carving and decorating. Well-carved examples, especially those of rare species, are appreciating rapidly, and those with original paint are more desirable. In the listings that follow, all decoys are solid-bodied unless noted hollow.

Key:
CG — Challenge Grade   OWP — original working paint
DG — Detroit Grade   PG — Premier Grade
MDF — Mason's Decoy Factory   SG — Standard Grade
OP — original paint   WDF — Wildfowler Decoy Factory
ORP — old repaint   WOP — worn original paint

Black Duck, B Graves, from Caswell rig, EX OP, 2 sm cracks..**7,250.00**
Black Duck, E Crowell, reattached bill, OP, mini, VG..............**550.00**
Black Duck, HV Shourds, ORP, tail chips/dings, 1880s...............**450.00**
Black Duck, J Heisler, hollow, ORP to body, 1920s, oversz, dents..**1,250.00**
Black Duck, MDF, PG, snakey head, NM OP, lightly shot.......**1,900.00**
Black Duck, R 'Turk' Lipensberger, sleeping, hollow, 1950s, M unused....**300.00**
Bluebill Drake, D Nichol, orig scratch pnt w/lt wear, mid-20th C...**600.00**
Bluebill Drake, MDF, CG, WOP, reset head, crack/shots **135.00**
Bluebill Drake, R McGaw, hairline crack, dtd 1937, NM **500.00**
Bluebill Hen, J McLoughlin, low head, EX OP, minor dents.......**600.00**
Bluebill Hen, Peterson Decoy Factory, NM OP, late 19th C **2,500.00**
Bluebill Hen, R McGaw, well cvd, pnt flake, dtd 1937, NM **550.00**
Brant, H Conklin, swimming/reaching, EX OP, mid 20th C.......**400.00**
Brant, MDF, CG, WOP, prof rpt to bill, sm crack........................**800.00**
Canada Goose, H Conklin, hollow, calling pose, EX OP, crack in neck..**1,300.00**
Canada Goose, Ward Bros, EX OP w/possible ORP to tail, rpr/crack, 1928 ..**8,000.00**
Canada Goose, WDF, hollow pine, preening, NM (crack in neck)...**450.00**
Canvasback Drake, E Crowell, feeding, chip on bill, dk pnt, mini **625.00**
Canvasback Drake, MDF, CG, snakey head, EX OP, dents/cracks .**1,400.00**
Canvasback Hen, J English, hollow, detailed cvg, dry EX OP **3,950.00**
Canvasback Hen, Ken Anger, NM OP **1,600.00**
Canvasback pr, B Graves, OP w/EX patina, sm rpr/dents.........**5,500.00**
Canvasback pr, WDF, EX OP, branded....................................**400.00**
Curlew, MDF, 2-pc body, long bill, NM OP, dents/shot **29,000.00**
Downy Woodpecker, E Crowell, on wood base, mini, NM OP ...**950.00**
Egret, H Conklin, hollow, EX OP, tiny dents............................**1,500.00**
Golden Plover, G Boyd, on wooden base, pnt flakes from metal legs ..**1,600.00**
Golden Plover, Nantucket area, hollow cvd, shoe-button eyes, NM OP...**3,750.00**
Goldeneye Hen, F Coombs, NM OP w/worn area under tail...**1,750.00**
Greenwing Teal Drake, MDF, SG, rstr pnt, rpl neck filler...........**250.00**
Harlequin Duck, DW Nichol, NM OP **1,800.00**
Mallard Drake, C McAlpin, trn head, M detailed pnt **1,000.00**
Mallard Drake, JM Hays..., Grand Prix model, EX OP, chips, 1900s.......**250.00**
Mallard Drake, MDF, CG, snakey head, EX OP w/minor RP, tight line.**800.00**
Mallard Drake, MDF, SG, glass eyes, NM OP, rpl neck filler/touchup **675.00**

Mallard Drake, Peterson Decoy Factory, NM OP, rpl filler, early..........1,300.00
Mallard Drake, R Elliston, EX OP w/varnish, sm crack in bill ..1,200.00
Mallard Hen, Charles Perdew, EX pnt detail/form, NM OP 2,000.00
Mallard pr, MDF, CG, from A Muhler rig, EX OP, cracks/rprs....800.00
Merganser Hen, A Verity, ORP, sm dents, crack in neck, 1920s.325.00
Merganser Hen, C 'Shang' Wheeler, feather pnt detail, NM OP, 17½".12,000.00
Old Squaw Hen, F Davis, prof rstr pnt, sm dents........................350.00
Pintail Drake, Dodge Decoy Factory, NM OP, crack in neck, 1890s..1,500.00
Pintail Drake, Hays Decoy Factory, SG, MOP, sm crack..........1,500.00
Pintail Drake, MDF, SG, glass eyes, EX OP, in-factory rpr, dents..1,000.00
Pintail Drake, MDF, SG, pnt eyes, EX OP, split, shot..................600.00
Redhead Drake, H Conklin, hollow, EX OP, 1960s.....................325.00
Redhead Drake, R McGaw (att), nontypical cvg, NMOP...........550.00
Redwing Teal Hen, R Elliston, NM OP, tiny shot mks 1 side...13,000.00
Swan, Herter's Factory, hollow, removable head, 1960s, M.........550.00
Wigeon Hen, WDF, balsa body, EX OP, dents, old stamp............400.00
Wood Duck Drake, C 'Shang' Wheeler, raised wing tips, NM OP, crack...15,000.00
Wood Duck Hen, C 'Shang' Wheeler, raised wing tips, NM OP....18,000.00
Yellowlegs, att WS Morton, shoe-button eyes, inserted bill, EX OP.4,000.00

Dedham Pottery

Originally founded in Chelsea, Massachusetts, as the Chelsea Keramic Works, the name was changed to Dedham Pottery in 1895 after the firm relocated in Dedham, near Boston, Massachusetts. The ware utilized a gray stoneware body with a crackle glaze and simple cobalt border designs of flowers, birds, and animals. Decorations were brushed on by hand using an ancient Chinese method which suspended the cobalt within the overall glaze. There were thirteen standard patterns, among them Magnolia, Iris, Butterfly, Duck, Polar Bear, and Rabbit, the latter of which was chosen to represent the company on their logo. On the very early pieces, the rabbits face left; decorators soon found the reverse position easier to paint, and the rabbits were turned to the right. (Earlier examples are worth from 10% to 20% more than identical pieces manufactured in later years.) In addition to the standard patterns, other designs were produced for special orders. These and artist-signed pieces are highly valued by collectors today.

Though their primary product was the blue-printed, crackle-glazed dinnerware, two types of artware were also produced: crackle glaze and flambe. Their notable volcanic ware was a type of the latter. The mark is incised and often accompanies the cipher of Hugh Robertson. The firm was operated by succeeding generations of the Robertson family until it closed in 1943. Our advisor for this category is Dale MacLean; he is listed in the Directory under Massachusetts. See also Chelsea Keramic Art Works.

Dinnerware

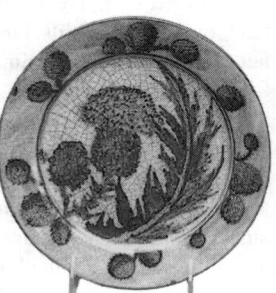

Plate, Thistle, Hugh Robertson, stamped/impressed, 8½", $2,700.00.

Ashtray, Rabbit, flat rim, invt slots, stamped/registered, 6¾"......250.00
Bacon rasher, Dolphin, Davenport rebus, stamped/registered, 10" ..950.00
Bowl, Butterfly, #6, stamped, 4½"..500.00

Bowl, Grape, #3, stamped, 3¼x7", VG 275.00
Bowl, Horse Chestnut, stamped/registered, 1¾x7¾", NM 250.00
Bowl, Lotus, misglaze at base, unmk, 5" 325.00
Bowl, mayonnaise; Elephant & Baby, stamped/1931, 5½" 850.00
Bowl, nappy; Azalea, #5, stamped, 6" 275.00
Bowl, nappy; Elephant & Baby, #2, imp, 10¾" 900.00
Bowl, nappy; Rabbit, #3, stamped, 9¾" 400.00
Bowl, nappy; Rabbit, #3, stamped/registered, 2½x11" 500.00
Bowl, Poppy, Chinese Cut #A, registered, 5¾x11" 1,500.00
Bowl, Rabbit, Davenport rebus, #1, stamped, 3¾x9", NM 450.00
Bowl, Rabbit, stamped/registered/imp, 9" 400.00
Bowl, Rabbit (clockwise), stamped, 3x8" 450.00
Bowl, Snowtree, #5, stamped, 2x5¼" 250.00
Bowl, whipped cream; Rabbit, flat rim, stamped, 2½x7½"..........375.00
Butter pat, Floral, hand-cut petals lined in bl, stamped/registered....375.00
Charger, Elephant & Baby, stamped/registered/imp, 12" 2,000.00
Charger, Rabbit, stamped, 12", NM..900.00
Coaster, Rabbit, stamped/registered, 4" 375.00
Creamer, Rabbit, #8, stamped, 3½x3¾" 400.00
Creamer, Turkey, #1, stamped, 3½x5½" 475.00
Creamer & sugar bowl, Azalea, w/lid, stamped/registered............450.00
Cup & saucer, coffee; Rabbit, stamped, 3x5" 250.00
Cup & saucer, coffee; Rabbit, stamped/registered, 2¼", 5" 250.00
Cup & saucer, Iris, stamped, 2⅛", 6" 250.00
Cup & saucer, Polar Bear, stamped/registered, 2⅛", 6" 475.00
Egg dish, Rabbit, w/lid, stamped registered, NM 900.00
Figurine, Swan on boot figural, stamped, 5x4¼" 850.00
Flower holder, Rabbit figural, domed holder base, stamped, 6¾" ..1,200.00
Flower holder, Turtle, stamped/registered, 3½" dia 600.00
Jar, marmalade; Swan, stamped, 4" 500.00
Jar, mustard; Rabbit, stamped, mini, 2¾" 425.00
Knife rest, Rabbit figural, all wht, stamped, 3¼" 375.00
Mug, child's; Lobster, stamped, 3" 700.00
Olive dish, Rabbit, EX color/art, stamped, 7¾" 500.00
Pitcher, Azalea, #6, stamped, 5x4" 500.00
Pitcher, Double Turtle, #6, stamped/incised DP, 5x4" 1,500.00
Pitcher, Grape, bulbous, #2, stamped, 5x4" 475.00
Pitcher, Horse Chestnut, #2, line/rust, stamped, 5x6" 275.00
Pitcher, Night & Day, stamped, 5x5¼" 550.00
Pitcher, Rabbit, #11, stamped/registered, 7" 500.00
Pitcher, Rabbit, #2, unmk, 5½x6", NM 450.00
Pitcher, Rabbit, sq mouth & sides, stamped, 4½x3½" 1,200.00
Pitcher, 1850s style #17, bulbous, scalloped, stamped, 5x3¾" 650.00
Plate, Azalea, stamped/imp, 8½" 300.00
Plate, Bird in The Potted Orange Tree, misglazes, imp, 10" 500.00
Plate, breakfast; Iris, stamped/imp, pre-1932, 8⅜" 300.00
Plate, butterfly, registered/imp, 9¾"..600.00
Plate, Chick, stamped/registered, 8½", NM..............................2,000.00
Plate, Crab, registered/1931/imp, 7½" 500.00
Plate, Day Lily, Davenport rebus, stamped, 6".............................800.00
Plate, Dolphin, CPUS, 10" 750.00
Plate, Double Turtle, stamped/imp, 8½" 950.00
Plate, Dove, nick/line, stamped, rare, 8½" 1,400.00
Plate, Duck, Davenport rebus, stamped/imp, 8¼"........................350.00
Plate, Elephant & Baby, stamped/registered/imp, 8½" 700.00
Plate, Horse Chestnut, stamped, 8½", pr 300.00
Plate, Iris, Davenport rebus, stamped/imp, 10"............................400.00
Plate, Lion Tapestry, stamped/imp, 8½" 1,500.00
Plate, Lobster, stamped/registered/1931, 7½", 6 for 2,500.00
Plate, Luna Moth, stamped, 6", NM..500.00
Plate, Magnolia, Davenport rebus, sm rstr, stamped/imp, 10"......350.00
Plate, Magnolia, stamped/imp, 8½"...275.00
Plate, Moth, Davenport rebus, stamped, 8½"................................550.00
Plate, Mushroom, stamped/imp, 10" 450.00

Plate, Nasturtium, stamped/imp, 8¾"..**2,700.00**
Plate, Peacock, imp, 6"..**3,000.00**
Plate, Polar Bear, Davenport rebus, stamped/imp, 10"................**750.00**
Plate, Pond Lily, Davenport rebus, stamped/imp, 10"..................**375.00**
Plate, Pond Lily, stamped/registered/imp, 6"..............................**250.00**
Plate, Poppy, stamped, 8¼"..**650.00**
Plate, Rabbit, Coat of Arms center, registered/1931/imp, 8¾"....**500.00**
Plate, Rabbit, stamp/imp, pre-1932, 8½", EX............................**225.00**
Plate, Rabbit, stamp/imp, 7¾", 6 for......................................**1,000.00**
Plate, Rabbit, stamped, 6", 6 for...**700.00**
Plate, Rabbit (clockwise), stamped, 8½", 6 for.......................**1,000.00**
Plate, San Francisco - Golden Gate, SF/Dec 21/MS/stamped, 20" ..**1,800.00**
Plate, Scottie Dog Pair, hairline, stamped/registered/1931, 8½" .**800.00**
Plate, Snowtree, Davenport rebus, warped, stamped/imp, 6".......**150.00**
Plate, Snowtree, stamped, 10", NM..**300.00**
Plate, Snowtree, stamped, 8½"..**275.00**
Plate, Swan, stamped/imp, 6"..**300.00**
Plate, Swan, stamped/imp, 8½"..**500.00**
Plate, Tufted Duck, imp, 10¼"..**400.00**
Plate, Turkey, Davenport rebus, stamped/imp, 6⅛"....................**375.00**
Plate, Turkey, stamped/imp, 8½"..**325.00**
Plate, Water Lily, Davenport rebus, stamped/imp, 6"..................**225.00**
Plate, Wild Rose, att Davenport, stamped, rare, 6" **1,500.00**
Platter, Grape, stamped/imp, 12"..**950.00**
Salt cellar, Walnut on Leaf, hand sgn DP in bl, 3".....................**600.00**
Saucer, Reverse Rabbit, stamped, 6¼"..**450.00**
Shakers, Rabbit, bulbous, long necks, mk DP, 3½", pr **400.00**
Sherbet, Rabbit, broad ped, unmk, 3¼x5½", NM........................**400.00**
Soup, Single Ear Rabbit, Davenport rebus, stamped/imp, 8¼"....**475.00**
Spoon, Elephant, stamped, 4 /12"...**1,100.00**
Star dish, Azalea, 5-sided, stamped/registered, 7½".....................**575.00**
Star dish, Rabbit, 5-sided, stamped/1931, 7½x7".......................**450.00**
Teacups & saucer, Rabbit, stamped, 6" dia, 6 for...................**12,500.00**
Tile, Horse Chestnut, stamped, 6⅛" dia.....................................**425.00**
Tile, Rabbit, stamped, 6", NM...**425.00**
Toothpick holder, Tulip, stamped, 2½"......................................**600.00**
Tureen, Azalea, w/lid, stamped, 5¾x9½"................................**1,200.00**

Miscellaneous

Book, Dedham Potteries, LE Hawes MD, hardcover, 1st ed, 1968, M...**300.00**
Bottle, gin; curved panels w/scrolled G in bl on wht, 8½" **700.00**
Catalog, w/history/listings of lines/etc, 38-pg, VG **500.00**
Snuffer, Elephant & Baby, unmk, 2" **1,100.00**
Vase, frothy brn & gr, volcanic/bulbous, Robertson, 9¾x5" **1,250.00**
Vase, volcanic gr/gray/teal/red/blk, HC Robertson, S, 6⅛", NM...**1,300.00**

Degenhart

The Crystal Art Glass factory in Cambridge, Ohio, opened in 1947 under the private ownership of John and Elizabeth Degenhart. John had previously worked for the Cambridge Glass Company and was well known for his superior paperweights. After his death in 1964, Elizabeth took over management of the factory, hiring several workers from the defunct Cambridge Company, including Zack Boyd. Boyd was responsible for many unique colors, some of which were named for him. From 1964 to 1974, more than twenty-seven different moulds were created, most of them resulting from Elizabeth Degenhart's work and creativity, and over 145 official colors were developed. Elizabeth died in 1978, requesting that the ten moulds she had built while operating the factory were to be turned over to the Degenhart Museum. The remaining moulds were to be held by the Island Mould and Machine Company, who (complying with her request) removed the familiar 'D in heart'

trademark. The factory was eventually bought by Zack's son, Bernard Boyd. He also acquired the remaining Degenhart moulds, to which he added his own logo.

In general, slags and opaques should be valued 15% to 20% higher than crystals in color.

Baby Shoe (Hobo Boot) Toothpick Holder, Gold....................**10.00**
Basket Toothpick Holder, Cobalt..**15.00**
Beaded Oval Toothpick Holder, Caramel................................**45.00**
Beaded Oval Toothpick Holder, Maverick...............................**45.00**
Bicentennial Bell, Butterscotch...**30.00**
Bicentennial Bell, Sapphire...**12.00**
Bird Salt & Pepper, Lavender Green Slag................................**60.00**
Bird Salt w/Cherry, Baby Blue..**15.00**
Bird Salt w/Cherry, Daffodil w/Green....................................**40.00**
Bird Salt w/Cherry, Tomato..**45.00**
Bow Slipper, Champagne **15.00**
Bow Slipper, Peach (clear) **15.00**
Buzz Saw Wine, Amber..**15.00**
Buzz Saw Wine, Emerald Green..**25.00**
Buzz Saw Wine, Red Carnival...**75.00**
Buzz Saw Wine, Sapphire..**20.00**
Chick Covered Dish, Mint or Lime Custard, 2", ea...............**50.00**
Chick Covered Dish, 2", Bluebell...**20.00**
Coaster, Shamrock...**8.00**
Colonial Drape Toothpick Holder, Light Custard (Mosser), hand-stamped......**25.00**
Daisy & Button Creamer & Sugar Bowl, Dk Cobalt Carnival, hand-stamped ...**100.00**
Daisy & Button Hat, Amethyst Carnival, rare..........................**45.00**
Daisy & Button Salt, Apple Green...**15.00**
Daisy & Button Salt, Red..**25.00**
Daisy & Button Toothpick Holder, Apple Green **20.00**
Daisy & Button Wine, Cobalt..**25.00**
Elephant Head Toothpick Holder, Amber...............................**20.00**
Elephant Head Toothpick Holder, Pink **25.00**
Forget-Me-Not Toothpick Holder, Blue & White Slag **30.00**
Forget-Me-Not Toothpick Holder, Ivory Slag **25.00**
Forget-Me-Not Toothpick Holder, Spring Green **20.00**
Forget-Me-Not Toothpick Holder, Zack Boyd Slag, rare **50.00**
Gypsy Pot Toothpick Holder, Dark Caramel............................**45.00**
Gypsy Pot Toothpick Holder, Red **35.00**
Hand, Crystal..**6.00**
Hand, Tomato..**25.00**
Heart & Lyre Cup Plate, Taffeta..**12.00**
Heart Jewel Box, Green Lavender Slag **45.00**
Heart Toothpick Holder, Blue Jay Slag...................................**30.00**
Heart Toothpick Holder, Lavender Slag **35.00**
Hen Covered Dish, Amethsyt, 5"...**50.00**
Hen Covered Dish, Bluebell, 3"...**45.00**
Hen Covered Dish, Heliotrope, 5"..**90.00**
Hen Covered Dish, Milk Blue, 5"...**60.00**
Hen Covered Dish, Persimmon, 5"...**60.00**
High Boot, Cobalt...**30.00**
High Boot, Persimmon **25.00**
Kat Slipper (Puss & Boots), Amber..**20.00**
Kat Slipper (Puss & Boots), Ivory...**40.00**
Lamb Covered Dish, Bernard Boyd's Ebony **85.00**
Lamb Covered Dish, Canary, 5"...**35.00**
Lamb Covered Dish, Pine Green, 5"..**65.00**
Mini Pitcher, Sapphire **15.00**
Mini Slipper w/o Sole, Mint Green **25.00**
Mini Slipper w/Sole, Vaseline **35.00**
Owl, Blue & White **50.00**
Owl, Champagne..**50.00**
Owl, Custard #1..**50.00**

Owl, Delft Blue Slag...75.00
Owl, Jim Dandy..200.00
Owl, Midnight Sun..50.00
Owl, Spice Brown...50.00
Pooch, Autumn 25.00
Pooch, Daffodil Slag, from $30 to..60.00
Pooch, Henry's Blue..25.00
Pooch, Light Daffodil..15.00
Portrait Plate, Blue & White Slag, rare...............................200.00
Portrait Plate, Crystal...35.00
Portrait Plate, Red..60.00
Pottie Salt, Amber..6.00
Priscilla, Bittersweet..150.00
Priscilla, Smoky Blue..95.00
Robin Covered Dish, Sapphire, 5".......................................50.00
Seal of Ohio Cup Plate, Bluebell..15.00
Star & Dew Drop Salt, Amberina...25.00
Stork & Peacock Child's Mug, Apple Green 25.00
Stork & Peacock Child's Mug, Henry's Blue 25.00

Texas Boot, Cobalt, 1974, 2⅝", $25.00. (Photo courtesy Earlene Wheatley)

Texas Boot, Red...25.00
Texas Creamer & Sugar, Red..100.00
Tomahawk (Hatchet), Crown Tuscan....................................50.00
Tomahawk (Hatchet), Peach Blo..25.00
Turkey Covered Dish, Bluina, 5" 125.00
Turkey Covered Dish, Ruby, 5" 90.00
Wildflower Candle Holder, Milk Blue..................................25.00

Delft

Old Delftware, made as early as the sixteenth century, was originally a low-fired earthenware coated in a thin opaque tin glaze with painted-on blue or polychrome designs. It was not until the last half of the nineteenth century, however, that the ware became commonly referred to as Delft, acquiring the name from the Dutch city that had become the major center of its production. English, German, and French potters also produced Delft, though with noticeable differences both in shape and decorative theme.

In the early part of the eighteenth century, the German potter, Bottger, developed a formula for porcelain; in England, Wedgwood began producing creamware — both of which were much more durable. Unable to compete, one by one the Delft potteries failed. Soon only one remained. In 1876 De Porcelyne Fles reintroduced Delftware on a hard white body with blue and white decorative themes reflecting the Dutch countryside, windmills by the sea, and Dutch children. This manufacturer is the most well known of several operating today. Their products are now produced under the Royal Delft label.

For further information we recommend *Discovering Dutch Delftware*,

Modern Delft and Makkum Pottery, by Stephen J. Van Hook (Glen Park Press, Alexandria, Virginia). Examples listed here are blue on white unless noted otherwise. See also specific manufacturers. Our advisor is Ralph Jaarsma; he is listed in the Directory under Iowa.

Bottle, Dutch, floral, ca 1879, mfg flaw, 3¼x2¼"......................255.00
Bowl, Dutch, bl & yel tulips, ca 1690, 2x8¾"........................1,050.00
Box, Dutch, floral, de Porceleyne Fles, ca 1905, 5" sq..............315.00
Charger, Dutch, landscape, sgn, Porcelyne Fles, ca 1894, 16"...575.00
Charger, Dutch, scene after J Israels, 1894, 15½"....................450.00
Charger, English, flowers & foliage, 18th C, 13"...................1,050.00
Figural group, English, Shepherd & Shepherdess on Rock, 1820, 11", NM...775.00
Figurine, Dutch, boy on cask mk Root, early 1800s, 5½".........535.00
Figurine, English, elk, late 1800s, 6¼x5", EX.........................235.00
Jar, Dutch, floral, dog finial, 6-sided, ca 1887, 16"..................285.00
Jug, Dutch, floral, bulbous, Porceleyne Fles, 1932, 7½x5".......155.00
Plate, Dutch, floral, sgn van Aalst, Porceleyne Fles, 1941, 11¼"...165.00
Plate, Dutch, Wan-Li style Chinese garden w/flower signs, 1700s, 9"..195.00
Plate, English, peacock & butterflies, mid-18th C, 9"...............215.00
Swan dish, Dutch, floral, 18th C, line, 4¾x4¾".....................465.00
Tea caddy scoop, English, rider's hat form, 19th C, 1¾x2½x1¾"....725.00
Tile, Dutch, bulldog, de Porceleyne Fles, ca 1920, 8¼".............355.00
Tile, Dutch, sailing ship, 18th C..185.00
Vase, Dutch, floral, stripes on bottle neck, 1882, 11½x5¼".......260.00
Vase, Dutch, man in rocky landscape, ca 1760, 18th C, 10", VG/EX..200.00

Depression Glass

Depression glass is defined by Gene Florence, author of several best-selling books on the subject, as 'the inexpensive glassware made primarily during the Depression era in the colors of amber, green, pink, blue, red, yellow, white, and crystal.' This glass was mass produced, sold through five-and-dime stores and mail-order catalogs, and given away as premiums with gas and food products.

The listings in this book are far from being complete. If you want a more thorough presentation of this fascinating glassware, we recommend *The Collector's Encyclopedia of Depression Glass*, *The Pocket Guide to Depression Glass*, *Elegant Glassware of the Depression Era*, and *Very Rare Glassware of the Depression Years*, all by Gene Florence, whose address is listed in the Directory under Kentucky. See also McKee; New Martinsville.

Key:
AOP — allover pattern   PAT — pattern at top

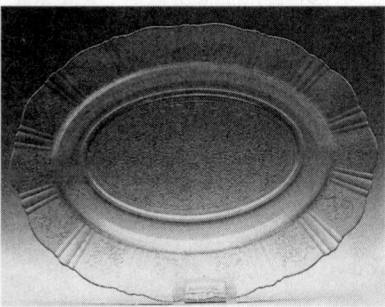

American Sweetheart, platter, pink, oval, 13", $60.00. (Photo courtesy Gene Florence)

Adam, bowl, dessert; pk or gr, 4¾".......................................22.00
Adam, bowl, gr, w/lid, 9"..45.00
Adam, butter dish, pk, w/lid..85.00
Adam, cake plate, pk, ftd, 10" 30.00
Adam, coaster, gr, 3¼" 20.00
Adam, pitcher, gr, 32-oz, 8"...325.00

Adam, tumbler, pk, 4½" 40.00
American Pioneer, bowl, crystal or pk, hdld, 9" 22.00
American Pioneer, coaster, crystal, pk or gr, 3½" 35.00
American Pioneer, goblet, wine; gr, 3-oz, 4" 55.00
American Pioneer, mayonnaise, gr, 4¼" 90.00
American Pioneer, saucer, crystal or pk 4.00
American Sweetheart, bowl, console; bl, 18" 1,250.00
American Sweetheart, bowl, flat soup; pk, 9½" 75.00
American Sweetheart, lamp shade, cremax....................495.00
American Sweetheart, plate, salver; monax, 12" 22.00
American Sweetheart, plate, salver; red, 12" 185.00
American Sweetheart, shakers, pk, ftd, pr......................575.00
American Sweetheart, sugar bowl, smoke & other trim, ftd, open....100.00
American Sweetheart, tidbit, pk or monax, 2-tier, 8" & 12".........60.00
Aunt Polly, bowl, bl, oval, 8⅜" 125.00
Aunt Polly, candy dish, gr or irid, 2-hdld, w/lid 75.00
Aunt Polly, plate, luncheon; bl, 8" 20.00
Aunt Polly, vase, bl, ftd, 6½" 55.00
Aurora, plate, cobalt or pk, 6½" 12.50
Aurora, tumbler, cobalt or pk, 10-oz, 4¾" 27.50
Avocado, bowl, pk, 2-hdld, oval, 8" 22.00
Avocado, cup, gr, 2-styles, ftd 40.00
Avocado, plate, sherbet; gr, 6⅜" 18.00
Avocado, saucer, pk, 6⅜" 22.00
Beaded Block, bowl, celery; crystal, pk, gr or amber, 8¼" 30.00
Beaded Block, bowl, crystal, pk, gr or amber, sq, 5½" 20.00

Beaded Block, vase, crystal, 6", $25.00. (Photo courtesy Gene Florence)

Block Optic, bowl, cereal; gr, 5¼" 15.00
Block Optic, candlesticks, pk, 1¾", pr.........................80.00
Block Optic, goblet, cocktail; gr or pk, 4" 40.00
Block Optic, saucer, gr, w/cup ring, 6⅛" 10.00
Block Optic, tumbler, gr or pk, 9½-oz, 3¾" 15.00
Block Optic, whiskey, gr or pk, 2-oz, 2¼" 32.00
Bowknot, cup, gr 9.00
Bowknot, sherbet, gr, low ftd...................................20.00
Cameo, bowl, sauce; crystal or platinum, 4¼" 6.00
Cameo, bowl, vegetable; yel, oval, 10" 42.00
Cameo, candy jar, gr, w/lid, 6½" 185.00
Cameo, creamer, pk, 4¼" 125.00
Cameo, goblet, wine; pk, 4" 225.00
Cameo, pitcher, juice; gr, 36-oz, 6" 65.00
Cameo, plate, dinner; pk, rimmed, 10½" 175.00
Cameo, tumbler, juice; gr, 5-oz, 3¾" 33.00
Cherry Blossom, bowl, berry; pk, 4¾" 20.00
Cherry Blossom, cake plate, gr, 3-legged, 10¼" 40.00
Cherry Blossom, pitcher, pk or gr, PAT, flat, 42-oz, 8" 60.00
Cherry Blossom, platter, pk or gr, divided, 13" 70.00
Cherry Blossom, tumbler, pk, flat, PAT, 4-oz, 3½" 22.00
Cherryberry, bowl, salad; crystal or irid, deep, 6½" 20.00

Cherryberry, creamer, pk or gr, sm 22.50
Cherryberry, pickle dish, crystal or irid, oval, 8¼" 9.00
Cherryberry, tumbler, pk or gr, 9-oz, 3⅝"...................38.00
Chinex Classic, bowl, vegetable; Brownstone, 9"...........11.00
Chinex Classic, butter dish, castle decal, w/lid 150.00
Chinex Classic, sugar bowl, w/decal 10.00
Circle, bowl, gr, 5¼" 10.00
Circle, cup, pk, 2 styles, ea 7.00
Circle, sherbet, pk, 3⅛" 10.00
Circle, tumbler, water; gr, 8-oz, 4" 9.00
Cloverleaf, ashtray, blk, match holder in center, 4" 65.00
Cloverleaf, bowl, cereal; gr or yel, 5" 50.00
Colonial, bowl, berry; gr, 4½" 20.00
Colonial, butter dish, crystal, w/lid.............................45.00
Colonial, pitcher, pk, 68-oz, 7¾" 70.00
Colonial, stem, cordial; gr, 1-oz, 3¾" 30.00
Colonial, tumbler, juice; crystal, 5-oz, 3" 15.00
Colonial, tumbler, pk, ftd, 3-oz, 3½" 17.00
Colonial Block, butter tub, pk or gr............................45.00
Colonial Block, creamer, wht......................................7.00
Colonial Block, tumbler, pk or gr, ftd, 5-oz, 5¼" 55.00
Colonial Fluted, bowl, cereal; gr, 6" 15.00
Colonial Fluted, saucer, gr 2.00
Columbia, bowl, soup; crystal, low, 8" 22.00
Columbia, butter dish, crystal, w/lid...........................20.00
Columbia, snack plate, crystal.....................................30.00
Coronation, bowl, berry; Royal Ruby, hdld, lg, 8" 18.00
Coronation, plate, sherbet; pk, 6" 3.00
Coronation, tumbler, pk, ftd, 10-oz, 5" 33.00
Cube, bowl, pk, deep, 4½"..8.00
Cube, butter dish, gr, w/lid...65.00
Cube, cup, gr 9.00
Cube, shakers, pk or gr, pr..35.00
Cube, tumbler, gr, 9-oz, 4" 75.00
Diamond Quilted, bowl, cereal; pk or gr, 5" 7.50
Diamond Quilted, candy jar, pk or gr, w/lid, ftd.............65.00
Diamond Quilted, goblet, cordial; pk or gr, 1-oz 12.00
Diamond Quilted, pitcher, pk or gr, 64-oz 50.00
Diamond Quilted, plate, dinner; pk or gr, 14" 15.00
Diamond Quilted, sherbet, bl or blk 16.00
Diana, bowl, cereal; crystal, 5" 6.00
Diana, bowl, pk, scalloped edge, 12" 30.00
Diana, coaster, amber, 3½"..10.00
Diana, platter, pk, oval, 12"...33.00
Diana, tumbler, crystal or amber, 9-oz, 4⅛" 30.00
Dogwood, bowl, berry; monax or cremax, 8½"..............40.00
Dogwood, cup, monax or cremax, thick 40.00
Dogwood, platter, pk, oval, rare, 12"...........................695.00
Dogwood, sherbet, gr, low ftd....................................115.00
Dogwood, tumbler, gr, decor, 10-oz, 4" 97.50
Doric, bowl, cream soup; gr, 5" 450.00
Doric, butter dish, gr, w/lid..85.00
Doric, pitcher, Delphite, flat, 32-oz, 5½" 1,200.00
Doric, plate, dinner; pk, 9" 18.00
Doric, sherbet, Delphite, ftd..9.00
Doric, tray, serving; gr, 8x8" 28.00
Doric & Pansy, bowl, berry; gr or teal, lg, 8" 85.00
Doric & Pansy, cup, pk or crystal................................12.00
Doric & Pansy, plate, salad; gr or teal, 7" 40.00
Doric & Pansy, sugar bowl, pk or crystal, open 85.00
English Hobnail, bottle, toilet; pk or gr, 5-oz 25.00
English Hobnail, bowl, nappy; turq or ice bl, rnd, 4½"...................30.00
English Hobnail, bowl, pickle; pk or gr, 8" 30.00
English Hobnail, cigarette box, pk or gr, w/lid, 4½x2½" 27.50

English Hobnail, cup, demi; pk or gr 55.00
English Hobnail, nut, pk or gr, ftd, ind............................18.00
English Hobnail, plate, pk or gr, rnd, 5½" 9.50
English Hobnail, stem, water goblet; turq or ice bl, ftd, sq, 8-oz ...50.00
English Hobnail, straw jar, pk or gr, 10" 100.00
English Hobnail, sugar bowl, turq or ice bl, ftd, hexagonal 45.00
Fire-King Philbe, bowl, cereal; pk or gr, 7¼" 80.00
Fire-King Philbe, cup, crystal 60.00
Fire-King Philbe, pitcher, bl, 56-oz, 8½" 1,175.00
Fire-King Philbe, saucer, pk or gr, 6"..............................65.00
Fire-King Philbe, tumbler, juice; bl, ftd, 3½" 175.00
Floral, butter dish, gr, w/lid......................................90.00
Floral, plate, dinner; Delphite, 9" 150.00
Floral, tumbler, gr, ftd, 3-oz, 3½" 175.00
Floral & Diamond Band, butter dish, gr, w/lid.....................130.00
Floral & Diamond Band, sherbet, pk 7.00
Floral & Diamond Band, tumbler, iced tea; gr, 5" 50.00
Florentine No 1, bowl, berry; crystal or gr, 5".....................12.00
Florentine No 1, bowl, cream soup; pk, 5" 20.00
Florentine No 1, butter dish, yel or pk, w/lid.....................160.00
Florentine No 1, plate, salad; crystal or gr, 8½" 8.00
Florentine No 1, sherbet, yel, ftd, 3-oz 14.00
Florentine No 1, tumbler, iced tea; crystal, ftd, 12-oz, 5¼" 28.00
Florentine No 1, tumbler, juice; yel or pk, ftd, 5-oz, 3¾" 25.00
Florentine No 2, bowl, cereal; crystal or gr, 6" 33.00
Florentine No 2, bowl, vegetable; yel, w/lid, oval, 9"..............85.00
Florentine No 2, candlesticks, crystal or gr, 2¾", pr 50.00
Florentine No 2, cup, amber 50.00
Florentine No 2, plate, dinner; crystal, gr or yel, 10".............16.00
Florentine No 2, platter (for gravy boat), yel, 11½"................45.00
Florentine No 2, sugar bowl, crystal or gr, w/lid...................25.00
Florentine No 2, tumbler, yel, ftd, 9-oz, 4½".......................35.00
Flower Garden w/Butterflies, bonbon, blk, w/lid, 6⅝" dia..........250.00
Flower Garden w/Butterflies, comport, canary yel, 4¼x4¾" 50.00
Flower Garden w/Butterflies, plate, amber, 2 styles, 8" 15.00
Flower Garden w/Butterflies, powder jar, pk or gr, ftd, 6¼"........135.00
Flower Garden w/Butterflies, vase, bl or canary yel, 6¼" 160.00
Flower Garden w/Butterflies, vase, blk, wall hanging, 9" 350.00
Fortune, candy dish, pk or crystal, w/lid, flat.....................25.00
Fortune, cup, pk or crystal 3.00
Fruits, tumbler, gr, 12-oz, 5" 150.00
Georgian, bowl, deep, 6½"...68.00
Georgian, creamer, gr, ftd, 4"......................................17.00
Hex Optic, bowl, berry; pk or gr, ruffled, 4¼" 7.00
Hex Optic, creamer, pk or gr, 2 styles of hdls, ea...................5.50
Hex Optic, pitcher, pk or gr, ftd, 48-oz, 9" 50.00
Hex Optic, platter, rnd, 11"...15.00
Hex Optic, saucer, pk or gr 2.50
Hex Optic, tumbler, pk or gr, ftd, 7-oz, 4¾" 7.50
Hobnail, bowl, salad; crystal, 7" 4.50
Hobnail, goblet, iced tea; crystal, 13-oz...........................10.00
Hobnail, sherbet, pk 3.50
Hobnail, whiskey, crystal, 1½-oz.....................................6.00

Homespun, butter dish, pk or crystal, w/lid.........................60.00
Homespun, platter, pk or crystal, closed hdls, 13" 20.00
Homespun, tumbler, iced tea; pk or crystal, 12½-oz, 5⅜"............33.00
Homespun, tumbler, pk or crystal, ftd, 15-oz, 6⅜" 33.00
Indiana Custard, bowl, vegetable; French Ivory, oval, 9½" 33.00
Indiana Custard, plate, bread & butter; French Ivory, 5¾"..........6.50
Indiana Custard, plate, luncheon; French Ivory, 8⅞"...............18.00
Indiana Custard, sugar bowl, French Ivory, w/lid 37.00
Iris, bowl, berry; irid, beaded edge, 8" 25.00
Iris, bowl, sauce; crystal, ruffled, 5" 9.00
Iris, butter dish, irid, w/lid......................................45.00
Iris, cup, demi; crystal 35.00
Iris, goblet, wine; crystal, 3-oz, 4½"..............................17.00
Iris, sherbet, crystal, ftd, 2½"....................................28.00
Iris, tumbler, irid, ftd, 6"...16.00
Jubilee, bowl, fruit; pk, flat, 11½"...............................195.00
Jubilee, mayonnaise & plate, pk, w/orig ladle 310.00
Jubilee, stem, oyster cocktail; yel, 4-oz, 4¾".....................75.00
Jubilee, vase, pk or yel, 12".......................................350.00
Lace Edge, bowl, crystal, 8¼".......................................12.00
Lace Edge, cup, pk..28.00
Lace Edge, plate, luncheon; pk, 8¼".................................25.00
Lace Edge, plate, relish; pk, 3-part, 10½".........................26.00
Lace Edge, relish dish, pk, 3-part, deep, 7½".......................65.00
Lace Edge, tumbler, pk, ftd, 10½-oz, 5".............................90.00
Laced Edge, bowl, fruit; bl or gr opal, 4⅜"-4¾"....................30.00
Laced Edge, bowl, soup; bl or gr opal, 7".............................85.00
Laced Edge, plate, bread & butter; bl or gr opal, 6½"..............18.00
Laced Edge, platter, bl or gr opal, 13".............................175.00
Laced Edge, tidbit, bl or gr opal, 2-tiered, 8" & 10" plates 100.00
Lake Como, creamer, wht w/bl scenes, ftd............................32.50
Lake Como, saucer, wht w/bl scenes 12.00
Laurel, bowl, berry; French Ivory, lg, 9"...........................28.00
Laurel, bowl, cereal; wht opal or Jade Green, 6"....................20.00
Laurel, creamer, Poudre Blue, tall 40.00
Laurel, platter, French Ivory, oval, 10¾"..........................30.00
Laurel, saucer, Poudre Blue...7.50
Lincoln Inn, bowl, colors other than cobalt or red, shallow, 9".....23.00
Lincoln Inn, bowl, fruit; cobalt or red, 5".........................11.50
Lincoln Inn, sherbet, colors other than cobalt or red, 4¾" 12.50
Little Jewel, bowl, crystal, 6½"....................................10.00
Little Jewel, creamer, colors 15.00
Little Jewel, pickle dish, crystal, 6½".............................12.50
Lorain, creamer, yel, ftd...27.50
Lorain, plate, dinner; crystal or gr, 10¼"..........................48.00
Lorain, saucer, yel..6.00
Madrid, bowl, console; pk, low, 11".................................11.00
Madrid, bowl, cream soup; amber, 4¾"................................18.00
Madrid, cookie jar, pk, w/lid.......................................30.00
Madrid, hot dish coaster, amber 50.00
Madrid, pitcher, amber, w/o ice lip, 80-oz, 8½"....................60.00
Madrid, shakers, gr, ftd, 3½", pr 110.00
Madrid, tumbler, bl, 5-oz, 3⅞".......................................40.00
Madrid, tumbler, gr, ftd, 10-oz, 5½"................................45.00
Manhattan, ashtray, crystal, 4½" sq.................................18.00
Manhattan, candlesticks, crystal, sq, 4½", pr.......................22.00
Manhattan, creamer, pk, oval 15.00
Manhattan, relish tray insert, crystal 5.50
Manhattan, saucer/sherbet plate, pk.................................75.00
Mayfair Federal, bowl, cream soup; amber, 5".......................20.00
Mayfair Federal, cup, crystal 5.00
Mayfair Federal, plate, grill; amber, 9½"..........................14.00
Mayfair Federal, sugar bowl, gr, ftd 16.00
Mayfair/Open Rose, bowl, gr, low, flat, 11¾".......................45.00

Holiday, pitcher, pink, 6¾", $38.00.

Mayfair/Open Rose, bowl, vegetable; bl, oval, 9"............................80.00
Mayfair/Open Rose, celery dish, pk, 10"..............................50.00
Mayfair/Open Rose, cup, bl..............................55.00
Mayfair/Open Rose, goblet, claret; gr, 4½-oz, 5¼" 950.00
Mayfair/Open Rose, plate, luncheon; pk, 8½"..............................33.00
Mayfair/Open Rose, relish, bl, 4-part, 8⅜"..............................75.00
Mayfair/Open Rose, sandwich server, gr, center hdl..............................40.00
Mayfair/Open Rose, saucer, gr or yel, 5¾"..............................90.00
Mayfair/Open Rose, tumbler, water; gr or yel, 11-oz, 4¾" 200.00
Miss America, bowl, crystal, curved in at top, 8"............................40.00
Miss America, coaster, pk, 5¾"..............................35.00
Miss America, cup, Royal Ruby..............................250.00
Miss America, goblet, water; Royal Ruby, 1-oz, 5½" 255.00
Miss America, plate, sherbet; pk, 5¾"..............................12.00
Miss America, relish, crystal, 4-part, 8¾"..............................11.00
Miss America, tumbler, juice; pk, 5-oz, 4"..............................55.00
Moderntone, bowl, cream soup; cobalt, 4¾"..............................25.00
Moderntone, plate, sherbet; cobalt, 5⅞"..............................6.50
Moderntone, platter, cobalt, oval, 11"..............................50.00
Moondrops, bowl, bl or red, tab hdls, 3-ftd, 5⅜"..............................75.00
Moondrops, bowl, console; colors other than bl or red, 3-ftd, 12" ...32.00
Moondrops, creamer, colors other than bl or red, regular, 3¾" 10.00
Moondrops, goblet, wine; bl or red, metal stem, 4-oz, 5½"...........20.00
Moondrops, plate, dinner; bl or red, 9½" 30.00
Moondrops, tumbler, shot, colors other than bl or red, 2-oz, 2¾".10.00
Mt Pleasant, bowl, fruit; pk or gr, ftd, sq, 4⅞"..............................13.00
Mt Pleasant, plate, pk or gr, scalloped, hdls, 7"..............................9.00
Mt Pleasant, sherbet, amethyst, blk or cobalt, 2 styles, ea............17.50
New Century, bowl, cream soup; gr or crystal, 4¾"..............................20.00
New Century, decanter, gr or crystal, w/stopper..............................65.00
New Century, pitcher, pk, w/ or w/o ice lip, 60-oz, 7¾" 35.00
New Century, plate, grill; gr or crystal, 10"..............................12.00
New Century, tumbler, gr, crystal, pk, cobalt or amethyst, 10-oz, 5" ...20.00
Newport, bowl, berry; amethyst, lg, 8¼"..............................40.00
Newport, bowl, cream soup; cobalt, 4¾"..............................22.00
Newport, plate, luncheon; cobalt, 8½"..............................16.00
Newport, sugar bowl, amethyst..............................14.00
No 610 Pyramid, bowl, crystal, oval, 9½"..............................30.00
No 610 Pyramid, tumbler, pk or gr, ftd, 2 styles, 8-oz..............................45.00
No 612 Horseshoe, bowl, cereal; yel, 6½"..............................35.00
No 612 Horseshoe, butter dish, gr, w/lid 800.00
No 612 Horseshoe, cup, yel..............................13.00
No 612 Horseshoe, plate, luncheon; gr, 9⅜"..............................14.00
No 616 Vernon, creamer, gr or yel, ftd 27.50
No 616 Vernon, plate, sandwich; crystal, 11½"..............................12.00
No 616 Vernon, tumbler, gr or yel, ftd, 5"..............................40.00
No 618 Pineapple & Floral, bowl, berry; crystal, 4¾"..............................25.00
No 618 Pineapple & Floral, creamer, amber, dmn shape..............................10.00
No 618 Pineapple & Floral, plate, sherbet; crystal, 8⅜"..............................4.00
No 618 Pineapple & Floral, tumbler, amber or red, 8-oz, 4¼" 25.00
Normandie, bowl, cereal; amber, 6½"..............................28.00
Normandie, pitcher, pk, 80-oz, 8"..............................175.00
Normandie, plate, grill; irid, 11" 9.00
Normandie, saucer, amber..............................2.00
Normandie, tumbler, juice; pk, 5-oz, 4"..............................90.00
Old Cafe, bowl, crystal or pk, tab hdld, 4½"..............................10.00
Old Cafe, candy dish, Royal Ruby, tab hdld, low, 8"..............................16.00
Old Cafe, olive dish, crystal or pk, oblong, 6"..............................9.00
Old Cafe, tumbler, water; Royal Ruby, 4"..............................32.00
Old English, bowl, fruit; pk, gr or amber, ftd, 9"..............................30.00
Old English, vase, pk, gr or amber, ftd, 4¼x8¼"..............................45.00
Ovide, bowl, berry; decor wht, 4¾"..............................7.00
Ovide, creamer, blk..............................6.50
Ovide, saucer, gr..............................2.50

Oyster & Pearl, bowl, crystal or pk, heart shape, hdl, 5¼"...........14.00
Oyster & Pearl, plate, sandwich; Royal Ruby, 13½"..............................50.00
Parrot, bowl, soup; gr, 7"..............................50.00
Parrot, butter dish, amber, w/lid..............................1,300.00
Parrot, hot plate, gr, pointed, 5"..............................895.00
Parrot, saucer, amber or gr..............................15.00
Parrot, tumbler, gr, 10-oz, 4¼"..............................175.00
Patrician, butter dish, pk, w/lid..............................225.00
Patrician, creamer, pk or gr, ftd..............................12.00
Patrician, plate, luncheon; amber, 9"..............................12.00
Patrician, saucer, amber, crystal, pk or gr..............................9.50
Patrician, tumbler, gr, 9-oz, 4¼"..............................25.00
Patrick, bowl, fruit; pk, hdld, 9"..............................175.00
Patrick, goblet; water; pk, 10-oz, 6"..............................80.00
Patrick, plate, luncheon; yel, 8"..............................27.50
Patrick, plate, sherbet; pk, 7"..............................20.00
Pebbled Rim, bowl, berry; all colors..............................8.00
Pebbled Rim, candle holder, all colors..............................20.00
Petalware, bowl, cereal; crystal, 5¾"..............................4.00
Petalware, plate, salver; red trim floral, 12"..............................40.00
Petalware, sherbet, cremax or monax (plain), low ft, 4½"..............8.00
Pillar Optic, pitcher, amber, gr or pk, w/o ice lip, 60-oz..............45.00

Pineapple & Floral, plate, crystal, 9⅜", $17.50.

Primo, bowl, yel or gr, 7¾"..............................35.00
Primo, plate, yel or gr, 6¼"..............................10.00
Primo, sugar bowl, yel or gr..............................12.00
Princess, bowl, berry; gr or pk, 4½"..............................30.00
Princess, coaster, topaz or apricot..............................115.00
Princess, pitcher, pk, 37-oz, 6"..............................65.00
Princess, platter, gr or pk, closed hdls, 12"..............................27.00
Princess, sugar bowl, topaz or apricot, w/lid..............................26.00
Princess, tumbler, pk, ftd, sq, 9-oz, 4¾"..............................60.00
Queen Mary, bowl, berry; crystal, #478, lg, 8¾"..............................15.00
Queen Mary, bowl, berry; crystal, 4½"..............................4.00
Queen Mary, bowl, berry; pk, flared, 5"..............................12.00
Queen Mary, pickle/celery dish, pk, #467, 5x10"..............................25.00
Queen Mary, plate, dinner; crystal, #426, 9¾"..............................18.00
Queen Mary, saucer, pk, w/cup ring..............................5.00
Queen Mary, tumbler, juice; crystal, 5-oz, 3½"..............................4.00
Radiance, bowl, bonbon; ice bl or red, ftd, 6"..............................32.00
Radiance, comport, ice bl or red, 6"..............................35.00
Radiance, mayonnaise, amber, 3-pc set..............................40.00
Radiance, tumbler, ice bl or red, 9-oz..............................30.00
Raindrops, bowl, berry; gr, 7½"..............................50.00
Raindrops, saucer, gr..............................2.00
Raindrops, tumbler, gr, 2-oz, 2⅛"..............................5.00
Ribbon, bowl, cereal; gr, 5"..............................40.00
Ribbon, cup, gr..............................5.00
Ribbon, plate, luncheon; blk, 8"..............................14.00
Ribbon, tumbler, gr, 10-oz, 6"..............................33.00

Ring, bowl, soup; crystal, 7"..................................10.00
Ring, goblet, cocktail; crystal, 3½-oz, 3¾"..................11.00
Ring, plate, sherbet; w/decor or gr, 6¼"......................2.50
Ring, saucer, crystal...1.50
Ring, tumbler, w/decor or gr, 5-oz, 3½"........................9.00
Ring, tumbler, water; crystal, ftd, 5½".........................6.00
Rock Crystal, bowl, crystal, scalloped edge, 4½"..............14.00
Rock Crystal, butter dish, crystal, w/lid......................335.00
Rock Crystal, candlesticks, colors other than red, 8", pr....150.00
Rock Crystal, lamp, red, electric.............................695.00
Rock Crystal, plate, bread & butter; red, scalloped edge, 6"...20.00
Rock Crystal, plate, crystal, scalloped edge, 11½"...........18.00
Rock Crystal, syrup, red, w/lid...............................750.00
Rock Crystal, vase, crystal, ftd, 11".........................60.00
Rose Cameo, bowl, berry; gr, 4½"..............................12.00
Rose Cameo, plate, salad; gr, 7"..............................14.00
Rosemary, bowl, berry; amber, 5"...............................6.00
Rosemary, plate, salad; gr, 6¾"................................8.50
Rosemary, tumbler, pk, 9-oz, 4¼"..............................60.00
Roulette, cup, crystal...4.00
Roulette, plate, sherbet; pk or gr, 6".........................4.50
Roulette, saucer, crystal......................................1.50
Roulette, tumbler, iced tea; pk or gr, 12-oz, 5⅛".............33.00
Round Robin, cup, gr, ftd......................................7.00
Round Robin, plate, luncheon; gr or irid, 8"...................4.00
Roxana, bowl, berry; yel, 5"..................................15.00
Roxana, tumbler, yel, 9-oz, 4¼"...............................22.00
Royal Lace, bowl, berry; crystal, 5"..........................15.00
Royal Lace, butter dish, gr, w/lid...........................275.00
Royal Lace, candlesticks, bl, ruffled edge, pr...............500.00
Royal Lace, plate, luncheon; crystal, 8½".....................8.00
Royal Lace, tumbler, bl, 5-oz, 3½"............................60.00
Royal Ruby, bowl, Coronation, hdld, 8".........................15.00
Royal Ruby, bowl, Sandwich, smooth, 4⅞".......................12.50
Royal Ruby, sherbet, Old Cafe, low ft.........................12.00
Royal Ruby, stem, ball stem...................................12.00
S Pattern, creamer, crystal, thick or thin.....................6.00
S Pattern, sugar bowl, crystal, thick or thin..................5.50
Sandwich, basket, amber or crystal, 10" H.....................35.00
Sandwich, bowl, console; pk or gr, 11½".......................50.00
Sandwich, bowl, teal bl, hexagonal, 6"........................14.00
Sandwich, cruet, teal bl, w/stopper, 6½-oz...................135.00
Sandwich, plate, bread & butter; amber or crystal, 7"..........4.00
Sandwich, plate, sandwich; red, 13"...........................35.00
Sandwich, tumbler, cocktail; amber or crystal, ftd, 3-oz.......7.50
Sandwich, wine, pk or gr, 4-oz, 3"............................25.00
Sharon, bowl, cream soup; amber, 5"...........................28.00
Sharon, butter dish, gr, w/lid................................90.00
Sharon, jam jar, amber, 7½"...................................40.00
Sharon, plate, salad; amber, 7½"..............................15.00
Sharon, tumbler, amber, thick, 12-oz, 5¼".....................65.00
Sharon, tumbler, pk, ftd, 15-oz, 6½"..........................57.50
Ships, cocktail shaker, bl & wht..............................38.00
Ships, plate, dinner; bl & wht, 9"............................35.00
Ships, plate, sherbet; bl & wht, 5⅞"..........................30.00
Ships, tumbler, roly poly; bl & wht, 6-oz.....................11.00
Sierra, bowl, berry; pk, lg, 8½"..............................35.00
Sierra, pitcher, gr, 32-oz, 6½"..............................135.00
Sierra, shakers, pk or gr, pr.................................45.00
Spiral, bowl, mixing; gr, 7"..................................10.00
Spiral, ice/butter tub, gr....................................27.50
Spiral, sherbet, gr..5.00
Spiral, vase, gr, ftd, 5¾"....................................50.00
Starlight, bowl, pk, closed hdls, 8½".........................20.00

Starlight, cup, crystal or wht.................................5.00
Starlight, plate, dinner; crystal or wht, 9"...................7.50
Starlight, shakers, crystal or wht, pr........................22.50
Strawberry, comport, pk or gr, 5¾"............................25.00
Strawberry, plate, sherbet; pk or gr, 6"......................12.00
Strawberry, tumbler, crystal or irid, 8-oz, 3⅝"...............20.00
Sunburst, bowl, berry; crystal, 4¾"............................8.00
Sunburst, plate, sandwich; crystal, 11¾".......................20.00
Sunflower, cake plate, pk or gr, 3-legged, 10"................15.00
Sunflower, plate, dinner; pk or gr, 9"........................22.00
Sunflower, sugar bowl, opaque.................................85.00
Swirl, bowl, console; ultramarine, ftd, 10½"..................30.00
Swirl, bowl, salad; pk, 9"....................................26.00
Swirl, creamer, Delphite, ftd.................................12.00
Swirl, plate, sherbet; Delphite, 6½"...........................6.00
Swirl, saucer, ultramarine.....................................4.00
Swirl, tumbler, pk, 13-oz, 5⅛"................................55.00
Tea Room, bowl, banana split; gr, ftd, 7½"....................85.00
Tea Room, candlesticks, gr or pk, low, pr.....................70.00
Tea Room, sherbet, gr, ftd, low...............................25.00
Tea Room, tumbler, gr, ftd, 8-oz, 5¼".........................33.00
Tea Room, vase, pk, ruffled edge, 11".........................295.00
Thistle, bowl, cereal; gr, 5½"................................30.00
Thistle, plate, grill; pk, 10¼"...............................25.00
Tulip, plate, amethyst or bl, 7¼".............................15.00
Tulip, tumbler, juice; crystal or gr, 2¾".....................22.00
Twisted Optic, basket, bl or canary yel, 10" H................95.00
Twisted Optic, candy jar, bl or canary yel, flanged edge, flat, w/lid...70.00
Twisted Optic, creamer, colors other than bl or canary yel.....7.50
Twisted Optic, mayonnaise, colors other than bl or canary yel.....20.00
Twisted Optic, preserve, colors other than bl or canary yel.....27.50
Twisted Optic, sherbet, colors other than bl or canary yel.....6.00
US Swirl, bowl, gr, hdld, 5½"..................................9.50
US Swirl, butter dish, gr or pk, w/lid.......................120.00
US Swirl, vase, pk, 6½".......................................20.00
Victory, bowl, blk or bl, flat edge, 12½".....................65.00
Victory, bowl, soup; amber, pk or gr, flat, 8½"...............20.00
Victory, plate, dinner; blk or bl, 9".........................55.00
Vitrock, bowl, fruit; wht, 6"..................................5.50
Vitrock, creamer, wht, oval....................................6.00
Waterford, bowl, berry; crystal, 4¾"...........................6.50
Waterford, cake plate, crystal, hdld, 10¼"....................10.00
Waterford, creamer, pk, oval..................................12.00
Waterford, pitcher, juice; crystal, tilted, 42-oz.............24.00
Waterford, sherbet, pk, ftd...................................18.00
Waterford, tumbler, crystal, ftd, 10-oz, 4⅞"..................14.00
Windsor, bowl, crystal, pointed edge, 5".......................6.00
Windsor, coaster, gr, 3¼".....................................20.00
Windsor, platter, crystal, oval, 11½".........................12.00
Windsor, sugar bowl, pk, w/lid................................30.00
Windsor, tumbler, red, 9-oz, 4"...............................55.00

Desert Sands

As early as the 1850s, the Evans family living in the Ozark Mountains of Missouri produced domestic clay products. Their small pot shop was passed on from one generation to the next. In the 1920s it was moved to North Las Vegas, Nevada, where the name Desert Sands was adopted. Succeeding generations of the family continued to relocate, taking the business with them. From 1937 to 1962 it operated in Boulder City, Nevada; then it was moved to Barstow, California, where it remained until it closed in the late 1970s.

Desert Sands pottery is similar to Mission Ware by Niloak. Various mineral oxides were blended to mimic the naturally occurring sand formations of the American West. A high-gloss glaze was applied to add intensity to the colorful striations that characterize the ware. Not all examples are marked, making it sometimes difficult to attribute. Marked items carry an ink stamp with the Desert Sands designation. Paper labels were also used.

Ashtray, 6½"	**22.00**
Bowl, console; hand thrown, 9½"	**45.00**
Bowl, incurvate rim, 3"	**18.00**
Bowl, inverted cylinder, 5"	**25.00**
Butter dish	**50.00**

Covered jar, 4½x4", $45.00.

Shakers, pr	**30.00**
Tumbler	**22.00**
Vase, cactus ink mk, 7"	**30.00**
Vase, flared rim, 3½"	**25.00**

Devon, Crown Devon

Devon and Crown Devon were trade names of S. Fielding and Company, Ltd., an English firm founded after 1879. They produced majolica, earthenware mugs, vases, and kitchenware. In the 1930s they manufactured an exceptional line of Art Deco vases that have recently been much in demand.

Pitcher, flowering trees on brn mottle, ribbed, 8⅞"	**225.00**
Toby jug, Happy John, yel waistcoat, musical, 9"	**190.00**
Toby jug, hat w/grapes & leaves on brim, red coat, 1900s, 11"	**110.00**
Vase, Wisteria & butterflies on cobalt, sm hdls, 5¾"	**150.00**

Documents

Although the word 'document' is defined in the general sense as 'anything printed or written, etc., relied upon to record or prove something. . .,' in the collectibles market, the term is more diversified with broadsides, billheads, checks, invoices, letters and letterheads, land grants, receipts, and waybills some of the most sought after. Some documents in demand are those related to a specific subject such as advertising, mining, railroads, military, politics, banking, slavery, nautical, or legal (deeds, mortgages, etc.). Other collectors look for examples representing a specific period of time such as colonial documents, Revolutionary, or Civil War documents, early western documents, or those from a specific region, state, or city.

Aside from supply and demand, there are five major factors which determine the collector-value of a document. These are:

1) Age — Documents from the eastern half of the country can be found that date back to the 1700s or earlier. Most documents sought by collectors usually date from 1700 to 1900. Those with twentieth-century dates are still abundant and not in demand unless of special significance or beauty.

2) Region of origin — Depending on age, documents from rural and less-populated areas are harder to find than those from major cities and heavily populated states. The colonization of the West and Midwest did not begin until after 1850, so while an 1870s billhead from New York or Chicago is common, one from Albuquerque or Phoenix is not, since most of the Southwest was still unsettled.

3) Attractiveness — Some documents are plain and unadorned, but collectors prefer colorful, profusely illustrated pieces. Additional artwork and engravings add to the value.

4) Historical content — Unusual or interesting content, such as a letter written by a Civil War soldier giving an eye-witness account of the Battle of Gettysburg or a western territorial billhead listing numerous animal hides purchased from a trapper, will sell for more than one with mundane information.

5) Condition — Through neglect or environmental conditions, over many decades paper articles can become stained, torn, or deteriorated. Heavily damaged or stained documents are generally avoided altogether. Those with minor problems are more acceptable, although their value will decrease anywhere from 20% to 50%, depending upon the extent of damage. Avoid attempting to repair tears with scotch tape — sell 'as is' so that the collector can take proper steps toward restoration.

Foreign documents are plentiful; and though some are very attractive, resale may be difficult. The listings that follow are generalized; prices are variable depending entirely upon the five points noted above. Values here are based upon examples with no major damage. Common grade documents without significant content are found in abundance and generally have little collector value. These usually date from the late 1800s to mid-1900s. It should be noted that the items listed below are examples of those that meet the criteria for having collector value. There is little demand for documents worth less than $5.00. For more information we recommend *Owning Western History* by our advisor Warren Anderson. His address and ordering information may be found in the Directory under Utah.

Key:
illus — illustrated   vgn — vignette

Application for franchise, Hudson Automobiles, ca 1949, unused	**35.00**
Bank draft, Whitewood Banking Co, SD, Devil's Tower vgn, 1897	**15.00**
Bill of sale, 4 slaves in New Orleans, 3-pg, 1855	**220.00**
Billhead, AZ & CA Lumber Co of Tucson, 1881, 7x8"	**20.00**
Billhead, CA wagonmaker, ornate heading, filled out, sgn, 1883, 8x14"	**25.00**
Billhead, Denver horseshoer, blksmith vgn, lists costs, 1891, 5x8"	**25.00**
Billhead, NYC Wells Fargo Office, 1860, 5x8", VG	**55.00**
Birth certificate/cradle roll, baby scenes/flowers, CM Burd, 1927	**47.00**
Business card, IL Metropolitan Hotel proprietor, 1890s, 2x4"	**9.00**
Certificate, Boiler Inspector's Office, MO, 3 signatures, 1893, 8x9"	**12.00**
Certificate, finding Confederate private disabled, 1864	**275.00**
Check, North Butte Mining Co, MT, bl logo on bl, 1916, 3x8"	**4.00**
Check, Park City Light Heat & Power Co, 1st Nat'l Bank, UT, 1899, 3x8"	**20.00**
Clothing order, handwritten to military store, 1857, 1-pg	**15.00**
Complaint, MT Territory, selling w/o license, 1879, 8x14"	**25.00**
Envelope, Hazard Powder, quacking mallard on left side, 1901 postmark	**100.00**
Fishing license, Andover MA, 1880, EX	**140.00**
Fishing license, CA, gr & blk paper, 1915, EX	**80.00**
Form letter, Holland Rod & Bait Co, ca 1910, EX	**30.00**
Furlough, Confederate soldier, sgn Geo C Brn, 1862	**110.00**
General orders, Major-Gen BF Butler, 1862	**195.00**
Indenture contract, Negro lady & boy child, MS, 1860s	**360.00**
Land deed, NM Territory, pre-printed, 1894, 1 legal-sz pg	**15.00**
Land grant, Dakota Territory, General Land Office issue, 1888	**35.00**
Land grant, 160 MI acres to soldier, emb seal, 1851, 10x16"	**35.00**
Land indenture, PA, 1772, 24¼x29⅝", EX	**330.00**
Ledger book, Union infantry accounts of purchases, 1862-63, EX	**100.00**

Letter, payment overdue on shares, CA, 1885, 5x8" **15.00**
Letter, preacher from Salem OR, consignment of goods, 1862, 2-pg..**25.00**
Letter, sale of married slaves (separate owners), Paris, 1833 ....**200.00**
Letter, Union soldier re: Chancellorsville battle, 12-pg, EX........**525.00**
Letter, WA Territory, extra charges for powder, 1878, 5x8", 2-pg..**25.00**
Letterhead, Agricultural Implements, 2 farming vgns, OR, 1883, 6x9"..**15.00**
Letterhead, Connel Co Sporting Goods, mc bass, 1927, EX **15.00**
Letterhead, Golden Eagle Mining Co, payment for interest, 1907, 8x10"....**20.00**
Letterhead, JA Folger & Co, CA, vgn, pre-printed, 1904 ....**12.00**
Letterhead, MT Territory Penitentiary, labor issues, 1882, 8x11"..**25.00**
Letterhead, Wyandotte CO, MO, courthouse vgn, 1897, 8x11"...........**9.00**
Money order, Bank of Red Oak, Indian Territory (OK), 1908, 3x8"..**9.00**
Muster roll, 2nd US Sharpshooters Co, 1863, sgn Albert Buxton, VG ..**200.00**
Order of confinement, Silver Bow Co MT, sgn by judge, 1911, 2-pg....**15.00**
Pay order, OR Territory, handwritten, services at jail, 1858, 3x8".**30.00**
Policy, Royal Insurance Co of Liverpool, $3,500 hotel, 1905, 17x20".......**30.00**
Proclamation of Emancipation, engraving, Kidder, NY, 1865, 22x18"....**575.00**
Program, organ recital; Mormon Tabernacle, w/Choir, 1936, 4-pg, 3x7" ..**15.00**
Promissory note, Glendale State Bank, AZ, pre-printed, 1912, 3x8" **15.00**
Prospectus, Banker's Oil Co, CA, red/blk print, 1902, 8-pg **20.00**
Ration book, WWII, TX, set of 12 ....**12.00**
Ration book, WWII WW, w/orig coupons for sugar/tires/etc, EX..**25.00**
Receipt, Crown King Mining Camp, AZ, pre-printed, 1895, 3x8" ..**20.00**
Receipt, farm implements (7) vgns, pre-printed, Sacramento CA, 1880.**25.00**
Receipt, fraternal, Tombstone, AZ Territory, pre-printed, 1905, 3x8" ...**20.00**
Receipt for slaves, matted w/letter of settlement, 1860 ....**150.00**
Steamboat pass, MA paddle wheeler, unused, 4x5"........................**70.00**
Tax log, Newbury MA, listing of 1755 towns people/collections, 8x10"...**115.00**

Dollhouses and Furnishings

Dollhouses were introduced commercially in this country late in the 1700s by Dutch craftsmen who settled in the East. By the mid-1800s, they had become meticulously detailed, divided into separate rooms, and lavishly furnished to reflect the opulence of the day. Originally intended for the amusement of adults of the household, by the latter 1800s their status had changed to that of a child's toy. Though many early dollhouses were lovingly hand fashioned for a special little girl, those made commercially by such companies as Bliss and Schoenhut are highly valued.

Furniture and furnishings in the Biedermeier style featuring stenciled Victorian decorations often sell for several hundred dollars each. Other early pieces made of pewter, porcelain, or papier-mache are also quite valuable. Certainly less expensive but very collectible, nonetheless, is the quality, hallmarked plastic furniture produced during the '40s by Renwal and Acme, and the '60s Petite Princess line produced by Ideal. In the listings that follow, dollhouses are litho paper on wood, unless otherwise noted. For more information, see *Schroeder's Collectible Toys, Antique to Modern.* Our advisor for this category is Barbara Rosen; she is listed in the Directory under New Jersey. See also Miniatures.

Furnishings

Bathinette, Renwal, bl, no decal **8.00**
Bathinette, Renwal, pk w/decal **15.00**
Bed, Jaydon, w/spread, reddish brn swirl.............................**18.00**
Bedroom set, Marx, hard plastic, dk ivory, 8 pcs **40.00**
Boudoir chase lounge, Ideal Petite Princess, bl **25.00**
Buffet, Ideal Young Decorator, marbleized maroon **20.00**
Buffet, Kilgore, CI, bl **50.00**
Buffet, Renwal, brn, w/opening drw **8.00**
Chair, barrel; Renwal, dk red w/brn base **12.00**
Chair, dining room; Plasco, brn w/striped seat **4.00**
Chest of drws, Grand Rapids, stained wood **20.00**

Clock, mantle, Renwal, ivory or red, ea **10.00**
Dining room set, Plasco, 8 pcs, MIB................................**55.00**
Dining room set, Tootsietoy, 12 pcs, MIB **225.00**
Doll, nurse; Renwal, EX **75.00**
Doll, sister; Renwal, yel dress, metal rivets, EX **25.00**
Dresser w/mirror, Wolverine **10.00**
Fireplace, Ideal **35.00**
Garden set, Irwin, MOC **75.00**
Highchair, Renwal, pk w/decal...**25.00**

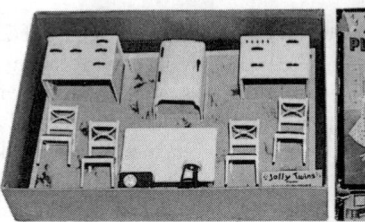

Jolly Twins Plastic Furniture Kitchen Set, Renwal, MIB, from $125.00 to $150.00. (Photo courtesy Judith Mosholder)

Kitchen bar, Tomy Smaller Homes **12.00**
Living room set, Strombecker, MIB.................................**75.00**
Mop, Renwal...**45.00**
Nursery set, Sally Ann; Kilgore, pnt CI, NMIB...................**700.00**
Pail, Irwin, dk bl **6.00**
Piano, Marx, hard plastic, red or yel, ea **15.00**
Picnic table, Ideal, wht...**20.00**
Potty chair, Ideal, bl **15.00**
Radio, floor; Ideal **10.00**
Refrigerator, Marx, soft plastic **3.00**
Refrigerator, Plasco, wht w/bl base **5.00**
Rocker, bentwood; Tomy Smaller Homes **8.00**
Sink, bathroom; Kilgore, CI, gr.......................................**60.00**
Sink/icebox, Mattel Littles, MIB **12.00**
Sofa, Marx, soft plastic, red or yel, ea **3.00**
Sofa, Renwal, ivory w/brn base **18.00**
Sofa, Sonia Messer, lt gr fabric **80.00**
Stove, Marx, hard plastic, ivory or wht, ea.........................**5.00**
Table, coffee; Marx, hard plastic, lt gr **10.00**
Table, coffee; Superior, bright yel....................................**8.00**
Table, dining; Renwal, brn, stenciled................................**20.00**
Table, kitchen; Plasco, lt bl **5.00**
Table, patio; Plasco, bl w/ivory legs.................................**4.00**
Vanity, Biedermeier, stenciled, w/mirror...........................**250.00**
Vanity, Blue Box, tan w/heart-shaped mirror......................**3.00**
Vanity & bench, Superior, yel...**10.00**
Washing machine, Renwal, bl or pk w/bear decal, ea **25.00**

Houses, Shops, and Single Rooms

Arcade, bathroom #681, 3-sided cb, CI furnishings, NMIB.....**2,200.00**
Arcade, laundry room #716, 3-sided cb, CI accessories, NMIB ..**2,500.00**
Bliss, 2-story Colonial, 2 columns/steps/dbl doors, 18x16", VG ..**325.00**
Fisher-Price, #250, 3-story w/5 rooms, 1978-80, M **40.00**
Germany, carriage house & carriage, litho/pnt wood, 17x36", EX ...**1,700.00**
Germany, grocery store, pnt wood, hinged sides, complete, 21x16", EX...**475.00**
Germany, 2-story, red brick/red gabled roof, 1900, 19x13", EX ...**900.00**
Jayline, 2-story w/5 rooms, tin, 1949, 15x19", VG **50.00**
Mansford, 2-story Victorian w/belvedere, CI fence/lions, 1800s, EX ..**2,800.00**
Marx, Newlyweds Kitchen #190, 3-sided litho tin, 1925, MIB.................**250.00**
Marx, 2-story w/attached garage, tin, w/40 pcs of furniture, NM ...**100.00**

Meritoy, Cape Cod, tin, ivory boards/gray stone, 1949, 21x14", M.**200.00**
Nuremberg, kitchen, tin, tin accessories, late 1800s, 15x35", EX .**2,100.00**
Schoenhut, 1-room bungalow, wood, 1920s, 11", VG **500.00**
Schoenhut, 2-story w/8 rooms & attic, 1923, 27", EX.............**2,400.00**
Thorne, drawing room, paneled walls, Chpndl, 1940s, 15x28", EX .**3,000.00**
Tootsietoy, 2-story w/6 rooms & attic, cb, furnished, 1927, EX...**650.00**
Wolverine, Country Cottage #800, 1986, ½" scale, EX................**50.00**

Dolls

To learn to invest your money wisely as you enjoy the hobby of doll collecting, you must become aware of defects which may devaluate a doll. In bisque, watch for eye chips, hairline cracks and chips, or breaks on any part of the head. Composition should be clean, not crazed or cracked. Vinyl and plastic should be clean with no pen or crayon marks. Though a quality replacement wig is acceptable for bisque dolls, composition and hard plastic dolls should have their originals in uncut condition. Original clothing is a must except in bisque dolls, since it is unusual to find one in its original costume.

It is important to remember that prices are based on condition and rarity. When no condition is noted, dolls are assumed to be in excellent condition with the exceptions of American Character and Madame Alexander, which are generally priced in mint condition. In relation to bisque dolls, excellent means having no cracks, chips, or hairlines, being nicely dressed, shoed, wigged, and ready to to be placed into a collection. For a more thorough study of the subject, refer to *Modern Collectible Dolls, Vols II, III* and *IV*, and *Doll Values, Antique to Modern, Fourth Edition*, by Patsy Moyer; *Collector's Guide to Dolls of the 1960s and 1970s* by Cindy Sabulis; *Talking Toys of the 20th Century* by Kathy and Don Lewis; and *Collector's Encyclopedia of American Composition Dolls, 1900 – 1950*, by Ursula R. Mertz. Several other book are referenced throughout this category. All are published by Collector Books. Except for the subcategories where another expert is noted, our general advisor for this category is author Patsy Moyer; she is listed in the Directory under New Mexico.

Key:
bjtd — ball jointed	OC — original clothes
blb — bent limb body	o/m — open mouth
bsk — bisque	p/e — pierced ears
c/m — closed mouth	pnt — painted
hh — human hair	pwt — paperweight eyes
hp — hard plastic	RpC — replaced clothes
jtd — jointed	ShHd — shoulder head
MIG — Made in Germany	ShPl — shoulder plate
NC — no clothes	SkHd — socket head
o/c/e — open closed eyes	str — straight
o/c/m — open closed mouth	trn — turned

American Character

Betsy McCall, vinyl socket head, blue sleep eyes, closed mouth, rooted red hair, original clothes, 1961, 30", EX, $275.00; Sandy McCall, vinyl socket head, blue sleep eyes, freckles, original clothes, 1959, 35", $525.00. (Photo courtesy McMasters Auctions)

AC or Petite, mama, compo/cloth, mohair or hh wig, crier, OC, 16"..**275.00**
Annie Oakley, hp walker, embr on skirt, 1954, OC, 14"............**400.00**
Campbell Kid, compo, jtd limbs, mk A Petite Doll, OC, 12" **350.00**
Freckles, face changes, 1966, OC, 13" **40.00**
Pre-teen Tressy, grow hair, Am Char 63, 1963, OC, 14" **300.00**
Puggy, jtd compo, scowling, pnt hair, cowboy OC, 13" **500.00**
Ricky Jr, vinyl baby boy, 1955-56, OC, 13" **125.00**
Sally, compo/cloth, crier, o/ce, OC, 16" **450.00**
Talking Marie, record player in body, battery-op, 1963, OC, 18"..**90.00**
Toodle-Loo, plastic, rooted hair, pnt eyes, c/m, OC, 1961, 18"...**190.00**
Toodles, vinyl, rooted hair, o/c/e, c/m, OC, 11" **285.00**
Vinyl head, mk Am Character, OC, 20" **80.00**

Annalee

Barbara Annalee Davis has been making her dolls since 1950. What began as a hobby, very soon turned into a commercial venture. Her whimsical creations range from tiny angels atop powder puff clouds to funky giant frogs, some 42" in height. In between there are dolls for every occasion (with Christmas being her specialty), all characterized by their unique construction methods (felt over flexible wire framework) and wonderful facial expressions. Naturally, some of the older dolls are the most valuable (though more recent examples are desirable as well, depending on scarcity and demand), and condition, as usual, is very important. To date your doll, look at the tag. If made before 1986, that date is only the copyright date. (Dolls made after 1986 do carry the manufacturing date.) Dolls from the '50s have a long white red-embroidered tag with no date. From 1959 to 1964, that same tag had a date in the upper right-hand corner. From 1965 until 1970, it was folded in half and sewn into the seam. In 1970, a satiny white tag with a date preceded by a copyright symbol in the upper right-hand corner was used. In '75, the tag was a long white cotton strip with a copyright date. This tag was folded over in 1982, making it shorter. Our advisor for Annalees is Jane Holt; she is listed in the Directory under New Hampshire.

1960, Christmas Choir girl or boy, gr, wht or red, 10", ea..............**75.00**
1967, nun, wht attire, 10" **125.00**
1967-79, mouse (7") in gr mitten..**25.00**
1968, donkey, holds vote button, 16" **250.00**
1969-72, nun w/skis & poles, blk attire, spectacles, 10" **150.00**
1971, monk bottle cover, 18" **175.00**
1974, elf, red, 22", riding reindeer (36"+antlers) **150.00**
1976, Santa in mechanical rocker, Mrs Claus (29") & kid stand by ...**200.00**
1977, elf, gr, 22" **65.00**
1981, mouse in Christmas stocking...**30.00**
1981, red fox, in Santa suit w/gr bag, 18" **250.00**
1983, Mr & Mrs Claus w/basket, 30", pr **155.00**
1984, snowman w/broom, 30"..**140.00**
1985, Santa (7") in sled (7"), w/3 reindeer................................**95.00**
1985, Society Logo Kid, boy w/sock & glass of milk...................**200.00**
1986, baby bear w/bee, 10"..**50.00**
1987, girl bunny, 7", in 10" 'carrot' balloon **100.00**
1987, kangaroo, baby in pouch, society animal, 7" **75.00**
1987, Mr & Mrs Tuckered w/2 PJ Kids, 30", 18", set of 4............**250.00**
1987, Mrs Santa w/muff, Victorian, wooden stand, 30"...............**125.00**
1987, New Hampshire State Police, wooden base, glass dome, 10"...**200.00**
1987, ornament, girl caroler on cloud, 3" **20.00**
1987, Victorian Santa, w/card holder sack, 18".............................**50.00**
1988, goose w/basket, Santa hat, gr scarf, 24" **100.00**
1988, Society Logo Kid, in raincoat w/umbrella **50.00**
1988, Thanksgiving turkey, lg...**60.00**
1989, Nativity: Mary & Baby Jesus, Joseph; on base, w/dome.....**150.00**
1989, Spring swan, 24", w/10" fairy...**75.00**
1990, angel, 30" **100.00**

1990, Jacob Marley from Dickens Series, w/lock & chain, 10" ...**125.00**
1990, Maid Marion mouse, 7" **25.00**
1990, PJ kid, boy w/blk hair, girl w/blond, 18", ea.................**50.00**
1990, Thorndike chicken, w/egg & sign, Society animal, 7" **50.00**
1995, Mr & Mrs Old World Santa, wooden bases, 30", pr **175.00**

Armand Marseille

Alma, ShHd, 15" **275.00**
AM, Floradora, ShHd, 20" **500.00**
AM, Floradora, SkHd, 27" **750.00**
AM, ShHd, boy, 14" **250.00**
AM, SkHd, 16" **275.00**
AM, Sunshine, ShHd, 1910, 24" **525.00**
AM 1894, boy SkHd, brn o/c/e, o/m w/teeth, rprs, RpC, 23"......**400.00**
AM 253, SkHd, googly eyes, 1915, 16" **2,100.00**
AM 255, SkHd, intaglio eyes, 7½" **900.00**
AM 320, SkHd, c/m, googly eyes, 6½" **650.00**
AM 3200, ShHd, some trn, 22" **450.00**
AM 323, SkHd, googly eyes, 9" **1,000.00**
AM 324, googly eyes, 7"...**465.00**
AM 328, baby, SkHd, closed dome, 1922, 14" **275.00**
AM 341, My Dream Baby, flange, c/m, 18" **550.00**
Am 347, SkHd, 1909, 16" **365.00**
AM 351, Rock-A-Bye Baby, flange, o/m, 6" **150.00**
AM 362, Teenie Weenie, baby, closed dome, wht, 15" **550.00**
AM 370, Floradora, ShHd, o/c/e, o/m/4 teeth, hh wig, RpC, 20" **425.00**
AM 370, 16½" **275.00**
AM 370n, Kiddiejoy, girl, SkHd, c/m, molded hair, 20".........**2,600.00**
AM 390, My Dearie, 23" **465.00**
AM 390n, SkHd, 1915, 27" **550.00**
AM 402, SkHd, pnt bsk, 14" **300.00**
AM 500, Infant Berry, molded hair, 1908, 8" **765.00**
AM 600, SkHd, flange, c/m, 1910, 10" **1,200.00**
AM 966, baby, SkHd, flirty eyes, 14".....................................**350.00**
AM 975, Sadie, baby, SkHd, 1914, 9" **250.00**
AM 990, Happy Tot, baby, SkHd, 1910, 16"............................**450.00**
AM 992, baby, SkHd, 1914, 22" **700.00**

Barbie Dolls and Related Dolls

Though the face has changed three times since 1959, Barbie is still as popular today as she was when she was first introduced. Named after the young daughter of the first owner of the Mattel Company, the original Barbie had a white iris but no eye color. These dolls are nearly impossible to find, but there is a myriad of her successors and related collectibles just waiting to be found.

For further information we recommend *The Story of Barbie, Second Edition*, by Kittarah B. Westenhouser; *The World of Barbie Dolls* and *The Wonder of Barbie, 1976 – 1986*, by Paris, Susan, and Carol Manos; *Barbie Exclusives, Books 1* and *2*, by Margo Rana; *A Decade of Barbie Dolls and Collectibles, 1981 – 1991*, by Beth Summers; *Thirty Years of Mattel Fashion Dolls* and *Collector's Encyclopedia of Barbie Doll Exclusives and More*, both by J. Michael Augustyniak; *The Barbie Doll Years* by Patrick C. and Joyce L. Olds; and *Skipper — Barbie Doll's Little Sister*, by Scott Arend, Karla Holzerland, and Trina Kent. *Barbie Fashion, Vol I* and *II*, by Sarah Sink Eames, gives a complete history of the wardrobes of Barbie, her friends, and her family. *Schroeder's Toys, Antique to Modern*, is another good source for current market values. You may also be interested in *Collector's Guide to Barbie Doll Vinyl Cases* by Connie Craig Kaplan. All these are published by Collector Books.

Allan, 1964-67, pnt red hair, str legs, MIB...................................**145.00**
Barbie, #1, 1959, blond hair, rpl liner, no stand, MIB.............**7,100.00**

Barbie, #1, 1959, brunette hair, MIB...**7,475.00**
Barbie, #2, 1959, blond or brunette hair, MIB, ea, from $6,325 to **6,500.00**
Barbie, #3, 1960, blond hair, orig swimsuit, MIB, minimum value **1,100.00**
Barbie, #3, 1960, brunette hair, orig swimsuit, MIB, minimum value..**1,150.00**
Barbie, #4, 1960, blond or brunette, orig swimsuit, MIB, ea **665.00**
Barbie, #5, 1961, blond hair, MIB **565.00**
Barbie, #5, 1961, red hair, orig swimsuit, MIB **640.00**
Barbie, #6, 1962, Ponytail, MIB..**530.00**
Barbie, 1964, Am Girl, platinum cheek-length hair, orig swimsuit, NM....**650.00**
Barbie, 1966, Color Magic, blond, orig swimsuit, MIB (plastic box).......**1,700.00**
Barbie, 1971, Growin' Pretty Hair, NRFB..................................**350.00**
Barbie, 1972, Busy, NRFB...**260.00**
Barbie, 1973, Newport, NRFB..**165.00**
Barbie, 1973, Sun Valley, NRFB...**100.00**
Barbie, 1973, Sweet Sixteen, NRFB...**100.00**
Barbie, 1977, Fashion Photo, MIB...**65.00**
Barbie, 1981, Golden Dreams, NRFB..**90.00**
Barbie, 1981, Scottish, Dolls of the World, NRFB **195.00**
Barbie, 1982, Eskimo, Dolls of the World, NRFB **165.00**
Barbie, 1983, Angel Face, NRFB...**45.00**
Barbie, 1985, Day-to-night, NRFB..**75.00**
Barbie, 1986, Astronaut, NRFB...**100.00**
Barbie, 1986, Blue Rapsody, porc, NRFB **800.00**
Barbie, 1986, German, Dolls of the World, NRFB **125.00**
Barbie, 1988, Holiday, red gown, NRFB, minimum value **775.00**
Barbie, 1988, Lilac & Lovely, Sears Exclusive, NRFB.................**60.00**
Brad, 1969, bendable legs, NRFB..**200.00**
Casey, 1967, Twist 'N Turn, blond or brunette, MIB, ea **275.00**
Chris, 1974, auburn hair, OC, EX..**75.00**
Christie, 1968, Twist 'N Turn, red hair, orig swimsuit, NM.........**250.00**
Francie, 1966, brunette hair, bendable legs, MIB.......................**370.00**
Francie, 1970, Growin' Pretty Hair, MIB....................................**300.00**
Ken, 1969, Spanish Talking, NRFB..**200.00**
Ken, 1972, Busy Talking, OC, VG **85.00**
Ken, 1983, Hawaiian Fun, MIB..**50.00**
Ken, 1987, Doctor, MIB...**35.00**
Ken, 1989, Animal Lovin', MIB..**35.00**
Ken, 1991, 30th Anniversary, NRFB..**225.00**
Midge, 1988, California Dream, MIB..**50.00**
Midge, 1990, Wedding Day, NRFB..**30.00**
PJ, 1970, Talking, MIB..**275.00**
PJ, 1983, Dream Date, MIB..**50.00**

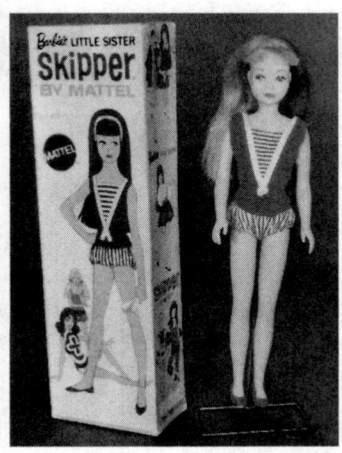

Skipper, 1970 brunette, straight-leg reissue, MIB, $225.00. (Photo courtesy Stefanie Deutsch)

Skipper, 1970-71, Twist 'N Turn, NRFB....................................**300.00**
Skipper, 1973-75, Quick Curl, NRFB, minimum value **125.00**
Skipper, 1976-77, Deluxe Quick Curl, NRFB, minimum value.....**75.00**
Skipper, 1982, Horse Lovin', NRFB..**40.00**

Skooter, 1976, Funtime, NRFB, minimum value **200.00**
Stacey, 1969, Twist 'N Turn, blond hair, replica swimsuit, 1969, MIB .**400.00**

Barbie Gifts Sets and Related Accessories

When no condition is indicated, the items listed below are assumed to be mint and in the original box or package (if one was issued). Items in only excellent condition may be worth 40% to 60% less.

Barbie Collector Series III, Silver Sensation, #7438, 1983, MIB (unopened), $40.00. (Photo courtesy Beth Summers)

Case, Barbie & Midge Travel Pals, 1963, blk, zipper closure, NM ...**50.00**
Case, Bubble Cut Barbie, Solo in Spotlight, 1963, NM, from $75 to....**85.00**
Clothes, Barbie, Best Buy Fashion Pack, #3362, 1972, MIP........**125.00**
Clothes, Barbie, Pink Sparkle, #1440, complete, M **150.00**
Clothes, Francie, Dance Party, #1257, complete, M **150.00**
Clothes, Francie, Two for the Ball, #1232, MOC **225.00**
Clothes, Skipper, All Over Felt, #3476, NRFB...........................**150.00**
Clothes, Skipper, Skating Fun, #1908, NRFB **175.00**
Furniture, Barbie, Starlight Bed, 1990, MIB.............................**30.00**
Furniture, Miss Barbie Furniture Set, Sears Exclusive, 1964, MIB..**75.00**
Furniture, Suzy Goose Hope Chest, 1961, EX **5.00**
Furniture, Sweet Roses Roll-Top Desk, 1990, NRFB **25.00**
Gift set, Barbie Loves Elvis, 1996, NRFB...................................**75.00**
Gift set, Chris Fun-Timers Set, Sears Exclusive, 1967, M **400.00**
Gift set, Francie Rise & Shine, 1971, NRFB, minimum value.**1,000.00**
Gift set, Loving You Barbie, 1984, NRFB....................................**65.00**
Gift set, Talking Barbie Pink Premier, 1969, MIB **500.00**
House, Barbie Deluxe Family House, 1966, complete, VG **135.00**
House, Fashion Plaza, 1975, complete, NMIB **100.00**
Playset, Barbie Boutique Playset w/Sound, 1994, MIB **100.00**
Vehicle, Barbie Motor Bike, 1983, NRFB **35.00**
Vehicle, Snowmobile, Montgomery Ward, 1972, MIB **65.00**

Belton

Concave head, 2 or 3 hole, EX bsk, o/c/m or c/m, w/wig, 8" **800.00**
Concave head, 2 or 3 hole, EX bsk, o/c/m or c/m, w/wig, 10"..**1,200.00**
Concave head, 2 or 3 hole, EX bsk, o/c/m or c/m, w/wig, 13"..**1,600.00**
Concave head, 2 or 3 hole, EX bsk, o/c/m or c/m, w/wig, 15"..**1,900.00**
Concave head, 2 or 3 hole, EX bsk, o/c/m or c/m, w/wig, 16"..**2,000.00**
Concave head, 2 or 3 hole, EX bsk, o/c/m or c/m, w/wig, 17"..**2,400.00**
Concave head, 2 or 3 hole, EX bsk, o/c/m or c/m, w/wig, 20"..**2,800.00**
Concave head, 2 or 3 hole, EX bsk, o/c/m or c/m, w/wig, 22"..**3,000.00**
Concave head, 2 or 3 hole, EX bsk, o/c/m or c/m, w/wig, 22"..**3,000.00**
Concave head, 2 or 3 hole, EX bsk, o/c/m or c/m, w/wig, 23"..**3,200.00**
Concave head, 2 or 3 hole, EX bsk, o/c/m or c/m, w/wig, 26"..**3,800.00**

Betsy McCall

Doll, Am Character, hp, rigid arms, all orig, 1957, 8", MIB........**400.00**

Doll, Am Character, vinyl, rooted hair, flirty eyes, 1959, 19", VG...**275.00**
Doll, Am Character, vinyl, swivel waist, OC, 14" **300.00**
Doll, Horsman, vinyl/hp, o/c/e, complete, 1974, 12½", MIB **75.00**
Doll, Horsman, vinyl/hp, o/c/e, rooted hair, c/m, 1974, 29", MIB...**275.00**
Doll, Ideal, P-90, vinyl/hp, o/c/e, c/m, OC, 1951, 14", MIB **725.00**
Doll, Ideal, vinyl head, hp strung Tony Body, OC, 14" **250.00**
Doll, Sandy McCall, Am Character, vinyl, o/c/e, OC, 1959, 39", M ...**350.00**
Doll, Uneeda, vinyl, rooted hair, o/c/e, nude, 1964, 11½", VG **25.00**
Doll, Uneeda, vinyl, rooted hair, o/c/e, OC, 1964, 11½", minimum..**95.00**

Boudoir Dolls

Boudoir dolls, often called bed dolls, French dolls, or flapper dolls were popular from the late teens through the 1940s. The era of the 1920s and 1930s was the golden age of boudoir dolls!

More common boudoir dolls are usually found with composition head, arms, and high-heeled feet. Clothes are nailed on (later ones have stapled-on clothes). Wigs are usually mohair, human hair, or silk floss. Smoking boudoir dolls were made in the late teens and early 1920s. More expensive boudoir dolls were made in France, Italy, and Germany, as well as the U.S. Usually they are all cloth with elaborate sewn or pinned-on costumes and silk, felt, or velvet painted faces. Sizes of boudoir dolls vary, but most are around 30". These dolls were made to adorn a lady's boudoir or sit on a bed. They were not meant as children's playthings! Our advisor for this category is Bonnie Groves; she is listed in the Directory under Texas.

Anita, compo head & hands, cloth body, nude, '20s, EX, from $75 to..**150.00**
Anita, compo head & hands, silk floss wig, OC/shoes, VG, $150 to.....**200.00**
Anita, nude, 30", VG, from $50 to..**135.00**
Anita, sleep eyes, all orig, EX, from $300 to **500.00**
Blossom, lady, all orig, 30", EX, from $300 to **600.00**
Blossom, lady w/toy, MIB, minimum value **600.00**
Cloth, music box inside, all orig, Fr, 30", EX, minimum value....**700.00**
Cloth, silk face, mohair wig, nude, shoes & stockings, 30", VG, $85 to...**150.00**
Compo, common carnival type, all orig, 1940s, 28", VG, $95 to....**160.00**
Compo, sleep eyes, bald, nude, 30", G, from $100 to **150.00**
Czech, bellhop, cloth, all orig, 24", EX **315.00**
Doll head on hat sand, VG, from $65 to.....................................**135.00**
Egg-head type, mask face, nude, 31", G **60.00**
Etta, all cloth, all orig, 30", VG, from $200 to...........................**450.00**
Finely pnt features, average clothes & quality, 28", from $85 to .**125.00**
Finely pnt features, average clothes & quality, 32", from $100 to..**150.00**
Finely pnt features, EX clothes/quality, glass eyes, 28", minimum..**200.00**
Finely pnt features, EX clothes/quality, glass eyes, 32", minimum...**250.00**
Finely pnt features, std quality, dressed, 16" **125.00**
Fr, cloth, all orig, 30", VG..**400.00**
Fr, harem lady, silk mask face, all cloth, fine clothes, 31", minimum ..**600.00**
Fr, mask face, all orig, G..**150.00**
Fr, silk face, bsk arms/legs, mini, 20", EX, from $200 to **350.00**
Fr, silk face, bsk limbs, OC, 30", VG, from $350 to....................**400.00**
Fr, silk face & costume, bsk arms/legs, 21", VG, from $150 to **200.00**
Fr, silk mask face, bsk arms/legs, OC, G **250.00**
Glass eyed, 27", EX, from $175 to **250.00**
Lenci, 18-26", minimum value **1,500.00**
Pierrot, mask face/swivel head, OC, Blossom, 1920s, 30", $400 to ..**600.00**
Shoes for doll, EX, minimum value **45.00**
Silk face, unmk, all orig, 30", EX...**300.00**
Smoker, Anita, head only, VG, from $50 to...................................**75.00**
Smoker, Blossom, Argentine costume, smoker, 30", EX, minimum value ...**650.00**
Smoker, cloth, 16"..**285.00**
Smoker, cloth, 25"..**475.00**
Smoker, compo, 28", minimum value...**375.00**
Smoker, jtd compo, all orig, EX, from $600 to **800.00**
Smoker, jtd compo, all orig, 25", G, from $300 to **800.00**

Smoker, jtd compo, crazed, all orig, VG costume, from $300 to .600.00
Smoker, jtd compo, faded costume/no shoes, 15", G 500.00
Smoker, jtd compo, nude/bald, 25", G-, from $100 to 200.00
Smoker, Lenci, salon lady, all orig, VG, minimum value 1,000.00
Standard pillow type (no legs), all orig, 24", VG 165.00
Sterling, compo jtd arms, OC, 26", VG 200.00
Sterling, Halloween lady, compo, all orig, 26", EX, minimum value...450.00
Sterling, jtd compo arms, nude, 26", VG 100.00
Sterling mk, compo, jtd arms, all orig, 26", VG, from $150 to....225.00
Unmk, silk face, wht mohair, RpC (old pattern), orig shoes, 30", EX..200.00
W-K-S, compo head, hands & ft, crazed/cracked, nude 45.00
W-K-S, compo head, hands & high-heeled ft, VG clothes, rpl hat, 30"...175.00
W-K-S Inc, common std doll, crazed, EX clothes, 28" 135.00
W-K-S Inc, compo ShPl, high-heeled ft, EX clothes, 30"...........175.00
1940s, all orig, 25", VG 95.00

Cabbage Patch

A, bl edition, 1978, MIB, minimum value...............................1,500.00
B, red edition, 1978, MIB...1,200.00
C, burgundy edition, 1979, MIB..900.00
D, purple edition, 1979, MIB, minimum value 1,200.00
Grand edition, 1980, MIB, minimum value 750.00
Indian edition, 1983, MIB 850.00
Popcorn hairdo, 1984-85, rare, MIB...200.00
Powder scent, bald, 1983, MIB 100.00
Powder scent, w/freckles, 1983, MIB 175.00
Single tooth, brunette w/ponytail, 1984-85, MIB, minimum value..165.00
Talking, 1987, MIB..140.00
World Class edition, 1984, MIB 175.00

Celebrity

Andy Gibb, Ideal, 1979, 7½", NRFB...50.00
Barbara Eden (Jeannie), Remco, 1972, 6½", NRFB 100.00
Brooke Shields, LJN, 1982, 1st issue, 11½", NRFB.....................50.00
Christy Brinkley, Real Models, Matchbox, 1989, 11½", NRFB 55.00
Desi Arnez (Ricky Ricardo), Applause, 1988, 17", MIB................50.00
Donna Douglas (Ellie Mae), jeans w/rope belt, 1965, MIB............65.00
Farrah Fawcett (Jill), jumpsuit & scarf, Hasbro, 1977, 8½", MOC..40.00
Fred Gwynn (Herman Munster), plush/vinyl, Presents, 1990, 12", MIB..35.00
Jimmy Osmond, Mattel, 1978, 9", MIB 75.00
Kate Jackson (Sabrina), jumpsuit & scarf, Hasbro, 1977, 8½", MOC...40.00

Louis Armstrong, molded plastic head and body, cloth suit, Effanbee, 15", EX in original box.

Lucille Ball (Lucy Ricardo), cloth, 1952, 26", rare, NRFB..........800.00
Mr T, bib overalls, 1st edition, Galoob, 1983, 12", MIB................60.00
Robin Williams (Mork), w/space pak, Mattel, 1979, 9", MIB.....450.00
Sonny Bono, Mego, 1976, 12", NRFB (orange box)...................150.00
Vanna White, ltd ed, wedding dress, Totsy Toys, 1990, rare, MIB ..125.00

China, Unmarked

Adelina Patti, center part, curls at temples, 1860s, 18" 450.00
Biedermeier or bald head, takes wig, RpC, 20" 700.00
Boy, #784, #9 on ShPl, pnt eyes, c/m, molded hair, bsk arms, 23", EX ..800.00
Common hairdo, blond or blk hair, RpC, after 1905, 8" 80.00
Common hairdo, blond or blk hair, RpC, after 1905, 12" 145.00
Covered Wagon style, sausage curls, leather arms, OC, 21", EX .700.00
Curly Top, loose ringlets, RpC, 1845-60s, 16" 500.00
Dolly Madison, modeled ribbon & bow, RpC, 1870-80s, 21"......600.00
Dolly Madison, modeled ribbon & bow, RpC, 1870-90s, 14"......275.00
Frozen Charlie, pnt eyes, c/m, pnt/molded hair, undies, 15½" 525.00
Glass eyes, various hairstyles, RpC, 1840s-70s, 14" 1,600.00
Man or Boy, glass eyes, side part, RpC, 14"..........................2,200.00
Man or Boy, pnt eyes, side part, RpC, 16" 1,400.00
Pet Name, molded shirtwaist w/name on front, RpC, 1905, 19".265.00
Pierced ears, various hairstyles, RpC, 18" 675.00

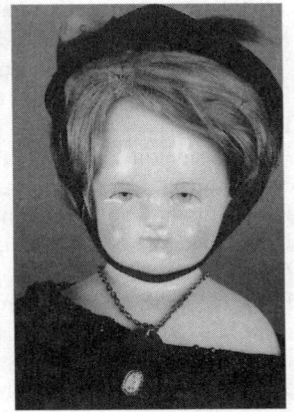

Solid dome china shoulder head with original human hair wig, painted blue eyes, closed mouth, china lower arms and legs with molded boots, in black taffeta outfit with jet trim, underclothing, 19", EX, $475.00. (Photo courtesy McMasters Auctions)

Spill curls, w/or w/o headband, RpC, 14" 400.00
Wood body, articulated/slim hips, RpC, 1840s-50s, 12" 1,600.00
Wood body, jtd hips, covered-wagon hairdo, 1840s-50s, 15" ...1,900.00

Cloth

A cloth doll in very good condition will display light wear and soiling, while one assessed as excellent will be clean and bright.

Alabama Indestructible, baby, 1900-25, 12", VG.........................750.00
Alabama Indestructible, Black baby, 1900-25, 20", EX 6,200.00
Alabama Indestructible, child, 1900-25, 15", G.........................800.00
Art Fabric Mills, color litho, 1899-1910+, 20", G 75.00
Babyland Rag, color litho, 1893-1928, 14½", EX 335.00
Beecher Missionary Ragbaby, silk jersey, HP, 1893-1910, 16", VG ..1,725.00
Bing Art, pnt hair, cloth or felt, 1921-32, 13", EX 550.00
Bing Art, wig, cloth or felt, 1921-32, 10", VG...........................175.00
Chad Valley, character, glass eyes, 1917-30+, 18", EX..............1,000.00
Chad Valley, child, glass eyes, 1917-30+, 14", VG 165.00
Chase, baby, OC, 1899-1930+, 16", EX 575.00
Columbian, HP features, stitched fingers & toes, 15", VG 2,225.00
Drayton, Chocolate Drop, yarn hair, 1923, Averill Mfg Co, 10", EX...400.00
Drayton, Dolly Dingle, printed features, Averill Mfg, 1923, 11", EX....385.00
Mammy style, pnt or embr features, 1910-20s, 12", EX 200.00
Mollye's, child, mask face, 1920-30+, 13", EX 130.00
Mollye's, lady, long dress, 1929-30+, 16", EX 175.00
Petzold, molded head, wig, sawdust filled, 1919-30+, 18", EX.....600.00
Raleigh, Shoebutton Sue, flat face, red sewn-on shoes, 1921, 15", VG...1,900.00
Wellings, child, pnt eyes, 1926-30+, 18", EX................................600.00

Effanbee

Bernard Fleischaker and Hugo Baum became business partners in 1910, and after two difficult years of finding toys to buy, they decided to manufacture dolls and toys of their own. The Effanbee trademark is a blending of their names, Eff for Fleischaker and bee for Baum. The company still exists today. For more information we recommend *Effanbee Dolls* by Pat Smith, and *Collector's Encyclopedia of American Composition Dolls, 1900 – 1950,* by Ursula R. Mertz.

Baby Effanbee, compo/cloth, OC, 12-13", EX..............................165.00
Baby Grumpy, compo ShHd, pnt eyes, c/m, cloth/compo body, OC, 14"..300.00
Betty Bounce, compo, o/m/2 teeth/tongue, skin wig, OC, 18"....375.00
Charlie McCarthy, compo ShHd, pnt eyes, string-op, OC, 17"..600.00
Charlie McCarthy, ShHd, pnt eyes, string-op, OC, 20" 775.00
Coquette, Naughty Marietta, compo/cloth, OC, 1915+, 12" 400.00
Honey Walker, hp, jtd knees/ankles, OC, 14"............................350.00
Ice Queen, compo, o/m, skater outfit, 17" 850.00
Lamkins, compo/cloth, crier, o/c/e, o/m, OC, 16" 475.00
Mary Ann, compo, o/c/e, o/m, wig, 1932+, OC, 19" 350.00
Mary Lee, compo, o/c/e, wooden limbs, OC, 20" 700.00
Mary Lee as Anne Shirley, compo, o/m/4 teeth, mohair wig, OC, 16"..500.00
Patricia as Ann Shirley, compo, o/c/e, c/m, hh wig, OC, 15", VG 450.00
Patsy, compo, pnt eyes, molded hair w/hair band, 1920s, OC, 13½"......550.00
Patsy, compo ShHd, tin o/c/e, o/m/4 teeth, hh wig, OC, 22" 450.00
Patsy Ann, compo, o/c/e, c/m, 5-pc body OC, 19" 600.00
Patsy Ann, jtd vinyl, rooted hair, o/c/e, freckles, OC, 15"..........250.00
Patsy Baby, compo, o/c/e, c/m, bent limbs, OC, 11" 350.00
Patsy Jr, compo, pnt eyes, c/m, molded/pnt hair, OC, 11"..........400.00
Patsy Jr, compo, tin o/c/e, c/m, molded pnt hair, OC, 11", VG...300.00
Patsy Lou, compo, o/c/e, c/m, molded hair/wig, OC, 22" 625.00
Patsy Lou, compo, o/c/e, c/m, pnt hair, 5-pc body, 22" 525.00
Patsy Ruth, ShPl, o/c/e, c/m, mohair wig, cloth/compo body, RpC, 26"...900.00
Patsyette, compo, pnt eyes, c/m, molded/pnt hair, OC, 9", MIB ..500.00
Skippy, compo/cloth, pnt eyes, c/m, molded/pnt hair, OC (soldier), 14"....525.00

Skippy Soldier (Black), all original, 14", $1,350.00.
(Photo courtesy McMasters Auctions)

Suzanne, jtd compo, o/c/e, wig, c/m, magnets in hands, OC, 14" ...325.00
Tinyette Quintuplets, FAO Schwartz..., compo, OC, 7", EX in case..1,750.00

Half Dolls

Half dolls were never meant to be objects of play. Most were modeled after the likenesses of lovely ladies, though children and animals were represented as well. Most of the ladies were firmly sewn on to pincushion bases that were beautifully decorated and served as the skirts of their gowns. Other skirts were actually covers for items on milady's dressing table. Some were used for parasol or brush handles or for tops to candy

containers or perfume bottles. Most popular from 1900 to about 1930, they will most often be found marked with the country of their origin, especially Bavaria, Germany, France, and Japan. You may also find some fine quality pieces marked Goebel, Dressel and Kester, KPM, and Heubach.

Germany, arms & hands attached, common type, 3" 35.00
Germany, arms & hands attached, common type, 5" 45.00
Germany, arms & hands attached, common type, 8" 75.00
Germany, arms & hands completely away, 3", from $85 to 145.00
Germany, arms & hands completely away, 5", from $100 to 285.00
Germany, arms & hands completely away, 8", from $165 to 650.00
Germany, arms & hands completely away, 12", from $675 to 900.00
Germany, arms extended, hands attached, 3"................................50.00
Germany, arms extended, hands attached, 5"................................85.00
Germany, arms extended, hands attached, 8"..............................125.00
Japan mk, 3"..20.00
Japan mk, 5"..30.00
Japan mk, 8"..50.00

Handwerck, Heinrich

Child, #109, o/m/4 teeth, p/e, mohair wig, OC, 22" 750.00
Child, #99, SkHd, o/m/4 teeth, p/e, synthetic wig, RPC, 23" 450.00
Child, bsk SkHd, o/c/e, o/m/4 teeth, jtd, RpC, 28" 850.00
Child, bsk SkHd, o/c/e, o/m/4 teeth, jtd wood/compo, RpC, 24", VG ..400.00
109, SkHd, o/c/e, o/m/4 teeth, p/e, hh wig, jtd, RpC, 17½"........450.00
109, SkHd, o/c/e, o/m/4 teeth, p/e, mohair wig, jtd, RpC, 19" 550.00
109, SkHd, o/c/e, o/m/4 teeth, p/e, synthetic wig, jtd, RpC, 26".750.00

Hertel, Schwab and Company

127, character child, dome w/molded hair, o/c/e, o/m, RpC, 15" ..1,350.00
131, character, solid dome, pnt c/m, RpC, 18" 1,300.00
136, character face, o/m, Made in Germany, RpC, 24" 1,100.00
140, character, glass eyes, o/m laughing, RpC, 12" 3,400.00
141, character, pnt eyes, o/c/m, RpC, 24" 7,500.00
142, bsk head, compo bent-leg baby, o/c/e, RpC, 9" 300.00
150, bsk head, toddler body, RpC, 14" 500.00
151, SkHd, o/c/e, o/m/2 teeth, RpC, 11"....................................400.00
154, bsk head, c/m, RpC, 21" 2,700.00
154, character, solid dome, molded hair, glass eyes, o/m, RpC, 20" ...1,900.00
167, K&H character, o/c/m or o/m, RpC, ca 1912, 15"............2,000.00

Heubach, Ernst

267, SkHd, glass eyes, o/m, 5-pc bent-leg body, RpC, 11"............240.00
275, ShHd, o/m, kid body, RpC, 09" 200.00
275, ShHd, o/m, kid body, RpC, 22" 550.00
300, baby, SkHd, o/c/e, o/m/teeth, 5-pc bent-limb body, RpC, 17"..250.00
321, SkHd, glass eyes, o/m, 5-pc bent-leg body, RpC, 20" 550.00
338, solid dome, glass eyes, c/m, pnt hair, cloth/compo body, RpC, 12" ...425.00
1900, glass eyes, o/m, kid or cloth body, horseshoe mk, RpC, 12" ..150.00
1900, pnt bsk, glass eyes, o/m, kid or cloth body, RpC, 16"........225.00

Heubach, Gebruder

Heubach (no mold #), adult, glass eyes, o/m, 14", VG.............3,350.00
Heubach (no mold #), o/c/m, dimples, RpC, 18" 4,450.00
5/0 D, solid dome, intaglio eyes, o/c/m/teeth/tongue, rpt, RpC, 7"...350.00
5636, glass eyes, o/c/m/teeth, RpC, 15" 2,000.00
5777, Dolly Dimple, o/m, for Hamburger & Co, RpC, 14" 2,300.00
6688, character child, ShHd, intaglio eyes, c/m, molded hair, RpC, 10" ..625.00
6736, pnt eyes, laughing mouth, RpC, 13" 1,100.00
6969, SkHd, glass eyes, c/m, sq mk, RpC, 12" 1,850.00

7247, glass eyes, c/m, RpC, 15" 3,500.00
7602, dome SkHd, intaglio eyes, pouty/m, bent limbs, RpC, 9½"....325.00
7622, intaglio eyes, c/m or o/c/m, RpC, 16" 1,200.00
7850, Coquette, o/c/m, RpC, 11" 750.00
7975, Baby Stuart, glass eyes, removable molded bsk bonnet, RpC, 13"..1,900.00
8381, Princess Juliana, molded hair w/ribbon, pnt eyes, c/m, RpC, 14" ...6,600.00
8420, glass eyes, c/m, sq mk, RpC, 15" 2,800.00
1010, Revalo, o/c/e, o/m, for Gebr Ohlhaver, RpC, 19" 700.00

Ideal

Two of Ideal's most collectible lines of dolls are Chrisy and Toni. For more information, refer to *Collector's Guide to Ideal Dolls, Second Edition,* by Judith Izen (Collector Books).

Baby Crissy, pk dress, 1973-76, EX.................................50.00
Baby Flatsy, EX 10.00
Cory Flatsy, silver pantsuit, complete, EX 40.00
Crissy, Country Fashion, 1982-83, MIB..........................45.00
Crissy, Magic Hair, 1977, EX..30.00
Crissy, Swirla Curla, 1973, EX 35.00
Flatsy Casey, NRFB...65.00
Pepper, MIB 65.00

Peter Playpal, vinyl, gold open/close eyes, freckles, original clothes, 1960 – 64, 38", M, $850.00. (Photo courtesy McMasters Auctions)

Play Time Flatsy, NRFB...75.00
Pos'n Dodi, M in plain box 75.00
Tammy, Grown Up, MIB..75.00
Tammy's Dad, MIB 65.00
Tara, Black, yel gingham outfit, 1976, MIB.....................85.00
Ted, MIB 65.00
Tony, hp/vinyl, o/c/e, c/m, nylon wig, OC, 14", w/tag, MIB........925.00
Velvet, Movin' Groovin', 1971, EX 35.00
Vicki Vanta, vinyl/magic skin, pnt eyes, c/m, OC, 9½" 175.00

Jumeau

The Jumeau factory became the best known name for dolls during the 1880s and 1890s. Early dolls were works of art with closed mouths and paperweight eyes. When son Emile Jumeau took over, he patented sleep eyes with eyelids that drooped down over the eyes. This model also had flirty (eyes that move from side to side) eyes and is extremely rare. Over 98% of Jumeau dolls have paperweight eyes. The less-expensive German dolls were the downfall of the French doll manufacturers, and in 1899 the Jumeau company had to combine with several others in an effort to save the French doll industry from German competition.

E 8 J, bsk SkHd, pwt eyes, c/m, p/e, hh wig, crier, period RpC, 19" ..5,200.00
E 8 J, SkHd, pwt eyes, p/e, wig, RpC, 15" 4,600.00
E 9 J/Medaille d'Or, SkHd, pwt eyes, c/m, p/e, hh wig, RpC, 20" 4,200.00
EJ Bebe, SkHd, pwt eyes, c/m, jtd body w/str wrists, RpC, 17" 10,250.00
Fashion type, swivel head, pwt eyes, c/m, p/e, kid body, RpC, 11"...2,450.00
O/m, mk Jumeau Medaille d'Or Paris, 24", EX 4,900.00
Princess Elizabeth, bsk SkHd w/EX color, flirty eyes, c/m, RpC, 30" .3,900.00
Tete Jumeau, Bebe, pwt eyes, c/m, p/e, mohair wig, OC, 14"...4,850.00
Tete Jumeau, Bebe (child), SkHd, glass eyes, c/m, RpC, 10" ...6,000.00
Tete Jumeau, pwt eyes, c/m, compo/wood body, RpC, 23"....4,600.00
Tete Jumeau, SkHd, pwt eyes, c/m, p/e, mohair wig, period RpC, 16½"...3,950.00
1907, mk Jumeau, o/c/e, o/m, jtd Fr body, RpC, 14"................1,850.00

Kammer and Reinhardt

K*R (no mold #), SkHd, glass eyes, o/m, RpC, 12" 550.00
17, SkHd, o/c/e, o/m/2 teeth, mohair wig, 5-pc compo body, RpC, 7" ..300.00
58, SkHd, o/c/e, o/m/4 teeth, p/e, mohair wig, RpC, 23" 700.00
62, SkHd, inset eyes, o/m/4 teeth, p/e, rpl wig, RpC, 25½" 500.00
85, SkHd, o/c/e, o/m/4 teeth, p/e, mohair wig, jtd, period RpC, 33" ..1,500.00
100, character baby, dome head, jtd body, o/c/m, RpC, 11" 650.00
100, SkHd, pnt eyes, o/c/m, bent-limb compo, RpC, 19", VG+ .800.00
101, boy or girl, pnt eyes, c/m (pouty), OC, 13½" 2,500.00
101, Peter or Marie, pnt eyes, c/m, RpC, 7-8", ea...................1,600.00
112, pnt o/c/m, RpC, 14" 9,700.00
114, Hans or Gretchen, pnt eyes, c/m, RpC, 10", ea.................2,900.00
115, solid dome, pnt hair, o/c/e, c/m, RpC, 15" 5,000.00
117A, glass eyes, c/m, RpC, 16" 5,000.00
121, toddler, SkHd, o/c/e, o/m w/teeth, jtd compo, 16"..............525.00
122, o/c/e, bent-leg baby, RpC, 11" 700.00
126, Mein Liebling, flirty eyes, bent-leg baby, RpC, 14" 750.00
126, SkHd, inset eyes, o/m/2 teeth, mohair wig, RpC, 9½" 675.00
126, SkHd, o/c/e, o/m/2 teeth/tongue, RpC, 10".....................440.00
126, SkHd, tin-lid flirty eyes, o/m/teeth/tongue, RpC, 24", VG .500.00
135, baby, o/c/e, o/m, RpC, 13" 850.00
191, Dolly face, o/c/e, o/m, jtd child, RpC, 17" 865.00
192, bsk SkHd, o/c/e, o/m/4 teeth, p/e, rpl wig, jtd, RpC, 20½" ..1,000.00
192, o/c/e, o/m, jtd child, RpC, 9"...................................1,000.00

Kestner

Johannes D. Kestner made buttons at a lathe in a Waltershausen factory in the early 1800s. When this line of work failed, he used the same lathe to turn doll bodies. Thus the Kestner company began. It was one of the few German manufacturers to make the complete doll. By 1860, with the purchase of a porcelain factory, Kestner made doll heads of china and bisque as well as wax, worked-in-leather, celluloid, and cardboard. In 1895 the Kestner trademark of a crown with streamers was registered in the U.S. and a year later in Germany. Kestner felt the mark was appropriate since he referred to himself as the 'king of German dollmakers.'

Century Doll, flange head, o/c/e, o/c/m/teeth/tongue, OC, 16" ..500.00
JDK 6, Baby Jean, dome Sk Hd, o/c/e, o/m/2 teeth/tongue, RpC, 11"...675.00
11, solid dome, inset eyes, o/m/2 teeth, JDK/MIG, RpC, 13½" ..325.00
19, dome SkHd, inset eyes, o/m/teeth/tongue, period RpC, 25"..800.00
112, googly eyes, watermelon/m, molded shoes, 1920s, 5", +3 outfits...3,225.00
128, SkHd, inset eyes, c/m, mohair wig, H/MIG/12, RpC, 19"...2,100.00
146, ShHd, o/c/e, o/m, mohair wig, fully jtd, old RpC, 31".......1,100.00
146, ShHd, o/c/e, o/m/4 teeth, hh wig, jtd wood/compo, RpC, 28"...865.00
146, SkHd, o/c/e, o/m/4 teeth, rpl wig, jtd wood/compo, RpC, 28", VG....500.00
154, ShHd, o/c/e, o/m/4 teeth, mohair wig, kid/compo body, RpC, 26" 500.00
160, SkHd, o/c/e, o/m/4 teeth, hh wig, period RpC, 16" 750.00
160, SkHd, o/c/e, o/m/4 teeth, rpl wig, jtd wood/compo, RpC, 30"....900.00
164, SkHd, o/c/e, o/m/2 teeth, rpl wig, RpC (antique undies), 16"....650.00

171, brn-pnt SkHd, o/c/e, o/m, rpl wig, jtd compo, RpC, 28", VG.....**700.00**
171, SkHd, o/c/e, o/m/4 teeth, hh wig, jtd compo, period RpC, 28" ..**600.00**
211, SkHd, o/c/e, o/c/m, mohair wig, K/MIG/14/JDK, RpC, 18" **550.00**
211, SkHd, o/c/e, o/m, mohair wig, jdt toddler body, RpC, 11", NM...**950.00**
257, SkHd, set eyes, o/m/2 teeth, mohair wig, crier, JDK, RpC, 15"....**700.00**
1070, Hilda, o/c/e, o/m/teeth, mohair wig, talker, RpC, 16" **1,400.00**

Lenci

Characteristics of Lenci dolls include seamless, steam-molded felt heads, quality clothing, childishly plump bodies, and painted eyes that glance to the side. Fine mohair wigs were used, and the middle and fourth fingers were sewn together. Look for the factory stamp on the foot, though paper labels were also used. Dolls under 10" are known as mascottes and usually sell for $150.00 to $200.00. The Lenci factory continues today, producing dolls of the same high quality. Values are for dolls in near mint condition — no moth holes, very little fading.

Aviator girl, felt helmet, 18"..**3,200.00**
Boy, pnt eyes, rooted mohair, OC w/sweater/leg warmers, 1920s, 17" ..**500.00**
Child, mini, 9"...**400.00**
Child, Oriental, 17" **3,600.00**
Child, 1920s-30s, softer face, elaborate costume, 13" **1,750.00**
Child, 1940s-50s, hard face, less intricate costume, 13" **400.00**
Child, 1940s-50s, hard face, less intricate costume, 17" **600.00**
Flower girl, ca 1930, 20"...**1,000.00**
Glass eyes variation, 16" **1,600.00**
Glass eyes variation (flirty), 20" **2,800.00**
Lady, flapper or boudoir body, long slim limbs, 17" **1,050.00**
Madame Butterfly, ca 1926, 17"...**3,200.00**

Mascotte girl holding pot with pink rose, original clothes, 8", EX, $400.00. (Photo courtesy McMasters Auctions)

Mascotte, swing legs, may have loop on neck, 8½", VG+..........**325.00**
Modestina, swivel head, pnt/e, o/c/m, mohair wig, OC, 20"....**1,750.00**
Pan, hooved ft, 10" **2,000.00**
Smoker, pnt eyes, 28"..**2,400.00**
Swivel-head girl, c/m, OC w/shawl/apron/hat/shoes, 17", EX w/tag..**1,200.00**

Liddle Kiddles

From 1966 to 1971, Mattel produced Liddle Kiddle dolls ranging in size from ¾" to 4". They were all poseable and had rooted hair that could be restyled. There were various series of the dolls, among them Animiddles, Zoolery Jewelry Kiddles, extraterrestrials, and Sweet Treats, as well as many accessories. Our advisor for this category is Paris Langford; she is listed in the Directory under Louisiana. Please send SASE for information or contact Paris by e-mail: bbean415@aol.com.

Aqua Funny Bunny, #3532, complete, EX................................**35.00**
Baby Din-Din, #3820, complete, M...**65.00**
Beach Buggy, #5003, NM...**50.00**
Bunson Bernie, #3501, complete, M..**85.00**
Cinderiddle's Palace, #5068, plastic window version, M..............**60.00**
Flower Charm Bracelet, #3747, MIP **50.00**
Frosty Mint Kone, #3653, complete, M....................................**75.00**
Greta Griddle, #3580, complete, M..**85.00**
Heart Ring Kiddle, #3744, MIP..**50.00**
Hot Dog Stand, #5002, M...**60.00**
Howard Biff Boodle, ##502, NRFP..**300.00**
Kiddle Komedy Theatre, #3592, EX..**50.00**
Kleo Kola, #3729, complete, M...**50.00**
Laffy Lemon, #3732, MIP...**85.00**
Liddle Biddle Peep, #3544, complete, M...................................**125.00**
Liddle Kiddles, Kottage, ##534, EX **40.00**
Liddle Kiddles 3-Story House, M..**55.00**
Lois Locket, #3541, complete, M..**85.00**
Lorelei Locket, #3679, complete, M **35.00**
Luana Locket, #3680, Gold Rush version, MIP **85.00**
Millie Middle, #3509, complete, M...**125.00**
Peter Paniddle, #3547, NRFP..**350.00**
Rapunzel & the Prince, #3783, MIP...**200.00**
Shirley Skediddle, #3766, MIP..**85.00**
Snap-Happy Living Room, #5173, NMIP................................**25.00**
Surfy Skediddle, #3517, complete, M.......................................**85.00**
Tessie Tractor, #3671, complete, NM..**150.00**
Vanilla Lilly, #2819, MIP **25.00**
World of Kiddles Beauty Bazaar, #3586, NRFB.........................**300.00**

Madame Alexander

Beatrice Alexander founded the Alexander Doll Company in 1923 by making an all-cloth, oil-painted face, Alice in Wonderland doll. With the help of her three sisters, the company prospered; and by the late 1950s there were over six hundred employees making Madame Alexander dolls. The company still produces these lovely dolls today. For more information, refer to *Collector's Encyclopedia of Madame Alexander Dolls* by Pat Smith; and *Madame Alexander Collector's Doll Price Guide* and *Madame Alexander Store Exclusives and Limited Editions*, both by Linda Crosey. All are published by Collector Books.

Active Miss, hp, Violet/Cissy, 1954 only, 18" **850.00**
Alexander-Kin, Maypole Dance, hp, str-leg walker, 1954-55 ......**550.00**
Alice in Wonderland, compo, Tiny Betty, 1930s, 7"....................**395.00**
Annabelle, hp, Maggie, 1951-52 only, 14-15", ea **575.00**
Annie Laurie, compo, Wendy Ann, 1937, 14"............................**650.00**
Baby Genius, compo/cloth, 1930s-40s, 11-12", ea, minimum value **225.00**
Barbara Jane, cloth/vinyl, 1952 only, 29" **500.00**
Betty, compo, 1935-42, 14"..**425.00**
Bonnie Toddler, cloth/hp head/vinyl limbs, 1950-51, 18" **175.00**
Brazil, hp, str leg, Wendy Ann, mk Alex, #0773, #573, 1973-1975, 8" ..**70.00**
Bridesmaid, hp, Cissie/Bonnie, 1955 only, 15" **325.00**
Canada, hp, bend-knee, Wendy Ann, #760, 1968-72, 8".............**100.00**
Changing Seasons (Spring, Summer, Autumn, Winter), 1993-94, 14", ea...**150.00**
Christening Baby, cloth/vinyl, 1951-54, 11-13", ea **135.00**
Cinderella, hp, Margaret, ballgown, 1950-51, 14", minimum value ..**850.00**
Cissy Bride, porc portrait, 1994 only, #52011, 21" **500.00**
Colonial, compo, Tiny Betty, 1937-38, 7" **300.00**
Cynthia, hp, Black Margaret, 1952 only, 15", minimum value ...**850.00**
Daisy, Portrette series, Cissette, wht over yel, #1110, 1987-89, 10"....**75.00**
Denmark, hp, Cissette, 1962-63, 10"..**650.00**
Dottie Dumbunnie, cloth/felt, 1930s, minimum value **800.00**
Elaine, hp, Cissy, 1954 only, 18", minimum value......................**1,600.00**

Elise, hp, jtd ankle/elbows/knees, bouffant hair, 1961, 16½".......375.00
English Guard, hp, bend-knee, Wendy Ann, #764, 1966-68, 8".350.00
Finland, hp, bend-knee, Wendy Ann, #767, 1968-72, 8"...........100.00
Flower Girl, compo, Princess Elizabeth, 1939, 1944-47, 16-18", ea 550.00
Geranium, vinyl toddler, red organdy dress & bonnet, 1953 only, 9" ...125.00
Godey Bride, hp, Margaret, long train, 1950, 14", minimum value...1,000.00
Grayson, Kathryn; hp, Margaret, 1949 only, 20-21", minimum value....5,500.00
Hamlet, Nancy Drew, Romance Series, 12" 125.00
Henie, Sonja; compo, Tiny Betty, 1939-42, 7" 425.00
Honeybea, vinyl, 1963 only, 12"..175.00
Hyacinth, vinyl toddler, bl dress & bonnet, 1953 only, 9" 150.00
Iris, hp, Cissette, pale bl, #1112, 1987-88, 10" 90.00
Jacqueline, Portrait, lace overskirt, plain veil, #2192, 1969, 21".725.00
Janie, toddler, #1156, 1964-66 only, 12"...............................275.00
Juliet, compo, Wendy Ann, 1937-40, 18", minimum value 1,275.00
Karen, hp, Margaret, 1948-49, 15-18", minimum value 850.00
Kitten, cloth/vinyl, 1962-63, 14-18", from $50 to.....................85.00
Lady in Waiting, hp, Wendy Ann, #487, 1955 only, 8", minimum value..1,600.00
Leslie, vinyl, Black Polly, wedding gown, 1966-71, 17" 300.00
Lind, Jenny; hp/plastic, Jacqueline, in pk w/no trim, 1969, 21" ..1,500.00
Lissy, hp, jtd knees & elbows, ballerina, 1956-58, 11½-12" 425.00
Little Shaver, cloth, 1940-44, 10", minimum value 450.00
Lollie Baby, rubber/compo, 1941-42 ....100.00
Lucy Bride, compo, Wendy Ann, 1937-40, 17" 550.00
Madeline, hp, jtd elbows & knees, 1950-53, 17-18", minimum value ..800.00
Maggie Mixup, hp, w/overalls & watering can, #610, 1960-61, 8"........750.00
Maggie Mixup, plastic/vinyl, 1961 only, 17", minimum value.....400.00
Margot Ballerina, hp/vinyl, Cissy, 1955 only, 15-18", from $375 to...475.00
Mary Muslin, cloth, pansy eyes, 1951 only, 19" 500.00
Melanie, compo, Wendy Ann, 1945-47, 21", minimum value.2,300.00
Mexico, compo, Tiny Betty, 1936, 7" 275.00
Miss America, compo, holds flag, 1941-43, 14", minimum value ..850.00
Muffin, cloth, sapphire eyes, 1965 only, 14".............................95.00
Nurse, compo, 1939, 1942-43, 9"...325.00
O'Brien, Margaret; hp, 1949-51, 14½", minimum value 900.00
O'Hara, Scarlett; compo, Tiny Betty, 1937-42, 7"......................475.00
O'Hara, Scarlett; hp/vinyl, gr velvet, #2240, 1979-85, 21" 350.00
Peggy Bride, hp, Margaret, very blond hair, 1950-51, 14-18", $950 to ..1,200.00
Peter Pan, hp, Margaret, 1953-54, 15", minimum value..............750.00

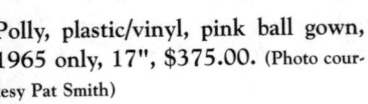

Polly, plastic/vinyl, pink ball gown, 1965 only, 17", $375.00. (Photo courtesy Pat Smith)

Polly, plastic/vinyl, ballgown, 1965 only, 17" 375.00
Prince Charles, Wendy Ann, #397, 1957 only, 8", minimum value ..750.00
Princess Rosetta, compo, Wendy Ann, 1939, 1946-47, 21", minimum value....2,300.00
Pumpkin, cloth/vinyl, 1967-76, 22"..125.00
Queen, hp, Margaret, wht gown/velvet cape, 1953 only, 18"...1,800.00
Randolph, Martha; Louisa, 1976-78 ....150.00
Red Riding Hood, compo, Tiny Betty, 1936-42, 7"....................275.00
Renoir, hp, Margaret, 1950 only, 14", minimum value 875.00
Rosebud, cloth/vinyl, 1952-53, 16-19" 150.00

Russia, hp, bend-knee, Wendy Ann, #774, 1968-72, 8" 100.00
Sailor, compo, Wendy Ann, 1942-45, 14"................................750.00
Skating Doll (untagged Sonja Henie), 1947-50, 16" 700.00
Snow White, compo, Princess Elizabeth, 1939-40, 18" 750.00
South American, compo, Tiny Betty, 1938-43, 7"......................275.00
Spanish Girl, hp, bend-knee walker, Wendy Ann, #779, 1964-68, 8"...375.00
Sweden (Swedish), hp, bend-knee walker, Wendy Ann, 1961-65, 8" ...125.00
Sweet Tears, vinyl, 1965-74, 9"...85.00
Teeny Twinkle, cloth, flirty eyes, 1946 only................................525.00
Thomas, Marlo; plastic/vinyl, Polly, 1967 only, 17", minimum value...600.00
Topsy-Turvy, compo, Tiny Betty heads, 1935 only.......................275.00
Violetta, Cissette, dk bl gown, #1116, 1987-88, 10" 70.00
WAAC, compo, Wendy Ann, 1943-44, 14", minimum value.....750.00
Wendy Kin Baby, vinyl 1-pc body, hp Little Genius head, 1954, 8"..375.00
Yolanda, Brenda Starr, 1965 only, 12" 375.00

Mattel

Baby Colleen, Sears Exclusive, 1965, 15½", MIB.......................100.00
Baby First Step, 1967, MIB...225.00
Baby Small Talk, 1968, MIB..125.00
Charmin' Chatty, auburn or blond hair, bl eyes, MIB.................275.00
Chatty Baby, brunette hair, red pinafore & wht romper, w/tag, MIB..250.00
Chatty Baby, open speaker, blond hair, bl eyes, M.....................250.00
Chatty Baby, open speaker, brunette hair, brn eyes, M 375.00
Chatty Cathy, later issue, open speaker, brunette hair, brn eyes, M...850.00
Chatty Cathy, mid-year/transitional, brunette hair, brn eyes, M.650.00
Chatty Cathy, porc, 1980, MIB 750.00
Downy Dilly, #3832, complete 75.00
Drowsy Sleeper-Keeper, 1966, MIB 125.00
Hi Dottie, Black, 1972, complete w/telephone, NM......................75.00
Miss Information, #3831, NRFB...150.00
Pudgy Fudgy, #3826, NRFB..150.00
Singin' Chatty, blond hair, M 250.00
Sister Belle, 1961, MIB..300.00
Teachy Talk, 1970, MIB 50.00
Tiny Chatty Baby, brunette hair, brn eyes, M 300.00

Papier-Mache

Boy, ShHd, glass eyes, o/m/teeth, molded hair, kid arms, 1840s, 26", G....435.00
Cloth body, bright coloring, wig, 1920s & later, RpC, 8" 80.00
Cloth body, wooden limbs, glass eyes, RpC, 1840s-60s, 24".....2,200.00
Cloth body, wooden limbs, long curls, RpC, 1840s-60s, 12" 650.00
Cloth body, wooden limbs, pnt eyes, RpC, 1840s-60s, 9"...........450.00
Clown, cloth body w/compo pnt features/molded hair, RpC, 8" .235.00
Clown, pnt features, 5-pc body, o/ or c/m, OC, 9".......................265.00
French, solid dome, nailed-on wig, teeth, glass eyes, RpC, 15"...1,350.00
French/French type, bamboo teeth, glass eyes, RpC, 15" 1,400.00
German, molded hair, pnt eyes, c/m, RpC, 1870-1900, 23" 475.00
German, pnt eyes, c/m, 1870s-90s, EX clothes, 18" 375.00
Greiner, ShHd, center part, pnt eyes, kid arms, 1858 label, 22", G...325.00
Kid body, wooden limbs, center part, sausage curls, RpC, 14".....575.00
Kid body, wooden limbs, molded comb, braided coronet, RpC, 16"..3,300.00
M&S Superior, ShHd, glass eyes, kid arms/boots, RpC, 12" 600.00
M&S Superior, ShHd, kid or leather arms/boots, RpC, 17" 425.00
M&S Superior, ShHd, molded hair, pnt eyes, RpC, 16"..............400.00
M&S Superior, ShHd, pnt eyes, molded hair, kid arms, undies, 36", VG ..315.00
Man, ShHd, pnt eyes, cloth body, period RpC, leather shoes, 1840s, 21"..750.00
Milliner's model, ShHd, pnt eyes, c/m, pnt hair, kid body, RpC, 14"....500.00
Motschmann type, wood & twill body, glass eyes, c/m, RpC, 16".........700.00
ShHd, center-part, pnt eyes, cloth body, leather arms, 1850s, RpC, 27"...300.00
ShHd, pupilless glass eyes, hh wig, early 1800s, RpC, 28", VG....485.00
ShHd, pupilless glass eyes, 10 molded curls, 1850s, RpC, 34" 750.00

Trn head, solid dome, glass eyes, c/m, compo lower arms, RpC, 18" ...**775.00**
Wooden limbs, long curls, 1840s-50s, EX clothes, 14".................**650.00**

Parian

Boy, trn ShHd, molded pnt hair, cloth/kid body, period clothes, 15" ..**400.00**
Common hair style, solid dome, pnt eyes, wig, 1850s, RpC, 18".**950.00**
Common hair style w/no decor, pnt eyes, RpC, 10" **165.00**
Countess Dagmar, head band, cluster curls on forehead, RpC, 25" ..**800.00**
Fancy hairdo w/jeweled tiara, glass eyes, p/e, fine RpC, 19".....**1,425.00**
Fancy hairdo w/ribbons/flowers etc, glass eyes, p/e, RpC, 20" ..**2,700.00**
Fancy hairdo w/ribbons/flowers/etc, glass eyes, p/e, RpC, 16" ..**1,700.00**
Fancy hairdo w/ribbons/flowers/etc, glass eyes, swivel neck, RpC, 15"...**2,625.00**
Fancy hairdo w/ribbons/flowers/etc, pnt eyes, p/e, RpC, 16" **900.00**

Fancy hairdo with ribbon, glass eyes, swivel neck, cloth body with leather lower arms, nicely dressed, 24", $3,200.00. (Photo courtesy McMasters Auctions)

Man, painted hair, cloth body, fancy tie/shirt, pnt eyes, RpC, 13" ...**557.00**
Man, pnt hair, glass eyes, cloth body, RpC, 16" **2,825.00**
Man w/parted pnt hair, glass eyes, cloth body, RpC, 16"..........**2,825.00**
Molded bodice, Irish Queen, Limbach, clover mk, #8552, RpC, 14"...**575.00**
Molded hat, pnt blond or blk hair, pnt eyes, RpC, 19" **2,900.00**
Molded hat, pnt hair, glass eyes, RpC, 14"..............................**2,400.00**
Molded hat, pnt hair, glass eyes, RpC, 16".............................**2,825.00**
Wigged, solid-dome head, molded ears, 1850s, RpC, 16" **850.00**

Schoenhut

Albert Schoenhut left Germany in 1866 to go to Pennsylvania to work as a repairman for toy pianos. He eventually applied his skills to wooden toys and later designed an all-wood doll which he patented on January 17, 1911. These uniquely jointed dolls were painted with enamels and came with a metal stand. Some of the later dolls had stuffed bodies, voice boxes, and hollow heads. Due to the changing economy and fierce competition, the company closed in the mid-1930s.

Schnickel-Fritz, cvd hair, o/c/m/teeth, lg ears, RpC, 15"..........**3,000.00**
Toddler walker, wooden SkHd, pnt eyes, c/m, mohair wig, OC, 14"...**600.00**
101, girl w/cvd bobbed hair, 1912-23, RpC, 14" **2,200.00**
102, girl, cvd braided hair, 1912-23, RpC, 14"........................**1,900.00**
105, girl, cvd bobbed hair & ribbon, 1912-23, RpC, 14-26"...**1,900.00**
107 or 107W (walker), bent-limb baby, nude, 1913-26, VG.......**375.00**
107 or 107W (walker), toddler, 1917-26, RpC, 11", EX.............**650.00**
108 or 108W, toddler, nude, 1917-26, 17", VG.........................**650.00**
108 or 108W (walker), bent-limb baby, 1913-26, RpC, 15"........**575.00**
109W, bent-limb baby, o/c/e, o/m, 1921-23, RpC, 13" **500.00**
110W, bent-limb baby, o/c/e, o/m, 1921-23, RpC, 15" **600.00**
207, boy, cvd curly hair, 1912-16, RpC, 14" **2,400.00**
307, girl, curly wig, smooth eye, nude, 1911-16, 15", VG **625.00**
310, girl w/face same as 105, long curly wig, 1912-16, RpC, 14-16"..**775.00**

312, girl, bobbed wig, 1912-24, RpC, 14"...................................**775.00**
407, boy w/wig, same face of 310 girl, 1912-16, RpC, 19-21"......**825.00**

SFBJ

By 1895 Germany was producing dolls at much lower prices than the French dollmakers could, so to save the doll industry, several leading French manufacturers united to form one large company. Bru, Raberry and Delphieu, Pintel and Godshaux, Fleischman and Bodel, Jumeau, and many others united to form the company Society Francaise de Fabrication de Bebes et Jouets (SFBJ).

20, molded pnt shoes & eyes, 5-pc body, Paris/12, 10" **365.00**
60, French WWI nurse, 5-pc body, SFBJ/13/10, 8½"................**475.00**
60, o/m w/teeth, o/c/e, hh wig, RpC, 12" **450.00**
60, SkHd, compo w/str legs, o/m, curved arms, 15" **650.00**
215, bsk swivel head over compo, c/m, inset eyes, 15" **1,800.00**
227, bsk swivel closed dome head, animal skin wig, 15" **1,900.00**
229, compo w/swivel head, o/c/m, inset eyes, 18" **5,000.00**
230, bsk SkHd, pwt, o/m/teeth, jtd wood/compo, wig, RpC, 24"..**1,000.00**
230, compo walker, p/e, o/m, inset eyes, 16" **1,600.00**
235, closed dome, molded hair, o/c/m & eyes, 16" **1,700.00**
236, laughing Jumeau, o/m, o/c/e, dbl chin, 13" **1,300.00**
236, laughing Jumeau, o/m, o/c/e, dbl chin, 20" **2,200.00**
238, compo w/swivel head, o/m, inset eyes, Paris/6, 15".........**3,800.00**
239, Poulbot, c/, street urchin, red wig, 17" **9,500.00**
245, boy, o/c/m, lg glass googly eyes, pnt shoes, 8" **1,400.00**
247, toddler, o/c/m w/2 inset teeth, 20" **2,900.00**
247, Twirp, SkHd, o/c/m & eyes, 2 teeth, 21".........................**3,000.00**
252, pouty, c/m, inset eyes, papier-mache body, 11" **2,800.00**
252, pouty, c/m, inset eyes, papier-mache body, 22" **7,800.00**
266, character, bsk head, closed dome, o/c/m, 20" **4,200.00**
301, bsk SkHd on compo, o/m, inset eyes, 22" **1,200.00**
301, bsk SkHd on compo, o/m, inset eyes, 28" **1,700.00**

Shirley Temple

Prices are suggested for dolls complete and in mint condition. Add up to 25% (depending on her outfit) if mint with box. A played-with doll in only very good condition would be worth only about half of listed values.

Bsk, 6", pnt, molded hair, unlicensed Japan, incomplete, played with...**65.00**
Celluloid, 5", unlicensed Japan, EX/M **185.00**
Celluloid, 8", unlicensed Japan, incomplete, played with..............**65.00**
Celluloid, 13", open crown, o/c/e, Dutch costume, 1937+, incomplete...**90.00**
Compo, 7½", Japan, molded curls, pnt eyes, o/c/m/teeth, EX/M **300.00**
Compo, 11", Ideal, all orig, EX/M...**975.00**
Compo, 17", Ideal, incomplete, played with **200.00**
Compo, 18", Baby Shirley, Ideal, EX/M **1,200.00**
Compo, 27", Ideal, EX/M...**1,750.00**
Compo, 27", Ideal, incomplete, played with **450.00**
Porc, 20", Danbury Mint, 1990+, MIB......................................**240.00**
Vinyl, 8", 1982-83, complete, NM/M **30.00**
Vinyl, 8", 1982-83, incomplete, EX..**8.00**
Vinyl, 12", Ideal, complete, EX/M **275.00**
Vinyl, 15", Ideal, 1958-61, complete, EX/M................................**375.00**
Vinyl, 17", Montgomery Wards reissue, 1972, M in plain box **225.00**
Vinyl, 35-36", jtd wrists, incomplete, played with **550.00**
Vinyl, 35-36", jtd wrists, 1960, complete, NM/M...................**2,000.00**

Simon and Halbig

Simon and Halbig was one of the finest German makers to operate during the 1870s into the 1930s. Due to the high quality of the makers, their dolls still command large prices today. During the 1890s a few Simon & Halbig heads were used by a French maker, but these are extremely rare and well marked S&H.

CM Bergmann, SkHd, o/m w/teeth, Simon & Halbig, RpC, 32" ..1,500.00
Handwerk, SkHd, o/m, 1895, G/S&H/1, 16" 450.00
409, SkHd, o/m, S&H, 24" 685.00
550, SkHd, o/c/e, o/m/4 teeth, synthetic wig, RpC, rpr, 22"........400.00
570, SkHd, o/c/e, o/m/4 teeth, mohair wig, jtd wood/compo, RpC, 23" ...500.00
719, SkHd, bjtd, o/m, S12H/DEP, rpl wig, RpC, 20" 3,300.00
769, SkHd, c/m, S&H DEP, 17" 2,600.00
890, SkHd, o/c/e, o/m/4 teeth, mohair wig, jtd bsk, mostly OC, 7".525.00
940, SkHd, swivel on ShPl, o/c/m, S 2 H, 14" 1,500.00
979, SkHd, inset eyes, o/m/teeth, p/e, hh wig, crier, RpC, 22", VG ..850.00
1010, ShHd, o/c/e, o/m/4 teeth, p/e, hh wig, kid body, RpC, 15" ..300.00
1039, SkHd, flirty bl eyes, jtd walker, p/e, wig, 22" 1,100.00
1039, SkHd, inset eyes, o/m/teeth, OC (ethnic), 16" 650.00
1078, SkHd, inset eyes, o/m/4 teeth, rpl wig, S&H 0, RpC, 9", VG.....300.00
1078, SkHd, o/c/e, o/m, p/e, mohair wig, fully jtd compo, RpC, 29".1,100.00
1078, SkHd, o/c/e, o/m/4 teeth, p/e, mohair wig, RpC, 27", VG ...575.00

1079-8½ DEP, bisque socket head, brown set eyes, open mouth with teeth, jointed body, antique human hair wig, in antique gingham dress and undies, replaced shoes and socks, 19", EX, $425.00. (Photo courtesy McMasters Auctions)

1079, SkHd, o/c/e, o/m/4 teeth, p/e, rpl wig, jtd, RpC, 27" 700.00
1079, SkHd, o/c/e, o/m/4 teeth, p/e, S&H/DEP/16/B, RpC, 34"...1,300.00
1498, SkHd, c/m, 5-pc baby body, period RpC, 13", EX 1,100.00

Steiner, Jules

Jules Nicholas Steiner established one of the earliest French manufacturing companies (making dishes and clocks) in 1855. He began with mechanical dolls with bisque heads and open mouths with two rows of bamboo teeth; his patents grew to include walking and talking dolls. In 1880 he registered a patent for a doll with sleep eyes. This doll could be put to sleep by turning a rod that operated a wire attached to its eyes.

A series, child, cb pate, c/m, pwt eyes, jtd, RpC, 9" 3,100.00
A or C series, bsk SkHd w/cb pate, wig, pwt eyes, c/m, RpC, 14" ..8,500.00
A series, Le Parisien, o/m, RpC, 23" 2,500.00
Bebe, unmk, bulgy pwt eyes, o/m/teeth, p/e, RpC, 1870s, 18" .5,500.00
Bourgoin, c/m, 1870s, RpC, 17" 5,200.00
C series, o/m w/teeth, pwt eyes, RpC, 23"................................6,200.00
Le Parisien, bsk SKHd w/cb pate, jtd compo, o/m, p/e, RpC, 10" ..3,600.00
Le Parisien, SkHd, pwt eyes, c/m, p/e, hh wig, RpC, 16½", VG.....3,400.00
Le Petit Parisien, bsk SkHd, glass eyes, c/m, p/e, RpC, 13" 3,500.00
Motschmann type, bsk head, twill body, glass eyes, c/m, RpC, 14" ...4,800.00
128, child, compo, o/c/e, o/m, 9", M...175.00
240, newborn, solid dome, c/m, o/c/e, RpC, 16" 600.00
246, character, dome, glass eyes, o/c laughing/m, teeth, OC, 9" 700.00

401, ShHd, dome, pnt eyes, o/c laughing/m/teeth/tongue, RpC, 15" ..475.00

Vogue

This is the company that made the Ginny doll. Composition was used during the '40s, but vinyl was the preferred material throughout the decade of the '50s. An original mint-condition composition Ginny would be worth a minimum of $450.00 on the market today (played-with about $90.00). The last Ginny came out in 1969. Another Vogue doll that is becoming very collectible is Jill, whose values are steadily climbing. For more information, we recommend *Collector's Guide to Vogue Dolls* by Judith Izen and Carol Stover. Our advisor for Jill dolls is Bonnie Groves; she is listed in the Directory under Texas.

Baby Dear One, 1973, 25", MIB...175.00
Binny Baby, 20", MIB..55.00
Ginny, hp, jtd walker, o/c/e, 1957, 8", M..................................150.00
Ginny, hp, molded lashes, walker, 1954-57, OC, minimum value ...300.00
Ginny, hp, pnt eyes, c/m, mohair wig, OC (overalls), 7½" 225.00
Ginny, hp, pnt lashes, strung, 1953, 8", MIB 325.00
Ginny as Davy Crockett, 1953, 8"...400.00
Ginny International, vinyl, 1977, OC, minimum value 45.00
Jan, all oirg, 10½", G...65.00
Jan, vinyl, basic bra & girdle, VG...54.00
Jan (Sweetheart), all orig, 12", MIB, minimum value................75.00
Jan/Jill, desk & chair, gr, VG, from $50 to...............................135.00
Jan/Jill wardrobe, gr, VG, from $50 to.....................................135.00
Jeff, in tuxedo, all orig, VG w/box..65.00
Jeff, nude, VG, from $25 to..45.00
Jeff, vinyl, bl suit, 10", VG..125.00
Jeff, vinyl, shorts outfit, 10", VG, from $65 to 85.00
Jill, hp, cotton street dress, all orig, 10½", from $85 to 135.00
Jill, hp, formal, 10½", EX, from $150 to..................................200.00
Jill, hp, leotard, 1957, 10½", MIB 250.00
Jill, hp, nude, haircut, 10½", G-...20.00
Jill, hp, 1957-62, 10½", MIB...190.00
Jill, in office dress, incomplete outfit, VG 75.00
Jill, peach flowered formal, all orig, from $135 to.......................200.00
Jill, toreador outfit, all orig, VG...85.00
Jill, vinyl, History Land, all orig, from $165 to 200.00
Jill, 1960 street dress, scarce, incomplete, from $65 to..................80.00
Jill bed, VG from $50 to...85.00
Jill chromium head pendant, MIP, from $50 to..........................80.00
Jill Coke bottle, accessory to jeans outfits, scarce, from $12 to 20.00
Jill cotton dress, from $35 to..50.00
Jill Dream Cozy Bed Set (bedding), MIP, from $35 to 50.00
Jill dress, semiformal, MIP, from $50 to 75.00
Jill felt coat, from $45 to..65.00
Jill hostess outfit set (no doll), #3311, 1960, MIB 160.00
Jill jewelry, MIP, from $35 to...50.00
Jill semiformal set (no doll), #7511, 1957, MIB..........................255.00
Jill shoes, MIP..25.00
Toddles Draf-Tee, compo toddler, pnt eyes, c/m, mohair wig, OC, 7½" ...350.00
Toodles Baby, compo, pnt eyes, OC: dress/coat/bonnet, 7" 265.00

Wax, Poured Wax

Alice in Wonderland style, molded headband, RpC, 16" 525.00
Bartenstein, 2-faced (laughing/crying), 1880-90s, RpC, 15" 900.00
Child, molded cap, 1860-80, RpC, 16"......................................325.00
Man, trn ShHd, molded top hat, set eyes, cloth/wood body, 17", VG.1,000.00
Poured ShHd, child, glass eyes, inserted hair, RpC, 13" 1,100.00
Poured ShHd, lady, glass eyes, inserted hair, RpC, 8" 770.00
Wax over compo, glass eyes, molded hair/shoes, wood limbs, RpC, 15" ...300.00

Wax over compo, ShHd, molded hair ribbon, c/m, p/e, 1870s, RpC, 15", G...**100.00**
Wax over compo or papier-mache, child, ShHd, glass eyes, RpC, 14" **1,000.00**
Wax over ShHd, glass eyes, c/m, molded/pnt hair, cloth body, RpC, 5" ...**775.00**
Wax over ShHd, set eyes, c/m, mohair, cloth/kid body, RpC, 26" ..**750.00**
Wax over SkHd, child, glass eyes, o/c/m, cloth body, RpC, 11" ..**200.00**

Door Knockers

Door knockers, those charming precursors of the doorbell, come in an intriguing array of shapes and styles. The very rare ones come from England. Cast-iron examples made in this country were often produced in forms similar to the more familiar doorstop figures.

Our listings are prices realized at auction. Most were in exceptional condition. See Doorstops for suggestions on pricing examples in lesser conditions.

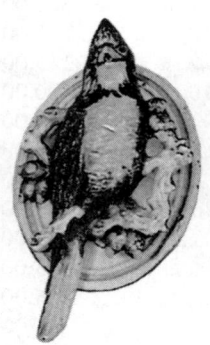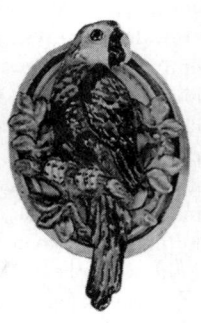

Cardinal on twigs, multicolor paint on cast iron, 5x3", M, $325.00; Parrot on twigs, multicolor paint on cast iron, 4½x3", M, $175.00; Parrot on branch, multicolor paint on cast iron, Hubley, 4¾x2¾", M, $175.00. (Photo courtesy Bertoia Auctions)

Basket of Daffodils, bl bow at top, 4¼x2½" **300.00**
Bathing Beauty, flapper style, Fish, rare, 5⅛x2½".......................**700.00**
Birdhouse w/Birds, ornate casting, Hubley, 3¾x1⅝" **400.00**
Bunch of Roses, mc w/pk bow at top of bking, 4¼x2¾" **345.00**
Castle, on mtntop w/clouds, #632, 4x2¾"....................................**265.00**
Flower Basket, mc w/purple, Hubley #124, 4x2¾".......................**715.00**
Hanging Basket, mc flowers, Hubley #205, 3x2⅛" **275.00**
Ivy Basket, Hubley #123, Made in USA, rare, 4½x2¼".............**135.00**
Morning Glory, 3¼x2¾"...**325.00**
Parrot in Hoop, 3¼x2½"...**200.00**
Peace Dove, w/olive branch in beak, 4x2¾"................................**375.00**
Pear, floral & leaf bking, 3¼x3" **300.00**
Poinsettia, Hubley #627, 3½x2½"..**350.00**
Rooster in Hoop, cast leaves, 4¼x3", EX **300.00**
Rooster in Ring, crowing, bright mc, 3¼x2⅞" **250.00**
Rose, w/sm branch & leaves, 5¼x3"..**330.00**
Spider, w/captured fly, rare, 3½x1¾"...**450.00**
Vase w/flowers, gold trim, 3¾x2¼" **275.00**
Woodpecker, pecking tree trunk bking, Hubley, #251, 3⅝x2¾".**150.00**
Zinnia, gold highlights, Pat Pend LVL, 3¾x2½" **325.00**

Doorstops

Although introduced in England in the mid-1800s, cast-iron doorstops were not made to any great extent in this country until after the Civil War. Once called 'door porters,' their function was to keep doors open to provide better ventilation. They have been produced in many shapes and sizes, both dimensional and flat-backed, and in the past few years have become a popular, yet affordable collectible. While cast-iron examples are the most common, brass, wood, and chalk were also used. An average price is in the $100.00 to $200.00 range, though some are valued at more than $400.00. Doorstops retained their usefulness and appeal well into the '30s.

The prices below were realized at Bertoia's auctions in the east where doorstops are at a premium. For other areas of the country, it may be necessary to adjust prices down about 25%. When no condition code is present, items are assumed to be in exceptional original condition, flat-backed unless noted full-figured, and cast iron unless another material is mentioned. To evaluate a doorstop in only very good to excellent paint, deduct at least 35%. Values for examples in poor to good paint drop dramatically. For further information we recommend *Doorstops, Identification and Values*, by Jeanne Bertoia.

Key: ff — full figured

Anchor w/Sailing Ship Scene, Bradley & Hubbard, 11½" **220.00**
Basset Hound, wrinkled brow, Hubley, 7x6½", VG/EX **770.00**
Bird of Paradise, plumed tail, LACS, 13½" **2,750.00**
Boston Terrier w/Paw Up, ff, varnished, 9½" **660.00**
Boxer, ff, Hubley, 8½x9" **660.00**
Boy in Tuxedo, w/top hat, c Jo, #1262, 7¼x4⅜", EX **385.00**
Boy w/Fruit Basket, w/top hat, 9¼" **880.00**
Bulldog, standing, ff, Hubley, 4⅝x5½"..**660.00**
Cat Licking Paw, Waverly Studio, 7⅝" **660.00**
Cat on Rug, recumbent, on semicircle, 7¼" L...........................**1,400.00**
Cat Scratch Fever, girl & kitten, Judd, c JO 1271, 8¾" **1,550.00**
Climbing Cat, Deco style, heavy casting, rare, 13¼" **1,875.00**
Clipper ship, full sails, wavy sea, Albany Foundry, 8⅛x10", EX....**90.00**
Clown, leaning against wall w/base, c Jo, 8x3½" **825.00**
Cockatoo, ff, perched on stump, 14x4½" **990.00**
Cockatoo, 3-D, on branch, rnd base, 7¼" **420.00**
Colonial Lawyer, yel long coat, gr pants, Waverly Studios, 9⅝", EX...**660.00**
Colonial Woman, full dress, 11½" **770.00**
Colonial Woman, pk dress, Pat Pending, 10½x5½" **500.00**
Colonial Woman w/Fan, yel dress, Waverly Studios, 9¾" **825.00**
Conestoga Wagon, orange spokes, bl body, mk 1930, 12" L, EX.**275.00**
Cosmos, Hubley, 17¾"...**1,850.00**
Cottage, red roof, towering grees, wedge, 7¼x8½", EX **330.00**
Cottage in Woods, trees & flowers, smoke at chimney, 8¼x7¼", EX ..**600.00**
Cottage w/Fence, many flowers on walls, National Foundry, 5¾x8" **330.00**
Dachshund, ff, Hubley Made in USA, 5½x9½" **530.00**
Dolly, girl w/baby doll, Hubley, 7¾x3¾", VG............................**385.00**
Duck Pecking Dog, Greenblatt, #11, c 1924, 9¾x8¾" **2,750.00**
Dutch Girl, classic attire, 2 flower baskets, Hubley, 9¼x5½".....**880.00**
Edgar Allen Poe House, Bradley & Hubbard, 5x7⅝" **2,000.00**
Elephant, trunk up, ff, 8¼x11½" **495.00**
Elk, standing on base, 11x10", EX **880.00**
Fireplace Scene, lady at spinning wheel, Eastern Specialty, 6¼x8"..**330.00**
Flowered Doorway, floral arch & bench at door, 7⅝x7½" **1,400.00**
Fruit Basket, bright colors, mk LACS 745-N, 11⅞x6" **660.00**
Fruit Basket, wicker basket w/pk bow, 9¾" **250.00**
Fruit Basket, wicker w/draped bow, gr base, 7½x6" **495.00**
Fruit Basket, wide base, Albany Foundry, 10⅛x7½" **300.00**
Geese, 3 facing left), Hubley, c Fred Everett, 8x8" **935.00**
Girl Holding Bouquet, Albany Foundry, 7⅝x4¾" **600.00**
Girl Holding Dress, rubber knobs intact, B&G 7798, 13x6¾" ..**2,100.00**
Girl Holding Flowers (as bridesmaid), rare, 8¼", EX................**825.00**
Girl Wearing Bonnet, w/flowers & blanket, Albany Foundry, 4¾"....**440.00**
Golfer, bag on shoulder, ff, rare, 6x3½"...................................**1,200.00**
Halloween Cat, frightened pose, Budd & Fender, 1915, 9¼x7¼"....**990.00**
Heron, EX details, Bradley & Hubbard, very rare, sm crack, EX..**3,500.00**

Heron on the Rocks, tall grasses, 10", EX 360.00
Jester on Trunk, Eastern Specialties, rare, 7¼" 1,300.00
Kittens in Basket, 3 in wicker basket, Rosenstein, c 1932, 10x7" ..825.00
Lady Holding Carpet Bag, Symonds, rare, 12", EX....1,650.00
Li'l Red Riding Hubley, Hubley, varnished, 9½x5", EX 825.00
Little Girl, ff, Judd, 7x4½", VG....200.00
Little Red Riding Hood, c 1930, Creation Co Pat No 100, 8⅞" ...935.00
Little Red Riding Hood & Wolf, NUYDEA, rare, 7½x9½" 2,200.00
Man Holding Package, hiding 2nd in jacket, ff, 5½", EX....275.00
Man Walking w/Cane, wedge, c Jo, #1256, 7⅜"....880.00
Mary Quite Contrary, w/water can, flowers, rake, rare, 15x8", EX.....1,050.00
Mountain-Top Mansion, winding road, Bradley & Hubbard, 9⅜", EX...1,750.00
Old Doorway, lady by fence at doorway, Symonds, 7½x8½"....6,600.00
Old Tom, Don't You Tell (on gr base), England, 17½x11", VG..525.00
Owl, rubber knobs intact, Bradley & Hubbard, 15½" 2,400.00
Parrot, colorful, detailed, c Jo, 8x3⅞"....330.00
Peasant girl, bl apron, red beads, mc flowers, c Jo, #1277, 11⅞"..1,750.00
Pekinese, lifelike details, Hubley, 14½x9" 1,550.00
Peter Rabbit, eating carrot, Hubley, 9½x4¾"....1,100.00
Pheasant, realistic, Hubley, c Fred Everett, 8½x7½" 660.00
Quail (3), Hubley, c Fred Everett, 7¼x6¼" 990.00
Rabbit, realistic, B&H #7900, rare, 15" 4,400.00
Rabbit, realistic, Bradley & Hubbard, rare, 12½x11½"....6,000.00
Rabbit Pushing Wheelbarrow, rare, 8¼x11" 4,625.00
Reaching Child, nude bkside view, 17", EX....3,100.00
Rooster, strutting, wht w/floral base, red comb, 10x6"....935.00
Ship, multi-sail/tall, Greenblatt Studios, 1925, 10x12" 530.00
Spanish Girl, w/fan, LACS, #760, 9⅞x5½" 1,200.00
Terrier, wedge, Spencer, rare, 4"....990.00
Turkey, detailed feathers, Bradley & Hubbard, 12½x11½" 6,000.00
Urn w/flowers, ornately cast, hdl at top, 8⅝"....330.00
Whimsical Dog, tongue out, Greenblatt Studio, c 1937, 9¾".....770.00
Whimsical Man, bow tie, head band, c Jo, #1258, 7x3½", EX....385.00
Windmill, ocean scene in bkground, 11½" L....2,200.00
Yawning Pup, ff, open mouth, very rare, 7x5" 770.00

Dorchester Pottery

Taking its name from the town in Massachusetts where it was organized in 1895, the Dorchester Pottery Company made primarily utilitarian wares, though other types of items were made as well. By 1940 a line of decorative pottery was introduced, some of which was painted by hand with scrollwork or themes from nature. The buildings were destroyed by fire in the late 1970s, and the pottery was never rebuilt. In the listings that follow, the decorations described are all in cobalt unless otherwise noted. Our advisor for this category is Dale MacLean; he is listed in the Directory under Massachusetts.

Key: CAH — Charles A. Hill (noted artist)

Bottle, scent; Whale, scroll stopper, CAH, 5"....200.00
Bowl, Apple, CAH, stamped, 1776-1976, 2x5¾" 100.00
Bowl, Blueberry, sgn CAH/N Ricci, stamped, 2x6½" 75.00
Bowl, cereal; Pine Cone, 6"....75.00
Bowl, Eagle & Star, Nixon Inauguration commemorative, hdls, CAH ..275.00
Bowl, Grape, CAH, stamped, 3⅛x7" 175.00
Bowl, Teardrop, CAH, stamped, 2¼x5¾"....150.00
Candle holder, Pine Cone, CAH, stamped, 2¼x5½", NM 150.00
Candy dish, Butterfly & Flower, sgn, stamped, 1½x6¼" 240.00
Candy dish, Clown, striped rim, CAH, 4" dia 150.00
Casserole, Half Scroll, CAH/N Ricci, stamped, 4¾x7¼" 225.00
Casserole, Whale, CAH/N Ricci, stamped, 4¾x8"....300.00
Charger, Ship, sgn JM/N Ricci, stamped, 12¼" 450.00
Coffee set, Blueberry, CAH, pot+mug+sugar bowl 200.00
Coffeecup, Pine Cone....60.00
Creamer & sugar bowl, Blueberry, CAH, 3", 3¼"....150.00
Creamer & sugar bowl, Whale, CAH, 3", 3½", EX....200.00
Cup, Blueberry, CAH, 3¾", 3 for 200.00
Cup & saucer, Pine Cone, CAH, stamped, 3", 6¼"....100.00
Jar, Sacred Cod, w/lid, CAH, stamped, 3½x3¾" 125.00
Jar, Whale, bulbous, C-hdl, 1950s, 5¼"....175.00
Mug, Bell, striped hdl, paper label, 4½x3⅜" 130.00
Mug, Clown, All Gone inside, CAH, stamped, 2¾" 175.00
Mug, Eight Bells, K Denisons, flake, 4¾"....125.00
Mug, Full Scroll, CAH, 4½"....100.00
Mug, Pussy Willow, sgn CAH, stamped, 2¾x4¾" 125.00
Nut dish, Striped & Scroll, CAH, 3¾", EX....75.00
Pitcher, dogwood flowers, CAH, C hdl, 1950s, w/lid, 5¾"....230.00
Pitcher, Pine Cone, CAH/N Ricci, stamped, 5½x4¼"....225.00
Pitcher, Plum Branch, CAH, raised rim, loop hdl, 1950s, 4¾" ...150.00
Pitcher, Pussy Willow, CAH/N Ricci, stamped, 5½x4¼"....225.00
Pitcher, waves at rim, hooks at middle, RT, 7⅛" 175.00
Pitcher, Whale, CAH/N Ricci, stamped, 5½x7" 250.00
Plate, Daffodil, swirled bl ground, CAH, 7¼"....225.00
Plate, Farm Mill & Landscape, K Denisons, stamped, 7½" 200.00

Plate, Whale, blended blue waves, N. Ricci/Fecit/CAH, 10½", $250.00.

Sugar bowl, Lighthouse, K Denisons, w/lid, 3½" 125.00
Sugar bowl, Pomegranate, blended bl, K Denisons, EX 125.00
Sugar jar, Lace, bulbous, JM, stamped, 3¼x3"....150.00
Syrup, Half Scroll, bulbous, 5¼x4½" 125.00
Toby jug, Quaker Oats replica, early orig label, 8x7½"....250.00
Vase, Pine Cone, trumpet shape, CAH, 3½x3" 125.00

Dorflinger

Christian Dorflinger was born in Alsace, France, and came to this country when he was ten years old. When still very young, he obtained a job in a glass factory in New Jersey. As a young man, he started his own glassworks in Brooklyn, New York, opening new factories as profits permitted. During that time he made cut glass articles for many famous people including President and Mrs. Lincoln, for whom he produced a complete service of tableware with the United States Coat of Arms. In 1863 he sold the New York factories because of ill health and moved to his farm near White Mills, Pennsylvania. His health returned, and he started a plant near his home. It was there that he did much of his best work, making use of only the very finest materials. Christian died in 1915, and the plant was closed in 1921 by consent of the family.

Dorflinger glass is rare and often hard to identify. Very few pieces were marked. Many only carried a small paper label which was quickly discarded; these are seldom found today. Identification is more accurately made through a study of the patterns, as colors may vary.

Cup & saucer, demitasse; Parisian, set of 4 ....1,400.00

Decanter, gr to clear, Dmn Point & oval cuttings, w/stopper **295.00**
Parfait, Renaissance, faceted teardrop stem, 6 for **195.00**
Plate, oyster; Kalana Art #17, etched, 9", 8 for...........................**275.00**
Sherbet, Renaissance, bl to clear, stemmed, pr **175.00**
Vase, sweet pea; Kalana, pansies, 3¼x6" **110.00**
Wine, Kalana Lily, 5", set of 6...**90.00**
Wine, Renaissance, cranberry to clear.......................................**185.00**

Dragon Ware

Dragon ware is fairly accessible and is still being made today. The new dragon ware is distinguishable by the lack of detail in the application of the dragon. In the older pieces, much care is given to the slipwork of the dragon itself, including the eyes, wings, scales, and pearl. The new ware tends to be flat, lacking personality and detail. Many pieces were made for souvenirs, so be aware of additional markings on the outside of the piece.

The colors that are mentioned refer to the primary color found on the piece. This usually tends to be the black or gray colors. Splashes of pink and blue are found on these pieces. The newer pieces tend to have more shine or gloss than their older counterparts (not including lustreware). Older colors tend to be more vibrant, while many of the newer colors run into the pastel range. In addition to the primary colors, splashes of other colors are often found, creating a cloud effect behind the dragon. At this writing, pieces that are older and not the typical black/gray colors are commanding slightly higher prices and attention then similar pieces in black.

The primary colors are applied in several ways, the most common being a wide band of color on the top and bottom of each piece. The 'cloud' effect is created when the primary color (and often the only color besides those of the dragon) is swirled on, creating a cloud-like background for the dragon. The lustreware look is achieved when the primary color is solid throughout the piece, creating a very shiny background. The solid color is entirely one color except for the dragon, clouds, and pearl.

Many cups have lithophanes consisting of the face of a geisha girl. Nude lithophanes can also be found, although they are scarce. The newer the lithophane, the less detail that it seems to have.

Items listed below are unmarked unless noted otherwise. Ranges are given to take into consideration the age and quality of the piece. Please examine the pieces carefully and note if the piece is old or new. The Internet auction sites are good places to see various pieces from different areas.

Key:
MIJ — Made in Japan   MIOJ — Made in Occupied Japan

Child's teapot+c/s, peach, from $35 to **60.00**
Compote, w/lid, gray, ornate hdls, MIJ, 7x7¾", from $125 to.....**200.00**
Condiment set w/lids & tray, gray, MIJ, 10-pc, from $150 to......**225.00**
Console set, gray, bowl+2 candlesticks, from $175 to..................**250.00**
Cup & saucer, blk, nude lithophane, 2¾", 5½", from $40 to........**75.00**
Cup & saucer, demi; bl, nude lithophane, 2x2", 3½", from $25 to ..**75.00**
Cup & saucer, gold, lithophane, 2x5", from $30 to........................**75.00**
Cup & saucer, gr cloud, MIOJ, from $25 to **60.00**
Cup & saucer, red, nude lithophane, MIJ paper, 2⅛", 4¾", $40 to **75.00**
Incense burner, blk, gold hdls & finials, 3x3¼", from $15 to **45.00**
Luncheon set, gray, lithophane, kidney-shaped plates, 13-pc, $150 to...**225.00**
Plate, gray, lattice, Japan, 6½", from $30 to **60.00**
Play, gray, gold hdl, Japan, 5½", from $15 to...............................**45.00**
Relish tray, gray, 4-part, wicker hdl, from $40 to..........................**75.00**
Rice soup bowl set w/spoons, gray, 4½x2¼", 12-pc, from $60 to ..**80.00**
Saki dispenser w/stopper, gray, whistling, Kutani, 6¼", from $35 to **60.00**

Saki set, gray, keg w/elephant stopper+6 cups, Japan, 9½", $125 to ..**225.00**
Saki set, orange cloud, lithophanes/whistle, MIJ, 5-pc, 5¾", $60 to..**125.00**
Shakers, gray, nodding on base, MIJ, 3-pc set, from $125 to **225.00**
Tea set, bl, MIJ, 23-pc, from $200 to **350.00**
Tea set, brn, w/serving plate, MIJ, 24-pc, from $175 to **350.00**
Tea set, demi; orange, lithophane, 15-pc, from $90 to.................**175.00**
Tea set, demi; red, lithophane, 15-pc, from $90 to **175.00**
Tea set, Satsuma style, MIJ, 24-pc, from $250 to **350.00**
Teapot set (dbl) w/lids & stands, gray, HP MIJ, 5x7", 5x8", $125 to...**175.00**
Tidbit tray, gray, 2-tier w/hdl, from $75 to..................................**150.00**
Vase, brn, ftd, 7½", from $35 to...**75.00**
Vase, brn, hdls, Nippon, 12½", from $175 to..............................**250.00**
Vase, gray, clear bl eyes, Nippon, 11¼", from $150 to...............**250.00**
Vase, gray, Nippon, mk #101, 5", from $75 to.............................**175.00**
Vase, gray, Noritake, 7¾", from $150 to......................................**225.00**

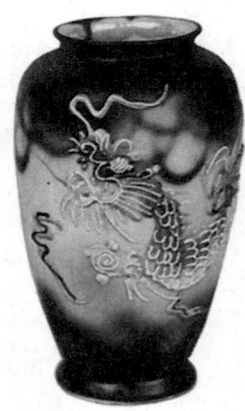

Vase, moriage Golden Gate Bridge, 5", from $25.00 to $50.00.

Vase, red & blk, hdls, 3¾x4x1", from $25 to **55.00**
Wall pocket, red/brn, MIJ, 5½", from $50 to **100.00**

Dresden

The term Dresden is used today to indicate the porcelains that were produced in Meissen and Dresden, Germany, from the very early eighteenth century well into the next. John Bottger, a young alchemist, discovered the formula for the first true porcelain in 1708 while being held a virtual prisoner at the palace in Dresden because of the King's determination to produce a superior ware. Two years later a factory was erected in nearby Meissen with Bottger as director. There fine tableware, elaborate centerpieces, and exquisite figurines with applied details were produced. In 1731, to distinguish their product from the wares of such potters as Sevres, Worcester, Chelsea, and Derby, the Meissen company adopted their famous crossed swords trademark. During the next century, several potteries were producing porcelain in the 'Meissen style' in Dresden itself. Their wares were often marked with imitations of Meissen's crossed swords.

The Carl Theime factory produced dinnerware as well as decorative pieces in the Meissen style from 1872 until 1972. Openwork pieces were their specialty. Their mark was an intertwined 'SP' with the word Dresden below. Other companies followed suit, and in 1883 began using the crown mark along with the Dresden indication. There were several variations of this mark employed over the years. Many of these companies produced Meissen-type wares well into the twentieth century. See also Meissen.

Bowl, 4 angels support ea corner, cobalt trim, 7x14x11½"..........**500.00**
Cache pot, rams' head hdls, 7x6" dia...**500.00**
Figurine, ballerina tying shoe, 8x7" **350.00**
Figurine, Beethoven, pianist & 5 figures, lace trim, 11x24x13"...**5,850.00**
Figurine, boy & girl picking apples, 5½x10" **485.00**

Figurine, boy tending sheep, 8x10x5" 300.00
Figurine, couple playing cards, 5½x6½x4" 285.00
Figurine, couple playing chess, 5½x6x4" 500.00
Figurine, Elizabeth, 10½" 375.00
Figurine, Flight to Egypt, 9x13x5" 1,500.00
Figurine, Kwan Yin, 9½" 450.00
Figurine, lady seated w/fan, lacy skirt, 7½x6" 265.00
Figurine, Language Lesson, lady w/parrot, 8½x8½x6" 345.00
Figurine, Le Seprano, 10x11x9" 750.00
Figurine, Royal Coach, wht horses, 5x12x5" 1,100.00
Figurine, St Petersburg Sleigh Ride, 7x16x7" 1,000.00
Figurine, Tea Time, 3 ladies, cobalt trim, 4x6x4" 450.00
Figurine, 2 ladies & man in garden, 9x13x7" 1,750.00
Mirror, appl florals, mc, 3-light, 33x17" 2,750.00
Mirror, Four Seasons, 17x24" 850.00
Ramekin, gold lattice on burgundy, 3¼" 55.00

Dresser Accessories

Dresser sets, ring trees, figural or satin pincushions, manicure sets — all those lovely items that graced milady's dressing table — were at the same time decorative as well as functional. Today they appeal to collectors for many reasons. The Victorian era is well represented by repousse silver-backed mirrors, brushes, and pincushions that were used to display ornamental pins for the hair, hats, and scarves. The hair receiver — similar to a powder jar but with an opening in the lid — was used to hold long strands of hair retrieved from the comb or brush. These were wound around the finger and tucked in the opening to be used later for hair jewelry and pictures, many of which survive to the present day. (See Hair Weaving.)

Celluloid dresser sets were popular during the late 1800s and early 1900s. Some included manicure tools, pill boxes, and buttonhooks, as well as the basic items. Because celluloid tends to break rather easily, a whole set may be hard to find today. (See also Plastics.) With the current interest in anything Art Deco, sets from the '30s and '40s are especially collectible. These may be made of crystal, Bakelite, or silver, and the original boxes just as lavishly appointed as their contents.

Blotter, Deco-floral, Nippon mk, 4¼" 200.00
Box, plain ivory-grained celluloid, 1930s, sm, from $15 to 20.00
Box, powder; floral, souvenir of Newport RI, Nippon gr mk, 3" .150.00
Brush, bonnet; celluloid w/long hdl, mk Keystone-French Ivory...18.00
Brush & comb, lt pk plastic w/HP gold & roses, unmk, 1930s 25.00
Clothes brush, celluloid w/1" horsehair bristles, from $8 to...........10.00
Hair receiver, floral on wht w/gold, 4 slim legs, Nippon, 4¾" L...80.00
Hair receiver, roses on gr, bl Nippon mk, 5" dia..............................85.00
Jar, potpourri; Deco floral on wht w/cobalt trim, Nippon mk, 5½" ..195.00
Jar, powder; ivory grained celluloid w/mc floral, 2¾x2⅞" 15.00
Letter box, tortoise shell w/ivory crest, 4x10x5", w/quill............880.00
Set, Am silver, mirror+3 brushes+silver-mtd comb, 5-pc 365.00
Set, ivory celluloid w/monogram, Parisian Ivory, ca 1910, 11-pc..125.00
Set, sterling repousse, S Kirk, 1905, 2 brushes+hand mirror 195.00
Set, wht w/pk Deco band, 6-sided shapes, Nippon, 5 pcs on 10" tray...350.00
Shoe horn, lady's leg shape, pk pearlescent celluloid w/rhinestones........35.00
Shoe horn, Navarre (floral) pattern, gr Lucite, ca 1930 ....12.00

Dryden

Dryden Pottery was founded in 1946 by WWII veteran Jim Dryden. Starting in a Quonset hut and selling molded products from his dad's hardware store, the small company was soon selling pottery to Macy's of New York and the Fred Harvey Restaurants on the Santa Fe Railroad.

He used tan Kansas clay and volcanic ash as a component of his very durable glossy glaze.

After ten years some six hundred stores stocked Dryden pottery. Direct sales to tourists offered the best profit against growing pottery imports from retooled Japan and Europe. Jim invented personalizing his pottery for tourists and companies using a dental drill. This handwork was appreciated by customers then and by collectors today.

To find a broader and larger tourist base, the pottery moved to Hot Springs National Park in 1956. Again, local clay and quartz for glazes were used to make the pottery initially. Then commercial clay, firing bone white, and controlled glazes were used for improved consistency. These improvements were used in a competitive move towards hand-turned original pottery made today. The ever-growing variety of unique shapes and glazes has made Dryden Pottery fascinationg for 55 years.

In 2001 The Book Stops Here will publish the first catalog and history of Dryden Pottery. The book will show the evolution of Dryden art pottery from molded ware to unique hand-thrown pieces; the studio illustrations will show the durable and colorful glazes that make Dryden special. The book will include a complete bibliography and price guide.

Kansas pieces have a golden tan clay base and were made between 1946 and 1956. Arkansas pieces, made after 1956, used bone white clay. Dryden is easily one of the major quality potteries yet unknown to many collectors and can be found in a variety of prices. A personalized piece with its original label commands about twice the price of the same piece plain. For one-of-a-kind and unusual items rarely seen for sale, prices can soar over $500.00. Dryden early figurines currently command the highest prices. Our advisor for this category is Ralph Winslow; he is listed in the Directory under Missouri.

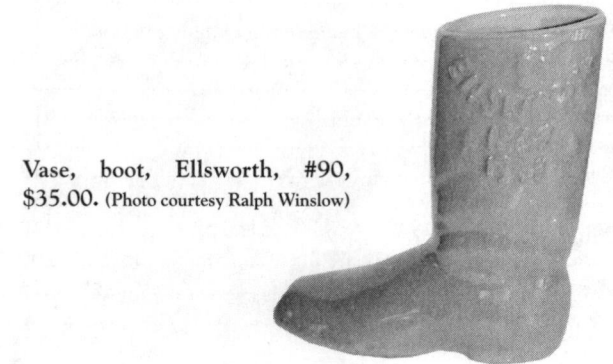

Vase, boot, Ellsworth, #90, $35.00. (Photo courtesy Ralph Winslow)

Kansas Dryden (1946 – 1956)

Ashtray, big-mouth fish, #91 ....35.00
Ashtray, rnd, Isis Temple 40.00
Bookends, Scotty dog, #80, pr..125.00
Bowl, Sundance WY, #105, 4½" 35.00
Bowl (candy dish), #7B, 2" 15.00
Cup, coffee; #2, 2½" 15.00
Dish, lg apple, #12 ....25.00
Dish, sm apple, #C2 ....16.00
Figurine, Aladdin's lamp...45.00
Figurine, buffalo, Abilene Kans 250.00
Figurine, circus elephants, #9 ....200.00
Figurine, donkey on stand, #Z...60.00
Figurine, elephant, #10, lg...175.00
Figurine, Girl Scout..100.00
Figurine, lion..175.00
Gravy boat, #7H 20.00
Jug, #H3, #H2 or #H1, ea..15.00
Pitcher, #49, 70-oz..45.00

Pitcher, bbl, #8P 40.00
Pitcher, Ellsworth Kans, #12, 3½" 45.00
Pitcher, ewer shape, #99, mini 18.00
Pitcher, fish, #62 ....75.00
Pitcher, Isis, narrow 35.00
Planter, #Y 35.00
Planter, cow (smiling) 50.00
Planter, hippo, 3314 ....130.00
Shakers, cube, #108A, pr. 35.00
Shakers, jugs, #70, pr 20.00
Stein, #7, bbl. 18.00
Stein, #7, emb nude 50.00
Vase, boot, Ellsworth, #90 ....35.00
Vase, donkey, #Z 75.00
Vase, ivy, #180, 4" 25.00
Wall pocket, octagon 50.00
Wall pocket, 3-leaf, #956 ....35.00
Wall pocket, 4-H clover 40.00

Arkansas Dryden (1956 to Present)

Ashtray, Ellsworth HS, 1981 ....15.00
Bowl, muted, 8½" 22.00
Cup, face, JK Dryden 12.00
Figurine, fighting cocks, mc, 11" 35.00
Mug, dragon hdl. 45.00
Mugs, faces, set of 5 ....50.00
Mugs, mc, set of 6 ....24.00
Nude. 45.00
Pitcher, folk art, 8½" 16.00
Planter, elephant. 12.00
Platter, fish, mc, 14" 25.00
Teapot, mc 35.00
Vase, cactus 12.50
Vase, Deco nude 75.00
Vase, hole in side 12.00
Vase, JK Dryden, Ark, 10" 57.00
Vase, mc, wheel thrown, 1979, 5" 30.00
Vase, twisted top, wheel thrown, 14" 100.00
Vase, wheel thrown, last kiln of 1999, 6" 75.00
Vase, wheel thrown, mini 20.00

Duncan and Miller

The firm that became known as the Duncan and Miller Glass Company in 1900 was organized in 1874 in Pittsburgh, Pennsylvania, a partnership between George Duncan, his sons Harry and James, and his son-in-law Augustus Heisey. John Ernest Miller was hired as their designer. He is credited with creating the most famous of all Duncan's glassware lines, Three Face. (See Pattern Glass.) The George Duncan and Sons Glass Company, as it was titled, was only one of eighteen companies that merged in 1891 with U.S. Glass. Soon after the Pittsburgh factory burned in 1892, the association was dissolved, and Heisey left the firm to set up his own factory in Newark, Ohio. Duncan built his new plant in Washington, Pennsylvania, where he continued to make pressed glassware in such notable patterns as Bagware, Amberette, Duncan Flute, Button Arches, and Zippered Slash. The firm was eventually sold to U.S. Glass in Tiffin, Ohio, and unofficially closed in August 1955.

In addition to the early pressed dinnerware patterns, today's Duncan and Miller collectors enjoy searching for opalescent vases in many patterns and colors, frosted 'Satin Tone' glassware, acid-etched designs, and lovely stemware such as the Rock Crystal cuttings. Milk glass was made in limited quantity and is considered a good investment. Ruby

glass, Ebony (a lovely opaque black glass popular during the '20s and '30s), and, of course, the glass animal and bird figurines are all highly valued examples of the art of Duncan and Miller.

Expect to pay at least 25% more than values listed for other colors, for ruby and cobalt, as much as 50% more in the Georgian, Pall Mall, and Sandwich lines. Pink, green, and amber Sandwich is worth approximately 30% more than the same items in crystal. Milk glass examples of American Way are valued up to 30% higher than color, 50% higher in Pall Mall. Chartreuse Canterbury is worth 10% to 20% more than crystal. Add approximately 40% to 50% to listed prices for opalescent items. Etchings, cuttings, and other decorations will increase values by about 50%. For further study we recommend *The Encyclopedia of Duncan Glass*, by Gail Krause; she is listed in the Directory under Pennsylvania. Several Duncan and Miller lines are shown in *Elegant Glassware of the Depression Era* by Gene Florence. Also refer to *Glass Animals and Figural Flower Frogs of the Depression Era* by Lee Garmon and Dick Spencer; they are both listed under Illinois. See also Glass Animals. Our advisor is Roselle Schleifman; she is listed in the Directory under New York.

Canterbury, crystal, ashtray, 3" 6.00
Canterbury, crystal, bowl, finger; 4½x2" 8.00
Canterbury, crystal, bowl, salad; 10x5" 30.00
Canterbury, crystal, bowl, 10¾x4¾" 27.50
Canterbury, crystal, lamp, hurricane; w/prisms, 15" ...95.00

Canterbury, crystal, pitcher, 64-ounce, $225.00 (if colored, from $250.00 to $275.00). (Photo courtesy Gene Florence)

Canterbury, crystal, shakers, pr. 22.50
Canterbury, crystal, tumbler, juice; flat, 5-oz, 3¾" 8.00
Canterbury, crystal, urn, 4½x4½" 15.00
Canterbury, crystal, vase, cloverleaf; 5" 25.00
Canterbury, crystal, vase, flower arranger; 7" 45.00
Caribbean, bl, bowl, console; flared edge, 12" 90.00
Caribbean, bl, bowl, 8½" 75.00
Caribbean, bl, plate, bread & butter; 6¼" 12.00
Caribbean, bl, relish, 4-part, oblong, 9½" 65.00
Caribbean, bl, stem, champagne; ball stem, ftd, 6-oz, 4" ...27.50
Caribbean, bl, vase, ball shape, flared edge, ftd, 7¼" ...70.00
Caribbean, crystal, ashtray, 4 indents, 6" 15.00
Caribbean, crystal, bowl, vegetable; hdld, 9¼" 30.00
Caribbean, crystal, cruet. 47.00
Caribbean, crystal, plate, salad liner; rolled edge, 12" ..24.00
Caribbean, crystal, shakers, metal lids, 5", pr 37.50
Caribbean, crystal, tumbler, flat, 5-oz, 3½" 20.00
Caribbean, crystal, vase, ftd, 10" 57.00
First Love, crystal, ashtray, #111, sq, 3½" 16.50
First Love, crystal, bowl, #115, crimped, 10½x5" 45.00
First Love, crystal, bowl, finger; #30, 4x1½" 32.00
First Love, crystal, candle, #30, 2-light, 6" 35.00
First Love, crystal, candy jar, #25, ftd, w/lid, 5x7¼" ...85.00
First Love, crystal, cocktail shaker, #5200, 14-oz 145.00
First Love, crystal, creamer, #111, 10-oz, 3" 18.00

First Love, crystal, mayonnaise, #111, hdld, w/7" tray 35.00
First Love, crystal, pitcher, #5200 ....175.00
First Love, crystal, plate, #111, 7½" 1,900.00
First Love, crystal, plate, #115, 8½" 20.00
First Love, crystal, relish, #115, 10½x7" 37.50
First Love, crystal, stem, juice; #5111½, ftd, 5-oz, 5¾" 24.00
First Love, crystal, tray, celery; #91, 8¾" 30.00
First Love, crystal, urn, #111, 4½x4½" 27.50
First Love, crystal, vase, #505, 8½x2¾" 110.00
Lily of the Valley, crystal, ashtray, 6" 25.00
Lily of the Valley, crystal, cheese & cracker 75.00
Lily of the Valley, crystal, mayonnaise liner 15.00
Lily of the Valley, crystal, plate, 9" 45.00
Lily of the Valley, crystal, stem, cocktail 22.00
Lily of the Valley, crystal, stem, water goblet 40.00
Nautical, bl, marmalade 65.00
Nautical, bl, tumbler, bar; 2-oz 25.00
Nautical, blue, ashtray, 3" 20.00
Nautical, crystal, plate, 10" 25.00
Nautical, crystal, tumbler, orange juice; ftd 15.00
Nautical, opal, candy jar, w/lid 650.00
Nautical, opal, decanter 650.00
Sandwich, crystal, basket, w/loop hdl, 11½" 250.00
Sandwich, crystal, bonbon, ftd, w/lid, 7½" 50.00
Sandwich, crystal, bowl, finger; 4" 12.50
Sandwich, crystal, bowl, gardenia; 11½" 45.00
Sandwich, crystal, bowl, nappy; w/ring hdl, 6" 18.00
Sandwich, crystal, bowl, salad; deep, 10" 75.00
Sandwich, crystal, butter dish, w/lid, ¼-lb 40.00
Sandwich, crystal, candlestick, 1-light, 4" 15.00
Sandwich, crystal, candy dish, sq, 6" 395.00
Sandwich, crystal, cigarette holder, ftd, 3" 27.50
Sandwich, crystal, comport, ftd, 4¼" 20.00
Sandwich, crystal, comport, 2¼" 15.00
Sandwich, crystal, creamer, ftd, 7-oz, 4" 9.00
Sandwich, crystal, jelly, ind, 3" 7.00
Sandwich, crystal, pitcher, metal lid, 13-oz 70.00
Sandwich, crystal, plate, dinner; 9½" 45.00
Sandwich, crystal, plate, finger bowl liner; 6½" 8.00
Sandwich, crystal, plate, hostess; 16" 125.00
Sandwich, crystal, relish, oval, 2-part, 7" 20.00
Sandwich, crystal, relish, 3-part, 12" 40.00
Sandwich, crystal, saucer, w/ring, 6" 5.00
Sandwich, crystal, shakers, w/glass lids, 2½", pr 18.00
Sandwich, crystal, stem, champagne; 5-oz, 5¼" 20.00
Sandwich, crystal, stem, cocktail; 3-oz, 4¼" 15.00
Sandwich, crystal, sugar bowl, 5-oz 7.50
Sandwich, crystal, tray, celery; oval, 10" 18.00
Sandwich, crystal, tray, pickle; oval, 7" 15.00
Sandwich, crystal, tumbler, iced tea; flat, 13-oz, 5¼" 21.50
Sandwich, crystal, vase, ftd, 10" 75.00
Spiral Flutes, amber, gr or pk, bowl, almond; 2" 13.00
Spiral Flutes, amber, gr or pk, bowl, baked apple; flanged, 7½" 22.50
Spiral Flutes, amber, gr or pk, bowl, console; cupped, 12" 32.50
Spiral Flutes, amber, gr or pk, bowl, nappy; 8" 17.50
Spiral Flutes, amber, gr or pk, cigarette holder, 4" 35.00
Spiral Flutes, amber, gr or pk, creamer, oval 8.00
Spiral Flutes, amber, gr or pk, lamp, countess; 10½" 295.00
Spiral Flutes, amber, gr or pk, plate, pie; 6" 3.00
Spiral Flutes, amber, gr or pk, platter, 11" 35.00
Spiral Flutes, amber, gr or pk, saucer 3.00
Spiral Flutes, amber, gr or pk, stem, parfait; 4½-oz, 5⅝" 17.50
Spiral Flutes, amber, gr or pk, sweetmeat, w/lid, 7½" 115.00
Spiral Flutes, amber, gr or pk, tumbler, ginger ale; 11-oz, 5½" 70.00

Tear Drop, crystal, ashtray, 5" 8.00
Tear Drop, crystal, basket, flower; loop hdl, 12" 145.00
Tear Drop, crystal, bowl, gardenia; 13" 35.00
Tear Drop, crystal, bowl, nappy; hdls, 5" 8.00
Tear Drop, crystal, bowl, salad; 9" 27.50
Tear Drop, crystal, candlestick, 4" 9.50
Tear Drop, crystal, celery dish, hdls, 11" 15.00
Tear Drop, crystal, comport, ftd, 4¾" 12.00
Tear Drop, crystal, creamer, 6-oz 7.00
Tear Drop, crystal, mustard jar, w/lid, 4¼" 35.00
Tear Drop, crystal, olive dish, 2-part, 6" 15.00
Tear Drop, crystal, plate, lemon; hdls, 7" 12.50
Tear Drop, crystal, plate, torte; 14" 37.00
Tear Drop, crystal, relish, hdls, 2-part, 7" 15.00

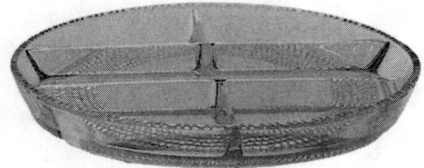

**Tear Drop, crystal, six-part relish, 12",
$30.00.** (Photo courtesy Gene Florence)

Tear Drop, crystal, relish, 5-part, rnd, 12" 35.00
Tear Drop, crystal, shakers, 5", pr 25.00
Tear Drop, crystal, stem, ale; 8-oz, 6¼" 15.00
Tear Drop, crystal, tumbler, iced tea; 14-oz, 6" 17.50
Tear Drop, crystal, tumbler, juice; ftd, 4½-oz, 4" 8.00
Tear Drop, crystal, tumbler, whiskey; flat, 2-oz, 2¼" 18.00
Tear Drop, crystal, vase, ftd, rnd, 9" 37.50
Terrace, cobalt or red, bowl, finger; #5111½, 4¼" 40.00
Terrace, cobalt or red, comport, w/lid, 8¾x5½" 425.00
Terrace, cobalt or red, pitcher 995.00
Terrace, cobalt or red, plate, cracker; w/ring, hdld, 11" 110.00
Terrace, cobalt or red, sugar bowl, 10-oz, 3" 45.00
Terrace, cobalt or red, urn, 10½x4½" 450.00
Terrace, crystal or amber, ashtray, sq, 3½" 17.50
Terrace, crystal or amber, bowl, ftd, flared rim, 10x3¾" 55.00
Terrace, crystal or amber, bowl, hdls, 2½x9½" 45.00
Terrace, crystal or amber, candle, low, 4" 25.00
Terrace, crystal or amber, mayonnaise, crimped, 5½x3½" 32.00
Terrace, crystal or amber, plate, sq, 7½" 19.00
Terrace, crystal or amber, plate, torte; rolled edge, 13" 57.50
Terrace, crystal or amber, stem, claret; #5111½, 4½-oz, 6" 45.00

Durand

Durand art glass was made by the Vineland Flint Glass Works of Vineland, New Jersey. Victor Durand Jr. was the sole proprietor. The division called the 'fancy shop' was geared to the production of fine hand-blown art glass in the style of Tiffany and Steuben. Lustered glass and opal glass were used as a base to create such patterns as King Tut, Heart and Vine, Peacock Feather, and Egyptian Crackle. Cased glass was used to produce cut designs. Production of art glass began in 1924 and continued until 1931. Although most of this art glass was unsigned, when it was, it was generally signed within the pontil 'Durand' or 'Durand' written across the top of a large letter V, all in silver script. The numbers that sometimes appear along with the signature indicate the shape and height of the object. Owner Victor Durand employed the owner and several workers from the failed Quezal Art Glass and Decorating Co. This is why early Durand may sometimes look similar to Quezal art glass. In 1926 Durand art glass was awarded a medal of honor at the Sesquicentennial International Exposition in Philadelphia, Pennsylvania. Our advisor for this category is Edward J. Meschi, author of *Durand — The Man and His Glass* (Antique Publications); he is listed in the Directory under New Jersey.

Vase, King Tut, gold lustre with blue, applied foot, 14", $1,750.00. (Photo courtesy Edward J. Meschi)

Bowl, feathers, red/opal on red over clear, 3x12½" 825.00
Bowl, finger; ambergirs w/gr trim, 2½x5", w/6½" underplate 225.00
Bowl, heart & vines, bl on dk bl, acorn form w/amber ft, 7"....1,700.00
Bowl, hearts & vines, wht on bl irid, 2x4¼" 575.00
Bowl, peacock feathers, opal/gr on gr over crystal, 4x9½" 650.00
Bowl, yel lustre, wht-trim ft, bl/wht crisscross bands, 4½x10½" .800.00
Candlesticks, ruby w/Spanish Yellow cup/stem, ruby ft, 6", pr 825.00
Champagne, Optic Ribbed, amethyst, 4" 175.00
Champagne, ruby flashed w/Spanish Yellow stem, ruby ft, 6" 325.00
Champagne, Spanish Yellow w/gr trim, 7" 150.00
Cocktail, peacock feathers, opal/red on red on crystal, 4½" 325.00
Compote, King Tut, bl w/gold irid int, 6½x6" 825.00
Compote, Optic Rib, ruby w/Spanish Yellow stem, ruby ft, 4x7½"..625.00
Creamer, peacock feathers, opal/ruby on ruby flashed, crystal hdl/ft .425.00
Darner, gr/red/gold pulled feathers w/gold irid dots 1,200.00
Flower spill, feathers, red/opal on crystal, 8" 925.00
Goblet, feathers, opal on red over crystal, crystal stem/ft, 6".......350.00
Goblet, feathers, opal on royal bl, amber stem/base, 7" 425.00
Goblet, geometric zipper, bl over crystal, crystal/stem/ft, 7" 450.00
Goblet, peacock feathers, opal/red on red to clear, yel stem/ft, 7"..350.00
Ice bucket, bl to clear, honeycomb vesicas/X-hatch dmns, SP rim/bail...675.00
Jar, bl irid w/bl threading, yel florette on lid, 9x10" 1,950.00
Jar, King Tut, gr w/gold decor, amber prunt on lid, 7" 3,100.00
Lamp base, gold irid w/overall gold threading, 18½x7" 325.00
Pitcher, red crystal crackle, appl hdl, 8½" 1,425.00
Plate, Optic Rib, bl, scalloped rim, 11½" 150.00
Plate, pulled feathers, opal on ruby w/frosted center, 8" 325.00
Shade, Egyptian Craquelle, ruby & wht over ambergris base, 5x7"..450.00
Sherbet, feathers, wht on Spanish yellow w/bl & wht trim, 4" ...425.00
Torchiere, leaves & vine gr/wht trumpet shade, CI base, 71", pr ..1,500.00
Tumbler, iced tea; ambergris w/gr trim, 6" 100.00
Tumbler, iced tea; feathers, gr/opal on gr on yel lustre, apple ft, 6" .375.00
Tumbler, lemonade; Optic Rib, ambergris w/gr trim, 5½" 125.00
Vase, amber w/gold irid, beehive form, #1978, ca 1925, 13" 925.00
Vase, Beehive, bl irid, #20177, 6½" 975.00
Vase, bl crystal crackle, hard ribbed, w/lustre, 10" 1,300.00
Vase, bl irid, amber rim-to-hip hdls, #2010-12", 12" 1,350.00
Vase, bl irid, cylindrical, polished pontil, 1968, 8"....................825.00
Vase, bl irid, waisted w/flared rim, 6¼" 850.00

Vase, bl irid w/bl threading, #1812-8, 7½", NM 875.00
Vase, bl irid w/gold & silver swirls, urn shape, orange int, 9¼" ..1,500.00
Vase, bl w/wht peacock feathers, disk ft, #2028½", 8", NM 950.00
Vase, clear w/controlled air trap, ovoid, #1995, 4x4" 200.00
Vase, coil decor, bl on gold, 10½" 1,200.00
Vase, cut o/l, red to clear, 9" 2,250.00
Vase, Egyptian Crackle, gr/wht on lustre-amber, 10x12" 1,875.00
Vase, feathers, opal & red on red to clear, appl ft, 12" 1,150.00
Vase, geometric cuttings, red to crystal, 10" 1,450.00
Vase, gold irid, ftd, flared rim, 10½" 450.00
Vase, heart & vine, bl irid on orange-gold, #1969-10, 9¾" 1,325.00
Vase, hearts & vines, opal on bl irid, can neck w/2 rings, 10" .1,750.00
Vase, hearts & vines, opal on bl irid, gold disk ft, 8x3" 1,200.00
Vase, hearts & vines, silver on cobalt irid, vasiform, 9½" 1,950.00
Vase, hearts & vines allover, opal on bl irid, #1812-7, 7½" 1,300.00
Vase, King Tut, bl irid w/bl-opal swirled veins, ruffled, 7" 1,000.00
Vase, King Tut, bl on gold lustre, #1710, 4¼" 1,250.00
Vase, King Tut, gr on orange, #1812-V-6, 6" 1,050.00
Vase, King Tut, wht on gold, 10" 875.00
Vase, Lady Gay Rose w/irid coils, squat/ftd w/long neck, 12½" ..3,100.00
Vase, marigold irid w/overall gold threading, stick form, 9½" 850.00
Vase, Optic Ribbed, amethyst w/appl ft, 8" 575.00
Vase, red hard-ribbed Moorish crackle w/lustre, 7½" 1,875.00
Vase, red ribbed crackle over crystal w/lustre, 6" 1,800.00

Easter

In the early 1900s to the 1930s, Germany made the first composition candy containers in the shapes of Easter rabbits, ducks, and chicks. A few were also made of molded cardboard. In the 1940s West Germany made candy containers out of molded cardboard. Many of these had spring necks to give a nodding effect. From the 1930s and into the 1950s, United States manufacturers made Easter candy containers out of egg-carton material (pulp) or pressed cardboard. Ducks and chicks are not as high in demand as rabbits. Rabbits with painted-on clothes or attached fabric clothes bring more than the plain brown or white rabbits. When no condition mentioned in the description, assume that values reflect excellent to near mint condition for all but paper items; those assume to be in near mint to mint condition. Our advisor for this category is Jenny Tarrant; she is listed in the Directory under Missouri.

Note: In the candy container section, measurements given for the rabbit and cart or rabbit and wagon containers indicate the distance to the tip of the rabbits' ears.

Candy Containers

German, begging rabbit, brn w/glass eyes, compo, 1900-30s, 5" 95.00
German, begging rabbit, brn w/glass eyes, compo, 1900-30s, 6" ..125.00
German, begging rabbit, brn w/glass eyes, compo, 1900-30s, 7" ..150.00
German, begging rabbit, brn w/glass eyes, compo, 1900-30s, 8" ..175.00
German, begging rabbit, brn w/glass eyes, compo, 1900-30s, 9" ..250.00
German, begging rabbit, mohair covered, compo, 1900-30s, 4" ..150.00
German, begging rabbit, mohair covered, compo, 1900-30s, 5" ..175.00
German, begging rabbit, mohair covered, compo, 1900-30s, 6" ..250.00
German, begging rabbit, mohair covered, compo, 1900-30s, 7" ..275.00
German, duck, yel w/glass eyes, compo, 1900-30s, 5" 110.00
German, duck or chick, pnt-on clothes, compo, 1900-30s, 3-4" ..125.00
German, duck or chick, pnt-on clothes, compo, 1900-30s, 5" 145.00
German, duck or chick, pnt-on clothes, compo, 1900-30s, 6" 185.00
German, duck or chick, pnt-on clothes, compo, 1900-30s, 7" 200.00
German, egg, molded cb, 1900-30, 3-7", from $65 to 85.00
German, egg, molded cb, 1900-30, 8"..100.00
German, egg, tin, 1900-10, EX, 2-3", from $65 to 75.00

German, rabbit (dressed) in car, compo, 1900-30s, from $250 to ..**325.00**
German, rabbit (dressed) in shoe, compo, 1900-30s, from $250 to ..**325.00**
German, rabbit (dressed) on egg, compo, 1900-30s, from $250 to ...**325.00**
German, rabbit (dressed) on log, compo, 1900-30s, from $200 to....**250.00**

German, Ma and Pa Rabbit, hand-painted molded card-board, heads remove for candy, 1920s, 10½", $340.00 each.

German, rabbit pulling wood cart, mohair covered, 1900-30s, 4"..**250.00**
German, rabbit pulling wood cart, mohair covered, 1900-30s, 5"..**275.00**
German, rabbit pulling wood cart, mohair covered, 1900-30s, 6"..**300.00**
German, rabbit pulling wood cart, mohair covered, 1900-30s, 7"..**375.00**
German, rabbit pulling wood wagon, brn compo, 1900-30s, 4"...**195.00**
German, rabbit pulling wood wagon, brn compo, 1900-30s, 5"...**250.00**
German, rabbit pulling wood wagon, brn compo, 1900-30s, 6"...**275.00**
German, rabbit pulling wood wagon, brn compo, 1900-30s, 7"...**325.00**
German, rabbit w/fabric clothes, compo, 1900-30s, 4" **250.00**
German, rabbit w/fabric clothes, compo, 1900-30s, 5" **300.00**
German, rabbit w/fabric clothes, compo, 1900-30s, 6" **350.00**
German, rabbit w/fabric clothes, compo, 1900-30s, 7" **400.00**
German, rabbit w/glass beading, compo, 1900-30s, 6" **150.00**
German, rabbit w/pnt-on clothes, compo, 1900-30s, 4" **150.00**
German, rabbit w/pnt-on clothes, compo, 1900-30s, 5" **200.00**
German, rabbit w/pnt-on clothes, compo, 1900-30s, 6" **250.00**
German, rabbit w/pnt-on clothes, compo, 1900-30s, 7" **300.00**
German, sitting rabbit, brn w/glass eyes, compo, 1900-30s, 5" **95.00**
German, sitting rabbit, brn w/glass eyes, compo, 1900-30s, 6" **110.00**
German, sitting rabbit, brn w/glass eyes, compo, 1900-30s, 7" **125.00**
German, sitting rabbit, mohair covered, compo, 1900-30s, 4" **150.00**
German, sitting rabbit, mohair covered, compo, 1900-30s, 5" **175.00**
German, sitting rabbit, mohair covered, compo, 1900-30s, 6" **225.00**
German, walking rabbit, brn w/glass eyes, compo, 1900-30s, 5"..**110.00**
German, walking rabbit, brn w/glass eyes, compo, 1900-30s, 6"..**125.00**
German, walking rabbit, brn w/glass eyes, compo, 1900-30s, 7"..**150.00**
German, walking rabbit, brn w/glass eyes, compo, 1900-30s, 8"..**175.00**
German, walking rabbit, brn w/glass eyes, compo, 1900-30s, 9"..**250.00**
German, walking rabbit, mohair covered, compo, 1900-30s, 4"..**195.00**
German, walking rabbit, mohair covered, compo, 1900-30s, 5"..**225.00**
German, walking rabbit, mohair covered, compo, 1900-30s, 6"..**250.00**
German, walking rabbit, mohair covered, compo, 1900-30s, 7"..**275.00**
German, walking rabbit, wht, compo, 1900-30s, 6" **125.00**
German, wht w/pnt-on clothes, compo, 1900-30s, 3" **125.00**
US, begging rabbit, pulp, 1940-50 ....**55.00**
US, sitting rabbit, pulp, brn w/glass eyes, Burk Co, 1930 ....**140.00**
US, sitting rabbit, pulp, no basket, 1940-50 ....**60.00**
US, sitting rabbit next to lg basket, pulp, 1930-50 ....**125.00**
US, sitting rabbit w/basket on bk, pulp, 1940-50 ....**95.00**
W German, egg, molded cb, 1940-60, 3-8", from $25 to **40.00**
W German/US Zone, dressed chick, cb, spring neck, 1940-50......**65.00**
W German/US Zone, dressed duck, cb, spring neck, 1940-50.......**65.00**
W German/US Zone, dressed rabbit, cb, spring neck, 1940-50.....**95.00**
W German/US Zone, plain rabbit, cb, spring neck, 1940-50 ....**75.00**

Miscellaneous

Celluloid chick or duck, dressed, 3-5", M...............................**45.00**
Celluloid chick or duck, dressed, 6-8" **75.00**
Celluloid chicken pulling wagon w/rabbit, M **125.00**
Celluloid rabbit, dressed, 3-5", M...**65.00**
Celluloid rabbit, dressed, 6-8", M...**75.00**
Celluloid rabbit, plain, 3-5", M..**20.00**
Celluloid rabbit, plain, 6-7", M..**30.00**
Celluloid rabbit & chick in swan boat, M..............................**150.00**
Celluloid rabbit driving car, M **150.00**
Celluloid rabbit pulling wagon, M **125.00**
Celluloid rabbit pushing or pulling cart, lg, M **125.00**
Celluloid rabbit pushing or pulling cart, sm, M......................**75.00**
Celluloid windup toy, Japan or Occupied Japan, M **150.00**
Celluloid windup toy, Japan or Occupied Japan, MIB **195.00**
Cotton batten rabbit w/paper ears, Japan, 1930-50, 2-5", $30 to ..**45.00**
Cotton batten rabbit w/paper ears, Japan, 1930-50, 6" **85.00**

Egg Cups

Egg cups, one of the fastest growing collectibles of the '90s, have been traced back to the ruins of Pompeii. Since then, they have been made in almost every country and in almost every conceivable material (ceramics, glass, metal, papier-mache, plastic, wood, ivory, even rubber and straw). Popular categories include Art Deco, Black Memorabilia, Chintz, Characters/Personalities, Golliwoggs, Railroadiana, Steamship, and Souvenir Ware.

Still being produced today in most countries, egg cups appeal to collectors on many levels. Prices can range from quite inexpensive to many thousands of dollars. Those made prior to 1840 are scarce and sought after, as are the character/personality egg cups of the 1930s.

For a more thorough study of egg cups we recommend that you refer to *Egg Cups: An Illustrated History and Price Guide* (Antique Publications) by Brenda Blake, our advisor for this category. You will find her address listed in the Directory under Maine.

Key:
bkt — bucket, a single cup
  without a foot
dbl — 2-sided with small
  end for eating egg in shell,
  large end for mixing egg
  with toast and butter
fig — figural, an egg cup
  actually molded into the
  shape of an animal, bird,
  car, person, etc.

hoop — hoop, a single open
  cup with waistline
inst. dbl — large custard cup shape
set — tray or cruet
  (stand, frame or basket)
  with 2 to 8 cups
sgl — single, with a foot;
  goblet shaped

American China/Pottery

Bkt, mustard ground, Paul Revere Pottery.............................**90.00**
Dbl, Arizona, Eva Zeisel, Hall, 1950s **28.00**
Dbl, Autumn Leaf, Hall's Autumn Leaf Collector's Club gift, 1997 ...**55.00**
Dbl, Brittany, Homer Laughlin **20.00**
Dbl, Chick, Juvenile, Roseville, ca 1917 ....**235.00**
Dbl, English Abbey, Taylor Smith & Taylor.............................**32.00**
Dbl, Homespun, plaid, Vernon Kilns, 1950s...........................**22.00**
Dbl, Lu Ray, pk **25.00**
Dbl, Norma, Blue Ridge **35.00**
Dbl, Polar Bear, Dedham...**550.00**
Dbl, Rustic Plaid, Blue Ridge, 1950s.......................................**25.00**
Dbl, Strawberry, Blue Ridge, 1950s...**45.00**

Inst dbl, Rosebud, Coors, 1940s **65.00**
Sgl, Desert Rose, Franciscan **32.00**
Sgl, Turquoise Blue, Lenox, ca 1911 ....**55.00**
Sgl, Vistosa, lt gr, Taylor Smith & Taylor, ca 1940 ....**38.00**
Sgl, Yellow Ware, no decor, ca 1880 ....**325.00**

Characters/Personalities

Bkt, Lone Ranger, molded face against stump, Keele St Pottery, 1961 ..**105.00**
Bkt, Marilyn Monroe, transfer, ca 1993 ....**3.50**
Bkt, Tonto, molded face against stump, Keele St Pottery, 1961 ....**80.00**
Dbl, Little Red Riding Hood, Columbia China **20.00**
Fig, Andy Gump, Germany **150.00**
Fig, Betty Boop, lustreware figural of face w/earrings, Japan, 1930s ..**325.00**
Fig, Mickey Mouse, knock off, blk ears, red bow tie, blk gloves, unmk ..**250.00**
Fig, Pink Panther, seated w/cup between legs, Royal Orleans **150.00**
Fig, Popeye, squatting, smoking pipe **115.00**
Fig, Ronald Reagan, Spitting Image, Luck & Flaw, 1980s **90.00**
Fig, Stan Laurel, face in relief, mk Foreign **185.00**
Set, Beatles, 4 buckets, blk/wht portrait sketches, Keele St Pottery ...**240.00**
Sgl, Basil Brush, Coalport, 1977 ....**35.00**
Sgl, Holly Hobbie w/bl bonnet, 1960s **20.00**
Sgl, Mickey Mouse, SP, w/attached figural **110.00**
Sgl, Teletubbies, w/box & chocolate egg **13.00**

Figurals

Bear, orange lustre, Foreign **48.00**
Bluebird, Lefton **40.00**
Boat, orange, Honiton **24.00**

Boy, marked Occupied Japan, 2⅜", $17.50.

Car, pk & blk, mouse driver, St James **40.00**
Cat, hdld, Portugal **15.00**
Cat salt attached to wht cup w/magnet, Rot Ceramic, Germany, 1980s ..**20.00**
Donkey pulling cart, cobalt, Italy **20.00**
Face, male, Au Grand Dud Bethune, R Fredric-Degeorges **35.00**
Golly, gr polka-dot tie, recent **56.00**
Grandmother, hdld, gray boots **15.00**
Man reading newspaper, soap egg **18.00**
Pig, seated, orange hat band & tie, Japan **65.00**
Quail, Goebel **35.00**
Rabbit, face molded on cup, gold lustre **16.00**
Rabbit, repro Dedham, The Potting Shed, 1990 ....**35.00**
Rabbit & cart, brn & gr trim **12.00**
Truck, aqua, transporting wht cup **18.00**
Whistler, train, lustre **120.00**

Foreign

Dbl, Alpine Peasant Ware, Germany **14.00**
Dbl, Azalea, Noritake **45.00**

Dbl, Breton, Quimper, recent **40.00**
Set, flowers & sprigs, 6 cups on stand, Royal Bonn, ca 1900 ....**195.00**
Sgl, Capo-di-Monte, emb figures, 19th C **175.00**
Sgl, Elfinware, Moss Ware **95.00**
Sgl, majolica, Onnaing, France **135.00**
Sgl, Oriole, Goebel, 1989 ....**21.00**
Sgl, Regina, Gouda, 1920s **115.00**
Sgl, Rothchild's Bird, Herend **72.00**
Sgl, stag, gr, HP, Gmunder, 1990s **20.00**
Sgl, Vieux Luxembourt, Villeroy & Boch **20.00**

Glass

Dbl, Ashburton, clambroth, ca 1850 ....**170.00**
Dbl, Cape Cod, crystal, Imperial Glass Co, ca 1932 ....**38.00**
Dbl, Chalaine Blue, McKee **24.00**
Dbl, Jade-ite Green **32.00**
Fig, bunny, Fenton **30.00**
Fig, chick, milk glass, hdld, Westmoreland **22.00**
Sgl, cameo, floral, Daum Nancy, ca 1900 ....**1,350.00**
Sgl, Flamingo, Heisey **50.00**
Sgl, Messena, Baccarat, 1970s **50.00**
Sgl, Moongleam, Heisey **40.00**
Sgl, Rock Crystal, McKee **14.00**

Railroad

Inst dbl, Milwaukee Traveler **55.00**
Inst dbl, Richmond, Fredericksburg & Potomac, Tri-Link pattern, 1927 ...**500.00**
Sgl, Chicago & Northwestern, 1985 ....**20.00**
Sgl, Denver & Rio Grande, recent **10.00**
Sgl, NYC Dewitt Clinton **175.00**
Sgl, Reading Railroad, SP, Rowley Mfg Co **300.00**
Sgl, Union Pacific, Desert Flower **78.00**

Souvenir

Bkt, British Airways, bl border, silver stripes, Royal Doulton **14.00**
Bkt, British navy, gold crown & anchor, Royal Tuscan, 1980s **15.00**
Bkt, Raffles, Churchill Hotelware, 1995 ....**12.00**
Dbl, Am Legion Auxilliary, maroon seal **25.00**
Dbl, McGill University, maroon seal, 1930s **35.00**
Dbl, Mt Rushmore Nat'l Memorial, transfer, Japan, 1930s **15.00**
Dbl, The Haverford School, maroon & gold crest **20.00**
Dbl, Wyoming Seminary, bl seal **18.00**
Dbl, Zeppelin Deutsche Aeromail, gold rim, bl stripe, Heinrich ...**1,200.00**
Fig, Harrods' Doorman, Wade, 1990s **40.00**
Inst dbl, Annapolis, 1930s **35.00**
Sgl, Channel Tunnel 1988-94, 1994 ....**16.00**
Sgl, Conservation Authorities Conference, Toronto, wooden, 1958 ..**15.00**
Sgl, Hotel Clarenden Seabreeze FL, Germany **16.00**
Sgl, Lazarus Stores 89th Anniversary, turq, Fiesta, 1940 ....**120.00**
Sgl, New York & Brooklyn Bridge, transfer, Germany, ca 1910 ....**40.00**
Sgl, Ritz Carlton Hotel, gr & pk criss-cross border, Rosenthal **25.00**
Sgl, Soldier's Monument, Gettysburg PA, transfer, Germany, ca 1900 ...**38.00**
Sgl, World's Fair, St Louis, transfer, 1904 ....**130.00**

Staffordshire

Bkt, bl polka dots & stripes on tan, Susie Cooper, 1930s **28.00**
Bkt, Golly, fluted, MacDonald, 1980s **25.00**
Dbl, Calyx Ware, Adams **22.00**
Dbl, Ferrara, red transfer, Wedgwood **36.00**
Dbl, Holland, flow bl, Johnson Bros, ca 1891 ....**70.00**

Dbl, Mr Snowman w/dish hat, Royal Doulton **90.00**
Dbl, Osborne, flow bl, Ridgways, ca 1905 ....**115.00**
Dbl, Troika, side-by-side, ca 1965 ....**100.00**
Dbl, Vincent, Wedgwood, 1951 ....**24.00**
Dbl, Vista, red, Masons..**35.00**
Set, Du Barry, chintz, James Kent.....................................**180.00**
Sgl, Bunnykins, sgn Vernon, Royal Doulton, ca 1937 ....**150.00**
Sgl, Cambridge, flow bl, New Wharf Pottery **80.00**
Sgl, Caneware, Wedgwood, ca 1820 ....**325.00**
Sgl, Castle, brn transfer, ca 1850 ....**125.00**
Sgl, Cottage, Watcombe Torquay......................................**30.00**
Sgl, Dainty Blue, 6-flute, Shelley......................................**75.00**
Sgl, Jasperware, Dance of the Hours, Wedgwood, 1995 ....**32.00**
Sgl, Pixie, Mabel Lucie Atwell **190.00**
Sgl, Real Old Willow, Booth...**40.00**
Sgl, 3 goats legs, triangle base, ca 1815 ....**375.00**

Steamship/Cruise Ship

Bkt, AF Klaveness & Co, red & bl swallowtail pennant **20.00**
Bkt, NAC, Cunard, bl & gold band, Porsgrund **22.00**
Dbl, Canadian Nat'l System, bl & red flag, Grindley **80.00**
Dbl, Dollar Steamships Lines, President Hoover pattern, ca 1930 .**85.00**
Dbl, United States Lines, Lamberton **78.00**
Hoop, British & Commonwealth..**55.00**
Hoop, Norddeutscher Lloyd Bremen, ca 1910 ....**200.00**
Hoop, Queen Mary, Booths & Colcloughs.........................**55.00**
Hoop, Union Steamship Co, Dunn Bennett & Co.....................**50.00**
Hoop, White Star, bl garland, ca 1915 ....**600.00**
Hoop, White Star Line, turq, repro, 1990s.........................**150.00**
Sgl, HMS Aquitania, SP, pierced/scalloped rim, enameled crest.**140.00**

Elfinware

Made in Germany from about 1920 until the 1940s, these miniature vases, boxes, salt cellars, and miscellaneous novelty items are characterized by the tiny applied flowers that often cover their entire surface. Pieces with animals and birds are the most valuable, followed by the more interesting examples such as diminutive grand pianos, candle holders, etc. Items covered in 'spinach' (applied green moss) can be valued at 75% to 100% higher than pieces that are not decorated in this manner. See also Salts, Open.

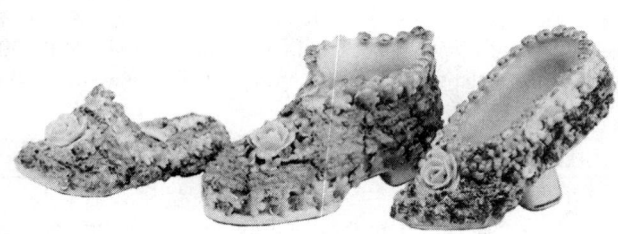

Slippers, applied flowers and green 'spinach,' various styles and sizes, ca 1920, $65.00 each. (Photo courtesy Earlene Wheatley)

Basket, appl flower, much spinach, 2x3x2"..............................**70.00**
Basket, criss-crossed hdls, appl flowers & spinach, 2¼x2½"..........**70.00**
Box, appl flowers & spinach, 4½x5½x4½"............................**50.00**
Chair, appl flowers, 2¾x1½"...**50.00**
Dog, appl spinach, 2¼", EX...**280.00**
Grand piano, appl flowers & spinach, 3½x6x4" **200.00**
Grand piano, appl roses/pansies/daisies/spinach, 5x6½" **260.00**

Salt cellar, swan w/appl flowers & spinach, 2¼" **65.00**
Shakers, appl flowers & spinach, NM, pr............................**200.00**
Shoe, pointed toe, appl flowers & spinach, Margate on side, 2¾" ...**60.00**
Shoe w/high-heel, rose on toe, appl flowers & spinach, 2x3".......**70.00**
Teapot, appl flowers & spinach, 2" **60.00**
Vase, appl flowers & spinach, hdls, 3¾".............................**150.00**

Epergnes

Popular during the Victorian era, epergnes were fancy centerpieces often consisting of several tiers of vases (called lilies), candle holders, dishes, or a combination of components. They were made in all types of art glass, and some were set in ornate plated frames.

Amethyst frost to clear, 1-lily; bronze-finish ft, 16x10" **365.00**
Clear opal w/cranberry rim, 3-lily, ruffled bowl, 15" **550.00**
Crystal overshot w/cranberry rim, 1-lily in 10" bowl **330.00**
Gr overshot bowl w/matching lily; ormolu base, 16½x9½".......**325.00**
Pk opal lilies (4); 3-ftd scrolling SP base, 16" **475.00**
Pk satin irid, 4-trumpet; SP griffin fr, 16"........................**4,250.00**
Rose o/l w/HP flroal, 1-lily, clear ruffle; ormolu fr, 11½" **250.00**

Erickson

Carl Erickson of Bremen, Ohio, produced hand-formed glassware from 1943 until 1960 in artistic shapes, no two of which were identical. One of the characteristics of his work was the air bubbles that were captured within the glass. Though most examples are clear, colored items were also made. Rather than to risk compromising his high standards by selling the factory, when Erickson retired, the plant was dismantled and sold.

Bowl, amber over crystal, paperweight, 8" **65.00**
Candlestick, gr, controlled bubbles, paperweight, tall, pr **137.50**
Compote, smoke, clear paperweight base, 9¾x7¼" **275.00**
Decanter, clear w/purple lining, 6"+bubble-filled stopper............**100.00**
Pitcher, gr to clear, 9½", +pr 4" old-fashioned tumblers..............**170.00**
Vase, smoke, clear paperweight base w/bubbles, 6½" **45.00**

Erphila

The Erphila trademark was used by Ebeling and Ruess Co. of Philadelphia between 1886 and the 1950s. The company imported quality porcelain and pottery from Germany, Czechoslovakia, Italy, and France. Pieces more readily found are from Germany and Czechoslovakia. A variety of items can be found and pieces such as figural teapots and larger figurines are moving up in value. There are a variety of marks, but all contain the name Erphila. One of the earlier marks is a green rectangle containing the name Erphila Germany. In general Erphila pieces are not easily found.

Ashtray, bird & 2 chicks on rim, oval................................**25.00**
Basket, porc, desert scene w/sphinx, Czech **56.00**
Basket, rust, sm, MIG, 4½"..**32.00**
Bookends, Colonial girl & boy, pk & wht, Czech, pr..................**60.00**
Bookends, man/woman, mc, MIG **75.00**
Cake plate, wht flowers, MIG **22.00**
Candlesticks, bl & wht, ea dbl, Czech, pr...........................**45.00**
Celery dish, leaf shape, wht, MIG...................................**27.50**
Charger, majolica, gr grapes in center, blk forest mk **120.00**
Cookie jar, coaching scene, egg shape, 8¼"........................**300.00**
Cookie jar, drinking scene on wht, 9½"............................**115.00**

Creamer, blk silhouette scene on yel, blk hdl, w/lid, 5½" 125.00
Creamer, gr & wht, dog hdl, MIG 72.50
Creamer, pig form, bk & blk, MIG, 8" 98.00
Dish, wheelbarrow shape w/child pushing, mc, MIG, 3x4" 50.00
Dresser doll, Madame Pompadour, yel dress, MIG, 5" 120.00
Dresser doll, Nancy Pert, bl, MIG 140.00
Figurine, beagle dog, mk Germany, 9" 55.00
Figurine, bear, gray, MIG, 1x3" 25.00
Figurine, bull terrier dog, MIG, 5" L 40.00
Figurine, cat, gray & blk, MIG, 3" 45.00
Figurine, cat, sitting, blk & wht, MIG, 4½" 40.00
Figurine, cat, wht w/gold ball, MIG, 12" L 150.00
Figurine, elephant, red, MIG, orig sticker, 3⅛" 53.00
Figurine, fighting cock, wht/mc, 6½x7", pr 100.00
Figurine, fox, wht & tan, MIG, pr 55.00
Figurine, goose, wings spread, wht & gray, MIG 35.00
Figurine, horse rearing, bl, Czech, 7" 30.00
Figurine, pheasant, mc, MIG, 8x10" 72.50
Inkwell, Ink Girls, 2 faces on 1 base, MIG 300.00
Pitcher, chicken figural, red/yel/blk, Czech, chip, 9" 90.00
Pitcher, man in cavalier costume on brn, 9", +3 mugs 235.00
Planter, lady in pleated dress, Czech, 8" 45.00
Planter, red flowers, ring hdls, Czech, 4" 30.00
Planter, woman & children blk silhouette on beige, ring hdls, 4¼" ..55.00
Plate, emb fruit, mc, 8" 25.00
Sprinkling can, wht, orange & gr flowers, 6½" 40.00
Syrup, poppies on wht w/orange trim, w/lid, 5¼" 50.00
Teapot, pig figural, pk & blk, MIG, 8" 150.00
Teapot, rabbit form, brn, MIG, 8½" 125.00
Toothbrush holder, lady figural, wht & bl dress, 8" 40.00
Vase, blk silhouette scene on yel, urn form, 8⅛" 90.00
Vase, wht w/yel rings, 3-leg, 4" 12.50

Eskimo Artifacts

While ivory carvings made from walrus tusks or whale teeth have been the most emphasized articles of Eskimo art, basketry and woodworking are other areas in which these Alaskan Indians excel. Their designs are effected through the application of simple yet dramatic lines and almost stark decorative devices. Though not pursued to the extent of American Indian art, the unique work of these northern tribes is beginning to attract the serious attention of today's collectors.

Basket, Hooper Bay, polychrome decor, ca 1900, 16x13", EX+, $850.00; Mask, hand carved with feather quill extensions, nineteenth century, 17x7", $300.00.

Adz, cvd bone, grooved at hilt end, 3x13", VG 80.00
Boots, sealskin high-top, handmade, gr trade-cloth trim, 1940s, 13" H ..150.00
Bowl, hand-wrought stone, 19th C, 11½" dia 225.00
Cribbage board, wolves' tusk ivory, whaling scene, 1900s, 24x3" .550.00
Cup, cvd from natural shape of whale jawbone, 1880s, 5x3x3" ..170.00
Doll, cvd wood, w/baby, in leather costume, 1900s, 15x4" 250.00
Mask, ivory & baleen, J Kokuluk, ceremonial, 1940s, 5" 300.00
Moccasins, sealksin w/puckered sole, beaded cross on toe, 1920s, 8" .40.00
Model, man in kayak w/harpoon paraphernalia, 1910s, 4x36" 300.00

Necklace, hand-cvd fossil ivory/bone/trade bead hunter's, 19th C, 27"...300.00
Sculpture, man, gr-blk stone, ca 1975, 11x7x3" 150.00
Seal skin separator, bone, 7⅛", G 40.00
Sled runner, bone, notched on both sides, early, 17¼x2¼", VG...80.00

Face Jugs, Contemporary

The most recognizable form of Southern folk pottery is the face jug. Rich alkaline glazes (lustrous greens and browns) are typical, and occasionally shards of glass are applied to the surface of the ware which during firing melts to produce opalescent 'glass runs' over the alkaline. In some locations clay deposits contain elements that result in areas of fluorescent blue or rutile; another variation is swirled or striped ware, reminiscent of eighteenth-century agateware from Staffordshire. Collector demand for these unique one-of-a-kind jugs is at an all-time high and is still escalating. Choice examples made by Burlon B. Craig and Lanier Meaders often bring over $1,000.00 on the secondary market. If you're interested in learning more about this type of folk pottery, contact the Southern Folk Pottery Collectors Society; their address is in the Directory under Clubs, Newsletters, and Catalogs. Our advisor for this category is Billy Ray Hussey; he is listed in the Directory under North Carolina.

China plate teeth, arched eyes, inserted pupils, LD Brown, 1991, 8" ...300.00
China plate teeth, coleslaw brows & mustache, Seagrove, 9¾".........3,325.00
China plate teeth, incised mustache, unglazed eyes, M Hewell, 6⅜"......50.00
China plate teeth, oriental w/mustache, gr/orange, BR Hussy, 1975, 8"....325.00
China plate teeth, pierced eyes, Albany slip glaze mix, 1976, 10" 950.00
China plate teeth, wht glaze eyes w/blk pupils, Hewell, 1993, 9½"........150.00
China teeth, pierced eyes, Albany slip glaze mix, BB Craig, 1976, 10"....950.00
China teeth, stitch scar, dk brn, Brown Pottery, 1930s, 6" 600.00
China teeth, wht clay eyes, single brow, CL Vale, 1986, 11⅜" ...250.00
Clay teeth, beard/mustache, pierced pupils, Cole Pottery, 1980s, 4" ...100.00
Dbl-face (husband/wife), china teeth, wht on red-brn, Brown, 1994, 9" ..175.00
Devil, china teeth w/tongue, streaky gloss, BH (Hussey), 1988, 9" 400.00
Devil, Coca-Cola crushed glass glaze, Craig, 1980s, 12¼" 1,600.00
Devil, curly horns, mustache, dk brn/cream, Allen Ham, 1988, 10⅛" 275.00
Devil, hairy brows/whiskers, dbl-dipped brn, R Brown, 1990s, 14" ..225.00
Devil, pig-style nose, blk/brn w/cream teeth, E Miller, 1980s, 9½"....100.00
Devil, streaky ovoid, pierced ears, Lanier Meaders, 1970s, 8⅞" .2,900.00
Devil, unglazed sharpened teeth, curly horns, Allen Hamm, 1988, 10"..275.00
Devil, wht clay eyes/teeth, red highlights, Anita Meaders, 7⅜" .120.00
Porc teeth & eyes, 1-pc eyebrows, Charles Lisk, 1985-86, 9⅛"....425.00
Rock teeth, pointed ears, appl brows, L Meaders, 1970, 9½"...1,800.00
Unglazed teeth & eyes, olive gloss, Reggie Meaders, 1980s, 9¾" .375.00
Wht clay teeth, cobalt pupils, heavy chin, L Meaders, 1980-82, 9⅝".950.00
Wht clay teeth/eyes, contorted features, mc & buff, B Hussey, 8½"....600.00

Fairings

Fairings are small, brightly colored nineteenth-century hard-paste porcelain objects, largely figural groups and boxes. Most figural fairings portray amusing (if not risque) scenes of courting couples, marital woes, and political satire complete with appropriate base captions.

Fairing boxes, also referred to as trinket boxes, sometimes had captions similar to figural fairings, and often the same figures on top. It was originally assumed that fairings were made in the Staffordshire area. They were referred to as Staffordshire fairings for many years. The European market soon followed producing fairings and boxes since they could be made very inexpensively. England encouraged these markets by not charging import duties. Both the figural fairings and the trinket box fairings were made with the same consumer in mind.

Conta & Boehme of Poessneck, Germany, became the leading maker of both types of fairings. Not all fairings were marked. Those that were had an incised model number, a Roman numeral size number and the painter's number. By 1850 the Conta shield was impressed or raised on the porcelain (with model #), followed by the paper label (1900s). Their mark depicts a bent arm holding a sword inside a shield. After 1891 all wares shipped into the U.S. had to be clearly marked with the country of origin, thus the word Germany was added. The words 'Made in...' were added in 1921.

For more information, we recommend *Victorian Trinket Boxes* by our advisors for this category, Janice and Richard Vogel, and their latest book *Conta & Boehme Porcelain*, published by the authors (see Directory, Florida). Other good 'out of print' references are *Victorian Fairings* by W.S. Bristoe and *Victorian Fairings and Their Values* by Margaret Anderson. Items listed below reflect values for items in very good to excellent condition.

Fairings

Every vehicle driven by a horse, mule, or ass 2d. Toll keeper at toll gate stopping a man riding a bicycle, minimum value, $400.00. (Photo courtesy Janice and Richard Vogel)

Can Can, #2897 ....230.00
Five o'clock tea, #3339.....................................112.00
Kiss me quick, #2865..125.00
Last in bed to put out the lights, #2581...................75.00
O' do leave me a drop, #3350..............................200.00
Returning at one o'clock in the morning, #2857 ....85.00
Sarah's young man, #2874...................................125.00
Shamming sick, #3358.......................................150.00
Tea Party, #3365...150.00
Tug of War, #3336..100.00
Twelve months after marriage, #2858.......................75.00
Walk in please, #2892......................................250.00
When a man is married his troubles begin, #3329 ....150.00
Who is coming?, #3382.......................................70.00
Who said Rats?, #3359......................................150.00

Trinket Boxes

Dresser, boy feeding chicken, #3536...........................175.00
Dresser, boy in bed putting on his trousers, 33576............175.00
Dresser, boy in washtub w/oars, 'Paddling his own canoe,' #3555 ...150.00
Dresser, boy sitting on box eating, dog on his bk, #3577.....150.00
Dresser, boy sitting w/dog, #3590.............................160.00
Dresser, cats (2), #3528.......................................130.00
Dresser, child in bed w/cat on covers, #3566..................175.00
Dresser, dog pulls child's nightshirt, 'Little John in trouble,' #3559 ...200.00
Dresser, dog sitting on pillow, #2959.........................125.00
Dresser, frogs (2) sitting on shell putting on boots, #2962...........175.00
Dresser, girl in bed putting on socks, #3572..................175.00
Dresser, girl on fireplace mantel, #2909......................150.00
Dresser, girl sitting w/kitten in basket, #3589...............90.00

Dresser, Jester sitting on drum, 33505 ....100.00
Dresser, Mary & her lamb, #3543 ....125.00
Dresser, monkey wearing top hat, #3567 ....250.00
Dresser, pug dog & frog, #2981 ....200.00
Dresser, swans (2) & frog, #3520................................50.00
Figural, girl sitting in chair w/ball, 'Grandma,' #2194 ....130.00
Figural, 2 cats in basket, 'After the race,' #3516.............175.00
Vintage, girl in chair, 2 chickens in front, #433.............125.00
Vintage, girl w/book, dog on cushion, #186 ....195.00
Vintage, Mary & her lamb, #255.................................50.00
3-spot, checker player w/1 onlooker, #2100.....................160.00

Fans

The Japanese are said to have invented the fan. From there it went to China, and Portuguese traders took the idea to Europe. Though usually considered milady's accessory, even the gentlemen in seventeenth-century England carried fans! More fashionable than practical, some were of feathers and lovely hand-painted silks with carved ivory or tortoise sticks. Some French fans had peepholes. There are mourning fans, calendar fans, and those with advertising.

Fine antique fans (pre-1900) of ivory or mother-of-pearl are highly desirable. Those from before 1800 often sell for upwards of $1,000.00. Examples with mother-of-pearl sticks are most desirable; least desirable are those with sticks of celluloid. Our advisor for this category is Vicki Flanigan; she is listed in the Directory under Virginia.

Dbl-image, bone brise, parrot scene/flowers, 1820s, 5½" 400.00
Dbl-image, pierced bone w/4 HP scenes, ca 1820, 6" 400.00
HP celluloid, couple w/flowers, gold ribbon & border, 6" closed ...95.00
HP gauze w/putti, MOP sticks, 1890s, 14".........................150.00
HP gauze w/roses, ca 1890, 13" 150.00
HP paper w/figures in garden, lacquered ivory sticks, 1860s, 10" ...350.00
HP peacock feathers w/florals, wood sticks, 22½" 50.00
HP silk cabriolet w/lovers, embr sequins, ivory sticks, 1890s, 12" ..425.00
HP silk scenic, ivory sticks, sequins & mine-cut dmn, 18th C, 12x21"...1,100.00
HP silk w/angel & roses, MOP sticks (damage), 1900s, 20" 215.00
HP silk w/couple reserve, artist sgn, eng celluloid hdl, Fr, NMIB ..135.00
HP silk w/lady & putti, Brussels lace inserts, MOP sticks, 1890s, 13" ...300.00
HP silk w/lady & 2 men in garden, ivory sticks, 17", EX+ 300.00
HP silk w/maidens in flower garden, MOP sticks, 1820-30s, 21", EX .500.00
HP silk w/peonies/fruit/etc, pierced ivory sticks, Canton, 1800, 11" ...600.00
HP woodcut of snow scene, ivory sticks, Japan, late 19th C, 10½" 400.00
HP/embr silk w/cvd ivory sticks, China Export, 1870s, 11"........865.00
Ivory brise, cvd/pierced w/figures/animals/etc, Canton, 1820s, 7" ...550.00
Marriage, HP silk w/lovers, pnt bone sticks, European, 1740s, 11".300.00
Silk w/machine lace trim, cvd/pnt wooden sticks, 1900s, 13" 150.00

Farm Collectibles

Country living in the nineteenth century entailed plowing, planting, and harvesting; gathering eggs and milking; making soap from lard rendered on butchering day; and numerous other tasks performed with primitive tools of which we in the twentieth century have had little first-hand knowledge. Our advisor for this category is Lar Hothem; his address is listed in the Directory under Ohio. See also Cast Iron; Lamps, Lanterns; Woodenware; Wrought Iron.

Bee smoker, late 1800s...30.00
Buckboard wagon, classic style 'pickup' bed, VG.................1,000.00
Buggy seat, maple & ash, 3 arched slats, trn arms, rfn, 1790s, 36" H...1,500.00
Corn planter, wood/leather, iron tip in bottom, dbl ftrest, 1800s..80.00

Corn sheller, Black Beauty, Durbin Durco Inc, St Louis MO, EX .45.00
Corn sheller, Black Hawk H-1903, CI, hand crank, EX 65.00
Corn sheller, Fulton, CI, hand crank, orig wood hdl, EX 45.00
Corn sheller, Jiffy, Ashland O, hand-held, EX 55.00
Corn sheller, Palm-Thumb, orig leather strap, wire thumb cover, EX ...60.00
Cow bell, sheet metal w/sq iron hdl, iron ball clapper, 7x5½x3" ..35.00
Curry comb, iron & brass w/decor, trn wood hdl, 7¾" 110.00
Duster/smoker, all pine w/G old dk patina, 25½" 275.00
Fork, hay; CI, spring-loaded trigger release, #430, 33" 32.00
Fork, hay; red oak, 3-prong, EX 50.00
Fork, shaking; wood, 3-prong, late 1800s, 50" 175.00
Grain probe, brass, early 1900s, 63" 65.00
Hay knife, orig red pnt on hdl, 36½" L, EX 32.00
Hay rack, CI, 19th C, 29x37x17", EX 300.00
Horse collar, EX leather, rpl straps 75.00
Implement seat, Bonanza, CI, 15" 170.00
Implement seat, Hocking Valley, CI, 13x6", EX 200.00
Implement seat, Massey-Harris, CI, 18" W 150.00
Implement seat, PP emb on CI heart shape, old wht pnt 195.00
Implement seat, Stoddard, CI, VG 65.00
Implement seat, Toledo, CI...245.00
Ladle, butchering; wrought iron w/copper rivets, 5½" bowl, 18" hdl ...40.00
Pump, hand; CI w/solid brass cartridge, onion bulb casting, 1880s....175.00
Pump, kitchen; orig gr pnt, 2 GH on hdl, EX 65.00
Rake, hay; all wood, 10-tine, 77" 85.00
Rake, wood, fitted w/8 wooden teeth, early red pnt, 70x25" 30.00
Roof ornament, zinc, full-bodied owl, glass eyes, 19th C, 28"..2,875.00
Rope maker, CI, 3-hook, crank type, dtd 1901, 10". EX..............135.00
Scoop, grain; wood w/orig bl pnt, 19th C, 12x7¾"....................300.00
Seed corn dryer, handmade, primitive metal, 26" L, 24 ears..........20.00
Shovel, grain; softwood, str front edge, arched hdl, 37x12", VG...45.00
Sickle, wrought iron, crescent-shaped blade, 21" L, VG..............25.00
Sieve, copper, rolled rim, ring for hanging, 2¾x13".....................55.00
Single tree, orig old red w/mustard pnt, 33" 25.00
Tool, horse singeing; tin & brass w/turn key, 13¾x5¼"...............25.00
Wagon, grain; Mitchell Co, wood w/old pnt & pinstriping, EX..750.00
Wagon seat, old blk rpt w/gold trim & date: 1776, 35" L............600.00
Wagon seat, rush seat, trn legs & posts, 30x36", EX...................550.00
Wagon seat, splint seat, sq crest, tapering spindles, 1850s, 34x17"...460.00
Yoke, oxen; wood w/old bl pnt, iron ring, 42" 35.00
Yoke, oxen; wood w/3¾" dia iron ring, dbl, 33", EX.....................65.00

Fenton

Frank and John Fenton were brothers who founded the Fenton Art Glass Company in 1906 in Martin's Ferry, Ohio. The venture, at first only a decorating shop, began operations in July of 1905 using blanks purchased from other companies. This operation soon proved unsatisfactory, and by 1907 they had constructed their own glass factory in Williamstown, West Virginia. John left the company in 1909 and organized his own firm in Millersburg, Ohio.

The Fenton Company produced over one hundred thirty patterns of carnival glass. They also made custard, chocolate, opalescent, and stretch glass. This company has always been known for its various colors of glass and has continually changed its production to stay attune with current tastes in decorating. In 1925 they produced a line of 'handmade' items that incorporated the techniques of threading and mosaic work. Because the process proved to be unprofitable, the line was discontinued by 1927. Even their glassware made in the past twenty-five years is already regarded as collectible. Various paper labels have been used since the 1920s; only since 1970 has the logo been stamped into the glass. For further information we recommend *Fenton Art Glass, 1907 – 39*, and *Fenton Art Glass Patterns, 1939 – 1980*, by Margaret and Kenn Whitmyer; *Fenton*

Glass, The Third Twenty-Five Years, by William Heacock (with 1998 value guide); and *Fenton Glass: The 1980s Decade* by Robert E. Eaton, Jr. (1997 values). For information concerning Fenton Art Glass Collectors of America, Inc., see the Clubs, Newsletters, and Catalogs section of the Directory. See also Carnival Glass; Custard Glass; Stretch Glass.

Hobnail, epergne, plum opalescent, three-lily, #371, made for LeVay in 1984, $375.00. (Photo courtesy Lee Garmon)

Apple Blossom Crest, candlestick, #7271 ....60.00
Apple Blossom Crest, vase, dbl-crimped, #7254, 4" 50.00
Aqua Crest, bowl, dbl-crimp, #7321, 11½" 75.00
Aqua Crest, mayonnaise, 3-pc 95.00
Aqua Crest, pitcher, 7" 67.50
Aqua Crest, tidbit tray, 2-tier...65.00
Baroque, candy dish, lav satin, w/lid, 7½" 95.00
Basketweave, basket, ruby, cupped bowl, 6" dia..........................24.00
Beaded Melon, rose bowl, gr o/l, 3 /12" 35.00
Beaded Melon, vase, gr cased, tulip form, sm 35.00
Beaded Melon, vase, gr o/l, 4¼" 40.00
Bicentennial, comport, Patriot, chocolate, w/lid........................195.00
Bicentennial, plate, Lafayette, chocolate 16.50
Big Cookies, basket, Mandarin Red, wicker hdl, 10½"...............170.00
Black Rose, vase, MOP, 10¾" 150.00
Block & Star, candlesticks, milk glass, #5670, pr 18.00
Blue Overlay, basket, #192, 6" 38.00
Burmese, pitcher, no decor, 4½" 50.00
Chinese Yellow, candlestick, #315, 3½", ea................................60.00
Coin Dot, basket, cranberry opal, #1925, 10½" 165.00
Coin Dot, bowl, bl opal, 10" 90.00
Coin Dot, bowl, lime opal, 7" 78.00
Coin Dot, candy jar, cranberry opal, #1522 ....180.00
Coin Dot, creamer, French opal, 4" 32.00
Coin Dot, lamp, French opal, w/chimney, 11" 240.00
Coin Dot, vase, cranberry opal, #3005, 7½"................................65.00
Coin Dot, vase, cranberry opal, 8¼" 130.00
Daisy & Button, bowl, bl, oval, 4-leg, 5½x4"..............................25.00
Daisy & Button, candlesticks, milk glass, 2-light, pr.....................60.00
Daisy & Fern, pitcher, water; cranberry opal...............................255.00
Daisy & Fern, pitcher, water; yel opal 275.00
Dancing Ladies, vase, Mongolian Green, flared rim, #901, 8½" .185.00
Diamond Optic, basket, mulberry, #192, 10½" 475.00
Diamond Optic, basket, ruby o/l, 7"...65.00
Diamond Optic, creamer, ruby o/l...20.00
Diamond Optic, pitcher, rosalene, 7½" 72.50
Diamond Optic/Beaded Melon, vase, cranberry opal, 8" 62.50
Dolphin, bowl, console; jade gr, hdls, oval, ftd, 10½"..................140.00
Dot Optic, cruet, cranberry opal w/pearlized finish, lg................120.00
Dot Optic, pitcher, cranberry opal, water sz 275.00
Dot Optic, pitcher, gr opal, 9" 250.00
Ebony, candlesticks, #449, 8½", pr 90.00
Emerald Crest, compote, low ftd, #7329 ....32.50

Fern Optic, vase, cranberry opal, dbl-crimped, 11" 175.00
Flame Crest, cake plate, stem...160.00
Gold Crest, compote, ftd, 6½x8" 30.00
Gold Crest, triangle bowl, #203, in metal fr................................45.00
Hobnail, basket, bl opal, 4" 70.00
Hobnail, bonbon, bl opal, 6" 36.00
Hobnail, bottle, cologne; cranberry opal, 4" 60.00
Hobnail, bowl, cranberry opal, dbl-crimped, 10" 110.00
Hobnail, bowl, French opal, dbl-crimped, ftd, 11" 90.00
Hobnail, bowl, plum opal, #3924, 9" 150.00
Hobnail, bowl, topaz opal, dbl-crimped, ftd, 11" 125.00
Hobnail, cake plate, French opal, ftd..80.00
Hobnail, candle holders, cranberry opal, hdl, pr 175.00
Hobnail, cruet, bl opal, 4" 95.00
Hobnail, cruet, cranberry opal, w/stopper, 4⅞" 110.00
Hobnail, epergne, bl opal, 3-lily, apartment sz 150.00
Hobnail, fan vase, topaz opal, 4" 45.00
Hobnail, hat vase, bl opa, 2½" 25.00
Hobnail, jug, cranberry opal, squat, #3965, 5½" 125.00
Hobnail, pitcher, juice; yel opal, +6 tumblers` 250.00
Hobnail, shakers, French opal, flat, pr.......................................45.00
Hobnail, shoe w/kitten, bl opal..45.00
Hobnail, tumbler, bl opal, flat bbl form, 4¾" 35.00
Hobnail, tumbler, juice; bl opal, flat, 3¼" 25.00
Hobnail, vase, bl o/l, 8" 82.50
Hobnail, vase, cameo opal, 4½" 42.50
Hobnail, vase, French opal, dbl-crimped, 6" 45.00
Hobnail, vase, topaz opal, dbl-crimped, 8" 95.00
Hobnail/Spiral Optic, vase, cranberry opal, 7" 75.00
Ivory Crest, bowl, cone shape, 7" 50.00
Ivory Crest, candle holder, cornucopia form, 6¼" 45.00
Jacqueline, shakers, gr, pr...27.50
Jade, vase, hand decor, w/ebony 5-ftd base, #612, 6¼" 250.00
Lilac, shell bowl, cased, #9020, 10" 120.00
Mandarin Red, console set, 10" bowl+2 6¾" candlesticks 185.00
Melon Rib, bottle, scent; mulberry, low, w/stopper, 9" 145.00
Melon Rib/Silver Crest, bottle, scent; w/stopper, 7" 45.00
Ming Green, bowl, octagonal, #750, 9", w/14" underplate 275.00
Orange Tree, jelly compote, crystal...20.00
Paisley, bell, Copper Rose, 7" 45.00
Peach Crest, pitcher, #192 ....90.00
Peach Crest, powder jar, w/2 colognes......................................160.00
Peach Crest, vase, triangular, narrow neck, 8" 42.50
Persian Medallion, compote, custard satin, 6½" 30.00
Persian Medallion, compote, Lime Sherbet, #8324......................40.00
Persian Medallion, lamp, fairy; Rose Burmese, #8408, 3-pc..........90.00
Plymouth, champagne, ruby, 4"...25.00
Polka Dot, butter dish, cranberry opal, milk glass base 160.00
Polka Dot, pitcher, cranberry opal, #2267, rare, 9" 400.00
Rosalene, paperweight, fish, 5"..65.00
Rose, bowl, console; Velva Blue..36.00
Rose, vase, Provincial Blue opal, ped ft, 9" 42.50
Rose Overlay, basket, #1924, 5"...55.00
Ruby Overlay, vase, tricorner, 6" 40.00
Scroll, vase, Lime Sherbet, 8" 67.50
Silver Crest, banana bowl, high std 45.00
Silver Crest, banana stand 125.00
Silver Crest, basket, 7½" 45.00
Silver Crest, bowl, salad, 9½" 55.00
Silver Crest, cake stand, 13" 55.00
Silver Crest, candle holders, low, pr...37.50
Silver Crest, candy box, ftd, tall 145.00
Silver Crest, plate, 10¼" 45.00
Silver Crest, plate, 8½" 20.00

Silver Crest/Melon Rib, vase, beaded, 5x3"...............................10.00
Silver Jamestown, vase, bl, #6056, 6" 45.00
Snow Crest, bowl, ruby, heart shape 35.00
Snow Crest, vase, aqua, #3153, 7½" 60.00
Snow Crest, vase, ruby, #1425, 8" 95.00
Spanish Lace, basket, cranberry opal, crimped, 8" 67.50
Spiral Optic, cruet, cranberry opal, clear twisted/reeded hdl.......125.00
Strawberry, basket, rosalene, ftd, 4½" 50.00
Stretch, candy dish, aquamarine, #531 ....38.00
Stretch/Velva Rose, candlestick, #316 ....22.00

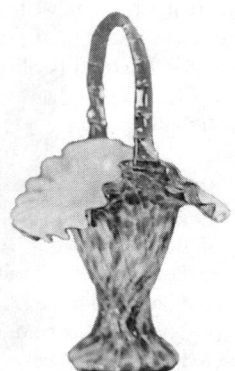

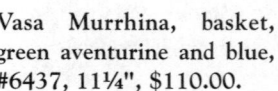

Vasa Murrhina, basket, green aventurine and blue, #6437, 11¼", $110.00.

Vasa Murrhina, basket, gr/bl, 7" 75.00
Vasa Murrhina, vase, gr/bl, dbl-crimp, #6454, 4" 48.00
Waffle, vase, gr opal, cupped, 4¼" 40.00
Water Lily, basket, custard satin...36.00
Water Lily, candlesticks, rosalene, pr..47.50
Water Lily, candy dish, rosaline, ftd, #8480, w/lid......................88.00
Water Lily, compote, Velva Rose, sm...35.00
Water Lily, jardiniere, custard satin, #8498 ....45.00
Water Lily, pitcher, wht satin, #8464, 30-oz..............................55.00

Fiesta

Fiesta is a line of dinnerware that was originally produced by the Homer Laughlin China Company of Newell, West Virginia, from 1936 until 1973. It was made in eleven different solid colors with over fifty pieces in the assortment. The pattern was developed by Frederick Rhead, an English Stoke-on-Trent potter who was an important contributor to the art-pottery movement in this country during the early part of the century. The design was carried out through the use of a simple band-of-rings device near the rim. Fiesta Red, a strong red-orange glaze color, was made with depleted uranium oxide. It was more expensive to produce than the other colors and sold at higher prices. During the '50s the color assortment was gray, rose, chartreuse, and dark green. These colors are relatively harder to find and along with medium green (new in 1959) command the highest prices.

Fiesta Kitchen Kraft was introduced in 1939; it consisted of seventeen pieces of kitchenware such as pie plates, refrigerator sets, mixing bowls, and covered jars in four popular Fiesta colors.

As a final attempt to adapt production to modern-day techniques and methods, Fiesta was restyled in 1969. Of the original colors, only Fiesta Red remained. This line, called Fiesta Ironstone, was discontinued in 1973.

Two types of marks were used: an ink stamp on machine-jiggered pieces and an indented mark molded into the hollow ware pieces.

In 1986 HLC reintroduced a line of Fiesta dinnerware in five colors: black, white, pink, apricot, and cobalt (darker and denser than the original shade). Since then yellow, turquoise, seafoam green, 'country' blue, lilac, persimmon, sapphire blue, chartreuse, gray, juniper, and cinnabar have been added. Collectors have found that the new line poses no threat to their investments.

In the listings below, 'original colors' indicates only three of the original six — light green, turquoise, and yellow (or those remaining after specific original colors have been priced). Red, ivory, and cobalt values are listed separately. Turquoise was the last original color to be introduced, so the items that were discontinued in 1946 are harder to find in that color (since it had a shorter production run), and values fall into the price range of red, cobalt, and ivory. These are designated with an asterisk.

For more information we recommend *The Collector's Encyclopedia of Fiesta, Harlequin, and Riviera, 9th Edition* (values updated in 2001), by Sharon and Bob Huxford (Collector Books).

Dinnerware

Ashtray, '50s colors	88.00
Ashtray, orig colors	47.00
Ashtray, red, cobalt or ivory	60.00
Bowl, covered onion soup; cobalt or ivory	725.00
Bowl, covered onion soup; red	750.00
Bowl, covered onion soup; turq, minimum value	8,000.00
Bowl, covered onion soup; yel or lt gr	600.00
Bowl, cream soup; '50s colors	72.00
Bowl, cream soup; med gr, minimum value	4,000.00
Bowl, cream soup; orig colors	42.00
Bowl, cream soup; red, cobalt or ivory	60.00
Bowl, dessert; '50s colors, 6"	52.00
Bowl, dessert; med gr, 6"	475.00
Bowl, dessert; orig colors, 6"	38.00
Bowl, dessert; red, cobalt or ivory, 6"	52.00
Bowl, fruit; '50s colors, 4¾"	40.00
Bowl, fruit; '50s colors, 5½"	40.00
Bowl, fruit; med gr, 4¾"	485.00
Bowl, fruit; med gr, 5½"	75.00
Bowl, fruit; orig colors, 4¾"	28.00
Bowl, fruit; orig colors, 5½"	28.00
Bowl, fruit; orig colors, 11¾"	300.00
Bowl, fruit; red, cobalt or ivory, 4¾"	35.00
Bowl, fruit; red, cobalt or ivory, 5½"	35.00
Bowl, fruit; red, cobalt or ivory, 11¾" *	300.00
Bowl, ftd salad; orig colors	300.00
Bowl, ftd salad; red, cobalt or ivory *	350.00
Bowl, ind salad; med gr, 7½"	105.00
Bowl, ind salad; red, turq or yel, 7½"	85.00
Bowl, nappy; '50s colors, 8½"	65.00
Bowl, nappy; med gr, 8½"	140.00
Bowl, nappy; orig colors, 8½"	40.00
Bowl, nappy; orig colors, 9½"	52.00
Bowl, nappy; red, cobalt or ivory, 8½" *	60.00
Bowl, nappy; red, cobalt or ivory, 9½" *	65.00
Bowl, Tom & Jerry; ivory w/gold letters	260.00
Bowl, unlisted salad; red, cobalt, or ivory	500.00
Bowl, unlisted salad; yel	105.00
Candle holders, bulb; orig colors, pr	95.00
Candle holders, bulb; red, cobalt or ivory, pr *	130.00
Candle holders, tripod; orig colors, pr	465.00
Candle holders, tripod; red, cobalt or ivory, pr *	600.00
Carafe, orig colors	250.00
Carafe, red, cobalt or ivory *	300.00
Casserole, '50s colors	300.00
Casserole, French; standard colors other than yel	650.00
Casserole, French; yel	300.00

Casserole, med gr	725.00
Casserole, orig colors	150.00
Casserole, red, cobalt or ivory	200.00
Coffeepot, '50s colors	350.00

Coffeepot, demitasse; red, cobalt, or ivory, $435.00; Original colors, $340.00; Cup, demitasse; red, cobalt, or ivory, $75.00; Original colors, $65.00; '50s colors, $350.00.

Coffeepot, orig colors	195.00
Coffeepot, red, cobalt or ivory	245.00
Compote, orig colors, 12"	148.00
Compote, red, cobalt or ivory, 12" *	185.00
Compote, sweets; orig colors	75.00
Compote, sweets; red, cobalt or ivory *	90.00
Creamer, '50s colors	40.00
Creamer, ind; red	250.00
Creamer, ind; turq or cobalt	345.00
Creamer, ind; yel	70.00
Creamer, med gr	80.00
Creamer, orig colors	22.00
Creamer, red, cobalt or ivory	35.00
Creamer, stick hdld, orig colors	45.00
Creamer, stick hdld, red, cobalt or ivory *	70.00
Egg cup, '50s colors	160.00
Egg cup, orig colors	58.00
Egg cup, red, cobalt, or ivory	70.00
Lid, for mixing bowl #1-#3, any color, minimum value	785.00
Lid, for mixing bowl #4, any color, minimum value	1,000.00
Marmalade, orig colors	230.00
Marmalade, red, cobalt or ivory *	285.00
Mixing bowl, #1, orig colors	170.00
Mixing bowl, #1, red, cobalt or ivory *	225.00
Mixing bowl, #2, orig colors	110.00
Mixing bowl, #2, red, cobalt or ivory *	125.00
Mixing bowl, #3, orig colors	120.00
Mixing bowl, #3, red, cobalt or ivory *	130.00
Mixing bowl, #4, orig colors	130.00
Mixing bowl, #4, red, cobalt or ivory *	155.00
Mixing bowl, #5, orig colors	155.00
Mixing bowl, #5, red, cobalt or ivory *	185.00
Mixing bowl, #6, orig colors	200.00
Mixing bowl, #6, red, cobalt or ivory *	265.00
Mixing bowl, #7, orig colors	280.00
Mixing bowl, #7, red, cobalt or ivory *	350.00
Mug, Tom & Jerry; '50s colors	100.00
Mug, Tom & Jerry; ivory w/gold letters	65.00
Mug, Tom & Jerry; orig colors	60.00
Mug, Tom & Jerry; red, cobalt or ivory	85.00
Mustard, orig colors	200.00
Mustard, red, cobalt or ivory *	250.00
Pitcher, disk juice; gray, minimum value	2,500.00
Pitcher, disk juice; Harlequin yel	62.00

Pitcher, disk juice; red 450.00
Pitcher, disk juice; yel 45.00
Pitcher, disk water; '50s colors 275.00
Pitcher, disk water; med gr, minimum value 1,150.00
Pitcher, disk water; orig colors 125.00
Pitcher, disk water; red, cobalt or ivory 165.00
Pitcher, ice; orig colors 140.00
Pitcher, ice; red, cobalt or ivory * 160.00
Pitcher, jug, 2-pt; '50s colors 150.00
Pitcher, jug, 2-pt; orig colors 90.00
Pitcher, jug, 2-pt; red, cobalt or ivory 120.00
Plate, '50s colors, 6" 9.00
Plate, '50s colors, 7" 13.00
Plate, '50s colors, 9" 22.00
Plate, '50s colors, 10" 52.00
Plate, cake; orig colors 755.00
Plate, cake; red, cobalt or ivory * 885.00
Plate, calendar; 1954 or 1955, 10" 45.00
Plate, calendar; 1955, 9" 50.00
Plate, chop; '50s colors, 13" 100.00
Plate, chop; '50s colors, 15" 115.00
Plate, chop; med gr, 13" 275.00
Plate, chop; orig colors, 13" 35.00
Plate, chop; orig colors, 15" 48.00
Plate, chop; red, cobalt or ivory, 13" 55.00
Plate, chop; red, cobalt or ivory, 15" 75.00
Plate, compartment; '50s colors, 10½" 75.00
Plate, compartment; orig colors, 10½" 40.00
Plate, compartment; orig colors, 12" 50.00
Plate, compartment; red, cobalt or ivory, 10½" 40.00
Plate, compartment; red, cobalt or ivory, 12" 60.00
Plate, deep; '50s colors 55.00
Plate, deep; med gr 120.00
Plate, deep; orig colors 40.00
Plate, deep; red, cobalt or ivory 60.00
Plate, med gr, 6" 20.00
Plate, med gr, 7" 32.00
Plate, med gr, 9" 45.00
Plate, med gr, 10" 110.00
Plate, orig colors, 6" 5.00
Plate, orig colors, 7" 9.00
Plate, orig colors, 9" 12.00
Plate, orig colors, 10" 32.00
Plate, red, cobalt or ivory, 6" 7.00
Plate, red, cobalt or ivory, 7" 10.00
Plate, red, cobalt or ivory, 9" 18.00
Plate, red, cobalt or ivory, 10" 40.00
Platter, '50s colors 58.00
Platter, med gr 140.00
Platter, orig colors 35.00
Platter, red, cobalt or ivory 45.00
Relish tray, gold decor, complete 250.00
Relish tray base, orig colors 65.00
Relish tray base, red, cobalt or ivory * 85.00
Relish tray center insert, orig colors 42.00
Relish tray center insert, red, cobalt or ivory * 55.00
Relish tray side insert, orig colors 40.00
Relish tray side insert, red, cobalt or ivory * 48.00
Sauce boat, '50s colors 78.00
Sauce boat, med gr 155.00
Sauce boat, orig colors 45.00
Sauce boat, red, cobalt or ivory 75.00
Saucer, '50s colors 6.00
Saucer, demi; '50s colors 95.00

Saucer, demi; orig colors..18.00
Saucer, demi; red, cobalt or ivory..............................22.00
Saucer, med gr...12.00
Saucer, orig colors..4.00
Saucer, red, cobalt or ivory..5.00
Shakers, '50s colors, pr...45.00
Shakers, med gr, pr...140.00
Shakers, orig colors, pr...22.00
Shakers, red, cobalt or ivory, pr..................................30.00
Sugar bowl, ind; turq..350.00
Sugar bowl, ind; yel..120.00
Sugar bowl, w/lid, '50s colors, 3¼x3½"......................72.00
Sugar bowl, w/lid, med gr, 3¼x3½".........................160.00
Sugar bowl, w/lid, orig colors, 3¼x3½"......................45.00
Sugar bowl, w/lid, red, cobalt or ivory, 3¼x3½".........55.00
Syrup, orig colors..325.00
Syrup, red, cobalt or ivory *.....................................400.00
Teacup, '50s colors...38.00
Teacup, med gr...58.00
Teacup, orig colors..25.00
Teacup, red, cobalt or ivory..35.00
Teapot, lg; orig colors...185.00
Teapot, lg; red, cobalt or ivory *..............................220.00
Teapot, med; '50s colors...325.00
Teapot, med; med gr, minimum value.....................1,000.00
Teapot, med; orig colors..160.00
Teapot, med; red, cobalt or ivory..............................200.00
Tray, figure-8; cobalt..90.00
Tray, figure-8; turq or yel...350.00
Tray, utility; orig colors...38.00
Tray, utility; red, cobalt or ivory *.............................42.00
Tumbler, juice; chartreuse, Harlequin yel or dk gr.....460.00
Tumbler, juice; orig colors..40.00
Tumbler, juice; red, cobalt or ivory............................45.00
Tumbler, juice; rose..65.00
Tumbler, water; orig colors...60.00
Tumbler, water; red, cobalt or ivory *........................85.00
Vase, bud; orig colors...80.00
Vase, bud; red, cobalt or ivory *...............................110.00
Vase, orig colors, 8"..600.00
Vase, orig colors, 10"..750.00
Vase, orig colors, 12", minimum value...................1,000.00
Vase, red, cobalt or ivory, 8" *.................................700.00
Vase, red, cobalt or ivory, 10" *...............................850.00
Vase, red, cobalt or ivory, 12", minimum value *....1,200.00

Kitchen Kraft

Covered jug, light green or yellow, $250.00; red or cobalt, $275.00.

Bowl, mixing; lt gr or yel, 6" 65.00
Bowl, mixing; lt gr or yel, 8" 82.00
Bowl, mixing; lt gr or yel, 10" 100.00
Bowl, mixing; red or cobalt, 6" 75.00

Bowl, mixing; red or cobalt, 8"	92.00
Bowl, mixing; red or cobalt, 10"	120.00
Cake plate, lt gr or yel	55.00
Cake plate, red or cobalt	65.00
Cake server, lt gr or yel	130.00
Cake server, red or cobalt	140.00
Casserole, ind; lt gr or yel	140.00
Casserole, ind; red or cobalt	155.00
Casserole, lt gr or yel, 7½"	85.00
Casserole, lt gr or yel, 8½"	100.00
Casserole, red or cobalt, 7½"	90.00
Casserole, red or cobalt, 8½"	110.00
Covered jar, lg; lt gr or yel	300.00
Covered jar, lg; red or cobalt	320.00
Covered jar, med; lt gr or yel	260.00
Covered jar, med; red or cobalt	280.00
Covered jar, sm; lt gr or yel	270.00
Covered jar, sm; red or cobalt	290.00
Covered jug, lt gr or yel	250.00
Covered jug, red or cobalt	275.00
Fork, lt gr or yel	100.00
Fork, red or cobalt	125.00
Metal frame for platter	26.00
Pie plate, lt gr or yel, 9"	40.00
Pie plate, lt gr or yel, 10"	40.00
Pie plate, red or cobalt, 9"	45.00
Pie plate, red or cobalt, 10"	45.00
Pie plate, Spruce gr	290.00
Platter, lt gr or yel	68.00
Platter, red or cobalt	78.00
Platter, spruce gr	350.00
Shakers, lt gr or yel, pr	95.00
Shakers, red or cobalt, pr	105.00
Spoon, ivory, 12", minimum value	500.00
Spoon, lt gr or yel	100.00
Spoon, red or cobalt	125.00
Stacking refrigerator lid, ivory	205.00
Stacking refrigerator lid, lt gr or yel	70.00
Stacking refrigerator lid, red or cobalt	80.00
Stacking refrigerator unit, ivory	195.00
Stacking refrigerator unit, lt gr or yel	45.00
Stacking refrigerator unit, red or cobalt	55.00

Fifties Modern

Postwar furniture design is marked by organic shapes and lighter woods and forms. New materials from war research such as molded plywood and fiberglass were used extensively. For the first time, design was extended to the masses and the baby-boomer generation grew up surrounded by modern shape and color, the perfect expression of postwar optimism. The top designers in America worked for Herman Miller and Knoll Furniture Company. These include Charles Eames, George Nelson, and Eero Saarinen.

Unless noted otherwise values are given for furnishings in excellent condition; glassware and ceramic items are assumed to be in mint condition. This information was provided to us by Richard Wright. See also Italian Glass.

Key:
alum — aluminum	lcq — lacquered
cntl — cantilevered	ss — stainless steel
fbrg — fiberglass	uphl — upholstered
lam — laminated	vnr — veneer

Lounge chair and ottoman, Charles Eames/Herman Miller, rosewood frame, tufted tan leather upholstery, $1,800.00.

Armchair, Eames/Miller, Alum Group, channeled uphl, 33", 4 for	1,200.00
Armchair, folding; McArthur/Mayfair, vinyl/alum, 22", 4 for	2,000.00
Armchair, Robsjohn-Gibbings, walnut fr w/dowel bk, orig uphl, 31"	1,000.00
Armchair, teak, wide curved bk & arms, rush seat, post legs, 30¾"	145.00
Armchair, Wegner, loose cushions, oak fr, 26x29¾x30", VG	225.00
Armchair, Wegner/Hansen, teak, rnd bk, caned seat, 30x24½", pr	3,000.00
Bed, Nelson, Thin Edge, birch fr, woven cane headrest, metal legs, VG	2,600.00
Bench, Knoll, slatted wood, wht metal fr, 15x55x20", VG	900.00
Bench, Nelson/Miller, primavera birch top, ebonized legs, 69"	950.00
Bench, Nelson/Miller, slatted top, ebonized wooden legs, 15x68x18"	950.00
Bench, Robsjohn-Gibbings, walnut dowel X-fr w/orig uphl seat, 22x34"	800.00
Bench, Wormley/Dunbar, fabric uphl seat, tag, 14½x66x18"	500.00
Bench, Wormley/Dunbar, Long John, walnut plank, hairpin legs, 84"	1,000.00
Bottle, Fantoni, wht semimatt drips on mustard, flask shape, 7x9"	275.00
Bowl, Fantoni, free-form w/incised figure, mc on wht crackle, 18" L	150.00
Box, TAXCO, brass & MOP, hinged lid, 5½x3½"	35.00
Buffet, Nelson/Miller, #5626, part ebonized/walnut, 40x40"	1,150.00
Cabinet, file; Aalto/Artek, birch vnr, 3-drw, 26x27x16"	600.00
Cabinet, Nelson/Miller, blond wood, 2-door, plank legs, 30x34"	450.00
Cabinet, Nelson/Miller, ebonized vnr, 5-drw, alum knobs, 40x40x19"	1,000.00
Cabinet, Nelson/Miller, walnut vnr, 4-drw, 30x34x18"	600.00
Cabinet, Nelson/Miller, walnut vnr/coral enamel front, 30x56x20"	1,500.00
Cabinet, Spence/Sweden, birch vnr, tambour top, 5-drw, 48x38"	1,800.00
Cabinet, stereo; Clairtone, rosewood/chrome, globe speakers, 82" L	950.00
Cabinet, Wormley/Dunbar, rosewood/mahog, 4-drw, 35x33"	800.00
Carpet, wool, abstract red on gray, 68x84", VG	150.00
Chair, Aarnio, wht fbrg ball w/ped base, brn ultra-suede uphl, 48"	1,800.00
Chair, Aznuso/Arflex, fabric over foam, brass fr, 32", VG	1,400.00
Chair, Baughman/Coggin, #1948, bbl shaped plywood, uphl cushion, pr	900.00
Chair, Bertoia/Knoll, dmn fr on chrome supports, gr fabric	375.00
Chair, captain's; Nakashima, walnut, curved bk/dowel legs/woven seat	1,200.00
Chair, club; Gehry, Grandpa Beaver, corrugated cb, 36x46x39"	6,000.00
Chair, dining; Emeco, cast aluminum, 34", 4 for	800.00
Chair, dyed molded seat & bk, chrome fr, screw-on ft, 29", pr	425.00
Chair, Eames/Miller, ash seat/bk/fr, early Evans version, 27"	1,100.00
Chair, Eames/Miller, Eiffel Tower, blk wire, screw-on ft pads, 4 for	1,200.00
Chair, Eames/Miller, Eiffel Tower, wire w/orig hopsack bikini pad, 31"	200.00
Chair, Eames/Miller, molded plywood, tubular chrome fr, 26", pr	1,200.00
Chair, Eames/Miller, rosewood seat & bk, chrome fr, 29", VG	950.00
Chair, Eames/Miller, Soft Pad, leather uphl, anodized fr, 32", pr	1,000.00
Chair, Eames/Miller, swivel, blk wire, wht pads, dowel legs, 32"	1,000.00
Chair, Jacobsen/Hansen, swivel, walnut plywood seat/bk, chrome fr, 34"	550.00
Chair, Komai, #939 variant, ash vnr, 4 ebonized legs, 27x21x21", G	400.00
Chair, lounge; Eames, fbrg shell, Eiffel Tower base, shock mts, 31", G	260.00
Chair, lounge; Eames/Miller, low rod base, gray shell, 26"	260.00
Chair, lounge; Eames/Miller, tigerwood vnr fr, leather uphl, +ottoman	2,700.00
Chair, lounge; Eames/Miller, Zenith, rope-edge shell, zinc legs, 26"	375.00
Chair, lounge; Engstrom, bentwood, lamb's wool uphl, 40x28x29"	600.00
Chair, lounge; Robsjohn-Gibbings/Widdicomb, walnut dowel fr & bk, 31"	800.00
Chair, Mathsson, Pernilla, birch plywood w/orig gray webbing, 36x40"	1,400.00

Chair, Nelson/Miller, Thin Edge, striped uphl, tilt arms, 28" ..**1,500.00**
Chair, patio; Hoffer, Spider Webb, gr webbing, blk metal fr, 33" dia.**650.00**
Chair, Robert John, curved arms, brass base, orig uphl, 27x33x31".....**120.00**
Chair, side; Cherner/Plycraft, bentwood w/leather pads, 30½" ...**650.00**
Chair, side; Eames/Miller, fbrg on zinc H base, 1956, 32", 6 for..**500.00**
Chair, Wormley/Dunbar, Janus, orange uphl, tufted bk, mahog legs, 29"..**850.00**
Chaise, wrought iron fr w/orig wood & rattan sling seat, 38"......**850.00**
Chest, Nakashima, walnut, 4-drw, recessed hdls, 30x36x20" ..**3,750.00**
Clock, Nelson/Miller, Asterisk, blk metal face/wht hands, 10" dia..**500.00**
Clock, Nelson/Miller, Atomic Ball, brass/blk enamel/wood, 1959, 14"..**700.00**
Clock, Nelson/Miller, Starburst, brass, ebonized arms, 18¼" dia ...**600.00**
Clock, Nelson/Miller, Starburst, brass & wood w/pnt hands, 18" dia ...**650.00**
Clock, Nelson/Miller, Starburst, walnut/wht enamel, 18¼" dia..**750.00**
Clock, Nelson/Miller, Starburst, wht enamel/walnut, mc hands, 18¼"...**550.00**
Clock, Nelson/Miller, Steering Wheel, all orig, 12" dia **475.00**
Clock, Nelson/Miller, Steering Wheel, brass/blk enamel/wht #s, 12" dia...**700.00**
Console, Parziner, lt bl w/silver trim, 2 doors, 32x45x19", VG..**3,500.00**
Credenza, Nelson/Miller, walnut w/Formica top, blk sliding doors, 60"...**650.00**
Daybed, Kagan, curved arms w/Lucite base, channel uphl, 67" ..**1,200.00**
Daybed, Nelson/Miller, birch/chrome, reuhpl cushion/bolsters, 80" ..**2,700.00**
Daybed, Nelson/Miller, nubby uphl, ebonized fr, 10½x75x33" ...**950.00**
Daybed, van der Rohe/Knoll, tufted blk leather uphl/bolster, steel fr ..**4,000.00**
Desk, Aalto/Artek, mahog top, 7 birch drw, 29x59x28" **600.00**
Desk, executive; Dunbar/Sprunger, #2040, rosewood vnr, suspended drws....**1,400.00**
Desk, Nelson/Miller, Home Office Action Series, oak tambour top **600.00**
Desk, Nelson/Miller, Modern Management Group, walnut/steel, 48"..**650.00**
Desk, Protzmann/Miller, vnr top/drw fronts, chrome fr, 30x65x33"......**130.00**
Dresser, Knoll, 3-pc rosewood vnr on brass base, 9-drw, 29x110" **2,500.00**
Dresser, Nakashima, free-form top, dvtl walnut, sliding doors, 72" W..**12,000.00**
Figurine, Wayland Gregory, fish, orange w/gold, 8¼x12" **425.00**
Headboard, Nakashima, free-form solid walnut, 37x82" **2,700.00**
Headboard, Wormley/Dunbar, rosewood/mahog, 39x80".............**500.00**
Highboy, Deskey/Widdicomb, rosewood & ebonized, ss trim, 51x30"..**3,000.00**
Lamp, desk; Light-o-lier, blk enamel shade, brass arm, 17x16" dia **200.00**
Lamp, floor, Laurel, wht opaque 12" shade on ss fr, 56".............**400.00**
Lamp, floor; Light-o-lier, gray/wht/rust shades, 3 brass arms, 69" ...**900.00**
Lamp, hanging; Nelson/Miller, Bubble, plastic over wire, 24" dia..**600.00**
Lamp, Raymor, chevrons, wht/texture, 2 stacked cylinders, 20x8"...**90.00**
Lamp, table; Chase, chrome C-arm w/blk enamel 10" shade, 15"...**175.00**
Lamp, table; Nesso/Artimede, mushroom shape orange fbrg, 14x21"...**175.00**
Lamp, von Nessen, Anywhere, yel enamel shade, cntl chrome, 14".....**1,000.00**
Lamp, von Nessen, cntl arm, brushed steel 20" shade, 60"..........**700.00**
Lounge, Wormley, Listen-to-Me, channeled uphl, birch/walnut fr, 74"..**10,000.00**
Ottoman, Bertoia, wht vinyl-coated steel rods, 17x24x17"........**270.00**
Planter, Kamball, gray fbrg on wrought-iron std, 16x15" dia.........**50.00**
Rocker, Eames/Miller, fbrg shell, zinc struts, birch runners, 27" ..**800.00**
Rocker, Eames/Miller, parchment fbrg shell, blk struts, birch runners ..**950.00**
Rocker, Eames/Miller, wht fbrg shell, Eiffel tower base, 26" **900.00**
Rocker, Eames/Miller, wire top, orig bikini pad, birch runners, 28" **950.00**
Rocker, Gehry, Easy Edges, lam cb w/masonite edge, 24x41x24", VG...**3,750.00**
Sculpture, Ceramicraft, cocktail glass, pk lustre/blk/mc bubbles, 10"....**125.00**
Sculpture, Fantoni, cubist-style seated figure, mc, 16x9x6" **2,000.00**
Sculpture, musical trio, steel, wall hanging, 36x42"..................**650.00**
Sculpture, Weinberg, golfer, wire & pnt metal, 42x21", VG.......**450.00**
Settee, Jacobsen/Hansen, #3300 Easy Chair, uphl in chrome fr, 39x49"..**2,600.00**
Sideboard, McCobb/Calvin, Irwin Collection, bleached mahog, 34x66"....**425.00**
Sideboard, McCobb/Calvin, walnut vnr, 3 drws, sliding doors, 36x66"....**1,000.00**
Sideboard, Wormley, mahog w/woven doors, 32½x81½x18" ..**3,750.00**
Sofa, Borsani, #D70 Techno, orange uphl, blk steel fr, 32x74½" ..**6,500.00**
Sofa, Dunbar, sq sides, channelled bk, reuphl, 88" **2,200.00**
Sofa, Eames/Miller, Alum Group, orig bl vinyl, 33x72" **2,500.00**
Sofa, Eames/Miller, bl vinyl slab seat & bk, #3743, 73" **4,500.00**
Sofa, Eames/Miller, uphl slab seat & bk, cast alum fr, #3743, 73"..**3,250.00**
Sofa, Stendig/ASKO, mc uphl, sq chrome legs, 27x71x24"........**550.00**

Sofa, Wegner, loose cushions, oak fr, 27x71½x31" **300.00**
Stand, sculpting; walnut, 3 corseted legs, circular top, 30x13" dia ...**1,000.00**
Stool, child's; Eames/Evans, bentwood mahog, 8½x15x11"....**2,000.00**
Stool, Eames/Miller, Time-Life, trn walnut, concave seat, 15x13"..**600.00**
Stool, Knoll, bentwood, gr wool seat, flared legs, 18x16x15"......**225.00**
Stool, McCobb, uphl cushion in brass fr w/X-stretchers, 17x21x21" ..**280.00**
Table, Bellman/Knoll, birch top, ebonized ash tripod, 19x24" dia ...**2,100.00**
Table, coffee; maple, tapered cylindrical legs, ca 1955, 16x32" dia......**115.00**
Table, coffee; Parisi/Singer & Sons, inlay burl/walnut/brass, 59"......**3,500.00**
Table, coffee; Platner, knoll, glass top, chromed wire fr, 16x40" dia..**475.00**
Table, coffee; Robsjohn-Gibbings/Widdicomb, Sorrel, X base, 16x58x21" ...**500.00**
Table, coffee; Saarinen/Knoll, walnut vnr, wht enamel base, 15x36" dia....**300.00**
Table, coffee; Tornenan, mc sqs pnt on top, blond fr, 29x54x22" ..**750.00**
Table, coffee; Wormley/Dunbar, Janus, walnut/tile insets, 20x38" dia **4,250.00**
Table, conference; Saarinen/Knoll, walnut top w/tulip support, 30x48"...**2,300.00**
Table, dinette; Nat'l Chair Co, red lam, metal, drop-leaf, 48" **100.00**
Table, Eames, La Fonda, blk slat top, alum base, 30" dia.............**100.00**
Table, Eames/Miller, molded walnut plywood, chrome legs, 16x34" dia...**500.00**
Table, game; Frankl/Johnson, wht lacquered cork top, mahog legs......**300.00**
Table, game; Wormley/Dunbar, walnut/rosewood, 8-sided, rfn, 25x50"...**2,000.00**
Table, gate-leg; Mathsson, walnut vnr, drop-leaf, 28½" H **1,000.00**
Table, Noguchi/Knoll, lam w/chrome struts, blk iron base, 48" dia ...**1,800.00**
Table, occasional; walnut vnr, blk metal column, alum ft, 29" dia...**60.00**
Table, side; Rohde, glass top, ebonized legs, brass caps, 22x28x19"..**500.00**
Table, side; Saarinen/Knoll, wht lam, pnt metal base, 20½x20" .**250.00**
Table, side; Wormley/Dunbar, formica top trns, walnut legs, 29" dia...**550.00**
Table, side; Wormley/Dunbar, mahog w/3 Tiffany tiles, 24x30x22" ...**3,000.00**
Table, side; Wormley/Dunbar, walnut vnr top, ebonized base w/shelf ..**450.00**
Table, Sorenson/Knoll, 2-tier, blond bentwood tops, 25x25x22" ...**700.00**
Table, Weber, blk laminate top & shelf, tubular chrome fr, 21x30x18" ..**1,000.00**
Vase, Dancause, mahog matt, pillow form, 11½x13½" **275.00**

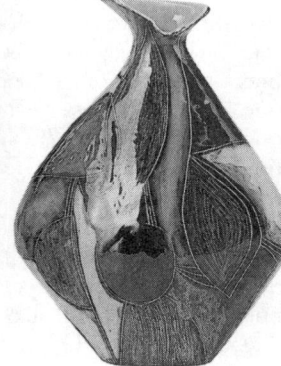

Vase, Fantoni free-form with abstract sgraffito and polychrome glazes, marked, 10¼x8", NM, $275.00.

Vase, Fantoni, teal & charcoal mottle, cylindrical, 11x4¼", NM..**200.00**
Vase, Fantoni/Raymor, gr & purple, organic ribs, 12x11" **125.00**
Vase, Gambone, bottle shape, dots/sqs, teal/eggplant, 5½x4¼" ..**100.00**
Vase, Lauger, HP pine boughs, mc on lt gr, classic shape, 12" **400.00**
Vase, Raymor, yel & brn organic ribs, label, 11½x10"...............**150.00**
Vase, Raymor, yel crackle, 2 openings, #108, 13x8", NM **90.00**

Finch, Kay

Kay Finch and her husband, Braden, operated a small pottery in Corona Del Mar, California, from 1939 to 1963. The company remained small, employing from twenty to sixty local residents who Kay trained in all but the most requiring tasks, which she herself performed. The company produced animal and bird figurines, most notably dogs, Kay's favorites. Figures of 'Godey' type couples were also made, as were tableware (consisting of breakfast sets) and other artware. Most pieces were marked, but ink stamps often came off during cleaning.

After Kay's husband, Braden, died in 1962, she closed the business. Some of her molds were sold to Freeman-McFarlin of El Monte, California, who soon contracted with Kay for new designs. Though the realism that is so evident in her original works is still strikingly apparent in these later pieces, none of the vibrant pastels or signature curliques are there.

Kay Finch died on June 21, 1993. Prices for her work have been climbing.

For further information we recommend *Kay Finch Ceramics, Her Enchanted World* (Schiffer), written by our advisors for this category, Mike Nickel and Cynthia Horvath; they are listed in the Directory under Michigan. Another fine reference is *Collectible Kay Finch* by Richard Marteniz and Jean Frick (Collector Books). *The New Kay Finch Ceramics Identification Guide* (published in 1996), containing many reprints of original catalog pages, is available from Frances Finch Webb; she is listed in the Directory under California. See also Clubs, Newsletters, and Catalogs.

Note: Original model numbers are included in the following descriptions — three-digit numbers indicate pre-1946 models. After 1946 they were assigned four-digit numbers, the first two digits representing the year of initial production. Prices below are for figurines decorated in multiple colors, not solid glazes.

Ashtray, Swan, #4958, 4½" **50.00**
Bank, Swiss Chalet, #4628, 6" **400.00**
Bank, Winkie, pig, #185, 3¾x4" **100.00**
Candlesticks, turkey figural, #5794, 3¾", pr **225.00**
Cookie jar, Cookie Puss, #4614, 11¾", minimum value...........**2,000.00**
Cup, Kitten Face Toby, 3" **100.00**
Figurine, Afghan Angel, #4911, 2½x2½" **375.00**
Figurine, Ambrosia, Persian cat, #155, 10¾", minimum value....**450.00**
Figurine, angel, #114a, #114b, or #114c, ea **40.00**
Figurine, Baby Cottontail, #152, 2½" **100.00**
Figurine, Big Mouth Fish, #6013, 3x4½" **500.00**
Figurine, Bride & Groom, #204, 6", 6½", pr **375.00**
Figurine, Butch & Biddy, rooster & hen, #177 & #178, he: 8½", pr...**100.00**
Figurine, Caress the Colt, #4806, 11" **325.00**
Figurine, Chinese Princess, #477, 23" **2,500.00**
Figurine, Choir Boy, #210, 7½" **75.00**
Figurine, cockatoo, Celadon Green glaze, #828, 13" **175.00**
Figurine, Cocker, cocker spaniel, #5260, 4½" **350.00**
Figurine, Cuddles, bunny, #4623, 11" **900.00**
Figurine, Dachshund Pup, #5320, 8" **750.00**
Figurine, Dalmatian/Coach Dog, #159, 17" **1,500.00**
Figurine, Doggie w/Silver Bell, poodle, #5001, 7½" **750.00**
Figurine, Godey Man & Lady, #160, 7½", pr **95.00**
Figurine, Happy, sitting monkey, #4903, 11", minimum value......**800.00**
Figurine, Harvey, rabbit w/bow, #4622, 21" **3,500.00**

Figurine, hippopotamus with bow, $450.00.

Figurine, Hoot Owl, #187, 8½" **150.00**
Figurine, Jezebel, recumbent cat, #179, 6" **150.00**
Figurine, Littlest Angel, #4803, on knees, 2½" **175.00**

Figurine, Mama Quail, #5984, 7" **425.00**
Figurine, Mermaid, #161, 6½" **500.00**
Figurine, Monkeyshines, monkey waving, #4962, 9½"............**1,250.00**
Figurine, Mr & Mrs Bird, pastels, #454 & #453, 4½", 3", pr.......**175.00**
Figurine, Muff & Puff, playful kittens, pastels, #182 & #182, pr.**100.00**
Figurine, Pajama Girl, #5002, 5½" **500.00**
Figurine, Parakeet on a Perch, #5164, 5¾" **350.00**
Figurine, Peanuts Elephant, #191, 8½" **225.00**
Figurine, Peep & Jeep Ducks, wht or yel, #178a & #178b, 3", pr..**75.00**
Figurine, Peke, recumbent pekingese, #154, 14" L..............**650.00**
Figurine, Pekingese, #156, 1½x3" **175.00**
Figurine, Perky, poodle, #5419, 16" **4,000.00**
Figurine, Pete, papa penguin, #466, 7½" **325.00**
Figurine, Pheasant, #5300, 10" **250.00**
Figurine, Piggy Wiggy, #5408, 1x1¼" **125.00**
Figurine, Puddin', Yorkshire Terrier, #158, 11x12" **3,500.00**
Figurine, Rearing Lamb, #109, 5½" **75.00**
Figurine, Rudiki, Afghan Hound, silver leaf glaze, #834, 13" **750.00**
Figurine, Sassy Pig, #166, 3¾" **75.00**
Figurine, Scandie Boy (#127) & Scandie Girl (#126), 5¼", pr...**100.00**
Figurine, Shih-tzu, #837, gold leaf glaze, 10x12" **475.00**
Figurine, Siamese Cat, #5103, 10" **650.00**
Figurine, Sitting Afghan, #5553, 5¼" **450.00**
Figurine, Sitting Angel, #4802, 4½" **180.00**
Figurine, Tootsie, #189, 3¾" **35.00**
Figurine, Tubby, playful bear, #4847, 4¼" **225.00**
Figurine, Vicki, cocker spaniel, #455, 11" **900.00**
Figurine, Violet, elephant, Queen of the Circus, #190, 17" **3,500.00**
Figurine, Western Prospector's Burro, #475, 10" **850.00**
Figurine, Windblown Afghan, #5757, 6x6" **400.00**
Figurine, Yorky Pups, #170 & #171, pr **450.00**
Figurines, Squirrel Family, #108A, B, & C, papa, mama & baby, set ..**175.00**
Fountain, Sea Horse, #6063, 42" **1,250.00**
Moon bottle, #5502, 13" **175.00**
Mugs, kissing; His in bl or Hers in pk emb, #B5415, 3½", ea......**100.00**
Planter, Animal Books or Animal Blocks series, ea **75.00**
Shaker, kitchen; Puss, cat, #4616, 6" **350.00**
Tureen, turkey, platinum & gray, w/feather-hdl ladle, #5361, 9" .**495.00**
Vase, South Sea Girl, #4912, 8¼" **180.00**
Wall plaque, Sea Horse, #5788, 16" L **225.00**
Wall pocket, Santa, #5373, 9½" **375.00**

Findlay Onyx and Floradine

Findlay, Ohio, was the location of the Dalzell, Gilmore, and Leighton Glass Company, one of at least sixteen companies that flourished there between 1886 and 1901. Their most famous ware, Onyx, is very rare. It was produced for only a short time beginning in 1889 due to the heavy losses incurred in the manufacturing process.

Onyx is layered glass, usually found in creamy white with a dainty floral pattern accented with metallic lustre that has been trapped between the two layers. Other colors found on rare occasions include a light amber (with either no lustre or with gilt flowers), light amethyst (or lavender), and rose. Although old tradepaper articles indicate the company originally intended to produce the line in three distinct colors, long-time Onyx collectors report that aside from the white, production was very limited. Other colors of Onyx are very rare, and the few examples that are found tend to support the theory that production of colored Onyx ware remained for the most part in the experimental stage. Even three-layered items have been found (they are extremely rare) decorated with three-color flowers. As a rule of thumb, using white Onyx prices as a basis for evaluation, expect to pay two to five times more for colored examples.

Floradine is a separate line that was made with the Onyx molds. A single-layer rose satin glassware with white opal flowers, it is usually priced in the general range of colored Onyx.

Chipping around the rims is very common, and price is determined to a great extent by condition. Our advisors for this category are Betty and Clarence Maier; they are listed in the Directory under Pennsylvania.

Floradine

Bowl, fluted, squat bulbous base, 4" 950.00
Celery vase, fluted cylinder neck, bulbous body, 6½", EX........1,000.00
Celery vase, NM...1,800.00
Creamer, bulbous, 4⅝" 950.00
Mustard pot, NM 1,550.00
Spooner, 4¾"..1,285.00
Sugar bowl, bulbous, w/lid, 5½" 1,200.00
Sugar shaker 1,500.00
Syrup pitcher...2,500.00
Toothpick holder, 2½"..1,500.00
Tumbler, slightly bulbous, 3⅝" 1,000.00

Onyx

Bowl, wht w/raspberry decor, fluted top, 2½x4½" 2,000.00
Bowl, wht w/silver decor, 2¾x8"................................350.00
Butter dish, wht w/silver decor, 3x6".........................1,250.00
Covered dish, wht w/silver decor, 5½"..........................1,000.00
Creamer, wht w/silver decor, 4½"...............................485.00
Lamp, oil; blk opaque base, sm rpr to collar, 7¼" 6,500.00
Mustard, wht w/raspberry decor, hinged metal lid, 3¼" 2,900.00
Pitcher, water; wht w/silver decor, 8" 1,200.00
Shaker, wht w/silver decor, minor wear, 2¾" 650.00
Shaker, wht w/silver decor, Pat 2/23/1889, 2⅝", NM 800.00
Spooner, wht w/orange decor, 3¾" 950.00
Spooner, wht w/silver decor, 4½x4" 525.00
Sugar bowl, wht w/silver decor, 5½", EX........................475.00
Sugar shaker, wht w/silver decor, 5½", from $450 to 550.00
Syrup, gr (unusual color) 3,000.00
Syrup, wht w/silver decor, 7¾", from $850 to..................1,150.00
Toothpick holder, wht w/silver decor, from $425 to 500.00
Tumbler, wht s/silver decor, thin str sides, 3¾", NM...........1,250.00
Tumbler, wht w/apricot decor, lt line unseen from w/in, bbl....2,300.00
Tumbler, wht w/silver decor, bbl shape, 3½", EX................450.00

Fire Marks

The earliest American fire marks date back to 1752 when 'The Philadelphia Contributionship for the Insurance of Houses From Loss by Fire' (the official name of this company, who is still in business) used a plaque to identify property they insured. Early fire marks were made of cast iron, sheet brass, lead, copper, tin, and zinc. The insignia of the insurance company appeared on each mark, and they would normally reward the volunteer fire department who managed to be the first on the scene to battle the fire. (Altercations occasionally broke out between firefighting companies vying for the chance to earn the reward!)

Fire marks were first used in Great Britain about 1780 and were more elaborate than U.S. marks. The first English examples were made of lead and carried a policy number. They were used to identify insured property to the fire brigades maintained by the insurance companies. Most copper and brass fire marks are of European origin.

During the latter half of the nineteenth century, municipalities replaced the volunteer fire companies and fire brigades with paid fire departments. No longer was there a need for fire marks, so the companies discontinued their use (though some companies still use fire marks

for advertising purposes). See *The Fire Mark Circle of America*, listed under Clubs, Catalogs, and Newsletters in the Directory.

Prices listed are for legitimate fire marks in good to excellent condition. Reproductions are identified when possible. Many fire marks have been and continue to be widely reproduced in cast iron and aluminum. They are sold legitimately as decorator items and collectible reproductions. Fantasy items, on the other hand, are not reproductions, as they depict items that never existed in the first place. They are twentieth century fabrications and never existed in their present form prior to this recent production. They appear in cast iron, aluminum, and other mediums.

Baltimore Equitable Society...MD, CI, old pnt, 1974, 9⅜x10" ...750.00
British, copper on brass, lion & shield, 8" dia.................110.00
Eagle in oval, gold & blk rpt, bk: Issued 1830 by Ins Co of NA, 11"..275.00
Eagle Ins Co Cin O, eagle above banner, CI w/gold on blk, 8x12".....850.00
Insured Home New York, tin, 5¼x8⅛", VG.........................80.00

London Assurance Co. A.D. 1720, tin, modern reproduction, 10x11¾", $25.00.

Mutual Assurance of Phila, gr tree type on wooden shield..........100.00
Mutual Assurance of Phila, gr tree type on wooden shield, repro .15.00
Phoenix, copper, many varieties, worn 90.00
Royal, copper or brass, crown above/bird below, pnt traces, 10x12" ..175.00
Tree form, CI, gr pnt, 11¼x8" 175.00
Valiant Hose #2, pnt CI, 10½", repro...........................18.00

Firefighting Collectibles

Firefighting collectibles have always been a good investment in terms of value appreciation. Many times the market will be temporarily affected by wild price swings caused by the supply and demand principle as related to a small group of aggressive collectors. These collectors will occasionally pay well over market value for a particular item they need or want. Once their desires are satisfied, prices seem to return to their normal range. It has been noticed that during these periods of high prices, many items enter the marketplace that otherwise would remain in collections. This may (it has in the past) cause a price depression (due again to the supply and demand principle of market behavior).

The recent phenomena of Internet buying and selling of firefighting collectibles and antiques has caused wild swings in prices for some fire collectibles. The cause of this is the ability to reach into vast international markets. It appears that this has resulted in a significant escalation in prices paid for select items.The bottom-line items still languish price wise but at least continue to change hands. This marketplace continues to be active, and many outstanding items have appeared recently in the fire antiques and collectibles field. But when all is said and done, the careful purchase of quality, well-documented firefighting items will continue to be an enjoyable hobby and an excellent investment opportunity.

Today there is a large, active group of collectors for fire department antiques (items over 100 years old) and an even larger group seeking related collectibles (those less than 100 years old). Our advisors for this category (except grenades) are H. Thomas and Patricia Laun; they are listed in the Directory under New York. (SASE required.)

Fire grenades preceded the pressurized metal fire extinguishers used today. They were filled with a mixture of chemicals and water and made of glass thin enough to shatter easily when thrown into the flames. Many varieties of colors and shapes were used. Not all the grenades listed contain salt-brine solution, some, such as the Red Comet, contain carbon tetrachloride, a powerful solvent that is also a health hazard and an environmental threat. (It attacks the ozone layer.) It is best to leave any contents inside the glass balls. The source of grenade prices are mainly auction results; current retail values will fluctuate. Our fire grenades advisor is Willy Young; he is listed in the Directory under Nevada.

Key:
ALF — American LaFrance   s&a — soda & acid
CCL4 — carbon tetrachloride

Alarm, Fire-Larm, steel cylinder w/CO2-powered whistle.............**15.00**
Axe, forged steel, ¾-sz, 25", w/wood hdl.............**40.00**
Axe, hand; steel w/wood hdl, sm.............**35.00**
Axe, parade; NP w/brass edge guard, blk-pnt hdl, 13".............**120.00**
Axe, red pnt traces, 27½".............**45.00**
Axe holder, brass, old style, 9¼x3¾".............**65.00**
Badge, Chief Fire Dept, bl enamel on 10k gold w/eagle.............**60.00**
Badge, custom die, larger fire dept w/member's ID number, from $65 to..**110.00**
Badge, generic/everyday type, sm community, general membership, $25 to..**35.00**
Badge, hat; LAFD, gold-tone metal, 1930s, 2".............**20.00**
Badge, presentation; Ex Foreman..., bl enamel on 14k gold.............**275.00**
Badge, presentation; gold w/dmns, from $450 to.............**1,000.00**
Badge, presentation; gold w/dmns from major lg city, from $900 to..**1,500.00**
Bell, apparatus; chrome, heavy, w/bracket.............**500.00**
Bell, Fire Cry Dayton OH, 8" dia.............**35.00**
Bell, pull type, 10" dia.............**90.00**
Belt, parade; Asst Engineer, VG.............**45.00**
Box, alarm; Gamewell, CI w/Cole key guard, full sz, EX.............**175.00**
Box, alarm; Peerless Pat'd 1916, mechanism only.............**50.00**
Box, ballot; walnut, 2-compartment, w/marbles.............**85.00**
Bucket, leather, clipper ship pnting, VG.............**275.00**
Bucket, leather, Fire Bucket GMT, VG.............**300.00**
Bucket, leather, orig pnt, Constitution, brass studs, 8½", EX.............**385.00**
Bucket, leather, red pnt w/partial decor, European, VG.............**100.00**
Bucket, leather, w/hdls, 10x9½", EX.............**170.00**
Cape, parade; red w/gold lettering, Monroe, VG.............**850.00**
Case, metal, held 5 CCL4 balls, Stemple St Louis, EX.............**100.00**
Case, Shur-Stop Kit, metal w/5 clear glass grenades, VG.............**80.00**
Catalog, Fire Alarm Telegraph Apparatus Star Electric Co, 1906..**350.00**
Catalog, Gamewell Fire Alarm Telegraph Co, 1904, 36-pg, VG.**225.00**
Catalog, Motor Fire Apparatus, AM LaFrance, 1916, EX.............**140.00**
Certificate, Southern NY Volunteers to Star Hose of NY, 1907, G..**35.00**
Engine seat, metal w/red pnt & gold-leaf trim, VG.............**300.00**
Extinguisher, American, tin tube, 22", G.............**20.00**
Extinguisher, Badgers, brass & copper, S&A, pony sz, 1½", VG...**85.00**
Extinguisher, Child's, copper w/riveted seams, S&A, 2½-gal.............**25.00**
Extinguisher, Fire Dust, tin tube, dry powder, 3x13¼", G.............**65.00**
Extinguisher, General Quick Aid, brass, CCL4, w/bracket.............**15.00**
Extinguisher, Indian, brass w/pump mechanism.............**60.00**
Extinguisher, Phister, copper & brass, CCL4, 3½-gal.............**45.00**
Extinguisher, Security...Hudson Mfg Sheridan MI, red pnt, 20" +bracket..**25.00**
Extinguisher, Shur-Spray, sprinkler head w/fuseable link, CCL4, G..**50.00**
Frontispc, leather, C Volunteer Assn (some letters missing), 8"..**125.00**
Frontispc, leather, 2 lg stars/Perkins 2, 1850s, 8".............**475.00**
Gauge, apparatus; ALF, reads to 400 lbs pressure, VG.............**80.00**
Gong, Gamewell, 6" chromed turtle, EX.............**95.00**
Gong, house; 10" brass pull-type bell, 11½x14", mtd on board...**130.00**

Gong/indicator, Gamewell, lacking internal mechanism, 15" bell...**1,750.00**
Grenade, Autofyrstop, glass ball, CCL4, w/bracket, EX.............**30.00**
Grenade, Dri-Gas, Dmn Quilt, w/orig bracket.............**125.00**
Grenade, Harden's Hand Fire...Patented, purple-bl, 4¾".............**375.00**
Grenade, Harden's Star, peacock bl, crack in neck.............**70.00**
Grenade, Harden's Star, turq bl, w/contents, 6⅝".............**95.00**
Grenade, Harden's...Pat #1 August 8 1871...1883, turq, w/contents..**135.00**
Grenade, Harden Star..., cobalt, sb, 6¾".............**185.00**
Grenade, Hayward's Hand Fire..., bright lav, tooled mouth, 6¼"..**1,100.00**
Grenade, Hayward's...NY, clear, smooth base, w/contents, 6".....**140.00**
Grenade, Hayward's...SF Hayward...NY, cobalt, #3 on base, 6⅛"..**200.00**
Grenade, Hazelton's High Pressure...Keg, med amber bbl, 11¼".**325.00**
Grenade, HNS, straw yel, smooth base, w/contents, 7⅛".............**210.00**
Grenade, HNS, yel, w/contents & orig labels.............**165.00**
Grenade, Magic Fire Extinguisher, yel-amber, 1880-90, 6¼".............**625.00**
Grenade, Miracle, glass ball, CCL4, EX.............**25.00**
Grenade, Red Comet, CCL4, ceiling mt.............**20.00**
Grenade, Star, sapphire bl, crude, NM.............**130.00**
Grenade, Star-Harden, turq bl, w/contents, 6¾".............**110.00**
Helmet, aluminum, Senator style, red pnt, Cairns, G.............**90.00**
Helmet, aluminum, Senator style, VG.............**120.00**
Helmet, leather, Gratacap brass eagle, w/liner, VG.............**475.00**
Helmet, leather, high eagle, #23 on fontispc, EX.............**300.00**
Helmet, leather, high eagle, Glen Cove 2nd Asst, G.............**275.00**
Helmet, leather, high eagle, H&L #10 on frontispc, VG.............**300.00**
Helmet, leather, high eagle, jockey style, VG.............**450.00**
Helmet, leather, high eagle, Mat-Tuck-FD, G.............**175.00**

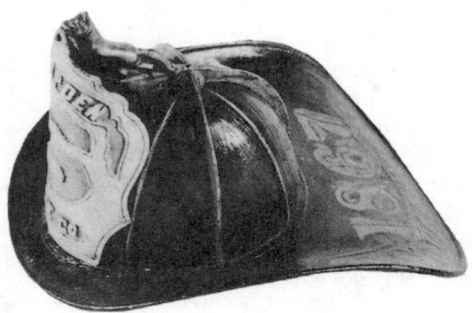

Helmet, leather, fox frontispiece, Hampden 6 Fire Co., black with gold trim combs, early, EX, from $750.00 to $950.00.

Helmet, leather, high eagle, Newburg NVFA, 60-comb, w/liner, EX...**475.00**
Helmet, leather, jockey style (scarce), greyhound frontispc, rpt..**600.00**
Helmet, leather, multiple combs, fireman frontispc holder, VG..**650.00**
Helmet, leather, New Yorker w/Bourke eye shield, Cairns, VG..**180.00**
Helmet, leather, pnt frontispc, lion finial, Miller of NY, 1860-70..**1,950.00**
Helmet, leather, silver forntispc w/S Am style holder, Jr H&T Co, EX..**800.00**
Helmet, leather, 142 Lieutenant front, Cairns, G.............**180.00**
Lantern, Dewey Mill, original blk pnt & brass tag, VG.............**90.00**
Lantern, Dietz Fire King Dept, tin, VG.............**175.00**
Lantern, Dietz King, removable sliding cage, tin, VG.............**225.00**
Lantern, Dietz King FD, brass & copper, red globe, Pat 1907, VG.**225.00**
Lantern, Dietz King Fire Dept, mustard pnt, incomplete.............**80.00**
Lantern, Dietz Mill, orig red pnt, VG.............**85.00**
Lantern, Ham's, brass, apparatus, complete, VG.............**600.00**
Lantern, hand; brass top, oil burner, clear globe, 1870s, VG.......**300.00**
Lantern, hand; Eclipse, ALF, clear globe, EX.............**1,200.00**
Lantern, porter's, wrist wring, candle count, EX.............**850.00**
Lantern, wrist; spring-loaded candle burner, fixed globe, 1870s..**650.00**
Lantern globe, 2-color, amber over clear (globe only).............**700.00**
Lantern globe, 2-color, cobalt over clear (globe only).............**650.00**

Lantern globe, 2-color, gr over clear (globe only).....................850.00
Lantern globe, 2-color, red over clear (globe only)....................850.00
Log, Amoskeag Steam Fire Engine Co #2, NJ, 1897-1898..........225.00
Nozzle, Akron Brass Mfg, 2½" 2-man type w/leather straps, 13½" L..175.00
Nozzle, brass, stand pipe, 1½" brass str tip.................................15.00
Nozzle, brass, str, removable top, early, 24".................................45.00
Nozzle, brass w/chrome ALF tip, complete.................................150.00
Nozzle, Larkin, 2-man w/flow control, brass, 19", VG................140.00
Nozzle, Underwriter's Test, brass & copper, string wrap.................50.00
Punch register, Gamewell Excelsior, w/take-upn reel..................300.00
Rattle, alarm; wooden, single reed, NBFD, VG 125.00
Ring, presentation; 20 Yrs Service, gold w/2 sm dmns................150.00
Shield, presentation; leather, dtd 1889, 24x16".......................3,000.00
Shield, presentation; leather, Presented....NJ, 1915, 23", NM....6,000.00
Siren, Sterling Siren Fire Horn, hand crank, VG 600.00
Torch, brass w/wood hdl, VG..675.00
Torch, parade; solid brass & copper, oak hdl, 36", EX 125.00
Trumpet, NP brass, VG..300.00
Trumpet, presentation; brass, much eng, 1908, 18" w/7" dia bell...850.00
Trumpet, presentation; SP w/much eng, old tassle cord, EX........850.00

Fireplace Accessories and Implements

In the colonial days of our country, fireplaces provided heat in the winter and were used year round to cook food in the kitchen. The implements that were a necessary part of these functions were varied and have become treasured collectibles, many put to new use in modern homes as decorative accessories. Gypsy pots may hold magazines; copper and brass kettles, newly polished and gleaming, contain dried flowers or green plants. Firebacks, highly ornamental iron panels that once reflected heat and protected masonry walls, are now sometimes used as wall decorations. By Victorian times the cook stove had replaced the kitchen fireplace, and many of these early utensils were already obsolete; but as a source of heat and comfort, the fireplace continued to be used for several more decades. See also Wrought Iron.

Andirons, brass, acorn/urn finials, iron knife blades, 24", pr 770.00
Andirons, brass, ball finials, fire dogs, Hunneman Boston, 16", pr...550.00
Andirons, brass, ball-top finials, baluster shaft, Am, 1795, 14", pr...635.00
Andirons, brass, Louis XVi-style, torches/wreaths, 20½", pr.......715.00
Andirons, brass, urn finials, early 1800s, 16", pr 500.00
Andirons, brass, urn finials, iron knife blades, 25", pr.............1,100.00
Andirons, brass, 2-lemon finial, ca 1800, 20½", pr.....................990.00
Andirons, brass w/CI legs (old rstr), 18", pr 165.00
Andirons, CI, classical busts of woman, 5½x9¾", pr..................330.00
Andirons, CI, Geo Washington, pnt traces, 14½", pr..................140.00
Andirons, CI, lion heads & bat wings, 2-tone bronze finish, 21", pr....275.00
Andirons, wrought iron, faceted finials, w/goosenecks, primitive, pr....525.00
Andirons, wrought iron, gooseneck style, EW Wade, 19th C, 17", pr...315.00
Andirons, wrought iron, rnd legs, pad ft, sq shaft, 15x13", pr 190.00
Coal hod, brass helmet shape, dvtl, 9", pr.................................110.00
Coal hod, hammered copper helmet shape, wrought iron mts, 21"..110.00
Crane, wrought iron, vertical bar w/rnded ends, 40" arm, 32" 200.00
Fender, brass, w/tool stands, 66", w/poker+shovel+tongs.............650.00
Fender, brass & wire, 4 ball ft, iron base fr, early 1800s, 17x48x15" ..925.00
Fender, brass & wire w/scrollwork, ca 1800, 18x40x16" 1,500.00
Fender, brass w/pierced sunburst decor, late 1800s, 18x45" 495.00
Fender, wrought iron w/serpentine front/scrolls, 18th C, 22x30"...275.00
Fender, wrought iron w/wire grill, brass top rail, 11x51x15"........685.00
Fire carrier, wrought iron, detailed, scrolled finial, 24" L............550.00
Gridiron, wrought iron, sq legs, scrolled ft, 2¼x9¼x11"+hdls.......75.00
Kettle shelf trivet, rtcl brass top, wrought-iron base, 11x14½" ...250.00
Kettle tilter, wrought iron, 2 scrolled hooks/bar, 10⅜x19½" L ...400.00

Screen, brass, scalloped fan shape when extended, 27x37" 100.00
Screen, folding brass fan shape in rococo fr on plinth base, 31"...450.00
Screen, wrought iron w/appl arabesques/woven mesh, 56".......2,100.00
Surround, CI semicircle w/marble shelf, chrome-plated, 47".......300.00
Tongs & shovel, iron w/brass hdls, urn-shape finials, 1800s, 31", 22"...180.00
Tools, brass & iron-belted, ball finials, early 1800s, 20", pr.........750.00
Trammel, wrought iron, 8 holes w/swivel loop, 19th C, 25½" 160.00
Trammel, wrought-iron ratchet type, 46½" 100.00
Trivet, brass/iron, pierced top, heart hdl, 19th C, 11x13x12" 575.00

Fishing Collectibles

Collecting old fishing tackle is becoming more popular every year. Though at first most interest was geared toward old lures and some reels, rods, advertising, and miscellaneous items are quickly gaining ground. Values are given for examples in excellent or better condition and should be used only as a guide. For more information we recommend *19th-Century Fishing Lures* by Arlan Carter; *The Fishing Lure Collector's Bible* by R.L. Streater with Dudley Murphy and Rick Edmisten; *Fishing Lure Collectibles* by Dudley Murphy and Rick Edmisten; and *Collector's Guide to Creek Chub Lures and Collectibles* by Harold E. Smith, MD. All are published by Collector Books. Our advisor for this category is Dave Hoover; he is listed in the Directory under Indiana.

Key:
GE — glass eyes
DLT — double line tie
PE — painted eyes
TE — tack eyes
2PCCB — 2-piece cardboard box

Book, Fishing Flies & Fly Tying, Wm Blades, 234 pgs, 1951, VG.50.00
Catalog, Abercrombie & Finch, ...Book of Fishing, 1968, VG+ ...65.00
Catalog, Creek Chub, color pgs, 22 pgs, 1950, NM.....................220.00
Catalog, Creek Chub, Tough One, 1927, 9x6", EX 895.00
Catalog, Heddon, fold-out pg, 1935, 10x7", EX...........................375.00
Catalog, Heddon, 43 pgs, 1939, NM 220.00
Catalog, Shakespeare, color, 51 pages, 1930, VG 110.00
Compass, brass, clip-on, Marble's...20.00
Creel, split cane w/leather trim & pocket, canvas straps, Campae, EX....95.00
Creel, willow & split rattan, leather fish-shaped latch, VG 110.00
Decoy, C Christenson, Northern Pike, GE, wooden tail, 9¾", EX....85.00
Display, Xd paddles w/dk gr canoe center, Old Town Canoe, EX..60.00
Fish grabber, Marble Arms, mechanically sound, 1920s, G 75.00
Float, casting; yel & blk decal, Montague, w/weight, EXIB.........165.00
Fly box, Hardy Neroda, w/24 flies, lg clips, 4x6", EX.................275.00
Lure, Creek Chub, Deluxe Wag Tail, GE, wht w/red head, EX...145.00
Lure, Creek Chub, Flip Flap, GE, silver flash, EX.......................250.00
Lure, Creek Chub, Giant Straight Pike, #6002, TE, wht w/red head, NIB..95.00
Lure, Creek Chub, Husky Jointed Pike, #3302, GE, M (2PCCB) ..125.00
Lure, Creek Chub, Husky Plunker, GE, silver flash, EX-.............165.00
Lure, Creek Chub, Injured Minnow, #1518, GE, M (2PCCB)......95.00
Lure, Creek Chub, Jigger, GE, red, scale, EX-...............................225.00

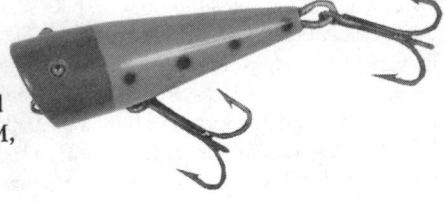

Lure, Creek Chub **Musky Plunker**, orange with black spots and red head, 3⅝", NM, $1,500.00.

Lure, Creek Chub, Pickerel Pike, #2600R, GE, M (2PCCB)......325.00

Lure, Creek Chub, Pike #2602, jtd, GE, M (2PCCB) **55.00**
Lure, Creek Chub, Plunker #9200 Ultra Light, perch, 1⅝", MIB.**25.00**
Lure, Creek Chub, Pop & Dunk, GE, wht w/red head, EX+ **75.00**
Lure, Creek Chub, Snook Pike #5501, jtd, perch, M (2PCCB)..**125.00**
Lure, Creek Chub, Wiggler 100, DLT, GE, chub, NM.................**150.00**
Lure, Creek Chub, Wiggler 200, DLT GE, EX **65.00**
Lure, Heddon, Crab Wiggler #1800, red & wht, GE, EX (G box)..**225.00**
Lure, Heddon, Crazy Crawler #2100, red & yel, 2-pc, EX-............**75.00**
Lure, Heddon, Deluxe Basser, wht w/red gill & eyes, EX............**155.00**
Lure, Heddon, Flap-Tail, vamp, wht w/red head & tail, GE, EX ...**75.00**
Lure, Heddon, Gamefisher, shiner scale, VG- **25.00**
Lure, Heddon, Go Deeper Crab #1900, PE, gr crackleback, MIB..**65.00**
Lure, Heddon, King Basser #8560, GE, pearl x-ray shore minnow, EX..**125.00**
Lure, Heddon, Luny Frog, bar rig, plain blk centers, EX...............**85.00**
Lure, Heddon, Punkinseed #730, bluegill, EX.........................**225.00**
Lure, Heddon, Sea Runt, PE, strawberry, VG+ **125.00**
Lure, Heddon, Zara Puppy, clear w/yel eyes, EX........................**10.00**
Lure, Heddon, Zig Wag, shiner scale, GE, 2-hook pattern, EX ...**145.00**
Lure, Heddon #100, GE, red head & tail w/wht middle, EX-......**375.00**
Lure, Heddon #200, wht w/blended red head, GE, 2-pc, EX- **225.00**

Lure, Heddon #400 Bucktail Surface Minnows: Yellow with sienna-yellow forehead, glass eyes, red flannel tail hook dressing, 2⅝", EX, $450.00; Early Rainbow finish, glass eyes, white bucktail dressed tail treble hook, 2⅝", VG, $325.00.

Lure, Heddon #1700 Near Surface Wiggler, GE, hump line tie, VG-..**85.00**
Lure, Hoage Magnetic Weedless, perch, w/wht lightning stripe, EX ..**55.00**
Lure, P&K Weedless Wonder Crab, brn, MOC **20.00**
Lure, Pflueger, All-in-One Minnow #3500, GE, 2 trebles, EX **225.00**
Lure, Pflueger, Conrad Frog, 1-hook, airbrushed, 1931, 3", EX **45.00**
Lure, Pflueger, Cyclone Spinner #3053, mk spinners, 1915, 1⅛", EX...**45.00**
Lure, Pflueger, Flocked Mouse, 2 trebles, 1950s, 2¾", EX **175.00**
Lure, Pflueger, Invincible Minnow, 2 trebles, 1900, 3¾", EX........**45.00**
Lure, Pflueger, Live-Wire #7600, 2 trebles, ca 1931, 3½", EX........**50.00**
Lure, Pflueger, Pal-O-Mine #5000, 2 trebles, ca 1924, 3¼", EX....**45.00**
Lure, Pflueger, Pearl Squid, single hook, no spinner blade, 1885, EX ..**35.00**
Lure, Shakespeare, Jack Smith, 2 trebles, 1935, 3¾", EX **65.00**
Lure, Shakespeare, Striped Bass Wobbler #6636, 2 lg trebles, '39, EX..**125.00**
Lure, Shakespeare, Swimming Mouse #578, 2 trebles, 1924, 3⅜", EX....**45.00**
Lure, Shurebite Glutton Trolling Spoon, MIB **25.00**
Lure, Shurebite Surf Spinner, MIB **10.00**
Lure, South Bend, Bass-Oreno, GE, pike scale, EX **125.00**
Lure, South Bend, Dive-Oreno #952 YP, TE, yel perch, MIB **55.00**
Lure, South Bend, Min-Buck Minnow #943, 3 trebles, 1914, 3", EX..**85.00**
Lure, South Bend, Musk-Oreno #976, 3 trebles, 1926, 4½", EX...**45.00**
Lure, South Bend, Underwater Minnow #903, 3 trebles, 1921, 3", EX..**65.00**
Lure, South Bend, Vacuum Bait (sm) #21, 3 trebles, 1925, 2", EX....**110.00**
Lure, South Bend, Worden Combination Minnow #933, 1914, 2⅝", EX..**75.00**
Lure, Wright & McGill, Flapper Crab, GE, gr w/red stripes, EX.**225.00**
Net, brass & aluminum, folding, triangular, Hardy, 30" hdl, EX....**30.00**
Net, No Snag, folding spring fr, leather belt case w/emb fish, VG ...**40.00**

Net, trout; Weber #29, laminated wood w/orig net, 23½" dia, EX...**50.00**
Plaque, Heddon, walleye pictured on tree slab, 6x9½", EX..........**95.00**
Prints, Denton, Lake Trout, Sea Bass, 9¼x12", EX, ea **35.00**
Reel, Abu #1750A, 1 end sandwiched, EX- **85.00**
Reel, Ambassadeur #2050, sandwich end plates, EX...................**95.00**
Reel, Ambassadeur #5000, red, grooved rims, 4-screw, VG **70.00**
Reel, Ambassadeur #6000, ridge rim, 4-screw, EX......................**90.00**
Reel, Mitchell Orca #70, MIB **45.00**
Reel, Shakespeare Criterion, level-wind, EXIB...........................**35.00**
Reel, Shakespeare Uncle Sam #23059, VG+ **35.00**
Rod, Leonard Model 50-DF Tournament Trout; 3-pc, 96" **430.00**
Rod, Orvis' Light Salmon, 3-pc, 102", EX (EX bag & tube) **165.00**
Rod, trout; Sharps' Scottie, 2-pc, 84", M (orig bag & tube)........**550.00**
Scale, J& & JS George, Pat 1878, NP brass, 10-lb, VG................**25.00**
Weight, casting; South Bend, wht, 3¾", EX- **25.00**

Flags of the United States

Over the past few years the popularity of vintage flags has grown dramatically, and prices have risen greatly as a result. The pending restoration of the Fort McHenry Flag (The Star Spangled Banner) has also created greater public interest in flag collecting.

The brevity and imprecise language of the first Flag Act of 1777 allowed great artistic license for America's early flag makers. This resulted in a rich variety of imaginative star formations which coexisted with more conventional row patterns. In 1912 inviolate design standards were established for the new 48-star flag, but the banners of our earlier history continue to survive:

The 'Great Star' pattern — configured from the combined stars of the union, appeared in various star denominations for about 50 years, then gradually disappeared in the post-Civil War years.

The utilitarian 'scatter' pattern — created through the random placement of stars, is traceable to the formative years of our nation and remained a design influence through most of the nineteenth century.

The 'wreath' pattern — first appearing in the form of simple single-wreath formations, eventually evolved into the elegant double- and triple-wreath medallion patterns of the Centennial period.

Acquisition of specific star denominations is also a primary consideration in the collecting process. Pre-Civil War flags of 33 stars or less are very scarce and are typically treated as 'blue chip' items. Civil War-era flags of 34 and 35 stars also stand among the most sought-after denominations. Market demand for 36-, 37-, and 38-star flags is strong but less broad-based, while interest in the unofficial 39-, 40-, 41-, and 42-star examples is largely confined to flag aficionados. The very rare 43 remains in a class by itself and is guaranteed to attract the attention of the serious collector.

Row-patterned flags of 44, 45, and 46 stars still turn up with some frequency and serve as a source of more modestly priced vintage flags. Ordinary 48-star flags flood the flea markets and are priced accordingly, while the short-lived 49 is regarded as a legitimate collectible. Thirteenth-star flags, produced over a period of more than 200 years, surface in many forms and must be assessed on a case-by-case basis.

Many flag buffs favor sizes that are manageable for wall display, while others are attracted to the more monumental proportions. Allowances are typically made for the normal wear and tear — it goes with the territory. But severe fabric deterioration and other forms of excessive physical damage are legitimate points of negotiation.

The dollar value of a flag is by no means based upon age alone. The wide price swings in the listing below have been influenced by a variety of determining factors related to age, scarcity, and aesthetic merit. In fact, almost any special feature that stands out as unusual or distinctive is a potential asset. Imprinted flags and inscribed flags; 8-point stars, gold stars, and added stars; extra stripes, missing stripes, tricolor stripes, and war stripes are all part of the pricing equation. And while political and military flags may rank above all others in terms of prestige and price, any flag with a significant and well-documented historical connection has 'star' potential (pardon the pun). Our advisor for this category is Ryan Cooper; he is listed in the Directory under Massachusetts.

13 stars, circular pattern, hand sewn, 1860s, 29x40" 1,800.00
13 stars, hand/machine sewn, Centennial, 60x86" 650.00
13 stars, printed glazed muslin, 1880s, 7x11" 100.00
13 stars, US Naval boat insignia, 1880, 50x96" 750.00
15 stars, Union Jack from War of 1812, rare, 35x62" 23,000.00
15 stars, 15 stripes, all machine sewn, ca 1912, 48x72" 375.00
16 stars, Great Star, hand sewn, 1850s, 54x78" 6,800.00
19 stars, 16 orig+3, sewn scrap fabric, 39x66" 6,500.00
20 stars, oval pattern, ship's flag, 1818, worn, 64x128" 6,500.00
21 stars, Commissioning pennant, ship 'Herald,' 1819, 50-ft ... 8,500.00
25 stars, oval pattern w/central star, ship's flag, 96x200" 6,700.00
25 stars, row pattern, Civil War, 90x175" 2,200.00
26 stars, Great Star, embr on sewn silk, 30x43" 7,500.00
29 stars, entirely hand sewn, poor condition, 43x68" 2,500.00
30 stars, gold stars/fringe, silk, delicate, 52x68" 3,500.00
31 stars, Great Star, hand-sewn silk, 14' 2,500.00
31 stars, row pattern, hand-stitched bunting, 104x247" 2,500.00
32 stars, dbl wreath of inset stars, hand sewn, 36x48" 5,200.00
33 stars, Great Star, hand-sewn muslin, 60x96" 4,200.00
33 stars, hand-/machine-sewn wool bunting, 66x92" 2,250.00
33 stars, in rows, printed bunting, 28x44", G- 700.00
34 stars, dbl-wreath pattern, printed silk, 18x28" 900.00
34 stars, Great Star, from Albany RR Depot, 116x175" 4,500.00
34 stars, printed linen, 3 sewn sections, 22x48" 600.00
34 stars, random pattern, hand sewn, 66x140" 1,200.00
35 stars, dbl-wreath pattern, printed, sized muslin, 19x28" 750.00
35 stars, recruiting flag, sewn bunting, 50x116" 1,300.00
35 stars, row pattern, hand/machine sewn, 96x180" 950.00
36 stars, cut-in, in rows, machined stripes, 25x50" 700.00
36 stars, inscr parade flag, muslin print, 6x9" 250.00
36 stars, sailing ship's, inscr & dtd, 75x142" 950.00
37 stars, medallion pattern, printed/sewn muslin, 48x87" 450.00
37 stars, printed silk, 32x40" 225.00
37 stars, row pattern, hand-sewn silk, poor, 60x80" 230.00
37 stars, row pattern, stitched bunting, 30x48" 450.00
38 stars, medallion-wreath pattern, printed cotton, 12x17" 225.00
38 stars, printed silk w/ribbon ties, 30x47" 250.00
38 stars, row pattern, clamp dyed in 3 sections, 60x120" 220.00
38 stars, row pattern, hand/machine-stitched bunting, 71x116" .250.00
38 stars, unique wreath pattern, sewn, 89x134" 500.00
38 stars, 1776-1876 pattern, printed linen, 27½x46" 1,800.00
39 stars, Centennial 'International Flag,' 16x24" 140.00
39 stars, row pattern, all machine-stitched bunting, 40x84" 350.00
39 stars, row pattern variation, printed silk, 12x24" 125.00
39 stars (6-5 pattern), printed gauze bunting, 19x34" 125.00
40 stars, row pattern, hand-sewn bunting, lg, 98x204" 270.00
40 stars, row pattern, printed/sewn British import, 55x106" 185.00
41 stars (rare), printed cotton sheeting, 15x24" 225.00
42 stars, sewn cotton, from Ft Hamilton NY, 120x177" 275.00
42 stars, 7-row pattern, printed cotton, 12x17" 125.00
43 stars, machine-sewn bunting, extremely rare, 29x70" 1,200.00
44 stars, machine-sewn cotton bunting, 53x82" 200.00
44 stars, triple-wreath pattern, printed cotton, 23x26" 175.00
45 stars, HP w/sewn stripes, 38x70" 120.00
45 stars, machine-sewn cotton bunting, 80x108" 55.00
45 stars, printed silk w/red ribbon ties, 32x46" 45.00
45 stars, row pattern variant, printed muslin, 9x13" 25.00
46 stars, machine-sewn wool bunting, 72x138" 60.00

46 stars, printed silk, GAR Post in gold, 32x45" 350.00
47 stars, unofficial, sewn bunting, 108x137" 350.00
48 stars, all crocheted, dtd 1941, 20x38" 85.00
48 stars, machine-sewn cotton bunting, 60x96" 30.00
48 stars, printed cotton w/GAR surprint, 11x16" 25.00
48 stars, sewn to form 'USA,' unauthorized WWI, 45x69" 300.00
48 stars, USN Union Jack, machine-sewn wool, 23x33" 35.00
48 stars in gold, sewn WWII casket flag, 58x118" 95.00
49 stars, embr, sewn stripes, 36x60" 45.00
49 stars, 3 uncut flags, printed cotton sheet, 37x36" 25.00
50 stars, early prototype 'June 1959,' 52x66" 220.00
50 stars, hand-knitted coverlet w/fringe, 30x51" 30.00
51 stars, printed flaglette for DC statehood, 4x6" 15.00

Florence Ceramics

Figurines marked 'Florence Ceramics' were produced in the '40s and '50s in Pasadena, California. The quality of the ware and the attention given to detail are prompting a growing interest among today's collectors. The names of these lovely ladies, gents, and figural groups are nearly always incised into their bases. The company name is ink stamped. Examples are evaluated by size, rarity, and intricacy of design. For more information we recommend *The Florence Collectibles* by Doug Foland, a coadvisor for this category. You will find him listed in the Directory under Oregon. Another source is *The Collector's Encyclopedia of California Pottery, Second Edition*, by Jack Chipman; he is listed in the Directory under California. Advise also came from Jerry Kline; he is listed in the Directory under Tennessee.

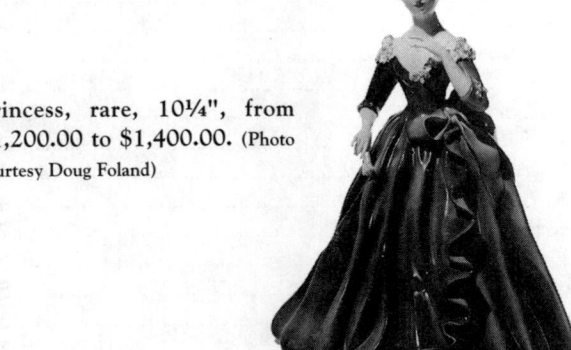

Princess, rare, 10¼", from $1,200.00 to $1,400.00. (Photo courtesy Doug Foland)

Adeline, bl or pk 295.00
Amber, 9¼" 700.00
Angel, 7¾" 140.00
Baby, flower holder, from $75 to 100.00
Barbara, child, 8½", from $200 to 250.00
Bea, from $100 to 150.00
Birthday Girl, 9", from $1,000 to 1,250.00
Blossom Girl, flower holder 125.00
Bryan, very rare, from $2,500 to 3,000.00
Camille, Godey style, from $175 to 250.00
Camille, hands, 8½" 325.00
Carol, rare, from $600 to 700.00
Catherine, 7¾" 700.00
Charles, 8¾" 325.00
Charmaine, hands away, 8½" 300.00
Cinderella & Prince Charming, from $2,500 to 3,000.00

Clarissa, hand w/articulated fingers, 7¾" 275.00
Cynthia, w/lace & fur, gold trim, 9¼" 750.00
Darleen, 8¼" 650.00
Dear Ruth, lamp, from $950 to 1,250.00
Deborah 750.00
Delia, hand showing, from $150 to 200.00
Diana, powder box, 6¼" 450.00
Diane, from $175 to 200.00
Edward, 7" 450.00
Elizabeth, red dress 450.00
Elizabeth, 8½x7", from $350 to 450.00
Ellen, from $120 to 125.00
Fern, flower holder/wall pocket, w/gold, 7", from $200 to 250.00
Gary, 8½" 200.00
Georgette, 10" 750.00
Gesille, from $900 to 1,000.00
Grandmother & I, rare, from $2,500 to 3,000.00
Her Majesty, 7" 200.00
Jeanette, fancy, 7¾" 225.00
Jim, 6¾" 80.00
Josephine, from $200 to 250.00
Joyce, 9" 500.00
Karla, ballerina, from $200 to 450.00
Kay, flower holder, 7" 60.00
Lavon, rare, 8½" 500.00
Leading Man, 10½" 475.00
Lillian, 7¼" 150.00
Little Princess, very rare, from $1,250 to 1,500.00
Louis XV and Madame Pompadour, pr 900.00
Louise, 7¼", from $135 to 145.00
Madame Du Barry, rare, from $300 to 450.00
Madame Pompadour, 12½" 450.00
Madeline, from $200 to 300.00
Marsie, from $350 to 400.00
Mary, seated, 7½" 600.00
Matilda, 8½" 175.00
Mikado, from $800 to 900.00
Musette, 8¾" 495.00
Pamela, 7¼" 325.00
Pat & Mike, pr, from $250 to 400.00
Pinky & Blue Boy, pr 750.00
Prima Donna, from $500 to 650.00
Priscilla & John Alden, pr 500.00
Rebecca, aqua dress w/violet trim, 7" 325.00
Rebecca, other colors, 7" 250.00
Rhett 395.00
Sarah, 7½" 130.00
Scarlett, hands away, fancy, 8¾" 300.00
Scarlett, no hand away, 8¾", from $200 to 275.00
Shirley, hands away, 8" 375.00
Story Hour w/Boy & Girl, 8" 1,250.00
Sue, 6" 75.00
Victor, 9¼", from $325 to 350.00
Victoria, lady on sofa, from $450 to 550.00
Violet, wall pocket, w/gold, 7", from $200 to 250.00
Vivian, 10" 395.00
Wood Nymph, from $300 to 450.00
Wynkin & Blykin, 5½", 5½", pr 500.00

Flow Blue

Flow Blue ware was produced by many Staffordshire potters; among the most familiar were Meigh, Podmore and Walker, Samuel Alcock, Ridgway, John Wedge Wood (who often signed his work Wedgewood), and Davenport. It was popular from about 1825 through 1860 and again from 1880 until the turn of the century. The name describes the blurred or flowing affect of the cobalt decoration, achieved through the introduction of a chemical vapor into the kiln. The body of the ware is ironstone, and Oriental motifs were favored. Later issues were on a lighter body and often decorated with gilt. For further information we recommend *The Collector's Encyclopedia of Flow Blue China* (1st and 2nd series) by Mary Frank Gaston (Collector Books).

Abbey, footed bowl, Petrus Regout, 4¾x8¼", $250.00.

Abbey, chocolate pot, Geo Jones, 10" 250.00
Abbey, teapot, Geo Jones, 6" 295.00
Alaska, bowl, oval, WH Grindley, 9" 125.00
Albany, bowl, vegetable; w/lid 275.00
Aldine, bone dish, Grindley, 6½" 50.00
Aldine, sugar bowl, w/lid, Grindley 145.00
Amoy, bowl, sauce; Davenport, 5¼" 100.00
Amoy, creamer, Davenport, 5x4¾" 550.00
Amoy, pitcher, att Adams, 7" 700.00
Amoy, plate, Davenport, 10½" 175.00
Amoy, plate, Davenport, 9" 115.00
Amoy, platter, Davenport, 17½x13½" 900.00
Amoy, relish, Davenport 265.00
Amoy, sugar bowl, ftd, w/lid, Davenport, 8x6¾" 750.00
Amoy, teapot, Davenport, 9½x10", EX 1,000.00
Anemone, plate, Minton, 10" 135.00
Argyle, bowl, vegetable; w/lid, Ford 400.00
Argyle, bowl, w/lid, 8-sided, Grindley 275.00
Argyle, butter pat 50.00
Argyle, gravy boat 150.00
Argyle, platter, Grindley, 19⅝" 500.00
Arundel, bowl, salad; silver rim, Doulton 250.00
Arundel, fork & spoon, salad; Doulton, pr 250.00
Ashburton, pitcher, Grindley, 2-qt 495.00
Asiatic Pheasants, butter dish, w/insert, Meir 495.00
Asiatic Pheasants, butter pat, Meir 60.00
Astoria, bowl, New Wharf Pottery, 9¼" 150.00
Astoria, pitcher, New Wharf Pottery, 6¾" 375.00
Athens, gravy boat, Charles Meigh, 5¼x8x3", EX 175.00
Athens, sauce tureen, w/lid, att Charles Meigh, 7x8x4", EX 450.00
Baltic, bowl, soup; Grindley 75.00
Baltic, butter pat, Grindley 35.00
Baltic, plate, Grindley, 8" 75.00
Belmont, creamer & sugar bowl, w/lid, Meakin 525.00
Belmont, wash bowl & pitcher, Grindley 1,800.00
Bentick, soup tureen, polychrome, Cauldon, w/lid, 1905-20 ....800.00
Burleigh, tureen, sauce; w/lid & tray, gold trim, Burgess & Leigh 550.00
California, plate, Podmore Walker, Wedgwood in banner, 1849, 10" 140.00
Canton, cup, demitasse; Maddock, 2½" 120.00
Cashmere, cup, Ridgway & Morley 135.00
Cashmere, plate, Ridgway & Morley, 7" 120.00
Cashmere, waste bowl, Ridgway & Morley, 3x5¼" 400.00

Celeste, platter, Alcock, 10x7" 400.00
Chapoo, bowl, vegetable; w/lid, Wedge Wood, rpr, 12x9½" 750.00
Chapoo, bowl, vegetable; Wedge Wood, ca 1850, 9½x7" 275.00
Chapoo, plate, Wedge Wood, 10½" 200.00
Chapoo, plate, Wedge Wood, 9" 175.00
Chapoo, plate, 12-sided, Wedge Wood, 8⅜", EX..............165.00
Chapoo, plate, 8-sided, T&B Boote, 7½" 125.00
Chapoo, teapot, Wedge Wood...............................1,000.00
Chinese, platter, well & tree; Dimmock, prof rpr, 15¾x12"......350.00
Chinese, vase, polychromed, Ridgways, 8¼" 275.00
Chiswick, plate, scalloped rim, Ridgways, 10" 85.00
Chiswick, saucer, smooth rim, Ridgways.....................25.00
Chusan, bowl, soup; Morely & Ashworth, flake, 10½" 200.00
Chusan, cup & saucer 125.00
Chusan, pitcher, ped ft, C Collinson & Co, 11"............1,200.00
Chusan, sugar bowl, w/lid, Clementson, 8" 700.00
Cleopatra, cake stand, att Walley, 2⅝x11¾".................800.00
Cleopatra, compote, fruit; Walley, 9x13" 1,200.00
Coburg, cup plate, Edwards, 4½" 110.00
Coburg, plate, Edwards, 8" 130.00
Coburg, plate, Edwards, 10½" 140.00
Colonial, cup & saucer 65.00
Colonial, plate, 7" 42.00
Conway, bowl, serving.....................................250.00
Conway, plate, New Wharf Pottery, 10" 90.00
Crescent, bowl, vegetable; rectangular, Grindley, 10x8".....140.00
Crescent, gravy boat w/underplate, Grindley, 4x9"..........175.00
Cyprus, bowl, Ridgway, Bates & Co, 10½" 160.00
Dahlia, sugar bowl, w/lid, att Challinor, 7½"..............550.00
Delmar, bowl, vegetable; w/lid, Grindley, 7½x11" 375.00
Doreen, wash bowl & pitcher, Grindley....................1,600.00
Dresden, platter, Johnson Bros, 12x6".....................140.00
Elsie, platter, New Wharf Pottery, 16½x14"................250.00
Fairy Villas, bowl, Adams, 6½"..............................50.00
Fairy Villas, bowl, vegetable; w/lid, Adams, 9½x12" 425.00
Fairy Villas, soap dish, att Adams, 5½x4" 75.00
Fairy Villas, soup, Adams, 9" 100.00
Florida, plate, Johnson Bros, 9"............................80.00
Gironde, bone dish, Grindley................................50.00
Gironde, gravy boat, Grindley 100.00
Gironde, soap dish, Grindley 110.00
Glenwood, creamer..90.00
Glenwood, teapot, Johnson Bros 695.00
Haddon, butter pat, Grindley 40.00
Haddon, platter, Grindley, 16¼x11½" 250.00
Hanley, plate, Meakin, 8½" 90.00
Hong Kong, bowl, soup; Charles Meigh, 10½" 225.00
Hong Kong, chamber pot, w/lid, Meigh, EX 700.00
Hong Kong, plate, Meigh, 8" 150.00
Hong Kong, platter, Meigh, 16x12", EX.....................700.00
Hong Kong, teapot, Meigh, ca 1845, rstr, 8½"..............600.00
Indian Vase, platter, S&EH, 12½x10".......................500.00
Iris, cheese dish, Doulton, 9½x9" 600.00
Iris, cup & saucer, Royal Pottery 50.00
Iris, plate, gold trim, Wilkinson, 9" 50.00
Iris, plate, sponged gold at rim, Cauldon, 10"..............90.00
Iris, platter, Wilkinson, 13x9½"...........................250.00
Iris, teapot...400.00
Jedo, wash bowl & pitcher, W Adams & Sons 1,895.00
La Belle, bowl, scalloped, oval, Wheeling, 9" 275.00
La Belle, bowl, vegetable; w/lid, Wheeling 495.00
La Belle, charger, Wheeling, 14½"..........................295.00
La Belle, chocolate pot, Wheeling, 10" 950.00
La Belle, creamer, Wheeling, 4½x6", EX 225.00

La Belle, custard ramekin, Wheeling........................295.00
La Belle, pitcher, Wheeling, 3-qt, 8" 795.00
La Belle, pitcher, Wheeling, 6¾x7½" 400.00
La Belle, sugar bowl, Wheeling, 4¾x5½".....................350.00
La Belle, syrup, w/metal lid & underplate, Wheeling 495.00
La Francaise, bowl, soup; French China, 9" 50.00
La Francaise, butter pat 22.00
La Francaise, gravy boat, w/underplate, French China 95.00
Lily, plate, Dimmock, 10".................................135.00
Lily, vase, gold tapestry & sponging, bulbous, Adderly, late 1800s, 9" ...500.00
Londsale, cup & saucer, Ridgways 110.00
Lonsdale, bowl, vegetable; rectangular w/gold, w/lid/tray, S Ford & Co....550.00
Lonsdale, plate, Ridgways, 9" 70.00
Lonsdale, plate, 10" 65.00
Lorne, bowl, vegetable; w/lid, oval, Grindley..............295.00
Lorne, plate, Grindley, 10" 100.00
Lorne, platter, Grindley, 12".............................200.00
Lorne, platter, Grindley, 14".............................275.00
Lorne, tureen, sauce; Grindley, w/lid 350.00
Lotus, tureen, w/lid, 8¾" dia, EX, +mismatched ladle.......150.00

Luneville, soup bowl, 8¾", $75.00.

Madras, plate, Doulton, 10½"..............................105.00
Madras, teapot, Doulton...................................700.00
Manilla, plate, Podmore Walker, 9¾" 195.00
Manilla, platter, 18" 795.00
Manilla, sugar bowl, Podmore Walker, 8½x6½" 500.00
Marechal Neil, bowl, cereal/fruit; Grindley, 6"............55.00
Marechal Neil, butter pat, Grindley 55.00
Marechal Neil, platter, Grindley, 16"......................215.00
Marechal Neil, sugar bowl, w/lid, Grindley 175.00
Melbourne, gravy boat, w/underplate, Grindley.............210.00
Melbourne, plate, 9" 65.00
Melbourne, platter, 16"...................................475.00
Melbourne, platter, 17"...................................240.00
Melrose, bowl, soup; New Wharf Pottery, 9" 65.00
Nankin, plate, Doulton, 10½"..............................100.00
Nankin, teapot, ped ft, att Cauldon, late 1800s..........1,000.00
Non-Pareil, butter dish, Burgess & Leigh 350.00
Non-Pareil, chop plate, Burgess & Leigh, 11½" 275.00
Non-Pareil, creamer, Burgess & Leigh, 5" 250.00
Non-Pareil, plate, Burgess & Leigh, 5¾" 35.00
Non-Pareil, sauce ladle, Burgess & Leigh, EX 200.00
Non-Pareil, saucer, extended side for spoon rest, Burgess & Leigh...125.00
Non-Pareil, tureen, w/lid, Burgess & Leigh, 7x12" 325.00
Normandy, bowl, Johnson Bros, 7⅝".........................60.00
Normandy, cup & saucer, Johnson Bros......................95.00
Normandy, plate, dessert; Johnson Bros, 7" 50.00
Normandy, plate, Johnson Bros, 10½"........................75.00
Normandy, platter, Johnson Bros, 9¾" 160.00
Old Castles, plate, Alcock, ca 1913, 10"..................150.00

Oregon, bowl, berry; Mayer......................................100.00
Oregon, sauce tureen, Mayer, w/lid & underplate, rstr 600.00
Oregon, teapot, ped ft, Mayer....................................1,000.00
Oriental, plate, Alcock, 10½".....................................140.00
Orleans, platter, Dimmock, 16x14" 500.00
Ormonde, toothbrush holder, Meakin, 5¾"..........................275.00
Ormonde, waste jar, w/lid, Meakin 800.00
Osborne, bowl, flanged, 9" 65.00
Paisley, bowl, soup; flat, Mercer, 7¼"............................40.00
Paisley, platter, Mercer, 14" 275.00
Paris, bowl, New Wharf Pottery, 8"................................55.00
Pearl, gravy, floral pattern, Upper Hanley 65.00
Pekin, butter pat, Jones..45.00
Pekin, cup & saucer, handleless; Dimmock, 2¾", 5¾" 160.00
Pekin, plate, border pattern only, Wilkinson, 8".................65.00
Pelew, plate, 9"...110.00
Penang, plate, 7"...65.00
Persian Spray, platter, Doulton, 19½x16½" 575.00
Poppy, plate, New Wharf Pottery, 8¾".............................75.00
Poppy, tureen, soup; w/lid & platter, Grindley, 5x13", 14x10" 500.00
Regent, plate, unknown mfg, after 1891, 9".......................75.00
Regent, platter, Meakin, 14" 350.00
Rhone, bowl, wash; Goodfellow, 4½x13¾", EX 400.00
Rhone, teapot, ped ft, Furnival................................1,000.00
Rock, plate, 9"..105.00
Roseville, compote, gold trim, Maddock & Sons, 4x9" 400.00
Roseville, platter, Maddock & Sons, 14½x10"......................275.00
Sabraon, creamer, 5¾"...375.00
Salisbury, wash bowl & pitcher, Ford & Sons 2,000.00
Scinde, bowl, vegetable; Alcock, 2x9½x7".........................300.00
Scinde, bowl, vegetable; Alcock, 8"..............................450.00
Scinde, creamer, Alcock, 5¼x5¼"..................................500.00
Scinde, plate, Alcock, 8¼".......................................100.00
Scinde, plate, Alcock, 9½".......................................135.00
Scinde, plate, Alcock, 10½", from $125 to 175.00
Scinde, platter, Alcock, 11x8½"..................................425.00
Scinde, soap dish, w/lid, floral border only, Alcock 350.00
Scinde, waste bowl, Alcock, 3¼x5¼" 500.00
Sevres, butter pat, Wood & Son....................................25.00
Shanghae, relish, shell shape, Furnival..........................225.00
Shanghae, sugar bowl, ped base, w/lid, Furnival 800.00
Shanghae, teapot, Furnival.....................................1,100.00
Shanghai, plate, Grindley, 9"....................................120.00
Shanghai, platter, Grindley, 13¾"................................200.00
Shapoo, coffeepot, 8-sided, T&R Boote, 9¾", EX...................650.00
Shapoo, plate, T&R Boote, 10"....................................160.00
Shell, plate, Challinor, 10¼"....................................135.00
Shell, teapot, Alcock..750.00
Strawberry Brushstroke, bowl, unmk, 9"...........................225.00
Strawberry Brushstroke, cup & saucer, handleless, NM............135.00
Temple, cup & saucer, handleless, Podmore Walker, 3", 6".........175.00
Temple, plate, Podmore Walker, 9" 125.00
Temple, relish, Podmore Walker...................................425.00
Tonquin, bowl, soup; Adams.......................................125.00
Tonquin, butter dish, Adams, 7" dia..............................500.00
Tonquin, plate, Adams, 10½"......................................185.00
Tonquin, plate, Adams & Sons, 8½"................................150.00
Tonquin, sugar bowl, Heath.......................................275.00
Touraine, bone dish..90.00
Touraine, bowl, vegetable; flanged rim, Alcock, 9½" 175.00
Touraine, bowl, vegetable; w/lid, Stanley, gold trim 495.00
Touraine, creamer, Stanley.......................................325.00
Touraine, cup & saucer, Stanley, from $120 to 150.00
Touraine, gravy boat & undertray, Stanley........................250.00

Touraine, pitcher, milk; Stanley, lg.............................950.00
Touraine, plate, Alcock, 8".......................................75.00
Touraine, plate, Alcock, 9".......................................95.00
Touraine, plate, 10"...110.00
Touraine, platter, 12"...185.00
Trilby, pitcher, hot water; Wood & Son...........................175.00
Turkey, plate, unmk, 9½"...125.00
Verona, plate, Ford & Sons, 9¾"...................................90.00
Virginia, butter pat, Maddock.....................................50.00
Virginia, platter, Maddock, 20"..................................750.00
Waldorf, bowl, serving; rnd, New Wharf Pottery...................175.00
Waldorf, creamer, New Wharf Pottery 350.00
Waldorf, cup & saucer, New Wharf Pottery 225.00
Waldorf, platter, ham/egg; New Wharf Pottery 160.00
Watteau, bowl, New Wharf Pottery.................................125.00
Watteau, bowl, ped ft, int/ext decor, dome lid, 10".............545.00
Watteau, mug, milk; New Wharf Pottery 285.00
Watteau, plate, Doulton, 10½"....................................120.00
Watteau, plate, New Wharf Pottery, 10½"..........................75.00
Watteau, platter, well & tree; Doulton, 17½x14".................795.00
Watteau, punch bowl, ped ft, Doulton, 14" 1,595.00
Waverly, bowl, vegetable; w/lid, Maddock 275.00
Waverly, plate, Grindley, 10".....................................95.00
Waverly, platter, Maddock, 17"...................................350.00
Waverly, soup tureen, w/lid & ladle, Maddock 575.00
Waverly, sugar bowl, w/lid, Grindley 250.00
Whampoa, pitcher, att Mellor Venables, 1830s, 7¼"................800.00

Flue Covers

When spring housecleaning started and the heating stove was taken down for the warm weather season, the unsightly hole where the stovepipe joined the chimney was hidden with an attractive flue cover. They were made with a colorful litho print behind glass with a chain for hanging. In a 1929 catalog, they were advertised at 16¢ each or six for 80¢. Although scarce today, some scenes were actually reverse painted on the glass itself. The most popular motifs were florals, children, animals, and lovely ladies. Occasionally flue covers were made in sets of three — one served a functional purpose, while the others were added to provide a more attractive wall arrangement. They range in size from 7" to 14", but 9" is the average.

For further information we recommend *Flue Covers, Collector's Value Guide*, by Jim Meckley II, available from Collector Books or your local bookstore.

Gypsy girl in green, 14" diameter, from $100.00 to $115.00.

Alice Blue, girl w/bl hat & jacket among flowers, 7¾", from $75 to..85.00
Asian Beauty, lady w/flowers & sticks in hair, 7", from $70 to......80.00
Autumn, pastoral scene, 6½x8¼", from $50 to............................60.00

Basket of Strawberries, spilling over, 7x8¼", from $75 to.............85.00
Dressed for Sunday, girl in finery, 7¾", from $50 to.....................60.00
Feline Love, lady w/rose in hair holds wht cat, 7¾", from $90 to..100.00
Fisherman, sailboat scene, 9¼", from $60 to.................................70.00
Flapper, lady in cloche hat w/flower, 7¾", from $75 to.................85.00
Frau & Frow, fine lady & maid servant, 9½", from $85 to...........95.00
Fun at the Pond, boy & girl skating, 9½", from $85 to................95.00
Fun Gathering Twigs, 3 smiling children, 9½", from $80 to..........90.00
Game of Croquet, puppy & kittens w/ball & mallet, 9½", $100 to..110.00
Garden Tease, blond girl points to butterfly, 7½", from $75 to.....85.00
Grandpa's Store, wht-bearded man reads to girl, 11¾", from $90 to...100.00
House by Creek, wide gold border, 10¼", from $50 to 60.00
In the Garden, 2 cherubs, 14", from $90 to.................................100.00
Jezebel, brunette w/fancy hair, irises at lower right, 8½x6½" 85.00
Lady w/Iris, dressed in yel & bl, 9½", from $85 to 95.00
Lavender Wisteria, 9¾", from $55 to...65.00
Mademoiselle, lady w/flowing brn hair, flower border, 9¼", $50 to...60.00
Matron, lady in fine plumed hat, 9½", from $90 to.....................100.00
Naive, lady in diaphanous gown, gold border, 9¼", from $55 to...65.00
Over the Fence, courting couple at fence, 9½", from $60 to.........65.00
Pansies, mc bouquet, 9½", from $75 to 85.00
Peck's Bad Boy, mischievous-looking boy, 9¾", from $75 to 85.00
Pet Goose, boy & girl w/wht goose, wide border, 7¾", from $55 to..65.00
Please Stay, Psyche & Cupid, 15½", from $110 to.......................120.00
Profile, lady in red cap w/flowing brn hair, red border, 11", $55 to..65.00
Resting w/Storm, lady leaning against horse, 9¼", from $65 to 75.00
Scholar, old man reading lg book, 10x8", from $80 to 90.00
St Nicholas, w/boy, girl & dog, 10", from $250 to 275.00
Storytime, girl in lg hat holds book, 9½", from $70 to 80.00
Summer Leisure, mother & daughter w/parasol & book, 9½", $85 to...95.00
Swallows, 3 birds on flowering branch, 9½", from $85 to.............95.00
Three Little Kittens, playing w/ball on rug, 9½", from $90 to 100.00
Under the Oak Tree, courting scene, 9¼", from $55 to.................65.00
Willameana, lady w/fan & roses sits beside table, 9½", from $80 to...90.00
Yellow Daisies, in wht woven box on shelf, 9½", from $85 to.......95.00

Folk Art

That the creative energies of the mind ever spark innovations in functional utilitarian channels as well as toward playful frivolity is well documented in the study of American folk art. While the average early settler rarely had free time to pursue art for its own sake, his creative energy exemplified itself in fashioning useful objects carved or otherwise ornamented beyond the scope of pure practicality. After the advent of the Industrial Revolution, the pace of everyday living became more leisurely, and country folk found they had extra time. Not accustomed to sitting idle, many turned to carving, painting, or weaving. Whirligigs, imaginative toys for the children, and whimsies of all types resulted. Though often rather crude, this type of early art represents a segment of our heritage and as such has become valued by collectors.

Values given for drawings, paintings, and theorems are 'in frame' unless noted otherwise. See also Baskets; Decoys; Frakturs; Samplers; Trade Signs; Weather Vanes; Wood Carvings.

Birdhouse, head-shape, open mouth holds twig nest, wood w/mc, 15"..160.00
Box, walnut w/chip-cvd decor/scratch cvd date: 1883, cut-out ft, 15"....330.00
Calligraphic drawing, birds/book/Bible/verse, 16x20"+oak fr 415.00
Calligraphic drawing, eagle flying, 18x23" 110.00
Calligraphic drawing, eagle w/banner, artist sgn, 24x30".............275.00
Calligraphic drawing, Lord's Paryer/Christ's head/branches/etc, 21x27"...195.00
Carving, cardinal, limestone, E (Popeye) Reed, 1976, 5½".........300.00
Drawing, charcoal/chalk on paper, hunting scene w/stag, fr: 30x44" 165.00
Drawing, graphite on paper, horse in landscape, L Pappe, 25x30"+fr....300.00

Drawing, pen/ink on paper, Hero of Bueno Vista, horseman, 23x18"+fr...1,045.00
Figurine, horse, laminated wood w/old blk & wht pnt, 12¼"........30.00

Figure, Uncle Sam, hand-painted composition, string jointed, early, 9", NM, $150.00.

Folding chair, forked tree branch w/bark, scenic flat surfaces, 1892....13,750.00
Oil on board, fruit still life, sgn Ream, 8x10"+ornate fr 935.00
Oil on board, primitive landscape of Hudson River Falley, 19x15"+fr...550.00
Oil on board, primitive mtn/lake landscape, ornate rpt fr, 16x12"..........375.00
Oil on board, 3-masted ship in rough sea, touch-up, in gilt fr: 17x20"...660.00
Painting on masonite, Sailing Ship..., artist sgn, OH, 18x28"+fr...275.00
Panel, wool/cotton animal/birds/etc appliqued on cotton, fr: 35x33" ..1,500.00
Plaque, 2 cvd deer heads w/twig antlers, pine cone/moss border, 14"......195.00
Theorem on paper, flowers in brn vase, oval format, 13x10" 485.00
Theorem on velvet, still life of fruit, old fr, 17x14" 660.00
Tinsel picture, mc flowers in vase on blk, shadowbox fr, 17x17".440.00
Watercolor on paper, man in frock coat, pen in hand, 4⅝x3½"+fr .220.00
Watercolor on paper, rooster, primitive style, 1812, 5½x6¾"+fr...1,750.00
Whirligig, Black lady washing clothes in tub, wood/tin/wire, 26", EX...110.00
Whirligig, Black man w/hat pumps water/Mammy does laundry, mc pnt, 27" 1,075.00
Whirligig, man sawing logs, tin/wood, mc pnt, 32¾" 150.00
Whirligig, tower (derrick like) w/facing roosters, mc pnt, 62" 110.00

Fostoria

The Fostoria Glass Company was built in 1887 at Fostoria, Ohio, but by 1891 it had moved to Moundsville, West Virginia. During the next two decades, they produced many lines of pressed patterned tableware and lamps. Their most famous pattern, American, was introduced in 1915 and was produced continuously until 1986 in well over two hundred different pieces. From 1920 to 1925, top artists designed tablewares in colored glass — canary (vaseline), amber, blue, orchid, green, and ebony — in pressed patterns as well as etched designs. By the late '30s, Fostoria was recognized as the largest producer of handmade glassware in the world. The company ceased operations in Moundsville in 1986.

Many items from both the American and Coin Glass lines have been reproduced by Lancaster Colony. In some cases the new glass is superior in quality to the old. Since the 1950s, Indiana Glass has produced a pattern called 'Whitehall' that looks very much like Fostoria's American, though with slight variations. Because Indiana's is not handmade glass, the lines of the 'cube' pattern and the edges of the items are sharp and untapered in comparison to the fire-polished originals. Three-footed pieces lack the 'toe' and instead have a peg-like foot, and the rays on the bottoms of the American examples are narrower than on the Whitehall counterparts. The Home Interiors Company offers several pieces of American look-alikes which were not even produced in the United States. Be sure of your dealer and study the books suggested below to become more familiar with the original line.

Coin Glass reproductions are flooding the market. Among items you may encounter are an 8" round bowl, 9" oval bowl, 8¼" wedding bowl, 4½" candlesticks, urn with lid, 6¼" candy jar with lid, footed comport, sugar and creamer; there could possibly be others. Colors in production are crystal, green, blue, and red. The red color is very good, but the blue is not the original color, nor is the emerald green. Buyer beware!

For further information see *Elegant Glassware of the Depression Era* by Gene Florence; *Fostoria Glassware, 1887 – 1982,* by Frances Bones; *Fostoria Stemware, The Crystal for America*, and *Fostoria Tableware, 1924 – 1943, Fostoria Tableware, 1944 – 1986, Fostoria, Useful and Ornamental,* by Milbra Long and Emily Seate; and *Fostoria, Books I* and *II*, by Ann Kerr. *Glass Animal Figural Flower Frogs of the Depression Era* by Lee Garmon and Dick Spencer offers an in-depth look at that particular aspect of Fostoria's production. (See also Glass Animals.) Their addresses are listed in the Directory under Illinois. Items with (+) at the end of the lines have been reproduced; prices are for original issues. Our advisor is Deborah Maggard; she is listed in the Directory under Ohio.

American, bell 425.00
American, bowl, float; 11½" 65.00
American, bowl, ftd, 8" 90.00
American, bowl, lemon; w/lid, 5½" 60.00
American, bowl, nappy; 5" 10.00
American, bowl, rose; 3½" 20.00
American, box, w/lid, 4½x4½" 225.00

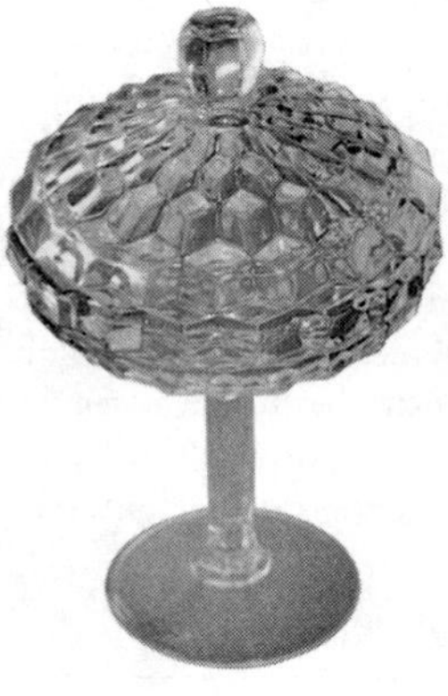

American, covered candy dish, 9½x5½", $37.50.

American, goblet, claret; #2056, 7-oz, 4⅞" 60.00
American, hat, tall, 4" 65.00
American, ice dish insert 10.00
American, mustard, w/lid 35.00
American, pitcher, ftd, 3-pt, ftd, 8" 70.00
American, plate, cake; 3-ftd, 12" 25.00
American, plate, salad; 8½" 12.00
American, sugar shaker 65.00
American, tray, rectangular, 5x2½" 80.00
American, tray, 12" dia 165.00
American, tumbler, water; #2056, ftd, 9-oz, 4⅞" 15.00
American, vase, flared, 8" 80.00
American, vase, str side, 12" 195.00
American, vase, sweet pea; 4½" 80.00
Baroque, bl, ice bucket 125.00
Baroque, bl, platter, oval, 12" 65.00
Baroque, bl, tray, oval, 11" 47.50
Baroque, crystal, bowl, fruit; 5" 15.00
Baroque, crystal, comport, 4¾" 15.00
Baroque, crystal, plate, cake; 10" 30.00
Baroque, crystal, stem, water; 9-oz, 6¾" 15.00
Baroque, yel, plate, 6" 10.00
Baroque, yel, sauce dish 40.00
Baroque, yel, vase, 6½" 110.00
Buttercup, bottle, salad dressing; #2083 .....250.00
Buttercup, bowl, salad; #2364, 11" 55.00
Buttercup, candlestick, #2324, 6" 32.50
Buttercup, celery, #2350, 11" 27.50
Buttercup, plate, #2337, 7½" 12.00
Buttercup, plate, #2337, 9½" 40.00
Buttercup, plate, sandwich; #2364, 11" 35.00
Buttercup, shaker, #2364, 2⅝" 32.50
Buttercup, stem, sherbet; #6030, high, 6-oz, 5⅝" 20.00
Buttercup, tumbler, juice; #6030, ftd, 5-oz, 4⅝" 22.00
Buttercup, vase, #2614, 10" 150.00
Camellia, bowl, hdld, 4½" 15.00
Camellia, butter dish, w/lid, ¼-lb 50.00
Camellia, ice bucket 75.00
Camellia, pitcher, 16-oz, 6⅛" 85.00
Camellia, plate, cake; hdld, 10" 30.00
Camellia, plate, luncheon; 8½" 15.00
Camellia, preserve, w/lid, 6" 65.00
Camellia, tray, center hdl, 11½" 38.00
Camellia, vase, #2657, ftd, 10½" 115.00
Camellia, vase, #6021, ftd, 6" 65.00
Century, ashtray, 2¾" 10.00
Century, bowl, lily pond; 9" 30.00
Century, bowl, snack; ftd, 6¼" 14.00
Century, candy, w/lid, 7" 37.50
Century, oil, w/stopper, 5-oz 45.00
Century, pitcher, 48-oz, 7⅛" 110.00
Century, plate, luncheon; 8½" 12.50
Century, platter, 12" 47.50
Century, stem, oyster cocktail; 4½-oz, 3¾" 20.00
Century, tray, for ind shakers, 4¼" 14.00
Century, vase, bud; 6" 18.00
Chintz, bowl, finger; #869, 4½" 65.00
Chintz, candlestick, #2496, 4" 20.00
Chintz, creamer, #2496½, ind 22.50
Chintz, plate, cake; #2496, hdld, 10½" 45.00
Chintz, plate, luncheon; #2496, 8½" 21.00
Chintz, platter, #2496, 12" 100.00
Chintz, stem, cordial; #6026, 1-oz, 3⅞" 47.50
Chintz, vase, #4143, ftd, 7½" 195.00
Coin, amber, ashtray, #1372/123, 5" 17.50
Coin, amber, oil lamp, coach; #1372/320, 13½" 135.00
Coin, amber, vase, bud; #1372/799, 8" 22.00
Coin, bl, ashtray, #1372/124, 10" 50.00
Coin, bl, lamp chimney, coach or patio; #1372/461 .....60.00
Coin, bl, urn, #1372/829, ftd, w/lid, 8" 125.00
Coin, crystal, bowl, #1372/179, rnd, 8" 25.00
Coin, crystal, nappy, #1372/495, 4½" 22.00
Coin, crystal, vase, #1372/818, ftd, 10" 45.00
Coin, gr, candle holder, #1372/316, 4½", pr 50.00
Coin, gr, pitcher, #1372/453, 32-oz, 6¼" 175.00
Coin, olive, salver, #1372/630, ftd, 6½" H 125.00
Coin, olive or crystal, cigarette urn, #1372/381, ftd, 3⅜" 20.00
Colony, bowl, cupped, 8" 35.00
Colony, bowl, finger; 4¾" 55.00
Colony, bowl, flared, 11" 40.00
Colony, comport, 4" 15.00
Colony, ice bucket 75.00
Colony, pitcher, w/ice lip, 2-qt 115.00
Colony, platter, 12" 50.00
Colony, tumbler, tea; 12-oz, 4⅞" 30.00
Colony, vase, cornucopia; 9" 70.00

Corsage, bowl, #2537, ftd, 9½" 145.00
Corsage, bowl, finger; #869 ....25.00
Corsage, bowl, sauce; #2440, oval, 6½" 75.00
Corsage, candlestick, #2535, 5½" 35.00
Corsage, celery, #2440 ....32.00
Corsage, plate, cake; #2440, hdld, 10½" 32.50
Corsage, plate, cake; #2496, hdld, 10" 35.00
Corsage, relish, #2496, 2-part 22.50
Corsage, stem, sherbet; #6014, low, 5½-oz, 4½" 16.00
Corsage, tumbler, juice; #6014, ftd, 5-oz, 4¾" 20.00
Corsage, vase, #2470, ftd, 10" 135.00
Fairfax #2375, amber, bonbon 9.00
Fairfax #2375, amber, plate, dinner; 10¼" 20.00
Fairfax #2375, amber, stem, claret; 4-oz, 6" 25.00
Fairfax #2375, gr or topaz, bowl, sweetmeat 16.00
Fairfax #2375, gr or topaz, cigarette box 25.00
Fairfax #2375, gr or topaz, relish, 11½" 13.00
Fairfax #2375, gr or topaz, whipped cream pail 30.00
Fairfax #2375, rose, bl or orchid, ashtray, 4" 17.50
Fairfax #2375, rose, bl or orchid, pitcher, #5000 ......300.00
Fairfax #2375, rose, bl or orchid, shakers, ftd, pr 70.00
Fuchsia, crystal, bonbon, #2470 ....33.00
Fuchsia, crystal, bowl, finger; #869 ....35.00
Fuchsia, crystal, stem, claret; #6004, 4-oz 45.00
Fuchsia, crystal, tumbler, #833, 5-oz 22.50
Fuchsia, wisteria, bowl, #2470, 12" 165.00
Fuchsia, wisteria, oyster cocktail, #6004, 4½-oz 35.00
Fuchsia, wisteria, stem, water; #6004, 9-oz 55.00
Fuchsia, wisteria, tumbler, #6004, ftd, 12-oz 57.50
Heather, basket, wicker hdld, 10¼x6½" 85.00
Heather, bowl, flared, 8" 32.50
Heather, candlestick, 4½" 22.00
Heather, comport, 4⅜" 30.00
Heather, pitcher, 48-oz, 7⅛" 165.00
Heather, plate, crescent salad; 7½" 45.00
Heather, plate, salad; 7½" 10.00
Heather, plate, snack tray; sm center, 10½" 30.00
Heather, relish, 2-part, 7⅜" 20.00
Heather, stem, cocktail; #6037, 4-oz, 5" 20.00
Heather, stem, cordial; #6037, 1-oz, 4" 42.00

Heather, three-part relish, 11", $35.00.

Heather, tidbit, 2-tier, metal hdl, 10¼" 45.00
Heather, tray, muffin; hdld, 9½" 33.00
Heather, tray, utility; hdld, 9⅛" 45.00
Heather, vase, bud; #6021, ftd, 6" 55.00
Heather, vase, oval, 8½" 85.00
Hermitage, amber, gr or topaz, bowl, cereal; #2449½, 6" 10.00
Hermitage, amber, gr or topaz, plate, crescent salad; #2449, 7⅜"..10.00
Hermitage, azure, candlestick, #2449, 6" 35.00
Hermitage, azure, relish, pickle; #2449, 8" 17.50

Hermitage, azure, tumbler, cocktail; #2449, 4-oz, 3" 14.00
Hermitage, crystal, ashtray, #2449 ....3.00
Hermitage, crystal, mug, #2449, ftd, 12-oz 15.00
Hermitage, crystal, stem, sherbet; #2449, 5½-oz, 3¼" 8.00
Hermitage, wisteria, ice tub, #2449, 6" 175.00
Hermitage, wisteria, relish, celery; #2449, 11" 50.00
Hermitage, wisteria, tumbler, #2449, ftd, 9-oz, 4⅛" ...25.00
Holly, bowl, baked apple; #2464 ....15.00
Holly, bowl, finger; #1769 ....35.00
Holly, candlestick, #2324, 4" 20.00
Holly, comport, #2364, 8" 32.00
Holly, pitcher, #2666, 32-oz 75.00
Holly, plate, cracker; #2364 ....25.00
Holly, plate, salad; #2337, 7½" 10.00
Holly, shakers, #2364, 3¼", pr 40.00
Holly, stem, claret/wine; #6030, 3½-oz, 6" 30.00
Holly, tumbler, juice; #6030, ftd, 5-oz, 4⅝" 15.00
Holly, vase, #2619½, 9½" 95.00
Horizon, Cinnamon, crystal or Spruce Green, bowl, fruit; 4½"......7.00
Horizon, Cinnamon, crystal or Spruce Green, cup, 8½-oz 10.00
Horizon, Cinnamon, crystal or Spruce Green, platter, oval, 12" ...22.00
Horizon, Cinnamon, crystal or Spruce Green, saucer 2.00
Jamestown, amber or brn, bowl, salad; #2719/211, 10" 21.00
Jamestown, amber or brn, salver, #2719/630, 17x10" dia.....60.00
Jamestown, amethyst, crystal or gr, celery, #2719/360, 9¼"....32.50
Jamestown, amethyst, tumbler, tea; #2719/63, ftd, 11-oz, 6".....10.00
Jamestown, bl, pk or ruby, pickle, #2719/540, 8⅜" 45.00
Jamestown, crystal, stem, sherbet; #2719/7, 6½-oz, 4¼".....12.50
June, crystal, ashtray 25.00
June, crystal, candlestick, 2" 14.00
June, crystal, decanter 425.00
June, crystal, plate, canape 20.00
June, crystal, plate, dinner; 10¼" 40.00
June, crystal, sugar pail 70.00
June, rose or bl, celery; 11½" 110.00
June, rose or bl, grapefruit 110.00
June, rose or bl, plate, salad; 7½" 18.00
June, rose or bl, platter, 15" 250.00
June, rose or bl, tray, service/lemon 350.00
June, topaz, bowl, soup; 7" 175.00
June, topaz, comport, #2400, 8" 80.00
June, topaz, plate, grill; 10" 75.00
June, topaz, saucer, AD...10.00
June, topaz, whipped cream pail.................................150.00
Kashmir, bl, bowl, baker; 9" 85.00
Kashmir, bl, candy, w/lid 150.00
Kashmir, bl, pitcher, ftd 425.00
Kashmir, bl, stem, whiskey; ftd, 2-oz 50.00
Kashmir, yel or gr, bowl, fruit; 5" 13.00
Kashmir, yel or gr, candlestick, 3" 20.00
Kashmir, yel or gr, grapefruit 50.00
Kashmir, yel or gr, shakers, pr 120.00
Kashmir, yel or gr, stem, water; 9-oz............................20.00
Lafayette, crystal or amber, almond, ind 15.00
Lafayette, Empire Green, plate, torte; 13" 110.00
Lafayette, Regal Blue or burgundy, cake plate, oval, hdls, 10½" ...60.00
Lafayette, rose, gr or topaz, bowl, cereal; 6" 25.00
Lido, bowl, bonbon; 3-ftd, 7⅜" 17.00
Lido, bowl, hdld, 4⅜" 14.00
Lido, candlestick, 4" 20.00
Lido, creamer 10.00
Lido, plate, dinner; 10¼" 45.00
Lido, plate, 7½" 9.00
Lido, relish, 3-part, 10"..30.00

Lido, stem, wine; #6017, 3-oz, 5½" 27.50
Lido, tumbler, sham; #4132, 12-oz, 4⅞" 15.00
Lido, tumbler, whiskey; #4132, 1½-oz, 2⅛" 25.00
Lido, vase, 5" 75.00
Mayflower, bowl, whip cream; #2560, hdld, 5" 22.50
Mayflower, candlestick, #2560½, 4" 27.50
Mayflower, creamer, #2560, ind 12.50
Mayflower, pitcher, #4140, flat, 60-oz, 7½" 265.00
Mayflower, plate, #2560, 7½" 10.00
Mayflower, plate, torte; #2560, 14" 50.00
Mayflower, stem, cocktail; #6020, 3½-oz, 4⅞" 18.00
Mayflower, vase, #2430, 8" 110.00
Meadow Rose, bowl, floating garden; oval, 10" 50.00
Meadow Rose, bowl, tricornered, 4⅝" 15.00
Meadow Rose, candlestick, dbl, 4½" 35.00
Meadow Rose, pitcher, #5000, ftd, 48-oz 350.00
Meadow Rose, plate, cracker; 11" 30.00
Meadow Rose, relish, #2419, 5-part, 13¼" 85.00
Meadow Rose, vase, #4108, 5" 75.00
Navarre, bowl, #2496, flared, 12" 70.00
Navarre, bowl, floating garden; #2496, oval, 10" 55.00
Navarre, celery, #2440, 9" 35.00

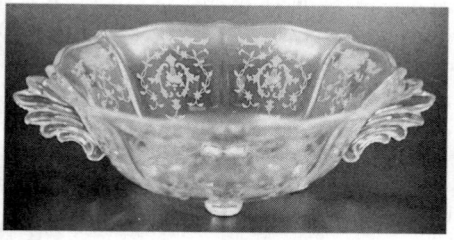

Navarre, console bowl, handled, footed, 10½", $65.00.

Navarre, creamer, #2496, ind 17.50
Navarre, dinner bell 60.00
Navarre, plate, bread & butter; #2440, 6" 11.00
Navarre, relish, #2419, 5-part, 13¼" 95.00
Navarre, sauce dish liner, #2496, oval, 8" 30.00
Navarre, stem, water; #6106, 10-oz, 7⅝" 32.00
Navarre, vase, #4108, 5" 110.00
New Garland, amber or topaz, bowl, cereal; 6" 12.00
New Garland, amber or topaz, cream soup 18.00
New Garland, amber or topaz, pitcher, ftd 225.00
New Garland, amber or topaz, tumbler, #4120, 5-oz ...12.00
New Garland, rose, bowl, finger; #4121 ....15.00
New Garland, rose, candlestick, 2" 20.00
New Garland, rose, stem, cordial; #6002 ....37.50
New Garland, rose, tumbler, #6002, ftd, 2-oz 22.00
Pioneer, azure or orchid, ashtray, deep, lg 25.00
Pioneer, bl, plate, service; 15" 35.00
Pioneer, crystal, amber or gr, ashtray, 3¾" 16.00
Pioneer, crystal, amber or gr, egg cup 20.00
Pioneer, crystal, amber or gr, platter, 12" 15.00
Pioneer, ebony, creamer, ftd 10.00
Pioneer, ebony, plate, salad; 7" 9.00
Pioneer, rose or topaz, comport, 8" 30.00
Rogene, creamer, #1851, flat 22.50
Rogene, jug, #318, 7" 135.00
Rogene, nappy, #5078, ftd, 6" 25.00
Rogene, plate, #2283, 6" 7.00
Rogene, plate, 11" 25.00
Rogene, stem, #5082, 9-oz 22.50
Rogene, stem, wine; #5082, 2½-oz 25.00
Romance, bowl, #2596, shallow, oblong, 11" 47.50

Romance, bowl, baked apple; #2364, 6" 20.00
Romance, candlestick, #2324, 4" 20.00
Romance, cigarette holder, #2364, blown, 2" 37.50
Romance, ice tub, #4132, 4¾" 70.00
Romance, plate, #2337, 9" 47.50
Romance, plate, cracker; #2364, 11¼" 25.00
Romance, stem, cocktail; #6017, 3½-oz, 4⅞" 21.50
Romance, tray, #2364, center hdl, 11⅛" 35.00
Romance, vase, #2470, ftd, 10" 115.00
Royal, amber or gr, bowl, #2324, ftd, 10" 45.00
Royal, amber or gr, bowl, finger; #869, 4½" 20.00
Royal, amber or gr, butter dish, #2350, w/lid 295.00
Royal, amber or gr, cup, #2350, flat 12.00
Royal, amber or gr, pickle, #2350, 8" 20.00
Royal, amber or gr, plate, chop; #2350, 13" 30.00
Royal, amber or gr, stem, cordial; #869, ¾-oz 70.00
Royal, amber or gr, sugar bowl, w/lid, flat 165.00
Royal, amber or gr, vase, #2324, urn style, ftd 100.00
Seascape, opal, bowl, shallow, 11½" 65.00
Seascape, opal, mayonnaise, 3-pc set 50.00
Seascape, opal, salver, ftd, 12" 125.00
Seascape, opal, tray, for ind creamer & sugar bowl ...25.00
Seascape, opal, tray, mint; ftd, 7½" 30.00
Seville, amber, bowl, console; #2371, oval, 13" 35.00
Seville, amber, comport, #2350, 8" 27.50
Seville, amber, stem, oyster cocktail; #870 ....16.50
Seville, gr, bowl, baker; #2350, oval, 9" 30.00
Seville, gr, butter dish, #2350, w/lid, rnd 250.00
Seville, gr, cup, #2350½, ftd 12.50
Seville, gr, plate, dinner; #2350, sm, 9½" 13.50
Seville, gr, sauce boat liner, #2350 ....30.00
Seville, gr, tumbler, #5084, ftd, 2-oz 40.00
Sun Ray, bonbon, hdld 16.00
Sun Ray, candelabrum, 2-light 45.00
Sun Ray, creamer, ftd 12.00
Sun Ray, nappy, hdld, regular 12.00
Sun Ray, relish, 3-part 20.00
Sun Ray, stem, goblet; 9-oz, 5¾" 16.00
Sun Ray, tumbler, tea; #2510½, 13-oz, 5⅛" 22.00
Trojan, rose, bowl, soup; #2375, 7" 125.00
Trojan, rose, celery, #2375, 11½" 42.00
Trojan, rose, grapefruit, #5282½ 60.00
Trojan, topaz, bowl, centerpc; #2394, ftd, 12" 70.00
Trojan, topaz, bowl, mint; #2394, 3-ftd, 4½" 22.00
Trojan, topaz, cup, AD; #2375 ....40.00
Trojan, topaz, oil, #2375, ftd 295.00
Versailles, bl, celery, #2375, 11½" 125.00
Versailles, bl, oil, #2375, ftd 595.00
Versailles, bl, shakers, #2375, ftd, pr 165.00
Versailles, bl, vase, #4100, 8" 295.00
Versailles, pk, gr or yel, bowl, baker; #2375, 9" 75.00
Versailles, pk, gr or yel, creamer, #2375½, ftd 20.00
Versailles, pk, gr or yel, grapefruit, #5082½ 75.00
Versailles, pk, gr or yel, platter, #2375, 15" 125.00
Versailles, pk, tumbler, tea; flat 110.00
Versailles, pk or gr, candlestick, #2394, 2", ea 28.00
Versailles, pk or gr, goblet, claret; #5098 or #5099, 4-oz, 6" ...110.00
Versailles, pk or gr, ice bucket, #2375 ....65.00
Versailles, yel, bowl, baker; #2375, 10" 60.00
Versailles, yel, sugar pail, #2378 ....165.00
Versailles, yel, whipped cream pail, #2378 ....175.00
Vesper, amber, bowl, #2267, low ftd, 7" 30.00
Vesper, amber, butter dish, #2350 ....850.00
Vesper, amber, cheese, #2368, ftd 25.00

Vesper, amber, oyster cocktail, #5100 ....30.00
Vesper, amber, stem, water goblet; #5093 ....32.00
Vesper, amber, tumbler, #5100, ftd, 2-oz 45.00
Vesper, amber or bl, candlestick, #2394, 9" 100.00
Vesper, bl, plate, dinner; #2350, sm, 9½" 40.00
Vesper, bl, stem, cocktail; #5093, 3-oz 50.00
Vesper, gr, ashtray, #2350, 4" 25.00
Vesper, gr, bowl, #2375, 3-ftd, 12½" 50.00
Vesper, gr, cup, #2350 ....15.00
Vesper, gr, platter, #2350, 15" 100.00
Vesper, gr, urn, lg 115.00

Fostoria Glass Specialty Company

The Fostoria Glass Specialty Company was founded in Fostoria, Ohio, in 1899. In 1910 they were purchased by General Electric. The new owners had an interest in developing a high-quality lustre-type art glass able to compete with the very successful glassware produced by Tiffany. They hired Walter Hicks, who had previously worked for Tiffany, to help develop the line they called Iris. Their efforts were extremely successful. The art glass they developed was cased and iridescent, very similar to Steuben's Aurene. Colors included green, tan, white, blue, yellow, and rose. It was made in several patterns, including Heart and Leaf, Leaf and Tendrils, Heart and Spider Webbing, and Lustred Dot. Although the main thrust of their production was lamp shades, vases and bowls were made as well. Iris was made for only four years, since gold was required in its production and manufacturing costs were very high. It was marked with only a paper label, without which identification is sometimes difficult. Look for a pronounced, well-finished pontil that shows the glass layers represented. Most items show a layer of white, which Fostoria called Calcite, as did Steuben. Very little has been written on the history of this company, but for more information refer to *The Collector's Encyclopedia of Art Glass* by John Shuman (Collector Books), and *Fostoria Ohio Glass, Vol II*, by Melvin L. Murray (self published).

Our advisor for this category is Frank W. Ford; he is listed in the Directory under Massachusetts.

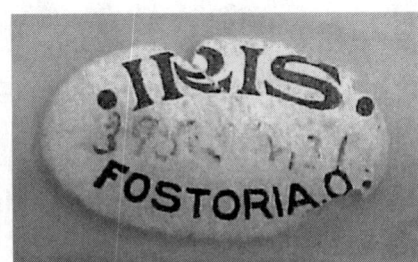

Paper label, one of two known to exist. (Photo courtesy Frank W. Ford)

Rose bowl, Iris, gold lustre leaves on opal, ovoid 500.00
Shade, festoons, gr on opal, 7" 250.00
Shade, leaves & vines, gr & gold on opal, 4-sided 250.00
Shade, leaves & vines on pearly wht, gold int, bell form, 4½" ...300.00
Vase, Iris, gold lustre, pinched-in sides, narrow neck, ftd, 4½" ...600.00
Vase, Iris, gold lustre w/gr leaves/vines, sq top, 12" 2,000.00

Frakturs

Fraktur is a German style of black letter text type. To collectors the fraktur is a type of hand-lettered document used by the people of German descent who settled in the areas of Pennsylvania, New Jersey, Maryland, Virginia, North and South Carolina, Ohio, Kentucky, and Ontario. These documents recorded births and baptisms and were used as book-

plates and as certificates of honor. They were elaborately decorated with colorful folk-art borders of hearts, birds, angels, and flowers. Examples by recognized artists and those with an unusual decorative motif bring prices well into the thousands of dollars; in fact, some have sold at major auction houses well in excess of $10,000.00. Frakturs made in the late 1700s after the invention of the printing press provided the writer with a prepared text that he needed only to fill in at his own discretion. The next step in the evolution of machine-printed frakturs combined wood-block-printed decorations along with the text which the 'artist' sometimes enhanced with color. By the mid-1800s, even the coloring was done by machine. The vorschrift was a handwritten example prepared by a fraktur teacher to demonstrate his skill in lettering and decorating. These are often considered to be the finest of frakturs. Those dated before 1820 are most valuable.

The practice of fraktur art began to diminish after 1830 but hung on even to the early years of this century among the Pennsylvania Germans ingrained with such customs. Our advisor for this category is Frederick S. Weiser; he is listed in the Directory under Pennsylvania. (Mr. Weiser has provided our text, but being unable to physically examine the frakturs listed below can not vouch for their authenticity, age, or condition. When requesting information, please include a self-addressed stamped evelope.) These prices were realized at various reputable auction galleries in the East and Midwest. Unless otherwise noted, values are for examples in excellent condition. Note: Be careful not to confuse frakturs with prints, calligraphy, English-language marriage certificates, Lord's Prayers, etc.

Key:
lp — laid paper   wc — watercolored
pr — printed   wp — wove paper
p/i — pen and ink

Birth Records

P/i/wc, bird on branch among flowers, PA, 19th C, 5¼x4" 2,000.00
P/i/wc, floral, M Breckall, PA, 1845, 11x16¼", EX 2,200.00
P/i/wc, flowers/text, 1842, 5¾x4⅛" +fr, VG 1,400.00
P/i/wc, Gerburts und Taufschein, Young, 1792, 12x15"+matt & fr ..3,600.00
P/i/wc, Gerburts und Taufschein, Young, 1835, 15x12⅜" +fr ..3,900.00
P/i/wc, heart/birds/flowers/text, Kuster, PA, 1866, 15x18" 1,800.00
P/i/wc, stars/lines/flowers, PA, 1792, 11x7" +fr, VG 1,300.00
P/i/wc, urns/text, Young, 15x12" +fr, G 950.00
P/i/wc, wreath/flowers/bow knots, PA, 1868, 9⅝x16½" +fr, G ...350.00
P/i/wc/lp, bird/branch/flowers, Ebersol, 1873, 7¼x9" 8,000.00
P/i/wc/lp, birds/leafy branch/butterfly, 3⅛x2⅝" 415.00
P/i/wc/lp, floral wreath, PA, 1775, 7¼x12¾"+old fr 1,150.00
P/i/wc/lp, flowers/hearts/birds, 1810, NJ, 8¼x10¼", VG 495.00
P/i/wc/lp, heart/bird/flowers/border, PA, 1830, 4x2¾" 2,300.00
P/i/wc/lp, tulips/flowers/text, PA, 1804, 6x8" 715.00
P/i/wc/wp, birds/flowers, 1849, 8x9", VG 275.00
P/i/wc/wp, eagle w/branch/2 stars/For a Good Boy, late, 7x10" ...330.00
P/i/wc/wp, heart/stars, trimmed, 1801, 3¼x3⅞" 300.00
P/i/wc/wp, hearts/flowers/foliage, PA, 6x7¾"+old fr 2,200.00
P/i/wc/wp, stars/figures/flowers, PA, 1852, 7⅜x12"+matt & fr ..8,500.00
Pr/i/wc, Gerburts und Taufschein, PA, 1952, 20x17"+bird's-eye fr..250.00
Pr/i/wc, heart, eagles/verse, PA, 1806, 12x15½"+newer fr...........475.00
Pr/i/wc/cut paper on lp, F Krebs, 1804, 12⅝x15⅜", VG 2,400.00
Pr/i/wc/lp, heart/flowers/vines, PA, 1795, 12½x15½" 635.00
Pr/p/i/wc, angels/birds/etc, Ruth, Rube & Young, PA, 1831, 15x19" ..200.00
Pr/p/i/wc/lp, Gerburts und Taufschein in heart, 1813, 13x15½" 1,100.00
Pr/p/i/wc/lp, verse/eagle, PA, 1812, 13x9"+fr, VG 385.00
Pr/wc, angels/cherub/birds, Ritter, PA, 1820s, 16x13", VG 200.00
Pr/wc, eagle/angels/branches, Heins, 1863, 17x14", G.................80.00
Pr/wc, flowers/leaves/reserve, PA, 12½x15¼"+fr 495.00

Pr/wc, Gerburts und Taufschein/angels, Ritter, PA, 19x16"+fr....**200.00**
Pr/wc, Ritter, PA, mid-1800s, 12⅜x15¾", VG **150.00**
Pr/wc, strong colors, PA, 1840, 8¼x13"+ornate old fr.............**660.00**

Miscellaneous

Award of merit, p/i/wc, florals/lines, PA, early 1800s, 5x4", EX ..**150.00**
Award of merit, p/i/wc/lp, flowers/borders, ca 1800, 5¼x3" **2,650.00**
Bookmark, p/i/wc, sawtooth border/flowers, PA, 1903, 8½x6½"...**5,200.00**
Bookplate, p/i/wc, bird/flower/verse, stains, 5½x3¾"+fr..............**330.00**
Bookplate, p/i/wc, floral, PA, 1798, 6¾x4⅛" **600.00**
Bookplate, p/i/wc, flower/scrolls, B Ebersol, 1879, 7x4¼", VG ..**400.00**
Bookplate, p/i/wc/wove paper, PA, 1833, 4x6½"+fr....................**825.00**
Family register, p/i/wc on paper, floral, old grpt fr, 13x16" **2,300.00**
Family register, p/i/wc/lp, flowers/hearts/etc, 1800s, 14x12" **910.00**
Family register, wc/lp, NH, ca 1823, 13½x16½" **1,600.00**
Reward of merit, p/i/wc, Engelhard, early 1800s, 3⅞x2⅞" **50.00**
Tauf Zedel, wc, floral, PA, 1850, 9x7"+old fr **100.00**
Vorschrift, p/i/wc/lp, scrolls/flowers, 1833, stains, fr, 16x20" **825.00**

Frames

Styles in picture frames have changed with the fashion of the day, but those that especially interest today's collectors are the deep shadow boxes made of fine woods such as walnut or cherry, those with Art Nouveau influence, and the oak frames decorated with molded gesso and gilt from the Victorian era. Our advisor for this category is Michael Hinton; he is listed in the Directory under Pennsylvania.

Note: Unless another date is given, frames described in the following listings are from the nineteenth century.

Brass, cast bow (at top) & decor, oval, easel bk, #2236, 6½x4¼" ..**85.00**
Brass, cast cherubs, 20x12"..**250.00**
Brass, cut filigree, Italy, 1700s, 9x6"................................**600.00**
Brass, glass jewels, velvet easel bk, 5x7" **98.00**
Brass, pierced scrolls & florals, easel bk, ca 1900, 7¾x5" **120.00**
Cast iron, pnt/cast pheasant & berries, #230, 9x7½" **360.00**
Cherry Emp, half-columns & corner blocks, old pnt, 17x13"......**450.00**
CI, floral swags, wht w/mc details, 14¼x8¾".......................**385.00**
CI, lion head & satyr head, gold rpt, 22" **195.00**
CI, Nouveau lady's profile & swans, 10¼x7¾" **275.00**
CI, ornate scrolled medallions, 9½x8".................................**275.00**
CI, overlapping florals, wht pnt, 9x6" **220.00**
CI, 2 Nouveau ladies w/flowers & butterflies, rpt, 14x11"...........**550.00**
Curly maple w/EX curl & color, 16x16" **385.00**
Figured walnut heart shape w/old varnish, scrolled arms on base, 7"......**195.00**
Giltwood/grpt Georgian Rococo, rocaille crest, appl rosettes, 49x47" .**3,500.00**
Pine, architectural, cut/cvd, fan at top, early 1900s, 18x11" **300.00**
Silverplate, crown & Cupid crest, scroll ft, easel bk, 8 12" **300.00**

Solid copper frame with hand-chased designs, slip-in holder for photo, knotted brass wire easel back, 1920s, 9x6", $125.00.
(Photo courtesy Michael Hinton)

Sterling, etched flowers ea corner, standing, 2x3" **80.00**
Walnut, beveled, 2" molding, 17x14" **150.00**
Walnut Am Renaissance w/gilt incising, 1870s, 38x38", pr **550.00**
Walnut cross-corner w/appl cutouts, 24x30" **140.00**

Frances Ware

Frances Ware, produced in the 1880s by Hobbs, Brockunier and Company of Wheeling, West Virginia, is a term refering to the decoration or finish used in the production of some of their glassware lines. Hobnail (Dewdrop) is the most commonly found of these lines, though Swirl and on occasion Quartered Block with Stars were also finished with the frosted surface and amber-stained band that defines the Frances Ware indication. Though in general collectors also tend to regard examples in crystal with simply an amber-stained band as Frances Ware, according to *Hobbs, Brockunier & Co. Glass* by Nelia and Tom Bredehoft (Collector Books), this is incorrect. The company called this finish 'decorated #7.' To evaluate examples in crystal with amber stain, deduct 10% from the values given below, which are strictly for the frosted finish. Our advisors for this category are Betty and Clarence Maier; they are listed in the Directory under Pennsylvania.

Hobnail, bowl, ftd, berry pontil, 6x10".............................**150.00**
Hobnail, bowl, no flange, 9" sq **85.00**
Hobnail, bowl, oblong, 8" **75.00**
Hobnail, bowl, sq, 7½" **70.00**
Hobnail, bowl, 2½x5½" **30.00**
Hobnail, bowl, 7½", from $65 to **75.00**
Hobnail, bowl, 8" dia..**75.00**
Hobnail, butter dish, from $80 to **120.00**
Hobnail, chandelier, amber font, brass fr, 14" dia **950.00**

Hobnail, creamer, from $40.00 to $60.00.

Hobnail, cruet, from $425 to **500.00**
Hobnail, finger bowl, 4", from $25 to **35.00**
Hobnail, pitcher, milk **175.00**
Hobnail, pitcher, water; sq top, 8½" **195.00**
Hobnail, sauce dish, sq, 4"...**28.00**
Hobnail, shakers, very rare, pr **300.00**
Hobnail, sugar bowl, w/lid, from $65 to..............................**80.00**
Hobnail, syrup, pewter lid **375.00**
Hobnail, toothpick holder/toy tumbler................................**60.00**
Hobnail, tray, cloverleaf, 12", from $90 to **125.00**
Hobnail, tumbler, water..**45.00**
Quartered Block w/Stars, bowl, oval, 10" **65.00**
Quartered Block w/Stars, butter dish **95.00**
Quartered Block w/Stars, goblet **140.00**
Quartered Block w/Stars, sugar bowl, w/lid **75.00**
Swirl, bowl, 4"...**25.00**
Swirl, cruet, from $250 to **295.00**

Swirl, mustard jar, from $90 to......................................125.00
Swirl, pitcher, water 225.00
Swirl, shakers, pr...165.00
Swirl, sugar bowl, w/lid...80.00
Swirl, sugar shaker, orig lid...195.00
Swirl, syrup, Pat dtd 295.00
Swirl, tumbler 45.00

Franciscan

Franciscan is a trade name used by Gladding McBean and Co., founded in northern California in 1875. In 1923 they purchased the Tropico plant in Glendale where they produced sewer pipe, gardenware, and tile. By 1934 the first of their dinnerware lines, El Patio, was produced. It was a plain design made in bright, attractive colors. El Patio Nouveau followed in 1935, glazed in two colors — one tone on the inside, a contrasting hue on the outside. Coronado, a favorite of today's collectors, was introduced in 1936. It was styled with a wide, swirled border and was made in pastels, both satin and glossy. Before 1940 fifteen patterns had been produced. The first hand-decorated lines were introduced in 1937, the ever-popular Apple pattern in 1940, Desert Rose in 1941, and Ivy in 1948. Many other hand-decorated and decaled patterns were produced there from 1934 to 1984.

Dinnerware marks before 1940 include 'GMcB' in an oval, 'F' within a square, or 'Franciscan' with 'Pottery' underneath (which was later changed to 'Ware.') A circular arrangement of 'Franciscan' with 'Made in California USA' in the center was used from 1940 until 1949. At least forty marks were used before 1975; several more were introduced after that. At one time, paper labels were used.

The company merged with Lock Joint Pipe Company in 1963, becoming part of the Interpace Corporation. In July of 1979 Franciscan was purchased by Wedgwood Limited of England, and the Glendale plant closed in October 1984.

Note: Due to limited space, we have used a pricing formula, meant to be only a general guide, not a mechanical ratio on each piece. Rarity varies with pattern, and not all pieces occur in all patterns. Our advisors for this category are Mick and Lorna Chase (Fiesta Plus); they are listed in the Directory under Tennessee. See also Gladding McBean.

Coronado

Both satin (matt) and glossy colors were made including turquoise, coral, celadon, light yellow, ivory, and gray (in satin); and turquoise, coral, apple green, light yellow, white, maroon, and redwood in glossy glazes. High-end values are for maroon, yellow, redwood, and gray. Add 10 – 15% for gloss.

Bowl, casserole; w/lid, from $85 to 125.00
Bowl, cereal; from $15 to 20.00
Bowl, cream soup; w/underplate, from $40 to................50.00
Bowl, fruit; from $12 to 18.00
Bowl, nut cup; from $16 to..18.00
Bowl, onion soup; w/lid, from $45 to.............................60.00
Bowl, rim soup; from $28 to 32.00
Bowl, salad; lg, from $35 to 50.00
Bowl, serving; oval, 10½", from $30 to...........................45.00
Bowl, serving; 7½" dia, from $20 to...............................25.00
Bowl, serving; 8½" dia, from $18 to...............................20.00
Bowl, sherbet/egg cup; from $15 to 18.00
Butter dish, from $35 to 45.00
Cigarette box, w/lid, from $75 to....................................90.00
Creamer, from $12 to..15.00
Cup & saucer, demitasse; from $28 to 45.00

Cup & saucer, jumbo...35.00
Demitasse pot, from $125 to 195.00
Fast-stand gravy, from $28 to..40.00
Jam jar, w/lid, from $65 to 80.00
Pitcher, 1½-qt, from $35 to..60.00
Plate, chop; 12½" dia, from $25 to 35.00
Plate, chop; 14" dia, from $35 to 45.00
Plate, crescent hostess; w/cup well, no established value
Plate, crescent salad; lg, no established value
Plate, ind crescent salad; from $25 to 35.00
Plate, 6½", from $6 to...10.00
Plate, 7½", from $9 to...12.00
Plate, 8½", from $12 to...15.00
Plate, 9½", from $15 to...18.00
Plate, 10½", from $20 to...25.00
Platter, oval, 10", from $20 to..25.00
Platter, oval, 13", from $30 to..45.00
Platter, oval, 15½", from $45 to......................................60.00
Relish dish, oval, from $20 to 35.00
Shakers, pr, from $20 to 35.00
Sugar bowl, w/lid, from $15 to 25.00
Teacup & saucer, from $12 to 15.00
Teapot, from $65 to 95.00
Tumbler, water; no established value
Vase, 8", no established value

Desert Rose

Ashtray, ind 20.00
Ashtray, oval..125.00
Ashtray, sq 295.00
Bell, Danbury Mint 125.00
Bell, dinner..125.00
Bowl, bouillon; w/lid..395.00
Bowl, cereal; 6"...15.00
Bowl, divided vegetable..45.00
Bowl, fruit..7.00
Bowl, mixing; lg...195.00
Bowl, mixing; med..185.00
Bowl, mixing; sm..175.00
Bowl, porringer...200.00
Bowl, rimmed soup...28.00
Bowl, salad; 10"...115.00
Bowl, soup; ftd...32.00
Bowl, vegetable; 8"...32.00
Bowl, vegetable; 9"...40.00
Box, cigarette...125.00
Box, egg...195.00
Box, heart shape...165.00
Box, rnd...165.00
Butter dish...45.00
Candle holders, pr...145.00
Candy dish, oval...295.00
Casserole, 1½-qt...85.00
Casserole, 2½-qt, minimum value 495.00
Coffeepot...125.00
Coffeepot, ind...395.00
Compote, lg..75.00
Compote, low..125.00
Cookie jar...295.00
Creamer, ind...40.00
Creamer, regular...22.00
Cup & saucer, coffee...85.00
Cup & saucer, demitasse..55.00

Cup & saucer, jumbo	65.00
Cup & saucer, tall	45.00
Cup & saucer, tea	15.00
Egg cup	35.00
Ginger jar	225.00
Goblet, ftd	195.00
Gravy boat	32.00
Heart	145.00
Hurricane lamp	495.00
Jam jar	125.00
Long 'n narrow, 15½x7¾"	495.00
Microwave dish, oblong, 1½-qt	285.00
Microwave dish, sq, 1-qt	215.00
Microwave dish, sq, 8"	245.00
Mug, bbl, 12-oz	50.00
Mug, cocoa; 10-oz	135.00
Mug, 7-oz	32.00
Napkin ring	65.00
Piggy bank	295.00
Pitcher, jug	195.00
Pitcher, milk	75.00
Pitcher, syrup	95.00
Pitcher, water; 2½-qt	125.00
Plate, chop; 12"	75.00
Plate, chop; 14"	175.00
Plate, coupe dessert	65.00
Plate, coupe party	195.00
Plate, coupe steak	195.00
Plate, divided; child's	195.00
Plate, grill	125.00
Plate, side salad	40.00
Plate, TV	175.00
Plate, 6½"	6.00
Plate, 8½"	12.00
Plate, 9½"	20.00
Plate, 10½"	18.00
Platter, turkey; 19"	295.00
Platter, 12¾"	45.00
Platter, 14"	65.00
Relish, oval, 10"	35.00
Relish, 3-section	75.00
Shaker & pepper mill, pr	295.00
Shakers, rose bud, pr	18.00
Shakers, tall, pr	75.00
Sherbet	25.00
Soup ladle	95.00
Sugar bowl, open, ind	125.00
Sugar bowl, regular	32.00
Tea canister	225.00
Teapot	125.00
Thimble	75.00
Tidbit tray, 2-tier	195.00
Tile, in fr	75.00
Tile, sq	45.00
Toast cover	195.00
Trivet, fluted, rnd	325.00
Tumbler, juice; 6-oz	55.00
Tumbler, 10-oz	32.00
Tureen, soup; flat bottom	495.00
Tureen, soup; ftd, either style	695.00
Vase, bud	75.00

For other hand-painted patterns, we recommend the following general guide for comparable pieces (based on current values of Desert Rose):

Daisy	-20%
October	-20%
Cafe Royal	Same as Desert Rose
Forget-Me-Not	Same as Desert Rose
Meadow Rose	Same as Desert Rose
Strawberry Fair	Same as Desert Rose
Strawberry Time	Same as Desert Rose
Fresh Fruit	Same as Desert Rose
Bountiful	Same as Desert Rose
Desert Rose	Base Line Values
Apple	+10%
Ivy	+20%
Poppy	+50%
Original (small) Fruit	+50%
Wild Flower	200% or more!

Apple Pieces Not Available in Desert Rose

There are several Apple items that are so scarce they command higher prices than fit the above formula. The Apple ginger jar is valued at $600.00+, the 4" jug at $195.00+, and any covered box in Apple is at least 50% more than Desert Rose.

There is not an active market in Bouquet, Rosette, or Twilight Rose, as these are scarce, having been produced only a short time. Our estimate would place Bouquet and Rosette in the October range (-20%) and Twilight Rose in the Ivy range (+40%).

El Patio, 1934 – 1954

This line includes a few pieces not offered in Coronado, and the colors differ; but per piece these two patterns are valued about the same.

Bowl, batter; minimum value	450.00
Bowl, str sides, lg	55.00
Bowl, str sides, med	45.00
Casserole, stick hdl & lid, ind	65.00
Coaster	65.00
Jam jar, redesigned	425.00
Shaker & pepper mill, wooden top, pr	395.00
½-apple baker, from $195 to	225.00

Franciscan Fine China

The main line of fine china was called Masterpiece. There were at least four marks used during its production from 1941 to 1977. Almost every piece is clearly marked. This china is true porcelain, the body having been fired at a very high temperature. Many years of research and experimentation went into this china before it was marketed. Production was temporarily suspended during the war years. More than 170 patterns and many varying shapes were produced. All are valued about the same with the exception of the Renaissance group, which is 25% higher.

Bowl, vegetable; serving, oval	50.00
Cup	20.00
Plate, bread & butter	18.00
Plate, dinner	30.00
Plate, salad	25.00
Saucer	12.00

Starburst

Ashtray, ind	20.00
Ashtray, oval, lg	50.00
Bonbon/jelly dish	35.00

Bowl, crescent salad..40.00
Bowl, divided, 8"...25.00
Bowl, fruit; ind..13.00
Bowl, salad; ind...25.00
Bowl, soup/cereal..13.00
Bowl, vegetable; 8½"...45.00
Butter dish..45.00
Candlesticks, pr, from $175 to..200.00
Casserole, lg...100.00
Coffeepot...150.00
Creamer..15.00
Cup & saucer...25.00
Gravy boat, from $20 to..30.00
Jug, water; 10"..90.00
Mug, sm..60.00
Mug, tall..95.00
Oil cruet..75.00
Pepper mill...150.00
Pitcher, water; 10"..85.00
Pitcher, 7½", from $50 to..75.00
Plate, chop; from $55 to...65.00
Plate, dinner..12.00
Plate, 6"...6.00
Plate, 8"...8.00
Plate, 11"...45.00

Platter, 15", $80.00; Gravy boat with attached undertray, $40.00, Gravy ladle, $30.00.

Shakers, bullet shape, lg, pr..50.00
Shakers, sm, pr..20.00
Snack/TV tray w/cup rest, 12½", from $75 to.................................100.00
Sugar bowl...25.00
Tumbler, 6-oz, from $40 to...50.00
Vinegar cruet..75.00

Frankart

During the 1920s Frankart, Inc., of New York City, produced a line of accessories that included figural nude lamps, bookends, ashtrays, etc. These white metal composition items were offered in several finishes including verde green, jap black, and gunmetal gray. The company also produced a line of caricatured animals, but the stylized nude figurals have proven to be the most collectible today. With few exceptions, all pieces were marked 'Frankart, Inc.' with a patent number or 'pat. appl. for.' All pieces listed are in very good original condition unless otherwise indicated. Our advisor for this category is Walter Glenn; he is listed in the Directory under Georgia.

Aquarium, 3 kneeling nudes encircle 10" fish bowl, 10½".......1,250.00
Ashtray, nude emerges from leaves to hold tray above, 25".....1,250.00
Ashtray, nude kneels on cushion, holds 3" pottery tray, 6"..........450.00
Ashtray, nude stands, 3" ashball on geometric base, 10"..............650.00

Ashtray, nude stands/leans against circle, tray at ft, 7"...............550.00
Ashtray, nudes bk to bk hold rack of 4 rnd ashtrays, 8"............750.00
Ashtray, satyr (striding) holds 3" ceramic tray, 8".......................450.00
Bookends, nude fan dancer holds books, 10", pr......................550.00
Bookends, nude sits atop metal book, 10", pr...........................550.00
Bookends, nude sits atop mushrooms, 8", pr 550.00
Bookends, nudes kneeling, bks support books, 6", pr.................450.00
Bookends, Roman inspired masks, 7½", pr..............................575.00
Candy dish, majorette, 1 knee supports dish, 10" 750.00
Cigarette box, nudes bk to bk hold 4" rectangular glass box, 9"..950.00
Lamp, nude holds rod above, glass panel hangs by rings, 13"...1,550.00
Lamp, nude silhouettes (standing) against rectangular glass panel, 11" ..1,050.00
Lamp, nude stands, arms bk, glass butterfly wings, 10¼" 1,800.00
Lamp, nudes (2) kneel bk-to-bk, 8" crackle globe between, 9"...1,450.00
Lamp, nudes (2) stand bk-to-bk, hold skyscraper globe, 21"....1,250.00
Lamp, nudes (2) stand either side sq glass cylinder, 13" 1,500.00
Lamp, nudes (2) stand either side 8" crackle globe, 9" 1,250.00
Wall plaque, Diana the Huntress, 8" sq....................................550.00
Wall sconce, nude sits on floral framework, 6"..........................650.00

Frankoma

The Frank Pottery, founded in Oklahoma in 1933 by John Frank, became known as Frankoma in 1934. The company produced decorative figurals, vases, and such, marking their ware from 1936 to 1938 with a pacing leopard 'Frankoma' mark. These pieces are highly sought. The entire operation was destroyed by fire in 1938, and new molds were cast — some from surviving pieces — and a similar line of production was pursued. The body of the ware was changed in 1955 from a honey tan (called 'Ada clay,' referring to the name of the town near the area where it was dug) to a red brick clay (known as Sapulpa), and this, along with the color of the glazes (over fifty have been used), helps determine the period of production. A Southwestern theme has always been favored in design as well as in color selection.

In 1965 they began to produce a limited-edition series of Christmas plates, followed by a bottle vase series in 1969. Considered very collectible are their political mugs, bicentennial plates, Teenagers of the Bible plates, and the Wildlife series. Their ceramic Christmas cards are also very popular items with today's collectors.

Frankoma celebrated their fiftieth anniversary in 1983. On September 26 of that same year, Frankoma was again destroyed by fire. Because of a fire-proof wall, master molds of all 1983 production items were saved, allowing plans for rebuilding to begin immediately.

Frankoma filed for Chapter 11 in April, 1990, and eventually sold to a Maryland investor in February of 1991, thereby ending the family-ownership era. For a more thorough study of the subject, we recommend that you refer to *Frankoma Treasures* and *Frankoma and Other Oklahoma Potteries* by Phyllis and Tom Bess, our advisors; you will find their address in the Directory under Oklahoma.

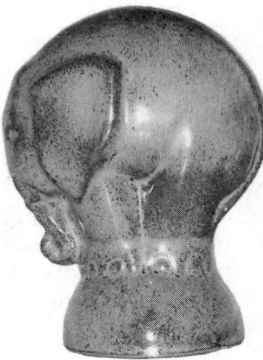

Sculpture, Elephant, #160, from $110.00 to $135.00.

Ashtray, Elephant, Prairie Green, #359, 1952....200.00
Ashtray, Sleeping Cocker Spaniel, Prairie Green, Ada clay, 1948-49..135.00
Bookend, Dreamer Girl, Prairie Green, #427, 5⅝", ea....250.00
Bookends, duck, Prairie Green, red clay, 4½", pr....350.00
Bookends, Irish Setter, Chocolate Brown, Sapulpa clay, pr....185.00
Bookends, Puma on Rocks, blk gloss, Sapulpa Clay, #119, pr....200.00
Bowl, Prairie Green, #5N, 5½x11"....45.00
Candle holders, Prairie Green, Ada clay, #300, 2½x3¾", pr....95.00
Canisters, Prairie Green, #25F/#25S/#25C/#25C, 4 for....185.00
Christmas card, 1944, from $400 to....500.00
Christmas card, 1947-48, from $95 to....115.00
Christmas card, 1949, from $85 to....95.00
Christmas card, 1950-51, from $125 to....150.00
Christmas card, 1952, Donna Frank, from $150 to....200.00
Christmas card, 1952, from $125 to....140.00
Christmas card, 1953, from $90 to....110.00
Christmas card, 1954....110.00
Christmas card, 1957....70.00
Christmas card, 1958-60....65.00
Christmas card, 1961-66....60.00
Christmas card, 1967-68....50.00
Christmas card, 1969-71....40.00
Christmas card, 1972....35.00
Christmas card, 1973-75....30.00
Christmas card, 1976-77....25.00
Christmas card, 1978-79....25.00
Christmas card, 1980-82....25.00
Jar, cvd, Prairie Green, Ada clay, #70, 1940s, 5"....85.00
Jug, Bar-B-Que, Prairie Green, 4"....65.00
Jug perfume, wht, missing rawhide hdl & cork stopper, 3½x3½"...210.00
Lazy susan, Wagon Wheel, Desert Gold, Sapulpa clay, complete..75.00
Mug, elephant, 1968, from $75 to....95.00
Mug, elephant, 1969, from $65 to....85.00
Mug, Elephant, 1974, Nixon/Ford....500.00
Mug, Elephant or Donkey, 1975-76, from $30 to....40.00
Mug, Elephant or Donkey, 1977-90, from $20 to....30.00
Mug, 1974, from $35 to....45.00
Pitcher, Guernsey, Peacock Blue, Ada clay, 5"....75.00
Pitcher, tea; Fawn Brown, Ada clay, pacing leopard mk, ca 1936, 7"...175.00
Plate, salad; Mayan Aztec, 7"....12.00
Platter, Plainsman, Prairie Green, 17"....70.00
Sculpture, Bronco, Osage Brown, Ada clay....210.00
Sculpture, Cat, Prairie Green, mini, 3"....110.00
Sculpture, Circus Horse, glossy brn, 4½"....175.00
Sculpture, Gardener Boy, Prairie Green, #702....125.00
Sculpture, Gardener Girl, Prairie Green, unglazed face/arms, Ada clay..125.00
Sculpture, Greyhound, Flame Orange, red clay, 14½" L....275.00
Sculpture, Horse, Prairie Green, Ada clay, 2½x3"....120.00
Sculpture, Indian Chief, glossy blk, Ada clay, 7½"....125.00
Sculpture, Nude & Puma, G Smith, Desert Gold, Sapulpa clay, 11¾" L...130.00
Sculpture, Panther, Prairie Green, 3⅛"....100.00
Sculpture, Ponytail Girl, Prairie Green, 10"....80.00
Shakers, Bull, Prairie Green, pr....175.00
Tumbler, Prairie Green, #5L....8.00
Vase, collector; V-1, from $125 to....150.00
Vase, collector; V-2, 1970, 12", from $80 to....90.00
Vase, collector; V-4, 1972....85.00
Vase, collector; V-5, 1973, 13"....85.00
Vase, collector; V-6, from $80 to....90.00
Vase, collector; V-7, 13"....80.00
Vase, collector; V-8, w/stopper, 13"....75.00
Vase, collector; V-9, w/stopper, 13"....75.00
Vase, collector; V-10 & V-11, ea, from $40 to....50.00
Vase, collector; V-12, 13"....65.00
Vase, collector; V-14, from $75 to....85.00
Vase, collector; V-15, 13", from $85 to....100.00
Vase, Double Nude, Desert Sand, Gerald Smith, #272, 11"....160.00
Vase, Duck, Prairie Green, Ada clay, 3¾x3¼", from $200 to....250.00
Vase, Fawn, #51, Deco form, 6¾x3¾"....215.00
Vase, Low Ring, Blue-Gray Jade, #13, 3¼"....150.00
Vase, Prairie Green, hdld urn form, 11"....85.00
Vase, Thunderbird, Osage Brown, Ada clay, mini, 3½"....135.00
Wall mask, Indian Maiden, Prairie Green, 4⅛"....55.00
Wall plaque, Peter Pan, Prairie Green, #100, 6x4¼"....100.00
Wall pocket, Billiken, Prairie Green, Ada clay, 1954, 7"....100.00
Wall pocket, Phoebe, Prairie Green, Ada clay, #730, 7½"....150.00

Fraternal Organizations

Fraternal memorabilia is a vast and varied field. Emblems representing the various organizations have been used to decorate cups, shaving mugs, plates, and glassware. Medals, swords, documents, and other ceremonial paraphernalia from the 1800s and early 1900s are especially prized. Our advisor for Odd Fellows is Greg Spiess; he is listed in the Directory under Illinois. Information on Masonic and Shrine memorabilia has been provided by David Smies, who is listed under Kansas. Assistance concerning Elks collectibles was provided by David Wendel; he is listed in the Directory under Missouri.

Elks

Badge, Fort Worth member at Dallas Reunion 1908, bronze, 2 part..50.00
Bookends, BPOE, gray metal, Ronson, 1922, 3¼", pr....75.00
Card, membership; 1925 Lakewood NJ, in leather holder, 3¼x4⅜"..22.50
Compact, silver, ornate flower decor, Portland OR eng, ca 1900s....165.00
Decanter, Elks Centennial, dtd 1968, made by Jim Beam Company..15.00
Medal, New York Elks, St Louis Reunion 1899, EX....85.00
Money safe, logo on front, mk Marathon inside, 1x2"....30.00
Mug, logo opposite hdl, mk Staten Island, 3¾"....35.00
Plate, tin w/advertising, BPOE, 1912....45.00
Postcard, Elks Club Room, Cleveland OH, unmailed, EX....10.00
Tip tray, 45th Annual Reunion...Los Angeles, 1909, 4", EX....95.00

Masons

Apron, wht silk w/emblems & brocade, ca 1885, 13x14½"....200.00
Bible, Holman; Mason Edition #3, c 1924, EXIB....25.00
Book, History of Supreme Council, 1801-1861, c 1964, EX....15.00
Book, Master's Lectures, 2nd printing 1961, 96 pgs, EX....10.00
Book, Poetry of Freemasonry, Robert Morris, 1884, 8x10½", VG+...35.00
Bookends, emblems, CI, Judd, ca 1928, 5¼", pr....50.00
Brooch, Eastern Star centered in 25 rhinestones in star shape, 1"...15.00
Carpet, red & blk, sun/eye/moon/tools/etc, 36x53", EX....125.00
Creamer, Eastern Star, hand-pnt star, gold trim, Lefton China, 3x4"..10.00
Glass, Mason Shriner Syria, Atlantic City 7/13/04, pnt decor, EX..60.00
Pin, Eastern Star High Princess Studded Cross & Gavel; ½"....15.00
Plate, Blue Delft, celebrates 50th Anniversary in 1903, 10"....55.00
Plate, SP, Gorham, ca 1903....50.00
Postcard, Masonic Temple, Cheyenne WY, divided bk, unused....5.00
Print on silk, Washington's Apron, presentation pc, fr, 14x11"..100.00
Shield, compass framing arm & gavel, cvd walnut, 1902, 20x18"...230.00

Odd Fellows

Badge, Emerald Lodge....45.00
Book, General Laws of the IOOF of Oklahoma, 7th edition, 1948, VG...12.00
Bookends, symbols, bronze, Vergne Artware, #119, ca 1935, 6¼", pr....125.00

Hat rack, pnt horseshoe shape w/5 ceremonial weapons, mc/gilt, 37".....**600.00**
Pin, representative; yel w/blk IOOF, 1920, EX................................**12.50**
Stickpin, gold wash, 3 rings w/enameled F, L, & T, EX.................**12.50**

Shrine

Fez, Oleika, Public Relations,
EX, from $20.00 to $25.00.

Book, Ritual...White Shrine of Jerusalem, 1924, EX.....................**30.00**
Cup, loving; 37th Imperial Council AAONMS, Rochester 1911, 4½"...**22.50**
Decanter, camel shape, Mr Boston Distilleries, 1975, EX **22.50**
Fez, red wool w/gold insignia, 1930s, NM...................................**15.00**
Mug, 59th Session, Atlantic City, Lenox, 1933 ....**75.00**
Plate, crystal w/emblems & HP flowers, emb scimitar, 1906, 6"....**20.00**
Plate, Pittsburgh Commandery, 1907, 8" **85.00**
Wristwatch, Bulova, Fez on dial, 17-jewel, running......................**45.00**

Miscellaneous

Am Legion, bookends, bronze, ca 1939, 8", pr **50.00**
Knights of Columbus, bookends, gray metal, Ronson, 1922, 3¼", pr ..**45.00**
Knights of Pythias, peephole, diecast metal, old, 7x4¼" **50.00**
Syria Temple, bookends, camel relief, gray metal, ca 1930, 5½", pr ...**50.00**

Fraunfelter

Charles Fraunfelter organized his company in Zanesville, Ohio, in 1915. It was known as the Ohio Pottery Company until 1923. During this period their main product was a line of utilitarian articles for chemical laboratories made of hard-paste porcelain. In 1918 they used the same body to produce a brown and white line called 'Petruscan.' By 1920 a line of hotel ware was added. The company organized in 1923 and became known and Fraunfelter China Company; but after the death of Fraunfelter in 1925, the business fell into hard times and eventually closed altogether in 1939.

Plaque, vase of flowers, rose/daisy gold border, Rhodes, 11x8" **350.00**
Trivet, HP roses w/much gold, #80, 6½" dia **50.00**
Vase, bl lustre, shouldered, #98, 5⅞", NM **50.00**
Vase, gr-gold lustre, shouldered, PHS, 1925, 5¾" **75.00**

Fruit Jars

As early as 1829, canning jars were being manufactured for use in the home preservation of foodstuffs. For the past twenty-five years, they have been sought as popular collectibles. At the last estimate, over four thousand fruit jars and variations were known to exist. Some are very rare, perhaps one-of-a-kind examples known to have survived to the present day. Among the most valuable are the black glass jars, the amber Van Vliet, and the cobalt Millville. These often bring prices in excess of $10,000.00 when they can be found. Aside from condition, values are based on age, rarity, color, and special features.

Our advisor for this category is John Hathaway; he is listed in the Directory under Maine.

Acme (on shield w/stars & stripes), qt..**2.00**
Acme Seal (script), lt sun-colored amethyst, qt............................**55.00**
Acme Seal (script), regular mouth, qt **50.00**
All Right Rev Patd Jan 26th 1868, repro closure, qt **118.00**
Amazon Swift Seal (in circle), bl, pt..**22.00**
American (over eagle & flags) Fruit Jar, lt gr, qt.........................**125.00**
Anchor (block letters, below slanted anchor), qt...........................**70.00**
Atlas (dropped), jelly glass, ½-pt...**6.00**
Atlas (4-leaf clover) Good Luck, ½-gal..**25.00**
Atlas E-Z Seal, amber, qt...**55.00**
Atlas E-Z Seal, gr, w/gr lid, pt or qt, ea.......................................**18.00**
Atlas E-Z Seal, ½-pt..**3.00**
Atlas Mason Improved Patd, gr, qt **25.00**
Atlas Mason's Patent, apple gr, qt...**20.00**
Atlas Mason's Patent, lt olive gr, pt...**45.00**
Atlas Mason's Patent, lt olive gr, qt...**25.00**
Atlas Strong Shoulder Mason, gr, qt...**20.00**
Ball Eclipse, wide mouth, ½-gal..**6.00**
Ball Ideal, sq, ½-gal...**3.00**
Ball Improved (dropped A), pt...**9.00**
Ball Mason, apple gr, qt..**35.00**
Ball Mason (disconnected underscore, dropped A), bl, pt.............**12.00**
Ball Perfect Mason, amber, 6 ribs, ½-gal **45.00**
Ball Perfect Mason, aquamarine, ½-gal..**25.00**
Ball Perfect Mason (no cross bar in A), bl, qt................................**15.00**
Ball Perfect Mason (offset to right), emerald gr, qt **75.00**
Ball Sanitary Sure Seal, bl, ½-gal..**50.00**
Ball Standard, aqua, wax sealer, tin lid, ½-gal...............................**20.00**
Banner (in stippled banner), ½-pt..**120.00**
Beaver Chewing a Log Over Beaver, lt gr, midget **225.00**
Bee, aqua, no closure, scarce, ½-gal...**600.00**
Boston Trade Mark Dagger (dagger) Brand, lt gr, qt....................**250.00**
Clark's Peerless, aqua, qt..**6.00**
Cohansey (arched), aqua, ½-gal **45.00**
Corona Jar Made in Canada, pt...**3.00**
Crown (crown), apple gr, clear insert, qt..**25.00**
Crown (no dot crown), sky bl, qt...**35.00**
Crown Crown (ring crown), aqua, qt..**17.00**
Daisy FE Ward & Co, aqua, qt..**10.00**
Dexter (circled by fruit & vegetables), aqua, qt **75.00**
Doolittle Patented Dec 3rd 1901 (on lid), ½-gal............................**50.00**
Drey Improved Ever Seal, pt...**2.00**
Eureka (script), base: Eureka Jar Co Boston Mass, ½-pt...............**40.00**
Excelsior, aqua, unlisted sz: ½-gal...**65.00**
Foster Sealfast, wide mouth, qt...**5.00**
Fruit Keeper, GCCo, aqua, pt, orig clamps **75.00**
Genuine (Mason script in flag), aqua, qt..**12.00**
Green Mountain (in fr), qt..**12.00**
Hazel Atlas E-Z Seal, aqua, qt..**20.00**
Hero, aqua, qt...**35.00**
Kerr 'Self Sealing' Mason, amber, qt...**40.00**
King (on banner below crown), pt..**8.00**
Knox (K in Keystone) Mason, w/correct Knox insert, ½-pt...........**40.00**
Leotric, aqua, sm mouth, qt...**5.00**
Mason's (cross) Improved Rev Circle, aqua, qt **25.00**
Mason's CFJ Patent Nov 30th 1858, apple gr, qt..........................**55.00**
Mason's Cross Improved Ghost Trade Mark, lt apple gr, qt...........**48.00**
Mason's Cross Patent Nov 30th 1858, lt apple gr, qt....................**69.00**
Mason's Crystal Jar, ½-gal...**35.00**
Mason's II Patent Nov 30th 1858, aqua, qt...................................**25.00**
Mason's Improved, aqua, ½-gal..**10.00**

Mason's Patent, teal, ½-gal 25.00
Mason's Patent Nov 30th 1858, apple gr, smooth lip, ½-gal 50.00

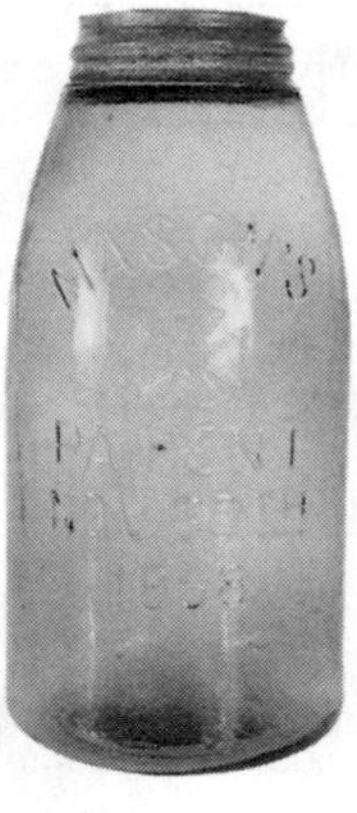

Mason's Patent Nov 30th 1858, golden yellow amber, Pat Nov 26 67 on smooth base, screw lid, half-gallon, M, $275.00.

Mason's Patent Nov 30th 1858, bl, qt 50.00
Mason's Patent Nov 30th 1858, reverse: UG Co, aqua, qt 15.00
Mason's Patent Nov 30th 1858, reverse: UG Co Ball, bl, qt 50.00
Mason's Patent Nov 30th 58, aqua, midget 60.00
Mason's 10 Patent Nov 30th 1858, aqua, qt 25.00
Mason Star Jar, qt 1.00
Mountain Mason, rnd, qt 22.00
Mrs Chapin's Mayonnaise Boston Mass, pt 6.00
Myer's Test Jar, orig lid, repro brass clamp, qt 175.00
Pearl Fruit Jar (on lid), pt 6.00
Presto Supreme Mason, reverse; Mfg by Owens-Illinois..., ½-pt ...15.00
Presto Supreme Mason, ½-gal 5.00
Princess, pt 18.00
Putnam (base), amber, qt 45.00
Putnam (base), aqua, 1½-pt 30.00
Queen (circled by pat dates), aqua, ground lip, qt 33.00
Safe Seal (in circle), bl, pt 5.00
Security Seal FG Co (in triangles), pt 6.00
Selco Surety Seal (in circle) Pat July 14 1908, bl, ½-gal 60.00
Smalley's Nu Seal (in dmns), pt 6.00
Sun, aqua, pt, orig clamp 150.00
Swayzee's Improved Mason, aqua, qt 6.00
The Gem (1 line), aqua, ½-gal 10.00
Trade Mark Lightning Registered US Patent Office, cornflower, qt....100.00
Trade Mark Mason's CFJ Improved, aqua, midget 35.00
Trademark Banner Registered (in banner), qt 10.00
Trademark Keystone Registered, pt 6.00
Victory in Shield on milk glass lid, qt 8.00
Wan-Eta Cocoa Boston, amber, qt 15.00

Fry

Henry Fry established his glassworks in 1901 in Rochester, Pennsylvania. There, until 1933 when it was sold to the Libbey Company, he produced glassware of the finest quality. In the early years they produced beautiful cut glass; and when it began to wane in popularity, Fry turned to the manufacture of occasional pieces and oven glassware. He is perhaps most famous for the opalescent pearl glass called 'Foval.' It was sometimes made with blue or jade green trim in combination. Because it was in production for only a short time in 1926 and 1927, it is hard to find. For more information we recommend *Collector's Encyclopedia of Fry Glassware* by the H. C. Fry Glass Society. Our advisor for this category is Ron Damaska; he is listed in the Directory under Pennsylvania. See also Kitchen Collectibles, Glassware.

Basket, pearl ovenware, oval, 13" 35.00
Bean pot, pearl ovenware, w/lid, 1924, 1-qt 120.00
Bowl, Pershing cutting, 3½x8" 215.00
Bowl, Sunbeam cutting, hobstar base, 1896-1915, 2¾x8¾" 225.00
Bowl, Wilhelm cutting, 9" 115.00
Candlesticks, cobalt, clear swirl ball in stem, 5", pr 210.00
Candlesticks, Foval, bl bobeche/threads, disk ft, 1926, 10⅜", pr.....350.00
Casserole, blk w/silver resist, w/lid, pre-1933, 1½-qt in NP fr.....215.00
Casserole, pearl ovenware, w/lid, 6-qt 85.00
Casserole, pearl ovenware, w/lid, 7" dia 75.00
Champagne, etched, Rose, hollow stem 45.00
Chicken roaster, pearl ovenware, #1946, 14" 60.00
Comport, St Louis Dmn cutting, rayed star ft, 10x6½" 265.00
Creamer, Foval, sm 35.00
Creamer & sugar bowl, cut, notched sgn hdls 165.00
Creamer & sugar bowl, Foval w/silver o/l, jade gr hdls, 3¼", 3"..250.00
Cup & saucer, Foval, gold floral border, gr hdl, 2¼", 5½" 125.00
Cup & saucer, Foval, jade hdls, 4 for 325.00
Cup & saucer, Fuchsia 50.00
Loaf pan, pearl ovenware, rectangular, 9" 30.00
Mug, lemonade; Foval, jade gr hdl 75.00
Percolator, Foval, glass insert 400.00
Pickle dish, brilliant cutting, 8x4" 85.00
Pie plate, Ovenglass, 11½" 60.00
Pitcher, lemonade; clear crackle, w/lid, 1922-27, 9¾" 40.00
Plate, Flower Basket cutting, 9" 95.00
Plate, Foval, bl rim, 8¼", 6 for 175.00
Plate, opal w/dk gr & blk rings at rim, 10½", 3 for 70.00
Platter, meat; 6-ftd, 1927, 12½" 40.00
Relish, Asteroid cutting, oblong, 13" 150.00
Sherbet, pk, Rib Optic w/gold Rambler Rose rim, 4x3¾" 35.00
Snack set, opal, 1930s, 6x9¼" tray+2" cup 57.50
Tazza, brillant cutting, rayed base, invt rim, 8x6¼" 210.00
Tea set, Foval w/silver o/l, pot+cr/sug+6 c/s, ca 1920 ....865.00
Trivet, inscribed Fry's Heat Resisting Glass, 3 sm ft, 8" 20.00
Tumbler, brilliant cutting, 4x3", 4 for 215.00
Tumbler, pk, Rib Optic, w/gold Rambler Rose border, 5¼" 15.00
Vase, cut, trumpet form, 12x4½", NM 135.00
Vase, Honeysuckle etch, slim, #811 line, 12" 125.00
Vase, Ivy cutting, slim, 14" 275.00
Vase, jack-in-the-pulpit; Foval, amethyst rim, 10" 400.00
Vase, opal, flared rim, 5x5½", 2" at bottom 20.00
Vase, reeded crystal w/emerald threading 90.00

Fulper

Throughout the nineteenth century (for perhaps as long as one hundred years) the Fulper pottery in Flemington, New Jersey, produced utilitarian and commercial wares. But it was during the span from 1909 to 1935 (the Arts & Crafts period in particular) that they became prominent producers of beautifully glazed art pottery. Although most pieces were cast and not hand decorated, their graceful, classical shapes together with wonderful experimental glaze combinations made each piece a true work of art.

The company also made dolls' heads, Kewpies, figural perfume lamps, and powder boxes. Examples prized most highly by collectors today are those that were produced before the devastating fire of 1929 and the subsequent takeover by Martin Stangl. (See Stangl Pottery.)

Several marks were used: a vertical in-line 'Fulper' being the most common, a horizontal mark, Flemington, Rafco, Prang, and paper labels (on earlier pieces). Most Fulper is marked although unmarked pots that surface can be identified by shape and glaze characteristics. Values are determined by size, desirability of glaze, and rarity of form. Lamps with colored glass inserts are rare and avidly sought by collectors. Our advisor for this category is Douglass White; he is listed in the Directory under Florida.

Bookends, eagle, Cucumber Crystalline matt, sm rstr, 9x7½", pr...950.00
Bottle, Cat's Eye flambe, salamander emb, 8x4" 1,600.00
Bowl, bl & gr crystalline, 8½"..130.00
Bowl, Cat's Eye flambe/speckled mustard, peacock feather form, 8"....175.00
Bowl, centerpc; effigy, Chinese Blue flambe over bl matt, 8½x10" 950.00
Bowl, centerpc; Ibis, caramel & bl, Flemington Green flambe int, 11" ..1,000.00
Bowl, centerpc; turq crystalline flambe, 3-ftd, 5x11¼"...............300.00
Bowl, Flemington Green flambe over mustard matt, collar neck, 4x10" ..900.00
Bowl, gr & Butterscotch flambe, emb fish, 3x11" 1,000.00
Bowl, gr crystalline, 3-ftd, incurvate rim, 10½", NM 475.00
Bowl vase, gr & brn flambe on brn & salmon, buttresses, 6" W .260.00
Candlesticks, Cat's Eye flambe, faceted, 10½x4" 500.00
Chamberstick, bl crystalline flambe over gr, 7" 200.00
Cooker, Room 11/JK, cobalt on salt glaze, 1908, 11¼", EX 450.00
Decanter, caramel flambe w/silver o/l, musical, 9¾" 925.00
Doorstop, cat, Butterscotch flambe crystalline, 3½x9", EX.........950.00
Flower frog, Egyptian man, gr & turq flambe, Kunzman, 1909, 7½", EX....700.00
Flower frog, lady in beached canoe, gray-gr mottle, 1917, 7½" L....500.00
Incense burner, gr crystalline matt, pierced lid, 4 buttresses, 4x5"....950.00
Lamp, boudoir; gr crystalline w/striated slag panels, L24, 14⅛"...10,925.00
Lamp, cafe-au-lait w/slag inserts, mushroom shape, 24", EX+..8,500.00
Lamp, Chinese Blue & Butterscotch flambe, mushroom shape, 24x15½"..11,000.00
Mug, bl drip in matt & gloss, 4¾" 700.00
Mug, tan mottle & gr drip, 4¾"..125.00
Pitcher, grapes/Room 11/JK/horseshoe, cobalt/salt glaze, 9x7".1,800.00
Sconce, gr w/charcoal spots, vasiform cup, rectangular bk, 14¼"..1,380.00
Urn, cobalt crystalline, 2 buttressed hdls, Vasekraft, rstr, 11¼" ..550.00

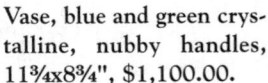
Vase, blue and green crystalline, nubby handles, 11¾x8¾", $1,100.00.

Vase, brn/bl/cream flambe, can neck, drill hole, 10" 260.00
Vase, bud; Butterscotch flambe, baluster, 9x2½"..........................275.00
Vase, Butterscotch flambe, baluster, 12x4½"..............................550.00
Vase, caramel & bl drip, 2 vertical buttresses, 9½" 625.00
Vase, Cat's Eye flambe, 16x5" 2,500.00
Vase, Chinese Blue & mirror brn flambe, drilled, 17x8" 1,500.00
Vase, Chinese Blue flambe, scratches, 10x10" 1,700.00
Vase, Chinese Blue flambe, teardrop shape, ring hdls, #574, 13x7½"...650.00
Vase, cobalt crystalline on periwinkle, ochre rim, 1915, 12".......635.00
Vase, Famille Rose flambe, 2 angular hdls, 9½x8"......................1,400.00
Vase, Flemington Green flambe, buttressed, 13½x10¼"..........2,750.00
Vase, gr & aqua crystalline, bulbous, flared rim, sm hdls, 4¾" 175.00
Vase, gr & bl flambe, orig label, 3½" 350.00
Vase, gr & brn flambe on brn & salmon, buttressed top, 6" 160.00
Vase, gr & Chinese Blue flambe, gourd shape, 3¾x6" 325.00
Vase, gr crystalline, integral hdls, 5" W 375.00
Vase, gr crystalline, sm angle hdls, 9½".....................................550.00
Vase, gr flambe, buttress hdls, #643, 7½" 1,035.00

Vase, gr/bl/purple flambe, hdls, 6½" 260.00
Vase, Leopard's Skin crystalline, classic shape, 9¾x6½" 600.00
Vase, maroon/gr/bl flambe, ribbed, hdls, 8½"...........................150.00
Vase, mirror blk crystalline, 4 rstr hdls, lines, 13x12" 700.00
Vase, mirrored gr/mahog/ivory flambe, 2-hdld urn form, 12x7½" 1,200.00
Vase, moss to rose (thick frothy), Oriental shape, 10x8".............550.00
Vase, mottled gr/cream/brn drip, stick neck, 5½" 200.00
Vase, pk matt w/gr streaks, 4 buttresses on flared cylinder, 8¼"..285.00
Vase, purple & bl matt, bulbous w/tapered neck, 7½".................350.00
Vase, purple-bl matt, raised rim, rim-to-hip hdls, 6" 460.00
Vase, Rose Famille, bulbous, #121, 6¼x3¼", ...1,300.00
Vase, Rouge Flambe, classic shape, 12x7"..................................650.00
Wall pocket, Pipes of Pan, Cucumber matt, ink mk, 10½x4¾" ..400.00
Wash bowl, grapes/G, cobalt on salt glaze, 1908, 7x9½", EX 700.00

Furniture

American seventeenth- and eighteenth-century furniture played an important role in our country's environment. Aside from its utility, furniture was a symbol indicating wealth, taste, and station in life of the owner. Each period brought about distinct design changes that created a recognizable form for that particular time frame. Our earliest furniture was handmade by the cabinetmaker with apprentices and journeymen who learned every phase of the craft from the master cabinetmaker. The end of the Civil War brought the Industrial Revolution and mechanization of furniture manufacturing. With it came the ornate Victorian period and the many revival styles. These were followed in the twentieth century by Art Deco and Art Nouveau and more revival of our earliest periods.

It is important for the buyer of antique and collectible furniture to approach each piece from the point of view of the prevailing taste of that particular time frame. Pieces from lesser cabinetmakers should be recognized simply as old furniture, as age alone does not equal value.

Indeed the marketplace has completely recovered from the recession. Equally important is the change in the marketplace. Victorian oak furniture is not as desirable or pricey as it was in years past. Ornate Victorian furniture in dark woods such as rosewood and walnut has not faired as badly and is still being pursued. Prices for case pieces of period furniture in formal and high country styles continue to top most auction houses estimates. Still on the rise are the sound mahogany pieces from the first half of the twentieth century in the traditional styling of Queen Anne, Chippendale, Sheraton, Hepplewhite, and Duncan Phyffe. Enjoying the popularity are English counterparts. Turn of the century European inlaid and carved furniture is still rising in value. Stronger in the marketplace is the 'decorator trade,' who realize this type of furniture is a sound value and can be refinished (without any loss of value) to suit the client's needs. Upholstered pieces that are 'floor ready' are bringing stronger prices at auction. Frames for sofas, chairs, and benches needing new upholstery and some work are being sold reasonably to eager collectors and dealers. They realize that when the work is completed, they have a unique, well made item at a reasonable price.

Items that have sold at auction for at least 25% lower than their normal market values will be designated with (*). Items listed in the lines that are designated with (**) are pieces in the best of form and of museum quality.

Please note: If a piece actually dates to the period of time during which it originated, we will use the name of the style only. For example: 'Hepplewhite' will indicate an American piece from roughly the late 1700s to 1815. The term 'style' will describe a piece that is far removed from the original time frame. 'Hepplewhite style' refers to examples from the turn of the century. When the term 'repro' is used it will mean that the item in question is less than thirty years old and is being sold on a secondary market. When only one dimension is given for blanket chests, dry sinks, tables, settees, sideboards, and sofas, it is length.

Condition is the most important factor to consider in determining value. It is also important to remember that *where* a piece sells has a definite bearing on the price it will realize, due simply to regional preference. Our advisor for this category is Suzy McLennan Anderson, ISA CAPP, of Heritage Antiques and Anderson Auctions, LLC, whose address is listed in the Directory under New Jersey. (Photo and SASE required; no phone appraisals.) To learn more about furniture, we recommend *The Collector's Encyclopedia of American Furniture* (there are three in the series) and *Furniture of the Depression Era* by Robert and Harriet Swedberg; *Heywood-Wakefield Modern Furniture* by Steve and Roger Rouland; *Antique Oak Furniture* by Conover Hill; *American Oak Furniture, Books I and II*, and *Victorian Furniture, Our American Heritage, Books I and II*, by Kathryn McNerney; and *Collector's Guide to Oak Furniture* by Jennifer George. See also Art Deco; Art Nouveau; Arts and Crafts; Fifties Modern; Nutting, Wallace; Shaker; Stickley.

Key:

Am — American	Geo — Georgian
bj — bootjack	grpt — grainpainted
brd — board	hdbd — headboard
Chpndl — Chippendale	hdw — hardware
Co — Country	Hplwht — Hepplewhite
cvd — carved	mar — marriage
cvg — carving	NE — New England
c&b — claw and ball	QA — Queen Anne
do — door	rswd — rosewood
drw — drawer	trn — turning, turned
Emp — Empire	uphl — upholstered/upholstery
Fed — Federal	vnr — veneer
Fr — French	Vict — Victorian
ftbd — footboard	W/M — William and Mary
G — good	: — over (example: 1 do:2 drw)

Armoires, See Also Wardrobes

Cherry in Fr taste, cornice:2 panel do:scalloped skirt, 1800s, 92" **21,000.00**
Circassian walnut Fr Restauration w/figured vnr, 2-do, 89x52x20" **1,750.00**
Grpt Am, pedimented cornice:do:base drw:bracket ft, 19th C, 85x42" .**990.00**
Mahog Am Fed, cornice:2 panel do:drw:ball ft, 1815-20, 90x58" **9,200.00**
Mahog Am Fed, dbl-do, brass ball ft, 1815, 91x55x19" **12,000.00**
Mahog Am Late Fed, 2 panel do, deep cornice, 1840s, 92x70" ..**2,000.00**
Mahog Am Late Fed w/cvg, 2 do, 1830s, 91x64x25" **3,300.00**
Mahog Bell Epoque Louis XVI style w/brass inlay, bevelled mirror, 93"..**1,400.00**
Rswd Am Rococo, cvd crest/do w/arched mirror:2 drw, 1850s, 98x46" .**3,850.00**
Walnut & burl Am Rococo, arched/molded/cvd cornice, 2 do:2 drw, 98" **2,750.00**
Walnut Fr Provincial, 2 panel do, reeded stiles, drw, pegged, 86" ...**2,875.00**

Beds

Victorian walnut bed with rosewood graining, turned feet and posts, paneled head and footboards with oval medallions and turned finials, 88x72x53", $500.00. (Photo courtesy Garth's Auctions)

Baby, walnut Jenny Lind, trn posts & spool-trn details, rpl slats, 30" ...**110.00**
Brass, stylized sunburst on hdbd/ftbrd, ca 1930, 42½x49" **500.00**
Day, mahog Am Fed, acanthus-cvd crest/stiles, 1825, 37x76x32" ..**3,575.00**
Day, mahog Am Late Fed, scroll/swan-cvd ends, 1830s, 86" **3,200.00**
Day, maple W/M, trn stretcher base w/8 legs, urn splat, rfn/rstr, 68" ..**2,200.00**
Half-tester, rosewood Am Rococo, cvd/incised/panelled, 1850s** ...**16,500.00**
Half-tester youth, mahog cvd Am Rococo, curved hdbd, 1850s.......**3,300.00**
Low post, mahog Fed, pineapple finials:spirals, 1820s, 60x50x72" **2,875.00**
Mahog Fr Emp style, paneled hdbd/ftbd, 20th C, rprs, 46x82x52" **495.00**
Murphy, oak, appl cvgs, brass hdw, mirror bk, 20x60x54" **1,800.00**
Pencil post, hardwood/poplar w/old red, canopy fr, 84x51x72" ...**250.00**
Rope, maple w/tight figure, trn trumpet finials, worn finish/rprs.**495.00**
Rope, maple/curly maple cannonball, trn legs, 69" rails **770.00**
Rope, poplar w/old red, trn posts/bell finials, orig rails, 54x71"...**140.00**
Rope, poplar/hardwood Co, trn posts, shaped hdbd, blanket rail, 59x76" ..**300.00**
Rope, tiger maple PA Sheraton, 1850s, rstr/rpl, 84x53x49" **500.00**
Sleigh, mahog & parcel-gilt Napoleon III Directoire-style, 54x60x56" ..**5,750.00**
Tall post, birch/maple Fed, arched hdbd, 19th C, 61x53x75"+tester ..**1,375.00**
Tall post, cherry, 4 8-sided pencil posts, flat tester fr, 1800s, 82" **1,800.00**
Tall post, curly maple/pine Sheraton, trn/reeded, rfn/rpl, 68x49x73" ..**1,750.00**
Tall post, mahog Transitional Emp to Vict, Gothic insets, 101" **6,875.00**
Tall post, walnut Vict, spool-trn posts, paneled/cvd hdbd, 75x54x76" ...**660.00**
Tester, mahog Am Rococo, cabochon crest/faceted posts, 1850s, 98".**4,675.00**
Vict, walnut w/rswd grpt, paneled hdbds/ftbds, 88x72x63".........**825.00**

Benches

Bucket, cupboard base, pnt softwood, PA, 1580s, 45x45x17" ..**1,900.00**
Bucket, old yel rpt, 3 dvtl drw in shelf:bench:2 panel do, 48x42" ..**4,400.00**
Bucket, pine, old red sq nails, 1-brd ends w/cutouts, 2-brd top, 48"...**660.00**
Bucket, pnt softwood, scrubbed top, splashboard, PA, 1850s, 49" ..**4,400.00**
Bucket, poplar w/old red, sq neels, gallery:4 shelves, 52x44x13" **2,200.00**
Cherry, bj ends, base shelf, wire nails, 23x30x14" **170.00**
Cobbler's, pine w/old rfn, 3-drw/4-compartment, ca 1820s, 20x36x14" ..**1,800.00**
Decorated, orig brn w/mc stripes & fruit/flower stencil, touchups, 78" **1,500.00**
Dk-finish Emp w/traces of orig decor, S scroll seat, spindle bk, 82"........**1,100.00**
Kneeling, pine w/orig grpt, arched cutouts, sq nails, 7½x45x6" ..**300.00**
Piano, oak flat-top w/height adjustment, Std Piano Bench Co ...**200.00**
Pine Co, old pnt layers, 1-brd cut-out ft mortised through top, 54" ..**415.00**
Pine w/old brn grpt on yel, cut-out legs mortised through, 15x36"....**300.00**
Pine w/old gr rpt, bj ends, age cracks, 22x24x9" **275.00**
Pine/walnut Co, fitted cushions, old mellow finish, 33x63x16" **250.00**
Pnt Am Sheraton, bamboo-trn spindled bk/arms/legs, rush seat, 29x24"...**660.00**
Settle, arrow-bk w/old gr pnt, blk & gold stripes, fruit decor, 60" **880.00**
Settle, bamboo Windsor, gr rpt w/yel striping, rprs, 78" **1,100.00**
Settle, dk pnt w/striping & floral decor, rpl baby guard, 45" **715.00**
Settle, worn gr rpt, spindle-bk:plank seat:trn legs, rpl arms, 78" .**275.00**
Settle, worn gr/brn grpt, mc floral crest/striping, ½-spindles, 82".**880.00**
Settle, ½-spindle bk w/shaped crest, S-curve arms, brn rfn, 71" .**770.00**
Walnut primitive, bj legs, age crack, old rfn, 16x62x12" **165.00**
Water, poplar Co w/worn red, 2-shelf top:drw:open shelf base, 60x42"...**2,400.00**

Blanket Chests, Coffers, Trunks, and Mule Chests

Dome top, poplar w/old red pnt & foliage decor, wear/cracks, 25" L.......**715.00**
Dower, walnut, box:2 drw:molded base:bracket ft, 1780s, 31x51x23".**1,380.00**
Immigrant's, dvtl pine w/old gr rpt, Mercer Co PA label, 44" **125.00**
Immigrant's, pine w/orig floral pnt, dvtl, till, wear, 23x45x24" **770.00**
Mixed hardwoods w/early PA-style rpt, dvtl drws, 2-brd top, 30x48" ...**660.00**
Oak English cvd, 6-brd, rose-head nails, old rfn, 25x41x14".......**715.00**
PA decor on pine (old rpt), strap hinges/bear trap lock, 53" ...**1,870.00**
Pine, 2 dvtl drw w/beading, bracket ft, old red rpt, 35x36x18" ...**2,500.00**
Pine Co QA w/brn-red pnt, 3 dvtl drw, rpl hinges, 52x38x18" ..**2,650.00**
Pine Co w/old red, 6-brd, cut-out ft, till, 22x40x15" **880.00**

Pine w/old decor rpt (some orig showing through), PA, 24x49x19"...**1,375.00**
Pine w/scratch geometrics, pintle hinges, 1690s, 21x39x16"....**8,000.00**
Pine/poplar w/brn grpt, 3 bl grpt drws, PA, sm rprs, 28x50x23"**...**9,900.00**
Pine/poplar w/pnt decor, dvtl case, till, PA, 21x38x18" **1,265.00**
Poplar cleaned down to old red grpt, dvtl, till, 26x44x21" **440.00**
Poplar w/orig brn grpt, 2 dvtl drw, till, PA, 23x38x19" **1,375.00**
Poplar w/red varnish/grpt traces, dvtl, walnut lid, 23x37x19" **220.00**
Vinegar grpt, hinged top:drw:bracket ft, rpl brasses, 1800s, 31x36"**...**7,475.00**
Wine/spirit, dvtl walnut, molded edge lid/strap hinges, rfn, 16x27x16" ..**1,200.00**

Bookcases

Burl walnut Am Renaissance, 2 arched do:2 drw, 1870s, 62x46x18"...**1,875.00**
Hardwood Co w/burned vintage on dk red, 1-pane dbl do, 61x41x17" ..**495.00**
Mahog Am Gothic Revival style, 4 do w/brass grills:4, 73" **4,950.00**
Mahog Irish Geo III Chpndl breakfront, pediment, 101x80"**...**22,000.00**
Oak, wide cornice w/appl moldings & lion-head cvgs, rfn, Am, 69x44"...**1,165.00**
Oak, 4 stacking sections, brass knobs, Hales...NY, 63x48x10" **675.00**
Oak European, cvd fruit/foliage/etc, 2 drw:dbl do, 51x47x16" **770.00**
Stack, mahog, 4-sections w/leaded glass top do, Globe Wernicke, 66"..**800.00**
Walnut Am, molded cornice:dbl glazed do:ogee plinth base, 19th C, 82"..**1,300.00**
Walnut Am Gothic, cvd arches/quatrefoils, 2-do, 1850s, 92x60"...**3,685.00**
Walnut Am Rococo, 2-do:2 drw, scroll & shell cvgs, 1840s, 98x67x21"...**5,465.00**
Walnut/chestnut Am cvd, 2 arched do:2 do, 2-part, 19th C, 103x54x20"....**2,600.00**

Bureaus, See Chests

Cabinets

China, mahog/oak Traditional style, Wms, Kimp & Co, 83x42x19", EX ..**990.00**
China, oak, swell-front glass do, curved glass sides, paw ft, 53x36" ...**1,395.00**

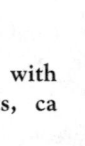

China, quartersawn oak with carved barley twist posts, ca 1895, $2,100.00.

Corner, cherry glaze, cornice:12-pane do:2 panel do, rfn/rprs, 86" **4,300.00**
Corner, mahog Irish Geo III w/inlay, bowfront, 1790s, 86x36"...**7,765.00**
Corner, 2 8-pane do:drw:dbl do:bracket ft, 1800s, 85x52x24" .**2,000.00**
Credenza, antiqued wht pnt w/florals/scenes, marble top, 41x43" **385.00**
Display, mahog Fr Neoclassical Revival, marble busts/columns, 89" **8,000.00**
Folio, mahog w/leather top, panel sides ea w/2 do, 1840s, 31x54x41"......**550.00**
Hoosier, oak, flour bin & glass sugar can swing out, ca 1910, 89x40" .**1,500.00**
Hoosier, oak, ft rprs, rpl tin in bins, rpl top do, 70x45x25" **900.00**
Mahog Fr Egyptian Revival, marble top, gilt capitols, drw/do, 30" **1,200.00**
On stand, mahog Late Vict, dbl do, relief cvgs, trn stiles, 79x41"......**1,150.00**
Press, mahog Am Late Fed, cornice:2 do:3 drws:brass ft, 1815, 90"**...**15,400.00**
Press, mahog Geo III, 2-part, panel dos:4 drw, 1780s, rprs, 88x50"..**3,300.00**

Spice, mahog Chpndl style, arched panel do, 7 int drws, 23x17x12" ...**990.00**

Candlestands

Birch Co, sq top:vase:trn ped:tripod cabriole legs, rfn, 76x17x17"..**635.00**
Birch Fed w/red pnt, 8-sided tilt-top, MA, 1810, 30x23x16"..**4,000.00**
Blk pnt, molded top w/scalloped edge, tripod legs, 1790s, 28x14"**...**9,775.00**
Cherry, sq top:drw:vase:tripod w/cabriole legs, 1790s, 28x19x18" ..**2,875.00**
Cherry Chpndl, ovolo corners/serpentine sides, 1780s, 28x19x19".....**1,000.00**
Cherry Co Chpndl, tripod w/snake ft, age cracks in top, rprs, 15" dia....**600.00**
Cherry Co w/old red, 2-brd top:tripod w/snake ft, 37x13" dia.....**990.00**
Cherry Hplwht, tilt top:tripod w/spider legs, rprs/rfn, 29x16" sq.**275.00**
Cherry Hplwht, 1-brd top w/gallery:trn column:tripod w/snake ft **770.00**
Cherry QA, scallop edge, tripod cabriole legs, rfn, 1790s, 29x14"**.6,900.00**
Cherry/maple Co, dished top:trn column:tripod, rprs/rfn, 37x14" dia...**385.00**
Hardwood primitive, trn column, adjustable arm w/2 sockets, 23" ...**990.00**
Mahog Chpndl, dish tilt-top:trn column:tripod base, rfn, 20x19" dia...**330.00**
Mahog Chpndl, 1-brd tilt-top:birdcage:tripod base, 29x22" dia.........**1,045.00**
Mahog Chpndl tilt-top, tripod w/shaped ft, cleaned down to roig, 21" ..**3,850.00**
Mahog Chpndl tilt-top w/overvarnish, birdcage, snake ft, rprs, 27x21"......**880.00**
Mahog QA, tilt-top on trn shaft, tripod legs, 28x24" dia **990.00**
Maple Co Chpndl, 1-brd top:tripod:snake ft, rprs/dk varnish, 16" sq...**385.00**
Pine/maple Co Hplwht, 1-brd top:tripod w/spider legs, rfn, 18" dia......**275.00**
Tiger maple Fed, canted corners, tripod, 1825, 39x17x22" **1,380.00**
Tiger maple Fed, shaped top:vase:tripod:ball ft, 29x19x16" **925.00**
Walnut Co Hplwht, 2-brd top:trn column:tripod base, rfn, 20" dia **300.00**

Chairs

Arm, bamboo Windsor, molded crest w/continuous arms, dk finish, 37"..**1,400.00**
Arm, bamboo Windsor, 7-spindle bk, shaped seat, old rfn, 40"....**330.00**
Arm, bamboo Windsor w/birdcage, 7-spindle (3 in crest), rfn, 35"* ...**500.00**
Arm, cherry Martha Washington Hplwht-style w/inlay, reuphl/rfn, 44".**330.00**
Arm, hardwood Louis XV-style w/walnut finish, reuphl, 1900s, 40"........**550.00**
Arm, mahog English Sheraton style, shield bk, slip seat, 19th C, rprs.....**200.00**
Arm, mahog Martha Washington style, print uphl, Hickory repro, 42"..**330.00**
Arm, oak Boston-style, trn spindles/legs/stretchers, saddle seat, 42" **175.00**
Arm, oak Elizabethan Revival, bobbin-&-ball trns, caned seat, 1860s....**395.00**
Arm, QA wing-bk w/cvg, reuphl, mid-20th C, 43" **250.00**
Arm, quartersawn oak, barley twists, reeding, uphl seat, 1920s, rstr........**250.00**
Arm, W&M-style, open scrolled arms, trn legs, reuphl, 20th C repro ...**415.00**
Arm, walnut Chpndl, vase splat, scrolled arms, reuphl slip seat, 40"...**1,850.00**
Arm, walnut Eastlake Vict w/burl vnr, cvd/trn details, cane seat, 37"........**75.00**
Arm, walnut Louis XVI Provincial Voltaire Metamorphique, reuphl **5,500.00**
Arm, walnut Vict, open arms/cvd flowers, reuphl, tufted bk, 38" ..**275.00**
Arm, Windsor, continuous arm, brace-bk, sgn AD Allen, ca 1820s, 39"..**2,400.00**
Arm, Windsor, PA bow-bk, alligatored blk, bamboo trns, rprs, 36".**935.00**
Arm, Windsor, spindled sack-bk, bowed crest rail, old rfn, 38" ...**440.00**
Arm, Windsor, spindled sack-bk w/trn arm posts, blk rpt, 38" .**2,860.00**
Arm, Windsor, 6-spindle bow-bk, splayed base w/trn legs, rfn, 37" **440.00**
Arm, Windsor, 7-spindle bow-bk, saddle seat, dk brn rpt, rprs, 39" ...**1,045.00**
Arm, Windsor, 7-spindle bow-bk, splayed base, trn posts, rfn, 38" **525.00**
Arm, Windsor, 7-spindle fan-bk, pnt, serpentine crest, 42"**...**51,750.00**
Arm, Windsor, 9-spindle bow-bk, PA blk w/yel striping rpt, 38" **550.00**
Arm, 4-arched slat ladderbk, woven seat, blk rpt, 47" **550.00**
Arm, 4-slat banister-bk, trn posts/legs/finials, old splint & pnt, 46"...**1,265.00**
Arm, 4-slat banister-bk w/old blk rpt, scrolled hand rests, 47" **685.00**
Corner, cherry Chpndl, 2 vasiform splats, rush seat, rfn...........**5,175.00**
Corner, English Sheraton, mahog, trn legs, orig slip seat w/rpl rush ...**1,100.00**
Corner, mahog English Chpndl style, rpl slip seat, rprs/rfn, 31x18" **385.00**
Corner, maple QA, scrolled arms, 3 trn legs, reuphl, 30" **1,400.00**
Corner, maple QA, trn posts, arched slats, curved arms, rpl seat, 31"....**495.00**
Easy, mahog Fed, arched crest:curved bk:scroll arms, 1815, 42"..........**3,450.00**
Kitchen, step-down crest:vase splat, plank saddle seat, 1910s, 32"........**150.00**

Platform rocker, mahog, cvd lion's heads on arms, cvd crest, reuphl.......**225.00**
Platform rocker, trn hardwood fr w/red stain, worn reuphl, Nat'l...NY..**200.00**
Rocker, Adirondack-style bentwood, stripped of bark, 42", G.....**165.00**
Rocker, golden oak, appl cvgs, 7 spindles:2 splats, caned seat, 1870s **275.00**
Rocker, plain & quartersawn oak, banister bk, uphl seat, ca 1900, 42"..**145.00**
Rocker, pnt florals, angel-wing crest, bj splat, PA, 43" **715.00**
Rocker, sewing; bamboo Windsor, spindle-bk/rabbit-ear posts, rfn, 30" ..**100.00**
Rocker/arm, bamboo Windsor, 9-spindle, D seat, rfn/rpr, 33" **200.00**
Side, bamboo Windsor, red/blk flame grpt w/stencil, step-down crest....**650.00**
Side, bamboo Windsor, 7-spindle bow-bk, rprs/old rfn, 38".........**330.00**
Side, golden oak, pressed crest, 7-spindle, rpl cane seat, 34" **175.00**
Side, hardwood banister-bk, trn legs, ½-trn spindles, rfn, 41".......**360.00**
Side, hardwood Co QA, vase splat/yoke crest, Spanish ft, rfn, 40" **525.00**
Side, mahog Chpndl-style, cvd splat, cabriole legs w/cvg, reuphl, 38"..**275.00**
Side, mahog English Chpndl, cabriole legs w/cvd knees/c&b ft, rprs....**825.00**
Side, mahog English Chpndl, cvd splat/crest, slip seat, rprs, 37".**350.00**
Side, maple ladder-bk, 6 arched slats, rush seat, rfn/rprs, 44" **660.00**
Side, maple QA, vasiform splat:slip seat:cabriole legs, 1740-60, 41"..**4,300.00**
Side, maple QA, yoked crest:vasiform splat/balloon seat:cabriole legs ..**4,300.00**
Side, oak, pressed crest:9 trn spindles:low slat w/reeding, cane seat **125.00**
Side, walnut Chpndl, serpentine crest rail, vasiform splat, 1760s...........**1,950.00**
Side, walnut Chpndl, serpentine crest w/cvd terminals, slip seat, rfn **3,150.00**
Side, walnut Chpndl, serpentine crest:pierced splat:slip seat, 40"..**9,200.00**
Side, walnut Chpndl, shell cvg:pierced splat w/C scrolls, old rfn ..**7,000.00**
Side, walnut English Transitional QA to Chpndl, slip seat, rpr ..**500.00**
Side, Windsor, 6-spindle bk w/step-down crest, rfn/rstr, 33".........**115.00**
Side, Windsor 7-spindle fan-bk w/rprs, saddle seat, 36" **195.00**
Side, 4-slat ladder-bk w/old blk, sausage trns, rush seat, 40".........**275.00**
Slipper, walnut European Baroque Revival, reuphl, tufted bk, 39"*....**140.00**
Wing-bk, mahog Chpndl style, reuphl, sq legs, 19th C, 35".........**375.00**

Chair Sets

Arm, walnut Dutch QA-style w/cvg, leather uphl seat, 19th C...**1,100.00**
Dining, blk rpt w/stenciling on splat & crest, OH, 33", 6 for......**990.00**
Dining, Captain's, yel w/red-brn grpt, stripes/stencil, 6 for..........**770.00**
Dining, Hitchcock-type Sheraton, orig red/blk grpt/stencil, 35", 6 for ...**715.00**
Dining, mahog Chpndl-style, reuphl seats, 20th C, 2 arm+6 side **2,850.00**
Dining, medallions/leaves/etc on gray, PA, 33", 4 for **1,500.00**
Dining, QA style w/orig blk pnt/stripes/flower baskets, 1900s, 4 for...**1,450.00**
Dining, tiger maple Fed, curved crests/slats, cane seat, 6 for **2,185.00**
Dining, tiger maple Fed, much cvg, cane seats, rfn, 1825, 5 for **1,500.00**
Dining, walnut Continental Rococo, much cvg, 2 arm+10 side **5,280.00**
Dining, Windsor, birdcage bk, old brn rpt w/yel stripes, 33", 4 for **990.00**
Dining, Windsor, bowed crest w/7 spindles, saddle seat, 35", 5 for...**1,450.00**
Dining, 4-slat ladder-bk, woven seat, ca 1900, 42", 2 arm+4 side ..**375.00**
Directoire, hardwood, tapered legs, reuphl slip seats, 34", 6 for ..**600.00**

Chests (Antique), See Also Dressers

Apothecary, pine, 18-drw, old mellow rfn, rprs, 24x45"...............**825.00**
Apothecary, poplar, 19-drw, sq nails, old finish, 25x21x7".......**1,045.00**
Cherry Chpndl, 4 drw in beaded fr:apron drop:bracket ft, rfn, 33x36" ..**3,400.00**
Cherry Co Emp, 4-drw w/beading, ring-trn pilasters, rpl/rfn, 41x41".....**550.00**
Cherry Co Hplwht w/inlay, 4 drw w/beading, rpl brasses, 44x44".....**4,800.00**
Cherry Fed D-front, 4 dvtl drw w/beading, rprs/rfn, 40x41" **880.00**
Cherry Fed w/figured mahog facade, rope-cvg, 6-drw, crest, 57x47".......**825.00**
Cherry Hplwht w/inlay, 1-drw:scalloped apron:Fr ft, rfn, 39x42x21"..**2,860.00**
Cherry inlaid bow-front, 4 grad drw:curved skirt:Fr ft, 1800s, 39".....**4,600.00**
Cherry Sheraton, 3 short:2:4 grad drw:trn ft, mellow rfn, 70x46"....**2,200.00**
Cherry Sheraton bow-front w/mahog vnr facade, 4-drw, att MA, 41x42"..**3,000.00**
Cherry Sherton bow-front, 4 dvtl drw w/beading, rpl/rfn, 39x42" **1,650.00**
Cherry/bird's-eye maple Fed, 6 dvtl drw, panel ends, trn legs, 46x43"....**770.00**
Cherry/curly maple Co Emp, crest:4 drw:trn ft, panel ends, rfn, 58"......**525.00**

Cherry/mahog Emp, 4-drw, chip-cvd columns, ring-trn pilasters, 46x42"....**450.00**
Cherry/maple Chpndl, 4 short drw w/central fan:6 grad drws, 63x37"**....**46,000.00**
Cherry/pine Chpndl, shaped 2-brd top:4 dvtl drw:rpr ft, 39x43" **1,100.00**
Cherry/walnut Hplwht w/inlay, cornice:8 drw:Fr ft, rpl, 65x38"...**6,000.00**
Cherry/walnut/curly maple Co Emp, 4-drw, dmn escutcheons, 50x43x20"...**600.00**
Curly birch Chpndl, cvd fan, 6 dvtl drw, scrolled apron, rfn, 52x39" ..**2,200.00**
Curly maple Chpndl, 5 dvtl grad drw, old brasses, rfn, 46x39" ...**3,575.00**
Curly maple vnr/cherry Co Sheraton, cornice:8-drw, rpl pulls/rfn, 67" ..**4,345.00**
Curly walnut Chpndl, 9-drw, fluted ¼-columns, old finish, 61x38".........**9,350.00**
Mahog Chpndl Serpentine, 4 grad drw, Boston, 1760-80, 32x36x20"..**34,500.00**
Mahog Chpndl style, 3:2:5 grad drw, 20th C, 70x43x22".........**2,100.00**
Mahog English Chpndl, 5 dvtl drw w/beading, rpl ft, 32x37" ..**2,200.00**
Mahog English Chpndl-style bow-front, Kittinger, 36x38x21" ...**825.00**
Mahog Fed, scroll bkbrd:2 short:4 drw, spiral cvd columns, 50x40" ..**2,400.00**
Maple Chpndl, 5 grad drw, rpl ft, rfn/rpl/rpl, 46x36x18"..........**1,450.00**
Maple Co Chpndl (some curl), 6 grad drw, rpl/rfn, 52x38x18"....**2,475.00**
Oak w/tilting beveled mirror:5-drw, panel sides, Am, 69x30" **600.00**
On base, tiger maple, cornice:7 drw, orig brass, old rfn, 18th C, 59"....**8,625.00**
On chest, cherry Chpndl, scroll top:3 sm:3 long drw, rfn, 84x34"......**13,800.00**
On chest, cherry Chpndl, 2-pc, 3 short:2:4 grad:3 drw, rprs/rpl, 79" ..**12,650.00**
On chest, grpt, hinged lid:well:2 drw:skirt:Fr ft, 1825-35, 37x43"......**63,000.00**
On chest, walnut/maple QA, 2 short:3 grad drw: long:3 short drw, 71"...**17,250.00**
On fr, mahog QA style, Kindel, Grand Rapids label, 58x35x21"...**550.00**
On fr, oak W&M, geometric cvg, 2 short/3 long drws:3 short, 1690s, 58"...**1,100.00**
Over drws, pine w/old grpt, 6-brd, high cut-out ft, 2-drw, 43x44x20"..**990.00**
Over drws, pine w/orig pnt, 6-brd, 2 dvtl drw, early, 43x43x19" ...**3,400.00**

Painted six-board chest, gold and burnt sienna graining, lidded till, New England, early 1800s, 18x36x15", $3,000.00.

Pine Co QA, dvtl, 2 short:4 drw, red stain, NE, rpr, 49x38" **1,045.00**
Pine Co Sheraton, 4 dvtl drw, orig brn-red grpt, NE, 44x39" ..**1,100.00**
Pine/poplar w/old red, 2 dvtl drw w/beading, rpl knobs, 20x24x12"....**1,375.00**
Spice, red wash w/gold lettering, 12-drw, wire nails, 12x16x5" ...**715.00**
Sugar, cherry & poplar Co, divided drw, brass hdls, age cracks, 12x11"..**1,200.00**
Sugar, cherry Am Fed, hinged lid, drw, trn legs, 1820s, 34x28x18" **3,000.00**
Sugar, cherry w/inlay, Fr ft, dvtl case, slant lid, KY, 30x30x14", VG ..**1,870.00**
Tiger Maple QA, 4 sm:2:4 grad drw, old rfn, ca 1750, 50x35x18"....**21,850.00**
Walnut Chpndl, 3:2:4 grad drw, PA, rfn/rpl/rprs, 57x40" **4,950.00**
Walnut Chpndl, 4 grad drw, rpl ogee ft, rfn/rprs, 35x36x21" ...**1,500.00**
Walnut Co Chpndl, 4 dvtl drw:rpl bracket ft, rfn/rpl brasses, 40x36"....**990.00**
Walnut Hplwht w/cherry inlay, 6-drw, rfn/rpl, 46x38x21" **2,400.00**
Walnut QA, X-banded drws (2 short:3), oak sides, 1710s, 36x38x22"...**4,000.00**

Cupboards, See Also Pie Safes

Cherry Co, 2 panel do:2 drw:2 panel do, 1-pc, rfn, 81x42".........**220.00**
Corner, cherry, 2 panel do, dvtl drw, handmade repro, 1-pc, 78x61" ..**385.00**
Corner, cherry Hplwht, 12-pane do:2 drw:2 panel do, 89x47".**7,425.00**
Corner, cherry/poplar Co, 2 panel do:2, dk rfn, 1-pc, 83x42" ..**2,000.00**
Corner, cherry/walnut Vict, scrolled top/bottom brackets, do, 29x17"......**220.00**
Corner, pine, cornice:arch w/3 shelves:do, stripped finish, 1730s, 77"...**4,000.00**

Corner, pine, orig grpt, 12-pane do:2 drw:2 do, 2-pc, 91x48"**..........**19,250.00**
Corner, pine Co, 9-pane do:drw:2 panel do, old red pnt, 1-pc, 43x39"...**3,400.00**
Corner, pine w/dk finish, cornice:9-pane do:2 panel do:rpl ft, 81x50"...**5,500.00**
Corner, pine w/old gr rpt, 1-pc, geometric glass do:panel do, 88x27".....**1,155.00**
Corner, poplar Co w/dk cherry stain, cut-out ft, panel dos, 74x46".......**1,200.00**
Corner, poplar Co w/old cherry, 12-pane do:3 drw:2 panel do, 81x39".**2,750.00**
Corner, poplar PA, 4 stepped raised-panel do, bl-gray rpt, 1-pc, 84"......**2,850.00**
Corner, poplar primitive, 2 panel do, 1-pc, rfn, 60x43" **385.00**
Corner, poplar w/old red, orig red inside, ca 1838, 48x28".......**2,150.00**
Corner, walnut Co, cornice:9-pane do:panel do:bracket ft, rprs, 84x41"...**3,200.00**
Corner, walnut Co, 2 1-pane do:2 panel do:scrolled apron, 1-pc, 82" **1,200.00**
Corner, walnut Co, 2 8-pane do:2 drw:2 panel do, bl-pnt int, 84x60" **4,000.00**
Corner, walnut Hplwht w/inlay, 12-pane do:drw:panel do, rfn/rpr, 96"...**2,850.00**
Jelly, cherry Co, gallery:2 drw:panel do, dk rfn, 58x46" **880.00**
Jelly, pine Co, 1-brd sides/top/dos, rfn pumpkin stain, rstr, 56x37"......**300.00**
Jelly, pine Co, 2 panel do w/beading:cut-out ft, old rfn, 44x40x18" **900.00**
Jelly, pine PA, molded cornice:4 panel do, 1-brd ends, pnt traces, 67"..**4,400.00**
Jelly, pine w/red-brn grpt, cornice:2 panel do:rpr ft, 66x45x17" **5,400.00**
Jelly, pine/poplar Co, panel do, butterfly hinges, dvtl/rprs/rfn, 48" **880.00**
Jelly, pine/poplar w/old red, 2 dvtl drw:2 panel do, rprs, 48x48".......**1,150.00**
Jelly, poplar Co w/layers of worn rpt, panel dos, age cracks, 50x36"....**935.00**
Jelly, poplar w/yel grpt:red & blk, 2 dvtl drws, gallery, 51x43x19"....**1,500.00**
Jelly, walnut Am, dbl do:2 molded drw, 1850s, 48x42x16".........**575.00**
Jelly, walnut Co w/red traces, 2 drw:2 2-panel do, 1-brd ends, 69x44"...**1,320.00**
Jelly, walnut/poplar Co w/old red pnt, 1-brd ends, 2 drw:2 do, 54"......**990.00**
Jelly, yel pine, raised panel dos, rstr/rfn, 57x42x11" **275.00**
Pewter, hardwood Co, 3-shelf, 1-brd dos, old finish, 81x36"........**1,450.00**
Pewter, hardwood primitive, red-brn stain, rprs, 59x42x13".........**440.00**
Pewter, pine, cut-out feet, 1 do, int shelf, 1-pc, rstr, 63x53x18"...**1,300.00**
Pewter, pine, open 2-shelf top:panel do, rfn/rstr, red int, 66x35"......**600.00**
Pewter, pine w/old brn rfn, 2 panel do, shallow top, rstr, 76x48".....**1,265.00**
Pine, old red rpt, panel do:panel do, Southern, rprs, 76x37x23" **2,000.00**
Pine Co, old red, 2 2-pane do:2 panel do, early pulls, PA, 48x44...**3,300.00**
Pine Co, 12-pane do:2 panel do, rprs/rfn, 2-pc, 84x48"..........**3,685.00**
Pine Co cleaned to old red, 4 panel do, OH, 2-pc, 89x46" **2,200.00**
Pine Co step-bk, dut-out ft, panel dos, dk rfn, 75x49x18" **1,100.00**
Pine Co step-bk, 2 16-pane do:shelf:2 drw:2 panel do, 84x50"...**2,850.00**
Poplar w/blk pnt, pnt stylized deer & abstract stripes, GA, 74x45"...**4,000.00**
Step-bk, oak Co w/old wht pnt traces, 2 1-pane do:drw:2 panel do, 1910...**975.00**
Step-bk, old bl pnt, 2 panel do:shelf:2 panel do, 1800s, 81x37x17"...**7,500.00**
Step-bk, pine Co, 8-pane dbl do:2 batten do, CI latches, rfn, 82x46"....**990.00**
Step-bk, pine Co w/old red, 2 panel do, beaded fr, 1-pc, 80x36".........**2,100.00**
Step-bk, pine w/brn flame grpt, open top:2 brd & batten do, 76x42"......**500.00**
Step-bk, poplar, 1-pc, 2 do, bj ends, sq nails, old gray, 68x33" **500.00**
Step-bk, walnut Co, 2 4-panel do:2 drw:2 panel do, 1-pc, rfn, 82x45"......**1,200.00**
Walnut Continental, appl molding, cvd panel dos, rprs, early, 61x39".........**770.00**
Walnut Dutch step-bk, 2 6-pane do:shelf:3 drw:2 panel do, PA, 83x60"..**7,500.00**

Desks

Birch Chpndl, slant lid, rpl brass, orig finish, 1780s, 42x38x20" **11,500.00**
Birch Chpndl, slant lid, 4 dvtl drw w/beading, old rfn/rpr, 42x40".........**2,475.00**
Birch/pine Co Chpndl, slant lid:4 dvtl drw, red rpt, 39x34x18" **3,750.00**
Butler's, mahog & burl vnr English Chpndl-style, 4-drw/pull-out shelf....**600.00**
Butler's, mahog English Chpndl-style, Williamsburg repro, 30".............**1,045.00**
Cherry Chpndl, slant lid:4 drw, old rfn, 39x35"........................**7,700.00**
Cherry Hplwht, slant lid, 4 dvtl drws w/beading, rpl, 44x42" ..**1,650.00**
Clerk's, cherry Co, slant lid:false drw:2 drw, rfn, 53x41x19" **825.00**
Clerk's, pine Co w/old red, dvtl top, 3 dvtl drw, rpl brasses, 49x34" **440.00**
Lady's, mahog/bird's-eye maple Fed w/rswd vnr, NH, 1810s, 58x41x20".**9,775.00**
Lawyer's, walnut/burl, Pat-action, pull-out:4 short drw & do, 1850s......**4,400.00**
Mahog Chpndl-style w/slant front, b&c ft, serpentine, 4-drw, 40x31"........**440.00**
Mahog flame birch/bird's-eye maple Fed, bookcase top, old rfn, 61x39"....**17,250.00**
Mahog Irish Chpndl knee-hole, 7 dvtl drw, rpl/rprs, 32x38"...**3,025.00**

Mahog traditional-style knee-hole, 20th C, 30x42x21"..............**110.00**
Maple Chpndl, slant lid, 4 grad drw:bracket base, 42x35x18" .**6,325.00**
Maple Co QA, lift top lid w/fitted int, rfn/sm rprs, 32x32x20"...**880.00**
Partner's, mahog Am, ped ends w/drws, much cvg, ball ft, 1900s, 68"...**8,625.00**
Plantation, golden oak, drop lid:long drw:2 short, brass hdw, 64" **1,400.00**
Plantation, poplar Co w/old red, drop-leaf, worn finish, 67x36" .**550.00**
S-roll top, oak, pull-out shelf, 4-drw, fitted int, 1880s, 44x43"..**2,000.00**
Table-top, burl/chestnut, dvtl, rprs, old finish, 9½x22x16"...**1,320.00**
Tiger maple Chpndl, drop front, bracket base............................**2,400.00**

Victorian walnut S roll-top desk, carved panels, liquor compartments, ca 1875 – 1885, EX, $3,500.00.

Walnut Chpndl, slant lid, 4 drw, fluted ¼-columns, rfn, 46x40" ..**2,600.00**
Walnut/burl vnr Eastlake Vict cylinder, do/4-drw base, sm **1,430.00**
Yel pine Southern Chpndl, slant front, 4-drw, rprs/rfn, 41x42" ..**1,650.00**

Dry Sinks

Hardwood Co, wht/bl alligatored pnt layers, 3-drw/2-do, 33x54x26"........**600.00**
Oak Co, 2-drw hutch top w/shelf:copper-lined well:2 panel do, 56x50"...**330.00**
Pine Co w/red pnt, 2 do, cut-out ft, early 1800s, 30x42x18".......**630.00**
Pine w/old rfn, cut-down, cut-out ft, panel dos, copper-lined top, 42"...**660.00**
Poplar Co, 2 dvtl drw, 2 panel do, hutch top, rstr/rfn, 49x54" **800.00**
Poplar w/red stain, well w/shelf:drw:panel do, sq nails, 34x54x18"......**700.00**
Poplar/chestnut w/brn pnt w/yel feathering, 2-pc, att Amish, 68x45"...**2,200.00**

Hall Pieces

Bench, oak w/blk stain, bk panel, pegged sides, lift seat, 34x33".....**150.00**
Chair, James II-style, trn legs/stretchers, antique uphl, 19th C ...**770.00**
Seat, walnut Continental in Renaissance taste, much cvg, 1890s, 48x52"..**1,200.00**
Stand, CI Coalbrookdale, ornate foliage/Welcome banner, 1870s, 88x52"...**9,900.00**
Table, mahog Emp, marble top, drw, bk splash w/floral tiles, 49x48" ..**550.00**
Tree, CI Rococo Revival w/blk rpt, umbrella stand in base, 78" .**990.00**
Tree, Mission oak, beveled mirror, ball ft, lift lid, rfn, 92x53x20"...**1,400.00**
Tree, walnut Vict w/burl panels, CI insets, marble top, drw, 87" **2,400.00**

Highboys

Cherry QA, cvd fans, 7-drw top:4 drw, rfn/old brasses, 86".......**4,400.00**
Cherry QA, 5 grad drw:4:scalloped apron:cabriole legs, NE, 76"**.....**14,850.00**
Curly maple QA-style, cabriole legs, 9 drw w/cvd fans, 63x30x17" **2,500.00**
Maple Co QA, 6-drw top:3 drw:cabriole legs, rpl brasses/rfn, 70x39"...**3,850.00**
Maple QA, cornice:2 short:4 grad:3 short drw:cabriole legs, 71"**.....**40,000.00**
Maple QA, split-top drw:4 drw:1 long:3 short drw, fan cvg, rfn, 75" ...**28,750.00**
Maple QA, 5 grad drw:1 long:3 short drw, rfn/rpl, 71x39"......**14,950.00**

Maple QA, 5-drw top:2-drw base:cabriole legs, rfn/rprs/rpl, 69".........**1,100.00**
QA style, mahog, 11-drw:cabriole legs, Henredon, 81x37x20", EX ..**1,500.00**
Walnut Chpndl-style w/inlay, 3 drw:3 grad:base, rfn/rpl, 68x39" **1,750.00**

Lowboys

Walnut Chippendale lowboy, thumb-molded drawer over shell-carved drawer flanked by two small drawers, brass handles, shell-carved cabriole legs, claw and ball feet, Philadelphia, ca 1770, 29x33x19", $12,000.00 (sold at least 25% below current market value).

Curly maple Co QA, 2 drw:apron:cabriole legs:slipper ft, 36x38x20" **1,750.00**
Oak Georgian, 3-drw, scalloped skirt, cabriole legs, 18th C, 38x32x20" .**1,650.00**
Walnut QA w/X-banded inlay top, drw, cabriole legs, 18th C, 28x32x19"..**3,000.00**
Walnut QA-style w/inlay, 4 dvtl drw, cabriole legs, late 1800s, 30x34"...**880.00**

Pie Safes

Cherry w/old red, punched tin panels, reeding/beading, 19th C, 46x32" ...**635.00**
Cherry/poplar Co, old gr rpt, punched tin, rprs/rpl, 65x58x24" ..**4,675.00**
Hanging, pine fr w/old red, punched tin all sides, 34x30x20" **935.00**
Oak, handmade w/screened dbl do, 3 shelves, brass hdw, 39x29x16" **650.00**
Pine, molded top:drw:2 hinged screen do, 3-shelf, rfn, NJ, 1800s, 54".....**2,645.00**
Pine Co, mortised & pinned fr, openings recovered w/screen, rpt, 48" **400.00**
Pine/poplar Co, sq corner posts, mortised, punched tin, drw, 58" ..**600.00**
Poplar Co w/old brn rpt, 2 drw:2 panel do, 2 punched panel sides, 53"..**1,045.00**
Poplar w/old bl-gr rpt, punched tin panels in dos & sides, 53x37" **745.00**
Poplar/walnut w/old pnt, sq corner posts, high ft, dvtl drw, 54x39".....**440.00**
Walnut step-bk, 2 punched tin do:2 drws:2 punched tin do, rpt, 80x40" ...**2,200.00**

Secretaries

Cherry Fed, 2 do:fold-out top:3 grad drw:Fr ft, old finish, 55x42" **1,800.00**
Cherry Hplwht w/inlay, 2 panel do:slant lid:4 drw:Fr ft, rfn, 80x41"..**4,500.00**
Ebony & ivory Italian Renaissance-style, fall front, 55x29x14"...........**2,100.00**
Hardwood Vict, press cvd, w/bookcase, worn finish, 73x42x13" .**465.00**
Mahog Am Late Classical, bookcase:2 drw:shelf:2 drw:2 do, 1840s, 89" ..**2,400.00**
Mahog Biedermeier w/ebonized panels, appl gilt decor, sm rprs, 77" **1,875.00**
Oak/walnut Vict, dbl do:slant lid:9 dvtl drw:knee-hole base, rprs, 81".........**990.00**

Settees

Fed, 5 decor crest rails/5 spindles:pnt rush seat:12 trn legs, 76"......**13,800.00**
Fr Louis XVI-style, trn/cvd fr w/cane seat & bk, reuphl cushion, 1900s.**880.00**
Louis XIV-style, much cvg, gold rpt, old reuphl, 42" **550.00**
Mahog Sheraton style, fluted arm supports & legs, torn uphl, 34x47"....**1,725.00**
Maple/pine Windsor w/bamboo trns, 21-spindle bk, 1810, 33x78x21"....**3,200.00**

Pnt Fed, crests:spindles w/medallions/urns:rush seat, gilt decor, 70"........**2,100.00**
Rswd Am Rococo, laminated/cvd Rosalie, att Belter, 1850s, 64"............**4,600.00**
Rswd Am Rococo (cvd/laminated), triple-bk, reuphl, att Belter, 90"...**13,000.00**
Sectional, cabriole legs w/b&c ft, velvet reuphl, curved, 44", pr.**200.00**
Walnut Eastlake Vict, tapestry reuphl, old finish, 46½" **275.00**
Walnut Eastlake Vict w/burl vnr, cvd center panel, reuphl, 48"..**220.00**

Settles, See Benches

Shelves

Corner wall, poplar w/old blk pnt, gold edging, w/bin & baffle, 34x16" ...**330.00**
Etagere, mahog, 3-tier, serpentine fronts, mirror bks, 43x22x13"....**500.00**
Etagere, walnut Vict Rococo Revival, mirror/shelves/marble/drw, 96x44"...**3,850.00**
Etagere, walnut/burl vnr Vict, marble top, do, shelves, mirror, 90x48" ...**2,650.00**
Hardwood, worn red rpt, 3 shelves, sq nails, 35x23x9½" **440.00**
Pine, old pnt layers, 13x6½x6½"...**300.00**
Wall, oak Co Vict, scrolled ends, screws, 31x21x7" **165.00**
Wall, oak w/worn blk pnt, shaped ends, 3 shelves, 19th C, 33x29x7" ...**110.00**
Wall, pine w/worn brn, 4 shelves, trn corner posts, 32x28x7" .**1,045.00**
Wall, poplar w/old red, 24 pigeonholes, edge damage, 24x56x9" .**550.00**
Wall, walnut, 4 grad shelves w/trn posts, cut-out bk splat, 35x30x10"...**330.00**
Wall, walnut Co, sq nails, fitted int, plate rail, rfn, 34x20x9" **300.00**

Sideboards

Cherry Am Late Fed, spindled gallery/scrolled crest, 3-drw:4 do, 61".......**3,500.00**
Mahog Am Late Fed w/cvg, 3 drw:4 panel do, reeded ½-columns, 73" .**3,300.00**
Mahog Emp, paw ft w/acanthus leaves, 2 fan-cvd do amid 2 panel, 47x68"..**2,300.00**
Mahog Emp w/figure, peaked crest:molded front drws:panel dos, 50x60"...**935.00**
Mahog English bow-front Sheraton, trn legs, blk pnt details, 41x66"......**3,650.00**
Mahog Fed, beading, serpentine center, cvgs, trn legs, rpl brass, 58" .**10,925.00**
Mahog Fed, brass inlay gallery:marble:2 do, stencil, 42x46" **4,300.00**
Mahog Fed, gallery:3 sm drw:3 do, cvd columns, 1815-25, 54x61".......**2,185.00**
Mahog Fed, serpentine, drw:2 1-shelf cupboards, 2 bottle drws, 80"....**23,000.00**
Mahog Fed, 3 short drw:4 do, free-standing columns, 1820s, 60"..........**4,850.00**
Mahog Fed w/inlay, ovolo top, cockbeaded drws/dos, old rfn, 40x73"**..**32,000.00**
Mahog Sheraton w/flame vnr, breakfront, trn ft, att Baltimore, 67" ..**2,200.00**
Mahog vnr Emp-style w/inlay, 6 drw, 2 do, 31x60x21" **250.00**
Mahog vnr Fed, concave drw amid 2 peds, 1820s, 81" **43,700.00**
Oak, shelf:mirror:2 sm drw by 2 cupboards:long drw, Leavens, 60x48" **400.00**
Oak Elizabethan Revival breakfront, heavy cvg, 4 do/4 drw, 41x83x25"...**2,200.00**
Oak Jacobean-style, G trn/cvd details, 6-drw, Kittinger, 72" **660.00**
Oak Vict, cvd free-standing griffins, fruit & foliage, 1890s, 81x81"...**3,300.00**
Walnut burl Fr Art Deco, marble top, 3-section, 43x67x18" ...**2,300.00**
Walnut burl Fr Art Deco, marble top:2 drw:dbl do, 43x48x20" ...**1,000.00**
Walnut Vict Rococo Revival, ornate top, marble:2 drw:2 do, 88x55x21" .**5,200.00**
Walnut/mahog Emp, 4 do, 7 dvtl drw, rfn/rpl crest, 42x71x20" ..**935.00**

Sofas

Beech cvd in Neoclassical Taste, serpentine bkrail, damask uphl, 75"...**3,000.00**
Biedermier, fruitwood vnr lyre fr, brocade reuphl, 81"* **880.00**
Chippendale-style camel-bk, much-cvd fr, worn uphl, 20th C repro, 80"......**2,250.00**
Chpndl-style, camel-bk, fine uphl, late 20th C, 81" **470.00**
Edwardian-style Chesterfield, rpl brn leather, 90" **1,450.00**
Mahog Am Fed w/brass inlay/dolphin cvgs, reuphl, 1815, 94"..**4,675.00**
Mahog Am Late Fed, curved bk, cvd arm supports, 1840s, 84" ..**6,050.00**
Mahog Chpndl camel-bk, shaped fr, velvet reuphl, 81" **1,155.00**
Mahog Fed, reeded crest, molded arms, old rfn, reuphl, 34x76"...**7,475.00**
Mahog Fed sq-bk w/maple inlay, reeded legs, reuphl, 33x76"...**2,500.00**
Mahog Fed style, cvd ft, reeded cuffs, velvet uphl, 32x74" **440.00**
Mahog Fed w/inlay, arched crest, bowed seat fr, reuphl, 1800s, 80"**..**17,250.00**
Mahog vnr Am Emp, lyre fr, ornately cvd ft, old reuphl, 92"...**1,265.00**

Mahog/mahog vnr Emp lyre fr, gold velvet reuphl, 35x77x27" **1,430.00**
Meridienne, mahog Fr Restauration w/cvd fr, hinged at lower end, 58" ...**990.00**
Meridienne style rswd Rococo laminated, John Belter, EX **8,250.00**
Rswd Fr, scalloped bk w/cvd crest, worn uphl, 41x60x27" **150.00**
Sheraton-style, mahog w/striped uphl, brass tacks on apron, 36x68" ..**770.00**
Walnut Vict Rococo Revival, EX detail, velvet reuphl, 74" **880.00**

Stands

Adirondack style, old dk finish w/blk & wht highlights, 31x14x14" **125.00**
Bedside, curly maple Co, 1-brd top:rpl drw:sq legs, rfn, 39x20x17" **550.00**
Bedside, hardwood/figured mahog w/inlay, 2 drw, trn legs, 39x22x18" .**440.00**
Birch Co Hplwht, 1-brd top:mortised & pinned apron:sq legs, 28x15" sq...**165.00**
Birch/chestnut Co Hplwht, 2-brd top:dvtl drw:tapered legs, 29x19x21" **525.00**
Canterbury, rswd Wm IV, pierced fretwork gallery, cvd facade, 34x22"..**2,400.00**
Canterbury, walnut, drw, trn legs, wire nails, rpl brasses, 24x23" **550.00**
Cherry Co Hplwht, 2-brd top:rpl drws:2 sq tapered legs, rfn, 28x18x20" **300.00**
Cherry Co Sheraton, dvtl drw, 2-brd top, rfn, 29x20x20" **275.00**
Cherry/poplar, red/blk grpt, 1-brd top, dvtl drw, PA, 22" sq, NM .**4,400.00**
Curly maple Co, 1-brd top:2 dvtl drw:trn legs, 31x19" sq **1,265.00**
Curly Maple Co w/EX figure & color, rnded drw front, 38x22x22" ..**1,375.00**
Mahog Fed, 1-drw w/beading, str skirt:4 sq legs, rfn, 38x17x16" **1,265.00**
Mahog Sheraton, 2-drw, rope-cvd legs, trn ft, rpl/rfn, 29x19x16"..**500.00**
Pine Co Sheraton w/bird's-eye maple top, worn red pnt, drw, 24x15" ...**300.00**
Plant, hardwood w/overall pressed florals, 28x21x18" **125.00**
Poplar Co Hplwht, 1-brd top, worn red-brn w/grpt on drw, 28x21x17"..**770.00**
Sewing, bird's-eye/tiger maple Sheraton, deep apron, 2 tiers dvtl drws..**650.00**
Sewing, walnut/cherry Vict, lyre base, 2 dvtl drw, 31x22x17" **500.00**

Stools

Footstool, mahogany base with needlepoint top, American Late Classical, carved base joined by turned stretcher, 1840s, 16x23", $550.00.

Co Shaker style w/red traces, woven splint seat, 18x13x13"* **50.00**
Curly maple Late Fed, trn tapering legs, reuphl top, 1830s, 19x23" ...**275.00**
Footstool, cherry, cut-out ft mortised through top, 7x13x7", EX.**195.00**
Footstool, cherry w/inlaid stars in top, alligatored finish, 7x7x12"..**500.00**
Footstool, Fr style, cabriole legs, cvd fr, uphl, 20th C, 7x13x9".....**50.00**
Footstool, hardwood horseshoe shape, worn velvet cover, 13½".**110.00**
Footstool, mc rpt w/striping & mc florals, 9½x18x8" **85.00**
Footstool, pine Co, hand-hold in top, 9x15x9"...........................**100.00**
Footstool, pine w/bj ft, chip-cvd top, rprs/worn varnish, 14" **80.00**
Footstool, Windsor, old red-brn w/yel striping, 33" **770.00**
Giltwood Italian Neoclassical w/cvd lion heads, paw ft, 22x30x18", pr...**1,300.00**
Gout, Neoclassical style w/much cvg, 19th C **165.00**
Kneeling, oak, rest for elbows, mass produced, 1880s, 26x18x17" **235.00**
Oak W/M, cvd stretchers w/cherubs flanking crown, cane seat ..**400.00**
Piano, cvd rswd, Am, 1850s..**165.00**
Pub, fruitwood English Regency, leather uphl, trn legs, 31x15x15" .**385.00**
Tavern, Iberian cvd elm & wrought iron, pr **500.00**

Tables

Banquet, mahog Fed, trn/reeded legs, figured top/apron, 89", pr*......**1,870.00**

Banquet, mahog Fed, 2-part, ea w/drop leaf, old rfn, 1800s, 29x84x43" ..**2,650.00**
Banquet, mahog Geo III-style, 3-part, 19th C, 30x140x56".....**8,250.00**
Banquet, mahog Hplwht, 3-part, 'D' end, banded inlay, rprs, 115" ..**1,450.00**
Banquet, oak, lion base, Hastings, 60" dia+6 leaves **6,600.00**
Breakfast/drop-leaf, Am Classical w/brass inlay, cvd legs w/paw ft ...**2,500.00**
Card, birch Sheraton w/figured mahog/bird's-eye maple on apron, 35x17"..**2,100.00**
Card, hardwood/mahog vnr Emp, trn/sq post legs, beading, swing top **500.00**
Card, mahog Fed w/inlay, serpentine front, Boston, 1810, 30x36x19"**..**19,550.00**
Card, mahog Hplwht w/flame grain vnr & inlay, 2-brd top, 29x36x18"........**1,650.00**
Center, mahog flame vnr Charles X, ped on plinth w/bun ft, 1830s, 47"..**2,400.00**
Center, mahog Fr Emp-style, 6-column base, ormolu, 31x55" dia...............**2,757.00**
Coffee, walnut Vict-style, red pnt base, wht oval marble top, 36x26"............**330.00**
Console, bird's-eye maple/mahog Classical, marble top, VT, 1820s, 40" **2,875.00**
Console, mahog European, marble top, 3-do, appl cvgs, 33x58" .**700.00**
Console-desserte; Louis XVI-style Kingwood Parquetry, marble top, 26" ..**1,450.00**
Cricket, pine, 2-brd top, stretcher base, putty rpr, 39x26" dia.....**550.00**
Demilune, mahog Hplwht-style, sq legs w/spade ft, hidden drw, 44"...........**440.00**
Demilune side, mahog, trn column/rear flank supports, marble top, 36" **300.00**
Dining, oak, rnd top:5 legs, Leavens label, 1915, 48"+4 12" leaves...............**700.00**
Dining, oak w/lg ped, scroll legs w/fruit cvgs, Am, 1880s, 62"+leaves **3,500.00**
Dining, quarter-sawn Golden Oak Era, hand-crank for leaves, 55"+leaf..**1,240.00**
Dressing, cherry Fed w/inlay, 2 short drw, 1815-20, 30x34x21"..**2,875.00**
Dressing, hardwood & poplar w/old yel rpt w/mc striping, 3-drw, 39x34" ...**330.00**
Dressing, pine Co Sheraton, crest:2-brd top:drw:trn legs, rfn, 29x32" ...**300.00**
Dressing, pnt Fed w/decor & gold, 2 short:1 drw, 1820-30, 40x36x17" **4,600.00**
Drop-leaf, cherry Co Sheraton, dvtl drw, 1-brd top, 35x19"+leaves.............**440.00**
Drop-leaf, cherry/walnut Chpndl w/maple swing leg, rfn, 48x16"+leaves..**935.00**
Drop-leaf, curly maple Co, trn legs, rstr/rfn, 29x38x23" **550.00**
Drop-leaf, mahog Chpndl, serpentine top & leaves, sq legs, old rfn, 31" ..**6,300.00**
Drop-leaf, mahog Hplwht w/inlay, scalloped edge & leaves, 35"+leaves **1,750.00**
Drop-leaf, mahog QA, shaped apron:cabriole legs, Santo Domingo, 48".**10,925.00**
Drop-leaf, mahog Sheraton, 2-brd scrubbed top, swing leg, 42"+leaves.......**385.00**
Drop-leaf, maple/birch Hplwht, dvtl drw, 1-brd top, rfn, 36"+2 leaves **880.00**
Drop-leaf, maple QA, cabriole legs, molded apron, rfn, 42"+2 leaves **3,000.00**
Drop-leaf, tiger maple, drw, sq tapered legs, scrubbed top, 1800s, 40".........**1,725.00**
Drop-leaf, tiger maple, str skirts, ring-trn legs, 30x38x41" **1,150.00**
Drop-leaf/work, mahog English Sheraton w/X-banding, rprs, 19"+leaves..**715.00**
Eating board, pine sawbuck, old natural, MA, 1800s, 32x82x21" ..**2,070.00**
Folding, oak w/trestle base, shoe ft, top folds flat, 40" dia **440.00**
Gate-leg, maple Baroque, drw, ring-trn legs, 1720-80, 48"+leaves.....**19,550.00**
Gate-leg, maple W&M, drop-leaf top, drw, rfn, 18th C, 22x53x42" ...**9,775.00**
Harvest, pine Co Hplwht w/red rpt, 2-brd breadbrd top, 28x83x24"...**1,750.00**
Harvest, pine 5-brd rfn top, birch base w/old red, ME, 55x42"...**1,650.00**
Harvest, pnt pine, drop-leaf, scrubbed top, ca 1800, 21x103x40"...**11,500.00**
Hutch, curly maple, sq nails, cut-out ft, 2-brd top, rfn, 60x40" ..**1,925.00**
Hutch, hardwood/softwood Co, 2-brd pine top, rfn, 29x43x34" .**825.00**
Hutch, pine/birch Co cleaned to old red, 3-brd top, 30x44x54" **2,100.00**
Library, Baroque Revival, rope-trn legs, cvd apron, drw, 20x40x24"......**500.00**
Library, oak Elizabethan Revival, much cvg/trestle/drw/marble top, 52"..**3,200.00**
Parlor, walnut Eastlake Vict, trn/cvd, porc casters, 32x20x28"....**360.00**
Parlor, walnut Vict, relief-cvd & trn detail, marble top, 31x29x21"....**500.00**
Parlor, walnut Vict w/burl vnr, cvgs, rpl marble top, rfn, 30x19x17"....**220.00**
Parlor, walnut w/burl vnr Eastlake Vict, marble top, 30x24x17".**300.00**
Primitive, pine, nailed drw/galleried shelf, rpl pull/rstr, 25x28x21" **440.00**
Rent, cherry/oak/maple, 8-sided top revolves, 4 drw, 1850s, 26" dia ...**3,000.00**
Sawbuck, pine, 1-brd top w/bread brd ends, rprs/frn, 41x20" **550.00**
Sawbuck, trough, X-legs, dk top:red stain base, ca 1800, 39x35x24"..**2,650.00**
Server, cherry/curly maple Co Sheraton, 2 drw: drw in shelf, rfn, 36" ...**1,200.00**
Sorting, pine, tray:drw:str skirt:tapered legs, wht over gr, 22x16"......**700.00**
Tavern, curly maple QA style, 3-brd oval top, handmade repro, 33x25"....**385.00**
Tavern, hardwood/pine Co QA, 2-brd top, apron, dvtl drw, rprs, 43x29" ..**110.00**
Tavern, maple/cherry Co Chpndl, drw, scrubbed, 28x36x20"......**990.00**
Tavern, maple/pine, Co QA, stretcher base w/ball ft, drw, rfn, 42x22" ..**1,750.00**
Tavern, pine Co Chpndl, stretcher base, apron, 2-brd top, 31x22" **715.00**

Tavern, pine/hardwood Co QA-style, trn legs, 2-brd top, rfn, 26x21x30"...**495.00**
Tea, cherry, 2-brd top: trn column w/chip cvg:tripod, old finish, 26".......**220.00**
Tea, mahog Chpndl-style tilt-top, tripod w/b&c ft, 20th C, 29x31"........**495.00**
Tea, mahog English Chpndl-style, 3-tier, tripod base w/snake ft, 43"...**1,350.00**
Tea, maple, tilt-top:birdcage:tripod w/cabriole legs, cvd knees, 29"......**2,000.00**
Tea, maple/pine Co Chpndl, tilt-top, snake ft, rfn, 28x31" dia ...**440.00**
Tea, walnut PA Chpndl, dish top:birdcage:tripod:3 shaped ft, rfn, 36"..**1,045.00**
Tea, walnut PA Chpndl, tilt-top:birdcage:tripod w/shaped ft, 36" dia......**825.00**
Tiered, mahog Chpndl-style, 2 dish shelves:tripod:snake ft, 32x17".........**165.00**
Trestle, oak English, mortise/peg, 2-brd top, rprs, old finish, 101".........**3,400.00**
Trestle, red pnt sawbuck, nailed, scrubbed top, 45x27x28".........**550.00**
Trestle, walnut, thick brds w/cut-out ends, handmade 20th C, 46".......**220.00**
Vitrine, mahog English Regency w/X-banded vnr, lift lid, 33x23" sq...**550.00**
Vitrine, mahog Fr w/ormolu, marble top, glass do, 20th C, 40" ...**770.00**
Walnut Continental Baroque, cabriole legs, dvtl drw, rprs, 30x22x28".......**550.00**
Wine tasting, mahog Chpndl-style, dish top:tripod base, 22x14" dia........**440.00**
Work, bird's-eye & tiger maple/cherry, 2-drw, trn legs, rfn, 29x22x19"....**1,600.00**
Work, hardwood/pine Co Chpndl w/blk pnt, 2-brd:dvtl drw, 28x48x29"....**800.00**
Work, mahog Fed, 2 drw: ped base w/4 cvd legs:paw ft, rfn, 30x21x18".....**880.00**
Work, walnut Co Hplwht, worn brn-gray, 2-brd top:2 drw:sq legs, 68"...**1,870.00**
Writing, mahog English Sheraton, 2-drw, molded apron, rpl brasses, 39"...**1,045.00**

Wardrobes

Kas, pine w/rosemaled floral decor, panel do:drw, ca 1800, 78x54"...........**4,400.00**
Linen press, mahog English Chpndl, dbl panel do:4 dvtl drw, 2-pc, 82"..**4,675.00**
Linen press, mahog Fed, flared cornice:panel dos:2 drw:2 do, 89"*...........**1,850.00**
Linen press, oak English, 4 grad drw, 2 mirrored do:2 drw, 88x79x23"......**6,600.00**
Linen press, walnut cvd Classical, 2 panel do, fluted columns, 88"...**10,825.00**
Poplar w/brn 'curly maple' grpt, panel do, wear, 85x56" **165.00**
Poplar w/mustard rpt, 2 raised-panel do:drw, rprs, 67x42"...........**2,750.00**
Poplar/pine Co, brn rpt, dvtl drw, Rockingham knob, fitted int, 84x40" ...**525.00**

Washstands

Butternut Co, lift lid:drw:dbl do:scrolled apron, 30x29x20"........**350.00**
Cherry Sheraton, dvtl drw, shelf, trn legs, rfn/rstr, 33x22x17" **520.00**
Cherrywood Southern Am, cut-out top:shelf:drw, 19th C, 31x18x17" **440.00**
Corner, mahog English Hplwht, dvtl drw in shelf, gallery, 38x24" **330.00**
Curly maple Co Sheraton w/EX figure, trn legs, dvtl drw, 33x20x17" **3,400.00**
Mahog Am early Vict, marble top/inserts, 3-drw, 1840s, 29x51x23".......**1,100.00**
Mahog Am Late Classical w/marble top, drw:2 do, 1840s, 30x35"..........**1,200.00**
Mahog Am Late Fed, hinged top:cupboard & drw:trn legs, 1820s, 31x22".**715.00**
Mahog Sheraton, base shelf w/drw, trn legs/posts, rpl pulls, 33x20x16"........**330.00**
Oak Grand Rapids factory-style, drw:2 do, shelves, casters, 29x31" **225.00**
Oak w/appl cvgs, decor splashbrd, brass pulls, Am, 58x38x20" **400.00**
Pine w/yel rpt w/brn/blk stripes, fruit/foliage crest, 36x16x14"...........**220.00**
Poplar Co, scalloped end aprons, 3 dvtl drws, rpl pulls, 33x30x16" .**220.00**
Rswd Am Rococo, marble bksplash/top, drw:cupboard, 1850s, 39x37"..**2,200.00**
Stained Fed, 1-brd top, 1 drw, trn legs, 1800s, 35x22x14"...........**465.00**
Walnut Co, crest & towel bars:drw:trn legs, worn, 39x26x13"...........**110.00**
Walnut w/old pnt traces, 2-brd top, 33x54x22"........................**3,300.00**

Miscellaneous

Bookmill, mahog Louis XVI-style w/brass mts, drw/shelves, 1910s, 48" ...**5,775.00**
Brackets, giltwood Fr Rococo-style, coquiform w/laurel band, pr...**575.00**
Cellarette, mahog Fed w/inlay, molded fr/fitted int, ca 1800, 22x18"**...**8,000.00**
Dinette set, plastic laminate/chrome table+2 vinyl/chrome chairs....**300.00**
Fainting couch, walnut Vict, velvet reuphl, tufted bk, 70"...........**550.00**
Firescreen, mahog & gilt metal Fr Emp-style, circular form, 41x22" ...**2,000.00**
Firescreen, pierced cvd Rococo style, floral panel..........................**880.00**
Pedestal, alabaster, intertwined dolphins column, 22x18" dia, VG....**250.00**
Pedestal, walnut & burl, marble top, cvd cartouch, drw, 1875, 38", pr..**3,300.00**

Peg board, pine w/worn dk finish, beaded edges, 9 pegs, 60".......**220.00**
Screen, cvd/gessoed giltwood w/pnt canvas panels, 19th C, 72x88"..**4,950.00**
Screen, mahog English Regency, brocade reuphl, rprs, 43x20"....**220.00**
Screen, oil-on-canvas pnt panels (4), reed/rocaille fr, 82x112" .**8,250.00**
Screen, pnt floral canvas panels (ea 68x18"), worn varnish, EX.**440.00**
Steps, library; mahog w/old varnish, 4 trn legs w/casters, 20th C, 67" ...**500.00**
Tray, butler's; English, dvtl mahog, folding base, rprs, 34x25x18"..**495.00**

Galena

Potteries located in the Galena, Illinois, area generally produced plain utility wares with lead glaze, often found in a pumpkin color with some slip decoration or splashes of other colors. These potteries thrived from the early 1830s until sometime around 1860. In the listings that follow, all items are made of red clay unless noted otherwise.

Churn, red-amber w/orange spots, appl hdls, tooled lines, mini, 4½" ..**1,400.00**
Jar, gr & orange mottle, minor glaze flakes, 10" **415.00**

Galle

Emile Galle was one of the most important producers of cameo glass in France. His firm, founded in Nancy in 1874, produced beautiful cameo in the Art Nouveau style during the 1890s, using a variety of techniques. He also produced glassware with enameled decoration, as well as some fine pottery — animal figurines, table services, vases, and other objets d' art. In the mid-1880s he became interested in the various colors and textures of natural woods and as a result began to create furniture which he used as yet another medium for expression of his artistic talent. Marquetry was the primary method Galle used in decorating his furniture, preferring landscapes, Nouveau floral and fruit arrangements, butterflies, squirrels, and other forms from nature. It is for his furniture and his cameo glass that he is best known today. All Galle is signed.

In the listings below, 'fp' indicates items that have been fire polished. Our advisor for this category is Don Williams; he is listed in the Directory under Missouri.

Cameo

Bottle, scent; berries/leaves, brn/yel, atomizer top (no ball), 9" ..**700.00**
Bottle, scent; foliage, purple/amber/frost, 4¼x4½" **900.00**
Bowl, flower branches, pk/yel-gr/amber, 4¼x7¾" **700.00**
Bowl, flowering myrtle, frost/yel/lav/bl, tricorner, 6" **800.00**
Bowl, sea fern, gr/frosted amber, 5x6" **750.00**

Box, leaves and berries, purple on frost, 3x7", $2,350.00.

Ceiling fixture, floral, amber on frost, 3-arm hanger, 3-light, 14" ...**4,480.00**
Flask, floral, brn/yel/amber, narrow neck, rnd body, 5¼x5" **1,200.00**
Lamp, apple blossom 11½" dome shade; matching std, 21¼"...**12,650.00**
Lamp, perfume; floral, burgundy/frosty citron w/gold, globular, 7" ...**2,000.00**

Tazza, clematis, amber-yel/maroon, ftd, 10¾", NM **1,150.00**
Tumbler, foliage, dk gr/citron, 3½" **450.00**
Vase, aspen branches w/seeds, pk/gr/brn, tapered oval, 8" **1,500.00**
Vase, berries, pk opaque/clear/olive, bulbous, 3½" **600.00**
Vase, berries cascading, smoky topaz/olive-gr, long neck, 16" **2,500.00**
Vase, berries/leaves, pk/olive gr, bulbous w/flared neck, 8" **400.00**
Vase, bud; foliage, orange/frost, ftd cylinder, 8" **650.00**
Vase, buds/leaves, dk royal bl/rose/frost, 4", NM **625.00**
Vase, carnations, ginger red/citron, slim, 7½" **1,500.00**
Vase, clematis, gray/yel/purple, invt trumpet form, 13" **975.00**
Vase, clematis, violet to milky wht, fp, ovoid, 4¾" **1,150.00**
Vase, columbines, frosted/yel/pk/mauve, cylinder w/broad base, 13"...**2,500.00**
Vase, crocuses, pk-purple/clear, stepped cylinder, 8" **1,265.00**
Vase, crocuses/leaves/sunset, bl/turq/yel, flask shape, 8¼" **6,250.00**
Vase, cyclamen/buds, red-brn/rust frost, 6" **1,200.00**
Vase, daffodils, yel/orange/gr, raised rim, ovoid, 4¾" **975.00**
Vase, fern fronds, gr jade to celadon tinged, cylindrical, 9⅞" ..**2,185.00**
Vase, fern fronds, lime gr on translucent, stick neck, 7" **1,100.00**
Vase, fern fronds/butterfly, gr on gray frost, stick neck, 5¾" **1,100.00**
Vase, ferns, gr on pk to wht frost, baluster, 5" **1,035.00**
Vase, ferns, yel/clear/frost, mk w/star, 10¾x3½" **1,435.00**
Vase, floral, amethyst/pk frost, 5¼" **450.00**
Vase, floral, apricot on gray frost, tapered cylinder, 18⅜" **2,600.00**
Vase, floral, burgundy/amber/frost, banjo shape, 6¾" **1,100.00**
Vase, floral, cut/pnt, amber/burgundy/orange/brn, 8¾x8½" **3,500.00**
Vase, floral, orange/bl, shouldered, fp, 7¼" **1,700.00**
Vase, floral, pk-lav/lt bl, flared rim, ovoid, 4¾" **700.00**
Vase, floral, royal bl/citron frost, flat sided, shouldered, ftd, 8" ...**2,400.00**
Vase, floral, yel splash on frost, 4" **395.00**
Vase, floral branches, gr/bl on milky frost, bulbous, 6¼", pr **3,000.00**
Vase, grape clusters, brn on gray to maroon frost, 7⅞" **1,725.00**
Vase, grapes/leaves, lav/amber/pk, ftd, 3¾" **525.00**
Vase, hydrangeas, frost/pk/periwinkle/gr, ovoid, 7⅞" **750.00**
Vase, hydrangeas, gray/pk/periwinkle/gr, long neck, 6½" **575.00**
Vase, irises, lt & dk bl/amber, cylindrical w/bulbous base, 9¾" ...**2,750.00**
Vase, irises, purple/lt bl on frost, tapered cylinder, 6¾" **1,450.00**
Vase, lake scene, amber on lemon frost, ovoid, 7½" **1,600.00**
Vase, lake/trees/mtns, amethyst/bl/gr/wht frost, bulbous, 7¾"..**1,800.00**
Vase, landscape, blush/gray/citron/brn, narrow mouth, 9" **1,725.00**
Vase, leafy branches, amber/frosted/lt gr/olive, ovoid, 13" **925.00**
Vase, leafy branches, pk/gray/wht/gr, stick neck, ca 1904, 7¾" ...**700.00**
Vase, leaves & pods, purple on citron, stick form, 13" **1,125.00**
Vase, lilies, bl/amber frost, stick neck, tricorner top, fp, 7½" ...**2,800.00**
Vase, magnolias, rose/pk/wht, cylindrical, 23½" **3,500.00**
Vase, mtn scene, gr/amber/frost, cylindrical, 6¼" **800.00**
Vase, nasturtiums/vines/pods, ochre/citron, invt trumpet form, 18" ..**1,800.00**
Vase, orchids, yel/clear/brn, long neck on flattened sphere, 7"....**525.00**
Vase, Persian Islamic pattern, cut/pnt, amber/red/brn, bbl shape, 5" ..**3,700.00**
Vase, poppies, gr/brn/bl/amber, bulbous, flared rim, 13" **2,200.00**
Vase, poppies, orang on frost, stick neck, 15" **1,350.00**
Vase, primroses, bl frost/purple/olive, flared rim, 5" **400.00**
Vase, seed pods, wht/yel/gr on peach, hexagonal baluster, 11⅝"..**2,200.00**
Vase, seed pods, wine/yel/gr on gray, flattened baluster, 10" **1,950.00**
Vase, ships/shore/islands, brn/dk brn/yel, stick neck, 20½"....**3,000.00**
Vase, spider mums, amber on frost, shouldered, slim, 10".........**1,350.00**
Vase, St Geo & dragon, eggplant/amber opal, flattened ovoid, ftd, 12" ...**9,775.00**
Vase, thistle, gr/citron/lt rose/pk, 5-pointed top, ftd, 4½" **800.00**
Vase, thistles, gr/lt pk/gr frost, 2½x3" **350.00**
Vase, thistles, lt gr on gray to peach, cylindrical, 17" **1,150.00**
Vase, trees/mtns/shore, dk, med & lt bl/frost/amber, urn shape, 14"..**6,750.00**
Vase, water lilies, pumpkin/yel/gr, 8" **2,000.00**
Vase, wildflowers, amber to yel, ftd, 5¾" **1,000.00**
Vase, wildflowers, frosted yel/aubergine, flattened oval, 5"..........**900.00**
Vase, wisteria pods/leaves, amethyst/pk/frost, 3" **300.00**

Enameled Glass

Bowl, grasshopper & floral branches, mc w/gold, triangular, 9¾"...**1,150.00**
Bowl, orchids (3), gold on gr, folded petal rim, 1¾x6" **475.00**
Cup, stylized flowers w/gold, 2⅝", pr.....................................**150.00**
Decanter, floral on lt amber, rpl stopper, 10¾x5½" **400.00**
Decanter, grasshopper/wildflowers, mc w/blk & gold, bulbous, 8½".**1,035.00**
Ewer, orchids/flowers, serpentine hdl, organic spout, 1880s, 20½"...**5,750.00**
Salt cellar, rain scene w/trees, 1x2", NM **2,000.00**
Vase, leaves/tendrils, mc on amber, sq, 4⅜" **700.00**

Marquetry, Wood

**Wall shelf, inlaid butterflies and fuchsia blossoms, open
form with central shelf, 24x42x10", $1,850.00.**

Box, country scene inlay, mixed woods, 14x8x5", VG **1,950.00**
Cabinet, mahog, cvd & inlaid florals & scenic, mk, 36x25" **4,675.00**
Table, occasional; 2-tier, foliate design, stretcher shelf, 39x23".**1,000.00**
Vitrine, flowers, top/sides/front panel, glass door, 53x24".........**6,500.00**

Pottery

Bowl, faience, flowers/shore HP int, foliate shape, gilt rim, 10¼"...**315.00**
Figurine, cat, yel w/bl & wht hearts, gr glass eyes, 13" **2,900.00**
Plaque, pastoral landscape in Limoges style, 12½".....................**800.00**
Vase, grasshopper on gr & brn w/gold, floriform top, 3½"...........**635.00**

Gambling Memorabilia

Gambling memorabilia from the infamous casinos of the West and
items that were once used on the 'Floating Palace' riverboats are especially sought after by today's collectors.

Box, wood w/SP tabs, ca 1900, 12", +chips/dominoes/game pcs, EX+...**700.00**
Card press, maple w/turq inlay roses, EX **275.00**
Case keeper, faro; celluloid strips/maple, Cowper, 1910, EX **550.00**
Case keeper, faro; walnut w/compo sliders, Will & Finck, 11¾".**600.00**
Cheating device, card trimmer, mk Will & Finck, brass & steel, EX..**850.00**
Cheating device, gaffed dealing box known as sand-tell, EX.......**925.00**
Chip, clay, assorted advertising, 1900s, 30 for..............................**150.00**
Chip, Golden Gate Casino, 25¢, inlaid...**70.00**
Chip, ivory w/fancy numeral cvgs, set of 5 ....**210.00**
Chip, ivory; #1, 1½"..**125.00**
Chip, Red Garter Las Vegas Nevada, $1, ca 1970s-80s, M..........**160.00**
Dice cage, NP brass & steel w/drum skin ends, bell & dice, 16".**210.00**
Game, Play Poker, cb sheet w/punch-out disks, Brady, 1949, 12x8"....**125.00**
Game, Top of Day, tin litho spinner+dice, CH Loper, ca 1920s, EXIB ...**200.00**
Playing cards, faro; Ruell & Morgan, dtd May 31, 81 on Ace, 52 ....**235.00**
Roulette watch, Roulette Ideal, beveled crystal, 1890s, EX.........**350.00**

Wheel, pnt plywood, G age, 14" dia..................................**220.00**
Wheel, roulette; mahog, table-top type, 22" dia, EX **560.00**
Wheel, roulette; NP CI w/in walnut fr, Balny Model Depose, 12", G..**125.00**
Wheel, roulette; wood, hinged side compartment, mini, 2x10x5" ...**375.00**
Wheel, roulette; wood w/old mc pnt, 36" dia, EX....................**175.00**
Wheel, wooden floor model, worn pnt, 73x42" dia, G **300.00**
Whist scorer, cvd ivory hand w/pointing finger, 1870s, 7 for **900.00**

Game Calls

Those interested in hunting and fishing collectibles are beginning to take notice of the finer specimens of game calls available on today's market.

Crow, Charles Perdew, made with chip in barrel, G, $200.00; Goose, David Fuller, small, VG, $325.00; Duck, James Reynolds, Bakelite, stopper screws into barrel, M, $475.00; Duck, Irv Redshaw, walnut with maple stopper, VG, $300.00.

Crow, Charles H Perdew, walnut bbl, stamped name, 4½", G **125.00**
Crow, FA Allen, maple & metal bbl, 4" (scarce length), VG **90.00**
Crow, Hoosier, cedar bbl, scratches/dings, 4½", G **15.00**
Crow, Tom Turpin, walnut bbl, 5", EX **70.00**
Deer, Dazy, mouth call, MIB **30.00**
Duck, Blackduck, Whiting IN, walnut bbl, plastic reed, 6¼", EX.**25.00**
Duck, Everett Baldridge, walnut bbl, cvd/fluted, 5½" **95.00**
Duck, Herter's 'Feeder,' walnut bbl, red rubber attachment, EX....**38.00**
Duck, Mark Weedman, AR, walnut bbl, plastic reed, 6¼", EX.....**45.00**
Duck, Tom Cando, ebony bbl & stopper, metal reed, 5¼", EX **45.00**
Goose, Herter's, walnut w/amber plastic stopper, metal reed, VG.**35.00**
Goose, walnut bbl & stopper, plastic reed, unknown mfg, 5⅝".....**30.00**
Predator, Herter's, Stage 1, EXIB **20.00**
Predator, Herter's World Famous, amber plastic stopper, EX **40.00**
Turkey, Dixie Yelper, walnut, Joyner Wood Products...Ala, 5", G.**30.00**
Turkey, Lloyd E Moon, hand-cvd bone, 5¾", EX.............................**30.00**
Turkey, Lynch's World Champion, altered w/6 drilled holes, VG..**45.00**

Gameboards

Gameboards, the handmade ones from the eighteenth and nineteenth century, are collected more for their folk art quality than their relation to games. Excellent examples of these handcrafted 'playthings' sell well into the thousands of dollars; even the simple designs are often expensive. If you are interested in this field, you must study it carefully. The market is always full of 'new' examples. Well-established dealers are often your best sources; they are essential if you do not have the expertise to judge the age of the boards yourself. Our advisor for this category is Louis Picek; he is listed in the Directory under Iowa.

Backgammon, inlaid dmn-shaped motif, hinged, 21x21"...............**70.00**
Checkers, arched top, red/yel pnt w/varnished appl edge, 12x19"...**257.00**

Checkers, blk/mustard checks w/mc linear decor, 19th C, 18" sq..**490.00**
Checkers, blk/red stained sqs w/gold band, 19th C, 19x21" **210.00**
Checkers, cherry/maple/pine w/inlay, late, 18x27" **250.00**
Checkers, dk red swirl & sponging on mustard, blk checks, 17" sq ...**1,950.00**
Checkers, dk/red/taupe pnt, 19th C, 18x32", VG........................**175.00**
Checkers, gr/blk pnt, 2-board w/tongue & groove, 19x30", EX...**165.00**
Checkers, gr/wht red on pine, 24x31" **360.00**
Checkers, maple & walnut inlay w/cherry edge, poplar bk, 17" sq..**140.00**
Checkers, mustard/wht pnt, 2-board w/nailed braces on bk, 14x27"**250.00**
Checkers, pine w/old red & wht rpt, appl gallery, 144 sqs, 20x32"...**360.00**
Checkers, pine w/red/wht/gr rpt, 144 sqs, 17x24" **220.00**
Checkers, poplar w/old blk/gr/maroon pnt, wear, 17x17½".........**635.00**
Checkers, red over gr w/blk, molded rim, age cracks, 18x29"......**330.00**
Checkers, red/blk pnt, chamfered edges, 1890s, 26x14" **750.00**
Checkers, 4-color pnt w/blk-lined sqs, ca 1900, 21x21" **925.00**
Checkers/backgammon, mc pnt, folds, 19th C, 15x17", EX........**350.00**
Checkers/backgammon, pine w/walnut inlay/pnt/varnish, 17x17" .**715.00**
Checkers/geometric unknown, old mc rpt, 13" sq........................**715.00**
Checkers/unknown, maroon/orange/gr/blk pnt, 24x25"..............**990.00**
Checkers/unknown, orig mc pnt on pine, 1-board, 16x16" **330.00**
Checkers/unknown, worn yel/gr pnt, stenciling, 2-board, 18x29" .**300.00**

Games

Collectors of antique games are finding it more difficult to find their treasures at shows and flea markets. Most of the action these days seems to be through specialty dealers and auctions. The appreciation of the art on the boards and boxes continues to grow. You see many of the early games proudly displayed as art, and they should be. The period from the 1850s to 1910 continues to draw the most interest. Many of the games of that period were executed by well-known artists and illustrators. The quality of their lithography cannot be matched today. The historical value of games made before 1850 has caused interest in this period to increase. While they may not have the graphic quality of the later period, their insights into the social and moral character of the early nineteenth century are interesting.

Twentieth-century games invoke a nostalgic feeling among collectors who recall looking forward to a game under the Christmas tree each year. They search for examples that bring back those Christmas-morning memories. While the quality of their lithography is certainly less than the early games, the introduction of personalities from the comic strips, radio, and later TV created new interest. Every child wanted a game that featured their favorite character. Monopoly, probably the most famous game ever produced, was introduced during the Great Depression.

For further information, we recommend *Schroeder's Collectible Toys, Antique to Modern*, available from Collector Books.

Across the Continent, Parker Bros, 1952, NM (EX box) **40.00**
American Boys, McLoughlin Bros, early 1900s, EXIB **200.00**
Animal Talk, Mattel, 1964, MIB...**150.00**
Auto Racing, Milton Bradley, 1930s, VG (VG box) **225.00**
Automobile Race, McLoughlin Bros, 1904, EXIB **1,800.00**
Bandersnatch, Mattel, 1969, NMIB..**70.00**
Baseball Pinball, Marx, 11", NM (EX box) **75.00**
Battle Line, Ideal, 1964, EXIB **40.00**
Battleship, Whitman, 1940, EXIB **65.00**
Beat the Clock, Milton Bradley, 1969, NM (EX box) **40.00**
Big Town News Reporting, Lowell, 1950s, rare, NMIB **75.00**
Blockade, Corey Games, 1941, VG (VG box) **85.00**
Boom or Bust, Parker Bros, 1951, EXIB **250.00**
Chiromagica, McLoughlin Bros, 1890, VG (VG wood/glass box) ..**300.00**
Civil War Game of 1863, Parker Bros, 1961, NMIB....................**50.00**
Concentration, Milton Bradley, 1959, 1st edition, EXIB..............**40.00**

Cowboy Game, Chaffee & Selchow, 1898, EXIB 400.00
Crazy Clock, Ideal, 1964, NMIB..100.00
Dice Ball, Milton Bradley, 1934, VG (VG box) 60.00
Direct Hit, Northwestern, 1950, EXIB 70.00
Down & Out, Milton Bradley, EX (worn box)..........................150.00
Dream Date, Transogram, 1963, EXIB 50.00
Dream House, Milton Bradley, 1968, rare, EXIB 100.00
FBI, Transogram Landmark Game Series, MIB 75.00
Fortune's Wheel, Parker Bros, 1903, EXIB 175.00
Funny Finger, Ideal, 1968, EXIB 25.00
Game of Crusaders, McLoughlin Bros, 1888, EX (G box) 30.00
Game of Mail Express or Accomodation, Milton Bradley, 1930s, EXIB...250.00
Game of Philippine, McLoughlin Bros, 1900, EXIB 300.00
Game of Steeple Chase, McLoughlin Bros, 1889, EX (worn box) ...350.00
Game of the Visit of Santa Claus, McLoughlin, 1890s, VG (VG box) ..1,600.00
Game of Up & Down, Whitman, 1859, EXIB 35.00
Game of Zulu, McLoughlin Bros, EXIB 1,100.00
Gay Purr-ee, Whitman, 1962, EXIB 70.00
Gee-Wiz Race, Wolverine, EXIB 85.00
Great American Game of Baseball, Hustler Toys, 1923, NM 300.00
Great Family Amusement Target, Rubber Top Co, 1900, EXIB..250.00
Gypsy Fortune Telling Game, Milton Bradley, 1920, NMIB 150.00
Heedless Tommy, McLoughlin Bros, 1893, 9½x20", EX..............400.00
Jumpy Tinker, Toy Tinkers, 1918, EX (worn box) 75.00
Kentucky Derby, Whitman, 1969, NMIB 30.00
Lost Heir, Milton Bradley, 1905, EX (VG box) 125.00
Magic Robot, J&L Randall LTD/England, 1950s, EXIB 125.00
Mammoth Hunt, Cadaco, 1962, EXIB 40.00
Mansion of Happiness, Ives, 1864, VG (VG box) 300.00
Marathon Tinker, Toy Tinkers, 1925, EXIB 150.00
Masquerade Party, Bettye-B, 1955, EXIB....................................65.00
Mouse Trap, Ideal, 1963, 1st edition, EXIB 65.00
Mystery Pistol Target Master, Ohio Art, 1960s, EXIB 100.00
Mystic Skull Game of Voodoo, Ideal, 1960s, EXIB 65.00
Picture Lotto, McLoughlin Bros, 1888, VG (VG wood box) 300.00
Pie in Your Eye, Ideal, 1966, EXIB..30.00
Pirate's Gold, All-Fair, 1946, EXIB 60.00
Pot O' Gold, All-Fair, 1940, EXIB 30.00
Pursuit, Aurora, 1973, EXIB..30.00
Ring My Nose, Milton Bradley, EXIB 50.00
Sea Raiders, Parker Bors, 1945, EXIB 55.00
Skatterbug, Parker Bros, 1952, EXIB 45.00
Skill-Drive Raceway, Tarco, 1960s, NMIB 45.00
Sonar Sub Hunt, Mattel, 1961, EXIB 65.00
Sports Arena, Milton Bradley, 1962, EXIB 50.00
Sprint, Holland Crafts, 1930s, EXIB..75.00
Spy Detector, Mattel, 1960, NMIB..40.00
Them Bones, Mego, 1976, NMIB..100.00
Think-A-Tron, Hasbro, 1961, EXIB 75.00
Tickle Bee, Schaper, 1959, EXIB 35.00
Tiger Island, Ideal, 1966, EXIB 50.00
Tinkerdux, Toy Tinkers, 1919, EX (worn box) 60.00
Top Secret, National Games, 1956, EXIB 75.00
Uranium Rush, Gardner, 1950s, EXIB 100.00
Whyoo, Milton Bradley, 1906, EXIB..100.00
Winner Boxing, GL Seibel, 1956, NMIB..................................100.00
Yacht Race, Parker Bros, 1961, VG (VG box) 100.00
Zoo Game, Milton Bradley, 1920s, EX (worn box) 55.00

Personalities, Movies, and TV Shows

Adventures of Popeye, Transogram, 1957, EXIB..........................50.00
Annie Oakley, Game Gems/T Chon, 1965, EXIB 50.00
Aquaman & the Justice League of America, Hasbro, 1967, NMIB...200.00

Bamm-Bamm Color Me Happy, Transogram, 1963, EXIB 65.00
Batman & Robin Target, Hasbro, 1966, MIB............................200.00
Batman's Cave Maze, Pressman, scarce, NMIB 350.00
Bewitched, Game Gems, 1965, rare, EXIB 145.00
Blondie & Dagwood Race for the Office, Jaymar, 1950, EXIB......50.00
Bullwinkle Fli-Hi Target, Parks, 1961, EXIB............................250.00

Dick Van Dyke Game, Standard Toykraft, 1964, EXIB, $75.00. (Photo courtesy Rick Polizzi)

Emmett Kelly's Circus, All-Fair, 1953, EXIB..............................60.00
Family Affair, Remco, 1968, MIB 100.00
Flying Nun, Milton Bradley, 1968, MIB 75.00
Garrison's Gorillas, Ideal, 1967, EXIB 75.00
Gilligan's Island, Game Gems/T Chon, 1965, EXIB 350.00
Godzilla, Ideal, 1963, EXIB 300.00
Green Acres, Standard Toykraft, 1965, MIB 100.00
Gumby & Pokey Playful Trails, MIB 100.00
Have Gun Will Travel, Parker Bros, 1959, EXIB 100.00
Honey West, Ideal, 1955, MIB 175.00
Howdy Doody TV Game, Milton Bradley, 1950s, EXIB............100.00
Huckleberry Hound Bumps, Transogram, 1960s, EXIB............100.00
Jackie Robinson Baseball, Gotham, 1950s, EXIB......................275.00
Jetsons Out of This World, Transogram, 1962, EXIB................125.00
Jonny Quest, Transogram, 1964, EXIB 800.00
King Leonardo & His Subjects, Milton Bradley, 1960, EXIB 75.00
Kojak Stakeout Detective Game, Milton Bradley, 1975, EXIB 25.00
Li'l Abner's Spoof, Milton Bradley, 1950, EXIB........................100.00
Little Lulu, Milton Bradley, 1946, EXIB 200.00
Little Orphan Annie, Milton Bradley, 1927, rare, MIB..............250.00
Lost in Space, Milton Bradley, 1965, EXIB 75.00
Magilla Gorilla, Ideal, 1964, EXIB..75.00
Man Hunt, Parker Bros, 1930s, EXIB 125.00
Mandrake the Magician, Transogram, 1966, NMIB..................100.00
Marlin Perkin's Zoo Parade, Cadaco, 1955, NMIB 60.00
McHale's Navy, Transogram, 1962, EXIB 50.00
Mickey's Tug-Boat, Chad Valley, 1948, EXIB 125.00
Mighty Mouse & His Pals, Milton Bradley, 1957, NMIB 65.00
Munsters Drag Race, Hasbro, 1965, EXIB................................700.00
Nancy & Sluggo, Milton Bradley, 1944, EXIB 75.00
Nancy Drew Mystery, Parker Bros, 1957, EXIB........................100.00
Nellie Bly, McLoughlin Bros, early 1900s, EXIB 325.00
Pebbles Flintstone, Transogram, 1962, NMIB............................65.00
Peter Pan, Selchow & Righter, 1927, EXIB 175.00
Petticoat Junction, Standard Toykraft, 1964, EXIB 100.00
Popeye the Sailor Shipwreck, Einson-Freeman, 1933, scarce, EXIB..200.00
Rifleman, Milton Bradley, 1959, EXIB 75.00
Road Runner, Milton Bradley, 1968, NMIB 50.00
Snow White & the Seven Dwarfs, Milton Bradley, 1937, rare, NMIB..200.00
Superman Radio Quiz Master, 1948, EXIB 65.00
Superman Speed, Milton Bradley, 1940, EXIB..........................200.00
Three Musketeers, Milton Bradley, 1950, NMIB 60.00
Touche Turtle, Transogram, 1962, EXIB 125.00
Treasure Island, Harett-Gilmar, 1950s, EXIB 100.00
Twiggy, Mitlon Bradley, 1967, EXIB..100.00

Underdog, Milton Bradley, 1964, EXIB..**50.00**
Wally Gator, Transogram, EXIB...**75.00**
Wanted Dead or Alive, Lowell, 1959, EXIB **100.00**
What's My Line?, Lowell, 1954, 1st edition, EXIB.........................**65.00**
White Shadow, Cadaco, 1970s, rare, EXIB....................................**85.00**
Winie the Pooh, Parker Bros, 1954, EXIB......................................**40.00**
Wonder Woman & the Justice League of America, Hasbro, 1976, MIB..**150.00**
Yogi Bear Go Fly a Kite, Transogram, 1961, NMIB **50.00**
Zany Zoo Adventures of Tennessee Tuxedo, Transogram, 1963, NMIB....**200.00**
Zorro Target, Superior/T Chon, 1960, EXIB **175.00**

G. A. R. Memorabilia

The 'The Grand Army of the Republic' was first conceived by Chaplain W.J. Rutledge and Major B.J. Stephenson early in 1864 when they were tent-mates during our own Civil War. These men vowed to each other that if they were spared they would establish an organization that would preserve friendships and memories formed during this time. Shortly after the war ended, Rutledge and Stephenson made their desires a reality. The first National Convention of the Grand Army of the Republic was held in Indianapolis, Indiana, on November 20, 1866. The purpose of the organization was to provide aid and assistance to the widows and orphans of the fallen Union dead and to care for the hospitalized veterans as needed. The last comrade of the G.A.R. died in 1949.

Many items are surfacing from the early encampments which were held on both state and national levels and resulted in a wide variety of souvenir items having been made.

Badge, Chaplain, flag on bl, 3⅝"...**235.00**
Badge, membership; eagle & star type III, Pat Dec 28, 1869.......**360.00**
Badge, membership; Type IV, eagle & star w/flag ribbon, EX **185.00**
Badge, officer's; silver eagle on purple, EX **155.00**
Badge, Post Commander, soldier & sailor, w/ribbon & eagle bar...**310.00**
Badge, representantive's, Golden Jubilee Encampment, 1916, NM..**190.00**
Badge, representative's; 70th Nat'l Encampment, 1936, EX........**170.00**
Badge, 1st MI Vet Vol Cavalry, mtd soldier, Pats 1892 & 1895, w/ribbon...**310.00**
Badge, 86 IL Vol Inf above acorn, early 1900s, 2x3¾" w/ribbon.**385.00**
Canteen, 33rd Nat'l Encampment, dtd 1899, 4½" dia **360.00**
Certificate, Resolution of Respect, to family, 1914, 7¾x10¼"+fr .**85.00**
Document, charter; NH post, 1880, EX in fr **300.00**
Invitation, reunion; sgn Gen WE Strong, 1868, w/ticket & envelope .**100.00**
Journal, proceedings of 39th (MO) Encampment, 1920, VG........**95.00**
Medal, lady's membership; bronze w/flag ribbon, EX **35.00**
Pin-bk, Texas State Fair, eagle/flag/star, red/wht/bl, 1908, 1¼"...**125.00**
Plaque, cast bronze, guns/swords/canons/etc, Rutzler of NY, 12" dia ...**135.00**
Poster, marching scene, Atlantic City, 44th Encampment, 1910...**260.00**
Print, memorial presentation, ca 1894, 32x24"+fr **155.00**
Program, Final Campfire, 83rd Annual Encampment, IN, 1949, EX..**140.00**
Scroll, lists major battles/etc, in 3½" tube mk Pat'd...1890, EX ..**135.00**
Sword, M1860 dress sabre, GAR brass grip w/weapons, 32" blade, VG+...**265.00**

Garden City Pottery

Founded in 1902 in San Jose, California, by the end of the 1920s this pottery had grown to become the largest in Northern California. During that period production focused on stoneware, sewer pipe, and red clay flowerpots. In the late '30s and '40s, the company produced dinnerware in bright solid colors of yellow, green, blue, orange, cobalt, turquoise, white, and black. Royal Arden Hickman, who would later gain fame for the innovative artware he modeled for the Haeger company, designed not only dinnerware but a line of Art Deco vases and bowls as well. The company endured hard times by adapting to the changing needs of the market and during the '50s concentrated on production of garden products. Foreign imports, however, proved to be too competitive, and the company's pottery production ceased in 1979.

Because none of the colored-glazed products were ever marked, to learn to identify the products of this company, you'll need to refer to *Sanford's Guide to Garden City Pottery* by Jim Pasquali, who is listed in the Directory under California. Values apply to items in all colors (except black) and all patterns, unless noted otherwise. Due to relative rarity 20% should be added for any item found in black.

Bowl, batter; solid color, 2-qt **65.00**
Bowl, mixing; wide ring, solid color, #5, lg................................**50.00**
Bowl, soup; plain, solid color...**25.00**
Bowls, nesting (Bulb Bowls); 1930s, set of 3 ....**150.00**
Candle holders, flared ft, solid color, 3", pr **45.00**
Carafe, Geometric, cobalt, w/lid..**65.00**

Carafe, plain, open, **$45.00**; Artichoke plate, **$35.00**. (Photo courtesy Jim Pasquali)

Churn, #3, cobalt on wht, 3-gal, lid missing **55.00**
Cookie jar, Deco style, solid color, 7½" **75.00**
Creamer, Geometric, solid color **15.00**
Cup & saucer, Diamond, solid color..**20.00**
Flowerpot, yel, 6" **25.00**
Pitcher, orange, Deco style, 3⅞" **95.00**
Plate, dinner; Ring, solid color, 9" **15.00**
Shakers, Deco 'Rocket,' solid color, 5", pr **45.00**
Sugar bowl, Swirl, solid color, w/lid **25.00**
Tumbler, wide ring, solid color **15.00**
Vase, blk gloss, ftd, 7⅛"...**295.00**
Vase, bud; hand-thrown tumbler shape, solid color, 5" **35.00**
Vase, yel, Deco style (Royal Hickman design), low, ftd...............**90.00**

Gas Globes and Panels

Gas globes and panels, once a common sight, have vanished from the countryside but are being sought by collectors as a unique form of advertising memorabilia. Early globes from the 1920s (some date back to as early as 1912), now referred to as 'one-piece globes,' were made of molded milk glass and were globular in shape. The gas company name was etched or painted on the glass. Few of these were ever produced, and this type is valued very highly by collectors today.

A new type of pump was introduced in the early 1930s; the old 'visible' pumps were replaced by 'electric' models. Globes were changing at the same time. By the mid-teens a three-piece globe consisting of a pair of inserts and a metal body was being produced in both 15" and 16½" sizes. Collectors prefer to call globes that are not one-piece or plastic 'three-piece glass' (Type 2) or 'metal body, glass inserts' (Type 3). Though metal-body globes (Type 3) were popular in the 1930s, they were common in the 1920s, and some were actually made as early as 1915. Though rare in numbers, their use spans many years. In the 1930s Type 2 and Type 3 globes became the replacements of the one-piece globe. The most recently manufactured gas globes are made with a plastic body that contains two 13½" glass lenses. These were common in the 1950s but were actually used as early as 1932.

Note: Standard Crowns with raised letters are one-piece globes that were made in the 1920s; those made in the 1950s (no raised letters), though one-piece, are not regarded as such by today's collectors. Our advisor for this category is Scott Benjamin; he is listed in the Directory under Ohio.

For more informaition we recommend *Value Guide to Gas Station Memorabilia* by B. J. Summers.

Type 1, Plastic Body, Glass Inserts (Inserts 13½") — 1931 – 1950s

D-X Marine, rare	1,000.00
Dixie, plastic band	250.00
DX Lubricating Gasoline, tan body	275.00
Frontier Gas, Rarin' To Go, w/horse	1,100.00
Kendal Deluxe, Capcolite body w/red pnt, 13½"	325.00
Kendall Polly Power, Capcolite body, 13½" dia, NM	375.00
Marathon, no runner	200.00
Never Nox Ethyl	450.00
Spur, Oval body	350.00
Texaco Diesel Chief, Capcolite body, 13½", NM	1,350.00
Viking, pictures Viking ship	1,750.00

Type 2, Glass Frame, Glass Inserts (Inserts 13½") — 1926 – 1940s

Aerio, gr gill ripple body, 13½" dia, NM	6,500.00
American, gill body, 12½", NM	400.00
Amoco, gill body, 13½", NM	400.00
Atlantic, glass body, 13½" dia, NM	325.00
Atlantic Imperial, gill body, 13½", EX	400.00

Bell, orange rippled body, metal base, 13½", $2,400.00.

Derby	450.00
Esso	325.00
Frontier Gas, Double Refined	350.00
Guyler Brand, milk glass, EX	850.00
Pitman Streamlined, bl gill rippled body, 13½", NM	6,500.00
Pure	500.00
Sinclair Dino, milk glass, EX	300.00
Sinclair Pennant	1,000.00
Sky Chief, gill body, 13½", NM	500.00
Standard Crown, gr or orange, ea	900.00
Standard Crown, wht, red or gold, ea	400.00
Standard Flame	400.00
Texaco Ethyl	1,500.00
White Flash, gill body	450.00
WNAX, w/radio station pictured	2,000.00

Type 3, Metal Frame, Glass Inserts (Inserts 15" or 16½") — 1915 – 1930s

Aero Mobilgas, new metal body, rare, 15", NM	2,500.00
Atlantic Ethyl, 16½"	750.00
Atlantic White Flash, 16½"	750.00
General Ethyl, 15" fr, complete	900.00
Kendal Gasoline, airplane, metal body, rare, 15", NM	6,000.00
Oil Creek Gas, drake well & derrick, 15", NM	3,000.00
Phillips Benzo, low profile metal body, 15", NM	3,500.00
Purol Gasoline, w/arrow, porc body	900.00
Red Crown Ethyl	950.00
Signal, old stoplight, 15", VG	4,500.00
Stanolined Aviation, rare, 16½", EX	5,000.00
Texaco Leaded, glass panels, complete globe	5,000.00
White Star, 15" fr, complete	1,100.00

Type 4, One-Piece Glass Globes, No Inserts, Co. Name Etched, Raised or Enameled — 1912 – 1931

Atlantic, chimney cap	3,000.00
Dixie, etched	2,000.00
Mobil Gargoyle, gargoyle pictured, oval	2,200.00
Pierce Pennant, etched	3,200.00
Republic, 3-sided	2,200.00
Shell, rnd, etched	800.00
Super Shell, clam shape	1,800.00
Super Shell, rnd, etched	3,800.00
Texaco Ethyl	2,100.00
That Good Gulf..., emb, orange & blk letters, EX	1,000.00
White Eagle, some feather detail, 20¾", EX	1,600.00
White Rose, boy pictured, pnt	2,800.00

Gaudy Dutch

Inspired by Oriental Imari wares, Gaudy Dutch was made in England from 1800 to 1820. It was hand decorated on a soft-paste body with rich underglaze blues accented in orange, red, pink, green, and yellow. It differs from Gaudy Welsh in that there is no lustre (except on Water Lily). There are seventeen patterns, some of which are War Bonnet, Grape, Dahlia, Oyster, Urn, Butterfly, Carnation, Single Rose, Double Rose, and Water Lily. For further information we recommend *The Collector's Encyclopedia of Gaudy Dutch and Welsh* by John A. Shuman III, available from Collector Books. Unless otherwise noted, values are given for items with minimal wear and no obvious damage.

Butterfly, coffeepot, 11"	4,400.00
Butterfly, cup plate	880.00
Butterfly, cup plate	880.00
Butterfly, pitcher, milk; 4", M	910.00
Butterfly, plate, butterfly center, unusual wide spread decor, 9⅞"	1,870.00
Butterfly, plate, butterfly on side, 7¼", M	825.00
Butterfly, plate, toddy; 4¼", rare	825.00
Butterfly, platter, 10½", NM	3,000.00
Butterfly, sugar bowl	1,870.00
Butterfly, tea bowl & saucer, butterfly on side	1,650.00
Carnation, plate, lg yel dot border, 10"	825.00
Carnation, plate, 7¼", M	605.00
Carnation, plate, 8⅜", M	850.00
Carnation, soup plate, 8½"	770.00
Carnation, sugar bowl	880.00
Cyupis, toddy plate, central butterfly, mk Cybis	175.00
Dahlia, creamer	990.00
Dahlia, plate, 8⅜"	990.00
Dahlia, sugar bowl	990.00
Dahlia, tea bowl & saucer	825.00
Double Rose, cup plate	770.00

Double Rose, plate, 8¾" 715.00
Double Rose, plate, 9", M 990.00
Double Rose, sugar bowl 880.00
Double Rose, toddy plate, 4½", rare 825.00
Double Rose, waste bowl, 6", M 690.00
Dove, creamer, helmet shape, rare 1,400.00
Dove, cup & saucer, bl band, M 620.00
Dove, plate, 9¾" 880.00
Dove, teapot, EX 880.00
Dove, toddy plate 700.00
Grape, cup & saucer 515.00
Grape, plate, soup; 8¾" 500.00
Grape, plate, 6", M 300.00
Grape, plate, 7", M 440.00
Grape, plate, 8", M 550.00
Grape, plate, 9¾" 660.00
Grape, waste bowl 400.00
Leaf, bowl, unusual shape, 8¾" 1,100.00
Leaf, tea bowl & saucer 800.00
Oyster, cup & saucer, EX 300.00
Oyster, cup & saucer, VG 140.00
Oyster, plate, 5⅝" 400.00
Oyster, plate, 8½" 515.00
Oyster, teapot 550.00
Primrose, plate, mk Riley, 8¾" 610.00
Primrose, sugar bowl 990.00
Single Rose, coffeepot 800.00

Single Rose, creamer, M, $925.00; War Bonnet, creamer, $660.00.

Single Rose, cup & saucer, chips 160.00
Single Rose, plate, deep, 8¼", M 440.00
Single Rose, plate, 6½", M 500.00
Single Rose, plate, 7¼", M 550.00
Single Rose, tea bowl & saucer 330.00
Strawflower, plate, mk Riley, 10", EX 1,015.00
Strawflower, plate, 8½" 900.00
Strawflower, toddy plate, mk Riley, rim chip, 4¾" 575.00
Sunflower, creamer 500.00
Sunflower, sugar bowl, w/lid, EX 600.00
Sunflower, tea bowl & saucer 880.00
Urn, creamer 385.00
Urn, cup plate 465.00
Urn, plate, 8¼", M 685.00
Urn, teapot 660.00
War Bonnet, coffeepot, old riveted rpr 990.00
War Bonnet, cup plate 715.00
War Bonnet, plate, shallow, 8⅛", M 1,000.00
War Bonnet, toddy plate, shows wear, 5¼" 275.00
War Bonnet, waste bowl, 5", M 1,100.00
Zinnia, plate, deep, 9¾" 1,245.00

Zinnia, plate, 6⅛" 660.00

Gaudy Welsh

Gaudy Welsh was an inexpensive hand-decorated ware made in both England and Wales from 1820 until 1860. It is characterized by its colors — principally blue, orange-rust, and copper lustre — and by its uninhibited patterns. Accent colors may be yellow and green. (Pink lustre may be present, since lustre applied to the white areas appears pink. A copper tone develops from painting lustre onto the dark colors.) The body of the ware may be heavy ironstone (also called Gaudy Ironstone), creamware, earthenware, or porcelain; even style and shapes vary considerably. Patterns, while usually floral, are also sometimes geometric and may have trees and birds. Beware! The Wagon Wheel pattern has been reproduced.

Our advisor for this category is Cheryl Nelson; she is listed in the Directory under Minnesota. For further information we recommend *The Collector's Encyclopedia of Gaudy Dutch & Welsh* by John A. Shuman III, available from Collector Books.

Note: Prices are rising. Each day more collectors enter. For the first time British auction houses are picturing and promoting Gaudy Welsh. Demand for Columbine, Grape, Tulip, Oyster, and Wagon Wheel is slow. We should also mention that the Bethedsa pattern is very similar to a Davenport jug pattern. No porcelain Gaudy Welsh was made in Wales.

Aberystwyth, jug, 6" 555.00
Asarina, cup & saucer 150.00
Bali, cup & saucer 150.00
Begonia, creamer 245.00
Brecon, mug, 6" 500.00
Caerleon, cup & saucer 130.00
Camellia, charger, 19" 990.00
Celyn, wash bowl & jug 1,800.00
Cherry Tree, mug, 3½" 495.00
Cheyenne, bowl, gr, 9" 675.00
Clover, plate, 9½" 250.00
Columbine, tea set, 17-pc 845.00
Cosmos, plate, 8" 165.00
Denbigh, mug, 6½" 395.00
Dyfed, mug, 6" 385.00
Floret, cup & saucer 85.00
Garland, plate, 9¾" 255.00
Glamorgan, jug, 5" 350.00
Grape, creamer 190.00
Grape, mug, 8" 275.00
Grape, teapot 480.00
Harmony, mug, gr, 6" 560.00
Herald, plate, 8" 270.00
Hexagon, teapot, Hildich 490.00
Japan, teapot 510.00
Llanarth, jug, 7" 375.00
Newgale, jug, 7¼" 490.00

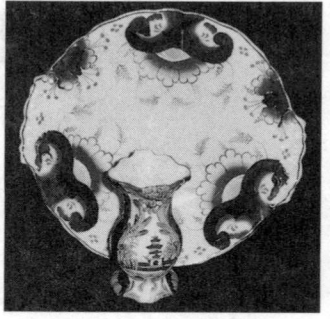

Oriental Pagoda, vase, 4¾", $675.00; Fountain, plate, 10", $365.00. (Photo courtesy Cheryl L. Nelson)

Palm House, jug, 3¾" 230.00
Panelled Daisy, cup & saucer 70.00
Pennoth, cup & saucer 130.00
Rocking Urn, plate, 6" 200.00
Scallop, mug, 2½" 135.00
Wings, mug, 3¼" 210.00

Geisha Girl

Geisha Girl Porcelain was one of several key Japanese china production efforts aimed at the booming export markets of the U.S., Canada, England, and other parts of Europe. The wares feature colorful, kimono-clad Japanese ladies in scenes of everyday Japanese life, surrounded by exquisite flora, fauna, and mountain ranges. Nonetheless, the forms in which the wares were produced reflected the late nineteenth and early twentieth-century Western dining and decorating preferences: tea and coffee services, vases, dresser sets, children's items, planters, etc.

Over a hundred manufacturers were involved in Geisha Girl production. This accounts for the several hundred different patterns, well over a dozen border colors and styles, and several methods of design execution. Geisha Girl Porcelain was produced in wholly hand-painted versions, but most were hand painted over stencilled outlines. Be wary of Geisha ware executed with decals. Very few decaled examples came out of Japan. Rather, most were Czechoslovakian attempts to hone in on the market. Czech pieces have stamped marks in broad, pseudo-Oriental characters. Items with portraits of Oriental ladies in the bottom of tea or sake cups are *not* Geisha Girl Porcelain, unless the outside surface of the wares are decorated as described above. These lovely faces, formed by varying the thickness of the porcelain body, are called lithophanes and are collectible in their own right.

The height of Geisha Girl production was between 1910 and the mid-1930s. Some post-World War II production has been found marked Occupied Japan.

The ware continued in minimal production during the 1960s, but the point of origin of the later pieces was Hong Kong. These productions are discerned by the pure whiteness of the porcelain; even, unemotional borders; lack of background washes and gold enameling; and overall sparseness of detail. A new wave of Nippon-marked reproduction Geisha emerged in 1996. If the Geisha Girl productions of the 1960s – 80s were overly plain, the mid-1990s repros are overly ornate. Original Geisha Girl porcelain was enhanced by brush strokes of color over a stenciled design; it was never the 'color perfectly within the lines' type of decoration found on current reproductions. Original Geisha Girl porcelain was decorated with color washes; the reproductions are in heavy enamels. The backdrop decoration of the current reproductions feature solid, thick colors, and the patterns feature too much color; period Geisha ware had a high ratio of white space to color. The new pieces also have bright shiny gold in proportions greater than most period Geisha ware. The Nippon marks on the reproductions are wrong. Some of the Geisha ware created during the Nippon era bore the small precise decaled green M-in-Wreath mark, a Noritake registered trademark. The reproduction items feature an irregular facsimile of this mark. Stamped onto the reproductions is an unrealistically large M-in-Wreath mark in shades of green ranging from an almost neon to pine green with a wreath that looks like it has seen better days, as it does not have the perfect roundness of the original mark. Reproductions of mid-sized trays, chunky hatpin holders, an ornate vase, a covered bottle, and a powder jar are among the current reproductions popping up at flea and antique markets.

Many of our descriptions contain references to border colors and treatments. This information is given immediately preceding the mark and/or size. Our advisor for this category is Elyce Litts; she is listed in the Directory under New Jersey.

Ashtray, Temple A, spade-shaped, mc 25.00
Basket, Parasol C: Parasol, red-orange border & hdl....................25.00
Biscuit jar, Baskets of Mums, melon ribbed, 3-ftd, red w/gold 49.00
Bonbon dish, Bamboo Trellis, red w/gold 15.00
Bowl, Boy's Processional, red-orange w/yel, 9½" 40.00
Bowl, carp, red w/gold, 6" 18.00
Bowl, Flower Gathering A, pine gr, 9" 25.00
Box, Mother & Daughter, gold rim, 2x5x4" 32.00
Butter pat, Fan A, red border, 4¼" 8.00
Cake platter, Fan A, floriate edge w/hole in ea petal, red-orange..45.00
Celery dish, Foreign Garden, bl border 45.00
Cookie jar, Checkerboard, cobalt, 3-ftd 85.00
Cracker jar, Spider puppet, ftd & lobed, cobalt w/gold border 65.00
Creamer, Boy w/Scythe, cobalt w/gold 15.00
Cup & saucer, tea; Bellflower, wavy red-orange border, gold below ..20.00
Cup & saucer, tea; Cloud B, red-orange w/yel 14.00
Dresser set, Porch, modern, red, 3-pc 25.00
Egg cup, dbl; Child Reaching for Butterfly, red w/gold 15.00
Ewer, Garden Bench H, red w/gold lacing 35.00
Gravy boat w/drip tray, Temple A, mc 72.00
Hatpin holder, Long-Stemmed Peony, ribbed hourglass form, cobalt/gold ...45.00
Humidor, Battledore, scalloped bl w/gold line, lg figures 100.00
Jug, Battledore, ribbed/fluted, yel-gr w/gold, 4¼" 25.00
Jug, Cherry Blossom, red-orange edge, 6½" 35.00
Manicure Box, Pointing F, swirl-ribbed body, apple gr w/gold 25.00
Match holder, hanging; Garden Bench A, bl-gr 30.00
Mint dish, Gardening, 4-lobed, cobalt w/gold 13.00
Mug, lemonade; Geisha in Sampan B, cobalt w/gold 10.00

Store premium mustard jar, Parasol variant, red border and gold buds, Hoover Furniture Co., Harrisburg, PA, $38.00. (Photo courtesy Elyce Litts)

Mustard pot, Lady in Rickshaw B, bl w/gold, w/lid & attached plate ..28.00
Nappy, Temple A, hand-fluted edge, single hdl, sea-gr border.......35.00
Nut dish, master; Basket, dk apple gr, 9-lobed, 3-ftd, 6" 25.00
Nut dish, master; Feather Fan, ftd, Nippon 48.00
Pitcher, Processional, red w/mc geometrics, gold hdl & base border..25.00
Plate, Bamboo Trellis, bl-gr w/gold buds, simple decor, 6½" 8.00
Plate, Basket, swirl fluted, scalloped edge, dk apple gr, 8½" 30.00
Plate, Butterfly Dancers, red w/gold, 7" 35.00
Plate, Courtesan Processional, bl, fluted, scalloped rim, 6½" 15.00
Plate, Geisha in Sampan A, brn w/gold, 9½" 25.00
Plate, Oni Dance A, swirl-fluted/scalloped, red w/gold lacing, 7¼" ..20.00
Puff box, Flower Gathering, ribbed, blk design, red-orange edge...18.00
Relish dish, Paper Carp, fluted edge, cut-out hdls, red...................15.00
Ring tree, Garden Bench Q, gold hand on decorated base............55.00
Sauce dish, Meeting B, dk apple gr...12.00
Talcum shaker, Parasol L: Miscellaneous, red-orange w/yel lacing..35.00
Tea set, River's Edge, gr 3-banded border w/gold, pot+cr/sug+6 c/s..125.00
Teapot, Kite A, brn w/gold...28.00
Toothpick holder, Circle Dance, cylindrical, red 15.00
Vase, bud; Watching the Carp, red-orange, 4½" 18.00

Georgia Art Pottery

In Cartersville, Georgia, in August 1935, W.J. Gordy first fired pottery turned from regional clays. By 1936 he was marking his wares 'Georgia Art Pottery' (GP) or 'Georgia Art Pottery' (GAP) and continued to do so until 1950 when he used a 'Hand Made by WJ Gordy' stamp (HM). Since 1970 he has signed his pottery. Known throughout the world for his fine glazes, he won the Georgia Governor's Award in 1983. Examples of his wares are on display in the Smithsonian. His father W.T.B. and brother D.X. are also well-known potters.

Basket, feldspathic sky bl, fluted rim, 2 hdls at sides, 3¼x7⅛".......90.00
Basket, red-like copper, fluted rim, side hdls, ca 1950, 3¼x7⅛".120.00
Jug, gunmetal Albany slip (uncommon) at top, mk WJG, 1935-36, 8¼"..250.00
Mug, Albany slip, bbl shape, ca 1937-39, 4½"...............................45.00
Pansy pot, sky bl gloss, sgn WJG, ca 1935-36, 4¾".........................60.00
Pitcher, feldspathic bright bl gloss, low, wide, 1940-60, 3¾".........80.00
Pitcher, Rebekah, feldspathic sky bl matt, ovoid, ca 1935-36, 9¼".......115.00
Pitcher, refrigerator; feldspathic sky bl, ovoid, rounded top hdl, 7".......200.00
Vase, chocolate & milk-color swirled clays, egg shape, glazed int, 6"....125.00
Vase, feldspathic sky bl, folded top, 1935-36, 8" 150.00

German Porcelain

Unless otherwise noted, the porcelain listed in this section is marked simply 'Germany.' Products of other German manufactures are listed in specific categories. See also Bisque; Pink Paw Bears; Pink Pigs; Elfinware.

Chocolate set, HP/decaled roses w/wht, gr lid, 9½", +4 cups......185.00
Cracker jar, floral panels, 1890s, 7x6" 255.00
Figurine, ballerina, arms/legs extended, bk bent, 4¾x9¼" 250.00
Figurine, child in monk's robe w/flowers, ca 1940, 8⅜", NM......210.00
Figurine, Deco-style nude w/brn braided hair, 3½", pr 615.00
Figurine, Egyptian Dancer, Boess design, ca 1917, 8¾" 295.00
Figurine, golfer, comic, 1920s, #1552 Germany, 8⅛"...................250.00
Figurine, lady sitting on cushion, ruffled dress, wht, 10½" 285.00
Figurine, youth & maiden in chairs, mc w/gold, mk, late, 8", pr.110.00
Mirror, appl cherubs & roses, ca 1870, 6½x8", EX 300.00
Plaque, Education of Virgin, after Batoni, late 1800s, 4x5"+fr....400.00

Gladding McBean and Company

This company was established in 1875 in Lincoln, California. They first produced only clay drainage pipes, but in 1883 architectural terra cotta was introduced, which has been used extensively in the United States as well as abroad. Sometime later a line of garden pottery was added. They soon became the leading producers of tile in the country. In 1923 they purchased the Tropico Pottery in Glendale, California, where in addition to tile they also produced huge garden vases. Their line was expanded in 1934 to included artware and dinnerware.

At least fifteen lines of art pottery were developed between 1934 and 1942. For a short time they stamped their wares with the Tropico Pottery mark; but the majority was signed 'GMcB' in an oval. Later the mark was changed to 'Franciscan' with several variations. After 1937 'Catalina Pottery' was used on some lines. (All items marked 'Catalina Pottery' were made in Glendale.) For further information we recommend *The Collector's Encyclopedia of California Pottery, Second Edition*, by Jack Chipman (Collector Books). See also Franciscan Ware.

Bowl, Cocinero, turq, #10, NM 140.00
Bowl, mottled Oxblood, blk int, 3¾x11¼"....................................240.00
Bowl, serving; gr satin, 1937-38, 11"...57.50
Bowl, serving; peach w/turq int, long oval, 3½" H 45.00
Bowl, soup; El Patio, gr...15.00
Bowl, turq w/emb floral swags, 6x7"..115.00
Bowl, wht gloss w/turq int, 4x9", NM...55.00
Bowl, wht satin matt, early CMCB mk, 4½x11".............................45.00
Candle holders, soft gr semimatt, 2¾x4", pr 50.00
Carafe, Rancho, cobalt w/wood hdl, no lid 35.00
Creamer, pk (scarce color), 1930s..45.00
Cup & saucer, demitasse; Oxblood, 1939-49, 2¼x2½", 4⅜".........50.00
Mug, blk, bbl shape, 4", 6 for 235.00
Pedestal, Neoclassical style w/palmettes, turq-gr, sq base, 35½"..575.00
Pedestal, turq, 35½x16x16 (at base), EX 225.00
Pitcher, dbl-dipped, WJ Gordy, 1960s-70s, 8¼"............................240.00
Plate, chop; Rancho, orange, 1937-41, 16" 32.00
Plate, dinner; Birchbark, 4 for 25.00
Ramekin, Coffee Brn, 2x4½" 12.00
Tea set, yel, 3-pc...85.00
Tile, Hermosa Art Ware, floral, 5-color, 6".....................................30.00
Tile, Hermosa Art Ware, Hawaiian lady leans on palm, 4¼"........60.00
Vase, bl semimatte, fluted, C-256, 5¼x5½"......................................32.00
Vase, Candy Apple Red, bulbous w/trumpet neck, 8½" 325.00
Vase, cobalt gloss, 1940s-50s, 4½x5"...65.00
Vase, Oxblood, bulbous, Catalina Pottery, 4¾x4" 160.00
Vase, Oxblood, bulbous, oval decal, 4"..225.00
Vase, Rebecca Jug, cobalt, WJG, 7⅜" (at top of hdl)...................190.00
Vase, Saguaro Art Ware, Catalina Pottery, 1938, 8½"...................67.50
Vase, swirl, Handmade by WJ Gordy, 1970s, 3" 60.00
Vase, Tropico Art Ware, wht, 6" 70.00

Glass Animals and Figurines

These beautiful glass sculptures have been produced by many major companies in America, in fact, some are still being made today. Heisey, Fostoria, Duncan and Miller, Imperial, Paden City, Tiffin, and Cambridge made the vast majority, but there were many others involved on a lesser scale. Some, but not all, marked their animals.

As many of the glass companies went out of business, molds were often sold to others still active who used them to reproduce their own line of animals. While some are easy to recognize, others can be very confusing. For example, Summit Art Glass now owns Cambridge's 6½", 8½", and 10" swan molds. We recommend *Glass Animals of the Depression Era* by Lee Garmon and Dick Spencer, if you're thinking of starting a collection or wanting to identify and evaluate the glass animals you already have. Both are our advisors for this category and are listed in the Directory under Illinois.

Note: Heisey Collectors of America stopped using the plug horse and have adopted the rabbit paperweight as the new yearly mascot.

Cambridge

Bashful Charlotte, flower frog, Dianthus, 6½" 175.00
Bashful Charlotte, flower frog, Moonlight Blue, 11½" 575.00
Bird, crystal satin, 2¾" L..35.00
Bird on stump, flower frog, gr, 5¼"...375.00
Blue jay, flower holder, crystal...160.00
Buddha, amber, 5½"..250.00
Draped Lady, flower frog, crystal frost, 13¼"...............................175.00
Draped Lady, flower frog, Dianthus, 8½".......................................175.00

Draped Lady, flower frog, Gold Krystol, 8½"......................250.00
Draped Lady, flower frog, gr frost, 8½"...........................150.00
Draped Lady, flower frog, lt emerald, 8½"........................175.00
Draped Lady, flower frog, Moonlight Blue, 13"..................860.00
Frog, crystal satin...35.00
Heron, crystal, lg, 12"..135.00
Mandolin Lady, flower frog, crystal...............................250.00
Mandolin Lady, flower frog, lt emerald...........................400.00
Melon Boy, flower frog, Dianthus....................................450.00
Rose Lady, flower frog, amber, 8½"................................225.00
Rose Lady, flower frog, Dianthus, 8½"...........................250.00
Rose Lady, flower frog, gr, 8½".......................................200.00
Scottie, bookends, crystal, hollow, pr..............................175.00
Sea gull, flower block, crystal...60.00
Swan, Apple Green, #1 style, 13½"..................................850.00
Swan, Carmen, 6½"..225.00
Swan, Crown Tuscan, 8½"...125.00
Swan, dk gr, #3 style, 8½"...175.00
Swan, ebony, 12½"...300.00
Swan, ebony, 8½"...165.00
Swan, milk glass, #3 style, 8½"...350.00
Swan, milk glass, 8½"...275.00
Swan, yel, 8½"..175.00
Turkey, gr, w/lid..475.00
Two Kids, flower frog, amber, oval base, 9¼"..................350.00
Two Kids, flower frog, amber satin, 9¼"..........................400.00

Duncan and Miller

Donkey, cart & peon, crystal, 3-pc set.............................525.00
Duck, ashtray, red, 7"...100.00
Duck, cigarette box, red, 6"...170.00
Heron, crystal..150.00
Heron, crystal satin, 7"..120.00
Mallard duck, cigarette box, crystal, #30, w/lid, 3½x4½"........60.00
Swan, candle holder, red, 7", ea..80.00
Swan, crystal, solid, 5"...35.00
Swan, wheat cutting, 11"..200.00
Swordfish, bl opal, rare...500.00
Sylvan swan, bl or pk, 5½"...125.00
Sylvan swan, yel opal, 7½"..140.00
Tropical fish, ashtray, pk opal, 3½"....................................50.00

Fenton

Airedale, Rosalene, 1992 issue for Heisey..........................95.00
Alley cat, Teal Marigold, 11"..85.00
Bunny, lt bl..16.00
Butterfly, candle holder, ruby carnival, 1989 souvenir, 7½", ea.....95.00
Cardinal head, ruby, 6½"..150.00

Elephant, flower bowl, black, #1618, 1928, $450.00. (Photo courtesy Margaret and Kenn Whitmyer)

Elephant, periwinkle, whiskey bottle, 8"..........................450.00
Filly, Rosalene, head front, 1992 issue for Heisey..............95.00

Fish, bookend, Rosalene, ea..65.00
Fish, red w/amberina tail & fins, 2½"..................................55.00
Gazelle, Rosalene...95.00
Happiness Bird, Rosalene..40.00
Hen, Rosalene, 1992 issue for Heisey.................................95.00
Plug Horse, HCA, Rosalene..50.00
Rabbit, paperweight, Rosalene, 1992 issue for Heisey........55.00

Fostoria

Buddha, bookends, blk, pr..525.00
Cat, lt bl, 3¾"...35.00
Chinese Lute, ebony w/gold, 12½"...................................300.00
Colt, Silver Mist, standing...45.00
Deer, milk glass, sitting or standing, ea.............................55.00
Duck, mama, crystal...30.00
Duckling, crystal, head down (+).......................................20.00
Elephant, bookend, ebony, 6½", ea..................................150.00
Horse, bookend, crystal, 7¾", ea..45.00
Lady bug, bl, lemon or olive gr, 1¼", ea.............................35.00
Madonna, Silver Mist, orig issue, 10" (+)...........................50.00
Mermaid, crystal, 11½"..125.00
Owl, bl, lemon or olive gr, 2¾"...35.00
Penguin, crystal, sq base, 4⅝"..75.00
Polar bear, topaz, 4⅝"..125.00
Sea horse, bookend, crystal, 8", ea...................................125.00
Squirrel, amber, running or sitting, ea...............................45.00
Squirrel, amber, sitting..45.00
Stork, bl, lemon or olive gr, 2", ea.....................................35.00

Heisey

Airedale, crystal..650.00
Bull, crystal, sgn, 4x7½"..1,800.00
Chick, crystal, head down or up, ea....................................95.00
Clydesdale, crystal, 7½x7"..475.00
Colt, amber, kicking..650.00
Colt, cobalt, kicking..1,500.00
Colt, crystal, kicking...200.00
Colt, crystal, rearing...200.00
Cygnet, baby swan, crystal, 2½"..225.00
Doe head, bookend, crystal, 6¼", ea.................................850.00
Dolphin, candlesticks, crystal, #110, pr...........................400.00
Dolphin, candlesticks, Moongleam, #110, pr....................800.00
Donkey, crystal..295.00
Duck, ashtray, crystal..100.00
Duck, flower block, crystal..140.00
Duck, flower block, Hawthorne..295.00
Elephant, amber, sm..1,650.00
Elephant, crystal, sm...275.00
Filly, crystal, head forward..1,000.00
Fish, bookend, crystal, ea...160.00
Fish, bowl, crystal, 9½"...450.00
Fish, candlestick, crystal, 5", ea.......................................200.00
Fish, match holder, crystal, 3x2¾"....................................180.00
Flying Mare, crystal...3,500.00
Frog, cheese plate, Marigold...285.00
Giraffe, crystal, head bk..275.00
Giraffe, crystal, head to side...275.00
Goose, crystal, wings half..100.00
Goose, crystal, wings up..130.00
Horse head, bookend, crystal, ea......................................175.00
Horse head, cigarette box, crystal, #1489, 4½x4"...............60.00
Irish setter, ashtray, crystal..30.00

Kingfisher, flower block, Flamingo............................225.00
Kingfisher, Moongleam, flower block 250.00
Mallard, crystal, wings half......................................200.00
Piglet, crystal, sitting...100.00
Plug horse, amber 600.00
Plug horse, cobalt...1,200.00
Rabbit, paperweight, crystal, 2¾x3¾"......................225.00
Ram head, stopper, crystal, 3½".............................160.00
Ringneck pheasant, crystal, 11¾"............................175.00
Rooster, crystal, 5½x5"..350.00
Rooster, Fighting; crystal frost, 7½x5½"...................200.00
Rooster head, cocktail, crystal..................................60.00
Rooster head, stopper, crystal, 4½"...........................45.00
Scotty, crystal..170.00
Show horse, crystal...1,250.00
Sow, crystal, 3x4½"..1,000.00
Sparrow, crystal..120.00
Swan, crystal...1,450.00
Swan, master nut, crystal, #1503..............................45.00
Swan, pitcher, crystal..1,400.00
Tropical fish, crystal, 12".....................................2,200.00
Wood duck, crystal, floating...................................175.00
Wood duck, crystal, mother....................................800.00
Wood duck, crystal, standing...................................200.00

Imperial

Angelfish, bookend, crystal or frosted, ea...................120.00
Bulldog-type pup, milk glass, 3½"..............................65.00
Chick, milk glass, head down....................................10.00
Chick, milk glass, head up..10.00
Clydesdale, Verde Green...170.00
Colt, amber, balking...140.00
Colt, amber, standing...125.00
Colt, Horizon Blue, kicking 35.00
Cygnet, blk, 2½"...55.00
Cygnet, Horizon Blue 25.00
Dog, Airedale, caramel slag.....................................115.00
Dog, Airedale, Ultra Blue..75.00
Donkey, caramel slag...55.00
Donkey, Meadow Green carnival................................65.00
Elephant, caramel slag, med......................................65.00
Elephant, Meadow Green carnival, #674, med 75.00
Elephant, Nut Brown, sm..120.00
Fish, bookend, ruby, ea...340.00
Fish, match holder, Sunshine Yellow satin, 3"..............20.00
Flying mare, amber, NI mk, extremely rare...............1,500.00
Gazelle, blk, 11" 300.00
Giraffe, amber, ALIG mk, extremely rare....................350.00
Mallard, caramel slag, wings down............................200.00
Mallard, caramel slag, wings half 35.00
Mallard, Horizon Blue, wings down, HCA, 4½"..............35.00
Marmote Sentinel (woodchuck), caramel slag, 4½"........60.00
Owl, Jade Green slag, shiny 85.00
Owl, jar, caramel slag, 16½".......................................75.00
Owl, milk glass..48.00
Piglet, amber, sitting...40.00
Piglet, amber, standing 40.00
Plug horse, pk, HCA, 1978 ....40.00
Ring-neck pheasant, amber, extremely rare.................320.00
Rooster, pk, fighting...175.00
Scolding bird, Cathay Crystal 175.00
Swan, purple slag, shiny 95.00
Terrier, Parlour Pup, Sunshine Yellow carnival 50.00

Tiger, paperweight, Jade Green slag, 8" L 95.00
Wood duck, caramel slag..65.00
Wood duck, Ultra Blue satin......................................55.00
Wood duckling, floating, Sunshine Yellow satin.............20.00
Wood duckling, standing, Sunshine Yellow satin............20.00

L.E. Smith

Cock, Fighting; bl, 9" 55.00
Elephant, crystal, 1¾"...20.00
Goose Girl, crystal, orig, 6" 25.00
Goose Girl, gr or flame, 6", ea...................................40.00
Horse, bookend, amber, rearing, ea............................38.00
Horse, bookend, ruby, rearing, ea..............................55.00
Horse, crystal, bookend, rearing, ea...........................35.00
King Fish, aquarium, gr, 7¼x15"...............................275.00
Rooster, butterscotch slag, ltd ed, #208 ....85.00

Scottie dog, frosted, 2½x6x5", $35.00. (Photo courtesy Candace Sten Davis and Patricia J. Baugh)

Scottie, pipe rest, fired-on blk, 5½" L........................20.00
Swan, milk glass w/decor, 8½" 45.00
Thrush, bl frost 20.00

New Martinsville

Bear, mama, crystal, 4x6".......................................225.00
Bear, papa, crystal frost..225.00
Bunny, crystal, head up, scarce, 1" H..........................60.00
Chick, orange-red...65.00
Gazelle, crystal w/frosted base, leaping, 8¼" 65.00
German shepherd, lamp base, pk..............................125.00
Hen, crystal, 5"..75.00
Horse, crystal, head up, 8".......................................95.00
Nautilus shell, bookend, crystal frost, 6", ea.................35.00
Pelican, crystal..95.00
Pig, mama, crystal...325.00
Porpoise on wave, orig...750.00
Rooster w/crooked tail, crystal, 7½" 85.00
Seal, candle holders, crystal, pr................................125.00
Seal, candlesticks, crystal, lg, pr...............................150.00
Seal w/ball, bookends, crystal, 7", pr.........................150.00
Starfish, bookends, crystal, pr..................................200.00
Swan, candle holders, ruby, pr...................................70.00
Swan, sweetheart candy dish, red, 5"..........................35.00
Tiger, crystal frost, head down, 7¼"...........................200.00
Wolfhound, crystal, 7"..95.00

Paden City

Bunny, cotton-ball dispenser, crystal frost, ears bk........110.00
Bunny, cotton-ball dispenser, milk glass, ears bk..........125.00
Bunny, cotton-ball dispenser, pk frost, ears up 200.00
Eagle, bookends, crystal, pr.....................................300.00

Pheasant, Chinese; bl 180.00
Pheasant, Chinese; crystal, 13¾" 100.00
Pheasant, crystal, head bk, 12" 110.00
Pheasant, lt bl, head bk, 12" 195.00
Polar bear on ice, crystal, 4½" 65.00
Pony, crystal, 12" 100.00
Rooster, Barnyard; bl, 8¾" 200.00
Rooster, Barnyard; crystal, 8¾" 85.00
Rooster, Chanticleer; bl, 9½" 200.00
Rooster, Elegant; lt bl, 11" 225.00
Squirrel on curved log, crystal, 5½" 65.00

Tiffin

Cat, blk satin, raised bumps, #9445, 6¼" 140.00
Cat, Sassy Suzie, milk glass 300.00
Fawn, flower floater, Copen Blue..........................500.00
Frog, candle holders, blk satin, pr 225.00
Pheasants, Copen Blue, paperweight bases, male & female pr 650.00

Viking

Angelfish, amber, 7x7" 125.00
Angelfish, blk, 6½" 150.00
Bird, candy dish, med gr, w/lid, 12" 75.00
Bird, med dk bl, 9½" 40.00
Bird, moss gr, tail up, 12" 40.00
Bird, orange, #1311, 10" 35.00
Bird, ruby, #1310, 12" 85.00
Dog, orange 45.00
Duck, crystal, fighting, head up or down, Viking's Epic Line, ea ...45.00
Duck, crystal, standing, Viking's Epic Line, 9" 35.00
Duck, dk teal, Viking's Epic Line, 9" 45.00
Duck, orange, rnd, ftd, 5" 35.00
Duck, vaseline, 5" 35.00
Egret, orange, 12" 45.00
Hound dog, crystal, 8" 45.00
Owl, amber, Viking's Epic Line 45.00
Owl, paperweight, amber.......................................50.00
Rabbit, amber, 6½" 45.00
Rooster, avocado, Viking's Epic Line 55.00

Rooster, orange, Viking's Epic Line, 1960s, 9½", from $60.00 to $65.00.

Swan, bowl, amber, 6" 45.00
Swan, orange, fluted, 6½x4" 45.00
Swan, Yellow Mist, paper label, 6" 50.00

Westmoreland

Butterfly, Blue Mist, 2½" 25.00
Butterfly, Green Mist, 2½" 25.00

Butterfly, pk, 2½" 25.00
Butterfly, Smoke, 3½" 25.00
Owl, dk bl, shiny eyes, 5½" 65.00
Pig, amberina 85.00
Porky Pig, milk glass, hollow, 3" L 25.00
Pouter pigeon, any color, 2½", ea 25.00
Robin, crystal, 5⅛" 20.00
Robin, red, 5⅛" 27.50
Turtle, ashtray, crystal 15.00
Turtle, cigarette box, crystal 45.00
Turtle, flower block, gr, 7 holes, 4" L 55.00
Wren, Crystal Mist, 2½" 20.00
Wren, lt bl, 2½" 25.00
Wren, red, 2½" 25.00
Wren, smoke, 2½" 25.00

Miscellaneous

American Glass Co, horse, crystal, jumping.............65.00
Co-Operative Flint, elephant, crystal, 13" 375.00
Co-Operative Flint, elephant, pk, 4½x7" 85.00
Haley, horse, crystal, jumping, 9½" L 65.00
Haley, horse, milk glass, jumping 75.00
Haley, Lady Godiva, bookend, crystal, 1940s, ea.......45.00
Haley, thrush, crystal 30.00
Haley, thrush, Robins' Egg Blue 85.00
Indiana, panther, amber, walking...........................300.00
Indiana, panther, bl, walking 400.00
LG Wright, trout, crystal.......................................150.00
LG Wright, turtle, amber 125.00
New Martinsville by Mirror Images, baby bear, ruby....95.00
New Martinsville by Mirror Images, mama bear, ruby....150.00
New Martinsville by Mirror Images, police dog, ruby....150.00
New Martinsville by Mirror Images, wolfhound, ruby carnival ...150.00

Glass Knives

Glass knives were manufactured from about 1920 to 1950, with distribution at its greatest in the late 1930s and early 1940s. Colors generally followed Depression glass dinnerware: crystal, light blue, light green, pink (originally called rose), and more rarely amber, forest green, and white (opal). Many glass knives were hand painted in fruit or flower designs. Knife blades were ground to a sharp edge. Today knives are usually found with blades nicked through years of use or bumping in silverware drawers or reground, which is acceptable to collectors as long as the original knife shape is maintained.

Many glass knives were engraved for gift-giving, personalized with the recipient's name and, on occasion, with a greeting. Originally presented in boxes, most glass knives were accompanied by a paper insert extolling the virtues of the knife and describing its care.

Boxes printed with World's Fair logos are fun to find, though not rare. Butter knives, which are smaller than other glass knives, typically were made in Czechoslovakia and sometimes match the handle patterns of glass salad sets. Knife lengths often vary slightly because the knives were snapped off the molded glass and the end ground during manufacture.

Several styles of knives (i.e. Vitex, Dur-X, Cryst-O-Lite) were manufactured by the thousands and are therefore found more often. Prices have become volatile due to the popularity of online, Internet auctions and the competition that results.

Our advisor for this category is Michele Rosewitz; she is listed in the Directory under California. Values reflect knives with minor blade roughness or resharpening.

Aer-Flo, crystal, 7½"...40.00
Aer-Flo, pk, 7½"..90.00
Block, crystal, 8¼"...25.00
Candlewick, crystal, 8½" 400.00
Dagger, crystal, 9¼"...150.00
Dur-X (3-leaf), pk, 8½-9"..40.00
Dur-X (5-leaf), gr, 8½"..45.00
Pinwheel, crystal...12.00
Plain hdl, crystal, 8½"..15.00
Plain hdl, gr, 8½"...35.00
Steelite, crystal, 8½"..35.00
Steelite, gr, 8½"...75.00
Stonex, dk amber, 8¼"...250.00
Stonex, gr, 8½"...80.00
Stonex, opal, 8½"..350.00
3 Star, bl, 8½"...35.00
3 Star, bl, 9¼"...35.00

Glass Shoes

Little shoes made of glass can be found in hundreds of styles, shapes, and colors. They've been made since the early 1800s by nearly every glasshouse, large and small, in America. To learn more about them, we recommend *Shoes of Glass II* (newly updated) by our advisor Libby Yalom, who is listed in the Directory under Maryland. Numbers in the listings refer to her book. Another reference is *Collectible Shoes of Glass, Second Edition,* by Earlene Wheatley, published by Collector Books. See also Boyd; Degenhart.

#10A, slipper, Daisy & Button, frosted bl, 5" L................50.00
#89A, slipper, frosted w/pnt flower decor, Gillinder, 5½" L...........70.00
#147A, boot, high-button w/horizontal ribs, frosted amber, 4¼" ..60.00
#169A, skate (high-top), waffle pattern, scalloped edge, teal, 4" ..40.00
#207A, bootee, knitted look, clear apple gr, King Glass Co, 3⅝" L..60.00
#240A, bootee, Daisy & Button, clear, Duncan, 4¼" L.................90.00
#264B, slipper, clear w/gold metal trim, 5" L...............120.00
#310A, pump, frosted w/clear decor on vamp, 6¼" L................150.00
#319A, clog, sm knob on bk, clear gr, 8¼" L 90.00
#324B, boot, cased, clear decor over opaque yel, 4"..........110.00
#388, slipper, sunburst design, clear, Sowerby, 7½" L 130.00
#395, boot match holder, flat-sided, wall mt, dk gr........................45.00

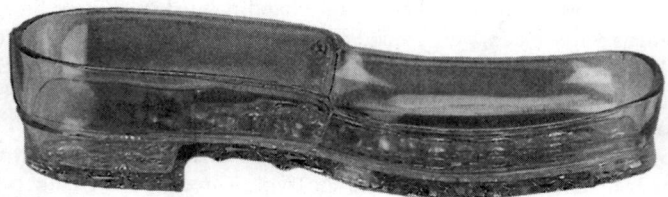

#412, Daisy and Button, Apple Green, Hobbs, Brockunier & Co., 1880s, 2½x11¾x4½", $165.00. (Photo courtesy Libby Yalom)

#569A, boot (man's riding type), ruby w/gold & enamel decor, 6⅞" ...75.00
#745, high-heel, flared open front, teal, Czech Republic, 8½" L ...300.00
#766, clog style, iridized, diamond, mold-blown, England, 7" L..175.00
#768, slipper, flat heel w/flat bow, amber, England, 9" L 175.00
#817, tennis shoe, clear, 5⅝" L..45.00

Glidden

Genius designer Glidden Parker established Glidden Pottery in

---

1940 in Alfred, New York, having been schooled at the unrivaled New York State College of Ceramics at Alfred University. Glidden pottery is characterized by a fine stoneware body, innovative forms, outstanding hand-milled glazes, and hand decoration which make the pieces individual works of art. Production consisted of casual dinnerware, artware, and accessories that were distributed internationally.

In 1949 Glidden Pottery became the second ceramic plant in the country to utilize the revolutionary Ram pressing machine. This allowed for increased production and for the most part eliminated the previously used slip-casting method. However, Glidden stoneware continued to reflect the same superb quality of craftsmanship until the factory closed in 1957. Although the majority of form and decorative patterns were Mr. Parker's personal designs, Fong Chow and Sergio Dello Strologo also designed award-winning lines.

Glidden will be found marked on the unglazed underside with a signature that is hand incised, mold impressed, or ink stamped. Interest in this unique stoneware is growing as collectors discover that it embodies the very finest of Mid-Century High Style. Our advisor is David Pierce; he is listed in the Directory under Ohio.

Ashtray, Fish (Fred Press), #275.............................17.00
Ashtray, Green Mesa, #274-U..................................30.00
Ashtray, Leaves (Fred Press), #274 ....22.00
Ashtray, Loop Artware, #904-U.................................45.00
Ashtray, Safex, dbl, sq...25.00
Bowl, cobalt, #23..30.00
Bowl, Counterpane, #622..25.00
Bowl, Early Pink, oval, #38.....................................37.50
Bowl, Plaid, #27...27.00
Bowl, Turquoise Matrix, #21....................................18.00
Bowl, Turquoise Matrix, #26....................................20.00
Bowl, Viridian, lug soup, #467.................................15.00
Bowl, Viridian, oval, #417......................................25.00
Candle bench, Afrikans...65.00
Canister, Garden, w/lid & bail, #601........................75.00
Casserole, Pear, w/lid, #165....................................40.00
Casserole, Ric Rac, yel, #167...................................25.00
Casserole, Turquoise Matrix, #162............................20.00
Casserole, Viridian, #165..35.00
Casserole, Will O' the Wisp, #167............................35.00
Coaster, Mexican Cock, #19......................................8.00
Creamer & sugar bowl, Feather, w/lid, #144/#143 ....50.00
Creamer & sugar bowl, Pear, w/lid, #144/#143.............60.00
Creamer & sugar bowl, Turquoise Matrix, w/lid, #1430/#1440 ....40.00
Creamer & sugar bowl, Yellowstone, w/lid, #1430/#1440 ....45.00
Cup & saucer, Boston Spice, #441A/#442.....................25.00
Cup & saucer, Feather, #441A/#442............................18.00
Cup & saucer, Turquoise Matrix, #141/#142 ....20.00
Pitcher, Turquoise Matrix, #617................................45.00
Planter, Charcoal & Rice, bird form.........................160.00
Planter, Sage & Sand, #122......................................15.00
Plate, Marine Fantasia, Lucent Green, #431 ....65.00
Plate, Mexican Cock, #35...18.00
Plate, Plaid, salad, #65..28.00
Plate, Turn of the Century, #35................................48.00
Teapot, Flourish, #140..65.00
Teapot, Yellowstone, #240.......................................55.00
Vase, cobalt, ball from, #49.....................................60.00
Vase, Early Pink, pillow from, #128...........................40.00

Goebel

F.W. Goebel founded the F&W Goebel Company in 1871, located

in Rodental, West Germany. They produced thousands of different decorative and useful items over the years, the most famous of which are the Hummel figurines first produced in 1935 based on the artwork of a Franciscan nun, Sister Maria Innocentia Hummel.

The Goebel trademarks have long been a source of confusion because *all* Goebel products, including Hummels, of any particular time period bear the same trademark, thus leading many to believe all Goebels are Hummels. Always look for the Hummel signature on actual Hummel figurines (these are listed in a separate section).

There are many, many other series — some of which are based on artwork of particular artists such as Disney, Charlot Byj, Janet Robson, Harry Holt, Norman Rockwell, M. Spotl, Lore, Huldah, and Schaubach. Miscellaneous useful items include ashtrays, bookends, salt and pepper shakers, banks, pitchers, inkwells, perfume bottles, etc. Figurines include birds, animals, Art Deco pieces, etc. The Friar Tuck monks and the Co-Boy elves are especially popular.

The date of manufacture of a particular piece is determined by the trademark. The incised date found underneath the base on many items is the *mold copyright* date. Actual date of manufacture may vary as much as twenty years or more from the copyright date.

Most Common Goebel Trademarks and Approximate Dates Used

1.) Crown mark (may be incised or stamped, or both): 1923 – 1950
2.) Full bee (complete bumble bee inside the letter 'V'): 1950 – 1957
3.) Stylized bee (dot with wings inside the letter 'V'): 1957 – 1964
4.) 3-Line (stylized bee with three lines of copyright info to the right of the trademark): 1964 – 1972
5.) Goebel bee (word Goebel with stylized bee mark over the last letter 'e'): 1972 – 1979
6.) Goebel (word Goebel only): 1979 – present

Our advisors for this category are Gale and Wayne Bailey; they are listed in the Directory under Georgia.

Cardinal Tuck (Red Monk)

Ashtray, flat, RF142	140.00
Bank	500.00
Calendar holder	325.00
Cigarette holder, RX110, TMK-3, 3"	225.00
Cookie jar, K29, TMK-3, from $1,750 to	2,000.00
Creamer, 4"	150.00
Mug, T741, 5¼x5"	260.00
Pipe stubber	295.00
Shakers, pr, w/Bibles	150.00
Sugar bowl, Z37, TMK-3, 4"	155.00

Charlot BYJ Redheads and Blonds

Barbeque, BYJ76, 1975, 4¼x6½"	145.00
Bird Watcher, BYJ84	105.00
Bless Us All	65.00
Bongo Beat, 5"	110.00
Girl standing on head w/dog, BYJ73, 4"	165.00
Girl w/2 dachshunds following her, BYJ25	120.00
Girl w/3 cats, BYJ3	115.00
Little girl sitting bkwards in chair w/dog underneath, BYJ23	110.00
Little Miss Coy, BYJ4, 4½"	125.00
Little Shopper, BYJ53	110.00
Off Key, BYJ22	105.00
Roving Eye, BYJ2	110.00
Sleepy Head, BYJ11	110.00
Springtime, BYJ10	115.00
Strike, BYJ1	110.00

Sunbonnet Girl, BYJ12	100.00
1-2 Ski-dooo, BYJ77, 2½x6	150.00

Co-Boy Figurines

Brad the Clockmaker, 7½x7"	280.00
Brum the Lawyer, w/owl	65.00
Chris the Shoe Cobbler, 2½x6"	85.00
Chuck the Chimney Sweep, 7¾"	255.00
Gil the Goalie, EX	65.00
Gilda, w/baby doll, 2x3½"	70.00
Jack the Pharmicist, 7½"	60.00
Kitchen Gnome, peeling carrot, 8"	70.00
Kitchen Gnome, Porz, offering mushroom, 7"	55.00
Mark the Gnome, ready for beach, 8"	50.00
Petri the Fisherman, 7½"	55.00
Rosi & Rolf, 3½x4¼"	110.00
Sepp, clock, #17 558 24, 10"	300.00
Ted the Gnome Tennis Player, EX	75.00
UTZ, bank, #17 516 18, 5½x7¼"	200.00
Walter the Jogger, w/tag	50.00

Friar Tuck (Brown Monk)

Bottle stopper, 2½x1½"	55.00
Bowl/ashtray, stylized bee, ZF42/II, 2½x4½" dia	65.00
Cigar stopper, 1¾"	75.00
Clock, 8½x7½"	235.00
Coin bank, SD29, 3x4½"	60.00

Cookie jar, full bee, from $375.00 to $475.00. (Photo courtesy Fred and Joyce Roerig)

Cordial set, KL91, stylized bee	350.00
Decanter, KL93, musical	500.00
Egg timer, 2 monks holds rope w/timer in middle, 3½"	125.00
Flask/cigarette holder, KL90/B, 10½"	165.00
Matchbox holder, RX-111, stylized bee, 3"	100.00
Mug, stylized bee, 5x7"	85.00
Napkin ring, X98, 1¾x1½" dia	85.00
Oil & vinegar cruets, M80, full bee, 5½"	325.00
Shakers, musicians, 5", pr	125.00
Toothpick holder, KL94, 1⅞"	45.00
Wine glass, 5"	60.00

Shakers

Bears, 3", pr	25.00
Beer steins, 3", pr	25.00
Dogs, 2½", pr	25.00
Googley-eyed couple, 3", pr	75.00
Lobsters, reddish-orange w/blk & gray trim, #18A, pr	38.00
Pelicans, yel w/bl on wings, 3⅛", pr	60.00

Peppers, 1 gr w/3 holes, 1 red w/2 holes, pr 31.00
Skunks, 1 sitting up, other on all 4s, pr 30.00

Miscellaneous

Bottle, bellboy w/letter, pnt porc, gold crown top, 4¾"...............250.00
Bottle, scent; lady holding fan, flowered dress, XF 133, 5" 200.00
Bowl, Huldah, lady figural, skirt forms bowl, #722, 5¾"...............170.00
Candelabra, dbl; angel in red holding candle cups, crown mk, 8½"..130.00
Cookie jar, Dog, Goebel W Germany, from $100 to.....................125.00
Cookie jar, Lion, Goebel W Germany, from $70 to......................100.00
Cookie jar, Owl, Goebel W Germany, 8½", from $70 to 125.00
Egg timer, girl & chick hold timer between them, E70, 3"...........185.00
Figurine, bird hanging upside down on branch, CV64, EX 40.00
Figurine, bunnies (2), brn & wht, #34, 6½x3¾" 45.00
Figurine, Dachshunds (2) running, #30090, 9½" L...................135.00
Figurine, German Shepherd, 11¼" 155.00
Figurine, Lady & the Tramp, Disney, 1940s, 4", M 210.00
Figurine, Mickey Mouse Going Hunting, ca 1955, EX 245.00
Figurine, mute swan, flying, #38-152-15, 1977, 10½x8x6".........145.00
Figurine, owl, #38373, 3x2½", EX 25.00
Figurine, praying Madonna, stylized bee, 8⅞", EX 50.00
Figurine, sparrow, head up, tail down, CV74, EX......................35.00
Figurine, Tinkerbell, Disney, #2126, 8½" 130.00
Half-doll, Marie Antoinette, #1208, Tea Cozy series, 10", EXIB ...235.00
Mug, owl, #74607, 4½x5" 30.00
Nativity set, complete w/manger w/star on top, MIB.................205.00
Toothbrush holder, bellhop holding flowers, EX..........................150.00

Goldscheider

The Goldscheider family operated a pottery in Vienna for many generations before seeking refuge in the United States following Hitler's invasion of their country. They settled in Trenton, New Jersey, in the early 1940s where they established a new corporation and began producing objects of art and tableware items. (No mention was made of the company in the Trenton City Directory after 1950, and it is assumed that by this time the influx of foreign imports had taken its toll.) In 1946 Marcel Goldscheider established a pottery in Staffordshire where he manufactured bone china figures, earthenware, etc., marked with a stamp of his signature. Larger artist-signed examples are the most valuable with the Austrian pieces bringing the higher prices.

A wide variety of marks has been found: 1.) Goldscheider USA Fine China; 2.) Original Goldscheider Fine China; 3.) Goldscheider USA; 4.) Goldscheider-Everlast Corp.; 5.) Goldscheider Everlast Corp. in circle; 6.) Goldscheider Inc. in circle; 7.) Goldcrest Ceramics Corp. in circle; 8.) Goldcrest Fine China; 9.) Goldcrest Fine China USA; 10.) A Goldcrest Creation; and 11.) Created by Goldscheider USA.

Our co-advisors are Randy and Debbie Coe (listed in the Directory under Oregon) and Darrell Thomas (listed under Wisconsin).

Bust of woman, porcelain and terra cotta, brown matt, mottled blue, orange, and white, original wooden base, 15½", $2,300.00.

Ashtray, duck, running, teal & brn, 9½"...................................75.00
Bust, boy, terra cotta w/bl curly hair, orange lips, mk, 1920s, 7".950.00
Busts, Javanese heads, Helen Lindloff, #225/#226, 7½", pr.........275.00
Busts, Mongol heads, sgn H Lindloff, #338/#339, 7½", 6½", pr..300.00
Figurine, bird w/nest of eggs, Myott & Sons, 3x5", from $125 to.150.00
Figurine, birds on limb, Myott & Sons, 4" W 145.00
Figurine, cardinal w/butterfly on base, detailed, #889, 7" 165.00
Figurine, Chinese Noble Lady, pk/cream/brn, K Urbach, #1258, 12" W ...175.00
Figurine, First Party, boy & girl, P Porscher, #871/#872, pr.........350.00
Figurine, Indian Dancer, hands up, lt bl & ivory, Kathy Urbach, 10" ..275.00
Figurine, lady w/fan, bl ballgown, 12", 10" base w/orig price tag.375.00
Figurine, Madame Butterfly, acting position, red/gold/teal, Latour........300.00
Figurine, man w/top hat, no face details, Doblinger, pre-1900, 14" ...1,800.00
Figurine, Old London, tan flowered dress, Peggy Porscher, 7".....155.00
Figurine, Pioneer Lady, bl, w/coat, picking flowers, 7", from $200 to ...250.00
Figurine, storks, purple/gray/copper lustre, #273/#274 14", pr 850.00
Figurine, toucans, Myott & Sons, 4", pr 265.00
Figurine, Yamadori, bl & gold w/red arms, open, Latour, mk 200.00
Vase, ship w/sails, bl, unusual, Myott & Sons, 9"......................195.00
Vase, purple w/bl feathers on base, USA mks, 14"....................250.00

Gonder

Lawton Gonder grew up with clay in his hands and fire in his eyes. Gonder's interest in ceramics was greatly influenced by his parents who worked for Weller and a close family friend and noted ceramic authority, John Herold. In his early teens Gonder launched his ceramic career at the Ohio Pottery Company while working for Herold. He later gained valuable experience at American Encaustic Tile Company, Cherry Art Tile, and the Florence Pottery. Gonder was plant manager at the Florence Pottery until fire destroyed the facility in late 1941.

After years of solid production and management experience, Lawton Gonder established the Gonder Ceramic Art Company, formerly the Peters and Reed plant, in South Zanesville, Ohio. Gonder Ceramic Arts produced quality art pottery with beautiful contemporary designs which included human and animal figures and a complete line of Oriental pottery. Accentuating the beautiful shapes were unique and innovative glazes developed by Gonder such as flambe (flame red with streaks of yellow), 24k gold crackle, antique gold, and Chinese crackle. (These glazes bring premium prices.)

All Gonder is marked with the company name and mold number. They include 'Gonder U.S.A' in block letters, 'Gonder' in script, 'Gonder Original' in script, and 'Gonder Ceramic Art' in block letters. Paper labels were also used. Some of the early Gonder molds closely resemble RumRill designs that had been manufactured at the Florence Pottery; and because some RumRill pieces are found with similar (if not identical) shapes, matching mold numbers, and Gonder glazes, it is speculated that some RumRill was produced at the Gonder plant. In 1946 Gonder started another company which he named Elgee (chosen for his initials LG) where he manufactured lamp bases until a fire in 1954 resulted in his shifting lamp production to the main plant. Operations ceased in 1957.

Our values are for items in mint condition, unless noted otherwise. Our advisor for this category is Ron Hoopes; he is listed in the Directory under Ohio.

Figurine, Balinese Water Bearer Man & Woman, maroon, 13½", pr ...110.00
Figurine, deer (2), red flambe, #690, 6½x11x3"...........................45.00
Figurine, panther, brn, #310, 19" 135.00
Figurine, panther, red flambe, #210, 19"...................................150.00
Ginger jar, bl crackle, #530 ....72.50
Jardiniere, gray w/emb floral, pk int, 5½x6½".............................50.00
Lamp base, horses, gray on wht crackle, 12½x8x4½"....................85.00

Pitcher, mottled burgundy gloss, w/lid, 8" 115.00
Pitcher, water; red flambe, #404, 7x5" 55.00
Vase, basketweave emb, mustard & brn, 4-sided, #594, 12" ...135.00
Vase, bird by stump, plum & wht, #541, scarce, NM 80.00
Vase, leaf pattern, maroon w/lt brn trim, #599, 15¾" 95.00
Vase, lt bl w/pk int, #537, 8¼", pr 37.50
Vase, mauve & mustard streaks, ribbon-like design, #594, lg 92.50
Vase, red flambe, #861, 11½" 55.00
Vase, red-brn on wht, ewer form, #410, 7¾" 35.00
Vase, Shell, gold crackle, J-60, 8¼x11" 100.00
Vase, swan, wht w/pk int, #511, 9" 115.00

Goofus Glass

Goofus glass is American-made pressed glass with designs that are either embossed (blown out) or intaglio (cut in). The decorated colors were aerographed or hand applied and not fired on the pieces. The various patterns exemplify the artistry of the turn-of-the-century glass crafters. The primary production dates were ca 1908 to 1918. Goofus was produced by many well-known manufacturers such as Northwood, Indiana, and Dugan.

When no condition is given, values are for items in mint original paint. Our advisor for this category is Steve Gillespie of the *Goofus Glass Gazette*; he is listed in the Directory under Missouri. See also Clubs, Newsletters, and Catalogs.

Bread tray, The Last Supper, 7x11", $65.00.

Bowl, Butterfly, pattern decor, Dugan, 9" 80.00
Bowl, Carnation, La Belle & Roses in the Snow, 5½" sq 12.00
Bowl, Carnation, La Belle & Roses in the Snow, 9" 15.00
Bowl, Cupids, 6½" 45.00
Bowl, Daisy & Plume, opal, ruffled edge, 9" 45.00
Bowl, Greek Key & Sunflower, gr glass, Northwood, 9" 65.00
Bowl, Hearts, 7" 45.00
Bowl, panel w/1" edge w/crossing Smooth Rope, Starburst center, 5" ...25.00
Bowl, panel w/1" rim band w/crossing Smooth Rope, Starburst center, 5" ...25.00
Bowl, pears/cherries/plums, crimped rim, EX orig pnt, 4x7" 37.50
Bowl, Rose, 6-sided (hard to find) 110.00
Bowl, Rose 4-Panel (uncommon), ftd, 8" sq..............................60.00
Bowl, Two Fruits & Olympic Torch, pattern decor, rare, 9" 130.00
Cake plate, Acorn & Leaf, 12" 30.00
Cake plate, Carnation, La Belle & Roses in Snow, 11" 15.00
Cake plate, Carnation, La Belle & Roses in Snow, 9" 15.00
Cake plate, Wild Flower, crackle glass border, 12" 25.00
Compote, Lightning Flower, clear, unsgn Northwood, 6½"............30.00
Compote, Lightning Flower, gr, unsgn Northwood, 6½" 35.00
Compote, Rose, 6" 35.00
Compote, Rose Perfect, 6"...30.00
Compote & saucer set, Poppy, crackle glass, 6" 40.00
Dish, flowered, heart shape, 6" 50.00
Dish, heart shape, cut or pressed pattern, 6" 70.00
Dish, Hearts, rolled rim, 10"..50.00

Lamp, Cabbage Rose, matching chimney, 12" 350.00
Lamp, oil; Nosegay, #2, EX orig pnt 250.00
Pitcher, water; Carnation, 7"...80.00
Plate, Butterfly, Dugan, rare, 11" 125.00
Plate, Carnation, La Belle & Roses in Snow, 4½" or 6", ea..........10.00
Plate, Carnation, La Belle & Roses in Snow, 9"........................15.00
Plate, Gibson Cameo (series), 8½" 30.00
Plate, Hearts, 10" 45.00
Plate, Holly, opal, 10½" 70.00
Plate, Lightning Flower, clear, unsgn Northwood, 7" 25.00
Plate, Lightning Flower, gr, unsgn Northwood, 7" 27.00
Plate, monk drinking from tankard, uptrn edges, 7" 40.00
Plate, Poppy, clear, unsgn Northwood, 7".................................27.00
Plate, Poppy, gr, unsgn Northwood, 7" 35.00
Plate, Rose & Lattice, 6" 15.00
Plate, Roses, Grapes & Apples, w/lattice edge (series), 8½" 23.00
Plate, Roses, Latticed Glass Edge Roses, 7" 25.00
Plate, Wheel & Block, opal, 9½" 45.00
Relish plate, flowered, glass hdls, 7" 45.00
Relish plate, Poppy, glass hdls, 7" 47.00
Relish plate, Rose, glass hdls, 7" 50.00
Slipper, lg, 7"...45.00
Sugar shaker, Grape, gold on milk glass, orig pnt/top, 4½" 37.50
Syrup, Cabbage Rose 150.00
Tray, Fruit, 8½" sq 90.00
Tumbler, Grape, gold on crackle, 4", NM................................50.00
Vase, Basketweave w/Peonies, narrow base, 7½"........................80.00
Vase, Basketweave w/Wild Rose, narrow neck & base, 9" 70.00
Vase, bl glass (hard to find), 14½"...160.00
Vase, Cabbage Rose, 15" 95.00
Vase, Dogwood, baluster, 15" 95.00
Vase, gr glass (hard to find), 14½".......................................150.00
Vase, Iris, milk glass, 7½" 65.00
Vase, lg roses allover (hard to find), clear, 5½" 50.00
Vase, lg roses allover (hard to find), opal, 7" 75.00
Vase, Magnolia Blossoms, filigree top & bottom, 9½" 75.00
Vase, Peacock in a Tree, red/gr/gold, 15" 225.00
Vase, Poppy, 5"..15.00
Vase, Poppy (1 lg) on front, 9"..80.00
Vase, Poppy Clusters on front, 9"...80.00
Vase, Tree Flowers (uncommon), 14½"..................................110.00
Vase, Victorian Vase & Rose Buds, 14½" 120.00
Vase, Vine & Flowers, w/neck, 10" 65.00

Goss and Crested China

William Henry Goss received his early education at the Government School of Design at Somerset House, London, and as a result of his merit was introduced to Alderman William Copeland, who owned the Copeland Spode Pottery. Under the influence of Copeland from 1852 to 1858, Goss quickly learned the trade and soon became their chief designer. Little is known about this brief association, and in 1858 Goss left to begin his own business. After a short-lived partnership with a Mr. Peake, Goss opened a pottery on John Street, Stoke-on-Trent, but by 1870 he had moved his business to a location near London Road. This pottery became the famous Falcon Works. Their mark was a spread-wing falcon (goss-hawk) centering a narrow, horizontal bar with 'W.H. Goss' printed below.

Many of the early pieces made by Goss were left unmarked and are difficult to discern from products made by the Copeland factory, but after he had been in business for about fifteen years, all of his wares were marked. Today unmarked items do not command the prices of the later marked wares.

Adolphus William Henry Goss (Goss's eldest son) joined his father's firm in the 1880s. He introduced cheaper lines, though the more expensive lines continued in production. Shortly after his father's death in 1906, Adolphus retired and left the business to his two younger brothers. The business suffered from problems created by a war economy, and in 1936 Goss assets were held by Cauldon Potteries Ltd. These were eventually taken over by the Coalport Group, who retained the right to use the Goss trademark. Messrs. Ridgeway Potteries bought all the assets in 1954 as well as the right to use the Goss trademark and name. In 1964 the group was known as Allied English Potteries Ltd. (A.E.P.), and in 1971 A.E.P. merged with the Doulton Group. Now it remains to be seen if Goss ware will ever be produced again. Values are all for items in mint condition.

Model of Lloyd George's Early home, Llanystymdwy with annex, 4" wide; Model of same without annex, 2⅜" wide, $175.00 each.

Abergavenny Jar, Holyhead, 2" 27.50
Ancient Cup, Grand Lodge of England, 2¼" 75.00
Ancient Earthen Jar, Pershore Abbey, 2¼" 30.00
Ancient Irish Wooden Noggin, Arms of Totland, 2½" 32.00
Bournemouth Pine Cone, Earl of Lancaster, 3½" 25.00
Cambridge Pitcher, Deganwy, 2½" 22.50
Carlisle Salt Pot, Shanklin, 1½" 22.00
Cup & saucer, Bournemouth, England, 1920s 22.50
Devizes Celtic Drinking Cup, Ryde, 2½" 25.00
Glastonbury Ewer, Argyll, 3" 20.00
Irish Mather, Deal, 3" 20.00
Jersey Fish Basket, Arms of Sir Walter Raleigh, 3x4" 35.00
Old Welsh Milk Can 24.00
Oolen Pot, Earl of Pembroke coat of arms....................67.50
Rochester of Bellarmine, Simon de Montfort, 2½"........35.00
Roman Vase, Deal, ca 1901, 2⅝" 25.00
Savoy, HMS Queen Elizabeth Battleship, City of Worcester........42.00
Silchester Vase, Towyn, 2" 22.00
Stockton Salt Pot, Eastborne, 3" 30.00

Crested China

Arcadian, Manx Cat, Isle of Man 55.00
Arcadian, tortoise, Lynton, 2½" L 20.00
Arcadian, trinket box, horseshoe, Allied flags, 1914 ......20.00
Carlton, Fourth Bridge, Wiltshire & Robinson, 6½" L.....72.50
Carlton, fruit basket, Barnsley, 3½" 31.00
Carlton, golf ball, Iver, 1½" dia 28.00
Carlton, ship (for 1918 surrender of German fleet), Maidenhead, 5" ..90.00
Carlton, Toby jug, pearl lustre, Hastings, 1930s, 2¾" 20.00
Fountains Abbey Cup, Bath Abbey, 1¾" 25.00
Grafton, egg cup, St Helena (HP not transfer) 17.50
Willow Art, bottle, shouldered; Longton, 3½" 10.00

Gouda

Gouda is an old Dutch market town in the province of South Hol-

land. Famous for its cheese, Gouda's ceramics industry had its beginnings in the early sixteenth century and was fueled by the growth in the popularity of smoking tobacco. Initially learning their craft from immigrant potters from England who had settled in the area, the clay pipe makers of Gouda were soon regarded as the best. While some authorities give 1898 (the date the Zuid-Holland factory began operations) as the initial date for the manufacturing of decorative pottery in Gouda, C.W. Moody, author of *Gouda Ceramics*, indicates the date was ca 1885. Gouda was not the only town in the Netherlands making pottery; Arnhem, Schoonhoven, and Amsterdam also had earthenware factories, but technically the term 'Gouda pottery' refers only to pieces made within the town of Gouda. Today, no Gouda-style factories are active within the city's limits, but in the first quarter of the twentieth century there were several firms producing decorative pottery there — the best known being Zuid, Regina, Zenith, Ivora, and Goedewaagen.

This information was provided to us by Adela Meadows; she is listed in the Directory under California.

For further information we recommend *The World of Gouda Pottery* by Phyllis T. Ritvo (Front & Center Press, Weston, Massachussets).

Ashtray, glossy, w/matchbook holder, Ponseau, date tree, 6" dia ..300.00
Bowl vase, floral on rust w/gold, wht int, Regina, 6¾x4" 240.00
Candle holder, bl floral w/gold, Dutch mk, 2½x6½" 110.00
Candlesticks, geometrics/Greek Key bands, #057, Orientale, 8" ..325.00
Clock, irises, mc w/gold, works mk J Unghans, 1900s, 9" dia......800.00
Compote, gr matt, int w/mc flowers, 5x9½" 175.00
Garniture, Nouveau flowers, clock mt+2 candle holders, Zuid, 1900s...2,875.00
Inkwell, Rhodian House mk 135.00
Jug, Ivora, floral, #120, 5¼" 330.00
Plate, rural autumn scene w/mother & children, fr, 6x12" 425.00
Vase, blk w/wide mc floral band, ftd gourd shape, mk, 6" 110.00
Vase, Deco floral, blk & mc on satin, mk, 6⅛x3¼" 110.00
Vase, fruit compote & villate scene, mk, 5½x16½", NM...........200.00
Vase, Nouveau florals, ca 1895, bl mk, 4⅝" 275.00
Vase, peasant woman, #7052 RR Holland/#1852R, 12½", NM ..350.00
Vase, repeating geometrics, WK Bagdad, 3½" 100.00
Vase, tulips, bl/gr/cream on gr, #091/1R, 7¾" 175.00
Wall pocket, wooden shoe, Holland mk, 9¼", EX......................100.00

Graniteware

Graniteware, made of a variety of metals with enamel coatings, derives its name from its appearance. The speckled, swirled, or mottled effect of the vari-colored enamels may look like granite — but there the resemblance stops. It wasn't especially durable! Expect at least minor chipping if you plan to collect.

Graniteware was featured in 1876 at Phily's Expo. It was mass produced in quantity, and enough of it has survived to make at least the common items easily affordable. Condition, color, shape, and size are important considerations in evaluating an item; cobalt blue and white, green and white, brown and white, and old red and white swirled items are unusual, thus more expensive. Pieces of heavier weight, seam constructed, riveted, and those with wooden handles and tin or matching graniteware lids are usually older. Pieces with matching granite lids demand higher prices than ones with tin lids.

For further study we recommend *The Collector's Encyclopedia of Graniteware, Book II*, by our advisor, Helen Greguire. It is available from the author and Collector Books. For information on how to order, see her listing in the Directory under South Carolina. For the address of the National Graniteware Society, see the section on Clubs, Newsletters, and Catalogs.

Note: Our values are for pieces in mint or near-mint condition unless noted otherwise; appropriate deductions must be made if damage is present.

ABC plate, M, $2,550.00; Coffee flask, M, $625.00; Oval shirred egg plate, marked, M, $195.00. All in gray mottle. (Photo courtesy Helen Greguire)

Bowl, bl & wht lg swirl, wht inside, rimmed, Columbian Ware, EX...155.00
Bowl, dough/salad; bl & wht fine mottle w/blk trim, EX 1,350.00
Bowl, fruit; cobalt & wht lg mottle, wht inside, ped ft, 7½x8" ...975.00
Bowl, vegetable; brn & wht lg swirl, wht inside, 1½x9½x7½" ...295.00
Bucket, berry; cream w/gr trim, seamless, 5x3½", VG 165.00
Can, cream (Boston); gr & wht relish w/cobalt trim 235.00
Can, milk; bl & wht lg swirl w/blk trim, seamed, 10½", VG 785.00
Can, milk; dk gr & wht med mottle w/blk, Chrysolite, 11½x6⅛"..650.00
Can, milk; gray lg mottle, seamed, wooden bail, sm 80.00
Canister, sugar; wht w/dk bl trim, recessed strap hdl on lid, EX 95.00
Carrier, coffee; bl & wht checkered w/red trim, wire ears, tin lid, EX.295.00
Carrier, stacking dinner, mc lg swirl w/cobalt, ltweight, 1950s, EX.395.00
Carrier, water; gray lg mottle, seamless, pouring lip, 8x8½" 295.00
Chamber pot, gr & wht swirl w/cobalt, Emerald Ware, 10½" dia, VG..395.00
Churn, floor dasher, bl-gr shading to wht, blk trim, 17½", VG ..875.00
Clothes boiler, wht w/red-brn letters, w/lid, sm 215.00
Coffee biggin, cobalt & wht checkered w/red trim, 3-pc 425.00
Coffee biggin, med gray mottle, tin biggin & spreader, 4-pc, 2-cup...495.00
Coffee biggin, red & wht med mottle, 4-pc 595.00
Coffee biggin, red & wht med mottle w/red trim, wht int, 4-pc, 9¼" ..595.00
Coffee boiler, cobalt & wht lg swirl 325.00
Coffee roaster, blk & wht med mottle, screen-style drum, lg.......425.00
Coffeepot, bl & wht wavy mottle, wht int, blk trim/hdl, seamed, 9¼"..425.00
Coffeepot, cobalt to lt bl w/blk, wht inside, seamless, 9¼", VG .295.00
Coffeepot, dk gr & wht lg swirl, Chrysolite.................................495.00
Coffeepot, gray mottle w/pewter trim, hinged spout, copper bottom ..325.00
Coffeepot, lav-cobalt & wht lg swirl, tin lid 385.00
Coffeepot, wht w/gr veins lg mottled, Elite Austria, G.................225.00
Colander, bl & wht lg mottle w/cobalt, ftd, 4½x9⅛" 195.00
Colander, gr veins of lg mottle w/gr trim, ftd, 5½x11¾" 135.00
Colander, gray lg mottle, ftd, shallow 165.00
Creamer, cobalt & wht lg swirl w/blk trim & hdl, squatty...........110.00
Cup, lt bl & wht swirl w/blk trim 70.00
Dbl boiler, bl & wht lg swirl, Lava Ware, EX 395.00
Dbl boiler, cobalt & wht lg swirl w/blk trim, seamless, Belle shape..525.00
Dipper, cocoa; wht w/tubular hollow hdl, hook at top of hdl, EX...165.00
Dipper, gr & wht lg swirl w/brn hollow hdl, flared, EX...............185.00
Dipper, Windsor; bl & wht lg swirl, blk hollow hdl 165.00
Dishpan, bl & wht lg mottle, wht side, eyelet, 4½x14½", VG ...110.00
Dishpan, wht, lt bl & gray swirl w/blk trim & hdls.......................135.00
Flask, coffee; gray lg mottle, seamed, Nesco Pure Graystone..., 6¼"....575.00
Funnel, 'old' red & wht lg mottle (Snow on Mtn) w/red trim, EX 425.00
Funnel, bl & wht lg swirl w/blk trim/hdl, Columbian Ware, 4½x3¼"..450.00
Grater, cream w/gr hdl, flat, 1x5½x4½" 180.00
Grater, solid cobalt, lg, EX 130.00
Griddle, gray med mottle, wire bail, riveted ears, 16¼" dia, VG.195.00
Jar, solid wht, w/wht lid, 3¼x3" 40.00
Jug, batter; gray lg mottle, tin lid, 2-seam body..........................395.00
Kettle, Berlin style, gr & wht lg swirl w/cobalt, Emerald Ware ...425.00

Kettle, preserving; bl & wht lg mottle w/blk trim, tipping hdl, lip...265.00
Kettle, preserving; gr & wht lg swirl w/cobalt, lip, Emerald Ware, EX...295.00
Ladle, soup; lt bl & wht lg mottle, wht inside, 14⅞", VG 60.00
Matchbox, bl & gray med swirl w/bl trim, emb fancy bk.............285.00
Measure, 'old' red & wht med mottle, seamed body, seamless lip, EX ..425.00
Measure, aqua-gr & wht lg swirl w/cobalt trim, wht inside, sm, EX......420.00
Measure, gray lg mottle, seamless, graduated lip, 4-cup 110.00
Measure, oyster; gray lg mottle, seamed, emb: 1 qt liq'd, 5⅜x4¼" ..395.00
Mold, lion form, solid wht, 4½x5⅛x7", VG 395.00
Mold, melon shape, gray mottle, No 30 (sm sz)..........................225.00
Mold, scalloped, gray lg mottle 75.00
Mold, tube; aqua & wht lg mottle w/blk trim, 8-sided................335.00
Mug, 'old' red & wht lg swirl w/cobalt, wht inside, seamless, 3⅛" ..950.00
Mug, dk gr & wht lg swirl w/bl trim, Chrysolite 165.00
Mug, gray med mottle..35.00
Mug, mush; brn & wht lg swirl w/cobalt, wht inside, 4⅝x6⅛", VG..325.00
Pan, baking; gr & wht lg swirl, seamless, Emerald Ware, 14¼" L .550.00
Pan, baking; lt bl & wht lg swirl w/blk trim, appl hdls, oblong...185.00
Pan, biscuit; brn & wht med mottle, Onyx Enamel Ware, 24-cup, VG .1,150.00
Pan, egg fry; cobalt, wht inside, riveted hdl, 10¼" dia, G 95.00
Pan, egg fry; solid red, hdl, 7 eyes, 1⅛x9⅞" dia 130.00
Pan, fry; lav-bl & wht lg swirl w/blk trim & hdl, med sz, EX 265.00
Pan, fry; red & wht lg swirl w/blk trim & hdl, ltweight, 1970s ...185.00
Pan, muffin; lav-cobalt & wht med swirl w/blk, wht inside, 8-cup..695.00
Pan, muffin; lt bl & wht lg swirl, 8-cup, EX 495.00
Pan, pudding; cobalt & wht lg swirl w/blk trim, wht inside, lg, EX 155.00
Pan, stew; bl & wht lg mottle w/blk trim & hdl, wht inside, deep, EX....195.00
Pitcher, body; dk bl & wht 'up & down' swirl w/cobalt, 13⅜x8" ...395.00
Pitcher, molasses; bl & wht swirl, cobalt hdl, Columbian Ware, 5½"..1,600.00
Pitcher, water; 'old' red & wht lg swirl w/cobalt trim, triple coated 5,775.00
Pitcher, water; bl & wht lg swirl w/blk trim & hdl, EX 325.00
Plate, dinner; bl & wht med swirl, ¾x10", VG 95.00
Plate, dinner; red & wht lg swirl w/blk trim, ltweight, 1960s 45.00
Plate, divided; yel & wht lg swirl w/blk trim, 1950s, 11⅛" 55.00
Plate, pie; cobalt & wht lg swirl w/blk trim, wht inside...............115.00
Plate, pie; dk sea gr to moss gr, wht inside, 9" 65.00
Rack, utility; gray & wht lg mottle, perforated bk, EX.................220.00
Roaster, bl & wht lg swirl w/blk trim/hdls, flat top, 3-pc.............375.00
Roaster, cream & gr, emb Savory, 8x17x10⅝", VG 85.00
Roaster, solid red ridged top, blk bottom, seamless, 9½" dia, VG .65.00
Salt box, wht w/lt bl veins (Chicken Wire), EX 395.00
Scoop, spice; med gray mottle, pieced bk, strap hdl, EX 325.00
Skimmer, cobalt & gray lg mottle, flat, perforated, hdld, EX 110.00
Skimmer, cobalt & wht med mottle w/gr veins, blk hdl (end of day) ..195.00
Skimmer, med gray mottle, perforated, lg......................................55.00
Spatula, gray med mottle, sm...125.00
Spoon, basting; bl & wht lg mottle, blk hdl, EX..........................110.00
Spoon, basting; cobalt & wht lg swirl, EX...................................135.00
Strainer, tea; bl & wht fine mottle, wht inside, EX 150.00
Strainer, tea; wht, screen insert...50.00
Syrup, gray lg mottle, pewter trim, hinged lid, squatty.............1,450.00
Tea steeper, brn & wht relish w/cobalt trim, wht inside, tin lid, EX....145.00
Teakettle, cobalt & wht lg mottle w/blk trim, seamed, 7½", VG....400.00
Teakettle, gr & wht relish, NP trim, Manning-Bowman, 10" 695.00
Teakettle, pk & wht marbleized w/blk, wht inside, 6¾x9" 525.00
Teapot, bl & wht lg swirl w/cobalt, seamless, Bl Dmn Ware, 9", VG ...395.00
Teapot, cobalt bl to wht w/cobalt floral w/gold, bulbous 165.00
Teapot, heron & rushes on wht, pewter trim, 5½" 595.00
Teapot, red & wht med swirl, flared cylinder, 1960s....................125.00
Teapot, wht & bl lg swirl w/blk hdl, seamless, 9x5½", VG..........225.00
Tray, gray lg mottle, oblong, L&G Mfg Co, 13⅜x9½" 185.00
Tray, gray med mottle, sq...165.00
Tray, red & wht lg swirl w/cobalt trim, ltweight, rnd, 1960s..........65.00
Trivet, aqua solid, 3 molded ft on CI, F&W ETI 75.00

Tub, foot; bl & wht lg swirl w/blk trim, oval, eyelet, EX 295.00
Tub, foot; dk gr & wht lg mottle w/blk, Chrysolite, 18½" L, VG....495.00
Tumbler, red-brn & wht lg swirl w/cobalt, wht inside, 4¾x3½" .350.00
Tureen, wht w/bl veining (Chicken Wire), ftd, hdls, w/lid, EX...325.00
Wash basin, cobalt & wht lg swirl, w/eyelet, EX.........................125.00
Wash bowl & pitcher, red w/blk trim & hdl, squatty, EX 225.00

Green Opaque

Introduced in 1887 by the New England Glass Works, this ware is very scarce due to the fact that it was produced for less than one year. It is characterized by its soft green color and a wavy band of gold reserving a mottled blue metallic stain. It is usually found in satin; examples with a shiny finish are extremely rare. Values depend to a large extent on the amount of the gold and stain remaining.

Bowl, EX mottling & gold, 3½x8"...995.00
Bowl, M stain & gold, 4x8" 1,150.00
Box, powder; EX stain & gold on bowl & lid, 4x6¼" 1,150.00
Celery vase, worn stain & gold, 6½" 450.00
Cruet, M stain & gold, orig stopper 1,950.00
Cruet, VG stain...1,500.00
Mug, EX stain & gold, 2¼"..500.00
Mug, M stain & gold, 2½"..700.00
Punch cup, M stain & gold...750.00
Punch cup, worn stain & gold, 2½"....................................225.00
Shaker, M stain & gold, 2½"...400.00
Toothpick holder, EX gold..900.00
Toothpick holder, M gold...1,150.00
Tumbler, EX stain & gold, 3½"...700.00
Tumbler, lemonade; w/hdl, M stain & gold, 5" 950.00

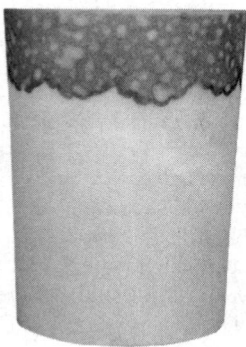

Tumbler, M stain and gold, 3½", $800.00.

Vase, flared, M stain & gold, 6" 900.00
Vase, 14-rib w/flaring rim, VG stain & gold, 6" 500.00

Greenaway, Kate

Kate Greenaway was an English artist who lived from 1846 to 1901. She gained worldwide fame as an illustrator of children's books, drawing children clothed in the styles worn by proper English and American boys and girls of the very early 1800s. Her book, *Under the Willow Tree*, published in 1878, was the first of many. Her sketches appeared in leading magazines, and her greeting cards were in great demand. Manufacturers of china, pottery, and metal products copied her characters to decorate children's dishes, tiles, and salt and pepper shakers as well as many other items.

What some collectors/dealers call Kate Greenaway items are not actual Kate Greenaway designs but merely look-alikes. Genuine Kate Greenaway items (metal, paper, cloth, etc.) must bear close resemblance

to her drawings in books, magazines, and special collections. See also Napkin Rings.

Almanac, 1884, London, Routledge, NM 140.00
Almanac, 1892, London, 1st ed, VG.......................................135.00
Biscuit jar, ceramic, boy w/tinted features, w/lid 165.00
Book, A Apple Pie, Warne, 1940, w/dust jacket, VG 28.00
Book, Birthday Book for Children, Greenaway illus, 1880, VG..160.00
Book, Day in a Child's Life, Routledge, 1st ed, VG 150.00
Book, Greenaway's Babies, Saalfield Muslin Book, 1907, G+ 40.00
Book, Kate Greenaway Pictures, London, Warne, 1st ed, 1921, VG ..300.00
Book, Kate Greenaway's Alphabet, London, 1880, EX................190.00
Book, Kate Greenaway's Book of Games, Routledge, 1st ed, 1889, NM...475.00
Book, Language of Flowers, Routledge, 1st ed, picture board, VG ...100.00
Book, Marigold Garden, Greenaway illus, London, 1888, VG......60.00
Book, Mother Goose, London, later print of 1st ed, VG 150.00
Book, Pied Piper of Hamlin, Greenaway illus, NM.......................85.00
Book, Under the Willow, Routledge, 1st ed, orig cloth 165.00
Bowl, Daisy & Button, amber; R&B SP fr w/girl & dog.............525.00
Butter pat, children playing transfer, pre-1910 ....40.00
Combination set, shakers/napkin ring/stand, Middlton Plate, $350 to..500.00
Engraving, Harper's Bazaar, Jan 1879, full-pg 25.00
Figurine, seated girl tugs on lg hat, bsk, pre-1910, sm.................75.00
Hatpin holder, SP, figural girl, Meriden, 4" 125.00
Inkwell, boy & girl, bronze...215.00
Match holder, ornate SP, girl in fancy clothes, Tufts 195.00
Paperweight, CI Victorian girl in lt bonnet, pre-1910, 3x2¾" 110.00
Pencil holder, pnt porc, pre-1910 ....100.00
Pickle castor, bl; SP fr w/2 girls, blown-out florals 455.00
Plate, ABC, girl in lg hat, Staffordshire, 7".............................105.00
Plate, children at play, fruits, birds & flowers, 9" 100.00
Salt cellar, Little People, bsk, arms over basket, 3¾"..................10.00
Scarf, Greenaway illus on silk, early, EX...................................65.00
Tea set, semi porc, floral motif, pre-1910, 3-pc, child sz 95.00
Toothpick holder, bsk, girl sits on stump, basket on bk.................40.00
Toothpick holder, clear glass, 2 girls by basket 100.00
Toothpick holder, SP, girl holds amberina cup, ornate base, 5" ...785.00
Wall pocket, ceramic, 6 girls on open book form, 6x9x3" 137.00

Greentown Glass

Greentown glass is a term referring to the product of the Indiana Tumbler and Goblet Company of Greentown, Indiana, ca 1894 to 1903. Their earlier pressed glass patterns were #75 (originally known as #11), a pseudo-cut glass design; #137, Pleat Band; and #200, Austrian. Another line, Dewey, was designed in 1898. Many lovely colors were produced in addition to crystal. Jacob Rosenthal, who was later affiliated with Fenton, developed his famous chocolate glass in 1900. The rich, shaded opaque brown glass was an overnight success. Two new patterns, Leaf Bracket and Cactus, were designed to display the glass to its best advantage, but previously existing molds were also used. In only three years Rosenthal developed yet another important color formula, Golden Agate. The Holly pattern was designed especially for its production. The dolphin covered dish with a fish finial is perhaps the most common and easily recognized piece ever produced. Other animal dishes were also made; all are highly collectible. There have been many repros — not all are marked! The symbol (+) at the end of some of the following lines was used to indicate items that have been reproduced.

Our advisors for this category are Jerry and Sandi Garrett; they are listed in the Directory under Indiana. See the Pattern Glass section for clear pressed glass; only colored items are listed here.

Animal dish, bird w/berry, amber (+)...325.00

Animal dish, bird w/berry, emerald gr (+)................325.00
Animal dish, bird w/berry, teal bl.........................375.00
Animal dish, cat on hamper, canary, low.................850.00
Animal dish, cat on hamper, canary, tall (+) 600.00
Animal dish, cat on hamper, cobalt, tall.................750.00
Animal dish, cat on hamper, opaque wht, tall 500.00
Animal dish, dolphin, beaded, amber......................800.00
Animal dish, dolphin, beaded, Golden Agate 1,000.00
Animal dish, dolphin, sawtooth, cobalt.................1,000.00
Animal dish, fighting cocks, amber.....................2,000.00
Animal dish, fighting cocks, cobalt....................2,400.00
Animal dish, hen, emerald gr.............................225.00
Animal dish, hen, opaque wht.............................200.00
Animal dish, rabbit, amber (+)...........................200.00
Animal dish, rabbit, cobalt..............................600.00
Austrian, bowl, canary, 8"...............................300.00
Austrian, butter dish, chocolate, child sz..............750.00
Austrian, compote, canary, 4½"...........................225.00
Austrian, creamer, emerald gr, 4¼".......................215.00
Austrian, plate, canary, sq..............................225.00
Austrian, punch cup, amber...............................225.00
Austrian, sugar bowl, chocolate, w/lid, 2½" dia.........175.00
Austrian, wine, emerald gr...............................200.00
Beehive, bud vase, amber.................................300.00
Beehive, tumbler, chocolate..............................550.00
Brazen Shield, butter dish, bl...........................275.00
Brazen Shield, compote, bl, w/lid, 6⅜"...................250.00
Brazen Shield, sauce bowl, bl, 3⅞".........................35.00
Brazen Shield, tumbler, bl................................90.00
Cactus, bowl, chocolate, 6¼".............................135.00
Cactus, creamer, chocolate, w/Dewey lid, 2¼"............135.00
Cactus, plate, chocolate, 7¼"............................115.00
Cactus, tumbler, bl-wht opal rim.........................350.00
Cord Drapery, bowl, cobalt, ftd, 6¼".....................175.00
Cord Drapery, butter dish, amber, 4¾" dia...............350.00
Cord Drapery, compote, emerald gr, w/lid, 4½".........240.00
Cord Drapery, goblet, amber..............................280.00
Cord Drapery, punch cup, cobalt..........................150.00
Cord Drapery, toothpick holder, amber...................350.00
Cupid, butter dish, wht opaque...........................150.00
Cupid, creamer, chocolate................................375.00
Cupid, spooner, chocolate................................350.00
Cupid, sugar bowl, Nile Green, w/lid.....................450.00
Dewey, bowl, emerald gr, 8"...............................90.00
Dewey, butter dish, canary, 5" dia.......................150.00
Dewey, creamer, chocolate, 5"............................450.00
Dewey, mug, amber...65.00
Dewey, plate, canary......................................85.00
Dewey, serpentine tray, emerald gr, sm....................60.00
Dewey, sugar bowl, cobalt, w/lid, 2½" dia...............225.00
Early Diamond, dish, amber, rectangular, 8x5"...........175.00
Early Diamond, tumbler, cobalt...........................200.00
Greentown Daisy, mustard pot, chocolate.................225.00
Herringbone Buttress, bowl, amber, 5¼"...................275.00
Herringbone Buttress, butter dish, emerald gr...........400.00
Herringbone Buttress, cordial, amber, 3"................400.00
Herringbone Buttress, cordial, olive gr, 3⅜"............200.00
Herringbone Buttress, shaker, emerald gr................325.00
Herringbone Buttress, tumbler, emerald gr, either style, ea........275.00
Holly, spooner, Rose Agate.............................9,000.00
Holly, toothpick holder, White Agate...................3,650.00
Holly Amber, bowl, rectangular, 10x4"..................1,500.00
Holly Amber, bowl, 8½"...................................700.00
Holly Amber, cake stand................................2,600.00

Holly Amber, compote, w/lid, 7¼"......................1,700.00
Holly Amber, creamer.....................................850.00
Holly Amber, plate, 7½"..................................800.00
Holly Amber, toothpick holder (+)........................450.00
Holly Amber, vase, 6"....................................850.00
Leaf Bracket, butter dish, cobalt......................1,300.00
Leaf Bracket, cruet, chocolate...........................200.00
Leaf Bracket, toothpick holder, chocolate...............350.00
Mug, Deer & Oak Tree, chocolate..........................750.00

Mug, Indoor Drinking Scene, chocolate, 8½", $550.00.

Mug, Indoor Drinking Scene, Nile Green, hdlless.........435.00
Mug, Serenade, cobalt, 4¾"...............................450.00
Novelty, Connecticut Skillet, Nile Green................650.00
Novelty, Corn vase, amber, 4⅝"...........................250.00
Novelty, hairbrush, Nile Green...........................650.00
Novelty, Scotch Thistle, chocolate.....................1,175.00
Novelty, wheelbarrow, teal bl............................175.00
Pattern #75, bowl, emerald gr, rectangular, 8x6½".......100.00
Pattern #75, relish tray, canary, 6" L..................200.00
Pleat Band, cordial, canary.............................250.00
Pleat Band, wine, canary................................200.00
Ruffled Eye, pitcher, chocolate.........................625.00
Ruffled Eye, pitcher, emerald gr........................200.00
Scalloped Flange, vase, chocolate........................95.00
Shuttle, bowl, chocolate, 8¼"...........................550.00
Shuttle, mug, cobalt....................................400.00
Shuttle, punch cup, chocolate...........................110.00
Shuttle, tankard creamer, chocolate......................90.00
Shuttle, tumbler, canary................................400.00
Teardrop & Tassel, bowl, chocolate, 8¼".................650.00
Teardrop & Tassel, creamer, opaque wht..................125.00
Teardrop & Tassel, pitcher, cobalt......................275.00
Teardrop & Tassel, sauce bowl, emerald gr, 4½"...........85.00
Teardrop & Tassel, tumbler, cobalt.......................85.00
Toothpick holder, Dog Head, chocolate (+)...............750.00
Toothpick holder, Dog Head, frosted bl..................350.00
Toothpick holder, Picture Frame, amber..................250.00
Toothpick holder, Witch Head, Nile Green (+)............200.00

Grueby

    William Henry Grueby joined the firm of the Low Art Tile Works at the age of fifteen and in 1894, after several years of experience in the production of architectural tiles, founded his own plant, the Grueby Faience Company, in Boston, Massachusetts. Grueby began experimenting with the idea of producing art pottery and had soon perfected a fine glaze (soft and without gloss) in shades of blue, gray, yellow, brown, and his most successful, cucumber green. In 1900 his exhibit at the Paris Exposition Universelle won three gold medals.

    Grueby pottery was hand thrown and hand decorated in the Arts and Crafts style. Vertically thrust stylized leaves and flowers in relief were the most common decorative devices. Tiles continued to be an important product, unique (due to the matt glaze decoration) as well as durable. Grueby tiles were often a full inch thick. 'En cuenca' refers to a decorative technique for tiles that is the equivalent of cloisonne. Instead of copper 'cloisonnes' however, the tiles have a pressed dust wall pushed into their surface. Then glazes of appropriate color are laid into the channels between them. This has the effect of stylizing the design in a way complementary to the Arts and Crafts style.

Incompatible with the Art Nouveau style, the artware production ceased in 1907, but tile production continued for another decade. The ware is marked in one of several ways: 'Grueby Pottery, Boston, USA'; 'Grueby, Boston, Mass.'; or 'Grueby Faience.' The artware is often artist signed. Our advisor for this category is David Rago; he is listed in the Directory under New Jersey.

Bowl, bl matt, mk/2 labels, 5½" 850.00
Paperweight, scarab, 4x2¾", from $600 to 700.00
Tile, angel, oatmeal matt on gray-bl, en cuenca, Le Boutillier, 8" 460.00
Tile, flower, mustard-yel on gr mottle, 6¼", in ftd copper fr 1,100.00
Tile, geometrics, gr matt, mustard yel, blk matt, 4½x6" 300.00
Tile, Grueby Tile & yel candle, en cuenca, 6x4½", in new fr ..4,000.00
Tile, knight, gray-bl on creamy yel, #655, 6" 545.00
Tile, knight on horsebk, yel on terra cotta, le Boutillier, #655, 6" ..200.00
Tile, rabbit in cabbage patch, yel & gr, 6", in new fr 3,000.00
Tile, stage beneath tree, brns/gr/bl, en cuenca, 4" in new fr 950.00
Tile, water lilies, gr/ivory/yel/dk gr, PS/label, 6", NM 2,200.00
Tile, 3-masted ship on water, 5-color, 8" 700.00
Tile frieze, Pines, mc, Addison le Boutillier, 1902, 6x42" 37,500.00
Vase, bl matt, cylindrical, incurvate rim, 7½" 550.00
Vase, gr, buds on long stems, can neck, bulbous, #22, 8", NM.3,165.00
Vase, gr, shouldered, flared rim, 3" 950.00
Vase, gr, tooled leaves, Ellen Farmington, nick, 7¼x4½" 2,600.00
Vase, gr, tooled/appl daffodils, R Erickson, label, 11x5¼" 19,000.00
Vase, gr, tooled/appl daffodils/buds, L Newman, #161, 12⅞".10,350.00

Vase, green, tooled and applied leaves with exceptional definition, double gourd form, 12½", $25,000.00. (Photo courtesy David Rago)

Vase, gr, tooled/appl leaves, bulbous, rstr rim, 22½x8" 12,000.00
Vase, gr, tooled/appl leaves, floriform rim, 7¾x4" 3,750.00
Vase, gr, tooled/appl leaves, R Erickson, 6¾x7¼" 25,000.00
Vase, gr, tooled/appl leaves & yel buds, R Erickson, 8" 20,000.00
Vase, gr, tooled/appl leaves/buds, M Seaman, #175, 7½", NM.3,250.00
Vase, gr, tooled/appl wht daffodils, bulbous, sm rpr, 11" 9,000.00
Vase, gr, vertical leaves, artist sgn, low, label, 4" dia 900.00
Vase, gr (leathery), tooled/appl leaves, W Post, rstr, 7¼x7¾" ..2,500.00
Vase, multi-tone bl matt, gourd shape, 5" 550.00
Vase, oatmeal (thick), cylindrical, 7x3" 850.00
Vase, speckled bl-gray, bulbous, collared/ribbed rim, 6¼x5" 800.00
Vase, spicy brn, 6 incised panels, closed-in rim, R Erickson, 11½" 3,250.00

Gustavsberg

Gustavsberg Pottery, founded near Stockholm, Sweden, in the late 1700s, manufactured faience, creamware, and porcelain in the English taste until the end of the nineteenth century. During the twentieth century, the factory has produced some inventive modernistic designs, often signed by their artists. Wilhelm Kage (1889 – 1960) is best remembered for Argenta, a stoneware body decorated in silver overlay, introduced in the 1930s. Usually a mottled green, Argenta can also be found in cobalt blue and white. Other lines included Cintra (an exceptionally translucent porcelain), Farsta (copper-glazed ware), and Farstarust (iron oxide geometric overlay). Designer Stig Lindberg's work, which dates from the 1940s through the early 1970s, includes slab-built figures and a full range of tableware. Some pieces of Gustavsberg are dated.

Box, Argenta, nude w/cigarette holder o/l on gr, #1125, 5⅜" L..250.00
Vase, Argenta, Deco silver mermaid & fish on turq, bulbous, 10" ...2,100.00
Vase, Argenta, gr mottle rocket shape w/silver o/l, 9x4½", pr..475.00
Vase, Argenta, man blowing horn/lady w/flowers silver o/l, 9"....375.00
Vase, nude man on chicken on wht, cylindrical, 8" 110.00
Vase, Selectra, turq/gray mottle, stick neck, sgn BF, 8½" 275.00

Hadley, M.A.

Founded by artist-turned-potter Mary Alice Hadley, this Louisville, Tennessee, company has been producing handmade dinnerware and decorative items since 1940. Their work is painted freehand in a folky style with barnyard animals, baskets, whales, and sailing ships in a pastel palette of predominately blues and greens. Each piece is signed with Hadley's first two initials and her last name. She is responsible for creating each design; among collectors, horses and pigs are popular subject matter. Older pieces are generally heavier and along with the more unusual items command the higher prices.

Bank, horse figural, 6½" 40.00
Bean pot, horse, Whoa inside, hdld, 7" 60.00
Bowl, flowers on lid, sgn inside lid & on bottom, 4x6".................50.00
Canister, sugar; Please Fill Me inside, 8½" 75.00
Casserole, cow & pig on lid, The End inside, 5x10" 45.00
Cooler crock, farmer, wife & pig, w/lid, 15x10" 135.00
Cup, farmer's; horse, 4¾" 50.00
Cup & saucer, tall ship, Low Tide inside, EX 18.00
Egg cup, farmer, 4x3" 45.00
Jewelry holder, Ring, 2¾x2" 17.00
Jug, cow, 4" 30.00
Mug, pig, The End in bottom, 4" 15.00
Pie plate, horse, 9½" 42.00
Pie plate, Way to a Man's Heart 35.00
Pitcher, character 'toby,' 6½" 30.00
Pitcher, cherub, 5-cup..35.00
Plaques, farmer & wife, 6½", 5½", pr 40.00
Plate, dinner; house, 11" 25.00
Plate, farmer & wife, 15" 90.00
Plate, Happy Birthday, birthday cake, 4" 12.50
Plate, luncheon; frog, 9" 40.00
Plate, rearing horse, 6¼" 14.00
Platter, Christmas, 12½" 45.00
Platter, farmer & wife, 15½" 95.00
Shakers, cow on salt, horse on pepper, 4½", pr 25.00
Tureen, cow & pig, 2-qt 65.00
Utensil jar, flowers, 5½x5" 55.00

Hagen-Renaker

Best known for their line of miniature animal figures, Hagen-Renaker was founded in Monrovia, California, in 1946. It is estimated that perhaps as many as eighty different dogs were produced. In addition to the animals, they made replicas of characters from several popular Disney films under license from the Disney Studio. The firm relocated in San Dimas in 1960, where they remain active to the present time. Their wares are sometimes marked with an incised 'HR,' a stamped 'Hagen-Renaker' or part of the name, or paper labels. For more information, we recommend *The Collector's Encyclopedia of California Pottery, Second Edition,* by Jack Chipman; *Charlton Standard Catalog of Hagen-Renaker, Second Edition; Disneyana Collector's Guide to Californian Pottery, 1938 – 1960,* by Devin Frick and Tamara Hodge; and *Hagen-Renaker Pottery: Horses and Other Figurines* by Nancy Kelly (Schiffer). Another source of information is Hagen-Renaker Collectors Club (HRCC), listed in the Directory under Clubs, Newsletters, and Catalogs.

Figurine, zebra mama and baby, $300.00. (Photo courtesy Gayle Roller)

Figurine, Adelaide, donkey w/hat, Monrovia, 5½x6" 135.00
Figurine, armadillo baby, ½" 10.00
Figurine, Beanbag, sitting dachshund, 2x3" 40.00
Figurine, Belle, standing beagle, 2" 25.00
Figurine, Bobby, bulldog puppy, 1955, 2x3" 40.00
Figurine, Brunhilda, dachshund, 1955, 4½" 60.00
Figurine, Champ, sitting boxer puppy, 5⅛" 37.50
Figurine, Cornball, sitting dachshund pup, sticker, 1¼x2" 40.00
Figurine, Country Mouse, DW sticker, 1950s, 3" 40.00
Figurine, Donald Duck, 1½" 140.00
Figurine, Elsa, scratching dachshund pup, sticker, 1¼x1¼" 40.00
Figurine, Heather, Morgan mare, wht matt, B-548, 5x6" 375.00
Figurine, Honey Girl, Cocker Spaniel, 1955, 5½x7½" 45.00
Figurine, Hymie, dachshund, 1955, 3" L 35.00
Figurine, Lady, from Lady & the Tramp, 1⅜" 40.00
Figurine, Lippett, Morgan stallion, Monrovia, 6½" 160.00
Figurine, Little Horrible #421, September Morn, 1950s, 1½" 75.00
Figurine, Madame Fluff, Persian cat, sticker, 5x3¾" 100.00
Figurine, Maggie, walking femal Boxer, 2¾" 40.00
Figurine, Mallard drake, wings out, early 1950s, mini, 2½" 25.00
Figurine, Miss Pepper, Morgan foal, red chestnut, #701, 2¾" 100.00
Figurine, Mother Goose, red or gr shawl, Fall 1990/Fall 1991, mini...20.00
Figurine, mountain lion, recumbent, DW sticker, 5x9" 250.00
Figurine, opossom baby, mini, ⅜" 10.00
Figurine, papa goat, brn, mini, 2½" 25.00
Figurine, Pedro, dog from Lady & Tramp, 1930s, 1¼" 85.00
Figurine, quail, w/metal legs & feather, mini, 1" 20.00
Figurine, quarterhorse mare, chestnut or gray, matt or gloss, #75, 8"...175.00
Figurine, Sassy, sitting tabby kitten, B-719, 1959, 3" 50.00
Figurine, Si, Siamese cat from Lady & the Tramp, 1955-59, 1¾".90.00
Figurine, Spooky, Dalmatian, 1954, 6" 75.00

Figurine, Squire, English setter, 1954, 5¾x10" 75.00
Figurine, Sun Cortez, horse, wht matt, San Marcos, DW sticker...150.00
Figurine, Tiger, dachshund puppy, paper label, 1½x2" 40.00
Figurine, Von, German Shepherd, 1954, 5¾x9½" 60.00

Hagenauer

Carl Hagenauer founded his metal workshops in Vienna in 1898. He was joined by his son Karl in 1919. They produced a wide range of stylized sculptural designs in both metal and wood.

Bowl, openwork male & female golfers w/2 caddies at base, brass...**475.00**
Bust, Deco lady, bronze w/blk & gold patina, 4½x3" **625.00**
Bust, Deco lady, cvd rosewood base, brass hair, 10x6" **300.00**
Compote, on ribbed oak ped, WHW/Made in Vienna Austria, 5½x10½"...**400.00**
Figure, African lady dancer, Deco style, bronze, sm grass skirt, 10" .**750.00**
Figure, dancing man, bronze, verdigris torso, 6¼x2½" **550.00**
Figure, elephant, blk w/golden tusks, 7x11" **750.00**
Figure, Jesus Christ, bronze, EX patina, 1920s-30s, 5x3¾" **375.00**
Figure, man & lady looking opposite directions, brass, 1920s, 9"...**665.00**
Figure, warrior w/arrows, bronze, 6" **335.00**
Figure, warrior w/bow & arrow, bronze & brass, mk, 7½x4¼" **300.00**
Figure, 3 natives paddle boat, bronze/brass/wood, 2½x7½" **565.00**
Mirror, chrome plated, Deco style, 1930s, 8x4¾" dia **475.00**
Pin tray, Scottie dog at side, SP bronze, 4" sq **395.00**

Hair Weaving

A rather unusual craft became popular during the mid-1800s. Human hair was used to make jewelry (rings, bracelets, lockets, etc.) by braiding and interlacing fine strands into hollow forms with pearls and beads added for effect. Wreaths were also made, often using hair from deceased family members as well as the living. They were displayed in deep satin-lined frames along with mementoes of the weaver or her departed kin. The fad was abandoned before the turn of the century. The values suggested below are for mint condition examples. Any fraying of the hair greatly lowers value. For further information, we recommend *Collector's Encyclopedia of Hairwork Jewelry* by C. Jeanenne Bell (Collector Books). See also Mourning Collectibles.

Key: p-w — palette work   t-w — table work

Brooch, p-w basketweave in gold navette shape, 1790-1820, 1⅞" L **475.00**
Brooch, p-w bouquet under rock crystal, half pearls, 1790-1820, 1⅜"..**650.00**
Brooch, p-w flowers & curls under glass, gold mt, 1850s, 1⅛x1" ...**350.00**
Brooch, p-w under crystal, coral cabochons surround, 1830s, ⅞" ..**350.00**
Brooch, p-w wheat sheaf under crystal, 1790-1810, 1¾x1" **575.00**
Brooch, t-w acorns & leaves, gold mts, 1850-60s, 1¾x1⅝" **395.00**
Brooch, t-w bow (plaid weave), gold mts, rprs, 1850-70s **400.00**
Brooch, t-w coiled snake w/gold head & garnets, ca 1840, 2x2¼"..**975.00**
Brooch, t-w lyre w/gold mts, ca 1860-80, 1⅛x⅞" **175.00**
Brooch, t-w 2-color bow w/gold mts, acorn drops, 1850-70s, 2x2½"..**475.00**
Brooch/pendant, t-w 2-tone hair w/gold mts, 1860-80s, 2x1⅜"..**350.00**
Earrings, gold hoops w/t-w hair, 1850-70s, 1⅜" dia, pr **575.00**
Earrings, t-w openweave acorns w/gold mts, 1850-70s, 1¼", pr ..**375.00**
Earrings, t-w openweave bells w/gutta-percha mts, 1850-70s, 1⅝", pr...**475.00**
Earrings, t-w openweave teardrop shapes, gold mts, 1840-70, 3¾"...pr**420.00**
Floral arrangement, on wood base, glass dome, 19th C, 10x10"..**110.00**
Necklace, t-w chain w/1⅝" anchor drop, gold mts, 1850-60.......**400.00**
Necklace, t-w flat chain w/gold clasp, 1850-60, choker style, 16"...**275.00**
Necklace, t-w flatweave crossover-style choker, gold mts, 1850s.**500.00**
Necklace, t-w multiple strands, gold mts, 1840-60, 12" **400.00**

Necklace, t-w twist weave w/2 acorn drops, gold mts, 1840-70, 15"..345.00
Necklace, t/w open-weave balls, gold mts & center shell w/garnet ...900.00
Ring, p-w hair under rock crystal, pearl surround, 1790s.............550.00
Ring, p-w weeping willow under glass, gold mts, 1780s...............850.00
Watch chain, spiraling tube weave, gold-filled mts, 1830s, 13"...150.00
Wreath, flowers & curls, mc hair, thick, in gilt 27" sq fr..........1,300.00
Wreath, 3-color, ca 1840, EX, in shadow-box fr, 12x16" 375.00

Hall

The Hall China Company of East Liverpool, Ohio, was established in 1903. Their earliest product was whiteware toilet seats, mugs, jugs, etc. By 1920 their restaurant-type dinnerware and cookingware had become so successful that Hall was assured of a solid future. They continue today to be one of the country's largest manufacturers of this type of product.

Hall introduced the first of their famous teapots in 1920; new shapes and colors were added each year until about 1948, making them the largest teapot manufacturer in the world. These and the dinnerware lines of the '30s through the '50s have become popular collectibles. For more thorough study of the subject, we recommend *The Collector's Encyclopedia of Hall China, Third Edition*, by Margaret and Kenn Whitmyer; their address may be found in the Directory under Ohio.

Flamingo, syrup pitcher, $125.00; Batter bowl, 8", $100.00.

Blue Bouquet, bowl, flared, 7¾".................................45.00
Blue Bouquet, bowl, fruit; D-style, 5½"........................10.00
Blue Bouquet, casserole, Thick Rim 45.00
Blue Bouquet, cup, D-style.....................................18.00
Blue Bouquet, jug, Medallion, #3...............................35.00
Blue Bouquet, plate, D-style, 9"...............................18.00
Blue Bouquet, platter, D-style, oval, 13¼"....................40.00
Blue Bouquet, saucer, D-style.................................2.50
Blue Bouquet, soup tureen....................................310.00
Blue Bouquet, tray, metal, rectangular.........................50.00
Cameo Rose, bowl, oval, 10½"..................................22.00
Cameo Rose, butter dish, E-style, ¼-lb.......................400.00
Cameo Rose, gravy boat, E-style, w/underplate..................32.00
Cameo Rose, platter, E-style, oval.............................25.00
Cameo Rose, shakers, E-style, pr..............................40.00
Christmas Tree & Holly, bowl, E-style, oval....................55.00
Christmas Tree & Holly, bowl, plum pudding; E-style, 4½" 25.00
Christmas Tree & Holly, cup...................................18.00
Christmas Tree & Holly, saucer, E-style........................4.00
Crocus, bowl, vegetable; D-style, rnd, 9¼"....................35.00
Crocus, casserole, Radiance...................................32.00
Crocus, drip jar, #1188, open.................................40.00
Crocus, gravy boat, D-style...................................30.00
Crocus, mug, tankard style....................................60.00
Crocus, plate, D-style, 9"....................................18.00
Crocus, soap dispenser, metal................................100.00
Crocus, teapot, Boston.......................................200.00

Five Band, cookie jar, colors other than red or cobalt 125.00
Five Band, syrup, red or cobalt................................75.00
Game Bird, cup, E-style.......................................22.00
Game Bird, mug, Irish coffee..................................60.00
Game Bird, plate, E-style, 10"................................60.00
Heather Rose, cake plate......................................15.00
Heather Rose, cup, E-style.....................................6.50
Heather Rose, plate, E-style, 10".............................10.00
Heather Rose, saucer, E-style..................................2.00
Homewood, bowl, flat soup; D-style, 8½".......................12.00
Homewood, cup, D-style...7.00
Homewood, saucer, D-style......................................1.50
Medallion, bowl, ruffled, Lettuce, 9¼".......................125.00
Medallion, stack set, ivory...................................50.00
Mums, bowl, fruit; D-style, 5½"................................5.50
Mums, creamer, Art Deco.......................................25.00
Mums, jug, Simplicity..200.00
Mums, mug, beverage...55.00
Mums, plate, D-style, 9"......................................10.00
Mums, platter, D-style, oval, 13¼"............................35.00
Mums, teapot, Rutherford.....................................225.00
No 488, bowl, fruit; D-style, 5½"..............................7.50
No 488, bowl, Radiance, 5"....................................20.00
No 488, creamer, Art Deco.....................................22.00
No 488, cup, D-style..14.00
No 488, custard, Radiance.....................................20.00
No 488, drip coffeepot, #691.................................400.00
No 488, platter, D-style, oval, 11¼"..........................32.00
Orange Poppy, bean pot, New England, #4......................125.00
Orange Poppy, bowl, flat soup; C-style, 8½"...................30.00
Orange Poppy, bread box, metal...............................100.00
Orange Poppy, drip jar, Radiance, w/lid.......................30.00
Orange Poppy, platter, C-style, oval, 13¼"....................40.00
Pastel Morning Glory, bowl, D-style, oval.....................40.00
Pastel Morning Glory, gravy boat, D-style.....................32.00
Pastel Morning Glory, plate, D-style, 10" 60.00
Pastel Morning Glory, pretzel jar............................200.00
Pastel Morning Glory, sugar bowl, New York, w/lid.............25.00
Primrose, bowl, flat soup; E-style, 8".........................10.00
Primrose, cake plate..15.00
Primrose, plate, E-style, 10".................................10.00
Primrose, sugar bowl, E-style, w/lid..........................14.00
Red Poppy, bowl, cereal; D-style, 6"..........................16.00
Red Poppy, bowl, Radiance, 9".................................22.00
Red Poppy, cake safe, metal...................................45.00
Red Poppy, custard..18.00
Red Poppy, gravy boat, D-style................................35.00
Red Poppy, plate, D-style, 10"................................65.00
Red Poppy, tumbler, clear glass...............................30.00
Sani-Grid, bean pot, tab hdls, Chinese Red....................60.00
Sears' Arlington, bowl, vegetable; E-style, w/lid 32.00
Sears' Arlington, creamer, E-style 9.00
Sears' Fairfax, bowl, fruit; 5¼"...............................4.50
Sears' Fairfax, plate, 7¼"....................................4.50
Sears' Fairfax, platter, oval, 13¼"...........................22.00
Sears' Monticello, bowl, flat soup; E-style, 8"...............11.00
Sears' Monticello, gravy boat, E-style, w/underplate..........25.00
Sears' Monticello, sugar bowl, E-style, w/lid.................15.00
Sears' Mount Vernon, bowl, cereal; E-style, 6¼"................8.00
Sears' Mount Vernon, casserole, w/lid.........................40.00
Sears' Mount Vernon, coffeepot, all-china....................200.00
Sears' Richmond/Brown-Eyed Susan, bowl, cereal; 6¼" 7.00
Sears' Richmond/Brown-Eyed Susan, cup..........................6.50
Serenade, bowl, D-style, rnd, 9¼".............................22.00

Serenade, cup, D-style	9.00
Serenade, pie baker	35.00
Serenade, teapot, New York	125.00
Silhouette, ball jug, #3	125.00
Silhouette, bowl, vegetable; D-style, rnd, 9¼"	32.00
Silhouette, casserole, Medallion	40.00
Silhouette, coaster	6.00
Silhouette, drip coffeepot, Kadota (all-china)	250.00
Silhouette, plate, D-style, 9"	18.00
Silhouette, shakers, Five Band, ea	18.00
Silhouette, tray, metal, oval	32.00
Springtime, cake plate	16.00
Springtime, creamer, Modern	11.00
Springtime, platter, D-style, oval, 15"	40.00
Springtime, sugar bowl, Modern, w/lid	18.00
Teapot, Airflow, gold decor, 8-cup	60.00
Teapot, Airflow, Indian Red, 6-cup	250.00
Teapot, Airflow, turq, 6-cup	65.00
Teapot, Aladdin, common solid colors, oval opening	55.00
Teapot, Aladdin, red or cobalt, rnd opening	145.00
Teapot, Albany, Gold Special, 6-cup	85.00
Teapot, Automobile, red or cobalt, 6-cup	650.00
Teapot, Bellvue, common solid colors, 10-cup	45.00
Teapot, Boston, Early Gold Design, 6-cup	50.00
Teapot, Football, colors other than red or cobalt	550.00
Teapot, French, common colors, 6-cup	32.00
Teapot, French, Old Gold Decorated, 8-cup	65.00
Teapot, French, red or cobalt	185.00
Teapot, Globe, red, 6-cup	350.00
Teapot, Hollywood, red, 5-cup	200.00
Teapot, Manhattan, colors other than red, 2-cup	55.00
Teapot, Moderne, common solid colors, 6-cup	30.00
Teapot, Moderne, red, 6-cup	175.00
Teapot, Parade, Gold Label, 6-cup	45.00
Teapot, Philadelphia, decal, 6-cup	125.00
Teapot, Streamline, common solid colors, 6-cup	60.00
Teapot, Surfside, Gold Special, 6-cup	225.00
Teapot, Windshield, Game Bird decal, 6-cup	165.00
Tulip, baker, French, fluted	20.00
Tulip, bowl, flat soup; D-style, 8½"	18.00
Tulip, bowl, Thick Rim, 8½"	30.00
Tulip, canister set, metal, 4-pc	100.00
Tulip, tidbit, D-style, 3-tier	55.00
Wildfire, casserole, tab hdls	32.00
Wildfire, coffee dispenser, metal	22.00
Wildfire, gravy boat, D-style	25.00
Wildfire, plate, D-style, 10"	50.00
Yellow Rose, bowl, vegetable; rnd, 9½"	30.00
Yellow Rose, drip jar, Radiance, w/lid	35.00
Yellow Rose, platter, oval, 13¼"	30.00

Zeisel Designs, Hallcraft

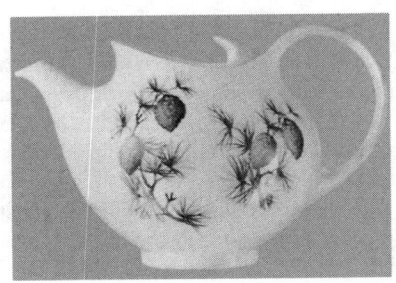

Tomorrow's Classic Pinecone, teapot, six-cup, $125.00.
(Photo courtesy Margaret and Kenn Whitmyer)

Century Fern, bowl, salad; 11¾"	25.00

Century Fern, butter dish	90.00
Century Fern, jug	28.00
Century Fern, platter, 15"	30.00
Century Sunglow, bowl, salad; 11¾"	30.00
Century Sunglow, casserole	55.00
Century Sunglow, relish, 4-part	35.00
Century Sunglow, teapot, 6-cup	155.00
Tomorrow's Classic Arizona, bowl, celery; oval	20.00
Tomorrow's Classic Arizona, bowl, salad; 14½"	32.00
Tomorrow's Classic Arizona, egg cup	45.00
Tomorrow's Classic Bouquet, baker, open, 11-oz	22.00
Tomorrow's Classic Bouquet, coffeepot, 6-cup	100.00
Tomorrow's Classic Bouquet, onion soup, w/lid	40.00
Tomorrow's Classic Bouquet, platter, 17"	40.00
Tomorrow's Classic Buckingham, bowl, fruit; ftd, lg	42.00
Tomorrow's Classic Buckingham, butter dish	160.00
Tomorrow's Classic Buckingham, gravy boat	42.00
Tomorrow's Classic Buckingham, plate, 11"	12.00
Tomorrow's Classic Caprice, bowl, fruit; 5¾"	7.50
Tomorrow's Classic Caprice, candlestick, 4½"	30.00
Tomorrow's Classic Caprice, gravy boat	35.00
Tomorrow's Classic Caprice, sugar bowl, w/lid	10.00
Tomorrow's Classic Fantasy, bowl, coupe soup; 9"	11.00
Tomorrow's Classic Fantasy, butter dish	165.00
Tomorrow's Classic Fantasy, jug, 3-qt	30.00
Tomorrow's Classic Fantasy, vase	65.00
Tomorrow's Classic Frost Flowers, bowl, celery; oval	17.00
Tomorrow's Classic Frost Flowers, casserole, 2-qt	45.00
Tomorrow's Classic Frost Flowers, onion soup, w/lid	35.00
Tomorrow's Classic Frost Flowers, platter, 12¼"	20.00
Tomorrow's Classic Harlequin, ball jug, #3	160.00
Tomorrow's Classic Harlequin, cup	9.00
Tomorrow's Classic Harlequin, egg cup	50.00
Tomorrow's Classic Harlequin, teapot, 6-cup	195.00
Tomorrow's Classic Holiday, baker, open, 11-oz	20.00
Tomorrow's Classic Holiday, candlestick, 8"	40.00
Tomorrow's Classic Holiday, plate, 11"	11.00
Tomorrow's Classic Holiday, platter, 17"	35.00
Tomorrow's Classic Lyric/Mulberry, bowl, fruit; 5¾"	8.00
Tomorrow's Classic Lyric/Mulberry, casserole, 2-qt	45.00
Tomorrow's Classic Lyric/Mulberry, onion soup, w.lid	37.00
Tomorrow's Classic Lyric/Mulberry, teapot, 6-cup	195.00
Tomorrow's Classic Peach Blossom, candlestick, 8"	35.00
Tomorrow's Classic Peach Blossom, cup	7.00
Tomorrow's Classic Peach Blossom, plate, E-style 9"	8.50
Tomorrow's Classic Peach Blossom, sugar bowl, open	12.00
Tomorrow's Classic Pinecone, butter dish	140.00
Tomorrow's Classic Pinecone, mug	25.00
Tomorrow's Classic Pinecone, plate, E-style, 9¼"	8.50
Tomorrow's Classic Pinecone, sugar bowl, w/lid	20.00
Tomorrow's Classic Spring, bowl, vegetable; open, 8¾" sq	22.00
Tomorrow's Classic Spring, creamer	12.00
Tomorrow's Classic Spring, marmite, w/lid	27.00

Hallmark

Hallmark introduced a line of artplas (molded plastic) ornaments in 1973 which quickly became popular with collectors. The Hallmark Keepsake Ornament Collectors' Club was organized in 1987 and offered exclusive limited edition ornaments to club members only. Hallmark has produced miniature ornaments since 1988 and added a line of Easter (now known as Spring) ornaments beginning in 1991. All these ornaments are very collectibles.

Our advice for this category is from the Baggage Car; you will find them listed in the Directory under Iowa. Values are for ornaments in mint condition and with their original boxes.

1991, QX 410-9, Hooked on Santa, Julia Lee, MIB, $20.00.

1973, 250XHD100-2, Betsy Clark (musicians), glass ball 85.00
1973, 250XHD102-2, Manger Ball, red 95.00
1973, 250XHD103-5, Elves, glass ball 99.00
1974, 250QX107-1, Snowgoose, glass ball...............................75.00
1974, 250QX107-1, Snowgoose, glass ball...............................75.00
1975, QX161-1, Drummer Boy, handcrafted 225.00
1975, 175QX123-1, Raggedy Andy, yarn, reissued in 1976 ....57.00
1975, 250QX135-1, Charmers, Mary Hamilton, dtd, glass ball, no box ..50.00
1976, 250QX203-1, Bicentennial '76 Commemorative, satin ball, dtd ..60.00
1976, 500QX181-1, Yesteryear Train, dtd, handcrafted 165.00
1977, 250QX158-2, Mountains, glass ball, spotted 45.00
1977, 350QX153-5, Charmers, satin ball, dtd 65.00
1978, 350QX269-6, 25th Christmas Together, glass ball, dtd........35.00
1978, 600QX149-6, Animal Home, handcrafted 175.00
1979, 350QX211-9, Granddaughter, satin ball, dtd 40.00
1979, 350QX352-7, Colors of Christmas, Star Over Bethlehem, acrylic ..85.00
1980, 300QX163-4, Snowman, yarn, reissued in 1981....................8.50
1980, 650QX139-4, A Heavenly Nap, handcrafted 55.00
1981, 550QX445-5, Snowman Chimes, metal 30.00
1981, 550QX501-5, Christmas Star, acrylic, dtd, handcrafted.......22.50
1981, 550QX505-5, First Christmas Together, acrylic, dtd 25.00
1982, 400QX300-3, Artic Penguin, acrylic 20.00
1982, 450QX211-3, First Christmas Together, glass ball, dtd 39.50
1983, 450QX207-9, Love, glass ball, dtd 70.00
1983, 450QX217-9, An Old-Fashioned Christmas, glass ball........34.50
1984, 1000QX443-1, Bell Ringer Squirrel, glass ball, handcrafted .40.00
1984, 450QX254-1, A Savior Is Born, glass ball 33.00
1985, 1575QLX711-2, Little Red School House, light 95.00
1985, 475QX261-2, First Christmas, bl glass ball, dtd 24.50
1985, 550X521-2, Engineering Mouse 25.00
1985, 775QX492-2, Sun & Fun Santa, dtd 40.00
1986, 1000QLX7076, Keep On Glowin' 50.00
1986, 475QX2723, glass ball, dtd..40.00
1986, 975QX424-6, Wynken, Blynken & Nod, handcrafted........43.00
1987, 1500QX465-9, Heavenly Harmony, musical 34.50
1987, 550QX542-9, Spots 'n Stripes, Dalmatian........................25.00
1988, 1175QXM566-1, Heavenly Glow, tree topper, brass angel ..23.00
1988, 475QX277-1, Grandparents, ball, dtd 20.00
1988, 850QLX7111, Cardinal, limited edition, acrylic 30.00
1989, 1350QLX7242, Little Drummer Boy, Christmas Classics #4, dtd...42.50
1989, 450QXM5742, Strollin' Snowman, ceramic, mini..............17.50
1989, 625QX489-5, Balancing Elf 23.00
1990, 1275QX4656, Greatest Story, 1st edition.........................25.00
1990, 475QX215-3, 10 Years Together, ball, dtd.........................23.00

Halloween

Though the origin of Halloween is steeped in pagan rites and superstitions, today Halloween is strictly a fun time, and Halloween items are fun to collect. Pumpkin-head candy containers of papier-mache or pressed cardboard, noisemakers, postcards with black cats and witches, costumes, and decorations are only a sampling of the variety available.

Here's how you can determine the origin of your jack-o'-lantern:

American
1940 – 1950s

German
1900 – 1930s

— items are larger
— made of egg-carton material
— bottom and body are one piece

— items are generally small
— made of cardboard or composition
— always has a cut-out triangular nose; simple, crisscross lines in mouth; blue rings in eyes
— have attached cardboard bottoms

For further information we recommend *More Halloween Collectibles, Anthropomorphic Vegetables and Fruits of Halloween,* by Pamela E. Apkarian-Russell (Schiffer). Other good reference books are *Halloween in America* by Stuart Schneider, and *Halloween Collectables* by Dan and Pauline Campanelli.

Our advisor for this category is Jenny Tarrant; she is listed in the Directory under Missouri. See Clubs, Newsletters, and Catalogs for information concerning *Trick or Treat Trader,* a quarterly newsletter. Unless noted otherwise, values are for examples in excellent to near mint condition except for paper items, in which case assume the condition to be near mint to mint.

American

Most American items were made during the 1940s and 1950s, though a few date from the 1930s as well. Lanterns are constructed either of flat cardboard or the pressed cardboard pulp used to make the jack-o-lantern shown on the left.

Jack-o'-lantern, pressed cb pulp w/orig face, 4" 95.00
Jack-o'-lantern, pressed cb pulp w/orig face, 4½".........................125.00
Jack-o'-lantern, pressed cb pulp w/orig face, 5" 145.00
Jack-o'-lantern, pressed cb pulp w/orig face, 5½".........................165.00
Jack-o'-lantern, pressed cb pulp w/orig face, 6" 185.00
Jack-o'-lantern, pressed cb pulp w/orig face, 6½".........................195.00
Jack-o'-lantern, pressed cb pulp w/orig face, 7" 225.00
Jack-o'-lantern, pressed cb pulp w/roig face, 8", minimum value ...275.00
Lantern, cat, pressed cb pulp w/orig face 245.00
Lantern, cat (full body), pressed cb pulp, 7x6½" 350.00
Lantern, cb w/tab sides, any 95.00

Lantern, pumpkin man (full body), pressed cb pulp 350.00
Plastic Halloween car..250.00
Plastic pumpkin stagecoach, witch & cat....................................450.00
Plastic witch holding blk cat w/wobbling head, 7" 150.00
Plastic witch on rocket, upright, 7" 450.00
Plastic witch on rocket, 4" 95.00
Plastic witch on rocket, 5" 350.00
Tambourine, tin litho/paper, Ohio Art, 1930s, 6" dia 75.00
Tin noisemaker, bell style...38.00
Tin noisemaker, can shaker 38.00
Tin noisemaker, clicker...35.00
Tin noisemaker, fry pan style...55.00
Tin noisemaker, horn..55.00
Tin noisemaker, sq spinner 38.00
Tin noisemaker, tambourine, Chein 150.00
Tin noisemaker, tambourine, Kirkoff 95.00

Celluloid (German, Japanese, or American)

Blk cat, plain, M..150.00
Egg-shape house, M 400.00
Long-leg veggie rattle, M 300.00
Owl, plain, M..150.00
Owl on pumpkin, M..175.00
Owl on tree, M..200.00
Pumpkin-face man, M 350.00
Pumpkin-face pirate, M 400.00
Scarecrow, M 175.00
Witch, plain, M...300.00
Witch in auto, M...450.00
Witch in corncob car, M 500.00
Witch pulling cart w/ghost, M 400.00
Witch pulling pumpkin cart w/cat, M 400.00
Witch sitting on pumpkin, M 350.00

German

As a general rule, German Halloween collectibles date from 1900 through the early 1930s. They were made either of composition or molded cardboard, and their values are higher than American-made items. In the listings that follow, all candy containers are made of composition unless noted otherwise.

Candy container, blk cat walking, glass eyes, head removes, 3-4" ...225.00
Candy container, blk cat walking, glass eyes, head removes, 5-6" ...250.00
Candy container, cat, glass eyes, 4-6", from $250 to.....................325.00
Candy container, cat, w/mohair, 5" 350.00
Candy container, cat, 3-5", from $175 to 285.00
Candy container, lemon-head man, pnt compo, 7" 575.00
Candy container, pumpkin-head man (or any vegetable), on box, 3"..175.00
Candy container, pumpkin-head man (or any vegetable), on box, 4"..185.00
Candy container, pumpkin-head man (or any vegetable), on box, 5"..225.00
Candy container, pumpkin-head man (or any vegetable), on box, 6"..275.00
Candy container, witch, pumpkin people, devil, ghost, etc, 3" ..225.00
Candy container, witch, pumpkin people, devil, ghost, etc, 4" ..300.00
Candy container, witch, pumpkin people, devil, ghost, etc, 5" ..375.00
Candy container, witch, pumpkin people, devil, ghost, etc, 6" ..425.00
Candy container, witch or pumpkin man, head removes, 4", $225 to ...275.00
Candy container, witch or pumpkin man, head removes, 5", $275 to ...325.00
Candy container, witch or pumpkin man, head removes, 6", $325 to ...365.00
Candy container, witch or pumpkin man, head removes, 7", $375 to ...425.00
Diecut, bat, emb cb, from $95 to 125.00
Diecut, cat, emb cb, from $55 to..95.00
Diecut, devil, emb cb, from $95 to 150.00

Diecut, jack-o'-lantern, emb cb..65.00
Diecut, pumpkin man or lady, emb cb, 7½" 125.00
Jack-o'-lantern, compo w/orig insert, 3" 225.00
Jack-o'-lantern, compo w/orig insert, 3½" 250.00
Jack-o'-lantern, compo w/orig insert, 4" 275.00
Jack-o'-lantern, compo w/orig insert, 4½" 325.00
Jack-o'-lantern, compo w/orig insert, 5" 350.00
Jack-o'-lantern, molded cb w/orig insert, 3" 110.00
Jack-o'-lantern, molded cb w/orig insert, 3½" 120.00
Jack-o'-lantern, molded cb w/orig insert, 4" 155.00
Jack-o'-lantern, molded cb w/orig insert, 4½" 165.00
Jack-o'-lantern, molded cb w/orig insert, 5" 200.00
Jack-o'-lantern, molded cb w/orig insert, 5½" 225.00
Jack-o'-lantern, molded cb w/orig insert, 6" 275.00
Jack-o'-lantern, molded cb w/orig insert, 6½", minimum value ..300.00
Lantern, cat, cb, molded nose, bow under chin, 3-5", from $275 to ..375.00
Lantern, cat, cb, simple rnd style..225.00
Lantern (ghost, skull, devil, witch, etc), molded cb, 3-4", minimum ..375.00
Lantern (ghost, skull, devil, witch, etc), molded cb, 5"+, minimum ...425.00
Lantern (skull, devil, witch, etc), compo, 3", minimum value 375.00
Lantern (skull, devil, witch, etc), compo, 4", minimum value 425.00
Lantern (skull, devil, witch, etc), compo, 5", minimum value 550.00
Noisemaker, cat (3-D) on wood rachet 150.00
Noisemaker, cb figure (flat) on rachet 125.00
Noisemaker, db paddle w/diecut face 95.00
Noisemaker, devil (3-D) on wood rachet 175.00
Noisemaker, pumpkin head (3-D) on wood rachet......................150.00
Noisemaker, tin frying pan paddle, 5" L 125.00
Noisemaker, tin horn, 3"...75.00
Noisemaker, veggie (3-D) horn (w/pnt face) 150.00
Noisemaker, veggie or fruit (3-D) horn (no face), ea....................65.00
Noisemaker, witch (3-D) on wood rachet 175.00
Noisemaker, wood & paper tambourine 250.00

Hampshire

The Hampshire Pottery Company was established in 1871 in Keene, New Hampshire, by James Scollay Taft. Their earliest products were redware and stoneware utility items such as jugs, churns, crocks, and flowerpots. In 1878 they produced majolica ware which met with such success that they began to experiment with the idea of manufacturing art pottery. By 1883 they had developed a Royal Worcester type of finish which they applied to vases, tea sets, powder boxes, and cookie jars. It was also utilized for souvenir items that were decorated with transfer designs prepared from photographic plates.

Cadmon Robertson, brother-in-law of Taft, joined the company in 1904 and was responsible for developing their famous matt glazes. Colors included shades of green, brown, red, and blue. Early examples were of earthenware, but eventually the body was changed to semiporcelain. Some of his designs were marked with an M in a circle as a tribute to his wife, Emoretta. Robertson died in 1914, leaving a void impossible to fill. Taft sold the business in 1916 to George Morton, who continued to use the matt glazes that Robertson had developed. After a temporary halt in production during WWI, Morton returned to Keene and re-equipped the factory with the machinery needed to manufacture hotel china and floor tile. Because of the expense involved in transporting coal to fire the kilns, Morton found he could not compete with potteries of Ohio and New Jersey who were able to utilize locally available natural gas. He was forced to close the plant in 1923.

Interest is highest in examples with the monochrome glazes, and it is the glaze, not the size or form, that dictates value. The souvenir pieces are not particularly of high quality and tend to be passed over by today's collectors.

Vase, steel blue neck with frothy mint green to cream mottle to light gray-pink below, base covered in Cereulean Blue with gray mottling, 9½x7½", $2,500.00.

Bowl, gr, #96, 2⅝x4¾" 300.00
Bowl, gr matt w/gray streaks, kiln pop, 2¾x4½" 150.00
Chamberstick, gr gloss, tricorner base, loop hdl, 3½x7" 230.00
Inkwell, gr matt, hollow form w/deep well, 2 openings, 3x4" 200.00
Lamp base, gr matt, verdigris to fittings, emb lily pads, 16x7" 900.00
Pitcher, gr matt, incised palms, #81, 9½" 425.00
Toothpick holder, Corn, early JST & Co, 2" 300.00
Vase, bl matt, shouldered, 12" 950.00
Vase, brn gloss, daisies, low, 4¼" dia 100.00
Vase, bud; gr matt, serpent head at opening, wrapping tail, 6"....325.00
Vase, Cerulean Bl mottle w/gray streaks, incised panels, #157, 7" .600.00
Vase, cucumber gr matt, Indian-like design, flat mouth, 8x7" 600.00
Vase, dk bl matt, buds & lotus leaves, C Robertson, #42, 19¼" .575.00
Vase, frothy mottled azure w/wht drips on Cerulean Bl, ovoid, #33, 7" .800.00
Vase, gr, integral hdls, 6" 350.00
Vase, gr matt, blade-like leaves, #98, 7¼" 800.00
Vase, gr matt, Greek key bands, rtcl hdls, #88, 15x9", NM......1,700.00
Vase, gr matt w/brn flecks, long neck, 6¾" 300.00
Vase, gr matt w/gray streaks, cylindrical, #63, 6x5".........200.00
Vase, gr to bl, cylindrical, flared rim, 12" 900.00
Vase, gunmetal blk, bowling-pin shape, #1-11, 9"...........225.00
Vase, Lightning Bolt, gr matt w/drips, 7¾" 650.00
Vase, mottled sea gr volcanic w/cobalt, triple floral, #68, 8¾x6" .3,000.00
Vase, steel to navy matt w/feather-like repeats, #121, 5¾"..........600.00

Handel

Philip Handel was best known for the art glass lamps he produced at the turn of the century. His work is similar to the Tiffany lamps of the same era. Handel made gas and electric lamps with both leaded glass and reverse-painted shades. Chipped ice shades with a texture similar to overshot glass were also produced. Shades signed by artists such as Bailey, Palme, and Parlow are highly valued.

Teroma lamp shades were created from clear blown glass blanks that were painted on the interior (reverse painted), while Teroma art glass (the decorative vases, humidors, etc. in the Handel Ware line) is painted on the exterior. This type of glassware has a 'chipped ice' effect achieved by sand blasting and coating the surface with fish glue. The piece is kiln fired at 800 degrees F. The contraction of the glue during the cooling process gives the glass a frosted, textured effect. Some shades are sand finished, adding texture and depth.

Both the glassware and chinaware decorated by Handel are rare and command high prices on today's market. Many of Handel's chinaware blanks were supplied by Limoges.

Key:
cb — counterbalance   chp — chipped/lightly sanded

Handel Ware

Unless noted china, all items in the following listing are glass.

Candlestick, windmill scene, sgn Broggi, #4213, 8½" 550.00
Humidor, cameo, geese/cattails, Rochette, #4238, 8½" 4,950.00
Humidor, horse & dog on brn to gr to amber, metal lid w/pipe hdl, 7" ...725.00
Humidor, hunting dog on gr, pipe finial, squat, #4060/B, 5" 550.00
Humidor, molded/pnt leafy scrolls, squat, #4050, 7¼" 550.00
Humidor, owl on branch, squat, #4038, 5" 600.00
Humidor, pointer dog on caramel, pipe finial, squat, #72/129, 5" ...550.00
Humidor, stag bellowing, Godwinn, oviform, #4091/J, 6½" 660.00
Humidor, yel shading to brn, pipe finial, melon form, #127, 4½" ...495.00
Jar, cigarette; dog w/game bird, cylindrical, hdls, #200/L, 3½" 385.00
Pitcher, tankard, palms, gr & gold on ivory, china, 11" 935.00
Plate, squirrels on limb, sgn Loehner, 9½" 400.00
Vase, birds in flight, ftd baluster, 11" 1,925.00
Vase, cameo floral, irid on textured frost, 8" 1,250.00
Vase, chrysanthemums on dk gr, flared ft, 12" 350.00
Vase, Teroma, autumn landscape, att Bailey, #4211, 10" 1,500.00
Vase, Teroma, mtns/trees/lake, Broggi, #4210, 8" 925.00
Vase, Teroma, trees/lake, Gubisch, baluster, ca 1925, 8" 1,150.00

Lamps

Base, bronze 3-socket cylinder w/mask hdls, mk, 23½" 975.00
Boudoir, HP 7" windmill scene #5882 shade; mk std 2,750.00
Boudoir, rvpt landscape elliptical #6672 shade; candlestick std, 14"..4,950.00
Boudoir, rvpt 5" floral #7175 shade; bronze baluster vase std, 15".....7,000.00
Boudoir, rvpt 6¾" Egyptian scene #6557 shade; trees std, 14½"....2,250.00
Boudoir, rvpt 7" desert scene 6-sided shade; bronze std, 15" 2,750.00
Boudoir, rvpt 7" lake/wood #6538 shade; coppered metal mk std, 14"..4,950.00
Boudoir, rvpt 7" parakeets #6905 shade; blk & gold mk std.....8,250.00
Boudoir, rvpt 7" woodland bell-shape #6231 shade; urn std.....4,125.00
Boudoir, rvpt/chp 7" parakeet shade; bronze std, 14½" 5,500.00
Boudoir, rvpt/chp 7" roses #6242 shade; chp base, 13½"..........3,750.00
Desk, chp 8½" floral shade; bronzed std adjusts, 14" 850.00
Desk, HP/chp 10" cornucopia/scroll shade; bronze swing-arm std, 12"..1,100.00
Desk, rvpt 8" mtns landscape shade; bronze dome-ft std 2,600.00
Desk, rvpt/chp roses #7076 shade; bronze bridge std, 13".........5,500.00
Desk, rvpt/chp 8" scenic #6326 shade; adjustable arm mk std, 13" ..2,400.00
Desk, slag 8" floral cutout shade, bronze std w/mushroom cutouts, 14"..4,750.00
Floor, chp 10" #6068 shade; bronzed bell harp std, 58" 2,000.00
Floor, chp 14" speckled brn shade; bronze harp std, 58"...........2,100.00
Floor, ldgl 10" floral shade; bronzed-metal std (cleaned), 57"..6,000.00
Floor, Mosserine 10" shade; bronzed-metal std, 57" 4,000.00
Floor, rvpt 10" floral #3060 shade; bronze mk std, 57¼".........2,300.00
Floor, rvpt/chp 8½x4" foliage #7173 shade; 1-socket std, 57"..2,860.00
Floor, 10" Steuben zig-zag shade; bronze metal base, 57" 4,000.00
Floor, 14" gold irid Steuben shade; bell-shaped harp, bronze std, 55"....2,900.00
Hanging, parrot & grapevines globe w/tassel, #7006, 6" dia, 28" drop ..2,500.00
Hanging, rvpt/chp 11" exotic birds mushroom #6997 shade, 28" 4,950.00
Night light, HP 8" roses oviform shade; pierced hardwood std...1,100.00
Pendant, rvpt/chp ice 10" birds in flight ball shade; all orig, 38" ..6,050.00
Piano, slag 6½" shade w/metal o/l; curved arm on weighted std, 8"..1,380.00
Table, etch/frost 10" birds #7721 shade; brass/marble 3-socket std...4,400.00
Table, HP 18" daffodils conical shade; bulbous mk std...........12,000.00
Table, HP 18" Oriental floral conical shade; exotic bird std ..68,750.00
Table, HP 18" scenic #7107 conical shade; bronze mk std, ca 1924..7,150.00
Table, HP/rvpt 18" scenic #5384 shade; bronze std 5,500.00
Table, ldgl rectangles in lozenge form shade; quatrefoil, 13"..650.00
Table, ldgl 16" slag dome gridwork shade; lobed std, 26" 4,000.00
Table, ldgl 16½" floral shade; bronzed metal std, 22"...............3,000.00
Table, ldgl 18" daffodils shade; bronze slim 2-socket std..........3,575.00
Table, ldgl 20" peacock feather shade; bronzed mk std, 24" 7,500.00
Table, ldgl 20" vintage shade; bronze urn mk std, 24" 1,400.00
Table, rvpt 14" Arts & Crafts #5488 dome shade; bronze std ..2,200.00
Table, rvpt 14" autumn scenic dome #7147 shade; bronze std .3,300.00

Table, rvpt 14" goldenrod conical #6177 shade; mk bronze std ...3,300.00
Table, rvpt 14" landscape #6720 shade; bronzed std, 22½" 3,250.00
Table, rvpt 14" parakeets conical shade; bronze std 5,775.00
Table, rvpt 16" butterfly border shade; bronzed std, 24" 9,500.00
Table, rvpt 16" floral shade; 3-socket bronze std, 26" 3,250.00
Table, rvpt 16" seashore #6814 dome shade; metal baluster std ..7,150.00
Table, rvpt 17" fleur-de-lis on slag panel shade; 3-socket std, 23" ..2,070.00
Table, rvpt 18" Arts & Crafts border dome shade; mk std 8,250.00
Table, rvpt 18" bird & flower shade; tripod std w/stepped base, 25" ..4,850.00
Table, rvpt 18" desert scene Bedigee shade; bronze std, 23½" ..23,000.00
Table, rvpt 18" exotic birds/floral branches dome shade; tripod std ...22,000.00
Table, rvpt 18" floral border #6750 shade; bronze baluster std, 24" 7,000.00
Table, rvpt 18" floral dome #7122 shade; bronze urn mk std .17,600.00
Table, rvpt 18" landscape #6957 shade; bronzed std, 23½" 4,250.00
Table, rvpt 18" landscape scalloped/paneled shade; ornate std ..7,700.00
Table, rvpt 18" pagoda & landscape dome shade; ebony std 7,975.00
Table, rvpt 18" parrots/butterfly/floral dome shade; tripod mk std ...14,850.00
Table, rvpt 18" roses dome shade; bronze tripod std 15,950.00
Table, rvpt 18" Treasure Island scene dome shade; bronze std ..13,200.00
Table, rvpt/chp 16" mums dropped-apron shade; bronze std 7,150.00
Table, rvpt/chp 18" floral #6688 dome shade; tripod std, 24" ..22,000.00
Table, rvpt/chp 18" scenic #6324 dome shade; tree trunk std, 25" 9,350.00
Table, slag 10" bent 8-panel shade w/fretwork o/l; #5339 std, 23" 4,000.00
Table, slag 14" geometric/woven-design shade; bronze std, 21" 4,250.00

Table lamp, 18" green and caramel slag with roses overlay eight-panel shade; bronzed metal base with EX original patina, 24", $4,250.00.

Table, slag 18" shade w/roses o/l; bronzed std w/EX patina, 24" ...4,250.00
Table, slag 19" shade w/metal o/l; 3-socket std w/4 bracket ft, 27" 4,300.00
Table, slag 20" petal shade; 4-socket copper shaft on lily-pad ft, 26" ..3,335.00
Table, slag 7" gr/ivory sq shell w/metal o/l; metal std, 22" 1,600.00
Table, textured 18" #d shade w/gold ferns; bronze ribbed std, 23" 3,300.00
Table, 18" citron crown #6884 shade w/floral border; brass std, 23" ..3,500.00
Torchere, rvpt 8" birds in flight cylindrical shade; bronze std, pr 4,675.00

Harker

The Harker Pottery was established in East Liverpool, Ohio, in 1840. Their earliest products were yellow ware and Rockingham produced from local clay. After 1900 whiteware was made from imported materials. The plant eventually grew to be a large manufacturer of dinnerware and kitchenware, employing as many as three hundred people. It closed in 1972 after it was purchased by the Jeannette Glass Company. Perhaps their best-known lines were their Cameo wares, decorated with white silhouettes in a cameo effect on contrasting solid colors. Floral silhouettes are standard, but other designs were also used. Blue and pink are the most often found background hues; a few pieces are found in yellow. For further information we recommend *The Best of Collectible*

Dinnerware by Jo Cunningham (Schiffer). Our advisor for this category is Ted Haun; he is listed in the Directory under Indiana.

Amy, plate, dinner...10.00
Apples & Nuts, plate, dinner..10.00
Basket of Flowers, bowl, vegetable.....................................15.00
Blue Grapes, pie baker..25.00
Cactus, pie baker...25.00
Calico Ribbon, bowl, mixing...40.00
Carnivale, salad fork server...20.00
Chesterton (Bermuda Blue), gravy boat.............................14.00
Chesterton (Pink Cocoa), plate, 6".......................................5.00
Chesterton (Teal), creamer & sugar bowl...........................20.00
Cock O'Morn, platter, Olympic...14.00
Colonial Lady, casserole & spoon set.................................25.00
Crayon Apples, batter jug..25.00
Dainty Flower, batter jug...28.00
Dainty Flower, swirl cup..10.00
Deco Dahlia, casserole, w/lid..36.00
Dogwood, plate, lunch..8.00
Donna, cake plate & lifter set..20.00
English Ivy, bowl, mixing..40.00
Forest Flower, plate, 6"...5.00
Gladiola, bowl, mixing...40.00
Green Blush, dresser tray, w/pk roses.................................20.00
Holly & Berries, plate, lunch...8.00
Ivy Vine, pie baker..25.00
Lovelace, cake lifter...13.00
Modern Tulip, jug, Modern Age, w/lid................................35.00
Old Carriages, plate, dinner...10.00
Pastel Tulip, casserole, w/lid...36.00
Petit Point, rolling pin...120.00
Provincial Tulip, cup & saucer..10.00
Red & Black Lines, teapot, Cameoware shape (squashed sides)....25.00
Red Apple, drips jar, Skyscraper..18.00
Republic, shaving mug, pastel roses....................................30.00
Rose, platter, Olympic..14.00
Rosebud, shakers, Skyscraper, pr..22.00
Shellridge, gravy boat, plain wht..20.00
Spanish Gold, plate, lunch...25.00
Sweet Pea, rolling pin..24.00
Vintage, platter..11.00
White Daisy, cup, wht w/yel int...5.00
Winter Asters, plate, dinner...15.00

Harlequin

Harlequin dinnerware, produced by the Homer Laughlin China Company of Newell, West Virginia, was introduced in 1938. It was a lightweight ware made in maroon, mauve blue, and spruce green, as well as all the Fiesta colors except ivory (see Fiesta). It was marketed exclusively by the Woolworth stores, who considered it to be their all-time bestseller. For this reason they contracted with Homer Laughlin to reissue Harlequin to commemorate their 100th anniversary in 1979. Although three of the original glazes were used in the reissue, the few serving pieces that were made were restyled, and collectors found the new line to be no threat to their investments.

The Harlequin animals, including a fish, lamb, cat, penguin, duck, and donkey, were made during the early 1940s, also for the dime-store trade. Today these are very desirable to collectors of Homer Laughlin china.

In the listings that follow, use the values designated 'high' for all colors other than turquoise and yellow. Unless priced, for medium green, double the 'high' values on all items other than flat items and small bowls. *The Collector's Encyclopedia of Fiesta* (Collector Books, 2001 values) by Sharon and Bob Huxford contains a more thorough study of this subject and includes specific pricing for many medium green examples.

Animals, maverick, gold trim	50.00
Animals, non-standard color	325.00
Animals, standard color	195.00
Ashtray, basketweave, high	60.00
Ashtray, basketweave, low	40.00
Ashtray, regular, high	53.00
Ashtray, regular, low	38.00
Ashtray/saucer, high	68.00
Ashtray/saucer, low	55.00
Bowl, '36s oatmeal; high	28.00
Bowl, '36s oatmeal; low	16.00
Bowl, '36s; high	40.00
Bowl, '36s; low	28.00
Bowl, cream soup; high	32.00
Bowl, cream soup; low	25.00
Bowl, cream soup; med gr, minimum value	900.00
Bowl, fruit; high, 5½"	11.00
Bowl, fruit; low, 5½"	8.00
Bowl, ind salad; high	42.00
Bowl, ind salad; low	28.00
Bowl, mixing; Kitchen Kraft, mauve bl, 8"	125.00
Bowl, mixing; Kitchen Kraft, red or lt gr, 6", ea	90.00
Bowl, mixing; Kitchen Kraft, yel, 10"	125.00
Bowl, nappy; high, 9"	40.00
Bowl, nappy; low, 9"	28.00
Bowl, oval baker, high	42.00
Bowl, oval baker, low	27.00
Butter dish, cobalt, ½-lb	300.00
Butter dish, high, ½-lb	135.00
Butter dish, low, ½-lb	115.00
Candle holders, high, pr	300.00
Candle holders, low, pr	250.00

Casserole, with lid, High, $160.00; Low, $95.00.

Creamer, high lip, any color, ea	135.00
Creamer, ind; high	35.00
Creamer, ind; low	20.00
Creamer, novelty, high	42.00
Creamer, novelty, low	28.00
Creamer, regular, high	20.00
Creamer, regular, low	14.00
Cup, demitasse; high	110.00
Cup, demitasse; low	42.00
Cup, lg, any color, ea	185.00
Cup, tea; high	11.00
Cup, tea; low	9.00
Egg cup, dbl, high	28.00
Egg cup, dbl, low	20.00
Egg cup, single, high	35.00

Egg cup, single, low	25.00
Marmalade, high	265.00
Marmalade, low	225.00
Nut dish, basketweave, high	20.00
Nut dish, basketweave, low	15.00
Perfume bottle, any color, ea	140.00
Pitcher, service water; high	105.00
Pitcher, service water; low	75.00
Pitcher, 22-oz jug, high	70.00
Pitcher, 22-oz jug, low	50.00
Pitcher, 22-oz jug, med gr	800.00
Plate, deep; high	30.00
Plate, deep; low	20.00
Plate, deep; med gr	90.00
Plate, high, 6"	5.50
Plate, high, 7"	8.00
Plate, high, 9"	14.00
Plate, high, 10"	40.00
Plate, low, 6"	4.00
Plate, low, 7"	6.00
Plate, low, 9"	10.00
Plate, low, 10"	24.00
Platter, high, 11"	27.00
Platter, high, 13"	34.00
Platter, low, 11"	20.00
Platter, low, 13"	24.00
Platter, med gr, 11"	210.00
Platter, med gr, 13"	300.00
Relish tray, mixed colors	335.00
Sauce boat, high	35.00
Sauce boat, low	22.00
Saucer, demitasse; high	30.00
Saucer, demitasse; low	18.00
Saucer, demitasse; med gr, minimum value	175.00
Saucer, high	4.00
Saucer, low	2.00
Shakers, high, pr	26.00
Shakers, low, pr	18.00
Sugar bowl, w/lid, high	32.00
Sugar bowl, w/lid, low	20.00
Sugar bowl, w/lid, med gr, minimum value	135.00
Syrup, red or yel	250.00
Syrup, spruce gr or mauve	340.00
Teapot, high	155.00
Teapot, low	90.00
Tumbler, car decal	65.00
Tumbler, high	58.00
Tumbler, low	45.00

Hatpin Holders

Most hatpin holders were made from 1860 to 1920 to coincide with the period during which hatpins were popularly in vogue. The taller types were required to house the long hatpins necessary to secure the large hats that were in style from 1890 to 1914. They were usually porcelain, either decorated by hand or by transfer with florals or scenics, although some were clever figurals. Glass examples are rare, and those of slag or carnival glass are especially valuable.

If you are interested in collecting or dealing in hatpins or hatpin holders, you will enjoy *Hatpins and Hatpin Holders* by Lillian Baker, with beautiful color illustrations and current market values. For information concerning the International Club for Collectors of Hatpins and Hatpin Holders, see the Clubs, Newsletters, and Catalogs section of the Directory. Our advisor for this category is Robert Larsen; he is listed in the Directory under Nebraska. (SASE required.)

Bsk, bear & tower form, Schafer & Vater mk, 4¾x3½" **325.00**

Carnival glass Butterfly and Berry hatpin holders, made in two colors: blue (more common) and marigold, attributed to the Fenton Glass Company, from $1,800.00 to $2,000.00 each. (Photo courtesy Robert Larsen)

Carnival glass, Grape & Cable, purple, 7x2½" **295.00**
China, dbl-face, lady 1 side/man on other, mk............................**425.00**
China, floral, hexagonal w/attached trinket box, RS Prussia mk ...**650.00**
China, mc roses, artist sgn, Bavaria **225.00**
China, windmill scene, bl & wht export, mk Japan, 4" **225.00**
Chocolate glass, emb florals, ftd, 7⅛x2⅝" **700.00**
Glass, Daisy & Button, clear, silver top w/pinholes, rare, 8" **375.00**
Moriage, gold butterflies on wht, Nippon mk, 5⅛x2¾" **250.00**
Pottery, brn shaded, H Richards, London, ca 1890....................**175.00**
Pottery, City of York crest, souvenir, Goss, 3½x2½" **275.00**
Royal Bayreuth, clover figural, bl mk......................................**900.00**
Royal Bayreuth, Nouveau lady figural, bl mk, 4½"..................**1,300.00**
Schafer & Vater, bl jasper, Kewpies, sgn O'Neill, 4"..................**900.00**
Silver, etched & eng, 16-hole, unmk, 1880s, 5½x2¾" **275.00**
Silver w/cherub figure at side, plush cushion, unmk, 4x2¾" **350.00**
Sterling golf bag form, 2 putters form legs, mk, 1895, 3" **375.00**

Hatpins

A hatpin was used to securely fasten a hat to the hair and head of the wearer. Hatpins, measuring from 4" to 12" in length, were worn from approximately 1850 to 1920. During the Art Deco period, hatpins became ornaments rather than the decorative functional jewels that they had been. The hatpin period reached its zenith in 1913 just prior to World War I, which brought about a radical change in women's head-dress and fashion. About that time, women began to scorn the bonnet and adopt 'the hat' as a symbol of their equality. The hatpin was made of every natural and manufactured element in a myriad of designs that challenge the imagination. They were contrived to serve every fashion need and complement the milliner's art. Collectors often concentrate on a specific type: hand-painted porcelains, sterling silver, commemoratives, sporting activities, carnival glass, Art Nouveau and/or Art Deco designs, Victorian gothics with mounted stones, exquisite rhinestones, engraved and brass-mounted escutcheon heads, gold and gems, or simply primitive types made in the Victorian parlor. Some collectors prefer the long pin-shanks while others select only those on tremblants or nodder-type pin-shanks.

If you are interested in collecting or dealing in hatpins, see the information in the Hatpin Holders introduction concerning a reference book and a national collectors' club. For further study we recommend *Hatpins and Hatpin Holders* by Lillian Baker, available at your local book-store or from Collector Books. Our advisor for this category is Robert Larsen; he is listed in the Directory under Nebraska. (SASE required.)

Key: cab — cabochon

Bakelite, marbled red w/wht band & navy balls, 2¾" **600.00**
Carnival glass, butterfly, gr irid..**275.00**
Celluloid, ivory 1¾" scallop shell, ca 1920 ....**125.00**
Celluloid, pierced or cut, Deco 2-mold design, 1920s.................**125.00**
Celluloid molded 2½" elephant head, ca 1920, on 5½" pin........**200.00**
Faux jade, cabachon cut, gilt brass Egyptian-style mt **230.00**
French ivory w/marbleized insert, 2¾" head, 1910s **175.00**
Gilt brass Egyptian decor w/faux topaz stone **275.00**
Gilt brass scarab w/pate-de-verre insert, hinged, 2¼" **425.00**
Gilt mt w/¾" oval aquamarine, ca 1895, on 8" wht pin **200.00**
Peacock-eye glass in sterling cage, Chas Homer **275.00**
Pk slag 1⅝" glass center w/gilt mt, 1900s, on wht pin **200.00**
Plastic, HP Art Deco pattern w/2¾" head, ca 1920....................**175.00**
Plastic ⅞" molded rose, Art Nouveau mt, 1900s, on wht pin **225.00**
Plique-a-jour butterfly, bl & gr, 1½" wingspan, 6½" shank **900.00**
Silver, oxidized lotus w/faux dmn & ruby.................................**275.00**
Sterling, thistle decor, mk Charles Horner................................**285.00**
Sterling, thistle w/faux topaz stone, English hallmk **275.00**

Haviland

The Haviland China Company was organized in 1840 by David Haviland, a New York china importer. His search for a pure white, non-porous porcelain led him to Limoges, France, where natural deposits of suitable clay had already attracted numerous china manufacturers. The fine china he produced there was translucent and meticulously decorated, with each piece fired in an individual sagger.

It has been estimated that as many as 60,000 chinaware patterns were designed, each piece marked with one of several company back-stamps. 'H. & Co.' was used until 1890 when a law was enacted making it necessary to include the country of origin. Various marks have been used since that time including 'Haviland, France'; 'Haviland & Co. Limoges'; and 'Decorated by Haviland & Co.' Various associations with family members over the years have resulted in changes in management as well as company name. In 1892 Theodore Haviland left the firm to start his own business. Some of his ware was marked 'Mont Mery.' Later logos included a horseshoe, a shield, and various uses of his initials and name. In 1941 this branch moved to the United States. Wares produced here are marked 'Theodore Haviland, N.Y.' or 'Made In America.'

Though it is their dinnerware lines for which they are most famous, during the 1880s and 1890s they also made exquisite art pottery using a technique of underglaze slip decoration called Barbotine, which had been invented by Ernest Chaplet. In 1885 Haviland bought the formula and hired Chaplet to oversee its production. The technique involved mixing heavy white clay slip with pigments to produce a compound of the same consistency as oil paints. The finished product actually resembled oil paintings of the period, the texture achieved through the application of the heavy medium to the clay body in much the same manner as an artist would apply paint to his canvas. Primarily the body used with this method was a low-fired faience, though they also produced stoneware. Numbers in the listings below refer to pattern books by Arlene Schleiger. For further information we recommend Mary Frank Gaston's *Encyclopedia of Limoges Porcelain, Third Edition* (the first two editions are out of print), which offers examples and marks of the Haviland Company.

Basket, rtcl bowl on ped ft w/magenta transfer & gold, Theo **450.00**
Bowl, roses form border w/gold, 1 gold hdl, H&Co, 9¼"...............**55.00**
Bowl, sm floral sprays form border w/gold, hdls, w/lid, H&Co, 10" sq..**200.00**
Bowl, vegetable; Old Blackberry w/gold, rectangular, w/lid, H&Co **350.00**
Chocolate set, 2-tone gold band emb w/classic designs, pot+4 c/s **250.00**
Coffee set, floral, mc on wht w/bl bands, H&Co, 9" pot+cr/sug....**600.00**

Coffeepot, floral sprays, anchor design w/braid hdl, H&Co, 9½" ..325.00
Coffeepot, roses w/pk flowers & brushed gold, H&Co, 9¾"........325.00
Compote, rose-colored bands on wht, Fabrique Par... mk, 1850s, 9" dia...650.00
Cup & saucer, bl floral w/gold, Napkin Fold shape, H&Co, from $75 to ...90.00
Cup & saucer, bouillon; Spanish Ware-style HP florals, Limoges, 1870s....150.00
Fish set, HP fish & seaweed w/gold, late 19th C, platter+12 rnd plates......450.00
Leaf bowl, red fruit, beetle & rabbit w/gold, Theo R Davis, 12" ..6,750.00
Pitcher, Oriental flowers/appl/pnt/cvd on bsk, #59, 10⅞" 800.00
Plate, Autumn Leaf, H&Co, 10", from $35 to 45.00
Plate, dinner; simple gold trim at inner & outer borders, Theo 50.00
Plate, fish & water scene (Oriental-style art), bl rim, H&Co, 8½"..235.00
Plate, floral center, lt pk border, H&Co mk, 9½", from $75 to...100.00
Plate, flower bouquets at random w/brushed gold, Theo, 10", $60 to....75.00
Plate, game birds, yel, teal or wine border, H&Co, 9", from $140 to ..165.00
Plate, mythological scene, Kauffman, lav border w/gold, 10" 375.00
Plate, oyster; 5 shell sections w/pk flowers & gold, H&Co, 7¼".235.00
Plate, rabbit & dog in woods, lt pk border w/gold, Theo, 9¼" 215.00
Platter, flower bouquets at random w/brushed gold, Theo, 12x7" ..165.00
Platter, pk floral, Ranson shape, H&Co, 13½", from $175 to.....225.00
Sauce tureen, floral w/gold, attached tray, w/lid, H&Co 155.00
Tea set, floral transfer w/gold, Ivy mold, H&Co mk, 3-pc, from $425 to....475.00
Tea set, Wedding Ring, H&Co mk, 3-pc, from $375 to 425.00
Teapot, bird & leaves, Basket-Weave mold, H&Co, 6", from $240 to..265.00
Teapot, brn flowers w/yel & gold, sponged gold hdl, H&Co, from $225 to..250.00
Vase, flowers on rust to wht, gold hdls, Marseille form, H&Co, 11" ..750.00
Vase, village scene w/figures, Morand, Limoges, S6, 3" 800.00

Hawkes

Thomas Hawkes established his factory in Corning, New York, in 1880. He developed many beautiful patterns of cut glass, two of which were awarded the Grand Prize at the Paris Exposition in 1889. By the end of the century, his company was renowned for the finest in cut glass production. The company logo was a trefoil form enclosing a hawk in each of the two bottom lobes with a fleur-de-lis in the center. With the exception of some of the very early designs, all Hawkes was signed. (Our values are for signed pieces.)

Bottle, vinegar; eng floral, sterling top, Pat 1916, 7½" 50.00
Bowl, allover eng, bulbous, ped ft, 5x7½" 120.00
Bowl, Chrysanthemum, 4½x10"...500.00
Bowl, Gladys, low, 8", pr 495.00
Bowl, Greek Key rim, 9⅜" 140.00
Butter pat, Star & T'print 40.00
Chalice, blazing stars w/dmn-faceted amber centers, 7¾" 160.00
Compote, Teardrop, notched prism stem, 7½x6", pr 550.00
Cordial, Middlesex, 3½"..80.00
Decanter, Gladys, orig faceted stopper, 11" 550.00
Dresser set, cut floral, 2 boxes+hair receiver+bottle+jar+tray .3,400.00

Inkstand, Gravic, deep cut and polished scrolls, central cavity with metal hinged lid of copper with silver steerhead crest, 4¼x5", $1,725.00.

Pitcher, cider; Brunswick, 6½" 475.00
Pitcher, Hobstar & Fan, 7½" 200.00
Plate, Verre de Soie, eng bows & swags, mk, ⅞x8"......................115.00
Tray, Holland, 13" dia 900.00
Vase, amber w/eng vintage, rnd disk base, 11", NM 300.00
Vase, amethyst, eng floral, deep ribbing, sterling ft, 12x4" 350.00
Vase, Navarre, trumpet form, 10" 400.00

Head Vases

Vases modeled as heads of lovely ladies, delightful children, clowns, Madonnas — even some animals — were once popular as flower containers. Today they represent a growing area of collector interest. Most of them were imported from Japan, although some American potteries produced a few as well.

For more information, we recommend *Head Vases, Identification and Values*, by Kathleen Cole; and *The World of Head Vase Planters* by Mike Posgay and Ian Warner.

Animal, #38, poodle head in bonnet w/neck bow, pk, gold trim, 6" ..65.00
Animal, #39, girl pig w/flower on head, hoof to snout, pk, 6" 65.00
Animal, Lefton #H1953, horse head, wht, 6"................................30.00
Baby, Enesco, girl w/kitten, bow in hair, 5½" 45.00
Baby, Enesco #2185, girl in bonnet w/phone to ear, pearl necklace, 5" ..45.00
Baby, Inarco #E4392, Hello Gran'pa! lettered on boy's bib, 6"......45.00
Baby, Relpo #K1866, blond girl in bonnet w/bow on top, 7".........65.00
Child, Geo Z Lefton #50416, wide eyes, bow/rose in hair, 6" 30.00
Child, Inarco #E2183, girl w/pigtails & bonnet on bk of head, 5½" ..45.00
Child, Inarco #E3155, Bavarian boy, eyes closed, 5½" 40.00
Child, Japan, girl holding gift, hat w/daisies, gold trim, 5½" 50.00
Child, Napcoware #C7094, boy w/neckerchief, brn hair, 4"..........38.00
Child, Reliable Glassware #K679B, girl w/open hand to face/bonnet, 6" ...45.00
Child, Relpo, boy in stocking cap/high ruffled collar, 5½" 45.00
Clown, Inarco #E5071, wht face w/red nose & mouth, sm blk hat, 4½"...40.00
Clown, Inarco #E6730, wht face, red hair, bl/yel hat & collar, 5½"..50.00
Clown, Napcoware #1988, cartoon features, lg neck bow, 4¾".....45.00
Geisha girl, Lee Wards (paper label), blk & wht w/gold trim, 5" ..50.00
Geisha girl, unmk, open fan to chin, gold eyelashes, 4¾" 45.00
Harlequin man or woman, Japan, blk masks, ruffled collars, 5½", ea 65.00
Lady, Acme Ware, pk bonnet w/bl chin bow, pk roses at shoulders, 6"...50.00
Lady, Atlas, eyes open, hat w/bow, puffy sleeves, updo, heavy gold, 6" ...50.00
Lady, Enesco, middle part w/upswept curls/lg bow in bk, 7½" 250.00
Lady, Inarco, #E-1069, updo w/gold crown, wht bodice/gold dots, 10"..300.00
Lady, Inarco #E1062, gloved hand w/closed fan to face, blond curls, 6" ..60.00
Lady, Inarco #E1062, updo w/gold tiara, blk bodice, pearls, 6"......75.00
Lady, Inarco #E190 E/L, hand to chin, blond, blk hat w/tulle, 8½"..250.00
Lady, Inarco #E2104, gloved hand to chin, wht/gold rose in hair, 7"..125.00
Lady, Inarco #E2104, hand to chin, hair over eye, 7" 250.00
Lady, Inarco #E2966, updo/bangs, blk scalloped bodice, eyes open, 11"..450.00
Lady, Inarco #E5626, hand to mouth, curls/bow, heart pendant, 7"....500.00
Lady, Japan, hand to cheek, updo w/hat, allover bl w/gold trim, 6½"....45.00
Lady, Lefton's #2251, gloved hand to chin, blond flip, picture hat, 6"....95.00
Lady, Lefton's #624, gloved hand up, eyes open, brn flip, 5½" 65.00
Lady, Napco #C1775B, cuffed hand to chin, brimmed hat w/bow, 7¼" .75.00
Lady, Napco #C3959A, polka-dot hat bow, upturned collar, 5½".50.00
Lady, Napco #C4553A, cut-out bangs, wide-brimmed hat, 6".......50.00
Lady, Napcoware #C5677, hand to mouth, beauty mk by eye, hat, 5½" .45.00
Lady, Napcoware #6986, updo/bow, bodice/high ruffled collar, 9"..........275.00
Lady, Parma #A219, frosted side flip, shoulder bows, eyes open, 8½" 300.00
Lady, Relpo #A1129, gloved hands up, floral pillbox hat, eyes open, 5"..55.00
Lady, Relpo #K1335, Colonial, wht curls, gold trim, eyes open, 8"........350.00
Lady, Rubens #4135, hooded blond head, turtleneck, 5½"............65.00
Lady, Rubens #495, gloved hands clasped at chin, flat-brim hat, 5¾"...65.00

Lady, Rubens #501, head turned, yel updo/cross braid, 6½" 50.00
Lady, unmk, Art Deco-style w/head bk, lg hat, allover tan, 9¼".150.00
Lady, unmk, glamour girl pose, wht w/bl airbrushing gold trim, 5¼".....20.00
Lady, unmk, wht hat w/polka-dot chin bow & trim, head tilted, 5½"..65.00
Lady, Vcagco, hooded head, 2 wht/gold daisies w/pearls, 5½" 70.00
Religious, Floret/Japan, Virgin Mary praying, 6" 22.50
Religious, Relpo #C1881, nun w/eyes closed, pale bl, 5" 28.00
Religious, unmk, monk w/child's features praying, 6" 45.00
Teen girl, Inarco #E1064, lt gr tam/blk hair, cowl collar, 4½" 45.00
Teen girl, Inarco #E2967, blond flip w/lt bl band, eyes open, 5½" ...65.00
Teen girl, Inarco #E6211, wide-eyed, high ruffled collar, 5" 55.00
Teen girl, Inarco #E6211, windswept hair, turtleneck sweater, 5"...55.00
Teen girl, Japan, mod hat w/bill & pom-pon, ponytails, turtleneck, 6"....60.00
Teen girl, Japan, short flip/bangs/bow, collar/bare shoulders, 5½" .55.00
Teen girl, Napcoware #C8493, hair bow, Peter Pan collar, 5½" 65.00
Teen girl, Rubens #4135, pigtails/flower, high collar w/2 buttons, 6"...75.00
Teen girl, Sonsco, blond flip, front hair bow, bl bodice w/gold, 4" ...35.00
Teen girl, unmk, glasses on top of head, 2 ponytails, 7½" 350.00
Teen girl, unmk, leopard-print hat w/bill, blond flip, 5" 55.00
Uncle Sam, unmk, allover gr, 6½" 30.00

Heisey

A.H. Heisey began his long career at the King Glass Company of Pittsburgh. He later joined the Ripley Glass Company which soon became Geo. Duncan and Sons. After Duncan's death Heisey became half-owner in partnership with his brother-in-law, James Duncan. In 1895 he built his own factory in Newark, Ohio, initiating production in 1896 and continuing until Christmas of 1957. At that time Imperial Glass Corporation bought some of the molds. After 1968 they removed the old 'Diamond H' from any they put into use. In 1985 HCA purchased all of Imperial's Heisey molds with the exception of the Old Williamsburg line.

During their highly successful period of production, Heisey made fine handcrafted tableware with simple, yet graceful designs. Early pieces were not marked. After November 1901 the glassware was marked either with the 'Diamond H' or a paper label. Blown ware is often marked on the stem, never on the bowl or foot.

For more information we recommend *Collector's Encyclopedia of Heisey Glass, 1925 – 1938*, by Neila Bredehoft and *Heisey Glass, 1896 – 1957* by Neila and Tom Bredehoft.

For information concerning Heisey Collectors of America, see the Clubs, Newsletters, and Catalogs section of the Directory. See also Glass Animals.

Cabochon, crystal, bowl, dessert; #1951, 4½" 4.00
Cabochon, crystal, bowl, floral/salad; #1951, 13" 18.00
Cabochon, crystal, candy, #1951, w/lid, 6¼" 38.00
Cabochon, crystal, plate, sandwich; #1951, 14" 18.00
Cabochon, crystal, stem, oyster cocktail; #6091, 3-oz 4.00
Cabochon, crystal, sugar bowl, #1951, w/lid.....................14.00
Cabochon, crystal, tumbler, beverage; #6092, blown, 10-oz 8.00
Charter Oak, crystal, comport, #3362, ftd, 7" 50.00
Charter Oak, crystal, plate, salad; #1246, Acorn & Leaves, 6".......5.00
Charter Oak, gr, candle holder, #130, Acorn, 1-light...............135.00
Charter Oak, marigold, comport, #3362, low ft, 6".................100.00
Charter Oak, marigold, tumbler, #3362, flat, 12-oz..............35.00
Charter Oak, orchid, stem, goblet; #3362, high ft, 8-oz.............95.00
Charter Oak, pk, candlestick, #129, Tricorn, 3-light, 5".............90.00
Charter Oak, pk, plate, dinner; #1246, Acorn & Leaves, 10½"....45.00
Chintz, crystal, bowl, cream soup.................................18.00
Chintz, crystal, bowl, floral; ftd, hdls, 8½" 35.00
Chintz, crystal, pitcher, dolphin ft, 3-pt 200.00

Chintz, cup and saucer, crystal, $18.00. (Photo courtesy Gene Florence)

Chintz, crystal, sugar bowl, 3 dolphin ft 20.00
Chintz, yel, bowl, mint; ftd, 6" 32.00
Chintz, yel, comport, oval, 7" 85.00
Chintz, yel, ice bucket, ftd 135.00
Chintz, yel, plate, dinner; sq, 10½" 85.00
Chintz, yel, tray, celery; 13" 45.00
Crystolite, crystal, ashtray/coaster, rnd, 4" 8.00
Crystolite, crystal, bottle, syrup; w/drip & cut top 135.00
Crystolite, crystal, bowl, preserve; hdls, 6" 20.00
Crystolite, crystal, bowl, salad; rnd, 10" 50.00
Crystolite, crystal, candlestick, 2-light 35.00
Crystolite, crystal, cigarette holder, oval 25.00
Crystolite, crystal, hurricane block, 1-light, sq 40.00
Crystolite, crystal, mayonnaise, hdld, oval, 6" 40.00
Crystolite, crystal, plate, coupe; 7½" 40.00
Crystolite, crystal, plate, shell torte; 13" 100.00
Crystolite, crystal, plate, torte; 14" 50.00
Crystolite, crystal, sugar bowl, regular..........................30.00
Crystolite, crystal, tumbler, #5003, pressed, 8-oz................60.00
Empress, Alexandrite, cup..115.00
Empress, Alexandrite, tray, celery; 10" 150.00
Empress, cobalt, candlestick, dolphin ft, 6" 260.00
Empress, cobalt, plate, 8".......................................70.00
Empress, gr, bowl, nappy; 8" 45.00
Empress, gr, plate, 7"...17.00
Empress, gr, stem, saucer champagne; 4-oz 60.00
Empress, gr, vase, flared, 8" 190.00
Empress, pk, marmalade, dolphin ft, w/lid........................200.00
Empress, pk, plate, hdls, sq, 13" 40.00
Empress, pk or yel, bowl, cream soup...........................30.00
Empress, pk or yel, saucer, AD..................................10.00
Empress, yel, bowl, relish; triplex, 10" 55.00
Empress, yel, plate, 4½"...15.00
Greek Key, crystal, bowl, almond; ftd, ind.......................45.00
Greek Key, crystal, bowl, nappy; 9"..............................70.00
Greek Key, crystal, bowl, str side, low ft, 7"....................90.00
Greek Key, crystal, candy, w/lid, 1-lb..........................170.00
Greek Key, crystal, coaster......................................20.00
Greek Key, crystal, jar, pickle; w/knob lid 160.00
Greek Key, crystal, plate, 4½"...................................20.00
Greek Key, crystal, puff box, #3, w/lid..........................175.00
Greek Key, crystal, stem, sherry; 2-oz..........................200.00
Greek Key, crystal, tray, oblong, 13".............................260.00
Greek Key, crystal, water bottle.................................220.00
Ipswich, Alexandrite, stem, goblet; knob in stem, 10-oz 750.00
Ipswich, crystal, bowl, finger; w/underplate......................40.00
Ipswich, crystal, tumbler, straight rim, flat bottom, 10-oz........70.00
Ipswich, gr, oil bottle, ftd, w/#86 stopper, 2-oz.................300.00
Ipswich, pk, tumbler, soda; ftd, 5-oz.............................45.00
Ipswich, pk, vase, candlestick centerpc; ftd, A prisms, complete ...300.00
Ipswich, yel, candy jar, w/lid, ½-lb.............................300.00
Ipswich, yel, plate, sq, 8".......................................55.00
Lariat, crystal, basket, bonbon; 7½" 100.00
Lariat, crystal, bowl, nappy; 7".................................20.00

Lariat, crystal, bowl, relish; 2-hdld, oblong, 11" 30.00
Lariat, crystal, cigarette box 55.00
Lariat, crystal, cup 20.00
Lariat, crystal, oil bottle, hdld, w/#133 stopper, 4-oz 180.00
Lariat, crystal, plate, cookie; 11" 35.00
Lariat, crystal, shakers, pr 200.00
Lariat, crystal, stem, sherbet; low, 6-oz 10.00
Lariat, crystal, stem, wine; pressed, 3½-oz 24.00
Lariat, crystal, vase, swung 135.00
Lodestar, Dawn, ashtray 95.00
Lodestar, Dawn, bowl, 8" 65.00
Lodestar, Dawn, candlestick, 1-light centerpc, 2" H, pr 130.00
Lodestar, Dawn, creamer, w/hdl 90.00
Lodestar, Dawn, relish, 3-part, 7½" 60.00
Lodestar, Dawn, vase, #1626, 8" 160.00
Minuet, crystal, bowl, relish; 5 o'clock, 2-part, 11" 80.00
Minuet, crystal, candlestick, #112, 1-light.....................................35.00
Minuet, crystal, comport, #5010, 5½" 40.00
Minuet, crystal, ice bucket, dolphin ft 160.00
Minuet, crystal, plate, luncheon; 8" 30.00
Minuet, crystal, plate, sandwich; #1511, Toujours, 15" 65.00
Minuet, crystal, stem, water; #5010, 9-oz 35.00
Minuet, crystal, sugar bowl, #1511, Toujours 60.00
Minuet, crystal, tumbler, tea; #5010, 12-oz 60.00
Minuet, crystal, vase, #4196, 8" 95.00
New Era, crystal, bottle, rye; w/stopper 155.00
New Era, crystal, cup, AD 70.00
New Era, crystal, relish, 3-part, 13" 32.00
New Era, crystal, stem, goblet; 10-oz 20.00
New Era, crystal, tumbler, soda; ftd, 8-oz 15.00
Octagon, crystal, basket, #500, 5" 100.00
Octagon, crystal, plate, 10½" 17.00
Octagon, Dawn, tray, variety; #500, 4-part, 12" 350.00
Octagon, Marigold, ice tub, #500 ....150.00
Octagon, Orchid, cup, #1231 ....35.00
Octagon, Orchid, tray, celery; 12" 50.00
Octagon, pk, bowl, jelly; #1229, 5½" 30.00
Octagon, pk, gr or Orchid, cheese dish, #1229, hdls, 6" 15.00
Octagon, pk, plate, 14" 25.00
Octagon, pk, yel or gr, tray, #500, oblong, 6" 15.00
Octagon, yel, bowl, comport; #1229, ftd, 8" 35.00
Octagon, yel or gr, saucer, #1231 ....10.00
Old Colony, yel, bowl, finger; #4075 ....15.00
Old Colony, yel, bowl, nappy; dolphin ft, 7½" 70.00
Old Colony, yel, creamer, ind 40.00
Old Colony, yel, plate, bouillon 15.00
Old Colony, yel, plate, rnd or sq, 7" 20.00
Old Colony, yel, plate, sandwich; hdls, rnd, 12" 70.00
Old Colony, yel, stem, claret; #3380, 4-oz 40.00
Old Colony, yel, stem, sherbet; #3390, 6-oz 25.00
Old Colony, yel, tray, celery; 10" 30.00
Old Colony, yel, tumbler, bar; #3380, ftd, 2-oz...............................20.00
Old Sandwich, cobalt, decanter, w/#98 stopper, 1-pt.....................425.00
Old Sandwich, cobalt, tumbler, bar; ground bottom, 1½-oz........100.00
Old Sandwich, crystal, mug, beer; 12-oz...35.00
Old Sandwich, crystal, parfait, 4½-oz 15.00
Old Sandwich, crystal, pilsner, 10-oz 16.00
Old Sandwich, crystal, tumbler, low ft, 10-oz 15.00
Old Sandwich, gr, stem, low ft, 10-oz 40.00
Old Sandwich, pk, bowl, finger..50.00
Old Sandwich, pk, plate, sq, 7" 27.00
Old Sandwich, pk or yel, stem, wine; 2½-oz 45.00
Old Sandwich, yel, bowl, floral; ftd, oval, 12" 70.00
Orchid, crystal, ashtray, 3" 30.00

Orchid, crystal, bow, gardenia; Queen Ann, 9" 65.00
Orchid, crystal, bowl, floral; ftd, 11"..115.00
Orchid, crystal, bowl, jelly; Queen Ann, hdls, 6" 37.50
Orchid, crystal, bowl, nappy; Queen Ann, 8" 70.00
Orchid, crystal, bowl, salad; 7" 60.00
Orchid, crystal, bowl, shallow, rolled edge, 11" 70.00
Orchid, crystal, butter dish, Waverly, w/lid, 6" 175.00
Orchid, crystal, candlestick, Waverly, 2-light..................................65.00
Orchid, crystal, cocktail shaker, #4225, 1-pt 275.00

Orchid, comport, crystal, low foot, 6" diameter, $55.00.

Orchid, crystal, ice bucket, Waverly, hdls 450.00
Orchid, crystal, mayonnaise, hdl, divided, 6½" 65.00
Orchid, crystal, plate, sandwich; hdld, rnd, 12" 70.00
Orchid, crystal, stem, claret; #5022 or #5025, 4½-oz.....................145.00
Orchid, crystal, vase, crimped top, 6" 125.00
Orchid, crystal, vase, 12"...395.00
Plantation, crystal, bowl, gardenia; ftd, 11½" 140.00
Plantation, crystal, bowl, relish; 4-part, rnd, 8" 70.00
Plantation, crystal, butter dish, oblong, w/lid, ¼-lb......................115.00
Plantation, crystal, candlestick, 1-light 100.00
Plantation, crystal, candy box, flat bottom, w/lid, 7" L 180.00
Plantation, crystal, cup 40.00
Plantation, crystal, plate, salad; 8" 35.00
Plantation, crystal, stem, claret; blown or pressed, 4½-oz..............65.00
Plantation, crystal, tumbler, pressed, 10-oz....................................95.00
Plantation, crystal, vase, flared, ftd, 9" 140.00
Pleat & Panel, crystal, bowl, chow chow; 4" 6.00
Pleat & Panel, crystal, cup 7.00
Pleat & Panel, crystal, plate, 6" 4.00
Pleat & Panel, crystal, stem, saucer champagne; 5-oz 5.00
Pleat & Panel, gr, compotier, high ftd, w/lid, 5" 80.00
Pleat & Panel, gr, plate, sandwich; 14" 40.00
Pleat & Panel, gr, vase, 8" 100.00
Pleat & Panel, pk, bowl, lemon; w/lid, 5" 45.00
Pleat & Panel, pk, pitcher, w/ice lip, 3-pt 140.00
Pleat & Panel, pk, plate, luncheon; 8" 12.50
Pleat & Panel, pk, sugar bowl, w/lid, hotel sz 30.00
Provincial, crystal, ashtray, sq, 3" 12.50
Provincial, crystal, cigarette box, w/lid 60.00
Provincial, crystal, mustard 110.00
Provincial, crystal, plate, cheese; ftd, 5" 20.00
Provincial, crystal, stem, sherbet/champagne; 5-oz 10.00
Provincial, crystal, stem, 10-oz 20.00
Provincial, crystal, tumbler, iced tea; flat, 13" 20.00
Provincial, Limelight Green, bowl, nappy; 5½" 40.00
Provincial, Limelight Green, creamer, ftd 95.00
Provincial, Limelight Green, plate, luncheon; 8"..............................50.00
Queen Ann, crystal, ashtray 30.00
Queen Ann, crystal, bowl, jelly; ftd, 2-hdld, 6"...............................15.00
Queen Ann, crystal, bowl, nappy; 8" 25.00
Queen Ann, crystal, bowl, pickle/olive; 2-part, 13" 20.00
Queen Ann, crystal, comport, oval, 7" 35.00

Queen Ann, crystal, oil bottle, 4-oz................................40.00
Queen Ann, crystal, plate, 12".......................................25.00
Queen Ann, crystal, plate, 7"...8.00
Queen Ann, crystal, saucer, sq.......................................5.00
Queen Ann, crystal, stem, sherbet; 4-oz........................15.00
Queen Ann, crystal, tray, celery; 10"...........................12.00
Queen Ann, crystal, vase, flared, 8".............................55.00
Ridgeleigh, crsytal, tray, oblong, 10½"..........................40.00
Ridgeleigh, crystal, ashtray, sq.....................................10.00
Ridgeleigh, crystal, bowl, floral; oval, 12"....................55.00
Ridgeleigh, crystal, bowl, jelly; hdls, 6" 30.00
Ridgeleigh, crystal, bowl, nut; 2-part, ind....................20.00
Ridgeleigh, crystal, cheese, hdls, 6"............................22.00
Ridgeleigh, crystal, comport, flared, low ftd, 6"...........25.00
Ridgeleigh, crystal, plate, sq, 7".................................26.00

Ridgleigh, three-part relish, crystal, 11", $45.00.

Ridgeleigh, crystal, salt dip, ind 13.00
Ridgeleigh, crystal, stem, cocktail; blown, 3½-oz.........35.00
Ridgeleigh, crystal, tumbler, soda; blown, 8-oz...........40.00
Rose, crystal, bowl, finger; #3309..............................110.00
Rose, crystal, bowl, floral; Waverly shape, 11" 70.00
Rose, crystal, bowl, jelly; Waverly shape, ftd, 6½" 45.00
Rose, crystal, candlestick, #112, 1-light......................45.00
Rose, crystal, candy, Waverly shape, ftd, w/lid, 5".....195.00
Rose, crystal, cigarette holder, #4035 ....125.00
Rose, crystal, cup, Waverly shape 55.00
Rose, crystal, oil, Waverly shape, ftd, 3-oz 185.00
Rose, crystal, saucer, Waverly shape 10.00
Rose, crystal, stem, cordial; #5072, 1-oz 150.00
Saturn, crystal, ashtray 10.00
Saturn, crystal, bowl, pickle; 7"..................................35.00
Saturn, crystal, bowl, salad; 11".................................140.00
Saturn, crystal, creamer 25.00
Saturn, crystal, oil bottle, 3-oz...................................55.00
Saturn, crystal, stem, saucer champagne; 6-oz 10.00
Saturn, crystal, tray, tidbit; 2 sides turned as fan 25.00
Saturn, Zircon or Limelight Green, bowl, finger............65.00
Saturn, Zircon or Limelight Green, marmalade, w/lid.....500.00
Saturn, Zircon or Limelight Green, shakers, pr............550.00
Saturn, Zircon or Limelight Green, vase, 10½" 260.00
Stanhope, crystal, ashtray, ind.....................................25.00
Stanhope, crystal, candy box, w/ or w/o rnd knob, w/lid, rnd......180.00
Stanhope, crystal, jelly dish, w/ or w/o rnd knob, hdl, 3-pt, 6"......25.00
Stanhope, crystal, stem, cocktail; #4083, pressed, 3½-oz...............25.00
Stanhope, crystal, stem, goblet; pressed, 9-oz 45.00
Stanhope, crystal, tumbler, soda; #4083, 8-oz.............22.50
Twist, Alexandrite, bowl, nasturtium; rnd, 8" 450.00
Twist, crystal, baker, oval, 9" 25.00
Twist, crystal, plate, ground bottom, 8"........................7.00

Twist, crystal, tumbler, iced tea; ftd, 12-oz...................20.00
Twist, Marigold, bowl, floral; 4-ftd, oval, 12" 90.00
Twist, Marigold or yel, tray, celery; 10" 40.00
Twist, pk, bowl, nut; ind...25.00
Twist, pk, plate, relish; 3-part, 13"..............................17.00
Twist, pk or gr, bowl, low ftd, 8"................................80.00
Twist, pk or gr, stem, wine; 2-block stem, 2½-oz.........50.00
Twist, yel, oil bottle, w/#78 stopper, 4-oz...................90.00
Victorian, crystal, candlestick, 2-light........................110.00
Victorian, crystal, creamer..30.00
Victorian, crystal, oil bottle, 3-oz...............................65.00
Victorian, crystal, plate, 8" 35.00
Victorian, crystal, relish, 3-part, 11" 50.00
Victorian, crystal, stem, oyster cocktail; 5-oz...............20.00
Victorian, crystal, tray, celery; 12" 40.00
Victorian, crystal, vase, 4"..50.00
Waverly, crystal, bowl, fruit; 9" 30.00
Waverly, crystal, bowl, lemon; w/lid, oval, 6"..............45.00
Waverly, crystal, box, chocolate; w/lid, 5"...................80.00
Waverly, crystal, candle holder, 2-light........................40.00
Waverly, crystal, cheese dish, ftd, 5½"........................20.00
Waverly, crystal, creamer & sugar bowl, ind, w/tray......50.00
Waverly, crystal, plate, luncheon; 8"............................10.00
Waverly, crystal, plate, sandwich; 14".........................35.00
Waverly, crystal, stem, sherbet/champagne; #5019, 5½-oz.............9.00
Waverly, crystal, vase, violet; 3½"...............................60.00
Yeoman, crystal, bowl, finger.......................................5.00
Yeoman, crystal, plate, soup; 8"...................................9.00
Yeoman, crystal, tumbler, tea; 12-oz.............................5.00
Yeoman, gr, stem sherbet; 5-oz.....................................9.00
Yeoman, Marigold, plate, 7"...22.00
Yeoman, Orchid, cup, AD..50.00
Yeoman, Orchid, sugar bowl, w/lid...............................70.00
Yeoman, pk, bowl, lemon; w/lid, rnd, 5".......................60.00
Yeoman, pk, platter, oval, 12" 17.00
Yeoman, pk, yel or gr, cologne bottle, w/stopper..........160.00
Yeoman, pk or yel, bowl, vegetable; 2-hdls, w/lid, 9"....60.00

Herend

Herend, Hungary, was the center of a thriving pottery industry as early as the mid-1800s. Decorative items as well as tablewares were made in keeping with the styles of the times. One of the factories located in this area was founded by Moritz Fisher, who often marked his wares with a cojoined MF. Items described in the following listings may be marked simply Herend, indicating the city, or with a manufacturer's backstamp.

Ashtray, HP flowers w/gold, chip, 6" dia.......................60.00
Cup & saucer, bouillon; Chinese Gr Bouquet, 1950s, from $150 to..200.00
Figurine, fish, bl & orange w/gold, 4⅜" H...................135.00
Figurine, sea horse, copper irid w/orange & yel, mk, 6¾" 235.00
Jar, HP birds & insects on basketweave, rose finial, 4¼".............250.00
Jar, mc butterflies/bird, appl 3-rose final, gold trim, 5½" 300.00
Sugar bowl, Victoria, rose finial 55.00

Heubach

Gebruder Heubach is a German company that has been in operation since the 1800s, producing quality bisque figurines and novelty items. They are perhaps most famous for their doll heads and piano babies, most of which are marked with the circular rising sun device containing an 'H' superimposed over a 'C.' Items with arms and hands positioned away from the body are more valuable, and color of hair and intaglio eyes affect price as well. Our advisor for this category is Grace Ochsner; she is listed in the Directory under Illinois. See also Dolls, Heubach.

Angry baby w/clenched hands before open eggshell, 5" **485.00**
Babies (2), in pk & bl, hands as if to clap, 5", pr **350.00**
Babies (4) in wicker basket, 8x8½x4½"....................................**1,200.00**
Baby playing w/toes, mk, 9" L..**460.00**
Baby w/bl intaglio eyes, seated, wht gown, sunburst mk, 6" **325.00**
Blond girl in pk pleated dress w/gr sash, 5¾" **425.00**
Boy, seminude w/2 fish baskets on bk, 7"................................**325.00**
Boy & girl dancing, rocky base, 12½" **550.00**
Boy w/red hat & eyeglasses sits w/arms Xd on chair bk, 7"..........**650.00**
Dog on haunches, wht w/tan collar, mk, 9x3⅝" **375.00**
Dutch girl seated w/hands at knees, bl dress, #3218, 5" **350.00**
Dutch girl sits before basket vase, hands across lap, sunburst mk, 5"...**325.00**
Girl holds gr pleated skirt to side, 6¼" **275.00**
Girl holds seashell to ear, sunburst mk, 11½" **315.00**
Girl in bunny costume before lg pk egg, eyes to side, 7½" **600.00**
Humidor, Jasper, gr, Indian chief on lid, 5" **295.00**
Lady seated beside wht egg w/gold heart, 4".............................**295.00**
Lady stands w/sm guardian angel at ft, #2832, 9"......................**300.00**
Lady w/blond hair, flowing dress & bl scarf, #9031, 8", pr...........**425.00**
Pup w/muzzle, impressed mk, 5"...**295.00**
Rooster peers in to empty egg shell, #9160, 5½" **325.00**
Vase, lady's profile w/in Nouveau floral reserve on bl, 4½" **415.00**
Vase, lilies on gr, tube-lined, invt rim, 8", NM **395.00**

Hickman, Royal Arden

Born in Willamette, Oregon, Royal A. Hickman was a genius in all aspects of design interpretation. Mr. Hickman's expertise can be seen in the designs of the lovely Heisey figurines, Kosta crystal, Bruce Fox aluminum, Three Crowns aluminum, Vernon Kilns, and Royal Haeger Pottery, as well as handcrafted silver, furniture, and paintings.

Because Mr. Hickman moved around during much of his lifetime, his influence has been felt in all forms of the media. Designs from his independent companies include 'Royal Hickman Pottery and Lamps' (sold through Ceramic Arts Inc., of Chattanooga, Tennessee), 'Royal Hickman's Paris Ware,' 'Royal Hickman — Florida,' and 'California Designed by Royal Hickman.' The following listings will give examples of pieces bearing the various trademarks. See also Garden City Pottery; Royal Haeger.

Bruce Fox Aluminum

Candle holders, triple; curved ribbon-like base, 5¾" high end, pr..**75.00**
Dish, lobster, sgn Bruce For-RH #37, lg..................................**85.00**
Leaf dish, long/slender, 4 cast ft, RH-5, 5½x26" **85.00**
Leaf tray, 5-lobe w/long stem (hdl), 5-ftd, 9½x11"+stem **80.00**
Lobster tray, RH20 Bruce Cox, 14" L **70.00**
2-acorn oak tray, 14½" **30.00**

California, Designed by Royal Hickman

Figurine, deer, apple gr w/wht spots, appl eyes, 15" **45.00**
Lamp base, flying geese, 17"..**250.00**
Swan, red & blk highlights, #643, #17 ....**125.00**

Miscellaneous Signatures

Vase, bl mottle, shouldered, Royal Hickman USA, #544, 11½" .**165.00**
Vase, fish figural, Petty Crystal Glaze, #467 ....**45.00**

Vase, sea horse figural, Royal Hickman USA, #468, 8" **35.00**
Vase, swan form, Petty Crystal Glaze, Royal Hickman USA #475, 16⅝"..**125.00**

Royal Hickman — Guadalajara, Mexico

Tray, silver, banana leaf hdls, 15" L **220.00**
Vase, 3 dolphin figures, 14k gold decor, gold crown label, 13" **200.00**
Vase, classic ftd shape w/very ornate hdls, pk mottle, #342, 12" .**145.00**

Higgins

Contemporary glass artists Frances and Michael Higgins designed high-quality glassware from the late 1940s until Michael's death on February 13, 1999. (Frances continues with her staff.) Their designs were often created by fusing layers of glass together, though sometimes colored ground glass was used to 'paint' the decoration onto the surface. Molds were used, and through a process called 'slumping,' the glass was fired to a very high temperature, causing it to soften and take on the predetermined shape. Their work is ultramodern and is more readily found in metropolitan areas.

The earliest mark was an engraved signature on the bottom of the glass — either 'Frances Stewart Higgins' or 'Michael Higgins' or both, which was dropped in favor of just 'Higgins' with a raised 'Higgins Man.' From approximately 1957 to 1964, the Higgins signature was embossed in gold on the top. After 1964 the signature again appeared on the bottom and was engraved in the glass. Recent items produced at the Higgins studio in Riverside, Illinois, are marked 'Higgins' and dated (Higgins 99 for example). For more information we recommend *Higgins, Adventures in Glass*, by Donald-Brian Johnson and Leslie Pina (Schiffer). Our advisor is Dennis Hopp; he is listed in the Directory under Illinois.

Ashtray, gold, yellow, blue, and teal rectangles on light blue, 7x5", $85.00.

Ashtray, birds, mc on clear, triangular, 14½x12" **175.00**
Ashtray, bl & yel checks, gold mk, 7x10", from $70 to................**90.00**
Ashtray, bl w/appl bl sqs, gold mk, 7x10" **50.00**
Ashtray, lock & keys, gold mk, 7x10"....................................**95.00**
Ashtray, purple w/bl & gr spikes, gold mk, 7x10", from $70 to **90.00**
Bowl, bl blob, etch mk, 10"..**110.00**
Bowl, emerald w/appl patches, stickman mk, 9½" **220.00**
Bowl, gr & orange dot ray, gold mk, 12½" **85.00**
Bowl, wht dot ray, gold mk, 12½", from $100 to **125.00**
Charger, bl/gr/gold ray, gold mk, 13½" sq **85.00**
Charger, gr w/chartreuse spikes, gold mk, 17½" **135.00**
Charger, orange spike, gold mk, 17" **110.00**
Dish, radiating rays, gr & orange on clear, 3-compartment, 20x7"...**100.00**
Pendant, w/F Lloyd Wright window design, etch mk, 2x3", from $50 to..**70.00**
Plate, bl scroll, gold mk, 13½" **85.00**
Plate, orange spike, gold mk, 12½" **55.00**
Plate, purple w/bl & gr spikes, gold mk/paper label, 12½"............**70.00**
Tray, bl & brn waves w/gold sand dollar, gold mk, 7x10", from $70 to ...**90.00**
Tray, bl seaweed w/gold stickman mk, 5x10"............................**75.00**
Tray, random sqs on emerald gr, 14x6¾" **800.00**

Tray, wht daisy, gold mk, 4½", from $40 to **50.00**
Tray, wht w/wildflowers, stickman & etch mks, 5" sq, from $70 to ...**90.00**

Historical Glass

Glassware commemorating particularly significant historical events became popular in the late 1800s. Bread trays were the most common form, but plates, mugs, pitchers, and other items were also pressed in clear as well as colored glass. It was sold in vast amounts at the 1876 Philadelphia Centennial Exposition by various manufacturers who exhibited their wares on the grounds. It remained popular well into the twentieth century.

In the listings that follow, L numbers refer to a book by Lindsey, a standard guide used by many collectors. Our advisor for this category is Darlene Yohe; she is listed in the Directory under Arkansas. See also Bread Plates; Pattern Glass.

Bank, Liberty Bell..**38.00**
Bottle, Granger, L-266 ....**110.00**
Bottle, Grant's Tomb, milk glass, no stopper **250.00**
Bust, Dewey, Manila 1898, 5" **145.00**
Butter dish, American Shield **195.00**
Butter dish, Garfield Drape **85.00**
Celery, Independence Hall **65.00**
Compote, Washington Centennial, ftd, open **40.00**
Cup, Harrison & Morton, bl **235.00**
Cup plate, Bunker Hill **30.00**
Flask, Blaine & Logan, oval, 6¾" **550.00**
Flask, John Paul Jones **20.00**
Flask, McKinley & Hobart, Distilled Protection, 7" **475.00**
Goblet, Emblem Centennial, L-61 ....**45.00**
Goblet, 3 Presidents, rare **325.00**
Hat, Uncle Sam, no pnt, L-110 ....**35.00**
Jar, apothecary; Statue of Liberty, blown **135.00**
Lamp, Emblem, L-62 ....**195.00**
Mug, Assassination **60.00**
Mug, Christopher Columbus, L-1 ....**45.00**
Mug, Martyr's Lincoln & Garfield, L-272................................**95.00**
Mug, McKinley **30.00**
Mug, shaving; Garfield & Lucretia Randolf Garfield, milk glass, 6" ..**250.00**
Mustard dish, Dewey bust, w/Xd flags on lid, milk glass, 4¼" **55.00**
Paperweight, Columbian Expo, lady w/upswept hair, US Glass, frosted ...**145.00**
Paperweight, Memorial Hall, frosted, L-495............................**150.00**
Paperweight, Moses in Bullrushes, frosted center, Gillinder **145.00**
Paperweight, Shakespeare, frosted, Gillinder **150.00**
Pickle dish, E Pluribus Unum...**45.00**
Pin tray, McKinley bust, frosted base, L-297 ....**110.00**
Pitcher, Garfield Drape, scarce **145.00**
Pitcher, Liberty Bell, John Hancock, milk glass **595.00**
Plate, Admiral Dewey, gr, lacy edge, 5½" **23.00**
Plate, Admiral Dewey, lacy edge, 5½" **17.00**
Plate, Bryan, flag/eagle/star border, milk glass, L-359............**85.00**
Plate, CA Gold Rush, Eureka **50.00**
Plate, Dewey, clear/frosted, sm **15.00**
Plate, For President Winfield S Hancock, 8" **110.00**
Plate, Grant, Patriot & Soldier, amber, sq, 9½" **50.00**
Plate, Indian, milk glass, L-14, 7½" **60.00**
Plate, McKinley **35.00**
Plate, Pope Leo, milk glass, L-240...**40.00**
Plate, Yankee Doodle, Egg & Dart border, 5¼" **35.00**
Shaker, Centennial, boot **27.00**
Spooner, Liberty Bell **50.00**
Spooner, Log Cabin, L-184 ....**115.00**

Statuette, Ruth the Gleaner, frosted, 1876 Phila Expo, Gillinder...**175.00**
Stein, Centennial **60.00**
Tumbler, Admiral Dewey, L-398 ....**50.00**
Tumbler, America, L-48 ....**25.00**
Tumbler, Hobson, in laurel wreath, frosted.............................**60.00**
Tumbler, Lincoln Tribute, L-282 ....**25.00**
Tumbler, McKinley, L-337..**50.00**
Tumbler, Rock of Ages, L-227..**25.00**
Tumbler, 5 stars & Flag w/13 stars & rifle **175.00**
Wine, Washington Centennial **65.00**

Hobbs, Brockunier, & Co.

Hobbs and Brockunier's South Wheeling Glass Works was in operation during the last quarter of the nineteenth century. They are most famous for their peachblow, amberina, Daisy and Button, and Hobnail pattern glass. The mainstay of the operation, however, was druggist items and plain glassware — bowls, mugs, and simple footed pitchers with shell handles.

For further information we recommend *Hobbs, Brockunier & Co. Glass, Identification and Value Guide*, by Neila and Tom Bredehoft (Collector Books). See also Frances Ware.

Bottle, scent; Daisy & Button, Marine Green, cut stopper...........**80.00**
Bowl, Daisy & Button, canary, 9½"..**70.00**
Bowl, finger; Craquelle, amber, melon ribs.............................**145.00**
Bowl, nappy, Dew Drop, canary, 4½".......................................**25.00**
Bowl, Snowstorm, rubena w/wht Craquelle o/l, crimped rim, 7".**400.00**
Bowl, waste; Swirl, ruby opal **125.00**
Canoe, Daisy & Button, crystal w/amber stain.........................**80.00**

Creamer, Dolphin, crystal with sand-blast decor, #305, $150.00.
(Photo courtesy Neila and Tom Bredehoft)

Creamer, Spangled, bl, melon ribs, appl hdl.............................**250.00**
Cup, custard; sapphire bl, shell hdl **10.00**
Molasses can, Polka Dot, ruby, #97, 12-oz..............................**175.00**
Salt cellar, Daisy & Button, yacht form, 3" **18.00**
Salt cellar, turtle shape..**75.00**
Shade, Dew Drop, dome shape, ruby opal, 10"........................**250.00**
Shade, Windows, sapphire opal, tulip form, 4" **425.00**
Sugar bowl, Craquelle, sapphire bl, #305................................**90.00**
Sugar bowl, Dew Drop, canary, w/lid.......................................**65.00**
Tankard, Daisy & Button, sapphire, 2-qt..................................**190.00**
Tumbler, Polka Dot, Old Gold, #236..**26.00**
Tumbler, Spangled..**140.00**
Tumbler, Venetian, wht loopings w/red threading, minimum value ..**850.00**
Water bottle, Dew Drop, sapphire **135.00**

Holt Howard

Novelty ceramics marked Holt Howard represent one of the newest areas of collectibles on today's market, and dealers report a good amount of market activity. Made from the '50s into the '70s, they're not only marked, but most are dated as well. There are several lines to reassemble — the rooster, the white cat, figural banks, Christmas angels and Santas, to name only a few — but the one that most Holt Howard collectors seem to gravitate toward is the pixie line. For more information see *Garage Sale and Flea Market Annual* (Collector Books). Our advisors for this category are Pat and Ann Duncan; they are listed in the Directory under Missouri.

Angel, cb cone body w/pk feathers, ceramic head, from $20 to	30.00
Ashtray, lady w/bottle	110.00
Ashtray/coaster, mouse	25.00
Bank, Dandy Lion, bobbing head, from $100 to	135.00
Bowl, cereal; Rooster, 6"	15.00
Bud vase, Rooster, figural, from $25 to	30.00
Butter dish, emb Rooster, ¼-lb	65.00
Candelabra, Santa trio, gift packages hold candles, 5x8"	60.00
Candle holder, Ponytail Princess on figure-8 base w/flower candle cup	60.00
Candle holders, angel figurines, pr	35.00
Candle holders, children dressed as Wise Men, 3½", set of 3	55.00
Candle holders, Santa w/climbing mouse, pr	35.00
Candlestick, Santa hdl	25.00
Candlestick, winking Santa-head candle cup on red saucer base	20.00
Chocolate pot, emb Rooster on front, tall & narrow w/flaring sides	70.00
Christmas tree, bottle-brush type w/fruit, foil ornaments & birds, 15"	40.00
Cocktail olives, Pixieware, winking gr head finial, from $120 to	135.00
Coffeepot, emb Rooster	85.00
Cookie jar, emb Rooster	150.00
Cookies/candy jar, roly-poly Santa figure, 3-pc, minimum value	150.00
Cottage cheese keeper, Kozy Kitten, cat knob on lid	100.00
Cruets, oil & vinegar; Sally & Sam, pr, minimum value	250.00
Decanter, whiskey; Pixieware, winking head stopper, minimum value	225.00
Desk accessory, eagle w/wings wide on marble base, holds 1 pen	100.00
Dish, Rooster, open-body receptacle	25.00
Dish, Rooster figural, open body receptacle	25.00
Dish, Santa head w/scalloped beard bowl	25.00
Head vase, girl w/drop earrings, holly head band, pearl necklace, 4"	85.00
Honey jar, Pixieware, rare, minimum value	500.00
Hors d'oeurve, Pixieware, pierced body, tall hairdo, minimum value	225.00
Instant coffee jar, Pixieware, scarce, from $150 to	250.00
Italian dressing bottle, Pixieware, from $160 to	175.00
Letter holder, Kozy Kitten w/coiled wire bk, from $45 to	60.00
Lipstick holder, Ponytail Princess, from $50 to	65.00
Mayonnaise jar, Pixieware, winking head finial, minimum value	250.00
Mug, Christmas tree w/Santa hdl	10.00
Mustard jar, emb Rooster on front, w/lid	50.00
Napkin holder, emb Rooster	35.00
Onion jar, Pixieware, flat onion-head finial, 1958, from $150 to	200.00
Onions jar, Onions If You Please on sign held by butler, minimum	200.00
Pitcher, Rooster, flaring sides, tail hdl, tall, from $50 to	60.00
Planter, camel	20.00
Planter, mother deer & fawn, wht w/gold bow	35.00
Powdered cleanser shaker, Kozy Kitten, full-bodied cat w/apron & broom	150.00
Razor bank, barber figure	30.00
Russian dressing bottle, Pixieware, from $165 to	175.00
Sewing box, Kozy Kitten figural w/tape measure tongue on lid, $150 to	175.00
Shakers, Christmas trees w/Santa's face on ea, S & P, 4½", pr	25.00
Shakers, holly girl w/poinsettia w/P or S at center, pr, from $15 to	20.00
Shakers, Kozy Kitten, tall, pr	40.00
Shakers, Pixieware, Salty & Peppy, flat heads, pnt wood hdls, pr	125.00
Shakers, Ponytail Princess	45.00
Shakers, Rooster figural, tall, pr, from $25 to	30.00
Shakers, 2 stacked gift boxes, Merry Xmas on top, pr	15.00
Soup tureen, tomato form, lg, from $85 to	100.00

Spice rack, Kozy Kitten, stacking, from $150 to	175.00
Spoon rest, apple form	15.00
Syrup, emb Rooster on front, tail hdl, from $50 to	65.00
Tape Measure, Kozy Kitten on cushion	85.00
Towel hook, Pixieware, flat head w/sm loop hanger, minimum value	200.00
Tray, dbl; Ponytail Princess between 2 flower cups	65.00
Tray, Rooster, facing left	20.00
Tray, Santa, beard forms tray, 7¾", from $25 to	30.00
Trivet, Rooster, tile in iron framework, from $40 to	50.00
Votive candle holder, Santa, dtd 1968, 3"	20.00

Homer Laughlin

The Homer Laughlin China Company of Newell, West Virginia, was founded in 1871. The superior dinnerware they displayed at the Centennial Exposition in Philadelphia in 1876 won the highest award of excellence. From that time to the present, they have continued to produce quality dinnerware and kitchenware, many lines of which are becoming very popular collectibles. Most of the dinnerware is marked with the name of the pattern and occasionally with the shape name as well. The 'HLC' trademark is usually followed by a number series, the first two digits of which indicate the year of its manufacture. For further information we recommend *The Collector's Encyclopedia of Fiesta, Ninth Edition*, by Sharon and Bob Huxford; *The Collector's Encyclopedia of Homer Laughlin China* by Joanne Jasper; and *Collector's Guide to Homer Laughlin's Virginia Rose* by Richard G. Racheter (all available from Collector Books). Another fine source of information is *Homer Laughlin, A Giant Among Dishes*, by Jo Cunningham (Schiffer). Our advisors for Virginia Rose are Jack and Treva Hamlin; they are listed in the Directory under Ohio.

Our values are base prices. Very desirable patterns on the shapes named in our listings may increase values by as much as 70%. See also Blue Willow; Fiesta; Harlequin; Riviera.

Priscilla, coffeepot, from $85.00 to $95.00.

Debutante

Casserole, w/lid, from $30 to	35.00
Nappy, 8", from $12 to	14.00
Pie server, from $20 to	30.00
Plate, chop; 15", from $16 to	20.00
Plate, 10", from $8 to	9.00
Plate, 9", from $7 to	8.00
Teacup, from $3 to	5.00
Teapot, from $35 to	45.00

Eggshell Georgian

Bowl, cream soup; from $18 to	22.00
Bowl, fruit; from $6 to	8.00
Bowl, oatmeal; 6", from $7 to	9.00
Bowl, 5", from $12 to	15.00

Egg cup, dbl; from $20 to 30.00
Plate, 10", from $12 to 15.00
Sauce boat stand, from $8 to.......................................12.00
Shakers, pr, from $24 to 40.00

Eggshell Nautilus

Baker, 9", from $18 to..24.00
Creamer, from $13 to...17.00
Nappy, 10", from $18 to...24.00
Plate, chop; 14", from $22 to.....................................32.00
Plate, rim soup; deep, from $9 to................................12.00
Plate, sq, 8", from $12 to...14.00
Platter, 11", from $18 to..24.00
Saucer, AD; from $4 to..6.00

Empress

Baker, 7", from $14 to..16.00
Boullion saucer, from $8 to 10.00
Bowl, fruit; 6", from $6 to..8.00
Coffee saucer, rare, from $6 to.....................................8.00
Creamer, ind, 4-oz, from $10 to 12.00
Dish, 14", from $25 to..28.00
Dish, 17", from $30 to..35.00
Egg cup, Boston, from $20 to 25.00
Nappy, 11", from $22 to...24.00
Plate, deep, 7", from $8 to..12.00
Sauce tureen, from $45 to...55.00
Teacup, from $6 to..8.00

Jade

Baker, 10", from $24 to...30.00
Butter dish, w/lid, from $50 to....................................65.00
Jug, from $40 to..50.00
Plate, rim soup; deep, from $10 to...............................12.00
Plate, 8", from $8 to...10.00
Sauce boat stand, from $8 to.......................................10.00
Tea saucer, from $4 to..6.00
Teapot, from $75 to...95.00

Marigold

Bowl, deep, 5", from $10 to...12.00
Casserole, w/lid, from $55 to......................................65.00
Nappy, 9", from $22 to 28.00
Plate, sq, 8", from $12 to..15.00
Plate, 7", from $6 to...8.00
Platter, 11", from $20 to..30.00
Sugar bowl, w/lid, from $22 to....................................26.00
Tea saucer, from $3 to...5.00

Nautilus

Baker, 10", from $20 to...26.00
Bowl, coupe soup; from $7 to..9.00
Bowl, fruit; from $3 to..6.00
Butter dish, w/lid, Jade, from $50 to............................65.00
Coffee mug, Baltimore, from $18 to.............................25.00
Creamer, from $12 to..16.00
Plate, 10", from $10 to..13.00
Plate, 6", from $5 to...7.00
Sauce boat, from $20 to...28.00

Teapot, from $65 to...85.00

Rhythm

Bowl, fruit; from $4 to..6.00
Casserole, w/lid, from $40 to......................................50.00
Dish, 13½", from $18 to..24.00
Plate, 7", from $5 to...7.00
Sauce boat, from $20 to...26.00
Sugar bowl, w/lid, from $16 to....................................20.00
Tea saucer, from $3 to...4.00
Tidbit tray, from $25 to...45.00

Swing

Bowl, fruit; from $6 to..8.00
Casserole, w/lid, from $45 to......................................65.00
Coffeepot, AD; from $45 to...65.00
Creamer, from $14 to..18.00
Egg cup, dbl; from $22 to..28.00
Plate, 7", from $7 to...9.00
Sauce boat, from $18 to...28.00
Sugar bowl, AD; from $12 to.......................................16.00

Wells

Baker, 8", from $16 to..18.00
Bowl, deep, 5", from $12 to...15.00
Creamer, from $14 to..18.00
Dish, 13", from $24 to..28.00
Egg cup, dbl; from $18 to..25.00
Jug, 24s, w/lid, from $65 to...85.00
Muffin cover, from $55 to..75.00
Plate, chop; from $24 to..32.00
Plate, 6", from $5 to...7.00
Saucer, AD; from $6 to...8.00

Yellowstone

Baker, 8", from $12 to..18.00
Bowl, fruit; 6s, from $5 to..7.00
Bowl, oyster; 5", from $12 to.......................................15.00
Creamer, from $10 to..16.00
Dish, 11", from $18 to..22.00
Jug, 36s, from $25 to...30.00
Nappy, 9", from $14 to...22.00
Plate, 10", from $12 to..15.00
Sauce boat, from $16 to...24.00
Teapot, from $45 to...75.00

Hull

    The A.E. Hull Pottery was formed in 1905 in Zanesville, Ohio, and in the early years produced stoneware specialities. They expanded in 1907, adding a second plant and employing over two hundred workers. By 1920 they were manufacturing a full line of stoneware, art pottery with both air-brushed and blended glazes, florist pots, and gardenware. They also produced toilet ware and kitchen items with a white semiporcelain body. Although these continued to be staple products, after the stock market crash of 1929, emphasis was shifted to tile production. By the mid-'30 interest in art pottery production was growing, and over the next fifteen years, several lines of matt pastel floral-decorated patterns were designed, consisting of vases, planters, baskets, ewers, and bowls in various sizes.

The Red Riding Hood cookie jar, patented in 1943, proved so successful that a whole line of figural kitchenware and novelty items was added. They continued to be produced well into the '50s. (See also Little Red Riding Hood.) Through the '40s their floral artware lines flooded the market, due to the restriction of foreign imports. Although best known for their pastel matt-glazed ware, some of the lines were high gloss. Rosella, glossy coral on a pink clay body, was produced for a short time only; and Magnolia, although offered in a matt glaze, was produced in gloss as well.

The plant was destroyed in 1950 by a flood which resulted in a devastating fire when the floodwater caused the kilns to explode. The company rebuilt and equipped their new factory with the most modern machinery. It was soon apparent that the matt glaze could not be duplicated through the more modern processes, however, and soon attention was concentrated on high-gloss artware lines such as Parchment and Pine and Ebb Tide. Figural planters and novelties, piggy banks, and dinnerware were produced in abundance in the late '50s and '60s. By the mid-'70s dinnerware and florist ware were the mainstay of their business. The firm discontinued operations in 1985.

Our advisor, Brenda Roberts, has compiled a lovely book, *The Collector's Encyclopedia of Hull Pottery*, with full-color photos and current values, available from Collector Books.

Special note to Hull collectors: Reproductions are on the market in all categories of Hull pottery — matt florals, Red Riding Hood, and later lines including House 'n Garden dinnerware.

Blossom Flite, console bowl, #T-10, 16½" 155.00
Blossom Flite, ewer, #T-13, 13½" 195.00
Blossom Flite, planter, unmk, 10½" 125.00
Bow-Knot, cornucopia, dbl; #B-13, 13" 425.00

Bow-Knot, ewer, B-1, 5½", from $190.00 to $260.00.

Bow-Knot, flowerpot w/attached saucer, #B-6, 6½" 275.00
Bow-Knot, teapot, #B-20, 6" 500.00
Bow-Knot, vase, #B-5, 6½" 250.00
Bow-Knot, vase, #B-8, 8½" 300.00
Bow-Knot, wall plaque, #B-28, 10" 1,400.00
Bow-Knot, wall pocket, pitcher form, #B-26, 6" 275.00
Butterfly, lavabo, matt, orig hanger, top #B-25/bottom #B-24 ..... 240.00
Butterfly, pitcher, matt, #B-11, 8¾" 195.00
Butterfly, serving tray, matt wht & turq w/gold trim, #B-23, 11½" .. 140.00
Calla Lily, bowl, 500/32, 10" 240.00
Calla Lily, candle holder, unmk, 2¼" 125.00
Calla Lily, console bowl, #590/33, 4x13" 210.00
Calla Lily, cornucopia, #570/33, 8" 150.00
Calla Lily, vase, #540/33, 6" 160.00
Cinderella Kitchenware (Blossom), casserole, #21, 7½" 45.00
Cinderella Kitchenware (Blossom), pitcher, #22, 64-oz 230.00
Cinderella Kitchenware (Blossom), teapot, #26, 42-oz 200.00
Cinderella Kitchenware (Bouquet), bowl, brn ink stamp, sq, 9¾" .. 125.00
Cinderella Kitchenware (Bouquet), grease jar, #24, #24, 32-oz 65.00

Cinderella Kitchenware (Bouquet), shakers, #25, 3½", ea 30.00
Classic, ewer, #6, 6" 25.00
Classic, vase, #4, 6" 25.00
Continental, bud vase, #66, 9½" 40.00
Continental, candle holder/planter, unmk, 4" 35.00
Crescent Kitchenware, casserole, #B-2, w/lid, 10" 50.00
Crescent Kitchenware, cookie jar, #B-8, 9½" 80.00
Crescent Kitchenware, mug, #B-16, 4¼" 20.00
Dogwood, console bowl, #511, 11½" 385.00
Dogwood, jardiniere, #514, 4" 145.00
Dogwood, teapot, #507, 6½" 450.00
Dogwood, vase, #513, 6½" 165.00
Dogwood, vase, #516, 4¾" 95.00
Dogwood, window box, #508, 10½" 295.00
Early Art, jardiniere, stoneware, circled H, 6½" 130.00
Early Art, pitcher, stoneware, #27 (w/circled H), 6½" 375.00
Early Art, vase, stoneware, #39 (w/circled H), 8" 150.00
Early Art, vase, stoneware, #40 (w/circled H), 7" 110.00
Early Utility, custard, #60 (w/circled H), 2½" 18.00
Early Utility, pitcher, #197, 4¾" 70.00
Early Utility, pretzel jar, circled H, 9½" 310.00
Early Utility, stein, emb elk, #499, 6½" 90.00
Ebb Tide, basket, unmk, 6¼" 165.00
Ebb Tide, console bowl, #E-12, 15¾" 195.00
Ebb Tide, sugar bowl, #E-16, w/lid, 4" 100.00
Heritageware, cookie jar, #-18, 9¼" 120.00
Heritageware, oil cruet, USA, 6¼" 30.00
Heritageware, shakers, 3½", ea 14.00
Imperial, basket/planter, carnation pk, #F-24, 12½" 32.00
Imperial, vase, carnation pk, #F-28, 9½" 15.00
Iris, bud vase, #410, 7½" 200.00
Iris, candle holder, #411, 5" 145.00
Iris, ewer, #401, 13½" 575.00
Iris, rose bowl, #412, 7" 210.00
Magnolia, gloss; basket, #H-14, 10½" 425.00
Magnolia, gloss; console bowl, #H-23, 13" 135.00
Magnolia, gloss; cornucopia, #H-10, 8½" 135.00
Magnolia, gloss; creamer, #H-21, 3¾" 55.00
Magnolia, gloss; ewer, #H-19, 13½" 450.00
Magnolia, gloss; sugar bowl, #H-22, w/lid, 3¾" 60.00
Magnolia, gloss; teapot, #H-20, 6½" 200.00
Magnolia, gloss; vase, #H-17, 12½" 290.00
Magnolia, gloss; vase, #H-2, 5½" 50.00
Magnolia, matt; basket, #10, 10½" 410.00
Magnolia, matt; console bowl, #26, 12" 235.00
Magnolia, matt; cornucopia, dbl; #6, 12" 225.00
Magnolia, matt; ewer, #5, 7" 205.00
Magnolia, matt; lamp base, 12½" 450.00
Magnolia, matt; vase, #13, 4¾" 60.00
Magnolia, matt; vase, #16, 15" 510.00
Magnolia, matt; vase, #2, 8½" 195.00
Mardi Gras, mixing bowl, unmk, 10¼" 55.00
Mardi Gras, vase, unmk, 6" 35.00
Mardi Gras/Granada, ewer, #66, 10" 175.00
Mardi Gras/Granada, planter, #204, 6" 60.00
Mardi Gras/Granada, vase, #47, 9" 75.00
Novelty, figurine, dachshund, 6x14" 225.00
Novelty, flower pot, #95, 4½" 20.00
Novelty, planter, basket girl, #954, 8" 45.00
Novelty, planter, dancing girl, #955, 7" 75.00
Novelty, planter, kitten, #61, 7½" 45.00
Novelty, planter, knight on horse, #55, 8" 120.00
Novelty, planter, lovebirds, #93, 6" 60.00
Novelty, planter, poodle form, #114, 8" 65.00

Novelty, vase, #108, 8" 100.00
Novelty, wall pocket, goose form, #67, 6½" 70.00
Nuline Bak-Serve, bean pot, #B-19, w/lid, 5½" 65.00
Nuline Bak-Serve, cookie jar, #D-20, 8" 200.00
Nuline Bak-Serve, custard, #B-14, 2¾" 15.00
Nuline Bak-Serve, pitcher, #C-29, 7" 105.00
Open Rose, cornucopia, #101, 8½" 200.00
Open Rose, ewer, #115, 8½" 315.00
Open Rose, hanging basket, #132, 7" 325.00
Open Rose, jardiniere, #114, 8¼" 380.00
Open Rose, planter, mermaid/shell, #104, 10½" 2,600.00
Open Rose, vase, #131, 4¾" 100.00
Open Rose, wall pocket, #125, 8½" 480.00
Orchid, basket, #305, 7" 850.00
Orchid, bookends, #316, 7", pr 1,350.00
Orchid, ewer, #311, 13" 775.00
Orchid, jardiniere, #310, 6" 265.00
Orchid, vase, #308, 4½" 145.00
Parchment & Pine, basket, #S-8, 16½" L 225.00
Parchment & Pine, console bowl, unmk, 16" L 135.00
Parchment & Pine, teapot, #S-15, 8" 215.00
Pinecone, vase, #55, 6½" 225.00
Poppy, basket, #601, 12" 1,200.00
Poppy, ewer, #610, 13½" 1,050.00
Poppy, vase, #605, 8½" 310.00
Poppy, vase, #612, 6½" 175.00
Rosella, basket, #R-12, 7" 215.00
Rosella, creamer, #R-3, 5½" 65.00
Rosella, vase, #R-15, 8½" 160.00
Rosella, wall pocket, #R-10, 6½" 180.00
Serenade, candle holders, #S-16, 6½", pr 160.00
Serenade, candy dish, #S-3, 8¼" 175.00
Serenade, pitcher, #S-21, 10½" 250.00
Serenade, teapot, #S-17, 5" 225.00
Sueno Tulip, basket, #102/33, 6" 395.00
Sueno Tulip, flowerpot w/attached saucer, #116-33, 6" 240.00
Sueno Tulip, jardiniere, #115/33, 7" 345.00
Sueno Tulip, vase, #107/33, 8" 200.00
Sueno Tulip, vase, #110/33, 6" 150.00
Sunglow, basket, #84, 6½" 135.00
Sunglow, bell, pk, unmk, 6½" 135.00
Sunglow, bell, yel, unmk, 6" 110.00
Sunglow, bowl, #50, 9½" 45.00
Sunglow, ewer, #90, 5½" 45.00
Sunglow, grease jar, #53, 5¼" 65.00
Sunglow, pitcher, #55, 7½" 185.00
Sunglow, shakers, #54, 2¾", ea 20.00
Sunglow, wall pocket, cup & saucer form, #80, 6¼" ...140.00
Thistle, vase, #53, 6½" 150.00
Tokay/Tuscany, basket, #11, 10½" 160.00
Tokay/Tuscany, candy dish, #9, 8½" 155.00
Tokay/Tuscany, creamer, #17 ....95.00
Tokay/Tuscany, sugar bowl, #18 ....95.00
Tropicana, basket, #55, 12¾" 750.00
Tropicana, vase, #54, 12½" 550.00
Water Lily, console bowl, #L-21, 13½" 300.00
Water Lily, ewer, #L-17, 13½" 550.00
Water Lily, ewer, #L-3, 5½" 125.00
Water Lily, jardiniere, #L-23, 5½" 145.00
Water Lily, lamp base, unmk, 7½" 350.00
Water Lily, teapot, #L-18, 6" 265.00
Water Lily, vase, #L-10, 9½" 255.00
Water Lily, vase, #L-6, 6½" 90.00
Water Lily, vase, #L-8, 8½" 265.00

Wildflower, basket, #W-16, 10½" 500.00
Wildflower, console bowl, #W-21, 12" 255.00
Wildflower, cornucopia, #W-10, 8½" 185.00
Wildflower, ewer, #W-11, 8½" 225.00
Wildflower, lamp base, #W-17, 12½" 400.00
Wildflower, vase, #W-14, 10½" 320.00
Wildflower, vase, #W-8, 7½" 125.00
Wildflower (# series), console bowl, #70, 12" 475.00
Wildflower (# series), creamer, #73, 4¾" 275.00
Wildflower (# series), ewer, #55, 13½" 1,100.00
Wildflower (# series), jardiniere, #64, 4" 160.00
Wildflower (# series), sugar bowl, #74, 4¾" 275.00
Wildflower (# series), vase, #51, 8½" 325.00
Woodland, gloss; basket, #W-22, 10½" 280.00
Woodland, gloss; console bowl, #W-29, 14" 300.00
Woodland, gloss; cornucopia, #W-10, 11" 100.00
Woodland, gloss; creamer & sugar bowl, #W-27/#W-28, 3½", ea 65.00
Woodland, gloss; teapot, #W-26, 6½" 180.00
Woodland, gloss; window box, #W-14, 10" 100.00
Woodland, matt; basket, #W-9, 8¾" 325.00
Woodland, matt; cornucopia, #W-10, 11" 210.00
Woodland, matt; ewer, #W-3, 5½" 155.00
Woodland, matt; hanging basket, #W-31, 5½" 295.00
Woodland, matt; vase, #W-1, 5½" 105.00
Woodland, matt; vase, #W-25, 12½" 775.00
Woodland, matt; vase, dbl bud; #W-15, 8½" 240.00
Woodland, matt; wall pocket, shell form, #W-13, 7½" ...275.00

Hummel

Hummel figurines were created through the artistry of Berta Hummel, a Franciscan nun called Sister M. Innocentia. The first figures were made about 1935 by Franz Goebel of Goebel Art Inc., Rodental, West Germany. Plates, plaques, and candy dishes are also produced, and the older, discontinued editions are highly sought collectibles. Generally speaking, an issue can be dated by the trademark. The first Hummels, from 1935 to 1949, were either incised or stamped with the 'Crown WG' mark. The 'Full Bee in V' mark was employed with minor variations until 1959. At that time the bee was stylized and represented by a solid disk with angled symetrical wings completely contained within the confines of the 'V.' The Three-Line mark, 1964 – 1972, utilized the stylized bee and included a three-line arrangement, 'c by W. Goebel, W. Germany.' Another change in 1972 saw the 'stylized bee in V' suspended between the vertical bars of the 'b' and 'l' of a printed 'Goebel, West Germany.' Collectors refer to this mark as the 'last bee' or 'Goebel bee.' The mark in use from 1979 to 1990 omits the 'bee in V.' The New Crown mark, in use from 1991 to 1999 is a small crown with 'WG' initials, a large 'Goebel,' and a small 'Germany' signifying a united Germany. The current millennium mark came into use in the year 2000. For further study we recommend *Hummel, An Illustrated Handbook and Price Guide*, by Ken Armke; *Hummel Figurines and Plates, A Collector's Identification and Value Guide*, by Carl Luckey; *The No. 1 Price Guide to M.I. Hummel* by Robert L. Miller; and *The Fascinating World of M.I. Hummel* by Goebel. These books are available through your local book dealer. See also Limited Edition Plates.

Key:

ce — closed edition	MM — millennium mark
CM — crown mark	NC — new crown mark
cn — closed number	oe — open edition
FB — full bee	SB — stylized bee
LB — last bee	tw — temporarily withdrawn
MB — missing bee	3L — three-line mark

#II/111, Wayside Harmony, table lamp, FB, ce, 7½" 325.00
#II/112, Just Resting, table lamp, SB, ce, 7½" 270.00
#III/110, Let's Sing, box, CM, ce, 6¼" 540.00
#III/58, Playmates, box, FB, ce, 6¾" 415.00
#1, Puppy Love, FB, ce, 5"-5¼" 395.00
#1/38/0, Joyous News w/Lute, Angel, SB, ce, 2"-2½" 65.00
#3/I, Book Worm, SB, ce, 5½" 340.00
#5, Strolling Along, CM, ce, 4¾"-5¾" 505.00
#6/0, Sensitive Hunter, CM, ce, 4¾" 470.00
#8, Book Worm, CM, ce, 4"-4½" 505.00
#9, Begging His Share, CM, ce, 5¼"-6" 540.00
#12/I, Chimney Sweep, FB, ce, 5½"-6½" 305.00
#14 A&B, Book Worms, Boy & Girl, bookends, FB, ce, 5½" 470.00
#16/I, Little Hiker, 3L, ce, 5½"-6" 215.00
#18, Christ Child, MB, tw, 3¼x6" 120.00
#20, Prayer Before Battle, SB, ce, 4"-4½" 180.00
#22/0, Angel w/Bird, font, CM, ce, 3x4" 180.00
#24/I, Lullaby, candle holder, CM, ce, 3½x5"-5½" 395.00
#26/0, Child Jesus, font, SB, ce, 2¾x5¼" 50.00
#28/II, Wayside Devotion, FB, ce, 7"-7½" 540.00
#30/0 A&B, Ba-Bee-Ring, 3L, ce, 4¾x5" 185.00
#32/0, Little Gabriel, FB, ce, 5"-5½" 215.00
#34, Singing Lesson, ashtray, 3L, ce, 3½x6¼" 145.00
#36/0, Child w/Flowers, font, CM, ce, 3¼x4¼" 160.00
#42/0, Good Shepherd, CM, ce, 6¼"-6½" 540.00
#44B, Out of Danger, table lamp, FB, ce, 8½"-9½" 305.00
#45/I, Madonna w/Halo, wht, FB, ce, 11½"-13¼" 70.00
#48/0, Madonna, plaque, FB, ce, 3¼"x4½" 125.00
#50 2/0, Volunteers, 3L, ce, 4¾"-5" 230.00
#52/I, Going to Grandma's, CM, ce, 6"-6¼" 900.00
#54, Silent Night, candle holder, CM, ce, 3½"-4¾" 610.00
#56/B, Out of Danger, SB, ce, 6¼"-6¾" 325.00
#60A&B, Farm Boy & Goose Girl, bookends, FB, ce, 4¾" 470.00
#63, Singing Lessons, SB, ce, 2¾"-3" 130.00
#65/0, Farewell, FB, ce, 4" 4,320.00
#67, Doll Mother, CM, ce, 4¼"-4¾" 470.00
#69, Happy Pastime, SB, ce, 3½" 180.00
#71, Stormy Weather, CM, ce, 6"-7" 790.00
#73, Little Helper, SB, ce, 4¼"-4½" 135.00
#74, Little Gardener, SB, ce, 4"-4½" 135.00
#79, Globe Trotter, FB, ce, 5"-5½" 270.00
#80, Little Scholar, CM, ce, 5¼"-5¾" 470.00
#82 2/0, School Boy, 3L, ce, 4"-4½" 145.00
#84/0, Worship, SB, ce, 5"-5½" 180.00
#86, Happiness, FB, ce, 4½"-5" 180.00
#89/I, Little Cellist, 3L, ce, 5¼"-6¼" 200.00
#91A&B, Angels at Prayer, font, CM, ce, 3¼x4½" 290.00
#93, Little Fiddler, plaque, CM, ce, 4½x5"-5x5½" 325.00
#94, Suprise, CM, ce, 5¾" 575.00
#97, Trumpet Boy, CM, ce, 4½"-4¾" 290.00
#99, Eventide, FB, ce, 4¼x5" 430.00
#100, Shrine, table lamp, CM, ce, 7½" 5,760.00
#104, Eventide, table lamp, CM, ce, 7½" 5,760.00
#107, Little Fiddler, plaque w/wood fr, CM, ce, 6x6" 2,160.00
#109, Happy Traveler, 3L, ce, 4¾"-5" 145.00
#114, Let's Sing, ashtray, FB, old style, ce, 3½x6¼" 430.00
#118, Little Thrifty, bank, CM, ce, 5"-5½" 360.00
#119, Postman, CM, ce, 5"-5½" 430.00
#124/0, Hello, SB, ce, 5¾"-6¼" 250.00
#126, Retreat to Safety, plaque, 3L, ce, 4¾x4¾" 160.00
#128, Baker, CM, ce, 4¾"-5" 430.00
#130, Duet, FB, ce, 5"-5½" 395.00
#132, Star Gazer, SB, ce, 4¾" 235.00
#134, Quartet, plaque, FB, ce, 5½x6¼" 380.00

#136/V, Friends, CM, ce, 10¾"-11" 2,160.00
#138, Tiny Baby in Crib, wall plaque, FB, cn, 2¼x3" 2,160.00
#140, The Mail is Here, plaque, CM, ce, 4¼x6¾" 470.00
#142/I, Apple Tree Boy, NC, oe, 6"-6⅞" 240.00
#143, Boots, FB, ce, 6¾" 470.00
#145, Little Guardian, CM, ce, 3¾"-4" 290.00
#147, Angel Shrine, font, SB, ce, 3x5" 60.00
#151, Madonna Holding Child, bl, CM, ce, 12½" 1,440.00
#152B, Umbrella Girl, CM, ce, 8" 2,880.00
#154/0, Waiter, CM, ce, 6"-6¼" 430.00
#163, Whitsuntide, FB, ce, 6½"-7" 610.00
#167, Angel w/Bird, font, FB, ce, 3¼x4⅛" 110.00
#169, Bird Duet, CM, ce, 3¾"-4" 305.00
#171 4/0, Little Sweeper, NC, oe, 3" 85.00
#173/0, Festival Harmony (flute), SB, ce, 8" 360.00
#174, She Loves Me, She Loves Me Not, FB, ce, 4¼" 250.00

#176, Happy Birthday, crown mark, U.S. Zone Germany stamped on bottom, 5½", **$610.00.** (Photo courtesy Marilyn and Fred Roberts)

#177/I, School Girls, SB, ce, 7½" 1,190.00
#179, Coquettes, CM, ce, 5"-5½" 575.00
#180, Tuneful Good Night, wall plaque, FB, ce, 5x4¾" 290.00
#183, Forest Shrine, FB, ce, 9" 720.00
#185, Accordion Boy, SB, ce, 5"-6" 215.00
#187, MI Hummel Plaque (English), FB, ce, 5½x4" 540.00
#188, Celestial Musician, FB, ce, 7" 610.00
#192, Candlelight, candle holder, FB, ce, 6¾"-7" 575.00
#195/I, Barnyard Hero, FB, ce, 5½" 430.00
#197/I, Be Patient, FB, ce, 6"-6¼" 360.00
#199/I, Feeding Time, 3L, ce, 5½"-5¾" 270.00
#201/I, Retreat to Safety, SB, ce, 5½"-5¾" 340.00
#203, Signs of Spring, CM, ce, 5¼" 540.00
#205, MI Hummel Dealer's Plaque (German), SB, ce, 5½x4¼" .610.00
#206, Angel Cloud, font, CM, ce, 3¼x4¾" 250.00
#217, Boy w/Toothache, SB, ce, 5¼"-5½" 230.00
#218 2/0, Birthday Serenade, FB, ce, 4¼"-4½" 430.00
#220 2/0, We Congratulate (w/base), FB, ce, 4" 340.00
#224/II, Wayside Harmony, table lamp, 3L, ce, 9½" 340.00
#226, The Mail Is Here, SB, ce, 4¼x6" 610.00
#229, Apple Tree Girl, table lamp, FB, ce, 7½" 650.00
#232, Happy Days, table lamp, LB, ce, 9¾" 360.00
#238A, Angel w/Lute, SB, ce, 2"-2½" 70.00
#239B, Girl w/Doll, SB, ce, 3½" 110.00
#240, Little Drummer, 3L, ce, 4"-4¼" 140.00
#246, Holy Family, font, SB, ce, 3⅛x4½" 70.00
#248/I, Guardian Angel, font, SB, ce, 2¾x6¼" 720.00
#256, Knitting Lesson, SB, ce, 7½" 630.00
#258, Which Hand?, SB, ce, 5¼"-5½" 450.00
#260A, Madonna (lg nativity set), 3L, ce, 9¾" 450.00
#260N, Moorish King (standing, lg nativityy set), MB, tw, 12¾" 405.00
#261, Angel Duet, 3L, ce, 5" 470.00
#262, Heavenly Lullaby, 3L, ce, 3½x5" 470.00

#264, Heavenly Angel, annual plate, 1971, 3L, ce, 7½" 360.00
#272, Singing Lesson, annual plate, 1979, LB, ce, 7½" 30.00
#277, Little Helper, annual plate, 1984, MB, ce, 7½" 35.00
#283, Feeding Time, annual plate, 1987, MB, ce, 7½" 185.00
#292, Meditation Plate, NC, ce, 7⅛" 70.00
#295, Suprise Plate, NC, oe, 7⅛" 70.00
#305, The Builder, SB, ce, 5½" 720.00
#308, Little Tailor, 3L, ce, 5¼"-5¾" 720.00
#311, Kiss Me, LB, ce, 6"-6¼" 250.00
#314, Confidentially, 3L, ce, 5¼"-5¾" 720.00
#317, Not for You, SB, ce, 5½" 540.00
#321, Wash Day, 3L, ce, 5½"-6" 290.00
#322, Little Pharmicist, SB, ce, 5¾"-6" 540.00
#327, Run-A-Way, 3L, ce, 5¼" 790.00
#328, Carnival, SB, ce, 5¾"-6" 540.00
#331, Crossroads, 3L, ce, 6¾" 540.00
#334, Homeward Bound, SB, ce, 5¼" 720.00
#337, Cinderella, 3L, ce, 4½" 1,080.00
#340, Letter to Santa Claus, 3L, ce, 7¼" 540.00
#345, A Fair Measure, 3L, ce, 5½"-5¾" 720.00
#348, Ring Around the Rosie, SB, ce, 6¾"-7" 2,880.00
#351, The Botanist, LB, ce, 4"-4¼" 1,080.00
#353/0, Spring Dance, 3L, ce, 5¼" 1,440.00
#355, Autumn Harvest, 3L, ce, 5" 720.00
#359, Tuneful Angel, 3L, ce, 2¾" 125.00
#361, Favorite Pet, SB, ce, 4½" 865.00
#364, Supreme Protection, MB, ce, 9"-9¼" 250.00
#367, Busy Student, SB, ce, 4¼" 610.00
#369, Follow the Leader, 3L, ce, 7" 1,225.00
#373, Just Fishing, LB, ce, 4¼"-4½" 720.00
#374, Lost Stocking, LB, ce, 4½" 135.00
#378, Easter Greetings, NC, oe, 5" 160.00
#380, Daisies Don't Tell, LB, ce, 5" 720.00
#383, Going Home, LB, ce, 5" 1,440.00
#386, On Secret Path, 3L, ce, 5¼" 720.00
#389, Girl w/Sheet of Music, 3L, ce, 2½" 125.00
#393, Dove, font, early sample, 3L, ce, 2¾x4¼" 1,440.00
#396, Ride Into Christmas, 3L, ce, 5¾" 1,440.00
#401, Forty Winks, early sample, LB, ce, 5¼" 2,160.00
#403, An Apple a Day, NC, oe, 6½" 240.00
#406, Pleasant Journey, MB, ce, 7⅛x6½" 1,980.00
#409, Coffee Break, MB, ce, 4" 215.00
#413, Whistler's Duet, MB, ce, 4¼" 360.00
#416, Jubilee, MB, ce, 6¼" 360.00
#418, What's New, NC, oe, 5¼" 240.00
#421, It's Cold, MB, ce, 5"-5¼" 250.00
#423, Horse Trainer, MB, ce, 4½" 185.00

Hutschenreuther

The Porcelain Factory C.M. Hutschenreuther operated in Bavaria from 1814 to 1969. After the death of the elder Hutschenreuther in 1845, his son Lorenz took over operations, continuing there until 1857 when he left to establish his own company in the nearby city of Selb. The original manufactory became a joint stock company in 1904, absorbing several other potteries. In 1969 both Hutschenreuther firms merged, and that company still operates in Selb. They have distributing centers in both France and the United States.

Bowl, vegetable; Revere Sylvia, wht w/gold trim, w/lid 250.00
Figurine, bears playing (2), wht, 4½" 110.00
Figurine, ducks, natural colors, #12, 3x3" 85.00
Figurine, First Waltz, dancing putti, wht, Tutter, 5" 110.00

Figurine, leopards (2) on base, 1930s, 9½" L, from $700 to 800.00
Figurine, mermaid, sgn Achtziger, lion in oval mk, 5¾x5" 275.00
Figurine, nude, head bk, arms reaching upward, paper label, 9"..235.00
Figurine, nude on ball, sgn Tutter, 8" 200.00
Figurine, nude standing on 1 ft, head bk, arms reaching, Tutter, 8"...185.00
Figurine, Playmates, Lorenz, 8x7" 195.00
Figurine, Ring Around the Rosey, 8", on separate 9" dia base.....265.00
Figurine, rooster/cat riding donkey, 7¾x6" 195.00
Figurine, sea gull in flight, wht, sgn Achtziger, 7x4½" 135.00
Nude, kneeling, hands at her head, Tutter, lion mk, 7" 165.00
Stein, tobacco pouch, inlaid lid, .5L 1,000.00
Tray, gold w/etched florals, Pickard style, gr mk/lion, 13" dia......155.00

Imari

Imari is a generic term which covers a broad family of wares. It was made in more than a dozen Japanese villages, but the name is that of the port from whence it was shipped to Europe. There are several types of Imari. The most common features a design with panels of birds, florals, or people surrounding a central basket of flowers. The colors used in this type are underglaze blue with overglaze red, gold, and green enamels. The Chinese also made Imari wares which differ from the Japanese type in several ways — the absence of spur marks, a thinner-type body, and a more consistent control of the blue. Imari-type wares were copied on the continent by Meissen and by English potters, among them Worcester, Derby, and Bow. Unless noted otherwise, our values are for Japanese ware.

Bowl, tree branch reserves, bamboo finial, w/hdls, 1900, 10" W.235.00
Bowl, 6 scenic panels, 1860s, sm mfg flaw, 3¾x9½" 250.00

Charger, multicolor Oriental scene with flowers and gold, nineteenth century, 25", $550.00.

Charger, florals/leaves w/gold, scalloped, 19th C, 12" 500.00
Charger, pine/bamboo/plum blossoms, 1850s, 14" 250.00
Charger, 3 foo dogs border (3X), floral center, late 19th C, 18"..525.00
Dish, Black Ship center, 7" dia 275.00
Flowerpot, phoenix/foliage panels, 3-ftd, 5¾x7¾" 225.00
Ginger jar, florals/leaves (3X), w/gold, ca 1950s, 12" 245.00
Plate, heron, paneled/foliate border, fan shape, 1800s, 10x10"....565.00
Plate, vase of flowers, scrolling floral border, Kangxi, 9" 365.00
Plate, water buffalo, phoenix border, Arita, early 18th C, 12".1,735.00
Plate, 3-lobe medallion, border: red/lt gr/gold reserves, 8½" 225.00
Platter, fish shape, 1800s, 15" L 575.00
Platter, lg cabbage-like central design, late 19th C, 11" L...........395.00
Vase, floral medallion/diapering, ribbed/fluted, 1800s, 9½" 1,100.00
Vase, lion/peony (2 wht panels) on cobalt, 6-sided, 1860s, 6" 235.00
Vase, wht cartouch (pine/rabbits/etc) on cobalt, dbl gourd, 1900, 9" ...225.00

Imperial Glass Company

The Imperial Glass Company was organized in 1901 in Bellaire,

Ohio, and started manufacturing glassware in 1904. Their early products were jelly glasses, hotel tumblers, etc., but by 1910 they were making a name for themselves by pressing quantities of carnival glass, the iridescent glassware that was popular during that time. In 1914 NuCut was introduced to imitate cut glass. The line was so popular that it was made in crystal and colors and was reintroduced as Collector's Crystal in the 1950s. From 1916 to 1920 they used the lustre process to make a line called Imperial Jewels. Free-Hand ware, art glass made entirely by hand using no molds, was made from 1922 to 1928.

The company entered bankruptcy in 1931 but was able to continue operations and reorganize as the Imperial Glass Corporation. In 1936 Imperial introduced the Candlewick line, for which it is best known. In the late thirties the Vintage Grape Milk Glass line was added, and in 1951 a major ad campaign was launched, making Imperial one of the leading milk glass manufacturers.

In 1940 Imperial bought the molds and assets of the Central Glass Works of Wheeling, West Virginia; in 1958 they acquired the molds of the Heisey Company; and in 1960 the molds of the Cambridge Glass Company of Cambridge, Ohio. Imperial used these molds, and after 1951 they marked their glassware with an 'I' superimposed over the 'G' trademark. The company was bought by Lenox in 1973; subsequently an 'L' was added to the 'IG' mark. In 1981 Lenox sold Imperial to Arthur Lorch, a private investor (who modified the L by adding a line at the top angled to the left, giving rise to the 'ALIG' mark). He in turn sold the company to Robert F. Stahl, Jr., in 1982. Mr. Stahl filed for Chapter 11 to reorganize, but in mid-1984 liquidation was ordered, and all assets were sold. A few items that had been made in '84 were marked with an 'N' superimposed over the 'I' for 'New Imperial.'

For more information, we recommend *Imperial Glass Encyclopedia*, *Vols I, II,* and *III,* edited by James Measell; and *Imperial Carnival Glass* by Carl. O. Burns. Our advisor is Joan Cimini; she is listed in the Directory under Ohio. See also Candlewick; Carnival Glass; Glass Animals and Figurines; Stretch Glass.

Ashtray, Cape Cod, crystal, #160/134/1, 4"	14.00
Ashtray, heart shape, #294, ruby slag, 4½"	25.00
Baked Apple, Traditional, crystal	8.00
Basket, Crocheted Crystal, 9"	37.50
Basket, Crocheted Crystal, 12"	60.00
Basket, ruby slag, #475, mini	45.00
Bottle, condiment; Cape Cod, crystal, #160/224, 6-oz	65.00
Bottle, cordial; Cape Cod, Ritz Blue, #160/256, 18-oz	250.00
Bottle, ketchup; Cape Cod, crystal, #160/237, 14-oz	210.00
Bowl, Cape Cod, crystal, hdls, #160/51F, 6"	33.00
Bowl, console; Crocheted Crystal, 11"	27.50
Bowl, Crocheted Crystal, Narcissus, 7"	40.00
Bowl, Dmn Quilt, blk, crimped, 7"	20.00
Bowl, heart; Cape Cod, crystal, hdld, #160/40H, 6"	20.00
Bowl, Hobnail; #641, purple slag, 8½"	95.00
Bowl, jelly; Beaded Block, bl opal, hdls	45.00
Bowl, mayonnaise; Crocheted Crystal, 5¼"	12.50
Bowl, Pipe, ruby slag, #1605, 7½"	40.00
Bowl, punch; Crocheted Crystal, 14"	65.00
Bowl, Rose, jade slag, #52c, 8"	65.00
Bowl, Rose, jade slag, #62c, 9"	75.00
Bowl, salad; Cape Cod, crystal, #7608A, 11"	90.00
Bowl, salad; Crocheted Crystal, 10½"	27.50
Bowl, soup; Katy, gr opal, 7"	80.00
Bowl, vegetable; Katy, bl opal, 9"	95.00
Box, dog, purple slag, #822	185.00
Box, squirrel, purple slag, #821, 5½"	180.00
Butter dish, Cape Cod, crystal, #160/161, 1/4-lb	45.00
Cake stand, Cape Cod, crystal, #150/103D, 11"	80.00
Cake stand, Crocheted Crystal, ftd, 12"	40.00

Candle holder, Cape Cod, crystal, #160/170, 3"	26.50
Candle holder, Crocheted Crystal, dbl, 4½"	17.50
Candle holder, Crocheted Crystal, Narcissus bowl shape	25.00
Candlestick, Free-Hand, heart/vine, wht on clear, bl cup, 10"	400.00
Candlesticks, Dolphin, caramel slag, 3779, 5", pr	65.00
Celery, Crocheted Crystal, oval, 10"	25.00
Celery tray, Huckabee, pk, oval, 8¼"	32.50
Champagne, Cape Cod, amber, #1602	25.00
Cheese & cracker, Crocheted Crystal, 12" plate, ftd dish	38.00
Cigarette holder, Cape Cod, crystal, ftd, #1602	12.50
Claret, Cape Cod, Azalea, #1602	20.00
Coaster, Cape Cod, crystal, flat, #160/1R, 4½"	9.00
Coaster, Cape Cod, crystal, w/spoon rest, #160/76	10.00
Cocktail, Cape Cod, crystal, #160b	12.00
Cocktail, Cape Cod, ruby, #160	27.00
Comport, Cape Cod, crystal, #160F, 5¼"	27.50
Comport, Katy, milk glass, 4¾"	45.00
Cookie jar, Cape Cod, crystal, wicker hdl, w/lid, #160/195, 6½"	100.00
Cordial, Collector's Crystal, crystal, #612	14.00
Cordial, Fancy Colonial, pk, #582, 1-oz	50.00
Creamer, Cape Cod, crystal, #160/30	12.00

Creamer and sugar bowl, Crocheted Crystal, flat bottoms, $25.00 each. (Photo courtesy Gene Florence)

Creamer, Crocheted Crystal, ftd	20.00
Cruet, Collector's Crystal, caramel slag, #505	50.00
Cruet, Octagon, jade, w/stopper, #505	75.00
Cup, punch; Crocheted Crystal, closed hdl	5.00
Cup, punch; Crocheted Crystal, open hdl	7.00
Cup & saucer, Pillar Flutes, lt bl	25.00
Decanter, bourbon; Cape Cod, crystal, #160/260	80.00
Decanter, Cask #1, Antique Blue	50.00
Decanter, Grape, Heather, #8	55.00
Egg cup, Cape Cod, crystal, #160/225	32.50
Goblet, Cape Cod, Evergreen, #160, 14-oz	55.00
Goblet, Chroma, amber (Maderia), #123	24.00
Goblet, Chroma, burgundy, #123	30.00
Ivy ball, Reeded (Spun), red, crystal ft, 4"	65.00
Jar, pokal; Cape Cod, crystal, #160/128, 11"	85.00
Ladle, mayonnaise; Crocheted Crystal	5.00
Ladle, punch; Cape Cod, crystal	30.00
Lamp, hurricane; Crocheted Crystal, w/shade, 11"	45.00
Mayonnaise, Katy, bl opal, w/underplate	120.00
Mayonnaise, Katy, gr opal, 3-pc	135.00
Mint dish, Cape Cod, crystal, heart shape, #160/49, 5"	25.00
Nappy, Pansy, caramel slag, hdl, 5"	35.00
Nut dish, Cape Cod, crystal, hdld, #160/184, 4"	30.00
Pitcher, Dew Drop, opal, #624, 56-oz	65.00
Pitcher, Windmill, red slag, satin	55.00
Plate, bread & butter; Cape Cod, crystal, #160/1D, 6½"	8.00
Plate, Crocheted Crystal, 13"	22.50
Plate, Crocheted Crystal, 14"	25.00
Plate, Crocheted Crystal, 17"	40.00
Plate, dinner; Cape Cod, crystal, #160/10D, 10"	37.50

Plate, salad bowl liner; Crocheted Crystal, 13"	22.50
Plate, salad; Crocheted Crystal, 8"	7.50
Plate, salad; Katy, bl opal, 8"	32.00
Plate, torte; Cape Cod, crystal, #1608F, 13"	37.50
Punch bowl, Crocheted Crystal, 14"	65.00
Relish, Cape Cod, crystal, 5-part, #160/102, 11"	70.00
Relish, Crocheted Crystal, 3-part, 11½"	25.00
Rose bowl, Wide Panel, marigold on milk glass	210.00
Salt cellar, ruby slag, 4-ftd, #61	16.00
Shakers, Cape Cod, crystal, #160/109, pr	20.00
Shakers, Cape Cod, Fern Green, #160/117, pr	60.00
Sherbet, Huckabee, pk, ftd	30.00
Stem, cocktail; Crocheted Crystal, 3½-oz, 4½"	12.50
Stem, parfait; Cape Cod, crystal, #1602, 6-oz	12.00
Stem, sherbet; Crocheted Crystal, 6-oz, 5"	10.00
Stem, water goblet; Crocheted Crystal, 9-oz, 7⅛"	14.00
Sugar bowl, Crocheted Crystal, ftd	20.00
Sugar bowl, Katy, bl opal	42.50
Toothpick holder, Octagon, caramel slag, #505	18.00
Tumbler, fruit juice; Crocheted Crystal, ftd, 6-oz, 6"	10.00
Tumbler, iced tea; Crocheted Crystal, ftd, 12-oz	15.00
Tumbler, Katy, gr opal, 9-oz	55.00
Tumbler, whiskey; Cape Cod, crystal, #160, 2½-oz	12.50
Vase, bud; Free-Hand, hearts/vines, lt gr on opal, 8½"	350.00
Vase, bud; peach & butterscotch w/lead lustre, 10"	200.00
Vase, Cape Cod, crystal, urn form w/hdls, #160/186, 10½"	165.00
Vase, Crocheted Crystal, 8"	20.00
Vase, Free-Hand, draped swags, gr-bl on marigold irid, 11½"	1,000.00
Vase, Free-Hand, gold lustre, swollen w/invt rim, ca 1921, 4¾", NM	300.00
Vase, Free-Hand, hearts/vines, orange on dk bl, 5¾"	900.00
Vase, Free-Hand, leaves, gr on cream w/gold irid, ca 1925, 10½"	800.00
Vase, Free-Hand, loops, bl on wht, baluster, att, ca 1925, 6¾"	300.00
Vase, Free-Hand, marigold irid, tapered w/flared rim, 6½"	175.00
Vase, Free-Hand, mc swirls in cobalt, orange int, stick neck, 9¾"	500.00
Vase, Free-Hand, orange w/deep orange throat, slender 10"	450.00
Vase, Free-Hand, peacock bl w/folded & stretched top border, 10½"	350.00
Vase, Free-Hand, swags, bl on opal, orange int, shouldered, 7½"	550.00
Vase, Free-hand, wht/bl/gray marbleized w/bl int, cylindrical, 9"	500.00
Vase, Katy, bl opal, #743n, 5½"	60.00
Vase, Katy, bl opal, #743x, 4½"	45.00
Vase, Katy, red, #743b, 5¼"	65.00
Vase, Mosaic, cobalt shaded & swirled w/opal, orange int, 6½"	490.00
Vase, Reeded, cobalt, squat, 5¾"	65.00
Vase, Reeded (Spun), red, 9"	75.00

Imperial Porcelain

The Blue Ridge Mountain Boys were created by cartoonist Paul Webb and translated into three-dimension by the Imperial Porcelain Corporation of Zanesville, Ohio, in 1947. These figurines decorated ashtrays, vases, mugs, bowls, pitchers, planters, and other items. The Mountain Boys series were numbered 92 through 108, each with a different and amusing portrayal of mountain life. Imperial also produced American Folklore miniatures, twenty-three tiny animals one inch or less in size, and the Al Capp Dogpatch series. Because of financial difficulties, the company closed in 1960.

American Folklore Miniatures

Cat, 1½", from $95 to	125.00
Cow, 1¾", from $95 to	125.00
Hound dogs, from $95 to	125.00
Plaque, store ad, Am Folklore Porcelain Miniatures, 4½"	450.00

Sow, from $95 to	125.00

Blue Ridge Mountain Boys by Paul Webb

Shakers, Ma and Old Doc, $115.00. (Photo courtesy Helene Guarnaccia)

Ashtray, #92, 2 men by tree stump, for pipes	125.00
Ashtray, #101, man w/jug & snake	120.00
Ashtray, #103, hillbilly & skunk	120.00
Ashtray, #105, baby, hound dog, & frog	135.00
Ashtray, #106, Barrel of Wishes, w/hound	115.00
Box, cigarette; #98, dog atop, baby at door, sq	165.00
Dealer's sign, Handcrafted Paul Webb Mtn Boys, rare, 9"	700.00
Decanter, #100, outhouse, man, & bird	125.00
Decanter, #104, Ma leaning over stump, w/baby & skunk	145.00
Decanter, man, jug, snake, & tree stump, Hispch Inc, 1946	125.00
Figurine, #101, man leans against tree trunk, 5"	125.00
Figurine, man on hands & knees, 3"	130.00
Figurine, man sitting, 3½"	145.00
Figurine, man sitting w/chicken on knee, 3"	130.00
Jug, #101, Willie & snake	95.00
Mug, #94, Bearing Down, 6"	95.00
Mug, #94, dbl baby hdl, 4¼"	95.00
Mug, #94, ma hdl, 4¼"	95.00
Mug, #94, man w/bl pants hdl, 4¼"	95.00
Mug, #94, man w/yel beard & red pants hdl, 4¼"	95.00
Mug, #99, Target Practice, boy on goat, farmer, 5¾"	95.00
Pitcher, lemonade	200.00
Planter, #81, man drinking from jug, sitting by washtub	95.00
Planter, #100, outhouse, man, & bird	125.00
Planter, #105, man w/chicken on knee, washtub	130.00
Planter, #110, man, w/jug & snake, 4½"	95.00

Miscellaneous

Items in this section that are designated 'IP' are miscellaneous novelties made by Imperial Porcelain; the remainder are of interest to Paul Webb collectors, though made by an unknown manufacturer. Prints on calendars and playing cards are signed 'Paul Webb.'

Artist board, babies or mtn women, sgn Paul Webb, 30x30"	275.00
Artist board, mtn boys only, sgn Paul Webb, 30x30"	275.00
Calendar, 1954, 12 sgn scenes, Brown & Bigelow, complete	65.00
Figurine, cat in high-heeled shoe, 5½" L	65.00
Hot pad, Dutch boy w/tulips, rnd, IP	30.00
Ink blotters, sgn scenes, ea	15.00
Mug, #29, man hdl, sgn Paul Webb, 4¾"	50.00
Planter, #106, dog sitting by tub, IP	95.00
Playing cards, ad: Rafe Oiling Gun, Brown & Bigelow, MIB	75.00
Shakers, pigs, 5", pr	95.00
Shakers, standing pigs, IP, 8", pr	110.00

Indian Tree

Indian Tree is a popular dinnerware pattern produced by various potteries since the early 1800s to recent times. Although backgrounds and borders vary, the Oriental theme is carried out with the gnarled, brown branch of a pink-blossomed tree. Among the manufacturers' marks, you may find represented such notable firms as Coalport, S. Hancock and Sons, Soho Pottery, and John Maddock and Sons. See also Johnson Brothers.

Bonbon, fluted, Coalport, 6¼" 20.00
Bowl, Aynsley, 2¾x8¾" 60.00
Bowl, cream soup; scalloped, Spode.......................................45.00
Bowl, fruit; Johnson Bros, 5" 9.00
Bowl, fruit; Morley, sm..8.00
Bowl, fruit; Spode, 5¼", set of 6 ....95.00
Bowl, Myott, 8"..20.00
Bowl, scalloped, Coalport, 1½x6" 40.00
Bowl, soup; Johnson Bros, 7¼" 13.00
Bowl, vegetable; John Maddock & Sons, ca 1935, w/lid, 8" dia 55.00
Bowl, vegetable; Johnson Bros, 8½" 25.00
Bowl, vegetable; Noritake, ca 1930s, w/hdls & lid, 10½" W 50.00
Butter pat, scalloped, #2/916, 4¼" 18.00
Candy dish, scalloped edge, gr mk, 5¼" L 20.00
Creamer & sugar bowl, Coalport, bone china mk, late.................40.00
Cup & saucer, AD; Minton...25.00
Cup & saucer, Spode 35.00
Dinner service, Coalport, serves 10+8 serving pieces, 144-pc 750.00
Egg cup, flat base, Johnson Bros, 1¾", set of 4 ....70.00
Gravy boat, w/attached underplate, Spode 88.00
Jar, Sadler, fancy shape, w/lid, 4½" 55.00
Pitcher, Coalport, 4¾" 65.00
Plate, cookie; Coalport, 10½" 55.00
Plate, Copeland Spode, 9", 12 for...425.00
Plate, dessert; ruffled rim, 8"..30.00
Plate, dinner; scalloped, Coalport, 10" 40.00
Plate, luncheon; Minton, #5185, 9¼", set of 8 ....100.00
Plate, Maddock, 8"..8.00
Plate, salad; scalloped, Coalport, 7¾", set of 6 ....85.00
Plate, sandwich; closed scroll hdls, Coalport, sq, 10" W 55.00
Plate, Staffordshire, 9" 12.00
Platter, Ashworth, 14½" 90.00

Platter, Buffalo China, 10½x7⅛", $100.00.

Platter, John Maddock & Son, 14" 35.00
Platter, well & tree, 21"...305.00
Tazza, scalloped ft, Coalport, 3¼x8" 75.00
Teacup & saucer, cone shape, scalloped, Coalport, gr mk............32.00
Teapot, Burgess & Lee 60.00
Tray, mc w/gold accents, Coalport, 10¾x8½" 85.00
Tray, octagonal, scalloped rim, Copeland, 8".............................65.00
Tray, serving; fluted, w/hdls, 10½", EX 48.00

Inkwells and Inkstands

Receptacles for various writing fluids have been used since ancient times. Through the years they have been made from countless materials — glass, metal, porcelain, pottery, wood, and even papier-mache. During the eighteenth century, gold or silver inkstands were presented to royalty; the well-known silver inkstand by Philip Syng, Jr., was used for the signing of the Declaration of Independence, and impressive brass inkstands with wells and pounce pots (sanders) were proud possessions of men of letters. When literacy vastly increased in the nineteenth century, the dip pen replaced the quill pen, and inkwells and inkstands were widely used and produced in a broad range of sizes in functional and decorative forms from ornate Victorian to flowing Art Nouveau and stylized Art Deco designs. However, the acceptance of the ballpoint pen literally put inkstands and inkwells 'out of business.' But their historical significance and intriguing diversity of form and styling fascinate today's collectors.

For further information we recommend *Collector's Encyclopedia to Inkwells, Books I* and *II,* by Veldon Badders (Collector Books). See also Bottles, Ink.

Blown, bl-gr, funnel-shaped opening, Am, mid-1800s, 2⅞x2⅝" dia 250.00
Blown, paperweight type, funnel opening, late 19th C, 4¼x2¾" dia ...275.00
Blown/cut glass, bl, faceted sq, brass mts, 2⅛x1⅜" sq 425.00
Blown/cut glass, vaseline, 3-tier w/facets, brass mts, 1890s, 2¾" ..550.00
Brass, pierced free-form base, hinged lid, sq cut glass well, 1900s.135.00
Britannia, pierced base, swirl glass well, European, 1800s 175.00
Bronze, Bacchante & grapevines before a thyrsus, Philippe, 12".920.00
Bronze, HP ruins landscape, dolphin finial, Fr, 1800s, 4⅜".........550.00
Bronze, Nouveau pendant branches, 2 wells w/hinged lids, 14" L...460.00
Cast brass, chestnut leaf & nut w/ladybug, glass insert, 1900s.....225.00
Cast brass w/hinged lid/fancy strapwork, 4 pen trays, Fr, 1900s, 4x6"...220.00
Ceramic, red glaze, 522.7 W Germany, 20th C, 2" sq, from $30 to....40.00
CI, Renaissance style, hinged lid, glass well, Am, 1890s, 4½" L.135.00
Cut glass, bl w/hinged brass mts, 8-sided, Am, 1900-10, 2¾" 450.00
Cut glass, cast wht metal lid w/gilt, 1900-15, 1½" sq....................55.00
Cut glass, mushroom-style top, Am, 1900-15, 2¼" sq...................95.00
Faience, HP Roman ruins, 2-hole, Sceaux France, ca 1900, 2⅛x4½"..185.00
Gilt dome top w/emb floral on cut/eng crystal base, ca 1890, 6½"...2,650.00
Patinated wht metal, Nouveau girl w/mandolin, Am, 1900s, 4½x7"...170.00
Pattern glass, brass mts, plastic lid, Am, early 1900s, 2½" 40.00
Pnt cast wht metal lion's head, hinged top, clear glass well, 3½"....210.00
Porc, floral w/gold, Rococo style, Germany, 1890s, 3½x3⅛" sq..175.00
Porc, foliate form w/gold surface, Fr, 1850-60, 5" W, from $150 to ..170.00
Porc, maroon w/gold Rococo, brass mts, dome lid, Fr, 1890, 2½" .85.00
Porc, pierced sides, bl bamboo, Japan, late 1800s, 2¼" sq...........185.00
Pottery, Rockingham, funnel type w/fluting, Am, 1850-60, 3" dia 125.00
Pottery, swan/egg/tree trunk on top, mc w/gold, Staffordshire, 1860s ...250.00
Pottery, thrown, circular contour, sgn KM, Am, 20th C, 3¼" dia....35.00
Pressed glass, Sawtooth, Bakelite insert, Am, ca 1900, 2⅝x3" dia ...90.00
Pressed glass/Bakelite, Aavis Automatic Inkstand, ca 1889, 3½x3" ...25.00
Sheet brass w/Nouveau-style pierced decor, porc insert, Am, 1900-15...95.00
Silver dome w/chased florals, cut/eng crystal base, 1850s, 6¼" ...1,750.00
Stoneware, old lady w/bonnet, tan w/brn details, 2¼", EX 275.00
Stoneware, tiered body, Am, ca 1850-60, 3", from $45 to 50.00
Trn wood, HP cherries, hinged lid, glass insert, early 1900s, 3½".135.00
Wood, cvd nut & leaf, Germany (?), 1890-1900, 5" L , from $125 to ..140.00

Insulators

The telegraph was invented in 1844. The devices developed to hold the electrical transmission wires to the poles were called insulators. The telephone, invented in 1876, intensified their usefulness; and by the turn of the century, thousands of varieties were being produced in pottery, wood, and glass of various colors. Even though it has been rumored that red glass insulators exist, none have ever been authenticated. There are amber-colored insulators that appear to have a red tint to the amber, and those are called red-amber. Many insulators are embossed with patent dates.

Of the more than 3,000 types known to exist, today's collectors evaluate their worth by age, rarity of color and, of course, condition. Aqua and green are the most common colors in glass, dark brown the most common in porcelain. Threadless insulators (for example, CD #701.1) made between 1850 and 1865, bring prices well into the hundreds, sometimes even the thousands, if in mint condition.

In the listings that follow, the CD numbers are from an identification system developed in the late 1960s by N.R. Woodward.

Those seeking additional information about insulators are encouraged to contact Line Jewels NIA #1380 (whose address may be found in the Directory under Clubs, Newsletters, and Catalogs) or attend a club-endorsed show. (For information see Directory under Florida for Jacqueline Linscott.) In the listings that follow those stating 'no name' have no company identification, but do have embossed numbers, dots, etc. Those stating 'no embossing' are without raised letters, dots, or any other markings.

Key:
* (asterisk) — Canadian
BE — base embossed
CB — corrugated base
CD — Consolidated Design
FDP — flat drip points
RB — rough base
RDP — round drip points
SB — smooth base
SDP — sharp drip points

Threaded Pin-type and Threadless Glass Insulators

CD 102, California, SB, bl 25.00
CD 1038, Cutter Pat April 26, 04, SB, aqua 300.00
CD 114, Hemingray/No 11, SDP, lt aqua 8.00
CD 114, Hemingray/No 11, SDP, red-amber 7,000.00
CD 114.2, The Standard Glass Insulator Co, BE, aqua...........2,000.00
CD 115, Whitall Tatum/No 3, SB, lt straw 2.00
CD 121, AM Tel & Tel Co, SB, lt gr 10.00
CD 121, C & P Tel Co, SB, aqua 8.00
CD 121, Gaynor/No 160, SDP, ice bl 12.00
CD 122, Lynchburg/No 30, RDP, aqua 8.00
CD 122*, Dominion-16, RDP, lt peach 2.00
CD 125, Hemingray/No 15, SDP, gr 75.00
CD 128, Armstrong CSC, SB, bl tint..2.00
CD 133, City Fire Alarm, SB, lt aqua 100.00
CD 134, Am Ins Co/Pat Sep 13 1881, BE, lt gr 40.00
CD 134, K C G W, SB, gr-aqua 18.00
CD 134, T-H E Co, SB, lt bl-aqua 10.00
CD 136, B&O, SB, gr-aqua 20.00
CD 140, Jumbo, SB, aqua 300.00
CD 145, G T P Tel Co, SB, Aqua 15.00
CD 145, Hawley PA/USA, SB, milky bl-aqua..................................25.00
CD 152, B, SB, aqua 1.00
CD 154, Hemingray-42, RDP, aqua 1.00
CD 154, Hemingray-42, SB, Hemingray Blue..................................30.00
CD 154, McLaughlin-42, SDP, emerald gr 75.00
CD 154*, Dominion-42, RDP, lt straw 4.00
CD 155, Hemingray-45, SB, clear..1.00
CD 157, Brookfield, SB, aqua 10.00
CD 160, Brookfield/New York, SB, gr...5.00
CD 161, California, SB, purple 30.00
CD 161, California, SDP, smoky peach..1,750.00
CD 162, Gaynor/No 36-190, SDP, aqua w/milk swirls.................75.00
CD 162, Maydwell-19, RDP, dk straw..2.00
CD 162*, 1678, RDP, lt gr 100.00

CD 162*, 1678, SDP, lt gr...150.00
CD 164, McLaughlin/No 20, SDP, aqua 5.00
CD 202, Hemingray-53, RDP, ice aqua 15.00
CD 203, Armstrong TW, SB, clear 1.00
CD 213, Hemingray/No 43, RDP, aqua 12.00
CD 228, Brookfield, SB, dk aqua..500.00
CD 231, Hemingray-820, CB, clear...25.00
CD 238, Hemingray-514, CB, honey-amber 325.00
CD 250, NEGM Co, SB, aqua..1,250.00
CD 252, No 2 Cable, RB, dk aqua..10.00
CD 252, No 2 Cable, RB, orange-amber 300.00
CD 262, No 2 Columbia, SB, lt bl-aqua...175.00
CD 267.5, NEGM Co, SB, emerald gr 200.00

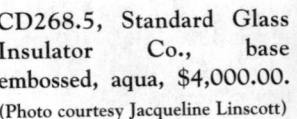

CD268.5, Standard Glass Insulator Co., base embossed, aqua, $4,000.00.
(Photo courtesy Jacqueline Linscott)

CD 297, FM Locke Victor NY/No 16, SB, dk aqua 15.00
CD 317, Chambers/Pat Aug 14 1877, SB, lt aqua 500.00
CD 327, Corning Pyrex TM Reg US Pat Off, SB, carnival.........150.00
CD 729.4, Mulford & Biddle/83 John St NY SB, aqua 1,250.00
CD 734.8*, no embossing, SB, olive blk glass 300.00
CD 735, Chester/NY, SB, aqua 600.00
CD 736, NY & ERR, SB, lt gr-aqua 3,000.00
CD 742.3, MTCo, BE, lt teal bl..600.00

Irons

History, geography, art, and cultural diversity are all represented in the collecting of antique pressing irons. The progress of fashion and invention can be traced through the evolution of the pressing iron.

Over seven hundred years ago, implements constructed of stone, bone, wood, glass, and wrought iron were used for pressing fabrics. Early ironing devices were quite primitive in form, and heating techniques included inserting a hot metal slug into a cavity of the iron, adding hot burning coals into a chamber or pan, and placing the iron directly on hot coals or a hot surface.

To the pleasure of today's collectors, some of these early irons, mainly from the period of 1700 to 1850, were decorated by artisans who carved and painted them with regional motifs typical of their natural surroundings and spiritual cultures.

Beginning in the mid-1800s, new cultural demands for fancy wearing apparel initiated a revolution in technology for types of irons and methods to heat them. Typical of this period is the fluter which was essential for producing the ruffles demanded by the nineteenth-century ladies. Hat irons, polishers, and numerous unusual iron forms were also used during this time, and provided a means to produce crimps, curves, curls, and special fabric textures. Irons from this era are characterized by their unique shapes, odd handles, latches, decorations, and even revolving mechanisms.

Also during this time, irons began to be heated by burning liquid and gaseous fuels. Gradually the new technology of the electrically heated iron replaced all other heating methods, except in the more rural areas and undeveloped countries. Even today the Amish communities utilize gasoline fuel irons.

In the listings that follow, prices are given for examples in best possible as-found condition. Damage, repairs, plating, excessive wear, rust, and missing parts can dramatically reduce value. For further information we recommend *Irons By Irons*, *More Irons By Irons*, and *Even More Irons by Irons* by our advisor Dave Irons; his address and information for ordering these books are given in the Directory under Pennsylvania.

Alcohol, Geo L Marion...NY, 1897, 6", w/trivet, from $150 to...**200.00**
Box, English, #10, brass, lift-up gate, mid-1800s, 7¾", $150 to ..**200.00**
Box, European, brass/iron, mid-1700s, 10", from $300 to **500.00**
Box, Germany, prancing lion on body, hinged at bk, ca 1900, 6½"...**250.00**
Box, India, brass, vent holes, front latch, bk hinge, late 1800s, 8"....**100.00**
Box, Scottish, C Mather, iron/brass, after 1850, 6", from $800 to ..**1,000.00**
Box w/thermometer, S Waterman...Wis...1889, 7⅜", from $300 to...**500.00**
Buttonhole, Pat June 1901 Iron Toy, movable hdl, 6½", from $300 to..**400.00**
Drop-in-bk, European, w/trivet, early 1800s, 6¼", from $300 to ...**500.00**
Flat, cold hdl w/holes & spike support, late 1800s, 6⅛", $100 to ..**150.00**
Flat, Fr, #2, cast, belled-out hdl, late 1800s, 6⅞", from $50 to **70.00**
Flat, Fr, brass posts, cutwork trivet, flower/urn top, 1800s, 6¼" ..**400.00**
Flat, Ober #6 Pat Mar 19 '12, cast, 6", from $70 to **100.00**
Flat, Russian, cast, late 1800s, 6½", from $100 to........................**150.00**
Flower, G Molla NY, brass base, iron top, late 1800s, 6¾", $100 to......**150.00**
Fluter, clamp-on, HB Adams Pat Pending, ca 1875, 3½" roll, $200 to.**300.00**
Fluter, combination, Patented, wooden tin-covered base, late 1800s ...**500.00**
Fluter, electric, C Vigneron...Ferry NJ, ca 1900, 6" roll, $500 to ...**750.00**
Fluter, H Sauerbier...1866, pinstriping, 6" roll, from $150 to **200.00**

Gas, Central Mfg. Co., chimney openings on sides, closed-in front, EX, $250.00.

Gasoline, Sunshine...Pat Pending, early 1900s, 7½", from $70 to...**100.00**
Goffering, European, CI, early 1900s, 8¼", from $100 to............**150.00**
Goffering, European, iron, tripod base, 1850s, 8¼", from $250 to....**300.00**
Goffering, European, wrought iron, sm monkey tail, tripod, 1800, 11"...**750.00**
Hat, R Raines & Co..., wood tolliker, late 1800s, 3⅛", from $100 to...**150.00**
Hat, toliker, Fr, CI, smooth bottom, late 1800s, 5¼", from $100 to......**150.00**
Little, cast swan, RM Harpel...PA, early 1900s, 3⅜", from $300 to **500.00**
Little, cylinder grip, ca 1900, 3¾", from $30 to **50.00**
Little, Grey Iron, rope hdl, right-hand twist, 1900s, 2¾", $200 to..**300.00**
Little, ox tongue, slug, European, brass, 1850s, 4⅞", w/trivet **300.00**
Little, slug, English, #2, all brass, lift-up gate, late 1800s, 3⅞"....**200.00**
Little, wire hdl, ca 1900, 4", from $50 to..**70.00**
Little, wood grip, Victor #10, J&E Stevens, ca 1900, 3", from $150 to..**200.00**
Movable chimney, Kimachi Pat, damper adjusts, after 1925, 6¾".**70.00**
Natural gas, Bless & Drake...Pat App For, early 1900s, 6¼", $150 to ..**200.00**
Ox tongue, European, wrought iron, hinged gate, 1700s, 10", $200 to ..**300.00**
Ox tongue, slug or gas jet, Aver Wein, lift-up gate, 1900s, 8¼"..**150.00**
Polisher, Keystone, Pat M Shimer...Sept 4 1883, 4⅞" **150.00**
Polisher, Mrs Streeters...Sept 6 87, movable hdl, 5½", from $150 to ..**200.00**
Seam, Lightning...'92 Bridgeport CT USA, 7", from $200 to **300.00**
Sleeve, Pat'd June 15 1897, long flat toe, 9⅞", from $150 to......**200.00**
Slug, English, brass/iron, lyre lift gate, late 1800s, 7⅞", minimum..**750.00**
Slug, European, brass cutwork, eng o/l plated top, 1850s, 7", minimum...**750.00**

Swan, CI, red w/yel pinstripes, 2¼", from $350 to......................**400.00**
Tailor, Wapak #12, cast, ca 1900, 9¼", from $70 to **100.00**
Tailor/steam, Koenig New Jersey, ca 1900, 11¼", from $70 to **100.00**
Tall chimney, E Bless R Drake...1852, vulcan face damper, 6¼".**150.00**

Ironstone

During the last quarter of the eighteenth century, English potters began experimenting with a new type of body that contained calcinated flint and a higher china clay content, intent on producing a fine durable whiteware — heavy, yet with a texture that would resemble porcelain. To remove the last trace of yellow, a minute amount of cobalt was added, often resulting in a bluish-white tone. Wm and John Turner of Caughley and Josiah Spode II were the first to manufacture the ware successfully. Others, such as Davenport, Hicks and Meigh, and Ralph and Josiah Wedgwood, followed with their own versions. The latter coined the name 'Pearl' to refer to his product and incorporated the term into his trademark. In 1813 a fourteen-year patent was issued to Charles James Mason, who called his ware Patented Ironstone. Francis Morley, G.L. Asworth, T.J. Mayer, and other Staffordshire potters continued to produce ironstone until the end of the century. While some of these patterns are simple to the extreme, many are decorated with in-mold designs of fruit, grain, and foliage on ribbed or scalloped shapes. In the 1830s transfer-printed designs in blue, mulberry, pink, green, and black became popular; and polychrome versions of Oriental wares were manufactured to compete with the Chinese trade. See also Mason's Ironstone. Our advise for this category comes from Home Place Antiques, whose address is listed in the Directory under Illinois.

Baker, oblong, scalloped rim, Johnson Bros, 1¼x7¼x5⅛" **20.00**
Bowl, syllabub; Gothic-type shape, Furnival, w/hdls, 6x11½" W ..**450.00**
Bowl, vegetable; Fig, Wedgwood, w/lid, 1856, 7¼x13⅜x9¼".....**150.00**
Bowl, vegetable; Wheat, Ceres shape, Elsmore & Forster, w/lid..**175.00**
Cake stand, allover emb creamware-type motif, 5x10" **165.00**
Child's set, no emb, 5¾" teapot+2 c/s & 6 4½" plates, EX **100.00**
Compote, fluted/scalloped rim, GP Co, 6¼x9½" **155.00**
Compote, Sydenham, 6-sided pyramid lid, TR Boote, 7½x10½".**565.00**
Compote, wheat emb at int rim, Hughes & Son, 3½x9½" **150.00**
Creamer, Chelsea, Meakin, 6"...**50.00**
Creamer, design emb at hdl, Cockson & Seddon, 6¼", NM.........**80.00**
Creamer, Sydenham, T&R Boote, 5½"..**130.00**
Creamer & sugar bowl, Red Cliff...**20.00**
Cup & saucer, Budded Vine, Meakin..**32.00**
Cup & saucer, Ivy Wreath, Meir...**45.00**
Cup & saucer, Prairie, Lively & Powell..**30.00**
Cup & saucer, Sydenham...**40.00**
Pitcher, Budded Vine, J&G Meakin, 12"..**145.00**
Pitcher, Cable & Ring, Cookson & Seddon, 9", NM **130.00**
Pitcher, Corn & Oats, dtd 1863, J Wedgwood, 12" **325.00**
Pitcher, Fig, paneled body, Wedgwood, 9"...................................**195.00**
Pitcher, Girard, paneled, Ridgway & Bates, slender, 12" **235.00**
Pitcher, leaves at top of beaded hdl, T&R Boote, 13" **175.00**
Pitcher, Oak Leaf & Acorn, Clarke, 13" **150.00**
Pitcher, rope trim at top of hdl, J&G Meakin, 13" **135.00**
Pitcher, Square Ridged, Johnson Bros, 8½".................................**165.00**
Plate, Bellflower, John Edwards, 10" **50.00**
Plate, Fern, Furnival & Sons, 10¾" **60.00**
Plate, Ivy Wreath, Meir & Son, 10½" **70.00**
Plate, Memnon, Meir & Son, 10" **40.00**
Plate, Prairie, J Clementson, 9½" **22.00**
Plate, Ribbed Grape, scalloped, W&E Corn, 9" **25.00**
Plate, Starflower, JW Pankhurst, 10" **38.00**
Plate, Sydenham, T&R Boote, 9½"..**35.00**

Plate, Virginia, Brougham & Mayers, 10" 32.00
Plate, Wheat & Clover, Turner & Tomkinson, 8" 30.00
Plate, Wheat & Clover, Turner & Tomkinson, 9" 45.00
Platter, plain, oval, Alcock, 10½x15½" 35.00
Platter, President, John Edwards, 15½" 110.00
Platter, Wheat, Turner, Goddard & Co, 18½x13½", EX..............75.00
Sugar bowl, Ceres, Elsmore & Forster, 7¾" 135.00
Sugar bowl, Full Ribbed, flower finial, Pankhurst 225.00
Sugar bowl, Paneled Grape, Furnival, 8" 145.00
Sugar bowl, paneled ovoid, ornate hdls, Maddock, 7x7" 160.00
Syrup pitcher, plain, pear shape, pewter lid, NM......................165.00
Teapot, Bordered Fuchsia, Shaw, 10" 350.00
Teapot, Ceres, Elsmore & Forster, EX.......................................180.00
Teapot, Laurel Wreath, Elsmore & Forster, knot finial, 9¾" 235.00
Teapot, Washington, emb floral, Meir, 9½" 265.00
Tureen, sauce; Ribbed Bud, Pankhurst, 8" L, +undertray 400.00
Tureen, sauce; Wheat, oval, Elsmore & Forster, +9⅛x7" undertray ..175.00
Tureen, soup; Ceres, Elsmore & Forster, 13" W, EX....................235.00
Tureen, soup; paneled, flower finial, +tray/ladle, Red Cliff, 12" H......165.00
Tureen, vegetable; Columbia, w/lid & hdls, ftd, Wooliscroft, 11" W..185.00
Tureen, vegetable; President, Edwards, w/lid, 8x9" dia 235.00

Patterned Ironstone

Bowl, vegetable; Carrare, pk transfer, unmk, 1⅝x7⅜x5⅞" 85.00
Coffeepot, Canella, brn transfer, Challinor, 14", EX.....................95.00
Coffeepot, Tyrol, purple transfer, Wedgwood, rpr, 10" 75.00
Compote, Summer Time, blk transfer, T&R Boote, 5½x9½", NM ...145.00
Creamer, Brentwood, cloverleaves, bl transfer, WM Adams & Sons..28.00
Cup & saucer, Cleopatra, brn transfer 25.00
Cup & saucer, Paradise, purple transfer, Livsley Powell 85.00
Pitcher, birds on branch, hummingbirds at rim, brn transfer, 7", NM ..130.00
Pitcher, milk; Tyrol, purple transfer, Wedgwood, 8¾", NM...........60.00
Plate, allover roses/leaves, red transfer, 10" 28.00
Plate, Corinthian, pk transfer, Challinor, 10"...............................20.00
Plate, Excelsior, gr transfer w/mc, 12-sided, Wolliscroft, 10" 50.00
Plate, Feather, gr transfer w/mc, W&C, 9⅜", NM.......................25.00
Plate, Indian Bridge, 12-sided, SA & Co, 10⅝", EX......................25.00
Plate, Montill, bl transfer, Davenport, 8" 32.00
Plate, pagodas/birds/flowers, HP/transfer, Adams, 8" 650.00
Plate, Pastoral, purple transfer, England, 1790, 10⅜" 30.00
Platter, Blantyre, brn transfer, Meigh & Son, 22x17" 185.00
Platter, butterflies/floral, mc, Ashworth, 20" 110.00
Platter, Eochara, blk transfer, canted corners, 12".......................165.00
Platter, Gipsy, bl transfer, 15x11¾" 80.00
Platter, Oriental design, mc, GL Ashworth, 15" 165.00
Platter, well & tree; Delft, bl transfer, Minton, 20" 110.00
Punch bowl, mc flower basket transfer w/gold, 1850s, 14¼" 250.00
Tureen, soup; Lahore, mc transfer, TR Boote, lid/ladle, 8x13" 175.00
Tureen, vegetable; boats/rope border, brn transfer, 12" L, EX......115.00
Waste bowl, Seaweed, bl transfer, Ridgeway, 3⅜x5⅝" sia 35.00

Italian Glass

Throughout the twentieth century, one of the major glassmaking centers of the world was the island of Murano. From the Stile Liberte work of Artisi Barovier (1890 – 1920s) to the early work of Ettore Sottsass in the 1970s, they excelled in creativity and craftsmanship. The 1920s to 1940s featured the work of glass designers like Ercole Barovier for Barovier and Toso and Vittorio Zecchin, Napoleone Martinuzzi and Carlo Scarpa for Venini. Many of these pieces are highly prized by collectors.

The 1950s saw a revival of Italy as a world-reknown design center for all of the arts. Glass led the charge with the brightly colored work of Fulvio Bianconi for Venini, Dino Martens for Aureliano Toso, and Ercole Barovier for Barovier and Toso. The best of these pieces are extremely desirable. The '60s and '70s have also seen many innovative designs with work by the Finnish Tapio Wirkkala, the American Thomas Stearns, and many other designers.

Unfortunately, amongst the great glass, there was a plethora of commercial ashtrays, vases, and figurines produced that, though having some value, do not compare in quality and design to the great glass of Murano.

Venini: The Venini company was founded in 1921 by Paolo Venini, and he led the company until his death in 1959. Major Italian designers worked for the firm, including Vittorio Zecchin, Napoleone Martinuzzi, Carlo Scarpa, and Fulvio Bianconi. After his death, his son-in-law, Ludovico de Santillana, ran the factory and employed designers like Toni Zucchieri, Tapio Wirkkala, and Thomas Stearns. The company is known for creative designs and techniques including Inciso (finely etched lines), Battuto (carved facets), Sommerso (controlled bubbles), Pezzato (patches of fused glass), and Fascie (horizontal colored lines in clear glass). Until the mid-'60s, most pieces were signed with acid-etched 'Venini Murano ITALIA.' In the '60s they started engraving the signatures. The factory still exists.

Barovier: In the late 1920s, Ercole Barovier took over the Artisti Barovier and started designing many different vases. In the 1930s he merged with Ferro Toso and became Barovier and Toso. He designed many different series of glass including the Barbarico (rough, acid-treated brown or deep blue glass), Eugenio (free-blown vases), Efeso, Rotallato, Dorico, Egeo (vases incorporating murrine designs), and Primavera (white etched glass with black bands). He designed until 1974. The company is still in existence. Most pieces were unsigned.

Aureliano Toso: The great glass designer Dino Martens was involved with the company from about 1938 to 1965. It was his work that produced the very desirable Oriente vases. This technique consisted of free-formed patches of green, yellow, blue, purple, black, and white stars and pieces of zanfirico canes fused into brilliantly colored vases and bowls. His El Dorado series was based on the same technique but was not opaque. He also designed pieces with alternating groups of black and white filigrana lines. Pieces are unsigned.

Seguso: Flavio Poli became the artistic director of Seguso in the late 1930s and remained until 1963. He is known for his Corroso (acid-etched glass) and his Valve series (elegant forms of two to three layers of colored glass with a clear glass casing).

Archimede Seguso: In 1946 Archimede Seguso left the Seguso Vetri D'Arte to open a new company and designed many innovative pieces. His Merlatto (thin white filigrana suspended three dimensionally) series is his most famous. The epitome of his work is where a colored glass (yellow or purple) is windowed in the merlotti. His Macchia Ambra Verde is yellow and spots on a gold base encased in clear glass. The A Piume series contained feathers and leaves suspended in glass. Pieces are unsigned.

Alfredo Barbini: Barbini was a designer known for his sculptures of sea subjects and his amorphic-shaped vases with an inner core of red or blue glass with a heavy layer of finely incised outer glass. He worked in the 1950s to the 1960s, and some pieces are signed.

Vistosi: Although this glassworks was started in the 1940s, fame came in the 1960s and 1970s with the birds designed by Allesandro Pianon and the early work of the Memphis school designer, Ettore Sottsass. Pieces may be signed.

AVEM: This company is known for its work in the 1950s and 1960s. The designer, Ansolo Fuga, did work using a solid white glass with inclusions of multicolored murrines.

Cenedese: This is a postwar company led by Gino Cenedese with Alfredo Barbini as designer. When Barbini left, Cenedese took over the design work and also used the free-lanced designs of Fulvio Bianconi. They are known for their figurines and vases with suspended murrines.

Cappellin: Venini's original partner (1921 – 25), Giacomo Cappellin, opened a short-lived company (1925 – 32) that was to become extremely important. His chief designer was the young Carlo Scarpa who was to create many masterpieces in glass both for Cappellin and then Venini.

Ettore Sottsass: Sottass founded the Memphis School of Design in the 1970s. He is an extremely famous modern designer who designed several series of glass for the Vistosi Glass Company. The pieces were created in limited editions, signed and numbered, and each piece was given a name.

Our advisor for this category is Howard Lockwood, publisher of *Vetri: Italian Glass News*. For further information concerning Mr. Lockwood or this publication, see the Directory under New Jersey.

Venini Glass

Paolo Venini, for Venini, Mosaico-zanfirico vase with slanted rim, turquoise with white netting, 14x3¾", $7,500.00. (Photo courtesy David Rago)

A Machie: vase, sgn, 9½" 11,073.00
A Pezzame: vase, red/bl/gr, sgn, 10½" 9,988.00
Battuto, vase, salmon, sgn, 8¾" 12,822.00
Battuto: vase, bl, 12" 6,994.00
Battuto: vase, red, sgn, 7½" 15,840.00
Canne: pitcher, red/yel/turq/clear, 5½" 539.00
Con Fiori: bowl, wht/blk interior flowers, sgn, 3¼" ..4,465.00
Coreano: vase, bl/gr, sgn, 14" 2,330.00
Corroso: bird, clear, sgn, 7" 863.00
Corroso: bowl, gr, sgn, 2½" 520.00
Corroso: vase, sq, 4½" 2,070.00
Egg: purple/gold spiral, sgn, 6¼" 140.00
Fasce Orrizontali: bottle, gr w/red band, sgn, 13½" ...3,497.00
Fasce Orrizontali: vase, 2 necks, blk/red stripes, sgn, 8½" 8,225.00
Fasce Verticale: bottle, bl/gr, sgn, 7¼" 3,760.00
Fasce Verticale: hurricane shades, sgn, 12", 3 for ...2,590.00
Fazzoletto: bl/gr/wht zanfirico, sgn, 3½" 113.00
Fazzoletto: blk exterior/wht interior, sgn, 7¾" 1,748.00
Fazzoletto: clear/wht zanfirico, sgn, 11½" 2,394.00
Fazzoletto: gr irid, sgn, 3½" 320.00
Fazzoletto: pk/wht zanfirico, sgn, 11" 1,840.00
Fazzoletto: stretched bl/wht/clear, sgn, 8¾" 4,935.00
Fazzoletto: turq, 6" 309.00
Fazzoletto: wht exterior/tan interior, sgn, 4" 219.00
Filigrana bird: wht/clear, 4¼" 6,463.00
Forato: vase, bl, 1 hdl, sgn, 10¾" 1,748.00
Forato: vase, bl w/pierced hole, sgn 1,540.00
Giada: bottle, gr w/stopper, sgn, 12" 1,840.00
Hourglass: gr/lav, 6¾" 229.00
Incalmo: fan vase, sgn 4,935.00
Inciso: stoppered bottle, bl, sgn, 7¼" 428.00
Inciso: stoppered bottle, red, 12" 1,183.00
Mezza Filigrana: leaf, sgn, 8" L 408.00

Mezza Filigrana: vase, 20½" 8,225.00
Morandi: bottle, gr stem, sgn, 14" 816.00
Occhi: vase, aubergine, sgn, 5½" 1,748.00
Occhi: vase, yel/blk, sgn, 1994, 12" 1,840.00
Pezzato: bottle vase, bl/wht/red/purple, 13" 17,625.00
Pezzato: vase, bl/gr/red/clear, sgn, 11" 6,564.00
Pezzato: vase, cigar shaped, sgn, 10½" 8,050.00
Pezzato: vase, red/bl/clear, sgn, 12" 5,513.00
Pezzato: vase, red/bl/gr/clear, sgn, 8¾" 7,107.00
Pezzato: vase, red/bl/straw/gr, sgn, 9½" 11,656.00
Soffiato: Libellula, sgn, 6" 1,632.00
Sommerso: vase, gr w/gold, sgn, 8½" 4,313.00
Tessuto: vase, yel/clear filigrana, sgn, 8" 4,954.00
Tumblers, red/gr/gray/bl/purple/yel, 4¼", 10 for 3,738.00
Zanfirico: vase, wht/bl, sgn, 7¼" 525.00

Non-Venini Glass

Archimede Seguso, bowl, turq-bl shell shape, 2½" H 117.00
Archimede Seguso, bowl: gr/silver/amethyst, ftd, 10½" 200.00
Archimede Seguso, bowl: spiral ribs, gold inclusions, 6¾" 175.00
Archimede Seguso, covered bowl, pk, wht bird finial, 10½" H ...233.00
Archimede Seguso, Losanghe: vase, red, cylindrical, label, 11" ..1,380.00
Archimede Seguso, Macchia Ambre Verde: ashtray, 6¾" H 699.00
Archimede Seguso, Merletto: bottle, bl, 8" 2,760.00
Archimede Seguso, Piume: vase, amber, 7 feathers, 10½" 6,325.00
Archimede Seguso, Polveri: vase, amethyst/gold, 3 openings, 9" ..1,725.00
Aureliano Toso, Aventurina: bird, 10½" 1,645.00
Aureliano Toso, Eldorado: vase, 12½" 15,275.00
Aureliano Toso, Mezza Filigrana: pitcher, bianca nera, 10¼" ..7,638.00
Aureliano Toso, Mezza Filigrana: vase, bianca nera, 11¼" 4,032.00
Aureliano Toso, Oriente: ashtray, 4" 520.00
Aureliano Toso, Oriente: Geltrude vase, 11½" 35,250.00
Aureliano Toso, Oriente: gooseneck vase, 16¾" 19,975.00
Aureliano Toso, Oriente: Nabucco vase, 9½" 7,200.00
Aureliano Toso, Oriente: vase, 9½" 8,225.00
AVEM, Anse Volante: vase, red, pierced hdl, 9½" 4,320.00
AVEM, Reazioni Policrome: bowl, 3x8" 115.00
AVEM, Rooster, sgn, 8¼" 280.00
AVEM, vase, wht w/red/bl disks & zanfirico canes, 15¾" 1,748.00
AVEM, vase, wht w/yel/bl/red cane patches, 13" 3,205.00
AVEM, vase, wht w/yel/red/bl cranes, 3-sided, 19" 3,656.00
AVEM, vase, zanfirico strips, canes, murrines, pierced hole, 15¾" ...2,914.00
Barbini, Corroso/Sommerso: vase, red, 5¼" 690.00
Barbini, Pezzato: vase, apricot/wht, sgn, 8¾" 1,150.00
Barbini, Scavo: vase, maritime scene, sgn, 10" 6,900.00
Barbini, Sommerso: vase, amber, 9½" 395.00
Barbini, Vetro Pesante: vase, ftd, 9½" 7,893.00
Barovier, Ambrato: bird, 7¾" 9,400.00
Barovier, Athena Cattedrale: vase, 7½" 6,994.00
Barovier, Barbarico: vase, pinched side, 9" 1,748.00
Barovier, Christian Dior: decanter, 9" 9,908.00
Barovier, Cordanato D'Oro: lamp base, 15" 229.00
Barovier, Cordonato D'Oro: bowl, 8½" 276.00
Barovier, Cordonato D'Oro: vase, gold, 8¾" 330.00
Barovier, Corniola: vase, serpent head, 6½" 3,450.00
Barovier, Crepuscolo: lamp base, 14½" 1,163.00
Barovier, Dorico Corniola: vase, 16" 13,987.00
Barovier, Egeo: vase, amethyst & wht, 26¾" 10,364.00
Barovier, Eugenio: gr vase, serpent hdl, 7" 2,875.00
Barovier, Gemmata: vase, marina series, 4½" 1,865.00
Barovier, Intarsio: bowl, red/gray triangles, 5" 1,748.00
Barovier, Oriente: bowl, 8½" 6,994.00
Barovier, Pezzato: vase, purple/opal, 9" 3,938.00

Barovier, Porpora Oro: bowl, 3" H................................169.00
Barovier, Sidereo: vase, appl rings, 13".......................2,040.00
Barovier, Spina: vase, gr/wht, 11½"............................9,200.00
Cenedese, Sommerso: momento vase, 10"......................3,105.00
Deguso Vetri D'Ar, Valva: vase, purple/red, 9¼"...........1,163.00
Fratelli Toso, Gocce: vase, yel w/red teardrops, 13½".....4,896.00
Fratelli Toso, Kiku: bl/wht murrines w/yel core, 10¾".....3,063.00
Fratelli Toso, Kiku: vase, red/blk w/yel core, 8½"........14,700.00
Fratelli Toso, Millefiori: vase, bl/yel/purple, 14"........2,875.00
Fratelli Toso, Millefiori: vase, red/wht murrines, 14".......460.00
Fratelli Toso, Murrine; pitcher, millefiori w/gr murrines, 7½"......518.00
Fratelli Toso, Murrine: vase, bl w/red/blk murrines, 14½".......1,410.00
Fratelli Toso, Murrine: vase, bl/pk/wht/gr murrines, 5".......1,610.00
Fratelli Toso, Murrine: vase, blk w/red/wht murrines, 9½".......1,838.00
Fratelli Toso, Nero Rosso: vase, red hdls, 13½".............2,875.00
Fratelli Toso, Nero Rosso: vase w/mica inclusions, 14".......920.00
Fratelli Toso, Nerox vase: lav/bl/wht/red murrines, 12½".......8,050.00
Fratelli Toso, Pezzato: vase, bl/clear, 8¾"..................2,205.00
MVM Cappellin, A Canne: covered bowl, red/bl, sgn, 9".......6,463.00
MVM Cappellin, Fenicio: vase, tan/gr, sgn, 14¾"...........32,375.00
MVM Cappellin, Fenicio: vase, wht/bl, 12"..................15,840.00
MVM Cappellin, Soffiato: bell shape w/3 appl threads, 6½".......410.00
MVM Cappellin, Soffiato: vase, bl, ftd, sgn, 7½".............821.00
Nason, Policrome Reazione: vase, 9"..........................4,025.00
Salviati, bowl: rose & bl fish shape, sgn, 16½" L..............104.00
Salviati, Sasso, vase, bl/gr, label, 6"........................5,527.00
Seguso Vetri D'Ar, Siderale: vase, gr/yel rings, 9".........47,000.00
Seguso Vetri D'Ar, Sommerso: bowl, gr/yel, 6½"..............1,748.00
Seguso Vetri D'Ar, Sommerso: vase, brn w/red line, 10¾".......1,715.00
Vistosi, bird: bl, J shaped, 11½".............................3,030.00
Vistosi, bird: bl, triangular, 7¼"............................2,623.00
Vistosi, bird: orange, globular, 8½"..........................1,487.00
Vistosi, bird: sq, 8½"...1,427.00
Vistosi, bird: violet w/bl murrines, elongated, 10½".........3,205.00

Ivory

Ivory has been used and appreciated since Neolithic times. It has been a product of every culture and continent. It is the second most valuable organic material after pearls. Ivory is defined as the dentine portion of mammalian teeth. Commercially the most important ivory comes from elephant and mammoth tusks, walrus tusks, hippo teeth, and sperm whale teeth. The smaller tusks of boar and warthog are often used whole.

Ivory has been used for artistic purposes as a palette for oil paints, as inlay on furniture, and especially as a medium for sculptures. Some are in the round, others in the form of plaques. Ivory also has numerous utilitarian uses such as cups and tankards; combs; handles for knives and medical tools; salt and pepper shakers; chess, domino, and checker pieces; billiard balls; jewelry; shoehorns; snuff boxes; brush pots; and fans.

There are a number of laws domestically and internationally to protect endangered animals including the elephant, walrus, and whale. However ivory taken and used before the various enactment dates is legal within the country in which it is located, and can be shipped internationally with a permit. Ivory from mammoths, hippopotamus, wart hog, and boar is excepted from all bans.

Prices have been stable for the last ten years, rising slightly in the last year. Prices are highest for European, Japanese, and Chinese ivories. Prices are lowest for African and Indian ivories. As with all collectibles, the very best pieces will appreciate most in the years to come. Small, poorly carved pieces will not appreciate to any extent. Our advisor for this category is Robert Weisblut; he is listed in the Directory under Maryland.

Bust of Voltaire on marble plinth, Fr, 19th C, 10"...........7,500.00

Communist Chinese-era cvg of children, 9½"..................1,250.00
Ear ornament, hornbill ivory, Borneo, early 20th C, 4"........750.00
Grouping of gods & children, Chinese, early 20th C, 10".......2,650.00
Hippo tooth cvg of village scene, Chinese, 1980s, 16" L.......325.00
Man defeating dragon & taking flaming pearl, Chinese, 9½".....950.00
Multi-armed goddess w/sitar, Indian, 20th C, 6½".............125.00
Shakers, narwhal tusk, scrimshawed, 2½", pr..................350.00
Snuff bottle, deep relief, China, 19th C, 5"...............1,250.00
Study of rose branch, Japan, early 20th C, 13" L...........1,750.00
Tusk (fully cvd), procession of people, African, mid-19th C.......775.00
Village scene, Japanese, ca 1900, 5½"......................2,000.00
Walrus sailing vessel w/full sails, Eskimo, 1950s, 10".......1,500.00
Woman w/flowers, polychromed, Chinese, mid 20th C, 9".......150.00
Woman w/knitting implements, Chinese, early 20th C, 9".......675.00

Jack-in-the-Pulpit Vases

Popular novelties at the turn of the century, jack-in-the-pulpit vases were made in every type of art glass produced. Some were simple, others elaborately appliquéd and enameled. They were shaped to resemble the lily for which they were named.

Opaline with ruby edge, Diamond Quilted base, 7", $135.00.

Mc spatter, clear appl ft, 8x4"..............................150.00
Pale bl crackle, long slender stem, 12½".....................65.00
Pk o/l w/mc flowers, ruffled top w/clear edge, 7½x5½".......175.00
Vaseline opal, wht ruffled rim, 7"............................60.00
Wht opal w/gr at rim, clear ft, 8½"...........................55.00

Jewelry

Jewelry as objects of adornment has always been regarded with special affection. Today prices for gems and gemstones crafted into antique and collectible jewelry are based on artistic merit, personal appeal, pure sentimentality, and intrinsic value. Note: In general, diamond prices have gone up more than 20% in the past year, and platinum is becoming popular again, so retail prices are rising. Diamond prices vary greatly depending on cut, color, clarity, etc., and to assess the value of any diamond of more than a carat in weight, you will need to have information about all of these factors. Values given here are for diamond jewelry with a standard commercial grade of diamonds that are most likely to be encountered.

Our advisor for fine jewelry is Rebecca Dodds; her address may be found in the Directory under Florida. Marcia 'Sparkles' Brown is our advisor for costume jewelry and the author of *Unsigned Beauties of Costume Jewelry* (Collector Books); she is also the host of the video *Hidden Treasures, A Collector's Guide to Antique and Vintage Jewelry of the 19th and 20th Centuries*. Mrs. Brown is listed in the Directory under Oregon. Other good references are *Collectible Costume Jewelry* by Cherri Simonds; *Costume Jewelry, A Practical Handbook & Value Guide*, and

Collectible Silver Jewelry by Fred Rezazadeh; Art Nouveau and Art Deco Jewelry, 100 Years of Collectible Jewelry, and Fifty Years of Collectible Fashion Jewelry by Lillian Baker; and Collector's Guide to Hair Combs, Identification and Values, by Mary Bachman (all available from Collector Books). See also American Painted Porcelain; Hair Weaving.

Key:

cab — cabochon	g-t — gold-tone
ct — carat	k — karat
dmn — diamond	plat — platinum
dwt — penny weight	r/stn — rhinestone
Euro — European cut	stn — stone
fl — filigree	tw — total weight
gf — gold filled	wg — white gold
gp — gold plated	yg — yellow gold
grad — graduated	ygf — yellow gold filled
gw — gold washed	

Bar pin, 10k rose & yg, .20ct mine-cut dmn among scrolls/leaves ..150.00
Bar pin, 14k wg w/sm dmn, Art Deco style 145.00
Bracelet, Arts & Crafts, hammered silver w/raised rib, 1¾" W...150.00
Bracelet, bangle; 14k yg w/21 sm opals...575.00
Bracelet, bangle; 9k yg w/4 .60ct peridot & 4 3.5mm pearls 265.00
Bracelet, charm; Spratling, sterling chevrons, amethyst cabs...1,000.00
Bracelet, cuff; gf w/geometric eng, 1880s, pr..............................350.00
Bracelet, cultured pearls, 2-strand, 14k gold clasp......................165.00
Bracelet, Tiffany, 14k gold links, hidden self-clasp, 52dwt 2,200.00
Bracelet, 18k yg, heavy links, Italian stirrup design 440.00
Bracelet, 18k yg links (4.6 ozs) w/84 rnd dmns 6.75ct tw 6,000.00
Brooch, Arts & Crafts, copper & nickel, emb geometrics/florals, 2¼"..60.00
Brooch, Carence Crafters, hammered silver w/inset jewel, 3¼" L.600.00
Brooch, Forest Craft Guild, hammered brass w/inset jewel, 2½"..550.00
Brooch, Georg Jensen, silver mythical deer w/wings, 2x2⅛".......545.00
Brooch, 14k yg, mine-cut SI J-K 3.75ct dmn solitaire 8,800.00

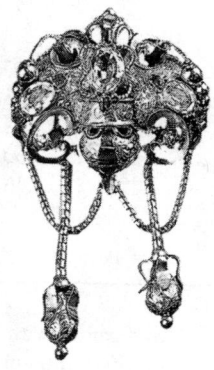

Brooch, 18kt gold with three oval faceted topaz, four fashion-cut rubies, swags, and ball drops, Victorian, in fitted case, $1,265.00.

Brooch, 18k yg abstract w/.35 dmn, plat/dmn spray accent.........700.00
Brooch, 18k yg starburst set w/sm dmns centering pearl.............350.00
Brooch/pendant, 10k yg w/seed pearl & enamel 175.00
Brooch/pendant, 14k yg heart w/pearls/.20ct mine-cut dmn 225.00
Buckle, Tiffany, 14k yg, 1950s, 2" W...750.00
Comb, brass fl, cut steel studs, ca 1860, 5x3¼", $35 to 45.00
Comb, coral-color celluloid, pierced work, 1880-1900, 7x4", $55 to...65.00
Comb, cream celluloid w/gr stones & pnt Nouveau flowers, 1900s, 5½"..55.00
Comb, dyed horn, much cutwork, 4x4", from $65 to.....................75.00
Comb, dyed horn, pierced cuttings, 5½x3", from $45 to 55.00
Comb, emb cut steel, ca 1810, 5x4", from $45 to 55.00
Comb, Fr jet, ca 1890, 3¼x4½", from $40 to.................................55.00
Comb, silver gilt, filigree, ca 1800-1810, 5x4¾", from $75 to.......85.00
Comb, tortoise shell, folding, 3 hinged leaves, 1850s, 3x5", $65 to...75.00
Comb, tortoise shell, pierced work, ca 1830, 2¼x5½", $300 to..400.00

Comb, tortoise shell w/numerous sm Bohemian garnets............375.00
Cuff links, gold w/emb florals, Am Art Nouveau, pr 85.00
Cuff links, ornate gold scroll repousse, pr................................200.00
Cuff links, 10k yg w/.50ct tw dmns, pr......................................130.00
Cuff links, 14k yg w/gr jade, bamboo form, pr...........................140.00
Earrings, Tiffany, 14k yg, basketweave design, ½" W 1,250.00
Earrings, 14k gold w/½ct tw dmns, pr......................................330.00
Earrings, 14k wg w/.30ct tw dmn studs, pr...............................165.00
Hairpin, celluloid w/clear paste stones, from $5 to........................7.50
Hairpin, celluloid/wire/Fr jet butterfly, ca 1920, from $45 to 55.00
Hairpin, horn w/fl & colored enamels, Deco style, 1920s, from $30 to ..35.00
Hairpin, sterling, butterfly motif, Nouveau styling, ca 1900, $70 to 75.00
Lavalier, sq peridot in scrolls, 4mm pearl+freshwater drop..........175.00
Necklace, Cartier, 14k yg snake links................................1,450.00
Necklace, cultured pearls, 1-strand, 6-6½mm, long, 14k yg clasp...550.00
Necklace, cultured pearls, 1-strand, 7½-8mm, 20" 575.00
Necklace, cultured pearls, 3-strand, 7-8mm, w/14k gold clasp 550.00
Necklace, 14k yg, Etruscan-style links, choker, 1870s 900.00
Necklace, 18k yg heavy links (12.7 ozs) w/200 rnd dmns 15ct tw .9,775.00
Pendant, wg w/pear-shaped emerald & 28 sm rnd dmns............660.00
Pendant, yg & amethyst, on gf chain, Victorian......................175.00
Pendant, yg Mercedes-Benz style fr w/.80ct mine-cut dmn+65 sm dmns..3,350.00
Pendant, 10k wg w/1.0ct mine-cut dmn & 8 sm stones (2.0ct tw)..2,400.00
Pendant, 14k wg cross w/full-cut dmn, 7 sapphires, 4 rubies 300.00
Pendant, 14k yg Byzantine-style cross w/3.50ct natural emeralds, 2"...770.00
Pendant, 18k yg heart w/15 full-cut .50ct tw dmns (VS-S1-GHI).......260.00
Ring, yg w/blk & wht onyx cameo of woman's profile.................165.00
Ring, yg w/fresh water pearl 85.00
Ring, yg w/synthetic ruby, bezel set, hand-hammered decor, man's..165.00
Ring, 10k yg w/emerald cut 10mmx8mm synthetic alexandrite 75.00
Ring, 14k wg, 16x11mm bl sapphire w/10 sm sapphires/14 sm dmns ..4,000.00
Ring, 14K wg, 3.35ct emerald-cut emerald, 4 sm baguette dmns ..3,450.00
Ring, 14k wg w/oval fct garnet solitaire 110.00
Ring, 14k wg w/2 Euro dmn tw .50ct..600.00
Ring, 14k yg, 15 pave rubies 2.50ct tw, 2 sm dmns ea side, modern250.00
Ring, 14k yg, 3 champagne-color dmns 1ct tw, man's.................300.00
Ring, 14k yg, 9 old mine-cut dmns (.65ct) in cluster 465.00
Ring, 14K yg free-form w/rnd 1.67ct dmn w/37 sm (2.00ct tw) dmns..2,000.00
Ring, 14k yg in form of dragon set w/jade, ruby & dmn eyes 220.00
Ring, 14k yg w/blk onyx cameo, twist shank................................110.00
Ring, 14k yg w/lg citrine, Etruscan design border 350.00
Ring, 14k yg w/marquise sapphires & .50ct tw dmns...................465.00
Ring, 14k yg w/10mm rnd cab opal w/much red...........................335.00
Ring, 14k yg w/7x9mm opal..175.00
Ring, 14k yg/wg, sm old mine-cut dmns, openwork scrollwork ...800.00
Ring, 18k plat, 7 sapphires w/8 sm dmns ea side 485.00
Ring, 18k yg w/lg faceted smoky topaz 140.00
Tie tack, 14k yg w/blk star sapphire 60.00

Costume Jewelry

Rhinestone jewelry is a very popular field of collecting. Rhinestones are foil-backed leaded crystal stones with a sparkle outshining diamonds. Copyrighting jewelry came into effect in 1955. Pieces bearing a copyright mark (post-1955) are considered 'collectibles,' while pieces (with no copyright) made before then are regarded as 'antiques.' Fur clips are two-pronged, used to anchor fur stoles. Dress clips have a spring clasp and are used at the dress neckline. Look for signed and well-made, unmarked pieces for your collections and preserve this American art form. Our advisor for costume jewelry is Marcia Brown (see introductory paragraphs for information on her books and videos).

Bracelet, Cini, 4 sterling sections: crest, lion, knight, lady, 7" 120.00

Bracelet, gold-/silver-tone w/aurora borealis & plastic seed beads .90.00
Bracelet, gold-tone w/molded/pnt plastic faces, red r/stns, 1¼" W ...200.00
Bracelet, gp chain links w/gr/bl plastic beads, ¾" W, $175 to 225.00
Bracelet, gp w/faux pearls/aurora borealis/amethyst r/stns, 1¼" W .135.00
Bracelet, hinged, dk amethyst fct r/stns w/lav stones 65.00
Bracelet, Hobé, floral filigree segments, mc r/stns, gilt metal, 7" ..600.00
Bracelet, Hobé, flower links, sterling w/aqua r/stns, 7" 70.00
Bracelet, mc pastel r/stns w/clear borders, 6 vertical rows.............80.00
Bracelet, pk r/stns in spaced rows, 2" W 95.00
Brooch, antiqued gp w/lav/plum/clear r/stns, 1960s, 3½x3½" 100.00
Brooch, Bakelite, bar, red w/cvd foliage, 3¾" 130.00
Brooch, Bakelite, carrots hang from cvd blk oval, 3½" 400.00
Brooch, Bakelite, hat form, butterscotch, HP band, appl flowers, 3"...500.00
Brooch, Bakelite, Swiss hat, butterscotch w/HP feather, 2½" 350.00
Brooch, ballerina, gold-tone w/enamel flowers in skirt 22.00
Brooch, bird, sterling silver w/gr navette r/stns, 1930s.................63.00
Brooch, Boucher, abstract floral, mc r/stns on sterling, 3¾".........500.00
Brooch, Boucher, bird, mc pearlized enamel, clear r/stns, 5½"....850.00
Brooch, Boucher, bird of paradise, etched gp w/r/stns, 4", $300 to..400.00
Brooch, Boucher, blueberries, r/stns, mc enamel, 2¾" 550.00
Brooch, Boucher, cherries, r/stns & mc enamel on silver-tone, 2¼" ...350.00
Brooch, Boucher, floral, mc enamel, faux pearls, r/stns, 3" 700.00
Brooch, Boucher, pearlized enamel & r/stns on silver-tone, 4¼" ..600.00
Brooch, Boucher, ribbon, turq stones, bl & clear r/stns, 2¼" 80.00
Brooch, bow, sterling, holds Lucite bbl w/watch inside..................98.00
Brooch, cat, blk enamel on pot metal w/clear r/stns 68.00
Brooch, Cini, Christmas tree, sterling w/gilt-sterling ornaments, 2" 90.00
Brooch, Coro, Am Indian, pave r/stns, HP details on silver-tone, 3"...325.00
Brooch, Coro, Duette masks, bl/clear r/stns, blk/red enamel, 2¼".........350.00
Brooch, Coro, floral cascade w/red r/stns, mc enamel on silver metal ..170.00
Brooch, Coro, grasshopper, r/stns & mc enamel on silver-tone, 3" 425.00
Brooch, Coro Craft, gilt sterling w/mc r/stns, 4", EX 250.00
Brooch, Coro Craft, lady in headdress, r/stns, gilt-sterling, 3".....400.00
Brooch, Coro Craft, Spanish lady & boy, mc on gilt sterling, 2¾"......300.00
Brooch, cushion, gp w/aurora borealis/bl r/stn, 1950s, 3¼", $225 to ...275.00
Brooch, Czech, gp spider w/2 purple r/stns, 8 gp legs 25.00
Brooch, Eisenberg, bow, gilt metal w/clear/red r/stns, 4½" 300.00
Brooch, Eisenberg, floral, silver metal w/faux pearls/clear r/stns, 4" .100.00
Brooch, feather, wht glass cabs & clear r/stones, +earrings............55.00
Brooch, flower, gp w/plastic magenta r/stn, 1950s, 3¼", from $75 to...100.00
Brooch, flower, Nouveau free-form flower w/r/stns 55.00
Brooch, Haskell, snowflake, cut glass & filigree, clear r/stns, 3½"...260.00
Brooch, Hobé, dbl heart, mc r/stns, gilt metal, att, 3¼" 800.00
Brooch, horse head, silver-tone w/aurora borealis & red r/stns, 2½" 100.00
Brooch, lizard, gp w/mc navettes...35.00
Brooch, Lucite & wood, hand w/cvd cuff, 3" 120.00
Brooch, Maltese cross, gold-tone w/mc r/stns.................................25.00
Brooch, ribbon cascade, clear & red r/stns, gilt sterling, 3" 270.00
Brooch, rose, porc, in English style, dainty.....................................25.00
Brooch, S Coventry, gp/plastic cabs/gr r/stns/faux pearls+earrings....120.00
Brooch, S Coventry, rhodium plated w/clear r/stn abstract cushion ...65.00
Brooch, snowflake, bl cab & lt bl chatons/clear r/stones, +earrings....45.00
Brooch, snowflake, SP w/chaton r/stns, very lg 55.00
Brooch, Staret, bow, clear r/stns on silver metal, 4¼" 180.00
Brooch, swirling ribbon, gp, faux citrine/emeralds/r/stns, 1930s, 3"..325.00
Brooch, Trifari, bumble bee, SP w/r/stns & mc enamel, 2".........200.00
Brooch, Trifari, Clip-Mates, floral, r/stns on silver-tone, 3".........150.00
Brooch, Trifari, horse/whip/horseshoe, mc on gold-tone, r/stns, 3" ..950.00
Brooch, Trifari, leaf, pave r/stns on silver metal, 2½" 160.00
Brooch, Trifari, penguin w/jelly belly, r/stns, gilt sterling, 2¼"....400.00
Brooch, Trifari, sailboat w/jelly belly, r/stns, gilt sterling, 2½" 850.00
Brooch, wheat, gp w/bl navettes 18.00
Brooch, 5-leaf clover, gp w/emerald gr chatons 48.00
Brooch & earrings, leaf, gilt-sterling w/red cabs & bl stones 300.00

Clip, Eisenberg, abstract gilt-metal w/red/bl/gr cabs, 4" 400.00
Clip, Eisenberg, flower, silver metal w/clear r/stns, 3" 140.00
Clip, Eisenberg, pk & clear pave r/stns on gilt sterling, 3" 270.00
Clip, fct irid r/stns & spray of topaz baguettes, from $250 to.......300.00
Clip, silver-metal flower bouquet w/mc r/stns, 2½" 800.00
Clip, Trifari, bird, silver-tone w/clear r/stns/mc enamel, 4" 230.00
Clip & earrings, starburst, gilt-sterling w/r/stns, 2½", ¾" 160.00
Earrings, A Scaasi, rhodium plated w/gr & clear r/stns, 3¼", pr .250.00
Earrings, bl chatons, navette & aurora borealis r/stns, pr..............28.00
Earrings, button, faux pearl w/floral decor edge, pr, from $20 to ...35.00
Earrings, cluster, aurora borealis r/stns, pr....................................38.00
Earrings, Eisenberg, hearts, clear r/stns on silver metal, ¾", pr......60.00
Earrings, emeralds on gp clips w/clear baguettes, pr 45.00
Earrings, gilt brass w/red glass teardrop, 1910s, 2½", from $40 to..70.00
Earrings, H Carnegie, crystal chandelier type, 2¾", pr, $175 to..225.00
Earrings, pearl stud w/grad pear drop, pr.......................................28.00
Earrings, strung pearl loops w/r/stn rondels & balls, pr 50.00
Necklace, aurora borealis form 1" W semi-collar, +earrings 62.00
Necklace, Bakelite, cream/med & dk gr pickles on chain, 15" ...3,500.00
Necklace, Bakelite, reverse-cvd 2" apple juice medallion on chain .275.00
Necklace, BK, gilt brass floral choker, prong-set mc stones, +earrings..100.00
Necklace, chromium plated w/blk & ivory compo beads, Deco fringe ..125.00
Necklace, Coro, gold-tone w/bright aqua r/stn dangle, 1940s 150.00
Necklace, dk gr chatons form chain, peridot drops, +earrings.......78.00
Necklace, Eisenberg Orig, clear r/stn links, safety chain, 13¾"....200.00
Necklace, gp yel r/stn choker in bow design, early 1950s, $50 to..75.00
Necklace, Haskell, 2-strand faux pearls w/seed pearl, r/stns, 15" .300.00
Necklace, Hattie Carnegie, aurora borealis & r/stn gp bib, +earrings ...600.00
Necklace, Hobé, 3 silver floral segments on dbl chain, 16".........250.00
Necklace, irid r/stn bib style, +earrings 75.00
Necklace, Kramer, gp yel r/stns in V shape, 1950s, from $250 to...350.00

Necklace, Krementz, rattail rolled gold-plate choker-length chain with three-dimensional roses and leaves, from $125.00 to $150.00.
(Photo courtesy Cherri Simonds)

Necklace, pk plastic flat-bk cabs on golden chain, +bracelet/earrings...45.00
Necklace, Reinad, chromium plated, faux pk star cabs/r/stns, 1930s...425.00
Necklace, Renoir, copper open-work links, 1950s,¾" W, +bracelet 165.00
Necklace, tourmaline fct chatons/fuchsia r/stns, +bracelet/earrings 400.00

Johnson Brothers

A Staffordshire-based company operating since well before the turn of the century, Johnson Brothers has produced many familiar lines of dinnerware, several of which are becoming very collectible. Some of their patterns were made in both blue and pink transfer as well as in polychrome. One of the more familiar patterns is Friendly Village, which is still being produced, though the pattern is much more limited than it once was.

Values below range from a low base price for patterns that are still in production (i.e., Friendly Village) or less collectible to a high that would apply to very desirable patterns such as Old Britain Castles, Wild

Turkeys, Strawberry Fair, Historic America, Rose Chintz, Chintz, etc. Mid-range lines include Coaching Scenes, Millsteam, Old English Countryside, Rose Bouquet (and there are others).

For more information on marks, patterns, and pricing, we recommend *Johnson Brothers Dinnerware Pattern Directory and Price Guide* by our advisor, Mary J. Finegan, who is listed in the Directory under North Carolina.

Bowl, cereal/soup; rnd, sq, or lug, ea, from $10 to	12.00
Bowl, soup; rnd or sq, 7", from $12 to	14.00
Bowl, vegetable; oval, from $30 to	40.00
Chop/cake plate, from $50 to	70.00

Coaching Scenes: Plate, 10", $18.00; Cup and saucer, $17.00.
(Photo courtesy Mary J. Finegan)

Coffee mug, from $15 to	25.00
Coffeepot, from $80 to	100.00
Covered butter dish, from $50 to	60.00
Demitasse set, 2-pc, from $20 to	24.00
Pitcher/jug, from $45 to	60.00
Plate, buffet; 10½-11", from $26 to	35.00
Plate, dinner; from $14 to	20.00
Plate, salad; sq or rnd, from $10 to	14.00
Platter, med, 12-14", ea, from $45 to	55.00
Sauce boat/gravy, from $40 to	48.00
Sugar bowl, open, from $30 to	35.00
Teacup & saucer, from $15 to	20.00
Teapot, from $80 to	100.00
Turkey platter, 20½", from $200 to	300.00

Josef Originals

Figurines of lovely ladies, charming girls, and whimsical animals marked Josef Originals were designed by Muriel Joseph George of Arcadia, California, from 1945 to 1985. Until 1960 they were produced in California, but costs were high and copies of her work were being made in Japan. To remain competitive, she and her partner, George Good, contracted with the Katayama Company in Japan to build a factory to produce her designs to her approval. Muriel retired in 1982; however, George Good continued production of her work as well as new ones of his staff's creation. The company was sold in late 1985; the name is currently owned by Applause, and a limited amount of figurines bear the name. Those made during the ownership of Muriel George are the most collectible. They can be recognized by these characteristics: The girls have a high-gloss finish, black eyes, and most are signed. Brown eyes date from 1982 to 1985. Applause uses a red-brown eye. The animals were mainly done in a matt finish and have labels. Later animals have a flocked coat. Prices are given for figurines (with black eyes unless specified otherwise) in perfect condition. Our advisors, Jim and Kaye Whitaker, are the authors of three books: *Josef Originals, Charming Figurines*; *Josef Originals, A Second Look*; and *Josef Originals, Figurines of Muriel Joseph George*, an informative book with no repeats of the two previous books. The Whitakers are listed in the Directory under Washington.

Aquarius, Zodiac Girls series, Japan, 4¾", from $32 to	40.00
Birthstone dolls, Jan through Dec, Japan, 3½", ea	20.00
Boxer dog, Champions series, Japan, 5"	18.00
Buggy Bugs series, various poses, wire antenna, Japan, 3¼", EX	12.00
Dalmatian, Kennel Club series, Japan, 3½"	8.00
Farmer's Daughter, girl w/hen & basket of eggs, Japan, 5"	40.00
Hawaii, Small World series, brn eyes, Japan, 4½"	32.00
Hunter, standing horse, Japan, 6"	28.00
Jeanne, Colonial Days series, Japan, 9"	110.00
Lipstick, First Time series, Japan, 4½", from $28 to	32.00
Mice, Christmas, Japan, 2¾", ea	10.00
Monkey dressed as doctor, Japan, 3"	8.00
Music box, Happy Anniversary, Japan, 7¼"	56.00
New Home, Special Occasions series, girl w/key, Japan, 4½"	28.00
Pixie, various poses, gr w/red & gold trim, Japan, 2-3¼", ea	24.00
Rose Garden series, brn eyes, Japan, 6 different, 5¼", ea	52.00
Ruby, Little Jewels series, girl w/ruby in crown, Japan, 3½"	28.00
Santa, kiss on forehead, Japan, 4¾"	48.00
Skunks w/wht hair tuft on head, Japan, 2½"	15.00
Sports Angels series, angels playing various sports, Japan, 2¾", ea	28.00
Tawny, Character Cat, Siamese, Japan, 4"	14.00
Three Kings, Japan, 8½-11", set of 3	56.00
Wee Ching & Wee Ling, Chinese boy & girl w/dog & cat (much copied), pr	60.00
Wee Folk, various poses, Japan, 4½", ea	10.00
Yorkshire, Kennel Klub series, Japan, 3", from $12 to	16.00

Judaica

The items listed below are representative of objects used in both the secular and religious life of the Jewish people. They are evident of a culture where silversmiths, painters, engravers, writers, and metal workers were highly gifted and skilled in their art. Most of the treasures shown in recently displayed exhibits of Judaica were confiscated by the Germans during the late 1930s up to 1945; by then eight Jewish synagogues and fifty warehouses had been filled with Hitler's plunder. Judaica is currently available through dealers, from private collections, and the annual auction held in Israel, New York City, and Boston.

Beaker, kiddush; silver, cylindrical, ball suports, WH, 1825-75, 3"	575.00
Beaker, kiddush; silver, emb scenes, B Dornhelm, 1900, 2⅝"	925.00
Beaker, passover; silver, lipped base, Augsburg, 1759-61, rprs, 2¾"	2,875.00
Box, charity; Burial Society, steel, European, 17th-18th C, 9¾"	3,000.00
Box, charity; Deco silver w/star, Germany, 1920s-30s, 5⅝"	9,200.00
Box, charity; silver, eng lid, St Petersburg, late 19th C, 3½"	1,500.00
Box, charity; silver, inscr lid, Birmingham, 1911, 3½"	1,100.00

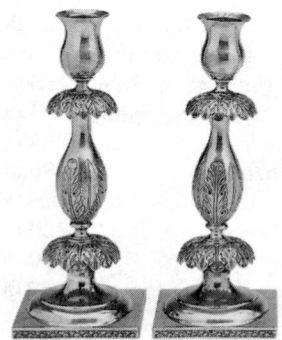

Candlesticks, Sabbath; Nast, Warsaw, silver, classic design with foliate skirts, rose vine design, 1830 – 50, 9⅜", $2,400.00 for the pair.

Candlesticks, sabbath; silver, eng foliage, mk MJ, late 1800s, 13", pr	575.00
Container, spice; silver apple form w/filigree, att Poland, 20th C, 4"	260.00
Container, spice; silver pear on leaves, Poland, ca 1900, 7½"	575.00

Container, spice; silver tower, eagles/lion, Austro-Hungary, 1800s, 8"..7,000.00
Container, spice; silver tower, openwork, 2-tier, Berlin, 1820s, 10" 1,150.00
Container, spice; silver tower, 3-tier, bell, Altona, 1800s, 8¼" ...5,500.00
Container, spice; silver/ivory, buds/leaves, Russia, 1880s, 8½" 800.00
Cup, kiddush; silver, chased flowers, inscription, PS, 1750s, 6" .5,750.00
Cup, kiddush; silver, eng scrolls/shields, Augsburg, 1737-39, rprs, 3" ...1,150.00
Cup, kiddush; silver, floral rococo, inscription, IGS, 1770s, 4½" .8,000.00
Cup, kiddush; silver tulip shape w/florals, Pogorelski, 1856, 4⅝"..800.00
Cup, bar mitzva; silver, eng inscription, Warsaw, 1919, 2¾" 975.00
Cup, presentation; silver, foliage, family crest, England, 1881, 7"..9,200.00
Cups, marriage; silver, bl/red agates, mk RC, ca 1900, 4", pr ..2,300.00
Etrog container, silver, emb scrolls/foliage, Poland, 19th C, 5½" 865.00
Etrog container, silver, houses/palms lid, Yemini, 1900s, 6½"..1,950.00
Goblet, presentation; silver, eng floral/medallion, London, 1813 ....12,650.00
Goblet, wine; silver, Deco flowers, hammered, Germany, 1920s, 8¾"..575.00
Lamp, hannukah, silver, mirhab motifs/lattice, 8-light, Tunisia, 12".2,850.00
Lamp, hannukah; brass, foliage, 8-light, Am, 1920s, 7½" 575.00
Lamp, hannukah; brass, foliage/birds, 8-light, Morocco, 1790s, 12" ..450.00
Lamp, hannukah; silver, decalogue/lions/crown, Germany, 19th C, 10"..1,500.00
Lamp, hannukah; silver, temple type, swans/flowers, Prague, 1826, 15".18,500.00
Lamp, sabbath; brass, 5-light, slender baluster, Poland, 19th C, 16" ...285.00
Plate, purim; faience, Hamman/Mordecai, Hungaria, 19th C, 12"..1,600.00
Torah breastplate, Nouveau silver w/star, bells, early 1900s, 5½"...450.00
Torah case, velvet covered, silver mts, Lebanon, 1950s, 38½" ...1,800.00
Torah finials, silver-gilt, chased foliage/bells, mk FB, 1800s, 14"..9,775.00
Torah pointer, silver, 4-sided panels, Continental, 18th C, 12½" 450.00
Torah pointer, silver w/gilt hand, Russia, mk AK, 1886, 10".......700.00
Torah shield, gilt-silver, emb lions/pillars/ark/etc, Katz, 1894, 13"..2,300.00
Tray, passover seder; SP, foods/pyramids, 20th C, 14", pr............450.00
Tray, passover; SP, men in chains, 20th C, 22¾" L.....................925.00

Jugtown

The Jugtown Pottery was started about 1920 by Juliana and Jacques Busbee, in Moore County, North Carolina. Ben Owen, a young descendant of a Staffordshire potter, was hired in 1923. He was the master potter, while the Busbees experimented with perfecting glazes and supervising design and modeling. Preferred shapes were those reminiscent of traditional country wares and classic Oriental forms. Glazes were various: natural-clay oranges, buffs, Tobacco-spit Brown, Mirror Black, white, Frog Skin Green, a lovely turquoise called Chinese Blue, and the traditional cobalt-decorated salt glaze. The pottery gained national recognition, and as a result of their success, several other local potteries were established. The pottery closed for a time in the late 1950s due to the ill health of Mrs. Busbee (who had directed the business after her husband died in 1947) but reopened in 1960. Jugtown is still in operation; however, they no longer use their original glaze colors which are now so collectible and the circular mark is slightly smaller than the original.

Bowl, Frog Skin Albany slip, B Owen, 1960s, 2x5" 50.00
Creamer & sugar bowl, Tobacco Spit Brown, 1940s, w/lid, 4" 130.00
Inkwell, Chinese Blue, conical, brn int, 1940s, 3" 375.00
Jar, bright orange, w/lid, early 1930s, 3½" 175.00
Jar, Chinese Blue, sm hdls, early 1940s, 7"..........................1,250.00
Jug, salt glaze, good orange-peel texture, stopper, 1983, 10⅜" 100.00
Pitcher, bright orange w/gr spots, Ben Owen, 1930s, 9¼" 175.00
Pitcher, cream; speckled orange-brn, early 20th C, 4½" 70.00
Pitcher, orange w/gr spots, Ben Owen, 1920s, 7⅜" 300.00
Pot, cobalt floral on salt glaze, Ben Owen/J Busbee, 1930s, 4¼" ...80.00
Teapot, Tobacco Spit Brown, Ben Owen, ca 1930, 6½", EX.......250.00
Vase, brn (multi-tone) gloss, shouldered, 3½" 110.00
Vase, celadon-style gr, bl & reduction red, 1930s, 3¼x4⅜" 350.00

Vase, Chinese Blue, appl dogwood blossoms, 1940s, 7⅝"...........950.00
Vase, Chinese Blue, bell shape, Ben Owen, 1930s, 3½x5"..........500.00
Vase, Chinese Blue, shouldered, sm opening at rim, 7" 450.00
Vase, Chinese Blue, shouldered, 1930s, 5" 700.00
Vase, Chinese Blue, shouldered, EX color, 6¼x7" 1,300.00
Vase, Chinese Blue, shouldered, 6x6½" 800.00
Vase, Chinese Blue, wide shoulder, 1930s, 3¾" 450.00
Vase, Chinese Blue, 1930s, 5½"...350.00
Vase, Chinese Blue, 1940s, 3⅞"...200.00
Vase, Chinese Blue, 3⅝x5¾"..450.00
Vase, Chinese White, Frogskin Albany slip int, 1930s, 5¼" 175.00
Vase, Frog Skin Green, hdls, 1920s, 5½"....................................850.00

K. P. M. Porcelain

The original KPM wares were produced from 1823 until 1847 by the Konigliche Porzellan Manfaktur, located in Berlin, Germany. Meissen used the same letters on some of their porcelains, as did several others in the area. In addition to the initials, the mark sometimes contains a crowned eagle with a scepter. Watch for items currently being imported from China; they are marked KPM with the eagle, but the scepter is not present. Our advisor for this category is Don Williams; he is listed in the Directory under Missouri.

Cup, burning building scene, gilt hdl/int, dtd July 29, 1817, 3½" 335.00
Plaque, children play/boy w/toy cannon, scepter mk, 10½x12½".5,500.00
Plaque, classical lady w/flower vase, 13x8"................................4,400.00
Plaque, Immaculate Conception, in ornate gilt fr, 17" 6,150.00

Plaque, lady with pearls, incised scepter, KPM and decorator's marks, 10½", in gilt frame, $3,500.00.

Plaque, Melon Corp, boys eating melon, 10x7½" 3,500.00
Plaque, men talking at table, Knoeller, 8½x10¾"+fr 4,500.00
Plaque, monk eating, Dietrich, 10¼x12¾"+fr.........................4,400.00
Plaque, monk looking at glass while eating, 10¼x12¾"+fr 4,850.00
Plaque, monk sitting in chair, 5¾x7¾"+fr 2,500.00
Plaque, monks at midday meal, Scherk, 12½x10½"+fr...........5,500.00
Plaque, violinist, 9x7" in giltwood fr.......................................3,000.00
Plate, wht Jasper mythological medallion on gray, mk, 11½", 8 for...485.00

Kayserzinn Pewter

J.P. Kayser Sohn produced pewter decorated with relief-molded Art Nouveau motifs in Germany during the late 1800s and into the twentieth century. Examples are marked with 'Kayserzinn' and the mold number within an elongated oval reserve. Items with three-dimensional animals, insects, birds, etc., are valued much higher than bowls, plates, and trays with simple embossed florals, which are usually priced at $100.00 to about $200.00, depending on size.

Basket, floral relief, 9x11½" 265.00
Bowl, Art Nouveau, leaf hdls, acorn finial, w/lid, #4037, 6½" 275.00
Chocolate set, Art Nouveau, duck-shaped pot+6 tumblers+8" tray ..275.00
Pitcher, oak leaves & acorns, long flaring neck, bulbous, 11" 315.00
Tea/coffee set, emb floral, 2 pots+cr/sug+19½" tray....................950.00
Vase, butterflies & flowers, 8"..260.00
Vase, emb fish (5 detailed), 2 open hdls, 6½"..........................275.00
Vase, emb geometrics & florals, unmk, 9", EX.........................150.00
Vase, tooled Arts & Crafts design, minor dents, 9" 100.00

Keeler, Brad

Keeler studied art for a time in the 1930s; later he became a modeler for a Los Angeles firm. By 1939 he was working in his own studio where he created naturalistic studies of birds and animals which were marketed through giftware stores. They were decorated by means of an airbrush and enhanced with hand-painted details. His flamingo figures were particularly popular. In the mid-'40s, he developed a successful line of Chinese Modern housewares glazed in Ming Dragon Blood, a red color he personally developed. Keeler died of a heart attack in 1952, and the pottery closed soon thereafter. For more information, we recommend *The Collector's Encyclopedia of California Pottery, Second Edition,* by Jack Chipman (Collector Books).

Figurine, exotic birds, #803, 13½", $225.00; #718, 11½", $175.00.
(Photo courtesy Lee Garmon)

Ashtray, trout & creel, #346, 4x7"..70.00
Cookie jar, rooster, NM..110.00
Figurine, canary on limb, female w/tail down, 6" 45.00
Figurine, Chinese man holding fish, #601, 6½".............................185.00
Figurine, flamingo, #1, 12", pr..250.00
Figurine, kitten at play, #772...50.00
Figurine, Little Boy Blue, #973, 3x6"..90.00
Figurine, rabbit, wht w/pk ears up, 1950s, 4½x2"...........................40.00
Figurine, rooster, #746 Made in USA, 18x11", from $335 to......350.00
Figurine, rooster & hen, #935 & #936, pr..65.00
Figurine, zebra, Pryde 'N Joy sticker, BAK mk, 5¾" 35.00
Leaf dish, bluebirds at side, 3-ftd, 1952, 3¼x8x6½"........................50.00
Mayonnaise set, lobster, #871B, 3-pc set, from $50 to 65.00
Planter, monkey, Pryde 'N Joy sticker, 5⅜"....................................45.00
Planter, sleigh, #915, 5x7½"...25.00
Shakers, lobster, 3⅝", pr..45.00
Sign, Ming Dragon Blood, 6x7¼" 550.00
Tray w/attached tomato-dipping bowl, mk, 11½" L 50.00
Tureen, lobster, #825, w/lid, 6x11x6½"...150.00
Tureen, lobster, leafy base, #616, 8½x14".......................................250.00
Tureen, lobster, w/lid & ladle, 8" L...85.00

Keen Kutter

Keen Kutter was the brand name chosen in 1870 by the Simmons

Firm for a line of high-grade tools and cutlery. The trademark was first applied to high-grade axes. A corporation was formed in 1874 called Simmons Hardware Company. In 1922 Winchester merged with Simmons and continued to carry a full line of hardware plus the Winchester brand. The merger terminated in March of 1929 and converted back to the original status of Simmons Hardware Co. It wasn't until July 1, 1950, that Simmons Hardware Co. was purchased by Shapleigh Hardware Company. All Simmons Hardware Co. trademark lines were continued, and the business operated successfully until its closing in 1962. Today the Keen Kutter logo is owned by the Val-Test Company of Chicago, Illinois. For further study we recommend *Collector's Guide to E.C.Simmons Keen Kutter Cutlery Tools,* an illustrated price guide by our advisors for this category, Jerry and Elaine Heuring, available from Collector Books. The Heurings are listed in the Directory under Missouri. See also Knives.

Axe, w/nail puller head, mk KK..25.00
Bit, expansion; w/KK emblem, 8" 20.00
Book, Want; Winchester-Simmons...50.00
Box openers, #2, KK logo & KK written out...............................25.00
Cabinet scraper, #K79..40.00
Calendar, axe-head shape w/waterfall scene, 1935, complete, 17", NM..450.00
Calendar, 1939, full pad...125.00
Concrete groover, brass, #K05, wood hdl, mk KK.......................80.00
Display, punch/chisel; red logo shape, mk KK............................90.00
Drill bit holder, yel, w/lid, mk KK...25.00
Emblem, for pedal grindstone, mk KK...25.00
Fishing reel, Keen Kaster, #SKK..50.00
Flashlight battery, Shapleigh Keen Kutter mk.............................50.00
Food chopper, w/wood hdl, mk KK..15.00
Garden trowel, mk KK...55.00
Glass cutter, mk KK..50.00
Hammer, bill poster; mk KK...50.00
Hammer, brick; mk KK, 7½"..35.00
Hammer, claw; curved, rubber hdl..45.00
Hammer, claw; str, w/KK original hdl, 10-oz...............................45.00
Hammer, tinner's; KK emblem, 8-oz (orig hdl) 30.00
Hay knife, Heath's pattern w/KK emblem on steel 75.00
Knife, farrier's; bone hdl, curved blade 75.00
Knife, linoleum; mk KK, M...35.00
Level, #KK0, mk KK..25.00
Level, cast aluminum, mk KK, 24"..30.00
Level, CI, #K612, no rust, mk KK, 12".......................................220.00
Level, wood, brass ends, #KK-30, mk KK, 28"............................60.00
Mitre box base only, cast w/dbl logos..250.00
Nail clippers, mk KK...45.00
Nail puller, mk KK..20.00
Oil bottle, emb glass, 4"..50.00
Plane, circular; #KK115..300.00
Plane, iron, emblem on lever cap, 10"..40.00
Plane, wood, mk KK, 15" 45.00
Plane, wood, smooth bottom, hdld, #K35, mk KK, 9" 45.00
Pliers, combination; #K160, mk KK...25.00
Plumb bob, hexagon, screw on top, 3½" L....................................90.00
Postcard, The Dog Doesn't Mind..., postmarked 1912, VG+ 130.00
Poster, The Dog Doesn't Mind, repro, 27x22"..............................10.00
Razor, Bakelite hdl, boxed w/2 pkgs of razors, 4x3x1", EX+ 35.00
Razor, straight; #5, mk KK..30.00
Razor hone, Junior, mk KK, aluminum box+papers 55.00
Razor strop, #K80, mk KK, ECS, 2½x24".....................................50.00
Router, #KK171½..135.00
Sandpaper, med flint, mk KK, 2 sheets...25.00
Saw, circular; electric, #K810..45.00
Saw, de-horning; mk KK..50.00

Saw, hack; #K48, mk KK 35.00
Saw, hand; axe-head button, mk KK, 20" blade 50.00
Scissors, stork figural, KK logo, 4" 175.00
Scissors holder, holds 4 prs, mk KK, in leather case 80.00
Scraper, long hdl, mk KK 40.00
Sheep shears, w/picture on blade, mk Simmons 90.00
Showcase, etched KK logos, 72x42x24", EX 1,200.00
Sign, porc emblem, EC Simmons...Cutlery..., red, dbl-sided, 12", EX..1,500.00
Sign, store; Omar Webb Hardware, Jasper MO, mk KK, 10x28"..85.00
Spading fork, emblem on hdl, mk KK, sm 40.00
Spoke shave, #K91 ....60.00
Spoke shave, concave cutter, K95 ....60.00
Staple puller, w/KK emblem in both hdls 30.00
Thermometer, metal on wood, 7", EX 90.00
Thermometer, wood, ECS, mk KK, 9" 90.00
Tin, Keen Kutter Kombination Razor Hone, #K20, 2x6", EX 65.00
Trimmer/edger, push-style, red pnt, mk KKT, rare..........90.00
Wrench, pipe; KK on hdl, 12" 30.00
Wrench, pipe; Stillson pattern, wood hdl, mk KK, 8" 30.00

Kellogg Studio

Stanley Kellogg (1908 – 1972) opened the Kellogg Studio in Petoskey, Michigan, in 1948. It remained in operation until 1976, producing a wide range of both decorative and functional ceramics including dinnerware, vases, and figurines. Most pieces are glazed in rich, solid colors and are marked 'Petoskey' as well as 'S. Kellogg Studio' or 'Kellogg's.' Stanley Kellogg began as a sculptor, and it was while working on an outdoor monument with the great Swedish-American sculptor, Carl Milles, that Stanley suffered the back injury which forced him to turn to studio work. In addition to naturalistic treatments of Michigan wildlife, Kellogg developed some angular, architectural forms in his molded art pottery. Our co-advisors for this category are Walter P. Hogan and Wendy L. Woodworth; they are listed in the Directory under Michigan. See Kellogg Studio website: www.emunix.emich.edu/~whogan/kellogg/index.html.

Ashtray, brn, leaf shape w/floral design, 5" 20.00
Ashtray, gr, sq w/personalized name 15.00
Bowl, bl w/wht int, 1" 8.00
Bowl, shadow type, gr, bulbous, cut-out chickadees, 7" 150.00
Box, metallic glaze, w/lid, 3x5" 50.00
Dish, teardrop shape, red w/tiny flower frog insert, 3½" 15.00

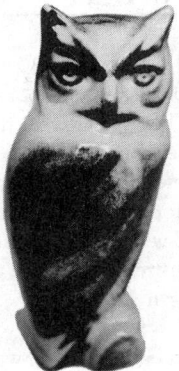

Figure, great-horned owl on branch, brown and ivory, 7¼", $65.00. (Photo courtesy Walter P. Hogan and Wendy L. Woodworth)

Figurine, owl chick standing, blk, 5" 95.00
Flower frog vase, wht, spherical, 3¼", w/separate rnd base, 4" 50.00
Pitcher, bl, curved hdl, 9" 40.00
Plate/charger, brn w/yel pears, 10" 45.00
Vase, blk gourd shape w/irregular vertical grooves, 16" 90.00

Kelva

Kelva was a trademark of the C.F. Monroe Company of Meriden, Connecticut; it was produced for only a few years after the turn of the century. It is distinguished from the Wave Crest and Nakara lines by its unique Batik-like background, probably achieved through the use of a cloth or sponge to apply the color. Large florals are hand painted on the opaque milk glass; and ormolu and brass mounts were used for the boxes, vases, and trays. Most pieces are signed. Our advisors for this category are Dolli and Wilfred Cohen; they are listed in the Directory under California.

Box, floral, pk on bl, 3x4" 500.00
Box, floral on rose lid, ornate metal bottom, 5" dia 550.00
Box, landscape panels on Crown mold, ormolu mts/ft, med 1,450.00
Box, rose (blown out), pk & wht on dk gr, 3½x4" 850.00
Fernery, floral on fuchsia, 4¼x7½" 550.00
Humidor, Cigars/flowers on bl, metal mt/lid/hdl, 4½x8¾" 1,250.00
Shakers, floral on gr, pr 850.00
Tray, floral on gr, Crown mold, ormolu collar/hdls, 6" dia..........650.00
Vase, floral on gr, ormolu hdls, 7¾" 875.00
Vase, floral on moss gr, ornate ormolu hdls/ft, 14" 1,350.00
Vase, floral spray on fuchsia, cone shape w/ormolu ft, 6x2"........650.00
Vase, wild roses on dk gr, ftd, 14x4" 1,150.00

Kenton Hills

Kenton Hills Porcelain was established in 1940 in Erlanger, Kentucky, by Harold Bopp, former Rookwood superintendent, and David Seyler, noted artist and sculptor. Native clay was used; glazes were very similar to Rookwood's of the same period. The work was of high quality, but because of the restrictions imposed on needed material due to the onset of the war, the operation failed in 1942. Much of the ware is artist signed and marked with the Kenton Hills name or cipher and shape number.

Ashtray, horse head form, brn/bl glossy, Seyler, #182, 6" 110.00
Vase, gazelles/geometrics on gr, Hentschel, 3134, 6½", NM 550.00
Vase, Teardrop, Wm Hentschel, #105, 4", NM 250.00

Kentucky Derby Glasses

Kentucky Derby glasses are the official souvenir glasses sold at Churchill Downs filled with mint juleps on Derby Day. Many folks from all over the country who attend the Derby take home the souvenir glass, and thus the collecting begins. The first glass (1938) is said to have either been given away as a souvenir or used for drinks among the elite at the Downs. This one, the 1939 glass, two glasses from 1940, the 1940 – 41 aluminum tumbler, the 'Beetleware' tumblers from 1941 to 1944, and the 1945 short, tall, and jigger glasses are the rarest, most sought-after glasses, and they command the highest prices. Some 1974 glasses incorrectly listed the 1971 winner Canonero II as just Canonero; as a result, it became the 'mistake' glass for that year. Also, glasses made by the Federal Glass Company (whose logo, found on the bottom of the glass, is a small shield containing an F) were used for extra glasses for the 100th running in 1974. There is also a 'mistake' and a correct Federal glass, making four to collect for that year.

The 1956 glass has four variations. On some 1956 glasses the star which was meant to separate the words 'Kentucky Derby' is missing making only one star instead of two stars. Also, all three horses on the glass were meant to have tails, but on some of the glasses only two have tails making two tails instead of three. To identify which 1956 glass you have, just count the number of stars and tails.

In order to identify the year of a pre-1969 glass, since it did not appear on the front of the glass prior to then, simply add one year to the last date listed on the back of the glass. This may seem to be a confusing practice, but the current year's glass is produced long before the Derby winner is determined.

The prices took a bit of a jump this year as more and more collectors are searching for the older glasses which are becoming extremely hard to locate. Our advisor for this category is Betty Hornback; she is listed in the Directory under Kentucky.

1938	4,000.00
1939	6,500.00
1940, aluminum	800.00
1940, French Lick, aluminum	800.00
1940, glass tumbler, 2 styles, ea, minimum value	10,000.00
1941-44, Beetleware, from $2,500 to	4,000.00
1945, jigger	1,000.00
1945, regular	1,600.00
1945, tall	450.00
1946-47, ea	100.00
1948, clear bottom	225.00
1948, frosted bottom	250.00

1949, He Has Seen Them All, green on frosted, $225.00.

1950	450.00
1951	650.00
1952, Gold Cup	225.00
1953	175.00
1954	200.00
1955	150.00
1956, 1 star, 2 tails	200.00
1956, 1 star, 3 tails	400.00
1956, 2 stars, 2 tails	200.00
1956, 2 stars, 3 tails	250.00
1957, gold & blk on frosted	125.00
1958, Gold Bar	175.00
1958, Iron Leige	225.00
1959-60, ea	100.00
1961	110.00
1962, Churchill Downs, red, gold & blk on clear	80.00
1963-64	50.00
1965	75.00
1966	60.00
1967-68, ea	60.00
1969	65.00
1970	70.00
1971	50.00
1972	45.00
1973	55.00
1974, Federal, regular & mistake, ea	200.00

1974, Libbey, mistake, Canonero in 1971 listing on bk	18.00
1974, regular, Canonero II in 1971 listing on bk	16.00
1975	16.00
1976	16.00
1976, plastic	16.00
1977	14.00
1978-79, ea	16.00
1980	22.00
1981	14.00
1982	14.00
1983-85, ea	12.00
1986	14.00
1986 (1985 copy)	20.00
1987-89, ea	12.00
1990-92, ea	10.00
1993-95, ea	9.00
1996-97, ea	8.00
1998-99, ea	6.00
2000-1001, ea	5.00

Keramos

Imported by the Everling and Reuss Co. of Philadelphia in the late 1920s to early 1950s, this company produced very high quality ceramic figurines with very detailed glazing similar to other firms in the Austrian country. Most pieces are marked and numbered, usually found with a shield and name mark on the bottom. Occasionally there will be another name listed with the shield mark, i.e. 'Knight Ceramics by Keramos of Austria,' or accompanied by a sticker with the Eberling & Reuss crown.

The more detailed the piece the more valuable it is. Artist-signed examples are not easily found. All pieces listed here are in excellent condition. Our advisor is Darrell Thomas; he is listed in the Directory under Wisconsin.

Figurien, Budgie parakeet, bright bl/wht/blk, sgn Lg, mk	425.00
Figurine, birds (3) on branch, bl/yel/gray, mk, E&R sticker	250.00
Figurine, chrous girl w/flowered dress & sheet music, Dakon mk, 8½"	350.00
Figurine, Deco lady w/dress fanned open, Dakon mk, #K-2118, 9x10"	595.00
Figurine, girl w/baby cart, detailed, Dakon Keramos mk, 9x5"	950.00
Figurine, lady on skis, mc, detailed, shield & knight mk, 12"	1,150.00
Figurine, newspaper boy w/hat & paper, Dakon Keramos mk, 9½"	350.00

Kew Blas

The Union Glass Company was founded in 1854, in Somerville, Massachusetts, an offshoot of the New England Glass Co. in East Cambridge. They made only flint glass — tablewares, lamps, globes, and shades. Kew Blas was a trade name they used for their iridescent, lustered art glass produced there from 1893 until about 1920. The glass was made in imitation of Tiffany and achieved notable success. Some items were decorated with pulled leaf and feather designs, while others had a monochrome lustre surface. The mark was an engraved 'Kew Blas' in an arching arrangement.

Bowl, feathers, gr/gold on wht, red-orange int, flared rim, 3⅞" H	525.00
Candlesticks, gold irid, swirled stems, 8", pr	765.00
Cordial, red-gold, distended stem, 5"	325.00
Tumbler, gold, pinched sides, 3"	275.00
Tumbler, gold irid, 4 pinched-in sides, 3½x3"	600.00
Vase, gold irid, dbl gourd form, 8½x5½"	435.00
Vase, trumpet; amber w/stretch gold irid int, disk ft, 12"	865.00

King's Rose

King's Rose was made in Staffordshire, England, from about 1820 to 1830. It is closely related to Gaudy Dutch in body type as well as the colors used in its decoration. The pattern consists of a full-blown, orange-red rose with green, pink, and yellow leaves and accents. When the rose is in pink, the ware is often referred to as Queen's Rose.

Plate, embossed line designs with green teardrops between form border, 1820 – 30, 5¼", $125.00. (Photo courtesy A&B Auctions Inc.)

Bowl, int w/wide pk band, deep, 5½"	500.00
Cake plate, Queen's Rose, floral rim band, rose in center, 10"	200.00
Coffeepot, dome lid, pearlware, 11¼"	650.00
Cup & saucer, handleless; red rose, vine border	245.00
Cup & saucer, Queen's Rose, pearlware, 2⅛x3⅜", 5½", EX	130.00
Pitcher, milk; pearlware, 5⅜"	300.00
Pitcher, petal band at top, draping wreath designs, 4⅛"	50.00
Plate, unmk, 7½"	150.00
Plate, pk band w/red stripes, 8⅛"	125.00
Plate, plain rim, vining border, #10, 7½", EX	125.00
Plate, Queen's Rose, unmk, 1820-30, 7¼"	125.00
Plate, unmk, 6¾"	125.00
Teapot, pk border, emb shell-design body, C hdl, 6⅛", EX	85.00

Kitchen Collectibles

During the last half of the 1850s, mass-produced kitchen gadgets were patented at an astonishing rate. Most were ingeniously efficient. Apple peelers, egg beaters, cherry pitters, food choppers, and such were only the most common of hundreds of kitchen tools well designed to perform only specific tasks. Today all are very collectible.

For further information we recommend *Kitchen Glassware of the Depression Years* and *Anchor Hocking's Fire-King & More, Second Edition*, both by Gene Florence; and *Kitchen Antiques, 1790 – 1940*, by Kathryn McNerney. See also Appliances; Butter Molds and Stamps; Cast Iron; Cookbooks; Copper; Glass Knives; Molds; Pie Birds; Primitives; Reamers; String Holders; Tinware; Trivets; Wooden Ware; Wrought Iron.

Key: TM — trade mark

Cast Kitchen Ware

Be aware that cast-iron counterfeit production is on the increase. Items with phony production numbers, finishes, etc., are being made at this time. Many of these new pieces are the popular miniature cornstick pans. To command the values given below, examples must be free from damage of any kind or excessive wear. Waffle irons must be complete with all three pieces and the handle. The term 'EPU' in the description lines refers to the **Erie PA, USA** mark. The term 'block mark' refers to the lettering in the large logo that was used ca 1920 until 1940; 'slant logo' refers

to the lettering in the large logo ca 1900 to 1920. Victor was Griswold's first low-budget line (ca 1875). Skillets #5 and #6 are uncommon, while #7, #8, and #9 are easy to find. For further information contact our advisor, Grant S. Windsor (SASE required); he is listed in the Directory under Virginia. See also Keen Kutter; Clubs, Newsletters, and Catalogs.

Breadstick pan, Griswold #21, from $125 to	175.00
Cake mold, rabbit, Griswold, Warning: heavily reproduced, from $250 to	300.00
Corn/wheat stick pan, Griswold #272, no ft, from $125 to	175.00
Cornstick pan, Griswold #283, from $125 to	175.00
Cornstick pan, Wagner #1319, tab hdls, Pat Pending, from $75 to	100.00
Danish cake pan/egg poacher, Griswold #32, Diamond TM, from $150 to	200.00
Dutch oven, Griswold #6, ERIE TM, rnd bottom, from $200 to	250.00
Dutch oven, Griswold #8, early tite-top, Block TMs, from $40 to	60.00
Dutch oven, Griswold #8, ERIE TM, rnd bottom, from $50 to	75.00
Dutch oven, Wagner #6, stylized TM, raised writing on lid, from $75 to	125.00
Gem pan, GF Filley #5, 8 oval cups, from $75 to	125.00
Gem pan, Griswold #1, marked No 1 & 940, 11 rnd cups, from $75 to	100.00
Gem pan, Griswold #11 French Roll, wide band, 12 cups, from $30 to	40.00
Gem pan, Griswold #19, fully mk, 6-cup golf ball, from $450 to	550.00
Gem pan, Griswold #5, mk No 5, 8 oval cups, from $150 to	250.00
Gem pan, Griswold #9, 'brownie cake pan,' from $125 to	150.00
Gem pan, Wagner 'B' popover pan, 11 cups, from $20 to	40.00
Griddle, bailed; Griswold #16, ERIE TM, from $75 to	100.00
Griddle, hdld; Griswold #8, Diamond TM, from $75 to	100.00
Griddle, hdld; Wagner #8, Stylized TM, from $20 to	30.00
Griddle, long; Griswold #11, Slant/Griswold's Erie TM, from $100 to	150.00
Griddle, long; Wagner #8, mk WAGNER Sidney O, from $35 to	45.00
Kettle, lipped; Wagner #7, mk WAGNER Sidney O, from $45 to	65.00
Kettle, low; Griswold #7, ERIE TM, from $50 to	75.00
Roaster, oval; Griswold #9, Block TMs/full writing lid, from $350 to	450.00
Saucepan, Griswold, ERIE TM, 4-qt, from $125 to	175.00
Skillet, bacon; Wagner, #1103, w/press, from $125 to	175.00
Skillet, Griswold #2, Block TM, no heat ring, from $300 to	400.00
Skillet, Griswold #2, Block TM, w/heat ring, from $1,600 to	2,600.00
Skillet, Griswold #3, Slant/EPU TM, w/heat ring, from $25 to	50.00
Skillet, Griswold #3, sm TM, grooved hdl, from $5 to	15.00
Skillet, Griswold #4, Block TM, no heat ring, from $40 to	60.00
Skillet, Griswold #4, Slant EPU TM, from $75 to	100.00
Skillet, Griswold #5, ERIE TM, from $450 to	550.00
Skillet, Griswold, 5-in-1 breakfast, from $140 to	160.00
Skillet, Griswold #6, Block TM, w/heat ring, from $75 to	100.00
Skillet, Griswold #6, sq fry, from $75 to	125.00
Skillet, Griswold #6, Victor, from $250 to	325.00
Skillet, Griswold #7, sm TM, early hdl, from $10 to	20.00
Skillet, Griswold #768, sq utility w/#769 iron lid, from $275 to	300.00
Skillet, Griswold #8, ERIE TM, outside heat ring, from $20 to	40.00
Skillet, Griswold #8, sm TM, grooved hdl, from $10 to	20.00
Skillet, Griswold #9, slant/ERIE TM, from $20 to	40.00
Skillet, Griswold #10, Block TM, no heat ring, from $40 to	60.00
Skillet, Griswold #10, sm TM, late hdl, from $25 to	45.00
Skillet, Griswold #11, Slant/EPU TM, from $250 to	300.00
Skillet, Griswold #12, Block TM, from $75 to	100.00
Skillet, Griswold #12, Slant/ERIE TM, from $100 to	150.00
Skillet, Griswold #14, Block TM, from $125 to	175.00
Skillet, Martin Stove & Range #14, from $125 to	175.00
Skillet, Wagner #14, stylized TM, w/inset heat ring, from $150 to	200.00
Skillet, Wagner #5, mk WAGNER Sidney O, from $20 to	30.00
Skillet, Wagner #7, National, from $25 to	50.00
Skillet, Wagner #7, pie logo, from $75 to	100.00
Skillet, Wagner #8, Stylized TM, no heat ring, from $15 to	25.00
Skillet, Wapak #3, Indian head medallion, from $100 to	150.00
Skillet cover, Griswold #10, high smooth dome, Block TM, from $40 to	60.00
Skillet cover, Griswold #3, low smooth dome, from $300 to	350.00

Skillet cover, Griswold #14, low dome, raised writing, from $475 to ..**525.00**
Wafer iron, Wagner #1451, w/wrought-iron hdls, from $125 to.**150.00**
Waffle iron, Griswold #12, 2 pans, from $450 to **550.00**
Waffle iron, Griswold #2, sq, from $650 to **750.00**
Waffle iron, Griswold #8, Victor, scissors hinge, from $200 to....**250.00**
Waffle iron, hearth; unmk, std grid, CI pans/wrought hdls, from $50 to...**150.00**
Waffle iron, Seldon & Griswold #8, full web pattern, from $200 to..**250.00**
Waffle iron, Wagner, Pat July 26 1892, 6¾" sq, from $75 to.......**100.00**
Yankee bowl, Griswold #2, Block TM, smooth sides, from $75 to..**100.00**

Egg Beaters

Egg beaters are unbeatable. Ranging from hand helds, rotary crank, and squeeze power to Archimedes up-and-down models, egg beaters are America's favorite kitchen gadget. A mainstay of any kitchenware collection, in recent years egg beaters have come into their own — nutmeg graters, spatulas, and can openers will have to scramble to catch up! At the turn of the century, everyone in America owned an egg beater. Every household did its own mixing and baking — there were no pre-processed foods. And every inventor thought he/she could make a better beater. Thus American ingenuity produced more than one thousand egg beater patents, dating back to 1856, with several hundred different models being manufactured over the years. As true examples of Americana, egg beaters have risen in value over the past couple of years, with a half dozen mixers valued at $2,750.00 and more, including the cast-iron, rotary crank 'Dodge Race Course egg beater.' But the vast majority stay under $50.00, while the values of the super rare beaters continue upward. And just when you think you've seen them all, new ones always turn up, usually at flea markets or garage sales. For further information, we recommend our advisor (author of the definitive book on egg beaters) Don Thornton, who is listed in the Directory under California. (SASE required.)

A&J, all metal, sm, 9¾" **10.00**
A&J, center drive, pk & gray wooden hdls, 12"............................**12.00**
Aluminum Beauty Pat'd April 20, 1920, rotary crank, 10½" **15.00**
Beats Eggs, Cream...No 825 Androck, hand-held fan type, 11".......**5.00**
Dover...Patd May 6th 1873...1891..., CI rotary crank, 11¼"....**55.00**
Express or 'Fly Swatter,' Pat Oct 25, 1887, 11½"......................**1,300.00**
Holt's Egg Beater & Cream Whip, CI, Pat August 22 '99-Apr 6 '00, 9"..**240.00**
Jaquette Phila PA, CI & wire, dbl hdls, Pat No 3, 10½"..........**1,000.00**
Jiffy Whip...Krasbert & Sons Mfg, rotary crank turbine, 11¾"......**25.00**
K-C (soap bubble), 1930s, 10" **42.00**
Keystone Mfg Pat Dec 15 '85, Philadelphia PA, wall mt, EX......**425.00**
Quik Whip Reg US Pat Off...Pending, metal, squeeze power, 11¾"...**295.00**
Star Egg Beater April 19 59 Oct 16 60, CI rotary crank, 10½" ..**1,000.00**
Turbine Beater Androck Made in USA, rotary crank, 11½".........**18.00**
Vandeusen Egg Whip, CA Chapman...1894, all metal, hand held, 11"..**15.00**
Whipwell...USA Pat Mch 23 1920..., rotary crank, wood hdl, 11"..**20.00**

Glass

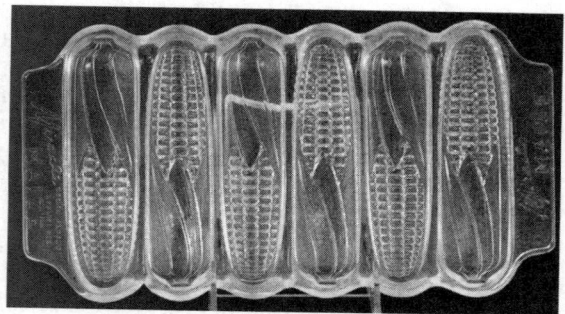

Miracle Maize cornstick pan, clear glass, 12x6¼", $65.00.

Ashtray holder, clear, Cambridge, from $30 to............................**35.00**
Batter jug, amber, Paden City, from $50 to **60.00**
Batter set, cobalt, New Martinsville, from $375 to....................**400.00**
Bottle, water; Forest Green, Hocking, w/top, from $70 to............**75.00**
Bowl, mixing; blk, 9⅜", from $65 to..**70.00**
Bowl, mixing; cobalt, 9⅝", from $50 to...................................**60.00**
Bowl, mixing; Delphite Blue, Jeannette, 9", from $80 to **100.00**
Bowl, mixing; fired-on color, Pyrex, set of 4, from $28 to.............**36.00**
Bowl, mixing; Jade-ite, Hocking, 9", from $22 to **25.00**
Boxl, mixing; gr, 6½"..**15.00**
Butter box, gr, Jeannette, 2-lb, from $175 to............................**200.00**
Butter dish, amber, Federal, ¼-lb, from $30 to...........................**35.00**
Cake plate, Snowflake, pk, from $22 to.....................................**25.00**
Canister, custard, Coffee in blk letters, sq sides, McKee, from $40 to..**50.00**
Canister, Delphite Blue, Sugar in blk letters, Jeannette, 40-oz....**400.00**
Canister, dk amber, emb Coffee, from $100 to.........................**125.00**
Coffeepot, Silex, red, from $175 to.......................................**200.00**
Cruet, oil/vinegar; gr, Cambridge, from $85 to..........................**95.00**
Egg cup, blk, from $18 to...**20.00**
Ice bucket, pk, Fry, w/lid, from $200 to **225.00**
Ice tub, Peacock Blue, from $35 to..**40.00**
Ladle, Chalaine Blue, screw-on hdl, from $200 to......................**225.00**
Measure, apothecary; dk amber, 1-oz.....................................**30.00**
Measuring cup, Chalaine Blue, 2-spout, from $800 to..............**900.00**
Measuring cup, dk amber, 1-cup, from $275 to.......................**300.00**
Measuring cup, gr, 3-spout, Federal......................................**45.00**
Measuring cup, red, 2-cup, from $12 to...................................**15.00**
Measuring cup, yel opaque, ftd, w/hdl, Mckee, 4-cup, from $125 to .**140.00**
Measuring pitcher, Delphite Blue, McKee, 2-cup, from $80 to **90.00**
Measuring pitcher, pk, ribbed, Hocking, 2-cup, from $50 to **55.00**
Mug, Chanticleer on wht, Anchor Hocking, from $12 to............**14.00**
Mug, gr clambroth, from $30 to **35.00**
Pitcher, Skokie Green, McKee, 4-cup, from $35 to **40.00**
Refrigerator dish, Chalaine Blue, 7¼" sq, from $125 to **140.00**
Refrigerator dish, pk, Federal, 8x8", from $35 to.......................**40.00**
Refrigerator jar, clear wedge shape w/Jade-ite lid, from $12 to......**15.00**
Rolling pin, blk glass, wear, 17"..**110.00**
Rolling pin, blown, golden yel-amber, pontil scar, 1820-35, 12¾"..**140.00**
Rolling pin, cobalt w/worn floral transfers, blown, 29"...............**110.00**
Rolling pin, green w/wht loopings, blown, 14" **195.00**
Rolling pin, wht clambroth, wooden hdls, from $100 to.............**125.00**
Salt shakers, lt Jade-ite, Jeannette, pr, from $17.50 to **20.00**
Scoop, bl, from $55 to..**60.00**
Straw holder, gr, tall, metal lid, from $400 to **450.00**
Sugar bowl, Emerald-Glo, w/liner, from $25 to **30.00**
Sugar shaker, Hex Optic, Jeannette, from $200 to......................**225.00**
Syrup jug, amber, Cambridge, from $50 to **55.00**
Vase, Chalaine Blue, 12", from $100 to....................................**125.00**

Miscellaneous

Apple peeler, CI w/wood hdl, Pat Oct 6 1863, 11¾" **125.00**
Apple peeler, Domestic...Landers Frary & Clark, CI, Pat 1873...**200.00**
Apple peeler, Geo R Thompson, CI, lever action **165.00**
Apple peeler, Goodell...Pat 1898, CI, turntable, EX....................**60.00**
Apple peeler, Hudson Improved, CI, Pat 1882, 9".....................**195.00**
Apple peeler, Larner & Seagrave Worcester Mass **300.00**
Apple peeler, Little Star, CI...**65.00**
Apple peeler, Reading Hdw, CI, last Pat May 22, 1877................**95.00**
Apple peeler, softwood w/wrought-iron peeler, on plank, ca 1850s..**295.00**
Apple peeler, Thompson, New England Butt Co, CI, Pat 1877..**175.00**
Apple peeler, Union, DH Wittemore Worcester...Pat...1866, 8½"...**180.00**
Apple peeler, wood & iron, 1860s, 4½x3¾" on board **195.00**
Apple peeler, 7" walnut wheel w/string pulleys on board, 1700s ..**400.00**

Asparagus buncher, Ellis Keystone AGL Wks, CI, mtd on board..**45.00**
Asparagus buncher, Philadelphia, CI, 5x5", mtd on board **65.00**
Biscuit cutter, Horsford's Baking Powder, tin, 4" **35.00**
Biscuit cutter, Stover's Pride, tin, 2½x3" **50.00**
Biscuit cutter, wood w/thin sharp cutting edge, wood hdl, 3¼x2¼" ..**45.00**
Biscuit pricker/cutter, tin box-like form, minor rust......................**50.00**
Biscuit/cookie cutter, Ballard's Flour, 2¾x2¼" **35.00**
Box, knife scouring; wood w/sq nails, 1840s, 14½" H................**110.00**
Bread maker, Universal #8, metal, Pat Dec 25, 1906................**75.00**
Cake turner/spatula, metal w/trn wood hdl, ca 1890, 14"........**22.50**
Can opener, Bon Acord Mackerel/Bon Acord Herring, w/fork & corkscrew...**110.00**
Can opener, Dazey, electric **28.00**
Can opener, Universal Dazey Americana, CI, wall mt **67.50**
Can opener, Vaughan's Easy Cutter, steel w/wood hdl, 1900s..........**7.00**
Candy hatchet, CI, ca 1900, 8¾" **25.00**
Cheese slicer, iron w/fine wire blade, 1920s, 6⅞" **18.00**
Cherry seeder, Duke, Reading Hdw, Pat Pend, ca 1890, 11" **95.00**
Cherry seeder, Home Cherry Stoner, Pat Aug 17 1917..., dbl pitter ..**30.00**
Cherry seeder, New Standard Wobbly Wheel...............................**110.00**
Chopper, iron, kidney-shaped 8½" blade, 22"..........................**85.00**
Chopper, Starrett, Pat 5/23/1865, iron/tin on wood base **350.00**
Chopper, W Marples & Son, 6x6½"..**40.00**
Chopper, wooden block w/wrought-iron pivoting chopper, 1890s, 10x13"..**50.00**
Chopper, wrought blade, cast tube iron hdl, Pat Feb 1887 ....**55.00**
Chopper, wrought iron, heart-shaped cut-out blade, 7⅛" L **225.00**
Chopper, wrought iron blade w/wood hdl, 1800s........................**55.00**
Chopper/grinder, Griswold #4, EX..**45.00**
Churn, Borden's, glass, 1-qt...**60.00**
Churn, Dazey #10, beveled edge, 1-qt.....................................**750.00**
Churn, Dazey #10, bull's eye, 1-qt...**700.00**
Churn, Dazey #20, ...**200.00**
Churn, Dazey #30, Pat 1922 ....**225.00**
Churn, Dazey #40 ....**140.00**
Churn, Dazey #60 ....**165.00**
Churn, Dazey #80 ....**250.00**
Churn, Lightning Butter Machine, Pat Feb 6, 1917, 2-qt **120.00**
Churn, syllabub; tin, rnd w/holes in bottom, tall **85.00**
Churn, unmk, glass, 1-gal..**75.00**
Clothesline reel, Cordomatic, 1950s, EX....................................**15.00**
Cork press, CI, hinged top, oblong w/long hdl, 19th C, 3x9⅜x4" ...**40.00**
Cream stirrer, Bennett...Co, tin/iron, 4¾" dia, 22" L....................**18.00**
Crimper/noodle cutter, brass, 1" dia wheel, steel shaft, 7¾" L.......**35.00**
Crimper/noodle cutter, brass & iron w/trn wood hdl, 7¼" L.........**60.00**
Egg cooker/poacher, Sunbeam, holds 5 eggs, 6½" **40.00**
Egg poacher, Comet, aluminum, holds 4 ....**20.00**
Egg poacher, Fries, tin, EX..**45.00**
Egg poacher, tin, holds 4, lt rust...**32.00**
Flour sifter, bentwood & wire, rod enforcements, gr pnt, 5x17"....**35.00**
Flour sifter, Bromwell's, apples, enamel on tin, 1950s, NM **30.00**
Flour sifter, cherry blossoms, enamel on tin, 6" **40.00**
Flour sifter, Duplex, tin, 5-cup...**45.00**
Flour sifter, lady & boy in kitchen, enamel on tin, 1950s, EX.......**38.00**
Flour sifter, Lee's Favorite Flour, tin, crank hdl, 6x5", EX.............**28.00**
Flour sifter, strawberries, enamel on tin, EX..............................**40.00**
Grater, All in One Pat Pend, tin, ca 1940, 10⅝x4¼" **25.00**
Grater, cheese; pine fr w/punched tin front, 12x8x4"+hdl **225.00**
Grater, cheese/nutmeg; tin, trifold, center slicer, Eve Ware..........**85.00**
Grater, coconut; Magic Cocoanut Grater Pat Pend, tin, 9½" **40.00**
Grater, nutmeg; Boyd...Pat Apl'd For, 5¾" **80.00**
Grater, nutmeg; Dominick & Haff, sterling, 5"........................**175.00**
Grater, nutmeg; Edgar, dtd 1891 & 1896, 8½x2¼" dia, EX **195.00**
Grater, nutmeg; Gem, Caldwell, CI/tin/wood, 1890s.................**125.00**
Grater, nutmeg; Gilmore Pat, japanned tin, half-rnd, 1800s, 9"....**15.00**
Grater, nutmeg; japanned tin cylinder w/hinged sides, 2½x1⅛".**100.00**

Grater, nutmeg; Pat Appld For, CI/tin/wood, 3¾x3½"................**65.00**
Grater, nutmeg; Pat Date Dec 26 77, crank hdl, spring loaded, EX...**175.00**
Grater, nutmeg; Snyder, 1904 ....**475.00**
Grater, nutmeg; tin oval, hinged, w/compartment, 7½" **270.00**
Grater, tin/nickel/wood, revolving drum type, 1930s, 8⅞" **25.00**
Grinder, herb; CI, disk blade, wood hdls, slant-sided trough, 19th C...**395.00**
Grinder/grater, CI/aluminum, Germany, clamps on, NM **28.00**
Kraut cutter, cut-out crest w/heart, EX patina, 22" L................**120.00**
Kraut cutter, nailed, single steel blade, 19th C, 1¾x20x8" **40.00**
Kraut cutter, walnut & hardwood w/heart cutout in hdl, 22"......**350.00**
Kraut cutter, walnut w/single steel blade, 1890s, 23x7" **60.00**
Kraut cutter, 3 metal blades mtd on oak board, 25x9" **55.00**
Lard press, Sensible Press, NR Streeter...NY, 2-qt, EX...............**65.00**
Lard/fruit press, Enterprise, CI cylinder, ca 1900, EX................**75.00**
Lard/fruit press, Enterprise, 4-qt..**115.00**
Lemon squeezer, Arcade NO 2, CI/wood/porc **45.00**
Lemon squeezer, hinged wood, EX patina, 11"..........................**40.00**
Lemon squeezer, Newman's Drum..., CI/wood, Pat 1883, 9".........**95.00**
Masher, iron bottom w/holes, wood hdl, 16" **20.00**
Masher, trn wood w/mushroom finial, 1800s, 10¾" **25.00**
Mixer, Robert's Lightning, glass bottom, w/dasher, Pat 1913.........**55.00**
Pan, chicken; Griswold #8, chrome, self-basting lid **60.00**
Pie crimper, bone wheel, wood hdl, 5¼" **30.00**
Pineapple corer, scissors type, 5½"..**20.00**
Raisin seeder, Black Lightning, CI, clamps on **95.00**
Raisin seeder, Enterprise, CI, Wet the Raisins, #36, Pat 4/2/1895....**150.00**
Raisin seeder, Everett, wood w/7 curved wires, 1889-93 ....**70.00**
Rolling pin, wht stoneware, maple hdls, 19x3" dia.....................**200.00**
Sieve, bean; wood w/slats, moves from sq to dmn shape **210.00**
Sieve, Foley Food Mill, tin w/wood hdls...................................**12.00**
Sifter, flour; tin/CI/Wood, Hunter's New..., table top, 23¼" **1,200.00**
Slicer, vegetable; Anthony Iske's Improved..., walnut/steel, Pat 1875 ..**250.00**
Slicer, vegetable; bird's-eye maple w/iron blade, 14x7" **90.00**
Slicer, vegetable; wood, 6 blades, wire pusher, 1898, 18"...............**95.00**
Spatula, Wholesome Baking Powder, open hdl, 11½" **12.00**
Sprinkler bottle, cat, marble eyes, ceramic, Am Bisque, from $250 to....**350.00**
Sprinkler bottle, Chinese man, towel over arm, ceramic, from $200 to..**300.00**
Sprinkler bottle, clothespin, red, yel & gr plastic, from $20 to **25.00**
Sprinkler bottle, elephant, trunk forms hdl, Am Bisque, from $250 to...**400.00**
Sprinkler bottle, iron, Fl souvenir, pk flamingo, ceramic, $225 to ..**250.00**
Sprinkler bottle, iron, gr ivy, ceramic, from $50 to **75.00**
Sprinkler bottle, Kitchen Prayer Lady, ceramic, from $300 to **400.00**
Sprinkler bottle, Mary Maid, any color, plastic, Reliance, from $15 to...**35.00**
Sprinkler bottle, rooster, mc details on wht, ceramic, from $125 to......**150.00**
Sugar nippers, wrought iron, pliers type, lines/rings, 10" **225.00**
Whip, cream; Fries **135.00**
Whip, mayonnaise; Universal, rare...**400.00**

Knife Rests

    Several scholars feel that knife rests originated in Germany and France with usage spreading to England and later America as travel between countries became more widespread. Knife rests have been documented from 1720 through 1839, and they're being made yet today by porcelain manufacturers and glasshouses to match their tableware patterns. Some of the present-day producers are located in France, Germany, and Poland.

    Knife rests of pressed glass, cut crystal, porcelain, sterling silver, plated silver, wood, ivory, and bone have been collected for many years. Signed knife rests are especially desired. It was not until the Centennial Exhibition in Philadelphia in 1876 that the brilliant new cut glass rests, deeply faceted and shining like diamonds, appeared in shops by the hundreds. There were sets of twelve, eight, or six; some came boxed. Sizes of knife rests vary from 1¼" to 3¼" for individual knives and from 5" to 6" for carving knives. Glass knife rests were made in many colors such as purple, blue, green, vaseline, pink, and cranberry. It is important to note that prices may vary from one area of the country to another and from dealer to dealer. For further information we recommend our advisor, Beverly Schell Ales; she is listed in the Directory under California.

Art France, glass horse, pr 100.00
Bing & Grondahl, sea horse, bl & wht, 1870-90, 3¾" H, lg 145.00
Cut crystal, dmns & clear bands w/star-cut ends, 4", NM 145.00
Cut crystal, overall Brilliant cuttings, knob ends, 5½" 185.00
Cut crystal, squash form 75.00
Cut crystal, w/star on end of ball, 3" 70.00
Gold-tone metal, horse on base, 2¾" L 75.00
Heisey, pressed glass, dmn & H mk, 3¼", from $100 to 150.00
Imperial, milk glass, marked IG 35.00
Lalique France, mk, frosted end 95.00
Meissen, mk X w/sword logo on end, pr 165.00
Metal, fruit & flowers, 3¾", set of 6 (ea different).........................85.00
Pressed glass, gr, 3½", pr 60.00
Quimper, #499, 1950s, from $40 to......................................65.00
Royal Copenhagen, 1/134, Denmark, bl & wht....................150.00
Sabino, bl glass w/duck end..50.00
SP, children hopping over stile 125.00
SP, sphinx ea end...75.00
SP, squirrel w/lg bar on tail, Simpson, Hall & Miller.................195.00
Val St Lambert Belquigue, amber glass, 1963.........................100.00
Verlys (unmk), bl glass, 4", from $100 to 150.00
Waterford, mk, lg..100.00

Knives

Knife collecting as a hobby began in earnest during the 1960s when government regulations required for the first time that knife companies mark their product with the country of origin. The few collectors and dealers cognizant of this change at once began stockpiling the older knives made before this law was enacted. Another impetus to the growing interest in this area came with the Gun Control Act of 1968, which severely restricted gun trading. Frustrated gun dealers transferred their attention to knives. Today there are collectors' clubs in many of the states.

The most sought-after pocketknives are those made before WWII. However, Case, Schrade, and Primble knives of a more recent manufacture are also collected. Most collectors prefer knives 'as found.' Do not attempt to clean, sharpen, or in any way 'improve' on an old knife.

The prices quoted here are for knives in mint condition. If a knife has been used, sharpened, or blemished in any way, its value decreases. Knives in excellent condition generally are valued at half the prices listed below. The newer the knife, the greater the reduction in value. For further information refer to *The Standard Knife Collector's Guide, 2nd Edition; Cattaragus Cutlery, Identification and Values;* and *The Big Knife Book* by Ron Stewart and Roy Ritchie (all published by Collector Books); and *Sargent's American Premium Guide to Knives and Razors, Identification and Values, 3rd Edition,* by Jim Sargent. Our advisor for this category is Bill Wright; he is listed in the Directory under Indiana.

Key:
bd — blade   jack — jackknife
imi — imitation

Case, C61050, gr bone hdl, 1-bd, Case Tested XX, 5⅜"..............600.00
Case, gr bone hdl, 2-bd, Tested XX, 3¼" 225.00
Case, M100, red cracked ice hdl, 1-bd, XX, 3¼" 120.00

Case, RM2028, Christmas tree hdl, 2-bd, Tested XX, 2⅞"..........400.00
Case, 06267, bone hdl, 2-bd, USA, 3¼" 75.00
Case, 1116SP, walnut hdl, 1-bd, XX, 3½" 45.00
Case, 2279 1/2, slick blk hdl, 2-bd, Tested XX, 3¼"...................125.00
Case, 31048SP, yel compo hdl, 1-bd, USA, 4⅛".........................50.00
Case, 31093, toothpick, yel compo hdl, 1-bd, Tested XX, 5" 250.00
Case, 33044HP, bird's eye, yel compo hdl, 3-bd, XX, 1964, 3¼"...75.00
Case, 4257, wht compo hdl, 2-bd, XX, 3¾" 40.00
Case, 5197L, SSP stag hdl, 1-bd, Case XX, USA w/dots, 5" 75.00
Case, 5260T, stag hdl, 2-bd, WR Case & Sons 225.00
Case, 61013, gr bone hdl, 1-bd, Tested XX, 3⅝" 200.00
Case, 61049LP, gr bone hdl, 1-bd, Case Tested XX, 4⅛".............500.00
Case, 6116 1/2, gr bone hdl, 1-bd, Tested XX, 1920-40, 3⅜"......175.00
Case, 6172, gr bone hdl, 1-bd, Tested XX, 5½" 1,400.00
Case, 62009, blk compo hdl, 2-bd, XX, 3⅞" 100.00
Case, 62089, gr bone hdl, 2-bd, Case Bradford PA, 3¾"..........1,200.00
Case, 62100, gr bone hdl, 2-bd, Tested XX, 1920-40, 4⅝".........900.00
Case, 6213LP, Rogers bone hdl, 2-bd, WR Case & Sons, 3⅞"..1,000.00
Case, 6235EO, blk imi jigged hdl, 2-bd, XX, 3¼".......................50.00
Case, 6249, copperhead, gr bone hdl, 2-bd, XX, 3⅞" 600.00
Case, 63063 1/2, gr bone hdl, 3-bd, Tested XX, 3⅛" 750.00
Case, 6339LP, Rogers bone hdl, 3-bd, Case Bradford PA, 3¾"..1,000.00
Case, 640045R, scout, blk plastic hdl, 4-bd, XX, 1940-50, 3⅝"..100.00
Case, 6592, transitional, gr bone hdl, 5-bd, Tested XX, 3⅞"......3,500.00
Case, 72006, tortoise shell hdl, 2-bd, Case Bradford PA, 2⅝".....300.00
Case, 8224, pearl hdl, 2-bd, WR Case & Sons, 3" 250.00
Case, 83047, pearl hdl, 3-bd, WR Case & Sons, 4"................1,000.00
Case, 83102F LP, cracked ice hdl, 2-bd, Tested XX 175.00
Case, 9165SAB, cracked ice hdl, 1-bd, Tested XX, 1920-40, 5¾"..500.00
Case, 9393, Fr pearl hdl, 3-bd, Case Bradford, 3⅞" 450.00
Keen Kutter, barlow, blk compo hdl, 2-bd, 3⅜" 50.00

Keen Kutter, E.C. Simmons, Coke bottle shape with Simmons picture in handle, clear celluloid, 5¼", $250.00.

Keen Kutter, equal end, walnut hdl, 2-bd, EC Simmons, 3⅝" 100.00
Keen Kutter, jack, brn bone hdl, 1-bd, EC Simmons, 3¼" 75.00
Keen Kutter, jack, brn bone hdl, 2-bd, EC Simmons, 3⅞"..........200.00
Keen Kutter, jack, cocobola hdl, 2-bd, EC Simmons, 3⅞"..........125.00
Keen Kutter, K1058, lock bk, brn bone hdl, EC Simmons, 4¼".450.00
Keen Kutter, K3463, whittler, pearl hdl, 3-bd, EC Simmons, 3⅜".300.00
Keen Kutter, Lobster Pen, pearl hdl, 2-bd, EC Simmons, 3" 100.00
Keen Kutter, muskrat, Christmas tree hdl, 2-bd, EC Simmons, 4"..350.00
Keen Kutter, Senator Pen, brn bone hdl, 2-bd, EC Simmons, 3⅜"...90.00
Keen Kutter, utility, brn bone hdl, 3-bd, EC Simmons, 3⅝".......250.00
Keen Kutter, whittler, pick bone hdl, 3-bd, EC Simmons, 3¼" ..200.00
Keen Kutter, 30, peanut, candy-stripe hdl, 2-bd, EC Simmons, 2⅞"...125.00
Keen Kutter, 801, Daddy Barlow, brn bone hdl, 1-bd, 5".............200.00
Keen Kutter, 828, barlow, brn bone hdl, 2-bd, 3⅜" 75.00
Keen Kutter, 2881, barlow, brn bone hdl, 2-bd, EC Simmons, 3⅜"....100.00
Queen, Rogers bone hdl, 2-bd, Queen City, 4½"......................200.00
Queen, 11EO, winterbottom bone hdl, 2-bd, Queen Steel, 4"......75.00
Queen, 15, winterbottom bone hdl, 2-bd, Queen, 3½" 50.00
Queen, 19, fisherman's, Rogers bone hdl, 2-bd, Big Q, 5" 100.00
Queen, 28, jack, winterbottom bone hdl, 2-bd, Queen Steel, 4½"..125.00
Queen, 33, congress, Rogers bone hdl, 4-bd, Big Q, 3½"............120.00
Queen, 36, lockback, winterbottom bone hdl, 1-bd, Queen, 4½"....125.00

Queen, 38, swell center jumbo, jigged bone hdl, 1-bd, Big Q, 5¼"..200.00
Queen, 57, smoked pearl hdl, 3-bd, Queen, 3⅜" 75.00
Queen, 7, imi blk bone hdl, 2-bd, Queen Big Q Carbon, 2½" 28.00
Queen, 8415, canoe, stag hdl, 2-bd, Queen, 500 made, 3⅝" 35.00
Remington, RB44, barlow (clip), brn bone hdl, 2-bd, 3⅜" 150.00
Remington, R111, redwood hdl, 3-bd, 3⅜"................................100.00
Remington, R1153, jack, brn bone hdl, 2-bd, 4½" 400.00
Remington, R1240, barlow, brn bone hdl, 1-bd, 5" 300.00
Remington, R1339, metal hdl, 2-bd, 3"..65.00
Remington, R1613, bone hdl, 1-bd, rnd shield, 5" 900.00
Remington, R165, jack, pyremite hdl, 2-bd, 3½" 125.00
Remington, R173, jack, brn bone hdl, 2-bd, teardrop bd, 3¾" ...375.00
Remington, R1783, jack teardrop, brn bone hdl, 2-bd, 3½" 125.00
Remington, R1823, brn bone hdl, 2-bd, long pull, 3⅝" 125.00
Remington, R3143, stockman, bone hdl, 5-bd, 4"....................5,000.00
Remington, R3555, stockman, pyremite hdl, 3-bd, 3⅞"..............350.00
Remington, R3557, stockman, imi ivory hdl, 3-bd, 4" 350.00
Remington, R3580, buffalo horn hdl, 3-bd, 4"............................500.00
Remington, R373, jack, bone hdl, 2-bd, 3¾"..............................300.00
Remington, R3855, pruner, imi ivory hdl, 2-bd, 4".....................350.00
Remington, R629, lobster, metal hdl w/bail, 3-bd, 2¾" 90.00
Remington, R653, bowtie, bone hdl, 1-bd, 3⅞" 500.00
Remington, R698, hawkbill, cocobola hdl, 1-bd, 4" 150.00
Remington, R963, scout/easy opener, bone hdl, 2-bd, 3½" 750.00
Remington, R995, jack, bl & wht compo hdl, 2-bd, 3¼" 125.00
Western States, lockbk, bone hdl, 1-bd, 5¼"..............................400.00
Western States, 2203, imi pearl hdl, 2-bd, drilled bolster, 5⅛" ...250.00
Western States, 2203B, gr sparkle hdl w/bail, 2-bd, 2½" 75.00
Western States, 3100, pearl overlay compo hdl, 1-bd, 5¼" 250.00
Western States, 422, bone hdl, 2-bd, shield, 3⅝" 200.00
Western States, 6211, barlow, bone hdl, 2-bd (spear), 3⅜".........125.00
Western States, 6212, jack, bone hdl, 2-bd, 3¼" 125.00
Winchester, 1920, folding hunter, bone hdl, 1-bd, 5⅜" 1,750.00
Winchester, 1936, toothpick, brn bone hdl, 1-bd, 5"..................500.00
Winchester, 2330, pen, pearl hdl, 2-bd, 3¼"..............................200.00
Winchester, 2847, pen, brn bone hdl, 2-bd, 3¼" 125.00
Winchester, 2853, gunstock, brn bone hdl, 2-bd, 3½"................500.00
Winchester, 2876, sm muskrat, brn bone hdl, 2-bd, 3¼"............300.00
Winchester, 2969, swell center, bone hdl, 2-bd, 3⅞"..................350.00
Winchester, 2991, peanut, brn bone hdl, 2-bd, 2⅞" 140.00
Winchester, 3002, whittler, gr celluloid hdl, 3-bd, 3¾" 350.00

Miscellaneous

Bowie, Alfred Hunter, 12" clip-point bd, 5" wood hdl, EX....15,000.00
Bowie, brass guard & pommel, walnut hdl, custom made, 8¾" bd, M ..75.00
Hunting, Marbles, 6" bd, stag hdl, EX 275.00
Sheath, 17" bd w/brass ferrule, cvd horn hdl, 23", +leather sheath..100.00
Skinning, Marbles, Woodcraft, leather hdl, EX 125.00
Trout, Marbles, all steel, early 1900s, 6", in orig leather sheath ..250.00
WWII theatre, 5" bd, aluminum hdl, EX...50.00
WWII theatre, 6" bd, plexiglass hdl, EX...85.00
WWII theatre, 7" bd, mc hdl, EX...150.00
WWII theatre, 8" bd, wood hdl, EX 100.00

Kosta

Kosta glassware has been made in Sweden since 1742. Today they are one of that country's leading producers of quality art glass. Two of their most important designers were Elis Bergh (1929 – 1950) and Vicke Lindstrand, artistic director from 1950 to 1973. Lindstrand brought to the company knowledge of important techniques such as Graal, fine figural engraving, Ariel, etc. He influenced new artists to experiment with these techniques and inspired them to create new and innovative designs. Today's collectors are most interested in pieces made during the 1950s and 1960s. Our advisor for this category is Abby Malowanczyk; she is listed in the Directory under Texas.

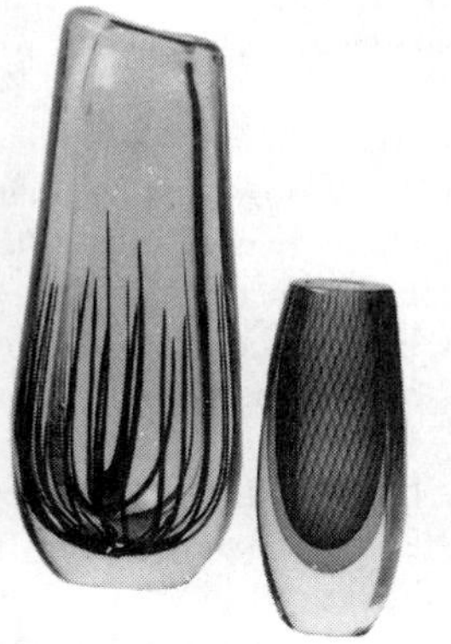

Vase, internally decorated vertical black canes, Lindstrand, LU2004, ca 1955, 13¾", $800.00; Vase, green cased over blue and clear with internal trails, Lindstrand, LH 1590, 8", $600.00.

Bowl, bl to red swags in clear, ftd, Warff/57456, 5".....................110.00
Bowl, clear w/cut ovals, Lindstrand Unik 1672, 3½x15½" 750.00
Bowl, gr & clear w/cut ovals, Lindstrand/56690, 7½x8¼" 365.00
Charger, goldfish, amber/yel, Hoff/77725, 12½"..........................300.00
Vase, aburgine spirals in clear, Lindstrand/LH 1384, 1955, 5½" .450.00
Vase, Ariel, seafoam gr/amethyst, Lindstrand/U1529, 5x5".........775.00
Vase, clear w/gr patches & oval windows, Lindstrand/46691, 8½"...700.00
Vase, clear w/purple/blk/wht crisscrosses, Lindstrand/LH1261 ....250.00
Vase, dk bl w/asymmetrical opening, Lindstrand, LH1606, 7" 190.00
Vase, gr & cobalt, Kosta LH1588, 6¾x4¾x2⅜"..........................635.00
Vase, Negress, Lindstrand/LS580, 1953, 16" 1,000.00
Vase, Ventana, orange/clear, Morales-Schildt/SS165/8, 4¾x3x1⅜" ..550.00

Kutani

Kutani, named for the Japanese village where it originated, was first produced in the seventeenth century. The early ware, Ko Kutani, was made for only about thirty years. Several types were produced before 1800, but these are rarely encountered. In the nineteenth century, kilns located in several different villages began to copy the old Kutani wares. This later, more familiar type has large areas of red with gold designs on a white ground decorated with warriors, birds, and flowers in controlled colors of red, gold, and black.

Bowl, bird & flowers, Meiji period, w/lid, 7x9"..........................160.00
Bowl, 1000 Cranes, Genuine Japan, 8⅝" 135.00
Can, condensed milk; geishas on cobalt, uptrn hdls, 5⅛x3½"+stand 235.00
Dinner ware, temple/mtns, 90-pc, EX..365.00
Figurine, cat, Maneki Neko, 7½x4"..400.00
Figurine, hen, late Meiji period, ca 1912, 5½", EX.......................400.00
Figurine, Hotei, 10"..135.00
Jar, ginger; floral on wht w/gold, Meiji, 5"..................................135.00
Sake set, carafe whistles when poured, 6 cups w/geisha lithophanes...150.00
Tea set, geishas in garden, Meiji period, 10-pc...........................150.00
Vase, flower bushes on wht w/much gold, Meiji period, 7"..........110.00
Vase, samurai/servants/rooster, bulbous, Meiji period, 9½" 235.00
Vase, waterfowl & flowers, 4 ped ft, Meiji period, 9½x9"............300.00

Labels

Before the advent of the cardboard box, wooden crates were used for transporting products. Paper labels were attached to the crates to identify the contents and the packer. These labels often had colorful lithographed illustrations covering a broad range of subjects. Eventually the cardboard box replaced the crate, and the artwork was imprinted directly onto the carton. Today these paper labels are becoming collectible — primarily for the art, but also for their advertising appeal. Our advisor for this category is Cerebro; their address is listed in the Directory under Pennsylvania.

Can, Abbey Brand Peaches, church ruins/peaches, VG.................**20.00**
Can, Black Horse Jams & Fruits, 2 peaches/blk horse, EX.............**25.00**
Can, Cycle Brand Salmon, Victorian woman on bike/salmon, M.**35.00**
Can, El Banquette Coffee, Mexican flag/senorita & coffee, EX **18.00**
Can, Ferndell Lima Beans, ferns/beans in pods, M.........................**12.00**
Can, Homestead Mushrooms, mushrooms/country home, M **18.00**
Can, Just Off the Cob Corn, lady cleaning ears of corn, M...........**12.00**
Can, Le Prince Leopold Pineapple, pineapple/Belgium/ports, VG...**15.00**
Can, Locust Grove Tomatoes, forest road/tomato, EX **20.00**
Can, Modac Bartlett Pears, Indian Chief/arrows/baskets/pears, M **20.00**
Can, Okeanos Marrow Peas, sea horse/Cupid standing on shell, M..**15.00**
Can, OT Ozark Trail, car on mountain road/fruits & vegetables, EX ..**40.00**
Can, Rose Bowl Pears, football players/bowl of pears, M **35.00**
Can, Tide Rim Oysters, ocean waves/2 oysters, M **20.00**
Cigar box, inner lid; Captain Corker, w/cigar, M **75.00**
Cigar box, inner lid; Dante, images from poem Divine Comedy, M..**125.00**
Cigar box, inner lid; Frontier, hunter w/buck/cabin, M..............**175.00**
Cigar box, inner lid; Grand Sachem, Indian & Spaniard, EX **75.00**
Cigar box, inner lid; Kitty Grey, blk cat/woman in red, M...........**40.00**
Cigar box, inner lid; La Puma, woman w/peacock feathers, VG ...**30.00**
Cigar box, outer; Carl Phelps, actor, EX **35.00**
Cigar box, outer; Fine Domestic, half-nude Indian maiden, EX..**100.00**
Cigar box, outer; Here's Luck, men at bar, EX **40.00**
Cigar box, outer; Press Club, men reading paper, M **85.00**
Cigar box, outer; Rosa Donita, woman holding lute, EX..............**15.00**
Cigar box, outer; Schutzen Konig, 2 men in top hats w/rifle, M ...**45.00**
Cigar box, outer; The Prairie King, buffalo hunt, G **50.00**
Crate, apple, Best Strike, baseball player, 1920, M **45.00**
Crate, apple, Good Stock, orchard scene/apples, M......................**55.00**
Crate, apple, Tom Tit, blue birds on apple blossoms, M **60.00**

Crate, apple, U Like Um, 1940s, 9x10½", $3.00.
(Photo courtesy Cerebro)

Crate, CA Orange, Black Hawk, bust of Indian brave, M...........**150.00**
Crate, CA Orange, Commonwealth, capital building, M..............**50.00**
Crate, CA Orange, Mountie, Mountie on horseback, VG **60.00**
Crate, CA Orange, Ranger, park ranger/mountain scenes, VG.....**45.00**
Crate, FL Citrus, Aunty, smiling Black woman, M **30.00**
Crate, FL Citrus, Florida Cowboy, cowboy on bucking horse, 1930, M...**10.00**
Crate, FL Citrus, Horseshoe, silhouette of race horses/shoe, EX .**125.00**
Crate, lemon, Basketball, women players, 1920, EX **50.00**
Crate, lemon, First American, Indian/tepee, 1916, M **150.00**
Crate, lemon, Southern Cross, San Fernando Mission/stars, 1930, M...**80.00**
Crate, pear, Buckingham, cowboy riding a wild pig, 1920, M..........**8.00**
Crate, pear, Grand Prize, California mission, 1915, M...................**15.00**

Crate, pear, McCurdy, silhouette view of Lick Observatory, 1920, M .**6.00**

Labino

Dominick Labino was a glass blower who until mid-1985 worked in his studio in Ohio, blowing and sculpting various items which he signed and dated. A ceramic engineer by trade, he was instrumental in developing the heat-resistant tiles used in space flights. His glassmaking shows his versatility in the art. While some of his designs are free-form and futuristic, others are reminiscent of the products of older glasshouses. Because of problems with his health, Mr. Labino became unable to blow glass himself; he died January, 10, 1987. Work coming from his studio since mid-1985 has been signed 'Labino Studios, Baker,' indicating ware made by his protegee, E. Baker O'Brien. In addition to her own compositions, she continues to use many of the colors developed by Labino.

Paperweight, Emergence, pk/bl int layers, 1990, 5" **140.00**
Pitcher, honey amber, appl hdl, 1967, 5¾" **260.00**
Sculpture, Emergence, clear, pk/orange veils, bubbles, 1971, 9¼" ..**6,325.00**
Sculpture, Emergence, clear, pk/orange veils, bubbles, 1972, 7" **4,890.00**
Sculpture, Emergence, Slab, cobalt to clear w/wht opal int, 1981, 5"..**75.00**
Vase, bl swirls cased to ruby, oviform, hdls, everted rim, 1971, 7"......**400.00**
Vase, bl w/opal & smoke encased w/in long prunts, 1966, 10¾".**475.00**
Vase, golden olive gr, free-form flanged lip, ribbed, 1965, 8¾" ...**275.00**
Vase, owl form, amber on clear w/other colors, 1968, 4½".........**250.00**
Vase, ruby irid urn form w/hdls, 1972, 5¼" **545.00**
Vase, tobacco-amber w/yel lip, teardrop form, 1967, 8½"............**435.00**

Lace, Linens, and Needlework

Two distinct audiences vie for old lace and linens. Collectors seek out exceptional stitchery like philatelists and numismatists seek stamps or coins — simply to marvel at its beauty, rarity, and ties to history. Collectors judge lace and linens like figure skaters and gymnasts are judged: artist impression is half the score, technical merit the other. How complex and difficult are the stitches and how well are they done? The 'users' see lace and linens as recyclables. They seek pretty wearables or decorative materials. They want fashionable things in mint condition, and have little or no interest in technique. Both groups influence price.

Undiscovered and underpriced are the eighteenth-century masterpieces of lace and needle art in techniques which will never be duplicated. Their beauty is subtle. Amazing stitches often are invisible without magnification. To get the best value in any lace, linen, or textile item, learn to look closely at individual stitches, and study the design and technique. The finest pieces are wonderfully constructed. The stitches are beautiful to look at, and they do a good job of holding the item together. Our advisor for this category is Elizabeth M. Kurella, author (Krause) of books related to this subject; she is listed in the Directory under Indiana.

Key: embr — embroidered

Ascot, Schiffli machine embr, ivory lace border, 16x18" **20.00**
Bedspread, Fr lace netting w/lg medallion, Victorian, 110x88" ...**265.00**
Bedspread, popcorn lace crochet, ca 1900, 72x96" **125.00**
Blanket, homespun wool, bl & natural wht, 2-pc, 70x84", VG .**165.00**
Blanket, homespun wool, bl & red plaid, 2-pc, rprs, 72x78" **200.00**
Blanket, homespun wool, blk checks & natural wht, 2-pc, 68x76", EX..**330.00**
Collar, Duchesse lace, ecru flowers/scrolls/etc, 53x5" **100.00**
Collar, hand-beaded jet on net, Victorian, 40x8½" **75.00**
Collar, mixed Brussels lace, Pointe de Gaze & Duchesse, handmade ..**85.00**
Collar, Rosaline lace, handmade, ca 1900, 5" at widest................**50.00**

Counterpane, off-wht woven peacock/cornucopias/cherubs, 70x80"..**75.00**
Counterpane, wht w/woven-in floral center & dmn border, 1890s, 80" sq ..**50.00**
Counterpane, wht woven florals surround woven dmns, 1880s, 68x70"..**50.00**
Curtain tiebacks, gilt & silk thread, tassel drops, 6 for **385.00**
Doily, Belgian bobbin lace, wht, 7" dia..........................**20.00**
Doily, crochet, flower bouquet, ecru, 10½x17" **25.00**
Doily, crochet, wht, for bread tray, 5x12" **20.00**
Doily, network handmade lace w/cherubs/animals/etc, 22" dia......**85.00**
Doily, tatted lace, 5" dia **15.00**
Doily, wht linen w/tatted lace border, 11" dia **32.00**
Fabric, bl & wht plaid homespun linen, 19th C, 40x55" **150.00**
Fabric, red & wht check homespun linen w/wht homespun bking, 58x62" ...**165.00**
Lace picture, filet, classic ladies dancing, 8x22" **65.00**
Lap robe, velvet & silk embr, Windmill Blades, 1885, 56x59"....**550.00**
Linen bed case, 3-color plaid homespun, w/fringe, 1894, 68x70"+bolster ..**2,100.00**
Needlepoint panel, still life on table, 21x46"+fr................**300.00**
Needlework, family crest, gold/silver bullion/silk/wool, 1900s, 14"..**250.00**
Needlework, figures in woods, 30x24", EX in bird's-eye maple fr...**715.00**
Needlework, lady & dog at well w/trees, silk, 19th C, 18x16" **515.00**
Needlework, lady & dog in landscape, HP sky, 10x12"+fr...........**545.00**
Needlework, lady plays harp beside urn/flowers/willow, 19th C, 15x18"...**800.00**
Needlework, lady w/roses in landscape, 9x6"+eglomise mat & fr....**400.00**
Needlework, landscape on silk, sgn/1786, 18x20".................**385.00**
Needlework, mc roses & rust border on beige, tapestry, 30x48"..**200.00**
Needlework, mc roses in ivory medallions on beige, tapestry, 48x70".**450.00**
Needlework, World w/All Modern Discoveries, silk on satin, 24x29"...**1,045.00**
Pillowcase, cotton w/applique eagle & flowers, late 1800s, 28x24"..**130.00**
Pillowcases, linen w/drawnwork pattern, 38x20", pr.............**65.00**
Pillowcases, linen w/floral crochet trim, 34", pr, +matching sheet...**42.50**
Runner, ecru linen w/wide filet lace border, 62x18"...............**65.00**
Runner, Fr lace w/embr florals, full table length: 90x10".........**265.00**
Runner, Grecian ladies & cherubs, ecru filet lace, 32x10"........**90.00**
Runner, lace, dainty floral pattern, oval, Czech Republic, 28x14"...**25.00**
Runner, linen w/cutwork/needle lace inserts/bobbin lace border, 70x17".**110.00**
Runner, needle lace w/flowers/acorns, deep ecru, 41½x17".........**80.00**
Runner, Normandy lace, mk Made in France, 44x17".................**110.00**
Tablecloth, Cluny lace, 80" dia..................................**195.00**
Tablecloth, crochet, wht, fancy, 58x78" **150.00**
Tablecloth, embr & cutwork linen, 70x116", +12 napkins..........**150.00**
Tablecloth, embr linen, gray on wht, 64x82", +8 napkins...........**125.00**
Tablecloth, filet lace sqs & cutwork sqs, hand embr, 86x88".......**150.00**
Tablecloth, floral drawnwork on linen, 88x110", +12 napkins+12 towels...**250.00**
Tablecloth, geometric drawnwork on linen, 88x162", EX **300.00**
Tablecloth, intricate lace openwork flowers & spiderwebs, 84x102"...**250.00**
Tablecloth, lace/cutwork/drawnwork/embr dragon/gamebirds/lion, 81x77"..**225.00**
Tablecloth, lacework & wht-on-wht embr, 72x100", +8 napkins ..**200.00**
Tablecloth, linen, cutouts/embr flowers & grapes, scalloped, 113x72"...**225.00**
Tablecloth, linen, eyelet roses w/embr vines, lt stain, 90x106" ...**120.00**
Tablecloth, linen, gray & natural woven chain & lattice, 82x116" .**125.00**
Tablecloth, linen, red/wht, Greek Key border, 56x82" **75.00**
Tablecloth, linen damask, 176x396", +12 napkins **400.00**
Tablecloth, machine-made floral ecru lace, 1940s, 60x88".........**265.00**
Tablecloth, organdy, Marghab Hortensia (floral), 112x72", +12 napkins...**536.00**
Tablecloth, Pointe de Venice needle lace, 1920s, 103x70".........**550.00**
Towel, embr cherub, Victorian, 36x27" **65.00**
Towel, hand; Marghab calla lilies, 21½x14", set of 3, MIB **127.50**
Towel, hand; Marghab yel roses on yel linen, 15x21" **54.00**

Lacy Glassware

Lacy glass became popular in the late 1820s after the development of the pressing machine. It was decorated with allover patterns — hearts, lyres, sheaves of wheat, etc. — and backgrounds were completely stip-

pled. The designs were intricate and delicate, hence the term 'lacy.' Although Sandwich produced this type of glassware in abundance, it was also made by other eastern glassworks as well as in the Midwest. By 1840, its popularity on the wane and a depressed economy forcing manufacturers to seek less expensive modes of production, lacy glass began to be phased out in favor of pressed pattern glass.

For more information refer to *Sandwich Glass* by Ruth Webb Lee. When no condition is indicated, the items listed below are assumed to be without obvious damage; minor roughness is normal. See also Salts, Open.

Plates, crosshatched hearts in center, sapphire blue, 5⅞", EX, $350.00; Roman Rosette, purple amethyst, 5½", VG, $275.00.

Bowl, Butterfly, ca 1835-50, 1x6¼x4½" **95.00**
Bowl, Industry, 6¼", EX **150.00**
Bowl, nappy, Iron Cross in Heart Box, 1835-50, rare, 2x10" ...**1,000.00**
Candlestick, Hexagonal Gothic, minor chips, 8¾" **100.00**
Compote, Heart, appl knop stem, 3½x4¾" **400.00**
Compote, Heart, bladed stem, rnd base w/pontil, 4x6" **425.00**
Creamer, Heart & Scale, 1838-45, 4½" **350.00**
Dish, bull's-eye rim, C scrolls/zigzags, star center, 8" **600.00**
Dish, Feather, 9½" **60.00**
Egg cup, Anthemion leaves, scalloped rim, 3⅜", EX **70.00**
Plate, Maple Leaf, sawtooth rim, Gillinder & Sons, 11" **105.00**
Plate, Midwestern rope border, 6" **70.00**
Plate, Pine Tree & Shield, opal, scalloped, 6" **350.00**
Sugar bowl, Gothic Arch, bright bl, 5¼"........................**1,200.00**
Taster, emerald gr, petal ft, 1¾" **425.00**
Taster, Sunflower, ftd, 2¼" **150.00**
Tureen, deep sapphire bl, w/lid, Sandwich, mini, 2x3" **400.00**

Lalique

Beginning his lengthy career as a designer and maker of fine jewelry, Rene Lalique at first only dabbled in glass, making small panels of cire perdue (wax casting) to use in his jewelry. He also made small flacons of gold and silver with his glass inlays, which attracted the attention of M.F. Coty, who commissioned Lalique to design bottles for his perfume company. The success of this venture resulted in the opening of his own glassworks at Combs-la-Ville in 1909. In 1921 a larger factory was established at Wingen-sur-Moder in Alsace-Lorraine. By the '30s Lalique was world renown as the most important designer of his time.

Lalique glass is lead based, either mold blown or pressed. Favored motifs during the Art Nouveau period were dancing nymphs, fish, dragonflies, and foliage. Characteristically the glass is crystal in combination with acid-etched relief. Later some items were made in as many as ten colors (red, amber, and green among them) and were occasionally accented with enameling. These colored pieces, especially those in black, are highly prized by advanced collectors.

During the '20s and '30s, Lalique designed several vases and bowls reminiscent of American Indian art. He also developed a line in the Art Deco style decorated with stylized birds, florals, and geometrics. In addition to vases, clocks, automobile mascots, stemware, and bottles, many other useful objects were produced. Most items made before his death in 1945 were marked 'R. Lalique'; later the 'R' was deleted even though some of the original molds were still used. Numbers found on the bases of some pieces are catalog numbers. Beware of fraudulent pieces that have begun to surface in increasing numbers. Our advisor for this category is John Danis; he is listed in the Directory under Illinois.

Key:
cl/fr — clear and frosted   RL — signed R. Lalique
L — signed Lalique   RLF — signed R. Lalique, France
LF — signed Lalique France

Vase, Sauterelles, grasshoppers, clear and frosted with blue and green stain, introduced in 1912, 10¼", $6,900.00.

Ashtray, Caravelle, sailing ship, cl/fr, ca 1930, 2½x4" 115.00
Ashtray, Serpent, coiled snake center, cl/fr, ca 1920, 4½" 800.00
Atomizer, abstract thorny vines, cl/fr, SP mts, 3¼" 425.00
Atomizer, Maison, fr w/bl wash, RL, 3⅜" 500.00
Basin, Cremieu, flower, opal, RLF, #400, 12" dia 925.00
Bottle, scent; Amèlie, overlapping leaves, fr, oblong, RL, 3" 750.00
Bottle, scent; Ambre, cl/fr blk, ca 1911, 5¼" 1,500.00
Bottle, scent; butterflies, cl/fr, RL, 2x3¼" 750.00
Bottle, scent; Camille, geometric sections, gr fr, 2¼" 1,500.00
Bottle, scent; Chypre, flower heads, cl/fr w/blk stain, D'Orsay, 3" ..865.00
Bottle, scent; Coeur Joie, fr flacon, LF, 6", +pk box...................500.00
Bottle, scent; D'Heraud, flat-sided ovoid, tan wash, RLF, 8x6" ..325.00
Bottle, scent; dahlias, cl/fr, LF, 8⅛" 500.00
Bottle, scent; Dans la Nuit, bl cl/fr, for Worth, '24, 9⅜" 700.00
Bottle, scent; Enfants, putti, cl/fr w/bl stain, ca '31, 3¾x3½" ..1,000.00
Bottle, scent; Flausa, cl/fr w/amber wash, Roger & Gallet, 4¾"..3,000.00
Bottle, scent; Fleur de France, cl, 3" 400.00
Bottle, scent; Hirondelles, swallows, cl/fr w/bl stain, 3½" 1,500.00
Bottle, scent; L'Aire du Temps, doves, cl/fr, N Ricci, 4½" 75.00
Bottle, scent; La Violette, flowers, cl w/violet enamel, 3¼".....1,500.00
Bottle, scent; Poesie d'Orsay, fr w/bl wash, RL, 6" 2,000.00
Bottle, scent; Success, fr snail shell/nude stopper, D'Orsay, 3¾"..1,900.00
Bottle, scent; Telline, bl-gray fr, RL, 3¾", NM 700.00
Bottle, scent; Vers le Jour, cl/fr orange to yel, 4½" 1,200.00
Bowl, Calypso, mermaids, cl/fr w/bl stain, ca 1930, 14" 5,175.00
Bowl, Dauphins, fish in ripples, cl/fr irid w/brn stain, ca '32, 9"...1,000.00
Bowl, Eglantine, flower sprays, bl, RLF, 1¾x9¾" 600.00
Bowl, finger; Tokyo, bubbles, cl, ca 1933, 4⅝"...........................300.00
Bowl, Nemours, flower heads, cl/fr w/blk enamel, #11010, 10" ...300.00
Bowl, Nonetes, birds in flight, cl/fr, RL, 2⅛x8⅝" 300.00
Box, Gui, mistletoe, cl/fr opal w/orange-red stain, ca 1920, 4" dia..425.00
Box, Pervenches, flowerheads, cobalt, egg form, RLF, 4½" L..3,500.00
Box, Quatre Papillons, butterflies, cl/fr, Lalique Depose, 2x3⅛" ..575.00
Champagne, Strasbourg, 2 male grape pressers form std, cl/fr, 6 for..600.00
Clock, Inseparables, lovebirds, cl/fr w/bl stain, ca 1926, 4¼" ..1,950.00
Clock, 2 sparrows ea side demilune case, cl/fr, 6⅛x8½"...........2,500.00
Decanter, Nippon, bubbles, cl, ca 1930, 9¾" 800.00

Figurine, Ara, cockatoo, fr, #11621 ....1,840.00
Figurine, cat, head forward, fr, LF, 4x9½" 700.00
Figurine, cock, fighting, LF, 8" 320.00
Figurine, Daneuse, nude female, fr, LF, 1960, 9¼" 375.00
Figurine, duck, LF, 9½x10" 375.00
Figurine, Ete Surtout Quatre Seasons, nude/wheat, cl/fr, 1939, 7¾"...1,950.00
Figurine, owl, LF, 3½" 60.00
Figurine, toad, fr/polished, mid-205h C, 3⅛" 230.00
Jar, dresser; Epines, thorny brambles, sepia wash, RLF, 3½" 345.00
Mascot, Chrysis, nude w/flowing hair, fr, RLF, #1183, 1932, 5¼"...3,000.00
Mascot, Cog Nain, rooster, smoke gray, RLF, #1135, 8" 1,500.00
Mascot, greyhound, cl/fr, RLF, 1928, 7¾" 1,725.00
Mascot, Perche, fish, cl/fr, LF, 6¼" 1,150.00
Mascot, Sanglier, boar, gr, RLF, #1157, 1932, 2¾" 1,500.00
Necklace, Fuchsia, cl fuchsia pendant w/alternating ovals/beads, 17"....2,875.00
Paperweight, Chrysis, woman kneeling, fr, LF, 5¼" 375.00
Paperweight, sparrow, cl/fr, RLF, 1930, 2½x5" 150.00
Paperweight, Tete de Paun, peacock's head, cl/fr on blk base, 7" ..5,750.00
Pendant, Guepes, wasps, cl/fr amethyst, ca 1920, 2⅜" 1,150.00
Pin, Deux Figurines Dos a Dos, 2 nudes, cl/fr, ca 1913, 2⅛"....2,750.00
Plate, grapes & vines, cl, LF, 9", 8 for 500.00
Plate, Sea Anemone, opal, RLF, 1933, 11".................................300.00
Sconces, Soliel, sunburst, cl/fr, corner type, ca 1926, 9", pr 2,000.00
Tumbler, Oleron, globular, fr, 4" 900.00
Vase, Acanthes, leaves, cl/fr red, ca 1921, 11"........................11,500.00
Vase, Albert, falcon-head hdls, topaz, RL, 6¾" 1,265.00
Vase, Bagatelles, sparrows on branches, fr, LF, after 1952, 6¾" ...700.00
Vase, berries on vine, cl/fr, LF, 6", pr 400.00
Vase, birds & branches, cl/fr, ovoid, RLF, 6½" 650.00
Vase, Borneo, birds & foliage, cl/fr, RLF, 9½", NM 2,645.00
Vase, Cariatides, 8 lady's torsos, cl/fr, RLF, 1930s, 7¾".............4,600.00
Vase, Chamarande, flower hdls, cl/fr opal, ca 1926, 7¾" 1,955.00
Vase, Daisy, opal w/bl wash, RL, 4½" 1,095.00
Vase, Davos, geometrics, clear plum-brn, ca 1932, 11"............5,465.00
Vase, Domremy, thistles, gr frost w/wht stain, ca 1926, 8¼" ...3,500.00
Vase, Esterel, stylized leaves, cl/fr amber, ca 1923, 6⅛".........2,300.00
Vase, Fougeres, leaves, bl fr w/wht stain, ca 1912, 6" 5,750.00
Vase, Grenade, flower petals, cl/fr w/bl stain, ca 1930, 4½".....1,380.00
Vase, Gui, mistletoe, emerald gr/fr, #948, 6½" 2,185.00
Vase, Gui, mistletoe, opal, spherical, RL, #948, 6¾" 800.00
Vase, hearts emb, LF, 7"..275.00
Vase, Marisa, trout, gray frost, RL, spherical, 9½" 2,600.00
Vase, Mesanges, birds & wreath, cl/fr, ca 1931, 11¾" 1,375.00
Vase, Milan, aspen branches, cl/fr, spherical, RL, 11⅛" 2,000.00
Vase, Monnaie dup Pape, branches, fr, RL/RLF, 9⅛" 2,500.00
Vase, Nanking, triangles, cl/fr w/gr stain, ca 1925, 13"............8,000.00
Vase, Ormeaux, leaves, cl/fr w/gr stain, ca 1926, 6⅝" 1,500.00
Vase, Oursin, sea urchin, cl/fr w/bl stain, ca 1935, 7¼" 1,495.00
Vase, Piriac, fish band, cl/fr w/bl stain, ca 1930, 7⅛" 2,300.00
Vase, Quatre Grupes de Lezards, cl/fr w/brn stain, ca 1912, 12"...4,600.00
Vase, Renoncules, flowers, cl/fr w/bl wash, RLF, 6"....................635.00
Vase, Ronces, thorny branches, cl/fr, ca 1921, 9¼" 2,415.00

Lamps

The earliest lamps were simple dish containers with a wick that hung over the edge or was supported by a channel or tube. Grease and oil from animal or vegetable sources were the first fuels used. Ancient pottery lamps, crusie, and Betty lamps are examples of these early types. In 1784 Swiss inventor Ami Argand introduced the first major improvement in lamps. His lamp featured a tubular wick and a glass chimney. During the first half of the nineteenth century, whale oil, burning fluid (a highly explosive mixture of turpentine and alcohol), and lard were the most common fuels used in North America. Many lamps were patented for specific use with these fuels.

Kerosene was the first major breakthrough in lighting fuels. It was demonstrated by Canadian geologist Dr. Abraham Gesner in 1846. The discovery and drilling of petroleum in the late 1850s provided an abundant and inexpensive supply of kerosene. It became the main source of light for homes during the balance of the nineteenth century and for remote locations until the 1950s.

Although Thomas A. Edison invented the electric lamp in 1879, it was not until two or three decades later that electric lamps replaced kerosene household lamps. Millions of kerosene lamps were made for every purpose and pocketbook. They ranged in size from tiny night or miniature lamps to tall stand or piano lamps. Hanging varieties for homes commonly had one or two fonts (oil containers), but chandeliers for churches and public buildings often had six or more. Wall or bracket lamps usually had silvered reflectors. Student lamps, parlor lamps (now called Gone-With-the-Wind lamps), and patterned glass lamps were designed to complement the popular furnishing trends of the day. Gaslight, introduced in the early nineteenth century, was used mainly in homes of the wealthy and public places until the early twentieth century. Most fixtures were wall or ceiling mounted, although some table models were also used.

Few of the ordinary early electric lamps have survived. Many lamp manufacturers made the same or similar styles for either kerosene or electricity, sometimes for gas. Top-of-the-line lamps were made by Pairpoint, Phoenix, Tiffany, Bradley and Hubbard, and Handel. See also these specific sections.

When buying lamps that have been converted to electricity, inspect them very carefully for any damage that may have resulted from the alterations; such damage is very common, and when it does occur, the lamp's value may be lessened by as much as 50%. Lamps seem to bring much higher prices in some areas than others, especially the larger cities. Conversely, in rural areas they may bring only half as much as our listed values. One of our advisors for lamps is Carl Heck; he is listed in the Directory under Colorado. Advise for miniature lamps comes from Bob Culver (who is listed in the Directory under Michigan), and Jeff Bradfield (in Virginia) is our advisor for pattern glass lamps. See also Stained Glass.

Aladdin Lamps, Electric

Bed, #2302SS, whip-o-lite fluted shade, from $200 to.................250.00
Boudoir, G-50, Alacite, 1952, from $40 to....................................50.00
Boudoir, M-158, metal, 1937, from $30 to 40.00
Bridge, #2058, from $200 to...275.00
Bridge, #7088, combination table lamp, no shade, from $250 to...300.00
Bridge, swing arm; #7011, wood, from $150 to 225.00
Figurine, G-16, lady, crystal, etched, from $600 to 700.00
Figurine, G-343, lady w/dog, from $375 to...................................475.00
Floor, #3510, oak, from $175 to..225.00
Floor, #3545S, IES reflector, candle arms, from $175 to..............250.00
Floor, #3602, reflector, candle arms, from $175 to.......................250.00
Floor, #3821, night light, Alacite ring, no candle arms, from $200 to...275.00
Floor, #3994, night light, Alacite ring, candle arms, from $250 to...350.00
Floor, fluorescent; #4898C, Circline, trigger ring, from $200 to...250.00
Floor, Junior; #J-120, amber glass bowl, from $250 to.................300.00
Floor, Junior; #1062, candle arms, from $175 to 225.00
Floor, torchere; #3761, from $350 to 400.00
Floor, torchere; #4598, from $250 to 300.00
Glass Urn, G-375, Dancing Ladies Urn, Alacite, from $1,100 to ..1,200.00
Glass Urn, G-378C, Hoppy Bullet, Alacite, from $300 to 350.00
Ranch House, G-378C, Alacite Bullet, illuminated urn, from $300 to ..350.00
Smoking stand, #7532, from $200 to...300.00
Table, #783G, vase lamp, gr, from $225 to...................................275.00
Table, G-189, tree trunk, opalique, from $400 to 500.00

Table, G-263A, Alacite, illuminated base, from $60 to................75.00
Table, G-311, Alacite, illuminated base, from $50 to....................75.00
Table, G-4, marble-like glass, from $350 to.................................400.00
Table, G-84, Velvex, from $550 to 600.00
Table, M-93, whip-o-lite shade, from $175 to 225.00
Table, MT-507, ceramic base, magic touch, from $300 to 350.00
Table, P-403, ceramic, from $50 to...60.00
Table, P-467, ceramic, from $30 to...50.00

Aladdin Lamps, Kerosene

From 1908 Aladdin lamps with a mantle became the mainstay of rural America, providing light that compared favorably with the electric light bulb. They were produced by the Mantle Lamp Company of America in over eighteen models and more than one hundred styles. During the 1930s to the 1950s, this company was the leading manufacturer of electric lamps as well. Still in operation today, the company is now known as Aladdin Mantle Lamp Co., located in Clarksville, Tennessee. For those seeking additional information on Aladdin Lamps, we recommend *Aladdin — The Magic Name in Lamps*, *Aladdin Electric Lamps Collector's Manual & Price Guide #3*, and *Aladdin Collector's Manual and Price Guide #19*, all written by our advisor for Aladdins, J. W. Courter; he is listed in the Directory under Kentucky. Mr. Courter has also published a book called *Angle Lamps, Collector's Manual and Price Guide*.

Caboose Model 21C, B-400, aluminum font, from $75 to...........150.00
Candle, Aladdinette, metal chimney, from $100 to......................150.00
Floor Model #12, #1250, bl & gold, 1928-29, from $200 to........350.00
Floor Model B, #1248, bronze, 1934-35, from $150 to 225.00
Floor Model B, B-294, bronze & gold lacquer, 1939-42, from $200 to ..250.00
Hanging Model #3, w/#203 shade, from $650 to 750.00
Hanging Model B, flat steel fr, parchment shade, from $200 to..275.00
Parlour, Practicus, polished brass or Old English, from $500 to ..600.00
Parlour Model #2, Old English or Jap bronze, from $600 to........750.00
Shelf Model 23 Lincoln Drape, 1975-82, clear, from $100 to 125.00

Model 12 table lamp, $95.00; With #601S shade, $375.00.
(Photo courtesy J.W. Courter)

Table Model #12, Crystal Vase #1242, Bengal Red, from $450 to ..550.00
Table Model #12, Crystal Vase #1247, Red Venetian Art-Craft, $550 to..650.00
Table Model #12, Florentine Vase #1237, rose moonstone, from $2,800 to..3,200.00
Table Model A, Venetian #103, rose, from $175 to.....................275.00
Table Model B, Cathedral #112, rose moonstone, 1934, from $400 to..500.00
Table Model B, Colonial #105, gr crystal, 1933, from $150 to....200.00
Table Model B, Corinthian B-125, wht & gr moonstone, from $250 to.300.00
Table Model B, Majestic B-120, wht moonstone, from $375 to..450.00
Table Model B, Queen B-97, gr moonstone, from $375 to..........425.00
Table Model B, Short Lincoln Drape B-610, amber opalique, $4,000 to..4,500.00
Table Model B, Simplicity B-29, gr, from $125 to 175.00
Table Model B, Vertique B-88, yel moonstone, 1938, from $600 to..700.00

Table Model B, Washington Drape B-49, amber crystal, from $350 to ...**400.00**
Table Model C, B-165, aluminum font, font lamp (no base), from $45 to.**75.00**
Table Model 23, B-2301, brass plated, 1974-77, from $75 to **100.00**
Table Model 23, Short Lincoln Drape, amber, from $75 to.........**100.00**
Wall Bracket, Practicus, w/font, burner, flame spreader, bracket.**450.00**
Wall Bracket Model #7 or #8, complete, from $500 to................**600.00**
Wall Bracket Model #9, complete, from $175 to **225.00**

Angle Lamps

The Angle Lamp Company of New York City developed a unique type of kerosene lamp that was a vast improvement over those already on the market; they were sold from about 1896 until 1929 and were expensive for their time. Nearly all Angle lamps are hanging lamps and wall lamps. Table models are uncommon. Our Angle lamp advisor is J.W. Courter; he is listed in the Directory under Kentucky. See the narrative for Aladdin Lamps for information concerning popular books Mr. Courter has authored.

Note: Old glass pieces for Angle lamps are scarce to rare; the lamp values that follow are for examples with no glass.

Barn lantern, #115, tin, complete **1,000.00**

Chandelier, #465, four-arm, polished brass, EX, with glass, 4,000.00. (Photo courtesy Bill and Treva Courter)

Hanging, #263, polished brass, EX...**375.00**
Hanging, #352, 3-burner, polished brass, EX................................**600.00**
Hanging, Classic #2, Antique Gold, EX **1,800.00**
Hanging, EG-22, nickel, EX **450.00**
Wall, #102, nickel, EX **350.00**
Wall, #125, pinwheel emb, 1-burner, NP brass, EX **400.00**
Wall, #285, antique brass, EX..**1,000.00**
Wall, clear globe, conical milk glass ribbed shade; NP burner, 14" ..**165.00**
Wall, clear mk globe, plain milk glass shade, NP, 14"..................**150.00**
Wall, Leaf & Vine, nickel, EX..**400.00**
Wall, Plain Grape, nickel, EX...**425.00**

Banquet Lamps

Banquet, Dmn cut, SP Egyptian stem/ft, foreign burner, 18".......**350.00**
Brass w/blk glazed ceramic ft, amber swirled globe, w/burner **150.00**
Brass w/lion head & Greek Key, etched shade w/yel-gr rim, 28".**220.00**
Cranberry w/emb ribs, blk stem, wht metal ft, foreign burner, 22", VG ..**400.00**
Cut clear/frosted ball shade, SP std, Hinks burner, 30½" **460.00**
Cut font, reeded stem, brass ft, foreign burner, 18" **300.00**
Cut gr font on gr onyx stem & ft, foreign burner, 20¾"..............**300.00**
HP milk glass ball globe, gilt CI/brass stepped base, 1895, 32"....**300.00**
Pk cased, 3-part, brass mts, plated ft, Consolidated, 25½", VG+ ...**460.00**
Violet-bl opaque base, clambroth font, scalloped ft, 14¾" **300.00**

Chandeliers

Art Nouveau, 9-light, w/8 sgn Quezal shades, rstr/electrified, 48x26" ...**6,000.00**

Baluster gilt-metal shaft w/12 arms, hex prisms, bobeches, 51x31" ..**4,675.00**
Bats (3) hold foliate fixture, bronze, 22x22" **7,200.00**
Crystal & silvered metal, 18-light, spring arms, prisms, 50x31" .**4,400.00**
Cut glass shades, 6-light, brass fr, prisms, 1850s, 42x30" **3,850.00**
Empire-style marble/bronze dore w/rams' heads/leaves, 6-light, 28x24" ..**825.00**
Georgian style, cut crystal, 10-light, att Waterford, 44x37"....**5,000.00**
Gilt brass Fr style w/porc inserts, 8 candle arms, 1900s, 28"........**990.00**
Giltwood & iron, 3-tier, 25-arm, electrified, ca 1800, 40x46"..**19,550.00**
Pressed/cut glass w/glass scroll arms, 5-light, prisms, 24x26" **575.00**
Rococo-style brass, 24-light, crystal prism swags, 60" H...........**1,045.00**
Rococo-style brass & molded glass, 6-arm w/pendant lamps, 36x38" ..**1,500.00**

Decorated Kerosene Lamps

When only one color is given in a two-layer cut overlay lamp description, the second layer is generally clear; in three-layer examples, the second will ususally be white, the third clear. Exceptions will be noted.

Key: col — cut overlay

Col (2-layer), amethyst, reeded stem, stepped marble base, 19"....**1,325.00**
Col (2-layer), bl, cut stem, marble base, cut/frosted ball shade, 21" .**575.00**
Col (2-layer), bl, matching stem, marble base, Sandwich, 21"....**11,000.00**
Col (2-layer), cranberry, brass stem, dbl-step marble base, 20"....**700.00**
Col (2-layer), emerald gr, brass stem, marble base, gold trim, 20" ..**3,795.00**
Col (2-layer), gr, stars/ovals/etc, marble base, Sandwich, 13" ..**1,150.00**
Col (2-layer), gr, worn gilt, 17".......................................**415.00**
Col (2-layer), powder bl, bl stem & ft, #1 burner, 9½" **1,150.00**
Col (3-layer), cranberry/wht, stars/ovals/etc, Sandwich, 11½"..**3,750.00**

Fairy Lamps

Apricot MOP, ruffled top base, 6 clear ft, 6" **550.00**
Bl frost w/cut flowers, clear ribbed Clarke cup, 4¾x3⅝".............**185.00**
Bl satin, Reverse Drape, Clarke cup, 5¾", EX **300.00**
Bl satin, ruffled base & top, vertical opaque stripes, 4½x5¾" **450.00**
Bl satin w/vertical opaque stripes, Clarke cup, 4½x5¼"..............**450.00**
Burmese, Clarke cup, 4¾x3⅞"..**295.00**
Burmese, Eden Lite insert, 4-ftd Rogers hdld fr, 9" **525.00**
Canary yel to wht MOP, Herringbone, ball shade, 5¼" **1,250.00**
Florentine Cameo, cranberry w/florals & geometrics, 4⅞".........**500.00**
Nailsea, bl, ruffled rim base w/clear Clarke cup, 5½x5½" **800.00**
Nailsea, citron, ruffled bowl base, 6¾x5" **600.00**
Rubena, Dmn Quilt, ruffled, clear Clarke cup, 6¼x3¾"............**225.00**
Spatter glass w/clear base, Cricklite Clark's Trademk, SI-250, 4½"..**200.00**

Gone-With-the-Wind Lamps

Baby Face, bl satin, orig burner/font/shade, CI floral base, 25x10"...**675.00**
Baby Face, gr satin, orig burner/font/shade, scroll base, 25x10" ..**785.00**
Beaded Crinkle, CI base, 18¾"...**300.00**
Bl satin w/HP vintage, brass drop-in font, electrified, 19"........**2,350.00**
HP milk glass ball shade, scrolled/plated CI base, Success burner, 24"...**300.00**
HP milk glass ball shade & font, CI ftd base, brass burner, 22½" ..**350.00**
HP milk glass w/lion's head motif, 24¼", EX............................**300.00**
Mobius Strip, milk glass w/HP & emb floral, 12½" **450.00**
Red satin, puffy Victorian pattern, electrified, 27"......................**500.00**
Yel cased, 5-part, P&A Victor burner, 18" **400.00**

Hanging Lamps

Clear globe w/cut floral, emb brass mts, smoke bell, 28" **600.00**
Cobalt w/smoke bell, orig brass foliate bezel, complete, 14x10" ..**990.00**

Cranberry Hobnail shade, rpl font, jewel fr, prisms, 15" dia........900.00
Cranberry swirl globe w/brass mts, 25x10" dia..........250.00
Peachblow melon-rib 14" shade/font, rtcl brass fr, Sandwich...2,000.00
Pk opal swirl shade in red brass fr, 11½"..........250.00
Rayo, brass, kerosene, gilt metal fr, 38x14", pr..........250.00

Lanterns

Brass bell shape w/blown & etched globe, 19th C, 18x9¾"........900.00
CI, Sheraton style, 6 glass panels, 30x13" dia, EX..........1,380.00
Dennis & Wheeler, tin, cylinder w/conical top, 1850s, 6½x3⅛".120.00
Minors Pat, folding, tin, 5¼x3x3⅝", VG..........100.00
Pierced tin, clear blown onion globe, 10", EX..........440.00
Pierced tin, cylindrical, hinged door, conical top, 16½"..........325.00
Skater's, tin w/gr glass globe, Am, late 1800s, 6½"..........375.00
Tin, 4 glass panels, pyramidal top, sliding do, 12½", EX..........165.00

Lard Oil/Grease Lamps

Betty, wrought iron, hinged lid, oval, w/wick pick, 4¾x3½x4½".220.00
Betty, wrought iron, ovoid w/flat bottom, arched bracket, 7⅝"..475.00
Betty, wrought iron w/hinged lid, complete, 4⅝x2⅞x4"..........240.00
Betty, wrought iron w/trn wooden stand, pitting, 12"+hanger....220.00
Crusie, dbl; wrought iron, long spike w/hook, 5⅜x4¾"..........110.00
Mathby Neal Pat, saucer base, ribbon-shaped hdl, 5½x5"..........150.00
Pan, wrought iron, low-arched flat bk, swivel pin, lg spike, 3¾"..140.00
Pan, wrought iron, triangular w/appl ft & bracket, 5¾x4x6"......125.00
Petticoat, japanned tin, acorn font, C hdl, 4¾x3"..........160.00
Rush, sq wood base, wrought iron shaft w/hinged top, EX..........280.00

Miniature Lamps, Kerosene

Miniature oil lamps were originally called 'night lamps' by their manufacturers. Early examples were very utilitarian in design — some holding only enough oil to burn through the night. When kerosene replaced whale oil in the second half of the nineteenth century, 'mini' lamps became more decorative and started serving other purposes. While mini lamps continue to be produced today, collectors place special value on the lamps of the kerosene era, roughly 1855 to 1910. Four reference books are especially valuable to collectors as they try to identify and value their collections: *Miniature Lamps* by Frank and Ruth Smith, Schiffer Publishing, 1968 (referred to as SI); *Miniature Lamps II* by Ruth Smith, Schiffer Publishing, 1982 (SII); *Miniature Victorian Lamps* by Margorie Hulsebus, Schiffer Publishing, 1996; and *Price Guide for Miniature Lamps* by Marjorie Hulsebus, Schiffer Publishing, 1998 (contains 1998 values for all the above books). References in the following listings correlate with each lamp's plate number in the Smith books. Our advisor is Bob Culver; he is listed in the Directory under Michigan.

Amberina w/amber shell leaves/ft, nutmeg burner, SI-536, 8½".3,735.00
Amethyst, paneled/emb, hornet burner, SI-262, 9"..........375.00
Beaded Drape, cranberry opal, SI-173, 10½"..........400.00
Bl cased w/emb swirled ribs, nutmeg burner, SI-421/SI-391, 7½".300.00
Bl opaline w/emb ribs & flowers, foreign burner, SI-408, 8"........450.00
Bl opaque w/emb decor, nutmeg burner, SI-240, 8¼"..........425.00
Bl opaque w/ribbed panels, nutmeg burner, SI-310, 8", EX.........425.00
Cathedral, amber, SI-199, 9¾"..........480.00
Cone, pink cased, nutmeg burner, SI-394, 8", VG..........350.00
Cranberry Optic w/crystal edge & rigaree, foreign burner, 9"..4,000.00
Cranberry w/emb beads & ribs, hornet burner, SI-367, 9", VG.....65.00
Cranberry w/wht opal swirls, nutmeg burner, SI-II-503, 8".........315.00
Cut Velvet Dmn Quilt, yel, frosted ft, nutmeg burner, SI-531, 8", VG.925.00
Dk pk to lt pk satin w/emb swirls, emb burner, SI-563, 11½"..2,000.00
Emerald gr, emb panels, hornet burner, SI-262, 9", EX..........350.00
Gold/dk ruby spatter w/emb beaded swirl, hornet burner, SI-369, 8".300.00
Gr, optic ribs/HP florals, nutmeg burner, SI-470, 7¼"..........400.00
Gr opaque w/emb decor, acorn burner, SI-234, 8"..........425.00
Gr opaque w/emb dmns & flowers, nutmeg burner, SI-229, 7½", EX.400.00
Gr w/clear leaves & shell ft, nutmeg burner, SI-536, 8½", EX+..575.00
Improved Banner, milk glass chimney, SI-44..........50.00
Little Duchess, cobalt, brass saucer, SI-32, 2½x4⅜"..........110.00
Milk glass, brass ped, ball shade, SI-33, 11"..........250.00
Milk glass w/emb dmn latticework & mc flowers, ball shade, SI-115...180.00
Milk glass w/vertical ribbed panels, nutmeg burner, SI-142, 9⅜"...150.00

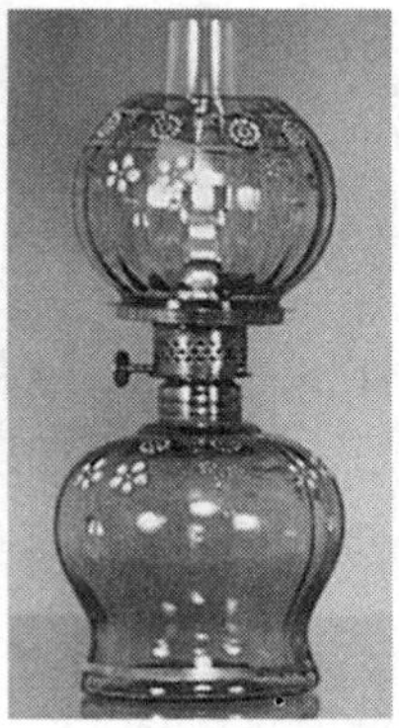

Optic Rib with painted florals and gold on green, nutmeg burner, S-470, 7¼", EX+, $400.00.
(Photo courtesy James D. Julia Inc.)

Pk cased, molded ball shade, Pat Feby 27, 1877, SI-167, 7½".....180.00
Pk cased w/emb decor, hornet burner, SI-374, 8½"..........575.00
Pk satin ped base w/matching tulip shade, Made in USA, SI-134, 10⅞"...650.00
Red & wht spatter, reverse swirl, nutmeg burner, SI-II-548, 8"...865.00
Red satin, hornet burner, SI-405, 9½"..........350.00
Yel cased, emb rose petal shade, sq base, nutmeg burner, SI-385, 7"..635.00

Motion Lamps

Animated motion lamps were made as early as 1920 and as late as the 1980s. They reached their peak during the 1950s when plastic became widely used. They are characterized by action created by the heat of a light bulb which causes the cylinder to revolve and create the illusion of an animated scene. Some of the better-known manufacturers were Econolite Corp., Scene in Action Corp., and LA Goodman Mfg. Co. As with many collectible items, prices are guided by condition, availability, and collector demand. Collectors should be aware that reproductions of cars, trains, sailing ships, fish, and mill scenes are being made. Values are given for original lamps in mint condition. Any damage or flaws seriously reduce the price. Our advisors for motion lamps are Kaye and Jim Whitaker; they are listed in the Directory under Washington.

For more information we recommend *Collector's Guide to Motion Lamps* by Sam and Anna Samuelian.

Aquarium, Scene in Action, #50, 1931, from $360 to..........440.00
Barber Shop Pole, LA Goodman, 1950s, from $160 to..........200.00
Bathing Beauties, LA Goodman, 1950s, from $145 to..........285.00
Birches, LA Goodman, 1956, from $200 to..........220.00
Buddha, Scene in Action, 1931, scarce, from $280 to..........320.00
Circus, Econolite, #655, 1958, scarce, from $280 to..........320.00
Dance at Dawn, Rev-o-Lite, #201, 1930s, from $160 to..........200.00
Fountain of Youth, Econolite, #861, 1950, from $80 to..........100.00
Jets, Econolite, #774, 1958, from $315 to..........360.00
Nature's Splendor, National, 1930s, from $240 to..........280.00
Niagara Falls, Scene in Action, #43, 1931, from $80 to..........100.00
Old Mill, Econolite, 1961, from $280 to..........320.00
Oriental Fantasy, LA Goodman, 1957, from $160 to..........200.00
Picture Frame Train, Econolite, #LP-3/PE, 1953, from $80..........95.00

Planets, LA Goodman, 1957, from $200 to **240.00**
Roadrunner & Coyote, Warner Bros, 1970, from $100 to...........**145.00**
Start Saving Now, Scene in Action, speedboat/plane, 1920s, $320 to ..**400.00**

Pattern Glass Lamps

The letter/number codes in the following descriptions refer to *Oil Lamps, Books I and II*, by Katherine Thuro (book, page, item number, or letter). Our advisor for this section is Jeff Bradfield who is listed in the Directory under Virginia.

Amity, stand lamp, T1-200a, 8", from $50 to........................**60.00**
Ava Font w/Dmn Base, stand lamp, T1-263l, 9¾".........................**95.00**
Bradford, stand lamp, T1-262d, 7½" **100.00**
Carlisle 1, stand lamp, T1-263, 7½" **75.00**
Columbia, ftd hand lamp, T1-273f, 5¾" **100.00**
Cord & Tassel, stand lamp, T1-208a, 7¼" **175.00**
Corn, hand lamp, dtd, T1-204b, 3¼" **200.00**
Dumbarton, stand lamp, T1-149, 9⅜"..**225.00**
Early Almond Thumbprint, stand lamp, T1-158b, 8".................**175.00**
Egyptian, stand lamp (figural stem), T1-261f, 12" **650.00**
Feline Fancy, stand lamp, T1-209e, 11¾".....................................**125.00**
Gloria, hand lamp, T1-196D, 3½"...**60.00**
Grape Leaf Band, stand lamp, T1-144c, 10¼" **125.00**
Hackle, ftd hand lamp, T1-272b, 4⅝"..**125.00**
Heart Top Panel, stand lamp, T1-167g, 11" **150.00**
Herringbone Band, stand lamp, T1-286c, 9"................................**100.00**
Hobbs Star, stand lamp, T1-153g, 8"...**150.00**
King Heart, ftd hand lamp, T1-247e **100.00**
Lady w/Urn, figural stem, T1-174a, 13½" **300.00**
Lomax Plain, all glass stand lamp, T1-178A, 9" **100.00**
Ohio, stand lamp, opaque base, T1-142a, 9⅜"..............................**200.00**
Perkins & House's 1860s, stand lamp, T1-190a, 9⅞" **150.00**
Pillow Encircled, stand lamp, T1-254a..**125.00**
Pillow Encircled, stand lamp, T1-254a, gr, bl or amber **275.00**
Rayed Dmn Flat Band font, Chevron stem, rnd ribbed base, T1-222b..**100.00**
Ripley Patent, hand lamp, T-184, 4½" **175.00**
Riverside Almond, stand lamp, T1-242a, 8" **70.00**
Riverside Rose, ftd hand lamp, T1-242c, 5⅝"..............................**175.00**
Sawtooth Band & Panel, stand lamp, iron base, T1-170b, 9½"..**175.00**
Scalloped Medallion, stand lamp, w/out shade, T1-166b, 10¾" .**190.00**
Sears, composite lamp, T1-218a, 11⅛" **100.00**
Shelley, stand lamp, opaque glass octagon base, T1-143h, 9"......**165.00**
Sherman, ftd hand lamp, T1-147..**150.00**
Stacked Thumbprints, stand lamp, T1-200e, 6¼"..........................**90.00**
Stipple & Leaf, stand lamp, T1-276b, 7⅝" **100.00**
Stippled Daisy & Leaf Band, stand lamp, T1-201l, 8" **90.00**
Thousand Eye, stand lamp, amber, T1-262c, 12⅜".......................**250.00**
Two Directional Rib, hand lamp, T1-196F, 3½"............................**75.00**
US Coin, stand lamp, T1-213f, 9⅜"...**550.00**

Peg Lamps

Gr frost w/mc floral, brass candlestick base, foreign burner, 12"..**285.00**
Gr irid w/HP decor, brass candlestick base, foreign burner, 12" ..**500.00**
Gr irid w/mc floral, orig trn brass candlestick, 15".......................**450.00**
Gr pressed glass, brass chamberstick base, ejector knob, 4x5⅝", VG...**85.00**
Mc floral shade/stem, SP ft, foreign burner, 12" **750.00**
Pk satin w/swirled ribs, strait rib font, brass 8" candlestick, 19" ..**975.00**
Yel satin w/emb decor, copper-color candlestick base, 17"...........**500.00**

Reverse-Painted Lamps

Classique, 18" floral domical shade; slim bronze std..................**7,150.00**

Jefferson, 16" landscape #2367 shade; bronze std w/melon ribs, 22" ..**1,500.00**
Jefferson, 16" mtns & lake scene shade; orig metal std, 23½"..**1,775.00**
Jefferson, 18" conical scenic shade; 2-socket 5-sided std, 22¾" ..**2,650.00**
Jefferson, 21" lakeside scenic dome shade; rstr std, 16" **1,265.00**
McKenny & Waterbury, 8" daffodil shade; patinated slim std, 13¾"..**1,150.00**
Moe Bridges, 17½" spring landscape shade; bronze std, 23".....**3,000.00**
Moe Bridges, 18" farmhouse bell-shape shade; urn-shaped std, 26"..**2,585.00**
Moe Bridges, 18" geese in flight conical shade; urn std...........**7,150.00**
Moe Bridges, 18" Greek ruins conical shade; matching rvpt std..**4,400.00**
Phoenix, 18" scenic dome shade; matching illuminated std.....**2,200.00**
Phoenix, 18" woodland dome shade; floral bronze std..............**2,200.00**
Pittsburgh, 7" Oriental decor 4-panel shade; pnt std, 15"...........**250.00**
Pittsburgh, 9½" shoreline scenic shade; patinated std, 14" **1,150.00**
Pittsburgh, 16" scenic dome shade; bronze std.........................**1,800.00**
Pittsburgh, 18" autumn leaves dome shade; bronze std.............**3,850.00**
Pittsburgh, 18" snowy scene 6-panel shade; bronzed rvpt std, 22" ..**1,600.00**
Unmk, 15" snow scene shade; dbl-hdld urn std w/paw ft, 18"..**1,400.00**
Unmk, 16" forest scene on burnt orange & citron; bronze std, 22"..**650.00**
Unmk, 17" multilevel trees (12) shade; copper-colored std, 23" ...**1,600.00**

Student Lamps, Kerosene

Berlin, NP brass, gr cased umbrella-shape shade, 1850s, 20⅛"....**325.00**
Brass w/adjustable milk glass shade, polished, electrified, 21" **330.00**
Cleveland Safety Library, brass, milk glass globe, 21" **440.00**
German Student Lamp Co, NP brass, rpl 7" gr cased shades (2) ..**1,265.00**
Kleeman, brass, 7" milk glass dome shade, dtd 1863, 21½".........**250.00**
Manhattan Brass Co, gr cased umbrella shade, brass top, 22½" ..**135.00**

Nickel-plated brass, single light with original green cased glass shade, reservoir and burner intact, 20½", EX, $675.00.

NP brass w/iron supports, clear chimney, milk glass shade, 23"...**160.00**
Post & Co Am Cincinnati, 2 milk glass shades, 24" **2,100.00**

TV Lamps

When TV viewing became a popular pastime during the 1940s, TV lamps were developed to provide just the right amount of light — not bright enough to compromise the sharpness of the picture, but just enough to prevent the eyestrain it was feared might result from watching TV in a darkened room. Most were made of ceramic, and many were figurals such as cats, owls, ducks and the like, or made in the shape of Conestoga wagons, sailing ships, seashells, etc. Some had shades and others were made as planters. Few were marked well enough to identify the maker without some study. *TV Lamps* by Tom Santiso (Collector Books) provides many photos and suggested value ranges for those who want more information.

Our advisors for this category are John and Peggy Scott who are listed in the Directory under Missouri. All lamps listed below are ceramic unless otherwise described. See also Maddux; Morton Pottery; Rosemeade; other specific manufacturers

Bluejay pr on stonework base w/gr leaves, natural colors, bsk **75.00**
Conestoga wagon, natuarl colors, light inside, Marcia of CA **110.00**
Cornucopia, woven, gr gloss, bulb inside, from $45 to...................**55.00**
Dancer (plaster) seated before (plastic) fan shade, wood base.......**95.00**
Deer & fawn heads before Fiberglas shade, from $75 to **95.00**
Duck, brn w/foamy gray wing tops, stylized, wood base **95.00**
Duck, wings wide, behind planter, natural colors, 13", from $100 to..**125.00**
Gazelle, Deco/leaping, plumes at base, lt lime gr, from $75 to.......**95.00**
Horse & carriage, metal w/glass insert, from $85 to.....................**100.00**
Horse head, blk w/wht mane, Deco style, light inside, from $75 to ..**95.00**
Horses (pr) facing/rearing, leafy molding between, tan...................**80.00**
Lady w/greyhound before planter, brn gloss, from $110 to...........**120.00**
Leaves & fruit w/planter, silver gray w/gold flecks, from $55 to **70.00**
Mermaid seated before Fiberglas shade, from $85 to....................**110.00**
Panther, blk on gr base, before red Fiberglas shade, from $65 to ...**75.00**
Panther crouching atop rectangular planter base, blk **65.00**
Rooster on fence, bright mc, Lane, from $95 to...........................**110.00**
Sailing ship, airbrushed decor, from $65 to **80.00**
Sampan w/Oriental ea end, wht/mc, rtcl windows, from $65 to....**75.00**
Siamese cats, 1 sitting/1 recumbent, plump, Kron, from $75 to **90.00**
Swan (sm) beside vase overlaid w/lg leaves, wht/gr, 8", from $50 to ..**95.00**
Swordfish w/planter, lime w/gold, from $95 to **110.00**
Yorkie dog, recumbent, plaster, Rock-O-Stone, from $75 to **85.00**

Whale Oil/Burning Fluid Lamps

Clear blown font, stepped pressed base w/wafer top, 10½", EX...**150.00**
Clear blown font w/wafers, pressed base w/lions' heads/flowers, 11" ..**385.00**
Clear blown pear font, pressed triangular paw-ft base, 10", pr.....**300.00**
Clear pressed Dmn Quilt font, opal base, prisms, 1850s, 11x6"...**700.00**
Dk amethyst, hexagonal, pewter collar, twin burners, 8" **2,300.00**
Pewter, conical base, cylindrical font, 2-tube, Am, 19th C, 7x4".**135.00**
Pewter, conical base w/tooled rings, dbl burners, unmk, 8", pr **250.00**
Pressed Lyre pattern, brass std, marble base, 1850s, 9", pr **250.00**

Miscellaneous

Argand, Messenger/Nones, Low & Ball, 2-arm, prisms, 1835, 18x18x8"..**3,000.00**
Astral, frosted/clear shade, brass font, gilt stem, marble base, 24" ..**1,850.00**
Astral, frosted/cut shade, bl to clear stem, marble base, 21¼" .**3,220.00**
Lace maker's, Invt T'print, cranberry, brass font, orig burner, 21x10" ...**965.00**
Marriage, DC Ripley Pat Pending, milk glass/clambroth, 12⅛"..**770.00**
Solar, Am Rococo gilt brass, tripodal, 1850s, electrified, 18" **975.00**
Solar, Cornelius & Baker, crimped/etched/frosted shades, 1845, 24", pr ..**3,300.00**
Solar, Cornelius & Co, bronze caryatid figures, 1845, 39" **4,000.00**
Solar, mercury glass w/etched grapes, rpl shade, 1850s, 17½x6" .**715.00**

Lang, Anton

Anton Lang (1875 – 1938) was a German studio potter and an actor in the Oberammergau Passion Plays early in the twentieth century. Because he played the role of Christ three times, tourists brought his pottery back to the U.S. in suitcases, which accounts for the prevalence of smaller examples today. During 1923 – 1924 Anton Lang and the other 'Passion Players' toured the U.S. selling their crafts. Lang would occasionally throw pottery when the cast passed through a pottery center such as Cincinnati, where Rookwood was located. The pots thrown at Rookwood are easy to identify as Lang hand signed the side of each piece and they have a 1924 Rookwood mark on the bottom. Lang visited the U.S. only once, and contrary to popular belief, he was never employed by Rookwood. His pottery, marked with his name in script, is fairly scarce and highly valued for its artistic quality. His son Karl (1903 – 1990), also a gifted potter, designed most of the Art Deco shapes and

conducted glaze experiments. Only pieces bearing a hand-written signature (not a facsimile) are certain to be Anton Lang originals instead of the work of Karl or the Langs' assistants. Anton and Karl also made pieces together; Karl might design a piece and Anton decorate it. Postcards, programs, prints, and photographs depicting Lang are also collectible. Karl was managing the day-to-day operations of the pottery by 1934, and he continued to operate it as Anton Lang Pottery after his father's death in 1938. The pottery is now owned and operated by Karl's daughter, Barbara Lampe, who took over for her father in 1975. The facsimile 'Anton Lang' signature was used until 1995 when the name was changed to Barbara Lampe Pottery. Her mark is an interlocked 'BL' in a circle. Pieces with a facsimile signature and an interlocked 'UL' in a circle were made by Lampe's former husband, Uli Lampe, and date from 1975 to 1982. The 'Anton Lang' mark is not sharp on pieces made in 1975 and later. The bottoms are brick red clay with three lighter circular tripod marks. The later pieces are considerably heavier than the earlier work. Our advisor for this category is Clark Miller; he is listed in the Directory under Minnesota.

Bowl, Deco-style, brilliant red/orange, 1x8" **95.00**
Bowl, deer, wht w/bl decor, 2x6" **65.00**
Bowl, floral, bl, gr & yel, 2x6" **70.00**
Bowl, turq w/yel int, 1¾x4" **66.00**
Box, brn & orange decor, 3¾x3¾"..**105.00**
Etching, Anton Lang shop, autographed, 1922, 14¾x10½" **200.00**
Ewer, bl matt w/yel int, pewter lid, & rim of ft, from $88 to.......**168.00**
Ewer, maroon w/turq int, hand sgn, 6" **125.00**
Figurine, cat w/ball, mirror blk, 8"..**800.00**
Figurine, dog, brn gloss, 9½"...**800.00**
Figurine, Joseph, Mary & Child, Deco style, mc, 12x8x5" **500.00**
Figurine candle holders, gargoyles, ornate, 7½x7½", pr **500.00**
Holy water font, raised dove decor, bl matt, hand sgn, 5½x3½".**105.00**
Lamp, Deco style, orange, 9x5½" **225.00**
Medallion, Lang/Jesus, 1922 Oberammergau, silver, hand sgn, 2x2"......**130.00**
Medallion, Lang/Jesus, 1924 Oberammergau in Am, metal, 1½x2", $36 to...**50.00**
Photo, Lang as Christ, autographed & hand dtd 1922, 9½x7½" ..**50.00**
Photo, Lang as Christ, autographed & hand dtd 1900, 6x4" **25.00**
Photo, Lang on Am tour, autographed & hand dtd 1924, 3½x5¼" ..**35.00**
Pitcher, ochre & yel w/gr & terra cotta, 4".....................................**50.00**
Pitcher, yel w/gr & brn decor, 5"..**84.00**
Postcard, photo portrait w/works, authentic signature, EX unused .**22.50**
Program, Oberammergau in Am tour, 1923-24, 8¼x11½" **52.00**
Stereoview card, Anton Lang as Christ w/Oberammergau view......**7.50**
Tile, deer, bl on cream, 4⅞x4⅞"...**25.00**
Tile, saint w/child, emb decor, bl on cream, 7½x7¾" **60.00**
Vase, bl matt, 2¾x2¾"...**35.00**
Vase, bl w/mc flower band, 5½x5½" **150.00**

Vase, blue with yellow flowers, hand signed, 15¾x6½", $1,250.00. (Photo courtesy Clark Miller)

Vase, Deco style, blk w/bl int, 7¾x7¼"...**275.00**
Vase, frog skin, 3x2¾"...**60.00**

Vase, gr drip, yel int, hand sgn, 5¼x5½" 175.00
Vase, maroon over tan flambe w/gr int, 12½x5¾" 263.00
Vase, pine boughs, gr & brn, hand sgn, 3¼x2¾" 65.00
Vase, turq, hand sgn, 4¼x5" 140.00
Vase, turq, 1¾x2½" 32.50
Vase, turq over maroon flambe w/yel int, hand sgn, 11¼x5¼" ...325.00
Wall plaque, angel, emb decor, brn, dtd 1934, 4¼" dia 42.00
Wall plaque/bowl, flowers, mc, 1¾x6" 115.00
Wall pocket, angel w/yel bowl on purple bkground, 4½x7", NM ..145.00
Wall pocket, Deco style, gr, 7½x3½" 175.00

Le Verre Francais

Le Verre Francais was produced during the 1920s by Schneider at Epinay-sur-Seine in France. It was a commercial art glass in the cameo style composed of layered glass with the designs engraved by acid. Favored motifs were stylized leaves and flowers or geometric patterns. It was marked with the name in script or with an inlaid filigrane. Our advisor for this category is Don Williams; he is listed in the Directory under Missouri.

Cameo

Lamp, floral, red/yel-orange mottle/clear, burgundy std, 8½" ...1,150.00
Vase, bars/floral pods, amethyst/lav/wht/aqua, onion base, 9¾" ...1,300.00
Vase, floral, cobalt/bl mottle, Charder, 7½" 675.00
Vase, floral, orange/purple mottle on lemon yel, tapered cylinder, 16" ..2,200.00
Vase, geometrics, cobalt on gr mottle, 4" 350.00
Vase, radiating rays/lozenges, orange on mottled orange to clear, 20" ..2,185.00
Vase, roses, pk/gr/pk frost, 5½" 500.00
Vase, seed pods, red & amethyst on frost & mottled amethyst, hdls, 14" ...2,125.00

Leeds, Leeds Type

The Leeds Pottery was established in 1758 in Yorkshire and under varied management produced fine creamware, often highly reticulated and transfer printed, shiny black-glazed Jackfield wares, polychromed pearlware, and figurines similar to those made in the Staffordshire area. Little of the early ware was marked; after 1775 the impressed 'Leeds Pottery' mark was used. From 1781 to 1820, the name 'Hartley Greens & Co.' was added. The pottery closed in 1898.

Today the term 'Leeds' has become generic and is used to encompass all polychromed pearlware and creamware, wherever its origin. Thus similar wares of other potters (Wood for instance) is often incorrectly called 'Leeds.' Unless a piece is marked or can be definitely attributed to Leeds by confirming the pattern to be authentic, 'Leeds-Type' would be a more accurate nomenclature.

Key:
cw — creamware   pw — pearlware

Coffeepot, cw, floral, pear shape, foliate spout, 1780s, 10⅛" 700.00
Coffeepot, cw, rose & flower spray, dome top, acanthus spout, 11" ..550.00
Creamer, pw, bl & gr vintage, imp leaf ends, 3⅝" 190.00
Creamer, pw, pk floral reserve, ca 1800, 4½x5½" 160.00
Cup plate, Lafayette, blk transfer on pw, 3¾", EX 600.00
Cup plate, Present For Martha, brn transfer, mc floral border, 4⅝" ..220.00
Mug, pw, cobalt flowers, stepped base, ca 1800, prof rstr, 6¼" 235.00
Mustard pot, pw, molded decor w/gr, 1790-1820, 2x2½", EX 150.00
Pitcher, milk; floral, 5-color, 5" 660.00
Plate, pw, floral swags, shell edge, ca 1790, 10", EX 225.00
Sugar bowl, mc flowers, 8-sided, swan finial, 6x5" 1,485.00
Sugar bowl, peacock in sponged tree, 5-color, mismatched lid, 4½" ...300.00

Tea bowl & saucer, pw, mc floral, EX 180.00
Teapot, cw, gr stripes, pierced rim, late 1700s, 5½" 435.00
Teapot, cw, HP florals/figures w/gold, globular, 1780s, 4½", EX ..750.00
Waste bowl, flowers/birds/fruit, blk transfer w/mc, 5¼", NM 175.00

Lefton China

The Lefton China Company was the creation of Mr. George Zoltan Lefton who migrated to the United States from Hungary in 1939. In 1941 he embarked on a new career and began shaping a business that sprang from his passion for collecting fine china and porcelains. Though his funds were very limited, his vision was to develop a source from which to obtain fine porcelains by reviving the postwar Japanese ceramic industry, which dated back to antiquity. As a trailblazer, George Zoltan Lefton soon earned the reputation as 'The China King.'

Counted among the most desirable and sought-after collectibles of today, Lefton items such as Bluebirds, Miss Priss, Angels, all types of dinnerware and tea-related items are eagerly acquired by collectors. As is true with any antique or collectible, prices may vary, dependent on location, condition, and availability. For additional information on the history of Lefton China, its factories, marks, products, and values, readers should consult the *Collector's Encyclopedia of Lefton China, Books I, II,* and *III,* and *Lefton Price Guide* by our advisor, Loretta DeLozier, who is listed in the Directory under Tennessee. All are published by Collector Books.

Planter, Leprechaun, #4313, 6¼", $22.00. (Photo courtesy Loretta DeLozier)

Angel, November, #1411, 4" 32.00
Angel, Sunday, #2554, 4" 35.00
Angel, Valentine Kissing Angels, #6770, 4", pr 22.00
Animal, bay colt, #2212, 4½" 50.00
Animal, bluegill, #1072, 4½" 42.00
Animal, chipmunks, #4753, 11" 125.00
Animal, cocker spaniel, #00412, 4½" 25.00
Animal, dachshund w/bkground, #1641 ....65.00
Animal, Palomino colt, #2212, 4½" 50.00
Animal, poodle, gray & wht, #6659, 6" 45.00
Animal, rabbits, #880 ....35.00
Animal, raccoon w/baby, #2149, 6" 95.00
Animal, red squirrel, #4492, 8" 95.00
Animal, reindeer, gr holly, #1187, 4" 40.00
Animal, skunk w/babies, #1311, 5½", complete set 400.00
Animal, Tabby cat, #6364, 4½" 28.00
Ashtray, leaf shape, wht holly, #6056, 7" 20.00
Ashtray, Miss Priss, #1524, 6" 60.00
Ashtray, swan, floral bsk bouquet, #4744 ....20.00
Bank, devil, Root of All Evil, #4923, 8" 65.00
Bank, graduate girl, College Fund, #5010, 6¾" 38.00
Bank, Miss Priss, #4916 ....400.00
Bell, bride & groom, musical: We've Only Just..., #04637, 5" 25.00

Bird, Bee Eater, on branch, #1707, 7½" 65.00
Bird, cockatoo, #1542, 7½" 90.00
Bird, egret, #1058, 9½" 140.00
Bird, goldfinch, #6609, 4½" 25.00
Bird, heron, #1541, 6½" 45.00
Bird, Indigo Bunting, on tree, #1706, 7" 110.00
Bird, peacock, tail spread, #2336, 6" 65.00
Bone dish, Rose Chintz, #627, 8" 18.00
Bookends, ducks, 32229, 5", pr 95.00
Bowl, Pink Clover, #2503, 6¼" 10.00
Box, candy; egg shape (2 kinds), #559, 5" 25.00
Box, candy; Green Heritage, ftd, #4053 ....50.00
Cigarette set, Elegant Rose, #088, 5-pc 200.00
Coaster, floral design (7 styles), #20128, ea 12.00
Coffeepot, Yuletide Hollyberry, #7802 ....135.00
Compote, Floral Chintz, #8043, 7" 22.00
Compote, Fruits of Italy, #1205, 8⅝" 12.00
Compote, latticed w/stones, #231, 8" 85.00
Cookie jar, Blue Country Charm, #4611 ....75.00
Cookie jar, Chef boy, #2361 ....350.00
Cookie jar, Little Pixie Baby w/flowers at neck, #1370 ....125.00
Cookie jar, Pear 'n Apple, #4335 ....55.00
Cookie jar, Pennsylvania Dutch, #3702 ....200.00
Cookie jar, Pink Clover, #2498 ....90.00
Cookie jar, Santa Claus, #2097, 7¼" 110.00
Cookie jar, Thumblina, #1692, 8" 250.00
Creamer & sugar bowl, Black Chintz, #1934 ....95.00
Cup & saucer, demi; Pink Cotillion, #3189 ....28.00
Cup & saucer, tea; floral design, #976 ....35.00
Dish, bonbon; rose design, #486, 6¾" 30.00
Dish, candy; Floral Mood, 3 colors, #4670, 6¼" 15.00
Dish, cookie; White Holly, #6051, 6" 15.00
Figurine, boy & girl w/cups, sitting, #3499, 5½" 125.00
Figurine, Colonial lady & man, dbl, #3074, 9" 175.00
Figurine, Gay Nineties, wht or pk, #8569, 6" 125.00
Figurine, I Had a Little Hen, Nursery Rhyme, #1473, 4½" 75.00
Figurine, Japanese Geisha girls, wht w/gr, #1433, 6", pr 145.00
Figurine, kissing couple, #10530, 4¼", pr 65.00
Figurine, lady, (3 kinds), #1460, 6" 70.00
Figurine, lady, Dubonnet, bl or turq, #5743, 7½" 150.00
Figurine, lady in gr dress, #4494, 8" 80.00
Figurine, Little Red Riding Hood, #471, 4" 25.00
Figurine, Siamese Dancers, #10293, 8½", pr 350.00
Figurine, Simple Simon, #1255, 6¼" 95.00
Figurine, Valentine girl, #7173, 4" 15.00
Figurine, Victorian lady, pk, #1570, 6¼" 145.00
Jam jar, Bossie the Cow, #6509 ....30.00
Jam jar, Cuddles, #1451 ....35.00
Jar, spice; Sweet Violets, #2876, 5" 22.00
Lamp, hurricane; Green Holly, #4229, 5½" 45.00
Mug, beer; Paul Bunyan, #609 ....22.00
Mug, Green Holly, #1366 ....15.00
Mug, Stonewall Jackson, #1112, 4½" 45.00
Night light, clown, #01890, 7" 48.00
Night light, mouse w/mushroom, #7920, 6" 28.00
Perfume set, Only a Rose, #385, complete 125.00
Pin holder, Magnetic Bobby, #993, 4½" 55.00
Pitcher, Misty Rose, #5692, 7" 135.00
Pitcher & bowl, Green Heritage, #4172, 5¼" 65.00
Planter, Baby ABC Block, #2128, 4" 12.00
Planter, clown holding puppy, brilliant red, #265, 8" 80.00
Planter, egg urn, Floral Bisque Bouquet, #5442, 3½" 15.00
Planter, Pilgrim boy & girl w/baskets, #5376, 6¼", pr 100.00
Planter, pink frog, #02680, 6" 15.00

Plate, Brown Heritage Floral, #1882, 7½" 25.00
Plate, Heirloom Elegance, #5388, 9" 38.00
Plate, Rose Chintz, #659, 9" 35.00
Shakers, brn dogs, #6087, 3¼", pr 18.00
Shakers, Mammy & Chef, #2046, 3¼", pr 35.00
Teapot, Cuddles, #1448 ....95.00
Teapot, Dainty Miss, #321 ....175.00
Teapot, demi; Green Vintage, #6711 ....45.00
Teapot, Elegant Rose, #866 ....65.00
Teapot, Fruits of Italy, #1175 ....65.00
Tumble-up, Miss Priss, #5697 ....125.00
Vase, bud; Rose Chintz, #679, 6¼" 32.00
Vase, Only a Rose, triple hdld, #392, 6" 65.00
Vase, wht w/lg pk roses, #263, 6¼" 60.00
Wall plaque, bellows, Country Squire, #1612, 7¾" 35.00
Wall plaque, cat face, pk or bl glaze, #150, 5½" 55.00
Wall plaque, horseshoe, Floral Bisque Bouquet, #7458 ....25.00
Wall pocket, girl w/basket, bl, #50264, 7" 150.00
Wall pocket, Sweet Violets, #2894, 6½" 18.00

Legras

Legras and Cie was founded in St. Denis, France, in 1864. Production continued until the 1930s. In addition to their enameled wares, they made cameo art glass decorated with outdoor scenes and florals executed by acid cuttings through two to six layers of glass. Their work is signed 'Legras' in relief and in enamel. Our advisor for this category is Don Williams; he is listed in the Directory under Missouri.

Cameo

Bowl, floral, rose/pk/lt & dk bl, cut/pnt, 4x6" 500.00
Vase, floral, tan/lav, slim flared cylinder, 13½" 850.00
Vase, fruit branches, olive gr/ochre/gray, cut/pnt, ovoid, 8¼" 450.00
Vase, hills/trees/sea/sky, gr/brn/orange/frost, rectangular, 6½" 500.00
Vase, holly berries/leaves, gr & red on peach to yel, 8½" 800.00
Vase, ivy, clear/fuchsia/frost, waisted, 5⅝" 350.00
Vase, lake/shore/sunset, cut/pnt, gr/orange/yel, stick, 15¾" 900.00
Vase, leafy stalks, bl/yel on textured frost, ovoid, 9¼" 900.00
Vase, oak leaves/vines, maroon/frost, stick neck, 8¾" 400.00
Vase, stylized ACB band, bl/gr/wht/brn, 8⅜" 630.00
Vase, trees along shore, gr/bl/rose, pillow form, 4¼x5½" 550.00
Vase, trees/lake/mtns, gr/orange frost/lt gr, sq, 7" 425.00
Vase, trees/lake/sky, gr to lav, slim, flared ft, 14", pr 1,550.00
Vase, vining floral, tan/lav, 13½" 850.00

Lenox

Walter Scott Lenox, former art director at Ott and Brewer, and Jonathan Coxon founded The Ceramic Art Company of Trenton, New Jersey, in 1889. By 1906 Cox had left the company, and to reflect the change in ownership, the name was changed to Lenox Inc. Until 1930 when the production of American-made Belleek came to an end, they continued to produce the same type of high-quality ornamental wares that Lenox and Coxon had learned to master while in the employ of Ott and Brewer. Their superior dinnerware made the company famous, and since 1917 Lenox has been chosen the official White House China. Our advisor for this category is Mary Frank Gaston. See also Ceramic Art Company.

Bowl, wht lotus w/bellflower base, ca 1920, 4½x7½" 100.00
Box, cigarette; leaf finial on wht, gr mks, +2 matching trays 65.00
Chocolate pot, Ming, 11" 400.00

Cup & saucer, Cattail, w/gold 30.00
Cup & saucer, Christie 22.00

Demitasse cup and saucer, loop handle, hand-painted plums by J. Nosek, 1930s, from $100.00 to $125.00.
(Photo courtesy Jim and Susan Harran)

Dinnerware, flower baskets w/gold on ivory w/bl rim, 36-pc set..350.00
Dinnerware, gold rim on wht, for LB King & Co, gr mk, 37-pc set...165.00
Figurine, Leda & Swan, ca 1929, 10x5½" 100.00
Honey pot, wht hive w/gold bees & trim, 1900-20, 5¼x4".........160.00
Lamp, pk urn w/wht swan hdls, orig wht shade, gr mk, 22", pr ...375.00
Mayonnaise set (bowl & tray), Ming, blk mk 85.00
Mug, ear of corn, artist sgn, 5x4" 110.00
Mug, floral, gr on gr, artist sgn, 1902, 5x4" 65.00
Pitcher, lemonade; grapes & leaves, artist sgn, 6" 335.00
Planter, bird w/open bk, gr mk, 5¼x6" 100.00
Plate, bread & butter; Flirtation 20.00
Plate, bread & butter; Golden Wreath 8.00
Plate, dinner; Country Garden 35.00
Plate, dinner; Meadowsong 18.00
Plate, dinner; Rhodora, 4 for 80.00
Plate, salad; Gaylord 13.00
Plate, salad; Tudor 13.00
Platter, gold hdls, old gold mk, 16½x12" 55.00
Platter, Kelly, lg 140.00
Stein, geometrics on dk gr, sgn, ca 1912, 7¼x4" 80.00
Teapot, quilted flowers on melon shape, 1930-53 gr mk, 6½" 80.00
Toby jug, Franklin D Roosevelt, elephant hdl, 1909, 8"..........1,550.00
Toby mug, William Penn, pk body, wht hdl, gr mk, 6½" 155.00
Vase, autumn flowers, slim, palette mk, 13½x4½" (at base) 135.00
Vase, Bracelet, cream on pk, old bl mk, 5⅛x6¾" 55.00
Vase, bright yel, Marshall Field & Co, 1930-53, 8".....................95.00
Vase, butterflies & spider webs w/gold, ca 1906-24, 11½x4⅛" ...365.00
Vase, Deco-style dragonflies on wht, 6-sided, palette mk, 6¼"......75.00
Vase, Fluted, lt pk/rose to creamy wht, 1950s, 9x6½" 80.00
Vase, Lenox Rose, gold hdls, ruffled rim, gr mk, 7".....................125.00

Letter Openers

Made in a wide variety of materials and designs, letter openers make an interesting collection, easy to display and easy on the budget as well. For further information we recommend *Collector's Guide to Letter Openers, Identification & Values*, by Everett Grist (Collector Books); Mr. Grist is listed in the Directory under Tennessee.

Aluminum, cut-out dogwood blossom on hdl.................................15.00
Antler/stainless steel, Nordic scene 15.00
Bakelite, orange/yel marbleized w/Peekskill NY lettered on hdl....25.00
Bakelite, saber form w/various pnt motifs on butterscotch hdl, ea..25.00
Bone, cut-out totem pole on hdl...20.00
Bone, walrus; cvd polar bear on end 45.00

Brass, armadillo hdl 12.00
Brass, contoured w/Art Nouveau holly motif 30.00
Brass, owl hdl 10.00
Brass, 3-D grasshopper paperweight hdl....................................20.00
Bronze, dragon hdl w/erotic scene on blade 35.00
Bronze, Masonic, Scottish Rite emblems....................................35.00
Bronze, 2 dachshund heads in relief, ca 1900, 10" 175.00
Cast iron, Amish head (man or woman), ad sticker on blade, ea..20.00
Cast iron, Civil War gun w/bayonet 18.00
Celluloid/steel, opener/pen knife, Kutmaster..............................25.00
Copper, pnt war bonnet...8.00
Copper, Scottie dog hdl w/very pointed blade.............................12.00
Enamel/chrome, sword w/mc dragon motif, green tassel 25.00
Ivory, cvd camel motif 60.00
Ivory, cvd crocodile hdl 85.00
Leather, brn tooled hdl & sheath w/steel blade...........................10.00
Lucite, fish form w/encapsulated seashells, w/souvenir label..........35.00
MOP, cvd stylized pineapple motif, Victorian 65.00
Pewter, buffalo hdl 10.00
Plastic, golfer figure hdl w/curved sword-like blade, Italy 12.00
Porc, pk rose motif, sgn R Riddle..45.00
Resin, hula girl hdl..6.00
Rhinestones, SP w/crown & shield fleur-de-lis..............................15.00
SP, bamboo-style hdl..10.00
SP, Mohawk Trail, Mohawk chief w/bow hdl 75.00
Sterling, Siam dancing god 45.00
White metal, golf clubs & bag, Metzke 1985 ....15.00
Wood, cvd saber form w/inlaid abalone design.............................15.00
Wood, cvd sleek duck hdl 20.00
Wood, primitive cvd/pnt Indian 25.00

Libbey

The New England Glass Company was established in 1818 in Boston, Massachusetts. In 1892 it became known as the Libbey Glass Company. At Chicago's Columbian Expo in 1893, Libbey set up a ten-pot furnace and made glass souvenirs. The display brought them worldwide fame. Between 1878 and 1918, Libbey made exquisite cut and faceted glass, considered today to be the best from the brilliant period. The company is credited for several innovations — the Owens bottle machine that made mass production possible and the Westlake machine which turned out both electric light bulbs and tumblers automatically. They developed a machine to polish the rims of their tumblers in such a way that chipping was unlikely to occur. Their glassware carried the patented Safedge guarantee. Libbey also made glassware in numerous colors, among them cobalt, ruby, pink, green, and amber. Our advisors for this category are Don and Anne Kier; they are listed in the Directory under Ohio.

Basket, cut, Am Brilliant period, 21" 3,500.00
Bottle, water; cut, Imperial 300.00
Bowl, cut, Eulalia, 10⅞" sq 400.00
Bowl, cut, New Brilliant, 1¾x8"..125.00
Bowl, cut, Sultana, 16-point hobstar base, 10"...........................460.00
Bowl, finger; floral etch 150.00
Bowl, nappy, cut, Heart, 7" 200.00
Bowl, punch; cut, Spillane, w/base 4,700.00
Bowl, vegetable; Primrose eng, 2½x9".......................................200.00
Candlesticks, camel, opal, 1930s-30s, 5¼x4", pr, NM 320.00
Candlesticks, cut, Prism, hollow stem, 10x4¾", pr.......................600.00
Candy dish, cut, fans in sqs, 1905-10, 7" 95.00
Carafe, cut, hobstars, fans & mitres...230.00
Compote, cut, geometric, scalloped rim, long std, 11½x6½" 225.00

Console set, clear w/sq ft throughout, 12" bowl+4 4" candlesticks...300.00
Decanter, cut, bulbous base, notch hdl, faceted stopper, 13" 500.00
Jug, milk; cut, Venetia, 2-qt, 7" 425.00
Maize, bowl, gr husks on wht opaque, 4x8¾" 275.00
Maize, butter dish, bl husks on irid 650.00
Maize, butter dish, gr husks on custard 165.00
Maize, celery vase, clear w/amber stain & bl husks, 6" 235.00
Maize, celery vase, gold leaves, 6½x4½" 225.00
Maize, celery vase, gr husks on custard 200.00
Maize, celery vase, gr husks on wht opaque 230.00
Maize, condiment set, custard, 3 pcs on tray w/metal lid............600.00
Maize, pickle castor, amber stain 595.00
Maize, pickle castor, gr husks on custard, SP fr 550.00
Maize, pitcher, bl husks on clear w/amber irid, clear hdls, 9" 600.00
Maize, pitcher, clear irid w/amber stain, 8½" 550.00
Maize, shakers, gold-edge, bl husks on custard, pr...................250.00
Maize, sugar shaker, yel/gold husks on custard, 5¾" 345.00
Maize, syrup, pewter lid, gold irid cob, bl husks, 6" 600.00
Maize, toothpick holder, gold-edge gr husks on custard.............400.00
Maize, tumbler, bl husks on irid 160.00
Maize, tumbler, gold irid w/bl eaves 195.00
Maize, tumbler, gr leaves w/gold on wht.................................175.00
Maize, tumbler, gr leaves w/yel-brn tips, 4" 100.00
Maize, vase, yel/gold husks on custard, 6½" 250.00
Pitcher, cut, Jewell, 3-pt 265.00
Stem, champagne, flute, bear stem, wht opal, 5½" 185.00
Stem, champagne, squirrel, wht opal, 6" 165.00
Stem, claret, bear, blk, 5½" 155.00
Stem, claret, Royal Fern, 1920s 350.00
Stem, cordial, Embassy, tall 100.00
Stem, cordial, monkey, blk 150.00
Stem, cordial, monkey, wht opal, 5" 140.00
Stem, cordial, whippet/greyhound, wht opal 175.00
Stem, goblet, cat, wht opal 200.00
Stem, goblet, monkey, wht opal, 1930s 160.00
Stem, sherbet, rabbit, 2½x4", 4 for 295.00
Stem, wine, giraffe, wht opal, 6" 120.00
Stem, wine, kangaroo, wht opal..230.00
Toothpick holder, Little Lob, wht satin.....................................200.00
Tray, cut, Neola, 12" 2,000.00
Tray, cut, Regis, 12" 775.00
Tray, ice cream; cut, Somerset, 12" 275.00
Tray, rnd, Senora, 12" 875.00
Tumbler, juice; cut, Corinthian variant 70.00
Vase, amberina, intaglio eng, #3000, Amberina 1917 Revival, 16" ...1,075.00
Vase, amberina, stick neck w/swirls from top to body, 11¾" 400.00
Vase, Chintz, caramel cased to brn, zipper decor, spherical, 6" ...230.00
Vase, cut, Feathers & Bull's Eyes, rayed base, bulbous, 7"...........175.00
Vase, cut, Star & Feather, 16" 1,300.00
Vase, floral intaglio, 14x4⅞" 200.00
Water set, cut, geometric floral, 8½" jug+4 3¾" tumblers..........625.00

Lightning Rod Balls

Used as ornaments on lightning rods, the vast majority of these balls were made of glass, but ceramic examples can be found as well. Their average diameter is 4½", but it can vary from 3½" up to 5½". Only a few of the many available pattern-and-color combinations are listed here. The most common measure 4½" and are found in sun-colored amethyst and milk glass. Our advisor is Rod Krupka, author of a book on this subject. Anyone interested in his book may write to him for more information; he is listed in the Directory under Michigan.

Hawkeye, 5¼" x 4½", in amber, $200.00, in blue opaque, $50.00.
(Photo courtesy Rod Krupka)

Amber, Doorknob, 4x4¼" 110.00
Amber, Quilt-Flat, copper caps, 5x5½" 80.00
Amber, Quilt-Raised, 5x5½" 90.00
Amber, Shinn-Belted, emb, copper end caps, 4⅜x5"...................45.00
Amber, sm copper caps, 4½" 27.00
Amethyst, Moon & Star, 4½x5" 80.00
Bl opaque, Mast, 5x5¾" 65.00
Bl opaque, med to dk swirls, 3½x3½" 30.00
Bl opaque, National Belted, copper caps, 4½x5¼" 90.00
Bl opaque, Pleat-Pointed, dk swirls, copper caps, 4½" 45.00
Cobalt, Pleat-Round, copper caps, 4½x5" 100.00
Gr opaque, lg aluminum caps, heavy, 4½" 95.00
Milk glass, Electra Cone, unemb, copper caps, 4½x5" 30.00
Milk glass, Maher, sm chip on bottom collar, 4½x5" 180.00
Orange opaque, swirling, sm copper caps, 4½" 400.00
Red, Didie Blitzen, 3¾x4" 210.00
Red, Ribbed Grape, aluminum caps, 4⅜x5" 475.00
Red, sm collars, 4½" 85.00
Red cased, Chestnut, old aluminum caps, 3⅞x4⅛" 200.00
Root beer, Dodd & Struthers, gold pnt aluminum caps, 5¾" 225.00

Limited Edition Plates

Current values of some limited edition plates have risen while others have fallen. Prices charged by plate dealers in the secondary market vary greatly; we have tried to suggest an average.

Since Goebel Hummel plates have been discontinued, values have started to decline. While those who are trying to complete the series continue to buy them, few seem interested in starting a collection. As for the Danish plates, Royal Copenhagen and Bing and Grondahl, more purchases are for plates that commemorate the birth year of a child or a wedding anniversary than to add to a collection.

Bing and Grondahl

1895, Behind the Frozen Window 6,250.00
1896, New Moon 2,300.00
1897, Christmas Meal of Sparrows 1,500.00
1898, Roses & Star 850.00
1899, Crows Enjoying Christmas...1,800.00
1900, Church Bells Chiming 1,200.00
1901, 3 Wise Men 495.00
1902, Gothic Church Interior...425.00
1903, Expectant Children..425.00
1904, View of Copenhagen From Fredericksberg Hill 210.00
1905, Anxiety of the Coming Christmas Night..........................205.00
1906, Sleighing to Church 135.00
1907, Little Match Girl...195.00
1908, St Petri Church 110.00
1909, Yule Tree 125.00
1910, Old Organist..125.00
1911, Angels & Shepherds 110.00
1912, Going to Church 110.00
1913, Bringing Home the Tree 110.00

1914, Amalienborg Castle......................................105.00
1915, Dog on Chain Outside Window 155.00
1916, Prayer of the Sparrows...............................105.00
1917, Christmas Boat..105.00
1918, Fishing Boat..105.00
1919, Outside the Lighted Window........................95.00
1920, Hare in the Snow 95.00
1921, Pigeons..95.00
1922, Star of Bethlehem...95.00
1923, Hermitage..95.00
1924, Lighthouse..105.00
1925, Child's Christmas 105.00
1926, Churchgoers..105.00
1927, Skating Couple..155.00
1928, Eskimos...95.00
1929, Fox Outside Farm.......................................105.00
1930, Tree in Town Hall Square 115.00
1931, Christmas Train..115.00
1932, Lifeboat at Work...115.00
1933, Korsor-Nyborg Ferry....................................95.00
1934, Church Bell in Tower....................................95.00
1935, Lillebelt Bridge..95.00
1936, Royal Guard...95.00
1937, Arrival of Christmas Guests........................115.00
1938, Lighting the Candles...................................175.00
1939, Old Lock-Eye, The Sandman.......................215.00
1940, Delivering Christmas Letters 265.00
1941, Horses Enjoying Meal.................................325.00
1942, Danish Farm on Christmas Night................275.00
1943, Ribe Cathedral..235.00
1944, Sorgenfri Castle...145.00
1945, Old Water Mill..165.00
1946, Commemoration Cross 135.00
1947, Dybbol Mill...165.00
1948, Watchman...115.00
1949, Landsoldaten 125.00
1950, Kronborg Castle at Elsinore........................155.00
1951, Jens Bang...125.00
1952, Old Copenhagen Canals & Thorsvaldsen Museum..........135.00
1953, Royal Boat..135.00
1954, Snowman..145.00
1955, Kaulundborg Church...................................145.00
1956, Christmas in Copenhagen...........................175.00
1957, Christmas Candles.......................................175.00
1958, Santa Claus..140.00
1959, Christmas Eve...155.00
1960, Village Church 205.00
1961, Winter Harmony 135.00
1962, Winter Night...125.00
1963, Christmas Elf..145.00
1964, Fir Tree & Hare 65.00
1965, Bringing Home the Tree...............................55.00
1966, Home for Christmas 45.00
1967, Sharing the Joy 45.00
1968, Christmas in Church 35.00
1969, Arrival of Guests..30.00
1970, Pheasants in Snow..27.00
1971, Christmas at Home.......................................27.00
1972, Christmas in Greenland 27.00
1973, Country Christmas 30.00
1974, Christmas in the Village...............................30.00
1975, The Old Water Mill......................................30.00
1976, Christmas Welcome......................................30.00
1977, Copenhagen Christmas 30.00

1978, A Christmas Tale..30.00
1979, White Christmas 40.00
1980, Christmas in the Woods................................40.00
1981, Christmas Peace...40.00
1982, The Christmas Tree.......................................57.00
1983, Christmas in Old Town.................................47.00
1984, Christmas Letter...75.00
1985, Christmas Eve, Farm....................................65.00
1986, Silent Night...70.00
1987, Snowman's Christmas...................................55.00
1988, In King's Garden..75.00
1989, Christmas Anchorage....................................60.00
1990, Changing Guards..65.00
1991, Copenhagen Stock Exchange 65.00
1992, Pastor's Christmas......................................105.00
1993, Father Christmas in Copenhagen................100.00

M. I. Hummel

The last issue for M.I. Hummel annual plates was made in 1995. Values listed here are for plates in mint condition with original boxes.

1971, Heavenly Angel...395.00

1972, Hear Ye, Hear Ye, $40.00.

1973, Glober Trotter...60.00
1974, Goose Girl..45.00
1975, Ride Into Christmas 47.00
1976, Apple Tree Girl...47.00
1977, Apple Tree Boy...55.00
1978, Happy Pastime 35.00
1979, Singing Lesson 35.00
1980, School Girl...40.00
1981, Umbrella Boy..70.00
1982, Umbrella Girl..85.00
1983, The Postman...125.00
1984, Little Helper...50.00
1985, Chick Girl...60.00
1986, Playmates...100.00
1987, Feeding Time...130.00
1988, Little Goat Herder...85.00
1989, Farm Boy..100.00
1990, Shepherd's Boy 165.00
1991, Just Resting...125.00
1992, Meditation..160.00
1993, Doll Bath..150.00
1994, Doctor..150.00
1995, Come Back Soon..170.00

Royal Copenhagen

1908, Madonna & Child 3,500.00
1909, Danish Landscape.......................................240.00

1910, Magi 185.00
1911, Danish Landscape 185.00
1912, Christmas Tree 185.00
1913, Frederik Church Spire 170.00
1914, Holy Spirit Church 195.00
1915, Danish Landscape 210.00
1916, Shepherd at Christmas 155.00
1917, Our Savior Church 135.00
1918, Sheep & Shepherds 135.00
1919, In the Park 135.00
1920, Mary & Child Jesus 130.00
1921, Aabenraa Marketplace 125.00
1922, 3 Singing Angels 125.00
1923, Danish Landscape 125.00
1924, Sailing Ship 150.00
1925, Christianshavn Street Scene................125.00
1926, Christianshavn Canal 115.00
1927, Ship's Boy at Tiller 175.00
1928, Vicar's Family....................................125.00
1929, Grundtvig Church 125.00
1930, Fishing Boats 155.00
1931, Mother & Child 150.00
1932, Frederiksberg Gardens 150.00
1933, Ferry & Great Belt 185.00
1934, Hermitage Castle 195.00
1935, Kronborg Castle..................................275.00
1936, Roskilde Cathedral 240.00
1937, Main Street of Copenhagen.................295.00
1938, Round Church of Osterlars 425.00
1939, Greenland Pack Ice 495.00
1940, Good Shepherd 595.00
1941, Danish Village Church 425.00
1942, Bell Tower..495.00
1943, Flight Into Egypt 650.00
1944, Danish Village Scene 395.00
1945, Peaceful Scene 565.00
1946, Zealand Village Church 275.00
1947, Good Shepherd 300.00
1948, Nodebo Church 275.00
1949, Our Lady's Cathedral..........................295.00
1950, Boeslunde Church 295.00
1951, Christmas Angel 450.00
1952, Christmas in Forest 175.00
1953, Frederiksberg Castle 170.00
1954, Amalienborg Palace 185.00
1955, Fano Girl 230.00
1956, Rosenborg Castle................................210.00
1957, Good Shepherd 150.00
1958, Sunshine Over Greenland 155.00
1959, Christmas Night 175.00
1960, Stag 140.00
1961, Training Ship 165.00
1962, Little Mermaid....................................265.00
1963, Hojsager Mill......................................75.00
1964, Fetching the Tree 70.00
1965, Little Skaters 55.00
1966, Blackbird 45.00
1967, Royal Oak...50.00
1968, Last Umiak...45.00
1969, Old Farmyard 55.00
1970, Christmas Rose & Cat.........................55.00
1971, Hare in Winter 35.00
1972, In the Desert......................................27.00
1973, Train Home Bound..............................37.00

1974, Winter Twilight 36.00
1975, Queens Palace 30.00
1976, Danish Watermill 45.00
1977, Immervad Bridge 30.00
1978, Greenland Scenery 32.00
1979, Choosing Tree....................................70.00
1980, Bringing Home Tree............................35.00
1981, Admiring Tree 45.00
1982, Waiting for Christmas 95.00
1983, Merry Christmas 75.00
1984, Jingle Bells 70.00
1985, Snowman 70.00
1986, Wait for Me 67.00
1987, Winter Birds 80.00
1988, Christmas Eve Copenhagen 82.00
1989, Old Skating Pond................................95.00
1990, Christmas in Tivoli..............................145.00
1991, St Lucia Basilica.................................75.00
1992, Royal Coach 80.00
1993, Arrival Guests by Train.......................95.00
1994, Christmas Shopping 90.00

Limoges

From the mid-eighteenth century, Limoges was the center of the porcelain industry of France, where at one time more than forty companies utilized the local kaolin to make a superior quality china, much of which was exported to the United States. Various marks were used; some included the name of the American export company (rather than the manufacturer) and 'Limoges.' After 1891 'France' was added. Pieces signed by factory artists are more valuable than those decorated outside the factory by amateurs. The listings below are hand-painted pieces unless noted otherwise.

For a more thorough study of the subject, we recommend you refer to *The Collector's Encyclopedia of Limoges Porcelain, Third Edition* (with beautiful illustrations and current market values), by our advisor, Mary Frank Gaston.

Plaque, couple in landscape, Barbotine faience, 23½" diameter, $975.00.

Basket, roses, mc on cream w/gold, Duval, 1890-1932 mk, 9" L .425.00
Bonbon, floral basket shape w/gold, 1908-13 mk, 7½" L.............225.00
Bottle, scent; flowers on pitcher form w/gold, orig stopper, 5½". 125.00
Bowl, mums, mc on cream w/gold, oval, gr circle mk, 1900s, 12"..275.00
Box, wht roses w/curling vines on wht, Beaux-Arts mk, 6" L......250.00
Chalice, grapes w/gold scrolls & medallions, 1890-1932 mk, 10½" ...275.00
Charger, roses, mc on pk to wht w/gold, T&V, 17", from $500 to 600.00
Chocolate pot, gold-paste florals & hdl, red mk, ca 1880s-1891, 9"..450.00
Chocolate pot, gold-paste florals & lt gr leaves, 1890-1907 mk, 10".550.00
Cup & saucer, berries w/gold on lt gr, Duval, 1890s mk 165.00
Cup & saucer, chocolate; gold flowers on cobalt, twig hdl, 1890-1914...125.00

Cup & saucer, mc vintage w/gold, gold int, 1880s 275.00
Gravy boat, fish scene w/gold, w/underplate, gr mk, 1891-1914 .300.00
Inkwell holder, floral on wht w/gold, 1900-20s mk, from $140 to...165.00
Pancake dish, floral, w/lid, GDA mks, early 1900s, 10" dia.........325.00
Pitcher, cider; HP cherries, Z Goodrick '15, B&Co mk, 6½".......400.00
Plaque, bird in flight w/gold, Dubois, Flambeau mks, 1890s, 9¾" ...250.00
Plaque, Cupid's Kiss, 1880-1900, in wood fr: 13x16"................1,650.00
Plaque, Indian brave portrait, sgn Luc, gr mk, ca 1906-20, 10"....550.00
Plate, Daisy on apple gr, mk HP, T&V, 8¼", from $70 to............85.00
Plate, dinner; floral border, 1930s mks, 9", from $100 to.............125.00
Plate, Eastern scene w/men & donkeys, pierced, 13" 295.00
Plate, mc dainty bouquets w/gold, Theodore Haviland, 10".........65.00
Plate, peacock on flowering limb w/gold, H&Co, dtd 1887, 8"...115.00
Stein, HP repeating design/verse, inlaid lid, ½-litre 880.00
Tray, George & Martha transfers, prof decor souvenir, T&V, 8x11" 200.00
Vase, cherub on pk w/gold, hdls, ftd, ca 1891-1900, 7", from $375 to ..425.00
Vase, cobalt w/silver poppies o/l, 8x4" 400.00
Vase, foil under wht opal/copper/gold/blk, C Faure, 8¾" 3,450.00
Vase, geometrics in foil, mc w/gold, C Faure, ovoid, 11½" 3,565.00
Vase, roses, pk & yel w/gr leaves, Bronssilon, 1906-20, 15" 1,500.00

Lithophanes

Lithophanes are porcelain panels with relief designs of varying degrees of thickness and density. Transmitted light brings out the pattern in graduated shading, lighter where the porcelain is thin and darker in the heavy areas. They were cast from wax models prepared by artists and depict views of life from the 1800s, religious themes, or scenes of historical significance. First made in Berlin about 1803, they were used as lamp shade panels, window plaques, and candle shields. Later steins, mugs, and cups were made with lithophanes in their bases. Japanese wares were sometimes made with dragons or geisha lithophanes. See also Dragon Ware; Steins.

Candle shield, lovers in boat, wood-caned fr, 9x7" 500.00
Fairy lamp, children (4 scenes), HP/gilt, Clarke cup, 4¼" 1,750.00
Firescreen, Wm Penn's Treaty w/Indians, 18th C, 17x10" 1,300.00
Lamp shade, 5 scenic panels, metal fr, Schierholz, 6½x9" 1,000.00
Panel, couple in woods/children at well, PPM, 7x5¾", pr...........275.00
Panel, foxes at den w/rooster, elk at stream, PPM948/932, 13x11", pr...375.00
Panel, man gives lady gift, child sleeps, PPM, 5x4¼" 375.00
Stein, 2 girls read letter (in base), tavern scene ext, 10" 250.00

Little Red Riding Hood

Though usually thought of as a product of the Hull Pottery Company, research has shown that a major part of this line was actually made by Regal China. The idea for this popular line of novelties and kitchenware items was developed and patented by Hull, but records show that to a large extent Hull sent their whiteware to Regal to be decorated. Little Red Riding Hood was produced from 1943 until 1957.

For further information we recommend *The Collector's Encyclopedia of Hull Pottery* by Brenda Roberts, and *The Collector's Encyclopedia of Cookie Jars* by Joyce and Fred Roerig. All are published by Collector Books.

Bank, standing, from $650 to...750.00
Butter dish, from $325 to 350.00
Canister, cereal...1,375.00
Canister, coffee, sugar or flour; ea from $600 to 700.00
Canister, salt..1,100.00
Canister, tea..700.00
Clock 375.00

Cookie jar, closed basket, from $375 to..400.00
Cookie jar, full skirt, from $750 to...850.00
Cookie jar, open basket, from $300 to..350.00
Cracker jar, unmk, from $575 to...650.00
Creamer, side pour, from $150 to...175.00
Creamer, top pour, no tab hdl, from $400 to.......................................425.00
Creamer, top pour, tab hdl, from $350 to...375.00
Lamp, from $1,500 to..1,800.00
Match holder, wall hanging, from $800 to 850.00
Mustard jar, no spoon..325.00
Mustard jar, w/orig spoon..425.00
Pitcher, 7", from $325 to...350.00
Pitcher, 8"...400.00
Planter, wall hanging, from $475 to...500.00
Shakers, Pat design 135889, med sz, pr (+), from $800 to...........900.00
Shakers, 3¼", pr, from $60 to..90.00
Shakers, 5½", pr, from $175 to..200.00
Spice jar, sq base, ea, from $650 to..750.00
String holder, from $1,800 to...2,500.00
Sugar bowl, crawling, no lid, from $300 to..350.00
Sugar bowl, standing, no lid, from $150 to...175.00
Sugar bowl, w/lid, from $300 to...425.00
Sugar bowl lid, minimum value 175.00
Teapot, from $325 to..375.00
Wolf jar, red base, from $925 to...975.00
Wolf jar, yel base, from $750 to..800.00

Liverpool

In the late 1700s Liverpool potters produced a creamy ivory ware, sometimes called Queen's Ware, which they decorated by means of the newly perfected transfer print. Made specifically for the American market, patriotic inscriptions, political portraits, or other American themes were applied in black with colors sometimes added by hand. (Obviously their loyalty to the crown did not inhibit the progress of business!) Before it lost favor in about 1825, other English potters made a similar product. Today Liverpool is a generic term used to refer to all ware of this type. In our listings, information following the slash mark describes the transfer on the reverse side.

Jug, Wine Cannot Cure the Pain I Endure for My Chloe, drinking scene, man playing flute for lady, black transfer, ca 1800, 7x4½", $1,000.00. (Photo courtesy Early Auction Co.)

Bowl, When This You See/ships & sailor, blk transfer, 3¾x8¾", EX ...715.00
Jug, John Adams/Plenty/Justice/Cupid, blk transfer w/mc, 9¾" 4,000.00
Jug, Masonic/ship w/Am flag, blk transfer, 10", NM..................1,200.00
Jug, milk; Lafayette/Ben Franklin, blk transfer, 5½", VG 600.00
Jug, Seal of US/Chain of States, blk transfer, 8¼", EX 750.00
Jug, Stephen Decator (sic)/Jacob Brown, blk transfer, 5½".......2,000.00
Jug, The John (Am warship)/By Virtue & Valor..., blk, rstr, 10".700.00

Jug, Washington's Glory-Am in Tears/eagle & ship, blk, 10", EX ..**1,700.00**
Plate, Am sailing ship, blk transfer, Herculaneum, 9⅞" **200.00**
Plate, British sailing ship, blk transfer w/mc, Neale, 9⅞" **120.00**

Lladro

Lladro porcelains are currently being produced in Labernes Blanques, Spain. Their retired and limited edition figurines are popular collectibles on the secondary market.

Afternoon Promenade, #7636, retired, 1995 ....**280.00**
Alice in Wonderland, #5740, 9" **500.00**
Anniversary Waltz, #1372, 12¼" **315.00**
Baffled Dog, #5111 ....**380.00**
Basket of Love, #7622, retired, 1995 ....**350.00**
Checking the Time..**430.00**
Christmas Bell, 1989 ....**50.00**
Circus Magic..**400.00**
Classic Spring, #1142, 16" **550.00**
Clown Bust, #5610, 9" **305.00**
Clown w/Alarm Clock, #5156, 12"..................................**540.00**
Collie, #1316, 5½" **330.00**
Debutante **225.00**
Donkey in Love, retired **375.00**
Embroiderer, #4865 ....**370.00**
Fall Cleanup, #5286, 13" **330.00**
Fishing w/Gramps, #5215 ....**580.00**
Girl on Carousel Horse, #1469, MIB..............................**570.00**
Hunter Puppet, #4971, 7½" **405.00**
Innocence in Bloom, #7644, retired, 1996 ....**250.00**
Jazz Drums, #5929..**405.00**
Jester's Serenade, #5932 ....**975.00**
King Balthasar, #1020, 16" **900.00**
Kiyoko, #1450G..**425.00**
Litter of Love, #1441, 5" **355.00**
Little Riders **300.00**
Love in Bloom, #5292 ....**230.00**
Medieval Lady, #4928, 14½" **510.00**
One More Try **675.00**
Oriental Girl..**350.00**
Pocket Full of Wishes, #7650, 11" **300.00**
Purr-Fect, #1444, 5¼" **475.00**
Singapore Dancers..**750.00**
Sister's Pride, #5878...**440.00**
Tailor Made...**140.00**
Team Player, #6185 ....**130.00**
Ten & Growing, retired, 1966, from $375 to **425.00**
Teruko, #1451, 10¼" **375.00**
Thai Dancer (Gres) **725.00**
Trick or Treat **225.00**
Virgo, #06215...**145.00**
Visit w/Granny, #5305, 9" **450.00**
Winter Frost, #5287G **315.00**

Lobmeyer

J. and L. Lobmeyer, contemporaries of Moser, worked in Vienna, Austria, during the last quarter of the 1800s. Most of the work attributed to them is decorated with distinctive enameling; favored motifs are people in eighteenth-century garb. Our advisor for this category is Don Williams; he is listed in the Directory under Missouri.

Beverage set, coats of arms, dtd 1860, pitcher+6 tumblers.......**1,500.00**
Box, intaglio lid w/nude & cornucopias, clear, 6" dia **750.00**
Goblet, Victorian figure & flowers, unsgn, 5½", pr **800.00**
Plate, Persian enameling **350.00**
Tumbler, courting couple scene, unsgn, 4½", 5 for **800.00**

Locke Art

By the time he came to America, Joseph Locke had already proven himself many times over as a master glass maker, having worked in leading English glasshouses for more than seventeen years. Here he joined the New England Glass Company where he invented processes for the manufacture of several types of art glass — amberina, peachblow, pomona, and agata among them. In 1898 he established the Locke Art Glassware Co. in Mt. Oliver, Pittsburgh, Pennsylvania. Locke Art Glass was produced using an acid-etching process by which the most delicate designs were executed on crystal blanks. Most examples are signed simply 'Locke Art,' often placed unobtrusively near a leaf or a stem. Other items are signed 'Jo Locke,' some are dated, and some are unsigned. Most of the work was done by hand. The business continued into the 1920s. For further study we recommend *Locke Art Glass, Guide for Collectors*, by Joseph and Janet Locke, available at your local bookstore.

Our advisor for this category is Richard Haigh; he is listed in the Directory under Virginia.

Champagne, Poppy, 6" **130.00**
Cup, punch; Poppy **95.00**
Goblet, Ivy...**125.00**

Goblets, Kaluna Poppy, 6½", NM, 12 for $865.00.

Pitcher, Rose etch, 8" **350.00**
Plate, Poinsettias etch, 7" **75.00**
Salt cellar, Vintage, ped ft, 2¼x1¼"...........................**100.00**
Sherbet, Ivy...**85.00**
Tray, ice cream; eng flowers, 16x8" **460.00**
Tumbler, eng sheaves of wheat, 2¾" **95.00**
Tumbler, Vintage **110.00**
Vase, Peonies etch, ruffled rim, 5" **375.00**
Vase, Poppies eng, 5x3" **270.00**
Vase, Rose etch, flared rim, 6¼" **375.00**

Locks

The earliest type of lock in recorded history was the wooden cross bar used by ancient Egyptians and their contemporaries. The early Romans are credited with making the first key-operated mechanical lock. The ward lock was invented during the Middle Ages by the Etruscans of Northern Italy; the lever tumbler and combination locks followed at various stages of history with varying degrees of effectiveness. In the eighteenth century the first precision lock was constructed. It was a device that utilized a lever-tumbler mechanism. Two of the best-known of the early nineteenth-century American lock manufacturers are Yale and Sargent, and today's collectors value Winchester and Keen Kutter locks very highly. Factors to consider are rarity, condition, and construction. Brass and bronze locks are generally priced higher than those of steel or iron. Our advisor for this section is Joe Tanner; he is listed in the Directory under Washington.

Key:
bbl — barrel   st — stamped

Brass Lever Tumbler

Anchor, 6-lever, emb, 3⅛" 38.00
Automatic, emb, flat key, 2⅛" 20.00
Belknap, emb, 3⅛" 25.00
Chubbs, Patent London, st, 6⅛" 350.00
Cleveland 4 Way, Cleveland 4 Way emb on front, 3⅝" 90.00
Cotterill, st High Security key, 5⅛x3⅛" 350.00
Cotterill Birmingham Eng, st, 5⅛" 400.00
Crusader, shield, swords emb on body, 2¾" 45.00
Duplex Yale & Towne Mfg Co, st, 2⅞" 200.00
Geo B Bahr & Co Lou Ky, st, 3⅛" 70.00
GW Co, 1929, emb, 3" 60.00
GW Nock, fancy etch, st, 2⅞" 200.00
JWM, emb, bbl key, 2⅝" 25.00
Mercury, Mercury emb on body, 2¾" 75.00
Our Very Best, OVB emb on body, 2⅞" 200.00
P Fister Cin O, st, 2½" 60.00
Romer & Co, Romer & Co st on dust cover, 3" 55.00
Ruby, Ruby emb in scroll on front, 2¾" 30.00
Siberian, Siberian emb on shackle, 2½" 110.00
Tower & Lyon NY, st, 3" 25.00
W Bohannan & Co, SW emb in scroll on front, 2⅜" 30.00
Watch, emb, flat key, 3" 30.00

Winchester, Winchester embossed on front and back, 2" wide, $170.00.

Winchester, Winchester emb on front, 3" 160.00
1898, emb, 2¾" 30.00

Combinations

Canton Lock Co, emb, iron, 3⅜" 425.00
Clark, st, brass, 2¼" 300.00
Edwards Mfg Co No-Key, st on lock, brass, 2¾" 60.00
Junkunc Bros Mfrs, all st on bk, brass, 1⅞" 35.00
Number or letter disk, st, 3-disk, brass, 2½" 100.00

Number or letter disk, st, 4-disk, brass, 3½" 170.00
Number or letter disk, st, 4-disk, iron, 4½" 275.00
Number or letter disk type (4 disks), brass, 2¾" 130.00
Sorel Limited Canada, st, brass, 3¼" 200.00
Sutton Lock Co st on body, 3" 200.00
Turman's Keyless, st, brass, 2¼" 160.00
Vulcana Push Lock Corp, st on lock case, 3¼" 50.00
WA Harrison, Inc, st, brass, 2½" 100.00
Your Own st on body, 3⅞" 400.00

Eight-Lever Type

Armory, brass, Armory 8-Lever st on front 30.00
Electric, steel, Electric st on front 30.00
Goliath, steel, Goliath 8-Lever st on front 25.00
Mastodon, st, steel, 4½" 15.00
Miller, steel, Miller 8-lever st on front 18.00
Samson, brass, 8-Lever st on front 18.00

Iron Lever Tumbler

Airplane, st, 2¾" 60.00
Automobile, st, 2⅞" 50.00
Bronco, emb, 3¼" 45.00
Bulldog, word Bulldog & face of dog emb on front, 2¾" 35.00
Caesar, emb, 2¾" 15.00
Dan Patch, Dan Patch emb on front, horseshoe on bk, 2¾" 150.00
Eagle, word Eagle emb on body, 4⅜" 40.00
HC Jones (trick lock), st, 4¼" 600.00
Indian Head, Indian head emb on front, 3" 140.00
King Korn, words King Korn emb on body, 2⅞" 40.00
Lever Buckle Co, emb, 4½" 90.00
Moose head, emb, 2¾" 20.00
Owl, emb, 2¼" 30.00
Red Chief, words Red Chief emb on body, 3¾" 150.00
Rough Rider (horse & rider), emb, 3" 90.00
S Andrews, st, 2⅝" 200.00
Thoroughbred, emb, 2⅛" 35.00
W Bohannon, Brook NY WB, st, 3¼" 35.00
W Hall & Co, st, 4½" 400.00
Yale & Towne, lion face emb on front, shackle mk Y&T, 3" 150.00

Lever Push Key

Achilles, emb, iron, 3⅝" 80.00
Aztec, emb 6-Lever, 2⅛" 100.00
California, emb, brass, 2½" 100.00
Celtic Cross, emb cross on face, brass, 2¼" 150.00
Columbia, emb Columbia 6-Lever, brass push-key type, 2¼" 35.00
Crescent, 4-Lever, emb, iron, 2" 40.00
Duke, emb 6-Lever, 2⅛" 65.00
Empire, emb, 6-Lever, brass, 2½" 20.00
Fordloc, emb, iron, 3¼" 40.00
HS&Co, 6-Lever, emb, brass, 2¼" 100.00
IXL, emb IXL on body, 2¼" 110.00
Jewett Buffalo, emb, brass, 2¼" 200.00
McIntosh, emb, 6-Lever, iron, 2½" 150.00
Morley, emb, iron, 2½" 150.00
Nugget 4-Lever, emb, brass, 2" 50.00
SB Co, emb SB Co on body, 3¼" 60.00
Smith & Egge Mfg Co, Smith & Egge st on front, 3" 75.00
Supplee, emb, iron, 2½" 100.00
Ten Star, emb Ten Star 6-Lever, 2¼" 60.00
Vulcan, emb, iron, 2¾" 20.00

Logo — Special Made

West Baking Co., embossed, brass, 2½", $200.00.

Anaconda, st, brass, 2⅞" 60.00
Brass pancake push key, emb US Internal Revenue, 2¼" 225.00
Canada Custom, emb, iron, 2¾" 200.00
City of Boston Dept of Schools, st, brass, 2⅞" 40.00
Coca-Cola, st, brass, 2⅝" 50.00
Conoco, st, brass, 2⅝" 25.00
Georgia Power Co, st, brass, 3" 15.00
Hawaiian Elec, st, brass, 3" 30.00
Heart-shape brass lever type, st Board Education, bbl key, 3½" 65.00
International Harvester Co, emb, brass, 2½" 100.00
John Deere, st, brass 50.00
Property of Syracuse Univ, st, brass, 2⅝" 40.00
Public Service Co, st, brass, 2⅞" 20.00
Sq Yale-type brass pin tumbler, st Shell Oil Co on body, 3⅛"........25.00
Sq Yale-type brass pin tumbler, st US/A/tree/Forest Svc, 2⅞" 200.00
Swift & Co, st, iron, 2¼" 20.00
Texaco, emb, brass, 2¾" 60.00
University of Okla, st, brass, 2⅞" 40.00
USBIA, st, brass, 3¾" 80.00
USGS, emb, iron, 2½" 40.00
USMC, st, brass, 2½" 100.00

Pin-Tumbler Type

Corbin, brass, Corbin in oval st on body, 3⅝" 25.00
Eagle, brass, Eagle st on body, 2⅞" 20.00
Eagle, emb, iron, 2¾" 20.00
Hickory, emb, iron, 2¾" 150.00
Hope, brass, emb Hope on body, 2½" 20.00
Il-A-Noy, emb, iron, 2¾" 40.00
Il-A-Noy, emb Il-A-Noy on body, 2½" 40.00
Pearl, brass, emb Pearl on body, 2⅛" 30.00
Sargent, brass, emb Sargent on body, 3" 15.00
Shapleigh, emb Shapleigh on body, 2⅝" 30.00
Simmons, emb, iron, 2⅝" 30.00
Yale, brass, emb Yale on body, Yale & Towne on shackle, 2⅝" 25.00
Yale, emb, iron, 2¼" 70.00

Scandinavian (Jail House) Type

Backalaphknck (Russian), st, iron, 5"....................400.00
Bull Dog, emb, brass, 2½" 150.00
JHW Climax Co, iron, 2⅞" 50.00
Nrarvck (Russian), st, iron, 4" 250.00
R&E Co, emb, iron, 3¼" 40.00
Star, emb line on bottom, iron, 3¾" 150.00

999 Miller, emb 999, brass, 2½"..............................70.00

Six-Lever Type

Bon-Ton, st, iron, 3" 15.00
Edwards, iron, Edwards st on body 18.00
Oak Leaf Six-Lever, st, iron, 3¼"..........................15.00
Olympiad Six-Lever, st, iron, 3¾".........................25.00
Safe, brass, Safe st on body 18.00
SHCo Simmons Six-Lever, emb, iron, 3⅞".............70.00

Story and Commemorative

AYPEX Seattle (Alaska Yukon Pacific Expo), emb tin/iron, 3" ..235.00
Canteen, US emb on lock, lock: canteen shape, 2" 700.00
CI, emb ornate scroll motif throughout body of lock, 3½"..........250.00
CQD/sinking ship Titanic & SOS waves emb on brass, 2¾" 120.00
Mail Pouch emb on lock, lock in shape of mail pouch, 3⅛" 225.00
National Hardware Co (NHCo), emb, iron, 2½" 200.00
National Hardware Co (NHCo), emb Mercury figure, iron, 2" ..250.00
National Hardware Co (NHCo), emb SK, iron, 3½" 600.00
Russell & Erwin (R&E), emb bird, iron, 2⅞" 500.00
Russell & Erwin (R&E), emb Ganesha form, iron, 3" 700.00
Russell & Erwin (R&E), emb mailbox, iron, 3⅛"....................600.00
Russell & Erwin (R&e), emb vase, iron, 3¼" 800.00
1901 Pan Am Expo, brass, emb w/buffalo, 2⅝" 450.00
1904 World's Fair, iron & brass, 3⅝"...................................400.00

Warded Type

Bramah's Patent VR, 5"......................................60.00
Cruso Chicken, emb, brass, 2¾" 35.00
G&B, st, brass, 3"...15.00
Globe, iron sq lock case, emb US on bk, 2⅜" 20.00
Jewel, emb, iron, 2½" 18.00
Kirby, emb, brass, 2¼" 20.00
Navy, iron pancake ward key, bk: scrolled emb letters, 2½" 40.00
Rex, steel case, emb letters, 2⅝" 18.00
Safe, brass sq case, emb letters, 1⅞" 8.00
Safety First, brass pancake type, emb letters, 2¾" ...15.00
Sprocket, brass oval shape, emb letters, 2⅛" 50.00
Texas, emb, brass, 2½" 50.00
Twister, st, brass, 2⅞" 12.00
Winchester, brass sq case, st letters, 2¾" 135.00

Wrought Iron Lever Type (Smokehouse Type)

Improved Warranted, 3½"....................................35.00
MW&Co, bbl key, 2⅝" 10.00
R&E, 4½" 40.00
S&Co, bbl key, 3" 8.00
VR, 3½" 30.00
Waines, 4⅜"..40.00
WT Patent, 3¼" 20.00

Loetz

The Loetz Glassworks was established in Klostermule, Austria, in 1840. After Loetz's death the firm was purchased by his grandson, Johann Loetz Witwe. Until WWII the operation continued to produce fine artware, some of which made in the early 1900s bears a striking resemblance to Tiffany's, with whom Loetz was associated at one time. In addition to the iridescent Tiffany-style glass, he also produced threaded glass and some cameo. The majority of Loetz pieces will have a polished pontil. Our advisor for this category is Don Williams; he is listed in the Directory under Missouri.

Bowl, gr encased w/crystal, bl-gr irid int, ruffled rim, 10" 250.00
Bowl, gr w/bl-gold oil spots, tricorner rim, 4¼x6½" 400.00
Bowl, marbleized mc w/HP Deco rim & gold, ftd, 5¾x7" 400.00
Bowl, peach w/oil spots & ruby pulls, 4 gold irid ft, unmk, 6⅝"..4,000.00
Compote, gold & crystal irid, thorny trunk base/stem, 9" bowl..1,200.00
Inkwell, gold irid w/amethyst trails, apple w/brass leaf cap, 2½".300.00

Inkwell, pulled design on iridized gold, purple, and red, hinged metal lid with red and iridescent cap with pulled decor, clear insert, 3", $3,500.00; Vase, silver overlay thistles on elongated oval body with gold spots, 10", $2,185.00.

Pitcher, bluerina irid, crystal hdl, sgn MK, cylindrical, 10½" 900.00
Pitcher, paperweight; Dmn Quilt, gr w/gold grasses & wht dots, 3¼" ..225.00
Planter, pig figural, gold irid, opening in bk, 4½x7½" 2,200.00
Rose bowl, gr w/faint irid, draped silver-bl threads, pinched, 3¼"...150.00
Rose bowl, silver-bl oil spots on cobalt, ruffled, 4x5¾" 325.00
Shades, amber bell form w/gold spots, fluted/scalloped, 6", pr.....800.00
Vase, amber irid, bronze snakes mt w/tulip bulbs fr, 5x9x6½"..1,725.00
Vase, amber w/rainbow oil spots, 2"..240.00
Vase, bl irid, dbl trumpet form, amber irid ft, cobalt int, 6¼" 700.00
Vase, bl irid w/oil spots & HP floral, trifold, pinched, 10¼" 700.00
Vase, bl w/oil spots & random pulled vines & leaves, 12x10"..1,500.00
Vase, bl-gold irid w/oil spots, sq, dimpled, 8¾" 475.00
Vase, cameo, geometrics, lt/dk amethyst, cylindrical, Beckart, 7¼"..2,250.00
Vase, cameo berries & fines, bl/pk frost, 11¾".......................1,750.00
Vase, cobalt w/bl oil spots, cylindrical neck, bulbous, 6" 485.00
Vase, floral, yel on bl irid w/oil spots, trifold top, slim neck, 10"..700.00
Vase, gold irid serpent circles rubena neck, chartreuse oil spots, 10"...225.00
Vase, gold irid w/oil spots & bl-gold pulled design, 10"............2,200.00
Vase, gold w/oil spots, clear seaweed supports over star-form base, 9"...1,265.00
Vase, gold w/pk irid/clear oil spots, trefoil mouth, pinched, 10⅝"...1,100.00
Vase, gold w/violet irid, 2 rows of dimples, ovoid, 6½"................700.00
Vase, gr irid Rusticana, melon ribs w/pigtail intrusions, 4¼x6½"..150.00
Vase, gr irid to pk at ruffled rim, ribs, mk (rare), 10¼"................750.00
Vase, gr irid w/mc pulled decor, tricorner rim, 7¾" 1,035.00
Vase, gr w/pulled magenta & pearl irid, gr bulbous top, 4¾", NM...1,000.00
Vase, gray irid w/3 appl gr tendrils, waisted/ruffled, 5¾" 260.00
Vase, Octopus, dk brn w/wht int, HP decor, 8x6½" 2,000.00
Vase, olive gr w/broad leaves of irid oil spots, ovoid, 8" 1,265.00
Vase, peach w/silvery irid pulls, 5 appl pads & trailings, 6⅛"..2,500.00
Vase, pk & purple swirls w/silver spots, pinched oviform, att, 4¼"..2,650.00
Vase, pk w/pulled & swirled silver irid, gold oil spots, 5½"......1,500.00
Vase, purple irid, 4-fold top, spiked pewter fr, 11" 1,500.00
Vase, red irid w/wht & irid chartreuse oil spots, waisted, 6" 500.00
Vase, red w/silvery bl oil spots, cylinder w/ovoid top, ftd, 9⅜"..1,150.00
Vase, red w/silvery irid pulls, trefoil mouth, pinched, 9⅛".......1,265.00
Vase, Silberis, gold w/bl irid, floriform, 10¼" 800.00
Vase, silver o/l, lt bl oil spots on dk gold lustre, shouldered, 7"..1,725.00
Vase, silver o/l floral on bl, pinched, trifold, silver o/l, 6" 2,800.00
Vase, silver o/l leaves on ambergris, tricorner rim, 8⅛", NM 575.00
Vase, silver o/l on gr irid to pearly bl, ca 1905, 6½" 750.00
Vase, silver o/l vintage on bl, silver hdl, cylindrical, 10½" 8,000.00

Vase, stretch irid, pinched sides, 6"..225.00

Longwy

The Longwy workshops were founded in 1798 and continue today to produce pottery in the north of France near the Luxembourg-Belgian border under the name 'Societe des Faienceries de Longwy et Senelle.' The ware for which they are best known was produced during the Art Deco period, decorated in bold colors and designs. Earlier wares made during the first quarter of the nineteenth century reflected the popularity of Oriental art, cloisonne enamels in particular. The designs were executed by impressing the pattern into the moist clay and filling in the depressions with enamels. Examples are marked 'Longwy,' either impressed or painted under glaze.

Bowl, floral w/birds at edge of water, 10½" 325.00
Bowl, floral w/birds nesting on roofs, much cobalt, 5½".............100.00
Box, ducks, cat & rabbit decor, mk, 4½" L, EX 150.00
Charger, birds & flower branches, mc on turq crackle, Chevalier, 15"..925.00
Compote, Deco-style geometrics, hairline, 10" 260.00
Pitcher, flowering plants on lt bl crackle, twist hdl, #1801, 10"..400.00
Plate, floral w/inset panels, much cobalt, mk, 14" 400.00
Trivet, geometric design w/shield, ftd, 8"...................................150.00
Vase, emb birds, on ped base (rstr) w/4 elephant-head supports, 10"..500.00
Vase, ivory (no decor), 8-sided, mk, 11½".................................120.00
Vase, Primavera, turq crackle, flared neck, flattened body, ftd, 12"..250.00

Lonhuda

William Long was a druggist by trade who combined his knowledge of chemistry with his artistic ability in an attempt to produce a type of brown-glazed slip-decorated artware similar to that made by the Rookwood Pottery. He achieved his goal in 1889 after years of long and dedicated study. Three years later he founded his firm, the Lonhuda Pottery Company. The name was coined from the first few letters of the last name of each of his partners, W.H. Hunter and Alfred Day. Laura Fry, formerly of the Rookwood company, joined the firm in 1892, bringing with her a license for Long to use her patented airbrush-blending process. Other artists of note, Sarah McLaughlin, Helen Harper, and Jessie Spaulding, joined the firm and decorated the ware with nature studies, animals, and portraits, often signing their work with their initials. Three types of marks were used on the Steubenville Lonhuda ware. The first was a linear composite of the letters 'LPCO' with the name 'Lonhuda' impressed above it. The second, adopted in 1893, was a die-stamp representing the solid profile of an Indian, used on ware patterned after pottery made by the American Indians. This mark was later replaced with an impressed outline of the Indian head with 'Lonhuda' arching above it. Although the ware was successful, the business floundered due to poor management. In 1895 Long became a partner of Sam Weller and moved to Zanesville where the manufacture of the Lonhuda line continued. Less than a year later, Long left the Weller company. He was associated with J.B. Owens until 1899, at which time he moved to Denver, Colorado, where he established the Denver China and Pottery Company in 1901. His efforts to produce Lonhuda utilizing local clay were highly successful. Examples of Denver Lonhuda are sometimes marked with the LF (Lonhuda Faience) cipher contained within a canted diamond form.

Bowl, floral, ivory/cream/brn, brn int, incurvate rim, 2¼x6" 360.00
Pitcher, daisies, 6", NM...250.00
Vase, blue berries & leaves, brn tones, bulbous, 8¼x4", NM 340.00
Vase, mums on brn, artist sgn, bulbous, flared rim, 1893, 9" 450.00

Lotton

Charles Lotton is a contemporary glass artist. He began blowing glass and developing original designs thirty years ago and now has work on display in many major glass museums and collections, among them the Smithsonian, the Art Institute of Chicago, the Museum of Glass, and the Chrysler Museum. He has become famous for his unique lamps. Every piece is signed and dated. His three sons, David, Daniel, and John, each work in their own studios. All four artists produce distinctive work. They sell their glass at antique shows and in their showroom in Crete, Illinois. For further information read *Lotton Art Glass* by Charles Lotton and Tom O'Conner; see the Directory under Illinois. The values that follow are actual prices realized from a recent auction.

Bowl, Multi Flora, ruby, Charles 1992, 7½x8" 750.00
Toothpick holder, cobalt irid, Charles 1981, 2½" 200.00
Vase, drapes, bl on opal, 1975, 7½" 400.00
Vase, drapes, irid purple oil spots & bl lustre, John 1983, 8".......250.00
Vase, drapes, silver on bl Cypriot, Charles 1981, 9" 500.00
Vase, feathers, gr & bl on opal, selenium red int, 1981, 8"..........450.00
Vase, feathers, irid, Charles 1983, 7"...450.00
Vase, fernery & swirls, ruby w/bl, gourd form, Charles 1987, 6¾"...450.00
Vase, ferns, bl lustre in opal, selenium red int, Charles 1983, 8½" .675.00
Vase, hearts/threaded vines, cobalt irid, Charles 1983, 8" 900.00
Vase, King Tut, bl lustre w/purple oil spots, John 1991, 3" 165.00
Vase, Lava, cobalt w/purple hues & silvery droplets, Charles 1977, 6" ..450.00
Vase, Lava draping, bl lustre in cobalt Cypriot, Charles 1987, 6" ..700.00
Vase, leaves, bl lustre in opal, purple int, David 1995, 5"............365.00
Vase, leaves, cobalt on alabaster irid, Charles 1979, 6¼" 300.00
Vase, leaves/vines, bl irid on selenium red, 1991, 5¾" 300.00
Vase, leaves/vines, bl lustre in neo-bl verre de soie, Charles '86, 5"...815.00
Vase, leaves/vines, irid on pk mottled opal, 1994, 8½"................280.00
Vase, leaves/vines, pk/gr/opal, purple irid rim, John 1990, 10" 550.00
Vase, leaves/vines, silvery bl & gr in neo-bl, David 1995, 5" 450.00
Vase, Multi Flora, pk in gr aventurine, Charles 1988, 10"...........725.00
Vase, Multi Flora, verre de soie, pk/bl/gr, Charles 1983, 8½"......550.00
Vase, vines (bl) appl to opal lustre, pinched/folded, 1972, 5½" ..250.00
Vase, zipper ribs, silver-bl w/wht & pk festoons, Charles 1977, 8½"..325.00

Lotus Ware

Isaac Knowles and Issac Harvey operated a pottery in East Liverpool, Ohio, in 1853 where they produced both yellow ware and Rockingham. In 1870 Knowles brought Harvey's interests and took as partners John Taylor and Homer Knowles. Their principal product was ironstone china, but Knowles was confident that American potters could produce as fine a ware as the Europeans. To prove his point, he hired Joshua Poole, an artist from the Belleek Works in Ireland. Poole quickly perfected a Belleek-type china, but fire destroyed this portion of the company. Before it could function again, their hotel china business had grown to the point that it required their full attention in order to meet market demands. By 1891 they were able to try again. They developed a bone china, as fine and thin as before, which they called Lotus. Henry Schmidt from the Meissen factory in Germany decorated the ware, often with lacy filigree applications or hand-formed leaves and flowers to which he added further decoration with liquid slip applied by means of a squeeze bag. Due to high production costs resulting from so much of the fragile ware being damaged in firing and because of changes in tastes and styles of decoration, the Lotus Ware line was dropped in 1896. Some of the early ware was marked 'KT&K China'; later marks have a star and a crescent with 'Lotus Ware' added. Our advisor for this category is Mary Frank Gaston.

Bonbon/nappy, sm floral on wht w/gold, ftd, 8" L..........................325.00
Bottle, scent; pierced/scrolled, twig hdls, folded rim, 3½" 650.00
Bowl, floral branches w/gold, fishscale shoulder, mk, 4¾" H.......400.00
Chocolate jug, gold-paste floral, 9"..750.00
Cup & saucer, AD; Mecca, lg geometrics w/gold, 2½", 5"...........135.00
Pin tray, draped nude, fan behind her, HP, rare, 6" L 1,300.00
Pitcher, molded bands, 5¼" 275.00
Pitcher, pk floral branches w/gold, bamboo hdl w/gold, 4½".......275.00
Rose jar, lt gr & wht accents, rtcl ball form, w/lid, 4" 700.00
Rose jar, wht w/allover bead swags & medallions, petal ft, 8"..1,700.00
Salt cellar, gold lustre int, ind 80.00
Shell tray, roses & gold transfer, 5x5½"..350.00
Teapot, fishnet on wht, 4", +cr/sug, ea 4".....................................225.00
Vase, Etruscan, appl flowers, filigree hdls, whtware, 10"...........1,350.00
Vase, HP purple clematis on lt bl & wht w/much gold, 7¼" 440.00
Vase, HP thistles, encrusted gold, AR Nov 7 '97, 8", NM..........600.00
Whiskey jug, Meredith's Diamond Club, Pure Rye Whiskey, 7½" ..150.00

Lu Ray Pastels

Lu Ray Pastels dinnerware was introduced in the early 1940s by Taylor, Smith, and Taylor of East Liverpool, Ohio. It was offered in assorted colors of Persian Cream, Sharon Pink, Surf Green, Windsor Blue, and Chatham Gray in complete place settings as well as many service pieces. It was a successful line in its day and is once again finding favor with collectors of American dinnerware. For further information we recommend *Collector's Guide to Lu Ray Pastels* by Bill and Kathy Meehan. Our advisor for this category is Shirley Moore; she is listed in the Directory under Oklahoma.

Coaster/nut dish, $65.00.

Bowl, '36s oatmeal..60.00
Bowl, coupe soup; flat...15.00
Bowl, cream soup..70.00
Bowl, fruit; Chatham Gray, 5" 16.00
Bowl, fruit; 5"..5.00
Bowl, lug soup; tab hdld..19.00
Bowl, mixing; 5½"...125.00
Bowl, mixing; 7"...125.00
Bowl, mixing; 8¾"...100.00
Bowl, mixing; 10¼"...150.00
Bowl, salad; any color other than yel...65.00
Bowl, salad; yel..55.00
Bowl, vegetable; oval, 9½"...20.00
Butter dish, any color other than Chatham Gray, w/lid...............50.00
Butter dish, Chatham Gray, rare color, w/lid..............................90.00
Calendar plates, 8", 9" & 10", ea 40.00
Casserole..125.00
Chocolate cup, AD; str sides..80.00

Chocolate pot, AD; str sides 400.00
Coffee cup, AD...20.00
Coffeepot, AD 200.00
Creamer...8.00
Creamer, AD, ind...40.00
Creamer, AD, ind, from chocolate set 92.00
Egg cup, dbl..24.00
Epergne 110.00
Gravy boat 28.00
Jug, water; ftd 125.00
Muffin cover 125.00
Muffin cover, w/8" underplate..145.00
Nappy, vegetable; rnd, 8½" 20.00
Pitcher, any color other than yel, bulbous w/flat bottom...................125.00
Pitcher, juice 200.00
Pitcher, yel, bulbous w/flat bottom 95.00
Plate, cake 70.00
Plate, Chatham Gray, rare color, 7" 16.00
Plate, chop; 15"..38.00
Plate, grill; compartment 35.00
Plate, 6" 3.00
Plate, 7" 12.00
Plate, 8" 20.00
Plate, 9" 10.00
Plate, 10" 20.00
Platter, oval, 11½" 16.00
Platter, oval, 13" 19.00
Relish dish, 4-part...95.00
Sauce boat, any other color than yel, fixed stand..........................35.00
Sauce boat, yel, fixed stand 22.50
Saucer, coffee; AD 8.50
Saucer, coffee/chocolate 30.00
Saucer, cream soup..28.00
Saucer, tea 3.00
Shakers, pr 16.00
Sugar bowl, AD; w/lid, from chocolate set 92.00
Sugar bowl, AD; w/lid, ind 40.00
Sugar bowl, w/lid 15.00
Teacup 8.00
Teapot, curved spout, w/lid 125.00
Teapot, flat spout, w/lid..160.00
Tray, pickle 28.00
Tumbler, juice 50.00
Tumbler, water 80.00
Vase, bud..400.00

Lunch Boxes

Early twentieth-century tobacco companies such as Union Leader, Tiger, and Dixie sold their products in square, steel containers with flat, metal carrying handles. These were specifically engineered to be used as lunch boxes when they became empty. (See Advertising, specific companies.) By 1930 oval lunch pails with colorful lithographed decorations on tin were being manufactured to appeal directly to children. These were made by Ohio Art, Decoware, and a few other companies. In 1950 Aladdin Industries produced the first 'real' character lunch box — a Hopalong Cassidy decal-decorated steel container now considered the beginning of the kids' lunch box industry. The other big lunch box manufacturer, American Thermos (later King Seely Thermos Company), brought out its 'blockbuster' Roy Rogers box in 1953, the first fully lithographed steel lunch box and matching bottle. Other companies (ADCO Liberty; Landers, Frary & Clark; Ardee Industries; Okay Industries; Universal; Tindco; Cheinco) also produced character pails. Today's collectors

often tend to specialize in those boxes dealing with a particular subject. Western, space, TV series, Disney movies, and cartoon characters are the most popular. There are well over five hundred different lunch boxes available to the astute collector. For further information we recommend *Collector's Guide to Lunch Boxes* by Carole Bess White and L.M. White (Collector Books), and *The Illustrated Encyclopedia of Metal Lunch Boxes* by Allen Woodall and Sean Brickell. Our advisor for this category is Allan Smith; he is listed in the Directory under Texas. In the following listings, lunch boxes are metal unless noted vinyl or plastic, and values include thermoses only when they are mentioned within the descriptions.

As indicated in the lines, our values are for examples in exceptional condition; remember to discount sharply for wear and damage beyond the stated conditions.

Early West, Pony Express, Ohio Art, 1982, M, with original price tag, $150.00.

A-Team, 1985, plastic, red, w/thermos, EX 25.00
Alf, 1987, plastic, red, w/thermos, NM....................................18.00
Alvin & the Chipmunks, 1963, vinyl, w/thermos, EX 125.00
Atom Ant, 1966, G...60.00
Batman & Robin, 1966, G...95.00
Bedknobs & Broomsticks, 1972, VG..30.00
Bee Gees, 1978, NM..80.00
Benji, 1974, plastic, VG 15.00
Beverly Hillbillies, 1963, w/thermos, M 500.00
Bionic Woman, 1978, EX..85.00
Black Hole, 1979, EX 70.00
Blondie, 1968, w/thermos, EX, from $130 to 165.00
Buck Rogers, 1979, w/thermos, M 135.00
Bugaloos, Aladdin, 1971, NM..125.00
Captain Astro, 1966, VG 150.00
Care Bears, 1983, bl rim, w/thermos, G....................................20.00
Cartoon Zoo, 1962, G..80.00
Chan Clan, 1973, w/thermos, EX 100.00
Charlie's Angels, 1978, w/thermos, M 200.00
Cracker Jack, 1979, VG+ 35.00
Davy Crockett/Kit Carson, 1955, VG 225.00
Dawn, M 75.00
Disney Express, 1979, w/thermos, M, from $50 to 75.00
Donnie & Marie, 1978, vinyl brunch bag, EX 125.00
Dr Dolittle, 1967, w/thermos, NM 175.00
Eighteen Wheeler, 1978, EX 50.00
Empire Strikes Back, 1980, w/thermos, VG 35.00
Evel Knievel, 1974, w/thermos, VG+ 75.00
Fall Guy, 1981, VG+ 50.00
Fat Albert, EX..50.00
Fess Parker, 1964, VG 150.00
Flipper, 1966, w/thermos, NM, from $160 to 200.00
Gentle Ben, 1968, VG..65.00
Globetrotters, 1959, dome top, VG..200.00
Gomer Pyle, 1966, VG...100.00

Gremlins, 1984, w/thermos, VG+..............................20.00
Gunsmoke, 1959, w/thermos, VG+............................250.00
Hogan's Heroes, 1966, dome top, EX........................300.00
Hot Wheels, 1965, w/thermos, VG.............................75.00
Howdy Doody, 1954, EX...300.00
HR Pufnstuf, Aladdin, 1971, EX, from $75 to............95.00
It's About Time, dome top, NM+, from $450 to........500.00
Jetsons, 1963, dome top, EX.....................................200.00
Jungle Book, 1966, VG..65.00
Kung Fu, 1974, EX...50.00
Liddle Kiddles, 1968, vinyl, NM...............................150.00
Little Dutch Miss, 1959, w/thermos, NM, from $250 to............300.00
Little House on the Prairie, 1978, EX........................55.00
Little Mermaid, plastic, EX...5.00
Lone Ranger, 1954, EX..400.00
Man From UNCLE, 1966, w/thermos, NM................200.00
Mickey Mouse Head, 1988, plastic, w/thermos, M....50.00
Mr T, 1984, plastic, orange, w/thermos, EX.............30.00
My Little Pony, 1989, plastic, bl, w/thermos, EX 12.00
Osmonds, 1973, w/thermos, NM...............................125.00
Pebbles & Bamm-Bamm, 1971, EX.............................80.00
Pete's Dragon, 1978, EX..45.00
Pinocchio, 1971, VG..60.00
Porky's Lunch Wagon, 1959, dome top, EX.............375.00
Pussycats, 1968, vinyl brunch bag, NM...................250.00
Snoopy, 1981, plastic, orange, dome top, w/thermos, EX..............35.00
Soupy Sales, 1960s, vinyl, bl w/red hdl, EX............300.00
Superfriends, 1976, w/thermos, EX.............................50.00
Superman, 1980, plastic, dome top, w/thermos, EX 40.00
Traveler, 1962, red rim, VG...45.00
Walt Disney School Bus, 1960s, dome top, EX, from $50 to........70.00
Welcome Back Kotter, 1977, NM, from $85 to 110.00
Wild Wild West, 1969, EX..225.00
Yellow Submarine, 1968, EX, from $275 to..............350.00
Yogi Bear Memos, 1974, NM, from $65 to..................85.00

Lutz

From 1869 to 1888, Nicholas Lutz worked for the Boston and Sandwich Company where he produced the threaded and striped art glass that was so popular during that era. His works were not marked; and since many other glassmakers of the day made similar wares, the term Lutz has come to refer not only to his original works but to any of this type.

Chalice, ruby, tall stem, flared ft, pr 800.00
Jar, clear w/pk threading, w/lid...............................250.00
Jug, clear w/pk threading, bulbous 250.00
Pitcher, lemonade; clear crackle w/pk threads..........275.00

Maddux of California

One of the California-made ceramics now so popular with collectors, Maddux was founded in the late 1930s and during the years that followed produced novelty items, TV lamps, figurines, planters, and tableware accessories.

#150, planter, swan, blk, 11"......................................18.00
#206A, planter, Chinese Bell Tower, 8".....................20.00
#221, vase, swan, wht, 12"...20.00
#225, vase, horse's head top, str-sided body, aqua, 12" 20.00
#300, figurine, puppy, 6x5½".....................................15.00

#400/401, flamingos, pr 50.00
#515, planter, flamingo, pk, 10½"...............................45.00
#519, TV lamp, rooster, orange, 13"...........................75.00
#528, planter, 2 birds in flight, pk & blk, 10"...........20.00
#529, vase, 2 flamingos, 5"...40.00
#612, cockatoo planter, pk & bl...................................24.00
#628, planter, swallow, pk & gray................................35.00

#718R, clock, astrology design, Westclox, 12", $75.00.
(Photo courtesy Lee Garmon)

#808, TV lamp, pearl-tone shell, 13".........................40.00
#810, TV lamp, stallion prancing on base, 12"...........65.00
#826, TV lamp, cockatoos...65.00
#829, TV lamp, deer (2) running, natural, 10½"..........45.00
#841, TV lamp, head of Christ, 3-D planter 45.00
#846, TV lamp, nativity scene, 3-D planter................45.00
#887, TV lamp, Persian Glory (horse head), 11½".....50.00
#892, TV lamp, Colonial ship, 10½".............................40.00
#895, TV lamp, dbl swan, 11½"....................................50.00
#897, TV lamp, mare & foal, wht porc.........................60.00
#912/913, Chinese pheasants, airbrushed colors, 11", pr 30.00
#923, swans (2), blk matt, 10½"..................................25.00
#928/929, mallards, male/female, natural, 9½", pr 40.00
#969, Early Birds, blk matt, tangerine, 14½", pr 25.00
#971, flamingo winging, natural colors, 12" 45.00
#982, horse prancing 20.00
#1019, swan console bowl (set), porc wht, 11½" 20.00
#1050, candlestick, triple 35.00
#1067, shell console bowl (set), pk, 16".....................15.00
#2015, Antique Gold, hdls, 12"....................................15.00
#2217, cream can, Paul Revere, Milc Co, Maddux 75.00
#3009, serving tray/lazy Susan, pearlized, 2-tiered, 6-pc...............25.00
#3051, bowl, red tomato w/gr dbl leaves, w/lid, 16" L..............35.00
#321L, serving tray, 2-tiered 20.00
#3302, bank, cat, yel...25.00
#7134, ashtray, fish, 6" L...20.00
Ashtray set, metal caddy w/6 ind ashtrays, yel & red......20.00
Bowl, cabbage leaf design, 4x13" L..............................25.00
Cockatoos on branch w/appl flowers, 11".....................40.00
Cookie jar, Chipmunk on stump, C Romanelli, from $130 to 145.00
Cookie jar, Green Ivy, #2112..35.00
Cookie jar, Koala..60.00
Cookie jar, Shopping Cat, from $135 to 155.00
Cookie jar, Snowman..75.00
Cookie jar, Walrus...50.00
Ducklings, 3 on grassy base 20.00
Flamingo Line, single flamingo planter, 6"..................20.00
Wall pocket, bird in metal holder (resembles cage), 7x7"+ cage...35.00

Magazines

Magazines are collected for their cover prints and for the information pertaining to defunct companies and their products that can be gleaned from the old advertisements. In the listings that follow, items are assumed to be in very good condition unless noted otherwise. Our advisor for this category is Charles Zayic; he is listed in the Directory under Maine. See also Movie Memorabilia; Parrish, Maxfield.

Key:
M — mint condition, in original wrapper
EX — excellent condition, spine intact, edges of pages clean and
     straight
VG — very good condition, the average as-found condition

Appleton's Magazine, 1905, December, Rose O'Neill illus, EX 25.00
Atlantic Monthly, 1933, November, Wyeth poster, EX 20.00
Ballou's Pictorial, 1856, September 6, St Louis, NM 20.00
Baseball Digest, 1943, September, Stan Musial, NM 18.00
Bohemian, 1908, January, postcard issue, NM............................30.00
Boys Life, 1969, June, Mickey Mantle, NM 25.00
Century, 1884, January, Palmer Cox illus, NM............................18.00
Chain Store Age, 1955, March, Buffalo Bill Jr, NM.......................18.00
Collier's Weekly, 1905, September, Maxfield Parrish cover art, VG .25.00
Cosmopolitan, 1903, August, Rose O'Neill illus, NM 25.00
Cosmopolitan, 1913, July, Harrison Fisher illus, NM....................25.00
Country Gentleman, 1925, September, NC Wyeth cover art, NM ..35.00
Country Song Roundup, 1957, August, Elvis, NM 25.00
Dynamite, 1955, June, Vol 1/No 1, NM 22.00
Esquire, 1939, December, Petty art/foldout, NM 50.00
Fashions, 1900, December, hats & dresses, NM 20.00
Favorite Westerns, 1960, August, John Wayne, NM 10.00
Forest & Stream, 1876, December 10, Vol 3/No 18, EX................25.00
Forest & Stream, 1876, February 3, EX..30.00
Fortune, 1932, Grant Wood illus, NM 12.00
Good Housekeeping, Coles Phillips cover art, NM.......................35.00
Harper's Bazaar, 1867, November 2, Winslow Homer illus, NM ...20.00
Inside Sports, 1980, April, Nolan Ryan, NM 28.00
Judge, 1891, July 4, baseball cartoons, NM 22.00
Knickerbocker, 1837, October, ballooning article, NM 30.00
Ladies' Home Journal, 1909, September, H Fisher cover art, NM.30.00
Ladies' Home Journal, 1927, April, Rose O'Neill kewpies, NM....18.00
Liberty, 1942, March 14, Disney cover art, EX.............................20.00
Life, 1937, May 3, Jean Harlow, EX..45.00
Life, 1938, July 11, Rudolph Valentino, EX 40.00
Life, 1939, September 4, Rosalind Russell, EX..............................20.00
Life, 1940, October 7, Gary Cooper, EX.......................................50.00
Life, 1941, Lana Turner & Clark Gable, EX..................................35.00
Life, 1942, June 1, Hedy Lamarr, EX 30.00
Life, 1943, January 1, Rita Hayworth, EX 30.00
Life, 1944, January 10, Bob Hope, EX 20.00
Life, 1945, April 23, Harry S Truman/baseball, EX......................25.00
Life, 1946, November 25, 10th Anniversary Issue, EX 30.00
Life, 1949, August 1, Joe DiMaggio, EX 65.00
Life, 1950, June 12, Hopalong Cassidy, EX..................................65.00
Life, 1956, August 20, Audrey Hepburn, EX................................25.00

Life, 1961, January 13,
Clark Gable cover, EX,
from $12.00 to $14.00.

Life, 1962, March 11, Batman, EX..30.00
Life, 1970, October 23, Muhammad Ali, EX.................................25.00
Life, 1981, October, Marilyn Monroe, EX.....................................45.00
Literary Digest, 1907, May 9, JC Leyendecker cover art, EX........28.00
Look, 1937, May, Vol 1/No 5, Jean Harlow article, NM...............40.00
Look, 1946, October, 15, Ted Williams, NM 75.00
Look, 1952, September 9, Marilyn Monroe, NM...........................60.00
Look, 1954, June 1, Jackie Gleason, NM.......................................15.00
Look, 1963, January 9, Beatle article, NM 30.00
McCall's, 1931, July, NC Wyeth illus, NM....................................25.00
McCall's, 1951, August, Betsy McCall paper dolls, NM 15.00
McCall's, 1960, April, Marilyn Monroe, NM.................................20.00
McCall's, 1968, May, Raquel Welch, NM..6.00
Metropolitan, 1918, July, Rolf Armstrong cover art, NM..............42.00
Modern Photography, 1956, September, Glamour Issue, NM........12.00
Motor World, 1953, June 19, Marilyn Monroe, NM......................80.00
Musical Digest, 1928, March, Louis Icart cover art, NM 72.00
Nation, 1912, February 22, Maxfield Parrish article, NM..............20.00
National Geographic, 1915-16, ea 15.00
National Geographic, 1917-24, ea 9.00
National Geographic, 1925-29, ea 8.00
National Geographic, 1930-45, ea 7.00
National Geographic, 1946-55, ea 6.00
National Geographic, 1956-57, ea 5.50
National Geographic, 1968-89, ea 4.50
National Geographic, 1990-present, ea 2.00
Navy Magazine, 1907, November, fleet & maps, NM....................18.00
Needlecraft, 1924, October, Rockwell Quaker Oats illus, NM......28.00
New Anvil, 1939, March, Vol 1/No 1, NM....................................22.00
Newsweek, 1933, February 17, Vol 1/No 1, NM 35.00
Newsweek, 1946, September 14, Ted Williams, NM 75.00
Peek, 1940, July, Betty Grable, NM...15.00
People's Home Journal, 1915, August, JC Leyendecker Kellogg's ad, NM....25.00
Photoplay, 1948, September, Alan Ladd, EX.................................25.00
Planet Stories, 1939, Winter, No 1, NM 20.00
Playboy, 1957, May, Dawn Richards, EX+....................................50.00
Playboy, 1960, Linda Gamble, NM..25.00
Playboy, 1963, August, Phyllis Sherwood, EX 27.50
Playboy, 1967, February, Kim Farber, NM 15.00
Playboy, 1982, April, Kym Malin, NM 6.50
Popular Magazine, 1909, March, JC Leyendecker cover art, NM..70.00
Popular Photography, 1937, May, Vol 1/No 1, Carrol Lombard, NM ..30.00
Publisher's Weekly, 1951, June 2, JD Sallinger, NM 40.00
Rave, 1953, April, Vol 1/NO 1, NM...20.00
Redbook, 1936, June, Tunney & Louis, NM 10.00
Redbook, 1954, November, Grace Kelly, NM................................15.00
Redbook, 1957, December, How the Grinch Stole Christmas, VG+ ..75.00
Rolling Stone, 1969, August 9, Brian Jones, EX 55.00
Rolling Stone, 1971, August 5, Jim Morrison memorial, EX.........62.50
Rolling Stone, 1972, May 11, David Cassidy, NM, from $40 to....55.00
Rolling Stone, 1981, September 3, Stevie Nicks, EX 60.00
Saturday Evening Post, 1900, November 10, H Fisher cover art, NM ..40.00
Saturday Evening Post, 1910, October, R Robinson cover art, VG+ 20.00
Saturday Evening Post, 1954, May 1, Stan Musial, NM 35.00
Screen Stories, 1959, May, Ricky Nelson, VG...............................20.00
Scribners, 1880, February, Edison's Light, NM.............................20.00
Sport, 1946, September, Joe DiMaggio, NM 100.00
Sport, 1948, April, Ted Williams, EX..50.00
Sport, 1959, December, Johnny Unitas, NM.................................12.00
Sporting News, 1957, January 23, Mickey Mantle, NM 20.00
Sports Illustrated, 1956, April 23, Billy Martin, NM....................28.00
Sports Illustrated, 1972, March 13, Johnny Bench, NM...............20.00
Stage, 1936, June, WC Fields, NM 38.00
Time, 1963, February 22, Cassius Clay, VG..................................30.00

Town & Country, 1948, July, Salvadore Dali, VG 30.00
True Love, 1940, May, Joan Fontaine, EX 12.00
True Story, 1935, April, Zoe Mozert cover art, NM 32.00
Vanity Fair, 1913, September, Babe Ruth, NM+ 80.00
Vogue, 1913, March 15, FX Leyendecker cover art, EX................75.00
Woman's Home Companion, 1925, October, Our Gang paper dolls, NM ..40.00
Woman's Home Companion, 1933, September, Charlie Chaplin, NM ..30.00
Woman's World, 1932, November, Rose O'Neill Oxydol ad, EX ..10.00
Youth's Companion, 1895, October 3, Mark Twain article, EX.....40.00

Majolica

    Majolica is a type of heavy earthenware, design-molded and decorated in vivid colors with either a lead or tin type of glaze. It reached its height of popularity in the Victorian era; examples from this period are found in only the lead glazes. Nearly every potter of note, both here and abroad, produced large majolica jardinieres, umbrella stands, pitchers with animal themes, leaf shapes, vegetable forms, and nearly any other design from nature that came to mind. Not all, however, marked their ware. Among those who sometimes did were Minton, Wedgwood, Holdcroft, and George Jones in England; Griffin, Smith and Hill (Etruscan) in Phoenixville, Pennsylvania; and Chesapeake Pottery (Avalon and Clifton) in Baltimore.

    Color and condition are both very important worth-assessing factors. Pieces with cobalt, lavender, and turquoise glazes command the highest prices. For further information we recommend *The Collector's Encyclopedia of Majolica* by Mariann Katz-Marks (see Directory, Pennsylvania). Unless another condition is given, the values that follow are for pieces in mint condition. Our advisor for this category is Hardy Hudson; he is listed in the Directory under Florida.

Umbrella stand, ostrich stands to side of naturalistic stand, 33x16", $2,800.00.

Basket, Pond Lily & Floral, Holdcroft, 7¾" 800.00
Bowl, centerpc; lion's mask medallion, mermaid hdls, 14x19x8" .700.00
Bowl, centerpc; 2 putto w/basket, #296, Minton 2,000.00
Bowl, Maple Leaf, EX color, 10" 225.00
Bowl, Shell, 3 shell ft, Holdcroft, 12½" 300.00
Bowl, Shell & Seaweed, Etruscan, 9" 400.00
Box, lady reclining on lid, WS&S 350.00
Butter dish, Shell & Seaweed, Albino, Etruscan 350.00
Butter dish, Water Lily, cobalt, bird finial 650.00
Butter dish, Wheat & Daisy, cobalt 600.00
Butter pat, Geranium, Etruscan 150.00
Butter pat, Maple Leaf 200.00
Butter pat, Pansy, cobalt & yel 200.00
Butter pat, Ribbon, Bow & Floral, Fielding 350.00
Butter pat, Shell & Seaweed, Albino, Etruscan 200.00

Butter pat, Shell & Seaweed, lav center, Wedgwood...................250.00
Cake stand, Cauliflower, Etruscan 500.00
Cake stand, Maple Leaves on pk, Etruscan 375.00
Cake stand, Morning Glory, Etruscan, scarce 550.00
Cake stand, Pond Lily, 3 herons around ped, 6x9½"..................650.00
Cake stand, Shell & Seaweed 900.00
Chamberstick, Pond Lily..400.00
Charger, nude riding sea serpent, Wedgwood, 1871, 15¼".........400.00
Cheese keeper, Bird on Branch, cobalt, 9½" H 1,000.00
Coffeepot, Bird in Flight, pewter lid, snail hdl 700.00
Compote, Blackberry, Clifton 300.00
Compote, Maple Leaves, lav, Etruscan 300.00
Compote, Wild Rose & Rope, cobalt 300.00
Creamer, Shell & Seaweed, 4" 350.00
Cup & saucer, Butterfly, Fielding 300.00
Cup & saucer, Cauliflower, Etruscan 450.00
Cup & saucer, Shell & Seaweed 300.00
Deep dish, Argenta Ware, emb florals, star fr, Wedgwood, 1882, 12"...350.00
Egg basket, good colors, 4 egg cups 650.00
Egg holder, chick figural, Portugal 300.00
Humidor, fat frog, Eichwald 500.00
Jardiniere, Magnolia, pk & yel, Wedgwood, 1887, 12¼".............800.00
Mug, Pond Lily, Holdcroft 300.00
Pitcher, bear w/drum figural, Holdcroft, 7½" 1,700.00
Pitcher, Bird & Fan, tricorner, 7"...400.00
Pitcher, Corn, pewter top, English Registry mk, 9"...................600.00
Pitcher, Corn, 9"...350.00
Pitcher, Dragonfly & Fan, cobalt, sq top, 8½" 500.00
Pitcher, Floral, cobalt, 4"..225.00
Pitcher, frog on lily pad figural, English Registry mk, 5½"........1,200.00
Pitcher, irises in relief, iris-form hdl, mk JS, 1890s, 7¼" 250.00
Pitcher, lizard figural, Palissy, Mafra Portugal, 13½".................1,250.00
Pitcher, monkey figural, bamboo hdl, 6½" 600.00
Pitcher, Morning Glory, Ribbon & Bow, Fielding, 4" 200.00
Pitcher, parrot figural, 9½"..475.00
Pitcher, Pineapple, pewter top, 7"..400.00
Pitcher, Shell, Fielding, 10", EX 225.00
Pitcher, Shell & Seaweed, Albino, Etruscan, 6½" 200.00
Pitcher, syrup; Bamboo, Etruscan 600.00
Pitcher, syrup; Corn, pewter lid, 6"..350.00
Pitcher, syrup; Sunflower, cobalt, Etruscan...............................600.00
Pitcher, train conductor figural, French, 10" 325.00
Planter, dove & flowers, turq, pk int, att Minton, 13" dia 3,250.00
Plaque, fish on bed of leaves surrounded by shells, Palissy, 11"...2,300.00
Plaque, snake, frog, & sea creatures, Palissy, 9½" 1,500.00
Plate, Cauliflower, Etruscan, 9"..350.00
Plate, Classical, Etruscan, 9" 150.00
Plate, Leaf & Floral, Continental 75.00
Plate, oyster; cobalt & pk w/mottled center, 10".........................400.00
Plate, oyster; pk & wht, 9½"...425.00
Plate, oyster; Water Lily, Holdcroft 2,200.00
Plate, Strawberry & Grape, yel, Wedgwood, 9", NM.................450.00
Plate, Strawberry & Napkin, pk, Geo Gones, 8" 650.00
Plate, vegetable; Argenta, Wedgwood, 8½" 400.00
Platter, Bamboo & Fern, cobalt, Wardle, 13½"..........................475.00
Platter, Banana Leaf, 12" dia 400.00
Platter, Basketweave & Floral...350.00
Platter, Fern, mottled w/lav rim 350.00
Platter, Geranium & Basketweave...400.00
Platter, Morning Glory & Basketweave, cobalt center 375.00
Platter, Picket Fence & Floral..425.00
Platter, Strawberry, Ribbon & Bow..400.00
Platter, Urn & Sunflower, Samuel Lear, 13"...............................550.00
Platter, Wild Rose & rope, cobalt, 15"...450.00

Salt cellar, bearded man w/knapsack & cat on bk, Minton, 5½" 850.00
Sauce boat, Asparagus, w/undertray, French 300.00
Spittoon, Pineapple, Etruscan..650.00
Spittoon, Sunflower, English Registry mk 600.00
Tea set, Shell & Seaweed, turq, Wedgwood, 3-pc 2,250.00
Teapot, Chinaman figural, Minton, 6x7" 4,500.00
Teapot, dragon figural, tan w/brn, Wedgwood...........................500.00
Teapot, Fan & Scroll, Fielding...450.00
Teapot, Leaf, turq, Waddle...350.00
Teapot, Morning Glory, Ribbon & Bow, Fielding.......................450.00
Teapot, Owl & Fan, tricorner, 7½"...650.00
Teapot, Shell & Seaweed, Etruscan...750.00
Tray, bread; Wheat..350.00
Tray, Geranium, hdls, Etruscan...350.00
Tray, Grape, Argenta, twig hdls, Wedgwood, 13" 500.00
Tray, oak leaf, Etruscan..350.00
Tray, squirrel on leaf...500.00
Tray, wedding; Ribbon & Floral, 3 bow ft, Argenta, Wedgwood, 13"...500.00
Tureen, boar's head, Continental, 8x16" 500.00
Umbrella stand, Argenta, St Louis pattern, Wedgwood, 1881, 22"...1,100.00
Undertray, Bamboo, Minton, 10¼" 200.00
Vase, Bird in Flight, cobalt, hdls, Eureka, 9½"..........................500.00
Vase, Geranium & Basketweave, Clifton, 6¼" 200.00
Vase, parrot on branch figural, 13" 250.00
Vase, Peacock, Continental, 17½x13" 1,200.00
Vase, Queens, cobalt/yel/gr, ram's head hdls, Minton, 27½" 7,500.00

Malachite Glass

Malachite is a type of art glass that exhibits strata-like layerings in shades of green, similar to the mineral in its natural form. Some examples have an acid-etched mark of Moser/Carlsbad, usually on the base. However, it should be noted that in the past fifteen years there have been reproductions from Czechoslovakia with a paper label.

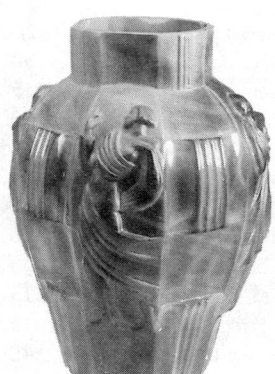

Vase, draped women and geometric panels, Ingrid, designed by Schlevogt, 9½", $400.00.

Bottle, scent; cherubs in pierced teardrop stopper, Czech, 7½"...130.00
Bottle, scent; elephant on globe, Czech, 5½" 5,225.00
Bottle, scent; Oriental figures relief, gr glass & gold metal lid, 3" ...220.00
Bottle, scent; stylized flowers & leaves, Ingrid, Czech, 6¾" 1,350.00
Box, cigarette; Deco-style nude in relief on lid, Czech, 5x4" 130.00
Vase, nudes (6) in relief, 5" 195.00

Mantel Lustres

Mantel lustres are decorative vases or candle holders made from all types of glass, often highly decorated, and usually hung with one or more rows of prisms. In the listings that follow, values are given for a pair.

Bl satin w/gilt sawtooth rim, spear prisms, late 19th C, 13½".....280.00
Bristol, bl opaque w/gold & glass jewels, prisms, 14½" 500.00
Cut crystal w/cross-cut dmns/mitres/fans, ca 1940s, 12¼" 365.00
Gr glass w/gilt & Albert prisms, 12½"....................................935.00
Ruby glass w/mc & gilt enameling, clear cut prisms, 15"............475.00
Ruby w/wht o/l, pnt florals, basal knobs, gold trim, late 1800s, 10"...450.00

Maps and Atlases

Maps are highly collectible, not only for historical value but also for their sometimes elaborate artwork, legendary information, or data that since they were printed has been proven erroneous. There are many types of maps including geographical, military, celestial, road, and railroad. Nineteenth-century maps, particularly of U.S. areas, are increasing in popularity and price. Rarity, area depicted (i.e. Texas is more sought after than North Dakota), and condition are major price factors. Our advisor for this category is Murray Hudson; he is listed in the Directory under Tennessee.

Key: hc — hand colored

Atlases

Cram's Universal..., NY, mc maps, 1888, 375-pg, EX 250.00
Cram's Unrivaled...World, Stebbins, 1887, 231 colored maps, VG.........195.00
Geo F Cram's Unrivaled Family...World, Chicago, 1883, 124-pg, EX.....235.00
HH Hardesty's Historical & Geographical Encyclopedia, 1884, 430-pg.550.00
Home & School..., AE Frye, Ginn & Co, Boston/London, 1896, 24 maps, EX ...85.00
Library...Modern Geography, Appleton/NY, 1892, 103 dbl-pg folding maps.......275.00
Lippincott Popular Family...World, Philadelphia, 1886, 26-pg, VG+ ...110.00
Mitchell's New General..., Wm M Bradley & Bro, 1885, leather bound ...750.00
New Popular Family...World, Loomis T Palmer, Chicago, 1891, 582-pg, EX...210.00
People's Illustrated & Descriptive Family...World, 1884, 366-pg, VG....225.00
Rand McNally & Co's Indexed...World, 1883, 93 maps, elephant folio 475.00
Rand McNally Standard...World, Chicago, 1890, 296-pg, EX 195.00
Winn & Hammond New Family...World, 1885, 55 color maps, sm scale, EX...150.00

Maps

Amerique Septintrionale, N Sanson, CA as island, hc, 1683, 8x12"..990.00
Antilles or W-India Island, Baldwin & Cradock, London, 1835, 13x16"...175.00
Carte de la Louisiane, Guillaume de la Haye, hc, 1752, 21x37"......1,500.00
Course of Mississipi from Balise to Fort Chartres, 1775, 46x17"......1,800.00
Cuba Sugar Plantations, Munson Steamship Lines, Cuba Review, 1930s....95.00
Dorchester & Milton MA, EJ Baker, Pendleton's Litho, 1831, 34x26"...255.00
Louisiana, Finley, Philadelphia, hc, 1826, 9¾x12¼" 230.00
Mexico/Central Am/New Granada/etc, hc, Pratt-Oakley, 1860s, 11x19"...110.00
PA Counties (4), from Atlas of PA, hc, ca 1880-1900, 18½x22½" .15.00
United States, hc, JH Young, J Finley Phila, 1826, 17x21½" 440.00
W Florida, eng from Gentleman's Magazine, 1771, 8x14⅝", EX ...140.00

Marblehead

What began as therapy for patients in a sanitarium in Marblehead, Massachusetts, has become recognized as an important part of the Arts and Crafts movement in America. Results of the early experiments under the guidance of Arthur E. Baggs in 1904 met with such success that by 1908 the pottery had been converted to a solely commercial venture. Simple vase shapes were sometimes incised with stylized animal and floral motifs or sailing ships. Some were decorated in low relief; many were plain. Simple matt glazes in soft yellow, gray, wisteria, rose, tobacco brown, and their most popular, Marblehead blue, were used alone or in combination. The Marblehead logo is distinctive — a ship with full sail and the letters 'M' and 'P.' The pottery closed in 1936.

Unless noted otherwise, all items listed below are marked and in the matt glaze.

Bookends, ship in full sail, mc on bl, rstr, 5½", pr 950.00

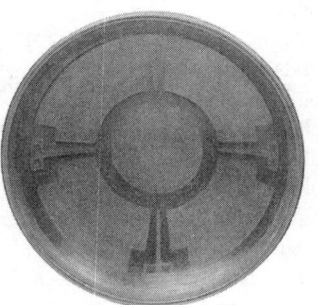

Bowl, black incised and painted geometrics on green, 8½", $2,100.00. (Photo courtesy Treadway Gallery, Inc.)

Bowl, cobalt, closed-in rim, squat, 2⅜x5" 375.00
Bowl, dk teal bl, tapered spherical form, 4½" 175.00
Bowl, geometrics, blk on gr, 8½" 2,000.00
Bowl, geometrics, dk brn on oatmeal, sgn HJ, 3½x7" 5,000.00
Bowl, linear decor, brn on gr, H Tutt, 2½" H 1,725.00
Bowl, teal-gr bands on mottled brn w/lustre, 4½" 375.00
Candlesticks, bl, orig labels, 6½", pr......................................400.00
Chamberstick, bl, saucer base, curved hdl, 8" 425.00
Plaque, Egyptian in relief, turq gloss, 7½x4⅝" 545.00
Tile, floral, mc, label, 6", +Arts & Crafts oak fr 1,000.00
Tile, medieval knight & horse emb, burnt orange, 9¼x9¼" 275.00
Tile, sailing ship, bl/brn/teal crackle, 4½" 325.00
Tiles, leaves, gr on cobalt & ochre, set of 4, ea: 9x4" 2,000.00
Vase, bl, cylindrical, 9" 850.00
Vase, bl mottle, cylindrical, mk, 4½x5" 750.00
Vase, bl mottle, cylindrical, 8¾x3¾" 850.00
Vase, bl-gray, tapered cylinder, 5½" 345.00
Vase, brn, sm angle hdls at shoulders, 7" 900.00
Vase, butterflies & flowers, bl/yel/pk/teal, 4½x4" 950.00
Vase, dk bl, oviform, flared rim, 7¾" 800.00
Vase, dk bl, ovoid, 9x4" 850.00
Vase, floral, 2-toned bl on gray, H Tutt, tapered, 6½" 4,500.00
Vase, flowers, H Tutt, swollen cylinder, 4¾".........................1,600.00
Vase, gr, cylindrical, 7" 600.00
Vase, gr mottle on gray, H Tutt, 11" 1,700.00
Vase, gray, tapered form, 6" 600.00
Vase, gray-mauve mottle, cylindrical, mk, 8¾x4" 750.00
Vase, lav, slightly-waisted cylinder, 9", NM...........................300.00
Vase, navy, sq shoulders, bl int, 4¾x6", NM.........................350.00
Vase, roses in 8 panels, brn/gr/yel, 6⅞" 12,500.00
Vase, roses repeat on mottled brn, rstr, 3½x5"....................1,100.00
Vase, trees, blk & bl on gray, H Tutt, 1905, 3⅝" 2,400.00
Vase, yel, tapered form, paper label, 6" 230.00
Vase, yel to brn, globular, 3½x5½" 650.00
Wall pocket, bl w/turq lining, 5¼" 300.00
Wall pocket, brn, ivory int, flared sides, label, 6x7" 400.00

Marbles

Marbles have been popular with children since the mid-1800s. They've been made in many types from a variety of materials. Among some of the first glass items to be produced, the earliest marbles were made from a solid glass rod broken into sections of the proper length which were placed in a tray of sand and charcoal and returned to the fire.

As they were reheated, the trays were constantly agitated until the marbles were completely round. Other marbles were made of china, pottery, steel, and natural stones. Below is a listing of the various types, along with a brief description of each.

Agates: stone marbles of many different colors — bands of color alternating with white usually encircle the marble; most are translucent.

Ballot Box: handmade (with pontils), opaque white or black, used in lodge elections.

Bloodstone: green chalcedony with red spots, a type of quartz.

China: with or without glaze, in a variety of hand-painted designs — parallel bands or bull's-eye designs most common.

Clambroth: opaque glass with outer evenly spaced swirls of one or alternating colors.

Clay: one of the most common older types; some are painted while others are not.

Comic Strip: a series of twelve machine-made marbles with faces of comic strip characters, Peltier Glass Factory, Illinois.

Crockery: sometimes referred to as Benningtons; most are either blue or brown, although some are speckled. The clay is shaped into a sphere, then coated with glaze and fired.

End of the Day: single-pontil glass marbles — the colored part often appears as a multicolored blob or mushroom cloud.

Goldstone: clear glass completely filled with copper flakes that have turned gold-colored from the heat of the manufacturing process.

Indian Swirls: usually black glass with a colored swirl appearing on the outside next to the surface, often irregular.

Latticinio Core Swirls: double-pontil marble with an inner area with net-like effects of swirls coming up around the center.

Lutz Type: glass with colored or clear bands alternating with bands which contain copper flecks.

Micas: clear or colored glass with mica flecks which reflect as silver dots when marble is turned. Red is rare.

Onionskin: spiral type which are solidly colored instead of having individual ribbons or threads, multicolored.

Peppermint Swirls: made of white opaque glass with alternating blue and red outer swirls.

Ribbon Core Swirls: double-pontil marble — center shaped like a ribbon with swirls that come up around the middle.

Rose Quartz: stone marble, usually pink in color, often with fractures inside and on outer surface.

Solid Core Swirls: double-pontil marble — middle is solid with swirls coming up around the core.

Steelies: hollow steel spheres marked with a cross where the steel was bent together to form the ball.

Sulfides: generally made of clear glass with figures inside. Rarer types have colored figures or colored glass.

Tiger Eye: stone marble of golden quartz with inclusions of asbestos, dark brown with gold highlights.

Vaseline: machine-made of yellowish-green glass with small bubbles.

Prices listed below are for marbles in near-mint condition unless noted otherwise. When size is not indicated, assume them to be of average size, ½" to 1". Polished marbles have greatly reduced values. (We do not list tinted marbles because there is no way of knowing how much color the tinting has, and intensity of color is an important worth-assessing factor.)

For a more thorough study of the subject, we recommend *Antique and Collectible Marbles, 3rd Edition*; *Machine-Made and Contemporary Marbles, 2nd Edition*; and *Big Book of Marbles, Second Edition*, all by Everett Grist (published by Collector Books); you will find his address in the Directory under Tennessee. Our advisors for this category are Robert and Stan Block; they are listed in the Directory under Connecticut.

Agate, contemporary, carnelian, 1¾" 20.00

Akro Agate, bl slag 1.00
Akro Agate, corkscrew 2.00
Akro Agate, Popeye corkscrew 25.00
Akro Agate, sparkler 45.00
Banded Opaque, gr & wht, 2" 1,200.00
Banded Opaque, red & wht, ¾" 125.00
Banded Opaque, red & wht, 1¾" 1,200.00
Banded Transparent Swirl, bl, ¾" 45.00
Banded Transparent Swirl, lt gr, 1¾" 300.00
Bennington, bl, ¾" 1.00
Bennington, bl, 1¾" 15.00
Bennington, brn, 1¾" 15.00
Bennington, fancy, ¾" 2.00
Bennington, fancy, 1¾" 40.00
China, decorated, glazed, apple, 1¾" 750.00
China, decorated, glazed, rose, 1¾" 750.00
China, decorated, glazed, wht w/geometrics, 1¾" ..75.00
China, decorated, unglazed, geometrics & flowers, ¾" 125.00
Christensen Agate, Bloodie 80.00
Christensen Agate, flame 400.00
Christensen Agate, Guinea 500.00
Christensen Agate, slag 25.00
Christensen Agate, swirl 25.00
Clambroth, opaque, bl & wht, ¾" 200.00
Clambroth, opaque, bl & wht, 1¾" 1,500.00
Comic, Andy Gump 80.00
Comic, Betty Boop 250.00
Comic, Cotes Bakery, advertising 900.00
Comic, Kayo, rare 450.00
Comic, Little Orphan Annie 150.00
Comic, Moon Mullins 300.00

Comic, set of 12, $1,500.00.

Comic, Skeezix 80.00
End of Day, bl & wht, 1¾" 450.00
Goldstone, ¾" 12.50
Indian Swirl, 1¾" 2,500.00
Indian Swirl Lutz-type, gold flakes, ¾" 1,200.00
Line Crockery, clay, 1¾" 20.00
Marble King, bumblebee 1.00
Marble King, watermelon 400.00
MF Christensen, bl opaque 250.00
MF Christensen, slag, bl 5.00
Mica, bl, ¾" 30.00
Mica, gr, 1¾" 500.00
Onionskin, w/mica, ¾" 110.00
Onionskin, w/mica, 1¾" 1,200.00
Onionskin, 16-lobe, unusual, 1¾" 3,000.00
Onionskin, ¾" 80.00
Onionskin, 4-lobe, 1¼" 450.00
Opaque Swirl, gr, ¾" 40.00
Opaque Swirl Lutz-type, bl, yel, gr, ¾" 325.00

Peltier Glass, Golden Rebel 500.00
Peltier Glass, National line 25.00
Peltier Glass, Peerless Patch 5.00
Peltier Glass, slag 15.00
Peltier Glass, Superman 150.00
Peppermint Swirl, opaque, red, wht & bl, ¾" 125.00
Peppermint Swirl, opaque, red, wht & bl, 1¾" ..2,000.00
Pottery, 1¾" 20.00
Ribbon Core Lutz-type, red, 1¾" 1,500.00
Solid Opaque, gr, 1¾" 300.00
Solid Opaque, ¾" 40.00
Sulfide, angel face w/wings, 1¾", M 1,200.00
Sulfide, baboon playing bass fiddle, 2⅛" 1,200.00
Sulfide, bear cub on all 4s, detailed, 1¼" 100.00
Sulfide, billy goat, 1½" 100.00
Sulfide, bird, 2" 100.00
Sulfide, boar, 1⅞" 165.00
Sulfide, camel, 1-hump, on grassy mound, 1½" 200.00
Sulfide, child sitting, 1¾", M 600.00
Sulfide, circus bear, 2" 140.00
Sulfide, crane w/fish, 1¾" 250.00
Sulfide, crucifix, 1¾", M 600.00
Sulfide, deer, 1¼" 175.00
Sulfide, dog howling, 1⅜", M 140.00
Sulfide, dog on grass mound, HP/3-color, pontil, 1¼" 3,500.00
Sulfide, dog w/bird in mouth, 1¾", M 400.00
Sulfide, dove, 1⅝", M 165.00
Sulfide, eagle w/closed wings, 1⅞" 200.00
Sulfide, elephant standing, sea gr glass, 1¾" ..400.00
Sulfide, elephant w/long trunk, 1¼" 140.00
Sulfide, fish, 1¾", M 175.00
Sulfide, fox, 1½", EX 130.00
Sulfide, George Washington, bust, 2⅜" 2,000.00
Sulfide, hen, 1⅛", M 150.00
Sulfide, horse rearing, 1⅞" 175.00
Sulfide, horse standing, 2", EX 130.00
Sulfide, lamb, 1¾" 125.00
Sulfide, lion, standing male, 1½" 125.00
Sulfide, Little Boy Blue, 1¾", M 450.00
Sulfide, monkey seated on drum, 1⅜", M 200.00
Sulfide, Nipper dog, 1¾", EX 200.00
Sulfide, owl w/closed wings, 1¾" 150.00
Sulfide, papoose, 1¾", M 300.00
Sulfide, parrot, 1½", EX 100.00
Sulfide, poodle on hind legs, 1⅛" 100.00
Sulfide, rabbit running, lg/offset/sm bubble, 1½", M- 110.00
Sulfide, razor-bk hog, 1½" 150.00
Sulfide, rooster, 1¾" 150.00
Sulfide, sheep grazing, 1¼" 150.00
Sulfide, squirrel standing, 1¾", EX 170.00
Sulfide, woman (Kate Greenaway), 1½" 300.00
Transitional, Leighton, 1" 1,000.00
Transitional, oxblood, ¾" 2,500.00

Marine Collectibles

Vintage tools used on sea-going vessels, lanterns, clocks, and memorabilia of all types are sought out by those who are interested in preserving the romantic genre that revolves around the life of the sea captains, their boats, and their crews; ports of call; and the lure of far-away islands. See also Steamship Collectibles; Telescopes; Scrimshaw; Tools.

Axe, boarding; wooden hdl, rusted head, ca 1800, 20" 125.00

Barometer/altimeter/thermometer/compass, Schwalb Hermanos, 2" dia ..400.00
Bell, ship's, solid brass, w/clapper, as found, 8x7¾"......................275.00
Binnacle, brass, compass mk: Baker Boston Pat Nov 1875...1875, 2".1,300.00
Binnacle, lifeboat; Sestrel, Henry Brown & Sons, 10½x7" dia ...185.00
Blubber spade, iron, 18½" unmtd 175.00
Book, Yankee Whaler, Clifford Ashley, 1926, VG 300.00
Cannon, CI on wheels, 11¼" bbl, 7¼" H, EX 150.00
Chest, grpt w/2 runners, iron strap hinges, lift hdls, till, EX........400.00
Chronometer, Hamilton Watch...PA Model 22, brass gimball, 5¾x6" sq ...800.00
Chronometer, WM Sheppard Liverpool in silvered dial, EX.......850.00
Chronometer/watch, Longines, 56-hr up/down indicator, mahog case..950.00
Clock, ship's bell; Chelsea, 6" dial, EX 425.00
Compass, dry card; brass, 2" dia, VG 200.00
Desk, captain's lap; MOP inlaid rosewood, 19th C, 9x14", VG ..500.00
Desk, captain's; many symbol inlays, 3 drws, 19x17x9½", VG ...1,700.00
Diving helmet, copper, 3 lights, carrying hdl, Russian, EX 1,300.00
Gauge, air pressure; Ashcroft Mfg, brass, 5½" dia 50.00
Globe, cased star globe, Russian origin, ca 1975, dvtl case.........425.00
Gun, harpoon, solid iron, CC Brand Mfg, ca 1850s, EX 850.00
Harpoon, dbl flute, hand-wrought iron, EX 200.00
Harpoon, dbl flute w/reverse withers, cleaned, 31½"..................850.00
Harpoon, Provincetown type, iron, 18½" 325.00
Hook, blubber; wrought iron, curved wood hdl, Am, 1850s, 44½" ..150.00
Instrument, Dalton Dead Reckoning Computer...G, w/strap, 6½" ...300.00
Instrument, plotting; L Morgan & Son...NY, wooden, Pat 1869, 17x2¼" ..150.00
Knife, diver's; Siebe Gorman & Co, EX in brass scabbard w/belt ..400.00
Knife, whaler's; steel blade, wood hdl w/brass wheel inlays, 7" 350.00
Knot board, red/wht/bl shield w/stars & stripes, 12x14½"...........110.00
Lance, whale keeling, sound but used & crusted, 1850s, 60".......850.00
Lantern, anchor; Perko, brass, clear ribbed lens, 13" 140.00
Lantern, bulkhead; brass, polished, EX 55.00
Lantern, masthead; brass, bl/red/clear lenses, 9", VG 225.00
Lantern, masthead; National Marine Lamp Co NY, 9" 110.00
Lantern, masthead; Wilcox & Crittendon Conn, brass, 6½" 110.00
Lanterns, brass & port; Perco, brass, 18"+hdl, pr 650.00
Microbarograph, Belfort Instrument...MD, 1950s, w/manual, NM....225.00
Model, sailing ship Whippet of 1773, fully rigged, well made 325.00
Name board, orig red/blk/gold pnt, 120x10", VG....................1,300.00
Octant, dbl-T, Wood Liverpool, EX in case w/2 eyepcs..............500.00
Octant, Spencer, Browning & Rust London, ebony & ivory, 1800s, 14" ...525.00
Octant, Vda de J Rosel Barcelona, brass w/ivory scales, scarce ...650.00
Pistol, flare; Sculler Signal Pistol, solid brass, EX 200.00
Protractor, Cole Course by Marine Compass Co, 1907, EX in case....80.00
Quadrant, H Duren NY, ebony/ivory/brass, ca 1930, 13", +case .700.00
Rudder indicator, blk & gold, w/wire hanger in bk, 13x14" 200.00
Rule, rolling; cast solid brass, 18x2½", +dvtl case 200.00
Sextant, C Frodsham London, ebony/ivory/brass, 1830-29, 11", +case...2,500.00
Sextant, E&GW Blunt NY, 19th C, EX in case 1,700.00
Sextant, J&I Hardy London, brass lattice fr, polished, 1810, 12"...950.00
Sextant, Spencer Browning & Rust London, dbl fr, 1800s, EX in case ...1,500.00
Sextant, TJ Williams Cardiff, brass, polished, dvtl case..............600.00
Sextant, US Navy Bunav-Mark II David White...Wis, EX in case ..300.00
Shears, sail maker's; Newark NJ mk, 13¼", EX.............................70.00
Sundial, Augsburg, brass, 8-sided, scalloped shoulders, 18th C...1,600.00
Telegraph, engine room; A Robinson...Liverpool...1760, 17¾" dia ...325.00
Timer, sand/glass, trn wood columns, 2-pc glass, 7", EX 2,000.00
Trumpet, speaking; brass, 19", VG 480.00
Wheel, oak w/brass fittings, Am, ca 1800, 41" dia.......................900.00
Wheel, wood w/brass hub, 2 thin inlays, pegged, 72", VG 950.00

Martin Bros.

The Martin Bros. were studio potters who worked from 1873 until 1914, first at Fulham and later at London and Southall. There were four brothers, each of whom excelled in their particular area. Robert, known as Wallace, was an experienced stonecarver. He modeled a series of grotesque bird and animal figural caricatures. Walter was the potter, responsible for throwing the larger vases on the wheel, firing the kiln, and mixing the clay. Edwin, an artist of stature, preferred more naturalistic forms of decoration. His work was often incised or had relief designs of seaweed, florals, fish, and birds. The fourth brother, Charles, was their business manager. Their work was incised with their names, place of production, and letters and numbers indicating month and year.

Though figural jars continue to command the higher prices, decorated vases and bowls have increased a great deal in value. Our advisor for this category is David Rago; he is listed in the Directory under New Jersey.

Bird vessel, grotesque, lg beak, gr/bl/blk, 1897, 10x8" 12,000.00
Figurine, imp singing w/music book, dk brn, on enamel stand, 4x4"..1,500.00

Humidor, bird figural with droopy beak and sleepy eyes, R.W. Martin..., on stand: 11½x5½", $9,500.00. (Photo courtesy David Rago)

Jar, impish creature w/brn scales, w/lid, 5½x3½".......................6,500.00
Jug, creature w/open mouth, tail hdl, dk brn/bl, rpr, RW Martin, 5" ..1,600.00
Jug, incised sea reptiles, indigo & amber, label, 9¾x5", NM ...1,600.00
Paperweight, lizard flying, blk/gr/beige, sm rstr, 2¼x4" 1,000.00
Pitcher, incised fish, brn on brn & gray, spherical, 1886, 2½x3" ...500.00
Pitcher, 2-faced, gunmetal brn, RW Martin, 6¼x6" 2,500.00
Pitcher, 2-faced, gunmetal brn/caramel mottle, RW Martin, 4½", EX...2,600.00
Vase, bud; incised fish, gr/cobalt on gray, line, 1913, 6x2", NM..850.00
Vase, incised fish, brn on gr, 1904, 2¼x1¾" 500.00

Mary Gregory

Mary Gregory glass, for reasons that remain obscure, is the namesake of a Boston and Sandwich Glass Company employee who worked for the company for only two years in the mid-1800s. Although no evidence actually exists to indicate that glass of this type was even produced there, the fine colored or crystal ware decorated with figures of children in white enamel is commonly referred to as Mary Gregory. The glass, in fact, originated in Europe and was imported into this country where it was copied by several eastern glasshouses. It was popular from the mid-1800s until the turn of the century. It is generally accepted that examples with all-white figures were made in the U.S.A., while gold-trimmed items and those with children having tinted faces or a small amount of color on their clothing are European. Though amethyst is rare, examples in cranberry command the higher prices. Blue ranks next; and green, amber, and clear items are worth the least. Watch for new glass decorated with screen-printed children and a minimum of hand painting. The screen effect is easily detected with a magnifying glass.

Box, dresser; bl, girl w/bouquet, sm..150.00

Pitcher, cranberry, maiden w/flower baskets, ribbed, 8" **275.00**
Pitcher, gr, boy among fern-like leaves, cylindrical, low hdl, 8½" ...**250.00**
Pitcher, gr, lady w/flower bowl, ribbed, reeded hdl, water sz **225.00**
Pitcher, tankard, gr, girl w/butterfly net, gold rim, 6¼" **375.00**
Tray, calling card; bl, girl w/flower garland, 6½x8½" **400.00**
Tumbler, gr, boy chasing bird, 3¾x2¾" **75.00**
Vase, blk, boy w/stick toy, shouldered, ca 1850s, 13" **385.00**
Vase, gr, boy & girl & birds in forest, fluted rim, 9x7" **185.00**
Vase, pk satin, girl among flowers & butterflies, stick neck, 9" ...**600.00**

Mason's Ironstone

In 1813 Charles J. Mason was granted a patent for a process said to 'improve the quality of English porcelain.' The new type of ware was in fact ironstone which Mason decorated with colorful florals and scenics, some of which reflected the Oriental taste. Although his business failed for a short time in the late 1840s, Mason re-established himself and continued to produce dinnerware, tea services, and ornamental pieces until about 1852, at which time the pottery was sold to Francis Morley. Ten years later, Geo. L. and Taylor Ashworth became owners. Both Morley and the Ashworths not only used Mason's molds and patterns but often his mark as well. Because the quality and the workmanship of the later wares do not compare with Mason's earlier product, collectors should take care to distinguish one from the other. Consult a good book on marks to be sure. The Wedgwood Company now owns the rights to the Mason patterns and is reproducing Vista. Note: Blue Vista is generally valued at 15% to 20% above prices for pink/red.

Bowl, Blue Pheasants, bl, 1813-25 mk, 1¼x7¾" **150.00**
Bowl, Mandarin, mc on wht, scalloped, 1818 mk, 1¼x11x7¾" ..**475.00**
Bowl, Nango, mc on wht, scalloped, 1812-25 mk, 11¼x7" **400.00**
Bowl, Vista, red, 1890-1900 mk, 2½x8" **150.00**
Bowl, Vista, red, 1890-1900 mk, 2¼x10¾x6½" **100.00**
Bowl, Vista, red, 6-sided rim, 1925-30 mk, 2¼x9" **175.00**
Box, Strathmore, mc, 1925-30 mk, 2x5¼x4¾" **275.00**
Butter dish, Vista, red, rectangular, 1925-30 mk, 7x3" **175.00**
Butter dish, Vista, red, 1925-30 mk, 5½" dia **150.00**
Cake plate, Vista, red, 1890-1900 mk, 12½" **275.00**
Casserole, American Marine, brn, Ashworth, 13¾x7" **150.00**
Cheese keeper, Vista, red, 1925-30 mk, 3¾" H lid, 7" tray **150.00**
Creamer, Vista, red, bulbous, 1925-30 mk, 3½" **60.00**
Creamer, Vista, red, late 1800s, 4x4" **50.00**
Egg cup, Strathmore, mc, 1925-30 mk, 3½x2½" **90.00**
Ginger jar, Pagoda Willow, red & wht, w/lid, 5x4¾" **80.00**
Jug, Classical Motif, mc, Ashworth, ca 1862+, 5x4" **175.00**
Jug, Classical Motif, mc, Ashworth, 6½" **225.00**
Jug, Classical Motif, mc, bulbous, Ashworth, 7¼x5½", NM **300.00**
Jug, Colored Bandana, ca 1840 blk printed mk, 5" **350.00**
Jug, Fountain Landscape, mc, 1890-1900 mauve mk, 4¾x5½" **80.00**
Jug, Fruit Basket, 8-sided, 1925-30 mk, 5½x6" **125.00**
Jug, Japan, mc, branch hdl, 1840 mk, 3⅛x3½" **225.00**
Jug, Japan, mc, serpent hdl, octagonal, unmk, ca 1840, 4¼" **150.00**
Jug, Pagoda Willow, bl & wht, 1890-1900 mk, 5x5" **90.00**
Jug, Spraying Fountain, red, 8-sided, 1890-1900, 6¼x6½" **125.00**
Jug, Vista, bl, 8-sided, 1925-30 mk, 4½x3¾" **100.00**
Jug, Vista, brn, 8-sided, 1925-30 mk, 7x5½" **125.00**
Jug, Vista, red, 8-sided, serpent hdl, 1925-30 mk, 6¼" **200.00**
Jug, Vista, red, 8-sided, 1890-1900 mk, 5½x4½" **150.00**
Jug, Vista, red, 8-sided, 1890-1900 mk, 6¼x5½" **200.00**
Jug, Vista, red, 8-sided, 1925-30 mk, 6¾x7¾" **250.00**
Plate, Bandana & Vase, Ashworth, ca 1862+, 6 for **325.00**
Plate, dinner; Vista, red, 1890-1900 mk, 10½", 3 for................**175.00**
Plate, Flying Bird, blk w/mc, 1890s mk, 9½", 6 for...................**150.00**

Plate, Vista, red, 1925-30 mk, 10¾", 4 for **100.00**
Platter, Vista, red, Made in England, 15¼x12¼" **100.00**
Relish, Landscape/Floral, bl & wht, Ashworth, 1873-1890 mk, 8½"...**80.00**
Sugar bowl, Vista, red, bulbous, 1925-30 mk, 4½" **90.00**
Sugar bowl, Vista, red, 1890-1900, 5¼x6" **100.00**
Tea caddy, Pagoda Willow, bl & wht, 1890-1900 mk, 6½" **100.00**
Teapot, Vista, red, 1890-1900 mk, 6¼" **300.00**
Teapot, Vista, red, 1925-30 mk, 7x9" **250.00**
Toast holder, Regency/Indian Grasshopper, mc, 1925-30 mk, 4¾"..**150.00**
Toothpick holder, Vista, red, 1890-1900 mk, 2¼" **90.00**
Tureen, sauce; Vista, bl, 1890-1900 mk, 8½", +8¾" underplate .**200.00**
Tureen, soup; Floral Medallion, mc, 1835 brn mk, 11½x13¼", EX .**500.00**

Massier

Clement Massier was a French artist-potter who in 1881 established a workshop at Golfe Juan, France, where he experimented with metallic lustre glazes. (One of his pupils was Jacques Sicardo, who brought the knowledge he had gained through his association with Massier to the Weller Pottery Company in Zanesville, Ohio.) The lustre lines developed by Massier incorporated nature themes with allover decorations of foliage or flowers on shapes modeled in the Art Nouveau style. The ware was usually incised with the Massier name, his initials, or the location of the pottery. Massier died in 1917.

Charger, Mediterranean bay scene with pines, gold and burgundy lustre, 13" diameter, $1,300.00.

Pitcher, satyr portrait, draped nude hdl, metallic lustre, 10" **1,495.00**
Vase, copper to gr to purple w/snake hdls, swollen cylinder, 9½"..**1,035.00**
Vase, stylized flowers, lustre/metallic, #100, 8¼" **950.00**
Vase, thistles, gourd shape, ca 1900, 7" **365.00**

Match Holders

John Walker, an English chemist, invented the match more than one hundred years ago, quite by accident. Walker was working with a mixture of potash and antimony, hoping to make a combustible that could be used to fire guns. The mixture adhered to the end of the wooden stick he had used for stirring. As he tried to remove it by scraping the stick on the stone floor, it burst into flames. The invention of the match was only a step away! From that time to the present, match holders have been made in amusing figural forms as well as simple utilitarian styles and in a wide range of materials. Both table-top and wallhanging models were made — all designed to keep matches conveniently at hand. The prices in this category are very volatile due to increased interest in this field and the fact that so many can be classified as a cross or dual collectible.

Caution: As prices for originals continue to climb, so do the number of reproductions. Know your dealer. Our advisor for this category is Ron Damaska; he is listed in the Directory under Pennsylvania. See also Advertising.

Advertising, Apollinaris Table Water, ceramic, striker neck, 3x4½"..**80.00**
Blk Forest, cvd wood, stag/weapons/pouch (for matches), 11½x5" ...**345.00**

Brass, coat of arms/flags/helmet/2 drums (holders), heavy 85.00
Brass, dog at window 65.00
Brass, Nouveau hammered design, J Hoffmann, ca 1904, 5" 615.00
Bronze, sentry w/musket, caped uniform & kepi, 19th C, EX 135.00
Bsk, boy w/butterfly net..50.00
Bsk, monkey in bow tie, hat at ft, striker on head, Germany 225.00
Bsk, street urchin on stump smoking cigar, pastels, 7½" 115.00
China, gaudy decor, wall mt, Japan..25.00
China chamberstick w/matchbox holder, Dresden.......................110.00
CI, admiral w/flags/cannons/stars/etc emb, ca 1870s-80s, 6x4"....250.00
CI, arched top, hinged lid, striker plate, hangs, 7x4x2⅛".............25.00
CI, eagle top, florals surround 2 dogs, wall hanging, 10x6" 85.00
CI, openwork scroll bk, 2 urn-shape holders, 1867, 5x7½x1¼"....65.00
CI, self-closing, Pat 12/20/1864, rare sm version............................90.00
CI, urn w/hdls, on sq saucer base, 3" 75.00
Clear glass, owl w/silver rim, w/striker, 2¾" 495.00
Compo, Indian in full headdress, mc pnt, 7½x4⅞x3½" 50.00
Glass, Miss Liberty's head, 4½", NM..100.00
Metal, hunting dog & tree stump, old bronze pnt, 2½x4½" 160.00
NP iron, hatchet, wall hanging, 1908..40.00
Pot metal, elk & stump, VG pnt, 4x6¼" 80.00
Redware, acorns & leaves, wht & gr, around pocket, 7" dia........165.00
Spelter, Dickens-like character w/oversz top hat extended, 5¾"....250.00
Tin, crest w/crimped & cut-out decor, pnt traces, 4x7", EX..........32.00
Walnut wood bbl w/leaded mechanical base, 5½x4¾x3" 85.00
Yellow ware, man leaning by stone well, early 1900s, 8x5½" 80.00

Match Safes

Before the invention of the safety match in 1855, matches were carried in small pocket-sized containers because they ignited so easily. Aptly called match safes, these containers were used extensively until about 1920, when cigarette lighters became widely available. Some incorporated added features (hidden compartments, cigar cutters, etc.), some were figural, and others were used by retail companies as advertising giveaways. They were made from every type of material, but silverplated styles abound. Both the advertising and common silverplated cases generally fall in the $50.00 to $100.00 price range.

Beware of reproductions and fakes; there are many currently on the market. Know your dealer. Our advisor for this category is Ron Damaska; he is listed in the Directory under Pennsylvania. See also Advertising.

Advertising, Phoenix Brewer, St. Louis, embossed brass, hinged lid, 3x1¼", EX, $220.00.

Advertising, Arm & Hammer, gutta percha..................................125.00
Brass, built-in striker on side, screw-on lid, 2½x2⅛" 45.00
Brass, Rober Bicycle advertising, 1½"..65.00
Brass, Victorian man, hinged hat, 3"..85.00
Brass w/overall emb florals, interior tip cutter, 2¼" 35.00
Celluloid, domino figural, 1⅛x1⅞" 165.00

Celluloid, Neverslips Horseshoes..125.00
MOP, Indian chief eng, brass mts..95.00
NP brass turtle form w/button latch, 2⅞x1⅝" 200.00
SP, Nouveau floral emb, EX 75.00
Sterling, Nouveau Cipid kissing sleeping maiden, ca 1900 ....200.00
Sterling, plain, w/monogram, 2½" 80.00
Sterling, sea nymph emb 95.00
Tin, White Star Line, 4-stack steamer, ⅞x2¼x1½", VG 265.00
Tin & NP brass, Nouveau reserves of deer & Gibson girl, 2¼".....40.00

Mauchline Ware

Mauchline ware is the generic name for small, well-made, and useful wooden souvenirs and giftware from Mauchline, Scotland, and nearby locations. It was made from the early nineteenth century into the 1930s. Snuff boxes were among the earliest items, and tea caddies soon followed. From the 1830s on, needlework, stationery, domestic, and cosmetic items were made by the thousands. Today, needlework items are the most plentiful and range from boxes of all sizes made to hold supplies to tiny bodkins and buttons. Napkin rings, egg cups, vases, and bowls are just a few of the domestic items available.

The wood most commonly used in the production of Mauchline ware was sycamore. Finishes vary. Early items were hand decorated with colored paints or pen and ink. By the 1850s, perhaps even earlier, transfer ware was produced, decorated with views associated with the place of purchase. These souvenir items were avidly bought by travelers for themselves as well as for gifts. Major exhibitions and royal occasions were also represented on transferware. An alternative decorating process was initiated during the mid-1860s whereby actual photos replaced the transfers. Because they were finished with multiple layers of varnish, many examples found today are still in excellent condition.

Tartan ware's distinctive decoration was originally hand painted directly on the wood with inks, but in the 1840s machine-made paper in authentic Tartan designs became available. Except for the smallest items, each piece was stamped with the Tartan name. The Tartan decoration was applied to virtually the entire range of Mauchline ware, and because it was favored by Queen Victoria, it became widely popular. Collectors still value Tartan ware above other types of decoration, with transferware being their second choice. Other types of Mauchline decorations include Fern ware and Black Lacquer with floral or transfer decorations.

When cleaning any Mauchline item, extreme care should be used to avoid damaging the finish! Mauchline ware has been reproduced for at least twenty-five years, especially some of the more popular pieces and finishes. Collectors should study the older items for comparison and to learn about the decorating and manufacturing processes.

Album, photo view & H Rothe quote on cover, 6 dbl-sided pgs, 1880s...135.00
Box, Ballochmyle Bridge/poem, hinged book form, 3¾" L..........150.00
Box, card; Chicester Cross medallion, cards border, 3½x4½" 120.00
Box, Dunkeled Birnam vignettes, 1½x3¾x2½", NM................127.50
Box, Edinburgh Castle From Grassmarket, 2x3" dia 130.00
Box, Katerskill Falls...NY, blk transfer, 1900s, 1¼x4x2¼" 132.00
Box, match; Summit of Mt Washington, 2⅜x1½" dia 120.00
Box, money; St Peter's Church Bournemouth, ca 1900, 1½x3x2".110.00
Box, photo lid w/harbor view, 2x4¼x2¾", EX............................145.00
Box, pill, Old Orchard House ME, 1¾" 115.00
Box, postal rates/ruler/calendar, Weyjmouth from the North scene, 9" L...170.00
Box, Rebekah at the Well, Tartan Ware, 2x7¼x2¼" 125.00
Box, ribbon; Whitehall From Ferry Cottage, ca 1900, 2x2" 160.00
Box, sewing; All Souls College Oxford, w/thimble & spool, 1900..115.00
Box, sewing; Jacob's Ladder, Mt Washington NH, jug form, EX .150.00
Box, sewing; Sir Walter Scott's Monument, empty beehive form, 1¾"...130.00
Box, stamp; Block Island RI, 2½" L...155.00

Box, stamp; Tam O'Shanter & Souter Johnny, worn, 1¼x2½x1¾" ..160.00
Box, thread; bluebirds & bamboo, teapot form, EX 115.00
Compass, Bunker Hill Monument, 2⅜" dia 95.00
Cradle, doll; Shakespeare's House scene, 4½x3½x2" 110.00
Egg timer, Mt Nonotuck MA, ca 1900, 3⅛" 150.00
Eraser holder, Ann Hathaway's Cottage...Avon, 1¾x1¼" 90.00
Glove stretcher, Melrose Abbey, ca 1890, 7" 100.00
Letter opener, Lift, Folkestone on blade, 12½x1½" 70.00
Letter rack, Front & Almondry Mount St Bernard's Abbey........110.00
Mirror, Prince Charlie Tartan Ware, 3½x2¾", VG 150.00
Napkin ring, Lighthouse View in MA 135.00
Page turner, Sarasota Springs, Grand Union Hotel, 9¼x1"..........60.00
Pincushion, Fern Ware, cylindrical, 1⅞x2" 110.00
Pincushion, MacBeth Tartan, ca 1860, 1½" dia 110.00
Pincushion, Pearl House, Orr's Island ME, drum form, 3 ball ft, 2½" ..95.00
Plate, New Hampshire transfer scenes on wood, late 1880s, 7"...185.00
Tape measure, Cromer town view, bbl form, 2" 80.00
Tape measure, Pearl House, Orr's Island ME, bell shape, 2" 130.00
Thimble holder, Burns' Monument, w/silver thimble, 1x1¾x1¼"..135.00
Vase, McDonald, Tartan Ware, old rpr, 4¼" 160.00
Watch stand, Sea Wall Parade Bridlington Quay, 8-sided, EX 165.00
Whistle, Wm Shakespeare, Shakespeare's Mont, Stratford on Avon, 3"....132.50

McCoy

The third generation McCoy potter in the Roseville, Ohio, area was Nelson, who with the aid of his father, J.W., established the Nelson McCoy Sanitary Stoneware Company in 1910. They manufactured churns, jars, jugs, poultry fountains, and foot warmers. By 1925 they had expanded their wares to include majolica jardinieres and pedestals, umbrella stands, and cuspidors, and an embossed line of vases and small jardinieres in a blended brown and green matt glaze. From the late '20s through the mid-'40s, a utilitarian stoneware was produced, some of which was glazed in the soft blue and white so popular with collectors today. They also used a dark brown mahogany color and a medium to dark green, both in a high gloss. In 1933 the firm became known as the Nelson McCoy Pottery Company. They expanded their facilities in 1940 and began to make the novelty art-ware, cookie jars, and dinnerware that today are synonymous with 'McCoy.' More than two hundred cookie jars of every theme and description were produced.

More than a dozen different marks have been used by the company; nearly all incorporate the name 'McCoy,' although some of the older items were marked 'NM USA.' For further information consult *The Collector's Encyclopedia of McCoy Pottery* (with recently updated values) by Sharon and Bob Huxford; or *McCoy Pottery Collector's Reference & Value Guide, Vol. I* and *II*, by Margaret Hanson, Craig Nissen, and Bob Hanson (all published by Collector Books). Also available is *Sanfords Guide to McCoy Pottery* by Martha and Steve Sanford. (Mr. Sanford is listed in the Directory under California.)

Alert! Stimulated by the high prices commanded by desirable cookie jars, a broad spectrum of 'new' cookie jars are flooding the marketplace in three categories: 1) Manufacturers have expanded their lines with exciting new designs to attract the collector market. 2) Limited editions and artist-designed jars have proliferated. 3) Reproductions, signed and unsigned, have pervaded the market, creating uncertainty among new collectors and inexperienced dealers. After McCoy closed its doors in the late 1980s, an entrepreneur in Tennessee tried (and succeeded for nearly a decade) to adopt the McCoy Pottery name and mark. This company reproduced old McCoy designs as well as some classic designs of other defunct American potteries, signing their wares 'McCoy' with a mark which very closely approximated the old McCoy mark. Legal action finally put a stop to this practice, though since then this compa-

ny has used other fraudulent marks as well: Brush-McCoy (the compound name was never used on Brush cookie jars) and B.J. Hull.

Note: At the present time, the cookie jar market is somewhat soft, so consider our values to be high end.

Cookie Jars

Animal Crackers 100.00
Apollo Age, minimum value 1,000.00
Apple, 1950-64 ....50.00
Apple, 1967 ....60.00
Asparagus 50.00
Astronauts, from $750 to 850.00
Bananas 125.00
Barnum's Animals 250.00
Baseball Boy 250.00
Basket of Eggs 40.00
Basket of Potatoes 40.00
Bear, cookie in vest, no 'Cookies', from $75 to 85.00
Black Kettle, w/immovable bail, HP flowers 40.00
Blue Willow Pitcher 75.00
Bobby Baker 65.00
Bugs Bunny, cylinder, from $165 to 200.00
Burlap Bag, red bird on lid 50.00
Caboose 150.00
Chairman of the Board (+) 550.00
Chef, donut (+) 250.00
Christmas Tree, minimum value 800.00
Churn, 2 bands 35.00
Circus Horse, blk 250.00
Clown Bust (+) 75.00
Clown in Barrel, yel, bl or gr 85.00
Clyde Dog 250.00
Coca-Cola Can 100.00
Coca-Cola Jug 85.00
Coffee Grinder 45.00
Coffee Mug 45.00
Colonial Fireplace 85.00
Cookie Bank, 1961 ....165.00
Cookie Boy 225.00
Cookie Jug, dbl loop 35.00
Cookie Jug, single loop, 2-tone gr rope 35.00
Cookie Jug, w/cork stopper, brn & wht 40.00
Cookie Log, squirrel finial, from $35 to 45.00
Cookie Mug 45.00
Cookie Pot, 1964 ....40.00
Cookie Safe 65.00
Corn, row of standing ears, yel or wht, 1977 ....85.00
Corn, single ear 175.00
Covered Wagon 95.00
Cylinder, w/red flowers 45.00
Dalmatians in Rocking Chair (+) 275.00
Dog on Basketweave, from $75 to 90.00
Drum, red 90.00
Duck on Basketweave, from $75 to 90.00
Dutch Boy 45.00
Dutch Girl, boy on reverse, rare 250.00
Eagle on Basket, from $35 to 50.00
Early American Chest (Chiffoniere) 85.00
Elephant 200.00
Elephant w/Split Trunk, rare, minimum value 300.00
Engine, blk 175.00
Flowerpot, plastic flower on top.......................................500.00
Football Boy (+), from $245 to...275.00

Forbidden Fruit, from $65 to 90.00
Freddy Gleep (+), minimum value 500.00
Friendship 7 ....200.00
Frog on Stump 75.00
Frontier Family 55.00
Fruit in Bushel Basket, from $65 to 80.00
Gingerbread Boy 75.00
Globe 275.00
Grandfather Clock 90.00
Granny 120.00
Hamm's Bear (+) 225.00
Happy Face 80.00
Hen on Nest, from $85 to 95.00
Hobby Horse (+), from $125 to 150.00
Hocus Rabbit 45.00
Honey Bear, rustic glaze, from $65 to 80.00
Hot Air Balloon 40.00
Ice Cream Cone 45.00
Indian, brn (+) 350.00
Indian, majolica 400.00

Jack-O'-Lantern, $600.00.
(Photo courtesy Joyce Roerig)

Kangaroo, bl 300.00
Kettle, bronze, 1961 ....40.00
Kissing Penguins, from $100 to 125.00
Kitten on Basketweave 90.00
Kittens (2) on Low Basket, minimum value 600.00
Koala Bear 85.00
Kookie Kettle, blk 35.00
Lamb on Basketweave 90.00
Leprechaun, minimum value (+) 1,800.00
Little Clown 75.00
Lollipops 80.00
Mac Dog 95.00
Mammy, Cookies on base, wht (+) 150.00
Milk Can, Spirit of '76 ....45.00
Modern 65.00
Monk 50.00
Mother Goose 175.00
Mouse on Clock 40.00
Mr & Mrs Owl, from $75 to 90.00
Mushroom on Stump 55.00
Nursery, decal of Humpty Dumpty, from $70 to 80.00
Orange 55.00
Owl 50.00
Pear, 1952 ....85.00
Pears on Basketweave 70.00
Penguin, yel or aqua, from $175 to 200.00
Pepper, yel 40.00
Picnic Basket, from $65 to 75.00
Pig, winking 300.00
Pineapple 80.00

Pineapple, Modern 90.00
Popeye Cylinder 200.00
Potbelly Stove, blk 30.00
Puppy, w/sign 85.00
Quaker Oats, rare, minimum value 700.00
Raggedy Ann 110.00
Red Barn, cow in door, rare, minimum value 350.00
Rooster, wht, 1970-1974 ....60.00
Round w/HP Leaves 45.00
Sad Clown 85.00
Snoopy on Doghouse (+), mk United Features Syndicate 200.00
Snow Bear, from $65 to 75.00
Stagecoach, minimum value 800.00
Strawberry, 1955-57 ....65.00
Teapot, 1972 ....60.00
Tepee, slat top 350.00
Tepee, str top (+) 300.00
Tilt Pitcher, blk w/roses 50.00
Timmy Tortoise 45.00
Tomato 60.00
Touring Car 100.00
Traffic Light 50.00
Tudor Cookie House 125.00
Turkey, gr, rare color 300.00
Turkey, natural colors 250.00
Upside Down Bear, panda 50.00
WC Fields 200.00
Wedding Jar 90.00
Windmill 100.00
Woodsy Owl, from $250 to 300.00
Wren House, side lid 175.00
Yosemite Sam, cylinder 200.00

Miscellaneous

Ashtray, bird at side of 5-petal flower, from $20 to 25.00
Basket, leaves & berries, wht, hanging, 6", from $25 to ...35.00
Beverage server, Sunburst gold, mk, 1957, 11", from $60 to ..80.00
Bookends, lily form, gr w/decor, 1948, 5x5½", pr, from $85 to ..125.00
Bookends, rearing horse, USA mk, 1940s, 8", pr, from $80 to ..100.00
Bookends, rearing horses, wht w/gold trim, unmk, 1942, 8", pr ..125.00
Candle holder, leaves, gr to brn, scalloped rim, unmk, 1930s 25.00
Candy boat, gondola shape, Sunburst gold, mk, 1957, 3½x11½" .65.00
Centerpiece, antelope on base w/4 openings, unmk, 1955, 8½x12" ..275.00
Dog feeder, Man's Best Friend His Dog, brn, yel or gr, 1930s, 7½" ..60.00
Ferner, Hobnail, pastel, NM mk, 1940s, 5½", from $20 to 30.00
Flower bowl ornament, peacock, wht, unmk, 4¾", from $40 to 60.00
Flower holder, elephant, unmk, 1490s, 5½x6½", from $20 to 25.00
Flower holder, Hands of Friendship (Praying Hands), NM mk, 3x4" ..50.00
Flower holder, swan, Sunburst Gold, NM mk, 3½x4¾", from $30 to ..40.00
Flower holder, turtle, yel or rose, 2x4¼", from $60 to 80.00
Jardiniere, Acorn, gr & brn matt, unmk, 4½", from $18 to 25.00
Jardiniere, blended glazes, 7½", from $30 to 50.00
Jardiniere, Brocade, cherry & gr, mk, 1956, 6½" sq, from $25 to ..30.00
Jardiniere, Hobnail, pastel matt, unmk, 1940s, 6", from $50 to ..50.00
Jardiniere, Holly, brn onyx, unmk, 1930s, 10½", from $85 to ...100.00
Jardiniere & pedestal, Basketweave, gr or wht, 8½", 12½" 250.00
Jardiniere & pedestal, Holly, brn & gr, 8½", 12½", from $200 to ..250.00
Matchbox holder, wht w/bl speckles, mk, 1970s, 5¾x3¼" 40.00
Oil jar, various glazes, mk NM, 4", ea from $20 to 25.00
Paperweight, baseball glove, football or basketball, 1940s, ea $85 to ..100.00
Pitcher, ball jug, glossy, unmk, 1950s, 7½", from $35 to 45.00
Planter, baseball glove, brn spray w/yel or gr, unmk, 1957, 6x6" .135.00
Planter, clown & pig, wht w/HP details, mk, 1951, 8½" L 75.00

Planter, cornucopia; McCoy mk, 1940s, 8", from $30 to **40.00**
Planter, Dragonfly, pastel matt, unmk, 1940s, 5¾", from $40 to.....**50.00**
Planter, fawn, opening in bk, pastel, NM mk, 1940s, 4½x5".........**50.00**
Planter, lamb, wht w/pk or bl pnt, mk, 1953, 7¼x8½" **50.00**
Planter, Mary Ann Shoe, pastel, NM mk, 1940s, 5" L, from $20 to...**35.00**
Planter, rabbit w/carrot, wht or yel w/cold pnt, mk, 1950s, 7¼" ...**90.00**
Planter, wheelbarrow, wht, gr or yel, mk, 1955, 7x10½", from $60 to ..**75.00**
Sand jar, Sphinx, wht, 1930s, 16", from $450 to..........................**600.00**
Spoon rest, penguin, yel w/decor, mk, 1953, 7x5", from $75 to ..**100.00**
Stretch animal, hound (Dachshund), pastel matt, unmk, 1940s, 5x8¼" ..**125.00**
Stretch animal, lion, pastel matt, unmk, 1940s, 7½x5½", $175 to ..**225.00**
Tankard, gr w/emb grapes, old mk, 8½", from $60 to.....................**75.00**
Teapot, daisies, brn to gr to wht, mk, 1940s, from $40 to **50.00**
Vase, Blossomtime, rectangular, 1946, 8", from $45 to **55.00**
Vase, Butterfly, std color (not including coral), hdls, USA mk, 10" ..**125.00**
Vase, cowboy boots, blk w/decor, mk, 1956, 6x7", from $40 to **50.00**
Vase, fruit & basketweave, gr & brn matt, unmk, 8", from $40 to...**60.00**
Vase, leaves & berries, gr, waisted cylinder, unmk, 1930s, 14" **100.00**
Vase, onyx, short neck, hdls, 1930s, 8", from $50 to......................**65.00**
Vase, Uncle Sam, various glossy colors, McCoy mk, 1940s, 7½" ..**60.00**
Vase, wht w/lizard hdls, 9", from $85 to **110.00**
Vase, Wild Rose, pk w/yel rose, mk, 1952, 4½", from $50 to **60.00**
Wall pocket, Butterfly, gr, wht or yel, NM mk, 6x7", from $200 to..**250.00**
Wall pocket, butterfly, pastel, NM mk, 7x6", from $200 to.........**250.00**
Wall pocket, cuckoo clock, burgundy & bl w/gold, from $150 to ..**200.00**
Wall pocket, fan, Sunburst gold, mk, 1950s, 8½x8", from $60 to .**75.00**
Wall pocket, lady w/bonnet, polka-dot scarf, mk, 1940s, 8", $40 to........**75.00**
Wall pocket, leaves & berries, glossy, unmk, 1940s, 7", from $150 to..**200.00**
Wall pocket, lily bud, pastel, NM mk, 1940s, 8", from $175 to...**225.00**

McCoy, J. W.

The J.W. McCoy Pottery Company was incorporated in 1899. It operated under that name in Roseville, Ohio, until 1911 when McCoy entered into a partnership with George Brush, forming the Brush-McCoy Company. During the early years, McCoy produced kitchenware, majolica jardinieres and pedestals, umbrella stands, and cuspidors. By 1903 they had begun to experiment in the field of art pottery and, though never involved to the extent of some of their contemporaries, nevertheless produced several art lines of merit. Their first line was Mt. Pelee, examples of which are very rare today. Two types of glazes were used, matt green and an iridescent charcoal gray. Though the line was primarily mold formed, some pieces evidence the fact that while the clay remained wet and pliable it was pulled and pinched with the fingers to form crests and peaks in a style not unlike George Ohr.

The company rebuilt in 1904 after being destroyed by fire, and other artware was designed. Loy-Nel Art and Renaissance were standard brown lines, hand decorated under the glaze with colored slip. Shapes and artwork were usually simple but effective. Olympia and Rosewood were relief-molded brown-glaze lines decorated in natural colors with wreaths of leaves and berries or simple floral sprays. Although much of this ware was not marked, you will find examples with the die-stamped 'Loy-Nel Art, McCoy,' or an incised line identification.

Corn Line, tankard, unmk, 1910, from $300 to **350.00**
Liberty Bell, umbrella stand, Cusick, unmk, 1910, 23", from $800 to ..**900.00**
Loy-Nel-Art, bowl, mk, 1905, 2", from $150 to **200.00**
Loy-Nel-Art, jardiniere, Halley's Comet, mk, 1910, 4", from $350 to..**400.00**
Loy-Nel-Art, vase, cylindrical, mk, 6", from $250 to...................**300.00**
Loy-Nel-Art, vase, rim-to-hip hdls, unmk, 1905, 8", from $250 to.......**300.00**
Marble Ware, jardiniere & pedestal, unmk, 1910, 39", from $700 to ...**800.00**
Olympia, pretzel bowl, unmk, 1905, from $400 to **500.00**

Olympia, punch bowl, 1905, from $500.00 to $600.00.

Olympia, vase, initialed S, 1905, 11", from $400 to **500.00**
Rosewood, vase, #41, 1905, 5", from $200 to................................**250.00**
Rosewood, vase, trumpet neck, unmk, pre-1903, 9", from $200 to ..**250.00**

McKee

McKee Glass was founded in 1853 in Pittsburgh, Pennsylvania. Among their early products were tableware of both the flint and non-flint varieties. In 1888 the company relocated to avail themselves of a source of natural gas, thereby founding the town of Jeannette, Pennsylvania. One of their most famous colored dinnerware lines, Rock Crystal, was manufactured in the 1920s. Production during the '30s and '40s included colored opaque dinnerware, Sunkist reamers, and 'bottoms up' cocktail tumblers as well as a line of black glass vases, bowls, and novelty items. All are popular items with today's collectors, but watch for reproductions. The mark of an authentic 'bottoms up' tumbler is the patent number 77725 embossed beneath the feet. The company was purchased in 1916 by Jeannette Glass, under which name it continues to operate. See also Animal Dishes with Covers; Depression Glass; Kitchen Collectibles; Reamers.

Batter jug, cobalt w/chrome trim **125.00**
Bottoms Up, coaster, cream ivory (custard), from $50 to **60.00**
Bottoms Up, coaster, Jade-ite...**225.00**
Bottoms Up, tumbler, butterscotch opal......................................**125.00**
Bottoms Up, tumbler, caramel **80.00**
Bottoms Up, tumbler, cream ivory (custard), from $90 to...........**100.00**
Bottoms Up, tumbler, Jade-ite, from $125 to **150.00**
Bottoms Up, tumbler, Jade-ite, split legs **285.00**
Bottoms Up, tumbler, lt opal, from $50 to **75.00**
Bottoms Up, tumbler & coaster, cream ivory (custard) **175.00**
Centerpiece, Honeycomb, pk, ftd **42.50**
Clock, Tambour Art Glass, pk or amber, 14" L............................**225.00**
Dresser set, Shari, pk 7" base+2 metal compacts+2 perfumes+lid..**190.00**
Lamp, Danse de Lumiere, pk frost, nude holds drape wide **700.00**
Pitcher, Prescutt, Utec 'Eclipse' **45.00**
Pitcher, Toltec, tankard, 8½" **110.00**
Punch bowl, Aztec, w/stand & 2 cups **60.00**
Punch bowl, Tom & Jerry; Jade-ite, w/6 matching mugs **430.00**
Stein, Serenade (Troubador), bl opaque, 4¾".............................**75.00**
Sugar bowl, Laurel, ivory...**32.50**
Tumbler, cream ivory (custard) **20.00**
Vase, Chalaine Blue, shouldered, scalloped rim, 11½" **110.00**
Vase, nudes (3 in panels), Jade-ite, 9½".....................................**125.00**
Vase, Pattern #410, cut floral decor, 10¼" **125.00**
Vase, Sarah, Delphite, 12" **150.00**
Window box, blk, 3½x9x5"..**100.00**

Medical Collectibles

The field of medical-related items encompasses a wide area from the primitive bleeding bowl to the X-ray machines of the early 1900s. Other closely related collectibles include apothecary and dental items. Many tools that were originally intended for the pharmacist found their way to the doctor's office, and dentists often used surgical tools when no suitable dental instrument was available. A trend in the late 1800s toward self-medication brought a whole new wave of home-care manuals and patent medical machines for home use. Commonly referred to as 'quack' medical gimmicks, these machines were usually ineffective and occasionally dangerous. Our advisor for this category is Jim Calison; he is listed in the Directory under New York.

Amputation saw, stainless steel blade w/brass holder, 1800s **65.00**
Bag, field; leather over wood, 3 compartments w/lids, 10x16x7"...**30.00**
Bleeder, folding, Stephen's Pat Nov 16, 1869, w/compo sleeve mk Rogers..**55.00**
Book, Pathogenesis of Corony Occulsion, Morgan, 1956, w/dust jacket...**45.00**
Book, Practical Medicine Series, Volume III, Head & Mix, c 1912, VG ..**17.50**
Chart, Venous & Nervous system, GH Michael...OH, 1910, 48x32", EX ..**125.00**
Cupping machine, electric, Vankey, ca 1950s, w/cups & extras ..**135.00**
Dose bottle, cobalt, John Wyeth, Pat May 16, 1899, 6½x2¼" sq .**17.50**
Dose glass, amethyst, FJ Kneeland...Gergus Falls Minn, 1890-1910........**60.00**
Dose glass, Guaranteed Cure...Bassett's Native herbs emb, 1890-1910...**55.00**
Dose spoon, glass, Phillip's Magnesia emb, graduated measures, 4" L......**30.00**
Drill, bone; stainless steel, chuck key in base of hdl, Zimmer/Jacobs **175.00**
Ear trumpet, tin w/old flaking pnt, 4¾" w/3¾" bell................**365.00**
Enema pump, Irrigateur Systeme...Eguisier..., 1858 ....**85.00**
Eye cup, glass, amber, bucket form, mk MAWS, 1930s................**90.00**
Eye cup, glass, cobalt, 1915................**365.00**
Eye cup, glass, emb ribs **155.00**
Eye cup, glass, Nedusa, 2¼" **315.00**
Eye cup, glass (free-blown), amber, ftd, England, 1850s **225.00**
Eye cup, milk glass, mk Optrex **180.00**
Eye cup, porc, bl & wht floral, 2", VG **775.00**
Eye cup, porc, bl & wht floral w/gold, 2" **1,225.00**
Fistula syringe, Fleming Co, Chicago Il, ca 1910 ....**27.50**

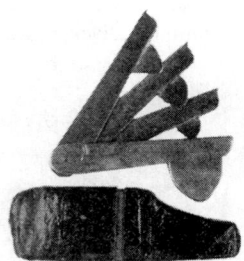

Fleam, three steel blades, brass handle, Browick Cast Steel lettered on shaft, 3½" when folded, EX in pressed paper case, $300.00.

Fleam, brass & steel, Proctor, 3¾", EX **60.00**
Forceps, dental; S Jackson Co, ca 1821-22 ....**40.00**
Forceps, obstetric; stainless steel w/Catalin hdls, #12, 15" L **90.00**
Jar, Ext: Glycyr label under glass, milk glass, 1880-1900, 4"........**110.00**
Jar, glass w/stainless steel lid, Kalon/Profex USA, 7¾x4", 5 for **75.00**
Kit, field; 20 tools in leather roll-up case, Will Corp...NY, 7x12" ...**130.00**
Mouth gag, chrome-plated, ratchet type, Jennings, late 1800s......**80.00**
Probe, ivory hdl, Civil War era **35.00**
Quack device, shock machine, Whitall Tatum...1885/FG Otto & Sons, EX ...**165.00**
Quack device, violet ray machine, Marvel Special, Pat Aug 26, 1924 ...**65.00**
Sterilizer cabinet, oak & glass, 3-shelf, old pnt, 12x12x8", EX......**60.00**
Stethoscope, Hewlett Packard...USA/Rappaport Sprague on ball, EX ...**30.00**
Tooth extractor, wrought iron, trn wood hdl, 5¾"................**130.00**

Meissen

The Royal Saxon Porcelain Works was established in 1710 in Meis-

sen, Saxony. Under the direction of Johann Frederick Bottger, who in 1708 had developed the formula for the first true porcelain body, fine ceramic figurines with exquisite detail and tableware of the highest quality were produced. Although every effort was made to insure the secrecy of Bottger's discovery, others soon began to copy his ware; and in 1731 Meissen adopted the famous crossed swords trademark to identify their own work. The term 'Dresden ware' is often used to refer to Meissen porcelain, since Bottger's discovery and first potting efforts were in nearby Dresden. See also Onion Pattern.

Candlesticks, rococo scrolls w/cherubs/flowers/gilt, mk, 14", pr ..**800.00**
Cup & saucer, floral swags, oval, 19th C, 3x5" **110.00**
Figurine, barefoot girl w/flowers in apron, Xd swords, 5½"..........**700.00**
Figurine, cherub, Coup Sur Coup, Xd swords, 5¾" **700.00**
Figurine, cherub w/scythe & wheat, Xd swords, 5" **585.00**
Figurine, child w/toy horse, newspaper hat dtd 1905, 6½" **675.00**
Figurine, Cupid fanning flame of lovers' hearts, 1877 mk, 7¼" ..**1,400.00**
Figurine, Cupid w/bow stands at attention, #0773-76, 6¼" **650.00**
Figurine, falconer on plinth, Xd swords, 8" **300.00**
Figurine, gardener, mc w/gold, mk, 5⅝", NM **300.00**
Figurine, girl feeding chickens, Xd swords mk, 4½" **525.00**
Figurine, Happy Family, couple admiring baby, 8½"................**1,900.00**
Figurine, lady in elegant attire, mc w/gilt, 1910 mk, rprs, 6" **275.00**
Figurine, lady sits at table listing her goods, rpr, 7" **1,250.00**
Figurine, man holding grapes, Xd swords mk, 4¾" **500.00**
Figurine, seated girl & cat, 1800s, 5" **900.00**
Figurine, Spring, seminude cherub w/grapes, Xd swords mk, 5" ..**650.00**
Plate, swans scene relief, floral & gold border, 8½" **260.00**
Stein, castle on hill, relief florals, bird finial, 1810s, 6½" **4,400.00**
Stein, HP repeating design, inlaid lid, 3L................**550.00**
Stein, Sachsen crest 1710-1910, sculpted pewter lid, ½-litre......**865.00**
Sweetmeat dish, recumbent lady holding oval bowl, #2858, 12½", NM ..**635.00**

Mercury Glass

Silvered glass, commonly called mercury glass, was a major scientific achievement of the nineteenth century. It was developed by the glass industry, who was searching for an inexpensive substitute for silver. Though very fragile, it was lightweight and would not tarnish. Mercury glass was made with two thin layers, either blown with a double wall or joined in sections, with the space between the walls of the vessel filled with a silvering compound, the perfecting of which involved much experimentation. Colored glass was also silvered. Green, blue, and amber were favored. Occasionally, colors were achieved using clear glass by adding certain chemicals to the compound. Besides hollow ware items, flat surfaces were silvered as well, through a process whereby small facets were cut on the underneath side, then treated with the silvering compound. Sometimes mercury glass was decorated by engraving; it was also hand painted. Besides decorative items such as vases and candlesticks, for instance, utilitarian items — doorknobs, curtain tiebacks, and reflectors for lamps — were also popular. Silvered Christmas ornaments were produced in large quantities.

Condition is an issue, though opinions are divided. While some prefer their acquisitions to be in mint condition, others accept items with flaked silvering. Watch for reproductions marked Made in China. In the listings that follow, all examples are silver unless noted another color.

Candlesticks, gold, HP leaves & rings, 7½", pr................**135.00**
Candlesticks, wht floral decor, baluster stem, rnd base, 12", pr...**300.00**
Compote, gold-amber int, knobbed stem, 8¼" **150.00**
Compote, 5½x7" **110.00**
Creamer & sugar bowl, etched vintage, w/lid **200.00**
Doorknobs, pr **70.00**

Match holder	70.00
Mug, clear appl hdl, 3"	40.00
Pitcher, water; etch lacy floral, bulbous, clear hdl, 1840s	350.00
Rolling pin	120.00
Salt cellar, gold int, etch floral, ftd, 2½x3"	85.00
Sugar bowl, floral decor, domed lid, low ft, 6¼x4¼"	55.00
Tie back, silver, etch decor, 3½" dia	75.00
Toothpick holder	50.00
Vase, HP stork among flowers, 10½x4"	155.00
Vase, bird decor, 7½"	70.00
Vase, gold, HP floral, shouldered, flat rim, 8¾", pr	250.00
Vase, gold, HP heron among trees, shouldered, 9¼"	145.00
Vase, gold, stepped shoulder, ftd, 9¼"	140.00
Vase, gold int, urn form, ped ft, 3"	130.00
Vase, gold int & center band, HP flowers, 7¼"	135.00
Vase, HP floral, waisted, ftd, 11"	200.00
Vase, pk roses, trumpet neck, ftd, 11¾"	220.00
Wine, HP/etched decor	65.00

Merrimac

Founded in 1897 in Newburyport, Massachusetts, the Merrimac Pottery Company primarily produced gardenware. In 1901, however, they introduced a line of artware that is now attracting the interest of collectors. Marked examples carry an impressed die-stamp or a paper label, each with the firm name and the outline of a sturgeon, the definition of the Indian word Merrimac.

Humidor, gr & gunmetal mottle, 3 sm hdls, rubs/rim chip, 7x6"	1,100.00
Vase, feathered gr, tooled/appl swirling leaves, closed-in rim, 7¾"	3,750.00
Vase, gr matt, broad shoulders, 9½"	1,900.00

Metlox

Metlox Potteries was founded in 1927 in Manhattan Beach, California. Before 1934 when they began producing the ceramic housewares for which they have become famous, they made ceramic and neon outdoor advertising signs. The company went out of business in 1989.

Well-known sculptor Carl Romanelli designed artware in the late 1930s and early 1940s (and again briefly in the 1950s). His work is especially sought after today.

Some Provincial dinnerware lines can be confusing. There are two 'rooster' lines, Red Rooster (red, orange, and brown) and California Provincial (dark green and burgundy), and there are three 'homestead' lines, Colonial Heritage (red, orange, and brown like the Red Rooster pieces), Homestead Provincial (dark green and burgundy like California Provincial), and Provincial Blue (blue and white). For further information we recommend *Collector's Encyclopedia of Metlox Potteries, Second Edition*, by our advisor Carl Gibbs, Jr.; he is listed in the Directory under Texas.

Cookie Jars

Apple, red, 3½-qt, 9½"	85.00
Barrel, w/squirrel & nuts lid (aka Squirrel Nut Barrel), 11"	150.00
Basket, natural, w/gr apple lid	50.00
Basket, wht, w/basket lid	45.00
Bear, Ballerina	150.00
Bear, Circus, minimum value	450.00
Bear, Panda, w/lollipop, minimum value	350.00
Bear, Panda, w/o lollipop	100.00
Bear, Teddy, brn	45.00
Beaver, Bucky	175.00

Calf, Ferdinand, minimum value	750.00
Cat, calico, gr w/pk ribbon	225.00
Chickadee, Cookie Creations series, 2-qt	85.00
Clown, wht w/bl accents, 3-qt	250.00
Cow, purple w/pk flowers & butterfly, yel bell, 2½-qt	700.00
Cow, yel w/butterfly & bell, no flowers, 2½-qt, minimum value	500.00
Dog, Fido, cream	225.00
Dog, Scottie, blk	150.00
Dutch Girl, minimum value	350.00
Flamingo, minimum value	500.00
Goose, Lucy	125.00
Granada Green, 3-qt	45.00
Happy the Clown, 11", minimum value	350.00
Hen & Chick, minimum value	350.00
Hippo, Bubbles, lt gray & gr, minimum value	350.00
Kangaroo, 11¼", minimum value	1,000.00
Lamb, wht	300.00
Lighthouse, minimum value	350.00
Mammy, Cook, red	850.00
Mammy, Scrub Woman, minimum value	2,000.00
Merry Go Round, bl, wht, gr	225.00
Miller's Sack	75.00
Mushroom Cottage	350.00
Owl, bl, 2½-qt	75.00
Owl, brn, 2½-qt	45.00
Parrot, minimum value	350.00
Pelican, Salty	250.00
Pig, Slenderella	150.00
Piggy, Little; plain wht	150.00
Pumpkin, boy on lid, minimum value	500.00
Rabbit, clover bloom finial	250.00
Rabbit, Easter Bunny, color glazed	325.00
Rabbit, Mrs Bunny holding carrot	125.00
Rabbit, w/carrot, glaze decor, minimum value	450.00
Raccoon, Cookie Bandit, bsk, 2¾-qt	100.00
Rag Doll, girl, 2½-qt	200.00
Santa, standing, Black, minimum value	750.00

Santa, standing, solid chocolate, minimum value, $900.00.
(Photo courtesy Joyce and Fred Roerig)

Santa Head, minimum value	350.00
Scout, Brownie, minimum value	750.00
Seal, Sammy, minimum value	500.00
Squirrel on Pine Cone, stain finish, 3-qt, 11"	95.00
Squirrel w/acorn, stain finish	325.00
Sun	250.00
Sunflowers, Cookie Creations series, 2-qt	85.00
Topsy, bl polka dots	575.00
Turtle, Flash, minimum value	375.00
Watermelon	325.00

Dinnerware

Antique Grape, gravy, fastand, 1-pt	40.00
Antique Grape, jam & jelly	55.00
Antique Grape, pitcher, sm, 1½-pt	40.00
Antique Grape, plate, luncheon; 9"	18.00
Autumn Berry, coffeepot, 8-cup	90.00
Autumn Berry, mug, 8-oz	20.00
Autumn Berry, plate, dinner; 10¾"	13.00
California Aztec, mug, cocoa	40.00
California Aztec, plate, salad	18.00
California Aztec, platter, 13"	65.00
California Confetti, bowl, vegetable; w/lid	100.00
California Confetti, coaster	25.00
California Confetti, plate, salad	14.00
California Confetti, teapot	125.00
California Freeform, cup, juice	45.00
California Freeform, flowerpot, 6"	80.00
California Freeform, pitcher, water	230.00
California Ivy, bowl, vegetable; rnd, w/lid, 11"	95.00
California Ivy, cup, jumbo	40.00
California Ivy, egg cup	35.00
California Ivy, gravy boat, 12-oz	35.00
California Ivy, plate, dinner; 10¼"	16.00
California Ivy, platter, med, oval, 11"	45.00
California Ivy, salt shaker & pepper mill, pr	85.00
California Provincial, bread server, 9½"	75.00
California Provincial, candle holder	55.00
California Provincial, hen on nest	130.00
California Provincial, pipkin set	250.00
California Provincial, pitcher, sm, 1½-pt	60.00
California Provincial, plate, dinner; 10"	20.00
California Provincial, tray, 3-tier, maple-finish divider	125.00
California Tempo, cup & saucer	12.00
California Tempo, tumbler, 10-oz	25.00
Colonial Heritage Provincial, bowl, vegetable; rnd, med	50.00
Colonial Heritage Provincial, coffee carafe	130.00
Colonial Heritage Provincial, egg cup	28.00
Colonial Heritage Provincial, plate, dinner	14.00
Colonial Heritage Provincial, platter, oval, X-lg	80.00
Colorstax, baker, oval, 13"	45.00
Colorstax, bowl, mixing; med, 44-oz	45.00
Colorstax, candlestick	28.00
Colorstax, gravy boat, 1-pt	30.00
Colorstax, plate, dinner; 10½"	14.00
Homestead Provincial, bowl, soup; 8"	28.00
Homestead Provincial, cookie jar	125.00
Homestead Provincial, plate, bread & butter; 6⅜"	10.00
Homestead Provincial, platter, oval, 16"	85.00
Homestead Provincial, soup tureen, w/lid	500.00
Homestead Provincial, sprinkling can	110.00
Homestead Provincial, turkey platter, 22½"	250.00
Lotus, bowl, vegetable, med, 10"	55.00
Lotus, cup, demitasse	28.00
Lotus, mug, 7-oz	25.00
Lotus, plate, dinner; 10½"	16.00
Navajo, bowl, divided vegetable; sm	45.00
Navajo, butter dish	65.00
Navajo, pitcher, 1-pt	40.00
Provincial Blue, ashtray, med, 6⅜"	25.00

Wells Fargo, 11x9"	550.00
Wheat Shock, 4-qt	125.00
Yellow w/daisy lid	75.00

Provincial Blue, butter dish	85.00
Provincial Blue, cigarette box	115.00
Provincial Blue, coffee carafe, 44-oz, 7-cup	145.00
Provincial Blue, cup & saucer, 6-oz	18.00
Provincial Blue, gravy boat, 1-pt	45.00
Provincial Blue, pepper mill	55.00
Provincial Blue, tumbler, 11-oz	45.00
Red Rooster Provincial, ashtray, 10"	35.00
Red Rooster Provincial, egg cup	32.00
Red Rooster Provincial, gravy boat, 1-pt	45.00
Red Rooster Provincial, kettle casserole, w/lid, 2-qt+12 oz	130.00
Red Rooster Provincial, pitcher, med, 1-qt	70.00

Red Rooster, plate, stamped mark, 10", from $13.00 to $15.00.

Red Rooster Provincial, sugar bowl, w/lid, 8-oz	30.00
Red Rooster Provincial, teapot, 42-oz, 6-cup	130.00
Sculptured Daisy, bowl, cereal; 7¼"	14.00
Sculptured Daisy, cup & saucer	14.00
Sculptured Daisy, plate, salad; 7½"	10.00
Sculptured Daisy, tumbler, 11-oz	30.00
Sculptured Grape, bowl, soup; 8⅛"	24.00
Sculptured Grape, salad fork & spoon	80.00
Sculptured Grape, tea canister	55.00
Tickled Pink (Vernonware), plate, dinner; 10"	12.00
Tickled Pink (Vernonware), platter, oval, 13½"	35.00
Tickled Pink (Vernonware), shakers, pr	24.00
Tickled Pink (Vernonware), teapot, 7-cup	90.00
True Blue (Vernonware), jam & jelly, 8¼"	45.00
True Blue (Vernonware), platter, oval, med, 12⅜"	35.00
True Blue (Vernonware), soup tureen, w/lid, 3-qt	165.00
True Blue (Vernonware), tumbler, 10-oz	28.00
Vernon Antiqua (Vernonware), cup & saucer	16.00
Vernon Antiqua (Vernonware), oval baker, 12⅛"	50.00
Vernon Antiqua (Vernonware), plate, luncheon	18.00
Vernon Antiqua (Vernonware), sugar bowl, w/lid, 10-oz	28.00
Woodland Gold, mug, 8-oz	22.00
Woodland Gold, plate, bread & butter; 6⅜"	8.00
Woodland Gold, shakers, pr	24.00

Disney Figurines

Alice in Wonderland	400.00
Bambi, jumbo	1,500.00
Bambi w/butterfly	250.00
Cinderella, as peasant	500.00
Dumbo, mini, 1¾"	200.00
Dumbo, standing	225.00
Dwarf (of 7 Dwarfs), 2"	250.00
Faline	165.00
Figaro (cat), sitting or standing	225.00
Hippo, Fantasia	400.00

Mamma Mouse, from Cinderella series..................................200.00
Pinocchio..450.00
Prince Charming..400.00
Snow White...500.00
Sprite, Fantasia...250.00
Three Little Pigs, 1¼", ea...200.00

Miniatures

Alligator, 9"..105.00
Bear, paw upraised, 5"..85.00
Burro, sitting, 3"..55.00
Caterpillar..35.00
Dog, Cubistic, prone, 5"...85.00
Elephant, Indian; Baby, walking, 6½"..125.00
Fawn, 5½"..55.00
Giraffe, 5¾"..140.00
Horse, Goofy, 4½"..75.00
Penguin, 3"..55.00
Sailboat, 2½"..45.00
Turtle, standing..55.00

Nostalgia Line

Reminiscent of the late nineteenth and early twentieth centuries, the Nostalgia line contained models of locomotives, gramophones, early autos, stage coaches, and baby carriages. There were also wagons and carts pulled by horses or donkeys, sometimes with separate drivers and passengers. The line was produced from the late 1940s through the 1960s.

American Royal Horse, colt, prone, 4¼x3"..................................70.00
American Royal Horse, Currier & Ives, 11x7¾"........................125.00
Cadillac..85.00
Coachman...70.00
Locomotive...65.00
Mail Wagon..80.00
Old Cannon..55.00
Santa..115.00
Stage Coach...100.00
Train set, 3-pc..165.00

Poppets

From the mid-'60s through the mid-'70s, Metlox produced a line of 'Poppets,' eighty-eight in all, representing characters ranging from royalty and professionals to a Salvation Army group. They came with a name tag; some had paper labels, others backstamps.

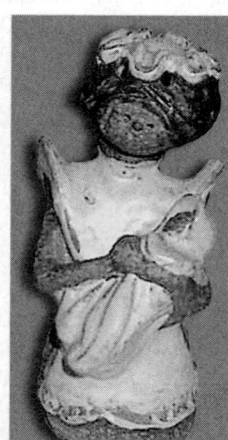

Penelope, nursemaid, 7¾", $35.00.

Betsy, goose girl, 8½"...60.00
Charlie, seated man, 5⅞"...55.00
Grace, princess..45.00
Jackie, choir boy #3..45.00
Lorna, standing girl, 7⅞"..45.00
Louisa, girl w/muff, 8½"...45.00
Mother Goose, 8"...55.00
Zelda, choral lady #2, 7⅝"..45.00

Romanelli Artware

Bookends, nude w/hounds, pr...450.00
Figurine, deer, 7"..125.00
Figurine/flower holder, nude, 8¾"...250.00
Vase, mermaid & fish..175.00
Vase, nude w/flamingo...300.00
Vase, swordfish, 9"..150.00
Vase, Zodiac series, set of 12, ea..160.00

Mettlach

In 1836 Nicholas Villeroy and Eugene Francis Boch, both of whom were already involved in the potting industry, formed a partnership and established a stoneware factory in an old restored abbey in Mettlach, Germany. Decorative stoneware with in-mold relief was their specialty, steins in particular. Through constant experimentation, they developed innovative methods of decoration. One process, called chromolith, involved inlaying colorful mosaic designs into the body of the ware. Later underglaze printing from copper plates was used. Their stoneware was of high quality, and their steins won many medals at the St. Louis Expo and early world's fairs. Most examples are marked with an incised castle and the name 'Mettlach.' The numbering system indicates size, date, stock number, and decorator. Production was halted by a fire in 1921; the factory was not rebuilt.

Key:
L — liter   PUG — print under glaze
POG — print over glaze   tl — thumb lift

#1032, coaster, PUG: dwarfs, 4¾", pr..225.00
#1044-991, plaque, PUG: dwarf picking grapes, Schlitt, 8".........415.00
#1062, stein, etch/glaze: repeating design, inlaid lid, .5L.............660.00
#1261, stein, etch/relief: repeating design, inlaid lid, .5L 550.00
#1385, plaque, warrior scene, sgn Schultz, dtd 1910, 14½".........850.00
#1410, plaque, etch/glaze: man in plumed hat, 35", NM..........8,150.00
#1508, stein, etch: Gasthaus scene, inlaid lid, .5L 465.00
#1526, stein, HP: barmaid w/bbl, relief pewter lid, lady tl, .5L....300.00
#1526, stein, HP: bowling crest 1906-09, relief pewter lid, .5L....200.00
#1526, stein, HP: Student Society, lg crest, pewter lid, 1L..........880.00
#1526, stein, PUG: 400 Yr Anniversary of Annaberg 1496-1896, .5L..340.00
#1526-1219, stein, PUG: students drink & smoke, crest lid, .5L, NM..275.00
#1530-580, stein, PUG: man w/rifle smoking, inlaid lid, .5L 415.00
#1541, vase, etch/glaze: repeating florals, 7¾" 285.00
#1593, stein, etch: jester, cavalier lid (rpl), rprs, 1.5L 1,870.00
#1675, stein, etch: Heidelburg, inlaid lid, .5L 465.00
#1677, plaque, relief: birds at lake, flower border, 15" 935.00
#1733, stein, etch: jockeys w/horses, cap lid, .5L......................1,300.00
#1786, etch/glaze: St Florian & fire, dragon hdl, pewter lid, 1L...1,300.00
#1795, stein, etch: City of Freiburg, inlaid lid, .5L 825.00
#1797, stein, etch: cards, gold coin inlaid lid, bent tl, .5L...........465.00
#1809, relief/glaze: 5 cavaliers/barmaid scenes, inlaid lid, 1L...1,375.00
#1861, stein, etch/PUG: Frederick II, brass lid, worn SP, .5L......495.00
#1861, stein, etch/PUG: Wilhelm I, inlaid lid, .5L.......................550.00

#1861, stein, etch/PUG: Wilhelm II, rpl tl, inlaid lid, .5L 415.00
#1875, vase, etch/glaze: repeating floral, 8¾".................................360.00
#1909-1177, stein, PUG: Musik, pewter lid, .5L.....................300.00
#1909-1271, stein, PUG: porter wheels drunken man, pewter lid, .5L ...465.00
#1932, stein, etch: cavaliers toasting, inlaid lid, Warth, .5L........415.00
#1946, stein, etch/relief: couple, lovebirds lid, .5L, EX...............450.00
#1972, stein, etch: 4 scenes of lady, inlaid lid, .25L...............415.00
#1994, stein, etch/glaze: repeating design, inlaid lid, .25L...........525.00
#1997, stein, etch/PUG: Nettlach-Saar w/Abbey, inlaid lid, rprs, .5L..990.00
#2001H, stein, etch/relief: forestry, inlaid lid, .5L................1,375.00
#2001K, stein, etch/relief: banking, inlaid lid, Mercury tl, .5L....685.00
#2002, stein, etch: Munchen skyline & verse, inlaid lid, 1L 880.00
#2013, plaque, etch/glaze: Imperial Eagle/crests, 27" 7,700.00
#2026, vase, etch/glaze: repeating design, pk int, 3¾" 355.00
#2031, stein, etch: military scene, inlaid lid, .5L 880.00
#2034, stein, etch/glaze: repeating geometrics, .3L 600.00
#2078, plaque, etch: Ulannen (2) on horsebk, Stocke, 15" 1,925.00
#2083, stein, etch: boar hunt, St Hubertus inlaid lid, .5L.........1,200.00
#2090, stein, etch: man at table, inlaid lid, Schlitt, .3L, NM......255.00
#2091, stein, etch: St Florian & fire, inlaid lid, Schlitt, .5L, EX.465.00
#2106, stein, etch/relief: caged monkeys, monkey hdl, inlaid lid, .4L..4,950.00
#2122, stein, etch: crusader & monk, Schlitt, relief inlaid lid, 3.8L.....4,400.00
#2134, stein, etch: dwarf in nest, inlaid lid, Schlitt, .5L 1,265.00
#2140-754, stein, PUG: 1 Garde-Regiment..., pewter lid, .5L.....990.00
#2140-764, stein, PUG: Regt Nr 16, pewter lid, .5L 1,075.00
#2140-814, stein, PUG: Kur Regt...No 2, weapons/flag lid, .5L...1,075.00
#2184-967, stein, PUG: dwarfs dancing, dwarf tl, inlaid lid, .3L...385.00
#2191, stein, etch: Etruscan scene, inlaid lid, Schlitt, .5L...........715.00
#2209, vase, scenes from Oohengrin opera & Siegfried, lady hdls, 17" ...2,750.00
#2235, stein, etch: Schutzenliesl, inlaid lid, .5L.........................715.00
#2262-1014, stein, PUG: Munich Child on globe, pewter lid, '03, 4.25L...1,485.00
#2279, vase, etch: Etruscan wedding scene, 13" 525.00
#2327-119, beaker, PUG: Gesang, .25L.......................................80.00
#2368, beaker, PUG: elks, .25L...80.00
#2381, stein, etch: Thirsty Rider, Schlitt, tower body, .5L.........685.00
#2416, vase, etch/glaze: Nouveau design, Hein, 6 hdls, rpr, 15½"...715.00
#2441, stein, etch: dice game, inlaid lid, music box....................745.00
#2472, vase, etch: floral, flaw, 4½" 450.00
#2502, punch bowl, cameo: woman w/children, w/underplate & Lid, NM ..600.00
#2518, plaque, etch: City of Meissen, 17½" 1,100.00
#2520, stein, etch: man w/barmaid, Schlitt, inlaid lid, .5L...........935.00
#2582, stein, etch: jester & crowd, jester lid, dwarf tl, 1L 715.00
#2583, stein, etch: Black Whale of Ascolon, inlaid lid, .5L........950.00
#2628, stein, cameo: bowling scene, Stahl, ball & pins lid, .5L ..770.00
#2632, plaque, etch: City of Heidelberg, 17½" 825.00
#2698, plaque, etch: dwarf reads under toadstools, Schlitt, 17½".....6,600.00
#2724, stein, etch/glaze: mason occupation, rpl inlaid lid, .5L 935.00
#2726, stein, etch/glaze: goldsmith occupation, rpl inlaid lid, .5L....880.00
#2752, stein, etch: man drinking, Schlitt, inlaid lid, .5L...........745.00
#2765, stein, etch: knight on wht horse, Schlitt, tower body, .5L ..1,870.00
#2778, stein, etch: carnival scene, Schlitt, inlaid lid, .5L 1,485.00
#280F, stein, HP/slight relief: Student Society, eng pewter lid, .5L ..575.00
#2887, stein, etch: knights drinking, inlaid lid, .5L 660.00
#2892, stein, etch: Art Nouveau, inlaid lid, .5L 575.00
#2917, stein, erch/relief: Munich Child, Pauson lid, 1L..........1,100.00
#2922, stein, etch: men at campfire, inlaid lid, .25L.................265.00
#2934, stein, etch: Art Nouveau, inlaid lid, .25L 798.00
#2938, stein, etch: hunter & dog, Quidenus, inlaid lid, .5L 770.00
#2994, stein, etch: Art Nouveau, sculpted, inlaid lid, .5L...........685.00
#3071, stein, relief: bowling scene, inlaid lid, .5L 285.00
#3088, punch bowl, Noah/animals/ark, Schlitt, w/lid/plate, NM..3,600.00
#3092, stein, etch: man w/goblet, Schlitt, inlaid lid, .5L.............825.00
#3138, stein, etch: Art Deco, inlaid lid, 2.4L, NM 825.00
#3139, stein, etch: Art Nouveau, inlaid lid, .5L 635.00

#3185-1280, stein, PUG: couple dancing, inlaid lid, .5L............330.00
#3288, stein, etch: bowling scene, inlaid lid, Bavaria, .5L...........660.00
#3335, stein, etch: drinking scene, inlaid lid, .4L....................1,100.00
#3350, stein, etch: men finger fighting, horn finial & tl, .4L...1,265.00
#5005-5188, stein, faience: man drinking, pewter lid, .5L...........465.00
#5016, stein, faience: woman w/dragon, HP birds/flowers, 1.35L..1,045.00
#7002, vase, Phanolith, woman w/children, 9¾".........................800.00
#7058, vase, Phanolith, 3 ladies either side, Stahl, 14¾".........1,100.00
#7079, plaque, Phanolith, man & woman on stumps w/sheep, 8x6" +fr....600.00

Microscopes

The microscope has taken on many forms during its 250-year evo-lutionary period. The current collectors' market primarily includes examples from England, surplus items from institutions, and continental beginner and intermediate forms which sold through Sears Roebuck & Company and other retailers of technical instruments. Earlier examples have brass main tubes which are unpainted. Later, more common exam-ples are all black with brass or silver knobs and horseshoe-shaped bases. Early and more complex forms are the most valuable; these always had hardwood cases to house the delicate instruments and their accessories. Instruments were never polished during use, and those that have been polished to use as decorator pieces are of little interest to most avid col-lectors. Our advisor for this category is Dale Beeks; he is listed in the Directory under Iowa.

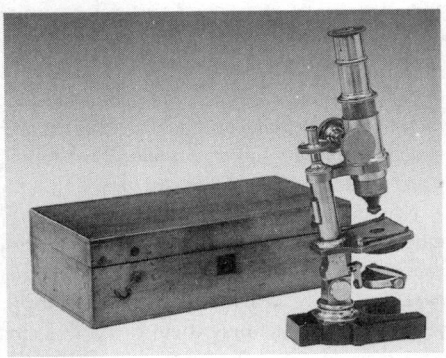

Student, Continental form, ca 1870, with case, 11", $350.00.

B Pike & Sons, NY, Barlimb, w/optics, 1870s, EX 550.00
Baker, 224 High Holborn London, brass, 1840s, 17" 1,200.00
Bausch & Lomb, brass, Pat Aug 24 '97, 12x4⅛x6", NM in crate..235.00
Bulloch, Chicago, brass, complex, Y base, 1880, 15", +case 1,100.00
English, student, brass, ca 1870, 12", +case/accessories 595.00
Gundlach, brass, Y base, 1879, 14", EX 325.00
Hartnack, Paris, brass, 1860s, mahog case, EX 900.00
Leitz, metallurgical polarizing, w/case/attachments, G.................450.00
Martin drum type, brass, rack & pinion, unmk, 1800s, w/case, EX ...1,100.00
Schrauer of NY, homeopathic, brass, 3 lenses, tools, 19th C ...1,200.00
Smith & Black, brass, binocular, L,ondon #3243, EX, +mahog box...1,350.00
Watson, English binoculars form, 1880, 18", EX, +case 1,250.00
Zeiss, w/reflected bright/dk field, w/stage, complete 1,000.00

Midwestern Glass

As early as 1814, blown glass was made in Ohio. By 1835 glasshous-es in Michigan were producing similar pattern-molded types that have long been highly regarded by collectors. During the latter part of the nineteenth century, all six of the states of the Northwest Territory were mass producing the pressed-glass tableware patterns that were then in vogue. Various types of art glass were produced in the area until after the turn of the century. Items listed here are attributed to the Midwest by certain physical characteristics known to be indigenous to that part of the country. See also Findlay Onyx; Greentown Glass; Libbey; Mantua; Zanesville Glass. Our advisor for this category is Mark Vuono; he is listed in the Directory under Connecticut.

Bottle, bl-aqua, rolled lip, globular, pontil scar, 3" **500.00**
Bottle, club; dk bl-aqua, 18 broken swirl ribs, pontil, 8" **140.00**
Bottle, dk bl-aqua, 24 left-swirl ribs, globular, 7⅞", NM **175.00**
Bottle, golden yel w/olive tint, 24 left-swirl ribs, globular, 7⅝" ..**1,750.00**
Bottle, gr-aqua, 16 vertical ribs, globular, pontil scar, 8⅛" **180.00**
Bottle, med golden amber, globular, mini, 3¼" **675.00**
Bottle, med orange-amber, 24 left-swirl ribs, globular, 8½" **475.00**
Bottle, med orange-amber, 24 right-swirl ribs, globular, 7¾".......**600.00**
Bottle, red-amber, 24 left-swirl ribs, globular, 7⅛" **450.00**
Bottle, root beer amber, rolled lip, globular, sm stain, 2⅜"..........**625.00**
Bottle, yel-amber, 24 left-swirl ribs, globular, pontil, 8"..............**475.00**
Bottle, yel-olive, 24 vertical ribs, globular, pontil, 8" **3,100.00**
Compote, cobalt base w/clear bowl, Att Central Glass, 7½x9¼" ..**280.00**
Flask, chestnut; golden yel, 24 vertical ribs, faint haze, 5⅝" **575.00**
Flask, chestnut; straw yel, 20 broken left-swirl ribs, 7" **5,000.00**
Lamp, cobalt base w/clear unpatterned font, brass collar, 9¼" **165.00**

Militaria

Because of the wide and varied scope of items available to collectors of militaria, most tend to concentrate mainly on the area or areas that interest them most or that they can afford to buy. Some items represent a major investment and because of their value have been reproduced. Extreme caution should be used when purchasing Nazi items. Every badge, medal, cap, uniform, dagger, and sword that Nazi Germany issued is being reproduced today. Some repros are crude and easily identified as fakes, while others are very well done and difficult to recognize as reproductions. Purchases from WWII veterans are usually your safest buys. Reputable dealers or collectors will normally offer a money-back guarantee on Nazi items purchased from them. There are a number of excellent Third Reich reference books available in bookstores at very reasonable prices. Study them to avoid losing a much larger sum spent on a reproduction. Our advisor for this category is Ron L. Willis; he is listed in the Directory under Florida.

Key: insg — insignia

Imperial German

Spiked helmet, steel, eagle hat plate, lobster-tail back, NM, $1,980.00. (Photo courtesy Jackson's Auctioneers & Appraisers)

Badge, Bavarian Pilot, worn SP **350.00**
Buckle, enlisted, gray metal, w/belt keeper....................................**30.00**

Cockade, spike helmet; Prussian officer, silvered wreath on blk....**25.00**
Helmet, Baden Infantry, gray metal furniture, dtd 1916, w/liner, EX ..**550.00**
Helmet, gilt spike; w/fluting, rampant lion w/crown insg, 10", EX...**660.00**
Helmet, spike (plated); eagle insg, chin strap, G **350.00**
Helmet, spike; Bavarian enlisted, complete, EX **350.00**
Helmet, spike; Prussian Guard Infantry inlisted, eagle frontplate, EX ..**625.00**
Helmet, spike; Prussian NCO, brass furniture, pre-1887 pattern, EX **300.00**
Medal, Baden WWI War Service, gray metal, w/ribbon **30.00**
Medal, Prussian 1915 War Service, gray metal, w/ribbon **30.00**
Medal, 1813 Iron Cross, 2nd class, silver fr, worn......................**850.00**
Shoulder boards, Beamte officer, silver trees on dk bl wool **50.00**
Tunic, Shooting Assoc, gr wool frock w/silver buttons, 1870s.....**350.00**
Waistcoat, Prussian Diplomatic official, bl wool, EX **550.00**

Third Reich

Armband, SS, swastika, blk on red & wht cotton **100.00**
Backpack, Army M1934, field gray canvas, fur-covered flap, EX ..**55.00**
Backpack, Army M1939, gray canvas, fur-covered flap.................**40.00**
Badge, General Assault, worn SP on gray metal, VG **45.00**
Badge, Luftwaffe Pilot combat, embr wreath on gray wool **75.00**
Badge, Tirolean 1943 Marksmanship, gilt w/eagle/target/wreath...**30.00**
Banner, dbl-sided, blk swastika on wht circle on red, 48x220"....**200.00**
Boots, riding; Army officer, blk leather, high-top, EX **125.00**
Boots, WWII Army officer, blk leather, EX **350.00**
Canteen, Army, wool over aluminum, Bakelite cup, screw cap, EX..**35.00**
Canteen, WWII, gr glass w/appl top, EX..................................**100.00**
Collar tab, Waffen SS enlisted, hand/scimitar/swastika on wool.**115.00**
Collar tabs, Luftwaffe Administration official, pr...........................**45.00**
Compass, wrist; WWII Air Force pilot, blk Bakelite, EX..............**45.00**
Coverall, Navy, blk leather, 1-pc w/zippers/pockets, Eagle over M mk.**450.00**
Gas mask, Army, eagle proof mk, w/canister/straps/etc **30.00**
Hat, visor; Army Infantry officer, gray wool, aluminum eagle **175.00**
Hat, visor; Luftwaffe Flak Artillery summer enlisted, EX **250.00**
Helmet, battlefield relic, M42 style, relic condition **45.00**
Helmet, pith; Africa Corps, gray felt, metal insg, VG...................**80.00**
Insignia, sleeve; Army Jager Troupes, oak leaves on gr oval **30.00**
Medal, Army Close Combat Bar, bronze, w/reverse plate, hallmk ..**125.00**
Medal, 25 Yr Civil Service Long Service, silver w/blk swastika **45.00**
Mess kit, WWII Army, aluminum w/worn blk, hinged hdl, dtd 1940...**75.00**
Metal, Luftschutz Service, 2nd Class, gray metal, ribbon missing .**25.00**
Plate, Luftwaffe mess hall, wht porc w/early eagle, 1940, 9½".......**25.00**
Postcard, Army, machine gun crew in winter scene, colored, EX..**25.00**
Rucksack, Luftwaffe, gray canvas, leather belting, w/straps, EX ...**30.00**
Scope, rifle; WWII sniper rifle, 6½", EX optics, w/bag & caps ...**250.00**
Shoulder boards, Motorized Rifle Unit, purple & olive drab wool, 1980s...**25.00**
Shoulder boards, WWII Medical Troops enlisted, brass snake, pr ..**55.00**
Telephone, field; WWII era, blk Bakelite case, Morse code key....**85.00**
Trousers, Army fatigue, natural linen, 2 side pockets, compo buttons..**150.00**
Tunic, Army Ordnance, field gray twill w/gr collar, breast eagle.**385.00**
Uniform, WWII Army enlisted, M1943 rubaha, shirt & breeches, rare...**900.00**
Uniform, WWII snow camo, drawstring hood & waist, EX **500.00**

Japanese

Bag, mail; khaki cotton twill w/brass grommets, 1960s.................**25.00**
Box, collar; lacquered wood, ca 1900, 6" dia...............................**195.00**
Canteen, WWII, aluminum w/Skelton webbing, EX **75.00**
Cover, blanket roll; WWII Army, waterproof canvas, rare..........**255.00**
Ensemble, Order of Rising Sun, 8th class, silver w/ribbon & lapel pin.**110.00**
Ensemble, Order of Sacred Treasure, silver, +ribbon/lapel pin/case.......**110.00**
Flag, silk, wht w/red sun & blk print, 33x27", EX.........................**80.00**
Headband, WWII Kamikaze, red printed ball & blk characters on wht...**350.00**
Medal, 1904/05 War, w/ribbon...**55.00**

Mess kit, WWII Army, aluminum w/NM khaki finish..................35.00
Pencil, mechanical; WWII officer, NP finish, metal body, EX 45.00
Uniform, WWII officer, navy & yel wool, brass buttons, complete, EX .550.00

Russia/Soviet

Backpack, Imperial Era Army, cotton/leather, 1915, EX 300.00
Badge, breast; Imperial Era, Order of St Vladimir, 4th class, 1917 ...450.00
Badge, WWII Best Artilleryman, brass, cannons/insg w/red wht enamel ...37.50
Beret, Army, blk wool w/gilt wreath/red star, 1970s....................27.50
Book, aircraft identification, silhouettes, dtd 1956, EX 35.00
Buckle, Army, brass w/star insg, ca 1970 ....25.00
Case, map; Army, waterproof material w/leather shoulder strap, 1950s..27.50
Flashlight, Army field, khaki pnt on metal, NP fittings, EX...........25.00
Hat, visor; Air Force officer, bl w/brass winged star/wreath, 1980s .35.00
Hat, visor; Soviet Border Guard, Kelly gr w/red piping, 1980s 35.00
Helmet, WWII battlefield relic, khaki gr pnt finish, G- 50.00
Medal, Imperial Era, Czar Nicholas 1896 Coronation, brass 28.00
Medal, Imperial Era, St George Medal for Bravery, 3rd class, silver ...45.00
Medallion, Imperial Era, Czar's 25th Wedding anniversary, EX 75.00
Photograph, Imperial officer in dress uniform w/epaulettes/etc, 1880s ..30.00
Poster, Occupied Estonia Concentration Camp propaganda, 1945, 32x24" ...200.00
Pouch, AK-47, khaki canvas, belt loops, ca 1970 ....25.00

United States

Backpack, WWI Army, khaki canvas, stenciled US, dtd 1918, EX....30.00
Badge, Army Expert Qualification, silver cross, rifle bar, hallmk ..15.00
Badge, Maltese Cross, Union 5th Corps, cloth, ca 1863, EX 350.00
Badge, WWI Army Expert Rifleman, bronze, Xd rifles, EX...........28.00
Belt, Civil War enlisted man, silver wreath buckle w/eagle, VG..350.00
Beret, USAF, blk wool, metal front insg Air Training Command, 1980s..25.00
Box, cap; Civil War enlisted man, SH Young & Co, ca 1862, VG ..200.00
Bullet mold, Colt's Patent, dbl cavity, .36 caliber, hinged, EX 75.00
Busby, blk lamb's wool, red wool crown, gold tassel, 1890s, EX ..145.00
Canteen, Civil War era, cadet gray cover, complete....................185.00
Cap, WWII Army overseas, khaki cotton twill, unused 10.00
Cap, WWII Navy sailor, dk bl wool, embr US Navy, NM.............15.00
Chevrons, WWI Coastal Artillery Crops, star/governor/wreath, EX..28.00
Coat, frock; Indian Wars era Army General, bl wool, 1880s, EX...900.00
Gauntlets, Civil War officer, buff-colored leather, pr, EX............350.00
Greatcoat, WWII Army officer, khaki, dbl-breasted, EX..............45.00
Hat, visor; Spanish-Am War era, dk bl wool w/gold bullion, VG .75.00
Helmet, artillery spike; Indian Wars Era enlisted, cork w/bl cover, EX..250.00
Helmet, Korean War era, Airborne liner w/side straps, EX............25.00
Helmet, WWII Army, olive drab finish, w/liner/chin strap/etc, EX ...35.00
Insignia, shoulder; Infantry Pioneer, Xd axes on bl, 1880s 27.50
Insignia, shoulder; WWII USO, eagle on red, scarce....................30.00
Jacket, Civil War Engineer, wool w/brass eagle buttons, G 200.00
Parachute, USAF, orange/gr/brn nylon, 1980s, EX.....................100.00
Trousers & tunic, Desert Storm era, desert pattern, M 25.00
Tunic, Korean War Era Marine Corps, 4-pocket, gr wool, EX.......35.00
Tunic, pre-WWI Infantry dress enlisted, navy wool, G 100.00
Tunic, WWI Army enlisted, khaki wool, NM 125.00
Uniform, WWII Red Cross women, cap+blouse+2 dresses+greatcoat, EX...150.00
Vest, Navy officer, bl twill, eagle buttons, 1940s 37.50

Miscellaneous

Argentina, helmet, Army, Fr Adrian style, w/top comb, EX 125.00
Austrian, badge; hat; Army, gilt crown w/sunrays, recent.............25.00
Canada, hat, visor; Cavalry, bl wool w/gr mohair band, 1980s, NM ..45.00
E Germany, cap, Army, gray wool, fur pile visor, 1970s 25.00
E Germany, medal, Civil Defense, silver w/burgundy & wht ribbon ..35.00

France, helmet, brass w/NP spike, ca 1880s, EX 150.00
France, helmet, WWII Army, G khaki finish, top comb, G-.........25.00
France, medal, WWII Resistance, bronze cross w/swords & ribbon ..30.00
France, metal, Combatant Cross, bronze, w/ribbon......................30.00
Great Britain, beret, Army, blk cotton twill, G............................25.00
Great Britain, helmet, spike; enlisted, bl wool w/gilt furniture, EX..150.00
Great Britain, helmet, WWII Army, khaki finish, G....................25.00
Great Britain, medal, India Service, Geo V profile, ca 1920.........35.00
Great Britain, medal, WWI Peace, gray metal, Britannia figure ...30.00
Italy, beret, Air Force, bl wool w/eagle & torch, 1960s................20.00
Italy, helmet, WWII, EX liner & chin strap................................50.00
Sweden, helmet, Army, 3-pad leather liner, 1940s.......................50.00

Milk Glass

Milk glass is the current collector's name for milk-white opaque glass. The early glassmaker's term was Opal Ware. Originally attempted in England in the eighteenth century with the intention of imitating china, milk glass was not commercially successful until the mid-1800s. Pieces produced in the U.S.A., England, and France during the 1870 – 1900 period are highly prized for their intricate detail and fiery, opalescent edges.

For further information we recommend *Collector's Encyclopedia of Milk Glass, An Identification & Value Guide*, by Betty and Bill Newbound. (CE numbers in our listings refer to this publication.) Another highly recommended book is *The Milk Glass Book* by Frank Chiarenza and James Slater. The newest reference, published in 2001, is *Milk Glass Imperial Glass Corporation* by Myrna and Bob Garrison. Our advisor for this category is Rod Dockery; he is listed in the Directory under Texas. See also Animal Dishes with Covers; Bread Plates; Historical Glass; Westmoreland.

Key:
CE — Newbound   G — Garrison
F — Ferson   MGB — Milk Glass Book

Plate, No Easter Without Us, Dithridge, CE-268C/F-592, ca 1900, 6¼", $55.00.

Ashtray set, trivet form, Imperial, G-1950/450, set of 4 ....40.00
Bottle, cologne; hobnail, CE-4, 6½"...12.00
Bowl, scroll pattern, scalloped, Imperial, G-1950/235, 8½" 20.00
Bread plate, Give Us This Day.., dmn grid, Atterbury, CE-338, 12" ..65.00
Butter dish, Lace & Dewdrop, w/lid, Kemple, CE-317, 6" H.........40.00
Candlesticks, figural dolphins, Westmoreland, CE-65, 9¼", pr....75.00
Candy dish, heart shape, 3-part, rope border on HP lid, CE-47, 7x8" ...50.00
Candy dish, 3-section, w/HP mc floral lid, CE-45, 6½" dia...........30.00
Cigarette box, emb Santa Maria ship, Consolidated, CE-50, 3¾x5" ...130.00
Compote, Lace & Dew Drop, w/lid, Kemple, CE-98, 8½".............40.00
Compote, scalloped nest w/leaves on bird ped, CE-87, 4⅛"..........50.00
Cookie jar, tufted w/pnt leaves, gold trim, Consolidated, CE-182, 9" .75.00
Covered dish, fainting couch, CE-57, old Westmoreland, 5" L...250.00
Covered dish, pie wagon, G-1950/377, Imperial, 6¼" L............225.00

Covered dish, prairie schooner form, KR Halley, F-409, 5⅞" L ..185.00
Covered dish, Remember the Maine battleship, MGB-177, rare, minimum ...500.00
Creamer, Crossed Fern, Atterbury, F-231 ....60.00
Creamer, Holly, MGB-330, rare..135.00
Creamer & sugar bowl, emb cow & wheat, ftd, CE-295, ea 125.00
Creamer & sugar bowl, owl form w/amber glass eyes, CE-303, ea .25.00
Decanter, wine; grape pattern, Imperial Glass, G-1950/163, 11½" 50.00
Dresser box, comma shaped, gold trim, McKee, CE-43, 2¼x3¾" ..20.00
Dresser tray, wagon wheel edge, gold trim, CE-351, 7⅜x10¼" 25.00
Figurine, chubby snub-nose dog seated w/neck bow, CE-191, 5" ...50.00
Figurine, swan w/open bk, pnt bill, LE Smith, CE-204, 9" 40.00
Goblet, Jewel & Dewdrop, Kemple, CE-218, 6"............................20.00
Lamp, hurricane; emb flowers/scrollwork/cross-hatching, ftd, CE-235 ..100.00
Leaf dish, Fenton, CE-339, 1955, 11½x10½" 25.00
Marmalade jar, pineapple form, w/lid & spoon, G-1950/567, Imperial, 6" ...45.00
Matchbox, butterfly form, gold trim, wall mt, CE-327, 3¾"..........60.00
Match safe, upright book form, CE-326, 3" 50.00
Mug, bird & wheat in gold, Atterbury, CE-212, 4⅛" 35.00
Novelty, false teeth, MGB-281, 1x3x2¼" 125.00
Pickle dish, Love's Request Is Pickles, Crystal or LaBelle, CE-332, 9"...40.00
Pin tray, hand form w/flower at wrist, McKee, CE-340, 5" 18.00
Pitcher, allover emb water lily decor, Fenton, CE-319, 7" 75.00
Pitcher, owl form w/amber glass eyes, CE-313, Challinor-Taylor, 7½"..185.00
Plate, eagle & shield, MarCor, CE-251, 15" 50.00
Plate, emb roses, scalloped edge, Imperial, G-1950/13D, 12" 30.00
Plate, HP roses w/gold trim, CE-259, 10" 30.00
Plate, moss rose, CE-252, 12" 25.00
Plate, Shell & Club border, emb Columbus w/1492-1892, CE-270, 9¾"..45.00
Salt box, emb lettering, wooden lid, CE-59, 5¾" 115.00
Shakers, emb tassels, CE-282, 3¼", pr..30.00
Shakers & tray, gold-pnt emb grapes, CE-284, 5½x2⅜" tray, 3-pc ..35.00
Toothpick holder, Bunch of Cigars 25.00
Toothpick holder, cup on bk of alligator form, Victorian, F-451, 3"....250.00
Tray, hand holding fan form, Atterbury, CE-331, 9¼"...................80.00
Vase, tri-panel w/beaded columns, 3-ftd, US Glass, CE-377, 9" 20.00

Millefiori

Millefiori was a type of art glass produced during the 1800s. Literally the term means 'thousand flowers,' an accurate description of its appearance. Canes, fused bundles of multicolored glass threads such as are often used in paperweights were cut into small cross sections, arranged in the desired pattern, refired, and shaped into articles such as cruets, lamps, and novelty items. It is still being produced, and many examples found on the market today are fairly recent in manufacture. See also Paperweights.

Bottle, barber; pontil, 7¾x3¾" 230.00
Bowl, 4" H, in silver wire basket fr, 7" H.....................................185.00
Door knob, far star cane bundles, brass fittings, 1⅞" 525.00
Lamp, mushroom shade & matching base in brass fr, 18½x12" ..425.00
Lamp, mushroom shade w/cobalt teardrop prisms (12 total), 11½x7" ...425.00
Toothpick holder, 2½x2" 100.00
Trade beads, wht, bl & red chevron, 50 form 26" strand 110.00
Tumbler, 6¼x3" 125.00
Vase, red base, flared cylinder, 10" 425.00

Miniatures

There is some confusion as to what should be included in a listing of miniature collectibles. Some feel the only true miniature is the salesman's sample; other collectors consider certain small-scale children's toys to be

appropriately referred to as miniatures, while yet others believe a miniature to be any small-scale item that gives evidence to the craftsmanship of its creator. For salesman's samples, see specific category; other types are listed below. See also Dollhouses and Furnishings; Children's Things.

Armoire, walnut, molded ogee cornice, panel doors, 1850s, 38x22" .9,500.00
Bench, settle; old gr rpt w/floral stencil, scalloped crest, 17x26x10" 935.00
Blanket chest, cherry Chpndl style, Guild of Shaker Crafts...MI, 16" ..165.00
Blanket chest, pine w/old olive pnt, stenciled florals, 14x30x13".600.00
Blanket chest, pine w/orig gr, dvtl, 1-brd top, sq legs, 10x16x10"......770.00
Blanket chest, poplar, trn ft, dvtl case, inlaid escutcheon, rfn, 14"....330.00
Blanket chest, poplar w/old mustard rpt, till, wire nails, 12x19x11"..550.00
Blanket chest, poplar w/orig grpt, dvtl case, bracket ft, 14x20" ..1,300.00
Blanket chest, poplar w/orig red pnt w/daubs of blk, 15x25x15" ...2,850.00
Box, dome top, grpt, initials in reserve, Am, 19th C, 5x11x7"...1,150.00
Box, writing; pine w/old patina, hinged lid, 1 drw, 4x9x7"..........440.00
Candle mold, tin, 2-tube, petticoat base, 5" 360.00
Chest, mahog, 4 dvtl drw w/beading, rfn, rpl pulls, 26x26"......1,500.00
Chest, mahog English Hplwht, 4 dvtl drw, Fr ft, trn knobs, 14x13x9"....660.00
Chest, mahog Hplwht style, 4-drw, Fr ft, porc pulls, 20th C, 15x11x7"..550.00
Chest, mahog veneer on pine, 3 dvtl drw, button ft, rprs, 8x10" ..195.00
Chest, mahog/pine/poplar, trn front ft, 3 dvtl drw, old finish, 15x14"...1,500.00
Chest, pine, cvd bksplash, 4 grad drws, bracket fr, 1850s, 20x9".575.00
Chest, walnut, 5 dvtl drw w/beveled edge fronts, brass pulls, 9½"....500.00
Chest over drawer, pnt pine, nailed, wire hinges, 19th C, 8x8x5" ...975.00
Desk, slant lid, leather hinges, 2 drws, brn pnt, 19th C, 10x8x7"..575.00
Jar, storage; lt gr, sq form, pontil scar, 1½" 400.00
Noah's ark, wood w/3-color pnt, 2 figures/43 animals, 2½x5⅝"..525.00
Safe, Queen, CI w/combination dial, wheels, EX pnt, 16½x13x10"....720.00

Sofa, serpentine back, stained wood with stenciled gold, embossed velvet upholstery, 10", VG, $500.00.

Utensil rack, wrought iron, 7½", +5 mini utensils.........................50.00
Wine glass, clear glass, appl ft, smooth rim, pontil scar, 2½".........50.00

Minton

Thomas Minton established his firm in 1793 at Stoke on Trent and within a few years began producing earthenware with blue-printed patterns similar to the ware he had learned to decorate while employed by the Caughley Porcelain Factory. The Willow pattern was one of his most popular. Neither this nor the porcelain made from 1798 to 1805 was marked (except for an occasional number series), making identification often impossible.

After 1805 until about 1816, fine tea services, beehive-shaped honey pots, trays, etc., were hand decorated with florals, landscapes, Imari-type designs, and neoclassic devices. These were often marked with crossed 'Ls.' It was Minton that invented the acid gold process of decorating (1863), which is now used by a number of different companies. From 1816 until 1823, no porcelain was made. Through the '20s and '30s, the ornamental wares with colorful decoration of applied fruits and florals and figurines in both bisque and enamel were usually left unmarked. As a result, they have been erroneously attributed to other potters. Some of the ware that was marked bears a deliberate imitation of Meissen's crossed swords. From the late '20s through the '40s, Minton made a molded stoneware line (mugs, jugs, teapots, etc.) with florals or figures in high relief. These were marked with an embossed scroll with an 'M' in the bottom curve. Fine parian ware was made in the late 1840s, and in the 1850s Minton experimented with and perfected a line of quality majolica which they produced from 1860 until it was discontinued in 1908. Their slogan was 'Majolica for the Millions,' and for it they gained widespread recognition. Leadership of the firm was assumed by Minton's son Herbert sometime around the middle of the nineteenth century. Working hand in hand with Leon Arnoux, who was both a chemist and an artist, he managed to secure the company's financial future through constant, successful experimentation with both materials and decorating methods. During the Victorian era, M.L. Solon decorated pieces in the pate-sur-pate style, often signing his work; these examples are considered to be the finest of their type. After 1862 all wares were marked 'Minton' or 'Mintons,' with an impressed year cipher.

Many collectors today reassemble the lovely dinnerware patterns that have been made by Minton. Perhaps one of their most popular lines was Minton Rose, introduced in 1854. The company itself once counted forty-seven versions of this pattern being made by other potteries around the world. In addition to less expensive copies, elaborate hand-enameled pieces were also made by Aynsley, Crown Staffordshire, and Paragon China. Solando Ware (1937) and Byzantine Range (1938) were designed by John Wadsworth. Minton ceased all earthenware production in 1939.

Dinnerware values given in the following listings are for items that were produced from 1870 to 1950. Current production pieces bring lower prices on the resale market. See also Majolica; Pate-Sur-Pate.

Bowl, berry; Ardmore, 5½", 8 for	70.00
Bowl, serving; Rose; shallow, hdls, 10x9"	70.00
Candlesticks, draped nudes hold columns, lt gr/celadon, 16½", pr	1,750.00
Cream soup & saucer, Rose	30.00
Creamer, Rose, sm	42.50
Cup & saucer, Cockatrice, 1916	65.00
Planter, Secessionist, stylized flowers, 1920s, 11x11¾"	400.00
Plate, dinner; Rose, ca 1921, 11", 3 for	85.00
Plate, Eurasian Bullfinch, Mitchell, rtcl rim, ca 1872, 9¾"	465.00
Plate, luncheon; Ardmore, 8"	40.00
Tray, Haddon Hall, 11¼"	35.00
Vase, pk floral 'cloisonne,' moon flask shape, ca 1900, 7¾"	1,175.00
Vase, squeezebag peacock feathers, gr/lav, ovoid, #2707, 13x5½"	1,900.00

Mirrors

The first mirrors were made in England in the thirteenth century of very thin glass backed with lead. Reverse-painted glass mirrors were made in this country as early as the late 1700s and remained popular throughout the next century. The simple hand-painted panel was separated from the mirrored section by a narrow slat, and the frame was either the dark-finished Federal style or the more elegant, often-gilded Sheraton.

Mirrors changed with the style of other furnishings; but whatever type you purchase, as long as the glass sections remain solid, even broken or flaking mirrors are more valued than replaced glass. Careful resilvering is acceptable if excessive deterioration has taken place. In the listings that follow, items are from the nineteenth century unless noted otherwise. The term 'style' (example: Federal style) is used to indicate a

mirror reminiscent of but made well after the period indicated. Obviously these retro styles will be valued much lower than their original counterparts. Our advisor for this category is Michael Hinton; he is listed in the Directory under Pennsylvania.

Key:
Chpndl — Chippendale
Emp — Empire
Fed — Federal
QA — Queen Anne
Vict — Victorian
vnr — veneer

Wall mirror, French Provincial, carved oak with fruit and grotesque motifs, 53x44", $1,300.00.

Brass emb over wood, faceted side lights, Dutch, 20x10½", pr	880.00
CI, openwork base w/column & vintage details, old pnt, 1830s, 25"	350.00
Courting, pine, worn blk/gold floral arabesque, rpl glass, 15x11"	1,500.00
Curly maple Chpndl style, ornate scrolls on crest, 45x21", VG	660.00
Gilt gesso cvd girandole, Am, ca 1810-20, rstr, 43x24"	5,500.00
Gilt gesso Fed, appl spherules, rvpt lady & child, 1815, 34x16"	700.00
Giltwood Continental in Baroque taste, foliage/scrolls, 52x34"	2,500.00
Giltwood Fed, molded rectangle, ca 1835, 38x26"	385.00
Giltwood Fed w/rvpt Neoclassical scene, MA, 19th C, 39½"	700.00
Giltwood Louis XV, floral basket crest, much cvg, 18th C, 38x22"	2,400.00
Giltwood Regency girandole, eagle crest/acanthus leaves, 1820s, 64x36"	14,300.00
Mahog & gilt gesso, eagle crest, old gold rpt, 36"	550.00
Mahog Am Late Fed, blocked corners, 1840s, 36x23"	550.00
Mahog architectural, reeded columns/corner blocks, rvpt scene, 37x20"	330.00
Mahog Chpndl scroll, molded crest, old rprs, 20x11"	165.00
Mahog Chpndl scroll, worn gilt liner/phoenix, rpl/rprs, 28x18"	550.00
Mahog Chpndl scroll, worn silvering, 18x11"	660.00
Mahog Chpndl scroll w/banded vnr & ebony inlay, 16x12"	300.00
Mahog Chpndl scroll w/compo eagle crest, molded fr w/gilt liner, 41"	3,500.00
Mahog Chpndl scroll w/gilt liner, rpr/rstr, 26x15"	440.00
Mahog Chpndl scroll w/inlay, old but not period, rprs, 39x21"	385.00
Mahog Chpndl-style scroll, EX details, some age, 22x13"	330.00
Mahog Chpndl-style scroll, figured vnr & gilt bird, 38x20"	500.00
Mahog Emp w/acanthus & rope-cvd pilasters, inlay ornaments, 50"	750.00
Mahog flame alligatored vnr, rvpt still life, 2-part, 34x18"	200.00
Mahog on pine Chpndl scroll, gilt liner/phoenix, 26x14"	3,500.00
Mahog vnr Chpndl scroll, gilt liner/phoenix, old rpt, rprs, 29x18"	660.00
Mahog vnr Chpndl scroll, gilt phoenix crest, old rpr, 32x18"	1,750.00
Mahog vnr Hplwht scroll w/inlay, rprs/rpl bkboard, 43x22"	475.00
Maple Chpndl-style scroll w/some curl & gilt, 20th C, 35x18"	500.00
Meissen-style porc w/M Antoinette portrait, appl cherubs, 1900s, 31"	2,200.00
Over-mantel, gilt gesso Fed, cvd rosettes, 3-part, 59x38"	2,400.00
Over-mantel, giltwood & gesso Louis Philippe, 1850s, 50x45"	2,000.00
Over-mantel, giltwood Am Fed, cvd ½-columns, 1820s, 61x34"	2,000.00
Over-mantel, giltwood cvd/ebonized Am Fed, 1820, 71x48"	8,250.00
Over-mantel, giltwood Louis XVI style, egg & dart cornice, 83x49"	3,750.00
Pier, giltwood floral bouquet cvd top, cvd appliques, 19th C, 82x54"	925.00
Pier, mahog & giltwood Chpndl style, phoenix crest, 59x27"	750.00
Pier, walnut Eastlake Vict, appl cvgs, marble shelf, 92x28"	1,150.00
Pier, walnut Renaissance Revival, 61x41"	400.00

Pier, walnut/burl Eastlake w/cvg, gold pnt, marble shelf, 100x30"....**660.00**
Pine Co architectural, reeded pilasters, rvpt top, rprs/rfn, 15x14"....**600.00**
Pine Fed architectural, fluted w/corner blocks, rvpt building, 21x13"..**250.00**
Pine fr/base, cvd walnut crest w/2 angels, 108x30"..................**2,500.00**
Shaving, mahog Co Sheraton w/inlay, 2 drw, rprs, 23x18x7½" ..**350.00**
Shaving, mahog Hplwht bowfront, shield, 3-drw, 38x35", VG..**1,500.00**
Tabernacle, gilt gesso Fed, 2-part, 1815-20, 52x29"..................**2,000.00**
Trumeau, pnt/gilt Louis XV/XVI style, 61x42" **2,100.00**
Walnut & gilt gesso Chpndl scroll, 1780s, England, 42x22"....**1,500.00**
Walnut QA, scrolled cornice/pendant, 18th C, 38x18" **1,500.00**
Walnut QA w/gesso Prince of Wales device, 1760s, 40x16"....**1,950.00**
Walnut vnr QA w/parcel gilt, old rfn, 1740-60, 39x17"...........**1,950.00**
Walnut vnr w/figure QA, scrolled crest, rpl glass, 16x9" **770.00**
Walnut w/scrolled crest & molded fr, Elliot Phila, 1786, 22x12"..**2,300.00**

Mocha

Mochaware is utilitarian pottery made principally in England (and to a lesser extent in France) between 1780 and 1840 on the then prevalent creamware and pearlware bodies. Initially, only those pieces decorated in the seaweed pattern were called 'Mocha,' while geometrically decorated pieces were referred to as 'Banded Creamware.' Other types of decorations were called 'Dipped Ware.' During the last thirty to forty years the term 'Mocha' has been applied to the entire realm of 'Industrialized Slipware' — pottery decorated by the turner on his lathe using coggle wheels and slip cups.

Mocha was made in numerous patterns — Tree, Seaweed or Dandelion, Rope (also called Worm or Loop), Cat's-eye, Tobacco Leaf, Lollypop or Balloon, Marbled, Marbled and Combed, Twig, Geometric or Checkered, Banded, and slip decorations of rings, dots, flags, tulips, wavy lines, etc. It came into its own as a collectible in the latter half of the 1940s and has become increasingly popular as more and more people are exposed to the rich colorings and artistic appeal of its varied forms of abstract decoration. (Please note: Values hinge to a great extent on vivid coloration, intricacy of patterns and unusual features.)

The collector should take care not to confuse the early pearlware and creamware Mocha with the later kitchen yellow ware, graniteware, and ironstone sporting mocha-type decoration that was produced in America by such potters as J. Vodrey, George S. Harker, Edwin Bennett, and John Bell. This type was also produced in Scotland and Wales and was marketed well into the twentieth century.

Bowl, blk band w/wht wavy lines, bl/tan/wht stripes, wear, 9¾".**715.00**
Bowl, waste, earthworm, wht & brn, bl & tan stripes, 3⅛x6¼", EX.......**350.00**
Bowl, waste; gr & blk bands encircle mc marbleized body, 3x5⅝", EX..**495.00**
Creamer, seaweed, blk on ochre, beaded/quilted gr bands, 4½", VG...**1,300.00**
Mug, balloons, blk & wht on rust band, zig-zag line at rim, rpr, 2" **1,750.00**
Mug, earthworm, bl & brn on olive/cream & ochre sunflowers, 5¾"..**2,400.00**
Mug, earthworm, 3-color on wht band on mustard w/blk & wht stripes, 6"..**550.00**
Mug, foliage bands w/gr/brn stripes, lt bl/ornate bands, 5" **715.00**
Mug, geometrics, blk on wht w/tooled gr bands, tan stripes, 5½"....**1,485.00**
Mug, geometrics, brn on cream w/brn & yel stripes, rprs, 5" **450.00**
Mug, seaweed, blk on cream, wht & dk brn stripes, 4⅝"..............**850.00**
Mug, wavy lines, brn on cream w/ochre stripes, cream dots, 4¾" ..**900.00**
Mug, wide wht slip band at top, molded C hdl, 19th C, 3½" **450.00**
Pepper pot, bl & tan stripes, brn check tooled bands, 4¼" **1,200.00**
Pepper pot, bl/wht/blk stripes, 4⅜", EX....................................**575.00**
Pepper pot, cat's eye, bl/ochre & cream on dk brn w/mc stripes, 5" ..**1,100.00**
Pepper pot, cat's eye, wht/cinnamon/brn on bl w/mc stripes, 4⅜"....**920.00**
Pepper pot, earthworm, blk/wht on tan, brn stripes, chip, 4⅜"...**385.00**
Pepper pot, earthworm, 3-color on bl w/gr beads, dome top, 5", EX ...**800.00**
Pepper pot, tobacco leaf, dk brn/ocher/ginger on cream, dome, 5" ..**1,950.00**
Pitcher, bl bands w/blk stripes on wht, wear/stain, 7⅝"..............**165.00**

Pitcher, cat's eye, brn/cream/ochre on bl, brn/wht stripes, 7"...**1,500.00**
Pitcher, cat's eye, 4-color on ochre, bl/cream stripes, 7¼" **3,500.00**
Pitcher, earthworm, bl/brn on celadon & ochre, 8x5"..............**2,200.00**
Pitcher, earthworm, bl/brn/wht on brn, gr bands, 6¼x4", EX..**1,000.00**
Pitcher, earthworm, bl/brn/wht on mc striped ground, 5½x4".**1,380.00**
Pitcher, earthworm, blk & wht, mc stripes, bl band, 5½", VG ...**330.00**
Pitcher, earthworm, lt bl/wht/brn on tan & dk brn, prof rpr hdl, 5"..**660.00**
Pitcher, earthworm, tan/wht, dk & lt brn stripes, rprs, 6"...........**385.00**
Pitcher, geometrics, brn on cream w/brn & bl bands, 7¼", EX...**925.00**
Pitcher, lt gr/brn/tan tooling & bands, leaf hdl, 6¾", EX.........**1,800.00**

Pitcher, marbled blue, brown, black, and white with blue band at rim, white handle (repaired), 7¾", $2,400.00; Mug, earthworm on orange and yellow stripes, green impressed band at top, repair/small chips, 5¾", $2,500.00.

Pitcher, seaweed, bl on orange band, blk & wht stripes, 5"......**1,870.00**
Pitcher, seaweed, blk & tan, bl bands at top & bottom, 6¼", EX..**550.00**
Pitcher, zigzag earthworm, wht & brn on gr w/brn/wht stripes, 6" ...**1,380.00**
Pitcher, 2 lt bl bands on wht, bbl shape, C hdl, 6⅜" **75.00**
Stein, eng wreath w/inscription/1816, mc tands/lines, pewter lid, 8" ..**990.00**
Sugar bowl, balloons, 3-color on cream w/brn/wht stripes, 3x4" **1,750.00**
Waste bowl, earthworm, bl & wht on gray band, brn stripes, 4¾" **500.00**

Molds

Food molds have become popular as collectibles — not only for their value as antiques, but because they also revive childhood memories of elaborate ice cream Santas with candy trim or barley sugar figurals adorning a Christmas tree. Ice cream molds were made of pewter and came in a wide variety of shapes and styles. Chocolate molds were made in fewer shapes but were more detailed. They were usually made of tin or copper, and then were nickel plated to keep them from tarnishing or rusting, and also for sanitary reasons. Hard candy molds were usually metal, although primitive maple sugar molds (usually simple hearts, rabbits, and other animals) were carved from wood. (Unless otherwise indicated, the hard candy molds in our listings are cast aluminum or stainless steel.) Cake molds were made of cast iron or cast aluminum and were most common in the shape of a lamb, a rabbit, or Santa Claus. Our advisors for this category are Dale and Jean Van Kuren; they are listed in the Directory under New York.

Chocolate Molds

Boy on sled, Letang & Fils #4652, 2-pc, w/clip............................**175.00**
Boy w/valentine, Gesetzl Germany #8141, 4¼" **80.00**
Bulldog, Anton Reiche #25420, hinged 2-pc, 12x9¾" **300.00**
Bunny w/basket, USA, 2 clips, 8¼x7¼" **60.00**
Cat w/boots, JKV Tilburg #16301, 2-part, 5x3".............................**65.00**
Chick coming out of egg, Anton Reiche, 3" **60.00**
Child on chicken, Anton Reiche #6531, 2-part, 4x3¼" **230.00**
Christmas bear w/tree, 2-pc, 3 clips, 5½" **85.00**

Doves (2), 2-pc, w/orig clips, 11x4½x6" 130.00
Father Christmas, Jaburg Bros, 2-pc, 4½x2" 100.00
Father Christmas w/2 children, #1023, 2-pc w/clip, 11" 415.00
Greyhound, Anton Reiche #24855, 2-part, 3x8½" 200.00
Horse, Sommet, 2-pc w/clips, 9x10" 240.00
Jack-o'-lanterns (5), Anton Reiche #17688, dtd 1929, 9¼" L 310.00
Keystone Cop, Anton Reiche #17541, 6½" 90.00
Pig playing horn, Anton Reiche #17595, 2-pc, hinged, 5½" 135.00
Rabbit bride, Anton Reiche #23957, 2-pc w/clips, 6¾" 275.00
Rabbit in house, Anton Reiche #25658, 2-pc, 6½x5" 225.00
Rabbit on scooter w/pack on bk, Germany, 2-pc, 8" 175.00
Rabbit w/jacket, Made in USA #4744, 2-pc, 9" 155.00
Santa on donkey, Letang, 5" 95.00
Santa w/bag, #3305, 2-part, 11x4¾" 395.00
Santa w/canes, toys, etc, Anton Reiche #25272, 13" 875.00
Teddy bear, Anton Reiche #17536, hinged, 1933, 4¾" 350.00
Turkeys (2), hinged, 4 clips, 6¼x9¾x2⅝" 80.00

Ice Cream Molds

Abraham Lincoln, #579, 4½" 65.00
Acorn, CC #816 BIS, 3¼x2¾x2" 135.00
Apple, S&Co #149, 2½x4" 40.00
Apple, 3" 25.00
Asparagus bunch, CC, 9½" 55.00
Basket, E&Co #1014, 4x3" 50.00
Boot, E&Co, #1230 ....45.00
Bride & groom, E&Co NY #M1201 ....115.00
Bride & groom in foliage fr, #468, 3¾" dia 75.00
Butterfly, #181, 5" 80.00
Christmas candle, 5" 130.00
Cow, 3-part, S&Co, #493, 3½x4½" 150.00

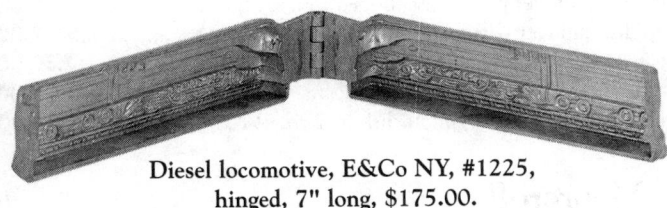

**Diesel locomotive, E&Co NY, #1225,
hinged, 7" long, $175.00.**

Fish, S&Co #??85, hinged, 4¾" 95.00
Flower, #495, 3x4¼" 57.50
Football, 3-pc, 2 hinges, pre-WWII, 3½" 50.00
George Washington, E-1099, 3¾" 75.00
Harp, E-116, 5½x3½" 110.00
King of Spades, E&Co, 4x2¾" 42.50
Lion's Club symbol, E&Co, 3¼" dia 47.50
Masonic, 5¾" 25.00
Melon, 2-part, 6½" 55.00
Monkey, E&Co 45.00
Palmer Cox Brownie, 5xx2¼" 90.00
Pumpkin, E&Co #309, hinged, 2½x3" 45.00
Rose, S&Co #554, 3½" 35.00
Santa, E-991, 4½" 110.00
Shield w/stars, S&Co #281 ....37.50
Teddy bear, 2-pc, hinged, E&Co, 5¾" 200.00
Train, #856, 4x7½" 155.00
Witch on broomstick, E-1153, 1950s, 5¼" 200.00

Maple Sugar Molds

Animals/birds/fish/etc, cvd maple, ca 1800s, 15½x7", EX 70.00

Beaver, hand cvd, EX detail, 5x9" 90.00
Heart, wood, iron hinge, pouring hole at top, 1890s, 5" 85.00
Heart w/face, hand-cvd wood, in orig tin case, 1800s, 5½" 300.00
House w/cvd-in windows & doors, separate sides & roof, 5½" 110.00
Openwork on rnd fluted cups, CI, 1840s, 12 in 11x16" fr 115.00
Rooster, cvd hardwood, 2-pc, ca early 1800s, 7¾x5¼" 195.00
Sq sections (9), cvd hardwood, 33x5¼" 80.00
Strawberry, deeply cvd pine, rectangle, 1830s, 1¾x5½x9" 165.00

Miscellaneous

CI, 3 squirrels seated eating nuts, #155, 2¾x7" 195.00
Stoneware, salt glaze, rnd w/scallop design inside, 10⅞" 140.00
Tin, chicken, 3-part, Germany, 9" 200.00
Tin, fish, oval, 2¾x10x5⅝" 75.00
Tin/copper, eagle in oval, 6" L 100.00
Tin/copper, fruit, 6½" dia 120.00
Tin/copper, star design, ribbed sides, 4½" dia 50.00
Tin/copper, wheat sheaf oval reserve on rectangle, 9" L 150.00

Monart

Scottish glassmaker, John Moncrief was fascinated by the technique of suspending colored enamels within the molten glass during the glass-making process. Recognizing the potential of the process (which he had observed while in France), he began his own business in Perth, Scotland, in 1924. The glassware he created was called Monart. Several commercial lines were along the fine artware pieces designed with scrolls or feathers suspended within the glass. Nearly all examples are unmarked, most having originally carried a paper label.

Bowl, gr/orange/aventurine in clear, yel-orange mottle rim, 10" .175.00
Vase, cluthra type, dk bl/med bl w/goldstone, 6x5" 150.00
Vase, earth tone mottle, opal spatter base, mk Scotland, 12" ..1,250.00
Vase, mauve mottled w/pale gr at top w/aventurine, ftd, 7" 225.00
Vase, red mottle w/maroon stripes & opal mottling, 4½" 130.00

Monmouth

The Monmouth Pottery Company was established in 1892 in Monmouth, Illinois. It was touted as the largest pottery in the world. Their primary products were utilitarian: stoneware crocks, churns, jugs, water coolers, etc. — in salt glaze, Bristol, spongeware, and Albany brown. In 1906 they were absorbed by a conglomerate called the Western Stoneware Company. Monmouth became their #1 plant and until 1930 continued to produce stoneware marked with their maple leaf logo. Items marked 'Monmouth Pottery Co.' were made before 1906. Western Stoneware Co. introduced a line of artware in 1926. The name chosen for the artware was Monmouth Pottery. Some stamps and paper labels add ILL to the name.

Bowl, salt glazed, brn inside, base mk, 2-gal 200.00
Churn, #5/maple leaf, cobalt on salt glaze, 5-gal 125.00
Churn, Bristol, 2-gal 250.00
Churn, salt glaze, mini, 4" 1,200.00
Churn, salt glazed, 3-gal 350.00
Churn, 2 Men in a Crock stencil, 5-gal 800.00
Churn #3/maple leaf, cobalt on salt glaze, 3-gal, 13" 50.00
Cookie jar 50.00
Cooler, ice water; bl & wht sponge, w/lid & spigot, 8-gal 2,000.00
Cooler, ice water; bl & wht sponge, 5-gal 2,000.00
Cow & calf, brn, mk Monmouth Pottery Co 2,000.00

Crock, Bristol, mini, 2½" 600.00
Crock, Bristol, 10-gal 100.00
Crock, Bristol, 20-gal 100.00
Crock, Bristol, 60-gal 1,500.00
Crock, early dull Bristol w/cobalt stencil.................300.00
Crock, salt glaze, unmk, 2-gal 60.00
Crock, salt glaze, 3-gal...150.00
Crock, salt glazed, hand decor, base mk, 2-gal 250.00
Crock, stencil, bl on dk brn Albany, 3-gal 300.00
Crock, stencil, bl on dk brn Albany, 6-gal 400.00
Crock, 2 Men in a Crock stencil, 10-gal 500.00
Hen on nest, bl & wht spongeware 1,200.00
Jug, bristol w/Albany top, mini, 2½" 500.00
Pig, brn, mk Monmouth Pottery Co............................1,000.00
Snuff or preserve jar, wax seal 350.00
Tobacco jar, monk, brn Albany 300.00
Vase, bl matt, incised shoulder band, 16x10" 495.00
Water cooler, bl & wht spongeware, mini....................1,000.00

Mont Joye

Mont Joye was a type of acid-cut French cameo glass produced by Cristallerie de Pantin in Paris around the turn of the century. It is accented by enamels. Our advisor for this category is Don Williams; he is listed in the Directory under Missouri.

Biscuit jar, floral, mc on frost, ormolu rim hdl & lid, 10" 800.00
Biscuit jar, floral, purple/gr/yel on frost, 10" 800.00
Bowl, chestnuts on branches, 3-color on icy ground w/gold, 8" ..525.00
Bowl, poppies, mc on red frost w/gold, invt rim, 9½"..............1,150.00
Vase, floral, purple/gold, gold leaves/silver buds as base, 19"....1,850.00
Vase, floral on textured gr w/gold, 9¾" 600.00

Moon and Star

Moon and Star was originally produced in the 1880s by John Adams & Company of Pittsburgh. In the 1960s, Joseph Weishar of Wheeling, West Virginia, owner of the Island Mould & Machine Company, reproduced some of the original molds and incorporated the pattern into approximately forty new and different items. Two of the largest distributors of this line were L.E. Smith of Mt. Pleasant, Pennsylvania, who pressed their own glass, and L.G. Wright of New Martinsville, West Virginia, who had theirs pressed by Fostoria, Fenton, and Westmoreland. Both companies carried a large and varied assortment of shapes and colors. Several other companies were involved in its manufacture as well, especially of the smaller items.

Over the years the glassware has been pressed in amberina (yellow shading to orange- or ruby-red), green, amber, crystal, light blue, and ruby. Pieces in ruby and light blue are most collectible and harder to find than the other colors, which seem to be abundant. Purple, pink, cobalt, amethyst, tan slag, and light green and blue opalescent were made, too, but on a lesser scale.

In 1992 the Weishar company introduced a new color, teal green, which was followed in 1993 with sapphire blue opalescent, and in 1994 with cranberry ice. These items carried the Weishar mark and were made primarily for collectors. Currently the company is producing water sets, salt and pepper shakers, creamers and sugars, spoon holders, and various relish trays in Delphite and Delphite carnival, Crown Tuscan and Crown Tuscan carnival, Colonial Blue, Millennium Rose (pink), and various other colors on a more limited basis.

Our values are given for vintage glassware in ruby and light blue; for amberina, green, and amber, deduct 20%.

Ashtray, allover pattern, scalloped rim, 4 rests, 8" dia 25.00

Ashtray, moons at rim, star in base, 6-sided, 5½" 18.00
Banana boat, allover pattern, scalloped rim, 12" 45.00
Basket, allover pattern, scalloped rim, solid hdl, 9", from $50 to ..65.00
Bowl, allover pattern, ftd, crimped rim, 7½", from $25 to...........35.00
Butter/cheese dish, patterned lid, plain base, 7" dia, from $50 to..65.00
Cake plate, allover pattern, low collared base, 13" dia, $50 to......60.00
Cake stand, allover pattern, removable plate, 2-pc, 11" dia 75.00
Candle bowl, allover pattern, ftd, 8", from $25 to 30.00
Candle holders, allover pattern, flared base, 4½", pr, $20 to........25.00
Candy dish, allover pattern on base & lid, ftd ball shape, 6".........25.00
Canister, allover pattern, 1-lb or 2-lb, from $12 to 15.00
Canister, allover pattern, 3½-lb or 5-lb, from $18 to....................22.00
Chandelier, ruffled dome shape w/allover pattern, amber, 10" 100.00
Cheese dish, patterned base, clear plain lid, 9½", from $65 to......70.00
Compote, allover pattern, ftd, flared crimped rim, 5", from $15 to..22.00
Compote, allover pattern, raised ft, patterned lid & finial, 10x8"..65.00
Compote, allover pattern, raised ft w/scalloped edge, 5¾x3" 35.00
Compote, allover pattern, scalloped rim, ftd, 5½x8" 35.00
Compote, allover pattern, scalloped rim, ftd, 5x6½" 20.00
Compote, allover pattern, scalloped rim, ftd, 7x10".....................45.00
Creamer & sugar bowl (open), disk ft, sm, from $25 to.................35.00
Epergne, allover pattern, 2-pc, 9", minimum value.....................65.00
Jardiniere, allover pattern, 9¾", minimum value 85.00
Jardiniere/tobacco jar, allover pattern, 6", minimum value...........45.00
Lamp, miniature; amber 145.00
Lamp, miniature; bl, from $185 to 225.00
Lamp, miniature; gr 185.00
Lamp, miniature; milk glass 245.00
Lamp, miniature; red 235.00
Light, allover pattern body, metal fittings, from $40 to 50.00
Nappy, allover patttern, crimped rim, 2¾x6", from $12 to...........18.00
Plate, patterned body & center, smooth rim, 8".........................35.00
Relish bowl, 6 lg scallops form allover pattern, 1½x8" 35.00
Salt cellar, allover pattern, scalloped rim, sm flat ft 8.00
Soap dish, allover pattern, oval, 2x6" 12.00
Sugar shaker, allover pattern, metal top, 4½x3½" 50.00
Syrup pitcher, allover pattern, metal lid, 4½x3½".......................75.00
Tumbler, no pattern at rim or disk ft, 7-oz, 4¼", from $12 to........15.00

Moorcroft

William Moorcroft began to work for MacIntyre Potteries in 1897. At first he was the chief designer but very soon took over their newly created art pottery department. His first important design was the Aurelian Ware, part transfer and part hand painted. Very shortly thereafter, around the turn of the century, he developed his famous Florian Ware, with heavy slip, done in mostly blue and white. Since the early 1900s there has been a succession of designs, most of them very characteristic of the company. Moorcroft left MacIntyre in 1913 and went out on his own. He had already well established his name, having won prizes and gold medals at the St. Louis World's Fair as well as in Paris. In 1929 Queen Mary, who had been collecting his pottery, made him 'Potter to the Queen,' and the pottery was so stamped up until 1949. William Moorcroft died in 1945, and his son Walter ran the company until recent years. The factory is still in existence. They now produce different designs but continue to use the characteristic slipwork. Moorcroft pottery was sold abroad in Canada, the United States, Australia, and Europe as well as in specialty areas such as the island of Bermuda.

Moorcroft went through a 'Japanese' stage in the early teens with his lovely lustre glazes, Oriental shapes and decorations. During the mid-teens he began to produce his most popular Pomegranate Ware, and Wisteria (often called 'Fruit'). Around that time he also designed the popular Pansy line as well as Leaves and Grapes. Soon he introduced a beautiful landscape series called variously Hazeldine, Moonlit Blue, Eventide, and Dawn. These wonderful designs along with Claremont (Mushrooms) seem to be the most sought after by collectors today. It would be possible to add many other designs to this list.

During the 1920s and 1930s, Moorcroft became very interested in highly fired Flambe (red) glazes. These could only be achieved through a very difficult procedure which he himself perfected in secret. He later passed the knowledge on to his son.

Dating of this pottery is done by knowledge of the designs, shapes, signatures, and marks on the bottom of each piece; an experienced person can usually narrow it down to a short time frame. Prices escalated for this 'rediscovered' pottery in the late 1980s but has now leveled off. This is true mainly of the pre-1935 designs of William Moorcroft, as it is items from that era that attract the most collector interest. Prices in the listings below are for pieces in mint condition unless noted otherwise; no reproductions are listed here. Advisors for this category are Wilfred and Dolli Cohen; they are listed in the Directory under California.

Biscuit barrel, Florian, floral on wht, SP mts, MacIntyre, 5"....1,400.00
Biscuit barrel, Florian, poppies, gr mk, 9" 1,950.00
Bowl, Eventide, sunset scene, WM, MIE, 3x8"........................1,400.00
Bowl, Moonlit Blue, trees on bl, mk, MIE, #195Y, 5½x7".......1,450.00
Bowl, pomegranates on cobalt, WM, #56, 1928-29, 3x7"............850.00
Box, anemones, lt to bl, cyclindrical, mk, 1945, 3½" H..............260.00
Coffeepot, Florian, floral, bl hdl/spout, MacIntyre 1,350.00
Creamer & sugar bowl, Lorne, cream/bl Florian w/gr band, 1st mk, 3" ...650.00
Cup & saucer, Florian, bl, MacIntyre 795.00
Cup & saucer, Florian, gr/brn leaves on wht, bl rim, MacIntyre .800.00
Egg cup, Florian, poppies, SP fr, mk, 4 for...............................1,100.00
Lamp base, grape & leaf flambe, unmk, 12"...............................1,200.00
Marmalade, Florian, floral on wht, SP fr, MacIntyre 700.00
Pitcher, orchids on gr, mk, 4½" 250.00
Pitcher, tankard, Florian, poppies, MacIntyre, 8" 1,350.00
Sweetmeat, Florian, bl poppies, silver fr, MacIntyre, 3½" 850.00
Tea set, floral band on teal, turq spout/hdls, pot+cr/sug 1,850.00
Teapot, Aurelian, bl/gr/wht, Registered 1898, MacIntyre............750.00
Teapot, Edward, floral, bl/gr/wht, bl hdl/spout, mk 700.00
Teapot, floral, bl/gr, bl hdl/spout, MacIntyre, 1898, 7", +trivet...1,500.00
Teapot, Lorne, tulips, bl/cream w/gr band, MacIntyre, 2-cup 850.00
Tray, pin; pansies, paper label, dtd 1953, 9" L 125.00
Vase, anemones, mauve/purple on cobalt, flared rim, bulbous, 3"..250.00
Vase, anemones, mc on cobalt, bulbous, 1947, 3¼"......................260.00
Vase, anemones on cobalt & gr, bulbous w/flared rim, 10"..........600.00
Vase, clematis, mc on red-orange flambe, mid-20th C, 7"...........400.00
Vase, clematis on tan to bl, WM, 6"...200.00
Vase, Florian, floral on bl w/butterflies, stick form, 1900s, 9" ..1,850.00
Vase, freesia, red flambe, WM, 12¾x7"......................................2,500.00
Vase, fruit, red/garnet on cobalt, chalice shape, paper seal, 9x5½" ..1,200.00
Vase, Hazeldine, trees, gr/gray on gr, mk, 1913, 4½x7".............1,600.00
Vase, pomegranates, mc on cobalt, early 20th C, rpr, 7⅝" 465.00
Vase, pomegranates on cobalt, fluted cylinder, 1913-16, 13" ...1,950.00
Vase, wisteria, mc on cobalt, shouldered, mid-20th C, 10" 900.00
Vase, wisteria on cobalt, MIE, #74, 12"....................................1,200.00
Vase, wisteria on cobalt, WM, 8⅛" 700.00

Moravian Pottery and Tile Works

The Moravian Pottery and Tile Works, Doylestown, Pennsylvania, was founded by Dr. Henry Chapman Mercer in 1898. He discovered the art and science of tile making on his own, without training from the existing American or European tile industry. This, along with his diverse talents as an author, anthropologist, historian, and artist, led Dr. Mercer to create something very unique. He approached tile design with an his-

toric point of view, and he created totally new production methods that ultimately became widely accepted by manufacturers of handcrafted tile. The subject matter for the designs he preferred included nature and the arts, colonial tools and artifacts, storytelling, and medieval themes. Both of these 'new' approaches (to design and production) allowed Dr. Mercer to become extremely influential in the development of pottery and tile in the Arts & Crafts Movement in America.

After Mercer's death in 1930, the Tile Works was managed by Frank Swain until 1954. In 1967 it was purchased by the Bucks County Dept. of Parks & Recreation. Tiles are being produced there today in the handmade tradition of Mercer; they are marked with a conjoined MOR and dated. Collectors look for the early tiles (mostly pre-1940), the preponderance of which bear no backstamps. These tiles were made using both red and white clays and are also referred to as 'Mercer' tiles. Our advisor for this category is Karen Guido; she is listed in the Directory under Connecticut.

Florence Nightingale's lamp, green and cream with red flush, 4", $70.00. (Photo courtesy Karen Guido)

Aquarius, Zodiac series, gr w/red flush high glaze, V border, 4".....75.00
Bounty, filigree border, bl/wht matt, 4"...70.00
Bounty, gr/cream w/red flush high glaze, 4"...................................90.00
Cow, self-fr, red clay/bl, 4"...80.00
Dragon, lg brocade, red clay w/bl semi-matt, 5x4"..........................90.00
Fire Starter, bl/wht matt, 4"..70.00
Gnome, brocade, smoked finish, 3½"..65.00
La Perouse ship, gr/cream w/red flush, high glaze, 4" 85.00
Literature, Arts series, gr/yel w/red flush high glaze, 4".................95.00
Montezuma (city), bl/cream w/red flush, high glaze, 4" 155.00
Organ, Musician series, brocade, mc, 7x5", VG.............................225.00
Pomegranate, brocade, dk gr high glaze, 4"...................................140.00
Scorpio, pierced & notched gr/yel high glaze, 4¼" 90.00
Sheep, red/gr, self-fr, 4", VG..70.00
Swan, red/gr, self-fr, 4"...85.00
Swan & tower, bl w/terra cottal, stove plate, 7¾" 350.00

Morgantown Glass

Incorporated in 1899, the Morgantown Glass Works experienced many name changes over the years. Today 'Morgantown Glass' is a generic term used to identify all glass produced there. Purchased by Fostoria in 1965, the factory was permanently closed in 1971.

Golf Ball is the most recognized design with crosshatched bumps equally distributed along the stem (very similar to Cambridge #1066, identified with alternating lines of dimples between rows of crosshatching). Color identification is difficult and further information is provided by Gene Florence in his book *Stemware Identification* (Collector Books). Prices for Golf Ball with ranges begin with lower values referring to colors other than Steigel Green, Spanish Red, or Ritz Blue with the high range reflecting values for those colors. For further information we also recommend *Elegant Glassware of the Depression Era, Ninth Edition*, by Gene Florence (Collector Books).

Golf Ball, candle, torch; 6", pr, from $225 to....300.00
Golf Ball, creamer....175.00
Golf Ball, pilsner, 11-oz, 9⅛", from $135 to....175.00
Golf Ball, stem, champagne; 5½-oz, 5", from $25 to....35.00
Golf Ball, stem, cordial; 1½-oz, 3½", from $40 to....50.00
Golf Ball, stem, sherry; 2½-oz, 4⅝", from $40 to....55.00
Golf Ball, tumbler, tea; ftd, 12-oz, 6¾", from $30 to....40.00
Golf Ball, tumbler, wine; ftd, 4⅜", from $17 to....25.00
Queen Louise, crystal w/pk, bowl, finger; ftd....200.00
Queen Louise, crystal w/pk, plate, salad....150.00
Queen Louise, crystal w/pk, stem, cocktail; 3-oz....350.00
Queen Louise, crystal w/pk, stem, sherbet; 5½-oz....300.00
Queen Louise, crystal w/pk, stem, water; 9-oz....385.00
Sunrise Medallion, bl, bowl, finger; ftd....85.00
Sunrise Medallion, bl, stem, cocktail; 6⅛"....55.00
Sunrise Medallion, bl, tumbler, ftd, 11-oz, 5½"....85.00
Sunrise Medallion, crystal, parfait, 5-oz....55.00
Sunrise Medallion, crystal, saucer....15.00
Sunrise Medallion, crystal, tumbler, flat, 4¼"....20.00
Sunrise Medallion, pk or gr, vase, bud; slender, 10"....295.00
Sunrise Medallion, pk or gr, plate, salad; 7½"....20.00
Sunrise Medallion, pk or gr, tumbler, ftd, 4-oz, 3½"....35.00
Tinkerbell, azure or gr, bowl, finger; ftd....75.00
Tinkerbell, azure or gr, plate, finger bowl liner....35.00
Tinkerbell, azure or gr, stem, cocktail; 3½-oz....95.00
Tinkerbell, azure or gr, stem, goblet; 9-oz....125.00
Tinkerbell, azure or gr, stem, sherbet; 5½-oz....85.00
Tinkerbell, azure or gr, stem, wine; 2½-oz....120.00

Moriage

The term 'moriage' refers to certain Japanese wares decorated with applied slipwork designs. There are several methods used to achieve the characteristic relief effect. The decorative devices may be designed separately and applied to the vessel, piped on in narrow ribbons of clay (slip-trailed), or built up by brushing on successive layers of liquefied slip. See also Dragon Ware; Nippon.

Ashtray, floral, 4¾"....60.00
Rose bowl, turq & wht slipwork, jewels, ftd, 5¾"....285.00
Tea set, floral reserve on wht band on bl, ca 1900, 3-pc....140.00
Vase, floral, mc on bl, slim w/flared base, early 1800s, 14½x6"...525.00
Vase, irises, mk US Pat Nbr9 2179, Feb 9, 1909, Japan, 6"....240.00

Mortars and Pestles

Mortars are bowl-shaped vessels used for centuries for the purpose of grinding drugs to a powder or grain into meal. The masher or grinding device is called a pestle.

Ash burl, G detail & finish, age crack, 6½"....60.00
Brass, eng H Poppenberg, sm edge splits, 3¾"....55.00
Burl, rfn, 4⅛", +pestle w/brass tip....100.00
Burl, 7", +plain wood pestle....480.00
Curly maple w/old varnish, 8"....330.00
Hardwood, w/old worn finish, 4⅜"....110.00
Hardwood w/old red, minor age cracks, 7¼"....275.00

Mortens Studio

Oscar Mortens was already established as a fine sculptural artist when he left his native Sweden to take up residency in Arizona. During the 1940s he developed a line of detailed animal figures which were distributed through the Mortens Studios, a firm he co-founded with Gunnar Thelin. Thelin hired and trained artists to produce Mortens' line, which he called Royal Designs. More than two hundred dogs were modeled and over one hundred horses. Cats and wild animals such as elephants, panthers, deer, and elk were made, but on a much smaller scale. Bookends with sculptured dog heads were shown in their catalogs, and collectors report finding wall plaques on rare occasions. The material they used was a plaster-type composition with wires embedded to support the weight. Examples were marked 'Copyright by the Mortens Studio' either in ink or decal. Watch for flaking, cracks, and separations. Crazing seems to be present in some degree in many examples. When no condition is indicated, the items listed below are assumed to be in near-mint condition, allowing for minor crazing.

Airedale, 5x6"....85.00
Arabian horse, wall plaque....125.00
Bay trotter horse....75.00
Bengal tiger, 6x8"....175.00
Boston terrier, wall plaque, foil sticker, 6", M....200.00
Boxer pup, recumbent, unclipped ears, 5½" L....65.00
Boxer pup, sitting, 3"....60.00
Brahma bull, blond version, #401....150.00
Bulldog, standing, 3½x6"....85.00
Chihuahua, wall plaque, 5x6"....260.00
Chihuahua pup, sitting, 3½x2¾"....60.00
Chow, red, standing, 5½"....110.00
Dalmatian, red collar, 5½x8½"....85.00
Doberman pinscher, #783, 7¼"....135.00
Doberman pinscher, sitting, 6½x5½"....145.00
English pointer, wht w/brn spots, 6½x10½"....190.00
English setter, gold foil label, mini....55.00
Fox terrier, red & wht, 5⅛x6¾"....170.00

Great Dane, 8½x8", $95.00.

Irish setter, brn, #720A, 6½"....110.00
Kerry blue terrier, 4¾x6"....110.00
Old English sheep dog, foil sticker, 6" L....150.00
Pekingese, #741, Royal Design sticker, 2½x3¾"....75.00
Persian cat, brn tabby, foil stickers, 4x4"....110.00
Persian cat, silver tabby, 3¾x4½"....100.00
Poodle, plaque, gray, 7x6"....100.00
Samoyed (Husky), 2¼"....50.00
Siamese cat, recumbent, 2¾x5½"....135.00
Siamese cat, standing, 5x8"....70.00
Spaniel, begging, 5¼"....70.00
St Bernard, 6½x8"....180.00
Swedish lady, bookends, #311, pr....145.00
Walking Black Saddlebred, horse, sticker....80.00
Wire-hair fox terrier, sitting, 3¼"....40.00

Wolfhound, 6¼x7¼"..145.00

Morton Pottery

Six potteries operated in Morton, Illinois, at various times from 1877 to 1976. Each traced its origin to six brothers who immigrated to America to avoid military service in Germany. The Rapp brothers established their first pottery near clay deposits on the south side of town where they made field tile and bricks. Within a few years, they branched out to include utility wares such as jugs, bowls, jars, pitchers, etc. During the ninety-nine years of pottery operations in Morton, the original factory was expanded by some of the sons and nephews of the Rapps. Other family members started their own potteries where artware, gift-store items, and special-order goods were produced. The Cliftwood Art Pottery and the Morton Pottery Company had showrooms in Chicago and New York City during the 1930s. All of Morton's potteries were relatively short-lived operations with the Morton Pottery Company being the last to shut down on September 8, 1976. For a more thorough study of the subject, we recommend *Morton's Potteries: 99 Years, Vols. I* and *II*, by Doris and Burdell Hall; their address can be found in the Directory under Illinois.

Morton Pottery Works — Morton Earthenware Co. (1877 – 1917)

Baker, deep yel ware, 8" dia..50.00
Bowl, mixing; yel ware, lattice w/wht slip lines, nested set of 5 ..280.00
Cuspidor, cobalt, 7" dia..75.00
Jug, Dutch, cobalt, 3-pt..130.00
Jug, milk; brn Rockingham, 8-pt..120.00
Milk boiler, brn Rockingham, 1½-pt..45.00
Mug, coffee; yel ware w/wht slip lines, 1-pt..85.00
Rice nappy, fluted, yel ware, 4½"..30.00
Rice nappy, plain, yel ware, 13"..85.00
Stein, German motto top/bottom, gr (rare color), 1-pt..90.00
Teapot, acorn shape, brn Rockingham, 3¾- to 4-cup..90.00
Teapot, globe shape, brn Rockingham, 5¼-pt..70.00
Teapot, Rebecca at the Well, brn Rockingham, 8½-pt..150.00
Teapot, std shape, yel ware, 1-cup..50.00

Cliftwood Art Potteries, Inc. (1920 – 1940)

Beer set, chocolate drip, bbl-shape pitcher+6 mugs..225.00
Bookends, elephant figurals, bl/gray drip, 4½x6", pr..125.00
Bookends, lion & lioness on Herbage Green bases, 4¼x6¼", pr ...150.00
Bowl, hdld batter; orchid/pk drip over wht, 9" dia..75.00
Candlesticks, blk semi-lustre, 7", pr..50.00
Card holder, elephant w/side pockets, cobalt, 5¾x4x5"..90.00
Clock, donut shape, Lux clock works, Herbage Green, 8½"..............95.00
Clock, octagonal, Lux clock works, chocolate drip, 8½"..............125.00
Creamer, cow figural, tail forms hdl, chocolate drip, 3¼x6½" 125.00
Figurine, elephant, trumpeting, Old Rose, 10½x7½"..50.00
Figurine, lioness, chocolate drip, 7x12"..85.00
Figurine, Police dog, chocolate drip, 5x8½"..80.00
Figurine, Scottie dog, cobalt, 8x5½"..55.00
Vase, peacock feather w/twig hdls, turq matt, 15½"..55.00
Vase, snake w/fish, figural hdls, chocolate drip, 18¼"..100.00
Vase, tree trunk w/3 open limbs at top, Herbage Green, 9"..........70.00

Midwest Potteries, Inc. (1940 – 1944)

Cow creamer, brn drip w/yel hdl, 5"..24.00
Figurine, canaries (2) on stump, yel/gold, 4¼"..30.00
Figurine, duck w/2 ducklings behind, yel/wht, 3x6½x1¼"..........24.00

Figurine, female nude, September Morn, 14k gold, 12"..............100.00
Figurine, geese (attached pr), wht/yel, 4x2¾"..20.00
Figurine, sunfish on seaweed base, yel/brn spray, 10½"..................40.00
Figurine, turkey, brn/tan spray w/red cold-pnt decor, 12"..............35.00
Miniature, dog, brn drip, 2x2"..14.00
Miniature, hen & rooster, bl/yel drip, 2¼x¾", pr..18.00
Miniature, lion, brn drip, 2½x1¾"..14.00
Miniature, polar bear, wht, 2½x1¾"..15.00
Miniature, swan, wht matt, 2¾x2¼"..12.00
Pitcher, duck figural w/cattail hdl, brn/gray spray, 10"..................40.00
Planter, bird & nest, bl, 6½x3½"..18.00
Planter, broken egg shell on tripod, 14k gold, 3¾"..20.00
Planter, Calico cat, bl/yel spatter, 8"..20.00
Planter, cat cactus holder, cactus forms tail, cobalt, 2x3"..............12.00
Planter, deer, recumbent, brn spray, 6½x5½"..18.00
Planter, Gingham dog, bl/yel spatter, 8"..20.00

Morton Pottery Company (1922 – 1976)

Bank, acorn, brn..35.00
Bank, bulldog, wht..25.00
Bank, hen, blk/wht..35.00
Bank, kitten, recumbent, yel/wht spray..20.00
Bank, log cabin school, brn..30.00
Bank, pig, blk/wht..50.00
Bank, pig, wall hanger, bl..30.00
Bowl, beater; A&J Double Action egg beater, brn..65.00
Bowl, mixing; Pilgrim Pottery line, bl, nested set of 6..............150.00
Bowl, mixing; Woodland spatterware, nested set of 4..............175.00
Bowl, mold, heart shape w/dogwood cluster in bottom, brn..........50.00
Bowl, plain nappy, Sears Roebuck, Vincent Price, bl spongeware .45.00
Creamer/sugar bowl, hen & rooster, wht w/brushed blk, red cold pnt...35.00
Figurine, buffalo, brn/blk spray, 10x7"..100.00
Figurine, cat, recumbent, wht/gray spray, 9x5½"..20.00
Figurine, Colonial lady, HP underglaze decor, 10"..40.00
Figurine, hound dog, wht/brn/blk, #583, 3¼x4½"..15.00
Figurine, pointer dog, brn spray, 6¾x4"..24.00
Figurine, Scottish terrier, wht/brn spray, 7½x7"..15.00
Figurine, seeing-eye dog, Leader Dog on collar, blk, 5¾"..............20.00
Pie bird, duckling, bl/pk/wht, 5½"..45.00
Pie bird, rooster, gr/pk/wht, 5¼"..75.00
Pie bird, yel/gr/red brushed decor, 5"..40.00
Pitcher, no drip type, groove under lip catches drips, any color 30.00
Pitcher, no drip type, hand decor w/gold & enamels..50.00
Stein, beer; bbl shape, advertising Old Heidelberg, brn, 5"..........25.00
Stein, beer; bbl shape, Happy Days Are Here Again, brn, 5"........30.00
Stein, beer; leaf design, brn Rockingham, 5"..18.00
Stein, beer; Parrot on Lattice, brn Rockingham, 5"..20.00

American Art Potteries (1947 – 1963)

Planter, lamb, white and pink, #456, 8½", $25.00.
(Photo courtesy Doris and Burdell Hall)

Doll parts, head/arms/legs, 3", set of 5 pcs 60.00
Doll parts, head/arms/legs, 7¼", set of 5 pcs 90.00
Figurine, deer, brn/wht spray, gr base, dk brn antlers, 12" 40.00
Figurine, Hampshire hog, blk w/wht ribbon, gr base, 5½x7½"......40.00
Figurine, Poland China hog, wht/gray spots, gr base, 5½x7½"......50.00
Figurine, wild horse, brn spray, 11½" 35.00
Planter, baby buggy, wht, decor, 5½x7" 20.00
Planter, bunny beside log, natural spray colors, 4¾" 20.00
Planter, elephant trumpeting, wht, 7½x2½" 30.00
Planter, swan, orchid/pk w/gold 25.00
Planter, Teddy bear on 3 building blocks, wht/pk/bl, 12x4x4".......24.00
TV lamp, Afghan hounds, blk, 15" 55.00
TV lamp, conch shell, gan/gr spray, 6½" 30.00
TV lamp, fish (2) on rectangular base, gr/yel spray, 6x8x3½" 25.00
Vase, bulbous w/molded flowers, brn/yel spray, 12¾" 45.00
Vase, cornucopia; dbl peacock feathers, brn/pk spray, 10½" 45.00
Vase, ewer form, pk, 14" 20.00
Vase, ruffled tulip form, brn/yel/pk spray, 9" 24.00

Moser

Ludwig Moser began his career as a struggling glass artist, catering to the rich who visited the famous Austrian health spas. His talent and popularity grew and in 1857 the first of his three studios opened in Karlsbad, Czechoslovakia. The styles developed there were entirely his own; no copies of other artists have ever been found. Some of his original designs include grapes with trailing vines, acorns and oak leaves, and richly enameled, deeply cut or carved floral pieces. Sometimes jewels were applied to the glass as well. Moser's animal scenes reflect his careful attention to detail. Famed for his birds in flight, he also designed stalking tigers and large, detailed elephants, all created in fine enameling.

Moser died in 1916, but the business was continued by his two sons who had been personally and carefully trained by their father. The Moser company bought the Meyr's Neffe Glassworks in 1922 and continued to produce quality glassware.

When identifying Moser, look for great clarity in the glass; deeply carved, continuous engravings; perfect coloration; finely applied enameling (often covered with thin gold leaf); and well-polished pontils. Our advisor for this category is Don Williams; he is listed in the Directory under Missouri. Items described below are enameled unless noted otherwise. If no color is mentioned in the line, the glass is clear.

Beaker, cranberry w/gold & florals, facet-cut body, 5½" 300.00
Bottle, scent; mc floral on vines, enameled stopper, 6", pr 600.00
Bowl, bl to orange, amber ft, mc floral, fold-over rim, 5x7½" 400.00
Champagne, heavy gold, set of 6 ....1,200.00
Creamer & sugar bowl, cranberry, extensive florals 1,150.00
Cruet, amethyst to clear, mc floral, 7¾" 500.00
Cruet, bl, wht/gold lilies of the valley, faceted stopper 325.00
Decanter, cranberry, cut/gold pattern, 14", +6 cordials 1,500.00
Decanter, gilt & enameled leaves, ovoid, cylinder neck, 12x5" ..500.00
Decanters, emerald w/gilt-decor, bulbous, teardrop stopper, 15", pr...1,100.00
Dresser set, emerald gr w/florals & gold, 4 pcs+10½" tray 1,200.00
Goblet, bl stain w/gilt floral, appl prunts on stem, 1890s, 8" 425.00
Goblet, cranberry stain w/gilt blown-out bowl, 1890s, 5" 300.00
Goblet, red, gilt floral, ca 1890, 6½" 365.00
Mug, cranberry, appl acorns/mc leafage 450.00
Pitcher, bl crackle, stork & landscape, angle hdl, 5½" 650.00
Pitcher, clear crackle, stork scene, cylindrical, 10" 700.00
Pitcher, florals, gold band, 2⅛" 200.00
Pitcher, topaz irid crackle w/grasshopper & dragonfly, 1880s, 6".550.00
Planter vase, amethyst, snow scene w/cabins, bk: oak branch, 7x12"..1,850.00
Shade, Coin Spot, amberina, mc leaves & 5 emb acorns, 5½x7½"...900.00

Vase, amber, relief gold band w/soliders, 5¾" 150.00
Vase, amber, ships/crowns/birds/sun/sunflower, 1920s, 8½" 130.00
Vase, amethyst, florals, appl gr snake hdls, gold dots/wheat, 10".575.00
Vase, amethyst, wheat stalks & flowers, snake hdls, 9½" 575.00
Vase, aqua to clear, pansies & grasses w/gold, ribbed, 13½" 950.00
Vase, clear over yel variegated w/floral & ruby-stain band, 15¾".....285.00
Vase, clear to gr w/geometric gold floral/scroll panels, trumpet, 17"...200.00
Vase, cobalt w/armed men in gold band, 5x4¾" 180.00
Vase, cranberry, mc flowers & gold at shoulder, 5" 200.00
Vase, gray-topaz, cameo florals w/cut lattice work w/gold, 12¼".500.00
Vase, mottled earth tones w/bronze o/l, appl acorns, att, 6" 600.00
Vase, olive craquelle, fish & plants, 4 appl pods, 6", NM...........300.00
Vase, Persian, lime gr cased to wht, shouldered, 6¾" 465.00
Vase, pk crackle, floral, ftd, 5" 425.00
Vase, ruby facets, unmk, 3⅞" 125.00
Vase, smoky gray, facet-cut panels in 4 horizontal bands, 1925, 10"..250.00
Vase, topaz crackle, fish in seascape, bulbous, 4¼" 325.00
Vase, trumpet; crystal to gr w/gold panels, florals, 17" 200.00
Wine, gr w/gold enamel decor, air-twist stem, 7" 200.00

Moss Rose

Moss Rose was a favorite dinnerware pattern of many Staffordshire and American potters of the mid-1800s. In America the Wheeling Pottery of West Virginia produced the ware in large quantities, and it became one of their bestsellers, remaining popular well into the '90s. The pattern was colored by hand; this type is designated 'old' in our listings to distinguish it from the more modern Moss Rose design of the twentieth century, which we've also included. It's not hard to distinguish between the two. The later ware you'll recognize immediately, since the pattern is applied by decalcomania on stark white backgrounds. It has been made in Japan to a large extent, but companies in Germany and Bavaria have produced it as well. Today, there is more interest in the twentieth-century items than in the older ware.

Bowl, Japan, 1950s, 4x7" 20.00
Cake/sandwich plate, Royal Albert.................................45.00
Candle holders, Japan, 3", pr..15.00
Cup & saucer, Japan, 2½", 5½" 10.00
Cup & saucer, Royal Albert 22.50

Creamer and sugar bowl, old Haviland & Co., 7" to finial, $90.00.

Dinnerware set, Japan, 1960s, child sz, 38-pc, MIB 165.00
Egg boiler, electric, NM...55.00
Lamp, oil; 2-hdl, Japan, 7½" 30.00
Mustache cup, gold accents, old Haviland, from $225 to...........275.00
Pitcher, gold trim, old Limoges, 8", from $250 to 300.00
Place setting, plate+bread plate+berry bowl+c/s, 5-pc set 30.00
Plate, dinner; Royal Albert, 11¼" 15.00
Plate, 12-sided, old Limoges, 9¼" 30.00
Platter, Ucagco, rare, 12", from $65 to 85.00
Shakers, Royal Albert, 3", pr..30.00

Soap dish, w/lid & drainer, gold trim, old Haviland, 5x4", from $175 to...**200.00**
Tea set, child sz, 29-pc, MIB **300.00**
Tea tile, old Haviland, 6½" dia, from $125 to............................**150.00**
Teapot, whistling, electric, Japan, 6"................................**15.00**
Tidbit, 2-tier, Japan..**20.00**

Mother-of-Pearl Glass

Mother-of-Pearl glass was a type of mold-blown satin art glass popular during the last half of the nineteenth century. A patent for its manufacture was issued in 1886 to Frederick S. Shirley, and one of the companies who produced it was the Mt. Washington Glass Company of New Bedford, Massachusetts. Another was the English firm of Stevens and Williams. Its delicate patterns were developed by blowing the gather into a mold with inside projections that left an intaglio design on the surface of the glass, then sealing the first layer with a second, trapping air in the recesses. Most common are the Diamond Quilted, Raindrop, and Herringbone patterns. It was made in several soft colors, the most rare and valuable is rainbow — a blend of rose, light blue, yellow, and white. Occasionally it may be decorated with coralene, enameling, or gilt. Watch for twentieth-century reproductions, especially in the Diamond Quilted pattern. Our advisors for this category are Betty and Clarence Maier; they are listed in the Directory under Pennsylvania. See also Coralene.

Basket, Herringbone, pk ruffled rim, frosted twist hdl, 5½" **300.00**
Bottle, scent; Peacock Eye, yel, stick neck, sterling cap, 7½"......**750.00**
Bottle, scent; wht, 24 vertical stripes, flip-top cap, 4" dia **400.00**
Bowl, Dmn Quilt, apricot, ruffled rim, 3½x8½" **200.00**
Bowl, Dmn Quilt, chartreuse, appl frosted ft, 5½x6" **275.00**
Box, lav-pk, leaves & scrolls, brass bail hdl, hinged lid, 4¾" **350.00**
Celery vase, lemon yel w/florals, ruffled, SP holder w/hdls, 9" **385.00**
Cookie jar, gr w/florals, SP hdl, lid & rim **230.00**
Cruet, Dmn Quilt, apricot, thorn hdl, frosted stopper, NM **350.00**
Cruet, Dmn Quilt, butterscotch, frosted thorn hdl, 6½" **550.00**
Cruet, Herringbone, bl, ruffled top, frosted hdl, 6" **500.00**
Cup & saucer, Raindrop, pk, 3", 5"..................................**285.00**
Ewer, Dmn Quilt, pk, melon-rib body, crimped mouth, 12" **475.00**
Pitcher, bl w/florals & foliage, frosted hdl, oval top, bulbous **390.00**
Pitcher, Dmn Quilt, pk, pinched top, camphor hdl, 7"...............**175.00**
Pitcher, Dmn Quilt, pk, ruffled rim, clear reeded hdl, 9"............**400.00**
Pitcher, Raindrop, bl to wht, tricorn spout, high loop hdl, 9" **325.00**
Rose bowl, Dmn Quilt, bl, att Webb, 2¾" **385.00**
Rose bowl, Dmn Quilt, chartreuse, appl frosted ft, 5½x6" **275.00**
Rose bowl, Dmn Quilt, rainbow, crimped top, 3¾x3¾".............**750.00**
Rose bowl, Ribbon, wht, 2½x3" **800.00**
Tumbler, Dmn Quilt, pk, daisies & leaves, 7⅞" **345.00**
Vase, Dmn Quilt, bl, ruffled rim, 5x4½" **225.00**
Vase, Dmn Quilt, chartreuse gr, ruffled rim, floral ormolu base, 10" ..**720.00**
Vase, Drape, pk, 7¼" **315.00**
Vase, Federzeichnung, brn on pk, bulbous, ftd, mk Pat/#d, 7¼"....**1,750.00**
Vase, Federzeichnung, chocolate, burnished gold tracery, 7x4½"..**2,500.00**
Vase, Herringbone, apricot, ruffled rim, 7¼"..........................**125.00**
Vase, Herringbone, bl, ruffled top, clear thorn hdls, 8½" **150.00**
Vase, Herringbone, bl, 4-fold crystal rim, shouldered, 8"............**175.00**
Vase, Pompeian Swirl, bl & pk air-trap ribbons, Stevens & Wms, 5½"..**545.00**
Vase, Raindrop, raspberry, trifold top, Pairpoint, 8" **150.00**
Vase, Ribbon, wht w/gold bows & garlands, 6½" **1,465.00**
Vase, Swirl w/air traps, brn, pale gr int, Harrach, 5½" **1,250.00**

Movie Memorabilia

Movie memorabilia covers a broad range of collectibles, from books and magazines dealing with the industry in general to the various promotional materials which were distributed to arouse interest in a particular film. Many collectors specialize in a specific area — posters, pressbooks, stills, lobby cards, or souvenir programs (also referred to as premiere booklets). In the listings below, a one-sheet poster measures approximately 27" x 41", three-sheet: 41" x 81", and six-sheet: 81" x 81". Window cards measure 14" x 22". Values are for examples in NM condition unless noted otherwise. See also Autographs; Cartoon Art; Magazines; Paper Dolls; Personalities; Rock 'n Roll Memorabilia; Sheet Music.

Insert, Baby Doll, Carroll Baker sucking thumb, 1956, VG+ **90.00**
Insert, Band of Angels, C Gable/Y DeCarlo, 1957, EX.................**50.00**
Insert, Bedtime Story, F March/L Young, 1941, EX....................**50.00**
Insert, Bringing Up Father, Maggie & Jiggs series, 1946.................**60.00**
Insert, Country Girl, G Kelly/W Holden/B Crosby, 1954............**50.00**

Insert, *Creature From the Black Lagoon,* **Richard Carlson, Julia Adams, 1954, $1,200.00.** (Photo courtesy Shwann Galleries)

Insert, Dangerous When Wet, Tom & Jerry scene, 1953 ....**85.00**
Insert, Doctor at Sea, Bardot pinup shot, 1956, rare, EX.............**65.00**
Insert, Father of the Bride, E Taylor/S Tracy, 1962 (reissue)..........**70.00**
Insert, Going My Way, Bing Crosby, 1944 ....**175.00**
Insert, Gypsy, N Wood/K Malden/R Russell, 1962.......................**50.00**
Insert, Happy Go Lucky, D Powell/B Hutton/M Martin/R Vallee, 1943...**65.00**
Insert, Her Husband's Affairs, Lucille Ball, 1947, VG+ **75.00**
Insert, Invitation to the Dance, Gene Kelly, 1956......................**65.00**
Insert, Iron Petticoat, K Hepburn/B Hope, 1956, VG+................**40.00**
Insert, Love in the Afternoon, A Hepburn/G Cooper, 1957.......**100.00**
Insert, Mad Wednesday, Harold Lloyd, 1950..........................**75.00**
Insert, Rob Roy, Disney film, Richard Todd, 1953 ....**50.00**
Insert, Twin Beds, J Bennett/G Brent, 1942............................**40.00**
Insert, What a Woman, Rosalind Russell/Brian Aherne, 1943 .....**60.00**
Insert, Whirlpool, Gene Tierney, 1950.................................**50.00**
Lobby card, College Holiday, Martha Raye, 1936, VG+ **75.00**
Lobby card, Dark City, Charlton Heston, 1950........................**30.00**
Lobby card, Guess Who's Coming to Dinner?, Tracy/Hepburn, 1967, VG ..**30.00**
Lobby card, Three Stooges Fun-O-Rama, Joe Besser as 3rd Stooge, 1959....**40.00**
Lobby card, Voice in the Night, Tim McCoy, 1934 ....**50.00**
Lobby card, Ziegfield Girl, Tony Martin, 1941...........................**25.00**
Lobby card set, Challange to Lassie, Lassie/E Gwenn, 1949 ....**50.00**
Lobby card set, Gigi, Leslie Caron/Louis Jourdan, 1958 ....**75.00**
Lobby card set, Hole in the Head, F Capra comedy, 1959, VG+ ..**50.00**
Lobby card set, Kismet, H Keel/A Blyth, 1956.........................**50.00**
Lobby card set, Let's Make It Legal, Marilyn Monroe, 1951........**175.00**
Lobby card set, Mr 880, B Lancaster/E Gwenn/D McGuire, 1950, EX...**50.00**
Lobby card set, The Spy Who Loved Me, Bob Peak artwork, 1977 ..**50.00**
Lobby card set, Wuthering Heights, Timothy Dalton, 1971 ....**35.00**
Poster, Aristocats, Disney animation, 1971, 1-sheet **125.00**
Poster, Bedtime Story, F March/L Young, 1941, 1-sheet, VG+......**65.00**
Poster, Boom, E Taylor/R Burton, 1968, 1-sheet **35.00**
Poster, Born To Be Bad, Joan Fontaine, 1950, 1-sheet, G+ **85.00**

Poster, Chain Gang, Douglas Kennedy, 1950, 1-sheet 40.00
Poster, Easy Come Easy Go, Elvis Presley, 1966, 3-sheet 100.00
Poster, Elmer Gantry, B Lancaster/J Simmons, 1960, 6-sheet......125.00
Poster, Enchantment, D Niven/T Wright, 1949, 3-sheet 100.00
Poster, Family Plot, Bruce Dern, 1976, 1-sheet 50.00
Poster, Fit for a King, Joe E Brown, 1947 (reissue), 1-sheet...........30.00
Poster, Forbidden Planet, W Pidgeon/etc, 1956, 1-sheet (linen bk) ...2,000.00
Poster, Girl Hunters, Mickey Spillane, 1963, 1-sheet 75.00
Poster, Go Go Mania, Beatles/Animals/etc, 1965, 1-sheet, VG+ ..75.00
Poster, Goldfinger, Sean Connery, 1964, 1-sheet (linen bk) 650.00
Poster, Grand Prix, J Garner/EM Saint, 1967, ½-sheet (rolled) 65.00
Poster, Grease, J Travolta/O Newton-John, 1978, 1-sheet............85.00
Poster, Hawaii, J Andrews/M von Sydow, 1966, 1-sheet...............35.00
Poster, High School Confidential, Jerry Lee Lewis, 1958, 1-sheet.....100.00
Poster, House on Haunted Hill, Vincent Price, 1958, 1-sheet, rare...850.00
Poster, If I Had My Way, Bing Crosby, 1940, 1-sheet 100.00
Poster, If You Knew Susie, E Cantor/J Davis, 3-sheet 150.00
Poster, King Solomon's Mines, 1962 (reissue), 1-sheet 50.00
Poster, Lady & the Tramp, Disney animation, 1955, 1-sheet 700.00
Poster, Lady Sings the Blues, Diana Ross, 1972, 1-sheet 40.00
Poster, Las Vegas Story, J Russell/V Mature, 1952, ½-sheet 150.00
Poster, Let's Go Steady, Mel Torme & the Meltones, 1944, 1-sheet...40.00
Poster, Magic Town, J Stewart/J Wyman, 1947, 3-sheet 100.00
Poster, Mame, Lucille Ball, Bob Peak artwork, 1974, 1-sheet........35.00
Poster, Man Called Adam, S Davis Jr/L Armstrong/O Davis, 1966, 1-sheet.....75.00
Poster, Miracle Worker, P Duke/A Bancroft, 1962, ½-sheet 50.00
Poster, Munster Go Home, 1966, 3-sheet, VG+ 150.00
Poster, Muscle Beach Party, F Avalon/A Funicello, 1964, 40x60"...100.00
Poster, One Million Years BC, Raquel Welch, 1966, 40x60" (rolled).......100.00
Poster, Palm Beach Story, C Cobert/J McCrea, 1942, 1-sheet (linen bk)....850.00
Poster, Pickup Alley, Anita Ekberg, 1957, 1-sheet......................125.00
Poster, Porgy & Bess, Gershwin musical, 1959, 1-sheet...............125.00
Poster, Prison Train, Fred Keating, 1937, 1-sheet 125.00
Poster, Private Affair, R Cummings/N Kelly, 1940, 1-sheet, VG+ ...50.00
Poster, Riverboat Rhythm, Leon Errol, 1945, 1-sheet..................50.00
Poster, Road to Nashville, Johnny Cash/etc, 1966, 1-sheet..........50.00
Poster, Roman Holiday, A Hepburn/G Peck, 1962 (reissue), 40x60"......100.00
Poster, Satchmo the Great, L Armstrong documentary, 1957, ½-sheet..150.00
Poster, Saturday Night Fever, John Travolta, 1977, 1-sheet...........65.00
Poster, Shock Corridor, Peter Breck, 1963, ½-sheet (rolled).........65.00
Poster, Single Room Furnished, J Mansfield, 1968, ½ sheet (rolled)...50.00
Poster, Slattery's Hurricane, V Lake/R Widmark/L Darnell, ½-sheet ..65.00
Poster, Small Town Girl, J Powell, 1953, 1-sheet.......................45.00
Poster, Song of Love, Katharine Hepburn, 1946, ½-sheet............75.00
Poster, Stolen Holiday, Kay Francis, 1937, 1-sheet (rstr on linen)...550.00
Poster, Strait Jacket, Joan Crawford, 1964, 1-sheet, Fair..............75.00
Poster, Sudden Fear, J Crawford/J Palance, ½-sheet (rolled), VG...100.00
Poster, Summer Storm, L Darnell/G Sanders, 1944, 1-sheet (linen bk) ...250.00
Poster, The Happening, Anthony Quinn, 1967, 1-sheet 35.00
Poster, The Strangler, Victor Buono, 1964, 1-sheet 100.00
Poster, Torn Curtain, P Newman/J Andrews, 1966, 3-sheet..........50.00
Poster, True to Life, D Powell/M Martin, 1943, 1-sheet 50.00
Poster, When Ladies Meet, J Crawford/R Taylor/G Garson, '41, ½ sheet ...150.00
Poster, Where the Boys Are, C Francis/G Hamilton, 1961, 1-sheet.........75.00
Poster, Where the Hot Wind Blows, Gina Lollobrigida, 1960, 1-sheet....35.00
Poster, Who's Afraid...Virginia Woolf, E Taylor/R Burton, '66, 1-sheet....50.00
Poster, Woman on Pier 13, R Ryan/L Day, 1950, 3-sheet............100.00
Poster, Yellow Rolls Royce, I Bergman/R Harrison, 1965, 1-sheet..50.00
Poster, You Can't Beat Love, J Fontaine/P Foster, 1937, 1-sheet ..250.00
Poster, Zulu, Michael Caine, 1963, 40x30" (rolled), rare 100.00
Program, Big Parade, John Gilbert, VG....................................55.00
Program, The Ten Commandments, DeMille film, 16 pgs, 1923, EX ...75.00
Souvenir book, Around the World in 80 Days, 1957..................25.00
Window card, Dragnet, Jack Webb, 1954...............................75.00

Window card, General Died at Dawn, G Cooper/M Carroll, 1936, rare..350.00
Window card, Having a Wonderful..., G Rogers/D Fairbanks Jr, 1937, G+..150.00
Window card, I'm No Angel, Mae West/Cary Grant, 1933, rare, EX ..750.00
Window card, Johnny Doughboy, Jane Withers, 1943 ....50.00
Window card, Littlest Rebel, Shirley Temple, 1935, VG+ 350.00
Window card, Peter Pan, Disney animation, 1958 (reissue), VG ..100.00
Window card, Prince Valiant, J Mason/J Leigh/R Wagner, 1954...75.00
Window card, Rose of the Rancho, G Swarthout/J Boles, 1935..125.00
Window card, The Working Man, George Arliss, 1933 ....200.00

Mt. Washington

The Mt. Washington Glass Works was founded in 1837 in South Boston, Massachusetts, but moved to New Bedford in 1869 after purchasing the facilities of the New Bedford Glass Company. Frederick S. Shirley became associated with the firm in 1874. Two years later the company reorganized and became known as the Mt. Washington Glass Company. In 1894 it merged with the Pairpoint Manufacturing Company, a small Brittania works nearby, but continued to conduct business under its own title until after the turn of the century. The combined plants were equipped with the most modern and varied machinery available and boasted a working force with experience and expertise rival to none in the art of blowing and cutting glass. In addition to their fine cut glass, they are recognized as the first American company to make cameo glass, an effect they achieved through acid-cutting methods. In 1885 Shirley was issued a patent to make Burmese, pale yellow glassware tinged with a delicate pink blush. Another patent issued in 1886 allowed them the rights to produce Rose Amber, or amberina, a transparent ware shading from ruby to amber. Pearl Satin Ware and Peachblow, so named for its resemblance to a rosy peach skin, were patented the same year. One of their most famous lines, Crown Milano, was introduced in 1893. It was an opal glass either free blown or pattern molded, tinted a delicate color and decorated with enameling and gilt. Royal Flemish was patented in 1894 and is considered the rarest of the Mt. Washington art glass lines. It was decorated with raised, gold-enameled lines dividing the surface of the ware in much the same way as lead lines divide a stained glass window. The sections were filled in with one or several transparent colors and further decorated in gold enamel with florals, foliage, beading, and medallions.

Our advisors for this category are Betty and Clarence Maier; they are listed in the Directory under Pennsylvania. See also Amberina; Cranberry; Salt Shakers; Burmese; Crown Milano; Mother of Pearl; Royal Flemish; etc.

Creamer and sugar bowl (3½" to top of finial), pansies on white opaque, $350.00.

Bowl, Butterfly & Daisy, pierced SP rim, 8½" 750.00
Bowl, cameo griffins/urns/garlands, pk on wht, 3½x9" 425.00
Goblet, Rose Amber, amberina...250.00
Lamp, oil; cameo floral, pk/wht, orig shade, NM.....................2,500.00
Mustard pot, flower garlands on wht, SP lid w/spike finial, 3¼".385.00
Pitcher, bl satin w/1893 WF, Mt WA, 2½".................................435.00
Plate, Butterfly & Daisy, 8" 200.00
Plate, 5 Grecian ladies on burmese (nonfactory), detailed border, 12"....950.00
Rose bowl, lustreless, mc cherubs, lg...430.00

Shaker, cockleshell, floral w/bl on opal to cream, 2½" 800.00
Shakers, bluerina, Hartford SP fr, pr..400.00
Shakers, daisies, gold & wht on cranberry, fig form, pr..............250.00
Shakers, floral, bl on yel to opal, lay-down egg form, pr.............400.00
Shakers, floral, red & gr on wht, fig form, pr 300.00
Shakers, floral on cockle shell form, 5", pr in SP donkey fr 3,300.00
Sugar shaker, autumn leaves on pnt burmese, 3x3½" 400.00
Sugar shaker, chrysanthemums on wht to bl w/gold, 4¼" 385.00
Sugar shaker, daisies, mc on wht sculptured body, fig form, 4x3¾"....1,600.00
Sugar shaker, daisies on lemon yel to wht satin, egg form, 4½" ..350.00
Sugar shaker, Strawberry Dmn & Fans, egg shape 600.00
Sugar shaker, violets & gold on lt gr satin, 4½" 385.00
Tankard, Greek Lady/figure w/wings, grotesque head under spout, 9" ..800.00
Toothpick holder, wht lustreless w/HP leaves, hat shape, 2⅛" 400.00
Vase, Lava, appl hdls, 4½x5" 2,500.00
Vase, Lava, blk w/mc chips, bulbous, flared rim, 5⅜x4⅛" 1,950.00
Vase, Lava, gr & bl irid, pinched top, quatrafold rim, 6½" 1,600.00
Vase, Napoli, chicks in the rain, 8¾" 1,400.00
Vase, Napoli, chrysanthemums, mc w/gold webbing, #837, 5¼x6½"...1,200.00
Vase, Napoli, 5 spider mums, mc w/gold, trumpet neck, #880, 10" ...1,350.00
Vase, Verona, floral, gold on deep rose on crystal, #932, 16¼x5" ...2,750.00
Vase, Verona, florals lined w/gold & silver on pk, #918, 9" 1,250.00

Mulberry China

Mulberry china was made by many of the Staffordshire area potters from about 1830 until the 1850s. It is a transfer-printed earthenware or ironstone named for the color of its decorations, a purplish-brown resembling the juice of the mulberry. Some pieces may have faded out over the years and today look almost gray with only a hint of purple. (Transfer printing was done in many colors; technically only those in the mauve tones are 'mulberry'; color variations have little effect on value.) Some of the patterns (Corean, Jeddo, Pelew, and Formosa, for instance) were also produced in Flow Blue ware. Others seem to have been used exclusively with the mulberry color. Our advisor for this category is Mary Frank Gaston.

Abbey, creamer 195.00
Abbey, pitcher, 8-sided, 7¼" 265.00
Abbey, teapot, Wm Adams, 10¼", EX 435.00
Athens, gravy boat, Meigh 85.00
Athens, sugar bowl..105.00
Aurora, bowl, vegetable; Morley, 2⅛x10⅞x8½" 125.00
Bochara, bowl, vegetable; Edwards, w/lid.................................375.00
Bochara, plate, Edwards, 9"..75.00
Bochara, tureen, Edwards, w/lid, underplate & ladle 650.00
Calcutta, teapot..275.00
Castle Scenery, pitcher, 8" 395.00
Corea, plate, 7¼"...55.00
Corea, platter, Clementson, 14x10½"...265.00
Corea, sauce tureen, Clementson, 6½".......................................145.00
Corean, pitcher, Podmore Walker, 5½"......................................165.00
Corean, plate, 7¾"...50.00
Corean, plate, 9¾"...65.00
Corean, platter, Podmore Walker, 13½"....................................225.00
Corean, platter, 16x12¼"...325.00
Corean, teapot...600.00
Cyprus, creamer, 8-panel, Davenport, 5⅝"................................145.00
Della, platter, MT&C, 18x13½"..195.00
Flora, creamer 170.00
Flora, platter, Thomas Walker, 15¼x12" 250.00
Hyson, sugar bowl...165.00
Jeddo, gravy boat, Adams...175.00

Jeddo, platter, 13x10" 250.00
Longport, plate, T&J Mayer, 9½" 25.00
Medina, cup & saucer..65.00
Panama, creamer, Challinor..245.00
Pelew, pitcher, water...195.00
Peruvian, cup & saucer, handleless...70.00
Rhone Scenery, pitcher, water; 10", EX....................................100.00
Rhone Scenery, platter, 13½" 175.00
Rhone Scenery, tureen, saucer; w/underplate............................250.00
Seine, platter, Wedgwood, 13½x10⅜" 160.00
Shannon, plate, 8"..20.00
Shapoo, cup plate 65.00
Strawberry, tea bowl & saucer, 3" cup......................................110.00
Temple, pitcher..125.00
Vincennes, bowl, vegetable; w/lid...380.00
Vincennes, plate, 9½"..75.00
Vincennes, platter, Alcock, 15½x11¾".......................................195.00
Vincennes, platter, 20x15½"..410.00
Vincennes, relish, 8-sided, scroll hdl...110.00
Washington Vase, bowl, serving; Podmore Walker, 3¾x9" 145.00
Washington Vase, pitcher, Podmore Walker, 5½" 135.00
Washington Vase, sugar bowl, lion's head hdls, Podmore Walker ...240.00
Washington Vase, teapot..525.00

Muller Freres

Henri Muller established a factory in 1900 at Croismare, France. He produced fine cameo art glass decorated with florals, birds, and insects in the Art Nouveau style. The work was accomplished by acid engraving and hand finishing. Usual marks were 'Muller,' 'Muller Croismare,' or 'Croismare, Nancy.' In 1910 Henri and his brother Deseri formed a glassworks at Luneville. The cameo art glass made there was nearly all produced by acid cuttings of up to four layers with motifs similar to those favored at Croismare. A good range of colors was used, and some later pieces were gold flecked. Handles and decorative devices were sometimes applied by hand. In addition to the cameo glass, they also produced an acid-finished glass of bold mottled colors in the Deco style. Examples were signed 'Muller Freres' or 'Luneville.' Our advisor for this category is Don Williams; he is listed in the Directory under Missouri.

Cameo

Bowl, raspberry branches, cut/pnt, red/butterscotch/gr/amethyst, 3" ...950.00
Lamp, Broken Pine, brn/gr/yel/frost, 12" base, 24½" overall 9,500.00
Vase, anemones/stems, fuchsia/opal frost w/mc inclusions, 7¾" 2,600.00
Vase, bleeding hearts/vines, rust/brn/red-pk/wht, sm shoulder, 7¾" ...2,000.00
Vase, flowering vines, bl/gr/yel/frosted mottle, bulbous, 8".......1,200.00
Vase, ginko leaves, dk gr/amethyst frost, red jewels, 5¼" 1,200.00
Vase, landscape, chocolate/peach/bl, globular, 10" 4,000.00
Vase, leopards (4) band over panels, cream to amber, 8⅞" 3,500.00
Vase, roses/leaves, 4-color, 10½x9" 4,600.00
Vase, tree/mtn/lake, brn/orange, 5¼x5½" 2,000.00
Vase, trees/mtn/lake, dk brn/orange, de Sevigne, 5¼x5½" 1,350.00
Vase, trees/mtns/lake, 4-color, internal decor sky, 11" 3,150.00
Vase, violets, burgundy/dk & lt gr/yel, bbl shape, 4¾" 1,400.00
Vase, wood nymphs/trees/lake, gr/salmon/bl/wht, 13¼" 3,250.00

Miscellaneous

Chandelier, frosted flower-form dome shade; 4 metal arms, 38" ...2,000.00
Lamp, autumn landscape dome shade, 3-arm, mk std, 11½" 2,300.00
Lamp, boudoir; bl/purple/orange mottled mushroom form, 1925, 12" ..800.00
Vase, frosted cobalt/orange/yel mottle, tapered ovoid, 11¼", NM.........635.00

Vase, orange mottle, ftd, hdls, 14¾".................................750.00

Muncie

The Muncie Pottery was established in Muncie, Indiana, by Charles O. Grafton; it operated there from 1922 until about 1935. The pottery they produced is made of a heavier clay than most of its contemporaries; the styles are sturdy and simple. Early glazes were bright and colorful. In fact, Muncie was advertised as the 'rainbow pottery.' Later most of the ware was finished in a matt glaze. The more collectible examples are those modeled after Consolidated Glass vases — sculptured with lovebirds, grasshoppers, and goldfish. Their line of Art Deco-style vases bear a remarkable resemblance to the Consolidated Glass Company's Ruba Rhombic line. Vases, candlesticks, bookends, ashtrays, bowls, lamp bases, and luncheon sets were made. A line of garden pottery was manufactured for a short time. Items were frequently impressed with MUNCIE in block letters. Letters such as A, K, E, or D and the numbers 1, 2, 3, 4, or 5 often found scratched into the base are finishers' marks.

Bookends, #257, w/owls, gr/rose, 5", pr.........................325.00
Canoe, #253, glossy blk, w/flower frog.........................275.00
Canoe, #253, w/o flower frog.................................200.00
Canoe flower holder w/flower frog, purple over gr matt, 2¼x11¼"..225.00
Chamberstick, #152, matt gr/rose...............................125.00
Dutch shoe, #U-20, matt gr/rose, 5".............................325.00
Ewer, #136, mat lt rose/wht, 12"...............................150.00
Lamp, gr & pk matt, I-A, 10½" (ceramic portion).................600.00
Vase, #189, gold fish, matt gr/lav, 9".........................425.00
Vase, #193, lovebird, lt bl matt, 9"...........................475.00
Vase, #194, katydid, matt wht/bl, 6½"..........................375.00
Vase, #259, gr matt, trumpet form, 9"..........................165.00
Vase, #278, Spanish 'Aorta,' matt gr, 5".......................265.00
Vase, #312, Rombic Star, matt bl, 5"...........................425.00
Vase, #432, hat form, lt matt gr, 5"...........................175.00
Vase, #446, sq top, rnd bottom, wht/rose, 8"...................135.00
Vase, gr over orange w/emb grasshoppers & grass, 5⅞".......300.00
Vase, pk & gr matt, hdls, 4½", NM...............................50.00
Vase, purple over pk, corseted, 12¼"...........................300.00
Vase, Ruba Rhombic, gr over orange matt, unmk, 4¼".............275.00
Vase, Ruba Rhombic, wht over bl, #312-5, 4⅛"...................425.00

Musical Instruments

The field of automatic musical instruments covers many different categories ranging from watches and tiny seals concealing fine early musical movements to huge organs and orchestrions which weigh many hundreds of pounds and are equivalent to small orchestras. Music boxes, first made in the early nineteenth century by Swiss watchmakers, were produced in both disc and cylinder models. The latter type employs a cylinder with tiny pins that lift the teeth in the comb of the music box (producing a sound much like many individual tuning forks), and music results. The value of a cylinder music box depends on the length and diameter of the cylinder, the date of its manufacture, the number of tunes it plays (four or six is usually better than ten or twelve), and its manufacturer. Nicole Freres, Henri Capt, LeCoultre, and Bremond are among the most highly regarded, and the larger boxes made by Mermod Freres are also popular. Examples with multiple cylinders, extra instruments (such as bells or an organ section), and those in particularly ornate cabinets or with matching tables bring significantly higher prices. While smaller cylinder boxes are still being made, the larger ones (over 10" cylinders) typically date from before 1900. Disc music boxes were introduced about 1890 but were replaced by the phonograph only twenty-five years later. However, during that time hundreds of thousands were made. Their great advantage was in playing inexpensive interchangeable discs, a factor that remains an attraction for today's collector as well. Among the most popular disc boxes are those made by Regina (USA), Polyphon, Mira, Stella, and Symphonion. Relative values are determined by the size of the discs they play, whether they have single or double combs, if they are upright or table models, and how ornate their cases are. Especially valuable are those that play multiple discs at the same time or are incorporated into tall case clocks.

Player pianos were made in a wide variety of styles. Early varieties consisted of a mechanism which pushed up to a piano and played on the keyboard by means of felt-tipped fingers. These use sixty-five note rolls. Later models have the playing mechanism built in, and most use eighty-eight note rolls. Upright pump player pianos have little value in unrestored condition because the cost of restoration is so high. 'Reproducing' pianos, especially the 'grand' format, can be quite valuable, depending on the make, the size, the condition, and the ornateness of the case. 'Reproducing' pianos have very sophisticated mechanisms and are much more realistic in the reproduction of piano music. They were made in relatively limited quantities. Better manufacturers include Steinway and Mason & Hamlin. Popular roll mechanism makers include Ampico, Duo-Art, and Welte. The market for all types of player pianos has been weak for several years.

Coin-operated pianos (orchestrions) were used commercially and typically incorporate extra instruments in addition to the piano action. These can be very large and complex, incorporating drums, cymbals, xylophones, bells, and hundreds of pipes. Both American and European coin pianos are very popular, especially the larger and more complex models made by Wurlitzer, Seeburg, Cremona, Weber, Welte, Hupfeld, and many others. These companies also made automatically playing violins (Mills Violin Virtuoso, Hupfeld), banjos (Encore), and harps (Whitlock); these are quite valuable.

Collecting player organettes is a fun endeavor. Roller organs, organettes, player organs, grind organs, hand organs — whatever the name — are a fascinating group of music makers. Some used wooden barrels or cobs to operate the valves, or metal and cardboard discs or paper strips, paper rolls, metal donuts, or metal strips. They usually played from fourteen to twenty keys or notes. Some were presser operated or vacuum type. Their heyday lasted from the 1870s to the turn of the century. Most were reed organs, but a few had pipes. Many were made in either America or Germany. They lost favor with the advent of the phonograph, as did the music box. Some music boxes were built with little player organs in them. Any player organette in good working condition with some music and in their original finish should be worth from $300.00 to $1,200.00, depending on the model. Generally the more keying it has and the larger and fancier the case, the more desirable it is. Rarity plays a part too. There are a handfull of individuals who make new music rolls for these player organs. Some machines are very rare, and music for them is nearly impossible to find. For further information on player organs we recommend *Encyclopedia of Musical Instruments* by Bowers.

Unless noted, prices given are for instruments in fine condition, playing properly, with cabinets or cases in well-preserved or refinished condition. In all instances, unrestored instruments sell for much less, as do those with broken or missing parts, damaged cases, and the like. On the other hand, particularly superb examples in especially ornate case designs and those that have been particularly well kept will often command more. Our advisor for mechanical instruments is Martin Roenigk; he is listed in the Directory under Arkansas.

Key:
c — cylinder   d — disc

Mechanical

Bird, automated, in cage, separate key, 22", unrstr...................1,400.00

Bird, automated, tortoise-shell case, fusee, Bruguier, ca 1865 ..3,500.00
Box, Criterion, 15½" d, dbl combs, w/matching base, EX........6,200.00
Box, Cuff; Capital Style B, w/8 cuffs, lt rstr.....................6,800.00
Box, Euphonia, paper rolls, glass windows expose mechanism, wood case ..580.00
Box, German Symphonion, 13¾" d, walnut veneer 22" case...2,700.00
Box, Imperial Symphonion, 15¾" d, mahog case w/cvg, EX....3,200.00
Box, Langdorf Longue Marche, 7 12½" c, EX 9,500.00
Box, Mandoline Quatour, 17¼" c, ornate 28" case................4,500.00
Box, Mermod Freres, 11¼" c, 2½" d, 10-tune 1,500.00
Box, Mira, 15½" dbl c, w/14 d, EX.................................3,800.00
Box, Mira, 18½" d, console w/decal case, rstr.....................11,000.00
Box, Orpheus, 12" d, Switzerland, 1880s..........................1,800.00
Box, Polyphon, tiger-sawn oak/yew/walnut, upright, 24½" d, 1900s....14,000.00
Box, Polyphon, upright, 19⅝" d, G..................................5,700.00
Box, Polyphon, 15½" d, coin-op, 23x34", EX.......................3,500.00
Box, Regina, oak upright, 27" d, gallery, single play..............13,500.00
Box, Regina, ornate cvd mahog, dbl comb, 15½" d 4,600.00
Box, Regina, 12" d, mahog cabinet 2,100.00
Box, Regina, 15½" d, heavily cvd case.............................4,500.00
Box, Regina, 15½" d, inlaid case w/paper label of children, EX...4,200.00
Box, Regina, 15½" d, single c, mahog case, EX 2,400.00
Box, Regina, 20¾" d, upright, rstr..................................5,500.00
Box, Regina, 27" d, single auto changer, walnut case, EX rstr ..21,000.00
Box, Reginaphone #240, 15½" d, mahog, w/horn/7 extra ds....10,500.00
Box, Stella, 15½" d, mahog case w/decor top, 13x25x19", VG ..3,500.00
Box, Stella, 17¼" d, console w/cvd cabinet, G.....................6,000.00
Box, Stella, 17¼" d, table model, G.................................4,500.00
Box, Swiss, rosewood case w/inlay, 12" c, 8-tune, 4 bells, rstr ..1,900.00
Box, Swiss, 11⅛" c, 4-tune, key wind, 1850s.......................1,700.00
Box, Symphonion, 11⅞" d, dbl comb, G 2,300.00
Box, Symphonion, 12" d, ornate cvd case w/angels, 20x12" +9 disks ..4,000.00
Calliope, National, 53-note, w/ext blower, EX orig.................7,900.00
Nickelodeon, Coinola Cupid, rstr 7,000.00
Nickelodeon, Nelson & Wiggins #5X, mahog, rstr, 58x38" 8,000.00
Nickelodeon, Peerless, 44-note, beveled glass front, rare, EX...17,000.00
Nickelodeon, Seeburg A, w/xylophone, rstr 5,500.00
Nickelodeon, Seeburg KT, eagle glass, oak case, rstr, 62x45".12,000.00
Nickelodeon, Seeburg L, rstr 7,000.00
Nickelodeon, Western Electric B, oak case, art glass, 1925, 62" ..6,000.00
Orchestrelle, Aeolian V, oak, EX orig 3,500.00
Orchestrelle, Aeolian W, EX, +200 rolls...........................4,900.00
Orchestrion, Coinola C-2, EX......................................27,000.00
Orchestrion, Coinola Style #0 Midget, oak case, art glass, rstr ...8,000.00
Orchestrion, Cremona J, rstr.......................................45,000.00
Orchestrion, Seeburg KT Special Replica, 1970s, M 15,000.00
Organ, Auto-Phone, paper roll/sheet unit w/bellows, NMIB 550.00
Organ, band; cvd pnt wood w/British Officer figure, late 1800s, 31"..5,750.00
Organ, band; Wurlitzer, #105, new case 9,000.00
Organ, band; Wurlitzer #125, partially rstr 20,000.00
Organ, bbl; Bacigalupo, 38-key, 90 pipes...........................6,600.00
Organ, Bijou Orchestrone, 20-note paper roll, Am, rstr.............800.00
Organ, concert roller; oak case, glass door, 18x12½", EX, +2 rolls...800.00
Organ, dance; Bursen, rstr 17,500.00
Organ, Dutch street; Limonaire, 47-key, w/music book/1 figure 22,000.00
Organ, fairground; Gasparini, 52-key, early 1900s, rstr 20,000.00
Organ, Grand Roller, 15" roller cob, 32-note 4,000.00
Organ, monkey; Molinari, 26-key, EX..............................4,500.00
Organ, pump; Aeolian Orchestrelle Reed, mahog, '03, EX+, +rolls...4,000.00
Organette, Amorette, zinc d, 16-note, Germany, 22.5 cm...........600.00
Organette, Concert Roller, 22-note, G, +5 6¾" wooden cobs 750.00
Organette, Organina, walnut case, paper rolls 375.00
Piano, baby grand; Baldwin Welte, mahog case, 38x61x56", EX ..2,000.00
Piano, barrel; Victor Chlappa, 34-key c (2), EX orig................1,200.00
Piano, grand; Knabe Ampico, art case, 68", EX orig 7,000.00

Piano, grand; Marshall & Wendall Ampico, 60", EX orig........1,800.00
Piano, grand; Wurlitzer/Apollo Ampico, art case, 73", rstr....11,000.00
Piano, Seeburg, dog race behind glass, oak case, 37x52x27", EX ..9,900.00
Piano, Steinway Duo-Art, walnut, 79", rstr 17,500.00
Piano, upright, Duo-Art, walnut, 1922, EX orig 1,250.00
Piano, upright; Chickering Ampico, EX orig 1,500.00
Piano/pipe organ, Reproduco, EX orig 6,500.00
Violano, Mills Virtuoso, single violin & piano, oak, G..........24,000.00

Non-Mechanical

Banjo, 5-string, 16 spread-wing eagle-head tensioners, 1860s, G ...300.00
Concertina, Koch Harmonica, pressed wood case, MOP buttons, EX ..50.00
Drum, Whaley Royce & Co/Toronto, brass body, 14½" dia, G...100.00
Guitar, Chet Atkins #6120 Gretsch, orig hard shell case, 1961, EX ...3,000.00
Guitar, Gibson L-1, flat top, 1926, EX in worn soft case..........1,450.00
Guitar, Gibson SG Deluxe, grainy mahog, 1971, M in case.....1,000.00
Guitar, Les Paul, blk w/emb logo humbucker pickups, 1972, EX ..1,350.00
Guitar, Martin D-18, str neck, 1952, EX............................2,000.00
Guitar, Martin D-35, Brazilian rosewood/Sitka spruce, 1965, EX .1,750.00
Guitar, PRS Standard, cherry w/moon inlays, EX orig................965.00
Harmonica, Hohner Caromatic, NP brass & wood, WWI era, 4¾", EX..175.00
Harmonica, Hohner 64 Charominaca...Professional Model, 1910s, 7" 185.00

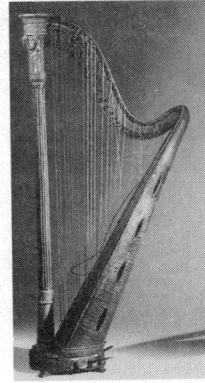

Harp, Gerard Menhers, Paris, carved giltwood, Neoclassical-style cap with rams' heads, paw feet, nineteenth century, 65¾", $1,000.00.

Harp, mixed woods, ornate gesso leaves at base, old rpt, 55", VG.......880.00
Piano, Am, rosewood, scrolled lyre music rest, 1860s, 38x80⅝" 1,650.00
Piano, baby grand; Schumann, Fr-style mahog w/inlay, 63", EX .935.00
Piano, Chickering, mahog w/late Classical influence, lg ivories ..1,250.00
Piano, grand; J Berger Inwein (Vienna), walnut/brass/MOP, 37x73x55" .5,000.00
Piano, grand; Steinway & Sons, cvd rosewood rococo, EX 3,850.00
Piano, grand; Steinway & Sons, ebonized, cvd knees, 1911, EX orig...7,500.00
Piano, Robert Fearn Jr, London, 1810, on stand, 23x65x23" ...2,300.00
Piano, Steinway & Sons, Pat 1859, rosewood Rococo, 36x80x40" ..4,400.00
Piano, upright; Geo Steck, rosewood, cvd keyboard support, 63x59" 500.00
Piano, upright; Henri Herz Model B, walnut, 1880s, 47x48" ...925.00
Violin, maple w/cvd whale-bone fittings, mid 1800s, pnt decor, 23"...2,100.00
Violin, traditional shape, handmade, Civil War era, G 400.00

Mustache Cups

Mustache cups were popular items during the late Victorian period, designed specifically for the man with the mustache! They were made in silverplate as well as china and ironstone. Decorations ranged from simple transfers to elaborately applied and gilded florals. To properly position the 'mustache bar,' special cups were designed for the 'lefties.' These are the rare ones!

Advertising slogan & floral transfer, Made in Germany..............100.00

Floral sprays, pk lustre, unmk Germany, from $65 to **85.00**
Floral transfer w/overpnt, scalloped, unmk Germany, ca 1890s, up to ...**100.00**
Flowers & ferns w/gold, 8-fluted, Japan, 1875-90, from $150 to .**200.00**
Forget-me-nots (non-factory), Limoges, 1893 ....**150.00**
Gold decor on wht, 8-flute, unmk Germany, from $60 to **75.00**
Gold flowers & leaves appl on yel lustre, unmk Germany, from $75 to..**100.00**
HP florals on bucket shape w/bamboo hdl, Worcester.................**300.00**
Longfellow's Wayside Inn reserve, mk Germany, from $75 to **70.00**
Remember Me & HP flowers, unmk Germany, #4522, from $100 to ..**125.00**
Roses transfer on pk to wht, Czechoslovakia, 1920s, from $150 to.......**175.00**
Stylized floral on gr lustre, unmk Germany, from $60 to **90.00**

Nailsea

Nailsea is a term referring to clear or colored glass decorated in contrasting spatters, swirls, or loops. These are usually white but may also be pink, red, or blue. It was first produced in Nailsea, England, during the late 1700s but was made in other parts of Britain and Scotland as well. During the mid-1800s a similar type of glass was produced in this country. Originally used for decorative novelties only, by that time tumblers and other practical items were being made from Nailsea-type glass. See also Lamps; Witch Balls.

Biscuit jar, cranberry w/wht loopings, silvered bail hdl, 6" **725.00**
Bottle, gemel; clear w/wht loopings, cobalt lip, 9¾" **165.00**
Darner, aqua-bl loops on alabaster, 6"....................................**400.00**
Darner, maize of royal bl lines over wht, 5¼" **375.00**
Darner, red loops on alabaster, 6" **375.00**
Darner, ribboned red/bl/wht/yel, brass end cover, 8½" **300.00**
Darner, royal bl swirls on wht, 6"..**375.00**
Decanter, cobalt w/wht loopings, ball form, 1880s, 7⅛"............**850.00**
Decanter, cobalt w/wht loopings, wht opal mouth, 7⅝"............**450.00**
Flask, clear w/wht loopings, 7⅜".......................................**195.00**
Flask, red w/wht loopings, pontil scar, rolled lip, 6⅝" **325.00**
Pitcher, clear w/wht loopings, pontil scar, 6¼", NM **200.00**

Nakara

Nakara was a line of decorated opaque milk glass produced by the C.F. Monroe Company of Meriden, Connecticut, for a few years after the turn of the century. It differs from their Wave Crest line in several ways. The shapes were simpler; pastel colors were deeper and covered more of the surface; more beading was present; flowers were larger; and large transfer prints of figures, Victorian ladies, cherubs, etc., were used as well. Ormolu and brass collars and mounts complemented these opulent pieces. Most items were signed; however, this is not important since the ware was never reproduced. Our advisors for this category are Dolli and Wilfred R. Cohen; their address is listed in the Directory under California.

Box, daisies on pink with beading, oval, footed, 4x6x4", EX, $595.00.
(Photo courtesy James D. Julia, Inc.)

Box, Bishop's hat, floral on pk to yel, 4x6" **650.00**
Box, cherubs on mauve, 6"..**750.00**
Box, daisies on bright pk, beaded center, 4x6x4".................**575.00**

Box, Greenway figures at picnic on bl, beading, 4x6"...............**975.00**
Box, iris on on gr stems on creamy beige, 6"........................**650.00**
Box, rose on lav to pk, mirror, hinged lid, 4x4½".................**675.00**
Box, Victorian lady on lt bl, wht beading, 2½x4½" **595.00**
Box, violets on yel, 3¾"...**350.00**
Box, 18th-C couple portrait medallion & flowers on pk, 4x6½" ..**1,000.00**
Hair receiver, children's tea party, lacy decor, dmn shape............**585.00**
Humidor, floral on bl to cream, Cigars in purple, 6x7" **1,295.00**
Humidor, roses, on gr to pk, Tobacco in purple, 7½x4½" **1,350.00**
Match holder, tiny beaded flowers on gr, ormolu rim, 2" dia.......**495.00**
Tray, dresser; daisies, pk/wht on gr, ormolu hdls, 6" dia **495.00**
Vase, wild roses on pk/yel, blown-out scrolls, dolphin hdls, 15"...**1,975.00**

Napkin Rings

Napkin rings became popular during the late 1800s. They were made from various materials. Among the most popular and collectible today are the large group of varied silverplated figurals made by American manufacturers. Recently the larger figurals in excellent condition have appreciated considerably. Only those with a blackened finish, corrosion, or broken and/or missing parts have maintained their earlier price levels. When no condition is indicated, the items listed below are assumed to be all original and in very good to excellent condition. Check very carefully for missing parts, solder repairs, marriages, and reproductions.

A timely warning: inexperienced buyers should be aware of excellent reproductions on the market, especially the wheeled pieces and cherubs. However, these do not have the fine detail and patina of the originals and tend to have a more consistent, soft pewter-like finish. These are appearing at the large, quality shows at top prices, being shown along with authentic antique merchandise. Beware! Our advisor for this category is Deborah Maggard; she is listed in the Directory under Ohio.

Key:
gw — gold washed   SH&M — Simpson, Hall &
R&B — Reed & Barton   Miller

Artist's palette supports ring, hammered finish, Sharick #239.....**350.00**
Baby in rocking cradle holder mk Mother, JW Tufts #1620, minimum....**500.00**
Badminton girl leaning on ring on flat rectangular base, R&B #1455......**500.00**
Beaver atop ring encircled by branch w/maple leaf base, Toronto #1110.**350.00**
Berries & leaves form hdl on leaf base w/ring, Middletown #141.**200.00**
Bird atop sq holder angled on plain rnd ped base, unmk, #64.....**200.00**
Bird w/hdld ring around neck on base, Rogers & Bro #158........**500.00**
Boy (Greenaway type) atop wooden post fence that forms holder, unmk ...**350.00**
Butterfly atop ring on fancy scroll-ftd base, unmk **200.00**
Camel next to ring on ball-ftd oval base, Meriden Britannia #269..**500.00**
Cat seated w/ring on bk, glass eyes, Meriden Britannia #235......**500.00**
Chair (Victorian balloon-bk) supports ring, R Strickland...........**200.00**
Cherub w/hat & sword straddles turtle on base w/ring, Middletown #71...**500.00**
Conquistador stands beside ring on fancy ftd base, Toronto #1137.....**500.00**
Cow on floral base stands beside bucket-shaped ring, Meriden #268..**350.00**
Dog barking at frog atop ring, unmk................................**350.00**
Dog seated on base w/ring holder in mouth, SH&M #14............**500.00**
Dog w/tassel collar sits beside ring w/beaded edge, FB Rogers #287 ..**350.00**
Elephant-head hdls on ring, ped base, JW Tufts #1567 ....**350.00**
Elves (2) balancing ring on fancy ped, R&B #1326, minimum value ..**500.00**
Fireman's hat against ring on rectangular base, Pairpoint #81, minimum ..**500.00**
Frog leaping w/ring on bk, leafy base, Southington #35 ....**350.00**
Giraffe feeding on branch on base, Rogers & Bro #239, minimum value ..**500.00**
Goat on scrolled base beside bright-cut ring, unmk, #560...........**350.00**
Goat pulling fancy cart w/ring, Meriden #212 ....**500.00**
Grapes draped over bbl ring on ped base, Standard #733...........**350.00**
Greenaway-type baby beside ring on ftd oval base, Derby #335..**500.00**

Greenaway-type baby pushing ring on base, Middletown #25.....**500.00**
Greenaway-type boy w/stick on bench leans on ring, Hartford #30 ..**500.00**
Greenaway-type girl atop wooden fence that forms holder, unmk.....**250.00**
Greenaway-type girl on dog-drawn cart w/ring, unmk, #1150, minimum....**500.00**
Greenaway-type lady stands beside ring, no base, Derby #381, minimum ...**500.00**
Horse heads (2) on sides of ring on ped base, Derby #326 ....**350.00**
Iron w/hdl forms holder eng w/scrolling flowers & leaves, Meriden......**200.00**
Jester leaning on ring while pointing, Meriden #258, minimum value ..**500.00**
Knight in armor beside ring on rnd base, Knickerbocker #198 ...**350.00**
Lizard w/ring on bk, Meriden #202..**350.00**
Monkey as workman w/bbl, Tufts, ca 1880, 4" **345.00**
Oriental fans (2) form holder on sq ftd base, SH&M #213 ....**350.00**
Owl on branch beside ring, no base, Middletown #112...............**200.00**
Parrot atop ring supported by sawhorse-like base, unmk.............**350.00**
Pear on leafy branch drapes ring on leaf base, Middletown #140...**350.00**
Pitcher-shaped bud vase w/open ring on base, R&B #1337.........**350.00**
Rabbit upright on ball-ft base beside ring, Meriden Britannia #233..**500.00**
Reindeer pulling child atop ring on base, SH&M #18 ....**500.00**
Rip Van Winkle w/ring on shoulder, SH&M #8, minimum value ..**500.00**
Saddlebags draped over ring resting on Xd swords, unmk, #291 .**350.00**
Spinx w/wings atop ring on ped base, Meriden Britannia #131 ..**350.00**
Squirrel w/nut on leafy branch that encircles ring, Toronto #1102..**350.00**
Top hat holder on hand on flat base w/cut-out corners, Meriden #225 ..**350.00**
Turtle w/ring on bk, Pairpoint #51 ....**500.00**
Violin & ring w/eng leaves on base eng Old Times, Wilcox #4393 .**350.00**

Nash

A. Douglas Nash founded the Corona Art Glass Company in Long Island, New York. He produced tableware, vases, flasks, etc. using delicate artistic shapes and forms. After 1933 he worked for the Libbey Glass Company.

Bottle, scent; Chintz, gr/bl/clear stripes, clear stopper, 5" **725.00**
Bowl, Chintz, red w/silver stripes, 4" **675.00**
Candlestick, gold irid, floriform rim, #650, 3¾x4" **550.00**
Chalice, pk/gold/platinum, fluted, #d, 4½" **750.00**
Compote, Chintz, gr, 4½x7½"...**350.00**
Goblet, Chintz, bl & silver, ped ft, 5"...**135.00**
Parfait, gold irid, #543, 4¼" **375.00**
Plate, Chintz, clear/orchid/chartreuse spirals, 6½".......................**200.00**
Vase, amber & violet irid, ribbed cylinder, G 577, 3¼", pr **575.00**
Vase, amber irid, flared rim, Nash-544, 4¼" **600.00**

Vase, Chintz, red with narrow vertical silver lustre stripes, Nash RD 66, 5½", $980.00.

Vase, Chintz, red w/brn strips around body, crystal ball collar, 9" ..**850.00**
Vase, gold irid, stretched rim, emb calyx leaves, #551, 5¼" **850.00**
Vase, gold irid w/emb calyx leaves, #567-1, 6" **450.00**
Vase, gold irid w/emb vertical veins, #535, 7¼".........................**800.00**
Vase, 8 ruby teardrops on crystal, bulbous, ftd, 8½x6".................**350.00**

Natzler, Gertrude and Otto

The Natzlers came to the United States from Vienna in the late 1930s. They settled in Los Angeles where they continued their work in ceramics, for which they were already internationally recognized. Gertrude created the forms; Otto formulated a variety of interesting glazes, among them volcanic, crystalline, and lustre. Our advisor for this category is Abby Malowanczyk; she is listed in the Directory under Texas.

Bottle, yel semi-matt over brn clay, 11x5¼" **2,600.00**
Bowl, dk brn metallic w/silvery crystalline, #H270, 2x6½".......**1,600.00**
Bowl, EX golden flambe, sm ft, 3x4¼" **1,700.00**
Bowl, frothy sky bl semimatt, ink mk, paper label: J097, 3x5" .**1,400.00**
Bowl, gunmetal/brn/turq/gr matt, shallow, 4½" **800.00**
Bowl, lav matt, flared rim, ink mk, 2x7" **1,300.00**
Bowl, turq over red clay, 3x4" **950.00**
Bowl, volcanic wht & brn, shallow, ink mk, 1½x6½"..............**2,600.00**
Bowl, wht matt w/red clay showing through, #J491, 2½x6" **1,000.00**
Cup, gray opal (mottled gray) on thin red clay, mk, 1¾" **150.00**
Dish, bl-gr & taupe mottle, ink mk, 6" dia..................................**600.00**
Vase, bl gr & umber crystalline, cylindrical, K384 tag, 6¼x3½"..**2,000.00**
Vase, dawn celadon reduction w/melt fissures, cylindrical, 5½"...**1,900.00**
Vase, gray-brn/blk volcanic on red clay, 5x6⅞" **3,200.00**

New England Glass Works

Founded in 1818 by Deming Jarves in Boston, Massachusetts, the New England Glass Company produced cut, blown three-mold, free-form, and pressed glass of the highest quality. They were recognized for their fine decorative accomplishments, using etching, gilding, and engraving to emphasize their wares. For more than fifty years, they produced prize-winning pressed glass dinnerware sets. Because they refused to compromise the quality of their product by using the cheaper lime-based glass that flooded the market in the 1860s, the company fell into financial trouble and by 1877 was forced to close. However, William Libbey, who had been the sales manager there since 1870, leased the premises and resumed operations with his father, Edward Drummond Libbey, as full partner. In 1892 the firm became known as The Libbey Glass Company. See also Libbey.

Bottle, scent; wht opaque, hexagonal w/emb dmns, 4¾", EX........**50.00**
Candlesticks, caryatid form, deep opal, att, 1875, 9", pr, EX....**2,500.00**
Candlesticks, dk golden yel, made in 1 pc, 1850s, 9", pr **500.00**
Candlesticks, lt bl opaque, baluster stem, 1850s, 7", pr, EX.........**750.00**
Cruet, wht opaque, 6" **850.00**
Vase, blown, teal gr & clear, flared rim, appl ring, 6½"............**2,500.00**

New Geneva

In the early years of the nineteenth century, several potteries flourished in the Greensboro, Pennsylvania, area. They produced utilitarian stoneware items as well as tile and novelties for many decades. All failed well before the turn of the century.

Bank, dk Albany slip w/flowers on gray/tan, wear/sm chips at slot, 7" .**1,870.00**
Pitcher, tan w/brn Albany slip floral, scalloped rim, strap hdl, 5" ..**800.00**
Pitcher, unglazed gray w/Albany slip decor, 1860, 1-qt, 8½".......**850.00**

New Martinsville

The New Martinsville Glass Company took its name from the town in West Virginia where it began operations in 1901. In the beginning years, pressed tablewares were made in crystal as well as colored and opalescent glass. Considered an innovator, the company was known for their imaginative applications of the medium in creating lamps made entirely of glass, vanity sets, figural decanters, and models of animals and birds. In 1944 the company was purchased by Viking Glass, who continued to use many of the old molds, the animal molds included. They marked their wares 'Viking' or 'Rainbow Art.' Viking recently ceased operations and has been purchased by Kenneth Dalzell, president of the Fostoria Company. They, too, are making the bird and animal models. Although at first they were not marked, future productions are to be marked with an acid stamp. Dalzell/Viking animals are in the $50.00 to $60.00 range. Values for cobalt and red items are two to three times higher than for the same item in clear. See also Depression Glass; Glass Animals and Figurines.

Janice, bl or red, bowl, flared, 11" 60.00
Janice, bl or red, bowl, flower; w/8 crimps, 5½" 35.00
Janice, bl or red, creamer, 6-oz 20.00
Janice, bl or red, ice tub, ftd, 6" 250.00
Janice, bl or red, plate, cheese; 11" 40.00
Janice, bl or red, sherbet..20.00
Janice, bl or red, vase, ftd, 7"..75.00
Janice, crystal, basket, 11"...65.00
Janice, crystal, bowl, 10"...37.50
Janice, crystal, candlestick, 1-light, 5" W, 5½" H.................30.00
Janice, crystal, ice pail, hdld, 10"...70.00
Janice, crystal, oil bottle, w/stopper, 5-oz.............................45.00
Janice, crystal, plate, torte; rolled edge, 15".........................50.00
Janice, crystal, tumbler..14.00
Janice, crystal, vase, ball shape, 9".......................................55.00
Lions (Heraldry), blk, cup..35.00
Lions (Heraldry), blk, plate, 8"...30.00
Lions (Heraldry), crystal, candle holder, #37.........................22.50
Lions (Heraldry), crystal, sugar bowl, #37.............................15.00
Lions (Heraldry), pk or gr, creamer, #34...............................45.00
Lions (Heraldry), pk or gr, saucer...6.50
Meadow Wreath, crystal, bowl, crimped, flat, 13"..................50.00
Meadow Wreath, crystal, bowl, flared, flat, 10"......................40.00
Meadow Wreath, crystal, candle, 2-light, rnd, ftd...................37.50
Meadow Wreath, crystal, cheese & cracker, #42/26, 11"........45.00
Meadow Wreath, crystal, compote, #4218/26, 10".................35.00
Meadow Wreath, crystal, ladle, punch; #4226.......................55.00
Meadow Wreath, crystal, plate, 11".......................................35.00
Meadow Wreath, crystal, salver, #42/26, ftd, 12"...................45.00
Meadow Wreath, crystal, vase, #42/26, flared, 10".................50.00
Moondrops, bl or red, ashtray...32.00
Moondrops, bl or red, bowl, vegetable; oval, 9¾"...................75.00
Moondrops, bl or red, candlesticks, triple light, 5¼", pr.........150.00
Moondrops, bl or red, cup..18.00
Moondrops, bl or red, goblet, wine; metal stem, 4-oz, 5¼"......20.00
Moondrops, bl or red, plate, salad; 7⅛"..................................15.00
Moondrops, bl or red, platter, oval, 12".................................50.00
Moondrops, bl or red, sugar bowl, 4"....................................16.00
Moondrops, bl or red, tumbler, 12-oz, 5⅛".............................32.00
Moondrops, bl or red, vase, Rocket bud; 8½".........................275.00
Moondrops, color other than bl or red, bowl, cream soup; 4¼"....35.00
Moondrops, color other than bl or red, casserole, w/lid, 9¾"......100.00
Moondrops, color other than bl or red, casserole, 3-ftd, 12".........32.00
Moondrops, color other than bl or red, compote, 4"...................18.00
Moondrops, color other than bl or red, decanter, sm, 7¾"..........40.00
Moondrops, color other than bl or red, plate, dinner; 9½".........20.00
Moondrops, color other than bl or red, plate, sherbet; 6⅛".........5.00
Moondrops, color other than bl or red, tumbler, hdld shot; 2¾"...11.00

Moondrops, color other than bl or red, tumbler, 9-oz, 4⅞" 15.00
Prelude, crystal, bonbon, 3-ftd, 6"...20.00
Prelude, crystal, bowl, 3-part, w/lid, 5¼x7½".........................65.00
Prelude, crystal, butter dish, 6½"..37.50
Prelude, crystal, candlestick, dbl, 5".......................................35.00
Prelude, crystal, candy box, open knob, 6½"...........................65.00
Prelude, crystal, compote, 3x5½"...30.00
Prelude, crystal, lazy susan, 3-pc set, 18"................................165.00
Prelude, crystal, oil bottle, 4-oz...50.00
Prelude, crystal, plate, hdld, 13"..40.00
Prelude, crystal, plate, salad; 8"..10.00
Prelude, crystal, platter, 14½"..65.00

Prelude, crystal, relish with handles, three-part, 10", from $30.00 to $40.00.

Prelude, crystal, relish, 5-part, 13" 45.00
Prelude, crystal, stem, cordial; 1-oz.......................................40.00
Prelude, crystal, stem, sherbet; ball stem, 6-oz........................12.00
Prelude, crystal, tray, center hdl, 11"......................................40.00
Prelude, crystal, tumbler, juice; ball stem, 5-oz.......................17.50
Prelude, crystal, vase, 8"...40.00
Radiance, amber, bonbon, ftd, 6"...17.50
Radiance, amber, celery bowl, 10"...18.00
Radiance, amber, cheese & cracker set, 11"............................35.00
Radiance, amber, creamer..15.00
Radiance, amber, plate, luncheon; 8".....................................10.00
Radiance, amber, punch cup, flat..7.00
Radiance, amber, tray, oval..24.00
Radiance, bl or red, bonbon, 6"..30.00
Radiance, bl or red, bowl, 2-part, 7".......................................35.00
Radiance, bl or red, candlesticks, 8", pr..................................225.00
Radiance, bl or red, compote, 6"..38.00
Radiance, bl or red, cup & saucer...26.50
Radiance, bl or red, pitcher, 64-oz...295.00
Radiance, bl or red, shakers, pr..95.00
Star & Leaf, crystal, water set, ca 1910-15, 8" pitcher+6 4" tumblers..85.00

Newcomb

The Newcomb College of New Orleans, Louisiana, established a pottery in 1895 to provide the students with first-hand experience in the fields of art and ceramics. Using locally dug clays — red and buff in the early years, white-burning by the turn of the century — potters were employed to throw the ware which the ladies of the college decorated. Until about 1910 a glossy glaze was used on ware decorated by carving and surface painting with earlier pieces having surface paint underglaze. After that a matt glaze was favored. Soft blues and greens were used almost exclusively, and decorative themes were chosen to reflect the beauty of the South. The matt-glaze period and the art-pottery era ended in 1930.

Various marks used by the pottery include an 'N' within a 'C,' sometimes with 'HB' added to indicate a 'hand-built' piece. The potter often incised his initials into the ware, and the artists were encouraged to sign their work. Among the most well-known artists were Sadie Irvine, Henrietta Bailey, and Fannie Simpson.

Newcomb pottery is evaluated to a large extent by era (early, transitional, matt), decoration, size, and condition. In the following listings, items are assumed matt unless noted otherwise. Our advisor for this category is David Rago; he is listed in the Directory under New Jersey.

Note: In the following descriptions, the decoration is slip painted unless noted carved within the line. The term 'transitional' defines a period of two to three years between earlier and later work, and signifies changes to the glazes, colors, and style of decoration.

Bowl, buds band, Sadie Irvine, hemispherical, 1927, 2½x4½" ...1,100.00
Chamberstick, gr drip over red clay, rstr hdl, 7x5¼" 425.00
Charger, 3 lg bl crabs, Sabrina Wells, 1904, YY64, 13" 25,000.00
Jar, Here Are Sweet Peas... on lid, floral band, MT Ryan, 1903, 8x6" ..37,500.00
Mug, smiling masks in mc band at rim, Marie Le Blanc, 1905, 5⅜" 4,125.00
Pitcher, floral above vertical ribs, mc on dk bl matt, AF Simpson, 5" 1,500.00
Pitcher, pine cones & needles, pk on purple to bl, H Bailey, #244, 6" 2,000.00
Planter, wild roses, S Irvine, Transitional, 1912, 5¼x6½" sq 700.00
Plate, stylized tulip & leaf border, L Nicholson, ca 1905, 8⅜".1,850.00
Poster, stylized flowers, for exhibit, ca 1940s, 30x13½" 750.00
Teapot, wild roses, A Mason, Transitional, 1911, #EG44, 4¼x5½" ..3,000.00
Trivet, floral, pk & gr on dk bl, AF Simpson, #QZ65, 5½" dia....1,500.00
Vase, bamboo, gr on bl, H Bailey/J Meyer, D34, 1909, 12" 42,500.00
Vase, bell-flower wreath on dk bl, AF Simpson, 1928, 8½x3¼"..3,250.00
Vase, bell-shaped flowers on cobalt, H Bailey, 1929, 3x3¾" 1,300.00
Vase, bud; floral, wht on bl, M DeHoa LeBlanc, corseted, 1909, 9½" ...6,000.00
Vase, buds & leaves, hdls, squat, illegible mk, 4¼x4¾" 1,700.00
Vase, cornstalks, gr/cobalt/bl, R Kennon, 1902, 9¾x4¾" 4,000.00
Vase, daffodils, lt & dk bl/gr on cream, H Joor, 3-hdl, #F85, rpr, 5" ..3,500.00
Vase, dk gr matt drips on lt gr, flared cylinder, 12½", NM 750.00
Vase, floral, cvd/pnt on gr to rose to bl, S Irvine, #KA54, 6½" ..4,000.00
Vase, floral, gr & yel w/red overglaze on bl, AF Simpson, #HQ20, 6"..1,500.00
Vase, floral, mc on bl matt, AF Simpson, #KC43, 3252, 6½" W..1,200.00
Vase, floral, mc on shaded bl, H Bailey, #IL8, #63, 6" 1,800.00
Vase, floral, mc on shaded bl, Sadie Irvine, #OM81, 6½"........1,800.00
Vase, floral, pk & yel touches on bl-gr, A Simpson, HQ16, 7½" ..2,800.00
Vase, floral, Sadie Irvine, Transitional, 1915, 11¼x4" 3,250.00
Vase, floral, wht w/gr stems on bl, AF Simpson, #TD70, 6"...1,600.00
Vase, floral, yel & blk on wht, Marie Ross, J59X, 6½" 7,000.00
Vase, floral, 4-color on shaded bl, 4-hdl, Irvine, #SF86, 5½" dia ...2,100.00
Vase, floral (4 repeats), lt bl on bl, SA Estelle, 6" 1,500.00
Vase, floral w/purple overglaze, AF Simpson, Transitional, 1915, 3x5"..1,200.00
Vase, gunmetal, mahog & gr glossy, hand-thrown, sgn, 3" 325.00
Vase, irises, AF Simpson, bulbous, Transitional, 1910, 8½x6".7,000.00
Vase, jonquils, cvd/pnt, wht/bl/gr, AF Simpson/J Meyer, #25, 6½"....4,000.00
Vase, jonquils, mc on shaded bl, Sadie Irvine, #256, 6½" W...1,600.00
Vase, lilies, wht/lt bl/yel on bl, M Ross, 1905, 4¼x4½" 6,500.00
Vase, magnolias, oxblood & bl, M De Hoa LeBlanc, 8⅛"........6,000.00
Vase, moon/moss/oaks, AF Simpson, 1922, 8¼x5"............8,500.00
Vase, moon/moss/oaks, AF Simpson, 4¾x3¾" 4,500.00
Vase, moon/moss/oaks, S Irvine, 1930, 5½x3", from $1,800 to ..2,750.00
Vase, moon/moss/oaks, Sadie Irvine, 1923, 11x6½" 5,500.00
Vase, moon/moss/oaks, Sadie Irvine, 1927, classic shape, 11x5" ...13,000.00
Vase, moon/moss/trees, AF Simpson, 1927, classic shape, 11x5" ...13,000.00
Vase, moon/moss/trees, sgn FHF, ca 1939, 5½x7", NM 3,000.00
Vase, moss/cypress, AF Simpson, 8, 1912, 8½x3½" 5,775.00
Vase, moss/oaks, cvd/pnt, gr/bl/pk, AF Simpson, 8½" 4,500.00
Vase, moss/oaks w/pk sky, AF Simpson, 3½" 2,000.00
Vase, mushrooms, lt gr gloss on shaded bl, A Roman, #BL28, 3½" dia...1,600.00
Vase, narcissus, Anna F Simpson, Transitional, 1914, 9x4½" ..3,750.00
Vase, narcissus, bl/gr/pk, J Meyer/H Bailey, LX66/#181, 6¼x4½"...2,750.00
Vase, narcissus on bl, corseted, IB Keep, 1903, line, 10¾x4¾" ..4,500.00
Vase, nasturtiums, bl & yel, NC/Leona Nicholson/AB95, 1904, 6½" ...8,800.00
Vase, palmetto fronds, Sadie Irvine/K Smith/TZ97, 7½x6¾" ..1,980.00
Vase, pines, Harriet Joor, 1902, minor rstr, 12¼x7½" 19,000.00
Vase, raspberry, NC/JM, 4x3¼" 450.00

Vase, sectioned abstract vertical design, Irvine, 1932, 3⅝x4"..1,870.00
Vase, sorghum plants on bl & gr, NC/M28/Q, 11½x8½" 21,000.00
Vase, strawberries, E Elliot, 1902, ER19, 3¾x3¼".....................8,000.00
Vase, stylized primrose, M Ryan, cylindrical, 1904, 7¼x3¼"...7,500.00
Vase, swans in water, L Nicholson, #5/22, Q, 9¾x11½"........18,700.00
Vase, tall pines, Sadie Irvine, Transitional, 1916, 4x3½" 800.00
Vase, wisteria, M Robinson, 1904, sm rstr, 8¾x4¾" 12,000.00
Vase, 3-panel, emblem, sorority logo & flowers, H Bailey, 5", rstr..4,000.00

Newspapers

People do not collect newspapers simply because they are old. Age has absolutely nothing to do with value — it does not hold true that the older the newspaper, the higher the value. Instead, most of the value is determined by the historic event content. In most cases, the more important to American history the event is, the higher the value. In over two hundred years of American history, perhaps as many as 98% of all newspapers ever published *do not* contain news of a significant historic event. Newspapers not having news of major events in history are called 'atmosphere.' Atmosphere papers have little collector value. (See price guide below.)

To learn more about the hobby of collecting old and historic newspapers, be sure to visit our mega-websight on the Internet at www.histo rybuff.com/. The e-mail address for the NCSA is help@historybuff.com/. See Newspaper Collector's Society of America in Clubs, Newsletters, and Catalogs for more information.

1800-1820, Atmosphere editions 7.00
1821-1859, Atmosphere editions 5.00
1836, Texas declares independence...60.00
1845, Annexation of Texas...35.00
1846, Start of Mexican War...30.00
1846-1847, Major battles of Mexican War..................................20.00
1847, End of Mexican War..30.00
1848, Gold discovered in California..60.00
1859, John Brown's raid on Harper's Ferry 45.00
1860, Lincoln elected 1st term..150.00
1861, Lincoln's inaugural address...175.00
1861-1865, Atmosphere editions: Confederate titles.....................50.00
1861-1865, Atmosphere editions: Union titles 7.00
1861-1865, Major battles of Civil War.......................................75.00
1862, Emancipation Proclamation..135.00
1863, Gettysburg Address..250.00
1865, April 29 edition of Frank Leslie's.....................................350.00
1865, April 29 edition of Harper's Weekly.................................300.00
1865, Capture & death of J Wilkes Booth 100.00
1865, Fall of Richmond..100.00
1865, NY Herald, Apr 15 (Beware: reprints abound) 900.00
1865, Titles other than NY Herald, Apr 15 ....400.00
1866-1900, Atmosphere editions 4.00
1876, Custer's Last Stand...150.00
1881, Billy the Kid killed...200.00
1881, Garfield assassinated..50.00
1881, Gunfight at OK Corral..225.00
1882, Jesse James killed...200.00
1898, Sinking of Maine..40.00
1901, McKinley assassinated..60.00
1903, Wright Brother's flight 300.00
1906, San Francisco earthquake, other titles................................30.00
1906, San Francisco earthquake, San Francisco title.....................500.00
1912, Sinking of Titanic...250.00
1915, Sinking of Lusitania..125.00
1927, Babe Ruth hits 60th home run 70.00

1927, Welcome Lindy, New York Journal, EX color graphics, from $75.00 to $100.00.

1929, St Valentine's Day Massacre 150.00
1929, Stock market crash 90.00
1931, Al Capone found guilty...35.00
1931, Jack 'Legs' Diamond killed..35.00
1933, Machine Gun Kelley captured 35.00
1934, Baby Face Nelson killed..40.00
1934, Bonnie & Clyde killed...125.00
1934, Dillinger killed...150.00
1934, Pretty Boy Floyd killed...35.00
1937, Hindenbergh explodes..65.00
1941, Honolulu Star-Bulletin, Dec 7, 1st extra (+) 600.00
1941, Other titles, Dec 7, w/Pearl Harbor news 35.00
1948, Chicago Daily Tribune, Nov 3, Dewey Defeats Truman 900.00
1961, Alan Shephard 1st astronaut in space 20.00
1961, Roger Maris hits 61st home run..25.00
1962, Death of Marilyn Monroe 30.00
1962, John Glenn orbits Earth...18.00
1963, JFK assassination, Nov 22, Dallas title 60.00
1963, JFK assassination, Nov 22, titles other than Dallas................8.00
1968, Assassination of Martin Luther King 7.00
1968, Assassination of Robert Kennedy..7.00
1969, Moon landing 10.00
1974, Nixon resigns 5.00

Nicodemus

Chester Nicodemus moved from Dayton, to Columbus, Ohio, in 1930 and started teaching at the Columbus Art School. During this time he made vases and commissioned sculptures, water fountains, and limestone and wood carvings. In 1941 Chester left the field of teaching to pursue pottery making full time, using local red clay containing a large amount of iron. Known for its durability, he called the ware Ferro-stone. He made teapots and other utility wares, but these goods lost favor, so he started producing animal and bird sculptures, nativity sets, and Christmas ornaments, some bearing Chester's and his wife, Florine's names as personalized cards for his customers and friends. Chester died in 1990.

His glaze colors were turquoise or aqua, ivory, green mottle (pink), pussy willow, and golden yellow. The glaze was applied so that the color of the warm red clay would show through, adding an extra dimension to each piece. Examples are usually marked with his name incised in the clay, but paper labels were also used. For more information, we recommend *Sanford Guide to Nicodemus, His Pottery and His Art*, by our advisor for this category, James Riebel; he is listed in the Directory under Ohio.

Ashtray, Kappa Kappa Gamma, 4½" 40.00
Ashtray, turq, #218 ....65.00
Figurine, bull, head lowered, 3x7" 155.00
Figurine, bunny, blk glossy eyes, wht tail, Ferro-stone sticker, 3x4"...78.00

Figurine, squirrel, sgn EJ, 3" 140.00
Figurine, wren, Ferro-stone sticker, mk, 2¼x3¼"..........................85.00
Flower frog, penguin, gr mottle on red clay, 6⅝" 235.00
Flower holder, kneeling girl, curdled bl, 6¾" 250.00
Leaf tray, mustard on red clay, 8½x7¼".......................................48.00
Pitcher, yel, Ferro-stone, arch mk, 6x6" 110.00
Teapot, gr mottle, 4x4" 35.00
Toothpick holder, elephant figural, brn tones, 2x2¼" 115.00
Vase, verdigris w/brn top, ovoid, 4½" 135.00

Niloak

During the latter part of the 1800s, there were many small utilitarian potteries in Benton, Arkansas. By 1900 only the Hyten Brothers Pottery remained. Charles Hyten, a second generation potter, took control of the family business around 1902. Shortly thereafter he renamed it the Eagle Pottery Company. In 1909 Hyten and former Rookwood potter Arthur Dovey began experimentation on a new swirl pottery. Dovey previously worked for the Ouachita Pottery Company of Hot Springs and produced a swirl pottery there as early as 1906. In March 1910 the Eagle Pottery Company introduced Niloak, kaolin spelled backwards. During 1911 Benton businessmen formed the Niloak Pottery corporation. Niloak, connected to the Arts and Crafts Movement and known as 'mission' ware, had a national representative in New York by 1913. Niloak's production centered on art pottery characterized by accidental, swirling patterns of natural and artificially colored clays. Many companies through the years have produced swirl pottery, yet none achieved the technical and aesthetic qualities of Niloak. Hyten received a patent in 1928 for the swirl technique. Although most examples have an interior glaze, some early Mission Ware pieces have an exterior glaze as well; these are extremely rare. Swirl/Mission Ware production continued steadily until the Depression when hard times and sagging sales caused Hyten to produce more traditional wares. In 1931 Niloak introduced Hywood Art Pottery, a glazed ware (sometimes similar in shape to Weller's Nile) of mostly hand-thrown vases. Soon thereafter, Niloak introduced castware as its primary production and renamed the line Hywood by Niloak. Throughout its existence, the company produced utilitarian items as well as artware.

In 1934 Hyten's company found itself facing bankruptcy. Hardy L. Winburn, Jr., along with other Little Rock businessmen, raised the necessary capital and were able to provide the kind of leadership needed to make the business profitable once again. Both lines (Eagle and Hywood) were renamed 'Niloak' in 1937 to capitalize on this well-known name. The pottery continued in production until 1947 when it was converted to the Winburn Tile Company, which exists to this day in Little Rock.

Be careful not to confuse the swirl production of the Evans Pottery of Missouri with Niloak. The significant difference is the dark brown matt interior glaze of Evans pottery. For further information we recommend *Collector's Encyclopedia of Niloak Pottery* by David Edwin Gifford (Collector Books). Our advisors for this category are Lila and Fred Shrader; they are listed in the Directory under California.

Mission Ware

Key:
N — N Mark   NI — Niloak (impressed) mark
NB — Niloak (block letters) mark   NL — Niloak (in low relief)

Bowl, incurvate rim, 2nd art mk, 8¾", from $275 to..................325.00
Bowl, w/flower frog, imp mk, 10" dia...250.00
Candlestick, attached saucer base, 1st art mk, 4", from $150 to..200.00
Candlestick, flared ft, 2nd art mk, 7", from $125 to 175.00
Cigarette jar, 1st art mk, 4¾x3¼", from $275 to 325.00

Ginger jar, stamped, 8½x5½" 1,200.00
Jardiniere, decor rim, paper label/stamped, 11¼x12½" 1,500.00
Jardiniere, decor rim, stamped, 8x9" 600.00
Jug, w/o hdl, 7" 340.00
Mug, cylindrical, mk Patent Pend'g, 5½", from $300 to............400.00
Vase, Benton Ark mk (die stamp), 7", from $225 to 275.00
Vase, bottle form, stamped, 10¼x4½" 425.00
Vase, bowl shape, mk Patent Pend'g, 4¼x5½" 235.00
Vase, bulbous, stamped, 13x7" 1,100.00
Vase, corseted, stamped, 12x5¼" 600.00
Vase, cylindrical, imp mk, 5½" 90.00
Vase, flared cylinder, mk Patent Pend'g, 10½", from $400 to......500.00
Vase, incurvate rim pierced to hold flowers, stamped, 5" dia.......275.00
Vase, low shoulder, early mk, 8¼", from $275 to 325.00
Vase, rolled rim, stamped, 10¼x5" 275.00
Vase, shouldered, flared rim, stamped, 18" 2,700.00
Vase, shouldered, slightly waisted (unusual shape), 6" 190.00
Vase, shouldered, 10½" 325.00
Vase, shouldered cylinder, 1st art mk, 10¼", from $300 to.........350.00
Vase, slightly bulbous, 1st art mk, 14", from $700 to 900.00
Vase, squat, 5" 160.00
Vase, teardrop shape, 1st art mk, 10", from $375 to...............425.00
Vase, trumpet neck, mk Patent Pend'g, 6¼", from $200 to.........250.00
Vase, waisted, 1st art mk, 10", from $400 to 500.00
Vase, wide bands of color, 2nd art mk, 3x3½" 88.00

Miscellaneous

Ball jug, Delft Blue, hi-gloss, Hywood, 5½", from $125 to..........175.00
Candlestick, Hywood by Niloak, 3x6" 36.00
Figurine, Southern Belle, Ozark Dawn II, 7¼", from $100 to 125.00
Figurine, Trojan horse, 2nd art mk, 8¾", from $125 to 175.00
Head vase, w/hat, emb mk, 7" 120.00
Jug, gr/tan mottle, spherical, 6" 210.00
Pitcher, hi-gloss, mini, 2½" to 3½", from $10 to................20.00
Planter, camel before planter, brn-tan, emb mk, 3¼", from $35 to.....45.00
Planter, hi-gloss, attached saucer, 5x4" sq.....................15.00
Tray, ivory, ruffled rim, unmk, 12½", from $25 to 50.00
Vase, cornucopia; hi-gloss, 7" 24.00
Vase, fan shape, Ozark Dawn, 14" 135.00
Vase, fine vertical ribbing, Ozark Dawn, 12" 85.00
Vase, gr & tan matt, hdls, Hywood, 5½", from $35 to.............45.00
Vase, maroon, incurvate rim, Hywood, 6⅛", from $75 to 100.00
Vase, Ozark Blue, Art Deco, Niloak block letters, 9½", from $100 to...150.00
Vase, Ozark Blue, unmk, 5¾", from $35 to 45.00
Vase, Peacock Blue, hdls, Hywood, 5¾", from $100 to 125.00
Vase, Pearled Green, hdls, unmk Hywood, 9½", from $500 to ...600.00
Vase, pk w/bl overspray, unmk, 5½", from $50 to.................75.00
Vase, Sea Green, 3-hdld, Hywood, 5½", from $300 to 400.00
Vase, tulip form, hi-gloss, mk, 7½" 29.00

Nippon

Nippon generally refers to Japanese wares made during the period from 1891 to 1921, although the Nippon mark was also used to a limited extent on later wares (accompanied by 'Japan'). Nippon, meaning Japan, identified the country of origin to comply with American importation restrictions. After 1921 'Japan' was the acceptable alternative. The term does not imply a specific type of product and may be found on items other than porcelains. For further information we recommend *The Collector's Encyclopedias of Nippon Porcelain* (there are six in the series) by our advisor, Joan Van Patten; you will find her address in the Directory under New York. In the following listings, items are assumed hand

painted unless noted otherwise. Numbers included in the descriptions refer to these specific marks:

Key:
#1 — China E-OH
#2 — M in Wreath
#3 — Cherry Blossom
#4 — Double T Diamond in Circle
#5 — Rising Sun
#6 — Royal Kinran
#7 — Maple Leaf
#8 — Royal Nippon, Nishiki
#9 — Royal Moriye Nippon

Basket, scenic tapestry, gold trim, 9", from $2,000.00 to $2,300.00. (Photo courtesy Jackson's Auctions)

Ashtray/match box holder, pastoral scene, gr #2, 3½" 275.00
Basket vase, gold on cobalt, #2, 7¾" 725.00
Basket vase, mc roses w/much gold on wht, unmk, 7" 425.00
Bottle, scent; pastoral scene, earth tones w/cobalt, bulbous, #2, 5" ..285.00
Bowl, berry; reserves in gr border w/gold, #7, +8¾" underplate ..265.00
Bowl, floral w/ornate gold rim, 3-leg, 6-sided, #2, 7¼" 145.00
Bowl, gold florals & swags on wht, RC mk, 8½" 265.00
Bowl, nut; floral & gold on wht, scalloped rim, #2, 7", +4 3" bowls ..195.00
Bowl, peanuts in relief, hdls, #2, 7" 150.00
Bowl, roses, ornate gold scalloped rim, #2, 12" 375.00
Bowl, roses on wht, tub hdls, #2, 7½" 250.00
Bowl, roses w/cobalt & gold scalloped rim, cobalt ft, #7, 4½"....525.00
Box, cigarette; Indian portrait on brn, #2, 4¼" L 275.00
Box, powder; floral band on wht w/gold, #2, 5½" 70.00
Box, powder; scenic w/gold beading, #7, 5¾" dia 350.00
Box, trinket; floral on wht heart shape, #2, sm 80.00
Cake plate, floral band w/gold, gr & red crown mk, 10½" 100.00
Candlestick, Deco floral on cobalt, 6-sided, gr #2, 9", pr 300.00
Cheese & cracker dish, sampan in sunset scenic, #7, 8½" 140.00
Cheese dish, Deco decor on wht w/cobalt slant lid, #2, 7¾" 175.00
Cheese dish, floral on wht w/bl & wht Wedgwood trim, slant lid, #2 ...500.00
Chocolate pot, roses on wht w/much gold, illegible mk, 11½", +4 c/s...875.00
Cookie jar, mc roses & cobalt w/gold, ftd, #7, 7¾" 900.00
Cracker jar, floral, bl & yel on wht w/gold, #2, 9½" w/hdls 250.00
Creamer & sugar bowl, gold on wht, w/lid, RC mk 75.00
Cup & saucer, gold on cobalt, unmk 100.00
Demitasse set, pk & gold band on wht, #5, 6" pot+cr/s+4 c/s+12" tray ..350.00
Egg cup, sampan in sunset scenic, #5, 2½" 65.00
Ewer, landscape tapestry band on gold, #7, 7" 1,350.00
Ewer, mixed floral reserve on patterned gold, waisted, #7, 9¾" ..475.00
Ewer, moriage flowers, ornate hdl, conical, unmk, 7½" 375.00
Ewer, roses on wht w/gold, melon ribs, bl #6, 9¼" 450.00
Ewer, roses on wht w/gold, melon ribs, bl #6, 9¼" 450.00
Ferner, floral, gold ruffled rim, wht int, #2, 4¼x7¾" 400.00
Ferner, sampan scenic, triangular, 3 sm gold ft, #2, 8" L 325.00
Humidor, deer in sunset scene, #2, 5½" 450.00
Humidor, fox hunt scenic band on green, #7, 6½" 925.00
Humidor, man on camel in relief, mc on brn tones, #2, 7½" ...1,500.00
Humidor, roses w/gold, #7, 8¼" 650.00
Humidor, 12 monks & animals in relief, brn wash, #7, 7½" 2,250.00
Humidor, 4 scenic reserves on sq Deco-motif body, #2, 5" 450.00

Jar, moriage palms scenic, triangular, #2, 6" **335.00**
Jug, whiskey; scenic reserve on brn bbl form, #2, 5½" **750.00**
Jug, wine; English coach scene reserve on gr, #7, 9½" **1,400.00**
Lamp, flowers w/gold beads, candlestick type, #7, 13" **365.00**
Lemon dish, bl birds on wht, sm hdls, #5, 5½" **25.00**
Mug, Cardinal portrait reserve, 5½" **1,100.00**
Mug, sampan in sunset, souvenir of Delaware Water Gap, #2, 5½" ..**300.00**
Pancake server, roses on wht w/gold, #7, 8¾" **230.00**
Pitcher, sampan scenic, brn trim & hdl, w/lid, #7, 7" **300.00**
Plaque, birds on flowering branch, #2, 10" **325.00**
Plaque, gulls swim along crest of ocean wave, gold rim, #7, 11½" ..**450.00**
Plaque, hunt scene w/riders & dogs on chase, #2, 8¾" **475.00**
Plaque, Indian chief on jumping horse in relief, #2, 10½" **900.00**
Plaque, irises in lav tones, gr #2, 10½" **350.00**
Plaque, lady's portrait, coralene border, US Pat mk, 11" **3,000.00**
Plaque, sampan scenic, earth tones, simple border, mk, 8½" **325.00**
Plaque, squirrel in relief, earth tones, #2, 10½" **900.00**
Plaque/charger palms in sunset, #2, 14" **450.00**
Plate, camel scenic, cobalt & gold rim, #2, 10" **425.00**
Punch bowl, mc grapes, ftd, hdls, gr #2, 12¾x13" **1,100.00**
Salt cellar, Capitol Building Washington DC reserve, #2, 2½" **40.00**
Shakers, floral on wht, pr in center-hdld fr, #5 ....**35.00**
Smoke set, camel in desert scenic, #2, 7½" tray+humidor+box ..**700.00**
Stein, pastoral cottage scene on brn, #2, 7" **650.00**
Stein, silhouettes in sunset scene, #2, 7" **650.00**
Tankard, coralene florals on shaded gr, unmk, 12" **1,700.00**
Tankard, fruit & flower on branch w/cobalt & gold, bl #7, 16½" ...**1,000.00**
Tankard, irises, gr & brn tones, #6, 12½" **925.00**
Tea set, palms scenic w/gold, bl #7, 5" pot+cr/sug w/lid **300.00**
Tray, scenic center w/6 reserves on cobalt w/gold, #7, 11¼" L **500.00**
Urn, bird on branch, much gold, ornate hdls, bolted, #7, 19½" ..**2,500.00**
Urn, mixed flowers, ornate gold hdls, bolted, #2, 18" **1,800.00**
Urn, swan scenic, artist sgn, #2, 19" **7,000.00**
Vase, airplane above pastoral scene, hdls, #2, 4" **300.00**
Vase, Am Indian in canoe, decor rim & ft, hdls, Imperial mk, 7" **385.00**
Vase, bird on flowering branch, sm angle hdls, Imperial mk, 10½" ..**315.00**
Vase, camel rider in desert scene, ornate hdls, mk, 6" **375.00**
Vase, classical ladies reserve on wht w/gold & pk, cylinder, #7, 16" **2,400.00**
Vase, coralene flowers w/cobalt & gold, hdls, bottle neck, mk, 11½" ..**1,400.00**
Vase, coralene water lilies & leaves, ornate hdls, mk, 6¾" **650.00**
Vase, cottage & stream scene, much gold, #2, 15¾" **2,300.00**
Vase, Countess Anna Potocka reserve on wht w/gold, hdls, #7, 7½" ...**900.00**
Vase, floral on brn w/gold at rim, 1 hdl, slim, #3, 11" **450.00**
Vase, floral on cobalt, low integral hdls, #7, 9½" **325.00**
Vase, floral reserve band w/much gold on cobalt, ftd, #2, 7½" **650.00**
Vase, flowers in relief, mc on bl, bottle neck, #7, 9½" **775.00**
Vase, gold o/l leaves on brn, bottle-necked cylinder, #7, 7½" **250.00**
Vase, gold o/l mums on cobalt, hdls, #7, 12¼" **950.00**
Vase, gold scenic reserve & band on cobalt, sm mouth, hdls, #7, 7½" ..**650.00**
Vase, grapes, yel & purple, bottle neck, #7, 10¼" **385.00**
Vase, irises & long leaves, 3 hdls, #2, 11½" **450.00**
Vase, lady w/flowers in vase reserve on cobalt & gold, #7, 7¾" ..**1,300.00**
Vase, lilies, wht on brn, sm hdls, #2, 9¾" **350.00**
Vase, Madame Lebrun portrait w/much gold, sm hdls, unmk, 9½" ..**1,150.00**
Vase, moriage birds, bottle neck, #7, 6½" **500.00**
Vase, moriage birds in flight, integral hdls, #7, 4½" **285.00**
Vase, moriage flowers on gr, bulbous, flared rim, bl mk, 4½" **300.00**
Vase, moriage trees & hdls, bulbous, sm mouth, #7, 9" **565.00**
Vase, mums on shaded brn, 4 angle hdls, sq sides, Imperial mk, 10¼" ..**275.00**
Vase, owls in relief, brn tones, #2, 7¾" **1,700.00**
Vase, pastoral scenic w/cobalt & gold, bottle neck, #7, 9" **600.00**
Vase, poppies on yel to wht, gold hdls, #2, 10½" **350.00**
Vase, river scenic, hdls, porc, gr #2, 9¾" **365.00**
Vase, roses, wht w/brn leaves on wht, sm gold hdls, #2, 8¾" **315.00**

Vase, roses (lg/mc) on brn w/gold, #7, 12" **600.00**
Vase, roses (pk) below cobalt w/much silver o/l, hdls, #7, 7" **450.00**
Vase, roses on shaded brn, 32, 9½" **265.00**
Vase, roses tapestry w/gold, sm gold hdls, #7, 6" **950.00**
Vase, scenic tapestry, cylindrical, #7, 6¼" **850.00**
Vase, silhouette of rider w/lariat in sunset, hdls, Imperial mk, 12" ..**900.00**
Vase, swan scenic, moriage grapes & leaves, sm hdls, bl mk, 10" ...**550.00**
Vase, swan scenic w/moriage trim & hdls, bottle neck, #7, 9" **450.00**
Vase, swans scenic w/moriage grapes & leaves, gr hdls, #7, 9½" .**625.00**
Vase, Wedgwood, cream on bl, hdls, #2, 8" **675.00**
Vase, windmill in sunset scenic, loving cup form, #2, 5½" **125.00**
Vase, windmill scenic, angle hdls w/rings, #2, 6" **140.00**
Vase, woodland scene, brn hdls, #2, 7¼" **800.00**
Vase, woodland scene, wht w/moriage trim, #2, 10" **700.00**

Nodders

So called because of the nodding action of their heads and hands, nodders originated in China where they were used in temple rituals to represent deity. At first they were made of brass and were actually a type of bell; when these bells were rung, the heads of the figures would nod. In the eighteenth century, the idea was adopted by Meissen and by French manufacturers who produced not only china nodders but bisque as well. Most nodders are individual; couples are unusual. The idea remained popular until the end of the nineteenth century and was used during the Victorian era by toy manufacturers. Our advisor for non-German nodders is Barry Larkins; he is listed in the Directory under Florida.

Astronaut/spaceman, blk helmet w/lightning bolts, air pack on bk **140.00**
Baseball player, Baltimore Orioles, 1961-61, wht base, rare, minimum **450.00**
Baseball player, Cleveland Indians, team mascot, 1961-62, sq wht base ..**600.00**
Basketball player, Harlem Globetrotters, 1962 ....**350.00**
Basketball player, Los Angeles Lakers, 1962 ....**225.00**
Black boy smoking cigar at side of tray, CI, Austria **85.00**
Black cat, flocking over molded hard plastic, 8x10" **40.00**
Cow, compo, gold horns, 5½x4", EX **37.50**
Football player, Atlanta Falcons, 1967, rnd gold base **75.00**
Football player, Green Bay Packers, 1967, gold base **150.00**
Football player, Washington Redskins, 1961-62, lt face, rnd wht base ..**400.00**
Football player, WSU Cougars, Japan, 6½" **200.00**
Hippopotamus, cast metal, 6¼" **110.00**
Hockey player, Detroit Redwings, 6¼", NM **130.00**
Hula dancer w/flower in hair, compo, 6¾" **50.00**
Hula dancer w/ukelele, ceramic, unmk, 7" **110.00**
Lady in bikini sitting in chair, leg kicks high, ceramic, mk Pat TT ...**110.00**
Lucy (Peanuts), Lego **110.00**
Mickey Mantle, 1961-62, scarce, NM **600.00**
Oriental man & lady, bsk, 6½", pr **175.00**
Oriental man & lady, noding heads/waving arms, Ardalt Japan, 7", pr **150.00**
Pluto, Walt Disney Productions, Made in Japan, 5½" **90.00**
Smokey the Bear, ceramic, 6" **40.00**

German Comic Characters

During the early 1930s, Germany produced a collection of small figure dolls, approximately 2" to 4" high, representing the most popular comic strip and cartoon characters of that time. They were made of bisque with brightly painted details and clearly stamped with their appropriate names and 'Germany' on their backs. Generally, their movable heads were attached with an elastic string going through their bodies, hence the name 'nodders,' but there were some characters produced earlier that were frozen with no movable parts. The most popular ones came in boxed sets, but the lesser-known characters were sold separately, making them rarer and harder to find today. We have listed the most valuable characters from the series here; those not mentioned below are valued at $125.00 and under. Our advisor for German character nodders is Doug Dezso; he is listed in the Directory under New Jersey. He will answer questions (as long as an SASE is included) on German character nodders only.

Perry Winkle, $100.00+, Winnie Winkle, $150.00. (Photo courtesy Hilma R. Irtz)

Ambrose Potts	350.00
Auntie Blossom	150.00
Auntie Mamie & Uncle Willie, ea	250.00
Avery	200.00
Bill	200.00
Buttercup	250.00
Chubby Chaney	250.00
Corky	475.00
Dinty Moor (frozen)	500.00
Dock	200.00
Fanny or Rudy Nebbs, ea	250.00
Ferina	350.00
Grandpa Teen	350.00
Happy Hooligan	625.00
Harold Teen	150.00
Jeff Regus, med or lg, ea	250.00
Jeff Regus, sm	175.00
Josie	425.00
Junior Nebbs	625.00
Lilacs	425.00
Lillums	150.00
Little Annie Rooney, movable arms, complete	350.00
Little Egypt	350.00
Lord Plushbottom	150.00
Ma & Pa Winkle, ea	350.00
Marjorie	425.00
Mary Ann Jackson	250.00
Max	200.00
Min Gump	150.00
Mr Bailey	150.00
Mr Bibb	400.00
Mr Wicker	250.00
Mushmouth	175.00
Mutt, med or lg, NM, ea	250.00
Mutt, sm	175.00
Nicodemus	350.00
Old Timer	350.00
Our Gang, 6-pc set, MIB	1,400.00
Pat Finegan	400.00
Patsy	425.00
Pete the Dog	250.00
Pop Jenks	200.00

Rudy Nebs	250.00
Scraps	250.00
Uncle Willy	250.00
Widow Zandor	400.00

Nordic Art Glass

Finnish and Swedish glass has recently started to develop a following, probably stemming from the revitalization of interest in forms from the 1950s. (The name Nordic is used because of the inclusion of Finnish glass — the term Scandinavian does not refer to this country.) Included here are Holmegaard, Hadeland, Benny Motzfeldt, Flygsfors, Maleras, and Strombergshyttan.

Our suggested prices are 'fair market values,' developed after researching the Nordic secondary markets, the current retail prices on items still being produced, and American auction houses and antique stores.

Our advisor for this category is William L. Geary; he is listed in the Directory under Colorado.

Flygsfors Glass Works, Sweden

Flygsfors Glass Works was established in 1888 and continued to operate until 1979 when the Orrefors Glass Group ceased operations at this factory.

Flygsfors is well known for art glass designed by Paul Kedelv, who joined the firm in 1949 with a contract to design light fittings, a specialty of the company. Other internationally known artist/designers include Prince Sigvard Bernadotte and the Finnish designer Helene Tynell.

Examples of the 'Coquille' series, which uses a unique overlay technique utilizing opaque, bright colors and 'flamingo,' have become hits on the secondary market.

Bowl, Coquille, oblong w/flared ends, cranberry/wht, Kedelv, 11"	95.00
Lamp, tall stem form, gr w/clear o/l, flared base, 11"	125.00
Vase, Coquille, flared wings, bl/red, Kedelv, 10¼"	150.00
Vase, Coquille, flared wings, maroon/gr, Kedelv, 13"	165.00
Vase, Flamingo, teardrop, gr/brn/wht threads w/in, Kedelv, 10½"	135.00

Hadeland Glassverk, Norway

Glass has been produced at this glass works since 1765. From the beginning, the main product was bottles. Since the 1850s they have made small items — drinking glasses, vases, bowls, jugs, etc., and for the last forty years, figurines, souvenirs and objects of art.

Important designers include Willy Johansson, Arne John Jutrem, Inger Magnus, Severin Broby, and Gro Sommerfelt.

Bowl, pk w/blk rim & ft, #10747, I Magnus, 8"	225.00
Bowl, presentation; clear, eng cranes/stylized leaves, 8x11½"	150.00
Plate, clear w/brn & bl, Jon Jutrem, #10814, 23½"	295.00
Plate, opal & amber center w/textured underside, Sommerfelt, 9½"	65.00
Vase, cranberry, teardrop form, Johansson, 11½"	50.00

Holmegaard Glassvaerk, Denmark

This company was founded in 1825. Because of a shortage of wood in Denmark, it became necessary for them to use peat, the only material available for fuel.

Their first full-time designers were hired after 1923. Orla Juul Nielson was the first. He was followed in 1925 by Jacob Band, an architect. Per Lukin became the chief designer in 1941. His production and art glass incorporates a simple yet complex series of designs. They continue to be popular among collectors of Scandinavian glass.

During 1965 the company merged with Kastrup and became Kastrup Holmegaard AS; a merger with Royal Copenhagen followed in 1975.

Bowl, wht w/orange o/l, flattened form, Michael Bang, 2x7" **25.00**
Flame vase, gr w/clear o/l, Per Lukin, 9⅛x3½" **100.00**
Jar, gr, sq w/short neck, Per Lukin, 6½x6" **35.00**
Vase, wht opal w/purple lines/2 musical notes, cylinder, Lukin, 6¾"..**50.00**
Vase, wht w/orange o/l, flared body, short neck, Otto Bauer, 4¾x6" ..**65.00**

Maleras Glass Works, Sweden

The first glass works at Maleras was founded in 1890. The city of Maleras was an important railway junction in Smaland, the Kingdom of Crystal, where articles from many of the glasshouses were shipped to the cities of Stockholm, Goteborg, and Malmo, Sweden.

During the 1940s Maleras Glass Works built a reputation throughout Sweden as one of the leading manufacturers of lead crystal.

In 1975 the company joined the Royal Krona Group. Six years later under the leadership of Mats Jonasson, the glass blowers and members of the community bought the factory from the existing management.

During the last twenty years, the company has produced first class, crystal sculptures of wildlife, which are sold around the world.

Mats Jonasson is the master designer for the factory, and his wildlife images and engraving techniques are superb. The artists Erika Hoglund and Lars Goran Tinback recently joined the company as designers.

Sculpture, Dolphins, ltd ed, Jonasson, #13303, 8½" **1,250.00**
Sculpture, Eagle, ltd ed, Jonasson, 313301, 12½" **1,250.00**
Sculpture, Giraffes, ltd ed, Jonasson, #33116, 9¾" **380.00**
Sculpture, Plura, E Hoglund, #25004, 9¼"................................**470.00**
Sculpture, Sharks, Jonasson, #33619, 7¼" **190.00**

Benny Motzfeldt, Norwegian Glass Artist

Benny Motzfeldt, a graduate of the Arts and Crafts School of Oslo, Norway, started her career in glass in 1954 by answering an advertisement for a designer of engraving and decoration at Christiania Glassmagasin and Hadeland Glassverk. After serveral years at Hadeland, she joined the Plus organization and managed their glass studio in Frederikstad. She is acknowledged as one of the leading exponents of Norwegian art glass and is recognized internationally. She challenged the rather sober Norwegian glass designs with a strong desire to try new ways, using vigorous forms and opaque colors embedded with silver nitrate following patterns.

Bottle, clear w/wht shards, short neck, sgn, 6" **65.00**
Bowl, bl & gr w/appl bubbles, wht & blk shards, 3x5" **85.00**
Bowl, orange w/internal bubbles, sgn, 9⅞x6⅛".............................**50.00**
Vase, wht underlay w/gold frit bands/vertical lines, 7¼x4¼" **95.00**
Vase, yel w/orange band at rim & ft, sgn, 7x7" **100.00**

Strombergshyttan, Sweden

The original factory, Lindefors, was started in 1876. Although the factory was modernized in the 1920s, it closed in 1931. In 1933 Edvard Stromberg bought the factory; Gerda Stromberg designed for the company until 1942. In 1945 the factory was purchased by Stromberg's son Eric and his wife Asta. She designed for them until 1976. Edvard worked with Eric, who was a chemist, and together they developed a new color of glass with a distinctive bluish-silver hue which became the factory's speciality.

Gunnar Nylund, famous for his copper wheel-engraved forms, was at the glassworks from 1952 until 1975.

After a renovation in 1962, the factory suffered a serious fire and due to economic conditions was sold to Orrefors Glass Works; it operated under that title until it closed in 1979.

Sculpture, cast crystal, girl & deer w/2 trees in bkground, 7x6" **65.00**
Vase, bl-silver teardrop w/eng girl & flying seed, Nylund, 10" **225.00**
Vase, dk gray, B963, Stromberg, 14½"......................................**110.00**
Vase, gray, Ariel technique, circles of air, B943, Stromberg, 5"...**210.00**

Noritake

The Noritake Company was first registered in 1904 as Nippon Gomei Kaisha. In 1917 the name became Nippon Toki Kabushiki Toki. The 'M in wreath' mark is that of the Morimura Brothers, distributors with offices in New York. It was used until 1941. The 'tree crest' mark is the crest of the Morimura family.

The Noritake Company has produced fine porcelain dinnerware sets and occasional pieces decorated in the delicate manner for which the Japanese are noted. (Two dinnerware patterns are featured below, and a general range is suggested for others.)

Authority Joan Van Patten has compiled a lovely book, *The Collector's Encyclopedia of Noritake*, with many full-color photos and current prices; you will find her address in the Directory under New York. In the following listings, examples are hand painted unless noted otherwise. Numbers refer to these specific marks:

Key:
#1 — Komaru   #3 — N in Wreath
#2 — M in Wreath

Azalea

The Azalea pattern was produced exclusively for the Larkin Company, who gave the lovely ware away as premiums to club members and their home agents. From 1916 through the 1930s, Larkin distributed fine china which was decorated in pink azaleas on white with gold tracing along edges and handles. Early in the '30s, six pieces of crystal hand painted with the same design were offered: candle holders, a compote, a tray with handles, a scalloped fruit bowl, a cheese and cracker set, and a cake plate. All in all, seventy different pieces of Azalea were produced. Some, such as the fifteen-piece child's set, bulbous vase, china ashtray, and the pancake jug, are quite rare. One of the earliest marks was the Noritake 'M in wreath' with variations. Later the ware was marked 'Noritake, Azalea, Hand Painted, Japan.' Our advisor for Azalea is Linda Williams; she is listed in the Directory under Massachusetts.

Basket, Dolly Varden...**265.00**

Syrup pitcher and underplate, $110.00. (Photo courtesy Linda Williams)

Basket, mint; Dolly Varden, #193 ....**140.00**
Bonbon, #184, 6¼" **50.00**
Bowl, #12, 10" **42.50**
Bowl, candy/grapefruit; #185..**195.00**
Bowl, cream soup; #363...**175.00**
Bowl, deep, #310..**68.00**
Bowl, fruit; shell form, #188, 7¾"..**385.00**

Bowl, oatmeal; #55, 5½" 28.00
Bowl, soup; #19, 7⅛" 25.00
Bowl, vegetable; divided, #439, 9½"...................295.00
Bowl, vegetable; oval, #101, 10½" 60.00
Bowl, vegetable; oval, #172, 9¼" 58.00
Butter chip, #312, 3¼" 120.00
Butter tub, w/insert, #54 ....48.00
Cake plate, #10, 9¾" 40.00
Candy jar, w/lid, #313 ....750.00
Casserole, gold finial, w/lid, #372 ....475.00
Casserole, w/lid, #16 ....95.00
Celery tray, closed hdls, 10" 330.00
Celery/roll tray, #99, 12" 55.00
Cheese/butter dish, #314 ....135.00
Child's set, #253, 15-pc 2,500.00
Coffeepot, AD; #182 ....600.00
Compote, #170 ....98.00
Condiment set, #14, 5-pc 65.00
Creamer & sugar bowl, #7 ....45.00
Creamer & sugar bowl, AD; open, #123, from $125 to ..140.00
Creamer & sugar bowl, gold finial, #401 ....155.00
Creamer & sugar bowl, ind, #449 ....395.00
Creamer & sugar shaker, #122 ....125.00
Cruet, #190 ....160.00
Cup & saucer, #2 ....20.00
Cup & saucer, AD; #183, from $150 to 160.00
Cup & saucer, bouillon; #124, 3½" 28.00
Egg cup, #120 ....40.00
Gravy boat, #40 ....48.00
Jam jar set, #125, 4-pc 155.00
Mayonnaise set, scalloped, #453, 3-pc 495.00
Mustard jar, #191, 3-pc 50.00
Pickle/lemon set, #121 ....24.50
Pitcher, milk jug; #100, 1-qt 260.00
Plate, #4, 7½" 10.00
Plate, bread & butter; #8, 6½" 10.00
Plate, breakfast; #98 ....28.00
Plate, dinner; #13, 9¾" 22.00
Plate, grill; 3-compartment, #38, 10¼", from $165 to .175.00
Plate, salad, 7⅝" sq 75.00
Plate, scalloped sq, salesman's sample 950.00
Platter, #17, 14" 60.00
Platter, #186, 16" 475.00
Platter, #56, 12" 58.00
Platter, cold meat/bacon; #311, 10¼" 195.00
Refreshment set, #39, 2-pc 48.00
Relish, #194, 7⅛" 85.00
Relish, oval, #18, 8½" 20.00
Relish, 2-part, #171 ....58.00
Relish, 2-part, loop hdl, #450, from $390 to 425.00
Relish, 4-section, #119, rare, 10" 160.00
Saucer, fruit; #9, 5¼" 10.00
Shakers, bell form, #11, pr 30.00
Shakers, bulbous, #189, 8" 115.00
Shakers, ind, #126, pr 27.50
Spoon holder, #189, 8" 115.00
Syrup, #97, w/underplate & lid 110.00
Tea tile 40.00
Teapot, #15 ....110.00
Teapot, gold finial, #400 ....495.00
Toothpick holder, #192, from $115 to 120.00
Vase, bulbous, #452 ....1,150.00
Vase, fan form, ftd #187 ....185.00
Whipped cream/mayonnaise set, #3, 3-pc 38.50

Tree in the Meadow

Another of their dinnerware lines has become a favorite of many collectors. Tree in the Meadow is a scenic hand-painted pattern which features a thatched cottage in a meadow with a lake in the foreground. The version accepted by most collectors will have a tree behind the cottage and will not have a swan or a bridge. The colors resemble a golden sunset on a fall day with shades of orange, gold, and rust. This line was made during the 1920s and 1930s and seems today to be in good supply. A fairly large dinnerware set with several unusual serving pieces can be readily assembled. Our advisor for Tree in the Meadow is Linda Williams; she is listed in the Directory under Massachusetts.

Basket, Dolly Varden 125.00
Bowl, cream soup; 2-hdl 35.00
Bowl, fruit; shell form, #210 ....300.00
Bowl, oatmeal 15.00
Bowl, oval, 10½" 45.00
Bowl, oval, 9½" 28.00
Bowl, soup 28.00
Bowl, vegetable; 9" 35.00
Butter pat 15.00
Butter tub, open, w/drainer 35.00
Cake plate, open hdl 35.00
Candy dish, octagonal, w/lid, 5½" 350.00
Celery dish 35.00
Cheese dish 75.00
Condiment set, 5-pc 45.00
Creamer & sugar bowl, demitasse 40.00
Cruets, vinegar & oil; cojoined, #319 ....325.00
Cup & saucer, breakfast 18.00
Cup & saucer, demitasse 35.00
Egg cup 30.00
Gravy boat 50.00
Jam jar/dish, 4-pc 70.00
Lemon dish 15.00
Mayonnaise set, 3-pc 48.00
Platter, 10" 135.00
Platter, 11¾x9" 50.00
Platter, 13¾x10¼" 60.00
Relish, divided 35.00
Sugar bowl, #204 ....25.00
Tea set, 3-pc 135.00

Miscellaneous

Vase, ships reserve on tan lustre, blue lustre at foot and rim, green and yellow birds perched along rim, green mark, 7", from $325.00 to $375.00. (Photo courtesy Joan Van Patten)

Ashtray, flowers on shaded cream, 4 rests, #2, 5¾" 50.00
Ashtray, Indian chief portrait, geometric rim, 6-sided, #2, 6½" ..160.00
Bowl, exotic birds on wht, Deco-style band, #2, 7¼" 90.00
Bowl, floral reserve w/orange lustre, bl rim, hdls, #2, 9¼" 65.00
Bowl, irises on wht, bl rim w/gold hdls, #2, 10½" 85.00

Bowl, river scenic, 8-sided, red #2, 6½"..............................**50.00**
Bowl, roses, pk on wht w/gold border & hdls, gr #2, 11" W........**150.00**
Bowl, 3 floral reserves w/gold on wht, 3 pierced hdls, #2, 6¼"....**50.00**
Candlesticks, exotic bird on branch, bl rims & ft, #2, 8¼", pr....**240.00**
Candy jar, river reserve & band on gold lustre, #2, 6½"............**225.00**
Celery tray, celery stalks on cream, #2, 12", +6 3¾" salts............**140.00**
Cheese dish, yel band w/Deco flowers on wht, slant lid, #2, 8" L..**100.00**
Chocolate pot, gold o/l on wht, #2, 9"..............................**200.00**
Chocolate set, exotic birds on wht w/gold, #2, 9½" pot+5 c/s....**300.00**
Cigarette holder, flowers on bell shape, bird finial, #2, 5"..........**250.00**
Compote, floral on cream w/gold hdls, ftd, #2, 9¾"................**80.00**
Compote, swans in river scenic, hdls, #2, 9" W..................**85.00**
Condensed milk container, Deco floral on wht w/gold, #2, 5¼"..**160.00**
Condiment set, exotic birds on red, #2, 3 pcs on 6¾" tray..........**150.00**
Egg cup, windmill & river scenic, earth tones, #2, 3½"............**40.00**
Humidor, camel scene at sunset, gr #2, 5¾"........................**375.00**
Humidor, owl on branch in relief, #2, 7"............................**775.00**
Jam jar, bl & gold lustre, rose finial, #2, w/spoon & tray, 5¼"......**80.00**
Lemon dish, flowering branch on yel, red #2, 6½" L..................**40.00**
Lemon dish, lemons & leaves, tan lustre rim, #2, 5¾"..............**40.00**
Mantel set, Deco floral on cream w/gold, #2, 9" bowl+pr sticks..**475.00**
Mustard set, roses, pk & yel on wht, #2, 3", 4-pc..................**35.00**
Napkin ring, mc roses, #2, 2¼" W..................................**45.00**
Nappy, roses, pastels on cream, 1-hdl, #2, 5"......................**40.00**
Night light, lady praying (figural,) lustre dress, #2, 9¾"..........**2,400.00**
Plaque, river scenic w/swans, earth tones, #2, 6½"................**115.00**
Plate, windmill & river landscape, bright colors, #2, 7½"..........**65.00**
Playing card holder, horse on tan lustre, ftd, #2, 3¾"..............**150.00**
Sauce dish, flowers & bird on wht w/tan lustre, #2, 4½", +spoon..**50.00**
Sauce dish, roses on tan w/orange lustre, #2, 5", +ladle & tray....**80.00**
Shakers, river scenic, earth tones, #2, 2½", pr....................**16.00**
Shaving mug, river scenic, earth tones w/gold, #2, 3¾"............**120.00**
Spooner, river scenic w/red-roofed cottage, #2, 8" L..............**70.00**
Sugar shaker, floral band on wht, gold top, #2, 6½"................**30.00**
Syrup, trees, river & red-roofed cottage scene, #2, 4¼"+tray......**85.00**
Tea set, river scenic, #2, child sz, 3½" pot+8 pcs..................**225.00**
Tile, river scenic, canted corners, #2, 5"..........................**55.00**
Toast rack, bl lustre w/bird finial, #2, 5½" L......................**125.00**
Tray, river scenic w/swans, bl #1, 12"..............................**80.00**
Vase, lg open roses, pastel tones w/gold, hdls, #2, 11¼"............**250.00**
Vase, peacock feathers on tan, ruffled rim, slim, #1, 8", pr........**180.00**
Vase, river scenic, jack-in-pulpit shape, #2, 7¾"..................**200.00**
Vase, roses on long stems on wht, hdls, #2, 8½"....................**165.00**
Vase, tulip figural, purple & gr, #2, 5¼"............................**300.00**
Vase, Wedgwood type, wht flowers on bl, hdls, #1, 9½"............**475.00**
Wall pocket, butterflies on tan lustre, red #2, 9"..................**125.00**

Various Dinnerware Patterns, ca. 1933 to Present

So many lines of dinnerware have been produced by the Noritake company that to list them all would require a volume in itself. In fact, just such a book is available — *The Collector's Encylopedia of Early Noritake* by Aimee Neff Alden (Collector Books). And while many patterns had specific names, others did not, so you'll probably need the photographs the book contains to help you identify your pattern. Outlined below is a general guide for the more common pieces and patterns. The high side of the range will represent lines from about 1933 until the mid-'60s (including those marked 'Occupied Japan'), while the lower side should be used to evaluate lines made after that period.

Bowl, berry; ind, from $8 to..**12.00**
Bowl, soup; 7½", from $12 to..**16.00**
Bowl, vegetable; rnd or oval, ca 1945 to present, from $28 to......**38.00**
Butter dish, 3-pc, ca 1933-64, from $40 to............................**50.00**

Creamer, from $18 to..**28.00**
Cup & saucer, demitasse; from $12 to..................................**17.50**
Gravy boat, from $35 to..**45.00**
Pickle or relish dish, from $18 to..**28.00**
Plate, bread & butter; from $8 to..**12.00**
Plate, dinner; from $15 to..**30.00**
Plate, luncheon; from $10 to..**18.00**
Plate, salad; from $10 to..**15.00**
Platter, 12", from $25 to..**40.00**
Platter, 16" (or larger), from $40 to....................................**60.00**
Shakers, pr, from $15 to..**25.00**
Sugar bowl, w/lid, from $18 to..**30.00**
Tea & toast set (sm cup & tray), from $18 to..........................**28.00**
Teapot, demitasse, chocolate or coffeepot, ea, from $45 to..........**60.00**

Norse

The Norse Pottery was established in 1903 in Edgerton, Wisconsin, by Thorwald Sampson and Louis Ipson. A year later it was purchased by A.W. Wheelock and moved to Rockford, Illinois. The ware they produced was inspired by ancient bronze vessels of the Norsemen. Designs were often incised into the red clay body. Dragon handles and feet were favored decorative devices, and they achieved a semblance of patina through the application of metallic glazes. The ware was marked with model numbers and a stylized 'N' containing a vertical arrangement of the remaining letters of the name. Production ceased after 1913. Our advisor for this category is John Danis; he is listed in the Directory under Illinois.

Bowl, band of cvd waves, 3 dragon-head ft, 4x7½"....................**325.00**
Bowl, blk w/bronze wash, incised decor, 3 faces form ft, #61, 5¾x7"..**275.00**
Bowl, incised rising sun, dragon-head hdls, #50, 7½" L..............**250.00**
Candlestick, blk w/gold snake looped at base, #54, 12", pr..........**275.00**
Candlestick, dk charcoal matt w/gr accents, #28, 7" W..............**300.00**
Jardiniere, incised snake, 3 Viking head ft, verdigris, #62, 7x9"..**500.00**

Jardiniere, salamander handles, three small animal-head feet, metal insert may have held an oil font and burner, #70, 4x6", **$500.00.** (This design is known to have been made in three sizes.)

Lamp base, appl ferns, verdigris, #29L, 10"........................**1,250.00**
Mug, blk w/bronze wash, incised decor, #51, 5"....................**150.00**
Pitcher, 1-stem plant w/incised leaves, gold wash, #90, 12"........**300.00**
Vase, geometrics, gr on brn to blk, hdls, #14, 11½"................**475.00**
Vase, geometrics at top, gold remains, #45, 4½"....................**95.00**
Vase, lg lizard on side, gold wash, #25, 12"........................**1,000.00**
Vase, slash mks at shoulder, #43, 9x1¾"............................**100.00**
Wall pocket, dmn shape w/lizards, #72, 11"..........................**1,000.00**

North Dakota School of Mines

The School of Mines of the University of North Dakota was established in 1890, but due to a lack of funding it was not until 1898 that Earle J. Babcock was appointed as director, and efforts were made to produce ware from the native clay he had discovered several years earlier.

The first pieces were made by firms in the east from the clay Babcock sent them. Some of the ware was decorated by the manufacturer; some was shipped back to North Dakota to be decorated by native artists. By 1909 students at the University of North Dakota were producing utilitarian items such as tile, brick, shingles, etc., in conjunction with a ceramic course offered through the chemistry department. By 1910 a ceramic department had been established, supervised by Margaret Kelly Cable. Under her leadership, fine artware was produced. Native flowers, grains, buffalo, cowboys, and other subjects indigenous to the state were incorporated into the decorations. Some pieces have an Art Nouveau–Art Deco style easily attributed to her association with Frederick H. Rhead, with whom she studied in 1911. During the '20s the pottery was marketed on a limited scale through gift and jewelry stores in the state. From 1927 until 1949 when Miss Cable announced her retirement, a more widespread distribution was maintained with sales branching out into other states. The ware was marked in cobalt with the official seal — 'Made at School of Mines, N.D. Clay, University of North Dakota, Grand Forks, N.D.' in a circle. Very early ware was sometimes marked 'U.N.D.' in cobalt by hand. For more information refer to *Collector's Encyclopedia of Dakota Potteries* by Darlene Hurst Dommel (Collector Books). Our advisor for this category is William M. Bilsland III; he is listed in the Directory under Iowa.

Bookends, windmills in relief, brn tones, 5½", pr, from $800 to ..**1,000.00**
Bowl, leaves cvd on gr, sgn BC, mk, 8" **350.00**
Charger, floral on burnt sienna, M Cable, #844, 1932, 9¾".........**900.00**
Figurine, chicken, brn, 3" W..**200.00**
Figurine, coyote, gr & brn hi-glaze, mk, 3½" **150.00**
Figurine, dog, ivory, 2½" L...**150.00**
Figurine, elephant, brn, North Dakota IGB on bk, 3⅛", EX **300.00**
Honey jar, bee emb on lid, gr on ivory, M Cable, 4¾" **200.00**
Pitcher, floral, bl & yel on gray, M Cable, mk, 5½" **275.00**
Trivet, fish, gr & ochre on lt yel, Julia Mattson, M58, 5" dia......**250.00**
Vase, brn to gr matt, cylindrical, sm flared rim, 5½" **230.00**
Vase, buffalo prs, bl/gray, J Mattson, #466, 3¾x4½" **1,700.00**
Vase, cowboy & lasso, Why Not Minot, J Mattson, #175, 5¾x2¾".....**375.00**
Vase, cowboy scene emb on chocolate brn, Flora Huckfield, 7¼x5".**1,500.00**
Vase, cowboys in chaps on brn & gr matt, Julia Mattson, 5x3".**1,300.00**
Vase, florals (cvd) on dk bl-gray matt, mk Pasque Flowers, 3½x6"....**400.00**
Vase, florals on lt brn to copper-chocolate, ovoid, 3¾", pr **920.00**
Vase, geometrics, gr matt, Arnegard, 1932, 3½x5" **700.00**
Vase, gr-brn matt, classic shape, Julia Mattson, flake, 9" **350.00**
Vase, haystacks on gr, F Huckfield, bulbous, #164, 4¼x3½" **900.00**
Vase, lantern, mustard yel on charcoal-bl gloss, RLH, 5½x6½" ..**5,000.00**
Vase, leaves, brn on bl, Julia Mattson, 7½"................................**550.00**
Vase, Meadowlark, birds, chartreuse, M Cable, squat, #155, 3¼".**600.00**
Vase, Native Am-style birds, Bentonite, Armstrong, 1948, 4¼x4¾".....**900.00**
Vase, North Dakota wheat, brn shades, F Huckfield, #1655, 4¾x7".**1,200.00**
Vase, oxen & covered wagons, brn matt, M Cable, #186, 5½x7¼" ..**1,300.00**
Vase, prairie roses, Huckfield & student, #4248, 4x5½" **700.00**
Vase, sheaves of wheat, purple-brn, Huckfield, 10x5½" **1,300.00**
Vase, stylized flowers, celadon semi-matt, #53H, 3¾x3¼" **500.00**
Vase, stylized flowers at shoulder, caramel matt, Sorbo, #196, 4¾" ..**450.00**
Vase, stylized thistles, Huck, #838, 6⅛"................................**1,500.00**
Vase, Viking ship, bls/grs, Julia Mattson, #149A, 5x4¾" **1,500.00**

North State

In 1924 the North State Pottery of Sanford, North Carolina, began small-scale production, the result of the extreme fondness Mrs. Rebecca Copper had for potting. With the help of her husband, Henry, and the abundance of suitable local clay, the pottery flourished and became well known for lovely shapes and beautiful glazes. They shared the knowledge they gained from their glaze experiments with the ceramic engineering department of North Carolina University; and during summer vacation, they often employed some of the university students. Salt glazed stoneware was produced in the early years but was quickly abandoned in favor of Henry's vibrant glazes. Colors of copper red, Chinese Red, moss green, and turquoise blue were used alone and combination, producing bands of blending colors. Some swirl ware was made as well. The pottery was in business for thirty-five years; most of its ware was sold in gift and craft shops throughout North Carolina.

Booklet, overview of production & merchandise, 10-pg, 1925-26, EX..**110.00**
Ewer, red/bl/beige drip, mk/label, 13½" **130.00**
Lamp, brn/gr/yel/orange drip ball base, pierced metal 19" shade, 21"....**600.00**
Pitcher, bl/gr/red, rim-to-hip hdl, 7" **125.00**
Pitcher, bright gr over feldspathic khaki, ca 1926-27, 6¾"..........**175.00**
Pitcher, multi-color dbl dip on wht, 1940s, 5"..............................**80.00**
Pitcher, Rebekah, bl matt over glossy blk-brn, 1930s, 13"..........**300.00**
Pitcher, Rebekah, Chinese Blue, 1940s, 8¼" **400.00**
Teapot, wht gloss & bl-violet, Walter Owen, 1930s, 6⅛x8¾" ..**400.00**
Vase, bl tones, 2 split hdls, 9x9½" **210.00**
Vase, blk matt w/indented sides, overal slight iridescence, 9" **110.00**
Vase, Chinese Blue & Flambe, hdls, 1930s, 18", NM..............**7,250.00**
Vase, Chinese Blue & gr dbl-drip on wht, 1940s, 9", NM..........**325.00**
Vase, dbl-dip bl mottle over Chinese Red, 4⅛" **100.00**
Vase, fan; Chinese Blue & turq, Walter Owen, 1930s, 3¼x5" **100.00**
Vase, glossy blackened gr variations, 1925-26, 5½" **350.00**
Vase, gr & brn mottle, hdls, 11¾"..**100.00**
Vase, gr drips on gr, 2-hdl trophy style, Walter Owen, 1940s, 7"...**40.00**
Vase, gr metallic over brn, hdls, 7⅝" **50.00**
Vase, mint over mint gr gloss, rim-to-hip hdls, Walter Owen, 9⅜"..**275.00**

Northwood

The Northwood Company was founded in 1896 in Indiana, Pennsylvania, by Harry Northwood, whose father, John, was the art director for Stevens and Williams, an English glassworks. Northwood joined the National Glass Company in 1899 but in 1901 again became an independent contractor and formed the Harry Northwood Glass Company of Wheeling, West Virginia. He marketed his first carnival glass in 1908, and it became his most popular product. His company was also famous for its custard, goofus, and pressed glass. Northwood died in 1923, and the company closed. See also Carnival; Custard; Goofus; Opalescent; Pattern Glass.

Bottle, dresser; Leaf Mold, vaseline spatter, shiny.........................**500.00**
Bowl, berry; Grape Frieze, gr w/gold, 11"...................................**230.00**
Bowl, berry; Posies & Pods, gr w/gold, lg+6 sm.........................**275.00**
Bowl, Cherry T'print, crystal w/ruby & gold, 4⅜x9¼" **55.00**
Bowl, Finecut & Roses, amethyst, 3-ftd, 4" H.............................**60.00**
Bowl, Memphis, gr w/gold, 4½x9" **67.50**
Bowl, sauce; Strawberry & Cable, w/ruby & gold, sm................**20.00**
Butter dish, Cherry T'print, crystal w/ruby & gold.....................**125.00**
Butter dish, Grape & Gothic Arches, gr w/gold............................**95.00**
Butter dish, Leaf Medallion, gr w/gold, 8" dia..........................**250.00**
Butter dish, Royal Oak, rubena...**375.00**
Butter dish, Royal Oak, rubena satin..**425.00**
Candy jar, Cherry T'print, crystal w/ruby & gold, 3¾x3⅞" **100.00**
Cordial, Cherry T'print, crystal w/ruby & gold, 4 for **120.00**
Creamer, Cherry T'print, w/ruby & gold **50.00**
Creamer, Leaf Medallion, gr w/gold..**85.00**
Creamer, Royal Ivy, rubena...**175.00**
Creamer & sugar bowl, Cherry T'print, crystal w/ruby & gold....**110.00**
Cruet, Leaf Mold, vaseline spatter, shiny **450.00**
Cruet, Leaf Umbrella, bl o/l, clear faceted stopper, 7" **250.00**

Cruet, Leaf Umbrella, Rose DuBarry 275.00
Decanter, Cornflower, gr w/gold, orig stopper, +4 wines.............125.00
Goblet, Cherry T'print, crystal w/ruby & gold, 5¾", 4 for 100.00
Jar, condiment; Leaf Mold, bl frost, NP top.........................75.00
Pickle castor, Panelled Sprig, cranberry w/HP decor; SP fr..........450.00
Pickle castor, Royal Oak, rubena frost; SP fr, w/tongs..............400.00
Pitcher, Cherry T'print, crystal w/ruby & gold, 7⅞x8½" 90.00
Pitcher, Oriental Poppy, gr, water sz, +6 tumblers..................750.00
Pitcher, water; Leaf Mold, vaseline, +4 tumblers 550.00
Pitcher, water; Leaf Umbrella, vaseline spatter frost 500.00
Pitcher, water; Peach, crystal w/ruby & gold 150.00
Pitcher, water; Royal Ivy, rubena craquelle satin..................250.00
Rose bowl, Brocade, opaline..35.00
Rose bowl, Leaf Mold, vaseline frost 285.00
Rose bowl, Quilted Phlox, mint gr..................................40.00
Rose bowl, Royal Ivy, rubena 150.00
Salt cellar, Cherry T'print, crystal w/ruby & gold, 1 lg+4 sm 165.00
Shakers, Alaska (Foggy Bottom), bl to wht opal, 2⅛", pr 150.00
Shakers, Circled Scroll, gr, 2⅞", pr..............................150.00
Shakers, Daisy & Fern, cranberry opal, 2¾", pr 170.00
Shakers, Leaf Umbrella, bl cased, 2⅞", pr 200.00
Shakers, Quilted Phlox, pastel gr cased, 3", pr 80.00
Shakers, Royal Ivy, cranberry satin, pr............................150.00
Shakers, Royal Oak, rubena, pr.....................................230.00
Shakers, S-Repeat, gr w/irid, 3", pr 70.00
Shakers, Shell, bl, 1¾", pr..80.00
Shakers, Spanish Lace, vaseline opal, bulbous, 2⅞", pr.............160.00
Spooner, Cherry T'print, crystal w/ruby & gold.....................50.00
Spooner, Grape & Gothic Arches, gr w/gold 50.00
Spooner, Peach, gr w/gold 95.00
Spooner, Royal Oak, rubena frost 135.00
Sugar bowl, Royal Ivy, rubena, w/lid...............................225.00
Sugar bowl, Teardrop Flower, gr w/gold.............................125.00
Sugar shaker, Lattice, ribbed cranberry opal.......................300.00
Sugar shaker, Leaf Mold, bl frost..................................295.00
Sugar shaker, Leaf Umbrella, bl cased, shiny.......................365.00
Sugar shaker, Leaf Umbrella, yel cased, ca 1890 ....265.00
Sugar shaker, Parian Swirl, gr opaque 125.00
Sugar shaker, Royal Ivy, rainbow cased.............................345.00
Sugar shaker, Royal Ivy, satinized, swirled body, 4½" 300.00
Syrup, Cherry T'print, crystal w/ruby & gold, 4"...................80.00
Syrup, Optic Ribbed, rubena..915.00
Syrup, Wild Rose...65.00
Toothpick holder, Cherry T'print, crystal w/ruby & gold, 2¾"......35.00
Toothpick holder, Leaf Mold, cranberry spatter 300.00
Toothpick holder, Leaf Umbrella, cranberry spatter 295.00
Toothpick holder, Royal Ivy, rubena 110.00
Toothpick holder, Royal Oak, rubena................................135.00
Tumbler, Cherry & Plum, crystal w/ruby & gold......................32.50
Tumbler, Invt Fan & Feather, gr w/gold.............................25.00
Tumbler, Leaf Medallion, amethyst w/gold, 4".......................42.50
Tumbler, Leaf Umbrella, cranberry spatter, 3⅞" 120.00
Tumbler, Memphis, gr w/gold..30.00
Tumbler, Oriental Poppy, amethyst..................................60.00
Tumbler, Royal Ivy, rubena frost 100.00

Nutcrackers

The nutcracker, though a strictly functional tool, is a good example of one to which man has applied ingenuity, imagination, and engineering skills. Though all were designed to accomplish the same end, hundreds of types exist in almost every material sturdy enough to withstand sufficient pressure to crack the nut. Figurals are popular collectibles, as

are those with unusual design and construction. Patented examples are also desirable. Our advisor for this category is Susan Otto; she is listed in the Directory under Ohio. For more information, we recommend *Ornamental and Figural Nutcrackers* by Judith A. Rittenhouse.

Black man in shirt and jacket, carved bone, ca 1875, 6¾", EX, $800.00.

Cat, cast brass, 1920s-30s, 5¼" 88.00
Dog, NP CI, 5x12", EX...50.00
Dog w/tail lever, CI w/old tan rpt, 11"..............................40.00
Dragon, CI, EX detail, 5½x4x14".....................................345.00
Eagle, cvd wood, glass eyes, Switzerland, 8" 200.00
Elephant, cvd wood, wood tusks, 8" 210.00
Elf, cvd wood, detailed face, early 1900s, 11"......................100.00
Face on log, 'Mr Wind,' cvd wood, Austria 56.00
Fish, CI, mk RD 751619, ca 1887, 8½"................................365.00
Harley-Davidson, CI, hdl on bk, #99237-00Z, Germany, 15½" ..235.00
Imp, CI, ca 1900, 4¼x6½x1¼" 85.00
Indian head, cvd wood, 19th C, 6½"..................................125.00
Lady w/basket & umbrella, cvd wood, Germany, 14¾" 65.00
Man, cvd/HP wood w/EX detail, ANRI, 7½" 135.00
Man w/beard, cvd oak, ca 1900, from $65 to 90.00
Pierrot (clown), cast brass, England, 20th C 80.00
Pliers type, CI, clamps on table, JA Hurley....CT, Pat 1909, 9½"..85.00
Rabbi, cvd wood, Swiss 650.00
Scottie dog, cvd wood, glass eyes, HP collar, 10" 100.00
Soldier, cvd/pnt wood, wht uniform, German Democratic Republic, 1980s ...60.00
Squirrel, brass, screw-in hdl, unmk 75.00
Squirrel, CI, 10½x6¾"...345.00
Squirrel, CI w/EX detail & finish, Pat May 28, 1879, 8½"+base ...300.00
West Point Cadet, cvd/pnt wood, Volkmar Matthes, W Germany, 12" ..60.00
William Shakespeare (emb portrait & house), cast brass, pliers type...35.00

Nutting, Wallace

Wallace Nutting (1861 – 1941) was America's most famous photographer of the early twentieth century. A retired minister, Nutting took more than 50,000 pictures, keeping 10,000 of his best and destroying the rest. His popular and bestselling scenes included exterior scenes (apple blossoms, country lanes, orchards, calm streams, and rural American countrysides), interior scenes (usually featuring a colonial woman working near a hearth), and foreign scenes (typically thatch-roofed cottages). His poorest selling pictures, which have become today's rarest and most highly collectible, are classified as miscellaneous unusual scenes and include categories not mentioned above: animals, architecturals, children, florals, men, seascapes, and snow scenes. Process prints are 1930s machine-produced reprints of twelve of Nutting's most popular pictures. These have minimal value and can be detected by using a magnifying glass.

Nutting sold literally millions of his hand-colored platinotype pictures between 1900 and his death in 1941. He started in Southbury,

Connecticut, and later moved his business to Framingham, Massachusetts. The peak of Wallace Nutting picture production was 1915 – 25. During this period Nutting employed nearly two hundred people, including colorists, darkroom staff, salesmen, and assorted office personnel. Wallace Nutting pictures proved to be a huge commercial success and scarcely an American household was without one by 1925.

While attempting to seek out the finest and best early American furniture as props for his colonial interior scenes, Nutting became an expert in early American antiques. He published nearly twenty books in his lifetime, including his ten-volume *State Beautiful* series and various other books on furniture, photography, clocks, stools, chairs, settles, settees, tables, stands, desks, mirrors, beds, chests of drawers, cabinet pieces, and treenware. He made furniture as well, which he clearly marked with a distinctive paper label that was glued directly onto the piece, or a block or script signature brand which was literally branded into the furniture.

The overall synergy of the Wallace Nutting name — on pictures, books, and furniture — has made anything 'Wallace Nutting' quite collectible.

Our advisor for this category is Michael Ivankovich, author of many books concerning Nutting. Those currently available are *The Collector's Guide to Wallace Nutting Pictures; The Wallace Nutting Expansible Catalog; The Alphabetical and Numerical Index to Wallace Nutting Pictures; The Guide to Wallace Nutting Furniture, Wallace Nutting General Catalog, Supreme Edition; Wallace Nutting: A Great American Idea; Wallace Nutting's Windsors: Correct Windsor Furniture;* and *The Guide to Wallace Nutting-Like Photographers of the Early 20th Century.* Also available through Mr. Ivankovich is *The History of The Sawyer Pictures* by Carol Begley Gray. Mr Ivankovich's address and ordering information are listed in the Directory under Pennsylvania.

Prices below are for pictures in good to excellent condition. Mat stains or blemishes, poor picture color, or frame damage can decrease value significantly.

Wallace Nutting Pictures

All the News & More, 18x22"	210.00
Arbor Arch, 13x16"	440.00
Autumn Grotto, 16x20"	175.00
Blossoms at the Bend, 10x13"	110.00
Boys at Positano, 13x15"	770.00
Bridesmaid's Procession, 10x12"	110.00
Charms of Home, 11x14"	175.00
Concord Banks, 11x14"	145.00
Cup That Cheers, 11x14"	105.00
Dandeline Fluff & Buttercup, 11x14"	325.00
Dell Dale Shadows, 13x16"	121.00
Dykeside Blossoms, 10x12"	165.00
Flume Falls, 11x14"	160.00
Garden of Larkspur, 13x16"	100.00
Gettysburg Crossing, 14x17"	390.00
Grandmother's China, 11x17"	100.00
Heifers by the Stream, 11x17"	400.00
Honeymoon Stroll, 10x12"	80.00
Interrupted Letter, 14x17"	75.00
La Jolla, 13x15"	155.00
Life of the Golden Age, 11x17"	235.00
Little River, 20x30"	200.00
Meadow Lilies, 13x16"	1,980.00
Morning Duties, 10x12"	155.00
Nap Time Stories, 10x12"	410.00
New Hampshire Roadside, 11x13"	95.00
Old Pasture, 9x14"	465.00
Paradise Portal, 9x11"	190.00
Pause at the Bridge, 9x11"	310.00
Pigeon Brook Banks, 13x15"	575.00
Pool of Delights, 9x11"	125.00
Rocks Off Portland, 11x14"	140.00
Rural Sweetness, 16x20"	170.00
Scotland Beautiful, 11x13"	175.00
Sea Song, 13x16"	220.00
Skirting Lake Como, 13x16"	425.00
Southern Colonial Room, 13x17"	265.00
Stony Brook Drive, 11x14"	105.00
Summer Stream, 18x22"	145.00
Three Chums, 10x12"	385.00
Turf Path, 9x11"	250.00
Vermont Road, 11x14"	100.00
Way Through the Orchard, 12x15"	75.00
White Way, 13x16"	190.00
Worcester Byway, 13x16"	65.00

Wallace Nutting Furniture

Armchair, fan-bk Windsor, old natural finish, brand/label, 44"	1,100.00
Butterfly table, #625	2,200.00
Comb-bk armchair, #415	1,050.00
Country Dutch maple armchair, #461	750.00
Cross base candlestand, #22	525.00
Dutch country chair, #461	400.00
Footstool, #292	275.00
Game table w/rotating top	850.00
Ladderback chair, #392	350.00
Maple bed, #809	600.00
Maple drop-leaf chair, #603	950.00
Maple drop-leaf table, #620	1,900.00
Maple slat-bk chair, #374	350.00
Maple slat-bk side chair, #377	525.00
NE ladderback armchair, #492	770.00
NE ladderback chair, #490	825.00
Ogee-top table, #609	625.00
Pembroke table, #628	1,600.00
Pennsylvania stool, #143	350.00
Pilgrim armchair, #493	1,050.00
Pilgrim side chair, #393	425.00
Stool, oval, #102	250.00
Trestle table	350.00
Wild Rose side chair, #365	440.00
Windsor side chair, #326	850.00
Windsor stand, 3-leg, $605	600.00
Windsor writing armchair, #451	1,600.00

Major Wallace Nutting-Like Photographers

Although Wallace Nutting was widely recognized as the country's leading producer of hand-colored photographs during the early twentieth century, he was by no means the only photographer selling this style of picture. Throughout the country literally hundreds of regional photographers were selling hand-colored photographs from their home regions or travels. The subject matters of these photographers was very comparable to Nutting's, including interior, exterior, foreign, and miscellaneous unusual scenes. The key determinants of value include the collectability of the particular photographer, subject matter, condition, and size. Keep in mind that only the rarest pictures in the best condition will bring top prices. Discoloration and/or damage to the picture or matting can reduce value significantly.

Several photographers operated large businesses, and although not as large or well known as Wallace Nutting, they sold a substantial volume of pictures which can still be readily found today. The vast majority of their work was photographed in their home regions and sold primarily to local residents or visiting tourists. It should come as little surprise that three of the major Wallace Nutting-like photographers — David Davidson, Fred Thompson, and the Sawyer Art Co. — each had ties to Wallace Nutting.

David Davidson: Second to Nutting in overall production, Davidson worked primarily in the Rhode Island and Southern Massachusetts area. While a student at Brown University around 1900, Davidson learned the art of hand-colored photography from Wallace Nutting, who happened to be the minister at Davidson's church. After Nutting moved to Southbury in 1905, Davidson graduated from Brown and started a successful photography business in Providence, Rhode Island, which he operated until his death in 1967.

Sawyer: A father and son team, Charles H. Sawyer and Harold B. Sawyer, operated the very successful Sawyer Art Company from 1903 into the 1970s. Beginning in Maine, the Sawyer Art Company moved to Concord, New Hampshire, in 1920 to be nearer their primary market of New Hampshire's White Mountains. Charles H. Sawyer briefly worked for Nutting in 1902 – 03 while living in southern Maine. Sawyer's production volume ranks #3 behind Wallace Nutting and David Davidson.

Fred Thompson: Frederick H. Thompson and Frederick M. Thompson were another father and son team that operated the Thompson Art Company (TACO) from 1908 to 1923, working primarily in the Portland, Maine, area. We know that Thompson and Nutting had collaborated because Thompson widely marketed an interior scene he had taken in Nutting's Southbury home. The production volume of the Thompson Art Company ranks #4 behind Nutting, Davidson, and Sawyer.

Carlock, Close-Framed Jefferson Memorial, 8x10"	25.00
Davidson, Birches & Reflections, 9x15"	50.00
Davidson, Canoeist's Delight, 13x16"	65.00
Davidson, Heart's Desire Facsimilie, 12x16"	40.00
Davidson, Jack Frost Palette, 10x12"	60.00
Davidson, Lambs May Feast, 5x7"	120.00
Davidson, Pergola Gate, 13x15"	95.00
Davidson, Profile Water Hazard, 12x15"	105.00
Davidson, Snow Bound Brook, 9x12"	155.00
Davidson, Spent Wave, 5x7"	65.00
Davidson, Stone Arch, 8x10"	70.00
Davidson, Vacation Seat, 12x16"	85.00
Gibson, Back Road, 11x14"	20.00
Gibson, Old Homestead, 7x8"	50.00
Gibson, Snow Path, 7x9"	50.00
Harris, Close-Framed Florida Scene, 6x16"	55.00
Harris, Florida Wilds, 6x10"	20.00
Haynes, Untitled Old Faithful, 8x13"	55.00
Haynes, Yellowstone Park Portfolio Set, 10x13"	60.00
Sawyer, Afterglow, 9x11"	50.00
Sawyer, At the Bend of the Road, 7x9"	45.00
Sawyer, Bridge of Flowers, 10x13"	175.00
Sawyer, Cloister, San Juan Capistrano, 13x16"	150.00
Sawyer, Cold Stream, Mohawk Trail, 13x16"	70.00
Sawyer, Echo Lake, 8x10"	35.00
Sawyer, Gates of Yosemite, 13x15"	265.00
Sawyer, Jordan Pond Road, 5x7"	40.00
Sawyer, Mt Lafayette, 7x8"	85.00
Sawyer, Old Man of the Mts, 7x9"	90.00
Sawyer, Rainbow & Horseshoe Falls, 8x10"	120.00
Thompson, Angry Surf, 8x15"	85.00
Thompson, Birch Road, 8x16"	40.00
Thompson, Calm of Autumn, 14x17"	60.00
Thompson, Gamecock, 5x7"	175.00
Thompson, Gay Head, 10x15"	300.00
Thompson, Lombardy Poplar, 13x16"	110.00
Thompson, Oceanside, 14x16"	120.00

Thompson, Paring Apples, 7x9"	60.00
Thompson, Portland Head, 8x13"	90.00
Thompson, Sunbonnet Days, 7x9"	175.00
Thompson, Whittier's Home, 8x13"	230.00

Minor Wallace-Like Photographers

Hundreds of other smaller local and regional photographers attempted to market hand-colored pictures comparable to Nutting's during the 1900 – 30s time period. Although quite attractive, most were not as appealing to the general public as Wallace Nutting pictures. However, as the price of Wallace Nutting pictures has escalated, the work of these lesser-known Wallace Nutting-like photographers have become increasingly collectible.

A partial listing of some of these minor Wallace Nutting-like photographers include Babcock; J.C. Bicknell; Blair; Ralph Blood (Portland, Maine); Bragg; Brehmer; Brooks; Burrowes; Busch; Carlock; Pedro Cacciola; Croft; Currier; Depue Bros; Derek; Dowly; Eddy; May Farini (hand-colored colonial lithographs); Geo. Forest; Gandara; Gardner (Nantucket, Bermuda, Florida); Gibson; Gideon; Gunn; Bessie Pease Gutmann (hand-colored colonial lithographs); Edward Guy; Harris; C Hazen; Knoffe; Haynes (Yellowstone Park); Margaret Hennesey; Charles Higgins; Hodges; Homer; Krabel; Kattleman; La Bushe; Lake; Lamson (Portland, Maine); M. Lightstrum; Machering; Rossiler Mackinae; Merrill; Meyers; William Moehring; Moran; Murrey; Lyman Nelson; J. Robinson Neville (New England); Patterson; Owen Perry; Phelps; Phinney; Reynolds; F. Robbins; Royce; Fred'k Scheetz (Phila., Pennsylvania); Shelton; Standley (Colorado); Stott; Summers; Esther Svenson; Florence Thompson; Thomas Thompson; M.A. Trott; Sanford Tull; Underhill; Villar; Ward; Wilmot; Edith Wilson; and Wright.

A very general breakdown of prices for works by these minor Wallace Nutting-like photographers would be as follows: larger pictures, greater than 14" x 17", from $75.00 to over $200.00; medium pictures, from 11" x 14" to 14" x 17", from $50.00 to $200.00; smaller pictures, 5" x 7" to 10" x 12", from $10.00 to $75.00.

The same pricing guidelines that apply to Wallace Nutting pictures typically apply to Wallace Nutting-like pictures.

1.) Exterior scenes are the most common.

2.) Some photographers sold colonial interior scenes as well.

3.) Subject, matter, condition, and size are all important determinants of value.

Bicknell, J Carleton; Double Head, 8x12"	30.00
Bicknell, J Carleton; Mirror w/Exterior Scene, 8x11"	85.00
Burrowes, Country Road, 8x10"	35.00
Carlock, Royal; Washington DC Monument, 5x7"	30.00
Edson, Norman; Mt Elephantic, 8x10"	45.00
Gardiner, H Marshall; Bermuda, 12x15"	65.00
Gardiner, H Marshall; Bermuda, 7x9"	45.00
Harris, Natural Bridge, VA, 12x22"	90.00
Harris, St Augustine, 9x16"	75.00
Harris, St Augustine City Gates, 8x10"	45.00
Haynes, Yellowstone Triptych, 10x23"	45.00
Higgins, Charles; Fireside Reflections, 7x11"	80.00
Higgins, Charles; Rare Christmas Card, 3x8"	65.00
Lamson, Apple Blossom, Time, 8x10"	35.00
Lamson, Willow Road, 8x15"	60.00
Martin, Fred; Spanish Mission, 6x11"	85.00
McLeod, N; Cabot Trail, Cape Breton, 10x16"	45.00
Moosilauke Studio, B&W Echo Lake, 8x10"	25.00
Neville, Sunset Glow, 14x16"	10.00
Petty, George B; Favorite Walk, 11x14"	35.00
Rogers, Stanley; Gay Head Cliffs, 8x18"	120.00
Smith, Nature's Mirror, 11x14"	25.00

Sunsene, Along Florida Coast, 10x12" 25.00
Thompson, Florence; Canyon, 6x12" 40.00
Tillinghast, untitled, cows, 9x11" 40.00
Vannatta, Singing Tower, Florida, 11x14" 25.00
Winslow, R; Outer Shore, Cape Cod, 11x14" 75.00

Occupied Japan

Items marked 'Occupied Japan' have become popular collectibles in the last few years. They were produced during the period from the end of World War II until April 18, 1952, when the occupation ended. By no means was all of the ware exported during that time marked 'Occupied Japan'; some was marked 'Japan' or 'Made In Japan.' It is thought that because of the natural resentment felt by the Japanese toward the occupation, only a fraction of these wares carried the 'Occupied' mark. Even though you may find identical 'Japan'-marked items, because of its limited use, only those with the 'Occupied Japan' mark are being collected to any great extent. Values vary considerably, based on the quality of workmanship. Generally, bisque figures command much higher prices than porcelain, since on the whole they are of a finer quality.

For those wanting more information, we recommend *Occupied Japan Collectibles* by Gene Florence; he is listed in the Directory under Kentucky. Our advisor for this category is Florence Archambault; she is listed in the Directory under Rhode Island. She represents the Occupied Japan Club, whose mailing address may be found in the Directory under Clubs, Newsletters, and Catalogs. All items described in the following listings are assumed ceramic unless noted otherwise.

Ashtray, house on lake scene, 6-sided, bl rim w/3 red rests............10.00
Ashtray, Wedgwood type, bl & wht, 2⅝" 10.00
Bell, Dutch girl figural, orange lustre skirt, sm 20.00
Bookends, Dutch boy & girl seated, deep colors, pr......................40.00
Bookends, penguins, 4", pr 25.00
Box, cigarette; appl roses (red) on wht w/gold trim 25.00
Box, cigarette; man carrying box w/dragon finial, 6⅜" 30.00
Candle holder, Colonial figure seated between 2 flower cups, 4", pr ..55.00
Cigarette lighter, metal, Indian chief's head shape 30.00
Cup & saucer, bird & floral on blk, Lenwile China, Ardalt 6194 .22.50
Cup & saucer, bl rimmed, floral int, Merit China........................20.00
Cup & saucer, chintz-like floral on wht, Merit China 20.00
Cup & saucer, flower on pk, Trimont China 22.00
Cup & saucer, vining floral on wht, Merit 20.00
Dinnerware, complete set for 12, w/all major serving pcs............500.00
Dinnerware, 3 szs of plates, service for 4 w/berries & soups+cr/sug ..200.00
Doll, celluloid, baby in pnt gr snowsuit, mk ft...........................35.00
Doll, celluloid, Betty Boop type, under 8" 50.00
Doll, celluloid, Kewpie, 2¾" 20.00
Doll, celluloid, Kewpie w/feathers, 8" 30.00
Doll, celluloid, pk crochet dress, 6" 40.00
Figure, celluloid, football player, jtd shoulders, 6" 20.00
Figure, celluloid, lamb, cow or goat, emb mk 10.00
Figurine, ballerina, net dress, 5¾"...40.00
Figurine, bird on stump w/leaves & flower, EX detail, 7⅛" 40.00
Figurine, Black band member, 2¾" 25.00
Figurine, Black boy fiddler, 5" 42.50
Figurine, boy in short pants w/suitcase, Maruyama, 5"..................20.00
Figurine, boy playing tuba, 3½"..6.00
Figurine, boy w/accordion, 2⅝" 5.00
Figurine, boy w/parrot, red mk, 5" 15.00
Figurine, boy w/saxophone, bl pants, red hair, 4⅝" 10.00
Figurine, boy w/skis over shoulder, bl pants, 3½" 10.00
Figurine, bride & groom on base, bsk, 6⅛" 50.00

Figurine, cat, sitting, gr circle T mk, 4½"....................................22.50
Figurine, cat w/fiddle, 2"...7.50
Figurine, Colonial couple at piano, 4" 22.50
Figurine, Colonial courting douple on base, Maruyama, 6" 55.00
Figurine, Colonial lady mandolin player, 10¼" 50.00
Figurine, Colonial lady w/duck & basket, man w/rabbit, 7¼", pr..65.00
Figurine, Colonial lady w/ruffled skirt holds basket, 5¾"...............15.00
Figurine, Colonial man & lady, fine attire w/gold, 7½", pr............60.00
Figurine, Colonial man w/red hair, yel pants, gr coat, Paulux, 9¾"..75.00
Figurine, Colonial man w/violin, bsk, 9" 60.00
Figurine, cow, 2¾x4" 10.00
Figurine, dog, seated spaniel, 4⅜" L..30.00
Figurine, dog beside lamp, 2"..4.00
Figurine, dog pushing 2 puppies in basket-like buggy, 3" 15.00
Figurine, Dolly Dimples w/rabbit or duck, cloverleaf/cross mk, 4" ..12.50
Figurine, Dutch girl w/milk can, red mk, 6" 22.50
Figurine, East Indian man & lady in wht, red mk, 6⅛", pr...........30.00
Figurine, elf w/log, 5"..20.00
Figurine, fisher boy w/basket & pole, Ucagco, 7" 40.00
Figurine, gardening boy & girl on base, Hummel type, Paulux, 5½"..60.00
Figurine, girl w/basket, Hummel type, 5½" 30.00
Figurine, girl w/doll buggy, 2½"..5.00
Figurine, girl w/song book, Ucagco China, 5¾"..........................40.00
Figurine, horse w/rider, bsk, mk Andrea HP, 10¼".....................250.00
Figurine, horses (jumping) on base, bl circle T mk, 5" 50.00
Figurine, lady bug w/vest, bl mk, 3½" 12.50
Figurine, lion pride (group of 4), 4⅛" 50.00
Figurine, Little Red Riding Hood, red mk, 4⅛" 15.00
Figurine, man beside lady playing cello, Maruyama, 3½" 25.00
Figurine, man woos lady w/mandolin on base, 4¾" 20.00
Figurine, Mexican boy on donkey, red mk, 8¼" 30.00
Figurine, newsboy, long stride, red mk, 5½" 20.00
Figurine, Oriental lady w/fan, 5" 20.00
Figurine, Oriental man w/stringed instrument, 9" 45.00
Figurine, Oriental warrior, raised hand, EX color, 8" 40.00
Figurine, peacock w/plume tail cascading down, 5" 20.00
Figurine, peasant man & lady by fence, red mk, 8⅛", pr............125.00
Figurine, Polynesian girl w/grass skirt, 4" 20.00
Figurine, Spanish girl w/guitar, red mk, 4¼" 12.50
Figurine, villain in blk hat w/mustache w/captive lady, 7½" 75.00
Incense burner, Oriental figure, 4¼"..20.00

Lamps, blue bonnets and leaves on ivory, 12¼" to top of socket, $100.00 for the pair. (Photo courtesy Florence Archambault)

Lamp base, Colonial couple, Chikuoa, 10¼" to top of socket.......40.00
Pencil holder, dog figural...10.00
Planter, baby buggy, bl, 5¼" 10.00
Planter, dog, comic look, 3⅝" 8.00
Planter, dog sticks out tongue beside top hat, 3⅝" 8.00
Planter, girl w/mandolin stands beside basket, brn mk, 3⅝".........10.00
Planter, Oriental girl stands before lg shell, red mk, 6⅛" 30.00
Plaque, mallard in flight, wings wide, 6½" 25.00
Plate, flower center, lattice rim, Rosetti Chicago USA, 6"............25.00

Shaker, Dutch girl, red mk, 3" 8.00
Shelf, corner; lacquerware, folding type, 9¼" 45.00
Stein, man & woman w/dog, brn vine hdl, 8½" 40.00
Toby pitcher, man holding 2 mugs, red mk, 4⅞" 40.00
Toby pitcher, 4⅞" 60.00
Tray, metal, emb White House, souvenir of Washington DC, 5x3½" ..6.50
Vase, snake charmer couple stand before vase, 5½" 30.00

Ohr, George

George Ohr established his pottery in the 1880s in Biloxi, Mississippi. The first pottery burned down and was subsequently rebuilt. Ohr, among other things, was a master of the wheel. This mastery enabled him to create unique forms of unbelievable thinness, verging at times on *Abstraction* and looking far ahead toward many art movements of the twentieth century. In addition to *Abstraction,* by studying Ohr, one can discover elements of *Expressionism* and *Fauvism* (the wild use of color often seemingly at odds with the piece being glazed) and *Dada* (meaning shock the bourgeosie). An Ohr piece may be rooted in the functional form of a teapot, but following his manipulation it becomes a sculpture for which the functional form serves only as a take-off point for the finished piece. Ohr was also a master of glazes. Highly esteemed are his volcanic and gunmetal glazes. He was not well received in his day and sold few pieces of his art pottery — a van Gogh-like tale. Ohr decorated his pieces with snakes and lizards and sometimes with asymmetrical handles. He believed that like all things on earth, no two things should be alike. This dictum was applied to his pottery making. He signed his pieces either in impressed letters or florid script. In the early 1900s Ohr ceased making pottery and became a motorcycle dealer and ultimately sold automobiles. His pottery was stored away to be rediscovered many years later. Ohr died in 1918.

Basket, gr/brn/gunmetal mottle, serrated rim, rstr, 3x6" 1,400.00
Bottle, dk brn, tapered cylinder, narrow top, 14¾x7¾" 3,750.00
Bowl, half: emerald to teal gr, 2nd half: beige caramel, 3¾" 1,200.00
Bowl, mirror brn/gr/clear amber, crimped, mfg flaw, 4x7" 1,500.00
Bowl, olive gr gloss w/copper dusting, mk, 4½" 500.00
Bowl vase, bsk, swirling brn & terra cotta, 5½" dia.....................550.00
Bowl vase, bsk w/4 indents, 5½" dia 600.00
Bowler hat, bl speckled w/gr int, 2x4½", NM 950.00
Egg cup, teal gr speckled, serrated rim, 1¼x1¾" 450.00
Floppy hat, blk w/gr int, 3x4½", NM 1,200.00
Inkwell, mule head by pot & tree, mc mottle, ear-tip rprs, 4x7x5" ..4,000.00
Mug, Here's Your Good Health..., Joe Jefferson, gourd shape, 6½" ..2,100.00
Mug, puzzle; brn rtcl circular pattern, rabbit hdl, twist base, 3½".....1,150.00
Mug, puzzle; pebbly mahog gloss w/incised suns, mk, 3¾" 1,000.00
Pitcher, amber/gr/gunmetal speckled, closed-in rim, squat, 3x5½" ...650.00
Pitcher, cobalt glossy, collapsed side, 4½x4¾" 9,500.00
Pitcher, marbleized bsk, free-form, pinched/folded, 3¾x5" ...5,500.00
Pitcher, mauve, chartreuse int, 4-sided/pinched, cut-out hdl, 2½"..2,000.00
Tall hat, chartreuse drips on wht clay, 3¼x3" 2,600.00
Tall hat, Saturday Night 9PM, curdled lav & yel, 1903, 4x4¾".......2,900.00
Teacup, mahog mottle, crenolated rim, hand-built hdl, 2½", NM...1,300.00
Teapot, brn/blk/gr/orange, in-twist body, serpent spout, 3⅞" ...6,750.00
Teapot, sheer mirrored gr, deeply twisted, 4x7½" 13,000.00
Teapot, volcanic chartreuse, serpent spout, 6x8½" 12,000.00
Vase, amber & gunmetal, dbl-gourd, 4½x3½" 950.00
Vase, blk mottle w/t'print base, crimped rim, cylindrical, 4¾" .1,375.00
Vase, bright/pk/bl/gr sponging, folded rim, 2½x4½"...............4,250.00
Vase, brn & gray sponging w/cobalt band, in-body twist, 5x4½" ..5,500.00
Vase, brn mottle on red w/t'print base, short neck, 2½" 1,150.00
Vase, brn/gunmetal/gr red gloss, dbl gourd, lg ft, 9½" 15,000.00
Vase, cadmium yel/lav/gr/pk volcanic, bulbous, 4x3¾" 2,700.00

Vase, charcoal & lt gr speckles on lt red clay, shouldered, 5"...2,100.00
Vase, cobalt gloss, cupped rim, in-body twist, 3½x3¾" 3,250.00
Vase, cobalt/amber/raspberry sponging, appl snake, dimpled, rstr, 7"..9,500.00
Vase, dk speckled olive gr, folded gunmetal rim, spherical, 4½" ..2,300.00
Vase, gr & purple w/gunmetal, tortured waist & top, 5"...........7,500.00
Vase, honey gold w/caramel swirls & orange speckles, mk, 2¾x3¾" 1,500.00
Vase, mirrored cobalt & gunmetal, dimpled/fluted, spherical base, 10"...8,500.00
Vase, pk w/sponged-on gr & gunmetal band, folded/scalloped, 6x5".....17,000.00
Vase, red & gunmetal sponging, ovoid, 3¾x3¾"...............1,500.00
Vase, speckled amber, collapsed/dimpled shoulder, 4¾x4¼"...3,250.00
Vase, speckled amber & gunmetal, folded rim/collapsed side, 4½" ..5,500.00
Vase, speckled umber, collared rim, dimpled, 4x3¾" 1,900.00
Vessel, brn & gr w/red spots, deeply twisted, 4¼x6½" 11,000.00
Vessel, gr & brn gloss w/lt irid, ribbed, appl hdl, 7" 3,500.00
Vessel, marbleized, pinched/folded, rstr chip, AE Harrison, 1907, 4x7" ...2,300.00
Vessel, mc sponging, Here's to Your...., Jefferson, 1896, 4x6" ...3,000.00

Old Ivory

Old Ivory dinnerware was produced during the late 1800s by Herman Ohme, of Lower Salzbrunn in Silesia. The patterns are referred to by the numbers stamped on the bottom of many items. (Though not every piece is numbered, the vast majority bears the tiny blue fleur-de-lis/crown mark with Silesia or Germany beneath. Handwritten numbers signify something other than pattern.) Patterns #16 and #84 are the easiest to find and come in a wide variety of table items. Values are about the same for both patterns. Other floral designs include pink, yellow, and orange roses; holly; and lavender flowers — all on the same soft ivory background. The ware was not widely marketed; its two main distribution points were in Maine and, to a lesser extent, Chicago. Our price ranges are intended to represent a nationwide average, though you may have to pay a little more in some areas. Minor damage and gold wear can lower these prices by as much as 25%. Holly pieces command from 25% to 50% more. Novice collectors should be aware of copy-cat versions from the turn of the century that are much heavier and of a coarser material. They are marked 'Old Ivory' without the blue trademark. They are not included in this listing.

In the past year prices for Old Ivory have skyrocketed. Record prices were set when a well-known collection crossed the auction block, and prices realized on the Internet now rival RS Prussia. Another area gaining in popularity is the vases from Ohme usually featuring portraits of Edwardian children. There are few other forms with portraits, and these are very pricey, with 4" to 5" vases going in the range of $250.00 to $400.00, and 8" and 9" vases about $500.00 to $900.00.

For further information we recommend *Collector's Encyclopedia of Old Ivory China, The Mystery Explored,* by Alma Hillman (our advisor), David Goldschmitt, and Adam Szynkiewicz (Collector Books). Ms. Hillman is listed in the Directory under Maine.

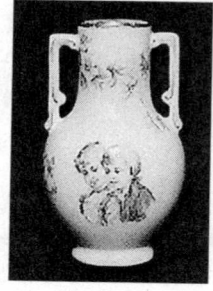

Vase, portrait, 4", from $250.00 to $400.00. (Photo courtesy Alma Hillman)

Bowl, cereal; #16 or #84, 16½", from $50 to 85.00
Bowl, ice cream; #4, 10", from $250 to..350.00

Bowl, vegetable; oval, #7, 9½", from $125 to 225.00
Butter dish, w/insert, #15, 7½", from $700 to 900.00
Butter pat, #28, 3¼", from $100 to 150.00
Cake plate, open hdls, #83, 10" or 11", ea, from $100 to 195.00
Chocolate pot, #75, 9½", from $400 to 600.00
Coffeepot, #84, 9", from $700 to 900.00
Compote, #137, 9", from $400 to 600.00
Cup, coffee; & saucer, #12, 3½", from $85 to 125.00
Cup & saucer, cider; #16, 3", from $250 to 350.00
Egg cup, #84, 2½", from $400 to 500.00
Hair receiver, #84, from $350 to 450.00
Jam jar, #200, 3½", from $200 to 300.00
Pitcher, water; #11, 8", from $800 to......................................1,100.00
Plate, coupe; #16, 6¼", from $50 to 75.00
Plate, dinner; #11, 9½" or 10", from $200 to 275.00
Plate, salad; #29, 7½", from $40 to 85.00
Platter, #15, 13½", from $200 to 300.00
Platter, #34, 21", from $500 to 600.00
Shakers, #75, 2¾", pr, from $100 to 150.00
Tray, bun; #92, 12", from $250 to 350.00

Old Paris

Old Paris porcelains were made from the mid-eighteenth century until about 1900. Seldom marked, the term refers to the area of manufacture rather than a specific company. In general, the ware was of high quality, characterized by classic shapes, colorful decoration, and gold application.

Basket (anneau d'or corbeille), rtcl, acanthus hdls, ftd, 8½x12".265.00
Bottle, liquour; floral bouquets, 19th C, 11x3¼" 130.00
Bottle, scent; female figure w/hand on bottle, mc, 10" 350.00
Bottle, scent; mc floral/puce & gilt panels, 8-sided, 7" 825.00
Bottle, scent; pastoral/scenic reserve, mc w/gold, w/stopper, 8"...700.00
Bowl, serving; floral & fruit spray, pk rim, pierced hdls, 14" L 150.00
Box, bejeweled hand (finial) atop stacked book form, 1830s, 3½x4x3" ...2,200.00
Cache pot, landscape cartouches/mc florals, cylindrical, 7¾" 500.00
Clock, mantel; Turk w/saber atop rockwork base, 1850s, 20"...5,775.00
Corbeilles, gilt trim, paw ft, tole-copper liners, 19th C, 5x9", pr...1,100.00
Cup & saucer, harbour scene, pk/cobalt/wht w/gold 330.00
Cup & saucer, lady's portrait reserve w/much gold, early 19th C...450.00
Cup & saucer, Neoclassical decor on lt pk, gold int, paw ft, 19th C ..350.00
Dessert service, mc fruit/florals/birds w/burgundy & gold, 24-pc.....1,300.00
Figurine, man & lady on base, in manner of J Petit, 19th C, 16" ..220.00
Inkwell, lady seated w/child on settee, w/ink pot & sand holder..165.00
Pitcher, floral w/gold, 8" 220.00
Pitcher & basin, floral on bl w/gold, 1850s, 8", 12¾" 1,650.00
Plate, Iroquois chief in ceremonial dress, ca 1820, 9½" 5,600.00
Plate, Italian figure in native dress, Denuelle, 1820, 9½", pr...3,300.00
Plate, Polonais/Hollandais in landscape, Denuelle, 1820s, 9½", pr..4,000.00
Soup plate, floral w/gold, 9", 7 for 360.00
Sweetmeat basket, pierced rim, HP floral sprays, 4¼", pr...........125.00
Sweetmeat stand, mc floral w/gold, 2-tier, 19th C, 11½x11" 300.00
Tea set, gilt foliage & scrolls, fruit finials, 1850s, 3-pc................150.00
Urn, classical profiles & Greek Key borders on gr, 19th C, 14" ..250.00
Urns, coastal scenes/flowers w/gold, mask hdls, 11x8½", pr.....1,650.00
Vase, birds' heads on sides, appl flowers, HP medallions, 10" 250.00
Vase, cornucopia w/landscape reserves & gold, figure at side, 17", pr...1,450.00
Vase, floral panels/appl flowers & leaves, much gold, rstr, 20", pr....1,050.00
Vase, floral reserve, gold trim, scalloped top, 1850s, 13x7x6", pr...465.00
Vase, floral w/bl & gold, trumpet shape, 1830s, 7½", pr...........1,400.00
Vase, garlands/birds/cornucopias w/gold, hdls, J Petit, 1845, 20"...4,000.00
Vase, hand holding cornucopia form, 19th C, 5½"......................165.00
Vase, ladies in landscape, appl floral hdls, much gold, 22x13", pr..4,000.00

Vase, mc floral panel w/gold, hdls, flared rim, 1845, 11½", pr 550.00
Vase, swan-form cornucopia base, scroll ft, J Petit, 1850s, 9x8" 1,265.00

Old Sleepy Eye

Old Sleepy Eye was a Sioux Indian chief who was born in Minnesota in 1780. His name was used for the name of a town as well as a flour mill. In 1903 the Sleepy Eye Milling Company of Sleepy Eye, Minnesota, contracted the Weir Pottery Company of Monmouth, Illinois, to make steins, vases, salt crocks, and butter tubs which the company gave away to their customers. A bust profile of the old Indian and his name decorated each piece of the blue and gray stoneware. In addition to these four items, the Minnesota Stoneware Company of Red Wing made a mug with a verse which is very scarce today.

In 1906 Weir Pottery merged with six others to form the Western Stoneware Company in Monmouth. They produced a line of blue and white ware using a lighter body, but these pieces were never given as flour premiums. This line consisted of pitchers (five sizes), steins, mugs, sugar bowls, vases, trivets, and mustache cups. These pieces turn up only rarely in other colors and are highly prized by advanced collectors. Advertising items such as trade cards, pillow tops, thermometers, paperweights, letter openers, postcards, cookbooks, and thimbles are considered very valuable. The original ware was made sporadically until 1937. Brown steins and mugs were produced in 1952. Our advisor for this category is Jim Martin; he is listed in the Directory under Illinois.

Banner, center portrait & western scenes, 22" sq, EX 1,450.00
Barrel, flour; orig paper label, 1920s..1,800.00
Barrel, grapevine-effect banding...3,500.00
Barrel, oak w/brass bands..4,500.00
Barrel label, Chief Strong Bakers..., 16", EX+............................170.00
Blanket, horse; w/logo, EX...2,500.00
Butter crock, Flemish bl & gray 750.00
Cabinet, bread display; Old Sleepy Eye etched in glass 950.00
Calendar, 1904, NM...375.00
Cookbook, Indian on cover, Sleepy Eye Milling Co, 4¾x4" 300.00
Cookbook, loaf of bread shape, NM 210.00
Coupon, for ordering cookbook...250.00
Dough scraper, tin/wood, To Be Sure, EX..................................435.00
Fan, diecut image of Old Sleepy Eye, EX+.................................200.00
Flour sack, cloth, mc Indian, red letters....................................345.00
Flour sack, paper, Indian in blk, blk lettering, NM....................125.00
Hot plate/trivet, bl & wht 4,500.00
Ink blotter..125.00
Letter opener, bronze...900.00
Match holder, pnt...1,000.00
Match holder, wht 1,050.00
Mug, bl & gray, 4¼"...360.00
Mug, bl & wht, 4¼"...220.00
Mug, verse, Red Wing, EX..1,625.00
Paperweight, bronzed company trademk 560.00
Pillow cover, Sleepy Eye & tribe meet President Monroe 750.00
Pillow cover, trademk center w/various scenes, 22", NM 1,800.00
Pin-bk button, Indian, rnd w/face...350.00
Pitcher, #1, 4" 300.00
Pitcher, #2..350.00
Pitcher, #3..315.00
Pitcher, #3, w/bl rim...1,375.00
Pitcher, #4..400.00
Pitcher, #5..435.00
Pitcher, bl & gray, 5"...400.00
Pitcher, bl on cream, 8", M 345.00
Pitcher, brn on yel, Sesquicentennial, 1981, from $100 to.........125.00

Pitcher, standing Indian, good color	1,560.00
Postcard, colorful trademk, 1904 Expo Winner	185.00
Ruler, wooden, 15"	700.00
Salt crock, Flemish bl & gray, 4x6½"	700.00
Sheet music, in fr	300.00
Sign, self-fr tin, Old Sleepy Eye Flour, 20x24"	3,000.00
Sign, sf tin, portrait w/multiple scenes around border, 24x20", G	2,300.00
Sign, tin litho die-cut Indian, ...Flour & Cereals, 13½"	1,650.00
Spoon, demitasse; emb roses in bowl, Unity SP	105.00
Spoon, Indian-head hdl	125.00
Stein, bl & wht, 7¾"	800.00
Stein, Board of Directors, all yrs, 40-oz	265.00
Stein, Board of Directors, 1969, 22-oz	550.00
Stein, brn, 1952, 22-oz	300.00
Stein, brn & wht	1,500.00
Stein, brn & yel, Western Stoneware mk	1,500.00
Stein, chestnut, 40-oz, 1952	325.00
Stein, cobalt	1,250.00
Stein, Flemish, bl on gray	700.00
Stein, ltd edition, 1979-84, ea	125.00
Sugar bowl, bl & wht, 3"	750.00
Thermometer, front rpl	800.00
Vase, cattails, all cobalt	1,450.00
Vase, cattails, bl & wht, good color, 9"	800.00
Vase, cattails, brn on yel, rare color	1,500.00
Vase, cattails, gr & wht, rare	5,000.00
Vase, Indian & cattails, Flemish, 8½"	470.00

O'Neill, Rose

Rose O'Neill's Kewpies were introduced in 1909 when they were used to conclude a story in the December issue of *Ladies' Home Journal*. They were an immediate success, and soon Kewpie dolls were being produced worldwide. German manufacturers were among the earliest and also used the Kewpie motif to decorate chinaware as well as other items. The Kewpie is still popular today and can be found on products ranging from Christmas cards and cake ornaments to fabrics, wallpaper, and metal items.

For further information we recommend *Doll Values, Antique to Modern*, by Patsy Moyer (Collector Books). In the following listings, 'sgn' indicates that the item is signed Rose O'Neill. Values are for examples in excellent condition with no chips. The copyright symbol, ©, is also a good mark on items. Unsigned items can be of interest to collectors; many are authentic and collectible, some are too small to sign.

Our advisors for this category are Don and Anne Kier; they are listed in the Directory under Ohio.

Box, dresser; bsk, Kewpie on lid, 4½", EX	165.00
Candy container, bsk, Kewpie, 4"	500.00
Clock, gr jasperware, Kewpies, c Rose O'Neill, 1910s, 4x4¾x1¾"	425.00
Inkwell, bsk, w/writer Kewpie, 4½"	500.00
Kewpie, bsk, Action Figure, arms folded, 6"	600.00
Kewpie, bsk, Action figure, Carpenter, w/tool apron, 8½"	1,100.00
Kewpie, bsk, Aviator, 8½"	850.00
Kewpie, bsk, Bride & Groom, 3½"	350.00
Kewpie, bsk, Confederate Soldier, 4"	400.00
Kewpie, bsk, Cowboy, mk #7863 on ft, 1960s, 6x4"	215.00
Kewpie, bsk, Drummer, mk on ft, 3½"	1,400.00
Kewpie, bsk, Fireman, #7863 on ft, 1960x, 6x4"	185.00
Kewpie, bsk, fly on ft, 3"	600.00
Kewpie, bsk, Huggers, 2½"	125.00
Kewpie, bsk, immobile, 2"	110.00
Kewpie, bsk, immobile, 4½"	150.00
Kewpie, bsk, immobile, 6"	275.00

Kewpie, bsk, Indian, #7863 on ft, 6x4"	245.00
Kewpie, bsk, Jester, wht hat on head, sgn, 4½", minimum value	850.00
Kewpie, bsk, jtd hips & shoulders, 5"	525.00
Kewpie, bsk, jtd hips & shoulders, 10"	1,000.00
Kewpie, bsk, jtd shoulders, molded clothing, 2½"	200.00
Kewpie, bsk, jtd shoulders, molded clothing, 8"	375.00
Kewpie, bsk, jtd shoulders, molded clothing, 10"	625.00
Kewpie, bsk, jtd shoulders, red heart label, Germany, 5¼"	160.00
Kewpie, bsk, jtd shoulders, 4½"	130.00
Kewpie, bsk, jtd shoulders, 8½"	400.00
Kewpie, bsk, jtd shoulders, 10"	625.00
Kewpie, bsk, kneeling, 4"	750.00
Kewpie, bsk, Mayor, arms folded, sgn, 6"	600.00
Kewpie, bsk, Mayor, seated in gr wicker chair, 4½"	950.00
Kewpie, bsk, Minister, 5"	250.00
Kewpie, bsk, on tummy, arms & legs out, sgn, 4"	450.00
Kewpie, bsk, on tummy, heart sticker, sgn, 4"	550.00
Kewpie, bsk, playing mandolin, mk on base of chair	850.00
Kewpie, bsk, Policeman, #7863 on ft, 1960s, 6x4"	225.00
Kewpie, bsk, Santa hat, hands on hips, Enesco, mk Jesco, 1993, 4", MIB	60.00
Kewpie, bsk, seated in fancy chair, 4"	400.00
Kewpie, bsk, sits w/chick, 2"	600.00
Kewpie, bsk, sitting, 'O' mouth, hands on ears, sgn, 3½"	1,850.00
Kewpie, bsk, Thinker, 4-5", ea	275.00
Kewpie, bsk, Traveler, w/umbrella & bag, sgn, 4" (common sz)	350.00
Kewpie, bsk, w/cat, 3"	300.00
Kewpie, bsk, w/Doodle dog	250.00
Kewpie, bsk, Writer, pen in hand, sgn, 2"	360.00
Kewpie, carnival chalk, jtd shoulders, sgn, 13", M	165.00
Kewpie, cast steel on sq base, 5½"	55.00
Kewpie, celluloid, Black, Germany, 2", from $95 to	100.00
Kewpie, celluloid, Bride & Groom, 4"	40.00
Kewpie, cloth, 1-pc, Kreuger, 12", EX w/tag	250.00
Kewpie, compo, Hottentot, heart decal, jtd arms, ca 1946, 11"	575.00
Kewpie, compo, jtd body, bl wings, 11"	375.00
Kewpie, hard plastic, ca 1950, 8½", NMIB	385.00
Kewpie, vinyl, hinged joints, 1960s, 15", M w/tag	185.00
Kewpie, vinyl, molded in 1-pc, sgn, 9"	25.00
Kewpie, vinyl, str legs, sgn ft, Cameo, 11", MIP	85.00
Soap figure, Kewpie, RO Wilson, 1917, 4"	110.00
Sugar bowl, wht w/gr lustre trim, Kewpies, sgn, 3¾"	80.00
Talcum container, Kewpie, celluloid, jtd shoulders, c O'Neill, Japan	285.00
Talcum container, Kewpie, compo, heart label on chest, 7"	65.00
Tea set, Kewpies, Rose O'Neill Kewpie Germany, 6" pot+cr/sug	425.00

Onion Pattern

The familiar pattern known to collectors as Onion acquired its name through a case of mistaken identity. Designed in the early 1700s by Johann Haroldt of the Meissen factory in Germany, the pattern was a mixture of earlier Oriental designs. One of its components was a stylized peach, which was mistaken for an onion; as a result, the pattern became known by that name. Usually found in blue, an occasional piece may also be found in pink and red. The pattern is commonly associated with Meissen, but it has been reproduced by many others including Villeroy and Boch and Royal Copenhagen.

Many marks have been used, some of them fraudulent Meissen marks. Study a marks book to become more familiar with them. In our listings, 'Xd swords' indicates first-quality old Meissen ware. Meissen in an oval over a star was a mark of C. Teichert Stove and Porcelain Factory of Meissen; it was used from 1882 until about 1930. Items marked simply Meissen were produced by the State's Porcelain Manufactory VEB after 1972. The crossed swords indication was sometimes added. Today's market abounds with quality reproductions.

Blue Danube is a modern line of Onion-patterned dinnerware produced in Japan and distributed by Lipper International of Wallingford, Connecticut. At least one hundred items are available in porcelain; it is sold in most large stores with china departments.

Bell, Blue Danube, 6" 25.00
Bowl, berry; Xd swords, ca 1870, 1½x4½" 100.00
Bowl, cream soup; w/lid, Blue Danube, from $30 to 35.00
Bowl, deep, Germany, 9" 60.00
Bowl, rim soup; England, late 25.00
Bowl, rim soup; Xd swords, ca 1870s, 9" 145.00
Bowl, rim w/4 shaped lobes, Meissen w/arrow, 6½" 75.00
Bowl, scalloped, Xd swords, 8" 245.00
Bowl, soup/cereal; Blue Danube, from $12 to 15.00
Bowl, wedding; w/lid, footed, sq, Blue Danube, 8½x5" 65.00
Cache pot, gold borders, Xd swords, 1890s, 5½" 245.00
Cache pot, w/hdls, Blue Danube, 8x8" 45.00
Cake pedestal, rtcl rim, 2-pc bolted, Xd swords, 2¾x8" 325.00
Cake server & knife, Blue Danube, from $25 to 30.00
Canister, Coffee on wht band, Xd arrows 'Blue Onion,' 9x4" 135.00
Cheese board, rectangular, hanging hole, 8x4½" 50.00
Cheese board, shaped top w/hanging hole, Xd swords, 10x6" 325.00
Cheese dish, Meissen, ca 1900, 7x9" 175.00
Clock, plate style, Hutschenreuther, #286, 13" dia 85.00
Coffeepot, emb/appl spout, ornate hdl, Blue Danube, 7½" 65.00
Creamer, ovoid, Blue Danube, 3½" 15.00
Creamer, Xd swords, 4" 135.00
Cup & saucer, angle hdl, scalloped rims, Blue Danube, from $7 to 9.00
Cup & saucer, Xd twig hdl, mk in gr: Germany, in bl: Xd swords 95.00
Egg cup w/attached saucer, Xd swords, 3x4½" 125.00
Funnel, loop hdl, lg 125.00
Grater, sled shape, 8½x4¼" 250.00
Gravy boat, dbl spout, w/undertray, Blue Danube, 3½x6" 40.00
Ink stand, 2 lidded inserts, shaped base, banner mk, Blue Danube, 9" ...300.00
Invalid feeder, Simplex #10, 4¼" 135.00
Jar, bbl shape, detailed knob, w/gold, unmk Meissen, 5" 150.00
Jar, instant coffee; Japan 24.00
Jar, rosebud finial, Xd swords, #43/477/038, 2¾" 250.00
Jug, water; w/pewter fittings, Xd swords, 12" 525.00
Lamps, Xd swords, 1870s, electrified, 12½x7", pr 545.00
Letter opener, brass blade, Germany 40.00
Measuring cup, dbl-ended, unmk Meissen, 3" 145.00
Measuring cup set, 4 on hanging rack, Japan, 12" L, from $75 to ...100.00
Meat cleaver, Germany 125.00
Meat tenderizer, 11" L 195.00
Pestle 150.00
Pie crimper, wooden hdl 150.00
Pitcher, bulbous w/flared rim, Blue Danube, 6¼" 40.00
Pitcher, ribbed band under rim, Schumann, 5" 135.00
Plate, Hutschenreuther, 7½" 9.00
Plate, lattice rim, Blue Danube, 8" 15.00
Plate, Meissen w/star, 10", 4 for 145.00
Plate, rtcl rim, med bl, Xd swords, 8" 165.00
Plate, scalloped, Xd swords, 10" 100.00
Plate, Xd swords, 9¾", 6 for 385.00
Platter, England dbl circle mk, 15½" L 160.00
Platter, oval, Staffordshire England/lion mk, 12" L 75.00
Platter, Xd swords, 13¾" 275.00
Rolling pin, heavy, old, EX quality, 18" 325.00
Rolling pin, Meissen, 6"+4" hdls 180.00
Salt box, rnd, wood hdl, wall mt, Made in Japan, 7" 100.00
Shakers, bbl shape w/cursive letters, old, 2½", pr 60.00
Soup tureen, w/tray, Blue Danube, from $225 to 250.00
Spoon, long wood hdl, 15x2½" 145.00

Spoon, silver hdl mk A Lewis Sheffield, 11½" L 75.00
Stein, metal lid, Hutchenreuther, 5¼" 50.00
Sugar bowl, ovoid, w/lid, Blue Danube, 5", from $20 to 25.00
Sugar bowl, rosebud finial, unmk Meissen, 2¾x2¼" 235.00
Sugar bowl, Xd swords, lg..195.00
Tea tile/trivet, Blue Danube, 6", from $18 to 25.00
Tea/coffeepot, pear shape w/gooseneck spout, Blue Nordic/Meakin, 9" ...50.00
Teapot, globular, Xd swords..425.00
Teapot, Vienna Woods, 10" W 50.00
Tray, bread; Xd swords, 16x11" 175.00
Tray, closed hdls, oval mk, 15x5" 110.00
Tray, open hdls, ornate scrolling rim, no mk, 10½" sq 75.00
Tray, ribbed rim, open fleur-de-lys hdls, Villery & Boch, 12½" L..95.00
Tureen, shell hdls, dome lid, 1900, 10½" H 665.00
Whisk...115.00

Opalescent Glass

First made in England in 1870, opalescent glass became popular in America around the turn of the century. Its name comes from the milky-white opalescent trim that defines the lines of the pattern. It was produced in table sets, novelties, toothpick holders, vases, and lamps. Note that American-made sugar bowls have lids; sugar bowls of British origin are considered to be complete without lids. For further information we recommend *The Standard Encyclopedia of Opalescent Glass, Third Edition,* by Bill Edwards and Mike Carwile (Collector Books).

Herringbone (Plain), tumbler, blue opalescent, $100.00. (Photo courtesy Bill Edwards and Mike Carwile)

(Beatty) Honeycomb, mug, bl...55.00
(Bubble) Lattice, butter dish, bl, w/lid 225.00
Abalone, bowl, bl 35.00
Ala-Bock, tumbler, vaseline or canary 30.00
Alaska, spooner, wht 50.00
Argonaut Shell (Nautilus), pitcher, bl..................................395.00
Argus (Thumbprint), compote, bl 90.00
Astro, bowl, gr 50.00
Baby Coinspot, syrup, wht 140.00
Barbells, bowl, vaseline or canary 45.00
Beaded Moon & Stars, banana bowl, bl, stemmed................85.00
Beaded Ovals in Sand, bowl, sauce; gr 30.00
Beaded Star Medallion, shade, wht......................................40.00
Beads & Bark, vase, gr, ftd 70.00
Beatty Rib, butter dish, bl, w/lid 175.00
Beatty Rib, mustard jar, wht..125.00
Beatty Swirl, pitcher, bl...185.00
Blossom & Web, bowl, bl, rare 65.00
Blossoms & Palms, bowl, bl...50.00
Blown Drape, sugar shaker, gr 375.00
Blown Twist, pitcher, vaseline or canary 375.00
Bulls-Eye, bowl, bl...50.00

Butterfly & Lily, epergne, bl..150.00
Buttons & Braids, pitcher, gr...175.00
Cane & Diamond Swirl, tray, vaseline or canary, stemmed..........70.00
Cherry, butter dish, bl, w/lid..95.00
Chippendale, pitcher, vaseline or canary...............................145.00
Chrysanthemum Base Swirl, celery vase, bl............................140.00
Chrysanthemum Base Swirl, straw holder, wht, w/lid............350.00
Chrysanthemum Swirl Variant, pitcher, teal, rare..................400.00
Circled Scroll, cruet, wht...275.00
Coinspot, pitcher, gr...175.00
Commonwealth, tumbler, wht..25.00
Consolidated Crisscross, creamer, wht.................................250.00
Contessa, pitcher, amber..325.00
Coral Reef, finger lamp, bl, stemmed...................................500.00
Corinth, vase, bl, 8"-13"...40.00
Coronation, pitcher, bl...200.00
Crocus, vase, vaseline or canary...350.00
Daisy & Fern, night lamp, bl...225.00
Daisy & Greek Key, bowl, sauce; gr, ftd.................................60.00
Daisy in Crisscross, syrup, bl..500.00
Daisy Intaglio, plate, wht...110.00
Dandelion, mug, bl, variant, rare..200.00
Diamond Maple Leaf, bowl, wht, hdld...................................45.00
Diamond Point Columns, vase, bl, scarce.............................200.00
Diamond Spearhead, pitcher, wht.......................................200.00
Diamond Stem, vase, aqua, 3 szs, rare..................................125.00
Diamonds, pitcher, rubina, 2 shapes...................................275.00
Dolphin & Herons, compote, bl, novelty, ftd.........................100.00
Double Greek Key, butter dish, wht, w/lid............................200.00
Dragon Lady, novelty bowl, bl...140.00
Drapery (Northwood's), vase, vaseline or canary.....................75.00
Dugan Intaglio Grape, plate, wht, rare, 12½"........................250.00
Dugan's Honeycomb, bowl, bl, various shapes, rare.................175.00
Dugan Strawberry Intaglio, bowl, wht, 9"...............................45.00
Ellipse & Diamond, pitcher, cranberry.................................500.00
Everglades, bowl, bl, oval, master......................................200.00
Fan, butter dish, bl, w/lid..350.00
Fancy Fantails, bowl, wht...25.00
Fenton #370, nappy, amber...55.00
Fern, butter dish, wht, w/lid...225.00
Finecut & Roses, novelty bowl, gr..50.00
Fish in the Sea, vase, gr, scarce...150.00
Flora, cruet, bl..750.00
Floral Eyelet, pitcher, wht..400.00
Fluted Scroll w/Vine, vase, vaseline or canary, ftd...................65.00
Frosted Leaf & Basketweave, sugar bowl, bl...........................175.00
Gonterman (Adonis) Swirl, cruet, bl...................................400.00
Grapevine Cluster, vase, bl, ftd..175.00
Harrow, creamer, bl...75.00
Hearts & Flowers, compote, wht...85.00
Hobnail (Hobbs), bride's basket, rubina...............................500.00
Hobnail (Northwood's), bowl, bl, master................................55.00
Hobnail in Square (vesta), butter dish, wht, w/lid..................150.00
Holly, bowl, wht..65.00
Honeycomb (Blown), cracker jar, bl.....................................325.00
Honeycomb & Clover, butter dish, wht, w/lid.........................150.00
Idyll, bowl, bl, master..60.00
Inside Ribbing, butter dish, bl, w/lid...................................225.00
Inside Ribbing, pitcher, wht..160.00
Intaglio, bowl, vaseline or canary, ftd, master.......................180.00
Intaglio (Dugan's), compote, wht, 8"-11"..............................150.00
Inverted Chevron, vase, gr...65.00
Inverted Fan & Feather, butter dish, bl, w/lid........................385.00
Inverted Fan & Feather, pitcher, wht...................................395.00

Iris w/Meander, butter dish, vaseline or canary, w/lid.............275.00
Jackson, candy dish, bl...55.00
Jazz, vase, gr..55.00
Jewel & Fan, banana bowl, emerald gr..................................135.00
Jewel & Flower, creamer, wht...65.00
Jewelled Heart, butter dish, bl, w/lid...................................300.00
Jewelled Heart, syrup, wht...350.00
Jolly Bear, bowl, gr, variant, rare.......................................250.00
Keyhole, rose bowl, gr...80.00
Late Coinspot, pitcher, bl..150.00
Leaf Chalice, novelty compote, cobalt..................................175.00
Lily Pool, epergne, vaseline or canary..................................300.00
Little Nell, vase, gr...35.00
Lotus, bowl, bl, w/underplate...90.00
Lustre Flute, bowl, gr, master...125.00
Many Loops, bowl, wht, deep, round......................................40.00
Maple Leaf, jelly compote, gr...100.00
National Swirl, pitcher, gr...275.00
Netted Roses, plate, bl...120.00
Northwood Block, celery vase, gr..55.00
Old Man Winter, basket, vaseline or canary, ftd, lg...............125.00
Opal Open (Beaded Panels), ring bowl, bl, hdld.....................100.00
Open O's, spittoon whimsey, gr..65.00
Overlapping Leaves (Leaf Tiers), plate, wht, ftd......................90.00
Palm Beach, butter dish, bl, w/lid.......................................300.00
Panelled Flowers, rose bowl, wht, ftd....................................45.00
Panelled Holly, sugar bowl, bl, very rare..............................325.00
Panelled Sprig, shakers, wht, pr..125.00
Piasa Bird, plate, bl, ftd...125.00
Pineapple & Fan, vase, vaseline or canary...............................85.00
Poinsettia, bowl, fruit; gr...110.00
Primrose (Daffodils Variant), pitcher, wht............................500.00
Princess Diana, bowl, salad; bl..55.00
Pump & Trough, pump, bl...130.00
Queen's Spill, vase, spill; vaseline or canary...........................90.00
Quilted Daisy, fairy lamp, bl..500.00
Rayed Heart, compote, wht..45.00
Regal (Northwood's), cruet, bl..400.00
Reverse Swirl, bowl, vaseline or canary, master........................55.00
Reverse Swirl, custard cup, wht..35.00
Reverse Swirl, toothpick holder, vaseline or canary.................125.00
Ribbed Lattice, bowl, sauce; cranberry....................................40.00
Ribbed Spiral, creamer, bl...100.00
Ribbed Spiral, toothpick holder, vaseline or canary.................175.00
Richelieu, creamer, vaseline or canary...................................60.00
Richelieu, pitcher, bl...160.00
Rose Show, bowl, bl, rare...200.00
Roulette, plate, wht...60.00
Rubena Verde, vase, cranberry...300.00
S-Repeat, pitcher, wht..200.00
Scottish Moor, pitcher, bl..350.00
Scroll w/Acanthus, shakers, vaseline or canary, pr..................200.00
Seaweed, bowl, bl, master..60.00
Serpent Threads, epergne, vaseline or canary, 23"...................300.00
Shell Beaded, creamer, gr...180.00
Simple Simon, compote, bl...65.00
Snowflake, night lamp, bl..1,300.00
Sowerby Salt, salt dish, gr...70.00
Spanish Lace, creamer, wht...100.00
Spanish Lace, tumbler, cranberry...125.00
Spool of Threads, compote, bl..60.00
Squirrel & Acorn, whimsey, wht...175.00
Strawberry, bowl, amethyst...125.00
Stripe, vase, wht..600.00

Sunk Hollyhock, bowl, vaseline or canary, scarce........................100.00
Swag w/Brackets, butter dish, bl, w/lid...................................200.00
Swag w/Brackets, shakers, gr...175.00
Swirl, shot glass, bl...80.00
Swirling Maze, tumbler, cranberry.......................................100.00
Thousand Eye, celery vase, wht..100.00
Thread & Ribbon, epergne, bl...500.00
Three Fruits, bowl, wht, scarce...145.00
Tokyo, butter dish, bl, w/lid..175.00
Trafalger Fountain, epergne, vaseline or canary....................300.00
Tree Stump, mug, wht...40.00
Twig, vase, gr, panelled, 7"...100.00
Twister, plate, bl...100.00
Victoria & Albert, butter dish, bl, w/lid...............................155.00
Vintage (Northwood/Dugan), bowl, wht................................30.00
Waffle, epergne, olive..750.00
Water Lily & Cattails, butter dish, wht, w/lid.......................175.00
Wild Bouquet, creamer, gr...95.00
Wild Rose, banana bowl, bl..70.00
William & Mary, sugar bowl, vaseline or canary, stemmed, open..65.00
Windows (Swirled), bowl, sauce; cranberry............................55.00
Windsor Stripe, vase, cranberry..125.00
Wishbone & Drapery, bowl, gr..45.00
Woven Wonder, rose bowl, bl...60.00
Zipper & Loops, vase, gr, ftd...70.00

Opaline

A type of semiopaque opal glass, opaline was made in white as well as pastel shades and is often enameled. It is similar in appearance to English bristol glass, though its enamel or gilt decorative devices tend to exhibit a French influence.

Bonbon, jade gr, emb ribs, w/lid, 1930s, 9½x9½"........................52.50
Bottle, cologne; jade gr w/scrolled floral ormolu o/l, 7"..............200.00
Bottle, scent; bl w/gold trim & bl serpentine enamel, 4x2" dia...135.00
Bowl, wht w/mc cranes/lake/etc, 4-fold rim, #1209/6P.533, 6"....200.00
Box, bl, brass mts, 4¼x5½x3½"...330.00
Box, bl, HP roses & scrolls on lid, hinged, Fr, 1⅝x2⅜" dia........125.00
Box, pk, bronze mts, Fr, 2½x3⅞" sq......................................215.00
Box, wht, bronze mts, Fr, ca 1860, 6½x2½x3"..........................345.00
Box, wht, etched Deco nude & cockatoo on lid, 2⅜x3½" sq.....110.00
Box, wht, gilt brass mts, curvilinear sides/beaded top, 1890s, 4x11x5"....1,450.00
Cup & saucer, wht w/etched design & gold Greek Key border...160.00
Decanter, turq threading at neck & teardrop stopper, 11¾", NM....250.00
Jar, powder; bl w/gold Deco-style vines, 4¼x3¾" dia.................60.00
Lamp base, wht, metal mts, 7¼"..195.00
Perfume set, peach, Murano label, 1960s, 7" bottle+4x4" dia box..100.00
Plate, gr w/gilt band, Fr, 19th C, 11", from $100 to.................150.00
Vase, gilt bronze Cupid on bl base beside sm bl vase, 7½".........265.00
Vase, wht w/amber rigaree, ca 1880, 10x6", pr.........................210.00

Orientalia

The art of the Orient is an area of collecting currently enjoying strong collector interest, not only in those examples that are truly 'antique' but in the twentieth-century items as well. Because of the many aspects involved in a study of Orientalia, we can only try through brief comments to acquaint the reader with some of the more readily available examples. We suggest you refer to specialized reference sources for more detailed information. See also specific categories.

Key:
Ch — Chinese
cvg — carving
drw — drawer
Dy — Dynasty
E — export
FR — Famille Rose
FV — Famille Verte
hdwd — hardwood
Jp — Japan
Ko — Korean
lcq — lacquer
mdl — medallion
rswd — rosewood
tkwd — teakwood

Blue and White Porcelain

Bottle vase, dbl-gourd; Immortals & sea, Late Ming Dy, 25".18,400.00
Bowl, 5 peonies w/foliage, Kangxi Dy, 8¾"..........................2,000.00
Brush box, peony scrolls & foliage, 16th C,⅝"........................700.00
Jar, ladies & figures on terraces, w/lid, mid-1600s, 14", pr........8,600.00
Jar, 2 dragons above waves, w/lid, 18th C, 15½".....................5,000.00
Lamp, scenic cartouches w/birds/lattice/flowers, 19th C, 24x7", pr...1,100.00
Plate, flowering tree & chrysanthemum decor, 19th C, 9", 6 for....460.00
Platter, peafowl, rocks & flowers, 18th C, 13½x16⅛"...............575.00

Bronze

Archer, Miyao-O style, parcel-gilt, Meiji, sealed Shojo, 12"+bow..3,700.00
Beauty holding lotus bud, ivory inlay, patinated, Meiji, 16¼".4,850.00
Bodhisattva on elephant, gilt lcq, Ming Dy, 10¼".....................635.00
Buddha on dbl lotus, ornate robes, Ch, 17th C, 10⅛"...............300.00
Censer, dragons in relief, foo dog hdls, 3-ftd, 8x7".................300.00
Censer, globular, flared mouth, lion mask hdls, Xuande mk, 3⅜"...250.00

Dish, carved on exterior with lotus petals, interior with cloud cluster surrounding dragon and pearl, Yuan Dynasty, fourteenth century, 16", $1,200.00.

Drum, invt bell form, Han Dy (206-BC-220AD), 19½x27"....7,300.00
Fertility figure, seated male, Philippines, ca 1900, 16"............300.00
Guanyin on dbl lotus, lcq, Ch, 16th/17th C, 15"......................700.00
Hand mirror, cranes & tortoise amidst pine, Edo, 4¾"..............300.00
Jardiniere, relief flowers/birds, splits, dk patina, 14x16"..........440.00
Kiwi perched on lily pad, gilt wash/gr patina, Jp, 1900, 5¼x7¾"...100.00
Louhan w/flowing robes, cold pnt, 19th C, 17¾"....................10,925.00
Manjusri on lotus flower, ornate diadem, Ming Dy, 10¼".........1,800.00
Musician seated, gilt traces, Ch, 12th C, 13⅛"......................1,150.00
Urn, phoenix panels, flared mouth & ft, dtd 1811, 11½"...........400.00
Warrior weilding jumonji yari, parcel gilt, Meiji, 13¼"............2,750.00
Yamantaka stands in yab-yum w/sakti on prostate bodies, 19th C, 7"...2,500.00

Furniture

Armchair, ebonized tkwd, cvd dragons, open arms, late 1800s, Ch, 53"..800.00
Armchair, MOP inlay & marble insets & seat, Ch, 19th C, 40x27x21"..350.00
Armchair, teak w/much cvg, mortised/pinned, bat & fruit splat, Ch, 39"...275.00
Bench, hdwd w/brn stain, paneled base, much cvg, Ch, rprs, 88"...550.00
Bench, rfn elm, trn legs, scrolled apron, Ch, 21x74x13".............200.00
Cabinet, oak w/blk lcq, cvd scenes w/mc, 3-drw, 20th C, 45x23"..200.00
Cabinet, plain wood w/moon-form brass mts, Ch, 19th C, 76x44x23"...1,100.00
Chest, blk & red lcq, swing doors w/pnt symbols, Tibetan, 40x50"...1,000.00

Chest, tkwd & camphorwood, EX cvgs, foo dog ft, 21x42x21", VG 300.00
Chest on base, eng brass binding, cvd base, Ko, 38x34x16" 110.00
Cupboard, Ch Xhanxi wedding, red-brn pnt, relief cvgs, 70x43", EX ..900.00
Cupboard, chinoiserie rpt, 2 doors w/rpl iron hinges, Ch, 48x30" 110.00
Cupboard, cvd/pierced upper doors, brass mts, Ch, rstr, 61x38" ..550.00
Cupboard, lcq w/mc decor & ivory inlay, Jp, rprs, 17x13x7" 215.00
Cupboard, tkwd/cedar w/ink decor on door panels, Ch, 2-pc, 78x40" ...495.00
Cupboard, tkwd/cedar w/ink decor on door panels, 2 drws, Ch, 47" 275.00
Curio cabinet, cvd tkwd, brass & ivory details, 78x50x16", VG .880.00
Mirror, tkwd w/cvd battle scenes, ivory inlay birds, E, 39x26" .1,000.00
Screen, cvd lcq w/gilt & polychrome, 4-panel, ea: 36x10½" 220.00
Screen, mixed metals, hammered landscape, Jp, ca 1874, 6-panel ...6,000.00
Screen, tkwd & lcq, 2-fold w/ivory mts, Jp, 72x64" 500.00
Screen, 4-part blk lcq fr w/pierced/cvd panels, gold over red, 34x53" ...200.00
Sofa, cvd tkwd fr, red silk upholstery, Ch, 20th C, 35x76" 750.00
Table, alter; hdwd w/worn red lcq, fretwork panels, Ch, 40x106x15" ...550.00
Table, alter; relief-cvd elm, drw/2 doors, Ch, rfn, 31x39x17" 300.00
Table, elm w/dk finish, molded legs, cvd apron, Ch, 22x55x18" .300.00
Table, Huanghuali, 2-drw, brass hdw, Ch, 19th C, 19x35" 300.00
Table, red lcq & pnt decor, Ch, ca 1900, nesting set of 4 ....300.00
Table, sewing; Ch E, lcq w/gilt, cvd ft, 1830s, 26x23x16" 715.00
Tansu, 2-part, 4-drw, dragon lock plates, ca 1900, 38x48x17" .1,345.00
Tray, cinnabar w/3-D MOP/ivory/stone inlay of temple scene, Ch, 24" 2,970.00
Wardrobe, calamander wood w/paktong mts, China trade, 18th C, 69" .12,650.00

Hardstones

Amber, pendant, curled feline, Han Dy, 1¼" L.............................500.00
Jade, Cong-form vessel, gr mottle, 19th C, 8½", w/stand 335.00
Jade, hasp, 2 monster-fish, dragons, Daoist & astrology signs, Ch, 7" .600.00
Jade, horse w/legs tucked underneath, head bk, Ming style, 24" L ...4,600.00
Jade, huang (pendant), face w/headdress, Shang Dy, 3" 2,875.00
Jade, plaque, spinach gr, mtn scene w/silver wire inlay, 15x24" ..1,850.00
Jade, table screen, wht, shou characters, in hdwd stand, sm........700.00
Rock crystal, vase, cvd Buddhist symbols, Qianlong, +lid/stand, 12" ..11,000.00
Tiger-eye, lady w/lg flower & mirror, Ch, 20th C, 8" 200.00

Lacquer

Lacquerware is found in several colors, but the one most likely to be encountered is cinnabar. It is often intricately carved, sometimes involving hundreds of layers built one at a time on a metal or wooden base. Later pieces remain red, while older examples tend to darken.

Box, aquatic plants, gilt hiramakie-ie & aogai, Meiji, 5x9x6" .1,300.00
Box, E, figures in garden on blk, Ch, 19th C, 4½x18x8¼" 115.00
Kobako, cranes/pines/Juji in gilt, 19th C, 3¾", NM.................2,600.00
Tea caddy, blk/gold w/figural panels, serpentine, 1850s 440.00

Netsukes

A netsuke is a miniature Japanese carving made with two holes called the Himitoshi, either channeled or within the carved design. As kimonos (the outer garment of the time) had no pockets, the Japanese man hung his pipe, tobacco pouch, or other daily necessities from his waist sash. The most highly valued accessory was a nest of little drawers called an Inro, in which they carried snuff or sometimes opium. The netsuke was the toggle that secured them. Although most are of ivory, others were made of bone, wood, metal, porcelain, or semiprecious stones. Some were inlaid or lacquered. They are found in many forms — figurals the most common, mythological beasts the most desirable. They range in size from 1" up to 3", which was the maximum size allowed by law. Many netsukes represented the owner's profession, religion, or hobbies. Scenes from the daily life of Japan at that time were

often depicted in the tiny carvings. The more detailed the carving, the greater the value.

Careful study is required to recognize the quality of the netsuke. Many have been made in Hong Kong in recent years; and even though some are very well carved, these are considered copies and avoided by the serious collector. There are many books that will help you learn to recognize quality netsukes, and most reputable dealers are glad to assist you. Use your magnifying glass to check for repairs. In the listings that follow, netsukes are ivory unless noted otherwise; 'stain' indicates a color wash.

Deer stands on rectangular base, unsgn, 19th C 1,150.00
Loquat (2) on fruited branch, sgn Mitsuhiro, late Edo period..1,150.00
Maiden & Fuden in clouds, lt stain, late Edo/Meiji period 1,250.00
Oni bathing in undersz tub, lt stain, sgn Sosonto, Meiji period ...3,100.00
Oni wearing loincloth w/cup in hand, horn inlay/partly colored, 1890s ..1,025.00
Ony scrubbing temple gong, unmk, 19th C 975.00
Raiden pnts drum, sgn Tomochika, late 19th C..........................700.00
Raiden squats by bag of wind & rprs hand fan, Gyokushu, 19th C..925.00
Sishi holding ball, lg himitoshi, att Kyoto, early 19th C..........1,000.00

Porcelain

Chinese export ware was designed to appeal to Western tastes and was often made to order. During the eighteenth century, vast amounts were shipped to Europe and on westward. Much of this fine porcelain consisted of dinnerware lines that were given specific pattern names. Rose Mandarin, Fitzhugh, Armorial, Rose Medallion, and Canton are but a few of the more familiar.

Basin, E, Imari palette floral, rolled rim, Kangxi (1662-1922), 10"....1,175.00
Bough pot, E, FR, rope hdls, ca 1770-80, 8¼" 2,300.00
Bowl, E, Armorial w/unicorn over lion shield, 18th C, 5x9".......375.00
Bowl, E, butterfly & chrysanthemum, ca 1880s, 11⅝" 250.00
Bowl, E, FR, figures & flowers in panels, Ch, 19th C, 4x24" 485.00
Bowl, E, grisaille decor, peacocks/trees/ships, 18th C, 5x12⅜"....460.00
Bowl, E, rose decor in Mandarin motif, 19th C, 10"..................150.00
Bowl, fruit; E, FR, peonies/birds, early 18th C, 10", EX...............300.00
Bowl, punch; E, butterfly & flowers w/gold, 19th C, w/lid & tray....350.00
Bowl, punch; E, FR, figures in panels, 5½x13", VG.................1,000.00
Bowl, serving; E, FR, uptrn rim, late 19th C, 10", EX.................200.00

Charger, Chinese Export, Armorial with floral spray border and gilt, eighteenth century, 13¾", $750.00.

Charger, E, FV, chrysanthemums, early 19th C, 15¼", EX..........450.00
Charger, E, Imari palette floral, Kangxi (1662-1722), 13⅝" 900.00
Charger, E, Thousand Butterfly, 19th C, 14⅝" 550.00
Creamer, E, hog snout w/brn eagle, red/wht/bl shield, 19th C, 3¼" 575.00
Cup & saucer, E, Armorial, arms of NY state/shields, late 18th C...345.00
Garden seat, E, bbl form, flowers/figures in panels, 1890s, 19", pr..1,400.00
Garden seat, FR, E, pictorial dbl panels/florals, hexagonal, 18½"...1,100.00
Gravy boat, E, flower baskets & swags, scalloped, 18th C, 3¾" H.....300.00
Jardiniere, Canton-style scene, lion mask hdls, staple rpr, 11⅜".300.00
Lamp, bride's FR, E, hexagonal w/rtcl panels, electrified, 14" 350.00

Plate, E, bird, dog on rock, peony & bamboo, 19th C, 13¾" 575.00
Plate, E, FV, women in garden, Kangxi (1662-1722), 9½", pr.....455.00
Plate, E, temple scene/king/Masonic symbols, rpr, ca 1800, 9"....375.00
Plate, luncheon; E, child on water buffalo/animals, 18th C, 8⅞"..230.00
Platter, Bl Fitzhugh, 19th C, 15x12", EX......................................575.00
Platter, E, Armorial, anchor/crown crest, 8-sided, 18th C, 10x12"...800.00
Platter, E, Armorial center w/mc floral sprays, 18th C, 16x13"...825.00
Platter, E, butterfly & floral w/gold trim, 19th C, 16x13", pr...1,200.00
Tazza, fruit; E, Rose Canton, dmn shape, 19th C, 14¼" 750.00
Urn, manor reserve/mc butterflies/etc, griffin hdls, 19th C, 15", pr...8,625.00
Urns, E, FR, mc flower basket reserves among bats & flowers, 12", pr...1,150.00
Vase, E, floral, bl on yel, 19th C, 13" 275.00
Vase, FR, baluster w/kylin hdls, ca 1870s, 18".........................980.00
Warming dish, E, Fitzhugh manner w/Mandarin & flowers, 1820-30, 16"....1,800.00
Water pot, Claire-de-Lune, incised decor on bl, Kangxi, 3¼" .2,800.00

Pottery

Bottle, Guan-type celadon, globular, long neck, Song Dy, 7⅝"..1,600.00
Bottle, sake; blk, no decor, teardrop shape, 1800s, 13" 150.00
Bowl, gray-streaked flambe w/flower cutouts, Song Dy, 6¼" 450.00
Brush pot, wht, rtcl wanzi roundel/vajira bolts, late Choson, 5"..2,350.00
Figure, warrior in armor, unglazed, Tang Dy, 21¾" 700.00
Figurine, horse standing on low base, Tang Dy, 14½" 700.00
Mortuary figure, court official, pnt details, Tang Dy, 13".........1,300.00
Teapot, terra cotta, squat melon form w/branch hdl, 1910 ....75.00
Vase, Guan-style crackleware, 8-sided, 18th C, 5¾"...................920.00

Rugs

Dagestan, ivory border, dk bl ground, minor damage, 43x67" 825.00
Gorovan, lt bl border on red, some wear, 102x137" 2,000.00
Hamadan, pk border, bl-gray spandrels on ivory, 93x123" 440.00
Heriz, dk bl border, ivory/rust spandrels on dk salmon, 121x138" 7,700.00
Heriz, red & blk w/ivory spandrels, 100x137"........................2,255.00
Karaja Heriz, bl border, salmon spandrels, ivory ground, 112x143"...2,475.00
Kashan, dk bl border & spandrels on red, 95x128" 825.00
Kazuk, ivory & dk bl borders, reddish ground, worn, 56x74" 660.00
Kuba, prayer, ivory border on blk, rprs, 40x86".....................1,550.00
Mahajarin Sarouk, dk bl border, red ground, 112x150"............3,025.00
Mahal Sarouk, dk bl border, mottled mauve ground, 50x73", VG+ ..550.00
Meshed, midnight bl border & plum ground, rpr, 120x154"......3,000.00
NW Persian, tan & pk borders w/gr & gray ground, wear, 42x113"....440.00
Pakistan, rust border w/mc diagonal striped ground, 59x70"....1,000.00
Persian Mahal, red border, blk ground, wear, 102x142"..............990.00
Sarouk, midnight bl/camel borders, floral on pink-red, 118x236"....4,700.00

Snuff Bottles

The Chinese were introduced to snuff in the seventeenth century, and their carved and painted snuff bottles typify their exquisite taste and workmanship. These small bottles, seldom measuring over 2½", were made of amber, jade, ivory, and cinnabar; tiny spoons were often attached to their stoppers. By the eighteenth century, some were being made of porcelain, others were of glass with delicate interior designs tediously reverse painted with minuscule brushes sometimes containing a single hair. Copper and brass were used but to no great extent.

Amethyst teardrop, ca 1900, 3¼" 350.00
Bubble suffused grown w/ruby o/l, 1800-60, 2⅛" 125.00
Malachite fish form, ca 1900, 2⅞"...200.00
Quartz, chalcedony w/relief-cvd horse, 19th C, 2⅛" 500.00
Rock crystal, rvpt landscape, sgn, 19th C, 2¼" 1,100.00
Rvpt glass, warriors on horsebk, 19th, C, 4"...............................225.00

Textiles

Kimono, embr wht silk w/swastikas & flowers, 1940s, EX...........315.00
Kimono, wedding; embr crane/flowers w/gold bullion, 1940s......225.00
Robe, priest's; silk brocade w/metallic/mc threads, ca 1800, 45"...500.00
Tapestry, 2 dragons & pearl, silk/metallic thread, 74x81".........2,185.00

Woodblock Prints, Japanese

Framed prints are of less value than those not framed, since it is impossible to inspect their condition or determined whether or not they have borders or have been trimmed.

Eishi, Geisha of Gr House, bijin in kimono w/drum, 1795, oban tate-e...1,100.00
Jun'ichiri Sekino, girl w/cat, 1957, 24½x12"...............................500.00
Kunisada, Whipping of Geisha Caught Stealing, 19th C, 14x9½" ..300.00
Kuniyoshi, figure & bird/seated couple, 1850s, 14x19¾" 350.00
Kuniyoshi, lady in flowing kimono, 19th C, 14½x10" 220.00
Toyokuni, samurai w/sword, 2nd w/teapot, 1850, diptich, 20x14", G....400.00
Toyokuni ga, Wife of Chushingura Merchant, oban tate-e 1,150.00

Orrefors

Orrefors Glassworks was founded in 1898 in the Swedish province of Smaaland. Utilizing the expertise of designers such as Simon Gate, Edward Hald, Vicke Lindstrand, and Edwin Ohrstrom, it produced art glass of the highest quality. Various techniques were used in achieving the decoration. Some were wheel engraved; others were blown through a unique process that formed controlled bubbles or air pockets resulting in unusual patterns and shapes. Our advisor for this category is Abby Malowanczyk; she is listed in the Directory under Texas.

Bowl, Sailor's Dream, painted sailors and nudes before dance band, Orrefors Expo 682-68 Gunnar Cyren, 7x9¼", $1,550,00.

Vase, Ariel, girl w/dove, Ohrstrom 957913, 1986, 7½x4½".....2,575.00
Vase, bl-gr, serpentine faceted panels, GA 276, 1930, 3¾" 145.00
Vase, chartreuse w/blk-lined fish, Graal, 1693D, Hald, 5"...........400.00
Vase, clear w/eng nude & 2 birds in flight, Palmquist AR, 5½x11"...435.00
Vase, dk bl (cased) bowl form, NU3953, 7" 200.00
Vase, Graal, blk fish, 2334C Edward Hald, 1951, 4¾x7¾" 525.00
Vase, Graal, fish & plants, Edward Hald, 198.E3, 6⅝" 460.00
Vase, Graal, lobster & crab, Edward Hald, N528, 7x6½".........1,100.00
Vase, Kraka, bl/gr swags in clear teardrop, Palmquist, 349, 5½"..650.00
Vase, purple w/eng nude dancer, Lindstrand 1359/33 (from 1935), 8½"..1,300.00
Vase, Tulpenglaser, goblet w/internal amber, Landberg ?79-58, 20"....2,000.00

Ott and Brewer

The partnership of Ott and Brewer began in 1865 in Trenton, New Jersey. By 1876 they were making decorated graniteware, parian, and 'ivory porcelain' — similar to Irish belleek though not as fine and of different composition. In 1883, however, experiments toward that end had reached a successful conclusion, and a true belleek body was introduced.

It came to be regarded as the finest china ever produced by an American firm. The ware was decorated by various means such as hand painting, transfer printing, gilding, and lustre glazing. The company closed in 1893, one of many that failed during that depression. In the listings below, the ware is belleek unless noted otherwise. Our advisor for this category is Mary Frank Gaston.

Bowl, cream soup; gold floral, gold twig hdls, 2½x3" **50.00**
Creamer & sugar bowl, gold ivy & turq jewels, rope hdl, ca 1885 ...**265.00**
Cup & saucer, demitasse; gold bamboo/dandelions/berries **225.00**
Pitcher, gold leaves on wht, twig hdl, 6⅜", EX..............................**250.00**
Pitcher, thistles w/fired-on gold, 5½" **190.00**
Plate, cake/sandwich; hummingbird & orchid, 3x8" sq **1,200.00**
Vase, bird & foliage in top band, obscured mk, 6" **450.00**
Vase, duck & dandelions, gold on coral, rtcl hdls, 10¼x7" **3,000.00**

Overbeck

The Overbeck Studio was established in 1911 in Cambridge City, Indiana, by four Overbeck sisters. It survived until the last sister died in 1955. Early wares were often decorated with carved designs of stylized animals, birds, or florals with the designs colored to contrast with the background. Others had tooled designs filled in with various colors for a mosaic effect. After 1937, Mary Frances, the last remaining sister, favored handmade figurines with somewhat bizarre features in fanciful combinations of color. Overbeck ware is signed 'OBK,' frequently with the designer's and potter's initials under the stylized 'OBK.'

Figurines, Bride and Groom, nineteenth-century clothes, OBK, 5", NM, $400.00 for the pair.

Chalice, camels & mtns, yel/gunmetal on raspberry, 6", EX **1,500.00**
Figurine, bl jay, bl & brn on wht, 3¼x5½" **145.00**
Figurine, dog, standing w/head up, dk brn matt, OBK, 3¾"........**300.00**
Figurine, girl w/pk bonnet/shawl, 3-color plaid skirt, 3½" **200.00**
Figurines, whimsical musicians, 4½", set of 5 ....**2,100.00**
Tumbler, crickets, gr on beige, 3¾x3" **1,300.00**
Vase, bud; lady figural, mc w/cvd flowers in skirt, prof rpr, 2⅝"..**700.00**
Vase, cut-bk/pnt birds in 3 panels on lt rose matt/dull gr, EH, 5½"...**3,500.00**
Vase, geometrics, gr on multi-tone brn, EF, 4" **1,600.00**

Overlay Glass

Art glass having layers of more than one type or color of glass is sometimes called overlay or cased glass. Very often glassware of this type has applied decorations such as fruit, flowers, leaves, or ruffles (rigaree), such as is commonly identified with Stevens and Williams. See also Stevens and Williams.

Biscuit jar, lav-pk w/HP decor, SP trim, 6⅝x4¾" **185.00**
Bowl, peachblow w/yel swags & branches forming ft, 5x7" **625.00**
Pitcher, gold satin w/emb swirl ribs, frosted reeded hdl, 5" **195.00**
Pitcher, orange, ruffled top, reeded hdl, 7¼x4¾" **165.00**
Rose bowl, bl, HP florals w/gold, 8-crimp, 3½x4¼" **110.00**

Vase, pk, ewer w/frosted hdl, HP flowers w/gold, 9¾x2¾" **125.00**
Vase, pk w/wht int, appl red/wht spatter flowers, ruffled rim, 8½" ...**150.00**
Vase, red, HP florals, cut scallops w/gold, gold hdls, 8½" **175.00**

Overshot

Overshot glass is characterized by the beaded or craggy appearance of its surface. Earlier ware was irregularly textured, while twentieth-century examples tend to be more uniform.

Basket, amberina, melon ribs, amber thorn hdl, fluted rim, 7½x6" ...**350.00**
Pitcher, cranberry, reeded hdl, water sz..**250.00**
Salt cellar, clear, in Reed & Barton SP fr **40.00**
Tumbler, clear w/gold rim, 6½x3¼" **30.00**
Tumbler, gr to clear, 3¾x2¾" **82.50**
Tumbler, rubena, swirled, 3¾" **165.00**

Owen, Ben

Ben Owen worked at the Jugtown Pottery of North Carolina from 1923 until it temporarily closed in 1959. He continued in the business in his own Plank Road Pottery, stamping his ware 'Ben Owen, Master Potter,' with many forms made by Lester Fanell Craven in the late 1960s. His pottery closed in 1972. He died in 1983 at the age of 81.

The pottery was reopened in 1981 under the supervision of Benjamin Wade Owen II. One of the principal potters was David Garner who worked there until about 1985. This pottery is still in operation today with Ben II as the main potter.

Bean pot, Frogskin Green, w/lid, att, 1960s, 6¾x8" **175.00**
Birdhouse, bright orange, earthenware, 1960s, 6¾" **30.00**
Bowl, rice; Mirror Black, Ben, 2x5" **100.00**
Bowl, rice; Mirror Black, early 1960s, 1⅞x4¾" **70.00**
Candlesticks, Chinese White, flared ft, 1960-62, 6⅛", pr **110.00**
Candlesticks, orange gloss, mk, 9", pr..**275.00**
Candlesticks, wht, cupped bobeches, Craven, 12½", pr **375.00**
Chamberstick, Tobacco Spit Brown, att Craven, 1¼x8" **60.00**
Inkwell, Frogskin Green, dome shape, Ben, early 1960s, 3x4" **175.00**
Jug, Frogskin Green, bulbous, hdl, 1960s, 7⅜"..............................**350.00**
Pie pan, Tobacco Spit Brown, 1960s, 2⅛x10⅞" **90.00**
Pitcher, buttermilk; Frogskin Green, 1960s, 8⅞" **250.00**
Sugar bowl, cobalt int & brush-stroke decor, 1960s, 2⅞x5½" **110.00**
Teapot, Tobacco Spit Brown, Craven, 1960s, 6x9" **225.00**
Vase, Chinese White, wide shoulder, mid-1960s, 7½"....................**60.00**
Vase, Frogskin & Mustard modified Albany slip, Ben III, 1992, 8¼" ...**110.00**
Vase, Frogskin Green, shouldered, 1960s, 4½" **70.00**
Vase, wht, Oriental translation, att Ben, early 1960s, 9" **200.00**

Owens Pottery

J.B. Owens founded his company in Zanesville, Ohio, in 1891, and until 1907, when the company decided to exert most of its energies in the area of tile production, made several quality lines of art pottery. His first line, Utopian, was a standard brown ware with underglaze slip decoration of nature studies, animals, and portraits. A similar line, Lotus, utilized lighter background colors. Henri Deux, introduced in 1900, featured incised Art Nouveau forms inlaid with color. (Be aware that the Brush McCoy Pottery acquired many of Owens' molds and reproduced a line similar to Henri Deux, which they called Navarre.) Other important lines were Opalesce, Rustic, Feroza, Cyrano, and Mission, examples of which are rare today. The factory burned in 1928, and the company closed shortly thereafter. Values vary according to the quality of the artwork and subject matter. Examples signed by the artist bring higher prices than those that are not signed. For further information we recommend *Owens Pottery Unearthed* by Kristy and Rick McKibben and Jeanette and Marvin Stofft. Mrs. Stofft is listed in the Directory under Indiana.

Aborigine, jug, pnt & slip decor, hdld, Owens #31 1864, 5⅛"....150.00
Aborigine, vase, slip trail decor at shoulder/collar, #29, 5⅜" 175.00
Henri Deux, jardiniere, Nouveau women, 8", NM......................600.00
Henri Deux, vase, sgraffito irises, mc on dk brn, 10¾x5¾", NM....450.00
Lightweight, cruet, roses, Cecil Excel, #868, 3¼"........................175.00
Lightweight, pillow vase, floral, Cecil Excel, #846, 4", EX..........250.00
Lotus, jardiniere, lotus blossoms, 6⅜", NM.................................375.00
Lotus, pitcher, water bird & water lily, 9"..................................700.00
Lotus, vase, mushrooms, F Ferrell, #1236, 6"...............................425.00
Malachite Opalesce Inlaid, tankard, Nouveau florals, unmk, 10"...1,100.00
Malachite Opalesce Inlaid, vase, Nouveau florals, 9⅞", NM...1,000.00
Malachite Opalesce Utopian, vase, nasturtiums, #1068, 12¼", NM ..1,500.00
Malachite Opalesce Utopian, vase, nasturtiums, flat sided, 10⅜" 850.00
Matt Green, mug, combed decor, #46, 3⅞" 200.00
Matt Green, vase, emb decor, hdls, #1112, 9¼" 550.00
Matt Green, vase, 4 buttressed ft, #1155, 5⅞" 400.00
Matt Utopian, vase, cherries, sgn, bottle neck, bulbous, 13".........475.00
Matt Utopian, vase, clovers, H Larzelere, #124, 13⅝", NM........500.00
Opalesce, pitcher, floral, ruffled rim, 10"...................................950.00
Opalesce, vase, floral, wide shoulders, bottle neck, 11" 950.00
Opalesce Inlaid, vase, Nouveau floral, #1123, 11⅞", NM........1,000.00
Oriental, box, wht w/bl beading, 3", NM....................................275.00
Parchment, vase, jonquils in heavy slip under crackle, #1073, 10¾" ..250.00
Semi-Glazed Etched, vase, irises, #123, 13¼", NM 1,200.00
Soudanese, lamp vase, cherries on blk, Lessell, unmk, 14" 800.00
Soudanese, vase, pansies on dk gloss, #202, 4", NM 450.00
Utopian, jug, tulips, T Steele, mk, 6½".......................................295.00
Utopian, lamp base, pansies, 10½", NM......................................225.00
Utopian, vase, Am Indian brave portrait, sgn, #1067, 14½", NM ...5,500.00
Utopian, vase, carnations, #832, 4⅞" 125.00
Utopian, vase, cherries, trumpet neck, 12"..................................350.00
Utopian, vase, clovers, bulbous, 8" 350.00
Utopian, vase, floral, stick neck, mk, 8" 175.00
Utopian, vase, floral, twist body, #120, 4⅜" 150.00
Utopian, vase, High Bear Sioux (Indian chief) portrait, 12" ...4,000.00
Utopian, vase, orchids, 5" 175.00
Utopian, vase, pansies, unmk, 5" 150.00
Utopian, vase, silver o/l roses on brn, #923, 6⅜" 150.00
Utopian, vase, wild roses, sgn, mk, 10½" 325.00
Utopian, vase, wild roses, slim, 11"..250.00

Pacific Clay Products

The Pacific Clay Products Company got its start in the 1920s as a consolidation of several smaller southern California potteries. The main Los Angeles plant had been founded in 1890 to make kitchen stoneware, ollas, and similar items. Terra cotta and brick were later produced. In 1932 Hostess Ware, a vividly colored line of dinnerware, was introduced to compete with Bauer's Ring Ware. Coralitos, a lighterweight, pastel-hued dinnerware line was first marketed in 1937, and a similar but less expensive line called Arcadia soon followed. Art ware including vases, figurines, candlesticks, etc., was produced from 1932 to 1942, at which time the company went into war-related work and pottery manufacture ceased. A limited amount of hand-decorated dinnerware was also made. For further information we recommend *The Collector's Encyclopedia of California Pottery, 2nd Edition*, by Jack Chipman; he is listed in the Directory under California.

Butter dish, Coralitos...60.00
Coffee carafe, Apache Red, 9½x7½"..95.00
Coffee carafe, yel, 9½x7½"...95.00
Coffee server, Coralitos, wood hdl 45.00
Coffee/teacup & saucer, Hostessware..25.00
Creamer, lilies & leaves form border at top, brn hdl....................35.00
Cup & saucer, demitasse; Coralitos...25.00
Egg cup, early design..45.00
Flowerpot, wht matt, Deco-style linear decor, #B02110, 5x5".......45.00
Planter, swan, pk, 6", NM...20.00
Plate, dinner; Coralitos, 10" 15.00
Teacup & saucer, Apache Red w/decor, minimum value 85.00
Tray, Hostessware, 15"..100.00
Tumbler, cobalt, #411, 4x3" 20.00
Vase, gazelle reserve on pk, 10x7½" sq....................................115.00
Vase, gr, #3005 USA, 1930s, 4½" 22.00
Vase, lime gr, trumpet form, emb leaves on flared ft, hdls, 8x5"..130.00
Vase, lt bl, fan form, 7½x6½" 65.00
Vase, lt pk, 8x5½" 55.00
Vase, swan form, bl, 1924, 9x11" 35.00

Paden City

Paden City Glass Mfg. Co. was founded in 1916 in Paden City, West Virginia. It made both mold-blown and pressed wares and is most remembered today for its handmade wares in bright colors with fanciful etchings. A great deal of Paden City's business was in supplying decorating companies and fitters with glass; therefore, Paden City never marked their glass with a trademark of any kind, and the company's advertisements were limited to trade, rather than retail publications. In 1948 the management of the company opened a second plant to make utilitarian machine-made wares such as tumblers and ashtrays, but the move was ill-advised due to a glut of similar wares already on the market. The company remained in operation until 1951 when it permanently closed the doors of both factories as a result of the losses incurred by 'Plant No. 2.' (To clear up an often-repeated misunderstanding, dealers and collectors alike should keep in mind that The Paden City Glass Mfg Co. had absolutely no connection with the Paden City Pottery Company, other than their identical locale.)

Today Paden City is best known for its numerous acid-etched wares sporting birds, but many other ornate etchings were also produced — some of which are well documented in print, while others have not been documented in widely available publications. Peacock and Rose, and Cupid are two of the most commonly found etched patterns. Currently, collectors especially seek out examples of Paden City's most detailed etching, Orchid, and its most appealing etching, Cupid. However, pieces bearing undocumented etchings or documented etchings on shapes and/or colors on which that etching has not previously been seen are fetching the highest prices from advanced collectors. Pieces in the company's plainer pressed dinnerware lines, however, have remained affordable, even though some patterns are quite scarce.

Below is a list of Paden City's colors. Names in capital letters indicate original factory color names where known, followed by a description of the color.

Amber — several shades
Blue — early 1920s color, medium shade, not cobalt
Cheriglo — pink
Copen, Neptune, Ceylon — various shades of light blue
Crystal — clear
Ebony — black
Emeraldglo — thinner dark green, not as deep as Forest Green
Forest Green — dark green

Green — various shades, from yellowish to electric green
Mulberry — amethyst
Opal — white (milk glass)
Primrose — amber with reddish tint (rare)
Rose — dark pink (rare)
Royal or Ritz Blue — cobalt
Ruby — red
Topaz — yellow

Collectors seeking more information on Paden City would do well to consult the following books: *Paden City, The Color Company,* by Jerry Barnett (out of print, privately published, 1979); *Colored Glassware of the Depression Era 2* by Hazel Marie Weatherman (Glassbooks, 1974); *Price Trends to Colored Glassware of the Depression Era 2* by Hazel Marie Weatherman (Glassbooks, Editions in 1977, 1979, and 1981).

Our advisor for this category is Michael Krumme; he is listed in the Directory under California. See also Clubs, Newsletters, and Catalogs.

Black Forest, batter jug, crystal 200.00
Black Forest, bowl, console; amber, 11" 75.00
Black Forest, candlestick, blk, mushroom style 75.00
Black Forest, comport, gr or pk, high ftd, 5½" 60.00
Black Forest, cup & saucer, red, 3 styles, ea 150.00
Black Forest, ice tub, ice bl, 2 styles, ea.......................195.00
Black Forest, plate, bread & butter; gr or pk, 6½" 25.00
Black Forest, shakers, crystal, pr 125.00
Black Forest, sugar bowl, blk, 2 styles, ea........................60.00
Black Forest, vase, ebony, #210, 9" 145.00
Black Forest, whipped cream pail, amber..........................95.00
Crow's Foot Round, bowl, console; cobalt, 3-ftd, flat rim...........125.00
Crow's Foot Round, plate, cracker; amber, amethyst or pk, 11" 22.50
Crow's Foot Round, plate, dinner; blk or bl, sm, 9¼"........40.00
Crow's Foot Square, bowl, amethyst or pk, 11"..................30.00
Crow's Foot Square, bowl, red, blk or bl, ftd, 10" 75.00
Crow's Foot Square, bowl, red, 4⅞" 25.00
Crow's Foot Square, cake plate, red, low ped ft.................85.00
Crow's Foot Square, candle holders, cobalt, single, mushroom style, pr .80.00
Crow's Foot Square, candlestick, blk or bl, 5¾"................30.00
Crow's Foot Square, candy dish, cloverleaf w/lid, in metal fr w/nudes...90.00
Crow's Foot Square, comport, crystal, wht or yel, 7¾x4¾"...........35.00
Crow's Foot Square, gravy boat, red, ped ft....................135.00
Crow's Foot Square, sandwich server, red, center hdl 45.00
Crow's Foot Square, sugar bowl, blk or bl 13.50
Crow's Foot Square, vase, amber, wht or crystal, cupped, 10¼" 45.00
Cupid, bowl, gr or pk, oval ft, 8½" 275.00
Cupid, cake stand, gr or pk, ftd, 2" H 215.00
Cupid, creamer, gr or pk, ftd, 5" 150.00
Cupid, cup, pk 300.00
Cupid, plate, gr or pk, 10½"..150.00
Cupid, syrup pitcher, gr, w/lid...................................1,500.00
Cupid, tray, gr or pk, oval ft, 10⅞" 250.00
Cupid, water bottle (w/tumbler), gr or pk 500.00
Delilah Bird, bowl, all colors, sq, 4⅞"..............................42.00
Delilah Bird, creamer, all colors, flat, 2¾".......................95.00
Delilah Bird, plate, luncheon; all colors, 8½"...................60.00
Delilah Bird, server, all colors, center hdld.......................75.00
Delilah Bird, vase, all colors, 10" 225.00
Gazebo, bowl, bl, bead hdls, 9" 75.00
Gazebo, candlestick, crystal, 5¼".....................................45.00
Gazebo, candy, bl, w/lid, sm, 10¼"................................110.00
Gazebo, creamer, crystal...22.50
Gazebo, mayonnaise liner, bl...225.00
Gazebo, plate, crystal, fan hdls, 13" 50.00
Gazebo, server, bl, center hdl, 11"..................................75.00

Gothic Garden, bowl, all colors, ftd, 10" 85.00
Gothic Garden, cake plate, all colors, ftd, 10½" 75.00
Gothic Garden, plate, all colors, tab hdld, 11"..................60.00
Gothic Garden, vase, all colors, 6½" 125.00
Largo, bowl, crystal, 7½" 20.00
Largo, cake plate, colors, ped...75.00
Largo, cheese dish, crystal, w/lid....................................65.00
Largo, creamer, colors, ftd...45.00
Largo, creamer & sugar bowl, amethyst..........................108.00
Largo, plate, crystal, 6⅝"..8.00
Largo, saucer, colors..10.00
Largo, tray, crystal, tab hdld..20.00
Lucy, candy dish, red, 3-ftd, w/lid..................................115.00
Orchid, bowl, yel, crystal, gr, pk or red, sq, 4⅞"...............25.00
Orchid, cake stand, red, blk or cobalt, sq, 2" H................150.00
Orchid, compote, crystal, low ft, flat rim, #412.................68.00
Orchid, creamer, yel, crystal, gr, amber or pk 50.00
Orchid, vase, red, blk or cobalt, 8" 275.00
Orchid, vase, red, flared, #412, 10"...............................480.00
Orchid, vase, yel, crystal, gr, amber or pk, 10" 125.00
Oriental Garden, crystal, elliptical, sm, 5" 98.00
Peacock & Rose, bowl, all colors, flat, 8½"....................125.00
Peacock & Rose, bowl, all colors, ftd, 8¾".....................175.00
Peacock & Rose, bowl, console; all colors, 14".................195.00
Peacock & Rose, cheese & cracker set, all colors 185.00
Peacock & Rose, pitcher, all colors, 5".............................265.00
Peacock & Rose, sugar bowl, all colors, rnd hdl, 4½".........55.00
Peacock & Rose, vase, all colors, 12" 295.00
Penny Line, creamer & sugar bowl, gr.............................30.00
Penny Line, creamer & sugar bowl, red............................25.00
Penny Line, stem, cordial; red, from $20 to......................25.00
Utopia, vase, blk or yel, 10¼".......................................195.00
Utopia, vase, rectangular, gr, 8" 210.00
Utopia, vase, rectangular, crystal, 8" 100.00

Paintings on Ivory

Miniature works of art executed on ivory from the 1800s are assessed by the finesse of the artist, as is any fine painting. Signed examples and portraits with identifiable subjects are usually preferred.

Napoleon, signed Delaroche, early 1900s, oval sight: 3¼x2½", in frame, $800.00. (Photo courtesy Neal Auctions)

Baby in wht gown & bonnet, bl bkground, w/hair lock, 2¾" 220.00
Baby in wht w/bl ribbon, dtd 1833, blk lacquered fr, 4¾" 250.00
Gentleman w/high collar, sgn Weinedel, 1837, 2¼x2", +pendant case ..900.00
Girl w/blond hair, lacy dress & bonnet, coral necklace, 2¼" 275.00
Girl w/long hair, embr/cutwork dress, gilt fr, 3¼", +case 440.00
Lady in blk w/pearl necklace, wht bonnet, brass fr, 2⅛".............770.00
Lady in low-cut dress w/lace, 2⅜"...................................330.00
Lady in straw hat, in burl fr, 6x6" 360.00

Lady in wht Empire dress, brn curly hair, 3⅝", +leatherized case ..**800.00**
Lady in wht w/pearls in hair, 2⅜".....................................**275.00**
Lady w/brn curly hair, 1⅝", +locket case w/machine tooling......**715.00**
Lady w/curls in bl dress, locket of hair on bk, brass fr, 2¼".........**275.00**
Man in bl frock coat, wht waist coat, 2", +rose gold colored case...**660.00**
Man in bl-gray waistcoat, gold-colored fr, 2⅜x1⅞"....................**415.00**
Man in blk frock coat, high collar, gesso fr w/appl compo swag, 4x4"..**275.00**
Man in uniform, gilt brass fr, 7⅝", VG................................**165.00**
Man w/stern look, blk coat, modern fr, 6⅝x5½"........................**300.00**

Pairpoint

The Pairpoint Manufacturing Company was built in 1880 in New Bedford, Massachusetts. It was primarily a metalworks whose chief product was coffin fittings. Next door, the Mt. Washington Glassworks made quality glasswares of many varieties. (See Mt. Washington for more information concerning their artware lines.) By 1894 it became apparent to both companies that a merger would be to their best interest.

From the late 1890s until the 1930s, lamps and lamp accessories were an important part of Pairpoint's production. There were three main types of shades, all of which were blown: puffy — blown-out reverse-painted shades (usually floral designs); ribbed — also reverse painted; and scenic — reverse painted with scenes of land or seascapes (usually executed on smooth surfaces, although ribbed scenics may be found occasionally). Cut glass lamps and those with metal overlay panels were also made. Scenic shades were sometimes artist signed. Every shade was stamped on the lower inside or outside edge with 1) The Pairpoint Corp., 2) Patent Pending, 3) Patented July 9, 1907, or 4) Patent Applied For. Bases were made of bronze, copper, brass, silver, or wood and are always signed.

Because they produced only fancy, handmade artware, the company's sales lagged seriously during the Depression, and as time and tastes changed, their style of product was less in demand. As a result, they never fully recovered; consequently part of the buildings and equipment was sold in 1938. The company reorganized in 1939 under the direction of Robert Gundersen and again specialized in quality hand-blown glassware. Isaac Babbit regained possession of the silver departments, and together they established Gundersen Glassworks, Inc. After WWII, because of a sharp decline in sales, it again became necessary to reorganize. The Gundersen-Pairpoint Glassworks was formed, and the old line of cut, engraved artware was reintroduced. The company moved to East Wareham, Massachusetts, in 1957. But business continued to suffer, and the firm closed only one year later. In 1970, however, new facilities were constructed in Sagamore under the direction of Robert Bryden, sales manager for the company since the 1950s.

In 1974 the company began to produce lead glass cup plates which were made on commission as fund-raisers for various churches and organizations. These are signed with a 'P' in diamond and are becoming quite collectible. See also Burmese; Napkin Rings.

Glass

Bell, wht opal, clear hdl w/wht decor, orig label, 10"...................**240.00**
Bishop's hat, cut, Baltic, 3x15", center bowl section: 8".............**565.00**
Bowl, berry; cut, floral & geometric, hobstar base, 3½x9"..........**155.00**
Box, cut, Pearl, worn SP trim, 5⅛"...................................**275.00**
Castor set, cut, 5 bottles w/fern-like leaves, SP fr revolves, 17"..**365.00**
Compote, cut, Butterfly & Daisy, scalloped rim, 6¼x9¼"..........**190.00**
Compote, cut, flowers/buds/plants/leaves, 6⅛x6¾", pr...............**235.00**
Pitcher, cut, Butterfly & Daisy, 10"..................................**325.00**
Vase, amethyst, trumpet neck, clear paperweight base, 9¾x5"......**85.00**

Lamps

Puffy boudoir, lilies invt cone shade; mk slim std **7,200.00**

Puffy 5" lilac/butterfly shade; tree-trunk base, rare **3,400.00**
Puffy 8½" rose/butterfly shade; stepped floriform std, 14¼".....**3,500.00**
Puffy 8½" rose/butterfly shade; gold-wash std, 13½".............**5,000.00**
Puffy 10" lotus (pk/gr) shade; std w/bun base, sm ft **11,000.00**
Puffy 12" grapes/leaves shade; mk std.............................**18,150.00**
Puffy 12" poppy shade; brass std w/repousse floral bands........**30,500.00**
Puffy 12" roses shade; eng bulbous gilt std w/hdls...............**20,350.00**
Puffy 14" butterflies/roses hanging shade; orig hdw **6,700.00**
Puffy 14" orange tree/butterflies shade; tree-trunk std, rare ...**60,000.00**
Puffy 14" Stratford hummingbird/roses shade; brass baluster std **11,600.00**
Puffy 16" begonia shade; slim std w/emb foliage/veins, rare....**67,000.00**
Puffy 16" roses/hummingbirds/scrolls shade; tree-trunk std...**21,450.00**
Rvpt boudoir, roses shade; bronzed std, 14" **2,000.00**
Rvpt 9" floral molded shade; gold-wash #B3048 std, 14" **1,035.00**
Rvpt 10" autumnal shade; patinated #C3064 std, 14½"...........**1,265.00**
Rvpt 12" Venice floral shade; bronze mk std.........................**6,600.00**
Rvpt 15" pastoral scenic shade; gold-wash #3070 std, 23".......**3,000.00**
Rvpt 16" Carlisle exotic bird shade; bronze tripod std............**7,150.00**
Rvpt 16" Garden of Allah Chesterfield shade; sqd SP std **13,000.00**
Rvpt 16" ribbed Chesterfield Persian carpet shade; mk gold-plate std....**15,950.00**
Rvpt 16" rose trellis shade; 4-arm stylized metal mk std, 22".....**4,000.00**
Rvpt 16½" butterfly/floral shade; 2-socket #C3066 std, 22½"...**3,500.00**
Rvpt 17" Exeter floral shade; brass std **4,400.00**
Rvpt 17" floral/urn shade; 3-socket urn-form std, att, 23½"......**2,300.00**
Rvpt 18" scenic Bombay shade; bronze std **3,575.00**
Rvpt 18" scenic Danver shade; SP mk std **3,300.00**
Rvpt 18" sea gulls/sailing ships shade, matching rvpt std **7,875.00**
Rvpt 20" Berkley woodland scene shade; brass std **4,950.00**
Rvpt 20" stylized border Lansdowne shade; bronze std............**3,300.00**
Rvpt 20½" Garden of Allah shade; brass-color urn-form std, 24" ..**8,500.00**
Rvpt 21" peach blossom shade; urn-shaped #D3016 std, 25" ...**6,500.00**

Pairpoint Limoges

Limoges china blanks were imported from France in strict accordance with Pairpoint specifications. They were decorated by Pairpoint in designs that ranged from simple to elaborate florals and scenics. Called Crown Pairpoint French China in old Pairpoint and Mt. Washington catalogs, these are easily identified. Look for the Pairpoint name over a crown with the Limoges name below. You may also find similar ware marked 'Pairpoint Minton.'

Compote, mc floral on cream w/gold, ftd, 6x10", from $550 to ..**650.00**
Ferner, mc flowers on cream, scrollwork, much gold, from $1,200 to ..**1,400.00**
Plate, sailboat in harbor, L Tripp, fuchsia-tinted rim, 7⅜" **385.00**
Vase, chrysanthemums w/gold, free-form hdls, #2008/262, 9½x7" ..**625.00**
Vase, Delft scenic reserves, pierced hdls, cylindrical, 13".........**2,250.00**
Vase, girl's portrait on red, gold scrolls/flowers, 14" **485.00**

Paper Dolls

No one knows quite how or when paper dolls originated. One belief is that they began in Europe as 'pantins' (jumping jacks). During the nineteenth century, most paper dolls portrayed famous dancers and opera stars such as Fanny Elssler and Jenny Lind. In the late 1800s, the Raphael Tuck Publishers of England produced many series of beautiful paper dolls; retail companies used them as advertisements to further the sale of their products. Around the turn of the century, many popular women's magazines began featuring a page of paper dolls.

Most familiar to today's collectors are the books with dolls on cardboard covers and clothes on the inside pages. These made their appearance in the late 1920s and early 1930s. The most collectible (and the most valuable) are those representing celebrities, movie stars, and comic-strip characters of the '30s and '40s.

When no condition is indicated, the dolls listed below are assumed to be in mint, uncut, original condition. Cut sets will be worth about half price if all dolls and outfits are included and pieces are in very good condition. If dolls were produced in die-cut form, these prices reflect such a set in mint condition with all costumes and accessories.

For further information we recommend *Tomart's Price Guide to Lowe and Whitman Paper Dolls*, by Mary Young, our advisor for this category; she is listed in the Directory under Ohio. We also recommend *Schroeder's Collectible Toys, Antique to Modern* (Collector Books).

Airline Stewardess, Lowe #2742, 1959, uncut, M 35.00
Alice in Wonderland, Whitman #928, 1930, stand-ups, uncut, M ..75.00
Ava Gardner, Whitman #2108, 1953, uncut, M, from $85 to 125.00
Baby Nancy, Whitman #1060, 1935, uncut, M 35.00
Baby Sparkle Plenty, Saalfield #2500, 1948, uncut, M 50.00
Baby Sue, Lowe #2786, 1969, uncut, M 15.00
Barbara Britton, Saalfield #4318, 1954, uncut, M, from $85 to ..150.00
Blondie, Whitman #967, 1948, uncut, M 125.00
Bridal Doll Book, Whitman #1986, 1978, uncut, M 16.00
Cathy Goes to Camp, Merrill #1562, 1954, uncut, M 35.00
Cinderella Steps Out, Lowe #1242, 1948, uncut, M 60.00
Claudette Colbert, Saalfield #322, 1943, uncut, M 75.00
Clothes Crazy, Lowe #1046, 1945, uncut, M 35.00
Coke Crowd, Merrill #3445, 1946, uncut, M 100.00
Debbie Reynolds, Whitman #1955, 1955, uncut, M 100.00
Donnie & Marie, Whitman #1991, 1977, uncut, M 35.00
Dy-Dee Baby Doll, Whitman #969, 1938, uncut, M 125.00

Elizabeth Taylor Authorized Edition, #968, 1949, M, $175.00.

Farmyard, Lowe #1254, 1943, stand-ups, uncut, M 10.00
Flying Nun, Saalfield #6069, 1969, uncut, MIB, from $50 to........60.00
Gene Autry, Merrill #3482, 1940, stand-ups, uncut, M 85.00
Gene Tierney, Whitman #992, 1947, uncut, M 175.00
Golden Girl, Merrill #1543, 1953, uncut, M 75.00
Gone With the Wind, Merrill #3404, 1940, uncut, M 350.00
Haley Mills in Moon-Spinners, Whitman, 1964, EX 40.00
Hello Patti, Lowe #1877, 1964, uncut, M 12.00
Jack & Jill, Lowe #9800, 1963, uncut, M 45.00
Janet Leigh, Lowe #2733, 1958, uncut, M 80.00
Joan's Wedding, Whitman #990, 1942, uncut, M 75.00
Josie & the Pussycats, Whitman #1982, 1971, EX 30.00
Karen Goes to College, Merrill #1564, 1955, uncut, M 50.00
Lennon Sisters, Whitman #1979, 1958, uncut, M 60.00
Let's Play House, Lowe #2708, 1957, uncut, M 20.00
Little Brothers & Sisters, Whitman #971, 1953, uncut, M............25.00

Little Women, Artcraft #5127, uncut, from $35 to......................50.00
Mary Poppins, Whitman #1982, 1964, uncut, M 40.00
Me & Mimi, Lowe #L144, 1942, uncut, M 40.00
Movie Starlets, Whitman #960, 1946, uncut, M 100.00
Natalie Wood, Whitman #1962, 1957, uncut, M 150.00
National Velvet, Whitman #1958, 1961, uncut, M 40.00
Nurses, Whitman #1975, 1963, uncut, M 50.00
Pepper Around the Clock, Whitman #4640, 1965, uncut, MIB ...50.00
Peter Rabbit, Saalfield #963, 1934, stand-ups, uncut, M 40.00
Princess Diana, Whitman #1530, 1985, uncut, M 50.00
Raggedy Ann & Andy, Whitman #1962, 1974, uncut, M............15.00
Rock Hudson, Whitman #2087, 1957, uncut, M 65.00
Sandra Dee, Saalfield #4417, 1959, uncut, M 65.00
Shirley Temple Dolls & Dresses, Saalfield #2112, 1934, uncut, M .250.00
Susan Dey as Laurie, Artcraft #4218, 1971, uncut, M 35.00
Tammy & Pepper, Whitman #1997, 1965, uncut, M, from $35 to ..45.00
Teddy Bear, J Ottmann, doll w/5 outfits, EX in envelope............200.00
Teen Queens, Lowe #2710, 1957, uncut, M 20.00
That Girl, Saalfield #4479, 1967, uncut, M, from $75 to...........100.00
Tiny Rescue Patrol, Whitman #1916-1, 1978, stand-ups, uncut, M .8.00
Twiggy, Whitman #1999, 1967, uncut, M 50.00
Virginia Mayo, Saalfield #4422, 1957, uncut, M........................125.00
Walt Disney's Fantasia, Whitman #950, 1940, stand-ups, uncut, M..200.00
Walt Disney's Mary Poppins, Whitman #1982, 1964, uncut, M....40.00
Wonder Woman, Whitman #1398, 1979, uncut, M 25.00
Ziegfield Girls, Merrill #3466, 1941, uncut, M 400.00

Paperweights

Glass paperweight collecting has become a feverish passion, growing in intensity in the past few years. Perhaps it is because there are many glass artists in the marketplace today who are creating beautiful examples, and a beginning collector can pick up these lovely objets d'art for under $100.00. Hundreds of glass artisans in the U.S. and factories in China, Italy, and Scotland produce 'gift range' paperweights. Collectors have the choice of forming their collections strictly in that price range, or can choose to select pieces that range in the thousands of dollars — and everything in between. Additionally, astute collectors are beginning to piece together collections of the old Chinese paperweights that were imported into this country first during the 1930s. These were basically unrefined imitations of the lovely and unique French weights of the mid-1800s. When viewed some seventy years later, however, one can appreciate the beauty and craftsmanship of these weights. Murano weights, especially those from the 1960s and 1970s, represent another area of concentrated interest. Prices are beginning to escalate in both categories. We note an increase of collectors interested in frit weights, Victorian portrait paperweights, and early advertising weights — all of which are still relatively inexpensive and abundant. Collectors who have a larger budget for these exquisite 'glass balls' may form their collection with only antique French paperweights from the classic period (1845 – 1860), the wonderful English or American weights from the 1850s, or choose to collect the high quality contemporary artistry of master glass artists. The door is wide open for everyone to begin collecting paperweights in whatever price range, and the Paperweight Collector's Association, Inc., with chapters in many states, can be of great assistance to collectors at all levels.

Baccarat, St. Louis, and Clichy, names synonymous with classic French paperweights, as well as some American factories stopped production of paperweights between the 1880s and 1910 due to a decline in popularity. In the 1950s Baccarat and St. Louis again began paperweight production and continue their lines of high quality, limited production weights. Other factories producing high quality millefiori and lampworked weights today include Perthshire and Caithness/Whitefriars (Scotland). In the 1960s many glass studios began to spring up due to the development of smaller glass furnaces, thereby allowing more freedom for the individual glassmaker to design and fabricate a piece of glass from the fire to the annealing kiln. Such success stories are evident in the creative glass produced by Landberg Studios, Orient and Flume, and Lotton Studios, to name but a few.

Many factors determine value, particularly of antique weights, and auction-realized prices of contemporary weights usually differ from issue price. Of course, competition among new collectors entering the field has greatly influenced prices as have Internet auction sales. As the number of collectors increases, available antique weights decrease per capita, forcing prices upwards. Antique paperweights have steadily increased in value as has the work of many now-deceased glass artists (i.e., Paul Ysart, Joe St. Clair, Charles Kazian, Del Tarsitano).

The dimension given at the end of the line is diameter. Prices are for weights in perfect or near-perfect condition, unless otherwise noted. Our advisors for this category are Betty and Larry Schwab, The Paperweight Shoppe; they are listed in the Directory under Illinois.

Key:
con — concentric   jsp — jasper
(d) — deceased   latt — latticinio
fct — faceted   mill — millefiori
gar — garland   o/l — overlay
grd — ground   sil — silhouette

Ayotte, Rick

Blk cherry bouquet, 1992, 3⅝" 700.00
Butterfly flying above flowering branch w/leaves, 1993, 2x3½" ..700.00
Hummingbirds/pk flowers/bl-gr leaves on bl mottle, 1997, 4" 800.00
Yel rose bouquet, 1995, 3¾" 1,500.00

Baccarat, Antique

White clematis with honeycomb cane center and bud on leafy stem, clear ground with ring of red and white canes, star-cut base, 1¾x2½", $1,600.00. (Photo courtesy Skinner, Inc.)

Clematis & bud, red/wht cane ring, star-cut base, 2½ 1,600.00
Clematis & gar w/bud, ribbed star-cut base, 2¾" 1,050.00
Close-pack mill w/animal canes, 1847, bruise, 3¼" 2,500.00
Dog Rose w/leaves & stem, star-cut base, 1⅞" 650.00
Looped gar of yel/red/gr/wht, 1-6 fcts, 3" 600.00
Pansy w/leaves & bud, stardust central cane, bubble, 2⅞" 650.00
Pompon in red/wht/bl gar, 1-6 fcts, watermelon-cut base, 2¾"...2,500.00
Primrose w/leaves & bud in gar, 1-6 fcts, 2¾" 3,500.00
Scattered mill w/sil of bee/elephant/etc, 1847, 2¾" 2,000.00

Wheatflower w/gr leaves in mc gar, 1-6 fcts, 2¾" 3,750.00

Baccarat, Modern

Gr/wht, dbl, 5 cut fcts, fireworks canes, cut base, 3"+, MIB 800.00
Gridel lovebirds, 1976, wht on blk w/purple & bl, 1976, 3x5x5" .600.00
Gridel squirrel w/outer ring of 18 Gridel sil canes, 1972, 3⅛" 600.00
Gridel stag, sm Gridel animals throughout, 1976, 3x5x5", NMIB .600.00
John F Kennedy, cobalt o/l, MIB 160.00
Red/wht dbl o/l mushroom, 1-5 fcts, 1972, 3⅛" 600.00
Sulphide, Will Rogers, gr/wht/clear 100.00

Banford, Bob

Bl flower w/posy ring, 3"..500.00
Salamander & flower on pebbly earth grd, 3¼" 800.00
Veined bl flower on amber grd, 1-6 fcts, 3⅛" 800.00

Banford, Ray

Cabbage rose bouquet on bl grd, 1-6 fcts, 3¼" 450.00
Irises (3 yel), grid-cut base, 3¼" 550.00
Red & wht rose bouquet on cobalt, 3⅛" 550.00

Clichy, Antique

Barber pole chequer mill w/filigree twists on lace grd, 2½"......3,500.00
Chequer, complex mill canes w/pk/gr rose, wht latt twists, 2¾" 1,265.00
Close-pack mill complex canes in turq/wht basket, 1850s, 2⅝" 1,200.00
End of day, close complex mill canes w/2 pk & gr roses, 3".........865.00
Pattern mill, mini, 1⅞" 300.00
Pattern mill star-cut base, 3⅛"......................................450.00
Rose amid complex mill con canes in clear, 3" 1,380.00
Spaced mill canes form star shape on clear, 2½" 450.00
Sulfide, Geo Washington on bl grd, 2¾", EX 700.00
6 pk/gr loops w/lg mc central cane on sodden snow grd, 3¼" ..1,500.00

Donofrio, Jim

Flowers & berries on earth grd, 1992, 3⅜"...........................325.00
Flowers on wood planks w/2 bottles, 1993, 3½".......................325.00
Gnome, 2 Indian pots & orange flowers on earth grd, 1992, 3½"...400.00
Horse & jockey, 1996, 3⅜" 450.00
Night scene w/horse on dk bl, 1996, 3⅜"..............................375.00
Rattlesnake w/yel cactus flower on rocky grd, 1992, 3⅜" 375.00

Kaziun, Charles

Spider lily w/leaves on dk bl aventurine, ped, 2⅞x1¼"...............550.00
6 Clichy-style pastry mold mill canes on burgundy, 1-8-8 fcts, mini ...800.00

New England Glass, Antique

Close con mill mc canes w/wht 10-point star cane, 19th C, 2½" ..350.00
Nosegay w/in mc gar on swirled latt, 2¾", NM 400.00
Pattern mill w/wht-star gar w/mc canes on latt grd, 2½" 500.00
Pear, chartreuse w/blush, clear cookie glass base, late 19th C, 3"...700.00
Poinsettia, bl/wht/gr, placed bubbles, 3" 600.00
Scrambled mill w/5 rabbit sil canes, 3⅛" 1,100.00

Perthshire

Crown, Christmas, 1985, ltd edition 300 ....600.00
Hollow swan, multi-fct, 1973..700.00

Rosenfeld, Ken

Bouquet on desert grd, 1992, 3⅜"..500.00
Chili peppers, 1995, mini, 2½"...250.00
Daffodils w/ladybugs on gr, 1997, 3⅜"................................550.00
Flowering cacti on sand w/rocks, 1993, 2½x3¼"..............650.00
Lizard w/flower on pebbled grd, 1996, 2½"........................275.00
Morning glories & buds w/lady bug on pk opaque grd, 1977, 3¼" ..600.00

Sandwich Glass

Dahlia, centered by complex mc cane, 2 gr leaves, 3"............1,200.00
Flowers (5) in wht latt basket w/in 6 gr leaves, 2½" 1,200.00
Fruit in basket, trapped bubbles, wht latt, 19th C, 2½"..............500.00
Pear w/gr leaf on clear base, 2⅛" 825.00
Pears (2) w/stems & leaves, 2½"...550.00
Poinsettia, bl w/gr stem, 3 jeweled leaves on wht latt, 2½" 1,000.00
Poinsettia, pk w/5 gr leaves on latt grd, 2⅝" 350.00
Poinsettia w/gr leaves, mill cane center, bubbles, 3¼"................750.00
Poinsettia w/rose cane center, clear glass & EX latt, 3¼", EX.....500.00
Poinsettia-like bl flower w/2 dk gr leaves, bubbles, 1875, 3" 460.00

St. Louis, Antique

Bouquet w/matchstick center, red & wht torsade, 13 fcts, 1850s, 3" ..1,300.00
Con mill mc canes surrounded by pk & gr mill on wht latt bed, 2½" ...900.00
Dahlia w/5 leaves on latt grd, 1-6 fcts, 1850s, 3⅛" 800.00
Mushroom w/lg canes in bl & wht torsade, 2⅞"......................1,200.00
Pansy/clematis, purple & wht w/leaves, grid-cut base, 3" 1,500.00
Pears (3) & cherries (3) w/leaves on dbl-swirl latt basket, 2¾" ..1,200.00

St. Louis, Modern

Doily on turq grd, 1972 ....700.00
Red cherries on latt cushion, 1975 ....500.00

Tarsitano, Debbie

Dahlia (purple) w/4 wht flowers, 3⅛" 700.00
Floral bouquet, mc w/gr stems, star-cut base, 3¾"....................575.00
Pansies (2) & 6 pk & yel blossoms on stems, 3¼" 925.00
Rose-like flowers (3) on leafy stems, 2¼x3½" 900.00

Ysart, Paul

Con mill on bl, 3" 400.00
Flower w/gar on bl & wht grd, 2¼" 600.00
Harlequin bubble, 2¼"...200.00
Striped flower & bubbles on lav grd, 2¾" 475.00
Striped flower on clear con mill 1,200.00

Miscellaneous

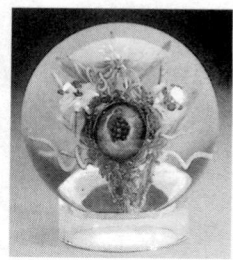

Cornflower, yellow flowers among leaves, green seed pod, sphagnum moss, ants, word canes, and spirit couple on reverse, 1998, 2¼x3⅛", $2,250.00.

Bohemian, con mill w/2 roses in 4-color torsade, 2¾", EX..........150.00

Bohemian, 8 colorful mill canes on lacy grd, 2⅞" 300.00
Gillinder, moving turtle in frosted hand..................................800.00
Lundberg, floral branch on cobalt, Salazar, 1988, 2¼x2¾" 265.00
Orient & Flume, dogwood blossoms on branch, 1985, ltd ed, 2¼" ..300.00
Smith, G; albino snake on mc grd, 1996, 3¼" 300.00
Smith, G; compound, upright underwater scene w/fish, 3¼" 475.00
Smith, G; dbl koi over sandy rocky grd, 1996, 3⅛" 500.00
Smith, Gordon; fish (2) in seascape, 1995, 3¼" 750.00
Whitefriars, close-pack mill, fcts, 1975, 1¾x3⅛" 400.00

Papier-Mache

The art of papier-mache was mainly European. It originated in Paris around the middle of the eighteenth century and became popular in America during Victorian times. Small items such as boxes, trays, inkwells, frames, etc., as well as extensive ceiling moldings and larger articles of furniture were made. The process involved building layer upon layer of paper soaked in glue, then coaxed into shape over a wood or wire form. When dry it was painted or decorated with gilt or inlays. Inexpensive twentieth-century 'notions' were machine processed and mold pressed. See also Christmas; Candy Containers.

Book stand, MOP inlay/gilt, HP florals, retracts/folds, 1850s, 7x13x5" ..440.00
Box, MOP star in lid, 1850s, 2½x3¼"................................200.00
Fire screen, HP decor on butterfly form, 1860s, 47" 375.00
Table, tilt-top, MOP inlaid flowers, allover gilt, tripod, 28x24" ..300.00
Tray, HP Jacobean scene, B Walton & Co, 1850s, 24x20", on stand..1,250.00
Wig stand, bust-length lady, pnt decor, late 1800s, 14½"............630.00

Parian Ware

Parian is hard-paste unglazed porcelain made to resemble marble. First made in the mid-1800s by Staffordshire potters, it was soon after produced in the United States by the U.S. Pottery at Bennington, Vermont. Busts and statuary were favored, but plaques, vases, mugs, and pitchers were also made.

Bust, classical female, highly detailed, unmk, 11", NM 140.00
Bust, 18th-C lady, mk Gille, Jne Fab, 11¾", EX 365.00
Busts, Apollo & Clytie, classical garb, 1850s, 10", pr 220.00
Figurine, classical goddess w/globe & calipers, 15½" 150.00
Figurine, gladiator dying, Bates, Brn-Westhead & Moore, 8½" ..700.00
Figurine, Mercury, Robinson & Leadbeater, late 1800s, 22⅜", EX...975.00
Figurine, nude lady in shackles, Copeland, 18½" 725.00

Parrish, Maxfield

Maxfield Parrish (1870 – 1966), with his unique abilities in architecture, illustrations, and landscapes, was the most prolific artist during 'the golden years of illustrators.' He produced art for more than one hundred magazines, painted girls on rocks for the Edison-Mazda division of General Electric, and landscapes for Brown & Bigelow. His most recognized work was 'Daybreak' that was published in 1923 by House of Art and sold nearly two million prints. Parrish began early training with his father who was a recognized artist, studied architecture at Dartmouth, and became an active participant in the Cornish artist colony in New Hampshire where he resided. Due to his increasing popularity, reproductions are now being marketed.

In our listings, values for prints apply to those that are in their original frames (or very nice and appropriate replacement frames) unless noted otherwise. For further information we recommend *Collector's Value*

Guide to Early 20th Century American Prints by Michael Ivankovich. Bobby Babcock, our advisor for this category, is listed in the Directory under Texas.

Ad, Saturday Evening Post, Edison/Mazda Lamps, full sheet, '24..**85.00**
Ad, Youth's Companion, Peter Peter Pumpkin Eater, full sheet, Feb 1919 ...**150.00**
Advertising postcard, Broadmoor, 1930-60, 4x6", ea **55.00**
Book, Arabian Nights, 12 plates, 1909, 1st ed **225.00**
Book, King Albert's Book, Dies Irae (color plate), 1914, NM.....**125.00**
Book, Knave of Hearts, hardbound, 1925, slightly scuffed, EX..**1,200.00**
Book, Tanglewood Tales, 1st edition, 1910, EX **225.00**
Book plate, Page, Knave of Hearts, fr, 1925, EX **75.00**
Book plate (King of Hearts), Bl & Yel Hose, chefs scene, 1925, 12x14" ...**95.00**
Book plate (Knave of Hearts), Manager Draws Curtain, 1925, 12x14"....**85.00**
Calendar, Ecstasy, Mazda, complete, 1930, 20½x14½", NM ...**2,150.00**
Calendar, New Moon, complete, 1958, 8½x6¾", EX.................**150.00**
Calendar, Old Glen Mill, 1954, 21½x16½", EX........................**450.00**
Calendar, Sunrise, Executive printing, 1955, 9x12"....................**275.00**
Calendar, Waterfall, Mazda, complete, 1931, 36x17", NM **2,000.00**
Calendar print, Sunrise, Brown & Bigelow, 20½x15" **375.00**
Magazine cover, Collier's, Boar's Head, Dec 16, 1905.................**175.00**
Magazine cover, Collier's, New Year's Number, Jan 6, 1906........**155.00**
Magazine cover, Collier's, permanent cover design, Aug 5, 1905..**35.00**
Magazine cover, Collier's, School Days, Sept 12, 1908.................**200.00**
Magazine cover, Ladies' Home Journal, Bud Below the Roses, May 1913 ...**115.00**
Magazine cover, Ladies' Home Journal, Shower of Fragrance, July 1912 ..**115.00**
Magazine cover, Life, A Man of Letters, Jan 5, 1922 ....**210.00**
Menu, Broadmoor Hotel, 1950-1960, 10x14" **175.00**
Playing cards, Dawn, Edison Mazda, MIB **525.00**
Playing cards, Ecstasy, Edison/Mazda, full deck, EX in box **325.00**
Playing cards, Waterfall, Edison/Mazda, full deck, EX in box.....**325.00**
Postcard; Pied Piper, 7x7" foldout, 1915....................................**225.00**
Postcard, The Tea Tray, 3½x5½" **400.00**
Poster, Century, nude in forest, orig fr, 1897, rare, 14x20" **1,730.00**
Print, Ancient Tree, massive oak, mtns beyond, 1952, 17x21" ...**400.00**
Print, Canyon, 1924, 12x15" **325.00**
Print, Christmas Morning, Brown/Bigelow, Executive print, 1948, 8x11"...**475.00**
Print, Circe's Palace, PF Collier, 1908, 9¼x11½"........................**175.00**
Print, Cleopatra, 1917, 24½x28"...**2,300.00**
Print, Daybreak, 1922, 6x10" **150.00**
Print, Dream Gardens, brochure for Curtis Publishing, 1915, 4x6¼"....**70.00**
Print, Errant Pan, hand-cvd fr, 1910, 11x9", NM **400.00**
Print, Fisherman & Genie, orig label, 1906, 9x11", NM.............**250.00**
Print, Garden of Allah, ornate fr, 1918, 15x30"..........................**550.00**
Print, Hilltop, Art Nouveau fr, 1927, scarce, 12x20".................**550.00**
Print, Hilltop, 1917, cvd fr, 18x30" **715.00**
Print, Lantern Bearers, 1910, 9x11"...**550.00**
Print, Lights of Welcome, Executive printing, 1945, 9x12" **300.00**
Print, Old King Cole, 1896, 6½x25" **1,200.00**
Print, Page, 1928, 10x12"...**175.00**
Print, Polly Put the Kettle On, Jell-O, 1923, 10x14"...................**100.00**
Print, Prince, 1928, 10x12"...**185.00**
Print, Valley of Enchantment, Brown & Bigelow, 1946, 5x6" **85.00**
Print, Waterfall, 1931, 8x10", EX **400.00**
Print, Winter Twilight, Executive print, 1941, 9x12" **350.00**

Pate-De-Verre

Simply translated, pate-de-verre means paste of glass. In the manufacturing process, lead glass is first ground, then mixed with sodium silicate solution to form a paste which can be molded and refired. Some of the most prominent artisans to use this procedure were Almaric Walter, Daum, Argy-Rouseau, and Decorchemont. See also specific manufacturers.

Vase, sleeping man, ruby/gr, shouldered, Despret, 6" L **875.00**
Vase, 3 pairs of intertwined salamanders/seaweed, Decorchement, 7" ...**3,750.00**

Pate-Sur-Pate

Pate-sur-pate, literally paste-on paste, is a technique whereby relief decorations are built up on a ceramic body by layering several applications of slip, one on the other, until the desired result is achieved. Usually only two colors are used, and the value of a piece is greatly enhanced as more color is added.

Charger, nymphs in water landscape, George Jones, signed Schenck, 12", $1,200.00.

Charger, maidens in woods, Schenk, Geo Jones, 1880s, 12" **1,265.00**
Plaque, putti/medallions, gr/wht/salmon, Alboin Birks, ca 1880s, 5" ..**300.00**
Plaque, Silver Age, female by plow, England, 19th C, 7⅛".........**700.00**
Plate, cherub cartouch, pierced rim w/gold, Minton, 1856, 9½", pr...**4,895.00**
Plate, Cupid medallion, A Birks, Minton, 10½" **1,800.00**
Salt cellar, HP decor in style of St Porchaire faience, Toft, 1879, 5" ..**1,100.00**
Stein, cavalier & older man at table, child w/boot on lid, .5L.**1,100.00**
Vase, angel w/ft bound below stars, Louis Solon, 1865, 7⅜" **525.00**
Vase, draped nymph w/poppy on dusty pk w/in wreath fr on MOP, 9½" ...**850.00**
Vase, foliate bands & lion masks, mc on plum to brn, C Toft, 14½"..**1,450.00**
Vase, pilgrim; grapes, foliate trim, Minton, 1885, 10¼" **925.00**
Vase, 2 scenes on gr w/gold, G Jones, late 19th C, 4".................**850.00**

Pattern Glass

Pattern glass was the first mass-produced fancy tableware in America and was much prized by our ancestors. From the 1840s to the Civil War, it contained a high lead content and is known as 'Flint Glass.' It is exceptionally clear and resonant. Later glass was made with soda lime and is known as non-flint. By the 1890s pattern glass was produced in great volume in thousands of patterns, and colored glass came into vogue. Today the highest prices are often paid for these later patterns flashed with rose, amber, canary, and vaseline; stained ruby; or made in colors of cobalt, green, yellow, amethyst, etc. Demand for pattern glass declined by 1915, and glass fanciers were collecting it by 1930. No other field of antiques offers more diversity in patterns, prices, or pieces than this unique and historical glass that represents the Victorian era in America.

Our advisor for this category is Darlene Yohe; she is listed in the Directory under Arkansas. For a more thorough study on the subject, we recommend *Field Guide to Pattern Glass* by Mollie Helen McCain; *Standard Encyclopedia of Pressed Glass, 1860 – 1930, Identification & Values*, by Bill Edwards and Mike Carwile; and *Early American Pattern Glass* and *Much More Early American Pattern Glass* by Alice Hulett Metz. All are available from Collector Books. See also Bread Plates; Cruets; Historical Glass; Salt and Pepper Shakers; Salts, Open; Sugar Shakers; Syrups; specific manufacturers such as Northwood.

Note: Values are given for open sugar bowls and compotes unless noted 'w/lid.'

Acorn, butter dish 85.00
Acorn Band, bowl 30.00
Acorn Band, wine 15.00
Actress, bowl, 6-9½", from $50 to 90.00
Actress, cheese dish 275.00
Actress, tumbler 80.00
Ada, celery dish 20.00
Admiral Dewey, See Dewey; See Also Greentown Dewey
Adonis, cake plate 25.00
Adonis, spooner 25.00
Alabama, butter dish, ruby stain 145.00
Alabama, nappy 30.00
Alaska, celery tray 70.00
Alaska, pitcher 85.00
Almond, tray, wine 30.00
Amazon, butter dish 55.00
Amazon, pitcher 65.00
Amberette, See Klondike
Amboy, butter dish 65.00
Amboy, goblet 35.00

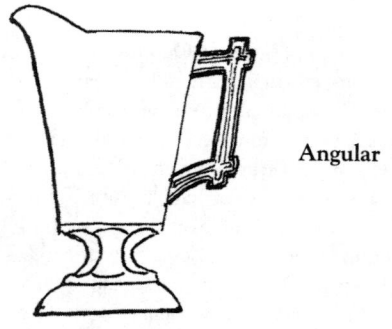

Angular

Angular, butter dish 65.00
Angular, tumbler 25.00
Arcadia Lace, candy dish, w/lid 35.00
Arcadia Lace, wine 20.00
Arch & Forget-Me-Not Bands, creamer 25.00
Arched Fleur-de-Lis, banana stand 35.00
Arched Fleur-de-Lis, pitcher 100.00
Arched Grape, butter dish, nonflint 48.00
Arched Grape, tumbler 20.00
Arched Ovals, plate 30.00
Arched Ovals, wine 20.00
Argent, bread plate, 13x9" 45.00
Argus, ale glass, flint 80.00
Argus, champagne 25.00
Arrowhead-in-Oval, basket 50.00
Arrowhead-in-Oval, celery dish 20.00
Art, banana stand 98.00
Art, goblet 40.00
Artichoke, bowl, 7-8" 35.00
Ashman, bread tray 30.00
Ashman, wine 15.00
Aurora, butter dish 75.00
Austrian, bowl, 8" 48.00
Austrian, pitcher 80.00
Baby Face, butter dish 275.00
Balder, See Pennsylvania
Baltimore Pear, bowl, 8" 22.00

Baltimore Pear, butter dish 75.00
Bamboo Beauty, butter dish 90.00
Bamboo Beauty, creamer or spooner 35.00
Banded Buckle, cordial 20.00
Banded Diamond Point, goblet 35.00
Banded Diamond Point, sugar bowl 25.00
Banded Star, celery vase 15.00
Banded Star, tumbler 20.00
Bar & Block, bowl, finger 15.00
Bar & Block, relish 25.00
Barrel Huber, See Huber
Beaded Band, compote 45.00
Beaded Band, creamer 32.00
Beaded Diamond, bowl, berry; sm 20.00
Beaded Diamond, sugar bowl 25.00
Beaded Grape, butter plate 25.00
Beaded Grape, sugar bowl 30.00
Beaded Tulip, butter dish 85.00
Beaded Tulip, goblet 38.00
Beaded Tulip, ice cream dish 20.00
Beaded Tulip, tumbler 15.00
Bearded Head, See Viking
Bethlehem Star, celery vase 20.00
Bethlehem Star, relish 15.00
Bird & Strawberry, bowl, flat, 9" 50.00
Bird & Strawberry, butter dish 100.00
Bird & Strawberry, plate, sandwich 100.00
Bleeding Heart, bowl, 8" 36.00
Bleeding Heart, honey dish 25.00
Block & Circle, butter dish 55.00
Block & Fan, biscuit Jar 50.00
Block & Fan, butter dish, ruby stain 90.00
Block & Fan, pitcher, milk 50.00
Blue Jay, See Cardinal Bird
Bow Tie, bowl, 7-11", from $15 to 55.00
Bow Tie, compote, high std, 7-11", from $35 to 85.00
Bow Tie, salt cellar, master 20.00
Brazen Shield, bowl, berry; sm 15.00
Brazen Shield, pickle dish 20.00
Brittanic, banana stand 85.00
Brittanic, custard cup 10.00
Broken Column, biscuit jar 80.00
Buckle w/Star, butter dish 75.00
Buckle w/Star, goblet 30.00
Buckle w/Star, relish tray 20.00
Bull's-Eye & Daisy, creamer or spooner 25.00
Bull's-Eye & Daisy, tumbler 20.00
Bull's-Eye & Fan, creamer 25.00
Bull's-Eye & Fan, pitcher 95.00
Bull's-Eye Band, See Reverse Torpedo
Bull's-Eye in Heart, See Heart w/Thumbprint
Button Arches, cake stand, ruby stain 175.00
Button Arches, compote, jelly 30.00
Button Panel, butter dish 60.00
Buzz-Star, bowl, berry; lg 45.00
Buzz-Star, salt cellar 15.00
Cabbage Rose, butter dish 65.00
Cabbage Rose, cake stand, 12½" 55.00
California, See Beaded Grape
Cane, celery vase 34.00
Cane, tumbler 20.00
Cannonball Pinwheel, butter dish 70.00
Cannonball Pinwheel, pitcher, milk 55.00
Cardinal Bird, butter dish 80.00

Cardinal Bird

Cardinal Bird, honey dish, w/lid 60.00
Cathedral, bowl, berry; 8" 42.50
Cathedral, tumbler 20.00
Centennial, See Liberty Bell
Chain, bowl, berry; sm 10.00
Chain, butter dish 45.00
Chain w/Star, cake stand 30.00
Chain w/Star, creamer 27.50
Chandelier, bowl, finger 35.00
Chandelier, creamer 35.00
Cherry & Cable, bowl, berry; sm 25.00
Church Windows, butter dish 65.00
Church Windows, sardine dish 25.00
Classic, compote, w/lid, 6½-12½", from $150 to 250.00
Clear Diagonal Band, butter dish 40.00
Clear Diagonal Band, pitcher 70.00
Cleopatra, See Egyptian
Coin, See US Coin
Comet, sugar bowl 25.00
Compact, See Snail
Connecticut, basket 35.00
Connecticut, plate 20.00
Cord Drapery, butter dish 55.00
Cord Drapery, creamer, bl 130.00
Cornucopia, bowl, berry; lg 50.00
Cornucopia, mug 30.00
Cosmos, creamer or spooner 20.00
Cottage, champagne 15.00
Cottage, pitcher, milk 45.00
Cottage, plate, 7" 22.50
Croesus, bowl, purple, 8" 155.00
Croesus, cake stand 60.00
Crow's Foot, See Yale
Crown Jewels, See Chandelier
Crystal Queen, basket 55.00
Crystal Wedding, celery 35.00
Crystal Wedding, salt cellar 20.00
Crystal Wedding, wine 98.00
Cube w/Fan, See Pineapple & Fan
Cupids, egg cup 30.00
Currier & Ives, creamer 35.00
Currier & Ives, tray, Balky Mule 75.00
Curtain Tie-Back, butter dish 45.00
Cut Log, banana stand 40.00
Cut Log, compote, w/lid, 5½-7½" 65.00
Cut Log, pitcher, water; ruby stain 250.00
Dahlia (Canton), cordial 20.00
Dahlia (Canton), wine 30.00
Daisy & Button (Hobbs), butter pat 30.00
Daisy & Button (Hobbs), ice tub 40.00
Daisy & Button w/Crossbars, bowl, 7-9" 30.00
Daisy & Button w/Crossbars, goblet 35.00
Daisy & Button w/V Ornament, bowl, finger 20.00
Daisy & Button w/V Ornament, celery vase 32.00

Daisy & Scroll, creamer or spooner 25.00
Daisy & Scroll, tumbler 20.00
Daisy-in-Square, bowl, berry; lg 35.00
Dakota, bottle, cologne 85.00
Dakota, celery tray 48.00
Dakota, goblet 50.00
Dart, bowl 25.00
Dart, compote, jelly 35.00
Deer & Dog, pitcher 175.00
Dew & Raindrop, goblet 35.00
Dew & Raindrop, sherbet 15.00
Dewdrop, cake tray, hdld 35.00
Dewdrop, sherbet 15.00
Dewey, breakfast set 75.00
Dewey, See Also Greentown Dewey
Diamond, compote 35.00
Diamond, pickle dish 15.00
Diamond Lattice, bowl, berry; lg 40.00
Diamond Lattice, plate 25.00
Diamond Medallion, See Grand
Diamond Spearhead, butter dish 65.00
Diamond Spearhead, rose bowl 25.00
Diamond Thumbprint, ale glass 90.00
Diamond Thumbprint, champagne 250.00
Diamond Thumbprint, wine 250.00
Dinner Bell, See Cottage
Doric, See Feather
Double Pinwheel, bowl, 7" 25.00
Double Pinwheel, pitcher 75.00
Egg in Sand, butter dish 65.00
Egg in Sand, goblet 35.00
Egg in Sand, sugar bowl 25.00
Egyptian, celery vase 85.00
Egyptian, sugar bowl 32.50
Egyptian, tray, rectangular 95.00
Elephant, See Jumbo
Emerald Green Herringbone, See Florida
English Colonial, claret 10.00
Esther, castor set 115.00
Esther, goblet 45.00
Etched Dakota, See Dakota
Eyewinker, banana dish 30.00
Eyewinker, compote, w/lid, 10-12½" 60.00
Eyewinker, plate, 7" sq 25.00
Fairfax Strawberry, See Strawberry
Falling Leaves, celery tray 25.00
Falling Leaves, pitcher, milk 45.00
Fancy Loop, bonbon 35.00
Fancy Loop, cracker jar, various, ea, from $25 to 45.00
Fandango, bottle, bar 35.00
Fandango, cookie jar, tall 50.00
Feather, cake stand, 8½" dia 42.50
Feather, plate, 10" 40.00
Feather Duster, egg cup 15.00
Festoon, compote, open 75.00
Festoon, plate, 7-9" 35.00
Festoon, tumbler 22.00
File, bottle, oil 70.00
File, rose bowl, 5½-7" 35.00
Fine Cut & Block, pitcher, amber 88.00
Fine Cut & Block, pitcher, milk 50.00
Fine Cut & Diamond, See Grand
Fine Cut & Fan, bowl, heart shape 30.00
Fine Cut & Fan, sugar bowl 25.00

Fine Cut & Feather, See Feather
Fishscale, bowl, 6" 38.00
Fishscale, butter dish 65.00
Fishscale, relish 20.00
Florida, celery vase 32.00
Flower Band, goblet 40.00
Flower Band, pitcher 85.00
Flower Pot, cake stand 50.00
Flower Pot, goblet 45.00
Flower Pot, tumbler 20.00
Flute & Cane, champagne 15.00
Flute & Cane, tumbler 15.00
Fringed Drape, vase, flat, 10-14" 45.00
Frosted Circle, butter dish 80.00
Frosted Circle, cake stand, 9½" 50.00
Frosted Circle, tumbler 20.00
Frosted Leaf, tumbler 45.00
Frosted Ribbon, See Ribbon
Frosted Stork, creamer or spooner 55.00
Frosted Stork, spooner 60.00
Frosted Stork, tumbler 35.00

Galloway

Galloway, butter dish 65.00
Galloway, champagne 70.00
Garfield Drape, pitcher, milk 65.00
Gem, See Nailhead
Good Luck, See Horseshoe
Gothic Windows, butter dish 65.00
Gothic Windows, sugar bowl 30.00
Grand, cake stand, 8-10" 35.00
Grand, decanter 70.00
Grand, spooner 20.00
Grape & Festoon, celery vase 30.00
Grape & Festoon, goblet 60.00
Grape & Festoon w/Shield, mug, 1⅞" 20.00
Grape w/o Vine, butter dish 65.00
Grape w/o Vine, tumbler 20.00
Grape w/Thumbprint, creamer 20.00
Grape w/Vine, bowl, lg 35.00
Grape w/Vine, compote 40.00
Grasshopper, butter dish 80.00
Grasshopper, celery vase 65.00
Hairpin, champagne, flint 78.00
Hand, cake stand 35.00
Hand, honey dish 35.00
Hand, pitcher 150.00
Hartley, goblet 50.00
Hartley, sugar bowl 25.00
Heart w/Thumbprint, bottle, barber 80.00
Heart w/Thumbprint, ice bucket 55.00
Herringbone Buttress, See Greentown, Herringbone Buttress
Hickman, compote, jelly 35.00

Hickman, pitcher, water 60.00
Hidalgo, cup & saucer 35.00
Hidalgo, tumbler 20.00
Hobnail w/Fan, butter dish 60.00
Hobnail w/Fan, pitcher 85.00
Hobstar & Feather, butter dish 200.00
Hobstar & Feather, tumbler 75.00
Holly, cake stand 140.00
Holly, egg cup 65.00
Holly Amber, See Greentown, Holly Amber
Honeycomb w/Star, celery vase 20.00
Honeycomb w/Star, pitcher 85.00
Honeycomb w/Star, sauce bowl, flat 10.00
Hops & Barley, See Wheat & Barley
Horseshoe, creamer 45.00
Horseshoe, plate, 8-10", ea 30.00
Huber, celery vase 40.00
Huber, decanter 65.00
Hummingbird, cheese plate 35.00
Hummingbird, wine 95.00
Idaho, See Snail
Illinois, box, puff 40.00
Illinois, olive dish 20.00
Indian Sunset, bowl, berry; lg 40.00
Indian Sunset, tumbler 20.00
Indiana, bowl, finger 20.00
Indiana, carafe 35.00
Inverted Feather, decanter 75.00
Inverted Strawberry, compote 50.00
Inverted Strawberry, goblet 60.00
Iris w/Meander, See Opalescent Glass
Jacob's Ladder, butter dish 80.00
Jacob's Ladder, honey dish 15.00
Jersey Swirl, butter dish, bl 70.00
Jersey Swirl, cake stand 35.00
Jersey Swirl, cup 10.00
Jewel & Dewdrop, cake stand 55.00
Jewel & Dewdrop, mug, 3½" 35.00
Job's Tear, See Art
Jubilee, celery tray 20.00
Jubilee, goblet 45.00
Jumbo, butter dish, elephant finial, rnd 725.00
Jumbo, pitcher 700.00
Jumbo, spoon rack 425.00
Kentucky, cake stand 40.00
Kentucky, tumbler 20.00
King's Crown, cake stand, 2 szs, ea 70.00
King's Crown, comote, open, 3 szs, ea, from $25 to 40.00
King's Crown, plate, 7" 15.00
King's Crown, saucer 15.00
Klondike, bowl, open, 7-8", from $60 to 80.00
Klondike, celery vase 90.00
Klondike, sugar bowl 125.00
Klondike, vase, frosted w/amber stain, trumpet form, 10" 300.00
Kokomo, casserole, w/lid 55.00
Kokomo, tumbler 25.00
La Clede, See Hickman
Lacy Dewdrop, bowl, berry; sm 20.00
Lattice, cake stand 35.00
Lattice, wine 15.00
Laverne, bowl, oval or rnd, ea, from $10 to 45.00
Leaf, See Maple Leaf
Leaf & Star, banana boat 40.00
Leaf & Star, goblet 50.00

Leaf Bracket, See Greentown, Leaf Medallion
Leaf Medallion, See Northwood, Leaf Medallion
Liberty Bell, butter dish................................165.00
Lincoln Drape, celery vase 80.00
Lincoln Drape, egg cup...................................70.00
Lincoln Drape, honey dish...............................35.00
Lincoln Drape, wine......................................150.00
Lion Head, compote, w/lid, 6-9", ea...............125.00
Lion Head, sugar bowl....................................75.00
Lion w/Cable, bread plate................................75.00
Lion w/Cable, jam jar.....................................70.00
Log Cabin, bowl, w/lid, 3⅝x9x5¼"...............120.00
Log Cabin, butter dish...................................325.00
Loop, bottle, bitters.......................................80.00
Loop, plate...30.00
Loop & Dart w/Diamond Ornament, egg cup....15.00
Loop & Dart w/Diamond Ornament, relish tray, oval 20.00
Manhattan, compote, 9½-10½", ea..................50.00
Manhattan, cup, punch...................................15.00
Manhattan, tumbler, iced tea...........................30.00
Maple Leaf, goblet, vaseline...........................160.00
Maple Leaf, tumbler.......................................20.00
Mardi Gras, cake stand...................................60.00
Mardi Gras, sherry...30.00
Maryland, cup...10.00
Maryland, pitcher, milk...................................50.00

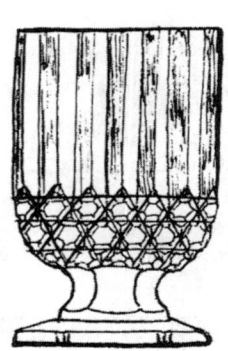

Masonic

Masonic, cake stand, 9-10", ea, from $35 to...........45.00
Masonic, relish..15.00
Massachusetts, butter dish...............................60.00
Massachusetts, goblet......................................40.00
Massachusetts, punch cup................................17.50
Medallion Sunburst, bowl, rnd or sq, ea.............25.00
Medallion Sunburst, tumbler............................15.00
Memphis, nappy..55.00
Memphis, punch bowl, w/base, regular.............350.00
Michigan, celery vase......................................25.00
Minerva, butter dish.......................................85.00
Minerva, pitcher, milk.....................................65.00
Minerva, waste bowl.......................................55.00
Minnesota, bowl, berry; lg...............................45.00
Minnesota, cup..17.50
Minnesota, mug...25.00
Missouri, cake stand.......................................35.00
Missouri, cordial..30.00
Missouri, sauce bowl, gr..................................12.50
Moon & Stars, bowl, salad...............................30.00
Moon & Stars, salt cellar.................................15.00
Moon & Stars, tumbler, flat..............................88.00
Nail, compote, berry.......................................30.00
Nail, goblet...55.00

Nailhead, bowl, berry; sm................................15.00
Nailhead, creamer..20.00
Nailhead, wine..38.00
New England Pineapple, champagne................190.00
New England Pineapple, egg cup......................45.00
New Hampshire, biscuit jar..............................45.00
New Hampshire, spooner..................................25.00
New Hampshire, wine, flared............................20.00
New Jersey, celery tray....................................25.00
New Jersey, olive dish.....................................25.00
Niagara, compote...30.00
Niagara, plate..25.00
Oaken Bucket, See Wooden Pail
Octagon, bowl, berry; lg..................................35.00
Octagon, pitcher, standard sz............................70.00
One Hundred & One, butter dish.......................65.00
One Hundred & One, creamer...........................55.00
One-O-One, See One Hundred & One
Optical Tube, See Tile
Oregon #1, carafe..45.00
Oregon #1, goblet..35.00
Oregon #1, mug..25.00
Palmette, cup plate...57.50
Palmette, tumbler, 2 szs, ea, from $35 to.............60.00
Panelled Diamond Blocks, sugar bowl.................25.00
Panelled Forget-Me-Not, butter dish...................50.00
Panelled Strawberry, bowl, berry; lg....................45.00
Panelled Strawberry, tumbler............................15.00
Panelled Thistle, butter dish.............................45.00
Pennsylvania, carafe.......................................50.00
Pennsylvania, goblet.......................................40.00
Persian, butter dish...65.00
Persian, cheese dish..65.00
Pigmy, See Torpedo
Pineapple & Fan, decanter...............................35.00
Pineapple & Fan, vase, trumpet form, 10"............35.00
Pioneer, See Westward Ho
Pleat & Panel, cake stand.................................35.00
Pleat & Panel, tray, water.................................25.00
Polar Bear, creamer......................................145.00
Polar Bear, ice bowl..95.00
Portland, basket...50.00
Portland, celery vase.......................................20.00
Portland, cup..20.00
Portland, pitcher, milk.....................................65.00
Portland, tray, water..35.00
Prayer Rug, See Horseshoe
Pressed Leaf, spooner......................................25.00
Pressed Leaf, wine..15.00
Priscilla, banana stand.....................................50.00
Priscilla, relish..15.00
Prism, champagne..15.00
Prism, egg cup..10.00
Prism, pitcher..60.00
Queen Anne, plate...20.00
Raindrop, butter dish......................................55.00
Raindrop, wine..15.00
Recessed Pillared Red Top, See Nail
Red Block, creamer or spooner, ea.....................70.00
Red Block, rose bowl......................................75.00
Red Top, See Button Arches
Reverse Torpedo, banana dish...........................35.00
Reverse Torpedo, cake stand, high standard..........80.00
Reverse Torpedo, fruit basket............................50.00

Rexford, butter dish 65.00
Rexford, goblet...50.00
Ribbed Palm, celery vase 20.00
Ribbed Palm, egg cup 15.00
Ribbon, cake stand 60.00
Ribbon, tumbler...30.00
Ribbon Candy, cake plate 35.00
Rising Sun, compote..45.00
Rising Sun, pitcher..75.00
Robin Hood, compote..35.00
Robin Hood, pickle dish......................................15.00
Rochelle, See Princess Feather
Roman Key, champagne 15.00
Roman Key, egg cup 20.00
Roman Rosette, cake stand, 2 szs, ea, from $35 to 45.00
Roman Rosette, creamer.......................................32.00
Roman Rosette, tumbler.......................................20.00
Romeo, See Block & Fan
Rose in Snow, compote, high or low, w/lid, ea, from $95 to........140.00
Rose in Snow, sweetmeat, w/lid............................100.00
Rose in Snow, tumbler..60.00
Rosette, champagne 42.50
Rosette, fish relish 35.00
Royal Ivy, See Northwood
Royal Oak, See Northwood
Ruby Diamond, sugar bowl...................................40.00
Ruby Diamond, tumbler.......................................20.00
Ruby Thumbprint, See King's Crown
S-Repeat, condiment tray, amethyst 40.00
S-Repeat, decanter...100.00
S-Repeat, sugar bowl 45.00
Saint Bernard, butter dish 65.00
Saint Bernard, tumbler...20.00
Sawtooth, carafe...55.00
Sawtooth, gas shade..60.00
Sawtooth, spill holder 20.00
Sawtooth, spooner, nonflint 60.00
Sawtooth Band, See Amazon
Scalloped Daisy Red Top, See Button Arches
Scroll w/Flowers, cake plate 40.00
Scroll w/Flowers, tumbler 20.00
Seneca Loop, See Loop
Sequoia, bowl, finger..20.00
Sequoia, tray, brandy 20.00
Sheaf & Block, creamer or spooner 25.00
Sheaf & Block, wine...15.00
Shell & Jewel, pitcher 90.00
Shell & Tassel, bowl, berry; sm 15.00
Shell & Tassel, oyster dish 235.00
Shelton Star, butter dish 50.00
Shelton Star, sugar bowl.......................................25.00
Sheraton, goblet...40.00
Sheraton, goblet, bl 48.00
Shuttle, cordial 15.00
Shuttle, goblet..65.00
Shuttle, mug...20.00
Snail, banana stand 160.00
Snail, bowl, finger..55.00
Snail, celery tray 35.00
Snow Flake, butter dish 65.00
Snow Flake, vase, 5-8¼", ea..................................35.00
Spirea Band, goblet..45.00
Star & Crescent, pickle dish 15.00
Star & Crescent, pitcher 65.00

Star & Feather, creamer 35.00
Star & File, custard cup..15.00
Star & File, tumbler, juice....................................15.00
Star in Bull's-Eye, butter dish 50.00
Star in Bull's-Eye, goblet 35.00
Star Medallion, tumbler.......................................15.00
Stars & Stripes, butter dish..................................65.00
Stars & Stripes, sugar bowl 25.00
Stars & Stripes, wine..18.00
States, cocktail...27.50
States, relish...25.00
Stippled Chain, cake stand 35.00
Stippled Chain, goblet..24.00
Stippled Chain, pitcher..85.00
Stippled Cherry, bowl, berry; lg...........................50.00

Stippled Forget-Me-Not

Stippled Forget-Me-Not, butter dish....................80.00
Stippled Medallion, cake plate.............................30.00
Stippled Medallion, plate.....................................20.00
Strawberry, butter dish...55.00
Strawberry, honey dish 15.00
Strawberry, salt cellar, gr......................................185.00
Strawberry & Cable, goblet...................................25.00
Strawberry & Cable, sweetmeat, w/lid, 2 styles, ea 95.00
Sunbeam, carafe..35.00
Sunbeam, tumbler...20.00
Sunk Daisy, carafe..35.00
Sunk Honeycomb, wine, eng................................20.00
Swag w/Brackets, cruet...160.00
Swirl & Ball, cake stand.......................................40.00
Swirl & Ball, candlestick.......................................30.00
Tarantem's Virginia, compote...............................35.00
Tarantem's Virginia, egg cup 15.00
Teardrop, bowl(s), sq, ea, from $20 to 45.00
Teardrop, pickle dish 15.00
Teardrop, pitcher 65.00
Teardrop & Tassel, pitcher....................................175.00
Teardrop & Tassel, relish.......................................36.00
Teasel, cracker jar...40.00
Texas, butter dish 50.00
Texas, creamer 50.00
Texas, horseradish, w/lid 55.00
Texas, tumbler..35.00
Theatrical, See Actress
Thousand Eye, butter dish....................................60.00
Thousand Eye, dish, sq, 5-10", ea, from $30 to 55.00
Thousand Eye, nappy, bl, 5" 45.00
Three Face, biscuit jar..350.00
Three Face, compote, low, w/lid, 6-10", ea............175.00
Three Face, cracker jar..1,350.00
Three Panel, goblet 35.00
Three Panel, spooner..16.00

Three-in-One, cake stand	55.00
Three-in-One, decanter, wine	70.00
Three-in-One, punch bowl	135.00
Thumbprint, See Argus	
Thumbprint Band, See Dakota	
Thunderbird, See Hummingbird	
Tile, cake stand	35.00
Tile, goblet	45.00
Tokyo, compote	25.00
Torpedo, banana stand	60.00
Torpedo, cup & saucer	25.00
Tree of Life, See Portland	
Tree of Life w/Hand, cake stand, frosted base, 11½"	130.00
Truncated Cube, celery vase	30.00
Truncated Cube, goblet	50.00
Tulip w/Sawtooth, creamer, flint	88.00
Twin Snowshoes, creamer or spooner	20.00
Twin Snowshoes, tumbler	25.00
Twinkle Star, See Utah	
Two Panel, mug	30.00
Two Panel, tray, hdld	35.00
Two Panel, wine	30.00
US Coin, bowl, berry; frosted, 7"	325.00
US Coin, cake stand	450.00
US Coin, claret	80.00
US Coin, goblet, 2 styles, ea	65.00
US Coin, tumbler	45.00
US Sheraton, dresser set, 3-pc	70.00
US Sheraton, plate, sq	20.00
US Sheraton, sundae dish	20.00
Utah, cake plate	25.00
Utah, creamer	32.00
Utah, tumbler	20.00
Valencia Waffle, bread plate	35.00
Valencia Waffle, goblet	40.00
Viking, butter dish	110.00
Viking, egg cup	35.00
Viking, jar, apothecary	75.00
Waffle & Fine Cut, butter dish	65.00
Waffle & Fine Cut, wine	20.00
Waffle Variant, cheese dish, w/lid	60.00
Westward Ho, celery vase	100.00
Westward Ho, marmalade jar	250.00
Wheat & Barley, cake stand	35.00
Wheat & Barley, shakers, pr	40.00
Wildflower, butter dish	47.50
Wildflower, salt cellar	10.00
Willow Oak, cake stand	45.00
Willow Oak, tumbler	20.00
Wisconsin, bonbon, hdls, 4"	25.00
Wisconsin, cup & saucer	35.00
Wisconsin, plate, 5-7", ea	20.00
Wooden Pail, cake stand	45.00
Wooden Pail, tumbler	60.00
X-Ray, butter dish	90.00
X-Ray, creamer or spooner	25.00
X-Ray, tray, cloverleaf	45.00
Yale, cake stand	55.00
Yale, celery vase	20.00
Yale, relish, oval	15.00
Zipper, compote, w/lid	55.00
Zippered Heart, creamer or sugar bowl, ind, ea	20.00
Zippered Heart, orange bowl, 12"	85.00
Zippered Heart, rose bowl, ped ft	90.00

Paul Revere Pottery

The Saturday Evening Girls were a social group of young Boston ladies who met to pursue various activities, among them pottery making. Their first kiln was bought in 1906, and within a few years it became necessary to move to a larger location. Because their new quarters were near the historical Old North Church, they chose the name Paul Revere Pottery. With very little training, the girls produced only simple ware. Until 1915 the pottery operated at a deficit, then a new building with four kilns was constructed on Nottingham Road. Vases, miniature jugs, children's tea sets, tiles, dinnerware, and lamps were produced, usually in soft matt glazes often decorated with incised, hand-painted designs from nature. Examples in a dark high gloss may also be found on occasion.

Several marks were used: 'P.R.P.'; 'S.E.G.'; or the circular device, 'Boston, Paul Revere Pottery' with the horse and rider.

The pottery continued to operate; and even though their product sold well, the high production costs of the handmade ware caused the pottery to fail in 1946.

Plate, Give Us This Day Our Daily Bread, white on blue, SEG II-21 FL, 9¾", NM, $550.00. (Photo courtesy David Rago)

Bowl, brn w/tan int, SEG, 2¾x8½"	170.00
Bowl, centerpc; flower band on navy, PRP logo/1-26/JMD, 2x10", NM	750.00
Bowl, centerpc; lotus flowers, wht on jade gr, 5-26/Edith Brn, 2x10"	750.00
Bowl, cereal; geese on bl, ...Her Bowl, SEG/8-17/EG, 2¼x5½"	700.00
Bowl, gr, invt rim, TMLM, 8" dia, NM	100.00
Bowl, lotus designs, wht on bl, SEG/AM/11, 2¼x5½"	700.00
Bowl, rabbits (3) at rim, wht on bl, hairline, 2¼x5⅜"	800.00
Creamer, squirrel band on wht, sm chip, SEG/2-7-12/G?, 3¼x3¼"	350.00
Creamer, stylized lotus flowers on yel, SEG/10-20/LM, 2"	125.00
Creamer, 2-tone bl, banded, 2¼"	110.00
Cup & saucer, floral border, mc on cream, SG91.7.12/92.7.12SEG	575.00
Cup & saucer, ivory/blk band on sage gr, SEG/1913/1915/EG, 2", 5½"	100.00
Cup & saucer, multi-tone bl matt bands, 2½", 5½", 3 for	160.00
Egg cup, chick on bl, unmk, early 1900s, 1¼"	250.00
Egg cup, mother hen & chick, unmk, early 1900s, 1¾"	450.00
Inkwell, gr semimatt, SEG/RB/1918, 2½"	275.00
Paperweight, sailing ship on yel, octagonal, SEG/JG/3-15, 2½"	350.00
Paperweight, swan face, ivory on bl & yel, SEG/3-15/JG, 2½"	375.00
Paperweight, windmill, brn on bl, octagonal, SEG/9-20/EW, 2½"	475.00
Pitcher, rabbit reserve on lt bl, Jane, 4½"	425.00
Pitcher, trees/sky/hills, minor rstr, SEG/1-11-11/FL, 5x3¾"	550.00
Plate, dinner; Give Us This Day... on bl, SEG/11-21/FL, 9¾", NM	550.00
Plate, Eate Thy Breade in... in wht band on pk, PRP/9-36/LS, 9½"	450.00
Plate, gunmetal & gr matt, 6"	60.00
Plate, lt bl, 7½", 3 for	100.00
Plate, pine cones & needles on ivory, SEG/6-17-/EG, 6¼"	225.00
Tile, mc geometrics, SEG, oak fr, 6"	750.00
Tile, Paul Revere on horse, mc on gr & bl, unmk, 3", VG	250.00
Trinket holder, tulips, mc on ivory, SEG/4-8-14/JG, 1½x3"	175.00
Vase, bl & gr matt drip, bulbous, flared rim, SEG, 6", NM	260.00

Vase, blk/gray/brn leopard skin, sgn RB, SEG, 6" **450.00**
Vase, bud; mocha brn satin, SEG/1913/SG, 4⅛" **325.00**
Vase, dk bl speckled gloss, stick neck, SEG/5-24/M, 7⅛" **345.00**
Vase, dove gray w/aqua speckles, ovoid, imp PRP mk, 5½x4" **125.00**
Vase, floral, yel & blk on cream, sgn EG, w/lid, sm rpr, 5" **400.00**
Vase, lotus band on bl-gray, SEG/AM/11-14, 4½x3¾" **1,100.00**
Vase, stylized petals, bl-gray & blk on dk bl semigloss, SEG, 8½"...**925.00**
Vase, trees band, bl semi-matt, ovoid, SEG/6/7/SG, 10¼x5"...**4,000.00**
Vase, tulips, yel & gr on bl, ovoid, 6½x5" **1,300.00**
Vase, tulips, yel on gr matt, stamp, illegible date, 5¾x4½" **1,100.00**
Vase, turq mottle, inverted rim, 1926, 7" **210.00**

Peachblow

Peachblow, made to imitate the colors of the Chinese Peachbloom porcelain, was made by several glasshouses in the late 1800s. Among them were New England Glass, Mt. Washington, Webb, and Hobbs, Brockunier and Company (Wheeling). Its pink shading was achieved through action of the heat on the gold content of the glass. While New England's peachblow shades from deep crimson to white, Mt. Washington's tends to shade from pink to blue-gray. Many pieces were enameled and gilded. While by far the majority of the pieces made by New England had a satin (acid) finish, they made shiny peachblow as well. Wheeling glass, on the other hand, is rarely found in satin. In the 1950s Gundersen-Pairpoint Glassworks initiated the reproduction of Mt. Washington peachblow, using an exact duplication of the original formula. Though of recent manufacture, this glass is very collectible. Our advisors for this category are Betty and Clarence Maier; they are listed in the Directory under Pennsylvania.

Bottle, scent; English, bulbous, sterling cap, 4¾x3½" **585.00**
Creamer, Wheeling, 3⅛" **885.00**
Creamer & sugar bowl, 1893 World's Fair, loop hdls, 3½x5", pr ..**925.00**
Cruet, Wheeling, faceted stopper, 6½", NM **900.00**
Cup, punch; NE Glass **385.00**
Pear, NE Glass, hollow stem, 4½", from $100 to **150.00**
Pitcher, ewer, Wheeling, appl rigaree at neck, conical body, 9½" ..**7,000.00**
Pitcher, tankard, Wheeling, amber hdl, 9½" **5,000.00**
Pitcher, Wheeling, quatreform, bulbous, amber hdl, 5¼"............**400.00**
Pitcher, Wheeling, shiny, sq top, 7" **1,400.00**
Pitcher, Wheeling, sq top, amber hdl, 5½", from $750 to........**1,100.00**
Pitcher, Wheeling, sq top, 7" **1,400.00**
Rose bowl, NE Glass, satin, ruffled rim, 5x9½" **150.00**
Rose bowl, NE glass, World's Fair 1893, 3¾x3¾" **325.00**
Rose bowl, Webb, gold floral & berry branches, scalloped, 3".....**375.00**
Sugar shaker, Wheeling, screw-on gunmetal-color lid, 5½" **1,950.00**
Toothpick holder, Mt WA, sq rim, 2¾" **1,300.00**
Tumbler, NE Glass..**225.00**
Tumbler, NE Glass, shiny, 3¾" **250.00**
Vase, lily; NE Glass, scarce sz, 7" **785.00**
Vase, lily; NE Glass, shiny, EX deep color, 18¾x7" **1,150.00**
Vase, lily; NE Glass, 8" **750.00**
Vase, Morgan; Wheeling, satin, 7¾" **500.00**
Vase, Morgan; Wheeling, plastic, 5-headed griffin holder, 10"..**1,000.00**
Vase, Morgan; Wheeling; orig 5-headed amber griffin holder, 10"...**2,700.00**
Vase, Mt WA, gourd shape, 8¼" **1,900.00**
Vase, Mt WA, shiny, tapered sides, rough pontil, 9¾" **1,700.00**
Vase, NE Glass, shiny, bulbous, sq top, 5" **125.00**
Vase, Webb, gold branches w/purple-bl plums, #579, 9", pr **450.00**
Vase, Webb, gold prunus, stick neck, 10¼" **485.00**
Vase, Webb, HP plums w/gold branches & leaves, #579/1 W134 II, 9"..**450.00**
Vase, Webb, ovoid, ftd, 9" **150.00**
Vase, Webb, stick neck, 10¾", NM..**350.00**

Vase, Wheeling, elongated oval, tapered base/rim, 13¾" **545.00**
Vase, Wheeling, shouldered, 8½" **750.00**
Vase, Wheeling, stick neck, 10½" **900.00**

Peking Cameo Glass

The first glasshouse was established in Peking in 1680. It produced glassware made in imitation of porcelain, a more desirable medium to the Chinese. By 1725 multilayered carving that resulted in a cameo effect lead to the manufacture of a wider range of shapes and colors. The factory was closed from 1736 to 1795, but glass made in Po-shan and shipped to Peking for finishing continued to be called Peking glass. Similar glassware was made through the first half of the twentieth century. See also Orientalia.

Belt buckle, Daoist scene, red on wht, rectangle, 1800s, 2¾" **875.00**
Bowl, prunus & rockwork, cobalt on wht, 1940s, 2½x4½" **55.00**
Cup, dragon panels in high relief, yel on wht, 1800s, 4½" **800.00**
Jar, ginger; faceted honeycomb-like cuttings, turq on wht, 4" **110.00**
Snuff bottle, cabbage form, gr to wht, 1950s, 2"............................**85.00**
Vase, floral, red on wht, late, 8¾" **225.00**
Vase, rams in landscape, lappet bands, cobalt on wht, 1800s, 9"...**1,750.00**

Peloton

Peloton glass was first made by Wilhelm Kralik in Bohemia in 1880. This unusual art glass was produced by rolling colored threads onto the transparent or opaque glass gather as it was removed from the furnace. Usually more than one color of threading was used, and some items were further decorated with enameling. It was made with both shiny and acid finishes.

Biscuit jar, bl w/mc strings, SP lid w/flowers & bird in flight, 7".**500.00**
Bowl, wht w/brn & yel strings, ribbed, 3 clear thorn ft, 6x6½"...**325.00**
Cruet, bl w/mc strings, swirl mold, faceted ball stopper, 7" **500.00**
Pitcher, water; yel w/mc strings, reeded hdl **675.00**
Vase, clear w/wht strings & HP flowers, shouldered, 6¼" **1,750.00**
Vase, pk w/mc strings, pinched middle, 3½x3x3⅞" **225.00**
Vase, wht w/mc strings, tricorner, 4x4¾" **295.00**

Pennsbury

Established in the 1950s in Morrisville, Pennsylvania, by Henry Below, the Pennsbury Pottery produced dinnerware and novelty items, much of which was sold in gift shops along the Pennsylvania Turnpike. Henry and his wife, Lee, worked for years at the Stangl Pottery before striking out on their own. Lee and her daughter were the artists responsible for many of the early pieces, the bird figures among them. Pennsbury pottery was hand painted, some in blue on white, some in multicolor on caramel. Pennsylvania Dutch motifs, Amish couples, and barbershop singers were among their most popular decorative themes. Sgraffito (hand incising) was used extensively. The company marked their wares 'Pennsbury Pottery' or 'Pennsbury Pottery, Morrisville, PA.'

In October of 1969 the company closed. Contents of the pottery were sold in December of the following year, and in April of 1971, the buildings burned to the ground. Items marked Pennsbury Glenview or Stumar Pottery (or these marks in combination) were made by Glenview after 1969. Pieces manufactured after 1976 were made by the Pennington Pottery. Several of the old molds still exist, and the original Pennsbury Caramel process is still being used on novelty items, some of which are produced by Lewis Brothers, New Jersey. Production of Pennsbury dinnerware was not resumed after the closing. Our advisor for this category is Shirley Graff; she is listed in the Directory under Ohio. Note: Prices may be higher in some areas of the country — particularly on the East Coast, the southern states, and Texas. Values for examples in the Rooster pattern apply to both black and red variations.

Dispensers, vinegar and oil; Pennsylvania Dutch man and woman stoppers, $150.00 for the pair.

Ashtray, Pennsbury Inn, 8" 45.00
Bowl, Dutch Talk, 9" 90.00
Butter dish, Folk Art, 5x4" 45.00
Candy dish, Hex, heart shape, 6x6" 35.00
Casserole, Hex, w/lid, 6½" 65.00
Charger, St George Slaying Dragon, 13½" 225.00
Chip & dip, Holly, 11" 100.00
Chip & dip, Red Rooster, 11" 85.00
Cigarette box, appl eagle, 3½x5" 40.00
Cruets, oil & vinegar; Black Rooster, pr................................150.00
Desk basket, Lafayette, 4" 50.00
Desk basket, Two Women Under Tree, 5" 60.00
Dresser tray, Tulip, 7½x4" 35.00
Figurine, Blue Jay, #108, 10½" 450.00
Figurine, Crested Chickadees, #101, 4", pr.............................150.00
Figurine, Nut Hatch, #110, 3½", pr..120.00
Figurine, rooster & hen, many variations, ea pr.....................450.00
Figurine, Wood Duck, #114, 10" 375.00
Letter holder, Neshaminy Woods...55.00
Mug, Amish, 3¼" 30.00
Mug, beer; Fisherman, 5" 45.00
Mug, Coast Guard, 3¼" 25.00
Mug, Hex, 3½" 22.00
Mug, Quartet, 3¼" 35.00
Pitcher, milk; Rooster, 4" 20.00
Plaque, Cambden & Amboy RR, John Bull, NM 45.00
Plaque, Central RR of NJ 1870 Star 95.00
Plaque, Eagle, #P214, 22" 175.00
Plaque, Eagle, sm 60.00
Plaque, Fisherman, 5" 28.00
Plaque, Making Pie, 6" 60.00
Plaque, Philadelphia & Reading RR, camel-bk 45.00
Plaque, Swallow the Insult, 6" dia...50.00
Plaque, The Flying Cloud, 9½x7" 75.00
Plaque, Toleware, brn, 5x7" 40.00
Plaque, Western & Atlantic RR General 45.00
Plate, Bible Reading, w/o primary colors, 9" 75.00
Plate, Blue Dowery, 10" 35.00
Plate, Boy & Girl, 11" 85.00
Plate, Christmas, Angel, 1970..35.00
Plate, Family, 11" 110.00
Plate, Give Us This Day Our Daily Bread, 7½" 35.00
Plate, Laurel Ridge...35.00
Plate, Pea Hen, 11"...85.00

Plate, Red Rooster, 6"...22.00
Pretzel bowl, Gay Nineties, 12x8"..95.00
Pretzel bowl, Red Barn, 12x8"...150.00
Snack set, Red Rooster 30.00
Tray, Horses, octagonal, 5x3" 30.00
Wall pocket, eagle in relief, bellows shape 50.00

Pens and Pencils

The first metallic writing pen was patented in 1809, and soon machine-produced pens with steel nibs gradually began replacing the quill. The first fountain pen was invented in 1830, but due to the fact that the ink flow was not consistent (though leakage was), they were not manufactured commercially until the 1880s. The first successful commercial producers were Waterman in 1884 and Parker with the Lucky Curve in 1888.

The self-filling pen of the early 1900s featured the soft, interior sack which filled with ink as the metal bar on the outside of the pen was raised and lowered. Variations of the filling mechanisms were tried until 1932 when Parker introduced the Vacumatic, a sackless pen with an internal pump.

For more information we recommend *Fountain Pens, Past & Present*, by Paul Erano (Collector Books). Our advisor for this category is Gary Lehrer; he is listed in the Directory under Connecticut. For those seeking additional information, catalogs are published by our advisor as well as the Pen Fanciers, whose address can be found in the Directory under Clubs, Newsletters, and Catalogs.

Key:
AF — aeromatic filler
BF — button filler
CF — capillary filler
CPT — chrome-plated trim
ED — eyedropper filler
GFM — gold-filled metal
GFT — gold-filled trim
GPT — gold-plated trim
HR — hard rubber
LF — lever filler
NPT — nickel-plated trim
PF — plunger filler
PIF — piston filler
PKF — push knob filler
TD — touchdown filler
VF — vacumatic filler

Ballpoint Pens

Christian Dior, 1985, blk lacquer, GPT, NM....................................20.00
Garland, 1960, chrome, Flair top, NM 20.00
Parker 75, 1985, gr lacquer, GF cap w/gr cabochon, M 110.00

Fountain Pens

Aikin Lambert #2 Capitol Cabinet, 1920, LF, blk chased HR, NM..50.00
Carter's #2, 1925, LF, lapis w/GFT, med nib, NM 175.00
Chilton #4, 1923, LF, red mottled HR, GFT, #4 fine nib, NM ...250.00
Conklin #2, 1926, LF, deep jade w/GFT, med flexible nib, NM..200.00
Conklin #2, 1935, LF, silver pearl w/blk veins & red specks, NPT, NM...150.00
Conklin #4, 1931, LF, blk w/GFT, fine flexible nib, EX 125.00
Conklin Endura, 1927, LF, jade, GFT, red cap/bbl bands, lg, NM....550.00
Conklin Endura, 1927, LF, sapphire bl w/GFT, red cap/bbl bands, NM...650.00
Conklin Endura Jr, 1926, LF, sapphire bl, GFT, red inlay cap/bands, NM..200.00
Conklin Endura Jr, 1927, LF, blk/bronze, GFT, yel inlay cap/bands, NM...200.00
Conklin Symetric, 1932, PIF, red & silver pearl w/view of ink, NM...275.00
Conway Stewart #338, 1939, bl marble, GFT, broad nib, NM....125.00
Conway Stewart #60 Executive, 1950, cracked ice, GFT, M w/label..275.00
Eclipse #2, 1920, LF, blk chased HR, wht derby, NPT, NM..........80.00
Esterbrook Dollar, 1935, LF, pearl gray w/red specks, CPT, NM....85.00
Esterbrook Pastel, 1950, LF, pk, CPT, med nib, NM 60.00
Esterbrook Relief #12, 1950, LF, silver pearl web, GFT, Italic nib, NM..250.00

Mabie Todd Blackbird Demonstrator, 1938, BF, yel plastic, GFT, NM ...**200.00**
Mabie Todd Swan #2, 1933, LF, bl marble, NPT, med nib, NM .**125.00**
Mabie Todd Swan 44 Eternal, 1924, LF, blk chased HR, GF band, NM.**150.00**
Mentmore #6 Sz Auto-Flow, 1945, BF, lav pearl, GFT, 14k nib, NM **95.00**
Montblanc 20 Masterpc, 1935, PKF, coral red, GFT, EX+ **550.00**
Montblanc 136, 1947, PIF, blk, long window, GFT, wartime nib, NM...**700.00**
Montblanc 142, 1955, PIF, gr stripe, GFT, med nib, NM **800.00**
Montblanc 234½, 1936, PIF, platinum, GFT, med nib, NM **975.00**
Montblanc 242, 1950, PIF, platinum, GFT, med nib, NM **1,000.00**
Montblanc 244, 1946, BF, gr marble, GFT, med nib, NM **400.00**
Moore #2, 1942, LF, bronze & silver pearl w/blk pinstripe, GFT, NM...**100.00**
Moore #2.0 Safety, 1905, blk HR, unrstr, NM **100.00**
Moore #3, 1925, LF, burgundy, GFT, fine point, NM **100.00**
Moore #5 Deluxe, 1945, LF, gr pearl web, GFT, med nib, NM ...**100.00**
Osmia #882, 1950, LF, red marble, GFT, broad flexible nib, NM..**90.00**
Parker Challenger, 1937, BF, golden herringbone, GFT, NM......**275.00**
Parker Duofold, 1942, BF, bl & silver pearl w/blk stripes, GFT, NM ...**90.00**
Parker Duofold Jr, 1923, BF, red HR, med-sz imprint, GFT, med nib, EX+...**250.00**
Parker Duofold Jr, 1928, BF, blk, GFT, broad nib, EX+ **95.00**
Parker Duofold Jr Deluxe, 1932, Sea Green, GFT, broad nib, EX+...**200.00**
Parker Duofold Sr, 1930, BF, blk/Pearl Moderne, GFT, NM........**350.00**
Parker Duofold Sr, 1930, BF, burgundy, GFT, fine point, EX+ **400.00**
Parker Duofold Sr, 1930, BF, lapis, GFT, broad point, NM **700.00**
Parker Duofold Vest Pocket, 1930, BF, blk, GFT, med nib, NM .**150.00**
Parker Lady Duofold, 1924, red HR w/sm imprint, med nib, EX+..**150.00**
Parker Lady Duofold, 1927, BF, lapis, GFT, med nib, NM...........**250.00**
Parker Vacumatic Debutante, VF, 1939, gr laminated, GFT, NM .**95.00**
Parker Vacumatic Jr, 1938, VF, golden web, GFT, NM................**250.00**
Parker Vacumatic Sr Maxima, 1937, gold laminated, dbl jeweled, GFT, NM.....**450.00**
Parker Vacumatic Standard, 1936, VF, silver laminated, NPT, NM....**150.00**
Parker Vacumatic Standard, 1937, VF, gr laminated, GFT, NM .**200.00**
Parker 1st Year Jotter, 1957, gray, ribbed nylon bbl, NM................**65.00**
Parker 41 Aerometric, 1950, salmon w/brushed Lustraloy cap, NM **175.00**
Parker 51 Aerometric, 1948, tan & brushed Lustraloy, GFT, NM **110.00**
Parker 51 Aerometric Demonstrator, clear plastic, Lustraloy, GFT, NM...**225.00**
Parker 51 Aerometric Mark II, 1950, gray, GF cap, NM **125.00**
Parker 51 Vacumatic, 1944, Cordovan Brn, dbl-jewel, GF cap, NM **225.00**
Pelikan 12 Silvexa, 1971, PIF, blk, stainless cap, M w/label **50.00**
Pelikan 100 N, 1950, PIF, gray striped, bbl mk Export, GFT, NM...........**400.00**
Pelikan 100CN, 1936, gr pearl, GFT, smooth knob, wartime nib, NM ..**300.00**
Pelikan 140, 1952, PIF, blk, GFT, med nib, NM **75.00**
Pelikan 400, 1950, PIF, brn striped, GFT, NM.................................**125.00**
Pelikan 400 NN, 1956, blk, GFT, med nib, NM..............................**175.00**
Sheaffer Lifetime, 1922, LF, blk-lined HR, GFT, med nib, lg, EX+ ...**325.00**
Sheaffer Lifetime, 1924, LF, deep jade, GFT, med nib, lg, NM ...**225.00**
Sheaffer PFM I Snorkel, 1959, bl, CPT, med nib, NM.................**175.00**
Sheaffer PFM IV Snorkel, 1959, gr, orig decal, chrome cap w/GFT, NM .**425.00**
Sheaffer PFM V Snorkel, 1959, burgundy, GFT, fine point, NM...**375.00**
Sheaffer Secretary, 1933, LF, Fire Engine Red, GFT, lg, EX+ **900.00**
Sheaffer Valiant Snorkel, 1952, salmon, GFT, M **175.00**
Sheaffer WASP, 1943, LF, red pearl, GFT, med nib, NM...............**80.00**
Sheaffer 3-25, 1923, LF, Cardinal HR, GFT, med nib, NM............**195.00**
Sheaffer 5-30 Balance, 1933, LF, gr marble, GFT, NM **65.00**
Wahl Eversharp Doric, 1935, LF, Silver Pearl, GFT, triple nib, NM...**175.00**
Wahl Eversharp Doric, 1939, LF, blk, GFT, adjustable nib, NM.**125.00**
Wahl Eversharp Equipoised #2, 1938, LF, Lobster (rare color), GFT, NM **175.00**
Wahl Eversharp Equipoised #2 Gold Seal, 1941, burgundy, GFT, NM......**95.00**
Wahl Eversharp Fifth Ave, 1943, LF, blk w/14k gold cap, med nib, NM....**150.00**
Wahl Eversharp Oversz Deco Band, 1929, blk, GFT, med nib, NM ...**500.00**
Wahl Eversharp Oversz Deco Band, 1929, gr & bronze, GFT, NM.....**850.00**
Wahl Eversharp Skyline, 1942, bl Modern stripe, GFT, NM **175.00**
Waterman Patrician, 1929, LF, onyx, lt ambering, GFT, NM ..**1,300.00**
Waterman Patrician, 1929, moss agate, GFT, NM **1,250.00**
Waterman 2, 1907, ED, taper cap in blk chased HR, GFT, med nib, NM..**175.00**

Waterman 2, 1949, LF, bl marble, GFT, stub nib, NM..................**90.00**
Waterman 3, 1932, LF, grey pearl w/red specks, CPT, NM **75.00**
Waterman 3V, 1933, LF, silver & bronze pearl, CPT, NM.............**75.00**
Waterman 13, 1906, ED, blk HR, fine nib, NM **100.00**
Waterman 52V, 1928, blk chased HR, NPT, broad nib, dipped o/w M....**75.00**
Waterman 94, 1930, LF, bl cream w/orange specks, CPT, NM....**250.00**
Waterman 94, 1930, LF, brn cream (mahog), GFT, Italic nib, NM .**200.00**
Waterman 100 Year Oversz, 1942, LF, blk, smooth cap/bbl, GFT, EX+ ..**300.00**
Waterman 441S Safety, sterling on blk HR, Sheraton pattern, EX ...**800.00**
Waterman 452, 1915, LF, silver o/l on Cardinal HR, NM **2,000.00**
Waterman 512½ VS Safety, 1920, GF, pinstripe pattern, EX......**225.00**
Waterman 552 LEC, 1920, LF, 18k chicken-wire pattern, NM...**750.00**
Waterman 552, 1915, LF, GF Sheraton pattern, dipped o/w M...**425.00**
Waterman 5116, 1939, LF, blk, GFT, calligraphy nib, NM **175.00**

Mechanical

Parker Challenger Jr, 1937, silver herringbone, CPT, NM **100.00**
Parker Duofold Jr, 1930, blk, GFT, minor brassing, o/w NM **75.00**
Parker Vacumatic Debutante, 1940, silver laminated, NPT, NM..**35.00**
Parker Vacumatic Standard, 1937, gr laminated, GFT, NM **50.00**
Parker 51, blk w/14k smooth cap, twist mechanism, NM............**160.00**
Wahl Eversharp Doric, 1935, repeater, silver web, CPT, NM **100.00**

Sets

Moore L-95, 1925, dk bl, GFT, med nib, NM **250.00**
Parker 51 Aerometric, 1948, tan, GF cap w/5 pinstripes, NM **150.00**
Parker 51 Aerometric, 1949, plum, brushed Lustraloy cap, NM .**250.00**
Parker 51 Aerometric, 1950, Forest Gr, Lustraloy cap, repeater pencil..**225.00**
Pelikan 455 ball pen & 350 repeater pencil, 1955, GFT, NM.....**125.00**
Wahl Eversharp Doric, 1935, LF, blk, GFT, med nib, NM **195.00**

Personalities, Fact and Fiction

One of the largest and most popular areas of collecting today is character-related memorabilia. Everyone has favorites, whether they be comic-strip personalities or true-life heroes. The earliest comic strip dealt with the adventures of the Yellow Kid, the smiling, bald-headed Oriental boy always in a nightshirt. He was introduced in 1895, a product of the imagination of Richard Fenton Outcault. Today, though very hard to come by, items relating to the Yellow Kid bring premium prices.

Though her 1923 introduction was unobtrusively made through only one newspaper, New York's *Daily News*, Little Orphan Annie, the vacant-eyed redhead in the inevitable red dress, was quickly adopted by hordes of readers nationwide, and before the demise of her creator, Harold Gray, in 1968, she had starred in her own radio show. She made two feature films, and in 1977 *Annie* was launched on Broadway.

Other early comic figures were Moon Mullins, created in 1923 by Frank Willard; Buck Rogers by Philip Nowlan in 1928; and Betty Boop, the round-faced, innocent-eyed, chubby-cheeked Boop-Boop-a-Doop girl of the early 1930s. Bimbo was her dog and KoKo her clown friend.

Popeye made his debut in 1929 as the spinach-eating sailor with the spindly-limbed girlfriend, Olive Oyl, in the comic strip *Thimble Theatre*, created by Elzie Segar. He became a film star in 1933 and had his own radio show that during 1936 played three times a week on CBS. He obligingly modeled for scores of toys, dolls, and figurines, and especially those from the '30s are very collectible.

Tarzan, created around 1930 by Edgar Rice Burroughs, and Captain Midnight by Robert Burtt and Willfred G. Moore, are popular heroes with today's collectors. During the days of radio, Sky King of the Flying Crown Ranch (also created by Burtt and Moore) thrilled boys and girls of the mid-1940s. Hopalong Cassidy, Red Rider, Tom Mix, and the Lone

Ranger were only a few of the other 'good guys' always on the side of law and order.

But of all the fictional heroes and comic characters collected today, probably the best loved and most well known is Mickey Mouse. Created in the late 1920s by Walt Disney, Micky (as his name was first spelled) became an instant success with his film debut, *Steamboat Willie*. His popularity was parlayed through wind-up toys, watches, figurines, cookie jars, puppets, clothing, and numerous other products. Items from the 1930s are usually copyrighted 'Walt Disney Enterprises'; thereafter, 'Walt Disney Productions' was used.

For more information we recommend *Schroeder's Collectible Toys, Antique to Modern*, by Sharon and Bob Huxford. For those interested in Disneyana, we recommend *Stern's Guide to Disney Collectibles* (there are three in the series), and *The Collector's Encyclopedia of Disneyana* by David Longest and Michael Stern. *Cartoon Toys & Collectibles* by David Longest; *Collector's Guide to TV Toys & Memorabilia, Second Edition*, by Greg Davis and Bill Morgan; *Roy Rogers and Dale Evans Toys and Memorabilia* by P. Allan Coyle; *Collector's Reference & Value Guide to the Lone Ranger* by Lee Felbinger; and *G-Men and FBI Toys and Collectibles* by Harry and Jody Whitworth are other great publications. All are available from Collector Books. See also Autographs; Banks; Big Little Books; Children's Books; Comic Books; Cookie Jars; Dolls; Games; Lunch Boxes; Movie Memorabilia; Paper Dolls; Pin-Back Buttons; Posters; Puzzles; Rock 'N Roll Memorabilia; Toys.

Alice in Wonderland, paint set, Hasbro, 1969, M (sealed) 50.00
Alice in Wonderland, phonograph, RCA-Victor, 1951, EX........150.00
Alice in Wonderland, tea set, litho tin, Ohio Art, 1982, 14 pcs, MIB 50.00
Alvin & the Chipmunks, dolls, plush, Knickerbocker, 1963, 14", ea.......50.00
Amos 'N Andy, figures, jtd wood, Jaymar, 1930s, 6", NM, pr......300.00
Andy Panda, bank, pnt compo figure, Crown Toy, 1939, 5", EX ...100.00
Annie Oakley, outfit, blouse/fringed skirt, Pla-Master, 1950, NMIB...200.00
Baby Huey & Papa, bop bag, vinyl, Doughboy, 1966, 54", EX 65.00
Barney Google & Spark Plug, figure, Barney, Syroco, 1944, 4", EX ...65.00
Barney Google & Spark Plug, pull toy, KFS, 1924, 8", NM 3,800.00
Barney Google & Spark Plug, Wa-Gee Walker, Spark Plug, 1924, 7", NM...600.00
Bat Masterson, Indian Fighter playset, Multiple, NMIB..............200.00
Batman, Activity Box, Whitman, 1966, complete, rare, EX 65.00
Batman, balloons, National Latex/NPPI, 1966, set of 8, MIP 75.00
Batman, Bat Grenade, plastic, Esquire, 1966, MOC....................125.00
Batman, Batcuffs, Ideal, 1966, 4", NM 100.00
Batman, Colorforms, 1966, complete, NMIB.................................55.00
Batman, doll, stuffed cloth w/plastic face, 1966, 27", NM...........150.00
Batman, Flying Batscout, Tarco, 1966, MOC................................50.00
Batman, periscope, Bar Zim, 1966, 19", EX...............................85.00
Batman, pinball machine, Marx, 1966, 22x10", EX.....................100.00
Batman, Sparkle Paints, Kenner, 1966, complete, EXIB...............75.00
Beany & Cecil, carrying case, vinyl, Bob Clampett, 1961, 9" dia, VG...50.00
Beany & Cecil, 3-D Mosaics, 1961, complete, EX (VG box)........65.00
Ben Casey, paint-by-number set, Transogram, 1962, MIB (sealed) ..125.00
Betty Boop, doll, compo/jtd wood, red dress, 13½", VG..........1,200.00
Betty Boop, tambourine, litho tin, 1930s, 6" dia, EX..................150.00
Big Bad Wolf, doll, Ross, 1934, NM..2,200.00
Big Bad Wolf, figure, bsk, Japan, 1930s, 3½", NM.....................100.00
Bionic Woman, slide-tile puzzle, APC, 1977, MOC....................35.00
Bionic Woman, wallet, pk or bl, Faberge/Canada, 1976, MIP, ea..40.00
Blondie & Dagwood, Blondie's Peg Set, KFS, 1930, NMIB, minimum value...100.00
Blondie & Dagwood, kazoo, tin sandwich shape, KFS, 1947, 6", NMIB....175.00
Bozo the Clown, Cartoon Kit, Colorforms, 1960, EXIB 50.00
Bozo the Clown, record player, Transogram, EX 65.00
Brer Rabbit, patch, cloth, BR w/hobo's bag, 1950s, 3" oval, EX 8.00
Buck Rogers, Chemical Laboratory, JE Dille, 1937, EXIB, from $700 to...900.00
Buck Rogers, helmet, rubber, Goodyear, 1930s, scarce, M...........525.00
Buck Rogers, Midget Caster Set, 1934, very rare, VG (VG box) ..750.00
Buck Rogers, ring, Saturn, 1940s, rare, EX...............................400.00

Buck Rogers, Solar Scouts, 1930s, EX 100.00
Buck Rogers, Stato-Kite, 1950, complete, EX (EX envelope) 150.00
Bugs Bunny, doll, as baseball player, 1950s, NM, from $300 to...400.00
Bugs Bunny, Skediddler, Mattel, 1969, 6", MIB............................85.00
Bugs Bunny, Toot-A-Tune, plastic, Warner Bros, NMIB, from $100 to..150.00
Bullwinkle, bank, vinyl vigure, Play Pal Plastics, 1973, 12", M.....75.00
Bullwinkle, doll, talker, Mattel, 1971, 11", EX...........................125.00
Buster Brown, pocketwatch, 1928, EX 175.00
Captain Kangaroo, doll, talker, Mattel, 1967, MIB 150.00
Captain Kangaroo, Finger Paint Set, Hasbro, 1956, EXIB.............55.00
Captain Marvel, Magic Blotter, NM..225.00
Captain Marvel, patch, glow-in-the-dark, rare, M......................500.00
Captain Midnight, ring, Whirlwind Whistle, 1941, scarce, M....450.00
Captain Video, ring, Flying Saucer, 1951, NM.........................1,200.00
Captain Video, ring, Photo, 1951, M 300.00
Casper the Friendly Ghost, kite, cb, Saalfield, 1960, MIP.............20.00
Charlie Brown, doll, vinyl, 1950s, 9", VG...................................75.00
Charlie Brown, megaphone, Chein, 1970, rare, EX 45.00
Charlie Chaplin, figure, chalkware, Hampton, 1915, rare, 7", VG 130.00
Charlie McCarthy, coloring set, Whitman, 1938, complete, NMIB...175.00
Charlie McCarthy, Radio Party, Chase & Sanborn, 1938, complete, NM..125.00
Charlie McCarthy, tumblers, set of 8, Libbey, 1930s, M (EX box) ...600.00
Charlie's Angels, Dresser Sets, Fleetwood, 1977, MOC, ea...........35.00
Charlie's Angels, target set, Placo Toys, 1977, MIB......................65.00
CHiPs, binoculars, 1970s, MIB..30.00
CHiPs, Police Set, Buddy L, 1981, NRFB..................................100.00
Cisco Kid, hobbyhorse, vinyl w/wood hdl, VG..............................50.00
Cisco Kid, ring, Saddle, rare, M..500.00
Dan Daring, Book of Magic Tricks, M (EX mailer)......................50.00
Daniel Boone, Fess Parker Cartoon Kit, Colorforms, 1964, MIB ..35.00
Daniel Boone, Fess Parker Super Slate, Whitman, 1964, NM.......50.00
Davy Crockett, doll, cloth/vinyl face, name on chest, 1950s, 27", EX...150.00
Davy Crockett, guitar, fiberboard, Peter Puppet, 25", EXIB 200.00
Davy Crockett, teepee, ...Official Fess Parker..., 1950s, 70", EX..225.00
Dennis the Menace, Dentist Set, Pressman, 1950s, EXIB 150.00
Dennis the Menace, Mischief Kit, Hasbro, 1955, EXIB................50.00
Dennis the Menace, wristwatch, 1960s, EX 75.00
Deputy Dawg, bop bag, Doughboy, 1961, 54", NM......................50.00
Dick Tracy, camera, 127mm, Seymour, 1950s, scarce, NMIB......100.00
Dick Tracy, Cartoon Kit, Colorforms, 1962, complete, EXIB.........75.00
Dick Tracy, Handcuffs for Junior, John Henry, 1940s, EX (on card)....75.00
Dick Tracy, mask, paper, Einson-Freeman, 1933, rare, EX...........100.00
Dick Tracy, ring, Hat, 1940s, EX..275.00
Donald Duck, bank, Donald w/life buoy, compo, WDE, 1938, 6½", VG...150.00
Donald Duck, doctor kit, WDP, 1940s, EXIB...............................125.00
Donald Duck, hairbrush, dk brn wood w/aluminum strip, 1930s, 4", EX ..50.00
Donald Duck, nodder, plastic, Marx, 2", EX.................................15.00
Donald Duck, roly poly, celluloid, long-billed/jtd, 1934, 7", EX....1,100.00
Donald Duck, watering can, train scene, Ohio Art, 1938, 3", NM..350.00
Donald Duck, Whirl-A-Tune Music Maker, Ideal, 1965, NMIB...75.00

Dopey bookends, Lamode, 1937, $375.00 for the pair.
(Photo courtesy Joel Cohen)

Dr Dolittle, bank, plastic figure w/monkey & dog, pk w/bl detail, NM ...50.00

Dr Dolittle, Cartoon Kit, Colorforms, 1967, NMIB, from $25 to..**35.00**
Dr Dolittle, Spelling & Counting Board, Bar-Zim, NMIP.............**35.00**
Dr Seuss, jack-in-the-box, Cat in the Hat, Mattel, 1970, EX........**65.00**
Dr Seuss, See 'N Say Talking Storybook, Mattel, 1970, NM.......**200.00**
Dumbo, Jingle Ball, vinyl, Vangard, 1950s, EX **30.00**
Dumbo, mask, starched linen, hat mk Dumbo, 1940s, EX..........**30.00**
Dumbo, salt & pepper shakers, ceramic, 1940s, 4½", EX, pr **30.00**
Elmer Fudd, nodder, papier-mache, NM, from $100 to **175.00**
Elmer Fudd, wristwatch, Sheffield, 1960s, NMIB **150.00**
Evil Kneivel, wristwatch, Bradley, 1976, EX.........................**150.00**
Felix the Cat, drum, litho tin, 1930s, scarce, NM.....................**200.00**
Felix the Cat, Pencil Coloring by Numbers, Hasbro, 1958, MIP...**50.00**
Felix the Cat, pull toy, tin, Nifty, 1925, rare, 8", NM **1,500.00**
Felix the Cat, tea set, lustreware, service for 6, M **900.00**
Flash Gordon, compass, silver plastic w/yel wristband, 1950s, MOC......**75.00**
Flintstones, bubble pipe, Bamm-Bamm, Transogram, 1963, MOC ..**25.00**
Flintstones, Cockamamies, 1961, complete, NMIB **35.00**
Flintstones, Fuzzy Felt Playset, Standard Toy, 1961, EXIB.............**75.00**
Flintstones, Stoneway Piano, Jaymar, 1961, rare, EXIB **200.00**
Flipper, Activity Box, Whitman, 1966, MIB...........................**40.00**
Flipper, ukelele, Mattel, 1968, MIP **100.00**
Fonzie, activity/coloring book, Grosset & Dunlap, 1976, EX **12.00**
Fonzie, beach towel, With Love From the Fonz, Franco, 1970s, 55", NM ...**45.00**
Fonzie, belt buckle, The Fonz, brass finish, 1976, from $15 to **20.00**
Fonzie, paint-by-number set, AAAA...Y The Fonz, Craftmaster, 1976, MIB...**25.00**
G-Man, Police Set, Pressman, complete, rare, EXIB **250.00**
Gabby Hayes, ring, Cannon, 1951, EX................................**185.00**
Garfield, doll, talker, Mattel, 1983, 10", VG+ **50.00**
Gene Autry, wallet, leather w/mc image on horse, ca 1950, NMIB....**125.00**
Gene Autry, wristwatch, New Haven, 1951, EX, from $300 to ..**400.00**
Geppetto, doll, wood w/cloth clothes, Chad Valley, orig tag, EX..**1,100.00**
Geppetto, figure, bsk, Multi-Products, 1940s, 2", NM **100.00**
Gilligan's Island, figure set (3), rubber, Playskool, 1977, MIB.......**35.00**
Gilligan's Island, Gilligan's Floating Island, Playskool, 1977, MIB...**150.00**
Goofy, figure, bsk, Japan, 1930s, 2", EX................................**60.00**
Goofy, figure, Jumpkins by Kohner, 1960s, 5", MOC....................**60.00**
Green Hornet, kite, Roalex, 1967, MIP **200.00**
Green Hornet, pennant, felt, Greenway Prod, 1966, 28", NM......**75.00**
Green Hornet, ring, Seal/Compartment, glow-in-the-dark, 1947, NM ..**900.00**
Green Hornet, walkie-talkies, Remco, 1966, 9", MIB **400.00**
Gumby & Pokey, Gumby's Jeep, w/figures, Lakeside, VG.............**150.00**
Gumby & Pokey, Modeling Dough, Chemtoy, 1967, unused, MIB...**50.00**
Heckle & Jeckle, figure, hard rubber, 1958, 8", NM **75.00**
Heckle & Jeckle, magic slate, Lowe, 1952, NM...........................**25.00**
Herman & Katnip, kite, cb, Saalfield, 1960, MIP **25.00**
Hopalong Cassidy, Bar 20 Ranch Horn, Perlins Prod, 1950s, EXIB....**250.00**
Hopalong Cassidy, membership kit, Savings Rodeo Club, EX (EX mailer) ..**250.00**
Hopalong Cassidy, photo album, brn leather/color image, 1950s, EX ..**150.00**
Hopalong Cassidy, Picture Gun Theater, Stephens, NMIB.........**300.00**
Hopalong Cassidy, wristwatch, w/saddle display, US Time, 1950, MIB...**625.00**
Howdy Doody, Bee-Nee Kit, 1950s, NMIB **65.00**
Howdy Doody, boxing gloves, Parvey, 1950s, 6", NMIB.............**325.00**
Howdy Doody, doll, plastic/cloth clothes, Beehler, 7", NMIB.....**250.00**
Howdy Doody, Phono Doodle, Shuratone, 1950s, EX, from $250 to **300.00**
Howdy Doody, ring, Jack-in-the-Box, plastic, 1950s, NM........**1,000.00**
Howdy Doody, swim ring, inflatable vinyl, 1950s, 24" dia, EX......**65.00**
Howdy Doody, tumblers, 6 different, Welch's, 1950s, ea, from $15 to...**20.00**
Howdy Doody, Venus Paradise Coloring Set, Kagran, 1950s, EXIB....**200.00**
Huckleberry Hound, bank, plastic figure, 1960, 10", EX................**35.00**
Huckleberry Hound, squeak figure in cowboy hat, vinyl, M........**150.00**
Incredible Hulk, Rub 'N Play, Colorforms, 1979, MIB **30.00**
Jack Armstrong, Bomb Sight, uncut, MIB **500.00**
Jack Armstrong, Sound Effects Kit, 1940s, MIB **300.00**
James Bond, Thunderball Paint Set, British, 1965, EX.................**175.00**

James Bond, 007 Electric Drawing Set, Lakeside, '66, EXIB, from $50 to...**75.00**
Jeep, doll, jtd wood, King Features, 1935, 13", EX....................**950.00**
Jeep, doll, jtd wood, King Features, 1937, 8", EX.....................**500.00**
Jetsons, Slate & Chalk Set, 1960s, unused, MIB **100.00**
Jiminy Cricket, figure, bsk, Japan, 1930s, 3¼", NM **100.00**
Jiminy Cricket, figure, bsk, Multi-Products, 1940s, 5", NM **100.00**
Jiminy Cricket, mug, plastic head, flasher eyes, 1960s, 4", EX.......**25.00**
Jonny Quest, paint-by-number set, Transogram, '65, EXIB, from $300 to...**400.00**
Krazy Kat, figure, jtd wood, Chein, 7", NM.............................**1,250.00**
Lassie, Trick Trainer, Mousely Inc, 1956, complete, scarce, NMIB ...**175.00**
Laurel & Hardy, dolls, Bend 'Em, Knickerbocker, 9", MIP, ea.......**45.00**
Laurel & Hardy, Stuff & Lace Dolls, Transogram, 1962, MIB, ea .**45.00**
Li'l Abner, bank, compo, Capp Enterprises, 1975, 7", M.............**100.00**
Little Audrey, nodder, papier-mache, 1960s, NM, from $100 to.**175.00**
Little Bo Peep, tea set, litho tin, Ohio Art, 1930s, 9 pcs, EX......**200.00**
Little Lulu, bank, Play Pal Plastics, 7½", NM **50.00**
Little Lulu, Cartoon-A-Kit, M Buell Kits Inc, 1948, NMIB........**200.00**
Little Orphan Annie, coin purse, vinyl/metal clasp, 1930s, 3x2", EX ...**25.00**
Little Orphan Annie, doll, stuffed, Knickerbocker, 1977, 15", MIB......**40.00**
Little Orphan Annie, toy stove, w/electric warmer, 1930s, NM .**200.00**
Little Red Riding Hood, tea set, tin, Ohio Art, 1960s, 11 pcs, NM **75.00**
Lone Ranger, alarm clock, Elgin/Bradley, 1981, MIB, from $100 to..**125.00**
Lone Ranger, bank, Lone Ranger on rearing Silver, plastic, NM .**125.00**
Lone Ranger, Bat-O-Ball, 1940, NM, from $75 to......................**125.00**
Lone Ranger, crayons, 1953, NM (NM tin box), from $75 to.....**100.00**
Lone Ranger, Deputy Kit, 1956, complete, NM, from $150 to....**175.00**
Lone Ranger, horseshoe set, rubber, Gardner Games, 1950, NMIB...**200.00**
Lone Ranger, microscope, Cheerios, 1947, NM, from $125 to....**150.00**
Lone Ranger, Picture Printing Set, 1938, NMIB **200.00**
Lone Ranger, Safety Club Kit, Bond Bread, 1940s, NM (NM mailer) ..**200.00**
Maggie & Jiggs, figures, celluloid, standing hand-in-hand, 6½", EX......**385.00**
Magilla Gorilla, pull toy, vinyl/plastic wagon, Ideal, 1964, EX......**65.00**
Mary Poppins, Deluxe Paint & Crayon Set, Hasbro, 1965, EXIB .**10.00**
Mickey & Minnie Mouse, pillow cover, Vogue Needlecraft #98, EX...**65.00**
Mickey Mouse, bank, Mickey/treasure, compo, Crown, 1938, 6", EX...**650.00**
Mickey Mouse, doll, cloth/compo, Knickerbocker, 1936, 12", EX....**600.00**
Mickey Mouse, Magic Transfers, Colorforms, 1978, MIP (sealed).**15.00**
Mickey Mouse, pencil box, diecut cb Mickey, Dixon, 1935, complete, EX ..**200.00**
Mickey Mouse, pencil sharpener, celluloid, Japan, prewar, 2¾", M .**275.00**

Mickey Mouse, ceramic pitcher, Japan, 1930s, 8", $125.00. (Photo courtesy Dunbar Gallery)

Mickey Mouse, riding toy, wood, Menge/WDE, 1930s, 16", EX..**650.00**
Mickey Mouse, scarf, cotton, Mickey/other characters, 1960s, 22", EX...**15.00**
Mickey Mouse, wash tub, tin, Chein, 1930s, rare, 5" dia, NM.......**225.00**
Mighty Mouse, alarm clock, w/bells, 1960s, NM.........................**85.00**
Mighty Mouse, figure, rubber w/cloth cape, 1955, 10", EX.............**75.00**
Mighty Mouse, How To Draw Cartoons Set, Gabriel, 1956, EXIB..**65.00**
Mighty Mouse, Presto-Paints, Kenner, 1963, EXIB.......................**65.00**
Minnie Mouse, doll, wood, Fun-E-Flex by Ideal, 7", EX.............**450.00**
Minnie Mouse, figurine, bsk, w/mandolin, Japan, 1930s, 3½", EX...**100.00**
Minnie Mouse, handkerchief, blk & bl on wht cloth, 9x9", VG...**15.00**
Minnie Mouse, tumbler, blk image, 1930s, 4½", EX.....................**40.00**
Moon Mullins, figure, bsk, 1930s, 7½", G.............................**125.00**

Mother Goose, magic slate set, Strathmore, 1945, EXIB.............35.00
Mother Goose, Peepul Pals Playset, Whitman, MIB.............50.00
Mr Green Jeans, doll, stuffed cloth, 1976, M 35.00
Nancy & Sluggo, dolls, cloth/vinyl, Georgene, 1944, 14", NMIB (2) ...1,400.00
Nancy & Sluggo, dolls, vinyl/cloth clothes, S&P, 1954, 16", ea .175.00
Phantom, membership kit, Pilot Patrol, 1930s, rare, NM (NM mailer)...2,000.00
Phantom, ring, Skull, brass w/red eyes, 1950s, NM 1,000.00
Pinocchio, Adventure Theatre, Holland, 1940s, complete, EX ..165.00
Pinocchio, Color Box, litho tin, Transogram/WDP, 1948, EX.....75.00
Pinocchio, coloring book, Whitman, 1954, 130 pgs, unused, NM...25.00
Pinocchio, doll, compo/wood, Ideal/WDP, 1939, 20", NM 900.00
Pinocchio, figure, bsk, Multi-Products, 1940s, 2", NM.............100.00
Pinocchio, figure, bsk, Multi-Products, 1940s, 5", NM.............125.00
Pinocchio, jack-in-the box, compo/cloth clothes, paper litho box, EX ..250.00
Pinocchio, Puppet Show, Whitman/WDE, 1939, complete, NMIB ..200.00
Pinocchio, push-button puppet, Kohner, 1970s-80s, EX.............12.00
Pluto, doll, Schuco, 1950s, 13", EX, minimum value..................350.00
Pluto, figure, rubber, Sieberling, 1930s, rare, 7", EX.............125.00
Pluto, Jingle Ball, vinyl, Vangard, 1950s, EX.............30.00
Pluto, roly poly, celluloid, Japan, prewar, 5", NM 250.00
Popeye, bank, sitting w/spinach can, vinyl, Alan Jay, 1958, 8", EX ..75.00
Popeye, boxing gloves, red, Everlast, 1950s, MIP.............75.00
Popeye, doll, cloth w/vinyl head & arms, Gund, 1957, 20", EX..150.00
Popeye, pocketwatch, Ingersoll, 1935, 2" dia, EX..................650.00
Popeye, Popeye Bingo, dexterity game, Bar-Zim, 1929, NM 100.00
Porky Pig, bank, Porky standing by tree, pot metal, EX.............100.00
Porky Pig, figure, bsk, Warner Bros, 1930s, EX.............150.00
Raggedy Ann, ball & jack set, Hallmark, MOC.............20.00
Raggedy Ann, doll, cloth/yarn hair, Georgene, 1938-45, 19", EX...350.00
Range Ryder, outfit, Pla-Master, 1950s, complete, MIB.............275.00
Red Ryder, Little Beaver Archery Set, 1950s, unused, EX (EX card) ...100.00
Rin-Tin-Tin, pen, blk plastic rifle, Nabisco, 1950s, EX.............50.00
Rin-Tin-Tin, ring, Magic Stamp, w/instructions, M..................450.00
Robin Hood, Colorforms, 1970, complete, NMIB 25.00
Rootie Kazootie, magic set, 1950s, NMIB 125.00
Roy Rogers, Crayon Set, Standard Toykraft, 1950s, VG (VG box) ..75.00
Roy Rogers, harmonica, Reed, 1955, NMOC 100.00
Roy Rogers, ring, Hat, sterling silver, 1950s, M 650.00
Roy Rogers, Trick Lasso, Knox-Reese, 1947, MIP (sealed)..........175.00
Sgt Preston, Ore Detector, w/instructions, Quaker, MIB.............100.00
Sgt Preston, pedometer, Quaker, 1954, unused, MIB.............125.00
Sky King, Secret Signal Scope, 1947, NM (NM mailer).............250.00
Sky King, stamp kit, complete, EX (EX mailer).............100.00
Sleeping Beauty, doll, Madame Alexander 1957, 16", EX 300.00
Sleeping Beauty, paint-by-number set, Transogram, 1959, MIB..100.00
Snoopy, alarm clock, w/tennis racket, Equity, 1968, 5" dia, EX.....30.00
Snoopy, bank, Snoopy on rainbow, compo, NM 25.00
Snoopy, kaleidoscope, Snoopy Disco, Determined, 1979, EX........20.00
Snoopy, skateboard, Snoopy as Joe Cool, 1970s, NM..............100.00
Snow White, Jingle Book, bread premium, 1938, EX 20.00
Snow White, pull toy, 2 dwarfs/Snow White, NN Hill Brass, 1938, NM ..700.00
Snow White, scrapbook, WDE, 1938, unused, EX.......................200.00
Snow White, tumblers, 8 different, verses on bk, ea, from $60 to ..80.00
Spider-Man, coloring book, Seeing Double, 1976, unused, EX 15.00
Spider-Man, doll, stuffed talker, Mego, 1974, 28", M 45.00
Spider-Man, kazoo, Straco, MOC.............50.00
Steve Canyon, Jet Helmet, Ideal, 1959, EXIB 100.00
Steve Canyon, school bag, canvas w/image, 1959, EX..................75.00
Straight Arrow, target set, EX (EX box).....................150.00
Superman, Building Set, Peter Puppet, 1954, EXIB, from $350 to...400.00
Superman, pin, Junior Defense League, EX.............200.00
Superman, playsuit, w/comic book, Funtime Playwear, 1954, EXIB ..500.00
Superman, ring, Crusader, 1940s, NM..................250.00
Sylvester the Cat, figure, w/squeaker, Sun Rubber, 1930s, rare, VG ..125.00

Tarzan, ring, Ape, 1930s, NM....................500.00
Three Little Pigs, figure set, bsk, minstrels, Borgfeldt, 3", NMIB .600.00
Three Little Pigs, watering can, litho tin, Ohio Art, 1930s, EX..200.00
Tom & Jerry, dolls, cloth, Georgene, 1949, 16" & 7", EX, pr......400.00
Tom & Jerry, jack-in-the-box, Mattel, M, from $75 to................100.00
Tom Corbett Space Cadet, Squadron Kit, Kellogg's, 1951-52, EX ..200.00
Tom Mix, badge, Dobie County Sheriff, w/siren, 1946, EX...........75.00
Tom Mix, jigsaw puzzle, Rexhall, 1920s, scarce, EX (EX envelope) ..150.00
Tom Mix, spurs, glow-in-the-dark, MIB 150.00
Tom Mix, watch fob, Gold Ore, 1940, NM.................100.00
Topo Gigio, nodder, papier-mache, w/or w/out fruit, NM, ea........75.00
Tweety Bird, charm, plastic, 1950s, ¾", NM.............15.00
Tweety Bird, figure, w/squeaker, Sun Rubber, 1930s, EX, from $75 to ...125.00
Wild Bill Hickok & Jingles, Ranch Bunkhouse Kit, 1950s, NMIP ..65.00
Winnie the Pooh, doll, bl shirt, Knickerbocker, 1963, 13", EX...100.00
Wonder Woman, wristwatch, Dabbs, 1977, EXIB.......................200.00
Woody Woodpecker, harmonica, plastic figure, early, 6", EX 30.00
Woody Woodpecker, TV Coloring Pencil Set, Conn Pencil, 1958, EXIB...35.00
Yogi Bear, Magic Rub-Off Pictures, Whitman, 1961, EXIB...........65.00
Yogi Bear, Play Fun Set, Whitman, 1964, NMIB 50.00
Zorro, Activity Box, Whitman, 1965, complete, EXIB.................40.00
Zorro, charm bracelet, gold-tone, photo/pistol/sword/whip, 1950s, EX...50.00
Zorro, gloves, logo on blk knit w/canvas trim, WDP, 1950s, EX ...65.00
Zorro, magic slate, Strathmore/WDP, 1955, EX 50.00
Zorro, Target Board, tin, complete, 15x23", MIB......................100.00

Peters and Reed

John Peters and Adam Reed founded their pottery in Zanesville, Ohio, just before the turn of the century, using the local red clay to produce a variety of wares. Moss Aztec, introduced about 1912, has an unglazed exterior with designs molded in high relief and the recesses highlighted with a green wash. Only the interior is glazed to hold water. Pereco (named for Peters, Reed and Company) is glazed in semi-matt blue, maroon, cream, and other colors. Orange was also used very early, but such examples are rare. Shapes are simple with in-mold decoration sometimes borrowed from the Moss Aztec line. Wilse Blue is a line of high-gloss medium blue with dark specks on simple shapes. Landsun, characterized by its soft matt multicolor or blue and gray combinations, is decorated either by dripping or by hand brushing in an effect sometimes called Flame or Herringbone. Chromal, in much the same colors as Landsun, may be decorated with a realistic scenic, or the swirling application of colors may merely suggest one. Vivid, realistic Chromal scenics command much higher prices than weak, poorly drawn examples. (Brush-McCoy made a very similar line called Chromart. Neither will be marked; and due to the lack of documented background material available, it may be impossible make a positive identification. Collectors nearly always attribute this type of decoration to Peters and Reed.) Shadow Ware is usually a glossy, multicolor drip over a harmonious base color but occasionally it is seen in overall matt glaze. When the base is black, the effect is often iridescent.

Perhaps the most familiar line is the brown high-glaze artware with the 'sprigged'-type designs. Although research has uncovered no positive proof, it has been generally accepted as having been made by Peters and Reed. However, this line has recently been re-attributed to Weller pottery by the Sanfords in their latest book on Peters and Reed pottery. This conclusion was drawn due to the overwhelming number of shapes proven to be Wellery pottery. Several other lines were produced including Mirror Black, Persian, Egyptian, Florentine, Marbleized, etc., and an unidentified line which collectors call Mottled-Marbleized Colors. In this high-gloss line, the red clay body often shows through the splashed-on colors.

In 1922 the company became known as the Zane Pottery. Peters and Reed retired, and Harry McClelland became president. Charles Chilcote designed new lines, and production of many of the old lines continued.

The body of the ware after 1922 was light in color. Marks include the impressed logo or ink stamp 'Zaneware' in a rectangle. See also Zaneware.

Bowl, centerpc; Wilse Blue, w/candlesticks.................................125.00
Bowl, Moss Aztec, emb dragonflies, 2¼x10"................................125.00
Bowl, Pereco, gr matt, emb leaves, 3½x9"..................................100.00
Jar, oil; Marbleized, emb ribs, flared rim, 24x15"........................550.00
Jar, sand; Marbleized, EX color & glaze, 23½", EX......................600.00
Jardiniere, Chromal scenic, 8"...750.00
Jardiniere, Moss Aztec, roses, 9x10", from $295 to....................350.00
Planter, Moss Aztec, classical figures, Ferrell, 5¼x12½", NM.....175.00
Vase, Chromal, tree & abstract mtns, lav/bl russet ground, 9½".350.00
Vase, Chromal (realistic), 13x7"...1,500.00
Vase, Chromal scenic (impressionistic), 11"..............................400.00
Vase, cream & brn w/emb grapes & leaves, 12".........................175.00
Vase, Italia, stylistic flowers, unmk, 6½x8"..............................250.00
Vase, Landsun, lt gr w/bl speckles over flame design base, 7¾x4"...165.00
Vase, Moss Aztec, blackberries, Zane Ware ink stamp, 8⅛".........150.00
Vase, Moss Aztec, brn w/gr wash, F Ferrell, 8"..........................165.00
Vase, Moss Aztec, emb Virginia Creepers, unmk, 8"...................125.00
Vase, Moss Aztec, ivy & berries, F Ferrell, 12x5½".....................195.00
Vase, Pereco, gr matt, emb floral, 6"...140.00
Vase, Pereco, swami w/crystal ball, opaque tan matt, 4¾"...........140.00
Vase, Shadow Ware, mc, 6½"...175.00
Vase, Shadow Ware, mc, 9"...250.00
Vase, Wilse Blue, #612, 8½"...80.00
Vase, Wilse Blue, corseted, 9"..80.00
Wall pocket, Egyptian figural, gr matt, 8"..................................275.00
Wall pocket, Moss Aztec, 3-D oak branches & leaves, unmk, 8½"..325.00

Pewabic

The Pewabic Pottery was formally established in Detroit, Michigan, in 1907 by Mary Chase Perry Stratton and Horace James Caulkins. The two had worked together since 1903, firing their ware in a small kiln Caulkins had designed especially for use by the dental trade. Always a small operation which relied upon basic equipment and the skill of the workers, they took pride in being commissioned for several important architectural tile installations.

Some of the early artware was glazed a simple matt green; occasionally other colors were added, sometimes in combination, one over the other in a drip effect. Later Stratton developed a lustrous crystalline glaze. (Today's values are determined to a great extent by the artistic merit of the glaze.) The body of the ware was highly fired and extremely hard. Shapes were basic, and decorative modeling, if used at all, was in low relief. Mary Stratton kept the pottery open until her death in 1961. In 1968 it was purchased and reopened by Michigan State University; it is still producing today. Several marks were used over the years: a triangle with 'Revelation Pottery' (for a short time only); 'Pewabic' with five maple leaves; and the impressed circle mark.

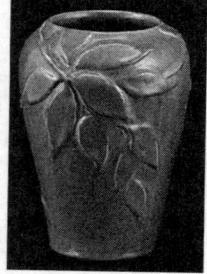

Vase, green matt with embossed leaves, impressed mark, 8x6", $5,750.00.

Bottle, leathery cobalt matt, gourd shape, 11x5¾"..................2,500.00
Bowl, turq drips on gunmetal, hemispherical, 3¾x6¾".............1,800.00

Candlestick, dk gr, wide saucer ft, 6"......................................350.00
Jardiniere, cobalt lustre, 8x9"...2,200.00
Tile, chamberstick emb, pk & gr irid, 2¼" sq..............................60.00
Vase, bl lustre & turq mottle, bulbous, 7¾x5½"......................1,200.00
Vase, bl/gray/red metallic, deeply ridged, hand thrown, 5½".......600.00
Vase, cobalt & gr lustre, flat shoulder, 3¾x3¾".........................650.00
Vase, cobalt & lt bl lustre, 2¾x4½"..650.00
Vase, dripping celadon & purple, pear shape, paper label, 6x4¼".750.00
Vase, frothy dripping celadon & gold lustre, drilled, 10½x5"..2,100.00
Vase, gr & red lustre, 2½x1½"..500.00
Vase, gunmetal & turq lustre, label, 2¼x3½"...........................1,200.00
Vase, horizontal band, ivory crackle, 1935, 10½x7"................1,000.00
Vase, mottled bl lustre, hand thrown, 5⅝".................................425.00
Vase, mustard drips on caramel at shoulder, emb nubs, 11x8½".10,000.00
Vase, orange matt, spherical, sm rstr, 5x5".................................400.00
Vase, pk, gray & gold lustre, spherical, 5x4½".........................1,400.00
Vase, pk crackle drips on bl lustre, 2½x2¼"..............................250.00
Vase, pulled cobalt & turq lustre, baluster, 9¾x6½"...............5,000.00
Vase, turq drips over gold, bottle shape, 4½x2½", NM............1,000.00
Vase, volcanic cobalt & celadon, squat, flat shoulder, 4¾x9¼"...4,750.00
Vase, yel & copper lustre, 2x2½"..800.00

Pewter

Pewter is a metal alloy of tin, copper, very small parts of bismuth and/or antimony, and sometimes lead. Very little American pewter contained lead, however, because much of the ware was designed to be used as tableware, and makers were aware that the use of lead could result in poisoning. (Pieces that do contain lead are usually darker in color and heavier than those that have no lead.) Most of the fine examples of American pewter date from 1700 to the 1840s. Many pieces were melted down and recast into bullets during the American Revolution in 1775; this accounts to some extent why examples from this period are quite difficult to find. The pieces that did survive may include buttons, buckles, and writing equipment as well as the tableware we generally think of.

After the Revolution makers began using antimony as the major alloy with the tin in an effort to regain the popularity of pewter, which glassware and china was beginning to replace in the home. The resulting product, known as britannia, had a lustrous silver-like appearance and was far more durable. While closely related, britannia is a collectible in its own right and should not be confused with pewter.

Key: tm — touch mark

Basin, London tm, ca 1800, 1¾x6⅞"..150.00
Basin, love & facing birds tm, ca 1800, 1¾x6¾"........................525.00
Basin, Nathaniel Austin eagle tm, wear/dents, 8".......................550.00
Basin, Richard Lee tm, slightly raised rim, wear/pitting, 2x8¾".575.00
Basin, TD (Thomas Danforth) eagle tm, flared rim, 12"..........1,150.00
Beaker, unmk Am, pitted bottom, 3"..55.00
Bowl, Ashbil Griswold eagle tm, wear/scratches, shallow, 11"....470.00
Bowl, Samuel Danforth tm (partial), wear/pitting, 13¼"...........440.00
Bowl, TD & eagle tm (Thomas Danforth), shallow, 11½", EX...850.00
Candlestick, H Hopper tm, 9½"..235.00
Candlestick, TBM Co tm, soldered rpr, 7½"................................85.00
Candlesticks, unmk Am, baluster w/domed base, pushup, rstr, 10", pr..330.00
Candlesticks, unmk Am, brass pushups, 7¾", unmatched pr......190.00
Candlesticks, unmk Am, reeded detail, 10¼"..............................250.00
Candlesticks, unmk but att Homan & Co, 9⅞", pr....................475.00
Chalice, I Trask tm, flared rim, stepped base, 5¾", pr..............1,025.00
Charger, London tm, minor scratches, 16½" dia..........................300.00
Charger, London tm w/flower & crown, hammered booge, sm rstr, 13½"..275.00
Charger, Love tm, wear/pitting, 12"...600.00

Charger, PDB & crowned rose tm, wear, 13¾" 275.00
Charger, SE (illegible)?? London, 13½" 350.00
Charger, Townsend & Compton tm, pitting/wear, 12¾" 160.00
Charger, Wm Johnson tm, molded rim, 18th C, 14⅞" 350.00
Coffeepot, R Dunham tm, trn ring ft/body, blk scroll hdl, 12" 465.00
Coffeepot, Roswell Gleason tm, paneled body, scrolled wood hdl, 10"..300.00
Dish, deep; Love & facing birds tm, ca 1800, 1x8⅝" 400.00
Flagon, I Trask tm, tapered sides, scroll hdl, domed lid, 12" 1,100.00
Flagon, Reed & Barton tm, tooled rings, scroll hdl, domed lid, 9⅝"......440.00
Flagon, Sheldon & Feltman Albany tm, step-down ft, domed lid, 11"..385.00
Ladle, unmk Am, att James Weekes, 7¼" 195.00
Lamp, chamber; E Smith tm, corroded, w/whale-oil burner, 5⅝"..195.00
Lamp, chamber; H Hopper tm, tooled lines, whale-oil burner, 1850s, 5"...190.00
Measure, Sanders & Sons tm, Quart, 6½" 150.00
Mug, Hartford & eagle tm, resoldered hdl, sm split, 4½" 450.00
Pitcher, Boardman & Hart New York tm, domed lid, rprs, 9¾"..385.00
Pitcher, Sellew & Co Cincinnati tm, cast ear hdl, 9" 360.00
Plate, Boardman & Co NY eagle tm, wear/scratches, 10¾" 275.00
Plate, G Lightner Baltimore eagle tm, minor dents, 8¾" 360.00
Plate, London tm, molded rim, ca 1800, 12" 180.00
Plate, Love & facing birds tm, early 19th C, 6" 450.00
Plate, Love & London tms, 8", VG 450.00
Plate, Nathaniel Austin eagle tm, battered/rim rpr, 9½" 220.00
Plate, S Ellis & crowned rose mk, wear/scratches, 8" 100.00
Plate, S Kilbourn eagle tm, wear/scratches, 7¾" 360.00
Plate, S Stafford Albany tm, hammered booge, scratches, 8⅞"..300.00
Plate, T Compton & Townsend tm, early 19th C, 12⅛" 250.00
Plate, TD & eagle tm, 7¾" 385.00
Plate, Thomas Danforth tm, wear/pitting, 9⅛" 160.00
Plate, Townsend & Compton tm, early 1800s, 8", pr 90.00
Porringer, cast crown hdl, New England, 5½"..............................300.00
Porringer, Richard Lee tm, pierced floral hdl, 3¾" 650.00
Porringer, TD&SB tm, crown hdl, minor pitting, 5" 440.00
Soup plate, Thistle tm, rim eng AS, 9¾" 135.00
Tablespoons, S&Co tm, sawtooth-like border hdls, early 1800s, 6 for...110.00
Tall pot, unmk Am, dents/minor damage, 11" 220.00
Tankard, London crowned X tm, bellied, crooked thumbpc, 12"...165.00

Tankard, T. Wildes, New York touch mark, stepped base with tooled rings at middle of body, old replaced domed lid, 8¼", $1,000.00; Tall pot, unmarked American, tapered body, domed lid, scrolled handle, light pitting, 11¼", $370.00.

Tankard, WH tm w/crown, hinged lid, ftd base, ca 1750s, 7¾x4¾"..890.00
Teapot, A Griswold eagle tm, domed lid, rpr hinge, 8¼" 250.00
Teapot, B&V tm, Queen Anne, wood hdl & wafer on finial, rpr, 6"..495.00
Teapot, Dixon & Sons tm, footed, fluted body, domed lid, rpr, 9"......165.00
Teapot, G Richardson Warranted tm, 7¼"....................................250.00
Teapot, H Yale & Co Wallingford tm, dents/rpr, 8" 200.00
Teapot, JW Cahill & Co, tooled lines, scalloped finial wafer, 7"..350.00
Teapot, partial JB Graves tm, 1850s, 9", EX 300.00
Teapot, TD&SB tm, pear shape, paneled spout, 8" 880.00

Pfaltzgraff

Pfaltzgraff has operated in Pennsylvania since the early 1800s making redware at first, then stoneware crocks and jugs, yellow ware and spongeware in the '20s, artware and kitchenware in the '30s, and

stoneware kitchen items through the '40s. To collectors, they're best known for their Gourmet Royal (circa 1950s), a high-gloss dinnerware line of solid brown with frothy white drip glaze around the rims, and their giftware line called Muggsy, comic-character mugs, ashtrays, bottle stoppers, children's dishes, pretzel jars, cookie jars, etc. It was designed in the late 1940s and continued in production until 1960. The older versions have protruding features, while the features of later examples were simply painted on.

Their popular Village line, an almond-glazed pattern with a brown-stenciled folk-art tulip design, was discontinued a few years ago, and is today becoming very collectible. Yorktown and Folk Art are manufactured today only on a very limited basis, so discontinued items in those lines are attracting much interest as well. (In general, use Village prices to help you evaluate those two lines.) For more information on their dinnerware, we recommend *The Flea Market Trader* and *The Garage Sale and Flea Market Annual*, both by Collector Books.

Gourmet Royale, baker, #321, oval, 7½", from $18 to..................20.00
Gourmet Royale, bean pot, #11-4, 4-qt..45.00
Gourmet Royale, bowl, cereal; #934SR, 5½", from $6 to 8.00
Gourmet Royale, bowl, mixing; 8", from $12 to............................14.00
Gourmet Royale, butter dish, #394, ¼-lb, stick type 12.00
Gourmet Royale, casserole, hen on nest, 2-qt, from $75 to 95.00
Gourmet Royale, casserole, stick hdl, 1-qt, from $15 to 18.00
Gourmet Royale, casserole-warming stand 10.00
Gourmet Royale, coffeepot, #303, 10-cup, from $35 to 45.00
Gourmet Royale, gravy boat, #426, 2-spout, lg, +underplate, $14 to...16.00
Gourmet Royale, mug, #391, 12-oz, from $6 to................................8.00
Gourmet Royale, plate, egg; holds 12 halves, 7¾x12½", $20 to ...22.00
Gourmet Royale, platter, #337, 16", from $25 to............................30.00
Gourmet Royale, roaster, #326, oval, 16", from $50 to..................60.00
Gourmet Royale, shirred egg dish, #360, 6", from $10 to 12.00
Village, baker, #236, rectangular, tab hdls, 2-qt, from $12 to 15.00
Village, baker, #240, oval, 7¾", from $6 to......................................8.00
Village, bowl, batter; w/spout & hdl, 8", from $35 to....................42.00
Village, bowl, mixing; #453, 1-qt, 2-qt & 3-qt, 3-pc set, $40 to....50.00
Village, bowl, serving; #010, 7", from $8 to....................................10.00
Village, bowl, vegetable; #011, 8¾", from $12 to............................15.00
Village, butter dish, #028..8.00
Village, casserole, w/lid, #315, 2-qt, from $18 to 25.00
Village, cookie jar, #540, 3-qt, from $18 to 25.00
Village, cup & saucer, #001 & #002..3.50
Village, gravy boat, #443, w/saucer, 16-oz, from $12 to................15.00
Village, onion soup crock, #295, stick hdl, sm, from $6 to 8.00
Village, pitcher, #416, 2-qt, from $20 to..25.00
Village, soup tureen, #160, w/lid & ladle, 3½-qt, from $40 to 45.00
Village, table light, #620, clear chimney, candle holder base, $12 to .14.00

Muggsy Line

Ashtray 125.00
Cigarette server..125.00
Clothes sprinkler bottle, Myrtle, Black, from $275 to..................375.00
Clothes sprinkler bottle, Myrtle, wht, from $250 to 350.00
Cookie jar, character face, minimum value 250.00
Jar, utility; Handy Harry, hat w/short bill as flat lid 200.00
Mug, action figure (golfer/fisherman/etc), any, from $65 to 85.00
Mug, shot sz, character face..50.00
Tumbler..60.00

Phoenix Bird

Blue and white Phoenix Bird china has been produced by various

Japanese potteries from the early 1900s. With slight variations the design features the Japanese bird of paradise and scroll-like vines of Kara-Kusa, or Chinese grass. Although some of their earlier ware is unmarked, the majority is marked in some fashion. More than one hundred different stamps have been reported, with 'Made in Japan' the one most often found. Coming in second is Morimura's wreath and/or crossed stems (both having the letter 'M' within). The cloverleaf with 'Japan' below very often indicates an item having a high-quality transfer-printed design. Among the many categories in the Phoenix Bird pattern are several shapes; therefore (for identification purposes), each has been given a number, i.e. #1, #2, etc. Newer items, if marked at all, carry a paper label. Compared to the older ware, the coloring of the new is whiter and the blue more harsh; the design is sparse with more ground area showing. Although collectors buy even 'new' pieces, the older is, of course, more highly prized and valued.

For further information we recommend *Phoenix Bird Chinaware, Books I – IV*, written and privately published by our advisor, Joan Oates; her address is in the Directory under Michigan. Join Phoenix Bird Collectors of America (PBCA) and receive the *Phoenix Bird Discoveries* newsletter, an informative publication that will further your appreciation of this chinaware. See Clubs, Newsletters, and Catalogs for ordering information.

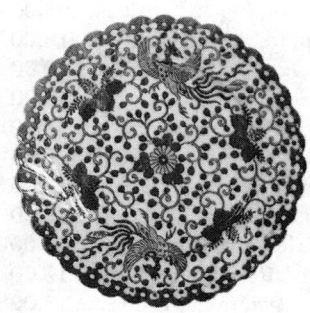

Dessert plate, scalloped and swirled (termed Ho-o because of heart-style border), 7¼", from $20.00 to $25.00. (Photo courtesy Joan Oates)

Bouillon cup & saucer, 2-hdl, from $25 to 30.00
Chocolate pot, style #1, bell-like, from $125 to..........................145.00
Chocolate pot, style #2, scalloped base, from $145 to 175.00
Coffee/tea cup & saucer, common farmer's sz, from $8 to.............10.00
Coffee/tea cups & saucer, common shape, from $5 to.....................8.50
Coffeepot, spray-can style #6, from $110 to 138.00
Condiment set, 3 triangular dishes w/orig box, from $250 to......350.00
Egg cup, dbl, top & bottom, from $15 to..22.00
Egg cup, single, ped ft, from $10 to..15.00
Gravy boat & underplate, common-style #4, from $45 to 55.00
Pitcher, buttermilk; rnd body, oval base, 6", from $75 to............110.00
Plate, dinner; 9¾", from $35 to 45.00
Plate, luncheon; 8¼", from $15 to...25.00
Platter, 12x8", from $45 to 65.00
Tea strainer, ftd, w/heart border, (Ho-o) style #6, from $45 to......55.00
Teapot & warmer, Takahashi-made, post-1970, from $35 to 45.00
Vegetable tureen & lid, rnd or oval, from $85 to.........................125.00

Phoenix Glass

Founded in 1880 in Monaca, Pennsylvania, the Phoenix Glass Company became one of the country's foremost manufacturers of lighting glass by the early 1900s. They also produced a wide variety of utilitarian and decorative glassware, including art glass by Joseph Webb, colored cut glass, Gone-With-the-Wind style oil lamps, hotel and barware, and pharmaceutical glassware. Today, however, collectors are primarily interested in the 'Sculptured Artware' produced in the 1930s and 1940s. These beautiful pressed and mold-blown pieces are most often found in white milk glass or crystal with various color treatments or a satin finish.

Phoenix did not mark their 'Sculptured Artware' line on the glass; instead, a silver and black (earliest) or gold and black (later) foil label in the shape of the mythical phoenix bird was used.

Quite often glassware made by the Consolidated Lamp and Glass Company of nearby Coraopolis, Pennsylvania, is mistaken for Phoenix's 'Sculptured Artware.' Though the style of the glass is very similar, one distinguishing characteristic is that perhaps 80% of the time Phoenix applied color to the background leaving the raised design plain in contrast, while Consolidated generally applied color to the raised design and left the background plain. Also, for the most part, the patterns and colors used by Phoenix were distinctively different from those used by Consolidated.

In 1970 Phoenix Glass became a division of Anchor Hocking which in turn was acquired by the Newell Group in 1987. Phoenix has the distinction of being one of the oldest continuously operating glass factories in the United States. For more information refer to *Phoenix and Consolidated Art Glass, 1926 – 1980*, written by our advisor, Jack D. Wilson, who is listed in the Directory under Arizona. See also Consolidated Glass.

Key: mg — milk glass

Bachelor Button, vase, tan w/brn shadow on flowers, 6" 275.00
Bachelor Button, vase, wht pearlized, 6" 225.00
Blackberry, compote, pk decor on mg..145.00
Bluebell, vase, deep burgundy pearlized, 7" 125.00
Bluebell, vase, florist gr (rare color), KR Haley, 1948, 7"...........250.00
Bluebell, vase, pearlized w/lt pk bkground, 7" 125.00
Bluebells, vase, beige on mg, silver label, 7½" 250.00
Cosmos, reverse-decor bl-gr on wht (strong colors), 7½" 275.00
Cosmos, vase, bl on mg, 7½" 200.00
Cosmos, vase, slate bl shadow, 7½" 185.00
Cosmos, vase, tan pearlized, 7½"..185.00
Daisy, vase, bl on mg, 9x9"...425.00
Daisy, vase, bl w/frosted flowers, 9"..325.00
Daisy, vase, yel w/pearlized flowers, 9".......................................435.00
Dancing Girls, vase, Florist Green (rare color), 12" 900.00
Dancing Girls, vase, frosted nudes on orange bkground, 12".......578.00
Dancing Girls, vase, gr over mg, 12"...475.00
Dancing Girls, vase, med bl over mg, 12" 650.00
Dancing Girls, vase, reverse Deco Blue on satin mg (rare color), 12" ..665.00
Dancing Girls, vase, wht mg on gray bkground, 12" 565.00
Diving Girl, bowl, bl on mg, 14" 330.00
Diving Girl, bowl, frosted nudes on orange bkground, 14"..........405.00
Diving Girl, oblong bowl, gr w/bl highlights, pearlized design, 14" ..350.00
Fern, vase, reverse decor pk & gr on wht (strong colors), 7".......280.00
Freesia, vase, aqua w/frosted design, fan shape, 8" 140.00
Freesia, vase, bl & frosted, 8"..295.00
Freesia, vase, bl chipped ice finish (rare), 8", from $1,375 to ..1,900.00
Freesia, vase, pk w/frosted design, 8" 150.00
Freesia, vase, reverse decor gr/yel on wht, fan form, 8"................330.00
Jewel, vase, bl pearlized, 4¾" 125.00
Jewel, vase, med gr on mg, 5"..100.00
Jewel, vase, tan & mg, 4¾"..100.00
Jonquil, tray, bl & frosted, 14" 320.00
Lacy Dewdrop, compote, pk decor on mg 145.00
Lily, vase, aqua wash, 3-crimp, 9" 225.00
Lily, vase, med bl, tri-crimped, 8½", EX......................................255.00
Lily, vase, purple w/frosted design, 9" 225.00
Line 700, vase, Reuben Blue (extremely rare color), 7" 525.00
Madonna, vase, brn shadow, 10"..275.00
Madonna, vase, Florist Green (rare), 10" 340.00
Madonna, vase, peach over mg, 10"..250.00
Madonna, vase, salmon pearlized, 10" 230.00

Philodendron, vase, brn shadow, 11½".............................200.00
Philodendron, vase, slate bl over mg, 11½"....................200.00
Phlox, ashtray, Reuben Blue (rare color), 5½x3"..........152.50
Phlox, ashtray, slate bl pearlized 225.00
Phlox, candy dish, bl shadow, w/lid 200.00
Phlox, candy dish, lt bl wash w/frosted design, w/lid 175.00
Primrose, vase, frosted w/bl bkground, 8¾"....................475.00
Primrose, vase, reverse decor yel & gr, 8¾", EX.............225.00
Spatter, vase, bl w/wht spatter, silver label, 3½x4" 230.00
Star Flower, vase, bl & mg, 7"..145.00
Star Flower, vase, blk stain over crystal, 7" 300.00
Star Flower, vase, brn over mg, 7" 150.00
Strawberry, candle holders, brn shadow, silver label, 4½" dia, pr .160.00
Thistle, umbrella vase, Florist Green (rare color), 18", NM........495.00
Thistle, vase, dk bl pearlized, 18"...................................550.00
Thistle, vase, lime gr pearlized, 18" 525.00
Thistle, vase, slate bl pearlized, 18"...............................550.00
Tiger Lily, bowl, amethyst frosted, 11½" 425.00
Tiger Lily, bowl, pk frosted, 11½".................................400.00
Wild Geese, matt mg geese on bl/purple bkground, 9x12" 225.00
Wild Geese, mg geese on slate bl bkground, 9x12"..........240.00
Wild Geese, vase, bl-gray w/frosted design, 9" 200.00
Wild Geese, vase, gr frosted, 9x12"................................225.00
Wild Rose, vase, brn shadow, 10½"................................175.00
Wild Rose, vase, wht frosted, 9" 100.00
Zodiac, vase, deep rose over mg, 10½"............................950.00
Zodiac, vase, tan over mg, 10½".....................................900.00
Zodiac, vase, wht frosted, 10½"......................................610.00

Phonographs

The phonograph, invented by Thomas Edison in 1877, was the first practical instrument for recording and reproducing sound. Sound wave vibrations were recorded on a tinfoil-covered cylinder and played back with a needle that ran along the grooves made from the recording, thus reproducing the sound. Very little changed to this art of record making until 1885, when the first replayable and removable wax cylinders were developed by the American Graphophone Company. These records were made from 1885 until 1894 and are rare today. Edison began to offer music on recorded wax cylinders in 1889. They continued to be made until 1902. Today they are known as brown wax records. Black wax cylinders were offered in 1902, and the earlier brown wax cylinders were discontinued. These wax two-minute records were sold until 1912. From 1912 until 1929, only four-minute celluloid blue amberol record cylinders were made. The first disc records and disc machines were offered by the inventor Berliner in 1894. They were sold in America until 1900, when the Victor company took over. In the 1890s, all machines played 7" diameter disc records; the 10" size was developed in 1901. By the early 1900s there existed many disc and cylinder phonograph companies, all offering their improvements. Among them were Berliner, Columbia, Zonophone, United States Phono, Wizard, Vitaphone, Amet, and others.

All Victor I's through VI's originally came with a choice of either brass bell, morning-glory, or wooden horns. Wood horns are the most valuable, adding $1,000.00 (or more) to the machine. Spring models were produced until 1929 (and even later). After 1929 most were electric (though some electric-motor models were produced as early as 1910). Unless another condition is noted, prices are for complete, original phonographs in at least fine to excellent condition. Note: Edison coin-operated cylinder players start at $7,000.00 and may go up to $20,000.00 each. All outside-horn Victor phonographs are worth at *least* $1,000.00 or more, if in excellent original condition. Machines that are complete, still retaining all their original parts, and with the original finish still in good condition are the most sought after, but those that have

been carefully restored with their original finishes, decals, etc., are bringing high prices as well. Unless noted, values are for examples in excellent condition, sold at popular, repeated buying prices.

Key:
cyl — cylinder	NP — nickel plated
mg — morning glory	rpd — reproducer

Mirophone, double-comb disk player, wooden horn, Jacot Music Box Co, NY, mahogany veneer case with applied carving, with sixteen 15½" discs, EX, $9,900.00 at auction. (Photo courtesy Stanton's Auctioneers and Realters)

Aretino, disc, orig gr mg horn, 3" center spindle 750.00
Berliner Trade Mark, disc, Clark Johnson rpd, brass horn........5,000.00
Bing Pigmyphone, disc, orig rpd, cone horn........................400.00
Brunswick, cvd upright case w/moldings, lg 350.00
Brunswick Queen Anne, console style, rpr motor, working........350.00
Busy Bee Q, cyl, VG..575.00
Cameraphone, disc, orig rpd, tortoise-shell resonator, oak 550.00
Cheney Talking Machine, disc, walnut, floor model 450.00
Columbia AA, cyl, eagle rpd, blk horn, oak 1,000.00
Columbia AH, disc, Columbia rpd, brass bell horn, no decal ..1,000.00
Columbia AZ, cyl, Lyric rpd, repro blk/brass horn 500.00
Columbia BG, cyl, chrome bedplate, brass bell horn, mahog...1,650.00
Columbia BI Sterling, disc, Columbia rpd, oak horn 2,250.00
Columbia BII, cyl, emb metal horn, EX finish & decal, NM...1,100.00
Columbia BK Jewel, cyl, Lyric rpd, orig horn, striping 450.00
Columbia B1, Dolcher control on rpd, NP horn 1,350.00
Columbia Graphophone B, cyl, sm gold-striped horn, long case, VG..450.00
Columbia Graphophone BE, cyl, lyre rpd, orig brass bell horn ...600.00
Columbia Graphophone BX, cyl, blk horn w/gold stripe, long case 375.00
Columbia Graphophone Q, blk horn w/gold trim, VG 350.00
Columbia K, disc, orig rpd, front mt 1,000.00
Columbia P Premium, disc, orig rpd, red horn 625.00
Columbia Q, cyl, Q rpd, repro cone horn, oak w/banner 350.00
Columbia Regent Desk, disc, Columbia rpd, inside horn, mahog ...400.00
Edison A-250, floor model 600.00
Edison Amberola VI, cyl, Dmn B rpd/inside horn, oak table top...450.00
Edison Amberola 10, cyl, prof rfn..525.00
Edison Amberola 30, cyl, Dmn C rpd, inside horn, oak, NM 375.00
Edison Amberola 50, cyl, all orig, M 700.00
Edison Concert, cyl, D rpd, brass horn/stand, 5" mandrel........2,500.00
Edison Concert A, cyl, automatic, rpr, 36" brass horn, w/stand 3,000.00
Edison Concert C, cyl, R rpd, 30" brass bell, floor stand, M 2,500.00
Edison Dmn Disc A100, DD rpd, inside horn, Moderne golden oak ..350.00
Edison Dmn Disc S-19, DD rpd, inside horn, oak, upright..........250.00
Edison Fireside A, cyl, Dmn B rpd, oak Music Master horn 2,250.00
Edison Fireside B, cyl, cygnet horn, rare rpd, VG.....................1,700.00
Edison Fireside B, cyl, Dmn B rpd, blk cygnet horn, 4-min 1,000.00
Edison Gem A, cyl, rpl horn & bracket, 1902-05 ....600.00
Edison Gem E Maroon, all orig...2,000.00
Edison Home, cyl, C rpd, bl mg horn w/bracket 725.00
Edison Home, cyl, H rpd, metal cygnet horn, 2/4-min 675.00
Edison Home A Suitcase, cyl, C rpd, 14" repro horn, decal........550.00
Edison Opera, mahog case & Music Master horn....................6,750.00
Edison Standard, cyl, C rpd, brass bell horn..............................475.00

Edison Standard, cyl, K rpd, no horn 700.00
Edison Standard D, cyl, C rpd, red mg horn 950.00
Edison Standard Flat Top, cyl, VG 600.00
Edison Triumph, cyl, O rpd, oak cygnet horn, NM 2,500.00
Edison Triumph E, cyl, no horn 900.00
Harmony #12, disc, EX orig 225.00
Kalamazoo Duplex, disc, Kalamazoo rpd, 2 blk/brass horns, rare...4,300.00
Klingsor, disc, Klingsor rpd, inside horn, ldgl doors..................2,000.00
Lakeside (Ward's), cyl, inside horn 750.00
Melodograph, disc, CI, G 175.00
Nirona box type, disc, Nirona rpd, sound reflector, red metal case, sm...550.00
Pathe Actuelle, disc, cone horn, mahog console 1,000.00
Puck Lyre, cyl, floating rdp, red mg horn 400.00
Regina Hexaphone #102, cyl, Hexaphone rpd, oak horn, rstr...7,500.00
Regina Hexaphone #104, cyl, Hexaphone rpd, oak horn, rstr...8,500.00
Standard A, disc, Standard rpd, bl mg horn, decal 650.00
Standard Talking Machine X2, bl horn, 1906, VG......................450.00
Standard X, disc, Standard rpd, front mt brass bell w/support.....600.00
Thorens Excalda, disc, Excalda rpd, internal horn, camera type.265.00
United Symphony, disc, United rpd, inside horn, table model ...250.00
Victor I, disc, Exhibition rpd, repro brass, bell, oak case 1,000.00
Victor II, disc, Exhibition rpd, brass bell horn 1,200.00
Victor IV, disc, Exhibition rpd, mahog horn & case.................4,000.00
Victor M Monarch Specialty, disc, Exhibition rpd, oak horn ..2,500.00
Victor R Royal, disc, Exhibition rpd, 9½" brass bell, oak.........1,000.00
Victor Schoolhouse XXF, disc, orig oak horn, oak upright.......3,000.00
Victor VI, disc, Exhibition rpd, mahog horn & case 5,000.00
Victor VV-VI, disc, Exhibition rpd, inside horn, oak table top...200.00
Victor VV-8-30, disc, Orthophonic rpd, inside horn, credenza...1,000.00
Victor Z, disc, Exhibition rpd, brass bell horn 1,400.00
Victrola Credenza, w/longest Victor horn, walnut, rare, VG.......800.00
Vitaphone, disc, w/horn, minimum value 1,000.00
Zonophone, disc, front mt w/horn, from $1,000 to 3,000.00
Zonophone Parlor, disc, brass bell horn, rear crank.................1,100.00
Zonophone Royal Grand, disc, lg NP horn...............................2,200.00

Photographica

Photographic collectibles include not only the cameras and equipment used to 'freeze' special moments in time but also the photographic images produced by a great variety of processes that have evolved since the daguerrean era of the mid-1800s. For the most part, good quality images have either maintained or increased in value. Poor quality examples (regardless of rarity) are not selling well. Interest in cameras and stereo equipment is down, and dealers report that average-priced items that were moving well are often completely overlooked. Though rare items always have a market, collectors seem to be buying only if they are bargain priced.

Our advisor for this category is John Hess; he is listed in the Directory under Massachusetts.

Albumen, Chinese man, hand colored, Shanghai label in English and Chinese characters, 1870s, 10x8", EX, $250.00.

Albumens

Street scene of crowd at post office in Nebraska, 1890s, 6x8½"..110.00
Theatrical lady in fancy costume & holding spear, 1890s, EX.......75.00
View of Admiral Porter's gunboats near Vicksburg, 5¼x7¼" 880.00
Warship USS Choctaw on Mississippi, Vicksburg beyond, 1863-4, 8x9½"...1,650.00

Ambrotypes

An ambrotype is a type of photograph produced by an early wet-plate process whereby a faint negative image on glass is seen as positive when held against a dark background.

4th-plate, man seated wearing vest & bow tie, EX, +8-sided case....225.00
4th-plate, OH Cavalryman in great coat, identified, EX, +Union case 415.00
4th-plate, storefront scene w/boy, Winchester NH, VG-.............200.00
6th-plate, boy sits on floor w/dog at side, VG+, +case 150.00
6th-plate, girl in fancy dress & much jewelry, EX, +Union case .165.00
6th-plate, Zoave w/pistol butt visible in belt, EX, +full case 300.00
9th-plate, African-Am lady in dress w/wht collar & brooch, +case 200.00

Cabinet Photos

Black baby in carriage, G Marr, OH, VG 35.00
Chester A Arthur, in civilian coat, identified, 1880s, VG 35.00
Crow family & teepees, 1890s, 6x4" 80.00
General Beauregard in Confederate uniform, 4x2¼" 60.00
Geronimo, J Pitcher Spooner, 1888, 6x4" 400.00
Lady banjo players seated together, MA, VG...............................125.00
Mad Bear (Am Indian), Kern Bros NY, 1890s, 6x4".................130.00
Man in fringed shirt, w/ammo belt, rifle, spurs, PA, VG+ 200.00
President Grover Cleveland in formal frock coat, identified, 6x4", EX....45.00
Wm Seward, Secretary of State, 1860s, EX 95.00

Cameras

Collecting antique cameras is very popular, and values have continued to move upward as the high-quality items have become harder to find. Most of the pre-1900 cameras will be found in the large format view cameras or studio camera types. There are quite a few of these that can be found in a well-worn condition, but there is a large difference in value between an average-wear item and an excellent or mint-condition camera. It is rare indeed to find one of these early cameras in mint condition.

The types of cameras are generally classified into — large format, medium format, early folding and box types, 35mm single-lens-reflex (SLR), 35mm rangefinders, twin-lens reflex (TLR), miniature or subminiature, novelty, and even a few others. Collectors may specialize in a type, a style, a time period, or even in high-quality examples of the same camera.

In the 1900 to 1940 period, large quantities of various makes of box cameras and folding bellows type cameras were produced by many manufacturers, and the popular 35mm camera was introduced in the 1930s. Most have low values because they were made in vast numbers, but mint-condition cameras are prized by collectors. In the 1930 to 1955 period, the 35mm rangefinders and the SLR's and TLR's became the cameras of choice. The most prized of these are the early German or Japanese rangefinders such as the Leica, Canon, or Nikon. Earlier, German optics were favored, but after WWII, Japanese cameras and optics rivaled and/or even exceeded the quality of many German optics.

Now there are thousands of different cameras to choose from, and collectors have many options when selecting categories. Quality is the major factor; values vary widely between an average-wear working camera and one in mint condition, or one still in the original box and unused. This brief list suggests average prices for good working cameras with average wear. The same camera in mint condition will be valued much higher, while one with excessive wear (scratches, dents, corrosion, poor optics, nonworking meters or rangefinders) may have little value.

Buying, selling, and trading of old and late vintage cameras on the Internet, both in direct transactions and via e-mail auctions, have affected the number of cameras that are available to collectors. As a result, values have fluctuated as well. Large numbers of old, mass-produced box cameras and folding cameras have been offered; many are in poor condition and have been put up for sale by persons who know nothing about quality. So in general, prices have dropped, except for the *mint* quality offerings. Many common models in poor to average condition can be bought for $1.00 to $10.00. The collector is advised to purchase only quality cameras that will enhance his collection.

Note: To date, no appreciable collector's market has developed for most old movie cameras or projectors. The Polaroid type of camera has little value, although a few models are gaining in popularity among collectors, and values are expected to increase. Note that many fakes and copies have been made of several of the classic cameras such as the German Leica, and caution is advised in purchasing one of these cameras at a price too good to be true. Consult a specialist on high-priced classics if good reference material is not available. Our advisor for this category is Gene Cataldo; he is listed in the Directory under Alabama (e-mail: genecams@aol.com). SASE required for information by mail.

Agfa, Billy, early 1930s	15.00
Agfa, Isolette	20.00
Agfa, Optima, 1960s, from $20 to	50.00
Aires, 35III, 1958	35.00
Ansco, Folding, Nr 1 to Nr 10, ea, from $10 to	40.00
Ansco, Memar, 1954-58	20.00
Ansco, Memo, 1927 type	100.00
Argus A2F, 1940	20.00
Argus C3, blk brick type, 1940-50, from $5 to	10.00
Asahiflex 1, 1st Japanese SLR	500.00
Bell & Howell Dial-35, from $25 to	50.00
Bell & Howell Foton, 1948	1,000.00
Canon J, 1939-44, from $4,500 to	6,000.00
Canon P, 1958-61	300.00
Canon S-II, 1947-49	375.00
Canon TX	60.00
Canon 7, 1961-64	450.00
Ciroflex, TLR, 1940s	30.00
Conley, 4x5 Folding Plate, 1905	150.00
Contex II or III, 1936	450.00
Eastman Folding Brownie Six-20	12.00
Eastman Kodak Bantam, Art Deco, 1935-38	35.00
Eastman Kodak Box Hawkeye No 2A	8.00
Eastman Kodak Medalist, 1941-48, from $140 to	200.00
Eastman Kodak No 3A Folding Pocket	30.00
Eastman Kodak Retina II	65.00
Eastman Kodak Retina IIIc, from $125 to	180.00
Eastman Kodak Retinette, various models, ea, from $20 to	50.00
Eastman Kodak Signet 80	60.00
Eastman Premo, many models exist, ea, from $30 to	200.00
Edinex, by Wirgen	30.00
FED 1, USSR, prewar, from $100 to	200.00
Fujica ST-701	70.00
Graflex Speed Graphic, various szs, ea, from $100 to	200.00
Leica II, 1963-67, from $300 to	450.00
Leica IID, 1932-38, from $250 to	400.00
Leica M3, 1954-66, from $600 to	1,400.00
Mamiyaflex, TLR, 1951, from $125 to	150.00
Minolta, SR-7	50.00
Minolta, XG-1, XG-7, XG-9, XG-A, ea, from $50 to	80.00
Minolta Autocord, TLR	100.00

Minolta-16, mini, various models, ea, from $15 to	30.00
Miranda Automex II, 1963	70.00
Nikon F, various finders & meters, ea, from $150 to	275.00
Nikon S2 Rangefinder, 1954-58, from $300 to	500.00
Olympus Pen EE, compact half-fr	35.00
Pax M3, 1957	40.00
Petri FT, FT-1000, FT-EE & similar models, ea	70.00
Plaubel-Makina II, 1933-39	200.00
Praktica, FX, 1952-57	40.00
Realist Stereo, 3.5 lens	100.00
Regula, King, various models, interchangeable lens, ea	75.00
Ricoh Singlex, 1965	80.00
Rolleicord II, 1936-50, from $70 to	90.00
Rolleiflex SL35M, 1978	100.00
Samoca 35, 1950s	25.00
Spartus Press Flash, 1939-50	10.00
Tessina, mini in colors, from $400 to	700.00
Topcon Uni	40.00
Tower 50, Sears, w/Cassar lens	20.00
Voigtlander Bessa, w/rangefinder, 1936	140.00
Voigtlander Vitessa L, 1954, from $150 to	300.00
Zeiss Ikon Nettar, folding, various szs, ea, from $20 to	35.00
Zorki, USSR, 1950-56	50.00

Carte De Visites

Among the many types of images collectible today are carte de visites, known as CDVs, which are 2¼" x 4" portraits printed on paper and produced in quantity. The CDV fad of the 1800s enticed the famous and the unknown alike to pose for these cards, which were circulated among the public to the extent that they became known as 'publics.' When the popularity of CDVs began to wane, a new fascination developed for the cabinet photo, a larger version measuring about 4½" x 6½". Note: A common portrait CDV is worth only about 50¢ unless it carries a revenue stamp on the back; those that do are valued at about $2.00 each.

Baptist Church, Colored, Petersburg VA, 1866, VG	125.00
Boy on hobby horse, F Gutenkunst Philadelphia, VG	80.00
Butcher w/lg knife & sharpener, OH, VG	80.00
Charles Sumner, abolitionist, VG+	35.00
Civil War officer w/Black orderly, Guay & Co, New Orleans, G	545.00
Civil War Union Captain (identified), signed/inscribed, 1863-64, VG	100.00
Colonel HR Lee & Staff, 27th MA Infantry, ca 1864-65, VG	200.00
Frederick Douglass, ¾-figure seated, EX	550.00
General Custer in uniform, ca 1864, VG+	775.00
Jefferson Davis, Matthew Brady/E Anthony, 1860-61, VG+	250.00
Sojourner Truth, I Sell the Shadow..., knitting in lap, ca 1864, VG	660.00
Stephen A Douglas as Presidential candidate, ca 1860, G	45.00
Winnebago Chiefs in Council, Whitney's...MN, VG	360.00

Daguerreotypes

Among the many processes used to produce photographic images are the daguerreotypes (made on a plate of chemically treated silver-plated copper) — the most-valued examples being the 'whole' plate which measures 6½" x 8½". Other sizes include the 'half' plate, measuring 4½" x 5½", the 'quarter' plate at 3¼" x 4¼", the 'sixth' plate at 2¾" x 3¼", the 'ninth' at 2" x 2½", and the 'sixteenth' at 1⅜" x 1⅝". (Sizes may vary slightly, and some may have been altered by the photographer.)

Full-case, boys (2) w/toys hold hands, G, +full case	225.00
Half-plate, old man w/lg hat in hand sits proudly, EX	675.00
6th-plate, brick building on sm knoll w/stone wall in foreground, EX	1,700.00
6th-plate, lady in bonnet & lg fishnet shawl, ca 1840s, +case	85.00

6th-plate, lady w/book & flowers, hand-tinted, EX 125.00
6th-plate, man in sports tunic w/looped chain, EX......................515.00
6th-plate, mother holds baby in pk-tinted gown, VG, +full case...110.00

Photos

Nez Perce chief in eagle headdress, 1900s, 9x7" 60.00
Photogravure, Chief of Desert Navajo, ES Curtis, sepia tone, 16x11"...500.00
Photogravure, Jicarilla Women, ES Curtis, sepia tone, 1904, 12x15"....500.00
Photogravure, Kutenai Duck Hunter, ES Curtis, sepia tone, 1910, 10x15"...950.00
Taos Pueblo NM feast day dance, 1940s, 11x14" 110.00
WWI enlisted man in campaign hat, 7½x4½" 25.00

Stereoscopic Views

Stereo cards are photos made to be viewed through a device called a stereoscope. The glass stereo plates of the mid-1800s and photo prints produced in the darkroom are among the most valuable. In evaluating stereo views, the subject, date, and condition are all important. Some views were printed over a thirty- to forty-year period; 'first generation' prices are far higher than later copies, made on cheap card stock with reprints or lithographs, rather than actual original photographs.

It is relatively easy to date an American stereo view by the color of the mount that was used, the style of the corners, etc. From about 1854 until the early 1860s, cards were either white, cream-colored, or glossy gray; shades of yellow and a dull gray followed. While the dull gray was used for a very short time, the yellow tones continued in use until the late 1860s. Red, green, violet, or blue cards are from the period between 1865 until about 1870. Until the late 1870s, corners were square; after that they were rounded off to prevent damage. Right now, quality stereo views are at a premium.

Abraham Lincoln, reprint of Anthony View, Keystone, EX- 250.00
Black waiters in elegant restaurant, FL, EX 40.00
Colored Troupes Taking Train Rest, WWI/1918, VG..................110.00
Horse-drawn baker's delivery sleigh loaded w/bread, EX 120.00
Lincoln funeral procession, street scene, VG 400.00
Nuns tending sick at Hotel Dieu Hospital, EX................................95.00
NY canal boat close-up, RR Abbott, VG+....................................35.00
Philadelphia street scene w/church, ca 1858, G 35.00
Pittsburgh GAR parade, crowd of veterans w/flags, Keystone, 1894...25.00
Printing Presses, US Bureau of Printing, Keystone #22343, EX 30.00
Raping of Black Hills, pioneer Quartz Mill, machinery, 1876, EX..95.00
Ship in San Francisco dry dock, USS China, Watkins #1719, VG..150.00
Steamship Pearl, Cleveland OH, VG..35.00

Tintypes

Tintypes, contemporaries of ambrotypes, were produced on japanned iron and were not as easily damaged.

4th-plate, Civil War Union private seated with arm on table, in Union case, VG, from $150.00 to $200.00.

Full-case, Black lady seated in chair, 1860s, VG, +case.............125.00
Half-plate, hunter w/shotgun & 3 ducks, EX 170.00
Whole plate, Civil War soldier wearing kepi, unfr, 8⅝x6½" ...190.00
4th plate, sailor in uniform w/hat & bosun whistle lanyard, EX .165.00
4th-plate, Civil War soldier in full view w/forage cap, EX, +case ..175.00
4th-plate, Union Corporal w/musket & bayonet, VG, +full case ..385.00
4th-plate, 5 armed soldiers at attention, EX, +half case 785.00
4th-plate, 8 soldiers w/stacked rifles/etc, outdoor scene, VG ...1,900.00
6th-plate, soldier w/rifle/pistol/sword, early 1860s, EX, +half case....450.00
6th-plate, well-dressed wht man centers 9 Black boys, 1880s, VG...140.00
6th-plate, young Union soldier w/knapsack & rolled blanket, EX ...330.00

Union Cases

From the mid-1850s until about 1880, cases designed to house these early images were produced from a material known as thermoplastic, a man-made material with an appearance much like gutta percha. Its innovator was Samuel Peck, who used shellac and wood fibers to create a composition he called Union. Peck was part owner of the Scoville Company, makers of both papier-mache and molded leather cases, and he used the company's existing dies to create his new line. Other companies (among them A.P. Critchlow & Company; Littlefield, Parsons & Company; and Holmes, Booth, & Hayden) soon duplicated his material and produced their own designs. Today's collectors may refer to cases made of this material as 'thermoplastic,' 'composition,' or 'hard cases,' but the term most often used is 'Union.' It is incorrect to refer to them as gutta percha cases.

Sizes may vary somewhat, but generally a 'whole' plate case measures 7" x 9⅛" to the outside edges, a 'half' plate 4⅞" x 6", a 'quarter' plate 3¾" x 4¾", a 'sixth' 3⅛" x 3⅝", a 'ninth' 2⅜" x 2⅞", and a 'sixteenth' 1¾" x 2". Clifford and Michele Krainik and Carl Walvoord have written a book, *Union Cases*, which we recommend for further study. Another source of information is *Nineteenth Century Photographic Cases and Wall Frames* by Paul Berg. Values are for examples in excellent condition unless noted otherwise.

Half-plate, WA Monument, K-4, couple ambrotype...................450.00
16th-plate, scroll, w/lady ambrotype, VG 45.00
4th-plate, Capture of Major Andre, S Peck & Co, ca 1856, EX .150.00
4th-plate, Parting of Hafed & Hinda, K-35, VG 200.00
4th-plate, Roger de Coverly & Gypsies, K-29, couple tintype, VG .100.00
6th-plate, Calmady Children, K-129, EX....................................200.00
6th-plate, Fireman Saving Child, K-118, EX 150.00
6th-plate, Geometric, K-224, w/2 tintypes 75.00
6th-plate, Shield, Crossed Cannon & Flags w/Liberty Cap, EX..175.00
9th-plate, American Gothic, K-374, EX...50.00
9th-plate, Chess Players, K-338, 2 children tintypes......................75.00
9th-plate, Chess Players, R-41 variant, NM 90.00
9th-plate, patriotic theme, K-368, EX 85.00
9th-plate, Scroll, Constitution & Laws, R-76, G.........................125.00

Miscellaneous

Album, celluloid, cherubs, w/music box, on stand, 1890s, EX 225.00
Album, celluloid, child w/kitten, rpl music box, 8x10" 200.00
Album, celluloid, classical lady beside irises, 16x7", minimum value 225.00
Case, daguerreotype or calotype, leather, hinged, 1850s, 10x12", NM..1,850.00
Magic lantern, metal w/pierced decor, Auguste Lapierre.............125.00
Megalethoscope (photograph viewer), Carlo Ponti, late 1860s, VG...570.00
Megalethoscope views, 39 views of Italy, Carlo Ponti, 1860s, EX 1,500.00
Phenakistiscope projector, hand-crank, 3½" disk, Germany, 1890s, VG ..345.00
Projector/magic lantern, 35mm, Carette/Germany, 1905, EXIB +12 slides ..345.00
Stanhope, alabaster bbl, Niagara Falls scene 30.00
Stanhope, Civil War bullet, Gettysburg views 50.00
Stanhope, cross, bone, WWI, troupes in trenches, ca 1914, EX....50.00

Stanhope, inkwell, ivory, chalet form, German views....................**50.00**
Stanhope, ring, man's, 2 female nude views, rare, EX.................**295.00**
Stanhope, tape measure, bbl form w/ivory finial, 1 view **65.00**
Stanhope, telescope, Stanton Secretary of War **400.00**
Stereo viewer, burl walnut, binocular-style eyepc, 7" **225.00**
Stereo viewer, figured walnut, Alex Beckets NY, 1857/1859, 18½"...**400.00**
Stereo viewer, walnut, folding stand, Pat 1866/1877/1878, 12½" ..**125.00**
Stereo-graphoscope, rosewood/brass, English, 1875, EX, +50 cards..**300.00**
Stereoscope, Am Novelty Co, Whiting's Sculptoscope, coin-op, 1920s, EX....**430.00**
Stereoscope, Brewster style, rosewood veneer, Fr, 1850s, EX.......**300.00**
Stereoscope, dbl; table-top, Beckers NY, ca 1860, EX+ **500.00**
Zoetrope on stand, metal drum w/13 slots, paper strips, 1870s, 11" ...**1,200.00**

Piano Babies

A familiar sight in Victorian parlors, piano babies languished atop shawl-covered pianos in a variety of poses: crawling, sitting, on their tummies, or on their backs playing with their toes. Some babies were nude, and some wore gowns. Sizes ranged from about 3" up to 12". The most famous manufacturer of these bisque darlings was the Heubach Brothers of Germany, who nearly always marked their product; see Heubach for listings. Watch for reproductions. These guidelines are excerpted from one of a series of informative doll books by Patsy Moyer, published by Collector Books. Values are for examples in excellent condition.

Blk, bsk, 4", EX quality...**400.00**
Blk, bsk, 4", med quality, unmk **135.00**
Blk, bsk, 8", EX quality...**525.00**
Blk, bsk, 8", med quality...**295.00**
Blk, bsk, 12", EX quality...**995.00**
Blk, bsk, 12", med quality...**400.00**
Blk, bsk, 16", EX quality...**925.00**
Blk, bsk, 16", med quality...**950.00**
Bsk, molded hair, unjtd, molded-on clothes, 4", EX quality, ea...**525.00**
Bsk, molded hair, unjtd, molded-on clothes, 4", med quality, ea.....**400.00**
Bsk, molded hair, unjtd, molded-on clothes, 8", EX quality, ea...**895.00**
Bsk, molded hair, unjtd, molded-on clothes, 8", med quality, ea.....**400.00**
Bsk, molded hair, unjtd, molded-on clothes, 12", EX quality, ea.**975.00**
Bsk, w/animal/pot/flowers/etc, 4", EX quality..............................**425.00**
Bsk, w/animal/pot/flowers/etc, 8", EX quality..............................**475.00**
Bsk, w/animal/pot/flowers/etc, 12", EX quality............................**800.00**
Bsk, w/animal/pot/flowers/etc, 16", EX quality, minimum value..**925.00**

Picasso Art Pottery

Pablo Picasso created some distinctive pottery during the 1940s, marking the ware with his signature.

Bowl, calligraphic bird, blk on wht, Madoura, 2½x5¾" **350.00**
Bowl, Don Quixote silhouette, blk on wht, Madoura, 3x5" **350.00**
Charger, 2 figures dancing, wht on blk, 4-sided, Madoura, 7½" sq...**650.00**
Plate, face, bl/wht/gray, #46...Madoura, 10" **1,200.00**

Pickard

Founded in 1895 in Chicago, Illinois, the Pickard China Company was originally a decorating studio, importing china blanks from European manufacturers. Some of these early pieces bear the name of those companies as well as Pickard's. Trained artists decorated the wares with hand-painted studies of fruit, florals, birds, and scenics and often signed their work. In 1915 Pickard introduced a line of 23k gold over a dainty floral-etched ground design. In the 1930s they began to experiment with the idea of making their own ware and by 1938 had succeeded in developing a formula for fine translucent china. Since 1976 they have issued an annual limited edition Christmas plate. They are now located in Antioch, Illinois.

The company has used various marks. The earliest (1893 – 1894) was a double-circle mark, 'Edgerton Hand Painted' with 'Pickard' in the center. Variations of the double-circle mark (with 'Hand Painted China' replacing the Edgerton designation) were employed until 1915, each differing enough that collectors can usually pinpoint the date of manufacture within five years. Later marks included the crown mark, 'Pickard' on a gold maple leaf, and the current mark, the lion and shield. Work signed by Challinor, Marker, and Yeschek is especially valued by today's collectors. For further information we recommend *Collector's Encyclopedia of Pickard China* by Alan B. Reed, available from Collector Books.

Bowl, Amaryllis & Etched Gold, Beutlich, 1905-10, Limoges blank, 10" ...**425.00**
Bowl, Fisher Pansies & Raised Gold, Charlotte shape, 1905-10, 8" ..**235.00**
Bowl, Hazelnuts, Montraux shape, 1903-05, Bavaria blank, 10¾" **425.00**
Bowl, Iris & Raised Gold w/Lustre, scalloped/ftd, 1903-05, 11"..**575.00**
Bowl, punch; Aura Mosaic, Corinthian shape, 1910-12, 10x10½" ..**3,400.00**
Bowl, Tulip Conventional, Gasper, 1903-05, JPL France blank, 9" **325.00**
Butter tub, Encrusted Gold, 1912-22, Z&S Co Bavaria blank, 3-pc.....**130.00**
Candlesticks, Iris Conventional, 1893-1803, Limoges blank, 8¾", pr..**500.00**
Celery dish, Tulip Conventional, 1903-05, 13" L **275.00**
Charger, Leon Poppies, sgn Leon, 1903-05, JPL France blank, 13"..**345.00**
Charger, Rean Pears, sgn Rean, 1903-05, JPL France blank, 13" ...**500.00**
Coffeepot, Carnation Conventional, sgn, 1903-05, T&V Limoges, +cr/sug ..**550.00**
Compote, Lilium Ornatum, sgn Yeschek, ftd, 1912-18, 6¼" **275.00**
Compote, raspberries w/gold, Stahl, scalloped/ftd, 1905-10, 3¾x6" ..**135.00**
Creamer & sugar bowl, Cyclamen, sgn RH, T&V Limoges blank.....**200.00**
Creamer & sugar bowl, Rose Bower, Leon, 1903-05, GDA France blank...**250.00**
Cup & saucer, Crocus Conventional, Roden, 1898-1903 mk, from $150 to ...**200.00**
Cup & saucer, demi; floral w/gold border, 1910-12, T&V Limoges blank...**150.00**
Cup & saucer, poppy, wht on gr, Hahn, 1903-05, Bavaria blank ...**175.00**
Cup & saucer, violets w/mc leaves, Sinclair, 1903-05, Limoges blank...**180.00**
Jug, Dorique, orange tree panels, 1903-05, T&V Limoges blank, 7¾" ..**425.00**
Jug, lemonade; Autumn Currants, wide mouth, 1905-10, Limoges blank, 7" ..**450.00**
Jug, whiskey; ears of corn on gr, Gifford, 1903-05, 7" **500.00**
Mug, cherry spray w/gold, Beitler, 1903-05, Limoges blank, 6" ...**375.00**
Mug, shaving; New Iris Conventional, sgn, 1903-05, T&V Limoges blank...**575.00**
Pitcher, Arabian, bamboo-style hdl, 1903-05, AD D France blank, 7¾" ...**675.00**
Pitcher, berries & blossoms on maroon band, Michel, 1898-1903 mk, 5"...**550.00**
Plaque, Cattle by Highland Lake, sgn, 1903-05, Limoges blank, 15⅜" ...**2,250.00**
Plate, Apple Blossom Bower, scalloped, 1903-05, Haviland blank, 8¾".....**185.00**
Plate, Autumn Border, Fisher, 1903-05, CA France blank, 8½" **150.00**
Plate, Butterfly, 1903-05, Limoges blank, 8¼" **235.00**
Plate, chrysanthemums, Brun, 1905-10, Limoges blank, 8¾" **85.00**
Plate, Gibson Pansies, scalloped, 1903-05, Limoges blank, 8½" .**165.00**
Plate, grape clusters on gold border, Challinor, 1903-05, 8¾".....**165.00**
Plate, hunting dogs scene, Heidrich, 1906-28, JPL France blank, 9¾" ..**275.00**
Plate, poppies on cream, Challinor, 1903, Haviland blank, 8½" ...**200.00**
Plate, The Seasons, Comyn, 1905-10, Haviland blank, 9" **155.00**
Platter, Cornflower & Royal Blue, Yeschek, 1905-10, 14x10"......**275.00**
Shakers, currants w/allover gilt, sgn Osbourne, 3½", pr................**55.00**
Sugar shaker, pansies on cream w/gold, 1905-10, 4¼" **135.00**
Teacup & saucer, Modern Conventional, R Hessler, 1912-18, from $200 to ...**250.00**
Vase, Arrow Root on Green Lustre, Gifford, 1905-10, 10¼" **350.00**
Vase, calla lilies, gr & wht w/gold, C Marker, cylindrical, 1900s, 16" ..**1,265.00**
Vase, Fruits Linear, sgn Tolpin, 1912-18, Noritake blank, 8½" ...**400.00**
Vase, Japanese Woman w/Comb, 1903-05, Willets blank, 12".**1,800.00**
Vase, narcissus on gr, Post, 1903-05, #3660 blank, 8" **400.00**
Vase, Praying Mohammedan, Farrington, 1903-05, Bavaria blank, 13½"....**2,750.00**
Vase, Rosa Emeraldus, sgn Coufall, Egyptian shape, 1905-10, 7" **300.00**

Vase, Roseland, sgn Marker, hexagonal, 1912-18, B&Co blank, 7" **450.00**

Pickle Castors

Pickle castors, which were both functional and decorative, became popular after the Civil War, reaching their peak about 1885. By 1900 they had virtually disappeared from factory catalogs. Numerous styles were available. They consisted of a decorated, silverplated frame that held either a fancy clear pressed-glass insert or one of decorated colored art glass — the latter being popular in the more affluent Victorian households and more desirable with collectors today.

In the listings below, the description prior to the semicolon refers to the jar (insert), and the remainder of the line describes the frame. Unless a color is mentioned, all glassware is clear. When no condition is indicated, the silverplate is assumed to be in very good to excellent condition, with the fork or tongs present. Glass jars are assumed near mint. Our advisor for this category is Deborah Maggard; she is listed in the Directory under Ohio.

Warning: Watch for reproduction frames from Taiwan!

Key: rsl — resilvered

Bl canoe; scrolling acanthus SP 10½x8½x8" fr, +tongs **975.00**
Bl w/HP daisies & gold; rstr SP #917 fr, 10", +tongs **700.00**
Bohemian irid overshot; Middletown fr, 11½" **250.00**
Cane, amber; fr w/rtcl 3-leaf hdl, +bird-ft tongs **300.00**
Coin Dot, amberina; 4-ftd Tufts fr, 10x8", +ornate tongs........**1,150.00**
Cranberry, vertical ribs; ftd Tufts fr w/side bail.........................**425.00**
Cranberry w/HP florals; ornate SP fr, +tongs **450.00**
Cranberry w/HP; Greenaway figure at base of Tufts #3063 fr...**1,350.00**
Cream opaque w/HP floral; SP Gothic arch fr w/raven's head, 13"..**550.00**
Cross in Diamond, vaseline, US Glass; orig SP fr, 1890s, 11" **415.00**
Crystal w/etched floral, star-cut bottom; rstr SP fr......................**465.00**
Cupid & Venus; rstr SP ornate fr, 11 /12", +tongs **375.00**
Daisy & Button, amber gondola; Homan #1068 wagon fr w/owls..**600.00**
Daisy & Button, amber; SP fr, +tongs **200.00**
Daisy & Button, bl; rstr SP fr & lid, 12", +tongs **350.00**
Daisy & Fern, bl; Rogers #94 fr, +fork **415.00**
Deer & Pine Tree; metal fr...**400.00**
Dk to lt bl w/HP daisies; Pairpoint #683 fr, +tongs **1,300.00**
Dmn Quilt, bl; SP Acme #302 fr, 10½" **325.00**
Dmn Quilt, rubena w/mc floral; ornate SP fr **700.00**
Florette, pk cased; orig SP fr **475.00**
Gr swirl w/gold; Cohannet #578 fr, 10" **800.00**
Heart Arches, wht satin w/HP floral; mk fr..................................**395.00**
Inverted Thumbprint, bl w/HP floral; Aurora B0656 fr, 10½" **565.00**
Inverted Thumbprint, cranberry w/HP floral; ornate SP fr, 11¾" ...**650.00**
Jacob's Ladder, Maltese Cross hdl; metal fr **200.00**
Mc spatter (cased); ornate Wilcox ftd fr..**495.00**
Panel Sprig, rubena; SP New Amsterdam fr, 11", +tongs **365.00**
Pk satin w/emb scrolls & gold; Pairpoint floral #B602 fr, 10½" ..**1,000.00**
Pk satin w/emb scrolls/HP floral, 4¼"; Pairpoint #668 fr, 10½" ..**875.00**
Pk satin w/HP florals; rstr US Silver #300 fr, 11".......................**935.00**
Raindrops, cranberry MOP; Rockford #1430 fr, 9¼" **1,125.00**
Sapphire bl w/floral, cylindrical; simple fr, 10½", +tongs **250.00**
Spanish Fern, cranberry opal; Meriden floral fr, 12", +tongs **400.00**
Swirl, emerald gr; rstr Birmingham #1424 fr, 11", +fork **600.00**
Yel to wht opal w/HP pk roses; Derby #405 fr w/birds, 12"..........**785.00**

Pie Birds

A pie bird or pie funnel (pie vent) is generally made of pottery, glazed inside and out. Most are 3" to 5" in height with arches at the base to allow steam to enter. The steam is then released through an exit hole at the top.

The English pie funnel was as tall as the special baking dish was deep and held the crust even with the dish's rim, thereby lifting the crust above the filling so it would stay crisp and firm. These dishes came in several different sizes, which accounts for the variances in the heights of the pie birds.

The first deviations from the basic funnels were produced in the mid-1930s to late 1940s: the Clarice Cliff (signed Midwinter or Newport) pie bird (reg. no. on white base) and the signed Nutbrown elephant. Shortly thereafter (1940s – 1960s), figures of bakers and colorful birds were created for additional visual baking fun. From the 1980s to present, many novelty pie vents have been added to the market for the enjoyment of both the baker and collector. These have been made by commercial (including Far East importers) and local enterprises in Canada, England, and the United States. A new category for the 1990s includes an array of holiday-related pie vents. Basic tip: older pie vents were air-brushed, not hand painted.

Incense burners (i.e., elephants and Oriental people), one-hole pepper shakers, dated brass toy bird whistle, egg timers (missing glass timer), and ring holders (i.e., elephant with clover on his tummy) should not be mistaken for pie vents.

Benny the Baker, with pie crimper and cake tester, Cardinal, from $150.00 to $175.00.

Bird, bl & wht on wht base, Royal Worcester, 2-pc, from $75 to ..**90.00**
Bird, blk on wht base, Royal Worcester, 2-pc, from $55 to............**65.00**
Bird, brn on wht base, Royal Worcester, 2-pc, from $150 to.......**175.00**
Bird, thin neck, Scotland, 1972, 4¼", from $75 to **90.00**
Bird, wht w/blk wings, unmk British Columbia, from $300 to **325.00**
Bird on log, Artone Pottery, England, 1950-95, 3¾", from $75 to...**85.00**
Bird w/gold beak, floral transfers on wht body, 4½", from $175 to...**200.00**
Bird w/gold beak, solid blk body, Chic Pottery, 4½" **125.00**
Bird w/gold beak, solid wht body, Chic Pottery, 4½" **125.00**
Bird w/2 heads, yel, Barn Pottery, England, 1985, from $65 to......**75.00**
Black bird on wht base, #d front, mk Midwinter..........................**30.00**
Blackbird, lg head, wide mouth, New Zealand, 4¾", from $75 to.**95.00**
Blackbird, wht head, teardrop eye, Australia, from $40 to............**50.00**
Blackbird on wht base, #d front, mk Newport Pottery...................**30.00**
Blackbird on wht base, Clarice Cliff, #d on front, 1933, from $30 to..**35.00**
Bluebird on gr stand w/wht bib, Josef, from $195 to **210.00**
Bluebird on nest w/babies, Artesian Galleries, Circled C, 5", $750 to...**800.00**
California Rooster, unmk Provincial Pottery, 1950s, from $50 to .**75.00**
Chef w/bl coat, wht hat, 1930-40s..**160.00**
Cobbler bird, 10 colors, Camark Pottery, 1950s, rare, 6⅝", $225 to...**250.00**
Dopey, Australia, old orig, rare, 4¼", (+)....................................**400.00**
Elephant on drum, solid pk base, mk CCC, from $325 to...........**350.00**
Funnel, brn, w/mouse, Haytown Pottery, from $65 to....................**75.00**
Funnel, clear glass, Pyrex, common, from $35 to **45.00**
Funnel, Grimwade Perfection, 1909, from $90 to **110.00**
Funnel, Roe's Patent Rosebud, pre-1900, from $90 to **110.00**
Funnel, wht, plain, from $10 to **12.00**
Gobbler's Mountain, Arkansas, solid colors, few made, 1994-95, $75 to ...**125.00**

Mammy w/outstretched arms, multi-purpose kitchen tool, 4¾", $150 to...175.00
Mushroom, w/smile on face, England, 4".................................135.00
Mushroom, wht w/red dots, grass on stem, Susie Cooper, from $75 to...80.00
Owl, wearing bow w/polka dots, Josef, from $225 to 250.00
Pagoda, Gourmet Pie Cup, 1901, from $75 to.........................80.00
Patches, rose, yel & turq on wing, Morton, common, 5", from $25 to....30.00
Pie Baker or Chef, Josef, 3⅝", from $85 to.............................95.00
Pie Chick, pk or bl beak & base, Shawnee (Pillsbury), common, 5¼"...45.00
Pie Duckling, bl, pk or yel, American Pottery Co, 5", from $55 to..65.00
Rooster, S neck, bl beak/base, pk comb, Pearl China, '30s, $75 to...85.00
Rooster, 3-color tail, V arch, Cleminson, 'b' in C mk, 4½", $45 to ..55.00
Servex Chef, Australia, 1938, from $150 to.............................165.00
Squab, funnel, Australia, from $95 to..................................100.00
Swan/duck head, brn w/yel beak, 4½", from $125 to...............150.00
Welsh dragon, bronze, Creigiau Pottery, from $300 to 325.00
Welsh dragon, copper lustre, Creigiau Pottery, from $625 to 650.00
Welsh lady, brn w/blk hat, Cymru, from $100 to 125.00
Wheat stalk, funnel, brn, from $150 to 175.00
Wheat stalk, funnel, wht, from $110 to 125.00
Yel chick w/pk lips, Josef, 3⅝", from $40 to.............................50.00
3 fruits series, peach, apple & cherries, Japan, 2½", ea, $350 to .400.00
3 fruits series, peach, apple & cherries, Japan, 2½", full set 1,500.00

Pierce, Howard

After Howard Pierce died on February 28, 1994, many values of his pieces increased greatly and items not seen before began to appear on the market. William Manker, a well-known ceramist, hired Mr. Pierce in 1936. This liaison lasted about three years and then Pierced opened a small studio in Laverne, California. He did not want to be in competition with Manker so he began making miniature animal figures, some of which he made into jewelry. Now, pewter miniature brooches, depending on the animal types, are selling for as much as $275.00. Howard married and he and his wife, Ellen (Van Voorhis), opened a small studio in Claremont, California, in 1941.

Polyurethane animals are high on collectors' lists as Howard, after creating in the early years only a few pieces using this material, realized he was allergic to it and had to discontinue its use. Polyurethane was used mostly to create a small number of roadrunners on bases, either standing or running, or birds on small, flat bases. The materials used by Pierce during his long career were varied, probably to satisfy his curiosity and many talents. He experimented with a Jasperware-type body, pewter, concrete, gold leaf, porcelain, Mt. St. Helens ash, and others. In November 1992, Pierce's health had continued to worsen and he and Ellen Pierce destroyed all the molds they had created over the years. Pierce began producing miniature versions of past porcelain wares and developing a few new items, also in miniature form. These pieces are stamp-marked simply 'Pierce.' It has been speculated that these items, over time, will command a higher value than their larger versions.

For further information we recommend *Collector's Encyclopedia of Howard Pierce Porcelain* by Darlene Hurst Dommel (Collector Books). Our advisor for this category is Susan Cox; she is listed in the Directory under California.

Bowl, blk bkground sprayed w/contrasting bl, 4x6¼" 125.00
Bowl, blk ext, aqua int w/sunburst effect, 2½x7½"....................100.00
Box, Art Deco gazelles, mint gr, 4x5"....................................150.00
Dish, brn ext w/sea gr mottled int, 12".................................125.00
Figurine, bear cub, high-gloss brn-gr, 4¾x5¼"..........................50.00
Figurine, birds (3) in tree, 15½x6"......................................300.00
Figurine, bison, unmk, 9"..210.00
Figurine, bull, high-gloss gray, 5½x3½".................................150.00
Figurine, circus horse w/sm center base, experimental bl, 7½x6½"..300.00
Figurine, dinosaur, brn w/wht, 5½x4½" 185.00

Figurine, dinosaur, experimental bl, 5½x4½" 250.00
Figurine, dog w/drooping ears, lt & dk brn, 1950s, 8x3", 6x2½", pr ..255.00
Figurine, dolphin riding wave, 9½x6½" 300.00
Figurine, duck, high-gloss blk, 4½x9"..................................85.00
Figurine, egret, standing, experimental bl, 9½" 355.00
Figurine, gazelle on base, #100P, 11¼x4".............................125.00
Figurine, girl w/dog, 4½x3¼"...85.00
Figurine, mountain sheep ram, 7¼x3"................................155.00
Figurine, pelican, brn, beak attached to body, 7½x4½".............155.00
Figurine, raccoon, textured, 5x5¼"...................................135.00
Figurine, rattlesnake, 3x6"...100.00
Figurine, robin w/orange breast, 4½x3½".............................100.00
Figurine, unicorn, 5¾x5½"..200.00
Magnet, roadrunner, brn, unmk, 6½"...................................120.00
Magnet, turtle, gray, unmk, 3¼"...125.00
Pencil holder, nude women, tan & brn, 1980 only, 3½x4¼"......210.00
Planter, leaf motif, mint gr matt, 2¼x6¾"............................95.00
Vase, brn & wht, flared top, 9x3½"....................................75.00

Pigeon Blood

Pigeon blood glass, produced in the late 1800s, may be distinguished from other dark red glass by its distinctive orange tint.

Bowl, berry; Torquay, sm..50.00
Bowl, lion head prunts, clear ft/hdls/rim, 7½" H 375.00
Bowl, master berry; Torquay...195.00
Butter dish, Torquay 595.00
Butter dish, Venecia, enamel decor................................5,000.00
Carafe, water; Torquay 325.00
Celery vase, Torquay, SP collar.......................................165.00
Condiment set, Torquay..1,150.00
Creamer, Torquay 125.00
Creamer, Venecia, enamel decor.......................................200.00
Humidor, Torquay...450.00
Pickle castor, Torquay..895.00
Pitcher, Bulging Loops, water sz.....................................525.00
Pitcher, clear hdl, 7"...225.00
Pitcher, cut strawberry dmns & panels, appl hdl, 6⅜" 165.00
Pitcher, water..395.00
Pitcher, water; Torquay...395.00
Shakers, Flower Band pattern, orig lids, pr.........................165.00
Shakers, Torquay, 3⅛", pr...225.00
Spooner, Torquay...125.00
Sugar bowl, Torquay..125.00
Sweetmeat jar, Torquay 450.00
Syrup, Torquay, squat..450.00
Syrup, Torquay, tall..1,200.00
Wine, 6"...50.00

Pigeon Forge

Douglas J. Ferguson and Ernest Wilson started their small pottery in Pigeon Forge, Tennessee, in 1946. Using red-brown and gray locally dug clay and glazes which they themselves formulate, bowls, vases, and sculptures are produced there. Their primary target is the tourist trade.

Bowl, wht w/gr squiggle inside, E Wilson, 2½x4" 45.00
Candle holder, gr mottle w/brn, hand built, Ferguson, 10", NM ...60.00
Figurine, fox, lt gray w/brn, DF, 11" L, on wooden base..............135.00
Figurine, mouse, wht on brn, D Ferguson, 2x2¾"...................35.00
Figurine, owl, cratered orange-peel wht/brn, stylized, 10½" 50.00

Figurine, owl, gray on brn, D Ferguson/dtd, 4" 35.00
Figurine, raccoon, gray/brn, D Ferguson, 5¼" 50.00
Pitcher, bl shading to brn rim, ewer style, Ferguson, 11" 45.00
Vase, bud; bl to brn, Huskey, 4½" 32.00
Vase, Tribal, wht slashes/markings on brn, Ferguson/1950, 6¾"...185.00
Vase, volcanic/cratered gray-bl/lav/burgundy, 2¾x3¼" 90.00

Pilkington

Founded in 1892 in Manchester, England, the Pilkington pottery experimented in wonderful lustre glazes that were so successful that when they were displayed at exhibition in 1904, they were met with critical acclaim. They soon attracted some of the best ceramic technicians and designers of the day who decorated the lustre ground with flowers, animals, and trees; some pieces were more elaborate with scenes of sailing ships and knights on horseback. Each artist signed his work with his personal monogram. Most pieces were dated and carried the company mark as well. After 1913 the company became known as Royal Lancastrian.

Their Lapis Ware line was introduced in the late 1920s, featuring intermingling tones of color under a matt glaze. Some pieces were very simply decorated while others were painted with designs of stylized leafage, scrolls, swirls, and stripes. The line continued into the '30s. Other pieces of this period were molded and carved with animals, leaves, etc., some of which were reminiscent of their earlier wares.

The company closed in 1938 but reopened in 1948. During this period their mark was a simple P within the outline of a petaled flower shape. Our advisor for this category is David Ehrhard; he is listed in the Directory under California.

Bowl vase, rust/bl flambe, ca 1920, 3½x6", NM 165.00
Tile, stylized floral, teal gr gloss, 6x6", EX 50.00
Tiles, Nouveau lady portrait formed by 3, EX in fr 300.00
Vase, dk rose w/bl speckles & ochre full-length drippings, unmk, 8"...250.00
Vase, exotic birds & flowers, Joyce, #2369, 1925, 9" 1,750.00
Vase, loopings, wine/aqua on lav, Gladys/ET Radford, 7x8"........200.00

Pillin

Polia Pillin was born in Poland in 1909. She came to the U.S. as a teenager and showed an interest and talent for art, which she studied in Chicago. She married William Pillin, who was a poet and potter. They ultimately combined their talents and produced her very distinctive pottery from the 1950s to the mid-1980s. She died in 1993.

Polia Pillin won many prizes for her work, which is always signed Pillin with the loop of the 'P' over the full name. Some undecorated pieces are signed W&P, due to her husband's collaboration.

Her work is prized for its art, not for the shape of her pots, which for the most part are simple vases, dishes, bowl, and boxes. Wall plaques are rare. She pictured women with hair reminiscent of halos, girls, an occasional boy, horses, birds, and fish. After viewing a few of her pieces, her style is unmistakable. Some of her early work is very much like that of Picasso.

Her pieces are somewhat difficult to find, as all the work was done without outside help, and therefore limited in quantity. In the last few years, more and more people have become interested in her work, resulting in escalating prices. Our advisors for this category are Dolli and Wilfred Cohen; they are listed in the Directory under California.

Bowl, stylized horses, mc on mauve, 7⅛" 550.00
Box, lady in wht robe, child in pk leotards, blk shirt, 5½x4" 495.00

Compote, frieze of lady's faces on lt marigold w/turq wash, 5x6" ...650.00
Goblet, bust portrait of lady, bl/gr/tan on brn, 9".........................750.00
Jug, blistered yel/brn gloss, 7¾x5½" 275.00
Pendant, female portrait on marigold, 3¼x2½" 500.00
Tray, ballerinas, 3 in leotards/1 center front in wht tutu on bl, 9x9" ...850.00
Tray, Madonna portrait on dk brn w/bl rim, rectangular, lg.........775.00
Tray, 2 women/bird, oval, 8½" L 925.00
Vase, avocado gr over lt seaweed gr, onion base, can neck, 6½".250.00
Vase, cat/rooster, trees & female dancers on marigold, 4½x3¾".665.00
Vase, fish, 6¼" 450.00
Vase, fish (9) on pastel sea, 6½x6" 495.00
Vase, ladies, mc on bl, rectangular, 9", NM...............................850.00
Vase, lady, horse & goose on brn, 6¼x5", NM 495.00
Vase, lady, various pastel-colored sqs as bkground, 6x4½"..........625.00
Vase, lady & birds/lady w/horse, bottle shape, 6½x2½" 550.00
Vase, lady holding bird, 2nd bird beside; bk: lady, 6¾"...............450.00
Vase, 2 lovely young women/2 roosters, 6⅞", EX.........................550.00

Pin-Back Buttons

Buttons produced up to the early 1920s were made of a celluloid covering held in place by a ring (or collet) to the back of which a pin was secured. Manufacturers used these 'cellos' to advertise their products. Many were of exceptional quality in both color and design. Buttons were produced in sets featuring a variety of subjects. These were given away by tobacco, chewing gum, and candy manufacturers, who often packed them with their product as premiums. Usually the name of the button maker or the product manufacturer was printed on a paper placed in the back of the button. Often these 'back papers' are still in place today. Much of the time the button maker's name was printed on the button's perimeter, and sometimes the copyright was added. Beginning in the 1920s, a large number of buttons were lithographed on tin; these are referred to as tin 'lithos.' Nearly all pin-back buttons are collected today for their advertising appeal or graphic design. There are countless categories to base a collection on.

The following listing contains non-political buttons representative of the many varieties you may find. Our advisor for this category is Michael J. McQuillen; he is listed in the Directory under Indiana.

Felix the Cat pep pin, NM, $55.00. (Photo courtesy Doug Dezso)

Ballisite & Empire/The Smokeless Powder, bull's-eye, ⅞", NM+..70.00
Beech-Nut Gum/Souvenir of...Autogiro 1931, w/scene, 1¾", EX...100.00
Ceresota/For Young or Old/The Best Flour Sold, 1¼", EX+..........85.00
Dead Shot Smokeless Powder, duck in flight, ⅞", NM+ 60.00
DuPont Shoot Powders, quail in landscape, ⅞", EX+..................350.00
DuPont Smokeless, 2 dogs/hanging birds/2 shotguns, 1", NM.....150.00
DuPont Smokeless Powder, quail on vivid ground, 1¼", NM+...135.00
Emancipation 1863-1963 Proud Americans, red/wht/bl, 1½", NM..300.00
Farmer Labor Festival, red/wht/bl, ca 1930s, 1x1½", VG+...........35.00
Fourth Alarm/All Talkie Thriller, fireman portrait, 1¼", NM 22.00
Frontier Days/Stockton Cal/June...1913, Let 'er Buck, 1½", EX ...50.00
High Admiral Cigarettes, Yellow Kid/goat, 1¼", EX 40.00
Kellogg's pep pin, Corky, NM 16.00
Kellogg's pep pin, Flash Gordon, NM...30.00
Kellogg's pep pin, Jiggs, NM...25.00
Kellogg's pep pin, Mamie, NM..15.00

Kellogg's pep pin, Phantom, NM 50.00
Kellogg's pep pin, Uncle Walt, NM 20.00
Kellogg's pep pin, Winnie Winkle, NM....................15.00
Laflin & Rand Infallible, flag in wreath, 1¼", NM+ 60.00
Let's Go To Luna Park, devil, Whitehead & Hoag, 1900, 1¾", EX+ ..75.00
Long Beach/Festival of the Sea, mermaid, 1908, 2", NM+..........850.00
Martin Luther King, blk & wht portrait, cello, ca 1968, 3"...........67.50
Miller High Life, diecut lady on logo hanger, 4x1¼", NM+ 100.00
Miller's Cocoa, Dutch windmill, Whitehead & Hoag, ⅞", NM....10.00
Orphan Annie Loves Red Cross Macaroni, portrait, 1¼", EX+ 57.00
Peters, duck flying through red P w/sky bkground, ⅞", NM+ 130.00
Peters, letter P in patriotic flag pattern , ⅞", NM+ 80.00
Peters, letter P over duck hunt scene, Bastian Bros, ⅞", EX+ 75.00
Peters Superior Cartridges, gold on blk, ⅞", EX+ 60.00
Pony Club Member, The Farmer's Wife, 1½", NM.....................139.00
Put America Bk To Work, red/wht/bl, 1390s, 1" oval, EX 30.00
St Thomas Rodeo Homecoming/Oct 18th 1940, Whoa Johnny, 2", NM..25.00
Tony (horse), Purina..15.00
UMC CO No 12 Arrow, emb brass resembling end of shell, ⅞", NM 40.00

Pine Ridge

In the mid-1930s, the Indian Bureau of Affairs and the Work Progress Administration offered the Native Americans living on the Pine Ridge Indian Reservation in South Dakota a class in pottery making. Originally, Margaret Cable (director of the University of North Dakota ceramics department) was the instructor and Bruce Doyle was director. By the early 1950s, pottery production at the school was abandoned. In 1955 the equipment was purchased by Ella Irving, a student who had been highly involved with the class since the late 1930s. From then until 1980 when it closed, Ella virtually ran the pot shop by herself.

The clay used in Pine Ridge pottery was red and the decoration reminiscent of early Indian pottery and beadwork designs. A variety of marks and labels were used. For more information we recommend *Collector's Encyclopedia of the Dakota Potteries* by Darlene Hurst Dommel (Collector Books).

Bowl, dk bl gloss, sgn Ramona W Knee, 2¾x4", from $50 to 75.00
Bowl, geometrics, cream on brn, N Firethunder, 2x10" 325.00
Creamer & sugar bowl, bl, Irving, 2", 2½", from $50 to 75.00
Cup & saucer, bl-gr gloss, Ella Cox, 2", 5½", from $50 to 75.00
Flower holder, gr & brn mottle, Julia Mattson, 1¾", from $40 to 50.00
Jardiniere, flowing earth tones, mk Sioux Indian, 4¾x9¼" 450.00
Shakers, geometrics, cream on brn, Talbot, 2½", pr, from $75 to ..100.00
Vase, avocado gr gloss, sgn FLH, 3½", from $50 to......................70.00
Vase, coiled, brn, mk SD-8, 3", from $50 to 75.00
Vase, geometric sgraffito, cream on red, Cottier, 7¼"..................375.00

Pink Lustre Ware

Pink lustre was produced by nearly every potter in the Staffordshire district in the late eighteenth and first half of the nineteenth centuries. The application of gold lustre on white or light-colored backgrounds produced pinks, while the same over dark colors developed copper. The wares ranged from hand-painted plaques to transfer-printed dinnerware.

Bowl, nine transfer scenes, overall wavy lines in pink lustre, Moore & Co., 10¼", $1,400.00.

Bowl, ivy, pk lustre int, 5½"...55.00
Bowl, lady/child w/badminton racquets, 5½", NM 85.00
Bowl, waste; heavy lustre English rose, 3½x6½"..........................65.00
Cake plate, pk rim band, mc florals/sprigs, #912, hdls, 10"...........85.00
Cup & saucer, leafage/berries, set of 6 ....150.00
Cup & saucer, pk rims, mc transfers: child/goat, girl/bird, EX 60.00
Cup & saucer, Queen Victoria/Prince Albert & family, 5½", EX ..100.00
Cup plate, long notched leaves spaced w/red flowers, 3¾" 35.00
Gravy boat, florals/leaves, lustre rim, 8" L.................................145.00
Mug, House, barn-like bldg in field w/shrubs, 3", NM................175.00
Mug, Sailor's Fairwell, 3-D frog in bottom, 4¾", VG 225.00
Pitcher, bands w/comma devices, bl/gr stylized vine, 3"..............90.00
Pitcher, House, sq bldg w/shrubs, pk band, o/w copper lustre, 4½" ...90.00
Plate, House, w/trees/clouds/flowers, 6⅛", EX 50.00
Plate, pk band, mc floral sprigs, 9¾", +6 6" plates, EX 70.00
Plate, pk rim band/florals, yel/gr accents, ¾x7"..........................80.00
Saucer, scenic view transfer, pk rim band 35.00
Sugar bowl, lg pk mums, gr sprigs, w/hdls & lid, 5½x6¾", VG 90.00
Teabowl & saucer, maroon transfer: boy hugging lamb................75.00

Pink Paw Bears

These charming figural pieces are very similar to the Pink Pigs described in the following category. They were made in Germany during the same time frame. The cabbage green is identical; the bears themselves are whitish-gray with pink foot pads. You'll find some that are unmarked while others are marked 'Germany' or 'Made in Germany.' In theory, the unmarked bears are the oldest, made prior to 1890 when the McKinley Tariff Act required imports to be marked with the country of origin. Those marked 'Made In' were probably produced after the revision of the Act in 1914.

1 by bean pot...135.00
1 by graphophone..150.00
1 by honey pot..145.00
1 by top hat..125.00
1 in front of basket..135.00
1 in roadster (car identical to pk pig car)..........................185.00
1 on binoculars...150.00
1 peaking out of basket..135.00
1 sitting in wicker chair..150.00
2 in hot air balloon..150.00
2 in purse...165.00
2 in roadster...165.00
2 on pin dish...120.00
2 on pin dish w/bag of coins...145.00
2 peering in floor mirror...150.00
2 sitting by mushroom..125.00
2 standing in wash tub..135.00
3 in roadster...190.00
3 on pin dish...145.00

Pink Pigs

Pink Pigs on cabbage green were made in Germany around the turn of the century. They were sold as souvenirs in train depots, amusement parks, and gift shops. 'Action pigs' (those involved in some amusing activity) are the most valuable, and prices increase with the number of pigs. Though a similar type of figurine was made in white bisque, most serious collectors prefer only the pink ones. They are marked in two ways: 'Germany' in incised letters, and a black ink stamp 'Made in Germany' in a circle. The unmarked pigs are the oldest, made prior to 1890 when the McKinley Tariff Act required imports to be marked with the country of origin. Those marked 'Made In' were probably produced after the revision of the Act in 1914.

1 beside gr drum, wall-mt match holder 95.00
1 beside shoe...115.00
1 beside stump, camera around neck, toothpick holder.............185.00
1 beside wastebasket...95.00
1 coming out of suitcase...95.00
1 coming through gr fence, post at sides, open for flowers...........125.00
1 driving touring car..185.00
1 going through purse..90.00
1 holding cup by fence...140.00
1 in case looking through binoculars..165.00
1 in gr suitcase bank, head 1 side, bk other, gold trim.................110.00
1 in Japanese submarine, Japan imp on both sides.......................125.00
1 in money sack bank...95.00
1 lg pig sitting behind 3" trough..95.00
1 on binoculars, gold trim..150.00
1 on chair..125.00
1 on gr trinket dish, leg caught in lobster claw............................125.00
1 on keg playing piano...185.00
1 on shoulder of gr ink bottle...115.00
1 playing accordion on side of tray, wht bear ea side..................185.00
1 pushing head through wooden gate..115.00
1 reclining on horseshoe ashtray..85.00
1 riding train, 4½"..190.00
1 sits, holds orange Boston Baked Beans pot match holder........125.00
1 sits by high-top boot..110.00
1 sitting on log, mk Germany...110.00
1 standing in front of cracked open egg......................................110.00
1 standing in gr tub...95.00
1 w/bean pot...85.00
1 w/front ft in 3-part dish containing 3 dice, 1 ft on dice............125.00
1 w/tennis racket stands beside vase, Lawn Tennis, 3¾"..............150.00
2, mother & baby in bl blanket in tub, rabbit on board atop......150.00
2, mother in tub gives baby a bottle, lamb looks on, 4x3½".......125.00
2, 1 at telephone booth, 1 inside, 4½"...165.00
2 behind trough, unmk..95.00
2 by eggshell...95.00
2 dancing, in top hat, tux & cane...135.00
2 in open trunk, 3¾"..125.00
2 in purse..115.00
2 on cotton bale, 1 peers from hole, 1 over top..........................135.00
2 on seesaw on top of pouch bank...135.00
2 on top hat..125.00
2 sitting at table playing card game 'Hearts'................................190.00
2 under toadstool...125.00
3, 2 sit in front of coal bucket, 3rd inside...................................125.00
3 at trough, 4½" L..110.00
3 dressed up on edge of dish..125.00
3 w/baby carriage, father & 2 babies, Wheeling His Own...........145.00

Pisgah Forest

The Pisgah Forest Pottery was established in 1920 near Mount Pisgah in Arden, North Carolina, by Walter B. Stephen, who had worked in previous years at other locations in the state — Nonconnah and Skyland (the latter from 1913 until 1916). Stephen, who was born in the mountain region near Asheville, was known for his work in the Southern tradition. He produced skillfully executed wares exhibiting an amazing variety of techniques. He operated his business with only two helpers. Recognized today as his most outstanding accomplishment, his

Cameo line was decorated by hand in the pate-sur-pate style (similar to Wedgwood Jasper) in such designs as Fiddler and Dog, Spinning Wheel, Covered Wagon, Buffalo Hunt, Mountain Cabin, Square Dancers, Indian Campfire, and Plowman. Stephen is known for other types of wares as well. His crystalline glaze is highly regarded by today's collectors.

At least nine different stamps mark his wares, several of which contain the outline of the potter at the wheel and 'Pisgah Forest.' Cameo is sometimes marked with a circle containing the line name and 'Long Pine, Arden, NC.' Two other marks may be more difficult to recognize: 1) a circle containing the outline of a pine tree, 'N.C.' to the left of the trunk and 'Pine Tree' on the other side; and 2) the letter 'P' with short uprights in the middle of the top and lower curves. Stephen died in 1961, but the work was continued by his associates. Our advisor for this category is R.J. Sayers; he is listed in the Directory under North Carolina.

Bowl, Christmas Carol cameos on gr, bright gr int, 195(?), 2½x5" 50.00
Bowl, Deer Hunter cameo on olive, rose int, Stephen, 1957, 5⅝"...400.00
Bowl, plum gloss, ivory matt int, 1934 mk, 4¾x8" 100.00
Cup, Spinning Wheel cameo on gr, Stephen, 1961, 3½"............250.00
Lamp, Buffalo Hunt cameo band, dk olive matt/aqua gloss, Stephen, 11"..1,350.00
Lamp base, Covered Wagon cameo on gr, 1930s, 9" 700.00
Pitcher, Covered Wagon cameo on sky bl, Stephen, 1946, 4¾" .275.00
Pitcher, turq crackle, rose int w/turq o/l, ca 1950, 5¾"................70.00
Pitcher, turq crackle, rose int w/turq o/l, 1953, 8⅛" 110.00
Teapot, Chinese Blue w/red/gr/bl highlights, 8" W......................200.00
Vase, Aubergine-Wine, classic shape, 1953, 6" 90.00
Vase, bl matt on gr, Stephen, 1946, 4¼x5¾"...............................110.00
Vase, Covered Wagon cameo, Stephen, 1953, 5½".......................275.00
Vase, Covered Wagon cameo on olive, rose int, Stephen, 195(?), 4"...275.00
Vase, crystalline, bl & wht striations, 1930s-40s, 5¼"..................225.00
Vase, crystalline, cobalt dbl drip on camel, porc, 1933, 7⅛".......500.00

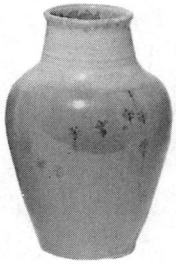

Vase, crystalline, olive and white with random blue bursts, broad shoulders, 1939, 6½", $300.00.

Vase, crystalline, wht on sky bl, bulbous, 1952, 5".......................300.00
Vase, gr & bl gloss, raised rim on tapered oval, hdls, 1932, 5" 115.00
Vase, ivory w/bl & pearl crystalline, can neck, Stephen/1946, 12" ..700.00
Vase, mint gr, yel-gray clay, clear int, 1926-27, 9¼" 250.00
Vase, mint to aqua, rose inside, ca 1938, 2¾x4" 70.00
Vase, multi-tone bl & gr w/red highlights, 1939, 5½" 90.00
Vase, Tobacco Spit Red, 1934, 9" 250.00
Vase, turq crackle, pale rose int w/turq o/l, 1952, 9¼" 125.00
Vase, turq crackle, rose int w/turq o/l, 1953, 4½x5⅝" 80.00
Vase, turq on aubergine-wine, ovoid, hdls, 1948, 6⅛"................225.00

Pittsburgh Glass

As early as 1797, utility window glass and hollow ware were being produced in the Pittsburgh area. Coal had been found in abundance, and it was there that it was first used instead of wood to fuel the glass furnaces. Because of this, as many as 150 glass companies operated there at one time. However, most failed due to the economically disastrous effects of the War of 1812. By the mid-1850s those that remained were producing a wide range of flint glass items including pattern-molded and free-blown glass, cut and engraved wares, and pressed tableware patterns.

Our advisor for this category is Mark Vuono; he is listed in the Directory under Connecticut.

Bottle, puce-amethyst, tapered, 16 right-swirl ribs, 7⅜" **350.00**
Celery vase, Pillar mold, baluster stem, flint, 9⅛" **220.00**
Compote, Pillar mold, 8-rib, flared rim, ftd, 1830s, 9x10⅛" **650.00**
Creamer, emerald gr, bulbous, rnd ft, pontiled, ca 1800, 4"........**850.00**
Decanter, cut, strawberry dmns & fans, hollow stopper, 9½" **170.00**
Lamp, 14" frosted amber Drapery shade; 2-socket floral std, 23"...**1,100.00**
Pitcher, cut, strawberry dmns, ovals & starbursts, 7¾" **450.00**
Tumbler, peacock bl w/amber streak, 9-panel, 3½" **230.00**
Tumbler, 6 arches over 6 panels, cobalt, sm chips, 3⅜" **90.00**
Wine, blown, bell-shaped bowl w/wht twisted thread, 6⅜"...........**115.00**

Plastics

Synthetic plastics were invented in 1868. Since then, many types have been developed, each with unique characteristics and uses. Among the earliest, those most familiar to us today are celluloid and French ivory; they were commonly used to make toiletry articles. In the early years of the century, buttons were made from Casein plastics, which could be made in a wide variety of colors and easily laminated and carved. The plastic jewelry that is so popular today had its heyday in the 1930s. The material used for its production was Phenol Formaldehyde. Two of the more recognizable tradenames for cast phenolics are Bakelite and Catalin. Buckles, buttons, radio and clock cases, cutlery handles, desk sets and novelties were also made from this type of plastic. Vinyl and Lucite, acrylic resins, were used during the period between the two World Wars. There were many applications for vinyl, which is still commonly used. Lucite items that are particular interesting to todays collectors are purses and jewelry. (See Jewelry.)

Today's collectors have adopted the term Bakelite to encompass any type of phenoic resin. There are two methods of testing used to identify genuine Bakelite: 1) using a cotton swab and Semichrome or 409, clean an inconspicuous area — oxidation on any color will tint the cotton ivory or light yellow; 2) hold the edge of item under very hot running water for at least twenty seconds; if it's genuine, it will smell like varnish or paint remover.

For more information we recommend *Celluloid Treasures of the Victorian Era* by Joan Van Patten and Elmer and Peggy Williams; *Celluloid Collectibles* by Shirley Dunn; and *Celluloid Collector's Reference and Value Guide* by Keith Lauer and Julie Robinson. All are published by Collector Books.

Bakelite

Ashtray, blk-speckled brn, Pullman Co, ca 1940s, 5½" dia **80.00**
Box, butterscotch, includes Gem razor & manual, in orig cb box...**350.00**
Box, ring; emerald gr w/striations, curved lid, 1¼x2¾" **175.00**
Box, 1933 Century of Progress, blk, 6" L, NM **11.00**
Buckle, belt, beige & taupe, 2 'wings,' 1 w/button fastner...........**145.00**
Buckle, latch type, mc, uncvd **25.00**
Buckle, latch type, 1-color, stylized floral or geometric.................**30.00**
Button, banana shape, orange w/blk, 2½x⅝" **130.00**
Buttons, card of 6, uncvd octagonal, amber, 1" dia **10.00**
Camera, Coronet Midget, gr, 2¼x1" **165.00**
Candle holders, brn marbleized, Deco style, Fr, 6½", pr **165.00**
Candlesticks, funerary; Deco style, inlaid stds, 52", pr.................**425.00**
Carving set, knife, fork, steel...**30.00**
Checkers, red & blk, full set, in box **35.00**
Chess set, pcs in wht or ivory, in poor orig box **400.00**
Cigar cutter, bust of man, put cigar in mouth, push down hat **95.00**

Cigarette box, chrome inserts, cylindrical, 4½" **45.00**
Cigarette box, half-cylinder, rotates open, dk brn.........................**45.00**
Cigarette dispenser, dk red w/celluloid lid, Trigerette, 3¾" **125.00**
Clock, mantel; wind-up alarm, Deco design, dk brn **60.00**
Corkscrew, chrome, red, gr or amber hdl, ea **12.50**
Crib toy, cat face w/metal bell w/in bell-shaped fr, 4x3", NM **110.00**
Crib toy, elephant, strung amber spools w/wht 3-D head, 3½" ...**265.00**
Crib toy, girl cat, strung butterscotch blocks, 3½", NM **110.00**
Crib toy, Humpty Dumpty, stung amber beads, wht egg head, 4½"..**210.00**
Crib toy, little girl, strung tan/butterscotch beads & chunks, 6" ...**95.00**
Crib toy, Tykie Toy, boy, girl, clown, kitten, etc, ea...................**195.00**
Dice, Caltex w/star on ivory, English, set of 5, MIB....................**70.00**
Dice cup, blk w/gold marbled bottom, 2" **80.00**
Drawer pull, butterscotch swirled, bar style w/chrome bars **15.00**
Figurine, greyhound, gray on gr marbled base, ca 1920s, 8" L **200.00**
Flashlight, Dyna-lite, ivory, streamline styling, EX in box **95.00**
Flatware, blk w/inlaid yel teardrop, GH Warranted, 6 sets in box ..**500.00**
Flatware, chrome plate, 1-color hdl **3.00**
Flatware, red hdls, service for 4 (4 pcs ea) **80.00**
Flatware, stainless, 1-color hdl **4.00**
Flatware, yel hdls, service for 6 (4 pcs ea), no serving pcs...........**100.00**
Gavel, lathe trn, ivory **25.00**
Gavel, mc rings, 7½", EX **100.00**
Gear shift knob/clock combo, blk/clear, New Haven, VG **100.00**
Hors d'oeuve set, butterscotch dice hdls, 8 forks in stand **200.00**
Inkwell, Carvacraft Great Britain, amber, dbl well **115.00**
Jar, amber w/blk & amber lid, emb horizontal rings, 4x3¼"........**165.00**
Letter opener, chrome/Catalin, Deco design **20.00**
Match holder, cvg of 4 frogs, butterscotch w/red base, 2x2"........**195.00**
Mold, cherry, mini **85.00**
Napkin ring, donkey, brn, cvd eyes/mouth **95.00**
Napkin ring, rocking horse, red w/gr eye, EX **65.00**
Napkin ring, Scottie dog, ivory, no eye **80.00**
Pen holder, blk Deco-style holder on red Lucite base, 3½" L........**55.00**
Pen holder, gr w/chrome accents, Deco styling, 3x2½x4" **135.00**
Pen holder, streamlined, blk **22.50**
Pencil sharpener, airplane, butterscotch w/2 insignias **55.00**
Pencil sharpener, Bambi, Walt Disney Productions, 1" dia............**55.00**
Pencil sharpener, bird, butterscotch marbled w/dk beak, 1½", EX..**100.00**
Pencil sharpener, Dopey, red w/litho Dopey, Dopey shape, WD .**100.00**
Pencil sharpener, Electro-Pointer, blk, electric, 5¾", NM...........**200.00**
Pencil sharpener, Goofy, rnd & fluted, 1½" **50.00**
Pencil sharpener, mantel clock, Germany 2"...............................**50.00**
Pencil sharpener, red marbled in brass bezel, Little Rascals, EX..**285.00**
Pencil sharpener, USA Army plane...**80.00**
Pencil sharpener, Walt Disney's train, figural, 1¾" **85.00**
Pencil sharpener, 1939 NY WF, butterscotch/blk fair symbols........**95.00**
Picture frame, red, gr or amber, 6" sq.......................................**35.00**
Poker chips, butterscotch swirled, 100 in orig box dtd 1932 ....**80.00**
Poker chips, red, gr & butterscotch, in marbled gr holder: 4x3x1⅜" ..**125.00**
Poker chips, 400 swirl-molded chips, in bl, tan, red, EX 14x8x3" case ..**450.00**
Powder box, amber & blk fluted cylinder, 2½" **50.00**
Powder jar, tortoise shell look, NM **95.00**
Radio, Astor, brn, chrome speaker bars, rstr, VG........................**215.00**
Radio, AWA Radiola, blk, tombstone-style case, EX **450.00**
Radio, AWA Radiolette, blk, 'Empire State,' EX **700.00**
Radio, Emerson, orange w/blk knobs & slats over speaker, 9" W, VG..**400.00**
Radio, Emerson Tombstone, ivory, nonworking, 10x7", NM **500.00**
Radio, Fada 1000, wine w/orange, EX **1,000.00**
Radio, Farnsworth BT50, brn, rnded corners, molded speaker bars, EX....**325.00**
Radio, Model #41 Kadette Jewel, blk w/scrollwork grill, EX **325.00**
Radio, Mullard, brn tombstone, bars/circles in grille, EX **250.00**
Radio/lamp combo, dk red orange, skyscraper form, brass base, 21", EX...**300.00**
Record player, RCA 45-EY-4, tube type, 11x13x8", EX **125.00**

Shakers, gr, bbl shape on flat/ftd 4" L stand, Japan, pr.................**125.00**
Shakers, red or butterscotch, pr fits bk to bk on 1¾" rnd tray.......**85.00**
Shakers, various colors, W Germany, miniature, ½", set of 4......**100.00**
Shakers, 3-pc barbell, shaker ea end, wine & yel, 4⅛" L............**125.00**
Shaving brush, red, gr or amber, w/holder **40.00**
Spoon, iced tea; chrome, w/Catalin knob, 6-pc set...................**25.00**
Swizzle stick, butterscotch, star finial, 5¼"...............................**30.00**
Table lighter, nude, pnt figure on bronze base, Dunhill **165.00**
Tray, Bartels Beer, orange lettering on blk.................................**165.00**

Celluloid

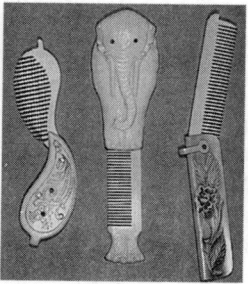

Folding novelty combs, Teardrop shape with incised florals and rhinestones, 2¼"; Elephant with green rhinestone eyes, pull feet to reveal comb; Rectangular with embossed florals and gold-tone paint, from $18.00 to $25.00 each. (Photo courtesy Keith Lauer and Julie Robinson)

Autograph album, Victorian lady, 4½x6", from $175 to.............**225.00**
Box, collar & cuff; lady's portrait, 6x6¼x6¼", from $300 to.......**350.00**
Box, handkerchief; Mucha print, 3x5½x5½", from $175 to **225.00**
Box, letter; Victorian girls, 2x5x7½", from $100 to....................**150.00**
Box, sewing; harvest scene, 4x9x7½", from $175 to...................**200.00**
Brush, Victorian lady bk, ornate hdl, 8½", from $90 to.............**125.00**
Glove case, Victorian scene, 3¼x11¼x3½", from $250 to **300.00**
Jewel case, mother/child reserve, gilt lock, 3x8x5", from $185 to ..**250.00**
Jewel case, Victorian children, velvet trim, musical, 4x10x6".....**250.00**
Manicure set, Victorian scene, 9-pc in 4x13x11" case, from $325 to....**400.00**
Mirror, hand; ornate bk, 9¾x4", from $100 to............................**150.00**
Mirror, shaving; emb classic figures, trifold, 12¼x20½" **500.00**
Photo album, Victorian child, musical, 12x9½", from $600 to ...**700.00**
Photo album, Victorian scene, upright, 8½x10½", from $450 to....**525.00**
Shaving set, ivoroid, 5-pc in 3½x9x7" box, from $350 to..........**400.00**
Whisk broom holder, lady in plumed hat, from $125 to..............**175.00**

Playing Cards

Playing cards can be an enjoyable way to trace the course of history. Knowledge of the art, literature, and politics of an era can be gleaned from a study of its playing cards. When royalty lost favor with the people, kings and queens were replaced by common people. During the periods of war, generals, officers, and soldiers were favored. In the United States, early examples had portraits of Washington and Adams as opposed to kings, Indian chiefs instead of jacks, and goddesses for queens.

Tarot cards were used in Europe during the 1300s as a game of chance, but in the eighteenth century they were used to predict the future and were regarded with great reverence.

The backs of cards were of no particular consequence until the 1890s. The marble design used by the French during the late 1800s and the colored wood-cut patterns of the Italians in the nineteenth century are among the first attempts at decoration. Later the English used cards printed with portraits of royalty. Eventually cards were decorated with a broad range of subjects from reproductions of fine art to advertising.

Although playing cards are becoming popular collectibles, prices are still relatively low. Complete decks of cards printed earlier than the first postage stamp can still be purchased for less than $100.00. In the listings, below decks are without boxes unless the box is specifically men-

tioned. Information concerning the American Antique Deck Collectors Club, 52 Plus Joker, may be found in the Directory under Clubs, Newsletters, and Catalogs.

Key:
AC — ad card	SC — score card
C — complete	std — standard
cts — courts	ws — wide scenic
J — joker	XC — extra card

Advertising

Alka Seltzer, Sammy Davis & Speedy bks, 1980 Olympics, dbl deck, MIB....**100.00**
Anheuser-Busch's Army & Navy, warships/officers, USPC, ca 1900, EXIB ...**250.00**
Bailey Banks & Biddle, eagle aces, 1915, 52+special J, VG, G box....**35.00**
Bar-Keeper's Friend, wide, special aces, 52+special J, VG..............**45.00**
Bernhart Altman Cashmere, Piatnik, Oriental cts, 1950, 52+2J, NM ..**75.00**
Cutty Sark Blended Scots Whisky, Waddington, clipper bks, 52+J, EXIB .**15.00**
Grand Imperial Sec, Germania Wine Cellars NY, 52noJ, EX+, VG box....**25.00**
Hamlet Mild Cigars, Benson & Hedges, 52+4J, NMIB **10.00**
La Tendencia Havana Cigars, 1902, 52+J+XC, NM, G box **150.00**
McConway & Torley, rail coupler bks, special aces, 52+SC, NMIB...**35.00**
Minolta, Carta Mundi, copiers on cts/aces, 52+3J, NMIB...........**100.00**
Old Master Coffee, USPC, special aces, 52+special J+2SC, VGIB .**95.00**
Park Lane Hotel Apartments, colorful bks, 1930, 52+J+XC+SC, NMIB...**45.00**
Philips Radio, Mesmaekers, Belgium, Deco cts, 1925, 52+J, EXIB....**200.00**
Scientific American, Rufus Porter, 1980s, MIB, sealed.................**22.00**
Tequila Sauza Alto Calidid, Clemente Jacques, roosters bks, 52+J, M.....**10.00**
Texaco, Pyramid PCC, special ads on bks, 1925, 52+XC, VG-, G box...**65.00**

Foreign Manufacturers

Australia, Vidette, cartoonish cts, WWI support, 1915, 52noJ, NMIB...**1,000.00**
Austria, Dante & Beatrice, Piatnik, Beatrice bks, 1923, NMIB..**125.00**
Austria, Winblad, Piatnik, fantasy cts, dbl deck, NMIB **16.00**
Austria-Hausermann Aluminum, Cocktail series, 1925, 52noJ, EXIB ..**1,200.00**
Belgium, Brepols, Turnhout/Liege, Skat deck, 1890, 32C, M......**120.00**
Belgium, Great Mogul, Genechten, 1890, 52C, NM **20.00**
Belgium, Luxus Skat Karte, Brepols, ca 1943, 32C, EX+, EX box.**30.00**
Canada, Imperial Club, Goodall, cigars/pipes bks, 1940s, MIB (sealed) ..**20.00**
England, Worshipful, Mexico Olympiad, bl bks, 1968, M in wrapper......**25.00**
Finland, Pelikortteja Speklort, Deco cts, 52noJ, NMIB...............**700.00**
France, Can Can, Philibert, orig ed, nonstd cts, 52+2J+blank, NMIB...**80.00**
France, Ciel de France, Draeger Freres, 1950, 52+J, NMIB...........**20.00**
France, Fantasy, Banco, gr/wht bks, 1952, 52+J, NMIB.................**20.00**
France, Paris Souvenir, Philibert, color photo bks, 1960, NM.......**30.00**
France, St Hubert's Bridge, Philibert, 1956, 52+2J, NMIB............**70.00**
Germany, Baronnesse #160, Dondorf, roses bks, 1895, 52+J, EX+, G box **40.00**
Germany, Das Kupferstichpiel, mc repro of 1617 Hoffmann deck, 48C, NM ..**85.00**
Germany, Heidborn & Wegener, plaid bks, c 1872, 32C?, EX- **50.00**
Ireland, Irish PC, Dechtire design, 52+leprechaun J+XC, MIB **40.00**
Italy, Centaurus, Modiano, Nouveau cts, 1910, 52noJ+XC, EX+ ..**350.00**
Italy, Italsider, Dal Negro, Constantini cts, red bks, 1964, NMIB....**50.00**
Italy, Morositas, cts/aces: soccor players/etc, 52+2J+XC, M **50.00**
Spain, Chinese Costumes, Fournier, 1984, dbl deck, MIB, sealed.**10.00**
Spain, Precolumbian America, Fournier, 1959, MIB, sealed **10.00**
Switzerland, La Suisse Historique #33, flower bks, 52+2J, NMIB .**18.00**

Older Narrow Decks

Alaskan Totem Pole, Russell Artcraft, 1930s, M, EX box..............**20.00**
Anma, Army/Navy/Marines/Air Corps suits, 52+Commander in Chief, EXIB ..**20.00**
Congress #606W, Dawn, whist sz, scenic bks, 52+J, VG, G- box ..**10.00**
Congress #606W, Rookwood, Indian head bks, 1925, EX-, G- box....**35.00**

Eagle 5-Suit Bridge, 5th suit is eagles, 1938, 65+J+XC, NMIB **10.00**
Golden Diamond, Hanzel, special color suits, 1923, 52+J+XC, NMIB.....**40.00**
Ideal Nonrevoke, Hurd & Co, gr dmns, brn clubs, 1928, 52C, NMIB......**50.00**
New Orleans Carnival, Mardi Gras figures on cts, 1925 orig, 52+J, VG..**40.00**
Pennant, USPC, 1910, 52noJ, VG+ **10.00**
Samuel Hart & Co, Indian & headdress bks, 1930s, 52noJ, VG+ ..**10.00**

Older Wide Decks

Allied Armies, Montreal Litho Co, 1916, 52+lion J+blank C, NM, G- box ...**250.00**
Am Steamboats, Am PCC, 1890, gr plaid bks, 52+steamer J, EX-, G box.......**100.00**
Apollo #33, Nat'l Card Co, 1895, 52noJ, VG, G box **10.00**
Bank Note #91, Std PCC, red bks, 1923, M (sealed), VG box **25.00**
Battle Axe Pinochle #622, Russell, bl bks, 1925, 48C, VGIB **12.00**
Bellevue, Parker Bros, sailing ship bks, 52+Bellevue J, VG-, G- box ...**50.00**
Bicycle #808, all wheel bl bks, c 1925, 52noJ, VG.................**30.00**
Bicycle #808, Cupid bl bks, 1922, 52+J, NM, G box **50.00**
Bicycle #808, model #2 bl bks, c 1925, 52noJ, VG **15.00**
Congress #606, Anticipation, 1902, 52+Anticipation J, EX-, G box ..**10.00**
Congress #606, Diana, c 1899, 52+Diana J, EX-, VG box.............**60.00**
Congress #606, Good Night, c 1900, 52noJ, VG, VG box **40.00**
Congress #606, Spring, 1903, 52noJ, VG-, G box **40.00**
Diavolo, Atlantin PCC, 1915, 52+devil J, EXIB **75.00**
Foster's Self-Playing Whist, Dougherty, 1889, 52+XC+pamphlet, EXIB..**70.00**
Gypsy Witches Fortune Telling, Standard PCC, river bks, 1903, NMIB ..**15.00**
Home Run, Pyramid PC, red bks, 1925, 52+Pyramid J+blank, VGIB.......**45.00**
Hungarian #32, Dougherty, red bks, 1910, 32C, G, G- box **30.00**
Indicator, Dougherty, cherubs bks, 1895, 52+rare J, EXIB...........**560.00**
Military Fortune Tellers, Loring, special suits, 1918, MIB, sealed..**25.00**
Moon Playing Cards #1, Dougherty, cherub bks, 1910, 52+moon J, VG ..**65.00**
Perfection, gold pattern bks, 1880, 52+Jolly J, VG-, snap case ...**100.00**
Pyramid Special, red pattern bk, 1920, 52+J, EX, G- box.............**25.00**
Red Seal #16, Dougherty, 1900, 52noJ, VGIB **30.00**
Success #28, Kalamazoo, lady w/violin bks, 1907, 52+J, VG+, VG box ..**45.00**
Tudor PC, Dougherty, red rose bks, 52+J, VG, G box **50.00**
Vanity Fair #41 Transformation, 1895, 52+devil J, VG+/torn box...**200.00**

Souvenir

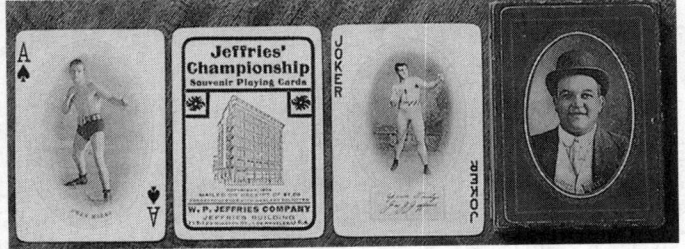

Jim Jeffries Championship, famous matches and fighters of the era, 1909, fifty-two cards, Joker, extra card, and booklet, NMIB, $550.00.

California, M Reider, 1907, 52+J+XC+booklet, NMIB.................**65.00**
California, RF Waters, type A oval photos, 1898-1900, 52+J, EX **20.00**
Cuba Souvenir, USPC, 1930, 52+J+XC, EXIB **50.00**
Forbidden City, Grimes Stassforth, photo cards, 1901, 50 of 52+J, EXIB..**200.00**
Great Southwest, F Harvey, aces show lookout, 1910, 52+J+map, EXIB **95.00**
Montreal & Quebec, Goodall, 1905, 52+J+XC, NM **15.00**
Nation's Capital, USPC, WA DC views, 52+J+XC, VG, G- box ..**40.00**
North Dakota Land of Opportunity, narrow, 1950s, dbl deck, VGIB ..**10.00**
North Shore MA, DRM Specialty, schooner bks, 1913, 52+J+SC, NMIB..**200.00**
NY City, USPC, Liberty bks, oval views, 51 of 52+J, VG, G box .**20.00**
O'Callaghan's...Chicago, Opera House bks, 1930, 52+J+XC+booklet, M ..**200.00**

Ocean to Ocean, Goodall, 1905, 52+J+EX, NM **15.00**

Transportation

Canadian National, Grand Trunk Pacific RR, 1900, 44 of 52+J, VG ...**75.00**
Canadian National Pacific, Grimaud, 6060 bks, 1982, M, sealed..**30.00**
Denver & Rio Grande RR, Interstate, 1915, 52+J, NMIB **20.00**
Mexicana Airlines, Las Alas de Oro 50th Anniversary, 1972, NMIB..**15.00**
Moore-McCormack Lines, Chicago, cruise ships bks, 1950s, VGIB......**10.00**
Motor Cargo Inc, Brown & Bigelow, 1960s, 52+2J, EXIB.............**10.00**
NY Central, Morning Along Hudson Bks/Engine 4028, 1948, M sealed..**10.00**
Southern Pacific, Barkalow Bros, 1937, 52+J+SC+booklet, NMIB..**45.00**
Union Pacific, Barkalow Bros, 1920, 52+J+XC+booklet, NMIB ..**20.00**
White Pass & Yukon Route, ca 1900, 52+J+2XC, NMIB **140.00**

Political

    The most valuable political items are those from any period which relate to a political figure whose term was especially significant or marked by an important event or one whose personality was particularly colorful. Posters, ribbons, badges, photographs, and pin-back buttons are but a few examples of the items popular with collectors of political memorabilia.

    Political campaign pin-back buttons were first mass produced and widely distributed in 1896 for the president-to-be William McKinley and for the first of three unsuccessful attempts by William Jennings Bryan. Pin-back buttons have been used during each presidential campaign ever since and are collected by many people. The scarcest are those used in the presidential campaigns of John W. Davis in 1924 and James Cox in 1920.

    Contributions to this category were made by Michael J. McQuillen, monthly columnist of *Political Parade*, which appears in *AntiqueWeek* newspapers; he is listed in the Directory under Indiana. Our advisor for this category is Paul J. Longo; he is listed under Massachusetts. See also Autographs; Broadsides; Historical Glass; Watch Fobs.

Badge, Democratic Convention Delegate, Chicago, 1932 ....**45.00**
Badge, Farmer's Alliance, FA&IU Unity & plow, 1890,¾", EX..**100.00**
Band, Votes for Women, bl lettering on yel felt, 1½x23", EX.....**145.00**
Bandana, Wm Henry Harrison on horsebk, 1850, 26x26½", EX...**500.00**
Banner, Wm Jennings Bryan, mc cloth, 1900, 24x35"................**250.00**
Book, Our Lenin, child's picture type, Shaw/Potamkin, 1934, EX...**45.00**
Book, Songs of Socialism, Co-op Printing Co, Chicago, 1911, 98-pg...**95.00**
Bubble gum cigar box, Win w/Dick, w/contents, 1x4½x8", NM+..**90.00**
Cane, FD Roosevelt base-metal finial, hardwood shaft, EX.........**350.00**
Cane, FD Roosevelt pot-metal crook hdl, hardwood shaft, brass ferrule...**225.00**
Cane, GC Wallace campaign, blond oak, Stick Up For..., 1960s .**125.00**
Cane, Gerald Ford for President on crook hdl, hardwood shaft, 1976 ....**125.00**
Cane, Jimmy Carter pot-metal hdl, hardwood shaft, plastic ferrule............**100.00**
Cane, McKinley 1896 presidential campaign, tin, horn mechanism, EX...**325.00**
Cane, Republican elephant pewter handle, bamboo shaft, ca 1890s, EX ...**200.00**
Cane, Wm McKinley pewter hdl, hardwood hdl, dtd 1896, EX..**225.00**
Card, Martin Van Buren, mechanical metamorphic, VG............**125.00**
Card, Nat'l Woman's Party membership, Statue of Liberty, 3x5" ..**35.00**
Card, Vote Socialist, Socialist Am Offers..., 1936, postcard sz **50.00**
Figure, Barry Goldwater, plastic, Remco, 1964, 5½", MIB **65.00**
Flyer, Then & Now, census figures, WF Ries, OH, 1860-1910, 3¼x6"...**20.00**
Invitation, inaugural; Kennedy/Johnson, 1961, 11x8½" **75.00**
Leaflet, Debs for President, 1900, 4-pg, 5½x8", G **95.00**
License plate, Al Smith the Happy Warrior, EX.........................**175.00**
Locket, Lincoln & Johnson portraits, gold-filled, ca 1864, EX **2,000.00**
Magazine, Sing Out!, Woody Guthrie cover, November 1953, EX...**35.00**
Medal, Geo WA Birth & Death, wht metal, edge clip, NM..........**30.00**
Medalet, GenAndrew Jackson, Nation's Good, brass, plain edge, EX ..**100.00**
Pamphlet, Blain the Proscriptionist..., mud slinging, 8-pg.............**50.00**

Pamphlet, Liberty, E Debs self-published speech, 1895, 5¼x7½"....100.00
Pennant, Vote Communist, silver letters on red paper, 1936, 17½"..325.00
Pocket mirror, McKinley & wife, bl & pk on sepia, ca 1900, VG.75.00
Postcard, Equal Suffrage - Woman's Birthright, unused, EX..........35.00
Postcard, Karl Marx Birthday, One Hundredth Anniversary, G....50.00
Postcard, western White House, Nixon estate................................4.00
Poster, Come Stop Wallace..., blk on yel card stock, 11x14", EX..40.00
Poster, Eugene V Debs, framed photo poster, 13½x9", EX..........250.00
Poster, Golden Gate Peace Rally, 1972, 14x19½", EX..................50.00
Poster, Internat'l Student Strike, red/wht/bl, 1968, 18x23"...........75.00
Poster, Vote Communist..., man w/sickle, Foster, 1924, 14x22", EX...1,200.00
Poster, Women's Liberation Movement, Pro-Arts, 1970, 21x33", EX......50.00
Poster stamp, Vote Communist, red/bl, Foster/Gitlow, 1929, 2x15".........75.00
Ribbon, Blaine & Logan, Independent Irish-Americans, 1884, 6x2¼".100.00
Scarf, Repeal Taft-Hartley Law, silk, brn tones, ca 1947, 33x33", EX......85.00
Silk, Andrew Jackson memorial, bl on cream, 1845, 7¾x3".......250.00
Silk, McKinley/Hobart jugate, yel, 7½x2¼", EX..........................100.00
Silk, Remember the Maine, red/wht/bl on cream, 1898, 6¾x2¾"..75.00
Silk, Sullivan-Fischer jugate, portrait/cabin, EX..........................300.00
Silk, Taft/Sherman jugate, bl on wht w/mc Am flag, 5½x2".......150.00
Silk, Wm Henry Harrison, Hero of Tippecanoe, portrait on wht.....230.00
Stickpin, Bryan, celluloid oval, mc..50.00
Tip tray, Taft-Sherman jugate, mc on tin, 1908, 4", EX...............150.00
Token, Lincoln 1864 campaign, copper, 1864, EX..........................60.00
Token, Republican Nat'l Convention, Lincoln portrait, 1940......30.00

Pin-back Buttons

For a People's Program - Vote Communist, mc, Slater, 1¾"..........30.00
LSD Not LBJ, bl on yel, 1¼"..22.50
Peace Flag, red & bl on wht, Vietnam War era, 1¼", EX..............15.00
Ratify ERA in 1975, red & wht, 3½", VG...................................15.00
Social Democratic Party, red flat, on wht, ca 1890, EX.................65.00
Stop Conscription, bl on wht cello, 1940, ¾", NM........................60.00
Stop Work - Stop War April 15, 1970, red/wht/bl, EX..................25.00
Students for Stevenson-Kefauver, bl & wht, 1956, 1"....................65.00
Vietnam March for Peace, Nov 27, bl on wht, 1", EX...................15.00
Welcome Theodore Roosevelt, ca 1910, 1¼", on red/wht/bl ribbon...100.00
Wilson-Pershing jugate, bl on cream, ca 1917-18, 1¼", EX...........100.00
World Youth Congress Against War & Fascism, red & wht litho, ¾".50.00
You Can't Pull a Wilson on US, red/wht/bl, cello, 1"...................60.00

Pomona

Pomona glass was patented in 1885 by the New England Glass Works. Its characteristics are an etched background of crystal lead glass often decorated with simple designs painted with metallic stains of amber or blue. The etching was first achieved by hand cutting through an acid resist. This method, called first ground, resulted in an uneven feather-like frost effect. Later, to cut production costs, the hand-cut process was discontinued in favor of an acid bath which effected an even frosting. This method is called second ground. Our advisors for this category are Betty and Clarence Maier; they are listed in the Directory under Pennsylvania.

Bowl, Cornflowers, 1st ground, scalloped base, 3½x8½"............650.00
Carafe, Cornflowers, 2nd ground, ribbed neck, T'print body, 8".385.00
Champagne, 2nd ground, EX amber stain, 5"..............................245.00
Cruet, Cornflowers, 2nd ground, amber stain, 7¼".....................335.00
Cruet, Invt T'print, 2nd ground, gold neck/hdls/stopper, 7"........385.00
Finger bowl, Cornflowers, 2nd ground, amber stain, 5½"............150.00
Pitcher, Honeycomb, 1st ground, HP floral, twist hdl, 7½"........700.00
Pitcher, Invt T'print, 1st grind, amber stain, 6"..........................600.00
Pitcher, tankard; 1st ground, leaves at rim, amber hdl, 9"...........325.00
Punch cup, 1st ground, amber hdl/rim, 2½"..................................85.00
Rose bowl, 2nd ground, bl flowers, 5x5¼"...................................450.00
Sugar bowl, Cornflowers, 1st ground, ruffled amber rim, 2¾".....175.00
Tumbler, Cornflowers, 1st ground, 6 for......................................400.00
Tumbler, Cornflowers, 2nd ground, amber & bl stain, 3⅝x2½".125.00
Tumbler, Dmn Quilt, bl & amber pansy & butterfly, 2nd ground, 3¾"..150.00
Tumbler, Dmn Quilt/Cornflowers, 2nd ground, bl stain, 3¾".....150.00
Vase, Baby T'print, 2nd ground, fan shape w/crimped rim, 3x5¾"...185.00
Vase, Invt T'print, 1st ground, ruffled, rigaree collar, 4½"..........170.00

Porcelier

The Porcelier Manufacturing Company, originally from East Liverpool, Ohio, started business in the late 1920s and moved to Greensburg, Pennsylvania, in the early 1930s. The company flourished until the late 1940s and finally closed its doors in 1954.

They produced an endless line of vitrified porcelain products including electric appliances, coffee makers, and light fixtures. These products were sold in many stores under a variety of names and carried over ten different types of marks and labels.

The prices below are for items in excellent condition with no chips, cracks, or excessive wear. For more information, we recommend *Collector's Guide to Porcelier China* by our advisor for this category, Susan E. (Grindberg) Lynn. If you have any questions or information regarding Porcelier, you may contact Mrs. Lynn; she is listed in the Directory under Nevada. (Queries require SASE.)

Bean pot, ind; Basketweave Cameo..12.00
Beverage cooler, bbl form, high or low, wht, ea...........................60.00
Boiler, Oriental Deco, 6-cup or 8-cup, ea......................................65.00
Canisters, Serv-All Line, gold or red/blk, #3016, ea.....................80.00
Casserole, Basketweave Cameo, w/lid, 8½"...................................85.00
Floral, 6-cup...25.00
Coffeepot, Beehive Floral Spray, 6-cup...35.00
Coffeepot, dbl; Black-Eyed Susan, 6-cup......................................120.00
Coffeepot, French Drip; Cameo Silhouette, 6-cup...........................45.00
Coffeepot, Nautical, 2-cup..40.00
Coffeepot, Scalloped Wild Flowers, 6-cup.......................................45.00
Creamer & sugar bowl, Flower Pot, ea..15.00
Creamer & sugar bowl, Nautical, ea...35.00
Lamp, dresser; Dutch Girl...55.00
Lamp, table; Antique Rose...45.00
Light fixture, dbl ceiling; Barock-Colonial.......................................60.00
Mug, pheasant, sailfish, dog or horse head, gold trim, ea..............40.00
Percolator, Antique Rose Platinum...60.00
Percolator, Cattail..140.00
Percolator, Lavender Bluebell Platinum...60.00
Percolator, Leaf & Shadow, short hdl...85.00
Pitcher, ball form, Mexican (Santa Fe)..80.00
Pitcher, batter; Barock-Colonial, Ivory, red or bl, #2014..............70.00
Pitcher, disc form, Hearth...85.00
Pitcher, hexagonal form, Field Flowers or Flower Pot, ea.............55.00
Pretzel jar, Serv-All Line, platinum..150.00
Sandwich grill, Scalloped Wild Flowers, from $300 to...............375.00
Shakers, Barock-Colonial, any color, #2020, ea.............................25.00
Teapot, Daisy Teardrop, gold trim, 4-cup.....................................110.00
Teapot, Serv-All Line, any color, #3011, ea...................................55.00
Toaster, Serv-All Line, gold or red/blk, #3002, from $1,000 to....1,200.00
Urn, Lavender Bluebell Platinum..75.00
Urn, Reversed Field Flowers Hostess or Platinum, ea......................75.00
Waffle iron, Silhouette, from $185 to...225.00
Wall sconce, Barock-Colonial...40.00

Postcards

Postcards are often very difficult to evaluate, since so many factors must be considered — for instance the subject matter or the field of interest they represent. For example: a 1905 postcard of the White House may seem like a desirable card, but thousands were produced and sold to tourists who visited there, thus the market is saturated with this card, and there are few collectors to buy it. Value: less than $1.00. However, a particular view of small town of which only five hundred were printed could sell for far more, provided you find someone interested in the subject matter pictured on that card. Take as an example a view of the courthouse in Hillsville, Virginia. This card would appeal to those focusing on that locality or county as well as courthouse collectors. Value: $3.00.

The ability of the subject to withstand time is also a key factor when evaluating postcards. Again using the courthouse as an example, one built in 1900 and still standing in the 1950s has been photographed for fifty years, from possibly a hundred different angles. Compare that with one built in 1900 and replaced in 1908 due to a fire, and you can see how much more desirable a view of the latter would be. But only a specialist would be aware of the differences between these two examples.

Postcard dealers can very easily build up stocks numbering in the 100,000s. Greeting and holiday cards are common and represent another area of collecting that appeals to an entirely different following than the view card. These types of cards range from heavily embossed designs to floral greetings and, of course, include the ever popular Santa Claus card. These were very popular from about 1900 until the 1920s, when postcard communication was the equivalent of today's quick phone call or e-mail. Because of the vast number of them printed, many have little if any value to a collector. For instance, a 1909 Easter card with tiny images or a common floral card of the same vintage, though almost one hundred years old, are virtually worthless. It's the cards with appeal and zest that command the higher prices. One with a beautiful Victorian woman in period clothing, her image filling up the entire card, could easily be worth $3.00 and up. Holiday cards designed for Easter, Valentines Day, Thanksgiving, and Christmas are much more common than those for New Year's, St. Patrick's Day, the 4th of July, and Halloween. Generally, then, they're worth less, but depending on the artist, graphics, desirability, and eye appeal, this may not always be true. The signature of a famous artist will add significant value — conversely, an unknown artist's signature adds none.

In summary, the best way to evaluate your cards is to have a knowledgeable dealer look at them. For a list of dealers, send a SASE to the International Federation of Postcard Dealers, P.O. Box 1765, Manassas, VA 20108. *Do not* expect a dealer to price cards from a list or written description as this is not possible. For individual questions or evaluation by photocopy (front and back), you may contact our advisor, Jeff Bradfield, 90 Main St., Dayton, VA 22821. You *must* include a SASE for a reply.

For more information we recommend *Collector's Guide to Post Cards'* by Jane Wood.

Posters

Advertising posters by such French artists as Cheret and Toulouse-Lautrec were used as early as the mid-1800s. Color lithography spurred their popularity. Circus posters by the Strobridge Lithograph Co. are considered to be the finest in their field, though Gibson and Co. Litho, Erie Litho, and Enquirer Job Printing Co. printed fine examples as well. Posters by noted artists such as Mucha, Parrish, and Hohlwein bring high prices. Other considerations are good color, interesting subject matter and, of course, condition. The WWII posters listed below are among the more expensive examples; 70% of those on the market bring less than $65.00. See also Movie Memorabilia; Rock 'N Roll.

Advertising

Anisetta Evangelesti Liquore..., monkey on yel, 1925, 55x39½" **1,200.00**
Cocnac Jacquet, peacock, Bouchet, stone litho, 1910, 61½x45½"...**1,200.00**
Cognac Albert Robin, Cappiello, 1906, 63x46", VG **1,200.00**
Cris-Craft, boat models, blk & wht, 1941, 25x18"+mat & fr, EX .**65.00**
Filver, clown w/suspenders & garters, D'Ylen, 90x43" **850.00**
Flexible Flyer, lady skiing, ca 1930s-40s, 32x24", EX...................**425.00**
Herculese Powder, Right in the Blind By Gosh!, 23x14", EX **350.00**
Jacob Hoffman Brewing Co, mc roses, ale & cigar, Ottmann, 31x21"...**185.00**
Jap Rose Soap, 2 children bathe doll, 35x31"+fr, G **400.00**
Je ne Fume que Nil Papier a Cigarettes, Cappiello, 1912, 44x60", VG...**900.00**
Keep Those Tips Up, risque lady skier, 30x21½", G **115.00**
Kendall's Spavin Cure, lady w/horse & beagles, 28x22"+fr, NM.**650.00**
Le Meilleur le Moins Cher, Michelin Tires, 12⅝x16¼", EX.......**285.00**
Le Nil, elephant, stone litho, Cappiello, ca 1920, 63x47"...........**900.00**
Lionel Line of All Time, 7 lg illustrations, 1930s-40s, 31x21" **175.00**
Maison du Robinson Ombrelles, Crusoe w/umbrella, 1900, 54x42" ..**300.00**
Maurin Quina, gr devil dancing w/bottle, Cappiello, 63x51"+fr **1,500.00**
NE Coast Industries, London & N Eastern Railway, Brangwyn, 1-sheet, EX **900.00**
Pez, girl w/Disney character dispensers, Brause, 1960s-70s, 33x23" ..**110.00**
Superlative Cigarettes, girl w/pansies, 17x12"+fr, VG **200.00**
Vermouth Perucchi, couple & Cupid, stone litho, 1930, 42½x30" ..**110.00**

Circus

B&B, Rare Zoological Features, 4 giraffes, 1909, 27x37", EX......**675.00**
Beatty-Cole Bros, lion & trainer, 36x21", NM **200.00**
Christiani Bros, circus parade, 28x42", w/attached streamer **300.00**
Cole Bros, Miss Christiani, mc, 28x21", EX **55.00**
Cole Bros, 24 performing elephants, 28x42", NM **300.00**
Downie Bros, action scenes, Epic Litho, 41x28", in metal fr.......**400.00**
Miller Bros, clown & elephants, 41x13", EX............................**20.00**
Miller Bros, girl shot from cannon, Temple Litho, 28x41" **250.00**
RB B&B, Dorothy Herbert on horse, 40x28", EX.......................**100.00**
RB B&B, Marcellous Troupe posed as statue, mc, 28x21" **150.00**

Magic

Alexander the Man Who Knows, 1930s-40s, 42x28", VG **450.00**
Carter Sweeps Secrets of Sphinx, Otis Litho, 1920, 28x40"........**500.00**
Fak Hongs, hooded mystic, 1910, 28x37", VG **250.00**
George, Triumphant Am Tour, Otis Litho, 1920s, 1-sheet..........**500.00**
Professor Alba, magician w/skeleton, 1920s, 31x16"...................**300.00**
Wizard, portrait of witchery, 1915, 42x79", VG..........................**850.00**

Theatrical

Primrose & Dockstader's Minstrels, Himself, man killing chicken, Strobridge, NY, 1901, EX, $415.00.

Antar, horseman in landscape, Rochegrosse, Maquet Paris, 32¾x26" ...**350.00**
Billy the Kid, saloon scene, US Litho, 1907, 27½x20", VG **185.00**
Blue Jeans, drama by Joseph Arthur, 1890s, 42x29", EX+ **175.00**

Grand Theatre de l'Expositon, lady in yel, Cheret, 15¾ x11⅜".......**245.00**
Human Hearts, winter scene, Russell Morgan, 1901, 42x80"......**135.00**
Little Eva's Temptation, Black girl & sunflower, 27x18", VG **300.00**
Papa de Francine, figures from operetta, stone litho, 31¼x23½" .**225.00**
Theatre de Madelaine/Club des Loufoques, Gesmar, 1920s, 37x32½"...**375.00**
3 Penny Opera, portrait of James Julia, 1976, 41x81", EX...........**650.00**

Travel

Algeria pictured at edge of desert, 1932, 40x25", EX...................**450.00**
Australia, Great Barrier Reef, fish w/coral, 1954, 39x25", EX+ ..**860.00**
Bermuda, couple on bikes/sailboat at night, 40x24", EX+...........**600.00**
Campagnie Generale Transatlantique, SS France, Bainbridge, 37x23" ...**225.00**
Central Hudson Line, couple watch shoreline, 1925, 46x30", NM.....**690.00**
Cunard Line, fleet at sea, 44x32", VG..**650.00**
Deauville, male diver against bl sky, 60½x46½", NM.................**400.00**
Holland for the Holidays, ship & dock, 39½x25", EX.................**290.00**
Norway Home of Ski-ing, couple rest on snow, 39x24", EX+ **950.00**
St Moritz, lg wht rabbit on dk bl ground, 50x36", NM.................**575.00**
Swiss Air, Winter Sports, family skis, 1950s, 40x25", EX **500.00**
Thermes de Cauterets, waterfalls/valleys, Pallandre, 1905, 39x29" ..**725.00**
United Air Lines, Hawaii, kayak in water, 40x20" **350.00**

War

WWI, Fight or Buy Bonds, HC Christy, 40x30" **550.00**
WWI, I Want You for the Navy, color litho, 1917, 40x26½" **900.00**
WWI, I Want Your...Army..., Uncle Sam, Flagg, 1917, 39x30", NM ..**1,800.00**
WWI, Liberty Bonds, red handprint, JA St John, 20x30", EX **100.00**
WWI, Red Cross nurse/wounded soldier, Fisher, 20x34", EX **330.00**
WWI, Uphold Our Honor Fight for Us, woman & flag, 42x28", NM..**230.00**
WWI, You Buy Liberty Bond Lest I Perish!, 1917, 20x18", EX...**195.00**
WWII, American All, color litho, 1918, EX................................**450.00**
WWII, Be a US Marine, marine before lg flag, 40x22", EX **100.00**
WWII, Do w/Less So They'll Have Enough!..., 40x28", M **125.00**
WWII, Guide the Fighter Planes, Join..., 28x20", EX..................**75.00**
WWII, Join the Navy, sailor riding torpedo, 40x28", VG **300.00**
WWII, Miles of Hell to Tokyo!, Work..., 26x18", G **100.00**
WWII, Save Rubber, GIs in jeep, 40x28", EX **100.00**
WWII, Tell It to Marines, red/wht/bl, 1942, 37x28", EX **175.00**
WWII, They Did Their Part, 5 Sullivan brothers, 28x22", G **150.00**
WWII, War Bonds, Squander Bug, Seuss, 14x46", EX..................**95.00**

Miscellaneous

Exposition D'Affiches, lady w/posters, Courvoisier, 1913, 35x25", EX ..**465.00**
Farewell to a Legend, Muhammad Ali, 4-color, 22x17" **115.00**
Hippodrome, figure on wht horse/cherubs, Cheret, 1880, 20¾x15¼"...**535.00**
Rue de Terrage Paris Emprunt National, J Carlu, 1930s, 32x47"......**625.00**
Venus Restored, blk/wht/pk, Man Ray, Valdonega, 1985, 27x17"....**185.00**
WMCA, His Home Over There, Herter, ca 1918, 40½x18", VG....**110.00**

Pot Lids

Pot lids were pottery covers for containers that were used for hair dressing, potted meats, etc. The most common were decorated with colorful transfer prints under the glaze in a variety of themes, animal and scenic. The first and probably the largest company to manufacture these lids was F. & R. Pratt of Fenton, Staffordshire, established in the early 1800s. The name or initials of Jesse Austin, their designer, may sometimes be found on exceptional designs. Although few pot lids were made after the 1880s, the firm continued into the twentieth century.

American pot lids are very rare. Most have been dug up by collectors searching through sites of early gold rush mining towns in California.

In the following listings, all lids are transfer printed; the color(s) mentioned describe the transfer. Minor rim chips are expected and normally do not detract from listed values. When no condition is given, assume that the value is based on an example in such condition.

American

Taylor's Saponaceous Compound..., man shaving, black transfer, ca 1845 – 60, 3¾", M, $375.00.

Bazin's Ambrosial Shaving Cream X Bazin..., purple, 3⅝", EX ...**200.00**
Bridges Dentifrice...Brooklyn NY, bl, 2⅝", M, +EX pot **425.00**
Burdell's Tooth Powder...San Francisco, mc, 3", NM.................**525.00**
Burdell's Tooth Powder...San Francisco, mc, 3", VG **150.00**
Chlorine Detergent & Orris Dentifrice..., blk, 3", from $650 to ..**800.00**
Cold Cream HP Wakelee...San Francisco, mc, 3".........................**200.00**
Cold Cream of Roses...Newport, red, 2½", +pot **150.00**
Compound Extract of Copaiba...Sent by Mail, blk, 3", NM........**675.00**
Cucumber Cream...NY City & Newport RI, blk, 3" **190.00**
Dr Boutmar's Celebrated...San Francisco, mc, 3¼" **1,500.00**
Dr EI Coxe's Extract...New Orleans, blk, 2⅞" **400.00**
Formodenta an Elegant Preparation...RI, blk, 2⅝" sq.................**145.00**
Genuine Bear's Grease HP Wakelee...San Francisco, mc, 3", EX....**700.00**
Hazard Hazard & Co...RI, blk, 2⅞", +pot **160.00**
Holloway's Ointment...the World, blk, 3⅞"..............................**200.00**
Improved Shaving Paste...Philadelphia, blk, 2⅝" **325.00**
Liston's Extract of Beef...Chicago IL, blk, 3¾", NM..................**125.00**
Massey's Elder Flower...Newport RI, red, 2⅞x2½" **160.00**
Odonto HP Wakelee Druggist, San Francisco, mc, 3", NM **700.00**
Odonto or Oak Bark Orris Tooth Paste... Boston, maroon, 3¼"..**250.00**
Perfumers HP & WC Taylor...WA Crossing Delaware, blk, 3⅜", EX .**200.00**
Phalton's Ambrosial Shaving Cream, purple, 3", +pot, EX **180.00**
Philcome HP Wakelee...San Francisco, mc, 3" **925.00**
R&GA Wright's Gold Medal Cold Cream Phila, blk, 2½" **210.00**
Saponaceous, E Phalon...Perfumer NY, girl/desk, blk, G **180.00**
Unequaled Cold Cream...Virginia NV, blk, 2¾", +G pot.............**800.00**
Ursina HP Wakelee Druggist..., mc, 3¼", NM............................**925.00**
Vinola...Shaving Soap for Sensitive Skins..., brn, 3¼" **200.00**
Wright's...Rose Shaving Cream, dog/fallen soldier, blk, 3½".......**925.00**
Wright's...Shaving Compound, man/mirror, blk, 4¼".................**650.00**

English

New St Thomas Hospital, mc, 4¼", NM **130.00**
On Guard, man sleeping at guard shack, mc, 4⅛", NM **110.00**
Pegwell Bay, Established 1760, mc, 4" **120.00**
Preparing for the Ride, 2 men prepare nobleman, 4"...................**140.00**
Residence of Anne Hathaway...Shottery Nr Stratford..., mc, 4".**100.00**
Room in Which Shakespeare Was Born....Avon, interior view, 4" ..**135.00**
Skewald Horse, 2 men/2 ladies w/horses, 4¼"............................**140.00**
Strasburg, village scene, mc, 4¾"...**145.00**
Transplanting Rice, Orientals at work, mc, 4" **135.00**
Uncle Toby, man examines lady's eye, 4½" **150.00**
Waterfall, scene, mc, 4", EX..**100.00**

Powder Horns and Shot Flasks

Though powder horns had already been in use for hundreds of years, collectors usually focus on those made after the expansion of the United States westward in the very early 1800s. While some are basic and very simple, others were scrimshawed and highly polished. Especially nice carvings can quickly escalate the value of a horn that has survived intact to as high as $400.00. Those with detailed maps, historical scenes, etc., bring even higher prices.

Metal flasks were introduced in the 1830s; by the middle of the century they were produced in quantity and at prices low enough that they became a viable alternative to the powder horn. Today's collector regards the smaller flasks as the more desirable and valuable, and those made for specific companies bring premium prices.

Flask, brass, Amelesk & Cap Co #8, emb game, VG 70.00
Flask, brass, hunter & dogs, plain bk, unmk, 8", VG 75.00
Flask, brass, Oak Leaf, G&JW Hawksley, 8", EX 100.00
Flask, copper, eagle atop bugle & US, graduated spout, ca 1830.400.00
Flask, copper, fouled anchor w/USN, Stimpson 1845 hallmk, EX ..900.00
Flask, copper, unmk, 10", VG 100.00
Flask, leather over brass, Sykes' Patent, 8", VG 35.00
Horn, cvd birds/flowers/church, dtd 1783, 6½", EX.................950.00
Horn, cvd decor (simple), wood base, orig cvd stopper, 6", G.......45.00
Horn, cvd geometrics (EX), spout plug missing, 21" 325.00
Horn, cvd sailing ship/bird/schooner/etc, octagonal, lg 325.00
Horn, cvd spout flange, flat base, short plug, ca 1880s, 5¾"..........45.00
Horn, dk w/sm cvd flange, oval cvd wood base, 1850s, 4¼".........35.00
Horn, eng eagle, leather strap, 19th C, 15x2" 120.00
Horn, eng name, OH, 1845, relief-cvd ring, sq nails, 9".............800.00
Horn, flat body, cvd wood base, orig stopper, 1870s, EX...............45.00
Horn, hammered brass cap, 19th C, 17x3".........................110.00
Horn, walnut plug, ca 1790-1800, 10¾" 100.00

Pratt

Prattware has become a generic reference for a type of relief-molded earthenware with polychrome decoration. Scenic motifs with figures were popular; sometimes captions were added. Jugs are most common, but teapots, tableware, even figurines were made. The term 'Pratt' refers to Wm. Pratt of Lane Delph, who is credited with making the first examples of this type, though similar wares were made later by other Staffordshire potters. Pot lids and other transfer wares marked Pratt were made in Fenton, Staffordshire, by F. & R. Pratt & Co. (See Pot Lids.)

Bottle, scent; figure reserve on orange peel, ca 1800, 3⅛" 260.00
Figurine, cradle, pearlware, typical palette, 11¾", EX.............2,415.00
Figurine, Winter allegory, cut-corner base, ca 1800, 9¼" 460.00
Pitcher, children in heart reserves, 5"............................375.00
Pitcher, pw, acanthus leaves & peacocks, gr/bl/brn/yel, 8¾", EX ..1,450.00
Toby jug, underglaze palette, minor hat rstr, 1790s, 8¼" 1,000

Primitives

Like the mouse that ate the grindstone, so has collectible interest in primitives increased, a little bit at a time, until demand is taking bites instead of nibbles into their availability. Although the term 'primitives' once referred to those survival essentials contrived by our American settlers, it has recently been expanded to include objects needed or desired by succeeding generations — items representing the cabin-'n-corn-patch existence as well as examples of life on larger farms and in towns.

Through popular usage, it also respectfully covers what are actually 'country collectibles.'

From the 1600s into the latter 1800s, factories employed carvers, blacksmiths, and other artisans whose handwork contributed to turning out quality items. When buying, 'touchmarks,' a company's name and/or location and maker's or owner's initials, are exciting discoveries.

Primitives are uniquely individual. Following identical forms, results more often than not show typically personal ideas. Using this as a guide (combined with circumstances of age, condition, desire to own, etc.) should lead to a reasonably accurate evaluation. For items not listed, consult comparable examples. Authority Kathryn McNerney has compiled several lovely books on primitives and related topics: *Primitives, Our American Heritage*; *Collectible Blue and White Stoneware*; and *Antique Tools, Our American Heritage*. You will find her address in the Directory under Florida. See also Butter Molds and Stamps; Boxes; Copper; Farm Collectibles; Fireplace Implements; Kitchen Collectibles; Molds; Tinware; Weaving; Woodenware; and Wrought Iron.

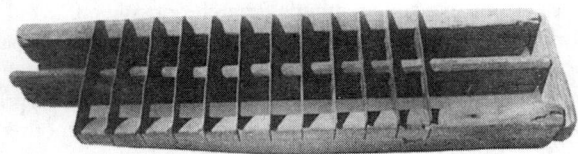

Lye soap cutter, pine lengths and iron strips, makes 22 bars, $110.00. (Photo courtesy Kathryn McNerney)

Bed warmer, brass, pierced lid, trn wood hdl, English, 43" 275.00
Bed warmer, brass w/tooled lid, trn wood hdl, 40" 250.00
Bed warmer, copper pan, tooled brass lid w/sunburst, wood hdl, 42"...275.00
Bed warmer, copper w/simple floral eng, trn hdl, dk brn rpt, 46" .215.00
Bed warmer, copper w/simple tooling on lid, polished, trn hdl, 44"...150.00
Bellows, turtle-bk w/orig pnt & stenciling, brass nozzle, 18", EX ...450.00
Broom, horsehair bristles, wood hdl w/orig pnt, 28" 250.00
Candle mold, pewter, 16-tube, pine fr, 14x13x9"..........................880.00
Candle mold, pewter, 6-tube, walnut fr, scrubbed, rpr, 12½x10x6"..........1,295.00
Candle mold, pewter, 18-tube, pine fr, W Webb NY; 28x22x6", EX.......1,200.00
Candle mold, pewter, 24-tube, pine/poplar, Humiston label, 17x22x7" ..1,375.00
Candle mold, redware, 24-tube, pine fr, cleaned patina, 25x25x9" 1,500.00
Candle mold, tin, 6-tube, conical ft, ear hdls, rprs, 12" 275.00
Candle mold, tin, 6-tube, half-candle sz, ear hdl, 6" 300.00
Candle mold, tin, 8-tube, curved foot, ear hdl, 11" 145.00
Candle mold, tin, 8-tube, wide curved base, 10¾", VG 165.00
Candle mold, tin, 11-tube (1 long row), 12x15"............................400.00
Candle mold, tin, 12-tube, conical finial w/ring hdl, 12", EX 500.00
Candle mold, tin, 12-tube, lg ear hdl, 8⅛"....................................275.00
Candle mold, tin, 12-tube (unusual placement), 4 conical ft, 11" ..350.00
Candle mold, tin, 24-tube, ear hdls, 10¾" 275.00
Candle mold, tin, 24-tube, half-candle sz, ear hdl, lt rust, 6" H..650.00
Candle mold, tin, 24-tube, pnt pine fr w/gold stencil label, 11x13x8"...1,600.00
Candle mold, tin, 25-tube, ear hdls, 12" H 550.00
Candle mold, tin, 36-tube, cherry fr w/dk patina, 16x23x14" ..1,550.00
Candle mold, tin, 36-tube, pine fr w/old red pnt, Walker label, 13" L..2,255.00
Candle mold, tin, 36-tube, walnut fr, bootjack ends, sq nails, 13"....825.00
Candle mold, tin, 48-tube, minor rpr, 1 hdl missing, 7x9x4" 625.00
Candle mold, tin, 50-tube, cherry fr, 10¼x17¼x7⅜" 990.00
Candle mold, tin, 72-tube, ear hdls, 10½" 935.00
Churn, poplar/ash w/blk grpt on red w/wht striping, 1868 Pat, 24".....770.00
Churn, staved wood, orig red, yel int, Bradley & Co, w/dasher, 46" ...440.00
Churn, staved/banded wood, old gray-gr pnt, w/dasher/lid, 47" .430.00
Cookie board, CI, almond shape w/bird on branch, 5¼" L 165.00
Cookie board, CI, flower basket in oval, 5½" 140.00
Cookie board, CI, oblong w/acorn & oak leaves, 5¾" L 195.00

Cookie board, CI, 12 segments w/animal/bird/etc, 5¼x7¾" 300.00
Dough bin, walnut w/EX patina, 1-board top, 10x24x13" 385.00
Foot warmer, hardwood & pine, sliding panel, bail hdl, rfn, 7x9x10" ..250.00
Foot warmer, mortised wood fr w/trn posts, punched tin, 9x8x6" ..275.00
Foot warmer, walnut w/starflower punched tin, 6x8x8", EX........200.00
Kindler, fire wick in soldered tin container, Pat 1871, VG............25.00
Rack, candle drying; 8 rotating arms, hardwood w/old gr pnt, 39" ...770.00
Rack, drying; iron butt hinges, 3 splats, late pnt, 1900s, 42x23x1" ..180.00
Rack, drying; mortised & pinned pine w/old blk, 2 sections, ea: 35x25" ..125.00
Rack, drying; pine, plank ft, vertical posts, 3 splats, 66x44x14"..275.00
Rack, drying; pine w/dk finish, shoe ft, rprs, 35x25" 85.00
Rack, drying; pine w/old red-brn stain, shoe ft, 2 X pcs, 30x26" .350.00
Tub, bath; wood & galvanized tin, zinc lined, 20x61x27" 150.00

Prints

The term 'print' may be defined today as almost any image printed on paper by any available method. Examples of collectible old 'prints' are Norman Rockwell magazine covers and Maxfield Parrish posters and calendars. 'Original print' refers to one achieved through the efforts of the artist or under his direct supervision. A 'reproduction' is a print produced by an accomplished print maker who reproduces another artist's print or original work. Thorough study is required on the part of the collector to recognize and appreciate the many variable factors to be considered in evaluating a print. Prices vary from one area of the country to another and are dependent upon new findings regarding the scarcity or abundance of prints as such information may arise. Although each collector of old prints may have their own varying criteria by which to judge condition, for those who deal only rarely in this area or newer collectors, a few guidelines may prove helpful. Staining, though unquestionably detrimental, is nearly always present in some degree and should be weighed against the rarity of the print. Professional cleaning should improve its appearance and at the same time help preserve it. Avoid tears that affect the image; minor margin tears are another matter, especially if the print is a rare one. Moderate 'foxing' (brown spots caused by mold or the fermentation of the rag content of old paper) and light stains from the old frames are not serious unless present in excess. Margin trimming was a common practice; but look for at least ½" to 1½" margins, depending on print size.

When no condition is indicated, the items listed below are assumed to be in very good to excellent condition. For more information we recommend *Collector's Value Guide to Early 20th Century American Prints* by Michael Ivankovich. See also Nutting, Wallace; Parrish, Maxfield.

Audubon, John J.

Audubon is the best known of American and European wildlife artists. His first series of prints, 'Birds of America,' was produced by Robert Havell of London. They were printed on Whitman watermarked paper bearing dates of 1826 to 1838. The octavo edition of the same series was printed in seven editions, the first by J.T. Bowen under Audubon's direction. There were seven volumes of text and prints, each 10" x 7", the first five bearing the J.J. Audubon and J.B. Chevalier mark, the last two, J.J. Audubon. They were produced from 1840 through 1844. The second and other editions were printed up to 1871. The bien edition prints were full size, made under the direction of Audubon's sons in the late 1850s. Due to the onset of the Civil War, only 105 plates were finished. These are considered to be the most valuable of the reprints of the 'Birds of America Series.'

In 1971 the complete set was reprinted by Johnson Reprint Corp. of New York and Theaturm Orbis Terrarum of Amsterdam. Examples of the latter bear the watermark G. Schut and Zonen. In 1985 a second reprint was done by Abbeville Press for the National Audubon Society.

Although Audubon is best known for his portrayal of birds, one of his less-familiar series, 'Vivaparous Quadrupeds of North America,' portrayed various species of animals. Assembled in corroboration with John Bachman from 1839 until 1851, these prints are 28" x 22" in size. Several octavo editions were published in the 1850s. In the following listing, all measurements are actual print size unless stated otherwise.

Azure Warbler, #48, Havell, elephant folio, plate: 19½x12⅛" ...1,200.00
Black or Surf Duck, Amsterdam, 23½x34" 575.00
Black Vulture, #106, Havell, 25½x37½" 5,500.00
Black-Headed Gull, #314, Havell, 1836, sight: 23½x35½".........650.00
Blue Winged Teal, #313, Havell, 18¾x13"+matt & fr............1,200.00
Boat-Tailed Grackle, #220, Bien, 1860, 32x22¼" 2,185.00
Carolina Squirrel, #7, Bowen, 7x11" 250.00
Chuck-Will's Widow, #52, Havell, 26x38" 14,000.00
Common Mouse, Bowen, 1842, Imperial folio, 22x28"..........20,000.00
Downy Squirrel, #25, Bowen, 1843, 26x20¼" 1,775.00
Goshawk, #141, 26x38" 16,000.00
Great Footed Hawk, #20, Bien, 27x39" 3,500.00
Grey Fox, Bowen, 1842, Imperial folio, 22x28" 25,000.00
Iceland Falcon, #366, Amsterdam, 26x39" 3,000.00
Key West Dove, #167, Havell, 26x35" 12,000.00
Lesser Tern, #319, Havell, 1836, 25¼x16" 2,645.00
Lg-Tailed Spermophile, #139, Bowen, 1848, sight: 19¼x17½" ...400.00
Mink, #33, Bowen, sight: 6x9½" 150.00
Oyster Catcher, #223, Havell, 26x38" 4,500.00
Painted Finch, #52, Amsterdam, 26x39" 660.00
Red-Breasted Snipe, #335, Havell, 1836, sight: 23½x35½".....1,500.00
Robin, #131, Amsterdam, 39x26"..725.00
Spermophilus Franklini, #84, Bowen, 1846, folio 800.00
Spermophilus Mexicanus, #124, Bowen, 1847, Imperial folio.....600.00
Summer Red Bird, #44, Havell, 1828, 38⅝x25½" 6,000.00
Western Duck, #429, R Havell, 1838, 13½x22½" 1,650.00
White Pelican, #311, Havell, 26x38".......................................95,000.00
White Weasel, Bowen, 1845, Imperial folio................................550.00
White Wolf, #27, Bowen, 22x27" 3,500.00

Currier and Ives

Nathaniel Currier was in business by himself until the late 1850s when he formed a partnership with James Merrit Ives. Currier is given credit for being the first to use the medium to portray newsworthy subjects, and the Currier and Ives views of nineteenth-century American culture are familiar to us all. In the following listings, 'C' numbers correspond with a standard reference book by Conningham. Values are given for prints in very good condition; all are colored unless indicated black and white. Unless noted 'NC' (Nathaniel Currier), all prints are published by Currier and Ives. Our advisors for this category are John and Barbara Rudisill (Rudisill's Alt Print Haus); they are listed in the Directory under Maryland.

Abigail, NC, 1846, C-9, sm folio...95.00
Accomodation Train, 1876, C-32, sm folio...............................450.00
American Autumn Fruits, 1865, C-106, lg folio......................2,000.00
American Game, 1866, C-163, lg folio 900.00
Arkansas Traveler, 1870, C-270, sm folio.................................275.00
Battle of Gettysburg..., undtd, C-407, sm folio 350.00
Bear Hunting, Close Quarters (summer); undtd, C-447, sm folio..750.00
Between Two Fires, 1879, C-511, sm folio................................300.00
Bird's Nest, undtd, C-533, sm folio...200.00
Black-Eyed Beauty, undtd, C-549, sm folio...............................75.00
Bound To Smash, 1877, C-633, sm folio 250.00
Burning of Clipper...Golden Light, NC, undtd, C-740, sm folio ..450.00
Butt of the Jokers, 1879, C-758, sm folio..................................200.00
Canal Scene, Moonlight; undtd, C-781, sm folio 350.00

Cares of a Family, NC, 1856, C-814, lg folio 3,500.00
Chicky's Dinner, undtd, C-1029, sm folio 175.00
City of NY, NC, 1855, C-1102, lg folio 3,000.00
Cottage Dooryard, Evening; NC, 1855, C-1265, med folio.........400.00
Darktown Yacht Club, Hard...Breeze; 1885, C-1439, sm folio 275.00
Declaration Committee, 1876, C-1530, sm folio 300.00
Dude Swell, 1883, C-1635, sm folio 250.00
Easter Flowers, 1869, C-1655, sm folio 50.00
El Capitan From Mariposa Trail, undtd, C-1681, sm folio..........650.00
English Winter Scene, undtd, C-1745, sm folio 525.00
First Ride, NC, 1849, C-1987, sm folio 150.00
Fording the River, NC, undtd, C-2081, med folio 650.00
Fruit Piece, undtd, C-2180, sm folio 200.00
Girl I Love, 1870, C-2376, sm folio 75.00
God Bless Our Home, undtd, C-2392, sm folio 250.00
Great Fire at Boston, undtd, C-2614, sm folio 350.00
Great St Louis Bridge Across Mississippi..., undtd, C-2648, sm folio ..600.00
Happy Little Pups, undtd, C-2717, sm folio 150.00
Harvesting, The Last Load; undtd, C-2750, sm folio 350.00
Home of the Deer, undtd, C-2867, med folio 550.00
Home on the Mississippi, 1871, C-2876, sm folio 600.00
Hudson River - Crow Nest, undtd, C-2978, sm folio................275.00
Hues of Autumn on Racquet River, undtd, C-2982, sm folio 300.00
Jay Eye See Record 2:10, 1883, C-3184, lg folio.....................1,500.00
Lake George, NY; undtd, C-3407, sm folio 250.00
Lakeside Home, 1869, C-3423, med folio 400.00
Life in the Country, Evening; 1862, C-3508, med folio.............850.00
Life in the Woods, Returning; 1860, C-3513, lg folio 3,500.00
Lincoln Family, 1867, C-3546, sm folio 100.00
Little Snowbird, undtd, C-3719, sm folio 250.00
Little Students, undtd, C-3720, sm folio 150.00
Loss of Steamboat Swallow, NC, 1845, C-3779, sm folio...........425.00
Lucy, NC, undtd, C-3835, sm folio 95.00
M'Donough's Victory on Lake Champaign, NC, 1846, C-4096, sm folio ...500.00
Maiden Rock, Mississippi River, undtd, C-3891, sm folio 450.00
Mill-Cove Lake, undtd, C-4123, sm folio................................375.00
Moose & Wolves, A Narrow Escape; undtd, C-4185, sm folio....300.00
Mother's Wing, 1866, C-4239, med folio 250.00
My Highland Boy, NC, undtd, C-4305, sm folio 95.00
New England Home, undtd, C-4417, sm folio 225.00
New Fashioned Girl, undtd, C-4422, sm folio 225.00
Old Mill in Summer, undtd, C-4571, sm folio 300.00
Old Mill-Dam, undtd, C-4572, sm folio................................375.00
On a Point, NC, 1855, C-4592, med folio 600.00
Parson's Colt, 1879, C-4706, sm folio...................................250.00
Partridge Shooting, 1870, C-4718, sm folio 400.00
Peaceful River, undtd, C-4736, sm folio 175.00
Perry's Victory on Lake Erie, C-4754, rpr, 9⅞x13⅞" 625.00
Pride of the Garden, 1873, C-4914, sm folio 200.00
Pursuit, NC, 1856, C-4974, lg folio......................................2,500.00
Puzzled Fox, 1872, C-4984, sm folio 350.00
Quail Shooting, NC, 1852, C-4989, lg folio...........................3,000.00
Robinson Crusoe..., 1874, C-5189, sm folio 200.00
Safe Sailing, undtd, C-5292, sm folio 200.00
See-Saw, undtd, C-5457, med folio 350.00
Southern Beauty, undtd, C-5630, sm folio 75.00
Stable Scene No 2, NC, undtd, C-5686, sm folio 500.00
Steam Ship Bothnia, undtd, C-5750, sm folio 325.00
Summer Landscape, Haymaking; undtd, C-5868, sm folio 425.00
Summer Time, undtd, C-5878, med folio 500.00
Sunrise at Lake Saranac, 1860, C-5895, lg folio......................2,800.00
Trotting Cracks at the Forge, 1869, C-6169, lg folio................8,000.00
United States Capitol, NC, undtd, C-6294, sm folio 375.00
Velocipede, 1869, C-6365, sm folio.....................................1,400.00

View of Harper's Ferry VA, undtd, C-6395, lg folio..................1,100.00
View on Rondout, undtd, C-6451, med folio 600.00
Virginia Water Windsor Park, undtd, C-6475, sm folio..............150.00
Washington at Princeton, NC, 1846, C-6518, sm folio..............450.00
White Squadron US Navy, 1893, C-6644, lg folio 1,200.00
Winter Morning - Feeding the Chickens, 1863, C-6741, lg folio...5,500.00
Wooding Up on the Mississippi, 1863, C-6776, lg folio..........9,500.00
Young Brood, 1870, C-6840, sm folio 250.00

Erte (Romain de Tirtoff)

Mah-Jongg, Chalk & Vermillion Fine Arts, NY, 34x26½" 800.00
Numerals Suite, 10 silkscreens, Circle Fine Art Corp, 1980, EX ..2,300.00
Opium, 1985, Chalk & Vermillion, NY, 31¼x42" 920.00
Portrait, Circle Fine Art Corp, Chicago, 1981, 24½x17½", VG ...460.00

Fox, R. Atkinson

A Canadian who worked as an artist in the 1880s, R. Atkinson Fox moved to New York about ten years later, where his original oils were widely sold at auction and through exhibitions. Today he is best known, however, for his prints, published by as many as twenty print makers. More than thirty examples of his work appeared on Brown and Bigelow calendars, and it was used in many other forms of advertising as well. Though he was an accomplished artist able to interpret any subject well, he is today best known for his landscapes. Fox died in 1935. Our advisor for Fox prints is Pat Gibson whose address is listed in the Directory under California.

Aces All, #557, 1929, 10x8" 285.00
An Approaching Storm, #169, 9x12"....................................175.00
Andrew Jackson, 1923 calendar, #742, 8x5"............................80.00
At the Foothills of Pikes Peak, #332, 9x7"..............................95.00
Dawn, #1, 10x18"...165.00
Day Dreams, #410, 10x14"...250.00
Departure of Columbus, #544, 8½x12".................................225.00
Dreamy Paradise, #329, 9x7"...95.00
Flanders Field, #76, 6x12" 95.00
Flowerland, #203, 18x30"...285.00
Garden of Contentment, #78, 10x18" 135.00
Garden of Hope, 10x12" 125.00
Girl of Golden West, sgn Geo White (pseudonym), 6x8" 85.00
Good Shepherd, #29, 12x20"...195.00
Guardian of the Valley, mountain puzzle, #591........................80.00
Heart's Desire, #55, 12x18"..185.00
Indian Summer, #35, 18x30" 285.00
Mirror Lake, #488, 5¼x3½"..95.00
Monarchs, lions, #442, 6x8" 285.00
Moonlight & Roses, #39, 14x18"..190.00
Mount Ranier, #524, 16x10" 180.00
Nature's Grandeur, #22, 14x22"..170.00
Nature's Treasures, #91, 18x30"..300.00
October Days, birches & flowers, #44, 6x8"..............................85.00
On Guard (dog & sheep), #588, 6x4".....................................150.00
Repairing of All Kinds, blksmith, #640, 13x10" 375.00
Russet Gems, #72, 16x20" 165.00
Seeking Protection, horses & fire, #363, 9½x8" 195.00
Sentry, bear, sgn, #373, 16x12" 200.00
Silvery Divide, George Turner pseudonym used, 6x8" 50.00
Spirit of Youth, #4, 10x18" 160.00
Sunny South, #69, 10x18" 140.00
Sunset Dreams, #23, 18x30" 320.00
When Evening Calls Them Home, cows by stream, #353, 9x7" .175.00
White Feather, Indian maiden, #309, 15x11" 450.00

Gutmann, Bessie Pease (1876 – 1960)

Delicately tinted prints of appealing children sometimes accompanied by their pets, sometimes asleep, often captured at some childhood activity are typical of the work of Gutmann; she painted lovely ladies as well and was a successful illustrator of children's books. Her career spanned the earlier decades of the 1900s. Our advisor for this category is Dr. Victor Christie; he is listed in the Directory under Pennsylvania.

Aeroplane, The; #266/#695, 14x21"	700.00
Always, #774, 1913, 18½x13½"	1,800.00
Annunciation, #705, 14x21"	900.00
Awakening, 14x21"	125.00
Baby's First Christmas, #158	500.00
Betty, #787, 14x21"	250.00
Blue Bird, The; #265/#666, 14x21"	600.00
Butterfly, #632, 14x18"	175.00
Call to Arms, A; #806, 14x21"	650.00
Chuckles, #799	125.00
Chums, #263, #665, 14x21"	300.00
Contentment, #781, oval fr, 4½x8"	90.00
Daddy's Coming, #644, 14x18"	450.00
Divine Fire, The; #722, 14x21"	500.00
Double Blessing, #643, 14x21"	500.00
Feeling, #19, 6x9", circular fr	200.00
Friendly Enemies, #215, 11x14"	155.00
Goldilocks, #771, 14x21"	900.00
Guest's Candle, #651, 14x18"	500.00
Hearing, #22, 6x9", circular fr	200.00
Home Builders, #233/#655, 14x18"	150.00

In Disgrace, 18x14", $175.00.
(Photo courtesy Michael Ivankovich)

In Slumberland, #786, 21x14"	100.00
Kitty's Breakfast, #805, 14x21"	250.00
Little Bit of Heaven, #650, 14x8"	125.00
Little Bo Peep, blk & wht, #200, 11x14"	150.00
Lorelei, #645, 14x18"	2,000.00
Love's Harmony, #791, 14x21"	350.00
May We Come In, #808, 14x21"	300.00
Message of Roses, #641, 14x20"	360.00
Mighty Like a Rose, #222/#642, 14x18"	155.00
Mischief Brewing, #152, 9x12"	1,700.00
Nitey Nite, #826, 14x18"	125.00
On Dreamland's Border, #150, 14x18"	165.00
On the Up & Up, #796, 14x18"	140.00
Our Alarm Clock, #150, 9x12"	220.00
Perfect Peace, #809, 14x21"	200.00
Popularity (Has Its Disadvantages), #825, 14x21"	125.00
Priceless Necklace, #744, 14x21"	1,000.00
Rosebud, #780, 14x21"	300.00
Seeing, #122, 11x14"	250.00

Snowbird, #777, 14x18"	500.00
Sunkissed, #818, 14x21"	100.00
Symphony, #702, 14x21"	500.00
Tom Tom the Piper's Son, #219, 11x14"	225.00
Touching, #210, 11x14"	125.00
Who's Sleepy, 14x21"	200.00
Winged Aureole, #700, 14x18"	450.00

Icart, Louis

Louis Icart (1888 – 1950) was a Parisian artist best known for his boudoir etchings in the '20s and '30s. In the '80s prices soared, primarily due to Japanese buying. The market began to readjust in 1990, and most etchings now sell at retail between $1,400.00 and $2,500.00. Value is determined by popularity and condition, more than by rarity. Original frames and matting are not important, as most collectors want the etchings restored to their original condition and protected with acid-free mats.

Beware of the following repro and knock-off items: 1. Pseudo engravings on white plastic with the Icart 'signature.' 2. Any bronzes with the Icart signature. 3. Most watercolors, especially if they look similar in subject matter to a popular etching. 4. Lithographs where the dot-matrix printing is visible under magnification. Some even have phony embossed seals or rubber stamp markings. Items listed below are in excellent condition unless noted otherwise. Our advisor is William Holland, author of *Louis Icart: The Complete Etchings,* and *The Collectible Maxfield Parrish;* he is listed in the Directory under Pennsylvania.

Bathers, 2 ladies beneath tree, 3rd wading, ca 1926, 21x17"	2,400.00
Belle Rose, 1933, 16x21", M	2,200.00
Carmen, 1927, 20¼x13⅞"	1,000.00
Casanova, 1928, 21x14"	1,265.00
Cinderella, 1927, 15x19"	1,650.00
Coursing II, 1929, 15¼x25¼"	3,575.00
Eve, 1928, 13x19"	1,750.00
Eve, 1928, 14x19", VG	1,800.00
Faust, 1928, 21¼x13¾", VG	1,450.00
Forsythia, 1925, 19½x15½"	1,265.00
French Doll, lady smoking, admiring doll, 14x18"	1,150.00
Gay Senorita, 1939, 18⅜x22⅛", VG	1,600.00
Gay Trio, 1936, 18½x11"	5,950.00
Guest, 1941, 17x11"	3,750.00
Hiding Place, 1927, 19x15"	1,850.00
Hydrangeas, 1929, 16¾x21½"	1,650.00
Lacquered Screen, 1922, 14½x8⅝"	1,500.00
Lady of the Camelias, 1927, 16¾x20½", VG+	1,450.00
Little Thieves, ca 1926, 16½x12"	1,850.00
Look, 1928, 19x14"	1,250.00
Madame Butterfly, 1927, 20x13"	1,495.00
Miss California, 1927, rpr, 21x16¾"	1,725.00
My Secret Love, 1927	1,250.00
Old Yarn, 1924, 17x21"	900.00
On the Champs Elysees, 1938, 15½x22¼", VG	2,450.00
On the Green, lady on grassy knoll w/parasol, 10½x15"	1,400.00
Paris Flowers, 1930, 15½x20"	1,459.00
Pink Lady, 1933, 8⅝x11"	1,200.00
Puff of Smoke, 1922, 19¼x13½"	1,265.00
Puppies, 1925, 17x22¼", VG+	1,950.00
Smoke, seminude w/cigarette, ca 1926, 19½x14¼"	2,200.00
Spanish Comb, 1922, 18x14¾", VG	1,150.00
Spanish Dance, 1929, 20⅞x14"	1,250.00
Springtime Promenade, 1948, 14½x19½"	2,000.00
Springtime Vision, 1914, 11¼x18½"	1,400.00
Teasing, 1926, 18¾x13⅞", VG	1,950.00
Venus, 1928, 13¾x19"	1,950.00

Venus, 1928, 14x19", VG **1,900.00**
Werther, lady by garden wall, 1928, 21x14"..................**2,000.00**
White Underwear, 1925, 15⅝x19¾", VG **1,950.00**
Winter Bouquet, 1924, 16½x11¾".............................**2,650.00**
Woman Reclining, 1948, sight: 16½x20½" **1,100.00**
Wounded Dove, 1929, 20¼x16¾", VG **1,450.00**

Kurz and Allison

Louis Kurz founded the Chicago Lithograph Company in 1833. Among his most notable works were a series of thirty-six Civil War scenes and one hundred illustrations of Chicago architecture. His company was destroyed in the Great Fire of 1871, and in 1880 Kurz formed a partnership with Alexander Allison, an engraver. Until both retired in 1903, they produced hundreds of lithographs in color as well as black and white.

Values in our listings are for large folio prints (image size 17½" x 25") in excellent condition.

Assault on Fort Sanders, lg folio **275.00**
Battle of Cedar Creek, Sheridan's Cavalry; lg folio....................**285.00**
Battle of Nashville, on board, rstr tears, 17½x25" **275.00**
Battle of New Orleans, on board, 17½x25", EX **325.00**
Capture of Fort Fisher, lg folio **260.00**
Colonel T Roosevelt, USV, blk/wht, w/Rough Riders, lg folio....**160.00**
General Joseph Hooker, blk/wht, bust view, lg folio **90.00**
Great Connemaugh...Disaster (Johnstown flood), lg folio..........**335.00**
Last Charge & Capture of Port Arthur, lg folio **200.00**
Siege of Vicksburg, lg folio..**275.00**
Trial of Robert Emmet, His Closing Remarks; lg folio................**200.00**
Wm McKinley, blk/wht, bust view w/facsimile sgn, lg folio..........**90.00**

McKenney and Hall

Unless otherwise noted, values are for 18x13" prints in excellent condition.

Ahyouwaighs Chief of 6 Nations, 1845, 8½x6½" **415.00**
Chittee-Yoholo, Seminole chief, 1845, 9¼x6" **200.00**
Encampment of Piekann Indians, 13¼x18¼" **1,750.00**
Hunting the Buffalo, Rose/Hart, JT Bowen, sight: 6¼x9" **715.00**
Katawabeda, Chippewa chief, Bowen, 1841, 18x13" **295.00**
Keduk Chief of Sacs & Foxes, Bowen, 1838, lg folio..................**900.00**
Little Crow, Sioux chief, Greenough, 1838, lg folio **200.00**
Mohongo, Greenough, 1841, sight: 17x12".....................**770.00**
Nah-Et-luc-Hopie, 1843, 16x10"+modern fr...................**350.00**
Nea-Math-La, Seminole war chief, Childs after King, 1833, 19x14" ...**400.00**
Neomonie, Iowa chief, Greenough, 1838, 18x13" **195.00**
Ne-Sow-a-quoit, Fox chief, 1836, 22x15½"....................**985.00**
Petalesharro, Pawnee brave, 1845, 9x6" **330.00**
Prairie on Fire, frontispc to Vol III, sight: 6¼x9".........**450.00**
Push-Ma-Ta-Ha, Chocktaw warrior, 1838, 18x13"........**935.00**
Takacon, Biddle, 1841, sight: 17x12" **715.00**
Tishcohan, Delaware chief, Biddle, 1937, 18x13" **145.00**

Mucha, Alphonse

Mucha became famous for his beautiful Art Nouveau lithographs featuring Sarah Bernhardt and Job cigarette papers, which he issued in the 1890s. Born in Prague in 1860, he studied there as well as in Paris and for a time taught at the New York School of Applied Design for women before returning to Prague.

Automne, 1903, 27¾x12" **6,400.00**
Biscuits Lefevre, metallic additions, Paris, 1896, 24x17⅜", VG ..**8,000.00**

Documents Decoratifs par AM Mucha, brn/blk print, 1901, 29x18", EX....**1,150.00**
Figures Decoratives, 1905, 14x10⅜".............................**300.00**
Flirt, linen-bk, 1900, 23x10", EX **2,500.00**
Job, metallic additions, Paris, split/tear, 1896, 20⅛x15⅜" ..**5,750.00**
L'Illustration Noel, ladies on mc ground, 1896, 16x12", EX........**600.00**
Monaco Monte-Carlo, maid w/in floral halo, 42x29"..............**9,200.00**
Precious Stones: La Topaz, 1900, 23¾x9½", VG **5,175.00**
Primevere et Plume, metallic additions, Paris, 1899, 29x11¼", VG...**7,475.00**
Russian Restinuenda, 1922, 30x17" **1,000.00**
Wiener Chic, lady in wht, 1900, 15x11", EX...................**1,000.00**
Zodiac La Plume, maid in profile, 1896, 25¾x19" **10,350.00**

Yard-Longs

Values for yard-long prints are given for examples in near mint condition, full length, nicely framed, and with the original glass. To learn more about this popular area of collector interest, we recommend *Those Wonderful Yard-Long Prints and More*, *More Wonderful Yard-Long Prints, Book 2*, and *Yard-Long Prints, Book 3*, by our advisors Bill and June Keagy, and Charles and Joan Rhoden. They are listed in the Directory under Indiana and Illinois respectively. A word of caution: Watch for reproductions; know your dealer.

Yard of Poppies, S. Clarkson, copyright 1892 by J.J. Ingalls, from $200.00 to $300.00. (Photo courtesy June and Bill Keagy)

Alluring, Pompeian Art, sgn B Krandall, lady in yel, man in tux ..**350.00**
Battle of Chicks, sgn Ben Austrian, c 1920..................**300.00**
Beatrice, ad for Belle of Drexel, Chicago's Best 5¢ Cigar, ca 1911 ..**450.00**
Bride, sgn Rolf Armstrong, Pompeian, c 1927 ....**400.00**
Carnations, flower-filled basket, Grace Barton Allen..................**250.00**
Easter Greetings, Paul DeLongpre, c 1894 ....**400.00**
Euthymol Girl, Parke Davis & Co, 1907.........................**400.00**
Flower Girl Souvenir, lady umbrella/flowers, Clay Robinson & Co, 1911 ..**450.00**
Hula Girl, lady dances/wears grass skirt, Gene Pressler..............**400.00**
In Grandmother's Garden, Charles C Curran, 1909 calendar at bottom ...**400.00**
ISTC by Alice Luella Fidler, The College Lad & Lassie series, c 1908.......**350.00**
Mother & Child, Nat'l Stockman & Farmer 'World's Greatest...,' c 1913 ..**400.00**
Mother cat & kittens (8), 1 w/book, 1 w/spool, 2 on mother, c 1903 ....**400.00**
Shower of Fruit, cherries/orange/apple/pear w/basket/plate/book/knife **250.00**
Stockman Bride, full attire, Nat'l Stockman & Farmer Magazine, 1912...**450.00**
Walk-Over Girl, lady seated in boat surrounded by water, 1912 .**400.00**
Walk-Over Shoe Co, girl in cowgirl outfit behind tree w/Walk-Over cvg .**450.00**
White & Purple Lilacs, Paul DeLongpre, c 1896 ....**300.00**
Yard of Dogs, 8 various breeds, 1 w/bird in mouth, c 1903 ....**300.00**
Yard of Kittens, sgn Guy Bedford.................................**350.00**
Yard of Pansies, sgn ME Hart.......................................**300.00**

Purinton

Founded in 1936 in Wellsville, Ohio, Purinton Pottery relocated in 1941 in Shippenville, Pennsylvania, and began producing hand-painted wares that are today attracting the interest of collectors of 'country-type' dinnerware. Using bold brush strokes of vivid color, simple yet attractive patterns such as Apple, Fruit, Tea Rose, and Pennsylvania Dutch were manufactured in tableware sets and accessory pieces. For more information we recommend *Purinton Pottery* by Susan Morris, our advisor for this category; she is listed in the Directory under Washington.

Ashtray, blindman's; Spatterware, 4½"	40.00
Baker, Pennsylvania Dutch, 7" dia.	45.00
Boot, miniature, 4½"	10.00
Bottle, vinegar; Fruit, cobalt trim, 1-pt, 9½"	35.00
Bowl, fruit; Apple, plain border, 12"	45.00
Bowl, fruit; Cactus Flower, 12"	150.00
Bowl, fruit; Maywood, 12"	35.00
Bowl, fruit; Provincial Fruit, 12"	50.00
Bowl, fruit; Ribbon Flower, 12"	50.00
Bowl, fruit; Saraband, 12"	25.00
Bowl, range; Saraband, w/lid, 5½"	20.00
Bowl, spaghetti; Normandy Plaid, 14½"	55.00
Bowl, vegetable; Apple, divided, 10½"	35.00
Bowl, vegetable; Normandy Plaid, open, 8½"	20.00
Bowl, vegetable; Pennsylvania, open, 8½"	40.00
Canister, Apple, red trim, oval, 9"	60.00
Canister, Daisy, flour, sugar, coffee or tea, cobalt trim, 9", ea	75.00
Coffeepot, Apple, w/drip filter, 8-cup, 11"	110.00
Coffeepot, Apple, 8-cup, 8"	90.00
Coffeepot, Ivy-Yellow Blossom, 8-cup, 8"	50.00
Cookie jar, Fruit, wooden lid, rnd, 8" H	70.00
Cookie jar, Intaglio, oval, 9½"	75.00
Cookie jar, rooster shape, 11", minimum value	400.00
Creamer, Fruit; 3"	15.00
Creamer, Heather Plaid, 3"	20.00
Creamer, Pennsylvania Dutch, creamer, 3½"	40.00
Creamer & sugar bowl, Fruit, 2" (both)	30.00
Cruets, oil & vinegar; Saraband, 5", pr	35.00
Cup & saucer, Fruit	13.00
Cup & saucer, Ming Tree	30.00
Cup & saucer, Tea Rose	28.00
Decanter, Mountain Rose, 5"	45.00
Dish, Apple, w/lid, 9"	65.00
Ewer, Cook Forest, souvenir, 9"	150.00
Gravy pitcher, Intaglio, TS&T mold, 3¾"	65.00
Honey jug, Pennsylvania Dutch, 6¼"	85.00
Jar, grease; Fruit, 5½"	45.00
Jar, grease; Heather Plaid, 5½"	60.00
Jardiniere, Pine Tree, 5"	40.00
Jug, honey; Apple, 6¼"	55.00
Jug, honey; Morning Glory, 6¼"	50.00
Jug, honey; Petals, 6¼"	45.00
Jug, Kent; Fruit, 1-pt, 4½"	30.00
Jug, Kent; Fuchsia, 1-pt, 4½"	35.00
Jug, oasis; Desert Scene, 9½", minimum value	500.00
Jug, Petals, 5-pt, 8"	85.00
Mug, beer; Normandy Plaid, 16-oz, 4¾"	40.00
Mug, beer; Spatterware, 16-oz, 4¾"	25.00
Mug, Clear Creek, jug style, souvenir, 8-oz, 4¾"	100.00
Mug, juice; Chartreuse, 6-oz, 2½"	15.00
Mug, Pennsylvania, souvenir, Intaglio style, 8-oz, 4"	75.00
Pickle dish, Pineapple, unusual sponged edge, 6" dia	35.00
Pitcher, beverage; Ivy-Red Blossom, 2-pt, 6¼"	55.00
Pitcher, gravy; Intaglio, TS&T mold, 3¾"	65.00
Pitcher, Peasant Garden, Rubel mold, 5"	150.00
Pitcher, Woodflowers, 6½"	65.00
Planter, Apple, rum jug shape, 6½"	55.00
Planter, basket; Blue Pansy, 6¼"	65.00
Planter, basket; Mountain Rose, 6¼"	50.00
Planter, Half-Blossom, rum jug shape, 6½"	55.00
Planter, Leaves, sprinkler can shape, 5½"	50.00

Planter, Ming Tree, 5"	35.00
Planter, Mountain Rose, rum jug shape, 6½"	65.00
Planter, Palm Tree, basket shape, 6¼"	100.00
Plate, Alpha Chalet, souvenir, 9¾", minimum value	175.00
Plate, Blessing; Fruits, sgn Dorothy Purinton, 12", minimum	350.00
Plate, breakfast; Apple, 8½"	12.00
Plate, chop; Amish Children, signed D Purinton, 12", minimum	400.00
Plate, chop; Apple, 12"	40.00
Plate, chop; Maywood, 12"	30.00

Chop plate, Mountain Rose. $85.00. (Photo courtesy Susan Morris)

Plate, chop; Peasant Garden, 12"	150.00
Plate, chop; Saraband, 12"	15.00
Plate, dinner; Maywood, 9¾"	15.00
Plate, dinner; Ming Tree, 9¾"	25.00
Plate, dinner; Turquoise, 9¾"	35.00
Plate, lap; Fruit, w/indent, 8½"	30.00
Plate, lap; Saraband, 8½"	15.00
Plate, salad; Saraband, 6¾"	8.00
Platter, grill; Maywood, 12"	35.00
Platter, meat; Provincial Fruit, 11"	40.00
Platter, meat; Tea Rose, 12"	50.00
Relish tray, Pennsylvania Dutch, 3-section, metal hdl, 10"	75.00
Roll tray, Intaglio, 11"	35.00
Roll tray, Maywood, 11"	20.00
Roll tray, Normandy Plaid, 11"	35.00
Shakers, Fruit, cobalt trim, range style, 4", pr	40.00
Shakers, Pour 'n Shake, Heather Plaid, 4¼", pr	60.00
Shakers, Seaform, 3", pr	55.00
Shakers, stacking; Provincial Fruit, 2¼", pr	35.00
Shakers, Tionesta Park, range style, souvenir, 4", pr	125.00
Sugar bowl, Pennsyvania Dutch, w/lid, 5"	50.00
Teapot, Crescent Flower, 6-cup, 6"	85.00
Teapot, Intaglio, 6-cup, 6½"	65.00
Teapot, Ming Tree, 2-cup, 5"	55.00
Teapot, Mountain Rose, 2-cup, 4"	45.00
Teapot, Saraband, 6-cup, 6½"	25.00
Tray, relish; Woodflowers, 8"	45.00
Tumbler, Chartreuse, 12-oz, 5"	20.00
Tumbler, Fruit, 12-oz, 5"	20.00
Tumbler, Normandy Plaid, 12-oz, 5"	20.00
Vase, cornucopia; Ivy-Red Blossom, 6"	25.00
Vase, Crescent Flower, hdld, 7½"	125.00
Vase, Palm Tree, 5"	75.00
Wall pocket, Apple, 3½"	40.00
Wall pocket, Mountain Rose, 3½"	65.00
Wall pocket, Pennsylvania Dutch, 3½"	65.00

Purses

Purses from the early 1800s are often decorated with small, brightly colored glass beads. Cut steel beads were popular in the 1840s and remained stylish until about 1930. Purses made of woven mesh date back to the 1820s. Chain-link mesh came into usage in the 1890s, followed by the enamel mesh bags carried by the flappers in the 1920s. Purses are divided into several categories by (a) construction techniques — whether beaded, embroidered, or a type of needlework; (b) material — fabric or metal; and (c) design and style. Condition is very important. Watch for dry, brittle leather or fragile material. For those interested in learning more, we recommend *Antique Purses, A History, Identification, and Value Guide, Second Edition,* by Richard Holiner; *More Beautiful Purses,* and *Combs and Purses,* both by Evelyn Haertigi of Carmel, California; and *Ladies' Vintage Accessories* by LaRee Johnson Bruton. An interesting related book is *Vintage Contemporary Purse Accessories* by Roselyn Gerson. Our advisor for this category is Veronica Trainer; she is listed in the Directory under Ohio. See also Plastics.

Key: W&D — Whiting & Davis

Beaded, bl loopy fringe allover, blk lining & drawstring, 5x7" **75.00**
Beaded, blk & wht stripes w/checks at top, looped fringe, 9x9"..**140.00**
Beaded, castle scene, blk fringe, SP fr, 7½x13½" **150.00**
Beaded, courting couple reserve, blk & tan, SP fr, 12½x7".........**250.00**
Beaded, exotic bird/flowers, mc on blk, fringe, silver-tone fr, 8x12"..**280.00**
Beaded, floral, mc on blk, drawstring, 5¾x10½" **140.00**
Beaded, floral, mc on cream, 3-color fringe, metal fr, 7½x10" **165.00**
Beaded, floral, mc on yel, gold-tone fr, Germany, 9¼x6¼" **120.00**
Beaded, geometric, blk/silver/gold, fringe, Fr, 4½x7½" **85.00**
Beaded, geometric, mc, blk fringe, drawstring, 7¾x11½" **245.00**
Beaded, mixed flowers, mc, blk & yel fringe, SP fr, 12¾x8½" ..**350.00**
Beaded, orange, ribbed, SP fr, 6¾x8" **135.00**
Beaded, roses on blk, mc fringe, SP fr, 7x11" **350.00**
Beaded, water & flower landscape, silver-tone fr, 6½x9½" **130.00**
Fabric, blk/cream DC logo canvas w/leather hdls, C Dior, med sz ..**250.00**
Fabric, brn Gucci logo w/red & gr leather stripes, 1970s, 8x15x4" .**295.00**
Leather, alligator, dk brn, 3 slit pockets, 2 hdls, 8x16x10½" **275.00**
Leather, alligator, Sac de Cordeliere, Hermes, 10x7", M **465.00**
Leather, alligator, wine, gold-tone closure, Lucille De Paris, 7x9"...**215.00**
Leather, Evans vanity, fitted int, w/hdl, 1940s, 9¾x10x3" **300.00**
Leather, silver w/Austrian crystals allover, J Leiber, 4x6½x3" **375.00**
Leather, stitchwork/piping/monogram, zippered pocket, Vuitton, 8x12x4"...**350.00**
Lucite, basket w/rhinestones in lid, Myles, 10" (top of hdl)x6"...**325.00**
Lucite, Beehive, bees/flowers on jeweled lid, Llewellyn, 1951, 6" L..**525.00**
Lucite, gray, rnd w/rhinestones, 5½" (+hdls)x7½" **235.00**
Lucite, gray marbleized coffin style w/silk orchids, 5x7½x4¾" **215.00**
Lucite, marbleized w/rhinestone trim, 4 sm wht fr, 6x8x4", NM.**265.00**
Mesh, blk & wht checks, Mandalian fr, 6x3¾" **80.00**
Mesh, butterflies & flowers, fringe, ornate Mandalian fr, 7x4" ...**95.00**
Mesh, circles in sqs, chain draws through rings, W&D, 7x4½".....**85.00**
Mesh, dbl blk & wht silver-tone vanity, W&D fr, 1920s, 3x8", $500 to...**800.00**
Mesh, dmn shapes, blk/gr, dk W&D fr, 7x4½" **100.00**
Mesh, dragon, zigzag fringe, W&D fr, 78x3¾" **165.00**
Mesh, exotic bird on branch, ornate W&D fr, 7x4" **165.00**
Mesh, floral, blk/gold/silver, fringe, ornate Mandalian fr, 7x3½" ...**100.00**
Mesh, floral, mc, fringe, W&D gold-tone fr, 7½x4" **125.00**
Mesh, floral, mc on gold, W&D fr, 7¼x5½" **130.00**
Mesh, floral, zigzag fringed bottom, Mandalian fr, 7x4" **95.00**
Mesh, geometric, blk & silver, zigzag bottom, W&D fr, 7x3½".....**85.00**
Mesh, geometric floral, bl/wht/gold, gold Mandalian fr, 7x4¾" ..**130.00**
Mesh, German silver extension gate-top vanity, 1920s, 1½" lid.**225.00**
Mesh, gold-tone, W&D Delysia, compartments, sapphire cabochon, 1920s....**650.00**
Mesh, gold-tone vanity, eng 2" lid, ca 1900, w/chain & tassel, $350 to..**450.00**
Mesh, gold-tone vanity, W&D Piccadilly, w/chain & bl cabochon, 1920s ..**25.00**
Mesh, rainbow-like design, W&D gold-tone fr, 5¼x4" **115.00**
Mesh, red, stylized red W&D fr, zigzag bottom, 7½x5½" **125.00**

Mesh, roses, zigzag fringe, Mandalian fr, 8¼x5" **180.00**
Mesh, tango chain vanity, 2½" cloisonne lid, 1900s, $500 to **700.00**
Mesh (fine), silver, fringe, SP W&D fr, 9¼x5¼" **75.00**
Petit-point, opera scene, gold-tone fr w/faux pearl, 1920s-30s **295.00**

Puzzles

'Jigsaw' puzzles have been around almost as long as games. The first examples were handcrafted from wood, and they are extremely difficult to find. Most of the early examples featured moral subjects just as the board games did. By the 1890s jigsaw puzzles had become a major form of home entertainment. During the Depression years jigsaw puzzles were set up on card tables in almost every home. The early wood examples are the most valuable.

Cube puzzles, or blocks, were often made by the same companies as the board games. Again, early examples display the finest quality lithography. While all subjects are collectible, some (such as Santa blocks) often command prices higher than games from the same period. In the listings all items are jigsaw puzzles unless noted otherwise.

Personalities, Movies, and TV Shows

Alice in Wonderland, fr-tray, Parker Bros, 1930s, set of 4, NMIB....**150.00**
Archies, jigsaw, Whitman, 1970, MIB...**25.00**
Barney Google & Snuffy Smith, fr-tray, Jaymar, 1940s-50s, NM...**40.00**
Ben Casey, jigsaw, Milton Bradley, 1962, 600 pcs, MIB (sealed)...**25.00**
Buck Rogers, jigsaw, Puzzle Craft/John Dille, 1945, set of 3, EXIB...**300.00**
Capt Marvel Rides Engine of Doom, jigsaw, 1940s, MIB **150.00**
Clarabelle, fr-tray, Whitman, 1954, NM **30.00**
Dr Strange, jigsaw, Third Eye, 1971, 500 pcs, MIB......................**100.00**
Eddie Canter, jigsaw, Einson, 1933, EXIB.......................................**45.00**
Family Affair, jigsaw, Whitman, 1970, 125 pcs, MIB....................**35.00**
Fantasy Island, jigsaw, HG Toys, 1977, MIB..................................**20.00**
Gulliver's Travels, fr-tray, Saalfield, 1930s, set of 8, EXIB **100.00**
Hoppity Hopper, fr-tray, Whitman, 1965, NM..............................**50.00**
Incredible Hulk, jigsaw, Third Eye, 1971, 500 pcs, MIB...............**100.00**
Journey to the Center of the Earth, jigsaw, Whitman, 1969, NMIB ..**25.00**
King Kong, jigsaw, Chad Valley, plywood, 200 pcs, NM (EX box) ..**600.00**
Lassie & Timmy, fr-tray, Whitman, EX..**25.00**
Lone Ranger, jigsaw, Jaymar, 1940, NMIB **125.00**
Mod Squad, jigsaw, Milton Bradley, 1969, MIB **70.00**
Nancy & Sluggo, jigsaw, Whitman, 1973, NMIB **15.00**
Pebbles Flintstone, fr-tray, Whitman, 1960s, NM **20.00**
Popeye's Comic Picture Puzzle, jigsaw, Parker Bros, set of 4, EXIB...**100.00**
Rootie Kazootie, jigsaw, Fairchild, 1950s, set of 3, NMIB.............**50.00**
Snagglepuss, jigsaw, Whitman Jr, 1962, MIB..................................**25.00**
Space Ghost, fr-tray, Whitman, 1967, complete, NM **50.00**
Superboy, fr-tray, Whitman, 1968, NM **50.00**
Superman Springs Into Action, jigsaw, Saalfield, 1940, EXIB.....**300.00**
Thunderbirds, jigsaw, Whitman, 1968, MIB....................................**30.00**
Tom Terrific, jigsaw, Jaymar, 1960s, rare, NMIB **100.00**
Uncle Wiggily, jigsaw, Milton Bradley, 1900, set of 3, NMIB **200.00**
Village People, jigsaw, APC, 1978, MIB, from $65 to....................**85.00**
Wacky Races, fr-tray, Whitman, 1969, EX **30.00**
Wyatt Earp, jigsaw, Whitman, 1960s, NMIB...................................**25.00**
Yogi Bear, fr-tray, Whitman, 1961, M...**20.00**
Zorro, fr-tray, Whitman, 1965, NM **25.00**

Miscellaneous

At Home & Abroad, plywood, J Straus/Royal, 1940-50, EXIB...**185.00**
Autumn Reflections, wood, early 1900s, EX (rpl box) **100.00**
Breath of Summer Days, pressed brd, B Nowell, 1930s, EXIB **75.00**

Castle in Spain, plywood, Milton Bradley/Premier, 1930s, EXIB ..**85.00**
Discussing the News, wood, Ingleside, 1909, EXIB.................**35.00**
Eiffel Tower, plywood, 1930s, EX (rpl box) **65.00**
French Town, plywood, Isabel Ayer, 1910s, EXIB..................**200.00**
Grand Canyon Arizona, plywood, J Straus, 1940-50, EXIB..........**35.00**
Hazy Hills, plywood, Parker Bros/Pastime, 1950s, EXIB..............**450.00**
In the Valley, wood, early 1900s, EX (rpl box)........................**80.00**
John Paul Jones at the Convention, plywood, F West, 1909, EXIB ..**70.00**
Little Bear at Home, pressed brd, Ryther Novelty, 1930s, EXIB....**25.00**
May Day, Mount Holy Cross, plywood, Sta-Put, 1930s, EXIB **125.00**
Nature's Vivid Trail, plywood, L Goff, 1930s, EXIB.......................**50.00**
Old Ironsides, plywood, Glengarry Puzzles, 1930s, EXIB **50.00**
Paradise Lake, plywood, James Browning, 1950s, EXIB..............**135.00**
Riders Going on Hunt, plywood, J Straus, 1930-40, EXIB **35.00**
Steamboat Natchez, plywood, J Straus, 1940s, EXIB **40.00**
Traveling Blacksmith, plywood, 1930s, EXIB.............................**300.00**
Venetian Silk Market, plywood, Parker Bros/Pastime, 1929, EXIB ..**175.00**
When Roses Climb, plywood, B Randall, 1931, EXIB.................**50.00**

Pyrography

Pyrography, also known as wood burning, Flemish art or poker work, is the art of burning designs into wood or leather and has been practiced over the centuries in many countries.

In the late 1800s pyrography became the hot new hobby for thousands of Americans who burned designs inspired by the popular artists of the day including Mucha, Gibson, Fisher, and Corbett. Thousands of wooden boxes, wall plaques, novelties, and pieces of furniture that they purchased from local general stores or from mail-order catalogs were burned and painted. These pieces were manufactured by companies such as The Flemish Art Company of New York and Thayer & Chandler of Chicago, who printed the designs on wood for the pyrographers to burn.

This Victorian fad developed into a new form of artistic expression as the individually burned and painted pieces reflected the personality of the pyrographers. The more adventurous started to burn between the lines and developed a style of 'allover burning' that today is known as Pyromania. Others not only created their own designs but even made the pieces to be decorated. Both these developments are particularly valued today as true examples of American folk art.

By the 1930s its popularity had declined. Like Mission furniture, it was neglected by generations of collectors and dealers. The recent appreciation of Victoriana, the Arts and Crafts Movement, the American West, and the popularity of turn-of-the-century graphic art has rekindled interest in pyrography which embraces all these styles.

An informative book, *The Burning Passion — Antique and Collectible Pyrography*, by Carole and Richard Smyth, our advisors for this category, is currently available from the authors; they are listed in the Directory under New York.

Key: hb — hand burned

Bedroom set, hb/pnt, Wm Rogers/Forusville PA, 1905-07, 3-pc ...**4,000.00**
Book rack, hb/pnt girl w/book, 5¾" W, extends to 15¾" L.........**150.00**
Box, flatware; factory burned/pnt poinsettias, Rogers, 9x11x5"...**195.00**
Box, floral decor, stamped design, 14½" sq...................................**40.00**
Box, lady w/flowing hair, Flemish Art Co, 1909, 11¼x4¼".........**120.00**
Chair-table, hb/pnt poinsettias, Rest-Ye... on chair bk, EX **950.00**
Checker/backgammon board, red & gr decor/glass bead insets, 30x15"..**1,550.00**
Chest, blanket; hb/pnt swans/lady's head/flowers/etc, ca 1890 ....**850.00**
Chest, medicine; hb/pnt Nouveau lady & vines, wall mt............**450.00**
Coat hanger, hb/pnt poppies & leaves, Mother Dearest **80.00**
Cue holder, hb pool-hall scene, folk art, unique **650.00**
Egg cup, hb/pnt, pr **60.00**

Etching set, Snow White, Disney/Marks, 1938, electric pen, complete ..**175.00**
Footstool, hb/pnt allover w/owl/branches/leaves..........................**125.00**
Frame, hb/pnt cherries, standing type, 7½x6", EX **85.00**
Frame, hb/pnt chrysanthemums, Thayer-Chandler, 10½x8", EX ..**85.00**
Frame, hb/pnt flower garland, Thayer-Chandler, 8" dia................**85.00**
Frame, owls in tree, 2 Is Company, 2 oval cutouts......................**145.00**
Gameboard, hb/pnt ea side/edges, Flemish Art, 15" sq (open)....**200.00**
Knife rack, hb Lizzie Borden w/axe, 5 hooks below, rare **550.00**
Magazine stand, 4-shelf, burned/pnt florals, Thayer-Chandler, 48"..**800.00**
Mirror, hand; hb/pnt lady's head w/flowing hair, 13¼x6¾" **180.00**
Nut bowl, hb/pnt squirrel on branch, Flemish Art Co #816, 5" **65.00**
Panel, basswood, burned/pnt orange, Thayer-Chandler, 16x30" .**465.00**
Panel, hb after painting: To the Feast, minor gold, 9x34" **500.00**
Pedestal, hb/pnt Nouveau flowers & vines, 45" **400.00**
Plaque, cvd/burned/pnt strawberry basket, 3-ply, 12" dia.............**70.00**
Plaque, girl bathing puppies, #854, 14½" **125.00**
Plaque, hb orange cat w/bow, paper 1912 calendar, 5¾" dia **50.00**
Plaque, Nouveau lady w/cherries, 19½" **150.00**
Plaque, Victorian couple, Parting by a Wall & flowers...............**145.00**
Ribbon holder, hb/pnt Sunbonnet babies (3), 5x12" **160.00**
Screen, birds & foliage, mc pnt, 3-part, 63x73" **400.00**
Spoon holder, geometric florals, wall hanging, 1915, 10x8" **45.00**
Tie rack, factory stamp, HP soldier/nurse/sailor, WWI motto **125.00**

Quezal

The Quezal Art Glass and Decorating Company of Brooklyn, New York, was founded in 1901 by Martin Bach. A former Tiffany employee, Bach's glass closely resembled that of his former employer. Most pieces were signed 'Quezal,' a name taken from a Central American bird. After Bach's death in 1920, his son-in-law, Conrad Vohlsing, continued to produce a Quezal-type glass in Elmhurst, New York, which he marked 'Lustre Art Glass.' Examples listed here are signed unless noted otherwise.

Vases, pedestal forms with pulled green feathers outlined with gold on ivory, gold feet, Left, smooth rim, 8", $800.00; Right, ruffled rim, 10½", $2,000.00.

Basket, bl irid, swirl prunts at hdl, #453, 7½x6½" **3,100.00**
Bowl, centerpc; bl-gold irid, flared rim, 4x10" **300.00**
Lamp, lily; 6 amber irid shades; stepped base, rprs, 22" **1,725.00**
Shade, feathers, gr on opal w/dots of gold, 5x4⅛" **375.00**
Shade, feathers, yel on opal, 5½x2⅞" **310.00**
Shades, feathers, opal on gold irid, flower from, 4x2½", pr **425.00**
Vase, amber w/gold irid, ribbed, bulbous, flared neck, #866, 3"...**700.00**
Vase, feathers, gold & gr on opal, ribbed gourd, 7".................**3,200.00**
Vase, feathers, gr & gold on yel/opal, globular, 4¾x5½" **750.00**
Vase, floriform; feathers, gr on opal, gold irid ft, #3, 8¾".........**3,450.00**
Vase, floriform; leaves, gr on wht w/gold at ruffled rim, 6" **350.00**
Vase, gold & bl irid swirls, bulbous, incurvate rim, 4½x5¾", NM ..**930.00**
Vase, gold irid w/bl & gr random pulls, 4" **700.00**
Vase, jack-in-the-pulpit; gold irid & pulled chartreuse, 8½".....**1,800.00**
Vase, King Tut, gold/bl/yel/opal, 11½" **2,500.00**
Vase, leaves, emerald gr w/gold tips pulled from opal base, K-202, 6"..**1,100.00**
Vase, leaves, gold on gr irid, gold irid neck, bulbous, 9"..........**4,600.00**
Vase, lily; gold w/bl irid, #K497, 4¼" (rare sz) **750.00**

Vase, silver o/l on muted rainbow irid, opal int, att, 5" **800.00**

Quilts

Quilts, while made of necessity, nevertheless represent an art form which expresses the character and the personality of the designer. During the seventeenth and eighteenth centuries, quilts were considered a necessary part of a bride's hope chest; the traditional number required to be properly endowed for marriage was a 'baker's dozen'! American colonial quilts reflect the English and French taste of our ancestors. They would include the classifications known as Lindsey-Woolsey and the central medallion appliqué quilts fashioned from imported copper-plate printed fabrics.

By 1829 spare time was slightly more available, so women gathered in quilting bees. This not only was a way of sharing the work but also gave them the opportunity to show off their best handiwork. The hand-dyed and pieced quilts emerged, and they are now known as sampler, album, and friendship quilts. By 1845 American printed fabric was available.

In 1793 Eli Whitney developed the cotton gin; as a result, textile production in America became industrialized. Soon inexpensive fabrics were readily available, and ladies were able to choose from colorful prints and solids to add contrast to their work. Both pieced and appliquéd work became popular.

Pieced quilts were considered utilitarian, while appliquéd quilts were shown with pride of accomplishment at the fair or used when itinerant preachers traveled through and stayed for a visit. Today many collectors prize pieced quilts and their intricate geometric patterns above all other types. Many of these designs were given names: Daisy and Oak Leaf, Grandmother's Flower Garden, Log Cabin, and Ocean Wave are only a few. Appliquéd quilts involved stitching one piece — carefully cut into a specific form such as a leaf, a flower, or a stylized device — onto either a large one-piece ground fabric or an individual block. Often the background fabric was quilted in a decorative pattern such as a wreath or medallions.

Amish women scorned printed calicos as 'worldly' and instead used colorful blocks set with black fabrics to produce a stunning pieced effect. To show their reverence for God, the Amish would often include a 'superstition' block which represented the 'imperfection' of Man!

One of the most valuable quilts in existence is the Baltimore album quilt. Made between 1840 and 1860 only three hundred or so still exist today. They have been known to fetch over $100,000.00 at prominent auction houses in New York City. Usually each block features elaborate appliqué work such as a basket of flowers, patriotic flags and eagles, the Oddfellow's heart in hand, etc. The border can be sawtooth, meandering, or swags and tassels.

During the Victorian period the crazy quilt emerged. This style became the most popular quilt ever in terms of sheer numbers produced. The crazy quilt was formed by random pieces put together following no organized lines and was usually embellished by elaborate embroidery stitches. Fabrics of choice were brocades, silks, and velvets.

Another type of quilting, highly prized and rare today, is trapunto. These quilts were made by first stitching the outline of the design onto a solid sheet of fabric which was backed with a second having a much looser weave. White was often favored, but color was sometimes used for accent. The design (grapes, flowers, leaves, etc.) was padded through openings made by separating the loose weave of the underneath fabric; a backing was added and the three layers quilted as one.

Besides condition, value is judged on intricacy of pattern, color effect, and craftsmanship. Examine the stitching. Quality quilts have from ten to twelve stitches to the inch. A stitch is defined as any time a needle pierces through the fabric. So you may see five threads but ten (stitches) have been used. In the listings that follow, examples rated excellent have minor defects, otherwise assume them to be free of any damage, soil, or wear. Values given here are auction results; retail may be somewhat higher. Our advisor is Craig Ambrose; he is listed in the Directory under Iowa.

Key:
hs — hand sewn, sewing
hq — hand quilted, quilting
mp — machine pieced
ms — machine sewn

Amish

Basket variant, 7-color w/wool indigo border, ca 1800, 92x71"...**550.00**
Octagons & 9-Patch, bl shades w/gr border, full sz, EX................**550.00**
Sq blk/royal bl/teal/gray patches, lav border, 1900s, 54x35".....**2,400.00**
Sunshine & Shade, purple/gr/red/pk/blk, 20th C, 80x86" **875.00**
Weathervane, blk/dk & lt bl/lav, 1940s, 80x102", EX **400.00**
9-Patch, blk sateen w/solid brn/red/bl/gr, OH, 48x40"................**440.00**

Appliquéd

Sunburst and Rose of Sharon with Birds (variant), red, green, and terra cotta on white, 1850s, 84x84", EX, $2,415.00.

Baskets (16), mc on wht, stains, 66x72".......................................**165.00**
Cherry & Oak Leaf, mc on wht cotton, fine hs, 72" sq, EX **300.00**
Dogwood, pks/grs/brns on wht, pk binding, hs/hq, 76x90", EX ...**300.00**
Dresden Plate, mc prints on wht, 73x82" **250.00**
Eagle in sunburst, gr/red/wht/gold, EX hq, PA, ca 1900, 80x80".**700.00**
Feathers/tulips/foliage, red/gr/yel/wht, Am, 19th C, 88x88", EX **2,000.00**
Floral medallions (stylized), pastels, lt wear/stains, 78x90"..........**300.00**
Floral medallions (9), goldenrod/gr/beige/wht, 80x82", EX **330.00**
Floral medallions (9), med bl/red/wht, fine hq, PA, 78x80" **770.00**
Floral medallions (9) w/vine border, gr calico/red/goldenrod, 95x100"..**470.00**
Floral medallions (9) w/vine border, red/pk/gr on wht, 75x76" ...**965.00**
Floral medallions w/swag & flower border on wht, 86x38"..........**500.00**
Floral w/vintage border, mc on wht, embr details, wear, 84x90" .**550.00**
Floral wreaths (9), mc on wht, sawtooth edge, 74x76" **415.00**
Flowers, meandering Princess Feather border, EX hq, 90x94", EX ...**500.00**
Flowers, pk & gr on wht, wear/some fading, 80x86" **360.00**
Flowers (9), red/yel/gr calico, trapunto pineapples, 92x92", VG .**300.00**
Flowers & buds, red/gr on wht, feather hq, gr border, 97x96" **600.00**
Flowers in pots (9), red/beige/goldenrod on wht, PA, 70x78" **550.00**
Friendship, embr names among flowers/stars/etc, some pc-work, 45x66"..**4,300.00**
Honey Bee, mc on wht, 78x78", NM **425.00**
Medallions (12) w/red dmns & gr leaves, ms binding, 73x86" **225.00**
Oak leaf medallions (10), red/gr/wht, rpl binding, 82x64" **385.00**
Oak leaf pinwheels & meandering flowers, red/goldenred/gr, 74" sq, EX ...**440.00**
Pinwheel flowers, floral trapunto, mc calicos/wht, sgn, 88" sq **965.00**
Pinwheels (9), red/gr calico on wht, feather hq, 1850s, 90x94" **1,265.00**
Princess Feather, red/bl/brn/wht/gold, PA, 1890s, 82x84", EX+ ..**2,500.00**
Rose wreaths, pk/gr/wht w/goldenrod flower centers, wear, 72x75"..**250.00**
Stars (16), gr calico/wht, trapunto flowers/foliage/etc, 94x96" **990.00**
Stars (9), pk/navy/rust/gr/wht, zigzag borders, 86x90" **3,300.00**
Sunbonnet Babies, mc on wht, ms, hand-embr, PA, 70x42" **110.00**
Sunbonnet Sue, mc on wht, blk outline stitches, 1930s, 72x88", M...**350.00**
Sunburst & Rose of Sharon w/birds, red/gr/tan/wht, 1850s, 84" sq ..**2,415.00**
Tulip medallions (9), gr/red/goldenrod/wht, scrolled hq, 78x80" ..**750.00**
Tulip medallions (9) & tulip border, mc on wht, EX hq, 104x84" ..**550.00**

Tulip pinwheels, tulip border, gr binding, fine hq, 72x86"..........**880.00**
Tulips & flowers, mc on wht, lt stains, 80x84"............................**715.00**
Vines/feather pinwheels/hearts, red/gr/wht, hq, wear, 62x79" **385.00**
Water lilies, wht/peach/gr on mint gr, embr, EX hq, 90x76" **400.00**

Pieced

Album (Friendship), 49 names in sqs, late 1800s, hs, 72" sq........**500.00**
Barn Raising, brn/bl prints, EX feather hq, 82x85"......................**825.00**
Basket, pk/wht, EX hq, 1930s, 74x92", NM..............................**435.00**
Basket w/sawtooth border, navy polka dots & wht, stains, 63x74"..**550.00**
Baskets, red/goldenrod/teal gr, faded spots, 94x82" **580.00**
Blazing Star, pastels/bl/wht/lav, 1930s, 68x76", EX **295.00**
Bow Tie, cotton prints/pk, fine hq, late 1920s, 74x88", EX.........**300.00**
Crazy, ginghams/cottons, brier stitching, tacked, 1920s, 64x74", EX.....**225.00**
Crazy, silk/satin/velvet/cotton, late 19th C, 79x63", EX..............**300.00**
Crazy, velvet/corduroy/felt, bl printed bk, dtd 1923, 72x82" **245.00**
Crown of Thorns, bl/blk calico on wht w/gr calico sqs, hs, 74x88".....**220.00**
Dbl Irish Chain, pk calico & wht, dbl borders, PA, 76x76", EX .**330.00**
Dbl Irish Chain Variant, pk/bl/mc print, pk/bl border, 89x92", EX..**495.00**
Dmn in Square, velvet & brocade, late 19th C, 76x65", EX.......**300.00**
Dmn Medallions (20) w/stars, red/teal/goldenrod/wht/bl, 73x91"...**715.00**
Dove in the Window, pk/wht/bl/checked gingham, 1930s, 74x90", M..**325.00**
Dresden Plate, mc prints in gr grid on wht, 1932, 81x100", EX..**360.00**
Drunkard's Path, bl print/wht, worn, 70x74"............................**250.00**
Flower Garden, mc cottons, late 1800s, 70x76"...........................**350.00**
Flower medallions (28), red/gr, minor damage, 70x82"................**350.00**
Flying Geese, navy/wht/ecru cottons, fine hq, 1899, 7x179", EX...**660.00**
Flying Geese variant, red/wht, hq except binding, 82x76" **350.00**
Geometric design, salmon/bl/wht, fine hq, stains, 80x102" **400.00**
Geometric pinwheels, red/blk/gr/gray, red flannel bk, heavy, 80x78".**360.00**
Goose Chase, bl indigo print & wht, lt wear, PA, 76x76"...........**660.00**
Grandmother's Flower Garden, mc prints & lemon yel, 62x78", EX.......**200.00**
Grandmother's Star, gray/red/bl/pk/wht, fine hq, 1920s, 68x82", NM......**350.00**
Improved 9-Patch, prints/percales/muslin, pk binding, '30s, 70x82", EX.**350.00**
Irish Chain, bl & wht, sawtooth border, hs, ca 1900, 90x92", EX+..........**500.00**
Irish Chain, med bl & mauve, feather design borders, 84x84", EX...........**465.00**
Irish Chain, red & wht w/quilted starflowers, 71x92", EX...........**330.00**
Joseph's Coat, 5-color, wide border, EX hq, PA, ca 1900, 84x86", NM..**2,300.00**
King's Crown, dk bl/wht, close hq, 1920s, 72x74", EX **500.00**
Lily, red/yel/gr chintz on wht, red border, 1850s, 85x85", EX......**700.00**
Linsey woolsey, indigo bl w/olive gr wool, wear/patches, 92x92" ..**1,675.00**
Log Cabin, bold colors/red sqs, red binding, minor stains, 84x82" ...**660.00**
Log Cabin, lt & dk cottons, late 1800s, 79x77", EX....................**250.00**
Log Cabin, mc calicos/solids on wht, homespun bk, ca 1829, 90x76"..**500.00**
Log Cabin, mc cotton prints, late 19th C, hq, 30x20" **200.00**
Log Cabin, silk/satin/velveteen, embr w/stars, 1890s, 50x60" **200.00**
Log Cabin reversing to sqs, prints/solids, ltweight, 37x45"..........**850.00**
Lone Star, bl/wht, EX hq, minor wear, ms binding, 84x72".........**300.00**
Lone Star, mc calicos on pk calico, wear, 39x52" **275.00**
Lone Star, mc cottons w/red & yel borders, EX hq, ca 1900, 82x80"...**1,400.00**
Lone Star, mc on wht, late 1800s, crib sz **925.00**
Lone Star, 4-color on wht, ms binding, 80x82"..........................**385.00**
Lyres (20), gr/goldenrod, EX hq, knit binding is ms, 86x82", EX...**715.00**
Monkey Wrench, mc calico/blk polka dots, polka-dot border, 80x68"..**465.00**
Monkey Wrench, mc prints, ms binding, stains/wear, 84x72".....**200.00**
Mosaic w/pinwheel stars, mc on lav, fishscale hq border, PA, 80x67"...**225.00**
Ocean Wave, red/blk/wht ginghams, close hq, 1920s, 68x78", EX **300.00**
Patchwork, ginghams/chambrays, red sashing, 1930s, 66x82", EX........**300.00**
Pine Tree, bl/gr/blk/brn/lav, ms binding, OH, 72x72"..................**300.00**
Pinwheel, lav & wht, stains, EX hq, 72x84" **360.00**
Pinwheel, red/bl/wht, ms red/wht/bl binding, EX........................**250.00**
Pinwheels, gr/wht print on wht, ca 1927, 70x83", EX **275.00**
Rob Peter To Pay Paul, indigo bl print/wht, PA, 73x74", EX.......**440.00**

Snail's Trail, purple/lav/bleached muslin, hq, 1930s, 66x72", EX .**295.00**
Snowflakes, navy bl/wht, dmn/circles/stars hq, 64x70"................**715.00**
Star, mc on wht, yel bk, 70x86"..**440.00**
Star, red/wht, stains/wear, 64x74"..**500.00**
Star & Tulip, mc cottons, scalloped border, 1950s, 100x97" **500.00**
Star medallions (20), mc wools/cottons/silks, wear/damage, 70x80" ...**275.00**
Star of Bethlehem, red/bl/wht, fitted for poster bed, 1890s, 79x93" **800.00**
Star w/sm stars in corners/sides, red/bl/yel/yel-gr/wht, 82x86", VG **360.00**
Star w/star border, pastels/lav, lav border, 83x88"......................**360.00**
Star Within a Star, pastels/lt brn, dbl-row hq, 1930s, 62x78", M .**300.00**
Stars (12) in grid, red/wht, some fading, 81x64".........................**300.00**
Stars (9), gr/yel/pk calico, dmn/stripes hq, 72x72" **385.00**
Stars in grid, mc on wht, KS, fine hq, 84x64"..........................**465.00**
Sunset Over Mtn, mc prints/blk & wht gingham, calico border, 65x84" ..**400.00**
Trip Around World, ginghams/reds/bls, close hq, 1920s, 70x70", EX..........**300.00**
Triple Irish Chain, pk/wht, pk binding, 1930s, 72x90", M **295.00**
Tumbling Block, mc cottons, dbl-printed, banded border, 1850s, 100x90"...**500.00**
Tumbling Block, mc prints/gr solid, hq, late 1800s, 78x70", NM...**525.00**
Washington's March, gr/red/wht, applique berries border, hq, 81x84"...**2,000.00**
Wedding Ring, bright prints/solids, scalloped edge, wear, 89x64"..**330.00**
Wedding Ring, lt prints/wht, gr/yel corners, hs, 1930s, 64x86", EX .**350.00**
Wedding Ring, mc prints on wht, lav ms binding, 80x94" **385.00**
Windmill, pk/gr/wht, gr binding, fine hq, 1940s, 70x82", M.......**300.00**
Yo-yo, mc solids/prints, scalloped edge, early 1900s, 102x94" **300.00**
Yo-yo, prints for 13 lg dmns, hs, 1930s, 88x96", EX...................**195.00**
6-Point Star, bright mc/wht, gr/wht check binding, 1930s, 68x86", EX..**300.00**
8-Point Star, prints/solids/mustard/pk, 1930s, 72x84", EX **300.00**
9-Patch w/sawtooth border, mc & wht, red/wht homespun bk, 76x80", EX...**550.00**
9-Square, mc w/solid purples w/quilted baskets, 1900s, 90x72" **275.00**

Quimper

Quimper pottery bears the name of the Breton town in northwestern France where it has been made for over three hundred years. Production began in 1690 when Jean-Baptiste Bousquet settled into a small workshop in the suburbs of Quimper, at Locmaria. There he began to make the hand-painted, tin enamel-glazed earthenware which we know today as faience. By the last quarter of the nineteenth century, there were three factories working concurrently: Porquier, de la Hubaudiere (the Grand Maison), and Henriot. All three houses produced similar wares which were decorated with scenes from the everyday life of the peasant folk of the region. Their respective marks are an AP or a P with an intersecting B (similar to a clover), an HB, and an HR (which became HenRiot after litigation in 1922).

The most desirable pieces were produced during the last quarter of the nineteenth century through the first quarter of the twentieth century. These are considered to be artistically superior to the examples made after World War I and II with the exception of the Odetta line, which is now experiencing a renaissance among collectors here and abroad.

Most of what was made was faience, but there was also a history of utilitarian gres ware (stoneware) having been produced there. In 1922 the Grande Maison HB revitalized this ware and introduced the line called Odetta, examples of which seemed to embody the bold spirit of the Art Deco style. The companion faience pieces of this period and genre are classified as Modern Movement examples and frequently bear the name of the artist who designed the mold.

Currently there are two factories still producing Quimper pottery. La Societe Nouvelle des Faienceries de Quimper is owned by Sarah and Paul Jenessens along with a group of American investors. Their mark is a stamped HB-Henriot logo. The other, La Faiencerie d'art Breton, is operated by the direct descendents of the HB and Henriot families. Their pieces are marked with an interlocked F and A conjoined with an inverted B. Other marks include HQF which is the Henriot Quimper

France mark and HBQ, the HB Quimper mark. If you care to learn more about Quimper, we recommend *Quimper Pottery: A French Folk Art Faience* by Sandra V. Bondhus, our advisor for this category, whose address can be found in the Directory under Connecticut.

Bell, lady's head w/ribboned coif forming hdl, Modern Movement, 4¾"....**160.00**
Bottle, Souvenir de...donut shape, bl croisille/geometrics, AP, 3".....**400.00**
Bowl, peasant lady/hydrangeas, shell shape, La Bernerie, AP, 4½".**225.00**
Bowl, salad; peasant man/florals, HQF, X, 3x10½", EX **175.00**
Bucket, peasant man/rose/flowers, HB Q, 19th C, w/lid & rattan hdl, 4" ..**325.00**
Butter dish, bagpipe shape, lady on rock, decor riche, HRQ, 5½x9" **475.00**
Butter dish, peasant man/flower garland, St Malo/#249MG5, 4x7½" ..**300.00**
Chamberstick, peasant lady w/bluets, leaf form, HQF 75, 6½", EX **235.00**
Charger, pansy, dbl garland/yel & bl bands, unmk, late 19th C, 11", EX ..**350.00**
Charger, peasant lady, scalloped border, HBQ, 11", NM **160.00**
Charger, Rouenesque quiver & torch/flowers/cornucopia, HB, 19th C, 20"...**1,050.00**
Cheese dish, peasant lady w/distaff on lid, hat shape, wheat hdl, HQ...**675.00**
Cigarette holder, camel ea side, HQ 82 F, 3x3½", NM................**300.00**
Creamer, fleur-de-lis, blk ermine tails, sponging, HB, 3¼"..........**240.00**
Cruet, dbl; ermine tails/fleur-de-lis, HB, 19th C, 7x9" **475.00**
Cruet, dbl; ivoire corbeille, Breton couple, head stoppers, HQ, 5x7" ...**375.00**
Cup & saucer, lady & bluets, dolphin hdl, HQF, 5", 6", EX **25.00**
Cup & saucer, peasant couple/florals, hexagonal, HQF 74 & 76...**65.00**
Cup & saucer, peasant man, dolphin hdl, HQF, 5", 6", EX............**60.00**
Egg cup, Breton boy w/basket (cup) figural, C Maillard, HQF, 3", NM...**100.00**
Egg cup, peasant lady w/open basket figural, Maillard, HQ, 2½" **210.00**
Egg cup, swan shape, bl wing feathers, striped neck, HQ, 2x3¼", NM ..**85.00**
Figurine, Breton man w/arms folded, EX detail, HBQx, 9" **350.00**
Figurine, Breton man w/cape & walking stick, HQF 140, 4", NM...**150.00**
Figurine, Loik, man leaning on walking stick, Modern Movement, HQ, 4"..**250.00**
Figurine, Saint Anne w/hand on daughter Mary, HQ, 4⅛".........**175.00**
Figurine, Vierge et l'Enfant, Madonna & Child, rare mold, HQF, 11½"...**500.00**
Frame, peasant couple/flower garlands, AP, 19th C, 8x6½" **1,200.00**
Jardiniere, peasant couple, decor riche, dragon hdls, Henriot, 8x15"...**1,500.00**
Jardiniere, peasant couple dance/Crest of Quimper, HR, 7x16"..**950.00**
Jardiniere, peasant lady/floral sprays, loop hdls, ftd, HB102/21, 5x9"..**800.00**
Jardiniere, peasant man w/flute/clover blossoms, HB 54, 7x17x8"...**1,350.00**
Mustard jar, peasant girl by churn figural, Galland, HQ, 5¼".....**200.00**
Pipe holder, duck figural, mc, opening in tail, PB, 3x5¼"..........**225.00**
Pitcher, biberon; floral, faded reds, HBQ, 6" **170.00**
Pitcher, biberon; Odetta, geometrics, greware, HBQ, 6¼".........**500.00**
Pitcher, geometric, wide lip & mouth, bl/yel/red/wht, HQ, 4x6" .**220.00**
Pitcher, geometric croisille, HQ, 5½", EX................**150.00**
Pitcher, lady w/water jug, bl lattice/red dots, HRQ, 5", NM **275.00**
Pitcher, peasant lady, HQF at hdl, 4¾", NM **100.00**
Pitcher, toby; F Pierce 1853-1857, US Presidential series, 2½"...**210.00**
Plaque, Breton bagpipe player, Crest of Brittany, 20th C, 9½x6½"...**125.00**
Plaque, Rumengol, Breton family praying, PB, w/hanger, 18¼x15" ..**875.00**
Plate, Breton lady entering church, bl PB mk, 19th C, 9" **1,800.00**
Plate, Breton man from Plougastel on shore, PB mk, 9½" **1,700.00**
Plate, butterfly, petal & dot garland, HB Q, 5½"................**220.00**
Plate, exotic bird on branches, faience populaire, 19th C, 8½", EX....**150.00**
Plate, Fishermen, peasant couple at shore, shells/bulls border, 9½"..**195.00**
Plate, Ivoire Corbeille, peasant girl, 8-sided, HQF 38, 9⅛" **250.00**
Plate, lady w/basket, chain border, unmk, 19th C, 9½"..............**180.00**
Plate, lady w/jug on head & milk pail, demi-fantasie, HRQ, 9½"..**270.00**
Plate, lady/floral sprays, HB, late 19th C, 9⅛"..................**275.00**
Plate, lady/sponge tree, a la touche florals, HB, 9".............**300.00**
Plate, man w/bagpipes, cottage beyond, bl PB mk, 19th C, 9", NM...**1,650.00**
Plate, Mary w/Infant Jesus & yel scepter, att HB, 19th C, 9¾"....**400.00**
Plate, Modern Movement geometric, HB, 9½"................**150.00**
Plate, peasant man/florals/bluets, HR, 8¼" **400.00**
Plate, peasants dance, acanthus border/Crest of Brittany, HQ, 10½"..**325.00**
Plate, pinwheel center/lattice/garland, unmk, 19th C, 9¾" **430.00**

Plate, soup; geometric snowflakes, bl/cream, HQ 90, 9" **75.00**
Platter, Botanique, carnations, PB (1st period), 9½"................**2,000.00**
Platter, Breton mother & grandmother w/toddler, PB 140, 12½"...**1,825.00**
Platter, man on stool beneath tree w/cider, HBQ, 13¼x10" **1,300.00**
Platter, peasant wedding procession, HenRiot 130, 20½x11"...**1,700.00**
Porringer, lady in pointed coif, att AP, 19th C, 3½x7½", EX **65.00**
Salt cellar, swan figural, peasant lady, HR, 2x3½" **140.00**
Salt shaker, Fr sailor's head, Modern Movement, HBQ, 4" **160.00**
Salt shaker, medieval bonneted lady, Modern Movement, Galland, 2½" ..**150.00**
Shoe, flower on toe, bluets, Souvenir de Brest, sm rstr, unmk AP, 4x4" **220.00**
Tankard, geometric bl w/sponging/lattice/swags, HB 97/1, 5½", EX...**300.00**
Teapot, Breton sailor & love at shore, Modern Movement, HB, 9"..**300.00**
Teapot, Fruits de la Mer, conch shell/seaweed, blk, Henriot, 9½x11" ..**275.00**
Tureen, man w/flute, croisille/demi-fantasie, w/lid, HRQ, 7x12", EX.**1,000.00**
Vase, Broderie Breton, courting scene, HBQ 510, 10¼" **425.00**
Vase, bud; lady/flowers, cornet shape, HQ, 4" **160.00**
Vase, demi-fantasie couple, bluets, tripod ft, prof rstr, HR, 12", pr...**1,250.00**
Vase, geometric, Modern Movement, Paul, Fouillen, 5".............**155.00**
Vase, peasant couple, decor riche, hdls, HBQ 792, 10½x10½" ..**1,450.00**
Vase, peasant ladies dance, HQ JE Sevellec, Modern Movement, 4x8½" ..**375.00**
Vase, peasant man w/bagpipes/Crest of Brittany/ermine tails, HR, 8x7"...**750.00**
Vase, quintal; ivoire corbeille, flowers, HQ 66, 3½" **75.00**
Vase, quintal; peasant lady w/egg basket/dogwood, HQF 160, 3¾" **230.00**
Wall pocket, bagpipe shape, dancing couple/flowers/ribbons, HR, 8" **400.00**
Wall pocket, envelope shape, peasant man (woman)/lattice, HR, 5", pr...**800.00**
Wall pocket, man w/walking stick, flower garlands, prof rstr, unmk, 7" **200.00**

Radford, Alfred

Pottery associated with Albert Radford (1882 – 1904) can be categorized by three periods of production. Pottery produced in Tiffin, Ohio (1896 – 1899), consists of bone china (no marked examples known) and high-quality jasperware with applied Wedgwood-like cameos. Tiffin jasperware is often impressed 'Radford Jasper' in small block letters. At Zanesville, Ohio, Radford jasperware was marked only with an incised, two-digit shape number, and the cameos were not applied but rather formed within the mold and filled with a white slip. Zanesville Radford ware was produced for only a few months before the Radford pottery was acquired by the Arc-en-Ciel company in 1903. Production in Zanesville was handled by Radford's father, Edward (1840 – 1910), who remained in Zanesville after Albert moved to Clarksburg, West Virginia, where the Radford Pottery Co. was completed shortly before Albert's death in 1904. Jasperware was not produced in Clarksburg, and the molds appear to have been left in Zanesville, where some were subsequently used by the Arc-en-Ciel pottery. The Clarksburg, West Virginia, pottery produced a standard glaze, slip-decorated ware, Ruko; Thera and Velvety, matt glazed ware often signed by Albert Haubrich, Alice Bloomer, and other artists; and Radura, a semimatt green glaze developed by Albert Radford's son, Edward. The Clarksburg plant closed in 1912.

Our advisor for this category is James L. Murphy; he is listed in the Directory under Ohio. For pottery marked E. Radford, see Radford, Edward.

Jasper

Bowl, muses & vintage, fluted rim, imp mk **295.00**
Box, classic figure, prof rstr chip, 5½" **100.00**
Box, figure w/cornucopia on lid, prof rpr, ca 1896, 5⅝" H **500.00**
Ewer, appl grapes/raspberries, Old Man Winter hdl, #17, 9" **350.00**
Letter holder, lady w/bow & target scene, bark trim, #61............**500.00**
Mug, vintage, gray, #25, 5"..**165.00**
Pitcher, tankard, vintage, lt bl, 326, 12".....................................**200.00**
Vase, bust of Gladstone ea side, twisted form, 3" **125.00**
Vase, bust of Washington, bk: eagle, bark trim, #12, 7"................**265.00**

Vase, cherubs on flying eagles, #23, 9½"..........................**475.00**
Vase, lady kneeling w/bird, gray, #24, 10½x4½"......................**250.00**
Vase, lady w/dog, #22, 10x6"..**250.00**
Vase, lady w/flowers, bk: grapes, #59, 4"..........................**165.00**
Vase, running girl, deep bl, flat & twisted, #53, 3½".................**100.00**

Miscellaneous

Jardiniere, Ruko, tulips, #10E, 9¼", EX..............................**130.00**
Jardiniere, Ruko, tulips, 8½x9".......................................**250.00**
Vase, Radura, 4-hdl, scalloped rim, 10"...............................**400.00**
Vase, Thera, floral, mc on gr, #1453, 12½"............................**700.00**
Vase, Thera, nasturtium, A Haubrich, ovoid, 13½", NM............**900.00**

Radford, Edward

Pottery marked 'E. Radford, Burslem,' or 'E. Radford, England,' includes a variety of earthenware designed by Edward Radford (1883 – 1968), first for H.J. Wood and later for himself in Burslem (production ending in 1948). A variety of floral patterns, cottage or tavern scenes, and Art Deco motifs distinguish this ware. His father, Edward Thomas Radford, worked at the Pilkington Tile and Pottery Co. in Manchester, England, and appears to have been a brother of Alfred Radford. Items in the following listings are hand painted unless noted otherwise.

Bowl, trees, earth tones on lt beige mottle, Burslem, 4½x4½"......**95.00**
Bowl, 3-D bird on nest, relief molded, pastels, 5x4¾", NM........**165.00**
Bowl vase, flower stalks, red/bl on pk mottle, Burslem, 2x4½"...**125.00**
Candle holders, floral, mc on ivory, #94-HZ-F, 3¾", pr..............**150.00**
Candle holders, violets on lt pk, 2¾", pr.............................**100.00**
Candy dish, morning glories, w/lid, 2x4"..............................**75.00**
Ewer, floral sprays, pastel on lt gr mottle, slim, England, 14"......**100.00**
Jug, butterflies/florals relief, str sides, Butterfly/England, 8½".......**60.00**
Jug, floral, red/gr on ivory mottle, 2KP/Burslem, 2½x5"............**100.00**
Jug, floral spray, mc on ivory, England, WG/H, 9½"..................**145.00**
Jug, poppies, bl/pk on lt beige mottle, waisted neck, Burslem, 4½"..**115.00**
Tray, dbl; poppy in ea well, Great Britain, 5¾" L....................**60.00**
Vase, clematis, EX color, 5"...**65.00**
Vase, floral, horizontal ridges, #672-JN, England, 8", NM............**60.00**
Vase, floral, pk/mc on pk mottle, Great Britain, 3½x3".............**85.00**
Vase, poppies, bl/purple on bl mottle, Burslem/232-JGB, 6"........**145.00**
Vase, Sgraffito, lg cvd floral, gr wash on mottled cream, 7½".....**225.00**
Vase, wisteria (4 repeats), red/bl on ivory, #180, England, 8"......**125.00**
Vase, 5-petal flowers, bl/rose on lt tan mottle, Burslem, 5½"........**70.00**
Wall pocket, floral spray, mc on pk, sqd cone shape, 7½"...........**125.00**

Radios

Vintage radios are very collectible. There were thousands of styles and types produced, the most popular of which today are the breadboard and the cathedral. Consoles are usually considered less marketable, since their size makes them hard to display and store. For those wishing to learn more about antique radios, we recommend *The Collector's Guide to Antique Radios, Volumes I through IV*, by Sue and Marty Bunis; and *Collector's Guide to Antique Radios, Fifth Edition*, by John Slusser, available from your local bookstore or Collector Books. Marty and Sue Bunis are also the authors of *A Collector's Guide to Transistor Radios, Second Edition*. For information on novelty radios, refer to *Collector's Guide to Novelty Radios, Books I and II*, by Marty Bunis and Robert Breed. Unless otherwise noted in the descriptions, values are given for radios in near mint to mint condition.

See also Plastics.

Key:
BC — broadcast
LW — long wave
pb — push button
phono — phonograph

R/P — radio-phonograph
s/r — slide rule
SW — short wave
tbl/m — table model

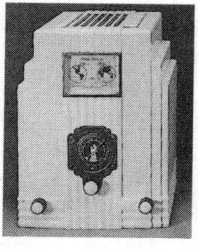

Air King, plastic skyscraper form with black and cream dial depicting Atlas, three knobs, encased Air King chrome plate with globes, stars, and stylized air waves, ca 1935, 11¾", EX, $2,875.00.

Addison, #A2A, tbl/m, plastic Deco style, AC, 1940.................**350.00**
Admiral, #940-11S, console, BC, SW, AC, 1937......................**125.00**
Air Castle, #2271, tbl/m, plastic, BC, 1950..........................**60.00**
Air Castle, #815 (Comet), tbl/m, wood, 1938.......................**60.00**
Airline, #GSL-1079-A, portable, leather, BC, SW, AC/DC, battery, 1955..**65.00**
Airline #5GCB-1541 (Lone Ranger), tbl/m, BC, AC/DC, 1952.....**750.00**
Airline, #17A80, R/P console, wood, 1941............................**90.00**
Airline, #25WG-1573A, tbl/m, plastic, BC, SW, AC, 1953.........**40.00**
Am Bosch, #16 (Amberola), tbl/m, wood/Bakelite, battery, 1925..**250.00**
Am Bosch, #76 (Cruiser), lowboy console, wood, battery, 1927.**125.00**
Arkay, #633, console, wood, 1934....................................**125.00**
Arvin, #243T, tbl/m, metal, BC, AC/DC, 1948.......................**85.00**
Arvin, #417 (Rhythm Boy), tombstone, wood, BC, SW, AC, 1936...**175.00**
Arvin, #8572, portable, leatherette, BC, AC/DC, battery, 1958...**35.00**
Atwater Kent, #46, console, AC, 1929................................**165.00**
Atwater Kent, #387, cathedral, wood, 1934.........................**275.00**
Automatic, #8-15, tbl/m, plastic Deco style, 1937..................**75.00**
Bendix, #112, tbl/m, walnut, BC, AC/DC, 1948.....................**40.00**
BF Goodrich, #92-523, tbl/m, plastic, BC, AC/DC, 1951............**35.00**
Brunswick, #1669, Hplwht side-tbl/m style, wood, AC, 1939.....**150.00**
Bulova, #100, tbl/m w/clock, plastic, BC, AC, 1957.................**40.00**
Capehart, #413P, R/P console, wood, BC, SW, FM, AC, 1949...**300.00**
Cavalier, #LK-447, cathedral, 2-tone wood, 1933...................**150.00**
Cisco, #9A5, tbl/m, plastic, BC, AC/DC, 1947.......................**75.00**
Clarion, #80, tombstone, wood, 1931.................................**175.00**
Clinton, #254, portable, leatherette, 1937............................**65.00**
Colonial, #16, tbl/m, wood, battery, 1925............................**125.00**
Concord, #1-403, tbl/m (streamline), plastic, BC, AC/DC, 1948.**65.00**
Coronado, #43-6321, tbl/m, wood, BC, battery, 1948..............**35.00**
Coronado, #43-7601, R/P console, wood, BC, SW, AC, 1946.....**80.00**
Crosley, #F-5RD, tbl/m, plastic, BC, AC, 1959.......................**65.00**
Crosley, #7H2, tombstone, wood, BC, SW, 1934....................**125.00**
Crosley, #127, tombstone, wood, 1931................................**260.00**
Crosley, #22CB, console, wood, BC, FM, AC, 1941..................**200.00**
Crosley, #56BP, portable, AC/DC, battery, 1946.....................**45.00**
Crosley, #63TA (Victory), wood, BC, SW, AC, 1946................**100.00**
Cutting & Washington, #12A, tbl/m, wood, battery, 1923.........**650.00**
David Grimes, #ADL, tbl/m, wood, battery, 1924...................**225.00**
Dearborn, #100, R/P tbl/m, wood, BC, AC, 1947....................**25.00**
Delco, #R-1230A, tbl/m, ivory plastic, BC, AC/DC, 1947...........**75.00**
Delco, #R-1254, R/P console, wood, BC, SW, FM, AC, 1948......**80.00**
Detrola, #4D, cathedral, wood, 1934.................................**190.00**
Detrola, #258EPC, R/P console, wood, 1938.........................**150.00**
Detrola, #281, tbl/m, Catalin, BC, SW, AC/DC, 1939, minimum value..**3,000.00**
Dewald, #A-501 (Harp), tbl/m, Catalin, BC, AC/DC, 1946, min value...**600.00**
Dewald, #550 Dynette, tbl/m, walnut w/inlay, AC/DC, 1933.......**90.00**
Dumont, #RA-354 (Beachcomber), portable, BC, AC/DC, battery, 1957..**35.00**
ECA, #204, portable, 'alligator,' BC, AC/DC, battery, 1948.........**30.00**

Echophone, #81, cathedral, wood, AC, 1931....................**275.00**
Edison, #C-4, R/P console, wood, 1929............................**350.00**
Emerson, #L-150, chairside, walnut, 2-band, 1935 ....**140.00**
Emerson, #17, tbl/m, plastic Deco style, AC/DC, 1935.............**125.00**
Emerson, #250-AW, tbl/m, burl wood, AC/DC, 1933.............**100.00**
Emerson, #747, portable, plastic, BC, battery, 1954............**175.00**
Espey, #31 (Roundabout), tbl/m, 2-tone plastic, BC, AC/DC, 1950...**150.00**
Eveready, #33, console, wood, AC, 1929 ....**185.00**
Fada, #20-W, tbl/m, plastic, BC, AC, 1938 ....**85.00**
Fada, #32, console, walnut, AC, 1929..............................**150.00**
Farnsworth, #AK-86, R/P console, wood, BC, SW, AC, 1940 ....**145.00**
Farnsworth, #GT-051, tbl/m, plastic Deco style, BC, AC/DC, 1948...**125.00**
Firestone, #4-A-86, R/P console, wood, BC, FM, AC, 1951 ....**80.00**
Firestone, #4-C-29, portable, plastic, BC, battery, 1956 ....**250.00**
Freshman, #5-F-2, tbl/m, wood, battery, 1925 ....**100.00**
Garod, #4A-1B, portable, BC, AM, battery, 1947 ....**45.00**
GE, #A-125, console, wood, AC, 1935 ....**185.00**
GE, #F-63, tbl/m, walnut streamline style, BC, SW, AC, 1937.....**85.00**
GE, #328, R/P console, blond wood, BC, FM, AC, 1949 ....**70.00**
GE, #417, R/P console, wood, BC, 2SW, 2FM, AC, 1947 ....**100.00**
Globe, #51, tbl/m, swirled plastic, BC, AC/DC, 1947 ....**85.00**
Grantline, #605, tbl/m, plastic streamline style, BC, AC/DC, 1946..**165.00**
Grunlow, #654, upright tbl/m, wood, BC, SW, AC, 1937 ....**100.00**
Horn, Riviera R, console, wood Deco style, 1935.....................**500.00**
Howard, #20, cathedral, wood, AC, 1931 ....**250.00**
Howard, #214, console, walnut, BC, SW, AC, 1937 ....**150.00**
Jewel, #502, tbl/m, wood w/inlay, BC, AC/DC, 1947 ....**40.00**
Kadette, #66X, tbl/m, wood, 1936 ....**50.00**
Kellogg, #504 (Wavemaster), tbl/m, wood, battery, 1925 ....**245.00**
Kennedy, #20, tbl/m, mahog, battery, 1925 ....**200.00**
King, #62, tbl/m, wood-tone, battery, 1926 ....**100.00**
Kodel, #C-14, tbl/m, wood, battery, 1924...........................**130.00**
Kolster, #6J, wood, AC, 1927..**135.00**
Lafayette, #D54, console, wood, BC, SW, AC, 1938.............**175.00**
Lyric, #546T, tbl/m, plastic, BC, AC/DC, 1946 ....**45.00**
Maguire, #661, tbl/m, plastic, BC, AC/DC, 1947 ....**55.00**
Majestic, #15, tombstone, wood, AC, 1932 ....**120.00**
Majestic, #886 (Park Avenue), console, 3-tone wood, 1933 ....**350.00**
Meck, #5A7-P11 (Trail Blazer), tbl/m, plastic, BC, AC/DC, 1948..**60.00**
Mohawk, #44, wood, battery, 1927 ....**100.00**
Motorola, #3A5, portable, metal/chrome, BC, AC/DC, battery, 1941 ...**40.00**
Motorola, #6-T, tbl/m, wood, BC, SW, AC, 1937.....................**85.00**
Musicaire, #576, tbl/m, wood/plastic, BC, AC, 1946....................**75.00**
National Union, #571, tbl/m, wood, BC, AC/DC, 1947 ....**30.00**
Olympic, #6-501, tbl/m, plastic, BC, AC/DC, 1946................**65.00**
Ozarka, #J-1 (Junior), tbl/m, wood, 1925 ....**325.00**
Perwal, #52, tbl/m, 2-tone wood, AC/DC, 1937 ....**70.00**
Philco, #E-675-124, portable, leather, BC, 1957..................**25.00**
Philco, #16B, tombstone, 2-tone wood, BC, SW, AC, 1933 ....**200.00**
Philco, #37-690, console, wood, BC, SW, AC, 1937.................**500.00**
Philco, #46, cathedral, wood, AC, 1931................................**325.00**
Pilot, #C-193, console, wood, BC, SW, AC, 1937......................**125.00**
Radiola, #61-5, tbl/m, BC, SW, AC/DC, 1947 ....**45.00**
RCA, #100, cathedral, wood, BC, AC, 1933...........................**175.00**
RCA, #6-T-2, tombstone, wood, BC, SW, 1936 ....**125.00**
RCA, #9K3, console, wood, BC, SW, AC, 1936 ....**130.00**
Roland, #5T1E, tbl/m, plastic, BC, AC/DC, 1953 ....**30.00**
Sentinel, #111, cathedral, wood, 1931 ....**250.00**
Setchell-Carlson, #23, tombstone, wood, BC, SW, battery, 1939..**60.00**
Silvertone, #1850, tombstone, wood Deco style, battery, 1935 ...**100.00**
Sonora, #LV-186, R/P console, wood, AC, 1942.....................**100.00**
Sterling, #8 (Concertone), console, wood, 1931....................**165.00**
Stewart-Warner, #A51T3 (Air Pal), tbl/m, plastic, BC, AC/DC, 1947..**100.00**
Stromberg-Carlson, #FR-506, R/P console, wood, AM, FM, AC, 1957....**70.00**

Temple, #G-419, tbl/m, metal, BC, AC/DC, 1947 ....**65.00**
Truetone, #D-2610, tbl/m, plastic, 1946 ....**75.00**
Tuska, #222, tbl/m, wood, battery, 1922 ....**450.00**
Unitone, #88, tbl/m, wood, BC, SW, AC/DC, 1946..................**40.00**
Vogue, #2554R, tbl/m, plastic, BC, AC/DC, 1946 ....**45.00**
Westinghouse, #H-169, R/P console, wood, BC, 2SW, FM, AC, 1948 ..**125.00**
Westinghouse, #H-343P5U, portable, plastic, BC, AC/DC, battery, 1951...**55.00**
Woolaroc, #3-1A, tbl/m, plastic streamline style, BC, AC/DC, 1946 ...**65.00**
Zenith, #M510-R, tbl/m, plastic, BC, AC/DC, 1955..............**40.00**
Zenith, #4-R, tbl/m, wood, battery, 1923 ....**375.00**
Zenith, #6-S-546, chairside, wood, BC, SW, AC, 1941.............**135.00**

Novelty Radios

Animal Crackers, box form w/cord hdl, NM....................**75.00**
Archie, jukebox form, Vanity Fair/Archie Co, 1977, 6", M...........**50.00**
Budweiser, Isis billboard, 4x12" L, NM............................**65.00**
Bullwinkle, 1969, 12", NM..**150.00**
Bumper Car, Playtime Concepts, 14" L, NM **125.00**
Cherry 7-Up, Popworks jukebox form, M...........................**75.00**
Computer Mouse, realistic form, FM only, China, M **35.00**
Del Monte Pineapple Chunks, can form, M.........................**75.00**
Ford 250 Camper, Philco-Ford model P-23, NM, from $300 to..**350.00**
Heinz's Tomato Soup, can form w/early label, Hong Kong, 3½", NM...**60.00**
Howdy Doody, cloth/vinyl, controls on front, 14", NM..............**50.00**
Hunt's Manwich, can form, AM/FM, NM...........................**40.00**
Incredible Hulk, Marvel Comics, 1978, 7", M....................**75.00**
Kellogg's Special K, box form, AM/FM, China, NM **50.00**
Mighty Mouse on Cheese, Vanity Fair/Via Com Int'l, 1978, 5", M...**150.00**
Mr Muscle Overnight Oven Cleaner, can form, NM **125.00**
Pepsi, analog wall-clock form, AM/FM, wht, 9x5½" dia, M..........**35.00**
Pink Panther, stuffed cloth, 12", NM.................................**35.00**
Popeye, plastic head figure, Hong Kong, 1960, EXIB **75.00**
Radio Peaches, can form, NM **100.00**
Ralston Purina Chuck Wagon, 8x6½" L, NM.....................**100.00**
Sears Easy Living Paint Can, Hong Kong, NM, from $35 to.........**50.00**
Shell Pendant, 3¼" clam shell w/24" chain, Hong Kong, NM ...**100.00**
Snow White & Seven Dwarfs, Syroco, Emerson, 1938, 7x11", NM ..**3,000.00**
Spider-Man, Marvel Comics/Hong Kong, 1979, 5", EX..............**50.00**
Sun-Drop, can form, NM **35.00**

Transistor Radios

Post-World War II baby boomers, now approaching their fiftieth year, are rediscovering prized possessions of youth, their pocket radios. The transistor wonders, born with rock 'n roll, were at the vanguard of miniaturization and futuristic design in the decade which followed their introduction to Christmas shoppers in 1954. The tiny receiving sets launched the growth of Texas Instruments and shortly to follow abroad, Sony and other Japanese giants.

The most desirable sets include the 1954 four-transistor Regency TR-1 and colorful early Sony and Toshiba models. Certain pre-1960 models by Hoffman and Admiral represented the earliest practical use of solar technology and are also highly valued. To avoid high tariffs, scores of two-transistor sets, boys' radios, were imported from Japan with names like Pet and Charmy. Many early inexpensive transistor sets could be heard only with an earphone. The smallest sets are known as shirt-pocket models while those slightly larger are called coat-pockets. Early collectible transistor radios all have civil defense triangle markings at 640 and 1240 on the frequency dial and nine or fewer transistors. Very few desirable sets were made after 1963. Model numbers are most commonly found inside. Our advisor for this category is Mike Brooks; he is listed in the Directory under California and welcomes questions. (Please include a SASE.)

Admiral, #7M18, horizontal, AM, battery, 1958......................**50.00**
Airline, #GEN-1202B, horizontal, 6 transistors, AM, battery, 1963...**35.00**
Aiwa, #AR-852, horizontal, 8 transistors, AM, battery, 1964 ....**30.00**
Blaupunkt, #22503, horizontal, 9 transistors, AM/FM, SW, battery, 1963 ...**45.00**
Braun, T3, 6 transistors, 1958 ....**40.00**
Bulova, #660, vertical, 8 transistors, AM, battery, 1959 ....**85.00**
Calrad, #60A183, vertical, 6 transistors, AM, battery, 1960 ....**125.00**
Columbia, #600G, vertical, 6 transistors, AM, battery, 1960 ....**35.00**
Crown, #TR-610, 6 transistors, 1959..................................**50.00**
Crown, #TR-875, horizontal, 8 transistors, AM, SW, battery, 1960...**60.00**
Delco, #980131, auto/portable, AM, 1958 ....**125.00**
Dewald, K-701, 6 transistors, 1956 ....**125.00**
Emerson, #555, horizontal, 4 transistors, AM, battery, 1959 ....**75.00**
Ever-Play, #1836A, vertical, 6 transistors, AM, battery, 1963 ....**35.00**
Falcon, #6THK, vertical, 6 transistors, AM, battery, 1964 ....**20.00**
GE, #676, horizontal, 5 transistors, AM, battery, 1955................**125.00**
Global, #GR-711, 6 transistors, 1959 ....**100.00**
Global, #GR-900, vertical, 9 transistors, AM, battery, 1963 ....**150.00**
Grundig, Prima-Boy, 9 transistors, AM/FM, LW, battery. 1061 .....**30.00**
Harpers, #GK-631, vertical, 6 transistors, AM, battery, 1962 .....**125.00**
Hi-Delity, #7TA-1X, horizontal, 8 transistors, AM, SW, battery, 1964...**100.00**
Hit Parade, 2 transistors, 1958 ....**70.00**
Hitachi, #TH-621, vertical, 6 transistors, AM, battery, 1959........**85.00**
Hoffman, #EP706, horizontal, 6 transistors, AM, battery, 1959 ..**300.00**
Honey Tone, #8TP-412, vertical, 8 transistors, AM, battery, 1963..**50.00**
Itt, #600, vertical, 6 transistors, AM, battery, 1963 ....**55.00**
Jaguar, #6T-250, vertical, 6 transistors, AM, battery, 1960..........**175.00**
Kowa, #KT-67, vertical, 6 transistors, AM, battery, 1961 ....**75.00**
Lafayette, #FS-91, vertical, 9 transistors, AM, battery..................**200.00**
Lefco, #6YR-15A, vertical, 6 transistors, AM, battery, 1961 ....**100.00**
Lido, TR-270, 2 transistors, 1960......................................**90.00**
Linmark, #T-25, vertical, 2 transistors, AM, battery, 1959 ....**100.00**
Loewe Opta, #5910, horizontal, 6 transistors, LW, AM, battery, 1960 ..**40.00**
Magnavox, #AM-62, vertical, AM, battery, 1963 ....**30.00**
Mantola, M4D, 4 transistors, 1956 ....**250.00**
Marvel, #6YR-05, vertical, 6 transistors, AM, battery, 1961 ....**75.00**
Motorola, #6X28B, horizontal, 6 transistors, AM, battery, 1959.**100.00**
NEC, NT-61, 6 transistors, 1960.......................................**100.00**
Nordmende, Mambo, horizontal, 7 transistors, LW, AM, battery, 1961 ....**40.00**
Norwood, #NA-1200, horizontal, 12 transistors, AM/FM, battery, 1964..**20.00**
Olympic, #766, vertical, 6 transistors, leather, AM, battery, 1959..**40.00**
Panasonic, #R-132, vertical, 8 transistors, AM, battery, 1966.......**25.00**
Philco, #T-3-130 (Veep), vertical, 3 transistors, AM, battery, 1959..**90.00**
Raytheon, #8TP-1, horizontal, 8 transistors, AM, battery, 1955.**175.00**
RCA, #1-BT-48, horizontal, 6 transistors, AM, battery, 1957 ....**35.00**
Realistic, #90L665, vertical, 6 transistors, AM, battery, 1962 ....**60.00**
Realtone, #TR-1971, vertical, 8 transistors, AM, battery, 1965 ....**25.00**
Regency, #TR-5, horizontal, leather, AM, battery, 1958................**55.00**
Roland, #6TR, vertical, 6 transistors, AM, battery, 1957 ....**50.00**
Saba, Sabinette 11, horizontal, 7 transistors, LW, AM, battery, 1960 ..**45.00**
Sharp, #TR-182, horizontal, AM, battery, 1959.......................**60.00**
Silvertone, #213, vertical, 6 transistors, AM, battery, 1959...........**40.00**
Sony, ICR-120, 3 transistors, 1968 ....**110.00**
Sony, TR-55, EX, 1965 ....**1,500.00**
Sylvania, #5P11R, horizontal, 5 transistors, AM, battery, 1960 ....**50.00**
Telefunken, #3061 (Mini-Partner), 6 transistors, AM, battery, 1960...**75.00**
Toshiba, #10TL-429F, horizontal, 10 transistors, AM/FM, battery, 1961...**55.00**
Toshiba, #3TP-315Y, vertical, 3 transistors, AM, battery, 1959 ..**150.00**
Trancel, #T-7, vertical, 6 transistors, AM, battery, 1959................**90.00**
Truetone, #DC3884, horizontal, 4 transistors, AM, battery, 1959.**25.00**
Universal, #PTR-62B, vertical, 6 transistors, AM, battery, 1963 ..**30.00**
Victoria, #TR-650, vertical, 6 transistors, AM, battery, 1961........**40.00**
Vulcan, #6T-160, Vulcan, horizontal, 6 transistors, AM, battery ..**80.00**
Westclox, #80002, horizontal, 6 transistors, AM, battery, 1962 ....**55.00**

Westinghouse, #H618P7, horizontal, 7 transistors, AM, battery, 1957...**75.00**
Wilco, #ST-6, horizontal, 6 transistors, AM, battery, 1962............**90.00**
Yashica, #YT-100, vertical, 6 transistors, AM, battery, 1961 ....**35.00**

Railroadiana

Collecting railroad-related memorabilia has become one of America's most popular hobbies. The range of collectible items available is almost endless; not surprising, considering the fact that more than 185 different railroad lines are represented. Some collectors prefer to specialize in only one railroad, while others attempt to collect at least one item from every railway line known to have existed. For the advanced collector, there is the challenge of locating rarities from short-lived railroads; for the novice, there are abundant keys, buttons, and passes. Among the most popular specializations are dining-car collectibles — flatware, glassware, dinnerware, etc., in a wide variety of patterns and styles. Railroad blankets are also collectible. Most common are Pullman blankets. The early ones had a cross-stitch pattern; these were followed by one in a solid cinnamon color; both are marked clearly with the Pullman name. These are now valued at $125.00 up to $175.00 in good condition. Pullman, in the 1920s, put out a blue blanket, marked Pullman, specifically for ethnic use. There is one in the Sacramento railroad museum. Other railroads had their own 'marked' blankets that are even more desirable, such as the Soo line, the Chessie, and one marked 'Pheasant' (which was a private car on the Milwaukee Line that was reserved to carry special parties for hunting trips).

Another name among railroad dining collectors is Fred Harvey. From 1893 until after WWII, Fred Harvey masterminded all the dining halls and dining cars on the Santa Fe Railroad System from Chicago to the West Coast. (A little known fact, he also had dining facilities on the Frisco railroad.) He had his famous Harvey girls, as portrayed by Judy Garland, and a lot of personal dining china, silver, and linens marked with his 'FH.' The Webster and Black Chain patterns have become highly collectible.

As is true in most collecting fields, scarcity and condition determine value. There is more interest in some railway lines than in others; generally speaking, it is greater in the region serviced by the particular railroad. Reproductions abound in railroadiana collectibles — from dinnerware and glassware to lanterns, keys, badges, belt buckles, timetables, and much more. Repro hand-executed, reverse-painted glass signs have been abundant throughout the country, most of them read 'Santa Fe,' but some say 'Whites Only.' Beware! Also railroad drumheads are coming out of collections. A drumhead is a large (approximately 24" diameter) glass sign in a metal case. They were used on the back end of all railroad observation cars to advertise a special train or a presidential foray, etc. They're now beginning to surface, and a good one like the Flying Crow from the Kansas City Southern Railroad will go for $2,500.00, as will many others. When items of this value come out, the counterfeiters are right there. It is important to 'know thy dealer.' For a more thorough study, we recommend *Railroad Collectibles, Fourth Revised Edition*, by Stanley L. Baker. The values noted for most of our dinnerware, glassware, linen, silverplate, and timetables are actual selling prices. However, because prices are so volatile, the best pricing sources are often monthly or quarterly 'For Sale' lists. Two you may find helpful may be ordered from Golden Spike, P.O. Box 422, Williamsville, NY 14221, and Grandpa's Depot, 6720 E. Mississippi Ave., Unit B, Denver, CO 80224. Our co-advisors for this category are Fred and Lila Shrader (See Directory, California), and John White (Grandpa's Depot, see Colorado).

Key:
BL — bottom logo	SL — side logo
BS — bottom stamped	SM — side mark
FBS — full back stamp	TL — top logo
NBS — no back stamp	TM — top mark

Dinnerware

Many railroads designed their own china for use in their dining cars or company-owned hotels or stations. Some railroads chose to use stock patterns to which they added their name or logo; others used the same stock patterns without the added identification. For more information we recommend *Restaurant China, Vols. I* and *II,* by Barbara J. Conroy.

Bowl, berry; D&RGW, Blue Adam, NBS, 5½" 18.00
Bowl, bouillon; IC, coral, no hdls, NBS, 3¼" 22.00
Bowl, salad; ATSF, Mimbreno, FBS, 3x7" 442.00
Butter pat, CB&Q, Burlington Route, Violets & Daisies, BS, 3" ..72.00
Butter pat, GN, Empire, NBS, 3" 27.00
Butter pat, SP&S, Am pattern, NBS 27.00
Chocolate pot, ATSF, California Poppy, NBS, 6" 135.00
Compote, N&W, Cavalier, TM, 2½x7" dia 865.00
Creamer, ind; Blue & Gold, no hdl, NBS, 2¾" 54.00
Creamer, ind; D&RGW, Blue Adam, no hdl, NBS, 3" 29.00
Creamer, ind; Pennsylvania, Purple Laurel, no hdl, BS, 3" 75.00
Cup & saucer, CNR, Queen Elizabeth, cup TL 47.00
Cup & saucer, demitasse; C&O, Homestead, SL 42.00
Cup & saucer, demitasse; PRR, Broadway, both BS 215.00
Cup & saucer, GN, Spokane Rose, saucer BS 78.00
Egg cup, GTW, Blue & Gold, SL, BS, 2⅞" 270.00
Gravy boat, B&O, Derby, NBS, 8" 44.00
Ice cream dish w/tab hdl, B&O, Derby, NBS, 6" 38.00
Plate, ACL, Palmetto, BS, TL, 7" sq w/notched corners 126.00
Plate, CMStP&P, Traveler, FBS, 9½" 195.00
Plate, CPR, Tremblant w/Railway, TL, 9" 58.00
Plate, IC, Coral, NBS, 9½" 80.00
Plate, NP, Monad, TL, NBS, 5" 51.00
Plate, service; IC, inner courtyard scene, NBS, 10½" 650.00
Platter, CM&StP, St Paul, TM, NBS, 5x8½" 235.00
Platter, UP, Portland Rose, FBS, 10x6½" 195.00
Relish dish, SR, Peach Blossom, TL, 12x6" 220.00
Sherbet, UP, Winged Streamliner, SL, 2½" 58.00
Teapot w/lid, GM&O, SM, 5¾" 668.00

Glass

Ashtray, NYC, 20th Century Limited, 5" 51.00
Ashtray, Rock Island, clear w/blk or red bearskin logo 15.00
Bottle, milk; ATSF, Santa Fe bl enamel logo, sq-ish, ½-pt, $16 to ..40.00
Bottle, milk; MP buzz saw logo, ½-pt, from $15 to 27.00
Carafe, Soo Line banner logo, cut neck, bulbous, 9" 195.00
Claret, GN, knob stem, frosted logo, 4¾" 45.00
Claret, NYC, 20th Century Limited, knob stem, 4¼" 35.00
Cordial, Alaska Railroad in cursive on ribbon logo, 3½" 255.00
Cordial, NP, etched Yellowstone Park Line logo, SM, 3¾" 100.00
Cordial, NYC System logo, plain stem, 4" 42.00
Cruet, GN, etched Great Northern & old goat logo, 5½" 250.00
Cruet & stopper, B&O etched capitol dome logo, 5½" 166.00
Decanter, Lehigh Valley flag logo wheel-cut, 8" 285.00
Goblet, UP, frosted shield logo, ball stem, 5½" 35.00
Goblet, UP wht enamel shield logo, ftd, 5½", from $12 to 21.00
Old fashioned, ICRR, Main Line of America, 4½" 25.00
Pitcher, M&StLRR, SP fr, #04266, Albert Pick & Co, 1928, water sz.350.00
Platter, ATSF, Chico w/train & US map in silver & blk, 14" 67.00
Roly-poly, CRI&P, Route of the Rockets in red, Golden State Route ..25.00
Roly-poly, CRI&P, Rock Island logo+Golden State oranges logo, 3" 14.00
Roly-poly, Wabash flag logo+Bluebird train, 3¼" 30.00
Sherbet, Canadian Nat'l System rectangular wht enamel logo, ped ft, 4" ...16.00
Sherbet, CNR, etched canted box logo, cut stem, SM, 4x3¼" 35.00
Shot glass, Pullman, etched SL, 2½" 65.00
Shot glass, UP, frosted shield logo, 2½" 18.00
Stem, wine, CMStP&P rectangular etched logo, 4⅛" 68.00
Swizzle stick, CMStP&P, The Hiawatha/Nothing Faster on Rails, 5" ..6.00
Tumbler, C&O For Progress in bl, SM, 4¾" 15.00
Tumbler, CPR, wht enamel shield w/beaver atop, SM, 4" 15.00
Tumbler, hi-ball; PRR, Madison Sq Garden, good gold, pre-1967, 5½" ..9.00
Tumbler, juice; CM&StP&P, etched box logo, SM, 3¾" 20.00
Tumbler, juice; GN, frosted logo, SM, 3½" 35.00
Tumbler, juice; Gulf, Mobile & Ohio enamel winged logo, 4" 15.00
Tumbler, NYC, 1964 World's Fair w/train in blk & gold, 6¾" 12.00
Tumbler, Santa Fe script in wht, 5½" 22.00
Tumbler, water; Western Pacific etched Feather River logo, 5¼" .75.00
Tumbler, whiskey; Lehigh Valley emb in bottom, 3¼" 203.00
Tumbler, whiskey; Pullman emb in bottom, 3", from $65 to 110.00
Wine, IC RR, frosted dmn logo, stemmed 17.50

Lanterns

Before 1920 kerosene brakemen's lanterns were made with tall globes, usually 5⅜" high. These are most desirable to collectors and are usually found at the top of the price scale. Short globes from 1921 through 1940 normally measure 3½" in height, except for those manufactured by Dietz, which are 4" tall. (Soon thereafter, battery brakemen's lanterns came into widespread usage; these are not highly regarded by collectors and are generally not railroad marked.)

All lanterns should be marked with the name or initials of the railroad — look on the top, the top apron, or the bell base (if it has one). Globes may be found in these colors (listed in order of popularity): clear, red, amber, aqua, cobalt, and two-color.

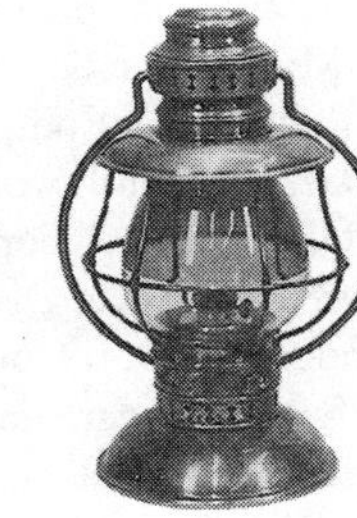

Conductor's, unmarked, half-colored green/clear globe, scarce, $350.00. (Photo courtesy Stanley Baker)

Adams & Westlake, CB&Q RR etched on red short globe 125.00
Adams & Westlake Adams, Santa Fe, clear unmk globe, 1909P ...375.00
Adlake, CMStP&P, short, clear unmk globe 75.00
Adlake, Indiana Harbor Belt, tall clear unmk globe 70.00
Adlake #250 Kero, ICRR on dome, short red globe, 1923 ....100.00
Adlake #250 Kero, SPCo on dome top, gr globe, 1923 ....125.00
Adlake Reliable, B&M, wire ring bottom, clear globe, 1913 ....160.00
Adlake Reliable, GTRy, bell bottom, amber globe, Pat 1913 ....250.00
Armspear, ERR Co on clear globe 130.00
Armspear, M&STL, wire ring bottom, clear globe, 1905 ....200.00
Dietz, NYO&W, short red unmk globe 165.00
Dressel, CMStP&P, no font, short unmk globe, flat ribs 70.00
Dressel, NP on lid, wire ring base, short red mk globe, Pat on bottom ..135.00
Handlan, ATSF, wire ring base, short red mk globe, dates on bottom ...135.00
Handlan, Burlington Rte, short, clear unmk globe 85.00
Handlan, Frisco top apron, short unmk globe, lt rust 75.00
Handlan, MOPAC, wire ring bottom, Safety First at bk, clear globe ...165.00
Handlan, PS in keystone on tall clear globe 165.00
Handlan-Buck, Frisco, clear 5½" globe, twisted bottom w/pot 375.00
Inspector's, Acme, C&A on hdl, w/globe & reflector 125.00
Inspector's, Dietz, ATSF, tin hood, reflector, kerosene burner 125.00
Inspector's, Dietz, no RR name, tall aqua globe, reflector 145.00
Inspector's, Dietz Ideal, clear globe mk Dietz Vesta, 11½", EX ...125.00

Inspector's, ICRR on hand, G globe w/reflector, rust....................**90.00**
Marker, Adlake, BR on side of vent, 4 lenses, sq top, blk finish .**245.00**
Marker, Adlake, GNRy on vent, sq top, 4 lenses, blk finish **265.00**
Marker, Dressel, Soo Line near base, 4 lenses, 5⅜" dia **275.00**
Oxweld, Model A Union Carbide, aluminum, clear lens, 11½" ...**75.00**
RR Signal Co, Boston & ME, clear unmk globe **65.00**
Semaphore, Adlake, CStPM&O, 2 clear lenses, oil font, 5⅜" dia ...**195.00**
Star Headlight Co....NY USA, clear globe, 9¾"...........................**300.00**
Switch-stand, Adlake, NP, cannonball type, 4 lenses, 5⅜" dia **60.00**
Switch-stand, GNRy #4, Adlake on sq top, 4 lenses, 6½" dia.....**235.00**
Track Walker's, unmk Dietz, 3" lens w/red slide, June 26, '09 .....**130.00**
Unmk Adlake, cannonball style, cast aluminum, 4 lenses...........**150.00**
Unmk mfg, CM&StP, sheet metal w/CI base, electric, red/gr lenses...**275.00**
Unmk mfg, NP brass, bell bottom, unmk globe, Pat May 11 1871 ....**600.00**
Wall, NP, kerosene burner, w/CI mt, bunk car, 4¼" dia **85.00**

Linens and Uniforms

Hat, C&O Ry Conductor, $225.00.

Blanket, C&NW, dk gr, gold edge, 56x82"...................................**250.00**
Blanket, CMStP&P, tan & brn wool, Hiawatha logo in center, 66x90"...**255.00**
Blanket, CMStP&P, tan & brn wool, Milwaukee Road logo, 68x90".......**178.00**
Blanket, Pullman, wht on cinnamon, 58x89" **175.00**
Blanket, UP, Pendleton wool, dbl-bed sz...................................**300.00**
Blanket, UP, Yermo Club, red on wht thick cotton, 35x64" **125.00**
Blanket, UP System over Overland logo, gray w/blk stripes, 60x77"...**250.00**
Coat, conductor's; B&O, blk wool, brass buttons, pre-1940........**185.00**
Hat, CN Super Continental, gr paper, unused **7.00**
Head rest seat cover, PRR, tan w/3" RR scene on bottom edge, 15x19"...**28.00**
Jacket, C&NW Commissary Dept, wht, ¾-sleeves, EX................**35.00**
Jacket, waiter; UP, wht w/color logo on left sleeve.....................**35.00**
Napkin, ATSF, Santa Fe in script, wht on wht, 22" sq **26.00**
Napkin, SP, Sunset logo woven in wht on wht, 21" sq **26.00**
Pillowcase, Burlington Rte, Pullman logo **12.00**
Pillowcase, CP, 35x16"...**12.00**
Sheet, berth; Pullman, twin sz..**12.00**
Sheet, berth; UP, shield logo sewn in red **14.00**
Tablecloth, MStP&SStM, Soo Lone logo in center, wht on wht, 57x66" ...**38.00**
Tablecloth, Pullman, wht on wht, 44x36" **45.00**
Tablecloth, UP, rust & cream w/UP woven on edge, 42" sq **35.00**
Towel, hand; Pullman - 1925 woven on bl center stripe.................**22.00**
Uniform, Louisville & Nashville, suit w/buttons, hat w/Flagman badge .**128.00**
Uniform, PRR, blk wool coat+vest+pants+hat+brass buttons+badge **185.00**

Locks

Brass switch locks (pre-1920) were made in two styles: heart-shaped and Keen Kutter style. Values for the heart-shaped locks are determined to a great extent by the railroad they represent and just how its name appears on the lock. Most in demand are locks with large embossed letters; if the letters are small and incised, demand for that lock is minimal. For instance, one from the Union Pacific line (even with heavily embossed letters) may go for only $45.00, while the same from the D&RG railroad could go easily sell for $250.00. Old Keen Kutter styles

(brass with a 'pointy' base) from Colorado & Southern and Denver & Rio Grande could range from $600.00 to $1,200.00.

Steel switch locks (circa 1920 on) with the initials of the railroad incised in small letters — for example BN, L&H, and PRR — are usually valued at $20.00 to $28.00.

Adams & Westlake, Rock Island **40.00**
Adlake, D&H, steel, w/chain & key...**45.00**
Adlake, D&RG, steel, rnd loop, chain **27.50**
Adlake, D&RGW, w/chain & EX mk key.................................**60.00**
Adlake, ICRR Signal, brass heart shape, w/fancy-head key...........**45.00**
Adlake, NPR, steel, w/chain **25.00**
Climax Mfg, UP on loop, brass heart shape **27.50**
Fraim, Reading Co Signal Service, brass, EX patina **35.00**
FS Hardware, UPMP&C, steel, w/key.....................................**55.00**
Keen Kutter, D&RG RR, w/chain & key..................................**365.00**
Safe, D&RG, brass heart shape, EX patina, 1870s, w/key...........**350.00**
So Pacific Co CS-44 Special, brass heart shape, w/chain, no key..**150.00**
Switch, NY O&W Ry, steel, w/brass key **65.00**
Yale, B&O Signal, brass, w/steel key...**32.00**

Silverplate

The value of silverplate, hollow ware, or flatware, is influenced by the location of the logo or railroad name and, of course, by condition. A side- or top-marked piece is preferable to one with a bottom mark. Examine a prospective purchase carefully. Some unmarked flatware has been 'enhanced' with a rather crude stamping of the railroad's name. Authentic railway markings were done at the time of manufacture and were generally executed in a flawless manner.

Butter pat, CRI&P, Wallace, BS, 3x3"......................................**38.00**
Butter pat, Illinois Central, R&B, TL, BS, 3¼"..........................**148.00**
Butter spreader, StL&SF, Commonwealth, R&B, Frisco Lines BS...**42.00**
Coffeepot, CRI&P Gorham, BS, 16-oz, 6"..................................**110.00**
Compote, NYC, ped w/o liner, BS, 2¾x7".................................**98.00**
Corn holders, ATSF, Phleghar, SM...**270.00**
Corn holders, CIL, monon SM..**110.00**
Creamer, B&O, R&B, BS, 2-oz, 2⅜"...**96.00**
Creamer, Pullman, hinged lid/attached underplate, Internat'l, BS, 6-oz ...**127.00**
Crumber, UP System, Sierra, R&B, TM, 12½" L **95.00**
Fork, dinner; CMStP&P, Ambassador (A), International, BS, 7¾"...**18.00**
Fork, dinner; Oregon & Washington RR, Westfield, Meriden, BS..**57.00**
Fork, seafood; D&RG, Clarenden, T&RG TM, R&B **55.00**
Horseradish holder, CMStP&P, glass insert & stopper, SL, 2-oz .**285.00**
Knife, dinner; CRI&P, Lexington, Rock Ilsand SM, 9½".............**56.00**
Knife, dinner; NYC, Century, Internat'l, SM............................**28.00**
Ladle, condiment; PRR, Kings, TM Keystone logo, R&B, 5"........**72.00**
Menu holder, Florida East Coast, Internat'l, SL, BS **126.00**
Plate, Pullman, Manning-Bowman, BS, 7".................................**85.00**
Spoon, bouillon; CMStP&P, Ambassador (A), Internat'l, BS.......**19.00**
Spoon, demitasse; MoPac, Century, BS, 4¾" **26.00**
Spoon, iced tea; Western Pacific, Cromwell, Internat'l, TM, 7½"..**32.00**
Spoon, mustard; NYC, Century, Internat'l, BS **52.00**
Sugar bowl, DL&W, w/lid, R&B, SL, BS, 3½x4½" **518.00**
Sugar bowl, SP, w/attached underplate & lid, R&B, SL, Bs, 4x7½" ..**142.00**
Sugar tongs, CCC&StL Ry, Windsor, R&B, TM, 5" **280.00**
Sugar tongs, Michigan Central, Windsor, R&B, TM, 5" **178.00**
Syrup, PRR, dripless type, hinged lid, R&B, SL, BS, 5½"...........**415.00**
Tablespoon, Santa Fe Route/F Harvey TM..................................**89.00**
Tea strainer, Canadian Pacific, U-shaped hdls, Internat'l, TM......**36.00**
Teapot, PRR, side Keystone logo, R&B, BS, 10-oz, 7"................**210.00**
Teaspoon, Seaboard, Century (B), Internat'l, TM **17.00**
Tray, ATSF, line & leaf border, Rogers, BS, 6" sq.......................**138.00**

Tray, change; NYC, Century, Internat'l, TM, 6½" **58.00**
Tureen, CB&Q, w/lid, R&B, SL, 16-oz, 5¼x7" **175.00**
Vase, bud; UP, Internat'l, early SL, 6¼" **115.00**

Switch Keys

Switch keys are brass with hollow barrels and round heads with holes for attaching to a key ring. They were used to unlock the padlocks on track-side switches when the course of the tracks had to be changed. (Switches were padlocked to prevent them from being thrown by accident or vandals, a situation that could result in a train wreck). A car key used to open padlocks on freight cars and the like is very similar to the switch key, except the bit is straighter instead of being specifically curved for a particular railroad and its accompanying switch locks. A second type of 'car' key was used for door locks on passenger cars, Pullmans, etc.; this type was usually of brass, but instead of having a hollow barrel, they were shaped like an old-fashioned hotel door key. In order for a key to be collectible, the head must be marked with a name, initials, or a railroad identification, with 'switch' generally designated by 'S' and 'car' by 'C' markings. Railroad, patina 'not polished,' and the presence of a manufacturer's mark other than Adlake all have a positive effect on pricing and collectibility.

A new precedent was set in 1995 when a Denver and South Park 'car' key went at a Missouri auction for $2,500.00. The key was marked DSP&P (an early Colorado road that stopped running in 1898); it was brass and had a hollow barrel and straight bit. Switch keys that only recently brought $15.00 to $17.00 are now bringing $35.00.

Adlake, B&O RR Co, EX patina **25.00**
Adlake, CMStP&P, EX patina **25.00**
Adlake, CWP&S **30.00**
Adlake, CWP&W, EX patina **38.00**
Adlake, IC, lg inscriptions, EX patina **25.00**
Adlake, ICRR, EX patina **27.00**
Adlake, NYC, Pittsburgh & Lake Erie cut, EX patina **35.00**
Adlake, PCRR, EX patina **24.00**
Adlake, WL&T Co, EX patina **27.50**
Fraim, DL&W, EX patina **27.50**
FS Hardware, MOPAC, EX patina **25.00**
FS Hardware, MP, MW (Maintenance of Way), EX patina...........**35.00**

Miscellaneous

Annual passes continue to be favored over trip and one-time passes. Their value is contingent upon the specific railroad, its length of run, and the appearance of the pass itself. Many were tiny works of art enhanced with fancy calligraphy and decorated with unique vignettes.

Timetables continue to gain in popularity and offer the collector vast information about the glory days of railroading. Pins and badges bearing the name or logo of a railroad are also popular collectibles. The novice needs to be cautious about signs (metal as well as cardboard) and belt buckles. Reproductions flourish in these areas.

Badge, Berkshire Street Railway 25, blue and white enameling on silver-tone metal, $65.00.

Agreement, ACL, RR Telegraphers, 1939 ....**5.00**
Ashtray, Am European Express, AEE in gold on wht ceramic, 4½" dia ...**22.00**
Ashtray, ATSF Super Chief, Turquoise Room, 3¾x4½", +orig box..........**22.00**
Ashtray, Burlington Rte, Denver Zephyr Chuck Wagon, blk glass, 9" L..**75.00**
Ashtray, PRR keystone shape, blk Bakelite, 4½" **19.00**
Ashtray, UP, smoky glass, 4" dia **14.00**
Attache case, red fabric w/top zipper, 11x16", M **10.00**
Attache pouch, CN, red plastic w/wht safety rules, zipper, M **7.00**
Badge, breast; Lehigh Valley, Police, 2x3" **148.00**
Badge, cap; Duluth, S Shore & Atlantic, brakeman, contour, silver-tone...**463.00**
Badge, cap; Erie logo in enamel, Trainman, contour, 4" L...........**198.00**
Badge, cap; UP, emb, Brakeman, contour, very early **325.00**
Bell, air-operated locomotive; replaced air-operated clapper, 12x9"...**168.00**
Bell, locomotive; brass on iron mt, 24" W bell+mt, 19" **1,125.00**
Bell, locomotive; CB&Q, NP brass, bell+mount, 24" **1,785.00**
Bell, locomotive; Sante Fe, w/cradle & welded-on stand, dtd 12-8-25...**2,200.00**
Blotter, Am Express Money Order, wht w/red & bl lettering, 3½x6"....**7.00**
Blotter, ATSF, Super Chief & SF cross logo, 3½x6" **10.00**
Blotter, CSS&SB RR, cheesecake-type, 1961 ....**37.00**
Blotter, GN, goat logo, 3½x6½" **12.00**
Blotter, UP, City of St Louis, Streamliner, 3½x6" **10.00**
Blotter, UP, Trains of Yesterday Today & Tomorrow, 4x9" **16.00**
Book, ACL Regulations, Relief Department, 1902 ....**5.00**
Book, N&W Ry - Pocahontas Coal Carrier, 1980, 8½x11" **115.00**
Book, operating rules; CN, gr cover, 1980, VG **4.00**
Book, Portrait of Silver Lady, CZ, MacGregor & Benson, 1977 .**167.00**
Book, rule; D&RG, Dining Car Department, 1948, 53-pg **25.00**
Book, safety rules; ATSF, gr cover, 1976, M....................................**4.00**
Book, UP, Rockies & Beyond, Strahorn, engravings, fold-out map, 1878..**165.00**
Book, UPRR Across Continent West From Omaha, 1868, 32-pg, 9x5¾", EX...**200.00**
Booklet, Burlington From Century of Progress...Expo..., 1933, 7x9"..**15.00**
Booklet, CMStP&P, Traveling on the Hiawatha, 1953, 18-pg **6.00**
Booklet, Florida Central & Peninsular, 1892, 47-pg **150.00**
Booklet, Gulf, CO&SF (w/TX Midland), Round Up of Facts, 1883 ..**225.00**
Booklet, Lehigh Valley, Land o' Lakes & Mtns, 1911, 6x9", 40-pg...**103.00**
Bookmark/calendar, SP, celluloid, Sunset logo+oranges, 1920, 5x1" **42.00**
Bottle, beer; PRR, Curve, brn short neck, EX label **17.50**
Brochure, ATSF, Welcome...El Capitan, lists meals, 1964, 4x8" ...**15.00**
Brochure, CB&Q, Frontier Shack, lists cars, 1936, 3x5" **17.00**
Brochure, Pullman, Economy & Dependability, many photos, 1935, 9x12"...**15.00**
Button, Boston, Lowell & Concord RR...................................**27.00**
Button, coat; New Haven, Waterbury, gold-tone **4.00**
Button, Delaware & Hudson, gold-tone dome, ⅝" **30.00**
Button, lapel; Star, Longevity Service, screw-on **5.00**
Button, Ottawa Electric Ry Co, silver-tone, ⅞" **13.00**
Button, Reading 'R Co,' silver-tone, N Snellenburg & Co, ⅞" **7.00**
Button, vest/sleeve; Milwaukee, gold-tone **3.00**
Button, vest/sleeve; Pullman, Scoville, gold-tone **3.00**
Calendar, C&O, Peake w/Army pack+pin-up, complete, 23x14"..**285.00**
Calendar, GN, Empire Builder, 1950, pocket-sz.........................**137.00**
Calendar, GNR, Tom Dawson pictured, 1950, 34", EX+ **70.00**
Calendar, MP, universal wall, month/day cards, 1940s/50s **66.00**
Calendar, NYC System, shows locomotive #4734, 1951, 28", EX.**55.00**
Calendar, Reading, 1932, pocket-sz **12.00**
Calendar & note pad, CMStP&P, 1932, 2½x5½" **26.00**
Calendar top, GN, Jim Blood, Glacier Nat'l Park, Reiss, 1932 .....**47.00**
Card, ATSF, Dining Car in Opposite Direction, bl on wht **17.00**
Card, CA Zephyr, Welcome To..., 3x5" **3.00**
Catalog, Shay Geared Locomotives, cb cover, 1921, 50-pg, 8x10¾" **61.00**
Catalog, Union Switch & Signal Co, hard cover, 1924, 400-pg, 6x9" .**202.00**
Chair, dining car; Santa Fe, wood, no arms, set of 4.................**300.00**
Check, CB&Q, lt letterhead, damage settlement, 1946 ....**10.00**
Cigar box, Fred Harvey, Niles & Moser, brn label, EX **75.00**
Cookbook, Dining Car Cookbook & Serving Instructions, UPRR, EX ..**35.00**

Cup, collapsible; Fred Harvey, shiny tin, w/lid, 2¼" 45.00
Dater die, PRR, New York 150.00
Dater die, Union Station, Toledo O 150.00
Fire extinguisher, B&O, brass, 24"......................................128.00
First-aid kit, wall mt, Southern Pacific emb on lid, metal, 9x6x3" ...129.00
Hanger, Pullman, wooden, logo 10.00
Hat band, RI Conductor, gold metal, w/2 hat buttons..................25.00
Jug, Rock Island Lines, stoneware, 1-gal sz.............................300.00
Letterhead, S Carolina & GA RR Co, insurance dispute, 1/4/1899 ..8.00
Letterhead, Wisconsin Central Lines, handwritten message, 5/8/1892....3.00
Magazine, C&O, July, 1942 ....15.00
Magazine, D&H, Bulletin, Nov 1930 ....15.00
Map, Fred Harvey, Servicemen's, mc pictures, 1943, 14x21".........17.50
Match holder to fit matchbook, PRR Keystone logo, brass 97.00
Match safe, Missouri-Kansas-Texas, logo shape, CI 165.00
Matchbook, CA Zephyr, silver w/blk lettering 5.00
Matchbook, Sante Fe, wht w/Chico..2.00
Matchbook, UP, Sun Valley Silver Anniversary, silver & red..........4.00
Medallion, Chicago RR Fair, gold color, 1949............................5.00
Medallion, inaugural; Am Orient Express, gold-tone, 2½", M in case ..20.00
Menu, B&A, Delegation to Columbian Expo, 1892, 5x5½".........49.00
Menu, Burlington Rte, breakfast, single card, 1969, 6½x10½".......7.50
Menu, C&O, snack, single card, bl, 5x9" 5.00
Menu, child's; UP, bear holding porridge bowl, 3x5" 10.00
Menu, D&H, Lake Champlain, blk/wht, map bk, 7x9" 7.00
Menu, Fred Harvey, Texas Chief, AT&SF Logo, 1942, 5½x9"......20.00
Menu, Fred Harvey, Western theme cover, 1947, 9½x6" 26.00
Menu, GN, Western Star, Indian Warfare cover by Russel, 1951, 7x10"..28.00
Menu, ICRR, Palm Grove Cafe, gray & gr, 1969, 12"...............12.00
Menu, New Haven, luncheon & dinner, 1932, 7¾x9"................36.00
Menu, Santa Fe by Fred Harvey, Indian child hunting, 1915, 4¾x6"..75.00
Menu, StL&SF, Thanksgiving, oyster shape, 1901, 4x4½"..........205.00
Menu card, NYC, Institute of Bankers, 1932, 7x9½" 16.00
Note pad, Santa Fe w/cb cover, unused, 5x2½"........................6.00
Paper clip, SMStP&P, spring-type, brass w/logo, early 1900s.........45.00
Paperweight, CGW, map+oak leaf under celluloid, 3" 125.00
Pass, annual; ATSF, curved blk lettering w/serifs, 1880 ....90.00
Pass, annual; ATSF RR & Leased Lines, Old English Lettering, 1879..90.00
Pass, annual; Milwaukee Rd, 1943-44 ....5.00
Pass, annual; Sante Fe, 1922 ....6.50
Pass, C&A, issued to Auditor of ORR&N Co, 1930 ....20.00
Pass, Copper Range RR, issued to President of MStP&SStM, 1930 ..24.00
Pass, Elkton & Guthrie RR, 1905 ....57.00
Pass, Louisville & Nashville, 1929 ....7.00
Pass, SP, 'not good on Sunset Ltd, 1896 ....25.00
Pencil, Fred Harvey Service in gold on bl, sharpened.....................3.00
Pencil, mechanical; Seaboard Air Line Ry logo+train on pearlized ..49.00
Pencil, Rock Island Lines in wht on gr, no eraser.......................1.50
Pencil, Santa Fe, bullet w/clip, 1930s 12.00
Photo, front view of Santa Fe #2907, 2¾x4"............................2.50
Photo, MP, locomotive & tender #5528 at Kansas City MO, 1934....15.00
Pin, lapel; UP in skeleton letters, screw bk, silver..........................4.00
Pin, Pacific Electric Ry, Balloon Route Trolley Trip, celluloid, 1"..38.00
Playing cards, AA RR, Souvenir of Inauguration, Carr Ferry '59 ..257.00
Playing cards, C&GW, 52 cards+case, 2¼" 7.00
Playing cards, Elgin, Joliet & Eastern, dbl-deck, 2¼" unopened case ..35.00
Playing cards, InterColonial Ry, scenics, case, 2½" 175.00
Playing cards, SAL RR, dbl-deck, 2¼" 95.00
Playing cards, WP&Y, 52+4 map, slipcase, 2½" 110.00
Pocketknife, Bessemer & Lake Erie Vet's Assoc, emb brass, 1929, 2¼" ...32.00
Pocketknife, Wabash logo, gold-tone scrolling, 2 blades+file, 3"..195.00
Poker chip, Santa Fe cross logo, bk: When the Chips Are..., plastic....3.50
Postcard, Argentine Central, Summit of Mt McClellan, unused.....2.50
Postcard, NYC, head-on engine collision, 1907...........................45.00

Poster, Steamboat Island in Hudson River, Fitchburg RR, 1887, 22x26" .150.00
Record, Rail Sounds, Steam & Diesel, 33½ rpm, in jacket 12.00
Schedule, Alaska Line, 1941..10.00
Schedule, CN, Chicago to Geneva, 1933, 4x7" 2.50
Sheet music, Freedrom Train, Irving Berlin, 1947 ....15.00
Sheet music, Pullman Porters Parade, marching cover, 1913 ....40.00
Sign, Amtrak, cb standup, Enjoy the Leaves..., 12x17"...............5.00
Sign, Amtrak, plastic standup, Tickets & Tours Sold Here, 11½x15"...15.00
Sign, Amtrak, shiny silver on heavy stock, standup, 44" L.............45.00
Sign, CP, The Canadian on plexiglass, 17x20" 245.00
Sign, MKT, porc emblem, 27", VG.......................................500.00
Sign, Trailways, rolled steel, red/wht w/sun logo, 24x48".............55.00
Spittoon, Frisco emb on top, 19 gauge aluminum, 6x8"..............85.00
Stationery, SF Super Chief in turq, pictures Turq Woman, 6x8½"..5.00
Step stool, D&RG (unmk) Conductor's, 9¾x9¼x9¼" 55.00
Step stool, ICRR, metal emb, Morton Mfg, 10x15x13½" 180.00
Swizzle stick, Fred Harvey in gold script, arrow shape, 5½" 10.00
Tag, baggage; Atlanta & West Point, Wilcox, brass......................40.00
Tape measure, Pacific Express Col, celluloid case, 6' tape, 1¾" dia..167.00
Telegraph key, NP on blk plastic base, EX..............................45.00
Telegraph resonator box w/sounder, CI base, pivoting arms 260.00
Ticket holder, Milwaukee Road, clear plastic, 2¾x3½" 3.00
Ticket punch, V on edge 20.00
Timetable, B&O, cap dome logo, blk/wht, 1922 ....15.00
Timetable, C&EI, yel & red, 1941, G....................................15.00
Timetable, employee; B&Me, Western Division, 1906 ....23.00
Timetable, employee; CN, 1994...2.50
Timetable, employee; RF&P, 1944, 48-pg..............................27.00
Timetable, GN, Empire Builder/Oriental Ltd, orange, 1948 ....17.50
Timetable, Nickel Plate, 1942, VG.......................................10.00
Timetable, PARR, 1965, G..10.00
Timetable, Portland Rose, w/western history, 1952, 3x5" 15.00
Timetable, public; D&RGW, 1946 ....13.00
Timetable, public; Gulf, Mobile & Ohio, 1944 ....38.00
Timetable, public; Louisville & Nashville, 1942, 39-pg................6.00
Timetable, public; Rome, Watertown & Ogdensburg, 8-panel, 1892 ..58.00
Timetable, public; West Jersey & Seashore RR, 1899.................90.00
Timetable, system; GN, color cover, 1966...............................12.00
Timetable, UP, gr tone w/lg Overland logo, 1893 calendar pg.......50.00
Timetable/brochure, PA Short Lines, 1897 ....50.00
Tool check, P&R, brass, emb logo & #, 1x1½" 12.00
Tool check, Reading, brass, Time Check 1832...Car Shop, 1½" dia..15.00
Tool check, UPRR Shop...Do Not Remove, 1⅛x1½" 10.00
Voucher, commission Wells Fargo, 1902, 7x9" 10.00
Wax sealer, CMStP&P, Agent, Exira IA, brass head, trn wood hdl...350.00
Wax sealer, LSMSRY, Agent, Irving NY, brass head, trn wood hdl...375.00
Whistle, steam; ICRR, 5-chime, step-up, brass, 23" 2,650.00

Razors

As straight razors gain in popularity, prices of those razors also increase. This carries with it a lure of investment possibilities which can encourage the novice or speculator to make purchases that may later prove to be unwise. We recommend that before investing serious money in razors, you become familiar with the elements which make a razor valuable. As with other collectibles, there are specific traits which are desirable and which have a major impact on the price of a piece.

The following information is based on the second edition of *The Standard Guide to Razors* by Roy Ritchie and Ron Stewart (available from R&C Books, P.O. Box 151, Combs, KY 41729, $9.95 +$2.50 S&H, autographed). It describes the elements most likely to influence a razor's collector value and their system of calculating that value. (Their book is a valuable reference guide to both the casual and serious collector of razors.)

There are four major factors which determine a razor's collector value. These are the brand and country of origin, the handle material, the art work found on the handles or blades, and the condition of the razor. Ritchie and Stewart freely admit that there are other factors that may come into play with some collectors, but these are the major players in determining value. They have devised a system of evaluation which is based on these four factors.

The most important factor is the value placed on the brand and country of origin. This is the price of a common razor made by (or for) a particular company. It has plain handles, probably made of plastic, no art work, and is in collectible condition. It is the beginning value. Hundreds (thousands?) of these values are provided in the 'Listings of Companies and Base Values' chapter in the book.

The second category is that of handle material. This covers a wide range of materials, from fiber on the low end to ivory on the high end. The collector needs to be able to identify the different handle materials when he sees them. This often takes some practice, since there are some very good plastics that can mimic ivory quite successfully. Also, the difference between genuine celluloid and plastic can become significant when determining value. A detailed chart of these values is supplied in the book. The listing below can be used as a general guide.

The third category is the most subjective. Nevertheless, it is an extremely important factor in determining value. This category is artwork, which can include everything from logo art to carving and sculpture. It may range from highly ornate to tastefully correct. Blade etching as well as handle artistry are to be considered. Perhaps what some call the 'gotta have it' or the 'neatness' factors properly fall into this category. You must accurately determine the artistic merits of your razor when you evaluate it relative to this factor. Again, the book we referenced earlier provides a more complete listing of considerations than is used here.

Finally, the condition is factored in. The book's scales run from 'parts' (10% +/-) to 'Good' (150% +/-). Average (100% +/-) is classified as 'Collectible.' See chart D for details concerning condition guidelines for evaluation.

Samplings from charts:

Chart A: Companies and Base Values:

Abercrombie & Finch, NY	14.00
Aerial, USA	24.00
Boker, Henri & Co, Germany	14.00
Brick, F, England	10.00
Chase Mfg Co, Spring Valley, NY	40.00
Chores, James	9.00
Dahlgren, CW; Sweden	14.00
Diane, Japan	10.00
Electric Co, NY	15.00
ERN, Germany	12.00
Fautless, Germany	11.00
Fox Cutlery, Germany	11.00
Griffon XX, GErmany	11.00
Henckels, Germany	15.00
Holly Mfg Co, CT	27.00
International Cutlery Co NY/Germany	11.00
IXL, Germany	12.00
Jay, John; NY	12.00
KaBar, Union Cut Co, USA	28.00
Kanner, J; Germany	11.00
Kern, R&W; Canada/England	12.00
LeCocltre, Jacque; Switzerland	12.00
Levering Razor Co, NY/Germany	18.00
McIntosh & Heather, OH	12.00
Merit Import Co, Germany	10.00
National Cut Co, OH	11.00

Oxford Razor Co, Germany	10.00
Palmer Brothers, Savannah, GA	20.00
Primble, John; Indian Steel Works, Louisville, KY	24.00
Queen City, NY	30.00
Quigley, Germany	12.00
Rattler Razor Co	10.00
Robeson Cut Co, USA	28.00
Salamander Works, Germany	11.00
Soderein, Ekilstuna, Sweden	11.00
Taylor, LM; Cincinnati OH	14.00
Tower Brand, Germany	16.00
Ulmer, Germany	11.00
US Barber Supply, TX	12.00
Vinnegut Hdw Co, IN	11.00
Vogel, Ed; PA	10.00
Wade & Butcher, England	24.00
Weis, JH; Supply House, Louisville, KY	15.00
Yankee Cutlery Co, Germany	11.00
Yazbek, Lahod, OH	11.00
Zacour Bros, Germany	10.00
Zepp Germany	10.00

Chart B, as described below, is an abbreviated version of the handle materials list in *The Standard Guide to Razors*. It is an essential category in the use of the appraisal system developed by the authors.

Ivory	550%
Tortoise Shell	500%
Pearl	400%
Stag	400%
Bone	300%
Celluloid	250%
Composition	150%
Plastic	100%

Chart C deals with the artistic value of the razor. As pointed out earlier, this is a very subjective area. It takes study to determine what is good and what is not. Taste can also play a significant role in determining the value placed on the artistic merit of a razor. The range is from superior to nonexistent. Categories generally are divided as follows:

Exceptional	650%
Superior	550%
Good	400%
Average	300%
Minimal	200%
Plain	100%
Nonexistant	0%

Chart D is also very subjective. It determines the condition of the razor. You must judge accurately if the appraisal system is to work for you.

Good	150%

Does not have to be factory mint to fall within this category. However, there can be no visible flaws if it is to be calculated at 150%.

Collectible	100%

May have some flaws that do not greatly detract from the artwork or finish.

Parts	10%

Unrepairable, valuable as salvageable parts.

Razors may fall within any of these categories, ie. collectible + 112%. Now to determine the value of your razor, multiply A times B, then multiply A times C. Add your two answers and multiply this sum times D. The answer you get is your collector value. See the example below.

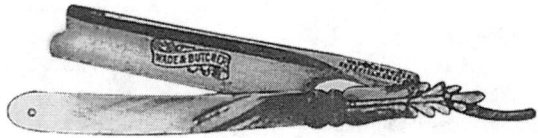

(a) Brand and Origin Base Value	(b) Handle Material % Value	(c) Artwork % Value	(d) Condition % Value	(e) Collector Value
Wade & Butcher England $24.00	Iridescent Pearl Handles 24 x 400% $96.00	Carved handles 24 x 500% $120.00	Cracked handle at pin Collectible- 80%	$96+$120=$216 $216 x 80%= $172.80

Reamers

The reamer market is very active right now, and prices are escalating rapidly. They have been made in hundreds of styles and colors and by as many manufacturers. Their purpose is to extract the juices from lemons, oranges, and grapefruits. The largest producer of glass reamers was McKee, who pressed their products from many types of glass — custard; Delphite and Chalaine Blue; opaque white; Skokie Green; black; caramel and white opalescent; Seville Yellow; and transparent pink, green, and clear. Among these, the black and the caramel opalescents are the most valuable.

The Fry Glass Company also made reamers that are today very collectible. The Hazel Atlas Crisscross orange reamer in pink is valued at $300.00 to $325.00 or more — the same in blue, $350.00. Hocking produced a light blue orange reamer and, in the same soft hue, a two-piece reamer and measuring cup combination. Both are considered rare and very valuable with currently quoted estimates at $1,000.00 and up for the former and $1,800.00 and up for the latter. In addition to the colors mentioned, red glass examples — transparent or slag — are rare and costly. Prices vary greatly according to color and rarity. The same reamer in crystal may be worth three times as much in a more desirable color.

Among the most valuable ceramic reamers are those made by American potteries. The Spongeband reamer by Red Wing is valued in excess of $500.00; Coorsite reamers with gold or silver trim are worth $300.00 and up. Figurals are popular — Mickey Mouse and John Bull may bring $600.00 to $1,000.00. Others range from $55.00 to $350.00. Fine china one- and two-piece reamers are also very desirable and command very respectable prices.

A word about reproductions: A series of limited edition reamers is being made by Edna Barnes of Uniontown, Ohio. These are all marked with a 'B' in a circle. Other reproductions have been made from old molds. The most important of these are Anchor Hocking two-piece two-cup measure and top, Gillespie one-cup measure with reamer top, Westmoreland with flattened handle, Westmoreland four-cup measure embossed with orange and lemons, Duboe (hand-held darning egg), and Easley's Diamonds one-piece.

Our advisor for this category is Dee Long; she is listed in the Directory under Illinois. For more information concerning reamers and reproductions, contact our advisor or the National Reamer Collectors Association (see Clubs, Newsletters, and Catalogs). Be sure to include an SASE when requesting information.

Ceramic

Baby's, chicks jumping rope, pk **150.00**

Baby's Orange, red & wht, Japan, 2-pc, 4½" 55.00
Clown, bl/yel/orange, Goebel saucer, 4½" 225.00
Clown, lime gr & wht, 4¾" 95.00
Clown, Sourpuss, w/saucer, 4¾" 135.00
Clown, 3-color on wht, Japan, 7½" 80.00
Clown Face Mug 80.00
Clown figural, mc, Japan, 6½" 95.00
Dog figural, beige w/red & blk trim, 2-pc, 8" 225.00
Duck, sm 95.00
Floral w/gold, Nippon, 2-pc 195.00
Girl face 135.00
House, beige w/tan & orange trim, Japan, 2-pc, 5½" 100.00
Mexican w/cactus figural, mc, Japan 200.00
Pail w/hdl form, tan & yel, Japan, 7¾" 70.00
Pear, yel & orange w/gr leaves, Japan, 4½" 60.00
Pitcher form, rust leaves, dk bl trim, 3½" 45.00
Puddinhead, 6" 175.00
Rose, pk w/gr leaves, Germany, 1¾" 225.00
Rose buds on gr, Japan, 2-pc 60.00
Sailboat form, yel or red, 3", ea 125.00
Saucer form, cream w/yel bees, Japan, 3¾" 45.00
Swan, 4" 125.00
Teapot, wht w/bl sailboat, Germany, 2-pc, 3¼" 80.00
Windmill form, Japan, 4½" 75.00

Glass

Anchor Hocking, gr, w/pitcher, 4-cup 40.00
Cambridge, amber, from $600 to 700.00
Cambridge, cobalt, from $2,500 to 2,750.00
Federal, gr, pointed cone, from $25 to 28.00
Federal, gr, seed dam, ribbed, tab hdl, from $25 to 28.00
Federal, pk, from $90 to 100.00
Federal, pk, ribbed, loop hdl, from $35 to 40.00
Fenton, Ming, gr, from $600 to 750.00
Fenton, red, w/pitcher, from $1,200 to 1,300.00
Foreign, dk amber, lemon sz, from $110 to 125.00
Fry, canary, fluted, from $325 to 350.00
Fry, emerald gr, fluted, from $500 to 550.00
Fry, lt gr, str side, from $25 to 28.00
Fry, pearl opal, str side, from $30 to 45.00
Hazel Atlas, cobalt, tab hdl, orange, from $275 to 295.00
Hazel Atlas, cobalt, tabl hdl, lemon, from $300 to 325.00
Hazel Atlas, gr, 2-pc, ftd, mk A&J, 4-cup 45.00
Hazel Atlas, yel, w/pitcher, 2-cup 375.00
Hazel Atlas, yel, 2-cup, w/pitcher, from $325 to 350.00
Indiana Glass, amber, spout opposite hdl, from $300 to 325.00
Indiana Glass, amber, 6-sided cone, vertical hdl 350.00
Indiana Glass, dk amber, from $300 to 325.00
Indiana Glass, pk, spout opposite hdl 95.00
Jeannette, Delphite Blue, lg, from $1,000 to 1,250.00
Jeannette, Delphite Blue, sm, from $85 to 95.00
Jeannette, gr, lg, from $22 to 25.00
LE Smith, pk, baby, from $200 to 250.00
Saunders, blk, from $1,250 to 1,400.00
Saunders, Skokie Green, from $1,250 to 1,450.00
Sunkist, blk, from $500 to 650.00
Sunkist, caramel, from $350 to 385.00
Tricia, blk, from $1,400 to 1,500.00
Tricia, pk, from $800 to 850.00
Unmk, Coke-bottle gr, w/pitcher, from $20 to 25.00
Unmk, frosted crystal, Baby's Orange, 2-pc, from $50 to 65.00
Unmk, gr, tab hdl, from $22 to 25.00
Unmk, red, tab hdl, from $12 to 15.00

US Glass, yel, w/pitcher, from $650 to	750.00
Valencia, dk amber, unemb, from $250 to	300.00
Westmoreland, amber, 2-pc, baby	225.00
Westmoreland, dk amber, 2-pc, from $175 to	200.00
Westmoreland, pk, 2-pc, baby	195.00
Westmoreland, pk frost, 2-pc, baby	130.00

Records

Records of interest to collectors are often not the million-selling hits by superstars. Very few records by Bing Crosby, for example, are of any more than nominal value, and those that are valuable usually don't even have his name on the label! Collectors today are most interested in records that were made in limited quantities, early works of a performer who later became famous, and those issued in special series or aimed at a limited market. Vintage records are judged desirable by their recorded content as well; those that lack the quality of music that makes a record collectible will always be 'junk' records in spite of their age, scarcity, or the obsolescence of their technology.

Records are usually graded visually rather than aurally, since it is seldom if ever possible to first play the records you buy at shows, by mail, at flea markets, etc. Condition is one of the most important determinants of value. For example, a nearly mint-condition Elvis Presley 45 of 'Milk Cow Blues' (Sun 215) has a potential value of over $1,500.00. A small sticker on the label could cut its value in half; noticeable wear could reduce its value by 80%. A mint record must show no evidence of use (record jackets, in the case of EPs and LPs, must be equally choice). Excellent condition denotes a record showing only slight signs of use with no audible defects. A very good record has noticeable wear but still plays well. Records of lesser grades may be unsaleable, unless very scarce and/or highly sought-after.

While the value of most 78s does not depend upon their being in appropriate sleeves (although a sleeveless existence certainly contributes to damage and deterioration!), this is not the case with most EPs (extended play 45s) and LPs (long-playing 33⅓ rpm albums), which *must* have their jackets (cardboard sleeves), in nice condition, free of disfiguring damage, such as writing, stickers or tape. Often, common and minimally valued 45s might be collectible if they are in appropriate 'picture sleeves' (special sleeves that depict the artist/group or other fanciful or symbolic graphic and identify the song titles, record label, and number), e.g. many common records by Elvis Presley, The Beatles, and The Beach Boys.

Promotional copies (DJ copies) supplied to radio stations often have labels different in designs and/or colors from their commercially issued counterparts. Labels usually bear a designation 'Not for Sale,' 'Audition Copy,' 'Sample Copy,' or the like. Records may be pressed of translucent vinyl; while most promos are not particularly collectible, those by certain 'hot' artists, such as Elvis Presley, The Beach Boys, and The Beatles are usually premium disks.

Many of the most desirable and valuable 45s have been 'bootlegged' (counterfeited). For example, there are probably more fake Elvis Presley *Sun* records in circulation than authentic copies — certainly in higher grades! Collectors should be alert for these often deceptive counterfeits.

Our advisor for this category is L.R. Docks, author of *American Premium Record Guide*, which lists 60,000 records by over 7,000 artists, soon to be in its sixth edition. He is listed in the Directory under Texas. In the listings that follow, prices are suggested for records that are in excellent condition; worn or abused records may be worth only a small fraction of the values quoted, and may not be saleable at all.

Blues, Rhythm and Blues, Rock 'n Roll, Rockabilly

Alabama Slim, Boar Hog Blues, Savoy 5553, 78 rpm	25.00
Anderson, Jimmie; Ko Ko Mo Blues, Broadway 5111, 78 rpm	400.00
Arkansas Shorty, Greyhound Bus, Bluebird 6545, 78 rpm	30.00
Arnold, Eddie; All-Time Favorites, RCA Victor 1223, LP	20.00
Atkins, Chet; Session, RCA Victor 1090, LP	30.00
Baker, Laverne; Sings Bessie Smith, Atlantic 1281, LP	40.00
Baxter, Helen; Scrubbin' Blues, Domino 3929, 78 rpm	30.00
Beatles, Ain't She Sweet, Atco 169, LP (stereo)	75.00
Bell, Ed; She's a Fool Gal, Columbia 14595, 78 rpm	125.00
Berry, Chuck; After School Session, Chess 1426 (blk/silver label), LP	50.00
Blind Joe Amos, C&O Blues, Vocalion 1116, 78 rpm	200.00
Bonds, Gary US; Dance 'Til Quarter to Three, Legrand 3001, LP	40.00
Boone, Pat; Pat, Dot 3050, LP	15.00
Cadets, Rockin' n' Rollin', Crown 5015, LP	50.00
Cameos, Lost Lover, Dean 504, 45 rpm	20.00
Campbell, Gene; Wandering Blues, Brunswick 7170, 78 rpm	120.00
Cardinals, She Rocks, Atlantic 972, 45 rpm	100.00
Catalinas, Speechless, Back Beat 513, 45 rpm	30.00
Classics, Blue Moon, Promo 1010, 45 rpm	10.00
Clayton, Peter J; Yo Yo Blues, Bluebird 6096, 78 rpm	40.00
Cline, Patsy; Walking After Midnight, Everlast 2020, 45 rpm	10.00
Coasters, Yakey Yak, Atco 6116, 78 rpm	30.00
Cooke, Sam; You Send Me, Keen 44013, 78 rpm	20.00
Country Jim, Old River Blues, Imperial 5073, 78 rpm	20.00
Darby, Teddy; My Laona Blues, Paramount 12828, 78 rpm	300.00
Darin, Bobby (& the Jaybirds); Bobby Darin, Atco 102, LP	20.00
Davis, Walter; Blue Sea Blues, Bluebird 5031, 78 rpm	80.00
Dickson, Tom; Worry Blues, Okeh 8570, 78 rpm	150.00
Dirty Red, Home Last Night, Aladdin 194, 78 rpm	15.00
Dixon, Mary; Black Dog Blues, Columbia 14459-D, 78 rpm	60.00
Drifters, Save the Last Dance for Me, Atlantic 8059, LP	30.00
Earls, Remember Me Baby, Old Town 104, LP	100.00
Edwards, Frank; Terraplane Blues, Okeh 06393, 78 rpm	15.00
Erby, Jack; Hot Peter, Columbia 14570, 78 rpm	50.00
Ervin, Leroy; Rock Island Blues, Gold Star 628, 78 rpm	20.00
Escorts, Sorry, Premium 407, 45 rpm	30.00
Fabres, Shelley; Things We Did Last Summer, Colpix 431, LP	30.00
Falcons, This Heart of Mine, Anna 1110, 45 rpm	20.00
Fender, Freddy; Wasted Days & Wasted Nights, Duncan 1001, 45 rpm	15.00
Five Satins, The Five Satins Sing, Ember 101, LP	200.00
Flamingos, Cross Over the Bridge, Chance 1154, 45 rpm	300.00
Fletcher, Napoleon; She Showed It All, Bluebird 5383, 78 rpm	150.00
Four Harmony Kings, Ain't It a Shame, Black Swan 2016, 78 rpm	20.00
Fuller, Bobby; I Fought the Law, Exeter 124, 45 rpm	15.00
Garland, Hattie; Strange Woman's Dreams, Black Patti 8005, 78 rpm	300.00
Garner, Cora; Wouldn't Stop Doing It, Columbia 14650-D, 78 rpm	100.00
Goldentones, Ocean of Tears, Hush 102, 45 rpm	15.00
Green, LC; Little Machine, Dot 1147, 78 rpm	20.00
Griffin, Tommy; Dream Book Blues, Bluebird 6756, 78 rpm	35.00
Hardin, Lane; Hard Time Blues, Bluebird 6242, 78 rpm	100.00
Harptones, Forever Mine, Bruce 109, 45 rpm	20.00
Henderson, Leroy; Good Scuffer Blues, Vocalion 02979, 78 rpm	50.00
Henry, Lena; Sinful Blues, Vocalion 14902, 78 rpm	30.00
Hicks, Edna; Just Thinkin; Ajax 17006, 78 rpm	50.00
Hill, Robert; Just Smilin', Bluebird 6680, 78 rpm	30.00
Holley, Rosa; Lookin' for the Blues, Vocalion 1179, 78 rpm	175.00
Holly, Buddy; Buddy Holly, Coral 57210 (maroon label), LP	75.00
Howard, John Henry; Black Snake, Gennett 3117, 78 rpm	40.00
Hudson, Hattie; Black Hand Blues, Columbia 14279-D, 78 rpm	100.00
Hunter & Jenkins, Meat Cuttin' Blues, Vocalion 02613, 78 rpm	20.00
Inspirations, Raindrops, Apollo 494, 45 rpm	30.00
Ivories, Alone, Jaguar 3019, 45 rpm	40.00
Jackson, Jim; My Monday Woman Blues, Victor 21236, 78 rpm	75.00
James, Jesse; Southern Casey Jones, Decca 7213, 78 rpm	30.00
James, Tommy & the Shondells; Hanky Panky, Snap 102, 45 rpm	20.00

Jan & Dean, Jan & Dean, Dore 101, LP 100.00
Jayhawks, Counting My Teardrops, Flash 105, 45 rpm 50.00
Joey & the Lexingtons, Bobbie, Dunes 2029, 45 rpm 15.00
Johnson, Babe; Worried 'Bout Him Blues, Silvertone 3562, 78 rpm...125.00
Johnson, Tommy; Canned Heat Blues, V38535, 78 rpm..........1,500.00
Jones, George; Salutes Hank Williams, Mercury 20596, LP 30.00
Jones, Grandpa; Strictly Country Tunes, King 625, LP.................20.00
Kalin Twins, The Kalin Twins, Decca 8812, LP 30.00
Keghouse, Keghouse Blues, Okeh 8583, 78 rpm..........................75.00
Kid Coley, Freight Train Blues, Victor 23369, 78 rpm...............500.00
Kinks, You Still Want Me, Cameo 348, 45 rpm............................100.00
Kodaks, Teenagers Dream, Fury 1007, 45 rpm..............................20.00
Laddins, Now You're Gone, Central 2602, 45 rpm 15.00
Lee, John; Rhythm Rockin' Boogie, JOB 114, 78 rpm 20.00
Liston, Virginia; House Rent Stomp, Okeh 8134, 78 rpm 40.00
Little David, Standing by a Lamppost, Decca 7211, 78 rpm.........25.00
Little Sister, My Back to the Wall, Varsity 6050, 78 rpm 20.00
Love Notes, Surrender Your Heart, Imperial 5254, 45 rpm 150.00
Lynn, Loretta; The Darkest Day, Zero 112, 45 rpm....................50.00
Mack, Bill; Play My Boogie, Imperial 8177, 45 rpm 30.00
Mary & Mack, Black, Bluebird 7908, 78 rpm...............................40.00
McClennan, Tommy; My Little Girl, Bluebird 8605, 78 rpm........15.00
McCoy, William; How Long Baby, Columbia 14393-D, 78 rpm ...75.00
Mellows, You're Gone, Candlelight 1011, 45 rpm 12.00
Midnight Ramblers, Down in the Alley, Vocalion 03517, 78 rpm...30.00
Miller, Carl; Rhythm Guitar, Lu 503, 45 rpm 40.00
Mississippi Mudder, Chanty Blues, Decca 7046, 78 rpm.............50.00
Moroccos, Pardon My Tears, United 188, 45 rpm......................100.00
Mullican, Moon; 16 Favorite Tunes, King 628, LP 30.00
Nelson, Willie; Night Life, Bellair 107 (red plastic), 45 rpm 20.00
Neons, Road to Romance, Tetra 4449, 45 rpm.............................15.00
Nichols, Nick; Frankie & Johnny, Columbia 2071-D, 78 rpm 50.00
Nutmegs, Key to the Kingdom, Herald 475, 45 rpm....................20.00
Old South Quartette, Watermelon Party, Broadway 7029, 78 rpm..125.00
Orbison, Roy; Crying, Monument 4007, LP 30.00
Orioles, Dare To Dream, Jubilee 5001, 78 rpm...........................15.00
Orlandos, Cloudburst, Cindy 3006, 45 rpm..................................40.00
Petway, Robert; My Little Girl, Bluebird 8786, 78 rpm 15.00
Pigmeat Terry, Black Sheep Blues, Champion 50043, 78 rpm.......40.00
Pinetop Slim, Applejack Boogie, Colonial 106, 78 rpm...............75.00
Playboys, Good Golly Miss Molly, Cat 115, 45 rpm 15.00
Presley, Elvis; King Creole, RCA Victor 1884, LP 50.00
Price, Lloyd; Stagger Lee, ABC Paramount 9972, 78 rpm............30.00
Quinns, Oh Starlight, Cyclone 111, 45 rpm 15.00
Ravens, Time Takes Care of Everything, Columbia 6-903, 45 rpm..100.00

Reb's Legion Club 45's, Steppin' High, Hollywood Record, $300.00.
(Photo courtesy Les Docks)

Red Devil, Huntsman Blues, Vocalion 03954, 78 rpm....................20.00
Rhodes, Walter; The Crowing Rooster, Columbia 14289-D, 78 rpm ...100.00
Ridley, Ethel; Get It Fixed, Ajax 17126, 78 rpm...........................50.00
Rivingtons, Doin' the Bird, Liberty 3282, LP................................40.00
Robinson & Mack, Booze, Okeh 8321, 78 rpm.............................75.00
Royals, Every Beat of My Heart, Federal 12064, 45 rom 200.00
Sam the Sham & the Pharoahs, Wooly Bully, XL 906, 45 rpm.....20.00

Sedaka, Neil; Ring-A-Rockin', Legion 133, 45 rpm 20.00
Sensations, Let Me In, Argo 4022, LP...30.00
Smith, Annie; Moonshine Blues, Harmograph 896, 78 rpm 120.00
Smith, Bessie; Baby Doll, Columbia 14147-D, 78 rpm 50.00
Smith, Susie; House Rent Blues, Ajax 17064, 78 rpm.................50.00
Strauss, Johnnie; Old Market Street Blues, Decca 7035, 78 rpm...50.00
Swan & Lee, Fishy Little Thing, Okeh 8732, 78 rpm...................75.00
Sylvester, Hannah; Midnight Blues, Emerson 10625, 78 rpm.......30.00
Tampa Kid, Keep On Trying, Decca 7278, 78 rpm......................30.00
Tate, Rose; Wild Woman Blue, Champion 15319, 78 rpm..........175.00
Teardrops, The Stars Are Out Tonight, Josie 766, 45 rpm...........75.00
Temptations, Dream Come True, Gordy 7001, 45 rpm 15.00
Terry, Don; Knees Shakin', Lin 5018, 45 rpm 40.00
Thomas, BJ; So Lonesome I Could Cry, Pacemaker 3001, LP.......50.00
Thomas, Washington; Time Enough, Champion 15489, 78 rpm...100.00
Thrillers, Lizabeth, Herald 432, 45 rpm.......................................75.00
Two Boys From Savannah, Messed Up Blues, Supertone 9529, 78 rpm...150.00
Tyus & Tyus, Dad's Ole Mule, Columbia 14638-D, 78 rpm.........150.00
Umbrian Glee Club, Rain Song, Vocalion 1013, 78 rpm.............30.00
Uniques, Tell the Angels, End 1012, 45 rpm 20.00
Vant, Louis; Do Right Blues, Okeh 8293, 78 rpm......................100.00
Velvetones, The Glory of Love, Aladdin 3372, 45 rpm.................50.00
Virgial, Otto; Bad Notion Blues, Bluebird 6213, 78 rpm.............25.00
Walker, Monroe; High Powered Mama, Columbia 14549-D, 78 rpm..60.00
Wallace, Minnie; Dirty Butter, Bluebird 5144, 78 rpm...............150.00
Wanderers, We Could Find Happiness, Savoy 1109, 45 rpm.........75.00
Washington, Booker T; Just Want To Think, Bluebird 8352, 78 rpm..20.00
Waters, Muddy; Little Anna Mae, Aristocrat 1302, 78 rpm..........50.00
Whitman, Slim; Bandera Waltz, Imperial 8144, 45 rpm 15.00
Willis, Mac; Pretty Woman, Elko 254, 78 rpm.............................20.00
Wooley, Sheb; The Purple People Eater, MGM 1607, EP 20.00
Yas Yas Girl, He May Be Your Man, Vocalion 04013, 78 rpm.......12.00
Young, Johnny; Woman Man Blues, Ora Nelle 712, 78 rpm.........20.00
Young, Nelson; Rock Old Sputnick, Lucky 0002, 45 rpm 40.00
Zebulons, Falling Water, Cub 9069, 45 rpm 20.00

Country and Western

Alabama Four, Looking This Way, Broadway 8209, 45 rpm..........25.00
Appalachian Vagabond, Peddler & His Wife, Vocalion 5450, 78 rpm...30.00
Arkansas Woodchopper, Little Green Valley, Gennett 7264, 78 rpm.....30.00
Baxter, Johnny; I Want My Rib, Superior 2811, 78 rpm...............30.00
Blue Boys, Memphis Stomp, Okeh 45314, 78 rpm.......................100.00
Boone, Jimmy; Crazy Blues, Superior 2638, 78 rpm....................50.00
Branch, Ernest; Lulu Love, Champion 16286, 78 rpm..................50.00
Buckeye Boys, Duck Foot Sue, Champion 16168, 78 rpm.............10.00
Carter Family, My Clinch Mountain Home, Bluebird 5301, 78 rpm..12.00
Dixie String Band, Atlanta Special, Paramount 3164, 78 rpm......75.00
Dodds, Johnny; The Railroad Boomer, Okeh 45417, 78 rpm........100.00
Ford & Grace, Kiss Me Cindy, Okeh 45157, 78 rpm 15.00
Fruit Jar Guzzlers, Old Joe Clark, Paramount 3148, 78 rpm 50.00
Georgia Pot Lickers, Up Jumped the Rabbit, Brunswick 595, 78 rpm...20.00
Harper & Hall, Life's Railway to Heaven, Superior 2799, 78 rpm ...20.00
Highlanders, Flop-Eared Mule, Paramount 3171, 78 rpm............50.00
Isabell, Wally & Tex; Sugar Cain Gal, Eddie's 1219, 78 rpm........12.00
Jennings, Waylon; Jole Bond, Brunswick 55130, 45 rpm...............75.00
Jones, Carl; My Tennessee Girl, Okeh 45540, 78 rpm..................30.00
Jones, Dempsey; Jack & May, Champion 16416, 78 rpm..............20.00
Justice, Dick; Henry Lee, Brunswick 367, 78 rpm 20.00
Kentucky Ramblers, Some Mother's Boy, Paramount 3300, 78 rpm...60.00
Kincaid, Bradley; The Little Mohee, Bluebird 6856, 78 rpm........20.00
Leake County Revelers, Johnson Gal, Columbia 15149-D, 78 rpm ...20.00
Major, Jack; Tennessee Mountain Girl, Brunswick 252, 78 rpm....20.00
Morrison Brothers Band, Dry & Dusty, Victor V40323, 78 rpm....50.00

Newman, Fred; San Antonio, Paramount 3177, 78 rpm...............15.00
Norris, Land; Groundhog, Okeh 40096, 78 rpm 20.00
Oakdale, Slim; No Hard Times, Crown 3461, 78 rpm 15.00
Parker, Dan & Bill; Fifty Years Repentin', Crown 3266, 78 rpm ...15.00
Perry County Music Makers, Vocalion 5425, 78 rpm.................30.00
Quadrillers, Drunk Man Blues, Paramount 3008, 78 rpm............20.00
Ray Brothers, Winona Rag, Victor 23713, 78 rpm..................100.00
Ritter, Tex; Down the Colorado Trail, Decca 5389, 78 rpm........10.00
Rogers, Roy; Hi-Yo Silver, Vocalion 04091, 78 rpm 12.00
Sons of the Pioneers, Cajon Stomp, Vocalion 04264, 78 rpm.......10.00
Stanton's Joy Boys, Huskin' Bee, Superior, 2671, 78 rpm 50.00
Steve's Hot Shots, Sour Apple Cider, Victor 23699, 78 rpm.........50.00
Texas Night Hawks, Possum Rag, Okeh 45363, 78 rpm 80.00
Turner, Cal; Only a Tramp, Champion 1558, 78 rpm 18.00
Uncle Bud & His Plowboys, Five Cent Cotton, Oriole 8170, 78 rpm...8.00
Vest, Billy; Billy's Blue Yodel, Columbia 15692, 78 rpm............15.00
Virginia Dandies, God's Getting Worried, Crown 3145, 78 rpm....20.00
Walker, Dave; Someone Owns a Cottage, Superior 2688, 78 rpm...30.00
Walker Family, Shaker Ben, Champion 16653, 78 rpm...............100.00
West Virginia Rail Splitter, The Habit, Champion 15990, 78 rpm...15.00
Yates, Ira & Eugene; Sarah Jane, Columbia 15581, 78 rpm...........50.00
Yellow Jackets, Medley, Gennett 7262, 78 rpm......................15.00
Zach & Glenn, Love's Old Sweet Song, Okeh 45240, 78 rpm 8.00

Jazz, Dance Bands, Personalities

Alabama Serenaders, Alabama Stomp, Champion 15140, 78 rpm ..30.00
Albert, Don & Orch; The Sheik of Araby, Vocalion 3411, 78 rpm ...15.00
All Star Californians, Cheerful Little Earful, Melotone 12000, 78 rpm...25.00
Andrews Sisters, Just a Simple Melody, Decca 1496, 78 rpm 12.00
Armstrong, Louis; Sweet Little Papa, Okeh 8379, 78 rpm 90.00
Astaire, Fred; Cheek to Cheek, Brunswick 7486, 78 rpm 10.00
Benny Benson's Orch; 'Taint No Sin, Champion 15886, 78 rpm..30.00
Boots & His Buddies, Georgia, Bluebird 6301, 78 rpm 12.00
Broadway Rastus, Rock My Soul, Paramount 12764, 78 rpm......150.00
Bucktown Five, Mobile Blues, Gennett 5405, 78 rpm.................150.00
Calloway, Cab & Orch; Scat Song, Brunswick 6272, 78 rpm........12.00
Campus Cut-Ups, Farewell Blues, Edison 11049, 78 rpm 50.00
Casa Loma Orch, White Jazz, Brunswick 6092, 78 rpm..............10.00
Coleman, EL; Steel String Blues, Okeh 8216, 78 rpm 75.00
Crosby, Bing; Sweet Georgia Brown, Brunswick 6320, 78 rpm 12.00
Dale, Flora; Jail House Blues, Domino 360, 78 rpm 30.00
Davis, Genevieve; I've Got Something, Victor, 20648, 78 rpm...100.00
Dixie Jazz Band, Icky Blues, Jewel 5547, 78 rpm 12.00
Ellington, Duke; Li'l Farina, Champion 15120, 78 rpm.................75.00
Finnie, Ethel; Hula Blues, Ajax 17027, 78 rpm........................30.00
Georgia Jumpers, California Blues, Columbia 14603-D, 78 rpm .125.00
Hall's Jazz Band, Look Who's Here!, Okeh 40410, 78 rpm 20.00
Holiday, Billie & Her Orch; Billie's Blues, Vocalion 3288, 78 rpm...12.00
Hollywood Shufflers, Low Down Rhythm, Vocalion 15837, 78 rpm ..150.00
Irvin, Kitty; Copenhagen, Gennett 5592, 78 rpm....................120.00
James, Jeanette; What's That Thing?, Paramount 12451, 78 rpm..200.00
Jazz Masters, Bees Knees, Black Swan 2109, 78 rpm 20.00
Jolson, Al; Pullman Porter's Parade, Columbia A-1374, 78 rpm ...40.00
Kansas City Frank, Jelly Roll Stomp, Brunswick 7062, 78 rpm....150.00
Kirby's Kings of Blues, Green River Blues, Bell 591, 78 rpm 30.00
Leroy's Dallas Band, Tampa Shout, Columbia 14402-D, 78 rpm.150.00
Marlow, Earl & His Orch; This Love, Parlophone PNY-34105, 78 rpm...25.00
Michigan Melody Makers, Indian Love Call, Pennington 1453, 78 rpm..30.00
Mills Musical Clowns, Wipin' the Pan, Perfect 15155, 78 rpm 12.00
Mississippi Trio, Doin' That Thing, Supertone 9528, 78 rpm 100.00
New Yorkers, Go Get 'Em Caroline, QRS 1002, 78 rpm...............30.00
Novelty Five, Bluin' the Blues, Aeolian-Vocalion 12117, 78 rpm.12.00
Original Jazz Hounds, Slow Down, Columbia 14094-D, 78 rpm .100.00

Pendleton, Andy; Thinking of You, Victor 23389, 78 rpm 125.00
Porter's Blue Devils, Steamboat Sal, Gennett 5249, 78 rpm..........15.00
Red Caps, Niagara Falls, Victor 23382, 78 rpm 150.00
Red Onion Jazz Babies, Brotherly Love, Silvertone 5024, 78 rpm ..100.00
Rollickers, Lonely Little Cinderella, Edison 52600, 78 rpm..........40.00
Searcy Trio, Kansas Avenue Blues, Okeh 8360, 78 rpm 75.00
Sepia Serenaders, Alligator Crawl, Bluebird 5803, 78 rpm...........20.00
Silver Slipper Orch, A Little Bit Closer, Challenge 801, 78 rpm ..200.00
Tennessee Tooters, Fallin' Down, Vocalion 15201, 78 rpm..........40.00
Thomas' Devils, Boot It, Boy, Brunswick 7064, 78 rpm.............150.00
Three Keys, Mood Indigo, Columbia 2706-D, 78 rpm................20.00
Travelers, Breakaway, Okeh 41260, 78 rpm...........................20.00
Tremer, George H; Some of These Days, Champion 15372, 78 rpm ..100.00
Varsity Eight, Mean Blues, Cameo 498, 78 rpm......................10.00
Virginians, Low Down, Victor 21680, 78 rpm 10.00
Wallace, Trixie; Copenhagen, Claxtonola 40393, 78 rpm..........120.00
Ward, Billy; Squeeze Me, Oriole 4472, 78 rpm 25.00
Washington, Buck; Old Fashioned Love, Columbia 2925-D, 78 rpm ...40.00
We Three, Plenty Off Center, Pathe-Actuelle 36492, 78 rpm 30.00
Whoopee Makers, Sister Kate, Columbia 14367-D, 78 rpm...........35.00
Wilson, Garland; Rockin' Chair, Okeh 41556, 78 rpm...............40.00
Yankee Six, Oh! These Eyes, Okeh 40335, 78 RPM....................50.00
Yellman, Duke & Orch; Fireworks, Edison 52328, 78 rpm 50.00
Zon-O-Phone Orchestra, Persian Lamb Rag, Zon-O-Phone 5320, 78 rpm...25.00

Red Wing

The Red Wing Stoneware Company, founded in 1878, took its name from its location in Red Wing, Minnesota. In 1906 the name was changed to the Red Wing Union Stoneware Company after a merger with several of the other local potteries. For the most part they produced utilitarian wares such as flowerpots, crocks, and jugs. Their early 1930s catalogs offered a line of art pottery vases in colored glazes, some of which featured handles modeled after swan's necks, snakes, or female nudes. Other examples were quite simple, often with classic styling. After the addition of their dinnerware lines in 1935, 'Stoneware' was dropped from the name, and the company became known as Red Wing Potteries, Inc. They closed in 1967.

The pottery was reopened several years ago, and handmade and decorated salt-glazed stoneware is again being produced. Each piece is stamped with the potters' initials and the year of production.

Our artware advisors are Wendy and Leo Frese (Three Rivers Collectibles); they are listed under Texas. For further study we recommend *Red Wing Stoneware, An Identification and Value Guide*, and *Red Wing Collectibles* by Dan and Gail DePasquale and Larry Peterson; and *Red Wing Art Pottery, Book II*, and *Collector's Encyclopedia of Red Wing Art Pottery*, by B.L. and R.L. Dollen. All are published by Collector Books. Another good reference is *Red Wing Art Pottery* by Ray Reiss (privately published).

Commercial Art Ware and Miscellaneous

Ash receiver, Pelican, wht, #880 ....175.00
Ash receiver, Scottie dog, wht, #877 ....225.00
Bank, bear form, Hamm's Beer, 1960s 225.00
Bowl, console; Regular Line, #852, 7½x12" 35.00
Candle holders, Magnolia, 2-light, #1029, pr....................55.00
Casserole, Fondoso, lt bl, w/lid.....................................25.00
Compote, Cherub, lav, #761 ....100.00
Figurine, cow w/nursing calf, brn, on base......................475.00
Flower frog, Fern, wht, #1046 ....175.00
Lamp, elephant hdls, gr, 9"...175.00
Magnolia, #1230 ....75.00
Pitcher, Gypsy Trail, cobalt w/wood hdl, #565.................100.00

Pitcher, Dutch Blue, dbl spout, #766	120.00
Planter, Ram Head, #739, 10"	125.00
Plate, African lady on lt bl, 14"	325.00
Soup, Fondoso, orange, ind, pr	20.00
Teapot, Lady, cobalt	175.00
Trivet, yel, 1858-1958	70.00
Vase, Acorn, Crackle Yellow, #173	100.00
Vase, Bamboo, maroon w/gray int, #400	50.00
Vase, gr & wht, #145, 9"	66.00
Vase, gr matt, #155, 15"	150.00
Vase, lady on a swing w/2 cherubs, #776, 12"	90.00
Vase, Lotus, HP decor, H-511, 10"	120.00
Vase, Pompeiian, #957, 10"	75.00
Vase, Prismatique, #794, 11"	105.00
Vase, Seafoam, #744	75.00
Wall clock, Mammy	125.00
Wall pocket, violin, #907	50.00
Wing, maroon, Red Wing Potteries	50.00

Cookie Jars

Be aware that there is a very good reproduction of the King of Tarts. Except for the fact that the new jars are slightly smaller, they are sometimes difficult to distinguish from the old.

Bob White, unmk	200.00
Carousel, unmk	350.00
Crock, wht	80.00
Dutch Girl (Katrina), yel w/brn trim	175.00
Friar Tuck, cream w/brn, mk	175.00
Friar Tuck, gr, mk	175.00
Friar Tuck, yel, unmk	150.00
Grapes, cobalt or dk purple, ea	275.00
Grapes, gr	135.00
Jack Frost, unmk, short	250.00
Jack Frost, unmk, tall	300.00
King of Tarts, mc, mk (+)	325.00
King of Tarts, pk w/bl & blk trim, mk	300.00
King of Tarts, wht, unmk	200.00
Peasant design, emb/pnt figures on aqua	110.00
Peasant design, emb/pnt figures on brn	120.00
Pierre (chef), bl, brn or pk, unmk, ea	150.00
Pineapple, yel	135.00

Dinnerware

Dinnerware lines were added in 1935, and today collectors scramble to rebuild extensive table services. Although interest is obvious, right now the market is so volatile, it is often difficult to establish a price scale with any degree of accuracy. Asking prices may vary from $50.00 to $200.00 on some items, which indicates instability and a collector market trying to find its way. (One guide currently on the market, for instance, lists Midnight Rose dinner plates at $15.00 to $20.00, while another terms them 'rare,' and values them at $145.00 each.) Sellers seem to be unfamiliar with pattern names and proper identification of the various pieces that each line consists of. There were many hand-decorated lines; among the most popular are Bob White, Tropicana, and Round-up. But there are other patterns that are just as attractive and deserving of attention. The Dollen books referenced above both have dinnerware sections, and Ray Reiss has published a book called *Red Wing Dinnerware, Price and Identification Guide*, which shows nearly one hundred patterns on its back cover alone.

Town and Country, designed by Eva Zeisel, was made for only one year in the late 1940s. Today many collectors regard Zeisel as one of the most gifted designers of that era and actively seek examples of her work. Town and Country was a versatile line, adaptable to both informal and semiformal use. It is characterized by irregular, often eccentric shapes, and handles of pitchers and serving pieces are usually extensions of the rim. Bowls and platters are free-form comma shapes or appear tilted, with one side slightly higher than the other. Although the ware is unmarked, it is recognizable by its distinctive shapes and glazes. White (often used to complement interiors of bowls and cups), though an original color, is actually more rare than Bronze (metallic brown, also called gunmetal), which enjoys favored status; Gray is unusual. Other colors include Rust, Dusk Blue, Sand, Chartreuse, Peach, and Forest Green. Pieces have also shown up in Mulberry and Ming Green and are considered quite rare. (These are Red Wing Quartelle colors!) Note: Eva Zeisel recently gave permission to reissue a few select pieces of Town and Country; these are being made by World of Ceramics. In 1996 salt and pepper shakers were reproduced in *new* colors not resembling Red Wing colors. In 1997 the mixing bowl and syrup were reissued. All new pieces are stamped EZ96 or EZ97 and are visibly different from the old, as far as glaze, pottery base, and weight.

Our advisor for this category is Brenda Dollen; she is listed in the Directory under Minnesota. Karen Silvermintz (see Texas) and Charles Alexander (see Indiana) advise on the Town and Country dinnerware.

Key:
c/s — cobalt on stoneware   RW — Red Wing
MN — Minnesota   RWUS — Red Wing Union
NS — North Star   Stoneware

Round-Up, platter, 13", $90.00; Water jug, 60-ounce, 12", $125.00.

Blossom Time, bowl, nappy	8.00
Blossom Time, chop plate	25.00
Blossom Time, plate, dinner; 10½"	18.00
Bob White, bowl, divided vegetable	50.00
Bob White, casserole, 2-qt	75.00
Bob White, cup & saucer	15.00
Bob White, relish, 3-part	50.00
Bob White, sauce bowl	15.00
Bob White, water jug, 60-oz	42.50
Brittany, coupe soup, 8"	24.00
Brittany, gravy boat	45.00
Brittany, plate, dinner; 10"	24.00
Capistrano, butter dish	27.50
Capistrano, plate, 7½"	10.00
Capistrano, trivet	27.50
Chrysanthemum, bowl, cereal	9.00
Chrysanthemum, cup & saucer, tea	12.50
Chrysanthemum, plate, 7"	8.00
Crocus, bowl, cereal	10.00
Crocus, bowl, fruit/sauce	10.00
Crocus, sugar bowl, w/lid	22.50
Desert Sun, bowl, sauce/fruit	10.00
Desert Sun, bread tray	50.00

Desert Sun, casserole, w/lid, 2½-qt 42.50
Desert Sun, cup & saucer, demitasse........................18.00
Desert Sun, plate, 7" 15.00
Driftwood, bowl, salad; lg 32.00
Driftwood, butter dish 50.00
Driftwood, cup & saucer, tea 12.50
Driftwood, platter, 15" 40.00
Fantasy, chop plate 40.00
Fantasy, creamer...12.50
Fantasy, cup, coffee 13.00
Fantasy, relish 22.50
Fantasy, teapot...75.00
Iris, bowl, divided vegetable 30.00
Iris, creamer 22.00
Iris, pitcher, water..50.00
Iris, supper tray..45.00
Lexington, celery tray..17.50
Lexington, plate, dinner; 10½"...............................12.50
Lexington, shakers, pr...16.00
Lotus, bowl, rim soup..12.50
Lotus, chop plate 32.50
Lotus, sugar bowl, w/lid 17.50
Lotus, teapot..65.00
Lute Song, bread tray..32.50
Lute Song, celery tray 15.00
Lute Song, creamer...20.00
Lute Song, platter, sm...30.00
Lute Song, teapot...70.00
Magnolia, bowl, cereal 8.00
Magnolia, bowl, nappy 12.50
Magnolia, butter dish..24.00
Magnolia, chop plate 32.50
Midnight Rose, bowl, salad; 5½" 40.00
Midnight Rose, bread tray 80.00
Midnight Rose, pitcher, water................................125.00
Midnight Rose, platter, 15" 100.00
Normandy, candle holders, pr 75.00
Normandy, plate, dinner; 10" 18.00
Normandy, shakers, pr..22.50
Normandy, water jug...70.00
Orleans, bowl, nappy, 9" 40.00
Orleans, creamer & sugar bowl, w/lid 65.00
Orleans, teapot...115.00
Pepe, bean pot 40.00
Pepe, bowl, divided relish 25.00
Pepe, bowl, salad; 10" 40.00
Pepe, plate, 6" 10.00
Pepe, shakers, pr 25.00
Pink Spice, bowl, cereal 15.00
Pink Spice, bowl, fruit/sauce 35.00
Pink Spice, creamer & sugar bowl, w/lid 45.00
Pink Spice, gravy boat 40.00
Random Harvest, butter dish 32.50
Random Harvest, pitcher, water; 2-qt 48.00
Random Harvest, plate, dinner; 10½" 22.00
Random Harvest, sugar bowl, w/lid.........................24.00
Random Harvest, teapot..85.00
Round-Up, bowl, divided vegetable..........................42.50
Round-Up, marmite, stick hdl, w/lid 70.00
Round-Up, plate, dinner; 10½" 55.00
Round-Up, shakers, pr...100.00
Round-Up, tray, 24" 160.00
Smart Set, bowl, rim soup 27.50
Smart Set, lazy susan, complete w/dishes & stand 195.00

Smart Set, plate, 6½"..8.00
Smart Set, shakers, pr 45.00
Spring Song, celery dish 22.50
Spring Song, creamer...12.50
Spring Song, egg plate, w/lid 89.00
Spring Song, spoon rest 45.00
Tampico, bowl, divided vegetable 27.50
Tampico, bowl, salad; 12" 37.50
Tampico, mug, coffee 40.00
Tampico, plate, 8½" 25.00
Town & Country, baker, 11x7½" 45.00
Town & Country, bean pot, Rust, w/lid, minimum value...........400.00
Town & Country, bowl, soup 27.50
Town & Country, creamer & sugar bowl, w/lid, minimum value ..60.00
Town & Country, cup & saucer, tea 27.50
Town & Country, lazy susan, mixed colors, complete w/stand 215.00
Town & Country, pitcher, 3-pt 100.00
Town & Country, plate, 10½"...................................45.00
Town & Country, platter, 15x11½" 70.00
Town & Country, shakers, Shmoo shape, mixed colors, pr...........75.00
Town & Country, syrup..65.00
Turtle Dove, ashtray 25.00
Turtle Dove, bowl, vegetable....................................24.00
Turtle Dove, platter, 15" 30.00
Turtle Dove, shakers, pr...24.00
Vintage, beverage server 90.00
Vintage, bowl, vegetable...32.50
Vintage, creamer...24.00
Vintage, plate, 10½"...28.00
Vintage, shakers, pr...30.00
Zinnia, bowl, rim soup...15.00
Zinnia, cup, coffee 10.00
Zinnia, pitcher, water..72.50
Zinnia, plate, 7½"...15.00

Stoneware

Bean pot, Albany slip, Boston style, RW, 1-gal 250.00
Bean pot, Albany slip, short neck, NS, 1-gal 140.00
Bowl, beater; Albany slip, RW, from $50 to 60.00
Bowl, shoulder; wht, RW, 1-pt..................................55.00
Churn, #4/P, c/s, RW, 4-gal 950.00
Churn, #5/oval adv logo, c/s, unsgn, 5-gal, from $3,000 to......3,500.00
Churn, #6/bird, c/s, unmk, 6-gal..........................1,500.00
Churn, #8, 2 birch leaves, c/s, unmk, 8-gal 800.00
Cooler, #3/Ice Water/birch leaves, c/s, wht, old shape........800.00
Cooler, #6/daisy, c/s, RW, 6-gal...........................2,000.00
Cooler, #8/Sanitary School Appliances adv, c/s, RW, 8-gal......1,500.00
Crock, #2/adv logo in rectangle, c/s, unmk, from $800 to.......1,000.00
Crock, #25/birch leaves, c/s, MN, 25-gal 1,200.00
Crock, #5/2 birch leaves, c/s, RWUS, 5-gal, from $1,000 to....1,200.00
Crock, #5/2 elephant ear leaves, c/s, unmk, 5-gal, from $1,200 to...1,400.00
Crock, #15/red wing, c/s, wht, RWUS, 15-gal...........100.00
Crock, butter; Albany slip, high style, NS, 1-qt..........150.00
Crock, butter; Albany slip, low style, RW, 1-lb 80.00
Crock, butter; wht, low style, MN, 10-lb...................50.00
Cuspidor, molded seam, Albany slip, unmk 125.00
Jar, preserve/snuff; Albany slip, MN, ½-gal...............60.00
Jar, wax sealer; Albany slip, MN, 1-qt......................60.00
Jug, bailed; half-moon adv, brn & salt glaze, MN, 1-gal 300.00
Jug, bailed; half-moon adv, brn & salt glaze, RW, ½-gal.........300.00
Jug, beehive; #4/red wing, c/s, RWUS, 4-gal 700.00
Jug, beehive; #5/birch leaf, c/s, RW, 5-gal.............2,500.00
Jug, common; Albany slip, bottom seam, MN, 1-gal 75.00

Jug, common; salt glaze, MN, 1-gal **325.00**
Jug, fancy; adv, wht w/brn ball top, RW, 2-gal, from $500 to **600.00**
Jug, fancy; wht w/brn ball top, MN, ¼-pt **225.00**
Jug, fancy; wht w/brn ball top, RW, 1-gal **200.00**
Jug, molded seam, Albany slip, bail hdl, RW, 1-gal **400.00**
Jug, molded seam, bl mottle, bail hdl, MN, 1-gal **1,300.00**
Jug, molded seam, wht, wide mouth, MN, ½-gal **70.00**
Jug, shoulder; #5/Indian adv logo, c/s, 5-gal, from $250 to ...**300.00**
Jug, shoulder; adv, brn & salt glaze, dome top, MN, 2-gal **225.00**
Jug, shoulder; adv, brn & salt glaze, funnel top, RW, ½-gal **200.00**
Jug, shoulder; advertising, RWUS, 5-gal, from $600 to **700.00**
Jug, shoulder; brn & salt glaze, cone top, RW, 2-gal **350.00**
Jug, shoulder; brn & salt glaze, dome top, MN, 1-gal, from $150 to ..**200.00**
Jug, shoulder; brn & salt glaze, funnel top, MN, ½-gal **200.00**
Jug, shoulder; Dr Bopps Hamburger Stomach Bitters, c/s, MN, 2-gal ...**750.00**
Jug, shoulder; Old Rose Pure Rye Whiskey, c/s, RW, ½-gal **400.00**
Jug, shoulder; RW Liquor Co adv, brn & salt glaze, ½-gal **600.00**
Jug, shoulder; salt glaze w/brn drips, pear top, NS, 2-gal **900.00**
Jug, shoulder; wht, funnel top, MN, 2-gal **75.00**
Pan, milk; wht, NS **100.00**
Pipkin, Albany slip or wht, unmk, 4-pt **90.00**
Pitcher, Russian; Albany slip, unmk, 1-gal **100.00**
Spittoon, salt glaze, RW **800.00**
Syrup, wht, shouldered, pouring spout, MN, 1-gal **60.00**
Umbrella stand, bl sponging, unsgn **1,400.00**

Redware

The term redware refers to a type of simple earthenware produced by the Colonists as early as the 1600s. The red clay used in its production was abundant throughout the country, and during the eighteenth and nineteenth centuries redware was made in great quantities. Intended for utilitarian purposes such as everyday tableware or use in the dairy, redware was simple in design and decoration. Glazes of various colors were used, and a liquid clay referred to as 'slip' was sometimes applied in patterns such as zigzag lines, daisies, or stars. Plates often have a 'coggled' edge, similar to the way a pie is crimped or jagged, which is done with a special tool. In the following listings, EX (excellent condition) indicates only minor damage. Our advisor for this category is Barbara Rosen; she is listed in the Directory under New Jersey.

Plate, orange-brown with yellow slip entwined and squiggled line decor, coggled rim, 10", EX, $250.00.

Bank, onion shape w/bird finial, yel slip stripes, rpr, 4⅛x2½" **260.00**
Bowl, dk brn sponging on dk orange, tooled band, rolled rim, 3¼x7" ..**440.00**
Bowl, milk; brn daubs on orange, tooled band, wear, 5½x13" **715.00**
Bowl, mixing; brn sponging at rim & in lines on sides, 5x11", EX ...**300.00**
Bowl, wht slip squiggles on dk brn, wear/old edge chips, 4x15" ..**1,980.00**
Bowl, yel slip w/cross & 4 dots, wear/chip, 8" **300.00**
Bust, man in long wig, brn glaze, hand molded, 10" **770.00**
Chamber pot, Gonic glaze, strap hdl, incised linear decor, 19th C, 6" ..**700.00**
Chamberstick, brn w/dk trim, 1938, minor rim flakes, 7" **30.00**
Charger, Pony Up the Cash in yel slip, coggled rim, 14", EX ...**18,700.00**

Charger, 4-line yel slip w/gr slip str lines, coggled rim, rpr, 12" ...**360.00**
Creamer, brn flecks, appl hdls, minor flakes, 3" **110.00**
Doorstop, brick w/molded star flower, brn & yel, chips, 5" **330.00**
Figurine, rooster, gr mottle, RR Stahl 11-4-50, 4¼" **220.00**
Figurine, Uncle Sam, worn/flaked mc, 4" **275.00**
Flowerpot, manganese splotches on orange, incised decor, 8¾x10", EX ...**130.00**
Flowerpot, yel slip on brn w/mc mottling, attached saucer, 5" **365.00**
Flowerpot, yel slip polka dots, trees & 1867, w/attached saucer, 9" ..**110.00**
Jar, apple butter; brn splotches on deep orange, tooled lines, hdl, 5" ..**580.00**
Jar, dk brn, ovoid, C Link, PA, late 1800s, chip, 3⅝" **55.00**
Jar, dk brn on orange-brn, hairline/flakes, 6⅜" **275.00**
Jar, dk splotches on orange w/mottled gr, galleried lip, 7⅜", EX .**825.00**
Jar, mottled amber/yel/gr w/dk brn daubs on gr, w/lid, 8" **1,485.00**
Jar, Net-like pattern, dk brn on burnt orange, 7½", EX **525.00**
Jug, blk splotches on brn, strap hdl, ovoid, 8¾", EX **300.00**
Jug, brn glaze, tapered oval, Am, 19th C, 8½" **150.00**
Jug, dk brn splotches, ME, 19th C, 7½", EX **635.00**
Jug, dk brn w/blk runs at shoulder & strap hdl, 8", EX **550.00**
Loaf pan, 3 yel slip lines, coggled edge, 3¼x15½x11½", EX **220.00**
Loaf pan, 4-line yel slip, coggled rim, chips, 14¼" **770.00**
Mold, fish, orange w/splotches, incised details, 2x12x4½", EX ...**425.00**
Mold, spiraled flutes w/scalloped rim, brn sponging on amber, 8" ...**140.00**
Mold, Turk's head, brn sponged rim, divided/fluted w/scallped rim, 8" ..**150.00**
Mold, Turk's head, yel slip rim, brn splotches on orange, 3x9", EX ...**330.00**
Mug, dk brn splotches on burnt orange, 3½", EX **140.00**
Mug, dk burnt orange w/brn streaks, ribbed hdl, 4⅞", EX **150.00**
Mug, mush; dk gr-amber, ribbed hdl, 3½", EX **90.00**
Novelty, doll's rocker, overall yel slip on brn speckles, 7¾" **465.00**
Pie plate, ABC & flourish in yel slip, coggled rim, 11¼", EX **195.00**
Pie plate, ABC script & flourish in yel slip, tooled rim, 11", EX ..**1,075.00**
Pie plate, bird on branch in yel slip, coggled rim, 10", EX+ **3,400.00**
Pie plate, brn daubs on orange, wear, 8¼" **1,150.00**
Pie plate, burnt orange, shiny, goggled rim, wear, 10½" **165.00**
Pie plate, seaweed in yel slip on bl, coggled rim, 10½", EX **1,625.00**
Pie plate, stylized flower in yel slip, coggled rim, wear, 11" **385.00**
Pie plate, W in bold script yel slip, coggled rim, 9", EX **935.00**
Pie plate, wavy yel slip lines, brn str line, tooled rim, 8½", EX ...**415.00**
Pie plate, yel slip flourish, coggled rim, wear/flakes, 12" **880.00**
Pie plate, yel slip on gr w/sgraffito peacock & inscription, 1934, 10" ...**115.00**
Pie plate, 3-line & dot yel slip, coggled rim, 9⅞", EX **385.00**
Pie plate, 3-line gr slip, coggled rim, 11¾", EX **880.00**
Pie plate, 3-line yel slip, coggled rim, minor chips, 7" **220.00**
Pie plate, 3-line yel slip, coggled rim, wear/chips, 10¼" **415.00**
Pie plate, 3-line yel slip, coggled rim, 11", EX **715.00**
Pie plate, 3-line yel slip, coggled rim, 11⅜", VG **415.00**
Pie plate, 3-line yel slip, coggled rim, 8", EX **385.00**
Pie plate, 3-line yel slip in bird's claw, coggled rim, 9½", EX **250.00**
Pitcher, brn splotches/flecks on orange, ribbed strap hdl, 7⅝", EX ..**660.00**
Plate, brn sponging on orange, minor chips, 4⅜" **330.00**
Plate, leaf design in brn slip on amber, coggled rim, 5½" **415.00**
Plate, med brn w/faint yel slip swags, coggled rim, chips, 9" **220.00**
Plate, sgraffito bird & foliage, yel slip & gr sponging, 20th C, 13" ...**250.00**
Plate, 2-line yel slip, minor wear, 7½" **465.00**
Plate, 3-line yel slip, coggled rim, wear, 9" **385.00**
Plate, 3-line yel slip, coggled rim, 8¼", EX **495.00**
Platter, marbleized w/mc slip, wht slip interior, appl hdl, 8⅛" **550.00**
Spittoon, dk brn, rnd w/flat bottom, 3¾x6⅛", EX **15.00**
Stove leveler, brn splotches on orange, chips, 2¾" **175.00**
Washboard, alkaline glaze w/dk gr sponging, wood fr, 1870s, 24x12" ...**600.00**

Regal China

Located in Antioch, Illinois, the Regal China Company open for business in 1938. Products of interest to collectors are Jim Beam decanters, cookie jars, salt and pepper shakers, and similar novelty items. The company closed its doors sometime in 1993. The Old MacDonald Farm series listed below is especially collectible, so are the salt and pepper shakers.

Note: Where applicable, prices are based on excellent gold trim. (Gold trim must be 90% intact or deductions should be made for wear.) See also Decanters.

Alice in Wonderland

Creamer, White Rabbit, from $625 to	650.00
Pitcher, King of Hearts, milk sz	650.00
Shakers, matching colors, rare, pr, from $600 to	675.00
Shakers, Tweedledee & Tweedledum, pr	850.00
Sugar bowl, White Rabbit, w/lid	600.00
Teapot, Mad Hatter	2,500.00

Cookie Jars

Cat, from $375 to	425.00
Churn Boy	275.00
Clown, gr collar, from $700 to	750.00
Davy Crockett, from $500 to	550.00
Diaper Pin Pig, from $500 to	600.00
Dutch Girl, from $675 to	725.00
FiFi Poodle, from $675 to	725.00
Fisherman, from $700 to	800.00
French Chef, from $400 to	450.00
Goldilocks (+)	375.00
Harpo Marx	1,200.00
Hobby Horse, from $275 to	300.00
Hubert Lion, from $800 to	950.00
Humpty Dumpty, red	325.00
Little Miss Muffet, from $350 to	385.00
Majorette, from $425 to	675.00
Oriental Lady w/Baskets, from $650 to	700.00
Peek-a-Boo (+), from $1,500 to	1,600.00
Quaker Oats	125.00
Three Bears	285.00
Toby Cookies, unmk, from $750 to	775.00
Tulip	300.00
Uncle Mistletoe	850.00

Old McDonald's Farm

Butter dish, cow's head	220.00
Canister, flour, cereal, coffee; med, ea, from $225 to	275.00
Canister, pretzels, peanuts, popcorn, chips, tidbits; lg, ea, $325 to	375.00
Canister, salt, sugar, tea; med, ea, from $225 to	275.00
Canister, soap, cookies; lg, ea, from $350 to	425.00
Cookie barn, from $295 to	325.00
Creamer, rooster, from $110 to	125.00
Grease jar, pig, from $200 to	250.00
Pitcher, milk; from $425 to	450.00
Shakers, churn, gold trim, pr	95.00
Shakers, feed sacks w/sheep, pr	195.00
Spice jar, assorted lids, sm, ea, from $100 to	150.00
Sugar bowl, hen	135.00
Teapot, duck's head, from $295 to	325.00

Shakers

A Nod to Abe, 3-pc nodder	300.00

Bendel, bears, wht w/pk & brn trim, pr	100.00
Bendel, bunnies, wht w/blk & pk trim, pr from $150 to	200.00
Bendel, kissing pigs, gray w/pk trim, lg, pr, from $400 to	450.00
Bendel, love bugs, burgundy, lg, pr, from $175 to	225.00
Bendel, love bugs, gr, sm, pr	65.00
Cat, sitting w/eyes closed, wht w/hat & gold bow, pr	225.00
Clown, pr	450.00
Dutch Girl, pr	275.00
FiFi, pr	450.00
Fish, mk C Miller, 1-pc	55.00
French Chef, wht w/gold trim, pr, from $250 to	350.00
Humpty Dumpty, pr	140.00
Peek-a-boo, red dots, lg, pr (+), from $450 to	500.00
Peek-a-boo, red dots, sm, pr, from $250 to	275.00
Peek-a-boo, wht solid, sm, pr	200.00
Pig, pk, mk C Miller, 1-pc	95.00
Tulip, pr	50.00
Van Tellingen, bears, brn, pr, from $25 to	28.00
Van Tellingen, boy & dog, wht, pr	68.00
Van Tellingen, bunnies, solid colors, pr, from $28	32.00
Van Tellingen, ducks, pr	38.00
Van Tellingen, Dutch boy & girl, from $45 to	50.00
Van Tellingen, Mary & lamb, pr	60.00
Van Tellingen, sailor & mermaid, pr, from $225 to	260.00

Relief-Molded Jugs

Early relief-molded pitchers (ca 1830s – 40s) were made in two-piece molds into which sheets of clay were pressed. The relief decoration was deep and well defined, usually of animal or human subjects. Most of these pitchers were designed with a flaring lip and substantial footing. Gradually styles changed, and by the 1860s the rim had become flatter and the foot less pronounced. The relief decoration was not as deep, and foliage became a common design. By the turn of the century, many other types of pitchers had been introduced, and the market for these early styles began to wane.

Watch for recent reproductions; these have been made by the slip-casting method. Unlike relief-molded ware which is relatively smooth inside, slip-cast pitchers will have interior indentations that follow the irregularities of the relief decoration. Values below are for pieces in excellent condition. Our advisor for this category is Kathy Hughes; she is listed in the Directory under North Carolina.

Key: Reg — Registered

Argos, gr, Brownfield, Apr 29, 1864, 8"	175.00
Bird & Butterfly, tan & wht, Minton, ca 1830, 6"	375.00
Bundle of Faggots, drabware, metal lid, Ridgway, Reg Oct 1, 1835, 8"	250.00
Cain & Abel, tan stoneware, Edward Walley, ca 1850, 10"	325.00
Chelsea Pensioners, wht stoneware, unknown, ca 1845	350.00
Chrysanthemum, gr & wht, Ridgway, ca 1860, 9¼"	275.00
Cupid at Play, buff & brn, Turner, ca 1800, 9½"	700.00
Diana, gr stoneware, Edward Walley, Reg June 21, 1850, 10"	425.00
Dilston family/instruments, bl smear/gilt, Alcock, 1840s, 7"	525.00
Garibaldi, unknown, ca 1870, 13"	250.00
Good Samaritan, buff & tan, Jones & Walley, 1841, 8"	375.00
Good Samaritan, wht stoneware, unknown, ca 1850, 9¾"	400.00
Idle Apprentices, wht & bl, unknown, 1840, 7"	250.00
Julius Caeser, gray, appl laurel wreath, Meigh, 1839, 8¼"	450.00
King Solomon, drabware, Wood & Brownfield, Reg Sept 30 1841, 7½"	350.00
Love & War, purple on wht parian, Samuel Alcock, ca 1845, 7¾"	425.00
Mermaid & Cupid, Minton, gr & wht parian, ca 1911, 6"	750.00
Naomi & Daughter-in-Law, lav on parian, Alcock, 1847, 8¾"	450.00

Now I'm Grandpapa, unknown, ca 1850, 8½" 450.00
Peel & Cobden, yel earthenware, unknown, ca 1846` 250.00
Princess Charlotte/Prince Leopold, gold/bl, 2¾" 300.00
Princess Charlotte/Prince Leopold, minor rstr, 6" 275.00
Punch, purple on wht parian, Samuel Alcock, ca 1845, 8¾" 600.00
Royal Children, bl earthenware, unknown, ca 1848 ....325.00
Shakespeare, wht on purple parian, Samuel Alcock, ca 1850, 6" ..600.00
Sir Robert Peel, tan earthenware, ca 1846 ....175.00
Sir Walter Scott commemorative, gray-gr, Minton, 8" 350.00
Slavery scenes, Ridgway & Abington, 1855, 7⅞", minimum value ..1,100.00
Stag, gray-gr, Enoch & Edward Wood, ca 1840, 9¼" 350.00
Stag, purple on wht parian, Samuel Alcock, ca 1845, 8⅛" 500.00
Tulip, bl & wht, Dudson, ca 1860, 7" 250.00
Tulip, wht stoneware, Dudson, ca 1860, 8" 250.00
Youth & Old Age, gray-gr, Copeland-Garret, ca 1845, 8¾" 300.00

Restraints

Since the beginning of time, many things from animals to treasures have been held in bondage by hemp, bamboo, chests, chains, shackles, and other constructed devices. Many of these devices were used to hold captives who awaited further torture, as if the restraint wasn't torturous enough. The study and collecting of restraints enables one to learn much about the advancement of civilization in the country or region from which they originated. Such devices at various times in history were made of very heavy metals — so heavy that the wearer could scarcely move about. It has only been in the last sixty years that vast improvements have been made in design and construction that afford the captive some degree of comfort. Our advisor for this category is Joseph Tanner; he is listed in the Directory under Washington.

Key:
bbl — barrel
d-lb — double lock button
K — key
Kd — keyed
lc — lock case
NST — non-swing through
ST — swing through
stp — stamped

Foreign Handcuffs

Australian, Saf Lock, ST, takes pin-tumbler K in side, stp 200.00
Czechalaviak, ST, Ralken flat key, modern ST 150.00
East German, aluminum, single lg hinge, ST, bbl key...................80.00
East German, heavy steel, NP single lg hinge, NST, bbl key.......120.00
English, Chubb Arrest, steel, ST, multi-bit solid K 250.00
English, Latrobe, aluminum alloy, center chain, ST, dbl-bit K....200.00
French Lapegy, ST, aluminum alloys, takes flat bitted K 75.00
French Revolved, oval, ST, takes 2 Ks: bbl & pin tumbler..........170.00
German, Swartiger, steel, NST, bbl K goes in at end of cuffs 500.00
German Clejuso, oval design, ST, dbl-cuff weight, 22-oz 100.00
German Darby, adjusts, well finished, NST, sm 120.00
German Hamburg 8, non-adjust NST, center bar/post w/K-way .275.00
Hiatt, solid state, 2 separate cuffs joined bk to bk, stp/#d...........190.00
Hiatt English non-adjust screw K Darby style, uses screw K 120.00
Hiatt Figure 8, swings open to insert/withdraw wrists................150.00
Plug 8, remove plug before inserting external threaded K 250.00
Russian modern ST, blued bbl key, unmk, crude 80.00
Spanish, stp Alcyon/Star, modern Peerless type, ST, sm bbl K......45.00

Foreign Leg Shackles

East German, aluminum, lg hinge, cable amid 4 cuffs, bbl key ...100.00
German Clejuso Darby type, adjusts/NST/plated, uses screw K ..160.00
Hiatt English combo manacles, handcuff/leg irons w/chain 325.00

Hiatt Plug leg irons, same K-ing as Plug-8 cuffs, w/chain 275.00

U.S. Handcuffs

Adams, teardrop lc, bbl Kd, NST, usually not stp 200.00
Bean Giant, sideways figure-8, solid center lc, dbl-bit K 550.00
Bean Patrolman, kidney-bean form, d-lb on lc, NST, stp T 130.00
Bean-Cobb, sm rnd lc, removable cylinder, d-lb, NST, 1899 ......100.00
Cavenay, looks like Marlin Daley but w/screw K, NST 180.00
Civil War padlocking type, various designs w/loop for lock 225.00
Colt, modern ST bow, sm bbl Kd, stp w/Colt & Co name 200.00
Flash Action Manacle, like Bean Giant w/ST, K-way center 400.00
Flexibles, steel segmented bows, NST Darby type, screw K.........250.00
H&R Super, ST, shaft-hinge connector takes hollow titted K 150.00
Harvard, takes sm bbl K, ST, stp Harvard Lock Co.....................65.00
Judd, NST, used rnd/internally triangular K, stp Mattatuck 150.00
Lilly Hand Iron, 2" strap iron (8" L), oval bands, NST, sq K 700.00
Marlin Daley, NST, bottle-neck form, neck stp, dbl-titted K 300.00
Mattatuck, NST, propeller-like K-way, stp Mattatuck/etc 130.00
Palmer, 2" steel bands, 2 K-ways (top & center), NST stp...........400.00
Peerless, ST, takes sm bbl K, stp Mfg'ered by Peerless Co............40.00
Peerless, ST, takes sm bbl K, stp Mfg'ered by S&W Co.................75.00
Peerless Big Guy, modern ST, bbl key.......................................50.00
Phelps, NST, twist chain between cuffs, Tower look-alike 400.00
Pratt combo, 1 cuff connnects w/nipper/claw, ST, mk Pratt 400.00
Providence Tool Co, stp, NST, Darby screw K style 350.00
Rankin, steel NST, mk screw K 300.00
Romer, NST, takes flat K, resembles padlock, stp Romer Co 300.00
S&W 94 Maximum Security, ST, takes Ace-type K, stp S&W...120.00
Strauss, ST, takes lg solid bitted K, stp Strauss Eng Co...............120.00
Tower, NST, bottom K, solid/flat-fitted K goes in cuff edge 200.00
Tower bar cuffs, cuffs separate by 10-12" steel bar......................300.00
Tower Dbl Lock, NST, takes bbl-bitted K, usually stp Tower 110.00
Tower Detective Pinkerton, NST, sq lc, bbl-bitted K, no stp 165.00
Tower Single Lock, NST, bbl-bit K, K-way slanted on lc, sm.......125.00
Tower-Bean, NST, sm rnd lc, takes tiny bbl-bitted K, stp...........130.00
Walden 'Lady Cuff,' NST, takes sm bbl K, lightweight, stp.........400.00

U.S. Leg Shackles

Slave iron leg shackles and chain, U-shaped, no key, worn links, EX, $550.00. (Photo courtesy Early Auction Company)

American Munitions, as handcuffs 55.00
Civil War or prison ball & chain, padlocking or rivet type.........500.00
Cloc spike, 30" L opening for ankle w/padlock & 2 spikes..........650.00
H&R Supers, as handcuffs 650.00
Harvard, as handcuffs 125.00
Judd, as handcuffs 155.00
Oregon boot, break-apart shackle on above ankle support.......1,200.00
Palmer, as handcuffs but w/detachable chain, NST 600.00
Providence Tool Co, stp, NST...250.00
Strauss, as handcuffs 200.00
Tower, bottom K, as handcuffs 150.00
Tower ball & chain, leg iron w/chain & 6-lb to 50-lb ball 500.00
Tower Dbl-Lock, as handcuffs 130.00
Tower Detective, as handcuffs..200.00

Various Other Restraining Devices

African slave Darby-style cuffs, heavy iron/chain, handmade 200.00
African slave Darby-style leg shackles, heavy/hand forged 220.00
African slave padlocking or riveted forged iron shackles.............170.00
Argus iron claw, twist T to open & close 60.00
Darby neck collar, rnd steel loop opens w/screw K 400.00
Gale finger cuff, knuckle duster, non-K, mk GFC 150.00
German nipper, twist hdl opens/closes cuff, stp Germany/etc........75.00
Hiatt High Security, hinged bbl K & pin-tumbler K (2 key) 150.00
Korean, hand chain model, blk, bbl key..60.00
Korean, hand hinged model, blk, bbl key..70.00
Mighty-Mite, thumb cuffs, solid body, ST, mk, bbl K 110.00
New Model Russian, chain bbl key, blued......................................125.00
New Model Russian, hinged, bbl key, blued..................................140.00
Thomas Nipper, claw, push button top to open 80.00
Tower Lyon, thumb cuffs, solid body, NST, dbl-bit center K 200.00

Reverse Painting on Glass

Verre eglomise is the technique of painting on the underside of glass. Dating back to the early 1700s, this art became popular in the nineteenth century when German immigrants chose historical figures and beautiful women as subjects for their reverse glass paintings. Advertising mirrors of this type came into vogue at the turn of the century.

Lady in bl w/red cape, gold trim, fancy hat, name in title bar, 10x8"....440.00
Lady in classical dress, alligatored, orig fr, 12x9¾" 220.00
Lady in mc turban & gr dress, flecks, fr, 14x11" 250.00
Lady in ornate dress & hat, flakes/touchups, orig fr: 12x9½" 140.00
Lady in plumed hat & Empire dress, rpt border, 19x15" 220.00
Lady in yel dress w/balloon sleeves, old fr: 11x9½" 220.00
Man in bl frock coat, identified, orig fr, 13⅜x10⅜" 250.00
Man in bl w/red vest, high collar, 10x8"...220.00
Napoleon on wht, flower border, rpr, old fr: 11x9¼" 220.00

Rhead

Associated with many companies during his career — Weller, Vance Avon, Arequipa, A.E. Tile, and finally Homer Laughlin China — Fredrick Herten Rhead organized his own pottery in Santa Barbara, California, ca 1913. Admittedly more of a designer than a potter, Rhead hired help to turn the pieces on the wheel but did most of the decorating himself. The process he favored most involved sgraffito designs inlaid with enameling. Egyptian and Art Nouveau influences were evidenced in much of his work. The ware he produced there was often marked with a logo incorporating the potter at the wheel and 'Santa Barbara.'

Tray, embossed buildings in bisque red clay with green trees and blue sky, 6¼x3¾", $1,750.00.

Vase, gr matt, Oriental shape, flake at ft, 10½" 1,300.00
Vase, multi-tone yel on red clay, cylindrical, att, 3", NM............100.00

Richard

Richard, who at one time worked for Galle, made cameo art glass in France during the 1920s. His work was often multilayered and acid cut with florals and scenics in lovely colors. The ware was marked with his name in relief. Our advisor for this category is Don Williams; he is listed in the Directory under Missouri.

Cameo

Atomizer, leaves, raspberry/pk, wafer ft, 7" 815.00
Bowl, floral, dk bl on yel, boat form, 2¾x3¾" 300.00
Vase, bell flowers & butterflies, purple on wht, 5" 335.00
Vase, floral, chartruse on wht, high waist, 5½" 460.00
Vase, mtn & lake, amethyst to wht, stick neck, 14" 600.00
Wall pocket, thistles, brn on yel, spear form, 7x1½" 700.00

Ridgway

As early as 1792, the Ridgway brothers, Job and George, produced fine quality earthenwares in Shelton, Staffordshire, marking their products 'Ridgway, Smith, & Ridgway,' and later 'Job & George Ridgway.' Around 1800 the brothers split, and each had his own firm, both at Shelton. They were joined in the business by various members of the Ridgway family, and, in fact, their descendants still operate there today.

The two firms created by the split were the Bell Works and the Cauldon Pottery. Bell produced stone china and earthenware decorated with blue transfer printing. Their mark was 'J. & W. Ridgway' or J. & W.R.' (John and William) until 1848 when 'William Ridgway' was used. The Cauldon Pottery made earthenware, stone china, and high quality porcelains fine enough to win them the distinction of being appointed potters to the Queen. From 1830 their wares attest to this fact, bearing the Royal Arms mark with 'J.R.' within the crest. In 1940 '& Co.' was added. Most examples of Ridgway's wares found today are transfer-printed historical scenes. See also Staffordshire, Historical; and Flow Blue.

Baking dish, Coaching Days, 11¼x6¼" 75.00
Biscuit jar, Coaching Days, brn rattan hdl, 6½" 245.00
Bowl, Coaching Days, 10" 65.00
Butter pat, Indus 40.00
Coffeepot, Coaching Days, 8" 135.00
Creamer & sugar bowl, Coaching Days, w/tray.............................210.00
Cup & saucer, Coaching Days...38.00
Cup & saucer, violets...25.00
Hot plate, Coaching Days, 6" dia 125.00
Mug, Coaching Days, Broken Trade, 4"...35.00
Pitcher, Coaching Days, 5½" 70.00
Pitcher, Coaching Days, 7½" 90.00
Plaque, Taking Up the Mails, yel, 12" 135.00
Plate, chop; Coaching Days, 13½" 150.00
Plate, Coaching Days, 8" 30.00
Plate, Coaching Days, 9" 35.00
Plate, Coaching Days, 10" 45.00
Plate, cup; giraffes w/floral & scroll border, 3¾" dia 210.00
Plate, Indus, crane & bamboo floral border w/birds, lt brn, 9¼"...60.00
Platter, Japan Flowers, brn transfer, Ridgway, Morley, Wear &Co, 13"..295.00
Platter, Liberty Cap & Flag, red transfer w/bl & gr, 12" 225.00
Tankard, Coaching Days, 5" 50.00
Teapot, Coaching Days, 5½"..175.00
Tray, Coaching Days, oval, 12" 90.00
Vase, Coaching Days, 5"...80.00

Riviera

Riviera was a line of dinnerware introduced by the Homer Laughlin China Company in 1938. It was sold exclusively by the Murphy Company through their nationwide chain of dime stores. Riviera was unmarked, lightweight, and inexpensive. It was discontinued sometime prior to 1950. Colors are mauve blue, red, yellow, light green, and ivory. On rare occasions, dark blue pieces are found, but this was not a standard color. For further information we recommend *The Collector's Encyclopedia of Fiesta* (2001 values) by Sharon and Bob Huxford, available from Collector Books.

Batter set, complete, from $290 to...315.00
Batter set, ivory, w/decals, complete, from $170 to......................185.00
Bowl, baker; 9", from $25 to...30.00
Bowl, cream soup; w/liner, ivory, from $75 to..........................80.00
Bowl, fruit; 5½", from $12 to...14.00
Bowl, nappy; 7¼", from $25 to...30.00
Bowl, oatmeal; 6", from $38 to...42.00
Bowl, utility; ivory, from $48 to...52.00
Butter dish, cobalt, ¼-lb, from $250 to 280.00
Butter dish, cobalt, ½-lb, from $300 to 325.00
Butter dish, colors other than cobalt, turq or ivory, ¼-lb, $135 to...150.00
Butter dish, colors other than cobalt, ½-lb, from $120 to 130.00
Butter dish, ivory, ¼-lb, from $175 to....................................185.00
Butter dish, turq, ¼-lb, from $290 to 310.00

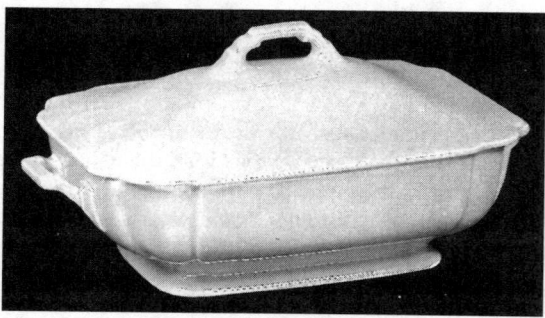

Casserole, from $110.00 to $130.00.

Creamer, from $11 to...13.00
Cup & saucer, demitasse; ivory, from $80 to 90.00
Jug, w/lid, from $130 to...145.00
Pitcher, juice; mauve bl, from $210 to......................................225.00
Pitcher, juice; yel, from $120 to...135.00
Plate, deep, from $22 to...25.00
Plate, 6", from $7 to...9.00
Plate, 7", from $10 to...14.00
Plate, 9", from $16 to...20.00
Plate, 10", from $55 to...65.00
Platter, closed hdls, 11¼", from $24 to.................................28.00
Platter, cobalt, 12", from $70 to...80.00
Platter, 11½", from $22 to...25.00
Platter, 15", from $55 to...65.00
Sauce boat, from $22 to...27.00
Saucer, from $4 to...5.00
Shakers, pr, from $18 to...20.00
Sugar bowl, w/lid, from $18 to...20.00
Syrup, w/lid, from $160 to...180.00
Teacup, from $8 to...11.00
Teapot, from $155 to...165.00
Tidbit, ivory, 2-tier, from $70 to...75.00

Tumbler, hdl, from $70 to...75.00
Tumbler, hdl, ivory, from $135 to...145.00
Tumbler, juice; from $52 to...55.00

Robertson

Fred H. Robertson, clay expert for the Los Angeles Pressed Brick Company and son of Alexander Robertson of the Roblin Pottery, experimented with crystalline glazes as early as 1906. In 1934 Fred and his son George established their own works in Los Angeles, but by 1943 they had moved operations to Hollywood. Though most of their early wares were turned by hand, some were also molded in low relief. Fine crackle glazes and crystallines were developed. Their ware was marked with 'Robertson,' 'F.H.R.,' or 'R.,' with the particular location of manufacture noted. The small pottery closed in 1952.

Vase, bl & gr crystalline on cream gloss, att, 5½"......................425.00
Vase, celadon w/tightly-packed crystals, classic shape, 7½x4¾"..3,250.00
Vase, gr/purple/rose/gray crystalline on lt lav, 6".....................1,400.00
Vase, multitoned gr matt, ped ft, 4"......................................400.00
Vase, wht crackle w/pk at top, 2"...110.00

Robineau

After short-term training in ceramics in 1903, Adelaide Robineau (with the help of her husband Samuel) built a small pottery studio at her home in Syracuse, New York. She was adept in mixing the clay and throwing the ware, which she often decorated by incising designs into the unfired clay. Samuel developed many of the glazes and took charge of the firing process. In 1910 she joined the staff of the American Women's League Pottery at St. Louis, where she designed the famous Scarab Vase. After this pottery failed, she served on the faculty of Syracuse University. Her work was and is today highly acclaimed for the standards of excellence to which she aspired.

Jar, mossy gr flambe, geometric floral bronze-glaze lid, 1920, 4½"...13,000.00
Vase, butterscotch flambe, 1904, bruise to rim, 2½x2" 2,100.00
Vase, cobalt crystalline, spherical, 3¾x4¾"..............................6,000.00
Vase, gr & bl matt crystalline, 1904, 2¼x2"............................1,700.00
Vase, turq/wht/gr/red frothy flambe, 1921, 5x5" 14,500.00

Robj

Robj was the name of a retail store that operated in Paris for only a few years, from about 1925 to 1931. Robj solicited designs from the best French artisans of the period to produce decorative objects for the home. These were executed mostly in porcelain but there were glass and earthenware pieces as well. The most well known are the figural bottles which were particularly popular in the United States. However, Robj also promoted tea sets, perfume lamps, chess sets, ashtrays, bookends, humidors, powder jars, cigarette boxes, figurines, lamps, and milk pitchers. Robj objects tend to be whimsical, and all embody the Art Deco style. Items listed below are ceramic unless noted otherwise. Our advisors for this category are Randall Monsen and Rod Baer; their address is listed in the Directory under Virginia.

Bookends, Pirogue Indienne, Indians in canoe, wht porc, faint mk...325.00
Bottle, bagpiper, cork stopper, 10¼"...300.00
Lamp, lady in evening gown, Aladdin Luxe Made in France, 14".........625.00
Lamp, perfume; Deco-style couple, perfume in her pocket, rpr, 8½" 275.00
Lamp, perfume; Pierrot w/censor (for perfume), Modele Depose..., 6x3"...550.00

Lamp base, Greek man (woman) w/gilt on wht, mk, 11", pr.......**460.00**
Powder jar, Art Deco lady, arms out to side, mc, 5½x5½" **635.00**

Rock 'N Roll Memorabilia

Memorabilia from the early days of rock 'n roll recalls an era that many of us experienced firsthand; these listings are offered to demonstrate the many and various aspects of this area of collecting. Beware of reproductions! Many are so well done even a knowledgeable collector will sometimes be fooled.

Our advisor for Elvis memorabilia is Rosalind Cranor, author of *Elvis Collectibles* and *Best of Elvis Collectibles* (Overmountain Press); she is listed in the Directory under Virginia. The remainder is under the advisement of Bob Gottuso, author of Beatles, Kiss, and Monkees sections in *Garage Sale Gold II* by Tomart; see Pennsylvania. For more information we recommend *Rock-N-Roll Treasures* by Joe Hilton and Greg Moore (Collector Books). See also Decanters.

Beatles, ring, black and white portrait on white, NM, from $50.00 to $75.00. (Photo courtesy Barbara Crawford, Hollis Lamon, and Michael Stern)

Allman Brothers, mobile, Wipe the Windows Check the Oil, M.**80.00**
Andy Gibb, fan club folder, complete, 10x8", 1980, M **125.00**
Andy Gibb, Wireless FM Microphone, LJN, 1978, MIB, from $55 to..**75.00**
Bangles, calendar, 1986, M...**50.00**
BB King-Moby Grape-Steve Miller Band, poster, Myers, 1967, 5x8"....**20.00**
Beach Boys, concert poster, Santa Barbara County Bowl, July, 1966, M **2,000.00**
Beach Boys, tour program, 1976, M..**30.00**
Beatles, apron, heavy paper w/blk & wht repeated design, US, 1964...**500.00**
Beatles, assignment book, Selecto-O-Pak, 1964, M **300.00**
Beatles, autograph book, photo image, 1964, unused, NM, from $500 to...**700.00**
Beatles, bank, bust figure, 4 different, Pride Creations, 8", EX, ea ..**600.00**
Beatles, book, Yellow Submarine, Max Wilk, hardcover, VG+ **90.00**
Beatles, book, Yellow Submarine, Max Wilk, paperbk, Signet, 4x7"..**18.00**
Beatles, bookmark, colorful cb figure of Ringo Star **12.00**
Beatles, calendar, Yellow Submarine, cartoon scenes, 12x12", VG ..**190.00**
Beatles, calendar, 1964, mc group photo, rare, EX **250.00**
Beatles, charm, faces on 1 side, metal, 1964, 1¼" **18.00**
Beatles, comb, Genuine Autographed Beatles Comb, Lido, 1964, 14", M.**250.00**
Beatles, concert flyer, Seattle, 1964, M **400.00**
Beatles, diecast vehicle, Yellow Submarine, Corgi, 1968, EX......**300.00**
Beatles, figures, lead, Magical Mystery Tour, set of 4, M.............**100.00**
Beatles, flasher button, portraits & 1st names on bl or red, 2½" ...**30.00**
Beatles, guitar, Junior by Selco, rare, 14", EX **1,500.00**
Beatles, guitar, Red Jet by Selco, rare, 31", NM.......................**1,800.00**
Beatles, headband, allover portraits & signatures, Dame, 1964, EX ...**85.00**
Beatles, key chain, flasher, Hong Kong, 1960s, NM **75.00**
Beatles, lamp, Yellow Submarine base, w/starfish shade, ca 1999 ..**45.00**
Beatles, lunch box, Yellow Submarine, VG+ **400.00**
Beatles, magazine, Official Yellow Submarine, 48-pg, VG.............**45.00**
Beatles, megaphone, portraits, NEMS, 1964, EX **600.00**
Beatles, mobile, cb characters, Sunshine Art Studios, 9¼x14¼", M....**180.00**
Beatles, mug, photo/names/The Beatles, Washington Pottery, 1964, M...**125.00**
Beatles, mug, Yellow Submarine, decal, Apple, ca 1987 ....**7.50**
Beatles, necklace, brass G-clef w/photo insert, Randall, 1964, MOC...**250.00**

Beatles, ornaments, glass figures w/plastic guitars, set of 4, MIB .**850.00**
Beatles, pen, Yellow Submarine moves past fish, ballpoint, 1980s ...**12.00**
Beatles, pen holder, ceramic, US Ceramic Co, 1964, M **1,000.00**
Beatles, pennant, I Love the Beatles, felt, 29", EX **200.00**
Beatles, pencil case, vinyl w/photos & autographs, SPP, EX........**200.00**
Beatles, pillow, red/wht/bl, Nordic House, 1964, 12", M w/tags ..**200.00**
Beatles, pin, guitar, plastic w/group photo under plastic **39.00**
Beatles, purse, faces/names on wht cloth, brass hdl, Dame, 1964, NM..**500.00**
Beatles, puzzle, Blue Meanies Attack, 650 pcs, EX (VG box) **200.00**
Beatles, puzzle, Meanies Invade Pepperland, 650 pcs, VG (VG- box)...**180.00**
Beatles, rug, woven, head images/instruments/musical notes, 1964, M..**450.00**
Beatles, scrapbook, The Beatles Scrap Book & head shots, 1964, M **85.00**
Beatles, sheet music, various songs, US, 1960s, EX, ea **25.00**
Beatles, stickpin, Yellow Submarine diecast, HP, ca 1968.............**38.00**
Beatles, tie clip, brass, 4 emb heads & The Beatles, 1" **70.00**
Beatles, tie tac, pewter, Ringo, on original blk & wht photo card.**35.00**
Beatles, tote bag, wht vinyl w/blk & wht photo image, Japan, 1966, M .**150.00**
Bee Gees, belt buckle, oval w/gold name on bl, gold trim, 1979, M...**35.00**
Bee Gees, bkpack, photo image, Factory, 1978, NM, from $50 to.**75.00**
Bee Gees, fan club kit, complete, 1979, NM, from $75 to **100.00**
Bee Gees, mirror, Sgt Pepper, M **50.00**
Bee Gees, mobile, Bee Gees Greatest, 1979 promo, rare, M **150.00**
Bee Gees, record case, 45 rpm, photo image, Vanity Fair, 1979, EX **50.00**
Bob Dylan, poster, Nobody Sings Dylan Like..., 1966 CBS promo, M...**600.00**
Bobby Darin, pen/record, Free Record w/Scripto..., 1958, MIP...**125.00**
Bobby Sherman, Love Beads, 1971, M, from $40 to **50.00**
Boy George & Culture Club, key chain, 1984, MIP **10.00**
Boy George & Culture Club, puffy stickers, set of 6, 1984, M.......**15.00**
Crosby Stills & Nash, whistle, Whistling Down the Wire, EX **20.00**
David Cassidy, fan club kit, complete, Laufer, 1972, M...............**100.00**
Dick Clark, doll, Juro, 1958, 24", MIB..**250.00**
Donny & Marie Osmond, camera & photo album, Gordy, 1976, MOC ..**35.00**
Donny & Marie Osmond, Poster Pen Set, Craft House, 1977, NRFB..**40.00**
Donny & Marie Osmond, record case, Peerless Vidtronic Corp, 1977, NM...**35.00**
Doors, concert poster, Santa Barbara, 1968, M......................**1,000.00**
Eagles, concert poster, Cerritos College, 1973, M........................**350.00**
Elton John, poster, Don't Shoot Me I'm Only the Piano Player, 1972, M...**400.00**
Elvis, alarm clock, Love Me Tender, Unique Time Co, NM..........**90.00**
Elvis, beach hat, orig photo hang tag, 1956, EX **150.00**
Elvis, car, diecast, T-Bird w/Elvis w/guitar, Corgi, 1957 ....**45.00**
Elvis, Christmas ornament, Hallmark, 1992....................................**20.00**
Elvis, earrings, Loving You, 1970s repro, MOC.............................**40.00**
Elvis, feather pen, Tickle Me, feather on top, 1965 promo...........**18.00**
Elvis, guitar, Lapin, 1984, MOC (sealed) **75.00**
Elvis, guitar, Selco, 1959, 32", rare, EXIB...................................**700.00**
Elvis, guitar (toy), Lapin, 1984, 29", MOC **75.00**
Elvis, key chain, Elvis Presley Blvd, plastic, 1980s **5.00**
Elvis, overnight case, images/signatures, EP Enterprises, 1956, EX....**650.00**
Elvis, pencil, Sincerely Elvis, 1956 ....**18.00**
Elvis, pillow, Love Me Tender, Elvis Presley Enterprises, 1956, NM .**400.00**
Elvis, ring, brass w/full-color image under clear bubble, 1956, EX.....**200.00**
Elvis, ring, flasher, 1957, EX, minimum value...............................**100.00**
Elvis, sheet music, Hound Dog, M **55.00**
Elvis, silk scarf, 1956, NM..**530.00**
Elvis, wallet, bl vinyl, EP Enterprises, 1956, EX, from $400 to ...**600.00**
Fats Domino & others, concert poster, South Salem High, 1957, M...**1,000.00**
Jackson Five, banner, I Love the Jackson 5, felt, 1960s-70s, 29", NM.......**35.00**
John Lennon, comb, mk John Lennon/Rock 'n Roll/SK 3419, M.**15.00**
KISS, ballpoint pen, 1978, MOC **125.00**
KISS, board game, On Tour, Aucoin, 1978, MIB **175.00**
KISS, fan club kit, KISS Army, complete, M **75.00**
KISS, school folder, unused, M..**50.00**
KISS, school notebook, spiral, unused, M **45.00**
KISS, waste can, Aucoin, 1977, M...**225.00**

Led Zeppelin, mirror, name & graphics, gold fr, sq, M 15.00
Led Zeppelin, photograph (fan club), 8x10", 1973, M 20.00
Led Zeppelin, t-shirt, 1977 US Tour (last US tour), M 50.00
Little Richard, concert poster, Crystal Garden, 1958, M 500.00
Madonna, bumper sticker, gold name on blk, MDI, 1994, M 15.00
Madonna, mask, by Caesar for Masquerade Novelty Co, 1989, M ...225.00
Madonna, Poster Book, w/9 posters, Button Up, 1990, M 30.00
Madonna, sports bottle, Express Yourself, Boy Toy, 1990, M 35.00
Madonna, stationery, Star Stationery, 1986, MIB (sealed) 75.00
MC Hammer, wallet, vinyl, Bustin' Productions, 1991, MOC 25.00
Michael Jackson, belt, various designs, 1984, ea, from $20 to 30.00
Michael Jackson, book, MJ King of Pop, hardbk w/dj, M 20.00
Michael Jackson, pillow, gold name/stars/crown design on blk, M .40.00
Michael Jackson, stamp set, complete, St Vincent, M 30.00
Michael Jackson, t-shirt, Heal the World concert, 1994, M..........25.00
Monkees, book, Monkees Annual, hardbk, Raybert Productions, 1967, NM..50.00
Monkees, book, Monkees Go Mod, softcover, 1967, EX 15.00
Monkees, fan club kit, complete, 1967, EX (EX mailer) 200.00
Monkees, ring, flasher, VG...25.00
New Kids on the Block, school kit, Big Step Productions, 1990, MIP ..15.00
Ricky Nelson, concert poster, Salem Armory, 1970, M 200.00
Rolling Stones, air freshener, Medo, 1983, MIP.........................15.00
Rolling Stones, ashtray, from Voodoo Lounge tour, M................25.00
Rolling Stones, book cover, Musidor, 1981, NM.......................15.00
Shaun Cassidy, record case, cb, Vanity Fair, 1978, EX 35.00
Supremes, handbill, w/The Lovin' Spoonfull..., 1960s, M 600.00
Turtles, poster, 1966, 5x7", VG 25.00
Van Halen, tour jacket, blk satin-like w/stiched graphics, 1984, M..250.00
Who, concert poster, Memorial Coliseum, Nov 22, 1970s, M 500.00
Yardbirds, concert flyer, 1966 tour, M...................................150.00
Young Rascals, concert flyer, 1967, M 50.00
ZZ Top, concert poster, Charger Stadium, 1973, M...................150.00

Rockingham

In the early part of the nineteenth century, American potters began to prefer brown- and buff-burning clays over red because of their durability. The glaze favored by many was Rockingham, which varied from a dark brown mottle to a sponged effect sometimes called tortoise shell. It consisted in part of manganese and various metallic salts and was used by many potters until well into the twentieth century. Over the past two years, demand and prices have risen sharply, especially in the east. See also Bennington.

Bank, circular building w/molded detail, OH, 5¼" 400.00
Bank, 2-story brick house w/chimneys, chips, 4¾" 165.00
Bean pot, dk tortoise-shell, flat lid w/mushroom finial, ca 1870, 5" ..95.00
Bed pan, oval w/spout 1 end, 5⅜x15x10⅜" 125.00
Boiler, milk; emb bands, dk brn, att Rapp Bros (IL), 4½", $45 to .60.00
Bowl, brn over yel ware, OH, 14", from $500 to.......................500.00
Bowl, columns & dots along rim, #195, ca 1860, 3½x10½", EX...95.00
Bowl, mottled, ca 1880, 4x9½" 75.00
Bowl, mush; rnd w/flat bottom, str sides, 3x11½" 50.00
Bowl, raised panel sides, hairlines at table ring, 6x13" 100.00
Bowl, ribbed band, heavy, 2½x7", from $50 to 65.00
Coffeepot, dk brn, curvilinear design, acorn finial, 10, from $450 to.....475.00
Cooler, brn w/gr streaks, att Woodward & Vodrey, 1848-1879, $350 to...700.00
Creamer, cow, chips, 5x7"..275.00
Crock, butter; bulbous, thin walls, no lid, 4¼", $75 to...............135.00
Crock, 2 lambrequin borders/plain band, ear hdls, OH, 1870s, 6½"..130.00
Crock (fruit jar), graduations in depth of color, 1870s, ½-gal, 7"...225.00
Cuspidor, brn runs w/bl-gr spots, paneled sides, scalloped rim, 9"..150.00
Custard, att J Patterson & Sons (OH), 6-oz, from $18 to............22.00

Custard cup, lt brn, ca 1870, 2¾" 20.00
Figurine, dog, seated, 10⅜" 475.00
Figurine, spaniel on base, mottled brn w/gr accents, 12x10x8", EX...525.00
Humidor, tortoise-shell glaze, flared top, paneled, 9", from $75 to.250.00
Inkwell, girl rests her head on stump, brn runs, 3½x4½x2½"....200.00
Jug, batter; ovoid, lipless, att OR Pottery Co, 1885-1895, 10" 100.00
Loving cup, appl man w/dogs & lantern/man at table, 7x12" at hdls, EX...300.00
Mold, Turk's head, rich pumpkin under brn, 8¾", from $100 to.150.00
Mug, dk brn, flower decal, ca 1930, 4¾", from $18 to...............125.00
Mug, dk brn, hand thrown, ca 1890, 5", from $45 to 100.00
Nappy, emb ft, 10½", from $100 to 125.00
Pie plate, controlled spatter of thick drops, thin body, 9½" 135.00
Pitcher, bbl design, ca 1900, 8½", EX.....................................125.00
Pitcher, horned cow w/in floral scroll, dk brn, 1½-pt, 7½" 235.00
Pitcher, hunt scene w/deer & dogs, hound hdl, ca 1860, 9¾".....400.00
Pitcher, hunt scene w/hanging game, 9" 250.00
Pitcher, iris & flower band, dk reddish-brn, ca 1900, 8¾"..........100.00
Pitcher, man smoking/woman w/snuff in medallions, w/lid, 9¼"...175.00
Pitcher, peacocks & palm trees, lt brn, OH, 1870-84, 8", from $125 to....275.00
Pitcher, pillar & scroll, 7¼" 150.00

Pitchers, rose, 9¾", G, $150.00; Cupid, 8¼", G, $150.00.

Pitcher, soldiers fighting/rifles & eagle w/snake reliefs, 9½"........330.00
Pitcher, tulip, ca 1890, 5"..150.00
Plate, berries & leaves, Hautin & Boulanger, 1880s, 8", from $35 to....65.00
Teapot, lt streaky brn, flower finial, att IL or OH, 1870s, 7¼"....250.00
Teapot, Rebekah at Well, domed lid, rosette finial, 19th C, 6"...125.00
Toby jug, Duke of Wellington...1859, 8", EX 195.00
Toby jug, seated man w/jug, ca 1880, 6" 150.00
Washboard, yel & brn, overall wear, East Liverpool Ohio origin, 22x12" ...600.00

Rockwell, Norman

Norman Rockwell began his career in 1911 at the age of seventeen doing illustrations for a children's book entitled *Tell Me Why Stories*. Within a few years he had produced the *Saturday Evening Post* cover that made him one of America's most beloved artists. Though not well accepted by the professional critics of his day who did not consider his work to be art but 'merely' commercial illustration, Rockwell's popularity grew to the extent that today there is an overwhelming abundance of examples of his work or those related to the theme of one of his illustrations.

The figurines described below were issued by the Rockwell Museum and Museum Collections Inc. (formerly Rockwell Museum). For Rockwell listings by Gorham see last year's edition of *Schroeder's Antiques Price Guide*. Our advisor for this category is Barb Putratz; she is listed in the Directory under Minnesota.

A Walkin' & a Whistlin', Museum Collections Inc, 1986 ....70.00
All Wrapped Up, 1984..100.00
America's Artist, ltd ed 5,000, 1983 ....195.00
Apple for the Teacher, Museum Collections Inc, 1986.................70.00
At the Circus, 1982...190.00
Baby's First Step, 1979..175.00
Bedtime, LCF series, ltd ed 1,000, 1982 ....225.00

Bicycle Boys, 1981..120.00
Birthday Party, 1980......................................150.00
Bored of Education, 1984..................................95.00
Boy Meets His Dog, 1986.................................100.00
Bride & Groom, 1981.....................................140.00
Celebration, 1982...190.00
Checking His List, 1980...................................90.00
Circus Comes to Town, 1982..............................125.00
Cobbler, LCF Series, ltd ed 1,000, 1982..................225.00
Collect Fine Porcelain Figures (ad stand), 1984...........140.00
Courageous Hero, 1982...................................185.00
Downhill Racer, 1981.....................................120.00
Dreams in the Antique Shop, Museum Collections Inc, 1986......80.00
Drummer's Friend, 1982..................................125.00
First Car in Town, ltd ed 2,500, 1985....................235.00
First Prom, 1979...125.00
For a Good Boy, 1980......................................90.00
Freedom of Speech, ltd ed 5,000, 1982...................350.00
Freedom of Worship, ltd ed 5,000, 1982.................350.00
Goin' Fishin', 1984.......................................95.00
Good Food, Good Friends, 1982..........................225.00
Helping Mother, 1982....................................120.00
High Stepping, 1982......................................110.00
Homerun Slugger, 1982..................................145.00
Late Night Dining, Museum Collections Inc, 1986...........80.00
Lighthouse Keeper's Daughter, LCF Series, ltd ed 1,000, 1982...225.00
Little Mother, 1980.......................................175.00
Little Salesman, 1982....................................185.00
Lovely in Lipstick, Museum Collections Inc, 1988..........75.00
Memories, 1980...90.00
Mom's Helper, ltd ed 15,000, 1986......................120.00
Music Lesson, 1980..90.00
Mysterious Malady, 1986.................................100.00
No Fishin', No Nothin', Museum Collections Inc, 1986......80.00
Out Fishin', Museum Collections Inc, ltd ed 25,000, 1985...100.00
Painter & the Pups, ltd ed 5,000, 1986..................205.00
Pest, 1982...125.00
Practice Makes Perfect, Museum Collections Inc, ltd ed 2,500, 1987..170.00
Puppy Love, 1983..95.00
Ringing in Good Cheer, 1981.............................125.00
Santa Takes a Break, Museum Collections Inc, ltd ed 3,500, 1987..110.00
Secrets, ltd ed 5,000, 1986..............................185.00
Soda Jerk, ltd ed 5,000, 1986...........................205.00
Space Pioneers, 1982....................................185.00
Spirit of America, ltd ed 5,000, 1982...................185.00
Stereoscope, 1986..100.00
Summer Fun, 1982..120.00
Surprise Treat, 1984......................................95.00
Sweet Sixteen, 1979......................................125.00
Tipping the Scale, Museum Collections Inc, 1986...........75.00
Toymaker, 1979...95.00
Vacation, 1982...115.00
Visiting the Vet, Museum Collections Inc, 1988............85.00
Washing Our Dog, 1981...................................140.00
Weighty Matters, ltd ed 5,000, 1986....................180.00
While the Audience Waits, 1981..........................100.00
Words of Wisdom, 1982..................................130.00

Rogers, John

John Rogers (1829 – 1904) was a machinist from Manchester, New Hampshire, who turned his hobby of sculpting into a financially successful venture. From the originals he meticulously fashioned of red clay,

he had bronze master molds made from which plaster copies were cast. He specialized in five different categories: theatrical, Shakespeare, Civil War, everyday life, and horses. His large detailed groupings portrayed the life and times of the period between 1859 and 1892. In the following listings, examples are assumed to be in very good to excellent condition. Our advisor for this category is George Humphrey; he is listed in the Directory under Maryland.

Balcony..1,500.00
Bubbles...2,000.00
Bushwacker...2,000.00
Chess..1,200.00

Coming to the Parson, 22", $375.00.

Council of War...1,100.00
Courtship in Sleepy Hollow, Pat date........................550.00
Fairy's Whisper, ca 1881..................................1,400.00
Favored Scholar...425.00
Fighting Bob, ca 1889....................................1,100.00
First Ride...725.00
Going for the Cows..450.00
Home Guard...800.00
Madam, Your Mother Craves a Word w/You....................700.00
Mail Day..2,000.00
Neighboring Pews..500.00
Parting Promise...475.00
Playing Doctor..500.00
Referee...600.00
Rip Van Winkle — At Home..................................325.00
Rip Van Winkle — Returned.................................425.00
Rip Van Winkle on the Mountain.............................425.00
Speak for Yourself John.....................................500.00
Taking the Oath & Drawing Rations, sgn, 23"................525.00
Tap on the Window..525.00
Village Schoolmaster..850.00
Washington...1,250.00
Watch on the Santa Maria.................................1,000.00
Wounded Scout, ca 1864.....................................750.00
Wounded to the Rear — One More Shot.......................550.00

Rookwood

The Rookwood Pottery Company was established in 1879 in Cincinnati, Ohio. Its founder was Maria Longworth Nichols Storer, daughter of a wealthy family who provided the backing necessary to make such an enterprise possible. Mrs. Storer hired competent ceramic artisans and artists of note, who through constant experimentation developed many lines of superior art pottery. While in her employ, Laura Fry invented the airbrush-blending process for which she was issued a patent in 1884. From this, several lines were designed that utilized blended backgrounds. One of their earlier lines, Standard, was a brown ware decorated with underglaze slip-painted nature studies, animals, portraits, etc. Iris and Sea Green were introduced in 1894 and Vellum, a transparent mat-glaze line, in 1904. Other lines followed: Ombroso in 1910 and Soft Porcelain in 1915. Many of the early artware lines were signed by the artist. Soon after the turn of the twentieth century, Rookwood manufactured 'production' pieces that relied mainly on molded designs and forms rather than freehand decoration for their esthetic appeal. The Depression brought on financial difficulties from which the pottery never recovered. Though it continued to operate, the quality of the ware deteriorated, and the pottery was forced to close in 1967.

Unmarked Rookwood is only rarely encountered. Many marks may be found, but the most familiar is the reverse 'RP' monogram. First used in 1886, a flame point was added above it for each succeeding year until 1900. After that a Roman numeral added below indicated the year of manufacture. Impressed letters that related to the type of clay utilized for the body were also used — G for ginger, O for olive, R for red, S for sage green, W for white, and Y for yellow. Artware must be judged on an individual basis. Quality of the artwork is a prime factor to consider. Portraits, animals, and birds are worth more than florals; and pieces signed by a particularly renowned artist are highly prized.

Aerial Blue

Vase, mother & child amidst waves, McDonald, 1895, #242D, 13x3" ..11,000.00
Vase, sailboat, bottle shape, Strafer, 1895, 5¾x2½" 3,700.00

Black Opal

Vase, cherry blossoms, HE Wilcox, #1358E, 1925, 7" 1,800.00
Vase, cherry blossoms (Deco), S Sax, #2918B, 1933, 11".........4,500.00
Vase, dogwood blossoms, K Shirayamadani, #2264E, 1925, 5½x6"...2,600.00
Vase, flowers (stylized), S Sax, #2996, 1927, 9x5½".................2,500.00
Vase, lilies (ornate/lg), HE Wilcox, #2785, 1928, 13" 7,500.00
Vase, roses (EX art), HE Wilcox, #2789, 1924, 11" 1,500.00
Vase, scenic, A Conant, #1873, 1921, 5⅜"..............................2,500.00

Cameo

Cup & saucer, floral on wht, A Valentien, #291, W, 1889, 3" 240.00
Jug, bird flying from pine branch, M Daly, 1886, 9x7½".........1,000.00
Vase, bird on pine branch, K Shirayamadani, #346B, 1881, 6x6¾"..1,600.00

Iris

Pocket vase, floral on mauve, S Sax, #90C W, 1910, 3¾"..........800.00
Vase, berries & leaves, S Sax, #860, 1901, bruise, 6½"...............400.00
Vase, cherry blossoms, L Asbury, #80E, 1909, line, 8" 550.00
Vase, clover blossoms, F Rothenbusch, #754, 1901, 6½x4½"..1,200.00
Vase, coreopsis, S Sax, #913C, 1906, W, 8½"...........................3,500.00
Vase, cvd/pnt roses & buds, SE Coyne, #922, 1907, flaw, 8"....1,200.00
Vase, cyclamen, C Todd, #1343, 1910, mfg flaw, 4½" 2,500.00
Vase, cyclamen, F Rothenbusch, #932D, 1906, 9"...................1,600.00
Vase, cyclamen, S Coyne, #1278D, W, 1907, 9¾" 3,200.00
Vase, daffodils, S Sax, #904CC, W, 1906, 9½"..........................4,000.00
Vase, fish swimming, ET Hurley, #902 D, W, 1906, 6¾" 3,300.00
Vase, fish swimming (4), SE Coyne, #1369e, 1911, 7"............2,200.00
Vase, flowering cactus, AR Valentien, #926A, 1902, 13" 11,000.00
Vase, flowers & leaves, I Bishop, #842d, 1907, X, 5½"................700.00
Vase, holly berries & leaves, S Sax, #922D, 1904, line, 7" 550.00
Vase, irises (EX art/color), C Schmidt, #901c, 1903, 9" 3,500.00
Vase, leafy branch, S Sax, #927E, 1901, W, 7", NM.................1,200.00
Vase, lilies of the valley, LE Lindeman, #925E, 1903, 6½".........1,200.00
Vase, magnolia blossoms, I Bishop, #80C, 1903, 6½x4"..............950.00
Vase, mushrooms (detailed), C Schmidt, #904D, 1902, 8" 3,250.00
Vase, narcissus (EX art), ET Hurley, #913D, 1928, 8" 3,250.00

Vase, nasturtiums, F Rothenbusch, #734D, 1903, 6¾x4"........1,300.00
Vase, pillow; sailboats, C Schmidt, #707AA W, X, 1902, 8¾"...3,500.00
Vase, poppies (EX art), C Schmidt, #1358B, 1908, X, 13"........4,750.00
Vase, poppies (fine art), K Shirayamadani, shouldered, 1907, 16"..32,500.00
Vase, Queen Ann's Lace, S Sax, #941, 1906, 9½x3½" 2,400.00
Vase, roses, E Diers, #926C, 1903, 8½x4½" 1,900.00
Vase, roses, F Rothenbusch, #907E W, 1903, 8⅜"..................2,000.00
Vase, sail boats, C Schmidt, #901C, 1904, X, 8½"...................2,700.00
Vase, thistles, SE Coyne, #904E, 1904, 6½"...........................1,000.00
Vase, thistles & leaves, S Sax, #909C, 1906, 8¾x5" 1,800.00
Vase, water lilies & lily pads, L Epply, #913D, 1902, 8" 2,000.00
Vase, wisteria (EX art), Ed Diers, #2720, 1925, 6½"..............2,400.00

Limoges

Pitcher, swallows among clouds, unknown artist, #123, 1882, 6¾"..425.00
Plate, floral w/gold, unsgn, #87, 1887, 6½" 220.00
Vase, 7 soaring birds w/gold flecks, M Rettig, #90, 1883, 8"........850.00
Vessel, winged beetle/reeds w/gold, AR Valentien, hdl, 1883, 10"...1,400.00

Mat

Note: Both incised mat and painted mat are listed here. Incised mat descriptions are indicated by the term 'cvd' within the line; the others are for the hand-painted mat ware.

Lamp, flowers, C Todd, 1910; 16" ldgl peacock shade, 22" 2,500.00
Plaque, irises (fine art), AR Valentien, #7BZ, 1901, 11" 12,000.00
Plaque, 3 geese along road, S Toohey, 4½x9"+orig oak fr 3,250.00
Vase, blueberries, F Rothenbusch, #969C, 1905, X, 6" 850.00
Vase, cvd calla lillies, A Pons, #1124D, 1907, 8½x3½"..........8,500.00
Vase, cvd stylized decor at shoulder, S Sax, #932E, 1905, 7x3" ..1,600.00
Vase, cvd/pnt flower band, C Todd, #270, 1917, 12".............4,000.00
Vase, cvd/pnt gr berries & leaves, S Sax, #4DZ, 1903, 7½", NM....600.00
Vase, cvd/pnt peacock feather, WE Hentschel, #77A8, 1914, 5"....950.00
Vase, cvd/pnt thistles (EX detail), K Shirayamadani, #299AZ, 1904, 15".7,000.00
Vase, dogwood blossoms, H Wilcox, #950B, 1906, 12¼x5".....3,750.00
Vase, floral, OG Reed, #1655E, 1911, 8x4" 1,300.00
Vase, mc geometrics, C Todd, 1919, 9" 950.00
Vase, trumpet flowers, K Shirayamadani, #2969, 1939, 8" 2,100.00
Vase, tulips & leaves, illegible signature, S, 1938, 11½" 1,000.00

Porcelain

Chalice, llamas, Jewel, J Jensen, 1933, 6x3¾" 2,100.00
Vase, animal figures (Deco style), E Barrett, #2193, 1944, 4½" ..950.00
Vase, cherry blossoms, Jewel, S Sax, #8903, 1920, 4x4"...........1,600.00
Vase, cvd/pnt floral, WE Hentschel, #S1904, 1914, X, 11"......1,200.00
Vase, cvd/pnt owls on branch, S Toohey, #614E, 1930, 8½" ...2,600.00
Vase, deer (EX art), J Jensen, #900C, 1931, 8½"......................4,000.00
Vase, deer & flowers, Jewel, J Jensen, 1933, 7¼x4"................2,100.00
Vase, floral, WE Hentschel, #1667, 1922, 11" 1,800.00
Vase, flowers, W Rehm, #2917E/#7006, 1945, 6½"..................850.00
Vase, fruit on thick limbs, E Barrett, #6891, 1945, 10" 1,500.00
Vase, macaw & foliage, Jewel, ET Hurley, #1667, 1922, 11"....3,750.00
Vase, magnolias, att L Holtkamp, #2984A, 1950, drilled, 16".....700.00
Vase, magnolias, Jewel, J Jensen, #2189, 1944, 6¾x5½".........1,300.00
Vase, swirl pattern on cobalt, Jewel, J Jenson, 1933, 5¾x5" ...1,600.00
Vase, Venetian scene at dusk, C Schmidt, #356E, 1922, 6½x3½" 4,250.00
Vase, wheat shocks, MH McDonald, hdls, 1936, S, 7½"............950.00

Sea Green

Vase, autumn leaves (detailed), S Laurence, #904c, 1901, 12"...6,000.00

Vase, cvd/pnt iris & leaves, MA Daly, #562, 1897, 9" 3,000.00
Vase, cvd/pnt irises & leaves, S Toohey, #829, G, 1898, 9½" ..4,750.00
Vase, frogs among grasses, AR Valentien, #786D, 1896, 8" 1,600.00
Vase, tulips, S Laurence, #907E, X, 1901, 8⅜" 2,600.00

Standard

Ewer, brn-eyed Susans, H Wilcox, #751C, 1894, 8x5½" 650.00
Pitcher, carp (Japanese style), M Daly, #220W, 1885, 8½x9¾"...1,400.00
Pitcher, gooseberry leaves, AR Valentien, #567W, 1891, 12x5¾" ...1,600.00
Pitcher, violets, CA Baker, #547, 1902, 3½" 350.00
Vase, acorns on leafy branch, L Asbury, #X240X, 1898, 10" 800.00
Vase, cherries & leaves, C Schmidt, #667, 1900, 6½" 500.00
Vase, cherries on branch, SE Coyne, #459C, 1900, 7¼" 500.00
Vase, cherry blossoms, E Noonan, #73C, 1906, paper label, 6½" ..450.00
Vase, clover & leaves, AM Valentien, #517D, 1892, 5½"...........550.00
Vase, Conquering Bear - Sioux portrait, A Sehon, #902C, 1901, 9"..7,000.00
Vase, daisies, K Shirayamadani, #401, 1888, glaze skip, 4" 350.00
Vase, day lilies w/silver o/l, EN Lincoln, #482, 1898, 9½", NM ..1,400.00
Vase, geese in flight, M Daly, #664B, 1898, 10½" 3,750.00
Vase, grapevine, E Diers, #734DD, 1900, 6½" 550.00
Vase, hydrangea, AR Valentien, #531D, 1891, rstr drill hole, 12x12"...2,800.00
Vase, maple leaves, I Bishop, #568E, 1900, 4½" 500.00
Vase, maple leaves/seed pods, K Shirayamadani, #S911, 1890, 13"...2,900.00
Vase, narcissus, E Lincoln, #900, 1903, 6¾" 500.00
Vase, orchids, AR Valentien, #702A, 1898, 13x5" 1,300.00
Vase, palm leaves, AR Valentien, special waisted shape, 1889, 29" ..5,000.00
Vase, pansies, S Markland, #553E, 1892, 6½", NM 450.00
Vase, peaches on branch, M Daly, #448F, 1890, 10x9".............1,600.00
Vase, poppies, faceted, L Asbury, #705, 1902, 8x4½" 1,000.00
Vase, poppies, M Nourse, #907C, 1900, 14x5" 2,300.00
Vase, Sitting Bull portrait, S Laurence, 1900, 11" 5,500.00
Vase, tulips, Mary Nourse, #904CC, 1903, 9¾x3¾" 1,000.00
Vessel, corn on husk, SE Coyne, #761, 1896, 4¾", NM.............300.00
Vessel, cyclamen w/silver o/l, S Toohey, #527, 1893, 4½" L 1,900.00

Tiger Eye

Vase, cvd/pnt egret & reeds, gold streaks, A Van Briggle, 1896, 7½"...1,600.00
Vase, red roosters, M Daly, #734D, 1894(?), 7".........................2,100.00

Vellum

Vase, Nouveau-style wild violets, Ed Diers, #5199C, 1930, 6x7⅞", $4,200.00.

Plaque, birches by river, ET Hurley, 1912, 11x9"+fr................7,000.00
Plaque, harbor scene, C Schmidt, ca 1920, 8x4"+orig fr 3,750.00
Plaque, sailboat scenic (detailed), C Schmidt, V, 1916, 9⅜x14½"..13,000.00
Plaque, Twilight, L Epply, 1917, 9x11" +orig fr 6,000.00
Plaque, Winter, landscape, S Coyne, 1918, 7x9" 3,900.00
Vase, Arts & Crafts landscape, S Coyne, #923E, 1920, 8" 3,500.00
Vase, birches at dusk, ET Hurley, #1550A, 1912, 16x6½" 6,500.00
Vase, birches by lake, CJ McLaughlin, #614, 1914, 8¾x4½"...2,100.00
Vase, cherry blossoms, CJ McLaughlin, #1918V, 1915, 9x5"....1,500.00
Vase, cherry blossoms, ET Hurley, #1110, 1925, 4" 850.00
Vase, cherry blossoms, L Epply, #949D, 1908, 9" 1,400.00

Vase, columbines, Ed Diers, #913D, 1931, 7¾x4½" 1,800.00
Vase, cyclamen, F Rothenbusch, #614E, 1908, 8½" 1,300.00
Vase, cyclamen & leaves, C Steinle, #1357E, 1901, 7" 900.00
Vase, daisies, E Lincoln, #614E, 1912, 8½x4" 1,200.00
Vase, daisies, MH McDonald, #901, 1913, 8x3½" 1,200.00
Vase, daisies w/long stems, M McDonald, #1655F, 1913, 6½".....950.00
Vase, dogwood blossoms, L Asbury, #911E, 1904, flaw, 4½" 550.00
Vase, fish swimming (Japanese style), ET Hurley, #1358, 1908, 7¼"...2,100.00
Vase, flowers & leaves, C Klinger, #919D, 1917, 5"...................650.00
Vase, flowers & stems, C Steinle, #939D, 1916, 8" 1,100.00
Vase, lake landscape, E Diers, #952E, 1918, 8x3½" 1,600.00
Vase, landscape (EX scene), E Hurley, #545C, 1927, 10" 3,750.00
Vase, landscape scene, ET Hurley, #6823, 1942, 8" 1,800.00
Vase, landscape scenic, E Diers, #951C, 1921, 10¾" 2,000.00
Vase, marsh landscape, S Sax, #904E, 1911, 7¼x3" 4,500.00
Vase, oak trees in meadow, E Diers, #604C, 1917, 10¼x7¼" ..3,750.00
Vase, peacock feathers, S Sax, #950E, 1910, 7½x3½" 2,400.00
Vase, poppies (EX art), S Sax, #30F, 1904, 6"......................1,100.00
Vase, sailboats in Venetian harbor, C Schmidt, #1121C, 1925, 10" ...6,500.00
Vase, snow scene, E McDermott, #939D, 1917, 8".................1,600.00
Vase, spring landscape, S Coyne, #932D, 1917, 10x3¾"..........1,400.00
Vase, trees in meadow, E Diers, #942E, 1919, 5x3¾" 1,300.00
Vase, trees in silhouette at sunset, S Sax, #2032C, 1920, 12½"..12,000.00
Vase, trees/lake/sunset, ET Hurley, #1667, 1909, 10½x4½" 800.00
Vase, 10 swans w/reflections, C Schmidt, #907C, 1915, 14" .20,000.00
Vase, 3 cicada on branch, E Diers, #942D, 1905, 9½x3¾" 4,250.00

Wax Mat

Bottle, chrysanthemums, E Lincoln, #2825A, 1926, 16½x7" ..3,750.00
Vase, abstract berries/flowers, K Jones, #215E, 1925, 7¼x3½"....950.00
Vase, abstract flowers, J Jenson, #906E, 1930, X, 9¼x4"..........1,400.00
Vase, abstract flowers, K Jones, 1925, #2441, 14x5½"..............1,500.00
Vase, apple blossoms, K Shirayamadani, #6148, 1937, 5½x4" .1,000.00
Vase, bachelor buttons, C Covalenco, #233, 1925, 8x3¾" 1,200.00
Vase, berries & leaves, S Coyne, ovoid, #917c, 1925, 8x4"......1,200.00
Vase, flowers, MH McDonald, #2966, 1930, 6½x3½" 700.00
Vase, water lilies, S Coyne, #614D, 1930, 10¾x5" 2,000.00

Miscellaneous

Ashtray, #2647, 1942, fox at side, yel hi-glaze, 7" dia.................200.00
Ashtray, #2765, 1942, frog at side, bl crystalline, 1¼x6¼" 250.00
Ashtray, #6026, 1930, clown w/legs wide at side of tray, mc, 4"..750.00
Ashtray, #6149, 1943, pelican at side, wht mat, 4"....................210.00
Bookends, #2655, 1946, owls, ivory hi-glaze, 5½", pr.................350.00
Bowl, #974D, 1923, mauve & gr mottle, glaze miss, 2¼" 225.00
Bowl, #2529, 1923, leaves, bl mat, 12"....................................260.00
Bowl, #2574C, 1960, blk mat w/wht slip, 13" 160.00
Bowl, #2803, 1925, gray mat, cloverleaf shape, 2¼x6" 80.00
Candlesticks, #2598, 1922, mauve hi-glaze, 10½", pr.................270.00
Candlesticks, #2661, 1923, dbl hdls, bl mat, 7½", pr.................240.00
Figurine, #6170, 1951, lamb, ivory hi-glaze, L Abel, 6" 170.00
Figurine, #6843, 1943, cockatoo, pk & ivory hi-glaze, 9" 300.00
Figurine, 1945, boxer dog, brn & gr hi-glaze, 10" 2,100.00
Flower frog, #2338, 1927, nudes, gr hi-glaze, C Beach, 6" 375.00
Flower frog, #2801, 1928, pelican, yel hi-glaze, 7⅛" 240.00
Mug, #345B, emb geometrics, dk gr mat, flaws, 5½" 180.00
Paperweight, #2677, 1923, monkey on book, brn mat, 3¾"........275.00
Paperweight, #2679, 1937, wolf, recumbent, brn mat, 5½".........650.00
Paperweight, #2792, 1930, Spanish galleon, X, 3¾"..................325.00
Paperweight, #6030, 1956, rooster, Violet Gray, 5"...................275.00
Paperweight, #6182, 1945, cat, caramel, #60 (L Abel), 6⅝".......650.00
Pencil holder, #1795, 1923, gr crystalline mat, 4¼" 250.00

Tile, landscape w/cloisonne technique, 12", in Arts & Crafts fr ...2,600.00
Tray, #1139, 1940, rook at side, ivory hi-glaze, 4x7" 200.00
Trivet, #2249, 1927, bird, yel & wht hi-glaze, 6" dia 200.00
Trivet, #3091, 1921, floral, yel & gr, 6" 230.00
Urn, #584B, 1912, Greek key, rose over chartreuse butterfat, 18x14" ...1,700.00
Vase, #63, 1933, turq & gr mottle, hdls, 4½" 140.00
Vase, #1267, 1910, Arts & Crafts style, 3x7" 230.00
Vase, #1795, 1922, rooks on 5-sided form, purple mat, 5" 400.00
Vase, #1795, 1944, rooks on 5-sided form, bl hi-glaze, 5" 220.00
Vase, #2013, 1917, floral, purple mat, flaw, 8" 325.00
Vase, #2088, 1928, leaves, turq & gr, 5½" 200.00
Vase, #2108, 1929, floral & leaf, purple mat, 6¼" 325.00
Vase, #2135, 1928, geometrics, bl mat, 6" 240.00
Vase, #2190, 1926, purple mat, 6½" 230.00
Vase, #2326, 1922, rooks, bl mat, 6" 260.00
Vase, #2741, 1930, emb leaves, lt gr mat, 4-sided, hdls, 3½" 110.00
Vase, #2762, 1928, yel mat, 3½" 200.00
Vase, #2859, 1930, emb leaves, 2-tone bl & gr, 6" 210.00
Vase, #4358C, 1924, bl mat, 11" 400.00
Vase, #5079, 1928, sang-de-beouf, Chinese-like shape, 18" 5,000.00
Vase, #6002, 1929, gr mottle, flared rim, 7" 220.00
Vase, #6035, 1928, floral, tan mat, 10", EX 18,000.00
Vase, #6254, 1931, multi-tone bl mat, hdls, 4½" 160.00
Vase, #6498, 1945, 4 molded donkeys, turq hi-glaze, 5" 150.00
Vase, #6547, 1934, ducks & grass, gr mat, 5" 260.00
Wall pocket, #1636, 1920, cicada form, gr mottle 1,000.00

Rorstrand

The Rorstrand Pottery was established in Sweden in 1726 and is today Sweden's oldest existing pottery. The earliest ware, now mostly displayed in Swedish museums, was much like old Delft. Later types were hard-paste porcelains that were enameled and decorated in a peasant style. Contemporary pieces are often described as Swedish Modern. Rorstrand is also famous for their Christmas plates.

Coffeepot, bl herringbone, ca 1960, 8½" 150.00
Figurine, dwarf w/horn, porc, Made in Sweden, Rorstrand, 8½".550.00
Vase, blk gloss w/turq geometrics, I Claussen, 1928-30, 8¼x6"..200.00
Vase, burnt ochre/brn rabbit skin, free-form, Nylund, 1955-56, 9x3"...300.00
Vase, butterflies, bl/purple/wht, 3½x3" 285.00
Vase, Chamotte ware, ball form, G Nylund, 1930s, 4¾" 250.00
Vase, fish in underwater scene, #772, 4½" 850.00
Vase, olive gr w/blk linear decor, bulbous, Stalhane, 1959, 6⅝".275.00
Vase, speckled ochre matt, collared rim, ribbed body, GN, 8¾x3"...500.00
Vase, wht w/varied gr rings, shouldered, Nylund, 5¼" 200.00

Rose Mandarin

Similar in design to Rose Medallion, this Chinese Export porcelain features the pattern of a robed mandarin, often separated by florals, ladies, genre scenes, or butterflies in polychrome enamels. It is sometimes trimmed in gold. Elaborate in decoration, this pattern was popular from the late 1700s until the early 1840s.

Bottle, water; rpr/flakes, w/lid, 14½" 1,150.00
Bowl, panorama, early 19th C, 3½x7⅞" 1,350.00
Bowl, 19th C, 4¾x11⅜" 1,495.00
Brush holder, cylindrical, 19th C, 4¾" 200.00
Dish, florals/foliage, oval, ftd mt w/swing hdl, 2½x12½x8½" 865.00
Garden seat, court scenes/butterflies/flowers, 19th C, 19", EX+..2,645.00
Mug, court scene, rope hdl, mid-19th C, 5¼x3¾" 550.00

Mug, cylindrical, entwined appl hdl, 19th C, 5⅛" 900.00
Pitcher, mandarin scenes, paneled, 7¼" 385.00
Plate, dessert; 19th C, 8", 4 for 700.00
Platter, 19th C, 15x12" 900.00
Platter, 19th C, 18¼x14½", NM 1,100.00
Platter, 19th C, 18¼x15¼" 1,600.00
Shrimp dish, 19th C, 10½" 700.00
Soup plate, 19th C, 10", 4 for 1,265.00
Teapot, 19th C, minor spout chip, 8¼" 800.00
Tureen, soup; w/lid, 19th C, 10½x14½x9" 3,000.00
Urn, dome lid w/foo dog finial & masks, baluster, 19th C, 16"....1,400.00
Vase, birds & roses, appl lizards, 19th C, 12" 350.00
Vase, cartouch panels of birds/flowers/domestic scenes, 19th C, 14"...795.00
Vase, foo dogs & kylins, baluster, 19th C, 17" 1,350.00
Vase, lizards, foo dog hdls, baluster, late 19th C, 14x7½", EX.....425.00

Rose Medallion

Rose Medallion is one of the patterns of Chinese export porcelain produced from before 1850 until the second decade of the twentieth century. It is decorated in rose colors with panels of florals, birds, and butterflies that form reserves containing Chinese figures. Pre-1850 ware is unmarked and is characterized by quality workmanship and gold trim. From about 1850 until 1860, the kilns in Canton did not operate, and no Rose Medallion was made. Post-1860 examples (still unmarked) can often be recognized by the poor quality of the gold trim or its absence. In the 1890s the ware was often marked 'China'; 'Made in China' was used from 1910 through the 1930s.

Basin, 19th C, 5¾x18¾", EX..800.00
Basket, fruit; floral, rtcl, w/undertray, 19th C, 14½x10x8½" ...1,600.00
Bowl, canted corners, late 19th C, 4¾x10½x10⅛" 465.00
Bowl, oval, 19th C, 2x18x11" 400.00
Bowl, punch; 19th C, 4½x10½" 865.00
Bowl, punch; 19th C, 5x11¾", NM 950.00
Bowl, punch; 19th C, 6¾x15½" 1,450.00
Bowl, rectangular, hdls, 19th C, 13⅞x7¼" 850.00
Bowl, vegetable; w/lid, mid-19th C, 5x8½x6½", EX 375.00
Bowl, vegetable; w/lid, 19th C, 2x9x7½" 375.00
Box, brush; divided int, late 19th C, 2⅞x7½x3¾" 635.00
Candlestick, w/drip ring, mid-19th C, 7", EX 350.00
Charger, 19th C, 19", NM 700.00
Compote, dmn shape, low, 19th C, 3x14x11" 750.00
Compote, 19th C, 3½x9½" 290.00
Cup & saucer, demitasse; 19th C, 8 for 400.00
Drainer, mid/late 19th C, 14½x12¼" 365.00
Garden seat, bbl form, paneled court scenes/florals, 19th C, 18" ..2,250.00
Garden seat, bbl form, 2 pierced sides, late 19th C, 18¾" 2,400.00

Jar, domed lid with bud finial, ovoid with leafy branch handles, nineteenth century, glaze flakes, 14½", $1,495.00.

Plate, 19th C, 6¼" 48.00
Plate, 19th C, 7¾" 65.00

Plate, 19th C, 8⅝" dia...75.00
Platter, tree & well; mid-19th C, 18x14", NM 2,225.00
Salt cellar, 19th C, 1½x4½x3¼", pr..............................900.00
Shrimp dish, 19th C, 9¾x10½".....................................450.00
Tea set, 19th C, teapot+2 sm cups, in wicker-lidded fitted basket ...120.00
Teapot, dome lid, 19th C, rstr spout, 8½".........................500.00
Teapot, dome lid, 19th C, 8¾", NM 1,250.00
Teapot, mid-19th C, 10½", EX....................................500.00
Teapot, mid-19th C, 6¾"...815.00
Tray, 19th C, 10¾x9", NM 365.00
Tureen, sauce; monogram, 19th C, w/lid, 6" H 2,645.00
Vase, gilt foo dogs & kylins, 19th C, 25", pr......................4,000.00
Vase, Ku form, 19th C, 13⅝", EX.................................430.00
Vase, Ku form, 19th C, 16x16", EX...............................700.00

Roselane

William and Georgia Fields began Roselane Pottery in their home in 1938. They moved several times over the years, but when William died in 1973, Georgia sold Roselane to Prather Engineering Corporation and the operation moved to Long Beach where it remained until its final closing in 1977.

Roselane had various lines that included several different glazes and treatments. Chinese-Modern is not as popular as some of Roselane's other products. Certain pieces of Chinese-Modern are plentiful and do not bring high values. In the mid-1940s until the early 1950s, Aqua Marine was a buffet serving line with pieces such as large, deep bowls and trays created in a sgraffito technique. The fish or snowflakes motifs are in demand today. The Sparkler series, created in the 1950s, was a popular product for the company. The airbrushed, decorated semi-porcelain children and animals fascinate collectors even though there are some reproductions on the market. Originally the Sparklers had rhinestone eyes, but the later ones were made of plastic. The deer and deer groups on a single base are sought after. Their muted glazes and their lifelike appearances have many collectors trying to amass all of them. William 'Doc' Fields created beautiful animals on walnut bases. The animals were generally a high-gloss white. When they became available the public did not buy them in any quantity and they were discontinued shortly after their introduction. Today collectors avidly look for items in this line and prices reflect that demand. Our advisor for this category is Susan Cox; she is listed in the Directory under California.

Bookends, Oriental design in bl, 4⅛x5", pr 110.00
Bowl, blk & turq w/fish, #27, 8".....................................75.00
Bowl, pk w/gray bkground w/snowflakes, #A9.........................90.00
Bowl, salad/pasta; fish, gray on pk, 14", w/matching spoon & fork ..78.00
Dish, maroon w/blk base, Art Deco design, ftd, 12x8x5"...............45.00
Figurine, Aladdin, wht w/hints of color, 7" 27.50
Figurine, bird, copper bronze lustre, on mk wood base, 6¼" 165.00
Figurine, boy seated & holding cookie jar, beige & brn, 3½"........25.00
Figurine, bulldog puppy, Sparkler, 1¾".............................20.00
Figurine, cat, modernistic, wht, 7½"................................50.00
Figurine, Chihuahua, sitting, Sparkler, 7".............................25.00
Figurine, deer, Art Deco design, aqua, 6½"..........................40.00
Figurine, deer (2) standing on base, dk brn, #210, 5¼" 45.00
Figurine, exotic bird on stump, gr w/lt brn accents, 12" 40.00
Figurine, fox, wht, on wood base, 9"................................225.00
Figurine, gazelle, Art Deco style, wht, 16"..........................115.00
Figurine, giraffe, speckled tan, #264, 8¾" & 7¼", pr...............78.00
Figurine, kangaroo mother w/2 babies in pouch, Sparkler, 4¼" 40.00
Figurine, mother & baby Siamese cats, Sparkler, 2¼", 4½", pr.....38.00
Figurine, puppy, aqua bl w/tan accents, Sparkler, #102, 3½" 30.00
Figurine, raccoon, crouched, Sparkler, 4¼"..........................30.00

Figurine, Scotty dog, tan w/pk highlights, Sparkler, 4½" L 30.00
Figurine, Siamese cat, Sparkler, 5"..................................28.00
Figurine, squirrel, Sparkler, 3¾"....................................25.00
Figurine, swan, #261, 8", pr...40.00
Pitcher, turq abstract design on blk, 6½"...........................65.00

Rosemeade

Rosemeade was the name chosen by Wahpeton Pottery Company of Wahpeton, North Dakota, to represent their product. The founders of the company were Laura A. Taylor and R.J. Hughes, who organized the firm in 1940. It is most noted for small bird and animal figurals, either in high gloss or a Van Briggle-like matt glaze. The ware was marked 'Rosemeade' with an ink stamp or carried a 'Prairie Rose' sticker. The pottery closed in 1961. Our advisor for this category is Bryce L. Farnsworth; he is listed in the Directory under North Dakota. For more information we recommend *Collector's Encyclopedia of Rosemeade Pottery* by Darlene Hurst Dommel (Collector Books).

Ashtray, Dekalb Corn, flying ear of corn, 5" 295.00
Ashtray, DeKalb Hybrid Sorghum emb on outer ridge, 4⅞x4½" ...265.00
Ashtray, Fenn's Walnut Crush Ice Cream, 8x5¾" 415.00
Ashtray, Lincoln on state of IL shape...................................80.00
Bank, bear, blk w/lt brn face, w/label & mk, 3¾x6" 450.00

Bank, buffalo, World's Largest — Jamestown ND, $400.00.

Bookends, Russian Wolfhounds, blk, 6¾", pr.........................325.00
Creamer & sugar bowl, tulip, mauve w/hint of yel, mini, pr 200.00
Creamer & sugar bowl, turkey.......................................175.00
Cup, mustache; emb man w/mustache, Blanchard...1856...1956, 3"...75.00
Figurine, Center of North America Monument.........................525.00
Figurine, elephant, creamy wht, 3"..................................165.00
Figurine, frog, gr, 1½"...175.00
Figurine, horse, pk, head up, 4¼".................................240.00
Figurine, monkey w/banana, creamy wht, 3"..........................400.00
Figurine, pheasant cock, 12½".....................................250.00
Figurine, roosters, fighting; 5x7", pr...............................285.00
Figurine, turkeys, Tom: 2", hen: 1½", pr............................135.00
Flower frog, fish, 3½"...80.00
Flower frog, squirrel, 4½" 80.00
Flower holder, heron, 6¾" 100.00
Hors d'ouvres, turkey, 6½"...200.00
Hors d'ouvres holder/server, turkey..................................175.00
Hors d'ouvres plate, pheasant, 9½"..................................135.00
Pitcher, wheat, gr, w/foil label, 5¾"................................60.00
Planter, sleigh, Dutch push-style, bl, 4x5¼".........................100.00
Plaque, Northern Pike, Pike Lake Resort, 3¾x6" 325.00
Shakers, Boston Terriers, pr 300.00
Shakers, buffalo, pr 175.00
Shakers, cactus, pincushion shape, pr 60.00
Shakers, colts, gr, pr 75.00
Shakers, coyotes, howling, 3½", pr 255.00
Shakers, fawns, leaping, pr 125.00
Shakers, fish, Muskellunge, pr......................................500.00

Shakers, Mallard drake & hen, pr..100.00
Shakers, mountain goats, 2", pr 160.00
Shakers, Palomino horse heads, pr......................................55.00
Shakers, Pekingese dogs, pr...100.00
Shakers, pelican, 3½", pr..80.00
Shakers, sailboats, pr 475.00
Shakers, skunk, lg, pr...80.00
Sugar bowl, Mallard duck hen, 2½x6" 120.00
Wall plaque vase, pooled & curdled gr, ink stamp/foil label, 4½"...125.00
Wall pocket, Egyptian, w/insert 400.00
Wall pocket, horse head...425.00

Rosenthal

In 1879 Phillip Rosenthal established the Rosenthal Porcelain Factory in Selb, Bavaria. Its earliest products were figurines and fine tablewares. The company has continued to operate to the present decade, manufacturing limited edition plates. Our advisor for this category is Raphael Wise; he is listed in the Directory under Florida.

Vase, lily on burnt orange, 14", $145.00.

Figurine, dancing nude, sgn R Kaesbach, ca 1940, 16½" 1,550.00
Figurine, Deco lady in cobalt dress w/swinging skirt, sgn, 9½"....765.00
Figurine, fox, gray, sgn Th Kaerner, #1538, ca 1940, 7⅝x16½" ..650.00
Figurine, greyhound, sgn Kaerner, #80, 3¼x6½" 815.00
Figurine, Nouveau man w/2 parrots, Liebermann, ca 1920, 6"....485.00
Figurine, pointer dog on plinth, sgn Diller, ca 1917, 7½x13¼" ..575.00
Figurine, putti on grasshopper, Caasman, ca 1912-13, 3¾" 450.00
Figurine, tiger, HP decor, sgn Kaerner, ca 1930, 8x8½"...............900.00
Figurine, 2 sleeping faun children, sgan Caasman, #174, 10", NM .850.00
Lamp, Oriental dancer (16"), C Holzer-Defanti, K 566 8, 25".2,000.00
Plate, dinner; encrusted gold rim on wht, 10½", 6 for..................50.00
Plate, fruit transfer w/HP decor, mc w/gilt, 8½" 27.50
Tankard, grape clusters w/gold, crown mk, 13½" +6 5" mugs, NM ..625.00
Tea set, Flash One, D Hafner, pot+cr/sug....................................200.00
Vase, cream medallions on burnt orange w/silver o/l floral, 6½".300.00

Roseville

The Roseville Pottery Company was established in 1892 by George F. Young in Roseville, Ohio. Finding their facilities inadequate, the company moved to Zanesville in 1898, erected a new building, and installed the most modern equipment available. By 1900 Young felt ready to enter into the stiffly competitive art pottery market. Roseville's first art line was called Rozane. Similar to Rookwood's Standard, Rozane featured dark blended backgrounds with slip-painted underglaze artwork of nature studies, portraits, birds, and animals. Azurean, developed in 1902, was a blue and white underglaze art line on a blue blended background. Egypto (1904) featured a matt glaze in a soft shade of old green and was modeled in low relief after examples of ancient Egyptian pottery. Mongol (1904) was a high-gloss oxblood red line after the fashion of the Chinese Sang de Boeuf. Mara (1904), an iridescent lustre line of magenta and rose with intricate patterns developed on the surface or in low relief, successfully duplicated Sicardo's work. These early lines were followed by many others of highest quality: Fudjiyama and Woodland (1905 – 06) reflected an Oriental theme; Crystalis (1906) was covered with beautiful frost-like crystals. Della Robbia, their most famous line (introduced in 1906), was decorated with designs ranging from florals, animals, and birds to scenes of Viking warriors and Roman gladiators. These designs were worked in sgraffito with slip-painted details. Very limited but of great importance to collectors today, Rozane Olympic (1905) was decorated with scenes of Greek mythology on a red ground. Pauleo (1914) was the last of the artware lines. It was varied — over two hundred glazes were recorded — and some pieces were decorated by hand, usually with florals.

During the second decade of the century until the plant closed forty years later, new lines were continually added. Some of the more popular of the middle-period lines were Donatello, 1915; Futura, 1928; Pine Cone, 1931; and Blackberry, 1933. The floral lines of the later years have become highly collectible. Pottery from every era of Roseville production — even its utility ware — attest to an unwavering dedication to quality and artistic merit.

Examples of the fine art pottery lines present the greatest challenge to evaluate. Scarcity is a prime consideration. The quality of artwork varied from one artist to another. Some pieces show fine detail and good color, and naturally this influences their values. Studies of animals and portraits bring higher prices than the floral designs. An artist's signature often increases the value of any item, especially if the artist is one who is well recognized.

The market is literally flooded with imposter Roseville that is coming into the country from China. An experienced eye can easily detect these fakes, but to a novice collector, they may pass for old Roseville. Study the marks. If the 'USA' is missing or appears only faintly, the piece is most definitely a reproduction. Also watch for lines with a mark that is not correct for its time frame; for example, Luffa with the script mark, and Woodland with the round Rozane stamp from the 1917 line.

For further information consult the newly revised *Collector's Encyclopedia of Roseville Pottery, First* and *Second Series,* by Sharon and Bob Huxford and Mike Nickel. (Collector Books). Other books on the subject include *Collector's Compendium of Roseville Pottery, Volumes I, II,* and *III,* by R.B. Monsen (see Directory, Virginia); and *Roseville in All Its Splendor With Price Guide* by Jack and Nancy Bomm (self-published).

Our advisor for this category is Mike Nickel; he is listed in the Directory under Michigan.

Apple Blossom, bowl, bl, #326-6, 2½x6½", from $175 to...........200.00
Artwood, planter, #1055-9, 7x9½", from $85 to 95.00
Artwood, planter, #1056-10, 6½x10½", from $85 to....................95.00
Autumn, jardiniere, no mk, 9½", from $600 to 700.00
Autumn, shaving mug, no mk, 4", from $275 to.........................325.00
Autumn, wash bowl, no mk, 14½", from $300 to........................350.00
Aztec, vase, no mk, 11", from $600 to..700.00
Azurean, candlestick, no mk, 9", from $550 to 650.00
Baneda, bowl, center; gr, no mk, #233, 3½x10", from $600 to ...700.00
Baneda, bowl, center; pk, no mk, #233, 3½x10", from $450 to ..525.00
Baneda, vase, gr, #596, sm silver paper label, 9", $1,500 to......1,750.00
Baneda, vase, pk, #596, sm silver paper label, 9", from $1,250 to 1,500.00
Baneda, vase, pk, #599, no mk, 12", from $2,000 to 2,500.00
Bittersweet, basket, #809-8, 8½", from $200 to 250.00
Bittersweet, candlesticks, #851-3, 3", pr, from $150 to 175.00
Blackberry, jardiniere, #623, 4", from $400 to.............................450.00
Blackberry, vase, #571, 6", from $550 to 600.00

Bleeding Heart, hanging basket, bl, #362, 8" W, from $375 to ...**425.00**
Bleeding Heart, hanging basket, pk or gr, #362, 8" W, from $325 to ..**350.00**
Bushberry, mug, bl or pk, #1-3½, 3½", from $200 to.................**225.00**
Bushberry, mug, gr, #1-3½, 3½", from $175 to.....................**200.00**
Bushberry, mug, orange, #1-3½, 3½", from $150 to.................**175.00**
Bushberry, vase, gr, #157-8, 8", from $225 to.....................**250.00**
Bushberry, vase, orange, #157-8, 8", from $200 to.................**225.00**
Carnelian I, flower frog, 4½", from $75 to **85.00**
Carnelian I, pillow vase, 5", from $90 to.........................**100.00**
Carnelian I, vase, 10", from $200 to.............................**250.00**
Carnelian II, bowl, no mk, 4x15", from $300 to **350.00**
Carnelian II, bowl, vase, silver paper label, 9", from $200 to **250.00**
Carnelian II, planter, sm blk paper label, 3x8", from $100 to **125.00**
Carnelian II, vase, no mk, 8", from $200 to **250.00**
Chloron, vase, no mk, 6½", from $450 to **500.00**
Chloron, vase, no mk, 12", from $1,100 to........................**1,200.00**
Chloron, vase, 9", from $800 to.................................**900.00**
Clemana, flower frog, tan, imp mk, #23, 4", from $150 to **175.00**
Clemana, vase, bl, #749-6, 6½", from $250 to.....................**275.00**
Clemana, vase, gr, impressed mk, #750-6, 6½", from $225 to **250.00**
Clematis, bowl, center; bl, #458-10, 14", from $200 to **250.00**
Clematis, bowl, center; gr or brn, #458-10, 14", from $175 to **200.00**
Clematis, flower arranger, bl, #102-5, 5½", from $100 to...........**125.00**
Clematis, vase, bl, #102-6, 6½", from $110 to.....................**130.00**
Colonial, bowl, no mk, 16", from $150 to **200.00**
Colonial, pitcher, no mk, 7½", from $100 to.......................**125.00**
Colonial, toothbrush holder, no mk, 5", from $85 to...............**95.00**
Columbine, cornucopia, pk, #149-6, 5½", from $175 to **200.00**
Columbine, vase, bl or tan, #17-7, 7½", from $175 to **225.00**
Columbine, vase, pk, #17-7, 7½", from $225 to **275.00**
Corinthian, bowl, ftd, no mk, 4½", from $100 to...................**125.00**
Corinthian, bowl, 3", from $75 to................................**95.00**
Corinthian, vase, no mk, 7", from $150 to **175.00**
Corinthian, vase, no mk, 8½", from $150 to **175.00**
Corinthian, wall pocket, no mk, 8", from $275 to **325.00**
Cornelian, pitcher, no mk, 4", from $50 to........................**60.00**
Cornelian, shaving mug, no mk, 4", from $65 to **75.00**
Cosmos, flower frog, gr, no mk, 3½", from $175 to.................**225.00**
Cosmos, flower frog, tan, no mk, 3½", from $150 to **175.00**
Cosmos, hanging basket, bl, #361, 7", from $400 to **425.00**
Cosmos, hanging basket, gr, #361, 7", from $375 to **425.00**
Crocus, letter receiver, no mk, 3½", from $400 to **500.00**
Crocus, vase, no mk, 9", from $600 to............................**700.00**
Crystalis, vase, 3½", from $600 to...............................**700.00**
Dahlrose, candlesticks, blk paper label, 3½", pr, from $175 to....**225.00**
Dawn, ewer, gr, #834-16, 16", from $650 to.......................**750.00**
Dawn, ewer, pk/yel, #834-16, 16", from $800 to...................**900.00**
Della Robbia, vase, narcissus, 12", from $15,000 to...............**17,500.00**
Della Robbia, vase, spade leaves, 10", from $6,000 to.............**7,000.00**
Dogwood I, tub, no mk, 4x7", from $125 to........................**150.00**
Dogwood II, hanging basket, no mk, 7", from $250 to **300.00**
Dogwood II, jardiniere, 8", from $150 to..........................**300.00**
Donatello, ashtray, no mk, 3", from $175 to **225.00**
Donatello, basket, imp seal, 7½", from $350 to **400.00**
Donatello, powder jar, no mk, 2x5", from $450 to.................**550.00**
Dutch, pin tray, no mk, 4", from $65 to...........................**75.00**
Dutch, sugar bowl, no mk, child's sz, 3", from $100 to **125.00**
Dutch, toothbrush holder, no mk, 4", $75 to **100.00**
Earlam, planter, #89, 5½x10½", from $400 to **450.00**
Earlam, vase, 6", from $450 to **500.00**
Egypto, pitcher, 7", from $700 to................................**750.00**
Egypto, pitcher vase, 11", from $1,750 to **2,000.00**
Falline, bowl, bl, #244, no mk, 11", from $500 to.................**600.00**
Falline, vase, bl, #650, sm silver label, 6", from $1,500 to........**1,750.00**

Falline, vase, tan, #650, sm silver label, 6", from $600 to............**700.00**
Ferella, lamp, any color, 10½", from $1,000 to.........................**1,250.00**
Ferella, vase, red, #505, no mk, 6", from $1,200 to **1,300.00**
Ferella, vase, tan, #505, no mk, 6", from $350 to....................**400.00**
Florane, basket, 8½", from $300 to **350.00**
Florane, bowl, 5", from $125 to **150.00**
Florane, vase, bud; dbl, 5", from $125 to **150.00**
Florentine, vase, blk paper label, 8", from $175 to **225.00**
Florentine, window box, sm ink stamp, 11½", from $300 to.......**350.00**
Foxglove, tray, bl, imp mk, #419, 8½", from $175 to **200.00**
Foxglove, tray, gr/pk, imp mk, #419, 8½", from $200 to............**225.00**
Foxglove, vase, pk, #47-8, 8½", from $225 to **275.00**
Freesia, basket, bl, #390-7, 7", from $250 to.......................**275.00**
Freesia, basket, gr, #390-7, 7", from $275 to.......................**300.00**
Freesia, vase, bl, #124-9, 9", from $250 to.........................**275.00**
Freesia, vase, tangerine, #124-9, 9", from $225 to **250.00**
Fuchsia, candlesticks, gr, imp mk, #1133-5, 5½", pr, $400 to.......**450.00**
Fuchsia, vase, bl, imp mk, #893-6, 6", from $250 to **300.00**
Fuchsia, vase, gr, imp mk, #893-6, 6", from $200 to **225.00**
Fudjiyama, jardiniere, ink stamp, 9", from $2,000 to...............**2,500.00**
Fudjiyama, vase, ink stamp, 9", from $1,500 to.....................**1,750.00**
Futura, bowl, center; #188, 4", from $700 to........................**800.00**
Futura, bowl, center; #195, 2½x10½", from $1,250 to...............**1,500.00**
Futura, vase, #189, 4", from $550 to................................**650.00**
Futura, vase, #380-6, 6", from $350 to..............................**450.00**
Futura, vase, #387, 7½", from $1,100 to.............................**1,200.00**
Futura, vase, #394, 12½", from $1,250 to............................**1,500.00**
Futura, vase, #403, 7", from $1,100 to..............................**1,200.00**
Futura, vase, #427, 8", from $1,250 to..............................**1,500.00**
Futura, window box, #376, 5x15½", from $1,750 to.................**2,000.00**
Gardenia, basket, #610-12, 12", from $350 to.......................**400.00**
Gardenia, vase, #683-8, 8", from $150 to............................**175.00**
Holland, mug, no mk, 4", from $65 to...............................**75.00**
Holland, pitcher, no mk, 12", from $400 to..........................**500.00**
Imperial I, basket, #7, 9", from $200 to.............................**250.00**
Imperial I, planter, no mk, 14x16", from $350 to....................**400.00**
Imperial I, vase, no mk, 12", from $350 to..........................**400.00**
Imperial II, vase, no mk, 6", from $1,000 to **1,250.00**
Imperial II, vase, no mk, 8½", from $1,200 to.......................**1,400.00**
Iris, basket, bl, imp mk, #355-10, 9½", from $475 to..................**550.00**
Iris, basket, pk or tan, imp mk, #355-10, 9½", from $425 to.......**475.00**
Iris, vase, bl, imp mk, #917-6, 6½", from $175 to...................**200.00**
Iris, vase, bl, imp mk, #924-9, 10", from $450 to...................**475.00**
Ivory II, hanging basket, 7", from $75 to...........................**100.00**
Ivory II, jardiniere, 6", from $50 to................................**75.00**
Ixia, bowl, console; imp mk, #330-7, 3½x10½", $100 to **125.00**
Ixia, vase, imp, #857-8, 8½", from $125 to..........................**150.00**
Jonquil, bowl, no mk, 3", from $175 to..............................**225.00**
Jonquil, candlestick, no mk, 4", from $450 to.......................**550.00**
Jonquil, vase, no mk, 4½", from $450 to.............................**550.00**
Jonquil, vase, no mk, 9½", from $600 to.............................**700.00**
Jonquil, vase, sm paper label, 8", from $500 to.....................**600.00**
Juvenile, creamer, bear, gr bands, no mk, 4", from $900 to **1,000.00**
Juvenile, creamer, duck w/boots, high gloss, 3", from $250 to.....**300.00**
Juvenile, creamer, pig, 4", from $1,000 to..........................**1,250.00**
Juvenile, cup & saucer, early duck w/hat, 2", 3", from $150 to ...**175.00**
Juvenile, cup & saucer, Sunbonnet girl, from $200 to.................**250.00**
Juvenile, custard, goose, no mk, 4", from $550 to....................**600.00**
Juvenile, mug, bear, no mk, 3½", from $900 to **1,000.00**
Juvenile, mug, early duck w/hat, 3", from $100 to **150.00**
Juvenile, mug, fancy cat, 3", from $1,000 to........................**1,250.00**
Juvenile, mug, plate, rabbit, rolled edge, 8", from $1,000 to **1,250.00**
Juvenile, mug, rabbit, 3", from $175 to.............................**200.00**
Juvenile, pitcher, fat puppy, no mk, 3½", from $600 to..............**700.00**

Juvenile, plate, rooster, rare, 8", from $1,500 to **2,000.00**
Juvenile, plate, Santa Claus, rolled edge, 8", from $1,250 to ...**1,500.00**
Juvenile, plate, skinny puppy, 8", from $125 to **150.00**
Juvenile, pudding dish, sitting rabbit, 1½x3½", from $250 to.....**275.00**
La Rose, vase, 4", from $125 to..**150.00**
Laurel, vase, gold, 10", from $550 to **650.00**
Laurel, vase, gr, 10", from $800 to **900.00**
Laurel, vase, russet, 10", from $650 to **750.00**
Lombardy, vase, no mk, 6", from $200 to **250.00**
Luffa, lamp, bl/rose glaze, no mk, 9½", from $1,200 to **1,400.00**
Luffa, vase, no mk, 8", from $650 to **750.00**
Magnolia, basket, #386-12, 12", from $200 to **225.00**
Magnolia, cornucopia, #184-6, 6", from $85 to......................**95.00**
Magnolia, planter, #388-6, 8½", from $85 to **90.00**
Mara, bowl, no mk, exceptional glaze, 4", from $2,000 to **2,500.00**
Matt Green, hanging basket, no mk, 9", from $150 to **200.00**
Matt Green, planter, no mk, 5½", from $300 to **350.00**
Mayfair, teapot, #1121, 5", from $125 to **150.00**
Mayfair, vase, #1104-9, 7", from $90 to **100.00**
Ming Tree, basket, #509-12, 13", from $275 to.....................**300.00**
Ming Tree, vase, #583-10, 10½", from $175 to **200.00**
Moderne, comport, imp, #297-6, 6", from $250 to **275.00**
Moderne, vase, imp mk, #787, 6½", from $175 to **225.00**
Mongol, vase, no mk, 2½", from $400 to **500.00**
Mongol, vase, paper label, 10½", from $1,250 to **1,500.00**
Montacello, vase, bl, no mk, 5", from $400 to **450.00**
Montacello, vase, tan, no mk, 5", from $350 to **400.00**
Morning Glory, candlesticks, ivory, #1102, 5", pr, from $600 to .**700.00**
Morning Glory, vase, pillow, ivory, #120, 7", from $400 to **450.00**
Morning Glory, vase, pillow; gr, #120, 7", from $550 to **600.00**
Moss, candlesticks, bl, imp mk, #1104, 2", pr, from $150 to........**175.00**
Moss, urn, pk/gr or orange/gr, imp mk, #290-6, 6", $350 to.........**400.00**
Mostique, comport, no mk, 7", from $125 to **150.00**
Mostique, vase, no mk, 6", from $175 to **225.00**
Old Ivory, jardiniere, no mk, 9", from $275 to.......................**325.00**
Orian, vase, red, imp mk, #733-6, 6", from $225 to...............**250.00**
Orian, vase, tan, imp mk, #733-6, 6", from $150 to...............**175.00**
Orian, vase, turq, imp mk, #733-6, 6½", from $175 to............**200.00**
Orian, vase, yel, imp mk, #733-6, 6½", from $200 to.............**225.00**
Pauleo, vase, broken glaze, no mk, 9", from $700 to...............**800.00**
Pauleo, vase, gray to lav, no mk, 16½", $1,200 to **1,500.00**
Pauleo, vase, ship, #340, 19", from $2,000 to **2,500.00**
Pauleo, vase, trees, no mk, 15½", from $3,000 to....................**3,500.00**
Peony, bookend, #11, 5½", ea, from $95 to...........................**110.00**
Peony, vase, #68-14, 14", from $250 to **300.00**
Persian, candlestick, no mk, 8½", ea, from $125 to.................**150.00**
Persian, jardiniere, mk in red ink, 5", from $350 to.................**400.00**
Pine Cone, bowl, mk in relief, #347-7, 4½", from $175 to.........**200.00**
Pine Cone, pitcher, #708-9, 9½", from $700 to.......................**800.00**
Pine Cone, planter, #124, 5", from $200 to............................**225.00**
Pine Cone, vase, #908-8, 8", from $250 to............................**275.00**
Pine Cone, vase, imp mk, #747-10, 10½", from $350 to...........**400.00**
Pine Cone, vase, imp mk, #907-7, 7", from $150 t..................**175.00**
Pine Cone, vase, silver paper label, #706, 8", from $225 to **250.00**
Poppy, bowl, gray/gr, imp mk, #642-3, 3½", from $100 to...........**125.00**
Poppy, bowl, pk, imp mk, #642-3, 3½", from $125 to................**150.00**
Poppy, ewer, pk, imp mk, #880-18, 18½", from $1,000 to.........**1,100.00**
Poppy, vase, pk, imp mk, #335-6, 6½", from $400 to **450.00**
Poppy, vase, pk, imp mk, #642-3, 3½", from $125 to................**150.00**
Poppy, vase, tan, imp mk, #335-6, 6½", from $600 to **675.00**
Primrose, vase, bl or pk, imp mk, #761-6, 6½", from $175 to **200.00**
Primrose, vase, tan, imp mk, #761-6, 6½", from $150 to............**175.00**
Raymor, bean pot, #195, from $50 to **60.00**
Raymor, bowl, salad; #161, 11½", from $35 to........................**40.00**

Raymor, bowl, vegetable; #160, 9", from $30 to......................**40.00**
Raymor, cup & saucer, #151, from $25 to...............................**30.00**
Raymor, gravy boat, #190, 9½", from $30 to...........................**35.00**
Raymor, plate, salad; #154, from $15 to.................................**20.00**
Raymor, shirred egg, #200, 10", from $45 to...........................**50.00**
Raymor, tumbler, coffee; hdl, 4", from $40 to..........................**50.00**
Raymor, water pitcher, #189, 10", from $100 to.......................**150.00**
Rosecraft Panel, vase, brn, 10", from $350 to..........................**400.00**
Rosecraft Panel, vase, brn, 6", from $150 to............................**175.00**
Rosecraft Panel, vase, gr, 10", from $450 to............................**500.00**
Rosecraft Panel, vase, gr, 6", from $200 to..............................**250.00**
Rozane Light, sugar bowl, floral, 4½", from $250 to....................**300.00**
Rozane Light, tankard, mug, berries, 5", from $300 to................**350.00**
Rozane Light, vase, floral, sgn Pillsbury, 8½", from $500 to........**600.00**
Rozane Light, vase, pillow; floral, 6½", from $450 to...................**550.00**
Rozane Royal, vase, floral, #840/6, 6½", from $200 to **225.00**
Rozane 1917, basket, bl glaze, 5", from $125 to **150.00**
Rozane 1917, bowl, no mk, 3½", from $100 to..........................**125.00**
Rozane 1917, bowl, no mk, 4½", from $125 to..........................**150.00**
Rozane 1917, vase, no mk, 8", from $150 to.............................**175.00**
Russco, vase, bud; dbl, 8½", from $100 to................................**175.00**
Russco, vase, heavy crystals, 7", from $175 to...........................**200.00**
Russco, vase, 9½", from $150 to..**175.00**
Silhouette, box, #740, 4½", from $150 to.................................**175.00**
Silhouette, vase, nude, #787-10, 10", from $750 to...................**850.00**
Snowberry, vase, bl or pk, #V-6, 6", from $90 to.......................**100.00**
Snowberry, vase, bl or pk, #1UR-8, 8½", from $225 to...............**250.00**
Snowberry, vase, gr, #V-6, 6", from $70 to...............................**85.00**
Snowberry, vase, gr, #1UR-8, 8½", from $175 to.......................**200.00**
Sunflower, candlesticks, no mk, 4", pr, from $400 to..................**450.00**
Sunflower, vase, no mk, 4", from $225 to.................................**250.00**
Sunflower, vase, no mk, 6", from $350 to.................................**450.00**
Sunflower, vase, no mk, 10", from $550 to...............................**650.00**
Sunflower, window box, no mk, 3½x11", from $350 to................**450.00**
Teasel, vase, dk bl or rust, imp mk, #888-12, 12", $550 to **600.00**
Thorn Apple, hanging basket, 7" W, from $350 to......................**400.00**
Thorn Apple, vase, imp mk, #820-9, 9½", from $175 to..............**225.00**
Topeo, bowl, no mk, 3x11½", from $115 to..............................**140.00**
Topeo, vase, no mk, 14", from $450 to....................................**550.00**
Topeo, vase, no mk, 15", from $500 to....................................**600.00**
Tourmaline, cornucopia, 7", from $75 to..................................**100.00**
Tourmaline, vase, spherical, 5½", from $80 to...........................**100.00**
Tourmaline, vase, w/hdls, 5½", from $100 to.............................**125.00**
Tourmaline, vase, 8", from $150 to...**175.00**
Tuscany, vase, gr/lt bl, blk paper label, 4", from $75 to...............**100.00**
Tuscany, vase, gray/lt bl, no mk, 9", from $150 to......................**175.00**
Tuscany, vase, pk, blk paper label, 4", from $100 to...................**125.00**
Velmoss, vase, no mk, 12½", from $350 to...............................**400.00**
Velmoss, vase, no mk, 14½", from $400 to...............................**500.00**
Velmoss Scroll, vase, no mk, 5", from $150 to...........................**175.00**
Velmoss Scroll, vase, no mk, 10", from $275 to.........................**325.00**
Vista, basket, no mk, 12", from $1,000 to **1,200.00**
Vista, vase, #121-15, 15", from $1,500 to................................**1,750.00**
Vista, vase, #134-18, 18", from $1,750 to................................**2,000.00**
Volpato, candlesticks, ivory, imp mk, 9½", pr, $250 to................**300.00**
Water Lily, flower frog, bl, #48, 4½", from $160 to **175.00**
Water Lily, vase, bl, #78-9, 9", from $325 to.............................**350.00**
Water Lily, vase, brn, #48, 4½", from $140 to............................**165.00**
Water Lily, vase, rose/gr, #78-9, 9", from $350 to......................**400.00**
White Rose, vase, #978-4, 4", from $80 to................................**90.00**
Wincraft, bowl, #227-10, 4x13½", from $150 to........................**175.00**
Wincraft, cornucopia, #221-8, 9x5", from $150 to **175.00**
Wincraft, vase, #274-7, 7", from $225 to.................................**250.00**
Windsor, bowl, bl, 3½x10½", from $150 to...............................**175.00**

Windsor, vase, bl, #546, no mk, 6", from $400 to 450.00
Windsor, vase, rust, #546, no mk, 6", from $300 to 350.00

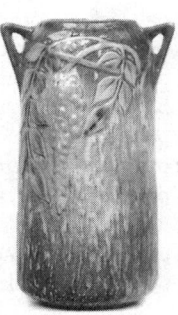

Wisteria vase, #639, 10½": in tan, from $750.00 to $850.00; in blue: from $1,250.00 to $1,500.00.

Wisteria, vase, bl, silver paper label, 10", from $1,250 to 1,500.00
Wisteria, vase, tan, silver paper label, 8½", from $700 to............800.00
Woodland, vase, no mk, 9", from $600 to 700.00
Woodland, vase, 11", from $700 to...800.00
Woodland, vase, 15", from $2,500 to 2,750.00
Zephyr Lily, vase, brn, #202-8, 8½", from $225 to......................250.00
Zephyr Lily, vase, fan; bl, #205-6, 6½", from $175 to 200.00
Zephyr Lily, vase, gr, #202-8, 8½", from $200 to 225.00

Rowland and Marsellus

Though the impressive back stamp seems to suggest otherwise, Rowland and Marsellus were not Staffordshire potters but American importers who commissioned various English companies to supply them with the transfer-printed crockery and historical ware that had been a popular import commodity since the early 1800s. Plates (both flat and with a rolled edge), cups and saucers, pitchers, and platters were sold as souvenirs from 1890 through the 1930s. Though other importers — Bawo & Dotter, and A. C. Bosselman & Co., both of New York City — commissioned the manufacture of similar souvenir items, by far the largest volume carries the R. & M. mark, and Rowland and Marcellus has become a generic term that covers all twentieth-century souvenir china of this type. Their mark may be in full or 'R. & M.' in a diamond. Though primarily made with blue transfers on white, other colors may occasionally be found as well. Our advisor for this category is David Ringering; he is listed in the Directory under Oregon.

Key:
r/e — rolled edge   v/o — view of
s/o — souvenir of

Creamer, Plymouth, mk as Burbank...45.00
Cup & saucer, Alaska-Yukon-Pacific Expo, 1909 ....120.00
Cup & saucer, Chicago, s/o 95.00
Cup & saucer, farmer's...45.00
Cup & saucer, Lemox MA, s/o...85.00
Cup & saucer, Niagara Falls NY, s/o 75.00
Fern pot, w/stand, lady's portrait by British artist, 11½"...............460.00
Pitcher, American Pilgrims, #527014, 6¼" 250.00
Pitcher, Discovery of America, lt bl, 7½"......................................275.00
Plate, Alaska-Yukan-Pacific Expo, 10"...65.00
Plate, Albany (NY), s/o, State Capital, r/e, 10" 60.00
Plate, Battle of Lake Erie, fruit & flower border............................50.00
Plate, Bermuda, 10" 80.00
Plate, Bethleham PA, Moravian College, v/o, 9" 35.00
Plate, Biltmore House, Ashville NC, fruit & flower border...........60.00
Plate, Bunker Hill Monument, Ye Olde Historical Pottery, 9" 35.00
Plate, Cape Cod, fisherman's portrait, 9".......................................50.00

Plate, Charles Dickens, r/e, 10" 65.00
Plate, Cincinnati OH, s/o, State Capital, r/e, 10" 65.00
Plate, coupe; American Poets, 7 portraits, v/o, 10" 50.00
Plate, coupe; Chicago, Marshall Field & Co, v/o, 6" 45.00
Plate, coupe; Denver, v/o, 10"...60.00
Plate, coupe; Early Missions of CA, s/o, Parmelee/Horham, 6" 40.00
Plate, coupe; Salem, v/o, witch & 5 scenes, Daniel Low, 6"..........65.00
Plate, coupe; Tucson AZ, 5 scenes, v/o, 6" 40.00
Plate, Denver CO, s/o, Capitol Building, r/e, 10" 65.00
Plate, Famous Musicians & Composers (9), 10"..............................75.00
Plate, Henry Addressing VA Assembly, fruit & flower border, 9¾" ..60.00
Plate, Hermitage, fruit & flower border, 9¾" 50.00
Plate, Jackson MS, s/o, New Capitol Building, r/e, 10".................65.00
Plate, Lake George, early home, 10" 50.00
Plate, Longfellow, 10"..80.00
Plate, Lookout Mountain TN, s/o, r/e, 10" 70.00
Plate, Los Angeles, 10¼"..75.00
Plate, Miami, s/o, Chief Osceola, 10" 70.00
Plate, Myles Standish, 10"..65.00
Plate, Nashville, v/o, State Capitol, r/e, 10"...................................80.00
Plate, Niagara Falls, 10"..50.00
Plate, Philadelphia, 10" 80.00
Plate, Plymouth MA, 10" 50.00
Plate, Richfield Springs, NY, 10" 60.00
Plate, Syracuse NY (Indian), s/o, r/e, 10¼" 140.00
Plate, Theodore Roosevelt, 10" 120.00
Plate, Waltham Watch factory, fruit & flower border 70.00
Plate, Whitlpool Rapids, fruit & flower border, 9¾"......................45.00
Sugar bowl, Plymouth, American Pilgrims 55.00
Tumbler, Ashville, mc, s/o..85.00
Tumbler, Fall River MA, v/o 85.00
Tumbler, Ottawa Canada...85.00
Tumbler, Thousand Islands, v/o 75.00
Tumbler, Views of Plymouth, 1906 ....65.00

Royal Bayreuth

Founded in 1794 in Tettau, Bavaria, the Royal Bayreuth firm originally manufactured fine dinnerware of superior quality. Their figural items, produced from before the turn of the century until the onset of WWI, are highly sought after by today's collectors. Perhaps the most abundantly produced and easily recognized of these are the tomato and lobster pieces. Fruits, flowers, people, animals, birds, and vegetables shapes were also made. Aside from figural items, pitchers, toothpick holders, cups and saucers, humidors, and the like were decorated in florals and scenic motifs. Some, such as the very popular Rose Tapestry line, utilized a cloth-like tapestry background. Transfer prints were used as well. Two of the most popular are Sunbonnet Babies and Nursery Rhymes (in particular, those decorated with the complete verse).

Caution: Many pieces were not marked; some were marked 'Deponiert' or 'Registered' only. While marked pieces are the most valued, unmarked items are still very worthwhile. Our advisors for this category are Larry Brenner from New Hampshire and Dee Hooks from Illinois; they are listed in the Directory under their home states.

Figurals

Ashtray, clown, bl mk 325.00
Ashtray, elk, bl mk 375.00
Ashtray, mtn goat, bl mk..460.00
Ashtray, oyster & pearl, bl mk 195.00
Basket, Art Nouveau lady, bl mk/Deponiert, 3x3½", NM........1,500.00

Bowl, elk head (dbl), bl mk, prof rstr antlers, bl mk, 4x10x6" 435.00
Bowl, radishes, gr leaf edge, bl mk, 2½x5" 200.00
Bowl, rose; Deponiert, 4½x8" 525.00
Bowl, salad; lobster, bl mk, lg 325.00
Box, card; Devil & Cards, bl mk..550.00
Candle holder, basset hound, bl mk, 4¼" 465.00
Candlestick, clown, low, bl mk 625.00
Candy dish, clown, bl mk..625.00
Candy dish, lobster, bl mk, 5½"..195.00
Celery tray, lobster, bl mk 200.00
Chamberstick, shell, MOP, saucer base, unmk, 6½x5½"............600.00
Compote, poppy, wht or orchid MOP, bl mk................................595.00
Covered dish, poppy, bl mk, sm..270.00
Cracker jar, grapes, bl mk...395.00
Cracker jar, poppy, stem hdl, bl mk, 8x7".....................................900.00
Cracker jar, strawberry, bl mk 600.00
Cracker jar, tomato w/gr leaf, stem finial, bl mk, 6¼"..................500.00
Cup, demitasse; rose, pk, bl mk..200.00
Cup & saucer, clover w/4-leaf saucer, bl mk, 1887-1902 ....450.00
Cup & saucer, demitasse; pear & gr leaf, bl mk...........................350.00
Cup & saucer, demitasse; rose, bl mk...375.00
Cup & saucer, rose, red, bl mk, NM..750.00
Gravy boat & undertray, tomato, bl mk 400.00
Hatpin holder, penguin, bl mk..750.00
Humidor, man's head w/turban, bl mk..550.00
Marmalade, grapes, gr, bl mk...300.00
Match holder, clown, bl mk, wall type 475.00
Match holder, Devil & Cards, full body, bl mk, 6x4" 1,400.00
Match holder, mountain goat, bl mk, wall hanging 825.00
Match holder, Santa w/red coat, bl mk, 4¾" 5,250.00
Mustard pot, orange, bl mk, w/lid...240.00
Mustard pot, red pepper, unmk, w/lid & spoon, leaf hdl...............375.00
Mustard pot, tomato, bl mk, no spoon...70.00
Nut dish, poppy, red, bl mk, sm..75.00
Pipe rest, Basset hound, bl mk 350.00
Pitcher, alligator, gr, bl mk, cream sz...350.00
Pitcher, apple, red, bl mk, cream sz..100.00
Pitcher, apple, red, bl mk, water sz...775.00
Pitcher, Art Nouveau, bl mk, cream sz..550.00
Pitcher, Art Nouveau, bl mk, water sz.......................................1,525.00
Pitcher, butterfly, closed wings, bl mk, cream sz..........................375.00
Pitcher, butterfly, open wings, bl mk, milk sz 675.00
Pitcher, cat, blk, bl mk, cream sz 230.00
Pitcher, chick, bl mk, cream sz, NM...230.00
Pitcher, clover, bl mk, cream sz 1,200.00
Pitcher, clown, bl mk, milk sz 625.00
Pitcher, clown, bl mk, water sz...925.00
Pitcher, coachman, bl mk, cream sz..425.00
Pitcher, coachman, bl mk, milk sz..395.00
Pitcher, dachshund, bl mk, cream sz...370.00
Pitcher, devil, red, bl mk, cream sz 550.00
Pitcher, Devil & Cards, bl mk, water sz..700.00
Pitcher, duck, bl mk, milk sz 325.00
Pitcher, duck, mk Registered, water sz, 6¾" 750.00
Pitcher, eagle, bl mk, cream sz 325.00
Pitcher, eagle, bl mk, milk sz..500.00
Pitcher, elk, bl mk, cream sz...150.00
Pitcher, elk, bl mk, water sz..500.00
Pitcher, fish head, bl mk, cream sz 225.00
Pitcher, geranium, bl mk, cream sz...495.00
Pitcher, grapes, bl mk, milk sz..295.00
Pitcher, lemon, bl mk, water sz 575.00
Pitcher, lobster, bl mk, cream sz...100.00
Pitcher, lobster, bl mk, water sz..325.00

Pitcher, melon, bl mk, cream sz 425.00
Pitcher, monkey, brn, bl mk, cream sz 525.00
Pitcher, mouse, unmk, cream sz, 4½x5" 1,125.00
Pitcher, oak leaf w/acorn hdl, pearlized, bl mk, cream sz 685.00
Pitcher, owl, bl mk, cream sz...650.00
Pitcher, oyster & pearl, bl mk, cream sz..200.00
Pitcher, pansy, pk & yel, bl mk, cream sz 350.00
Pitcher, parakeet, bl mk, cream sz...425.00
Pitcher, pig, pk, bl mk, cream sz...750.00
Pitcher, pig, red, bl mk, cream sz..650.00
Pitcher, platypus, bl mk, cream sz..1,275.00
Pitcher, poodle, gray, bl mk, cream sz 475.00
Pitcher, poppy, red, bl mk, cream sz...295.00
Pitcher, robin, bl mk, cream sz..270.00
Pitcher, snake, gr & wht w/gold scales, pearlized, water sz, rare 5,000.00
Pitcher, spikey shell, wht MOP, bl mk, cream sz, 4x5".................300.00
Pitcher, watermelon, bl mk, milk sz..525.00
Plate, corn, bl mk..250.00
Relish, radish, bl mk 250.00
Sauce boat w/underplate, oak leaf, bl mk 450.00
Shakers, grapes, purple, bl mk, pr...200.00
Shakers, tomato, bl mk, pr...75.00
Shaving mug, elk, bl mk..625.00
Sugar bowl, lemon, bl mk..250.00
Sugar bowl, lobster, w/lid, bl mk..180.00
Sugar bowl, rose, w/lid, bl mk 525.00
Sugar bowl, shell, bl mk..175.00
Tea strainer, apricot, bl mk 395.00
Teapot, pansy, purple, bl mk..625.00
Teapot, poppy, red, bl mk, 4¾" 415.00
Teapot, strawberry, bl mk..385.00
Toothpick holder, bell ringer, bl mk..695.00
Toothpick holder, elk, bl mk..295.00
Toothpick holder, spikey shell, MOP, bl mk 200.00
Tray, pin; Santa sitting, red, bl mk 3,500.00
Vase, kangaroo w/joey in pouch, bl mk, 3¼" 585.00
Wall pocket, shell, pearlized, bl mk..355.00
Wall vase, grapes, wht MOP, bl mk..550.00

Nursery Rhymes

Bell, Jack & the Beanstalk, w/rhyme, w/clapper, bl mk 350.00
Candlestick, Jack & Jill, w/verse, ring hdl, bl mk 235.00
Cup & saucer, Jack & the Beanstalk, w/verse, bl mk....................235.00
Pitcher, Jack & the Beanstalk, bl mk, water sz.............................350.00
Pitcher, Little Boy Blue, w/verse, bl mk, 3½"...............................275.00
Pitcher, Little Jack Horner, bl mk, 3½"..250.00
Plate, Little Bo Peep, no verse, bl mk, 6¼"..................................200.00
Plate, Ring Around the Rosies, no verse, bl mk, 6"......................125.00
Sugar bowl, Little Bo Peep, hdls, w/lid, bl mk.............................275.00
Sugar bowl, Little Boy Blue, no verse, bl mk 215.00

Scenics and Action Portraits

Ashtray, sheep in meadow, bl mk...65.00
Bell, Beach Babies, wooden clapper, bl mk...................................325.00
Box, musicians, unmk, 2x4" dia...110.00
Candle holder, Brittany Girl, shield bk, bl mk 350.00
Candle holder, elk by lake, bl mk, 5"..300.00
Coffeepot, Brittany girl w/draft horse, bl mk, 8" 600.00
Coffeepot, hunt scene, bl mk, mini..560.00
Humidor, ship scene, bl mk...350.00
Pitcher, Arab on horse, gold hdl, bl mk, 3⅛", from $125 to 150.00
Pitcher, cavalier, bl mk, water sz...250.00

Pitcher, girl w/dog, boat shape, bl mk, cream sz, 3½" 250.00
Pitcher, highland cattle, bl mk, dbl hdl, cream sz, 3¾" 225.00
Pitcher, highland sheep, bl mk, cream sz, 3½" 175.00
Pitcher, ship scene, bl mk, water sz, 8" 265.00
Plate, hunter & dog, gold trim, bl mk, 9¼", NM.......................285.00
Tea tile, Snow Babies, bl mk..145.00
Vase, candle girl, pk rim, bl mk, 4½"......................................180.00
Vase, cows, tab hdls, bl mk, 3¼x1⅞"......................................125.00
Vase, pastoral scene w/cows, bl mk, 10"...................................350.00

Sunbonnet Babies

Teapot, cleaning, long spout, blue mark, 5¾", $650.00.

Basket, 1 sweeping, 1 washing, unmk, 3" 355.00
Bonbon, heart shape, bl mk 350.00
Box, 3-legged, 3¼x4" 625.00
Candle holder, fishing, shield bk, bl mk 775.00
Candlesticks, bl mk, 4¼", pr...700.00
Creamer & sugar bowl, bl mk..800.00
Feeding dish, bl mk..600.00
Pitcher, fishing, bl mk, 3"...325.00
Pitcher, ironing, bl mk, 3½"...275.00
Pitcher, sweeping, bl mk, cream sz...275.00
Pitcher, 1 washing, 1 sweeping, unmk, cream sz, 3¼"...............250.00
Plate, washing, bl mk, 9"..240.00
Sugar bowl, washing, w/lid, bl mk..350.00
Toothpick holder, sewing, 3-ftd, pie-crust edge, unmk, 2½"........600.00

Tapestries

Basket, Rose Tapestry, 3-color, bl mk, 4¾x5¼" 395.00
Biscuit jar, lady w/horse, bl mk 850.00
Box, jewel; Rose Tapestry, pk, clam shape, bl mk, 2x5¼"...........450.00
Candle holders, Rose Tapestry, 3-color, bl mk, #1251, pr 750.00
Creamer & sugar bowl, Rose Tapestry, bulbous, w/lid, bl mk 550.00
Flowerpot, Rose Tapestry, 3-color, w/liner, bl mk, 3x4" 295.00
Hatpin holder, floral, mks dating from 1902, ftd, 4½" 545.00
Match holder, Rose Tapestry, bl mk...450.00
Match holder, sheep, wall hanging, bl mk, #1059......................485.00
Pitcher, bathers, bl mk, cream sz..400.00
Pitcher, Rose Tapestry, pk, pinched spout, bl mk, 4" 400.00
Plate, Rose Tapestry, 3-color, bl mk, 7½" 190.00
Powder jar, Rose Tapestry, ftd 395.00
Relish, Rose Tapestry, open hdls, bl mk, 8" 250.00
Sugar bowl, Rose Tapestry, pk, shape #1310............................250.00
Tray, dresser; Prince & His Lady, bl mk, 7x9¼" 500.00
Tray, dresser; Rose Tapestry, bl mk, 9¾x7¼".............................265.00
Vase, castle scene, bl mk, 4"..375.00
Vase, The Bathers, bl mk, 8¼" 525.00

Royal Bonn

Royal Bonn is a fine-paste porcelain, ornately decorated with scenes, portraits, or florals. The factory was established in the mid-1800s in Bonn, Germany; however, most pieces found today are from the latter part of the century.

Clock, L'Empire, mc w/gold, Ansonia, 1881, 14½x12x6½" 2,475.00
Clock, La Bretagne, 8-day, gong strike, Ansonia, 1904, 15" ...1,200.00
Clock, La Fontaine, rare bl, Ansonia, 11½x9x4¾" 525.00
Clock, La Grace, 8-day, gong strike, Ansonia, ca 1904, 11½" 465.00
Clock, La Meyenne, jeweled, w/key & pendulum, Ansonia........675.00
Clock, La Normandie, 8-day, gong strike, Ansonia, 1904, 13", NM....1,500.00
Clock, La Plata, open escapement, pendulum, crest, Ansonia, 12¾" ..1,100.00
Jardiniere & ped, floral w/gold, seashells & dolphin details, 30".850.00
Urn, mc floral w/much gold, hdls, w/lid & base, 29½" 900.00
Vase, lady's portrait, artist sgn, sm hdls, ca 1900, 17x12" 650.00
Vase, lady's portrait, Sticher, emb floral ft/rim, mk, 12½" 700.00
Vase, Nouveau floral w/gold above woodland landscape, 1900s, 10½"..550.00
Vase, Nouveau florals, mk Old Dutch..., #2556Z, 5½" 300.00
Vase, Nouveau irises, early 1900s, 11x3", pr.............................350.00

Royal Copenhagen

The Royal Copenhagen Manufactory was established in Denmark in about 1775 by Frantz Henrich Muller. When bankruptcy threatened in 1779, the Crown took charge. The fine dinnerware and objects of art produced after that time carry the familiar logo, the crown over three wavy lines. For further information we recommend *Royal Copenhagen Porcelain, Animals and Figurines,* by Robert J. Heritage (Schiffer). See also Limited Edition Plates.

Bowl, pickles; Flora Danica, #20/3542, 6½x3".........................475.00
Bowl, 200th Anniversary of Declaration of Independence, 13" ..665.00
Cake stand, Flora Danica, 1975-1979, 5½x8"............................865.00
Cream cup, Flora Danica, w/lid & undertray, 3½", 4" 735.00
Figurine, Amager girl, standing, #1251, 7½"............................175.00
Figurine, boy w/teddy, #3468, 7"..175.00
Figurine, bricklayer, #4377, 10"...185.00
Figurine, catfish, #464, 1½x7¼"..125.00
Figurine, children walking hand-in-hand, #1737, 7¾" 335.00
Figurine, cocker spaniel, #3116, 5"..130.00
Figurine, dormouse, #2644, 2½"...65.00
Figurine, Fano (girl), overglaze, #12413, 5½" 650.00
Figurine, Flight to America, boy & girl, #1761, 8" 350.00
Figurine, flycatcher, #2144, 3" 175.00
Figurine, French bulldog, #956, 6¾"..235.00
Figurine, geese (2), #2068, 8½"...335.00
Figurine, Gossips, 2 peasant ladies, #1319, 11" 625.00
Figurine, Henrik & Else, #3049, 17"...735.00
Figurine, lady kissing beast, wht gloss, 11x8¾"........................685.00
Figurine, Lippizzanner horse, #4752, 7½"................................325.00
Figurine, nude girl on rock, #4027, 5½"...................................145.00
Figurine, owl, brn, #2999, 5"...135.00
Figurine, Pan w/grapes, #2361, 5½"...260.00
Figurine, Pan w/lion cub, #2852, 5" 335.00
Figurine, Pekingese, recumbent, #442, 6x21"...........................585.00
Figurine, Pekingese, sitting, #1772, 4½"...................................135.00
Figurine, Pointer puppy, #1311, 2"..60.00
Figurine, polar bear cubs at play, #1107, 5" 145.00
Figurine, Princess & Hans Clodhopper, #1473, 9" 950.00
Figurine, rabbit scratching ear, #378, 4¼"................................125.00
Figurine, seminude Island girl putting flowers in her hair, 27" 575.00
Figurine, stag, recumbent, #756, 5½x6" 115.00
Figurine, Windswept, horse, #1362, 7½x12".............................450.00
Paperweight, snail, ca 1900, 5½x3½" 750.00
Plate, luncheon; Flora Danica, 8¾"..500.00

Vase, gr & red mottle, bulbous w/notched neck, rstr, 12x9½" **800.00**
Vase, seaweed on 2-tone brn, sgn KB, 6¼x3" **775.00**

Royal Copley

Royal Copley is a decorative type of pottery made by the Spaulding China Company in Sebring, Ohio, from 1942 to 1957. They also produced two other major lines — Royal Windsor and Spaulding. Royal Copley was primarily marketed through five-and-ten cent stores; Royal Windsor and Spaulding were sold through department stores, gift shops, and jobbers. Items trimmed in gold are worth 25% to 50% more than the same item with no gold trim.

For more information we recommend *Collector's Guide to Royal Copley Plus Royal Windsor & Spaulding, Books I and II,* by our advisor for this category, Joe Devine; he is listed in the Directory under Iowa.

Figurines, large Royal Windsor Chickens, 10½" rooster and 10" hen, from $400.00 to $450.00 for the pair. (Photo courtesy Glenn Hovinga)

Bank, Farmer Pig, paper label, 5½", from $70 to **80.00**
Bank, rooster, brn breast or w/cobalt tail, 8", from $75 to **90.00**
Candy dish, leaf form, mk USA, from $20 to...............................**25.00**
Coaster, antique automobile, unmk, from $35 to...........................**40.00**
Creamer & sugar bowl, leaf hdl, emb mk, 3", ea, from $34 to.......**45.00**
Figurine, Airedale dog, paper label, 6½", from $30 to **35.00**
Figurine, Banty rooster, paper label, 6½", from $90 to **100.00**
Figurine, Blackamoor, down on 1 knee, paper label, 8½", from $35 to ..**40.00**
Figurine, cockatoo, bl, paper label, 7¼", from $40 to **45.00**
Figurine, cockatoo, full bodied, 8¼", from $45 to.........................**50.00**
Figurine, dove, full bodied, paper label, 5", from $12 to **15.00**
Figurine, flycatcher, HP claws/bk of neck, paper label, 8", from $40 to ..**45.00**
Figurine, kingfisher, red, bl or yel, 5", from $45 to **50.00**
Figurine, swallow w/extended wings, paper label, 7", from $80 to.**90.00**
Figurine, thrush, full body, paper label, 6½", from $20 to.............**24.00**
Figurine, wren, paper label, 6¼", from $20 to **24.00**
Lamp, birds in bower, paper label, 8", from $50 to.........................**60.00**
Pitcher, Floral Beauty, pk, gr stamp, 8", from $50 to **60.00**
Pitcher, Pome Fruit, bl, gr mk, 8", from $55 to **65.00**
Planter, barefoot boy or girl, paper label, 7½", ea, from $35 to **40.00**
Planter, deer & fawn, paper label, 8¼", from $30 to.......................**35.00**
Planter, finch beside apple, paper label, 6½", from $30 to..............**35.00**
Planter, girl w/pigtails, emb mk, 7", from $45 to **50.00**
Planter, hat (lg), made to hang or rest on table, emb mk, 7", $40 to...**45.00**
Planter, Indian boy & drum, paper label, 6½", from $20 to **25.00**
Planter, kitten & book, paper label, 6½", from $30 to...................**35.00**
Planter, kitten w/ball of yarn, 8¼", from $35 to............................**40.00**
Planter, lady w/bare shoulder, paper label, 6", from $50 to **60.00**
Planter, Oriental boy w/lg basket, paper label, 8", from $40 to **45.00**
Planter, ram head, paper label, 6½", from $25 to...........................**30.00**
Planter, rooster, low tail, common, paper label, 7⅛", from $30 to ...**35.00**
Planter, rooster & wheelbarrow, paper label, 8", from $135 to **150.00**
Planter, Siamese cats, paper label, 9", from $150 to....................**175.00**
Planter, Spooks, label, 4", from $10 to.......................................**14.00**
Planter, Teddy bear, paper label, 6¼", from $40 to **45.00**
Planter, Teddy bear clinging to stump, paper label, 8¼", $35 to ...**40.00**
Planter/wall pocket, Cocker spaniel head, emb mk, 5", from $28 to ..**34.00**

Planter/wall pocket, girl in wide-brim hat, 7½", from $40 to........**45.00**
Planter/wall pocket, salt box, emb mk, 5½", from $35 to.............**40.00**
Plaque/planter, fruit, emb mk, 6¾", from $30 to **35.00**
Plaque/planter, The Mill, Ruysdael, 8", from $60 to **70.00**
Razor blade bank, barber pole, paper label, 6¼", from $70 to **75.00**
Vase, bud; warbler, gr mk or raised letters, 5", from $18 to..........**20.00**
Vase, Harmony, autumn leaf, tricolor, paper label, 7½", $50 to **55.00**
Vase, Ivy, gr on ivory, ftd, paper label, 7", from $10 to **12.00**
Vase, rooster, flowing tail, paper label, 7⅛", from $40 to.............**45.00**
Vase, stylized leaves, paper label, 8¼", from $12 to **15.00**
Vase, trailing leaf & vine, paper label, 8½", from $25 to..............**30.00**
Vase/planter, fish, yel & blk w/brn stripe, paper label, 6", $50 to ..**60.00**
Vase/planter, nuthatch beside stump, paper label, 5½", from $30 to ..**35.00**

Royal Crown Derby

The Royal Crown Derby company can trace its origin back to 1848. It first operated under the name of Locker & Co. but by 1859 had become Stevenson, Sharp & Co. Several changes in ownership occurred until 1866 when it became known as the Sampson Hancock Co. The Derby Crown Porcelain Co. Ltd. was formed in 1876, and these companies soon merged. In 1890 they were appointed as a manufacturer for the Queen and began using the name Royal Crown Derby.

In the early years, considerable 'Japan ware' decorated in Imari style, using red, blue, and gold in Oriental patterns was popular. The company excelled in their ability to use gold in the decoration, and some of the best flower painters of all time were employed. Nice vases or plaques signed by any of these artists will bring thousands of dollars: Gregory, Mosley, Rouse, Gresley, and D'esir'e Leroy. We have observed porcelain plaques decorated with flowers signed by Gregory selling at auction for as much as $12,000.00. If you find a signed piece and are not sure of its value, if at all possible, it would be best to have it appraised by someone very knowledgeable regarding current market values.

As is usual among most other English factories, nearly all of the vases produced by Royal Crown Derby came with covers. If they are missing, deduct 40% to 45%. There are several well illustrated books available from antique booksellers to help you learn to identify this ware. The back stamps used after 1891 will date every piece except dinnerware. The company is still in business, producing outstanding dinnerware and Imari-decorated figures and serving pieces. They also produce custom (one only) sets of table service for the wealthy of the world.

Bowl, fruit; Mikado..**52.00**
Bowl, Saran pattern, scroll hdls, lions' heads at corners, 4x11x9" ...**440.00**
Box, sailboat scene, artist sgn, crown mk, 4¼" **140.00**
Cup & saucer, coffee; Imari pattern, can shape w/loop hdl, 1915 .**85.00**
Cup & saucer, demi; floral on wht, can shape w/scalloped rim, 1933 ..**55.00**
Cup & saucer, demi; Old Imari **75.00**
Cup & saucer, Mandarin **60.00**
Heart dish, Saran or Oriental pattern, mc w/cobalt & gold, 9x10" ..**300.00**
Jar, potpourri; floral on ivory, ornate lid, #544/2658, 1880s, 8¾" ...**885.00**
Plate, hawk portrait, bl rim w/gold, 9½" **350.00**
Tureen, soup; Imari-style pattern, 16½" L, +undertray.............**1,275.00**
Vase, bud; wild roses, gold on brick red, mk, 7" **175.00**
Vase, bulbous, Tiffany & Co silver trim & hdls, 1885, 9½" **1,200.00**
Vase, flowers & butterfly, gold on mauve, hdls, ca 1880, 5½" **195.00**
Vase, gold enamel on pk, 3-hdl, 8½" **375.00**
Vase, wildflowers, gold on mauve, crown mk, 4"...........................**150.00**

Royal Doulton, Doulton

The range of wares produced by the Doulton Company since its inception in 1815 has been vast and varied. The earliest wares produced in the tiny pottery in Lambeth, England, were salt-glazed pitchers, plain and fancy figural bottles, etc. — all utility-type stoneware geared to the practical needs of everyday living. The original partners, John Doulton and John Watts, saw the potential for success in the manufacture of drain and sewage pipes and during the 1840s concentrated on these highly lucrative types of commercial wares. Watts retired from the company in 1854, and Doulton began experimenting with a more decorative product line. As time went by, many glazes and decorative effects were developed, among them Faience, Impasto, Silicon, Carrara, Marqueterie, Chine, and Rouge Flambe. Tiles and architectural terra cotta were an important part of their manufacture. Late in the nineteenth century at the original Lambeth location, fine artware was decorated by such notable artists as Hannah and Arthur Barlow, George Tinworth, and J.H. McLennan. Stoneware vases with incised animal drawings, gracefully shaped urns with painted scenes, and cleverly modeled figurines rivaled the best of any competitor.

In 1882 a second factory was built in Burslem which continues even yet to produce the famous figurines, character jugs, series ware, and table services so popular with collectors today. Their Kingsware line, made from 1899 to 1946, featured flasks and flagons with drinking scenes, usually on a brown-glazed ground. Some were limited editions, while others were commemorative and advertising items. The Gibson Girl series, twenty-four plates in all, was introduced in 1901. It was drawn by Charles Dana Gibson and is recognized by its blue and white borders and central illustrations, each scene depicting a humorous or poignant episode in the life of 'The Widow and Her Friends.' Dickensware, produced from 1911 through the early 1940s, featured illustrations by Charles Dickens, with many of his famous characters. The Robin Hood series was introduced in 1914; the Shakespeare series #1, portraying scenes from the Bard's plays, was made from 1914 until World War II. The Shakespeare series #2 ran from 1906 until 1974 and was decorated with featured characters. Nursery Rhymes was a series that was first produced in earthenware in 1930 and later in bone china. In 1933 a line of decorated children's ware, the Bunnykin series, was introduced; it continues to be made to the present day. About 150 'bunny' scenes have been devised, the earliest and most desirable being those signed by the artist Barbara Vernon. Most pieces range in value from $60.00 to $120.00.

Factors contributing to the value of a figurine are age, demand, color, and detail. Those with a limited production run and those signed by the artist or marked 'Potted' (indicating a pre-1939 origin) are also more valuable. After 1920 wares were marked with a lion — with or without a crown — over a circular 'Royal Doulton.' Our advisor for this category is Nicki Budin; she is listed in the Directory under Ohio.

Animals and Birds

Bull dog, K-2, 2x2"	200.00
Cairn dog, begging, HN2589	80.00
Cat, Lucky, K-12	200.00
Drake, HN806, flambe, sm	160.00
Elephant, HN2644, 5½"	225.00
Fox Terrier, eating from plate, HN1158	75.00
Fox Terrier, sitting, K-7	125.00
Penguin, K-22	265.00
Persian cat, HN999, blk & wht	165.00
Piglet, HN2653	235.00
Scottie, sitting on bk legs, K-18, 2½"	150.00
Welch Corgi, K-16, 2½x2½"	150.00

Bunnykins

Aerobic, DB40	225.00
Astro, DB20	145.00

Aussie Surfer, DB133	150.00
Australian Sidney, DB195	275.00
Autumn Days, DB5	365.00
Banjo, DB184	160.00
Bathtime, DB148	65.00
Be Prepared, DB56	65.00
Bedtime, DB55	45.00
Beefeater, DB163	295.00
Bogey, DB32	135.00
Boy Skater, colorway, DB187	150.00
Boy Skater, DB152	45.00
Bridesmaid, DB173	45.00
Britannia, DB219	175.00
Cheerleader, DB142, red	235.00
Cheerleader, DB143, yel.	250.00
Clarinet, DB182	160.00
Clean Sweep, DB6	85.00
Cowboy, DB201	165.00
Detective, DB193	165.00
Double Bass, DB185	175.00
English Athlete, DB216	175.00
Family Photo, DB1, bl	125.00
Family Photo, DB67, pk	195.00
Father, DB154	75.00
Father, Mother, Victoria, DB68	75.00
Fortune Teller Jug, #7157	299.00
Gardener, DB156	45.00
Girl Skater, DB153	65.00
Good Night, DB157	45.00
Guardsman	650.00
Happy Birthday, DB21	45.00
Harry, DB73	75.00
Helping Mother, DB2	85.00
Homerun, DB43	85.00
Indian, #202	175.00
Irishman, DB178	195.00
Jester, DB161	350.00
Jockey, DB169	295.00
Jogging, DB22	95.00
Joker, DB171	225.00
Juggler, DB164	295.00
King John, DB45	125.00
Minstrel, DB211	175.00
Mother Bunnykins, DB189	45.00
Mountie, DB135	850.00
Mr Bunnybeat, DB16	225.00
Mrs Easter Bunny, DB19	95.00
New Baby, DB158	45.00
Nurse, DB74, red cross	295.00
Olympic, DB28	195.00
Out for a Duck, DB160	325.00
Partners in Collecting, DB151	125.00
Playtime Higbees, DB80	175.00
Rainy Day, DB147	55.00
Rise & Shine, DB11	125.00
Sailor, DB166	60.00
Santa, DB17	85.00
Saxophone Player, DB186	160.00
Schoolmaster, DB60	65.00
Scotsman, DB180	160.00
Seaside, DB177	55.00
Sixtieth Anniversary, DB137	55.00
Sleepytime, DB15	55.00
Sleigh Ride, DB81	150.00

Springtime, DB7	350.00
Susan, DB70	75.00
Sweetheart, DB139	65.00
Tally Ho, DB12	115.00
Touchdown, DB29	145.00
Tourist Bunnykins, DB190	75.00
Uncle Sam, colorway, DB175	250.00
Welsh Lady, DB172	225.00
William, DB69	85.00

Character Jugs

North American Indian, John Sinclair Limited Edition, large, $150.00.

'Arriet, D6208, lg	140.00
'Arriet, D6250, mini	65.00
'Arry, D6207, lg	140.00
Antique Dealer, lg	165.00
Apothecary, D6574, sm	65.00
Aramis, D6441, lg	145.00
Athos, D6439, lg	145.00
Auld Mac, D5824, sm	45.00
Bacchus, D6499, lg	125.00
Beefeater, D6206, lg	140.00
Capt Ahab, D6506, sm	55.00
Capt Cuttle, D5842, odd sz	165.00
Capt Henry Morgan, D6469, sm	65.00
Capt Hook, D6597, lg	490.00
Capt Morgan, D6469, sm	65.00
Cardinal, D5033, A mk, sm	75.00
Cardinal, D6129, mini	55.00
Cavalier, D6173, sm	75.00
Cook & Cheshire Cat, lg	275.00
D'Artagnan, D6691, lg	130.00
Dick Turpin, D6528, horse hdl, lg	150.00
Dick Turpin, D6535, horse hdl, sm	50.00
Dick Whittington, D6375, lg	350.00
Dox Quixote, D6455, lg	125.00
Elephant Trainer, D6841, lg	275.00
Farmer John, sm	75.00
Fat Boy, D5840, odd sz	225.00
Fortune Teller, D6874, lg	450.00
Friar Tuck, D6321, lg	450.00
Gondolier, D6589, lg	550.00
Gone Away, D6531, lg	125.00
Gone Away, D6538, sm	65.00
Granny, D5521, lg	115.00
Guardsman of Williamsburg, D6568, lg	150.00
Henry VIII, D6642, lg	150.00
Isaac Walton, D6404, lg	150.00
Jester, D6446, sm	125.00
John Peel, D5612, lg	150.00
John Peel, D5731, sm	75.00
Lawyer, D6498, lg	150.00
Lobster Man, D6617, lg	125.00

Lord Nelson, D6336, lg	375.00
Louis Armstrong, D6707, lg	150.00
Lumberjack, D6610, lg	125.00
Macbeth, D6667, lg	160.00
Mad Hatter, D6598, lg	225.00
Mikado, D6501, lg	550.00
Mine Host, D6488, lg	125.00
Mine Host, D6513, mini	50.00
Mr Micawber, D5843, odd sz	165.00
Mr Pickwick, D5839, odd sz	185.00
Old Charley, D5527, sm	55.00
Old King Cole, D6036, lg	295.00
Old Mac, D5823, mini, A	40.00
Othello, D6673, lg	150.00
Paddy, D5042, mini, A	45.00
Parson Brown, D5529, sm	60.00
Pied Piper, D6403, lg	145.00
Pied Piper, D6514, mini	60.00
Porthos, D6440, lg	130.00
Punch & Judy Man, D6590, lg	550.00
Red Queen, D6777, lg	160.00
Robinson Crusoe, D6539, sm	65.00
Sairey Gamp, D5528, sm	55.00
Sam Johnson, D6289, lg	335.00
Sam Weller, D5841, sm	80.00
Sam Weller, D6140, mini	40.00
Sancho Panza, D6456, lg	145.00
Scaramouche, D6558, lg	775.00
Shakespeare, lg	115.00
Simon Cellarer, D5616, sm	75.00
Simple Simon, D6374, lg	675.00
Sir Henry Doulton, sm	95.00
Smuggler, D6616, lg	125.00
Snake Charmer, lg	250.00
St George, D6618, lg	295.00
Tam O'Shanter, D6632, lg	125.00
Tam O'Shanter, D6636, sm	65.00
Tony Weller, D5530, sm	45.00
Touchstone, D5613, lg	225.00
Town Crier, D6530, lg	175.00
Trapper, D6604, lg	150.00
Uncle Tom Cobbleigh, D6337, lg	350.00
Veteran Motorist, D6633, lg	135.00
Viking, D6502, sm	110.00
Walrus & Carpenter, D6600, lg	195.00
Walrus & Carpenter, D6608, mini	65.00
Witch, D6893, lg	200.00

Figurines

Abdullah, HN1410	495.00
Ascot, HN2356	165.00
Autumn Breezes, HN2147, wht skirt	450.00
Autumn Time, HN3231	250.00
Blithe Morning, HN2065, red	200.00
Blue Beard, HN2105, 2nd version	450.00
Bridesmaid, M30	275.00
Captain, HN2260, 2nd version	250.00
Cavalier, HN2716, 2nd version	195.00
Chief, HN2892	225.00
Chloe, HN1765, bl	400.00
Choir Boy, HN2141	125.00
Christine, HN2792, 2nd version	225.00
Clarinda, HN2724	175.00

Clarissa, HN2345 ....155.00
Country Lass, HN1991 ....150.00
Debbie, HN2385 ....95.00
Denise, HN2273, 1st edition 275.00
Diana, HN1986 ....150.00
Doctor, HN2858 ....250.00
Elegance, HN2264 ....155.00
Emily, HN3806 ....100.00
Eventide, HN2814 ....150.00
Fair Lady, NJ2832 ....145.00
Fiona, HN2694 ....200.00
Foaming Quart, HN2162 ....200.00
Fragrance, HN2334 ....175.00
Francine, HN2422 ....95.00
Homecoming, HN3295 ....250.00
Isadora, HN2938 ....250.00
Jane, HN2806 ....175.00
Janet, HN1916, 5¼" 180.00
Janine, HN2461 ....175.00
Jester, HN2016 ....300.00
Kathleen, HN3100 ....195.00
Lady Betty, HN1967 ....350.00
Laird, HN2361 ....175.00
Laura, HN2960 ....195.00
Lawyer, HN3041 ....200.00
Lily, HN1798 ....125.00
Lizzie, HN1749 ....160.00
Lunchtime, HN2485 ....175.00
Mask Seller, HN2103 ....225.00
Master, HN2325 ....175.00
Melanie, HN2271 ....165.00
Milkmaid, HN2057 ....195.00
Miss Demure, HN1402 ....275.00
Mother & Daughter, HN2841 ....100.00
October, HN2693 ....175.00
Old King, HN2134 ....650.00
Omar Khayyam, HN2247 ....175.00
Pauline, HN2441 ....165.00
Pearly Boy, HN2035 ....200.00
Piper, HN2907 ....225.00
Polly, HN3178 ....150.00
Potter, HN1493 ....485.00
Premiere, HN2343 ....165.00
Prince of Wales, HN2883 ....450.00
Prince Philip Duke of Edinburgh, HN2386 ...450.00
Professor, HN2281 ....175.00
Rest Awhile, HN2728 ....165.00
Reverie, HN2306 ....225.00
Romance, HN2430 ....155.00
Salome, HN3267, from $1,200 to 1,250.00
Sandra, HN2275 ....150.00
Silversmith of Williamsburg, HN2208 ......200.00
Skater, HN3439 ....225.00
Sleepy Darling, HN2953 ....160.00
Solitude, HN2810 ....225.00
Sophie, HN3257 ....225.00
Stephanie, HN2807 ....150.00
Stitch in Time, HN2352 ....155.00
Summertime, HN3137 ....140.00
Toymaker, HN2250 ....375.00
Vanity, HN2475 ....125.00
Veneta, HN2772 ....155.00
Votes for Women, HN2816 ....225.00
Wizard, HN2877 ....225.00

Flambe

Figurine, Brindle bulldog, HN1244 ....300.00
Figurine, Dog of Foo, #3819, 1982, 4¾" ...175.00
Figurine, fox, sitting, #14 ....160.00
Figurine, penguin, 6" 175.00
Figurine, pigs laying together, rare..........1,295.00
Figurine, rabbit, recumbent, 4" 120.00
Vase, cottage, trees & flowers, rouge, #7168, 6⅞" ...325.00
Vase, landscape, rouge, ink stamp, 11" 250.00
Vase, landscape, rouge, paper label, 8⅞" ...200.00
Vase, Sung, Noke & Moore, 5½" 300.00

Series Ware

Vase, Kingsware, monks, early twentieth century, 10¾", $525.00.

Ashtray, Gnomes, bl underglaze 250.00
Bowl, Coaching Days, men, carriage & horses, #d, 1½x7¾" 85.00
Candlestick, King Arthur's Knights, mc, D2961, 1924, 6½" 110.00
Chop plate, Under the Greenwood Tree, 13½" 270.00
Coffeepot, Moorish Gate, merchants, 7x3¾" ...150.00
Cup & saucer, Mad Hatter 125.00
Flask, Kingsware, Sporting Squire, Dewar's, 8½" 475.00
Jug, whiskey; Kingsware, Pipe Major, Dewar's, 1900-10, 8¼" 120.00
Mug, King Arthur's Knights, mc, D2961, dtd 1921, 5½" 265.00
Pitcher, Cavaliers, Better So Than Worse, 8" 95.00
Pitcher, Dogberry's Watch, man w/lantern, 7¾" 150.00
Plaque, Babes in Woods, girl w/basket, P Jones, 9¾x7¾" 1,525.00
Plate, burns, Here's a Help to Them..., 10½" 90.00
Plate, Deer, under tree, D5193, 10¼" 120.00
Plate, Dickensware, Cap'n Cuttle, 10" 125.00
Plate, Flowers: Nasturtiums, D3786, dtd 1915, 8½" ...135.00
Plate, Home Waters, barges at pier, Grace, 1913, 8¼" 60.00
Plate, Pan, flute player, D4794, 10¼" 125.00
Tray, Dickensware, Cap'n Cuttle, 10½x5⅝" 125.00
Tray, Shakespeare, Katharine, 15½" 165.00
Tumbler, Nursery Rhymes, Little Bo Peep 95.00
Vase, Babes in woods, children w/dogs, mk, 4½" 275.00
Vase, Babes in Woods, mother & child, #9889, 12" 1,075.00
Vase, Blue Children, 3 girls outdoors, 8x8½" 675.00
Vase, Kingsware, squire at table, 6-line verse, hdls, 10½" 450.00

Stoneware

Candlestick, scrolling decor, gr/bl/brn, Lambeth, #3924, 5¾" 300.00
Jar, lions, SP lid/mts, Lambeth, ca 1876-77, 5¼" 500.00
Jardiniere, geometric floral, brn on tan, Lambeth/Slater's Pat, 7⅝" ...350.00
Vase, incised deer band, tooled foliage borders, Lambeth, rpr, 7" ...195.00

Toby Jugs

Cap'n Cuttle, D6266 ....165.00

Cap'n Cuttle, sm..45.00
Falstaff, D6062...125.00
Falstaff, D6063...85.00
Fat Boy, D6264..225.00
Happy John, D6031...125.00
Huntsman, D6319...120.00
Mr Micawber, D6262...225.00
Mr Pickwick, D6261..225.00
Sairey Gamp, D6263...225.00
Sherlock Holmes, D661..120.00
Sir Frances Drake, D6660..120.00
Squire, D6319..450.00

Miscellaneous

Fairy Lamp, burmese shade on Arabian sgn Burslem base, 6x8x5"....1,350.00
Jug, Dewar's Scotch Whisky (sic), dk gr/brn on tan, 6¼"............300.00
Jug, Special Highland Whisky (sic), sailing ship, Greenlees Bros, 7"...2,100.00
Vase, cows & barn in twilight, Burslem, 10½"............................650.00
Vase, floral, bl w/gr stems & leaves on wht, 8", NM..................350.00
Vase, irises & daisies, shouldered, Lambeth, 20⅝"...................1,500.00
Vase, stylized slip-trail flowers, cylindrical, #6943, 9¾"............250.00
Vase, Titanian, Egyptian figures, Tutankahamen's..., 4⅞"...........225.00
Vase, Titanian, stork/flowers/moon, Allen, 5¾".......................600.00

Royal Dux

The Duxer Porzellan Manufactur was established by E. Eichler in 1860. Located in what is now Duchcov, Czechoslovakia, the area was known as Dux, Bohemia, until WWI. The war brought about changes in both the style of the ware as well as the mark. Prewar pieces were modeled in the Art Nouveau or Greek Classical manner and marked with 'Bohemia' and a pink triangle containing the letter 'E.' They were usually matt glazed in green, brown, and gold. Better pieces were made of porcelain, while the larger items were of pottery. After the war the ware was marked with the small pink triangle but without the Bohemia designation; 'Made in Czechoslovakia' was added. The style became Art Deco, with cobalt blue a dominant color.

Centerpiece, maiden stands on wave crest holding fishing net, two large shells at sides, pink triangle mark, ca 1900, 16¾", $1,750.00.

Bowl, centerpc; 4 maidens' heads/floral branches, #833 13, rstr, 19"...750.00
Figurine, boy w/stick & coat over shoulder, w/dog, #1853, 13½".350.00
Figurine, clown playing accordion, bls & grs, 12".....................550.00
Figurine, Dutch girls pulling in fishing net, #9903-32, 10"............30.00
Figurine, girl carrying basket on head stands beside jug, 7".........200.00
Figurine, goat & cart, 14x7"...225.00
Figurine, hound, recumbent, dk brn on wht base, 11" L, from $175 to...225.00
Figurine, lady sits w/legs bent, holding bottle, wht porc, 8".........275.00
Figurine, maiden on ped w/gown flowing to form 12" basin, 15"..1,350.00
Figurine, mother holding daughter, 21".................................1,200.00
Figurine, Noveau lady w/torch stand, #39/897, 15"..................1,500.00

Figurine, nude running w/Borzoi dog, #717-260, 14¼".............350.00
Figurine, nude sits on horse w/arms up, wht porc, 13"................375.00
Figurine, Statue of David, 21"...1,000.00
Figurine, woman being kissed by angel, 8"............................250.00
Figurine, woman w/boy playing flute, #2408, 8".......................300.00
Vase, nude coming out of flower bud w/leaves, #5518II, 17".......360.00

Royal Flemish

Royal Flemish was introduced in the late 1880s and was patented in 1894 by the Mt. Washington Glass Company. Transparent glass was enameled with one or several colors and the surface divided by a network of raised lines suggesting leaded glasswork. Some pieces were further decorated with enameled florals, birds, or Roman coins. Our advisors for this category are Betty and Clarence Maier; they are listed in the Directory under Pennsylvania.

Biscuit jar, mc panels, lion on shield, gold scrolls, 5x7½"........3,800.00
Ewer, 16 bl medallions/gold flowers, frosted hdl, 12x5½", NM...7,500.00
Ginger jar, gold-winged dragon, 7"....................................1,950.00
Sugar shaker, Queen Anne's Lace, clear satin, ovoid..................850.00
Vase, peacock, gold w/jewels on bl, #594, 13¼x7"................15,000.00
Vase, peafowls/dmns/stars/etc, mc w/gold on earth tone, 4½x4½"...1,850.00
Vase, roses, mc w/gold, dbl-bulbed, ca 1894, 9½".................3,335.00
Vase, snow geese in flight, violet/bl-gr/bl/gold, 14½"..............7,000.00
Vase, violets & scrolls on clear frost, sm hdls, #0583, 6½x6"..2,200.00
Vase, 3 medallions, gold foliage, burgundy dmns on earth tones, 11"..2,100.00

Royal Haeger, Haeger

In 1871 David Henry Haeger, a young son of German immigrants, purchased a brick factory at Dundee, Illinois. David's bricks rebuilt Chicago after their great fire in 1871. Many generations of the Haeger family have been associated with the ceramic industry, up to the present time. Haeger progressed to include artware in their production as early as 1914. That was only the beginning. In the '30s they began to make a line of commercial dinnerware that was marketed through Marshall Fields. Not long after, Haeger's artware was successful enough that a second plant in Macomb, Illinois, was built.

Royal Haeger was their premium line beginning in 1938 and continued in to modern-day production. The chief designer in the '40s was Royal Arden Hickman, a talented artist and sculptor who also worked in mediums other than pottery. For Haeger he designed a line of wonderfully stylized animals, birds, high-style vases, and human figures, all with extremely fine details. His designs are highly regarded by collectors today.

Paper labels have been used throughout Haeger's production. Some items from the teens, '20s, and '30s will be found with 'Haeger' in a diamond shape in-mold script mark. Items with 'RG' (Royal Garden) are part of their Flower-Ware line (also called Regular Haeger or Genuine Haeger). Haeger has produced a premium line (Royal Haeger) as well as a regular line for many years, it just has changed names over the years.

Collectors need to be aware that a certain glaze can bring two to three times more than others. Items that have Royal Hickman in the mold mark or on the label are usually higher valued than without his mark. The current collector trend has leaned more towards the mid-century modern styled pieces of artware. The most desired items are ones done by glaze designers Helmut Bruchman and Alrun Osterberg Guest (presently employed by Haeger). These items are from the late '60s into the very early '80s.

For those wanting to learn more about this pottery, we recommend *Haeger Potteries Through the Years* by our advisor for this category, David Dilley (L-W Books); he is listed in the Directory under Indiana.

#H-608, pitcher w/rooster hdl, Persian Blue, 6¾x9" 40.00
#R-108, pouter pigeon planter, Mauve Agate, 11⅞x8½" 75.00
#R-130, pheasant, Green Agate, 11¼x6" 30.00
#R-185, flower & leaf candle holders, lt bl w/lt gr accents, pr....65.00
#R-186, Bird of Paradise, Cloudy Blue, 9x13⅛" 65.00
#R-235, colt flower holder, Green Briar, 7x12½" 45.00
#R-246, dbl cornucopia vase, Mauve Agate, 14x8¼" 45.00
#R-271, sailfish planter, Peach Agate, 13x9" 45.00
#R-281, sphere w/3 feather plumes, Mauve Agate, 9" 125.00
#R-284, trout planter, Pearl Carnival w/gold fins, 8x9¼" 100.00
#R-287, wren house, Mauve Agate, 7¼x4¼x9½" 100.00
#R-293, violin bowl planter, Mallow, 16x1⅝" 100.00
#R-303, laurel wreath bow vase, Mauve Agate, 7¾x12" 75.00
#R-304, fish candle holder, Mauve Agate, 3¼x2x4¼", pr....50.00
#R-313, tiger, Pearl Gray Drip 125.00
#R-314, tigress, amber, 10¼x4¼x11" 125.00
#R-318, Russian Wolfhound, head down, Green Briar, 11½x6¼" 75.00
#R-334, fan-tail pouter pigeon planter, Peach Agate, 9x8x8" 75.00
#R-363, woman riding fish flower block, Green Agate....65.00
#R-370, Dutch cup bowl, Green Agate, 3½x18½" 45.00
#R-382, peasant man, Green Agate, 5" sq base, 17" H....125.00
#R-386, basket vase, Mauve Agate, 13¼x8½" 75.00
#R-393, Pegasus head vase, bl, 8½x11¼" 100.00
#R-421, bowl w/clusters, Silver Spray & chartreuse, 14½x7" 70.00
#R-422, butterfly vase, Mauve Agate, 9x5½" 40.00
#R-424, Bucking Bronco, amber, 13" 200.00
#R-426, cornucopia vase w/nude, chartreuse, 7½x8" 35.00
#R-442, bowl w/floral relief, Mauve Agate, 18¼x4¾" 45.00
#R-452, Morning Glory vase, Mauve Agate, 16½" 90.00
#R-455, bow vase, wht w/bl bow, 5x14" 75.00
#R-481, seashell on base, Silver Spray & chartreuse, 9¾x10½" ...75.00
#R-482, 3-feather plume vase, Mallow, 9½x14½" 75.00
#R-483, upright shell planter, Mallow, 10½x10½" 75.00
#R-515, swan planter, Mauve Agate, 18x8¼" 85.00
#R-516, swan candle holder, Mauve Agate, 3⅝x8", pr....50.00
#R-641, stallion bookend planter, chartreuse, 5½x8¾", pr 50.00
#R-657, gondolier planter, Green Agate, 19x8½" 65.00
#R-685, horse head cigarette box, Green Agate, 6¾x5" 75.00
#R-707, standing deer vase, ebony, 7x15¼" 40.00
#R-766, Rudolph the Red Nosed Reindeer planter, Desert Red, 9¼" 100.00
#R-869, gazelle planter, Antique, 17x13¾" 65.00
#R-967, starfish bowl, Pearl Gray Drip, 14½x2⅜" 45.00
#R-1131, leopard, chartreuse, 7½x7¾" 75.00
#R-1253, little sister holding basket, wht w/blk trim, 6x11½" 85.00
#R-1293, acanthus planter, Green Agate, 11x5¾" 35.00
#R-1504 & R-1505, lion's head lavabo, turq-bl, set....175.00
#R-1510, bull, Mandarin Orange, 18x8¼" 225.00
#R-1679-S, pitcher, turq-bl, 10¼x3¾" dia 65.00
#R-1734, goat planter, Sable, 13x9½" 45.00
#R-1752W, eccentric vase, wht w/turq, 16¾" 40.00
#R-1761, turkey planter, 14x10x12" 150.00
#RT-63, compote, Green Gold Tweed, sq, 4x4x7" 25.00
#25, 3-ftd bowl, dk & lt bl, 3¼x6" dia....60.00
#34, candle holder, stemmed, Mint Green, 5¼x10½", pr....50.00
#47, vase, dk & lt gr, 15½x6" dia....75.00
#77, bathing nude flower frog, wht, 7" 200.00
#135, ashtray, Purple Jewel Tone, 12x7½x1½" 10.00
#153, ashtray, Mandarin Orange, 10¾x1½" 15.00
#167, planter, yel, 5¼x6½" dia 20.00
#186, vase w/leaf design, bl & wht, 11¼x9" dia 150.00
#318-H, bowl, Amethyst Crackle, 11¾x5" 40.00
#329-H, pheasant bowl, Gold Tweed, 21¼x5½" 50.00
#335, compote, Blue Crackle w/gr accents, 10x4¾" 25.00
#514, mermaid w/bowl, Gold Tweed, 13¾x10⅜" 100.00
#612, rooster figurine, Burnt Sienna, 8½x4x11" 50.00
#616, teddy bear planter, chartreuse, 7x4¾" 15.00
#650, dove, wings spread up & bk, 9½" 50.00
#726-H, horse canister, Rust Brown, 4¼x3" dia....35.00
#777, cocker spaniel, brn w/blk tail, 5½x3" 50.00
#812, lady head, wht, 2½" sq base, 7" H 300.00
#815-H, candle holder compote, Gold Tweed, 15¼" 75.00
#873-H, egg-serving plate, chicken shape, Reseda Yellow, 14¾"...75.00
#2125X, ashtray, Earth Graphic Wrap, Fern Agate, 7¾" dia....15.00
#3003, compote, Cotton White & turq, 12x4½" 20.00
#3003, lady head lamp base, gr w/brn accents, 3½x14" 300.00
#3061, cornucopia planter, wht, 12x5½" 50.00
#3068, triple candle holder dish, brn w/wht accents, 12¼x3" 45.00
#3106, oblong vase planter, chartreuse, 11½x6¼" 25.00
#3122-A, ribbed bowl, gr, 2½x7" dia....15.00
#3130, ped planter, Earth Graphic Wrap, wht, 7x11" dia....50.00
#3182, pitcher, Sunset, 10x9½" dia....100.00
#3208, fish vase, wht, 4½x5½" 40.00
#3220, rooster vase, wht, 7x4x14" 75.00
#3227, dbl shell vase, Green Agate, 19x7" 75.00
#3314, horse planter, wht, 7½x6" 45.00
#3427-AM, musical Madonna planter, wht, plays Ave Marie, 11" ..75.00
#3532, flower girl w/bowl, brn & cream, 8½x9¾" 75.00
#4020, planter, gray, 7½x3½" 15.00
#4149, vase w/leaves in relief, Green Marigold, 12⅛" 40.00
#4233-X, vase, Earth Graphic Wrap, brn, 5x11" 60.00
#5000, planter, Earth Graphic Wrap, 8¼x12½" dia 100.00
#5073, racoon w/bucket planter, Bennington Brown Foam, 9x5½" ...45.00
#5190, Bucking Bronco w/cactus finial, 26" 250.00
#5205, girl on turtle table lamp, turq, 13x10x19" 250.00
#5240, horse head wall lamp, ebony, 9¼x5¼" dia base....200.00
#5473, 2-deer abstract TV lamp, oxblood & wht, 8x5x15½" 175.00
#6424S-TV, angel fish TV lamp, Antique, 13¾" 75.00
#8061, sugar canister, bl & wht, gold trim, 6½x5" dia....65.00
#8170, dish w/rooster on lid, Roman Bronze, 9x5x3" 150.00
#8198, Gleep cookie jar, yel-orange....500.00
#8237, vase, 2-tone gr, early logo, 7¾x6½" dia 100.00
#8300, toe tapper w/flute, brn, 4¼x8" 35.00

Royal Rudolstadt

The hard-paste porcelain that has come to be known as Royal Rudolstadt was produced in Thuringia, Germany, in the early eighteenth century. Various names and marks have been associated with this pottery. One of the earliest was a hay-fork symbol associated with Johann Frederich von Schwarzburg-Rudolstadt, one of the first founders. Variations, some that included an 'R,' were also used. In 1854 Earnst Bohne produced wares that were marked with an anchor and the letters 'EB.' Examples commonly found today were made during the late 1800s and early 1900s. These are usually marked with an 'RW' within a shield under a crown and the words 'Crown Rudolstadt.' Items marked 'Germany' were made after 1890.

Centerpiece, three winged cherubs support bowl with applied florals and gold trim, 1854 – 1900 mark, 5x10", $300.00.

Bowl, lt pk roses, 4 shaped lobes, sgn J Hahn, 8¾" 60.00
Bowl, wht & pk roses, floral border w/2 gold bands, 4 shaped lobes, 6" ...35.00
Butter/cheese dish, lt pk roses, w/lid, 7x5½x4" 65.00
Creamer & sugar bowl, purple violets, gold trim.........................110.00
Creamer & sugar bowl, wht w/Golliwogs, children's sz 85.00
Figurine, lady w/boy playing bagpipes, ornate lace, 6" 210.00
Plate, lt pk roses, sgn J Hahn, 8¾"..50.00
Plate, purple flowers, palette shape, 8½"..................................210.00
Plate, serving; purple flowers, gold rim, 10¼".............................60.00
Plate, violets, gold rim, 8½"...65.00
Powder dish, purple roses, w/lid, 4½" dia...................................75.00
Teapot, Golliwogs, child sz..75.00
Tidbit, wht roses, 2-tier, 3x9" dia..50.00
Vase, Cupid the Rascal, cobalt, dbl-hdld, sgn Celli, 12¾" 250.00

Royal Vienna

In 1719 Claude Innocentius de Paquier established a hard-paste porcelain factory in Vienna where he made highly ornamental wares similar to the type produced at Meissen. Early wares were usually unmarked; but after 1744, when the factory was purchased by the Empress, the Austrian shield (often called 'beehive') was stamped on under the glaze. In the following listings, values are for hand-painted items unless noted otherwise. Decal-decorated items would be considerably lower.

Note: An influx of Japanese reproductions on the market have influenced values to decline on genuine old Royal Vienna. Buyer beware! On new items the beehive mark is over the glaze, the weight of the porcelain is heavier, and the decoration is obviously decaled. Our advisor for this category is Madeleine France; she is listed in the Directory under Florida.

Candlesticks, scenes on maroon & gold, Kauffman, 5½", pr.......525.00
Charger, Armors Triumph scene, geometric borders, 1860s, 13¼"..1,400.00
Charger, children at play, mc w/much gold, beehive mk, 14" ..1,700.00
Cup & saucer, Fatima portrait on cobalt, early 1900s, 4½", 5" ..220.00
Pitcher, rnd portrait reserve on cobalt, ornate shape/hdl, 6½"....435.00
Plate, classical lady w/harp, Wagner, beehive mk, 9½" 785.00
Plate, Lady Scheffield portrait, Wagner, beehive mk, 10" 1,125.00
Plate, Rape of Europa, Wagner, #27255, 9½" 1,400.00
Plate, Waldesflustern, lady sits, cherub on shoulder, Wagner, 9½"...475.00
Stein, lovers kissing/flowers, inlaid lid, beehive mk, 5" 1,750.00

Roycroft

Near the turn of the twentieth century, Elbert Hubbard established the Roycroft Printing Shop in East Aurora, New York. Named in honor of two seventeenth-century printer-bookbinders, the print shop was just the beginning of a community called Roycroft, which came to be known worldwide. Hubbard became a popular personality of the early 1900s, known for his talents in a variety of areas from writing and lecturing to manufacturing. The Roycroft community became a meeting place for people of various capabilities and included shops for the production of furniture, copper, leather items, and a multitude of other wares which were marked with the Roycroft symbol, an 'R' within a circle below a double-barred cross. Hubbard lost his life on the Lusitania in 1915; production at the community continued until the Depression.

Interest is strong in the field of Arts and Crafts in general and in Roycroft items in particular. Copper items are evaluated to a large extent by the condition and type of the original patina. The most desirable patina is either the dark or medium brown; brass-wash, gunmetal, and silver-wash patinas follow in desirability. The acid-etched patina and the smooth (unhammered) surfaced Roycroft pieces are later (after 1925) developments and tend not to be attractive to collectors. Furniture was manufactured in oak, mahogany, bird's-eye maple, and occasionally walnut or ash; collectors prefer oak. Books with Levant binding, tooled leather covers, Japan vellum, or hand illumining are especially collectible; suede cover and parchment paper books are of less interest to collectors as they are fairly common. In the listings that follow, values reflect the worth of items in excellent original condition unless noted to the contrary. Our advisor for this category is Bruce Austin; he is listed in the Directory under New York.

Key: h/cp — hammered copper

Lamp, hammered copper, 8" Steuben brown aurene shade, 14", EX, $5,500.00.

Armchair, dining; vertical bk slat, short arms, rpl seat, 41", VG 3,500.00
Armchair, narrow slats, leather seat, orig finish, 39x32x25" ...1,800.00
Armchair, short arm slats, Mackmurdo ft, rpl seat, rfn, 47x29x27" ...2,700.00
Ashtray, h/cp, match holder held by 4 riveted straps, orb, 29x8" dia....375.00
Ashtray, h/cp riveted to tooled/weighted leather strap, 2¼x14" .275.00
Bench, Ali-Baba, split ash log on oak trestle base, orig finish, 42" 9,500.00
Bench, hall; even-arm form, 10-slat bk, 2 drws under seat, rfn, 60"...8,000.00
Book, Dreams, Schreiner, c E Hubbard, 1901, 10¼x8½" 60.00
Book, guest; tooled red leather cover, blank pgs, 6½x8½" 120.00
Book, sample; 50 mottos, many hand-illumined, split spine 2,000.00
Book, Walt Whitman, hand colored, leather cover, VG 110.00
Bookcase, #84, 1 door/low drw, script name/orb at top, rfn, 74x39" 12,000.00
Bookcase, 1-pane door, low drw, script at top, 61x31x16" 15,000.00
Bookends, brass, stylized geometric trees, arched top, 4x5", pr....230.00
Bookends, h/cp, owl, M orig patina, 4x6½", pr....................475.00
Bookends, h/cp, owls, riveted corners, EX patina, 5x5½", pr 400.00
Bookends, h/cp, Secessionist, riveted strap hinge & ring pull, pr .450.00
Bookends, h/cp, trefoil decor, orig dk patina, 5x3¾", pr.............250.00
Bookends, h/cp w/emb poppy, EX patina, 5x5", pr......................800.00
Bookends, hammered-on brass patina, cutouts, mk, 8½", pr 170.00
Bookends, leather covered w/lotus decor, early mk, 6x5", pr.......750.00
Bookstand, Little Journeys, mortise & tenon, rfn, 24½" W 600.00
Bowl, centerpc; h/cp, ftd, probably cleaned, 5x13"...................1,500.00
Bowl, h/cp, flattened broad form, EX orig patina, 10½" 600.00
Bowl, nut; h/cp, M orig patina, 4x10½"................................1,500.00
Bowl, silver-washed h/cp, lt wear, 3¾x10" 425.00
Box, h/cp, hinged quatrefoil lid, M orig patina, 1¾x7x3½" 900.00
Bracelet, cuff; sterling, emb dogwood blossom on hammered ground .900.00
Calendar, Dard Hunter art, mottos, 1908, mtd on board, 7½x9½" 750.00
Candlesticks, brass-washed h/cp, twisted shaft, EX patina, 12", pr 700.00
Catalog, books/metalwork/leather, color cover, 1912, 52-pg, 7½" L....250.00
Chair, straddle; #029, wide bk board over 2 slats, rpl seat, rfn, 34" ..2,600.00
Chamberstick, h/cp, flared base & bobeche, EX patina, 3½x4½" 375.00
Chamberstick, h/cp, orig polychrome patina, mk, 6" W.............250.00
Chandelier, h/cp w/domed wht glass shade, 27x15" dia 4,500.00
Chandelier, heavy wrought iron, 5 shades, 25x19½" dia.........8,500.00

Chest, 5-drw, paneled sides, cvd signature on bk splash, 56x48"....**14,000.00**
Chiffonier, mahog, 2 half drws, 4 grad long drws, 52x41x24", EX ...**3,750.00**
Clock, h/cp, orig brass wash, mk, 5", EX **650.00**
Compote, h/cp w/brass wash, emb floral, 2¾x8¾" **600.00**
Compote, h/cp w/silver wash, W Jennings, lt wear, 5" **170.00**
Desk organizer, h/cp w/brass wash, orig patina, 5" dia **110.00**
Dinner gong, wrought iron, orig patina, 12" **800.00**
Frame, Little Journeys, 6 renderings of famous artists, 11x38" .**2,500.00**
Humidor, h/cp, riveted hdl, EX orig patina, mar on lid, 3¾x4¾" ...**475.00**
Humidor, h/cp, Trillium, EX recent patina, 5½" **600.00**
Knife & fork, from Roycroft Inn, orb/cross mk on hdls, 9", pr...**375.00**
Lamp, h/cp, radial hammering, orig patina, recent mica, 13½" ..**2,000.00**
Lamp, helmet, h/cp, med patina, 1919, 14¼" **1,850.00**
Lamp, table; brass-washed h/cp, gr/lav leaded glass, Hunter, 23½"...**20,000.00**
Lamp, table; h/cp w/brass wash, acanthus 10" dome shade, 14½".......**2,300.00**
Lantern, porch; h/cp, slag glass, Dard Hunter, 1912, 9½x7"..**25,000.00**
Magazine pedestal, #080, 5 shelves under thick top, 64x18x18" ..**15,000.00**
Mat, tooled leather in brn tones, 6" dia **325.00**
Menu, hand-colored by Dard Hunter, 7x5½", EX....................**100.00**
Motto, hand illumined, Creed, Elbert Hubbard, 8¾x5¾"............**250.00**
Motto, hand illumined, Happiness Comes to Those Who Serve, 12x9" ...**900.00**
Motto, hand illumined, I Love You Because..., matted in fr: 28x26" **550.00**
Motto, hand illumined, Resolve, EX orig finish, in orig fr: 19x15" **500.00**
Mousetrap, missing cheese holder, 8½", VG **260.00**
Note pad holder, tooled/molded leather, att, 4½x2½" **40.00**
Nut spoon, h/cp, Trillium design, EX patina, 6½" L...................**110.00**
Pamphlet, Roycroft Inn, D Hunter cover, flaws, 8" L, VG **300.00**
Rocker, open arms, 5 vertical bk slats, rp leather seat, 36".......**1,500.00**
Rocker, sewing; vertical slats, tacked-on seat, 34", VG **1,000.00**
Rocker, vertical slat bk, orig leather seat/tacks, orb mk, 36" **1,600.00**
Shakers, china, wht w/gr/red/blk decor, mk, 3", pr.....................**350.00**
Spoon, sterling, emb grapes, orb in bowl, 6" **160.00**
Stand, plant; tapered posts, paneled box, orig finish, 29x14" sq.....**4,250.00**
Stand, sewing; lift-top, 3 sm drws, 2 storage bins, rfn, 29x30x17"..**3,750.00**
Table, #073 (similar), deep apron, X-stretcher, orb mk, 30x30" **3,750.00**
Table, library; #072, deep apron, legs shortened, 29½x36" dia **2,100.00**
Table, library; str apron, lower stretchers, rstr finish, 74" **6,500.00**
Table, side; shelf, Mackmurdo ft, rfn, 28x30x22".....................**4,250.00**
Table, sq top, tapered legs, rfn, 18½x12" sq...........................**1,100.00**
Tile, motto, in metal fr, mk, 6" sq...**160.00**
Tray, brass-washed h/cp, 2 riveted hdls, dents, 15½" dia **225.00**
Tray, fruit; stylized rim decor, 1918, 9¾" dia **525.00**
Tray, h/cp, 2-hdl, lightly cleaned, 18" **475.00**
Tray, Trillium, brass-washed h/cp, bent rim/wear, 10" **100.00**
Vase, Am Beauty, h/cp, EX orig patina, 21½" **2,500.00**
Vase, Am Beauty, h/cp, for Grove Park Inn, orig patina, 21x8½" ..**4,500.00**
Vase, Am Beauty, h/cp, orig patina, 19" **2,000.00**
Vase, Am Beauty, h/cp, stick neck, orig patina, 7¼x3½"...........**2,500.00**
Vase, h/cp, bulbous w/curled rim, EX patina, 8½x3¾"...........**1,600.00**
Vase, h/cp, flared riveted base, normal wear, 10¾x6¼" **2,500.00**
Vase, h/cp, orig polychrome patina, mk, 6½" W, VG................**475.00**
Vase, h/cp, tooled florals, worn orig patina, 9½"......................**550.00**
Vase, NP h/cp, geometric band at top, EX patina, 5" **950.00**
Vase, silver-washed h/cp, leaf-like prongs, gr Steuben liner, 6x3¾" ...**700.00**
Wall sconces, h/cp w/brass wash, EX patina, 12½", pr................**700.00**

Rozenburg

Some of the most innovative and original Art Nouveau ceramics were created by the Rozenburg factory at the Hague in The Netherlands between 1883 and 1914, when production ceased. (Several of their better painters continued to work in Gouda, which accounts for some pieces being similar to Gouda.) Rozenburg also made highly prized eggshell

ware, so called because of its very thin walls; this is eagerly sought after by collectors. T.A.C. Colenbrander was their artistic leader, with Samuel Schellink and J. Kok designing many of the eggshell pieces. The company liquidated in 1917. Most pieces carry a date code. Our advisor for this category is Ralph Jaarsma; he is listed in the Directory under Iowa.

Bowl, Nouveau floral, ped ft, earthenware, 4¼x7¼" **450.00**
Plaque, man w/farm animals, sgn, ca 1908, 9¾x13"+rpl fr.......**1,650.00**
Plaque, 5 flowers on bl, cobalt trim, 1890s, rstr, 18" **600.00**
Vase, stylized lotus, naturalistic colors, 3669, 6½x6¾"...............**600.00**

Rubena

Rubena glass was made by several firms in the late 1800s. It is a blown art glass that shades from clear to red. See also Art Glass Baskets; Cruets; Sugar Shakers; Salts; specific manufacturers.
Basket, candy ribbon rim, twist hdl, ca 1880, sm.........................**150.00**

Shaker, Optic, reverse coloring with painted floral spray, curved barrel shape, two-piece metal top, 1885 – 1890, 2⅞", from $150.00 to $160.00. (Photo courtesy Mildred and Ralph Lechner)

Bottle, scent; cut body, faceted stopper, 5⅜" **145.00**
Cheese dish, 7x10½" **230.00**
Compote, Honeycomb, ftd, 4x8½" **250.00**
Cookie jar, melon ribs, 9" **385.00**
Cup, punch; reeded hdl **55.00**
Ice bucket, enamel decor, silver bail hdl **125.00**
Pitcher, HP daisies **210.00**
Pitcher, water; fine ribs, ruffled top..**135.00**
Sugar shaker, melon ribs, bulbous, orig lid **165.00**
Syrup, threaded, orig tin lid **480.00**
Tumbler, Invt T'print, enameled..**100.00**

Rubena Verde

Rubena Verde glass was introduced in the late 1800s by Hobbs, Brockunier, and Company of Wheeling, West Virginia. Its transparent colors shade from red to green. See also Art Glass Baskets; Cruets; Sugar Shakers; Salts. For more information we recommend *Hobbs, Brockunier and Co. Glass* by Neila and Tom Bredehoft.

Bowl, finger; Hobnail, ruffled rim, 4¼" dia **110.00**
Bowl, finger; threaded **125.00**
Bowl, Hobbs, 2¾x4½" **125.00**
Butter dish **175.00**
Cheese dish, Coin Spot lid, gr Daisy & Button base, 7¼" **200.00**
Cruet, Invt T'print, teepee shape, 7" **550.00**
Pitcher, Hobnail, bulbous, sq top, vaseline hdl, 8" **400.00**
Pitcher, Invt T'print, reeded hdl, sq rim, 7¾" **250.00**
Syrup, Hobnail, orig lid..**150.00**
Vase, Drape, gr ruffled rim, 11"..**435.00**

Vase, gilt panel w/HP scrolls & flowers, 8".................300.00
Vase, HP floral on melon ribs, crimped rim, ftd, 6½" 450.00
Vase, jack-in-the-pulpit; HP floral/butterflies, 11½"..........500.00
Vase, jack-in-the-pulpit; HP June bugs, cylindrical, 9½"..........400.00
Vase, jack-in-the-pulpit; 12".................................250.00
Wine, Invt T'print, 4¼".......................................150.00

Ruby Glass

Produced for over one hundred years by every glasshouse of note in this country, ruby glass has been used to create decorative items such as one might find in gift shops, utilitarian bottles and kitchenware, figurines, and dinnerware lines such as were popular in the Depression era. For further information and study, we recommend *Ruby Glass of the 20th Century* by our advisor, Naomi Over; she is listed in the Directory under Colorado.

Basket, Barred Oval, Fenton, 1965-86, 7½" 35.00
Bonbon, swan form w/crystal neck, New Martinsville, 8½" 25.00
Bookends, goose girl, LE Smith, 1979, 8", ea 45.00
Bowl, cereal; Old Cafe, Anchor Hocking, 1940s, 5½" 12.00
Bowl, Dmn pattern, rounded edge, Imperial, 1920-30, 9"............25.00
Bowl, ruffled edge, Blenko, 1932-53, 15"..........................60.00
Box, treasure chest form, pnt rose decor, Westmoreland, 1980, 4⅛"..30.00
Butter dish, Eye Winker, dome lid, LG Wright, 1960s, from $65 to...75.00
Cake stand, Avon Cape Cod, 1991, 10½"..............................50.00
Candle holder, Ring-Stem pattern, 1-light, Cambridge, 1949-53, 5"..65.00
Candlestick, Teardrop, #44, New Martinsville, 6" 65.00
Candy dish, Daisy & Button, 6-sided, LE Smith, 1950s, 4¾"........15.00
Candy dish, Everglade, Cambridge, 1930s, 3" 15.00
Decanter, crackle glass, fluted top, w/stopper, Blenko, 1930-53, 11"..75.00
Figurine, bulldog, #75, Westmoreland, 1980, 3½"...................12.00
Figurine, clown seated on barrel, Mosser, 1982, 4½" 20.00
Goblet, Penny Line, #991, Paden City, 1932, 8-oz 20.00
Ice bucket, Plymouth, #1620, Fenton, 1933, 5¾" dia................125.00
Jar, jam; Eye Winker, LG Wright, 1960s, 4¾".......................45.00
Lamp, Wildflower & Lace, clear base, Westmoreland, 1982, 6½".65.00
Pickle dish, Royal Ruby, Anchor Hocking, 1940s, 7" 15.00
Pie server, ruby hdl, Avon Cape Cod, 1981-84, 8", from $18 to ...22.00
Pitcher, crystal hdl & stem, Paden City, 1932, 16-oz, 10¼"........195.00
Pitcher, Royal Ruby, Anchor Hocking, 1940, 80-oz.................40.00
Plate, Fleur-de-Lis, Viking, 1984, 7¼".............................35.00
Plate, heart, pnt girl fishing (Mary Gregory), Westmoreland, 1983, 8"..75.00
Platter, Simplicity, #700, oval, Paden City, 1930s................40.00
Shakers, English Hobnail, Westmoreland, 1980, 4½".................90.00
Tumbler, juice; Beaded Rings, Hocking, 1927-32, 4-oz.............15.00
Tumbler, Swirl, Cambridge, 1949-53, 12-oz.........................35.00
Urn, emb dancing nudes, Imperial, 1971-73, 8½" 85.00
Wine glass, crystal ball in stem, Morgantown, 1930s, 5½-oz.........25.00
Wine glass, Rosette base, Blenko, 1930-50, 4-oz 8.00

Ruby-Stained Glass

Ruby-flashed or ruby-stained glass was made through the application of a thin layer of color over clear. It was used in the manufacture of some early pressed tableware and from the Victorian era well into the twentieth century. These items were often engraved on the spot with the date, location, and buyer's name.

Creamer, Heart Band, Compliments of... in gold lettering, 4".......35.00
Creamer, Quadruped, Souvenir of Millersburg PA in silver, 4¼".35.00
Creamer, Ruby Thumbprint, scalloped rim, World's Fair 1893, 3" .45.00

Decanter, red, grape clusters, tooled mouth, 1890-1915, 7½" 150.00
Goblet, Plain Milton, Souvenir of Granville in silver, 6" 35.00
Goblet, Ruby Thumbprint, Souvenir of Pittsburg in silver, 5¾" ...35.00
Mug, Button Arches, Atlantic City 1901, 3⅝x2⅞"....................28.00
Pitcher, etched grapes & leaves, 1840s, 8¾" 315.00
Pitcher, tankard; Button Arches, eng name & 1899, 10⅝".........165.00
Toothpick holder, Beaded Swag, Gettysburg 1863, 2"...................35.00
Tumbler, Button Arches, eng Mt Gretna, 3¾x2⅞" 40.00
Tumbler, Button Arches, Louisana Purchase Expo 1904, 3⅞".......35.00
Wine, Button Arches, Bloomsburg Fair 1918, 4x1⅞"...................25.00

Rugs, Hooked

Hooked rugs are treasured today for their folk-art appeal. Rug making was a craft that was introduced to this country in about 1830 and flourished its best in the New England states. The prime consideration when evaluating one of these rugs is not age but artistic appeal. Scenes with animals, buildings, and people; patriotic designs; or whimsical themes are preferred. Those with finely conceived designs, great imagination, interesting color use, etc., demand higher prices. Condition is, of course, also a factor. Marked examples bearing the stamps of 'Frost and Co.,' 'Abenakee,' 'C.R.,' and 'Ouia' are highly prized. Note: The rugs listed here are made of rag unless noted otherwise. See also Orientalia, Rugs.

Geometric and stylized floral design, multicolor on blue, minor wear, 39½x27", $635.00.

Blk cat & kitten, floral border, ca 1900, 29x24" 550.00
Carriage w/horse, driver, passenger & footman, mc on beige, 25x46"..275.00
Changing colors in stripes form dmn pattern, mc, 25x51", EX ...250.00
Dog w/leaf border, mc, minor damage, 25x41"............................165.00
Floral center w/stylized leaves, mc, fading, 32x53" 100.00
Flowering tree, mc on blk, 25x46".....................................330.00
Geometric, red/lt & dk gr/bl/gray, minor wear, 26x46" 200.00
Geometric dmns/ovals/circles, brn/bl/blk/gray, lt wear, 27x43" ...500.00
Geometric expanding dmns in gr/rose/tan/brn, ca 1900, 53x30".465.00
Geometric floral, mc on gray-olive w/blk border, 32x42" 175.00
Geometric medallion, olive gr/bl/red/wht, minor wear, 59" sq 935.00
Geometric sqs, gr/bl/wht/yel/red, 27x60", some damage, EX 330.00
Home Sweet Home & flowers, mc w/red scroll border, 28x40"...200.00
House (scenic view), mc borders, ca 1900, 22x41" 325.00
House on lake w/pines, bridge & road in oval, EX colors, 19x32"....200.00
Lion in forest, deep mc, Ebenezer Ross, 1922, 33x63", EX.......1,400.00
Logs & leaves, gr/red/brn/gray/cream, old rebinding, 30x55" 165.00
Mixed flowers w/gr foliage on wht, ca 1950, 70x39"...................150.00
Noah's Ark scene, mc on gray mottle, 53x33" 1,375.00
Penny, mc, hexagonal, 1890s, 37x25"..................................315.00
Poppies, red/gr/brn/yel, foliage scroll border, 22x37"...................165.00
Puppy, chickens & ducks, mc w/blk borders, 28x44", mtd on fr..850.00
Sailing ship at sea, navy/red/bl/rust/taupe/cream, 39x29" 200.00
Squirrel on log eating acorns from tree, mc, wear, 28x40" 935.00
Stag in winter scene, owl in tree, mc, 35x37"..........................1,150.00
Vines (gr/brn/yel) on gray w/brn border, 60x96" 360.00

RumRill

George Rumrill designed and marketed his pottery from 1933 until his death in 1942. During this period of time, four different companies produced his works. Today the most popular designs are those made by the Red Wing Stoneware Company from 1933 until 1936 and Red Wing Potteries from 1936 until early 1938. Some of these lines include Trumpet Flower, Classic, Manhattan, and Athena, the Nudes.

For a period of months in 1938, Shawnee took over the production of RumRill pottery. This relationship ended abruptly, and the Florence Pottery took over and produced his wares until the plant burned down. The final producer was Gonder. Pieces from each individual pottery are easily recognized by their designs, glazes, and/or signatures. It is interesting to note that the same designs were produced by all three companies. They may be marked RumRill or with the name of the specific company that made them. You will find information on RumRill in these books: *Red Wing Art Pottery Book II*, and *Collector's Encyclopedia of Red Wing Art Pottery*, by B.L. and R.L. Dollen (Collector Books). Our advisors for this category are Wendy and Leo Frese; they are listed in the Directory under Texas.

Ball jug, brn & orange, #547, 7" 45.00
Ball jug, gr mottle, #547 ....45.00

Bookends, polar bears, black, #396, $350.00 for the pair. (Photo courtesy Wendy and Leo Frese)

Bowl, console; #414 ....40.00
Bowl, console; wht, #271 ....50.00
Bowl, cream matt, #311-7 ....50.00
Bowl, Pompeian, w/deer, #526 ....50.00
Candlesticks, wht, #529, pr 30.00
Ewer, #455 ....40.00
Ewer, Indian, brn & orange mottle, #184, 7" 50.00
Log, pk 35.00
Urn, ivory, #277 ....50.00
Vase, bl mottle, #633 ....55.00
Vase, Fluted, Dutch Blue, #300, 8½" 60.00
Vase, gr, #587 ....40.00
Vase, gr drip, #H-54 ....30.00
Vase, Neoclassic, slate bl, #697, 7½" 110.00
Vase, Ripe Wheat, #355 ....35.00
Vase, trumpet flower, #491, 10" 145.00
Vase, wht w/gr int, #271 ....75.00
Vase, yel, hdls, #706 ....25.00
Wall pocket, well, gr 45.00
What not, Violet, #323, 4" 50.00

Rushmore

Ivan House studied sculpture and fine arts at the University of Oregon. He gained valuable experience in the potting field, first by producing terra cotta architectural sculptures and later through the work he did with the carvers on Mt. Rushmore. In 1933 he purchased a tract of land near Mt. Rushmore where he built his own pottery. Using the especially adaptable clay he found there, he produced a line of decorative items until 1941, after which he went into the teaching field. His wares are characterized by the natural shading of the clay which he allowed to show through the glazes.

Ashtray, pk matt, 2 rests, sgn Hauser, 4½" dia 32.00
Bowl, serving; creamy yel, sgn Ivan House 80.00
Figurine, owl, seafoam gr & lilac, mk, 3¼x1½" 120.00
Pitcher, pk matt, 5½x4½" 75.00
Pitcher, turq, flared rim, appl hdl, 3½" 67.50
Vase, cattails HP on celery gr, 5⅞" 75.00
Vase, dk caramel, sgn Lang, 4¼" 80.00
Vase, rust-brn semigloss, shouldered, 5¾x4½" 85.00
Vase, variegated turq w/pools at shoulder, 4¼x2¾", pr 55.00

Ruskin

This English pottery operated near Birmingham from 1889 until 1935. Its founder was W. Howson Taylor, and it was named in honor of the renowned author and critic, John Ruskin. The earliest marks were 'Taylor' in block letters and the initials 'WHT,' the smaller W and H superimposed over the larger T. Later marks included the Ruskin name.

Candlestick, pk lustre, cylindrical cup on tapered stem, 1921, 6½"...385.00
Cup & saucer, demitasse; turq, 2x2", 4¼" 85.00
Lamp base, mottle & crystalline, tan/gr/bl, 6-sided, 1920s, 10½" ..300.00
Plate, crystalline, bl, 6" 75.00
Vase, bl/cream/ochre crystalline, hexagonal, sgn Taylor, 6½".....265.00
Vase, crystalline, bl/yel/ochre/cream, hexagonal, 9x5"................385.00
Vase, crystalline (int/ext), bl, WH Taylor, 4¾x4"........................450.00
Vase, crystalline (int/ext), orange, WH Taylor, 9x5¾"...............625.00
Vase, lustre (mc mottle), can neck, flared rim, H Taylor, 1925, 9¼"...535.00
Vase, lustre (orange), ovoid, flared rim, 1914, 9⅝x5⅝" 165.00
Vase, lustre (yel), shouldered, 1930, 8x4½" 350.00

Russel Wright Dinnerware

Russel Wright, one of America's foremost industrial designers, also designed several lines of ceramic dinnerware, glassware, and aluminum ware that are now highly sought-after collectibles. His most popular dinnerware then and with today's collectors, American Modern, was manufactured by the Steubenville Pottery Company from 1939 until 1959. It was produced in a variety of solid colors in assortments chosen to stay attune with the times. Casual (his first line sturdy enough to be guaranteed against breakage for ten years from date of purchase) is relatively easy to find today — simply because it has held up so well. During the years of its production, the Casual line was constantly being restyled, some items as many as five times. Early examples were heavily mottled, while later pieces were smoothly glazed and sometimes patterned. The ware was marked with Wright's signature and 'China by Iroquois.' It was marketed in fine department stores throughout the country. After 1950 the line was marked 'Iroquois China by Russel Wright.' For those wanting to learn more about the subject, we recommend *The Collector's Encyclopedia of Russel Wright, Second Edition*, by our advisor, Ann Kerr. She is listed in the Directory under Ohio.

American Modern

To calculate values for American Modern, double the values listed for these colors: Canteloupe, Glacier Blue, Bean Brown, and White. Chartreuse is represented by the low end of our range; Cedar, Black Chutney, and Seafoam by the high end; and Coral and Gray near the middle.

Bowl, vegetable; open, from $25 to..30.00
Creamer, from $12 to..15.00
Lug soup, from $15 to..20.00
Mug (tumbler), scarce, from $75 to..100.00
Pickle dish, from $18 to..20.00
Pitcher, w/lid, rare, from $225 to..250.00
Plate, chop; from $50 to..60.00
Plate, salad; 8", rare, from $12 to..15.00
Shakers, ea, from $6 to..8.00
Sugar bowl, from $15 to..20.00
Teapot, 6x10", scarce, from $135 to..165.00

Casual

To price Brick Red, Aqua, and Canteloupe, double our values; for Avocado, use the low end of the range. Oyster and Charcoal are valued at 50% more than the prices listed.

Bowl, cereal; 5" from $12 to..15.00
Casserole, 2-qt, 8", from $60 to..70.00
Creamer, stacking, from $15 to..18.00
Cup & saucer, tea; from $10 to..12.00
Gumbo, flat soup; 21-oz, from $40 to..55.00
Mug, restyled, scarce, from $90 to..115.00
Plate, chop; 13⅞", from $50 to..60.00
Plate, dinner; 10", from $10 to..12.00
Plate, party; w/cup, from $100 to..150.00
Shakers, stacking, from $20 to..25.00
Sugar, stacking, from $15 to..18.00

Glass

Unless otherwise described, values are given for glassware in coral and Seafoam; other colors are 10% to 15% less.

Imperial Flair, tumbler, iced tea; 14-oz, from $65 to......................70.00
Imperial Flair, tumbler, juice; 6-oz, from $50 to 75.00
Imperial Flair, tumbler, water; 11-oz, from $65 to 70.00
Imperial Pinch, tumbler, iced tea; 14-oz, from $50 to 75.00
Imperial Pinch, tumbler, juice; 6-oz, from $45 to 60.00
Imperial Pinch, tumbler, water; 11-oz, from $50 to 60.00
Imperial Twist, tumbler, iced tea; from $45 to 50.00
Imperial Twist, tumbler, juice; from $45 to 60.00
Imperial Twist, tumbler, old-fashioned; from $60 to 85.00
Imperial Twist, tumbler, water; from $35 to...................................50.00
Old Morgantown/Modern, cocktail, 3-oz, 2½", from $30 to 40.00
Old Morgantown/Modern, cordial, 2-oz, 2", from $50 to..............65.00
Old Morgantown/Modern, tumbler, dbl old-fashioned; 3½", from $45 to ..60.00
Old Morgantown/Modern, tumbler, juice; 8-oz, 3¾", from $30 to .40.00
Theme Formal, cordial, from $250 to....................................300.00
Theme Formal, goblet, 8-oz, 5", from $200 to.......................275.00
Theme Formal, highball, 7", from $200 to.............................250.00
Theme Formal, wine, 6-oz, 7", from $150 to..........................200.00

Highlight

Bowl, salad or vegetable; rnd, ea, from $75 to............................100.00
Bowl, soup/cereal; 2 szs, from $50 to.......................................75.00
Bowl, vegetable; oval, from $100 to 125.00
Creamer, from $50 to...75.00

Cup, from $25 to..50.00
Plate, bread & butter; from $10 to..15.00
Plate dinner; from $25 to..30.00
Platter, oval, lg, from $75 to..125.00
Platter, oval, sm, from $50 to..75.00
Platter, rnd, sm, from $60 to..70.00
Shakers, 2 szs, pr, from $75 to..125.00
Sugar bowl, from $45 to..60.00

Spun Aluminum

Russel Wright's aluminum ware may not have been especially well accepted in its day — it tended to damage easily and seems to have had only limited market appeal — but today's collectors feel quite differently about it, as is apparent in the suggested values noted in the following listings.

Bun warmer, from $80 to..110.00
Cheese knife, from $100 to..125.00
Ice fork, from $75 to..100.00
Peanut scoop, from $100 to..115.00
Relish rosette, med..125.00
Relish server (cold), w/glass inserts/ice pool bottom, from $225 to..250.00
Sandwich humidor, from $125 to..150.00
Tidbit, dbl, from $150 to..200.00

Sterling

Ashtray, scarce, from $100 to..125.00
Bouillon, 7-oz, from $15 to..20.00
Celery, 11¼", from $30 to..35.00
Cup, 7-oz, from $10 to..15.00
Pitcher, water; 2-qt, rare, from $150 to 175.00
Plate, dinner; 10¼", from $10 to 15.00
Plate, luncheon; 9", from $9 to..14.00
Plate, service; from $16 to..20.00
Platter, oval, 10½", from $15 to..20.00
Relish, divided, 16½", from $75 to..100.00
Sauce boat, 9-oz, from $30 to..40.00
Sugar bowl, w/lid, 10-oz, from $25 to 40.00

Miscellaneous

Bauer, ash bowl, #10A, 5½", from $500 to..700.00
Bauer, centerpiece bowl w/candlestick ends, #15A, from $700 to..1,000.00
Country Garden, bowl, serving; lg, from $200 to......................225.00
Country Garden, creamer, from $75 to......................................100.00
Country Garden, cup & saucer, from $100 to 125.00
Country Garden, pitcher, 5-cup, from $325 to..........................350.00
Country Garden, platter, from $150 to......................................175.00
Country Garden, sugar bowl, w/spoon lid, from $250 to 300.00
Country Garden, tray, bread; from $125 to 150.00
Flair, bowl, vegetable; deep, oval, from $20 to 25.00
Flair, bowl, vegetable; divided, from $25 to 30.00
Flair, plate, bread & butter; from $5 to....................................10.00
Harker White Clover, bowl, vegetable; open, 8¼", from $35 to..50.00
Harker White Clover, cup, from $12 to......................................15.00
Harker White Clover, pitcher, Clover decor, w/lid, 2-qt, from $100 to....150.00
Harker White Clover, plate, chop; Clover decor, 11", from $50 to....75.00
Home Decorator, creamer, from $12 to......................................15.00
Home Decorator, cup, from $8 to 10.00
Home Decorator, plate, dinner; from $10 to 12.00
Home Decorator, tumbler, from $18 to......................................20.00
Ideal Adult Kitchen Ware, bowl, salad; from $25 to....................30.00
Ideal Adult Kitchen Ware, dish, freezing; from $20 to 25.00

Ideal Adult Kitchen Ware, tumbler, 2 szs, from $25 to 30.00
Ideal Children's Toy Dishes, boxed set, from $150 to 250.00
Ideal Children's Toy Dishes, place setting item, from $15 to.........20.00
Ideal Children's Toy Dishes, serving pc, from $20 to 25.00
Knowles Esquire, cup, from $8 to..10.00
Knowles Esquire, pitcher, 2-qt, from $175 to 200.00
Knowles Esquire, plate, dinner; 10¾", from $15 to 20.00
Knowles Esquire, platter, oval, 13", from $40 to.............................50.00
Knowles Esquire, saucer, from $5 to...8.00
Meladur, bowl, cereal; from $10 to 12.00
Meladur, bowl, fruit; from $8 to 10.00
Meladur, bowl, soup; 12-oz, from $12 to 14.00
Meladur, plate, dessert; 6¼", from $8 to 10.00
Oceana serving item, candy box, shell covered, from $1,000 to ..2,000.00
Oceana serving item, flat shell salad bowl, from $800 to 1,500.00
Oceana serving item, leaf relish tray, from $800 to 1,500.00
Pinch cutlery, fork, from $75 to 85.00
Pinch cutlery, knife, from $100 to 150.00
Pinch cutlery, serving pcs, any, ea, from $150 to...........................200.00
Pinch cutlery, spoon, from $75 to 88.00
Residential, bowl, fruit; from $15 to 16.00
Residential, lug soup, from $12 to...15.00
Residential, sugar bowl, w/lid, from $15 to......................................20.00
Theme Formal, bowl, from $150 to 165.00
Theme Formal, coffeepot, no established value
Theme Formal, cup & saucer, after dinner; no established value
Theme Formal lacquerware, bowl, rice; from $350 to..................400.00
Theme Formal lacquerware, plate, from $175 to...........................200.00
Theme Informal, bowl, fruit; from $75 to..100.00
Theme Informal, mug, from $150 to 165.00
Theme Informal, plate, salad; 7", from $95 to................................125.00
Theme Informal, sugar bowl, w/lid, from $225 to 275.00

Russian Art

Before the Revolution in 1917, many jewelers and craftsmen created exquisite marvels of their arts, distinctive in the extravagant detail of their enamel work, jeweled inlays, and use of precious metals. These treasures aptly symbolized the glitter and the romance of the glorious days under the reign of the Tsars of Imperial Russia. The most famous of these master jewelers was Carl Faberge (1852 – 1920), goldsmith to the Romanovs. Following the tradition of his father, he took over the Faberge workshop in 1870. Eventually Faberge employed more than five hundred assistants and set up workshops in Moscow, Kiev, and London as well as in St. Petersburg. His specialties were enamel work, clockwork automated figures, carved animal and human figures of precious or semiprecious stones, cigarette cases, small boxes, scent flasks, and his best-known creations, the Imperial Easter Eggs — each of an entirely different design. By the turn of the century, his influence had spread to other countries, and his work was revered by royalty and the very wealthy. The onset of the war marked the end of the era. Very little of his work remains on the market, and items that are available are very expensive. But several of his contemporaries were goldsmiths whose work can be equally enchanting. Among them are Klingert, Ovchinnikov, Smirnov, Ruckert, Loriye, Cheryatov, Kuzmichev, Nevalainen, Adler, Sbitnev, Third Artel, Wakewa, Holmstrom, Britzin, Wigstrom, Orlov, Nichols, and Plincke. Most of them produced excellent pieces similar to those made by Faberge between 1880 and 1910.

Perhaps the most important bronze Russian artist was Eugenie Alexandrovich Lanceray (1847 – 87). From 1875 until 1887, he modeled many equestrian groups of falconers and soldiers ranging in height from about 20" to 30". Some of them bear the Chopin foundry mark; they are presently worth from $4,000.00 up. Other excellent artists were Schmidt Felling

(nineteenth century), who specialized in mounted figures of cossacks wearing military uniforms, and Nicholas Leiberich (late nineteenth century), who also specialized in equestrian groups. Most of the pieces made by the above artists were signed and had the foundry mark (Chopin, Woerfell, etc.).

Russian porcelain is another field where Imperial connections have undoubtedly added to the interest of collectors and museums worldwide. The most important factories were Imperial Russian Porcelain, St. Petersburg (or Petrograd or Leningrad, 1744 – 1917); Gardner, Moscow (1765 – 1872); Kuznetsoff, St. Petersburg and Moscow (1800 – 1900); Korniloff, St. Petersburg (1800 – 1900); and Babunin, St. Petersburg (1800 – 1900).

Beaker, Bicentennial of St Petersburg, porc, Saltykov, 1903, 3½" 500.00
Beaker, Czar Nicholas II coronation, ceramic, Kuznetzov, 1896, 4¾" ..500.00
Beaker, Nicholas II coronation, enameled, rstr, 4" 500.00
Box, lacquer, peasant girl w/water, att Fedoskino, ca 1900, 3½" .165.00
Box, pill; silver w/HP foliage, hinged lid w/thumbpc, 2" dia 565.00
Box, pill; silver w/translucent red, champleve bands, MS mk, 1⅜"...535.00
Box, silver w/HP floral on bl, Yegorov, Moscow 84, 1908, 2x2¼"....1,125.00
Buckle, gilt-silver & enamel, 2-pc, St Petersburg 84, ca 1900, 3¼"....335.00
Buckle, silver & niello foliage, Kiev 84, MRM mk, 1908, 3¼" 650.00
Charka, silver-gilt & enamel, ornate pierced hdl, PO, 2x3¾" .1,850.00
Cigarette case, silver w/mc HP foliage, Moscow 84, 1908, 3x4" .725.00
Cup, silver w/enamel floral, scroll hdl, 3x3¼" 700.00
Easter egg, gilt-silver w/mc foliage/turq beads, Moscow 84, DN, 2"...1,675.00
Egg, enamel on silver w/gold wash, Ovchinnikov, 19th C, 2¾x2"....1,380.00

Icon, overlaid with silver and enamel riza, ca 1900, 12x10", $20,000.00. (Photo courtesy Jackson's Auctioneers and Appraisers)

Icon, Deisis, cast bronze triptych w/gilt/enamel, 19th C, 6x16" ..500.00
Icon, Holy Mother & Child, gilt repousse o/l w/MOP, early 1900s, 9x7" .1,265.00
Icon, Kazan Mother of God, seed pearls/paste stones, 17th C, 11x13"...4,500.00
Icon, Lord Almighty, silver-gilt riza, ca 1900, 9½x8" 1,125.00
Icon, New Testament Trinity, incised gold-leaf ground, 1900s, 12x10"...895.00
Icon, St George on horse w/dragon beneath him, 19th C, 12½x14"...1,000.00
Icon, St John Forerunner, silver-gilt riza, Moscow, ca 1907, 11x14" 3,650.00
Icon, St Nicholas, silver-gilt riza, Fetisov, 19th C, 7x5¾".........1,100.00
Icon, Venerable Evdokia, incised gold-leaf ground, 1890s, 10½x9"...815.00
Kovsh, gilt-silver, mc cloisonne, Moscow 84, 1908, 3½" 1,000.00
Kovsh, silver-gilt foliage, bl beads, Moscow 84, 5" 1,250.00
Lampada, mc cloisonne, 3-arm, smoke bell, GS, 1890s, 21" 2,250.00
Mug, toasting; cut glass w/silver ring at mouth, Faberge, 4¾" .1,100.00
Oil on board, Peasant Girl, Bogdanov-Eelsky, dtd 1901, 28x16½" 8,900.00
Oil on canvas, Portrait of Devushka, Kuznetsov, 1924, 12x8½"...........2,350.00
Plaque, Returning Conquering Heroes, gilt-brass repousse, 1897, 7x10" ..450.00
Plate, 2 shepherdesses, porc, Gardner/Imperial Warrant, 19th C, 6".......115.00
Samovar, VA Volkova, brass & hardwood, w/warming kettle, 1887, 22"...590.00
Stein, bbl design, silver, St Petersburg, ca 1858, 7¼" 3,500.00
Stein, silver, eng city scene/lady figural lid, 1861, 6½" 2,400.00
Tray, floral pnt on metal, ca 1900, 26½x21" 315.00
Vase, amethyst amphora shape w/cutwork, gilt-metal fr, 1890s, 12x7"...2,400.00
Vase, chased silver, dome base, Mosco 84, mk PB, ca 1900, 8" ...225.00

Watercolor on paper on card, Archangel Michael, Nesterov, 1920, 6x4"..**3,350.00**
Watercolor over pencil, Prince Vladimir, Bilibin, 1925, 4½x7" ..**6,000.00**
Wax seal, silver dancing bear form, Smirnov, Moscow 84, 1¾"..**365.00**

Sabino

Sabino art glass was produced by Marius-Ernest Sabino in France during the 1920s and 1930s. It was made in opalescent, frosted, and colored glass and was designed to reflect the Art Deco style of that era. In 1960, using molds he modeled by hand, Sabino once again began to produce art glass using a special formula he himself developed that was characterized by a golden opalescence. Although the family continued to produce glassware for export after his death in 1971, they were never able to duplicate Sabino's formula.

Bottle, Petalia, cascading petals overall, 5x3" **95.00**
Bottle, scent; Fleurs, flowers, 7½x3¾" **190.00**
Bottle, scent; Frivolites, nudes & swans, 6".................................**130.00**
Bottle, scent; Gaite, nudes/garlands/scarves, 6"...........................**110.00**
Figurine, Argentina, dancer w/tambourine, 11x4"...................**2,300.00**
Figurine, bear on its bk w/paws up, 4¾"...................................**300.00**
Figurine, butterfly w/open wings, 6x4" **375.00**
Figurine, Chante Clair, rooster, EX details, 8x7" **795.00**
Figurine, crane, head up, 8x3" **350.00**
Figurine, draped nude w/long flowing scarves, 7¾x4½"...........**325.00**
Figurine, Egyptian Goddess, w/2 fans, 5x2".............................**150.00**
Figurine, elephant, trunk up, 4½x2½"....................................**100.00**
Figurine, gazelle, 4½x6"...**240.00**
Figurine, goldfish, Deco-style, opal, label, 4½".........................**130.00**
Figurine, hen, 3¼"..**50.00**
Figurine, Hesitation, 8¾x2"..**695.00**
Figurine, Isadora, 9½x6½"..**1,100.00**
Figurine, L'idole, lady meditating, 6½x4"...............................**2,200.00**
Figurine, Lady & Doves, 6x3" **500.00**
Figurine, Lady & Lamb, nude w/lamb draped around her neck, 7x3" ..**325.00**
Figurine, snail, 3" L...**42.00**
Figurine, squirrel, tail up, 3", from $50 to................................**60.00**
Figurine, swan, 1¾" **42.00**
Figurine, Venus, 2¾" **50.00**
Lamp, gr opal, cascade/waterfall shade, 14", from $2,200 to **2,500.00**
Tray, cherub seated at side of rippling pond, 1½x5¾x3¼"..........**120.00**

Salesman's Samples and Patent Models

Salesman's samples and patent models are often mistaken for toys or homemade folk art pieces. They are instead actual working models made by very skilled craftsmen who worked as model-makers. Patent models were made until the early 1900s. After that, the patent office no longer required a model to grant a patent. The name of the inventor or the model-maker and the date it was built is sometimes noted on the patent model. Salesman's samples were occasionally made by model-makers, but often they were assembled by an employee of the company. These usually carried advertising messages to boost the sale of the product. Though they are still in use today, the most desirable examples date from the 1800s to about 1945.

Many small stoves are incorrectly termed a 'salesman's sample'; remember that no matter how detailed one may be, it must be considered a toy unless accompanied by a carrying case, the indisputable mark of a salesman's sample.

Boiler, Round Oak Moist Air Heating System, CI, 18", VG.......**275.00**
Boots, Candee vulcanized rubber high tops, 5¼", NM, pr............**50.00**

Case, fishing lures, Palsa, 42 lures, 1950s, wood hinged case.......**265.00**
Chair, barber's; Koken, NP brass/blk leather, 16x8x9½" **2,300.00**
Chair, barber's; Victorian adirondack style, oak, unmk, 12½" .**4,600.00**
Clothes wringer, Horse Shoe Brand, complete, 2½x5x10½", EX ..**120.00**
Toboggan, wood w/over 100 tiny screws, 20½x4½", EX.............**460.00**
Washing machine, Apex, electrified, working, 8x12", +orig case ..**635.00**

Salt Glaze

As early as the 1600s, potters used common salt to glaze their stoneware. This was accomplished by heating the salt and introducing it into the kiln at maximum temperature. The resulting gray-white glaze was a thin, pitted surface that resembles the peel of an orange.

Oval dish, press molded with raised dot and diaper, star, diaper, and basketweave within scroll-bordered panels, 1850s, 10¼", $435.00.

Teapot, dmn band w/border, dragon hdl, mask-head spout, 1760s, 5½"...**1,600.00**
Teapot, flower landscape, globular, crabstock hdl/spout, 1760, 4" **700.00**
Teapot, mc bird & foliage, crabstock hdl & spout, ca 1760, 4½", EX **500.00**
Tureen, emb dots/stars/basketweave, 3 lion/paw ft, 8½", EX.......**435.00**

Salt Shakers

The screw-top salt shaker was invented by John Mason in 1858. Around 1871 when salt became more refined, some ceramic shakers were molded with perforated tops.

Today's Victorian glass salt shaker collectors' interests primarily encompass art glass of all types and colored glass, with preference given to hand-painted cranberry and ruby glass forms. Also, examples in rubena, opalescent, and custard glass are very desirable in both decorated and undecorated styles.

If you would like to learn more about Victorian glass salt shakers, we recommend *The World of Salt Shakers, Second* and *Third Editions,* written by Mildred and Ralph Lechner; their address may be found in the Directory under Virginia. (Mildred and Ralph deal only in Victorian glass shakers. Please do not contact them with questions pertaining to novelty types; written queries require a long self-addressed stamped envelope.) Values listed are for old, original shakers in excellent condition unless otherwise noted in the description.

Victorian Glass

Amberette, amber stain, Duncan, 1885, 2¾" **80.00**
Aster, Tall; bl opaque, New Martinsville, 1902-05, 3½"...............**42.00**
Atterbury Twin, wht opaque Cryolite, Pat 1873, Atterbury, 3⅛" ...**175.00**
Banded Shells, gr opaque, mold blown, Challinor Taylor, 1890, 1⅞"..**70.00**
Beaded Panel, Vertical; gr opaque, Consolidated, 1895-1903, 2⅝"...**37.00**
Beaded Panels, Six; bl opaque, Dithridge & Co, 1897-1901, 3⅝".**55.00**
Beaded Twist, wht opalware, Gillinder & Sons, 1890, 3¾"............**23.00**
Bow & Tassel, wht opalware w/gold, Eagle, 1899-1901, 3⅛".........**18.00**
Broken Column w/Red Dots, ruby stain, Columbia, 1893, 2⅞"..**150.00**

California (Beaded Grape), gr, US Glass, 1899, 2¾".....................80.00
Chrysanthemum Base, cranberry opal, Buckey, 1888-91, 2⅜" 165.00
Chrysanthemum Leaf, chocolate opaque, Indiana, 1901-03, 2⅝"...325.00
Clinging Vine, gr opaque, Fostoria, 1901-05, 3¾" 50.00
Cord & Tassel, Dbl; pk opaque to wht, Consolidated, 1894-1900, 2" ...85.00
Corn, custard opaque, Dithridge & Co, 1894-1901, 3⅛" 90.00
Cottage, bl, mold blown/pressed, Adams, ca 1874, 2⅛" 110.00
Daisy, Long Petal; gr opaque, Consolidated, 1904, 3½" 90.00
Diamond & Sunburst Vt, ruby stain, US Glass, 1892, 2¾" 70.00
Double Fan Band, pk opaque, Dithridge & Co, 1894-1900, 3⅜" ..60.00
Empress, emerald gr w/gold, Riverside, 1898-99, 3¼" 100.00
Epaulette, wht opalware w/gold clovers, Eagle, 1900-05, 2⅜" 20.00
Eye Winker, Dalzell Gilmore & Leighton, 1889-95, 3" (+)...........36.00
Fish Pond, bl w/appl fish & enameling, Moser, 1900-10, 3¾".....450.00
Flora, emerald gr w/emb gold floral, Beaumont, 1895, 3⅛".........135.00
Flower Band, pigeon blood satin, Lancaster, 1901-02, 2⅝".........180.00
Flower Bouquet, bl opaque, mold blown, Challinor Taylor, 1891, 3"...55.00
Flower Panel, McKee's; gr opaque, ca 1904-10, 2¾" 32.00
Georgia Gem, opaque custard w/HP floral, Tarentum, 1900-04, 2½"...115.00
Grape, Four Leaf; red & gold goofus pnt, Eagle, 1899-1906, 3½" .36.00
Half Cone, pk satin cased, Consolidated, 1895-1900, 2⅛" 145.00
Hobnail in Square, crystal & wht opal, Aetna, ca 1887, 2⅞" 72.00
Horseshoe & Aster, vaseline, mold blown, Challinor Taylor, 3½"...135.00
Knobby, opalware w/pk flower on shaded bl, Fostoria, 1898-1904, 3¼"...47.00
Leaf, Cabbage; opalware w/gr shading, Fostoria, 1905-11, 3⅛" 40.00
Leaf, Standing; custard opaque, Dithridge & Co, 1894-96, 2½" ...85.00
Liberty Bell, blown/pressed, hdld lid, Central Glass, 1875-77, 2¼" .145.00
Mario, amber stain, US Glass, ca 1891, 2⅝"................................180.00
New Jersey (Loops & Drops), ruby stain, US Glass, ca 1900, 2⅝"...115.00
Opal Coin Spot, cranberry opal, Hobbs Brockunier & Co, 1888-91, 3⅝" ..190.00
Palmette Band, bl opaque, New Martinsville, 1902-06, 2¾" 55.00
Panel, Christmas; Electric Blue, ca 1877, 3" (average)................210.00
Panelled Grape, rose & gr stain, Kokomo, 1903-05, 2¾" 95.00
Pineapple, pk opaque & wht variegated, Consolidated, 1894-98, 3"...105.00
Pineapple & Fan, ruby stain, Heisey, 1896-97, 2⅞"....................110.00
Rib, Corner; wht opalware w/gold, Eagle, 1906-12, 2¾" 18.00
Rib & Scroll, lime gr opaque, Consolidated, 1904-05, 3" 70.00
Ribbed Thumbprint, ruby stain, Jefferson, 1905-07, 2⅞" 45.00
Sphinx, Imperial, 1910-20, 2¼" 170.00
Sunset, pk opaque, Dithridge & Co, 1894-97, 2⅞" 75.00
Swirl, Blossom; wht opalware w/gold, Eagle, 1898-1903, 3⅝".......35.00
Teardrop & Tassel, Indiana, ca 1900, 2⅞"....................................55.00
Texas, US Glass, ca 1900, 2¾"..65.00
Tiptoe (Ramona), McKee, Pat 1904, 3⅛" 50.00

Novelty Shakers

Those interested in novelty shakers will enjoy *Salt and Pepper Shakers, Volumes I, II, III, and IV*, by Helene Guarnaccia; and *The Collector's Encyclopedia of Salt and Pepper Shakers, Figural and Novelty, Volumes I and II*, by Melva Davern. Both are available at your local library or from Collector Books. Note: 'Mini' shakers are no taller than 2". Instead of having a cork, the user was directed to 'use tape to cover hole.' Our advisor for novelty salt shakers is Judy Posner; she is listed in the Directory under Pennsylvania. See also Regal; Rosemeade; Occupied Japan; Shawnee; other specific manufacturers.

Novelty Advertising

Big Boy & hamburger, pottery, he: 4½", Special 1995 ltd ed, pr......49.00
Budweiser-Anheuser Busch, ceramic steins, 3⅝", pr......................29.00
Eveready Battery, metal batteries w/jumping cat, 2½", pr..............39.00
Falstaff Beer bottles, ceramic w/metal lid, Muth of Buffalo NY, 4", pr....29.00
Fingerhut truck, ceramic, 1¾x3¾", 2-pc set 29.00

Ft Pitt Beer, glass w/metal lids, 3", pr...15.00
Kellogg Snap & Pop, ceramic, Japan ink stamp, 2½", pr..............59.00
KenLRation Cat & Dog, plastic, F&F, 1950s, pr...........................35.00
Kool Cigarettes penguins Willie & Millie, plastic, F&F, 3½", pr ..35.00
Magic Chef, milk glass, red plastic lid, 3½", pr.............................85.00
Nabisco Premium Plus Saltine Crackers, plastic boxes, 3½", pr....39.00
Old Gluek's Beer, glass w/decal labels, metal lids, 4", pr..............55.00
Peerless Beer men, hard plastic, Hartland, 1950s, 5", pr...............95.00
Pure Oil Co gas pumps, hard plastic, 2¾", pr..............................225.00
Samovar Vodka, clear glass bottles w/emb dbl eagles on bks, 5", pr....24.00
Schlitz Beer bottles, glass w/paper labels, metal lids, 4¼", pr 28.00
Smokey Bear, ceramic, Norcrest Japan foil labels, 3⅞", pr, NM....55.00
Strasburg RR Engineer & Conductor, ceramic, Japan, 4¼", pr 28.00
Tappan Chefs, pottery, Japan, 4¼", pr...29.00
Tee-Eff Tastee Freeze Ice Cream guys, pottery, Japan, 3¾", pr.......45.00
Texaco Gas Station, milk glass, metal lids, 3¾", pr 50.00

Novelty Animals, Fish, and Birds

Ballerina bears, ceramic, mk PY, 3½", pr.....................................24.00
Bear driving car, ceramic, blk Japan mk, 3¾x3¾", 2-pc set 39.00
Cat & mouse, realistic, pottery, unmk USA, cat: 3¼" L 28.00
Cats in Boots, ceramic, souvenir stickers, unmk Japan, 3½", pr....25.00
Dachshund (2-pc) dog w/bee on tail, ceramic, 1590s, 3¼x5½" 29.00
Dachshunds, ceramic, realistic, Japan labels, 2¾x5", pr 36.00
Fish, jumping, porcelain, red Japan mk, 2¾", pr 28.00
Flamingos, ceramic, Sarsaparilla Co, 1986, 4", pr.........................28.00
Hippopotamus, ceramic, Japan, 1½x3½", pr 29.00
Monkey driving car, dressed up, ceramic, Japan, 1950s, 4½", 2-pc ..49.00
Patriotic eagles, chalkware, Denver souvenir, WWII era, 2⅝", pr...39.00
Piggy-bk pigs, clothed, ceramic, red Japan mk, 4½" when stacked ..35.00
Piggy-bk Teddy bears, dressed, ceramic, Japan, 4¼" when stacked...20.00
Pigs, hugging, ceramic, Japan mk, 2¾", pr...................................22.00
Pigs, lustreware, Germany, #849, 3½", pr....................................125.00
Pigs dressed as musicians, ceramic, Japan, 2¼", pr.......................26.00
Poodle, ceramic, appl pk flowers & spaghetti, Japan, 4", pr...........22.00
Purple cow, on 3-pc wire fr, ceramic, Japan, 4x5" 39.00
Rooster & hen, glass w/pottery heads, Czechoslovakia, 3", pr.......29.00
Scotties, blk & wht, ceramic, WWII era, 2½", pr...........................29.00
Sea horses, ceramic, Leyden Arts, California, 4¼", pr....................22.00
Skunks, ceramic, blk & wht gloss, Japan, 2¾", pr.........................22.00
Turkeys, ceramic, realistic, unmk Japan, 3¾", pr..........................22.00
Wall-Eye fish, ceramic, realistic, Made in Japan, 1950s, 5½" L, pr ..34.00

Miscellaneous

Comic, Mammy and Pappy Yokum (Al Capp characters), ceramic, $125.00 for the pair. (Photo courtesy Helen Guarnaccia)

Alamo, metal building replicas, Japan, 1¾x2½", pr.......................49.00
Alkatraz prison inmates, ceramic, Japan label, 4½", pr.................34.00
Babies playing baseball, ceramic, unmk Japan, 3⅝", pr 65.00
Baseball batter & catcher, pottery, souvenir, USA, '50s, 3¼", pr ..85.00
Boston University logo, porc, unmk, 3x3", pr...............................35.00

Bride & groom (turnabout), ceramic, Japan label, 4½", pr...........27.00
Child in top hat, stacking, ceramic, Japan, 5", 2-pc set 45.00
Colonial couple, ceramic, Japan, 3½", pr 17.00
Couple (smiling/frowning) turnabout, ceramic, gold trim, Japan, 5", pr..25.00
Eisenhower 'Ike' busts, ceramic, 1930s, 3½", pr 69.00
Flower girl (anthropomorphic), ceramic, PY Japan, 3", NM 49.00
Gift packages, pottery, fancy bows, unmk USA, 1950s, pr 18.00
Golf bag & ball, ceramic, unmk USA, 3¼" bag, pr 22.00
Hemisfair '68 Tower, ceramic, 5½", pr..................................49.00
Hula girls (in relief), ceramic, Japan, 1950s-60s, 2⅞", pr 28.00
Lousiana state & cotton ball, ceramic, Parkcraft, 1950s, pr...........49.00
McGuffy's reader & school bell, ceramic, 1950s, 2¼", 2½", pr 26.00
Mermaids, bsk, Japan label, 3½", pr.....................................35.00
Monk, cartoon-like, shiny porc, gr #s, 3½", pr.........................22.00
Nebraska (state) & cowboy boot, ceramic, state mk Parkcraft, pr....49.00
Nude man in bathtub, pottery, unmk USA, 1950s, 2½x3¼", 2-pc..69.00
Nude w/pearls on barrel, ceramic, Japan, 1950s, 5", pr 36.00
Oriental couple, cvd stone, Korea 67-68, 4⅜", pr, NM 59.00
Pipe on pipe holder, ceramic, Trevewood, 2x3¾", 2-pc set 22.00
Pixie baseball batter & catcher, ceramic, Japan, 3½", pr 75.00
Pixie chefs, comic, ceramic, Ucago Ceramics Japan, 4½", pr........39.00
Pixie heads, ceramic, mk #6891 Japan, 3¼", pr 32.00
San Francisco cable car, metal, Japan, 2x2¼", pr......................24.00
Scarecrow couple, ceramic, unmk Am, 3", pr...........................28.00
Schoolhouse & desk, ceramic, unmk USA, 2", 4x4x5", pr............19.00
Singing Tower Lake Wales Fla, silver-tone metal, 3½", pr...........55.00
St Lawrence Seaway ship, stacks are shakers, ceramic, 1950s, 3-pc....49.00
Tiki figures, Tiki restaurant, ceramic, MOC Japan label, 4¼", pr..29.00
Washington Monument, Bakelite, 4¼", pr.............................55.00
West Point souvenir, ceramic, Made in USA, 2⅞", pr 18.00
Western boots & saddle, ceramic, unmk USA, 1950s, 3½", pr.......22.00
Wood plane & sq rule, ceramic, unmk USA, 1¾x3", pr 22.00
Zodiac girls, creamic, Japan, 4½", pr.....................................55.00

Salts, Open

Before salt became refined, processed, and free-flowing as we know it today, it was necessary to serve it in a salt cellar. An innovation of the early 1800s, the master salt was placed by the host and passed from person to person. Smaller individual salts were a part of each place setting. A small silver spoon was used to sprinkle it onto the food.

If you would like to learn more about the subject of salts, we recommend 5,000 Open Salts, written by William Heacock and Patricia Johnson, with many full-color illustrations and current values. Our advisor for this category is Chris Christensen; he is listed in the Directory under California. In the listings below, the numbers refer to 5,000 Open Salts by Johnson and Heacock and Pressed Glass Salt Dishes by L.W. and D.B. Neal. Lines with 'repro' within the description reflect values for reproduced salts.

Key:
EPNS — electroplated nickel silver HM — hallmarked

Animals, Figurals, and Novelties

Bandmaster's cap, US Glass, H&J-3738 ....90.00
Bird & Berry, McKee, amber or bl vase, H&J-997, ea 45.00
Bird & Berry, unsgn Degenhart, H&J-933....................................20.00
Chickens, dbl, milk glass, sgn Vallerystahl, H&J-4447 ....55.00
Dog pulling cart, amber, H&J-2102..100.00
Dresser, salt & pepper, H&J-4742...150.00
Duck, heavy crystal, European, H&J-4677, 2¼" 45.00

Figural hdl, dbl, clear, European, H&J-3777 ....55.00
Horseshoe, 'Good Luck,' H&J-3742, master 100.00
Rabbit, covered, sgn Vallerystahl, H&J-3750...............................55.00
Sleigh, amber glass, ca 1900, H&J-3734....................................95.00
Sleigh, Fostoria, ca 1940, H&J-3735..55.00
Swan, gr, sgn Cambridge, H&J-935 ....35.00
Turtle, clear, H&J-3758..40.00
Wagon, clear, ca 1890, H&J-3739..55.00
Wildflower on turtle base, amber, H&J-506.................................140.00

Art Glass

Cranberry glass, ruffled rigaree, tulip top, SP holder....................135.00
Daum, enameled windmills, tub shape 1,100.00
Daum Nancy, floral, sgn, 7" 900.00
Daum Nancy, windmill scenic, sgn, H&J-10...............................995.00
Legras, floral, sterling gold-washed base, sgn, H&J-12 ....1,250.00
Monot & Stumpf, ormolu holder, stones....................................350.00
Monot & Stumpf, rnd, H&J-19-22...100.00
Mt WA, shiny, unsgn, H&J-46..175.00
Quezal, #18, 1" dia 300.00
Spatterware, wht cased, clear rigaree, appl ft, H&J-134 ....150.00
Steuben, Calcite, ped ft, H&J-34...275.00
Steuben, Jade Green w/Alabaster ped ft, H&J-2041...................250.00
Tiffany, bl, ruffled top edge, sgn, H&J-30...................................475.00
Tiffany, ruffled top edge, sgn, H&J-32..225.00
Wave Crest, tulip-molded sides, enamel decor, rnd, H&J-47 ......175.00

China

Austria, HP, rnd, sgn, H&J-1272, ind...15.00
Celery salt, HP, EX quality, H&J-1720 ....12.00
Elfinware, Germany, basket shape, H&J-1253.............................15.00
Elfinware, Germany, bird hdls, H&J-1261...................................25.00
Elfinware, Japan, H&J-1222..10.00
German Dresden, appl flowers, sgn, H&J-1689, ind 45.00
Haviland, pattern decor, H&J-1400, ind.....................................30.00
Japan, HP, H&J-1443, ind...20.00
Limoges, HP china, rnd, sgn, H&J-1275, ind..............................15.00
Meissen, sgn, ca 1890, H&J-1812-1814 ....125.00
Nippon, celery salt, H&J-1714...12.00
Nippon, HP, rnd, 3-ftd, H&J-1365, ind.......................................10.00
Royal Bayreuth, ped ft, HP scenic, sgn, H&J-1666.....................125.00
Royal Copenhagen, ca 1890, H&J-1201....................................55.00

Cut Glass

Buzz Star, H&J-3127...15.00
Canoe shape, cane cutting, 3"L..55.00
Cranberry, etched, ped ft, ca 1890, H&J-123 ....85.00
Diamond Points, gr to clear, ped ft 95.00
Hawkes, cut lower section, top eng, rnd, sgn, H&J-3083 ....55.00
Notched Prism, H&J-3727..15.00
Tub w/tab hdls, eng, H&J-3318 ....20.00
Waterford, boat, oval, ped ft, H&J-3698 ....90.00

Lacy Glass

Barlow/Kaiser #1464, sapphire blue boat embossed Lafayet - B&S/Glass Co - Sandwich, 2½x3½", $950.00.

Neal BF-1F, opal, Basket of Flowers, NM 200.00
Neal BT-2, med bl, boat, att Stourbridge, EX 450.00
Neal BT-4d, opal, Sandwich, NM 2,000.00
Neal BT-5, med bl, Lafayette boat 950.00
Neal BT-9, opal, boat shape, EX 250.00
Neal CT-1, silvery opaque bl, chariot, EX 750.00
Neal EE-8A, eagle w/ships, rnd, NM 250.00
Neal GA-4a, med bl, Gothic Arch, Sandwich.................500.00
Neal HN-13, med bl, Greek Key around bottom, NM 300.00
Neal LE-1, opal, Sandwich....................................700.00
Neal NE-1, fiery opal, mk NE Glass Co, NY 400.00
Neal OG-4, Pittsburgh area 100.00
Neal OL-11, citron, NM 300.00
Neal OL-17, med amethyst, NM 450.00
Neal OO-2, oval 125.00
Neal OP-4, cobalt, chip 400.00
Neal OP-8, grass gr, slight roughness 850.00
Neal OP-12, aqua opaque, NM 500.00
Neal OP-20, EX 75.00
Neal PO6, dk bl opal, Sandwich, NM 650.00
Neal RD-22a, purple-bl, Sandwich, EX+ 800.00
Neal RP-3, silvery bl opaque 700.00
Neal RP-4, bl opal, Sandwich, sm chips 500.00
Neal SD-9, dk cobalt, Sandwich 225.00
Neal WN-1A, wagon, VG 200.00

Pottery, Porcelain, Semiporcelain

Austrian, HP, ruffled edge, rnd...............................25.00
Celery salt, HP, oval platter..................................15.00
Chinese Export, bl & wht, trencher, 18th C.................350.00
Doulton Lambeth, rtcl base w/birds, sgn Fanny Clark, ca 1870s, 3½" ...400.00
Haviland, H&J-1613 ....35.00
Lenox, Belleek, HP, rnd, H&J-1290, sm 15.00
Meissen, oval w/scrolling ft, H&J-1812......................125.00
Nippon, HP, rnd, 3 sm ft, simple style 15.00
Nippon, HP w/gold trim, ped ft 25.00
Royal Bayreuth, poppy figural, H&J-1790 ....95.00
Royal Doulton, pottery w/gold swirls, bl int 75.00
Royal Worcester, snail-type shell, ivory stained 95.00

Pressed Pattern Glass, Clear

Alexis, Fostoria, H&J-2631 ....10.00
Applied Bands, H&J-2934, ind 25.00
Arched Leaf, master 20.00
Atlanta (Lion), H&J-2758, ind 45.00
Atlanta (Lion), master 55.00
Beatty Rib, old, H&J-3387 ....10.00
Buckle, H&J-3608, master 35.00
Butterfly & Cattails, H&J-3568 ....35.00
Diamond Point Disk, H&J-2930 ....15.00
Diamond Rosette, H&J-3407, master 30.00
Diamond Shield, H&J-3600....................................25.00
Grasshopper, H&J-3573 ....35.00
Harp, H&J-3601, master 40.00
Heisey Pillows, sgn, H&J-2697 ....35.00
Illinois, plain, H&J-2760, ind 15.00
Jacob's Ladder, H&J-3580 ....30.00
King's Crown, plain, H&J-2776...............................25.00
Lincoln Drape, H&J-3619.....................................45.00
Medallion Sunburst, H&J-2543 ....10.00
Open Plaid, H&J-3567..20.00
Plain Band, Heisey, H&J-2560...............................22.00

Sawtooth Circle, H&J-3540...................................30.00
Serrated Rib & Fine Cut, H&J-2535, ind 10.00
Snail, H&J-2656, ind 20.00
Tree of Life, 'Salt,' H&J-3582, master 85.00
Washington, H&J-2504, ind 27.00
Washington Centennial, H&J-2518, ind.....................20.00

Pressed Pattern Glass, Colored

Amber, triangular, H&J-524 ....15.00
Blk amethyst, honeycomb, H&J-2047 ....18.00
Bohemian, clear w/red flashing 45.00
Boyd, hen on nest, various colors 12.00
Degenhart, bl, sgn, H&J-931 ....45.00
Intaglio, polo players, gr, H&J-224 ....18.00
Milk glass, crossed logs, H&J-4473 ....40.00
Sowerby's #1350, custard glass, rnd w/sq hdls, H&J-4629 ...90.00
Swan, Cambridge, H&J-935 ....45.00
Swan, Crown Tuscan, unsgn, H&J-936 ....55.00
Swan, Mosser 12.00

Silverplate

Clear glass liner, H&J-3918, Victorian 75.00
Dog pulling open salt, mk Hall & Elton, Walkinford CT 375.00
English, David Hannel, ca 1754, sm dents, pr 350.00
Fluted, ped ft, H&J-4022 ....35.00
Heart shaped, rim decor 25.00
Meriden, egg w/chick's head, on wishbone, H&J-4284......45.00
Oblong, ftd, Meriden Co, H&J-4050, worn 15.00
Overshot glass in holder, H&J-4215 ....75.00
Pairpoint, dolphin supporting shell...........................45.00
Ped ft, Meriden Co, H&J-3948, worn 25.00
Reed & Barton, Roman Key, H&J-4132......................27.00
Ruby liner, Derby hallmk holder, H&J-319 ....75.00
Salt & pepper, English, ca 1890, H&J-4134 ....45.00

Sterling, Continental Silver, and Enamel

American, lattice w/glass liner, ca 1900, ind 25.00
English, gr liner, ca 1920, ind................................75.00
English, rectangular, Birmingham 1911 ....75.00
English, shell, 3 ball ft, H&J-4279, ind 20.00
English, trencher, Rockefeller repro, spoon, H&J-4227 .....75.00
English, tureen shape, heavy Baroque, ca 1890 ....95.00
European, cobalt in 800 silver holder, ca 1850, H&J-676 ...125.00
European, reindeer pulling sleigh, H&J-4748 ....425.00
French, cobalt, dbl, ped ft, ca 1850, H&J-761 ....140.00
French, ornate, ca 1800, master..............................225.00
French, ornate, ca 1845, H&J-3935, w/spoon, ind...........150.00
French, ornate, ca 1890, H&J-3937, w/spoon, ind...........125.00
French, sq w/glass insert, H&J-3946, w/spoon, ind 95.00
German, glass insert, ca 1880, H&J-3938, ind 35.00
German, swan w/liner, 800 silver, H&J-4294, ca 1890, w/spoon...95.00
German, wheelbarrow, 800 silver, H&J-4229, ca 1800 ......150.00
German, 3 swans hold salt, H&J-714, ca 1890 ....225.00
Gorham, Oriental-style etching, ped ft.......................75.00
Gorham, rnd bowl supported by 3 griffins 175.00
Jensen, Georg; acorn design, bl enameling, w/spoon 175.00
Mexico, simple rnd shape, H&J-4125........................20.00
Pierced holder, w/garlands, ftd, cobalt liner 125.00
Plique-a-jour filigree rim, enamel bowl, Scandinavia 650.00
Reed & Barton, ca 1890, H&J-4226, master, pr 175.00
Rnd, plain, H&J-3997-4000, sm 12.00

Russian, H&J-3936, not old, w/spoon..**45.00**
Russian enamel, H&J-2008, ca 1970, w/spoon............................**75.00**
Russian enamel, H&J-2022, ca 1896, chipped............................**350.00**
Sheffield, boxed presentation set of 4, matching spoons **250.00**
Shreve & Co holder, Lenox insert, H&J-3856.............................**45.00**
Swan, all silver, Germany...**80.00**
Swan, glass w/sterling wings, H&J-4289, ca 1920 ....**45.00**
Towle, H&J-4238, modern, w/spoon, ind **35.00**
Viking ship, 830 silver, H&J-4260, recent, w/spoon **45.00**

Other Types

Amethyst glass, grape leaf, Fostoria, ca 1940............................**35.00**
Amethyst glass, Pairpoint, H&J-416, ca 1880 ....**85.00**
Amethyst glass, tureen shape, Chippendale hdl, sgn Sowerby, H&J-385..**85.00**
Blue glass, rnd, cut & faceted, H&J-3891..................................**15.00**
Blue glass, tub shape, sgn Vallerystahl, H&J-501 ....**55.00**
Blue glass, tureen shape, Chippendale hdl, sgn Sowerby, H&J-385.**125.00**
Celluloid, Viking ship, ivory, w/pepper, H&J-207 ....**35.00**
Cobalt glass, ped ft, H&J-629, ca 1860, master.........................**125.00**
Cranberry glass, rnd, 3 clear appl ft, H&J-280, sm.....................**30.00**
Cranberry glass, sterling o/l, H&J-271 ....**125.00**
Green glass, opal, sgn Baccarat, H&J-360, ca 1885 ....**65.00**
Intaglio, cut & beveled, clear, H&J-3418, sm chips....................**12.00**
Intaglio, cut & beveled, color, H&J-227 ....**18.00**
Intaglio, pnt animal center, butterfly, sgn, H&J-156...................**65.00**
Intaglio, pressed, clear, H&J-2462, sm chips.............................**10.00**
Intaglio, pressed, color, H&J-219, sm chips...............................**14.00**
Mercury glass, cobalt, H&J-655, master **55.00**

Samplers

American samplers were made as early as the colonial days; even earlier examples from seventeenth-century England still exist today. Changes in style and design are evident down through the years. Verses were not added until the late seventeenth century. By the eighteenth century, samplers were used not only for sewing experience but also as an educational tool. Young ladies, who often signed and dated their work, embroidered numbers and letters of the alphabet and practiced fancy stitches as well. Fruits and flowers were added for borders; birds, animals, and Adam and Eve became popular subjects. Later houses and other buildings were included. By the nineteenth century, the American eagle and the little red schoolhouse had made their appearances.

Many factors bear on value: design and workmanship, strength of color, the presence of a signature and/or a date (both being preferred over only one or the other, and earlier is better), and, of course, condition.

ABC panels/churches/flowers/wreath, homespun, 1847, 17x14½", VG **1,000.00**
ABC panels/Federal building/birds/verse/etc, homespun, 1847, 19x19".....**1,150.00**
ABC panels/flower baskets/verse/wave border, homespun, 1832, 15x17"..**1,495.00**
ABC panels/flowers/geometrics/verse, homespun, 1834, 16x13", VG.......**1,265.00**
ABC panels/verse/flower border, homespun, 1811, 15½x19½", G.............**450.00**
ABC panels/wreath/flowers/verse, homespun, 1823, 17¼x17¼" ..**1,955.00**
ABCs, gr floss on openwork mesh, some damage, 11½x7½" **330.00**
ABCs, homespun, old gilt fr, 10½x9"...**350.00**
ABCs, homespun, sgn, 1837, fading/stain, fr: 17x10" **400.00**
ABCs/angels/crucifix/people/etc, homespun, faded, 14x16"+fr ...**140.00**
ABCs/birds/crown/trees, homespun, 1778, fr: 20x17", G.............**440.00**
ABCs/birds/dogs/flowers/verse, homespun, EX color, 19"+fr....**1,100.00**
ABCs/birds/lowers, homespun, wear/staining, fr: 13x8"...............**385.00**
ABCs/birds/trees/hearts/butterfly/flowers, 1822, 22x17" **850.00**
ABCs/borders, homespun, sgn/1824, fr: 18x17".........................**220.00**
ABCs/flower baskets/birds, homespun, sgn/1845, 12¼x12".........**880.00**

ABCs/flowers/crowns/symbols, homespun, England, 1760, 14x14", G.**575.00**
ABCs/flowers/house, homespun, handmade lace border, 22x12". G.....**220.00**
ABCs/fruit basket/wreath/verse, homespun, 1827, 19x14", VG ..**350.00**
ABCs/geometrics/flower borders, homespun, rpr, 17x14"+fr **935.00**
ABCs/geometrics/parrot/flowers/verses, homespun, 1789, 17x14" ..**1,150.00**
ABCs/house/fence/birds/trees, homespun, sgn, 15x12"+fr, EX.**1,000.00**
ABCs/house/fence/trees/verse, homespun, 1823, 18x15"+fr........**990.00**
ABCs/house/yard/flowers, homespun, 1834, fr: 17x17", EX **2,400.00**
ABCs/name, homespun, 1835, some fading, fr: 18x11" **600.00**
ABCs/numbers, homespun, sgn/1809, VA, 9x7"+fr **415.00**
ABCs/numbers/verses, homespun, 1815, fading/stains, 12x16"+fr....**525.00**
ABCs/trees/flowers/verse, homespun, sgn/1832, 21x21"+alligatored fr....**1,500.00**
ABCs/verse, homespun, 1813, 7¾x7¼", G **440.00**
ABCs/verse/flower baskets, floral border, homespun, 1820, 24x23" ..**2,100.00**
ABCs/verse/flowers, homespun, OH, 1828, fr: 18x19" **2,200.00**
ABCs/verse/flowers, homespun, PA, 1835, 17x17"+fr **2,000.00**
ABCs/verse/house/fence/birds/flowers, homespun, sgn/1829, OH, 17x18"....**7,700.00**
ABCs/vines/birds/flowers, homespun, bleeding/holes, fr: 21x17" ...**440.00**
ABCs/vines/lines, sgn/1826, fading, 8x16" **465.00**
ABCs/vines/verse, homespun, EX color, 1818, 14x12"+fr, pr...**3,000.00**
Adam & Eve/ABCs/crucifix/people/animals/etc, homespun, 1776, 36x10"...**2,300.00**
Adam & Eve/angels/flowers/verse/etc, homespun, 1814, 17x20"+fr....**2,000.00**
Birds/trees/flowers/verse, homespun, 1820s, 21x13", EX...........**1,150.00**
Eagle/flowers in pots, homespun, 1845, damage/stain, 10x17" **330.00**
Flowers in pots/birds/circles, gauze, 1794, damage, 9x8"...........**1,485.00**
Flowers/animals, cutwork lace, homespun, tears, 9¾x7½"........**5,500.00**
Flowers/Masonic symbols/In God We Trust, homespun, 1849, fr, 28" sq ..**4,400.00**
Flowers/verse/Federal house/animals, homespun, 1808, 17x12", VG..**1,380.00**
Mourning verse/flowers, homespun, 1775, losses/fading, 12x17".**700.00**
Sampler, verse & leaf border, canvas, damage, 1865, 17x12¾"...**385.00**
Verse/birds/flowers/trees, homespun, EX color, 1817, fr: 19x18" .**965.00**
Verse/boy & dog/trees/house/flowers, homespun, 1841, rprs, 24x22".**550.00**
Verse/building/birds/trees/flowers, homespun, 1832, 25x21", EX...**1,300.00**
Verse/couple/animal/flowers, homespun, 1809, 20x18" **1,500.00**
Verse/house/birds/flowers, homespun 183_, in fr: 29x25", EX..**1,750.00**
Verses (2)/symbolic devices, homespun, 1828, 14½x12½", VG..**750.00**

Sandwich Glass

The Boston and Sandwich Glass Company was founded in 1820 by Deming Jarves in Sandwich, Massachusetts. Their first products were simple cruets, salts, half-pint jugs, and lamps. They were attributed with being one of the first to perfect a method for pressing glass, a step toward the manufacture of the 'lacy' glass which they made until about 1840. Many other types of glass were made there — cut, colored, snakeskin, hobnail, and opalescent among them. After the Civil War, profits began to dwindle due to the keen competition of the Western factories which were situated in areas rich in natural gas and easily accessible sand and coal deposits. The end came with an unreconcilable wage dispute between the workers and the company, and the factory closed in 1888.

In 1907 the vacant glasshouse was purchased and refurbished by the Alton Manufacturing Company. They specialized in lighting fixtures, but under the direction of an ex-Tiffany glassblower and former Sandwich resident James H. Grady, they also produced a line of iridescent art glass called Trevaise, examples of which are very rare today. It was often decorated with pulled feathers, whorls, leaves, and vines similar to the glassware produced by Tiffany, Quezal, and Durand. Examples that surface on today's market range in price from $1,500.00 to $2,000.00. Trevaise was made for less than one year. Due to financial problems, the company closed in 1908. (This information was provided by the Sandwich Glass Museum.) See also Cup Plates; Lacy Glass; Salts, Open; other specific types of glass.

Bottle, scent; milk glass, t'print w/herringbone corners, 9" 220.00
Candlestick, Acanthus Leaf, dk bl socket/clambroth stem & base, 9¾"..475.00
Candlestick, amber, hexagonal, 7½" 450.00
Candlestick, amethyst, hexagonal, lg base, 7½"..........................600.00
Candlestick, canary yel, wafered font, lg hexagonal base, 6½" ...275.00
Candlestick, clambroth, dolphin/single-step base, 10¼" 540.00
Candlestick, gr, crucifix form, 11½"..735.00
Candlesticks, canary, dbl-step dolphin bases, 9¼", pr 1,100.00
Charger, tortoise shell, polished pontil, 11¼" 200.00
Creamer, GIII-24, violet-bl, flared-tooled rim, rayed pontil, 4¾"..300.00
Creamer & sugar bowl, GI-7 type 3, wht opaque, att, 3", 2¾"....150.00
Hat, GII-8, rolled rim, pontil scar, 2¼" 100.00
Jug, ruby threading, etched wheat/ferns/bees, bbl form, 6¾".......185.00
Smoke bell, Hobnail, cranberry w/clear ring, ruffled, 6" 160.00
Smoke bell, milk glass w/cobalt ruffle, pontil scar, 7⅛" 150.00
Tankard, amber w/amber threads, eng lilies & cattails, 7¼"........425.00
Tieback knob, cranberry to clear over mercury 110.00
Toothpick holder, blown, threaded & rainbow swirled, 2" 325.00
Tumbler, lemonade; canary w/canary threads, needle etching, 5½"...200.00
Vase, Loop, emerald gr, gauffered rim, 8-sided std, 1850s, 9¼" ...2,645.00

Santa Barbara Ceramic Design

Established in 1976 by current director Raymond Markow following three years of refining his decorative process, Santa Barbara Ceramic Design arose with less auspicious beginnings than the 'Ohio' potteries — no financial backing and no machinery beyond that available to ancient potters: wheel, kiln, brushes, and paint.

The company produced intricate, colorful, hand-painted flora and fauna designs on traditional pottery forms, primarily vases and table lamps. Although artistically aligned with turn-of-the-century art potteries, the techniques used were unique and developed within the studio.

Vibrant glaze stains with wax emulsion were applied by brush over a graduated multicolor background, followed by elaborate sgraffito detailing on petals and leaves. In the early 1980s a white stoneware body was incorporated to further brighten the color palette, and during the last few years sgraffito was replaced by detailing with a fine brush.

Early pieces were thrown. Mid-1980 saw a transition to casting, except for experimental or custom pieces. Artists were encouraged to be creative and often given individual gallery exhibitions. Custom orders were welcomed, and experimentation occurred regularly; the resulting pieces are the most rare and seldom appear today. Limited production lines evolved including the Collector Series that featured an elaborate ornamental border designed to enhance the primary design. The Artist's Collection was a numbered series of pieces by senior artists, usually combining flora and fauna.

The company's approach to bold colors and surface decoration influenced many contemporary potters and inspired imitation in both pottery and glass during the craft renaissance of the 1970s and 1980s. Several artists successfully made use of the studio's designs and techniques after leaving. Authentic pieces bear the artist's initials, date, and 'SBCD' marked in black stain and if thrown, the potter's inscription.

Markow employed as many as three potters and twelve decorators at a given time. The ware was marketed through craft festivals and wholesale distribution to art and craft galleries nationwide. An estimated 100,000 art pottery pieces were made before a transition in the late 1980s to silk-screened household and garden items which remain in production today.

Though less than 30 years old, Santa Barbara Ceramic Design's secondary market has seen upwards of 1,000 pieces change hands; these are often viewed as bargains compared to their Rookwood and Weller Hudson counterparts. For artist/potter marks from 1979 to 1989, e-mail john tasha@aol.com. Our advisor is John Guthrie; he is listed in the Directory under South Carolina.

Platter, Calla Lily, RB111, Collector Series, Laurie Linn Ball, ca 1985, 16", $425.00. (Photo courtesy John Guthrie)

Lamp, Iris, Gary Ba-Han, #7125, 1984, 31" 375.00
Lamp, Iris/Gladiola, Laurie Linn Ball, #5119xl, 1982, 29" 495.00
Lamp, Poppy, Laurie Linn Ball, #7115, 1986, 26" 395.00
Platter, Oriental, Itoko Takeuchi, #4118(?), 1984, 15" 243.00
Vase, Bouquet, Itoko Takeuchi, #7116c, 1986, 12" 325.00
Vase, Daffodil, Laurie Coscao, #5102, 1982, 9" 125.00
Vase, Daffodil, Margaret Gilson, #5104, 1984, 14" 225.00
Vase, Fuchsia/Hummingbird, DK Hutchinson, #6112/7, 1984, 10"..425.00
Vase, Tiger/Tiger Lily, Shannon Sargent, #7116ss, 1984, 12" 650.00
Vase, Tulip, unsgn (Itoko Takeuchi?), #5101, 7" 60.00

Sarreguemines

Sarreguemines, France, is the location of Utzschneider and Company, founded in 1770, producers of majolica, transfer-printed dinnerware, figurines, and novelties which are usually marked 'Sarreguemines.'

Basket, chestnuts lid, 6x9¼" 400.00
Basket, fruit lid, 5x7½" 365.00
Cup & saucer, orange form, gr leafy hdl, leaf saucer, 6 for..........250.00
Humidor, 4 scenes w/maiden ea corner, bronze finish, #88, 12", NM...225.00
Pitcher, court jester figural, loop hdl, 7½"...................................440.00
Pitcher, dog's head, #4024, prof rstr, 6¾x9" 325.00
Pitcher, gr crystalline, angle hdl, slim, 11" 250.00
Pitcher, man's face, obvious toothache, #3321, ca 1905, 7¼" 700.00
Pitcher, man w/red-brn hair & beard, lg nose, 7" 350.00
Pitcher, monkey, old rpr to fingers (spout), 8x8¼" 450.00
Pitcher, pig, pk, tail hdl, #3318...185.00
Pitcher, ram's head, late 1800s, 9" 450.00
Plate, Czar Nicholas II (Princess Alexandra), 8½", EX, pr 225.00
Plate, oyster; barbotine, 6 shells w/center bowl, 9⅜", 6 for 325.00
Plate, strawberries, 1868-90, 8¼" 165.00
Platter, fruit, ca 1920, 10¾" 185.00
Sauce dish, corn, 1920s, EX 100.00
Stein, etched Darmstadt city crest, pewter lid, 1-litre 1,265.00
Stein, Nouveau leaves & thumblift, snail inlaid lid, .5-litre........700.00
Stein, relief: drunk at lightpost w/monkey/cat, deer lid, #2888, 1-litre....1,600.00
Stein, relief: man w/baby, pewter lid, #2889, .5-litre, EX 800.00
Stein, relief: repeating decor, silver lid, #904, ½-litre.................300.00
Stein, relief: stag, Waidmann's Heil!, fox hdl, #2783, 1-litre, EX..1,075.00
Teapot, man's face, lg nose (spout), #3878, 5½x8½" 450.00
Vase, spill; bird figural, 5"...300.00

Satin Glass

Satin glass is simply glassware with a velvety matt finish achieved through the application of an acid bath. This procedure has been used by many companies since the twentieth century, both here and abroad, on many types of colored and art glass. See also Mother-of-Pearl; Webb.

Bowl, red, Bead & Drape, 3¾x9"...165.00

Cracker jar, pk, HP florals & scrolls, SP trim, 7½x5½".............250.00
Ewer, tan w/bl matsu-no-ke, camphor trim, mc/gold leaves, 6"...395.00
Rose bowl, bl, HP floral, 8-crimp, 3¼x4⅜" 140.00
Vase, apricot, hummingbird/branch, egg form, camphor ft, 6½".150.00
Vase, chartreuse gr o/l, ruffled fan form, HP florals, 5½x3".........135.00

Satsuma

Satsuma is a type of fine cream crackle-glaze pottery or earthenware made in Japan as early as the seventeenth century. The earliest wares, made at the original kiln in the Satsuma province, were enameled with only simple florals. By the late eighteenth century, a floral brocade (or nishikide design) was favored, and similar wares were being made at other kilns under the direction of the Lord of Satsuma. In the early part of the nineteenth century, a diaper pattern was added to the florals. Gold and silver enamels were used for accents by the latter years of the century. During the 1850s, as the quality of goods made for export to the Western world increased and the style of decoration began to evolve toward becoming more appealing to the Westerners, human forms such as Arhats, Kannon, geisha girls, and samurai warriors were added. Today the most valuable pieces are those marked 'Kinkozan,' 'Shuzan,' 'Ryuzan,' and 'Kozan.' The genuine Satsuma 'mon' or mark is a cross within a circle — usually in gold on the body or lid, or in red on the base of the ware. Character marks may be included.

Caution: Much of what is termed 'Satsuma' comes from the Showa Period (1926 to the present); it is not true Satsuma but a simulated type, a cheaper pottery with heavy enamel. Collectors need to be aware that much of the of the 'Satsuma' today is really Satsuma style and should not carry the values of true Satsuma.

Bowl, butterflies & flowers, Meiji era, 2⅛x5" 475.00
Bowl, Thousand Flowers on gold ground, scalloped, 7" 325.00
Bowl, 100+ figures inside & out, late 1800s, 3x7½" 465.00
Box, floral, mc on gold, lift-off lid, 19th C, 1x3"........................275.00
Cup & saucer, figures in landscape, Seikozan, 1900s 350.00
Figurine, Buddha w/money bag & children, ca 1880, 16x14" on wood base....2,575.00
Incense burner, 4 scenes, Meiji, 4½x4¼", EX..........................2,550.00
Jar, butterflies & mums on yel w/gold & brn, 8¼x7½" 375.00
Tray, Rakhans, goddess/figures, much gold, Meiji, 5½x5½" 525.00
Vase, butterflies w/much gold, late 1800s, 6x3" 500.00
Vase, figural panels, hexagonal baluster, late 1800s, 12" 1,000.00
Vase, figures (30+) along sides, EX details, trumpet neck, 6", NM...800.00
Vase, floral, mc & gilt on cream, ftd, Meiji, drilled, 10½x9" ...1,600.00
Vase, silver mums on lid, gods/goddesses/etc, 5½x3½" 1,250.00

Scales

In today's world of pre-measured and pre-packaged goods, it is difficult to imagine the days when such products as sugar, flour, soap, and candy first had to be weighed by the grocer. The variety of scales used at the turn of the century was highly diverse; at the Philadelphia Exposition in 1876, one company alone displayed over three hundred different weighing devices. Among those found today, brass, cast-iron, and plastic models are the most common. Fancy postal scales in decorative wood, silver, marble, bronze, and mosaic are also to be found.

A word of caution on the values listed: These values range from a low for those items in fair to good condition to the upper values for items in excellent condition. Naturally, items in mint condition could command even higher prices, and they often do. Also, these are *retail* prices that suggest what a collector will pay for the object. When you sell to a dealer, expect to get much less. The values noted are averages taken from various auction and other catalogs in the possession of the Society mem-

bers. Among these, but not limited to, are the following: Joel L. Malter & Co., Inc., Encino, CA; Auktion Alt Technic, Auction Team, Koln, Germany.

For those seeking additional information concerning antique scales we recommend *Scales, A Collector's Guide*, by Bill and Jan Berning (Schiffer). You are also encouraged to contact the International Society of Antique Scale Collectors, whose address can be found in the Directory under Clubs, Newsletters, and Catalogs.

Key:
ap — arrow pointer
bal — balance
bm — base metal
br — brass
Brit — British
Can — Canadian
Col — Colonial
CW — Civil War
cwt — counterweight
Engl — English
eq — equal arm
Euro — European
FIS — Fairbanks Infallible Scale Co.
h — hanging
hcp — hanging counterpoise
hh — hand held
l+ — label with foreign coin values
lb w/i — labeled box with instructions
lph — letter plate or holder
pend — pendulum
PP — Patent Pending
st — sterling
tt — torsion type
ua — unequal arm
wt — weight

New England encased balance scale, brass pans suspended from painted tin arm, two paper and ink registers in grain-painted pine case, single drawer, nineteenth century, 18x12½", $1,265.00. (Photo courtesy Skinner, Inc.)

Analytical (Scientific)

Am, eq, mahog w/br & ivory, late 1800s, 14x16x8", $200 to......400.00

Assay

Am, eq, mahog box w/br & ivory, plaque/drw, 1890s, $400 to.1,000.00

Coin: Equal Arm Balance, American

Blk japanned metal, eagle on lid, late 19th C, $300 to 400.00
Col, oak 6-part box, Col moneys, Boston, 1720-75, $600 to ...1,200.00
Post Col to CW, oak 6-part box, l+, 1843, $400 to..................1,000.00

Coin: Equal Arm Balance, English

Charles I, wooden box w/11 Brit wts, 1640s, $900 to..............1,500.00
1-pc wood box, rnd wts, label, Freeman, 1760s, $250 to 450.00
6-pc oak box, coin wts label, Thos Harrison, 1750s, $200 to......450.00

Coin: Equal Arm Balance, French

Solid wood box, 12 sq wts, J Reyne, Bourdeau, 1694, $400 to.1,000.00
Solid wood box w/recesses, 5 sq wts, A Gardes, 1800s, $250 to..800.00
1-pc oval box, nested/fractional wts, label, 18th C, $250 to 400.00
1-pc oval box, no wts, label of Fr/Euro coins, 18th C, $150 to ...250.00

1-pc walnut box, nested wts, Charpentier label, 1810, $275 to...**675.00**

Coin: Equal Arm Balance, Miscellaneous

Amsterdam, 1-pc box, 32 sq wts, label, late 1600s, $850 to.....**2,500.00**
Cologne, full set of wts & full label, late 1600s, $1,200 to.......**2,800.00**
German, wood box, 13+ wts beneath main wts, label, 1795, $650 to ...**900.00**

Counterfeit Coin Detectors, American

Allender Pat, lb w/i, cwt, Nov 22, 1855, 8½", $350 to **650.00**
Allender PP, rocker, labeled box, cwt, 1850s, 8½", $450 to **750.00**
Allender PP, rocker, no box or cwt, 1850s, 8½", $250 to **375.00**
Allender PP, space for $3 gold pc, lb w/i, cwt, 1855, $350 to......**750.00**
Allender PP, space for $3 gold pc, no box or cwt, 1855, $275 to **375.00**
Allender Warranted, rocker, no box or cwt, 1850s, 8½", $350 to ..**475.00**
McNally-Harrison Pat 1882, rocker, cwt, JT McNally, $275 to ..**500.00**
McNally-Harrison Pat 1882, rocker, cwt & box, FIS, $400 to **750.00**
McNally-Harrison...1882, rocker, CI base, no cwt/box, $250 to .**400.00**
Thompson, Z-formed rocker, Berrian Mfg, 1877 Pat, $175 to **350.00**

Counterfeit Coin Detectors, Dutch

Rocker, Ellinckhuysen, brass, +copy of 1829 Patent, $250 to **350.00**

Counterfeit Coin Detectors, English

Folding, Guinea, self-rising, labeled box, 1850s, $175 to.............**225.00**
Folding, Guinea, self-rising, wood box/label, ca 1890s, $125 to..**175.00**
Folding, Guinea, self-rising, wooden box, pre-1800, $175 to **275.00**
Rocker, simple, no maker's name or cb, end-cap box, $85 ......**125.00**
Rocker, w/maker's name & cb, end-cap box, $120 to **150.00**

Postal

In the listings below an asterisk (*) was used to indicate that any one of several manufacturers' or brand names might be found on that particular set of scales. Some of the American-made pieces could be marked Pelouze, Lorraine, Hanson, Kingsbury, Fairbanks, Troemner, IDL, Newman, Accurate, Ideal, B-T, Marvel, Reliance, Howe, Landers-Frary-Clark, Chatillon, Triner, American Bank Service, or Weiss. European/U.S.-made scales marked with an asterisk (*) could be marked Salter, Peerless, Pelouze, Sturgis, L.F.&C., Alderman, G. Little, or S&D. English-made scales with the asterisk (*) could be marked Josh. & Edmd. Ratcliff, R.W. Winfield, S. Mordan, STS (Samuel Turner, Sr.), W.&T. Avery, Parnall & Sons, S&P, or H.B. Wright. There may be other manufacturers as well.

Brit/Can Bal, eq, br or CI on base, *, 4"-15", $100 to **750.00**
Engl Bal, eq/Roberval, gilt or st, on stand, *, 3"-8", $500 to....**2,500.00**
Engl Bal, eq/Roberval, plain to ornate, *, 3"-8", $100 to **2,500.00**
Engl Spring, candlestick, br or st, *, 3½"-15", $100 to..............**500.00**
Engl Spring, CI, br or NP fr, Salter, ozs/lbs, 7"-10", $25 to..........**200.00**
Engl Steelyard, ua, 1- or 2-beam, h lph, *, 4"-15", $100 to......**1,500.00**
Euro pend, gravity, br, CI or NP fr on base, oz/grams, $75 to......**350.00**
Euro pend, gravity, 2-arm, bm, br or NP, *, 6"-9", $50 to **300.00**
Euro/US Spring, br or NP, pence/etc, h or hh, *, 4"-17", $10 to.**100.00**
US Pend, gravity, metal, pnt face, ap, hcp, sm, $20 to **100.00**
US Spring, pnt base metal, *, 2½"-8", $10 to **80.00**
US Spring, pnt bm, *, mtd on inkstand, 2½"-8", $75 to.............**250.00**
US Spring, pnt bm, rnd glass-covered face, *, 8"-10", $25 to......**100.00**
US Spring, SP, oblong base, *, 2½"-8", $100 to...........................**200.00**
US Spring, st, oblong base, *, 2½"-8", $200 to...........................**500.00**
US Steelyard, ua, CI, *, 5"-13" beam, 4½"-12" base, $25 to.......**100.00**

Schafer and Vater

Established in 1890 by Gustav Schafer and Gunther Vater in the Thuringia region of southwest Germany, by 1913 this firm employed over two hundred workers. The original factory burned in 1918 but was restarted and production continued until WWII. In 1972 the East German government took possession of the building and destroyed all of the molds and the records that were left.

You will find pieces with the impressed mark of a nine-point star with a script 'R' inside the star. On rare occasions you will find this mark in blue ink under glaze. The items are sometimes marked with a four-digit design number and a two-digit artist mark. In addition or instead, pieces may have 'Made in Germany' or in the case of the Kewpies, 'Rose O'Neill copyright.' The company also manufactured items for sale under store names, and those would not have the impressed mark.

Schafer and Vater used various types of clays. Items made of hard-paste porcelain, soft-paste porcelain, jasper, bisque, and majolica can be found. The glazed bisque pieces may be multicolored or have an applied colored slip wash that highlights the intricate details of the modeling. Gold accents were used as well as spots of high-gloss color called jewels. Metallic glazes are coveted. You can find the jasper in green, blue, pink, lavender, and white. New collectors gravitate toward the pink and lavender shades.

Since Schafer and Vater made such a multitude of items, collectors have to compete with many cross-over collections. These include shaving mugs, hatpin holders, match holders, figurines, figural pitchers, Kewpies, tea sets, bottles, naughties, etc.

Reproduction alert: In addition to the crudely made Japanese copies, some English firms are beginning to make figural reproductions. These seem to be well marked and easy to spot. Our advisor for this category is Joanne M. Koehn; she is listed in the Directory under Minnesota.

Figurines, Castle Walk, 5½", $240.00; Grizzly Bear, #9870, 6", $220.00.

Bottle, Santa w/Christmas tree & bottle, 6"...................................**265.00**
Candle holder, fish, #4534 ....**185.00**
Creamer, cow in dress w/lace collar, #6517, 3¾", EX..................**85.00**
Figurine, baby in chair, MIG, 3½"...**160.00**
Figurine, ballerina, mk, 5½"..**200.00**
Figurine, cat, #7029, mk, 5¾"...**160.00**
Figurine, Miss Proper Lady, #1094, unmk, 5" **160.00**
Flask, Cook, mk/MIG, 6"..**185.00**
Flask, I Am Always Full, mk, 5¼", NM...**250.00**
Flask, Present From the Isle of Man, mk, 7⅜" **255.00**
Match holder, Cricket Player, mk, 4¾"..**100.00**
Match holder, Gentleman Goose, #22, unmk, 6¼" **185.00**
Match holder, man's head w/bug on nose, unmk, 4½" **230.00**
Match holder, Peter, unmk, 3½"...**195.00**
Match holder, sailor & woman, mk, 3" **240.00**
Match holder/ashtray, Speak No, Hear No..., #8839, mk, 3¼" ...**100.00**
Match holder/striker, bulldog, If a Match..., #8480, mk, 3¼" **550.00**
Nodder, man sitting, ft swing, mk, 4¼"...**125.00**
Nodder, Oriental man holds spoon, lower jaw nods, 4¾" **315.00**
Nodder match holder, hungry monk, #8080, mk, 4¼" **450.00**
Pitcher, Oriental lady & baby, #6821, mk, 5¼" **185.00**
Toothpick holder, children (2) w/hands in air, 3½x4".................**85.00**

Wine set, Dutchman & keg decanter+2 smiling shots on tray....**200.00**

Scheier

The Scheiers began their ceramics careers in the late 1930s and soon thereafter began to teach their craft at the University of New Hampshire. After WWII they cooperated with the Puerto Rican government in establishing a native ceramic industry, an involvement which would continue to influence their designs. In the '50s they retired and moved to Mexico; they currently reside in Arizona.

Bottle, abstract faces on dk brn & mottled, 9¼x4" **600.00**
Bottle, children & fish sgraffito on bl & taupe crystalline, 7¾"..**500.00**
Bowl, male/female/fish figures, clear glazed bsk, 7⅜" **345.00**
Bowl, mask-like faces & fish, cuerda ceca ochre & plum, rstr, 6½"..**100.00**
Bowl, stylized human/fish/animal sgraffito, mottled brn, 4⅜" **575.00**
Bowl, zigzags, tan & brn, ftd, ca 1965, 5" H..............................**285.00**
Charger, faces & fish in sgraffito & slip, wht/gr on indigo, 11"...**2,100.00**
Lamp base, geometric sgraffito, brn & blk, wooden base, 15" ..**1,600.00**
Mug, bird (peafowl?) on vine, blk on wht gloss, 1950s, 5½" **165.00**
Vase, figures/faces/fish sgraffito, tan & brn, 1965, 9⅝" **450.00**
Vase, free-form brush strokes, brn on shaded pk/brn/tan, 1965, 6"..**285.00**
Vase, human faces/figures/fish sgraffito, tan/brn/bl, 7⅜" **545.00**
Vase, sea serpents band, olive semimatt, teardrop, #60, 4¾x4"...**250.00**

Schlegelmilch Porcelain

For information about Schlegelmilch Porcelain, see Mary Frank Gaston's books: *R. S. Prussia Popular Lines* which addresses R. S. Prussia molds and decorations, and *The Collector's Encyclopedia of R. S. Prussia, Fourth Series*, which contains information on the other Schlegelmilch marks, such as Erdman Schlegelmilch (E. S.), Oscar Schlegelmilch (O. S.), and the other R. S. marks (R. S. Germany, R. S. Suhl, R. S. Poland, and R. S. Tillowitz). Both books contain full-color illustrations and current values. Mold numbers appearing in some of the listings refer to these books. Assume that all items described below are marked unless noted otherwise.

E.S. Germany

Fine chinaware marked 'E.S. Germany' or 'E.S. Prov. Saxe' was produced by the E.S. Schlegelmilch factory in Suhl in the Thuringia region of Prussia from sometime after 1861 until about 1925.

Bowl, flowers & ferns, shell mold, mk, 4¾x8¼" **155.00**
Bowl, Left Hand Bear, American Indian portrait, 1x6x4½"........**175.00**
Cake plate, cherub in cart pulled by 3 maidens, gold rim, mk **235.00**
Candy dish, 4 portrait medallions, Recamier center, 7"...............**195.00**
Chamberstick, bl flowers, cobalt inner border, 2x6" **135.00**
Chocolate pot, Napoleon portrait...**375.00**
Plate, lady's portrait, scalloped gold rim, hdls, 9½"......................**195.00**
Plate, man between 2 ladies, burgundy & gold floral rim, 8¼" **175.00**
Vase, classical scene, gold/enamel jewels, Royal, 8"......................**300.00**
Vase, lady w/peacock, lady w/doves on verso, 10"........................**900.00**

R.S. Germany

In 1869 Reinhold Schlegelmilch began to manufacture porcelain in Suhl in the German province of Thuringia. In 1894 he established another factory in Tillowitz in upper Silesia. Both areas were rich in resources necessary for the production of hard-paste porcelain. Wares marked with the name 'Tillowitz' and the accompanying 'R.S. Germany' phrase are attributed to Reinhold. The most common mark is a wreath

and star in a solid color under the glaze. Items marked 'R.S. Germany' are usually more simply decorated than R.S. Prussia. Some reflect the Art Deco trend of the 1920s. Certain hand-painted floral decorations and themes such as 'Sheepherder,' 'Man With Horses,' and 'Cottage' are especially valued by collectors — those with a high-gloss finish or on Art Deco shapes in particular. Not all hand-painted items were painted at the factory. Those with an artist's signature but no 'Hand Painted' mark indicate that the blank was decorated outside the factory.

Bowl, flowers & scrollwork, unmk, 3x10½", NM **200.00**
Bowl, lady w/cows near cottage, hdls, 10" **250.00**
Bowl, vegetable; orange poppy **55.00**
Cake plate, poppies on gray, pierced hdls, unmk, 10" **90.00**
Celery tray, floral, pierced hdls, 10" L..**75.00**
Chocolate pot, Holly, 9" **275.00**
Chocolate pot, peach & wht flowers, 10½" **195.00**
Chocolate set, cotton plant, 9½" pot+8½" plate+4 c/s **550.00**
Demitasse set, pk roses w/gold, 9" pot+4 c/s.............................**375.00**
Hair receiver, roses w/gold, 2x4" **65.00**
Hatpin holder, wht roses w/gr leaves & gold trim, 7" **200.00**
Plate, daffodils, gold trim, 8⅜" **65.00**
Plate, shepherd & flock in landscape, Kolb, 8¾", NM **235.00**
Tray, roses, red mk, 11x7½" **265.00**
Vase, church scene, salesman's sample, 4" **110.00**
Vase, lilies, wht on gr, hdls, 5½" **110.00**

R.S. Poland

'R.S. Poland' is a mark attributed to Reinhold Schlegelmilch's factory in Tillowitz, Silesia. It was in use for a few years after 1945.

Bowl, Rembrandt's Nightwatch on gray-gr, 1½x5⅜"..................**155.00**
Ewer, golden pheasants, left handed, 6¼" **475.00**
Plate, roses w/gold, 7" **42.00**
Relish, roses on shaded wht, pierced hdls, 8x4", NM....................**60.00**

Sugar bowl, pink roses on white, flower finial, R.S. Prussia mold #704, 4½", $125.00.
(Photo courtesy Mary Frank Gaston)

Tray, bird on branch, floral/geometric border, 14".......................**135.00**
Vase, crowned cranes, salesman's sample, 3½x1½"......................**835.00**
Vase, hummingbird, unmk, 4"..**390.00**
Vase, lions (tigers), 5", NM, pr..**2,050.00**

R.S. Prussia

Art porcelain bearing the mark 'R.S. Prussia' was manufactured by Reinhold Schlegelmilch in the early 1900s in a Germanic area known until the end of WWI as Prussia. The vast array of mold shapes in combination with a wide variety of decorations is the basis for R.S. Prussia's appeal. Themes can be categorized as figural (usually based on a famous artist's work), birds, florals, portraits, scenics, and animals.

Bowl, barnyard animals & pheasant, Icicle mold, 11", from $800 to..**1,000.00**
Bowl, Lebrun I portrait w/gold, 10 petal ft, Lily mold, 10½" ...**2,300.00**

Bowl, mc roses, roses reserves w/gold, mold #55, 10½", $275 to .325.00
Bowl, mc roses on wht, Acorn mold, 10¼", from $325 to...........375.00
Bowl, mc roses on wht to gr w/gold, mold #25, 10¼", from $375 to...475.00
Bowl, pk & wht roses (2) on pearlized, Carnation mold, 10½" ..325.00
Bowl, pk roses & roses reserves w/gold, mold #79, 10½", $300 to 350.00
Bowl, Potacka portrait w/gold, mold #29, unmk, 10¼", $1,100 to 1,300.00
Bowl, Recamier portrait on Tiffany finish w/gold, mold #29, 10" 1,300.00
Bowl, red & wht roses (2) on cream to dk gr, mold #2, 11", $350 to ...400.00
Bowl, snowbird scene, oval, Icicle mold, 13½" L, from $1,600 to 1,800.00
Bowl, swans on lake, Icicle mold, 11", from $550 to 650.00
Bowl, 12 scattered swallows on pearl lustre, mold #157, 11", $375 to 475.00
Bowl, 4 seasons portrait medallions (Summer twice), mold #88, 10¾" ..2,600.00
Cake plate, Autumn portrait, pierced hdls, Lily mold, 10¼" ...2,300.00
Cake plate, poppies on wht w/gold, hdls, mold #151, 12", $200 to 250.00
Cake plate, roses & snowballs w/cobalt & gold, mold #82, 9¾" .400.00
Cake plate, roses w/ladies' portrait medallions at beaded rim, 11"............1,100.00
Cake plate, swans & wht shadow flowers, mold #202, 11½", $225 to 275.00
Celery tray, lg pk roses on watered silk, Stippled Floral mold, 12" 250.00
Celery tray, magnolias on cream to gr w/gold, mold #28, 13"......275.00
Chocolate pot, lg roses w/gold shields, mold #608, 10", from $600 to..700.00
Chocolate pot, magnolia on wht, mold #452a, 10", from $450 to...550.00
Chocolate pot, roses on satin, opal jewel at top, mold #642, 12" 650.00
Chocolate pot, roses on satin w/gold, Iris mold, 11", from $700 to 800.00
Chocolate pot, roses/shadow flowers on gr to wht, mold #550, 11½" ..475.00
Chocolate pot, snowbird scene w/blk & gold, mold #631, 9½" ..1,900.00
Chocolate pot, swans on lake on wht satin, mold #452, 10", $700 to..900.00
Coffeepot, Winter portrait w/gold & cobalt, mold #664, 8".....3,600.00
Cracker jar, floral, wht on lt gr, RM 200.00
Creamer & sugar bowl, Lebrun II portrait w/gold, mold #517, 5"...1,300.00
Creamer & sugar bowl, mill/castle scenes, mold #644, 3½", pr...550.00
Demitasse pot, mc roses, no decor on spout or hdl, mold #632, 9"...700.00
Ferner, swans on lake w/gold, mold #882, 4x9", from $550 to.....650.00
Hatpin holder, mill scene & swallows, 6-sided, mold #728, 4½" ..450.00
Hatpin holder, swallows w/gold, 6-sided, mold #728, 4½", $225 to......275.00
Pitcher, cider; Melon Eaters on lav, mold #82, 6x6", from $3,000 to...3,500.00
Pitcher, lemonade; Old Man in Mtn & swans, w/blk & gold, mold #631...1,100.00
Pitcher, roses & snowballs, Ribbon & Jewel variation w/gold, 9½"...525.00
Plaque, Old Man in Mtn, mold #426, 8½", from $700 to 800.00
Plate, mc roses on dk gr w/wht shadow flowers & gold, mold #403, 9"...275.00
Plate, mill scene, ornate floral rim w/gold, Iris mold, 9½"...........900.00
Plate, Spring, lady's portrait, floral border, mold #343, 9" 2,100.00
Relish, Spring portrait, Iris mold, 9¾x4¼", from $1,200 to.....1,400.00
Syrup, swan reserve, swallows/roses/gold, mold #631, 6", from $325 to...375.00
Tankard, roses w/Tiffany finish base, mold #643, 15", from $1,000 to..1,200.00
Teapot, poppies on satin, mold #507, 6½", from $300 to 350.00
Tray, pk flowers on satin, cut-out hdls, red mk, 11½" 220.00
Urn, 1 boy from Dice Throwers, jewels/gold, mold #963, w/lid, 9¼"...2,750.00
Vase, Dice Throwers, bulbous, mold #907, unmk, 6", from $450 to........550.00
Vase, mill scene w/swallows, bottle neck, mold #909, 5½"..........550.00
Vase, Old Man in Mtn w/swans, ornate hdls, mold #940, 11", $800 to.1,000.00
Vase, pheasant on yel to rust, bottle neck, mold #909, unmk, 5¼".........550.00
Vase, roses on lav to cream w/gold hdls, mold #944, 9", from $550 to......650.00
Vase, turkeys (3) on rust, mold #901, 8¼", from $600 to 700.00

R.S. Suhl, Suhl

Porcelains marked with this designation are attributed to Reinhold Schlegelmilch's Suhl factory.

Cake plate, floral w/floral border, hdls, 10" 155.00
Coffee set, Angelica Kauffmann scene, 9" pot+cr/sug+6 c/s 1,700.00
Cup & saucer, Nightwatch, brn tones 110.00
Vase, Melon Eaters, flared sides, 9½" 1,175.00
Wall plaque, daisies, 10½" 140.00

R.S. Tillowitz

R.S. Tillowitz-marked porcelains are attributed to Reinhold Schlegelmilch's factory in Tillowitz, Silesia.

Bowl, berry; open roses, pk w/gold on wht, 1⅛x5", 6 for...............50.00
Bowl, floral, cut-out hdls w/gold, 1½x7½" 35.00
Bowl, lilacs w/bl & gold tracing, oval, 10"....................................70.00

Bowl, pheasants in landscape, marked, 6¾x10", $275.00. (Photo courtesy Mary Frank Gaston)

Bowl, roses, pk on gr w/gold, ftd, 1930s-40s, 2x7⅜" 40.00
Creamer & sugar bowl, floral w/gold, w/lid 125.00
Creamer & sugar bowl, lilies, wht on shaded gr 145.00
Flower frog, Deco flower, 4x5", EX 60.00
Nut dish, peonies & snowballs on cream, openwork, 6" 110.00
Plate, pansies on pale mc, dtd 1928, 7¼" 25.00
Tea set, floral on wht w/gold, 3-pc...125.00
Tray, floral, bl on gr w/much gold, pierced hdls, 4x8" 55.00
Vase, golden pheasant, plain mold, 6" 275.00

Schneider

The Schneider Glass Company was founded in 1914 at Epinay-sur-seine, France. They made many types of art glass, some of which sandwiched designs between layers. Other decorative devices were appliqué and carved work. These were marked 'Charder' or 'Schneider.' During the '20s commercial artware was produced with Deco motifs cut by acid through two or three layers and signed 'LeVerre Francais' in script or with a section of inlaid filigrane. Our advisor for this category is Don Williams; he is listed in the Directory under Missouri. See also Le Verre Francais.

Bowl, brn to yel, 2½x4½" 235.00
Compote, rust w/amethyst neck, raspberry ft, 8¼" 650.00
Compote, tangerine & burgundy mottle, blk stem, ftd wrought base, 6" ..850.00
Lamp, orange & red swirl bell shades (2), wrought iron base, 14"......575.00
Plafonnier, gray/pk mottled dome shade w/gr rim, w/chain hanger, 16"....865.00
Tazza, wht to mottled amethyst & bl at invt rim, dbl-bulbed stem, 8" 865.00
Vase, clear to mint gr mottle, ribbed cylinder, ftd, 11½" 925.00
Vase, etched leaf band at shoulder, 2 appl florals on smoky topaz, 14" ..980.00
Vase, molded red/purple/gr/orange in wrought floral fr, 16½" ..1,000.00
Vase, orange (clear/mottled) w/yel top, burgundy ft, conical, 11" ...865.00
Vase, orange/yel mottle w/bl & gray inserts at rim, 19"............1,650.00
Vase, pk mottle to dk red w/appl dk red flower, ftd, 15½" 3,000.00
Vase, purple & pk swirls, rion base w/leaf design & amber beads, 15" .1,150.00
Vase, splotchy orange top over lt orange body, ovoid, 14" 1,150.00
Vase, wht shading to dk brn, ACB linear decor, 12¼x3¼".........215.00

Schoolhouse Collectibles

Schoolhouse collectibles bring to mind memories of a bygone era when the teacher rang her bell to call the youngsters to class in a one-room schoolhouse where often both the 'hickory stick' and an apple occupied a prominent position on her desk. Our advisor for this category is Kenn Norris; he is listed in the Directory under Texas.

Atlas, McNally, An Improved System of Geography, 1858, 31 maps...**165.00**
Atlas, Mitchell's New School..., 1858, 9¾x11¾" format, EX **150.00**
Bell, brass, trn wood hdl w/incised rings, heavy, 10".....................**185.00**
Bell, brass, wood hdl, EX patina, 8½"..**65.00**
Bell, brass cone muffin, dbl chime, 7½x3¼", EX.........................**235.00**
Bell, CI, Lakeside Foundry Chicago #4, 1886, 13, in 26" yoke stand ...**450.00**
Bench, wood & CI, folding type, 1880s, 36" L.............................**135.00**
Book, Dick & Jane, Art Stories, Book Two, 1935, 168-pg, EX ...**130.00**
Book, Dick & Jane, Guess Who, hardbk, 1951, EX **90.00**
Book, Dick & Jane, More Fun w/Our Friends, 1962, NM **85.00**
Book, Dick & Jane, New Friends & Neighbors, 1956, NM.........**185.00**
Book, Dick & Jane, We Come & Go, 1956, 72-pg, M **345.00**
Book, Dick & Jane, Your Child Learns To Read, guide for parents, 1953..**395.00**
Book, Fun w/Dick & Jane, bl hardbk, 1947-48, EX.....................**150.00**
Book, Fun w/Dick & Jane, teacher's edition, 1951, NM..............**175.00**
Book, McGuffey's Eclectic Reader, 1920s revised editions 1-5, VG ...**30.00**
Book bag, Davy Crockett, 1950s, M..**235.00**
Book carrier, metal w/wood hdl, woven cloth straps, EX **30.00**
Cards, Sally, Dick & Jane Our Big Book, 20½x19½", set of 16..**210.00**
Crossing sign, girl, 1950s, 49½x18" on 24" dia base, EX **175.00**
Desk, child's, wood shelf top w/swivel chair on CI fr...................**115.00**
Desk, child's; CI & wood, seat folds, American SE Co #3, rfn, 27" .**135.00**
Desk, child's; wood & lacy CI, American SE Co #5....NY, rstr ...**125.00**
Desk, master's, rfn walnut, lift lid, gallery, 37x37x24" **275.00**
Desk, master's; pnt softwood, pegged, hinged lid, 1800s, 36x32x22" ...**750.00**
Desk chair, herman Miller, upholstered chair, laminated shelf......**75.00**
Globe, Cram's Unrivaled Terrestrial 12", mahog stand, 1930s, EX ..**285.00**
Globe, J Wilson & Sons, Albany NY, 1826, mahog, on brass stand, 35" **11,275.00**
Globe, mahog stand, Replogle 12" Reference, Chicago, 1940s, 34".......**315.00**
Globe, mahog tripod w/paw ft & CI fr, Replogle...Chicago, 25".............**825.00**
Inkwell, glass, cork stopper w/embellished wood top, 2" H............**45.00**
Letter jacket, all leather, zip front, 1950s, EX **185.00**
Letter sweater, Wilson, 1930s, EX...**55.00**
Light fixture, ceiling mt, milk glass globe, 1930s, 13x14", EX.....**100.00**
Magazine, Musical Truth, Conn LTD, band edition, 1936, 9x12", EX....**125.00**
Maps, pull-down from oak wall bracket, Denoyer-Geppert 1942, 8 for...**110.00**
Pen holder, 4 rows of pen slots on softwood board, ca 1900, 14x5½" **45.00**
Photograph, Black teacher/pupils/building, ca 1900, 4½x6½" **110.00**
Poster, Courage, Scottie saves drowning girl, Keller, 1932, 13x17".....**55.00**
Slate board, oak fr, 1860s, 13x9½", EX+.......................................**185.00**
Slate board, wood fr w/wrapped leather, 1860s, 8x11" **65.00**

Pencil Boxes

Among the most common of school-related collectibles are the many types of pencil boxes. Generally from the period of the 1870s to the 1940s, these boxes were made in hundreds of different styles. Materials included tin, wood (thin frame and solid hardwood) and leather; fabric and plastics were later used. Most pencil boxes were in a basic, rectangular configuration, though rare examples were made to resemble other objects such as rolling pins, ball bats, nightsticks, etc. They may still be found at reasonable prices, even though collectors have recently taken a keen interest in them. All boxes listed below are in very good to near mint condition. Our advisors for pencil boxes are Sue and Lar Hothem, authors of School Collectibles of the Past; they are listed in the Directory under Ohio.

Burlington Zephyr Streamliner & Trans-Pacific sea plane, 1934, EX ..**155.00**
Charlie Chaplin on cover, tin litho, 7¾x2⅛x¾", EX...................**58.00**

Felix the Cat & 2 kittens, heavy cb, Am Pencil Co, 1939, 8¼" ...**55.00**
Lacquered papier-mache, Eiffel tower on lid, NY ad on bottom, 8" L ...**65.00**
Little Red Riding Hood litho top on wood fr, lift-lid, jtd corners, 8" **55.00**
Mauchline, wood, St Vincent Rocks Clifton decal, lift lid, 9" L..**110.00**
Peters Weatherbird Shoes, heavy cb w/tin threaded top, 8", EX ..**42.50**
Red cb, gold emb planes/trains/etc, 1850-1931, snap closure, 8½" L..**35.00**
Red plastic, Playmate Pencil Box, Gilmark, 4x¾x8" **30.00**
Uncle Sam silhouette, orig contents, Ozark...St Louis, 10½" **75.00**
Wood w/paper-covered top, Olympic Winner..., swivel lid, 1932, 9" L..**40.00**
Wood w/pyrographic decor, Am Pencil Co of London & NY, 8½" **75.00**
Wooden lady figural w/red & bl pnt, 7x1¾" dia, EX **40.00**

Schoop, Hedi

In the 1940s and 1950s one of the most talented artists working in California was Hedi Schoop. Her business ended in 1958 when a fire destroyed her operation. It was at that time that she decided to do freelance work for other companies such as Cleminson Clay. Schoop was probably the most imitated artist of the time and she answered some of those imitators by successfully suing them. Some imitators were Kim Ward, Ynez, and Yona. Schoop was diversified in her creations, making items such as shapely women, bulky-looking women and children with fat arms and legs, TV lamps, and animals as well as planters and bowls. Schoop used many different marks including the stamped or incised Schoop signature and also a hard-to-find sticker. 'Hollywood, Cal.' or 'California' were occasionally used in conjunction with the Hedi Schoop name. For further information we recommend The Encyclopedia of California Pottery, Second Edition, by Jack Chipman; he is listed in the Directory under California. Our advisor for this category is Susan Cox, also listed in California.

Bookends, poodle, sitting, gray w/blk highlights, on base, 12", pr **170.00**
Box, butterfly finial, maroon/pk/gray-gr, mk #218, 3½x5½" **30.00**
Box, poodle (pk/wht) on lid, blk base, triangular, 1¾x8" **155.00**
Candle holder, mermaid holds 2 shell cups aloft, 1950s, rare, 13½"....**500.00**
Canister, Darner Doll, #807, 12"..**85.00**
Casserole, brn, conical, w/lid, #510, 13½".......................................**55.00**
Cookie jar, Darner Doll, wht w/bl & gr apron, mk, 12"................**400.00**
Cookie jar, Queen, rare **600.00**
Figurine, anbel boy, from waist up, 8"..**110.00**
Figurine, circus clown lifting barbell, 12x12"................................**295.00**
Figurine, clown, ft wide apart, holds barbell aloft, 13".................**250.00**
Figurine, Conchita w/hat & 2 baskets, 12½"................................**175.00**
Figurine, dancing girl, bl dress w/HP florals, wht basket, 12" **165.00**
Figurine, Debutante, flower holder, 12½" **150.00**
Figurine, Debutante, handmade flowers, 1943, 12½" **195.00**
Figurine, drummer boy w/drumsticks, 13¼" **135.00**
Figurine, Dutch lady in gr w/wht flower vase, 9½".......................**50.00**
Figurine, fan dancer, in wht w/teal trim, HP yel-brn roses, 13"...**120.00**
Figurine, Fantasy dancers, pk w/gold, 13", 12½", pr.....................**200.00**
Figurine, girl standing, bell-shaped skirt, sunflower-shaped face, 9" .**125.00**
Figurine, gypsy dancer, yel dress & scarf w/gold trim, 10"............**200.00**
Figurine, Josephine, skirt & bandeau top, scarf over hair, 13½" .**135.00**
Figurine, lady, hat w/bow, plaid shawl on shoulders, head up, 13"...**135.00**
Figurine, lady in cream dress w/appl flowers, holds 2 baskets, 12"...**150.00**
Figurine, lady w/flowers, cream/brn/yel/peach, 13" **140.00**
Figurine, lady w/flowers on chest, 2 flowerpots in bk, 11½" **65.00**
Figurine, lady walking poodle, gray, blk & wht, 10" **145.00**
Figurine, Margueritta, sm glaze flaw, 13" **125.00**
Figurine, Oriental girl w/umbrella, gr, #200, 12"..........................**125.00**
Figurine, Repose, lady seated, holding bowl, tinted bsk, 12" **200.00**
Figurine, Repose, seated female holding bowl, bsk & high gloss .**185.00**
Figurine, senorita w/basket on head, mk #100, 12½" **210.00**

Figurine, Spanish lady dancer, 9½".........................95.00
Figurine, Western cowboy & cowgirl dancing, 1-pc, 11"...........250.00
Figurine, woman standing w/full mirror behind her, 10¾x12" 350.00
Figurine, woman w/umbrella in windstorm, 14½" 230.00
Figurine/planter, Dutch girl w/yel braids, opening in apron, 11" ...65.00
Figurine/planter, fan dancer, leaning against pot, 13½"...............165.00
Figurine/planter, lady w/2 open baskets, #121, 11½" 95.00
Figurine/planter, peasant girl, kneeling, opening in apron, 8½"..110.00
Figurine/planter, rooster crowing w/head up, 14½" 85.00
Jardiniere, wht w/gold trim, Asian theme, rnd, 7½" 110.00
Lamp, TV; Comedy & Tragedy, gr & blk 475.00
Planter, horse, wht w/gr trim, must have mk, 7½" 95.00
Planter, pinched irregular rim, 12" L..75.00
Plate, Old Crow mascot, blk/wht/gray, mk Hedi Schoop orig, 11x7½"...125.00
Plate, poodle (blk/wht) w/flower on head/tail, gold edge, 7½" sq .75.00
Tray, lady figural, skirt forms tray..215.00
Vase, butterfly, brn/lav/pk w/gold, 6x9" 60.00
Vase, duck form 75.00
Vase, stylized chicken, 9", pr...155.00
Wall pocket, angel w/finger up to mouth, 8" 85.00

Schramberg

The Schramberg factory was founded in the early nineteenth century in Schramberg Wuttemberg, Germany. The pieces most commonly seen are those made by Schramberger Majolika Fabrik (SMF) dating from 1912 until 1989.

Some pieces are stamped with the pattern name (i.e. Gobelin) and the number of the painter who executed it. The imprinted number identifies the shape. Marks may also include these names: Wheelock, Black Forest, and Mepoco.

Perhaps the most popular examples with collectors are those from the Gobelin line. Such pieces have a gray background with as many as ten other colors used to create that design. For example, Gobelin 3 pieces will be painted with green and orange leaves and yellow eyes along with other colors specific to that design.

Little is known of the designers who worked for Schramberg; however, Eva Zeisel was employed at the factory for nearly two years starting in the fall of 1928. Her duties included design, production, and merchandising. Our advisors for this category are Ralph Winslow who is listed in the Directory under Missouri and Ann Burton who is listed under Michigan.

Bowl, Gobelin 6, 10½"..65.00
Candlestick, floral, 5½"..34.00
Luncheon set, 18-pc 80.00
Pitcher, daisies, 4"..12.00

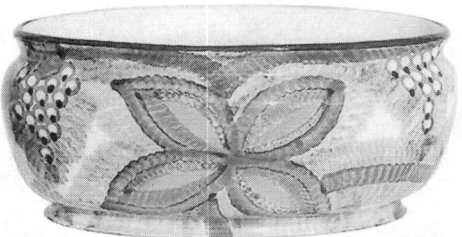

Planter, Gobelin 6, 10", $52.00.
(Photo courtesy Ralph Winslow)

Pitcher, floral, 5½"..45.00
Planter, daisies, 9"..50.00
Teapot, bulbous, 4¼"...65.00
Teapot, mc 98.00
Trivet, floral 13.00

Vase, blk forest, 4"...15.00
Vase, floral, 4¼"...28.00
Vase, Gobelin 2, 4½"...35.00
Vase, Gobelin 5, w/frog, 4" 75.00
Vase, Gobelin 5, 6"...29.00
Vase, leaves, 4¼"...45.00
Vase, mtn scene, 4½"...60.00
Wall pocket, peasants, 4¼"..20.00

Scouting Collectibles

Boy Scouts

Scouting was founded in England in 1907 by a retired Major General, Lord Robert Baden-Powell. Its purpose is the same today as it was then — to help develop physically strong, mentally alert boys and to teach them basic fundamentals of survival and leadership. The movement soon spread to the United States, and in 1910 a Chicago publisher, William Boyce, set out to establish scouting in America. The first World Scout Jamboree was held in 1911 in England. Baden-Powell was honored as the Chief Scout of the World. In 1926 he was awarded the Silver Buffalo Award in the United States. He was knighted in 1929 for distinguished military service and for his scouting efforts. Baden-Powell died in 1941. For more information you may contact our advisor, R.J. Sayers, author of *Guide to Scouting Collectibles*, whose address (and ordering information regarding his book) may be found in the Directory under North Carolina. (Correspondence other than book orders requires an SASE please.)

Armband, 1973 Nat'l Jamboree, OA Staff 20.00
Bank, Scout w/staff, CI, gray pnt 45.00
Beadcraft kit, beads, loom & cord, #1164.....................................20.00
Belt buckle, 1955 World Jamboree, Max Silber issue, 700 made...70.00
Belt buckle, 1957 Nat'l Jamboree, dbl lock 20.00
Blotter, 1937 Nat'l Jamboree, NY Council, section numbers 10.00
Book, A Patch Collectors Handbook, Myers, 1971.......................5.00
Book, Comprehensive Guide to Eagle Scout Award, Grove, 1991..6.00
Book, Nat'l Jamboree Insignia Checklist, Ellis, 1988 ....8.00
Book, The Scout in Aviation, Hyman, 1982...................................10.00
Bookends, Official 1960 Nat'l Jamboree souvenir, pr....................15.00
Bookmark, First Class enameled on top, 1950s 4.00
Camera, Official BSA, 1940s Seneca #2, box type 40.00
Canteen, plastic w/plastic screw top, 1970s.................................4.00
Cap, Official BSA, red barret w/patch...3.00
Cards, Christmas, w/envelopes in red box, set of 25 ....10.00
Cards, Ogdens Cigarette Cards, 1930s scouts, English, set of 50...85.00
Cigarette lighter, 1964 Nat'l Jamboree, Staff pc, w/logo 10.00
Compass, First Class in center, rnd, ca 1930 ....15.00
Compass, red plastic, 8-point side, ca 1930 ....12.00
Cup, collapsible; Tenderfoot logo on top, 1930-50s 7.00
Decal, Full First Class, silver, 1930s 3.00
Decals, Nat'l Regions 1-13, set of 13 ....40.00
Decals, 1937 Nat'l Jamboree, lg, set of 3 ....75.00
Drum, scouts along border, tin, Pat 1908, sm...............................100.00
Figurine, hiker w/staff, hollow...20.00
Figurine, scout frying eggs, hollow 30.00
Figurine, scout hiking, iron, full pnt 15.00
Fire Starting kit, flint & steel, in sm pouch.................................5.00
Flag, Cub Scout, local pack #s sewn on, bl wool, 1940.................25.00
Flag, Explorer Post, red & bl w/logo in center, 1960....................35.00
Game, Boy Scout Progress; board type, 1926...............................50.00
Game, Boy Scout 10 Pins, bowling type.....................................30.00
Game, Kiddie Camper, mechanical, 1920s....................................120.00
Handkerchief, bl w/Cub Scout Promise 4.00

Hatchet, Plumb, decal on hdl, Anchor brand 25.00
Hatchet, Tru-Temper, oak hdl, 1950s 12.50
Jacket, Philmont; red, wool 25.00
Leathercraft kit, makes a belt, 1930s, boxed 25.00
Money clip, Nat'l Staff, sterling silver w/pin-logo, 1950s 45.00
Mustache cup, scout on side, ceramic, ca 1915 ....50.00
Neckerchief, Nat'l Staff, sq w/emblem, limited edition 50.00
Paper dolls, 1930s-50s, EXIB...50.00
Paperweight, campaign hat, pnt CI, 1920s, 3" 25.00
Pedometer, Hikemeter, New Haven CT, w/belt loop holder 20.00
Pencil box, full color scene of camp activities, 1930s 25.00
Pennant, 1935 Nat'l Jamboree Official, bl felt, w/lg logo 100.00
Pin, First Class, TH Foley, safety-clasp bk, 2" 200.00
Plaque, Boy Scout Creed, fr, 1924..15.00
Plate, Am Boy Scout, scout in center, ceramic, 9" 75.00
Plate, Young Doctor, Rockwell-Gorham, ceramic 30.00
Postcard, Blazing a Trail, full color, #4 in series, 1914 ....10.00
Postcard, The Hero of the Day, scout w/flag, 1920........................7.00
Postcard, 1937 World Jamboree, Jesus w/scout, full color 10.00
Postcard, 1959 Official World Jamboree, w/logo 5.00
Poster, Follow Me Boys, set of 6 lobby cards................................40.00
Poster, Henry Aldridge Boy Scout, set of 6 lobby cards 50.00
Poster, John Glenn, Space Scout, 1960s 10.00
Poster, 50th Anniversary, heavy board 10.00
Record, Sousa's Boy Scout Marches, BSA approved, 78-rpm 15.00
Ring, onyx, Tenderfoot logo, sterling...8.00
Ring, 1957 Nat'l Jamboree special souvenir issue, sterling............40.00
Signal set, Official Heliograph, #1526 ....50.00
Tie bar, Camp Ranger, clip-on, w/logo...5.00
Woodburning kit, w/wood & cord 20.00

Girl Scouts

Collecting Girl Scout memorabilia is a hobby that is growing nationwide. When Sir Baden-Powell founded the Boy Scout movement in England, it proved to be too attractive and too well adapted to youth to limit its great opportunities to boys alone. The sister organization, known in England as the Girl Guides, quickly followed and was equally successful. Mrs. Juliette Low, an American visitor to England and a personal friend of the father of scouting, realized the tremendous future of the movement for her own country, and with the active and friendly cooperation of the Baden-Powells, she founded the Girl Guides in America, enrolling the first patrols in Savannah, Georgia, in March 1912. In 1915 national headquarters were established in Washington, D.C., and the name was changed to Girl Scouts. The first national convention was held in 1914. Each succeeding year has shown growth and increased enthusiasm in this steadily growing army of girls and young women who are learning in the happiest ways to combine patriotism, outdoor activities of every kind, skill in every branch of domestic science, and high standards of community service. Today there are over 400,000 Girl Scouts and more than 22,000 leaders. Mr. Sayers is also our Girl Scout advisor.

Armband, Girl Scout Farm Aid 15.00
Badge, Wing Scouting, cloth...20.00
Book, The Ralley, Vol 1 #1, first edition 100.00
Bookends, composition, 1940s, pr 15.00
Brownie Wings, 1926 ....15.00
Camera, Official Univex, 1937 ....50.00
Certificate, Brownie Law, emb, 1920..15.00
Cookie box, autographed by Babe Ruth, 1940s 200.00
Cup, collapsible; aluminum, 1950 ....5.00
Doll, Brownie 2-pc uniform, compo doll, 1930, 13" 100.00
Manual, Brownie; for Jr Scouts, Fed 1922 ....25.00

Pin, Brownie, elf shape, plastic & metal, 1920.............................20.00
Pin, Guard; for Brownie Girl Scout Leaders 15.00
Pin, Official Brownie Pow Wow, metal, 1922 ....200.00
Postcard, child by lake, Brownie, 1930s.......................................10.00
Poster, 1923 Cookie Drive, color litho 100.00
Trivet, CI, pierced insignia, 50th Anniversary..............................27.50
Uniform, Girl Scout-Brownie, w/middy & bloomers, 1918 ....200.00

Scrimshaw

The most desirable examples of the art of scrimshaw can be traced back to the first half of the nineteenth century to the heyday of the whaling industry. Some voyages lasted for several years, and conditions on board were often dismal. Sailors filled the long hours by using the tools of their trade to engrave whale teeth and make boxes, pie crimpers (jagging wheels), etc., from the bone and teeth of captured whales. Eskimos also made scrimshaw, sometimes borrowing designs from the sailors who traded with them.

Beware of fraudulent pieces; fakery is prevalent in this field. Many carved teeth are of recent synthetic manufacture (examples engraved with information such as ship's or captain's names, dates, places, etc., should be treated with extreme caution) and have no antique or collectible value. A listing of most of these plastic items has been published by the Kendall Whaling Museum in Sharon, Massachusetts. If you're in doubt or a novice collector, it's best to deal with reputable people who *guarantee* the items they sell. Our advisor for this category is John Rinaldi; he is listed in the Directory under Maine. See also Powder Horns.

Awl, tapered steel w/whale-tooth hdl, EX patina, 1850s, 8½" 375.00
Awl, trn whalebone, 4¾" 190.00
Block, whale ivory sheaves, copper/brass pins, 1830-40, 2¾x2x1" 495.00
Box, ditty; baleen, pierced cvg, pinwheel design, 1840s, 3¼x5¼" 1,275.00
Busk, whalebone, 3 cvd panels: ships/flag/angels/etc, 19th C, 13¾"..3,475.00
Case, whale ivory, silver hinge & band, 19th C, 1½x3¾x2¾" ...1,750.00
Cribbage board, pan bone, harbor scene center, deep cvg, 19th C..4,950.00
Crimper, sea horse, whale ivory, ca 1830-40, 5⅝", VG+ 10,750.00
Crimper, whale ivory, 4-wheel, 3 pierced cvgs, 1850s, 4¾"......1,500.00
Crimper, whale ivory w/abalone inlays, 1850s, 1½" wheel, 5½" L ...795.00
Crimper, whalebone, intricate trnings, 1830s, 2" dia, 8" L 595.00
Crimper, 3-tine fork finial, whale ivory w/wood spacers, 1840s, 7½" ..865.00
Fid, cvd geometric bone hdl, steel point, 5½"..............................150.00
Fid, tapered, octagonal top, ca 1850, 6⅜" 110.00
Jawbone section, girl w/gr bow on dress, pin-prick style, 1883, 5½"...675.00
Knife, 1830-40, 8¼" steel blade, 4" whale tooth hdl w/cvg, ...1,175.00
Pan bone panel, dramatic whaling scene w/11 whales, 1840s, EX ...9,500.00
Pan bone panel, ship at sea, fishing boat off stern, ca 1840, 3x16", VG..2,400.00

Pepper pot, whale ivory, hand turned, red, green, and black scribed lines, 1¾", $500.00.

Rolling pin, teak w/trn whale ivory hdls, 1840-50, 14x2" dia 695.00
Rolling pin, wooden center w/walrus ivory ends, 1840s, 2¼x14" ..985.00
Tooth, Am frigate/sailor at canon, EX art, 20th C, 4½x2+" 485.00
Tooth, Am ships ea side, mc stain, 1840-50, 5¾x2⅝" 2,800.00
Tooth, Elizabeth of London, att Edward Burdett, ca 1828, 5x2" ...14,750.00

Tooth, girl named Barbara/flowers/banners, G Ellison, 19th C, 6½x3" **2,300.00**
Tooth, lady in fancy gowns/bonnet ea side, 19th C, 9¼x3⅝"..**3,650.00**
Tooth, lady leans on anchor w/ship beyond, bk: lady angel, 1830s, 7"..**3,450.00**
Tooth, lady w/fancy hairdo & dress, 1850-60, 5½".................**1,185.00**
Tooth, Queen Victoria, bk: unknown man, pin-prick style, 1850s, 6"..**795.00**
Tooth, sailor prays/wounded, bk: palms/lighthouse/etc, 1840s, 6½" ..**3,450.00**
Tooth, sailor w/lg Am flag, bk: girl w/rose, mc, 19th C, 4½x2½"......**1,125.00**
Tooth, ship scene w/identity & date of 1843, lightly eng, 7" **975.00**
Tooth, sperm whale, Scottish tribal warrior in relief, att Bifer, 7" ..**5,875.00**
Tooth, whaling scene ea side (1 w/captured whale), 1840s, 8x3" ...**8,250.00**
Tusk, Am frigate w/3 ladies holding flowers, mc, 1850s, 23"....**3,450.00**
Walking stick, narwhal, w/ivory knob, wide silver band, 1850s, 34½"..**5,000.00**

Sebastians

Sebastian miniatures were first produced in 1938 by Prescott W. Baston in Marblehead, Massachusetts. Since then more than six hundred have been modeled. These figurines have been sold through gift shops all over the country, primarily in the New England states. In 1976 Baston withdrew his Sebastians from production. Under an agreement with the Lance Corporation of Hudson, Massachusetts, one hundred designs were selected to be produced by that company under Baston's supervision. Those remaining were discontinued. In the time since then, the older figurines have become very collectible. Price is determined by three factors: 1) in production/out of production; 2) labels — color of oval label, i.e. red, blue, green, etc.; Marblehead label, a green and silver palette-shaped label used until 1977; or no label; 3) condition. If there is no label and the varnish coat is quite yellowed, then it is considered to be of the Marblehead era. Dates are merely copyright dates and have no particular significance in regard to value. The signature 'P.W. Baston' should only have impact on price when it is an actual autograph. Most pieces are manufactured with an imprinted 'P.W. Baston' on the base. Baston died in 1984; the miniatures are now being done by P.W. Baston, Jr. Our advisor for this category is Jim Waite; he is listed in the Directory under Illinois.

Bob Crachit & Tiny Tim...**25.00**
Family Picnic **40.00**
Family Reads Aloud...**30.00**
Geo Washington w/cannon..**35.00**
Mr X Obocell, Prescott Baston, Marblehead, 1950.............**450.00**
Old Covered Bridge, Marblehead, 1954, 2½x3⅞x3" **50.00**
Peter Stuyvesant **24.00**
Savin Sandy **24.00**
Snow Days Boy & Girl, pr..**30.00**
Uncle Sam **24.00**

Sevres

Fine-quality porcelains have been made in Sevres, France, since the early 1700s. Rich ground colors were often hand painted with portraits, scenics, and florals. Some pieces were decorated with transfer prints and decalcomania; many were embellished with heavy gold. These wares are the most respected of all French porcelains. Their style and designs have been widely copied, and some of the items listed below are Sevres-type wares.

Bowl, court figures on bl w/gold, 12½", NM **385.00**
Box, courting couple/floral reserve, metal fr w/gold, 4x7" **200.00**
Coffee can & saucer, cherubs reserves on bl, pearl jewels, 1880s..**400.00**
Cup & saucer, swan form hdl, wings form cup's sides, 1806, 4½x5" ..**440.00**
Dinner service, Pose Pompadour w/gilt, serves 12, 72-pc **6,000.00**
Tray, mc floral, ormolu fr w/3 dolphin ft, scroll hdls, 1845, 4x6" ...**200.00**

Urn, romantic scenes, cobalt & gilt, 8-sided base, 19th c, 30".**1,500.00**
Vase, couple at well in heart medallion, hdld urn form, metal mts, 17" ..**500.00**

Sewer Tile

Whimsies, advertising novelties, and other ornamental items were sometimes made in potteries where the primary product was simply tile.

Pitcher, tooled bark, simple tooled face on spout, 6½", $150.00; Lion-head ashtray, artist signed, 4x5", $120.00; Squirrel with nut, 6", $215.00; Lion on rectangular base, molded with tooled details, 6¼x9¼", $385.00. (Photo courtesy Garth's Auctions, Inc.)

Bank, boy's head, 4½" **400.00**
Bank, dog, some detail, flakes, OH, 10½" **220.00**
Cat, seated, shiny copper speckles in glaze, chips/ft missing, 7" ..**330.00**
Dog, incised details, lt brn glaze, 10½"......................................**330.00**
Dog, molded/tooled, minor chips, 5½"..**195.00**
Dog, seated, cut-out front legs, molded/tooled, 8¾" **440.00**
Dog, seated, molded details, hollow, 5⅝" **165.00**
Dog, seated, molded w/punched collar, lt wear/flakes, 11½" **250.00**
Dog, seated, molded/tooled, 10½" **195.00**
Dog, seated, primitive head, molded/tooled, 9"...........................**360.00**
Lion on base, hollow-molded/tooled, 8¼", EX.............................**300.00**
Lion on oblong solid 2-tier base, much tooling, 7¼" L **1,400.00**
Lion on oval base, molded/tooled, brn matt, rpr, 15".................**600.00**
Lion on plinth, ca 1934, 5¼x8⅜x4⅛" **275.00**
Lion on rectangular base, OH, 5" L **385.00**
Lion on scalloped base, G detail/color, 10½", EX **415.00**
Lion on scalloped rectangular base, EX detail, 10", EX **635.00**
Owl, on tree trunk base, made in 2 pcs, 12¾" **550.00**
Spaniel, dk brn-red, incised collar & chain, 8¼", EX...................**275.00**
Spaniel, molded/tooled, incised EJE, 7½" **330.00**
Stump planter, tooled bark, 5 molded & appl ducks, 19x9¾" **465.00**
Stump planter, 4 branches, EX detailed bark, 17x10"................**330.00**
Stump planter, 8 branches, tooled bark, sm chips, 15" **330.00**
Train engine, molded details, artist sgn, OH, 19¼" **660.00**
Umbrella stand, tree trunk w/appl roses, chips, 25½"................**330.00**

Sewing Items

Sewing collectibles continue to intrigue collectors, and fine nineteenth-century and earlier pieces are commanding higher prices due to increased demand and scarcity. Complete needlework boxes and chatelaines in original condition are rare, but even incomplete examples can be considered prime additions to any collection, as long as they meet certain criteria: boxes should contain fittings of the period; the chains of the chatelaine should be intact and contemporary with the style; and the individual holders should be original and match the brooch. As nineteenth-century items become harder to find, new trends in collecting develop. Needle books, many of which were decorated with horses, children, beautiful ladies, etc., have become very popular. Some were giveaways printed with advertisements of products and businesses. Even early pins are collectible; the first ones were made in two parts with the round head attached separately. Pin disks, pin cubes, and other pin holders also make interesting additions to a sewing collection.

Tape measures are very popular — especially Victorian figurals. These command premium prices. Early wooden examples of transferware and Tunbridge ware have gained in popularity, as have figurals of vegetable ivory, celluloid, and other early plastics. From the twentieth century, tatting shuttles made of plastics, bone, brass, sterling, and wood decorated with Art Nouveau, Art Deco, and more modern designs are in demand — so are darning eggs, stilettos, and thimbles. Because of the decline in the popularity of needlework after the 1920s (due to increased production of machine-made items), novelty items were made in an attempt to regain consumer interest, and many collectors today also find these appealing.

Watch for reproductions. Sterling thimbles are being made in Holland and the U.S. and are available in many Victorian-era designs. But the originals are usually plainly marked, either in the inside apex or outside on the band. Avoid testing gold and silver thimbles for content; this often destroys the inside marks. Instead, research the manufacturer's mark; this will often denote the material as well. Even though the reproductions are well finished, they do not have manufacturers' marks. Many thimbles are being made specifically for the collectible market; reproductions of porcelain thimbles are also found. Prices should reflect the age and availability of these thimbles. For more information we recommend *Sewing Tools and Trinkets* by Helen Lester Thompson and *Antique and Collectible Thimbles and Accessories* by Averil Mathis. Our advisor for this category is Kathy Goldsworthy; she is listed in the Directory under Washington.

Box, mahog Neoclassical, HP scene on hinged lid, 10x7x4¾"......**1,100.00**
Box, step-down w/old mustard rpt, 5-drw w/brass pulls, 6½x11x11"...**225.00**
Box, wooden w/lion inlay, cushion top, drw, ca 1860, 9x4x8".....**865.00**
Caddy, Pease ware, 3-part w/metal rods, lt wear/chips, 5¾" **300.00**
Case, thimble; vegetable ivory, cvd acorn shape, 2¾x1½" **55.00**
Clamp, hand-cvd ivory, incised florals, metal thumbscrew, 5¼"..**1,495.00**
Clamp, ivory C-shape w/spool top, 5¾" **110.00**
Clamp, ivory/horn horse figural, brass eyes, 19th C, 4½" **800.00**
Clamp, screw top cvd of man's head, clamp resembles set of teeth, EX ..**700.00**
Clamp, wooden C-shape w/urn top holding cushion, 7⅛" **120.00**
Darner, blown, amethyst...**65.00**
Darner, pink & wht ribs encased in clear egg, 2⅝" **80.00**
Gauge, dressmaker's; metal, Picken, c 1915, 6", EX **12.50**
Measure, advertising, Hoover vacuum cleaner **45.00**
Measure, advertising, Stromberg, carburetor/anti-shock brakes, 1½"..**165.00**
Measure, celluloid, Black man w/cigarette, 1½", EX **190.00**
Measure, celluloid, cat w/mouse in mouth, tongue pulls, EX **300.00**
Measure, celluloid, flower basket, Germany **85.00**
Measure, celluloid, sewing machine, EX.......................................**265.00**
Measure, gold-pnt metal, royal coach, tape at side, 1890s, 1½x3" ...**565.00**
Measure, metal, egg & fly...**85.00**
Measure, plated metal, flat iron, EX **200.00**
Measure, vegetable ivory, acorn shape w/red fabric tape, 2x1", EX....**45.00**
Measure, vegetable ivory, bbl shape w/fabric tape, EX **45.00**
Needle book, Bestmaid, complete w/needles & threader, Japan, M.......**10.00**
Needle book, S&H Green Stamps, Made in Germany, complete, NM ..**7.50**
Needle case, ivory, tubular w/overall cvg, 4¾x¾" dia....................**85.00**
Needle case, rolled leather, ribbon ties, red fabric lining, 4" L **75.00**
Needle case, vegetable ivory, cylinder w/acorn-shaped ends, 2⅞".**20.00**
Pin/needle holder, sterling pig, Victorian **135.00**
Pincushion, china, flower basket, Lake Tahoe souvenir, Japan, 3" ..**7.50**
Pincushion, cvd ivory, bbl-like top w/velvet cushion ea end, 1⅝"..**40.00**
Pincushion, hand-sewn floral print dog, glass bead eyes, 1900s, EX ...**30.00**
Pincushion, leather pointed shoe, 1890s, sm................................**22.50**
Pincushion, porc, lady beside cushion, Occupied Japan, 3" **40.00**
Pincushion, vegetable ivory, ped ft, fabric cushion, 3⅝" **230.00**

Sewing bird, brass, rpl cushion, dtd 1853, EX **150.00**
Sewing bird, brass, 1860, 5x3" **185.00**
Sewing bird, cast metal, C-clamp, spring mechanism, ca 1880s, 4¾"...**250.00**
Sewing bird, cI w/gilt bird form w/dbl cushion, EX......................**225.00**
Sewing bird, wrought iron & brass, C-clamp base, 4x3" **370.00**
Sheath, knitting needle; bl cloth w/quill insert, 1850s, 3 4/8" L ..**75.00**
Shuttle, sterling, Victorian...**125.00**
Spool caddy, trn cherry w/metal posts, cushion top, dtd 1954, 7".**165.00**
Thimble, pewter, Golliwog in purple coat, 1¼" **28.00**

Thimble, sterling, Muhr crown hallmark, Philadelphia, $135.00 (because of unusual 'embroidery'-type knurling).

Thimble, sterling silver, fancy scalloped rim, lt wear **38.00**
Thimble, sterling silver, plain rim, USA **28.00**
Thimble holder, vegetable ivory, w/thimble, ball finial, 2⅜".........**50.00**
Thimble holder, 800 silver, strawberry..**85.00**
Thimble/needle case, Bakelite, Germany **40.00**
Thimble/needle case, sterling, oval...**95.00**
Tracing wheel, Bakelite Hdl, mk Dritz Tracing Wheel on metal stem...**7.50**
Tracing wheel, Singer mk on metal stem, plastic hdl, 6" **10.00**
Tracing wheel, yel Bakelite hdl...**12.50**

Sewing Machines

The fact that Thomas Saint, an English cabinetmaker, invented the first sewing machine in 1790 was unknown until 1874 when Newton Wilson, an English sewing machine manufacturer and patentee, chanced upon the drawings included in a patent specification describing methods of making boots and shoes. By the middle of the nineteenth century, several patents were granted to American inventors, among them Isaac M. Singer, whose machine used a treadle. These machines were ruggedly built, usually of cast iron. By the 1860s and 1870s, the sewing machine had become a popular commodity, and the ironwork became more detailed and ornate.

Though rare machines are costly, many of the old oak treadle machines (especially these brands: Davis, Home, Household, National, New Home, Singer, Weed, Wheeler & Wilson, and Willcox & Gibbs) have only nominal value. Machines manufactured after 1875 are generally very common as most were mass produced. Values for these later sewing machines range from $50.00 to $100.00. Refer to *Toy and Miniature Sewing Machines, Books I and II*, by Glenda Thomas for more information. Our advisor for this category is Peter Frei; he is listed in the Directory under Massachusetts. In the listings that follow, unless noted otherwise, values are suggested for machines in excellent working order.

Child's, Artcraft, Jr Miss, metal on wood base, 1940s-50s, from $50 to ..**75.00**
Child's, Baby Brother, gray-gr metallic, Japan, 1960s, from $75 to........**100.00**
Child's, Britain's Petite, pk plastic, 1980s, 8¾x10⅛x8¾" **40.00**
Child's, Casige, Deco decor, cam drive, MIG-British Zone, $75 to ...**100.00**
Child's, Diana, bl plastic, battery or hand operated, China, $15 to **30.00**
Child's, Gateway, red-pnt lightweight steel **50.00**
Child's, Ideal, CI & oak treadle type, 30½", G........................**2,000.00**
Child's, KAYanEE Sew Master, hand-operated, wood base............**50.00**

Child's, Little Worker, New Home, hand-operated, 1910s, 10½" L..**150.00**
Child's, Marx Sew Big, die-cast metal w/plastic table, 1960s.........**75.00**
Child's, Peerless Automatic, CI, w/wooden box...........................**495.00**
Child's, Sew-Ette, bl-crinkle metal, battery, 1960s, 7⅞" L............**50.00**
Child's, Strawberry Shortcake, pk plastic, 1980s, 8¼" **45.00**
Essex, highly chromed, wood base, 1940s-50s, 8" L **130.00**
Florence, CI, belt driven, Pat Nov 12, 1850, plain stand, EX **260.00**
New Home, Orange MA, 1903, EX..**185.00**
Shaw & Clark, 'Skinny Pillar,' 1864, EX **2,599.99**
Singer, leather sewing, floor model, heavy, EX..........................**300.00**
Singer Featherweight #221, all gold intact, w/all attachments, NM ...**400.00**
Singer Portable #3, hand-crank, dome case, 1898, NM.............**150.00**
Wilcox & Gibbs, early, sm **60.00**

Shaker Items

The Shaker community was founded in America in 1776 at Niskeyuna, New York, by a small group of English 'Shaking Quakers.' The name referred to a group dance which was part of their religious rites. Their leader was Mother Ann Lee. By 1815 their membership had grown to more than one thousand in eighteen communities as far west as Indiana and Kentucky. But in less than a decade, their numbers began to decline until today only a handful remain. Their furniture is prized for its originality, simplicity, workmanship, and practicality. Few pieces were signed. Some were carefully finished to enhance the natural wood; a few were painted.

Although other methods were used earlier, most Shaker boxes were of oval construction with overlapping 'fingers' at the seams to prevent buckling as the wood aged. Boxes with original paint fetch triple the price of an unpainted box; number of fingers and overall size should also be considered.

Although the Shakers were responsible for weaving a great number of baskets, their methods are not easily distinguished from those of their outside neighbors, and it is nearly impossible without first-hand knowledge to positively attribute a specific example to their manufacture. They were involved in various commercial efforts other than woodworking — among them sheep and dairy farming, sawmilling, and pipe and brick making. They were the first to raise crops specifically for seed and to market their product commercially. They perfected a method to recycle paper and were able to produce wrinkle-free fabrics. Our advisor for this category is Nancy Winston; she is listed in the Directory under New Hampshire. Standard two-letter state abbreviations have been used throughout the following listings.

Key:
CB — Canterbury   ML — Mt. Lebanon
EF — Enfield   SDL — Sabbathday Lake
NL — New Lebanon   WV — Watervliet

Apple corer & slicer, wood, 4-blade, riveted, CB, 5x4⅝"............**350.00**
Barrel, wooden staves, all wood, 16¼x17¼"............................**360.00**
Basket, blk ash, ear hdls, wrapped rim, CB, 5½x14x12½" **175.00**
Basket, sewing; woven poplarware, SDL, 2⅝x15½x2" **200.00**
Basket, wool gathering; picket-fence style, child's, ca 1890, 5x7⅝"..**385.00**
Basket, woven splint, bentwood hdl, oblong, 3½x6½x5¼" **165.00**
Basket, woven splint, bentwood hdl, SDL, 7¾x16" dia..............**198.00**
Bench, foot; #0, slanted sq top on trn legs, dk varnish, ML, 1875 ...**230.00**
Bench, kneeling; rfn poplar w/red stain, SDL, 6½x41x6" **275.00**
Box, bentwood pine, copper tacks, old varnish, 8¾" **295.00**
Box, handkerchief; poplarware, kidskin & ribbon trim, 1950s....**300.00**
Box, pine, sq corner posts, drw, bin-like top w/hinged lid, 38" L ...**880.00**
Box, pine/ash, bl-gr pnt, str seam, iron tacks, 4x8½"..................**450.00**
Box, sewing; mixed woods w/red stain, drw, compartment, 6⅝" .**550.00**

Box, sewing; 3-finger, copper tacks, SDL, 8" **295.00**
Box, 2-finger, pine/maple, orange stain, CB, 3⅛x5⅛x3¼" **1,500.00**
Box, 3-finger, hardwood/pine, copper tacks, 6⅛" L **395.00**
Box, 3-finger, hardwood/pine, gr pnt splashes, copper tacks, 10½" ..**350.00**
Box, 3-finger, old red varnish, copper tacks, 1850s+, 1¾x4⅝x3" ..**995.00**
Box, 3-finger, orig mustard pnt, copper tacks, sm split, 2x5½" ...**4,000.00**
Box, 3-finger, orig varnish, att ML, early 1900s, 2¼x7x4" **325.00**
Box, 3-finger, pine/maple, red pnt, copper tacks, 10¼" dia.........**995.00**
Box, 4-finger, old varnish, copper tacks, age crack, 10½".............**440.00**
Box, 5-finger, HP birds on lid, dk stain, 1800s, 15", EX **395.00**
Bucket, berry; old putty wht pnt w/EX patina, ML, ca 1870-90, 4½"...**800.00**
Bucket, staved wood, 2 bentwood bands, fine dk patina, 12x13"...**275.00**
Bucket, tapered staves, 3 bentwood bands, copper rivets, ML, 7", NM ...**265.00**
Bucket, utility; staved w/wire/metal bands, gr pnt, w/lid, 17x16"...**925.00**
Carrier, sewing; 3-finger, silk lined, w/lid, 1850s, 3½x9½"..........**700.00**
Carrier, 2-finger, copper tacks, bentwood hdl, 7x13x9½", VG....**350.00**
Carrier, 3-finger, pine/birch, stained, swing hdl, 6⅜" L **495.00**
Carrier, 4-finger, copper rnd-head tacks, red traces, 11" L...........**400.00**
Carrier, 4-finger, pine/ash w/stain, copper tacks, CB, 13" L **425.00**
Chair, side; #3, dk stain, orig tape seat, ML, ca 1870, 34"..........**650.00**
Chair, side; #4, low bk, tape seat, ML, ca 1900, 28" **515.00**
Chair, side; maple, 3-slat bk, mc tape seat, CB, 40½" **750.00**
Chair, side; maple, 3-slat bk, splint seat, ML, 37" **115.00**
Chair, side; 3-arch slat-bk, tape seat, trn legs, rfn, 1850s, 41" **920.00**
Chest, blanket; pine, dvtl drw, bracket ft, rfn, ML, 18x38".......**1,500.00**
Cupboard, butternut, 2 doors & 10 drw, EF, 1850s, 104x62" ...**2,500.00**
Cupboard, hanging; pine, red pnt, panel door, 1850s, 34x19" .**1,000.00**
Cupboard, panel door over 3 drws, old brn pnt, ML, rstr, 1830s, 63x25"...**2,300.00**
Cupboard, pine step-bk w/3 panel doors, WV, 1830s, 84x43x16" ...**2,500.00**
Cupboard, tool; pine, walnut drw fronts, gray pnt, MA, 45x39" **1,955.00**
Dipper, heavy gauge tin, long hdl w/D-shaped ring, CB, 13" **250.00**
Drying rack, cherry, 3 bars on trestle ft, rfn, 37x30" **300.00**
Foot warmer, dvtl walnut, tin int, velvet cover, ML, 7x8" **595.00**
Footstool, #1, tape seat, trn stretchers, ML, 9½x13x9½" **485.00**
Footstool, pine, brn stain, nailed, 5-brd, 9½x15x8" **750.00**
Lamp filler, tin conical form, CB, 19th C, 8", EX........................**150.00**
Measure, grain; oak/pine, ME stencil, 1880-96, 4x7½" **235.00**
Niddy noddy, old finish, ML, 18½"...**95.00**
Photo, teacher & pupils, CB, 1880s, VG....................................**160.00**
Pincushion, saddle-shaped wood w/velvet cushion, CB, 3x3½"..**340.00**
Rocker, arm; #1, maple, tape seat/bk, acorn finials, ML, 28".......**575.00**
Rocker, arm; #1, tape seat, ML label, 29", EX.............................**935.00**
Rocker, arm; #3, tape bk & seat, acorn finials, ML, 33½"...........**500.00**
Rocker, arm; #5, uphl bk/seat, trn stiles/acorn finials, ML, 38" ...**500.00**
Rocker, arm; #5, 4-slat bk, trn stiles, rpl tape seat, ML, 1880-1930...**1,650.00**
Rocker, arm; #6, tape seat, orig dk finish, ML, 41½"...................**880.00**
Rocker, arm; #6, w/bar, tape seat, NL, 1880-1900, 43" **750.00**
Rocker, arm; #7, orig dk varnish, rpl seat, ML, 41" **1,045.00**

Rocking chair, #7, acorn finials, taped back and seat, double stretchers, turned front legs, Mt. Lebanon, old finish, ca 1900, 42", $575.00.

Rocker, arm; banister bk, 1800s, poor splint seat, 1800s, 41" **325.00**
Rocker, arm; 4 arched slats, taped seat, old blk pnt, CB, 1840s, 45"...**2,185.00**
Rocker, armless; #3, old finish w/decal, NY, ca 1900, 33" **230.00**
Rocker, armless; #7, orig varnish, ML, 42" **500.00**
Rug, shag; mc knitted woolens on cotton ground, 1890s, 24x40"..**250.00**
Rug, sheared, concentric mc circles, 41½" **200.00**
Rug whip, wood & wire, ML, 26" **335.00**
Seed sower, pine/poplar w/galvanized metal, red pnt, EF, 10" **220.00**
Stove, CI, canted sides, 3-leg w/penny ft, 17x33x13" **500.00**
Stove set (shovel & tongs), wrought iron, att CB, 18", 22", pr...**500.00**
Swift, maple, table type, 19th C, 25x30" dia, EX.......................**230.00**
Swift, trn maple, simple styling, EX patina, 19th C, 21" open **165.00**
Table, birch, 1-drw, CB, 24½x28x17" **9,350.00**
Table, drop leaf; pine/ash/birch, red traces, CB, 72" L.............**2,000.00**
Table, work; Hplwht, breadboard top, stain traces, 56x40" **600.00**
Teapot, tin, side spout, 8½" **165.00**
Tub, rnd staves w/wooden bands, worn patina, 6¾x18" **275.00**

Shaving Mugs

Between 1865 and 1920, owning a personalized shaving mug was the order of the day, and the 'occupationals' were the most prestigious. The majority of men having occupational mugs would often frequent the barber shop several times a week, where their mugs were clearly visible for all to see in the barber's rack. As a matter of fact, this display was in many ways the index of the individual town or neighborhood.

During the first twenty years, blank mugs were almost entirely imported from France, Germany, and Austria and were hand painted in this country. Later on, some china was produced by local companies. It is noteworthy that American vitreous china is inferior to the imported Limoges and is subject to extreme crazing.

Artists employed by the American barber supply companies were for the most part extremely talented and capable of executing any design the owner required, depicting his occupation, fraternal affiliation, or preferred sport. When the mug was completed, the name and the gold trim were always added in varying degrees, depending on the price paid by the customer. This price was determined by the barber who added his markup to that of the barber-supply company. As mentioned above, the popularity of the occupational shaving mug diminished with the advent of World War I and the introduction by Gillette of the safety razor. Later followed the blue laws forcing barber shops to close on Sundays, thereby eliminating the political and social discussions for which they were so well noted.

Occupational shaving mugs are the most sought after of the group which would also include those with sport affiliations. Fraternal mugs, although desirable, do not command the same price as the occupationals. Occasionally, you will find the owner's occupation together with his fraternal affiliation. This combination could add anywhere between 25% to 50% to the price, which is dependent on the execution of the painting, rarity of the subject, and detail. Some subjects can be done very simply; others can be done in extreme detail, commanding substantially higher prices. It is fair to say, however, that the rarity of the occupation will dictate the price. Mugs with heavily worn gold lose between 20% and 30% of their value immediately. This would not apply to the gold trim around the rim, but to the loss of the name itself. Our advisor for this category is Burton Handelsman; he is listed in the Directory under New York.

Advertising, ...Antiseptic Soap Used Here, Germany, M **160.00**
Comic, frog smoking pipe while fishing, 3⅜" **450.00**
Comic, man & woman on bench, My Mind Rebels at Stagnation, Germany......**350.00**
Decorative, bird holds banner w/name & flowers, 3¾", M............**75.00**
Decorative, bust of pretty lady in reserve, D&Co on base, 3½" ..**250.00**

Decorative, crane & owl in separate floral frames, Kern, M........**200.00**
Decorative, drapery & flowers, Limoges, M....................................**75.00**
Decorative, drapery & hanging flower basket, T&V Limoges, 3⅝", M **100.00**
Decorative, florals & fancy gold name, D&Co France, 4".........**185.00**
Decorative, owl on branch w/smiling moon, Am, 3⅝".........**375.00**
Decorative, snow scene w/cottage & birds, Kern, 3⅞" **100.00**
Decorative, 2 horses in field during lightning storm, Koken, M..**150.00**
Decorative, 3 lg flowers, Limoges, 3⅝", M............................**170.00**
Fraternal, B of LF & E, locomotive & tender, Germany, M **135.00**
Fraternal, Jr Order of United Auto Mechanics, Vienna Austria, M ..**135.00**
Fraternal, Knights of Columbus, emblem, ca 1900, Austria, 3⅝" ..**150.00**
Fraternal, Knights of Golden Eagle, emblem, Germany, 3⅝" **250.00**
Fraternal, Knights of Pythias, emblem, T&V Limoges...................**50.00**
Fraternal, Knights of Templar, emblem, ca 1908, 3⅝" **200.00**
Fraternal, Odd Fellows, emblem/Bible/sword, 3⅝" **150.00**
Fraternal, POS of A (Patriotic Order of Sons of Am), emblem, 3½"...**135.00**
Hotel, 13 (room number) & flowers w/gold, unusual **150.00**
Occupational, American Express surrounds Am shield, M **1,250.00**
Occupational, baker, detailed bakery scene.............................**475.00**
Occupational, baker, man w/horse-drawn delivery wagon, 1885-1925, M..**650.00**
Occupational, bartender, bar scene, 4" **425.00**
Occupational, bicyclist, racing bicycle, Germany, 3¼".............**675.00**
Occupational, blacksmith, anvil & tools, Germany, 4" **200.00**
Occupational, brakeman w/caboose, PRR, Limoges, 3⅝".........**550.00**
Occupational, brick mason at wall, Am, 1885-1925, M **450.00**
Occupational, bull running, much gold, JPL France, M.............**425.00**
Occupational, carpenter planing wood, EX art, 3¾" **575.00**
Occupational, clerk waiting on lady, floral fr, 3⅝"....................**400.00**
Occupational, conductor, trolley w/crew, 1881-1925, T&V Limoges **600.00**
Occupational, druggist, mortar & pestle, 3⅝"...........................**160.00**
Occupational, farmer w/horse-drawn plow, Germany, 3⅝" **350.00**
Occupational, Habaneros, cigar bundle, Austria, 3⅝", M **525.00**
Occupational, horse beside fence, Am, 1885-1925, M **150.00**
Occupational, horse breeder/trainer, horse standing, Germany...**200.00**
Occupational, locomotive (BCRR) & tender, Vienna, lg, M......**250.00**
Occupational, man driving early motorcar, Germany, 3¾", NM ..**1,450.00**
Occupational, man w/horse-drawn wagon of cartons, 1885-1925, M..**400.00**
Occupational, man working on lg boiler, 1885-1925, VG **1,000.00**

Occupational, man on porch of large Victorian house (fine detail), ca 1890 – 1925, KPM Germany, 3⅝", $1,000.00.

Occupational, oilman, derrick & steam engine, Limoges, 3⅝" ...**725.00**
Occupational, painter, bucket & brushes, prof rpr, 4"............**350.00**
Occupational, Statue of Liberty & flowers, 3½", M **425.00**
Occupational, steer's head, Germany, 3⅞", M...........................**90.00**
Occupational, stemmed glass filled w/beer, 3⅝", M....................**210.00**
Occupational, tailor at bench, prof rpr, 3¾" **200.00**
Occupational, telegraph key, Am, 1885-1925, 4", M..................**400.00**
Occupational, tinsmith, furnace & tools, Germany, 3¼" **150.00**
Occupational, tobacco bundle, PHL Vienna, 3⅞", M...............**500.00**
Occupational, trainman, locomotive & tender, maroon wrap, 4" **200.00**
Occupational, turbine w/much detail, Vienna Austria/P Eisemann, M ..**525.00**
Occupational, violin w/bow, T&V Limoges France, 3⅝", M **525.00**

Occupational, 2 bucking goats, name in gold, minor pnt rstr, 3⅜" ..**160.00**

Occupational, 2 men on railroad hand car, Am, 1885-1925, M ...**1,600.00**

Patriotic, eagle & crossed Am flags, Germany, 1929, 3⅝" **220.00**

Patriotic, eagle/shield/flags, full bl wrap, 3¾".....................**325.00**

Patriotic, soldier w/Am flag, encampment, WWI era, M **2,500.00**

Photographic, reserve of named gentleman, 4", M **1,250.00**

Photographic, steam engine & man standing along side, T&V France ..**875.00**

Sportsman, dog w/bird in mouth, rifle, fishing equipment, Limoges, M..**200.00**

Sportsman, hunter w/dog on point, Limoges, Koken, 4", M........**325.00**

Sportsman, 2 men in canoe w/stringer of fish, sm prof rpr...........**135.00**

Shawnee

The Shawnee Pottery Company operated in Zanesville, Ohio, from 1937 to 1961. They produced inexpensive novelty ware (vases, flowerpots, and figurines) as well as a very successful line of figural cookie jars, creamers, and salt and pepper shakers.

They also produced three dinnerware lines, the first of which, Valencia, was designed by Louise Bauer in 1937 for Sears & Roebuck. A starter set was given away with the purchase of one of their refrigerators. Second and most popular was the Corn line. The original design was called White Corn. In 1946 the line was expanded and the color changed to a more natural yellow hue. It was marketed under the name Corn King, and it was produced from 1946 to 1954. Then the colors were changed again. Kernels became a lighter yellow and shucks a darker green. This variation was called Corn Queen. Their third dinnerware line, produced after 1954, was called Lobsterware. It was made in either black, brown, or gray; lobsters were usually applied to serving pieces and accessory items.

For further study we recommend these books: *The Collector's Guide to Shawnee Pottery* by Janice and Duane Vanderbilt, who are listed in the Directory under Indiana; and *Shawnee Pottery, An Identification and Value Guide*, by Jim and Bev Mangus, who are listed in Ohio.

Cookie Jars

Note: The prices in the following listings should be considered minimum values.

Puss 'n Boots, short tail, flowers and gold trim, marked Patented Puss 'n Boots USA, $550.00; Muggsy, with flowers and gold trim, marked Patented Muggsy USA, $1,000.00. (Photo courtesy Ermagene Westfall)

Basketweave, decal, mk USA **120.50**

Cottage, mk USA #6 ....**1,500.00**

Drum Major, mk USA #10 ....**575.00**

Fruit Basket, mk Shawnee #84 ....**225.00**

Jack, bl pants, wht top, mk USA **100.00**

Jack, striped pants, gold & decals, mk USA........................**400.00**

Jack, striped pants, mk USA **200.00**

Jill, bl skirt, bl trim on wht top, mk USA **100.00**

Jill, tulip on skirt, mk USA..**250.00**

Jill, yel skirt, bl trim on wht top, mk USA.........................**125.00**

Jo Jo the Clown, mk Shawnee #12 ....**475.00**

Little Chef, mc, mk USA..**150.00**

Little Chef, yel, mk USA..**175.00**

Muggsy, mk Pat Muggsy USA..**550.00**

Owl, gold & decals, mk USA..**350.00**

Owl, mk USA **150.00**

Pennsylvania Dutch, mk USA...**275.00**

Puss 'n Boots, long tail, mk Pat Puss 'n Boots **200.00**

Smiley the Pig, bl neckerchief, mk USA.............................**175.00**

Smiley the Pig, chrysanthemums, mk USA **400.00**

Smiley the Pig, roses, gold & decals, mk USA.....................**700.00**

Winnie the Pig, bl collar, mk USA **375.00**

Corn Line

When a range of values is given, use the low side to evaluate Queen Corn.

Bowl, cereal; King or Queen, mk #94 ....**50.00**

Bowl, fruit; King or Queen, mk #92..................................**48.00**

Bowl, mixing; King or Queen, mk #5, 5", from $22 to **25.00**

Bowl, mixing; King or Queen, mk #8, 8", from $35 to **45.00**

Bowl, vegetable; King or Queen, mk #95 ....**55.00**

Butter dish, King or Queen, mk #72, w/lid.........................**55.00**

Casserole, King, mk #74...**40.00**

Casserole, Queen, mk #74...**50.00**

Cookie jar, King or Queen, mk #66 ....**350.00**

Corn roast set, Queen, #108 ....**175.00**

Creamer, King, w/gold, mk #70 ....**95.00**

Creamer, King or Queen, mk #70 ....**25.00**

Creamer, White, mk USA **30.00**

Cup, King or Queen, mk #90, from $30 to **32.00**

Mug, King or Queen, mk #69...**50.00**

Pitcher, King or Queen, mk #71, from $60 to **70.00**

Pitcher, White, mk USA..**65.00**

Pitcher, White, w/gold, mk USA.......................................**120.00**

Platter, King or Queen, mk #96, 12"................................**55.00**

Popcorn set, Queen, mk #100 ....**200.00**

Relish, King or Queen, mk #79, from $30 to **40.00**

Shakers, King Indian, pr...**80.00**

Shakers, King or Queen, lg, pr **40.00**

Shakers, King or Queen, sm, pr **28.00**

Shakers, White, w/gold, sm, pr..**35.00**

Sugar bowl, King or Queen, mk #78, w/lid.........................**36.00**

Sugar bowl, White, gold trim, mk USA, w/lid **75.00**

Sugar shaker, White...**70.00**

Sugar shaker, White, w/gold..**110.00**

Teapot, King or Queen, mk #65, 10-oz.............................**175.00**

Teapot, White, gold trim, mk USA, 30-oz **85.00**

Kitchenware

Coffeepot, Pennsylvania Dutch, mk USA 52 ....**270.00**

Creamer, Elephant, wht w/gold trim, mk Pat USA **210.00**

Creamer, Puss 'n Boots, all gold, mk Pat Puss 'n Boots...............**480.00**

Creamer, Puss 'n Boots, gr & yel, mk Shawnee #85 ....**55.00**

Creamer, Smiley the Pig, clover bud on chest, mk Pat Smiley....**165.00**

Jug, ball; Snowflake, mk USA..**45.00**

Jug, ball; tulip, mk USA...**115.00**

Pitcher, Bo Peep, gold trim, mk Shawnee #47, 30-oz **175.00**

Pitcher, Bo Peep, mk Pat Bo Peep **90.00**

Pitcher, Chanticleer, all gold, mk Chanticleer....................**450.00**

Pitcher, Chanticleer, plain, mk Pat Chanticleer **90.00**

Pitcher, Smiley the Pig, emb clover, mk Pat Smiley USA..........**200.00**

Shakers, Bo Peep & Sailor Boy, gold trim, sm, pr **95.00**

Shakers, Chanticleer, lg, pr...**50.00**

Shakers, Dutch Boy & Girl, gold trim, lg, pr............................75.00
Shakers, fruit, mc, mk USA, lg, pr..40.00
Shakers, jugs, wht, lg, pr..25.00
Shakers, milk can, sm, pr..35.00
Shakers, Muggsy, gold trim, sm, pr...200.00
Shakers, Puss 'n Boots, sm, pr 35.00
Shakers, Smiley, gr bib w/gold & decals, lg, pr........................180.00
Shakers, Smiley, peach bib, sm, pr..50.00
Shakers, wheelbarrows, sm, pr..226.00
Shakers, Winnie & Smiley, bl neckerchiefs, lg, pr.....................135.00
Teapot, elephant, mk USA, 5-cup..135.00
Teapot, Granny Ann, mk USA..175.00
Teapot, heart-shaped flower decor, mk USA..............................50.00
Teapot, Pennsylvania Dutch, mk USA #27, 27-oz......................80.00
Teapot, Tom Tom, mk Tom The Piper's Son Pat USA...............120.00

Lobsterware

Baker, open, #915...40.00
Bean pot, #925..750.00
Butter dish, w/lid, #927...110.00
Casserole, Fr; #904, 2-qt..30.00
Creamer, jug style, #921...50.00
Hors d' oeuvre holder, #932..280.00
Plate, compartment; #912..100.00
Range set, #906, 4-pc...70.00
Shakers, claw, pr..40.00
Shakers, full body, pr..225.00
Spoon holder, dbl, #935...250.00

Valencia

Ashtray..24.00
Bowl, fruit; 5"..17.00
Bowl, mixing; 7"...22.00
Bowl, mixing; 9"...22.00
Candle holders, bulb, pr..35.00
Coffeepot, AD or regular...38.00
Cup, coffee; AD..22.00
Cup, cream soup...14.00
Fork, 9½"...35.00
Jug, 2-pt...30.00
Pie plate, 9¼"...20.00

Pitcher, with lid, two quart, $45.00.
(Photo courtesy Duane Vanderbilt)

Plate, 6½"...12.00
Refrigerator set, 3-pc..75.00
Shakers, pr...30.00
Sugar bowl, w/lid..25.00
Teapot, 8-cup...65.00
Tray, relish; compartment..135.00

Tray, utility; 10½"...18.00
Vase, flower; 8"...14.00

Miscellaneous

Bank, bull dog..250.00
Bank, tumbling bear..240.00
Figurine, Pekingese, gold & decals, mini................................175.00
Figurine, puppy dog, gold & decals, mini...............................175.00
Goblet, gold, mk Hand Decorated 24k Gold.............................60.00
Pie bird...50.00
Sock darner, mk USA..95.00
Sugar bowl, bucket form, w/lid, mk USA..................................50.00
Sugar bowl, fruit-basket style, w/lid, mk Shawnee #83..............65.00
Sugar bowl, Pennsylvania Dutch, tab hdls, w/lid, mk USA........120.00
Sugar bowl, Sunflower, w/lid, mk USA.....................................80.00

Shearwater

Since 1928 generations of the Peter, Walter, and James McConnell Anderson families have been producing figurines and artwares in their studio at Ocean Springs, Mississippi. Their work is difficult to date. Figures from the '20s and '30s won critical acclaim and have continued to be made to the present time. Early marks include a die-stamped 'Shearwater' in a dime-sized circle, a similar ink stamp, and a half-circle mark. Any older item may still be ordered in the same glazes as it was originally produced, so many pieces on the market today may be relatively new. However, the older marks are not currently in use. Currently produced Blacks and pirates figurines are marked with a hand-incised 'Shearwater' and/or a cipher formed with an 'S' whose bottom curve doubles as the top loop of a 'P' formed by the addition of an upright placed below and to the left of the S. Many are dated, '93, for example. These figures are generally valued at $35.00 to $50.00 and are available at the pottery or by mail order. New decorated and carved pieces are very expensive, starting at $400.00 to $500.00 for a 6" pot.

Bowl, emb peppers, 1¼" H...50.00
Figurine, sea gull, bl & teal crackle w/incising, 1940s, 5½x10½"...1,200.00
Figurines, Black group: fiddler father, dancer mother, son w/accordion ...60.00
Goblet, waves, Walter Anderson/Peter Anderson, 1955, 4¾" .1,100.00
Pitcher, gr matt w/metallic-like sheen, 1940s, 5⅛".................120.00
Teapot, gr & bl drip, Peter Anderson, 1930, 6x8½" 400.00
Vase, fish/sea plants sgraffito on cobalt, MA & PA, 10¾x6½" 3,000.00
Vase, gr & gunmetal, bulbous, flared rim, 6½".........................250.00
Vase, Mayan motif under bl & amber flambe, 7x7".................1,200.00
Vase, primrose under bl & pk semimatt, pierced shoulder, 5¼x6" ...750.00
Vase, turq & gr, cylinder w/can neck, 1930s, 5¾".....................330.00
Vase, Zodiac icons, ivory on gunmetal, 12x7½"......................1,750.00

Sheet Music

Sheet music is often collected more for its colorful lithographed covers, rather than for the music itself. Transportation songs (which have pictures or illustrations of trains, ships, and planes), Ragtime and Blues, Comic Characters (especially Disney), Sports, Political, and Expositions are eagerly sought after. Much of the sheet music on the market today is valued at under $5.00; some of the better examples are listed here. For more information refer to *Sheet Music Reference and Price Guide, Second Edition,* by Anna Marie Guiheen and Marie-Reine A. Pafik. Values are given for examples in excellent to near-mint condition unless otherwise noted.

After the Battle, Paul Dresser, 1905......................................**15.00**
All By Myself, Irving Berlin, 1921 ....**10.00**
America First, Howard Kocain, 1916......................................**15.00**
And the Band Played On, Palmer & Ward, 1895 ....**15.00**
Around the World in 80 Days, Adamson & Young, Movie: same, 1956...**5.00**
Atlantic City Pageant, John Philip Sousa, 1927......................**15.00**
Ballad of Davy Crockett, George Gruns, Photo: Fess Parker **5.00**
Beautiful Thoughts of Love, Jerome Heller, 1910......................**10.00**
Best Man, Alfred & Wise, Photo: Nat King Cole Trio, 1946 ....**5.00**
Blue Orchids, Hoagy Carmichael, 1939......................................**5.00**
Brazil, Bob Russell, Movie: Saludos Amigos (Disney), 1939 ....**15.00**
Bye Bye Blackbird, Dixon & Henderson, Photo: Gus Edwards, 1926...**5.00**
Caravan of Dreams, Fred Ahlert, Photo: Bing Crosby, 1947 ....**5.00**
Cherry Leaf Rag, Ed Cota, 1909 ....**10.00**
Cohen Owes Me, Irving Berlin, 1915......................................**15.00**
Cossack Love Song, George Gershwin, 1926 ....**10.00**
Curse, Paul Dresser, 1887 ....**15.00**
Dashing Cavaliers, ET Paull, 1938......................................**35.00**
Dixie Daisy, Halsey Mohr, 1911......................................**10.00**
Don't Forget Your Mother, Herndon Pence, 1934......................**5.00**
Down by the Erie Canal, George M Cohan **15.00**
Dreamy South Sea Moon, Hoyt, Cover Artist: Pfeiffer, 1929.........**10.00**
Entertainer's Rag, Jay Roberts, 1912 ....**20.00**
Eyes of the Army, Richard A Whiting, 1918 ....**15.00**
Fire & Rain, James Taylor, Photo: James Taylor, 1969 ....**5.00**
For Your Boy & My Boy, Kahn & Van Alstyne, 1918 ....**15.00**
Gasoline Gus & His Jitney Bus, Gay, 1915 ....**30.00**
Girl on the Automobile, Nathan, 1905......................................**15.00**
Golden Brown Blues, WC Handy, 1927......................................**10.00**
Good Morning Dixieland, Marshall, 1916......................................**10.00**
Guy Is a Guy, Oscar Brand, Photo: Doris Day, 1952 ....**5.00**
Hats Make the Woman, Victor Herbert, 1905......................**10.00**
He's Got My Goat, Smith, Cover Artist: Pfeiffer, 1912 ....**10.00**
Heat Wave, Irving Berlin, Musical: Easter Parade, 1933 ....**10.00**
Holiday Inn, Irving Berlin, 1942......................................**5.00**
Honored Dead, John Philip Sousa, 1896 ....**20.00**
I Beg of You, Elvis Presley, 1957......................................**20.00**
I Didn't Raise My Ford To Be a Jitney, Jack Frost, 1915 ....**25.00**
I Hate You Darling, Cole Porter, Movie: Let's Face It, 1943.............**5.00**
I'll Be a Soldier Boy, James Thatcher, 1915......................**10.00**
I'll See You Again, Noel Coward, Musical: Bitter Sweet, 1929.....**15.00**
I Love You Honolulu, Harry Lauder, Photo: Harry Lauder, 1915 ..**10.00**

I'm Building a Sailboat of Dreams, Cliff Friend & Dave Franklin, Guy Lombardo cover, 1939, $5.00.

I'm in Love Again, Cole Porter, 1925......................................**5.00**
I Sent My Wife to the 1,000 Islands, Al Jolson, 1916 ....**10.00**
I Want To Hold Your Hand, Beatles, 1978......................**25.00**
I Wonder Why She Kept on Saying Si-Si, Al Jolson, 1918..........**10.00**
If I Had You, Irving Berlin, 1914 ....**10.00**
If the Man In the Moon Were a Coon, Fred Fisher, 1905 ....**20.00**
In a Kingdom of My Own, George M Cohan......................**10.00**
In Philadelphia, Gus Edwards, 1909 ....**15.00**

In the Navy, Howard, 1918......................................**10.00**
Irish Eyes of Love, Ernest Ball, 1914......................................**5.00**
It's Home, Jack Yellen & Jay Gorney, Movie: Home, 1924.............**5.00**
It's Time To Close Your Drowsy Eyes, Henry Frantzen, 1910.........**10.00**
It's Too Late Now, Wm Tracey & Albert Von Tilzer, 1914.............**10.00**
Jockey Hat & Feather, Julia Brodwig, 1860......................**50.00**
Jolly Sailor, Harry J Lincoln, 1908......................................**15.00**
Kansas City Rag, James Scott, 1907......................................**10.00**
King Cotton March, John Philip Sousa, 1898......................**30.00**
Let It Snow, Sammy Cahn & Jule Styne, Photo: Perry Como, 1945....**5.00**
Lindy, Lindy!, Eisenbourg, Flight Map From USA-France, 1927 ..**50.00**
Little Toot, Allie Wrubel, Movie: Melody Time, Disney, 1948 .....**10.00**
Lizzie, R Barclay Brown, Musical: The Jail Birds, 1925................**10.00**
Love Dreams, George M Cohan **10.00**
Magna Carta, John Philip Sousa, 1927......................................**20.00**
Man I Love, Ira/George Gershwin, Movie: Strike Up the Band, 1945...**10.00**
Massa'a in the Cold Cold Ground, Stephen Foster, 1852.............**50.00**
Me & My Teddy Bear, Winters & Coots, Photo: Rosemary Clooney, 1950..**10.00**
Monkey Doodle Doo, Irving Berlin, Cover Artist: Pfeiffer, 1913 ..**15.00**
Motor Girl, Gus Edwards, 1909 ....**20.00**
My Little Book of Poetry, Irving Berlin, 1921 ....**10.00**
My Mother's Waltz, Dave Franklin, Photo: Bing Crosby, 1945 ....**5.00**
Nelly Bly, Stephen Foster, 1st edition, 1849......................**50.00**
Nobles of the Mystic Shrine March, John Philip Sousa, 1923.......**20.00**
Oh, That Cello, Charlie Chaplin, 1916......................................**15.00**
Oklahoma Hills, Jack & Woody Gunthrie, Photo: Jack Gunthrie...**10.00**
Ole Bossy Cow, Hattie Starr......................................**10.00**
One Boy, Adams & Strouse, Movie: Bye Bye Birdie, 1960.............**5.00**
Original Pags, Scott Joplin, 1899......................................**50.00**
Please Learn To Love, BC Hilliam, Musical: Buddies, 1919 ....**10.00**
Poor Jud, Rodgers & Hammerstein II, Musical: Oklahoma, 1943 ...**5.00**
Real Slow Rag, Scott Joplin, 1903......................................**50.00**
Rockabye Baby, Irving Berlin, 1924, Music Box Revue 1925 ....**10.00**
School of Ragtime, Scott Joplin, 1908......................................**50.00**
She Knows It, Al Jolson, 1921......................................**10.00**
She's Drivin' Me Wild, Gerald Marks & Buddy Fields, 1925.........**5.00**
Sky Anchors, Waring, 1942 ....**10.00**
Solace, Scott Joplin, Cover Artist: Shaw, 1909......................**50.00**
Some of These Days, Shelton Brooks, Photo: Sophie Tucker, 1937...**15.00**
Son of the Sheik, Photo: Rudolph Valentino, 1926......................**15.00**
St Louis Tickle, Barney & Seymour, 1904......................................**15.00**
Sugar Cane Rag, Scott Joplin, 1908......................................**50.00**
Sweet & Low-Down, Ira/George Gershwin, Musical: Tip Toes, 1925 ..**5.00**
Swipsey Cake Walk, Arthur Marshal & Scott Joplin, 1900...........**50.00**
Thanksgivin', Hoagy Carmichael & Johhny Mercer, 1932 ....**5.00**
There's a Girl in Havana, Irving Berlin, 1911......................**10.00**
Till There Was You, Meredith Wilson, Movie: The Music Man, 1950...**5.00**
Uncle Ned, Stephen Foster, 1945 ....**50.00**
Waltz of Memory, John Burger, Movie: It Happens on Ice, 1951 ....**5.00**
Welcome Song, Kermit Goell & Fred Spielman, 1945 ....**5.00**
When I Kissed the Blarney Stone, Walter Scanlan, Irish, 1923 ......**5.00**

Shell-Work Collectibles

Not long after the natural beauty of the shell was discovered, man began to use them for decorative purposes of many types. Shells were used to decorate clothing and household items as well as jewelry, personal gifts, and souvenirs. Remains of shell necklaces have been found that date to a time prior to the great flood!

During Victorian times shell work became a hobby for the middle class. Shell-work jewelry became popular at that time, but very little has survived due to its delicate nature. Examples of love tokens, souvenirs, and whimsies from that era are listed below. For further information we recommend *Neptune's Treasures, A Study and Value Guide*, available from our advisors, Carole and Richard Smyth (see their listing in the Directory under New York for ordering information).

Box, cushion top, fancy shell borders & sides, from $175 to **250.00**
Box, decor top & borders w/sm ship scene, rectangular, from $150 to...**300.00**
Box, desk; Victorian lady litho on lid, shell borders, from $125 to.........**300.00**
Box, heart shape, shell border & sides, cushion top, from $150 to.........**300.00**
Box, lg cowrie on lid w/overall decor, w/ or w/o ft, from $150 to **400.00**
Box, mussel shells form stylized flower, overall decor, 1800s, $150 to...**400.00**
Box, sailing scene top, fancy shell borders, from $150 to **400.00**
Framed picture, chromolitho under flat glass, from $150 to **500.00**
Hand mirror, lady's, shells on bk & hdl, Victorian, from $100 to ..**200.00**
Handbag, rectangular w/woven hdl, overall decor, souvenir, $150 to..**400.00**
Horseshoe, scene under glass in center, from $125 to **300.00**
Inkstand, ship scene, overall decor, souvenir, from $50 to...........**300.00**
Letter holder, chromolitho print & overall shells, from $125 to .**300.00**
Love token, anchor shape (symbol of dependability), Victorian .**350.00**
Miniature, dresser, overall decor, lift-lid w/cushion, from $175 to ..**400.00**
Miniature bellows, overall decor, from $50 to **300.00**
Miniature chest, overall decor, ftd, Made in England, from $150 to ...**250.00**
Paperweight, inscr w/name of town or vacation area, from $50 to **180.00**
Pin holder, decor front, bk: love message, pins around edge, $50 to....**150.00**
Pincushion, crown shape, shell & silk, Victorian, EX, from $125 to..**300.00**
Purse, hinged shell, tiny chain hdl, souvenir, mini, from $50 to .**100.00**
Roundel, litho scene under glass w/layered shells, from $125 to .**300.00**
Shoe, overall decor, from $150 to **300.00**
Star, print under glass, shells/mosses/grasses on points, $125 to ..**300.00**
Symbol of faith, mini shrine, etc, ea, from $50 to........................**250.00**

Shelley

In 1872 Joseph Shelley became partners with James Wileman, owner of Foley China Works, thus creating Wileman & Co. in Stoke-on-Trent. Twelve years later James Wileman withdrew from the company, though the firm continued to use his name until 1925 when it became known as Shelley Potteries, Ltd. Like many successful nineteenth-century English potteries, this firm continued to produce useful household wares as well as dinnerware of considerable note. In 1896 the beautiful Dainty White shape was introduced, and it is regarded by many as synonymous with the name Shelley. In addition to the original Dainty (six-flute) design, other lovely shapes were produced: Ludlow (fourteen-flute), Oleander (petal shape), Stratford (twelve-flute), Queen Anne (with eight angular panels), Ripon (with its distinctive pedestal), and the 1930s shapes of Vogue, Eve, and Regent.

Though often overlooked, striking earthenware was produced under the direction of Frederick Rhead and later Walter Slater and his son Eric. Many notable artists contributed their talents in designing unusual, attractive wares: Rowland Morris, Mabel Lucie Attwell, and Hilda Cowham, to name but a few.

In 1966 Allied English Potteries acquired control of the Shelley Company, and by 1967 the last of the exquisite Shelley China had been produced to honor remaining overseas orders. In 1971 Allied English Potteries merged with the Doulton group.

It had to happen: Shelley forgeries! Chris Davenport, author of *Shelley Pottery, The Later Years*, reports seeing Mocha-shape cups and saucers with the Shelley mark. However, on close examination it is evident that the mark has been applied to previously unmarked wares too poorly done to have ever left the Shelley pottery. This Shelley mark can actually be 'felt,' as the refiring is not done at the correct temperature to allow it to be fully incorporated into the glaze. (Beware! These items are often seen on Internet auction sites.)

Some Shelley patterns (Dainty Blue, Bridal Rose, Blue Rock) have been seen on Royal Albert and Queensware pieces. These companies are part of the Royal Doulton Group.

Note: Measurements for objects with lids are measured to the top of the finial unless stated otherwise. It should also be made known that Rose Spray and Bridal Rose are the same pattern. Our advisors for this category are Lila and Fred Shrader; they are listed in the Directory under California.

Key:
LF — Late Foley
MLA — Mabel Lucie Attwell
QA — Queen Anne shape
R&RD — Rose & Red Daisy
RPFMN — Rose, Pansy, Forget-Me-Not
Trio — Cup, saucer, and 8" plate unless stated otherwise
W — Wileman, pre-1910

Advertising ashtray, Ellis's ginger ale, soda water, 6 sided, 5½".....**48.00**
Advertising figure, Shelley Lady seated on pedestal, 11½" **4,500.00**
Advertising sign, oval, Shelley in script **445.00**
Ash box, Melody Chintz, 4 rests, 2¾" sq, w/rolled-in edge, 1¼" ..**48.00**
Ash tray, Dainty Green, Mauve or Yellow, 3½" dia, from $55 to..**85.00**
Bowl, fruit, Begonia, Blue Rock, Regency, Dainty shape, 5½", $25 to **40.00**
Bowl, rim soup, Begonia/Blue Rock/Regency, Dainty shape, 8½", $35 to.**50.00**
Bowl, vegetable; Blue Rock or Regency, Dainty shape, 4x9".......**225.00**

Bowl, vegetable; Violets, with dome lid and handles, 6x9", **$515.00.**

Butter pat, Bridal Rose or Pansy (repeat), 3⅛" **35.00**
Butter pat, Campanula or Violets, 3⅛"..**45.00**
Butter pat, Pansy, lg, Dainty shape, 3⅞".....................................**95.00**
Cake plate, Green Daisy Chintz, tab hdls, 8x10½"......................**72.00**
Cake plate, Wild Flowers, Dainty shape, tab hdls, 8x10½" **62.00**
Candy dish, Dainty Blue, tab hdls, 4½x5½" **48.00**
Candy dish, Primrose Chintz, Dainty shape w/10 flutes, 4½"........**43.00**
Children's ware, egg cup, dbl; Old King Cole, 3⅝".......................**66.00**
Children's ware, milk jug shell w/seaweed hdl & base by Hilda Cowham...**495.00**
Children's ware, MLA potty, Boo-Boo, girl & mushrooms **493.00**
Children's ware, teapot, tent, Hilda Cowham, 5¼" **750.00**
Coffeepot, Begonia or Campanula, Dainty shape, 7¾"................**235.00**
Coffeepot, Sheraton or Wreath of Leaves, Gainsborough shape, 7½" ...**179.00**
Condiment set, Harmont, 2 shakers+covered mustard on fitted tray.......**85.00**
Creamer, Harebell, Oleander shape, 3"...**45.00**
Creamer & sugar bowl, Rambler Rose, Dainty shape, +7¼" oval tray...**155.00**
Creamer & sugar bowl, Violets, Dainty shape, +7¼" oval tray ...**148.00**
Creamer & sugar bowl, Wild Anemone, Dainty shape **78.00**
Creamer & sugar bowl, Woodland, Henley shape..........................**58.00**
Crested ware, figurine, bulldog in doghouse, Wrexham, 4" **23.00**
Crested ware, figurine, elephant, Llanelly **43.00**
Crested ware, figurine, Some Pup, Arbroath, 4" **125.00**
Crested ware, model, Sir Walter Scott's Torquay crest, 2½".........**33.00**
Crested ware, pill box, Guernsey crest, Wileman, 2⅛" dia...........**42.00**
Cup & saucer, Bailey's Pink & Grey Flowers, #2462, Dainty shape...**114.00**
Cup & saucer, Begonia, Henley shape w/pk Laurel trim.................**58.00**
Cup & saucer, Blue Pansy Chintz int, bl ext & saucer, Boston shape ..**125.00**
Cup & saucer, Bridal Rose, Westminster shape, mini, 1¼".........**143.00**

Cup & saucer, Chevrons, pnt fruit w/truncated J, Mode shape ...**182.00**
Cup & saucer, Dainty Mauve, from $95 to ...**119.00**
Cup & saucer, demitasse; Bridal Rose or Rosebud, Ludlow shape, $48 to...**55.00**
Cup & saucer, demitasse; Campanula, Rosebud or R&RD Dainty shape...**55.00**
Cup & saucer, demitasse; Harebell, Oleander shape ...**60.00**
Cup & saucer, demitasse; RPFMN or Lilac Time, Dainty shape, $55 to..**65.00**
Cup & saucer, Maytime int, pk ext & saucer, ftd Oleander, $120 to...**151.00**
Cup & saucer, Petunia, Snowdrop shape, Wileman, 1890s to 1910...**78.00**
Cup & saucer, Primrose Chintz, Canterbury shape, mini, 1⅝" ...**407.00**
Cup & saucer, Violets, Canterbury shape, mini, 1⅝" ...**145.00**
Cup & saucer, Wine Grape, Westminster shape, mini, 1⅛"...**246.00**
Cup & saucer, Yellow Wild Flower w/gray crystals, #13793, Dainty shape...**60.00**
Egg cup, Dainty Green, Mauve, Pink or Yellow, 2½", from $65 to ...**95.00**
Egg cup, Dainty white w/yel polka dots, Dainty shape, 2½"...**122.00**
Egg cup, dbl; RPFMN, R&RD, Dainty shape, 3¾", from $50 to...**68.00**
Egg cup, R&RD, Stocks, Violets, Dainty shape, 2½", from $32 to ..**40.00**
Egg cup set, Lily of the Valley, Dainty shape, stand+4 cups, 1¾" ..**285.00**
Figurine, bird, Blue Creeper, 4¼" ...**135.00**
Figurine, Boo-Boo on dog, MLA, 2¾", from $375 to ...**525.00**
Food mold, angular design w/indented center, oval, 7¾x3" ...**76.00**
Gravy boat, Blue Rock, Rosebud, Regency, Dainty shape, +liner, $100 to ...**135.00**
Gravy boat, Harebell, Oleander shape, +liner ...**125.00**
Horn (tall mug w/hdl), Dainty White w/pk polka dots, 4" ...**177.00**
Horn (tall mug w/hdl), Primrose, R&RD or Stocks, 4", from $58 to ...**75.00**
Jam/honey pot, Wild Anenome, Dainty shape, notched lid & 4½" liner ..**138.00**
Mustard pot, Dainty Blue, notched lid, 2¼" ...**127.00**
Napkin ring, Blue Rock, Bridal Rose or Rosebud...**90.00**
Napkin ring, Primrose Chintz ...**137.00**
Plate, Begonia/Blue Rock/Celandine/Rambler Rose, Dainty shape, 6", $10..**15.00**
Plate, Blue Rock/Primrose/Rose Spray/R&RD, Dainty shape, 7", $12 to..**20.00**
Plate, Bridal Rose/Celandine/Harebell/R&RD, Dainty shape, 8", $35 to..**50.00**
Plate, Countryside Chintz, 6"...**65.00**
Plate, Maytime Chintz, 10¼"...**76.00**
Platter, Dainty Blue, 13x10½" ...**325.00**
Platter, Harebell, Oleander shape, 13x10½" ...**148.00**
Relish dish, RPFMN, Dainty shape, oval, 7x4"...**88.00**
Shakers, Blue Rock, cylindrical, Dainty shape, unmk, 2¾"...**125.00**
Smoke set, Primrose, Dainty shape, 2" cigarette holder+2 3" ashtrays ..**65.00**
Sugar bowl, Blue Rock, Dainty shape, ind sz...**19.00**
Tea & toast set, Dainty Green, oval plate w/indentation+cup, 5x8" ...**176.00**
Tea & toast set, Stocks, Dainty shape, plate w/indentation+cup, 5x8"...**88.00**
Teapot, Anenome Bunch, Regent shape, 6"...**135.00**
Teapot, Bridal Rose, Dainty shape, 6¾" ...**376.00**
Teapot, Dainty Mauve, 5½"...**676.00**
Teapot, Dainty White, 6"...**177.00**
Teapot, Dubarry, Gainsborough shape, 5¼" ...**165.00**
Teapot, Pink Harlequin, Carlisle shape, 6"...**95.00**
Teapot, Pink Moss Rose, #2436, Dainty shape, 5¼" ...**299.00**
Teapot, Rosebud, Dainty shape, 5½" ...**265.00**
Teapot, Rosebud, Dainty shape, 6¾" ...**360.00**
Teapot, Woodland, Henley shape, 5¾" ...**135.00**
Toast rack, Dainty Blue, 3 bars, 5¾x4" ...**460.00**
Toast rack, Maytime Chintz, 3 panels, 5" ...**138.00**
Tray, Begonia/Regency, Dainty shape, shell-like hdls, 9½x5", $85 to...**110.00**
Tray, Trees & Sunset, rtcl hdl, 10x4½"...**118.00**
Trio, Cape Gooseberry, #12299, Regent shape, plate: 5½" sq...**66.00**
Trio, Crabtree, #11651, Queen Anne shape, plate: 5½"...**135.00**
Trio, Melody, Ripon shape w/rich gold ped...**200.00**
Trio, My Garden, #11607, Queen Anne shape, plate: 6" ...**120.00**
Trio, Pink Moss Rose, #2424, Dainty shape ...**128.00**
Trio, Regency, Dainty shape, from $45 to...**85.00**
Trio, Sunrise & Tall Trees, #11678, Queen Anne shape, plate: 6" ...**148.00**
Trio, Thistle, Violets, Dainty shape ...**145.00**
Trio, Woodland, Richmond shape ...**110.00**
Vase, Balloons & Flashes, cylindrical, 8½x3½" ...**145.00**
Vase, Black Crackle, 6-sided, 7½" ...**76.00**
Vase, Blue Dragon Chintz w/gold trim, sq w/ped ft, 13" ...**375.00**
Vase, Green Dragon Chintz, 6-sided, 7" ...**335.00**
Vase, Green Dragon Chintz w/narrow neck, 5¾" ...**250.00**
Vase, Kingfisher, 5½"...**52.00**

Shenandoah

The Shenandoah Valley, extending from Virginia to Pennsylvania is well known for the fine pottery made there from the early 1800s until the turn of the century. It is characterized by bright, clear glazes in a variety of colors or in combination. Many small potteries were involved. Items marked 'Bell' indicate one of the larger companies.

Bank, brn sponging, bird finial w/nest & eggs, minor rstr, 5¾" ...**965.00**
Egg cup, wht slip on gr pebble glaze, 3", EX...**495.00**

Silhouettes

Silhouette portraits were made by positioning the subject between a bright light and a sheet of white drawing paper. The resulting shadow was then traced and cut out, the paper mounted over a contrasting color and framed. The hollow-cut process was simplified by an invention called the Physiognotrace, a device that allowed tracing and cutting to be done in one operation. Experienced silhouette artists could do full-length figures, scenics, ships, or trains freehand. Some of the most famous of these artists were Charles Peale Polk, Charles Wilson Peale, William Bache, Doyle, Edouart, Chamberlain, Brown, and William King. Though not often seen, some silhouettes were completely painted or executed in wax. Examples listed here are hollow-cut unless another type is described and assumed to be in excellent condition unless noted otherwise.

Key:
c/p — cut and pasted
p — profile
fl — full length

Full-figure cut silhouette of Charles Burrall Hoffman, artist signed, lithographed background, ca 1837, framed, VG, $1,265.00. (Photo courtesy Skinner, Inc.)

Child in dress, fl, c/p, gold/wht highlights, pencil details, fr: 8x6"...**1,265.00**
Girl, p, pencil details, identified 5-yr-old, 1822, 5x4"+fr...**495.00**
Lady, p, c/p, added oval mat, 7x5"+old blk fr...**195.00**
Lady, p, ink details, dress & collar cut from emb lt gr paper, 5x4" ..**250.00**
Lady, p, ink details, oval eglomise mat, 4x3¼" giltwood fr...**545.00**
Lady, p, low-cut neckline/jewelry, gilt detail on fiberboard, 9x8" ..**70.00**
Lady w/book, fl, fabric bk, pnt details, 3¾x2⅛"+fr ...**1,380.00**
Lady w/hair comb, p, puff sleeves, gilt fr, 7x6" ...**440.00**
Lady w/ribbon on bonnet, p, c/p, 4¾x3½"...**275.00**
Lady wearing hat, p, c/p, 3¼x2"...**50.00**
Man, p, c/p, ink details, 6x5⅛"...**300.00**

Man, p, ink details, sawtooth borders, tin fr, 3⅞x3" **440.00**
Man, p, label: Cut...Master Hubard, 6¼x5¼"+old gilt fr **300.00**
Man, p, late, in daguerreotype gutta percha case, 3¾x3½" **110.00**
Man & lady, p, c/p, ink details, domed glass/gilt fr, 5½x8⅝" **330.00**
Man in coat w/ruffled sleeves & cane, fl, blk fr/gilt liner, 12x9⅝" ..**110.00**
Man in high collar, p, sgn, old wood fr, 4x3⅜" **275.00**
Man w/lg crown flanked by flowers, p, c/p, PA, 7x6"+fr...............**330.00**
Man w/neck scarf, p, gray wash bkground, blk fr, 6½x5½" **100.00**

Silver

Coin Silver

During colonial times in America, the average household could not afford items made of silver, but those fortunate enough to have accumulations of silver coins (900 parts silver/100 parts alloy) took them to the local silversmith who melted them down and made the desired household article as requested. These pieces bore the owner's monogram and often the maker's mark, but the words 'Coin Silver' did not come into use until 1830. By 1860 the standard was raised to 925 parts silver/75 parts alloy and the word 'Sterling' was added. Coin silver came to an end about 1900.

Key:
AS — all solid silver   t-oz — troy ounce
gw — gold washed

A Rasch, Philadelphia; beaker, molded rims, eng, ca 1807, 3x3"...**485.00**
Adolphe Himmel, New Orleans; baby cup, eng name, ca 1870, 3½" ..**935.00**
AE Warner, Baltimore; fish slice, pierced blade, 12" **220.00**
AJ & FA Leslie, baby's cup, eng shield/name, 3¼" **770.00**
Am, cup, communion; str sided, eng w/in cut swag, dtd 1802, 8-t-oz..**1,380.00**
Am, mug, presentation; tapered cylinder, eng/dtd 1851, 5-t-oz...**175.00**
C&D, Plat Bros, NY; tea set, urn-form bodies w/florals, 1820s, 4-pc ..**2,300.00**
Clemens Oskamp, OH; punch ladle, bright-cut hdl & bowl, 12½" **440.00**
Davis, Palmer & Co, Boston; punch ladle, Fiddle hdl, 1838-45, 4-t-oz..**230.00**
Duhme, Cincinnati OH; cake slice, Medallion, monogram, 19th C, 10¾"...**715.00**
E&D Kinsey, Cincinnati OH; beaker, reeded top/bottom, 3½", 5-t-oz..**400.00**
E&D Kinsey, Cincinnati OH; tablespoons, Fiddle Tipped, 1850s, 6 for..**220.00**
EA Tyler, tablespoons, 1850s, 4 for..**165.00**
Eoff & Shepherd/Ball, Black & Co, NY; 4-pc presentation set, 1825 ..**1,265.00**
Farrington & Hunnewell, Boston; fish slice, chased fish, 1830s, 12" **250.00**
FS Blackman, teaspoons, Fiddle, 1830, 3 for **85.00**
G Boyce, NY; creamer, baluster w/appl floral band, 1820-57, 8-t-oz..**460.00**
G Boyce, NY; presentation mug, baluster, foliage, 1815, 5¼" **865.00**
Gorham, baby cup, Medallion, eng name/Christmas 1865, 3½" .**700.00**
Gorham & Co, tray, gadrooning, eng vases/florals, 1848-65, 12x9"...**375.00**
H Wishart, NY; 4-pc tea set, shield crest/eagles, 1784..............**3,750.00**
Henry Harland, New Orleans; soup ladle, Fiddle, early 1800s, 14"...**1,100.00**
Hyde & Goodrich, New Orleans; tablespoons, Fiddle, 19th C, 12 for ..**715.00**
J Foster, cream jug, oval w/appl rim, strap hdl, 4¾" **485.00**
J Moulton, cream jug, early 19th C, 5½" **415.00**
Melville & Co, New Orleans; tablespoon, Fiddle Thread, 1850s, 3 for **110.00**
N Taylor & Co, NY; tea set, pot+cr/sugar+waste bowl, 1825, 72 t-oz....**1,725.00**
S Edwards, Boston; tablespoon, emb shell bowl, 1705-62, 8" **630.00**
Samuel Ayers, KY; sauce ladle, Fiddle, eng initials, 1815, 7½" ...**1,100.00**
Samuel T Crosby, Boston; fish slice, Olive, pierced/eng blade, 1850s...**440.00**
Susan Turk, New Orleans; dinner fork, inscribed Wren, 1856-60..**248.00**
Taylor & Hinsdale, NY; punch ladle, fiddle hdl, monogram **260.00**
WG & pseudo hallmks, stuffing spoon, early 19th C **220.00**
Wm Gale & Son, NY: pitcher, gadroon borders, acanthus hdl, 20-t-oz..**1,650.00**
Wood & Hughes, NY; pitcher, invt ovoid body, beaded bands, 1850s, 14"..**2,650.00**
WP Loomis, Frankfort KY; punch laddle, Fiddle Tipped, 1850s, 12¾" ..**935.00**

Flatware

Silver flatware is being collected today either to replace missing pieces of heirloom sets or in lieu of buying new patterns, by those who admire and appreciate the style and quality of the older ware. Prices vary from dealer to dealer; some pieces are harder to find and are therefore more expensive. Items such as olive spoons, cream ladles, lemon forks, etc., once thought a necessary part of a silver service, may today be slow to sell; as a result, dealers may price them low and make up the difference on items that sell more readily. Many factors enter into evaluation. Popular patterns may be high due to demand though easily found, while scarce patterns may be passed over by collectors who find them difficult to reassemble. If pieces are monogrammed, deduct 20% (for rare, ornate patterns) to 30% (for common, plain pieces). Place settings generally come in three sizes: dinner, place, and luncheon, with the dinner size generally more expensive. In general, dinner knives are 9½" long, place knives, 9" to 9⅛", and luncheon knives, 8¾" to 8⅞". Dinner forks measure 7⅜" to 7½", place forks, 7¼" to 7⅜", and luncheon forks, 6⅞" to 7⅛". Our advisor for this category is Rick Spencer; he is listed in the Directory under Utah.

Acanthus 212-piece service, Georg Jensen, 260 ounces of weighable silver, $18,700.00 at auction.

Athene, Amston, cream soup spoon...**35.00**
Athene, Amston, lettuce fork **80.00**
Athene, Amston, olive spoon **45.00**
Athene, Amston, place setting, 4-pc...**110.00**
Atlantas, Tiffany, carving set, 3-pc **400.00**
Atlantas, Tiffany, place knife **180.00**
Atlantas, Tiffany, sugar sifter...**525.00**
Blackberry Vine, Tiffany, jelly server **695.00**
Blackberry Vine, Tiffany, nut cracker...**1,200.00**
Blossom, Jensen, gravy ladle..**595.00**
Blossom, Jensen, pie server, AS...**595.00**
Bridal Veil, ind butter spreader, flat hdl...**23.00**
Bridal Veil, International, cocktail fork..**23.00**
Bridal Veil, International, tablespoon..**60.00**
Bridal Veil, International, 4-pc place-sz setting...............................**95.00**
Calvert, Kirk, pierced serving spoon...**68.00**
Calvert, Kirk, salad fork **35.00**
Calvert, Kirk, sugar tongs...**45.00**
Canterbury, Towle, punch ladle **425.00**
Canterbury, Towle, 4-pc dinner-sz setting **175.00**
Carnation, Wallace, nut pick **42.00**
Carnation, Wallace, pie server...**58.00**
Chrysanthemum, Durgin, asparagus fork **825.00**
Chrysanthemum, Durgin, fish fork **150.00**
Chrysanthemum, Durgin, ice tongs..**1,100.00**
Chrysanthemum, Durgin, salad-serving set, AS..............................**825.00**
Chrysanthemum, Durgin, waffle knife..**825.00**
Chrysanthemum, Durgin, 4-pc place-sz setting **230.00**

Colonial Fiddle, Tuttle, gumbo soup spoon 40.00
Colonial Fiddle, Tuttle, jelly server 36.00
Dancing Flowers, Reed & Barton, gravy ladle...........................60.00
Dancing Flowers, Reed & Barton, salad-serving set, AS 120.00
Edward VII, Alvin, bouillon soup spoon.....................................38.00
Edward VII, Alvin, serving spoon...75.00
English Shell, Lunt, cold-meat fork..62.00
English Shell, Lunt, iced-tea spoon 34.00
English Shell, Lunt, 4-pc place-sz setting 90.00
Fiddle, Porter Blanchard, cold-meat fork....................................135.00
Fiddle, Porter Blanchard, pie server, AS.....................................225.00
Fiddle, Porter Blanchard, teaspoon..45.00
Fontaine Bleau, Gorham, cheese scoop 125.00
Fontaine Bleau, Gorham, sugar spoon 90.00
Heiress, Oneida, grill fork...30.00
Heiress, Oneida, grill knife..30.00
Heiress, Oneida, horseradish scoop 42.00
Imperial Queen, Whiting, fish-serving set...................................560.00
Imperial Queen, Whiting, pickle fork, long hdl...........................120.00
Imperial Queen, Whiting, ramekin fork 59.00
Imperial Queen, Whiting, strawberry fork....................................50.00
Imperial Queen, Whiting, teaspoon..25.00
Jenny Lind, Weidlich, bacon fork...75.00
Jenny Lind, Weidlich, cake breaker..60.00
Jonquil, Unger, pastry tongs 325.00
King Christian, Wallace, place soup spoon 35.00
King Christian, Wallace, 4-pc place-sz setting 100.00
Labors of Cupid, Dominick & Haff, asparagus fork.....................425.00
Labors of Cupid, Dominick & Haff, dinner knife 85.00
Labors of Cupid, Dominick & Haff, tomato server 225.00
Lasting Spring, Oneida, butter spreader, hollow hdl 20.00
Lasting Spring, Oneida, lemon fork 24.00
Lasting Spring, Oneida, steak-carving set, 2-pc 85.00
Lily, Whiting, cream soup..76.00
Lily, Whiting, soup ladle...800.00
Lily, Whiting, stuffing spoon, pierced...400.00
Lily, Whiting, 4-pc place-sz setting..200.00
Mary Chilton, Towle, fruit knife 36.00
Mary Chilton, Towle, ice cream fork 38.00
Mary Chilton, Towle, lettuce fork 70.00
Mary Chilton, Towle, nut spoon...45.00
Mary Chilton, Towle, salt spoon...20.00
Mary Chilton, Towle, sardine fork 89.00
Mary Warren, Manchester, baby spoon 26.00
Mary Warren, Manchester, olive spoon, Ideal..............................38.00
Mothers, Gorham, coffee spoon..18.00
Mothers, Gorham, fish fork...36.00
Mothers, Gorham, mayonnaise ladle...36.00
Mothers, Gorham, mustard ladle 36.00
Newport Shell, Frank Smith, dinner fork......................................39.00
Newport Shell, Frank Smith, dinner knife 39.00
Newport Shell, Frank Smith, salad fork...54.00
Orchid, Watson, almond scoop..325.00
Orchid, Watson, chocolate muddler...170.00
Orchid, Watson, cucumber server..230.00
Orchid, Watson, fish serving set, lg..1,250.00
Palm Beach, Buccellati, breakfast fork..30.00
Palm Beach, Buccellati, breakfast knife...30.00
Palm Beach, Buccellati, breakfast/egg spoon 30.00
Palm Beach, Buccellati, iced-tea spoon 45.00
Pyramid, Jensen, place soup spoon...85.00
Pyramid, Jensen, salad fork...95.00
Pyramid, Jensen, teaspoon..80.00
Raphael, Alvin, berry spoon 850.00

Raphael, Alvin, cheese scoop 840.00
Raphael, Alvin, gravy ladle, lg 1,100.00
Raphael, Alvin, sardine fork 530.00
Raphael, Alvin, teaspoon...86.00
Regency, Lunt, berry spoon...95.00
Regency, Lunt, sugar spoon...29.00
Regency, Lunt, tomato server..80.00
Saint Dunston, Tiffany, demitasse spoon 36.00
Saint Dunston, Tiffany, egg spoon 69.00
Saint Dunston, Tiffany, grapefruit spoon 66.00
Saint Dunston, Tiffany, ice tongs...500.00
Saint Dunston, Tiffany, preserve spoon, lg 125.00
Savoy, Buccellati, iced-tea spoon 70.00
Savoy, Buccellati, place knife..70.00
Savoy, Buccellati, salad fork..79.00
Sea Sculpture, Gorham, 4-pc place-sz setting 110.00
Sweetheart Rose, Lunt, junior set, 3-pc 89.00
Sweetheart Rose, Lunt, olive spoon..44.00
Tea Rose, Weidlich, bouillon spoon..30.00
Tea Rose, Weidlich, butter spreader, flat hdl.................................23.00
Tea Rose, Weidlich, sugar spoon...32.00
Theseum, International, cocktail fork 27.00
Theseum, International, ice-cream fork 36.00
Theseum, International, melon spoon...36.00
Theseum, International, sauce ladle..40.00
Theseum, International, 4-pc dinner-sz setting.............................125.00
Tulip, Fessenden, pierced sardine fork...125.00
Wadefield, Kirk, grapefruit spoon...38.00
Wadefield, Kirk, jelly server..45.00
Wildflower, Royal Crest, cold-meat fork.......................................60.00
Wildflower, Royal Crest, cream soup...32.00
Wildflower, Royal Crest, salad fork..32.00
Wildflower, Royal Crest, sugar spoon..30.00
Williamsburg Shell, Stieff, butter pick...50.00
Williamsburg Shell, Stieff, 4-pc dinner-sz setting........................149.00
Windham, Tiffany, baby spoon, bent hdl.......................................62.00
Windham, Tiffany, breakfast knife, hollow hdl 62.00
Windham, Tiffany, steak knife 75.00
Young Love, Oneida, lemon fork 24.00
Young Love, Oneida, master butter spreader, hollow hdl..............27.00
Young Love, Oneida, pierced serving spoon 65.00
Young Love, Oneida, 4-pc place-sz setting 85.00

Hollow Ware

Until the middle of the nineteenth century, the silverware produced in America was custom made on order of the buyer directly from the silversmith. With the rise of industrialization, factories sprung up that manufactured silverware for retailers who often added their trademark to the ware. Silver ore was mined in abundance, and demand spurred production. Changes in style occurred at the whim of fashion. Repousse decoration (relief work) became popular about 1885, reflecting the ostentatious preference of the Victorian era. Later in the century, Greek, Etruscan, and several classic styles found favor. Today the Art Deco styles of this century are very popular with collectors.

In the listings that follow, manufacturer's name or trademark is noted first; in lieu of that information, listings are by country or item. Weight is given in troy ounces. See also Tiffany, Silver.

Key: t-oz — troy ounce

Amable Brasier, Philadelphia; pitcher w/lid, foliate hdl, 1835, 4½" ..465.00
Atlantas, Tiffany, place fork..120.00
Bailey & Co, Philadelphia; pitcher, rose & bird repousse, 8½" .1,300.00

Bailey & Co, Philadelphia; tureen, repousse/openwork, w/lid, 1847, 11".....**1,300.00**
Ball Black & Co, NY; milk jug, repousse floral, 6", 12-t-oz **260.00**
Barbour, chocolate pot, flared cylinder, entwined ribbon decor, 7" ..**375.00**
Birmingham, salver, pie-crust edge, floral eng, 8" dia, 7.2-t-oz....**300.00**
Black, Star & Frost, pitcher, invt fluting, 1900s, 11" **715.00**
Continental, cream pitcher, helmet, strap hdl, appl decor, 7-t-oz..**330.00**
Crichton Bros, London & NY; tea/coffee service, 2 pots+cr/sug ...**2,400.00**
Dominick & Haff, tray, Virginia, 1912, 14" dia.......................**350.00**
FW Whiting, lady's flask, stylized leaf form, 1920s, 4" **300.00**
Georg Jensen, bowl, openwork vintage, 6x7¾", 20-t-oz.......**2,400.00**
Georg Jensen, tray, Danish floral hdls, 13¼", 20-t-oz..............**2,500.00**
Gorham, basket, rtcl oval, 12x9½", 12-t-oz **300.00**
Gorham, gravy boat, chased florals, C-scroll hdl, 1899, 4½x7½" ..**300.00**
Gorham, salver, eng vintage, emb beadwork, guilloche border, ftd, 11" ..**600.00**
Gorham, tea set, bachelor; reeded lids w/wood finial, 1898, 4-pc..**750.00**
Gorham, tea set, 8-sided urn forms, 5-pc, 68-t-oz.................**675.00**
Gorham, tureen, scroll/floral repousse, tall finial, 6x11"..............**450.00**
Gorham, waste bowl, Zodiac, 2½x5"...................................**150.00**
H Bateman, London; salver, Geo III, 14" dia, 40-t-oz **3,300.00**
Henry Vincent, London; milk pitcher, urn form w/strap hdl, 1800, 4" ..**200.00**
International, bread tray, Royal Danish.....................................**245.00**
John Williams, Dublin; gravy boat, Irish Georgian, 1770s, 10½-t-oz ...**1,045.00**
Kalo, bowl, floriform w/5 petal-like panels, hammered, 7" **400.00**
Kalo, bowl, hammered floriform, rolled rim, 20th C, 1⅞x7⅛" **400.00**
Kalo, bowl, 5-petal form w/invt rim, M323, 1¾x9¾"..................**400.00**
Katherine Pratt, bowl, hammered floriform, 2x4" **200.00**
Kirk, service plate, repousse **395.00**
Lebruecher & Co, nesting coffee set, pot+cr/sug, 12 t-oz **375.00**
London, mustard pot, hinged lid, strap hdl, ribbed middle, 1811...**250.00**
London hallmk for 1759, pitcher, Geo II, pear form, 4", 3-t-oz...**325.00**
Mary P Winlock, ladle, pierced hdl, champleve floral, 5" **350.00**
Mt Vernon Co, powder sifter, repousse flowers, 1910, 4x1½" **200.00**
Reed & Barton, lady's flask, cherub/florals, hinged lid, 5½".......**525.00**
Reed & Barton, salad servers, muse & putto terminals, pr **520.00**
Reed & Barton, tray, Francis I, monogram, 17", 36-t-oz..............**715.00**
S Kirk & Son, tray, castellated repousse pattern, 1890s, 21x14"..**2,850.00**
SC Young & Co, egg cruet on stand, Geo III, 6 cups/spoons/stand, 1817 ..**2,860.00**
Shreve, Crump & Low; bowl, 8", 12½-t-oz **150.00**
T Robins, London; box, Geo III, crested/hinged lid, 1812, 5x3½"...**880.00**
Towle, pitcher, water; Louis XIV, 10", 24-t-oz **550.00**
Wallace, coffee service, AD; pot+cr/sug+tray, 32-t-oz **700.00**
Wallace, creamer & sugar bowl, Grande Baroque........................**350.00**
Watson & Co, pitcher, emb florals/scrolls, ped base, 11", 28-t-oz ..**935.00**
Wm Smiley, London; hip flask, machine tooled, w/cap, 1869-70, 3¾"...**145.00**
Wm Spratling, box, trunk form w/dome lid, 2¼x3¼" **800.00**
Wood & Hughes, shakers, hand-chased allover repousse, pr **325.00**
WT Binder, bowl, serving; trefoil base w/3 hdls, repousse leaves, 12" ..**1,150.00**

Silver Lustre and Silver Resist

    Much of the ware known as silver lustre was produced in the 1800s in Staffordshire, England. This type of earthenware was entirely covered with the metallic silver glaze. It was most popular prior to 1840 when the technique of electroplating was developed and silverplated wares came into vogue. Later in the century, artisans used silver lustre to develop designs on vases and other decorative ware

    The process for decorating pottery with the silver-resist method involved first coating the design or that portion of the pattern that was to be left unsilvered with a water-soluble solution. The lustre was applied to the entire surface of the vessel and allowed to dry. Before the final firing, the surface was washed, removing only the silver from the coated areas. This type of ware was produced early in the 1800s by many English potteries, Wedgwood included.

Jug, floral medallions, ribbed/molded body, chip, 6¾" **165.00**
Jug, vining flowers, flakes/wear, 4½".......................................**140.00**
Pitcher, flowers & vines on wht, 8¾", EX..................................**250.00**
Teapot, EX allover lustre & finish, English, 9½" **100.00**

Silver Overlay

    The silver overlay glass made since the 1880s was decorated with a cut-out pattern of sterling silver applied to the surface of the ware.

Bottle, scent; cobalt w/leafy o/l, orig stopper, 9¼" **395.00**
Bowl, crystal, silver o/l & frosted flowers, 12½"...........................**100.00**
Honey jar, crystal, floral o/l, mk Rockwell **130.00**
Pitcher, cobalt, o/l decor, water sz, +6 tumblers.......................**1,200.00**
Pitcher, gr, vintage o/l, 11½" **475.00**

Vases: Engraved floral on green glass, Mathews Co., 6", $495.00; Engraved floral over favrille-type glass, Mermod & Jaccard, 5¼", $1,045.00.

Vase, blk amethyst, Baroque o/l on 2 sides, 10¼" **250.00**
Vase, emerald gr, scrolls & lattice o/l, 12" **650.00**
Vase, gr, Nouveau o/l, mk Gorham, 16" **670.00**

Silverplate

    Silverplated flatware is becoming the focus of attention for many of today's collectors. Demand is strong for early, ornate patterns, and prices have continued to rise steadily over the past five years. Our values are based on pieces in excellent or restored/resilvered condition. Serving pieces are priced to reflect the values of examples in complete original condition, with knives retaining their original blades. If pieces are monogrammed, deduct from 20% (for rare, ornate patterns) to 30% (for common, plain pieces). Our advisor for this category is Rick Spencer; he is listed in the Directory under Utah. For more information we recommend *Standard Encyclopedia of American Silverplate* by Frances M. Bones and Lee Roy Fisher and *Silverplated Flatware, Revised Fourth Edition,* by Tere Hagan.

    See also Railroadiana, Silverplate.

Flatware

Aldine, 1895, Rogers/Aurora, bouillon spoon **8.00**
Aldine, 1895, Rogers/Aurora, cocktail fork....................................**12.00**
Aldine, 1895, Rogers/Aurora, demitasse spoon...............................**12.00**
Alton, Rogers 1901, gravy ladle **16.00**
Alton, Rogers 1901, master butter spreader, twist hdl....................**20.00**
Arlington, 1894, Pairpoint Mfg, CF **10.00**
Beaded, 1896, Niagara, strawberry fork.......................................**14.00**
Bernice, 1900, Oneida, cream ladle **10.00**
Bernice, 1900, Oneida, ind butter spreader **7.00**
Blenheim, 1898, Rogers, berry spoon...**25.00**
Blenheim, 1898, Rogers, olive fork **15.00**
Blenheim, 1898, Rogers, soup ladle **65.00**
Blenheim, 1898, Rogers, strawberry fork **18.00**
Blossom, 1909, Wallace, aspic server...**24.00**
Blossom, 1909, Wallace, teaspoon..**6.00**

Bradford, 1915, Gorham, iced-tea spoon 6.00
Bradford, 1915, Gorham, jelly server 9.00
Bradford, 1915, Gorham, oval soup spoon 5.00
Bradford, 1915, Gorham, tomato server 19.00
Cardinal, 1887, Rogers, luncheon fork 12.00
Cardinal, 1887, Rogers, master salt spoon 22.00
Cardinal, 1887, Rogers, nut pick 9.00
Carolina, 1895, Gorham, cold meat fork 22.00
Cashmere, 1889, Reed & Barton, berry spoon 20.00
Cashmere, 1889, Reed & Barton, pastry fork 14.00
Cedric, 1906, International, fish serving fork 18.00
Cedric, 1906, International, salad fork 16.00
Coronet, 1926, Wm A Rogers, dinner knife, hollow hdl ...6.00
Coronet, 1926, Wm A Rogers, fruit spoon 7.00
Coronet, 1926, Wm A Rogers, gravy ladle 18.00
Coronet, 1926, Wm A Rogers, youth spoon 7.00
Daisy, 1910, International, cake server, hollow hdl 25.00
Daisy, 1910, International, dinner fork 6.00
Daisy, 1910, International, oyster ladle 45.00
Desoto, Rogers Meriden, sugar shell 5.00
Desoto, Rogers Meriden, viande fork 5.00
Desoto, Rogers Meriden, viande knife 6.00
Eastlake/Lyonnaise, 1879, Wm Rogers, cocktail fork 15.00
Eastlake/Lyonnaise, 1879, Wm Rogers, fish-serving fork ...40.00
Empress, 1870, Webster Mfg, oval soup 12.00
Empress, 1870, Webster Mfg, teaspoon 7.00
Exeter, 1913, Reliance, pickle fork 10.00
Exeter, 1913, Reliance, tablespoon 8.00
Exeter, 1913, Reliance, 5 o'clock spoon 5.00
Fair Oaks, 1909, Rockford, beef fork 16.00
Fair Oaks, 1909, Rockford, bouillon spoon 8.00
Florida, 1894, Rogers, gravy ladle 24.00
Florida, 1894, Rogers, tablespoon 12.00
Florida, 1894, Rogers, teaspoon 6.00
Garland, 1910, Oxford, cocktail fork 8.00
Garland, 1910, Oxford, dinner fork 8.00
Garland, 1910, Oxford, pie server, flat hdl 30.00
Glasgow aka Regent, 1894, International, beef fork 18.00
Glasgow aka Regent, 1894, International, demitasse spoon ...10.00
Glasgow aka Regent, 1894, International, fruit spoon 8.00
Glasgow aka Regent, 1894, International, pastry fork 12.00
Hiawatha, 1886, Holmes & Edwards, dinner knife, flat hdl ...12.00
Hiawatha, 1886, Holmes & Edwards, pastry fork 16.00
Imperial, 1893, Rogers & Bros, butter pick 35.00
Imperial, 1893, Rogers & Bros, cream ladle 12.00
Imperial, 1893, Rogers & Bros, strawberry fork 20.00
Iris, 1902, EHH Smith, dinner fork 14.00
Iris, 1902, EHH Smith, oyster fork 12.00
Iris, 1902, EHH Smith, preserves spoon 18.00
Iris, 1902, EHH Smith, salad fork 16.00
Legacy, 1928, 1847 Rogers, cream-soup spoon...............7.00
Legacy, 1928, 1847 Rogers, ice-cream fork 15.00
Legacy, 1928, 1847 Rogers, teaspoon 4.00
Lexington, 1904, Rogers, sherbet spoon 15.00
Lexington, 1904, Rogers, tablespoon 10.00
Linden, 1891, 1847 Rogers, Victorian pie knife 45.00
Linden/Endora, 1900, 1881 Rogers, punch ladle...........100.00
Louvain, 1918, 1847 Rogers, fruit knife, flat hdl 8.00
Louvain, 1918, 1847 Rogers, iced-tea spoon..................9.00
Lufbarry, 1915, Rogers & Bro, place fork 6.00
Lufbarry, 1915, Rogers & Bro, sugar tongs 16.00
Lufberry, 1915, Rogers & Bro, cake serving fork 20.00
Lufberry, 1915, Rogers & Bro, ice-cream fork 14.00
Lufberry, 1915, Rogers & Bro, tomato server.................18.00

Minerva, 1911, SL & GH Rogers, cold-meat fork 15.00
Minerva, 1911, SL & GH Rogers, salad fork.................12.00
Minerva, 1911, SL & GH Rogers, soup ladle 75.00
Minerva, 1911, SL & GH Rogers, teaspoon 5.00
Monarch, 1889, Meriden, olive fork............................20.00
Monarch, 1889, Meriden, sorbet spoon 14.00
Nassau, 1899, Holmes & Edwards, cream-soup spoon 10.00
Nassau, 1899, Holmes & Edwards, soup ladle 60.00
Nassau, 1899, Holmes & Edwards, strawberry fork 18.00
Newton aka Raleigh, 1900, cheese scoop, flat hdl 40.00
Norman, 1903, Tiffany, luncheon fork..........................10.00
Oregon, 1900, American, cold meat fork 20.00
Oregon, 1900, American, ind butter spreader 9.00
Oregon, 1900, American, pickle fork 16.00
Paisley, 1922, Rogers & Bros, breakfast knife, hollow hdl ...9.00
Paisley, 1922, Rogers & Bros, jelly server......................8.00
Portland, 1891, Wallace, dinner fork 10.00
Portland, 1891, Wallace, nut pick 9.00
Portland, 1891, Wallace, oval soup 10.00
Portland, 1891, Wallace, sugar tongs 32.00
Princess Louise, 1881, Gorham, cocktail fork................10.00
Princess Louise, 1881, Gorham, gravy ladle 30.00
Princess Louise, 1881, Gorham, soup ladle 70.00
Queen Elizabeth, 1908, National, bonbon server............10.00
Queen Elizabeth, 1908, National, cream soup spoon 4.00
Queen Elizabeth, 1908, National, salad fork....................6.00
Queen Elizabeth, 1908, National, sugar shell 7.00
Romance, 1925, Holmes & Edwards, breakfast knife, hollow hdl ...9.00
Romance, 1925, Holmes & Edwards, casserole spoon, sm ...14.00
Romance, 1925, Holmes & Edwards, luncheon knife, hollow hdl ..6.00
San Diego, 1889, Rogers & Bros, cream ladle 24.00
San Diego, 1889, Rogers & Bros, fruit spoon 14.00
San Diego, 1889, Rogers & Bros, soup ladle 75.00
Shakespeare, 1924, Stratford, youth fork......................10.00
Shakespeare, 1924, Stratford, youth knife 10.00
Unique, 1879, Reed & Barton, fish knife, flat hdl 14.00
Unique, 1879, Reed & Barton, Victorian pie knife 38.00
Vanity Fair, 1924, Gorham, cold-meat fork, lg...............20.00
Vanity Fair, 1924, Gorham, fruit knife, hollow hdl 12.00
Vanity Fair, 1924, Gorham, tablespoon 8.00
Vanity Fair, 1924, Gorham, teaspoon............................4.00
Verona, 1910, Rogers & Bros, cheese scoop 40.00
Washington, 1910, Holmes & Edwards, salad fork...........5.00
Washington, 1910, Holmes & Edwards, sugar tongs 16.00
Yorktown, 1913, Stratford, fish fork..............................9.00
Yorktown, 1913, Stratford, ice-cream fork.....................15.00

Hollow Ware

Biscuit bbl, floral medallions, rtcl base, Elkington, 19th C, 17"..300.00
Bowl, beaded/eng foliage, hdls, Richard Richardson, 19th C, 11" .345.00
Breakfast tureen, revolving top, James Dixon & Sons, 7x14" 300.00
Cafe-au-lait pot, att Casimir Rouyer, left-handed, wood hdl, 10" ..275.00
Candelabra, 2-arm, mk SGEP (English), 1900s, 16½", pr, EX 375.00
Candlesticks, Georgian-style, cut hurricane shade, 15½", pr 495.00
Candlesticks, orig bobeches, sq base/scroll corners, English, 10", pr ..550.00
Coffee/tea set, Georgian style, Birmingham Silver, 4-pc 350.00
Coffeepot, repousse florals/chased geometrics, Reed & Barton, 22"...110.00
Covered dish, Reflection, 1847 Rogers, 1959, 8x13" 60.00
Entree dish, telescoping dome lid, English, 8½x13½" 450.00
Hot water urn, classical shape, w/burner, Internat'l....................135.00
Lazy Susan, 2-tier, scrolled border, scroll chasing, Am 175.00
Meat dome, eng crest, beaded edge, fluted, English, 19th C, 9x14x11" ..385.00
Pepper castor, baluster, Crispin Fuller London, 1795, 6" 500.00

Pitcher, Nouveau lady's profile, scroll hdl, WMF, 1890s, 18"...**1,150.00**
Platter, well & tree; Paul Revere, Oneida, 1927 ....**65.00**
Sugar bowl, w/spoon rack, Toronto, 1890s, w/lid, 9½" **65.00**
Sweetmeat basket, rtcl/emb flowers, cobalt glass int, unmk, 7x7" ...**180.00**
Syrup pitcher, heavy emb flowers, emb lid, Wilcox, 4½" **100.00**
Tea/coffee set, Marie Louise, Internat'l, 2 pots+cr/sug+bowl+tray ..**750.00**
Tea/coffee set, Scroll, Towle, 2 pots+tray+kettle+cr/sug+bowl...**650.00**
Tray, Georgian style, serpentine edge/hdls, Reed & Barton, 25" .**375.00**

Sheffield

Bacon dish, crested eng lid, trn wood hdl, 19th C.......................**360.00**
Basket, bread; wirework boat form w/rope twist swing hdl, 11"..**330.00**
Basket, cake; gadroon base w/acanthus openwork hdl, 1830s, 16" .**495.00**
Basket, cake; gadroon border, swing hdls, 1810-20, 12"..............**220.00**
Basket, cake; openwork wire w/gadroon edge, swing hdl, 1810, 10½"...**195.00**
Basket, cast eng detail, 4½(+hdl)x11½x13¾" **165.00**
Bowl, center; gadroon border, ram's heads hdls, 1820s, 8x11x7".**385.00**
Candelabra, acanthus chased scrollwork columns, 1830s, 20x18", pr..**2,100.00**
Candelabra, cast rococo, partial touch mks, 17½", pr **330.00**
Candelabra, egg & dart banding, flame finial, 2-arm, 1820s, 21", pr...**825.00**
Candelabra, 3 gadrooned cups w/cast bobeches, 21x18", pr......**1,650.00**
Candlesticks, scroll & floral banding, 1830s, 9¾", pr **500.00**
Coffeepot, Georgian, acorn finial, vasiform w/pearwood hdl, 8½" .**300.00**
Entree dishes, scallops, acanthus hdls, eng crest, w/lid, 13", pr **1,045.00**
Epergne, revolving stand w/paw ft, lg cut bowl+4 sm, 1810s, 16x19"..**2,100.00**
Ewer, wine; Georgian, eng motto/crest w/greyhound, ca 1800, 12" **550.00**
Tankard, segmented bbl w/dome lid, rpr, 1800s, 5½x3¾" **400.00**
Tea caddy, emb musicians scenes, worn, 4⅝" **100.00**
Tea caddy, panelled navette form, divided int, 1800s, 7x7x5".....**440.00**
Tea/coffee set, gadrooned navette forms, hardwood hdls, 1830s, 4-pc..**1,200.00**
Tureen, shell hdls, gadroon border, w/lid, early 1800s, 5x8¼"....**275.00**
Urn, hot water; in Adam Taste, acorn finial, pistol-grip hdls, 20"..**1,155.00**
Venison dome & tray, oval, 1820s **500.00**
Wine cooler, Georgian, eng crest, 1800s, 8x8¼" **1,650.00**
Wine cooler, Georgian urn-shaped body w/gadrooning, 12x11"..**495.00**

Sinclaire

In 1904 H.P. Sinclaire and Company was founded in Corning, New York. For the first sixteen years of production, Sinclaire used blanks from other glassworks for his cut and engraved designs. In 1920 he established his own glassblowing factory in Bath, New York. His most popular designs utilize fruits, flowers, and other forms from nature. Most of Sinclaire's glass is unmarked; items that are carry his logo: an 'S' within a wreath with two shields.

Vase, floral on electric blue, shouldered, flared rim, 11", $250.00.

Bowl, canary yel, floral etch, rolled rim, 13" **230.00**
Bowl, fruit; brilliant cut, 5x8" **460.00**

Candlestick, lt gr, swirled ribs, 10¼" **95.00**
Champagne, Ivy...**70.00**
Compote, glossy blk w/Ivorene edge, 7" **420.00**
Flowerpot, intaglio border, geometric cutting **330.00**
Lamp, Flower Basket (cut), 17" **1,500.00**
Pitcher, cut & eng, ped ft, 9" **3,000.00**
Teapot, Rose **1,465.00**
Tray, crosscuts, fans & hobstars, oval, 10x7" **325.00**
Vase, Lily, amethyst to clear, 6" **300.00**
Vase, Stratford, 16" **500.00**
Vase, tulips etch, 13½"...**550.00**

Sitzendorf

The Sitzendorf factory began operations in East Germany in the mid-1800s, adopting the name of the city as the name of their company. They produced fine porcelain groups, figurines, etc., in much the same style and quality as Meissen and the Dresden factories. Much of their ware was marked with a crown over the letter 'S' and a horizontal line with two slash marks.

Bowl, rtcl crown shape, floral w/gold, 1887-1900, 2⅜x8¾x5¾".**140.00**
Candelabra, cherub & flowers amid 2 holders, 6¾x8", pr...........**350.00**
Centerpc, sea monsters & nymphs on boat shape, #198, 12x12x5"...**495.00**
Figurine, musical grouping of man/lady/child, 1850-70, 10x20x11" ..**550.00**

Skookum Dolls

Representing real Indians of various tribes, stern-faced Skookum dolls were designed by Mary McAboy of Missoula, Montana, in the early 1900s. The earliest of McAboy's creations were made with air-dried apple faces that bore a resemblance to the neighboring Chinook Indian tribe. The name Skookum is derived from the Chinook/Siwash term for large or excellent (aka Bully Good) and appears as part of the oval paper labels often attached to the feet of the dolls.

In 1913 McAboy applied for a patent that described her dolls in three styles: a female doll, a female doll with a baby, and a male doll. In 1916 George Borgman and Co. partnered with McAboy, registered the Skookum trademark, and manufactured these dolls which were distributed by the Arrow Novelty Co. of New York and the HH Tammen Co. of Denver. The Skookum (Apple) Packers Association of Washington state produced similar 'friendly faced' dolls as did Louis Ambery for the National Fruit exchange.

The dried apple faces of the first dolls were replaced by those made of a composition material. Plastic faces were introduced in the 1940s, and these continued to be used until production ended in 1959. Skookum dolls were produced in a variety of styles, with the most collectible having stern, lined faces with small painted eyes glancing to the right, colorful Indian blankets pulled tightly across the straw- or paper-filled body to form hidden arms, felt pants or skirts over wooden legs, and wooden feet covered with decorated felt suede or masking tape.

Skookums were produced in sizes ranging from a 2" souvenir mailer with a cardboard address tag to 36" novelty and advertising dolls. Collectors highly prize 21" to 26" dolls as well as dolls that glance to the left. Felt or suede feet predate the less desirable brown plastic feet of the late 1940s and 1950s. Our advisor is Glen Rairigh; he is listed in the Directory under Michigan.

Baby, looks left, cradle brd, beaded body/head covering, 10½"...**1,100.00**
Baby, mc blanket, leather headband w/pnt decor, 4" **30.00**
Baby, wrapped in mc blanket, feather in headband, 3½x3".........**200.00**
Baby mailer, 1½¢ postcard attached, feather/ribbon binding, 4".**100.00**

Baby mailer, 1½¢ postcard attached, rattan binding, 4" 105.00
Baby/child in loop basket, blanket wrap, necklace, 14" 200.00
Baby/child in loop blanket, blanket wrap, unbraided hair, 12"....225.00
Boy, brn ft w/pnt decor, Bully Good label, 6½" 100.00
Boy, brn suede ft w/decor, headband, 10" 150.00
Boy, mc blanet, felt pants, leather shoes, 6½", VG....................50.00
Boy, w/blanket/felt pnats, brn plastic ft w/mk, wood beads, 9½" ...85.00
Chief, w/headdress, paper shoes w/decor, 12½"........................250.00
Family, chief w/mc feathers, 15", female w/baby, clothes match, 14" ..600.00
Family, man w/exposed right arm, 13½", female w/baby, 12½" ...900.00
Female w/baby, floral skirt, glass bead necklace, 11½" 300.00
Female w/baby, w/blanket, purple felt ft/skirt, necklace, 11½"....200.00
Female w/baby, w/blanket, worn paper ft, 12½", VG....................150.00
Girl, cotton-wrapped legs, beaded ft decor, headband, 9½" 150.00
Girl, cotton-wrapped legs, pnt suede ft covers, Bully Good, 6½"..100.00
Girl, w/blanket, felt skirt, decor felt ft, bandana, 10"....................85.00
Girl, w/blanket/skirt, leather shoes, feather, label, 6½" 125.00
Mailer, baby in bl & yel cotton, Grand Canyon 10-1-52...............25.00
Mailer, baby in patterned cotton on yel cb.................................25.00
Mailer, baby in red bandana on yel cb..55.00
Mailer, clay child in leather pouch, Yel Stone Park 6-22-39 ....35.00

Slag Glass

Slag glass is a marbleized opaque glassware made by several companies from about 1870 until the turn of the century. It is usually found in purple or caramel (see Chocolate Glass), though other colors were also made. Pink is rare and very expensive. It was revived in recent years by several American glassmakers, L.E. Smith, Westmoreland, and Imperial among them.

For more information refer to *American Slag Glass* by Ruth Grizel (Collector Books). The listings below reflect values for items with excellent color. Our advisor for this category is Sharon Thoerner; she is listed in the Directory under California.

Almond, coal bucket, LE Smith #125a, 5" 25.00
Almond, swan vase, LE Smith #15a, 4½" 20.00
Blue, pitcher, Kanawha #265ED, 4¼" 25.00
Blue, Rose Slipper, Kanawha #829ED, 6" 30.00
Caramel, compote, Imperial #48, 7" 75.00
Caramel, creamer & sugar bowl, Imperial #30 ....65.00
Caramel, tray, shell shape, Imperial #297, 7½" 45.00
End-of-Day, rooster, w/lid, Kemple, 7½" 300.00
Green, Diamond Dot vase, Kanawha #315ED, 5¼"......................45.00
Green marble, hen on nest, Westmoreland #1, 7½" 200.00
Jade, sugar bowl, open, 2-hdld, Imperial #600...........................40.00
Pink, Invt Fan & Feather, bowl, berry; 6½" 1,000.00
Pink, Invt Fan & Feather, butter dish, 6" dia..........................1,500.00
Pink, Invt Fan & Feather, comport, jelly; ped ft, 5" 685.00
Pink, Invt Fan & Feather, creamer 500.00
Pink, Invt Fan & Feather, cruet..900.00
Pink, Invt Fan & Feather, pitcher, 7½" 1,200.00
Pink, Invt Fan & Feather, punch cup, from $285 to...................315.00
Pink, Invt Fan & Feather, sauce dish, ball ft, 2½x4⅝".................165.00
Pink, Invt Fan & Feather, shakers, rare, pr 1,200.00
Pink, Invt Fan & Feather, spooner, 4¼"....................................425.00
Pink, Invt Fan & Feather, toothpick holder...............................500.00
Pink, Invt Fan & Feather, toothpick holder, ftd, 2⅜" 1,500.00
Pink, Invt Fan & Feather, tumbler, 4" 300.00
Pink, Invt Fan & Feather, sauce dish, shell ft, 3½" 600.00
Pink, Invt Fan & Feather; sugar bowl, w/lid, 4"......................1,000.00
Purple, alley cat, Fenton #5177PS, 10" 150.00
Purple, bumpy-neck swan, A&A Imports....................................20.00

Purple, fox on nest, Westmoreland #1.......................................195.00
Purple, Happiness Bird, #5197PS, 7" 65.00
Purple, swan, Imperial #400, 8" 100.00
Ruby, ashtray, heart shape, Imperial #294, 4½" 25.00
Ruby, box, rnd, w/lid, Imperial #759...95.00
Ruby, Grape & Cable tobacco jar, Fenton #9188rx 195.00
Ruby, vase, cornucopia; Imperial #123, 3" 25.00

Smith Bros.

Alfred and Harry Smith founded their glassmaking firm in New Bedford, Massachusetts. They had been formerly associated with the Mt. Washington Glass Works, working there from 1871 to 1875 to aid in establishing a decorating department. Smith glass is valued for its excellent enameled decoration on satin or opalescent glass. Pieces were often marked with a lion in a red shield. Our advisors for this category are Betty and Clarence Maier; they are listed in the Directory under Pennsylvania.

Biscuit jar, leaves & stalks, gr/yel/rust, metal hdl & lid, 7¼" 450.00
Biscuit jar, mc grapes/gold branches on melon ribs, #405 on lid, 6" W ...750.00
Bottle, cologne; rampant lion stamp, 10¾x5¾" 475.00
Bowl, berry; floral on cream, bl dotted rim, 5" 175.00
Creamer & sugar bowl, melon ribs, HP/jewel decor, mk, 4x4", EX ..350.00
Humidor, pansies on cream, SP lid w/molded pipe, 7x5".............800.00
Jar, powder; allover daisies, melon ribs, 2¾x3¾" 250.00
Rose bowl, Compliments of the Season in gold, rampant lion mk...475.00
Sugar shaker, columbines on wht, melon ribs, SP lid, 3x4" 550.00
Sweetmeat, pansies w/raised gold, rampant lion mk 585.00
Vase, chrysanthemums w/gold on cream to gr, dbl bulb, 8½" ..1,150.00
Vase, daisy garland on cream, 3-sided, bottle neck, 4¾" 445.00
Vase, florals/emb foliage on cream, bulbous, 8½" 450.00
Vase, Santa Maria on flask shape, 8½"....................................1,500.00
Vase, Season's Greetings in gold, ribbed, 2½" 385.00

Snow Babies

During the last quarter of the nineteenth century, snow babies — little figurals in white snowsuits — originated in Germany. They were made of sugar candy and were often used as decorations for Christmas cakes. Later on they were made of marzipan, a confection of crushed almonds, sugar, and egg whites. Eventually porcelain manufacturers began making them in bisque. They were popular until WWII. These tiny bisque figures range in size from 1" up to 7" tall. Quality German pieces bring very respectable prices on the market today. Beware of reproductions. Our advisor for this category is Linda Vines; she is listed in the Directory under California.

Baby riding polar bear, 1930s, Germany, 2½", $175.00. (Photo courtesy Linda Vines)

Babies, 1 pulling another on sled, Germany, 2" 185.00
Babies, 2 dancing the cha-cha, Germany, 2" 150.00

Baby hiding under snow ledge, snow bear on top, Germany, 3"..**190.00**
Baby holding soccer ball on shoulder, Germany, 2" **140.00**
Baby inside igloo, Santa on top, Germany, 2".......................**165.00**
Baby inside igloo, Santa on top, Japan, 2".............................**60.00**
Baby on red or silver airplane, Germany, 2"........................**145.00**
Baby playing musical instrument, Germany, 2"....................**125.00**
Baby pulling 3 penguins on sled, Germany, 2"......................**285.00**
Baby sitting, snow on hand & ft, Germany, early, 2" **165.00**
Baby standing or sitting, Germany, 1" **40.00**
Baby w/seal & red ball, Germany, 2" **150.00**
Bear playing w/colorful ball, Germany, 1" **65.00**
Child, no snow, pushing lg snowball, Germany, 2" **145.00**
Child skater (girl or boy), snow on sweater & hat, Germany, 2" ...**110.00**
Children (2) sliding down brick wall, Germany, 2½" **95.00**
Penguins (3) walking down brick wall, Germany, 2½" **75.00**
Pixies (2) sit on hobby horse, wood stick legs, Germany, 2" **145.00**
Santa atop elephant, Germany, 2" **175.00**
Santa driving yel car, toys in bk, Germany, 2" **150.00**
Santa riding on snow bear, Germany, 2½" **175.00**
Santa riding yel train, pixie in bk, Germany, 3"..................**165.00**
Snow angel sits w/arms out, pk wings, loop in bk, Germany, 1½"...**200.00**
Snow cat, dog or rabbit, Germany, 1", ea **60.00**
Snowman sitting, red hat w/pompom, Germany, 1½" **75.00**

Snuff Boxes

As early as the seventeenth century, the Chinese began using snuff. By the early nineteenth century, the practice had spread to Europe and America. It was used by both the gentlemen and the ladies alike, and expensive snuff boxes and bottles were the earmark of the genteel. Some were of silver or gold set with precious stones or pearls, while others contained music boxes. In the following listings, the dimension noted is length. See also Orientalia, Snuff Bottles.

Horn w/silver top, prong-mt lg citrine, 2x1¼" **915.00**
Silver sedan chair form, Switzerland, 1⅜x1⅞" **250.00**
Sterling, sliding top, orig hinge, MacDonald Taylor mk, 1780s, 2" ..**455.00**
Sterling w/bright cut eng, 19th C..**200.00**
Tortoise shell w/gilt metal mts, 1830s...**450.00**
Trn wood w/gilt Napoleon medallion under glass, 1869, 3½" dia ..**350.00**
Wood w/silver shield inlay top, GA Civil War officer's presentation ...**525.00**
Wooden shoe form, 2-cover opening, Fr, ca 1900, 5" L **255.00**

Soap Hollow Furniture

In the Mennonite community of Soap Hollow, Pennsylvania, the women made and sold soap; the men made handcrafted furniture. Rare today, this furniture was stenciled, grain painted, and beautifully decorated with inlaid escutcheons. These pieces are becoming very sought after. When well kept, they are very distinctive and beautiful. The items described in these listings were recently sold through Merle S. Mishlers Auctions, RD 2, Hollsopple, Pennsylvania. All are in excellent condition unless otherwise noted. Our advisor for this category is Anita Levi; she is listed in the Directory under Pennsylvania.

Blanket chest, red/gr pnt w/yel stripes/stencil, SH, 1868, 24x49" ..**19,250.00**
Chest, blanket; grpt w/blk lid, fruit/florals w/gold, 1882 ....**2,900.00**
Chest, blanket; poplar, orig red pnt w/blk/gold, att, 22x42".....**3,850.00**
Chest, blanket; red & blk, gold stencil, MH/1871, 25x15x10", VG...**6,200.00**
Chest, blanket; rose decals, blk & brn grpt, LK/1890...............**5,000.00**
Chest, 4 lg/3 sm drws, stencil, enamel pulls, sgn, 1883, EX+ ...**5,400.00**
Chest, 6-drw, cherry w/red stain/ebonized trim, 45x37" **2,750.00**

Chest, six-drawer; red with mustard trim and florals, black sides and top, manufactured by John Sala, legs cut down, 47x37x20", EX, $1,900.00. (Photo courtesy Anita Levi)

Chest, 6-drw, no pnt or decor, EX wood, G **475.00**
Chest, 7-drw, foliate stenciling, 1851, 55x41" **1,350.00**
Chest, 7-drw, maroon w/blk top & sides, rpt, CKM/1879, G **550.00**
Chest of drws, brn grpt w/stencil, pnt pulls, 1883, EX+ **5,400.00**
Chest of drws, floral decals/fruit gilt stencil/grpt, MH, 1879....**2,750.00**
Chest of drws, rosewood, 1841..**750.00**
Cradle, gilt stencils, mustard trim, maroon grpt **1,100.00**
Cupboard, Dutch; 4 doors/2 drws, stencil/old rpt, 1875, 84x65" ..**8,000.00**
Cupboard, poplar w/orig red & gr pnt/striping/stencil, 2-pc, 87x64" .**35,200.00**
Cupboard, top only, 2 glass doors, no decor, 40x42x13"..........**3,500.00**
Frame, cross pcs, gr/yel striping, 15½x19¾" **1,000.00**
Rope bed, cherry, red & brn finish, rare.................................**2,300.00**

Soapstone

Soapstone is a soft talc in rock form with a smooth, greasy feel from whence comes its name. (It is also called Soo Chow Jade.) It is composed basically of talc, chlorite, and magnetite. In colonial times it was extracted from out-croppings in large sections with hand saws, carted by oxen to mills, and fashioned into useful domestic articles such as foot-warmers, cooking utensils, inkwells, etc. During the early 1800s, it was used to make heating stoves and kitchen sinks. Most familiar today are the carved vases, bookends, and boxes made in China during the Victorian era. For further information we recommend *Collector's Digest of Soapstone* by L-W Book Sales.

Ashtray, floral vine, 4¾x3" **25.00**
Bowl, baby dragon, 2¾x2x2"..**35.00**
Figurine, pig & piglets on wood base, 6¾x2¾x5"........................**325.00**
Figurine, rooster & hen on tree branch, on 4-ftd ped, 3½x7½" **80.00**
Figurine, 3 monkeys, Speak, Hear & See No Evil, 4½x1x3".........**65.00**
Lamp pull, dbl fish, 1¾x⅛x1⅛" **10.00**
Match holder, w/bat & bird, 5½x1½x2¾" **40.00**
Toothpick holder, Speak, See & Hear No Evil Monkeys, 1¾x3" ..**35.00**
Vase, floral vines, birds & 2 sm planters, 8½x6x14½"................**450.00**
Vase, floral w/2 planters, monkey & bird, 6x3½x6"......................**100.00**

Soda Fountain Collectibles

The first soda water sales in the United States occurred in the very late 1790s in New York and New Haven, Connecticut. By the 1830s soda water was being sold in drug stores as a medicinal item, especially the effervescent mineral waters from various springs around the country. By this time the first flavored soda water appeared at an apothecary shop in Philadelphia.

The 1830s also saw the first manufacturer (John Matthews) of devices to make soda water. The first marble soda fountain made its appearance in 1857 as a combination ice shaver and flavor-dispensing apparatus. By the 1870s the soda fountain was an established feature of the neighborhood drug store.

The fountains of this period were large, elaborate marble devices with druggists competing with each other for business by having fountains decorated with choice marbles, statues, mirrors, water fountains, and gas lamps.

In 1903 the fountain completed its last major evolution with the introduction of the 'front' counter service we know today. (The soda clerk faced the customer when drawing soda.)

By this time ice cream was a standard feature being served as sundaes, ice cream sodas, and milk shakes. Syrup dispensers were just being introduced as 'point-of-sale' devices to sell various flavorings from many different companies. Straws were commonplace, especially those made from paper. Fancy and unusual ice cream dippers were in daily use, and they continued to evolve, reaching their pinnacle with the introduction of the heart-shaped dipper in 1927.

This American business has provided collectors today with an almost endless supply of interesting and different articles of commerce. One can collect dippers, syrup dispensers, glassware, straw dispensers, milk shakers, advertising, and trade catalogs. (Note: The presence of a 'correct' pump enhances the value of a syrup dispenser by 25%.)

Collectors need to be made aware of decorating pieces that are actually fantasy items: copper ice cream cones, a large copper ice cream dipper, and a copper ice cream soda glass. These items have no resale value. Our advisors for this category are Joyce and Harold Screen; they are listed in the Directory under Maryland. See also Advertising; Coca-Cola.

Bottle, Cherry Smash, rvpt label, orig metal cap, 12½" 500.00
Bottle, Tame Cherry, rvpt label depicts flared glass, 13"...........1,000.00
Bowl, crushed fruit, 2 qts, Aztec pattern 400.00
Candy jar, glass ped cylinder w/dmn-pattern lid, 18x4" dia, VG.460.00
Dipper, Dover Clipper, #20, 11", EX...200.00
Dipper, Gilchrist #31, 12", EX 45.00
Dipper, Gilchrist #33, brass lever, 8", NM+ 65.00
Dipper, Hamilton Beach/Nopac #31, 9", NM 50.00
Dispenser, Birchola, ceramic ball form, w/pump, 14", G 1,800.00
Dispenser, Birchola, Drink...5¢, horizontal ceramic bbl, 16", EX ..2,650.00
Dispenser, Cardinal Cherry, ceramic, ca 1910, 9", VG.............3,000.00
Dispenser, Cherry Smash, ceramic, 3-cherry version, w/pump, 15", EX ...2,500.00
Dispenser, Cherry Smash, ceramic, 5¢ Flared Glass version, w/pump, 15" 3,100.00
Dispenser, Cherry Smash, red glass bowl/metal lid & spigot, 9", NM...575.00
Dispenser, Dr Swett's, ceramic stump w/silhouette logo, 14", VG 3,200.00
Dispenser, Ginger-Mint Julep, stoneware bbl, w/pump, 14", VG ...700.00
Dispenser, Grape Ola, textured glass top/milk glass base, 13", G ...250.00
Dispenser, ice cream cone; The Handy, metal/glass, 1937, 33x7" dia 575.00
Dispenser, Jersey Creme, red & gr letters, ca 1910, 15½" 1,600.00
Dispenser, Lash's Grapefruit, textured glass globe, 12", NM........200.00
Dispenser, Liberty Root Beer, wooden bbl, 13", EX+...................300.00
Dispenser, Middleby Root Beer, brn glass mug shape, 12", VG ...600.00
Dispenser, Moxie Fountain Syrup, jug on glass base, 18", G 375.00
Dispenser, Murray's Root Beer, ceramic bbl on stump, 12½" 425.00
Dispenser, Pepsi, ceramic, scenic, emb letters, 19", NM...........3,950.00
Dispenser, Rochester Root Beer, ceramic keg on stump, 12", NM+....325.00
Dispenser, Sterns Root Bear, ceramic bbl on stump, 15", EX 495.00
Dispenser, Ward's Lemon-Crush, ceramic lemon, w/ball pump, 14", EX ...1,750.00
Dispenser, Ward's Lime-Crush, ceramic lime form, w/pump, 14", G 2,250.00
Dispenser, Ward's Orange-Crush, ceramic orange, repro pump, 15"...........1,300.00
Dispenser, Wine-Dip 5 Cent, glass bbl on earthenware base, 19", VG....200.00
Menu, Fountain Menu/We Serve Chapell's Ice Cream, celluloid, 7x5", NM....350.00
Menu board, Dr Pepper, tin w/blkboard bottom, 23x17", EX......225.00
Mixer, milk shake; Greene, 3 units, w/malt dispenser 2,000.00
Mixer, milk shake; Horlicks Dumore, w/lighted base 1,000.00
Mixer, milk shake; Meyer's Double w/malt dispenser 2,000.00
Mixer, milk shake; Multimixer, model 9B, 18", G 350.00

Mixer, milk shake; Red Rooster, by Pick 300.00
Mixer, milk shake; The Aerator...300.00
Straw holder, CI, Drink Hires, 1911, 5x9¾x4½" 2,400.00
Straw holder, glass cylinder, metal base/lid, 12½", VG.............170.00
Straw holder, glass w/Greek key bands top/bottom, open, G.......250.00
Straw holder, paneled cut glass, brass-plated lid & mechanism, 12"..315.00
Straw holder, 1-2-3 Pick-up, glass, metal top/base, 12½", VG 185.00
Tray, Haines CeBrook Ice Cream, girl w/sundae, blk/red, 15x11", EX...165.00

Spangle Glass

Spangle glass, also known as Vasa Murrhina, is cased art glass characterized by the metallic flakes embedded in its top layer. It was made both abroad and in the United States during the latter years of the nineteenth century, and it was reproduced in the 1960s by the Fenton Art Glass Company.

Vasa Murrhina was a New England distributor who sold glassware of this type manufactured by a Dr. Flower of Sandwich, Massachusetts. Flower had purchased the defunct Cape Cod Glassworks in 1885 and used the facilities to operate his own company. Since none of the ware was marked, it is very difficult to attribute specific examples to his manufacture. See also Art Glass Baskets; Fenton.

Creamer, mc/cranberry spatter, crimped rim, melon ribs, 5¼" 165.00
Creamer & sugar bowl, pk to wht o/l w/mica, wafer ft, 4", 3" 135.00
Ewer vase, bl w/mica, clear appl thorn hdl, 7⅜x3⅜"..................115.00
Pitcher, Drape, pk, 4-lobe rim, clear reed hdl, 8½".....................300.00
Ring tree, orange & wht w/mc enameled dots & gold, 3½x3¼"...65.00
Rose bowl, beige/pk/oxblood w/mica, 8-crimp, 3⅜x3¾" 100.00
Rose bowl, pk spatter, ribbed, wht int, petal ft, 3¾"..................110.00
Rose bowl, rose o/l w/heavy mica, 8-crimp, 3¾x3¼" 100.00
Vase, jack-in-the-pulpit; amber/red/wht, blown, 4¾x7¾x6¼"......85.00
Vase, pk, melon ribbed, crimped/ruffled rim, 6" 90.00
Vase, pk & brn w/crimped & ruffled rim w/amber trim, 10"........135.00

Spatter Glass

Spatter glass, characterized by its multicolor 'spatters,' has been made from the late nineteenth century to the present by American glasshouses as well as those abroad. Although it was once thought to have been made entirely by workers at the 'end of the day' from bits and pieces of leftover scrap, it is now known that it was a standard line of production. See also Art Glass Baskets.

Cheese dish, red, blue, and yellow cased in white, clear finial, 10" diameter base, $250.00.

Creamer, mc/cranberry spatter, crimped rim, melon ribs, 5¼" 165.00
Pitcher, Reverse T'print, clear/cranberry/wht, fluting, 8½" 85.00
Pitcher, water; pk & wht w/gold vines & flowers, cased, ruffled rim ...475.00
Pitcher, water; 4-color, clear hdl, pinched spout, 9⅜" 110.00
Ring tree, orange & wht w/mc enameled dots & gold, 3½x3¼" 65.00
Tumbler, Invt T'print, orange & wht spatter w/mica, 3¾" 40.00

Tumbler, lemonade; cream & brn w/emb swirls, ca 1880-1900......**40.00**
Vase, mc w/HP bird & flowers, clear hdls, 7x4½"......................**165.00**
Vase, pk/yel/aqua/wht, clear hdls, fan-shape rim, stick neck, 10½"..**175.00**

Spatterware

Spatterware is a general term referring to a type of decoration used by English potters as early as the late 1700s. Using a brush or a stick, brightly colored paint was dabbed onto the soft-paste earthenware items, achieving a spattered effect which was often used as a border. Because much of this type of ware was made for export to the United States, some of the subjects in the central design — the schoolhouse and the eagle patterns, for instance — reflect American tastes. Yellow, green, and black spatterware is scarce and highly valued by collectors.

In the descriptions that follow, the color listed after the item indicates the color of the spatter. The central design is identified next, and the color description that follows that refers to the design. Our advisor is Diane Patalano; she is listed in the Directory under New Jersey.

Plate, red, Peafowl, four-color, 9¼", EX, $715.00; Tea bowl, blue, Rooster, four-color, miniature, $600.00; Pitcher, blue, Peafowl, four-color, molded handle, 7⅜", NM, $3,600.00; Tea bowl, Rainbow, three-color, flakes, miniature, $440.00; Plate, red, Peafowl, four-color, flakes, body of bird unglazed, 9", $275.00.

Creamer, bl, Clipper Ship, gr/red/blk, paneled, 5⅝".................**3,350.00**
Creamer, bl, Fort, red/blk/gr/yel, hairline in hdl, 5⅝".................**990.00**
Creamer, bl, Holly Berry, red/gr/bl, 4"..**660.00**
Creamer, red, flower, red/bl/blk, chips, 4¾"................................**330.00**
Creamer, red, Peafowl, red/bl/gr/blk, hairline, 4¼"....................**770.00**
Pitcher, bl, Peafowl, gr/yel/blk/red, leaf detail on hdl, 7⅜", NM..**3,600.00**
Pitcher, bl, Peafowl, red/yel/gr/blk, paneled, hairline, 6¼"..........**745.00**
Pitcher, red, Peafowl, 4-color, paneled, 9", NM...........................**990.00**
Plate, bl, Cock's Comb, red & gr, wear/stains, 8½"....................**900.00**
Plate, bl, Peafowl, yel/red/blk/gr, octagonal, 8¼x6", NM.........**1,400.00**
Plate, bl, Pomegranate, red/bl/blk/gr, Meakin, prof rpr, 7¼"......**440.00**
Plate, bl, Teepee, 6½"...**440.00**
Plate, bl, Tree, gr/blk, Best Goods, wear/rprs, 9".......................**165.00**
Plate, gr/red, Columbine w/rosebud & thistle, 4-color, 9¾"........**275.00**
Plate, Rainbow (red/bl/gr), Adams, lt wear, 9⅜".........................**600.00**
Plate, Rainbow (red/bl/gr), 9½"..**500.00**
Plate, red, Peafowl, bl/red/gr/blk, 7¾", NM.............................**1,265.00**
Plate, red, Peafowl, bl/yel/blk/gr, 8¼", EX.................................**275.00**
Plate, red, Peafowl, 4-color, 9½"..**1,265.00**
Plate, red, Thistle, red/gr, 8¼", NM..**1,155.00**
Plate, red/bl, Peafowl (chick), bl/yel/gr/blk, 6½".......................**880.00**
Plate, yel, Cock's Comb, red/gr/blk, 8½".................................**3,100.00**
Saucer, brn, Thistle, gr/red/blk...**550.00**
Sugar bowl, bl, Fort, blk-gray/red/gr, chip/flake, 4¼"................**770.00**
Sugar bowl, bl, Rooster, 4-color, prof rpr, 4¼"...........................**880.00**
Sugar bowl, red, Fort, red/blk/gr, stains, mismatched lid, 4⅛".....**360.00**
Tea bowl, Rainbow (bl & red), red rose w/gr & blk......................**600.00**
Tea bowl, Rainbow (bl/red/gr), sm flakes.....................................**440.00**

Tea bowl, red spatter along rim, no other decor, EX **55.00**
Tea bowl & saucer, bl, Berry & Bird, bl/red/gr/blk.......................**880.00**
Tea bowl & saucer, bl, Cock's Comb, red/gr/blk.......................**1,155.00**
Tea bowl & saucer, bl, Dove, yel ochre/bl/gr/blk.......................**2,750.00**
Tea bowl & saucer, bl, Fort, blk/red/gr.......................................**660.00**
Tea bowl & saucer, bl, Mourning Tulip, yel/gr/blk, NM..............**4,300.00**
Tea bowl & saucer, bl, Pansy, red/bl/gr/blk, NM.......................**3,850.00**
Tea bowl & saucer, bl, Rose, red/gr/blk, mini, EX........................**330.00**
Tea bowl & saucer, bl, Schoolhouse, red/gr/blk, rprs...................**990.00**
Tea bowl & saucer, bl, Star w/Forget-Me-Not, bl/red/gr/blk.....**3,200.00**
Tea bowl & saucer, bl, Umbrella Flower, red & gr, prof rpr.........**440.00**
Tea bowl & saucer, brn, mini, EX..**110.00**
Tea bowl & saucer, dk red, Acorn & Oak leaves, gr/brn/blk, prof rpr..**1,100.00**
Tea bowl & saucer, lilac, Peacock & Bar, yel/bl/gr/red/blk.......**2,300.00**
Tea bowl & saucer, lt gr, Peacock & Bar, yel/bl/gr/red/blk........**1,650.00**
Tea bowl & saucer, Rainbow (bl & gr) **1,485.00**
Tea bowl & saucer, Rainbow (bl & yel), NM..............................**2,100.00**
Tea bowl & saucer, Rainbow (purple & blk)................................**580.00**
Tea bowl & saucer, Rainbow (red & bl), rstr................................**440.00**
Tea bowl & saucer, Rainbow (red & yel), Thistle, red & gr **1,875.00**
Tea bowl & saucer, Rainbow Drape (red/bl) **2,100.00**
Tea bowl & saucer, red, Fort, bl/blk/red/gr, rare......................**2,000.00**
Tea bowl & saucer, red, Guinea Hen, red/bl/gr/blk, prof rpr....**1,550.00**
Tea bowl & saucer, red, Peafowl, bl/blk/yel/gr...........................**880.00**
Tea bowl & saucer, red, Schoolhouse, red/bl/yel/blk................**1,750.00**
Tea bowl & saucer, red, Teepee..**600.00**
Tea bowl & saucer, yel, Thistle, red/gr/blk, NM........................**3,400.00**
Teapot, bl, Parrot, 3-color, minor stains/prof rpr, 6¾"............**2,500.00**
Teapot, bl w/paneled sides, hairline, 9".....................................**330.00**
Teapot, purple, Tree, gr & blk, prof rpr, 6"...............................**2,000.00**
Teapot, red, Peafowl, red/bl/blk/gr, paneled, domed lid, 9".......**2,400.00**

Cut-Sponge

Bowl, red/bl, florets on blk vine, Staffordshire, 3⅝x7", EX **95.00**
Creamer, bl dmns, vertical pleatings, scalloped............................**145.00**
Cup & saucer, red & gr designs & florets, dk bl band..................**100.00**
Plate, bl/red/gr/brn/yel, brn rabbits & frog transfer, 9¾".............**415.00**
Plate, red & gr flowers w/bl stems, 3-color leaves, Adams, 9"........**60.00**
Soup plate, red & gr, leaves, bl flowers, lt wear, 10½" **110.00**

Spelter

Spelter items are cast from commercial zinc and coated with a metallic patina. The result is a product very similar to bronze in appearance, yet much less expensive

Bookends, draped nude, marble base, Le Verrier/France, 8⅜".....**545.00**
Bust, Queen Victoria, H MacCarthy RCA Sculptor Reg'd 1897, 16x10"...**700.00**
Figure, dancing lady & musician, 14", 15", pr.............................**400.00**
Figure, horse, Miller & Sons, 9x9"..**120.00**
Figure, Irish retriever catching bird, 3x7½x4" **125.00**
Figure, lady w/emb flowers in dress, hood-type hat, 1800s, 11"...**425.00**
Figure, Nouveau lady w/flowers, 30" **350.00**
Figurine, 2 greyhounds on cvd stone base, Deco-style, Masson, 22"...**1,725.00**
Inkwell, dbl; cherub w/urn of water, ornate scrollwork, 6½x9½"...**200.00**
Lamp, Blackamoor, cold pnt, #533FFN inside base, 22" overall..**235.00**
Lamp, boy & girl by tree, HP details, Moreau, 1930s, 46" overall, pr...**775.00**

Spode-Copeland

The Spode Works was established in 1770 in England by Josiah

Spode I and continued to operate under that title until 1843. Their earliest products were typical underglaze blue-printed patterns. After 1790 a translucent porcelain body was the basis for a line of fine enamel-decorated dinnerware. Stone China was introduced in 1805, often in patterns reflecting an Oriental influence. In 1833 William Taylor Copeland purchased the company, having been Spode's business partner. Copeland continued the business in much the same tradition as the Spode-Copeland partnership. Spode was the Royal Potter for years, providing many exquisite items for the Royal Families. They employed paintresses to decorate the merchandise by hand. Most of the Spode-Copeland wares were marked with one of several variations that incorporate the firm's name, making identification possible. The Spode Company merged with Worcester Royal Porcelain Company in 1976 and became Royal Worcester Spode Limited. This company was then purchased by Derby International in 1988. The two firms separated in 1989. The holding company is the Porcelain and Fine China Companies Limited, a division of Derby International. Spode china is still being manufactured today at exactly the same location where Josiah Spode I began in 1770. Robert Copeland, a descendent of William Taylor Copeland, resides in England. He writes books and gives lectures on Spode. Our advisor for this category is Don Haase; he is listed in the Directory under Washington.

The price quotes listed in these three categories of Spode are for twentieth-century pre-1965 dinnerware in pristine condition — no cracks, chips, crazing, or stains. Minor knife cuts do not constitute damage unless extreme.

The patterns in the first group are the most common and popular earthenware lines. The second group contains the rarer and higher priced pattern; they are both earthenware and stoneware. Bone china patterns comprise the third group.

First Group:

Ann Hathaway, Billingsley Rose, Buttercup, Byron, Camilla Pink, Chelsea Wicker, Chinese Rose, Christmas Tree (green), Cowslip, Fairy Dell, Fleur de Lis (blue/brown), Florence, Gadroon, Gainsborough, Hazel Dell, Indian Tree, Jewel, Moss Rose, Old Salem, Raeburn, Reynolds, Romney, Rosalie, Rose Brier, Rosebud Chintz, Tower Blue, Valencia, Wickerdale, Wickerdell, Wickerlane

Bowl, cereal; 6½"	32.00
Bowl, fruit; 5¼"	28.00
Bowl, waste; 6"	35.00
Coffeepot, 8-cup	265.00
Creamer, lg	75.00
Creamer, sm	65.00
Cup & saucer, demitasse	45.00
Cup & saucer, low/tall	39.00
Plate, bread & butter; 6¼"	28.00
Plate, butter pat	28.00
Plate, chop; rnd, 13"	185.00
Plate, luncheon; rnd, 8-9"	35.00
Plate, salad; 7½"	32.00
Platter, oval, 13"	140.00
Platter, oval, 15"	160.00
Platter, oval, 17"	180.00
Sauce boat, w/liner	145.00
Soup, cream; w/liner	55.00
Soup, rim, 7½"	35.00
Soup, rim, 8½"	45.00
Sugar bowl, w/lid, lg	75.00
Sugar bowl, w/lid, sm	65.00
Teapot, 8-cup	265.00
Vegetable, oval, 10-11"	165.00
Vegetable, oval, 9-10"	155.00
Vegetable, sq, 8"	145.00
Vegetable, sq, 9"	155.00
Vegetable, w/lid	265.00

Second Group:

Aster, Buchart, Christmas Tree (magenta), Italian, Mayflower, Herring Hunt (green/magenta), Patricia, Tower Pink, Wildflower (blue/red), Delhi, Fitzhugh (blue/red/green), Gloucester (blue/red), Ruins (blue/pink/brown), Tradewinds (blue/red).

Bowl, cereal; 6¼"	39.00
Bowl, fruit; 5½"	35.00
Bowl, waste; 6"	45.00
Coffeepot, 8-cup	375.00
Creamer, lg	95.00
Creamer, sm	85.00
Cup & saucer, demitasse	55.00
Cup & saucer, low/high	65.00
Plate, bread & butter; 6¼"	35.00
Plate, butter pat	35.00
Plate, chop; rnd, 13"	295.00
Plate, dinner; 10½"	65.00
Plate, luncheon; rnd, 8-9"	49.00
Plate, luncheon; sq, 8½"	65.00
Plate, salad; 7½"	39.00
Platter, oval, 13"	165.00
Platter, oval, 15"	180.00
Platter, oval, 17"	225.00
Sauce boat, w/liner	185.00
Soup, rim, 7½"	45.00
Soup, rim, 8½"	55.00
Sugar bowl, w/lid, lg	95.00
Sugar bowl, w/lid, sm	85.00
Teapot, 8-cup	395.00
Vegetable, oval, 10-11"	195.00
Vegetable, oval, 9-10"	175.00
Vegetable, sq, 8"	165.00
Vegetable, sq, 9"	185.00
Vegetable, w/lid	395.00

Third Group:

Billingsley Rose Savoy, Bridal Rose, Carolyn, Chelsea Garden, Christine, Claudia, Colonel, Dimity, Dresden, Rose Savoy, Fleur de Lis (gray/red/blue), Geisha (blue/pink/white), Irene, Maritime Rose, Primrose (pink), Shanghai, Savoy

Bowl, cereal; 6¼"	45.00
Bowl, fruit; 5½"	42.00
Bowl, waste; 6"	55.00
Coffeepot, 8-cup	445.00
Creamer, lg	120.00
Creamer, sm	110.00
Cup & saucer, demitasse	65.00
Cup & saucer, low/tall	75.00
Plate, bread & butter; 6¼"	45.00
Plate, butter pat	39.00
Plate, chop; rnd, 13"	315.00
Plate, dessert; 8"	55.00
Plate, dinner; 10½"	69.00
Plate, luncheon; rnd, 9"	59.00
Plate, luncheon; sq, 8½"	69.00
Plate, salad; 7½"	49.00
Platter, oval, 13"	195.00

Platter, oval, 15"	225.00
Platter, oval, 17"	295.00
Sauce boat, w/liner	145.00
Soup, cream; w/liner	145.00
Soup, rim, 7½"	65.00
Soup, rim, 8½"	75.00
Sugar bowl, w/lid, lg	120.00
Sugar bowl, w/lid, sm	115.00
Teapot, 8-cup	445.00
Vegetable, oval, 10-11"	235.00
Vegetable, oval, 9-10"	215.00
Vegetable, sq, 8"	245.00
Vegetable, sq, 9"	275.00
Vegetable, w/lid	425.00

Spongeware

Spongeware is a type of factory-made earthenware that was popular during the last quarter of the nineteenth century and into the first quarter of the twentieth century. It was decorated by dabbing color onto the drying ware with a sponge, leaving a splotched design at random or in simple patterns. Sometimes a solid band of color was added. The vessel was then covered with a clear glaze and fired at a high temperature. Blue on white is the most preferred combination, but green on ivory, orange on white, or those colors in combination may also occasionally be found. As with most pottery, condition is a major factor in establishing value. For further information we recommend *Collector's Encyclopedia of Salt Glaze Stoneware* by Terry Taylor, our advisor for this category, and Terry and Kay Lowrance, available from Collector Books.

Bank, bl/wht, Bank stenciled on side surrounded by sponging, rare, 3"	1,200.00
Bank, gr/brn, pig figural, pierced eyes, 3½x6"	200.00
Bowl, bl/wht, emb ribs, faint hairline, 4½x11"	75.00
Bowl, bl/wht, scalloped edge, 1½x9"	175.00
Bowl, bl/wht, 3½x10½"	175.00
Bowl, bl/wht repeating pattern, 4½x9", M, from $85 to	105.00
Bowl, bl/wht w/2 bl bands, stain, 6¼x14"	100.00
Bowl, mixing; bl/wht w/emb Heart pattern, 5½x10", M, from $175 to	225.00
Bowl, serving; bl/wht, emb columns, 6½x13¼"	300.00
Bowl, serving; bl/wht, 3x9½", M, from $75 to	125.00
Bowl, soup; bl/wht, 2¾x8¼", M, from $75 to	125.00
Chamber pot, bl/wht, 5x8½", M, from $225 to	250.00
Chamber pot, bl/wht bear paw pattern w/bl bands, 5x8½", M, $250 to	275.00
Chamber pot, bl/wht w/bl bands, orig domed lid, bail hdl, 12", M	575.00
Cookie jar, bl/wht, ftd ball shape, orig lid, 9"	45.00
Cooler, bl/wht, orig brass spigot, w/rpl lid, 3-gal, 10"	225.00
Crock, bl/wht chicken wire, Butter stencil, chips, 3¾"	175.00
Crock, bl/wht w/Butter stencil, 4x5½", M	250.00
Crock, milk; bl/wht, 5 sm ft, bail hdl, 5x10", M, from $300 to	350.00
Cup, bl/wht, hairline, 2¾"	50.00
Cup, bl/wht, w/matching saucer w/gold rim, EX	110.00
Honey pot, bl/wht (dk), ftd, orig lid, 4½", EX	250.00
Mug, bl/wht, 5x3½", M, from $175 to	200.00
Mug, bl/wht w/blk bands top & bottom, 3½", EX	200.00
Pitcher, batter; bl/wht, rare form, 8x8", M, from $1,700 to	2,000.00
Pitcher, bl/gray, bl bands top & bottom, bulbous, 9¾"	635.00
Pitcher, bl/wht, Child & Dog, design in oval ea side, 9", NM	875.00
Pitcher, bl/wht, emb daisy & vine w/gold, hairline, 9½"	165.00
Pitcher, bl/wht, hairline, 9"	300.00
Pitcher, bl/wht, Leaping Deer medallion, M, 8x5½"	1,250.00
Pitcher, bl/wht, strong color & pattern, 9", M	525.00
Pitcher, bl/wht chain-link pattern, 9", M, from $550 to	600.00
Pitcher, bl/wht close pattern, 10x7", M, from $275 to	375.00

Pitcher, bl/wht repeating pattern, Old Fashioned Garden Rose, 9", M	825.00
Pitcher, bl/wht repeating pattern, ovoid, sm pulled lip, 9x5½", M	350.00
Pitcher, bl/wht repeating pattern, 7x5", M, from $225 to	250.00
Pitcher, bl/wht repeating pattern, 9x5", M, from $300 to	350.00
Pitcher, bl/wht w/bl band, bulbous, 7x5½", M, from $275 to	325.00
Pitcher, bl/wht/gr, bl bands top & bottom, chip, 6½"	110.00
Pitcher, blw/ht, Pine Cone pattern, M, 9"	875.00
Pitcher, brn/bl on pumpkin, emb flower, 7¼", VG	90.00
Pitcher, brn/gr, emb lattice, surface chips, 9¼"	88.00
Pitcher, brn/gr chicken wire, mini, 3"	220.00

Pitcher, cobalt sponging on light gray, American, ca 1890, 8¾", M, from $325.00 to $350.00.

Pitcher, gr patterned, emb grapes, 8"	55.00
Pitcher, hot water; bl/wht, 7x5½", M, from $225 to	300.00
Pitcher, syrup; bl/wht paw prints, 5½x4", M, from $350 to	400.00
Plate, red/gr/brn repeated pattern, overall staining, ca 1880, 8½"	125.00
Soap dish, bl/wht, 5x3½", M, from $125 to	150.00
Soap dish, rnd circle w/raised grooves, 4"	125.00
Spittoon, bl/wht w/bl bands, 5x7½", M, from $175 to	225.00
Spittoon, bl/wht w/bl bands at rim & shoulder, 4½", EX	100.00
Teapot, bl/wht, 8½x8½", M, from $1,200 to	1,500.00
Vase, bl/wht, emb ribbon, sm chip, 7½"	110.00
Washbowl & pitcher, bl/wht, 5x14", 10x7½", M, from $650 to	750.00

Spoons

Souvenir spoons have been popular remembrances since the 1890s. The early hand-wrought examples of the silversmith's art are especially sought and appreciated for their fine craftsmanship. Commemorative, personality-related, advertising, and those with Indian busts or floral designs are only a few of the many types of collectible spoons. In the following listings, spoons are sorted by city, character, or occasion. For further information we recommend *Collectible Souvenir Spoons, Identification & Values*, by Wayne Bednersh (Collector Books).

Key:
B — bowl	ff — full figure
emb — embossed	H — handle
eng — engraved	HR — handle reverse

Black boy eating watermelon in B; squirrel finial; Watson, from $95 to	125.00
Brooklin Bridge eng in B; Stuyvesant ff H; Shepard, from $50 to	70.00
CA on H w/basket of bounty finial; HR: 1933, plain B; Watson	45.00
Chicago H w/ornate finial; plain B; Manchester/Baker, from $20 to	40.00
Chimney Rock, Wisconsin Dells on H; plain B, from $10 to	20.00
Christ ascending in B; cross finial H; Wallace, from $100 to	150.00
Christmas tree in B; Santa ff H; Johnston & Co, from $100 to	150.00
Daniel Boone portrait in rnd cast B; tobacco leaf finial; Gorham	100.00
Denver Capitol emb in B; Summit of Pikes Peak on H; from $25 to	40.00
Detroit MI & scene eng in B; skyline H; Paye & Baker, from $50 to	90.00

French Lick Hotel in B; devil ff H; bronzing, from $100 to **150.00**
Hastings MN, Spiral Bridge eng in B; Gorham, from $50 to.........**70.00**
Hear No...See No...Speak No Evil ff H; plain B; Paye & Baker, $40 to ..**80.00**
High Water Mark, Gettysburg eng in B; Baronial H; Frank Smith Co....**55.00**
House of Betsy Ross, Philadelphia PA on H; plain B; Robbins, $20 to....**40.00**
Indian in canoe finial; made w/various Bs; Lunt, from $20 to **45.00**
Indian w/bow ff H; eng date of 12-11-11 in B; Nat'l Silver Co...**175.00**
Indianapolis 500 on H; plain B; unmk, demi, from $15 to **25.00**
Kodiak bears ff H; plain B; unmk, from $125 to **175.00**
Madison State Capitol eng in B; Old English H; Towle, from $25 to.....**50.00**
Marietta OH Courthouse eng in B; Irving pattern H; Wallace, $30 to ..**50.00**
Marsailles IL Public Library eng in B; state H; Paye & Baker, $40 to.....**60.00**
Masonic Temple Chicago eng in B w/EX detail; unmk, from $30 to......**50.00**
Memphis & emb scene in B; skyline H; Shepard, from $70 to......**90.00**
Mission San Xavier, Tucson AZ on H; plain B; Robbins, from $20 to....**40.00**
Monmouth IL, Willett's School eng in B; Melrose H; Gorham, from $15 to ...**40.00**
Mt Ranier eng in B; lady rider ff H; Meyer Bros, from $200 to...**250.00**
NY Flatiron Building emb in B; H can vary; from $20 to..............**75.00**
Old Spanish Palace, Santa Fe...1590 eng in B; Versailles H; Gorham **60.00**
Passaic Falls Paterson NJ eng in B; Chantilly H; Gorham, from $30 to ..**50.00**
Pike's Peak Signal Station emb in B; mule finial on twisted H; demi **17.50**
Pine tree ff H; plain B; Watson, from $75 to **150.00**
Prickly pear ff H; Mexican coin B; Shrever, from $60 to.............**100.00**
Renovo PA & train eng in B; Shepard, from $30 to.....................**50.00**
Richmond IN, Reid Memorial Church eng in B; Fessenden, from $20 to ..**40.00**
Rochester MN H; St Mary's Hospital eng in B; Alvin, from $30 to...**50.00**
Scranton PA Post Office eng in B; Manchester/Baker, from $30 to ..**50.00**
Steer rider ff H; plain B; Meyer Bros, from $75 to **100.00**
Sutters Fort Sacramento Cal eng in B; Shepard, from $25 to........**50.00**
Uncle Sam ff H w/mc enamel, unmk, ca 1909, from $250 to......**325.00**
USS New York battleship eng in B; unknown mfg, from $30 to...**50.00**
Virginia IL eng in B; Irving pattern H; Wallace, from $30 to.........**50.00**
Washington ff H; Spokane Falls eng in B; Shepard, from $75 to...**125.00**
Wentworth Hall, Jackson NH in B; #52 pattern H; Shepard, from $40 to ..**60.00**
Whale in B; whaling ship finial; Gorham, from $75 to **100.00**
Woman in bathing suit (risque) ff H; Paye & Baker, from $75 to...**125.00**

Sports Collectibles

When sports cards became so widely collectible several years ago, other types of related memorabilia started to interest sports fans. Now they search for baseball uniforms, autographed baseballs, game-used bats and gloves, and all sorts of ephemera. Although baseball is America's all-time favorite, other sports have their own groups of interested collectors. Our advice for this category comes from Paul Longo Americana. Mr. Longo is listed in the Directory under Massachusetts. See also Target Balls; Tennis Rackets.

Key: sig — signature

Bag, golf; alligator leather, Spalding, brn w/gold trim, EX...........**425.00**
Ball, golf; Jack Nicklaus, 65-dimple, Uniroyal, M in sealed wrapper..**50.00**
Balls, tennis; Dunlop Championship..., 1950s, M in 8" can........**100.00**
Balls, tennis; Slazenger, red, ca 1950s, set of 3, NM in can.........**150.00**
Baseball, Detroit Tigers, team autographed, 1964, NMIB............**150.00**
Baseball, Reach brand, late 1950s-early 1960s, MIB (sealed)......**175.00**
Bat, James W Brine Co, ca 1920, 34", EX+ **250.00**
Bat, Joe DiMaggio H&B #125J, Trade Mark Reg, 1940s, 33", EX+...**265.00**
Bat, Kren's Bot-L-Bat, sm crack in hdl, 34".................................**150.00**
Bat, Kren's Special, Wal-O-Per trademk, 1920s, 35", EX **250.00**
Bat, Spalding Ring #53, ca 1880-1900, scarce, EX **300.00**
Book, Satchel Page's Own Story, 3-color cover, 1948, 96-pg, 5x7" ..**65.00**
Book, sketch; NY Yankees, 1953 ....**125.00**

Club, golf; Callaway 50-degree wedge, hickory shaft, steel core....**50.00**
Club, golf; Spaulding brass-headed putter, leather grip, wood shaft...**175.00**
Glove, baseball; D&M, Billy Myers, horsehide lining, 1950s, EX .**75.00**
Glove, baseball; mk Bing Miller & Red Reach in palm, 1920s, VG ...**200.00**
Glove, baseball; 5-finger, Wilson Professional #607, blk leather.**125.00**
Glove, hockey goalie; leather, Cooper GM21 Jr, right hand, EX ..**40.00**
Helmet, football; Baltimore Colts, Rawlings, 1960s, G **60.00**
Helmet, football; Dandux, 1930s-40s, leather, complete, EX **40.00**
Helmet, football; Hutch of Cincinnati H-18, EX.........................**80.00**
Hockey mask, goalie; Cooper/Weeks HM5, 1960s, EX...............**100.00**
Hockey stick, Dallas Blackhawks, Sher-wood #5073, ...**40.00**
Jacket, baseball; NY Yankees, wool & leather, Delong. EX **90.00**
Jacket, baseball; Varsity, wool & leather, Butwin, 1961, VG.........**90.00**
Jacket, Imperial 10X, tan, 1940s shooting patches, VG.................**45.00**
Jacket, tennis warmup; zipper front, Gucci, 1970s, EX...............**50.00**
Jersey, hockey; Gerry Cosby, Madison Sq Gardens, EX.............**55.00**
Knee pads, basketball; leather & wool, 1910s-20s, EX................**35.00**
Knickers, golf; Sporthaus Schuster, M **60.00**
Pants, football; leather, ankle laces, button-up fly, EX................**90.00**
Photo, basketball team, 7 players w/coach, 1917, EX in fr...........**40.00**
Pistol, flare; Winchester/Olin 25 mm, blk pnt, EX **85.00**
Plate, 1928 Olympic Games commemorative, brass, emb tennis player, 11"....**200.00**
Postcard, 1912 Indianapolis 500, winner w/car, EX **50.00**
Program, Army-Navy football game, 1950, 200 pgs **65.00**
Shoes, basketball; Adidas, Patrick Eweing, EX...........................**60.00**
Shoes, basketball; Nike Air Jordan, ca 1990, EX **75.00**
Shoes, football; canvas/rubber, Chuck Taylor, Converse, EX, pr ...**50.00**
Trophy, baseball, mk 1933 AMW Newark NJ, 10½"................**250.00**
Trophy, golf; President's Cup, SP, 1932, 11¾", EX+ **265.00**
Uniform, baseball; Akron, Spaulding, wool, 1920s-30s, EX **250.00**
Yearbook, NY Mets, 1975..**40.00**

St. Clair

The St. Clair Glass Company began as a small family-oriented operation in Elwood, Indiana, in 1941. Most famous for their lamps, the family made numerous small items of carnival, pink and caramel slag, and custard glass as well. Later, paperweights became popular production pieces; many command relatively high prices on today's market. Weights are stamped and usually dated, while small production pieces are often unmarked. Lamps are in big demand (prices depend on size and whether or not they are signed) as are items signed by Paul or Ed St. Clair. For further information we recommend *St. Clair Glass Collector's Book* by Bonnie Pruitt, available from our advisor, Ted Pruitt, who is listed in the Directory under Indiana.

Paperweight, kitten with butterfly on tail, sulfide, signed Joe St. Clair, 1985, from $140.00 to $165.00. (Photo courtesy Marbena "Jean" Fyke)

Animal dish, dolphin, bl, Joe St Clair...............................**175.00**
Bell, Christmas, from $100 to **125.00**

Bell, Holly Carillon, cobalt carnival, sgn 35.00
Bird, bl & clear, lg, from $75 to 95.00
Bowl, pk slag, ped ft, from $150 to 175.00
Candle holder, sulfide, mc floral, from $75 to 85.00
Cordial, any color, from $50 to 65.00
Covered dish, Reclining Colt, cobalt custard, from $135 to........160.00
Creamer, Holly Band, aqua opal 85.00
Creamer & sugar bowl, Grape & Cable, red carnival, from $150 to ...200.00
Doorstop, mallard 375.00
Goblet, Hobstar, ice bl 25.00
Goblet, Wildflower, amethyst carnival 45.00
Insulator, red, red carnival or marigold carnival, ea.....................110.00
Kewpie, chocolate carnival 110.00
Lamp, 3-ball, sgn Joe & Bob St Clair 1,500.00
Paperweight, cameo, windowed, from $250 to 300.00
Paperweight, Kewpie, windowed, from $175 to 200.00
Paperweight, sulfide, Betsy Ross, Joe St Clair 350.00
Paperweight, sulfide, James Madison on cobalt bl, 1971 ....150.00
Paperweight, sulfide, Scottie 145.00
Plate, Kewpie, cobalt carnival...198.00
Plate, Lyndon B Johnson, from $20 to 25.00
Plate, Mt St Helen, from $20 to 25.00
Ring holder, clear w/yel flower...50.00
Ring holder, teapot form, from $75 to 85.00
Statue, Scottie dog, dk amethyst (blk), Bob St Clair..................300.00
Toothpick holder, Bicentennial sq, any color, from $27.50 to 30.00
Toothpick holder, Cactus, wht carnival..35.00
Toothpick holder, Indian, bl & wht slag, sgn Joe St Clair 75.00
Toothpick holder, Indian, yel carnival..25.00
Toothpick holder, paneled, red carnival...25.00
Toothpick holder, Shriner's hat (fez), red, from $125 to..............150.00
Toothpick holder, sulfide, flower, from $65 to................................75.00
Toothpick holder, Swans, any color, from $35 to 45.00
Toothpick holder, witch, chocolate, from $50 to 75.00
Tumbler, Grape & Cable, red...30.00
Tumbler, Holly Band, marigold carnival, from $30 to.....................35.00
Vase, paperweight base, clear trumpet neck, from $75 to 85.00
Wine, Hobstar, crystal carnival, from $40 to.................................45.00

Staffordshire

Scores of potteries sprang up in England's Staffordshire district in the early eighteenth century; several remain to the present time. (See also specific companies.) Figurines and groups were made in great numbers; dogs were favorite subjects. Often they were made in pairs, each a mirror image of the other. They varied in heights from 3" or 4" to the largest, measuring 16" to 18". From 1840 until about 1900, portrait figures were produced to represent specific characters, both real and fictional. As a rule these were never marked.

The Historical Ware listed here was made throughout the district; some collectors refer to it as Staffordshire Blue Ware. It was produced as early as 1820, and because much was exported to America, it was very often decorated with transfers depicting scenic views of well-known American landmarks. Early examples were printed in a deep cobalt. By 1830 a softer blue was favored, and within the next decade black, pink, red, and green prints were used. Although sometimes careless about adding their trademark, many companies used their own border designs that were as individual as their names.

This ware should not be confused with the vast amounts of modern china (mostly plates) made from early in the century to the present. These souvenir or commemorative items are usually marketed through gift stores and the like. (See Rowland and Marcellus.) See also

specific manufacturers. Our advisors for this category are Dave and Anne Middleton; they are listed in the Directory under New Jersey.

Key:
blk — black   l/b — light blue
gr — green   m/b — medium blue
d/b — dark blue   m-d/b — medium dark blue

Figures and Groups

Benjamin Franklin with document and tricorn hat, incorrectly titled G. Washington, 16", $900.00.

Balmoral Castle, bocage & gold, ca 1860, 9¾x9¾" 995.00
Circus pony, sponge decor, separate front legs & tail, 1860s, 5½"...700.00
Dog, seated, glass eyes, brn & gray w/gold collar, 13½" 360.00
Dog, 4 open legs, mc pnt, glass eyes, sm rpr, 15" 275.00
Drummer boy w/dog & flag, mc, 1860s, 9" 795.00
Eva & Uncle Tom on base, mc w/gold, crazing, rpr, 8½" 195.00
Greyhound, recumbent, quill holder, ca 1860, 5x6½" 300.00
Hen on nest, covered dish, 1860s, 8x10", EX...............................800.00
Jean Jacques Rousseau stands beside pedestal, ornate base, 8¼" .600.00
John Wesley holding bible, gold trim, 1870s, 6" 265.00
King Charles spaniel, blk & wht, w/leafy hat, wine pitcher, 10¾" 660.00
King John signing Magna Carta, 1860s, 12½", NM 800.00
Mother goose, HP details, fine details, ca 1860, 7" 895.00
Prince & princess w/tabby cat & bird, mc w/gold, 1860s, 5½"....550.00
Princess on pony, cobalt & gold, 1860s, 5½" 650.00
Pug dog, separate front legs, ca 1875, 10"...................................550.00
Putti (2) & cockerels in arbor, mc, 1850s, 7¼", NM..................600.00
Sheep (pr), recumbent, mc details w/gold, oval bases, 5x3", pr...550.00
Sir James W Dundas, cobalt uniform jacket, 1860s, 15½" 950.00
Spaniel, separate front legs, EX coloring & gold, 1860s, 8½", pr...950.00
Spaniel w/begging pup, cobalt base, gold details, 1860s, 8" 900.00
Uncle Tom w/Little Eva on his shoulder, mc, crazing, 10⅜" 440.00
Victoria (young) on horsebk, mc w/cobalt & gold, ca 1850, 6½"..500.00
Zebra, mc, lt wear/crazing, 8¾"..495.00
Zebra, mc, rpr, late, 5" 140.00

Historical

Bidet, Beauties of Am, d/b, Ridgway, rstr, 4½x18"......................690.00
Bowl, Abbey Ruins, purple, scalloped, Mayer, 1½x10½" 100.00
Bowl, fruit; Capitol, Washington, d/b, Tams Anderson & Tams, 5x11"...1,850.00
Bowl, fruit; Landing of Lafayette at Castle Garden, d/b, rtcl, 11" L...3,000.00
Bowl, vegetable; Blantyre, l/b, shell finial, ftd, Alcock, 7¾x10"...400.00
Bowl, vegetable; Windsor Castle, d/b, unmk (Clews), 12½" L ...415.00
Bowl, waste; Lion Antique, m/b, Wm Smith, 4"............................80.00
Coffeepot, Lafayette at Franklin's Tomb, d/b, rpr spout, 13" 3,300.00
Coffeepot, Ruins, m/b, rstr, 11½" 225.00
Creamer, St Catherine's Hill..., d/b, Clews, 5", EX......................125.00
Pepper pot, Landing of Gen Lafayette, d/b, dome lid, 4⅝", NM...2,750.00
Pitcher, Am & Independence, d/b, chips, 6⅞" 660.00

Pitcher, English castle view, d/b, Clews States border, 11" **1,150.00**
Pitcher, Landing of Gen Lafayette, d/b, scroll hdl, 6¼", EX **1,750.00**
Pitcher, NY Insane Asylum & City Hall, d/b, Clews, 9", NM .**1,800.00**
Pitcher, Residence of Late Richard Jordan, blk, 6½", EX...........**250.00**
Pitcher, wash; Sirius, l/b, att Edwards, 10¼x9", EX **350.00**
Plate, Arms of NY, d/b, sm chip, 10" **495.00**
Plate, B&O Railroad (level), d/b, shell border, Wood, 10⅛" **935.00**
Plate, Boston State House, m/b, 5½" **200.00**
Plate, Canterbury Cathedral, d/b, 10¼" **225.00**
Plate, Catskill House Hudson River, d/b, Wood, 6½", NM........**190.00**
Plate, Catskill Mountain House, lt gr, Wood's cat border, 9" **800.00**
Plate, City Hall NY, m/b, 9¾" **225.00**
Plate, Commodore MacDonnough's Victory, d/b, Wood, 8⅜", NM ..**360.00**
Plate, cup; Cadmus, d/b, trefoil border, 3¾" **225.00**
Plate, cup; cottage in woods (untitled), d/b, Wood, 3⅝" **165.00**
Plate, cup; Customs House Philadelphia, d/b, prof rpr, 3½" **350.00**
Plate, cup; Landing of Lafayette, d/b, Wood, lines, 3¾" **150.00**
Plate, cup; Octagon Church Boston, mismk Staughton's Church, d/b, 4"...**550.00**
Plate, cup; Winter View of Pittsfield MA, d/b, Clews, 4⅝", EX..**190.00**
Plate, Dadmus, d/b, shell border, Wood, 10⅛" **495.00**
Plate, Elephant, blk, gr grass & emb border, 4¾" **275.00**
Plate, Faulkbourn Hall, m-d/b, Stevenson, 10", EX **195.00**
Plate, Hartford CT, purple, Jackson, 10¼" **120.00**
Plate, Kent East Indiaman, d/b, shell border, Wood, crazing, 9¼"....**340.00**
Plate, Kirkstall Abbey Yorkshire, d/b, Adams, 9¾" **180.00**
Plate, Lady of the Lake, unmk (att Carey's), 10¼", EX **150.00**
Plate, Landing of Gen Lafayette, d/b, Clews, 8⅞", NM **350.00**
Plate, Marine Hospital Louisville KY, d/b, Wood, 9¼", EX **400.00**
Plate, Palestine, d/b, Stevenson, 6" **100.00**
Plate, Park Scenery, purple, scalloped, 10½" **100.00**
Plate, Peace & Plenty, d/b, Clews, 10¼", NM **500.00**
Plate, Peace & Plenty, d/b, Clews, 7¾", EX **150.00**
Plate, Peace & Plenty, d/b, floral border, Clews, 9⅞" **330.00**
Plate, Pittsfield Elm, d/b, Clews, 5½", EX **250.00**
Plate, Residence of Late Richard Jordan, brn, 6¾" **110.00**
Plate, Table Rock, Niagara, d/b, Wood, 10⅛" **700.00**
Plate, toddy; girl playing harp, m/b, 4¾" **100.00**
Plate, Transylvania University Lexington, d/b, 9⅛", NM **300.00**
Plate, View of Canal...Mohawk River, red, Jackson, 10⅜" **225.00**
Plate, Winter View of Pittsfield MA, d/b, Clews, chips, 8" **150.00**
Plate, Winter View of Pittsfield MA, m/b, flake, 6⅞" **100.00**
Platter, Avenue, l/b, Edwards, 20½x15¾" **425.00**
Platter, Birds & Floral, l/b, illegible mk, 15½x12" **250.00**
Platter, Detroit, d/b, prof rpr to bk of rim, 18½" **3,000.00**
Platter, E Pluribus Unim/eagle/shield, d/b, Hammersley, 13½", EX...**300.00**
Platter, Eagle w/Shield, l/b, Ridgway, nicks, 15¾" **300.00**
Platter, Hannibal Crossing Alps, m/b, 19½x15¾", EX................**250.00**
Platter, Harper's Ferry, red, scalloped rim, 15⅜" **440.00**
Platter, India Temple, d/b, Stone China JWR, wear, 21¼" **500.00**
Platter, Lake George NY, d/b, Wood's shell border, 16½x13", VG ..**1,900.00**
Platter, Landing of Gen Lafayette, d/b, Clews, 19x14¼", NM.**2,100.00**
Platter, Landing of Gen Lafayette, d/b, floral border, Clews, 15¼" ..**1,300.00**
Platter, Mendenhall Ferry, d/b, Stubbs eagle border, 16½", EX...**1,800.00**
Platter, Niagara Falls From Am Side, d/b, Wood, 14¾" **600.00**
Platter, Penitentiary in Allegheny..., purple, 15¼", NM **350.00**
Platter, St Paul's Church Boston, d/b, Ridgway, 9½x6½"............**865.00**
Platter, Winter View of Pittsfield MA, d/b, Clews, 14½x12"...**1,400.00**
Saucer, City Hall NY, d/b, Stubbs, minor wear/chip, 6¼" **100.00**
Soup, Cadmus, d/b, Wood, 10" **450.00**
Soup, Fair Mount Near Philadelphia, m-d/b, 9⅞", EX **275.00**
Soup, Vue de Chateau de Coucy, d/b, scalloped rim, Wood, 8" .**165.00**
Sugar bowl, Landing of Gen Lafayette, d/b, w/lid, 6¼", EX **600.00**
Sugar bowl, MacDonnough's Victory, d/b, Wood, rpr, 6¾" **600.00**
Tea bowl & saucer, Beaded Frame, d/b, unmk, 2½", 3¾" **125.00**

Tea bowl & saucer, Castle Towards, d/b, Hall & Sons, 2¼", 5¼" ...**125.00**
Tea bowl & saucer, Cliffs of Dover, d/b, Wood, EX.......................**60.00**
Tea bowl & saucer, Franklin's Tomb, d/b, Phillips **285.00**
Tea bowl & saucer, Going to the Well, d/b, Clews NM **140.00**
Tea bowl & saucer, MacDonnough's Victory, d/b, Woods...........**330.00**
Tea bowl & saucer, Palestine, pk, Adams, EX **55.00**
Teapot, bird & nest, d/b, unmk, sm rpr, 7½" **220.00**
Teapot, Franklin's Tomb, d/b, Wood & Sons, rprs, 8" **500.00**
Tray, View From Ruggles House..., l/b, Ridgeway, 10¾", EX **150.00**
Tureen, Alms House Boston, d/b, w/lid, Ridgway, 9½x12¾", EX..**3,300.00**
Tureen, Dix Cove on Gold Coast Africa, d/b, w/lid, 11x15" ..**3,500.00**
Tureen, soup; NW View of LaGrange, d/b, w/lid & tray, 15½", NM..**6,100.00**
Undertray, Pass in Catskill Mtns, d/b, Wood, 8", NM.................**440.00**

Miscellaneous

Bowl, mottled brn creamware w/gr & yel int, late 1700s, 11" dia ..**1,265.00**
Jug, puzzle; bl transfer floral, rtcl neck, 1830s, rpr, 7", VG **180.00**
Ladle, woman & child by cottage in bowl, d/b, 7½" L **600.00**
Plate, Cabbage Rose, red w/yel & red sm flowers, scalloped, 8" ..**250.00**
Teapot, bl/gr/brn mottle, crabstock hdl, 1780s, rstr, 6" **135.00**
Vase, castle form, mc, late, 5" **180.00**

Stained Glass

There are many factors to consider in evaluating a window or panel of stained glass art. Besides the obvious factor of condition, intricacy, jeweling, beveling, and the amount of selenium (red, orange, and yellow) present should all be taken into account. Remember, repair work is itself an art and can be very expensive. Our advisor for this category is Carl Heck; he is listed in the Directory under Colorado.

Lamps

Chicago Mosaic, 12" floral-border shade, Morel; tree-trunk std...**2,750.00**
Chicago Mosaic, 18" floral dome shade, simple bronze std **3,575.00**
Duffner-Kimberly, 16" geometric gr shade, mk std....................**7,150.00**
Duffner-Kimberly, 18" gr slag-segments shade; Corinthian std, 25" **2,000.00**
Duffner-Kimberly, 18" mc shell dome shade; ornate bronze mk std..**22,000.00**
Duffner-Kimberly, 19½" slag-segment shade; 3-socket std, 24"...**2,185.00**
Duffner-Kimberly, 28" down-trn shade w/sm uptrn center, hanging..**23,000.00**
HA Best, 14" floral/geometric shade; 2-socket metal std, 19½"...**1,725.00**
Miller, 21" caramel slag w/mc ribbon-border shade; 3-socket std, 59"......**3,250.00**
Morgan, 24" jeweled vintage shade; tree-form std w/gr patina, 65" **23,000.00**
Wilkinson, 20" parasol-shaped shade w/dropped apron; Seuss std, 24"....**4,000.00**

Windows

American stained and jeweled window with satin glass field, color-phased opalescent flowers, hand-faceted jewels, ripple border, 27x33", $1,500.00.
(Photo courtesy Carl Heck)

Arched design w/pillars & flowers, panel in base, oak fr: 65x25"..**1,500.00**

Dutch lady w/shoulder yoke/girl at gate, fr: 50x52", EX **1,500.00**
Figure in toga w/in landscape, scrolled frwork, Am, 1890s, 76x55" ..**5,500.00**
Fleur-de-lis & floral medallions, att Belcher, 32x16"+fr...........**2,000.00**
Fleur-de-lis/banner, mc beaded border, fr: 14x25" **600.00**
Flying swallows, cobalt & orange w/trees on bl & tan slag, 37x30" ..**1,250.00**
Grapevines, gr & purple on clear field, 96x53", pr **5,500.00**
Grapevines, gr/bl/brn on gr mottled ground, 65x20", EX, pr....**3,250.00**
Grapevines, purple/gr/brn on caramel slag, 3-panel, ea: 30x34" **2,500.00**
Lady w/book flanked by pillars, mc, 1890s, 45x25"+fr.............**5,000.00**
Medallion, sailboat & flowers, amethyst border, clear panels, 34x18" ..**550.00**
Prairie School, geometric w/central chevron, 32x21" **750.00**
Prairie School, rectilinear w/central chevron, 35x19", VG **800.00**
Prairie School chevrons, gr/gold on clear ground, 76x26", pr ..**3,000.00**
Scarab over 2 columns flanked by lotus flowers, 53x26", 3 for.**7,000.00**
Scarab over 2 rows stylized papyrus, mc slag/clear panels, 56x31"..**3,000.00**
St Martin, ca 1900, outside wood fr: 69½x37¾" **600.00**
Trees mc medallion, cranberry/ruby border w/opal blocks, 22x28"..**475.00**

Stanford

The Stanford Pottery Co. was founded in 1945 in Sebring, Ohio. One of the founders was George Stanford, a former manager at Spaulding China (Royal Copley). They continued in operations until the factory was destroyed by a fire about 1961. They produced a Corn Line, similar to that of the Shawnee Company, that is today very collectible. Most examples are marked (either Stanford Sebring Ohio or with a paper label), so there should be no difficulty in distinguishing one line from the other.

In addition to their Corn line, they produced planters and figurines, many of which were black trimmed with gold, made to be sold as pairs or sets. Wall pockets and vases were made as well. In 1949 they introduced a line called Tomato Ware, consisting of a cookie jar, grease jar, salt and pepper shakers, creamer and sugar bowl, mustard jar, marmalade jar, etc. These were shaped as bright red tomatoes with green leaves and stems (often used as lid finials), and were marketed under the name 'The Pantry Parade.' Our advisor for this category is Joe Devine; he is listed in the Directory under Iowa.

Ashtray, free-form, orange w/wht 'stucco,' #270-D, mk, 10x7"......**12.00**
Corn Line, butter dish **60.00**
Corn Line, casserole, 8" L **50.00**
Corn Line, cookie jar **100.00**
Corn Line, creamer & sugar bowl **60.00**
Corn Line, cup **20.00**
Corn Line, pitcher, 7½" **65.00**
Corn Line, plate, 9" L..**35.00**
Corn Line, relish tray **45.00**
Corn Line, shakers, sm, pr **30.00**
Corn Line, shakers, 4", pr **35.00**
Corn Line, spoon rest **30.00**
Corn Line, teapot **75.00**
Corn Line, tumbler..**35.00**
Planter, Dutch boy or girl by tulip, blk w/gold trim, ea................**20.00**
Planter, marching drummer, boy or girl, 7", ea **22.00**
Planter, teddy bear, wht w/pk & bl trim, paper label, 7" **35.00**
Tomato Ware, casserole, w/lid, 6x9" **60.00**
Tomato Ware, cookie jar, 8" **80.00**
Tomato Ware, creamer **30.00**
Tomato Ware, grease jar, w/lid **38.00**
Tomato Ware, marmalade jar **35.00**
Tomato Ware, mustard jar **35.00**
Tomato Ware, pitcher, 6½" **65.00**
Tomato Ware, sugar bowl **30.00**

Wall pocket, bird, bl & cobalt w/gold trim, 7", from $40 to **45.00**
Wall pocket, cherry branch, red pie-crust edge, #299, mk, 6¼" **28.00**

Stangl

Stangl Pottery was one of the longest-existing potteries in the United States, having as its beginning in 1814 the Sam Hill Pottery, becoming the Fulper Pottery which gained eminence in the field of art pottery (ca 1860), and then coming under the aegis of Johann Martin Stangl. The German-born Stangl joined Fulper in 1910 as chemical engineer, left for a brief stint at Haeger in Dundee, Illinois, and rejoined Fulper as general manager in 1920. He became president of the firm in 1928. Although Stangl's name was on much of the ware from the late '20s onward, the company's name was not changed officially until 1955. J.M. Stangl died in 1972; the pottery continued under the ownership of Wheaton Industries until 1978, then closed. Stangl is best known for its extensive Birds of America line, styled after Audubon; its brightly colored, hand-carved, hand-painted dinnerware; and its great variety of giftware, including its dry-brushed gold lines. For more information we recommend *Collector's Encyclopedia of Stangl Dinnerware* by Robert Runge, Jr. (Collector Books). Another good reference is *Stangl Pottery* by Harvey Duke; for ordering information refer to the listing for Nancy and Robert Perzel, Popkorn Antiques (our advisors for this category), in the Directory under New Jersey. Soon to be available: *Encyclopedia of Stangl Artware, Lamps, and Birds* by Robert Runge, Jr. (Collector Books); and *Stangl Pottery, White-Bodied Artware, 1924 – 1942*, by Peter Meissner (Schiffer).

Animals

#3243, Wire-Haired Terrier, 3¼" **275.00**
#3244, Draft Horse, 3"..**200.00**
#3245, Rabbit, 2" **350.00**
#3246, Buffalo, 2½" **300.00**
#3247, Gazelle, 3¾" **300.00**
#3248, Giraffe, 2½" **600.00**
#3249, Elephant, Antique Gold, 5" **125.00**
#3249, Elephant, 3" **350.00**
#3277, Colt, 5" **1,500.00**
#3278, Goat, 5" **1,500.00**
#3279, Calf, 3½" **900.00**
#3280, Dog, sitting, 5¼" **350.00**
Cat, Siamese, sitting, decor, 8½" **600.00**
Cat, sitting, Granada Gold, 8½"..**300.00**

Birds

#3518D,   **White Crowned Pigeons pair, blue with white heads, 8x14", $1,000.00.**

#3250A, Standing Duck, 3¼" **115.00**
#3250D, Gazing Duck, 3¾" **115.00**
#3273, Rooster, 5¾" **1,000.00**
#3274, Penguin, 6" **475.00**
#3275, Turkey, 3½", from $375 to **400.00**

#3281, Duck, mother, 6" 650.00
#3285, Rooster, early, 4½" 100.00
#3286, Hen, late, 3¼" 50.00
#3400, Lovebird, old version, 4" 100.00
#3400, Lovebird, revised, 4" 65.00
#3401, Wren, dk brn, revised, 3½" 50.00
#3401D, Wren pr, tan, old version 700.00
#3402, Oriole, beak down, 3½" 110.00
#3402, Oriole, revised, 3¼" 50.00
#3405, Cockatoo, 6" 50.00
#3406, Kingfisher, 3½" 60.00
#3406D, Kingfisher pr, 5" 150.00
#3407, Owl, 5½x2½" 350.00
#3420D, Oriole pr, revised, w/leaves, 5½" 125.00
#3432, Duck, running, 5" 750.00
#3432, Duck, standing, brn 775.00
#3432, Duck, standing, grayish wht w/blk spots 1,200.00
#3433, Rooster, 16", minimum value 3,000.00
#3443, Flying Duck, gray, 9" 325.00
#3444, Cardinal, revised, glossy pk, 7" 90.00
#3445, Rooster, gray, 10" 250.00
#3446, Hen, yel, 7" 150.00
#3447, Prothonotary Warbler 55.00
#3448, Blue-Headed Vireo, 4¼", from $70 to 70.00
#3449, Parrot, 5½" 175.00
#3450, Passenger Pigeon, 9x18" 1,700.00
#3452, Painted Bunting, 5" 120.00
#3454, Key West Quail Dove, single wing up, 10" 275.00
#3454, Key West Quail Dove, wings spread 1,800.00
#3457, Pheasant, walking, 7¼x15" 2,600.00
#3458, Quail, 7½" 1,500.00
#3491, Hen Pheasant, 6¼x11" 200.00
#3492, Cock Pheasant 200.00
#3543, Mountain Bluebird, 6⅛" 1,250.00
#3580, Cockatoo, med, 8⅞", from $150 to 125.00
#3581, Chickadees, brn/wht, group of 3, 5½x8½" 210.00
#3582D, Parakeet pr, bl, 7" 250.00
#3582D, Parakeet pr, gr, 7" 250.00
#3583, Parula Warbler, 4¼" 65.00
#3585, Rufous Hummingbird, 3" 100.00
#3586, Della Ware Pheasant, natural colors 2,000.00
#3586, Pheasant (Della Ware), terra rose, gr 700.00
#3589, Indigo Bunting, 3½" 85.00
#3590, Carolina Wren, 4½" 160.00
#3591, Brewer's Blackbird, 3½" 175.00
#3592, Titmouse, 3" 55.00
#3593, Nuthatch, 2½" 65.00
#3594, Red-Faced Warbler, 3" 120.00
#3595, Bobolink, 4¾" 160.00
#3596, Gray Cardinal, 5" 70.00
#3597, Wilson Warbler, yel & blk, 3" 55.00
#3598, Kentucky Warbler, 3" 30.00
#3599D, Hummingbird pr 350.00
#3626, Broadtail Hummingbird w/bl flower 170.00
#3628, Rieffer's Hummingbird 170.00
#3629, Broadbill Hummingbird, 4½" 150.00
#3635, Gold Finches (group) 250.00
#3715, Blue Jay, w/peanut, 10¼" 650.00
#3746, Canary (right), rose flower, 6¼" 275.00
#3749, Western Tanager, red matt, 4¾" 500.00
#3750, Scarlet Tanager, 8½" 525.00
#3750D, Western Tanager pr, 8" 525.00
#3751, Red-Headed Woodpecker, glossy pk, 6¼" 475.00
#3751, Red-Headed Woodpecker, red matt, 6¼" 475.00

#3752D, Red-Headed Woodpecker pr, glossy pk, 7¼" 525.00
#3754, White-Wing Crossbill (single) 4,000.00
#3754D, White-Wing Crossbill pr, glossy pk, 9x8" 450.00
#3755, Audubon Warbler, 4¼" 475.00
#3757, Scissor-Tailed Flycatcher, 11" 800.00
#3758, Magpie-Jay, 10¾", from $1,300 to 1,500.00
#3810, Blackpoll Warbler, 3½" 175.00
#3811, Chestnut-Backed Chickadee, 5" 165.00
#3812, Chestnut-Sided Warbler, 4½" 165.00
#3813, Evening Grosbeak, 5" 150.00
#3814, Black-Throated Green Warbler, 3" 165.00
#3815, Western Bluebird, 7" 425.00
#3848, Golden-Crowned Kinglet, 4¼" 125.00
#3849, Goldfinch 150.00
#3851, Red-Breasted Nuthatch, 3¾" 70.00
#3852, Cliff Swallow, 3½" 150.00
#3853, Golden-Crowned Kinglets, 5½x5" 750.00
#3921, Yellow-Headed Verdin, 4½" 1,800.00
#3922, European Finch 1,000.00
#3923, Vermillion Fly-Catcher, 5¾" 2,300.00
#3924, Yellow-Throated Warbler, 6" 550.00
#3925, Magnolia Warbler 3,000.00

Dinnerware

Amber-Glo #3899, butter dish 35.00
Amber-Glo #3899, creamer 15.00
Amber-Glo #3899, gravy boat 15.00
Amber-Glo #3899, plate, 9" 10.00
Amber-Glo #3899, sugar bowl (open) 22.00
Antique Gold #1902, plate, chop; 14½" 60.00
Antique Gold #1902, plate, 11" 25.00
Antique Gold #1902, teapot 125.00
Apple Delight #5161, bowl, lug soup 18.00
Apple Delight #5161, coffeepot, 6-cup 75.00
Apple Delight #5161, pitcher, 2-qt 60.00
Bittersweet #5111, bowl, divided vegetable; oval 30.00
Bittersweet #5111, gravy boat 15.00
Bittersweet #5111, mug, stacking 35.00
Blueberry #3770, ashtray, rectangular 40.00
Blueberry #3770, bowl, fruit; from $15 to 18.00
Blueberry #3770, casserole, skillet shape, 8" 50.00
Blueberry #3770, creamer 25.00
Blueberry #3770, egg cup 25.00
Blueberry #3770, plate, chop; 12½" 75.00
Blueberry #3770, platter, oval, 11½" 125.00
Blueberry #3770, teapot 125.00
Chicory #3809, bowl, vegetable; 8" 45.00
Chicory #3809, cigarette box 125.00
Chicory #3809, gravy boat 35.00
Chicory #3809, plate, 9" 20.00
Cosmos #3339, bowl, fruit 12.00
Cosmos #3339, cup, AD 18.00
Cosmos #3339, plate, chop; 14½" 110.00
Cosmos #3339, teapot 130.00
Country Garden #3943, bowl, cereal 22.00
Country Garden #3943, bowl, divided vegetable; oval 40.00
Country Garden #3943, cake stand 30.00
Country Garden #3943, creamer 15.00
Country Garden #3943, pitcher, ½-pt 30.00
Country Garden #3943, plate, 11" 40.00
Country Garden #3943, platter, Casual, 13¾" 85.00
Country Garden #3943, teapot 100.00
Country Life #3946, bowl, fruit; rooster 40.00

Country Life #3946, cup, hen 25.00
Country Life #3946, plate, chop; barn, 14½", from $250 to........350.00
Country Life #3946, plate, cow, 8" 100.00
Daisy #1870, bowl, salad; 9" 60.00
Daisy #1870, creamer...20.00
Daisy #1870, plate, 10" 35.00
Daisy #1870, teapot...175.00
Dogwood #3668, bowl, salad; 10" 75.00
Dogwood #3668, plate, 8" 25.00
Dogwood #3668, sugar bowl 25.00
Festival #3677, bowl, salad; 10" 75.00
Festival #3677, candy dish..45.00
Festival #3677, plate, 11" 35.00
Festival #3677, sherbet 35.00
Festival #5072, bowl, fruit 15.00
Festival #5072, cake stand 25.00
Festival #5072, pitcher, 2-qt 100.00
Festival #5072, plate, 9" 25.00
Festival #5072, platter, Casual, 13¾"...............................75.00
Floral #3342, ashtray 20.00
Floral #3342, carafe, w/hdl 120.00
Floral #3342, plate, 9" 25.00
Fruit & Flowers #4030, bowl, divided vegetable; oval 50.00
Fruit & Flowers #4030, cigarette box, from $100 to 125.00
Fruit & Flowers #4030, egg cup 25.00
Fruit & Flowers #4030, pitcher, 6-oz, from $20 to 25.00
Fruit & Flowers #4030, plate, 6", from $8 to 10.00
Fruit #3697, bowl, coupe soup 35.00
Fruit #3697, bowl, salad; 10", from $55 to 65.00
Fruit #3697, bowl, vegetable; w/lid, 8", from $140 to 160.00
Fruit #3697, coffeepot, 8-cup, from $100 to 120.00
Fruit #3697, mug, coffee 50.00
Fruit #3697, pickle dish, from $25 to 30.00
Fruit #3697, plate, 9", from $20 to 25.00
Fruit #3697, tidbit, 10", from $10 to 15.00
Garden Flower #3700, bowl, cereal; from $20 to 25.00
Garden Flower #3700, bowl, lug soup; from $15 to 20.00
Garden Flower #3700, casserole, w/lid, 8" 75.00
Garden Flower #3700, coffeepot, from $225 to 250.00
Garden Flower #3700, cup & saucer, from $13 to 18.00
Garden Flower #3700, plate, 9", from $15 to 20.00
Golden Blossom #5155, creamer 8.00
Golden Blossom #5155, mug, 2-cup 30.00
Golden Blossom #5155, plate, 6" 4.50
Golden Blossom #5155, platter, oval, 14¾" 25.00
Golden Harvest #3887, bowl, salad; 10" 40.00
Golden Harvest #3887, casserole, w/lid, 6", from $20 to 25.00
Golden Harvest #3887, coffeepot, 8-cup 50.00
Golden Harvest #3887, cruet, w/stopper 35.00
Golden Harvest #3887, pickle dish 20.00
Golden Harvest #3887, pitcher, 1-qt 45.00
Golden Harvest #3887, tumbler, 12-oz, from $60 to 75.00
Grape #3865, casserole, ind; 4", from $25 to 30.00
Grape #3865, plate, 10" 50.00
Grape #3865, shakers, pr 40.00
Harvest #3341, bowl, lug soup; 5" 22.00
Harvest #3341, bowl, oval, 9", from $45 to 55.00
Harvest #3341, plate, 10" 45.00
Harvest #3341, shakers, pr 20.00
Holly #3869, bowl, salad; 13" 150.00
Holly #3869, cup 25.00
Holly #3869, cup, punch; from $50 to 60.00
Holly #3869, plate, 8"...45.00
Holly #3869, tidbit, from $15 to 20.00

Kiddieware, bowl, cereal; Flying Saucer #5018, 1960, from $275 to 300.00
Kiddieware, bowl, cereal; Indian Campfire #3916, 1955, from $125 to ..145.00
Kiddieware, bowl, cereal; Running Dog, 1941, from $300 to 350.00
Kiddieware, cup, Little Bo Peep #3434, 1942, from $80 to 110.00
Kiddieware, cup, Peter Rabbit #3882, 1953, from $75 to 90.00
Kiddieware, cup, Woman-in-the-Shoe #5208, 1968, from $100 to ..125.00
Kiddieware, divided dish, Bluebird #3827, 1950, from $300 to ...350.00
Kiddieware, divided dish, Cookie Twins #3960, 1957, from $200 to...250.00
Kiddieware, plate, Goldilocks #3764, 1946, 9", from $200 to 250.00
Kiddieware, plate, Mother Goose (pk or bl), 1962 ....400.00
Magnolia #3870, bowl, coupe soup 30.00
Magnolia #3870, bread tray, from $25 to 30.00
Magnolia #3870, coaster/ashtray 20.00
Magnolia #3870, mug, coffee 30.00
Magnolia #3870, pitcher, 1-qt 60.00
Orchard Song #5110, bread tray, from $30 to 35.00
Orchard Song #5110, mug, 2-cup, from $30 to 35.00
Orchard Song #5110, plate, 11", from $20 to 25.00
Prelude #3769, bowl, vegetable; 8", from $25 to 35.00
Prelude #3769, plate, 10" 18.00
Prelude #3769, shakers, pr 15.00
Provincial #3966, bowl, fruit 15.00
Provincial #3966, creamer 15.00
Provincial #3966, mug, 2-cup, from $35 to 45.00
Provincial #3966, plate, 9", from $12 to 18.00
Ranger #3304, bowl, fruit; from $110 to 145.00
Ranger #3304, creamer, from $100 to 125.00
Ranger #3304, cup, coffee; from $60 to 70.00
Ranger #3304, plate, 8", from $160 to 185.00
Rooster #5223, bowl, coupe soup; from $25 to 35.00
Rooster #5223, pitcher, 1-qt, from $65 to 75.00
Rooster #5223, plate, 10" 35.00
Rooster #5223, sugar bowl, from $15 to 20.00
Star Flower #3864, bowl, salad; 10", from $40 to 50.00
Star Flower #3864, cup & saucer, from $13 to 16.00
Star Flower #3864, gravy boat & undertray 30.00
Star Flower #3864, plate, 8", from $10 to 15.00
Thistle #3847, bowl, cereal 25.00
Thistle #3847, bowl, divided vegetable; oval 50.00
Thistle #3847, butter dish, from $50 to 60.00
Thistle #3847, casserole, ind; 4", from $20 to 25.00
Thistle #3847, coffeepot, ind; from $125 to 130.00
Thistle #3847, gravy boat, from $20 to 25.00
Thistle #3847, plate, grill; 9", from $45 to 55.00
Thistle #3847, plate, 11", from $30 to 35.00
Thistle #3847, relish 30.00
Thistle #3847, sugar bowl, Casual 50.00
Tiger Lily #3965, bread tray, from $40 to 50.00
Tiger Lily #3965, cup, from $10 to 12.00
Tiger Lily #3965, plate, 10" 25.00
Tiger Lily #3965, shakers, pr, from $20 to 24.00
Town & Country #5287, baking dish, bl, 7x10", from $100 to ...125.00
Town & Country #5287, bowl, soup/cereal; blk or crimson, from $20 to ...30.00
Town & Country #5287, bowl, vegetable; bl, 8" 60.00
Town & Country #5287, butter dish, brn, gr, honey or yel, $25 to ...35.00
Town & Country #5287, flowerpot, bl, 5", from $35 to 45.00
Town & Country #5287, mug, stacking; brn, gr, honey or yel, $20 to...35.00
Town & Country #5287, sugar bowl, blk or crimson, from $25 to 30.00
Tulip #3365, bowl, rim soup; from $20 to 25.00
Tulip #3365, sugar bowl, from $30 to 35.00
Tulip #3365, teacup, from $10 to 15.00
White Dogwood #5167, bowl, cereal 20.00
White Dogwood #5167, plate, chop; 12½", from $35 to 45.00
White Dogwood #5167, plate, 6" 7.00

White Dogwood #5167, tidbit, 2-tier, from $20 to 25.00
Wild Rose #3929, bowl, lug soup 15.00
Wild Rose #3929, butter dish 45.00
Wild Rose #3929, cake stand, from $20 to 25.00
Wild Rose #3929, coffeepot, 8-cup 110.00
Wild Rose #3929, mug, 2-cup, from $40 to 45.00
Wild Rose #3929, plate, 8" 15.00
Yellow Tulip #3637, bean pot/cookie jar 75.00
Yellow Tulip #3637, bowl, divided vegetable; oval 45.00
Yellow Tulip #3637, creamer 15.00
Yellow Tulip #3637, egg cup 20.00
Yellow Tulip #3637, pitcher, 2-qt, from $80 to 90.00
Yellow Tulip #3637, plate, 10", from $20 to 25.00

Stanley Tools

The Stanley company was founded in Connecticut in 1854, and over the years has absorbed more than a score of tool companies already in existence. By the second decade of the twentieth century, having long since solidified their position as *the* source for tools of the highest grade, the company enjoyed worldwide prestige. Through both World Wars, they were recognized as one of the nation's premier producers of wartime goods. Industrial arts classes introduced baby boomers to Stanley tools and provided yet another impetus to expansion and recognition. Overall, the company's growth and development has kept an easy pace along with the economy of the nation, and it continues today as a leader in the field of tool production.

Three factors to consider when evaluating a tool are these: age, completeness, and condition. One of their earliest trademarks (1854 – 1857) is 'A. Stanley,' found only on rulers. In the early '20s, their now-familiar 'sweetheart' trademark, the letters SW and a heart shape within the confines of a modified rectangle, was adopted. They continued to use this trademark until it was discontinued in 1936. Many other variations were used as well, some of which contain a patent date. A study of these marks will help you determine the vintage of your tools. Condition is extremely important, and though a light cleaning is acceptable, you should never attempt to 'restore' a tool by sanding, repainting, or replacing parts that may be damaged or missing. Tools listed below are for those in average 'as found' condition, ranging from very good to excellent. Note: Any common number $20.00 rule with the A. Stanley trademark is easily worth $500.00 plus!

For more information, we recommend *Antique and Collectible Stanley Tools*, written by our advisor, John Walter, who is listed in the Directory under Ohio.

Architect's rule, #86½ 800.00
Awl, Hurwood scratch; #7 .... 50.00
Bit brace, Four Square, #1151 .... 125.00
Breast drill, #722 .... 75.00
Carpenter's caliper rule, #32½ 85.00
Carpenter's plumb & level, #33 .... 400.00
Carpenter's rule, #68A 25.00
Engineer's hammer, #88 .... 50.00
Gauge, butt & rabbet; #93 .... 75.00
Hacksaw, #33 .... 150.00
Hard board fluting tool, #198 .... 150.00
Level, #36, iron, 95% finish, EX 55.00
Level, torpedo; #261 .... 35.00
Plane, #45, complete w/accessories & orig box, NM 360.00
Plane, block; #25, type #1 .... 700.00
Plane, bull nose block; #101½ 850.00
Plane, butcher block; #64, w/both cutters 2,500.00
Plane, circular; Victor #20, EX 150.00

Plane, dado; #39-1 .... 275.00
Plane, door & router; #171, PAT 12-26-11, EX 420.00
Plane, dovetail; #444 .... 1,500.00
Plane, jointer; #8C 200.00
Plane, jointer; Liberty Bell, #132 .... 200.00
Plane, scrub; #40, curved cutter, VG+ 75.00
Plane, Victor combination; #14 .... 4,500.00
Router, #71, w/3 cutters, orig box, EX 100.00
Screwdriver, Victor Special; #50 .... 50.00
Spoke shave, dbl cutter, #60 .... 75.00
Square, mitre 150.00
Tape measure, #636W 35.00
Trammel point, #6 .... 500.00
Veneer scraper, #12½ 75.00

Statue of Liberty

Long before she began greeting immigrants in 1886, the Statue of Liberty was being honored by craftsmen both here and abroad. Her likeness was etched on blades of the finest straight razors from England, captured in finely detailed busts sold as souvenirs to Paris fairgoers in 1878, and presented on colorfully lithographed trade cards, usually satirical, to American shoppers. Perhaps no other object has been represented in more forms or with such frequency as the universal symbol of America. Liberty's keepsakes are also universally accessible. Delightful souvenir models created in 1885 to raise funds for Liberty's pedestal are frequently found at flea markets, while earlier French bronze and terra cotta Liberties have been auctioned for over $100,000.00. Some collectors hunt for the countless forms of nineteenth-century Liberty memorabilia, while many collections were begun in anticipation of the 1986 Centennial with concentration on modern depictions. Our advisor for this category is Mike Brooks; he is listed in the Directory under California.

Smoking stand with electric lighter, ashtrays, and cigarette receptacle, light in torch, 1930s, 27x10½" diameter at base, $250.00. (Photo courtesy James Flanagan)

Booklet, Rays From Liberty's Torch, 1890 .... 30.00
Bookmark, silk, Bartholdi Souvenir, 1886 .... 75.00
Bottle, seltzer; etched Liberty, A Doeink, Liberty, NY 35.00
Box, porc figural, flag at base, Limoges, 4¼x1" 55.00
Card, admission to inauguration, 1886 .... 70.00
Cigar box label, Victory Day, WWII 6.00
Container, Yourex Silver Saver, rnd, cb, ca 1930 .... 27.00
Cup, sterling, Windsor Club, 1907, 2" 22.00
Flyer, Statue of Liberty steamboat excursions, 1890s 25.00
Harper's Weekly, various litho prints, 1880s, ea, from $10 to 25.00
Lamp, figural, bronze-tone metal, electric, 11" 130.00
Letter, teen to military father re: parade on Broadway, 1886 .... 95.00

Magazine, Harper's Weekly, Liberty centerfold, Nov 6, 1886, EX ...**125.00**
Medal, Belgium relief, bronze, 1916..**70.00**
Medal, Central Valley Nat'l Bank..**18.00**
Napkin holder, sterling..**15.00**
Pennant, felt, 1930s..**25.00**
Pin, enamel, 77th Div, WWI..**12.00**
Pipe, glazed clay, 1880s..**90.00**
Plates, various makers, 1980s, ea, from $10 to..**20.00**
Pocketwatch, Elgin, 1890s..**175.00**
Poster, DeLand, WWI..**150.00**
Radio speaker stand, wht metal casting, Palcone, 17"..**175.00**
Reverse painting on glass, in plaster fr w/orig pnt, 25x19", EX **75.00**
Scarf, head of Liberty, red/wht/bl, Hermes, 35" sq, NM..**150.00**
Scissors, emb metal, Liberty 1 side/Woolworth building on reverse, 6" ..**55.00**
Snow dome, figural, Atlas Crystal Works, 1920s..**55.00**
Statue, American Committee Model, 12", EX..**400.00**
Statue, cast metal on marble base, June 13, 1885..**1,000.00**
Statue, Wenck perfume, 1908..**325.00**
Straight razor, Liberty-etched blade, Sheffield, ca 1880..**75.00**
Ticket, admission to platform for inauguration, 1886..**60.00**
Ticket, lg souvenir of Gauthier et Cie (Liberty foundry), 1883...**105.00**
Trade card, Haas' Remedy, 1880s..**40.00**
Trade card, satirical, A&C Hams, 1880s..**70.00**
Vase, frosted Liberty hand, Gillinder, 1876 Centennial..**70.00**

Steamship Collectibles

For centuries, ocean-going vessels with their ventursome officers and crews were the catalyst that changed the unknown aspects of our world to the known. Changing economic conditions, unfortunately, have now placed the North American shipping industry in the same jeopardy as the American passenger train. They are becoming a memory. The surge of interest in railroad collectibles and the railroad-related steamship lines has lead collectors to examine the whole spectrum of steamship collectibles.

Reproduction (sometimes called 'Replica') and fantasy dinnerware has been creeping into the steamship dinnerware collecting field. Some of the 'replica' ware is quite well done so one should practice caution and... 'know thy dealer.' Our advisors for this category are Lila and Fred Shrader; they are listed in the Directory under California. For more information we recommend *Restaurant China, Vols. I* and *II,* by Barbara J. Conroy.

Key:
BS — back stamped   TL — top logo
SL — side logo   TM — top mark

Clipper ship card, Malay, Samuel Nesbitt & Co., ca 1860, 6¼x4", EX, $600.00.

Dinnerware

Bowl, fruit; Alaska SS Co, TM, 5" dia..**54.00**
Bowl, fruit; American Mail Line, flag in dbl circle, TL, 5"..**24.00**
Bowl, fruit; Colonial Lines, Lexington, TL, 5"..**65.00**

Bowl, fruit; Inland SS Co, Philip D. Block, TL on red dmn, 4½"..**17.00**
Bowl, oatmeal; United States Lines, Gray Star, BS, 6"..**52.00**
Bowl, soup, Seaboard Air Line Railway, Old Bay Line, SL, no hdl, 3¾..**65.00**
Butter pat, American President Lines, Eagle, TL, 3"..**55.00**
Butter pat, Detroit & Cleveland...Co, City of Detroit, TL, 3"..**112.00**
Butter pat, Oceanic SS Co of Savannah, Savannah Line, TL, 3"..**74.00**
Butter pat, United Fruit Lines, Castilla, TL, 2⅞"..**55.00**
Butter pat, United States Lines, Gray Star, BS, 3¼"..**25.00**
Creamer, American Export Lines, SL w/flag & dbl circle, 4½"..**26.00**
Creamer, Cunard White Star..., floral pattern, Cube style, BS, 3"..**38.00**
Creamer, Eastern Steamship Lines, Eastern Green, hdl, 3¾"..**78.00**
Creamer, Matson, Matsonia SL w/M flag, hdl, 3½"..**50.00**
Cup, Baltimore Mail Line, City of Baltimore, SL..**68.00**
Cup, The Texas Company, Texaco Michigan, SL..**219.00**
Cup & saucer, Am Export Lines, Independence, both BS..**45.00**
Cup & saucer, bouillon; Moore-McCormack Lines, Rio, hdls, BS..**67.00**
Cup & saucer, demitasse; Hamburg American Line, SL cup, TL saucer..**44.00**
Cup & saucer, French Line, Ile de France, SL cup, TM saucer..**96.00**
Egg cup, Union Castle Line, Edinburgh Castle belt logo, 2"..**59.00**
Egg cup, United States Line, Gray Star, 3¾"..**112.00**
Hot food cover, Northern Navigation Co, Port Arthur SL, 7"..**196.00**
Mug, coffee; The Texas Co, Texaco Michigan, SL..**218.00**
Pitcher, US Shipping Board, Centennial State, SL 7"..**96.00**
Plate, Alaska SS Co, TL, 5"..**28.00**
Plate, Canadian Pacific, Empress of Ireland, TM, 9½"..**640.00**
Plate, Grace Line TL w/¼" cobalt pinstripe, BS..**38.00**
Plate, Italian Line, Roma, TL, 8"..**58.00**
Plate, Johnson Line, Stockholm, TL house flag, 7"..**19.00**
Plate, Luckenbach Line, TL Edgar Luckenbach, 9½"..**85.00**
Plate, Moore-McCormack Lines, Rio, BS, 6"..**10.00**
Plate, New England Steamship Co, TL, 9"..**48.00**
Plate, Pere Marquette, Autoferry, TL, 6"..**87.00**
Plate, Pickands-Mather & Co, house flag TL, 7"..**37.00**
Plate, rim soup; Pacific Coast SS Co, TL belt logo w/flag, 9"..**63.00**
Plate, United States Lines, Kosher Service, TL, 7½"..**77.00**
Platter, NY&CMSS Co, TM+Ward Line house flag, 8½x5"..**84.00**
Platter, United States Shipping Board, TL Centennial State, 8x5¾"...**12.00**

Glassware

Ashtray, French Line w/CGT TL, green opaque, 2⅝x3¼"..**21.00**
Ashtray, United States Lines, 6 rests, 6-sided, 4¾"..**32.00**
Condiment container, Hamburg-Amerika, metal holder+porc lid, TL..**41.00**
Stem, cocktail; Norwegian American Line, enamel NAL SL..**18.00**
Stem, cordial; Matson, enamel SL encircled in stars..**22.00**
Stir rod, American Export Lines, cobalt, gold lettering, 5"..**11.00**
Tumbler, Northern Navigation Co, SL etched house flag, 4"..**35.00**
Tumbler, Swedish-American Line, SL cut, Orrefors, 5½"..**16.00**

Linens and Uniforms

Blanket, Hamburg-Amer Line, Hamburger Wohlfahrsonstalten, wool, 1950...**59.00**
Hat, officer's, Pacific Far East Lines, w/gold bear badge..**140.00**
Mat, bath; Matson, woven company logo, wht on wht, 29x19"..**45.00**
Napkin, American Mail Line logo, wht on wht, 34 woven on border, 19"...**16.00**
Napkin, United States Lines logo, wht on wht, 21" sq..**19.00**
Towel, bath; Matson, woven company logo, wht on wht, 46x24"..**79.00**
Towel, hand; American President Line woven on bl stripe..**5.00**
Towel, hand; Eastern Steamship woven on gr stripe..**7.00**
Towel, hand; Northern SS Co, Northern woven on both ends, wht on wht ...**11.00**

Paper

Binder, Matson, Procedures & Regulations, 1966, hinged metal, much inf......**66.00**

Book, War Vessels, 64 pages, 1917, 6x9" **51.00**
Booklet, French Lines, SS Paris, 1926 passenger list, general info ...**60.00**
Brochure, United Fruit Company, 1940, 14-pg **10.00**
Luggage sticker, United States Lines, unused, 3½" **4.00**
Luggage tag, Bermuda Line, 3x6" **12.00**
Magazine, June 30, 1952, Newsweek, newly christened SS United States ...**20.00**
Menu, American Republic Lines, SS Argentina, 9/19/39 ....**10.00**
Menu, Homes Lines, Homeric, 1972, 8½x11" **10.00**
Menu, RMS Queen Mary, 8/28/37, Knight cover, emb White Star logo ..**32.00**
Menu card, kosher, QEII, 1983 ....**9.00**
Pamphlet, Blk Ball Line Puget Sound Nav Co Ferries, info map, '40-50s ..**6.00**
Pass, annual; Alaska Pacific SS, 1910............................**33.00**
Pass, annual; Alaska SS, issued to VP of Lehigh Valley RR, cb, 1928......**22.00**
Pass, annual; Goodrich Trans, issued to VP/Lehigh Valley RR, cb, 1928..**27.00**
Pass, annual; Los Angeles SS Co, cb, 1925 ....**5.00**
Pass, New England SS Co, 1917 ....**19.00**
Pass, Portland, Bangor & Machias Steamboat Co, cb, 1880..........**20.00**
Passenger list, Hamburg-American Line, Normannia, 1894 ....**46.00**
Passenger list, Normandie, 16-pg, September 1939................**67.00**
Passenger list, RMS Mauretania, March 1934......................**28.00**
Playing cards, dbl deck, Royal Netherland SS Co, blk leather case....**16.00**
Playing cards, Lamport & Holt Line, TSS Vandyck, 1932, MIB...**47.00**
Playing cards, Moore-McCormack logo, unopened cellophane **6.00**
Pocket mirror, Pacific Coast SS, ship's portrait, celluloid, 3¼" **54.00**
Postcard, RMS Olympic main staircase, postmark illegible **67.00**

Silverware

Bowl, finger; Grace Line, SL, BS, 2x4".............................**62.00**
Bowl, serving; Detroit & Cleveland Navigation Co, hdls, SL, BS, 8½" ...**130.00**
Butter icer, White Star Lines, SL, BS, 3-pc, liner: 7" dia **175.00**
Coffeepot, Holland-Amerika w/SL belt logo+NASM, BS, 7" **90.00**
Creamer, Inter-Island Navigation Co, hinged lid+tray, SL, 4¾" ...**47.00**
Fork, Atlantic Transport Line, BS belt logo **12.00**
Knife, butter; Dollar SS Line, SL **21.00**
Ladle, Norddeutscher Lloyd, TM, Wilkens, Bremen, 13½"...........**36.00**
Napkin ring, White Star Line TL house flag, Elkington **174.00**
Pitcher, Clyde Lines, SL, Reed & Barton, 9" **154.00**
Pitcher, French Line, deep style, ebony-like hdl, BS, 9½" **118.00**
Spoon, iced tea; American Export Lines, TM **3.00**
Spoon, sugar; Dollar Lines, TM & BS **34.00**
Teaspoon, White Star, Adriatic, TL, Elkington **80.00**

Miscellaneous

Ashtray, Alaska SS Co, copper, TL, 3½"...........................**34.00**
Ashtray, Hamburg Am Line, Am flag/swastika, 5 rests, ceramic, 5½" ...**50.00**
Ashtray, Holland America Line, NASM TL, 2 rests, ceramic, 3½" dia .**40.00**
Ashtray, North German Lloyd, brn Bakelite w/picture of Europa on bull...**53.00**
Ashtray, Swedish American Line, 3 rests, rich gold, ceramic, 3½" ..**27.00**
Ashtray/matchbox holder, Am Banner Line, cermic, 2¼x4½" dia..**34.00**
Badge, hat; Lehigh Valley SS logo, enamel on metal, screw-bk **42.00**
Badge, hat; United Fruit Co, cloth logo, sew on **41.00**
Bell, ship's, brass w/hanging bracket, all original, 12x10½" dia...**415.00**
Calendar, perpetual; Queen Mary, metal fr, complete card set **43.00**
Calendar, pocket; Pacific Mail, SS Mongolia, celluloid, 1908.......**20.00**
Clock w/14" oak ship's wheel case, 7" face, Seth Thomas **215.00**
Coat hanger, Cunard's Mauretania, wood..........................**29.00**
Compass, Ritchie, Boston, compass bowl: 4½x10½" dia, +wood box ...**238.00**
Diving helmet, copper/brass/glass, w/shoulder & breastplate, Mark V ...**675.00**
Lamp, oil; Sherwood, Buckingham, onion style, 1864, 19" **290.00**
Lantern, ferry boat; brass+, red/gr lenses, oil burners, 26" **199.00**
Life jacket, Detroit & Cleveland Navigation Co..., cork fill, 1930s **38.00**
Loving cup, Atlantic Transport Line, appl enamel insignia on SP body.......**80.00**

Loving cup, French Line, Ile de France, '62 ping-pong champion, 7½" **125.00**
Luggage tags, Northern Trans Co, leather straps, 1880s, 1½x2", pr...............**53.00**
Newspaper, New York Journal, 8/17/12, 8th ed, Titanic disaster .**280.00**
Paperweight, Upper MI Towing Corp, Tugboat, Harriet Ann, metal, 5½"...**22.00**
Photo album, Queen of Bermuda, 50+ 1939 cruise photos+notations....**260.00**
Porthole, brass, fitted w/mirror, 11½" **30.00**
Souvenir, letter opener, Peninsular & Occidental SS house flag, 7"....**19.00**
Souvenir, pennant, Matson, 5x3½" **7.00**
Souvenir, plate, SS Christopher Columbus, Chicago-Milwaukee, 8½" ..**33.00**
Souvenir, pocketknife, SS United States, celluloid, 2 blades, 3¼"...**32.00**
Souvenir, spoon, D. Kaiser Wilhelm II, enamel bowl & house flag finial...**233.00**
Souvenir, spoon, RMS Doric, pierced, enameled White Star house flag....**285.00**
Souvenir, trinket box, Panama Mail Co, metal treasure chest, 5" L **50.00**
Thermos, United States Lines, SL, metal, w/stopper, 9½".............**22.00**
Whistle, bosun's; SP, 16" braided string lanyard, 4½" **65.00**

Steins

Steins have been made from pottery, pewter, glass, stoneware, and porcelain, from very small up to the four-liter size. They may be decorated by etching, in-mold relief, decals, and occasionally they may be hand painted. Some porcelain steins have lithophane bases. Collectors often specialize in a particular type — faience, regimental, or figural, for example — while others limit themselves to the products of only one manufacturer. See also Mettlach.

Key:
L — liter   tl — thumb lift
lith — lithophane

Pottery, golfer scene, pewter lid (torn), Hauber & Reuther, .5-liter, $1,200.00.

Anti-Semitic, pottery, relief: scene, Dumler & Breiden, .5L....**1,100.00**
Brewery, pottery, transfer/HP: Tigerbrau, logo lid, hairlines, .4L .**265.00**
Brewery, stoneware, eng: Mathaser-Brau, combed, pewter lid, 1L...**900.00**
Brewery, stoneware, transfer/HP: Schwabingerbrau, logo lid, .4L...**475.00**
Character, alligator wraps around, porc, E Bohne & Sohne, .5L.**715.00**
Character, Alpine Jager, porc, chamois tl, lith, sm rpr, .5L..........**635.00**
Character, Black man w/lg hat, pottery, #737, .5L...............**635.00**
Character, cat, pottery, #1000, .5L..............................**465.00**
Character, Cleopatra, pottery, #431, rpr, .5L....................**660.00**
Character, clown, stoneware, bl & purple salt glaze, .5L **775.00**
Character, dog, porc, Schierholz, new, .5L **275.00**
Character, eagle-hawk, stoneware, MP Sch & Co Ulm, inlaid lid, .5L...**850.00**
Character, fox, porc, porc lid, Schierholz, .5L............................**265.00**
Character, Hamburg sailor, pottery, #1821, sm chips, .5L............**440.00**
Character, hunter, pottery, #422, .5L.................................**650.00**
Character, monk, stoneware, inlaid lid, strong cobalt, 3L........**1,200.00**
Character, monkey, porc, inlaid lid, E Bohn & Sohne, .3L, NM **3,000.00**

Character, Munich Child, porc, inlaid lid, lith, rpr strap, .3L.....**265.00**
Character, Munich Child, porc, inlaid lid, Reinemann, rpr, 4¼"....**575.00**
Character, Munich Child, porc, Martin Pauson, .5L **525.00**
Character, Munich Child, pottery, inlaid lid, .5L **525.00**
Character, Munich Child, pottery, inlaid lid, #298, 5" **198.00**
Character, Munich Child, pottery, inlaid lid, Reinemann, 5¼"..**135.00**
Character, Nurnberg Tower, stoneware, pewter lid, mk TW, 2L **1,265.00**
Character, pig, porc, inlaid lid, E Bohne & Sohne, prof rpr, .5L**1,700.00**
Character, Roly Poly Bar Maid, pottery, inlaid lid, #1571, .5L....**600.00**
Character, skull, porc, inlaid lid, E Bohne & Sohne, .5L **425.00**
Character, skull on book, porc, inlaid lid, E Bohne & Sohne, .3L...**575.00**
Character, snowman, porc, sm pewter rpr, Schierholz, .3L.......**3,600.00**
Character, soccer ball, pottery, inlaid lid, #1774, .5L **1,000.00**
Character, stag, porc, porc lid, Schierholz, .5L...........................**275.00**
Character, tower, pottery, #1541, rprs, .5L **880.00**
Character, woman, pottery, inlaid lid, #702, .5L **440.00**
Faience, cold pnt: floral on yel, pewter ring, Schrezheim, 1820s, 1L...**375.00**
Glass, blown, amber, HP: cavaliers, inlaid lid, .5L **355.00**
Glass, blown, appl bl bands/knobs on amber, SP base, man hdl, 1L **715.00**
Glass, blown, bl opaline, matching inlaid lid, closed hinge, 1850, .5L .**385.00**
Glass, blown, eng: Deco design, pewter lid, WFM #265, .5L, NM **465.00**
Glass, blown, eng: vulter/stag, cobalt o/l, 1850s, .5L, EX **1,595.00**
Glass, blown, heavy cut decor, porc inlaid Gambrinus lid, .5L....**450.00**
Glass, blown, HP: floral on milk glass, pewter lid/ring, 1800s, 10"...**1,250.00**
Glass, blown, HP: lady on bicycle, amber, pewter lid, rpr, .5L....**660.00**
Glass, blown, HP: man in red coat, Ringer, pewter lid, .5L.........**625.00**
Glass, blown, HP: man on bicycle, fluted, pewter lid, .5L.........**635.00**
Glass, blown, HP: Nouveau fish/floral, ribs, pewter lid, .5L, NM..**1,750.00**
Glass, blown, wheel eng: couple scene, inlaid lid, 1850s, .5L......**500.00**
Glass, blown, wht & purple o/l cut to clear, set-on lid, 1850s, .5L **660.00**
Glass, blown, wht HP o/l, cut/gold, ivory eagle finial, 1850s, .5L.....**1,750.00**
Glass, blown, wht o/l, cut dmns, Nouveau silver lid, .5L.............**500.00**
Glass, blown, wht opaline, HP gold/wht, gr/clear beads, 1850s, .5L ...**550.00**
Glass, blown w/red o/l, cut/frosted, porc inlaid lid, HP scene, .5L..**3,200.00**
Glass, HP: doe & fawn, Hohlwein, cut base, pewter lid, .5L.......**965.00**
Glass, mold blown, cobalt, relief/HP: flowers, horsehead tl, .5L.**465.00**
Ivory, deer hunting scene w/riders, brass hdl/lid, 1890s, 4½"..**2,850.00**
Occupational, glass, blown: shoemaker, pewter lid, 1L.................**715.00**
Occupational, glass, HP: men loading truck, pewter lid, .5L, NM ..**635.00**
Occupational, porc, transfer/HP: artist scenes, lion tl, .5L, NM..**880.00**
Occupational, porc, transfer/HP: blacksmith, lion tl, king lith, .5L...**965.00**
Occupational, porc, transfer/HP: carpenter, couple lith, rpr, .5L.**550.00**
Occupational, porc, transfer/HP: cook, couple lith, .5L **1,450.00**
Occupational, porc, transfer/HP: dairyman, lion finial, lith, .5L..**1,400.00**
Occupational, porc, transfer/HP: fireman, lith, man tl, 1L.........**550.00**
Occupational, porc, transfer/HP: glazier, inlaid lid, lith, .5L **880.00**
Occupational, porc, transfer/HP: miner, lith, rprs, .5L **1,550.00**
Occupational, porc, transfer/HP: shoemaker, pewter lid, lith, .5L....**650.00**
Occupational, porc, transfer/HP: train scenes, wheel tl, lith, .5L **935.00**
Occupational, porc, trnasfer/HP: wallpaperer, lith, pewter lid, 1L, NM....**825.00**
Occupational, stoneware, transfer/HP: potter, pewter relief lid, 1L..**600.00**
Pewter, relief: eagle/2 bicyclists, Munich Child lid, putti tl, 12" **550.00**
Porc, HP: monks w/tankard & bbl, cobalt/gold/silver, .5L **2,400.00**
Porc, HP: windmill & harbor, windmill lid, lith, .5L...................**350.00**
Porc, HP: 2 ladys/putti, cobalt/gold, inlaid lid, .5L, NM **2,200.00**
Porc, transfer/HP: Gambrinus, couple lith, rpr, .5L....................**275.00**
Pottery, etch: doctor teaching, bone hdl, inlaid lid, #1518, .5L **1,050.00**
Pottery, etch: dwarfs party/frog band, Hauber & Reuther, .5L, EX...**415.00**
Pottery, etch: dwarfs w/king, dwarf lid, Germscheid, #172, .5L...**415.00**
Pottery, etch: laundresses, pewter lid, Hauber & Reuther, #412, .5L...**360.00**
Pottery, etch: man leaves tavern, inlaid lid, Gerz, #1217, .5L **240.00**
Pottery, etch: people on path, Hauber & Reuther, #406, .5L **355.00**
Pottery, relief: coins, inlaid lid w/coin finial, #1262, .5L **440.00**
Pottery, relief: fish, cat hdl, monkey lid, sgn KB, #1245, .5L.......**495.00**

Pottery, relief: frogs scenes, frog figural lid, #1171, .5L **495.00**
Pottery, relief: hikers in mtns, 9 'peak' faces, #1264, .5L **360.00**
Pottery, transfer/HP: Munich Child, skyline pewter lid, lion tl, .5L ..**300.00**
Pottery, transfer/HP: ocean liner, porc flag inlay lid, #1023, .5L.**415.00**
Pottery, transfer/HP: 4F Turner design, pewter lid, .5L, NM **285.00**
Regimental, Inft Rgt W...1902-04, bird tl, lith, .5L, EX **265.00**
Regimental, Kgl Sach...1902-04, Sachsen tl, lith, .5L **600.00**
Regimental, 1 Jager Bat...1901-03, porc, lion tl, .5L...................**950.00**
Regimental, 4 Komp Inf...1913-14, eagle tl, stanhope, lith, .5L, NM.........**880.00**
Regimental, 8 Inf Rgt...1909-11, monument lid, stanhope, lion tl, .5L......**525.00**
SP, relief: ladies allegoricals, serpent hdl, Elkington, 2.5L........**3,500.00**
Stoneware, combed, pewter ring & lid, 4-horse tl, 1890s, 1L......**635.00**
Stoneware, diagonal ribs, pewter ring/lid, Bunzlau, 1755, 2L...**1,155.00**
Stoneware, eng: star, floral sides, pewter lid, 1820, 8½", VG **880.00**
Stoneware, relief: Nouveau design, Magnussen, ca 1899, .5L......**450.00**
Stoneware, relief: repeating decor, 2-hdl, Annaburg, 1680s, 5¼", VG....**3,400.00**
Stoneware, transfer/HP: Am Society...Engineers...1913, Ringer, 1L **495.00**
Stoneware, transfer/HP: lady w/stein before target, pewter lid, 1L....**465.00**
Stoneware, transfer/HP: Lowenbrau, pewter lid, 2¾" **135.00**
Stoneware, transfer/HP: men w/flowers & lady, figural lid, .5L ...**220.00**
Stoneware, transfer/HP: Munich Child/city, pewter lid, rpr, 1L ..**330.00**
Stoneware, transfer/HP: Schutzenlust, man w/rifle, 1936, 1L......**440.00**
Stoneware, transfer/HP: shooting festival, Munich Child tl, 1906, .5L...**360.00**
Stoneware, transfer/HP: shooting festival, pewter lid, blister, .5L..**265.00**
Student Society, porc, HP: man w/sword & flag, lith, 1890, 1L...**1,980.00**
Third Reich, porc, transfer: Hitler portrait, Hitler lith, .5L.........**880.00**
Third Reich, pottery: transfer/HP: soldiers in raft, pewter lid, .5L....**600.00**
Third Reich, stoneware, transfer/HP: gun/flags, helmet lid, .5L..**525.00**
Third Reich, stoneware, transfer/HP: target/flags/swastikas, 1937, 1L...**800.00**
Wood, cvd: animals in forest, wood hdl/lid, rpl pin, 1860s, 8" **880.00**

Steuben

Carder Steuben glass was made by the Steuben Glass Works in Corning, New York, while under the direction of Frederick Carder from 1903 to 1932. Perhaps the most popular types of Carder Steuben glass are Gold Aurene which was introduced in 1904 and Blue Aurene, introduced in 1905. Gold and Blue Aurene objects shimmer with the lustrous beauty of their metallic iridescence. Carder also produced other types of 'Aurenes' including Red, Green, Yellow, Brown, and Decorated, all of which are very rare. Aurene also was cased with Calcite glass. Some pieces had paper labels.

Other types of Carder Steuben include Cluthra, Cintra, Florentia, Rosaline, Ivory, Ivrene, Jades, Verre de Soie; there are many more.

Frederick Carder's leadership of Steuben ended in 1932, and the production of colored glassware soon ceased. Since 1932 the tradition of fine Steuben art glass has been continued in crystal.

Our advisor for this category is Thomas P. Dimitroff; he is in the Directory under New York. In the following listings, examples are signed unless noted otherwise.

Key: ACB — acid cut back

Basket, Blue Aurene, #453, 7½x6½" **3,100.00**
Basket, Gold Aurene, arched hdl, pinched rim, #453, 5x4½".....**700.00**
Basket, Gold Aurene, swirl prunts at hdl, #453, 8x8" **1,700.00**
Basket, Verre-de-Soie, flaring flattened rim, tall hdls, 10"...........**400.00**
Bonbon, Gold Aurene w/Calcite ruffled top, 2½x5" **275.00**
Bottle, scent; Blue Aurene, #1414, flame stopper, 7½" **900.00**
Bottle, scent; Blue Aurene, floral stopper, #2758, ca 1920, 4¼" ...**1,200.00**
Bottle, scent; Gold Aurene, melon ribs, ball stopper, #1455, 6¾"....**700.00**
Bottle, scent; Green Jade/Alabaster, ftd, teardrop stopper, 7½" ..**600.00**
Bottle, scent; lt gr opal, 8-lobed melon, teardrop stopper, 5" **450.00**

Bottle, scent; Rosaline, Alabaster ft, #6412, 5⅜" **450.00**

Bottle, scent; silver flecks/gr cintra/bubbles, #6917, 7¼" **4,600.00**

Bottle, scent; Verre-de-Soie, Cintra stopper, #2835, 3¾" **475.00**

Bottle, scent; Verre-de-Soie, melon ribs, bl flame stopper, 4½" **400.00**

Bottle, scent; wht/blk cluthra/bubbles, eng decor, #6917, 7"......**4,300.00**

Bowl, Alabaster, flared/shaped rim, #6415, 1925, 4¾x8" **1,500.00**

Bowl, Blue Aurene, ruffled rim, mk Aurene Haviland w/in, 6" dia ...**750.00**

Bowl, Celeste Blue, wide optic swirl ribs, #112, ftd, 16" **400.00**

Bowl, centerpc; Blue Aurene, ftd, #2852, 3¼x9"...................**900.00**

Bowl, centerpc; Bristol Yellow, ribbed, ruffled rim w/blk threads, 15"...**350.00**

Bowl, centerpc; Celeste Blue, swirled optic ribs, rolled rim, 16" .**400.00**

Bowl, centerpc; Gold Aurene w/Calcite ft, 2x13¼" **750.00**

Bowl, Dmn Optic w/bl thread around rim, like #6778, 1930s, 5⅜"...**230.00**

Bowl, Gold Aurene, ftd, #d, 3½x9½" **500.00**

Bowl, Gold Aurene, sgn F Carder, flared rim, 2¼x6" **550.00**

Bowl, Gold Aurene on Calcite, stepped oval bowl, 1925, 10" **275.00**

Bowl, Gold Aurene on Calcite, 2¾x9⅝" **250.00**

Bowl, Green Jade, bulbous, ftd, 4x11¼" **515.00**

Bowl, Grotesque, Ivory, #7535, 11½" **550.00**

Bowl, Ivory, 4 dbl-rib panels, incurvate, #7337, 9½" **450.00**

Bowl, Yellow Jade, flared rim, 2½x4⅝" **550.00**

Box, Dmn Quilt, blk threads on clear, fleur-de-lis mk, 6½" **400.00**

Candlestick, amethyst, ½-twist stem, #686, 12" **350.00**

Candlestick, Green Jade flower form, Alabaster base, #7317, 10"...**1,500.00**

Candlestick, Rosaline bowl w/Alabaster stem, 11¾" **400.00**

Candlestick, Topaz, #6384, 5½" **100.00**

Candlesticks, Celeste Blue, appl foliate-form bobeche & cups, 12", pr ...**2,300.00**

Candlesticks, gr, dbl ped base, 3-ball stem, #2956, 8", pr **400.00**

Candlesticks, Green Jade/Alabaster, dbl-ball stem, #2956, 10", pr...**850.00**

Candlesticks, Optic Rib, amethyst, dbl-ball stem, 11¾", pr.....**2,850.00**

Candlesticks, Pillar eng, #7093, 8¼", pr **1,000.00**

Compote, bl w/yel threading, long stem on folded ft, 7" **300.00**

Compote, clear w/gr threading, bubbles, stemmed/ftd, 4⅞x7¼" .**200.00**

Compote, clear w/red threading, #6886, 7x7" **300.00**

Compote, Gold Aurene, stemmed, #2642, 8x6" **775.00**

Compote, Green Jade & Alabaster, 2¾x7" **350.00**

Compote, Silverina, pinched rim, amethyst stem w/mica, ca 1925, 5x7"....**950.00**

Cordial, Gold Aurene, twist stem, 32361, 4¾", 6 for..............**2,500.00**

Creamer & sugar bowl, Gold Aurene, #252 ....**600.00**

Cup & saucer, Gold Aurene, #616, cup: 3" dia.......................**250.00**

Darner, Blue Aurene, 7"..**550.00**

Flower frog, clear w/bl trim, mushroom form, 5" dia...................**225.00**

Goblet, Jade Green & Alabaster, twist stem, #5154, 6" **110.00**

Goblet, Poppy, pk opal w/swirled optic ribs, opal stem/ft, 5¾"....**400.00**

Lamp, ACB bl irid textured on Dk Jade, ormolu base w/swans, 24"...**2,500.00**

Lamp, Green Jade w/etch chrysanthemums, #7008, ca 1925, 32½"...**925.00**

Lamp base, Alabaster, grape etch, SP mts, #8006, 14" **1,300.00**

Lamp base, Cluthra, wht, etch Deco flowers, gilt-metal mts, 12½"...**2,000.00**

Lamp base, Gold Aurene/Yellow Jade/blk, Pegasus, 33" overall..**5,500.00**

Lamp base, Green Jade w/Alabaster threading, SP mts, 11"........**800.00**

Lamp base, Moss Agate, purple/bl/red, gilt-metal mts, #8023, 10¼"..**2,500.00**

Lamp base, Plum Jade, Belgrade etch, gilt-metal mts, #7001, 12"..**2,500.00**

Lamp base, purple Moss Agate, #8023, 10", +gild-metal mts...**2,400.00**

Parfait, Green Jade, Alabaster base, #1060, 4½", pr **225.00**

Parfait, Rosaline/Amber, conical, similar to #3152, 2½x4¾"......**175.00**

Pitcher, Spanish Green, angle hdl, disk ft, #6665, 9" **450.00**

Plate, Bristol Yellow, folded rib, faint ribs, #3579, 2x14¼" **175.00**

Plate, luncheon; Celeste Blue, leaf/dot eng rim, set of 12 ....**600.00**

Plate, luncheon; Kensington variant eng, 8½", 12 for..............**700.00**

Salt cellar, Blue Aurene, #3067, 1½x2½" **450.00**

Shade, Gold Aurene, 10-rib bell w/invt flared rim, 1915, 4⅛" H..**230.00**

Shade, Ivrene, etched medallions & swags, 4½x3½" **125.00**

Sherbet, Blue Aurene, stick stem, #2680, 3¾", on 6¼" tray **750.00**

Sherbet, Blue Aurene/Calcite, 3¾", matching 6" undertray **650.00**

Sherbet, Verre-de-Soie, 4¾" **65.00**

Tazza, Dmn Quilt, crystal, rose reeded rim/stem, Dmn Quilted ft, 7x7" ...**225.00**

Tumbler, iced tea; Amber w/Celeste Blue Mat-su-no-ke, hdl, #3329, 6"..**250.00**

Urn, aquamarine, ftd, #938, 11¼" **250.00**

Urn, Bristol Yellow & Green, conical finial, optic base, 9x4".....**260.00**

Vase, Black Cluthra, #2683, 6⅜" **1,100.00**

Vase, Blue Aurene, #2648, mini, 2¾" **550.00**

Vase, Blue Aurene, flared top, #2636 ....**950.00**

Vase, Blue Aurene, flared/ruffled rim, #1980, 7½" **750.00**

Vase, Blue Aurene, ftd trumpet form, #2909, 10" **1,700.00**

Vase, Blue Aurene, ovoid, short waisted neck, everted rim, #2683, 10"...**1,500.00**

Vase, Blue Aurene, spiral rope-like neck, sq/dimpled body, #799, 11"......**1,200.00**

Vase, Blue Jade, flared body, Alabaster ft, 5" **950.00**

Vase, Bristol Yellow, swirled cylinder, ftd, 7x6¾" **225.00**

Vase, bud; Blue Aurene, #2556, 8½" **400.00**

Vase, bud; crystal, long neck on swollen base, #7947, ca 1947, 6¾" ...**200.00**

Vase, Cluthra, royal bl & wht, sm trapped bubbles, #2683, 6¼" **1,035.00**

Vase, cornucopia; Ivrene, #6120, 6x8" **775.00**

Vase, Dmn Quilt, clear w/blk threading, #6777, 10"................**200.00**

Vase, fan; French Blue, random bubbles, threaded rim, #6287, 8½"..**550.00**

Vase, fan; Green Jade w/Alabaster disk ft, #6287 variant, 1920, 6"..**800.00**

Vase, free-form oval w/pillar lines, #7654, 6¼x8¼"................**635.00**

Vase, Gold Aurene with blue peacock feathers, #261, 8", $4,500.00.

Vase, Gold Aurene, #723, 9" **800.00**

Vase, Gold Aurene, #2683, ca 1928, 12" **3,750.00**

Vase, Gold Aurene, amphora w/4 appl prunts, #7097, 11¾" ...**2,200.00**

Vase, Gold Aurene, bulging collar midway stick neck, #170, 5¾" ...**800.00**

Vase, Gold Aurene, Dmn Quilt, invt rim, 2¼x3¼" **275.00**

Vase, Gold Aurene, gr pulled loops, #209, 4¾" **1,000.00**

Vase, Gold Aurene, ruffled rim, #723, 9x9" **1,100.00**

Vase, Gold Aurene, stump form, #2741, 6" **500.00**

Vase, Gold Aurene, trumpet form, #1585, 10" **550.00**

Vase, Gold Aurene, 12x11" **1,500.00**

Vase, Gold Aurene w/millefiori decor, #573, 5" **4,100.00**

Vase, gold ruby to clear ft, spiral trumpet form, flake, 9½"..........**400.00**

Vase, grasses/stars eng, Teague design, #7500, 10½" **575.00**

Vase, Green Cluthra, shouldered, ovoid, 10¼" **700.00**

Vase, Green Cluthra shading to wht, wide mouth, angular body, 5x7"...**800.00**

Vase, Green Jade, ribbed, #7437, 10" **650.00**

Vase, Green Jade, swirled cylinder, wide mouth, ftd, 6⅞x6⅞"....**375.00**

Vase, Green Jade on Ivory, ACB floral, ovoid, 9¾" **1,265.00**

Vase, Grotesque, amethyst, floriform, appl disk ft, ca 1930, 9¼" ...**525.00**

Vase, Grotesque, Flemish Blue to clear, ftd, 9" **400.00**

Vase, Ivory, ball stem, cupped ped ft, #7316, 9¼" **325.00**

Vase, Ivory, gourd form w/waisted rim, #5133, 5x6" **300.00**

Vase, Ivory, ruffled top, similar to #2081, 7¾" **350.00**

Vase, Ivrene, flared rim, #8453, ca 1920, 8" **800.00**

Vase, Ivrene, wide mouth flared rim, sgn F Carder, 5x5" **345.00**

Vase, Ivrene, 6-ruffle top, #723, 8x10" **350.00**

Vase, lt bl w/bl threading on top border, flared rim, 3"...............**150.00**

Vase, Oriental Poppy, shouldered w/flaring rim, no mk, 5" **1,120.00**

Vase, Rosaline & Alabaster, ACB florals, conical, 12"..............**1,000.00**

Vase, Strawberry Mansion, flared bulb/sq plinth/M hdls, #7389, 13x9" ...1,035.00
Vase, Swirl, amber, ftd, #6031, 7" 175.00
Vase, Verre de Soie, eng floral, eng rim, flared ft, 8x4"...............460.00
Vase, Verre de Soie, red threaded, ruffled/flared rim, #6813, 8" ..260.00
Vase, Verre de Soie, stretched irid on swirled gr, #676, 11½" ..2,185.00
Vase, Verre de Soie w/bl reeding, bulbous, flared rim, 3¼x4" 125.00
Vase, White Cluthra, appl M hdls, #8508, 10" 1,300.00
Vase, Yellow Jade, appl hdls w/suspended rings, #5007, 7" 2,000.00
Wall pocket, Cluthra, blk & wht, gilt-metal fr, 8x15½"..............500.00
Whiskey, clear w/blk beading, Dmn Quilt, 2½" 65.00

Stevengraphs

A Stevengraph is a small picture made of woven silk resembling an elaborate ribbon, created by Thomas Stevens in England in the latter half of the 1800s. They were matted and framed by Stevens, usually with his name appearing on the mat or often with the trade announcement on the back of the mat. He also produced silk postcards and bookmarks, all of which have 'Stevens' woven in silk on one of the mitered corners. Anyone wishing to learn more about Stevengraphs is encouraged to contact the Stevengraph Collectors' Association, whose address can be found in the Directory under Clubs, Newsletters, and Catalogs.

Are You Ready?, EX 300.00
Called to the Rescue, Heroism at Sea, EX 250.00
Coventry, 2 blk & wht scenes, fr, pr 110.00
Crystal Palace (inside), orig matt, G 385.00
Declaration of Independence, woven at Columbian Exhibition .225.00
Dick Turpin's Last Ride on His Black Bess, Hogarth, VG 150.00
First Point 80.00
First Train Built by Geo Stephenson in 1825, 8⅞x11⅝" 150.00
Full Cry, w/matt...120.00
Good Old Days, coach & 4, matted & fr, 7½x10½", M.............195.00
Grace Darling, EX 200.00
Kenilworth Castle, orig matt & fr, 15½x22½"........................175.00
Landing of Columbus, NM 250.00
London & York Mail Coach, 1879 Expo................................120.00
Mrs Cleveland, VG 135.00
Park in Coventry 75.00
Rescue at Sea, fr, VG 220.00
Start, NM..175.00
Struggle 80.00
Water Jump, fr, EX 225.00

Miscellaneous

Bookmark, A Wish O May You E'er in Peace Abide..., 11⅜x2⅛"...50.00
Bookmark, Behold the Man, blk, fr, G 50.00
Bookmark, Friend's Blessings...45.00
Bookmark, Geo Washington, made for Philadelphia Expo, 12x2"...175.00
Bookmark, Home Sweet Home..75.00
Bookmark, Love's Remembrance, VG 75.00
Bookmark, To My Dear Sister...60.00
Bookmark, To My Sons, G...40.00
Postcard, Ann Hathaway's Cottage......................................40.00
Postcard, RMS Lusitania, VG...75.00
Postcard, Shakespeare's Birthday..45.00

Stevens and Williams

Stevens and Williams glass was produced at the Brierly Hill Glassworks in Stourbridge, England, for nearly a century, beginning in the 1830s. They were credited with being among the first to develop a method of manufacturing a more affordable type of cameo glass. Other lines were also made — silver deposit, alexandrite, and engraved rock crystal, to name but a few. Our advisor for this category is Don Williams; he is listed in the Directory under Missouri.

Basket, pk o/l, amber ft, cranberry rigaree, mc leaves, 10"..........400.00
Bottle, scent; dk amber to gr satin, swirls, silver cap, att, 4¾"....635.00
Bottle, scent; Pompeian Swirl, gold/rust w/turq int, 6½x4".........895.00
Bowl, finger; & tray, Jewell, golden amber, crimped/fluted, 3", 6¾"....375.00
Bowl, matsu-no-ke, 36 florets on thorny branch on yel satin, 3x6"....985.00
Bowl, MOP Swirl, red & yel w/aqua tint, 3-ftd, 4½x5½"........1,100.00
Pitcher, yel/pk opal stripes on clear, ribbed, 6"......................225.00
Rose bowl, gold prunus on brn satin egg shape, pleated top, 5" ..375.00
Tumbler, bl swirled satin cased in wht, sq top, 3¾" 300.00
Vase, bronze to lt bl cased to yel, gourd shape, att, 7⅛" 300.00
Vase, cameo, cherry tree branch, pk/yel, scalloped, 5½"..........1,450.00

Vase, cameo, honeysuckle branches, butterfly in flight on reverse, white on turquoise, elongated neck, 13", $5,750.00.

Vase, mc pull-ups in crystal w/pk int, stick neck, 7¾" 1,350.00
Vase, Pompeian Swirl, rose satin, wht int, dbl gourd, 8" 900.00
Vase, rubena verde Swirl MOP, bulbous w/cup neck, 9¾" 1,500.00

Stickley

Among the leading proponents of the Arts and Crafts Movement, the Stickley brothers — Gustav, Leopold, Charles, Albert, and John George — were at various times and locations separately involved in designing and producing furniture as well as decorative items for the home. (See Arts and Crafts for further information.) The oldest of the five Stickley brothers was Gustav; his work is the most highly regarded of all. He developed the style of furniture referred to as Mission. It was strongly influenced by the type of furnishings found in the Spanish missions of California — utilitarian, squarely built, and simple. It was made most often of oak, and decoration was very limited or non-existent. The works of his brothers display adaptations of many of Gustav's ideas and designs. His factory, the Craftsman Workshop, operated in Eastwood, New York, from the late 1890s until 1915, when he was forced out of business by larger companies who copied his work and sold it at much lower prices. Among his shop marks are the early red decal containing a joiner's compass and the words 'Als Ik Kan,' the branded mark with very similar components, and paper labels.

The firm known as Stickley Brothers was located first in Binghamton, New York, and then Grand Rapids, Michigan. Albert and John George made the move to Michigan, leaving Charles in Binghamton (where he and an uncle continued the operation under a different name). After several years John George left the company to rejoin Leopold in New York. (These two later formed their own firm called L. & J.G. Stickley.) The Stickley Brothers Company's early work produced furniture featuring fine inlay work, decorative cutouts, and leaned strongly toward a style of Arts and Crafts with an English influence. It was tagged with a paper label 'Made by Stickley Brothers, Grand Rapids,' or with a brass plate or decal with the words 'Quaint Furniture,' an English term chosen to refer to their product. In addition to furniture, they made metal accessories as well.

The workshops of the L. & J.G. Stickley Company first operated under the name 'Onondaga Shops.' Located in Fayetteville, New York, their designs were often all but copies of Gustav's work. Their products were well made and marketed, and their business was very successful. Their decal labels contained all or a combination of the words 'Handcraft' or 'Onondaga Shops,' along with the brothers' initials and last name. The firm continues in business today. Our advisor for this category is Bruce Austin; he is listed in the Directory under New York. Note: When only one dimension is given for tables, it is length. Cleaning diminishes values; ours are for furniture and metals with excellent original finishes unless noted otherwise.

Key:
b — brand	hdw — hardware
brd — board	n — no mark
d — red decal	p — paper label
h/cp — hammered copper	t — Quaint metal tag

Charles Stickley

Bookcase, 16-pane do, copper bk-plate, rfn, att, 56x36x13" **3,000.00**
Settee, drop arms, slat bk w/wide center slat, d, 37x59", VG...**2,800.00**

Gustav Stickley

Wine cooler, #400, hammered copper, riveted handles, lightly cleaned patina, 13x22", $10,000.00.

Armchair, #2592, 4 bk slats (arch top), leather seat, d, '02-04, 41"...**4,000.00**
Armchair, 5 vertical slats, rewoven seat w/loose cushion, d, 37"........**1,500.00**
Armchair, 5 vertical slats ea side, rstr leather seat, b, 42" **2,600.00**
Armchairs, #310½, 3-slat ladder-bk, orig leather seat, 36", VG, pr...**1,400.00**
Bed, day; #216, 5 slats ea end, key tenons, reuphl/rfn, 78"........**2,800.00**
Bookcase, #715, 16-pane door, h/cp pull, slab sides, 56x36x13" **7,500.00**
Bookcase, #717, 2 8-pane doors, V pulls, rfn, remnant p, 56x48" **5,300.00**
Bookcase, #718, 2 12-pane doors, key & tenon, orig finish, 56x57x13"..**9,500.00**
Bookcase, #719, 2 12-pane doors, slab sides, key tenons, p, 56x54"........**9,500.00**
Bookrack, tabletop extension; 3 slats ea side, b, closed: 7x12x7", M..**1,100.00**
Bowl, h/cp, lightly cleaned, 8" **650.00**
Box, deed; h/cp & oak, orig leather bottom, EX patina, 12½" L......**6,000.00**
Box, shirtwaist; rectangular, cedar lined, h/cp hdls, b, 16x32x17"...**9,775.00**
Cabinet, china; #815, 2 8-pane do, str toe brd, b, 65x42x15" **9,500.00**
Cabinet, china; #822, gallery top, 16-pane door, h/cp pull, 59x35x13" ..**5,500.00**
Chair, #396, high bk, notched top rail, worn leather seat, b, 43".....**1,800.00**
Chair, #398, short H-bk, rstr drop-in seat, 33x16x16" **500.00**
Chair, Morris; #2341, 2 slats under arms, rpl seat, 38x30x34", VG...**5,000.00**
Chair, Morris; #332, flat arms w/5 slats below, worn leather, 40" ...**11,000.00**
Chair, Morris; #332, vertical slats under arms, rstr/rfn, 38" **6,500.00**
Chair, Morris; #367, 19 spindles under arms, sling seat, d......**12,000.00**
Chair, Morris; #369, 5-slats under slant arm, reuphl seat, 40", VG ...**7,500.00**

Chair, Morris; spindle sides, 4-slat bk, drop-in seat, unmk, 37" ..**7,500.00**
Chair, Morris: bow-arm, 4-slat bk, red leather seat, rprs, d, 42" ..**6,000.00**
Chair, side; #306½, 3-slat bk, rpl rush seat, rfn, 36", pr...............**700.00**
Chair, side; #335, tiger maple, 3 vertical bk slats w/inlay, rfn, d...**4,000.00**
Chair, side; 3-slat ladderbk, brn leather seats, 36", 6 for **3,700.00**
Chair, writing arm; 3 vertical slats, rfn, d, 45x28x25" **900.00**
Chest, #906, 2 drws over 4 grad, thru tenons, 49x41x21", EX **10,000.00**
Chest, bride's; recessed panels, CI hinges, rpl corbel, d, 35x18x20".....**15,000.00**
Desk, drop-front; copper/pewter/wood inlay, gallery, shelf, 44", VG..**25,000.00**
Desk, fall-front, #518, iron strapwork, open shelves, rfn, 52x26" ..**6,000.00**
Desk, knee-hole; 9-drw, keyed-through shelf, rfn top, d, 53" ...**5,500.00**
Desk, writing; #650, single drw, lower shelf, p, 30x36x24" **925.00**
Desk, writing; #720, organizer bk, 2 drws, d, 1904, 37x38x22" ..**3,250.00**
Desk, 5 drws, wood knobs, key tenons, early form ca 1902, rfn, 55"........**6,500.00**
Dresser, #905, 2 half-drws over 3 full, key tenons, mirror, 66x47"........**9,000.00**
Dresser, #915, maple, 3 drws amid 2 doors over 3 drws, d, 42x42x20"..**16,000.00**
Footstool, #301, reuhpl leather seat, tapered legs, rfn, 17x20x16" **200.00**
Footstool, #302, brn leather top, b, 4½x12¼x12¼", VG...........**400.00**
Footstool, dk brn orig leather, partial p, splinters, 5x12x12" **500.00**
Inkwell, h/cp, lightly cleaned, 5½" W...**325.00**
Lamp, desk; oak base, wrought-iron support for shade, 18½"..**4,750.00**
Lamp, table; #440, trumpeted stretcher, key tenons, recoated, 30" dia....**2,700.00**
Lantern, hanging; h/cp w/slag glass inserts in cutouts, 33x11" sq..**4,500.00**
Mirror, #916, peaked top, orig glass, d, 24x30", VG **1,600.00**
Rocker, #2627, 5 curved slats at bk, arched top rail, reuphl, 31".**750.00**
Rocker, #309½, 3-slat ladder-bk, rpl seat, d, 32" **600.00**
Rocker, #365, 3 vertical slats, worn leather seat, b, 38x26x30"...**800.00**
Rocker, flat-arm, slatted sides, leather seat, rfn, d, 39½"..........**2,200.00**
Rocker, V-bk w/5 vertical slats, leather seat, b, 34½" **750.00**
Rocker, 4 vertical slats, orig leather seat w/caned base, n, 38"..........**800.00**
Rocker, 5 vertical slats, corbels under flat arms, rpl seat **2,100.00**
Sconces, h/cp, spade-shape bks, buttressed shafts, 11x2½", pr.**1,400.00**
Screen, #91, nail-head cut-out design, leather inserts, d, 69x66"...**15,000.00**
Seat, window; #152 manor hall, trn legs/cvg, leatherette seat, 30" .**1,400.00**
Server, #819, 3 short drw, iron pulls, low shelf, recoated, 39x48".....**4,250.00**
Settle, #171, 5-leg, horizontal bk brd, key tenons, 1902, d, 78".**8,500.00**
Sideboard, #814½, 3 doors amid 2 doors over long drw, d, 48x56" **7,000.00**
Sideboard, #819, 3 short/1 long drw, iron hdw, d, 39x48x20"..................**4,250.00**
Sideboard, #955, 2 drws over shelf over single drw, d, 44x60x24" **50,000.00**
Stand, magazine; #72, 3 open shelves, arched panel sides, p, 49x29".....**2,900.00**
Stand, magazine; overhanging top, 3-shelf, apron, p, 42x22x13" ...**7,000.00**
Stand, plant; #660, cut-corner top, wide apron, p, 20x18x18", VG.....**1,500.00**
Stand, telephone; #605, sq top, shelf, d, p, 30x14x14" **850.00**
Table, #436, stacked X-stretcher, key tenons, rfn, d, 24" dia....**3,750.00**
Table, #511, cut-corner top, shelf, key tenons, rfn, n, 29x44x24" **2,400.00**
Table, #603, arched X-stretchers, p, 20x18" dia.........................**1,100.00**
Table, drop leaf; #673, oval w/stretcher, key tenons, cleaned, 44"........**2,100.00**
Table, lamp; #626, stretcher base, key tenons, wear, 30x40" dia.......**4,250.00**
Table, library, #456, 2 hidden drws, flush tenons, rfn, 29x36x24" **2,500.00**
Table, library; #675, 2-drw, copper pulls, 30x48x30", EX **1,850.00**
Table, library; spindle sides, shelf, 3-drw, d, p, 32x54x29".........**7,500.00**
Table, occasional; sq legs, arched stretchers, d, 1902, 29x36" dia **2,750.00**
Table, tea; #5, 4 splayed legs, key-tenon stretchers, 24x24" dia........**11,000.00**
Table, tea; #608, rnd top, X-stretchers, cleaned, d, 26x24" dia, VG..**2,500.00**
Table, tea; #699, rnd top, cloud lift, p, 30x50" **3,000.00**
Table, trestle; #637, leather top, key tenons, shelf, 39x48x30" **3,500.00**
Table, trestle; key tenons, shelf, overcoated finish, d, 48" **2,200.00**
Tray, h/cp, repousse poppy pads, orig patina, n, 15" **2,200.00**
Tray, h/cp, repousse spades, orig patina, n, 16" **1,300.00**
Wardrobe, #920, 2 panel doors, fitted int, 4 drws, p, 1910, 60x34" ..**14,950.00**

L. & J.G. Stickley

Armchair, #388, orig leather bk/seat/tacks, d, 37x27x42" **4,250.00**

Armchair, #422, U-bk over 6 vertical slats, uphl seat, d, 38" **750.00**
Armchair, fixed-bk, new seat & bk cushion, b, 42x32x36" **4,000.00**
Bookcase, #647, 3 12-pane doors, h/cp hdw, key tenons, 55x72"..**16,000.00**
Bookcase, single door, gallery, key tenons, d, 55x40x12" **7,500.00**
Bookcase, 2 12-pane doors, dbl-key tenons, n, 55x52x12" **6,500.00**
Cabinet, china; #727, 9-pane door, h/cp pull, recoated, l, 55x34"..**4,250.00**
Cabinet, china; #746, 2 doors w/ldgl panels, arched toe brd, 62x44"..**8,500.00**
Chair, Morris; #470, wide arms, thru posts, reuphl seat, rfn, 38" ..**2,200.00**
Chairs, dining; 8 vertical spindles, rpl leather seat, 40", 7 for..**4,750.00**
Chairs, side; #1340, 3 vertical slats, rstr seats, rfn, 35", 4 for ..**1,100.00**
Clock, grandfather; copper face, beveled top, w, 80x25x15"..**35,000.00**
Desk, #500, flat top, 5-drw, orig hdw, b, 30x42x26" **1,100.00**
Footstool, rpl leather top, arched apron, n, 16x19x15" **1,100.00**
Rocker, #421, 3-slat bk, uphl seat/bk cushion, d **865.00**
Rocker, #423, 6-slat bk, leather reuphl, 36" **900.00**
Rocker, slatted sides, curved slatted bk, orig seat, rfn, p, 31" ..**3,500.00**
Settle, #263, 7-slat bk, drop arms, rpl cushions, d, 37x70" **6,900.00**
Settle, #281, even-arm w/slats, orig spring seat, d, 34x76x31" .**7,500.00**
Sideboard, #735, 4-drw & 2 doors above long drw, 45x56x23", VG ..**2,400.00**
Sideboard, 2 doors flank 4 drws, linen drw, rpl rack, d, 72" **4,500.00**
Stand, magazine; #345, 4-shelf, gallery, chamfered bk, l, 46x19x12" **1,700.00**
Stand, magazine; #47, 4-shelf, arched support sides, n, 45x21x12" **1,500.00**
Stand, magazine; slatted sides, 4-shelf, worn finish, p, 42x21x12" ..**1,700.00**
Table, #561, clip corners, str apron, arched stretchers, 20x18" **1,400.00**
Table, clip corners, arched X-stretchers, rfn top, t, 29x24x24"....**750.00**
Table, lamp; #573, lower shelf, arched S stretchers, rfn, 29x24" dia..**1,400.00**
Table, library; #568, 2 drws, h/cp pulls, rfn, 54" **2,700.00**
Table, library; key-tenon shelf, 1 drw, rfn top, 42"...................**1,800.00**
Torchere, h/cp w/buttressed base & bobeche, EX patina, att, 54x11" ..**8,000.00**

Stickley Bros.

Bookcase, 2 1-pane doors, gallery, copper pull, t, 50x36x12" ...**3,500.00**
Cart, tea; removable tray w/rpl mirror, recoated, l, 30x30x17"....**650.00**
Chair, arm; vertical slat sides/(fixed) bk, rstr seat, t, 40" **1,600.00**
Chair, Morris; single slat under flat arms, canvas seat/cushions, 38" ...**1,200.00**
Chair, 5-slat bk, notched top rail, rpl seat, child sz, 29" **120.00**
Chamberstick, #48, h/cp, bobeche, 4½" **500.00**
Desk, #6178, 1-drw, organizer bk, 4-slat sides, t, 34x34x22" **1,200.00**
Dresser, #9032, 2 half drws, 4 full drw, orig knobs, d, 50x38x22"..**2,100.00**
Hall seat, #3822, 10 vertical slats, solid seat, lt recoat, 34x42" ...**2,400.00**
Rocker, #567, spindled bk, orig leather seat, b, p, 36x29" **1,400.00**
Rocker, 2 wide vertical slats at bk/arms, thru tenons, reuphl, 33" **2,000.00**
Settle, #3719, trapezoidal w/cut-out slats at bk/sides, rpl seat, 72" ...**3,750.00**
Stand, magazine, #4706, 4-shelf, recoated, t, 40x27x13" **1,500.00**
Stand, magazine, #4703, 3-shelf, 3 spindles ea side, t, 31x26x13"....**750.00**
Stand, magazine; 5-shelf, slatted sides/bk, p, 47x16x12" **1,200.00**
Table, #314½", 3-leg, flush tenons, key-tenon base, 18x15" dia....**1,200.00**
Table, lamp, #2894, X-stretchers, key tenons, t, 30x24" dia.....**1,700.00**
Table, lamp; #2882, 3-spindle sides, thru tenons, t, 30x30x28"..**1,300.00**
Table, library; #2860, 3 drws, thru tenons, 39x26" **2,500.00**
Table, side; #2501, rnd top, sq shelf, thru tenons, recoated, 29x26"..**1,200.00**
Table, sq top, 4 flared legs w/X stretcher, rfn, 19x12" **600.00**

Stiegel

Baron Henry Stiegel produced glassware in Pennsylvania as early as 1760, very similar to glass being made concurrently in Germany and England. Without substantiating evidence, it is impossible to positively attribute a specific article to his manufacture. Although he made other types of glass, today the term Stiegel generally refers to any very early ware made in shapes and colors similar to those he is known to have produced — especially that with etched or enameled decoration. It is gen-

erally conceded, however, that most glass of this type is of European origin. Our advisor for this category is Mark Vuono; he is listed in the Directory under Connecticut.

Bottle, scent; med amethyst, 20 ogival pattern over flutes, 6" **1,200.00**
Flask, chestnut; med amethyst, 21 dmns over flutes, pontil, 6½"...**675.00**
Tumbler, enameled hearts/hands/German writing/1708, pontil, 3½" ...**600.00**

Stocks and Bonds

Scripophily (scrip-awfully), the collecting of 'worthless' old stocks and bonds, gained recognition as an area of serious interest around the mid-1970s. Today there are an estimated 5,000 collectors in the United States and 15,000 worldwide. Collectors who come from numerous business fields mainly enjoy its hobby aspect, though there are those who consider scripophily an investment. Some collectors like the historical significance that certain certificates have. Others prefer the beauty of older stocks and bonds that were printed in various colors with fancy artwork and ornate engravings. Even autograph collectors are found in this field, on the lookout for signed certificates.

Many factors help determine the collector value: autograph value, age of the certificate, the industry represented, whether it is issued or not, its attractiveness, condition, and collector demand. Certificates from the mining, energy, and railroad industries are the most popular with collectors. Other industries or special collecting fields include banking, automobiles, aircraft, and territorials. Serious collectors usually prefer only issued certificates that date from before 1910. Unissued certificates are usually worth one-fourth to one-tenth the value of one that has been issued. Inexpensive issued common stocks and bonds dated between the 1930s and 1980s usually retail between $1.00 to $10.00. Those dating between 1890 and 1930 usually sell for $10.00 to $50.00. Those over one hundred years old retail between $25.00 and $100.00 or more, depending on the quantity found and the industry represented. Some stocks are one of a kind while others are found by the hundreds or even thousands, especially railroad certificates. Autographed stocks normally sell anywhere from $50.00 to $1,000.00 or more. A formal collecting organization for scripophilists is known as The Bond and Share Society with an American chapter located in New York City.

Our advisor for this category is Warren Anderson; he is listed in the Directory under Utah. In many of the following listings, two-letter state abbreviations immediately follow company name. All are in fine condition unless noted otherwise.

Key:
I/C — issued/cancelled   U — unissued
I/U — issued/uncancelled   vgn — vignette

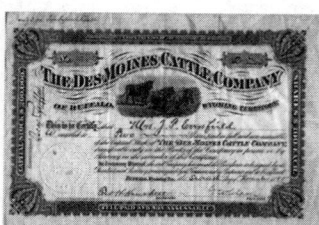

Des Moines Cattle Co, Wyoming Territory, 1885, cattle vignette, signed and recorded, VG+, $145.00 at auction. (Photo courtesy American Social History and Social Movements)

Allen Sarsaparilla, ME/1893, State Arms, dog & deer vgns, I/C...**80.00**
Bank of NC, NC/1864, reapers & portraits vgns, ABNCo, I/C ..**135.00**
Bingham Copper Boy Mining, UT/1903, minors vgn, ornate banner, I/U...**30.00**
Chemical Hand Fire Extinguisher, Portland ME/1880s, U, M.......**30.00**
Cincinnati Peru & Chicago RR, vgns, WC Hannah, 1856.........**150.00**
Clarion River Oil Co, horse/sailboats vgns, PA, 1865, 7x11"......**100.00**

Cold Crescent Mines, CO/1930, miners in tunnel, I/U **15.00**
Coleman Farm Mill, NY/1859, farming vgns, Hatch Litho, I/C **55.00**
Columbus & Indianapolis RR, OH/1864, train vgn, ornate title, I/C ...**40.00**
Crown Head Gold Mining, ME/1889, seal vgn, blk/wht, I/U **30.00**
Diamondless Core Drilling, AZ/1913, multiple scenes vgns, I/U ..**20.00**
Fame Mutal Insurance, PA/1860, lady w/trumpet vgn, I/C **30.00**
Fishhawk Timber Co, OR/1918, ornate banner, blk/wht, gold seal, I/U..**35.00**
Fort Pitt Petroleum Corp, DE/1919, 3 vgns, blk/wht, I/U **15.00**
Franklin Silver Mining, B Franklin/miners vgns, Philadelphia, 1867...**120.00**
Grand River Valley RR, MI/1903, station vgn, ABNCo, I/C **35.00**
Highland Oil Co, shepherds & frontiersman vgns, PA, 1865, 7½x11" ...**150.00**
IL Mining & Milling, UT/1903, miners vgn, 6 miners along borders, I/C....**25.00**
Indian Oil Co, Indian vgns, PA, 1865, 7x11" **245.00**
Internat'l Mining & Milling, NV/1933, Gold Bullion Debenture, I/U ..**10.00**
Internat'l Mining & Milling, NV/1936, ornate banner, I/U **8.00**
Ione Mining & Milling, UT/1904, miners vgn, I/U **25.00**
Kora Temple, ME/1908, Magi on camel, 3-color border, NM........**70.00**
Markeen Copper Co, WV/1902, 3 miners in shaft vgn, ABNCo, I/U..**45.00**
Massey Oil, TX/1926, 8" oilfield vgn w/wells, orange border, I/U .**15.00**
MO/KS/TX Railway, NY/1887, bold title, cattle vgn & cherubs, I/C..**35.00**
Oceanic Chemical Co, WA/1935, torch vgn, gr border/seal, I/U **8.00**
Oxford Linen Mills, ME/1910, machine vgn, I/U **20.00**
Pierce-Arrow Car, NY/1935, man & emblem vgns, ABNCo, I/C....**135.00**
Pittsburgh & Lake Erie RR, PA/1926, 3 vgns w/lg Pittsburgh scene, I/C..**20.00**
Price River Irrigation, UT/1918, prosperous valley vgn, I/U **20.00**
Rutland Oil & Gas, AZ Territory/1905, oil-wagon vgn, I/U **20.00**
Silver Leaf Metals Inc, CO/1927-30, silver leaf vgn, I/U..............**20.00**
St Lucie Rod & Gun Club, FL/1928, State arms, seal, I/C **50.00**
Tenderfoot Copper Mining, MT/1918, Lincoln portrait vgn, gold seal ..**15.00**
Upper Potomac Steamboat Co, VA/1875, PH Troth, 11x13", EX ...**22.50**
US Dehydrator Corp, SD/1917, 8" valley vgn, I/U **15.00**
UTCO Uranium Co, CO/1958, bald eagle vgn, orange seal, I/U **9.00**
Western Coal Oil & Gas Co of Durant, OK/1916, eagle vgn, I/U .**15.00**
World Exploration Co, DE/1927, gr/brn on wht, I/U.....................**10.00**
Zee Development, WA/1935, Miss Liberty vgn, gold seal, I/U **8.00**

Stoneware

There are three broad periods of time that collectors of American pottery can look to in evaluating and dating the stoneware and earthenware in their collections. Among the first permanent settlers in America were English and German potters who found a great demand for their individually turned wares. The early pottery was produced from red and yellow clays scraped from the ground at surface levels. The earthenware made in these potteries was fragile and coated with lead glazes that periodically created health problems for the people who ate or drank from it. There was little stoneware available for sale until the early 1800s, because the clays used in its production were not readily available in many areas and transportation was prohibitively expensive. The opening of the Erie Canal and improved roads brought about a dramatic increase in the accessibility of stoneware clay, and many new potteries began to open in New York and New England.

Collectors have difficulty today locating earthenware and stoneware jugs produced prior to 1840, because few have survived intact. These ovoid or pear-shaped jugs were designed to be used on a daily basis. When cracked or severely chipped, they were quickly discarded. The value of handcrafted pottery is often determined by the cobalt decoration it carries. Pieces with elaborate scenes (a chicken pecking corn, a bluebird on a branch, a stag standing near a pine tree, a sailing ship, or people) may easily bring $1,000.00 to $12,000.00 at auction.

After the Civil War there was a need and a national demand for stoneware jugs, crocks, canning jars, churns, spittoons, and a wide variety of other pottery items. The competition among the many potteries

reached the point where only the largest could survive. To cut costs, most potteries did away with all but the simplest kinds of decoration on their wares. Time-consuming brush-painted birds or flowers quickly gave way to more quickly executed swirls or numbers and stenciled designs. The coming of home refrigeration and Prohibition in 1919 effectively destroyed the American stoneware industry.

Investment possibilities: 1) Early nineteenth-century stoneware with elaborate decorations and a potter's mark is expensive and will continue to rise in price. 2) Late nineteenth-century hand-thrown stoneware with simple cobalt swirls or numbers is still reasonably priced and a good investment. 3) Mass-produced stoneware (ca. 1890 – 1920) is available in large quantities, inexpensive, and slowly increases in price over the years.

Skillfully repaired pieces often surface; their prices should reflect their condition. Look for a slight change in color and texture. The use of a black light is also useful in exposing some repairs. Buyer beware! Hint: Buy only from reputable dealers who will guarantee their merchandise.

In the following listings, 'c/s' means 'cobalt on salt glaze'; all decoration described before this abbreviation is in cobalt. See also Bennington, Stoneware. Assume that values are for examples in near mint condition with only minimal damage unless another condition code is given in the description.

Batter pail, AL Hyssong Bloomsburg PA, c/s, tin lid, ca 1891, 12" ..**415.00**
Butter churn, #4/lily, c/s, Hart Bros...NY, 1880s, 16", EX **275.00**
Churn, #4/geometrics, c/s, Whites Utica, ca 1865, 15½" **200.00**
Churn, #6/bird on flower branch, c/s, J Burger Jr, ca 1885, 20" ..**4,400.00**
Cooler, water; #6/wreath/accents, c/s, Ottman Bros, rpr, 1870s, 17"..**120.00**
Crock, #1/birds (2), c/s, Holmes & Purdy...NY, line, 1850s, 9" ...**495.00**
Crock, #1/duck in pond, c/s, MacQuoid & Co NY, 1860s, 7"..**1,150.00**
Crock, #1/swan, c/s, att Pottery Works NY, 1870s, 7½" **1,045.00**
Crock, #12/orchid (entire front), c/s, NA White, 1870s, 21" ..**2,000.00**
Crock, #2/bird on plume, c/s, S Taft & Co...NH, 1880s, 9½" **715.00**
Crock, #2/chicken pecking corn, c/s, Brady & Ryan...NY, ca 1885, 9"..**770.00**
Crock, #2/leaf, AB Wheeler & Co, c/s, dbl hdls, stain, 10" **150.00**
Crock, #2/lovebirds, c/s, S Hart Fulton, prof rstr, ca 1875, 9" **800.00**
Crock, #2/multiflower, c/s, Cortland, rim chip, 1870s, 9½" **360.00**
Crock, #2/plume, c/s, F Woodworth...VT, ca 1872-95, rpr, 10½"..**90.00**
Crock, #2/vine, c/s, NA White...NY, chip/stain, 1870s, 9" **145.00**
Crock, #3/bird (bold), c/s, S Hart Fulton, spider, ca 1877, 10½"..**575.00**
Crock, #3/bird on leaf, c/s, Ottman Bros, line, 1870s, 10½" **600.00**
Crock, #3/C Miller Groceries...NY, c/s, tight line, 1860s, 9½" ...**1,300.00**
Crock, #3/man's profile, unmk (Midwest), old rpr, 1850s, 11" **965.00**
Crock, #3/star, c/s, unidentified, 13"...**300.00**
Crock, #4/bird on plume, c/s, Whites Utica NY, rpl ear/rstr, 11½"..**120.00**
Crock, #4/bird w/shield & medallion, c/s, 12"..............................**465.00**
Crock, #4/leaf, c/s, Haxtun & Co...NY, 1870s, 11"......................**220.00**
Crock, #5/bird on plume (lg), c/s, Riedinger & Caire NY, 1870s, 12"...**900.00**
Crock, #5/drooping flower, c/s, dbl-ear hdls, 13x12"....................**330.00**
Crock, #5/grape cluster, c/s, WA MacQuoid...NY, line, ca 1865, 12"..**1,300.00**
Crock, #5/parrot on plume, c/s, FB Norton...Mass, ping, 1870s, 12" **700.00**

Crock, #6/eaglet with outstretched wings, Harrington & Burger Rochester, late nineteenth century, 14¾", $5,500.00.

Crock, #6/bird on stump, c/s, JA&CW Underwood...NY, ca 1865, 13", EX ...1,150.00
Crock, #6/flower, c/s, J Mantell Penn Yan, prof rstr, 1860s, 14"..660.00
Crock, cake; #5/dog among ground cover, c/s, West Troy, 1880s, 13"..2,750.00
Jar, #1/flower, c/s, Cowden & Wilcox, pings, 1870s, 9½" 525.00
Jar, #1/stylized leaf, c/s, Edmands & Co, 1870s, 9½" 190.00
Jar, #2/bird & triple flower, c/s, L Lehman...NY, 1860s, 15".....1,485.00
Jar, #2/bird on plume, c/s, FB Norton...Mass, 1870s, 11½" 1,100.00
Jar, #2/cabbage-style flower, c/s, N Clark..., rstr, 1850s, 12" 800.00
Jar, #2/flowers (dbl), c/s, Lyons, 1860s, 11" 525.00
Jar, #3/parrot & plume, c/s, FB Norton...Mass, rstr, 1870s, 13" ...1,200.00
Jar, oyster; Cowden & Wilcox, c/s, ca 1870, 1-qt, 8" 90.00
Jar, preserve; #1/plume, c/s, Lyons, prof rstr, 1860s, 9½"...........250.00
Jar, preserve; #2/wreath, c/s, T Harrington Lyons, 1860s, 11½" ..635.00
Jar, preserve; #4/hands shaking, c/s, Somerset Pottery Works, 15", EX.415.00
Jar, preserve; tulip & hands, c/s, emb lid w/eagle & slot, 7" 630.00
Jug, #1/bell flower, c/s, Cortland, chips/line, 1870s, 11"...........300.00
Jug, #1/flower, brn ochre, unmk, 1830s, 11".................................880.00
Jug, #1/leaf, c/s, WH Farrar...NY, 1840s, 10½"...........................300.00
Jug, #1/pine tree, c/s, NA White...NY, lt stain, 1870s, 10½" 145.00
Jug, #2/bird, c/s, I Seymour Troy, ca 1825, 13½", EX 1,700.00
Jug, #2/bird (very lg), c/s, West Troy, 1880s, 14", EX.................635.00
Jug, #2/bird on perch, c/s, NY Stoneware, 1870s, 14½" 770.00
Jug, #2/bird on twig, c/s, JA&CW Underwood, ca 1865, 15"......210.00
Jug, #2/flower, c/s, F Stetzenmeyer...NY, rare 1857 mk, 15" 1,925.00
Jug, #2/leaf & flower, c/s, I Seymour Troy, prof rstr, ca 1827, 14"...600.00
Jug, #2/parrot on plume, c/s, FB Norton...Mass, 1870s, 14", EX...990.00
Jug, #2/poppy flower, c/s, N White...Binghamton, prof rstr, 11½"...275.00
Jug, #2/snowflake, c/s, Clark & Co Rochester, 1850s, 14½"........715.00
Jug, #2/sunflower, c/s, John Burger Rochester, ca 1865, 14½" 900.00
Jug, #2/vine, c/s, C Crolius NY, ca 1800, 12½"...........................425.00
Jug, #3/flower (drooping), c/s, Whites Utica, ca 1875, 15", EX...300.00
Jug, #3/oak leaf, c/s, F Stetzenmeyer...NY, rpr, 1860s, 16" 1,300.00
Jug, syrup; #2/bird on plume, NY Stoneware, prof rstr, 1880s, 14" ...385.00
Jug, tulip, c/s, IM Mead Mogadore OH, flake, 14½"....................700.00
Pail, #2/flower (dancing), c/s, Harrington & Burger, rstr, ca 1853, 9"...360.00
Pitcher, #1/tulip, Burger & Lang...NY, wear/chips, 1870s, 10" 600.00
Pitcher, #2/flower, c/s, John Burger Rochester, rpr/lines, 11".......800.00
Pot, cream; #1/flower (triple), c/s, Cowden & Wilcox, line, 8"...385.00
Pot, cream; #3/star face design, c/s, T Harrington Lyons, line, 12"...3,500.00

Store

Perhaps more so than any other yesteryear establishment, the country store evokes feelings of nostalgia for folks old enough to remember its charms — barrels for coffee, crackers, and big green pickles; candy in a jar for the grocer to weigh on shiny brass scales; beheaded chickens in the meat case outwardly devoid of nothing but feathers. Today mementos from this segment of Americana are being collected by those who 'lived it' as well as those less fortunate! Our advisor for this category is Charles Reynolds; he is listed in the Directory under Virginia. For more information we recommend *General Store Collectibles, Vols. I and II,* by David L. Wilson. See also Advertising; Scales.

Bag holder, wooden sq post w/4 attachments to hold bags, 46x10" 70.00
Bill clip/clip board, solid brass clip w/emb boy & box, 7½x3¼" ...75.00
Bin, coffee; worn pine w/blk stenciling, 32x22x17", VG.............330.00
Bin, poplar w/worn gray rpt over yel, cut-out ends, hinged lid, 38x38"...220.00
Cabinet, grain/seed storage; oak, 24 drws w/glass fronts, 2-pc, 84"....995.00
Cabinet, oak step-bk, glass doors, 4 drws, 2-pc, 96x96"............1,150.00
Case, oak & glass, marble top insert, oak base w/NP CI legs, 56x20x20" ..650.00
Cash drw, Alsworth, wood, brass pull/drop slot, 1920, 6x7x18", EX...30.00
Cash drw, McCaskey, wood w/metal drw front, 6x15x21", EX 120.00
Cash drw, oak, w/ledger shelf, 9x16x24", EX 150.00

Counter, oak, 8-door front, 34x118x22", VG 1,725.00
Counter, seed; oak, 6 tin drws, glass sample windows, 34x33x31"...865.00
Dispenser, Bromo Seltzer, cobalt glass base & bottle, 17x4½x6".....125.00
Dispenser, perfume; oak, w/atomizer bottle, 1920s, 12x5x3", NM...350.00
Display stand, Teaberry Gum, vaseline glass, 3½x7x4¾", NM......85.00
Jar, candy, globe shape, smooth base, 11¾" 185.00
Jar, candy; globe shape, w/lid, 15"..200.00
Jar, candy; smooth base, tooled mouth, glass stopper, 1900s, 10"...425.00
Jar, Franklin Caro Co emb on lid finial, 4-sided, 12", VG............70.00
Jar, HO Foss & fleur-de-lis on front panel, 9½", EX 75.00
Jar, smooth base, tooled mouth, glass stopper, 1910s, 20"............700.00
Lamp, B&H, brass, hangs, Pat Appl For, electrified, 34½" H 250.00
Paper cutter, CI, Nixon, 20x28", G 70.00
Spice dispenser, AB Davis, litho & HP tin, 8-drw, 21x12x32", EX+ ..700.00

Stoves

Antique stoves' desirability is based on two criteria: their utility and their decorative merit. It's the latter that adds an 'antique' premium to the basic functional value that could be served just as well by a modern stove. Sheer age is usually irrelevant. Decorative features that enhance desirability include fancy, embossed ornamentation, nickel-plated trim, mica windows, ceramic tiles, and (in cooking stoves) water reservoirs and high warming closets rather than mere high shelves. The less sheet metal and the more cast iron, the better. Look for crisp, sharp designs in preference to those made from worn or damaged and repaired foundry patterns. Stoves with a pastel porcelain finish can be very attractive; blue is a favorite, white is least desirable. Chrome trim, rather than nickel, dates a stove to circa 1933 or later and is a good indicator of a post-antique stove. Though purists prefer the earlier models trimmed in nickel rather than chrome, there is now considerable public interest in these post-antique stoves as well, and some people are willing to pay a good price for these appliance-era 'classics.' (Note: Remember, not all bright metal trim is chrome; it is important to learn to distinguish chrome from the earlier, more desirable nickel plate.)

Among stove types, base burners (with self-feeding coal magazines) are the most desirable. Then come the upright, cylindrical 'oak' stoves, kitchen ranges, and wood parlors. Cannon stoves approach the margin of undesirability; laundries and gasoline stoves plunge through it.

There's a thin but continuing stream of desirable antique stoves going to the high-priced Pacific Coast market. Interest in antique stoves is least in the Deep South. Demand for wood/coal stoves is strongest in areas where firewood is affordable and storage of it is practical. Demand for antique gas ranges has become strong, especially in metropolitan markets, and interest in antique electric ranges is just starting to surface. The market for antique stoves is so limited and the variety so bewildering that a consensus on a going price can hardly emerge. They are only worth something to the right individual, and prices realized depend very greatly on who happens to be in the auction crowd. Even an expert's appraisal will usually miss the realized price by a substantial percent.

In judging condition look out for deep rust pits, warped or burnt-out parts, unsound fire bricks, poorly fitting parts, poor repairs, and empty mounting holes indicating missing trim. Search meticulously for cracks in the cast iron. Our listings reflect auction prices of completely restored, safe, and functional stoves, unless indicated otherwise.

Base Burners

Art Garland 250, Michigan Stove Co, 1920, rstr 1,250.00
Art Garland 58, Michigan Stove Co, ca 1910, rstr 8,000.00
Ideal Garland 200, wood/coal, no urn ca 1898, rstr.................1,300.00
Imperial Universal 50, Cribben & Sexton, Chicago, 1913, rstr...4,000.00
Noble Crown, ca 1920, dismounted from base, rstr 1,300.00

Radiant Stewart 34, Fuller & Warren, Milwaukee, ca 1900, rstr ..**5,000.00**
Retort 218, Marion IN, soft coal, 3 mica doors, 1914, rstr.......**2,400.00**
Wehrle 100, Wehrle Co Newark OH, 1911, 14", rpl parts/rstr....**4,000.00**
Wehrle 100, Wehrle Co Newark OH, 1911, 18", rstr.............**9,000.00**

Parlor

The term 'parlor stove' as we use it here is very general and encompasses at least eight distinct types recognized by the stove industry: cottage parlor, double-cased airtight, circulator, cylinder, oak, base burner, Franklin, and the fireplace heater.

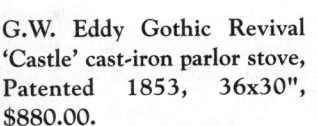
G.W. Eddy Gothic Revival 'Castle' cast-iron parlor stove, Patented 1853, 36x30", $880.00.

Estate Oak F-316, no urn, ca 1915, G **425.00**
Fr enamel, Neoclassical ormolu mts, ca 1880s, 30½x22½" **500.00**
Golden-Mist, Mitchell, Stevenson & Co, Pittsburgh PA, CI, 40", EX..**500.00**
Ideal Garland 220, wood/coal, no urn, ca 1898, rstr.................**1,300.00**
Ideal Heater 417, Gem City Stove...Quincy IL, oak stove, 1925, G ...**175.00**
Marion Retort 218, cased oak, 3 mica doors, ca 1905, rstr.......**2,400.00**
Peoria Oak, Culter & Proctor, oak stove, 1920, unrstr **25.00**
Round Oak D-18, 1901, complete, unrstr **300.00**
Round Oak D-18, 1904, complete, unrstr **300.00**
Round Oak 18-T-31, 1940, G **225.00**
Round Oak 18-0-2, 1916, unrstr.................................**100.00**
Violet #4, Campbell Ellison & Co...OH, CI, 4 sliding doors, 1856, 28" ...**500.00**

Ranges (Gas)

Alcazar, Milwaukee, 4-burner/1-oven, 1928, G.................**50.00**
Chambers, wht, 4-burner, ca 1949, G.................**250.00**
Cribben & Sexton Universal, cream & gr, 4-burner/1 oven, 1927, VG....**300.00**
Magic Chef, wht, 6-burner/2-oven, high closet, 1938, rstr, up to...**12,000.00**
Magic Chef, wht, 6-burner/2-oven, high closet, 1938, unrstr ..**1,000.00**
O'Keefe & Merritt, 4-burner, cabinet base, ca 1929, G.................**110.00**
Quick Meal, 4-burner, bl, cabinet style, 1919, G.................**925.00**
Quick Meal, 4-burner, gray, canopy/high closet, 1924, unrstr **375.00**
Quick Meal, 4-burner/1-oven, 1928, unrstr.................**300.00**
Roper, 4-burner/1-oven, 1929, unrstr **300.00**

Ranges (Wood and Coal)

Alpine Bride, CI, blk, ca 1920, rstr **300.00**
Brilliant Universal, bl, high closet, no reservoir, 1917, G **200.00**
Garland 1925, CI, Pat 1876, EX.................................**4,000.00**
Glenwood F 107, high shelf, 1910, rstr **1,100.00**
Globe, Kokomo IN, gray, ca 1925, G **150.00**

Kalamazoo Peerless, gray & wht, wood/coal/gas, G.................**875.00**
Magee 88, 2-oven/8-hole, CI, high closet/no reservoir, 1880, rstr ..**5,500.00**

Stove Manufacturers' Toy Stoves

Buck's Jr Range, St Louis MO, new body/pnt/recast parts, 26"....**850.00**
Charter Oak #503, GF Filley, St Louis MO, 14x12x25", EX..**2,050.00**
Dainty, Reading Stove Works, PA, 7x13x8", VG **150.00**
Estate Fresh Air Oven, blk/wht enamel, NP, working gas range, 15"..**2,400.00**
Karr, Qualified, bl porc w/NP, Belleville IL, 1925, EX.............**2,500.00**
Karr Qualified Range, aluminum/tin, dial on door, 21½x13", EX **775.00**
Karr Range, Belleville IL, bl porc, older model, 21½x13x9"....**3,100.00**
Little Eva T Southard, NYC, 8½x14x11", G **350.00**
Little Fanny, CI, minor rust, EX **300.00**
Royal American, Bridgeford, Louisville KY, 14x12x10", G **950.00**

Toy Manufacturers' Toy Stoves

Arcade Hotpoint Range, pnt CI, tan & gr, VG **150.00**
Arcade Roper Range, pnt CI, gas type, door opens, 4½", EX........**70.00**
Bing, cookstove, bl steel, brass trim, 16½", VG **600.00**
Crescent, cookstove, plated CI & steel, 4-hole, 11½", EX..........**230.00**
Eagle, Hubley, Lancaster PA, NP, recast parts, rstr.................**450.00**
Eagle, Kenton, CI, heavily scrolled, 4-ft, 11½x10", G.................**125.00**
Eclipse, CI, EX.................................**175.00**
Kenton Royal, CI & steel, 4-hole, ornate, 10", VG.................**100.00**
Lionel, porc & CI, cream & gr, 4-leg, 32x26", EX.................**550.00**
Little Giant, unmk/unidentified, 7½x8½x11", EX orig.............**675.00**
Novelty, Kenton Hdwe, bl pnt/NP trim, rfn, 13x6½x8½" **600.00**
Pet, The Young Bros, Albany NY, 10½x6x8½" **165.00**
Rival, J&E Stevens, Cromwell CT, 14x9x16", M, +2 kettles...**1,350.00**
Rival, no shelves, 12" L, EX.................................**900.00**
Royal, Kenton, CI & steel, 4-hole/working grates, rpt, 10", G......**50.00**
Royal, plated CI, stovepipe, shield shape, 16", G.................**85.00**
Triumph, Kenton Hdwe, OH, 14x8½x19", G.................**195.00**

Stretch Glass

Stretch glass, produced from circa 1916 through 1935, was made in an effort to emulate the fine art glass of Tiffany and Carder. The pressed or blown glassware was sprayed with a metallic salts mix while hot, then reshaped, causing a stretch effect in the iridescent finish. Pieces which were not reshaped had the iridized finish without the stretch, as seen on Fenton's #222 lemonade set and #401 guest set. Northwood, Imperial, Fenton, Diamond, Lancaster, Jeannette, Central, Vineland Flint, and the United States Glass Company were the manufacturers of this type of glass.

For more information we recommend *American Iridescent Stretch Glass* by John Madeley and Dave Shetlar (Collector Books). See also specific companies.

Bowl, amber (marigold), flared, 3-ftd, Jeannette, 3x9" **45.00**
Bowl, Aztec (marigold), flared rim, Lancaster, 2¾x10" **45.00**
Bowl, bl, flared rim, US Glass, 1⅞x12" **60.00**
Bowl, cobalt, flared rim, Vineland Flint Glass Works, 4x7½" **170.00**
Bowl, dk gr w/marigold irid, ruffled, Diamond Glass Co, 2¾x7½"...**165.00**
Bowl, Florentine Green, cupped rim, Fenton, #109, 2x3¾" **25.00**
Bowl, gr, cupped rim, Diamond Glass Co, 2⅞x5¾" **35.00**
Bowl, Iris Ice (crystal), 10-panel, wide flared rim imp, 4½x12¾" .**80.00**
Bowl, Jade Blue, 27-rib, cupped rim, Northwood, #638, 2½x6½".**50.00**
Bowl, lt purple, low ft, flared, US Glass, #314, 4¼x6¾" **100.00**
Bowl, olive; pk smoke decal decor, hdls, Imperial, #615, 2⅝" L .**125.00**
Bowl, Pearl Blue (bl slag), openwork rim, US Glass, #8076, 11⅛" ..**350.00**
Bowl, Pearl Silver (dk purple), 4-crimp, Imperial, #70, 3¾x8" ...**140.00**

Bowl, ruby, 3-ftd, crimped, Fenton, #603, 5¼x10⅜" 800.00
Bowl, topaz, 28 optic rays, ftd, Northwood, #682, 5¾x9¼" 150.00
Candlesticks, dk purple, Vineland Flint Glass Works, 6¾", pr....80.00
Candlesticks, Green Ice (bl-gr), hex bases, Imperial, #6009, 9", pr..175.00
Candlesticks, Harding Blue w/wht trim, Diamond Glass Co, 9x4⅜", pr ..125.00
Candlesticks, Trumpet Twist, bl, Northwood, 6⅜", pr....180.00

Candy jar, After Glow (pink), Diamond Glass, 5¼x6⅜", $150.00. (Photo courtesy John Madeley and Dave Shetlar)

Candy jar, Optic Rays, Iris Ice (crystal), 3-ftd, Lancaster, 7⅛"....95.00
Cheese & cracker, topaz w/blk, US Glass, #320, 3⅜x4⅝", 9⅝"....60.00
Cigarette holder, Velva Rose (pk), Fenton, #554, 3¼x4¾" 150.00
Comport, Celeste Blue, flared oval, Fenton, #103, 3x4x4¾" 75.00
Comport, topaz, high ft, cupped rim, US Glass, 4⅝x7½"....50.00
Lamp shade, gr w/marigold, ruffled, unknown mfg, 2⅝x8"....70.00
Mayonnaise, bl, flattened rim, Northwood, #704, 4x6⅜"....40.00
Pitcher, Adams Rib, Harding Blue, Diamond Glass Co, 9⅞"....500.00
Pitcher, bl w/topaz hdl, slim, unknown mfg, 10½x4¼" 400.00
Plate, cake; pk, ftd, US Glass, #310, 3⅛x12½"....80.00
Plate, Celeste Blue, Fenton, #757, octagon, laurel leaf, 7½" 35.00
Plate, lt bl, 12 optic panels, US Glass, 9" 25.00
Plate, Topaz, Worthwood, #630, 8¾" 30.00
Server, amber (marigold), narrow shovel hdl, Jeannette, 4½x10".50.00
Sherbet, Florentine, GA, Fenton, #408, 3¼"....35.00
Sherbet, Optic Rays, red, Imperial, #499, 3½"....75.00
Sherbet, Russet w/gold, 8-panel, flared, Northwood, 3½x3¾" 65.00
Vase, Florentine Green, Fenton, 11½x3¼"....120.00
Vase, Jade Green (gr opaque), slightly waisted, US Glass, 6¼x2⅛" 65.00
Vase, lt purple, crimped rim, US Glass, #179, 5⅞x7½"....75.00
Vase, Rose Ice (lt marigold), flared rim, Imperial, #693, 8x6½"...80.00
Vase, Sweet Pea, Rose Ice (dk marigold), rolled rim, Lancaster, 5½"...100.00
Vase, topaz, US Glass, #151, 11⅞" 75.00

String Holders

Today, if you want to wrap and secure a package, you have a variety of products to choose from: cellophane tape, staples, etc. But in the 1800s, string was about the only available binder; thus the string holder, either the hanging or counter type, was a common and practical item found in most homes and businesses. Chalkware and ceramic figurals from the 1930s and 1940s contrast with the cast and wrought-iron examples from the 1800s to make for an interesting collection. Our advisor for this category is Charles Reynolds; he is listed in the Directory under Virginia. See also Advertising.

Apple, many variations, chalkware, ea, from $25 to 50.00
Bananas, chalkware, from $85 to 95.00
Beehive, CI, orig tan pnt, lg....95.00
Beehive, CI, 1800s, 5x6¼", EX....60.00
Bird on branch, scissors in head, ceramic, from $85 to....100.00
Black child w/pk bandana, ceramic 195.00
Bonnet girl, chalkware, EX pnt, 8½x7", from $60 to....75.00
Boy, top hat & pipe, eyes to side, chalkware, from $50 to....60.00
Bride & bridesmaids, ceramic, from $100 to 125.00
Cat, chalkware, bright colors, 6x5", EX....65.00
Cat atop ball of red string, chalkware, 7" 45.00
Chef, pressed paper, Nadine Wendon 1941 Made in USA, EX....75.00
Colonial lady in rocking chair, PY/Japan 100.00
Dog w/chef's hat, chalkware, from $300 to 350.00
Fruit (mixed), chalkware, EX orig pnt, Chicago Copyright 194- ..65.00
Glass dome w/cobalt band at rim, eng flowers, 1850s....175.00
Granny in rocking chair, ceramic, Py, from $100 to 150.00
Jester, chalkware, from $125 to....175.00
Kitten on ball of yarn, ceramic, w/scissors, unmk, 6x4" 75.00
Mammy, ceramic, full figure, hands folded, 1930s-40s, 6½x7", EX....145.00
Mammy, chalkware, bright bandana w/polka-dots, gold earrings, 5" ...135.00
Man between 2 Southern belles, ceramic 50.00
Moon face, chalkware, from $300 to 350.00
Penguin, ceramic, from $85 to....100.00
Pig face, pottery....125.00
Porter, ceramic....95.00
Prince Pineapple, chalkware, from $300 to....350.00
Rooster & flowers on heart shape, ceramic, String Along..., 7x6" ...48.00

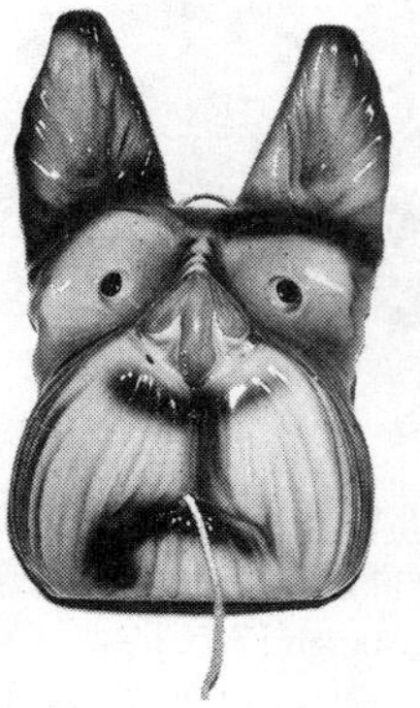

Schnauzer dog, ceramic, from $100.00 to $125.00. (Photo courtesy Ellen Bercovici)

Scottie, ceramic, side view, Made in Japan, NM....125.00
Senora, chalkware, from $125 to 200.00
Teapot, wooden, red pnt, decal front, 6x4½" 25.00
Woman in turban, chalkware, from $125 to 150.00

Sugar Shakers

Sugar shakers (or muffineers, as they were also called) were used during the Victorian era to sprinkle sugar and spice onto breakfast muffins, toast, etc. They were made of art glass, in pressed patterns, and in china. See also specific types and manufacturers (such as Northwood). Our coadvisors for this category are Jeff Bradfield and Dale MacAllister; they are listed in the Directory under Virginia.

Acorn, gr w/decor....275.00
Acorn, shaded pk w/enamel & gold 240.00
Argus Swirl, clear satin 130.00
Argus Swirl, Peach Bloom....230.00
Beatty Honeycomb, bl opal....250.00
Block & Fan....50.00
Blown Twist, gr opal, wide waist....350.00
Bubble Lattice, wht opal 225.00
Bulging Loops, bl cased, glossy....450.00
Challinor's Forget-Me-Not, gr opaque....225.00
Chrysanthemum Swirl, cranberry satin opal, 4½" 495.00
Coin Dot, bl opal, 9-panel 185.00
Coin Dot, cranberry opal 225.00
Cone, gr opaque....125.00

Cone, pk cased, tall 175.00
Cranberry w/cut panels, metal top, 6" 125.00
Creased Teardrop, translucent bl slag 160.00
Daisy & Fern, bl opal, wide waist 225.00
Daisy & Fern, cranberry opal, bulbous...........................375.00
Fern, bl opal...350.00
Guttate, cranberry (+)...495.00
Hobbs Swirl, cranberry opal 400.00
Inverted Thumbprint, amber, tapered 125.00
Leaning Pillar, bl opaque...110.00
Medallion Sprig, bl to clear..500.00
Netted Oak, milk glass, decor, Northwood......................125.00
Parian Swirl, cranberry...250.00
Parian Swirl, gr...185.00
Quilted Phlox, pk cased 225.00
Reverse Swirl, bl opal...250.00
Ribbed Lattice, cranberry opal.......................................300.00
Ribbed Pillar..185.00
Ring Neck, pk & wht spatter, brass lid, 4¾", EX 160.00
Ring Neck Optic, gr 225.00
Spanish Lace, bl opal, bulbous 225.00
Spanish Lace, vaseline opal..285.00
Tomato, wht satin w/decor, Mt WA 375.00
Venetian Diamond, cranberry...225.00
West Virginia, optic ribbed milk glass w/HP florals 95.00
Windows, bl opal..350.00

Sunderland Lustre

Sunderland lustre was made by various potters in the Sunderland district of England during the eighteenth and nineteenth centuries. It is often characterized by a splashed-on application of the pink lustre, which results in an effect sometimes referred to as the 'cloud' pattern. Some pieces are transfer printed with scenes, ships, florals, or portraits.

Creamer, allover pk lustre w/wht motif at neck, Gray's, 2¾" 30.00
Jug, Mariner's Arms/ship/shailors/lighthouse/verse/etc, 1850s, 7" ..635.00
Jug, shipwreck/To a Friend/Bridge at Sunderland/verses, 7⅜", EX ..500.00
Jug, West View...Bridge at Sunderland/verses, rprs, 7⅛" 225.00

Mug, Mariner's compass, 5", $375.00.

Pitcher & bowl, sailing ships/compass/verse/etc, 19th C, 6", 11" ...800.00
Plaque, Behold God will not cast way...., 7½x8¾" 425.00

Surveying Instruments

The practice of surveying offers a wide variety of precision instruments primarily for field use, most of which are associated with the recording of distance and angular measurements. These instruments were primarily made from brass; the larger examples were fitted with tripods and protective cases. These cases also held accessories for the instruments, and these can sometimes play a key part in their evaluation. Instruments in complete condition and showing little use will have much greater values than those that appear to have had moderate or heavy use. Instruments were never polished during use, and those that have been polished as decorator pieces are of little interest to most avid collectors. Our advisor for this category is Dale Beeks; he is listed in the Directory under Iowa.

Alidade, Dietzgen Geological #7008, complete, 18" base, NMIB ...475.00
Alidade, Keuffel & Esser #76-0000, w/orig tripod & oak case.....375.00
Alidade, Otto Fennel Sohne in Cassel #8050, ca 1909, 11½x16x6"..1,000.00
Chain, Gunter's, iron, wire swivel hdls, 33-ft............................365.00
Chain, Gurley, 50-link, brass tally tags & hdls, 19th C...............365.00
Clinometer, J Casatelli Manchester England, 1880, EX in case ..300.00
Clinometer, Kilpatrick & Co London, ca 1900, 5" L, EX in pouch 100.00
Compass, Benjamin Pike NY, polished brass, 1841-64, 14¾" L, w/case.....1,150.00
Compass, E&GW Blunt, brass, mid-1800s, 14⅝" L, EX 1,075.00
Compass, Lerebours & Secretan, ca 1845-55, missing scope, w/case 425.00
Compass, WC Davis NY, eng silvered face, 1840-50s, 14½" plate, EX..1,275.00
Cross, H Morin Paris, w/Jacob's Staff fitting, ca 1870, 6¼".........135.00
Level, brass & ebony, whole glass insert (no fluid), Sheffield, 9" ..50.00
Level, dumpy; Keuffel & Esser, 18", EX in case.......................215.00
Level, hand; Keuffel & Esser, 1949, 6", w/leather holder, MIB......45.00
Level, wye; Gurley, brass, spirits active, 23", no accessories, w/case .300.00
Level, wye; Gurley, brass w/orig pnt, minor wear, 19¼", w/case..350.00
Level transit, Bubb & Buff, 1928, w/tripod & case 650.00
Plummet, optical; Fuji-KOh, w/tripod & circular leval, Seco adapter ..200.00
Scope, Brandis Teckritz, brass & copper, 19", 1800s, EX in case .210.00
Transit, Bausch & Lomb, 1906, EX orig................................575.00
Transit, Buff & Buff, Pat Nov 13 1900, Soltman compass, w/case....750.00
Transit, Geier & Bluhm Troy NY, G&B Patents, 9", w/tripod 295.00
Transit, W&LE Gurley, ca 1900, EX in wooden case w/strap hdl.625.00

Swarovski Crystal

The Swarovski family has been perfecting the glassmaker's art in Wattens, Austria, since 1895. Collectible figurines and desk items were introduced in 1977, and the Swarovski Collectors Society (SCS) was created in 1987. Featuring lead content of 30%+, these 'Silver Crystal' limited edition decorative accessories have attracted a following of over 500,000 dedicated collectors worldwide. Some designs were distributed regionally, making pursuit of retired items an interesting challenge that spans the globe. Most items have an etched mark on the underside. The first mark was a block-style SC. In 1989 the mark was changed to a Swan. Marks on larger items also include the name Swarovski. SCS figurines are further identified with the year and designer's initials. As the vigilance of Swarovski collectors has grown, their interest in all items of Swarovski manufacture has increased. In addition to Swarovski Silver Crystal, collectors also seek Trimlite, Giftware Suite, Swarovski Selections, Ebeling & Reuss, and private label productions by the Swarovski company. Prices listed below reflect the presence of complete original packing and enclosures, without which prices are compromised 10% to 35%.

DO1X881, woodpeckers, #2, from $1,550 to 1,875.00
DO1X901, dolphins, #4, from $910 to.....................................1,130.00
DO1X901S, dolphins, #4, sgn, from $1,250 to 1,650.00
DO1X931, elephant, #7, from $1,250 to.................................1,395.00
DO1X951S, lion, #9, sgn, from $625 to 935.00
DO1X981WS, pegasus, #12, w/stand, from $440 to 625.00
D01X971ST, dragon stand, from $75 to 95.00
SDW001W/S, jeweled Mickey Mouse, w/stand, ltd ed, $565 to .700.00

003-0004417, Cenetary swan brooch, from $120 to **145.00**
69303, bald eagle head, Ebeling & Reuss **375.00**
7433NR80, Chaton paperweight, lg, from $215 to **325.00**
7464NR50, treasure box, rnd, flower, from $300 to **370.00**
7470NR50, bird's nest, from $160 to..**200.00**
7472NR030, mushrooms, from $60 to **70.00**
7473NR000002, airplane, from $175 to **215.00**
7474NR000021, Chrystal City cathedral, from $160 to.............**195.00**
7475NR000009, nativity angel, from $165 to............................**180.00**
7475NR200000, nativity wise men, from $220 to **250.00**
7504NR060G, apple photo stand, gold, king sz, from $680 to **690.00**
7505NR76G, beetle bottle opener, gold, from $1,500 to **2,250.00**
7522NR100, hummingbird, gold, from $1,250 to.....................**1,625.00**
7550NR30015G, grapes, gold, lg, from $2,625 to.....................**3,370.00**
7600NR104C, candle holder, #104C, from $280 to **325.00**
7610NR000001V1, from $425 to **500.00**
7626NR055000, hippopotamus, sm, from $110 to.....................**130.00**
7637NR112, bear, giant sz, from $2,500 to **3,750.00**
7638NR65, pig, lg, from $475 to **565.00**
7639NR55V1, butterfly, blk & rhodium, from $420 to **495.00**
7640NR35V4, Dumbo, Disney/Arribas Bros, variation #4, 1988, $3,750 to....**5,000.00**
7644NR41, blowfish, lg, from $170 to......................................**280.00**
7645NR100V1, falcon head, lg, variation #1, from $2,750 to .**3,800.00**
7646NR85V2, seal, silver wiskers, lg, from $145 to **200.00**
7677NR055, fox, running, mini, from $80 to **105.00**
9404NR50088, 50 mm rnd paperweight, Bermuda Blue, from $180 to ..**370.00**
9440NR000004, toucan on thimble (pine cone), from $110 to..**120.00**
9443NR960001, Memories angel, 1966, from $75 to.................**88.00**
980NR000009, Ricci candlesticks (1000), Daniel Swarovski, $1,875 to....**2,375.00**

Swastika Keramos

Swastika Keramos was a line of artware made by the Owens China Company of Minerva, Ohio, around 1902 – 04. It is characterized either by a coralene type of decoration (similar to the Opalesce line made by the J. B. Owens Pottery Company of Zanesville) or by the application of metallic lustres, usually in simple designs. Shapes are often plain and handles squarish and rather thick, suggestive of the Arts and Crafts style.

**Vase, tree in red, gold, and bronze, small repair, 7¼", $160.00;
Handled vessel, tree in red, gold, and bronze, 7", $230.00.**

Tankard, Nouveau florals, att Lessell, unmk, 10⅜".....................**275.00**
Vase, metallic floral, sgn, 8", NM **300.00**

Syracuse

Syracuse was a line of fine dinnerware and casual ware which was made for nearly a century by the Onondaga Pottery Company of Syracuse, New York. Early patterns were marked O.P. Company. Collectors

of American dinnerware are focusing their attention on reassembling some of their many lovely patterns. In 1966 the firm became officially known as the Syracuse China Company in order to better identify with the name of their popular chinaware. Many of the patterns were marked with the shape and color names (Old Ivory, Federal, etc.), not the pattern names. By 1971 dinnerware geared for use in the home was discontinued, and the company turned to the manufacture of hotel, restaurant, and other types of commercial tableware.

Alpine, coffeepot, w/lid...**125.00**
Apple Blossom, coffeepot, w/lid..**135.00**
Arcadia, bowl, vegetable; w/lid..**115.00**
Arcadia, cup & saucer **40.00**
Arcadia, platter, med **65.00**
Bombay, cup & saucer, gold trim...**30.00**
Bracelet, bowl, vegetable; w/lid...**175.00**
Bracelet, cream soup & saucer **55.00**
Bracelet, gravy boat, detailed gold rim......................................**115.00**
Bracelet, platter, rnd...**110.00**
Briarcliff, platter, med...**110.00**
Calhoun, casserole, w/lid...**100.00**
Champlaine, coffeepot, w/lid...**125.00**
Cliftondale, teapot, w/lid..**125.00**
Dorian, coffeepot, w/lid..**120.00**
Greenwood, bowl, vegetable; w/lid..**100.00**
Jefferson, bowl, vegetable; w/lid...**135.00**
Jefferson, coffeepot, w/lid...**125.00**
Jefferson, cup & saucer **32.00**
Jefferson, plate, chop..**115.00**
Jefferson, platter, med...**105.00**
Jefferson, teapot, w/lid..**135.00**
Jewel Tree, coffeepot, w/lid **120.00**
Kent (Gold), bowl, vegetable; w/lid...**100.00**
Lady Mary, plate, dinner; 9¾"..**22.00**
Lady Mary, platter, lg..**90.00**
Lady mary, sugar bowl...**36.00**
Lilac Rose, coffeepot, w/lid...**250.00**
Madame Butterfly, bowl, oval, 10¼"..**30.00**
Madame Butterfly, gravy boat, attached underplate **40.00**
Madame Butterfly, plate, 10"...**15.00**
Marlene, bowl, vegetable; w/lid **100.00**
Meadow Breeze, cup & saucer..**50.00**
Meadow Breeze, gravy boat..**140.00**
Minuet, cup & saucer **32.00**
Minuet, plate, salad **17.50**
Monticello, bowl, vegetable; w/lid..**100.00**
Monticello, gravy boat...**130.00**
Portland, bowl, vegetable; w/lid..**100.00**
Radcliffe (Maroon), gravy boat..**120.00**
Romance (Green), bowl, vegetable; w/lid...................................**110.00**
Shellridge (White), coffeepot, w/lid..**150.00**
Sherwood, bowl, vegetable; w/lid..**140.00**
Sherwood, cream soup & saucer **30.00**
Sherwood, gravy boat...**115.00**
Sherwood, plate, bread & butter..**6.00**
Sonja, teapot, w/lid...**120.00**
Suzanne, bowl, Federal shape, oval, 10½" **50.00**
Suzanne, bowl, vegetable; w/lid, gold trim **205.00**
Suzanne, cup & saucer, Federal shape..**25.00**
Suzanne, gravy boat...**115.00**
Suzanne, platter, gold trim, sm..**110.00**
Suzanne, platter, lg..**155.00**
Sweetheart, cup & saucer...**26.00**
Sweetheart, sugar bowl, w/lid..**45.00**

Victoria, gravy boat 130.00
Victoria, platter, med...130.00
Victoria, platter, sm..110.00
Vogue (Blue), coffeepot, w/lid.....................................120.00
Wayne (Maroon), gravy boat w/underplate.....................130.00

Syrups

Values are for old, original syrups. Beware of reproductions and watch handle area for cracks! See also various manufacturers (such as Northwood) and specific types of glass. Our coadvisors are Jeff Bradfield and Dale MacAllister; they are listed in the Directory under Virginia. See also Pattern Glass.

Acorn, gr..275.00
Atlanta, frosted..225.00
Aztec Medallion, gr opal swirl, orig NP lid 900.00
Bulging Loops, pk cased 375.00
Button Arches, ruby stain..275.00
Coin Spot & Swirl, bl..150.00
Cord Drapery, amber 425.00
Coreopsis, pigeon blood 400.00
Currier & Ives, amber 215.00
Daisy & Button w/Crossbars, bl 175.00
Diamond Spearhead, vaseline opal 575.00
Empress, gr...425.00
Fleur-de-Lis...115.00
Hercules Pillar, bl...175.00
Hexagon Block, ruby flashed..225.00
Honeycomb, wht opal, pewter lid 130.00
Invt T'print, cranberry, tapered....................................325.00
Invt T'print, gr, tapered..200.00
Nail, ruby stain 250.00
O'Hara Diamond, ruby stain...425.00
Open Heart Arches, cobalt...425.00
Paneled Herringbone, gr 195.00
Priscilla, gr w/EX gold, pewter lid 465.00
Reverse Swirl, bl opal 350.00
Ring Neck Coin Spot, bl opal..325.00
Rosette...280.00
Spanish Lace, bl...200.00
Sunk Honeycomb, ruby stain..225.00
Tree of Life, chartreuse opaque, w/orig copper lid.............350.00
Valencia Waffle, amber 150.00
Windows Swirled, bl opal..525.00
Windows Swirled, wht opal..250.00
X-Ray, gr, EX gold 550.00
Zipper Border, ruby stain, etched 300.00

Target Balls

Prior to 1880 when the clay pigeon was invented, blown glass target balls were used extensively for shotgun competitions. Approximately 2¾" in diameter, these balls were hand blown into a three-piece mold. All have a ragged hole where the blowpipe was twisted free. Target balls date from approximately 1840 (English) to World War I, although they were most widely used in the 1870 – 1880 period. Common examples are unmarked except for the blower's code — dots, crude numerals, etc. Some balls were embossed in a dot or diamond pattern so they were more likely to shatter when struck by shot, and some have names and/or patent dates. When evaluating condition, bubbles and other minor manufacturing imperfections are acceptable; cracks are not. The prices below are for mint condition examples.

Boers & CR Delft Flesschen Fabriek, lt gr, rare, 2⅝" 500.00
Bogardus' Glass Ball Pat'd April 10 1877, amber, Am.............350.00
Bogardus' Glass Ball Pat'd April 10 1877, cobalt, 2¾" 800.00
Bogardus' Glass Ball Pat'd April 10 1877, gr, 4-dot variant 1,600.00
Bogardus' Glass Ball Pat'd April 10 1877, olive gr, 2⅝" 1,150.00
C Newman, Dmn Quilt, amber, rare, 2⅝" 825.00
CTB Co, blk pitch, Pat dates on bottom, Am 250.00
Dmn Quilt w/o center band, yel-amber, 2¾" 250.00
Dmn Quilt w/plain center band, clear, ground top, Am..............150.00
Dmn Quilt w/plain center band, cobalt, 2⅝" 250.00
Dmn Quilt w/shooter emb in 2 panels, clear, English 300.00
Dmn Quilt w/shooter emb in 2 panels, cobalt, English 725.00
Dmn Quilt w/shooter emb in 2 panels, deep moss gr, English 575.00
Dmn Quilt w/shooter emb in 2 panels, gr or purple, English........500.00
Dmn Quilt w/shooter emb in 2 panels, med gr, English 375.00
EE Eaton Guns & C 53 State St Chicago, yel-amber, 2⅝" ...1,000.00
For Hockey's Pat Trap, gr, English 850.00
Glashutten Dr A Frank Charlottenburg, yel-olive, 2⅝"...........1,200.00
Glashuttenewotte Un Charlottenburg, clear, emb dmns, 2⅝" 700.00
Gurd & Son, London, Ontario, amber, Canadian 500.00
Hobnail w/horizontal ribs along seams, yel-amber, 2¾"..............800.00
Horizontal or vertical ribs, amber, either style 150.00
Horizontal ribs (2) intersect w/2 vertical, cobalt, 2⅝"................120.00
Horizontal ribs (7), root beer amber, 3-pc mold, 2⅝"................725.00
Ilmenau (Thur) Sophiehutte, amber, Dmn Quilt, Germany 425.00
Ira Paine's Filled Ball Pat Oct 23 1877, amber, Am................250.00
Ira Paine's Filled Ball Pat Oct 23 1877, cobalt, w/orig feathers...4,000.00
NB Glass Works Perth, other than pale gr, English 200.00
NB Glass Works Perth, pale gr, English...........................100.00
Plain, amber w/mold mks 65.00
Plain, clear w/mold mks..1,000.00
Plain, cobalt w/mold mks...150.00
Plain, dk grape amethyst w/mold mks, 2¾" dia....................250.00
Plain, dk teal gr w/mold mks, 2¾"..................................300.00
Plain, olive-yel w/mold mks 375.00
Plain, pk amethyst w/mold mks, 2⅝" 250.00
T Jones, Gunmaker, Blackburn, cobalt, English, 2⅝" 450.00
T Jones, Gunmaker, Blackburn, pale bl, English..................150.00
Van Cutsem A St Quentin, cobalt, 2¾" dia 100.00
WW Greener, St Mary's Works, various colors, English, ea 350.00

Related Memorabilia

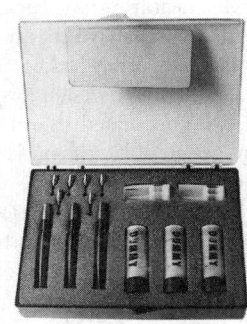

Remington functional dummy shell set, $100.00.

Ball thrower, dbl; old red pnt, ME Card, Pat...78, 79, VG 900.00
Clay birds, Winchester, Pat May 29 1917, 1 flight in box...........100.00
Pitch bird, blk DUVROCK...1.00
Shell, dummy, w/single window, any brand 35.00
Shell, dummy shotgun, Winchester, window w/powder, 6" 125.00
Shell set, dummy, Gamble Stores, 2 window shells, 3 cut out.....125.00
Shell set, dummy, Winchester, 5 window shells 175.00
Shell set, dummy shotgun, Peters, 6 window shells+full box.......175.00

Shotshell loader, rosewood/brass, Parker Bros, Pat 1884 ....50.00
Target, Am, sheet metal, rod ends mk Pat Feb 8 '21, set 25.00
Target, blk japanned sheet metal, Bussey Patentee, London.........50.00
Target, BUST-O, blk or wht breakable wafer 20.00
Trap, Chamberlain Cartridge...Nov 7th 05...USA, CI, 21½" L, EX...1,500.00
Trap, DUVROCK, w/blk pitch birds 250.00
Trap, MO-SKEET-O, w/birds 150.00

Tea Caddies

Because tea was once regarded as a precious commodity, special boxes called caddies were used to store the tea leaves. They were made from various materials: porcelain, carved and inlaid woods, and metals ranging from painted tin or tole to engraved silver. Our advisor for this category is Tina Carter; she is listed in the Directory under California.

Figured walnut and rosewood with silver and mother-of-pearl medallion, canted corners, brass ball feet, England, 1830s, 7x10½x6", $1,200.00.

Fruitwood w/shell inlays, variegated trim on lid, rfn, 5x7x5" 425.00
Mahog, dvtl/wire nails, gold stenciling, brass bail, rpr, 6¼" 275.00
Mahog English Regency, sarcophagus form, compartments, 5x8x5" ...330.00
Mahog Late Georgian w/inlay, sarcophagus, ball ft, 1820s, 8x12x6" ...330.00
Mahog veneer w/inlay, ogee ft, orig brass bail, 9¾", VG 150.00
Mahog w/rope-banded edge inlay, stepped lid, 5⅜x9½x5½" 415.00
Pear-shaped fruitwood, 18th C, 6½", EX.................................2,400.00
Regency silver, oval w/gadrooning, HS hallmks, 1810s, 4x3x4" ..330.00
Rosewood veneer, beaded brass trim, 2-compartment, worn, 8¾" ..275.00

Tea Leaf Ironstone

Tea Leaf Ironstone became popular in the 1880s when middle-class American housewives became bored with the plain white stone china that English potters had been exporting to this country for nearly a century. The original design has been credited to Anthony Shaw of Longport, who decorated the plain ironstone with a hand-painted copper lustre design of bands and leaves. Originally known as Lustre Band and Sprig, the pattern has since come to be known as Tea Leaf Lustre. It was produced with minor variations by many different firms both in England and the United States. By the early 1900s, it had become so commonplace that it had lost much of its appeal.

Items marked Red Cliff are reproductions made from 1950 until 1980 for this distributing and decorating company of Chicago, Illinois. Hall China provided many of the blanks.

Our advice for this category comes from Home Place Antiques, whose address is listed in the Directory under Illinois.

Baker, Wilkinson, 9½x6¾" 30.00
Bone dish, scalloped, Meakin...75.00
Bowl, rice; Meakin, 4¾"...70.00
Bowl, vegetable; Cable, w/lid, Burgess...235.00
Bowl, vegetable; Fish Hook, bracket ft, w/lid, Meakin, 11x7".....195.00

Bowl, vegetable; medallion finial & hdl, Mellor-Taylor............225.00
Brush box, Cable, Burgess..295.00
Butter dish, Fish Hook, Meakin, w/drain 175.00
Butter dish, Little Cable, Furnival..200.00
Butter pat, Meakin, 2¾" sq 14.00
Butter pat, Meakin, 3¼"..15.00
Chamber pot, Bamboo, w/lid, Alfred Meakin 345.00
Coffeepot, Bamboo, Meakin, 9"...225.00
Coffeepot, Fish Hook pattern, Meakin, steam hole in lid 195.00
Creamer, Adams Microtex 60.00
Creamer, Bamboo, Meakin, 6½"...195.00
Creamer, Wedgwood, 5¼"...165.00
Cup & saucer, handleless; Paneled, Shaw 110.00
Cup & saucer, Lily of the Valley, Shaw 125.00
Cup & saucer, Morning Glory, Tunstall 125.00
Cup plate, unmk, 3½" 60.00
Cup plate, Wilkinson, 3¼"..60.00
Egg cup, Boston, Meakin...350.00
Gravy boat, Fish Hook, Meakin, 2¾x8"..75.00
Gravy boat, simple sq, unmk...65.00
Pitcher, Lily of the Valley, Shaw, 7"...295.00
Pitcher, milk; Bamboo, Meakin, 7½"..265.00
Plate, Chinese shape, Shaw, 9½"...45.00
Plate, Meakin, 7½"..14.00
Plate, Meakin, 9" 35.00
Plate, Morning Glory, 9¾"...45.00
Plate, Red Cliff, 8¼"...22.00
Plate, Teaberry, 8" 35.00
Plate, Wedgwood, 8¼"..18.00
Platter, Brocade, Meakin, 12¾x9⅛"...75.00
Platter, rectangular, Meakin, 14"..75.00
Platter, Wedgwood, 14x10¼"...65.00
Relish, oval, Shaw 75.00
Sauce tureen, Bamboo, Meakin, w/lid, ladle & underplate 365.00
Shaving mug, leaf at hdl, Shaw 200.00
Soap dish, Cable, Anthony Shaw, w/drain insert.........................275.00
Soap dish, flanged, Meakin, 8¾" 30.00
Soap dish, Lily of the Valley, Shaw, w/liner 425.00
Sugar bowl, Bamboo, Grindley..95.00
Sugar bowl, Morning Glory, Portland shape, Elsmore & Forster.225.00
Teapot, Fish Hook, 8½" 225.00
Toothbrush holder, Mellor-Taylor...145.00
Tureen, gravy; Thomas Elsmore, w/underplate & ladle, 8" 425.00
Wash bowl, Meakin, 14¾"..235.00
Wash bowl & pitcher, Bishop & Stonier, 12", 14¾" dia 200.00
Wash bowl & pitcher, Cable, Shaw..485.00

Teapots

Teapots have become popular collectibles in recent years with a surge in tea shops featuring tea and teapots, and serving afternoon tea. Collectors should be aware of modern teapots which imitate older, similar versions. Study the types of pottery, porcelain, and china, as well as the marks. Multicolored, detailed marks over the glaze represent modern pieces. Teapots made in the last thirty years are quite collectible but generally don't demand the same prices as their antique counterparts.

A wide range of teapots can be found by the avid collector. Those from before 1880 are more apt to be found in museums or sold at quality auction houses. Almost every pottery and porcelain manufacturer in Asia, Europe, and America have produced teapots. Some are purely decorative and whimsical, while others are perfect for brewing a pot of tea. Tea drinkers should beware of odd-shaped spouts which sputter and drip. Reproductions to be aware of: majolica styles with modern marks, Blue

Willow which has been made continuously for almost two centuries, and those marked Made in China (older teapots have 'chop marks' in Chinese).

Refer to various manufacturers' names for further listings. Our advisor for this category is Tina M. Carter, listed in the Directory under California. Her book, *Teapots*, is available at bookstores or direct from the author.

Japan, cat figural, 11" wide, $45.00.

Advertising, McCormick & Co...Banquet Teas..., turq, Hall, 1930s-40s ...50.00
ALB, dripless, mottled, England, ca 1920......................................52.00
Barge, brn, emb mk, Derbyshire, England, lg 75.00
Ben Franklin figural, ceramic w/metal hdl.....................................65.00
Charles & Diana, brn pottery, Wales CM, 2½" 78.00
Charles & Diana commemorative, emb design on brn, 1981, CM Wales, sm..95.00
Cook's Hotel & Restaurant Supply, NY, Jackson China, yel to wht...35.00
Copper, Art Deco style, enamel decor, ball ft, China 38.00
Copper lustre, wht & copper poppies in band, Wade, 4" 45.00
Coralene, brn w/gold decor, Made in Japan, ca 1950 ....22.00
Cube, HP, Made in Japan, ca 1940 ....20.00
Dogwood blossoms on pk pearlized, unmk RS Prussia 350.00
Ebeling & Reuss, Santa, musical, from $75 to 125.00
Father Christmas, HP detail, pottery, Sadler, 1930s-40s 150.00
Fern & berries on wht bone china, Wedgwood Made in England, 1930s..175.00
Fitz & Floyd, King Wenceslas & forest creatures, from $80 to 135.00
Floral, purple on wht, rattan hdl, Asuka Fine China, Japan..........30.00
Floral band at top & rim of lid on shiny wht, Noritake, 5½"........45.00
Gold dragon, gr Japan mk, 5"..35.00
Goldcastle, floral yel & mc lustre, red mk, 6½" 50.00
Granny, Queensware, modern 35.00
Lefton, cozy set, violets, ca 1950 ....32.00
Lewis & Clark Expo, scene on cobalt, unmk Germany 40.00
Lipton's, rnd, various colors, Hall China Co 30.00
Lipton's, tan lustre w/blk hdl & finial, Noritake, ind, 3¼"..........250.00
Little Old lady, HP decor, HJ Wood, England, 1930-50s, from $85 to ..125.00
Lustreware, amber mottled, blk Japan mk, 4¾"............................65.00
Man in tux forms hdl, lady forms pot, ceramic, unmk, modern.....35.00
Meakin, Alfred; blk trim, china relief, England 38.00
Meito, floral reserve on tan lustre, blk hdl, red mk, w/matching tile...65.00
Nippon, floral tapestry w/beadwork, 6⅛".....................................525.00
Oriental garden scene w/appl trees/figures, wht, Ardalt/Japan, 8" ..50.00
Pottery, pk, mk Ford, USA, 1-cup...25.00
Pyrex, squat, blown glass hdl, mk Pyrex USA, ca 1925-40..........125.00
Red flowers on wht, bud finial, pottery, mk Italy, 1950s-60s, $45 to ..60.00
Rough glaze, buff sharkskin, tan, slip decor, Japan, 1920s...........28.00
Sadler, Dickens Christmas scenes from Christmas Carol, up to.....80.00
Sadler, Folklore, Robin Hood/King Arthur/etc, ca 1990................35.00
Salada Tea, promotional item, USA, 1-cup...................................25.00
Sherlock Holmes figural, Schrekengost, Hall China, 1988, w/pamphlet....250.00
Sigma, Star Wars, rare 215.00
Snow White w/Dwarfs, musical, Walt Disney Prod........................75.00
Snowman holding broom & snowball, hat is lid, Fitz & Floyd......75.00
Sylvestri, Victorian Skating Couple, from $125 to 200.00
Tiffin, tea liqueur, depot decanter, Germany, 1960 ....95.00
Windmill, HP under glaze, mk Japan, 1940s-50s..........................45.00

WWII, Esc to US by Royal Navy or Allied Fleets, brn, England ..45.00

Teco

Teco artware was made by the American Terra Cotta and Ceramic Company, located near Chicago, Illinois. The firm was established in 1886 and until 1901 produced only brick, sewer tile, and other redware. Their early glaze was inspired by the matt green made popular by Grueby. 'Teco Green' was made for nearly ten years. It was similar to Grueby's, yet with a subtle silver-gray cast. The company was one of the first in the United States to perfect a true crystalline glaze. The only decoration used was through the modeling and glazing techniques; no hand painting was attempted. Favored motifs were naturalistic leaves and flowers. The company broadened their lines to include garden pottery and faience tiles and panels. New matt glazes (browns, yellows, blue, and rose) were added to the green in 1910. By 1922 the artware lines were discontinued; the company was sold in 1930.

Values are dictated by size and shape, with architectural and organic forms being more desirable. Teco is usually marked with a vertical impressed device comprised of a large 'T' to the left of the remaining three letters.

Bowl, gr, emb floral at top, 9½" dia.......................................350.00
Bowl, gr, low, #350, 4½" 260.00
Bowl, gr, low Prairie form w/4-sided ft, 9½"......................1,900.00
Bowl, gr, 3 sm ft, 3¾", NM..300.00
Bowl, Roman Salad Bowl, gr, 4 buttressed ft, #400, 5¾x11¾" ...3,000.00
Box, gr w/charcoaling, squat, w/lid, bruise, 2¼x3½x2½" 700.00
Chamberstick, gr, angle hdl, mks/label, 5"............................550.00
Chamberstick, gr, stylized flowers & leaves, paper label, 10¾x5" ..800.00
Chamberstick, ivory, angle hdl, label, flaw in making, 5"............475.00
Ewer, aventurine, 4" 275.00
Jardiniere, gr, 4 buttressed legs, 7x11".............................6,000.00
Pitcher, gr, bulbous, integral hdl, rpr, 4½"............................400.00
Pitcher, gr, corseted w/wishbone hdl, firing flaw, 9x3½" 1,000.00
Pitcher, gr w/charcoaling, sinewy hdl, 8½x5" 750.00
Vase, brn, tapered form, 4"...400.00
Vase, brn aventurine, slim flared neck, bulbous body, 11¼", NM....2,000.00
Vase, dove gray, faint emb petals, scalloped mouth, 5¼x4".........350.00
Vase, gr, broad shoulders, 5"...425.00
Vase, gr, bulbous, protruding mouth, mk twice, 5⅛x4½" 550.00
Vase, gr, bullet shape w/buttresses, 8¾x4"...........................3,750.00
Vase, gr, calla lillies (4), rstr to sm drill hole, sm nick, 17½" ..25,000.00
Vase, gr, cylindrical, flakes, 5"..425.00
Vase, gr, emb tulips, rstr, paper label, 8½x4"........................800.00
Vase, gr, finger ridges, 4½"...350.00
Vase, gr, flat shoulders, #336, 7⅞"..500.00
Vase, gr, fluted neck, squat, rstr rim, 16½x8".....................1,500.00
Vase, gr, long flared rim, rolled rim, 7½"...............................650.00
Vase, gr, open hdl (1), emb ribs, 6½".....................................500.00
Vase, gr, ovoid, pronounced lip, mini, 4½x3¾".......................400.00
Vase, gr, petals & buds, waisted cylinder, #273, ca 1910, 13¼" ..2,875.00
Vase, gr, rim-to-hip angular hdls, slim, sm rpr, 11½"..............1,000.00
Vase, gr, rim-to-hip hdls, flared rim, 8" 1,800.00
Vase, gr, scalloped top, bulbous, 5"..650.00
Vase, gr, shouldered, label, 4½"...700.00
Vase, gr, spherical, sm flared rim, 6¾"..................................475.00
Vase, gr, tapered cylinder, 4¾"..450.00
Vase, gr, tulips w/openwork leaves, Dodd, #151, 11¼", NM 7,500.00
Vase, gr, 2 buttressed hdls at rim, paper label, 3x2¼" 850.00
Vase, gr, 3-sided, 8"..950.00
Vase, gr, 4 buttresses, flower-shaped top, 12¼x5"..............4,500.00
Vase, gr, 4 buttresses, minor rpr, 6½".....................................900.00

Vase, gr, 4 curled leaves at rim, #272, sm rstr, 6x9½"............**24,000.00**
Vase, gr, 4 indents, #356, 4"..**550.00**
Vase, gr, 4 swag buttressed legs, 9x3½" **1,000.00**
Vase, gr, 4-sided top, indented body, 4½"..........................**600.00**
Vase, gr (slightly curdled), sq shoulders, 4½x4" **500.00**
Vase, gr microcrystalline w/emb tall leaves, #343, rstr, 22x8½" ...**5,500.00**
Vase, gr w/charcoal speckles, dimpled, #519, 3¾x3¼" **550.00**
Vase, gr w/charcoaling, 4 open buttresses, 12" dia.........**5,000.00**
Vase, gr w/lt charcoaling, leaves, 4 open hdls & 12 cutouts, 6½" ..**3,500.00**
Vase, gray, bulbous, sm neck, 4½".......................................**180.00**
Vase, gray, cylindrical neck, flared base, 13¼x5¼" **1,500.00**
Vase, gray, shouldered cylinder, 6", NM **375.00**
Vase, mauve, 4 swag buttressed legs, 9x4" sq....................**7,000.00**
Vase, med brn, corseted, 6⅝"...**475.00**
Vase, pk to beige, pierced at top & shoulder, 4 open hdls, 6" ..**2,500.00**

Teddy Bear Collectibles

The story of Teddy Roosevelt's encounter with the bear cub has been oft recounted with varying degrees of accuracy, so it will suffice to say that it was as a result of this incident in 1902 that the teddy bear got his name. These appealing little creatures are enjoying renewed popularity with collectors today. To one who has not yet succumbed to their obvious charms, one bear seems to look very much like another. How to tell the older ones? Look for long snouts, jointed limbs, large feet and felt paws, long curving arms, and glass or shoe-button eyes. Most old bears have a humped back and are made of mohair stuffed with straw or excelsior. Cute expressions, original clothes, a nice personality, and, of course, good condition add to their value. Early Steiff bears in mint condition may go for a minimum of $100.00 per inch (for a small bear) up to $200.00 per inch (for one 20" high or larger). These are easily recognized by the trademark button within the ear. Our advisor for this category is Candace Gunther; she is listed in the Directory under California. For further information we recommend *Teddy Bear Treasury* by Ken Yenke; and *Teddy Bears, Annalee's & Steiff Animals*, by Margaret Fox Mandel. Both are available from Collector Books. See also Toys, Steiff.

Key: jtd — jointed

Bears

Am, gold bristle mohair, button eyes, twill nose, overalls, 13"....**325.00**
Bing, red-brn mohair, squeaker, embr nose, lg ft pads, '20, 9", EX....**2,000.00**
Bruin, cinnamon mohair, squeeze voice, glass eyes, 1907, 14", M....**3,000.00**
Chad Valley, long mohair, glass eyes, jtd, 1950s, 28", NM **750.00**
Chad Valley, mohair, velvet pads, lg ears, 24", EX......................**425.00**
Chiltern, mohair, fully jtd, squeaker, 16", EX+ **450.00**
Clemens, wht mohair, growler, glass eyes, chest tag, 1948, 15", M........**500.00**
Electric Eye, mohair, flashlight-bulb eyes, fully jtd, 1914, 26", EX+ ..**1,500.00**
German, cotton plush, rubber claws, performs w/ball, 1930s, 8", M **375.00**
Hahn & Amberg, mohair, long conical nose, cork stuffed, 12", NM....**2,000.00**
Hermann, growler, lt mohair, button eyes, straw filled, 1900s, 18", G ...**465.00**
Ideal, blond mohair, button eyes, felt pads, orig sweater, 1907, 12"....**1,500.00**
Ideal, long blond mohair, button eyes, jtd, ca 1905, 12", M.....**2,000.00**
Jopi, pk mohair, glass eyes, Swiss music box inside, 1925, 16", NM ...**3,000.00**
Knickerbocker, mohair, glass eyes, embr mouth/nose/pads, 1930s, 24" ..**535.00**
Knickerbocker, mohair, glass eyes, jtd, velvet pads, 1930s, 18", VG **250.00**
Knickerbocker, wht mohair, glass eyes, cord nose, 1920-30s, 15", M..**1,500.00**
Schuco, brn mohair, glass eyes, vertical-stitched nose, 1930s, 12" **1,000.00**
Schuco, gr (rare color), fully jtd, 1930s, 2½" **350.00**
Schuco, Janus Bear, 2 faces, cinnamon, 1950s, 3½", M................**750.00**
Schuco, yel w/glass eyes, 1920s, 12", VG **350.00**
Schuco, Yes/No Tricky Bear, tan, ribbon/tag, 1948, 13", M **1,200.00**

Steiff, beige mohair, blk bead eyes, ear button, 1905, 3½", EX ...**800.00**
Steiff, Bendy, reddish brn, bear-head chest tag, 1950s, 3", M......**125.00**
Steiff, Bendy, wht, all ID, 1980, 3½", M **65.00**
Steiff, cinnamon mohair, shoe-button eyes, FF button, 18", EX....**9,500.00**
Steiff, dense wht mohair, embr floss nose, button, 1907, 12", NM..**2,500.00**
Steiff, gold mohair, glass eyes, ribbon/button, 1950s, 13", NM **500.00**
Steiff, Jackie Bear, button/remnant tag, 1950s, 9½", EX **900.00**
Steiff, Orig Teddy, caramel mohair, jtd, button, 1950s, 5½", VG ..**200.00**
Steiff, Orig Teddy, gold mohair, all ID, 8", M................................**565.00**
Steiff, Orig Teddy, tan mohair, all ID, 1968, 13", M....................**225.00**
Steiff, Orig Teddy, tan mohair, all ID, 9", M **175.00**
Steiff, Teddy Baby, dk brn mohair, glass eyes, all ID, 1948, 9", EX....**1,100.00**
Steiff, Teddy Baby, gold mohair/velvet trim, all ID, 1950s, 3", NM ..**1,650.00**
Steiff, Zotty, caramel mohair, plastic eyes, ribbon/tag, 6½", M ...**245.00**
Steiff, Zotty, tan mohair, glass eyes, ribbon/tag, 7", M **365.00**
Unmk, gold moahir, bead eyes, jtd, embr details, 13", G.............**275.00**
Unmk, gold mohair, glass eyes, jtd, embr details, rprs, 16" **250.00**
Unmk, gold mohair w/wht felt, glass eyes, jtd, 13", G **75.00**
Unmk, golden mohair, fully jtd, squeaker (silent), 14", EX..........**525.00**
Unmk, growler (silent), hump, long arms, rprs, 18", VG.............**275.00**
Unmk, hump, blond mohair, glass eyes, fully jtd, 20", VG..........**265.00**
Unmk, taupe mohair, glass eyes, excelsior stuffing, jtd, 1920s, 23"...**350.00**
Unmk English, silky mohair, squeaker, glass eyes, 1930s, 18", VG...**425.00**

Telephones

Since Alexander Graham Bell's first successful telephone communication, the phone itself has undergone a complete evolution in style as well as efficiency. Early models, especially those wall types with ornately carved oak boxes, are of special interest to collectors. Also of value are the candlestick phones from the early part of the century and any related memorabilia.

Western Electric Company early candlestick telephone, black, label at speaker: Freehold 8-1064, 11¼", EX, $50.00.

Am Bell candlestick, nickle finish, 1904, NM **185.00**
American Electric, str shaft desk stand, 1903, 11", VG.............**135.00**
Grammont/Eurielt Paris candlestick, 2nd ear phone, 1950s?......**425.00**
Kellogg, candlestick, Bakelite & metal, blk finish, 12"................**110.00**
Leich, deck model, crank in place of dial, 1940s, VG...................**50.00**
Manhattan Electric Intercom, walnut, 1899, 5¾x5x3½", EX.....**150.00**
North Electric H-6, blk, 'Bogart' phone, EX **85.00**
Stromberg-Carlson, candlestick type, Pat Sept 12, 1905, 10½", EX..**175.00**
Unmarked walnut wall-mt, crank & bell system, 26", VG..........**200.00**
Viaduct Mfg, 3-box wall type, Blake transmitter, 1883, EX **1,800.00**
Western Electric, candlestick, Pat Jan 26/15 through Sept 21/20, 12"...**135.00**
Western Electric, crank type, wall-mt, rstr finish, 32½".............**285.00**
Western Electric #202, E-1 handset, ca 1930-37, EX...................**165.00**
Western Electric #259W, wall-mt, moving speaker, 32x11", EX .**400.00**
Western Electric #500, blk cradle type, 1950s, EX **15.00**
Western Electric Interphone, wall type, watch case receiver.........**75.00**
Western Electrick, dial, desk stand, 1930s, 12", EX **250.00**

Blue Bell Paperweights

First issued in the early 1900s, bell-shaped glass paperweights were used as 'give-aways' and/or presented to telephone company executives as tokens of appreciation. The paperweights were used to prevent stacks of papers from blowing off the desks in the days of overhead fans. Over the years they have all but vanished — some taken by retiring employees, others accidentally broken. The weights came to be widely used for advertising by individual telephone companies; and as the smaller companies merged to form larger companies, more and more new paperweights were created. They were widely distributed with the opening of the first transcontinental telephone line in 1915. The bell-shaped paperweight embossed 'Opening of Trans-Pacific Service, Dec. 23, 1931,' in peacock blue glass is very rare, and the price is negotiable. (Weights with 'open' in the price field are also rare and impossible to accurately evaluate.) In 1972 the first Pioneer bell paperweights were made to sell to raise funds for the charities the Pioneers support. This has continued to the present day. These bell paperweights have also become 'collectibles.' For further study we recommend *Blue Bell Paperweights, 1992 Revised Edition*, and its accompanying *1995 Addendum* by Jacqueline C. Linscott; she is listed in the Directory under Florida.

American Bell Association 25th Anniversary, cobalt..................150.00

Bell System Ches. and Pot. Tel. Company and Associated Companies, ice blue, $550.00. (Photo courtesy Jacqueline Linscott)

Bell System/Local and Long Distance, Peacock Blue...................225.00
Bell System/Universal Service, Peacock Blue 115.00
Break-Up of the Bell System, 1984, Pioneer Green.......................20.00
Diamond Jubilee, 1911-1986, 1984, dk Peacock Blue...................65.00
Diamond Jubilee 1911-1986, 1987, Bermuda Blue.......................65.00
First 50 Years NJ Bell, 1977, Jersey Green....................................30.00
Nevada Bell, blk glass..100.00
Pacific Bell, Nevada Bell, blk glass 75.00
Plain (no embossing), Ice Blue 40.00
Region 10 Assembly, 1984, bl..100.00
Save Time...Telephone/Save Steps...Telephone, Ice Blue 95.00
Southern Bell Telephone and Telegraph Company, cobalt..........200.00
TPA, Neodymium..50.00
TPA, 1978, aqua 25.00
TPA, 1983, clear..20.00
TPA, 1985, yel...20.00
TPA, 1989, Lime Green 40.00

Novelty Telephones

Batmobile (Batman Forever), MIB, from $35 to 50.00
Bugs Bunny, Warner Exclusive, MIB, from $60 to 70.00
Cabbage Patch Girl, 1980s, EX, from $65 to..................................75.00
Charlie Tuna, 1987, MIB, from $50 to 65.00
Darth Vader, 1983, MIB..195.00
Little Green Sprout, EX 75.00

Mario Bros, 1980s, MIB...50.00
Oscar Mayer Weiner, EX..65.00
Snoopy & Woodstock, Am Telephone Corp, 1976, touch-tone, EX..100.00
Snoopy as Joe Cool, 1980s, MIB...55.00
Spider-Man climbing down chimney, NM, from $165 to 200.00
Strawberry Shortcake, M...55.00
Superman, early version w/rotary dial, M 500.00

Telescopes

Antique telescopes were sold in large quantities to sailors, astronomers, voyeurs, and the military but survive in relatively few numbers because their glass lenses and brass tubes were easily damaged. Even scarcer are antique reflecting telescopes, which use a polished metal mirror to magnify the world. Telescopes used for astronomy give an inverted image, but most old telescopes were used for marine purposes and have more complicated optics that show the world right-side up. Spyglasses are smaller, hand-held telescopes that collapse into their tube and focus by drawing out the tube to the correct length. A more compact instrument, with three or four sections, is also more delicate, and sailors usually preferred a single-draw spyglass. They are almost always of brass, occasionally of nickel silver or silver plate, and usually covered with leather, or sometimes a beautiful rosewood veneer. Solid wood barrel spyglasses (with a brass draw tube) tend to be early and rare. Before the middle of the 1800s, makers put their names in elaborate script on the smallest draw tube, but as 1900 approached, most switched to plain block printing. British instruments from World War I made by a variety of makers are commonly found, sharing a format of a 2" objective, 30" long with three draws extended, a tapered main tube, and sometimes having low- and high-power oculars and beautiful leather cases. U.S. Navy WWII spyglasses are quite common but have outstanding optics and focus by twisting the eyepiece, which makes them weather-proof. The Quartermaster (Q.M.) 16x spyglass is 31" long, with a tapered barrel and a 2½" objective. The Officer of the Deck (O.D.D.) is a 23" cylinder with a 1½" objective. Very massive, short, brass telescopes are usually gun sights or ship equipment and have little interest to most collectors. World War II marked the first widespread use of coated optics, which can be recognized by a colored film on the objective lens. Collectible post-WWII telescopes include early refractors by Unitron or Fecker and reflectors by Cave or Questar. Modern spotting scopes often use a prism to erect the image and are of great interest if made by the best makers, including Nikon and Zeiss. Several modern makers still use lacquered brass, and many replica instruments have been produced.

A telescope with no maker's name is much less interesting than a signed instrument, and 'Made in France' is the most common mark on old spyglasses. Dollond of London made instruments for two hundred years and this is probably the most common name on antiques; but because of their important technical innovations and very high quality, Dollond telescopes are always valuable. Bardou, Paris, telescopes are also of very high quality. Bardou is another relatively common name, since they were a prolific maker for many years, and their spyglasses were sold by Sears. Alvan Clark and Sons were the most prolific early American makers, in operation from the 1850s to the 1920s, and their astronomical telescopes are of great historical import.

Spyglasses are delicate instruments that were subject to severe use under all weather conditions. Cracked or deeply scratched optics are impossible to repair and lower the value considerably. Most lenses are doublets, two lenses glued together, and deteriorated cement is common. This looks like crazed glaze and is fairly difficult to repair. Dents in the tube and damaged or missing leather covering can usually be fixed. The best test of a telescope is to use it, and the image should be sharp and clear. Any accessories, eyepieces, erecting prisms, or quality cases can add significantly to value. The following prices assume that the telescope is in very good to fine condition and give the objective lens (obj.) diameter, which is the most important measurement of a telescope.

Our advisor for this category is Peter Abrahams, who studies and collects telescopes and other optics. Please contact him, especially to exchange reference material. (See his comments concerning online auctions under Binoculars; they are applicable to telescopes as well.) Mr. Abrahams is listed in the Directory under Oregon. (Please include SASE with questions.)

Key:
obj — objective lens   ODD — Officer of the Deck

Mid-nineteenth century terrestrial telescope, no signature, leather-covered brass, rack and pinion and sliding tube focus, 2½" aperture, $600.00.

Adams, George; 2" dia reflecting, brass cabriole tripod............3,000.00
Bardou & Son, Paris, 4-draw, 50 mm obj, leather, 36"................250.00
Bausch & Lomb, 1-draw, 45mm obj, wrinkle pnt, 17" 90.00
Brashear, 3½" obj, brass, tripod, w/eyepcs 4,200.00
Cary, London (script), 2" obj, tripod, w/3 eyepieces.................2,500.00
Clark, Alvan; 4" obj, 48", iron mt on wood legs......................5,500.00
Criterion RV-6 Dynascope, 6" reflector, 1960s..........................500.00
Dallmeyer, London (script), 5-draw, 2½" obj, SP, 49" 500.00
Dolland, London (script), 2-draw, 2" obj, leather cover 200.00
Dollond, London (block), 2-draw, 2" obj, leather cover 290.00
Dollond, London (script), brass, 3" obj, 40", on tripod 2,900.00
Dollond, London (script), 2-draw, 2" obj, leather cover 380.00
France or Made in France, 3-draw, 30mm obj, lens cap 80.00
McAlister (script), brass, 3½" obj, 45", tripod.......................3,000.00
Mogey, brass, 3" obj, 40", on tripod, w/4 eyepieces.................2,600.00
Negretti & Zambra, 2.5" obj, equatorial mt, 36", tripod...........2,500.00
Plossl, Wien, 2.5" obj, Dialytic optics, 24", tabletop tripod 3,200.00
Queen & Co (script), 6-draw, 70mm obj, wood veneer, 50" 700.00
Questar, reflecting, on astro mt, 1950s, 3½" dia 2,200.00
R & J Beck, 2" obj, 24", tabletop tripod w/cabriole legs...........2,200.00
Short, James; 3" dia reflecting, brass cabriole tripod.................3,500.00
Tel Sct Regt Mk 2 S; (many maker's names), UK, WWI 120.00
Unitron, 4" obj, wht, 60", on tripod, many accessories 1,800.00
Unmk, brass, 2" obj, spyglass, leather cover, from $150 to 300.00
Unmk, brass, 2" obj, stand w/cabriole legs 1,200.00
US military, brass, very heavy, from $100 to 300.00
US Navy, QM Spyglass, 16X, Mk II, in box................................220.00
US Navy (ODD), Bu. Ships, Mk II, 10-Power, 1943...................125.00
Vion, Paris, 40 Power, 3-draw, 21", 40mm obj, leather................110.00
Wollensak Mirroscope, 1950s, 12x2" dia, leather case.................200.00
Wood bbl, rnd taper, 1½" obj, sgn, 1800s.................................350.00
Wood bbl, 8-sided, 1½" obj, 1700s, 30" 1,500.00
Zeiss, brass, 60mm obj, w/eyepcs & porro prism, tripod 1,700.00
Zeiss Asiola, 60mm obj, prism spotting scope, pre WWII 450.00

Televisions

Many early TVs have escalated in value over the last few years. Pre-1943 sets (usually with only one to five channels) are often worth $500.00 to $5,000.00. Unusually styled small-screen wooden 1940s TVs are 'hot'; but most metal, Bakelite, and large-screen sets are still shunned by collectors. Color TVs from the 1950s with 16" or smaller tubes are valuable;

larger color sets are not. One of our advisors for this category is Harry Poster, author of *Poster's Radio & Television Price Guide 1920 – 1990, 2nd Edition*; he is listed in the Directory under New Jersey. Another source of information is *Collector's Guide to Vintage Televisions* by Bryan Durbal and Glenn Bubenheimer (Collector Books).

Key: t/t — tabletop

Admiral, 16R12, console, Bakelite, 1950, 16" screen 50.00
Admiral, 19A11, brn or blk Bakelite, Chinese grill, 1948, 7" screen ..125.00
Admiral, 24R12, console, Bakelite, 1950, 14" screen 75.00
Arvin, #3120CB, console, blond, chassis #TE-272, 1949, 12" screen ...50.00
Arvin, #5206CB, console, blond, chassis #TE-300, 1950, 20" screen ...50.00
DuMont, #RA-102, t/t, mahog, Club, 1947, 15" screen 400.00
DuMont, #RA-112, console, mahog, TV/radio, 1950, 15" screen ...125.00
Emerson, #624, t/t, mahog, 1948, 10" screen 120.00
Emerson, #639, t/t, reverse gold pnt bezel, 1949, 7" screen 120.00
GE, #12T7, t/t, mahog, 1949, 12" screen...................................60.00
GE, #16T15, t/t, mahog, rectangular tube, 1950, 16" screen 25.00
Hallicrafters, #515, console, mahog, 1949, 10" screen 85.00
JVC, #3020, t/t, red & wht plastic, transistor, 1978, 5" screen........35.00
Majestic, #12T3, t/t, wood, 1950, 12" screen.............................75.00
Motorola, #17T5, t/t, Bakelite, 1950, 17" screen 35.00
Motorola, #27K2, console, walnut, 1953, 27" screen....................35.00
Olympic, #DX-214, t/t, wood, 1949, 12" screen..........................55.00
Olympic, #TV-944, t/t, Beverly, 1949, 12" screen 75.00
Panasonic, #TR-003, portable, plastic, TV/radio, 1975, 3" screen ...75.00
RCA, #2T51, t/t, metal, 1950, 12" screen...................................90.00
RCA, #630TCS, console, mahog, 1946, 10" screen......................250.00
RCA, #7T124, console, mahog, 1951, 17" screen..........................25.00
Regal, #1007, t/t, mahog, 10" screen..90.00
Scott, #800BT, console, wood, TV/radio/phono, 1949, projection ..400.00
Sentinel, #405, t/t, wood, 19948, 7" screen................................125.00

Philco Predictas and Related Items

Made in the years between 1958 and 1960, Philco Predictas have become one of the most sought after lines of televisions in the post-war era. Predictas are now over forty years old, yet their atom-age styling is just as futuristic today as it was in 1958. As we move into the new millenium, the Predicta line will continue to be highly collectible. Philco Predictas feature a swivel or separate enclosed picture tube and radical cabinet designs.

The values given here are for as-found, average, clean, complete, unrestored sets, running or not, that have good picture tubes. Predictas that are missing parts or have damaged viewing screens will have a lower value. Above average Predictas will have much higher values. Please keep in mind that Predictas that have been completely professionally restored to as new in appearance as well as electronically can easily bring four to five times the stated values. Our advisor for Predicta televisions is David Weddington; he is listed in the Directory under Tennessee.

G4242 Holiday 21" t/t, wood cabinet, blond finish 455.00
G4242 Holiday 21" t/t, wood cabinet, mahog finish....................400.00
G4654 Barber-Pole 21" console, boomerang front leg, blond......725.00
G4654 Barber-Pole 21" console, boomerang front leg, mahog 650.00
G4710 Tandem 21" seperate screen w/25' cable, mahog finish ...625.00
G4720 Stereo Tandem w/matching 1606S phono/amp, mahog..1,100.00
G64270 Stereo Tandem 21" separate screen, 4 brass legs, mahog..900.00
H3406 Motel 17" t/t, metal cabinet, cloth grill, no antenna 275.00
H3408 Debutante 17" t/t, cloth grill, w/antenna, charcoal 375.00
H3410 Princess 17" t/t, metal grill, plastic tuner window.............400.00
H3410 Princess 17" t/t, w/orig metal stand, red finish 500.00
H3412 Siesta 17" t/t, w/clock-timer above tuner, gold finish...............550.00

H4730 Danish Modern 21" console, 4 fin-shaped legs, mahog finish...**950.00**
H4744 Townhouse 21" room-divider, walnut shelves, brass finish.....**1,400.00**
17DRP4 picture tube, MIB, replacement for all 17" t/t Predictas..........**175.00**
21EAP4 or 21FDP4 picture tube, MIB, replacement for all 21" Predictas .**275.00**

Tennis Rackets

Early tennis rackets (pre-1940) generally exhibit these characteristics: head shape — may be oval, flat-top, transitional flat-top, triangular (or other); throat wedge — the triangular section of wood at the junction of the head and the handle may be concave, convex, solid, or laminated; handle — most from this era are not covered by leather and are either combed (grooved) or checkered wood, and some may have cork handles or enlargements at the butt end. Values vary, dependent on age, rarity, style, and condition. Brand and model are important, and all identifying decals should be legible and in good condition. Rackets from 1880 to 1940 range in price from $300.00 to $600.00 for rare models like the Hazel's Streamline down to $10.00 to $20.00 for more common models.

Our advisor for this category is Donald Jones; he is listed in the Directory under Georgia. In the listings that follow, values apply to examples in excellent condition.

Key:
cx-lam — convex laminated   tran — transitional
cx-s — convex solid

AJ Reach, Driver, concave wedge, combed hdl, over head, 1920..**75.00**
E Kent, Duchess, concave wedge, bulbous hdl, over head, 1930.**120.00**
Hazel's, Streamline, branched wedge, leather hdl, over head, 1935......**500.00**
Horsman, Elberton, concave wedge, smooth hdl, flat-top head, 1885..**350.00**
Iver Johnson, Special, ex-s wedge, bulbous hdl, tran head, 1900 ...**175.00**
Magnon, Superior, concave wedge, combed hdl, over head, 1928 ...**75.00**
Slazenger, Demon, cx-lam wedge, fishtail hdl, oval head, 1910 ..**250.00**
Spaulding, Park, cx-s wedge, combed hdl, flat-top head, 1895....**450.00**
Wright-Ditson, Hub, cx-s wedge, checkered hdl, oval head, 1890...**175.00**
Wright-Ditson, Octagon, concave head, combed hdl, oval head, 1895..**120.00**
Wright-Ditson, Star, cx-s wedge, combed hdl, oval head, 1904 ..**135.00**

Teplitz

Teplitz, in Bohemia, was an active art pottery center at the turn of the century. The Amphora Pottery Works was only one of the firms that operated there. (See Amphora.) Art Nouveau and Art Deco styles were favored, and much of the ware was hand decorated with the primary emphasis on vases and figurines. Items listed here are marked 'Teplitz' or 'Turn,' a nearby city.

Bust, lady w/ornate headpc, purple outfit w/caplet, Stellmacher, 18"...**1,700.00**
Ewer, bird on branch, winged dragon hdl, 10" **460.00**
Ewer, grapes & leaves w/ornate gold, invt cone shape, ca 1900, 11½" ..**110.00**
Figurine, boy w/pig, Stellmacher, 7½" **300.00**
Figurine, couple playing flutes, gold matt glaze, 12" **875.00**
Figurine, lion attacking Arab & camel, 13x15½".....................**1,200.00**
Teapot, winged dragon spout & hdl, 2 entwined dolphins finial, 12" ..**1,090.00**
Vase, dk bl/gr forest bkground w/mushrooms at bottom, 7⅛"......**620.00**
Vase, mc floral on wht, ornate gold rim-to-hip hdls, RSK red mk, 13"..**250.00**
Vase, Nouveau lady w/wings at top, gold florals, ca 1900, 17x11"....**400.00**

Terra Cotta

Terra cotta is a type of earthenware or clay used for statuary, architectural facings, or domestic articles. It is unglazed, baked to durable hardness, and characterized by the color of the body which may range from brick red to buff.

Bust of Louis XIV, 43", on 46" faux marble sq ped **4,200.00**
Desk caddy, girl w/puppy by basket & bed of flowers, Am, 1900s, 8x6"...**75.00**
Figure, Nouveau maiden, molded floral base, 20th C, 25½x13" .**495.00**
Jardiniere, lion's head medallions, verdigris, 14x15x16", pr.........**440.00**
Urn, Neoclassical satyr masks & grapes, tall plinth base, 86x32", pr..**3,300.00**

Thermometers

Few objects man has invented have been so eloquently expressed both functionally and artistically as the ubiquitous thermometer. Developed initially by Galileo as a scientific device, thermometers slowly evolved into decorative objet d'art, functional household utensils, and eye-catching advertising specialties. Most American thermometers manufactured early in the twentieth century were produced by Taylor (Tycos), and today their thermometers remain the most plentiful on the market. Decorative thermometers manufactured before 1800 are now ensconced in the permanent collections of approximately a dozen European museums. Because of their fragility, few devices of this era have survived in private collections. Nowadays most antique thermometers find their way to market through estate sales.

Insofar as sheer beauty, uniqueness, and scientific accuracy, decorative thermometers are far superior to the ordinary and inexpensive versions which carry advertising. Decorative thermometers run the gamut from plain tin household varieties to the highly ornate creations of Tiffany and Bradley and Hubbard. They have been manufactured from nearly every conceivable material — oak, sterling, brass, and glass being the favorites — and have tested the artistry and technical skills of some of America's finest craftsmen. Ornamental models can be found in free-hanging, wall-mounted, or desk/mantel versions.

Since 1994 instrument prices have been escalating at a rate of 35% annually. This is due to their relative scarcity, infrequent trading and absence of a 'knock-off' (retro) market. Look for this trend to continue indefinitely.

Thermometer prices are based on age, ornateness, and whether mercury or alcohol is used as the filler in the tube. A broken or missing tube will cut at least 40% off the value. Virtually all American-made thermometers available today as collectors' items were made between 1875 and 1940. The golden age of decoratives ended in the early 1940s as modern manufacturing processes and materials robbed them of their natural distinctiveness.

Key:
br — brass	Rea — Reaumer
Cen — Centigrade	sc — scale
Fah — Fahrenheit	stl — stainless
mrc — mercury in tube	strl — sterling
pmc — permacolor	VR — very rare
R — rare	

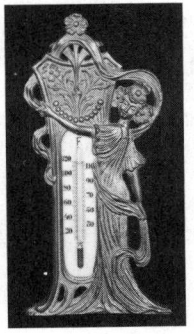

Westminster desk model, bronze Art Nouveau goddess, mercury in bulb, ca 1910, 10x4", $150.00.

Amadio, Fah, Corn Hill, desk, ivory pillar/compass, mrc, 1890, 10"...850.00
Anonymous, cvd wood squirrel, glass Rea sc, mrc, 1905, 10"......800.00
Anonymous, desk, br conquistador figural, br sc, mrc.................650.00
Anonymous, pendant, strl case, ivory Fah sc, mrc, 1880, 5"....1,250.00
Anonymous, sesk, love scene, silver metal, br Rea/Cen sc, mrc, 8" .830.00
Anonymous, wall, giltwood fr, ivory Fah sc, 1790, 10x3½".....3,100.00
Blk/Starr/Frost, desk, barometer, stl, Fah/Cen, mrc, '10, 11"....2,200.00
Bradley & Hubbard, desk, br fr & Fah sc, mrc, 1895, 13x6"....2,800.00
Calley, desk, strl inkwell fr, porc Rea sc, mrc, 1899, 5x6" 3,200.00
Capendium, desk, handmade br/porc fr, Fah/Cen sc, rnd mrc, 4" ..850.00
Carpenter & Westley, desk, ivory w/glass dome mrc, 1880, 6"...950.00
Casella London, wall, maxi/minimum, 2 units, wood, plastic sc .430.00
Cheshire Silversmiths, desk, br candelabra, mrc, 1875, 10".....4,500.00
Chevallier, L'ingre, wall, ivory/mahog, Rea/Cen sc, 1880, 11x3" .2,350.00
Clark, desk, ivory ped, crown, mrc, 1904, 7"................................400.00
Cloister, inkwell, stl bk & base w/angels at side, 1901 ....1,050.00
Creswel, travel, ivory/case/mirror, removable sc, mrc, 2½" 2,800.00
CW Wilder...NH, desk, Deco women, br Fah sc, mrc, R, 8"....1,300.00
Desk, cvd walrus tusk, 2-tier disk base, inlay sc, 1860, 9"...........430.00
Diamond, wall, br Fah sc on wood, R, 7½x1½"........................525.00
Dixie, W (London); desk, gilt/br, Gothic, SP sc, mrc, 8" 790.00
Dollard London, desk, strl, br sc, mrc, 1908, R, 6" 750.00
Dollard London, hanging, mahog fr, strl sc, mrc, 1810, 18".....4,600.00
Dring & Fage, desk, marble, ivory sc, mrc, 1880, 6" 1,500.00
England, desk, glass obelisk/8-sided, br Fah sc, mrc, 1880........1,260.00
England, desk, marble ped fr, Cen, mrc, 1885, 6½" 930.00
England, wall, br game bag fr, Fah sc, mrc, 1890, 9x5".............1,650.00
England, wall, rect wood fr, porc Cen sc, mrc, 1905, 5" 1,350.00
Farley, travel, walnut base mt, ivory Fah/Cen sc, mrc, 5" 900.00
Freeborn, desk, bronze w/3 lead decor, br sc,. mrc, 8".................180.00
G Cooper, desk, bell shape w/cupola, strl, dial, 2x3".....................400.00
Gilbert & Co, travel, silver eng sc, mrc, 1850, 8".........................630.00
Gloucenter Scientific, stl case, glass front, pmc, 42"..................1,500.00
Heath & Wing, figural calendar, br w/porc sc, mrc, 1870.............930.00
J Waldstein, wall, br Rea sc on wood, mrc, 1900s, VR, 10½" 920.00
Kendal, desk, strl obelisk, br Fah sc, mrc, 1890, 8", $1,350 to .1,850.00
Moreau, desk, mahog, Rea/Cen, spiral tube, mrc, 1860, 6½x5½" 1,725.00
Pairpoint, desk, strl picture fr, mrc, 1907, 5".............................650.00
Reau, desk, sq incline base, floral top, mrc, 1895 ....180.00
Rowley & Sons, travel, ivory sc, mrc, 1894, 4", +case.................350.00
Standard, wall, ivory Fah sc on ebony, mrc, 9" 750.00
Standard..., wall, br fr, enamel dial Fah sc, 1885, 9" dia 950.00
Taylor, ped, 3-sided, Fah sc, alcohol, 1900, R, 6"......................3,200.00
Thermindex Switzerland, desk, Bakelite stand, Fah sc, 5"...........725.00
Tiffany, desk, strl tetrahedron fr & Fah sc, mrc, 1910, 2x4"......4,000.00
Tiffany, gr glass w/pine needles, br sc/mrc, 1902, 8x12"..........2,800.00
Tycos, maxi/minimum, japanned tin/br, mrc, T-5452, 8".........125.00
Unknown, cvd wood squirrel, glass Rea sc, mrc, 1905, 10", VR .800.00
Unknown, desk, alabaster w/eagle, Rea/Cen sc, mrc, 1895 ....875.00
Unknown, desk, love scene, silver metal, br Rea/Cen sc, mrc, 8" 830.00
Unknown, wall, giltwood fr, ivory Fah sc, 1790, 10x3½".........3,100.00
VJD Inc, wall, clip Fah br sc, mrc, VR, 4"................................1,650.00
W Pratt, desk, wood inlays, ivory sc, mrc, 1900, 6" 350.00
Warren Foundries, wall, umbrella w/dragon hdl, br sc, mrc, 12"...220.00
West, desk, Gothic design, br, 1900, 12".................................1,360.00
WG Loveday, wall, Clearside, Fah sc, 5" dia 725.00
Whitehead & Hoag, Lambrecht's Polymeter, mrc, 9".............1,200.00
Zeradatha, desk, cast metal w/rotate sc, 1926, 7"........................140.00

1000 Faces China

So named because of its many hand-painted faces, much of this chinaware was made during the '30s through the '50s (some even earli-

er). Though many pieces are unmarked, others are marked 'Made in Japan.' There are two primary patterns, 'Black Face' and the 'Gold' pattern, and variations exist. Both designs employ many colors. Dinner plates usually are decorated with an outer-most 'ring of color' (two or three hues) containing a simple design which is often flowers. The inner ring is usually comprised of many colors radiating from the center circle which may be done in a primary color (red, for instance) with a design such as a dragon or clouds painted in gold. 'Black Face' is distinguishable by its range of colors — primarily red, white, and yellow with some green and blue — and the black hand-painted faces. The 'Gold' pattern is also multicolored but is dominated by the gold throughout the design, and the faces themselves are gold as well. Other variations include '1000 Men in Robes' and '1000 Faces' with black or blue rims on the saucers and cups. These pieces seem to be very scarce. In the listings that follow, all items are marked 'Made in Japan' (MIJ) unless noted otherwise. Our advisor for this category is Suzi Hibbard; she is listed in the Directory under California.

Cup and saucer, dessert plate, black faces, 1940s, MIJ, $45.00 for the set. (Photo courtesy Suzi Hibbard)

Bowl, gold faces, petal shape, 6"...20.00
Cup & saucer, blk faces 40.00
Cup & saucer, demitasse; gold faces....................................25.00
Cup & saucer, gold faces, from $30 to 50.00
Cup & saucer, 1000 Geishas, MIJ 40.00
Egg cup, bl faces, from $15 to..30.00
Ginger jar, gold faces, from $75 to......................................100.00
Lamp, gold faces, 8" vase base, from $100 to........................150.00
Plate, blk, 10", from $30 to 50.00
Plate, blk/gold, 6", from $7.50 to 15.00
Salt cellar, bl faces, from $5 to..10.00
Shakers, bl faces, pr, from $10 to 25.00
Snack set, blk faces, kidney shape, from $20 to......................25.00
Soup set, blk faces, 3-pc, from $50 to 80.00
Sweetmeat, blk faces, 9-pc set in lacquer box, from $150 to 200.00
Sweetmeat set, gold faces, 15-pc, serves 6 ....175.00
Tea set, blk faces, dragon spout, 7", from $50 to 75.00
Tea set, gold faces, 21-pc, MIJ, from $175 to 250.00
Teapot, gold faces, dragon spout, 7", from $30 to...................75.00
Teapot, Men in Robes, 6-sided, Japanese mk, from $40 to 75.00
Vase, blk faces, MIJ, 8", from $50 to....................................75.00
Vase, gold, 8", from $50 to 100.00

Tiffany

Louis Comfort Tiffany was born in 1848 to Charles Lewis and Harriet Young Tiffany of New York. By the time he was eighteen, his father's small dry goods and stationery store had grown and developed into the world-renowned Tiffany and Company. Preferring the study of art to joining his father in the family business, Louis spent the next six years under the tutelage of noted artists. He returned to America in 1870 and until 1875 painted canvases that focused on European and North

African scenes. Deciding the more lucrative approach was in the application of industrial arts and crafts, he opened a decorating studio called Louis C. Tiffany and Co., Associated Artists. He began seriously experimenting with glass, and eschewing traditionally painted-on details, he instead learned to produce glass with qualities that could suggest natural textures and effects. His experiments broadened, and he soon concentrated his efforts on vases, bowls, etc., that came to be considered the highest achievements of the art. Peacock feathers, leaves and vines, flowers, and abstracts were developed within the plane of the glass as it was blown. Opalescent and metallic lustres were combined with transparent color to produce stunning effects. Tiffany called his glass Favrile, meaning handmade.

In 1900 he established Tiffany Studios and turned his attention full time to producing art glass, leaded-glass lamp shades and windows, and household wares with metal components. He also designed a complete line of jewelry which was sold through his father's store. He became proficiently accomplished in silverwork and produced such articles as hand mirrors embellished with peacock feather designs set with gems and candlesticks with Favrile glass inserts.

Tiffany's work exemplified the Art Nouveau style of design and decoration, and through his own flamboyant personality and business acumen he perpetrated his tastes onto the American market to the extent that his name became a household word. Tiffany Studios continued to prosper until the 1920s when due to changing tastes his influence began to diminish. By the early 1930s the company had closed.

Serial numbers were assigned to much of Tiffany's work, and letter prefixes indicated the year of manufacture: A – N for 1896 – 1900, P – Z for 1901 – 1905. After that, the letter followed the numbers with A – N in use from 1906 to 1912; P – Z from 1913 to 1920. O-marked pieces were made especially for friends and relatives; X indicated pieces not made for sale.

Our listings are primarily from the auction houses in the east where Tiffany sells at a premium. All pieces are signed unless noted otherwise.

Glass

Bowl, amber irid, ruffled, appl disk ft, 2¼x6¼" 450.00
Bowl, amber irid, 10-rib, scalloped, nicks, 3x8" 925.00
Bowl, amber w/gold irid, 8-rib, ruffled, 4½", EX, 6 for 1,725.00
Bowl, amber w/violet irid, ruffled rim, #1496, 5⅝", +6½" plate .460.00
Bowl, centerpc; gold irid, ribbed, rolled rim, 3x7½" 1,100.00
Bowl, centerpc; gold irid, scalloped, 4x9¾" 3,900.00
Bowl, finger; gold irid, ruffled, 2¼x4¾", +6" tray 750.00
Bowl, finger; gold irid, 2½x4¼" 650.00
Bowl, finger; gold irid w/flower millefiori, gold heart & vines, 4" ...1,300.00
Bowl, finger; gold irid w/pulled pigtail decor, 2½x4½" 600.00
Bowl, finger; hearts & vines, gr on crystal, 2x4" 400.00
Bowl, finger; Optic Rib, clear opal w/aqua irid, #1777, 1⅞x5" ...700.00
Bowl, fruit; gold irid, ribbed, rolled rim, 3x7½" 1,100.00
Bowl, gold irid, 10-rib, scalloped, X-129, 2½x7¼" 485.00
Bowl, gold irid w/8 trailing prunts over threaded band, 2¼x4½" ..575.00
Bowl, gr irid w/gold pulls on opal, #04250, 2½x4¼" 2,750.00
Bowl, gr stretch opal w/ferns/eng insects in border, #1925, 12" .1,380.00
Bowl, leaves & vines, gold irid on clear, #4034K, 12½" 1,000.00
Bowl, leaves & vines intaglio on gold irid, 2¾x6¼" 635.00
Bowl, nut; bl-gold irid, waisted, melon ribs, 1½x2¼", pr 500.00
Bowl, nut; gold irid, ribbed, flared rim, 3" 300.00
Bowl, nut; gold irid, ruffled rim, 4¾" 500.00
Bowl, vines/heart-shaped leaves, blk on bl irid, 2½x3½" 1,900.00
Candlesticks, gold irid, spiral-ribbed shafts, 20th C, 5", pr 1,375.00
Compote, cobalt lustre w/stretched irid at rim, ftd, 3x9" 800.00
Compote, gold irid, folded ped ft, label, 2x7¾" 635.00
Compote, gold irid, scalloped, ribbed disk ft, 3¾x6" 1,100.00
Compote, gold irid w/cobalt ft, shallow, 2⅛x8" 1,250.00

Compote, gold irid w/2 eng butterflies w/in, ped ft, #1149, 4".1,150.00
Compote, leaves, opal on shaded turq, #5-1578, 4x10¼" 1,200.00
Compote, shrimp; feathers, sage gr on crystal, #698T, 6½" 375.00
Cordial, gold irid, 4 pinched sides, 1¾" 375.00
Covered dish, gold lustre, spiral finial, ftd, #2319J, 6x5¾" 1,150.00
Decanter, pulled pods/trailing stems, gold irid, G1588, 11" 2,300.00
Goblet, amber w/gold threading, pulled prunts, swollen cylinder, 5"...865.00
Plate, clear to wht opal w/stretched gr irid at rim, #1775, 8" 635.00
Plate, gold irid, scalloped, #R3691, 6½" 350.00
Salt cellar, gold irid, ruffled rim, 2¾" 250.00
Sconce, gold irid, dbl arms, scalloped border, 12x12", pr 3,000.00
Toothpick holder, gold irid, flared/pinched rim, 2" 315.00
Tumbler, gold irid, bulbous, flared rim, 3¾" 400.00
Vase, amber w/gold irid appl trailing prunts, #G1691, 4" 300.00
Vase, amber w/violet irid, tapered cylinder, trumpet-form top, 12"....1,725.00
Vase, amber-red to dk red top, label, #7113A, 6" 3,100.00
Vase, bl irid, wide pinched shoulders, ruffled rim, #1071, 4¾" ...1,000.00
Vase, bl irid, 10-rib gourd form, flared/ruffled, disk ft, 10¼" 1,500.00
Vase, bl w/pinched sides, #08172, 3" 600.00
Vase, blossoms/leaves/stems, gr/wht/amber on amber, #2889C, 5" ..2,200.00
Vase, bud; gold irid slim cylinder on bronze saucer base, 12" ...1,850.00
Vase, bud; leaves, gr on gold irid, ftd, #2201K, 7¾" 1,250.00
Vase, bud; leaves, gr on gold irid; scrolled bronze base, #714, 16" ..1,000.00
Vase, bud; turq bl cased in wht, sm mouth, ovoid, #6476N 1,000.00
Vase, cameo leaves, red/yel, red cameo-cvd holder, #4197A, 4½"....11,000.00
Vase, Cypriote, gold irid w/mc hues, brn dots, pulled bands, #1519, 6" .3,200.00
Vase, feathers, red & gold lustre on bl irid, #E550, 20¼"..........2,250.00
Vase, floriform; bl, emb ribs, waisted/scalloped rim, #1035H, 15¼" ..3,300.00
Vase, floriform; citron opal; combed leaves at yel opal rim, 11" ..4,100.00
Vase, floriform; dragonflies on pk w/crystal ft, #1900, 14¼" 1,500.00
Vase, floriform; gold to amber w/violet irid, #5139, 12⅝" 1,600.00
Vase, gold irid, ftd/ribbed cylinder, #1547-5690N, 11½" 900.00
Vase, gold irid, narrow neck w/fold-in rim, #7625L, 2¾" 425.00
Vase, gold irid, pinched/ruffled rim, 2½x4½" 285.00
Vase, gold irid, pulled loop hdls, #U4830, 2¼", NM 650.00
Vase, gold irid, ribbed/pinched hexagon, #G2899, 2⅞" 450.00
Vase, gold irid, tapered w/knob stem, flared rim, #5032B, 7¾"...1,300.00
Vase, gold irid, urn form, #1025 541K, 6¾" 1,025.00
Vase, gold irid bowl on bronze stick stem w/rnd base, #1686, 16" .3,300.00
Vase, gold irid w/bl irid at base, 8 swirls, #9320, 2⅞" 520.00
Vase, gold pulled work/red & gold bands, ovoid, sm mouth, #2032A, 3" .3,500.00
Vase, gold to bl irid, stick form, #1029-2437N, 6½" 1,100.00
Vase, gold w/gold Diatreta threads, wide mouth, ftd, #3694E, 3¾x4"...1,200.00
Vase, hearts & vines, amber w/gold irid, #840B, 8½" 1,950.00
Vase, hearts & vines, opal-gr on cobalt w/purple irid, 6¼" 2,185.00
Vase, hearts & vines, royal bl on bl irid, #244G, 7½" 3,200.00
Vase, hearts & vines on amber irid, #5603G, 9" 1,850.00
Vase, hearts/vines/millefiori, bl irid on bl to blk, Y3578, 4½"..4,000.00
Vase, jack-in-pulpit; gold irid, #1534-8802M, 10½" 1,600.00
Vase, jack-in-pulpit; gold irid, #7221, 19¾x10½" 14,000.00
Vase, leaves, amber w/gold irid on emerald gr, #W6639, 4¾"..2,400.00
Vase, leaves, gr & gold on opal, cylindrical w/bulbous base, 8¾"..1,250.00
Vase, leaves, gr on gold irid, ovoid, #4038B, 4½" 635.00
Vase, leaves, gr on gold irid, reverse trumpet, #3489 K, 8".......1,100.00
Vase, leaves, gr on opal, gold irid int/bronze base w/disk ft, 18½" ..6,325.00
Vase, leaves, gr on opal w/gold int, gold ft, #79E, 4½x5½" 1,100.00
Vase, leaves, gr variegated on almond, #9340D, 13½" 3,600.00
Vase, paperweight; floral, coral/gr on opal, #8490, ca 1907, 4½" ...8,625.00
Vase, paperweight; trailing leaves, mc on reactive cream to bl, 5" .7,000.00
Vase, petal blossom, peach opal on lt amber, ftd, M1142, 9½"...1,950.00

Lamps

Lamp prices seem to be getting stronger, especially for leaded lamps with brighter colors (red, blue, purples). Bases that are unusual or rare have brought good prices and added to the value of the more common shades that sold on them. Bases with enamel or glass inserts are very much in demand. Our advisor for Tiffany lamps is Carl Heck; he is listed in the Directory under Colorado.

Key: c-b — counterbalance

Base, bridge; c-b arm, swivel socket, 5 spade ft, #468, 55" **3,750.00**
Base, candlestick; gold w/violet irid, spiral ribs, boboche, 8".......**750.00**
Base, enameled metal, bulbous, electrified, #98942, 13½x8"...**5,500.00**
Base, radiating ribs, bronze, #684, 52¾".................................**2,000.00**
Boudoir, gr intaglio leaves on gold irid shade & base, #5594L, 16" ...**8,500.00**
Bridge, kapa shell shade on dbl S arm w/c-b, #468, 57" **3,000.00**
Candle, gold irid w/bl lustre at base, wht stem w/gr leaves, 13" ...**1,265.00**
Chandelier, bronze flush mt w/center dome, #972, 3 floriform shades **3,750.00**
Chandelier, daffodils & spiked leaves, invt dome, 16" dia, 21" drop.....**32,200.00**
Chandelier, ldgl 22" dia shade, 6-socket fixture, 58" drop **41,400.00**
Chandelier, 5-light w/floriform irid shades; brn-gr patina, 33".**4,500.00**
Desk, Am irid glass shade; c-b gilt-bronze mk std, 13¾"..........**2,250.00**
Desk, damascene 7" shade; paneled harp std w/wide base **8,500.00**
Desk, damascene 7" shade; 1-arm c/b bronze base **7,000.00**
Desk, gold irid bell shade on #419 gold-tone harp std.............**1,650.00**
Desk, gold pulled feathers shade; #661 harp std.....................**3,350.00**
Desk, Pine Needle open metalwork shade; stepped base, #724, 14¾" ...**2,750.00**
Floor, ldgl 20" acorn-band shade; 6-ftd bun base...................**27,500.00**
Floor, 10" gold irid shade; bronze harp #682 std, 55"...............**8,500.00**
Floor, 10" rvpt geometric shade; bronze harp std w/floral ft, 54" ...**2,700.00**
Hanging, ldgl 16" gridwork shade w/turtle bk tile center.......**24,000.00**
Hanging, ldgl 28" clematis shade; 6 Perkins sockets, rpl hdw...**55,000.00**
Lily, 12-light, amber irid shades; lily pad base **22,500.00**
Lily, 3 calyx-form sockets w/irid mk shades; #319 std, 12⅞" **3,165.00**
Lily, 4-light (3 down/1 up), bronze std w/ornate leaves............**7,700.00**
Lily, 8 calyx-form sockets w/irid shades; #381 std, 19½" **14,950.00**
Mantel, 8-sided cream shade w/mc pulled petals; gilt-bronze std, 8" ..**1,150.00**
Shade, ldgl, acorn band, hemispherical, 5¾x14" **5,000.00**
Shade, ldgl, leaves at top, metal rim w/16 thorns, tag, 6⅛x7½" .**1,200.00**
Shade, ldgl vine band shade, grs & amber, 16" **4,500.00**
Student, twisted central font amid dbl-post fr, 2-burner, D896, 29" **3,750.00**
Student, 10" wht opal w/wavy gold irid #S2881 shade; #1539 std, 25".**6,775.00**
Table, damascene 7" platinum/pk shade; bronze std, 18"..........**3,000.00**
Table, ldgl 14" acorn shade; gold doré #d std, 20"....................**9,500.00**
Table, ldgl 14" arrow-root shade; rare std w/openwork ferns..**22,500.00**
Table, ldgl 15" geometric shade; bronze organic mk std, 23" .**13,500.00**
Table, ldgl 16" acorn-band shade; ftd std w/fluted bun base...**13,000.00**
Table, ldgl 16" acorn-band shade; lily pad #26536 std, 19½"...**9,775.00**
Table, ldgl 16" acorn-band shade; 4-leg kerosene egg-form base ..**6,775.00**
Table, ldgl 16" daffodils shade; ftd bun base, str stem.............**22,000.00**
Table, ldgl 16" pomegranate leaf-band shade; urn std...............**8,500.00**
Table, ldgl 16" rose-band shade; bullet font in 3-prong mt **30,000.00**
Table, ldgl 16" tulip shade; lg urn base w/4 upright supports .**35,000.00**
Table, ldgl 16" turtle-bk #1470-4" shade; 4-ftd #533 std, 21" ...**18,000.00**
Table, ldgl 17" dragonfly shade; ovoid std w/oil canister, 18½" ...**23,000.00**
Table, ldgl 18" gridwork shade; Tiffany pottery bulbous base....**22,500.00**
Table, ldgl 18" peony shade; ftd fluted std/wide dome base #1475 ..**40,000.00**
Table, ldgl 20" daffodil shade; fluted std/wide ftd base **42,500.00**
Table, ldgl 20" dragonfly w/filigree shade; std w/blown-in glass ..**55,000.00**
Table, ldgl 20" gridwork cone shade; ftd Library base w/leaves ...**15,000.00**
Table, ldgl 20½" gr sq tile #434 shade; mk bronze std, 30"....**32,000.00**
Table, ldgl 22" nasturtium shade; 4-ftd std w/leaves & stems.**72,500.00**
Table, ldgl 22½" geometric shade; 4-socket bronze #532 std, 29" ..**19,550.00**
Table, linen-fold 12" 8-sided shade; gold doré geometric std, 18" **7,000.00**
Table, linen-fold 15" 12-sided amber shade; 3-socket #d std, 24", pr ...**15,000.00**
Table, Nautilus, shell shade, wide bun base **22,500.00**

Metal Work

Items are bronze unless noted otherwise.

Ashtray, 2 linear-etched loop hdls, #1711,⅞x4" **400.00**
Bookends, vegetation & shield elements, arched top, gold doré, pr ..**925.00**
Bookends, Venetian, gilt bronze w/mc enameling, #1683, 6¼", pr....**900.00**
Bowl, gilt bronze w/foliate border, #1677, 6½" **145.00**
Bowl, orig gold doré patina, 4½" **270.00**
Box, Bookmark, hexagonal, typographical mks/foliate panels, #905, 3" ...**315.00**
Box, cigar; Zodiac, mc enameling, cedar lining, #1655, 2½x6½x6" ...**1,600.00**
Box, cigarette; gilt bronze & enamel, cedar-lined, #130, 6¼" L..**750.00**
Box, desk; arabesques/curlicues/enameling, #2035, 1⅝x5⅝"........**375.00**
Box, glove; Grapevine w/striated gr slag inserts, ball ft, 3x13½x5" ..**980.00**
Box, stamp; Zodiac, 3-compartment, brn-gr patina, 1x3½x2".....**375.00**
Box, Zodiac, gilt bronze, #166, 2x4½x3½" **925.00**
Candle holder, lattice w/blown-in glass, long stem, #21100, 19½"..**1,450.00**
Candlestick, Queen Anne's Lace, corseted/rtcl, glass inserts, 21".....**3,750.00**
Candlestick, root base, gr glass cup w/gold feather, 12½" **2,600.00**
Candlestick, 4 paw ft, gr glass shade w/pulled feathers, 16" **3,250.00**
Candlesticks, bulbous cup on 3 prongs, gilded, #1213, 16", pr.**2,500.00**
Charger, Abalone, emb flowers, MOP dots, 14"............................**500.00**
Compote, allover etching on gilt bronze, #527, 4¼x6" **400.00**

Desk set, Grapevine, etched metal and green slag glass with bronze patina, seven-piece set, $1,950.00.

Desk set, Pine Needle, 3-tier stand+inkwell+paper clip+box+blotter ...**1,600.00**
Desk set, Pine Needle, 7-pc...**2,070.00**
Desk set, Zodiac, orig patina, 6-pc..**2,200.00**
Frame, Abalone, EX patina, 10x7½"...**3,250.00**
Frame, gr insects on gilt-metal, #600, 5½x4¼" **1,850.00**
Frame, Grapevine, glass inserts, orig patina, 6½x7".....................**700.00**
Frame, Grapevine, gr & ivory glass inserts, 10x8" **1,800.00**
Frame, Heraldic, brn patina, easel bk, 12x10¼".........................**1,000.00**
Frame, mottled pattern, EX orig patina, 12x10" **2,600.00**
Frame, ornate florals, EX patina, 6½x6".......................................**550.00**
Frame, Pine Needle, mc mottled glass inserts, #916, 14x12" ...**2,875.00**
Frame, Pine Needle, multitone gr glass inserts, 9½x8".............**2,100.00**
Frame, Pine Needle, yel & wht glass inserts, 7x8½" **1,600.00**
Frame, Spider Webb, slag glass inserts, 9½x8" **1,300.00**
Frame, Zodiac, gold doré, mk, 8½x7", EX................................**1,200.00**
Inkwell, Zodiac, opal glass insert, #1072, 6¼" **600.00**
Letter holder, Bookmark, 2-tier, #1020, spotting, 5¼x9¼x2¼"....**500.00**
Letter opener, scrollwork hdl, EX patina, ca 1910, 8½" **115.00**
Letter scale, Vintage o/l on gr slag, EX patina, #872, 3¼"...........**485.00**
Magnifying glass, Zodiac, brn patina, #928, 8¾" **700.00**
Money clip, St Louis World's Fair/eagle/flag, 1904, 1x2"...........**300.00**
Note paper holder, geometric border w/mc inlay, #610, 4⅛x7⅝" ...**260.00**
Tazza, Greek Key & foliage w/gr enamel inserts, 2½x7¼" **700.00**
Thermometer, Grapevine, gr patina & slag glass, easel stand, 8¾" ...**1,500.00**
Toothpick holder, spider web design, cleaned patina, 2½" **250.00**
Tray, fire-polished random design, rolled rim, #9064, 14¾" dia ..**980.00**
Tray, gilt bronze w/mc floral cloisonne hdls, #512, 9⅞" dia.........**450.00**
Tray, incised leaves, cleaned patina, 11½"...................................**170.00**
Tray, pen; Zodiac, brn patina, minor discoloration, 10x3¼" **200.00**

Twine holder, Bookmark, 6-sided, reddish patina, 3" 1,000.00

Pottery

Vase, blk crystalline drip on gr matt, 3¼" 800.00
Vase, cobalt & gr mottle, shouldered, chips to rim, 6¼x10¾" ...1,000.00
Vase, emb vines/berries under Old Ivory, closed-in rim, EP22Y, 5x8" ..6,000.00
Vase, overlapping leaves, yel-gr & ivory matt, #7, rpr, 11".......2,600.00
Vase, tulips & foliage emb on biscuit, gr int, BP 308, 16⅜" 2,975.00

Silver

Key: t-oz — troy ounces

Bonbon, pierced/beaded rims, monogrammed, 1900s, 2x4x2", 6 for .635.00
Bowl, bread; pierced/chased/emb clover blossoms, 1891-1902, 10" ...770.00
Bowl, copper leaf inlay, closed-in rim, 1950s, 3x7¾" 700.00
Bowl, hammered, hexagonal lobed outline w/appl rim, 2½x8½"..635.00
Bowl, vegetable; scrolls/leaves/flowers, 7x10", 36.5 t-oz 1,550.00
Box, pill; in form of gift package, heavy weight 110.00
Cake stand, eng floral & foliate border, 12" dia 700.00
Napkin ring, emb shells, ca 1920, 2½x1⅞" 265.00
Vase, rtcl body w/cobalt glass liner, Arts & Crafts style, 1910, 18" ..1,450.00

Tiffin Glass

The Tiffin Glass Company was founded in 1887 in Tiffin, Ohio, one of the many factories comprising the U.S. Glass Company. Its early wares consisted of tablewares and decorative items such as lamps and globes. Among the most popular of all Tiffin products was the black satin glass produced there during the 1920s. In 1959 U.S. Glass was sold, and in 1962 the factories closed. The plant was re-opened in 1963 as the Tiffin Art Glass Company. Products from this period were tableware, hand-blown stemware, and other decorative items.

Those interested in learning more about Tiffin glass are encouraged to contact the Tiffin Glass Collectors' Club, whose address can be found in the Directory under Clubs, Newsletters, and Catalogs. See also Black Glass; Glass Animals.

Ashtray, red & crystal, #6590, 11"..100.00
Basket, Jungle Assortment, any color, #151, 6" 85.00
Bell, Fuchsia, crystal, #15083, 5"..75.00
Bowl, bonbon; Flanders, pk, 2-hdld 65.00
Bowl, console; red satin Kimberly, 8½" 195.00
Bowl, June Night, crystal, crimped, 12" 65.00
Bowl, salad; Fuchsia, crystal, 10" 65.00
Cake stand, Ritz Carlton, Royal Blue w/gold, #74, 10" 150.00
Candlestick, Cellini, Copen Blue, #17423, pr............................325.00
Candlestick, cut, Sky Blue, bell bottom, 11" 100.00
Celery, Flanders, crystal, 11" 30.00
Cigarette box, Fuchsia, crystal, w/lid, #9305, 4x2¾" 120.00
Comport, blk satin etch, 7"..135.00
Compote, Ritz Carlton, satin, twisted stem, #15315, 7" 95.00

Creamer, Classic, crystal, $25.00.
(Photo courtesy Gene Florence)

Creamer, Classic, flat, pk...75.00
Creamer, Fontaine, amber, gr or pk, ftd, #4.............................35.00
Cup, Classic, crystal...60.00
Decanter, Jungle Assortment, any color, w/stopper.....................125.00
Dresser set, Dancing girl, pk, bl or gr, #9313.............................650.00
Flower arranger, cobalt, #6552, 8"...225.00
Grapefruit, Flanders, yel, w/liner..100.00
Icer, Cherokee Rose, crystal...110.00
Jug, Julia, amber, ftd, w/lid...295.00
Lamp, hurricane; crystal, #6408...85.00
Nut dish, Fuchsia, crystal, 6¼"...40.00
Parfait, Flanders, pk, hdld, 5⅝"..180.00
Pitcher, June Night, crystal...295.00
Plate, dinner; Fuchsia, crystal, #5902, 9½"................................65.00
Plate, Fontaine, Twilight, #8814, 6"..20.00
Plate, salad; Julia, amber..14.00
Relish, June Night, crystal, 3-part, 12½".....................................65.00
Rose bowl, gr & crystal, #6576, 6"...175.00
Saucer, Cadena, pk or yel..20.00
Saucer, Flanders, pk..15.00
Shakers, Fuchsia, crystal, #2, pr...145.00
Stem, claret; Flanders, yel...95.00
Stem, claret; Fontaine, amber, gr or pk, #033............................60.00
Stem, sherry; Cherokee Rose, crystal, 2-oz.................................35.00
Stem, wine; Cadena, crystal, 6"...35.00
Sugar bowl, Fontaine, Twilight, ftd, #4.......................................65.00
Sugar bowl, Fuchsia, crystal w/pearl edge...................................45.00
Tumbler, Flanders, pk, ftd, 10-oz, 4¾"...45.00
Tumbler, seltzer; Julia, amber, ftd..20.00
Vase, bud; Cherokee Rose, crystal, 6"...25.00
Vase, Smoke & Twilight, #6560, 16"..225.00
Wall vase, blk satin, #16258 ....110.00
Whipped cream, Fuchsia, crystal, #310, 3-ftd.............................40.00

Tiles

The history of tile making dates back to ancient Egypt and Assyria. For centuries tiles have played an important role as a decorative art form, as well as having a utilitarian function. Places such as palace walls, Islamic mosques, Roman floors, and medieval English churches were all adorned with tiles or glazed ceramic surfaces. Remnants of these tile installations can still be seen throughout the world.

The heyday of tile making in England and the United States dates back to circa 1860 through 1930 and envelops the Victorian, Art Nouveau, and Arts & Crafts Movements in both countries. These tiles comprise most of those seen on today's market.

Tiles are being collected today as individual art objects and are increasingly used as decorative accessories. They are also sought in order to restore homes, buildings, and furniture to original period condition. Many people are now incorporating antique and collectible tiles into their home-rebuilding projects for gardens, kitchens, bathrooms, fireplaces, stair risers, and floors.

Tiles must be judged on an individual basis. The condition of the tile face; the quality of the design; the rarity of the artist, company, or series; and the size of the tile or tile panel are just some of the factors to consider when assessing value. People, animals, and scenes are generally more desirable than florals and geometrics. Some glaze colors, such as true pale pink or bright red majolica, add value to Victorian tiles. Tiles may be more difficult to find than many other antiques or collectibles, partly because many were permanently installed. Unfortunately many installations have been destroyed. These factors all have influence on the tile market, and it is not unusual for prices to vary greatly. See also Moravian; Grueby; Rookwood; other specific manufacturers. Our advisor for this category is Karen Guido; she is listed in the Directory under Connecticut.

Key:
maj — majolica glaze   tbld — tube lined
pr mld — press molded   tp — transfer printed
srs — series

American

Attributed to Owens, three-tile frieze of nine marching geese, 11x25", NM in frame, $2,900.00. (Photo courtesy Treadway Auction Gallery)

AETCO, bird nest & eggs, brn maj, pr mld, 3" 80.00
AETCO, Miss Muffett, mc, cuenca, 4"..................................250.00
AETCO, Pres McKinley, bl intaglio, 3", VG 125.00
AETCO, profile male warrior, bl maj pr mld, 6" 285.00
AETCO, Woman in Renassaince garb gr maj, 18x6", VG 425.00
Arequipa, leaf & vine, mc, cuenca, 6" 1,200.00
Arequipa, leaves, mc matt, pr mld, 6", VG 550.00
Batchelder, man & dog w/spear, red clay, gr engobe, 4"..............200.00
Batchelder, trees/fruit, buff w/bl engobe, 4-tile panel, 6x24" 650.00
Batchelder, Viking ship, gr engobe, pr mld, 5¾"........................475.00
BFAT, George Washington, mauve maj, pr mld, 11¾", VG........985.00
Boston Terra Cotta, leaves & candle holder, terra cotta, 6" 165.00
Brown County Pottery, girl w/hat, mc, incised, 5½"...................150.00
C Pardee, Duchess & baby, mc, incised, 4½" 725.00
California Art Tile, paddle boat & scenic, mc, pr mld, 5⅝", VG ..300.00
California Faience, gargoyle, bl/yel, cuenca, hairline, 6" 345.00
Catalina, poinsettias, mc, cuerda seca, 6 tiles form circle, G.......500.00
Claycraft, Spanish house & scenic, mc matt, 12x8", G 650.00
Claycraft, stone arch bridge w/rocks & trees, mc matt, 12x4".....650.00
Enfield, shield on diagonal, mc, pr mld, 4½" 85.00
Flint Faience, Dutch boy tending ducks, mc, cuenca, 6" dia 800.00
Hamilton, woman & Cupid, mauve maj, pr mld, 6 tiles, 12x18" ...1,350.00
Kensington, greyhound, brn maj, pr mld, 6" 265.00
Low, profile, gr maj, sgn Arthur Osborne, 4"...........................275.00
Low, Summer & female face, bl maj, 6x4" 425.00
Marblehead, oak tree, dk gr crystalline, 6¼", fr.....................3,250.00
Mosaic, duck, bl/wht/yel, pr mld, 4", VG 185.00
Mueller, Viking ship, rose/gray, pr mld, 6"..............................350.00
San Jose Potteries, cactus, mc, Mexican A&C mk, 8"................600.00
San Jose Potteries, woodpecker on tree, mc, 2 tile vertical panel ...500.00
SEG, goat on grapevine, gr tones, incised, firing crack, 6" 925.00
Taylor, flower & leaves, mc, pr mld, Monaco line, 6" dia, G.......150.00
Trent, Art Nouveau floral, mc maj, 9x6"................................170.00
Walrich, floral, yel/br/bl, 5"...425.00
Wheatley, geometric, mc, pr mld, 3".....................................105.00

English

Brown, Westhead & Moore; dancing women, HP, 6" 250.00

England, male/female cow profiles, matched maj, ca 1895, 6", pr ...950.00
England, 3 tomatoes, caramel maj intaglio, ca 1890, 6" 105.00
H Richards, Art Nouveau floral, mc maj, 6", VG......................125.00
Malkin Edge, Games & Pastimes, brn/wht tp, 6" 200.00
Minton Hollins, Arts & Sciences srs, Painting, brn/wht tp, 6" ...125.00
Mintons ChWks, Aesop's Fables, Eagle & Tortoise, bl/wht, 6"....125.00
Mintons ChWks, horses in field, Wm Wise, bl/wht tp, 6", NM..140.00
Royal Doulton, house/landscape, HP, sgn E Louis, 17x15½" ...2,800.00
Sadler, Pretty Mantuamaker, tin glazed, red/wht, ca 1775, 5", VG....275.00
Sherwin & Cotton, geraniums, gr/purple maj, pr mld, 6"............105.00
T&R Boote, fire w/woman, brn/wht tp, 6"................................100.00
Wedgwood, floral barbotine, mc, ca 1880, 6", VG......................75.00
William De Morgan, stylized flower, mc, 8", NM 850.00

Other Countries

Belgian, Art Nouveau floral, mc, tbld, 6x3"................................85.00
De Porceleyne Fles, flying geese, mc, pr mld, vertical, 9x5"........150.00
De Porceleyne Fles, Viking ship, mc, ca 1920, 4"......................125.00
De Porceleyne Fles, winged bug, mc, ca 1920, 4"......................125.00
Mexico, man wearing sombrero in scene, sgn, mc, 5½" 150.00
Mexico, Pack mule, mc sgn Rugerio, 5½"................................100.00
Mexico, turkey, cactus & house, sgn Uriarte, mc, 5⅝"...............180.00

Tinware

In the American household of the seventeenth and eighteenth centuries, tinware items could be found in abundance, from food containers to foot warmers and mirror frames. Although the first settlers brought much of their tinware with them from Europe, by 1798 sheets of tin plate were being imported from England for use by the growing number of American tinsmiths. Tinwares were often decorated either by piercing or painted designs which were both freehand and stenciled. (See Toleware.) By the early 1900s, many homes had replaced their old tinware with the more attractive aluminum and graniteware.

In the nineteenth century, tenth wedding anniversaries were traditionally celebrated by gifts of tin. Couples gave big parties, dressed in their wedding clothes, and reaffirmed their vows before their friends and families who arrived bearing (and often wearing) tin gifts, most of which were quite humorous. Anniversary tin items may include hats, cradles, slippers and shoes, rolling pins, etc. See also Primitives and Kitchen Collectibles.

Anniversary, knife & fork, oversz, diagonal ribbed hdls, 22", 13", pr ..635.00
Anniversary, spoon, long ribbed hdl w/bent rod hanger, 41", G..375.00
Anniversary, top hat, band w/bow, 6½" 1,300.00
Box, cash; folding, HP decor w/gold striping, brass hasp, 7x8x4" ..40.00
Canister, worn old yel pnt, 32x18" 165.00
Coffeepot, bbl shape, removable lid, stick spout, 19th C, 9" 65.00
Coffeepot, G detail, pewter knob on lid, 9½"...........................250.00
Coffeepot, gooseneck, hinged lid, brass finial, 9⅞"....................120.00
Coffeepot, wood hdl, 8", EX..30.00
Colander, conical w/ftd base, appl arched hdls, ca 1900, 5¼x9½"...35.00
Dustpan, stamped dmn decor, punched flower, 19th C, 14x12"..270.00
Sconce, crimped pans, oval reflector, minor rprs, 1850s, 8", pr..1,300.00
Sconce, crimped piecrust edge & bobeche, 19th C, 9¾" dia 465.00
Sconce, rnded crest w/crimped edge, 11½", pr...........................850.00
Sconce, shelf w/3 sockets & reflector bk, emb dmns, 11x14"......465.00
Sconce, 2-light, crimped arched tops, mirror bk, 1850s, 17x6x4"..125.00
Sieve, cheese, dbl hdls, 4½x5" dia...155.00
Sieve, cheese; punched heart shape, 5¾x6½" 200.00
Sieve, dk patina, punched heart shape w/3 ft, ring hanger, 15x14"..635.00
Sieve, heart shape, punched lines/holes, 3-ftd, w/hanger, 3⅝x4½"..300.00
Skimmer, pierced sides, tubular stick hdl, 4½x8" dia, 22" hdl.......40.00

Tinder box, w/removable damper, candle socket, dk patina, 3¼" ...**300.00**

Tobacciana

Tobacciana is the generally accepted term used to cover a field of collecting that includes smoking pipes, cigar molds, cigarette lighters, humidors — in short, any article having to do with the practice of using tobacco in any form. Perhaps the most valuable variety of pipes is the meerschaum, hand carved from hydrous magnesium, an opaque white-gray or cream-colored mineral of the soapstone family. (Much of this is today mined in Turkey which has the largest meerschaum deposit in the world, though there are other deposits of lesser significance around the globe.) These figural bowls often portray an elaborately carved mythological character, an animal, or a historical scene. Amber is sometimes used for the stem. Other collectible pipes are corn cob (Missouri Meerschaum) and Indian peace pipes of clay or catlinite. (See American Indian Art.)

Chosen because it was the Indians who first introduced the white man to smoking, the cigar store Indian was a symbol used to identify tobacco stores in the nineteenth century. The majority of them were hand carved between 1830 and 1900 and are today recognized as some of the finest examples of early wood sculptures. When found they command very high prices.

For further information on lighters, refer to *Collector's Guide to Cigarette Lighters* by James Flanagan. Ashtray collectors will enjoy *Collector's Guide to Ashtrays, Second Edition*, by Nancy Wanvig. See also Advertising; Snuff Boxes.

Cigar store figure, William Penn holding cigars, papier-mache with wooden base, National Papier Mache Works, Milwaukee Wis., 1919, 65", EX+, $2,850.00.

Ashtray, Amish couple, pnt CI, Wilton, 4" sq **24.00**
Ashtray, beer stein form w/emb scenes, ceramic, plunger type, Germany ...**60.00**
Ashtray, blk amethyst glass, Sapulpa OK ad, Bartlett Collins, 4" sq......**15.00**
Ashtray, brass w/enameled flowers on bright bl, 3 rests, 5" L.........**13.00**
Ashtray, cut glass, cobalt to crystal, 2 rests, 3⅛" dia.....................**50.00**
Ashtray, dog at side of tray, lustreware, Japan, 3" **25.00**
Ashtray, Dutch shoe, ceramic, Delft, 5" L **15.00**
Ashtray, hobo w/top hat & umbrella figural, ceramic, Japan, 6¼" ...**57.00**
Ashtray, Manchu pattern, Mason's Ironstone, pre-1960s, 3½" sq......**8.00**
Ashtray, Queen Mary, Royal Ruby, Hocking, 1950s, 3½" dia..........**5.00**
Ashtray, silver-colored metal ball on ped, etched decor, 3" **8.00**
Ashtray, Victor Silver Co, emb Art Nouveau lady, 8x6", EX **115.00**
Book for smoking items, The Courtship of Lady Nicotine, Coltrock, NM...**180.00**
Change receiver, rvpt glass, Cu-Rey, pictorial, 6" dia, EX+.........**150.00**
Change receiver, rvpt glass, Universal Victor, Brunoff, 6½" dia .**150.00**
Cigar cutter, brass pocket sz, Pfeiering Solingen, 1940s-50s, EX ...**50.00**
Cigar cutter, CI, emb Enterprise Mfg Co, ca 1890, 4x19x7", EX ..**40.00**
Cigar cutter, CI swing-arm, w/advertising, Brunoff, 1906, 9", EX...**1,225.00**
Cigar cutter, guillotine, wood/brass, 1920s-30s, EX.....................**750.00**

Cigar cutter, keywind, Las Amantes, rvpt glass, wood base, EX ..**575.00**
Cigar cutter, keywind, Muriel Cigar, rvpt glass, wood base, EX...**480.00**
Cigar cutter/match dispenser, Uwanta 5¢, CI, 9x6x8", NM........**825.00**
Cigar lighter/lamp, tin shade w/punched ads, filigree base, 18", EX ..**500.00**
Cigar mold, wooden, makes 20, Paul F Beck, Stuttgart, #8523, 24" **70.00**
Cigar server, 12 trn brass cups w/figural cherub, 10", NM **235.00**
Cigar server, 8" compo Blk figure on 4x6" plaster-over-wood box, NM ..**80.00**
Cigar snuffer, Old General figure, pot metal, 7", EX....................**400.00**
Cigar vendor, Bennett, wood & glass case w/tongs, 12x18x23", EX...**1,500.00**
Cigarette case, chromium, eng decor, Talco, ca 1921, 2⅞x3⅞" **35.00**
Cigarette lighter, brass & enamel, Evans, ca 1934, 3½x2¼" **35.00**
Cigarette lighter, chromium, butane, Strato Flame, 1952, 1¾x2¼" **35.00**
Cigarette lighter, Electro-Match, blk plastic w/gold, Korex, 1950s ..**20.00**
Cigarette lighter, elephant form, chromium strike type, Ronson, 1935...**100.00**
Cigarette lighter, gold-plated, Evans, ca 1934, 2x1½" **55.00**
Cigarette lighter, Lucky Strike, pnt chromium, Japan, 1950s, 4⅜" ...**35.00**
Cigarette lighter, rocket ship, metal/plastic, battery/butane, 8½" **75.00**
Cigarette lighter, Typhoon, eng concrete truck, Ronson, 1960s, 2¼" ...**25.00**
Counter display, Dutch Masters, wood/glass dbl box, EX..............**65.00**
Counter display, Eden + 4 others, wood w/easel stand, 3x19x17", NM.**435.00**
Counter display, Hav-A-Tampa Cigar, tin/glass, 7x11x8", EX.....**190.00**
Counter display, La Fendrich, oak/glass, ca 1920, 42x26x36", EX....**775.00**
Honor box, brass ½-penny vendor for snuff/tobacco, early, 10x5", EX ..**250.00**
Humidor, ceramic, Turkish man, ¾-figure, mc, Japan **100.00**
Humidor, majolica, bowler figural, ¾-figure, bl & wht, 6" **300.00**
Humidor, porc, man's head, brn & flesh tones, #d, 6"....................**70.00**
Humidor, pottery, monk figural, brn & tan, 9"..............................**195.00**
Humidor, walnut w/brass inlay plaque on lid, English, 7x14x9" ..**550.00**
Humidor, wood, cherry-type w/brass trim, curved top/drw, 7x8x11", EX **55.00**
Lighter, cigar; Duralectric, 40 watt, wood-grained tin, 10x5x5", EX ...**125.00**
Lighter, cigar; Egyptian w/basket, brass, electric, 1930, 7", EX+....**60.00**
Lighter, cigar; Eldred, wood/tin, brass swing arm, 1915, 15x10x8", EX..**225.00**
Lighter, cigar; Midland Jump Spark, wood, 1909-20s, 15x8x8", EX.......**360.00**
Lighter, cigar/lamp; brass w/ruby glass globe, ca 1900, 8", NM....**200.00**
Lighter, cigar/paperweight; brass w/burgundy finish, 1930, 5½", EX..**110.00**
Match dispenser, Sellem, CI Art Nouveau w/emb dolphins, 1915, 13", EX...**550.00**
Match holder/ashtray, Elverso/Felice Cigars, CI Art Nouveau dish, EX ...**160.00**
Match holder/pipe rest, Art Nouveau bronze figure, mk JB 478, 6", EX **50.00**
Pipe rest, bronzed Art Nouveau-look lady, ca 1940-50, 7", NM....**40.00**
Tobacco tag, Red Letter, octagonal, red on yel, EX.......................**38.00**
Tobacco tag, Rough Rider (T Roosevelt), EX..............................**175.00**
Tobacco tag, Sky Light, crescent shape, red on yel, EX **37.00**
Tobacco tag, True Chew, bl, EX..**75.00**
Tobacco tag, Uncle Essex, EX...**323.00**
Tobacco tag, Yum Yum, Yellow Kid, EX **40.00**

Pipes

Briarwood w/cvd Viking head, ebonite stem, early 1900s, EX.....**110.00**
C Dunhill Rootbriar 1972 Made in England 17 on bowl, M.......**325.00**
Don Carlos Fatta a Mano, NM w/brochure/suede case & orig box ..**135.00**
Dunhill Shell 5 Made in England 59, EX.................................**235.00**
Ivory, cvd bust of Blackamoor, Continental, 1850s, NM in orig case ..**1,200.00**
Jobey Perlatta, Author model, #160, 6", MIB.............................**55.00**
Meerschaum, baby pulling cat's tail cvg, 4½", EX in case **215.00**
Meerschaum, cvd leaves & flowers, amber stem, 4".....................**160.00**
Meerschaum, hunter beside horse, amber stem, silver band **55.00**
Parker Super Briarbark, Made in London England 22 Pat..., 5⅝" ...**145.00**
Peterson's, Mark Twain label, sterling silver band, Ireland, EX **75.00**

Toleware

The term 'toleware' originally came from a French term meaning 'sheet iron.' Today it is used to refer to paint-decorated tin items, most popular from 1800 to 1850s. The craft flourished in Pennsylvania, Connecticut, Maine, and New York state. Early toleware has a very distinctive look. The surface is dull and unvarnished; background colors range from black to cream. Geometrics are quite common, but florals and fruits were also favored. Items made after 1850 were often stenciled, and gold trim was sometimes added.

American toleware is usually found in practical, everyday forms — trays, boxes, and coffeepots are most common — while French examples might include candlesticks, wine coolers, jardinieres, etc. Be sure to note color and design when determining date and value, but condition of the paint is the most important worth-assessing factor. Unless noted otherwise, values are for very good examples with average wear.

Bin, storage; floral & geometrics, early 1800s, 8½x8½", VG **200.00**
Box, document; cherries/leaves, mc on wht, dome top, 6x9x5", VG ..**250.00**
Box, document; floral, mc on blk, 19th C, 7½x13x8½", VG **460.00**
Box, document; floral, mc on blk japanning, dome top, 8¾", EX **500.00**
Box, document; fruit, mc on blk japanning, ca 1900, 7x9⅝x6½", NM ..**1,150.00**
Box, document; fruit bowl, mc on alligatored yel, dome top, 10", NM **750.00**
Box, document; fruit/foliage, mc on red japanning, dome top, 10", NM....**900.00**
Box, spice; gold stencil labels/striping on blk, 3-part, 9½" L........**110.00**
Canister, cherries & leaves, mc on red japanning, 19th C, 6x6¼" **400.00**
Coffeepot, birds/pomegranates, mc on bl, gooseneck spout, 19th C, 11"..**800.00**
Coffeepot, floral, mc on blk japanning, minor touchups, 10½" ..**525.00**
Coffeepot, floral, mc on blk japanning, 19th C, 8½", EX **450.00**
Coffeepot, floral on dk japanning, yel brush mks ea side, 11", NM...**1,200.00**
Coffeepot, fruit in dmn, mc on blk japanning, early 1800s, 10", EX **865.00**
Creamer, floral, mc on dk japanning, very worn, 4¾", G **85.00**
Deed box, floral, mc on blk, dome top, w/hasp, 8⅛", EX **600.00**
Jardiniere, floral, mc on gr w/gold lip, 19th C, 5x10½x8½" **465.00**
Mug, floral, mc on blk w/wht band, some wear, G color, 4½".....**660.00**
Mug, floral, mc on brn japanning, 5¾", VG.......................**385.00**
Mug, floral, red & yel on dk japanning, 5¾", VG **250.00**
Sugar bowl, floral, mc on blk, japanning, 3¾", EX **385.00**
Tea caddy, floral, mc on blk, japanning, dents, 7", G **195.00**
Tray, bread; floral, mc on dk japanning, wear, 8x14¼" **440.00**
Tray, floral, mc on blk, 19th C, 12½x8¼", EX.....................**350.00**
Tray, floral, mc on blk japanning, 14" dia, VG **165.00**
Tray, floral on blk w/gilt traces, English, 19th C, 30x23", VG **330.00**
Tray, shells, red & gold on blk, Greek-key borders, 1820s, 28x21", EX ...**660.00**

Tools

Before the Civil War, tools for the most part were handmade. Some were primitive to the point of crudeness, while others reflected the skill of those who took pride in their trade. Increasing demand for quality tools and the dawning of the age of industrialization resulted in tools that were mass produced. Factors important in evaluating antique tools are scarcity, usefulness, and portability. Those with a manufacturer's mark are worth more than unmarked items. When no condition is indicated, the items listed here are assumed to be in excellent condition. Our advisor for this category is Jim Calison; he is listed in the Directory under New York. See also Keen Kutter; Stanley; Winchester.

Ax, goose-wing; hand-wrought, ca 1800, 28" L **230.00**
Blut, oak w/iron band, oversz **18.00**
Carriage jack, oak w/iron teeth, minimum value **100.00**
Chisels, Mayhew, 1918, from 4½" to 7", 10-pc set........................**35.00**
Crate opener, claw & hammer ends, Nox Tox Bridgeport Hdw, 9½" ..**25.00**
Cutter, leather harness; scribe w/blade, Barnsley & Sons **25.00**
Drill, chain; Millers Falls #718, automatic feed, MIB **52.50**
Gauge, mortise; boxwood & brass, AW Lockwood, 1880s, 7½" **10.00**

Hoop setter, all wood, concave base **55.00**
Jack, Conestoga wagon; wrought iron & wood, 22½x6x8½" **150.00**
Level, initialed rosewood, brass bound, Pat 1872, lg...................**110.00**
Nail holder, CI, 2-pc, rnd top, 8 compartments, ca 1800, 8⅜" dia ..**45.00**
Plane, block; Thistle Brand, Auburn Tool Co, 16" **25.00**
Plane, molding; wood & brass, thumbscrews, S Post #102, 8¾"...**220.00**
Plane, rabbet; maple, corner grooving **45.00**
Plumb bob, brass, very heavy, 4½" L **110.00**
Rule, logging; wooden, Hitchcock, 36", EX **50.00**
Spoke shave, AC Bachelder, 1867, 10⅜" **35.00**
Try square, cherry, polished iron, brass bound, inlays...................**45.00**
Witchet, combined hardwood, brass-lined throat, dbl hdls, 1850s...**250.00**
Wrench, adjusts, hammer head, Sis Wrench Co/Perfect Handle..., 6½".....**45.00**
Wrench, bicycle/monkey; Ganz-Stahl DRGM Made in Germany, 4½".....**55.00**
Wrench, Crestoloy Steel Made in USA, Crescent Tool...NY, 6", NMIB ...**45.00**

Toothbrush Holders

Most of the collectible toothbrush holders were made in prewar Japan and were modeled after popular comic strip, Disney, and nursery rhyme characters. Since many were made of bisque and decorated with unfired paint, it's not uncommon to find them in less-than-perfect paint, a factor you must consider when attempting to assess their values. Our advisor for this category is Marilyn Cooper, author of *Pictorial Guide to Toothbrush Holders*; she is listed in the Directory under Texas. Plate numbers in the descriptions that follow refer to her book.

Moon Mullins, copyright FAS Moon Mullins, 5", $95.00; Old King Cole, with original cellophane-wrapped toothbrush, 5", $100.00.
(Photo courtesy Carole Bess White)

Annie Oakley, Japan, plate #11, 5¾", 5¾", from $100 to **145.00**
Baby Bunting, Germany, plate #1, 6¾" **375.00**
Baby Deer, mk Brush Teeth Daily, Japan, plate #12, 4", from $110 to..**140.00**
Betty Boop w/Toothbrush & Cup, KFS, plate #261, 4¾", from $85 to..**100.00**
Bonzo w/Sidetray, Germany, plate #23, 5⅝", from $135 to **160.00**
Boy in Knickers Next to Mailbox, Japan, 4¼", EX **60.00**
Boy in Top Hat, Japan, plate #29, 5½", from $75 to **100.00**
Boy Seated w/Umbrella, Japan, plate #46, 4¾", from $65 to.........**90.00**
Boy w/Violin, Goldcastle/Japan, plate #30, 5½", from $75 to **90.00**
Bulldog Seated w/Tongue Out, plate #264, 3½", from $50 to **70.00**
Cat (Calico), Japan, plate #37, 5½", from $90 to **110.00**
Cat on Pedestal, Diamond T/Japan, plate #225, 5⅞", from $125 to ...**175.00**
Clown Holding Mask, Japan, plate #62, 5½", from $115 to...........**160.00**
Cowboy Next to Cactus, Japan, plate #70, 5½", from $80 to **100.00**
Dachshund, Japan, plate #71, 5¼", from $80 to **120.00**
Dalmatian, Germany, plate #202, 4", from $150 to **195.00**
Doctor w/Satchel, Japan, plate #206, 5¾", from $90 to **110.00**
Dog w/Basket, Japan, plate #72, from $90 to **120.00**
Donald Duck, Japan, prewar, plate #247, 4½", from $400 to **425.00**
Flapper, plate #230, 4¼", from $125 to **150.00**
Frog w/Mandolin, Goldcastle/Japan, plate #209, 6", from $85 to....**110.00**
Indian Chief, Japan, plate #115, 4½", from $225 to **275.00**
Lion, Japan, plate #118, 6", from $75 to..**95.00**
Little Orphan Annie & Sandy Seated on Couch, Japan, plate #267, 3¾" ...**135.00**

Mary Poppins, Japan, plate #119, 6", from $125 to......................150.00
Mexican Boy, Japan, plate #120, 5½", from $80 to.....................110.00
Peter Pumpkin Eater, Japan, plate #129, 4⅞", from $85 to.........115.00
Pluto, Japan, plate #133, 4½", from $300 to 350.00
Schnauzer, Germany, plate #283, 3⅛", from $100 to................130.00
Skippy w/Jointed Arms, plate #245, 5⅝", from $100 to 125.00

Toothpick Holders

Once common on every table, the toothpick holder was relegated to the china cabinet near the turn of the century. Fortunately, this contributed to their survival. As a result, many are available to collectors today. Because they are small and easily displayed, they are very popular collectibles. They come in a wide range of prices to fit every budget. Many have been reproduced and, unfortunately, are being offered for sale right along with the originals. These 'repros' should be priced in the $10.00 to $30.00 range. Unless you're sure of what you're buying, choose a reputable dealer. In addition to pattern glass, you'll find examples in china, bisque, art glass, and various metals. For further information we recommend *Glass Toothpick Holders, Identification & Values*, by Neila and Tom Bredehoft and Jo and Bob Sanford.

Toothpick holders in the listings that follow are glass unless noted otherwise. Values here are for originals. Our advisor for this category is Judy A. Knauer; she is listed in the Directory under Pennsylvania.

See also specific companies (such as Northwood) and types of glassware (such as Burmese, cranberry, etc.).

Apollo 30.00
Atlas 24.00
Aztec 32.00
Beaded Grape, gr 65.00
Beaded Loop 75.00
Beatty Honeycomb, wht opal 45.00
Bohemian, gr w/EX gold..135.00
Button Arches, frosted band 27.50
Button Arches, ruby stain 25.00
China, floral, 2-hdl, RS Prussia.....................................165.00
China, girl w/geese, 3-hdl, Royal Bayreuth mk 145.00
China, swirl mold w/floral decor, Germany 30.00
Colorado, bl w/EX gold 50.00
Colorado, gr w/gold 35.00
Cord Drapery 100.00
Croesus, gr w/gold...95.00
Croesus, purple w/EX gold...135.00
Daisy & Button, bl, fan shape 42.50
Daisy & Button w/V Ornament, amber 37.50
Darwin (aka Monkey), bl..65.00
Darwin (aka Monkey), vaseline 65.00
Delaware, gr w/EX gold 75.00
Dew Drop/Dbl Eye Hobnail, Columbia Glass Co, 1887, 2⅜".......35.00
Diamond & Sunburst 42.00
Diamond Quilt, amberina, pie-crust rim 475.00
Diamond Quilt, amberina, sq top 275.00
Diamond Quilt, burmese satin, tricorner top 575.00
Diamond Ridge, Duncan & Miller, 1901, 2½" 45.00
Diamond Spearhead, gr opal 75.00
Diamond Spearhead, vaseline opal 80.00
Ellipses, rose stain, Beaumont Glass Co, 1902, 2⅜" 225.00
Empress, gr 95.00
Esther, amber stain 150.00
Esther, emerald gr w/gold, Riverside, 1896, 2½" 125.00
Feather 75.00

Fernland, Cambridge, 1907, 2¼" 45.00
Fine Cut, bl 27.50
Florette, clear irid, Consolidated Lamp & Glass, 1894, 2" 200.00
Gaelic, clear w/stain, Indiana Glass, 1908, 2" 35.00
Galloway (+) 20.00
Hickman, clear w/gold 60.00
Hobnail, bl 27.50
Illinois 47.50
Iris w/Meander, amethyst 45.00
Iris w/Meander, gr opal 80.00
Ivanhoe, Dalzelle, Gilmore & Leighton Glass Co, 1897, 2⅝" 125.00
Kentucky 65.00
Kentucky, gr 140.00
Kentucky, ruby stained 220.00
King's Crown/Ruby Thumbprint, clear w/ruby stain, Adams & Co, 2½" ...35.00
Klondike, frosted w/amber stain.....................................375.00
Lacy, gr (+) 30.00
Maine, pk stain...450.00
Maryland 140.00
Massachusetts 50.00
Minnesota, gr, 3-hdl 100.00
Minnesota, 3-hdl 30.00
Monkey on Stump, Bryce Bros, 2½" (+) 25.00
New Jersey, clear w/EX gold 70.00
Old Oaken Bucket/Wooden Pail, Bryce Bros, 1885 ....35.00
Peek-A-Boo, amber, McKee, 1904, 3¾" (+) 45.00
Pennsylvania, clear w/EX gold 60.00
Pomona, sq top, decor 350.00
Portland 28.00
Portland, pk stain 65.00
Reverse Swirl, bl speckled 95.00
Reverse 44, gold or platinum stain..................................85.00
Ruby Thumbprint, eng...45.00
S-Repeat, sapphire bl (+) 60.00
Silverplate, repousse floral, Derby 55.00
Silverplate, top hat & violin, Wilcox 145.00
Simplicity Scroll, gr frosted, metal band..........................50.00
Sunk Daisy, HP floral, Co-operative Flint Glass, 1897, 2⅜"....58.00
Sunk Honeycomb, ruby stain 45.00
Swirl, clear opal, 1890, 2⅛" 95.00
Tacoma, ruby stain...98.00
Teepee 35.00
Texas 32.50
Texas Star/Star Base Swirl, Steimer, 1905, 2½" 75.00
Touraine, Heisey, 1902, 2⅜" 265.00
Tree of Life, apple gr 128.00
Wisconsin..42.00
Witch's Kettle 15.00
Zippered Swirl & Diamond, US Glass, 1895, 2⅜" 42.00

Torquay Pottery

Torquay is a unique type of pottery made in the South Devon area of England as early as 1867. At the height of productivity, at least a dozen companies flourished there, producing simple folk pottery from the area's natural red clay. The ware was both wheel turned and molded and decorated under the glaze with heavy slip resulting in low-relief nature subjects or simple scrollwork. Three of the best-known of these potteries were Watcombe (1867 – 1962); Aller Vale (in operation from the mid-1800s, producing domestic ware and architectural products); and Longpark (1890 until 1957). Watcombe and Aller Vale merged in 1901 and operated until 1962 under the name of Royal Aller Vale and Watcombe Art Pottery.

A decline in the popularity of the early classical terra-cotta styles (urns, busts, figures, etc.) lead to the introduction of painted and glazed terra-cotta wares. During the late 1880s, white clay wares, both turned and molded, were decorated with colored glazes (Stapleton ware, grotesque molded figures, ornamental vases, large jardinieres, etc.). By the turn of the century, the market for art pottery was diminishing, so the potteries turned to wares decorated in colored slips (Barbotine, Persian, Scrolls, etc.).

Motto wares were introduced in the late nineteenth century by Aller Vale and taken up in the present century by the other Torquay potteries. This eventually became the 'bread and butter' product of the local industry. This was perhaps the most famous type of ware potted in this area because of the verses, proverbs, and quotations that decorated it. This was achieved by the sgraffito technique — scratching the letters through the slip to expose the red clay underneath. The most popular patterns were Cottage, Black Cockerel, Multi-Cockerel, and a scroll-work design called Scandy. Other popular decorations were Kerswell Daisy, ships, kingfishers, applied bird decorations, Art Deco styles, Egyptian ware, and many others. Aller Vale ware may sometimes be found marked 'H.H. and Company,' a firm who assumed ownership from 1897 to 1901. 'Watcombe Torquay' was an impressed mark used from 1884 to 1927.

Our advisors for this category are Jerry and Gerry Kline; they are listed in the Directory under Ohio. If you're interested in joining a Torquay club, you'll find the address of The North American Torquay Society under Clubs, Newsletters, and Catalogs.

Art Pottery

Biscuit barrel, parrots on branches on bl, wrapped hdl, 6" 125.00
Biscuit barrel, Polka Dot, Royal Watcombe, post-war, wicker hdl....125.00
Biscuit Barrel, porc, apple blossom, unmk, 6½" 256.00
Bottle, scent; Devon Lilies, crown top, 3½" 75.00
Bottle, scent; Hill's English Lavender, pitcher shape, 2¾"............95.00
Bottle, scent; rose, pk on bl, att Watcombe, 3" 80.00
Bottle, scent; violet bouquet shape, mk, Ye Old Devon Violets, 3" 95.00
Bowl, Blarney Castle, Watcombe, hdls, ftd, 4½x4¼" 75.00
Candlesticks, Scroll, Aller Vale, 7¾", pr...............................225.00
Canoe, Kingfisher, Royal Torquay, 2x9" 88.00
Cat, gr, Aller Vale, 6"...375.00
Ewer, Apple Blossom, unmk, 6½"..140.00
Face jug, Mr Punch, Exeter, 3"...75.00
Jug, floral on gr (K2 pattern code), Aller Vale, pinched, 4" 75.00
Mug, Lindisfarne Castle Holy Island, Watcombe, 2½" 55.00
Plate, windmill, Aller Vale, 1891-1910, 6½" dia........................125.00
Tobacco jar, Tintern Abby, unmk, 5⅝ hx4¾" dia..........................298.00
Tray, dresser, windmill, Aller Vale, no motto, 10½x7" 424.00
Vase, B3 scrolling pattern, Aller Vale, bulbous, ruffled rim, 4¼" ..80.00
Vase, Daffodil, Longpark, 4⅜", pr......................................135.00
Vase, Persian, Aller Vale, bulbous, 5¾" 85.00
Vase, swan on gr tricorn shape, ca 1900, 4½" 130.00
Wall pocket, flowers on horn shape, Exeter, 6½x4½" 175.00

Devon Motto Ware

Vase, Cockerel, with motto, 8", $175.00.

Basket, Multi-Cockerel, Longpark, 2¾x5x3¼" 95.00
Biscuit barrel, cottage, Watcombe, 'God Hath Often'.................244.00
Bottle, scent; Scandy, Watcombe, 'Frame Your Heart...' 3½".....125.00
Bowl, junket, Scandy, 'Help Yourself...,' 6⅞x3⅜" deep 159.00
Box, Scandy, Longpark, Hair Pins, St John's Chapel souvenir, 1920s...130.00
Butter dish, Black Hen, Aller Vale, 'Be Canny w/the Butter,' 5" .100.00
Candlestick, Kerswell Daisy, Aller Vale, 'I Slept And...,' 10"......188.00
Chamberstick, Cottage, Watcombe, 2½x5x4" 75.00
Chamberstick, Multi-Cockerel, Longpark, 'Don't the Day...,' 4¾" ..88.00
Chamberstick, Multi-Cockerel, Longpark, 'Hear All...,' 3⅛x3¼"....65.00
Chamberstick, Sailboat, 'Great Yarmouth, Last in Bed...,' 3½".....68.00
Chamberstick, Scandy, 'Many Are Called...' 70.00
Chamberstick, Scandy, Watcombe, 'Safe Conscience Makes...,' 4½" 60.00
Cheese scoop, Cottage, att Watcombe, 'Help Yourself to the Cheese'....80.00
Cheese server, 2 pc, bl, Cockerel, Longpark, 'Cheese,' 6¾x5¼".230.00
Coffeepot, Black Cockerel, Longpark, 'Be Happy While...,' 8", NM...175.00
Creamer & sugar bowl, Shamrock, Watcombe, mini, 2", 1½".......60.00
Cruet, Caernarvon, St Mary's Church, 'Cymru am Byth,' 5½" 55.00
Egg cup, Black Cockerel, Longpark, 'Laid Today,' saucer base.......55.00
Egg cup, Cockerel, Longpark, 'Fresh Laid,' 2½" 50.00
Egg cup, Cockerel (standing amid 2 holders), Royal Torquay, 6x5¼"....75.00
Gypsy pot, Shamrock, Aller Vale, 'Chosen Leaf of Bard...,' 4½"...85.00
Hat pin holder, Cockerel, 'Keep Me On Dressing,' 4¾" 150.00
Hot water pot, Cockerel, Longpark, 'Half the World's...,' 7".......250.00
Hot water pot, Scandy, Longpark, 'Whichever Way the Wind...,' 7" ...135.00
Humidor, Black Cockerel, Longpark, 'Dawnt'ee Be Fraid...,' 5¼"...175.00
Inkwell, Scandy, 'We're Aye Prood Tae Hear Frae Ye,' 3x2¾" 60.00
Inkwell, Scandy, Aller Vale, 'A Word Wi Ye...,' 3¾" W................60.00
Jar, swearing; 'My Worst Word Is Welcome & Welcome Again,' 7"....60.00
Jardiniere, Shamrock, Aller Vale, 'Old Erin's Native Shamrock,' 3" ...65.00
Jug, puzzle; Cottage, Dartmouth, 'Fit for Parson...,' 4½"............80.00
Jug, puzzle; Primrose, Exeter, 'Within This Jug...' 210.00
Jug, Scandy, Longpark, 3-hdld, 'Niver Zay Die...,' 3¼".............110.00
Match holder w/striker, Watcombe, 'Match for Any Man,' 3" 80.00
Pitcher, Cockerel, 'Make New Friends But...,' 5½", EX.............125.00
Pitcher, Cottage, 'Help Yourself Don't Be Shy,' 5¼x4½"............100.00
Pitcher, Kerswell Daisy, Aller Vale, 'Freely Drink...,' 4" 95.00
Pitcher, Sailboat, unmk, flared cylinder, 10", NM...................95.00
Plate, Cockerel, Longpark, Ca Canny & Flee Laigh, 5", NM........95.00
Plate, Cockerel, Royal Torquay, 'Put a Stout Heart...,' 8⅞", EX.150.00
Plate, Cottage, Dartmouth, 'Never Say Die...,' 5⅝"..................42.00
Plate, Cottage, Watcombe, 'Do Not Burden...,' 6"......................55.00
Plate, Cottage, Watcombe, 'Kind Words Are...,' 8"...................120.00
Plate, Watcombe, 'Don't Make a Toil of Pleasure,' 5".................62.50
Server, Cottage, 3 section, 'If You Can't Be Aisy,' 7¼" 130.00
Shakers, Cottage, Watcombe, 'Hot & Strong/Pass the Salt'..........75.00
Shaving mug, Cockerel, Longpark, 'Guide Folks...,' 4⅛" 279.00
Tea strainer, Cottage, St Mary Church, 'Buckfast,' 3½".............60.00
Teapot, Black Cockerel, 'Tak a Cup o Kindness...,' 5½".............125.00
Teapot, Black Cockerel, Longpark, 'Daunt'ee Be Fraid...,' 4½" 95.00
Teapot, Cottage, Allervale, 'Due Cum in an 'Ave...,' 4"............120.00
Teapot, Cottage, Babbacombe, 'Do What You Can...Glow...,' 4" ..75.00
Teapot, Sailboat, 'Droon Yer Sorrows...,' 5" 70.00
Teapot, Scandy w/Seaweed border, Aller Vale, 'Fellow Feeling...,' 7" ...110.00
Teapot, Shamrock, unmk Watcombe, Carrickfergus, 3"................62.50
Teapot, Thistle, Longpark, 'It's Unco Refreshin,' 4½", NM 85.00
Tile, lamp; Scandy, Longpark, 'O List...Ladies Fair...,' 5x7½".....260.00
Toast rack, Cottage, Dartmouth, 'Elp Yersel' to More,' 6½" 65.00
Toothpick holder, Cottage, 'Many Friends Few Helpers,' 2¾x3" ..55.00
Tray, Cottage, Watcombe, 'Greatest Troubles...,' 8¾x6" 165.00
Tray, dresser, Cottage, Longpark, 'Work On Hope On,' 11x7½".295.00
Tray, pen; Scandy, Exeter, 'Send Us a Scrape...,' 9⅛" L.............90.00
Tray, pin; Cottage, Watcombe, 'Still Waters...,' 5¼" L 60.00
Vase, udder; Scandy, Aller Vale, 'Actions Speak...'.....................85.00

Tortoise Shell Glass

By combining several shades of glass — brown, clear, and yellow — manufacturers of the nineteenth century were able to produce an art glass that closely resembled the shell of the tortoise. Some of this type of glassware was manufactured in Germany. In America it was made by several firms, the most prominent of which was the Boston and Sandwich Glass Works.

Bowl, sq w/fold-in top, HP florals, att Moser, 3x4¼" 125.00
Finger bowl & underplate, 3¼", 6" 275.00
Vase, gold bamboo/ferns/birds, pinched, ruffled, 8½" 300.00

Toys

Toys can be classified into at least two categories: early collectible toys with an established history, and the newer toys. The antique toys are easier to evaluate. A great deal of research has been done on them, and much data is available. The newer toys are just beginning to be studied; relative information is only now being published, and the lack of production records makes it difficult to know how many may be available. Often warehouse finds of these newer toys can change the market. This has happened with battery-operated toys and to some extent with robots. Review past issues of this guide. You will see the changing trends for the newer toys. All toys become more important as collectibles when a fixed period of manufacture is known. When we know the numbers produced and documentation of the makers is established, the prices become more predictable.

The best way to learn about toys is to attend toy shows and auctions. This will give you the opportunity to compare prices and condition. The more collectors and dealers you meet, the more you will learn. There is no substitute for holding a toy in your hand and seeing for yourself what they are. If you are going to be a serious collector, buy all the books you can find. Read every article you see. Knowledge is vital to building a good collection. Study all books that are available. These are some of the most helpful: *Collecting Toys, Collecting Toy Soldiers,* and *Collecting Toy Trains, An Identification & Value Guide #3,* by Richard O'Brien; and *Toys of the Sixties, A Pictorial Guide,* by Bill Bruegman. Other informative books (published by Collector Books) are *Schroeder's Collectible Toys, Antique to Modern,* by Sharon and Bob Huxford; *Collector's Guide to Tinker Toys* by Craig Strange; *The Golden Age of Automotive Toys, 1925 – 1941,* by Ken Hutchinson and Greg Johnson; *Collector's Encyclopedia of Disneyana* by David Longest and Michael Stern; *Modern Toys, American Toys, 1830 – 1980,* by Linda Baker; *Cartoon Toys & Collectibles* by David Longest; *Collectible Male Action Figures* by Paris and Susan Manos; *G-Men and FBI Toys and Collectibles* by Harry and Jody Whitworth; *Breyer Animal Collector's Guide* by Felicia Browell; *Collector's Guide to TV Toys and Memorabilia, 1960s & 1970s, Second Edition,* by Greg Davis and Bill Morgan; *Collector's Guide to Tootsietoys, Second Edition,* by David Richter; *Fisher-Price Toys* by Brad Cassity; and *Matchbox Toys, 1974 – 1998, Third Edition,* and *Collector's Guide to Diecast Toys and Scale Models, Second Edition,* both by Dana Johnson. In the listings that follow, toys are listed by manufacturer's name if possible, otherwise by type. Measurements are given when appropriate and available; if only one dimension is noted, it is the greater one — height if the toy is vertical, length if it is horizontal. See also Children's Things; Personalities. For toy stoves, see Stoves.

Key:
b/o — battery operated
cl — celluloid
jtd — jointed
NP — nickel plated
w/up — wind-up

Toys by Various Manufacturers

Marx, dump truck with high side extensions, heavy pressed steel, MIB, $300.00.
(Photo John Turney)

Alps, Acrocycle, w/up, tin, 6", NMIB 500.00
Alps, Arthur-A-Go-Go Drummer, b/o, 1960s, 10", NM.............475.00
Alps, Coney Island Rocket Ride, b/o, tin, 1950s, rare, M 800.00
Alps, Honey Bear, w/up, tin/plush/cloth clothes, 7", MIB...........200.00
Alps, Mexicalli Pete, b/o, 1960s, MIB...325.00
Alps, Musical Marching Bear, b/o, tin/plush, 1950s, 11", MIB....675.00
Arcade, Ford Tudor, CI w/NP driver, 6", NM 700.00
Arcade, Mack Coal Truck, CI w/NP driver, 10½", VG 900.00
Arcade, Mack Ice Truck, CI, w/driver, 11", EX 2,500.00
Arnold, Military Motorcycle, w/up, tin, w/driver/rider, 7½" 1,700.00
ATC, Oldsmobile, friction, tin, 2-tone, 12½", EXIB................1,200.00
Bandai, Air Control Tower, b/o, litho tin, 1960s, 11", EX..........400.00
Bandai, Aircraft Carrier, friction, tin, w/7 Navy jets, 16", EX...250.00
Bandai, Cadillac Convertible, friction, tin/chrome, 11½", EXIB...375.00
Bandai, Ford T-Bird, friction, tin/chrome detail, 11½", EXIB.....475.00
Bandai, Sea Bear B-313, friction, tin, 9½", EX 250.00
Bandai, Snowmobile, b/o, tin w/vinyl figure, 1960s, NMIB 175.00
Bandai, Typewriting Dog, w/up, tin/plush, 4", EXIB....................300.00
Bing, Ocean Liner, clockwork, pnt & litho tin, 11", EXIB 1,300.00
Bing, Touring Car, w/up, tin, no driver, 1915, 12½", EX 1,600.00
Bliss, Battleship Maine, paper litho on wood, rare, EX 1,600.00
Breyer, Arabian Foal, alabaster, 1973-82, NM................................30.00
Breyer, Clydesdale Stallion, woodgrain, 1960-65, NM.................250.00
Breyer, Quarter Horse Gelding, glossy bay, 1959-66, NM 150.00
Breyer, Ruffian, matt bay, 1977-90, NM..35.00
Breyer, Western Prancer, matt bay, 1961-71 ....75.00
Buddy L, Air Cruiser, 4-prop, 27" W, EX 500.00
Buddy L, Fire Chief Car, wood, 18½", NM.....................................750.00
Buddy L, School Bus, mk School District..., 1920s, 29", G 1,700.00
Buddy L, Transport Plane, 27" W, VG..275.00
Chein, Barnacle Bill Floor Puncher, 1930s, 7", EX 700.00
Chein, Big Top Tent, 1961, 10", EXIB 200.00
Chein, Fish, 1940s, NM 125.00
Chein, Native on Turtle, 1930s, 8", NM..350.00
Chein, Popeye Waddler, 1932, 6½", NM......................................1,300.00
CK, Uncle Wiggily Car, w/up, tin/cl, 7½", rare, NM 1,300.00
Cor Cor, Crysler Airflow, pressed steel, 1934, 16½", rstr 1,100.00
Corgi, Air Canada Concorde, #653, MIB 325.00
Corgi, Chrysler Imperial, #246, red, MIB.......................................110.00
Corgi, The Saint's Volvo, #201, MIB 150.00
Corgi, Transporter Set, #28, MIB...800.00
Corgi, VW Police Car, #489 ....30.00
Cragstan, Skater Bunny, w/up, tin/cloth clothes, 9", NMIB......125.00
Cragstan/MT, Tugboat Rover, b/o, tin, 14½", VG (VG box)......125.00
Cragstan/S&E, Teddy the Manager, b/o, 1950s, 8", EXIB........650.00
Dakin, Bullwinkle, Jay Ward, 1976, MIB 40.00
Dakin, Daffy Duck, Warner Bros, 1968, EX 30.00
Dakin, Dudley Do-Right, Jay Ward, 1976, MIB..............................75.00

Dakin, Fred Flintstone, Hanna-Barbera, 1970, EX......................40.00
Dakin, Jack-in-the Box, bank, 1971, EX 25.00
Dakin, Speedy Gonzales, Warner Bros, MIB........................50.00
Dakin, Underdog, Jay Ward, 1976, MIB............................150.00
Dinky, Corvette Stingray, #221.......................................60.00
Dinky, Fun A'Hoy Set, #125, MIB...................................250.00
Dinky, M*A*S*H Bell Police Helicopter, #732, MIB..........100.00
Dinky, NASA Space Shuttle, w/booster, #364, MIB...........100.00
Dinky, Sam's Car, gold, red or bl, MIB..........................160.00
Dinky, Sam's Car, silver, MIB.......................................120.00
Dinky, Trojan Van Cydrax, #454, MIB.............................175.00
Dinky, VW Deutsch Bundepost, #260..............................185.00
Distler, Motorcycle w/Sidecar, w/up, tin, driver/child, 7½", EX...2,500.00
Distler, Racing Track, w/up, tin, 9½" dia, EX................1,300.00
Fischer, Hi-Way Henry, w/up, tin, 10", EX 3,000.00
Fischer, Toonerville Trolley, w/up, tin, 1922, 5", NM..........800.00
Fisher-Price, Bucky Burro, #166, 1955-57, EX 250.00
Fisher-Price, Dr Doodle, #100, 1931, EX........................700.00
Fisher-Price, Dr Doodle, #132, 1957-60, EX.....................85.00
Fisher-Price, Magnetic Chug-Chug, #168, 1964-69, EX 50.00
Fisher-Price, Scoop Loader, #300, 1975-77, EX..................25.00
Fisher-Price, Teddy Tooter, #150, 1940-41, EX.................400.00
Fleischmann, Ocean Liner, clockwork, pnt tin, 16", NM 1,500.00
Gilbert, Erector Set #5½", complete, MIB.......................175.00
Gilbert, Erector Set #7, EX (EX wooden box)....................250.00
Girard, Pierce Arrow Coupe, pressed steel, b/o lights, 14", EX...1,000.00
Gunthermann, Granny w/Basket, w/up, pnt tin, 6", G.........350.00
Gunthermann, Tango Dancers, w/up, pnt tin, 8", VG..........700.00
Hartland Plastics, Annie Oakley, w/horse, NM.................275.00
Hartland Plastics, Brave Eagle, w/horse, NMIB................300.00
Hartland Plastics, Gil Favor, prancing, NM.....................650.00
Hartland Plastics, Rifleman, w/horse, NMIB....................350.00
Hartland Plastics, Seth Adams, w/horse, NM...................275.00
Hubley, Harley Hill Climber, CI, w/integral driver, 6", VG 300.00
Hubley, Indian Crash Car, CI, w/integral driver, 6½", VG 525.00
Hubley, Mr Magoo Car, b/o, tin/cloth top, 1961, 9", MIB......375.00
Ichida, Kissing Couple, b/o, 1950s, 10", MIB..................400.00
Ichiko, Renault Floride, friction, tin w/chrome trim, 8", EXIB ...150.00
Ideal, Clancy the Great, b/o, 1960s, MIB........................375.00
Irwin, Racing Car, w/up, plastic, 12½", scarce, MIB...........285.00
Ives, Cuzner Trotter, w/up, tin, Pat Mar 7 1871, 11½", EX......2,500.00
Ives, Steamboat King, tin, single funnel, 10½", VG............400.00
K, All Stars Mr Baseball Jr, tin, 8", NM (EX box) 1,000.00
K, Cyclist Clown, remote control, tin/cloth, 7", NMIB 700.00
K, Merry Rabbit, b/o, 1950s, 11", NM...........................200.00
Kenner, Girder & Panel Build-A-Home, complete, NMIB 50.00
Keystone, Circus Truck, w/3 cages & animals, 26½", EX........2,800.00
Keystone, Packard Moving Van, 1920s, 26", EX...............2,500.00
Keystone, Ride 'Em Fighter Plane #293, 27½" W, VG 1,100.00
Keystone, Steam Shovel, 20", NM................................400.00
Kilgore, Dump Truck, CI, lever-action dump, 8½", G.............700.00
Kilgore, Travel Air Mystery Plane, CI, 7" W, NM..............850.00
Kingsbury, Cannon Truck, pressed steel, clockwork, 15", EX 150.00
Kingsbury, Crysler Airflow, pressed steel, w/up, lights, 14", G.....400.00
Kingsbury, Greyhound Bus, pressed steel, bl/cream, 18", EX 400.00
Kingsbury, Roadster, pressed steel, clockwork, lights, 13", VG..1,100.00
KO, Mystery Police Car, friction, tin, 6", NMIB................450.00
Lehmann, Adam the Porter, litho tin, 8", NM 1,750.00
Lehmann, Crocodile, litho tin, 9", NM (VG box)..............1,000.00
Lehmann, Gustav the Miller, litho tin, 18", NM................500.00
Lehmann, Masuyama Rickshaw, litho tin, 7", NM............3,000.00
Lehmann, UHU Amphibious Car, litho tin, 9", EX..............650.00
Lindstrom, Dancing Dutch Boy, w/up, EXIB.....................275.00
Linemar, Androcles Lion, w/up, plush over tin, 6", EXIB............100.00

Linemar, Ball Playing Dog, b/o, tin/plush, 1950s, 9", M 125.00
Linemar, Banjo Player, w/up, tin, 5", NM........................200.00
Linemar, Casper the Ghost, w/up, tin, 5", VG..................250.00
Linemar, Casper Turnover Tank, w/up, tin, 4", NM............400.00
Linemar, Clarabelle the Clown, w/up, tin, 5", NMIB...........450.00
Linemar, Donald Duck Dipsy Car, w/up, tin, 5½", NMIB...1,100.00
Linemar, Ham 'N Sam, w/up, tin, 5½", VG+....................800.00
Linemar, Mickey the Magician, b/o, tin, 11", NM (EX box) ...2,400.00
Linemar, Moby Dicks Whaling Boat, remote control, 1950s, NM...200.00
Linemar, Nutty Nibs, b/o, pnt tin/paper skirt, 1950s, 12", EX.....875.00
Linemar, Smoking Popeye, b/o, tin, 1950s, 9½", rare, NM 2,500.00
Linemar, Superman Tank, b/o, tin, 1958, 10", rare, NMIB 3,500.00
Lionel, Mickey Mouse Handcar, w/up, 9", EXIB..............1,100.00
Marklin, Submarine, w/p, pnt tin, 16", EX....................1,100.00
Marusan, Cadillac, friction, tin/chrome detail, wht-walls, 13", NM....850.00
Marusan, Queen Mary, b/o, tin, 14", EX........................250.00
Marx, Babyland Nursery Playset #3379, 1955, EXIB...........350.00
Marx, Battle of the Blue & Gray Playset #4758, EXIB.........400.00
Marx, Brewster the Rooster, b/o, tin, 1950s, 9½", EX 250.00
Marx, Electric Convertible, b/o, 1950s, EX......................300.00
Marx, Funny Flivver, w/up, tin, 1925, 7½", NM (EX box)...1,500.00
Marx, Hi Way Express Truck, pressed steel, 16", NM...........350.00
Marx, Iwo Jima Playset #4147, 1954, EX (worn box)............350.00
Marx, Jungle Playset #3705, VG (VG box)......................550.00
Marx, Micky the Musician, w/up, tin/plastic, 12", NMIB..........750.00
Marx, Mighty King Kong, remote control, plush/tin, 1950s, 11", EX...500.00
Marx, Municipal Aeroplane Hangar, tin, 3½x6", NM (G box)...1,400.00
Marx, Railway Express Truck, pressed steel, 20", NM (EX box) .700.00
Marx, Roy Rogers Rodeo Ranch Playset #3985, 1955, MIB........550.00
Marx, Seascape Tugboat, b/o, 1950s, tin, 1950s, 6½", EX 100.00
Marx, Superman Rollover Plane, w/up, bl version, 6½", EX...1,000.00
Marx, Superman Rollover Plane, w/up, silver version, 6½", EX ...1,500.00
Marx, Walking Popeye, w/up, tin, 1935, 8½", MIB.............1,000.00
Marx, Zorro Playset #3753, NMIB..............................1,100.00
Matchbox, Cadillac Ambulance, #54-C, Super Fast, wht, 1970, NM+....22.00
Matchbox, Cadillac Sixty Special, #27-C, metallic gr/wht, 1960, MIP ..300.00
Matchbox, Dodge Stake Truck, #4-E, Super Fast, 1970, MIP........20.00
Matchbox, Esso Road Tanker, #11-B, red w/gray plastic tires, MIP....35.00
Matchbox, Mustang Fastback, #8-E, orange, 1966, MIP 125.00
Mattel Hot Wheels, Custom T-Bird, red line, gold (rare), 1968, NM...100.00
Mattel Hot Wheels, Evil Weevil, red line, red, #6 tampo, NM.....35.00
Mattel Hot Wheels, Odd Job, 1973, red line, lt bl, NM.............150.00
Mattel Hot Wheels, Super Van, 1975, blk walls, blk/flame tampo, EX....15.00
Mego, Baby Bertha the Watering Elephant, b/o, 1960s, 10", NMIB...1,100.00
Metalcraft, Plee-Zing Tow Truck, pressed steel, 10"...............500.00
Metalcraft, Pure Oil Co Truck, pressed steel, 14½", rstr.............475.00
Metalcraft, Toy Town Grocery Truck, pressed steel, 11", G 1,600.00
Milton Bradley, Terrytoon Fun Kit, 1958, NMIB...................75.00
MT, Mischievious Monkey, b/o, tin, MIB........................475.00
MT, Shooting Gorilla, b/o, 9", MIB..............................475.00
Nifty, Jiggs Jazz Car, w/up, tin, 1924, 6", scarce, VG 1,200.00
Nifty, Rudy the Ostrich, w/up, pnt tin, 1924, 8½", VG 350.00
Nylint, U-Haul Maxi-Mover, pressed steel, 20", MIB...........350.00
Ohio Art, Airport, w/up, tin, 9", NM (EX box) 250.00
Orkin, Battleship B2, clockwork, pressed steel, 37", EX...........3,800.00
Orkin, Cabin Cruiser, w/up, pressed steel, 1940s, 28", EX 1,100.00
Orkin, Dreadnaught US Nevada, clockwork, pressed steel, 22", EX..1,500.00
Reed, Battleship Philadelphia, paper on wood, 30", EX, $1000 to 1,500.00
Remco, Whirlybird Helicopter, b/o, 1960s, 25", NMIB.............250.00
Rosko, Lite-O-Wheel Lincoln, b/o, tin, 1950s, 10½", EX..........300.00
Rosko, Pretty Peggy Parrot, b/o, tin/plush, 10", EXIB............425.00
SAN, Smoking Grandpa, b/o, eyes open, 1950s, 9", MIB...........300.00
Sanyo, Taxi Cab, friction, tin, 1960s, 6", NMIB.................100.00
Schuco, Curvo 1000 Motorcycle, w/up, tin, 5", NMIB.............550.00

Schuco, Donald Duck, w/up, tin/felt jacket, 1935, 6", VG..........350.00
Schuco, Juggling Clown, w/up, tin/plastic/cloth clothes, 5", NMIB....300.00
Schuco, Teddy Bear on Scooter, friction, 1920s-30s, 6", NM ..1,000.00
Steelcraft, Army Scout NX-110, pressed steel, 22½" W, rstr.......600.00
Steelcraft, Bucket Truck, pressed steel, 26", scarce, EX 2,600.00
Steelcraft, Gasoline Tanker, pressed steel, C-cab, 1920s, 26", rstr ..1,000.00
Sturditoy, American LaFrance Pumper Truck, pressed steel, 34", rstr ..1,000.00
Sturditoy, Pumper Truck, pressed steel, friction, 20", G...............150.00
Sturditoy, US Army Truck, pressed steel, 27", EX+ 3,600.00
SY, USAF F-51 Fighter Plane, friction, litho tin, 7", NMIB 175.00
Taiyo, M-4 Combat Tank, b/o, tin, 11½", MIB............................225.00
Taiyo, Speed Jack Hot Rod, b/o, tin/plastic, 11", NMIB.............100.00
Technofix, Trick Motorcycle, w/up, tin, 7", NMIB 500.00
TN, Autocycle, friction, tin, w/driver, 5", NMIB.......................600.00
TN, Circus Jet, b/o, tin, 1960s, MIB.......................................200.00
TN, Popcorn Vendor Truck, b/o, tin, 9", EX.............................300.00
TN, Raja Rey the Indian Prince, b/o, 1960s, 12", NM 700.00
TN, Turn-O-Matic Gun Jeep, b/o, tin, 1960s, 10½", EX............200.00
TN, Waltzing Matilda, b/o, rare, MIB.....................................900.00
Tonka, Ace Stores Delivery Truck, 1954, M..............................600.00
Tonka, Cement Truck, #620, 1963, M.....................................200.00
Tonka, Dump Truck, #180, 1949-53, NM..................................275.00
Tonka, Wrecker, #250, 1953, EX..250.00
Tootsietoy, Army Set, #5220, complete, EXIB...........................500.00
Tootsietoy, Bi-Plane, #4650, 3", EX.......................................135.00
Tootsietoy, Delta Jet, 1954-55, silver, NM................................35.00
Tootsietoy, Graham Ambulance, #808, 4", NM.........................185.00
Tootsietoy, Rol-ezy Vehicle set, complete, NMIB......................450.00
Tootsietoy, Steam Roller, #4648, red, 3", EX............................175.00
Toy Tinkers, Miss Tilly Tinker, 1917-24, complete, EXIB 125.00
Toy Tinkers, Tinker Fish, 1927, complete, EX (worn box) 50.00
TPS, Calypso Joe the Drummer, w/up, tin, 6", NMIB 400.00
TPS, Champs on Ice, w/up, tin, 9" L, EX..................................350.00
TPS, Fishing Bear, w/up, tin, 7", NM (EX box) 250.00
Transogram, Federal Agent Fingerprint Outfit, 1938, MIB 200.00
TY, New Motorcycle, friction, tin, 5", NMIB 325.00
Unique Art, Hee-Haw, w/up, tin, 10½", G...............................200.00
Unique Art, Jazzbo Jim, w/up, tin, 1921, 10", VG 350.00
Unique Art, Kiddie-Go-Round, w/up, tin/plastic, 10", VG 250.00
Wolverine, Sulky Racer, w/up, plastic, 9", EXIB........................150.00
Wyandotte, Humphery Mobile, w/up, tin, 1950, 8½", NMIB.....800.00
Wyandotte, Ride 'Em Cowboy, w/up, tin, 7", EXIB 500.00
Wyandotte, Star Cruiser, pressed steel, 1940s, 13" W, G.............150.00
Y, Cragston Crapshooter, b/o, tin, 1950s, 9", MIB 175.00

Farm Toys

Bale throw wagon, John Deere, Ertl, #5755, 1/64th scale, MIB.......4.00
Baler, New Holland, Ertl, #337, 1/64th scale, MIB 3.00
Combine, Case IH, Ertl, #655, 1/64th scale, MIB 100.00
Combine, Massey-Ferguson 8680, Ertl, #230, 1/64th, MIB 10.00
Cotton picker, John Deere, Ertl, #1000, 1/80th scale, MIB.........100.00
Disc harrow, Caterpillar Challenger 65, Joal, #253, 1/50th scale, M ..22.00
Forge harvester, New Holland, Ertl, #372, 1/64th scale, MIB.........4.00
Hay rake, Case IH, Ertl, #210, 1/64th scale, MIB.........................3.00
Planter, Case IH, #478, 1/64th scale, MIB....................................3.00
Row crop, Case IH 5130, Ertl, #229, 1991, 1/64th scale, MIB 10.00
Row crop, John Deere 6400, Ertl, #5566, 1/16th scale, MIB.........40.00
Skid steer loader, John Deere, Ertl, #5622, 1/64th, MIB.................5.00
Spreader, McCormick-Deering #200 Precision, Ertl, #4201, MIB...100.00
Tractor, Allis Chalmers 220, Ertl, #4655, 1/16th scale, MIB.........30.00
Tractor, Case 400, Yoder, #19, 1/16th scale, M 275.00
Tractor, Caterpillar DC5, Joal, #174, 1/50th scale, M.................15.00
Tractor, Farmall H, Ertl, #4441, 1/16th scale, MIB 25.00

Tractor, Ford TW-35, Siku, #2855, 1/32nd scale, M 20.00
Tractor, New Holland 8360, Ertl, #3037, 1/16th scale, MIB 38.00
Tractor w/hay trailer, Massey-Ferguson MF 284, Siku, #2227, M....100.00
Wagon, hay; wood w/spoke wheels & horse fork, old bl pnt, 22½" ...110.00

Guns: Cast-Iron Cap Guns (Caution: Some reproductions exist.)

In years past, virtually every child played with toy guns, and the survival rate of these toys is minimal, at best. The interest in these charming toy guns has recently increased considerably, especially those with western character examples, as collectors discover their scarcity, quality, and value. Toy gun collectibles encompass the early and the very ornate figural toy guns and bombs through the more realistic ones with recognizable character names, gleaming finishes, faux jewels, dummy bullets, engraving, and colorful grips. This section will cover some of the most popular cast-iron and diecast toy guns from the past one hundred years. Recent market trends have witnessed a decline of interest in the earlier (1900 – 40) single-shot cast-iron pistols. The higher collector interest is for known western characters and cap pistols from the 1960 – 65 era. Generic toy guns such as Deputy, Pony Boy, Marshal, Ranger, Sheriff, Pirate, Cowboy, Dick, Western, Army, etc., generate only minimal collector interest.

Our advisor is James Schleyer, internationally recognized collector and appraiser of toy guns. He has authored numerous books, articles and newsletters on antique toy guns and holsters. He is the former editor for *Toy Gun Purveyors*, an international newsletter that fostered the collecting of these valuable and rare toys. His current book, *Backyard Buckaroos — Collecting Western Toy Guns*, contains nearly 2,500 photographs. Toy gun inquiries that include a SASE will be gracious answered. Send to: Jim Schleyer, Box 243-M, Burke, VA 22015.

In the listings below (*) designates a classic example.

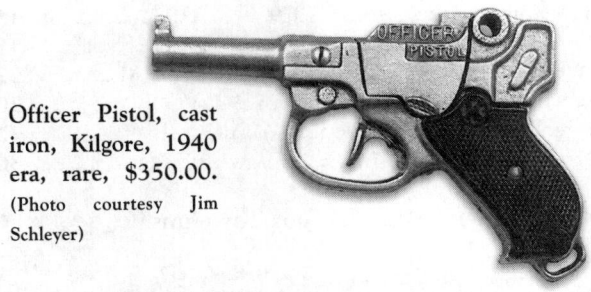

Officer Pistol, cast iron, Kilgore, 1940 era, rare, $350.00. (Photo courtesy Jim Schleyer)

American, cylinder revolves, Kilgore, 1940, 9⅜", EX (*) 450.00
Army 45 Auto, Hubley, 1945, 6½", M (*)..................................125.00
Atta Boy, single shot, Hubley, 1935, 4", G-................................35.00
Bango, eng, jewels, Stevens, 1940, 7½", VG................................70.00
Big Bill, single shot, Kilgore, 1935, 4⅞", M 35.00
Big Horn, cylinder revolves, Kilgore, 1940, 8⅝", M (*).............500.00
Big Scout, single shot, Stevens, 1930, 9⅜", G-..........................100.00
Billy the Kid, single shot, Stevens, 1940s, 6¾", G- 100.00
Border Patrol, automatic, Kilgore, 1935, 4½", VG........................50.00
Buc-A-Roo, single shot, Kilgore, 1940, 7¾", M...........................85.00
Buffalo Bill, single shot, Stevens, 1890, 11¾", rare, G-..............200.00
Bull's Eye, eng, Kenton, 1940, 6½", M....................................200.00
Bulldog, single shot, Hubley, 1935, 6", G 35.00
Bunker Hill, single shot, National, 1925, 5¼", M........................90.00
Captain, automatic, Kilgore, 1940, 4¼", VG...............................85.00
Champ, automatic, star medallion, Hubley, 1940, 5", EX..............70.00
Chief, single shot, Dent, 1935, 7½", VG....................................45.00
Colt, single shot, Stevens, 1900, 5½", EX...................................45.00
Cowboy, Hubley, 1940, 8", VG..100.00
Cowboy King, Stevens, 1940, 9", M (*)....................................250.00

Dick, automatic, Hubley, 1930, 4⅛", VG......................35.00
Doughboy, automatic, Kilgore, 1920, 4⅞", VG...............100.00
Eagle, single shot, Hubley, 1935, 8½", VG....................150.00
Federal, automatic, clip, Kilgore, 1940, 4⅞", M.............145.00
G-Man, automatic, Kilgore, 1935, 6", rare, M (*)............165.00
Gene Autry, eng, Kenton, 1951, 6½", rare, VG...............450.00
Gene Autry, eng, Kenton, 1951, 8⅜", rare, M.................550.00
Gene Autry, repeater, nickel, Kenton, 1940, 8⅜", EX (*)...250.00
Guard, bl finish, Kilgore, 1935, 6¼", EX......................100.00
Invincible, Kilgore, 1935, 5¼", G-...............................45.00
Lasso Em Bill, cylinder revolves, Kilgore, 1930, 9", EX.....225.00
Lawmaker, nickel, Kenton, 1940, 8⅜", rare, M (*)...........250.00
Lone Eagle, cylinder revolves, Kilgore, 1930, 5¼", EX......130.00
Lone Ranger, nickel, Kilgore, 1940, 8¼", rare, M (*)........325.00
Long Boy, single shot, Kilgore, 1920, 11⅛", VG..............115.00
Long Tom, cylinder revolves, Kilgore, 1940, 10⅜", M (*)...650.00
Mohican, single shot, Dent, 1930, 6¼", EX.....................60.00
National Automatic, National, 1915, 3¾", G-...................25.00
Officer's Pistol, automatic, Kilgore, 1940, 6", rare, M (*)....350.00
Patrol, Hubley, 1935-40, 6", M....................................75.00
Pawnee Bill, Stevens, 1940, 7⅝", VG (*)......................200.00
Peacemaker, gold, Stevens, 1940, 8½", M.....................150.00
Pirate, dbl bbl, Hubley, 1940, 8⅜", M (*).....................125.00
Police Chief, plastic grip, Kenton, 1940, 4⅝", EX...........100.00
Presto, automatic, Kilgore, 1940, 5⅛", VG.....................65.00
Rodeo, single shot, Hubley, 1940, 7", EX.......................45.00
Roy Rogers, Kilgore, 1940, 10¼", rare, EX (*)............1,750.00
Scout, single shot, Stevens, 1890, 7", VG......................55.00
Six Shooter, cylinder revolves, Kilgore, 1940, 6½", VG......75.00
Spitfire, automatic, Kilgore, 1940, 4⅝", EX...................65.00
Texan, CI/nickel, cylinder revolves, Hubley, 1940, 9¼", M (*)..175.00
Texan Jr, Hubley, 1940, 8⅛", VG (*)...........................100.00
Trooper, Safety, repeater, Kilgore, 1925, 10¼", M...........120.00
Two Time, rubber band, Kenton, 1929, 9¼", VG.............150.00
Warrior, nickel, repeater, Kilgore, 1920s, 9", EX.............175.00
Wild West, single shot, Kenton, 1920s, 11½", rare, M......225.00
101 Ranch, single shot, Hubley, 1930, 11½", VG.............200.00
2 In 1, rubber band, Stevens, 1930, 9¼", VG................125.00
49-er, Stevens, 1940, 9" (+)......................................300.00

Guns: Diecast and Miscellaneous Toy Guns

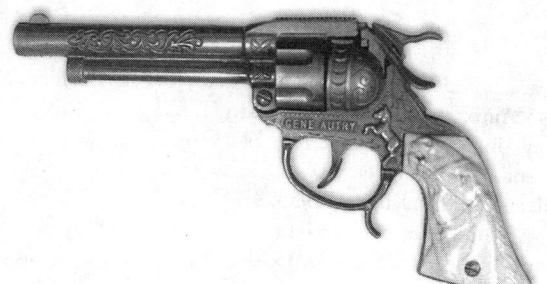

Gene Autry, nickel, Leslie-Henry, 9", M, $175.00.
(Photo courtesy Jim Schleyer)

Alan Ladd, Geo Schmidt, 10¼", rare, EX.....................300.00
Annie Oakley, gold, Leslie-Henry, 9", very rare..............650.00
Army 45 Automatic, compo, Hubley, 1940, nonworking......35.00
Atomic Disintegrator, space gun, Hubley, 8", VG............400.00
Bonanza, cylinder revolves, Leslie-Henry 44, 10½", M.....150.00
Bronco, cylinder revolves, Kilgore, 9¼", VG...................75.00
Buck'n Bronc, Geo Schmidt, 10½", EX........................100.00
Buckle Gun, derringer, Mattel, 3", VG..........................65.00

Burke's Law Snub Nose, blk, Lone Star, 5", M.................85.00
Champion, Leslie-Henry, 9", VG...............................125.00
Colt, Hubley Snub Nose Detective, mini, M....................30.00
Colt 44 1860, cylinder revolves, ivory grips, Hubley, 14", M...200.00
Colt 45, cylinder revolves, bullets, Hubley, 14", VG.........115.00
Cowboy, cylinder revolves, Hubley, 12", M...................145.00
Cowboy, gold, cylinder revolves, Hubley, 12", rare, EX.....200.00
Cowhand 250, Nichols, 8½", VG.................................70.00
Coyote, Hubley, 8¼", M..45.00
Dale Evans, jewels, Geo Schmidt, 10½", rare, VG...........350.00
Davy Crockett, Flintlock Buffalo Rifle, Hubley, 25", EX.....175.00
Deputy-BB, copper grips, Schmidt, sm, 8½", EX..............75.00
Dick Tracy, blk w/decal, steel clicker, Marx, EX..............65.00
Dick Tracy Siren Pistol, red finish, Marx, VG..................70.00
Dick Tracy Squad Shotgun, cap & water, pump, Mattel.....125.00
Eagle, nickel, cylinder revolves, Kilgore, 8", M..............100.00
Fanner 'Shootin' Shell,' bullets, Mattel, 9", M...............150.00
Fanner 45 'Shootin' Shell,' bullets, Mattel, 9", M...........150.00
Fanner 50, nickel, cylinder revolves, Mattel, 10⅝", EX.....165.00
Flip Rifleman Ring Rifle, Hubley, 32", VG.....................250.00
G-Boy, pressed steel, Acme Novelty Co, 7", M................65.00
G-Man, Sparking Wind-Up, steel pistol, Marx, 5", VG........55.00
G-Man, Sparkling Machine Gun, tin, Marx, 26", VG.........225.00
G-Man, tin clicker pistol w/jewel, Marx, 1935, M.............55.00
Gene Autry, nickel, Leslie-Henry, 9", M.......................175.00
Gray Ghost, nickel, silver grips, Lone Star, 9", rare, EX.....550.00
Grizzly, gold, cylinder revolves, Kilgore, 10¼", M...........250.00
Hawk, automatic, amber grips, Hubley, 5", VG................35.00
Hawkeye, automatic, Kilgore, 4¼", M...........................45.00
Hopalong Cassidy, cameo grips, Geo Schmidt, 9", EX.......300.00
Hopalong Cassidy, gold, Wyandotte, 9", M....................450.00
Hopalong Cassidy, nickel, Wyandotte, 9", VG................300.00
Indian Scout Rifle, bullets, Mattel, 30", M...................225.00
Lone Ranger, antique bronze, Actoy, 10", VAG...............175.00
Lone Ranger, tin clicker w/jewel, Marx, 8", M................65.00
Maire's Leg, Winchester lever-pistol, Marx, 14", EX.........135.00
Marshal, cylinder revolves, bullets, Halco, 10½", M.........125.00
Mattel Snub-Nosed Detective, chrome, shootin' shell, EX...90.00
Maverick, Leslie-Henry, 10½", VG..............................120.00
Maverick 45, cylinder revolves, Halco, 11", M...............300.00
Me & My Buddy, tin clicker, Wyandotte, 1935-40, VG......100.00
Model 61, cylinder revolves, steel-bl finish, Nichols, rare, M...350.00
Mountie, automatic, blk finish, Kilgore, 6", M................45.00
Mustang 500, nickel, Nichols, 12¼", EX.......................175.00
Pal, nickel, single shot, Kilgore, 1945-60, sm, M..............5.00
Paladin, nickel, repeater, Leslie-Henry, 9", rare, EX.........285.00
Pet, nickel, Hubley, 1945-60, M...................................5.00
Pioneer, nickel, blk grips, Hubley, 10¼", M..................100.00
Pirate, over-under bbls, Hubley, 1960, VG.....................45.00
Pony Boy, nickel, Esquire-Actoy, 10", EX......................50.00
Rebel Scattergun, dbl bbl, Marx, 21", rare, M...............900.00
Red Ranger, Wyandotte, 7¾", VG................................45.00
Remington 36, cylinder revolves, bullets, Hubley, 8¼", EX...85.00
Ric-O-Shay, cylinder revolves, bullets, Hubley, 12¼", M....100.00
Roy Rogers, copper girps, Geo Schmidt, 10¼", EX..........225.00
Roy Rogers, gold, Leslie-Henry, 9", EX........................275.00
Roy Rogers, nickel, diecast, Kilgore, 8", M...................185.00
Scout Rifle, nickel, lever action, Hubley, 1960, EX...........125.00
Sharps Carbine, Civil War Model, Marx, 1960, rare, EX....150.00
Stallion 32, Nichols, 8", VG......................................35.00
Stallion 38, cylinder revolves, bullets, Nichols, 9½", EX.....115.00
Stallion 45 Mk II, gold, cylinder revolves, Nichols, 12", rare, EX...1,500.00
Star, nickel, single shot, Hubley, 7", MIB......................20.00
Sure Shot, nickel, Hubley, 8", EX................................30.00

Tex, single shot, Hubley, sm, M.................................5.00
Texan Jr, diecast, break action, Hubley, 9", VG 65.00
Texan Jr, diecast, side opener, Hubley, 9½", M............65.00
Thundergun, nickel, eng, Marx, 12½", M............170.00
Tightrope Snub Nose, nickel, Lone Star, EX.............85.00
Trooper, nickel, snub snose, Hubley, 1950-60, EX.............25.00
US Marshal, antique bronze/cylinder trns, Leslie-Henry, 11¼", VG...125.00
Wagon Train, antique bronze, Leslie-Henry 44, 11¼", VG.........135.00
Wells Fargo, nickel, Actoy, 11", M............155.00
Western, nickel, Hubley, 9", M............55.00
Wild Bill Hickok, Leslie-Henry, 9", VG............150.00
Wild Bill Hickok, Leslie-Henry 44, 11¼", EX 150.00
Winchester Carbine, shootin' shell, Mattel, 26", M 165.00
Winchester Saddle Gun, Mattel, 33", M............185.00
Wyatt Earp, nickel, long bbl, Hubley, 11", M 165.00
2 in 1, 2 interchanging bbls, Hubley, 6", EX 45.00

Guns: Early-Style Figural Guns and Bombs (Caution: reproductions exist.)

Admiral Dewey Bomb, CI, Grey Iron, 1900, 1¾", VG...............200.00
Butting Match, CI, Ives, 1885, 5", EX 400.00
Cannon, CI, Kenton, 1900, 4⅞", VG 400.00
Chinese Must Go, CI, Ives, 1880, 4¾", EX 400.00
Clown on Powder Keg, CI, Ives, 1890s, 3¾", VG 500.00
Devil's Head Bomb, CI, 22 blank, Ives, 1880, 2¼", VG 325.00
Dog's Head Bomb, CI, Ives, 1880, 2⅛", EX 245.00
Double-Face Man, CI, Ives, 1890, 1⅝", VG 125.00
George Washington Bomb, CI, 1900, 1¼", EX 350.00
Hobo Bomb, CI, Ideal, 1890s, 2", G-............100.00
Liberty Bell Bomb, CI, 1876, 2⅜", EX 200.00
Lightening Express, CI, Kenton, 1900, 5", EX 650.00
Punch & Judy, CI, Ives, 1880s, 5¼", EX 850.00
Sea Serpent, CI, Stevens, 1890, 3½", G-............875.00
Yellow Kid Bomb, CI, Grey Iron, 1900, 1½", VG 170.00

Model Kits

Addar, Evel Knievel's Wheelie, 1974, MIB............125.00
Addar, World Wildlife, Outlaw Mustang, 1975, MIB 35.00
Airfix, Coldstream Guardsman, 1960s, MIB 20.00
Airfix, Datsun 280-ZX Champion, 1980, MIB............40.00
AMT, Get Smart Sunbeam Car, 1967, MIB............100.00
AMT, Man in Space Set, 1969, MIB (sealed)............250.00
AMT, Star Trek, USS Enterprise, 1967, MIB 200.00
Aurora, Captain America, 1966, MIB............400.00
Aurora, Dracula, 1969, glow-in-the-dark, MIB............100.00
Aurora, Dracula's Dragster, 1964, MIB............325.00
Aurora, Famous Fighters, Viking, 1958, MIB............350.00
Aurora, Incredible Hawk, 1966, MIB............250.00
Aurora, King Kong, 1964, MIB............400.00
Aurora, Spider-Man, 1966, MIB............250.00
Aurora, Wolfman, 1962, MIB 300.00
Aurora, Wolfman, 1972, MIB............125.00
Bachmann, Animals of the World, Lion, 1959, MIB............50.00
Bachmann, Dogs of the World, Pointer, 1959, MIB 40.00
Bandai, Godzilla, 1984, MIB............50.00
Eldon, Moon Survey, 1966, MIB............50.00
Hawk, Cherokee Sports Roadster, 1962, MIB 35.00
Hawk, Monte Carlo Sports Roadster, 1962, MIB............75.00
ITC, Launcher w/Soviet BB-1 Missile, 1960, MIB 145.00
ITC, Neanderthal Man, 1959, MIB............50.00
Lindberg, Coo Coo Clock, 1965, MIB............40.00
Monogram, Ghost of the Red Baron, 1969, MIB............200.00

Monogram, Rascal Missile, 1958, MIB............400.00
Monogram, Speed Shift, 1965, MIB............300.00
MPC, Mannix Roadster, 1968, MIB............150.00
MPC, Space: 1999, Alien Creature & Vehicle, 1976, MIB............50.00
Palmer, African Tribal Mask, 1950s, MIB............75.00
Pyro, Ghost Rider, 1970, MIB............50.00
Revell, Apollo Astronaut on Moon, 1970, MIB............100.00
Revell, Ed 'Big Daddy' Roth, Angel Fink, 1965, MIB 200.00
Revell, Moon Ship, 1957, MIB............225.00
Strombecker, Disneyland Stagecoach, 1950s, MIB 200.00
Superior, Seeing Eye, 1959, MIB............35.00

Pedal Cars and Ride-On Toys

Air Pilot, American National, pressed steel, 50", restored, $2,300.00.

Champion Roadster, Murry, rstr............1,250.00
Champion Wrecker, Murray, working boom, 46", rstr............1,250.00
Chrysler, Steelcraft, 1941, rstr............2,500.00
Dipside Champion, Murray, 1953, rstr............1,100.00
Dump Truck, BMC, 1940s, 39", rstr............500.00
FD Hook & Ladder Truck, AMF, complete, 48", NM orig condition..130.00
Fire Chief Car, Gendron, spoke wheels, 44", EX orig condition..4,500.00
Fire Engine, Murray, mk City Fire Dept, complete, rstr............150.00
Ford, Steelcraft, 1936, 36", rstr............1,800.00
Jordan Car, Gendron, w/parking brake, EX, from $3,000 to 4,000.00
King 8, Gendron, 1914, 45", EX orig condition 4,400.00
Lincoln Zephyr, Steelcraft, 1940, 44", rstr............300.00
Nash Tandem Car, Gendron Pioneer Line, 66", EX orig condition...12,000.00
Navy Patrol Plane, Steelcraft, 48", rstr............3,000.00
Packard, Gendorn, w/luggage rack, rstr, from $4,000 to............5,000.00
Ranchero, Murray, 1958, VG orig condition............400.00
Silver King Roadster, Toledo, EX orig condition, from $3,500 to ..4,500.00
Skipper Boat, Murray, 47", rstr............1,350.00
Thunderbolt, BMC, 1949, rstr............900.00
Tin Lizzy, Garton, 34", rstr............1,150.00
Woody Station Wagon, Steelcraft, 1941, rstr............2,300.00

Penny Toys

Airplane, Distler, 4-prop, w/orig pull string, EX 1,200.00
Armored gun car, Germany, inertia mechanisim, 3", EX............300.00
Boy at school desk, Meier, top slides out, 2½", EX............800.00
Boy playing bugle on rocking horse, Meier, EX............900.00
Delivery truck, Fischer, mk 245, w/driver, 3½", EX 175.00
Double-decker bus, Distler, rear stairs, 4½", EX............350.00
Dump truck, Fischer, w/driver, VG............125.00
Elephant cart, Fischer, nodding head, 5", EX............100.00

Express parcel delivery truck, Distler, w/driver, 3¾", VG............**175.00**
Fire ladder truck, Meier, fireman on open bench seat, 3½", EX..**225.00**
Giraffe on wheeled platform, Meier, 4", VG **250.00**
Girl on swing, Distler, 2½", NM..**250.00**
Goat on platform, Meier, 3", EX..**300.00**
Horse-drawn cab, Meier, dapple gray horse, 4½", EX **325.00**
Horse-drawn landau, Meier, w/driver, 4¾", EX **250.00**
Motorcycle, Kellerman, inertia wheels, w/driver, 4", VG+ **1,150.00**
Ocean liner, Meier, 2 stacks, 4½", VG+..................................**450.00**
Sedan, Fischer, center door, 4", EX..**150.00**
Toadstool w/butterfly, Fischer, EX...**650.00**
Touring car, Meier, w/lady passenger & driver, EX.....................**800.00**
Vis-A-Vis, Meier, w/driver, 3", VG **300.00**
Watering can, Meier, spring-loaded lid, 3", VG **250.00**
Zeppelin, Gesch, w/passengers in 2 open gondola, 4", EX...........**950.00**

Pull Toys

Boxers on platform, Rich, pnt wood & metal, 8" L, EX **175.00**
Buffalo Bill on platform, Fallows, pnt tin w/CI wheels, 9", VG..**3,600.00**
Clown & poodle bell toy, Gong Bell, 8", VG **600.00**
Dog on platform bell toy, Am, pnt tin, 14", EX **825.00**
Duck, Hubley, CI, waddles & mouth opens, 9½", VG **850.00**
Elgin street sweeper w/driver, Hubley, pnt CI, 1930, 8½", NMIB ..**9,500.00**
Goat cart w/driver, Harris, pnt CI, spoke wheels, 9", EX...........**750.00**
Graf zeppelin, Steelcraft, silver-pnt pressed steel, 25", EX...........**375.00**
Grasshopper, Hubley, pnt CI, 12", NM **2,400.00**
Horse cart w/girl & lions bell toy, Bergman, tin, 13", EX.........**4,500.00**
Horse-drawn spring cart w/driver, Geo Brown, pnt tin, 9", NM ...**1,900.00**
Horse-drawn sulky, Gibbs, litho-on-wood horse/metal cart, 7", EX..**200.00**
Jonah the Wale on platform, NH Hill Brass, CI, 6", EX **1,500.00**
Jumbo the Elephant, Hubley, compo, 5", NMIB.......................**200.00**
Lamb on platform bell toy, Fallows, pnt tin, 8", NM...............**1,400.00**
Monkey on tricycle, CI, rubber tires w/NP spokes, 7", NM **5,200.00**
Patriotic boy bell ringer, Bergmann, pnt tin, 1880, 9", EX.......**4,950.00**
Uncle Sam & the Don bell toy, Gong Bell, 7½", NM **6,200.00**

Robots

Atlas Robot, Argentina, w/up, tin/plastic, 7", EX (VG box).......**250.00**
Atomic Man, Japan, clockwork, litho tin, 5", VG **500.00**
Busy Cart Robot, SH, b/o, tin/plastic, 11½", NMIB **1,100.00**
Chief Robot Man, KO, 1950s, b/o, litho tin, 12", rare, MIB....**1,400.00**
Drumming Robot, TN, 1950s, remote control, tin, 8", rare, VG..**1,300.00**
Earth Man, TN, remote control, tin, 9", NMIB **1,200.00**
Flashy Jim, mk R-7, remote control, tin, 7½", rare, EXIB........**2,200.00**
Gear Robot, SH, b/o, tin/plastic, 11", NMIB **500.00**
High-Wheel Robot, KO, w/up, tin/plastic, 10", EXIB **250.00**
Jupiter Robot, Japan, w/up, plastic w/tin face, 7", NMIB **300.00**
Lavender Robot, Modern Toys, b/o, bump-&-go, 15", rare, NMIB..**5,600.00**
Mars King, SH, b/o, tin, 9", NMIB...**400.00**
Mister Flash, Cragstan, b/o, plastic, 8", NMIB..........................**400.00**
Mr Robot the Mechanical Brain, Alps, b/o, tin, 8", EXIB **1,100.00**
NASA Astronaut w/Razor, Japan, w/up, tin, 6", NMIB **200.00**
Omnibot 2000 Robot, remote control, plastic, w/accessories, 24", NM..**2,000.00**
Pete the Spaceman, Bandai, b/o, 1960s, MIB **225.00**
Piston Action Robot, TN, b/o, 1950s, tin/rubber hands, 8", NM **1,100.00**
Radicon Robot, Modern Toys, b/o, tin, 15", rare, NMIB **9,500.00**
Roto-Robot, Horikawa, b/o, tin w/plastic guns, 9", NMIB **300.00**
Smoking Spaceman, Linemar, b/o, tin, 12", rare, NMIB..........**3,000.00**
Swinging Baby Robot, Japan, clockwork, tin, 6", NMIB **500.00**
Talking Robot, Y, b/o, tin, 11", NM (NM box) **1,100.00**
Thunder Robot, A1, b/o, tin, 11", rare, NMIB.......................**3,200.00**
Winky Robot, Y, w/up, tin, 9½", scarce, NM **1,500.00**

X-70 Space Robot, Nomura, b/o, tin/plastic, 12", NMIB.........**2,000.00**

Schoenhut

Our advisor for Schoenhut toys is Keith Kaonis, who has collected these toys for over twenty years. Because of his involvement with the publishing industry (currently *Antique DOLL Collector*, and during the '80s, *Collectors' SHOWCASE*), he has visited collections across the United States, produced several articles on Schoenhut toys, and served a term as president of the Schoenhut Collectors' Club. Keith is listed in the Directory under New York.

The listings below are for Humpty Dumpty Circus pieces. All values are based on rating conditions of good to very good, i.e., very minor scratches and wear, good original finish, no splits or chips, no excessive paint wear or cracked eyes, and of course completeness and condition of clothes (if dressed figures).

Clowns with two-part heads (a cast face applied to a wooden head) were made from 1903 to 1912 and are most desirable — condition always is important. There have been nine distinct styles in fourteen different costumes recorded. Only eight costume styles apply to the two-part headed clowns. The later clowns had one-part heads whose features were pressed wood, and the costumes on the later ones, circa 1920+, were no longer tied at the wrists and ankles.

Comic characters, ca 1920s: Bonzo, very rare, from $500.00 to $1,200.00; Happy Hooligan, rare, from $1,000.00 to $2,000.00; Felix, 6", rarest size, from $800.00 to $1,200.00 (4", scarce but available, from $150.00 to $250.00; 8", from $400.00 to $750.00); KoKo the Inkwell Clown, King Features by Max Fleisher, extremely rare, from $2,500.00 to $5,000.00; Boob McNutt, rare, from $1,000.00 to $2,000.00; Jiggs and Maggie, from $500.00 to $1,400.00 for the pair. Condition dictates value. (Photo courtesy Keith and Donna Kaonis)

Humpty Dumpty Circus Clowns and Other Personel

Black Dude, reduced sz, from $300 to...**600.00**
Black Dude, 1-part head, purple coat, from $250 to **700.00**
Black Dude, 2-part head, blk coat, from $500 to **800.00**
Chinese Acrobat, 1-part head, from $200 to................................**600.00**
Chinese Acrobat, 2-part head, rare, from $400 to....................**1,500.00**
Clown, early, G, from $150 to **500.00**
Clown, reduced sz, 1925-53, from $75 to **150.00**
Gent Acrobat, bsk head, rare, from $300 to.................................**700.00**
Gent Acrobat, 2-part head, very rare, from $600 to.................**1,500.00**
Hobo, reduced sz, from $300 to **600.00**
Hobo, 1-part head, from $200 to **500.00**
Hobo, 2-part head, curved toes, blk coat, from $500 to **1,000.00**

Hobo, 2-part head, facet toe ft, from $400 to............................800.00
Lady Acrobat, bsk head, from $300 to....................................600.00
Lady Acrobat, 1-part head, from $200 to.................................400.00
Lady Rider, bsk head, from $250 to.......................................500.00
Lady Rider, 1-part head, from $200 to...................................400.00
Lady Rider, 2-part head, very rare, from $600 to....................1,500.00
Lion Tamer, bsk head, rare, from $350 to...............................750.00
Lion Tamer, 2-part head, early, very rare, from $600 to...........1,500.00
Ring Master, bsk, ca 1912-14, from $400 to............................650.00
Ring Master, 1-part head, from $200 to..................................450.00
Ring Master, 2-part head, early, very rare, from $500 to..........1,500.00

Humpty Dumpty Circus Animals

Humpty Dumpty Circus animals with glass eyes, ca. 1903 – 1914, are more desirable and can demand much higher prices than the later painted-eye versions. As a general rule, a glass-eye version is 30% to 40% more than a painted-eye version. (There are exceptions.) The following list suggests values for both GE (glass-eye) and PE (painted-eye) versions and reflects a *low PE price* to a *high GE price*.

There are other variations and nuances of certain figures: Bulldog — white with black spots or Brindle (brown); open- and closed-mouth zebras and giraffes; ball necks and hemispherical necks on some animals such as the pig, leopard, and tiger, to name a few. These points can affect the price and should be judged individually. Condition and rarity affect the price most significantly and the presence of an original box virtually doubles the price.

Alligator, GE/PE, from $200 to...500.00
Arabian Camel, 1 hump, GE/PE, from $250 to 900.00
Bactrian Camel, 2 humps, GE/PE, from $200 to 1,500.00
Brown Bear, GE/PE, from $200 to...900.00
Buffalo, cloth mane, GE/PE, from $300 to...........................1,000.00
Buffalo, cvd mane, GE/PE, from $200 to 1,200.00
Bulldog, GE/PE, from $400 to 1,600.00
Burro (made to go w/chariot & clown), GE/PE, from $200 to 800.00
Cat, GE/PE, rare, from $600 to..3,000.00
Cow, GE/PE, from $250 to..900.00
Deer, GE/PE, from $300 to..1,200.00
Donkey, GE/PE, from $75 to...200.00
Donkey w/blanket, GE/PE, from $90 to 400.00
Elephant, GE/PE, from $90 to 300.00
Elephant w/blanket, GE/PE, from $200 to 600.00
Gazelle, GE/PE, rare, from $700 to.....................................3,000.00
Giraffe, GE/PE, from $200 to...900.00
Goat, GE/PE, from $150 to...400.00
Goose, PE only, from $200 to...600.00
Gorilla, PE only, from $1200 to..3,500.00
Hippo, GE/PE, from $300 to...900.00
Horse, wht, platform, GE/PE, from $125 to 400.00
Hyena, GE/PE, very rare, from $1000 to..............................4,000.00
Kangaroo, GE/PE, from $400 to 1,500.00
Lion, cloth mane, GE, from $500 to 1,200.00
Lion, cvd mane, GE/PE, from $250 to....................................900.00
Monkey, 1-part head, PE only, from $250 to............................450.00
Monkey, 2-part head, wht face, from $300 to 900.00
Ostrich, GE/PE, from $200 to...900.00
Pig, 5 versions, GE/PE, from $200 to......................................700.00
Polar Bear, GE/PE, from $500 to...1,500.00
Poodle, cloth mane, GE only, from $300 to 500.00
Poodle, PE, from $100 to...300.00
Rabbit, GE/PE, very rare, from $1000 to..............................3,000.00
Rhino, GE/PE, from $250 to..1,000.00
Sea lion, GE/PE, from $400 to..1,500.00

Sheep (lamb) w/bell, GE/PE, from $200 to 800.00
Tiger, GE/PE, from $250 to..1,000.00
Wolf, GE/PE, very rare, from $600 to..................................5,000.00
Zebra, GE/PE, from $250 to...900.00
Zebu, GE/PE, rare, from $1000 to.......................................2,500.00

Humpty Dumpty Circus Accessories

There are many accessories: wagons, tents, ladders, chairs, pedestals, tight rope, weights, and more.

Menagerie tent, early, ca 1904, from $1500 to........................2,500.00
Menagerie tent, later, ca 1914-20, from $1200 to...................2,000.00
Oval litho tent, 1926, from $4000 to....................................8,000.00
Sideshow panels, 1926, pr, from $2000 to.............................6,000.00

Steiff

Margaret Steiff began making her stuffed felt toys in Germany in the late 1800s. The animals she made were tagged with an elephant in a circle. Her first teddy bear, made in 1903, became such a popular seller that she changed her tag to a bear. Felt stuffing was replaced with excelsior and wool; when it became available, foam was used. In addition to the tag, look for the 'Steiff' ribbon and the button inside the ear. For further information we recommend *Teddy Bears and Steiff Animals*, a full-color identification and value guide by Margaret Fox Mandel, available from Collector Books or your public library. See also Teddy Bears.

Baby Chick, spotted Dralon, all ID, 1971, 4", NM 85.00
Bazi Dog, seated, mohair, all ID, 1950, 7", NM 200.00
Bison, mohair w/felt horns, all ID, 1950, 8", M 225.00
Boar, blk w/brn face, all ID, 1950s, 11", M............................165.00
Clownie Clown, orig outfit, chest tag, 5", M 100.00
Collie, laying down, all ID, 1960s, 9", M 200.00
Cosy Camel, Dralon, all ID, 1968, 10½", M 125.00
Crabby Lobster, felt w/airbrushing, all ID, 4½", M 350.00

Dog, Revue Susi, long and short blond mohair, straw stuffed, jointed head, glass eyes, squeaker, ca 1960 – 1970, 11" (scarce size), $200.00.

Donkey, velvet/rope tail/harness, button/tag, 1959-67, 4½", M ..165.00
Dormy Dormouse, mohair/Dralon, all ID, 1968, 7½", M 125.00
Electrola Fox Dog, Dralon/mohair ears, tag, 1968, 4½", rare, NM 900.00
Elephant, ride-on, mohair/steel fr, 24½", EX 450.00
Floppy Kitty, sleeping, ribbon/tag, 8", EX..............................100.00
Foxy Dog, ribbon/tag, 1950, 3", EX 110.00
Hansi Parakeet, velvet/plastic ft, all ID, 1968, 3½", EX 125.00
Hoppy Rabbit, mohair, ribbon/bell, all ID, 1968, 9", NM 200.00
Jocko Monkey, mohair/felt, glass eyes, all ID, 11", M 225.00
Lizzy Lizard, velvet, glass eyes, no ID, 1959-61, 12", EX.............385.00
Manni Rabbit, mohair, glass eyes, no ID, 1950s, 16", NM 750.00
Moosy Moose, mohair/felt, glass eyes, all ID, 5", rare, NM 425.00
Orig Camel, all ID, 1950, 11", NM...250.00

Peky Dog, plush/felt, chest tag, 1950, 3", EX..................75.00
Pony, mohair, glass eyes, saddle/reins, chest tag, 1950s, 5", NM .125.00
Snobby Poodle, puppet, all ID, 1955-58, 9", NM......................100.00
Squirrel, puppet, mohair/felt, glass eyes, 8½", NM 75.00
Susi Cat, mohair, plastic eyes, all ID, 1960s, 5", NM.................200.00
Tucky Turkey, mohair/felt/velvet, glass eyes, all ID, 1952, 4", M ...365.00
Woolie Cat, gray & wht, ribbon/button/tag, 1970-74, 2½", M 65.00
Woolie Fish, gr & yel, button/tag, 1968, 1½", NM.......................35.00
Yuku Gazelle, all ID, 1963, 7½", rare, NM.................................325.00
Zicky Goat, mohair, glass eyes, ribbon/bell/tag, 6", EX..............100.00

Toy Soldiers and Accessories

Among the better-known manufacturers of 'dimestore' soldiers are Barclay, Manoil, and Jones, all of whom made hollow cast-lead figures; Grey Iron, who used cast iron; and Auburn, who made figures of rubber. They measured about 3" to 3½" tall, and often accessories such as trucks, tents, tanks, and airplanes were designed to add to the enjoyment of staging mock battles, parades, encampments, etc.

Britains is a very popular line, smaller and usually more detailed than the 'dimestores.' They've been made in England since 1893, and most of their boxed sets sell for a minimum of $100.00.

Some examples are very rare and therefore expensive, but condition is the driving force in making a value assessment. Percentages in the description lines refer to the amount of original paint remaining. Our advisors for this category are Stan and Sally Alekna; they are listed in the Directory under Pennsylvania. To learn more about this subject, we recommend *Collecting Toy Soldiers* by Richard O'Brien (Krause).

Barclay, officer's car with megaphone, very scarce, 95%, $300.00. (Photo courtesy Stan and Sally Alekna)

Auburn Rubber, Collie dog, lg, 95%..................................17.00
Auburn Rubber, machine gunner, 99% 21.00
Auburn Rubber, observer w/binoculars, 96%....................23.00
Auburn Rubber, piglet, 98%..8.00
Auburn Rubber, US Infantry officer, khaki, 94%..............14.00
Auburn Rubber, White Guard officer, yel or red trim, M 40.00
Barclay, ammo carrier, 97%...23.00
Barclay, aviator, 98%..29.00
Barclay, boy skater, 99%...18.00
Barclay, bull, NM..19.00
Barclay, cavalryman in khaki, gray horse, 1930, 97% 33.00
Barclay, cop on motorcycle, scarce, NM...........................57.00
Barclay, cowboy (masked) w/pistol on horse, 99% 48.00
Barclay, cowboy w/lasso, 98%...23.00
Barclay, horse grazing, 97%..15.00
Barclay, Indian w/bow & arrow, M 20.00
Barclay, Indian w/tomahawk & shield, 97%.....................22.00
Barclay, jockey on gold horse, #9, 99%.............................33.00
Barclay, knight w/shield, 99%...23.00
Barclay, machine gunner lying flat, 96% 26.00

Barclay, mailman, 99%..20.00
Barclay, man passenger w/overcoat, 98%..........................20.00
Barclay, newsboy, 97%..17.00
Barclay, officer w/sword, short stride, 97%.......................28.00
Barclay, parachute jumper, 98%..34.00
Barclay, pirate w/red outfit, 97%, scarce 33.00
Barclay, sailor in wht, 98%...24.00
Barclay, sentry, 97%..29.00
Barclay, sheep resting, M...20.00
Barclay, small Santa on sled, 99%.....................................50.00
Barclay, soldier ammo carrier, 97%...................................23.00
Barclay, soldier charging, gr, M 23.00
Barclay, soldier on crutches, gr, 98%, scarce 47.00
Barclay, soldier pigeon handler, 99% 37.00
Barclay, soldier telephone operator, 95%..........................26.00
Barclay, soldier w/range finder, 95%.................................27.00
Grey Iron, aviator, orange harness, prewar, 93%, very scarce 84.00
Grey Iron, Black man digging, prewar, 98%, scarce 32.00
Grey Iron, cadet, right shoulder arms, prewar, 94% 29.00
Grey Iron, Colonial officer in red tunic, postwar, 98%.................29.00
Grey Iron, Colonial officer on horse, prewar, 96%.......................47.00
Grey Iron, Ethiopian chief, prewar, 94%, scarce 66.00
Grey Iron, flagbearer, prewar, 98%.................................46.00
Grey Iron, garageman in gr, postwar, 98%, scarce 23.00
Grey Iron, holdup man, blk, postwar, M 39.00
Grey Iron, Indian brave shielding eyes, prewar, 97%.................35.00
Grey Iron, Legion drum major, prewar, 97%.....................28.00
Grey Iron, Legion flagbearer, prewar, 97%........................39.00
Grey Iron, machine gunner sitting, prewar, 94% 16.00
Grey Iron, man in traveling suit, postwar, M 17.00
Grey Iron, old man sitting, prewar, 99%............................14.00
Grey Iron, pirate boy, prewar, 95%, scarce 46.00
Grey Iron, sailor, dk bl, prewar, 92% 16.00
Grey Iron, US Doughboy charging, prewar, 98%...............23.00
Grey Iron, US Doughboy Sentry, prewar, 97%..................29.00
Grey Iron, US Infantry Officer, prewar, 97% 23.00
Grey Iron, woman w/basket, prewar, 97% 16.00
Jones, British Guardsman of 1921, NM, scarce 21.00
Jones, British Marine of 1775 firing musket at angle, 94%............24.00
Jones, mule, 99%...12.00
Jones, Scot Highlander of 1814, 54mm, 98%, scarce 28.00
Jones, Waynes Legion Soldier on guard w/bayonet, 54mm, M, scarce ..32.00
Manoil, antiaircraft machine gunner, 98%.........................31.00
Manoil, blacksmith making horseshoes, 97%.....................27.00
Manoil, bull, 98%..24.00
Manoil, carpenter sawing lumber, 98%..............................28.00
Manoil, cow feeding, 97%..22.00
Manoil, farmer cutting corn, 98%......................................28.00
Manoil, girl in sleeveless dress, 94%..................................11.00
Manoil, girl picking berries, 92%, scarce 56.00
Manoil, lady w/pie, 96%..26.00
Manoil, lineman on pole, 97%, scarce 120.00
Manoil, man chopping wood, 95%.....................................25.00
Manoil, man planting tree, 99%...63.00
Manoil, motorcycle rider, 99%, scarce 63.00
Manoil, nurse, 96%..27.00
Manoil, observer, 94%...34.00
Manoil, officer, hollow base, 94%, very scarce 80.00
Manoil, parachutist landing, yel harness, 96%...................55.00
Manoil, sniper, camouflaged, red & wht flowers, 99%................38.00
Manoil, soldier, wounded, standing....................................32.00
Manoil, soldier sitting w/rifle, scarce, 95%........................41.00
Manoil, woman watering flowers, 98%...............................28.00
Mignot, Grenadier Guards mounted, 6-pc, MIB...............490.00

Mignot, Guarde Imperiale De Russe, #228, 6-pc, M (G box) 350.00
Mignot, Prussian Infantry of 1914, 12-pc, MIB...........................275.00

Trains

Electric trains were produced as early as the late nineteenth century. Names to look for are Lionel, Ives, and American Flyer. Identification numbers given in the listings below actually appear on the item.

Am Flyer, Boxcar #00633, EX..50.00
Am Flyer, Burlington Locomotive 4-4-0 & Tender #21166, M...100.00
Am Flyer, Caboose #24603, EX 45.00
Am Flyer, DC Northern Locomotive & Tender #00332, G 250.00
Am Flyer, Log Car #00905, M 70.00
Am Flyer, Rio Grande Cookie Boxcar #24039, EX....................175.00
Dorfan, NYC Locomotive #51, EX...150.00
Ives, Caboose #195, EX 200.00
Ives, Flat Car #196, EX 175.00
Ives, Locomotive & Tender #1122 w/Cars #135/#136, VG......1,000.00
Ives, Locomotive 4-4-0 & Tender #1132, steam-powered, EX .2,900.00
Ives, Major Seagraves Special Set, EXIB.................................6,200.00
Ives, Stock Car #193, NM 200.00
Knapp, Fast Freight Merchandise Car #234, EX 850.00
Lionel, Baggage Car #2602, NMIB...275.00

Lionel, Bild-A-Loco #381E with coaches Illinois, Colorado, California, and New York, green, pre-war, largest and most elaborate of all Lionel 4-4-4 locomotives, complete, NM, $6,500.00.

Lionel, Blue Streak Set #0249/#617/#618/#619, EX.................2,400.00
Lionel, Boxcar #2814, VG (VG box).......................................1,300.00
Lionel, Cherry Picker #6512, EXIB 150.00
Lionel, Crossing Gate #0252, EXIB..25.00
Lionel, Denver & Rio Grande Pa-1 ABA Set #18107, MIB.......600.00
Lionel, Fire Car w/Ladders #16688, M....................................65.00
Lionel, Frisco Boxcar #19230, NM 50.00
Lionel, Liberty Bicentennial Set #1577, MIB..........................650.00
Lionel, MKT Boxcar #6464-350, NMIB 500.00
Lionel, Sante Fe F-3 ABA Set #11711, MIB............................500.00
Lionel, Southern Crescent Dining Car #19001, MIB.................100.00
Lionel, SS Rio Grande Set #01450, MIB.................................450.00
Lionel, Union Pacific Set #0636/#673/#638, VG....................4,400.00
Marx, Union Pacific Set, complete, NMIB...............................500.00
Williams, Norfolk & Western 4-8-4 Locomotive & Tender #5601, MIB..325.00

Trade Signs

Trade signs were popular during the 1800s. They were usually made in an easily recognizable shape that one could mentally associate with the particular type of business it was to represent, especially appropriate in the days when many customers could not read!

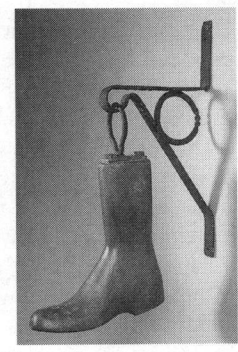

Bootmaker, zinc boot with wrought-iron bracket, golden brown paint, nineteenth century, 22½", EX, $1,380.00.

Anvil, cvd wood, orig blk pnt, 9x21", VG 275.00
Boot, tin w/worn patina, Repair in red, 20th C, 34", EX............470.00
Cigar, pnt/trn wood, Papa's Best, losses, ca 1890s, 37" L 400.00
Drugstore, raised lettering on dk bl asphaltum in wood fr, 19x72"...2,300.00
Eagle shape, cvd wood, old pnt traces, ca 1800, 16½x34x6" ...2,500.00
Key, cvd wood, much orig pnt, chain hanger, 34".....................315.00
Keys Made, 2-sided tin-litho key, 15x31", EX 100.00
Notary Public, brass, emb lettering, w/chain, 5x7".....................50.00
Optometrist, eyeglasses, CI & zinc w/mc pnt, dbl-sided, 12x27"...4,300.00
Pocketwatch, cast & sheet zinc, Roman numerals, gilt traces, 20"...350.00
Pocketwatch, pnt tin, silver dial, blk numerals, 1890s, 35x25" ...400.00
Rifle (resembles Henry), cvd wood w/gesso & old rpt, 70" L 935.00
Shoe, laminated wood, worn/weathered mc pnt, ca 1900, 25".2,300.00
Straight razor shape, pnt wood, Razors Ground, 14½x31" 860.00

Tramp Art

'Tramp' is considered a type of folk art. In America it was primarily made from the end of the Civil War through the 1930s, though it employs carving and decorating methods which are much older, originating mostly in Germany and Scandinavia. 'Trampen' probably refers to the itinerant stages of Middle Ages craft apprenticeship. The carving techniques were also used for practice. Tramp art was spread by soldiers in the Civil War and primarily practiced where there was a plentiful and free supply of materials such as cigar boxes and fruit crates. The belief that this work was done by tramps and hobos as payment for room or meals is generally incorrect. The larger pieces especially would have required a lengthy stay in one place.

There is a great variety of tramp art, from boxes and frames which are most common to large pieces of furniture and intricate objects. The most common method of decoration is chip carving with several layers built one on top of another. There are several variations of that form as well as others such as 'Crown of Thorns,' an interlocking method, which are completely different. The most common finishes were lacquer or stain, although paints were also used. The value of tramp art varies according to size, detail, surface, and complexity. The new collector should be aware that tramp art is being made today. While some sell it as new, others are offering it as old. In addition, many people mistakenly use the term as a catchall phrase to refer to other forms of construction — especially things they are uncertain about. This misuse of the term is growing, and makes a difference in the value of pieces. New collectors need to pay attention to how items are described.

For further information we recommend *Tramp Art: A Folk Art Phenomenon* by Helaine Fendelmam, Jonathan Taylor (Photographer)/Stewart Tabori & Chang; and *Hobo & Tramp Art Carving: An Authentic American Folk Tradition* by Adolph Vandertie, Patrick Spielman/Sterling Publications. Our advisors are Matt Lippa and Elizabeth Schaaf; they are listed in the Directory under Alabama.

Box, chip-cvd, heavy decor, 8" cross on top, 2 drw, 15x9½x6½"..1,037.00

Box, chip-cvd, old gr pnt int, porc knob, 4x13½x9", EX **587.00**
Box, chip-cvd, secret storage compartment in lid, 9½x12x8"..**1,312.00**
Box, comb; chip-cvd, scalloped top edge, 9½x8⅛x3½" **100.00**
Box, comb; eagle finial, notch-cvd star, layered strips, 16x9x4"..**300.00**
Box, sewing, notch/cvd dmns, drw, cushion top, dtd 1905, 6x7x7"..**230.00**
Box, sewing; 3-drw, notch-cvd border, cushion top, 7½x10x7"...**190.00**
Box, 3-tier, appl cvd lady & man, tall bk board, 20x6x4" **330.00**
Cabinet, chip-cvd, several layers, glass door front, 22x13x4½" ..**1,275.00**
Chest, chip-cvd, appl cut-out hearts, from cigar boxes, 13x9x7½" ..**1,075.00**
Chest, chip-cvd notches allover, dk finish, lift lid, 17x18x18" ...**1,712.00**
Clock stand, chip-cvd layers, drw, 4 bracket ft, 15x11x6"........**1,312.00**
Dressing stand, 5-tier, swivel mirror, 4 drws, chip cvd, 19th C, 31"..**1,675.00**
Frame, chip-cvd, old varnish, 8x7", EX **587.00**
Frame, chip-cvd, 4 appl cvd hearts, dk varnish, 14½x9" **437.00**
Frame, chip-cvd, 5-layer, 23x17¾" **462.00**
Frame, chip-cvd, 6-layer, ca 1910-20, 33x27", pr.....................**1,125.00**
Frame, chip-cvd, 6-layer, metal stars at corners, 29x26" **787.00**
Frame, Crown of Thorns, dk wood, 19½x17½", EX+ **262.00**
Frame, cvd dmns/pyramids overall, 30x26", VG **650.00**
Frame, cvd interlocking sections on pine, arched crest, 44x28"..**660.00**
Frame, Xd corners, pyramidal layered chip cvgs, 23x21", G........**165.00**
Lamp, floor; chip-cvd, 21" sq chip-cvd shade w/prisms, 72".....**7,200.00**
Mirror, rectangular/sq layered chip-cvgs, wht pnt, 23x17" **300.00**
Mirror, Xd corners, chip-cvd corners, rosettes, old pnt, 11x8" **210.00**
Puzzle bank, from 6 pcs of wood, stained, 20th C, 4¼" sq...........**100.00**

Traps

Though of interest to collectors for many years, trap collecting has gained in popularity over the past ten years in particular, causing prices to appreciate rapidly. Traps are usually marked on the pan as to manufacturer, and the condition of these trademarks are important when determining their value. Grading is as follows:

Good: one-half of pan legible.
Very Good: legible in entirety, but light.
Fine: legible in entirety, with strong lettering.
Mint: in like-new, shiny condition.

Our advisor for this category is Boyd Nedry; he is listed in the Directory under Michigan. Prices listed here are for traps in fine condition.

Sabo (for fox, raccoon, skunk, etc.) 1917, 13" long, with setting tool, $135.00. (Photo courtesy Russ Trading Post)

Abbey-Mc Leod, #4 rnd base **475.00**
Adirondak, instant death trap, wire trigger **350.00**
Anti-cat, automatic mousetrap **65.00**
Arrow, #2 single under spring......................................**65.00**
Aurouze, wire cage, mousetrap.....................................**65.00**
Bakers Automatic, wood & tin, mousetrap **135.00**
Bergs Automatic Ketchall, tin drowner, fits on pail of water........**50.00**
Blake & Lamb, #0, single long spring..............................**20.00**
Blake & Lamb, #44, dbl long spring **50.00**
Blizzard Cold Day, wood snap, mouse trap........................**20.00**

Buffalo, wood snap rat trap...**22.00**
Champion, #2, dbl long spring.......................................**35.00**
Clayton, killer..**120.00**
Clincher, #1½, single long spring..................................**80.00**
Coghill, WC mousetrap, fits on fruit jar............................**45.00**
Cortland, #0, single long spring....................................**235.00**
Cyclone, wood snap, mousetrap......................................**22.00**
Dalgren, Compensator, sm..**35.00**
Diamond, #21½, single long spring.................................**15.00**
Diamond, #4, coil spring..**35.00**
Dodd hair trigger, wood snap, mousetrap.........................**35.00**
Duke, #1½, coil spring..**7.00**
Dwight, #1, single long spring.....................................**425.00**
Eclipse, folding trap...**65.00**
Economy, #1½, single long spring..................................**25.00**
Ejector, Oneida NY, wood snap, mousetrap.......................**18.00**
Elenchik, #2, dogless, coil spring...................................**45.00**
Elgin, metal, mousetrap...**22.00**
End-O-Mice, cb snap..**20.00**
Eureka, Buel Bros, Detroit MI, wood snap, rat trap...............**21.00**
EZ Set, wood snap, mousetrap.......................................**20.00**
EZ Trip, mole trap...**30.00**
Fairy, w/exercise wheel, mousetrap.................................**85.00**
Fatal, Grip, single long spring, killer..............................**365.00**
Faultless, metal, snap rat trap..**40.00**
Flip-Trap, metal, squeeze to set, mousetrap.......................**30.00**
Gibbs, hawk trap, complete...**425.00**
Gibbs #0 King Bee, single coil spring...............................**75.00**
Gibbs #4, dope trap, dbl long spring.............................**575.00**
Good, wood snap, rat trap...**35.00**
Gurney's, gopher trap...**18.00**
Half Moon, tin, mousetrap..**85.00**
Halls, spear type, gopher trap, from $40 to........................**45.00**
Hawley & Norton, #2, dbl long spring **20.00**
Hellcat, metal, mousetrap...**20.00**
Henderson, mole trap..**440.00**
Herters, #0, single long spring.....................................**125.00**
Herters #1 Stoploss, single under spring............................**75.00**
Ideal, claw type, gopher trap..**525.00**
Intruder, gray plastic, mousetrap....................................**12.00**
Jackfrost, Never Lose #1, coil spring................................**40.00**
JVJ, Crete NB, gopher trap..**45.00**
Ketchum, tile trap...**45.00**
Kliflock, #1 killer..**40.00**
Kompakt, #0, under spring..**25.00**
Kriket, #1, single under spring.......................................**12.00**
Lastword, wood snap, mousetrap.....................................**20.00**
LicLure, metal snap, rat trap..**20.00**
Little Champ, 1-hole wht plastic choker, mousetrap **50.00**
Lomar, #3, coil spring..**35.00**
Macabee, gopher trap...**20.00**
Montgomery, #1½, dbl long spring.................................**10.00**
Montgomery, #2, butterfly pan.......................................**80.00**
Montgomery Digger, #2, dbl coil spring...........................**250.00**
Mouse House, cb live trap...**20.00**
Murry Hill, wood snap, rat trap......................................**35.00**
Muscatine, L-shape, wood, killer.....................................**25.00**
Nash, choker type, mole trap...**15.00**
Nelson Boode, Trailsend #5, long spring..........................**450.00**
Nesbit, #4, dbl long spring...**1,100.00**
Newhouse, #150, bear trap...**550.00**
Newhouse #4, dbl long spring..**35.00**
Nox, wood snap, mousetrap...**15.00**
Oneida, #14, w/teeth, under spring.................................**14.00**

Oneida, #3, dbl under spring......................................45.00
Out-O-Sight, wood snap, mousetrap.........................20.00
P-S-&-W, #0, cast pan, long spring...........................45.00
Pat Trap, Detroit Mich, tin box, mousetrap 38.00
Pioneer, #3, single long spring.................................8.00
Prott, #1¼, jumper, single long spring.....................40.00
PS Mfg Co, #2, dbl long spring...............................35.00
Rentokil, trap ease, plastic live mousetrap................15.00
Rival, Joliette Ill, wood snap, rat trap......................20.00
Roy, mole trap...20.00
Runway, tin, mousetrap..40.00
Sargent, #12, single long spring 45.00
Sargent, #24, dbl long spring 125.00
Snappy, metal, mousetrap.......................................25.00
Stephens Snow Trap, #2.......................................575.00
Sure Catch, wood & screen, roach trap.....................55.00
Sure Shot, mousetrap, fits on fruit jar......................35.00
Tornado, wood snap, rat trap..................................40.00
Triumph, #34X, master grip, coil spring 445.00
Triumph, #4 Kangaroo, coil....................................25.00
Unique, glass, fly trap 85.00
Victor, #0, long spring..7.00
Webley, 31, Disheye, springs 22.00
White House, wood snap, mousetrap.........................18.00

Trenton

Trenton, New Jersey, was an area that supported several pottery companies from the mid-1800s until the late 1960s. A consolidation of several smaller companies that occurred in the 1890s was called Trenton Potteries Company. Each company produced their own types of wares independent of the others.

Blade bank, HP English horseman on wht, wall hanging, 2½x1½" 125.00
Cup & saucer, NJ Battle Field of Revolution 1775-1875, Glasgow mk ...175.00
Vase, bl gloss, shouldered, mk, 12", from $185 to 200.00
Vase, bl gloss, spherical, 3 emb lines at center, 7x9"....................160.00
Vase, bl matt, hdls, 8x9½" 415.00
Vase, burgundy, TAC in circle mk, 10" 145.00
Vase, burgundy, 3 stepped circles design, mk Pat Pend, 9" dia.......98.00
Vase, gr, shouldered, flared rim, TEPECO mk, 12½"....................250.00
Vase, ivory/tan gloss, urn form, 6" 155.00
Vase, lt brn, 1940s, 8½x9" 200.00
Vase, wht gloss, Deco style, 10½x6¼x2¾"..................................65.00

Trivets

Although strictly a decorative item today, the original purpose of the trivet was much more practical. They were used to protect table tops from hot serving dishes, and irons heated on the kitchen range were placed on trivets during use to protect work surfaces. The first patent date was 1869; many of the earliest trivets bore portraits of famous people or patriotic designs. Florals, birds, animals, and fruit were other favored motifs. Watch for remakes of early original designs. Some of these are marked Wilton, Emig, Wright, Iron Art, and V.M. for Virginia Metalcrafters. However, many of these reproductions are becoming collectible. Expect to pay considerably less for these than for the originals, since they are abundant.

Brass

Horseshoe w/1888 in center, w/hdl...................................95.00

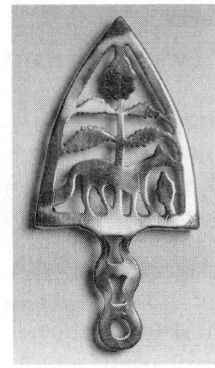

Fox and tree on sadiron shape, highly polished, 7¼x4x1", $135.00.

Kings Arms Trivet, 2 lions/unicorn, Metalcrafters, c 1953, 6".......45.00
Odd Fellows, heart in hand, 4 ft, 8½x5½".............................155.00
Rosette, ca 1900, 8½x3½"...50.00
Rtcl w/gallery, trn hdl, 14"...275.00
Spade shape w/hearts & dmn cutouts, 10"..............................110.00
Tripod base w/Queen Anne snake ft, mid-18th C, 13" H...........165.00

Cast Iron

Almond shape, circled rosette, NP, 7¼x3¾ 28.00
Geo Washington bust, shield shape, 9½" 75.00
Good Luck to All Who Use This Stand, 6-point star, 8x4¾".......40.00
Horseshoe shape, 1886 in lg numerals, ¾x9x4⅜" 45.00
Jenny Lind, 10"...165.00
LaClede, shield shape, 6x4"...50.00
Odd Fellows, heart in hand, 4 ft, 8½x5½.................................90.00
Texas star, 11x4½"...50.00

Wrought Iron

Circles & crescent incisings, scroll ft, 5⅛" dia.......................165.00
Curled scroll ft, 2½x9½x6½"..55.00
Heart, 19th C, 1¼x5¾x3¾" 175.00
Rnd, 3-leg, 18th C, 3x6" dia, +6" hdl....................................90.00
Shield shape w/cross in center, scrolled heart finial, 9" L.........360.00
Shield shape w/3 undulating iron bands, 1¾x4⅜x10".............120.00

Tuthill

The Tuthill Glass Company operated in Middletown, New York, from 1902 to 1923. Collectors look for signed pieces and those in an identifiable pattern. Condition is of utmost importance, and examples with brilliant cutting and intaglio (natural flowers and fruits) combined fetch the highest prices.

Bottle, scent; Primrose, shouldered, prism stopper, 4½x3" 315.00
Bowl, Tuthill Rex, 3x8" 1,700.00
Bowl, Vintage, 4x8", NM..700.00
Compote, Vintage, rolled rim, 4½x8½" 775.00
Creamer & sugar bowl, etched floral band, cut base, pr 225.00
Creamer & sugar bowl, Primrose w/cut geometrics, pr...............335.00
Pitcher, lemonade; Vintage, 7¾x5¾" 525.00
Pitcher, milk; dmns/hobstars/fans/scallops, 3-notch hdl, 8¾".....915.00
Plate, Vintage, hobstars at galleried rim, 1½x9¾" 475.00
Toothpick holder, Primrose, ftd, 2¼x1¾" 235.00
Tray, Hobstar, Prism, Fan & X-hatching, 14x8" 225.00
Vase, bud; floral eng, very slim, flared ft, 12" 160.00
Vase, floral eng, brilliant cuttings, cylindrical, 12x4" 300.00
Vase, floral eng, Hobstar & Star in bottom, 10x4¼" 275.00
Vase, Primrose, 3 vertical panels, frosted bull's-eyes, 10x4½".....250.00

Twin Winton

Twin brothers Don and Ross Winton started this California-based company during the mid-1930s while still in high school. In the mid-1940s they shut it down while in the armed forces and started up again in the late 1940s, when older brother Bruce Winton joined them and bought them out in the early 1950s. The company became a major producer of cookie jars, kitchenware, and household items sold nationally until it closed its San Juan Capistrano location in 1977.

Beside their extensive line of very collectible cookie jars, they're also well known for their Hillbilly line — mugs, pitchers, bowls, lamps, ashtrays, decanters, and other novelty items, which evolved from the late 1940s through the early 1970s with a variety of decorating methods still being discovered. Don Winton was the only designer for Twin Winton and created literally thousands of designs for them and hundreds of other companies. He is still sculpting in Corona del Mar, California, and collectors and dealers are continuing to find and document new pieces daily. To learn more about this subject, we recommend *Collector's Guide to Don Winton Designs* (Collector Books) by our advisor, Mike Ellis; he is listed in the Directory under California or visit the collector club website at www.twinwinton.com.

Bank, Elf, #408, 8"..50.00
Bank, Kitten, #415, 8"...50.00
Bank, Pirate Fox, #414, 8"...65.00
Bank, Ranger Bear, #404, 8"..50.00
Bank, Volkswagen, 5x8½"..125.00
Bank, Woolly Mammoth, 5"...125.00
Bowl, salad; Artist Palette Line, rare, 13" dia, minimum value...250.00
Candle holder, Strauss (short), #502S, 4½x6".....................12.00
Candy jar, Nut, squirrel finial, #353, 8x9".........................75.00
Candy jar, Sailor Elephant, #356, 6x9"..............................65.00
Candy jar, Turtle, #350, 8x10"...85.00
Canister, Coffee House, #103, 4x8"...................................75.00
Canister, Sugar Bucket, #61, 6x7"....................................40.00
Canister, Sugar Dairy, #112, 4x8"....................................55.00
Cocktail napkin holder, Rabbit, #452, 6x4".......................150.00
Cookie jar, Bambi, w/squirrel finial, #54, 8x10".................125.00
Cookie jar, Barrel, mouse finial, #62, 7½x9".......................75.00
Cookie jar, Cable Car, #98, 7x12"....................................75.00
Cookie jar, Cookie Barn, Collector Series, #241, 8x12".........150.00
Cookie jar, Cookie Coach, #99, 9x11"..............................200.00
Cookie jar, Cookie Elf, #59, 8½x12"..................................65.00
Cookie jar, Cow, #69, 8½x13½"...75.00
Cookie jar, Donkey, #88, 8x13"...65.00
Cookie jar, Duckling, #93, 8x11".....................................250.00
Cookie jar, Elf Bakery, elf finial, #50, 8¾x12"......................75.00
Cookie jar, Fire Engine, #56, 7x12"...................................85.00
Cookie jar, Grandma, #58, 7x10".....................................200.00
Cookie jar, Gunfighter Rabbit, #87, 8x13"...........................75.00
Cookie jar, Happy Bull, sitting, #95, 8½x12"........................75.00
Cookie jar, Hen on Basket, #61, ½x8½"..............................100.00
Cookie jar, Kangaroo, #99, 7½x13"...................................250.00
Cookie jar, Little Lamb, #66, 8x13"....................................40.00
Cookie jar, Modern Head, #98, 8x13"................................400.00
Cookie jar, Mother Goose, Collector Series, #275, 7x14".......225.00
Cookie jar, Pirate Fox, #46, 8½x11"...................................75.00
Cookie jar, Porky Pig, #76, 7½x12"....................................85.00
Cookie jar, Raccoon, #92, 8x11½".....................................50.00
Cookie jar, Sailor Elephant, #86, 9½x12"............................40.00
Cookie jar, Sailor Mouse, #63, 7x12".................................50.00
Cookie jar, Snail, w/elf on bk, #37, 7½x12".........................200.00
Cookie jar, Tugboat, #43, 7x12"......................................350.00

Creamer, Artist Palette line, 4" dia...................................40.00
Decanter, Frenchman, mk, 12x4"....................................100.00
Decanter, Robin Hood, mk, 10½x4⅜"................................100.00
Decanter, Southern Colonel, mk, 11x4"............................100.00
Expanimals, Kitten, #126, 7½"..250.00
Figurine, angel playing flute, 4".......................................35.00
Figurine, Black boy football player, #T-10, 5½"...................100.00
Figurine, BooBoo Bear by stump, 4"..................................75.00
Figurine, boy shot-putting in Yale shirt, 3".........................150.00
Figurine, boy skier, 7"...225.00
Figurine, cat standing on hind legs, 3"...............................30.00
Figurine, chipmunk in top hat, 3"......................................70.00
Figurine, cowboy on stick-horse, arched logo, 5¼"...............200.00
Figurine, deer lying down, dtd 1940-43, 3x5".......................75.00
Figurine, elf in shoe, 6"...120.00
Figurine, elf on turtle, 5"..75.00
Figurine, football player & girl, 5x6"................................275.00
Figurine, girl playing in the sand, #T-12, Twinton, 3½".........150.00
Figurine, hunting dog, #601, 11".......................................85.00
Figurine, little girl playing w/teddy, 4"...............................35.00
Figurine, mare, #317, sitting, mini, 1"..................................7.00
Figurine, Mickey Mouse the Sorcerer, 8".............................150.00
Figurine, Pan sitting on stump, 6½"..................................100.00
Figurine, quarterback in gr jersey, arched logo, 4½"..............175.00
Figurine, Quick Draw McGraw, 7".....................................75.00
Figurine, rabbit, sitting, #301, mini, 2"................................9.00
Figurine, rabbit crouching by basket eating carrot, 5x8".........85.00
Figurine, rabbit w/cart, 7x10"..85.00
Figurine, Sam the Eagle, 12"..200.00
Figurine, skunk, sitting, #203, mini, ¾".................................5.00
Figurine, Snagglepuss, 6"...60.00
Figurine, Snoopy Bear bud vase, 3x4".................................65.00
Figurine, squirrel holding stomach, 2½x4"...........................30.00
Figurine, squirrel w/mallet, dtd 1940-43, 3x5"......................40.00
Figurine, Yogi Bear sitting on stump, 5"............................150.00
Ice bucket, Bottoms Up, #32, 7½x14"...............................150.00
Lamp, Hotei, #257, 12"..250.00
Lamp, Kitten, #258, 13"...250.00
Men of the Mountain, mug, #H-102, 5"................................30.00
Men of the Mountain, pitcher, #H-101, 7½"...........................85.00
Men of the Mountain, punch cup, #H-111, 3".........................15.00
Mug, Bamboo, 6"...20.00
Mug, Owl, #501, 3¼"...85.00
Mug, Wood Grain, rope & spur hdl, 4".................................40.00
Napkin holder, Dobbin, #487, 7x5"....................................65.00
Napkin holder, Lamb, #482, 7x5".......................................75.00
Napkin holder, Owl, #472, 7x5"...65.00
Plate, dinner; Wood Grain, 10"...20.00
Shakers, Artist Palette, 3½", pr...65.00
Shakers, Barn, #141, pr...40.00
Shakers, Bull, #195, pr..40.00
Shakers, Butler, #160, pr...80.00
Shakers, Cookie Pot, #158, pr...30.00

Shakers, Cow, wood stain with hand-painted details, $40.00 for the pair. (Photo courtesy Lee Garmon)

Shakers, Dobbin, #180, pr 45.00
Shakers, Dutch Girl, #147, pr 35.00
Shakers, Foo Dog, #151, pr 125.00
Shakers, Gunfighter Rabbit, #187, pr 45.00
Shakers, Hen, #161, pr 50.00
Shakers, Jack-in-the-Box, #148, pr 175.00
Shakers, Owl, #191, pr 30.00
Shakers, Shoe, #182, pr 50.00
Shakers, Tommy Turtle, #177, pr 75.00
Stein, Bamboo, 8" 35.00
Tumbler, Wood Grain, 4" 20.00
Tumbler, Wood Grain, 7" 40.00

Typewriters

The first commercially successful typewriter was the Sholes and Glidden, introduced in 1874. By 1882 other models appeared, and by the 1890s dozens were on the market. At the time of the First World War, the ranks of typewriter-makers thinned, and by the 1920s only a few survived.

Collectors informally divide typewriter history into the pioneering period, up to about 1890; the classic period, from 1890 to 1920; and the modern period, since 1920. There are two broad classifications of early typewriters 1) Keyboard machines, in which depression of a key prints a character and via a shift key prints up to three different characters per key 2) Index machines, in which a chart of all the characters appears on the typewriter; the character is selected by a pointer or dial and is printed by operation of a lever or other device. Even though index typewriters were simpler and more primitive than keyboard machines, they were none-the-less a later development, designed to provide a cheaper alternative to the standard keyboard models that were selling for upwards of $100.00. Eventually second-hand keyboard typewriters supplied the low-price customer, and index typewriters vanished except as toys. Both classes of typewriters appeared in a great many designs.

It is difficult, if not impossible, to assign standard market prices to early typewriters. During the past decade, competition from a handful of wealthy overseas collectors has drastically affected the American market, and prices have become inflated on the rarer models. Some auction-realized prices have been astronomical. It is predicted that the market will drop again when this small group of collectors is satisfied and this atypical activity subsides. For now, we have updated values to reflect current market activity. Also, condition is a very important factor, and typewriters can vary infinitely in condition. A third factor to consider is that an early typewriter achieves its value mainly through the skill, effort, and patience of the collector who restores it to its original condition, in which case its purchase price is insignificant. Some unusual-looking early typewriters are not at all rare or valuable, while some very ordinary-looking ones are scarce and could be quite valuable. No general rules apply.

For further information we recommend *Antique Typewriters & Office Collectibles* by Darryl Rehr (Collector Books). See Clubs, Newsletters, and Catalogs in the Directory for information on the Early Typewriter Collectors Association. When no condition is indicated, the items listed below are assumed to be in excellent, unrestored condition. Our advisor for this category is Mike Brooks; he is listed in the Directory under California.

Bennett, NY, 1908, leatherette hard cover, 11" L 300.00
Blickensderfer #6, aluminum, 1890s, EX, w/tools/oil/etc 265.00
Blinkensderfer #5, G in orig case 245.00
Blinkensderfer #7, EX in case 210.00
Densmore #5, orig pnt & pinstriping, EX orig 345.00
Draper, CI, made for Sears Roebuck, VG 325.00

Franklin #7, curved keyboard, Pat 1891, EX in case 475.00
Hall, NY model, index, 72 characters, Pat 1881, EX in walnut case ...525.00

Hall #1, curved front, 1881, $600.00. (Photo courtesy Mike Brooks)

Hall #8017, EX orig in oak case 450.00
Hammond #2, semicircular keyboard, 1883, EX 325.00
Klein-Adler #1, ca 1913, VG 185.00
LC Smith Corona, fine decals, EX orig 225.00
Merritt, index, Pat Pending (Pre 1890), VG+ 425.00
Mignon, multilingual, indicator type, ca 1904, EX in case 180.00
Mignon #3, 1913, VG in case 450.00
Molle #3, 1914, EX in case 300.00
New Yost #1, VG+ in wooden case 750.00
Odell #4, index, 1892 ....250.00
Perkins Braille, w/manual/braille alphabet/etc, NM 265.00
Postal #5, 1902 ....225.00
Royal #1, NM in case 155.00
Royal Quiet Deluxe, portable, 1948-49, NM 215.00
Simplex, 1892 ....215.00
Smith Premier #10A, EX finish & NP, w/case 245.00
Victor #2, silver front decals, VG 235.00
Victor #3, 1909, EX 175.00

Uhl Pottery

Founded in Evansville, Indiana, in 1849 by German immigrants, the Uhl Pottery was moved to Huntingburg, Indiana, in 1908 because of the more suitable clay available there. They produced stoneware — Acorn Ware jugs, crocks, and bowls — which were marked with the acorn logo and 'Uhl Pottery.' They also made mugs, pitchers, and vases in simple shapes and solid glazes marked with a circular ink stamp containing the name of the pottery and 'Huntingburg, Indiana.' The pottery closed in the mid-1940s. Those seeking additional information about Uhl pottery are encouraged to contact the Uhl Collectors' Society, whose address is listed in the Directory under Clubs, Newsletters, and Catalogs.

Ashtray, Acorn, blk 210.00
Bank, Army tank, brn 750.00
Bank, pig figural, wht, sm 210.00
Beanpot, dk brn w/tan int, 3" 65.00
Churn, w/lid, 3-gal 80.00
Cooler, polar bear, blk & gr, 2-gal 230.00
Disc, Uhl logo, brn 220.00
Jug, Cumberland Falls, brn & wht, bellied, dbl hdls 200.00
Jug, Greetings From Uhl Pottery, brn & wht, ca 1938 ....360.00
Jug, polar bear, bl, missings stopper 300.00
Jug, shoulder; Dalton Ohio 1932, brn & wht 350.00
Mug, Compliments of Meyer & Dunzinger, bbl, mini 175.00
Pitcher, bl, lg, NM 500.00
Pitcher, bl & wht spongeware, 1-gal 500.00

Pitcher, Christmas 1943 ....1,100.00
Pitcher, Grape, bl, 5½" 130.00
Pitcher, Hill-Top Gift Shop...KY, pk, mini 145.00
Shoe, military boot, bl, mini 100.00
Shoes, baby's, bl, mini, pr 250.00

Unger Brothers

Art Nouveau silver items of the highest quality were produced by Unger Brothers, who operated in Newark, New Jersey, from the early 1880s until 1909. In addition to tableware, they also made brushes, mirrors, powder boxes, and the like for milady's dressing table as well as jewelry and small personal accessories such as match safes and flasks. They often marked their products with a circle seal containing an intertwined 'UB' and '925 fine sterling.' In addition to sterling, a very limited amount of gold was also used. Note: This company made no pewter items; Unger designs may occasionally be found in pewter, but these are copies. Items dated in the mark or signed 'Birmingham' are English (not Unger).

Ashtray, man-in-moon smoking pipe, profile of lady in curling smoke, 4x6⅞", $775.00.

Brooch, flowers, lily pads & lady's profile, ca 1905, 1¼" W 255.00
Brooch, lady w/flowing hair, ca 1904, ⅞" dia 125.00
Brooch, veiled head of lady in plumed hat, att, 2⅜" 925.00
Brooch, 4 faces of woman w/flowing hair, ca 1900, 2⅛x1⅝" 415.00
Brush & mirror, Nouveau lady w/flowing hair, mk, 1903, 9½", 10¼" ..325.00
Buckle, mermaid & sea creature, 1⅜x1½" 285.00
Carving set, ornate repousse, knife+fork+steel, 1900s 165.00
Flask, man in moon smoking pipe & Nouveau lady, faint mk 625.00
Jar, dresser; Love's Dream, 3½x3¾" 350.00
Lorgnette, floral decor, ca 1904, 5½", w/chain 555.00
Match safe, Nouveau lady, 2¾x1⅝" 145.00
Match safe, sea horses & fish, roaring monster at top, 2½" 515.00
Mirror, hand; ornate emb decor, ca 1889-90, 5" dia, 9½" L 315.00
Nail buffer, lady w/flowing hair & flowers, 1¾x4¼" 120.00
Pen holder, hinged, w/pen, eng name, Nouveau filigree, 4½" L..140.00

Universal

Universal Potteries Incorporated operated in Cambridge, Ohio, from 1934 to 1956. Many lines of dinnerware and kitchen items were produced in both earthenware and semiporcelain. In 1956 the emphasis was shifted to the manufacture of floor and wall tiles, and the name was changed to the Oxford Tile Company, Division of Universal Potteries. The plant closed in 1976. Our advisor for this category is Ted Haun; he is listed in the Directory under Indiana.

Baby's Breath, bowl, cereal; lug hdld, 6⅞" 15.00
Baby's Breath, plate, bread & butter 12.00
Ballerina, bowl, fruit 7.00
Ballerina, bowl, vegetable 35.00

Ballerina, cake plate 25.00
Ballerina, cup 10.00
Ballerina, plate, bread & butter 8.00
Ballerina (Mist), creamer 25.00
Ballerina (Mist), plate, chop; tab hdld 25.00
Ballerina (Mist), plate, dinner 18.00
Ballerina (Mist), platter, rnd 25.00
Ballerina (Mist), shakers, pr 20.00
Ballerina (Mist), sugar bowl, w/lid 35.00
Bittersweet, bowl, mixing; lg 20.00
Bittersweet, bowl, mixing; sm 30.00
Bittersweet, bowl, vegetable; open, rnd 45.00
Calico Fruit, creamer 11.00
Cattail, bowl, fruit/dessert 10.00
Cattail, bowl, vegetable; w/lid 30.00
Cattail, cake plate, Mt Vernon 25.00
Cattail, cake tray & cover, 10½x5¾" 50.00
Cattail, cup & saucer 12.00
Cattail, plate, luncheon 14.00
Cattail, platter, med, 13½" 30.00
Circus, platter, 13½" 25.00
Circus, saucer 3.00
Harvest, bowl, fruit/dessert 10.00
Harvest, cup & saucer 19.00
Harvest, pitcher 23.00
Highland, bowl, cereal 11.00
Highland, gravy boat 35.00
Highland, plate, dinner 12.00
Highland, plate, salad 10.00
Iris, creamer, 4½" 25.00
Iris, pie plate, 10" 38.00
Laurella (Coral), bowl, vegetable; open 19.00
Rose Bouquet, pie server 20.00
Woodvine, cup & saucer 8.00
Woodvine, pitcher, milk; 6½" 35.00

Val St. Lambert

Since its inception in Belgium at the turn of the nineteenth century, the Val St. Lambert Cristalleries has been involved in the production of high-quality glass, producing some cameo. The factory is still in production.

Punch bowl, ruby cut to clear, faceted circles and panels, 7¼x12", $450.00.

Cameo

Box, wisteria, lav/clear/frost, faceted finial, 1920s, 3¾x6½" 865.00
Box, wisteria vines, lav/frost, faceted finial, 1920s, 4x9" dia 975.00
Vase, elderberry plants, amethyst to clear, stick neck, 10" 800.00
Vase, irises, purple to wht frost, baluster, 16½" 1,850.00
Vase, roses, cobalt to clear w/gold geometrics, cylindrical, 10"....500.00

Valentines

It is time to address the big 'Internet' question. Yes, prices have changed dramatically since the auctions have become a reality on the web. Some values have gone down and the good news is some values have skyrocketed. The Internet has helped to validate the scarcity of some cards, i.e., Wonder Woman, Cracker Jack valentines, etc. The Internet cannot be ignored when putting values on your cards. The seven specifications still apply: age, category, size, manufacturer, artist signature, condition, and location.

Please note: When counting the dimensions on a card, the background is included in the count. Our advisor for this category is Katherine Kreider, author of *Valentines With Values*, *One Hundred Years of Valentines*, and *Valentines For the Eclectic Collector*. She is listed in the Directory under Pennsylvania.

Key:
dim — dimension/dimensional   HCPP — honeycomb paper puff
mech — mechanical

Dim, 1D, car, emb, PIG, early 1900s, 7x6x1½", EX........................**50.00**
Dim, 2D, African Am children/blk board, Tuck, 1900s, 5¼x6x½", EX...**50.00**
Dim, 2D, big-eyed child in front of castle, 6x3x2½", EX................**45.00**
Dim, 2D, child bringing basket of flowers, 7x4x2½", EX...............**35.00**
Dim, 2D, Longhorn steer, PIG, 5½x3x½", EX............................**35.00**
Dim, 3D, bicycle motif, PIG, 1920s, 7x4x3, EX.............................**125.00**
Dim, 3D, carousel, 1950s, Am Greetings/Italy, 8x10x4", EX.........**35.00**
Dim, 3D, costumed couples, PIG, early 1900s, 6x4x2", EX **45.00**

Dimensional, 3D, daffodils, air brushed, printed in Germany, chromolitho die-cut scraps, early 1900s, 9x7½x3½", EX, $175.00. (Photo courtesy Katherine Kreider)

Dim, 4D, boy w/wheelbarrow, PIG, early 1900s, 8x4x3", EX.........**55.00**
Flat, Art Deco Father card, 1920s 4x6", EX **15.00**
Flat, Buster Brown, heart shape, Outcault, Tuck, ca 1900, 8x8½"..**75.00**
Flat, Knight of Carnation, Nister, early 1900s, 5x4", EX **30.00**
Flat, Navy cat, Germany, early 1900s, 6x3", EX.............................**35.00**
Flat, Picketer, USA, 1950s, 4½x2", EX **5.00**
Flat, postcard type, message on bk, emb, late 1800s, 5x4", EX **15.00**
Flat, roadster, emb, air brushed, 1920s, 5x9", EX **75.00**
Flat, Russian officer, USA, 1940s, 6x5", EX **10.00**
Flat, Victorian Lady series, Nister, early 1900s, 4x2", EX **30.00**
Folded flat, hanging heart, train motif, Tuck, 8x8", EX...............**150.00**
Folded flat, magic, 1940s, 5x6", EX...**10.00**
Folded flat, vanity dresser, 1940s, 6x3½", EX................................**10.00**
Folded flat, walnut & nutcracker, 1940s, 5x3½", EX.....................**15.00**
Greeting card, Art Deco, for girlfriend, 6x5½", EX **15.00**
Greeting card, booklet, A Note of Joy, 1800s, 8x3½", EX..............**35.00**
Greeting card, fan, Rust Craft, 1930s, 6x8½", EX..........................**35.00**
Greeting card, fringed, Prang, late 1800s, 6x4½", EX....................**35.00**
Greeting card, Gibson Girl, Gibson Art Co, 7½x4", EX..................**45.00**

Greeting card, poppies, emb paper lace, cat, early 1900s, 6x5", EX...**15.00**
Greeting card, real photo, goat, emb, 5x3¾", EX **25.00**
HCPP, airplane motif, 1920s, 5¾x5x2", EX **50.00**
HCPP, big-eyed kid, tea party, PIG, ca 1920s, 7½x6x3", EX.........**75.00**
HCPP, dirigible, Los Angeles, PIG, 1920s, 8x13x3¾", EX..........**350.00**
HCPP, emb alligator brief case, PIG, ca 1920s, 4½x3x2", EX......**40.00**
HCPP, Persian cat motif, early 1900s, 8x3½x3", EX.......................**50.00**
Hold-to-light, cherubs, 5D, chromolitho, PIG, ca 1900, 8x4½x3"...**250.00**
Hold-to-light, gazebo, 6D, PIG, 1920s, 10½x12x4", EX...............**250.00**
Hold-to-light, mini hand-holding motif, early 1900s, 2D, 5x3x3", EX...**35.00**
Mech-flat, cherub climbing up to damsel, PIG, ca 1883, 5x3", EX **50.00**
Mech-flat, child sitting in heart-shaped wreath, HB, 1900s, 4x3", EX ...**25.00**
Mech-flat, crying baby, PIG, early 1900s, 6½x6", EX....................**35.00**
Mech-flat, delivery man, Edwin Boese, USA, 7x4", EX **45.00**
Mech-flat, drummer, Edwin Boese, USA, 7x4", EX **45.00**
Mech-flat, parrot, HB w/easel back, Gabrielle, 7x5", EX..............**45.00**
Novelty, banjo, Proxylin, early 1900s, 19x8½x2", EX **500.00**
Novelty, bank of true love, eng litho, 1850s, 7x3", EX................**350.00**
Novelty, bookmark, wood, cameo emb paper, 7x2½" **250.00**
Novelty, button boy, easel bk, 1920s, 3½x3½", EX......................**25.00**
Novelty, cob web valentine, Burke, 1840s, 10x8", EX................**350.00**
Novelty, elephant w/metal cymbals, PIG, 7x3¾", EX..................**45.00**
Novelty, full brush, toilet water, tennis player, USA, 5x2", EX.....**75.00**

Vallerysthal

Fine glassware has been produced in Vallerysthal, France, since the middle of the nineteenth century.

Candle holder, pk, beading on tapered stem & rim, 9".................**65.00**
Hand vase, milk glass w/HP mc flowers & gold, 6x2"...................**85.00**
Plate, amber w/emb florals & scrolls, 8½" **50.00**
Vase, orchids cameo, mc on frost, appl raindrops on stick neck, 13"...**3,500.00**

Van Briggle

The Van Briggle Pottery of Colorado Springs, Colorado, was established in 1901 by Artus Van Briggle, whose early career had been shaped by such notables as Karl Langenbeck and Maria Nichols Storer. His quest for several years had been to perfect a completely flat matt glaze, and upon accomplishing his goal, he opened his pottery. His wife, Anne, worked with him, and they, along with George Young, were responsible for the modeling of the wares. Their work typified the flow and form of the Art Nouveau movement, and the shapes they designed played as important a part in their success as their glazes. Some of their most famous pieces were Despondency, Lorelei, and Toast Cup. Increasing demand for their work soon made it necessary to add to their quarters as well as their staff. Although much of the ware was eventually made from molds, each piece was carefully trimmed and refined before the glaze was sprayed on. Their most popular colors were Persian Rose, Ming Blue, and Mustard Yellow.

Van Briggle died in 1904, but the work was continued by his wife. New facilities were built; and by 1908, in addition to their artware, tiles, gardenware, and commercial lines were added. By the '20s the emphasis had shifted from art pottery to novelties and commercial wares. Reproductions of some of the early designs continue to be made. The double AA mark has always been in use, but after 1920 the dates and/or shape numbers were dropped. Mention should be made here as well that the Anna Van Briggle glaze is a later line which was made between 1956 and 1968. Our advisor for this category is Michelle Ross; she is listed in the Directory under Michigan.

Bookends, lamb, bl/burgundy, post-1930s, 5", pr.........................**300.00**

Bottle, morning glory, frothy chartreuse matt, #208, 1904, 11¾"...**2,000.00**

Bowl, gr matt, 1907-12, 6½"...**190.00**

Bowl, lt turq matt, #50B, 1905, 3x6"...**800.00**

Bowl vase, leaves, gr/brn, low closed form, 1915, 6" W...............**700.00**

Bowl vase, leaves at shoulder, 2-tone bl, 1918, 10" W.................**900.00**

Figurine, dog, recumbent, bl/aqua, post-1930s, 5"......................**100.00**

Figurine, donkey, bl/aqua, post-1930s, 4"......................................**60.00**

Figurine, elephant, bl/aqua, post-1930s, 2½"..............................**120.00**

Leaf dish, Anna Van Briggle...**40.00**

Paperweight, horned toad, gr on mustard base, 1913, 1½x4¾"..**1,300.00**

Pitcher, Persian Rose, waisted, 8¾"...**175.00**

Pitcher (10") & 6 mugs, Anna Van Briggle **175.00**

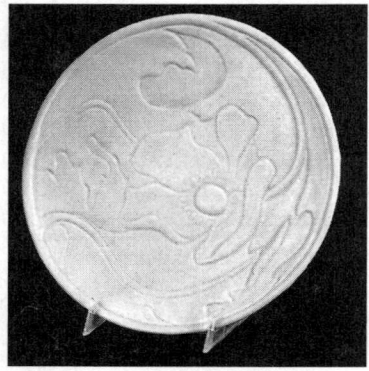

Plate, incised poppies on bright green, marked AA/Van Briggle/1902/III, 8½", $1,400.00.

Vase, Am Indian heads (3), gr/brn, ca 1920-30, 11"....................**550.00**

Vase, brn, spherical, #200, 1908, 6"..**485.00**

Vase, brn/gr (leathery), bottle form, #A320, 1905, 5½x2¾".......**650.00**

Vase, bud; floral, bl/burgundy, post-1930s, 7" **80.00**

Vase, bud; high gloss, Anna Van Briggle, 6"..................................**55.00**

Vase, buds & stems, brn, 1915, 6"..**400.00**

Vase, butterflies, cobalt/turq, 1916, 7x6½"..................................**500.00**

Vase, butterflies, gr/red, 1908-11, 3¾x5".....................................**450.00**

Vase, conch shell, bl/aqua, post-1930s, 3½"...................................**40.00**

Vase, cornflowers, bl-gray/gr, 2 sm hdls, #49, 1903, 9½x7"......**4,000.00**

Vase, cornflowers, oatmeal brn, 1906, 8½x4½"...........................**2,600.00**

Vase, crocus, gr/pk, ovoid, #823, 1910, 5¼x3½"..........................**450.00**

Vase, daffodils, corseted, #120, 1920s, 9x4".................................**550.00**

Vase, daffodils, gr, #25/III, 1902, 10½", M...............................**21,000.00**

Vase, daffodils, Persian Rose, 1915, 10½x4¼"..............................**700.00**

Vase, Despondency, nude male atop vase, bl, post-1930s, 16½"....**1,500.00**

Vase, Despondency, nude male atop vase, gr, 1909, 13".........**19,000.00**

Vase, dk mulberry w/plum overspray, incised band, hdls, 7¼".....**225.00**

Vase, dragonflies, bl/red, post-1920s, 7".......................................**290.00**

Vase, dragonfly, turq, 7"...**280.00**

Vase, emb vertical ribs, frothy gray/pk, 1907-12, 7x3¾"..........**1,200.00**

Vase, floral, bl, post-1930s, 3"..**60.00**

Vase, floral, burgundy, post-1930s, 5¼"...**70.00**

Vase, floral, maroon/bl, 1920s, 9½"...**500.00**

Vase, floral, multi-tone bl, incurvate rim, slim, 1915-20, 7½" **425.00**

Vase, floral, multi-tone gr, 1907-12, 2½"......................................**750.00**

Vase, floral, multi-tone gr on lt yel clay, 1907-12, 4" **1,600.00**

Vase, floral, plum, #845, 1916, 4⅛x5¼", NM................................**400.00**

Vase, floral, purple/gray/gr, 1907-12, 4" **650.00**

Vase, floral, purple/maroon, #753, 1915, 10½" **950.00**

Vase, floral (long stems), gr/bl/brn, spherical, 1915, 4"..............**450.00**

Vase, gr, low broad form, ca 1905, 5½" W **800.00**

Vase, gr (leathery), ovoid, 1903, 11x3¾"...................................**2,300.00**

Vase, gr to tobacco, low hdls, #242/V, 1904, 5" **1,000.00**

Vase, gr w/brn clay showing, tapered, 1905, 5½" **700.00**

Vase, gr/burgundy w/melt fissures, sm hdls, #224, 1904, 11" **2,200.00**

Vase, gray/lav (leathery), #339, 1905, 4½x5¼" **1,100.00**

Vase, jonquils, pk (leathery), #367, 1906, drilled, 9¼x4¼" **2,100.00**

Vase, Lady of the Lily figural, brn/gr, 1930s, 11x9½" **1,900.00**

Vase, lady slippers, bl/purple/gr marbleized, 1914, 9½x4", NM.**1,100.00**

Vase, lav, classic form, 1905, 8½x3½"..**1,500.00**

Vase, leaf, gr/tan, 1930s, 4½"...**160.00**

Vase, leaves, bl-gr, bulbous, 1908-11, 4¾x3¾".............................**475.00**

Vase, leaves, bl-gr, post-1930s, 5" **110.00**

Vase, leaves, copper clad, dk patina, #151, 1908-11, 4x4¾" **3,500.00**

Vase, leaves, maroon/bl, bulbous, 1920-30, 4½" **250.00**

Vase, leaves, tobacco/gr, 1918, 8" **450.00**

Vase, leaves (swirling), bl/burgundy, 1930s, 7½".........................**170.00**

Vase, leaves & vines, yel, III, 1903, 5½" W................................**1,500.00**

Vase, leaves w/swirling stems, gr, 1907, 3½x5"............................**550.00**

Vase, leaves/buds/stems, gr w/rose wash, #145/III, 1903, 4½" W.**3,750.00**

Vase, Lorelei, blk, post-1930s, 10½" **750.00**

Vase, Lorelei, Robin's Egg Blue, 1919, 9½x4", NM.................**2,300.00**

Vase, mistletoe, gr/pk, closed-in rim, 1906, 4½x10¾" **2,400.00**

Vase, mistletoe & berries, gr/mauve, #179, 1903, 2¾x2½"......**2,500.00**

Vase, mustard, #825, 1908-11, 5¾x3¾"...**700.00**

Vase, papyrus plants, gr/rose matt, 1916, 6½x4½", EX.............**1,900.00**

Vase, peacock feathers, olive gr/purple, cylindrical, #12, 1905, 13" ...**3,000.00**

Vase, popppies on whiplash stems, gr on dk brn clay, 1907, 4½".......**1,300.00**

Vase, poppy, 2-tone bl on brn clay, #20, 1920, 7½".....................**475.00**

Vase, poppy pods, gr-blk, #24, 1902, 4¼x3"..............................**4,250.00**

Vase, poppy pods, purple, #18, 1903, rstr, 9x6"........................**2,600.00**

Vase, Queen Anne's lace, maroon/bl, 1907-12, 10".................**1,500.00**

Vase, spade-shaped leaves, purple/bl-gray, #104V, 1904, 4½"...**1,600.00**

Vase, spade-shaped leaves & buds, brn/gr speckled, 1916, 7¼x3¾" **800.00**

Vase, trefoils, fine curdled brn, 1907-11, 3x3".............................**500.00**

Vase, tulips, dk maroon, invt rim, shouldered, mid-20th C, 10" .**260.00**

Vase, tulips, 2-tone bl crystalline, #736, 1907-12, 5½"...............**850.00**

Vase, tulips & leaves, multi-tone bl, 1915-20, 7½".......................**475.00**

Vase, turq (frothy), 1906, 4x6"...**450.00**

Vase, turq matt, classic shape, #269, 1906, 8x5½".......................**950.00**

Vase, turq matt, spherical, 1903, 3¾x4½".....................................**800.00**

Vase, twisted, 3-lobe top, bl/burgundy, 7"......................................**70.00**

Vase, vertical panels, burgundy, post-1920s, 5½" **90.00**

Vase, wheat sheaves, gr (leathery), trumpet form, 1905, 6x4" .**1,900.00**

Vase, yucca plants, lt gr (mottled), #139, 1906, 12¾x5½", NM...**2,000.00**

Vance/Avon Faience

Although pottery had been made in Tiltonville, Ohio, since about 1880, the ware manufactured there was of little significance until after the turn of the century when the Vance Faience Company was organized for the purpose of producing quality artware. By 1902 the name had been changed to the Avon Faience Company, and late in the same year, it and three other West Virginia potteries incorporated to form the Wheeling Potteries Company. The Avon branch operated in Tiltonville until 1905 when production was moved to Wheeling. Art pottery was discontinued.

From the beginning, only skilled craftsmen and trained engineers were hired. Wm. P. Jervis and Fredrick Hurten Rhead were among the notable artists responsible for designing some of the early artware. Some of the ware was slip decorated under glaze, while other pieces were molded with high-relief designs. Examples with squeeze-bag decoration by Rhead are obviously forerunners of the Jap Birdimal line he later developed for Weller. Ware was marked 'Vance F. Co.'; 'Avon F. Co., Tiltonville'; or 'Avon W. Pts. Co.'

Jardiniere, Nouveau flowers & trees, Rhead, #1014, 7⅞" **1,500.00**

Vase, buds/leaves, wht squeeze bag on dk bl, Rhead, 9"..............**500.00**

Vase, Nouveau trees on brn, Rhead, 4⅛".......................................**850.00**

Vase, stylized flowers, slip trailed/cvd, Avon, #166/#1005, 5¾" ..**475.00**
Vase, trees landscape, gr/brn on amber, #157, 11¼x4½".........**1,500.00**

Vaseline

Vaseline, a greenish-yellow colored glass produced by adding uranium oxide to the batch, was produced during the Victorian era. It was made in smaller quantities than other colors and lost much of its popularity with the advent of the electric light. It was used for pressed tablewares, vases, whimseys, souvenir items, oil lamps, perfume bottles, drawer pulls, and doorknobs. Pieces have been reproduced, and some factories still make it today in small batches. Vaseline glass will fluoresce under an ultraviolet light.

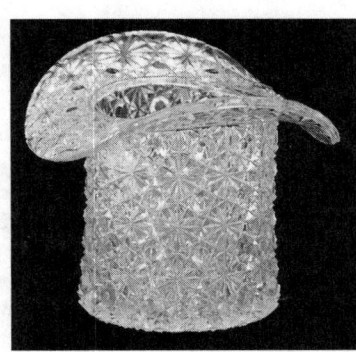

Vase, Daisy and Button top-hat form, 5", $35.00.

Bottle, scent; pressed, w/pointed stopper, 6¾" **200.00**
Bowl, invt rim w/stretch irid to int of rim, 1922, 11½" **115.00**
Candlestick, flint, Sandwich or NE Glass, 10½x5" **140.00**
Celery yacht, Daisy & Button, Hobbs & Brockunier, 2x14" **125.00**
Coaster, starfish form **30.00**
Egg cup, satin **35.00**
Mug, Cat & Dog...**35.00**
Sweetmeat, appl ruby loop edge, metal fr, 8x10"........................**125.00**
Tankard, Coin Spot, 3-strand air-twist hdl, Hobbs & Brockunier, 8½"...**500.00**
Toothpick holder, Hobnail, 10-row, pontil..................................**115.00**
Vase, swirl w/opal rice-like pattern, dimpled, ruffled, 4¾"............**95.00**
Wine, Rose, satin...**35.00**

Verlys

Verlys art glass, produced in France after 1931 by the Holophane Company of Verlys, was made in crystal with acid-finished relief work in the Art Deco style. Colored and opalescent glass was also used. In 1935 an American branch was opened in Newark, Ohio, where very similar wares were produced until the factory ceased production in 1951. French Verlys was signed with one of three mold-impressed script signatures, all containing the company name and country of origin. The American-made glassware was signed 'Verlys' only, either scratched with a diamond-tipped pen or impressed in the mold. There is very little if any difference in value between items produced in France and America. Though some seem to feel that the French should be higher priced (assuming it to be scarce), many prefer the American-made product.

In June of 1955, about sixteen Verlys molds were leased to the A.H. Heisey Company. Heisey's versions were not signed with the Verlys name, so if an item is unsigned it is almost certainly a Heisey piece. The molds were returned to Verlys of America in July 1957. Fenton now owns all Verlys molds, but all issues are marked Fenton.

Our advisor for this category is Don Frost; he is listed in the Directory under Washington.

Ashtray, Swallow, crystal etched, 4¾" **85.00**
Bonbon, serpentine, frosted, w/lid, 6½x4" **150.00**
Bookends, elephants, opaline, 4⅛x5¾", pr **425.00**
Bowl, Birds & Bees, Directoire Blue, 2¼x11⅝"...............................**350.00**
Bowl, Birds & Bees, frosted opal, 2x11¾" **425.00**
Bowl, Chrysanthemum, 6¼x10⅛"..**385.00**
Bowl, Cupid, clear frosted, 2x6"..**145.00**
Bowl, Pine Cone, opal...**225.00**
Bowl, Poissons (fish), crystal etched, 11¾x7⅞x19¼" **800.00**
Bowl, Poissons (fish), Directoire Blue opal, 11¾x7⅞x19¼"....**1,500.00**
Bowl, Thistle, topaz..**250.00**
Bowl, Wild Duck **175.00**
Bowl, 3 swallows amid bee swarm, opal, shallow, shaved rim, 11¾"..**230.00**
Box, Chrysanthemums, topaz, 5¼"..**375.00**
Figurine, pheasant, opaline, 18⅛" **500.00**
Figurine, pigeon, eating or pouting, frosted, 5⅛", ea **150.00**
Figurine, pigeon, preening, 4⅜"..**125.00**
Figurine, pigeon, relaxing, opaline, 4¼"..**200.00**
Vase, Alpine Thistle, opal, shouldered, 9" **625.00**
Vase, crested bird pr/berries leaves, bl, cylinder, 7¾"..................**450.00**
Vase, Dancer, flared, frosted, 7¾x6¼"..**300.00**
Vase, Eglantine, opal..**350.00**
Vase, Gems, amber, w/frog, 6½x5½" **350.00**
Vase, Lovebirds, clear frosted, w/sticker, 4½x6½".........................**225.00**
Vase, Lovebirds, flat-sided U-form, clear/frost, 5" **145.00**
Vase, Planets, frosted, 11½x11¾"...**350.00**
Vase, Seasons, wheat Autumn/dancer Spring, Schmitz, 8x5" ..**1,000.00**
Vase, Sirens, shouldered, frosted, 9¼x7¼" **325.00**
Vase, Sunflower, pk enamel, ovoid, 9" **375.00**
Vase, Thistle, fiery opal, mk, 9¾", NM **550.00**
Vase, Thistle, topaz, 9¾"..**450.00**

Vernon Kilns

Vernon Potteries Ltd. was established by Faye G. Bennison in Vernon, California, in 1931. The name was later changed to Vernon Kilns; until it closed in 1958, dinnerware, specialty plates, artware, and figurines were their primary products. Among its wares most sought after by collectors today are items designed by such famous artists as Rockwell Kent, Walt Disney, Don Blanding, Jane Bennison, and May and Vieve Hamilton. Our advisor is Maxine Nelson, author of *Collectible Vernon Kilns* (now out of print); you will find her listed in the Directory under Arizona.

Anytime Shape

Patterns you will find on this shape include Tickled Pink, Heavenly Days, Anytime, Imperial, Sherwood, Frolic, Young in Heart, Rose-A-Day, and Dis 'N Dot.

Bowl, chowder; 6", from $8 to...**10.00**
Bowl, vegetable; rnd, 7½", from $10 to **12.00**
Butter pat, ind, 2½", from $15 to...**18.00**
Casserole, w/lid, 8", from $25 to **40.00**
Creamer, from $7 to..**10.00**
Pitcher, 1-pt, from $15 to...**18.00**
Plate, salad; 7½", from $5 to **9.00**
Plate, snack; indent for tumbler, scarce, 12x8", from $35 to..........**40.00**
Platter, 11", from $12 to **18.00**
Relish dish, 3-part, from $20 to **25.00**

Teapot, w/lid, from $25 to **45.00**

Chatelaine Shape

This designer pattern by Sharon Merrill was made in four color combinations: Topaz, Bronze, decorated Platinum, and Jade.

Bowl, serving; Topaz & Bronze, 9", from $25 to **35.00**
Cup, coffee; flat base, decor Platinum & Jade, from $20 to **25.00**

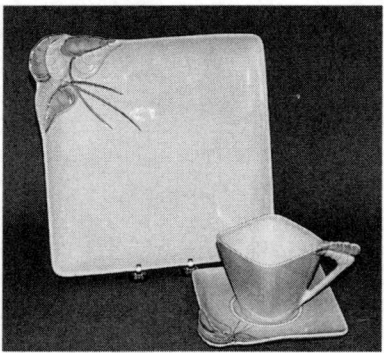

Dinner plate, decorated Jade, $25.00; Coffee cup (flat bottom) and saucer, decorated Jade, $25.00.

Plate, bread & butter; Topaz & Bronze, 6½", from $10 to **12.00**
Plate, chop; decor Platinum & Jade, 14", from $55 to **65.00**
Platter, Topaz & Bronze, 16", from $55 to **65.00**
Teapot, decor Platinum & Jade, w/lid, from $250 to **300.00**

Lotus and Pan American Lei Shape

Patterns on this shape include Lotus, Chinling, and Vintage. Pan American Lei was a variation with flatware from the San Marino line. To evaluate Lotus, use the low end of our range as the minimum value; the high end of values apply to Pan American Lei.

Ashtray, 5½", Pan American Lei only **45.00**
Bowl, fruit; 5½", from $7 to **12.00**
Bowl, mixing; Pan American Lei only, 9" **65.00**
Bowl, soup coupe; Pan American Lei only, 8½" **35.00**
Butter tray, oblong, w/lid, from $35 to......................................**75.00**
Casserole, w/lid, 8", from $35 to **85.00**
Mug, 9-oz, from $16 to **35.00**
Pepper mill, wooden cased, Pan American Lei only, 4½"..............**45.00**
Plate, coupe; Pan American Lei only, 7½" **25.00**
Plate, offset; Lotus only, 10½", from $12 to...............................**15.00**
Platter, coupe; Pan American Lei only, 13½" **65.00**
Sauce boat, from $18 to...**40.00**
Tumbler, style #5, 14-oz, from $18 to **35.00**

Melinda Shape

Patterns found on this shape are Arcadia, Beverly, Blossom Time, Chintz, Cosmos, Dolores, Fruitdale, Hawaii (Lei Lani on Melinda is two and a half times base value), May Flower, Monterey, Native California, and Philodendron. The more elaborate the pattern, the higher the value.

Bowl, fruit; 5½", from $6 to **8.00**
Bowl, rim soup; 8", from $12 to **18.00**
Butter tray, oblong, w/lid, from $35 to......................................**45.00**

Coffeepot, w/lid, 8-cup, from $35 to...**75.00**
Creamer, short or tall, from $12 to **20.00**
Egg cup, from $18 to...**25.00**
Jam jar, w/lid, from $55 to **65.00**
Pitcher, 2-qt, from $35 to **65.00**
Plate, dinner; 10½", from $12 to...**20.00**
Plate, salad; 7½", from $7 to **15.00**
Platter, 12", from $15 to **35.00**
Platter, 16", from $45 to **65.00**
Relish, leaf shape, 2-part, 11", from $30 to.................................**50.00**
Sauce boat, from $25 to **45.00**
Sugar bowl, short or tall, w/lid, from $15 to................................**25.00**
Teapot, w/lid, 6-cup, from $45 to..**75.00**

Montecito Shape (and Coronado)

This was one of the company's most utilized shapes — well over two hundred patterns have been documented. Among the most popular are the solid colors, plaids, the florals, westernware, and the Bird and Turnbull series. Bird, Turnbull, and Winchester 73 (Frontier Days) are two to four times base values. Disney hollow ware is seven to eight times base values. Plaids (except Tweed and Calico), solid colors, Brown-eyed Susan are represented by the lower range.

Ashtray, rnd, 5½", from $12 to **15.00**
Bowl, rim soup; 8½", from $12 to **15.00**
Butter pat, ind, 2½", from $20 to..**30.00**
Casserole, w/lid, ind, 4", from $20 to..**35.00**
Cup, custard; scarce, 3", from $20 to...**25.00**
Lemon server, center brass hdl, 6", from $20 to **25.00**
Pitcher, disk; plain or decor, 2-qt, from $45 to............................**75.00**
Plate, bread & butter; 6½", from $5 to **8.00**
Platter, 14", from $35 to **45.00**
Spoon holder, from $40 to **50.00**
Sugar bowl, angular, open, ind, from $18 to................................**20.00**
Teapot, angular or rnd, w/lid, from $45 to..................................**65.00**
Tidbit, 3-tier, wooden fixture, from $25 to..................................**40.00**

San Fernando Shape

Known patterns for this shape are Desert Bloom, Early Days, Hibiscus, R.F.D., Vernon's 1860, and Vernon Rose.

Bowl, fruit; 5½", from $8 to **10.00**
Bowl, mixing; RFD only, 6", from $19 to....................................**22.00**
Bowl, mixing; 8", RFD only, from $25 to....................................**30.00**
Bowl, rim soup; 8", from $12 to **20.00**
Bowl, serving; oval, 10", from $20 to...**25.00**
Casserole, w/lid, 8" (inside dia), from $35 to..............................**65.00**
Coaster, ridged, 3¾", RFD only, from $18 to...............................**22.00**
Creamer, regular, from $12 to...**15.00**
Egg cup, dbl; RFD only, from $15 to **20.00**
Lamp, kerosene; converted teapot, from $100 to **125.00**
Mug, 9-oz, RFD only, from $16 to..**22.00**
Olive dish, oval, 10", from $20 to..**35.00**
Plate, chop; 14", from $35 to **45.00**
Plate, salad; 7½", from $7 to **12.00**
Platter, 12", from $18 to **25.00**
Platter, 16", from $45 to **65.00**
Sauce boat, fast-stand, from $25 to..**45.00**
Spoon holder, RFD only, from $30 to **35.00**
Sugar bowl, w/lid, from $15 to **20.00**
Tumbler, style #5, 14-oz, RFD only, from $20 to **25.00**

San Marino Shape

Known patterns for this shape are Barkwood, Bel Air, California Originals, Casual California, Gayety, Hawaiian Coral, Heyday, Lei Lani (two and a half times base values), Mexicana, Pan American Lei (two and a half times base values), Raffia, Shadow Leaf, Shantung, Sun Garden, and Trade Winds.

Ashtray, 5½", from $15 to......................................20.00
Bowl, chowder; 6", from $9 to..............................12.00
Bowl, fruit; 5½", from $6 to...................................8.00
Bowl, mixing; 6", from $15 to...............................22.00
Bowl, mixing; 7", from $20 to...............................28.00
Bowl, mixing; 9", from $28 to...............................35.00
Bowl, salad; 10½", from $35 to..............................45.00
Bowl, serving; rnd, 9", from $15 to.......................20.00
Butter tray, oblong, w/lid, from $25 to..................40.00
Casserole, w/lid, ind, 4", from $15 to...................20.00
Coaster, ridged, 3¾", from $12 to.........................15.00
Creamer, regular, from $10 to...............................12.00
Custard, 3", from $18 to..22.00
Egg cup, dbl; from $15 to......................................18.00
Flowerpot, w/saucer, 3", from $30 to....................40.00
Flowerpot, w/saucer, 5", from $40 to....................50.00
Mug, 9-oz, from $15 to..20.00
Pitcher, 1-qt, from $20 to......................................25.00
Pitcher, 2-qt, from $30 to......................................35.00
Plate, bread & butter; 6", from $4 to......................7.00
Plate, chop; 13", from $18 to................................30.00
Plate, dinner; 10", from $12 to..............................15.00
Platter, 11", from $12 to..18.00
Platter, 13", from $15 to..25.00
Sauce boat, from $18 to..22.00
Spoon holder, from $30 to.....................................35.00
Teacup, from $8 to..12.00
Teapot, w/lid, 8-cup, 11" L, from $40 to................50.00
Tumbler, style #5, 14-oz, from $15 to...................22.00

Ultra Shape

More than fifty patterns were issued on this shape. Nearly all the artist-designed lines (Rockwell Kent, Don Blanding, and Disney) utilized Ultra. The shape was developed by Gale Turnbull, and many of the elaborate flower and fruit patterns can be credited to him as well; use the high end of our range as a minimum value for his work. For Frederick Lunning, use the mid range. For other artist patterns, use these formulae based on the high end: Blanding — 2X (Aquarium 3X); Disney, 7 – 8X; Kent — Moby Dick and Our America, 2½X, Salamina, 5 – 7X.

Bowl, cereal; 6", from $12 to................................20.00
Bowl, coupe soup; 7½", from $12 to.....................20.00
Bowl, mixing; 5", from $15 to...............................20.00
Bowl, mixing; 8", from $30 to...............................35.00
Comport, ftd, from $65 to.....................................85.00
Egg cup, from $15 to...20.00
Jam jar, notched lid, from $55 to...........................65.00
Jug, open, 1-pt, 4½", from $25 to..........................45.00
Mug, 8-oz, 3½", from $20 to..................................30.00
Pitcher, w/lid, 2-qt, from $65 to............................75.00
Plate, chop; 12", from $20 to................................50.00
Plate, chop; 17", from $45 to................................95.00
Plate, luncheon; 8½", from $12 to.........................20.00
Shakers, pr, from $15 to..25.00
Teacup, from $12 to..18.00

Teapot, 6-cup, from $45 to....................................75.00
Tureenette, notched lid, 7", from $65 to................95.00

Year 'Round Shape

Patterns on this shape include Country Cousin, Lollipop Tree, and Blueberry Hill.

Bowl, fruit; 5½", from $4 to....................................6.00
Butter tray, w/lid, from $25 to...............................35.00
Casserole, w/lid, 8", from $25 to...........................40.00
Creamer, from $7 to..12.00
Mug, 12-oz, from $12 to..20.00
Plate, dinner; 10", from $8 to................................12.00
Shakers, pr, from $12 to..18.00
Trio buffet server, from $50 to..............................70.00

Fantasia

Black Baby Pegasus #19, from $250 to.................400.00
Bowl, Winged Nymph, #122..................................350.00
Centaur #31, from $900 to................................1,200.00
Centaurrette #18, from $750 to...........................900.00
Donkey Unicorn #16, from $500 to.....................650.00
Pegasus #21, from $300 to...................................400.00
Shakers, Hippos, pr, from $400 to........................500.00
Vase, Winged Pegasus decor, #127, rare...........1,200.00

Souvenir Plates

Camino Real, 14"...40.00
Chicago IL, 10½"...16.00
Chinatown, San Francisco CA, 10½"...................17.50
Cocktail Hour Bicardi, 8½"..................................45.00
Florida, 10½"...12.00
Liszt, 8½"..25.00
St Louis Commemorative, Van Gelder, 1945, 10½"...12.50
Texas Foley's Store, mc, 10½".............................27.50
Williamsburg VA, mc, 10½".................................15.00

Vistosa

Vistosa was produced from about 1938 through the early 1940s. It was Taylor, Smith, and Taylor's answer to the very successful Fiesta line of their nearby competitor, Homer Laughlin. Vistosa was made in four solid colors: mango red, cobalt blue, light green, and deep yellow. 'Pie crust' edges and a dainty five-petal flower molded into handles and lid finials made for a very attractive yet nevertheless commercially unsuccessful product. For further information, we recommend *Collector's Guide to Lu-Ray Pastels* by Kathy and Bill Meehan (Collector Books). Our advisor for this category is Ted Haun; he is listed in the Directory under Indiana.

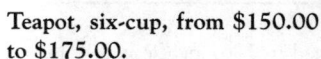
Teapot, six-cup, from $150.00 to $175.00.

Bowl, cream soup; from $20 to..............................25.00

Bowl, fruit; from $10 to **15.00**
Bowl, nappy; from $40 to **50.00**
Bowl, salad; ftd, 12", from $175 to..**200.00**
Bowl, soup; lug hdl, from $25 to **30.00**
Chop plate, 12"..**40.00**
Chop plate, 15", from $40 to..**50.00**
Coffee cup, AD; from $40 to...**50.00**
Coffee saucer, AD; from $20 to..**25.00**
Creamer...**20.00**
Egg cup, ftd, from $25 to...**35.00**
Jug water; 2-qt..**85.00**
Plate, 6", from $10 to...**15.00**
Plate, 7", from $12 to...**18.00**
Plate, 9", from $15 to...**20.00**
Plate, 10", from $50 to...**60.00**
Sauce boat, from $150 to **175.00**
Shakers, pr **32.00**
Sugar bowl, w/lid **25.00**
Teacup, from $10 to..**15.00**

Volkmar

Charles Volkmar established a workshop in Tremont, New York, in 1882. He produced artware decorated under the glaze in the manner of the early barbotine work done at the Haviland factory in Limoges, France. He relocated in 1888 in Menlo Park, New Jersey, and together with J.T. Smith established the Menlo Park Ceramic Company for the production of art tile. The partnership was dissolved in 1893. From 1895 until 1902, Volkmar located in Corona, New York, first under the name Volkmar Ceramic Company, later as Volkmar and Cory, and for the final six years as Crown Point. During the latter period he made art tile, blue under-glaze Delft-type wares, colorful polychrome vases, etc. The Volkmar Kilns were established in 1903 in Metuchen, New Jersey, by Volkmar and his son. Wares were marked with various devices consisting of the Volkmar name, initials, or 'Crown Point Ware.'

Bowl, centerpc; Persian Blue crackle, turq bl, 1928, 6½x13½"...**700.00**
Cider set, gr mottle w/mustard to brn int, 9" pitcher+4¾" mugs ...**600.00**
Vase, blk gunmetal, 8-sided, 4" **300.00**
Vase, dk gray to blk matt, 8-sided, 4", NM................................**200.00**
Vase, gr matt, bulbous, mk V, 5½" **225.00**

Vontury

Located in New Jersey, F.J. Von Tury is primarily a designer of architectural artware, tile, and murals in particular, but he also produces a line of vases, bowls, and other decorative items. These are signed 'Vontury' in script. Impressionistic florals are favored.

Bowl, chocolate matt w/frothy speckled int, 2¾x7½" **95.00**
Figurine, bird on fruited branch, HP mc, 1940s, 9¼" **185.00**
Tray, clover-leaf shape, misty bl w/HP decor, &"............................**50.00**

Wade

The Wade Potteries was established in 1867 by George Wade and his partner, a man by the name of Myatt. It was located in Burslem, England, the center of that country's pottery industry. In 1882 George Wade bought out his partner, and the name of the pottery was changed to Wade and Sons. In 1919 the pottery underwent yet another name change and became known as George Wade & Son Ltd. The year 1891

saw the establishment of another Wade Pottery — J & W Wade & Co., which in turn changed its name to A.J. Wade & Co. in 1927. At this time (1927) Wade Heath & Co. Ltd. was also formed.

The three potteries plus a new Irish pottery named Wade (Ireland) Ltd. were incorporated into one company in 1958 and given the name The Wade Group of Potteries. In 1990 the group was taken over by Beauford PLC. and became Wade Ceramics Ltd. It sold again in early 1999 to Wade Management and is now a private company.

For those interested in learning more about Wade pottery, we recommend *The World of Wade* and *The World of Wade Book 2* by Ian Warner and Mike Posgay; Mr. Warner is listed in the Directory under Canada.

Animal Figurine, Baby Panda, Geo Wade, 1930s **170.00**
Animal Figurine, Squirrel, Wade Heath from pre-war mold..........**95.00**
British Character, Lawyer, ca 1959, 2⅞" **250.00**
British Character, Pearly Queen, ca 1959, 3⅞"..........................**200.00**
Cat & Puppy Dishes, Alsatian Puppy, 1974-81 ....**25.00**
Cat & Puppy Dishes, Yorkshire Terrier Puppy, 1974-81................**40.00**
Circus Animal Set, Poodle, 1978-79, 1¾x⅝"................................**10.00**
Connoisseur's Collection, Kingfisher, 1980, 7" **375.00**
Disney, Copper, 1980s, 1⅝" **30.00**
Disney Blow-Up, Scamp, 1961-65, 4⅛x5" **230.00**

Disney Blow Up, Si, Siamese cat from 'Lady and the Tramp,' 1961 – 65, $250.00. (Photo courtesy Marbena 'Jean' Fyke)

Dogs & Puppies Series, Alsatian (adult), 1969-82, 2½" **25.00**
Dogs & Puppies Series, Corgi (puppy), 1969-82, 1⅝" **25.00**
Farmyard Set, Goose, 1982-83, 1⅜"...**8.00**
Hanna-Barbera Cartoon Character, Huckleberry Hound, 1959-60, 2⅜"...**125.00**
Hanna-Barbera Cartoon Character, Yogi Bear, 1959-60, 2½" **140.00**
Happy Families Series, Elephant (parent), 1978-86, 1¼" **18.00**
Happy Families Series, Giraffe (baby), 1978-86, ⅝" **15.00**
Happy Families Series, Kitten, 1978-86, 1⅜" **18.00**
Nursery Favourite, Old Woman (in Shoe), 1972-81, 2½"............**130.00**
Nursery Favourite, Willie Winkie, 1972-81, 1¾"..........................**28.00**
Nursery Rhyme Figurine, Goldilocks, 4" **300.00**
Nursery Rhyme Figurine, Thief, 3" **250.00**
Nursery Rhyme Figurine, Tinker, 2½" **250.00**
Red Rose Tea (Canada), Bluebird...**10.00**
Red Rose Tea (Canada), Kitten **8.00**
Red Rose Tea Promotion (USA), Pelican......................................**25.00**
Safari Set, Lion, 1976-77, 1⅛x1¾" **12.00**
Snow White & 7 Dwarfs, Bashful, 1981-86, 3¼" **180.00**
Snow White & 7 Dwarfs, Snow White, 1981-86, 3¾"..................**200.00**
Spirit Container, Baby Chick, ca 1961, 3⅜x2" dia **45.00**
Spirit Container, Cockatoo, 5x2½" dia.......................................**120.00**
Survival Set, Gorilla, 1984-85, 1½"...**10.00**
Whappas, Elephant, 1976-81, 2⅛" **25.00**
Whappas, Fox, 1976-81, 1¼x2½"...**40.00**
Whimsie, Bullfrog, 1978, ⅞x1" **20.00**
Whimsie, Crocodile, 1955, ¾x1⅝" **80.00**
Whimsie, Duck, 1972, 1¼x1½" **8.00**

Whimsie, Horse, 1953, 1½" **42.00**
Whimsie, Kitten, 1954, 1⅜" **50.00**
Whimsie - Land Series, Goat, 1985, 1¼" **20.00**
Whimsie - Land Series, Lion, 1984, 1¼" **16.00**
Whimsie - Land Series, Retriever, 1984, 1¼" **16.00**
Whoppas, Polar Bear, 1976-81, 1½" **25.00**
Wildlife Set, Partridge, 1980-81, 1⅛" **20.00**
World of Survival Series, Black Rhinoceros, 4½x9½" **450.00**

Wallace China

Dinnerware with a Western theme was produced by the Wallace China Company, who operated in California from 1931 until 1964. Artist Till Goodan designed three lines, Rodeo, Pioneer Trails, and Boots and Saddle, which they marketed under the package name Westward Ho. When dinnerware with a western theme became so popular just a few years ago, Rodeo was reproduced, but the new trademark includes neither 'California' or 'Wallace China.'

This ware is very heavy and not prone to chips, but be sure to examine it under a strong light to look for knife scratches, which will lessen its value to a considerable extent when excessive. Our advisor for this category is Marv Fogleman; he is listed in the Directory under California. If you'd like to learn more about this company, we recommend *The Collector's Encyclopedia of California Pottery* by Jack Chipman.

Banana Leaf, bowl, salad **35.00**
Boots & Saddle, ashtray, 5½", from $45 to.........................**50.00**
Boots & Saddle, pitcher, water **525.00**
Boots & Saddle, plate, chop; 13" **200.00**
Boots & Saddle, plate, dinner; 10½" **80.00**
Boots & Saddle, plate, luncheon; 9" **70.00**
Boots & Saddle, shakers, pr **125.00**
Chuck Wagon, bowl, dtd 1955, 6¾" **35.00**
Chuck Wagon, butter pat...**50.00**
Chuck Wagon, coffee cup..**72.50**
Chuck Wagon, cup & saucer..**75.00**
Chuck Wagon, plate, 9" **43.00**
El Rancho, bowl, 5" **45.00**
El Rancho, chop plate, 13½" **130.00**
El Rancho, cup & saucer **65.00**
El Rancho, plate, dinner; 10½" **100.00**
El Rancho, plate, 5½" **30.00**
Rodeo, ashtray, 5½", w/orig packing box...............................**100.00**
Rodeo, bowl, vegetable; oval, 12" **250.00**
Rodeo, creamer & sugar bowl, ind...**140.00**
Rodeo, cup & saucer, 7½-oz..**100.00**
Rodeo, pitcher, cream...**50.00**
Rodeo, plate, bread & butter; 7¼", from $55 to...................**65.00**
Rodeo, plate, dinner; 10¾" **100.00**
Rodeo, plate, luncheon; 9" **120.00**
Rodeo, shakers, lg, pr...**125.00**
Rodeo, sugar bowl, w/lid, lg..**125.00**
Westward Ho, ashtray, Mark Twain **75.00**
Westward Ho, bowl, mixing; 10¼" **650.00**
Westward Ho, plate, chop; Pioneer Trails, 13" **200.00**
49ers, plate, dinner; 10½" **85.00**

Walley

The Walley Pottery operated in West Sterling, Massachusetts, from 1898 to 1919. Never more than a one-man operation, Walley himself handcrafted all his wares from local clay. The majority of his pottery was simple and unadorned and usually glazed in matt green. On occasion, however, you may find high- and semi-gloss green, as well as matt glazes in blue, cream, brown, and red. The rarest and most desirable examples of his work are those with applied or relief-carved decorations. Some pieces are marked 'WJW.'

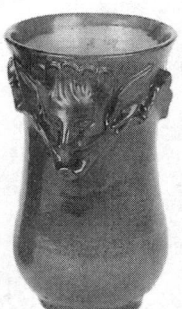

Mug, embossed devil's head, glossy green, repair to rim, 7½x6", $500.00.

Candlestick, bl drip, 14"..**260.00**
Vase, brn & gold mottle, mk, sm chips, 7¼x3¼" **1,200.00**
Vase, frothy gr semi-matt, bulbous, flake, 7½x5½" **1,300.00**

Walrath

Frederick Walrath was a studio potter who worked from around the turn of the century until his death in 1920. He was located in Rochester, New York, until 1918 when he became associated with the Newcomb Pottery in New Orleans, Louisiana.

Bowl, brn matt, mk, 8"...**325.00**
Mug, Arts & Crafts decor, brn & gr on shaded brn, 4"...............**160.00**
Scarab, gr matt, 3½x2¼"...**350.00**
Vase, floral, peach/brn on brn-purple, w/lid, 5½" W **1,800.00**
Vase, frothy ivory drips over celedon, bl & red, sm chips, 3¾" ...**550.00**
Vase, trees/clouds/moon in band on gr, cylindrical, 7x4¼" **13,000.00**

Walter, A.

Almaric Walter was employed from 1904 through 1914 at Verreries Artistiques des Freres Daum in Nancy, France. After 1919 he opened his own business where he continued to make the same type of quality objets d'art in pate-de-verre glass as he had earlier. His pieces are signed A. Walter, Nancy H. Berge Sc.

Bowl, cobalt-splashed gray glass w/dog/cat hdls, 9", NM..........**4,885.00**
Dish, nymph stands over oval form, lt gr to emerald, 7½" **2,875.00**
Figure, Buddha, jade gr, ca 1925, 3" **1,200.00**
Figure, rabbit, reclining, 1 ear up, celery gr on brn base, 3⅛"..**1,035.00**
Lamp, 3-petal flowers on thin stalks cone shade; wrought std, 9"..**2,000.00**
Pen tray, stag beetle on banana leaf form, 9¾" **2,875.00**
Pendant, chamelion, bl on gr w/amber florettes, triangular, 2¼"...**1,400.00**
Pendant, lizard in triangle, bl/gr/gray, 2⅜" **500.00**
Vase, floral, gr streaked w/bl, 6½" **2,850.00**
Vase, stylized flowers, mc on amber-tan, bell form, 4x4½".......**1,500.00**

Wannopee

The Wannopee Pottery, established in 1892, developed from the reorganization of the financially insecure New Milford Pottery Company of New Milford, Connecticut. They produced a line of mottled-glazed pottery called 'Duchess' and a similar line in porcelain. Both were marked with the impressed sunburst 'W' with 'porcelain' added to indicate that particular body type.

In 1895 semiporcelain pitchers in three sizes were decorated with relief medallion cameos of Beethoven, Mozart, and Napoleon. Lettuce-leaf ware was first produced in 1901 and used actual leaves in the modeling. Scarabronze, made in 1895, was their finest artware. It featured simple Egyptian shapes with a coppery glaze. It was marked with a scarab, either impressed or applied. Production ceased in 1903.

Candlestick, brn majolica, twist stem, 12⅜" **175.00**

Lamp, tobacco, green, and black flambe, eight-paneled 13" slag glass shade, EX, **$1,400.00.**

Vase, brn gloss, concave cylinder w/3 diagonal appl hdls, 8".......**230.00**
Vase, gr/brn streaks w/irid, cylinder neck, snake hdls, 27"...........**325.00**
Vase, Scarabronze, caramel, 6 integral shoulder hdls, 20x12" ..**2,250.00**

Warwick

The Warwick China Company operated in Wheeling, West Virginia, from 1887 until 1951. They produced both hand-painted and decaled plates, vases, teapots, coffeepots, pitchers, bowls, and jardinieres featuring lovely florals or portraits of beautiful ladies done in luscious colors. Backgrounds were usually blendings of brown and beige, but ivory was also used as well as greens and pinks. Various marks were employed, all of which incorporate the Warwick name. For a more thorough study of the subject, we recommend *Warwick, A to W*, a supplement to *Why Not Warwick* by our advisor, Donald C. Hoffmann, Sr.; his address can be found in the Directory under Illinois. In an effort to inform the collector/dealer, Mr. Hoffmann now has a video available that identifies the company's decals and their variations by number.

Bouquet #1, vase, brn w/floral decor, A-21, 11¾" **295.00**
Bouquet #1, vase, brn w/floral decor, A-24, 11¾" **285.00**
Bouquet #1, vase, brn w/floral decor, A-27, 11¾" **225.00**
Bouquet #2, vase, brn w/portrait, Anna Potocka, A-17, 10½"....**315.00**
Bouquet #2, vase, brn w/portrait, Gypsy w/Bow in Hair, A-17, 10½" ..**295.00**
Bouquet #2, vase, brn w/portrait, Gypsy w/Turban, A-17, 10½"..**290.00**
Bouquet #2, vase, brn w/portrait, Lady w/Violets, A-17, 10½" ...**335.00**
Bouquet #2, vase, brn w/portrait, Old Blonde, A-17, 10½" **295.00**
Bouquet #2, vase, brn w/portrait, Young Blonde, A-17, 10½".....**285.00**
Bouquet #2, vase, red overglaze, Anna Potocka, E-1, 10½" **330.00**
Bouquet #2, vase, red overglaze, floral decor, E-2, 10½".............**280.00**
Bouquet #2, vase, red overglaze, Gypsy w/Bow in Hair, E-1, 10½"....**290.00**
Bouquet #2, vase, red overglaze, Madame LeBrun, E-1, 10½".....**320.00**
Bouquet #2, vase, red overglaze, Madame Recamier, E-1, 10½"..**330.00**
Carnation, vase, brn w/floral decor (poppy), A-6, 10½" **175.00**
Carnation, vase, brn w/floral decor (roses), A-23, 10½" **170.00**

Carnation, vase, gr w/floral decor (roses), F-2, 10½"..................**195.00**
Chicago, vase, brn w/floral decor (hibiscus), A-27, 8"................**225.00**
Chicago, vase, gr w/floral decor (roses), F-2, 8" **315.00**
Chicago, vase, pk w/portrait, H-1, 8"..**475.00**
Clematis, vase, brn w/portrait, A-17, 10½"................................**350.00**
Clematis, vase, charcoal w/floral decor, C-5, 10½".....................**325.00**
Cuba, vase, brn w/floral decor (hibiscus), A-27, 7½"..................**290.00**
Cuba, vase, matt finish w/portrait, Gypsy, M-1, 7½" **330.00**
Dainty, vase, brn w/floral decor (poppy), A-6, 4½" **275.00**
Duchess, vase, wht w/bird decor (herons), D-1, 7½" **290.00**
Egyptian, vase, brn w/floral decor (hibiscus), A-27, 11¾"..........**290.00**
Egyptian, vase, brn w/floral decor (peonies), A-21, 11¾" **300.00**
Flower, vase, brn w/floral decor (poppy), A-27, 12"...................**115.00**
Flower, vase, brn w/portrait, A-17, 12".....................................**235.00**
Flower, vase, charcoal w/floral decor (poppy), C-6, 12".............**150.00**
Gem, vase, brn w/floral decor, A-16, 12" **270.00**
Gem, vase, charcoal w/portrait, C-1, 12"...................................**300.00**
Gem, vase, matt finish w/acorn decor, M-4, 12" **295.00**
Helene, vase, brn w/floral decor, A-16, 12"...............................**300.00**
Helene, vase, brn w/floral decor, A-27, 12"...............................**290.00**
Lily, vase, brn w/floral decor, A-27, 9½" **300.00**
Lily, vase, charcoal w/floral decor, C-2, 9½".............................**345.00**
Lily, vase, red overglaze w/floral decor, E-2, 9½".......................**325.00**
Magnolia, vase, wht w/bird decor (herons), D-1, 10½" **325.00**
Monroe, vase, matt finish w/nut decor (pine cones), M-6, 10½"...**350.00**
Oriental, vase, brn w/floral decor (peonies), A-21, 11" **370.00**
Pansy, vase, charcoal w/floral decor, C-5, 4" **120.00**
Queen, vase, charcoal w/portrait, C-1, 12"................................**400.00**
Regency, vase, charcoal w/floral decor, C-2, 11" **400.00**
Roberta, vase, red overglaze w/portrait (fisherman), E-3, 10"......**450.00**
Roman, vase, brn w/floral decor (peonies), A-21, 11½"..............**380.00**
Rose, vase, red overgalze w/floral decor (poinsettias), E-2, 8" **200.00**
Senator #1, vase, brn w/floral decor (hyacinths), A-16, 13" **250.00**
Senator #2, vase, brn w/floral decor (hibiscus), A-27, 13" **225.00**

Wash Sets

Before the days of running water, bedrooms were standardly equipped with a wash bowl and pitcher as a matter of necessity. A 'toilet set' was comprised of the pitcher and bowl, toothbrush holder, covered commode, soap dish, shaving dish, and mug. Some sets were even more elaborate. Through everyday usage, the smaller items were often broken, and today it is unusual to find a complete set.

Porcelain sets decorated with florals, fruits, or scenics were produced abroad by Limoges in France; some were imported from Germany and England. During the last quarter of the 1800s and until after the turn of the century, American-made toilet sets were manufactured in abundance. Tin and graniteware sets were also made.

Bridgewood & Sons (England), floral on wht, 7-pc set **750.00**
Davenport, Aquatic, bl-gray on wht, ca 1870s, 12" pitcher+16" bowl...**125.00**
Ironstone, Leaf emb, Meakin, 12" pitcher+14" bowl **135.00**
Mariborough Royal Porcelain, Wood & Son, flow bl, pitcher+bowl ..**800.00**
Paris, porc, floral on blk w/gold, 8-sided, pitcher+bowl..............**825.00**
Royal Doulton, Rosetti, pitcher+bowl...**250.00**
Wedgwood, Festoon, med bl transfer, pitcher+bowl, EX **150.00**

Watch Fobs

Watch fobs have been popular since the last quarter of the nineteenth century. They were often made by retail companies to feature their products. Souvenir, commemorative, and political fobs were also produced. Of special interest today are those with advertising, heavy equipment in particular. Some of the more pricey fobs are listed here, but most of those currently available were produced in such quantities that they are relatively common and should fall within a price range of $3.00 to $10.00. Our advisor for this category is Tony George; he is listed in the Directory under California. When no material is mentioned in the description, assume the fob is made of metal.

Boston Herald Newspaper, embossed metal, paint wear, $75.00; Kellogg's Toasted Corn Flakes, embossed metal, red and black lettering on gold, light wear, rare, $135.00.

Advance Threshers, Banner Boy logo, mc on celluloid, EX w/strap ...**315.00**
Allis Chalmers, Union mks on reverse, NP, 1½x1¾" **140.00**
Am Furnace & Foundry, brass & bl enameling, 1⅜x1¾" **60.00**
Arrowhead shape w/emb Indian & bowl, brass **40.00**
Aultman-Taylor Machine Co, Whitehead & Hoag **155.00**
Birdsell Clover Huller Co, 1920s, worn finish **135.00**
Bucyrus Revolving Shovels, celluloid, 1½x1⅝", NM **550.00**
Cincinnati Horseshoe & Iron Co **85.00**
Cyrus McCormick, brass **45.00**
De Laval, lady & machine, cloisonne & enamel inlay on metal, 1¼"..**140.00**
Gaar-Scott Tiger Thresher, Richmond IN; Bastian Bros **200.00**
Galloway of Waterloo Divides the Melon..., celluloid, EX **300.00**
Golden Sun Coffee, boy w/steaming cup, celluloid insert **130.00**
Heinz, brass plated, 57 on 1 side, factory on reverse, 1½x1¾" **50.00**
IN Nat'l Guard, Spanish-Am War era, NP brass, EX....................**75.00**
Indian Motorcycles, copper flashed, Bastian Bros, 1915, M **130.00**
John Deere, deer & lg D on brass, EX patina **160.00**
Lewis & Mann Livestock Commission, OK; 1¾x1½"................**160.00**
Marion Shovel Model 28, 2-color enamel on porc, 1910-20.......**375.00**
Milburn Wagon, Toledo OH; celluloid insert, EX **350.00**
Old Reliable Coffee **65.00**
Purity Brand Salt...Milwaukee, enameled, 1900s **120.00**
Ruff Brewing, Quincy IL; enameled..**160.00**
Sinclaire Sinco Oils, gr & wht enameling, 1½", NM on strap....**360.00**
State Farm, w/vintage car, red & blk enameling, EX **160.00**
Texas & Pacific 610, engine & boxcar, 2"................................**100.00**
Waterloo Boy, boy & tractor..**435.00**

Watch Stands

Watch stands were decorative articles designed with a hook from which to hang a watch. Some displayed the watch as the face of a grandfather clock or as part of an interior scene with figures in period costumes and contemporary furnishings. They were popular products of Staffordshire potters and silver companies as well.

Bronze, Nouveau lady by arched case, after Burschner, 8"..........**765.00**
CI, leafy scrollwork w/eagle, blk pnt traces, lt rust, 10¼" **90.00**
Gilt CI w/eagle & rococo decor, wht marble base, 7"................**140.00**
Hutch, chip-cvd decor, scalloped top, Am, 19th C, 6½" **750.00**
Staffordshire, Scottish couple w/hound, 19th C, 8½"................**175.00**

Watches

First made in the 1500s in Germany, early watches were actually small clocks, suspended from the neck or belt. By 1700 they had become the approximate shape and size we know today. The first watches produced in America were made in 1810. The well-known Waltham Watch Company was established in 1850. Later, Waterbury produced inexpensive watches which they sold by the thousands.

Open-face and hunting-case watches of the 1890s were often solid gold or gold-filled and were often elaborately decorated in several colors of gold. Gold watches became a status symbol in this decade and were worn by both men and women on chains with fobs or jeweled slides. Ladies sometimes fastened them to their clothing with pins often set with jewels. The chatelaine watch was worn at the waist, only one of several items such as scissors, coin purses, or needle cases, each attached by small chains.

Most turn-of-the-century watch cases were gold-filled; these are plentiful today. Sterling cases, though interest in them is on the increase, are not in great demand. For more information we recommend *Complete Price Guide to Watches, No. 21,* by Cooksey Shugart, Richard E. Gilbert, and Tom Engle (Collector Books).

Our advise for this category comes from Maundy International Watches, Antiquarian Horologists, price consultants, and researchers for many watch reference guides and books on Horology. Their firm is a leading purveyor of antique watches of all kinds. They are listed in the Directory under Kansas. For character-related watches, see Personalities.

Key:
adj — adjusted	k/s — key set
brg — bridge plate design	k/w — key wind
d/s — double sunk dial	l/s — lever set
fbd — finger bridge design	mvt — movement
g/f — gold-filled	o/f — open face
g/j/s — gold jewel setting	p/s — pendant set
h/c — hunter case	r/g/p — rolled gold plate
HCI#P — heat, cold,	s — size
isochronism & position	s/s — single sunk dial
adjusted	s/w — stem wind
j — jewel	w/g/f — white gold-filled
k — karat	y/g/f — yellow gold-filled

Patek Philippe pocketwatch, 18kt yellow gold, open face, Arabic numerals, ca 1900 – 10, M in original fitted box, $2,400.00 (EX without box, $1,450.00). (Photo courtesy Neal Auction Company)

Am Watch Co, 0s, 7j, #1891, 14k, h/c, Am Watch Co, M **325.00**
Am Watch Co, 12s, 21j, #1894, 14k, h/c, M **425.00**

Am Watch Co, 16s, 11j, #1872, p/s, silver h/c, Park Road, M 275.00
Am Watch Co, 16s, 15j, #1899, y/g/f, h/c, M 195.00
Am Watch Co, 16s, 16j, #1884, 5-min, 14k, Repeater, M 4,750.00
Am Watch Co, 16s, 17j, #1888, Railroader, M.................1,250.00
Am Watch Co, 16s, 19j, #1872, 14k, h/c, Am Watch Woerd's Pat, M ..5,000.00
Am Watch Co, 16s, 21j, #1888, h/c, 14k, Riverside Maximus, M...1,550.00
Am Watch Co, 16s, 21j, #1908, y/g/f, o/f, Grade #645, M 295.00
Am Watch Co, 16s, 23j, #1908, o/f, 18k, Premier Maximus, MIB ...11,950.00
Am Watch Co, 16s, 23j, #1908, y/g/f, o/f, adj, RR, Vanguard, M ..395.00
Am Watch Co, 16s, 23j, #1908, y/g/f, o/f, Vanguard Up/Down, EX...575.00
Am Watch Co, 18s, #1857, silver h/c, Samuel Curtiss k/w, M ...3,950.00
Am Watch Co, 18s, 11j, #1857, k/w, 1st run, PS Barlett, M....5,000.00
Am Watch Co, 18s, 11j, #1857, silver h/c, k/w, DH&D, EX ...1,200.00
Am Watch Co, 18s, 11j, #1857, silver h/c, k/w, s/s, Wm Ellery, EX ..225.00
Am Watch Co, 18s, 15j, #1877, k/w, RE Robbins, M.................425.00
Am Watch Co, 18s, 15j, #1883, y/g/f, 2-tone, Railroad King, EX 425.00
Am Watch Co, 18s, 17j, #1883, y/g/f, o/f, Crescent Street, M 175.00
Am Watch Co, 18s, 17j, #1892, HC, Canadian Pacific Railway, M ..950.00
Am Watch Co, 18s, 17j, #1892, y/g/f, o/f, Sidereal, rare, M.....2,400.00
Am Watch Co, 18s, 17j, 25-yr, y/g/f, o/f, s/s, PS Bartlett, M 135.00
Am Watch Co, 18s, 21j, #1892, y/g/f, o/f, d/s, Crescent St, M....395.00
Am Watch Co, 18s, 21j, #1892, y/g/f, o/f, Grade #845, EX 150.00
Am Watch Co, 18s, 21j, #1892, y/g/f, o/f, Pennsylvania Special, M ..2,850.00
Am Watch Co, 18s, 7j, #1857, silver case, k/w, CT Parker, M 3,000.00
Am Watch Co, 6s, 7j, #1873, y/g/f, h/c, Am Watch Co, M 85.00
Auburndale Watch Co, 18s, 7j, k/w, l/s, Lincoln, M 1,450.00
Aurora Watch Co, 18s, 11j, k/w, silver h/c, M.................275.00
Aurora Watch Co, 18s, 15 ruby j, y/g/f, s/w, 5th pinion, M 1,295.00
Ball (Elgin), 18s, 17j, o/f, silver, Official RR Standard, M 495.00
Ball (Hamilton), 16s, 21j, #999, g/f, o/f, l/s, M................450.00
Ball (Hamilton), 16s, 23j, #998, y/g/f, o/f, Elinvar, M 1,500.00
Ball (Hampden), 18s, 17j, o/f, adj, RR, Superior Grade, M ...1,650.00
Ball (Illinois), 12s, 19j, w/g/f, o/f, M................250.00
Ball (Waltham), 16s, 17j, y/g/f, o/f, RR, Commercial Std, M......250.00
Ball (Waltham), 16s, 21j, o/f, Official RR Standard, M 425.00
Columbus, 18s, 11-15j, k/w, k/s, M.................395.00
Columbus, 18s, 15j, o/f, l/s, M.................150.00
Columbus, 18s, 15j, y/g/f, o/f, Jay Gould on dial, G 800.00
Columbus, 18s, 21j, y/g/f, h/c, train on dial, Railway King, M 775.00
Columbus, 18s, 23j, y/g/f, h/c, Columbus King, M.................1,800.00
Columbus, 6s, 11j, y/g/f hc, M.................150.00
Cornell, 18s, 15j, s/w, JC Adams, EX.................240.00
Cornell, 18s, 15j, silver h/c, k/w, John Evans, EX.................275.00
Dudley, 12s, #1, 14k, o/f, flip-bk case, Masonic, G.................2,500.00
Elgin, 10s, 18k, h/c, k/w, k/s, s/s, Gail Borden, M.................425.00
Elgin, 12s, 15j, 14k, h/c, EX.................225.00
Elgin, 12s, 17j, 14k, h/c, GM Wheeler, M.................325.00
Elgin, 16s, 15j, doctor's, 4th model, 18k, 2nd sweep hand, h/c, M...1,650.00
Elgin, 16s, 15j, 14k, h/c, EX.................450.00
Elgin, 16s, 21j, y/g/f, g/j/s, o/f, BW Raymond, EX.................185.00
Elgin, 16s, 21j, y/g/f, g/j/s, 3 fbd, M.................395.00
Elgin, 16s, 21j, 14k, 3 fbd, grade #91, scarce, M.................3,500.00
Elgin, 16s, 23j, up/down indicator, BW Raymond, EX.................1,075.00
Elgin, 17s, 7j, k/w, orig silver case, Leader, M.................150.00
Elgin, 18s, 11j, silver, h/c, k/w, gilded, MG Odgen, M.................200.00
Elgin, 18s, 15j, o/f, d/s, k/w, silveroid, RR, BW Raymond 1st run, M ..1,450.00
Elgin, 18s, 15j, silver, k/w, k/s, h/c, HL Culver, M.................295.00
Elgin, 18s, 15j, silver h/c, Penn RR dial, BW Raymond k/w mvt, M...5,400.00
Elgin, 18s, 17j, silveroid h/c, BW Raymond, M.................225.00
Elgin, 18s, 21j, y/g/f, o/f, Father Time, G.................165.00
Elgin, 18s, 23j, y/g/f, o/f, 5-position, RR, Veritas, M.................495.00
Elgin, 6s, 11j, 14k, h/c, M.................275.00
Fredonia, 18s, 11j, y/g/f, h/c, k/w, M.................395.00
Hamilton, #4992B, 16s, 22j, o/f, steel case, G.................175.00

Hamilton, #910, 12s, 17j, 20-yr, y/g/f, o/f, s/s, EX 50.00
Hamilton, #920, 12s, 23j, 14k, o/f, M.................550.00
Hamilton, #922MP, 12s, 18k case, Masterpiece (sgn), M.........1,150.00
Hamilton, #925, 18s, 17j, y/g/f, h/c, s/s, l/s, M.................250.00
Hamilton, #928, 18s, 15j, y/g/f, o/f, s/s, EX.................200.00
Hamilton, #933, 18s, 16j, h/c, nickel plate, low serial #, M 675.00
Hamilton, #940, 18s, 21j, nickel plate, coin silver, o/f, M.........295.00
Hamilton, #946, 18s, 23j, y/g/f, o/f, g/j/s, M.................975.00
Hamilton, #947 (mk), 18s, 23j, 14k, h/c, orig/sgn, EX 4,250.00
Hamilton, #950, 16s, 23j, y/g/f, o/f, l/s, sgn d/s, M.................1,400.00
Hamilton, #965, 16s, 17j, 14k, p/s, h/c, brg, scarce, M.............1,275.00
Hamilton, #972, 16s, 17j, y/g/f, g/j/s, o/f, d/s, l/s, adj, EX...........135.00
Hamilton, #974, 16s, 17j, 20-yr, y/g/f, o/f, s/s, EX.................65.00
Hamilton, #992, 16s, 21j, y/g/f, o/f, adj, d/s, dbl roller, M...........250.00
Hamilton, #992B, 16s, 21j, y/g/f, o/f, l/s, Bar/Crown, M...........375.00
Hampden, 12s, 17j, w/g/f, o/f, thin model, Aviator, M 125.00
Hampden, 16s, 17j, y/g/f, h/c, s/w, M.................95.00
Hampden, 16s, 21j, g/j/s, y/g/f, NP, h/c, Dueber, ¾-mvt, M.......300.00
Hampden, 18s, 15j, k/w, mk on mvt, Railway, M.................995.00
Hampden, 18s, 15j, s/w, gilded, JC Perry, M.................150.00
Hampden, 18s, 21j, y/g/f, g/j/s, h/c, New Railway, M.................300.00
Hampden, 18s, 21j, y/g/f, o/f, d/s, l/s, N Am Railway, M 325.00
Hampden, 18s, 23j, y/g/f, o/f, d/s, adj, New Railway, M 350.00
Hampden, 18s, 23j, 14k, h/c, Special Railway, M.................925.00
Hampden, 18s, 7-11j, k/w, gilded, Springfield Mass, NM.................150.00
Howard, E; 16s, 15j, s/w, 14k h/c, L sz, M.................1,150.00
Howard, E; 18s, 15j, h/c, silver case, k/w, Series I, N sz, M....4,500.00
Howard, E; 18s, 15j, 18k h/c, k/w, Series II, N sz, M.................4,500.00
Howard, E; 18s, 17j, 25-yr, y/g/f, o/f, orig case, split plate, NM...800.00
Howard (Keystone), 12s, 23j, 14k, h/c, brg, Series 8, M.............675.00
Howard (Keystone), 16s, 17j, y/g/f, o/f, Series 9, M.................195.00
Howard (Keystone), 16s, 23j, y/g/f, o/f, Series 0, jeweled bbl, M.....695.00
Illinois, 0s, 7j, 14k, l/s, h/c, EX.................225.00
Illinois, 12s, 17j, y/g/f, o/f, d/s dial, EX.................40.00
Illinois, 16s, 17j, y/g/f, o/f, d/s, Bunn, EX.................175.00
Illinois, 16s, 21j, g/j/s, h/c, Burlington, M.................295.00
Illinois, 16s, 21j, o/f, d/s, Santa Fe Special, M.................475.00
Illinois, 16s, 21j, y/g/f, o/f, d/s, Bunn Special, M.................375.00
Illinois, 16s, 23j, y/g/f, stiff bow, o/f, Sangamo Special, EX.........875.00
Illinois, 18s, 11j, #3, o/f, s/w, l/s, Comet, G.................90.00
Illinois, 18s, 11j, Forest City, G.................85.00
Illinois, 18s, 15j, #1, adj, y/g/f, k/w, h/c, gilt, Bunn, M 675.00
Illinois, 18s, 15j, #1, k/w, k/s, silver hunter, Stuart, G 450.00
Illinois, 18s, 15j, k/w, k/s, gilt, Railway Regulator, M 875.00
Illinois, 18s, 17j, h/c, s/w, nickel plate, coin silver, Bunn, M.......300.00
Illinois, 18s, 17j, o/f, d/s, adj, silveroid case, Lakeshore, G 75.00
Illinois, 18s, 17j, o/f, s/w, 5th pinion, Miller, EX.................135.00
Illinois, 18s, 21j, g/j/s, g/f, o/f, A Lincoln, M.................395.00
Illinois, 18s, 21j, 14k, g/j/s, h/c, Bunn Special, M.................995.00
Illinois, 18s, 23j, g/j/s, Bunn Special, EX.................595.00
Illinois, 18s, 24j, g/j/s, adj, o/f, Chesapeake & Ohio, M.........2,800.00
Illinois, 18s, 24j, g/j/s, o/f, Bunn Special, EX.................595.00
Illinois, 18s, 26j, g/j/s, o/f, Ben Franklin USA, G.................5,000.00
Illinois, 18s, 26j, 14k, Penn Special, M.................8,000.00
Illinois, 18s, 7j, #3, o/f, Interior, G.................65.00
Illinois, 18s, 7j, #3, silveroid, America, G.................65.00
Illinois, 18s, 9-11j, o/f, k/w, s/s, silveroid case, Hoyt, M.................150.00
Ingersoll, 16s, 7j, wht base metal, Reliance, G.................20.00
Lancaster, 18s, 7j, o/f, k/w, k/s, eng silver case, EX 125.00
Marion US, 18s, h/c, k/w, k/s, ¾-plate, Asa Fuller, M.................395.00
Melrose Watch Co, 18s, 7j, k/w, k/s, G.................225.00
New York Watch Co, 19j, low sz #, wolf's teeth wind, M.........1,675.00
Patek Philippe, 12s, 18j, 18k, o/f, EX.................2,500.00
Patek Philippe, 16s, 20j, 18k, h/c, M.................2,450.00

Rockford, 16s, 17j, y/g/f, h/c, brg, dbl roller, EX...........................**90.00**
Rockford, 16s, 21j, #515, y/g/f, M **495.00**
Rockford, 16s, 21j, g/j/s, o/f, grade #537, rare, M...............**1,500.00**
Rockford, 16s, 23j, 14k, o/f, mk Doll on dial/mvt, M.............**2,500.00**
Rockford, 18s, 15j, o/f, k/w, silver case, EX **295.00**
Rockford, 18s, 17j, y/g/f, o/f, Winnebago, M **250.00**
Rockford, 18s, 21j, o/f, King Edward, M **425.00**
Seth Thomas, 18s, 17j, #2, g/j/s, adj, Henry Molineux, EX **595.00**
Seth Thomas, 18s, 17j, Edgemere, G **40.00**
Seth Thomas, 18s, 25j, g/j/s, g/f, Maiden Lane, EX **2,395.00**
South Bend, 12s, 21j, dbl roller, Grade #431, M........................**195.00**
South Bend, 12s, 21j, orig o/f, d/s, Studebaker, M **250.00**
South Bend, 18s, 21j, 14k, h/c, M **950.00**
Swiss, 18s, 18k, h/c, 1-min, Repeater, High Grade, M **3,775.00**

Waterford

The Waterford Glass Company operated in Ireland from the late 1700s until 1851 when the factory closed. One hundred years later (in 1951) another Waterford glassworks was instituted that produced glass similar to the eighteenth-century wares — crystal, usually with cut decoration. Today Waterford is a generic term referring to the type of glass first produced there.

Bowl, Aran Isles, 10" **350.00**
Bowl, dessert; Lismore, ftd..**65.00**
Brandy, Alana **70.00**
Candelabrum, Master Cutter, 3-light, prisms, 20".......................**450.00**
Champagne flute, Lismore..**59.50**
Chandelier, faceted shaft on circular base, 17x7½" dia **400.00**
Claret, Lismore **59.50**
Cordial, Lismore **47.50**
Decanter, Colleen, 11½x4½" **298.00**
Decanter, cut dmns, bulbous ewer form, 5" faceted stopper, 12" .**550.00**
Goblet, water; Alana, lg, 6 for **60.00**
Goblet, water; Colleen **89.00**
Goblet, water; Lismore **59.50**
Goblet, water; Sheila, 7x4" **85.00**
Goblet, water; Slane, 7⅝" **80.00**
Ice pail, Russborough, swags/dmns/vertical wedges/etc, ltd ed.....**425.00**
Old-fashioned, Lismore **52.50**
Rose bowl, cross-cut dmns/prismatic rings/printies, ftd, 9x5½" ...**600.00**
Saucer champagne, Colleen, 5-oz, ea..**89.00**
Sherbet, Boyne, 3⅜", 6 for **480.00**
Stauette, Tinkerbell, 1997 ltd ed **200.00**
Tumbler, juice; Alana, 10-oz **75.00**
Tumbler, Kenmare, 12-oz..**85.00**
Tumbler, Lismore, 12-oz **62.50**
Vase, Winter Wonderland, ltd ed **795.00**
Wine, Kinsale, 6"...**100.00**
Wine, Sheila **85.00**
Wine, Slane **80.00**

Watt Pottery

The Watt Pottery Company was established in Crooksville, Ohio, on July 5, 1922. From approximately 1922 until 1935, they manufactured hand-turned stone containers — jars, jugs, milk pans, preserve jars, and various sizes of mixing bowls, usually marked with a cobalt blue acorn stamp. In 1936 production of these items was discontinued, and the company began to produce kitchen utility ware and ovenware such as mixing bowls, spaghetti bowls and plates, canister sets, covered casseroles, salt and pepper shakers, cookie jars, ice buckets, pitchers, bean pots, and salad and dinnerware sets. Most Watt ware is individually hand painted with bold brush strokes of red, green, or blue contrasting with the natural buff color of the glazed body. Several patterns were produced: Apple, Autumn Foliage, Cherry, Dutch Tulip, Morning Glory, Rio Rose, Rooster, Tear Drop, Starflower, and Tulip, to name a few. Much of the ware was made for advertising premiums and is often found stamped with the name of the retail company.

Tragedy struck the Watt Pottery Company on October 4, 1965, when fire completely destroyed the factory and warehouse. Production never resumed, but the ware they made has withstood many years of service in American kitchens and is today highly regarded and prized by collectors. The vivid colors and folk art-like execution of each cheerful pattern create a homespun ambiance that will make Watt pottery a treasure for years to come.

For further study we recommend *Watt Pottery, An Identification and Price Guide*, by our advisors for this category, Sue and Dave Morris; they are listed in the Directory under Washington. For the address of the *Watt's News* newsletter, see the section on Clubs, Newsletters, and Catalogs.

Apple, baking dish, rectangular, hdls, 2¼x10x5¼" **1,500.00**
Apple, bowl, #05, ribbed, w/lid, 4x5" dia **145.00**
Apple, bowl, #55, 4x11¾" dia **250.00**
Apple, bowl, #67, w/lid, 6½x8½" dia..**125.00**
Apple, bowl, mixing; #7, 4x7" dia...**55.00**
Apple, bowl, spaghetti; #44, ind, 1½x8" dia **400.00**
Apple, casserole warmer, electric, 2x7"....................................**1,000.00**
Apple, ice bucket, w/lid, 7¼x7½" dia **275.00**
Apple, mug, #121, 3¾x3" dia **185.00**
Apple, platter, #31, 15" dia **350.00**
Apple, teapot, #505, 5¾x9"...**3,000.00**
Apple (reduced decor), bowl, mixing; #63, 4x6½" dia **85.00**
Autumn Foliage, bowl, #73, 4x9½" dia **85.00**
Autumn Foliage, fondue, w/lid, 3x9" **275.00**
Autumn Foliage, pitcher, #15, 5½x5¾" **65.00**
Basketweave, mug, #806, brn, 5¼x3¼" dia **10.00**
Blue/White Banded, casserole, 4½x8¾" dia..................................**45.00**
Cherry, bowl, cereal/salad; #23, 5¾" **50.00**
Cherry, pitcher, #17, 8x8½" **275.00**

Cherry, platter, #31, 15" diameter, $145.00.
(Photo courtesy Sue and Dave Morris)

Cherry, platter, #31, 15" dia **145.00**
Cherry, shaker, bbl shape, holes form 'S,' part of popcorn set, 4" ..**90.00**
Dutch Tulip, bowl, #67, w/lid, 6½x8½" dia **250.00**
Dutch Tulip, casserole, Fr; #18, ind, 4x8"....................................**275.00**
Eagle, bowl, cereal; 2x5½" dia **85.00**
Kitch-N-Queen, pitcher, w/ice lip; #17, 8x8½" **200.00**
Kla Ham'rd, bowl, 4½x6½" dia..**25.00**
Kla Ham'rd, casserole, hdls, #43, 6x9" dia.....................................**60.00**
Morning Glory, cookie jar, #95, 10¾x7½" dia..............................**400.00**
Morning Glory, pitcher, #96, 8x8½" **375.00**

Pansy (Cut-Leaf), bowl, spaghetti; 1½x8" 35.00
Pansy (Cut-Leaf), pie plate, 1½x9" dia 150.00
Pansy (Cut-Leaf), platter, Bull's Eye, 15" dia 110.00
Pansy (Old), pitcher, #15, 5½x5¾" dia..225.00
Pansy (Old), platter, #49, 12" dia..85.00
Pansy (Old), platter, Cross-Hatch Pansy, 15" dia.......................175.00
Rooster, bowl, #73, 4x9½" dia 145.00
Rooster, bowl, spaghetti; 3x13" dia 375.00
Rooster, ice bucket, w/lid, 7¼x7¾" dia 275.00
Rooster, pitcher, #15, 5½x5¾" 145.00
Speckled Watt Ware, bowl, salad; #106, 3½x10¾" dia 25.00
Starflower, bean pot, hdls, #76, 6½x7½" dia 175.00
Starflower, bowl, #73, 4x9½" dia 65.00
Starflower, casserole, #18, stick hdl, ind, 3¾x7½" 125.00
Starflower, cookie jar, #21, w/lid, 7½" 185.00
Starflower, pitcher, #17, 4-petal version, w/ice lip, 8x8½" 225.00
Starflower (Green-on-Brown), cookie jar, #21, w/lid, 7½x7" 125.00
Starflower (Green-on-Brown), tumbler, #56, 4½" 100.00
Starflower (Pink-on-Black), sugar bowl, hdls, 2¾x6½" 75.00
Starflower (Pink-on-Green), cup & saucer......................................65.00
Starflower (White-on-Green), bowl, spaghetti; 3x13" dia...........100.00
Tear Drop, bowl, #66, 3x7" dia...45.00
Tear Drop, casserole, Fr; #18, ind, 4x8" 225.00
Tulip, bowl, #73, 4x9½" dia 150.00
Tulip, pitcher, #15, 5½x5¾" 550.00
White Daisy, bowl, mixing; #5, 2¾x5" dia 85.00
White Daisy, plate, salad; 8½" dia 65.00
Woodgrain, bowl, #608W, w/lid, 7½x9" 65.00
Woodgrain, pitcher, #613W, 5¾x4½" 75.00

Box, Baroque Shell, flowers on pk, 4¼x4¾".................................450.00
Box, Baroque Shell, Moorish Fantasy, gold scrolls, 3¾x7¼"....1,250.00
Box, Baroque Shell, primroses in scrolled border, wht dots, 5" ...375.00
Box, Baroque Shell, violets, orig lining, 7"...................................550.00
Box, bl flowers, orig satin lining & puff, hinged lid, 4x4½" 400.00
Box, blown-out shell, dainty flowers, 3".......................................250.00
Box, cherub & daisies on yel & opal, 5" sq 550.00
Box, Cigar Band, 2½x3¾" 650.00
Box, Egg Crate, roses on gr w/purple & gold, 5¾x5½"................750.00
Box, Egg Crate, Tobacco & spring flowers, 4x5x5" 750.00
Box, gondolas & canal street, 4¾" W 495.00
Box, Swirl, blackberries on opal & lt turq w/gold, 5" 500.00
Box, Swirl, daisies on mauve to lt bl, 4-ftd, 6x7" 850.00
Box, Swirl, floral sprays on lt bl to opal, 5½" 450.00
Box, Swirl, roses, pk & gr on clear, 4½x7"....................................700.00
Box, Swirl, roses on bl, lion ft, 6x8¼" 975.00
Cigar holder, floral, pk/gr/yel, gold ormolu ft & rim, 3¾" 375.00
Clock, floral, molded scrolls, gilt fr, Pat Jan 13 1891, easel bk, 7"....2,350.00
Cracker jar, bl flowers, bbl shape, 12x6".......................................495.00
Cracker jar, Egg Crate, pk & wht clovers, orig mts, 11x5" 595.00
Creamer & sugar bowl, Swirl, floral on pk, 5", 4½" 500.00
Humidor, Egg Crate, spider mums, Tobacco in purple, 4½x5½" .635.00
Letter holder, Egg Crate, mums, ornate ormolu, 4¼x6" 450.00
Shakers, chrysanthemums, metal lids, 2½", pr 285.00
Sugar shaker, Swirl, floral/rococo swags, 3x3¼" 585.00
Tray, pin; Egg Crate, floral on bl, 2-hdl ormolu rim, 2x3" 200.00
Tray, pin; floral, metal collar, 4" 100.00
Vase, lady riding butterfly on pk w/gold, blown-out scrolls, 12¾x5" ..2,950.00
Vase, wild roses, pk w/gold on lt bl, gold beading, 9¾x4"........1,000.00

Wave Crest

Wave Crest is a line of decorated opal ware (milk glass) patented in 1892 by the C.F. Monroe Co. of Meriden, Connecticut. They made a full line of items for every room of the house, but they are probably best known for their boxes and vases. Most items were hand painted with various levels of decoration, but more transfers were used in the later years prior to the company's demise in 1916. Floral themes are common; items with the scenics and portraits are rarer and more highly prized. Many pieces have ornately scrolled ormolu and brass handles, feet, and rims. Early pieces were unsigned (though they may have had paper labels); later, about 1898, a red banner mark was used. The black mark is probably from about 1902 – 03. However, the glass is quite distinctive and has not been reproduced, so even unmarked items are easy to recognize. Our advisors for this category are Dolli and Wilfred Cohen; they are listed in the Directory under California. Note: There is no premium for signatures on Wave Crest. Values are given for hand-decorated pieces (unless noted 'transfer') that are *not* worn.

Weapons

Among the varied areas of specialization within the broad category of weapons, guns are by far the most popular. Muskets are among the earliest firearms; they were large-bore shoulder arms, usually firing black powder with separate loading of powder and shot. Some ignited the charge by flintlock or caplock, while later types used a firing pin with a metallic cartridge. Side arms, referred to as such because they were worn at the side, include pistols and revolvers. Pistols range from early single-shot and multiple barrels to modern types with cartridges held in the handle. Revolvers were supplied with a cylinder that turned to feed a fresh round in front of the barrel breech. Other firearms include shotguns, which fired round or conical bullets and had a smooth inner barrel surface, and rifles, so named because the interior of the barrel contained spiral grooves (rifling) which increased accuracy. For further study we recommend *Modern Guns, Thirteenth Edition,* by Russell Quertermous and Steve Quertermous, available from Collector Books. All weapons are under the advisement of Steve Howard, see the Directory under California. Unless another condition is noted in the line, our values are for examples in excellent condition. See also Militaria.

Box, forget-me-nots on pastel, 3½x5½", $550.00.

Key:
bbl — barrel
cal — caliber
conv — conversion
cyl — cylinder
f/l — flintlock
ga — gauge
hdw — hardware
mag — magazine

mod — modified
oct — octagon
O/U — over/under
p/b — patch box
perc — percussion
/s — stock
Spec O — Special Order

Ash receiver, roses on dk gr, 2½x6½" at hdls 385.00

Carbines

Austrian Fruwirth, 69 cal, 14½" bbl, G....................................400.00

Gallagher Civil War, 50 cal, std model, p/b, G..........................1,100.00
Joslyn 1864 Civil War, 52RF cal, 22" rnd bbl, sling bar/ring, EX+...1,750.00
Merrill Civil War, 54 cal, 21½" rnd bbl, p/b, G 1,000.00
North 1842 Hall, 54 cal, 21" bbl, G 800.00
Robinson Confederate Sharps, 54 cal, 22" bbl, rprs, G 7,000.00
Ruger Deerslayer, 44 mgn, 18" bbl, integral receiver sight, scope 425.00
Sharps & Hankins, 52 cal, 24" leather-covered bbl, std mks, VG+...1,000.00
Sharps & Hankins 1862 Naval, 52RF cal, 24" leather-covered bbl, G+ ..1,100.00
Sharps Conv, 50-70 cal, 22" bbl, inspector mks, rstr 1,750.00
Springfield 1899, 30-40 cal, 22" rnd bbl, walnut/s, VG 700.00
Starr Civil War, 54 cal, 21" rnd bbl, std mks on lock/receiver, VG...1,500.00
Winchester Ltd Ed II Commemorative Deluxe, 30-30 cal, M.....650.00
Winchester 1866 Saddle Ring, 44 cal, 20" bbl, full mag, VG ..2,000.00
Winchester 1876 NW Mounted Police Saddle Ring, 45-75 cal, 22" bbl...1,950.00
Winchester 1892, 38WCF cal, 20" bbl, full mag, std sights, VG.550.00
Winchester 1892 Saddle Ring, 25-20 cal, 20" bbl, full mag, str/s, VG.1,200.00
Winchester 1894, 32 cal, std 20" bbl, button mag 300.00
Winchester 1894, 32 cal, std 20" bbl, pistol grip, half mag, VG..400.00
Winchester 1894, 32 cal, 16" bbl, full mag, gumwood/s 750.00
Winchester 1894 Saddle Ring, 30 cal, 20" bbl, ⅔ mag, VG........300.00
Winchester 1894 Saddle Ring, 38-55 cal, std 20" bbl, full mag...900.00
Winchester 1894 Saddle Ring, 38-55 cal, 20" bbl, half mag, VG ...550.00
Winchester 1894 Trapper Saddle Ring, 30 cal, 16" bbl, full mag, VG...500.00

Muskets

Ballard Military, 52RF cal, 30" bbl, sling swivels, str/s, G............900.00
Barstow Exeter 1808, f/l, 69 cal, 43" bbl, VG 2,750.00
Barstow Exeter 1808, f/l, 69 cal, 44" bbl, G- 700.00
British Enfield Conv, 75 cal, 39" bbl, altered from f/l, G.............550.00
Harper's Ferry 1821, f/l, 69 cal, 42" bbl, rpl ramrod, VG 750.00
New England Fowler, f/l, 75 Flint cal, 47" part oct bbl, G+.....1,300.00
Norwich 1861 Contract, 58 cal, 40" bbl, leather sling, dtd 1863, G ..1,150.00
Remington 1816 Conv, 69 cal, 42" bbl, lock dtd 1855, G...........825.00
S Norris & WT Clements 1863, 58 cal, 40" bbl, VG...............1,700.00
Springfield 1842, 75 cal bored smooth, 42" bbl, lock dtd 1849, G-..600.00
Wickham Model 1816, f/l, 69 cal, 42" bbl, G- 600.00
Winchester High Wall Winder, 22LR cal, 28" rnd bbl, str/s, VG.650.00
Winchester 1885 Hi-Wall, 22 short cal, 28" bbl, G....................550.00

Pistols

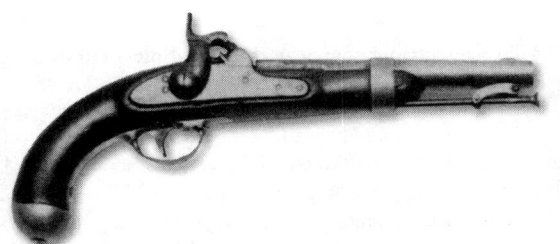

US Model 1842 percussion pistol by Henry Aston, 54 caliber, smooth bore single shot, 8½" round barrel, walnut stock, dated 1850, G, $600.00 to $800.00.

Allen & Thurber Pepperbox, 32 cal, 6-shot, 3½" fluted bbls, VG..........700.00
Beretta M1934 Semi-auto, 32 cal, 3⅜" bbl, postwar, NM, w/holster......175.00
Browning High Power Semi-Auto, 9mm, blued finish, 2 orig mags, NM...400.00
Colt 1903 Pocket, 32ACP, 3¾" bbl, late production, VG 180.00
Colt 1903 Semi-Auto, 32 cal, bbl bushing/long slide, compo grips, EX+...750.00
Colt 1908 Vest Pocket, 25 cal, silver/pearl grips, NM in box......650.00
Colt 1911 Commercial Govt, 45 cal, walnut grips, 1914, VG, +holster...800.00
Colt 1911 Navy Semi-Auto, 45 cal, US Property on side fr, 1911, VG....550.00

Colt 1911 Semi-Auto, 45 cal, checkered grips, military mag, 1918.......1,600.00
Colt 1911 Semi-Auto, 45 cal, checkered grips, 2-tone mag, 1917 ....1,350.00
Hammond Bulldog, 44 cal, 4" bbl, Pat Oct 25 1864 on breechblock, EX+ ..675.00
Luger, 30 cal, 11¾" bbl, later drum mag, rpl grips, VG+..........6,900.00
Luger byf/41 Black Widow, 9mm, orig blk, compo grips, unmk mag...900.00
Mauser 1914 Semi-Auto, 32 cal, 3⅜" bbl, VG, w/holster 100.00
Mauser 1930 Broomhandle w/Stock, 30 cal, 5½" rnd bbl 1,600.00
Remington Type II 3rd Variation Dbl Derringer, 41RF cal, pearl grips.......800.00
Remington 2nd Model Dbl Derringer, 41RF cal, 3" bbls/rosewood grips....550.00
Sharps 2A 4-Bbl, 32 cal, 3" bbls, rpl parts, G..............................300.00
Smith & Wesson 35, 35 cal, 3½" bbl, walnut grips w/gold logos, EX+ 650.00
Smith & Wesson 39-2 Semi-Auto, 7.65 Luger cal, walnut logo grips ...1,600.00

Revolvers

Colt Bisley Single-Action, 44-40 cal, 7½" bbl, dtd 1910, NM ...1,200.00
Colt Lightning, 41LC cal, 4½" bbl, worn grips, G.....................350.00
Colt Single-Action Army, 38-40 cal, 5½" bbl, dtd 1896, VG .1,425.00
Colt Single-Action Army, 44-40 cal, 5½" bbl, dtd 1894, G 1,200.00
Colt Single-Action Army, 44-40 cal, 7½" bbl, dtd 1884, VG .1,800.00
Colt Single-Action Army, 45 cal, early fr, 7½" bbl, ivory grips, G...2,500.00
Colt Single-Action Army, 45LC cal, 6½" bbl, dtd 1929, NM.4,250.00
Colt Single-Action Pre-War, 45 cal, 5½" bbl, pearl grips, EX+ 4,750.00
Colt 2nd Generation Single Action Army, 45 cal, 5½" bbl, VG+ ..850.00
Colt 3rd Generation Single Action Army, 45 cal, 4¾" bbl.........750.00
Smith & Wesson 1st Model Lady Smith, 22 cal, 3½" bbl, compo grips.....625.00
Smith & Wesson 1st Model 3rd Issue Tip Up, 22S cal, NP, walnut grips ..450.00
Smith & Wesson 1917 Army, 45 cal, 5½" bbl, factory eng.........550.00
Smith & Wesson 5th Model Safety Hammerless, 38 cal, NP, 4" keyhole bbl....250.00

Rifles

Belgian Browning Grade I Auto, 22 LR cal, 19" bbl, pistol-grip/s....325.00
Colt Burgess Lever Action, 44 cal, 25" oct bbl, full mag, VG..1,700.00
Colt Burgess Spec O, 44 cal, 22" part rnd bbl, half mag 1,400.00
Colt Med Fr Lightning, 32-20 cal, Std Grade, 26" oct bbl, full mag........700.00
Colt Sauer African Big Game, 458 mag cal, 24" rnd bbl, w/scope, MIB..1,200.00
Colt Sauer Bolt Action Sporting Deluxe, 30-06 cal, 24" rnd bbl, NM ...850.00
Enfield Custom 1917 Bolt Action, 30 cal, 24" rnd bbl, pistol grip...........500.00
Henry, 44RF cal, std 24" bbl, crescent butt plate, ca 1864.................15,000.00
Krag 1898 Military, 30-40 cal, 30" bbl, f/s, cartouch dtd 1900, VG........450.00
Marlin Golden 39A Lever Action, 22 cal, 24" rnd bbl, full mag 175.00
Marlin 1881 Lever Action, 40-60 cal, 28" oct bbl, full mag, VG....800.00
Marlin 1893 Lever Action Take Down, 38-55 cal, 26" oct bbl, full mag...1,100.00
Marlin 1897 Lever Action, 22 cal, 24" oct bbl, full mag 550.00
Mauser Lt Sporting, 22LR cal, half/s, 23½" rnd bbl, 5-rnd mag..600.00
Mauser 1871, 11mm cal, 33½" bbl, dtd 1879, +bayonet 500.00
Mauser 27 Code G98, 8mm cal, 24" rnd bbl, dtd 1939 on receiver ring, G ...450.00
Mossberg M24M Bolt Action, 22 cal, 22" rnd bbl, full/s, M4 scope....150.00
Obendorf Mauser Model M Bolt Action, 8mm, 20" rnd bbl, 4X scope, rstr...450.00
Obendorff Mauser Sporting, 8x57 cal, 24" rnd bbl, factory eng 1,000.00
Remington M1903A3 Military, 30-06 cal, str/s, bbl dtd 2-43......375.00
Remington M4 Take-Down Single Shot, 22 cal, 22" oct bbl, str/s, G ...250.00
Remington M740 Semi-Auto, 30-06 cal, Std grade, 22" bbl.......225.00
Remington Zouave, 54 perc cal, 32" blued bbl, 1863 on lockplate, EX+ .3,250.00
Rock Island 1903 Bolt Action Military, 30-06 cal, bbl dtd 12-27, VG........375.00
Rock Island 1903 Military, 30-06 cal, pistol grip/s, bbl dtd 44, VG+ 425.00
Savage M110FP Left Hand Tactical, 308 cal, 24" bbl, Kevlar/s, NM...........575.00
Springfield 1884 Trapdoor, 45-70 cal, 32" bbl, VG....................450.00
Springfield 1903 Converted by AO Neidner, 22 cal, 20" rnd bbl 600.00
Springfield 2nd Allen Conv, 50-70 cal, 36½" bbl, G 450.00
Steyr Mannlicher-Schoenauer 1908 Sporting, 8mm, 20" bbl 750.00
Winchester Custom Eng 1895, 30-06 cal, 22" rnd bbl, walnut/s...3,500.00
Winchester Model 07 Semi-Auto, 351 cal, 20" bbl, semi-pistol grip, VG...350.00

Winchester M62A Pump, 22 cal, 23" bbl, ¾ mag, str/s, G..........**325.00**
Winchester Spec O 1886 Take-Down, 45-70WCF cal, 26" rnd bbl, VG.**1,700.00**
Winchester Spec O 1894, 38-55 cal, 21¾" oct bbl, half mag, G.**275.00**
Winchester Spec O 1894 Take-Down, 22-35 cal, 24" oct bbl **600.00**
Winchester Spec O 1894 Take-Down, 32 cal, std 26" rnd bbl, VG **450.00**
Winchester Spec O 1894 Take-Down, 38-55 cal, 26" oct bbl..**2,450.00**
Winchester Spec O 1895 Take-Down Pistol Grip Deluxe, 30 cal, NM..**2,250.00**
Winchester 1876 2nd Model, 45-75WCF cal, 28" oct bbl, full mag..**1,750.00**
Winchester 1886, 38-56WCF cal, 26" oct bbl, full mag...........**1,200.00**
Winchester 1886, 45-70 cal, std 26" rnd bbl, full mag..............**4,000.00**
Winchester 1886 Fifty Express, 50EX cal, 26" rnd bbl, full mag, EX+ ...**6,500.00**
Winchester 1886 Lever Action, 40-82 cal, 26" oct bbl, full mag...........**3,250.00**
Winchester 1894, 32-40 cal, std 26" oct bbl, button mag, VG....**500.00**
Winchester 1894, 38-55 cal, std 26" bbl, full mag, walnut/s....**1,350.00**
Winchester 1894, 38-55 cal, std 26" rnd bbl, full mag, G............**350.00**
Winchester 1894 Deluxe Take-Down, 30 cal, cvd walnut/s, prof rstr...**1,350.00**
Winchester 1895 Deluxe, 35 cal, std 24" rnd bbl, checkered/s ..**1,200.00**
Winchester 55 Take-Down, 30 cal, std 24" bbl, half mag, VG....**450.00**
Winchester 64, 219 zipper cal, std 26" rnd bbl, half mag, NM.**2,000.00**

Shotguns

Am Arms Side Opening Hammer Dbl Bbl, 10 ga, 30" Damascus bbls, G...**250.00**
Bertuzzi Hammer Self-Cocking Dbl Bbl, 20 ga, 28" bbls, NMIB ...**11,500.00**
Charles Daly O/U Skeet, 20 cal, 28" bbls, eng receiver...............**900.00**
Charles Daly O/U Trap, 12 ga, 32" bbls, beavertail forearm, M .**850.00**
Harrington & Richardson Hammerless Dbl Bbl, 10 ga, Field Grade, G+....**350.00**
Ithaca Flutes Dbl Bbl, 12 ga, 26" bbls, dbl triggers, G **150.00**
Ithaca Grade 2 Dbl Bbl, 12 ga, 30" bbls, dbl triggers, eng receiver...**450.00**
Mossberg M9200A1 Tactical, 12 ga, synthetic/s, 18½" cyl bbl, M ...**375.00**
Parker DHE Dbl Bbl, 12 ga, pistol grip/s, eng receiver, EX+ **1,750.00**
Parker GH Damascus Dbl Bbl, 10 ga, 30" steel bbls, #3 fr, eng, EX+...**1,700.00**
Parker PH Dbl Bbl, 12 ga, 1 1/2 fr w/26" bbls, full/mod choke, VG........**900.00**
Parker Trojan Dbl Bbl, 12 ga, 28" bbls, pistol grip/s, VG.............**600.00**
Parker VH Dbl Bbl, 12 ga, 1 1/2-fr w/18" bbls, full/mod choke, VG **750.00**
Stevens M59-A Bolt Action, 410 cal, 24" bbl w/mag tube below, VG...**90.00**
Winchester M12 Deluxe Pump, 20 ga, style 4 eng w/gold inlay **1,600.00**
Winchester M12 Pump, 12 ga, Field grade, 28" plain mod bbl, EX+ **450.00**
Winchester M42 Pump, 410 cal, 26" plain full choke bbl, VG ...**575.00**
Winchester 1897 Riot, 12 ga, 20" bbl, walnut/s, sling swivel, G .**700.00**
Winchester 1901 Lever Action, 10 ga, 30" bbl, full choke, EX+ **900.00**
WW Greener Damascus Hammer Dbl Bbl, 12-ga, eng lockplates, VG ..**350.00**

Swords

All swords listed below are priced 'with scabbard,' unless otherwise noted.

Ames US Musicians 1840, metal blade, brass hdl, 1860, VG......**100.00**
Ames 1832 Pattern Short Artillery, Roman-style, 19" blade, G..**300.00**
Ames 1860 Cavalry, brass officer's buckle on hanger, 1862 ....**875.00**
Cavalry, 36" blade, ⅜" thick at handguard, leather-wrapped hdl, VG..**425.00**
Civil War Presentation, 1842 Pattern ft officer's, 30" blade, EX+ **1,450.00**
Clauberg Civil War foot officer's, 31¾" etch blade, VG+........**1,550.00**
Confederate Naval Cutlass, dbl-edge 20" blade, eagle pommel, EX+ **1,500.00**
Leech & Rigdon Confederate, 31" blade w/unstopped fullers, EX+ **12,250.00**
Yataghan, 22½" blade, brass hdl, attached w/iron pin, G............**200.00**

Weather Vanes

The earliest weather vanes were of handmade wrought iron and were generally simple angular silhouettes with a small hole suggesting an eye. Later copper, zinc, and polychromed wood with features in relief were fashioned into more realistic forms. Ships, horses, fish, Indians,

roosters, and angels were popular motifs. In the nineteenth century, silhouettes were often made from sheet metal. Wooden figures became highly carved and were painted in vivid colors. E.G. Washburne and Company in New York was one of the most prominent manufacturers of weather vanes during the last half of the century. Two-dimensional sheet metal weather vanes are increasing in value due to the already heady prices of the full-bodied variety. Originality, strength of line, and patina help to determine value. When no condition is indicated, the items listed below are assumed to be in excellent condition.

Arrow, copper, allover verdigris w/gilt traces, late 1800s, 18x42"..**2,000.00**
Arrow, copper, on pole, 12x54" **500.00**
Arrow & banner, gilt zinc, weathered, 12x68"..........................**2,000.00**
Arrow on sphere, sheet & cast copper w/old gr patina, rprs, 36x32".**1,375.00**
Banner, cvd/pnt wood, old weathered wht pnt, 19th C, 39x60"........**1,380.00**
Black Hawk, molded copper, verdigris w/gilt traces, 1890s, 19x33"...**6,550.00**
Bull, sheet copper, silhouette, EX gr patina, 24" **440.00**
Bull, sheet metal silhouette, battered, old blk rpt, 25" L **385.00**
Car, cvd/pnt wood & copper, roadster, early 20th C, 12x23", EX **6,900.00**
Cow, copper hollow body w/cast zinc head, rpr/bullet hole, 28" L ...**2,750.00**
Cow, gilt copper, full body, weathered, 19th C, 21x33x8" **13,800.00**
Eagle, copper & cast zinc w/later worn gilt, new base, 16x19" **385.00**
Eagle, hollow-bodied copper w/emb detail, EX patina, rprs, 20x23"....**880.00**
Eagle w/wings spread, sheet lead, 30x57" **385.00**
Fish, pnt zinc, flat sheet, appl fins, glass eyes, 19th C, 14x16".**1,000.00**
Horse leaping, 2 riveted sheets of tin, blk pnt, damage, 22x35"..**550.00**
Horse prancing, sheet iron, old pitting/pnt, bullet holes, 27x32" .**715.00**
Horse running, copper w/gray-gr patina, hollow body, 31".......**3,100.00**
Horse running, gilt copper, w/directionals, late 19th C, 15x25" **2,500.00**
Horse running, hollow copper w/CI head, rpr, 29"+pole & directionals.**1,900.00**
Horse running, sheet iron, pitting/blk pnt traces, bullet holes, 49".............**935.00**
Horse running, zinc head/copper body, full body, pnt traces, 19x41".......**6,500.00**

Horse trotting, copper with bullet holes, tail missing, EX patina, $1,350.00.

Hunter taking aim, sheet iron, ca 1900, 26½x25"....................**1,265.00**
Initials in banner, copper w/gilt traces, rprs, 29x72" **575.00**
Jockey on running horse, Cushing & White, old pnt/gilt traces, 16x27".**13,800.00**
Rooster, ark-welded steel, blk rpt w/mc details, wood base, 26" ..**140.00**
Rooster, cast metal, old rstr, CI directionals, old pnt, 59x26x24".....**715.00**
Rooster, copper, hollow body w/flat tooled tail, rpr, 19", VG **440.00**
Rooster, hollow-bodied zinc w/emb details, pnt traces, 20th C, 23" ...**1,100.00**
Rooster, sheet iron, riveted strapwork, Am, 37x28"....................**975.00**
Sailing ship, gilt copper & iron, 3 directionals only, 32x25"....**2,300.00**
Scrolled banner, 6 stylized C scrolls in strapwork fr, bronze, 21x50"..**750.00**
Stag leaping, gilt copper, att Harris, 1890s, 26x30"+CI stand ..**16,000.00**
Sulky w/horse & driver, molded copper, Fiske, late 1800s, 50" L..**17,250.00**

Weaving

Early Americans used a variety of tools and a great amount of time to produce the material from which their clothing was made. Soaked and dried flax was broken on a flax brake to remove waste material. It was then tapped and stroked with a scutching knife. Hackles further removed waste and separated the short fibers from the longer ones. Unspun fibers were placed on the distaff on the spinning wheel for processing into yarn. The yarn was then wound around a reel for measuring. Three tools used for this purpose were the niddy-noddy, the reel yarn winder, and the click reel. After it was washed and dyed, the yarn was transferred to a barrel-cage or squirrel-cage swift and fed onto a bobbin winder.

Today flax wheels are more plentiful than the large wool wheels since they were small and could be more easily stored and preserved. The distaff, an often-discarded or misplaced part of the wheel, is very scarce. French spinners from the Quebec area painted their wheels. Many have been stripped and refinished by those unaware of this fact. Wheels may be very simple or have a great amount of detail, depending upon the owner's ethnic background and the maker's skill.

Flax wheel, hardwood, old soft finish, bone trim, European, 28"..**165.00**
Hackle, hardwood w/scratch cvgs, old red/blk stain, 30", EX **330.00**
Niddy-noddy, tapered shaft, pegged, early 1800s, 18x15" **85.00**
Niddy-noddy, walnut, chip-cvd decor, dtd 1798, 14x17½" **400.00**
Spool winder, 3-spool holder w/ivory finials, 19th C, 6½" **800.00**
Swift, CI cup w/rtcl flowers, CI base w/man & woman figures, 17x20".**285.00**
Swift, mahog shaft, whalebone disks, ivory peg, 19th C, 17x22" dia **500.00**
Swift, scrimshaw, baleen shaft, ivory clamp, cushion top, 1850, 8"........**700.00**
Swift, whalebone & ivory, colored trnings, 1850s, 14" **1,000.00**
Swift, wood w/HP floral decor, Am, 19th C, 22½".....................**575.00**
Wheel, Arcadian hardwood & wrought iron, cvd spindles, 1850s, 36x29"...**385.00**
Yarn winder, hardwoods w/worn old red, EX detail, 20x26" dia ..**140.00**
Yarn winder, maple w/curly maple base, old patina, 43" **110.00**
Yarn winder, rfn hardwood, splayed legs, 6 trn arms, 25" reel......**175.00**
Yarn winder, 2-pc harvest table model, old red & blk pnt, 21" ...**275.00**

Webb

Thomas Webb and Sons have been glassmakers in Stourbridge, England, since 1837. Besides their fine cameo glass, they have also made enameled ware and pieces heavily decorated with applied glass ornaments. The butterfly is a motif that has been so often featured that it tends to suggest Webb as the manufacturer. Our advisor for this category is Don Williams; he is listed in the Directory under Missouri. See also specific types of glass such as Alexandrite, Burmese, Mother of Pearl, and Peachblow.

Cameo

Vases: Buds and flower, butterfly, white on blue, 5½", $2,500.00; Sunflowers, butterfly, white on raisin, 6", $3,750.00. (Photo courtesy Early Auction Company)

Bottle, scent; butterfly/ferns, lt bl on Prussian Bl, silver cap, 4" **2,200.00**
Bottle, scent; floral, rose/wht/citron, flip lid, 2¾" **1,300.00**
Bottle, scent; floral spray, wht on red, SP foliate cap, 2¼".......**1,100.00**
Bottle, scent; pussy willow twigs, citron/wht/red, silver lid, 6¼" ...**2,500.00**

Bottle, scent; shells/seaweed, wht on red, dome lid, 3⅛" **2,000.00**
Bottle, scent; trumpet flowers, Chinese Red on yel, teardrop form, 4" ..**2,750.00**
Bowl, floral branch/butterfly, bl/wht/gold, L/6107, 1¼x6"...........**985.00**
Bowl, morning glories, wht on bl, Gem, 7"...............................**1,685.00**
Bowl, swallows/trees/flowers, wht/purple on bl, Gem, 9" **28,000.00**
Flask, swan's head, red/wht, #11109, gold-washed sterling cap, 5⅜"...**6,500.00**
Jar, citron; berry pods, wht on red, silver lid, 4¼" **1,650.00**
Jar, potpourri; Ivory, acorns/leaves, bk: butterfly, 6" **2,500.00**
Rose bowl, brambles/rose bushes/butterfly/caterpillar, wht on red, 6" ..**2,875.00**
Toothpick holder, holly/berries, wht on citron frost, 2½" **1,500.00**
Vase, buds on thorny branch, wht on Prussian Bl, dbl borders, 5¼"...**1,800.00**
Vase, cherries/flowers/leaves, wht on amber, 9½" **2,200.00**
Vase, floral stems/butterfly, wht on red, baluster, 10½" **1,850.00**
Vase, floral/butterfly, wht on peachblow, dbl-gourd form, 7"....**2,750.00**
Vase, flowers/butterfly, wht on bl, ornate border, 5½" **2,500.00**
Vase, fuchsia, linear borders, wht on red, 3½" **1,265.00**
Vase, fuchsia/leaves/butterfly, chartreuse on wht, att, 5" **575.00**
Vase, gingko leaves/stems, wht on bl, bulbous, flared rim, 6¼" ..**1,800.00**
Vase, Ivory, foxglove spires, slim neck, 10½" **1,250.00**
Vase, Ivory, oak leaves/acorns w/gold, bottle form, Gem, 5" ...**1,265.00**
Vase, leaves/flowers/pods, wht on brn, cylindrical, 6½" **1,800.00**
Vase, narcissus/grasses, clear/ruby/wht opal, 7½" **2,750.00**
Vase, orchid lilies/butterfly, yel/wht on red, bulbous, 5¾"........**2,400.00**
Vase, raspberries, rose-red on wht, bamboo cylinder, 8¾x2½" ...**1,850.00**
Vase, wild roses/leaves, wht on red, 2¾x4" **1,750.00**

Miscellaneous

Bottle, lay-down; bl MOP Dmn Quilt, teardrop from, 5½" **600.00**
Compote, ruby w/clear stem, threaded ft/ruffled, Patent, 5½x8½"...**600.00**
Jardiniere, cranes/gilt/jeweled flowers on satin, 12x13" **665.00**
Sweetmeat, heavy gold florals on aqua, SP lid/etc, 5x3⅜" **300.00**
Vase, heavy gold prunus on ivory opaque, stick form, 7½"..........**185.00**
Vase, prunus/pine needles, gold on shaded brn, 5½x5¼" **435.00**
Vase, ruby cased w/gold fernery & decor, stick form, 13"...........**250.00**
Vase, yel cased w/pk, gilt flowers/insects, #7686, 8" **300.00**

Wedgwood

Josiah Wedgwood established his pottery in Burslem, England, in 1759. He produced only molded utilitarian earthenwares until 1770 when new facilities were opened at Etruria for the production of ornamental wares. It was there he introduced his famous Basalt and Jasperware. Jasperware, an unglazed fine stoneware decorated with classic figures in white relief, was usually produced in blues, but it was also made in ground colors of green, lilac, yellow, black, or white. Occasionally three or more colors were used in combination. It has been in continuous production to the present day and is the most easily recognized of all the Wedgwood lines. Jasper-dip is a ware with a solid-color body or a white body that has been dipped in an overlay color. It was introduced in the late 1700s and is the type most often encountered on today's market.

Though Wedgwood's Jasperware was highly acclaimed, on a more practical basis his improved creamware was his greatest success, due to the ease with which it could be potted and because its lighter weight significantly reduced transportation expenses. Wedgwood was able to offer 'chinaware' at affordable prices. Queen Charlotte was so pleased with the ware that she allowed it to be called 'Queen's Ware.' Most creamware was marked simply 'WEDGWOOD.' ('Wedgwood & Co.' and 'Wedgewood' are marks of other potters.) From 1769 to 1780, Wedgwood was in partnership with Thomas Bentley; artwares of the highest quality may bear the 'Wedgwood & Bentley' mark indicating this partnership. Moonlight Lustre, an allover splashed-on effect of pink intermingling with gray, brown, or yellow, was made from 1805 to 1815. Porcelain was made, though not to any great extent, from 1812 to 1822. Bone china was produced before 1822 and after 1872. These types of wares were marked 'WEDGWOOD' (with a printed 'Portland Vase' mark after 1872). Stone china and Pearlware were made from about 1820 to 1875. Examples of either may be found with a printed or impressed mark to indicate their body type. During the late 1800s, Wedgwood produced some fine parian and majolica. Creamware, hand painted by Emile Lessore, was sold from about 1860 to 1875. From the twentieth century, several lines of lustre wares — Butterfly, Dragon, and Fairyland (designed by Daisy Makeig-Jones) — have attracted the collector and, as their prices suggest, are highly sought after and admired.

Nearly all of Wedgwood's wares are clearly marked. 'WEDG-WOOD' was used before 1891, after which time 'ENGLAND' was added. Most examples marked 'MADE IN ENGLAND' were made after 1905. A detailed study of all marks is recommended for accurate dating. See also Majolica.

Key:
WW — WEDGWOOD   WWMIE — WEDGWOOD Made
WWE — WEDGWOOD England   in England

Biscuit jar, Jasper, 3-color, SP trim, WW, late 1800s, 5¾", NM..**500.00**
Boquetiere, Queen's Ware, brn basketweave, pierced lid, WW, 10"..**1,380.00**
Bough pot, Jasper, yel, cherubs, appl bl relief, WW, 5"............**1,600.00**
Bough pot, Pearlware w/mottled buff & gray bands, w/lid, WW, 11"....**430.00**
Bowl, Fairyland Lustre, Castle on Road/Fairy in Cage, Z5125, WW, 9"....**4,000.00**
Bowl, Lustre K'ang Hsi, butterflies on MOP, Z4832, WW, 8⅛"..**600.00**
Bowl, Queen's Ware, vintage borders, scalloped rim, WW, 1914, 11⅝"..**315.00**
Box, music; Jasper medallions on walnut vnr casket, 4-tune, WW, 8½"...**575.00**
Bust, Basalt, Byron, WW, 8½"..**575.00**
Bust, Basalt, Mercury, waisted socle, WW, 18¼"......................**2,100.00**
Bust, Basalt, Venus, WW, 14"..**2,100.00**
Candelabrum, Jasper, dk bl, classical figures w/gilt, 5-light, WW, 20".**460.00**
Candlestick, Basalt, foliage & figures w/gilt, WW, 9½"...........**1,265.00**
Candlesticks, Basalt, dolphin on base w/shell border, WWE, 9", pr...**1,100.00**
Candlesticks, Bone China, Powder Blue lustre, mc fruit, WW, 8", pr..**550.00**
Candlesticks, Jasper, lilac, medallions/festoons, WW, 1850s, 6"....**1,375.00**
Chandelier, Jasper, bl, classical relief, 6-light, unmk, 1890s, 22".**635.00**
Chimney ornament, Queen's Ware, Emile Lessore, children, WW, 1875, 7"..**1,035.00**
Cigar rest, Jasper, yel, appl bl classical relief & border, WW, 4"..**500.00**
Clock, mantel; Queen's Ware, landscapes, arched top w/verse, WW, 13"..**575.00**
Clock case, Jasper, dk bl, rpl movement, WWE, 6"......................**375.00**
Coffee can & saucer, Jasper, bl, classical panels, WW, 1800s, 5"......**1,035.00**
Condiment stand, Queen's Ware, fisherman, molded ends, WW, 10¼"..**515.00**
Cup & saucer, tea; Caneware, red anthemion band/children in relief, WW.....**865.00**
Figurine, Basalt, Cleopatra, nude on rock, WW, 8¾".................**975.00**
Figurine, Basalt, Faun & Flute, WW, 16⅝"............................**2,185.00**
Figurine, Basalt, Mercury, blk, gilt title, WWE, 1975, 11¼".........**1,300.00**
Figurine, Basalt, Nymph at Well, WW, 11"............................**2,400.00**
Figurine, Basalt, Winter, circular base, WW, 10"......................**1,035.00**
Foot bath, Pearlware, pk & gr panels, hdls, WW, early 1800s, 17½"....**450.00**
Incense burner, Drabware, dolphin tripod base, WW, 1830s, 5⅞"........**500.00**
Incense burner, Rosso Antico, dolphin base, pierced lid, WW, 5⅛".**2,415.00**
Inkpot, Jasper, gr, classical figures, WW, 1900, insert missing, 6"...**315.00**
Inkstand, Drabware, bird-head hdls, center candle holder, WW, 8"...**1,100.00**
Inkstand, Jasper, lt bl, foliage, WW, 1790s, 2"............................**925.00**
Jardiniere, brn stonware, Oriental florals, gilt mask hdls, WW, 6".......**700.00**
Jardiniere, Jasper, crimson, classical figures, WW, 1920s, 8" **2,400.00**
Jardiniere, Jasper, lilac, Muses, lion masks/rings, WW, 19th C, 8" ...**700.00**
Jug, Basalt, Bacchanalian boys, mask hdl, silver mt, WW, 7¾"...**1,725.00**
Jug, Jasper, crimson, classical figures, WW, 1920s, 6½"..............**900.00**
Jug, Jasper, yel, classical figures/florals, WW, ca 1900, 4⅝".........**575.00**
Jug, Queen's Ware, red bird & garden transfer, Doric style, WW, 12"..**200.00**
Jug, Silver Jubilee; Jasper, 3-color, Diceware, WWE, 1977, 4¾".**250.00**

Lamp, oil; Queen's Ware, E Lessore, cherubs, WW, 1869, 5⅞"...**635.00**
Medallion, Basalt, John Wesley, w/crown & angel border, WW, 3½".**315.00**
Mug, Basalt, molded oak leaves, silver mts, WW, 3" **630.00**
Mug, Jasper, bl, Drink Faire..., vintage border, WW, 1900s, 5¼"..**315.00**
Pipe stand, Jasper, bl, Xd pipes/pouch, WW, late 1800s, 5¼"......**260.00**
Planter, Jasper, bl, Muses w/foliate frs, WW, 19th C, 6¼"...........**500.00**
Plaque, Basalt, Judgement of Hercules, WW, 11¾" L **1,600.00**
Plaque, Basalt, Lioness & Cupids, WW, 10⅞"......................**2,300.00**
Plaque, Basalt, Vulcan Forging Armour of Achilles, WWE, 6x10"+fr...**700.00**
Plaque, Jasper, bl, classical man, oval, WW, 6½x8½" **1,600.00**
Plaque, Jasper, bl, Muses, rectangular, WW, 19th C, 4x10".........**500.00**
Plaque, Jasper, gr, Hector Taking Leave of Andromache, WW, 6x18".**2,750.00**
Plate, Jasper, Am Bicentennial, 5-color, WWE, 1976, 8⅞".........**460.00**
Shade, Bone China, vintage intaglio on bl, lithophane, WW, 1900s, 12"..**1,100.00**
Shade, Bone China, 4-panel, lithophane, WW, late 1800s, 3¾" H **175.00**
Strawberry dish, Queen's Ware, Pattern #1029, WW, 1800s, 10½" **575.00**
Tea canister, Jasper, lt bl, classical children, WW, 1790s, 5⅜"....**435.00**
Tea set, Jasper, bl, Geo VI/Queen Elizabeth, WWE, 5" pot+cr/sug ..**250.00**
Tea set, Jasper, gr, classical figures, WW, mini, 4-pc **500.00**
Teakettle, Basalt, bamboo molded, ca 1897, 6¼"........................**575.00**
Teapot, smear-glaze wht stoneware, floral band, spaniel finial, WW, 5"....**200.00**
Tile picture, allegorical female, Marsden's Pat, WW, 1880, 18x6"............**865.00**
Tray, pin; Jasper, yel, oak/acorn border, WW, 1850s, 5⅞" **350.00**
Vase, Basalt, classical figures, WW, 9"..................................**1,035.00**
Vase, Basalt, classical medallions & festoons, WW, 8¼".............**515.00**
Vase, bud; Basalt w/silver o/l, WW, 6"..................................**460.00**
Vase, Flambe, Chinese shape, WW, early 1900s, 10"..................**345.00**
Vase, Jasper, bl, Blind Man's Bluff, WW, late 1700s, 10¾" **1,100.00**
Vase, Jasper, bl, classical figures, Portland, 19th C, 10"............**2,100.00**
Vase, Jasper, bl, classical medallions, WWE, 1968, 11½" **400.00**
Vase, Jasper, bl, uptrn hdls, Cupid finial, WW, 8"......................**575.00**

Vase, Jasper, black, Dancing Hours (relief design), Bacchus head handles, missing lid, WWE, ca 1905, EX, 20", $1,500.00.

Vase, Jasper, blk, Dancing Hours, Bacchus-mask hdls, WW, 9¼" **1,500.00**
Vase, Jasper, gr, classical figures, hdls, WW, 10"........................**850.00**
Vase, Jasper, terra cotta, appl blk muses, WWE, 1957, 11¾" **975.00**
Vase, Lindsay Ware, HP peacock, hdls, WW, 1910s, 8⅞"........**4,000.00**
Vase, spill; Jasper, yel, appl bl foliage, WW, 1850s, 3⅞" **975.00**
Vase, Terra Cotta, wht w/gr & brn hoops, WW, 9" **1,600.00**

Weil Ware

Max Weil came to the United States in the 1940s, settling in California. There he began manufacturing dinnerware, figurines, cookie jars, and wall pockets. American clays were used, and the dinnerware was all hand decorated. Weil died in 1954; the company closed two years later. The last backstamp to be used was the outline of a burro with the words 'Weil Ware — Made in California.' Many unmarked pieces found today originally carried a silver foil label; but you'll often find a four-digit handwritten number series, especially on figurines. For further study we recommend *The Collector's Encyclopedia of California Pottery* by Jack Chipman (Collector Books).

Ashtray, gold flecks, heavy 25.00
Bowl, divided vegetable; Malay Bambu 42.50
Box, Ming Tree, w/lid, 5x5" 55.00
Butter dish, Malay Bambu, w/lid 25.00
Butter dish, Malay Blossom 25.00
Candle holders, Malay Bambu, 2", 4⅛" sq base, pr 40.00
Cup, Malay Blossom, sq..10.00
Cup & saucer, Rose 18.00
Figurine, girl in yel dress w/bl flowers, yel hat, 7½" 45.00
Figurine, lady in bl dress w/hands in yel muff, 10" 60.00
Flower holder, Asian boy w/2 sm containers on shoulder, 11".......25.00
Flower holder, girl in yel dress holds bl basket, hand on hip, 6½".35.00
Flower holder, girl kneeling beside planter, 7½" 55.00
Flower holder, lady in pk dress holds umbrella before planter, 10" ...70.00
Gravy bowl, Rose, attached underplate, 3¼x6½" 38.00
Pitcher, Roses, w/ice lip, 7" 35.00
Plate, dinner; Birchwood, 4 for 25.00
Plate, Malay Blossom, 9¾" sq 15.00
Platter, Malay Blossom 22.50
Platter, Rose, sq, 13½" 27.50
Vase, Ming Tree, slanted top, 11" 40.00
Vase, 2-toned gr, fan form, 7¼x8½" 25.00
Wall pocket, lady's head, brn hair, bl eyes, 6".....................60.00

Weller

The Weller Pottery Company was established in Zanesville, Ohio, in 1882, the outgrowth of a small one-kiln log cabin works Sam Weller had operated in Fultonham. Through an association with Wm. Long, he entered the art pottery field in 1895, producing the Lonhuda Ware Long had perfected in Steubenville six years earlier. His famous Louwelsa line was merely a continuation of Lonhuda and was made in at least five hundred different shapes until 1924. Many fine lines of artware followed under the direction of Charles Babcock Upjohn, art director from 1895 to 1904: Dickens Ware (1st Line), under-glaze slip decorations on dark backgrounds; Turada, featuring applied ivory bands of delicate openwork on solid dark brown backgrounds; and Aurelian, similar to Louwelsa, but with a brushed-on rather than blended ground. One of their most famous lines was 2nd Line Dickens, introduced in 1900. Backgrounds, characteristically caramel shading to turquoise matt, were decorated by sgraffito with animals, golfers, monks, Indians, and scenes from Dickens novels. The work is often artist signed. Sicardo, 1903, was a metallic lustre line in tones of rose, blue, green, or purple with flowing Art Nouveau patterns developed within the glaze.

Frederick Hurten Rhead, who worked for Weller from 1903 to 1904, created the prestigious Jap Birdimal line decorated with geisha girls, landscapes, storks, etc., accomplished through application of heavy slip forced through the tiny nozzle of a squeeze bag. Other lines to his credit are L'Art Nouveau, produced in both high-gloss brown and matt pastels, and 3rd Line Dickens, often decorated with Cruikshank's illustrations in relief. Other early artware lines were Eocean, Floretta, Hunter, Perfecto, Dresden, Etched Matt, and Etna.

In 1920 John Lessel was hired as art director, and under his supervision several new lines were created. LaSa, LaMar, Marengo, and Besline attest to his expertise with metallic lustres. The last of the artware lines and one of the most sought after by collectors today is Hudson, first made during the early 1920s. Hudson, a semimatt glazed ware, was beautifully artist decorated on shaded backgrounds with florals, animals, birds, and scenics. Notable artists often signed their work, among them Hester Pillsbury, Dorothy England Laughead, Ruth Axline, Claude Leffler, Sarah Reid McLaughlin, E.L. Pickens, and Mae Timberlake.

During the '30s Weller produced a line of gardenware and naturalistic life-sized figures of dogs, cats, swans, geese, and playful gnomes. The Depression brought a slow, steady decline in sales, and by 1948 the pottery was closed. For a more thorough study we recommend *The Collector's Encyclopedia of Weller Pottery* by Sharon and Bob Huxford, available at your local library or from Collector Books.

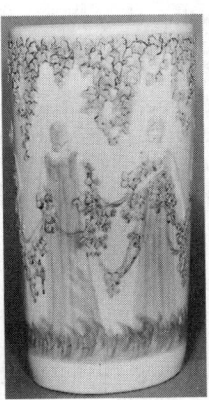

Zona, umbrella stand, young women holding garlands, glossy, 20½", $1,500.00.

Alvin, vase, tree trunk form, hdld, 12" 95.00
Arcadia, vase, #A-4, 5½" 40.00
Arcola, lamp base, berry branch, hdld, 10" 175.00
Arcola, planter, roses, ruffled rim, hdld, 5x9" 150.00
Ardsley, bulb bowl, 5" 125.00
Ardsley, candle holders, 3", pr 150.00
Ardsley, fan vase, cattails, 8" 175.00
Ardsley, vase, 3-sided, iris, 7" 250.00
Atlas, candle holders, #C-12, pr 110.00
Atlas, dish, #C-2, w/lid, 3½" 175.00
Aurelian, ewer, stag, sgn Abel, 12".......................................1,250.00
Aurelian, vase, floral, tapered, sgn RA, 13" 1,100.00
Baldin, vase, long neck w/bulbous bottom, apple branch, 7" 75.00
Barcelona, ewer, stylized floral, bulbous, 9½" 275.00
Blossom, vase, bulbous, hdld, 14" 225.00
Blossom, vase, dbl; #G-24, 12½" 175.00
Blue & Decorated, cylindrical, 8½" 225.00
Blue & Decorated, vase, hexagonal, 9½" 250.00
Blue & Decorated, vase, 4-sided, 9½" 200.00
Blue Drapery, bowl, 3" 65.00
Blue Drapery, jardiniere, 5½" 95.00
Blue Ware, comport, fruit swag, 5½" 275.00
Blue Ware, jardiniere, 2 angels, 8½" 300.00
Blue Ware, vase, tapering cylinder, classical dancer, 8½" 250.00
Bonito, candle holder, hdld-dish form w/ped ft, 3½" 125.00
Bonito, vase, floral, rim hdls, sgn NC, 10" 400.00
Bouquet, vase, #B-5, 8" 95.00
Breton, bowl, emb floral band, 4" 95.00
Brighton, bluebird on apple stump, wings spread, 7½" 700.00
Brighton, canary, 2½" 200.00
Brighton, crow, 6½" 900.00
Brighton, flamingo, 6" 500.00
Brighton, parrot on hanging perch, 15" 2,500.00
Brighton, rooster, wht, 9½" 1,500.00
Brighton, woodpecker, 6½" 400.00
Burntwood, plaque, bird on tree branch, 12" dia 400.00
Burntwood, urn, birds & flowers, pot form, 6½" 225.00
Burntwood, vase, flowers on stems, hexagonal, 5" 125.00
Camelot, vase, geometric design, genie-type bottle form, 8" 250.00

Cameo, basket, ball shape, ftd, 7½"..............85.00
Cameo, vase, sq, 8½"..............75.00
Cameo Jewel, umbrella stand, cameos/jewels, cylindrical, 22".1,250.00
Candis, hanging basket, scrolls & flowers/stepped panels, 5½"...125.00
Chase, vase, bl, bulbous, 12"..............650.00
Chengtu, ginger jar, ped ft, w/lid, 12"..............275.00
Chengtu, urn, rnd pot form, 5½"..............115.00
Clarmont, bowl, hdld, 3"..............60.00
Classic, plate, 11½"..............70.00
Classic, wall pocket, 7½"..............125.00
Claywood, mug, floral, 4½"..............115.00
Claywood, spittoon, 4½"..............150.00
Claywood, vase, floral, pot form w/angled shoulder, 3"..............75.00
Claywood, vase, pine cones, flared base, 6½"..............110.00
Coppertone, ashtray, frog, 6½"..............225.00
Coppertone, basket, emb floral, twig hdl, 8½"..............225.00
Coppertone, candle holder, turtle, 3"..............275.00
Coppertone, vase, ftd trumpet form w/scalloped rim, 6½"..............200.00
Copra, basket, floral, 11"..............275.00
Cornish, candle holder, berries & leaves, 3½"..............45.00
Creamware, hanging basket, rtcl pattern, 11½"..............200.00
Creamware, mug, HP floral, 5"..............125.00
Creamware, planter, 4-sided, hdld, 3"..............65.00
Creamware, vase, fan shape, Ethel, 6"..............70.00
Creamware, vase, grape motif, 11½"..............400.00
Darsie, vase, tassel swag, scalloped rim, 5½"..............70.00
Delsa, basket, emb floral, ftd, 7"..............95.00
Dickens I, mug, bust image of admiral, 5"..............1,000.00
Dickens I, mug, floral, sgn MM, 4½"..............150.00
Dickens II, cherubs (2), 4-sided, ftd, 11½"..............1,750.00
Dickens II, ewer, mermaid, shell-formed lip, 10½"..............700.00
Dickens II, mug, grapes, 5"..............300.00
Dickens II, tankard, monk, semi-gloss, sgn FF & Ferrell, 12½"..2,750.00
Dickens II, vase, Chief Hollowhorn Bear, sgn AD, 13"..............2,750.00
Dickens II, vase, lady golfer, sgn DS, ped ft, 8"..............1,750.00
Dickens II, vase, peasant girl w/baskets, tapered, sm neck, 13"...1,500.00
Dickens II, vase, rabbit by pond, cylindrical, sgn, 17"..............2,250.00
Dickens II, vase, scenic/figure, cvd cylinder, sgn RGT, 12½"..2,500.00
Dickens II, vase, shepherd & flock, 15"..............2,500.00
Dickens III, creamer, Charles Dickens on disk, #003, 4"..............250.00
Dickens III, mug, Colonial man w/pipe, dbl hdld, 4"..............300.00
Dickens III, mug, Master Belling, #7, 5"..............600.00
Dickens III, vase, lady in bonnet (bust), sm hdls at neck, 6"..............300.00
Dupont, planter, sq, topiary/doves, 3½"..............50.00
Dupont, vase, rose motif, cylindrical, 10"..............125.00
Elberta, bowl, 3-part, 3½"..............85.00
Elberta, cornucopia, 8"..............95.00
Elberta, nut dish, 3"..............65.00
Eocean, basket, floral, ped ft, 6½"..............550.00
Eocean, bud vase, floral, 6½"..............135.00
Eocean, candlestick, berries & leaves, sgn FF, 9"..............600.00
Eocean, vase, floral, bottle form, sgn LJB, 11½"..............850.00
Eocean, vase, floral, pot w/hdls at rim, gray to wht, sgn MS, 6"..350.00
Eocean, vase, floral, sgn AH, 13½"..............800.00
Eocean, vase, poodle, flask shape, ftd, sgn L Blake, 7½"..............1,700.00
Eocean (Late Line), vase, bulbous, sgn MT, 10½"..............450.00
Etna, pitcher, floral, lt pk/gr on gray to wht, 6½"..............225.00
Etna, vase, grape branch, shouldered/tapering, gray/wht, 15"..............850.00
Etna, vase, lizard, 4½"..............800.00
Evergreen, candle holder, triple; 7½"..............115.00
Fairfield, vase, band of cherubs w/fluted bottom, tapered, 9½"...125.00
Flemish, basket tub, roses, tapered, hdld, 4"..............115.00
Flemish, inkwell, bird motif, 4½x7"..............600.00
Flemish, jardiniere, geometric w/flowers in circles & panels, 8"..145.00

Flemish, jardiniere, peony stems, 8"..............350.00
Flemish, vase, shape #8, bl, 10"..............300.00
Fleron, bowl, #J-6, 3"..............100.00
Fleron, vase, bulbous, hdld, 8"..............175.00
Florala, bud vase, dbl; gate form, 5"..............85.00
Florala, wall pocket, paneled, 10"..............225.00
Florenzo, vase w/frog cover, fluted, ftd, 7"..............150.00
Florenzo, window box, floral swag, scalloped rim, 3"..............70.00
Floretta, ewer, emb grapes, gray to wht, 6"..............200.00
Floretta, ewer, floral, bulbous, brn, 4½"..............150.00
Floretta, mug, emb grapes, brn, 5"..............150.00
Floretta, vase, emb floral, bulbous, pk on brn to cream, 5½"..............325.00
Floretta (Matt), tankard, apples on a branch, sgn CD, 13½"..............800.00
Floretta (Matt), tankard, pears on a branch, 10½"..............550.00
Forest, basket, 8½"..............300.00
Forest, jardiniere, 7"..............400.00
Forest, pitcher, glossy, 5"..............250.00
Forest, planter, tub form, #3, 3½"..............95.00
Forest, window box, 5½x14½"..............500.00
Fruitone, bud vase, tall thin neck w/bulbous bottom, 11½"..............150.00
Fruitone, vase, hexagonal, 8½"..............175.00
Fudzi, stylized flowers, 4-sided, 10x3¾"..............2,600.00
Glendale, bowl w/frog, birds/nest w/eggs, 15½"..............550.00
Glendale, vase, shore bird, cylindrical, 6"..............400.00
Gloria, ewer, #G-12, 9"..............100.00
Gloria, vase, iris on tree trunk form, ftd, 12½"..............125.00
Golbrogreen, lamp base, 12"..............250.00
Golbrogreen, wall vase, 8½"..............225.00
Goldenglow, candle holder, triple; 7½"..............175.00
Greenbriar, pitcher, 10"..............275.00
Greenbriar, vase, high/low hdls, 7½"..............175.00
Greora, vase, angled hdls at plain rim & shoulder, 9"..............200.00
Greora, vase, cylindrical, 11½"..............275.00
Hobart, bowl, ftd, 3x9½"..............85.00
Hobart, candle holder, kneeling nude, 6"..............300.00
Hudson, vase, lg iris, cylindrical, sgn Axline, 8½"..............550.00
Hudson, vase, scenic, cylindrical, sgn Timberlake, 8½"..............800.00
Hudson, vase, swans/willow, cylindrical, sgn Pillsbury, 14½"...3,000.00
Hudson, vase, tiger in grass, slightly angled, plain rim, 8"..............2,500.00
Hudson-Perfecto, vase, Arab on horseback, 13"..............4,000.00
Hudson-Perfecto, vase, mums, bulbous pot form, sgn C Leffler, 9½"..950.00
Hunter, vase, birds in flight, #413, sgn UJ, 7½"..............950.00
Hunter, vase, stag, #343, 6½"..............750.00
Ivoris, basket, 5"..............95.00
Ivoris, powder box, rnd, 4"..............50.00
Ivory (Clinton Ivory), jardiniere, squirrels in tree, 6½"..............150.00
Ivory (Clinton Ivory), vase, corn-like pattern, bulbous bottom, 5"...85.00
Ivory (Clinton Ivory), vase, paneled leaf pattern, cylindrical, 10"...85.00
Jap Birdimal, pitcher, bird in flight, 4"..............400.00
Jap Birdimal, vase, geisha seated playing instrument, 4"..............400.00
Jap Birdimal, vase, geisha standing, sgn VMH, 13"..............2,000.00
Kenova, vase, blossom branch, pot form, 5½"..............350.00
Kenova, vase, morning glories, incurvate rim, 6½"..............400.00
Klyro, fan vase, flowers & berries, 8"..............50.00
Klyro, planter, flower swag, sq, 4"..............60.00
Klyro, wall pocket, flowers & berries, 7½"..............150.00
Knifewood, bowl, daisies, 3"..............100.00
Knifewood, tobacco jar, dog pointing, 7"..............600.00
L'Art Nouveau, bank, corn shape, 8"..............600.00
L'Art Nouveau, bud vase, iris form, 7½"..............600.00
L'Art Nouveau, ewer, floral lip, 12½"..............475.00
L'Art Nouveau, vase, corn shape, 4½"..............300.00
La Sa, vase, cross & flowers, pot form, 3½"..............150.00
La Sa, vase, scenic, pyramidal, 6½"..............200.00

Lamar, vase, scenic, shouldered, tapered, sm lipped rim, 6".........200.00
Lavonia, candle holders, hexagonal, 4", pr.........150.00
Lavonia, vase, champagne glass form w/3 low hdls at ft, 9".........150.00
Lido, planter, leaf form, 2x9".........30.00
Lido, vase, cylindrical, 12".........95.00
Lorbeek, bowl vase, 5".........125.00
Lorbeek, candle holders, 2½", pr.........95.00
Loru, vase, emb leaf decor on scalloped panels, 11".........110.00
Louella, hair receiver, 3".........125.00
Louella, vase, bulbous w/ruffled rim, ring hdls, 8".........130.00
Louwelsa, bowl, floral, 2½".........125.00
Louwelsa, candle holder, floral, jug form w/hdl, sgn MH, 4½"....175.00
Louwelsa, clock, mantel; floral, 10½x12½".........1,250.00
Louwelsa, ewer, floral w/silver overlay, 4-sided, 9".........2,500.00
Louwelsa, ewer, monk's portrait, sgn LJ Burgess FM, 12½".........1,500.00
Louwelsa, jardiniere, floral, ruffled rim, 9½".........350.00
Louwelsa, lamp, ball form, ftd, sgn, 10".........1,250.00
Louwelsa, mug, floral, sgn EA, 6".........225.00
Louwelsa, pitcher, bulbous, ftd, sgn MT, 5".........195.00
Louwelsa, umbrella stand, tropical foliage, cylindrical, 21".........900.00
Louwelsa, vase, cavalier's portrait, sgn LJ Burgess, 16".........3,000.00
Louwelsa, vase, floral, bulbous, sm neck, sgn EA, 5½".........225.00
Louwelsa, vase, floral, pillow form, ftd, sgn M, 4".........165.00
Louwelsa, vase, Indian in full headdress, Burgess, 11½".........2,750.00
Louwelsa, vase, pansies, 3-hdld/3-ftd, 6½".........225.00
Louwelsa (Blue), vase, floral, cylindrical, 10½".........1,100.00
Lustre, basket, gathered fabric look, 6½".........125.00
Malverne, circle vase, 8".........200.00
Malverne, jardinere & ped, mottled w/emb branch w/buds & leaves, 34"..950.00
Malverne, wall pocket, 11".........250.00
Mammy Line, cookie jar, 11".........2,000.00
Mammy Line, syrup pitcher, 6".........700.00
Manhattan, pitcher, emb flowers & leaves, hdl at rim, 10".........125.00
Marbleized, bowl, incurvate rim, 1½x5½".........50.00
Marbleized, comport, tall ped w/flared bottom, 8".........250.00
Marbleized, vase, 4-sided, 4".........115.00
Marengo, vase, trees & mountains, hexagonal, 8".........350.00
Marvo, vase, emb garden motif, cylindrical, 10".........115.00
Marvo, wall pocket, emb garden motif, 8½".........200.00
Melrose, basket, grapes & flowers, branch hdl, 10".........250.00
Melrose, vase, berry branch, twig hdls at ruffled rim, 8½".........125.00
Minerva, vase, flamingos, cylindrical, 8½".........600.00
Mirror Black, bud vase, trumpet form, 5½".........40.00
Mirror Black, wall pocket, trumpet form, 8".........150.00
Monochrome, comport, 10".........95.00
Muskota, boy fishing from rock, 6½".........375.00
Muskota, fish wrapped around stump, 5".........225.00
Muskota, flower frog, 2 geese on pond base, 6".........450.00
Muskota, girl w/watering can, 7".........500.00
Muskota, incense burner, Foxy Grandpa, 4".........575.00
Muskota, nude on rock, 8".........325.00
Noval, candle holder, roses & apples, tower form, 9½".........150.00
Noval, comport, apples, 5½".........115.00
Novelty, ashtray, Three Pigs, 4".........150.00
Novelty, jar, emb stylized facial features, 6".........250.00
Novelty, planter, frog & lotus blossom, 4".........95.00
Oak Leaf, basket, #G-1, 7½".........110.00
Oak Leaf, ewer, 14".........175.00
Panella, ginger jar, emb floral, w/lid, 6½".........125.00
Paragon, bowl vase, floral, 4½".........175.00
Parian, wall pocket, floral tile-like design, 10".........250.00
Patra, basket, 5½".........225.00
Patra, bowl, #13, ftd, 3".........125.00
Patra, vase, #15, 8".........200.00

Patricia, planter, duck, 6½".........200.00
Patricia, swan, 3½".........70.00
Pearl, bowl, str-sided, pearl swag, 3".........140.00
Pearl, vase, pearl swags/band of roses, 4 sm rim hdls, 9".........200.00
Pearl, wall pocket, pearls draped on band of roses, 7".........225.00
Pumila, console plate, 3x12".........125.00
Pumila, wall pocket, 7".........150.00
Ragenda, vase, drapery swag, cylindrical, 12".........135.00
Roba, ewer, emb blossom branch, 11".........175.00
Roba, wall pocket, emb floral, 10".........225.00
Roma, ashtray, ribbed w/band of roses & leaves, 2½".........110.00
Roma, basket, floral swag, 7½".........250.00
Roma, bud vase, roses & bl ribbon, cylindrical, 5".........45.00
Roma, candlestick, triple; flower & paneled leaves, 9".........200.00
Roma, console bowl, floral swags, 4½x16".........275.00
Roma, jardiniere, rose swags, 4-sided, 8½".........225.00
Roma, jardiniere, roses & bl ribbon swag, 5".........700.00
Roma, tobacco jar, pipe motif, 7½".........300.00
Roma, vase, pine cones, 4-sided, 10".........175.00
Rosemont, jardiniere, paneled fruit basket motif, 8".........250.00
Rudlor, vase, cylindrical, high-low hdls, 6½".........50.00
Sabrinian, basket, 7".........300.00
Sabrinian, bowl, ftd, 3½".........180.00
Sabrinian, candle holders, ftd, 2", pr.........125.00
Scandia, vase, cylindrical, 6".........95.00
Senic, planter, #S-17, 5½".........95.00
Senic, vase, #S-14, 10".........175.00
Sicardo, mug, cylindrical, 3½".........500.00
Sicardo, plaque, bamboo, 10½".........2,750.00
Sicardo, vase, flat-sided heart shape, ftd, sgn, 2½".........300.00
Sicardo, vase, twisted form w/ruffled neck, sgn, 12".........200.00
Silvertone, basket, berry branch, fan shape, 13".........450.00
Silvertone, bud vase, dbl; blossom w/branch hdl, 6".........175.00
Silvertone, candle holders, blossom branch, 3", pr.........125.00
Softone, ewer, 9½".........60.00
Softone, planter, 4x8".........45.00
Souevo, tobacco jar, geometric design, 6".........275.00
Sydonia, cornucopia, 8½".........100.00
Sydonia, planter, 4".........50.00
Tivoli, vase, cylindrical/flared rim, floral banded ftd base, 8½"...125.00
Turada, mug, mk 562/7, 6".........325.00
Turkis, vase, angled bowl w/angled hdls, 5½".........150.00
Turkis, vase, ruffled rim, 8".........175.00
Tutone, basket, 7½".........150.00
Tutone, candle holders, triangular, ftd, 2½", pr.........125.00
Tutone, vase, 3-sided, ftd, 6".........85.00
Voile, jardiniere, fruit trees, scalloped rim, ftd, 6".........150.00
Warwick, jardiniere, branch & wood tone, 7".........150.00
Warwick, vase, branch on wood tone, hdld, 4-ftd, 6½".........165.00
White & Decorated, bowl, 4".........200.00
White & Decorated, vase, hexagonal, 11".........275.00
Wild Rose, candle holder, triple; 6".........100.00
Wood Rose, bowl, roses on wooden bucket, 2½x8½".........85.00
Wood Rose, jardiniere, roses on wooden bucket, 7".........175.00
Wood Rose, wall pocket, roses on wooden bucket, 6".........125.00
Woodcraft, ashtray, tree stump w/oak leaves, 3".........150.00
Woodcraft, bowl, cut-out branch design, ftd, 3½".........125.00
Woodcraft, comport, bowl on tree-trunk ped base, 10".........400.00
Woodcraft, mug, fox family in tree trunk, 6".........300.00
Woodcraft, planter, fox family in tree stump, 5½".........350.00
Zona, baby plate, squirrels, alphabet rim, 7½".........150.00
Zona, jardiniere, roses on wht lattice on lt bl, blk rim, 6½".........225.00
Zona, mug, rabbit/bird on branch, 3".........125.00
Zona, pitcher, apples on branch, branch hdl, 6".........125.00

Zona, vase, apple on branch, sm twig hdls, rolled rim, 9".............175.00

Western Americana

The collecting of Western Americana encompasses a broad spectrum of memorabilia. Examples of various areas within the mainstream would include the following fields: weapons, bottles, photographs, mining/railroad artifacts, cowboy paraphernalia, farm and ranch implements, maps, barbed wire, tokens, Indian relics, saloon/gambling items, and branding irons. Some of these areas have their own separate listings in this book. Western Americana is not only a collecting field but is also a collecting era with specific boundries. Depending upon which field the collector decides to specialize in, prices can start at a few dollars and run into the thousands.

Our advisor for this category is Bill Mackin, author of *Cowboy and Gunfighter Collectibles* (order from the author); he is listed in the Directory under Colorado.

Belt, tooled leather w/brass bosses, leather slide, 1890s, EX 30.00
Blanket, Jacob's (Pendleton competitor), Indian design, 1920s, 78x54"..75.00
Blanket, Pendleton, crisp geometrics, 1920s, 66x54", EX............135.00
Blanket, Pendleton Glacier Park (like Hudson Bay), 1920s, 84x60" ..175.00
Chaps, gray leather w/NP fittings & roller buckle, working type, 1940s ..225.00
Holster w/cartridge belt, for Colt revolver, 3-loop stype, ca 1880 ..450.00
Longhorns, mtd set, 1920s, 30x12" 70.00
Saddle, side; Emanuel Schaeffer, tooled leather, fabric skirt, EX.250.00
Saddle roll, tooled leather, lacing holes, early 1800s, 17" L, EX..150.00
Spur, forged iron w/lt eng, pinwheel rowel, w/strap, 1870s, EX 75.00
Spurs, Crockett, silver o/l, 1½" rowels, Ex, pr...............................395.00
Spurs, North & Judd, dots & stars on bands, anchor marks, pr, EX 235.00
Spurs, unmk, chrome-plated, dbl-chain heel strap, 1940s, EX 125.00
Spurs, unmk CA style w/silver inlay, 2¼" 14-point rowels, pr, EX..850.00
Spurs, unmk lady's leg, silver & copper o/l, 1⅜" rowels, pr 360.00

Western Pottery Manufacturing Company

This pottery was originally founded as the Denver China and Pottery Company; William Long was the owner. The company's assets were sold to a group who in 1905 formed the Western Pottery Manufacturing Company, located at 16th Street and Alcott in Denver, Colorado. By 1926, 186 different items were being produced, including crocks, flowerpots, kitchen items, and other stoneware. The company dissolved in 1936.

Seven various marks were used during the years, and values may be higher for items that carry a rare mark. Numbers within the descriptions refer to specific marks, see the line drawings. Prices may vary depending on demand and locale. Our advisors for this category are Cathy Segelke and Pat James; they are listed in the Directory under Colorado.

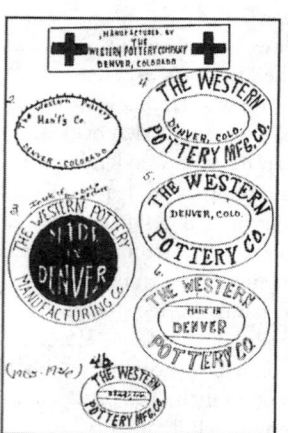

Churn, #2, hdl, 4-gal, M...75.00
Churn, #2, hdl, 5-gal, M...65.00
Churn, #2, no lid, 5-gal, G...80.00
Crock, #4, bail lip, 4-gal, G..55.00
Crock, #4, hdl, no lid, 8-gal, M..90.00
Crock, #4, ice water; bl/wht sponge pnt, 3-gal, NM 30.00
Crock, #4, 6-gal, EX..72.00
Crock, #4b, 20-gal, M..200.00
Crock, #4b, 22x17½", 15-gal, NM 150.00
Crock, #5, bail lip, 1½-gal, M...45.00
Crock, #5, no lid, 6-gal, M...70.00
Crock, #6, wire hdl, 10-gal, NM...100.00
Crock, #6, 3-gal, M..40.00
Crock, #6, 4-gal, M..50.00
Crock, #6, 5-gal, NM...60.00
Foot warmer, #6, M...60.00
Jug, #6, brn/wht, 1-gal, EX..25.00
Jug, #6, brn/wht, 5-gal, M...75.00
Rabbit feeder, #1, EX..25.00
Rabbit waterer, #1, M..25.00

Western Stoneware Co.

The Western Stoneware Co., Monmouth, Illinois, was formed in 1906 as a merger of seven potteries: Monmouth Pottery Co., Monmouth, IL; Weir Pottery Co., Monmouth, IL; Macomb Pottery Co. and Macomb Stoneware Co., Macomb, IL; D. Culbertson Stoneware Co., Whitehall, IL; Clinton Stoneware Co., Clinton, MO; and Fort Dodge Stoneware Co., Fort Dodge, IA.

Western Stoneware Co. manufactured stoneware, gardenware, flowerpots, artware, and dinnerware. Some early crocks, jugs, and churns are found with a plant number in the Maple Leaf logo. Plants 1 through 7 turn up. In 1926 an artware line was introduced as the Monmouth Pottery Artware. One by one each branch of the operation closed, and today one branch remains. Western Stoneware Co. is still in operation in Monmouth, Illinois, on the site of the Weir Pottery Co. Our advisor for this category is Jim Martin; he is listed in the Directory under Illinois. See also Old Sleepy Eye.

Bowl, bl banded, w/advertising...85.00
Chicken waterer, complete, 1-gal 125.00
Churn, flowers on side, 3-gal 200.00
Churn, Maple Leaf mk, mini..1,000.00
Churn, Maple Leaf mk, oval, 2-gal...175.00
Churn, Maple Leaf mk, 2-gal..200.00
Combinet, w/lid & hdl, mini..350.00
Cooler, #2, dk brn sponging on cream bristol, ca 1920, 9" 385.00
Crock, Maple Leaf mk, 60-gal 1,000.00
Custard cup, Colonial 250.00
Hot water bottle, pig, bl tint..225.00
Jar, Maple Leaf & oval mk, 2-gal..50.00
Jardiniere, Egyptian motif, brn-glazed int, 7"................................75.00
Jug, Monmouth advertising, 1-qt...125.00
Pitcher, Cattail, bl & wht, 1-qt..150.00
Shakers, 2nd Nat'l Bank, pr 30.00
Vase, cvd/pnt leaves, bl matt, 16", EX..150.00
Wall pocket, Egyptian, Burntwood, #312 ....60.00
Water cooler, Cupid, wht w/advertising 500.00
Water cooler, Egyptian motif, 9¼x11", M....................................450.00
Water cooler, Maple Leaf mk, no lid or spigot, 2-gal.................400.00

Westmoreland

Originally titled the Specialty Glass Company, Westmoreland

began operations in East Liverpool, Ohio, producing utility items as well as tableware in milk glass and crystal. When the company moved to Grapeville, Pennsylvania, in 1890, lamps, vases, covered animal dishes, and decorative plates were introduced. Prior to 1920 Westmoreland was a major manufacturer of carnival glass and soon thereafter added a line of lovely reproduction art glass items. High-quality milk glass became their speciality, accounting for about 90% of their production. Black glass was introduced in the 1940s, and later in the decade ruby-stained pieces and items decorated in the Mary Gregory style became fashionable. By the 1960s colored glassware was being produced, examples of which are very popular with collectors today. Early pieces were marked with a paper label; by the 1960s the ware was embossed with a superimposed 'WG.' The last mark was a circle containing 'Westmoreland' around the perimeter and a large 'W' in the center. The company closed in 1985, and on February 28, 1996, the factory burned to the ground.

For more information, we recommend *Westmoreland Glass* by Charles West Wilson.

Note: Though you may find pieces very similar to Westmoreland's, their Della Robbia has no bananas among the fruits relief. In the descriptions that follow, items in this pattern described as 'crystal with trim' refers to those pieces with the colored lustre stains. Our advisor for this category is Philip Rosso, Jr. He is listed in the Directory under Pennsylvania. See also Animal Dishes with Covers; Carnival Glass.

Beaded Edge, creamer, ftd, plain 11.00
Beaded Edge, platter, plain, tab hdls, 12" 40.00
Beaded Edge, relish, 3-part, plain 50.00
Beaded Edge, shakers, decor, pr 55.00
Beaded Edge, sherbet, ftd, plain 6.50
Beaded Edge, tumbler, ftd, decor, 8-oz 18.00
Della Robbia, basket, crystal w/decor, 9" 195.00
Della Robbia, bowl, crystal w/decor, ftd, 12" 135.00
Della Robbia, bowl, nappy; crystal w/decor, 1-hdl, 6½" 35.00
Della Robbia, comport, sweetmeat; crystal w/decor, belled, 8" 110.00
Della Robbia, plate, bread & butter; crystal w/decor, 6⅛" 15.00
Della Robbia, plate, crystal w/decor, 18", from $150 to 200.00
Della Robbia, saucer, crystal w/decor 15.00
Della Robbia, tumbler, water; crystal w/decor, 8-oz 25.00
English Hobnail, ashtray, turq or ice bl, 4½" 22.50
English Hobnail, bowl, pk or gr, 6" 18.00
English Hobnail, bowl, turq or ice bl, hdls, hexagonal, ftd, 8" 65.00
English Hobnail, cocktail, pk or gr, 3-oz 20.00
English Hobnail, cup, pk or gr 18.00
English Hobnail, pitcher, pk or gr, 23-oz 150.00
English Hobnail, sherbet, pk or gr 14.00
English Hobnail, tumbler, iced tea; pk or gr, 12-oz 30.00
Fruits, punch bowl set, milk glass, bowl/base/12 cups/ladle 175.00
Fruits, sherbet, gr 10.00
Old Quilt/#500, bowl, banana; milk glass, ftd, 11" 125.00
Old Quilt/#500, butter/cheese dish, milk glass, rnd 45.00
Old Quilt/#500, cake salver, milk glass, skirted, bell ft, 12" 125.00
Old Quilt/#500, plate, milk glass, 10½" 50.00
Panelled Grape, basket, milk glass, 8" 77.50
Panelled Grape, bowl, milk glass, oval, lipped, ftd, 11", $65 to 85.00
Panelled Grape, butter dish, milk glass, ¼-lb 25.00
Panelled Grape, cake salver, milk glass, skirted 85.00
Panelled Grape, candlesticks, milk glass, gold trim, pr 40.00
Panelled Grape, cheese dish, milk glass, dome lid, from $45 to 50.00
Panelled Grape, compote, milk glass, crimped, 4½" 30.00
Panelled Grape, egg tray, milk glass, metal center hdl, 10" 65.00
Panelled Grape, pitcher, milk glass, 32-oz 37.50
Panelled Grape, relish, milk glass, 3-part, 9" 40.00

Panelled Grape, sugar bowl, milk glass, 6½" 14.00
Panelled Grape, tumbler, juice; milk glass, 5-oz 24.00
Panelled Grape, vase, milk glass, 15" 30.00
Thousand Eye, basket, crystal, hdld, oval, 8" 45.00
Thousand Eye, bowl, crystal, belled, 11" 35.00
Thousand Eye, bowl, crystal, triangular, 11" 45.00
Thousand Eye, comport, crystal, high ftd, 5" 22.50
Thousand Eye, jug, crystal, ½-gal 75.00
Thousand Eye, shaker, crystal, ftd 15.00
Thousand Eye, stem, cordial; crystal, 1-oz 15.00
Thousand Eye, stem, crystal, 8-oz 10.00
Thousand Eye, tumbler, whiskey; crystal, 1½-oz 10.00

Wheatley, T. J.

In 1880 after a brief association with the Coultry Works, Thomas J. Wheatley opened his own studio in Cincinnati, Ohio, claiming to have been the first to discover the secret of under-glaze slip decoration on an unbaked clay vessel. He applied for and was granted a patent for his process. Demand for his ware increased to the point that several artists were hired to decorate the ware. The company incorporated in 1880 as the Cincinnati Art Pottery, but until 1882 it continued to operate under Wheatley's name. Ware from this period is marked 'T.J. Wheatley' or 'T.J.W. and Co.,' and it may be dated.

Matt green pieces dominate today's marketplace and will bring much more than the decorated pieces. The matt green pieces are seldom, if ever, marked or dated.

Vases: leaves and buds under dark leathery green, angular buttressed handles, 20x10", $4,000.00; embossed ribbed leaves on mottled green, 6¾x5", $850.00; embossed leaves and buds under leathery green, 16½x10½", NM, $3,500.00. (Photo courtesy David Rago)

Bowl vase, leaves & buds emb, gr matt, #638, 9" W 1,200.00
Jardiniere, feathery gr matt, 12¼x20⅞" 1,200.00
Lamp base, gr matt, 4 buttressed ft, #610, 7¼" 2,500.00
Vase, apple blossom branch on dk bl, ca 1880, 6⅝x4" 185.00
Vase, arches & windows emb, dk gr matt, unmk, 13¼" 2,200.00
Vase, arrowhead leaves emb, gr matt, flaws, 12½x6" 1,600.00
Vase, fiddlehead ferns emb & as hdls, gr matt, unmk, 11½" 2,500.00
Vase, floral on mc ground, sq, sm ft, 6½", NM 220.00
Vase, gr gloopy matt, gourd form, 11" 1,000.00
Vase, gr gloopy matt (very dk), stepped shoulder, 10½" 1,200.00
Vase, gr matt, elliptical, unmk, 11½", EX 550.00
Vase, gr matt, organic form w/4 elongated hdls, #615, 14" 3,800.00
Vase, gr matt, rim-to-base buttresses (4), unmk, 8⅛" 2,000.00
Vase, leaves & buds emb, gr gloopy matt, 12⅝", NM 2,400.00
Vase, leaves & buds emb, gr matt, unmk, 20⅛" 4,000.00
Vase, leaves & buds emb, thick gloopy gr matt, 7¾" 1,200.00
Vase, leaves emb, gr matt, faint mk, 8⅛" 1,200.00
Vase, leaves emb, leathery gr matt, gourd shape, 13x9", NM ...3,500.00

Vase, rows of leaves emb, frothy lt gr & amber, ribbed neck, 7¼" ..**800.00**
Vase, wild roses on mc, oval pillow form, 1880, 12x7¾" **500.00**

Whieldon

Thomas Whieldon was regarded as the finest of the Staffordshire potters of the mid-1700s. He produced marbled and black Egyptian wares as well as tortoise shell, a mottled brown-glazed earthenware accented with touches of blue and yellow. In 1754 he became a partner of Josiah Wedgwood. Other potters produced similar wares, and today the term Whieldon is used generically.

Bowl, tortoise shell, 1780, 4⅝", w/5¾" stand...............................**300.00**
Jug, tortoise shell w/emb figures/lion mask, ftd pear form, 1770s, 5" ...**265.00**
Plate, emb roses/moth/flower basket, brn & gr-mustard, 18th C, 9"....**515.00**
Platter, brn sponging w/gr splotches on cream, scalloped, 17", EX...**1,265.00**
Teapot, globular, bird finial, crabstock hdl, paw ft, 1770, 3¾" **550.00**

Wicker

Wicker is the basket-like material used in many types of furniture and accessories. It may be made from bamboo cane, rattan, reed, or artificial fibers. It is airy, lightweight, and very popular in hot regions. Imported from the Orient in the eighteenth century, it was first manufactured in the United States in about 1850. The elaborate, closely woven Victorian designs belong to the mid- to late 1800s, and the simple styles with coarse reedings usually indicate a post-1900 production. Art Deco styles followed in the '20s and '30s. The most important consideration in buying wicker is condition — it can be restored, but only by a professional. Age is an important factor, but be aware that 'Victorian-style' furniture is being manufactured today.

Key:
HB — Heywood Bros.   H/W — Heywood Wakefield

Photographer's chair, Heywood Wakefield, painted white, spider cane and curlicues on back, 44x31", EX, $1,000.00.

Armchair, circular bk, serpentine arms, splint seat, cushion, 42"...**150.00**
Armchair, tight-weave fan bk, caned seat, sm rprs, 61" **300.00**
Baby carriage, bk/ft adjusts, scroll-shaped sides, 33x45" **675.00**
Chair, ornate curlicue bk, cane seat, armless, HW, late 1800s, EX...**400.00**
Chair, reception; bk w/openwork rectangle, 3 rows of spindles ...**400.00**
Chaise lounge, roll-arm, serpentine styling, ca 1900, 38x68", EX...**325.00**
Chaise lounge, uphl cushions, H/W, 1940s, 37x66x25", EX........**485.00**
Crib, tight weave w/pnt flower swags & bows, 1930s, 44x53x28" **300.00**
Desk, writing; kidney shape w/apron, ca 1900, w/sm lady's chair, EX...**425.00**
Hall seat, lift-up seat, orig pnt, ca 1900, 78x48x20", EX..........**3,950.00**
Lamp, floor; woven dome shade, splayed leg base, 68x18" dia **850.00**
Loveseat, str bk w/2 tight-weave bands, scrolls under arms, 40"..**450.00**
Loveseat, tight-weave skirt, curlicues, HB, 39½x50" **2,100.00**

Magazine rack, 4 ball finials, curlicues, ca 1910, 30x19x15", NM ...**325.00**
Photographer's bench, openweave bk/sides/apron, H/W............**500.00**
Photographer's bench, stick & ball decor, elaborate, 1-arm........**840.00**
Rocker, peacock fan openwork, heavy shaped bk/arms, ornate ...**800.00**
Rocker, rnd bk w/circular inset, w/arms...........................**400.00**
Rocker, sq bk, flat arms, similar to Stickley style, 32"................**200.00**
Rocker, wheel design/scrollwork bk, w/arms........................**400.00**
Sewing basket, 2-tier, scrolled brackets, H/W **340.00**
Sewing stand, 2-tier, carbiole legs, dome top, HB label **535.00**
Stand, elaborate openwork apron, wooden lower shelf...............**800.00**
Stand, 3 wooden shelves, curlicues at bk, H/W, 37x17x13" **785.00**
Stool, 4 legs, ea w/scrolled capital **225.00**
Stroller, curls & curlicues, CI fr, late 1800s, doll sz, 26" L..........**235.00**
Table, lamp; cabriole legs w/scroll trim, 30" dia **600.00**
Table, lamp; heavy cabriole legs, wide apron, shelf, 22" sq..........**900.00**
Table, oak base w/wicker top, orig pnt trim, 1920s, 29x29x19"...**215.00**
Table, sewing; basket top, hinged center compartment, shelf, 1890s..**350.00**
Table, sewing; woven drw, 1 full shelf, 2 smaller, H/W, 42", NM...**500.00**
Tea cart, glass tray, spoke wheels, old brn stain, 33x34x20", EX **385.00**
Wastebasket, oak base, cylindrical, H/W, 16x12"........................**500.00**

Will-George

In 1934, after years of working in the family garage, the Will-George company was founded by William and George Climes in Los Angeles, California. They manufactured high-quality art china of porcelain and earthenware. Both brothers, motivated by their love of art pottery, had extensive education and training in manufacturing and decoration. In 1940 actor Edgar Bergen, a collector of pottery, developed a relationship with the brothers and invested in their business. With this new influx of funds, the company relocated to Pasadena. There they produced an extensive line of art pottery, but they excelled in their creation of bird and animal figurines. In addition they molded a large line of human figurines similar to Royal Doulton. The brothers, now with a staff of decorators, precisely molded their pieces with great care and emphasis on originality and detail, creating high quality works of art that were only carried by exclusive gift stores.

In the late 1940s, after a split with Bergen, the company moved to San Gabriel to a larger, more modern location and renamed themselves The Claysmiths. There they mass produced many items, but due to the cheap, postwar imports from Italy and Japan that were then flooding the market, they liquidated the business in 1956. Our advisor for this category is Marty Webster. He is listed in the Directory under Michigan.

Bowl, flamingo pond, gr sides w/rose int, 14x9" **65.00**
Bowl, serving; red onion form, 2x13x10"................................**65.00**
Box, Oriental figure kneeling on lid, 1x4x4"..............................**50.00**
Candle holder, lily design, pr **120.00**
Figurine, artist holding a palette, mc, 8"...............................**95.00**
Figurine, Baltimore Oriole **155.00**
Figurine, boy holds frog, mc, on base, 9" **95.00**
Figurine, cardinal on branch, 10".......................................**75.00**
Figurine, cardinal on branch, 12½" **150.00**
Figurine, dachshund, 6½x9" **200.00**
Figurine, eagle on rock, wht/brn, 10"..................................**150.00**
Figurine, faun (satyr) seated on stump, birds at ft, 1 in hand, 7½"...**110.00**
Figurine, flamingo, head facing bk, 7½"...............................**150.00**
Figurine, flamingo, head turned, 10" **200.00**
Figurine, flamingo, preening, 10"..**200.00**
Figurine, flamingo, wings spread, 15½" **275.00**
Figurine, flamingo beside stump, head down, 4½" **140.00**
Figurine, flamingo beside stump, 7¼".................................**180.00**
Figurine, flamingo stradling stump, beak by neck, 11½" **230.00**

Figurine, giraffe, 14½" 150.00
Figurine, girl holding doll, mc, on base, 9" 125.00
Figurine, hula dancer, wht skirt, 12" 155.00
Figurine, Mallard duck, wings wide, 7x11" 195.00
Figurine, monk, brn bsk, 4½" 50.00
Figurine, monk, brn bsk, 5½" 75.00
Figurine, pheasant, red breast, 6x14" 255.00
Figurine, pheasant hen 110.00
Figurine, Polynesian seated female, 5½" 80.00

**Parrot on perch, bright colors, 14½",
$110.00.** (Photo courtesy Marty Webster)

Pitcher, chicken figural, mc, 7" 125.00
Plate, dinner; red onion form, 10½x12¼" 12.00
Plate, luncheon; red onion form, 10¼" L, NM 10.00
Snack set, rooster, feathers along rim, rooster at ft of cup 60.00
Tumbler, chicken figural, mc, 4½" 50.00
Vase, Chinese girl seated in front, pillow form, 5" 85.00
Wine glass, chicken figural, mc, 5" 55.00

Willets

The Willets Manufacturing Company of Trenton, New Jersey, produced a type of belleek porcelain during the late 1880s and 1890s. Examples were often marked with a coiled snake that formed a 'W' with
'Willets' below and 'Belleek' above. Not all Willets is factory decorated.
Items painted by amateurs outside the factory are worth considerably
less. High prices usually equate with fine artwork. In the listings below,
all items are belleek unless noted otherwise. Our advisor for this category is Mary Frank Gaston; she is listed in the Directory under Texas.

Bowl, allover gold & bl flowers, 2¼x3¼" 45.00
Bowl, HP peaches & flowers w/gold, sgn EN Rewalt, ca 1885 ....225.00
Bowl, vintage, gold on wht, 3x8" 190.00
Charger, floral, ca 1895, 15" 375.00
Cup & saucer, demitasse; silver deposit decor, ped ft 75.00
Ewer, Nautilus Shell, coral-shaped hdl, ca 1890, 7¾" 365.00
Hair receiver, gold berries & branches, scalloped, 2" 135.00
Mug, no decor, lizard hdl, mk, 5½" 115.00
Pitcher, blkberries & blossoms w/gold, factory decor, 10¼" 400.00
Tankard, grapes, sgn Skillman, gold scroll hdl, 14" 375.00
Tankard, monk drinking/resting on dk gr, 15" 195.00
Teacup & saucer, gold-paste leaves w/jewels, 1885-1909, $175 to ..200.00
Vase, Am Beauty roses on mc, artist sgn, oviform, 15" 435.00
Vase, floral, artist sgn, cylindrical, 1880s-1909, 16" 400.00
Vase, lg flowers at top, gold banding, mk, 12½" 240.00
Vase, mc orchids w/gr leaves on mc ground, mk, 30" 600.00
Vase, narcissus flowers on gr, invt rim, ca 1895, 10" 345.00

Vase, roses w/trailing brn stems, Snyder, cylindrical, 8" 250.00
Vase, 2 egrets on pk & blk, tapering shape, 11⅝" 350.00
Vase, 4 Seasons, pastel w/gold, bulbous, flared rim, brn mk, 16" ..525.00

Winchester

The Winchester Repeating Arms Company lost their important
government contract after WWI and of necessity turned to the manufacture of sporting goods, hardware items, tools, etc., to augment their
gun production. Between 1920 and 1931, over 7,500 different items,
each marked 'Winchester Trademark U.S.A.,' were offered for sale by
thousands of Winchester Hardware stores throughout the country. After
1931 the firm became Winchester-Western. Collectors prefer the prewar
items such as we have listed below. Unless noted otherwise, values are
for examples in excellent condition.

Concerning current collecting trends: Oil cans that a short time ago
could be purchased for $2.00 to $5.00 now often sell for $25.00, some
over $50.00, and demand is high. Good examples of advertising posters
and calendars seem to have no upper limits and are difficult to find. Winchester fishing lures are strong, and the presence of original boxes
increases values by 25% to 40%. Another current trend concerns the
price of 'die cuts' (cardboard stand-ups, signs, or hanging signs). These
are out pricing many other items. A short time ago the average value of
a 'die cut' ranged from $25.00 to $45.00. Current values for most are in
the $200.00 to $500.00 range, with some approaching $1,000.00. Our
advisor for this category is James Anderson; he is listed in the Directory
under Minnesota. See also Knives.

Aerosol spray can, New Gun Oil, red/yel/blk, 5½-oz, EX 45.00
Baseball bat, #2408, EX 360.00
Baseball glove, Youth's Model Fielder's, EX 505.00
Battery, #3516, 4½ volt 190.00
Bicycle, boy's, 26" tires, rstr 725.00
Box w/product, New Rival Shells, #4 shot, 1892, full, EX+ 170.00
Box w/product, Nublack, 12 gauge, 1917, full, NM+ 450.00
Box w/product, Ranger Super Skeet Load, full, NM+ 175.00
Box w/product, 32 Gauge Paper Shot Shells, full, EX+ 160.00
Boxing gloves, Winchester, VG 825.00
Calendar, 1895, AB Frost art, 27", EX+ 1,100.00
Calendar, 1914 Winchester, complete, EX 2,800.00
Calendar, 1915, Lynn Bogue Hunt art, G 1,500.00
Calendar, 1916, PR Goodwin art, 30", EX+ 1,750.00
Calendar, 1922, H.C. Edwards art, 26", EX 875.00
Calendar, 1924, duck hunter, 13", VG 750.00
Calendar, 1926, PR Goodwin art, 27", VG+ 925.00
Calendar, 1928, Protection, 21", EX+ 550.00
Calendar, 1929, family waving at Pony Express rider, 21", EX+ ..325.00
Cartridge board, 1902 dbl-W graphics, wood fr, 40x58", EX+ ..4,200.00
Catalog, 1899, VG+ 625.00
Chisel, #4009, 7" 40.00
Chisel, wood; #4033, 5½" 40.00
Cover, Repeating Rifles..., mtn man/rifle, sepia, unused, NM+ ..185.00
Cover, Repeating Shotguns, game/gun intwined in red W, unused, EX+ ..100.00
Cover, Rifles & Shotguns, winter trapper, EX 130.00
Cover, Self-loading Shotguns, hunter w/game & gun, 1915, unused, NM+ ..85.00
Fan, pleated paper w/wooden hdl, The Winchester Store, 15x9", NM 50.00
File, bastard 75.00
Fishing line, Sea Maid, #8393 ....165.00
Fishing lure, #9574 ....85.00
Five panel wooden display w/inserts, EX 1,200.00
Framing sq, metal, #9650, 24", EX 100.00
Golf club, #6560 ....160.00
Golf club, lady's, mid-iron 95.00

Hammer, tack; #6212 ....80.00
Ice pick, wood & metal, #9502, G 50.00
Ice skates, American Club, EX...75.00
Knife, butcher; #7331 ....65.00
Knife, grapefruit; #4021, VG, from $45 to.........................65.00
Knife, paring; #4263, G 45.00
Knife, pruning; #1610 ....50.00
Knife, putty; #2862, EX...180.00
Lantern, Trail Blazer..55.00
Lawn mower, reel-cut push type, #WL16, EX 550.00
Level, iron, #9816, NM..310.00
Meat cleaver, #7814...50.00
Meat fork, #7728, G 30.00
Meat grinder, #W110, NM..100.00
Miner's light, G...45.00
Oil can, The Winchester Store, #WS-88, 7", VG+ 240.00
Pamphlet, Nublack Loaded Black Powder Shells, graphics, 6x7", NM...350.00
Pin-back button, W encircled by phrase, Whitehead & Hoag, 1", EX+ ...40.00
Pipe wrench, 14", G...60.00
Plane, grooved bottom, 9", G, from $55 to........................85.00
Plane, grooved bottom, 14" 90.00
Plane, grooved bottom, 22"..115.00
Plane, wood, #3005, G 60.00
Pliers, #2499, 10", G 35.00
Pliers, side cutting, G 35.00
Poster, Special, nude blond putting on T-shirt, 26x13", NM+ 426.00
Potato fork, VG 90.00
Rifle barrel reflector, brass, for model 1892, NM+ 160.00
Roller skates, #3831, in orig box..260.00
Ruler, folding; 4-fold, #F9562A, 24", G............................75.00
Saw, hand; #10, VG..80.00
Scissors, #9022, VG 35.00
Scoop shovel, orig hdl, #12, EX..300.00
Scraper, adjustable, #3075...150.00
Screwdriver, #7123, 4", G...25.00
Screwdriver, #7127, 10", G...40.00
Shell box, Winchester, 2-pc, Repeater Oval, EX 300.00
Sign, cb, Hunter's Choice/New Rival Shells, w/graphics, 10x17", EX.......900.00
Sign, cb, sf, group of men in cabin w/duck decoys, 1954, 21x28", EX+ 50.00
Sign, cb, Shoot Them & Avoid the Trouble, 1908, fr, 26x34", EX+ ...300.00
Sign, cb diecut, #22 shape (Model 61 & Model 63), 1940s, 10x9", EX+ ..325.00
Sign, cb stand-up, Canada geese in flight above text, 11x9", EX+.............500.00
Sign, cb stand-up, From the Grizzly to the Squirrel, 22", EX+ 785.00
Sign, cb stand-up, man shooting in circle, 1953, 18x17", NM....160.00
Sign, cb stand-up, Silvertip display, ca 1950, unused, 20x24", NM ...130.00
Sign, cb stand-up, The Man/The Gun/The Shells, 22x10", EX+ ...3,900.00
Sign, cb stand-up, 1800-1920 Winchester Guns & Ammunition..., 11", NM..120.00
Sign, paper-on-cb hanger, quail/shells/box, 9x14", EX+ 2,300.00
Sign, poster, deer on snowy mountain, Phillip R Goodwin art, 30", NM ..675.00
Sign, poster, hunter in snow w/attacking wolves, c 1906, 29x16", VG..3,300.00
Sign, poster, The Kind That Gets 'Em, 1904, banded, 26x16", EX........2,550.00
Sign, tin, 1892 Winchester, 2-sided, VG+ 2,400.00
Sign, tin-on-cb stand-up, rider/horse, PR Goodwin art, 9x12", EX+ ..100.00
Sign, 4 hunting dogs, HR Poore, oak fr: 41x32", VG+ 5,000.00
Sliding T-square, #9756 ....40.00
Square, #9655, EX 270.00
Square, steel, #W22..75.00
Stove, camp; Trail Blazer..65.00
Straight razor, #8533, in orig box, G...................................75.00
Straight razor, ivory-colored Bakelite hdls, #8534, leather pouch ..180.00
Talc tin, Winchester After Shave Talc, red w/hunt scene, 5", EX+ ...300.00
Tennis racket, Berkeley, VG 350.00
Tent, Trail Blazer 65.00
Three-hook wooden bait, EX 750.00

Trade card, diecut shell shape, New Rival, 2x6", EX 130.00
Whistle, official; #1806, EX..500.00
Yard stick, wooden, EX..125.00

Windmill Weights

Windmill weights made of cast iron were used to protect the windmill's plunger rod from damage during high winds by adding weight that slowed down the speed of the blades.

Bull, Boss Bull, worn pnt, 32-lb...................................1,800.00
Bull, Fairbury, no pnt, 18¼x24½x1¼" 750.00
Bull, old wht pnt, 18x24½"...600.00
Horse, bobtail, pnt traces, ca 1910, 17x17"....................300.00
Horse, long-tailed, mc layers of old pnt, ca 1910, 17x17" 400.00
Moon crescent, Fairbanks Morse, 1900, 22-lb, 11x6⅝"...........185.00

Rooster, Elgin (attributed), red comb and wattle, white body with rainbow tail (later paint), ca 1880, 18¾", $1,200.00.

Rooster, Hummer, Elgin Wind Power..., 13½"+wood base..........600.00
Rooster, Mogul; Elgin, hollow body, old blk pnt, 21".............2,300.00
Spear, Challenge, CI, no pnt, 35-lb, 24" 800.00
Squirrel, Elgin, old dk tan pnt, lt rust, 17½"......................1,650.00
Star, H37 Halladay Standard, worn wht pnt, 14" 660.00

Wire Ware

Very primitive wire was first made by cutting sheet metal into strips which were shaped with mallet and file. By the late thirteenth century, craftsmen in Europe had developed a method of pulling these strips through progressively smaller holes until the desired gauge was obtained. During the Industrial Revolution of the late 1800s, machinery was developed that could produce wire cheaply and easily; and it became a popular commercial commodity. It was used to produce large items such as garden benches and fencing as well as innumerable small pieces for use in the kitchen or on the farm. Beware of reproductions. Our advisor for this category is Rosella Tinsley; she is listed in the Directory under Kansas.

Basket, bread, wire in sm sqs, oval, 2 hdls 75.00
Basket, fruit; rnd openwork designs, ca 1900, 5x14" 90.00
Basket, onion; wire in circles, bulged-out sides 90.00
Basket, ornate twisted wire, ftd, 1850s, 5"..........................110.00
Bottle carrier, holds 6 twisted hdl, 4x9x14".........................50.00
Bottle holder, circular, top hdl, ftd 60.00
Bucket, heavy wire in dmn design, flared top, bail hdl, 12x12"....60.00
Comb holder, twisted, fancy top, hangs...............................105.00
Compote, triangular basket w/trn-down rim, ped ft, 7x9"........70.00
Egg cooker, 6-compartment, simple style............................35.00
Egg tongs, heavy oval circular wire, squeeze hdl, 11" L 50.00

Fork, meat; heavy wire, 3 sharp prongs, loop hdl, 1800s, 15" 20.00
Lifter, fruit jar; collapsible, jar fits inside 25.00
Napkin ring, twisted wire, fancy design, pr 115.00
Pie rack, 4-tier 75.00
Plant stand, scrolled ft, arched base, old pnt, Victorian, 32x19" dia....250.00
Rolling pin holder, fine twisted wire, 2 hearts, old, EX........75.00
Rug beater, wood hdl mk Kleen-e-ze Bristol Eng...1928, 21" 25.00
Soap saver, oblong screen-wire shape, wire & wood hdl........22.00
Sponge holder, heavy, hooks on side of tub, EX........50.00
Tea ball, wire screen, tin banding, lock fastener, 2¼" oval........30.00
Trivet, fine wire in circles, ftd, 14" dia........80.00
Trivet, triangular, dbl wire at sides, loop hdl, 3-ftd........40.00
Trivet, woven dmn center, 8" dia........20.00
Whisk, tined loop w/twisted hdl, Germany, 8", EX........20.00

Wisecarver, Rick

Rick Wisecarver is a contemporary ceramic artist from Ohio who is well known not only for his renderings of Indian portraits and brown-glaze ware reminiscent of similar lines made by earlier Ohio potteries but for his figural cookie jars as well, most of which have a Black theme.

Cookie jar, Beauty & the Beast........250.00
Cookie jar, Black Santa & child, sgn, 1984 ....300.00
Cookie jar, Christmas Day, from $200 to 225.00
Cookie jar, Cookstove Mammy, from $150 to........200.00
Cookie jar, Hill Folk, from $200 to 225.00
Cookie jar, Indian Maid........180.00
Cookie jar, Mammy w/Cookies, pk, sgn 165.00
Cookie jar, Saturday Bath, from $175 to........235.00
Cookie jar, Snow White, from $200 to 250.00
Vase, deer in snow, 18x10"........295.00
Vase, gladiator w/helmet, mc w/gold on brn, 14" 100.00
Vase, Indian, 13" 350.00
Vase, Native Am Chief, full headdress, mc on brn, 17" 450.00
Vase, old prospector, mc on yel to wht, 7½" 60.00

Witch Balls

Witch balls were a Victorian fad touted to be meritorious toward ridding the house of evil spirits, thus warding off sickness and bad luck. Folklore would have it that by wiping the dust and soot from the ball, the spirits were exorcised. It is much more probable, however, considering the fact that such beautiful art glass was used in their making, that the ostensive Victorians perpetrated the myth rather tongue-in-cheek while enjoying them as lovely decorations for their homes.

Amethyst, 6½", +matching trumpet vase, free-blown, 13" 1,600.00
Clear w/wht loopings, att Millville Glassworks, 5⅜", +8" stand .578.00
Clear w/wht opaque loopings, 7" 495.00
Free-blown, deep smoke, pontil scaled w/glob of glass, 5"........75.00
Ruby flashed in striated ruby-flashed bowl, clear ft, 4" dia 850.00
Sugar bowl, aqua, witch-ball lid, appl hdl, South Jersey, 3¼" ..3,300.00

Wood, Beatrice

A multitalented artist, Beatrice Wood is especially well known for her ceramics which are displayed in the Smithsonian and the Metropolitan Museum of Art as well as several other museums around the world. She was also famous for her work in other mediums, especially painting and photography. She studied drama in Europe at the age of eighteen, returning to America where she became involved in the revolutionary Dada art movement in New York. She moved to California in the late 1920s and in 1937 opened her own studio. Nicknamed Bea or Beato, she developed wonderful lustre glazes for which she is highly acclaimed. Her style is modernistic, and her work ranges from sedate teapots and vases to whimsical sculptures. She died in 1998 at the age of 105. Her fascinating experiences led her to write her autobiography which so captured the attention of Titanic director James Cameron that he fashioned the role of Rose around her.

Bowl, bl gray over terra-cotta tone, ftd cylinder, 3⅞" H 2,500.00
Bowl, blk, shallow, incurvate rim, ftd, 2¾x6½" 920.00
Bowl, copper red w/turq & tan streaks, flared ft, 3½x6¾" 2,100.00
Bowl, marbleized tan & cream w/violet shades, cylindrical, 4" ...3,165.00
Bowl, pale turq irid over terra-cotta tone, 4⅛x10⅛", EX........575.00
Bowl, tan w/copper magenta splotches & vertical stripes, ftd, 6½" ...1,150.00
Bowl, turq over terra-cotta tone, ftd, 3⅞x11⅛"........750.00
Bowl, turq over terra-cotta tone, shallow, 13⅝" dia, EX 1,100.00
Bowl, turq over terra-cotta tone w/drips, low, 11½", EX 345.00
Bowl, turq w/radiating blk streaks, ftd, 3x11½", EX 575.00
Bowl, volcanic bl-gr, ftd, 2½x5¾"........1,600.00
Bowl, volcanic lt bl, ftd, Beato, 3¼x7½", NM 1,100.00
Bowl, volcanic mustard, Beato, 2¼x6½" 1,100.00
Chalice, gold craters w/violets & bl-gr, conical, appl discs, 8" .3,165.00
Chalice, gold shaded w/turq, 3 appl worm-like devices, 7¼" ...1,840.00
Chalice, gold-gr to violet, conical on baluster stem, 7" 2,875.00
Chalice, gr & violet craters, stepped stem w/nodules, 6¾" 2,585.00
Chalice, ruby w/irregular fissures exposing turq, 6½" 2,185.00
Coffee set, blk lustre, 10½" pot+cr/sug+5¼" mug 1,850.00
Goblet, ruby w/irregular fissures exposing turq, bulbous knop, 5½" ...925.00
Goblet, ruby w/irregular fissures exposing turq, 6⅞"........1,095.00
Plaque, 3 floating angels, gr & gold w/purple over terra cotta, 10x6" ..2,875.00
Sculpture, eel, gr lustre w/coffee-bean eyes, sm fleck, 2x14" 1,600.00
Sculpture, figure on Tang Dynasty-style horse, gr w/gold & violet, 17"...5,175.00
Vase, fish & sea life w/bubbles, yel ochre w/violet, bbl shape, 6" ..2,585.00
Vase, red volcanic w/gr splotches, tapered cylinder, 15⅝" 3,165.00
Vase, seafoam gr w/violet tinge, globular, 13" 3,735.00
Vase, tan & rust red drip, tapered cylinder, rstr, 12⅞"........975.00
Vase, thick lime gr on brn clay, mk, 2½" 425.00

Wood Carvings

Wood sculptures represent an important section of American folk art. Wood carvings were made not only by skilled woodworkers such as cabinetmakers, carpenters, etc., but by amateur 'whittlers' as well. They take the form of circus-wagon figures, carousel animals, decoys, busts, figurines, and cigar store Indians. Oriental artists show themselves to have been as proficient with the medium of wood as they were with ivory or hardstone. See also Carousel Animals; Decoys; Tobacciana.

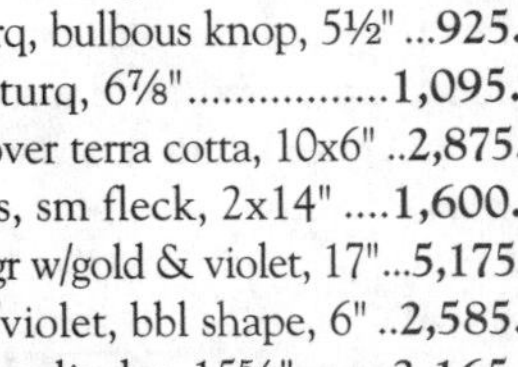

Eagle, mahogany with old finish, fine details, three-dimensional, 27", $3,400.00.

Deer, half-body, laminated, glass eyes, old pnt, 53" L 220.00

Eagle, architectural ornament, gilt traces, some damage, 16" wingspan..550.00
Eagle, detailed wings spread, fish in claws, on tree-root base, 15"...........250.00
Eagle, old pnt & gilt, Am, 19th C, 12½x19¼" 2,300.00
Eagle, pine w/worn gilt, red beak, age, 11x19" 440.00
Eagle, wht pnt (worn), Am, ca 1900, 5¾x21⅛"............................2,300.00
Eagle plaque, bold cvd feathers, gold pnt, old rpr, 10x18".............275.00
Gnome, old brn finish, used as garden ornament, 41" 220.00
Horse, orig buckskin-colored pnt, rpr, 7x11" on driftwood base..110.00
Horse, worn mc pnt, rpl fiber tail, age cracks, 16" 195.00
Indian, bright pnt, 'Smokem' on pipe, 14" 140.00
Lion, putty filled, old rpt over weathered surface, rprs, 42"........1,100.00
Owl, glass eyes, EX details & orig pnt, unsgn, 20th C, 9½" 55.00
Panel, relief-cvd gargoyles, oak, primitive style, 8x17" 150.00
Pike, pine w/orig pnt, artist sgn, 36" 195.00
Putto, polychrome & gold, 6¾" 450.00
Roadrunner, realist orig pnt, glass eyes, 8¾x13½" 250.00
Rooster, old mc pnt, 20th C, 14½"...110.00
Rooster, old natural finish, EX cvg, 20th C, 7" 315.00
Uncle Sam (Black), red/wht/bl pnt, cane missing, 11", EX......5,775.00
Whale, smiling, Am, 19th C, 6½x6½" dia 385.00

Woodenware

Woodenware (or treenware, as it is sometimes called) generally refers to those wooden items such as spoons, bowls, food molds, etc., that were used in the preparation of food. Common during the eighteenth and nineteenth centuries, these wares were designed from a strictly functional viewpoint and were used on a day-to-day basis. With the advent of the Industrial Revolution which brought with it new materials and products, much of the old woodenware was simply discarded. Today original handcrafted American woodenwares are extremely difficult to find. See also Primitives.

Bowl, burl walnut, carved rim, American, ca 1750, 4½x18½", $1,650.00.

Bowl, ash burl, dk finish, age crack in rim, 3½x8"........................220.00
Bowl, ash burl, elliptical w/cut-out hdls, minor cracks, 8x20" .2,750.00
Bowl, ash burl, EX patina, age hairline, 3¼x5"..........................180.00
Bowl, ash burl, scrubbed, old putty rpr, 8½x21" 1,650.00
Bowl, ash burl, trn ftd form w/shaped rim, 19th C, 3x5¼"..........315.00
Bowl, ash burl w/EX figure, cvd hdls, sm rpr, 8x20x17" 7,700.00
Bowl, ash burl w/EX figure, dk patina, trn ft & ring, 1⅝x5" 385.00
Bowl, ash burl w/EX figure, early trning, rim crack, 6x15".......1,800.00
Bowl, ash burl w/EX figure, putty rprs, varnish, 5¾x16¾".......1,100.00
Bowl, ash burl w/G figure, deeply trn, 6x14" 1,650.00
Bowl, ash burl w/G figure, EX old patina, age cracks, 6x20" ...1,500.00
Bowl, ash burl w/G figure, red traces, detailed ft, rolled rim, 6x18"...1,980.00
Bowl, ash burl w/G figure, scrubbed, trn ft, tight crack, 5x14"....1,595.00
Bowl, ash burl w/G figure & wold worn patina, rpr in bottom, 5x17"...1,100.00
Bowl, ash burl w/G patina, thinly trn, raised rim, 2½x7¼".........385.00
Bowl, bird's-eye maple, old rfn (G color), lt wear, 4¼x15x14" ...220.00
Bowl, maple, shallow, 3 shaved spoke legs, dk red pnt, 14x16½"...460.00
Bowl, maple, trn, mellow rfn, EX figure, 13"...............................275.00
Bowl, maple burl w/old honey-colored finish, 2x4" 140.00
Bowl, poplar, dull yel pnt on exterior, 12x13"..............................225.00

Bowl, poplar w/red stain, varnish inside, 7x22"............................330.00
Bowl, poplar w/worn pnt exterior, rpr/crack/worm holes, 7½x24"....300.00
Bowl, trn, silver-gray patina, 7x21x20"..195.00
Bucket, steel bands, wire bail w/wood hdl, old pnt, 10½x12½"..330.00
Butter paddle, ash burl w/horse-head hdl, EX, 9¼"....................825.00
Butter paddle, maple w/burl in bowl, curl in hdl, dk, 7¼" L.......195.00
Cage, vegetable washing; several spindles rpl, 23½" dia..............300.00
Carry-all, pine w/old red rpt, dvtl & nailed, 7x15x7"+hdl 440.00
Charger, scrubbed, old metal rprs, 24x25½"...............................315.00
Cookie board, Indian w/gun, pineapple, old patina, 5x8"............825.00
Cookie board, mahog w/cvd eagle/E Pluribus.../Liberty/WA/etc, 8x12" ...4,600.00
Cookie board, man on 1 side/woman on other, 17x5¾"..............250.00
Cookie board, man w/gun 1 side/lady w/flower basket on bk, 27x10"....1,000.00
Corn cutter, trn legs, old dk finish, 28x36x41" 100.00
Cutting board, pine w/oiled finish, cut-out heart hdl, 14x7".......275.00
Egg carrier, poplar w/red & blk stencil labels, OH, 11x14x12" ...275.00
Firkin, staved, copper tacks, tan pnt, rpr, 14".............................275.00
Firkin, staved, late blk pnt, 6¼" 220.00
Firkin, staved, lt gray-bl pnt, 10" 250.00
Firkin, staved, old yel pnt, 7½"..350.00
Firkin, staved, single finger bands, copper tacks, old rpt, 10x10" ...330.00
Firkin, staved, steel tacks, old gr pnt, bail hdl, 7" 525.00
Firkin, staved, steel tacks, orig gr pnt w/traces on hdl, 13".........440.00
Firkin, staved, warm varnish, 11¾x12" 250.00
Jar, Pease, dk patina, wood hdl w/wire bail, 9½x12"..................627.00
Jar, Pease, trn body, sloping shoulders, lt wear, 7x6½".................495.00
Match holder, bbl form w/brn & tan sponge pnt, Am, 1800s, 2⅛"..115.00
Peel, rnd plate w/long hdl w/pierced end, 18th C, 56½".............375.00
Pie carrier, poplar w/old varnish, 2 lift-out shelves, 20x23x13"...200.00
Pitcher, haystack; staved, iron bands, hdl & lip, dk finish, 16" ...495.00
Rundlet, trn bbl form, lt red pnt over gray, 19th C, 5" H............175.00
Soap dish, ash burl, rectangular w/canted sides, EX patina, 1⅝x5x4"....550.00
Spoon, pierced hdl, cvd hook, shallow bowl, 19th C, 8".............545.00
Tray, cutlery; dvtl cherry, 2-compartment, cutout hdls, 6x15x9".300.00
Trencher, hand hewn, oblong w/old red pnt, age crack, 22x13x5"....440.00
Tub, staved, trn lid & knob, label: Cedar Ware...MA, 4¼x5⅞" .250.00

Woodworking Machinery

Vintage cast-iron woodworking machines are monuments to the highly skilled engineers, foundrymen, and machinists who devised them, thus making possible the mass production of items ranging from clothespins, boxes, and barrels to decorative moldings and furniture. Though attractive from a nostalgic viewpoint, many of these machines are bought by the hobbyist and professional alike, to be put into actual use — at far less cost than new equipment. Many worth-assessing factors must be considered; but as a general rule, a machine in good condition is worth about 65¢ a pound (excluding motors). A machine needing a lot of restoration is not worth more than 35¢ a pound, while one professionally rebuilt and with a warranty can be calculated at $1.10 a pound. Modern, new machinery averages over $3.00 a pound. Two of the best sources of information on purchasing or selling such machines are *Vintage Machines — Searching for the Cast Iron Classics*, by Tom Howell, and *Used Machines and Abused Buyers* by Chuck Seidel from *Fine Woodworking*, November/December 1984. Prices quoted are for machines in good condition, less motors and accessories. Our advisor for this category is Mr. Dana Martin Batory, author of *Vintage Woodworking Machinery, An Illustrated Guide to Four Manufacturers*. See his listing in the Directory under Ohio for further information. No phone calls, please.

American Saw Mill Machinery Company, 1931

Band saw, Monarch Line, #X25, 30" built-in ball-bearing motor .770.00

Mortiser, Monarch Line, #XI, hollow chisel, motorized 345.00
Sander, Monarch Line, #X8, ball-bearing drum & disc 560.00

Delta Manufacturing Company, 1939

Band saw, #890, 14" 70.00
Belt sander, #1400, 6" 35.00
Drill press, bench, #999, 14" 50.00
Drill press, floor, #1370, 17" 200.00
Drill press, floor, high speed, #1370-H, 17" 200.00
Jointer, ball bearing, #390, 4" 35.00
Lathe, timken bearing, #955, 9" 35.00
Scroll saw, 4-speed, #1200, 24" 40.00
Shaper, ball bearing, reversible, 31180 ....30.00
Unisaw, tilting-arbor, #1450, 10" 175.00

F.H. Clement Co., 1896

Band saw, 28", Improved 1,040.00
Band saw, 34", Patent Improved 635.00
Band saw, 42" 1,430.00
Jointer, Perfection, 8" 620.00
Lathe, pattern maker's; iron bed, Improved, 20" 815.00
Planer, #2½, dbl belted, Improved, 24" 1,465.00
Planer, #3, dbl surface, 26" 3,000.00
Sand belt machine, Improved 425.00
Sander, #1, spindle & drum 520.00
Sanding machine, surface; Improved 650.00
Shaper, #1, reversible, Improved 650.00
Table saw, dbl arbor, Improved, 16" 815.00

Hoyt & Brother Company, 1888

Band saw & resawing machine, #1194, 20" 1,700.00
Jointer, Perfection, 8" 450.00
Planer, matcher & surfacer, New Combined, #2, 24" 5,200.00
Sand-papering machine, The Boss, #5, 24" 1,600.00
Shingle machine, Grand Mogul, 2-block, automatic feed 2,210.00
Tenoning machine, #2 ....650.00

J.D. Wallace Company, 1940s

Band saw, 16" 210.00
Grinder & sander, disk, Wonder, 16" 165.00
Jointer, 4" 15.00
Saw, circular (table saw); Universal, 7" 75.00
Saw, circular; plain, 7" 65.00

Levi Houston Co., 1897

Dovetailing machine, #2, sash 520.00
Moulder, new 4", 4-sided 650.00
Moulding machine, 4-headed, 10" 2,400.00
Panel raising machine, Pat Improved 650.00
Saw, heavy swing 910.00
Saw, new #1, improved variety, 14" 650.00
Saw, new combination, bench 910.00
Sticker, open-sided, door 500.00
Sticker, special, door 520.00
Tenoning machine, new stile, #3 ....585.00

Powermatic, Inc., 1965

Band saw, #141, 14" 145.00

Jointer, #50, 6" 110.00
Lathe, #45, 12" 230.00
Mortiser, #10, hollow chisel 375.00
Planer, #100, 12" 200.00
Planer, #180, 18" 685.00
Planer, #225, 24" 1,600.00
Sander, #33, 6" belt 90.00
Scroll saw, #95, 24" 100.00
Table saw, #62, 10" 135.00
Table saw, #72, 12" 515.00

The Sidney Machine Tool Co., 1916 (Famous Woodworking Machinery)

Bandsaw, No 1, 36", new 1,100.00
Bandsaw, 27" 535.00
Bandsaw, 32" 715.00
Jointer, Cyclone, 12" 525.00
Jointer, 20" 1,220.00
Jointer, 8" 615.00
Lathe, pattern maker's, 14" 275.00
Lathe, pattern maker's, 20" 325.00
Mortiser, hollow chisel 650.00
Mortiser & tenoner, combined 575.00
Planer, dbl-belted, 26x8" 1,755.00
Planer, 18" 880.00
Planer, 24" 975.00
Saw, combination; No 4, 16" 485.00
Saw, combination; No 5, 16" 525.00
Saw, Variety, No 2, 20" 875.00
Saw, Variety, No 6, 16" 780.00
Saw, Variety, No 8, 20" 650.00
Shaper, dbl spindle 1,300.00
Shaper, single spindle 650.00
Woodworker, portable, hand 485.00
Woodworker, Universal, Improved, No 14 ....1,525.00
Woodworker, Universal (5 machines in 1, No 30 or No 31, ea..2,015.00

Worcester Porcelain Company

The Worcester Porcelain Company was deeded in 1751. During the first or Dr. Wall period (so called for one of its proprietors), porcelain with an Oriental influence was decorated in underglaze blue. Useful tablewares represented the largest portion of production, but figurines and decorative items were also made. Very little of the earliest wares were marked and can only be identified by a study of forms, glazes, and the porcelain body, which tends to transmit a greenish cast when held to light. Late in the 1750s, a crescent mark was in general use, and rare examples bear a facsimile of the Meissen crossed swords. The first period ended in 1783, and the company went through several changes in ownership during the next eighty years. The years from 1783 – 1792 are referred to as the Flight period. Marks were a small crescent, a crown with 'Royal,' or an impressed 'Flight.' From 1792 – 1807 the company was known as Flight and Barr and used the trademark 'F&B' or 'B,' with or without a small cross. From 1807 to 1813 the company was under the Barr, Flight, and Barr management; this era is recognized as having produced porcelain with the highest quality of artistic decoration. Their mark was 'B.F.B.' From 1813 to 1840 many marks were used, but the most usual was 'F.B.B.' under a crown to indicate Flight, Barr, and Barr. In 1840 the firm merged with Chamberlain, and in 1852 they were succeeded by Kerr and Binns. The firm became known as Royal Worcester in 1862. The production was then marked with a circle with '51' within and a crown on top. The date of manufacture was incised into the bottom or stamped with a letter of the alphabet, just under the circle. In 1891 Royal Worcester England was added to the circle and crown. From that point on, each piece is dated with a code of dots or other symbols. After 1891 most wares had a blush-color ground. Prior to that date it was ivory. Most shapes were marked with a unique number.

During the early years they produced considerable ornamental wares with a Persian influence. This gave way to a Japanesque influence. James Hadley is most responsible for the Victorian look. He is considered the 'best ever' designer and modeller. He was joined by the finest porcelain painters. Together they produced pieces with very fine detail and exquisite painting and decoration. Figures, vases, and tableware were produced in great volume and are highly collectible. During the 1890s they allowed the artists to sign some of their work. Pieces signed on the face by the Stintons, Baldwyn, Davis, Raby, Austin, Powell, Sedgley, and Rushton (not a complete list) are in great demand. The company is still in production. There is an outstanding museum on the company grounds in Worcester, England.

Note: Most pieces had lids or tops (if there is a flat area on the top lip, chances are it had one), if missing deduct 30% to 40%.

Key:
BFB — Barr, Flight, and Barr   FBB — Flight, Barr, and Barr

Bowl, insects & birds on bl scales, scalloped/molded, shallow, 10" 275.00
Bowl, reserves w/gold on bl scales w/flowers & wheat, 1½x7½"...550.00
Bowl, Sabrina Porcelain, fish, WH Austin, 1926, 2¾x9¼" 1,000.00
Coffeepot, mc floral w/verdigris & gilt, ca 1888, 14" 725.00
Cup & saucer, chinoiserie, FBB, 1820s..165.00
Ewer, blkberries/butterflies, much gold, dragon hdl, 1883, 11⅛"..800.00
Ewer, floral w/gold, emb hdl/neck, ca 1888, 8"...........................165.00
Ewer, floral w/gold, stag-horn hdl, ca 1886, 10" 145.00
Ewer, floral w/gold, 1889 printed mk, 9½".....................................200.00
Ewer, highland cattle scene, shield mk, 12" 2,450.00
Ewer, spider mums, emb bamboo hdl, crown circle mk, ca 1889, 9½"...400.00
Jar, rtcl body w/jeweled florets, ca 1906, 3" 485.00
Jar & undertray, floral on cream w/gold, melon shape, 7x7½" 330.00
Jardiniere, floral/acanthus emb on wht, gr crown circle mk, 6½"..75.00
Jug, bl floral, bamboo hdl, crown circle mk, 1889, 10½"...............115.00
Jug, lizard figural, stag horn hdl w/verdigris & gold, 1900s, 7" 165.00
Pitcher, mc Oriental decor, emb elephant hdl, ca 1875, 8".........140.00
Pitcher, wild roses, gr crown circle mk, ca 1884, 7" 175.00
Plate, Pine Cone, underglaze bl, scalloped, 18th C, 6¼", pr 315.00

Plate, scalloped and pierced basketwork border, multicolor flower garlands, brown stem-like handles, unmarked, late 1800s, 11¾", NM, $3,450.00.

Teapot, flowers & butterflies, crescent mk, 5¾", VG 195.00
Tray, leaf form w/HP florals, ca 1888, 14" L 120.00
Urn, gilt ferns between rtcl bands, 2-pc/bolted, shield mk, 11½" ..400.00
Vase, cornucopia on bk of swan, ca 1870, rstr, 6⅛", pr................350.00
Vase, dragon encircles gourd body, jewel eyes, ca 1887, 17½" .1,000.00
Vase, horn shape w/female masks/acanthus leaves, tripod, 1840s, 6½"..485.00
Vase, hummingbird & flowers on cream w/gold, uptrn hdls, 1860s, 9"..300.00
Vase, Islamic style, rtcl scrolls, 1891 mk, lt wear, 14" 700.00
Vase, lotus form, patent metallic decor, late 1800s, rstr, 9⅜" 635.00

Vase, mc wildflowers, pierced neck band, hdls, ftd, ca 1885, 12½" ...300.00
Vase, rtcl globe w/cobalt center, trumpet neck, ca 1900, 10⅜" ...650.00

World's Fairs and Expos

Since 1851 and the Crystal Palace Exhibition in London, World's Fairs and Expositions have taken place at a steady pace. Many of them commemorate historical events. The 1904 Louisiana Purchase Exposition, commonly known as the St. Louis World's Fair, celebrated the 100th anniversary of the Louisiana Purchase agreement between Thomas Jefferson and Napoleon in 1803. The 1893 Columbian Exposition commemorated the 400th anniversary of the discovery of America by Columbus in 1492. (Both of these fairs were held one year later than originally scheduled.) The multitude of souvenirs from these and similar events have become a growing area of interest to collectors in recent years. Many items have a 'crossover' interest into other fields: i.e., collectors of postcards and souvenir spoons eagerly search for those from various fairs and expositions. For additional information collectors may contact World's Fairs Collectors Society (WFCS), whose address is in the Directory under Clubs, Newsletters, and Catalogs, or our advisor, Herbert Rolfes. His address is listed in the Directory under Florida.

Key:
T&P — Trylon & Perisphere   WF — World's Fair

1893 Columbian, Chicago

Coin, half-dollar, commemorative, NM 15.00
Elongated cent, 1869 Indian head penny 20.00
Portfolio, The Magic City, Historical Fine Art Series, 250 pgs 25.00
Trade card, Enterprise Congress-World's Fair, 5x3½"....................25.00

1894 California Mid-Winter, San Francisco

Pincushion, shoe shape, 4x1¼x1½" 65.00
Trade card, Mechanical Arts Bldg, Otea Cereal by Laumeister Mills....30.00

1898 Trans-Mississippi

Book, Snap Shots of 1898 Trans-Mississippi Expo, 48-pg, VG+....30.00
Cup, eng, New Amsterdam Silver CO Quadruple Plate, 2¾".......25.00
Medal, lady w/staff & scenes from Omaha, SD Childs & Co, 2½" dia...55.00
Paperweight, photographic image of Agricultural Bldg, glass, 4"...55.00

1901 Pan American

Award certificate, Honorable Mention, Potato/Onions, 15x18", $300 to....500.00
Book, illus by CD Arnold, Official Photographer, 115-pg, 10x7"..75.00
Booklet, Latest Edition Pan American...Niagara, 100 views, VG .25.00
Bookmark, pansy over logo, Libbey McNeill CO-Food Products, 5x1½" ...20.00
Cane, pewter buffalo L-hdl opens for pipe w/clay bowl, EX 1,600.00
Cup, emb images of Expo, silver, 3½"..35.00
Cup, ruby glass, mk Eugene Schreiber 1901 Pan American, EX....30.00
Encased cent, 1901 Indian head, Lucky Penny Pocket Piece, EX 25.00
Frying Pan, image of buffalo w/Am flag, mini, 2¾ 30.00
Letter opener, buffalo on hdl, dtd 1901, from $25 to 50.00
Magazine, Cosmopolitan, souvenir edition, EX+ 20.00
Paperweight, full-figure buffalo on 3" base, metal, 2¼" H 85.00
Paperweight, Machinery & Transportation Bldg, glass, 4x2¾"......50.00
Pin-bk, buffalo & Indian in center, 1¼" dia.................................50.00
Pin-bk, shows woman flying over buffalo, Whitehead & Hoag, 1¼"....65.00
Silk cloth, Liberal Arts Bldg, 20x20", VG.....................................48.00
Spoon, Indian & boar on hdl, waterfall on bk, SS, 5½" 47.00

Stereoview, On the Merry Midway, Kilburn #14469, VG............15.00
Ticket, children's souvenir, 3½x2¼", NM.................................20.00

1904 St. Louis

Book, The World's Work, Library Edition, #179 of 1,000, EX.......75.00
Bowl, cobalt w/Palace of Arts, gold trim, hdls, MIG, 2½x3½" 63.00
Flue cover, Administration Bldg under glass, metal fr/cb bk..........50.00
Guide, Official Guide to the Louisiana Purchase, 200-pg, EX.......50.00
Jewelry chest, Electricity Bldg, gold trim, 4-ftd, 3" H 290.00
Match safe, Machinery Bldg on lid, SP, EX................................100.00
Mug, Machinery Bldg, wht porc w/gold trim, mk Victoria, 4".....100.00
Paperweight, photo of Festival Hall & Cascades under glass, 3" dia...50.00
Pocket mirror, Observation Wheel, celluloid, 2¼", VG.............130.00
Salt shaker, Palace of Liberal Arts, 2¾", VG 50.00
Shot glass, brass, enameled bldg, 1⅞"......................................40.00
Trinket box, Palais de Gouvernement rvpt, beveled glass, 3x3x2¾"..125.00
Tumbler, ruby flash, World's Fair 1904 eng, 3⅞" 50.00

1905 Lewis and Clark

Badge, Elks Day w/enameled US Flag & Elks Flag, 3¼x2" 90.00
Book, 180 Glimpes...Exposition, 85+ pgs, softcover, 5x7" 35.00
Booklet, Sights & Scenes..., 96-pg, 5x7", EX 55.00
Elongated cent, Forestry Bldg, copper, 1⅜x¾".............................30.00
Seashell, Lewis & Clark Exposition 1905 cvg, 3⅜x2½", VG........50.00
Ticket, souvenir; Portland Day, Lewis/Clark/Portland, EX 33.00
Token, Forestry Bldg/Lewis & Clark, brass, ¾" dia 36.00
Watering can, Liberal Arts Bldg, teal w/gold trim, unmk, 3" 190.00

1909 Alaska Yukon Pacific

Medal, Virgin Utah Copper, seal of Utah, 1½" dia......................25.00
Plate, OR State Bldg, mc w/gold on china, 8", VG 90.00
Postcard, You'll Like Tacoma, unmailed, 3½x5½", EX 15.00
Season pass, Joy Wheel Pay Streak, yel, 2¼x4", EX 38.00
Trade coin, $1, EX..105.00

1915 Panama Pacific

Pin-back button, Independent Order of Foresters, Tower of Jewels, multicolored cello, 53mm, NM, $30.00.

Badge, BPOE, mk J Jessop & Sons, 3½x2¼"...................................42.00
Card, California Invitation Day, Cabrillo bridge image, 4½x7" 38.00
Paperweight, rvpt of tower at Expo, 3x5" 35.00
Plate, Liberty Bell PPIE 1915 on front, HP, gold trim, 6¼"..........30.00
Souvenir, Tower of Gems, glass amethyst nova gem in brass.........80.00
Spoon, Jeweled Tower in bowl, 1915 cvd in hdl, sterling mks, 5½" ...32.00

1933 Chicago

Banner, Electrical Bldg Exhibit, 8" (widest point), 26" L, EX 13.00
Book, A Century...Exposition 1933, Donnelley, 13x10", EX.........50.00
Bracelet, copper, logo & skyline scenes, Greek key border, EX 25.00
Car emblem, chrome w/enameling, 6½x2½", MIB.......................335.00
Compact, Federal Bldg/Hall of Science/T&T Bldg, metal, 3x2" ..55.00

Elongated coin, Skyride, EX...20.00
Figurine, dog, pnt CI, Expo tag at neck, 2x2", EX 95.00
Paperweight, paper under glass, ¾x3x4", NM 40.00
Playing cards, logo front/scenes on face, Western Playing Co, EX...48.00
Powder jar, gr vaseline satin glass, Sphere w/Tower, 6" H.............90.00
Tape measure, silver & blk w/logo/T&T Bldg, cloth tape, VG......50.00
Thermometer, key shape, metal, 9" L 40.00
Umbrella, bamboo/paper, mc graphics, 29" L, 31" open dia, EX, $50 to...100.00

1939 New York

Bullet camera, black and brass metal case with Trylon and Perisphere medallion, Kodak, in original paper box, M, $750.00.

Bookends, cvd T&P design in Syroco wood, 4½x6", pr 58.00
Cigarette tin, bl w/orange logo, lid slides, VG 125.00
Flag, orange/wht/bl rayon, 3 tie strings, 34x58", VG 150.00
Ink holder, 3D T&P Bldg, polished chrome, 5x3" 115.00
Pin dish, wht metal w/chrome, World of Tomorrow Today Bldg, EX ..60.00
Plate, T&P in center, red/wht/bl, hdld, Knowles, 11½" dia 175.00
Plate, T&P w/fair scenes, tab hdls, Cronin China, 10½" dia 100.00
Playing cards, T&P design w/fireworks, M (orig cellophone wrap) 75.00
Snowdome, Administration Bldg, glass, on Bakelite base, 3" dia 145.00
Thermos, Universal Super Vac, bl w/orange logo, VG (orig box) ...235.00

1939 San Francisco

Ashtray, Tower of Sun, fair scene border, Homer Laughlin, 6¼" ..36.00
Catalog, History of Am Paintings, Trumbull, 12-pg, EX................20.00
Program, Grand...Show Takarazuka girls..., geisha cover, EX.........37.50
Sticker, Oakland...Invites You, red/wht/bl, 1⅞x2½", M 5.00
Table, folding; Tower of Sun w/city skyline bkground, 30x30"....155.00

1962 Seattle

Booklet, Paris Spectakular Wax Museum, 12-pg, 11x8½", EX 17.00
Creamer, wht w/Space Needle & logos, gold trim, 5½".................38.00
Film, Visit...Fair, Columbia Pictures, 8mm, M (NM box) 45.00
Guide book, Northwest Coast Indian Art, 101-pg, softcover, EX .21.00
Kit, Space Needle, wood, Whitechester Heating, M (NM box) ...45.00
Medal set, Official Medals...Century 21 Expo, M (NM folder)...130.00
Mug, Bargreen's Cafe, Expo logo, Homer Laughlin, 2⅝".............35.00
Music box, Space Needle, ceramic, 7" H.....................................42.00
Pennant, red w/mc WF scenes, felt, 12" L, EX 23.00
Shakers, wht w/Space Needle & logo, 4½", pr.............................36.00
Shirt, gr w/Space Needle & logo, cotton, men's med sz, EX..........37.00

1964 New York

Keychain, Unisphere, w/light, Mallory Battery, 6¼x4", MOC......57.00
License plate, bl & orange w/logo in center, US Steel, EX............50.00
Model, Unisphere, chrome w/plastic base, US Steel, 3x3½"..........25.00

Playing cards, logo on bks, M (cards in cellophane, box open).....**38.00**
Tablecloth, mc fair images, cotton, 64x54", VG+ **75.00**

Wright, Frank Lloyd

Born in Richland Center, Wisconsin, in 1869, Wright became a pioneer in architectural expression, developing a style referred to as 'prairie.' From early in the century until he died in 1959, he designed houses with rooms that were open, rather than divided by walls in the traditional manner. They exhibited low, horizontal lines and strongly projecting eaves, and he filled them with furnishings whose radical aesthetics complemented the structures to perfection. Several of his homes have been preserved to the present day, and collectors who admire his ideas and the unique, striking look he achieved treasure the stained glass windows, furniture, chinaware, lamps, and other decorative accessories made by Wright.

Key:
drw — drawer   reuphl — reupolstered
H — Heritage Henredon

Chair, Heritage Henredon, olive green naugahyde, refinished, 41x22x22", VG, $1,000.00.

Architectural drawing, pen/pencil, electrical work, 26½x42½" **2,900.00**
Armchair, red leather & cast aluminum, executive style, 1956, 33"..**9,500.00**
Blueprints, general plan for house, sheet 4 (elevations), 1954, EX........**900.00**
Blueprints, plans for house heating/plumbing, 1954, 36½x25", VG **750.00**
Breakfront, H, hutch w/center glass door, cabinet base, 83x66".........**3,000.00**
Cabinet, H, cradle base, 2 doors, 26x34" **4,000.00**
Cabinet, H, 2 doors, recessed hdls, 25x31x17" **2,700.00**
Cabinet, H, 2 shelves, 2 drws, 25x20x20"................................**1,600.00**
Chair, child's, slab bk, cushion seat, rfn, 1912, 31x17x15"..........**425.00**
Chairs, dining; H, #2002, rfn, reuphl, 32", 4 for......................**2,700.00**
Chairs, dining; H, high-bk, reuphl, 40", 2 arm+4 side **4,000.00**
Chairs, side; H, 8-sided bk, cantilevered seat, pr.........................**450.00**
Chest, H, 2 half over 2 full drws, 25x33", G..............................**425.00**
Credenza, H, #2004/#2000, 2-part, ca 1956.............................**2,185.00**
Drawing, colored pencil rendering of CA house, 1951, 12x22", VG .**5,500.00**
Drawing, ink/pencil, 3 elevations of house, 28½x44½" **3,000.00**
Dresser, 11 graduated drws w/recessed hdls, 38x62x20"...........**1,600.00**
Fabric sample, Damask, attached color chart, 26x24"....................**70.00**
Fabric sample, linear design, red & gray, Schumaker, 1954, 51x27"....**550.00**
Fabric sample, silk & rayon, interlocking circles, ca 1954, 51x37" ..**1,600.00**
Frame, cvd in style of L Sullivan, weathered/losses, 1894, 49x47"...**4,000.00**
Headboard, H, #2001, mahog, 39x79", VG **1,500.00**
Magazine, Architectural Forum, 1938, devoted to his work........**175.00**
Night stand, H, drw, 2 open shelves, 25x21x18", VG..............**1,000.00**
Print, Wasmuth series, floor plan of Fuller house, 14x22", EX **600.00**
Print, Wasmuth series, Vorort house illustration, matted/fr, 25x13"....**550.00**
Stool, H, uphl swivel top on cruciform base, 25" dia...............**1,600.00**
Table, coffee; H, dropped sides, 14x50x20"................................**2,100.00**

Table, coffee; H, hexagon, 3-slab base, 48" dia **1,600.00**
Table, coffee; H,#450C, mitered drop leaves, rfn, 14x60x20" ..**1,600.00**
Table, dining, dbl V base, 2 leaves, 64x42" **1,100.00**
Table, dining; H, #2002, V slab base, rfn, 64", G........................**500.00**
Table, drop-leaf; gate-leg base, rfn top, 29x43x26"+2 20" leaves ...**425.00**
Table, end; H, hexagonal top, tri-form base, 17x20x20" **1,800.00**
Table, end; H, low shelf & drw, 23x27x21" **1,200.00**
Table, end; H, recessed top, shelf, drw, dbl-slab base, 33" **1,500.00**
Table, end; H, triangular on tri-form base, 15x22" **1,500.00**
Table, end; plywood, triangular, w/apron & shelf, 25x46x21"..**1,300.00**
Table, H, burled cube base, 13x26" sq..**2,200.00**
Table, H, hexagonal, 3-slab base, rfn top, 25" dia....................**1,800.00**
Table, H, rnd w/copper Taliesin edge, 24x54"+leaf.....................**900.00**
Table, H, sq top, low shelf & drw, 23x26x27".............................**1,400.00**
Table, library; trestle legs, board stretcher, 1946, 28x96x48" ...**6,000.00**

Wrought Iron

Until the middle of the nineteenth century, almost all the metal hand forged in America was made from a material called wrought iron. When wrought iron rusts it appears grainy, while the mild steel that was used later shows no grain but pits to an orange-peel surface. This is an important aid in determining the age of an ironwork piece. See also Fireplace Implements.

Heart spatula, 14½", $575.00; Beetlenut pick, birdhead crest, 5½", $45.00; Wedding spatula, two Distlefinks, incised decor, $550.00; Sugar nippers, 7½", $125.00; Pipe tongs, hinged support arm, with reamer and tamper, 18", $625.00. (Photo courtesy Aston Americana Auctioneers & Appraisers)

Brackets, open scrollwork & quatrefoil motifs, 32x34", pr **770.00**
Broiler, adjustable rack, tripod base, 27" H **990.00**
Broiler, rotary; medallion hdl terminal, penny ft, 24" **220.00**
Broiler, rotary; pinwheel-like, 12½" dia....................................**400.00**
Broiler, rotary; 7 parallel rods at top, tripod base, 4x16" dia........**190.00**
Broiler, 8-rod top, 4-ftd, 1800s, 8x8"+16" hdl..........................**250.00**
Fork, 3-tine, cast brass ovoid finial, 44"......................................**75.00**
Fork, 3-tine, hook finial, ca 1900, 28½".....................................**35.00**
Hinges, curved terminals, 19th C, 10½x11⅜", pr **130.00**
Peel, brass inlays in hdl w/eng initials, heart & 1827, 21"..........**350.00**
Peel, ram's horn finial, 37"..**165.00**
Toaster, T-shaped tripod base, 5x13x17½".................................**220.00**
Trammel, scalloped & scrolled finials, eng detail w/cross & 1890, 60" ..**495.00**
Utensil rack, scrolled detail, 5 hooks, 16" L................................**495.00**

Yellow Ware

Ranging in color from buff to deep mustard, yellow ware which almost always has a clear glaze can be slip banded, plain, Rockingham decorated, flint enamel glazed, or mocha decorated. Black or red mocha decorated pieces are the most desirable. Although blue mocha decorated pieces are the most common, green decorated pieces command the lowest prices. Pieces having a combination of two colors are the rarest. The majority of pieces are plain and do not bear a manufacture's mark. Primarily produced in the United States, England, and Canada this utilitarian ware was popular from the mid-nineteenth century until the early twentieth century. Yellow ware was first produced in New York, Pennsylvania, and Vermont. However, the center for yellow ware production was East Liverpool, Ohio, a town which once supported more than thirty potters. Yellow ware is still being produced today in both the United States and England. Because of websites and Internet auctions, prices have tended to become uniform throughout the United States. The use of this pottery as accessories in decorating and its exposure in country magazines has caused prices to rise, especially for the more utilitarian forms such as plates and bowls. Note: Because this is a utilitarian ware, it is often found with damage and heavy wear. Damage does have a negative impact on price, especially for the common forms. For further information we recommend *Collecting Yellow Ware: An Identification and Value Guide* written by our advisor John Michel and Lisa McAllister, and *Collector's Guide to Yellow Ware* by Lisa McAllister. Mr. Michel's address is in the Directory under New York. See also Rockingham.

Amimal dish, hen on nest, brn band at base, ca 1900, 2¼x2x2" 280.00
Bowl, mixing; seaweed, bl on cream w/2 narrow bl bands, 1870s, 14" 470.00
Bowl, mixing; seaweed on cream band w/brn borders, hairline, 5x11⅝" ..385.00
Bowl, mixing; seaweed on wht bnad w/brn borders, chip, 7x14¾" 330.00
Bowl, seaweed on wht band w/bl stripes, wear/stains, 4¼x8½" ...385.00
Chamber pot, seaweed, wht w/bl bands, appl ribbed hdl, 5¾x9" ...220.00
Colander, cream bristol w/relief arched panels, hairline, 5¼x12" ..175.00
Colander, wht bristol, relief dmns & panels, 4x9¼" 250.00
Figurine, dog, yel/brn runs, 8-sided base, Geo Diehl...1870, 7⅝" ..4,400.00
Flask, emb morning glories & eagle, chips, 7⅜" 1,200.00
Jar, canning, w/lid, 5¾" 250.00
Jar, molded design, wax lip, 8" 250.00
Jar, seaweed on wht band w/bl stripes, close mismatch lid, 8½" ..495.00
Jar, seaweed on wht band w/bl stripes, w/lid, 6" 600.00
Mold, ear of corn, scalloped rim, 3¼x7¾x5⅞", EX 65.00
Mold, rabbit, late 1800s, 3¾x8x4⅞", EX 95.00
Nappy, 4 molded relief lines, ca 1850, 3½x14" 110.00
Pie plate, overall staining, ca 1850, 1¾x12" 200.00

Pitcher, colored rings under clear glaze, 7¼", $800.00.

Pitcher, wht bands, ribbed hdl, rpr to spout, 8½" 550.00
Pitcher, wht bands & brn stripes, strap hdl, 5½" 550.00
Rolling pin, trn maple hdls, late 1800s, 15x3" dia 525.00
Shaker, seaweed on wht band w/bl stripes, 4⅜", NM..............1,320.00
Soap dish, some wear, 5⅝" dia...550.00
Toby bottle, man w/fiddle, crazing/lines, 8½" 715.00

Zanesville Glass

Glassware was produced in Zanesville, Ohio, from as early as 1815 until 1851. Two companies produced clear and colored hollow ware pieces in five characteristic patterns: 1) diamond faceted, 2) broken swirls, 3) vertical swirls, 4) perpendicular fluting, 5) plain, with scalloped or fluted rims and strap handles. The most readily identified product is perhaps the whiskey bottles made in the vertical swirl pattern, often called globular swirls because of their full, round bodies. Their necks vary in width; some have a ringed rim and some are collared. They were made in several colors; amber, light green, and light aquamarine are the most common. Our advisor for this category is Mark Vuono; he is listed in the Directory under Connecticut.

Chestnut flask, amber, ten-diamond pattern with good impression, 4½", $1,870.00.

Bottle, globular, amber, 24 swirled ribs, bruise, 8¼" 275.00
Bottle, globular, med to dk amber, 24 vertical ribs, 7⅞" 1,650.00
Flask, chestnut; med red-amber, 24 vertical ribs, 6½" 240.00
Flask, med amber, 10-Dmn, pontil scar, sm scratches, 5¼" 725.00

Zell

The Georg Schmider United Zell Ceramic Factories has a long and colorful history. Affectionately called 'Zell' by those who are attracted to this charming German-Dutch type tin-glazed earthenware, this type of ware came into production in the latter part of the nineteenth century.

While Zell has created some lovely majolica-like examples (which are beginning to attract their own following), it is the German-Dutch scenes that are collected with such enthusiasm. Typical scenes are set against a lush green background with windmills on the distant horizon. Into the scenes appear typically garbed girls (long dresses with long white aprons and lowland bonnet head-gear) being teased or admired by little boys attired in pantaloon-type trousers and short rust-colored jackets, all wearing wooden shoes. There are variations on this theme, and occasionally a collector may find an animal theme or even a Kate Greenaway-like scene.

A similar ware in both theme, technique, and quality but bearing the mark Haag or Made in Austria is included in this listing.

While Zell produced a wide range of wares and even quite recently (1970s) introduced an entirely hand-painted hen/rooster line, it is this early charming German-Dutch theme pottery that is coveted by increasing numbers of devoted collectors. Our advisors for this category are Fred and Lila Shrader; they are listed in the Directory under California.

Key:
KG — Kate Greenaway style   MIA — Made in Austria

Teapot, marked Haag Austria, $150.00.

Bowl, boy giving fish to cats, flat, MIA/Haag, 5½" dia	35.00
Bowl, Dutch scene, resemblse mini chamber pot, Baden, 2½"	96.00
Bowl, girl tending geese, flat, Baden, 5½" dia	39.00
Bowls, mixing; Dutch scenes, nested set of 3: 5½", 7", 9"	325.00
Candlestick, costumed animals parading, Haag, 6½"	165.00
Canister, Dutch theme, Baden, w/lid, 6½"	195.00
Canister, hen & rooster theme, w/lid, 7"	87.00
Chamberstick, han & rooster, w/finger ring, 6" dia	22.00
Chamberstick, windmill scene, w/finger ring, Baden, 6" dia	180.00
Child's warmer/feeding dish, girls & geese, Baden, 8" dia	110.00
Chocolate pot, girls teased by boys, windmill beyond, German, 6"	175.00
Compote, floral (majolica-like), ped ft, 3½x9¼"	160.00
Creamer, boys strolling, windmill beyond, 3¼"	32.00
Creamer, costumed cats, MIA, 3¼"	51.00
Creamer, girl in wagon, +geese, Haag, 3¾"	58.00
Cup & saucer, basketweave & florals (majolica-like)	20.00
Cup & saucer, Dutch theme, from $38 to	55.00
Egg cup, girl chasing geese, dbl, MIA, 4⅛"	65.00
Egg cup, hen & rooster, single, 2¾"	26.00
Mug, grandpa in garden, KG, Baden, 3½"	62.00
Pitcher, boys teasing girls in cart, Germany, 32-oz, 9"	135.00
Plaque, boy & girl kiss by wall, brass rtcl fr, 4½" dia	99.00
Plate, abstract flowers, HP leaves (Quimper-like), 9"	24.00
Plate, cherries, leaves & butterfly (majolica-like), Baden, 10½"	55.00
Plate, daisy-type flower (majolica-like), 6½"	11.00
Plate, grandpa, wheelbarrow & children, KG, Baden, 8½" dia	88.00
Plate, hen &k rooster, 10" dia	32.00
Plate, proverb: Variety's the Spice of Life, MIA, 9"	78.00
Salt box, hen & rooster, wall hanging, hinged wooden lid	69.00
Sugar bowl, boy in garden, bl trim, hdls, MIA, w/lid	64.00
Sugar bowl, boy strolling, windmill beyond, Germany, 3¼" dia	31.00
Trivet, boy & girl strolling, 6 sided, Baden, 6" dia	80.00
Trivet, girl feeding lamb, Baden, 6" sq	62.00
Tumbler, girls strolling, windmill beyond, Baden, 4½"	49.00
Vase, basketweave w/dandelions (majolica-like), Germany, 7"	28.00

Zsolnay

Only until the past decade has the production of the Zsolnay factory become more correctly understood. In the beginning they produced only cement; industrial and kitchen ware manufacture began in the 1850s, and in the early 1870s a line of decorative architectural and art pottery was initiated which has continued to the present time.

The city of Pecs (pronounced Paach) is the major provincial city of southwest Hungary close to the Yugoslav border. The old German name for the city was Funfkirchen, meaning 'Five Churches.' (The 'five-steeple' mark became the factory's logo in 1878.)

Although most Americans only think of Zsolnay in terms of the bizarre, reticulated examples of the 1880s and 1890s and the small 'Eosine' green figures of animals and children that have been produced since the 1920s, the factory went through all the art trends of major international art potteries and produced various types of forms and decorations. The 'golden period,' circa 1895 – 1920, is when its Art Nouveau (Sezession in Austro-Hungarian terms) examples were unequaled. Vilmos Zsolnay was a Renaissance man devoted to innovation, and his children carried on the tradition after his death in 1900. Important sculptors and artists of the day were employed (usually anonymously) and married into the family, creating a dynasty.

Nearly all Zsolnay is marked, either impressed 'Zsolnay Pecs' or with the 'five steeple' stamp. Variations and form numbers can date a piece fairly accurately. For the most part, the earlier ethnic historical-revival pieces do not bring the prices that the later Sezession and second Sezession (Deco) examples do. Our advisor for this category is John Gacher; he is listed in the Directory under Rhode Island.

Jardiniere, thistles, majolica, #5454, ca 1899, 18", NM, $6,500.00. (Photo courtesy the Zsolnay Store)

Basket, emb snowberry reserves, bl irid, #8880, 8x11x9"	850.00
Bowl, floral on wht, 3 lg rtcl incurvate extensions, 9"	200.00
Bowl, lobster in relief on scalloped rim, Eosine, 6"	75.00
Figurine, buffalo (resting), Eosine, 1940, 4¼x8¼"	240.00
Figurine, deer entwined (2), Eosine, 6½" L	110.00
Figurine, kneeling nude, wht w/brn hair, gr drape, '30s, 9x6"	85.00
Figurine, owl, gr w/streaky bl, Pecs/Made in Hungary, 1920s, 6¼"	350.00
Figurine, polar bear, Eosine, gold & maroon, 1890-1910, Pecs, 4½"	900.00
Figurine, Puli, dog, Eosine, ca 1930-40, Pecs, 6⅝"	350.00
Jardiniere, rtcl grillwork panels w/gold beadwork, #2214, 7⅛", NM	300.00
Jug, turq w/heavy texture, 4 rtcl bosses, #1379 Pecs, 9x6"	135.00
Lamp base, birds/flowers on crackle, ftd metal mts, 5-steeple mk	350.00
Lamp base, floral on wht, 6 lg rtcl/jeweled teardrops, w/gold, 10"	325.00
Pitcher, marbleized red & bl, 6¼"	600.00
Plate, scalloped/5-lobe floral center, scalloped/rtcl rim, 12"	785.00
Vase, emb floral, Eosine, spherical, 3x3½"	65.00
Vase, floral, mc on cobalt, dbl-walled w/rtcl wht top, 9x5"	345.00
Vase, tree-lined landscape, mc w/gold, elongated oviform, #5572, 10"	1,600.00

Advisory Board

The editors and staff take this opportunity to express our sincere gratitude and appreciation to each person who has in any way contributed to the preparation of this guide. We believe the credibility of our book is greatly enhanced through their efforts. See each advisor's directory listing for information concerning their specific areas of expertise.

You will notice that at the conclusion of some of the narratives the advisor's name is given. This is optional and up to the discretion of each individual. Simply because no name is mentioned does not indicate that we have no advisor for that subject. Our board grows with each issue and now numbers nearly 450; if you care to correspond with any of them or anyone listed in our Directory, you must send a SASE with your letter. If you are seeking an appraisal, first ask about their fee, since many of these people are professionals who must naturally charge for their services. Because of our huge circulation, every person who allows us to publish their name runs the risk of their privacy being invaded by too many phone calls and letters. We are indebted to every advisor and very much regret losing any one of them. By far, the majority of those we lose give that reason. Please help us retain them on our board by observing the simple rules of common courtesy. Take the differences in time zones into consideration; some of our advisors tell us they often get phone calls in the middle of the night. For suggestions that may help you evaluate your holdings, see the Introduction.

AAA Antique Shop
Nappanee, Indiana

Peter Abrahams
Lake Oswego, Oregon

Charles and Barbara Adams
South Yarmouth, Massachusetts

Geneva D. Addy
Winterset, Iowa

Stan and Sally Alekna
Lebanon, Pennsylvania

Beverly L. Ales
Pleasanton, California

Charles Alexander
Indianapolis, Indiana

Craig Ambrose
Des Moines, Iowa

James Anderson
New Brighton, Minnesota

Suzy McLennan Anderson
Holmdel, New Jersey

Tim Anderson
Provo, Utah

Warren R. Anderson
Cedar City, Utah

Dan Andrews
Rancho Palos Verdes, California

Dorothy Malone Anthony
Fort Scott, Kansas

Bruce A. Austin
Pittsford, New York

Bobby Babcock
Austin, Texas

Veldon Badders
Hamlin, New York

Rod Baer
Vienna, Virginia

Wayne and Gale Bailey
Dacula, Georgia

Jim Barker
Allentown, Pennsylvania

Kit Barry
Brattleboro, Vermont

Henry Bartsch
Rockaway, Oregon

Mark Bassett
Lakewood, Ohio

Dana Martin Batory
Crestline, Ohio

D.R. Beeks
Mt. Vernon, Iowa

Scott Benjamin
LaGrange, Ohio

Phyllis and Tom Bess
Tulsa, Oklahoma

Robert Bettinger
Mt. Dora, Florida

John E. Bilane
Union, New Jersey

William M. Bilsland III
Cedar Rapids, Iowa

Brenda Blake
York Harbor, Maine

Robert and Stan Block
Trumbull, Connecticut

Clarence H. Bodine, Jr.
New Hope, Pennsylvania

Sandra V. Bondhus
Unionville, Connecticut

Clifford Boram
Monticello, Indiana

Jeff Bradfield
Dayton, Virginia

Shane Branchcomb
Fairfax, Virginia

Larry Brenner
Manchester, New Hampshire

Mike Brooks
Oakland, California

Jim Broom
Effingham, Illinois

David L. Brown
Victoria, British Columbia, Canada

Marcia Brown
White City, Oregon

Rick Brown
Newspaper Collector's Society of America
Lansing, Michigan

Nicki Budin
Worthington, Ohio

Donald A. Bull
Wirtz, Virginia

Ann Burton
Decatur, Michigan

Robert C. Butz
Newbury Park, California

Jim Calison
Wallkill, New York

Tina M. Carter
El Cajon, California

Gene Cataldo
Huntsville, Alabama

Cerebro
East Prospect, Pennsylvania

Mick and Lorna Chase
Cookeville, Tennessee

Pat and Chris Christensen
Costa Mesa, California

Victor J.W. Christie, Ed. D.
Ephrata, Pennsylvania

Joan Cimini
Belmont, Ohio

Debbie and Randy Coe
Lafayette, Oregon

Wilfred and Dolli Cohen
Santa Ana, California

Marilyn Cooper
Houston, Texas

Ryan Cooper
Yarmouthport, Massachusetts

J.W. Courter
Kevil, Kentucky

Susan N. Cox
El Cajon, California

Rosalind Cranor
Blacksburg, Virginia

Bob Culver
Northville, Michigan

Ron Damaska
New Brighton, Pennsylvania

John Danis
Rockford, Illinois

Patricia M. Davis
Portland, Oregon

Hal & Meredith DeGood
Des Moines, Iowa

Loretta DeLozier
Knoxville, Tennessee

Joe Devine
Council Bluffs, Iowa

Doug Dezso
Maywood, New Jersey

David Dilley
Indianapolis, Indiana

Thomas P. Dimitroff
Corning, New York

Ginny Distel
Tiffin, Ohio

Rod Dockery
Ft. Worth, Texas

L.R. 'Les' Docks
San Antonio, Texas

Rebecca Dodds
Coral Springs, Florida

Brenda Dollen
Avoca, Iowa

Ron Donnelly
Tuscaloosa, Alabama

Robert A. Doyle, C.A.I., I.S.A.
Pleasant Valley, New York

James Dryden
Hot Springs National Park, Arkansas

Louise Dumont
Leesburg, Florida

Pat and Ann Duncan
Cape Fair, Missouri

Ken and Jackie Durham
Washington, DC

William Durham
Belvidere, Illinois

Rita and John Ebner
Columbus, Ohio

Bill Edwards
Madison, Indiana

J. David Ehrhard
Tujunga, California

Michael L. Ellis
Costa Mesa, California

Dr. Robert Elsner
Boynton Beach, Florida

Barbara Endter
Rochester, New York

Elaine Ezell
Pasadena, Maryland

Bryce Farnsworth
Fargo, North Dakota

Arthur M. Feldman
Highland Park, Illinois

Linda Fields
Dover, Tennessee

Mary J. Finegan
Boone, North Carolina

Paul Fink
Kent, Connecticut

Vicki Flanigan
Winchester, Virginia

Gene Florence
Lexington, Kentucky

Marv Fogleman
Santa Ana, California

Jenny Tarrant
St. Peters, Missouri

Terry Taylor
East Bend, North Carolina

Bruce Thalberg
Weston, Connecticut

Sharon Thoerner
Bellflower, California

Darrell Thomas
Nevah, Wisconsin

Chuck Thompson
Houston, Texas

Don Thornton
Moss Beach, California

Rosella Tinsley
Osawatomie, Kansas

Marlena Toohey
Longmont, Colorado

Veronica Trainer
Cleveland, Ohio

Dan Tucker
Toledo, Ohio

Valerie and Richard Tucker
Argyle, Texas

Robert Tuggle
New York, New York

Hobart D. Van Deusen
Watertown, Connecticut

Jean and Dale Van Kuren
Clarence Center, New York

Joan F. Van Patten
Rexford, New York

Linda L. Vines
Burbank, California

Stephen Visakay
West Caldwell, New Jersey

Janice and Richard Vogel
Ocala, Florida

Mark Vuono
Stamford, Connecticut

John W. Waddell
Mineral Wells, Texas

Jim Waite
Farmer City, Illinois

John Walter
Marietta, Ohio

Judith and Robert Walthall
Huntsville, Alabama

Ian Warner
Brampton, Ontario, Canada

Marty Webster
Saline, Michigan

David Weddington
Murfreesboro, Tennessee

Robert Weisblut
Wheaton, Maryland

Pastor Frederick S. Weiser
New Oxford, Pennsylvania

BA Wellman
Westminster, Massachusetts

David Wendel
Poplar Bluff, Missouri

Kaye and Jim Whitaker
Lynnwood, Washington

Douglass White
Orlando, Florida

John 'Grandpa' White
Denver, Colorado

Margaret and Kenn Whitmyer
Gahanna, Ohio

Steven Whysel
Plantation, Florida

Robert Wieland
Ormond Beach, Florida

Don Williams
Kirksville, Missouri

Linda Williams
Chicopee, Massachusetts

Ron L. Willis
Matlacha, Florida

Roy M. Willis
Lebanon Junction, Kentucky

Jack D. Wilson
Prescott, Arizona

Grant S. Windsor
Richmond, Virginia

Ralph Winslow
Camdenton, Missouri

Nancy Winston
Northwood, New Hampshire

Jo Ellen Winther
Arvada, Colorado

Raphael C. Wise
West Palm Beach, Florida

Dannie Woodard
Weatherford, Texas

Bill Wright
New Albany, Indiana

Libby Yalom
Adelphi, Maryland

Darlene Yohe
Stuttgart, Arkansas

Mary Young
Kettering, Ohio

Willy Young
Reno, Nevada

Charles S. Zayic
Ellsworth, Maine

Audrey Zeder
North Bend, Washington

Auction Houses

We wish to thank the following auction houses whose catalogs have been used as sources for pricing information. Many have granted us permission to reproduce their photographs as well.

A-1 Auction Service
2042 N. Rio Grande Ave., Suite 'E,' Orlando, FL 32804; 407-839-0004. Specializing in American antique sales; e-mail: a1auc@gateway.net

A&B Auctions, Inc.
17 Sherman St., Marlboro, MA 01752-3314; 508-480-0006 or (fax) 508-460-6101. Specializing in English ceramics, flow blue, pottery, and Mason's Ironstone

Absolute Auction & Realty, Inc.
Absolute Auction Center
Robert Doyle
PO Box 1739, Pleasant Valley, NY 12569. Antique and estate auctions twice a month at Absolute Auction Center; free calendar of auctions; www.absoluteauctionrealty.com

Allard Auctions Inc.
Col. Doug Allard
PO Box 460, #1 Museum Lane, St. Ignatius, MT 59865-0460; 406-745-2951 or (fax) 406-745-2961; www.allardauctions.com

America West Archives
Anderson, Warren
PO Box 100, Cedar City, UT 84721; 435-586-9497; Publishes 26-page illustrated catalog 6 times a year that includes auction section of scarce and historical early western documents, letters, autographs, stock certificates, and other important ephemera, subscription: $15 per year; e-mail: warren@americawestarchives.com

Americana Auctions
c/o Glen Rairigh
12633 Sandborn, Sunfield, MI 48890. Specializing in Skookum dolls, art glass, and art auctions

Anderson Auctions
Heritage Antiques & Appraisal Services
Suzy McLennan Anderson
65 E. Main St., Holmdel, NJ 07733; 908-946-8801 or (fax) 908-946-1036. Specializing in American furniture and decorative accessories

Andre Ammelounx
The Stein Company
PO Box 136, Palatine, IL 60078-0136; 847-991-5927 or (fax) 847-991-5947. Specializing in steins, catalogs available

Aston Americana Auctioneers & Appraisers
2825 Country Club Rd., Endwell, NY 13760-3349; phone/fax: 607-785-6598. Specializing in and appraisers of Americana, folk art, other primitives, furniture, Shaker, fine art, porcelain, and china; also have auctions on the Internet: eBay (folkman 2) and ehammer (folkman@stnylrun.com)

Bider's
397 Methuen St., Lawrence, MA 01843; 978-688-4347 or 978-688-0948. Antiques appraised, purchased, and sold on consignment; www.biders-auction.com

Bill Bertoia Auctions
1881 Spring Rd., Vineland, NJ 08360; 856-692-1881 or (fax) 856-692-8697. Specializing in toys, dolls, advertising, and related items; e-mail: Bill@BertoiaAuctions.com; www.bertoiaauctions.com

Block's Box
PO Box 51, Trumbull, CT 06611; 203-261-0057 or 203-926-8448; Buy and sell marbles in online auctions; www.blocksite.com

Buffalo Bay Auction Co.
5244 Quam Circle, Rogers, MN 55374; 612-428-8480; or (fax) 612-428-8879; Specializing in advertising, tins, and country store items; e-mail: buffalobay@hotmail.com; www.buffalobayauction.com

Butterfield & Butterfield
220 San Bruno Ave., San Francisco, CA 94103; 415-861-7500 or (fax) 415-861-8951. Also located at: 7601 Sunset Blvd., Los Angeles, CA 90046; 213-850-7500 or (fax) 213-850-5843 and 441 West Huron St., Chicago, IL 60610; 312-377-7500 or (fax) 312-377-7501. Fine art auctioneers and appraisers since 1865; e-mail: info@butterfields.com or www.butterfields.com

Butterfield, Butterfield & Dunning
755 Church Rd., Elgin, IL 60123; 847-741-3843 or (fax) 847-741-3589; www.butterfields.com

Cerebro
PO Box 327, E. Prospect, PA 17317-0327; 717-252-2400 or 800-69-LABEL; fax: 717-252-3685; Specializing in antique advertising labels, especially cigar box labels, cigar bands, food labels, firecracker labels; holds semiannual auction on tobacco ephemera; consignments accepted; e-mail: Cerebro@Cerebro.com

Charles E. Kirtley
PO Box 2273, Elizabeth City, NC 27096; 919-335-1262. Specializing in World's Fair, Civil War, political, advertising, and other American collectibles; e-mail: ckirtley@erols.com

Cincinnati Art Gallery
635 E. Main, Cincinnati, OH 45202; 513-381-2128. Specializing in American art pottery, American and European fine paintings, watercolors; www.cincinnatiartgalleries.com

Collector's Auction Services
R.D. 2, Box 431, Oil City, PA 16301-9426; 814-677-6070. Specializing in advertising, oil and gas, toys, rare museum and investment-quality antiques; e-mail: director@caswel.com; www.caswel.com

Country Girls Estate & Appraisal Service
Diane Patalano
PO Box 376, Saddle River, NJ 07458

Craftsman Auctions
1485 W Housatonic (Rt 20); Pittsfield, MA 01201; 413-448-8922. Specializing in Arts & Crafts furniture and accessories as well as American art pottery; color catalogs available; www.artsncrafts.com or www.ragoarts.com

Dargate Auction Galleries
5607 Baum Boulevard, Pittsburgh, PA 15206; 412-362-3558 or (fax) 412-362-3574. Specializing in estate auctions featuring fine art, antiques, and collectibles; e-mail: dargate@dargate.com; www.dargate.com

David Rago
20th Century Design
Auction hall: 333 N. Main, Lambertville, NJ 08530; 609-397-6780 or (fax) 609-397-6790. Specializing in American art pottery and Arts and Crafts; e-mail: rago@ragoarts.com; www.ragoarts.com

Du Mouchelles
409 Jefferson Ave., Detroit, MI 48226-4300; 313-963-6255 or (fax) 313-963-8199; www.dumouchelle.com

Dunbar's Gallery
Leila and Howard Dunbar
76 Haven St., Milford, MA 01757; 508-634-8697 or (fax) 508-634-8698; e-mail: Dunbars@mediaone.net or www.dunbarsgallery.com

Early American History Auctions
Dana Linett, President
PO Box 3341, La Jolla, CA 92038; 858-459-4159 or (fax) 858-459-4373; www.earlyamerican.com

Early Auction Co.
123 Main St., Milford, OH 45150-1121; 513-831-4833 or (fax) 513-831-1441; e-mail: info@EarlyAuctionCo.com; www.EarlyAuctionCo.com

Flying Deuce Auctions & Antiques
1224 Yellowstone Ave., Pocatello, ID 83201-4323; 208-237-2002 or (fax) 208-237-4544; e-mail: flying2@nicoh.com; www.flying2.com

Fontaine's Auction Gallery
1485 W. Housatonic St., Pittsfield, MA 01201; 413-448-8922 or (fax) 413-442-1550. Fine quality antiques; important twentieth century lighting, clocks, art glass; color catalogs available; www.fontaineauction.com

Frank's Antiques & Auctions
2405 N. Kings Rd., Hilliard, FL 32046-3332; 904-845-2870 or (fax) 904-845-4000. Specializing in antique advertising, country store items, rec room and restaurant decor as well as sporting collectibles, pottery, and stoneware; catalogs issued

Freeman Fine Arts Co. of Philadelphia, Inc.
1808 Chestnut St., Philadelphia, PA 19103; 215-563-9275 or (fax) 215-563-8236; www.freemansauction.com

Garth's Auctions Inc.
2690 Stratford Rd., Box 369, Delaware, OH 43015; 740-362-4771; e-mail: info@garths.com or www.garths.com

Glass-Works Auctions
102 Jefferson, East Greenville, PA 18041-11623; 215-679-5849 or (fax) 215-679-3068. America's leading auction company in early American bottles and glass and barber shop memorabilia; e-mail: glswrk@enter.net

Hanna-Whysel Auctioneers & Appraisers
Steven Whysel
3403 Bella Vista Way, Bella Vista, AR, 72714; 501-855-9600. Antiques and art auctions

Harmer Rooke Galleries
32 E. 57th St, 11th Floor, New York, NY 10022-2513; 212-751-1900 or (fax) 212-758-1713

Henry/Pierce Auctioneers
1456 Carson Court, Homewood, IL 60430-4013; 708-798-7508 or (fax) 708-799-3594. Specializing in bank auctions

High Noon
9929 Venice Blvd., Los Angeles, CA 90034-5111; 310-202-9010 or (fax) 310-202-9011. Specializing in cowboy and western collectibles; www.freemansauction.com

History Buff's Auctions
6031 Winterset, Lansing, MI 48911. Specializing in paper collectibles spanning 5 centuries; www.historybuff.com

Horst Auctioneers
Horst Auction Center
50 Durlach Rd. (corner of Rt. 322 & Durlach Rd., West of Ephrata), Ephrata, Lancaster County, PA 17522-9741; 717-859-1331 or 717-738-3080. Voices of Experience; www.horstauction.com

Jack Sellner
Sellner Marketing of California
PO Box 308, Fremont, CA 94536-0308; 415-745-9463

Jackson's, Auctioneers & Appraisers of Fine Art
2229 Lincoln St., Cedar Falls, IA 50613; 319-277-2256 or (fax) 319-277-1252; Specializing in American and European art pottery and art glass, American and European paintings, Russian works of art, decorative arts, toys, and jewelry. e-mail: jacksons@jacksonsauction.com; www.jacksonsauction.com

James D. Julia
PO Box 830, Rt. 201, Skowhegan Rd., Fairfield, ME 04937-0830; 207-453-7125 or (fax) 207-453-2502; e-mail: jjulia@juliaauctions.com or www.juliaauctions.com

John Toomey Gallery
818 North Blvd., Oak Park, IL 60301-1302; 708-383-5234 or (fax) 708-383-4828. Specializing in furniture and decorative arts of the Arts & Crafts, Art Deco, and Modern Design movements; modern design expert: Richard Wright; e-mail: arts@oprf.com; www.treadwaygallery.com

Joy Luke Auctioneers & Appraisers
The Gallery
300 East Grove St., Bloomington, IL 61701-5290; 309-828-5533 or (fax) 309-829-2266; e-mail: joyluke@aol.com; www.joyluke.com

Kit Barry Ephemera Auctions
136 High St., Brattleboro, VT 05301; 802-254-3634. Tradecard and ephemera auctions, fully illustrated catalogs with prices realized; consignment inquiries welcome; www.tradecards.com/kb

Kurt R. Krueger
160 N. Washington St., PO Box 275, Iola, WI 54945-0275; 715-445-3845 or (fax) 715-445-4100

L.R. 'Les' Docks
Box 691035, San Antonio, TX 78269-1035. Providing occasional mail-order record auctions, rarely consigned; the only consignments considered are exceptionally scarce and unusual records; e-mail: docks@texas.net; www.docks.home.texas.net

Lang's Sporting Collectibles, Inc.
31R Turtle Cove, Raymond, ME 04071; 207-655-4265

Lloyd Ralston Toys
109 Glover Ave., Norwalk, CT 06850; 203-845-033 or (fax) 203-845-0366; e-mail: lrt@lloydralstontoys.com; www.lloydralstontoys.com

Lowe, James Lewis
PO Box 8, Norwood, PA 19074; Specializing in Kate Greenaway, postcards; e-Bay: JLewisLowe@juno.com

Majolica Auctions
Michael G. Strawser
200 North Main, PO Box 332, Wolcottville, IN 46795-0332; 219-854-2859 or (fax) 219-854-3979. Issues color catalogs; e-mail: michael@strawserauctions.com; www.fiestaauctions.com

Manion's International Auction House, Inc.
PO Box 12214, Kansas City, KS 66112-0214; 913-299-6692 or (fax) 913-299-6792. Specializing in international militaria, particularly the US, Germany, and Japan; extensive catalogs in antiques and collectibles, sports, transportation, political, and advertising memorabilia, and vintage clothing and denim; publishes 9 catalogs for each of the 5 categories per year; request a free sample of past auctions, 1 issue of current auction for $7 or a 6-catalog subscription for $35; e-mail: manions@qni.com; www.manions.com

Maritime Auctions
935 US Rt. 1, PO Box 322, York, ME 03909-0322; 207-363-4247 or (fax) 353-1415; www.maritiques.com or auction: www.eswap.com

McMasters Doll Auctions
PO Box 1755, 5855 Glenn Highway, Cambridge, OH 43725-8768; 740-432-4419 or (fax) 740-432-3191; or 800-842-3526; e-mail: mcmasters@jadeinc.com; www.mcmastersauctions.com

Michael Ivankovich Auctions, Inc.
PO Box 1536, Doylestown, PA, 18901; 215-345-6094 or (fax) 215-345-6692. Specializing in early hand-colored photography and prints; auction held 4 times each year, providing opportunity for collectors and dealers to compete for the largest variety of Wallace Nutting, Wallace Nutting-like pictures, Maxfield Parrish, Bessie Pease Gutmann, R. Atkinson Fox, Philip Boileau, Harrison Fisher, etc.

Michael John Verlangieri
PO Box 844, Cambria, CA 93428; 805-927-4428. Specializing in fine California pottery; cataloged auctions (video tapes available); www.calpots.com

Monsen & Baer, Annual Perfume Bottle Auction
Monsen, Randall; and Baer, Rod
Box 529, Vienna, VA 22183; 703-938-2129 or (fax) 703-242-1357. Cataloged auctions of perfume bottles; will purchase, sell, and accept consignments; specializing in commercial, Czechoslovakian, Lalique, Baccarat, Victorian, crown top, factices, miniatures

Neal Auction Company
4038 Magazine St., New Orleans, LA 70115; 504-899-5329 or 1-800-467-5329; fax: 504-897-3803; www.nealauction.com

New England Absentee Auctions
16 6th St., Stamford, CT 06905-4610;
203-975-9055. Specializing in Quimper pottery

Noel Barrett Antiques & Auctions
PO Box 1001, 6183 Carversville Rd.,
Carversville, PA 18913; 215-297-5109
or (fax) 215-297-0457

Norman C. Heckler & Company
79 Bradford Corner Rd., Woodstock
Valley, CT 06282-2002; 860-974-1634
or (fax) 860-974-2003. Auctioneers and
appraisers specializing in early glass and
bottles; e-mail: heckler@neca.com;
www.hecklerauction.com

Nostalgia Co.
21 S. Lake Dr., Hackensack, NJ
07601-3098; 201-488-4536; www.
nostalgiapubs.com

Pacific Glass Auctions
1507 21st St., Ste. 203, Sacramento, CA
95814; 916-443-3296 or (fax) 916-443-
3199; www.pacglass.com

Past Tyme Pleasures
Steve Howard
PMB #204, 2491 San Ramon Blvd., #1,
San Ramon, CA 94583; 925-484-4488 or
(fax) 925-484-2551. Offers 2 absentee
auction catalogs per year pertaining to old
advertising items; e-mail: pasttyme@
excite.com; www.pasttyme.com

Phillips
406 E. 79th St., New York, NY 10021-
1498; 212-570-4830; www.phillips-
auctions.com

Postcards International
Martin J. Shapiro
2321 Whitney Ave., Suite 102, PO Box
185398; Hamden, CT 06518-0398;
203-248-6621 or (fax) 203-248-6628;
e-mail: quality@vintagepostcards.com;
www.vintagepostcards.com

Richard Opfer Auctioneering, Inc.
1919 Greenspring Dr., Timonium, MD
21093-4113; 410-252-5035; fax: 410-252-
5863; e-mail: info@opferauction.com;
www.opferauction.com

Roan Bros. Auction Gallery
R.R. 4, Box 118, Cogan Station, PA
17728; e-mail: roaninc@srlink.net

Schoolmaster Auctions and Real Estate
Kenn Norris
PO Box 4830; 513 N. 2nd St., Sanderson, TX 79848; 915-345-2640. Specializing in school-related items, barbed wire
and related literature, and L'il Abner

Skinner, Inc.
Auctioneers & Appraisers of Antiques
and Fine Arts
The Heritage on the Garden, 63 Park
Plaza, Boston, MA 02116-3925; 617-
350-5400 or (fax) 617-350-5429. Second address: 357 Main St., Bolton,
MA 01740; 978-779-6241 or (fax)
978-779-5144; www.skinnerinc.com

Smith & Jones, Inc.
12 Clark Lane, Sudbury, MA 01776;
508-443-5517 or (fax) 508-443-8045.
Specializing in Dedham dinnerware,
Buffalo china, and important American
art pottery; full-color catalogs available

SOLDUSA.COM (formerly Dixie
Sporting Collectibles)
1206 Rama Rd., Charlotte, NC 28211-
4345; 704-364-2900 or 877-SoldUSA;
(fax) 704-364-2322; Specializing in fine
sporting collectibles; e-mail:
gun1898@aol.com or www.Soldusa.com

Sotheby's
1334 York Ave., New York, NY 10021;
212-606-7000; www.sothebys.com

Stanton's Auctioneers & Realtors
144 S. Main St., PO Box 146, Ver-
montville, MI 49096-0146; 517-726-
0181 or (fax) 517-726-0060.
Specializing in all types of property, at
auction, anywhere; www.stantons-auc-
tions.com

Steffen's Historical Militaria
Roger S. Steffen
14 Murnan Rd., Cold Springs, KY
41076; 859-431-4499 or Fax: 859-431-
3113. Specializing in quality militaria,
military art, rare books, antique
firearms; www.steffensmilitaria.com

Superior Galleries
9478 West Olympic Boulevard, Beverly Hills, CA 90212-4246; 310-203-
9855 or (fax) 310-203-0496.
Specializing in manuscripts, decorative and fine arts, Hollywood memorabilia, sports memorabilia, stamps, and
coins; www.superiorsc.com

Swann Galleries, Inc.
104 E. 25th St., New York, NY 10010;
312-254-4710 or (fax) 212-979-1017;
www.swanngalleries.com

Three Rivers Collectibles
Wendy and Leo Frese
PO Box 551542, Dallas, TX 75355; 214-
341-5165. Annual Red Wing and Rum-
Rill pottery and stoneware auctions

Toy Scouts, Inc.
137 Casterton Ave., Akron, OH
44303-1543; 330-836-0668 or (fax)
330-869-8668; Specializing in baby-
boom era collectibles; e-mail:
toyscouts@toyscouts.com;
www.toyscouts.com

Tradewinds Auctions
Henry Taron
PO Box 249, Manchester-By-The-Sea,
MA 01944-0249; 508-768-3327;
www.tradewindantiques.com

Treadway Gallery, Inc.
2029 Madison Rd., Cincinnati, OH
45208-3218; 513-321-6742 or (fax) 513-
871-7722. Specializing in American Art
Pottery; American and European art
glass; European ceramics; Italian glass;
fine American and European paintings
and graphics; and furniture and decorative arts of the Arts & Crafts, Art Nouveau, Art Deco, and Modern Design
Movements; modern design expert:
Thierry Lorthioir; members: National
Antique Dealers' Association, American
Art Pottery Association, International
Society of Appraisers, American Ceramic Arts Society, Ohio Decorative Arts
Society, Art Gallery Association of
Cincinnati; www.treadwaygallery.com

Vogel Auction
4720 S.E. Fort King St., Ocala, FL
34470-1501; 352-694-5776. Specializing in souvenir china; e-mail:
Vogels@atlantic.net

Vicki and Bruce Waasdorp
PO Box 434; 10931 Main St.; Clarence,
NY 14031; 716-759-2361. Specializing in
decorated stoneware. www.antiques-
stoneware.com

Weschler's
Adam A. Weschler & Son
905 E. St. N.W., Washington, DC
20004-2006; 202-628-1281

William Doyle Galleries
Auctioneers & Appraisers
175 East 87th St., New York, NY
10128; 212-427-2730 or (fax) 212-
369-0892; e-mail: info@doylegalleries.
com or www.doylegalleries.com

Willis Henry Auctions
22 Main St., Marshfield, MA 02050-
2808; 781-834-7774 or (fax) 781-826-
3520; www.willishenry.com

York Town Auction Inc.
1625 Haviland Rd., York, PA 17404;
717-751-0211; (fax) 717-767-7729;
Specializing in the sale of antiques, art,
collections, fine furnishings, and real
estate; e-mail: yorktownauction@cyberia.
com; www.yorktown.com

Directory of Contributors

When contacting any of the buyers/sellers listed in this part of the Directory by mail, you must include an SASE (stamped, self-addressed envelope) if you expect a reply. As hectic as our lifestyles are, the time it saves them is probably worth more to them than the price of a stamp. Not only that, but trying to decipher someone's handwritten name and address can be very frustrating. Sometimes even zip codes are unreadable, and even more time is required to double check zip code numbers. And in the end, if 'Rosen' becomes 'Rirer' and 'Ave. 5' becomes 'Ave. S,' even if the person you contacted was gracious enough to answer you, you probably won't ever know he did. Many of these people are professional appraisers and there will be a fee for their time and service. Find out up front. Include a clear photo if you want an item identified. Most items cannot be described clearly enough to make an identification without a photo.

If you call and get their answering machine, when you leave your number so that they can return your call, tell them to call back collect. And please take the differences in time zones into consideration. 7:00 AM in the Midwest is only 4:00 AM in California! And if you're in California, remember that even 7:00 PM is too late to call the East Coast. Most people work and are gone during the daytime. Even some of our antique dealers say they prefer after-work phone calls. Don't assume that a person who deals in a particular field will be able to help you with related items. They may seem related to you when they are not.

Please, we need your help. This book sells in such great numbers that allowing their names to be published can create a potential nightmare for each advisor and contributor. Please do your part to help us minimize this, so that we can retain them on our board and in turn pass their experience and knowledge on to you through our book. Their only obligation is to advise us, not to evaluate your holdings. Many of our people tell us that even with the occasional problem, they feel that the good outweighs the bad and makes all their hard work worthwhile.

Alabama

Cataldo, Gene
C.E. Cataldo
4726 Panorama Dr., S.E., Huntsville, 35801; 256-536-6893; Specializing in classic and used cameras; e-mail: genecams@aol.com

Donnelly, Ron
Saturday Heroes
6302 Championship Dr., Tuscaloosa, 35405. Specializing in Big Little Books, movie posters, premiums, western heroes, Gone With the Wind, character collectibles, early Disney; inquiries require SASE; no free appraisals

Lippa, Matt; and Schaaf, Elizabeth
Artisans
PO Box 256, Mentone, 35984; 256-634-4037. Specializing in folk art, quilts, painted and folky furniture, tramp art, whirligigs, windmill weights; e-mail: artisans@folkartisans.com; www.folkartisans.com

Walthall, Judith and Robert
PO Box 4465, Huntsville, 35815; 256-881-9198. Judith founded Peanut Pals in 1978. Robert has served two terms as president of Peanut Pals. Specializing in Planters Peanuts memorabilia; also Old Crow collectibles

Arizona

Nelson, Maxine
7657 E. Hazelwood St., Scottsdale, 85251. Specializing in Vernon Kilns; author of *Collectible Vernon Kilns* (out of print). SASE appreciated for inquiries.

Roberts, Fred and Marilyn
Bah Humbug Collectibles
PO Box 5733, Lake Montezuma, 86342. Specializing in Hummel figurines

Wilson, Jack D.
1514 Eagle Ridge Road, Prescott, 86301-5418; 520-445-5137. Specializing in Phoenix and Consolidated glass; buying Ruba Rombic; author of *Phoenix and Consolidated Art glass: 1926 – 1980*; e-mail: jdwilson1@earthlink.net; www.home.earthlink.net/~jdwilson1/

Arkansas

Dryden, James
Dryden Pottery
PO Box 603, Hot Springs National Park, 71902; 501-627-4201. Specializing in hand-thrown artware vases, mugs, ovenware, etc.

Freyaldenhoven, Tony
PO Box 1295, Conway, 72033; 501-329-0628. Specializing in Camark pottery; e-mail: camarket@swbell.net

Musgrave, Marge
Look Nook Antiques
10757 Hwy. 5-S, Salesville, 72653-9698; 870-499-5283. Specializing in colored Victorian and art glass

Roenigk, Martin
Mechantiques
Crescent Hotel & Spa
75 Prospect St., Eureka Springs, 72632; 800-671-6333. Specializing in mechanical musical instruments, music boxes, band organs, musical clocks and watches, coin pianos, orchestrions, monkey organs, automata, mechanical birds and dolls, etc.; e-mail: mroenigk@aol.com; www.mechantiques.com

Yohe, Darlene
Timberview Antiques
PO Box 343, Stuttgart, 72160; 870-673-3437. Specializing in American pattern glass, historical glass, Victorian pattern glass, carnival glass, and custard glass

California

Ales, Beverly Schell
4046 Graham St., Pleasanton, 94566-5619; 925-846-5297. Specializing in knife rests and editor of *Knife Rests of Yesterday and Today*; e-mail: Beverlyales@hotmail.com

Andrews, Dan
27105 Shorewood Rd., Rancho Palos Verdes, 90275; 310-541-5149. Specializing in beer cans, breweriana; e-mail: brewpub@earthlink.net

Berg, Paul
PO Box 8895, Newport Beach, 92620. Author of *Nineteenth Century Photographica Cases and Wall Frames*

Brooks, Mike
7355 Skyline, Oakland, 94611; 510-339-1751 (evenings). Specializing in typewriters, transistor radios, early televisions, Statue of Liberty

Carter, Tina M.
882 S. Mollison, El Cajon, 92020-6506; 619-440-5043. Specializing in teapots, tea-related items, tea tins, children's and toy tea sets, plastic cookie cutters, etc.; book on teapots available; send $16 (includes postage) or $17 for CA residents, Canada: add $5, to above address

Chipman, Jack
California Spectrum
PO Box 1079, Venice, 90294-1079. Specializing in California ceramics; author of *Collector's Encyclopedia of California Pottery*, and *Collector's Encyclopedia of Bauer Pottery*, autographed copies available from author; either book: $28.45 ppd., +(CA) tax of $2.35

Christensen, Pat and Chris
1067 Salvador St., Costa Mesa, 92626. Specializing in open salts

Cohen, Wilfred and Dolli
Antiques & Art Glass
PO Box 27151, Santa Ana, 92799; 714-545-5673. Specializing in Wave Crest (C.F. Monroe); French cameo glass; Victorian-era art and pattern glass (salt shakers, toothpick holders, syrups, cruets, sugar shakers, tumblers, biscuit jars, table and pitcher sets); art glass and cameo glass open salts; custard and ruby-stained glass; burmese, peachblow and amberina glass; pottery by Moorcroft (pre-1935 only); Buffalo (Deldare and Emerald ware); Polia Pillin; Shelley China; Chintz China; and Clarice Cliff. Please include SASE for reply; a photo is very helpful for identification. e-mail: antsandartglass @aol.com

Conroy, Barbara J.
PO Box 2369, Santa Clara, 95055-2369. Specializing in commercial china; author and historian; e-mail: restaurantchina@earthlink.net

Cox, Susan N.
800 Murray Drive, El Cajon, 92020; 619-697-5922. Specializing in California pottery and Frankoma; e-mail: antiqfever@aol.com

Ehrhard, J. David
Psycho-Ceramic Restorations
7212 Valmont St., Tujunga, 91042. Specializing in restoration of ceramics, collects Susie Cooper and other British pottery, Mabel Lucie Attwell, 'Old Bill' china by Grimades, etc., artist: Bruce Bairnsfather

Ellis, Michael L.
266 Rose Ln., Costa Mesa, 92627; 949-646-7112 or (fax) 949-645-4919. Author (Collector Books) of *Collector's Guide to Don Winton Designs, Identification & Values*; specializing in Twin Winton

Enge, Delleen
Franciscan Dinnerware Matching Service
323 E. Matilija, Ste. 112, Ojai, 93023

Fogleman, Marv
Marv's Memories
73 Waterman, Irvine, 92602. Specializing in American and English dinnerware

George, Tony
22431-B160 Antonio Pkwy., #252, Rancho Santa Margarita, 92688; 714-589-6075. Specializing in watch fobs

Gibson, Pat
38280 Guava Dr., Newark, 94560; 510-792-0586. Specializing in R.A. Fox

Gunther, Candace (Candelaine)
Specializing in Steiff and Schuco bears and animals; send SASE for list; phone: 626-796-4568 or (fax) 626-796-7172; e-mail: candelaine@aol.com

Harrison, Gwynne
PO Box 1, Mira Loma, 91752-0001; 951-685-5434. Specializing in Autumn Leaf (Jewel Tea); e-mail: morgan99@pe.net

Hibbard, Suzi
WanderWares

Howard, Steve
Past Tyme Pleasures
PMB #204, 2491 San Ramon Valley Blvd., #1, San Ramon, 94583; 925-484-4488 or (fax) 925-484-2551. Specializing in antique American firearms, bowie knives, Western Americana, old advertising, vintage gambling items, barber and saloon items; e-mail: pasttyme@excite.com; www.pasttyme.com

Krumme, Michael
PO Box 48225, Los Angeles, CA 90048-0225; 323-937-1470. Specializing in Paden City Glass. e-mail: mkrumme@pacbell.net

Langtree, Elizabeth
PO Box 1616, Santa Ynez, CA 93460. Collector of Borsato figures
Main Street Antique Mall
237 E Main St., El Cajon, 92020; 619-447-0800

Maurer, Oveda L.
Oveda Maurer Antiques
34 Greenfield Ave., San Anselmo, 94960; 415-454-6439. Specializing in 18th-century and early 19th-century American furniture, lighting, pewter, hearthware, glass, folk art, and paintings

The Meadows Collection
Mark and Adela Meadows
PO Box 819, Carnelian Bay, 96104; 530-546-5516. Specializing in Gouda and Quimper; lecturers, authors of *Quimper Pottery, A guide to Origins, Styles, and Values*, serving on the board of directors of the Associated Antiques Dealers of America; please include SASE for inquiries; e-mail: meadows@cwo.com

Needham, Leonard
MacAdam's Antiques
707-748-4286. Specializing in advertising; e-mail: DB1918@msn.com; www.tias.com/stores/macadams

Pardini, Dick
3107 N. El Dorado St., Dept. SAPG, Stockton, 95204-3412; 209-466-5550 (recorder may answer). Specializing in California Perfume Company items dating from 1886 to 1928 and 'go-with' related companies: buyer and information center; not interested in items that have Avon, Perfection, or Anniversary Keepsake markings; California Perfume Company offerings must be accompanied by a photo, photocopy, or sketching along with a condition report and, most importantly, price wanted; inquiries require large SASE and must state what information you are seeking; not necessary if offering items for sale

Pasquali, Jim
479 Church #4, San Francisco, 94114; 415-861-4184. Author of *Sanfords Guide to Garden City Pottery, A Hidden Treasure of Northern California*

Roller, Gayle
PO Box 222, San Marcos, 92079-0222. Specializing in Hagen-Renaker

Rosewitz, Michele
3165 McKinley, San Bernardino, 92404; 909-862-8534. Specializing in glass knives manufactured in the USA during the 1920s through the 1950s; all requests for information should include a SASE; e-mail: rosetree@sprintmail.com

Sanford, Steve and Martha
230 Harrison Ave., Campbell, 95008; 408-978-8408. Authors of 2 books on Brush-McCoy and *Sanfords Guide to McCoy Pottery* (available from the authors); www.sanfords.com.

Shrader, Fred and Lila
Shrader Antiques
2025 Hwy. 199, Crescent City, 95531. Specializing in railroad, steamship, and other transportation memorabilia; Shelley china (and its predecessor, Foley China); Buffalo china and Buffalo Pottery including Deldare; Niloak, and Zell (and Haag)

Stella's Collectibles
Pieces of the Past
19032 S. Vermont Ave., Gardena, (Space 11), 90248; 310-316-7198; Westchester Faire Mall (Space 320); Enchanted Treasures, Lake Elsinore (Space 25); Collector's Corral, Lake Elsinore. Specializing in quality glass and china

Stillwell, Liz
Our Attic Antiques & Belleek
PO Box 1074, Pico Rivera, 90660; 323-257-3879 or 562-949-0592. Specializing in Irish and American Belleek

Tanner, Joseph and Pamela
Wheeler-Tanner Escapes
6442 Canyon Creek Way, Elk Grove, 95758-5431; 916-684-4006. Specializing in handcuffs, leg shackles, balls and chains, restraints and padlocks of all kinds (including railroad), locking and non-locking devices; also Houdini memorabilia: autographs, photos, posters, books, letters, etc.

Thoerner, Sharon
15549 Ryon Ave., Bellflower, 90706; 562-866-1555. Specializing in covered animal dishes, powder jars with animal and human figures, slag glass

Thornton, Don
PO Box 57, Moss Beach, 94038; 650-728-7978. Specializing in egg beaters and apple parers; author of *The Eggbeater Chronicles, 2nd Edition* ($50.45 ppd.); and *Apple Parers* ($59 ppd.); e-mail: thorntonhouse.com

Vines, Linda
311 N. Buena Vista, Apt. 214, Burbank, 91505; 818-848-7519. Specializing in Snow Babies, all holidays (Christmas, Easter, Halloween), dolls, toys, and Steiff

Webb, Frances Finch
1589 Gretel Lane, Mountain View, 94040. Specializing in Kay Finch ceramics

Canada

Brown, David L.
Stevengraph Collectors Assn.
2103-2829 Arbutus Rd., Victoria, British Columbia, V8N 5X5; 250-477-9896. Specializing in Stevengraphs

Melis, Mirko
Marcelle Antiques
Box 270, Waterdown, Ontario, LOR 2H0; 905-689-1648. Specializing in American and European art glass, Russian works of art (enamels, porcelains, silver, etc.), English and Continental glass and china; member of Antique Appraisal Association of America, Inc., and AADA (Associated Antique Dealers of America, Inc.)

Warner, Ian
PO Box 93022, 499 Main St. S., Brampton, Ontario, L6Y 4V8; 905-453-9074 or (fax) 905-453-2931. Specializing in Wade porcelain and Swankyswigs, author of *The World of Wade, The World of Wade Book 2, Wade Price Trends*, and *The World of Head Vase Planters*, co-author: Mike Posgay

Colorado

Geary, William L.
Glass Appraiser (American & European Art Glass)
PO Box 2247, Colorado Springs 80901; Telephone/Fax:719-527-0810. Specializing in Nordic art glass; e-mail: nordglass@aol.com.

Heck, Carl
Carl Heck Decorative Arts
Box 8416, Aspen, 81612; phone/fax: 970-925-8011. Specializing in original Tiffany lamps, art glass, windows, and chandeliers; also reverse-painted and leaded-glass table lamps, stained and beveled glass windows, bronzes, paintings, etc.; buy and sell; fee for written appraisals; please include SASE for reply; www.carlheck.com

Mackin, Bill
Author of *Cowboy and Gunfighter Collectibles*; available from author: 1137 Washington St., Craig, 81625; 970-824-6717, paperback: $25; other titles available. Specializing in old and fine spurs, guns, gun leather, cowboy gear, Western Americana (collection in the Museum of Northwest Colorado, Craig)

Over, Naomi L.
8909 Sharon Lane, Arvada, 80002; 303-424-5922. Specializing in ruby glassware, author of *Ruby Glass of the 20th Century, Book I*, autographed copies available from author for $25.00 softbound or $32.50 hardbound, ppd.; Book II available (1999 values) for $32.50 softbound or $42.50 hardbound, ppd. Naomi will attempt to make photo identifications for all who include a SASE with correspondence.

Segelke, Cathy; and James, Pat
970-847-3759 (Pat). Specializing in crocks, Western Pottery Mfg. Co. (Denver, CO)

Toohey, Marlena
703 S. Pratt Pky., Longmont, 80501; 303-678-9726. Specializing in black amethyst and black opaque glass (buy, sell, or trade); books available from author: Book 1 (over 600 colored pictures, descriptions and price guide), $23 ppd.; Book 2 (over 1,200 colored pictures, descriptions and price guide), $33 ppd. for soft bound ($43 ppd. for hard bound)

White, John 'Grandpa'
Grandpa's Depot
6720 E. Mississippi Ave., Unit B, Denver, 80224; 303-758-8540 or (fax) 303-321-2889. Specializing in railroad-related items; catalogs available

Winther, Jo Ellen
8449 W. 75th Way, Arvada, 80005; 800-872-2345 or 303-421-2371. Specializing in Coors

Connecticut

Block, Robert and Stan
Block's Box
PO Box 51, Trumbull, 06611; 203-926-8448; Specializing in marbles; e-mail: blockschip@aol.com.

Bondhus, Sandra V.
Box 100, Unionville, 06085; 860-678-1808. Author of *Quimper Pottery: A French Folk Art Faience*; specializing in Quimper pottery

Fink, Paul
Fun & Games
PO Box 488, Kent, 06757; 860-927-4001. Specializing in board games

Guido, Karen M.
Karen Michelle
PO Box 489, Bridgewater, 06752. Specializing in tiles; buy & sell; books on tiles available, many out of print; fee for written appraisal; please include SASE for inquiries

Kilbride, Mrs. Richard J.
81 Willard Terrace, Stamford, 06903; 203-322-0568. Has available for sale: *Art Deco Chrome, The Chase Era*, and *Art Deco Chrome, Book 2, A Collector's Guide, Industrial Design in the Chase Era*

Lehrer, Gary
16 Mulberry Road
Woodbridge 06525-1717. specializing in pens and pencils; Catalog available; www.gopens.com.

MacSorley, Earl
823 Indian Hill Rd., Orange, 06477; 203-387-1793 (after 7:00 p.m.). Specializing in nutcrackers, Bessie Pease Gutmann prints, figural lift-top spittoons

Postcards International
Martin J. Shapiro
2321 Whitney Ave., Suite 102, PO Box 185398, Hamden, 06518;203-248-6621 or (fax) 203-248-6628. Specializing in vintage picture postcards; www.vintagepostcards.com

Thalberg, Bruce
Mountain View Dr., Weston, 06883; 203-227-8175. Specializing in canes and walking sticks: novelty, carved, and Black

Van Deusen, Hobart D.
28 The Green, Watertown, 06795; 860-945-3456. Specializing in Canton, SASE required when requesting information; e-mail: rtn.hoby@snet.net

Vuono, Mark
16 6th St., Stamford, 06905; 203-357-0892 (10 a.m. to 5:30 p.m. E.S.T.). Specializing in historical flasks, blown 3-mold glass, blown American glass

District of Columbia

Durham, Ken and Jackie (By appointment)
909 26 St. N.W., Suite 502, Washington, D.C. 20037. Specializing in slot machines, jukeboxes, arcade machines, trade stimulators, vending machines, and service manuals; www.GameRoomAntiques.com

Florida

Bettinger, Robert
PO Box 333, Mt. Dora, 32756; 352-735-3575. General antiques, specializing in American art pottery and glass; rgbett@aol.com

Dodds, Rebecca
Silver Flute
PO Box 670664, Coral Springs, 33067. Specializing in jewelry

Dumont, Louise
318 Palo Verde Dr., Leesburg 34748. Specializing in cookie jars, Abingdon

Elsner, Dr. Robert
29 Clubhouse Lane, Boynton Beach, 33436; 561-736-1362. Specializing in antique barometers and nautical instruments

France, Madeleine
PO Box 15555, Ft. Lauderdale, 33318; 954-584-0009. Specializing in top-quality perfume bottles: Rene Lalique, Steuben, Czechoslovakian, DeVilbiss, Baccarat, Commercials; French dore bronze, and decorative arts

Hudson, Hardy
Our Antiques Market
5453 Lake Howell Rd., Winter Park, 32792; 407-657-2100 from 11:00 a.m. to 6:00 p.m. or (Home) 407-647-3454. Specializing in majolica, American art pottery (buying one piece or entire collections); also buying Weller (garden ornaments, birds, Hudson, Sicard, Sabrinian, Glendale, or animal related), Roseville, Grueby, Newcomb, Overbeck, Kay Finch, Clewell, Tiffany, etc.; e-mail: todiefor@mindspring.com

Joyce, Harriet
415 Soft Shadow Lane, DeBary, 32713. Specializing in Cracker Jack and Checkers (a competitor) early prizes and advertising; Also Flossie Fisher items

Kamm, Dorothy
PO Box 7460, Port St. Lucie, 34985-7460; 561-465-4008 or (fax) 561-460-9050. Specializing in American painted porcelain; Author of *American Painted Porcelain: Identification & Value Guide* (Collector Books), and *Comprehensive Guide to American Painted Porcelain* (Antique Trader Books). Publishes *Dorothy Kamm's Porcelain Collector's Companion*, bimonthly newsletter, subscription: $30 per year; e-mail: dorothykamm@usa.net

Kuritzky, Louis
4510 NW 17th Place, Gainesville, 32605; 352-377-3193. Author (Collector Books) of *Collector's Guide to Bookends*

Linscott, Jacqueline C.
Line Jewels
3557 Nicklaus Dr., Titusville, 32780; 321-267-9170. Specializing in glass insulators and other telephone items; distributor of the only known set of books dealing with insulators, *North American Glass Insulators* (2 volumes), and accompanying Price Guide; LSASE required for information; e-mail: bluebellwt@aol.com.

McNerny, Kathryn
118 Creek Hollow Lane, Middleburg, 32068. Author (Collector Books) on blue and white stoneware, primitives, tools

Posner, Judy
October – May: PO Box 2194 SC, Englewood, FL 34295, fax: 941-475-2645. Specializing in Disneyana, Black memorabilia, salt and pepper shakers, souvenirs of the USA, character and advertising memorabilia, figural pottery; buy, sell, collect; informal appraisals: $5+LSASE and photo of item; e-mail: judyandjef@aol.com or www.judyposner.com

Rodgers, Joanne
c/o Stretch Glass Society
508 Turnberry Lane, St. Augustine, 32084. Membership, $22 (US) or $24 (Canada; Quarterly newsletter with color photos; annual spring convention

Rolfes, Herbert
Yesterday's World
PO Box 398, Mt. Dora, 32756; 352-735-3947. Specializing in World's Fairs and Expositions; e-mail: NY1939@aol.com

Shaw, John
2201 Scenic Ridge Court, Mt. Flora, 32757 (November to May, See Maine listing for remaining months); 352-735-3831. Specializing in dairy bottles

Snyder-Haug, Diane
PO Box 815, St. Petersburg, 33731. Specializing in women's clothing, 1850 – 1940

Supnick, Mark
2771 Oakbrook Manor, Ft. Lauderdale, 33332; author of *Collecting Hull Pottery's Little Red Riding Hood* ($12.95 ppd.). Specializing in American pottery

Vogel, Janice and Richard
4720 S.E. Fort King St., Ocala, 34470-1501; 352-694-5776. Authors of *Victorian Trinket Boxes* and *Conta & Boehme Porcelain*. Specializing in Conta and Boehme German porcelain

White, Douglass
Classic Interiors & Antiques
2042 N. Rio Grande Ave., Suite E, Orlando, 32804; 407-839-0004. Specializing in Fulper, Arts & Crafts furniture (photos helpful); e-mail: a1auction@cfl.rr.com

Whysel, Steven
7867 N.W. 11th St., Plantation, 33322. Specializing in Art Nouveau, 19th- and 20th-century art

Wieland, Robert
American Antique Prints
33 South St. Andrews Drive, Ormond Beach, 32174; 904-672-9972. Specializing in early American prints: Currier & Ives, Kurz & Allison, and McKenny & Hall

Willis, Ron L.
PO Box 278, Matlacha, 33993; 941-282-5567. Specializing in military collectibles

Wise, Raphael C.
The Collector's Stop
12018 Suellen Circle, West Palm Beach, 33414; 561-793-0986. Specializing in Wedgwood Jasper Ware, Rosenthal (dogs & cats only), Moorcroft, Buffalo Deldare and Emerald Ware, Heisey, contemporary paperweights, English porcelains

Georgia

Bailey, Wayne and Gale
3152 Fence Rd., Dacula, 30019; 770-963-5736. Specializing in Goebels (Friar Tuck)

Glenn, Walter
Geode Ltd.
3393 Peachtree Rd., Atlanta, 30326. Specializing in Frankart

Hoefs, Steven
PO Box 1024, Avalon, 90704; 310-510-2623. Specializing in Catalina Island Pottery

Joiner, John R.
Aviation Collectors
173 Green Tree Dr., Newnan, 30265; 770-502-9565. Specializing in commercial aviation collectibles; e-mail: propJoiner@mindspring.com.

Jones, Donald
107 Rivers Edge Dr., Savannah, 31406; 912-354-2133. Specializing in vintage tennis collectibles; SASE with inquiries please

Illinois

Broom, Jim
Box 65, Effingham, 62401. Specializing in opalescent pattern glassware

Danis, John
11028 Raleigh Ct., Rockford, 61115; 815-877-2410 or fax: 815-877-6042. Specializing in R. Lalique and Norse pottery; e-mail: danis6033@aol.com

Feldman, Arthur M.
Arthur M. Feldman Gallery
1815 St. Johns Ave., Highland Park, 60035; 847-432-8858 or (fax) 847-266-1199. Specializing in Judaica, fine art, and antiques; www.JudaicaConnection.com

Frizzell, Doris
5687 Oakdale Dr., Springfield, 62707; 217-529-3873. Specializing in Royal Haeger and Maddux of California; co-author (Collector Books) of Royal Haeger book; SASE required when requesting information

Garmon, Lee
1529 Whittier St., Springfield, 62704; 217-789-9574. Specializing in Royal Haeger, Royal Hickman, glass animals; co-author (Collector Books) of *Glass Animals and Figural Flower Frogs of the Depression Era*

Griffith, Woody
PO Box 408277, Chicago, 60640. Specializing in De Vilbiss perfumes and perfume lamps

Hall, Doris and Burdell
B&B Antiques
210 W. Sassafras Dr., Morton, 61550-1254. Authors of *Morton's Potteries: 99 Years* (Vols. I and II); specializing in Morton pottery, American dinnerware, early American pattern glass, historical items

Hastings, Mary Jane
310 West 1st South, Mt. Olive, 62069; Phone/fax: 217-999-1222. Specializing in Chintz dinnerware

Hoffmann, Pat and Don, Sr.
1291 N. Elmwood Dr., Aurora, 60506-1309; 630-859-3435. Authors of *Warwick, A to W*, a supplement to *Why Not Warwick?*; video regarding Warwick decals currently available. P.C.: e-mail: warwick@fayetteville.net

The Home Place Antiques
Durham, William; Galaway, William
615 S. State St., Belvidiere, 61008; 815-544-0577. Specializing in Tea Leaf ironstone and white ironstone

Hooks, Dee
13050 Blackstump Rd., Percy, 62272; 618-965-3832. Specializing in R.S. Prussia, Royal Bayreuth, Haviland, other fine china

Hopp, Dennis Carl
Midcentury
Chicago, 773-935-7872. Specializing in 20th-century design, glass, pottery, metal, art

Long, Dee
112 S. Center, Lacon, 61540. Specializing in reamers

Martin, Jim
R.R. 1, 1091 215th Ave., Monmouth, 61462; 309-734-2703. Specializing in Old Sleepy Eye, Monmouth pottery, Western Stoneware

Miller, Larry; and Strickfaden, Dick
218 Devron Circle, E. Peoria, 61611-1605. Specializing in German and Czechoslovakian Erphila

Ochsner, Grace
Grace Ochsner Doll House
1636 E. County Rd. 2700, Niota, 62358; 217-755-4362. Specializing in piano babies, bisque German dolls and figurines

Rastello, Lisa
Milkweed Antiques
5N531 Ancient Oak Lane, St. Charles, 60175; 630-377-4612. Specializing in Depression-era collectibles

Rhoden, Joan and Charles
Rhoden Books & Publishing
8693 N. 1950 East Rd., Georgetown, 61846-6264; 217-662-8046. Specializing in new reference books on antiques and collectibles, Heisey and other Elegant glassware, spice tins, lard tins and Yard-Long Prints; co-authors of *Those Wonderful Yard-Long Prints and More*, and *More Wonderful Yard-Long Prints, Book II*, and *Yard-Long Prints, Book III*, illustrated value guides; e-mail: rhoden@soltec.net; www/antiqueref.com

Schwab, Betty and Larry
The Paperweight Shoppe
2507 Newport Dr., Bloomington, 61704; 309-662-1956. Specializing in glass paperweights; e-mail: PAPERWGT1@aol.com

Spencer, Dick
Glass and More (Shows only)
1203 N. Yale, O'Fallon, 62269; 618-632-9067. Specializing in Cambridge, Fenton, Fostoria, Heisey, etc.

Spiess, Greg
230 E. Washington, Joliet, 60433; 815-722-5639. Specializing in Odd Fellows lodge items; e-mail: spiessantq@aol.com

Stifter, Craig
218 S. Adams St., Hinsdale, 60521; 630-789-5780; mobile phone: 847-924-7828. Specializing in Coca-Cola, Pepsi-Cola, Orange Crush, Dr. Pepper, Hires, and other soda-pop brand collectibles; e-mail: cocacola@enteract.com

TV Guide Specialists
Box 20, Macomb 61455; 309-833-1809

Waite, Jim
112 N. Main St., Farmer City, 61842; 800-842-2593. Specializing in Sebastians

Yester-Daze Glass
c/o Illinois Antique Center
320 S.W. Commercial St., Peoria, 61604; 309-347-1679. Specializing in glass from the '20s, '30s, and '40s; Fiesta; Hall; Pie Birds; Sprinkler Bottles; and Florence figurines

---
Indiana

AAA Antique Shop
US 6 West, Nappanee, 46550; 219-773-4912. Specializing in trunks

Alexander, Charles
221 E. 34th St., Indianapolis, 46205; 317-924-9665. Specializing in American dinnerware

Boram, Clifford
Antique Stove Information Clearinghouse
Monticello; free consultation by phone only: 219-583-6465

Dilley, David
PO Box 225, Indianapolis, 46206; 317-251-0575. Specializing in Royal Haeger and Royal Hickman; e-mail: glaze bears@aol.com or bearpots@aol.com

Edwards, Bill
620 W. 2nd, Madison, 47250. Author (Collector Books) on carnival glass

Freese, Carol and Warner
House With the Lions Antiques
On the Square, Covington, 47932. General line

Garrett, Jerry and Sandi
Jerry's Antiques (Shows only)
1807 W. Madison St., Kokomo, 46901; 765-457-5256. Specializing in Greentown glass, old postcards

Haun, Ted
2426 N. 700 East, Kokomo, 46901; 765-628-7028. Specializing in American pottery and china, '50s items, Russel Wright designs; e-mail: Sam17@webtv.net

Highfield, James
6301-D University Commons, South Bend, 46635; 219-272-4200. Specializing in relief-style Capo-di-Monte-style porcelain (Doccia, Ginori, and Royal Naples)

Heiss, Virginia
7777 N. Alton Ave., Indianapolis, 46268; 317-875-6797. Specializing in Muncie, AMACO, Marblehead, Kenton Hills

Hoover, Dave
1023 Skyview Dr., New Albany, 47150. Specializing in fishing collectibles, publishes fixed-price catalog; also miniature boats and motors

Keagy, William and June
PO Box 106, Bloomfield, 47424; 812-384-3471. Co-authors of *Those Wonderful Yard-Long Prints and More*, *More Wonderful Yard-Long Prints, Book II*, and *Yard-Long Prints, Book III*, illustrated value guides

Kurella, Elizabeth
The Lace Merchant
Box 244, Whiting, 46394; 219-659-1124. Publisher of books on lace and lines; specializing in lace and linens; e-mail: ekurella@home.com

Leslie, Beverly
Secretary/Treasurer of Uhl Collectors Society
801 Poplar St., Boonville, 47601; 812-897-3681. Contact for newsletter and membership information

McQuillen, Michael J. and Polly
McQuillen's Collectibles
PO Box 50022, Indianapolis, 46250-0022; 317-845-1721. Writer of column, *Political Parade*, which appears monthly in *AntiqueWeek* other newspapers; specializing in political advertising, pin-back buttons, and sports memorabilia; buys and sells; e-mail: michael@politicalparade.com or www.politicalparade.com

Pruitt, Ted
3350 W. 700 N., Anderson, 46011. *St. Clair Glass Collector's Book,* available ($15 each) from Ted at above address

Ricketts, Vicki
Covington Antiques Company
6431 W US Highway 136; Covington 47932. General line

Scowden, Virgil
Williamsport, 47993; 765-762-3178. Antiques museum, general line, tours

Slater, Thomas D.
Slater's Americana
1325 W. 86th St., Indianapolis, 46260; 317-257-0863. Specializing in political and sports memorabilia

Webb's Antique Mall
over 400 Quality Dealers
200 W. Union St., Centerville, 47330

Wright, Bill
325 Shady Dr., New Albany, 47150. Specializing in knives: Bowie, hunting, military, and pocketknives

---
Iowa

Addy, Geneva D.
Winterset, 50273; 515-462-3027

Ambrose, Craig
3717 6th Ave., Apt. 244, Des Moines, 50313; 515-288-4595. Specializing in quilts; author of *Picture Book and Price Guide to Antique Quilts*, available from author for $45 +postage

The Baggage Car
Hal and Meredith DeGood
3100 Justin Dr., Ste. B; Des Moines 50322; 515-270-9080. Specializing in Hallmark ornaments, cookie cutters, etc.; publishes Hallmark newsletter and list; e-mail: baggagecar@aol.com

Beeks, Dale
PO Box 117, Mt. Vernon, 52314; 319-895-0506. Specializing in instruments of science technology and medicine, also surveying instruments and microscopes; e-mail: dbeeksci@aol.com

Bilsland, William M., III
PO Box 2671, Cedar Rapids, 52406-2671; 319-368-0658. Specializing in American art pottery

Devine, Dennis, Norman, and Joe
D & D Antique Mall
1411 3rd St., Council Bluffs, 51503; 712-323-5233 or 712-328-7305. Specializing in furniture, phonographs, collectibles, general line; Joe Devine: Royal Copley and other types of pottery (collector), author of *Collector's Guide to Royal Copley Plus Royal Windsor & Spaulding*, Books I and II

Dollen, Brenda
210 Benton St., Council Bluffs, IA 51503-3135. Specializing in Red Wing pottery; co-author (with R.L. Dollen) of *Red Wing Art Pottery*, Books I and II (Collector Books)

Jaarsma, Ralph
De Pelikaan Antieks
812 Washington St., c/o Red Ribbon Antique Mall, Pella, 50219. Specializing in Dutch antiques; SASE required when requesting information

Picek, Louis
Main Street Antiques
110 W. Main St., Box 340, West Branch, 52358. Specializing in folk art, country Americana, the unusual

---
Kansas

Anthony, Dorothy Malone
World of Bells Publications
2401 S. Horton, Fort Scott, 66701; 316-223-3404. Specializing in publishing and selling books on all types of small bells

Maundy International
PO Box 13028-GG, Shawnee Mission, 66282; 1-800-235-2866. Specializing in watches — antique pocket and vintage wristwatches

Old World Antiques
4436 State Line Rd., Kansas City, 66103; 913-677-4744 or (fax) 913-677-4879. Specializing in 18th- and 19th-century furniture, paintings, accessories, clocks, chandeliers, sconces, and much more

Smies, David
Pops Collectibles
Box 522, 315 So. 4th, Manhattan, 66502; 785-776-1433. Specializing in coins, stamps, cards, tokens, Masonic collectibles

Street, Patti
Currier & Ives (China) Quarterly Newsletter
PO Box 504, Riverton, 66770; 316-848-3529. Subscription: $12 per year (includes 2 free ads)

Tinsley, Rosella
105 15th St., Osawatomie, 66064; 913-755-3237. Specializing in primitives, kitchen, woodenware, and miscellaneous (phone calls only, no letters please)

Kentucky

Courter, J.W.
3935 Kelley Rd., Kevil, 42053; 270-488-2116. Specializing in Aladdin lamps; author of *Aladdin — The Magic Name in Lamps, Revised Edition*, hardbound, 304 pages; *Aladdin Electric Lamps*, softbound, 229 pages; and *Angle Lamps Collectors Manual & Price Guide*, softbound, 48 pages

Florence, Gene
Box 7186H, Lexington, 40522. Author (Collector Books) on Depression glass, Occupied Japan; Elegant glass, kitchen glassware

Hornback, Betty
Betty's Antiques
707 Sunrise Lane, Elizabethtown, 42701; 270-765-2441. Specializing in Kentucky Derby glasses; detailed Derby, Preakness, Belmont, Breeder's Cup, and others glass information and pictures available in a booklet for $15 ppd. e-mail: bettysantiques@kvnet.org

Johnson, Wes, Sr.
3606 Glenview Ave., Glenview, 40025. Specializing in Cracker Jack: toys, point of sale, packages, etc.; Checkers Confection, Schoenhut toys, Victor Toy Oats, Universal Theatre (Chicago), old toys; please include SASE

Ritchie, Roy B.
197 Royhill Rd., Hindman, 41822; 606-785-5796. Co-author of *Standard Knife Collector's Guide; Standard Guide to Razors; Cattaraugus Cutlery, Identification and Values*; and *The Big Knife Book*; specializing in razors and knives, all types of cutlery

Stewart, Ron
PO Box 151, Combs, 41729; 606-435-2412. Co-author of *Standard Knife Collector's Guide; Standard Guide to Razors; Cattaraugus Cutlery, Identification and Values*; and *The Big Knife Book*; specializing in razors and knives, all types of cutlery

Willis, Roy M.
Heartland of Kentucky Decanters and Steins
PO Box 428, Lebanon Jct., 40150; Huge selection of limited edition decanters and beer steins — open showroom; include large self-addressed envelope (two stamps) with correspondence; fee for appraisals; decanter price guide (listings only, no pictures, information on marketing decanters): $9.50 ppd; www.ka.net/heartlandky

Louisiana

Langford, Paris
Kollecting Kiddles
415 Dodge Ave., Jefferson, 70121; 504-733-0667. Specializing in all small vinyl dolls of the '60s and '70s; author of *Liddle Kiddles Identification and Value Guide* (now out of print); please include SASE when requesting information; contact for information concerning Liddle Kiddle convention; e-mail: bbean415@aol.com

Maine

Blake, Brenda
Box 555, York Harbor, 03911; 207-363-6566. Specializing in egg cups; e-mail: Eggcentric@aol.com

Hathaway, John
Hathaway's Antiques
3 Mills Rd., Bryant Pond, 04219; 207-665-2214. Specializing in fruit jars; mail order a specialty

Hillman, Alma
Antiques at the Hillman's
362 E. Main St., Searsport, 04974; 207-548-6658. Co-author (Collector Books) of *Collector's Encyclopedia of Old Ivory China, The Mystery Explored, Identification & Values*; specializing in Old Ivory China; e-mail: oldivory@acadia.net

Rinaldi, John
Nautical Antiques and Related Items
Box 765, Dock Square, Kennebunkport, 04046; 207-967-3218. Specializing in nautical antiques, scrimshaw, naval items, marine paintings, naval items, etc.; fully illustrated catalog: $5

Shaw, John
43 Ridgecrest Dr., Wilton, 04294 (June to October, See Florida listing for remaining months); 207-645-2443. Specializing in dairy bottles

Zayic, Charles S.
Americana Advertising Art
PO Box 57, Ellsworth, 04605; 207-667-7342. Specializing in early magazines, early advertising art, illustrators

Maryland

Ezell, Elaine; & Newhouse, George
Cruets Cruets Cruets
PO Box 1609, Pasadena, 21123-1609; 410-551-4101 (daytime) or 410-255-6777. Specializing in cruets and glass

Humphrey, George C.
4932 Prince George Ave., Beltsville, 20705; 301-937-7899. Specializing in John Rogers groups

Katz, Jerome R.
Katz Collectibles
Antique Station, Frederick, 21702; 301-695-0888. Specializing in technological artifacts; please include SASE when requesting information

Meadows, John, Jean, and Michael
Meadows House Antiques
919 Stiles St., Baltimore, 21202; 410-837-5427. Specializing in antique wicker furniture (rustic, twig, and old hickory), quilts, and tramp art

Rudisill's Alt Print Haus
Rudisill, John and Barbara
PO Box 199, Worton, 21678; 410-778-9290. Specializing in Currier & Ives; calls for information will be taken in return for a contribution (honor system) to the American Heart Association; e-mail: rudi@dmv.com; chesapeake-bay.com/altprinthaus

Screen, Harold and Joyce
2804 Munster Rd., Baltimore, 21234; 410-661-6765. Specializing in soda fountain 'tools of the trade' and paper: catalogs, 'Soda Fountain' magazines, etc., e-mail: hscreen@home.com

Weisblut, Robert
International Ivory Society
11109 Nicholas Dr., Wheaton, 20902; 301-649-4002. Specializing in ivory carvings and utilitarian objects; e-mail: RWeisblut@yahoo.com

Welsh, Joan
7015 Partridge Pl., Hyattsville, 20782; 301-779-6181. Specializing in Chintz; author of *Chintz Ceramics*

Yalom, Libby
The Shoe Lady
PO Box 7146, Adelphi, 20783-2758; 301-422-2026. Specializing in glass and china shoes; author of book

Massachusetts

Adams, Charles and Barbara
South Yarmouth, 02664; 508-760-3290 or (business) 508-587-5640. Specializing in Bennington (brown only)

Cooper, Ryan
205 White Rock Rd., Yarmouthport, 02675; 508-362-1604. Specializing in flags of historical significance and exceptional design; e-mail: rcmaritime@capecod.net

Dunbar's Gallery
Leila and Howard Dunbar
76 Haven St., Milford, 01757; 508-634-8697 or (fax) 508-634-8698. Specializing in advertising and toys; e-mail: Dunbars@mediaone.net; www.dumbarsgallery.com

Ford, Frank W.
237-26 South Street; Shrewsbury, 01545. Specializing in Fostoria Specialty Company glassware

Frei, Peter
PO Box 500, Brimfield, 01010; 1-800-942-8968. Specializing in sewing machines (pre-1875, non-electric only), adding machines, typewriters, and hand-powered vacuum cleaners; SASE required with correspondence

Hess, John A.
Fine Photographic Americana
PO Box 3062, Andover, 01810. Specializing in 19th-century photography

Longo, Paul J.
Paul Longo Americana
Box 5510, Magnolia, 01930; 978-525-2290. Specializing in political pins, ribbons, banners, autographs, old stocks and bonds, baseball and sports memorabilia of all types

MacLean, Dale
183 Robert Rd., Dedham, 02026; 781-326-3010 or 781-329-1303 (evenings). Specializing in Dedham and Dorchester potteries

Morin, Albert
668 Robbins Ave. #23, Dracut, 01826; 978-454-7907. Specializing in miscellaneous Akro Agate and Westite; e-mail: akroal@mediaone.net

Steinbock, Nancy
Nancy Steinbock Posters
800-438-1577. Specializing in posters: travel, literary, advertising; Charter member of the IVPDA (International Vintage Poster Dealers Association)

Wellman, BA
PO Box 673, Westminster, 01473-0673. Specializing in *all* areas of American ceramics, dinnerware, figurines, and art pottery; e-mail: BA@dishinitout.com

Williams, Linda
46 Columba St, #4D, Chicopee, 01020. Specializing in glass & china, general line antiques; e-mail Sito1845@aol.com

Michigan

Brown, Rick
Newspaper Collector's Society of America
Lansing, 517-887-1255. Specializing in newspapers; e-mail: help@historybuff.com; www.historybuff.com

Burton, Ann
43779 Valley Rd., Decatur, 49045. Specializing in Schramberg

Culver, Bob
Night Light Club
38619 Wakefield Ct., Northville, 48167; 248-473-8575. Specializing in miniature oil lamps

Haas, Norman
264 Clizbe Rd., Quincy 49802; 517-639-8537. Specializing in American art pottery

Hogan & Woodworth
Walter P. Hogan and Wendy L. Woodworth
520 N. State, Ann Arbor, 48104; 313-930-1913. Specializing in Kellogg Studio, www.emunix.emich.edu/~whogan/kellogg/index.html

Iannotti, Dan
212 W. Hickory Grove Rd., Bloomfield Hills, 48302-1127S; 248-335-5042. Specializing in modern mechanical cast-iron banks; Member of The Mechanical Bank Collectors of America; e-mail: modernbanks@prodigy.net

Krupka, Rod
2615 Echo Lane, Ortonville, 48462; 248-627-6351. Specializing in lightning rod balls

Marsh, Linda K.
1229 Gould Rd., Lansing, 48917. Specializing in Degenhart glass

Nedry, Boyd W.
728 Buth Dr., Comstock Park, 49321; 616-784-1513. Specializing in traps (including mice, rat, and fly traps) and trap-related items; please include SASE when requesting information

Nickel, Mike
A Nickel's Worth
PO Box 456, Portland, 48875; 517-647-7646. Specializing in American Art Pottery: Roseville, Weller, Rookwood, Kay Finch, Stangl and Pennsbury birds, Ceramic Art Studio, and Florence figurines; e-mail: mandc@voyager.net

Oates, Joan
685 S. Washington, Constantine, 49042; 616-435-8353. Specializing in Phoenix Bird chinaware; e-mail: koates120@earthlink.net

Rairigh, Glen
Americana Auctions
12633 Sandborn, Sunfield, 48890; 800-919-1950. Specializing in Skookum dolls and antique auctions

Ross, Michelle
PO Box 94, Berrien Center, 49102; 616-925-1604. Specializing in Van Briggle and American pottery; e-mail: motherclay@cs.com

Webster, Marty
6943 Suncrest Drive, Saline, 48176; 313-944-1188. Specializing in California porcelain and pottery, Orientalia

Minnesota

Anderson, James
Box 120704, New Brighton, 55112; 651-484-3198. Specializing in old fishing lures and reels, also tackle catalogs, posters, calendars, Winchester items

Harrigan, John
1900 Hennepin, Minneapolis, 55403; 612-660-2794 or (in winter) 561-732-0525. Specializing in Battersea (English enamel) boxes, Moorcroft, and Toby jugs

Ketcham, Steve
Steve Ketcham Antiques (Shows and mail order only)
Box 24114, Edina, 55424; 952-920-4205. Specializing in and buying early American bottles; Red Wing stoneware (no dinnerware); advertising signs, trays, trade cards, pocket mirrors, etched beer, and shot glasses; please include SASE for reply; e-mail: s.ketcham@unique-software.com

Koehn, Joanne M.
Temple's Antiques
PO Box 46237, Eden Prairie, 55344; 612-941-7641. Specializing in Victorian glass and china

Miller, Clark
4444 Garfield Ave., Minneapolis, 55409-1847; 612-827-6062. Specializing in Anton Lang pottery, American art pottery, Scandinavian glass and pottery

Nelson, C.L.
Box 222, Spring Park, 55384; 612-473-5625. Specializing in 18th-, 19th-, and 20th-century English pottery and porcelain, among others: Gaudy Welsh, ABC plates, relief-molded jugs, Staffordshire transfer ware

Putratz, Barb
Spring Lake Park, 763-784-0422. Specializing in Norman Rockwell

Schoneck, Steve
HG Handicraft Guild, Minneapolis
PO Box 56, Newport, 55055; 651-459-2980. Specializing in American art pottery, Arts & Crafts, HG Handicraft Guild Minneapolis

Missouri

Duncan, Pat and Ann
Box 175, Cape Fair, 65624; 417-538-2311. Specializing in Holt Howard, Lefton, Roseville, etc.

Gillespie, Steve, Publisher
Goofus Glass Gazette
400 Martin Blvd, Village of the Oaks, 64118; 888-452-5554 or (fax) 816-452-554. Specializing in Goofus glass, curator of 'Goofus Glass Museum,' had 4,000+ piece collection of Goofus glass; buy, sell & collect Goofus for 30+ years; expert contributor to forums on Goofus glass; contributor to website for Goofus glass; e-mail: goofus@mid-west.net

Heuring, Jerry
28450 US Highway 61, Scott City, 63780; 573-264-3947. Specializing in Keen Kutter

Scott, John and Peggy
Scotty's Antiques
4640 S. Leroy, Springfield, 65810; 417-887-2191. Specializing in Florence ceramics, Cambridge glassware, TV lamps

Siegel, Brenda and Jerry
Tower Grove Antiques
3308 Meramec, St. Louis, 63118; 314-352-9020. Specializing in Ungemach pottery

Tarrant, Jenny
Holly Daze Antiques
4 Gardenview, St. Peters, 63376. Specializing in early holiday items, Halloween, Christmas, Easter, etc.; always buying Halloween collectibles (except masks and costumes) and German holiday candy containers; e-mail: JennyJOL@aol.com; holiday for sale; www.holly-days.com

Wendel, David
F.E.I., Inc.
PO Box 1187, Poplar Bluff, 63902-1187; 573-686-1926. Specializing in Fraternal Elks collectibles

Wiesehan, Doug
D & R Farm Antiques
4535 Hwy. H, St. Charles, 63301. Specializing in salesman's samples and patent models, antique toys, farm toys, metal farm signs

Williams, Don
PO Box 147, Kirksville 63501; 660-627-8009 (between 8 a.m. and 6 p.m. only). Specializing in art glass; SASE required with all correspondence

Winslow, Ralph
PO Box 478, Camdenton, 65020. Specializing in Dryden Pottery

Nebraska

Larsen, Robert V.
3214 19th St., Columbus, 68601. Specializing in old hatpins and hatpin holders; please include SASE when requesting information

Nevada

Lynn, Susan (Grindberg)
1412 Pathfinder Rd., Henderson, 89014; 702-898-7535. Collector Books author of *Collector's Guide to Porcelier China, Identification and Values*; e-mail: sue@porcelierconnection.com; www.porcelierconnection.com

Young, Willy
80 Promontory Pointe, Reno, 89509; 775-745-0922. Specializing in fire grenades

New Hampshire

Apakarian-Russell, Pamela
Halloween Queen Antiques
PO Box 499, Winchester, 03470. Specializing in Halloween (and other holidays) and postcards

Brenner, Larry
Brenner Antiques
1005 Chestnut St., Manchester, 03104; 603-625-8203. Specializing in Royal Bayreuth; e-mail: elberenee@aol.com

Holt, Jane
Jane's Collectibles
PO Box 115, Derry, 03038. Specializing in Annalee Mobilitee Dolls

Winston, Nancy
Willow Hollow Antiques
648 1st N.H. Turnpike, Northwood, 03261; 603-942-5739. Specializing in Shaker smalls, primitives, iron, copper, stoneware, and baskets

New Jersey

Anderson, Suzy McLennan, ISA CAPP
Heritage Antiques & Appraisal Services
65 E. Main St., Holmdel, 07733; 908-946-8801 or (fax) 908-946-1036. Specializing in American furniture and decorative accessories; please include photo and SASE when requesting information; appraisals and identification are impossible to do over the phone

Bilane, John E. (Mail order only)
2065 Morris Ave., Apt. 109, Union, 07083. Specializing in antique glass cup plates

Dezso, Doug
864 Paterson Ave., Maywood, 07607-2119; 201-488-1311. Specializing in nodders (comic German), glass candy containers, Tonka; SASE required for information

Doorstop Collectors of America
Doorstopper Newsletter
Jeanie Bertoia
2413 Madison Ave., Vineland, 08630; 609-692-4092. Membership: $20 per year, includes 2 newsletters and convention; send 2-stamp SASE for sample

George, Dr. Joan M.
ABC Collector's Circle Newsletter
67 Stevens Ave., Old Bridge, 08857; (fax) 732-679-6102. Specializing in educational china (particularly ABC plates and mugs); e-mail: drgeorge@nac.net

Harran, Jim and Susan
208 Hemlock Dr., Neptune, 07753; 732-922-2825. Specializing in English and Continental porcelains with emphasis on antique cups and saucers; author of *Collectible Cups and Saucers, Identification and Values, Book I & II* (Collector Books); available for $20.95 ppd.; www.tias.com/stores/amit

Litts, Elyce
PO Box 394, Morris Plains, 07950; 973-361-4087. Author (Collector Books) of *Collector's Encyclopedia of Geisha Girl Porcelain* (out of print; ask your reference librarian or used bookstore to secure you a copy); e-mail: happy-memories@worldnet.att.net

Lockwood, Howard J.; Publisher
Vetri: Italian Glass News
Box 191, Fort Lee, 07024; 201-969-0373. Specializing in Italian glass of the 20th century

Meschi, Edward J.
129 Pinyard Rd., Monroeville, 08343; 856-358-7293 or (fax) 856-358-7789. Specializing in Durand art glass, Icart etchings, Maxfield Parrish prints, Rookwood pottery, occupational shaving mugs, oil paintings, and other fine arts; author of *Durand — The Man and His Glass*, available from author for $43 ppd. e-mail: ejmeschi@aol.com

Middleton, Dave and Anne
Pot O' Gold Antiques
PO Box 124, Allenwood, 08720; 732-528-6648. Specializing in epergnes, historical and figural Staffordshire, Flow Blue, fine glass

Patalano, Diane. I.S.A.
Appraisals, Liquidations, and Auctions
PO Box 376, Saddle River, 07458. Specializing in banks, Black Americana, furniture, spatterware, various antiques and collectibles

Perzel, Robert and Nancy
Popkorn
3 Mine St. (near Main St.), PO Box 1057, Flemington, 08822; 908-782-9631. Specializing in Stangl dinnerware, birds, and artware; American pottery and dinnerware

Poster, Harry
Vintage TVs
Box 1883, S. Hackensack, 07606; Days: 201-794-9606. Writes *Poster's Radio and Television Price Guide*; specializes in vintage televisions, transistor radios, 3-D stereo cameras; catalog available online: www.harryposter.com

Rago, David
333 N. Main St., Lambertville, 08530; 609-397-6780 or fax: 609-397-6790. Specializing in Arts & Crafts, art pottery; e-mail: ragoarts@ragoarts.com; www.ragoarts.com

Rash, Jim
135 Alder Ave., Egg Harbor Township, 08234. Specializing in advertising dolls

Rosen, Barbara
6 Shoshone Trail, Wayne, 07470. Specializing in figural bottle openers and antique dollhouses

Visakay, Stephen
Vintage Cocktail Shakers (by appt.)
PO Box 1517, W. Caldwell, 07007-1517. Author of book and specializing in vintage cocktail shakers and bar ware; e-mail: SVisakay@aol.com

New Mexico

Hardisty, Don
Artistic Restorations
3020 E. Majestic Ridge, Las Cruces, 88011; For information and questions: 505-522-3721; fax: 505-522-7909. Specializing in Bossons, Hummels, postcards, rare coins. Don's Collectibles carries a full line of current issues and most discontinued Bossons and Hummel figurines of all marks. Postcard inventory includes over 500,000 with many original photo cards and all current issues of Legend (lot purchase offers now being accepted). When mail ordering Bossons and Hummels, you may dial toll free 800-Bossons (267-7667). The book *The Imagical World of Bossons* (there are 2 volumes) is also available. e-mail: don@donsbossons.com; www.dons bossons.com

Manns, William
PO Box 6459, Santa Fe, 87502; 505-995-0102; Co-author of *Painted Ponies*, hardbound (226 pages), available from author for $46 ppd.; specializing in carousel art and cowboy antiques; e-mail: zon@nets.com

Moyer, Patsy
PO Box 311, Deming, 88031; fax: 419-730-6970; Collector Books author on dolls; e-mail: moddoll@yahoo.com

Nelson, Scott H.
PO Box 6081, Santa Fe, 87502-6081. Specializing in ethnographic art

New York

Austin, Bruce A.
1 Hardwood Hill Rd., Pittsford, 14534; 716-387-9820 (evenings); 716-475-2879 (week days). Specializing in clocks and Arts & Crafts furnishings and accessories including medalware, pottery, and lighting; e-mail: baagll@rit.edu

Badders, Veldon
692 Martin Rd., Hamlin, 14464; 716-964-3360. Author (Collector Books) of *Collector's Guide to Inkwells, Identification & Values*; specializing in inkwells

Calison, Jim
Tools of Distinction
Wallkill, 12589; 914-895-8035. Specializing in antique and collectible tools, buying and selling

Dimitroff, Thomas P.
Dimitroff's Antiques (Appointment only)
140 E. First St., Corning, 14830; 607-962-6745. Specializing in Steuben and cut glass; e-mail: tdimi1@aol.com

Doyle, Robert A.
Absolute Auction & Realty, Inc.
Absolute Auction Center
PO Box 1739, Pleasant Valley, 12569. Antique and estate auctions twice a month at Absolute Auction Center; free calendar of auctions available; www.absoluteauctionrealty.com

Endter, Barbara
29 Sandalwood Dr., Rochester, 14616-1513; 716-621-1433. Specializing in Chase Brass & Copper Company

Gerson, Roselyn
PO Box 40, Lynbrook, 11563; 516-593-8746. Author/collector specializing in unusual, gadgetry, figural compacts, vanity bags and purses, solid perfumes, and lipsticks

Handelsman, Burton
18 Hotel Dr., White Plains, 10605; 914-428-4480 (home) and 914-761-8880 (office). Specializing in occupational shaving mugs, accessories

Kaonis, Keith; Manager
Antique Doll Collector Magazine
6 Woodside Ave., Suite 300, Northport, 11768 or PO Box 344, Center Port, NY 11721-0344; 631-261-4100 or 631-361-0982 (evenings). Specializing in Schoenhut toys

Laun, H. Thomas and Patricia
Little Century
215 Paul Ave., Syracuse, 13206; 315-437-4156. Summer residence: 35109 Country Rte. 7, Cape Vincent, 13618; 315-654-3244. Specializing in firefighting collectibles; **all appraisals are free, and we will respond only to those who include a self-addressed stamped envelope (photograph is requested for accuracy)**

Malitz, Lucille
Lucid Antiques
Box KH, Scarsdale, 10583; 914-636-7825. Specializing in lithophanes, kaleidoscopes, stereoscopes, medical and dental antiques

Michel, John and Barbara
Iron Star Antiques
200 E. 78th St., 18E, New York City, 10021; 212-861-6094. Specializing in yellow ware, cast iron, tramp art, shooting gallery targets, and blue feather-edge

Rifken, Blume J.
Author of *Silhouettes in America — 1790 – 1840 — A Collector's Guide*. Specializing in American antique silhouettes from 1790 to 1840

Russ, William A.
Russ Trading Post
23 William St., Addison 14801-1326. Animal lure manufacture; hunting and trapping supply; catalog $1

Safir, Charlotte F.
1349 Lexington Ave., 9-B, New York City, 10128-1513; 212-534-7933. Specializing in cookbooks, children's books (out-of-print only)

Schleifman, Roselle
Ed's Collectibles/The Rage
16 Vincent Rd., Spring Valley, 10977; 845-356-2121. Specializing in Duncan & Miller, Elegant glass, Depression glass

Smyth, Carole and Richard
Carole Smyth Antiques
PO Box 2068, Huntington, 11743. Authors of *The Burning Passion — Antique and Collectible Pyrography*, available from authors at above address for $23.90 ppd. (New York: add 8.25% state sales tax)

Tuggle, Robert
105 W. St., New York City, 10023; 212-595-0514. Specializing in John Bennett, Anglo-Japanese china

Van Kuren, Jean and Dale
Ruth's Antiques, Inc.
PO Box 152, Clarence Center, 14032; 716-741-8001. Specializing chocolate molds, Buffalo pottery, Deldare ware; e-mail: ruthsantq@aol.com

Van Patten, Joan F.
Box 102, Rexford, 12148. Author (Collector Books) of books on Nippon and Noritake

Weitman, Stan and Arlene
PO Box 1186; N. Massapequa, 11758; author of book on crackle glass (Collector Books)

North Carolina

Finegan, Mary
Marfine Antiques
PO Box 3618; Boone 28607; 828-262-3441; Specializing in Johnson Brothers dinnerware; replacement service; author of book ($14 +$3 postage and handling); e-mail: marfine@boone.net

Hughes, Kathy (Mrs. Paul)
Tudor House Galleries
4126 Park Road, Suite E, Charlotte, 28209; 704-676-4871; fax: 704-676-5197. Specializing in relief-molded jugs, 18th- and 19th-century English pottery and 19th-century oil paintings. e-mail: paulh65304@aol.com or www.tudorhouse.com

Hussey, Billy Ray
Southern Folk Pottery Collector's Society, Shop, and Museum
1828 N. Howard Mill Rd., Robbins, 27325; 910-464-3961 or (fax:)910-464-2530. Specializing in historical research and documentation, education and promotion of the traditional folk potter (past and present) to a modern collecting audience

Iannantuoni, Jean-Paul
4179 Brownwood Lane, Concord, 28027-4501. Discontinued Dinnerware Shopping Service; send $2 for Royal Doulton list; Appraisals $2 each; www.freeyellow.com/members/royal-doulton/home.html

Kirtley, Charles E.
PO Box 2273, Elizabeth City, 27096; 919-335-1262. Specializing in monthly auctions and bid sales dealing with World's Fair, Civil War, political, advertising, and other American collectibles

Newbound, Betty
2206 Nob Hill Dr., Sanford, 27330. Author (Collector Books) on Blue Ridge dinnerware, milk glass, wall pockets, figural planters, and vases; specializing in collectible china and glass

Sayers, R.J.
Southeastern Antiques & Appraisals
305 N. Main St., Hendersonville, 28792; 828-697-6064. Specializing in Boy Scout collectibles, Pisgah Forest pottery, primitive American furniture; author of *Guide to Scouting Collectibles, Revised 1996 Edition*, available from author for $32.95 ppd.; member New England Appraisers Assn.

Taylor, Terry
3648 Prides Rd., East Bend, 27018. Co-author of *Collector's Encyclopedia of Salt Glaze Stoneware* (Collector Books); specializing in salt glaze stoneware

North Dakota

Farnsworth, Bryce
1334 14 1/2 St. South, Fargo, 58103; 701-237-3597. Specializing in Rosemeade pottery; if writing for information, please send a picture if possible, also phone number and best time to call

Ohio

Bassett, Mark
PO Box 771233, Lakewood, 44107; 216-221-6025. Buying and selling Ohio art pottery (including Roseville, Cowan, Weller, Rookwood, others), Cleveland arts and crafts, Art Deco, and other 20th century design movements; author of *Introducing Roseville Pottery* (1999), *Cowan Pottery and the Cleveland School* (1997), *Introducing Roseville Pottery* (revised and expanded 2nd edition, 2001), and *Bassett's Roseville Prices* (2001), for ordering information send e-mail to: markbassett@angelfire.com.

Batory, Mr. Dana Martin
402 E. Bucyrus St., Crestline, 44827. Specializing in antique woodworking machinery, old and new woodworking machinery catalogs; author of *Vintage Woodworking Machinery, an Illustrated Guide to Four Manufacturers*, currently available from Astragal Press, PO Box 239, Mendham, NJ 07945 for $25.45 ppd. In order to prepare a definitive history on American manufacturers of woodworking machinery, Dana is interested in acquiring (by loan, gift, or photocopy) catalogs, manuals, photos, personal reminiscences, etc., pertaining

to woodworking machinery and/or their manufacturers. Also available for $7.50 money order: 30+ page list of catalogs, owner's manuals, parts lists, company publications, etc. (updated quarterly). No phone calls please.

Benjamin, Scott
PO Box 556, LaGrange, 44050-0556; 440-355-6608. Specializing in gas globes; co-author of *Gas Pump Globes* and several other related books, listing nearly 4,000 gas globes with over 1,800 photos, prices, rarity guide, histories, and reproduction information (currently available from author); also available: *Petroleum Collectibles Monthly* magazine; www.oilcollectibles.com or www.gasglobes.com

Blair, Betty
Golden Apple Antiques
216 Bridge St., Jackson, 45640; 614-286-4817. Specializing in art pottery, Watt, cookie jars, chocolate molds, Beanie Babies, general line

Budin, Nicki
Curio Cabinet
679 High St., Worthington, 43085; 614-885-1986. Specializing in Royal Doulton

China Specialties, Inc.
Box 471, Valley City, 44280. Specializing in Autumn Leaf

Cimini, Joan
67183 Stein Rd., Belmont, 43718-9715. Specializing in Imperial glass; Candlewick matching service

Distel, Ginny
Distel's Antiques
4041 S.C.R. 22, Tiffin, 44883; 419-447-5832. Specializing in Tiffin glass

Ebner, Rita and John
Columbus. Specializing in door knockers, cast-iron bottle openers, Griswold

Forsythe, Ruth A.
Box 327, Galena, 43021. Author of *Made in Czechoslovakia*, books I and II; SASE required

Graff, Shirley
4515 Grafton Rd., Brunswick, 44212. Specializing in Pennsbury pottery

Guenin, Tom
Box 454, Chardon, 44024. Specializing in antique telephones and antique telephone restoration

Hamlin, Jack and Treva
145 Township Rd. 1088, Proctorville, 45669; 740-886-7644. Specializing in Currier and Ives by Royal China Co. and Homer Laughlin China; e-mail: trevajo@ezwv.com

Hothem, Lar
Hothem House
Box 458, Lancaster, 43130. Author of books on Indians and artifacts

Kao, Fern Larking
PO Box 312, Bowling Green, 43402; 419-352-5928. Specializing in jewelry, sewing implements, ladies' accessories

Kerr, Ann
PO 437, Sidney, 45365; 937-492-6369. Author (Collector Books) of *Collector's Encyclopedia of Russel Wright Designs*; specializing in work of Wright; interested in 20th-century decorative arts

Kier, Anne and Don
202 Marengo St., Toledo, 43614-4213; 419-385-8211. Specializing in glass, china, autographs, Brownies, Royal Bayreuth, 19th-century antiques, general line; e-mail: d.a.k.@dorldnet.att.net

Kitchen, Lorrie
Toledo, 419-475-1759. Specializing in Depression-era glass, Hall china, Fiesta, Blue Ridge, Shawnee

Klender, James and Grace
Town & Country Antiques & Collectibles
PO Box 447, Pioneer, 43554; 419-737-2880. Specializing in pattern glass, and general line

Kline, Mr. and Mrs. Jerry and Gerry
The Founding Members of North American Torquay Society and Members of Torquay Pottery Collectors' Society
604 Orchard View Dr., Maumee, 43537; 419-893-1226. Specializing in collecting Torquay pottery

Maggard, Deborah
P.O Box 211, Chagrin Falls, 44022. Specializing in elegant glassware, china, Victorian art glass, and Victorian silverplate; e-mail: debmaggard@worldnet.att.net

Mathes, Richard
PO Box 1408, Springfield, 45501-1408; 513-324-6917. Specializing in buttonhooks

Millman, Tom and Linda
231 S. Main St., Bethel, 45106; phone/fax: 513-734-6884 (after 9 p.m.). Specializing in perfume lamps, other antique and unique lighting

Moore, Carolyn
445 N. Prospect, Bowling Green, 43402. Specializing in primitives, yellow ware, graniteware, collecting stoneware

Murphy, James L.
1023 Neil Ave., Columbus, 43201; 614-297-0746. Specializing in American Radford, Vance Avon; e-mail: jlmruphy@columbus.rr.com.

National Imperial Glass Collectors' Society, Inc.
PO Box 534, Bellaire 43906. Dues: $15 per year (plus $1 for each additional member in the same household); quarterly newsletter; convention every June

Otto, Susan; Editor
Nutcracker Collectors' Club and Newsletter
12204 Fox Run Dr., Chesterland, 44026

Pierce, David
PO Box 248, Danville, 43014; 614-599-6394. Specializing in Glidden pottery; fee for appraisals

Rees, Debbie
Zanesville. Specializing in Watt, Roseville juvenile and other Roseville pottery, Zanesville area pottery, cookie jars, and Steiff

Riebel, James; Krause, Terry
Pottery Peregrinators
Zanesville, 740-452-7687. James is author of *Sanford's Guide to Nicodemus*, available from the author; specializing in American art pottery, Nicodemus, and carnival glass and Millersburg glass

Roberts, Brenda
Specializing in Hull pottery and general line; author of *Collector's Encyclopedia of Hull Pottery*, *Roberts' Ultimate Encyclopedia of Hull Pottery*, and *The Companion Guide to Roberts' Ultimate Encyclopedia of Hull Pottery*, all with accompanying price guides

Shields, Lorne
PO Box 211, Chagrin Falls, 44022-0211; 440-247-5632. Specializing in bicycles; e-mail: vintage@globalserve.net

Trainer, Veronica
Bayhouse
Box 40443, Cleveland, 44140; 440-871-8584. Specializing in beaded and enamelled mesh purses

Tucker, Dan
Toledo, 419-478-3815. Specializing in Depression-era glass, Hall china, Fiesta, Blue Ridge, Shawnee

Walter, John
The Old Tool Shop
208 Front St., Marietta, 45750; 740-373-9973; fax: 740-373-9059. Specializing in all types of antique tools; for detailed information on Stanley tools, John Walter's *Antique & Collectible Stanley Tools Guide to Identity and Value* is highly recommended, 885 pages, over 1500 crisp photos and engravings, current values, softcover: $35 ppd., hardcover: $45 ppd.; *2000 Stanley Pocket Price Guide:* $12 ppd; e-mail: toolmerchant@sprynet.com (Website coming soon: www.stanleytoolcollectors.org)

Whitmyer, Margaret and Kenn
Box 30806, Gahanna, 43230. Author (Collector Books) on children's dishes; specializing in Depression-era collectibles

Wilkins, Juanita
The Bird of Paradise
Wapakoneta. Specializing in R.S. china, Old Ivory china, colored pattern glass, lamps, and jewelry

Young, Mary
Box 9244, Wright Brothers Branch, Dayton, 45409; 937-298-4838. Specializing in paper dolls; author of several books

Oklahoma

Bess, Phyllis and Tom
14535 E. 13th St., Tulsa, 74108; 918-437-7776. Authors of *Frankoma Treasures*, and *Frankoma and Other Oklahoma Potteries*; specializing in Frankoma and Oklahoma pottery

Moore, Art and Shirley
4423 E. 31st St., Tulsa, 74135; 918-747-4164 or 918-744-8020. Specializing in Lu Ray Pastels, Depression glass

Scott, Roger R.
4250 S. Oswego, Tulsa, 74135; 918-742-8710 or (fax) 918-583-1226. Specializing in Victor and RCA Victor trademark items along with Nipper

Oregon

Abrahams, Peter
1948 Mapleleaf Rd., Lake Oswego, 97034; 503-636-2988. Specializing in telescopes, binoculars, microscopes; Peter studies and collects optics: telescopes, binoculars, hand magnifiers, and microscopes and especially seeks reference material on these subjects, including books, catalogs, repair manuals, and histories; e-mail: telscope@europa.com; www.europa.com/~telescope/binotele.htm

Bartsch, Henry
Antique Registers
Box 444, Rockaway, 97136; 503-355-2932. Specializing in servicing antique cash registers (by appointment)

Brown, Marcia
Sparkles
PO Box 2314, White City, 97503; 541-826-3039 or (fax) 541-830-5385. Author of *Unsigned Beauties of Costume Jewelry* (Collector Books); co-author and host of 7 volumes: *Hidden Treasures* videos; specializing in rhinestone jewelry; please include SASE if requesting information

Coe, Debbie and Randy
Coe's Mercantile
Lafayette School House Mall #2, 748 3rd (Hwy. 99W), Lafayette, 97127; specializing in Elegant and Depression glass, art pottery

Davis, Patricia M.
Antique and personal property appraisals
4326 N.W. Tam-O-Shanter Way, Portland, 97229-8738; 503-645-3084; e-mail: pam10davis@aol.com

Foland, Doug
PO Box 66854, Portland, 97290. Author of *The Florence Collectibles, an Era of Elegance*, available at your local bookstore or from Schiffer publishers

Hirshman, Susan and Larry
Everyday Antiques
2011 E. Main St., Medford, 97504. Specializing in china, glassware, kitchenware

Main Antique Mall
30 N. Riverside, Medford, 97501. Quality products and services for the serious collector, dealer, or those just browsing

Medford Antique Mall
Jim & Eileen Pearson, Owners
1 West 6th St., Medford 97501

Miller, Don and Robbie
541-535-1231. Specializing in milk
bottles, TV Siamese cat lamps, seltzer
bottles, red cocktail shakers

Morris, Thomas G.
Prize Publishers
PO Box 8307, Medford, 97504.
Author of *The Carnival Chalk Prize*,
Books I and II, pictorial price guides
on carnival chalkware figures with
brief histories and values for each; e-
mail: chalkman@cdsnet.net

Ringering, David
Kay Ring Antiques
4063 Durbin Ave., S.E., Salem, 97301;
503-364-0464 or Pager: 503-588-3747.
Specializing in Rowland & Marsellus
and other souvenir/historical china
with scenes of buildings, parks, and
other tourist attractions of the 1890s –
1930s. Feel free to contact David if
you have any questions about Rowland and Marsellus or other souvenir
china. He will be happy to answer
questions about souvenir china. e-
mail: AR1480@aol.com

Pennsylvania

Alekna, Stan and Sally
732 Aspen Lane, Lebanon, 17042-
9073; 717-228-2361 or fax: 717-228-
2362. Specializing in American
Dimestore Toy Soldiers

Barker, Jim
Toastermaster Antique Appliances
PO Box 746, Allentown, 18105; 610-
439-0751. Specializing in early electric
toasters and fans, Porcelier and Royal
Rochester; unusual electric toasters
always wanted; e-mail: jbar@enter.net

Barrett, Noel
Rosebud Antiques
PO Box 1001, Carversville, 18913;
215-297-5109. Specializing in toys

Bodine, Clarence H., Jr., Proprietor
East/West Gallery
41B West Ferry St., New Hope, 18938.
Specializing in antique Japanese woodblock prints, netsuke, inro, porcelains

Cerebro
PO Box 327, E. Prospect, 17317-0327;
717-252-2400 or 800-69-LABEL; Fax:
717-252-3685. Specializing in antique
advertising labels, especially cigar box
labels, cigar bands, food labels, firecracker labels; e-mail: Cerebro@Cerebro.com

Christie, Dr. Victor J.W.;
Author/Appraiser/Broker
1050 West Main St., Ephrata, 17522;
717-738-4032. Specializing in Bessie
Pease Gutmann & other Gutmann
artists; e-mail: smiller1@redrose.net;
signed copy of *Bessie Pease Gutmann,
Her Life and Works*, available from
author for $17.50 at above address

Damaska, Ron
738 9th Ave., New Brighton, 15066;
724-843-1393. Specializing in Fry cut
glass, match holders; SASE required
when requesting information

Gottuso, Bob
Bojo
PO Box 1403, Cranberry Township,
16066-0403; phone/fax: 724-776-
0621. Specializing in Beatles, Elvis,
KISS, Monkees, licensed Rock 'n Roll
memorabilia

Hain, Henry F., III
Antiques & Collectibles
2623 N. Second St., Harrisburg,
17110; 717-238-0534. Lists available
of items for sale

Hinton, Michael C.
246 W. Ashland St., Doylestown,
18901; 215-345-0892. Owns/operates
Bucks County Art & Antiques Company and Chem-Clean Furniture
Restoration Company; specializing in
quality restorations of a wide range of
art and antiques from colonial to contemporary; also owns Trading Post
Antiques, 532 Durham Rd., Wright-
stown, PA, 18940, a 60-dealer
antiques co-op with 15,000 square feet
— something for everyone in antiques
and collectibles; e-mail: oldstuff
@worldnet.att.net

Holland, William
William Holland Fine Arts
1554 Paoli Pike, West Chester, 19380-
6123; 610-344-9848 or (fax) 610-344-
0651. Specializing in Louis Icart
etchings and oils, Art Nouveau and
Art Deco items; author of *Louis Icart:
The Complete Etchings*, *The Collectible
Maxfield Parrish*, and *Louis Icart Eroti-
ca*; e-mail: bill@hollandarts.com;
www.hollandarts.com

Irons, Dave
Dave Irons Antiques
223 Covered Bridge Rd., Northamp-
ton, 18067; 610-262-9335 or (fax) 610-
262-2853. Author of *Irons By Irons*,
More Irons By Irons, and *Even More
Irons by Irons)*, available from author,
(each contains pictures of over 1,600
irons, current information and price
ranges, collecting hints, news of trends,
and information for proper care of
irons); specializing in pressing irons,
country furniture, primitives, quilts,
accessories; www.ironsantiques.com

Ivankovich, Michael
Michael Ivankovich Auctions, Inc.
PO Box 1536, Doylestown, 18901.
Specializing in early 20th-century
hand-colored photography and prints;
author of *The Collector's Value Guide to
Popular Early 20th Century American
Prints*, (1998) $19.95; *The Collector's
Guide to Wallace Nutting Pictures*,
$18.95; *The Alphabetical and Numerical
Index to Wallace Nutting Pictures*,
$14.95; and *The Guide to Wallace Nut-
ting Furniture*, $14.95; also available:
*Wallace Nutting General Catalog,
Supreme Edition* (reprint), $13.95; *Wal-

lace Nutting: A Great American Idea*
(reprint), $13.95; and *Wallace Nut-
ting's Windsor's: Correct Windsor Furniture* (reprint), $13.95; related available
book: *The History of Sawyer Pictures* by
Carol Begley Gray, $14.95. All these
books are currently available at the
above address. Shipping is $4.25 for
the first item ordered and $1.50 for
each additional item.

Knauer, Judy A.
National Toothpick Holder Collectors
  Society
1224 Spring Valley Lane, West
Chester, 19380-5112; 610-431-3477.
Specializing in toothpick holders and
Victorian glass

The Krauses
Krause, Gail
97 W. Wheeling St., Washington,
15301; 412-228-5034. Author of book
on Duncan glass

Kreider, Katherine
Kingsbury Antiques
PO Box 7957, Lancaster, 17604-7957;
717-892-3001. Author of *Valentines
With Values*, available for $22.90 ppd.
($24.09 PA residents); *One Hundred
Years of Valentines*, available for $28.90
ppd. ($30.40 PA residents); and *Valen-
tines for the Eclectic Collector* ($28.90
ppd. ($30.40 PA residents; no free
appraisals; stop by Booth #315 in
Stroudtburg Antique Center (formerly
Black Angus), in Adamstown, PA,
Sundays only; e-mail: Kingsbry
@aol.com

Levi, Anita
Allegheny Mountain Antique Gallery
5151 Clear Shade Dr., Windber,
15963; 814-467-8539. Specializing in
novelty clocks, advertising tins, primitives, holiday decorations, quilts, purses, Black memorabilia, linens,
stoneware, Roseville, kitchenware,
Art Deco

Lindsay, Ralph
PO Box 21, New Holland, 17557. Specializing in target balls; SASE required
with correspondence

Lowe, James Lewis
Kate Greenaway Society
PO Box 8, Norwood, 19074. Specializ-
ing in Kate Greenaway; e-mail:
JLewisLowe@juno.com

Maier, Clarence and Betty
Mail order: The Burmese Cruet
Box 432, Montgomeryville, 18936;
215-855-5388. Specializing in Victorian art glass. e-mail: burmesecruet@
erols.com; www.burmesecruet.com

Merchants Square Mall
Jim & Annetta Vitez, Managers
1901 S. 12th St., Allentown, 18103;
610-797-7743

Posner, Judy
June – September: R.D. 1 Box 273
SC, Effort 18330, fax: 717-629-
0521. Specializing in Disneyana,

Black memorabilia, salt and pepper
shakers, souvenirs of the USA.,
character and advertising memorabilia, figural pottery; buy, sell, collect; informal appraisals, $5 LSASE
and photo of item; e-mail: judyand
jef@aol.com

Reimert, Leon
121 Highland Dr., Coatesville, 19320;
610-383-6969. Specializing in Boehm
porcelain

Rosso, Philip J. and Philip Jr.
Wholesale Glass Dealers
1815 Trimble Ave., Port Vue, 15133;
412-678-7352. Specializing in Westmoreland glass

Weiser, Pastor Frederick S.
55 Kohler School Rd., New Oxford,
17350-9210; 717-624-4106. Specializing in frakturs and other Pennsylvania
German documents; SASE required
when requesting information; no telephone appraisals/ must see original or
clear colored photocopy

Rhode Island

Gacher, John
The Zsolnay Store
152 Spring St., Newport, 02840; 401-
841-5060. Specializing in Zsolnay, Fischer, Amphora, and Austro-Hungarian
art pottery; www.drawrm.com

The Occupied Japan Club
c/o Florence Archambault
29 Freeborn St., Newport, 02840-
1821. Publishes bimonthly newsletter,
*The Upside Down World of an O.J. Col-
lector*; SASE required when requesting
information; e-mail: florence@aicon-
nect.com

South Carolina

Greguire, Helen
Helen's Antiques
216 Mountain View Rd, Landrum,
29356; 864-457-7340. Specializing
in graniteware (any color), carnival
glass lamps and shades, carnival
glass lighting of all kinds; author
(Collector Books) of *The Collector's
Encyclopedia of Graniteware, Colors,
Shapes & Values* (updated values
$28.70 ppd.); second book on gran-
iteware now available with prices
updated to 2000 (same price); also
available is *Carnival in Lights*, featuring carnival glass, lamps, shades, etc.
($13.45 ppd.); and *Collector's Guide
to Toasters and Accessories, Identification & Values* ($21.95 ppd.); all
available from author; please include
SASE when requesting information;
looking for people interested in collecting toasters to form a national
club

Guthrie, John
1524 Plover Ave., Mount Pleasant,
29464; 843-884-1873. Specializing in
Santa Barbara Ceramic Design

Roerig, Fred and Joyce
1501 Maple Ridge Rd., Walterboro, 29488; 843-538-2487. Specializing in cookie jars; authors of *Collector's Encyclopedia of Cookie Jars, An Illustrated Value Guide*, (three in the series), publishers of *Cookie Jarrin' with Joyce: The Cookie Jar Newsletter*

Tennessee

Chase, Mick and Lorna
Fiesta Plus
380 Hawkins Crawford Rd., Cookeville, 38501; 931-372-8333. Specializing in Fiesta, Harlequin, Riviera, Franciscan, Metlox, Lu Ray, Bauer, Vernon, other American dinnerware

DeLozier, Loretta
PO Box 50201, Knoxville, 37950-0201. Author (Collector Books) of *Collector's Encyclopedia of Lefton China, Identification & Values*, Books I, II, and III and Price Guide; specializing in Lefton China; buy, sell, and consign; fee for written appraisals

Fields, Linda
158 Bagsby Hill Lane, Dover, 37058; 931-232-5099 after 6 p.m. Specializing in pie birds; e-mail: Fpiebird@compu.net

Foil, Richard and Sue
Serendipity Antiques
at Antiques Unlimited; State St., Birstol; 540-628-8315. Authors of book on Cumbow China

Grist, Everett
PO Box 91375, Chattanooga, 37412-3955; 423-510-8052. Specializing in covered animal dishes and marbles

Hudson, Murray
Murray Hudson Antiquarian Books & Maps
109 S. Church St., Box 163, Halls, 38040; 901-836-9057 or 800-748-9946; Fax: 901-836-9017. Specializing in antique maps, globes, and books with maps, atlases, explorations, travel guides, geographies, surveys, etc.

Kline, Jerry
Florence Showcase
3063 Sugarwood Dr., Kodak, 37764; 865-933-9060; fax: 865-933-4492. Specializing in Florence Ceramics of California, Rookwood pottery, Shelley English china, English chintz

Weddington, David
Predicta Sales & Service
2702 Albany Ct., Murfreesboro, 37129; 615-890-7498. Specializing in vintage Philco Predicta TVs

Texas

Babcock, Bobby
Jubilation Antiques
5108 Saddleridge Cove, Austin, 78759; 512-418-9373. Specializing in Maxfield Parrish, Black memorabilia, and brown Roseville Pine Cone; e-mail: jubantique@aol.com.

Cooper, Marilyn
8408 Lofland Dr., Houston, 77055-4811; 713-465-7773 or Summer address: PO Box 755, Douglas, MI 49406. Specializing in figural toothbrush holders, Pez, candy containers

Dockery, Rod
4600 Kemble St., Ft. Worth, 76103; 817-536-2168. Specializing in milk glass; SASE required with correspondence

Docks, L.R. 'Les'
Shellac Shack; Discollector
Box 691035, San Antonio, 78269-1035. Author of *American Premium Record Guide*; specializing in vintage records; e-mail: docks@texas.net; www.docks.home.texas.net

Frese, Leo and Wendy
Three Rivers Collectibles
Box 551542, Dallas, 75355; 214-341-5165. Specializing in RumRill, Red Wing pottery and stoneware

Gibbs, Carl, Jr.
PO Box 131584, Houston, 77219-1584; 713-521-9661. Author of *Collector's Encyclopedia of Metlox Potteries*, autographed copies available from author for $27.95 ppd.; specializing in American ceramic dinnerware

Groves, Bonnie
402 North Ave. A, Elgin, 78621. Specializing in boudoir dolls

Knight, Suzanne
Abilene, 79602-4634; 915-673-9115. Specializing in Alamo and Gilmer potteries; e-mail: knight@camalott.com

Malowanczyk, Abby and Wlodek
Collage-20th Century Classics
2820 N. Henderson, Dallas, 75206; Phone/fax: 214-828-9888; 214-880-0020. Specializing in architect-designed furniture and decorative arts from the modern movement; e-mail: txcollage@aol.com; www.collageclassics.com

Norris, Kenn
Schoolmaster Auctions & Real Estate
PO Box 4830, 513 N. 2nd St., Sanderson, 79848-4830; 915-345-2640. Specializing in school-related items, barbed wire, related literature, and L'il Abner (antique shop in downtown Sanderson)

Pringle, Joyce M.
Antiques and Moore
3708 W. Pioneer Pkwy., Arlington, 76013. Specializing in Boyd, Summit, and Mosser glass; e-mail: chip@antiquesandmoore.com; www.Antiquesandmoore.com/glas

Rosen, Kenna
Rosen Estate Sales & Appraisals, Inc.
9138 Loma Vista, Dallas, 75243; 972-503-1436. Specializing in Bluebird china, quality estate sales; e-mail: kerosen@swbell.net

Silvermintz, Karen
6164 Ravendale Lane, Dallas, 75214; 214-826-1107. Specializing in American dinnerware

Smith, Allan
1806 Shields Dr., Sherman, 75092; 903-893-3626. Specializing in children's lunch boxes, Coca-Cola, Dr. Pepper, Pepsi-Cola, RC Cola, western stars' items, character tin windup toys, and most character collectibles

Thompson, Chuck
Chuck Thompson & Associates
10802 Greencreek Dr., Suite 203, Houston, 77070-5365. Chuck's *Antiques and Quotes* is a series of stories about traditional and sacred quotes found on samplers and other antiques. His column is featured monthly in *MidAtlantic Antiques* Magazine.

Tucker, Richard and Valerie
Argyle Antiques
PO Box 262, Argyle, 76226; 940-464-3752. Specializing in windmill weights, shooting gallery targets, figural lawn sprinklers, cast-iron advertising paperweights, and other unusual figural cast iron; e-mail: lead1234@gte.net or rtucker@jw.com

Turner, Danny and Gretchen
Running Rabbit Video Auctions
PO Box 701, Waverly, 37185; 615-296-3600. Specializing in marbles

Waddell, John
2903 Stan Terrace, Mineral Wells, 76067. Specializing in buggy steps

Woodard, Dannie; Publisher
The Aluminist
PO Box 1345; Weatherford, 76086; 817-594-4680. Specializing in aluminum items, books & newsletters about aluminum

Utah

Anderson, Tim
Box 461, Provo, 84603. Specializing in autographs; buys single items or collections — historical, movie stars, US Presidents, sports figures, and pre-1860 correspondence. Autograph questions? Please include photocopies of your autographs if possible and enclose a SASE for guaranteed reply. www.AutographsOfAmerica.com

Anderson, Warren R.
America West Archives
PO Box 100, Cedar City, 84721; 435-586-9497. Specializing in old stock certificates and bonds, western documents and books, financial ephemera, autographs, maps, photos; author of *Owning Western History*, with 75+ photos of old documents and recommended reference guide available ($20 ppd., soft cover) from author at the above address; e-mail: warren@americawestarchives.com

Spencer, Rick
Salt Lake City, 801-973-0805. Specializing in American silverplate and sterling flatware, hollow ware, Shawnee, Van Telligen, salt and pepper shakers; appraisals available at reasonable cost

Vermont

Barry, Kit
136 High St., Brattleboro, 05301; 802-254-3634. Author of *Reflections 1* and *Reflections 2*, reference books on ephemera; specializing in advertising trade cards and ephemera in general

Virginia

Bradfield, Jeff
Jeff's Antiques
90 Main St., Dayton, 22821; 540-879-9961. Also located in The Factory Antique Mall (I-81), Exit 227B, Verona, and Rolling Hills Antique Mall, I-81, Exit 247B, Harrisonburg. Specializing in candy containers, toys, postcards, sugar shakers, lamps, furniture, pottery, and advertising items

Branchcomb, Shane
5523 Sideburn Rd., Fairfax, 22032. Specializing in antique coffee mills, send SASE for reply; e-mail: acmeman@erols.com

Bull, Donald A.
PO Box 596, Wirtz, 24184; 540-721-1128. Author of *The Ultimate Corkscrew Book, Boxes Full of Corkscrews, Bull's Pocket Guide to Corkscrews, Just for Openers* (with John Stanley), and *Soda Advertising Openers*; specializing in corkscrews

Cranor, Rosalind
PO Box 859, Blacksburg, 24063. Specializing in Elvis collectibles; author of *Elvis Collectibles* (out of print) and *Best of Elvis Collectibles*, available from author for $21.70 ppd.

Flanigan, Vicki
Flanigan's Antiques
PO Box 1662, Winchester, 22604. Specializing in antique dolls, hand fans, and Hawaiian dolls; please include SASE with correspondence; fee for appraisals, thank you

Haigh, Richard
PO Box 29562, Richmond 23242; 804-741-5770. Specializing in Locke Art, Steuben, Loetz, Fry, Italian; SASE required for reply

Lechner, Mildred and Ralph
Box 554, Mechanicsville, 23111; 804-737-3347. Author (Collector Books) on glass salt shakers; specializing in art and pattern glass salt shakers circa 1870-1940; directors of Antique and Art Glass Salt Shakers Collectors Society Club, 1991 – 92. **Please note: Mildred and Ralph have absolutely NO involvement or dealings concerning novelty salt shakers or their values.**

MacAllister, Dale
PO Box 46, Singers Glen, 22850. Specializing in sugar shakers and syrups

Monsen, Randall; and Baer, Rod
Monsen & Baer
Box 529, Vienna, 22183; 703-938-2129. Specializing in perfume bottles, Roseville pottery, Art Deco

Reynolds, Charles
Reynolds Toys
2836 Monroe St., Falls Church, 22042; 703-533-1322. Specializing in limited-edition mechanical and still banks, figural bottle openers; e-mail: reynoldstoys@erols.com

Schleyer, Jim
Box 243, Burke, 22015. Former editor of the newsletter, *Toy Gun Purveyors* and author of *Backyard Buckaroos — Collecting Western Toy Guns*, which contains nearly 2,500 photographs and value guide. Toy gun inquiries that include a SASE will be graciously answered.

Windsor, Grant S.
PO Box 72606, Richmond, 23235-8017; 804-320-0386. Specializing in Griswold cast-iron cookware. SASE required for inquiries. Grant currently has a reprint of Griswold Catalog S, dated November 1, 1895, 20 pages. It contains much information and illustrations of several items not seen in catalogs previously known. Information is revealed which specifically dates the 'World's Fair' griddle; currently available for $11.50 each (ppd.); for orders of 10 or more: $7.50 each (ppd.).

Washington

Frost, Donald M.
Country Estate Antiques (Appointment only)
14800 N.E. 8th St., Vancouver, 98684; 360-604-8434. Specializing in art glass and earlier 20th-century American glass

Goldsworthy, Kathy
Past Glories
425-488-8871. Specializing in vintage needlecraft accessories and textiles; www.tias.com/stores/pastglories

Haase, Don (Mr. Spode)
The Spode Shop
D&D Antiques
PO Box 818, Mukilteo, 98275; 425-348-7443. Specializing in Spode-Copeland China; e-mail: mrspode@aol.com or Don@mrspode.com; www.mrspode.com

Jackson, Denis C., Editor
The Illustrator Collector's News
PO Box 1958, Sequim, 98382; 360-452-3810; Copy of recent sample: $3. Specializing in old magazines & illustrations such as Rose O'Neill, Maxfield Parrish, pinups, Marilyn Monroe, Norman Rockwell, etc.; e-mail: ticn@olypen.com

Morris, Sue and Dave
PO Box 1684, Port Orchard, 98366. Specializing in Watt pottery and Purinton pottery; author of *Watt Pottery — An Identification and Value Guide*, and *Purinton Pottery — An Identification and Value Guide*

Payne, Sharon A.
Antiquities & Art
PO Box 528, Granite Falls, 98252. Specializing in Cordey. e-mail: hotel_california94546@yahoo.com

Weldin, Bob
Miner's Quest
W. 3015 Weile, Spokane, WA 99208; 509-327-2897. Specializing in mining antiques and collectibles (mail-order business)

Whitaker, Jim and Kaye
Eclectic Antiques
PO Box 475 Dept. S, Lynnwood, 98046. Specializing in Josef Originals and motion lamps; SASE required; www.eclecticantiques.com

Zeder, Audrey
1320 S.W. 10th Street #S, North Bend, 98045 (appointment only). Specializing in British Royalty Commemorative souvenirs (mail-order catalog available); author (Wallace Homestead) of *British Royalty Commemoratives*

West Virginia

Fostoria Glass Society of America, Inc.
Box 826, Moundsville, 26041. Specializing in Fostoria glass

Wisconsin

Helley, Phil
Old Kilbourne Antiques
629 Indiana Ave., Wisconsin Dells, 53965; 608-254-8770. Specializing in premiums, German and Japanese tin toys, Cracker Jack, toothbrush holders, radio premiums, pencil sharpeners, and comic strip toys

Knapper, Mary
Phoneco, Inc.
207 E. Mill Rd., PO Box 70, Galesville, 54630; 608-582-4124. Specializing in telephones, antique to modern

Matzke, Gene
Gene's Badges & Emblems
455 Big Horn Ct., Hancock, 54943; phone/fax: 715-249-5695. Specializing in police badges, leg irons, old police photos, fire badges (old), patches, old handcuffs, and memorabilia

Rice, Ferill J.
302 Pheasant Run, Kaukauna, 54130. Specializing in Fenton art glass

Thomas, Darrell
Knomus Antiques
1738 Golf Bridge Dr. #8, Nevah, 54956. Specializing in art pottery, ceramics, Deco ware

Clubs, Newsletters, and Catalogs

ABC Collectors' Circle (16-page newsletter, published 3 times a year)
Dr. Joan M. George
67 Stevens Ave., Old Bridge, NJ 08857; e-mail: drjgeorge@nac.net or (fax) 732-679-6102. Specializing in ABC plates and mugs

Abingdon Pottery Collectors Club
Elaine Westover, Membership and Treasurer
210 Knox Hwy. 5, Abingdon, IL 61410; 309-462-3267. Dues $8 for single, $10 per couple. Specializing in collecting and preservation of Abingdon pottery

Akro Agate Collectors Club and *Clarksburg Crow* quarterly newsletter
Roger Hardy
10 Bailey St., Clarksburg, WV 26301-2524; 304-624-4523 (evenings) or West End Antiques, 97 Milford St., Clarksburg, WV 26301; 304-624-7600 (week days). Annual membership fee: $25; Club www.akro-agate.com

The Akro Arsenal, quarterly catalog
Larry D. Wells
6301 Walnut Valley Dr., Ft. Wayne, IN 46818; 219-489-5842

The Aluminist
Dannie Woodard, Publisher
PO Box 1346, Weatherford, TX 76086.
Subscription: $20 (includes membership)

America West Archives
Anderson, Warren
PO Box 100, Cedar City, UT 84721; 435-586-9497. 26-page illustrated catalogs issued 6 times a year; has both fixed-price and auction sections offering early western documents, letters, stock certificates, autographs, and other important ephemera; subscription: $15 per year; e-mail: warren@americawestarchives.com

American Antique Deck Collectors
52 Plus Joker Club
Clear the Decks, quarterly publication
Larry Lubliner, Membership
3814 N. Freemont #3, Chicago, IL 60613 ($25 in US and Canada, $35 foreign). Specializing in antique playing cards; www.52plusjoker.org; e-mail: Joker1854@aol.com

American Bell Association, Int., Inc.
c/o The Bell Tower
PO Box 19443, Indianapolis, IN 46219. Dorothy Malone Anthony, past president; annual dues: $22 ($25 per couple); information e-mail: joanforman@earthlink.net

American Cut Glass Association
Kathy Emmerson, Executive Secretary
PO Box 482, Ramona, CA 92065-0482; 760-789-2715 or (fax) 760-789-7112. Membership dues (includes subscription to newsletter, *The Hobstar*: $45 (bulk mail) or $55 (first class & international); e-mail: ACGAKATHY@aol.com; www.cutglass.org

American Hatpin Society
Virginia Woodbury, President
20 Montecillo, Rolling Hills Estates, CA 90274; 310-326-2196. Newsletter published quarterly; meetings also quarterly; membership: $30; www.collectoronline.com/AHS/

Antique and Art Glass Salt Shaker Collectors' Society (AAGSSCS)
17460 Caloosa Trace Circle, Ft. Myers, FL 33912

Antique & Collectors Reproduction News
Antiques Coast to Coast
Mark Chervenka, Editor
PO Box 12130, Des Moines, IA 50312-9403; 515-274-5886 or (subscriptions only) 800-227-5531. 12 monthly issues: $32 per year in US; $41 in Canada; $59 all other foreign; e-mail: acrn@repronews.com

Antique Advertising Association of America (AAAA)
PO Box 1121, Morton Grove, IL 60053; 708-466-0904. Publishes *Past Times* Newsletter; subscription: $35

Antique Bottle & Glass Collector Magazine
Jim Hagenbuch, Publisher
102 Jefferson St., PO Box 180, East Greenville, PA 18041. Subscription: (12 issues) $21 in US ($24 in Canada)

Antique Journal
Michael F. Shores, Publisher
Jeffrey Hill, Editor/General Manager
2329 Santa Clara Ave., #207, Alameda, CA 94501; 800-791-8592

Antique Journal Northwest
Michael F. Shores, Publisher
Jeffrey Hill, Editor/General Manager
3439 North East Sandy Blvd., Suite #275, Portland, OR 97232; 888-845-3201

Antique Purses Catalog: $4
Bayhouse
PO Box 40443, Cleveland, OH 44140; 216-871-8584. Includes colored photos of beaded and enameled mesh purses

Antique Radio Classified (ARC)
PO Box 2, Carlisle, MA 01741; 978-371-0512

Antique Souvenir Collectors News
Gary Leveille, Editor
PO Box 562, Great Barrington, MA
01230

Antique Stove Association
Macy Stern, Editor of *Antique Stove
Association Quarterly*, 2617 Riverside
Dr., Houston, TX 77004; 713-528-
2990

Antique Telephone Collectors Assoc.
Box 94, Abilene, KS 67410; 785-263-
1757. An international organization
associated with the Museum of Independent Telephony; www.atcaon-
line.com

Antique Trader Weekly
Nancy Crowley, Editor
PO Box 1050, Dubuque, IA 52004-
1050. Featuring news about antiques
and collectibles, auctions and events;
listing over 165,000 buyers and sellers
in every edition; subscription: $37 (52
issues) per year; toll free for subscriptions only: 800-258-0929; e-mail: col-
lect@krause.com; www.collect.com

Antique Wireless Association
Ormiston Rd., Breesport, NY 14816

Appraisers National Association
120 S. Bradford Ave., Placentia, CA
92870; 714-579-1082. Founded in
1982 by Dr. David Long, Ph.D., President of the College for Appraisers, to
provide for a standardization of educational requirements for certification of
its appraiser members and assure the
public that A.N.A. appraisers not only
have a broad range of knowledge in
personal property valuation, but are
held to the highest ethical and professional standards in the industry.

Arman's Collectors Sales & Services
PO Box 6, Pomfret Center, CT 06259;
860-794-7008 or fax: 860-974-7010; e-
mail: Collectors.sales@snet.net

Association of Coffee Mill Enthusiasts
c/o Lucy Fullinwider, Treasurer
PO Box 5761, Midland, TX 79704.
Quarterly newsletter, annual convention; dues are $30 ($40 outside the
continental US and Canada), covers
cost of quarterly newsletter and copy
of membership roster

Auction Times for the West
Michael F. Shores, Publisher
Jeffrey Hill, Editor/General Manager
2329 Santa Clara Ave., Suite 207,
Alamedo, CA 94501; 800-791-8592

Autograph Times
2303 N. 44th St., #225, Phoenix, AZ
85008; 602-947-3112 or (fax) 602-
947-8363. Subscription: $15 (US) per
year

Autographs of America
Tim Anderson
PO Box 461, Provo, UT 84603; 801-
226-1787 (please call in the afternoon);
www.AutographsOfAmerica.com

Autumn Leaf
Bill Swanson, Editor
807 Roaring Springs Dr., Allen, TX
75002-2112; 972-727-5527
Gwynne Harrison, President
PO Box 1, Mira Loma, CA 91752-
0001; 951-685-5434

Avon Times Newsletter
c/o Dwight or Vera Young
PO Box 9868, Dept. P., Kansas City,
MO 64134. Inquiries should be
accompanied by LSASE

Beatlefan
PO Box 33515, Decatur, GA 30033.
Subscription: $7 (US) for 6 issues or
$21 (Canada and Mexico)

Black Memorabilia Illustrated Sales
     List ($2 and LSASE)
Judy Posner
June – September: R.D. 1, Box 273
SC, Effort, PA 18330, fax: 717-629-
0521; October – May: PO Box 2194
SC, Englewood, FL 34295, fax: 941-
475-2645. Buy-sell-collect; e-mail:
judyandjef@aol.com; www.judypos-
ner.com

Bojo
PO Box 1403, Cranberry Township,
PA 16066-0403. Send $3 for 38 pages
of Beatles, toys, dolls, jewelry, autographs, Yellow Submarine items, etc.

Bookend Collector Club
c/o Louis Kuritzky, M.D.
4510 NW 17th Place, Gainesville, FL
32650; 352-377-3193; Quarterly full-
color glossy newsletter, $25 per year; e-
mail: lkuritzky@aol.com

Bossons Briefs, quarterly newsletter
Available through membership of
International Bossons Collectors Soci-
ety, 1317 N. San Fernando Blvd, Suite
#325, Burbank, CA 91504

Boyd's Art Glass Collectors Guild
PO Box 52, Hatboro, PA 19040-0052

Boyd's Crystal Art Glass
*Jody & Darrell's Glass Collectibles
     Newsletter*
PO Box 180833, Arlington, TX
76096-0833. Publishes 6 times a year;
subscription includes an exclusive
glass collectible produced by Boyd's
Crystal Art Glass; LSASE for current
subscription rates; sample copy of
newsletter: $3

British Royal Commemorative Sou-
     venirs Mail Order Catalog
Audrey Zeder
1320 SW 10th St. #S, North Bend,
WA 98045

Buckeye Marble Collectors Club
Brenda Longbrake, Secretary
e-mail: brenda@wcoil.com

The Buttonhook Society
Box 287, White Marsh, MD 21162.
Publishes bimonthly newsletter *The
Boutonneur*, which promotes collecting
of buttonhooks and shares research and
information contributed by members

Candy Container Collectors of America
The Candy Gram Newsletter
Betty MacDuff, Membership Chairman
2711 De La Rosa St, The Villages, FL
32159
or Contact: Jeff Bradfield
90 Main St., Dayton, VA 22821
Membership: $18 per family;
www.candycontainer.org

The Cane Collector's Chronicle
Linda Beeman
15 2nd St. N.E., Washington, D.C.
20002; $30 for 4 issues

Cane Collectors Club
PO Box 1004, Englewood Cliff, NJ
07632; 201-886-8826; e-mail:
liela@walkingstickworld.com

The Carnival Pump
International Carnival Glass Assoc.
Lee Markley
Box 306, Mentone, IN 46539; Dues:
$20 per family per year in US and
Canada or $25 overseas, payable each
July 1st

The Carousel News & Trader
87 Parke Ave. W., Suite 206, Mansfield, OH 44902. A monthly magazine
for the carousel enthusiast. Subscription: $22 per year; sample: $3

The Carousel Shopper Resource Catalog
Box 47, Dept. PC, Millwood, NY
10546; only $2 (+50¢ postage); a full-
color catalog featuring dealers of
antique carousel art offering single figures or complete carousels, museums,
restoration services, organizations, full-
size reproductions, books, cards, posters,
auction services, and other hard-to-find
items for carousel enthusiasts

Cast Iron Marketplace
PO Box 16466, Saint Paul, MN
55116. Available to hobbyists/dealers
on a monthly basis to buy/sell/trade
products made by the great foundries
from our industrial past; subscription:
$30 per year (includes free ads up to
200 words per issue)

A Catalog Collection
Kenneth E. Schneringer
271 Sabrina Ct., Woodstock, GA
30188-4228; 770-926-9383. Specializing in catalogs, promochures, view
books, labels, trade cards, special paper
needs; e-mail: trademan68@aol.com

Central Florida Insulator Collectors
3557 Nicklaus Dr., Titusville, FL
32780-5356; 407-267-9170; Dues: $10
per year for single or family membership (checks payable to Jacqueline C.
Linscott). Dues covers the cost of
Newsnotes, the club's monthly
newsletter, which informs members of
meetings and shows, articles of interest
on insulators and other collectibles.
Members are invited to use free advertising of items for sale or trade. The
club meets quarterly in members'
homes and hosts a show each January
which is open to the public. For club
information send SASE to above
address; e-mail: bluebellwt@aol.com.

Ceramic Arts Studio Catalog Reprints
Wellman, BA
PO Box 673, Westminster, MA
01473-0673. Also offers many other
catalog reprints from dinnerware to art
pottery; specializing in all areas of
American ceramics, art pottery, dinnerware, and figurines; e-mail:
BA@dishinitout.com

Ceramic Arts Studio Collector's Assoc.
PO Box 46, Madison, WI 53701;
608-241-9138. Annual membership:
$15; inventory record and price guide
available

*Chicagoland Antique Amusements Slot
     Machine & Jukebox Gazette*
Ken Durham, Editor
909 26 St., N.W., Suite 502, Washington, D.C. 20037. 20-page newspaper
published twice a year; subscription: 4
issues for $30; sample: $10; send SASE
for free list of books; www.Game-
RoomAntiques.com

China Specialties, Inc.
Fiesta Collector's Quarterly Newsletter
PO Box 471, Valley City, OH 44280

Chintz Connection Newsletter
PO Box 222, Riverdale, MD 20738.
Dedicated to helping collectors share
information and find matchings; subscription: 4 issues per year for $25

The Cola Clan
Alice Fisher, Treasurer
2084 Continental Dr., N.E., Atlanta,
GA 30345

Collector's Life
The World's Foremost Publication for
     Steiff Enthusiasts
Beth Savino
PO Box 798; Holland, OH 43528; 1-
800-862-TOYS; fax: 419-473-3947;
www.toystorenet.com

Collector Glass News
Box 308, Slippery Rock, PA 16057
724-946-2838 or (fax) 724-946-9012.
An international publication providing current news to collectors of cartoon, fast-food, and promotional
glassware; e-mail: cgn@glassnews.com;
www.glassnews.com

Collectors of Findlay Glass
PO Box 256, Findlay, OH 45840. An
organization dedicated to the study
and recognition of Findlay glass;
newsletter *The Melting Pot*, published
quarterly; annual convention; membership: $10 per year ($15 per couple)

Compact Collectors
Roselyn Gerson
PO Box 40, Lynbrook, NY 11563;
516-593-8746 or (fax) 516-593-
0610. Publishes *Powder Puff*
Newsletter, which contains articles
covering all aspects of compact collecting, restoration, vintage ads,
patents, history, and articles by members and prominent guest writers;
seeker and sellers column offered free
to members; e-mail: compact
lady@aol.com

Cookie Crumbs
Cookie Cutter Collectors Club
Ruth Capper, Secretary/Treasurer
1167 Teal Road S.W., Dellroy, OH
44620. Subscription $12 per year (4
issues); Payable to CCCC

Cookie Jarrin' With Joyce: The Cookie Jar Newsletter
1501 Maple Ridge Rd., Walterboro, SC 29488

Cookies
Rosemary Henry
9610 Greenview Lane, Manassas, VA
20109-3320. Subscription: $12 per
year (6 issues); payable to Cookies

The Copley Courier
1639 N. Catalina St., Burbank, CA 91505

Cowan Pottery Museum Associates
For information write: CPMA, PO
Box 16765, Rocky River, OH 44116 or
contact Victoria Naumann Peltz,
Curatorial Associate, Cowan Pottery
Museum at Rocky River Public
Library, 1600 Hampton Rd., Rocky
River, OH 44116; 440-333-7610, ext.
214. Annual dues: $35, includes sub-
scription to biannual *Cowan Pottery
Journal* Newsletter; please visit our
Website at www.cowanpottery.org

Cracker Jack® Collector's Assoc.
The Prize Insider Newsletter
Theresa Richter, Membership Chairman
5469 S. Dorchester Ave., Chicago, IL
60615. Subscription/membership: $20
per year (single) or $24 (family); e-
mail: WaddyTMR@aol.com; www.col-
lector online.com/CJCA/

Creamers, quarterly newsletter
PO Box 11, Lake Villa, IL 60046-
0011. Subscription: $5 per year

Currier & Ives Catalog
Rudisill's Alt Print Haus
PO Box 199, Worton, MD 21678.
Please include LSASE; e-mail:
rudi@dmv.com or chesapeake-
bay.com/altprinthaus

(Currier & Ives) C&I Dinnerware
Collector Club
E.R. Aupperle, Treasurer
29470 Saxon Road, Toulton, IL
61483; 309-896-3331 or (fax) 309-
856-6005

Czechoslovakian Collectors Guild
International
Alan Badia
15006 Meadowlake St., Odessa, FL
33556-3126; www.czechartglass.com/ccgi

The DAZE, Inc. (formerly *The Depression Glass DAZE*)
Teri Steele (Cox), Publisher
The Nation's Marketplace and Meet-
ingplace for American glass, china,
and pottery collectors, Box 57,
Otisville, MI 48463; e-mail:
dgdaze@aol.com or call 800-336-9927
for trial subscription offer

*The Dedham Pottery Collectors Society
Newsletter*
Jim Kaufman, Publisher
248 Highland St., Dedham, MA
02026-5833; 800-283-8070; e-mail:
DedhamPottery.com

Disneyana Illustrated Sales List ($2
and LSASE)
Judy Posner
June - September: R.D. 1, Box 273 SC,
Effort, PA 18330, fax: 717-629-0521.
October - May: PO Box 2194 SC, Englewood, FL 34295, fax: 941-475-2645. Buy-
sell-collect; e-mail: judyandjef@aol.com
or www.judyposner.com

Docks, L.R. 'Les'
Shellac Shack
Box 691035, San Antonio, TX 78269-
1035. Send $2 for a 72-page catalog of
78s that Docks wants to buy, the prices
he will pay, and shipping instructions;
e-mail: docks@texas.net; www.docks.
home.texas.net

Doorstop Collectors of America
Doorstopper Newsletter
Jeanie Bertoia
2413 Madison Ave., Vineland, NJ
08630; 609-692-4092. Membership: $20
per year, includes 2 newsletters and convention; send 2-stamp SASE for sample

*Dorothy Kamm's Porcelain Collector's
Companion*
PO Box 7460, Port St. Lucie, FL
34985-7460; 561-465-4008 or (fax)
561-460-9050. Published bimonthly,
subscription: $30 per year; e-mail:
dorothy.kamm@usa.net

Drawing Room of Newport
Gacher, John
152 Spring St., Newport, RI 02840;
401-841-5060. Book on Zsolnay available; www.drawrm.com

Early Typewriter Collectors Assoc.
ETCetera newsletter
Chuck Dilts & Rich Cincotta, Co-editors
P.O. Box 286; Southborough, MA
01772; 508-229-2064; e-mail:
etcetera@writeme.com; www.type-
writer.rydia.net/etcetera.html

Ed Taylor Radio Museum
245 N. Oakland Ave., Indianapolis,
IN 46201-3360; 317-638-1641

Eggcup Collector's Corner
67 Stevens Ave., Old Bridge, NJ
08857. Issued quarterly; subscription:
$18 per year (payable to Joan George);
sample copy: $5

The Elegance of Old Ivory Newsletter
Box 1004, Wilsonville, OR 97070
Fenton Art Glass Collectors of America

Butterfly Net Newsletter
Kay Kenworthy, Editor
PO Box 384, 702 W. 5th St.,
Williamstown, WV 26187. Dues $20
per year for full membership, $5 for
each associate membership; children
under 12 free; e-mail:
kkenworthy@foth.com; www.collec-
toronline.com/club-FAGCA.html

Fiesta Collector's Quarterly Newsletter
PO Box 471, Valley City, OH 44280.
Subscription: $12 per year; www.chi-
naspecialties.com/fiesta.html

Figural Bottle Opener Collectors
Linda Fitzsimmons, 9697 Gwynn Park
Dr., Ellicott City, MD 21042; 410-465-
9296. Please include SASE when
requesting information

Florence Collector's Club Newsletter
Rita Bee, Editor
Beth Dunigan, Publisher
c/o Membership Chairman
PO Box 122, Richland, WA 99353.
Subscription: (6 issues per year) $20

Fostoria Glass Society of America
PO Box 826, Moundsville, WV 26041.
Membership: $16; www.fostoriaglass.org

Frankoma Family Collectors Assoc.
c/o Nancy Littrell
PO Box 32571, Oklahoma City, OK
73123-0771. Membership dues: $25
(includes quarterly newsletter); annual
convention

Friends of Degenhart
c/o Degenhart Museum
PO Box 186, Cambridge, OH 43725;
740-432-2626. Membership: $5 ($10
for family) includes *Heartbeat*
Newsletter (printed quarterly) and
free admission to museum

H.C. Fry Society
PO Box 41, Beaver, PA 15009. Founded in 1983 for the sole purpose of
learning about Fry glass; publishes
Shards, quarterly newsletter

The Glass Menagerie newsletter
Susan Candelaria, Editor
5440 El Arbol, Carlsbad, CA 92008

Goofus Glass Gazette
Steve Gillespie, Publisher
400 Martin Blvd., Village of the Oaks,
MO 64118; 888-452-5554 or (fax)
816-452-5554; e-mail: goofus@mid-
west.net

The Gonder Collector
917 Hurl Dr.
Pittsburgh, PA 15236

Grandpa's Depot
John 'Grandpa' White
6720 E. Mississippi Ave., Unit B, Denver, CO 80224; 303-758-8540 or (fax)
303-321-2889. Publishes catalogs on
railroad-related items

Griswold & Cast Iron Cookware Assoc.
Grant Windsor
PO Box 72606, Richmond, VA 23235-
2606; 804-320-0386. Membership:
$15 (for single) or $20 (for 2 members
per address) payable to club

Haeger Pottery Collectors of America
Lanette Clarke
5021 Toyon Way, Antioch, CA
94509; 925-776-7784. Newsletter published 6 times per year; dues: $20

*The Hagen-Renaker Collector's Club
Newsletter*
c/o Jenny Palmer
3651 Polish Line Rd., Cheboygan, MI
49721-9045

Hall China Collector's Club Newsletter
PO Box 360488, Cleveland, OH 44136

Head Hunters Newsletter
c/o Maddy Gordon
PO Box 83H, Scarsdale, NY 10583. Subscription: $24 yearly (quarterly issues)

Homer Laughlin China Collectors
Association (HLCCA)
The Dish magazine (a 16-page quarterly included with membership); PO
Box 26021; Crystal City, VA 22215-
6021. Single: $25, couple/family: $40;
www.hlcca.org

Ice Screamer
c/o Duvall Sollers
PO Box 132, Monkton, MD 21111.
Published quarterly; Dues: $15 per
year; annual convention held in late
June in Lancaster, PA

Ideal Collectors Club
c/o Judith Izen
PO Box 623, Lexington, MA 02173.
Membership: $20 per year, includes a
quarterly newsletter; subscribers get
free wanted/for sale ads in each issue;
e-mail: jizenres@aol.com

The Illustrator Collector's News
Denis C. Jackson, Editor
PO Box 1958, Sequim, WA 98382.
Subscription: $18 per year; $3 for sample copy of bimonthly publication;
publishes price and identification
guides on various illustrators and old
magazines, write for further information; e-mail: ticn@olypen.com

Indiana Historical Radio Society
245 N. Oakland Ave., Indianapolis,
IN 46201-3360; 317-638-1641

International Association of Calcula-
tor Collectors
International Calculator Collector
Newsletter
Guy Ball, Co-editor
PO Box 345, Tustin, CA 92781-0345.
Subscription: $16 per year ($20 for-
eign); sample copy: $3; e-mail:
mrcalc@usa.net

International Association of R.S.
Prussia, Inc.
Theresa Newcomer, Secretary
PO Box 446, Mount Joy, PA 17522.
Membership: $30 per household; year-
ly convention; www.rsprussia.com

International Club for Collectors of
Hatpins and Hatpin Holders (ICC
of H&HH)
Audrae Heath, Managing Editor
PO Box 1009. Bonners Ferry, ID
83805-1009. Bimonthly *Points*
newsletter and *Pictorial Journal*

International Golliwog Collector Club
Beth Savino
PO Box 798; Holland, OH 43528; 1-
800-862-TOYS or (fax) 419-473-
3947; toystorenet.com

International Ivory Society
Robert Weisblut, Co-Founder
11109 Nicholas Dr., Wheaton, MD
20902; 301-649-4002. $10 annual
membership fee includes 4 newsletters

International Match Safe Association
PO Box 791; Malaga, NJ 08328; 856-
694-4167. Quarterly newsletter and
annual convention; e-mail:
IMSAoc@aol.com; www.matchsafe.org

International Nippon Collectors Club
c/o David Przech
1531 Independence Ave. S.E., Washington, D.C. 20003. Publishes
newsletter 6 times a year; Holds annual convention; membership: $30;
www.nipponcollectorsclub.com

International Perfume and Scent Bottle Collectors Association
Randall Monsen
PO Box 529, Vienna, VA 22183 or
(fax) 703-242-1357.
or Coleen Abbot
396 Croton Rd., Wayne, PA 19087-
2038. Membership: $40 (USA) or $50
(Foreign); Newsletter published quarterly

International Rose O'Neill Club
Contact Karen Stewart
PO Box 668, Branson, MO 65616.
Publishes quarterly newsletter *Kewpi-
esta Kourier*; membership: (includes
newsletter) $10 (single) or $12 (family); www.kewpieroseoneillclub.com

International Society of Antique
Scale Collectors
Jan Macho, Executive Secretary
3616 Noakes St., Los Angeles, CA
90023; 323-263-6878. Publishes *Equi-
librium* Magazine; quarterly newsletter;
annual membership directory and out-
of-print scale catalogs; annual convention; membership: $65; please include
SASE when requesting information;
w w w . c o l l e c t o r o n l i n e . c o m /
clubs/ISASC

International Vintage Poster Dealers
Association (IVPDA)
Nancy Steinbock, Charter Member
800-438-1577. Specializing in posters

John F. Rinaldi
Nautical Antiques and Related Items
(Appointment only)
Box 765, Dock Square, Kennebunkport,
ME 04046; 207-967-3218; or (fax) 207-
967-2918. Illustrated catalog: $5

Josef Originals Newsletter
Jim and Kaye Whitaker
PO Box 475, Dept. S, Lynnwood, WA
98046. Subscription (4 issues): $10 per
year

Knife Rests of Yesterday and Today
Beverly L. Ales
4046 Graham St., Pleasanton, CA
94566-5619. Subscription: $20 per
year for 6 issues

Lang's Sporting Collectables, Inc.
14 Fishermans Lane, Raymond, ME
04071; phone/fax: 207-655-4265. Specializing in fishing tackle and related
accessories

The Laughlin Eagle
Joan Jasper, Publisher
Richard Racheter, Editor
1270 63rd Terrace S., St. Petersburg,
FL 33705. Subscription: $14 (4 issues)
per year; sample: $4

Les Amis de Vieux Quimper (Friends
of Old Quimper)
c/o Mark and Adela Meadows
PO Box 819, Carnelian Bay, CA
96140. SASE required for written
reply; e-mail: meadows@cwo.com

License Plate Collectors Hobby Magazine
Drew Steitz, Editor
PO Box 222, East Texas, PA 18046;
phone/fax: 610-791-7979. Bimonthly
publication with many photographs,
classifieds, etc.; $18 per year (1st class,
US); sample: $2

Liddle Kiddle Konvention
Paris Langford
415 Dodge Ave. Jefferson, LA 70121;
e-mail: BBEAN415@AOL.COM or
send SASE for information about
upcoming Liddle Kiddle Convention,
also send additional SASE for Liddle
Kiddle Newsletter information

Line Jewels, NIA #1380
3557 Nicklaus Dr., Titusville, FL 32780

Mabel Lucie Attwell Catalogs
J. David Ehrhard
7212 Valmont St., Tujunga, CA 91042

Majolica International Society
Suite #103, 1275 First Ave., New
York, NY 10021; 212-969-0025 or
(fax) 212-744-1124. Membership: $35
per year, includes annual meeting and
quarterly newsletter *Majolica Matters*;
www.majolicasociety.com

Marble Collectors' Society of America
Claire Block, Secretary
PO Box 222, Trumbull, CT 06611.
Publishes *Marble Mania*; gathers and
disseminates information to further
the hobby of marbles and marble collecting; $12 adds your name to the
contributor mailing list ($21 covers 2
years); e-mail: BlockMCSA@aol.com
or www.blocksite.com

Marble Collectors Unlimited
PO Box 206, Northboro, MA 01532

Martha's Kidlit Newsletter
Martha Rasmussen, Editor/Publisher
Box 1488, Ames IA 50014; 515-292-
9309. For children's book lovers and
collectors; subscription: $30 in US, all
others: $31; e-mail: mart515@aol.com

Midwest Open Salt Society
c/o Ed Bowman
2411 W. 500 North, Hartford City, IN
47348. Dues: $10 ($6 for spouse)

Midwest Sad Iron Collector Club
c/o Lynette Conrad, Secretary
24 Nob Hill Dr., St. Louis, MO 63138-
1458; 314-741-4171

Miniature Bottle Club of the Great Lakes
19745 Woodmont, Harper Woods, MI
48225. Dues $5 per year; 4 meetings
per year

Mt. Washington Art Glass Society
PO Box 107, Hyde Park, NY 12538-
1122. Publishes *MWAGS Review*, to
educate, inform, and provide helpful
information to anyone interested in art
glass; holds annual convention; sub-
scription/membership: $30 (single) or
$40 for (2 persons in 1 household)

Murray Hudson Antiquarian Books
and Maps
109 S. Church St., Box 163, Halls, TN
38040; 800-748-9946 or 901-836-9057;
fax: 901-836-9017. Buyer and seller of
antiquarian maps (especially pocket,
wall, US Civil War, and railroad maps)
and books with maps (atlases, travel
guides, geographies, gazetteers, explorations, land surveys, etc.), especially of
Southeastern and Southwestern US
prior to 1900; also world globes, map
jigsaw puzzles and game boards prior to
1950; contact for catalog

Mystic Lights of the Aladdin Knights,
bimonthly newsletter
c/o J.W. Courter
3935 Kelley Rd., Kevil, KY 40253-9532;
270-488-2116. Information requires
LSASE; www.aladdinknights.org

National Association of Avon Collectors
c/o Connie Clark
6100 Walnut, Dept. P, Kansas City, MO
64113. Information requires LSASE

National Association Breweriana
Advertising
2343 Met-To-Wee Lane, Wauwatosa,
WI 53226; 414-257-0158. Membership: $25 (US), $30 (Canada) or $40
(Overseas); publishes *The Breweriana
Collector* and membership directory;
holds annual convention;
www.nababrew.org

National Association of Watch &
Clock Collectors, Inc. (NAWCC)
514 Poplar St., Columbia, PA 17512-
2130; 717-684-8261. Benefits include
annual subscriptions to two publications, free research, participation in
national and regional meetings, and
the camaraderie of 35,000 fellow collectors worldwide; membership $45
(US, single) or $55 (US, household);
www.nawcc.org

National Autumn Leaf Collectors' Club
Bill Swanson, Newsletter Editor
807 Roaring Springs Dr., Allen, TX
75002-2112; 972-727-5527 or (fax) 972-
727-2107; e-mail: bescom@home.com
or Gwynne Harrison, President
PO Box 1, Mira Loma, CA 91752-0001;
909-685-5434 or (fax) 909-681-1652;
membership: $20, payable to NALCC,
c/o Dianna Kowales, PO Box 900968,
Palmdale, CA 93590-0968; e-mail:
morgan99@pe.net; www.nalcc.org

National Blue Ridge Newsletter
Norma Lilly
144 Highland Dr., Blountville, TN 37617.
Subscription: $15 per year (6 issues)

National Bobbin Head Club
Larkins, Barry
PO Box 9297, Daytona Beach, FL
32120; 904-253-7040; www.national-
bobbinheadclub.com

National Cambridge Collectors, Inc.
PO Box 416, Cambridge, OH 43725-
0416; 740-432-4245 or (fax) 740-439-
9223; membership: $20 (Associate
member: $3); e-mail: NCC-Crystal-
Ball@compuserve.com; www.Cam-
bridgeglass.org

National Cuff Link Society
c/o Eugene R. Klompus
PO Box 5700, Vernon Hills, IL 60061;
Phone/fax: 847-816-0035; e-mail:
g e n e k @ c u f f l i n k . c o m ;
www.cufflink.com. $30 annual dues
includes subscription to *The Link*, a
quarterly magazine; write for free
booklet *The Fun of Cuff Link Collecting*

National Depression Glass Association
Anita Woods
PO Box 69843, Odessa, TX 79769;
915-337-1297. Publishes *News and
Views*; membership: $17;
www.glassshow.com/NDGA

National Graniteware Society
PO Box 9248, Cedar Rapids, IA
52409-9248. Membership: $20;
www.graniteware.org

National Greentown Glass Assoc.
1807 W. Madison, Kokomo, IN 46901.
Membership: $20

National Imperial Glass Collectors'
Society, Inc.
PO Box 534, Bellaire, OH 43906.
Membership: $15 per year (+$3 for
each associate member); quarterly
newsletter; convention every June;
www.imperialglass.org

National Insulator Association
1315 Old Mill Path, Broadview
Heights, OH 44147. Membership:
$12; www.nia.org

National Milk Glass Collectors' Society & *Opaque News* newsletter
c/o Helen T. Storey
46 Almond Dr., Cocoa Townes, Her-
shey, PA 17033. Please include SASE;
membership: $18; www.nmgcs.org

National Reamer Association
c/o Debbie Gillham
47 Midline Ct., Gaithersburg, MD
20878. Membership: $25 per house-
hold; e-mail: reamers@erols.com;
www.reamers.org

National Shaving Mug Collectors
Association
Penelope G. Nader, President
320 S. Greenwood St., Allerton, PA
18104; 610-437-2534. To stimulate
the study, collection, and preservation
of shaving mugs and all related barbering items; provides quarterly newsletter, bibliography, and directory; holds
2 meetings per year; dues: $15 per year

National Shelley China Club
Rochelle Hart, Secretary/Treasurer
591 West 67th Ave., Anchorage, AK
99518-1555. Membership: $35 per
year, 4 quarterly newsletters plus many
other benefits and publications, 11
years old; e-mail: imahart@alaska.net

National Society of Lefton Collectors
c/o Loretta DeLozier
PO Box 50201, Knoxville, TN 37950-0201. Quarterly newsletter; dues: $25 per year; e-mail: leftonlady@aol.com

National Toothpick Holder Collectors
   Society
Membership Chairperson
PO Box 852, Archer City, TX 76351. Dues: $15 (single) or $20 (couple); includes 10 *Toothpick Bulletin* newsletters per year; annual convention held in August; exclusive toothpick holder annually; e-mail: tpinfo@glass-works.com

National Valentine Collectors Assoc.
Evalene Pulati
PO Box 1404, Santa Ana, CA 92702; 714-547-1355. Specializing in Valentines and love tokens

New England Society of Open Salt
   Collectors
Chuck Keys
21 Overbrook Lane, East Greenwich, RI 02818; Dues: $7 per year

Newspaper Collector's Society of America
Rick Brown
Lansing, MI, 517-887-1255. An extensive, searchable, 300,000-word reference library of American history with an emphasis on newspapers publishing speeches; interactive crossword puzzles; regular auctions of ephemera, historic documents, and newspapers; a mall with over one hundred different online catalogs of paper collectibles; and much, much more; e-mail: help@historybuff.com; www.historybuff.com

Night Light Club
Bob Culver
38619 Wakefield Ct., Northville, MI 48167; 248-473-8575. Specializing in miniature oil lamps

NM (Nelson McCoy) Express
Carol Seman, Editor
8934 Brecksville Rd., Suite 406, Brecksville, OH 44141-2318; 440-526-2094 (Voice & Fax); e-mail: McCjs@aol.com; www.members.aol.com /nmXpress/

North American Torquay Society
Jerry and Gerry Kline, 2 of the founding members and archivists; Also members of Torquay Pottery Collectors' Society
604 Orchard View Dr., Maumee, OH 43537. Quarterly newsletter sent to members; information and membership form requires #10 SASE

North American Trap Collectors'
   Association
c/o Tom Parr
PO Box 94, Galloway, OH 43119-0094. Dues: $15 per year; publishes bimonthly newsletter

North Dakota Pottery Collectors Society and Newsletter
Sandy Short, Membership Chairman
Box 14, Beach, ND 58621. Membership: $15 (includes spouse); annual convention in June; quarterly newsletters

Novelty Salt & Pepper Shakers Club
Lula Fuller
PO Box 679388, Orlando, FL 32867-7388; 407-678-1219. Publishes quarterly newsletter; holds annual convention; dues: $20 per year in US, Canada, and Mexico ($5 extra for couple)

Nutcracker Collectors' Club and
   Newsletter
Susan Otto, Editor
12204 Fox Run Dr., Chesterland, OH 44026. Membership: $15 ($17 foreign) includes quarterly newsletters, free classifieds

The Occupied Japan Club
c/o Florence Archambault
29 Freeborn St., Newport, RI 02840-1821. Publishes *The Upside Down World of an O.J. Collector*, a bimonthly newsletter; information requires SASE; e-mail: florence@ aiconnect.com

Old Sleepy Eye Collectors Club of
   America, Inc.
PO Box 12, Monmouth, IL 61462. Membership: $10 per year with additional $1 for spouse (if joining)

Old Stuff
Donna and Ron Miller, Publishers
2115 McDonald Lane, PO Box 1084, McMinnville, OR 97540. Published 6 times annually; copies by mail: $3.50 each; annual subscription: $18 ($32 in Canada)

On the LIGHTER Side Newsletter
(bimonthly publication)
International Lighter Collectors
Judith Sanders, Editor
136 Circle Dr., Quitman, TX 75783; 903-763-2795 or (fax) 903-763-4953. · Annual convention held in different cities in the US; subscription fees: overseas rate, US and Canada rate, and a junior and senior citizen rate; please include SASE when requesting information

Open Salt Collectors of the Atlantic
   Regions (O.S.C.A.R.)
Wilbur Rudisill, Treasurer
1844 York Rd., Gettysburg, PA 17325. Dues: $5 per year

Open Salt Seekers of the West, Northern California Chapter
Sara Conley
84 Margaret Dr., Walnut Creek, CA 94596. Dues: $7 per year

Open Salt Seekers of the West, Southern California Chapter
Janet Hudson
2525 E. Vassar Court, Visalia, CA 93277. Dues: $5 per year

Pacific Northwest Fenton Association
PO Box 881, Tillamook, OR 97141; 503-842-4815. Newsletter subscription: $20 per year (published quarterly, includes annual piece of glass made only for subscribers); e-mail: jshirley@pacifier.com; www.glasscastle.com/pnwfa.htm

Paden City Glass Collectors Guild
Paul Torsiello, Editor
42 Aldine Road, Parsippany, NJ, 07054. Publishes newsletter; for subscription information; e-mail: pcguild1@yahoo.com

Paper Collectors' Marketplace
PO Box 128, Scandinavia, WI 54977-0128; 715-467-2379 or (fax) 715-467-2243. Subscription: $19.95 in US (12 issues); e-mail: pcmpaper@gglbbs.com or www.pcmpaper.com

Paper Pile Quarterly Magazine
Ada Fitzsimmons, Editor
PO Box 337, San Anselmo, CA 94979; 415-454-5552 or (fax) 415-454-2947. Sales and features magazine for paper buyers & sellers since 1980; quarterly cataloged sales of paper items, large for-sale, and wanted sections, auction results, book reviews, quarterly price guide & show schedule; subscription: $20 per year (shipped 1st class); sample copy: $5 (returnable as credit toward subscription or advertising); e-mail: apaperpile@aol.com or www.paperpilecollectibles.com

Paperweight Collectors' Assoc.
PO Box 40, Barker, TX 77413-0040. Membership: for 1 or 2 people at 1 US address is $40 per year; $35 for non-US addresses; sustaining membership for 1 or 2 people at 1 US address is $55 per year and includes a copy of the Annual Bulletin; sustaining membership for 1 or 2 people at 1 non-US address is $55 per year if the Annual Bulletin is sent surface ($65 for airmail); publishes 4 newsletters a year; the Annual Bulletin is now hardcover, the next convention will be in 2001 in Corning, NY

Peanut Pals
Judith Walthall, Founder
PO Box 4465, Huntsville, AL 35815; 205-881-9198. Associated collectors of Planters Peanuts memorabilia, bimonthly newsletter *Peanut Papers*; annual directory sent to members; annual convention and regional conventions; primary membership: $20 per year (associate memberships available); membership information: PO Box 652, St. Clairsville, OH, 43950; sample newsletter: $2

Pen Collectors of America
PO Box 821449, Houston, TX 77282-1449; phone/fax: 713-496-2290. Quarterly newsletter, *Pennant*; annual membership: $25 (includes newsletter and access to reference library); www.pencollectors.com

Pen Fancier's Club
1169 Overcash Dr., Dunedin, FL 34698; 727-734-4742 or fax: 727-738-0476. Publishes quarterly catalog of vintage pens and mechanical pencils, books, parts, and information; subscription: $20 per year; sample: $4; e-mail: penfanc@aol.com

Pepsi-Cola Collectors Club Express
Bob Stoddard, Editor
PO Box 817; Claremont, CA 91711

Perrault-Rago Gallery
17 S. Main St., Lambertville, NJ 08530. Specializing in 20th-century decorative arts, particularly art pottery and decorative tiles

Petroleum Collectibles Monthly
Scott Benjamin and Wayne Henderson, Publishers
PO Box 556, LaGrange, OH 44050-0556; 440-355-6608; www.pcmpublishing.com (visit website or call). Subscription: $29.95 per year US, Canada $38.50, International $65.95, Samples $5. Scott advises Gasoline Globes and is devoted to gas and oil collectibles.

Phoenix and Consolidated Glass Collectors' Club
Tom Jiamachello, Secretary
41 River View Drive, Essex Junction, VT 05452; 802-878-2682. Membership: $25 (single), $35 (family) per year; please make checks payable to club; e-mail: TOPofVT@aol.com

Phoenix Bird Collectors of America
685 S. Washington, Constantine, MI 49042; 616-435-8353; e-mail: koates120@earthlink.net. Membership: (payable to Joan Oates) $15 per year, includes *Phoenix Bird Discoveries*, published 3 times a year; also available: 1996 Updated Value Guide to be used in conjunction with Books I – IV: $6 ppd.

Pickard Collectors Club, Ltd.
Membership office: 300 E. Grove St., Bloomington, IL 61701; 309-828-5533 or (fax) 309-829-2266. Membership (includes newsletter): $20 a year (single) or $25 (family); www.pickardcollectors.org

Pie Birds Unlimited Club & Newsletter
Linda Fields
158 Bagsby Hill Lane, Dover, TN 37058; 931-232-5099 after 6 p.m.; e-mail: Fpiebird@compu.net

Political Collectors of Indiana Club
Michael McQuillen
PO Box 50022, Indianapolis, IN 46250-0022; 317-845-1721. Official APIC (American Political Items Collectors) Chapter comprised of over 100 collectors of presidential and local political items; e-mail: michael@politicalparade.com; www.politicalparade.com

Porcelain Collector's Companion
c/o Dorothy Kamm
PO Box 7460, Port St. Lucie, FL 34985-4760; 561-464-4008 or (fax) 561-460-9050

Powder Puff Compact Collectors'
   Chronicle
Roselyn Gerson
PO Box 40, Lynbrook, NY 11563; 516-593-8746 or (fax) 516-593-0610; e-mail: compactlady@aol.com

The Prize Insider Newsletter for Cracker Jack Collectors
Larry White
108 Central St., Rowley, MA 01969; 508-948-8187; e-mail: larrydw@erols.com

Purinton News & Views
PO Box 153, Connellsville, PA 15425. Newsletter for Purinton pottery enthusiasts; Subscription: $16 per year

R. Lalique
John Danis
11028 Raleigh Ct., Rockford, IL 61115; 815-877-2410 or (fax) 815-877-6042; e-mail: danis6033@aol.com

R.A. Fox Collector's Club
c/o Pat Gibson
38280 Guava Dr., Newark, CA, 94560; 510-792-0586

Ribbon Tin News Newsletter
Hobart D. Van Deusen, Editor
28 The Green, Watertown, CT 06795; 860-945-3456. $30 per year for 24+ color plates. For collectors of typewriters, typewriter ribbon tins, and go-withs; indexed subscribers' list and participation in occasional mail/phone auctions; e-mail: rtn.hoby@worldnet.att.net

Rose Bowl Collectors
Johanna S. Billings, Co-Founder
P.O. Box 244; Danielsville, PA 18038-0244; 610-261-4775 or (fax) 610-261-4782. Issues quarterly newsletter; e-mail: bankie@concentric.net

Rosevilles of the Past Newsletter
Nancy Bomm, Editor
PO Box 656, Clarcona, FL 32710-0656. $19.95 per year for 6 newsletters

Saint Patrick Notes Newsletter
Chuck Thompson, Editor
10802 Greencreek Dr., Suite 203, Houston, TX 77070-5365. For everyone interested in the legends, myths, and lore of this great missionary. This free publication is also of interest to collectors of St. Patrick cards and memorabilia. New issues every March. Requests filled all year. To receive a copy, send name and address with 2 postage stamps.

Salt & Pepper Illustrated Sales List ($2 and LSASE)
Judy Posner
June - September: R.D. 1, Box 273 SC, Effort, PA 18330; fax: 717-629-0521; October - May: PO Box 2194 SC, Englewood, FL 34295, fax: 941-475-2645. Buy-Sell-Collect. e-mail: judyandjef@aol.com or www.judyposner.com

Schoenhut Collectors Club
c/o Pat Girbach
1003 w. Huron St., Ann Arbor, MI 48103-4217 for membership information

Shawnee Pottery Collectors' Club
PO Box 713, New Smyrna Beach, FL 32170-0713. Monthly nation-wide newsletter; SASE (c/o Pamela Curran) required when requesting information; $3 for sample of current newsletter

Shot Glass Exchange
PO Box 219, Western Springs, IL 60558; 708-246-1559. Primarily pre-prohibition glasses; subscription: (includes 2 semi-annual issues, available in US only) $13 per year, single copy $8

Society of Inkwell Collectors
5136 Thomas Ave. South, Minneapolis, MN 55410. Membership: $25.00 per year, includes subscription to *The Stained Finger*, a quarterly publication. e-mail: soic@concentric.net; www.soic.com

Southern California Marble Club
18361-1 Strothern St., Reseda, CA 91335

Southern Folk Pottery Collectors Society
Society headquarters: 220 Washington St., Bennett, NC 27208; 336-581-4246 or (fax) 336-581-4247 (Wednesday through Saturday, 10:00 to 5:00). Specializing in historical research and documentation, education and promotion of the traditional southern folk potter (past and present) to a modern collecting audience; membership dues includes biannual absentee auction catalogs (at discounted prices), access to member pieces, opportunities to meet potters, participate in events, newsletter information, various printings, and more

Southern Oregon Antiques & Collectibles Club
PO Box 508, Talent, OR 97540; 541-535-1231 or (fax) 541-535-5109. Meets 1st Wednesday of the month; promotes 2 shows a year in Medford, OR

Stangl/Fulper Collectors Club
PO Box 538, Flemington, NJ 08822. Yearly membership: $25 (includes quarterly newsletter); annual auction in June; American pottery and dinnerware show and sale in October; www.stanglfulper.com

Stevengraph Collectors Assn.
David L. Brown
2103-2829 Arbutus Rd., Victoria, British Columbia, Canada, V8N 5X5; 250-477-9896

Still Bank Collectors Club of America
c/o Larry Egelhoff
4175 Millersville Rd., Indianapolis, IN 46205. Membership: $35

Stretch Glass Society
508 Turnberry Lane, St. Augustine, FL, 32084. Membership: $22 (US) or $24 (Canada); quarterly newsletter with color photos; annual spring convention

Style: 1900 The Quarterly Journal of the Arts & Crafts Movement
David Rago
333 N. Main St., Lambertville, 08530; 609-397-4104.
Surveyors Historical Society Identification Committee

D.R. Beeks
PO Box 117, Mt. Vernon, IA 52314; 391-895-0506; e-mail dbeeksci@aol.com

Susie Cooper Catalogs
J. David Ehrhard
7212 Valmont St., Tujunga, CA 91042

Swan Seekers Network
9470 Campo Rd., #134, Spring Valley, CA 91977; 619-462-5517. Business hours: 9:00 a.m. - 5:00 p.m. Pacific Time, Monday - Thursday; publishes *Swan Seekers News* and *Swan Seekers Crystal Gallery* periodicals ($30 US, $45 foreign); specializing in retired Swarovski crystal; e-mail: jimer@swanseekers.com; www.swanseekers.com

Table Toppers
1340 West Irving Park Rd., PO Box 161, Chicago, IL 60613; 312-769-3184. Membership: $18 (single) per year, which includes *Table Topics*, a bimonthly newsletter for those interested in tabletop collectibles

The Tanner Restraints Collection
6442 Canyon Creek Way, Elk Grove, CA 95758-5431; 916-684-4006. 40-page catalog of magician/escape artist equipment from trick and regulation padlocks, handcuffs, leg shackles, and straight jackets to picks and pick sets; books on all of the above and much more; catalog: $3

Tarrant, Jenny
Holly Daze Antiques
4 Gardenview, St. Peters, MO 63376. Specializing in Halloween, Christmas, Easter, etc.; buying & selling Halloween and holiday items; e-mail: JennyJOL@aol.com; antique holiday for sale; www.holly-days.com

Tea Leaf Club International
Maxine Johnson, Membership
PO Box 377, Belton, MO 64012. Publishes *Tea Leaf Readings* Newsletter; membership: $20 (single) or $25 (couple); www.tealeafclub.com

Tea Talk
Tina M. Carter, Teapot Columnist
Diana Rosen/Lucy Roman, Editors
PO Box 860, Sausalito, CA 94966

The TeaTime Gazette
Linda Ashley Leamer
PO Box 40276, St. Paul, MN 55104

THCKK
The Hardware Companies Kollector's Klub
For information contact Jerry Heuring, 28450 US Highway 61, Scott City, MO 63780; 573-264-3947. Membership: $15 per year

Thermometer Collectors' Club of America
Richard Porter, Vice President
PO Box 944, Onset, MA 02558

Thimble Collectors International
Kay Conners, Membership Chairperson
3230 E. Upper Haden Lake Rd., Hayden, ID 83835. Membership: $25 US ($30 International); www.thimblecollectors.com

Three Rivers Depression Era Glass Society
Meetings held 1st Monday of each month at 6:00 p.m. at Old Country Bouffet, Heidleburg, PA
For more information call: Edith A. Putanko at John's Antiques & Edie's Glassware, Rte. 88 & Broughton Rd., Bethel Park, PA 15102; 412-831-2702

Tiffin Glass Collectors
PO Box 554, Tiffin, OH 44883. Meetings at Seneca County Museum on 2nd Tuesday of each month; Tiffin Glass Museum, 25 S. Washington, Tiffin, OH, Wednesday - Sunday from 1:00 p.m. - 5:00 p.m.

Tins 'n Signs
Box 440101, Aurora, CO 80044. Subscription: $25 per year

Tops & Bottoms Club (Rene Lalique perfumes only)
c/o Madeleine France
PO Box 15555, Ft. Lauderdale, FL 33318

Toy Shop
Mark Williams, Publisher
700 E. State St., Iola, WI 54990-0001; 715-445-2214 or (fax) 715-445-4087. Subscription $33 (26 issues) in US; www.toyshopmag.com

Trick or Treat Trader
PO Box 499, Winchester, NH 03470; 603-239-8875. Subscription: $15 per year for 4 quarterly issues

TW List (Typewriters)
Chuck Dilts/Rich Cincotta
PO Box 286, Southboro, MA 01772; 508-229-2064; e-mail: typewriters@writeme.com or visit www.typewriter.rydia.net/etcetera.htm

Twin Winton Collectors Club
266 Rose Lane, Costa Mesa, CA 92627; www.TwinWinton.com

Uhl Collectors' Society
3704 W. Old Rd. 64, Huntingburg, IN 47542. Membership: $12 per family

Dave and Donna Swick, Newsletter
506 Martin St., Newton, IL 62488; 618-783-3455; www.uhlcollectors.org

Vaseline Glass Collectors, Inc.
Madolyn Courter
PO Box 125
Russellville, MO 65074; e-mail: mcourter@socketis.net. An organization whose sole purpose is to unify vaseline glass collectors; newsletter *Glowing Report* published bimonthly; convention held annually; membership: $20; www.vaselineglass.org

Vaseline Glass Newsletter
Jerry Chambers
2163 Pomona Place, Fairfield, CA 94533; 707-425-6166 after 4:30 p.m. P.S.T.

Vernon Views, newsletter for Vernon Kilns collectors
PO Box 24234, Tempe, AZ 85285. Published quarterly beginning with the Spring issue, $10 per year

Vetri: Italian Glass News
Howard Lockwood, Publisher
PO Box 191, Fort Lee, NJ 07024; 201-969-0373. Quarterly newsletter about 20th-century Italian glass

Vintage Fashion & Costume Jewelry Newsletter/Club
PO Box 265, Glen Oaks, NY 11004; 718-939-3095 or (fax) 718-939-7988. Subscription (4 issues): $15 US, $20 Canada, $25 International: back issues available at $5 each; e-mail: VFCJ@aol.com

Vintage TVs
Harry Poster
Box 1883, S. Hackensack, 07606; Days: 201-794-9606. Specializes in vintage TVs, transistor radios, 3-D stereo cameras; catalog www.harry poster.com

The Wade Watch
Wade Watch Ltd.
8199 Pierson Ct., Arvada, CO 80005; 303-421-9655 or 303-424-4401; fax 303-421-0317. Year's subscription (4 issues): $8 in US; $14 International; articles and photos welcome, but if to be returned, enclose SASE

Walking Stick Notes
Marilyn Vlahos, Editor
2611 Catalpa Ave., Pascagoula, MS 39567-1806. Please write to Marilyn Vlahos at the above address for information about her publication plans.

The Wallace Nutting Collector's Club
PO Box 22475, Beachwood, OH 44122. Established in 1973, holds annual conventions, usually in the northeastern portion of the country; generally recognized national center of Wallace Nutting-like activity are Michael Ivankovich's Wallace Nutting & Wallace Nutting-Like Specialty Auctions, held 4 times each year. These auctions provide the opportunity for collectors and dealers to compete for the largest variety of Wallace Nutting and Wallace Nutting-Like pictures available anywhere. These auctions also give sellers the opportunity to place their items in front of the country's leading enthusiasts. When writing for information please include a close-up photograph which includes the picture's frame and a SASE. www.wallacenutting.com

Warwick China Collectors Club
Pat & Don Hoffmann, Sr.
1291 N. Elmwood Dr., Aurora, IL 60506-1309; 630-859-3435; e-mail: warwick@fayetteville.net

Watt's News Newsletter
Watt Collectors Association
PO Box 30561, Winston Salem, NC 27130. Subscription: $12 per year; quarterly newsletter, annual convention

Wave Crest Collectors Club
c/o Whitney Newland
PO Box 2013, Santa Barbara, CA 93120. Membership dues: $25 (includes quarterly newsletter); annual convention; whntique@gte.net

The Wedgwood Society of New York
7 Palatine Ct., Syosset, NY 11791-1105. Membership: $30 (single) or $35 (family); publishes newsletter (6 times per year) and a scholarly magazine, *Ars Ceramica*, of original articles published by the society; 6 meetings per year; www.wsny.org

Westmoreland Glass Collector's Newsletter
PO Box 143, North Liberty, IA 52317; Subscription: $16 per year. This publication is dedicated to the purpose of preserving Westmoreland Glass and its history.

Westmoreland Glass Society
Steve Jensen
PO Box PO Box 2883, Iowa City, IA 52240-2883. Membership: $15 (single) or $25 (household)

The Whimsey Club
c/o Lon Knickerbocker
PO Box 312, Dansville, NY, 14437. *Whimsical Notions*, quarterly newsletter with colored photos; dues: $8 per year; annual get-together

The White Ironstone China Assn, Inc.
Diane Dorman, Membership
PO Box 855, Fairport, NY 14450-0855. Newsletter available for: $25 (single) or $30 (2 individuals at same address); www.whiteironstone.com

Willow Review
PO Box 41312, Nashville, TN 37204. Send SASE for information

World's Fair Collectors' Society, Inc.
Fair News Newsletter (bimonthly publication for members)
Michael R. Pender, Editor
PO Box 20806, Sarasota, FL 34276-3806; 941-923-2590. Dues: $20 per year in US and Canada, $30 overseas

The Zsolnay Store
152 Spring St., Newport, RI 02840; 401-841-5060. Zsolnay book available; www.drawrm.com

Index

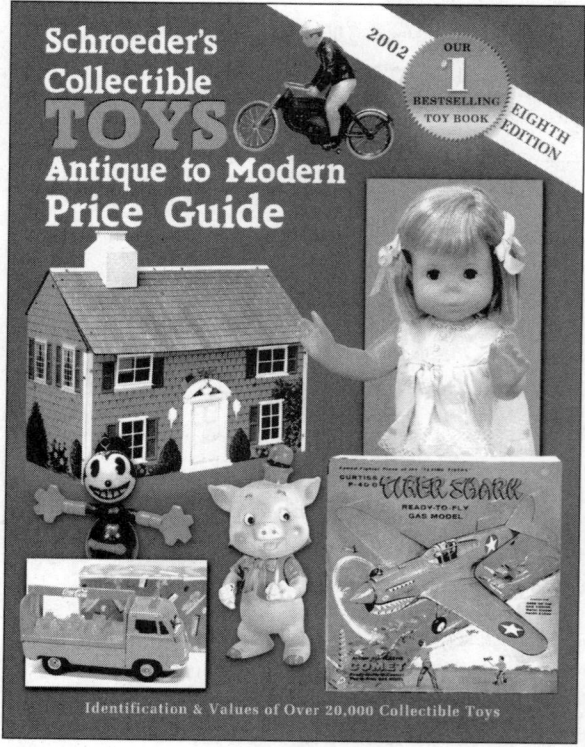